W9-BSP-330

FOR REFERENCE

Do not take from this room

THE OXFORD
DICTIONARY OF
QUOTATIONS

THE OXFORD
DICTIONARY OF
QUOTATIONS

FOURTH EDITION

Edited by
ANGELA PARTINGTON

Oxford   New York

OXFORD UNIVERSITY PRESS

Oxford University Press, Walton Street, Oxford OX2 6DP
Oxford New York Toronto
Delhi Bombay Calcutta Madras Karachi
Kuala Lumpur Singapore Hong Kong Tokyo
Nairobi Dar es Salaam Cape Town
Melbourne Auckland Madrid
and associated companies in
Berlin Ibadan

Oxford is a trade mark of Oxford University Press

Published in the United States by
Oxford University Press Inc., New York

Selection and arrangement © Oxford University Press 1979, 1992

First edition 1941
Second edition 1953
Third edition 1979
Fourth edition 1992

All rights reserved. No part of this publication may be reproduced,
stored in a retrieval system, or transmitted, in any form or by any means,
without the prior permission in writing of Oxford University Press.
Within the UK, exceptions are allowed in respect of any fair dealing for the
purpose of research or private study, or criticism or review, as permitted
under the Copyright, Designs and Patents Act, 1988, or in the case of
reprographic reproduction in accordance with the terms of the licences
issued by the Copyright Licensing Agency. Enquiries concerning
reproduction outside these terms and in other countries should be
sent to the Rights Department, Oxford University Press,
at the address above

This book is sold subject to the condition that it shall not, by way
of trade or otherwise, be lent, re-sold, hired out or otherwise circulated
without the publisher's prior consent in any form of binding or cover
other than that in which it is published and without a similar condition
including this condition being imposed on the subsequent purchaser

British Library Cataloguing in Publication Data
Data available

Library of Congress Cataloging in Publication Data
Data applied for

ISBN 0-19-866185-1

3 5 7 9 8 6 4

Text processing by Oxford University Press
Typeset by Latimer Trend & Co. Ltd.
Printed in Great Britain
on acid-free paper
at the Bath Press, Avon

Memorial Library
Mars Hill College
Mars Hill, N. C.
DISCARD

THE OXFORD DICTIONARY OF QUOTATIONS

PROJECT TEAM

MANAGING EDITOR Sara Tulloch

EDITOR Angela Partington

ASSISTANT EDITOR Susan Ratcliffe

EDITORIAL ASSISTANT Charles Brayne

STAFF RESEARCHERS Gwen Hampshire, Helen McCurdy

ADDITIONAL RESEARCH Melinda Babcock, Nancy Balz, George Chowdharay-Best
Daphne Gilbert-Carter, Katie Field, Sally Hinkle, Sarah Hutchinson, Rita Keckeissen
Adriana Orr, Clare Senior

FOREIGN LITERATURES Patrick Goldsmith, Dr I. Grafe, Christopher King
Helen McCurdy, Tamsin Simmill

DATA CAPTURE AND VALIDATION Kay Pepler, Trish Stableford
Sara Triggs, Helen DeWitt

SPECIALIST ADVISERS

Jonquil Bevan *Reader in English Literature, The University of Edinburgh*

Christopher Butler *Tutor in English, Christ Church, Oxford*

Sir Anthony Kenny *Warden, Rhodes House, Oxford*

G. H. L. Le May *Emeritus Fellow, Worcester College, Oxford*

H. G. Pitt *Emeritus Fellow, Worcester College, Oxford*

Jeremy Trevett *Lecturer, New College, Oxford*

Stephen Wall *Fellow, Keble College, Oxford*

John Wilders *Professor of the Humanities, Middlebury, Vermont, USA*

Karina Williamson *Supernumerary Fellow, St Hilda's College, Oxford*

ADDITIONAL CONTRIBUTORS

Colin Matthew, David Oderberg, Richard Rutherford, Jeffery Triggs

Reference
808.88
O980 4

930627

Memorial Library
Mars Hill College
Mars Hill, N. C.

Preface to the Fourth Edition

THIS, the fourth edition of the *Oxford Dictionary of Quotations*, is a new, thoroughly revised selection of writings and sayings from the past and present, drawn from every aspect of our culture.

A team of distinguished advisers, united by scholarship in particular literary periods and subject fields, coupled with great breadth of reading and variety of outlook, enabled us to pick our way through the *embarras des richesses* offered both by the previous 1979 edition of the *Dictionary* and the more recently issued *Oxford Dictionary of Modern Quotations*. In so doing, space was created for a generous intake of new material.

Additions, substitutions, and deletions were made where these were demanded by shifts in contemporary tastes, expectations, and cultural stimuli. New authors were introduced, and some older ones relinquished; others were retained, but represented by different sayings or different facets of their work. The resulting selection amounts to some 17,500 quotations from roughly 2,500 authors.

A major area for expansion was the representation of non-English authors, thinkers, and public figures. In 1979, Flaubert, for instance, rated only two quotations, as did Sartre: they now run to nine and fifteen respectively. Tolstoy and Chekhov were the sole representatives of Russian literature, whereas now they are joined by more than a dozen others, including Dostoevsky, Pushkin, Gogol, Goncharov, Akhmatova, Pasternak, Solzhenitsyn, and Yevtushenko.

American authors put in a much more substantial appearance than before. 'The Adams Family'—John, John Quincy, Henry, and the formidable Abigail ('It is not in the still calm of life that great characters are formed')—make an impressive opening with quotations which display the prodigious range of their activities. American politicians in general remain well represented and recently updated ('Read my lips: no new taxes') while American authors, and especially poets, enjoy substantial new representation: Richard Wilbur, Sylvia Plath, Hart Crane, Theodore Roethke, and many more, not forgetting Alice Walker ('Expect nothing. Live frugally on surprise'). Expansion has occurred also in non-literary fields. New or improved entries for philosophers and psychologists include Aristotle, Socrates, Plato, Hegel, Weber ('The concept of the "official secret" is bureaucracy's specific invention'), de Tocqueville ('History is a gallery of pictures in which there are few originals and many copies'), Chomsky, Wittgenstein, and many more.

Among those newly representing the sciences are Richard Dawkins ('However many ways there are of being alive . . . there are vastly more ways of being dead') and Arthur Eddington ('Science is an edged tool with which men play like children, and cut their own fingers'). Economists featuring in the *Dictionary* for the first time include J. R. Hicks ('The best of all monopoly profits is a quiet life') and David Ricardo ('Rent is that part of the earth, which is paid to the landlord for the use of the original and indestructible powers of the soil').

Social observers are well represented also, with pertinent quotations such as this from Thorstein Veblen: 'The thief or swindler who has gained great wealth by his delinquency has a better chance than the small thief of escaping the rigorous penalty of the law', and this from Samuel Smiles: 'Middle class people are apt to live up to their incomes, if not beyond them: affecting a degree of "style" which is most unhealthy in its effects upon society at large.'

Many quotations have been added from previously neglected authors, especially early women poets, some of whom are now belatedly receiving recognition: Mary Leapor on the importance of marrying well ('In spite of all romantic poets sing, This gold, my dearest, is an useful thing'), Hetty Wright (née Wesley) on the death of a new-born infant ('Smiling wonder of a day'), Esther Lewis voicing a complaint still common among women authors and publishers after two hundred and fifty years ('Why are the needle and the pen Thought incompatible by men?').

Hymns and songs make a welcome reappearance in the *Dictionary*, having been suppressed in the 1979 edition on the grounds that 'if the words cannot be said without the tune coming to mind, they are *not* quotations in the same sense as the others'. Given that verse forms in general enjoy a very much lower profile than once was the case, this policy seemed to exclude two of the richest and most heavily worked seams in our culture. Hymns especially provide us with some of the finest poetry in the language— 'Love to the loveless shown, That they might lovely be', 'Let holy charity Mine outward vesture be'—and for many in an increasingly secular society, their only remaining link with the sacred world.

Songs, too, are a rich source of lyrical, ironic, and satiric observation—'When the deep purple falls over sleepy garden walls', 'You've got to be taught to be afraid Of people whose eyes are oddly made', 'Ev'rything free in America For a small fee in America!'— their quality often overshadowed by the music for which they are best remembered, but for which they should not only be remembered. Some may throw up their hands in disbelief, but popular songs assuredly will feature in the verse anthologies of tomorrow, and a dictionary of this kind, which essentially is a mirror of the age, must acknowledge merit in whatever form it takes.

As with all mirrors, however, what we see and how significant it appears to us is determined by the angle at which the mirror is held. 'What *is* a quotation?' we ask ourselves. According to the *Concise Oxford Dictionary*, it is 'a passage or remark quoted', which strictly means that any of us could be candidates for inclusion in such a dictionary if only our friends could be persuaded to repeat the more felicitous of our utterances. We could claim grounds for inclusion, like M. Jourdain in *Le Bourgeois Gentilhomme*: 'For more than forty years I have been speaking prose without knowing it.'

Fame (or notoriety—'He would, wouldn't he?'), memorability, significance, importance—all, rightly, have claimed their place among the many criteria for inclusion in such a work. Among the more pressing is the combination of that which is both dateless and indisputably true, so that when we discover just how old a quotation is ('Man is by nature a political animal') we marvel that it was not written yesterday, and when we discover just how new it is ('Damaged people are dangerous; they know they can survive') we wonder that it was not always with us.

Ideally, a quotation should be able to float free from its moorings, remaining buoyant when detached from its original context. It should be apposite, pithy, wise, and of universal application—'To thine own self be true . . . Thou canst not then be false to any man'—much quoted, and easily remembered. If it is witty as well—'History just burps, and we taste again that raw-onion sandwich we swallowed centuries ago'—all to the good.

Much that falls into this category, however, more properly belongs in the realm of aphorism than of quotation, and some of it sounds better than in fact it is: style is found to have overtaken content, a high gloss masking what is little more than platitude. But judgements of this kind are fluid at best, one generation finding insight and moral uplift in observations which strike another as merely banal. For this and other reasons, the *Dictionary* requires regular revision and updating.

Inevitably such revisions will reflect differing social attitudes and political perspectives, as well as literary tastes. In the last century Gladstone, for instance, even at the height of his powers was widely considered a bore ('He speaks to me as if I was a public meeting'— Queen Victoria), endlessly droning on about Home Rule. Hindsight, however, coupled with a decline in imperialistic values, has considerably enhanced his standing, and though by 1953 he rated only eleven entries, dropping to just nine in 1979, he now rises again to eighteen.

Conversely, Elizabeth Barrett Browning in her day would have called for much larger representation than her husband Robert, whose talents, unbelievably as it seems to us now, were overshadowed by those of his wife; but by 1979 she ran to just over one column, whereas he weighed in at fifteen. As Pope remarked, on the altered tastes of his own day, 'Who now reads Cowley? if he pleases yet, His moral pleases, not his pointed wit.'

New characters edge in at the corners, others take on unexpected significance: Gerard Manley Hopkins's 'Binsey Poplars' ('Ten or twelve, only ten or twelve Strokes of havoc unselve') chimes so well with the mood of the times that it is hard to believe that it has not appeared in these pages before. On the same theme, 'We'll to the woods no more, The laurels all are cut', a long-term resident of the *Dictionary*, takes on added and yet more ominous significance. On a lighter note, we all thought—well, the editor thought—an 'ology' was the brainchild of 'Beattie', British Telecom's tame subscriber, the one with the telephone grafted to her ear ('You got an ology? You got an ology, you're a scientist!') but it was there in the *Dictionary* all the time: 'Maidservants, I hear people complaining, are getting instructed in the "ologies"' (Carlyle, 1866).

It would be good to think that 'Beattie' was nudging us into an acknowledgement of her wide field of cultural reference: more likely it was by happy accident that she hit on the same word as Carlyle. Often when we quote, or allude to a quotation, we do so without knowing we have done so: we are perhaps vaguely aware of expressing some well-worn idiom, but we think of it perhaps more in terms of a cliché than as being or belonging to a saying with a known source. 'There's method in my madness,' we say, or 'I'm not my brother's keeper!', drawing as we think on a common stock of language. It is both the distinction and the fate of some of our best known language (notably that of Shakespeare and of the Bible) that over time it is absorbed into our common vocabulary, becoming intrinsic to the way in which we express ourselves, and even to the way in which we think. We know what we can say: how we say it not only articulates our meaning, but shapes it, too. Language influences thought, acting favourably or unfavourably upon our nervous systems, as much as thought is reflected in language.

The reader wishing to check that his latest *bon mot* or happy turn of phrase is really his own creation and not that of some sixteenth-century wit, need only consult the index. To brush up on general knowledge, he can glance at the brief author descriptions, new to this edition, which in some cases make sense of the following quotation for the first time. (Anyone wondering what 'Win one for the Gipper' actually means, will discover that 'the Gipper' was an American football legend.)

In this edition, full bibliographical references are given for every quotation for which there is a known printed source.

Explanatory notes have been offered, where possible and where it has been felt that they would add to the interest or enjoyment of a quotation. Virtually all literary quotations from foreign literatures are offered in their original language, as are most of the philosophical and many of the political quotations from foreign sources. Translations, where not otherwise acknowledged, are intended as a faithful rendering of the original.

Every effort has been made to check sources of new quotations, and of old quotations where they gave grounds for doubt. Errors will have crept in, and will have remained in, and no doubt we shall be indebted, as before, to vigilant readers who take the trouble to write to us and point them out. It is a pleasure to acknowledge here the lively correspondence we enjoy with those who, in this way, give generously of their time and efforts to share with us the fruits of their own knowledge and scholarship, contributing in no small measure to the steady flow of good new quotations added to each successive edition of the *Dictionary*.

The selections made will not be to everyone's taste, or reflect everyone's judgement. They, and any other deficiencies, reflect the limitations of the editor, compounded by pressure of time and the usual economic and practical constraints incumbent upon producing a work of such substance at a price which the general reader can afford. Hymns and songs always will seem idiosyncratic in their selection; nursery rhymes and carols, however, were omitted for reasons of space and because they are comprehensively collected elsewhere. Many authors remain unrepresented, for the reason that from our considerable database they were found not to be quoted, and a specific reading programme would have been necessary to do justice to their undoubted merits.

Omissions which the editor would have wished to repair perforce remain unrepaired in some cases, or at best temporarily patched—most notably our relationship to the natural world in all its forms. It is to be hoped that in the not too distant future, and by a perfectly natural process of selection, we shall have a noticeably greener *Dictionary*—one indeed which reflects a stemming of the trend observed as early as 1879: 'Forests keep disappearing, rivers dry up, wildlife's become extinct.'

Its faults notwithstanding, the Fourth Edition has endeavoured to reflect that which is most pithy, most witty, and most treasurable in the cultures to which those of us in the English-speaking world have access. May it be for many a source of 'fireside enjoyments, home-born happiness'.

ANGELA PARTINGTON

Oxford, April 1992

Contents

How to Use the Dictionary

THE sequence of entries is by alphabetical order of author, usually by surname but with occasional exceptions such as imperial or royal titles, authors known by a pseudonym ('Saki') or a nickname (Caligula). In general authors' names are given in the form by which they are best known, so we have George Eliot (not Mary Ann Evans), and T. S. Eliot (not Thomas Stearns Eliot). Collections such as Anonymous, Ballads, the Bible, the Book of Common Prayer, the Missal, and so forth, are included in the alphabetical sequence.

Within each author entry, quotations are arranged by alphabetical order of the titles of the works from which they are taken: books, plays, poems. These titles are given in italic type; titles of pieces which comprise part of a published volume or collection (e.g. essays, short stories, poems not published as volumes in their own right) are given in roman type inside inverted commas. For example, *Paradise Lost*, but 'Ode to Autumn'; often the two forms will be found together, e.g. *Cautionary Tales* (1907) 'Matilda'.

Quotations from diaries, letters, speeches, and so on are given in chronological order, and normally follow the literary or other published works quoted; in the case of political figures, for instance, speeches appear first, just as poetry quotations precede those in prose for poets, and vice versa for writers whose principal work was in prose. Quotations cited from secondary sources—biographies and other writers' works—are found towards the end of an author's entry, in alphabetical order of author, editor, or title of work (newspaper, journal, etc.). 'In' preceding a source, such as *The Times*, indicates that the quotation is cited there; where a reference reads, for instance, '*Guardian* 26 February 1972', this indicates the *origin* of the quotation.

All numbers in source references are given in arabic, with the exception of lower-case roman numerals denoting quotations from prefatory matter, whose page numbering is separate from that of the main text. The numbering itself relates to the beginning of the quotation, whether or not it runs on to another stanza or page in the original. Where possible, chapter numbers have been offered for prose works, since pagination varies from one edition to another. In very long prose works with minimal subdivisions, attempts have been made to provide page references to specified editions.

A date in brackets indicates first publication in volume form of the work cited. Unless otherwise stated, the dates thus offered are intended as chronological guides only and do not necessarily indicate the date of the text cited; where the latter is of significance, this has been stated. Where neither date of publication nor of composition is known, an approximate date (e.g. '*c.*1625') indicates the likely date of composition. Where there is a large discrepancy between date of composition (or performance) and of publication, in most cases the former only has been given (e.g. 'written 1725', 'performed 1622').

Spellings have been Anglicized and modernized except in those cases, such as ballads, where this would have been inappropriate; capitalization has been retained only for personifications; with rare exceptions, verse has been aligned with the left hand margin. Italic type has been used for all foreign-language originals.

Sub-headings have been used as a guide to novel titles under Dickens, for the names of books under the Bible (arranged canonically, not alphabetically, and followed by the Vulgate), and for plays and poems under Shakespeare.

THE INDEX

Both the keywords and the entries following each keyword, including those in foreign languages, are in strict alphabetical order. Singular and plural nouns (with their possessive forms) are grouped separately: for 'some old lover's ghost' see 'lover'; for 'at lovers' perjuries' see 'lovers'. Variant forms of common words (honey/hunny, luve/love) are grouped under a single heading: 'honey', 'love'.

The references show the author's name, usually in abbreviated form (SHAK/Shakespeare), followed by the page number and the number of the quotation on that page: 183:15 therefore means quotation 15 on page 183.

THE OXFORD
DICTIONARY OF
QUOTATIONS

Quotations

Peter Abelard 1079–1142

French scholar, theologian, and philosopher

1 *O quanta qualia sunt illa sabbata,*
Quae semper celebrat superna curia.

O what their joy and glory must be,
Those endless sabbaths the blessèd ones see!
Hymnarius Paraclitensis bk. 1, pars altera 'Hymni Diurni'
no. 29 'Sabbato. Ad Vesperas' (translated by J. M. Neale,
1854)

Dannie Abse 1923–

Welsh-born doctor and poet

2 I know the colour rose, and it is lovely,
But not when it ripens in a tumour;
And healing greens, leaves and grass, so springlike,
In limbs that fester are not springlike.
'Pathology of Colours' (1968)

3 So in the simple blessing of a rainbow,
In the bevelled edge of a sunlit mirror,
I have seen visible, Death's artifact
Like a soldier's ribbon on a tunic tacked.
'Pathology of Colours' (1968)

Accius 170–c.86 BC

Latin poet and dramatist

4 *Oderint, dum metuant.*

Let them hate, so long as they fear.
From *Atreus*, in Seneca *Dialogues* bks. 3–5 *De Ira* bk. 1,
sect. 20, subsect. 4

Goodman Ace 1899–1982

American humorist

5 TV—a clever contraction derived from the words
Terrible Vaudeville . . . we call it a medium because
nothing's well done.
Letter to Groucho Marx, in *The Groucho Letters* (1967)
p. 114

Dean Acheson 1893–1971

American politician

6 Great Britain has lost an empire and has not yet found
a role.
Speech at the Military Academy, West Point, 5 December
1962, in *Vital Speeches* 1 January 1963, p. 163

7 The first requirement of a statesman is that he be dull.
In *Observer* 21 June 1970

8 I will undoubtedly have to seek what is happily
known as gainful employment, which I am glad to say
does not describe holding public office.
In *Time* 22 December 1952

9 A memorandum is written not to inform the reader
but to protect the writer.
In *Wall Street Journal* 8 September 1977

Lord Acton (John Emerich Edward Dahlberg, 1st Baron Acton) 1834–1902

British historian

10 Power tends to corrupt and absolute power corrupts
absolutely.
Letter to Bishop Mandell Creighton, 3 April 1887, in Louise
Creighton *Life and Letters of Mandell Creighton* (1904) vol. 1,
ch. 13. Cf. Pitt 515:8

Abigail Adams 1744–1818

Wife of John Adams, 2nd President of the USA

11 In the new code of laws which I suppose it will be
necessary for you to make I desire you would
remember the ladies, and be more generous and
favourable to them than your ancestors. Do not put
such unlimited power into the hands of the husbands.
Remember all men would be tyrants if they could.
Letter to John Adams, 31 March 1776, in Butterfield et al.
(eds.) *The Book of Abigail and John Adams* (1975) p. 121

12 It is really mortifying, sir, when a woman possessed of
a common share of understanding considers the
difference of education between the male and female
sex, even in those families where education is attended
to . . . Nay why should your sex wish for such a
disparity in those whom they one day intend for
companions and associates. Pardon me, sir, if I cannot
help sometimes suspecting that this neglect arises in
some measure from an ungenerous jealousy of rivals
near the throne.
Letter to John Thaxter, 15 February 1778, in *Adams Family
Correspondence* vol. 2 (1963) p. 391

13 These are times in which a genius would wish to live.
It is not in the still calm of life, or the repose of a
pacific station, that great characters are formed . . .
Great necessities call out great virtues.
Letter to John Quincy Adams, 19 January 1780, in
Butterfield et al. (eds.) *The Book of Abigail and John Adams*
(1975) p. 253

Charles Francis Adams 1807–86

American lawyer and diplomat

14 It would be superfluous in me to point out to your
lordship that this is war.
Dispatch to Earl Russell, 5 September 1863, in C. F. Adams
Charles Francis Adams (1900) ch. 17

Douglas Adams 1952–

English science fiction writer

1 The Answer to the Great Question Of . . . Life, the
Universe and Everything . . . [is] Forty-two.
   The Hitch Hiker's Guide to the Galaxy (1979) ch. 27

Frank Adams and Will M. Hough

2 I wonder who's kissing her now.
   Title of song (1909)

Franklin P. Adams 1881–1960

American journalist and humorist

3 When the political columnists say 'Every thinking
man' they mean themselves, and when candidates
appeal to 'Every intelligent voter' they mean
everybody who is going to vote for them.
   Nods and Becks (1944) p. 3

4 Years ago we discovered the exact point, the dead
centre of middle age. It occurs when you are too
young to take up golf and too old to rush up to the
net.
   Nods and Becks (1944) p. 53

5 Elections are won by men and women chiefly because
most people vote against somebody rather than for
somebody.
   Nods and Becks (1944) p. 206. Cf. Fields 282:23

Henry Brooks Adams 1838–1918

American man of letters

6 Politics, as a practice, whatever its professions, has
always been the systematic organization of hatreds.
   The Education of Henry Adams (1907) ch. 1

7 Accident counts for much in companionship as in
marriage.
   The Education of Henry Adams (1907) ch. 4. Cf. Ustinov
   707:12

8 Women have, commonly, a very positive moral sense;
that which they will, is right; that which they reject,
is wrong; and their will, in most cases, ends by
settling the moral.
   The Education of Henry Adams (1907) ch. 6

9 All experience is an arch to build upon.
   The Education of Henry Adams (1907) ch. 6

10 A friend in power is a friend lost.
   The Education of Henry Adams (1907) ch. 7

11 The effect of power and publicity on all men is the
aggravation of self, a sort of tumour that ends by
killing the victim's sympathies.
   The Education of Henry Adams (1907) ch. 10

12 These questions of taste, of feeling, of inheritance,
need no settlement. Everyone carries his own
inch-rule of taste, and amuses himself by applying it,
triumphantly, wherever he travels.
   The Education of Henry Adams (1907) ch. 12

13 [Charles] Sumner's mind had reached the calm of
water which receives and reflects images without
absorbing them; it contained nothing but itself.
   The Education of Henry Adams (1907) ch. 13

14 Chaos often breeds life, when order breeds habit.
   The Education of Henry Adams (1907) ch. 16

15 A teacher affects eternity; he can never tell where his
influence stops.
   The Education of Henry Adams (1907) ch. 20

16 One friend in a lifetime is much; two are many; three
are hardly possible. Friendship needs a certain
parallelism of life, a community of thought, a rivalry
of aim.
   The Education of Henry Adams (1907) ch. 20

17 What one knows is, in youth, of little moment; they
know enough who know how to learn.
   The Education of Henry Adams (1907) ch. 21

18 Morality is a private and costly luxury.
   The Education of Henry Adams (1907) ch. 22

19 Practical politics consists in ignoring facts.
   The Education of Henry Adams (1907) ch. 22

20 Nothing in education is so astonishing as the amount
of ignorance it accumulates in the form of inert facts.
   The Education of Henry Adams (1907) ch. 25

21 Symbol or energy, the Virgin had acted as the greatest
force the Western world had ever felt, and had drawn
man's activities to herself more strongly than any
other power, natural or supernatural, had ever done.
   The Education of Henry Adams (1907) ch. 25

22 Modern politics is, at bottom, a struggle not of men
but of forces.
   The Education of Henry Adams (1907) ch. 28

23 We combat obstacles in order to get repose, and, when
got, the repose is insupportable.
   The Education of Henry Adams (1907) ch. 29

24 No one means all he says, and yet very few say all
they mean, for words are slippery and thought is
viscous.
   The Education of Henry Adams (1907) ch. 31

John Adams 1735–1826

2nd President of the USA; father of John Quincy Adams

25 Liberty cannot be preserved without a general
knowledge among the people, who have a right . . .
and a desire to know; but besides this, they have a
right, an indisputable, unalienable, indefeasible, divine
right to that most dreaded and envied kind of
knowledge, I mean of the characters and conduct of
their rulers.
   A Dissertation on the Canon and Feudal Law (1765), in M. J.
   Kline (ed.) *Papers of John Adams* vol. 1 (1977) p. 120

26 There is danger from all men. The only maxim of a
free government ought to be to trust no man living
with power to endanger the public liberty.
   Notes for an Oration at Braintree (Spring 1772), in *Diary
   and Autobiography of John Adams* vol. 2 (1960) p. 59

27 A government of laws, and not of men.
   Boston Gazette (1774) no. 7, 'Novanglus' papers; later
   incorporated in the Massachusetts Constitution (1780)

28 I agree with you that in politics the middle way is
none at all.
   Letter to Horatio Gates, 23 March 1776, in R. J. Taylor
   (ed.) *Papers of John Adams* 3rd series (1979) vol. 4, p. 59

1 The happiness of society is the end of government.
Thoughts on Government (1776)

2 Fear is the foundation of most governments.
Thoughts on Government (1776)

3 You and I ought not to die before we have explained ourselves to each other.
Letter to Thomas Jefferson, 15 July 1813, in L. J. Cappon (ed.) *The Adams–Jefferson Letters* (1959) vol. 2, p. 358

4 The fundamental article of my political creed is that despotism, or unlimited sovereignty, or absolute power, is the same in a majority of a popular assembly, an aristocratic council, an oligarchical junto, and a single emperor.
Letter to Thomas Jefferson, 13 November 1815, in P. Wilstach (ed.) *Correspondence of John Adams and Thomas Jefferson* (1925) p. 117

John Quincy Adams 1767–1848

6th President of the USA

5 Think of your forefathers! Think of your posterity!
Oration at Plymouth 22 December 1802, p. 6

6 *Fiat justitia, pereat coelum* [Let justice be done, though heaven fall]. My toast would be, may our country be always successful, but whether successful or otherwise, always right.
Letter to John Adams, 1 August 1816, in A. Koch and W. Peden (eds.) *The Selected Writings of John and John Quincy Adams* (1946) p. 288

Samuel Adams 1722–1803

American revolutionary leader

7 What a glorious morning is this.
On hearing gunfire at Lexington, 19 April 1775; in J. K. Hosmer *Samuel Adams* (1886) ch. 19 (traditionally quoted 'What a glorious morning for America')

8 We cannot make events. Our business is wisely to improve them . . . Mankind are governed more by their feelings than by reason. Events which excite those feelings will produce wonderful effects.
In J. N. Rakove *The Beginnings of National Politics* (1979) ch. 5

9 A nation of shop-keepers are very seldom so disinterested.
Oration in Philadelphia 1 August 1776 (the authenticity of this publication is doubtful). Cf. Napoleon 490:5, Smith 651:1

Sarah Flower Adams 1805–48

English hymn-writer

10 Nearer, my God, to thee,
Nearer to thee!
E'en though it be a cross
That raiseth me:
Still all my song would be,
'Nearer, my God, to thee,
Nearer to thee!'
'Nearer My God to Thee' in W. G. Fox *Hymns and Anthems* (1841)

Harold Adamson 1906–80

American songwriter

11 Comin' in on a wing and a pray'r.
Title of song (1943); words derived from the contemporary comment of a war pilot, speaking from a disabled plane to ground control. See Sheila Davis *The Craft of Lyric Writing* (1985) p. 279

Joseph Addison 1672–1719

English poet, playwright, and essayist; co-founder of The Spectator

12 He more had pleased us, had he pleased us less.
An Account of the Greatest English Poets (1694, of Cowley)

13 'Twas then great Marlbro's mighty soul was proved.
The Campaign (1705) l. 279

14 And, pleased th' Almighty's orders to perform,
Rides in the whirl-wind, and directs the storm.
The Campaign (1705) l. 291

15 And those who paint 'em truest praise 'em most.
The Campaign (1705) l. 476

16 'Tis not in mortals to command success,
But we'll do more, Sempronius; we'll deserve it.
Cato (1713) act 1, sc. 2, l. 43

17 'Tis pride, rank pride, and haughtiness of soul;
I think the Romans call it stoicism.
Cato (1713) act 1, sc. 4, l. 82

18 Were you with these, my prince, you'd soon forget
The pale, unripened beauties of the north.
Cato (1713) act 1, sc. 4, l. 134

19 The woman that deliberates is lost.
Cato (1713) act 4, sc. 1, l. 31

20 Curse on his virtues! they've undone his country.
Such popular humanity is treason.
Cato (1713) act 4, sc. 1, l. 205

21   What pity is it
That we can die but once to serve our country!
Cato (1713) act 4, sc. 1, l. 258

22 Content thyself to be obscurely good.
When vice prevails, and impious men bear sway,
The post of honour is a private station.
Cato (1713) act 4, sc. 1, l. 319

23 It must be so—Plato, thou reason'st well!—
Else whence this pleasing hope, this fond desire,
This longing after immortality?
Or whence this secret dread, and inward horror,
Of falling into naught? Why shrinks the soul
Back on herself, and startles at destruction?
'Tis the divinity that stirs within us;
'Tis heaven itself, that points out an hereafter,
And intimates eternity to man.
Eternity! thou pleasing, dreadful thought!
Cato (1713) act 5, sc. 1, l. 1

24 From hence, let fierce contending nations know
What dire effects from civil discord flow.
Cato (1713) act 5, sc. 1 *ad fin.*

25 I should think my self a very bad woman, if I had done what I do, for a farthing less.
The Drummer (1716) act 1, sc. 1

1 There is nothing more requisite in business than dispatch.
The Drummer (1716) act 5, sc. 1

2 For wheresoe'er I turn my ravished eyes,
Gay gilded scenes and shining prospects rise,
Poetic fields encompass me around,
And still I seem to tread on classic ground.
Letter from Italy (1704)

3 A painted meadow, or a purling stream.
Letter from Italy (1704)

4 Music, the greatest good that mortals know,
And all of heaven we have below.
'A Song for St Cecilia's Day' (1694)

5 Should the whole frame of nature round him break,
In ruin and confusion hurled,
He, unconcerned, would hear the mighty crack,
And stand secure amidst a falling world.
Translation of Horace *Odes* bk. 3, no. 3. Cf. Horace 350:1,
Pope 519:26

6 A reader seldom peruses a book with pleasure until he knows whether the writer of it be a black man or a fair man, of a mild or choleric disposition, married or a bachelor.
The Spectator no. 1 (1 March 1711)

7 In all thy humours, whether grave or mellow,
Thou'rt such a touchy, testy, pleasant fellow;
Hast so much wit, and mirth, and spleen about thee,
There is no living with thee, nor without thee.
The Spectator no. 68 (18 May 1711). Cf. Martial 449:16

8 As Sir Roger is landlord to the whole congregation, he keeps them in very good order, and will suffer nobody to sleep in it [the church] besides himself; for if by chance he has been surprised into a short nap at sermon, upon recovering out of it, he stands up, and looks about him; and if he sees anybody else nodding, either wakes them himself, or sends his servant to them.
The Spectator no. 112 (9 July 1711)

9 Sir Roger told them, with the air of a man who would not give his judgement rashly, that much might be said on both sides.
The Spectator no. 122 (20 July 1711)

10 It was a saying of an ancient philosopher, which I find some of our writers have ascribed to Queen Elizabeth, who perhaps might have taken occasion to repeat it, that a good face is a letter of recommendation.
The Spectator no. 221 (13 November 1711). Cf. Publilius Syrus 531:1

11 I have often thought, says Sir Roger, it happens very well that Christmas should fall out in the Middle of Winter.
The Spectator no. 269 (8 January 1712)

12 A true critic ought to dwell rather upon excellencies than imperfections, to discover the concealed beauties of a writer, and communicate to the world such things as are worth their observation.
The Spectator no. 291 (2 February 1712). Cf. Horace 347:16

13 These widows, Sir, are the most perverse creatures in the world.
The Spectator no. 335 (25 March 1712)

14 Mirth is short and transient, cheerfulness fixed and permanent . . . Mirth is like a flash of lightning that breaks through a gloom of clouds, and glitters for a moment: cheerfulness keeps up a kind of day-light in the mind, and fills it with a steady and perpetual serenity.
The Spectator no. 381 (17 May 1712)

15 The Knight in the triumph of his heart made several reflections on the greatness of the British Nation; as, that one Englishman could beat three Frenchmen; that we could never be in danger of Popery so long as we took care of our fleet; that the Thames was the noblest river in Europe; that London Bridge was a greater piece of work than any of the Seven Wonders of the World; with many other honest prejudices which naturally cleave to the heart of a true Englishman.
The Spectator no. 383 (20 May 1712)

16 Wide and undetermined prospects are as pleasing to the fancy, as the speculations of eternity or infinitude are to the understanding.
The Spectator no. 412 (23 June 1712)

17 Through all Eternity to Thee
A joyful Song I'll raise,
For oh! Eternity's too short
To utter all thy Praise.
The Spectator no. 453 (9 August 1712)

18 We have in England a particular bashfulness in every thing that regards religion.
The Spectator no. 458 (15 August 1712)

19 The spacious firmament on high,
With all the blue ethereal sky,
And spangled heavens, a shining frame,
Their great Original proclaim.
The Spectator no. 465 (23 August 1712) 'Ode'

20 In Reason's ear they all rejoice,
And utter forth a glorious voice,
For ever singing, as they shine:
'The hand that made us is divine.'
The Spectator no. 465 (23 August 1712) 'Ode'

21 A woman seldom asks advice before she has bought her wedding clothes.
The Spectator no. 475 (4 September 1712)

22 Our disputants put me in mind of the skuttle fish, that when he is unable to extricate himself, blackens all the water about him, till he becomes invisible.
The Spectator no. 476 (5 September 1712)

23 If we may believe our logicians, man is distinguished from all other creatures by the faculty of laughter.
The Spectator no. 494 (26 September 1712)

24 'We are always doing', says he, 'something for Posterity, but I would fain see Posterity do something for us.'
The Spectator no. 583 (20 August 1714)

1 There is sometimes a greater judgement shewn in deviating from the rules of art, than in adhering to them; and ... there is more beauty in the works of a great genius who is ignorant of all the rules of art, than in the works of a little genius, who not only knows but scrupulously observes them.

The Spectator no. 592 (10 September 1714). Cf. Pope 521:7

2 I remember when our whole island was shaken with an earthquake some years ago, there was an impudent mountebank who sold pills which (as he told the country people) were very good against an earthquake.

The Tatler no. 240 (21 October 1710)

3 See in what peace a Christian can die.

Dying words to his stepson Lord Warwick, in Edward Young *Conjectures on Original Composition* (1759)

George Ade 1866–1944

American humorist and playwright

4 After being turned down by numerous publishers, he had decided to write for posterity.

Fables in Slang (1900) p. 158

5 R-E-M-O-R-S-E!
Those dry Martinis did the work for me;
Last night at twelve I felt immense,
Today I feel like thirty cents.
My eyes are bleared, my coppers hot,
I'll try to eat, but I cannot.
It is no time for mirth and laughter,
The cold, grey dawn of the morning after.

The Sultan of Sulu (1903) act 2, p. 63

6 'Whom are you?' he asked, for he had attended business college.

'The Steel Box' in *Chicago Record* 16 March 1898

Alfred Adler 1870–1937

Austrian psychologist and psychiatrist

7 The truth is often a terrible weapon of aggression. It is possible to lie, and even to murder, for the truth.

The Problems of Neurosis (1929) ch. 2

8 To be a human being means to possess a feeling of inferiority which constantly presses towards its own conquest ... The greater the feeling of inferiority that has been experienced, the more powerful is the urge for conquest and the more violent the emotional agitation.

In Heinz and Rowens Ansbacher (eds.) *The Individual Psychology of Alfred Adler* (1956) ch. 4, sect. 3

Polly Adler 1900–62

American writer

9 A house is not a home.

Title of book (1954)

Æ (*George William Russell*) 1867–1935

Irish poet and essayist

10 In ancient shadows and twilights
Where childhood had strayed,
The world's great sorrows were born
And its heroes were made.
In the lost boyhood of Judas
Christ was betrayed.

'Germinal' (1931)

Aeschylus *c*.525–456 BC

Greek tragedian

11 ἑλέναυς ἕλανδρος ἑλέπτολις.

Hell to ships, hell to men, hell to cities.

Of Helen (literally 'Ship-destroyer, man-destroyer, city-destroyer') in *Agamemnon* l. 689

12 ποντίων τε κυμάτων ἀνήριθμον γέλασμα.

Countless chuckles of the waves of the sea.

Prometheus Bound l. 89

Herbert Agar 1897–1980

American poet and writer

13 The truth which makes men free is for the most part the truth which men prefer not to hear.

A Time for Greatness (1942) ch. 7

James Agate 1877–1947

British drama critic and novelist

14 My mind is not a bed to be made and re-made.

Ego 6 (1944) 9 June 1943

Agathon b. *c*.445 BC

Athenian tragic poet

15 μόνου γὰρ αὐτοῦ καὶ θεὸς στερίσκεται ἀγένητα ποιεῖν ἄσσ' ἂν ᾖ πεπραγμένα.

Even a god cannot change the past.

In Aristotle *Nicomachaean Ethics* bk. 6, 1139b 10–11 (literally 'The one thing which even God cannot do is to make undone what has been done')

Spiro T. Agnew 1918–

American politician

16 A spirit of national masochism prevails, encouraged by an effete corps of impudent snobs who characterize themselves as intellectuals.

Speech in New Orleans, 19 October 1969, in *Frankly Speaking* (1970) ch. 3

Maria, Marchioness of Ailesbury d. 1902

1 My dear, my dear, you never know when any
beautiful young lady may not blossom into a Duchess!
  In Duke of Portland *Men, Women, and Things* (1937) ch. 3

Alfred Ainger 1837–1904

English lecturer

2 No flowers, by request.
  Summarizing the principle of conciseness for contributors to
  the *Dictionary of National Biography*, in *Supplement
  1901–1911* (1912) p. 27

Arthur Campbell Ainger 1841–1919

English schoolmaster

3 God is working his purpose out as year succeeds to
  year;
God is working his purpose out and the time is
  drawing near;
Nearer and nearer draws the time, the time that shall
  surely be,
When the earth shall be filled with the glory of God as
  the waters cover the sea.
  'God is working his purpose out' (1894 hymn)

Max Aitken

See LORD BEAVERBROOK

Mark Akenside 1721–70

English poet and physician

4 Mind, mind alone, bear witness, earth and heaven!
The living fountains in itself contains
Of beauteous and sublime.
  The Pleasures of Imagination (1744) bk. 1, l. 481

5   Nor ever yet
The melting rainbow's vernal-tinctured hues
To me have shone so pleasing, as when first
The hand of science pointed out the path
In which the sun-beams gleaming from the west
Fall on the wat'ry cloud.
  The Pleasures of Imagination (1744) bk. 2, l. 103

Anna Akhmatova 1889–1966

Russian poet

6 Все расхищено, предано, продано,
Черной смерти мелькало крыло.

All has been looted, betrayed, sold; black death's wing
flashed ahead.
  'All has been Looted' (1921) (translated by Dmitri
  Obolensky)

7 Меня, как реку,
Суровая эпоха повернула.
Мне подменили жизнь. В другое русло,
Мимо другого потекла она,
И я своих не знаю берегов.

As if I were a river
The harsh age changed my course,
Replaced one life with another,
Flowing in a different channel
And I do not recognize my shores.
  'As if I were a River' (1944) (translated by Amanda
  Haight)

8 Есть в близости людей заветная черта,
Ее не перейти влюбленности и страсти,
Пусть в жуткой тишине сливаются уста,
И сердце рвется от любви на части.

In human intimacy there is a secret boundary; neither
the experience of being in love nor passion can cross
it, though lips be joined together in awful silence, and
the heart break asunder with love.
  'In Human Intimacy' (1915) (translated by Dmitri
  Obolensky)

9 Я над будущим тайно колдую,
Если вечер совсем голубой,
И предчувствую встречу вторую,
Неизбежную встречу с тобой.

Yet I secretly cast spells over the future, whenever the
evenings are quite blue, and I have a foreboding of a
second meeting, an inevitable meeting, with you.
  'I Think of you Seldom' (1923) (translated by Dmitri
  Obolensky)

10 Есть три эпохи у воспоминаний.
И первая — как бы вчерашний день.
Душа под сводом их благословенным,
И тело в их блаженствует тени.

Memories have three epochs,
And the first is like yesterday.
The soul is under their blessed vault,
and the body is in the bliss of their shadow.
  Northern Elegies (1953) (translated by Richard McKane)

11 Это было когда улыбался
Только мертвый, спокойствию рад.

It was a time when only the dead smiled, happy in
their peace.
  Requiem (1935–40) (translated by Richard McKane)

12 Звезды смерти стояли над нами,
И безвинная корчилась
Под кровавыми сапогами
И под шинами черных марусь.

Stars of death stood over us,
and innocent Russia squirmed
under the bloody boots,
under the wheels of black Marias.
  Requiem (1935–40) (translated by Richard McKane)

Zoë Akins 1886–1958

American poet and playwright

13 The Greeks had a word for it.
  Title of play (1930)

William Alabaster 1567–1640

English divine and Latin poet

1 Away, fear, with thy projects, no false fire
Which thou dost make can aught my courage quail,
Or cause me leeward run or strike my sail.
What if the world do frown at my retire,
What if denial dash my wished desire . . .
Tell them, my soul, the fears that make me quake:
The smouldering brimstone and the burning lake,
Life feeding death, death ever life devouring,
Torments not moved, unheard, yet still roaring,
God lost, hell found,—ever, never begun.
Now bid me into flame from smoke to run!
  'Away, fear, with thy projects' (written 1597–8)

Alain (Émile-Auguste Chartier) 1868–1951

French poet and philosopher

2 *Rien n'est plus dangereux qu'une idée, quand on n'a qu'une idée.*

Nothing is more dangerous than an idea, when you have only one idea.
  Propos sur la religion (1938) no. 74

Alain-Fournier (Henri Alban) 1886–1914

French novelist

3 *Mais quelqu'un est venu qui m'a enlevé à tous ces plaisirs d'enfant paisible. Quelqu'un a soufflé la bougie qui éclairait pour moi le doux visage maternel penché sur le repas du soir. Quelqu'un a éteint la lampe autour de laquelle nous étions une famille heureuse, à la nuit, lorsque mon père avait accroché les volets de bois aux portes vitrées. Et celui-là, ce fut Augustin Meaulnes, que les autres élèves appelèrent bientôt le grand Meaulnes.*

But someone came and put an end to these mild and childish pleasures. Someone blew out the candle which illumined for me the sweet maternal face bent over the evening meal. Someone extinguished the lamp around which we had been a happy family group at night-time when my father had closed all the wooden shutters. And that someone was Augustin Meaulnes, whom in no time the other boys began to call le grand Meaulnes.
  Le Grand Meaulnes (1912) pt. 1, ch. 2 (translated by Frank Davison)

4 *Quand on a, disait-il, commis quelque lourde faute impardonnable, on songe parfois, au milieu d'une grande amertume: 'Il y a pourtant par le monde des gens qui me pardonneraient'. On imagine de vieilles gens, des grandparents pleins d'indulgence, qui sont persuadés à l'avance que tout ce que vous faites est bien fait.*

When you've done something inexcusable, you try to ease your conscience by telling yourself that someone, somewhere would forgive you. You think of old people, perhaps indulgent grandparents, who are convinced that whatever you do is right.
  Le Grand Meaulnes (1912) pt. 1, ch. 14 (translated by Frank Davison)

5 *Notre aventure est finie. L'hiver de cette année est mort comme la tombe. Peut-être quand nous mourrons, peut-être la mort seule nous donnera la clef et la suite et la fin de cette aventure manquée.*

Our adventure is ended. The winter of this year is as dead as the grave. Perhaps when we come to die, death will provide the meaning and the sequel and the ending of this unsuccessful adventure.
  Le Grand Meaulnes (1912) pt. 2, ch. 12 (translated by Frank Davison)

6 *Un homme qui a fait une fois un bond dans le paradis, comment pourrait-il s'accommoder ensuite de la vie de tout le monde?*

How can a man who has once strayed into Heaven ever hope to make terms with the earth!
  Le Grand Meaulnes (1912) pt. 3, ch. 4 (translated by Frank Davison)

7 *C'est d'abord comme une voix tremblante qui, de très loin, ose à peine chanter sa joie . . . Cet air que je ne connais pas, c'est aussi une prière, une supplication au bonheur de ne pas être trop cruel, un salut et comme un agenouillement devant le bonheur.*

It is at first like some far-away tentative voice intimidated by an excess of joy . . . This melody, which I've never heard before, is a kind of prayer to happiness, an entreaty asking fate not to be too cruel, a salutation to happiness and at the same time a genuflexion.
  Le Grand Meaulnes (1912) pt. 3, ch. 7 (translated by Frank Davison)

Edward Albee 1928–

American playwright

8 I have a fine sense of the ridiculous, but no sense of humour.
  Who's Afraid of Virginia Woolf? (1962) act 1

Prince Albert (Albert Francis Charles Augustus Emmanuel of Saxe-Coburg-Gotha) 1819–61

Consort of Queen Victoria from 1840

9 The works of art, by being publicly exhibited and offered for sale, are becoming articles of trade, following as such the unreasoning laws of markets and fashion; and public and even private patronage is swayed by their tyrannical influence.
  Speech at the Royal Academy Dinner, 3 May 1851, in *Addresses* (1857) p. 101

Scipione Alberti

10 *I pensieri stretti ed il viso sciolto* [Secret thoughts and open countenance] will go safely over the whole world.
  On being asked how to behave in Rome, quoted in letter from Sir Henry Wotton to John Milton, 13 April 1638, prefixed to *Comus* in Milton *Poems* (1645 ed.)

Mary Alcock c.1742–98

English poet

1 A masquerade, a murdered peer,
His throat just cut from ear to ear—
A rake turned hermit—a fond maid
Run mad, by some false loon betrayed—
These stores supply the female pen,
Which writes them o'er and o'er again,
And readers likewise may be found
To circulate them round and round.
   'A Receipt for Writing a Novel' l. 65

Alcuin c.735–804

English scholar and theologian

2 *Nec audiendi qui solent dicere, Vox populi, vox Dei, quum tumultuositas vulgi semper insaniae proxima sit.*

And those people should not be listened to who keep saying the voice of the people is the voice of God, since the riotousness of the crowd is always very close to madness.
   Letter 164 in *Works* (1863) vol. 1, p. 438

Richard Aldington 1892–1962

English poet, novelist, and biographer

3 Patriotism is a lively sense of collective responsibility. Nationalism is a silly cock crowing on its own dunghill.
   The Colonel's Daughter (1931) pt. 1, ch. 6

Brian Aldiss 1925–

English science fiction writer

4 Keep violence in the mind
Where it belongs.
   Barefoot in the Head (1969) 'Charteris' *ad fin.*

Henry Aldrich 1647–1710

English scholar; Dean of Christ Church, Oxford, from 1689

5 If all be true that I do think,
There are five reasons we should drink;
Good wine—a friend—or being dry—
Or lest·we should be by and by—
Or any other reason why.
   'Reasons for Drinking' (1689)

Thomas Bailey Aldrich 1836–1907

American writer

6   The fair, frail palaces,
The fading alps and archipelagoes,
And great cloud-continents of sunset-seas.
   'Miracles' (1874)

'Buzz' Aldrin (Edwin Eugene Aldrin Jnr) 1930–

American astronaut; second man on the moon

7 Houston, Tranquillity Base here. The Eagle has landed.
   In *The Times* 21 July 1969, p. 1

Alexander the Great 356–323 BC

King of Macedon from 336 BC

8 εἰ μὴ Ἀλέξανδρος ἤμην, Διογένης ἂν ἤμην.
If I were not Alexander, I would be Diogenes.
   In Plutarch *Parallel Lives* 'Alexander' ch. 14, sect. 3

Cecil Frances Alexander 1818–95

Irish poet

9 All things bright and beautiful,
All creatures great and small,
All things wise and wonderful,
The Lord God made them all.
   'All Things Bright and Beautiful' (1848)

10 The rich man in his castle,
The poor man at his gate,
God made them, high or lowly,
And ordered their estate.
   'All Things Bright and Beautiful' (1848)

11 Once in royal David's city
Stood a lowly cattle-shed,
Where a mother laid her baby
In a manger for his bed:
Mary was that mother mild,
Jesus Christ her little child.
   'Once in royal David's city' (1848)

12 With the poor and mean and lowly
Lived on earth our saviour holy.
   'Once in royal David's city' (1848)

13 Christian children all must be
Mild, obedient, good as he.
   'Once in royal David's city' (1848)

14 For he is our childhood's pattern
Day by day like us he grew,
He was little, weak, and helpless,
Tears and smiles like us he knew;
And he feeleth for our sadness,
And he shareth in our gladness.
   'Once in royal David's city' (1848)

15 I bind unto myself to-day
The strong name of the Trinity,
By invocation of the same
The Three in One and One in Three.
   Translation of 'St Patrick's Breastplate' (1889)

16 There is a green hill far away,
Without a city wall,
Where the dear Lord was crucified,
Who died to save us all.

We may not know, we cannot tell,
What pains he had to bear,
But we believe it was for us
He hung and suffered there.
   'There is a green hill far away' (1848)

Sir William Alexander, Earl of Stirling
c.1567–1640
Scottish poet and courtier

1 The weaker sex, to piety more prone.
   'Doomsday' 5th Hour (1637)

Alfonso 'the Wise' 1221–84
King of Castile and León from 1252

2 Had I been present at the Creation, I would have
   given some useful hints for the better ordering of the
   universe.
   On studying the Ptolemaic system (attributed)

Alfred the Great AD 849–99
King of Wessex from AD 871

3 Ða ic ða gemunde hu sio lar Lædengeðiodes ær ðissum
   afeallen wæs giond Angelcynn, ond ðeah monige cuðon
   Englisc gewrit arædan, ða ongan ic on gemang oðrum
   mislicum ond manigfealdum bisgum ðisses kynerices ða
   boc on Englisc ðe is genemned on Læden Pastoralis, ond
   on Englisc Hierdeboc, hwilum word be worde, hwilum
   andgit of andgite.

   When I recalled how knowledge of Latin had
   previously decayed throughout England, and yet many
   could still read things written in English, I then began,
   amidst the various and multifarious afflictions of this
   kingdom, to translate into English the book which in
   Latin is called *Pastoralis*, in English 'Shepherd-book',
   sometimes word for word, sometimes sense for sense.
   Preface to the Anglo-Saxon version of St Gregory's *Pastoral
   Care* (translated by S. Keynes and M. Lapidge, 1983)

Nelson Algren 1909–
American novelist

4 A walk on the wild side.
   Title of novel (1956)

5 Never play cards with a man called Doc. Never eat at
   a place called Mom's. Never sleep with a woman
   whose troubles are worse than your own.
   In *Newsweek* 2 July 1956

Muhammad Ali (Cassius Clay) 1942–
American boxer

6 Float like a butterfly, sting like a bee.
   Summary of his boxing strategy, in G. Sullivan *Cassius Clay
   Story* (1964) ch. 8 (probably originated by Drew 'Bundini'
   Brown). *See* W. Sheed *Muhammad Ali* (1975) p. 51

Abbé d'Allainval 1700–53
French playwright

7 L'embarras des richesses.
   The embarrassment of riches.
   Title of comedy (1726)

Fred Allen (John Florence Sullivan)
1894–1956
American humorist

8 Committee—a group of men who individually can do
   nothing but as a group decide that nothing can be
   done.
   Attributed

Woody Allen (Allen Stewart Konigsberg)
1935–
American film director, writer, and actor

9 That [sex] was the most fun I ever had without
   laughing.
   Annie Hall (1977 film, with Marshall Brickman)

10 Don't knock masturbation. It's sex with someone
   I love.
   Annie Hall (1977 film, with Marshall Brickman)

11 Is sex dirty? Only if it's done right.
   Everything You Always Wanted to Know about Sex (1972
   film)

12 If it turns out that there is a God, I don't think that
   he's evil. But the worst that you can say about him is
   that basically he's an underachiever.
   Love and Death (1975 film)

13 My brain? It's my second favourite organ.
   Sleeper (1973 film, with Marshall Brickman)

14 A fast word about oral contraception. I asked a girl to
   go to bed with me and she said 'no'.
   Woody Allen Volume Two (Colpix CP. 488) side 4, band 6

15 It's not that I'm afraid to die. I just don't want to be
   there when it happens.
   Death (1975) p. 63

16 Money is better than poverty, if only for financial
   reasons.
   Without Feathers (1976) 'Early Essays'

17 If only God would give me some clear sign! Like
   making a large deposit in my name at a Swiss bank.
   'Selections from the Allen Notebooks' in *New Yorker*
   5 November 1973

18 On bisexuality: It immediately doubles your chances
   for a date on Saturday night.
   New York Times 1 December 1975, p. 33

19 I don't want to achieve immortality through my work
   . . . I want to achieve it through not dying.
   In Eric Lax *Woody Allen and his Comedy* (1975) ch. 12

Margery Allingham 1904–66
English crime fiction writer

20 Once sex rears its ugly 'ead it's time to steer clear.
   Flowers for the Judge (1936) ch. 4. Cf. Ayckbourn 40:7

William Allingham 1828–89

Irish poet

1 Up the airy mountain,
  Down the rushy glen,
  We daren't go a-hunting,
  For fear of little men.
  'The Fairies' (1850)

2 Four ducks on a pond,
  A grass-bank beyond,
  A blue sky of spring,
  White clouds on the wing:
  What a little thing
  To remember for years—
  To remember with tears!
  'A Memory' (1888)

Joseph Alsop b. 1910

American journalist

3 Gratitude, like love, is never a dependable
  international emotion.
  In *Observer* 30 November 1952

Robert Altman 1922–

American film director

4 What's a cult? It just means not enough people to
  make a minority.
  In *Guardian* 11 April 1981

St Ambrose c.339–97

French-born bishop of Milan

5 *Ubi Petrus, ibi ergo ecclesia.*

  Where Peter is, there must be the Church.
  'Explanatio psalmi 40' in *Corpus Scriptorum Ecclesiasticorum
  Latinorum* (1919) vol. 64, p. 250

6 *Cum Romanum venio, ieiuno Sabbato; cum hic sum, non
  ieiuno: sic etiam tu, ad quam forte ecclesiam veneris, eius
  morem serva, si cuiquam non vis esse scandalum nec
  quemquam tibi.*

  When I go to Rome, I fast on Saturday, but here
  [Milan] I do not. Do you also follow the custom of
  whatever church you attend, if you do not want to
  give or receive scandal.
  In *St Augustine: Letters* vol. 1 (translated by Sister W.
  Parsons, 1951) 'Letter 54 to Januarius' (AD c.400). Cf.
  Taylor 679:17

Leo Amery 1873–1955

British Conservative politician

7 For twenty years he has held a season-ticket on the
  line of least resistance and has gone wherever the
  train of events has carried him, lucidly justifying his
  position at whatever point he has happened to find
  himself.
  On Herbert Asquith, in *Quarterly Review* July 1914, p. 276

8 Speak for England.
  Said to Arthur Greenwood in House of Commons,
  2 September 1939, in *My Political Life* (1955) vol. 3, p. 324

Fisher Ames 1758–1808

American politician

9 A monarchy is a merchantman which sails well, but
  will sometimes strike on a rock, and go to the bottom;
  whilst a republic is a raft which would never sink, but
  then your feet are always in the water.
  Attributed to Ames, speaking in the House of
  Representatives, 1795; quoted by R. W. Emerson in *Essays*
  (2nd series, 1844) no. 7, but not traced in Ames's speeches

Sir Kingsley Amis 1922–

English novelist and poet

10 'Promise me you'll always treat me as a person' . . .
   Experience had brought him to see that this kind of
   thing was nothing more than the levying of cock-tax
   . . . [he] had likened it in the past to the proclamations
   of a dictator, full of talk about ethnic integrity and his
   historic mission, when all he wanted was to seize the
   industry and mineral wealth of some helpless,
   peaceable neighbouring state.
   Difficulties with Girls (1988) ch. 9

11 The delusion that there are thousands of young people
   about who are capable of benefiting from university
   training, but have somehow failed to find their way
   there, is . . . a necessary component of the
   expansionist case . . . More will mean worse.
   Encounter July 1960

12 If there's one word that sums up everything that's
   gone wrong since the War, it's Workshop.
   Jake's Thing (1979) ch. 14

13 The light did him harm, but not as much as looking at
   things did; he resolved, having done it once, never to
   move his eyeballs again. A dusty thudding in his head
   made the scene before him beat like a pulse. His
   mouth had been used as a latrine by some small
   creature of the night, and then as its mausoleum.
   Lucky Jim (1953) ch. 6

14 Alun's life was coming to consist more and more
   exclusively of being told at dictation speed what he
   knew.
   The Old Devils (1986) ch. 7

15 Outside every fat man there was an even fatter man
   trying to close in.
   One Fat Englishman (1963) ch. 3. Cf. Connolly 216:17,
   Orwell 499:23

16 He was of the faith chiefly in the sense that the
   church he currently did not attend was Catholic.
   One Fat Englishman (1963) ch. 8

17 At the end of the line today was a creature looking
   like a giant mad sheep that had just been bundled into
   a coat of the colour Jenny called depressing red . . . If
   that was a mother, nobody ever needed lose hope of
   anything.
   Take a Girl Like You (1960) ch. 2

18 Should poets bicycle-pump the human heart
   Or squash it flat?
   Man's love is of man's life a thing apart;
   Girls aren't like that.
   'A Bookshop Idyll' (1956). Cf. Byron 170:13

1 We men have got love well weighed up; our stuff
Can get by without it.
Women don't seem to think that's good enough;
They write about it.
'A Bookshop Idyll' (1956)

2 Women are really much nicer than men:
No wonder we like them.
'A Bookshop Idyll' (1956)

3 Death has got something to be said for it:
There's no need to get out of bed for it;
Wherever you may be,
They bring it to you, free.
'Delivery Guaranteed' (1979)

4 The women of that ever-fresh terrain,
The night after tonight.
'A Dream of Fair Women' (1956)

Anacharsis

Scythian prince of the sixth century BC

5 Written laws are like spider's webs; they will catch, it
is true, the weak and poor, but would be torn in
pieces by the rich and powerful.
Plutarch *Parallel Lives* 'Solon' bk. 5, sect. 2. Cf. Shenstone
644:14, Swift 673:5

Anatolius

8th-century hymn-writer

6 Fierce was the wild billow,
Dark was the night;
Oars laboured heavily,
Foam glimmered white;
Trembled the mariners,
Peril was nigh:
Then said the God of God,
'Peace! it is I.'
'Fierce was the wild billow' (translated by John Mason
Neale, 1862)

Hans Christian Andersen 1805–75

Danish novelist and writer of fairy stories

7 'But the Emperor has nothing on at all!' cried a little
child.
Danish Fairy Legends and Tales (1846) 'The Emperor's New
Clothes'

Maxwell Anderson 1888–1959

American playwright

8 But it's a long, long while
From May to December;
And the days grow short
When you reach September.
'September Song' (1938 song; music by Kurt Weill)

Maxwell Anderson 1888–1959 *and* Lawrence Stallings 1894–1968

American playwrights

9 What price glory?
Title of play (1924)

Robert Anderson 1917–

American playwright

10 All you're supposed to do is every once in a while give
the boys a little tea and sympathy.
Tea and Sympathy (1957) act 1

Lancelot Andrewes 1555–1626

*English preacher and writer of sermons; bishop,
successively, of Chichester, Ely, and Winchester*

11 What shall become of me (said Righteousness)? What
use of Justice, if God will do no justice, if he spare
sinners? And what use of me (saith Mercy), if he spare
them not? Hard hold there was, inasmuch as, *Perii,
nisi homo moriatur* (said Righteousness) I die, if he die
not: And *Perii, nisi Misericordiam consequatur* (said
Mercy) if he die, I die too.
Of the Nativity (1616) Sermon 11. Cf. Milton 470:17

12 *Verbum infans*, the Word without a word, not able to
speak a word . . . He, that . . . taketh the vast body of
the main Sea, turns it to and fro, as a little child, and
rolls it about with the swaddling bands of darkness;
He, to come thus into clouts, himself!
Of the Nativity (1618) Sermon 12

13 It was no summer progress. A cold coming they had
of it, at this time of the year; just, the worst time of
the year, to take a journey, and specially a long
journey, in. The ways deep, the weather sharp, the
days short, the sun farthest off *in solstitio brumali*, the
very dead of Winter.
Of the Nativity (1622) Sermon 15. Cf. Eliot 271:17

14 The nearer the Church the further from God.
Of the Nativity (1622) Sermon 15

Sir Norman Angell 1872–1967

English pacifist

15 The great illusion.
Title of book (1910) on the futility of war, first published as
'Europe's optical illusion' (1909)

Anonymous

English

16 An abomination unto the Lord, but a very present
help in time of trouble.
Definition of a lie, an amalgamation of Proverbs 12.22 and
Psalms 46.1, often attributed to Adlai Stevenson. See Bill
Adler *The Stevenson Wit* (1966) p. 84

17 Absence makes the heart grow fonder.
In T. H. Bayly *Isle of Beauty* (revised ed., 1850); Sextus
Propertius *Elegies* bk. 2, no. 33, l. 43 has *Semper in absentes
felicior aestus amantes*

18 Adam
Had 'em.
On the antiquity of microbes (claimed to be the shortest
poem)

19 All human beings are born free and equal in dignity
and rights.
Universal Declaration of Human Rights (1948) article 1

1 All present and correct.
  King's Regulations (*Army*) Report of the Orderly Sergeant to the Officer of the Day

2 All this buttoning and unbuttoning.
  18th-century suicide note

3 The almighty dollar is the only object of worship.
  Philadelphia Public Ledger 2 December 1836

4 Along the electric wire the message came:
  He is not better—he is much the same.
  Parodic poem on the illness of the Prince of Wales, later King Edward VII, in F. H. Gribble *Romance of the Cambridge Colleges* (1913) p. 226; sometimes attributed to Alfred Austin (1835–1913), Poet Laureate

5 Any officer who shall behave in a scandalous manner, unbecoming the character of an officer and a gentleman shall . . . be CASHIERED.
  Articles of War (1872) 'Disgraceful Conduct' Article 79; the Naval Discipline Act, 10 August 1860, Article 24, uses the words 'conduct unbecoming the character of an Officer'

6 Appeal from Philip drunk to Philip sober.
  Paraphrase of the words of an unidentified woman in Valerius Maximus *Facta ac Dicta Memorabilia* (AD *c.*32) bk. 6, ch. 2

7 Are we downhearted? No!
  Expression much taken up by British soldiers during the First World War. Cf. Chamberlain 189:5

8 A-roving! A-roving!
  Since roving's been my ru-i-n
  I'll go no more a-roving
  With you fair maid.
  'A-roving' (traditional song)

9 A was an apple-pie;
  B bit it;
  C cut it.
  In John Eachard *Some Observations* (1671) p. 140

10 A bayonet is a weapon with a worker at each end.
  British pacifist slogan (1940)

11 A beast, but a just beast.
  Describing Dr Temple, Headmaster of Rugby School, 1857–69. See F. E. Kitchener *Rugby Memoir of Archbishop Temple 1857–1869* (1907) ch. 3

12 Be happy while y'er leevin,
  For y'er a lang time deid.
  Scottish motto for a house. See *Notes and Queries* 9th series, vol. 8, 7 December 1901, p. 469

13 The best defence against the atom bomb is not to be there when it goes off.
  Contributor to *British Army Journal*, in *Observer* 20 February 1949

14 Better red than dead.
  Slogan of nuclear disarmament campaigners, late 1950s

15 Between a rock and a hard place.
  US colloquial phrase, meaning to be in difficulty without a satisfactory alternative. See *Dialect Notes* (1921) no. 5, p. 113

16 Bigamy is having one husband too many. Monogamy is the same.
  In Erica Jong *Fear of Flying* (1973) ch. 1 (epigraph)

17 A bigger bang for a buck.
  Charles E. Wilson's defence policy, in *Newsweek* 22 March 1954

18 Black is beautiful.
  Slogan of American civil rights campaigners, mid-1960s

19 Burn, baby, burn.
  Black extremist slogan in use during the Los Angeles riots, August 1965

20 Careless talk costs lives.
  Second World War security slogan (popularly inverted as 'careless lives cost talk')

21 The children in Holland take pleasure in making
  What the children in England take pleasure in breaking.
  Nursery rhyme

22 The cloud of unknowing.
  Title of mystical prose work (14th century)

23 Collapse of Stout Party.
  Standard dénouement in Victorian humour. See R. Pearsall *Collapse of Stout Party* (1975) introduction

24 Come, landlord, fill the flowing bowl
  Until it doth run over . . .
  For to-night we'll merry be,
  To-morrow we'll be sober.
  'Come, Landlord, Fill the Flowing Bowl' (traditional song)

25 Come lasses and lads, get leave of your dads,
  And away to the Maypole hie,
  For every he has got him a she,
  And the fiddler's standing by.
  For Willie shall dance with Jane,
  And Johnny has got his Joan,
  To trip it, trip it, trip it, trip it, trip it up and down.
  'Come Lasses and Lads' (traditional song, *c.*1670)

26 A committee is a group of the unwilling, chosen from the unfit, to do the unnecessary.
  Various attributions (origin unknown)

27 A Company for carrying on an undertaking of Great Advantage, but no one to know what it is.
  The South Sea Company Prospectus (1711), in Virginia Cowles *The Great Swindle* (1963) ch. 5

28 Conduct . . . to the prejudice of good order and military discipline.
  Army Discipline and Regulation Act (1879) Section 40

29 Coughs and sneezes spread diseases. Trap the germs in your handkerchief.
  Second World War health slogan (1942)

30 Crisis? What Crisis?
  Sun headline, 11 January 1979, summarizing James Callaghan's remark of 10 January 1979: 'I don't think other people in the world would share the view [that] there is mounting chaos'

31 Death [is] nature's way of telling you to slow down.
  American life insurance proverb, in *Newsweek* 25 April 1960, p. 70

32 Defence, not defiance.
  Motto of the Volunteers Movement (1859)

33 Do not fold, spindle or mutilate.
  Instruction on punched cards (found in this form in the 1950s, and in differing forms from the 1930s)

34 Early one morning, just as the sun was rising,
  I heard a maid sing in the valley below:
  'Oh, don't deceive me; Oh, never leave me!
  How could you use a poor maiden so?'
  'Early One Morning' (traditional song)

1 Earned a precarious living by taking in one another's washing.

> Attributed to Mark Twain by William Morris, in *The Commonweal* 6 August 1887

2 The eternal triangle.

> Book review title, in *Daily Chronicle* 5 December 1907

3 Every country has its own constitution; ours is absolutism moderated by assassination.

> Ernst Friedrich Herbert, Count Münster, quoting 'an intelligent Russian', in *Political Sketches of the State of Europe, 1814–1867* (1868) p. 19

4 Everyman, I will go with thee, and be thy guide,
In thy most need to go by thy side.

> *Everyman* (*c*.1509–19) l. 522 (lines spoken by Knowledge)

5 Every picture tells a story.

> Advertisement for Doan's Backache Kidney Pills (early 1900s)

6 Expletive deleted.

> *Submission of Recorded Presidential Conversations to the Committee on the Judiciary of the House of Representatives by President Richard M. Nixon* 30 April 1974, appendix 1, p. 2

7 Exterminate . . . the treacherous English, walk over General French's contemptible little army.

> Annexe to BEF [British Expeditionary Force] Routine Orders of 24 September 1914, in Arthur Ponsonby *Falsehood in Wartime* (1928) ch. 10 (allegedly 'a copy of Orders issued by the German Emperor' [Kaiser Wilhelm II] but most probably fabricated by the British)

8 Faster than a speeding bullet! . . . Look! Up in the sky! It's a bird! It's a plane! It's Superman! Yes, it's Superman! Strange visitor from another planet . . . Who can change the course of mighty rivers, bend steel with his bare hands, and who—disguised as Clark Kent, mild-mannered reporter for a great metropolitan newspaper—fights a never ending battle for truth, justice and the American way!

> *Superman* (US radio show, 1940 onwards) preamble

9 The fault is great in man or woman
Who steals a goose from off a common;
But what can plead that man's excuse
Who steals a common from a goose?

> In *The Tickler Magazine* 1 February 1821

10 A form of statuary which no careful father would wish his daughter, or no discerning young man his fiancée, to see.

> On Jacob Epstein's sculptures for the former BMA building in the Strand, London, in *Evening Standard* 19 June 1908

11 Frankie and Albert were lovers, O Lordy, how they could love.
Swore to be true to each other, true as the stars above;
He was her man, but he done her wrong.

> 'Frankie and Albert', in John Huston *Frankie and Johnny* (1930) p. 95 (St Louis ballad later better known as 'Frankie and Johnny')

12 From ghoulies and ghosties and long-leggety beasties
And things that go bump in the night,
Good Lord, deliver us!

> 'The Cornish or West Country Litany', in Francis T. Nettleinghame *Polperro Proverbs and Others* (1926) 'Pokerwork Panels'

13 From shirtsleeves to shirtsleeves in three generations.

> In Nicholas Murray Butler *True and False Democracy* (1907) ch. 2 (often attributed to Andrew Carnegie (1835–1919) but not found in his writings)

14 A gentleman haranguing on the perfection of our law, and that it was equally open to the poor and the rich, was answered by another, 'So is the London Tavern'.

> *Tom Paine's Jests* (1794) no. 23; also attributed to John Horne Tooke (1736–1812) in W. Hazlitt *The Spirit of the Age* (1825) 'Mr Horne Tooke'. Cf. Mathew 453:17

15 Give me a child for the first seven years, and you may do what you like with him afterwards.

> Attributed as a Jesuit maxim, in *Lean's Collectanea* vol. 3 (1903) p. 472

16 God be in my head,
And in my understanding;

God be in my eyes,
And in my looking;

God be in my mouth,
And in my speaking;

God be in my heart,
And in my thinking;

God be at my end,
And at my departing.

> *Sarum Missal* (11th century)

17 God gave Noah the rainbow sign,
No more water, the fire next time.

> *Home in that Rock* (Negro spiritual)

18 God save our gracious king!
Long live our noble king!
God save the king!

> 'God save the King', attributed to various authors, including Henry Carey; see Percy Scholes *God save the King* (1942). Cf. Hogg 341:17

19 Confound their politics,
Frustrate their knavish tricks.

> 'God save the King'

20 Good at a fight, but better at a play,
Godlike in giving, but—the devil to pay!

> Lines written on a cast from Sheridan's hand, in Thomas Moore *Memoirs of the Life of . . . Richard Brinsley Sheridan* (1825) ch. 21, p. 712

21 Great Chatham with his sabre drawn
Stood waiting for Sir Richard Strachan;
Sir Richard, longing to be at 'em,
Stood waiting for the Earl of Chatham.

> 'At Walcheren, 1809'; attributed to Joseph Jekyll (1753–1837)

22 Greensleeves was all my joy,
Greensleeves was my delight,
Greensleeves was my heart of gold,
And who but Lady Greensleeves?

> 'A new Courtly Sonnet of the Lady Greensleeves, to the new tune of "Greensleeves"', in *A Handful of Pleasant Delights* (1584)

1 Happy is that city which in time of peace thinks of war.

> Inscription found in the armoury of Venice, in Robert Burton *The Anatomy of Melancholy* (1621–51) pt. 2, sect. 3, member 6. Cf. Vegetius 710:1

2 Have you heard? The Prime Minister has resigned and Northcliffe has sent for the King.

> Joke circulating in 1919, on Lord Northcliffe succeeding Lloyd George as Prime Minister; in Hamilton Fyfe *Northcliffe, an Intimate Biography* (1930) ch. 16

3 He may be one of its [the Church's] buttresses, but certainly not one of its pillars, for he is never found within it.

> Said of John Scott, Lord Eldon (1751–1838), in H. Twiss *Public and Private Life of Eldon* (1844) vol. 3, p. 489 (later attributed to Lord Melbourne)

4 Here lies a poor woman who always was tired,
For she lived in a place where help wasn't hired.
Her last words on earth were, Dear friends I am going
Where washing ain't done nor sweeping nor sewing,
And everything there is exact to my wishes,
For there they don't eat and there's no washing of dishes . . .
Don't mourn for me now, don't mourn for me never,
For I'm going to do nothing for ever and ever.

> Epitaph in Bushey churchyard, before 1860; destroyed by 1916

5 Here lies a valiant warrior
Who never drew a sword;
Here lies a noble courtier
Who never kept his word;
Here lies the Earl of Leicester
Who governed the estates
Whom the earth could never living love,
And the just heaven now hates.

> Attributed to Ben Jonson in Silvester Tissington *A Collection of Epitaphs and Monumental Inscriptions* (1857) p. 377

6 Here lies Fred,
Who was alive and is dead:
Had it been his father,
I had much rather;
Had it been his brother,
Still better than another;
Had it been his sister,
No one would have missed her;
Had it been the whole generation,
Still better for the nation:
But since 'tis only Fred,
Who was alive and is dead,—
There's no more to be said.

> In Horace Walpole *Memoirs of George II* (1847) vol. 1, p. 436

7 Here's tae us; wha's like us?
Gey few, and they're a' deid.

> Scottish Toast, probably of 19th-century origin. The first line appears in T. W. H. Crosland *The Unspeakable Scot* (1902) p. 24 n.; various versions of the second line are current

8 He talked shop like a tenth muse.

> On Gladstone's Budget speeches, in G. W. E. Russell *Collections and Recollections* (1898) ch. 12

9 He tickles this age that can
Call Tullia's ape a marmasyte
And Leda's goose a swan.

> 'Fara diddle dyno', in Thomas Weelkes *Airs or Fantastic Spirits* (1608); reprinted in N. Ault *Elizabethan Lyrics* (1925)

10 Hierusalem, my happy home
When shall I come to thee?
When shall my sorrows have an end,
Thy joys when shall I see?

> 'Hierusalem' (*c.*1600 hymn)

11 The holly and the ivy,
When they are both full grown,
Of all the trees that are in the wood,
The holly bears the crown:
The rising of the sun
And the running of the deer,
The playing of the merry organ,
Sweet singing in the choir.

> 'The Holly and the Ivy' (traditional carol)

12 How different, how very different from the home life of our own dear Queen!

> Comment overheard at a performance of Cleopatra by Sarah Bernhardt, in Irvin S. Cobb *A Laugh a Day* (1924) (probably apocryphal)

13 I can not eat but little meat,
My stomach is not good:
But sure I think, that I can drink
With him that wears a hood.
Though I go bare, take ye no care,
I am nothing acold:
I stuff my skin, so full within,
Of jolly good ale and old,
Back and side go bare, go bare,
Both foot and hand go cold:
But belly God send thee good ale enough,
Whether it be new or old.

> *Gammer Gurton's Needle* (1575) act 2 'Song', the play being attributed to William Stevenson (*c.*1530–75) and also to John Still (1543–1608), the song possibly of earlier origin

14 I don't like the family Stein!
There is Gert, there is Ep, there is Ein.
Gert's writings are punk,
Ep's statues are junk,
Nor can anyone understand Ein.

> Rhyme current in the USA in the 1920s, in R. Graves and A. Hodge *The Long Weekend* (1940) ch. 12

15 I feel no pain dear mother now
But oh, I am so dry!
O take me to a brewery
And leave me there to die.

> Parody of 'The Collier's Dying Child'. Cf. Farmer 280:5

16 If he only knew a little of law, he would know a little of everything.

> Said of Lord Brougham, in Ralph Waldo Emerson *Letters and Social Aims* (1877) 'Quotation and Originality'

17 If it moves, salute it; if it doesn't move, pick it up; and if you can't pick it up, paint it.

> 1940s saying, in Paul Dickson *The Official Rules* (1978) p. 21

1 I'll sing you twelve O.
Green grow the rushes O.
What is your twelve O?
Twelve for the twelve apostles,
Eleven for the eleven who went to heaven,
Ten for the ten commandments,
Nine for the nine bright shiners,
Eight for the eight bold rangers,
Seven for the seven stars in the sky,
Six for the six proud walkers,
Five for the symbol at your door,
Four for the Gospel makers,
Three for the rivals,
Two, two, the lily-white boys,
Clothed all in green O,
One is one and all alone
And ever more shall be so.

> 'The Dilly Song', in G. Grigson (ed.) *The Faber Book of Popular Verse* (1971). See Revd S. Baring-Gould and Revd H. Fleetwood Sheppard *Songs and Ballads of the West* (1891) no. 78 for a variant version

2 I'm armed with more than complete steel—The justice of my quarrel.

> *Lust's Dominion* (1657) act 4, sc. 3 (attributed to Marlowe, though of doubtful authorship)

3 I married my husband for life, not for lunch.

> Origin unknown

4 I met wid Napper Tandy, and he took me by the hand,
And he said, 'How's poor ould Ireland, and how does she stand?'
She's the most disthressful country that iver yet was seen,
For they're hangin' men an' women for the wearin' o' the Green.

> 'The Wearin' o' the Green' (*c*.1795 ballad)

5 In good King Charles's golden days,
When loyalty no harm meant;
A furious High-Churchman I was,
And so I gained preferment.
Unto my flock I daily preached,
Kings are by God appointed,
And damned are those who dare resist,
Or touch the Lord's Anointed.
And this is law, I will maintain,
Unto my dying day, Sir,
That whatsoever King shall reign,
I will be the Vicar of Bray, sir!

> 'The Vicar of Bray' in *British Musical Miscellany* (1734) vol. 1

6 I saw my lady weep,
And Sorrow proud to be exalted so
In those fair eyes where all perfections keep.
Her face was full of woe;
But such a woe, believe me, as wins more hearts,
Than Mirth can do with her enticing parts.

> Lute song set by John Dowland, in *New Oxford Book of Sixteenth-Century Verse* (1991)

7 It became necessary to destroy the town to save it.

> Statement by unidentified US Army Major, referring to Ben Tre in Vietnam, in Associated Press Report, *New York Times* 8 February 1968

8 It'll play in Peoria.

> Catch-phrase of the Nixon administration (early 1970s) meaning 'it will be acceptable to middle America', but originating in a standard music hall joke of the 1930s

9 It's taking your face in your hands.

> On the dangers of sitting for one's portrait to John Singer Sargent, in W. Graham Robertson *Time Was* (1931) ch. 21

10 It's that man again . . . ! At the head of a cavalcade of seven black motor cars Hitler swept out of his Berlin Chancellery last night on a mystery journey.

> Headline in *Daily Express* 2 May 1939; the acronym ITMA became the title of a BBC radio show, from September 1939

11 Jacques Brel is alive and well and living in Paris.

> Title of musical entertainment (1968–72) which triggered numerous imitations

12 John Brown's body lies a mould'ring in the grave,
His soul is marching on.

> Song (1861), variously attributed to Charles Sprague Hall, Henry Howard Brownell, Thomas Brigham Bishop, and inspired by the hanging of John Brown, an abolitionist, on 2 December 1859

13 Just when you thought it was safe to go back in the water.

> *Jaws 2* (1978 film) advertising copy

14 The King over the Water.

> Jacobite toast (18th-century)

15 King's Moll Reno'd in Wolsey's Home Town.

> US newspaper headline on Wallis Simpson's divorce proceedings in Ipswich, in Frances Donaldson *Edward VIII* (1974) ch. 7

16 Let's get out of these wet clothes and into a dry Martini.

> Line coined in the 1920s by Robert Benchley's press agent and adopted by Mae West in *Every Day's a Holiday* (1937 film). See Howard Teichmann *Smart Alec* (1976) ch. 9

17 Liberty is always unfinished business.

> Title of 36th Annual Report of the American Civil Liberties Union, 1 July 1955–30 June 1956

18 Life is a sexually transmitted disease.

> Graffito found on the London Underground, in D. J. Enright (ed.) *The Faber Book of Fevers and Frets* (1989) p. 345

19 Like a fine old English gentleman,
All of the olden time.

> 'The Fine Old English Gentleman' (traditional song)

20 Like Caesar's wife, all things to all men.

> Impartiality, as described by a newly-elected mayor, in G. W. E. Russell *Collections and Recollections* (1898) ch. 30

21 Little Englanders.

> *Westminster Gazette* 1 August 1895, p. 2 (phrase used to describe persons opposed to imperialism). *See Pall Mall Gazette* 16 September 1884, p. 1, for an early use of the phrase 'little England'

22 Lizzie Borden took an axe
And gave her mother forty whacks;
When she saw what she had done
She gave her father forty-one!

> Popular rhyme in circulation after the acquittal of Lizzie Borden, in June 1893, from the charge of murdering her father and stepmother at Fall River, Massachusetts on 4 August 1892

23 Lloyd George knew my father,
My father knew Lloyd George.

> Two-line comic song, sung to the tune of 'Onward, Christian Soldiers' and possibly by Tommy Rhys Roberts (1910–75)

24 London, thou art of townes *A per se.*

> 'London' (poem of unknown authorship, previously attributed to William Dunbar, *c*.1465–*c*.1530)

1 London, thou art the flower of cities all!
Gemme of all joy, jasper of jocunditie.
'London' l. 16

2 Fair be their wives, right lovesom, white and small.
'London' l. 46

3 Lousy but loyal.
London East End slogan at George V's Jubilee (1935)

4 Love me little, love me long,
Is the burden of my song.
'Love me little, love me long' (1569–70)

5 The lower organs of the Party in Britain must make
still greater efforts to penetrate the backward parts of
the proletariat.
In H. J. Eysenck *Rebel with a Cause* (1990)

6 Mademoiselle from Armenteers,
Hasn't been kissed for forty years,
Hinky, dinky, parley-voo.
Song of the First World War, variously attributed to Edward
Rowland and to Harry Carlton

7 CHILD: Mamma, are Tories born wicked, or do they
grow wicked afterwards?
MOTHER: They are born wicked, and grow worse.
In G. W. E. Russell *Collections and Recollections* (1898)
ch. 10

8 The man you love to hate.
Billing for Erich von Stroheim in the film *The Heart of
Humanity* (1918)

9 Matthew, Mark, Luke, and John,
The bed be blest that I lie on.
Four angels to my bed,
Four angels round my head,
One to watch, and one to pray,
And two to bear my soul away.
Traditional (the first two lines in Thomas Ady *A Candle in
the Dark*, 1656)

10 The ministry of all the talents.
Name given ironically to William Grenville's coalition of
1806, and also applied to later coalitions, in G. W. Cooke
The History of Party (1837) vol. 3, p. 460

11 Miss Buss and Miss Beale
Cupid's darts do not feel.
How different from us,
Miss Beale and Miss Buss.
Of the Headmistress of the North London Collegiate School
and the Principal of the Ladies' College, Cheltenham,
c.1884

12 Most Gracious Queen, we thee implore
To go away and sin no more,
But if that effort be too great,
To go away at any rate.
Epigram on Queen Caroline, quoted in a letter from Francis
Burton to Lord Colchester, 15 November 1820; in *Diary
and Correspondence of Lord Colchester* (1861) vol. 3, p. 181

13 Multiplication is vexation,
Division is as bad;
The Rule of Three doth puzzle me,
And Practice drives me mad.
In *Lean's Collectanea* vol. 4 (1904) p. 53 (possibly
16th-century)

14 My Love in her attire doth show her wit,
It doth so well become her:
For every season she hath dressings fit,
For winter, spring, and summer.
No beauty she doth miss,
When all her robes are on;
But beauty's self she is,
When all her robes are gone.
'Madrigal', in F. Davison (ed.) *Poetical Rhapsody* (1602)

15 My name is George Nathaniel Curzon,
I am a most superior person.
The Masque of Balliol (c.1870), in W. G. Hiscock *The Balliol
Rhymes* (1939) p. 19. Cf. Beeching 59:7, Spring-Rice
661:11

16 My sledge and anvil lie declined
My bellows too have lost their wind
My fire's extinct, my forge decayed,
And in the dust my vice is laid
My coals are spent, my iron's gone
My nails are drove, my work is done.
Blacksmith's epitaph in Nettlebed churchyard,
commemorating William Strange, d. 6 June 1746

17 The nature of God is a circle of which the centre is
everywhere and the circumference is nowhere.
Said to have been traced to a lost treatise of Empedocles;
quoted in the *Roman de la Rose*, and by St Bonaventura in
Itinerarius Mentis in Deum ch. 5 *ad fin.*

18 The nearest thing to death in life
Is David Patrick Maxwell Fyfe,
Though underneath that gloomy shell
He does himself extremely well.
In E. Grierson *Confessions of a Country Magistrate* (1972)
p. 35 (said to have been current on the Northern circuit in
the late 1930s)

19 *Nil carborundum illegitimi.*
Cod Latin for 'Don't let the bastards grind you down', in
circulation during the Second World War, though possibly
of earlier origin; often quoted '*nil carborundum*' or '*illegitimi
non carborundum*'

20 The noise, my dear! And the people!
Of the retreat from Dunkirk, May 1940. See Anthony
Rhodes *Sword of Bone* (1942) ch. 22 *ad fin.*

21 No more Latin, no more French,
No more sitting on a hard board bench.
No more beetles in my tea
Making googly eyes at me;
No more spiders in my bath
Trying hard to make me laugh.
Children's rhyme for the end of school term, in Iona and
Peter Opie *Lore and Language of Schoolchildren* (1959) ch. 13
(variants include 'No more Latin, no more Greek, / No
more cares to make me squeak')

22 Nostalgia isn't what it used to be.
Graffito (taken as title of book by Simone Signoret, 1978)

23 Not so much a programme, more a way of life!
Title of BBC television series, 1964

24 Now I lay me down to sleep;
I pray the Lord my soul to keep.
If I should die before I wake,
I pray the Lord my soul to take.
First printed in a late edition of the *New England Primer*
(1781)

1 O Death, where is thy sting-a-ling-a-ling,
O grave, thy victory?
The bells of Hell go ting-a-ling-a-ling
For you but not for me.

'For You But Not For Me', in S. Louis Giraud (ed.) *Songs That Won the War* (1930). Cf. I Corinthians 101:15

2 O God, if there be a God, save my soul, if I have a soul!

Prayer of a common soldier before the battle of Blenheim, in *Notes and Queries* vol. 173, no. 15 (9 October 1937) p. 264. Quoted in John Henry Newman *Apologia pro Vita Sua* (1864)

3 An old song made by an aged old pate,
Of an old worshipful gentleman who had a great estate.

'The Old Courtier', in Percy's *Reliques of Ancient Poetry* (1765) series 2, bk. 3, no. 8

4 Once again we stop the mighty roar of London's traffic.

In Town Tonight (BBC radio series, 1933–60) preamble

5 One Cartwright brought a Slave from Russia, and would scourge him, for which he was questioned: and it was resolved, That England was too pure an Air for Slaves to breathe in.

'In the 11th of Elizabeth' (17 November 1568–16 November 1569), in John Rushworth *Historical Collections* (1680–1722) vol. 2, p. 468. Cf. Cowper 223:19

6 One Friday morn when we set sail,
And our ship not far from land,
We there did espy a fair pretty maid,
With a comb and a glass in her hand.
While the raging seas did roar,
And the stormy winds did blow,
And we jolly sailor-boys were all up aloft
And the land-lubbers lying down below.

'The Mermaid' (traditional song)

7 On Waterloo's ensanguined plain
Full many a gallant man was slain,
But none, by sabre or by shot,
Fell half so flat as Walter Scott.

On Scott's poem 'The Field of Waterloo' (1815), in U. Pope-Hennessy *The Laird of Abbotsford* (1932) ch. 9

8 O ye'll tak' the high road, and I'll tak' the low road,
And I'll be in Scotland afore ye,
But me and my true love will never meet again,
On the bonnie, bonnie banks o' Loch Lomon'.

'The Bonnie Banks of Loch Lomon' (traditional song)

9 A place within the meaning of the Act.

Usually taken to be a reference to the Betting Act 1853, sect. 2, which banned off-course betting on horse-races

10 Please do not shoot the pianist. He is doing his best.

Printed notice in a dancing saloon, in Oscar Wilde *Impressions of America* 'Leadville' (c.1882–3)

11 Please to remember the Fifth of November,
Gunpowder Treason and Plot.
We know no reason why gunpowder treason
Should ever be forgot.

Traditional rhyme on the Gunpowder Plot (1605)

12 Power to the people.

Slogan of the Black Panther movement, from c.1968 onwards

13 *Puella Rigensis ridebat*
Quam tigris in tergo vehebat;
Externa profecta,
Interna revecta,
Risusque cum tigre manebat.

There was a young lady of Riga
Who went for a ride on a tiger;
They returned from the ride
With the lady inside,
And a smile on the face of the tiger.

In R. L. Green (ed.) *A Century of Humorous Verse* (1959) p. 285

14 The [*or* A] quick brown fox jumps over the lazy dog.

Used by keyboarders to ensure that all letters of the alphabet are functioning. See R. Hunter Middleton's introduction to *The Quick Brown Fox* (1945) by Richard H. Templeton Jr.

15 The rabbit has a charming face:
Its private life is a disgrace.
I really dare not name to you
The awful things that rabbits do.

'The Rabbit', in *The Week-End Book* (1925) p. 171

16 Raise the stone, and there thou shalt find me, cleave the wood and there am I.

Oxyrhynchus Papyri, in B. P. Grenfell and A. S. Hunt (eds.) *Sayings of Our Lord* (1897) Logion 5, l. 23

17 Says Tweed to Till—
'What gars ye rin sae still?'
Says Till to Tweed—
'Though ye rin with speed
And I rin slaw,
For ae man that ye droon
I droon twa'.

'Two Rivers' (traditional rhyme)

18 See the happy moron,
He doesn't give a damn,
I wish I were a moron,
My God! perhaps I am!

Eugenics Review July 1929

19 Seven wealthy towns contend for HOMER dead
Through which the living HOMER begged his bread.

Epilogue to *Aesop at Tunbridge; or, a Few Selected Fables in Verse* By No Person of Quality (1698). Cf. Heywood 338:6

20 She was poor but she was honest
Victim of a rich man's game.
First he loved her, then he left her,
And she lost her maiden name . . .
It's the same the whole world over,
It's the poor wot gets the blame,
It's the rich wot gets the gravy.
Ain't it all a bleedin' shame?

'She was Poor but she was Honest' (sung by British soldiers in the First World War)

21 Since first I saw your face, I resolved to honour and renown ye;
If now I be disdained, I wish my heart had never known ye.
What? I that loved and you that liked, shall we begin to wrangle?
No, no, no, my heart is fast, and cannot disentangle.

Song set by Thomas Ford in *Music of Sundry Kinds* (1607)

1 The singer not the song.
  From a West Indian calypso; taken as the title of a novel
  (1959) by Audrey Erskine Lindop

2 So cryptic as to be almost meaningless. If there is a
meaning, it is doubtless objectionable.
  The British Board of Film Censors, banning Jean Cocteau's
  film *The Seashell and the Clergyman* (1929). See J. C.
  Robertson *Hidden Cinema* (1989) ch. 1

3 Some talk of Alexander, and some of Hercules;
  Of Hector and Lysander, and such great names as
  these;
  But of all the world's brave heroes, there's none that
  can compare
  With a tow, row, row, row, row, row, for the British
  Grenadier.
  'The British Grenadiers' (traditional song)

4 So much chewing gum for the eyes.
  Small boy's definition of certain television programmes, in
  James Beasley Simpson *Best Quotes of '50, '55, '56* (1957)
  p. 233

5 Sticks nix hick pix.
  Front-page headline on the lack of enthusiasm for farm
  dramas among rural populations, in *Variety* 17 July 1935

6 Sumer is icumen in,
  Lhude sing cuccu!
  Groweth sed, and bloweth med,
  And springth the wude nu.
  'Cuckoo Song' (*c.*1250), sung annually at Reading Abbey
  gateway and first recorded by John Fornset, a monk of
  Reading Abbey

7 The Sun himself cannot forget
  His fellow traveller.
  Wit's Recreations (1640) epigram no. 146 (on Sir Francis
  Drake)

8 Swing low, sweet chariot—
  Comin' for to carry me home;
  I looked over Jordan and what did I see?
  A band of angels comin' after me—
  Comin' for to carry me home.
  Negro spiritual (*c.*1850)

9 Therefore let us sing and dance a galliard,
  To the remembrance of the mallard:
  And as the mallard dives in pool,
  Let us dabble, dive, and duck in Bowl.
  Oh! by the blood of King Edward,
  Oh! by the blood of King Edward,
  It was a swapping, swapping mallard.
  All Souls College, Oxford Song (possibly of Tudor date), in
  The Oxford Sausage (1764) p. 83

10 There is a lady sweet and kind,
  Was never face so pleased my mind;
  I did but see her passing by,
  And yet I love her till I die.
  Found on the reverse of leaf 53 of 'Popish Kingdome or
  reigne of Antichrist', in Latin verse by Thomas Naogeorgus,
  and Englished by Barnabe Googe; printed in 1570.
  Sometimes attributed to Thomas Forde

11 There is a tavern in the town,
  And there my dear love sits him down,
  And drinks his wine 'mid laughter free,
  And never, never thinks of me.
  Fare thee well, for I must leave thee,
  Do not let this parting grieve thee,
  And remember that the best of friends must part.

  Adieu, adieu, kind friends, adieu, adieu, adieu,
  I can no longer stay with you,
  I'll hang my harp on a weeping willow-tree,
  And may the world go well with thee.
  'There is a Tavern in the Town' (traditional song)

12 There is one thing stronger than all the armies in the
world; and that is an idea whose time has come.
  Nation 15 April 1943. Cf. Hugo 354:15

13 There is so much good in the worst of us,
  And so much bad in the best of us,
  That it hardly becomes any of us
  To talk about the rest of us.
  Attributed, among others, to Edward Wallis Hoch
  (1849–1945) on the grounds of it having appeared in his
  Kansas publication, the *Marion Record*, though in fact
  disclaimed by him ('behooves' sometimes substituted for
  'becomes')

14 There's no such thing as a free lunch.
  Colloquial axiom in US economics from the 1960s, much
  associated with Milton Friedman, q.v.; first found in printed
  form in Robert Heinlein *The Moon is a Harsh Mistress*
  (1966) ch. 11

15 There was a faith-healer of Deal
  Who said, 'Although pain isn't real,
  If I sit on a pin
  And it punctures my skin,
  I dislike what I fancy I feel.'
  In *The Week-End Book* (1925) p. 158

16 They come as a boon and a blessing to men,
  The Pickwick, the Owl, and the Waverley pen.
  Advertisement by MacNiven and H. Cameron Ltd. (*c.*1920);
  almost certainly inspired by J. C. Prince 'The Pen and the
  Press' in E. W. Cole (ed.) *The Thousand Best Poems in the
  World* (1891): 'It came as a boon and a blessing to men, /
  The peaceful, the pure, the victorious PEN!'

17 Thirty days hath September,
  April, June, and November;
  All the rest have thirty-one,
  Excepting February alone,
  And that has twenty-eight days clear
  And twenty-nine in each leap year.
  Stevins MS (*c.*1555)

18 This is a rotten argument, but it should be good
enough for their lordships on a hot summer afternoon.
  Annotation to a ministerial brief, said to have been read out
  inadvertently in the House of Lords, in Lord Home *The Way
  the Wind Blows* (1976) p. 204

19 Though I yield to no one in my admiration for Mr
Coolidge, I do wish he did not look as if he had been
weaned on a pickle.
  Anonymous remark, in Alice Roosevelt Longworth *Crowded
  Hours* (1933) ch. 21

20 *Hige sceal þe heardra, heorte þe cenre,*
  mod sceal þe mare, þe ure mægen lytlað.

  Thought shall be the harder, heart the keener,
  courage the greater, as our might lessens.
  The Battle of Maldon (translated by R. K. Gordon, 1926)

1 Three acres and a cow.

Associated with Jesse Collings and his land reform propaganda (*Hansard* 26 January 1886, col. 444), although used earlier by Joseph Chamberlain in a speech at Evesham (*The Times* 17 November 1885, p. 10), by which time it was already proverbial

2 To err is human but to really foul things up requires a computer.

Farmers' Almanac for 1978 'Capsules of Wisdom'

3 Too small to live in and too large to hang on a watch-chain.

Chiswick House described by a guest, in Cecil Roberts *And so to Bath* (1940) ch. 4

4 Wall St. lays an egg.

Crash headline, *Variety* 30 October 1929

5 War will cease when men refuse to fight.

Pacifist slogan, from *c.*1936 (often quoted 'Wars will cease ... ')

6 Weep you no more, sad fountains;
What need you flow so fast?

Lute song (1603) set to music by John Dowland, in *New Oxford Book of Sixteenth-Century Verse* (1991)

7 We hold these truths to be self-evident, that all men are created equal, that they are endowed by their Creator with certain unalienable rights, that among these are life, liberty and the pursuit of happiness.

The American Declaration of Independence, 4 July 1776. Cf. Jefferson 364:2

8 We're here
Because
We're here.

Sung to the tune of 'Auld Lang Syne', in John Brophy and Eric Partridge *Songs and Slang of the British Soldier 1914–18* (1930)

9 Were you there when they crucified my Lord?

Title of Negro spiritual (1865)

10 We shall not be moved.

Title of labour and civil rights song (1931) adapted from an earlier gospel hymn

11 We shall not pretend that there is nothing in his long career which those who respect and admire him would wish otherwise.

On Edward VII's accession to the throne, in *The Times* 23 January 1901, leading article

12 We shall overcome.

Title of song, originating from before the American Civil War, adapted as a Baptist hymn ('I'll Overcome Some Day', 1901) by C. Albert Tindley; revived in 1946 as a protest song by black tobacco workers, and in 1963 during the black Civil Rights Campaign

13 We want eight, and we won't wait.

On the construction of Dreadnoughts. See George Wyndham's speech in *The Times* 29 March 1909

14 Western wind, when will thou blow,
The small rain down can rain?
Christ, if my love were in my arms
And I in my bed again!

'Western Wind' (published 1790) in *New Oxford Book of Sixteenth-Century Verse* (1991)

15 What wee gave, wee have;
What wee spent, wee had;
What wee kept, wee lost.

Epitaph on Edward Courtenay, Earl of Devonshire (d. 1419) and his wife, at Tiverton, in Thomas Westcote *A View of Devonshire in 1630* (ed. G. Oliver and P. Jones, 1845); variants appear in Tristram Risdon *Survey of the County of Devon* (1714) and Edmund Spenser *The Shepherd's Calendar* (1579)

16 When Israel was in Egypt land,
Let my people go,
Oppressed so hard they could not stand,
Let my people go.
Go down, Moses,
Way-down in Egypt land,
Tell old Pharaoh
To let my people go.

'Go Down, Moses' (Negro spiritual). Cf. Exodus 72:5

17 When I was a little boy, I had but a little wit,
'Tis a long time ago, and I have no more yet;
Nor ever ever shall, until that I die,
For the longer I live the more fool am I.

Wit and Mirth, an Antidote against Melancholy (1684 ed.)

18 Where is the man who has the power and skill
To stem the torrent of a woman's will?
For if she will, she will, you may depend on't;
And if she won't, she won't; so there's an end on't.

Inscription on the pillar erected on the mount in the Dane John Field, Canterbury, in *Examiner* 31 May 1829

19 Whilst Adam slept, Eve from his side arose:
Strange his first sleep should be his last repose.

'The Consequence'

20 Who dares wins.

Motto of the British Special Air Service regiment, from 1942. See J. L. Collins *Elite Forces: the SAS* (1986) introduction

21 Whose finger do you want on the trigger?

Daily Mirror 21 September 1951; headline alluding to the atom bomb, apropos the failure of both the Labour and Conservative parties to purge their leaders of proven failures. See Hugh Cudlipp *Publish and be Damned* (1953) ch. 40

22 A willing foe and sea room.

Naval toast in the time of Nelson, in W. N. T. Beckett *A Few Naval Customs, Expressions, Traditions, and Superstitions* (1931) 'Customs'

23 With a heart of furious fancies,
Whereof I am commander;
With a burning spear,
And a horse of air,
To the wilderness I wander.

'Tom o' Bedlam'

24 Would you like to sin
With Elinor Glyn
On a tigerskin?
Or would you prefer
To err
With her
On some other fur?

1907 rhyme, in A. Glyn *Elinor Glyn* (1955) bk. 2, sect. 30

1 Yankee Doodle came to town
Riding on a pony;
Stuck a feather in his cap
And called it Macaroni.

> 'Yankee Doodle' (song, 1755 or earlier). See Nicholas Smith
> *Stories of Great National Songs* (1899) ch. 2

2 Yet, if his majesty our sovereign lord
Should of his own accord
Friendly himself invite,
And say 'I'll be your guest tomorrow night',
How should we stir ourselves, call and command
All hands to work!

> From Christ Church MS

3 But at the coming of the King of Heaven
All's set at six and seven:
We wallow in our sin.
Christ cannot find a chamber in the inn.
We entertain Him always like a stranger,
And as at first still lodge Him in the manger.

> From Christ Church MS

4 The young Sahib shot divinely, but God was very
merciful to the birds.

> In G. W. E. Russell *Collections and Recollections* (1898)
> ch. 30

5 You should make a point of trying every experience
once, excepting incest and folk-dancing.

> Sir Arnold Bax (1883–1953), quoting 'a sympathetic Scot'
> in *Farewell My Youth* (1943) p. 17

French

6 *Ça ira.*

> Refrain of 'Carillon national', popular song of the French
> Revolution (*c.* July 1790), translated 'Things will work out'
> by William Doyle in his *Oxford History of the French
> Revolution* (1989) p. 129; the phrase is believed to originate
> with Benjamin Franklin, who may have uttered it in 1776
> when asked for news of the American Revolution

7 *Cet animal est très méchant,*
Quand on l'attaque il se défend.

This animal is very bad; when attacked it defends
itself.

> 'La Ménagerie' (1868 song) by 'Théodore P. K.'

8 *Chevalier sans peur et sans reproche.*

Fearless, blameless knight.

> Description in contemporary chronicles of Pierre Bayard
> (1476–1524)

9 *Honi soit qui mal y pense.*

Evil be to him who evil thinks.

> Motto of the Order of the Garter, originated by Edward III,
> probably on 23 April of 1348 or 1349

10 *Ils ne passeront pas.*

They shall not pass.

> Slogan used by the French army at the defence of Verdun
> in 1916; variously attributed to Marshal Pétain and to
> General Robert Nivelle, and taken up by the Republicans in
> the Spanish Civil War in the form 'No pasarán!' Cf. Ibarruri
> 358:15

11 *Il y avait un jeune homme de Dijon,*
Qui n'avait que peu de religion.
Il dit: 'Quant à moi,
Je déteste tous les trois,
Le Père, et le Fils, et le Pigeon.'

There was a young man of Dijon,
Who had only a little religion,
He said: 'As for me,
I detest all the three,
The Father, the Son, and the Pigeon.'

> *The Norman Douglas Limerick Book* (1969, privately printed,
> 1928, as *Some Limericks*) introduction

12 [RIDDLE:] Je suis le capitaine de vingt-quatre soldats,
et sans moi Paris serait pris?
[ANSWER:] A.

[RIDDLE:] I am the captain of twenty-four soldiers,
and without me Paris would be taken?
[ANSWER:] A [i.e. 'Paris' minus 'a' = *pris* taken].

> In Hugh Rowley *Puniana: or, Thoughts wise and otherwise*
> (1867) p. 42. The saying 'With twenty-six lead soldiers [the
> characters of the alphabet set up for printing] I can conquer
> the world' may derive from this riddle, but probably arose
> independently

13 *Je suis Marxiste—tendance Groucho.*

I am a Marxist—of the Groucho tendency.

> Slogan found at Nanterre in Paris, 1968

14 *La grande phrase reçue, c'est qu'il ne faut pas être plus
royaliste que le roi. Cette phrase n'est pas du moment;
elle fut inventée sous Louis XVI: elle enchaîna les mains
des fidèles, pour ne laisser libre que le bras du bourreau.*

The big catch-phrase is that *you mustn't be more of a
royalist than the king.* This expression is not new; it
was coined under Louis XVI: it chained up the hands
of the loyal, leaving free only the arm of the
hangman.

> François René, Vicomte de Chateaubriand *De la monarchie
> selon la charte* (1816) ch. 81

15 *Laissez-nous-faire.*

Allow us to do [it].

> Remark dating from *c.*1664, in *Journal Oeconomique* Paris,
> April 1751: 'M. Colbert assembla plusieurs Deputés de
> commerce chez lui pour leur demander ce qu'il pourroit faire
> pour le commerce; le plus raisonnable et le moins flatteur
> d'entre eux, lui dit ce seul mot: "Laissez-nous-faire."
> [Monsieur Colbert assembled several deputies of commerce
> at his house to ask what could be done for commerce; the
> most rational and the least flattering among them answered
> him in one word: "Laissez-nous-faire"]'. Cf. d'Argenson
> 24:18, Quesnay 534:8

16 *L'amour est aveugle; l'amitié ferme les yeux.*

Love is blind; friendship closes its eyes.

> Proverbial saying

17 *Le monde est plein de fous, et qui n'en veut pas voir
Doit se tenir tout seul, et casser son miroir.*

The world is full of fools, and he who would not see it
should live alone and smash his mirror.

> Adaptation from an original form attributed to Claude Le
> Petit (1640–65) in *Discours satiriques* (1686)

1 *Liberté! Égalité! Fraternité!*

Freedom! Equality! Brotherhood!

> Motto of the French Revolution, but of earlier origin. The Club des Cordeliers passed a motion, 30 June 1793, '*que les propriétaires seront invités . . . de faire peindre sur la façade de leurs maisons, en gros caractères, ces mots: Unité, indivisibilité de la République, Liberté, Égalité, Fraternité ou la mort* [that owners should be urged to paint on the front of their houses, in large letters, the words: Unity, indivisibility of the Republic, Liberty, Equality, Fraternity or death]'; in *Journal de Paris* no. 182 (from 1795 the words '*ou la mort*' were dropped). Cf. Chamfort 189:16

2 *L'ordre règne à Varsovie.*

Order reigns in Warsaw.

> After the brutal suppression of an uprising, the newspaper *Moniteur* reported, 16 September 1831, '*L'ordre et la tranquillité sont entièrement rétablis dans la capitale* [Order and calm are completely restored in the capital]'; on the same day Count Sebastiani, minister of foreign affairs, declared: '*La tranquillité règne à Varsovie* [Peace reigns in Warsaw]'

3 *Nous n'irons plus aux bois, les lauriers sont coupés.*

We'll to the woods no more,
The laurels all are cut.

> Old nursery rhyme, quoted by Théodore de Banville in *Les Cariatides, les stalactites* (1842–6); translated by A. E. Housman in *Last Poems* (1922) introductory

4 *Revenons à ces moutons.*

Let us get back to these sheep [i.e. 'Let us get back to the subject'].

> *Maistre Pierre Pathelin* l. 1191 (often quoted '*Retournons à nos moutons* [Let us return to our sheep]')

5 *Si le Roi m'avait donné,*
Paris, sa grand'ville,
Et qu'il me fallût quitter
L'amour de ma mie,
Je dirais au roi Henri:
'*Reprenez votre Paris:*
J'aime mieux ma mie, au gué,
J'aime mieux ma mie.'

If the king had given me Paris, his great city, and if I were required to give up my darling's love, I would say to King Henry: 'Take your Paris back; I prefer my darling, by the ford, I prefer my darling.'

> Popular song, attributed to Antoine de Navarre (1518–62). See Dupré *Encyclopédie des citations* (1959) p. 9; quoted in this form by Molière in *Le Misanthrope* act 1, sc. 2

6 *Taisez-vous! Méfiez-vous! Les oreilles ennemies vous écoutent.*

Keep your mouth shut! Be on your guard! Enemy ears are listening to you.

> Official notice in France, 1915

7 *Toujours perdrix!*

Always partridge!

> Attributed to a confessor of Henri IV, who rebuked the king for his sexual liaisons and thereafter was served nothing but partridge; in G. Büchmann *Geflügelte Worte* (1874 ed.) p. 240

8 *Tout passe, tout casse, tout lasse.*

Everything passes, everything perishes, everything palls.

> Charles Cahier *Quelques six mille proverbes* (1856) no. 1718

German

9 *Arbeit macht frei.*

Work liberates.

> Words inscribed on the gates of Dachau concentration camp, 1933, and subsequently on those of Auschwitz

10 *Ein Reich, ein Volk, ein Führer.*

One realm, one people, one leader.

> Nazi Party slogan, early 1930s

11 *Kommt der Krieg ins Land*
Gibt's Lügen wie Sand.

When war enters a country
It produces lies like sand.

> Epigraph to Arthur Ponsonby *Falsehood in Wartime* (1928) p. 11. Cf. Johnson 368:8

12 *Vorsprung durch Technik.*

Progress through technology.

> Audi motors (advertising slogan, from 1986)

Greek

13 γνῶθι σεαυτόν.

Know thyself.

> Inscribed on the temple of Apollo at Delphi; Plato, in *Protagoras* 343 b, ascribes the saying to the Seven Wise Men

14 μηδὲν ἄγαν.

Nothing in excess.

> Inscribed on the temple of Apollo at Delphi, and variously ascribed to the Seven Wise Men

15 ὅταν δ' ὁ δαίμων ἀνδρὶ πορσύνῃ κακά,
τὸν νοῦν ἔβλαψε πρῶτον, ᾧ βουλεύεται.

Whenever God prepares evil for a man, He first damages his mind, with which he deliberates.

> Scholiastic annotation to Sophocles's *Antigone* l. 622. Cf. Duport 264:8

16 ἀγεωμέτρητος μηδεὶς εἰσίτω.

Let no one enter who does not know geometry [mathematics].

> Inscription on Plato's door, probably at the Academy at Athens, in Elias Philosophus *In Aristotelis Categorias Commentaria* p. 118, l. 18; in A. Busse (ed.) *Commentaria in Aristotelem Graeca* (1900) vol. 18, pt. 1

Italian

17 *Se non è vero, è molto ben trovato.*

If it is not true, it is a happy invention.

> Common saying from the 16th century

Latin

18 *Adeste, fideles,*
laeti triumphantes;
venite, venite in Bethlehem;
natum videte regem angelorum . . .
venite, adoremus Dominum.

O come, all ye faithful,
Joyful and triumphant,
O come ye, O come ye to Bethlehem;
Come and behold him,
Born the King of angels:
O come, let us adore him . . . Christ the Lord!

> French or German hymn (c.1743) in *Murray's Hymnal* (1852); translation based on that of F. Oakeley (1841)

1 *Ad majorem Dei gloriam.*

To the greater glory of God.

Motto of the Society of Jesus

2 *Ave Caesar, morituri te salutant.*

Hail Caesar, those who are about to die salute you.

Gladiators saluting the Roman Emperor. See Suetonius *Lives of the Caesars* 'Claudius' ch. 21

3 *Ave Maria, gratia plena, Dominus tecum: Benedicta tu in mulieribus, et benedictus fructus ventris tui, Jesus.*

Hail Mary, full of grace, the Lord is with thee: Blessed art thou among women, and blessed is the fruit of thy womb, Jesus.

'Ave Maria', also known as 'The Angelic Salutation', dating from the 11th century

4 *Ave verum corpus,*
natum ex Maria Virgine.

Hail the true body, born of the Virgin Mary.

Eucharistic hymn, probably dating from the 14th century

5 *Caveant consules ne quid res publica detrimenti caperet.*

Let the consuls see to it that no harm come to the state.

Senatorial 'ultimate decree' in the Roman Republic. See, for example, Cicero *Pro Milone* ch. 70

6 *Cras amet qui nunquam amavit, quique amavit cras amet!*

Let those love now, who never loved before:
Let those who always loved, now love the more.

Pervigilium Veneris (translated by Thomas Parnell, 1722)

7 *Et in Arcadia ego.*

And I too in Arcadia.

Tomb inscription, of disputed meaning, often depicted in classical paintings. *See* E. Panofsky 'Et in Arcadia ego' in R. K. Klibansky and H. J. Paton (eds.) *Philosophy and History: Essays Presented to E. Cassirer* (1936)

8 *Gaudeamus igitur,*
Juvenes dum sumus
Post jucundam juventutem,
Post molestam senectutem,
Nos habebit humus.

Let us then rejoice,
While we are young.
After the pleasures of youth
And the burdens of old age
Earth will hold us.

Medieval students' song, traced to 1267, but revised in the 18th century

9 *Meum est propositum*
In taberna mori,
Ut sint vina proxima
Morientis ori.
Tunc cantabunt laetius
Angelorum chori:
'Sit Deus propitius
Huic potatori!'

I desire to end my days in a tavern drinking,
May some Christian hold for me the glass when I am shrinking;
That the Cherubim may cry, when they see me sinking,
'God be merciful to a soul of this gentleman's way of thinking.'

The Arch-poet (fl. 1159–67) 'Estuans intrinsecus ira vehementi' (translated by Leigh Hunt)

10 *Nemo me impune lacessit.*

No one provokes me with impunity.

Motto of the Crown of Scotland and of all Scottish regiments

11 *Per ardua ad astra.*

Through struggle to the stars.

Motto of the Mulvany family, quoted and translated by Rider Haggard in *The People of the Mist* (1894) ch. 1; still in use as motto of the R.A.F., having been proposed by J. S. Yule in 1912 and approved by King George V in 1913

12 *Post coitum omne animal triste.*

After coition every animal is sad.

Post-classical saying

13 *Quidquid agis, prudenter agas, et respice finem.*

Whatever you do, do cautiously, and look to the end.

Gesta Romanorum no. 103

14 *Salve, regina, mater misericordiae,*
Vita, dulcedo et spes nostra, salve!
Ad te clamamus exsules filii Evae,
Ad te suspiramus gementes et flentes
In hac lacrimarum valle.
Eia ergo, advocata nostra,
Illos tuos misericordes oculos ad nos converte.
Et Iesum, benedictum fructum ventris tui,
Nobis post hoc exsilium ostende,
O clemens, o pia,
O dulcis virgo Maria.

Hail holy queen, mother of mercy, hail our life, our sweetness, and our hope! To thee do we cry, poor banished children of Eve; to thee do we send up our sighs, mourning and weeping in this vale of tears. Turn then, most gracious advocate, thine eyes of mercy towards us; and after this our exile show unto us the blessed fruit of thy womb, Jesus, O clement, O loving, O sweet virgin Mary.

Attributed to various 11th century authors. See *Analecta Hymnica* vol. 50 (1907) p. 318

15 *Sic transit gloria mundi.*

Thus passes the glory of the world.

Said during the coronation of a new Pope, while flax is burned to represent the transitoriness of earthly glory; used at the coronation of Alexander V in Pisa, 7 July 1409, but earlier in origin. Cf. Thomas à Kempis 692:3

16 *Si monumentum requiris, circumspice.*

If you seek a monument, gaze around.

Inscription in St Paul's Cathedral, London, attributed to the son of Sir Christopher Wren, its architect

17 *Te Deum laudamus: Te Dominum confitemur.*

We praise thee, God: we own thee Lord.

'Te Deum'; hymn traditionally attributed to St Ambrose and St Augustine in AD 387, though more recently to St Niceta (d. *c*.414). Cf. Book of Common Prayer 118:12

18 *In te Domine, speravi: non confundar in aeternum.*

Lord, I have set my hopes in thee, I shall not be destroyed for ever.

'Te Deum'. Cf. Book of Common Prayer 118:14

19 *Tempora mutantur, et nos mutamur in illis.*

Times change, and we change with them.

In William Harrison *Description of Britain* (1577) bk. 3, ch. 3; attributed to the Emperor Lothar I (795–855) in the form '*Omnia mutantur, nos et mutamur in illis* [All things change, and we change with them]'

1 *Vox et praeterea nihil.*

A voice and nothing more.

Describing a nightingale. See Plutarch *Moralia* sect. 233a, no. 15

Jean Anouilh 1910–87

French playwright

2 *Dieu est avec tout le monde ... Et, en fin de compte, il est toujours avec ceux qui ont beaucoup d'argent et de grosses armées.*

God is on everyone's side ... And, in the last analysis, he is on the side of those with plenty of money and large armies.

L'Alouette (1953) p. 120. Cf. de Bussy-Rabutin 165:19, Voltaire 716:20

3 *Maintenant le ressort est bandé. Cela n'a plus qu'à se dérouler tout seul. C'est cela qui est commode dans la tragédie. On donne le petit coup de pouce pour que cela démarre.*

The spring is wound up tight. It will uncoil of itself. That is what is so convenient in tragedy. The least little turn of the wrist will do the job. Anything will set it going.

Antigone (1944, translated by Lewis Galantiere, 1957) p. 34

4 *C'est propre, la tragédie. C'est reposant, c'est sûr.*

Tragedy is clean, it is restful, it is flawless.

Antigone (1944, translated by Lewis Galantiere, 1957) p. 34

5 *Il y a l'amour bien sûr. Et puis il y a la vie, son ennemie.*

There is love of course. And then there's life, its enemy.

Ardèle (1949) p. 8

6 *Vous savez bien que l'amour, c'est avant tout le don de soi!*

You know very well that love is, above all, the gift of oneself!

Ardèle (1949) p. 79

7 *La mort est belle. Elle seule donne à l'amour son vrai climat.*

Death is beautiful. It alone gives love its true habitat.

Eurydice (1942) act 4

8 *C'est très jolie la vie, mais cela n'a pas de forme. L'art a pour objet de lui en donner une précisément et de faire par tous les artifices possibles—plus vrai que le vrai.*

Life is very nice, but it has no shape. The object of art is actually to give it some and to do it by every artifice possible—truer than the truth.

La Répétition (1950) act 2

9 *Mourir, mourir ... Mourir ce n'est rien. Commence donc par vivre. C'est moins drôle et c'est plus long.*

Dying, dying ... Dying is nothing. So start by living. It's less fun and it lasts longer.

Roméo et Jeannette (1946) act 3

10 *Il y a aura toujours un chien perdu quelquepart qui m'empêchera d'être heureux.*

There will always be a lost dog somewhere that will prevent me from being happy.

La Sauvage (1938) act 3

Christopher Anstey 1724–1805

English writer

11 If ever I ate a good supper at night,
I dreamed of the devil, and waked in a fright.

The New Bath Guide (1766) Letter 4 'A Consultation of the Physicians'

12 You may go to Carlisle's, and to Almack's too;
And I'll give you my head if you find such a host,
For coffee, tea, chocolate, butter, and toast:
How he welcomes at once all the world and his wife,
And how civil to folk he ne'er saw in his life.

The New Bath Guide (1766) Letter 13 'A Public Breakfast'

F. Anstey (Thomas Anstey Guthrie) 1856–1934

English writer

13 Drastic measures is Latin for a whopping.

Vice Versa (1882) ch. 7

Guillaume Apollinaire 1880–1918

French poet

14 *Les souvenirs sont cors de chasse
Dont meurt le bruit parmi le vent.*

Memories are hunting horns
Whose sound dies on the wind.

'Cors de Chasse' (1912)

15 *Sous le pont Mirabeau coule la Seine.
Et nos amours, faut-il qu'il m'en souvienne?
La joie venait toujours après la peine.
Vienne la nuit, sonne l'heure,
Les jours s'en vont, je demeure.*

Under Mirabeau Bridge flows the Seine.
And our loves, must I remember them?
Joy always came after pain.
Let night come, ring out the hour,
The days go by, I remain.

'Le Pont Mirabeau' (1912)

16 *On ne peut pas porter partout le cadavre de son père.*

One can't carry one's father's corpse about everywhere.

In *Les peintres cubistes* (1965) 'Méditations esthétiques: Sur la peinture' pt. 1

Sir Edward Appleton 1892–1965

English physicist

17 I do not mind what language an opera is sung in so long as it is a language I don't understand.

In *Observer* 28 August 1955

Thomas Gold Appleton 1812–84

American epigrammatist

18 A Boston man is the east wind made flesh.

Attributed

19 Good Americans, when they die, go to Paris.

In Oliver Wendell Holmes *The Autocrat of the Breakfast Table* (1858) ch. 6

Arabian Nights Entertainments, or the Thousand and one Nights

A collection of stories written in Arabic

1 Who will change old lamps for new ones? . . . new lamps for old ones?
'The History of Aladdin'

2 Open Sesame!
'The History of Ali Baba'

William Arabin 1773–1841

English judge

3 If ever there was a case of clearer evidence than this of persons acting together, this case is that case.
In H. B. Churchill *Arabiniana* (1843) p. 9

4 They will steal the very teeth out of your mouth as you walk through the streets. *I know it from experience.*
On the citizens of Uxbridge, in Sir W. Ballantine *Some Experiences of a Barrister's Life* (1882) vol. 1, ch. 6

5 Prisoner, God has given you good abilities, instead of which you go about the country stealing ducks.
See Sir Frederick Pollock *Essays in the Law* (1922) p. 298, where attribution to a Revd Mr Alderson is preferred

Louis Aragon 1897–1982

French poet, essayist, and novelist

6 *Ô mois des floraisons mois des métamorphoses*
Mai qui fut sans nuage et Juin poignardé
Je n'oublierai jamais les lilas ni les roses
Ni ceux que le printemps dans ses plis a gardé.

O month of flowerings, month of metamorphoses,
May without cloud and June that was stabbed,
I shall never forget the lilac and the roses
Nor those whom spring has kept in its folds.
'Les lilas et les roses' (1940)

John Arbuthnot 1667–1735

Scottish physician and pamphleteer

7 He warns the heads of parties against believing their own lies.
The Art of Political Lying (1712) p. 19 (*He* the writer)

8 Law is a bottomless pit.
The History of John Bull (1712) title of first pamphlet

9 Hame's hame, be it never so hamely.
The History of John Bull (1712) 'John Bull Still in His Senses' ch. 3

10 Curle (who is one of the new terrors of Death) has been writing letters to every body for memoirs of his life.
Letter to Jonathan Swift, 13 January 1733, in H. Williams (ed.) *The Correspondence of Jonathan Swift* vol. 4 (1965) p. 101. Cf. Lyndhurst 433:14, Wetherell 729:22

Archilochus

Greek poet of the 7th century BC

11 πόλλ' οἶδ' ἀλώπηξ, ἀλλ' ἐχῖνος ἕν μέγα.
The fox knows many things—the hedgehog one *big* one.
E. Diehl (ed.) *Anthologia Lyrica Graeca* (3rd ed., 1949–52) vol. 1, p. 241, no. 103. Cf. Berlin 66:2

Archimedes *c.*287–212 BC

Greek mathematician and inventor

12 εὕρηκα.
Eureka! [I've got it!]
In Vitruvius Pollio *De Architectura* bk. 9, preface, sect. 10

13 δός μοι ποῦ στῶ καὶ κινῶ τὴν γῆν.
Give me but one firm spot on which to stand, and I will move the earth.
On the action of a lever, in Pappus *Synagoge* bk. 8, proposition 10, sect. 11

Hannah Arendt 1906–75

American political philosopher

14 It was as though in those last minutes he [Eichmann] was summing up the lessons that this long course in human wickedness had taught us—the lesson of the fearsome, word-and-thought-defying *banality of evil*.
Eichmann in Jerusalem (1963) ch. 15

15 Only crime and the criminal, it is true, confront us with the perplexity of radical evil; but only the hypocrite is really rotten to the core.
On Revolution (1963) ch. 2, pt. 5

16 The most radical revolutionary will become a conservative on the day after the revolution.
New Yorker 12 September 1970, p. 88

17 Under conditions of tyranny it is far easier to act than to think.
In W. H. Auden *A Certain World* (1970) p. 369

Marquis d'Argenson (René Louis de Voyer d'Argenson) 1694–1757

French politician and political essayist

18 *Laisser-faire.*
No interference.
Mémoires et Journal Inédit du Marquis d'Argenson (1858 ed.) vol. 5, p. 364. Cf. Anonymous 20:15, Quesnay 534:8

Comte d'Argenson (Marc Pierre de Voyer d'Argenson) 1696–1764

French statesman; founder of the École Militaire, Paris

19 ABBÉ GUYOT DESFONTAINES: *Il faut que je vive.*
D'ARGENSON: *Je n'en vois pas la nécessité.*

DESFONTAINES: I must live.
D'ARGENSON: I do not see the necessity.
On Desfontaines having produced a pamphlet satirizing D'Argenson, his benefactor. *See* Voltaire *Alzire* (1736) 'Discours Préliminaire' in *Oeuvres Complètes Théâtre* vol. 2 (1877) p. 381

Ludovico Ariosto 1474–1533
Italian poet and playwright

1 Natura il fece, e poi roppe la stampa.

Nature made him, and then broke the mould.
   Orlando Furioso (1532) canto 10, st. 84

Aristophanes *c.*450–*c.*385 BC
Athenian comic dramatist

2 βούλει Νεφελοκοκκυγίαν;

How about 'Cloudcuckooland'?
   Naming the capital city of the Birds in *The Birds* (414 BC)
   l. 819

3 εἶναι ... φασιν ἄμφω τὼ λόγω
   τὸν κρείττον', ὅστις ἐστί, καὶ τὸν ἥττονα.
   τούτοιν τὸν ἕτερον τοῖν λόγοιν, τὸν ἥττονα,
   νικᾶν λέγοντά φασι τἀδικώτερα.

This Second Logic then, I mean the Worse one,
They teach to talk unjustly, and—prevail.
   The Clouds (423 BC) l. 113 (translated by B. B. Rogers). Cf.
   Milton 469:13

4 ὁ δ' εὔκολος μὲν ἐνθάδ', εὔκολος δ' ἐκεῖ.

But he was contented there, is contented here.
   On Sophocles in *The Frogs* (405 BC) l. 82 (*there* on earth;
   here in Hades)

5 βρεκεκεκὲξ κοὰξ κοάξ.

Brekekekex koax koax.
   Cry of the Frogs in *The Frogs* (405 BC) l. 209 and *passim*

Aristotle 384–322 BC
Greek philosopher

00 Σχεδὸν γάρ, περὶ ὧν βουλεύονται πάντες καὶ περὶ ἃ
   ἀγορεύουσιν οἱ συμβουλεύοντες, τὰ μέγιστα τυγχάνει
   πέντε τὸν ἀριθμὸν ὄντα· ταῦτα δ' ἐστὶ περί τε πόρων, καὶ
   πολέμου καὶ εἰρήνης, ἔτι δὲ περὶ φυλακῆς τῆς χώρας, καὶ
   τῶν εἰσαγομένων καὶ ἐξαγομένων, καὶ περὶ νομοθεσίας.

Now, we may say that the most important subjects
about which all men deliberate and deliberative
orators harangue, are five in number, to wit: ways
and means, war and peace, the defence of the
country, imports and exports, legislation.
   The Art of Rhetoric bk. 1, 1359b 19–23

7 Πᾶσα τέχνη καὶ πᾶσα μέθοδος, ὁμοίως δὲ πρᾶξίς τε καὶ
   προαίρεσις, ἀγαθοῦ τινος ἐφίεσθαι δοκεῖ· διὸ καλῶς
   ἀπεφήναντο τἀγαθόν, οὗ πάντ' ἐφίεται.

Every art and every investigation, and likewise every
practical pursuit or undertaking, seems to aim at some
good: hence it has been well said that the Good is
That at which all things aim.
   Nicomachean Ethics bk. 1, 1094a 1–3

8 ὥστε τοῦτ' ἂν εἴη τἀνθρώπινον ἀγαθόν.

Therefore, the good of man must be the end [i.e.
objective] of the science of politics.
   Nicomachean Ethics bk. 1, 1094b 6–7

9 τὸ ἀνθρώπινον ἀγαθὸν ψυχῆς ἐνέργεια γίνεται κατ' ἀρετήν
   ... ἔτι δ' ἐν βίῳ τελείῳ· μία γὰρ χελιδὼν ἔαρ οὐ ποιεῖ,
   οὐδὲ μία ἡμέρα· οὕτω δὲ οὐδὲ μακάριον καὶ εὐδαίμονα μία
   ἡμέρα οὐδ' ὀλίγος χρόνος.

The Good of man is the active exercise of his soul's
faculties in conformity with excellence or virtue ...
Moreover this activity must occupy a complete
lifetime; for one swallow does not make spring, nor
does one fine day; and similarly one day or a brief
period of happiness does not make a man supremely
blessed and happy.
   Nicomachean Ethics bk. 1, 1098a 16–20

10 πολεμοῦμεν ἵν' εἰρήνην ἄγωμεν.

We make war that we may live in peace.
   Nicomachean Ethics bk. 10, 1177b 5–6 (translated by M.
   Ostwald). Cf. Vegetius 710:1

11 ἔστι δὲ καὶ ἡ τοῦ πολιτικοῦ ἄσχολος, καὶ παρ' αὐτὸ τὸ
   πολιτεύεσθαι περιποιουμένη δυναστείας καὶ τιμὰς ἢ τήν γε
   εὐδαιμονίαν.

Politicians also have no leisure, because they are
always aiming at something beyond political life itself,
power and glory, or happiness.
   Nicomachean Ethics bk. 10, 1177b 12–14

12 ἔστιν οὖν τραγῳδία μίμησις πράξεως σπουδαίας καὶ
   τελείας μέγεθος ἐχούσης ... δι' ἐλέου καὶ φόβου
   περαίνουσα τὴν τῶν τοιούτων παθημάτων κάθαρσιν.

Tragedy is thus a representation of an action that is
worth serious attention, complete in itself and of some
amplitude ... by means of pity and fear bringing
about the purgation of such emotions.
   Poetics ch. 6, 1449b 24–8

13 διὸ καὶ φιλοσοφώτερον καὶ σπουδαιότερον ποίησις
   ἱστορίας ἐστίν.

So poetry is something more philosophical and more
worthy of serious attention than history.
   Poetics ch. 9, 1451b 5–6

14 προαιρεῖσθαί τε δεῖ ἀδύνατα εἰκότα μᾶλλον ἢ δυνατὰ
   ἀπίθανα.

Probable impossibilities are to be preferred to
improbable possibilities.
   Poetics ch. 24, 1460a 26–7

15 ἄνθρωπος φύσει πολιτικὸν ζῷον.

Man is by nature a political animal.
   Politics bk. 1, 1253a 2–3

16 ὁ δὲ μὴ δυνάμενος κοινωνεῖν ἢ μηθὲν δεόμενος δι'
   αὐτάρκειαν ... ἢ θηρίον ἢ θεός.

He who is unable to live in society, or who has no
need because he is sufficient for himself, must be either
a beast or a god.
   Politics bk. 1, 1253a 27–9

17 ἡ φύσις μηθὲν μήτε ἀτελὲς ποιεῖ μήτε μάτην.

Nature does nothing without purpose or uselessly.
   Politics bk. 1, 1256b 20–1

18 ὅπου οἱ μὲν πολλὰ σφόδρα κέκτηνται οἱ δὲ μηθέν, ἢ
   δῆμος ἔσχατος γίγνεται ἢ ὀλιγαρχία ἄκρατος ἢ τυραννὶς
   δι' ἀμφοτέρας τὰς ὑπερβολάς.

Where some people are very wealthy and others have
nothing, the result will be either extreme democracy
or absolute oligarchy, or despotism will come from
either of those excesses.
   Politics bk. 4, 1296a 1–3

1 αὕτη μὲν οὖν ἐστι τοῖς νηπίοις ἁρμόττουσα τῶν παιδίων,
ἡ δὲ παιδεία πλαταγή τοῖς μείζοσι τῶν νέων.

Whereas then a rattle is a suitable occupation for
infant children, education serves as a rattle for young
people when older.
  Politics bk. 8, 1340b 29–31

2 ἐρωτηθεὶς τί ἐστι φίλος, ἔφη, ᾿μία ψυχὴ δύο σώμασιν
ἐνοικοῦσα.᾿᾿

When he was asked 'What is a friend?' he said 'One
soul inhabiting two bodies.'
  In Diogenes Laertius *Lives of Philosophers* bk. 5, sect. 20

3 *Amicus Plato, sed magis amica veritas.*

Plato is dear to me, but dearer still is truth.
  Latin translation of a Greek original ascribed to Aristotle

Lewis Addison Armistead 1817–63

American army officer

4 Give them the cold steel, boys!
  Attributed during the American Civil War, 1863

Harry Armstrong 1879–1951

American songwriter

5 There's an old mill by the stream, Nellie Dean,
Where we used to sit and dream, Nellie Dean.
And the waters as they flow
Seem to murmur sweet and low,
'You're my heart's desire; I love you, Nellie Dean.'
  'Nellie Dean' (1905 song)

John Armstrong 1709–79

Scottish poet and physician

6   Much had he read,
Much more had seen; he studied from the life,
And in th'original perused mankind.
  The Art of Preserving Health (1744) bk. 4, l. 231

7 'Tis not for mortals always to be blest.
  The Art of Preserving Health (1744) bk. 4, l. 260

8 Of right and wrong he taught
Truths as refined as ever Athens heard;
And (strange to tell!) he practised what he preached.
  The Art of Preserving Health (1744) bk. 4, l. 303

9 'Tis not too late to-morrow to be brave.
  The Art of Preserving Health (1744) bk. 4, l. 460

Louis Armstrong 1901–71

American singer and jazz musician

10 All music is folk music, I ain't never heard no horse
sing a song.
  In *New York Times* 7 July 1971, p. 41

11 If you still have to ask . . . shame on you.
  When asked what jazz is, in Max Jones et al. *Salute to
  Satchmo* (1970) p. 25 (sometimes quoted 'Man, if you gotta
  ask you'll never know')

Neil Armstrong 1930–

American astronaut; first man on the moon

12 That's one small step for man, one giant leap for
mankind.
  In *New York Times* 21 July 1969, p. 5 (interference in the
  transmission obliterated 'a' between 'for' and 'man')

Sir Robert Armstrong (Baron Armstrong)
1927–

Head of the British Civil Service, 1981–7

13 It contains a misleading impression, not a lie. It was
being economical with the truth.
  Referring to a letter during the 'Spycatcher' trial, Supreme
  Court, New South Wales, in *Daily Telegraph* 19 November
  1986. See Edmund Burke *Two letters on Proposals for Peace*
  (1796) pt. 1, p. 137: 'Falsehood and delusion are allowed
  in no case whatsoever: But, as in the exercise of all the
  virtues, there is an economy of truth.'

Sir Edwin Arnold 1832–1904

English poet and journalist

14 Nor ever once ashamed
So we be named
Press-men; Slaves of the Lamp; Servants of Light.
  'The Tenth Muse' (1895) st. 18

George Arnold 1834–65

American humorist

15 The living need charity more than the dead.
  'The Jolly Old Pedagogue' (1866)

Matthew Arnold 1822–88

English poet and essayist

16 And we forget because we must
And not because we will.
  'Absence' (1852)

17 Only—but this is rare—
When a belovèd hand is laid in ours,
When, jaded with the rush and glare
Of the interminable hours,
Our eyes can in another's eyes read clear,
When our world-deafened ear
Is by the tones of a loved voice caressed—
A bolt is shot back somewhere in our breast,
And a lost pulse of feeling stirs again.
The eye sinks inward, and the heart lies plain,
And what we mean, we say, and what we would, we
know.
  'The Buried Life' (1852) l. 77

1 The Sea of Faith
  Was once, too, at the full, and round earth's shore
  Lay like the folds of a bright girdle furled.
  But now I only hear
  Its melancholy, long, withdrawing roar,
  Retreating, to the breath
  Of the night-wind, down the vast edges drear
  And naked shingles of the world.

  Ah, love, let us be true
  To one another! for the world, which seems
  To lie before us like a land of dreams,
  So various, so beautiful, so new,
  Hath really neither joy, nor love, nor light,
  Nor certitude, nor peace, nor help for pain;
  And we are here as on a darkling plain
  Swept with confused alarms of struggle and flight,
  Where ignorant armies clash by night.
     'Dover Beach' (1867) l. 21

2 Be neither saint nor sophist-led, but be a man.
     Empedocles on Etna (1852) act 1, sc. 2, l. 136

3 Is it so small a thing
  To have enjoyed the sun,
  To have lived light in the spring,
  To have loved, to have thought, to have done.
     Empedocles on Etna (1852) act 1, sc. 2, l. 397

4 Because thou must not dream, thou needst not then
     despair!
     Empedocles on Etna (1852) act 1, sc. 2, l. 426

5 Come to me in my dreams, and then
  By day I shall be well again!
  For then the night will more than pay
  The hopeless longing of the day.
     'Faded Leaves' (1855) no. 5 (first published, 1852, as
     'Longing')

6 Come, dear children, let us away;
  Down and away below!
     'The Forsaken Merman' (1849) l. 1

7 Now the great winds shorewards blow;
  Now the salt tides seawards flow;
  Now the wild white horses play,
  Champ and chafe and toss in the spray.
     'The Forsaken Merman' (1849) l. 4

8 Sand-strewn caverns, cool and deep,
  Where the winds are all asleep;
  Where the spent lights quiver and gleam;
  Where the salt weed sways in the stream;
     'The Forsaken Merman' (1849) l. 35

9 Where great whales come sailing by,
  Sail and sail, with unshut eye,
  Round the world for ever and aye.
     'The Forsaken Merman' (1849) l. 43

10 This truth—to prove, and make thine own:
   'Thou hast been, shalt be, art, alone.'
      'Isolation. To Marguerite' (1857) l. 29

11 Creep into thy narrow bed,
   Creep, and let no more be said!
   Vain thy onset! all stands fast.
   Thou thyself must break at last.

   Let the long contention cease!
   Geese are swans, and swans are geese.
   Let them have it how they will!
   Thou art tired; best be still.
      'The Last Word' (1867)

12 Calm soul of all things! make it mine
   To feel, amid the city's jar,
   That there abides a peace of thine,
   Man did not make, and cannot mar.
      'Lines written in Kensington Gardens' (1852)

13 He spoke, and loosed our heart in tears.
   He laid us as we lay at birth
   On the cool flowery lap of earth.
      'Memorial Verses, April 1850' (1852) l. 47 (of
      Wordsworth)

14 Ere the parting hour go by,
   Quick, thy tablets, Memory!
      'A Memory Picture' (1849)

15 With aching hands and bleeding feet
   We dig and heap, lay stone on stone;
   We bear the burden and the heat
   Of the long day, and wish 'twere done.
   Not till the hours of light return,
   All we have built do we discern.
      'Morality' (1852). Cf. St Matthew 91:28

16 Say, has some wet bird-haunted English lawn
   Lent it the music of its trees at dawn?
      'Parting' (1852) l. 19

17 Hark! ah, the Nightingale!
   The tawny-throated!
   Hark! from that moonlit cedar what a burst!
   What triumph! hark—what pain!
      'Philomela' (1853) l. 1

18 Eternal Passion!
   Eternal Pain!
      'Philomela' (1853) l. 31

19 Cruel, but composed and bland,
   Dumb, inscrutable and grand,
   So Tiberius might have sat,
   Had Tiberius been a cat.
      'Poor Matthias' (1885) l. 40

20 Her cabined ample Spirit,
   It fluttered and failed for breath.
   To-night it doth inherit
   The vasty hall of death.
      'Requiescat' (1853)

21 Not deep the Poet sees, but wide.
      'Resignation' (1849) l. 214

22 Yet they, believe me, who await
   No gifts from chance, have conquered fate.
      'Resignation' (1849) l. 247

23 Not milder is the general lot
   Because our spirits have forgot,
   In action's dizzying eddy whirled,
   The something that infects the world.
      'Resignation' (1849) l. 275

1 Coldly, sadly descends
  The autumn evening. The Field
  Strewn with its dank yellow drifts
  Of withered leaves, and the elms,
  Fade into dimness apace,
  Silent;—hardly a shout
  From a few boys late at their play!
  'Rugby Chapel, November 1857' (1867)

2 Go, for they call you, Shepherd, from the hill.
  'The Scholar-Gipsy' (1853) l. 1

3 All the live murmur of a summer's day.
  'The Scholar-Gipsy' (1853) l. 20

4 Tired of knocking at Preferment's door.
  'The Scholar-Gipsy' (1853) l. 35

5 Crossing the stripling Thames at Bab-lock-hithe,
  Trailing in the cool stream thy fingers wet,
  As the slow punt swings round.
  'The Scholar-Gipsy' (1853) l. 74

6 Rapt, twirling in thy hand a withered spray,
  And waiting for the spark from heaven to fall.
  'The Scholar-Gipsy' (1853) l. 119

7 The line of festal light in Christ Church hall.
  'The Scholar-Gipsy' (1853) l. 129

8 Thou waitest for the spark from heaven! and we,
  Light half-believers in our casual creeds . . .
  Who hesitate and falter life away,
  And lose to-morrow the ground won to-day—
  Ah, do not we, Wanderer, await it too?
  'The Scholar-Gipsy' (1853) l. 171

9 O born in days when wits were fresh and clear,
  And life ran gaily as the sparkling Thames;
  Before this strange disease of modern life,
  With its sick hurry, its divided aims,
  Its heads o'ertaxed, its palsied hearts, was rife—
  Fly hence, our contact fear!
  'The Scholar-Gipsy' (1853) l. 201

10 Still nursing the unconquerable hope,
   Still clutching the inviolable shade.
   'The Scholar-Gipsy' (1853) l. 211

11 Resolve to be thyself: and know, that he
   Who finds himself, loses his misery.
   'Self-Dependence' (1852) l. 31

12 Others abide our question. Thou art free.
   We ask and ask: Thou smilest and art still,
   Out-topping knowledge.
   'Shakespeare' (1849)

13 And thou, who didst the stars and sunbeams know,
   Self-schooled, self-scanned, self-honoured, self-secure,
   Didst tread on Earth unguessed at.—Better so!
   All pains the immortal spirit must endure,
   All weakness which impairs, all griefs which bow,
   Find their sole speech in that victorious brow.
   'Shakespeare' (1849)

14 Curled minion, dancer, coiner of sweet words!
   'Sohrab and Rustum' (1853) l. 458

15 No horse's cry was that, most like the roar
   Of some pained desert lion, who all day
   Hath trailed the hunter's javelin in his side,
   And comes at night to die upon the sand.
   'Sohrab and Rustum' (1853) l. 501

16 Truth sits upon the lips of dying men.
   'Sohrab and Rustum' (1853) l. 656

17 But the majestic river floated on,
   Out of the mist and hum of that low land,
   Into the frosty starlight.
   'Sohrab and Rustum' (1853) l. 875

18 Oxus, forgetting the bright speed he had
   In his high mountain cradle in Pamere,
   A foiled circuitous wanderer—till at last
   The longed-for dash of waves is heard, and wide
   His luminous home of waters opens, bright
   And tranquil, from whose floor the new-bathed stars
   Emerge, and shine upon the Aral Sea.
   'Sohrab and Rustum' (1853) l. 886

19 For rigorous teachers seized my youth,
   And purged its faith, and trimmed its fire,
   Showed me the high, white star of Truth,
   There bade me gaze, and there aspire.
   'Stanzas from the Grande Chartreuse' (1855) l. 67

20 Wandering between two worlds, one dead,
   The other powerless to be born,
   With nowhere yet to rest my head,
   Like these, on earth I wait forlorn.
   'Stanzas from the Grande Chartreuse' (1855) l. 85

21 What helps it now, that Byron bore,
   With haughty scorn which mocked the smart,
   Through Europe to the Aetolian shore
   The pageant of his bleeding heart?
   That thousands counted every groan,
   And Europe made his woe her own?
   'Stanzas from the Grande Chartreuse' (1855) l. 133

22 Ah! two desires toss about
   The poet's feverish blood.
   One drives him to the world without,
   And one to solitude.
   'Stanzas in Memory of the Author of "Obermann" ' (1852)
   l. 93

23 Still bent to make some port he knows not where,
   Still standing for some false impossible shore.
   'A Summer Night' (1852) l. 68

24 The signal-elm, that looks on Ilsley downs,
   The Vale, the three lone weirs, the youthful Thames.
   'Thyrsis' (1866) l. 14

25 And that sweet City with her dreaming spires,
   She needs not June for beauty's heightening.
   'Thyrsis' (1866) l. 19

26 So have I heard the cuckoo's parting cry,
   From the wet field, through the vext garden-trees,
   Come with the volleying rain and tossing breeze:
   'The bloom is gone, and with the bloom go I.'
   'Thyrsis' (1866) l. 57

27 Too quick despairer, wherefore wilt thou go?
   Soon will the high Midsummer pomps come on,
   Soon will the musk carnations break and swell.
   'Thyrsis' (1866) l. 61

28 For Time, not Corydon, hath conquered thee.
   'Thyrsis' (1866) l. 80

29 The foot less prompt to meet the morning dew,
   The heart less bounding at emotion new,
   And hope, once crushed, less quick to spring again.
   'Thyrsis' (1866) l. 138

1 Who saw life steadily, and saw it whole:
  The mellow glory of the Attic stage;
  Singer of sweet Colonus, and its child.
  'To a Friend' (1849) (of Sophocles)

2 France, famed in all great arts, in none supreme.
  'To a Republican Friend—Continued' (1849)

3 Yes! in the sea of life enisled,
  With echoing straits between us thrown,
  Dotting the shoreless watery wild,
  We mortal millions live *alone*.
  'To Marguerite—Continued' (1852) l. 1

4 A God, a God their severance ruled!
  And bade betwixt their shores to be
  The unplumbed, salt, estranging sea.
  'To Marguerite—Continued' (1852) l. 22

5 Nor bring, to see me cease to live,
  Some doctor full of phrase and fame,
  To shake his sapient head and give
  The ill he cannot cure a name.
  'A Wish' (1867)

6 And sigh that one thing only has been lent
  To youth and age in common—discontent.
  'Youth's Agitations' (1852)

7 Our society distributes itself into Barbarians,
  Philistines, and Populace; and America is just
  ourselves, with the Barbarians quite left out, and the
  Populace nearly.
  Culture and Anarchy (1869) preface

8 The pursuit of perfection, then, is the pursuit of
  sweetness and light ... He who works for sweetness
  and light united, works to make reason and the will of
  God prevail.
  Culture and Anarchy (1869) ch. 1. Cf. Swift 673:4

9 The men of culture are the true apostles of equality.
  Culture and Anarchy (1869) ch. 1

10 When I want to distinguish clearly the aristocratic
   class from the Philistines proper, or middle class, [I]
   name the former, in my own mind *the Barbarians*.
   Culture and Anarchy (1869) ch. 3

11 That vast portion ... of the working-class which, raw
   and half-developed, has long lain half-hidden amidst
   its poverty and squalor, and is now issuing from its
   hiding-place to assert an Englishman's heaven-born
   privilege of doing as he likes, and is beginning to
   perplex us by marching where it likes, meeting where
   it likes, bawling what it likes, breaking what it
   likes—to this vast residuum we may with great
   propriety give the name of Populace.
   Culture and Anarchy (1869) ch. 3

12 Hebraism and Hellenism—between these two points of
   influence moves our world.
   Culture and Anarchy (1869) ch. 4

13 'He knows' says Hebraism, 'his Bible!'—whenever we
   hear this said, we may, without any elaborate defence
   of culture, content ourselves with answering simply:
   'No man, who knows nothing else, knows even his
   Bible.'
   Culture and Anarchy (1869) ch. 5

14 Nothing could moderate, in the bosom of the great
   English middle class, their passionate, absorbing,
   almost blood-thirsty clinging to life.
   Essays in Criticism First Series (1865) preface

15 Beautiful city! so venerable, so lovely, so unravaged
   by the fierce intellectual life of our century, so serene!
   ... whispering from her towers the last enchantments
   of the Middle Age ... Home of lost causes, and
   forsaken beliefs, and unpopular names, and impossible
   loyalties!
   Essays in Criticism First Series (1865) preface (of Oxford)

16 'Our unrivalled happiness';—what an element of
   grimness, bareness, and hideousness mixes with it and
   blurs it; the workhouse, the dismal Mapperly
   Hills,—how dismal those who have seen them will
   remember;—the gloom, the smoke, the cold, the
   strangled illegitimate child! ... And the final
   touch,—short, bleak and inhuman: *Wragg is in
   custody*. The sex lost in the confusion of our unrivalled
   happiness; or (shall I say?) the superfluous Christian
   name lopped off by the straightforward vigour of our
   old Anglo-Saxon breed!
   Essays in Criticism First Series (1865) 'The Function of
   Criticism at the Present Time' (prompted by a newspaper
   report of the murder of her illegitimate child by a girl
   named Wragg)

17 I am bound by my own definition of criticism: *a
   disinterested endeavour to learn and propagate the best
   that is known and thought in the world.*
   Essays in Criticism First Series (1865) 'The Function of
   Criticism at the Present Time'

18 Philistinism!—We have not the expression in English.
   Perhaps we have not the word because we have so
   much of the thing.
   Essays in Criticism First Series (1865) 'Heinrich Heine'

19 The great apostle of the Philistines, Lord Macaulay.
   Essays in Criticism First Series (1865) 'Joubert'

20 The absence, in this country, of any force of educated
   literary and scientific opinion.
   Essays in Criticism First Series (1865) 'The Literary
   Influence of Academies'

21 In poetry, no less than in life, he is 'a beautiful and
   ineffectual angel, beating in the void his luminous
   wings in vain'.
   Essays in Criticism Second Series (1888) 'Shelley' (quoting
   from his own essay on Byron in the same work)

22 More and more mankind will discover that we have to
   turn to poetry to interpret life for us, to console us, to
   sustain us. Without poetry, our science will appear
   incomplete; and most of what now passes with us for
   religion and philosophy will be replaced by poetry.
   Essays in Criticism Second Series (1888) 'The Study of
   Poetry'

23 The difference between genuine poetry and the poetry
   of Dryden, Pope, and all their school, is briefly this:
   their poetry is conceived and composed in their wits,
   genuine poetry is conceived and composed in the soul.
   Essays in Criticism Second Series (1888) 'Thomas Gray'

24 Poetry is at bottom a criticism of life.
   Essays in Criticism Second Series (1888) 'Wordsworth'

25 His expression may often be called bald ... but it is
   bald as the bare mountain tops are bald, with a
   baldness full of grandeur.
   Essays in Criticism Second Series (1888) 'Wordsworth'

26 I am past thirty, and three parts iced over.
   Howard Foster Lowry (ed.) *The Letters of Matthew Arnold to
   Arthur Hugh Clough* (1932) 12 February 1853

1 Terms like grace, new birth, justification . . . terms, in short, which with St Paul are literary terms, theologians have employed as if they were scientific terms.
  Literature and Dogma (1873) ch. 1

2 The true meaning of religion is thus not simply morality, but morality touched by emotion.
  Literature and Dogma (1873) ch. 1

3 Conduct is three-fourths of our life and its largest concern.
  Literature and Dogma (1873) ch. 1

4 But there remains the question: what righteousness really is. The method and secret and sweet reasonableness of Jesus.
  Literature and Dogma (1873) ch. 12

5 So we have the Philistine of genius in religion—Luther; the Philistine of genius in politics—Cromwell; the Philistine of genius in literature—Bunyan.
  Mixed Essays (1879) 'Lord Falkland'

6 Wordsworth says somewhere that wherever Virgil seems to have composed 'with his eye on the object', Dryden fails to render him. Homer invariably composes 'with his eye on the object', whether the object be a moral or a material one: Pope composes with his eye on his style, into which he translates his object, whatever it is.
  On Translating Homer (1861) Lecture 1

7 Of these two literatures [French and German], as of the intellect of Europe in general, the main effort, for now many years, has been a *critical* effort; the endeavours, in all branches of knowledge—theology, philosophy, history, art, science—to see the object as in itself it really is.
  On Translating Homer (1861) Lecture 2

8 He [the translator] will find one English book and one only, where, as in the *Iliad* itself, perfect plainness of speech is allied with perfect nobleness; and that book is the Bible.
  On Translating Homer (1861) Lecture 3

9 Nothing has raised more questioning among my critics than these words—noble, the grand style . . . I think it will be found that the grand style arises in poetry, when a noble nature, poetically gifted, treats with simplicity or with severity a serious subject.
  On Translating Homer. Last Words (1862)

10 People think that I can teach them style. What stuff it all is! Have something to say, and say it as clearly as you can. That is the only secret of style.
  In G. W. E. Russell *Collections and Recollections* (1898) ch. 13

Samuel James Arnold

English organist and composer

11 England, home and beauty.
  'The Death of Nelson' (1811 song)

Thomas Arnold 1795–1842

English historian; Headmaster of Rugby School from 1828

12 My object will be, if possible, to form Christian men, for Christian boys I can scarcely hope to make.
  Letter to Revd John Tucker, 2 March 1828, on appointment to the Headmastership of Rugby School, in Arthur Penrhyn Stanley *The Life and Correspondence of Thomas Arnold* (1844) vol. 1, ch. 2

13 What we must look for here is, 1st, religious and moral principles: 2ndly, gentlemanly conduct: 3rdly, intellectual ability.
  Address to the Praeposters of Rugby School, in Arthur Penrhyn Stanley *The Life and Correspondence of Thomas Arnold* (1844) vol. 1, ch. 3

14 As for rioting, the old Roman way of dealing with that is always the right one; flog the rank and file, and fling the ringleaders from the Tarpeian rock.
  From an unpublished letter written before 1828, quoted by Matthew Arnold in *Cornhill Magazine* August 1868 'Anarchy and Authority'

Raymond Aron 1905–

French sociologist and political journalist

15 *La pensée politique, en France, est rétrospective ou utopique.*
  Political thought, in France, is retrospective or utopian.
  L'opium des intellectuels (1955) ch. 1

Antonin Artaud 1896–1948

French actor, director, and dramatic theorist

16 *Il faut nous laver de la littérature. Nous voulons être hommes avant tout, être humains.*
  We must wash literature off ourselves. We want to be men above all, to be human.
  Les Oeuvres et les Hommes (unpublished MS, 17 May 1922)

George Asaf 1880–1951

British songwriter

17 What's the use of worrying?
  It never was worth while,
  So, pack up your troubles in your old kit-bag,
  And smile, smile, smile.
  'Pack up your Troubles' (1915 song)

Roger Ascham 1515–68

English scholar, writer, and courtier

18 I said . . . how, and why, young children, were sooner allured by love, than driven by beating, to attain good learning.
  The Schoolmaster (1570) preface

1 There is no such whetstone, to sharpen a good wit and encourage a will to learning, as is praise.

  The Schoolmaster (1570) bk. 1

2 *Inglese Italianato, è un diavolo incarnato*, that is to say, you remain men in shape and fashion, but become devils in life and condition.

  The Schoolmaster (1570) bk. 1 (of Englishmen travelling in Italy)

3 He that will write well in any tongue, must follow this counsel of Aristotle, to speak as the common people do, to think as wise men do; and so should every man understand him, and the judgement of wise men allow him.

  Toxophilus (1545) 'To all gentlemen and yeomen of England'

Daisy Ashford 1881–1972

English child author

4 Mr Salteena was an elderly man of 42.

  The Young Visiters (1919) ch. 1

5 I am not quite a gentleman but you would hardly notice it but can't be helped anyhow.

  The Young Visiters (1919) ch. 1

6 You look rather rash my dear your colors dont quite match your face.

  The Young Visiters (1919) ch. 2

7 Bernard always had a few prayers in the hall and some whiskey afterwards as he was rarther pious but Mr Salteena was not very addicted to prayers so he marched up to bed.

  The Young Visiters (1919) ch. 3

8 Oh this is most kind said Mr Salteena.
  Minnit closed his eyes with a tired smile. Not kind sir he muttered quite usual.

  The Young Visiters (1919) ch. 5

9 It was a sumpshous spot all done up in gold with plenty of looking glasses.

  The Young Visiters (1919) ch. 5

10 Oh I see said the Earl but my own idear is that these things are as piffle before the wind.

  The Young Visiters (1919) ch. 5

11 The bearer of this letter is an old friend of mine not quite the right side of the blanket as they say in fact he is the son of a first rate butcher but his mother was a decent family called Hyssopps of the Glen so you see he is not so bad and is desireus of being the correct article.

  The Young Visiters (1919) ch. 5

12 My life will be sour grapes and ashes without you.

  The Young Visiters (1919) ch. 8

13 Take me back to the Gaierty hotel.

  The Young Visiters (1919) ch. 9

Isaac Asimov 1920–92

Russian-born biochemist and science fiction writer

14 The three fundamental Rules of Robotics ... One, a robot may not injure a human being, or, through inaction, allow a human being to come to harm ... Two ... a robot must obey the orders given it by human beings except where such orders would conflict with the First Law ... three, a robot must protect its own existence as long as such protection does not conflict with the First or Second Laws.

  I, Robot (1950) 'Runaround'

Anne Askew 1521–46

English martyr

15 Like as the armèd knight
  Appointed to the field,
  With this world will I fight,
  And faith shall be my shield ...

  I am not she that list
  My anchor to let fall,
  For every drizzling mist
  My ship substantial.

  'The Ballad which Anne Askew made and sang when she was in Newgate' (1546)

Herbert Asquith (1st Earl of Oxford and Asquith) 1852–1928

British Liberal politician; Prime Minister, 1908–16

16 We had better wait and see.

  Phrase used repeatedly in speeches in 1910, referring to the rumour that the House of Lords was to be flooded with new Liberal peers to ensure the passage of the Finance Bill. See Roy Jenkins *Asquith* (1964) ch. 14

17 We shall never sheath the sword which we have not lightly drawn until Belgium recovers in full measure all and more than all that she has sacrificed, until France is adequately secured against the menace of aggression, until the rights of the smaller nationalities of Europe are placed upon an unassailable foundation, and until the military domination of Prussia is wholly and finally destroyed.

  Speech at the Guildhall, London, 9 November 1914, in *The Times* 10 November 1914

18 It is fitting that we should have buried the Unknown Prime Minister [Bonar Law] by the side of the Unknown Soldier.

  In Robert Blake *The Unknown Prime Minister* (1955) p. 531

19 [The War Office kept three sets of figures:] one to mislead the public, another to mislead the Cabinet, and the third to mislead itself.

  In Alistair Horne *Price of Glory* (1962) ch. 2

Margot Asquith (Countess of Oxford and Asquith) 1864–1945

Political hostess; wife of Herbert Asquith

20 Kitchener is a great poster.

  More Memories (1933) ch. 6

1 The *t* is silent, as in *Harlow*.
> To Jean Harlow, who had been mispronouncing her name, in T. S. Matthews *Great Tom* (1973) ch. 7

2 Lord Birkenhead is very clever but sometimes his brains go to his head.
> In *Listener* 11 June 1953 'Margot Oxford' by Lady Violet Bonham Carter

3 She tells enough white lies to ice a wedding cake.
> Of Lady Desborough, in *Listener* 11 June 1953 'Margot Oxford' by Lady Violet Bonham Carter

4 He can't see a belt without hitting below it.
> Of Lloyd George, in *Listener* 11 June 1953 'Margot Oxford' by Lady Violet Bonham Carter

Mary Astell 1668–1731
English poet and feminist

5   Their sophistry I can control
Who falsely say that women have no soul.
> 'Ambition' (written 1684) l. 7

6 Happy am I who out of danger sit,
Can see and pity them who wade thro it;
Need take no thought my treasure to dispose,
What I ne'er had I cannot fear to lose.
> 'Awake my Lute' l. 18

7 Our opposers usually miscall our quickness of thought, fancy and flash, and christen their own heaviness by the specious names of judgement and solidity; but it is easy to retort upon them the reproachful ones of dullness and stupidity.
> *An Essay in Defence of the Female Sex* (1696) p. 19

8 Fetters of gold are still fetters, and the softest lining can never make them so easy as liberty.
> *An Essay in Defence of the Female Sex* (1696) p. 25

9 If all men are born free, how is it that all women are born slaves?
> *Some Reflections upon Marriage* (1706 ed.) preface

Sir Jacob Astley 1579–1652
English soldier and royalist

10 O Lord! thou knowest how busy I must be this day: if I forget thee, do not thou forget me.
> Prayer before the Battle of Edgehill, in Sir Philip Warwick *Memoires* (1701) p. 229

Nancy Astor (Viscountess Astor) 1879–1964
British Conservative politician

11 I married beneath me, all women do.
> In *Dictionary of National Biography 1961–1970* (1981) p. 43

Brooks Atkinson 1894–1984
American journalist and critic

12 After each war there is a little less democracy to save.
> *Once Around the Sun* (1951) 7 January

E. L. Atkinson 1882–1929 *and* Apsley Cherry-Garrard 1882–1959
British polar explorers

13 Hereabouts died a very gallant gentleman, Captain L. E. G. Oates of the Inniskilling Dragoons. In March 1912, returning from the Pole, he walked willingly to his death in a blizzard to try and save his comrades, beset by hardships.
> Epitaph on cairn erected in the Antarctic, 15 November 1912, in Apsley Cherry-Garrard *The Worst Journey in the World* (1922) p. 487

Clement Attlee (1st Earl Attlee) 1883–1967
British Labour politician; Prime Minister, 1945–51

14 The voice we heard was that of Mr Churchill but the mind was that of Lord Beaverbrook.
> Speech on radio, 5 June 1945, in Francis Williams *A Prime Minister Remembers* (1961) ch. 6

15 I think the British have the distinction above all other nations of being able to put new wine into old bottles without bursting them.
> Speech, *Hansard* 24 October 1950, col. 2705

16 Few thought he was even a starter
There were many who thought themselves smarter
But he ended PM
CH and OM
An earl and a knight of the garter.
> Describing himself in a letter to Tom Attlee, 8 April 1956; in Kenneth Harris *Attlee* (1982) p. 545

17 [Russian Communism is] the illegitimate child of Karl Marx and Catherine the Great.
> Speech at Aarhus University, 11 April 1956, in *The Times* 12 April 1956

18 Democracy means government by discussion, but it is only effective if you can stop people talking.
> Speech at Oxford, 14 June 1957, in *The Times* 15 June 1957

19 A monologue is not a decision.
> To Winston Churchill, who had complained that a matter had been raised several times in Cabinet, in Francis Williams *A Prime Minister Remembers* (1961) ch. 7

Henriette Auber 1773–1862
English hymn-writer

20 Our blest Redeemer, ere he breathed
His tender last farewell,
A Guide, a Comforter, bequeathed
With us to dwell.

He came in tongues of living flame,
To teach, convince, subdue;
All-powerful as the wind he came,
As viewless too.
> 'Our blest Redeemer, ere he breathed' (1829 hymn)

John Aubrey 1626–97

English antiquary and biographer

1 The Bishop sometimes would take the key of the wine-cellar, and he and his chaplain would go and lock themselves in and be merry. Then first he lays down his episcopal hat—*There lies the Doctor.* Then he puts off his gown—*There lies the Bishop.* Then 'twas, *Here's to thee, Corbet,* and *Here's to thee, Lushington.*
   Brief Lives 'Richard Corbet'

2 How these curiosities would be quite forgot, did not such idle fellows as I am put them down.
   Brief Lives 'Venetia Digby'

3 He had read much, if one considers his long life; but his contemplation was much more than his reading. He was wont to say that if he had read as much as other men, he should have known no more than other men.
   Brief Lives 'Thomas Hobbes'

4 As they were reading of inscribing and circumscribing figures, said he, I will show you how to inscribe a triangle in a quadrangle. Bring a pig into the quadrangle and I will set the college dog at him, and he will take the pig by the ear, then I come and take the dog by the tail and the hog by the tail, and so there you have a triangle in a quadrangle; *quod erat faciendum.*
   Brief Lives 'Ralph Kettel'

5 The Dr [Ralph Kettel] tastes the wine:—'What,' said he, 'didst thou take this drink out of a ditch?' and when he saw the cheese-cakes:—'What have we here, *crinkum crankum?'*
   Brief Lives 'Ralph Kettel'

6 His harmonical and ingenious soul did lodge in a beautiful and well proportioned body. He was a spare man.
   Brief Lives 'John Milton'

7 Oval face. His eye a dark grey. He had auburn hair. His complexion exceeding fair—he was so fair that they called him the *lady of* Christ's College.
   Brief Lives 'John Milton'

8 He pronounced the letter R (*littera canina*) very hard—a certain sign of a satirical wit.
   Brief Lives 'John Milton'

9 Sciatica: he cured it, by boiling his buttock.
   Brief Lives 'Sir Jonas Moore'

10 She was when a child much against the Bishops, and prayed to God to take them to him, but afterwards was reconciled to them. Prayed aloud, as the hypocritical fashion then was, and was overheard.
   Brief Lives 'Katherine Philips'

11 Sir Walter, being strangely surprised and put out of his countenance at so great a table, gives his son a damned blow over the face. His son, as rude as he was, would not strike his father, but strikes over the face the gentleman that sat next to him and said 'Box about: 'twill come to my father anon'.
   Brief Lives 'Sir Walter Raleigh'

12 He was a handsome, well-shaped man: very good company, and of a very ready and pleasant smooth wit.
   Brief Lives 'William Shakespeare'

13 Anno 1670, not far from Cirencester, was an apparition; being demanded whether a good spirit or a bad? returned no answer, but disappeared with a curious perfume and most melodious twang. Mr W. Lilly believes it was a fairy.
   Miscellanies (1696) 'Apparitions'

Auctoritates Aristotelis

A compilation of medieval propositions drawn from diverse classical and other sources (ed. J. Hamesse, 1974)

14 *Consuetudo est altera natura.*
   Habit is second nature.

15 *Contra negantem principia non est disputandum.*
   You cannot argue with someone who denies the first principles.

16 *Deus et natura nihil faciunt frustra.*
   God and nature do nothing in vain.

17 *Ignorantia excusat peccatum.*
   Ignorance excuses from sin.

18 *Melius est esse quam non esse.*
   It is better to be than not to be.

19 *Natura dat unicuique quod sibi conveniens est.*
   Nature gives to each what is appropriate.

20 *Natura desiderat semper quod melius est.*
   Nature always desires what is better.

21 *Non est idem bonus homo et bonus civis.*
   A good man and a good citizen are not the same thing.

22 *Omnes homines naturaliter scire desiderant.*
   All men naturally desire to know.

23 *Oportet inquisitores veritatis non esse inimicos.*
   There should be no enmity among seekers after truth.

24 *Parentes plus amant filios quam e converso.*
   Parents love their children more than children love their parents.

25 *Signum scientis est posse docere.*
   The touchstone of knowledge is the ability to teach.

26 *Silentium mulieri praestat ornatum.*
   Silence is a woman's finest ornament.

27 *Tempus est mensura motus rerum mobilium.*
   Time is the measure of movement.

W. H. Auden (*Wystan Hugh Auden*) 1907–73

English poet

28 Sob, heavy world,
   Sob as you spin
   Mantled in mist, remote from the happy.
   The Age of Anxiety (1947) pt. 4 'The Dirge'

1 In a garden shady this holy lady
With reverent cadence and subtle psalm,
Like a black swan as death came on
Poured forth her song in perfect calm:
And by ocean's margin this innocent virgin
Constructed an organ to enlarge her prayer,
And notes tremendous from her great engine
Thundered out on the Roman air.

Blonde Aphrodite rose up excited,
Moved to delight by the melody,
White as an orchid she rode quite naked
In an oyster shell on top of the sea.

Anthem for St Cecilia's Day (1941) pt. 1; set to music by
Benjamin Britten, to whom it was dedicated, as *Hymn to St
Cecilia* op. 27 (1942)

2 Blessed Cecilia, appear in visions
To all musicians, appear and inspire:
Translated Daughter, come down and startle
Composing mortals with immortal fire.

Anthem for St Cecilia's Day (1941) pt. 1

3 I'll love you, dear, I'll love you
Till China and Africa meet
And the river jumps over the mountain
And the salmon sing in the street,

I'll love you till the ocean
Is folded and hung up to dry
And the seven stars go squawking
Like geese about the sky.

'As I Walked Out One Evening' (1940)

4 O plunge your hands in water,
Plunge them in up to the wrist;
Stare, stare in the basin
And wonder what you've missed.

The glacier knocks in the cupboard,
The desert sighs in the bed,
And the crack in the tea-cup opens
A lane to the land of the dead.

'As I Walked Out One Evening' (1940)

5 At the far end of the enormous room
An orchestra is playing to the rich.

'At the far end of the enormous room' (1933)

6 August for the people and their favourite islands.
Daily the steamers sidle up to meet
The effusive welcome of the pier.

'August for the people and their favourite islands' (1936)

7 The desires of the heart are as crooked as corkscrews
Not to be born is the best for man
The second best is a formal order
The dance's pattern, dance while you can.
Dance, dance, for the figure is easy
The tune is catching and will not stop
Dance till the stars come down with the rafters
Dance, dance, dance till you drop.

'Death's Echo' (1937). Cf. Sophocles 656:14

8 Happy the hare at morning, for she cannot read
The Hunter's waking thoughts.

Dog beneath the Skin (with Christopher Isherwood, 1935)
act 2, sc. 2

9 To save your world you asked this man to die:
Would this man, could he see you now, ask why?

'Epitaph for the Unknown Soldier' (1955)

10 Perfection, of a kind, was what he was after,
And the poetry he invented was easy to understand;
He knew human folly like the back of his hand,
And was greatly interested in armies and fleets;
When he laughed, respectable senators burst with
laughter,
And when he cried the little children died in the
streets.

'Epitaph on a Tyrant' (1940). Cf. Motley 487:3

11 Altogether elsewhere, vast
Herds of reindeer move across
Miles and miles of golden moss,
Silently and very fast.

'The Fall of Rome' (1951)

12 To us he is no more a person
now but a whole climate of opinion.

'In Memory of Sigmund Freud' (1940) st. 17

13 He disappeared in the dead of winter:
The brooks were frozen, the airports almost deserted,
And snow disfigured the public statues;
The mercury sank in the mouth of the dying day.
What instruments we have agree
The day of his death was a dark cold day.

'In Memory of W. B. Yeats' (1940) pt. 1

14 You were silly like us; your gift survived it all:
The parish of rich women, physical decay,
Yourself. Mad Ireland hurt you into poetry.
Now Ireland has her madness and her weather still,
For poetry makes nothing happen: it survives
In the valley of its saying where executives
Would never want to tamper, flows on south
From ranches of isolation and the busy griefs,
Raw towns that we believe and die in; it survives,
A way of happening, a mouth.

'In Memory of W. B. Yeats' (1940) pt. 2

15 Earth, receive an honoured guest:
William Yeats is laid to rest.
Let the Irish vessel lie
Emptied of its poetry.

In the nightmare of the dark
All the dogs of Europe bark,
And the living nations wait,
Each sequestered in its hate;

Intellectual disgrace
Stares from every human face,
And the seas of pity lie
Locked and frozen in each eye.

'In Memory of W. B. Yeats' (1940) pt. 3

16 In the deserts of the heart
Let the healing fountain start,
In the prison of his days
Teach the free man how to praise.

'In Memory of W. B. Yeats' (1940) pt. 3

17   There is no love;
There are only the various envies, all of them sad.

'In Praise of Limestone' (1951) l. 58

1 ... This land is not the sweet home that it looks,
  Nor its peace the historical calm of a site
  Where something was settled once and for all: A
    backward
  And dilapidated province, connected
  To the big busy world by a tunnel, with a certain
  Seedy appeal.
    'In Praise of Limestone' (1951) l. 61

2 I see it often since you've been away:
  The island, the veranda, and the fruit;
  The tiny steamer breaking from the bay;
  The literary mornings with its hoot;
  Our ugly comic servant; and then you,
  Lovely and willing every afternoon.
    'I see it often since you've been away' (1933)

3 Let the florid music praise,
  The flute and the trumpet,
  Beauty's conquest of your face:
  In that land of flesh and bone,
  Where from citadels on high
  Her imperial standards fly,
  Let the hot sun
  Shine on, shine on.
    'Let the florid music praise' (1936)

4 Look, stranger, at this island now
  The leaping light for your delight discovers,
  Stand stable here
  And silent be,
  That through the channels of the ear
  May wander like a river
  The swaying sound of the sea.
    'Look, stranger, at this island now' (1936)

5 Lay your sleeping head, my love,
  Human on my faithless arm;
  Time and fevers burn away
  Individual beauty from
  Thoughtful children, and the grave
  Proves the child ephemeral:
  But in my arms till break of day
  Let the living creature lie,
  Mortal, guilty, but to me
  The entirely beautiful.
    'Lullaby' (1940)

6 About suffering they were never wrong,
  The Old Masters: how well they understood
  Its human position; how it takes place
  While someone else is eating or opening a window or
    just walking dully along.
    'Musée des Beaux Arts' (1940)

7 They never forgot
  That even the dreadful martyrdom must run its course
  Anyhow in a corner, some untidy spot
  Where the dogs go on with their doggy life and the
    torturer's horse
  Scratches its innocent behind on a tree.
    'Musée des Beaux Arts' (1940)

8 To the man-in-the-street, who, I'm sorry to say,
  Is a keen observer of life,
  The word 'Intellectual' suggests straight away
  A man who's untrue to his wife.
    New Year Letter (1941) l. 1277 n.

9 This is the Night Mail crossing the Border,
  Bringing the cheque and the postal order,
  Letters for the rich, letters for the poor,
  The shop at the corner, the girl next door.
  Pulling up Beattock, a steady climb:
  The gradient's against her, but she's on time.
  Past cotton-grass and moorland border,
  Shovelling white steam over her shoulder.
    'Night Mail' (1936) pt. 1

10 Letters of thanks, letters from banks,
   Letters of joy from girl and boy,
   Receipted bills and invitations
   To inspect new stock or to visit relations,
   And applications for situations,
   And timid lovers' declarations,
   And gossip, gossip from all the nations.
    'Night Mail' (1936) pt. 3

11 And make us as Newton was, who in his garden
    watching
   The apple falling towards England, became aware
   Between himself and her of an eternal tie.
    'O Love, the interest itself' (1936)

12 Private faces in public places
   Are wiser and nicer
   Than public faces in private places.
    Orators (1932) dedication

13 Out on the lawn I lie in bed,
   Vega conspicuous overhead.
    'Out on the lawn I lie in bed' (1936)

14 O what is that sound which so thrills the ear
   Down in the valley drumming, drumming?
   Only the scarlet soldiers, dear,
   The soldiers coming.
    'O what is that sound' (1936)

15 O it's broken the lock and splintered the door,
   O it's the gate where they're turning, turning;
   Their boots are heavy on the floor
   And their eyes are burning.
    'O what is that sound' (1936)

16 Some thirty inches from my nose
   The frontier of my Person goes,
   And all the untilled air between
   Is private *pagus* or demesne.
   Stranger, unless with bedroom eyes
   I beckon you to fraternize,
   Beware of rudely crossing it:
   I have no gun, but I can spit.
    'Prologue: the Birth of Architecture' (1966) postscript

17 At Dirty Dick's and Sloppy Joe's
   We drank our liquor straight,
   Some went upstairs with Margery,
   And some, alas, with Kate.
    'The Sea and the Mirror' (1944) pt. 2 (Master and
    Boatswain)

18 My Dear One is mine as mirrors are lonely.
    'The Sea and the Mirror' (1944) pt. 2 (Miranda)

19 I and the public know
   What all schoolchildren learn,
   Those to whom evil is done
   Do evil in return.
    'September 1, 1939' (1940)

1 All I have is a voice
To undo the folded lie,
The romantic lie in the brain
Of the sensual man-in-the-street
And the lie of Authority
Whose buildings grope the sky:
There is no such thing as the State
And no one exists alone;
Hunger allows no choice
To the citizen or the police;
We must love one another or die.
    'September 1, 1939' (1940)

2 Out of the air a voice without a face
Proved by statistics that some cause was just
In tones as dry and level as the place.
    'The Shield of Achilles' (1955)

3 A shilling life will give you all the facts.
    Title of poem (1936)

4 A poet's hope: to be,
like some valley cheese,
local, but prized elsewhere.
    'Shorts II' (1976)

5 Sir, no man's enemy, forgiving all
But will his negative inversion, be prodigal:
Send to us power and light, a sovereign touch
Curing the intolerable neutral itch,
The exhaustion of weaning, the liar's quinsy,
And the distortions of ingrown virginity.
    'Sir, No Man's Enemy' (1930)

6 Harrow the house of the dead; look shining at
New styles of architecture, a change of heart.
    'Sir, No Man's Enemy' (1930)

7 To-morrow for the young the poets exploding like
    bombs,
The walks by the lake, the weeks of perfect
    communion;
To-morrow the bicycle races
Through the suburbs on summer evenings: but to-day
    the struggle.
    'Spain 1937' (1937) st. 20

8 The stars are dead; the animals will not look:
We are left alone with our day, and the time is short
    and
History to the defeated
May say Alas but cannot help or pardon.
    'Spain 1937' (1937) st. 23

9 To ask the hard question is simple.
    Title of poem (1933)

10 Let us honour if we can
The vertical man
Though we value none
But the horizontal one.
    'To Christopher Isherwood' (1930)

11 Our researches into Public Opinion are content
That he held the proper opinions for the time of year;
When there was peace, he was for peace; when there
    was war, he went.
    'The Unknown Citizen' (1940)

12 Was he free? Was he happy? The question is absurd:
Had anything been wrong, we should certainly have
    heard.
    'The Unknown Citizen' (1940)

13 The sky is darkening like a stain;
Something is going to fall like rain,
And it won't be flowers.
    'The Witnesses' (1935) l. 67

14 All sin tends to be addictive, and the terminal point of
addiction is what is called damnation.
    A Certain World (1970) 'Hell'

15 Man is a history-making creature who can neither
repeat his past nor leave it behind.
    The Dyer's Hand (1963) 'D. H. Lawrence'

16 The true men of action in our time, those who
transform the world, are not the politicians and
statesmen, but the scientists. Unfortunately poetry
cannot celebrate them, because their deeds are
concerned with things, not persons, and are,
therefore, speechless. When I find myself in the
company of scientists, I feel like a shabby curate who
has strayed by mistake into a drawing room full of
dukes.
    The Dyer's Hand (1963) 'The Poet and the City'

17 Some books are undeservedly forgotten; none are
undeservedly remembered.
    The Dyer's Hand (1963) 'Reading'

18 What do you think about England, this country of
ours where nobody is well?
    The Orators (1932) 'Address for a Prize-Day'

19 My face looks like a wedding-cake left out in the rain.
    In Humphrey Carpenter W. H. Auden (1981) pt. 2, ch. 6

20 Art is born of humiliation.
    In Stephen Spender World Within World (1951) ch. 2

Émile Augier 1820–89
French poet and playwright

21 MARQUIS: *Mettez un canard sur un lac au milieu des
cygnes, vous verrez qu'il regrettera sa mare et finira par
y retourner.*
MONTRICHARD: *La nostalgie de la boue!*
MARQUIS: Put a duck on a lake in the midst of some
    swans, and you'll see he'll miss his pond and
    eventually return to it.
MONTRICHARD: Longing to be back in the mud!
    Le Mariage d'Olympe (1855) act 1, sc. 1

St Augustine of Hippo AD 354–430
Early Christian theologian

22 *Nondum amabam, et amare amabam . . . quaerebam quid
amarem, amans amare.*
I loved not yet, yet I loved to love . . . I sought what I
might love, loving to love.
    Confessions (AD 397–8) bk. 3, ch. 1

23 *Et illa erant fercula, in quibus mihi esurienti te
inferebantur sol et luna.*
And these were the dishes wherein to me,
hunger-starven for thee, the sun and moon were
served up.
    Confessions (AD 397–8) bk. 3, ch. 6

24 *Da mihi castitatem et continentiam, sed noli modo.*
Give me chastity and continency—but not yet!
    Confessions (AD 397–8) bk. 8, ch. 7

1 *Tolle lege, tolle lege.*

Take up and read, take up and read.

Confessions (AD 397–8) bk. 8, ch. 12

2 *Sero te amavi, pulchritudo tam antiqua et tam nova, sero te amavi! et ecce intus eras et ego foris, et ibi te quaerebam.*

Too late came I to love thee, O thou Beauty both so ancient and so fresh, yea too late came I to love thee. And behold, thou wert within me, and I out of myself, where I made search for thee.

Confessions (AD 397–8) bk. 10, ch. 27

3 *Continentiam iubes; da quod iubes et iube quod vis.*

You command continence; give what you command, and command what you will.

Confessions (AD 397–8) bk. 10, ch. 29

4 *Salus extra ecclesiam non est.*

There is no salvation outside the church.

De Baptismo contra Donatistas bk. 4, ch. 17, sect. 24. Cf. Cyprian 229:8, 229:10

5 *Audi partem alteram.*

Hear the other side.

De Duabus Animabus contra Manicheos ch. 14

6 *Dilige et quod vis fac.*

Love and do what you will.

In Epistolam Joannis ad Parthos (AD 413) tractatus 7, sect. 8 (often quoted 'Ama et fac quod vis')

7 *Multi quidem facilius se abstinent ut non utantur, quam temperent ut bene utantur.*

To many, total abstinence is easier than perfect moderation.

On the Good of Marriage (AD 401) ch. 21

8 *Cum dilectione hominum et odio vitiorum.*

With love for mankind and hatred of sins.

Letter 211 in J.-P. Migne (ed.) *Patrologiae Latinae* (1845) vol. 33 (often quoted 'Love the sinner but hate the sin')

9 *Roma locuta est; causa finita est.*

Rome has spoken; the case is concluded.

Traditional summary of words found in *Sermons* (Antwerp, 1702) no. 131, sect. 10

10 *De vitiis nostris scalam nobis facimus, si vitia ipsa calcamus.*

We make ourselves a ladder out of our vices if we trample the vices themselves underfoot.

Sermon no. 176 ('On the Ascension of the Lord' no. 1) in J.-P. Migne (ed.) *Patrologiae Latinae* (1845) vol. 38

Augustus 63 BC–AD 14

First Roman emperor

11 *Quintili Vare, legiones redde.*

Quintilius Varus, give me back my legions.

In Suetonius *Lives of the Caesars* 'Divus Augustus' sect. 23

12 *Festina lente.*

Make haste slowly.

In Suetonius *Lives of the Caesars* 'Divus Augustus' sect. 25

13 *Iure sit gloriatus marmoream se relinquere, quam latericiam accepisset.*

He could boast that he inherited it brick and left it marble.

In Suetonius *Lives of the Caesars* 'Divus Augustus' sect. 28 (referring to the city of Rome)

14 *Ad Kalendas Graecas soluturos.*

That they would pay at the Greek Kalends.

In Suetonius *Lives of the Caesars* 'Divus Augustus' sect. 87 (meaning never)

Marcus Aurelius AD 121–80

Roman emperor from AD 161

15 πᾶν μοι συναρμόζει ὃ σοὶ εὐάρμοστόν ἐστιν, ὦ κόσμε. οὐδέν μοι πρόωρον οὐδὲ ὄψιμον ὃ σοὶ εὔκαιρον. πᾶν μοι καρπὸς ὃ φέρουσιν αἱ σαὶ ὧραι, ὦ φύσις· ἐκ σοῦ πάντα, ἐν σοὶ πάντα, εἰς σὲ πάντα. ἐκεῖνος μέν φησιν. "ὦ πόλι φίλη Κέκροπος". σὺ δὲ οὐκ ἐρεῖς· "ὦ πόλι φίλη Διος";

Everything is fitting for me, my universe, which fits thy purpose. Nothing in its good time is too early or too late for me; everything is fruit for me which thy seasons, Nature, bear; from thee, in thee, to thee, are all things. The poet sings 'Dear city of Cecrops', and you will not say 'Dear city of God'?

Meditations bk. 4, sect. 23

16 Ποταμός τίς ἐστι τῶν γινομένων καὶ ῥεῦμα βίαιον ὁ αἰών· ἅμα τε γὰρ ὤφθη ἕκαστον καὶ παρενήνεκται, καὶ ἄλλο παραφέρεται, τὸ δὲ ἐνεχθήσεται.

There is a sort of river of things passing into being, and Time is a violent torrent; no sooner is a thing brought to sight than it is swept by and another takes its place, and this too will be swept away.

Meditations bk. 4, sect. 43

17 Οὐδὲν οὐδενὶ συμβαίνει, ὃ οὐχὶ πέφυκε φέρειν.

Nothing happens to anybody which he is not fitted by nature to bear.

Meditations bk. 5, sect. 18

18 πᾶν τὸ ἐνεστὼς τοῦ χρόνου στιγμὴ τοῦ αἰῶνος. πάντα μικρά, εὔτρεπια, ἐναφανιζόμενα.

Every instant of time is a pinprick of eternity. All things are petty, easily changed, vanishing away.

Meditations bk. 6, sect. 36

19 ὁ τὰ νῦν ἰδὼν πάντα ἑώρακεν, ὅσα τε ἐξ ἀιδίου ἐγένετο καὶ ὅσα εἰς τὸ ἄπειρον ἔσται.

He who sees what is now has seen all things, whatsoever comes to pass from everlasting and whatsoever shall be unto everlasting time.

Meditations bk. 6, sect. 37

20 Μέμνησο, ὅτι καὶ τὸ μετατίθεσθαι καὶ ἕπεσθαι τῷ διορθοῦντι ὁμοίως ἐλεύθερόν ἐστιν.

To change your mind and to follow him who sets you right is to be nonetheless the free agent that you were before.

Meditations bk. 8, sect. 16

1 οἱ ἄνθρωποι γεγόνασιν ἀλλήλων ἕνεκεν· ἢ δίδασκε οὖν ἢ φέρε.

Mankind have been created for the sake of one another. Either instruct them, therefore, or endure them.
Meditations bk. 8, sect. 59

2 ὅ τι ἄν σοι συμβαίνῃ, τοῦτό σοι ἐξ αἰῶνος προκατεσκευάζετο καὶ ἡ ἐπιπλοκὴ τῶν αἰτίων συνέκλωθε τήν τε σὴν ὑπόστασιν ἐξ ἀϊδίου καὶ τὴν τούτου σύμβασιν.

Whatever befalls you was prepared for you beforehand from eternity, and the thread of causes was spinning from everlasting both your existence and this which befalls you.
Meditations bk. 10, sect. 5

3 ἄνθρωπε, ἐπολιτεύσω ἐν τῇ μεγάλῃ ταύτῃ πόλει· τί σοι διαφέρει, εἰ πέντε ἔτεσιν ἢ πεντήκοντα;

Man, you have been a citizen in this world city, what does it matter whether for five years or fifty?
Meditations bk. 12, sect. 36

Jane Austen 1775–1817

English novelist

4 Miss Bates stood in the very worst predicament in the world for having much of the public favour; and she had no intellectual superiority to make atonement for herself, or frighten those who might hate her, into outward respect.
Emma (1816) ch. 3

5 An egg boiled very soft is not unwholesome.
Emma (1816) ch. 3

6 One half of the world cannot understand the pleasures of the other.
Emma (1816) ch. 9

7 With men he can be rational and unaffected, but when he has ladies to please, every feature works.
Emma (1816) ch. 13

8 The folly of people's not staying comfortably at home when they can! . . . five dull hours in another man's house, with nothing to say or to hear that was not said and heard yesterday, and may not be said and heard again tomorrow . . . four horses and four servants taken out for nothing but to convey five idle, shivering creatures into colder rooms and worse company than they might have had at home.
Emma (1816) ch. 13

9 The sooner every party breaks up the better.
Emma (1816) ch. 25

10 Surprises are foolish things. The pleasure is not enhanced, and the inconvenience is often considerable.
Emma (1816) ch. 26

11 One has no great hopes from Birmingham. I always say there is something direful in the sound.
Emma (1816) ch. 36

12 One of Edward's Mistresses was Jane Shore, who has had a play written about her, but it is a tragedy and therefore not worth reading.
The History of England (written 1791)

13 Nothing can be said in his vindication, but that his abolishing Religious Houses and leaving them to the ruinous depredations of time has been of infinite use to the landscape of England in general.
The History of England (written 1791)

14 It was too pathetic for the feelings of Sophia and myself—we fainted Alternately on a Sofa.
Love and Freindship (written 1790) 'Letter the 8th'

15 She was nothing more than a mere good-tempered, civil and obliging young woman; as such we could scarcely dislike her—she was only an Object of Contempt.
Love and Freindship (written 1790) 'Letter the 13th'

16 There is not one in a hundred of either sex who is not taken in when they marry. Look where I will, I see that it *is* so; and I feel that it *must* be so, when I consider that it is, of all transactions, the one in which people expect most from others, and are least honest themselves.
Mansfield Park (1814) ch. 5

17 We do not look in great cities for our best morality.
Mansfield Park (1814) ch. 9

18 A large income is the best recipe for happiness I ever heard of. It certainly may secure all the myrtle and turkey part of it.
Mansfield Park (1814) ch. 22

19 Shakespeare one gets acquainted with without knowing how. It is part of an Englishman's constitution. His thoughts and beauties are so spread abroad that one touches them everywhere, one is intimate with him by instinct.
Mansfield Park (1814) ch. 34

20 Let other pens dwell on guilt and misery. I quit such odious subjects as soon as I can.
Mansfield Park (1814) ch. 48

21 'Oh! it is only a novel! . . . only Cecilia, or Camilla, or Belinda:' or, in short, only some work in which the most thorough knowledge of human nature, the happiest delineation of its varieties, the liveliest effusions of wit and humour are conveyed to the world in the best chosen language.
Northanger Abbey (1818) ch. 5

22 Oh! who can ever be tired of Bath?
Northanger Abbey (1818) ch. 10

23 Where people wish to attach, they should always be ignorant. To come with a well-informed mind, is to come with an inability of administering to the vanity of others, which a sensible person would always wish to avoid. A woman especially, if she have the misfortune of knowing any thing, should conceal it as well as she can.
Northanger Abbey (1818) ch. 14

24 From politics, it was an easy step to silence.
Northanger Abbey (1818) ch. 14

1 Remember the country and the age we live in. Remember that we are English, that we are Christians ... Does our education prepare us for such atrocities? Do our laws connive at them? Could they be perpetrated without being known, in a country like this, where social and literary intercourse is on such a footing; where every man is surrounded by a neighbourhood of voluntary spies, and where roads and newspapers lay every thing open?
Northanger Abbey (1818) ch. 34

2 Sir Walter Elliot, of Kellynch-hall, in Somersetshire, was a man who, for his own amusement, never took up any book but the Baronetage; there he found occupation for an idle hour, and consolation in a distressed one.
Persuasion (1818) ch. 1

3 She had been forced into prudence in her youth, she learned romance as she grew older—the natural sequel of an unnatural beginning.
Persuasion (1818) ch. 4

4 She ventured to hope he did not always read only poetry; and to say, that she thought it was the misfortune of poetry, to be seldom safely enjoyed by those who enjoyed it completely; and that the strong feelings which alone could estimate it truly, were the very feelings which ought to taste it but sparingly.
Persuasion (1818) ch. 11

5 'My idea of good company, Mr Elliot, is the company of clever, well-informed people, who have a great deal of conversation; that is what I call good company.'
'You are mistaken,' said he gently, 'that is not good company, that is the best.'
Persuasion (1818) ch. 16

6 Men have had every advantage of us in telling their own story. Education has been theirs in so much higher a degree; the pen has been in their hands.
Persuasion (1818) ch. 23. Cf. Hardy 324:7

7 All the privilege I claim for my own sex ... is that of loving longest, when existence or when hope is gone.
Persuasion (1818) ch. 23

8 It was, perhaps, one of those cases in which advice is good or bad only as the event decides.
Persuasion (1818) ch. 23

9 It is a truth universally acknowledged, that a single man in possession of a good fortune, must be in want of a wife.
Pride and Prejudice (1813) ch. 1. Cf. Burney 160:16

10 She was a woman of mean understanding, little information, and uncertain temper.
Pride and Prejudice (1813) ch. 1

11 May I ask whether these pleasing attentions proceed from the impulse of the moment, or are the result of previous study?
Pride and Prejudice (1813) ch. 14

12 Mr Collins had only to change from Jane to Elizabeth—and it was soon done—done while Mrs Bennet was stirring the fire.
Pride and Prejudice (1813) ch. 15

13 From this day you must be a stranger to one of your parents.—Your mother will never see you again if you do *not* marry Mr Collins, and I will never see you again if you *do*.
Pride and Prejudice (1813) ch. 20

14 Without thinking highly either of men or matrimony, marriage had always been her object; it was the only honourable provision for well-educated young women of small fortune, and however uncertain of giving happiness, must be their pleasantest preservative from want.
Pride and Prejudice (1813) ch. 22

15 What is the difference in matrimonial affairs, between the mercenary and the prudent move? Where does discretion end, and avarice begin?
Pride and Prejudice (1813) ch. 27

16 Loss of virtue in a female is irretrievable ... one false step involves her in endless ruin.
Pride and Prejudice (1813) ch. 47

17 Are the shades of Pemberley to be thus polluted?
Pride and Prejudice (1813) ch. 56

18 You ought certainly to forgive them as a Christian, but never to admit them in your sight, or allow their names to be mentioned in your hearing.
Pride and Prejudice (1813) ch. 57

19 For what do we live, but to make sport for our neighbours, and laugh at them in our turn?
Pride and Prejudice (1813) ch. 57

20 An annuity is a very serious business.
Sense and Sensibility (1811) vol. 1, ch. 2

21 On every formal visit a child ought to be of the party, by way of provision for discourse.
Sense and Sensibility (1811) vol. 2, ch. 6

22 A person and face, of strong, natural, sterling insignificance, though adorned in the first style of fashion.
Sense and Sensibility (1811) vol. 2, ch. 11

23 It is not time or opportunity that is to determine intimacy; it is disposition alone. Seven years would be insufficient to make some people acquainted with each other, and seven days are more than enough for others.
Sense and Sensibility (1811) vol. 2, ch. 12

24 We met ... Dr Hall in such very deep mourning that either his mother, his wife, or himself must be dead.
Letter to Cassandra Austen, 17 May 1799, in R. W. Chapman (ed.) *Jane Austen's Letters* (1952)

25 How horrible it is to have so many people killed!—And what a blessing that one cares for none of them!
Letter to Cassandra Austen, 31 May 1811, after the battle of Albuera, 16 May 1811, in R. W. Chapman (ed.) *Jane Austen's Letters* (1952)

26 3 or 4 families in a country village is the very thing to work on.
Letter to Anna Austen, 9 September 1814, in R. W. Chapman (ed.) *Jane Austen's Letters* (1952)

1 What should I do with your strong, manly, spirited sketches, full of variety and glow?—How could I possibly join them on to the little bit (two inches wide) of ivory on which I work with so fine a brush, as produces little effect after much labour?

   Letter to J. Edward Austen, 16 December 1816, in R. W. Chapman (ed.) *Jane Austen's Letters* (1952)

2 Single women have a dreadful propensity for being poor—which is one very strong argument in favour of matrimony.

   Letter to Fanny Knight, 13 March 1817, in R. W. Chapman (ed.) *Jane Austen's Letters* (1952)

3 He and I should not in the least agree of course, in our ideas of novels and heroines;—pictures of perfection as you know make me sick and wicked.

   Letter to Fanny Knight, 23 March 1817, in R. W. Chapman (ed.) *Jane Austen's Letters* (1952)

J. L. Austin 1911–60
English philosopher

4 In such cases we should not know what to say. This is when we say 'words fail us' and mean this literally. We should need new words. The old ones just would not fit. They aren't meant to cover this kind of case.

   On being asked how one might describe the predicament of the character in Kafka's *Metamorphosis* who wakes to find himself transformed into a giant cockroach; Isaiah Berlin 'Austin and the Early Beginnings of Oxford Philosophy' in *Essays on J. L. Austin* (1973)

5 When asked to state his 'criterion' of philosophical correctness, [he] replied that, well, if you could get a collection of 'more or less cantankerous colleagues' all to accept something after argument, that, he thought, would be 'a bit of a criterion'.

   G. J. Warnock 'Saturday Mornings' in *Essays on J. L. Austin* (1973)

Earl of Avon
See SIR ANTHONY EDEN

Revd Awdry (Wilbert Vere Awdry) 1911–

6 You've a lot to learn about trucks, little Thomas. They are silly things and must be kept in their place. After pushing them about here for a few weeks you'll know almost as much about them as Edward. Then you'll be a Really Useful Engine.

   Thomas the Tank Engine (1946) p. 46

Alan Ayckbourn 1939–
English playwright

7 My mother used to say, Delia, if S-E-X ever rears its ugly head, close your eyes before you see the rest of it.

   Bedroom Farce (1978) act 2. Cf. Allingham 9:20

8 This place, you tell them you're interested in the arts, you get messages of sympathy.

   Chorus of Disapproval (1986) act 2

9 Do you realize, Mrs Foster, the hours I've put into that woman? When I met her, you know, she was nothing. Nothing at all. With my own hands I have built her up. Encouraging her to join the public library and make use of her non-fiction tickets.

   How the Other Half Loves (1972) act 2, sc. 1

10 If you gave Ruth a rose, she'd peel all the petals off to make sure there weren't any greenfly. And when she'd done that, she'd turn round and say, do you call that a rose? Look at it, it's all in bits.

   Table Manners (1975) act 1, sc. 2

11 I always feel with Norman that I have him on loan from somewhere. Like one of his library books.

   Table Manners (1975) act 2, sc. 1

A. J. Ayer (Sir Alfred Jules Ayer) 1910–89
English philosopher

12 The criterion which we use to test the genuineness of apparent statements of fact is the criterion of verifiability. We say that a sentence is factually significant to any given person, if, and only if, he knows how to verify the proposition which it purports to express—that is, if he knows what observations would lead him, under certain conditions, to accept the proposition as being true, or reject it as being false.

   Language, Truth, and Logic (1936) ch. 1

13 If now I . . . say 'Stealing money is wrong,' I produce a sentence which has no factual meaning—that is, expresses no proposition which can be either true or false. It is as if I had written 'Stealing money!!'—where the shape and thickness of the exclamation marks show, by a suitable convention, that a special sort of moral disapproval is the feeling which is being expressed.

   Language, Truth, and Logic (1936) ch. 6

14 We offer the theist the same comfort as we gave to the moralist. His assertions cannot possibly be valid, but they cannot be invalid either. As he says nothing at all about the world, he cannot justly be accused of saying anything false, or anything for which he has insufficient grounds. It is only when the theist claims that in asserting the existence of a transcendent god he is expressing a genuine proposition that we are entitled to disagree with him.

   Language, Truth, and Logic (1936) ch. 6

15 Why should you mind being wrong if someone can show you that you are?

   Attributed

Pam Ayres 1947–
English writer of humorous verse

16 Medicinal discovery,
   It moves in mighty leaps,
   It leapt straight past the common cold
   And gave it us for keeps.

   'Oh no, I got a cold' (1976)

Sir Robert Aytoun 1570–1638

Scottish poet and courtier

1 I loved thee once. I'll love no more,
Thine be the grief, as is the blame;
Thou art not what thou wast before,
What reason I should be the same?
'To an Inconstant Mistress'

W. E. Aytoun 1813–65

Scottish lawyer and writer of ballads

2 'He is coming! he is coming!'
Like a bridegroom from his room,
Came the hero from his prison
To the scaffold and the doom.
'The Execution of Montrose' (1849) st. 14

3 The grim Geneva ministers
With anxious scowl drew near,
As you have seen the ravens flock
Around the dying deer.
'The Execution of Montrose' (1849) st. 17

4 They bore within their breasts the grief
That fame can never heal—
The deep, unutterable woe
Which none save exiles feel.
'The Island of the Scots' (1849) st. 12

5 The earth is all the home I have,
The heavens my wide roof-tree.
'The Wandering Jew' (1867) l. 49

Charles Babbage 1792–1871

English mathematician and inventor; pioneer of machine computing

6 Every moment dies a man,
Every moment $1\frac{1}{16}$ is born.
Parody of Tennyson's 'Vision of Sin' in an unpublished
letter to the poet. See *New Scientist* 4 December 1958,
p. 1428. Cf. Tennyson 690:5

Isaac Babel 1894–c.1939

Russian short-story writer

7 Фраза рождается на свет хорошей и дурной в
одно и то же время. Тайна заключается в
повороте, едва ощутимом. Рычаг должен лежать
в руке и обогреваться. Повернуть его надо один
раз, а не два.

A phrase is born into the world both good and bad at
the same time. The secret lies in a slight, an almost
invisible twist. The lever should rest in your hand,
getting warm, and you can only turn it once, not
twice.
Guy de Maupassant (1932)

8 Никакое железо не может войти в человеческое
сердце так леденяще, как точка, поставленная
вовремя.

No iron can stab the heart with such force as a full
stop put just at the right place.
Guy de Maupassant (1932)

9 В субботние кануны меня томит густая печаль
... О, истлевшие талмуды моего детства! О,
густая печаль воспоминания!

On Sabbath eves I am oppressed . . . O the rotted
Talmuds of my childhood! O the dense melancholy of
memories!
Red Cavalry (1926) 'Gedali' (translated by Walter Morison)

10 А за окном стоит ночь, как черная колонна ...
Земля выложена сумрачным сиянием, ожерелья
светящихся плодов повисли на кустах.

Beyond the window, night stands like a black column
. . . A shadowy radiance lies on the earth, and
hanging from the bushes are necklaces of gleaming
fruit.
Red Cavalry (1926) 'Pan Apolek' (translated by Walter
Morison)

11 Пчела скорби укусила его в сердце.

The bee of sorrow had stung his heart.
Red Cavalry (1926) 'Pan Apolek' (translated by Walter
Morison)

12 Она пошла к начдиву, неся грудь на высоких
башмаках, грудь, шевелившуюся, как животное в
мешке.

She went over to the Commander, bearing her bosom
on her high heels, a bosom that stirred like an animal
in a bag.
Red Cavalry (1926) 'The Story of a Horse' (translated by
Walter Morison)

13 Мы оба смотрели на мир, как на луг в мае, как на
луг, по которому ходят женщины и кони.

Both of us looked on the world as a meadow in
May—a meadow traversed by women and horses.
Red Cavalry (1926) 'The Story of a Horse' (translated by
Walter Morison)

Francis Bacon (1st Baron Verulam and Viscount St Albans) 1561–1626

English lawyer, courtier, philosopher, and essayist

14 For all knowledge and wonder (which is the seed of
knowledge) is an impression of pleasure in itself.
The Advancement of Learning (1605) bk. 1, ch. 1, sect. 3

15 So let great authors have their due, as time, which is
the author of authors, be not deprived of his due,
which is further and further to discover truth.
The Advancement of Learning (1605) bk. 1, ch. 4, sect. 12

16 If a man will begin with certainties, he shall end in
doubts; but if he will be content to begin with doubts,
he shall end in certainties.
The Advancement of Learning (1605) bk. 1, ch. 5, sect. 8

17 [Knowledge is] a rich storehouse for the glory of the
Creator and the relief of man's estate.
The Advancement of Learning (1605) bk. 1, ch. 5, sect. 11

18 Antiquities are history defaced, or some remnants of
history which have casually escaped the shipwreck of
time.
The Advancement of Learning (1605) bk. 2, ch. 2, sect. 1

1 Poesy was ever thought to have some participation of divineness, because it doth raise and erect the mind, by submitting the shows of things to the desires of the mind; whereas reason doth buckle and bow the mind unto the nature of things.

The Advancement of Learning (1605) bk. 2, ch. 4, sect. 2

2 The knowledge of man is as the waters, some descending from above, and some springing from beneath; the one informed by the light of nature, the other inspired by divine revelation.

The Advancement of Learning (1605) bk. 2, ch. 5, sect. 1

3 They are ill discoverers that think there is no land, when they can see nothing but sea.

The Advancement of Learning (1605) bk. 2, ch. 7, sect. 5

4 Words are the tokens current and accepted for conceits, as moneys are for values.

The Advancement of Learning (1605) bk. 2, ch. 16, sect. 3

5 A dance is a measured pace, as a verse is a measured speech.

The Advancement of Learning (1605) bk. 2, ch. 16, sect. 5

6 But men must know, that in this theatre of man's life it is reserved only for God and angels to be lookers on.

The Advancement of Learning (1605) bk. 2, ch. 20, sect. 8

7 Did not one of the fathers in great indignation call poesy *vinum daemonum*?

The Advancement of Learning (1605) bk. 2, ch. 22, sect. 13 (*vinum daemonum* the wine of devils)

8 All good moral philosophy is but an handmaid to religion.

The Advancement of Learning (1605) bk. 2, ch. 22, sect. 14

9 It is in life as it is in ways, the shortest way is commonly the foulest, and surely the fairer way is not much about.

The Advancement of Learning (1605) bk. 2, ch. 23, sect. 45

10 That all things are changed, and that nothing really perishes, and that the sum of matter remains exactly the same, is sufficiently certain.

Cogitationes de Natura Rerum Cogitatio 5 in J. Spedding (ed.) *The Works of Francis Bacon* vol. 5 (1858) p. 426

11 *Antiquitas saeculi juventus mundi.*

Ancient times were the youth of the world.

De Dignitate et Augmentis Scientiarum (1623) bk. 1 (translated by Gilbert Watts, 1640)

12 *Divitiae bona ancilla, pessima domina.*

Riches are a good handmaid, but the worst mistress.

De Dignitate et Augmentis Scientiarum (1623) bk. 6, ch. 3, pt. 3 'The Antitheta of Things' no. 6 (translated by Gilbert Watts, 1640)

13 *Nil moderatum vulgo gratum est.*

No term of moderation takes place with the vulgar.

De Dignitate et Augmentis Scientiarum (1623) bk. 6, ch. 3, pt. 3 'The Antitheta of Things' no. 30 (translated by Gilbert Watts, 1640)

14 *Silentium, stultorum virtus.*

Silence is the virtue of fools.

De Dignitate et Augmentis Scientiarum (1623) bk. 6, ch. 3, pt. 3 'The Antitheta of Things' no. 31 (translated by Gilbert Watts, 1640)

15 I hold every man a debtor to his profession.

The Elements of the Common Law (1596) preface

16 Why should a man be in love with his fetters, though of gold?

Essay of Death para. 4 in *The Remaines of . . . Lord Verulam* (1648)

17 He is the fountain of honour.

An Essay of a King (1642); attribution doubtful

18 Prosperity is the blessing of the Old Testament, adversity is the blessing of the New.

Essays (1625) 'Of Adversity'

19 The pencil of the Holy Ghost hath laboured more in describing the afflictions of Job than the felicities of Solomon.

Essays (1625) 'Of Adversity'

20 Prosperity is not without many fears and distastes; and adversity is not without comforts and hopes.

Essays (1625) 'Of Adversity'

21 Prosperity doth best discover vice, but adversity doth best discover virtue.

Essays (1625) 'Of Adversity'

22 I had rather believe all the fables in the legend, and the Talmud, and the Alcoran, than that this universal frame is without a mind.

Essays (1625) 'Of Atheism'

23 A little philosophy inclineth man's mind to atheism, but depth in philosophy bringeth men's minds about to religion.

Essays (1625) 'Of Atheism'

24 They that deny a God destroy man's nobility; for certainly man is of kin to the beasts by his body; and, if he be not of kin to God by his spirit, he is a base and ignoble creature.

Essays (1625) 'Of Atheism'

25 Virtue is like a rich stone, best plain set.

Essays (1625) 'Of Beauty'

26 That is the best part of beauty, which a picture cannot express.

Essays (1625) 'Of Beauty'

27 There is no excellent beauty that hath not some strangeness in the proportion.

Essays (1625) 'Of Beauty'

28 He said it that knew it best.

Essays (1625) 'Of Boldness' (referring to Demosthenes)

29 In civil business; what first? boldness; what second and third? boldness: and yet boldness is a child of ignorance and baseness.

Essays (1625) 'Of Boldness'. Cf. Danton 230:22

30 Boldness is an ill keeper of promise.

Essays (1625) 'Of Boldness'

31 Mahomet made the people believe that he would call a hill to him, and from the top of it offer up his prayers for the observers of his law. The people assembled: Mahomet called the hill to come to him again and again; and when the hill stood still, he was never a whit abashed, but said, 'If the hill will not come to Mahomet, Mahomet will go to the hill.'

Essays (1625) 'Of Boldness' (proverbially 'If the mountain will not come . . . ')

32 Houses are built to live in and not to look on; therefore let use be preferred before uniformity, except where both may be had.

Essays (1625) 'Of Building'

1 Light gains make heavy purses.
Essays (1625) 'Of Ceremonies and Respects'

2 He that is too much in anything, so that he giveth another occasion of satiety, maketh himself cheap.
Essays (1625) 'Of Ceremonies and Respects'

3 Books will speak plain when counsellors blanch.
Essays (1625) 'Of Counsel'

4 There be that can pack the cards and yet cannot play well; so there are some that are good in canvasses and factions, that are otherwise weak men.
Essays (1625) 'Of Cunning'

5 In things that are tender and unpleasing, it is good to break the ice by some whose words are of less weight, and to reserve the more weighty voice to come in as by chance.
Essays (1625) 'Of Cunning'

6 I knew one that when he wrote a letter he would put that which was most material in the postscript, as if it had been a bymatter.
Essays (1625) 'Of Cunning'

7 Nothing doth more hurt in a state than that cunning men pass for wise.
Essays (1625) 'Of Cunning'

8 Men fear death as children fear to go in the dark; and as that natural fear in children is increased with tales, so is the other.
Essays (1625) 'Of Death'

9 There is no passion in the mind of man so weak, but it mates and masters the fear of death. And therefore death is no such terrible enemy, when a man hath so many attendants about him that can win the combat of him. Revenge triumphs over death; love slights it; honour aspireth to it; grief flieth to it.
Essays (1625) 'Of Death'

10 It is as natural to die as to be born; and to a little infant, perhaps, the one is as painful as the other.
Essays (1625) 'Of Death'

11 Above all, believe it, the sweetest canticle is *Nunc dimittis*, when a man hath obtained worthy ends and expectations. Death hath this also, that it openeth the gate to good fame, and extinguisheth envy.
Essays (1625) 'Of Death'

12 If you dissemble sometimes your knowledge of that you are thought to know, you shall be thought, another time, to know that you know not.
Essays (1625) 'Of Discourse'

13 I knew a wise man that had it for a by-word, when he saw men hasten to a conclusion. 'Stay a little, that we may make an end the sooner.'
Essays (1625) 'Of Dispatch'

14 To choose time is to save time.
Essays (1625) 'Of Dispatch'

15 Riches are for spending.
Essays (1625) 'Of Expense'

16 A man ought warily to begin charges which once begun will continue.
Essays (1625) 'Of Expense'

17 There is little friendship in the world, and least of all between equals.
Essays (1625) 'Of Followers and Friends'

18 Chiefly the mould of a man's fortune is in his own hands.
Essays (1625) 'Of Fortune'

19 If a man look sharply, and attentively, he shall see Fortune: for though she be blind, yet she is not invisible.
Essays (1625) 'Of Fortune'

20 It had been hard for him that spake it to have put more truth and untruth together, in a few words, than in that speech: 'Whosoever is delighted in solitude is either a wild beast, or a god.'
Essays (1625) 'Of Friendship'. Cf. Aristotle 25:16

21 A crowd is not company, and faces are but a gallery of pictures, and talk but a tinkling cymbal, where there is no love.
Essays (1625) 'Of Friendship'

22 It redoubleth joys, and cutteth griefs in halves.
Essays (1625) 'Of Friendship'

23 As if you would call a physician, that is thought good for the cure of the disease you complain of but is unacquainted with your body, and therefore may put you in the way for a present cure but overthroweth your health in some other kind; and so cure the disease and kill the patient.
Essays (1625) 'Of Friendship'

24 God Almighty first planted a garden; and, indeed, it is the purest of human pleasures.
Essays (1625) 'Of Gardens'

25 The inclination to goodness is imprinted deeply in the nature of man: insomuch, that if it issue not towards men, it will take unto other living creatures.
Essays (1625) 'Of Goodness, and Goodness of Nature'

26 If a man be gracious and courteous to strangers, it shows he is a citizen of the world.
Essays (1625) 'Of Goodness, and Goodness of Nature'

27 Men in great place are thrice servants: servants of the sovereign or state, servants of fame, and servants of business.
Essays (1625) 'Of Great Place'

28 It is a strange desire to seek power and to lose liberty.
Essays (1625) 'Of Great Place'

29 The rising unto place is laborious, and by pains men come to greater pains; and it is sometimes base, and by indignities men come to dignities. The standing is slippery, and the regress is either a downfall, or at least an eclipse.
Essays (1625) 'Of Great Place'

30 Severity breedeth fear, but roughness breedeth hate. Even reproofs from authority ought to be grave, and not taunting.
Essays (1625) 'Of Great Place'

31 All rising to great place is by a winding stair.
Essays (1625) 'Of Great Place'

32 As the births of living creatures at first are ill-shapen, so are all innovations, which are the births of time.
Essays (1625) 'Of Innovations'

33 He that will not apply new remedies must expect new evils; for time is the greatest innovator.
Essays (1625) 'Of Innovations'

1 The speaking in a perpetual hyperbole is comely in nothing but in love.
  Essays (1625) 'Of Love'

2 It has been well said that 'the arch-flatterer with whom all the petty flatterers have intelligence is a man's self.'
  Essays (1625) 'Of Love'

3 He that hath wife and children hath given hostages to fortune; for they are impediments to great enterprises, either of virtue or mischief.
  Essays (1625) 'Of Marriage and the Single Life'. Cf. Lucan 431:7

4 A single life doth well with churchmen, for charity will hardly water the ground where it must first fill a pool.
  Essays (1625) 'Of Marriage and the Single Life'

5 Wives are young men's mistresses, companions for middle age, and old men's nurses.
  Essays (1625) 'Of Marriage and the Single Life'

6 He was reputed one of the wise men that made answer to the question when a man should marry? 'A young man not yet, an elder man not at all.'
  Essays (1625) 'Of Marriage and the Single Life'. Cf. Punch 531:7

7 Nature is often hidden, sometimes overcome, seldom extinguished.
  Essays (1625) 'Of Nature in Men'

8 It is generally better to deal by speech than by letter.
  Essays (1625) 'Of Negotiating'

9 New nobility is but the act of power, but ancient nobility is the act of time.
  Essays (1625) 'Of Nobility'

10 Nobility of birth commonly abateth industry.
  Essays (1625) 'Of Nobility'

11 The joys of parents are secret, and so are their griefs and fears.
  Essays (1625) 'Of Parents and Children'

12 Children sweeten labours, but they make misfortunes more bitter.
  Essays (1625) 'Of Parents and Children'

13 Fame is like a river, that beareth up things light and swollen, and drowns things weighty and solid.
  Essays (1625) 'Of Praise'

14 Age will not be defied.
  Essays (1625) 'Of Regimen of Health'

15 Revenge is a kind of wild justice, which the more man's nature runs to, the more ought law to weed it out.
  Essays (1625) 'Of Revenge'

16 A man that studieth revenge keeps his own wounds green.
  Essays (1625) 'Of Revenge'

17 Defer not charities till death; for certainly, if a man weigh it rightly, he that doth so is rather liberal of another man's than of his own.
  Essays (1625) 'Of Riches'

18 The four pillars of government ... (which are religion, justice, counsel, and treasure).
  Essays (1625) 'Of Seditions and Troubles'

19 The surest way to prevent seditions (if the times do bear it) is to take away the matter of them.
  Essays (1625) 'Of Seditions and Troubles'

20 Money is like muck, not good except it be spread.
  Essays (1625) 'Of Seditions and Troubles'

21 The remedy is worse than the disease.
  Essays (1625) 'Of Seditions and Troubles'

22 The French are wiser than they seem, and the Spaniards seem wiser than they are.
  Essays (1625) 'Of Seeming Wise'

23 Studies serve for delight, for ornament, and for ability.
  Essays (1625) 'Of Studies'

24 To spend too much time in studies is sloth.
  Essays (1625) 'Of Studies'

25 They perfect nature and are perfected by experience.
  Essays (1625) 'Of Studies'

26 Read not to contradict and confute, nor to believe and take for granted, nor to find talk and discourse, but to weigh and consider.
  Essays (1625) 'Of Studies'

27 Some books are to be tasted, others to be swallowed, and some few to be chewed and digested; that is, some books are to be read only in parts; others to be read but not curiously; and some few to be read wholly, and with diligence and attention. Some books also may be read by deputy, and extracts made of them by others.
  Essays (1625) 'Of Studies'

28 Reading maketh a full man; conference a ready man; and writing an exact man.
  Essays (1625) 'Of Studies'

29 Histories make men wise; poets, witty; the mathematics, subtile; natural philosophy, deep; moral, grave; logic and rhetoric, able to contend.
  Essays (1625) 'Of Studies'

30 There is a superstition in avoiding superstition.
  Essays (1625) 'Of Superstition'

31 Suspicions amongst thoughts are like bats amongst birds, they ever fly by twilight.
  Essays (1625) 'Of Suspicion'

32 There is nothing makes a man suspect much, more than to know little.
  Essays (1625) 'Of Suspicion'

33 Neither is money the sinews of war (as it is trivially said).
  Essays (1625) 'Of the True Greatness of Kingdoms'. Cf. Cicero 204:10

34 Neither will it be, that a people overlaid with taxes should ever become valiant and martial.
  Essays (1625) 'Of the True Greatness of Kingdoms'

35 Travel, in the younger sort, is a part of education; in the elder, a part of experience. He that travelleth into a country before he hath some entrance into the language, goeth to school, and not to travel.
  Essays (1625) 'Of Travel'

36 What is truth? said jesting Pilate; and would not stay for an answer.
  Essays (1625) 'Of Truth'. Cf. St John 97:24

37 A mixture of a lie doth ever add pleasure.
  Essays (1625) 'Of Truth'

1 It is not the lie that passeth through the mind, but the lie that sinketh in, and settleth in it, that doth the hurt.
Essays (1625) 'Of Truth'

2 The inquiry of truth, which is the love-making, or wooing of it, the knowledge of truth, which is the presence of it, and the belief of truth, which is the enjoying of it, is the sovereign good of human nature.
Essays (1625) 'Of Truth'

3 All colours will agree in the dark.
Essays (1625) 'Of Unity in Religion'

4 It was prettily devised of Aesop, 'The fly sat upon the axletree of the chariot-wheel and said, what a dust do I raise.'
Essays (1625) 'Of Vain-Glory'

5 In the youth of a state arms do flourish; in the middle age of a state, learning; and then both of them together for a time; in the declining age of a state, mechanical arts and merchandise.
Essays (1625) 'Of Vicissitude of Things'

6 Be so true to thyself as thou be not false to others.
Essays (1625) 'Of Wisdom for a Man's Self'. Cf. *Hamlet* 573:4

7 It is the nature of extreme self-lovers, as they will set a house on fire, and it were but to roast their eggs.
Essays (1625) 'Of Wisdom for a Man's Self'

8 It is the wisdom of the crocodiles, that shed tears when they would devour.
Essays (1625) 'Of Wisdom for a Man's Self'

9 Young men are fitter to invent than to judge, fitter for execution than for counsel, and fitter for new projects than for settled business.
Essays (1625) 'Of Youth and Age'

10 For they thought generally that he was a Prince as ordained, and sent down from heaven to unite and put to an end the long dissensions of the two houses; which although they had had, in the times of Henry the Fourth, Henry the Fifth, and a part of Henry the Sixth on the one side, and the times of Edward the Fourth on the other, lucid intervals and happy pauses; yet they did ever hang over the kingdom, ready to break forth into new perturbations and calamities.
History of King Henry VII (1622) para. 3 in J. Spedding (ed.) *The Works of Francis Bacon* vol. 6 (1858) p. 32

11 I have rather studied books than men.
A Letter of Advice . . . to the Duke of Buckingham, When he became Favourite to King James (1661)

12 I have taken all knowledge to be my province.
'To My Lord Treasurer Burghley' (1592) in J. Spedding (ed.) *The Letters and Life of Francis Bacon* vol. 1 (1861) p. 109

13 Opportunity makes a thief.
'A Letter of Advice to the Earl of Essex . . . ' (1598) in J. Spedding (ed.) *The Letters and Life of Francis Bacon* vol. 2 (1862) p. 99

14 Universities incline wits to sophistry and affectation.
Valerius Terminus of the Interpretation of Nature ch. 26 in *Letters and Remains of the Lord Chancellor Bacon* (collected by Robert Stephens, 1734) p. 450

15 *Nam et ipsa scientia potestas est.*
For also knowledge itself is power.
Meditationes Sacrae (1597) 'Of Heresies'

16 I would live to study, and not study to live.
Memorial of Access to King James I (c.1622) in *Letters, Speeches, Charges, Advices, etc. of Francis Bacon* (1763) p. 325

17 God's first Creature, which was Light.
New Atlantis (1627)

18 The end of our foundation is the knowledge of causes, and secret motions of things; and the enlarging of the bounds of human Empire, to the effecting of all things possible.
New Atlantis (1627)

19 *Quod enim mavult homo verum esse, id potius credit.*
For what a man would like to be true, that he more readily believes.
Novum Organum (1620) bk. 1, Aphorism 49 (translated by J. Spedding). Cf. Caesar 174:15

20 *Magna ista scientiarum mater.*
That great mother of sciences.
Novum Organum (1620) bk. 1, Aphorism 80 (translated by J. Spedding) on natural philosophy

21 *Vim et virtutem et consequentias rerum inventarum notare juvat; quae non in aliis manifestius occurrunt, quam in illis tribus quae antiquis incognitae, et quarum primordia, licet recentia, obscura et ingloria sunt: Artis nimirum Imprimendi, Pulveris Tormentarii, et Acus Nauticae. Haec enim tria rerum faciem et statum in orbe terrarum mutaverunt.*

It is well to observe the force and virtue and consequence of discoveries, and these are to be seen nowhere more conspicuously than in those three which were unknown to the ancients, and of which the origins, though recent, are obscure and inglorious; namely, printing, gunpowder, and the magnet [Mariner's Needle]. For these three have changed the whole face and state of things throughout the world.
Novum Organum (1620) bk. 1, Aphorism 129 (translated by J. Spedding). Cf. Carlyle 180:17

22 *Natura enim non imperatur, nisi parendo.*
Nature cannot be ordered about, except by obeying her.
Novum Organum (1620) bk. 1, Aphorism 129 (translated by J. Spedding)

23 Books must follow sciences, and not sciences books.
Resuscitatio (1657) 'Proposition touching Amendment of Laws'

24 Wise nature did never put her precious jewels into a garret four stories high: and therefore . . . exceeding tall men had ever very empty heads.
J. Spedding (ed.) *The Works of Francis Bacon* vol. 7 (1859) 'Additional Apophthegms' no. 17

25 Hope is a good breakfast, but it is a bad supper.
J. Spedding (ed.) *The Works of Francis Bacon* vol. 7 (1859) 'Apophthegms contained in *Resuscitatio*' no. 36

26 Anger makes dull men witty, but it keeps them poor.
J. Spedding (ed.) *The Works of Francis Bacon* vol. 7 (1859) 'Baconiana' (often attributed to Queen Elizabeth I from a misreading of the text)

27 The world's a bubble; and the life of man
Less than a span.
The World (1629)

28 Who then to frail mortality shall trust,
But limns the water, or but writes in dust.
The World (1629)

1 What is it then to have or have no wife,
But single thraldom, or a double strife?
  The World (1629)

2 What then remains, but that we still should cry,
Not to be born, or being born, to die?
  The World (1629)

3 For my name and memory, I leave it to men's
charitable speeches, and to foreign nations, and the
next ages.
  His last will (19 December 1625) in J. Spedding (ed.) *The
  Letters and Life of Francis Bacon* vol. 7 (1874) p. 539

Robert Baden-Powell (1st Baron Baden-Powell) 1857–1941

English soldier; founder of the Boy Scouts, 1908

4 The scouts' motto is founded on my initials, it is: BE
PREPARED, which means, you are always to be in
a state of readiness in mind and body to do your DUTY.
  Scouting for Boys (1908) pt. 1

Karl Baedeker 1801–59

German publisher

5 Oxford is on the whole more attractive than
Cambridge to the ordinary visitor; and the traveller is
therefore recommended to visit Cambridge first, or to
omit it altogether if he cannot visit both.
  Great Britain (1887) Route 30 'From London to Oxford'

6 The traveller need have no scruple in limiting his
donations to the smallest possible sums, as liberality
frequently becomes a source of annoyance and
embarrassment.
  Northern Italy (1895) 'Gratuities'

7 PASSPORTS. On arrival at a Syrian port the traveller's
passport is sometimes asked for, but an ordinary
visiting-card will answer the purpose equally well.
  Palestine and Syria (1876) 'Passports and Custom House'

Joan Baez 1941–

American singer and songwriter

8 The only thing that's been a worse flop than the
organization of non-violence has been the
organization of violence.
  Daybreak (1970) 'What Would You Do If?' Cf. Péguy
  511:7

Walter Bagehot 1826–77

English economist and essayist

9 A constitutional statesman is in general a man of
common opinion and uncommon abilities.
  Biographical Studies (1881) 'The Character of Sir Robert
  Peel'

10 He believes, with all his heart and soul and strength,
that there *is* such a thing as truth; he has the soul of
a martyr with the intellect of an advocate.
  Biographical Studies (1881) 'Mr Gladstone'

11 The mystic reverence, the religious allegiance, which
are essential to a true monarchy, are imaginative
sentiments that no legislature can manufacture in any
people.
  The English Constitution (1867) 'The Cabinet'

12 In such constitutions [as England's] there are two
parts . . . first, those which excite and preserve the
reverence of the population—the *dignified* parts . . . and
next, the *efficient* parts—those by which it, in fact,
works and rules.
  The English Constitution (1867) 'The Cabinet'

13 No orator ever made an impression by appealing to
men as to their plainest physical wants, except when
he could allege that those wants were caused by some
one's tyranny.
  The English Constitution (1867) 'The Cabinet'

14 The Crown is, according to the saying, the 'fountain
of honour'; but the Treasury is the spring of business.
  The English Constitution (1867) 'The Cabinet'. Cf. Bacon
  42:17

15 A cabinet is a combining committee—a *hyphen* which
joins, a *buckle* which fastens, the legislative part of the
state to the executive part of the state.
  The English Constitution (1867) 'The Cabinet'

16 It has been said that England invented the phrase,
'Her Majesty's Opposition'; that it was the first
government which made a criticism of administration
as much a part of the polity as administration itself.
This critical opposition is the consequence of cabinet
government.
  The English Constitution (1867) 'The Cabinet'

17 *The Times* has made many ministries.
  The English Constitution (1867) 'The Cabinet'

18 The great qualities, the imperious will, the rapid
energy, the eager nature fit for a great crisis are not
required—are impediments—in common times.
  The English Constitution (1867) 'The Cabinet'

19 It has been said, not truly, but with a possible
approximation to truth, that in 1802 every hereditary
monarch was insane.
  The English Constitution (1867) 'Checks and Balances'

20 The soldier—that is, the great soldier—of to-day is not
a romantic animal, dashing at forlorn hopes, animated
by frantic sentiment, full of fancies as to a love-lady or
a sovereign; but a quiet, grave man, busied in charts,
exact in sums, master of the art of tactics, occupied in
trivial detail; thinking, as the Duke of Wellington was
said to do, *most* of the shoes of his soldiers; despising
all manner of *éclat* and eloquence; perhaps, like Count
Moltke, 'silent in seven languages'.
  The English Constitution (1867) 'Checks and Balances'

21 The order of nobility is of great use, too, not only in
what it creates, but in what it prevents. It prevents
the rule of wealth—the religion of gold. This is the
obvious and natural idol of the Anglo-Saxon.
  The English Constitution (1867) 'The House of Lords'

22 A severe though not unfriendly critic of our
institutions said that 'the cure for admiring the House
of Lords was to go and look at it.'
  The English Constitution (1867) 'The House of Lords'

23 Nations touch at their summits.
  The English Constitution (1867) 'The House of Lords'

1 As soon as we see that England is a disguised republic we must see too that the classes for whom the disguise is necessary must be tenderly dealt with.
  The English Constitution (1867) 'Its History'

2 The best reason why Monarchy is a strong government is, that it is an intelligible government. The mass of mankind understand it, and they hardly anywhere in the world understand any other.
  The English Constitution (1867) 'The Monarchy'

3 The characteristic of the English Monarchy is that it retains the feelings by which the heroic kings governed their rude age, and has added the feelings by which the constitutions of later Greece ruled in more refined ages.
  The English Constitution (1867) 'The Monarchy'

4 Women—one half the human race at least—care fifty times more for a marriage than a ministry.
  The English Constitution (1867) 'The Monarchy'

5 Royalty is a government in which the attention of the nation is concentrated on one person doing interesting actions. A Republic is a government in which that attention is divided between many, who are all doing uninteresting actions. Accordingly, so long as the human heart is strong and the human reason weak, Royalty will be strong because it appeals to diffused feeling, and Republics weak because they appeal to the understanding.
  The English Constitution (1867) 'The Monarchy'

6 Throughout the greater part of his life George III was a kind of 'consecrated obstruction'.
  The English Constitution (1867) 'The Monarchy'

7 Above all things our royalty is to be reverenced, and if you begin to poke about it you cannot reverence it . . . Its mystery is its life. We must not let in daylight upon magic.
  The English Constitution (1867) 'The Monarchy (continued)'

8 The Sovereign has, under a constitutional monarchy such as ours, three rights—the right to be consulted, the right to encourage, the right to warn.
  The English Constitution (1867) 'The Monarchy (continued)'

9 No real English gentleman, in his secret soul, was ever sorry for the death of a political economist.
  Estimates of some Englishmen and Scotchmen (1858) 'The First Edinburgh Reviewers'

10 Writers, like teeth, are divided into incisors and grinders.
  Estimates of some Englishmen and Scotchmen (1858) 'The First Edinburgh Reviewers'

11 To a great experience one thing is essential, an experiencing nature.
  Estimates of some Englishmen and Scotchmen (1858) 'Shakespeare—the Individual'

12 One of the greatest pains to human nature is the pain of a new idea.
  Physics and Politics (1872) 'The Age of Discussion'

13 The most melancholy of human reflections, perhaps, is that, on the whole, it is a question whether the benevolence of mankind does most good or harm.
  Physics and Politics (1872) 'The Age of Discussion'

14 He describes London like a special correspondent for posterity.
  National Review 7 October 1858 'Charles Dickens'

15 Wordsworth, Tennyson and Browning; or, pure, ornate, and grotesque art in English poetry.
  The National Review November 1864, essay title

Philip James Bailey 1816–1902
English poet

16 We should count time by heart-throbs.
  Festus (1839) sc. 5

17 America, thou half-brother of the world;
With something good and bad of every land.
  Festus (1839) sc. 10

Bruce Bairnsfather 1888–1959
British cartoonist

18 Well, if you knows of a better 'ole, go to it.
  Fragments from France (1915) p. 1

Sir Henry Williams Baker 1821–77
English clergyman and hymn-writer

19 Lord, thy word abideth,
And our footsteps guideth;
Who its truth believeth
Light and joy receiveth.
  'Lord, thy word abideth' (1861 hymn)

20 The King of love my shepherd is,
Whose goodness faileth never;
I nothing lack if I am his
And he is mine for ever . . .

Perverse and foolish oft I strayed,
But yet in love he sought me,
And on his shoulder gently laid,
And home, rejoicing, brought me.
  'The King of love my shepherd is' (1868 hymn)

21 O praise ye the Lord, all things that give sound;
Each jubilant chord re-echo around;
Loud organs, his glory forth tell in deep tone,
And, sweet harp, the story of what he hath done.
  'O praise ye the Lord!' (1875 hymn)

Michael Bakunin 1814–76
Russian revolutionary and anarchist

22 *Die Lust der Zerstörung ist zugleich eine schaffende Lust!*

The urge for destruction is also a creative urge!
  Jahrbuch für Wissenschaft und Kunst (1842) 'Die Reaktion in Deutschland' (under the pseudonym 'Jules Elysard')

23 We wish, in a word, equality—equality in fact as corollary, or rather, as primordial condition of liberty. From each according to his faculties, to each according to his needs; that is what we wish sincerely and energetically.
  Declaration signed by forty-seven anarchists on trial after the failure of their uprising at Lyons in 1870, in J. Morrison Davidson *The Old Order and the New* (1890). *See North British Review* (1849) vol. 10, p. 269: 'The formula of Communism, as propounded by Cabet, may be expressed thus:—"the duty of each is according to his faculties; his right according to his wants." 'Cf. Marx 452:5

James Baldwin 1924–87

American novelist and essayist

1 Children have never been very good at listening to
their elders, but they have never failed to imitate
them. They must, they have no other models.
> *Nobody Knows My Name* (1961) 'Fifth Avenue, Uptown:
> a letter from Harlem'

2 Anyone who has ever struggled with poverty knows
how extremely expensive it is to be poor.
> *Nobody Knows My Name* (1961) 'Fifth Avenue, Uptown:
> a letter from Harlem'

3 Freedom is not something that anybody can be given;
freedom is something people take and people are as
free as they want to be.
> *Nobody Knows My Name* (1961) 'Notes for a Hypothetical
> Novel'

4 Money, it turned out, was exactly like sex, you
thought of nothing else if you didn't have it and
thought of other things if you did.
> *Esquire* May 1961 'Black Boy looks at the White Boy'. Cf.
> Brenan 140:12

5 If the concept of God has any validity or any use, it
can only be to make us larger, freer, and more loving.
If God cannot do this, then it is time we got rid of
Him.
> *New Yorker* 17 November 1962 'Down at the Cross'

6 If they take you in the morning, they will be coming
for us that night.
> *New York Review of Books* 7 January 1971 'Open Letter to
> my Sister, Angela Davis'

7 It comes as a great shock around the age of 5, 6 or 7
to discover that the flag to which you have pledged
allegiance, along with everybody else, has not pledged
allegiance to you. It comes as a great shock to see
Gary Cooper killing off the Indians and, although you
are rooting for Gary Cooper, that the Indians are you.
> Speaking for the proposition that 'The American Dream is
> at the expense of the American Negro' at the Cambridge
> Union, England, 17 February 1965; in *New York Times
> Magazine* 7 March 1965, p. 32

Stanley Baldwin (Earl Baldwin of Bewdley) 1867–1947

*British Conservative politician; Prime Minister, 1923–4,
1924–9, 1935–7*

8 A platitude is simply a truth repeated until people get
tired of hearing it.
> Speech, *Hansard* 29 May 1924, col. 727

9 I think it is well also for the man in the street to
realize that there is no power on earth that can
protect him from being bombed. Whatever people may
tell him, the bomber will always get through. The
only defence is in offence, which means that you have
to kill more women and children more quickly than
the enemy if you want to save yourselves.
> Speech, *Hansard* 10 November 1932, col. 632

10 Since the day of the air, the old frontiers are gone.
When you think of the defence of England you no
longer think of the chalk cliffs of Dover; you think of
the Rhine. That is where our frontier lies.
> Speech, *Hansard* 30 July 1934, col. 2339

11 I shall be but a short time tonight. I have seldom
spoken with greater regret, for my lips are not yet
unsealed. Were these troubles over I would make
a case, and I guarantee that not a man would go into
the lobby against us.
> Speech, *Hansard* 10 December 1935, col. 856, on the
> Abyssinian crisis (usually quoted 'My lips are sealed')

12 Do not run up your nose dead against the Pope or the
NUM!
> In Lord Butler *The Art of Memory* (1982) 'Iain Macleod'.
> Cf. Macmillan 440:10

13 They [parliament] are a lot of hard-faced men who
look as if they had done very well out of the war.
> In J. M. Keynes *Economic Consequences of the Peace* (1919)
> ch. 5

14 There are three classes which need sanctuary more
than others—birds, wild flowers, and Prime Ministers.
> In *Observer* 24 May 1925

15 The intelligent are to the intelligentsia what
a gentleman is to a gent.
> In G. M. Young *Stanley Baldwin* (1952) ch. 13

Arthur James Balfour (1st Earl of Balfour) 1848–1930

British Conservative politician; Prime Minister, 1902–5

16 Christianity, of course . . . but why journalism?
> Replying to Frank Harris, who had claimed that 'all the
> faults of the age come from Christianity and journalism', in
> Margot Asquith *Autobiography* (1920) vol. 1, ch. 10

17 [Our] whole political machinery pre-supposes a people
so fundamentally at one that they can safely afford to
bicker.
> In Walter Bagehot *The English Constitution* (World Classics
> ed., 1928) introduction

18 I thought he was a young man of promise, but it
appears he is a young man of promises.
> Describing Churchill, in Winston Churchill *My Early Life*
> (1930) ch. 17

19 It is unfortunate, considering that enthusiasm moves
the world, that so few enthusiasts can be trusted to
speak the truth.
> Letter to Mrs Drew, 19 May 1891, in L. March-Phillips and
> B. Christian (eds.) *Some Hawarden Letters* (1917) ch. 7

Ballads

20 There was a youth, and a well-beloved youth,
And he was an esquire's son,
He loved the bailiff's daughter dear,
That lived in Islington.
> 'The Bailiff's Daughter of Islington'

21 All in the merry month of May,
When green buds they were swellin',
Young Jemmy Grove on his death-bed lay,
For love of Barbara Allen.
> 'Barbara Allen's Cruelty'

22 O mother, mother, make my bed,
O make it saft and narrow:
My love has died for me to-day,
I'll die for him to-morrow.
> 'Barbara Allen's Cruelty'

1 It fell about the Lammastide,
When the muir-men win their hay,
The doughty Douglas bound him to ride
Into England, to drive a prey.
‘Battle of Otterburn’

2 Ye Highlands and ye Lawlands,
O where hae ye been?
They hae slain the Earl of Murray,
And hae laid him on the green.
‘The Bonny Earl of Murray’

3 He was a braw gallant,
And he played at the gluve;
And the bonny Earl of Murray,
O he was the Queen’s luve!

O lang will his Lady
Look owre the Castle Downe,
Ere she see the Earl of Murray
Come sounding through the town!
‘The Bonny Earl of Murray’

4 Is there any room at your head, Sanders?
Is there any room at your feet?
Or any room at your twa sides,
Where fain, fain I would sleep?

There is na room at my head, Margaret,
There is na room at my feet;
My bed it is the cold, cold grave;
Among the hungry worms I sleep.
‘Clerk Sanders’

5 She hadna sailed a league, a league,
A league but barely three,
Till grim, grim grew his countenance
And gurly grew the sea.
‘The Daemon Lover’

6 ‘What hills are yon, yon pleasant hills,
The sun shines sweetly on?’—
‘O yon are the hills o’ Heaven,’ he said,
‘Where you will never won.’
‘The Daemon Lover’

7 Let me have length and breadth enough,
And under my head a sod;
That they may say when I am dead,
—Here lies bold Robin Hood!
‘The Death of Robin Hood’

8 There were three lords drinking at the wine
On the dowie dens o’ Yarrow;
They made a compact them between
They would go fight tomorrow.
‘Dowie Dens of Yarrow’

9 O well’s me o’ my gay goss-hawk,
That he can speak and flee!
He’ll carry a letter to my love,
Bring another back to me.
‘The Gay Goss Hawk’

10 A ship I have got in the North Country
And she goes by the name of the Golden Vanity,
O I fear she will be taken by a Spanish Ga-la-lee,
As she sails by the Low-lands low.
‘The Golden Vanity’

11 He bored with his augur, he bored once and twice,
And some were playing cards, and some were playing dice,
When the water flowed in it dazzled their eyes,
And she sank by the Low-lands low.
‘The Golden Vanity’

12 I am a man upon the land,
I am a selkie in the sea;
When I am far and far from land,
My home it is the Sule Skerry.
‘The Great Selkie of Sule Skerry’

13 I wish I were where Helen lies,
Night and day on me she cries;
O that I were where Helen lies,
On fair Kirkconnell lea!

Curst be the heart that thought the thought,
And curst the hand that fired the shot,
When in my arms burd Helen dropt,
And died to succour me!
‘Helen of Kirkconnell’

14 Blair Atholl’s mine, Jeanie,
Little Dunkeld is mine, lassie,
St Johnston’s bower, and Huntingtower,
And all that’s mine is thine, lassie.
‘Huntingtower’

15 Where are your eyes that looked so mild
When my poor heart you first beguiled?
Why did you run from me and the child?
Och, Johnny, I hardly knew ye!
‘Johnny, I hardly knew Ye’

16 I was but seven years auld
When my mither she did die;
My father married the ae warst woman
The warld did ever see.

For she has made me the laily worm
That lies at the fit o’ the tree
And my sister Masery she’s made
The machrel of the sea.

An’ evry Saturday at noon
The machrel comes to me
An’ she takes my laily head
An’ lays it on her knee;
An’ she kaims it wi’ a siller kaim
An’ washes ’t in the sea.
‘The Laily Worm and the Machrel’

17 ‘What gat ye to your dinner, Lord Randal, my Son?
What gat ye to your dinner, my handsome young man?’
‘I gat eels boil’d in broo’; mother, make my bed soon,
For I’m weary wi’ hunting, and fain wald lie down.’
‘Lord Randal’

18 This ae nighte, this ae nighte,
—Every nighte and alle,
Fire and fleet and candle-lighte,
And Christe receive thy saule.
‘Lyke-Wake Dirge’

1 From Brig o' Dread when thou may'st pass,
    —Every nighte and alle,
To Purgatory fire thou com'st at last;
And Christe receive thy saule.

If ever thou gavest meat or drink,
    —Every nighte and alle,
The fire sall never make thee shrink
And Christe receive thy saule.
    'Lyke-Wake Dirge'

2 When captains courageous whom death could not
    daunt,
Did march to the siege of the city of Gaunt,
They mustered their soldiers by two and by three,
And the foremost in battle was Mary Ambree.
    'Mary Ambree'

3 For in my mind, of all mankind
I love but you alone.
    'The Nut Brown Maid'

4 For I must to the greenwood go
Alone, a bànished man.
    'The Nut Brown Maid'

5 Marie Hamilton's to the kirk gane
Wi' ribbons on her breast;
The King thought mair o' Marie Hamilton
Than he listen'd to the priest.
    'The Queen's Maries'

6 Yestreen the Queen had four Maries,
The night she'll hae but three;
There was Marie Seaton, and Marie Beaton,
And Marie Carmichael, and me.
    'The Queen's Maries'

7 'O what is longer than the wave?
And what is deeper than the sea?

What is greener than the grass?
And what is more wicked than a woman once was?'

'Love is longer than the wave,
And hell is deeper than the sea.

Envy's greener than the grass,
And the de'il more wicked than a woman e'er was.'

As soon as she the fiend did name,
He flew awa' in a bleezing flame.
    'Riddles Wisely Expounded'

8 There are twelve months in all the year,
As I hear many men say,
But the merriest month in all the year
Is the merry month of May.
    'Robin Hood and the Widow's Three Sons'

9 Fight on, my men, sayes Sir Andrew Bartton,
I am hurt but I am not slain;
Ile lay mee downe and bleed a while
And then Ile rise and fight againe.
    'Sir Andrew Bartton'

10 The king sits in Dunfermline town
Drinking the blude-red wine.
    'Sir Patrick Spens'

11 I saw the new moon late yestreen
Wi' the auld moon in her arm;
And if we gang to sea master,
I fear we'll come to harm.
    'Sir Patrick Spens'

12 O lang, lang may the ladies sit,
Wi' their fans into their hand,
Before they see Sir Patrick Spens
Come sailing to the strand!

And lang, lang may the maidens sit
Wi' their gowd kames in their hair,
A-waiting for their ain dear loves!
For them they'll see nae mair.

Half-owre, half-owre to Aberdour,
'Tis fifty fathoms deep;
And there lies good Sir Patrick Spens,
Wi' the Scots lords at his feet!
    'Sir Patrick Spens'

13 And she has kilted her green kirtle
A little abune her knee;
And she has braided her yellow hair
A little abune her bree.
    'Tam Lin'

14 But what I ken this night, Tam Lin,
Gin I had kent yestreen,
I wad ta'en out thy heart o' flesh,
And put in a heart o' stane.
    'Tam Lin'

15 She's mounted on her milk-white steed,
She's ta'en true Thomas up behind.
    'Thomas the Rhymer'

16 And see ye not yon braid, braid road,
That lies across the lily leven?
That is the Path of Wickedness,
Though some call it the Road to Heaven.
    'Thomas the Rhymer'

17 It was mirk, mirk night, there was nae starlight,
They waded thro' red blude to the knee;
For a' the blude that's shed on the earth
Rins through the springs o' that countrie.
    'Thomas the Rhymer'

18 There were three ravens sat on a tree,
They were as black as they might be.
The one of them said to his make,
'Where shall we our breakfast take?'
    'The Three Ravens'

19 God send every gentleman
Such hounds, such hawks, and such leman.
    'The Three Ravens' (*leman* sweetheart)

20 As I was walking all alane,
I heard twa corbies making a mane:
The tane unto the tither did say,
'Where sall we gang and dine the day?'

'—In behint yon auld fail dyke
I wot there lies a new-slain knight;
And naebody kens that he lies there
But his hawk, his hound, and his lady fair.

'His hound is to the hunting gane,
His hawk to fetch the wild-fowl hame,
His lady's ta'en anither mate,
So we may make our dinner sweet.

'Ye'll sit on his white hause-bane,
And I'll pike out his bonny blue e'en:
Wi' ae lock o' his gowden hair
We'll theek our nest when it grows bare.'
    'The Twa Corbies' (*corbies* ravens; *fail* turf; *hause* neck;
    theek thatch)

1 The wind doth blow to-day, my love,
  And a few small drops of rain;
  I never had but one true love;
  In cold grave she was lain.

  I'll do as much for my true-love
  As any young man may;
  I'll sit and mourn all at her grave
  For a twelvemonth and a day.
  'The Unquiet Grave'

2 O waly, waly, up the bank,
  And waly, waly, doun the brae,
  And waly, waly, yon burn-side,
  Where I and my Love wont to gae!

  I leaned my back unto an aik,
  I thocht it was a trustie tree;
  But first it bowed and syne it brake—
  Sae my true love did lichtlie me.

  O waly, waly, gin love be bonnie
  A little time while it is new!
  But when 'tis auld it waxeth cauld,
  And fades awa' like morning dew.
  'Waly, Waly'

3 But had I wist, before I kist,
  That love had been sae ill to win,
  I had locked my heart in a case o' gowd,
  And pinned it wi' a siller pin.

  And O! if my young babe were born,
  And set upon the nurse's knee;
  And I mysel' were dead and gane,
  And the green grass growing over me!
  'Waly, Waly'

4 Tom Pearse, Tom Pearse, lend me your grey mare,
  All along, down along, out along, lee.
  For I want for to go to Widdicombe Fair,
  Wi' Bill Brewer, Jan Stewer, Peter Gurney, Peter
    Davey, Dan'l Whiddon, Harry Hawk,
  Old Uncle Tom Cobbleigh and all.
  Old Uncle Tom Cobbleigh and all.
  'Widdicombe Fair'

Whitney Balliett 1926–
American writer

5 A critic is a bundle of biases held loosely together by
  a sense of taste.
  Dinosaurs in the Morning (1962) introductory note

6 The sound of surprise.
  Title of book on jazz (1959)

Pierre Balmain 1914–82
French couturier

7 The trick of wearing mink is to look as though you
  were wearing a cloth coat. The trick of wearing a cloth
  coat is to look as though you are wearing mink.
  In *Observer* 25 December 1955

Honoré de Balzac 1799–1850
French novelist

8 *L'homme n'est ni bon ni méchant, il naît avec des instincts
  et des aptitudes.*
  Man is neither good nor bad; he is born with instincts
  and abilities.
  La Comédie Humaine (1842) vol. 1, foreword

9 *La haine est un tonique, elle fait vivre, elle inspire la
  vengeance; mais la pitié tue, elle affaibli encore notre
  faiblesse.*
  Hatred is a tonic, it makes one live, it inspires
  vengeance; but pity kills, it makes our weakness
  weaker.
  La Peau de Chagrin (1831) ch. 1

10 *Le despotisme fait illégalement de grandes choses, la liberté
   ne se donne même pas la peine d'en faire légalement de très
   petites.*
   Despotism accomplishes great things illegally; liberty
   doesn't even go to the trouble of accomplishing small
   things legally.
   La Peau de Chagrin (1831) ch. 3

George Bancroft 1800–91

11 Calvinism [in Switzerland] . . . established a religion
   without a prelate, a government without a king.
   History of the United States (1855 ed.) vol. 3, ch. 6

Richard Bancroft 1544–1610
English prelate

12 Where Christ erecteth his Church, the devil in the
   same churchyard will have his chapel.
   Sermon at Paul's Cross, 9 February 1588. Cf. Becon 58:6,
   Luther 432:12

Théodore Faullain de Banville 1823–91
French poet

13 *Jeune homme sans mélancolie,
   Blond comme un soleil d'Italie,
   Garde bien ta belle folie.*
   Young man untroubled by melancholy, fair as an
   Italian sun, take good care of your fine carelessness.
   'A Adolphe Gaiffe' (1856)

14 LICENCES POÉTIQUES. *Il n'y en a pas.*
   POETIC LICENCE. There's no such thing.
   Petit traité de poésie française (1872) ch. 4

Imamu Amiri Baraka (Everett LeRoi Jones) 1934–
American poet and playwright

15 A man is either free or he is not. There cannot be any
   apprenticeship for freedom.
   Kulchur Spring 1962 'Tokenism'

16 God has been replaced, as he has all over the West,
   with respectability and airconditioning.
   Midstream (1963) p. 39

Yevgeny Baratynsky 1800–44

Russian poet

1 Дало две доли провидение
На выбор мудрости людской:
Или надежду и волнение,
Иль безнадежность и покой.

Providence has given human wisdom the choice
between two fates: either hope and agitation, or
hopelessness and calm.

'Two Fates' (1823) (translated by Dmitri Obolensky)

Anna Laetitia Barbauld 1743–1825

English poet and literary editor

2 If e'er thy breast with freedom glowed,
And spurned a tyrant's chain,
Let not thy strong oppressive force
A free-born mouse detain.

'The Mouse's Petition to Doctor Priestley Found in the Trap
where he had been confined all Night' (1773) l. 9

3 Beware, lest in the worm you crush
A brother's soul you find.

'The Mouse's Petition' (1773) l. 33

4 Yes, injured Woman! rise, assert thy right!

'The Rights of Woman' (written c.1795, published 1825)
l. 1

Mary Barber c.1690–1757

Irish poet

5 What is it our mammas bewitches
To plague us little boys with breeches?

'Written for My Son, and Spoken by Him at His First
Putting on Breeches' (1731) l. 1

6 A husband's first praise is a Friend and Protector:
Then change not these titles for Tyrant and Hector.

'Conclusion of a Letter to the Revd Mr C—' (1734) l. 67

John Barbour c.1320–95

Scottish poet

7 Storys to rede ar delitabill,
Suppos that thai be nocht bot fabill.

The Bruce (1375) bk. 1, l. 1

8 A! fredome is a noble thing!
Fredome mayse man to haiff liking.

The Bruce (1375) bk. 1, l. 225

Alexander Barclay c.1475–1552

Scottish poet and priest

9 Thy bread is black, of ill sapour and taste,
And hard as flint because thou none should waste,
That scant be thy teeth able it to break.
Dip it in pottage if thou no shift can make,
And though white and brown be both at one price,
With brown shalt thou feed lest white might make
thee nice.
The lords will alway that people note and see
Between them and servants some diversity,
Though it to them turn to no profit at all;
If they have pleasure, the servant shall have small.

Eclogues (1514) no. 2, l. 785

R. H. Barham ('Thomas Ingoldsby')
1788–1845

English clergyman

10 Though I've always considered Sir Christopher Wren,
As an architect, one of the greatest of men;
And, talking of Epitaphs,—much I admire his,
'Circumspice, si Monumentum requiris';
Which an erudite Verger translated to me,
'If you ask for his Monument, Sir-come-spy-see!'

The Ingoldsby Legends (First Series, 1840) 'The Cynotaph'.
Cf. Anonymous 22:16

11 What *was* to be done?—'twas perfectly plain
That they could not well hang the man over again;
What *was* to be done?—The man was dead!
Nought *could* be done—nought could be said;
So—my Lord Tomnoddy went home to bed!

The Ingoldsby Legends (First Series, 1840) 'Hon. Mr
Sucklethumbkin's Story'

12 The Jackdaw sat on the Cardinal's chair!
Bishop, and abbot, and prior were there;
Many a monk, and many a friar,
Many a knight, and many a squire,
With a great many more of lesser degree,—
In sooth a goodly company;
And they served the Lord Primate on bended knee.
Never, I ween,
Was a prouder seen,
Read of in books, or dreamt of in dreams,
Than the Cardinal Lord Archbishop of Rheims!

The Ingoldsby Legends (First Series, 1840) 'The Jackdaw of
Rheims'

13 And six little Singing-boys,—dear little souls!
In nice clean faces, and nice white stoles.

The Ingoldsby Legends (First Series, 1840) 'The Jackdaw of
Rheims'

14 He cursed him in sleeping, that every night
He should dream of the devil, and wake in a fright.

The Ingoldsby Legends (First Series, 1840) 'The Jackdaw of
Rheims'

15 Never was heard such a terrible curse!
But what gave rise
To no little surprise,
Nobody seemed one penny the worse!

The Ingoldsby Legends (First Series, 1840) 'The Jackdaw of
Rheims'

16 Heedless of grammar, they all cried, 'That's him!'

The Ingoldsby Legends (First Series, 1840) 'The Jackdaw of
Rheims'

17 Here's a corpse in the case with a sad swelled face,
And a 'Crowner's Quest' is a queer sort of thing!

The Ingoldsby Legends (First Series, 1840) 'A Lay of St
Gengulphus' (in later editions: 'a Medical Crowner's a
queer sort of thing!')

18 So put that in your pipe, my Lord Otto, and smoke it!

The Ingoldsby Legends (First Series, 1840) 'The Lay of St
Odille'

19 A servant's too often a negligent elf;
—If it's business of consequence, DO IT YOURSELF!

The Ingoldsby Legends (Second Series, 1842) 'The Ingoldsby
Penance!—Moral'

Maurice Baring 1874–1945
English man of letters

1 In Mozart and Salieri we see the contrast between the genius which does what it must and the talent which does what it can.
Outline of Russian Literature (1914) ch. 3

Sabine Baring-Gould 1834–1924
English clergyman

2 Onward, Christian soldiers,
Marching as to war,
With the cross of Jesus
Going on before.
'Onward, Christian Soldiers' (1864 hymn)

3 Through the night of doubt and sorrow
Onward goes the pilgrim band,
Singing songs of expectation,
Marching to the Promised Land.
'Through the night of doubt and sorrow' (1867 hymn);
translated from the Danish of B. S. Ingemann (1789–1862)

Frederick R. Barnard

4 One picture is worth ten thousand words.
Printers' Ink 10 March 1927

Julian Barnes 1946–
English novelist

5 What does this journey seem like to those who aren't British—as they head towards the land of embarrassment and breakfast?
Flaubert's Parrot (1984) ch. 7

6 The writer must be universal in sympathy and an outcast by nature: only then can he see clearly.
Flaubert's Parrot (1984) ch. 10

7 Do not imagine that Art is something which is designed to give gentle uplift and self-confidence. Art is not a *brassière*. At least, not in the English sense. But do not forget that *brassière* is the French for life-jacket.
Flaubert's Parrot (1984) ch. 10

8 Books say: she did this because. Life says: she did this. Books are where things are explained to you; life is where things aren't . . . Books make sense of life. The only problem is that the lives they make sense of are other people's lives, never your own.
Flaubert's Parrot (1984) ch. 13

9 All novelists know their art proceeds by indirection. When tempted by didacticism, the writer should imagine a spruce sea-captain eyeing the storm ahead, bustling from instrument to instrument in a catherine wheel of gold braid, expelling crisp orders down the speaking tube. But there is nobody below decks; the engine-room was never installed, and the rudder broke off centuries ago.
A History of the World in 10½ Chapters (1989) 'Parenthesis'

10 Does history repeat itself, the first time as tragedy, the second time as farce? No, that's too grand, too considered a process. History just burps, and we taste again that raw-onion sandwich it swallowed centuries ago.
A History of the World in 10½ Chapters (1989) 'Parenthesis'. Cf. Marx 452:7

11 Love is just a system for getting someone to call you darling after sex.
Talking It Over (1991) ch. 16

Peter Barnes 1931–
English playwright

12 CLAIRE: How do you know you're . . . God?
EARL OF GURNEY: Simple. When I pray to Him I find I'm talking to myself.
The Ruling Class (1969) act 1, sc. 4

William Barnes 1801–86
English poet

13 An' there vor me the apple tree
Do leän down low in Linden Lea.
Hwomely Rhymes (1859) 'My Orcha'd in Linden Lea'

14 But still the neäme do bide the seäme—
'Tis Pentridge—Pentridge by the river.
Hwomely Rhymes (1859) 'Pentridge by the River'

15 My love is the maïd ov all maïdens,
Though all mid be comely.
Poems of Rural Life in the Dorset Dialect (1862) 'In the Spring'

Richard Barnfield 1574–1627
English poet

16 The waters were his winding sheet, the sea was made his tomb;
Yet for his fame the ocean sea, was not sufficient room.
The Encomion of Lady Pecunia (1598) 'To the Gentlemen Readers' (on the death of Sir John Hawkins)

17 My flocks feed not, my ewes breed not,
My rams speed not, all is amiss;
Love in dying, Faith is defying,
Heart's renying, causer of this.
'The Unknown Shepherd's Complaint' in Nicholas Ling (ed.) *England's Helicon* (1600)

18 Man's life is well compared to a feast,
Furnished with choice of all variety;
To it comes Time; and as a bidden guest
He sets him down, in pomp and majesty;
The three-fold Age of man the waiters be.
Then with an earthen voider (made of clay)
Comes Death, and takes the table clean away.
'Man's life' (1598)

Phineas T. Barnum 1810–91
American showman

19 There's a sucker born every minute.
Attributed

Sir J. M. Barrie 1860–1937

Scottish writer and playwright

1 His lordship may compel us to be equal upstairs, but there will never be equality in the servants' hall.
The Admirable Crichton (performed 1902, published 1914) act 1

2 It's my deserts; I'm a second eleven sort of chap.
The Admirable Crichton (performed 1902, published 1914) act 3

3 The life of every man is a diary in which he means to write one story, and writes another; and his humblest hour is when he compares the volume as it is with what he vowed to make it.
The Little Minister (1891) vol. 1, ch. 1

4 It's grand, and you canna expect to be baith grand and comfortable.
The Little Minister (1891) vol. 1, ch. 10

5 Facts were never pleasing to him. He acquired them with reluctance and got rid of them with relief. He was never on terms with them until he had stood them on their heads.
The Greenwood Hat (1937) 'Love Me Never or For Ever'

6 When the first baby laughed for the first time, the laugh broke into a thousand pieces and they all went skipping about, and that was the beginning of fairies.
Peter Pan (1928) act 1

7 Every time a child says 'I don't believe in fairies' there is a little fairy somewhere that falls down dead.
Peter Pan (1928) act 1

8 To die will be an awfully big adventure.
Peter Pan (1928) act 3. Cf. Frohman 294:5

9 Do you believe in fairies? Say quick that you believe! If you believe, clap your hands!
Peter Pan (1928) act 4

10 That is ever the way. 'Tis all jealousy to the bride and good wishes to the corpse.
Quality Street (performed 1901, published 1913) act 1

11 One's religion is whatever he is most interested in, and yours is Success.
The Twelve-Pound Look (1921)

12 Charm ... it's a sort of bloom on a woman. If you have it, you don't need to have anything else; and if you don't have it, it doesn't much matter what else you have.
What Every Woman Knows (performed 1908, published 1918) act 1

13 There are few more impressive sights in the world than a Scotsman on the make.
What Every Woman Knows (performed 1908, published 1918) act 2

14 The tragedy of a man who has found himself out.
What Every Woman Knows (performed 1908, published 1918) act 4

15 Every man who is high up loves to think that he has done it all himself; and the wife smiles, and lets it go at that. It's our only joke. Every woman knows that.
What Every Woman Knows (performed 1908, published 1918) act 4

Ethel Barrymore 1879–1959

American actress

16 For an actress to be a success, she must have the face of a Venus, the brains of a Minerva, the grace of Terpsichore, the memory of a Macaulay, the figure of Juno, and the hide of a rhinoceros.
In George Jean Nathan *The Theatre in the Fifties* (1953) p. 30

Roland Barthes 1915–80

French writer and critic

17 *Ce que le public réclame, c'est l'image de la passion, non la passion elle-même.*
What the public wants is the image of passion, not passion itself.
Mythologies (1957) 'Le monde où l'on catche'

18 *Je crois que l'automobile est aujourd'hui l'équivalent assez exact des grandes cathédrales gothiques : je veux dire une grande création d'époque, conçue passionnement par des artistes inconnus, consommée dans son image, sinon dans son usage, par un peuple entier qui s'approprie en elle un objet parfaitement magique.*
I think that cars today are almost the exact equivalent of the great Gothic cathedrals: I mean the supreme creation of an era, conceived with passion by unknown artists, and consumed in image if not in usage by a whole population which appropriates them as a purely magical object.
Mythologies (1957) 'La nouvelle Citroën'

Bernard Baruch 1870–1965

American financier and presidential adviser

19 Let us not be deceived—we are today in the midst of a cold war.
Speech to South Carolina Legislature 16 April 1947, in *New York Times* 17 April 1947, p. 21 (the expression 'cold war' was suggested to him by H. B. Swope, former editor of the *New York World*)

20 To me old age is always fifteen years older than I am.
In *Newsweek* 29 August 1955

21 Vote for the man who promises least; he'll be the least disappointing.
In Meyer Berger *New York* (1960)

22 A political leader must keep looking over his shoulder all the time to see if the boys are still there. If they aren't still there, he's no longer a political leader.
In *New York Times* 21 June 1965, p. 16

Jacques Barzun 1907–

American historian and educationist

23 If it were possible to talk to the unborn, one could never explain to them how it feels to be alive, for life is washed in the speechless real.
The House of Intellect (1959) ch. 6

William Basse d. *c.*1653

English poet

1 The first men that our Saviour dear
Did choose to wait upon him here,
Blest fishers were; and fish the last
Food was, that he on earth did taste:
I therefore strive to follow those
Whom he to follow him hath chose.
　'The Angler's Song' (1653)

2 Renownèd Spenser, lie a thought more nigh
To learnèd Chaucer, and rare Beaumont lie
A little nearer Spenser, to make more room
For Shakespeare, in your threefold, fourfold tomb.
　'On Mr Wm. Shakespeare' (1633)

Thomas Bastard 1566–1618

English poet

3 Age is deformed, youth unkind,
We scorn their bodies, they our mind.
　Chrestoleros (1598) bk. 7, epigram 9

Edgar Bateman and George Le Brunn

British songwriters

4 Wiv a ladder and some glasses,
You could see to 'Ackney Marshes,
If it wasn't for the 'ouses in between.
　'If it wasn't for the 'Ouses in between' (1894 song)

Katherine Lee Bates 1859–1929

American writer and educationist

5 America! America!
God shed His grace on thee
And crown thy good with brotherhood
From sea to shining sea!
　'America the Beautiful' (1893)

Charles Baudelaire 1821–67

French poet and critic

6 *Le poète est semblable au prince des nuées
Qui hante la tempête et se rit de l'archer;
Exilé sur le sol, au milieu des huées,
Ses ailes de géant l'empêchent de marcher.*

The poet is like the prince of the clouds, who rides out the tempest and laughs at the archer. But when he is exiled on the ground, amidst the clamour, his giant's wings prevent him from walking.
　Les fleurs du mal (1857) 'L'Albatross'—'Spleen et idéal' no. 2

7 *Hypocrite lecteur,—mon semblable,—mon frère.*

Hypocrite reader—my likeness—my brother.
　Les fleurs du mal (1857) 'Au Lecteur'

8 *La nature est un temple où de vivants piliers
Laissent parfois sortir de confuses paroles;
L'homme y passe à travers des forêts de symboles
Qui l'observent avec des regards familiers.*

Nature is a temple, where, from living pillars, confused words are sometimes allowed to escape; here man passes, through forests of symbols, which watch him with looks of recognition.
　Les fleurs du mal (1857) 'Correspondances' no. 4

9 *Là, tout n'est qu'ordre et beauté,
Luxe, calme et volupté.*

Everything there is simply order and beauty, luxury, peace and sensual indulgence.
　Les fleurs du mal (1857) 'L'Invitation au voyage'—'Spleen et idéal' no. 56

10 *Quelle est cette île triste et noire? C'est Cythère,
Nous dit-on, un pays fameux dans les chansons,
Eldorado banal de tous les vieux garçons.
Regardez, après tout, c'est un pauvre terre.*

What sad, black isle is that? It's Cythera, so they say, a land celebrated in song, the banal Eldorado of all the old fools. Look, after all, it's a land of poverty.
　Les fleurs du mal (1857) 'Un voyage à Cythère'—'Les fleurs du mal' no. 121

11 *Nous voulons, tant ce feu nous brûle le cerveau,
Plonger au fond du gouffre, Enfer ou Ciel, qu'importe?
Au fond de l'Inconnu pour trouver du nouveau!*

We want, this fire so burns our brain tissue, to drown in the abyss—heaven or hell, who cares? Through the unknown, we'll find the new.
　Les fleurs du mal (1857) 'Le voyage' no. 126 (translated by Robert Lowell)

12 *Il y a dans tout changement quelque chose d'infâme et d'agréable à la fois, quelque chose qui tient de l'infidélité et du déménagement. Cela suffit à expliquer la Révolution Française.*

There is in all change something at once sordid and agreeable, which smacks of infidelity and household removals. This is sufficient to explain the French Revolution.
　Journaux intimes (1887) 'Mon coeur mis à nu' no. 4 (translated by Christopher Isherwood)

13 *La croyance au progrès est une doctrine de paresseux, une doctrine de Belges. C'est l'individu qui compte sur ses voisins pour faire sa besogne.*

Belief in progress is a doctrine of idlers and Belgians. It is the individual relying upon his neighbours to do his work.
　Journaux intimes (1887) 'Mon coeur mis à nu' no. 9 (translated by Christopher Isherwood)

14 *Il faut épater le bourgeois.*

One must astonish the bourgeois.
　Attributed. Also attributed to Privat d'Anglemont (*c.*1820–59) in the form '*Je les ai épatés, les bourgeois* [I flabbergasted them, the bourgeois]'

L. Frank Baum 1856–1919

American writer

15 The road to the City of Emeralds is paved with yellow brick.
　The Wonderful Wizard of Oz (1900) ch. 2

Vicki Baum 1888–1960

German novelist

1 *Verheiratet sein verlangt immer und überall die feinste Kunst der Unaufrichtigkeit zwischen Mensch und Mensch.*
Marriage always demands the finest arts of insincerity possible between two human beings.
    Zwischenfall in Lohwinckel (1930) p. 140 (translated by Margaret Goldsmith as *Results of an Accident* (1931) p. 140)

Sir Beverley Baxter 1891–1964

British journalist and Conservative politician

2 Beaverbrook is so pleased to be in the Government that he is like the town tart who has finally married the Mayor!
    In Sir Henry Channon *Chips: the Diaries* (1967) 12 June 1940

Thomas Haynes Bayly 1797–1839

English poet and playwright

3 Oh! no! we never mention her,
    Her name is never heard;
    My lips are now forbid to speak
    That once familiar word.
    'Oh! No! We Never Mention Her' (1844)

Beachcomber

See J. B. MORTON

James Beattie 1735–1803

Scottish philosopher and poet

4 Some deemed him wondrous wise, and some believed him mad.
    The Minstrel bk. 1 (1771) st. 16

5 Fancy a thousand wondrous forms descries
    More wildly great than ever pencil drew,
    Rocks, torrents, gulfs, and shapes of giant size,
    And glittering cliffs on cliffs, and fiery ramparts rise.
    The Minstrel bk. 1 (1771) st. 53

6 In the deep windings of the grove, no more
    The hag obscene, and grisly phantom dwell;
    Nor in the fall of mountain-stream, or roar
    Of winds, is heard the angry spirit's yell.
    The Minstrel bk. 2 (1774) st. 48

David Beatty (1st Earl Beatty) 1871–1936

British Admiral of the Fleet, 1916–19

7 There's something wrong with our bloody ships today, Chatfield.
    At the Battle of Jutland, 1916, in Winston Churchill *The World Crisis 1916–1918* (1927) pt. 1, p. 129

Topham Beauclerk 1739–80

English dandy

8 Then he does not wear them out in practice.
    On hearing that a certain person was 'a man of good principles', in James Boswell *The Life of Samuel Johnson* (1934 ed.) vol. 3, p. 281 (14 April 1778)

Pierre-Augustin Caron de Beaumarchais 1732–99

French playwright

9 *Aujourd'hui ce qui ne vaut pas la peine d'être dit, on le chante.*
Today if something is not worth saying, people sing it.
    Le Barbier de Séville (1775) act 1, sc. 2

10 *Je me presse de rire de tout, de peur d'être obligé d'en pleurer.*
I make myself laugh at everything, for fear of having to weep at it.
    Le Barbier de Séville (1775) act 1, sc. 2

11 *Boire sans soif et faire l'amour en tout temps, madame, il n'y a que ça qui nous distingue des autres bêtes.*
Drinking when we are not thirsty and making love all year round, madam; that is all there is to distinguish us from other animals.
    Le Mariage de Figaro (1785) act 2, sc. 21

12 *Parce que vous êtes un grand seigneur, vous vous croyez un grand génie! ... Vous vous êtes donné la peine de naître, et rien de plus.*
Because you are a great lord, you believe yourself to be a great genius! ... You took the trouble to be born, but no more.
    Le Mariage de Figaro (1785) act 5, sc. 3

Francis Beaumont 1584–1616

English poet and playwright

13 Nose, nose, jolly red nose,
    Who gave thee this jolly red nose? ...
    Nutmegs and ginger, cinnamon and cloves,
    And they gave me this jolly red nose.
    The Knight of the Burning Pestle (c.1607) act 1

14   What things have we seen,
    Done at the Mermaid! heard words that have been
    So nimble, and so full of subtil flame,
    As if that every one from whence they came,
    Had meant to put his whole wit in a jest,
    And had resolved to live a fool, the rest
    Of his dull life.
    'Letter to Ben Jonson'

15 Here are sands, ignoble things,
    Dropt from the ruined sides of kings;
    Here's a world of pomp and state,
    Buried in dust, once dead by fate.
    'On the Tombs in Westminster Abbey'

Francis Beaumont 1584–1616 *and* John Fletcher 1579–1625
English playwrights

1 Those have most power to hurt us that we love.
   The Maid's Tragedy (written 1610–11) act 5

2 PHILASTER: Oh, but thou dost not know
   What 'tis to die.
   BELLARIO: Yes, I do know, my Lord:
   'Tis less than to be born; a lasting sleep;
   A quiet resting from all jealousy,
   A thing we all pursue; I know besides,
   It is but giving over of a game,
   That must be lost.
   Philaster (written 1609) act 3

3 There is no other purgatory but a woman.
   The Scornful Lady (1616) act 3

4 It would talk: Lord how it talk't!
   The Scornful Lady (1616) act 4

See also JOHN FLETCHER

Lord Beaverbrook (*Max Aitken, 1st Baron Beaverbrook*) 1879–1964
Canadian-born British newspaper proprietor and Conservative politician

5 The Flying Scotsman is no less splendid a sight when it travels north to Edinburgh than when it travels south to London. Mr Baldwin denouncing sanctions was as dignified as Mr Baldwin imposing them.
   Daily Express 29 May 1937

6 [Lloyd George] did not seem to care which way he travelled providing he was in the driver's seat.
   The Decline and Fall of Lloyd George (1963) ch. 7

7 Now who is responsible for this work of development on which so much depends? To whom must the praise be given? To the boys in the back rooms. They do not sit in the limelight. But they are the men who do the work.
   Listener 27 March 1941

8 With the publication of his Private Papers in 1952, he [Earl Haig] committed suicide 25 years after his death.
   Men and Power (1956) p. xviii

9 Our cock won't fight.
   Said to Winston Churchill, of Edward VIII, during the abdication crisis of 1936, in Frances Donaldson *Edward VIII* (1974) ch. 22

Carl Becker 1873–1945
American historian

10 The significance of man is that he is that part of the universe that asks the question, What is the significance of Man? He alone can stand apart imaginatively and, regarding himself and the universe in their eternal aspects, pronounce a judgement: The significance of man is that he is insignificant and is aware of it.
   Progress and Power (1936) ch. 3

Samuel Beckett 1906–89
Irish playwright, novelist, and poet

11 It is suicide to be abroad. But what is it to be at home, Mr Tyler, what is it to be at home? A lingering dissolution.
   All That Fall (1957) p. 10

12 We could have saved sixpence. We have saved fivepence. (*Pause*) But at what cost?
   All That Fall (1957) p. 25

13 CLOV: Do you believe in the life to come?
   HAMM: Mine was always that.
   Endgame (1958) p. 35

14 Let us pray to God . . . the bastard! He doesn't exist!
   Endgame (1958) p. 38

15 Personally I have no bone to pick with graveyards, I take the air there willingly, perhaps more willingly than elsewhere, when take the air I must.
   First Love (1973) p. 8

16 There is no use indicting words, they are no shoddier than what they peddle.
   Malone Dies (1958) p. 19

17 If I had the use of my body I would throw it out of the window.
   Malone Dies (1958) p. 44

18 Where I am, I don't know, I'll never know, in the silence you don't know, you must go on, I can't go on, I'll go on.
   The Unnamable (1959) p. 418

19 Nothing to be done.
   Waiting for Godot (1955) act 1

20 One of the thieves was saved. (*Pause*) It's a reasonable percentage.
   Waiting for Godot (1955) act 1

21 ESTRAGON: Charming spot. Inspiring prospects. Let's go.
   VLADIMIR: We can't.
   ESTRAGON: Why not?
   VLADIMIR: We're waiting for Godot.
   Waiting for Godot (1955) act 1

22 Nothing happens, nobody comes, nobody goes, it's awful!
   Waiting for Godot (1955) act 1

23 He can't think without his hat.
   Waiting for Godot (1955) act 1

24 All my lousy life I've crawled about in the mud! And you talk to me about scenery!
   Waiting for Godot (1955) act 2

25 VLADIMIR: That passed the time.
   ESTRAGON: It would have passed in any case.
   VLADIMIR: Yes, but not so rapidly.
   Waiting for Godot (1955) act 1

26 We always find something, eh, Didi, to give us the impression that we exist?
   Waiting for Godot (1955) act 2

27 We are not saints, but we have kept our appointment. How many people can boast as much?
   Waiting for Godot (1955) act 2

28 We all are born mad. Some remain so.
   Waiting for Godot (1955) act 2

1 They give birth astride of a grave, the light gleams an instant, then it's night once more.
  Waiting for Godot (1955) act 2

2 The air is full of our cries. (*He listens*) But habit is a great deadener.
  Waiting for Godot (1955) act 2

William Beckford 1759–1844

English writer and collector

3 When he was angry, one of his eyes became so terrible, that no person could bear to behold it; and the wretch upon whom it was fixed, instantly fell backward, and sometimes expired. For fear, however, of depopulating his dominions and making his palace desolate, he but rarely gave way to his anger.
  Vathek (1782; 3rd ed., 1816) opening para.

4 He did not think, with the Caliph Omar Ben Adalaziz, that it was necessary to make a hell of this world to enjoy Paradise in the next.
  Vathek (1782; 3rd ed., 1816) para. 2

5 Your presence I condescend to accept; but beg you will let me be quiet; for, I am not over-fond of resisting temptation.
  Vathek (1782; 3rd ed., 1816) para. 215

Thomas Becon 1512–67

Chaplain to Thomas Cranmer

6 For commonly, wheresoever God buildeth a church, the devil will build a chapel just by.
  Catechism (1560, ed. J. Ayre, 1844) p. 361. Cf. Bancroft 51:12, Luther 432:12

7 When the wine is in, the wit is out.
  Catechism (1560, ed. J. Ayre, 1844) p. 375

Thomas Lovell Beddoes 1803–49

English poet and playwright

8 If thou wilt ease thine heart
Of love and all its smart,
Then sleep, dear, sleep.
  Death's Jest Book 1825–8 (1850) act 2, sc. 2 'Dirge'

9 But wilt thou cure thine heart
Of love and all its smart,
Then die, dear, die.
  Death's Jest Book 1825–8 (1850) act 2, sc. 2 'Dirge'

10 I have a bit of FIAT in my soul,
And can myself create my little world.
  Death's Jest Book 1825–8 (1850) act 5, sc. 1, l. 39

11 King Death hath asses' ears.
  Death's Jest Book 1825–8 (1850) act 5, sc. 4, l. 245

12 If there were dreams to sell,
What would you buy?
Some cost a passing bell;
Some a light sigh,
That shakes from Life's fresh crown
Only a rose-leaf down.
If there were dreams to sell,
Merry and sad to tell,
And the crier rung the bell,
What would you buy?
  'Dream-Pedlary' (written 1830, published 1851)

The Venerable Bede AD 673–735

English historian and scholar; monk of Jarrow

13 *Talis, inquiens, mihi videtur, rex, vita hominum praesens in terris, ad conparationem eius, quod nobis incertum est, temporis, quale cum te residente ad caenam cum ducibus ac ministris tuis tempore brumali, . . . adveniens unus passerum domum citissime, pervolaverit; qui cum per unum ostium ingrediens, mox per aliud exierit. Ipso quidem tempore, quo intus est, hiemis tempestate non tangitur, sed tamen parvissimo spatio serenitatis ad momentum excurso, mox de hieme in hiemem regrediens, tuis oculis elabitur. Ita haec vita hominum ad modicum apparet; quid autem sequatur, quidve praecesserit, prorsus ignoramus.*

'Such,' he said, 'O King, seems to me the present life of men on earth, in comparison with that time which to us is uncertain, as if when on a winter's night you sit feasting with your ealdormen and thegns,—a single sparrow should fly swiftly into the hall, and coming in at one door, instantly fly out through another. In that time in which it is indoors it is indeed not touched by the fury of the winter, but yet, this smallest space of calmness being passed almost in a flash, from winter going into winter again, it is lost to your eyes. Somewhat like this appears the life of man; but of what follows or what went before, we are utterly ignorant.'
  Ecclesiastical History of the English People (translated by B. Colgrave, 1969) bk. 2, ch. 13

Harry Bedford and Terry Sullivan

British songwriters

14 I'm a bit of a ruin that Cromwell knocked about a bit.
  'It's a Bit of a Ruin that Cromwell Knocked about a Bit' (1920 song; written for Marie Lloyd)

Barnard Elliott Bee 1823–61

American general

15 There is Jackson with his Virginians, standing like a stone wall. Let us determine to die here, and we will conquer.
  Referring to General T. J. ('Stonewall') Jackson at the battle of Bull Run, 21 July, 1861 (in which Bee himself was killed), in B. Perley Poore *Perley's Reminiscences* (1886) vol. 2, ch. 7

Sir Thomas Beecham 1879–1961

English conductor

16 There are two golden rules for an orchestra: start together and finish together. The public doesn't give a damn what goes on in between.
  In Harold Atkins and Archie Newman *Beecham Stories* (1978) p. 27

17 Like two skeletons copulating on a corrugated tin roof.
  Describing the harpsichord, in Harold Atkins and Archie Newman *Beecham Stories* (1978) p. 34

18 A kind of musical Malcolm Sargent.
  Describing Herbert von Karajan, in Harold Atkins and Archie Newman *Beecham Stories* (1978) p. 61

1 Why do we have to have all these third-rate foreign conductors around—when we have so many second-rate ones of our own?
In L. Ayre *Wit of Music* (1966) p. 70

2 The musical equivalent of the Towers of St Pancras Station.
Describing Elgar's 1st Symphony, in Neville Cardus *Sir Thomas Beecham* (1961) p. 113

3 Too much counterpoint; what is worse, Protestant counterpoint.
Describing Bach, in *Guardian* 8 March 1971

4 All the arts in America are a gigantic racket run by unscrupulous men for unhealthy women.
In *Observer* 5 May 1946

5 Madam, you have between your legs an instrument capable of giving pleasure to thousands—and all you can do is scratch it.
To a cellist (attributed)

H. C. Beeching 1859–1919

English divine

6 Not when the sense is dim,
But now from the heart of joy,
I would remember Him:
Take the thanks of a boy.
In a Garden and Other Poems (1895) 'Prayers'

7 First come I; my name is Jowett.
There's no knowledge but I know it.
I am Master of this college:
What I don't know isn't knowledge.
The Masque of Balliol (composed by and current among members of Balliol College in the late 1870s) in W. G. Hiscock (ed.) *The Balliol Rhymes* (1939). Cf. Anonymous 16:15, Spring-Rice 661:11

Sir Max Beerbohm 1872–1956

English critic, essayist, and caricaturist

8 Mankind is divisible into two great classes: hosts and guests.
And Even Now (1920) 'Hosts and Guests'

9 They so very indubitably *are*, you know!
Christmas Garland (1912) 'Mote in the Middle Distance'

10 A swear-word in a rustic slum
A simple swear-word is to some,
To Masefield something more.
Fifty Caricatures (1912) no. 12

11 I was not unpopular [at school] ... It is Oxford that has made me insufferable.
More (1899) 'Going Back to School'

12 Undergraduates owe their happiness chiefly to the consciousness that they are no longer at school. The nonsense which was knocked out of them at school is all put gently back at Oxford or Cambridge.
More (1899) 'Going Back to School'

13 Enter Michael Angelo. Andrea del Sarto appears for a moment at a window. Pippa passes.
Seven Men (1919) 'Savonarola Brown' act 3

14 The fading signals and grey eternal walls of that antique station, which, familiar to them and insignificant, does yet whisper to the tourist the last enchantments of the Middle Age.
Zuleika Dobson (1911) ch. 1. Cf. Arnold 29:15

15 The dullard's envy of brilliant men is always assuaged by the suspicion that they will come to a bad end.
Zuleika Dobson (1911) ch. 4

16 Women who love the same man have a kind of bitter freemasonry.
Zuleika Dobson (1911) ch. 4

17 Deeply regret inform your grace last night two black owls came and perched on battlements remained there through night hooting at dawn flew away none knows whither awaiting instructions Jellings.
Zuleika Dobson (1911) ch. 14

18 Prepare vault for funeral Monday Dorset.
Zuleika Dobson (1911) ch. 14

19 The Socratic manner is not a game at which two can play.
Zuleika Dobson (1911) ch. 15

20 Most women are not so young as they are painted.
The Yellow Book (1894) vol. 1, p. 67

21 Fate wrote her a most tremendous tragedy, and she played it in tights.
The Yellow Book (1894) vol. 3, p. 260 (of Queen Caroline of Brunswick)

Ethel Lynn Beers 1827–79

American poet

22 All quiet along the Potomac to-night,
No sound save the rush of the river,
While soft falls the dew on the face of the dead—
The picket's off duty forever.
'The Picket Guard' (1861) st. 6. Cf. McClellan 437:2

Ludwig van Beethoven 1770–1827

German composer

23 *Muss es sein? Es muss sein.*
Must it be? It must be.
String Quartet in F Major, Opus 135, epigraph

Mrs Beeton (*née Isabella Mary Mayson*) 1836–65

English writer on the domestic arts

24 A place for everything and everything in its place.
The Book of Household Management (1861) ch. 2, sect. 55 (often attributed to Samuel Smiles)

Brendan Behan 1923–64

Irish playwright

25 He was born an Englishman and remained one for years.
Hostage (1958) act 1

26 PAT: He was an Anglo-Irishman.
MEG: In the blessed name of God what's that?
PAT: A Protestant with a horse.
Hostage (1958) act 1

1 Meanwhile I'll sing that famous old song, 'The Hound that Caught the Pubic Hare'.
  Hostage (1958) act 1

2 When I came back to Dublin, I was courtmartialled in my absence and sentenced to death in my absence, so I said they could shoot me in my absence.
  Hostage (1958) act 1

3 I am a sociable worker. Have you your testament?
  Hostage (1958) act 2

4 Go on, abuse me—your own husband that took you off the streets on a Sunday morning, when there wasn't a pub open in the city.
  Hostage (1958) act 2

5 We're here because we're queer
  Because we're queer because we're here.
  Hostage (1958) act 3. Cf. Anonymous 19:8

6 There's no such thing as bad publicity except your own obituary.
  In Dominic Behan *My Brother Brendan* (1965) p. 158

Aphra Behn (née Johnson) 1640–89

English playwright, poet, and novelist

7 Oh, what a dear ravishing thing is the beginning of an Amour!
  The Emperor of the Moon (1687) act 1, sc. 1

8 Love ceases to be a pleasure, when it ceases to be a secret.
  The Lover's Watch (1686) 'Four o' Clock. General Conversation'

9 Since man with that inconstancy was born,
  To love the absent, and the present scorn,
  Why do we deck, why do we dress
  For such a short-lived happiness?
  Why do we put attraction on,
  Since either way 'tis we must be undone?
  Lycidus (1688) 'To Alexis, in Answer to his Poem against Fruition'

10 I owe a duty, where I cannot love.
  The Moor's Revenge (1677) act 3, sc. 3

11 Be just, my lovely swain, and do not take
  Freedoms you'll not to me allow;
  Or give Amynta so much freedom back
  That she may rove as well as you.

  Let us then love upon the honest square,
  Since interest neither have designed.
  For the sly gamester, who ne'er plays me fair,
  Must trick for trick expect to find.
  Poems upon Several Occasions (1684) 'To Lysander, on some Verses he writ, and asking more for his Heart than 'twas worth'

12 A brave world, Sir, full of religion, knavery, and change: we shall shortly see better days.
  The Roundheads (1682) act 1, sc. 1

13 Variety is the soul of pleasure.
  The Rover pt. 2 (1681) act 1

14 Come away; poverty's catching.
  The Rover pt. 2 (1681) act 1

15 Money speaks sense in a language all nations understand.
  The Rover pt. 2 (1681) act 3

16 Do you not daily see fine clothes, rich furniture, jewels and plate are more inviting than beauty unadorned?
  The Rover pt. 2 (1681) act 4

17 The soft, unhappy sex.
  The Wandering Beauty (1698) para. 1

John Hay Beith

See IAN HAY

Clive Bell 1881–1964

English art critic

18 Art and Religion are, then, two roads by which men escape from circumstance to ecstasy. Between aesthetic and religious rapture there is a family alliance. Art and Religion are means to similar states of mind.
  Art (1914) pt. 2, ch. 1

19 I will try to account for the degree of my aesthetic emotion. That, I conceive, is the function of the critic.
  Art (1914) pt. 3 ch. 3

20 Only reason can convince us of those three fundamental truths without a recognition of which there can be no effective liberty: that what we believe is not necessarily true; that what we like is not necessarily good; and that all questions are open.
  Civilization (1928) ch. 5

Hilaire Belloc 1870–1953

British poet, essayist, historian, novelist, and Liberal politician

21 Child! do not throw this book about;
  Refrain from the unholy pleasure
  Of cutting all the pictures out!
  Preserve it as your chiefest treasure.
  A Bad Child's Book of Beasts (1896) dedication

22 When people call this beast to mind,
  They marvel more and more
  At such a little tail behind,
  So large a trunk before.
  A Bad Child's Book of Beasts (1896) 'The Elephant'

23 I shoot the Hippopotamus
  With bullets made of platinum,
  Because if I use leaden ones
  His hide is sure to flatten 'em.
  A Bad Child's Book of Beasts (1896) 'The Hippopotamus'. Cf. Forster 289:19

24 The Tiger, on the other hand, is kittenish and mild,
  He makes a pretty play fellow for any little child;
  And mothers of large families (who claim to common sense)
  Will find a Tiger well repay the trouble and expense.
  A Bad Child's Book of Beasts (1896) 'The Tiger'

25 Believing Truth is staring at the sun
  Which but destroys the power that could perceive.
  So naught of our poor selves can be at one
  With burning Truth, nor utterly believe.
  'Believing Truth is staring at the sun' (1938)

1 Physicians of the Utmost Fame
Were called at once; but when they came
They answered, as they took their Fees,
'There is no Cure for this Disease.'
Cautionary Tales (1907) 'Henry King'

2 And always keep a-hold of Nurse
For fear of finding something worse.
Cautionary Tales (1907) 'Jim'

3 In my opinion, Butlers ought
To know their place, and not to play
The Old Retainer night and day.
Cautionary Tales (1907) 'Lord Lundy'

4 Sir! you have disappointed us!
We had intended you to be
The next Prime Minister but three:
The stocks were sold; the Press was squared;
The Middle Class was quite prepared.
But as it is! . . . My language fails!
Go out and govern New South Wales!
Cautionary Tales (1907) 'Lord Lundy'

5 Matilda told such Dreadful Lies,
It made one Gasp and Stretch one's Eyes;
Her Aunt, who, from her Earliest Youth,
Had kept a Strict Regard for Truth,
Attempted to Believe Matilda:
The effort very nearly killed her.
Cautionary Tales (1907) 'Matilda'

6 For every time She shouted 'Fire!'
They only answered 'Little Liar!'
And therefore when her Aunt returned,
Matilda, and the House, were Burned.
Cautionary Tales (1907) 'Matilda'

7 A Trick that everyone abhors
In Little Girls is slamming Doors.
Cautionary Tales (1907) 'Rebecca'

8 She was not really bad at heart,
But only rather rude and wild:
She was an aggravating child.
Cautionary Tales (1907) 'Rebecca'

9 Of Courtesy, it is much less
Than Courage of Heart or Holiness,
Yet in my Walks it seems to me
That the Grace of God is in Courtesy.
'Courtesy' (1910)

10 I said to Heart, 'How goes it ?' Heart replied:
'Right as a Ribstone Pippin!' But it lied.
'The False Heart' (1910)

11 I'm tired of Love: I'm still more tired of Rhyme.
But Money gives me pleasure all the time.
'Fatigued' (1923)

12 Strong brother in God and last companion, Wine.
'Heroic Poem upon Wine' (1926)

13 John Henderson, an unbeliever,
Had lately lost his Joie de Vivre
From reading far too many books . . .
MORAL
The moral is (it is indeed!)
You mustn't monkey with the Creed.
Ladies and Gentlemen (1932) 'The Example'

14 Remote and ineffectual Don
That dared attack my Chesterton.
'Lines to a Don' (1910)

15 Dons admirable! Dons of Might!
Uprising on my inward sight
Compact of ancient tales, and port
And sleep—and learning of a sort.
'Lines to a Don' (1910)

16 Whatever happens we have got
The Maxim Gun, and they have not.
The Modern Traveller (1898) pt. 6

17 The Llama is a woolly sort of fleecy hairy goat,
With an indolent expression and an undulating throat
Like an unsuccessful literary man.
More Beasts for Worse Children (1897) 'The Llama'

18 The Microbe is so very small
You cannot make him out at all.
But many sanguine people hope
To see him through a microscope.
More Beasts for Worse Children (1897) 'The Microbe'

19 Oh! let us never, never doubt
What nobody is sure about!
More Beasts for Worse Children (1897) 'The Microbe'

20 Lord Finchley tried to mend the Electric Light
Himself. It struck him dead: And serve him right!
It is the business of the wealthy man
To give employment to the artisan.
More Peers (1911) 'Lord Finchley'

21 Like many of the Upper Class
He liked the Sound of Broken Glass.
New Cautionary Tales (1930) 'About John'. Cf. Waugh
723:11

22 And even now, at twenty-five,
He has to WORK to keep alive!
Yes! All day long from 10 till 4!
For half the year or even more;
With but an hour or two to spend
At luncheon with a city friend.
New Cautionary Tales (1930) 'Peter Goole'

23 A smell of burning fills the startled Air—
The Electrician is no longer there!
'Newdigate Poem' (1910)

24 The accursed power which stands on Privilege
(And goes with Women, and Champagne, and Bridge)
Broke—and Democracy resumed her reign:
(Which goes with Bridge, and Women and
    Champagne).
'On a Great Election' (1923)

25 I am a sundial, and I make a botch
Of what is done much better by a watch.
'On a Sundial' (1938)

26 When I am dead, I hope it may be said:
'His sins were scarlet, but his books were read.'
'On His Books' (1923)

27 Pale Ebenezer thought it wrong to fight,
But Roaring Bill (who killed him) thought it right.
'The Pacifist' (1938)

28 When I am living in the Midlands
That are sodden and unkind . . .
And the great hills of the South Country
Come back into my mind.
'The South Country' (1910)

1 Do you remember an Inn,
   Miranda?
   Do you remember an Inn?
   And the tedding and the spreading
   Of the straw for a bedding,
   And the fleas that tease in the High Pyrenees
   And the wine that tasted of the tar?
      'Tarantella' (1923)

2 Balliol made me, Balliol fed me,
   Whatever I had she gave me again:
   And the best of Balliol loved and led me.
   God be with you, Balliol men.
      'To the Balliol Men Still in Africa' (1910)

3 From quiet homes and first beginning,
   Out to the undiscovered ends,
   There's nothing worth the wear of winning,
   But laughter and the love of friends.
      Verses (1910) 'Dedicatory Ode'

4 Is there no Latin word for Tea? Upon my soul, if I had
   known that I would have let the vulgar stuff alone.
      On Nothing (1908) 'On Tea'

5 Gentlemen, I am a Catholic ... If you reject me on
   account of my religion, I shall thank God that He has
   spared me the indignity of being your representative.
      Speech to voters of South Salford, 1906, in R. Speaight *Life
      of Hilaire Belloc* (1957) ch. 10

Saul Bellow 1915–

American novelist

6 If I am out of my mind, it's all right with me, thought
   Moses Herzog.
      Herzog (1961) opening sentence

7 A novel is balanced between a few true impressions
   and the multitude of false ones that make up most of
   what we call life. It tells us that for every human
   being there is a diversity of existences, that the single
   existence is itself an illusion in part ... it promises us
   meaning, harmony, and even justice.
      Speech on receiving the Nobel Prize, 1976, in *The American
      Scholar* Summer 1977, no. 46, p. 25

8 Art has something to do with the achievement of
   stillness in the midst of chaos. A stillness which
   characterizes prayer, too, and the eye of the storm ...
   an arrest of attention in the midst of distraction.
      In George Plimpton *Writers at Work* (1967) 3rd series,
      p. 190

De Belloy (Pierre-Laurent Buirette du Belloy) 1725–75

French playwright

9 *Plus je vis d'étrangers, plus j'aimai ma patrie.*

   The more foreigners I saw, the more I loved my
   homeland.
      Le Siège de Calais (1765) act 2, sc. 3

Robert Benchley 1889–1945

American humorist

10 My only solution for the problem of habitual accidents
   ... is to stay in bed all day. Even then, there is always
   the chance that you will fall out.
      Chips off the old Benchley (1949) 'Safety Second'

11 In America there are two classes of travel—first class,
   and with children.
      Pluck and Luck (1925) p. 6

12 It took me fifteen years to discover that I had no talent
   for writing, but I couldn't give it up because by that
   time I was too famous.
      In Nathaniel Benchley *Robert Benchley* (1955) ch. 1

13 STREETS FLOODED. PLEASE ADVISE.
      Telegraph message on arriving in Venice, in R. E. Drennan
      (ed.) *Wits End* (1973) 'Robert Benchley'

Julien Benda 1867–1956

French philosopher and novelist

14 *La trahison des clercs.*

   The treachery of the intellectuals.
      Title of book (1927)

Stephen Vincent Benét 1898–1943

American poet and novelist

15 I have fallen in love with American names,
   The sharp, gaunt names that never get fat,
   The snakeskin-titles of mining-claims,
   The plumed war-bonnet of Medicine Hat,
   Tucson and Deadwood and Lost Mule Flat.
      'American Names' (1927)

16 I shall not rest quiet in Montparnasse.
   I shall not lie easy at Winchelsea.
   You may bury my body in Sussex grass,
   You may bury my tongue at Champmédy.
   I shall not be there, I shall rise and pass.
   Bury my heart at Wounded Knee.
      'American Names' (1927)

17 We thought we were done with these things but we
      were wrong.
   We thought, because we had power, we had wisdom.
      'Litany for Dictatorships' (1935)

William Rose Benét 1886–1950

American poet

18 Blake saw a treefull of angels at Peckham Rye,
   And his hands could lay hold on the tiger's terrible
      heart.
   Blake knew how deep is Hell, and Heaven how high,
   And could build the universe from one tiny part.
      'Mad Blake' (1918)

Tony Benn (*Anthony Wedgwood Benn*) 1925–

British Labour politician

1 In developing our industrial strategy for the period ahead, we have the benefit of much experience. Almost everything has been tried at least once.
Hansard 13 March 1974, col. 197

2 It is as wholly wrong to blame Marx for what was done in his name, as it is to blame Jesus for what was done in his.
In Alan Freeman *The Benn Heresy* (1982) 'Interview with Tony Benn'

George Bennard 1873–1958

3 I will cling to the old rugged cross,
And exchange it some day for a crown.
'The Old Rugged Cross' (1913 hymn)

Alan Bennett 1934–

English actor and playwright

4 The real solvent of class distinction is a proper measure of self-esteem—a kind of unselfconsciousness. Some people are at ease with themselves, so the world is at ease with them. My parents thought this kind of ease was produced by education . . . they didn't see that what disqualified them was temperament—just as, though educated up to the hilt, it disqualifies me. What keeps us in our place is embarrassment.
Dinner at Noon (BBC television, 1988)

5 I don't want to give you the idea I'm trying to hide anything, or that anything unorthodox goes on between my wife and me. It doesn't. Nothing goes on at all . . . No foreplay. No afterplay. And fuck all in between.
Enjoy (1980) act 1

6 I have never understood this liking for war. It panders to instincts already catered for within the scope of any respectable domestic establishment.
Forty Years On (1969) act 1

7 Memories are not shackles, Franklin, they are garlands.
Forty Years On (1969) act 2

8 FRANKLIN: Have you ever thought, Headmaster, that your standards might perhaps be a little out of date?
HEADMASTER: Of course they're out of date. Standards are always out of date. That is what makes them standards.
Forty Years On (1969) act 2

9 We started off trying to set up a small anarchist community, but people wouldn't obey the rules.
Getting On (1972) act 1

10 The asylums of this country are full of the sound of mind disinherited by the out of pocket.
The Madness of George III (performed 1991)

11 We were put to Dickens as children but it never quite took. That unremitting humanity soon had me cheesed off.
The Old Country (1978) act 2

12 Here I sit, alone and sixty,
Bald, and fat, and full of sin,
Cold the seat and loud the cistern,
As I read the Harpic tin.
'Place Names of China'

Arnold Bennett 1867–1931

English novelist

13 His opinion of himself, having once risen, remained at 'set fair'.
The Card (1911) ch. 1

14 'What's he done? Has he ever done a day's work in his life? What great cause is he identified with?' 'He's identified . . . with the great cause of cheering us all up.'
The Card (1911) ch. 12

15 Englishmen act better than Frenchmen, and Frenchwomen better than Englishwomen.
Cupid and Commonsense (1909) preface

16 'With people like you, love only means one thing.' 'No,' he replied. 'It means twenty things, but it doesn't mean nineteen.'
Journal (1932) 20 November 1904

17 Pessimism, when you get used to it, is just as agreeable as optimism. Indeed, I think it must be more agreeable, must have a more real savour, than optimism—from the way in which pessimists abandon themselves to it.
Things that have Interested Me (1921) 'Slump in Pessimism'

18 The price of justice is eternal publicity.
Things that have Interested Me (2nd series, 1923) 'Secret Trials'

19 A cause may be inconvenient, but it's magnificent. It's like champagne or high heels, and one must be prepared to suffer for it.
The Title (1918) act 1

20 Being a husband is a whole-time job. That is why so many husbands fail. They cannot give their entire attention to it.
The Title (1918) act 1

21 Literature's always a good card to play for Honours. It makes people think that Cabinet ministers are educated.
The Title (1918) act 3

Jill Bennett 1931–90

English actress; former wife of John Osborne

22 Never marry a man who hates his mother, because he'll end up hating you.
In *Observer* 12 September 1982 'Sayings of the Week'

A. C. Benson 1862–1925

English writer

23 Land of Hope and Glory, Mother of the Free,
How shall we extol thee who are born of thee?
Wider still and wider shall thy bounds be set;
God who made thee mighty, make thee mightier yet.
'Land of Hope and Glory' written to be sung as the Finale to Elgar's *Coronation Ode* (1902)

Stella Benson 1892–1933

English novelist

1 Call no man foe, but never love a stranger.
   This is the End (1917) p. 63

Jeremy Bentham 1748–1832

English philosopher

2 Right . . . is the child of law: from real laws come real
   rights; but from imaginary laws, from laws of nature,
   fancied and invented by poets, rhetoricians, and
   dealers in moral and intellectual poisons, come
   imaginary rights, a bastard brood of monsters.
   Anarchical Fallacies in J. Bowring (ed.) *Works* vol. 2 (1843)
   p. 523

3 Natural rights is simple nonsense: natural and
   imprescriptible rights, rhetorical nonsense—nonsense
   upon stilts.
   Anarchical Fallacies in J. Bowring (ed.) *Works* vol. 2 (1843)
   p. 501

4 The greatest happiness of the greatest number is the
   foundation of morals and legislation.
   The Commonplace Book in J. Bowring (ed.) *Works* vol. 10
   (1843) p. 142, in which Bentham claims to have acquired
   the 'sacred truth' either from Joseph Priestley (1733–1804)
   or Cesare Beccaria (1738–94). Cf. Hutcheson 357:6

5 The Fool had stuck himself up one day, with great
   gravity, in the King's throne; with a stick, by way of a
   sceptre, in one hand, and a ball in the other: being
   asked what he was doing? he answered '*reigning*'.
   Much of the same sort of reign, I take it would be that
   of our Author's [Blackstone's] Democracy.
   A Fragment on Government (1776) ch. 2, para. 34,
   footnote (e)

6 All punishment is mischief: all punishment in itself is
   evil.
   Principles of Morals and Legislation (1789) ch. 13, para. 2

7 Prose is when all the lines except the last go on to the
   end. Poetry is when some of them fall short of it.
   In M. St. J. Packe *The Life of John Stuart Mill* (1954) bk. 1,
   ch. 2

8 He rather hated the ruling few than loved the
   suffering many.
   Referring to James Mill, in H. N. Pym (ed.) *Memories of Old
   Friends, being Extracts from the Journals and Letters of
   Caroline Fox* (1882) p. 113, 7 August 1840

Edmund Clerihew Bentley 1875–1956

English writer

9 When their lordships asked Bacon
   How many bribes he had taken
   He had at least the grace
   To get very red in the face.
   Baseless Biography (1939) 'Bacon'

10 The Art of Biography
   Is different from Geography.
   Geography is about Maps,
   But Biography is about Chaps.
   Biography for Beginners (1905) introduction

11 Chapman & Hall
   Swore not at all.
   Mr Chapman's yea was yea,
   And Mr Hall's nay was nay.
   Biography for Beginners (1905) 'Chapman & Hall'

12 What I like about Clive
   Is that he is no longer alive.
   There is a great deal to be said
   For being dead.
   Biography for Beginners (1905) 'Clive'

13 Sir Humphrey Davy
   Abominated gravy.
   He lived in the odium
   Of having discovered Sodium.
   Biography for Beginners (1905) 'Sir Humphrey Davy'

14 It looked bad when the Duke of Fife
   Left off using a knife;
   But people began to talk
   When he left off using a fork.
   Biography for Beginners (1905) 'The Duke of Fife'

15 Edward the Confessor
   Slept under the dresser.
   When that began to pall,
   He slept in the hall.
   Biography for Beginners (1905) 'Edward the Confessor'

16 John Stuart Mill,
   By a mighty effort of will,
   Overcame his natural *bonhomie*
   And wrote 'Principles of Political Economy'.
   Biography for Beginners (1905) 'John Stuart Mill'

17 Sir Christopher Wren
   Said, 'I am going to dine with some men.
   If anybody calls
   Say I am designing St Paul's.'
   Biography for Beginners (1905) 'Sir Christopher Wren'

18 George the Third
   Ought never to have occurred.
   One can only wonder
   At so grotesque a blunder.
   More Biography (1929) 'George the Third'

Eric Bentley 1916–

19 Ours is the age of substitutes: instead of language, we
   have jargon; instead of principles, slogans; and,
   instead of genuine ideas, Bright Ideas.
   New Republic 29 December 1952

Richard Bentley 1662–1742

English classical scholar

20 It is a pretty poem, Mr Pope, but you must not call it
   Homer.
   When pressed by Pope to comment on 'My Homer' [i.e. his
   translation of Homer's *Iliad*], in John Hawkins (ed.) *The
   Works of Samuel Johnson* (1787) vol. 4 'The Life of Pope'
   p. 126 n.

21 It would be port if it could.
   His judgement on claret, in R. C. Jebb *Bentley* (1902)
   ch. 12

1 I hold it as certain, that no man was ever written out of reputation but by himself.

> In William Warburton (ed.) *The Works of Alexander Pope* (1751) vol. 4, p. 159 n.

Pierre-Jean de Béranger 1780–1857

French poet

2 *Nos amis, les ennemis.*

Our friends, the enemy.

> 'L'Opinion de ces demoiselles' (written 1815) in *Chansons de De Béranger* (1832)

3 *Il était un roi d'Yvetot*
Peu connu dans l'histoire.

There was a king of Yvetot
Little known to history.

> 'Le Roi d'Yvetot' (written 1813) in *Chansons de De Béranger* (1832)

Lord Charles Beresford 1846–1919

British politician

4 Very sorry can't come. Lie follows by post.

> Telegraphed message to the Prince of Wales, on being summoned to dine at the eleventh hour; Ralph Nevill claims Beresford as the originator of this much imitated witticism in *The World of Fashion 1837–1922* (1923) ch. 5. Cf. Proust 530:15

Henri Bergson 1859–1941

French philosopher

5 *Le présent ne contient rien de plus que le passé, et ce qu'on trouve dans l'effet était déjà dans la cause.*

The present contains nothing more than the past, and what is found in the effect was already in the cause.

> *L'Évolution créatrice* (1907) ch. 1

6 *L'élan vital.*

The vital spirit.

> *L'Évolution créatrice* (1907) ch. 2 (section title)

George Berkeley 1685–1753

Irish philosopher and Anglican bishop

7 They are neither finite quantities, or quantities infinitely small, nor yet nothing. May we not call them the ghosts of departed quantities?

> *The Analyst* (1734) sect. 35 (on Newton's infinitesimals)

8 [Tar water] is of a nature so mild and benign and proportioned to the human constitution, as to warm without heating, to cheer but not inebriate.

> *Siris* (1744) para. 217. Cf. Cowper 223:31

9 Truth is the cry of all, but the game of the few.

> *Siris* (1744) para. 368

10 The same principles which at first lead to scepticism, pursued to a certain point bring men back to common sense.

> *Three Dialogues between Hylas and Philonous* (1734) Dialogue 3

11 We have first raised a dust and then complain we cannot see.

> *A Treatise Concerning the Principles of Human Knowledge* (1710) introduction, sect. 3

12 All the choir of heaven and furniture of earth—in a word, all those bodies which compose the mighty frame of the world—have not any subsistence without a mind.

> *A Treatise Concerning the Principles of Human Knowledge* (1710) pt. 1, sect. 6

13 Westward the course of empire takes its way;
The first four acts already past,
A fifth shall close the drama with the day:
Time's noblest offspring is the last.

> 'On the Prospect of Planting Arts and Learning in America' (1752) st. 6. See John Quincy Adams *Oration at Plymouth* (1802): 'Westward the star of empire takes its way'

Irving Berlin (Israel Baline) 1888–1989

American songwriter

14 There's no business like show business.

> *Annie Get Your Gun* (1946) title of song

15 Must you dance ev'ry dance
With the same fortunate man?
You have danced with him since the music began.
Won't you change partners and dance with me?

> *Carefree* (1938) 'Change Partners'

16 There may be trouble ahead,
But while there's moonlight and music and love and romance,
Let's face the music and dance.

> *Follow the Fleet* (1936) 'Let's Face the Music and Dance'

17 God bless America,
Land that I love,
Stand beside her and guide her
Thru the night with a light from above.
From the mountains to the prairies,
To the oceans white with foam,
God bless America,
My home sweet home.

> 'God Bless America' (1939 song)

18 I'm dreaming of a white Christmas,
Just like the ones I used to know,
Where the tree-tops glisten
And children listen
To hear sleigh bells in the snow.

> *Holiday Inn* (1942) 'White Christmas'

19 A pretty girl is like a melody
That haunts you night and day.

> 'A Pretty Girl is like a Melody' (1919 song)

20 The song is ended (but the melody lingers on).

> Title of song (1927)

21 Heaven—I'm in Heaven—And my heart beats so that I can hardly speak;
And I seem to find the happiness I seek
When we're out together dancing cheek-to-cheek.

> *Top Hat* (1935) 'Cheek-to-Cheek'

Sir Isaiah Berlin 1909–

British philosopher

1 Injustice, poverty, slavery, ignorance—these may be
cured by reform or revolution. But men do not live
only by fighting evils. They live by positive goals,
individual and collective, a vast variety of them,
seldom predictable, at times incompatible.
   Four Essays on Liberty (1969) 'Political Ideas in the
   Twentieth Century'

2 There exists a great chasm between those, on one side,
who relate everything to a single central vision . . .
and, on the other side, those who pursue many ends,
often unrelated and even contradictory . . . The first
kind of intellectual and artistic personality belongs to
the hedgehogs, the second to the foxes.
   The Hedgehog and the Fox (1953) sect. 1. Cf. Archilochus
   24:11

3 Rousseau was the first militant lowbrow.
   Observer 9 November 1952

4 Liberty is liberty, not equality or fairness or justice or
human happiness or a quiet conscience.
   Two Concepts of Liberty (1958) p. 10, n.

5 It is this—the 'positive' conception of liberty: not
freedom from, but freedom to—which the adherents of
the 'negative' notion represent as being, at times, no
better than a specious disguise for brutal tyranny.
   Two Concepts of Liberty (1958) p. 16

Georges Bernanos 1888–1948

French novelist and essayist

6 Le désir de la prière est déjà une prière.
   The wish for prayer is a prayer in itself.
   Journal d'un curé de campagne (1936) ch. 2

7 L'enfer, madame, c'est de ne plus aimer.
   Hell, madam, is to love no more.
   Journal d'un curé de campagne (1936) ch. 2

St Bernard 1090–1153

French theologian; Abbot of Clairvaux

8 Liberavi animam meam.
   I have freed my soul.
   Epistles no. 371

Bernard of Chartres d. c.1130

French philosopher

9 Bernard of Chartres used to say that we are like
dwarfs on the shoulders of giants, so that we can see
more than they, and things at a greater distance, not
by virtue of any sharpness of sight on our part, or any
physical distinction, but because we are carried high
and raised up by their giant size.
   John of Salisbury *The Metalogicon* (1159) bk. 3, ch. 4,
   quoted in R. K. Merton *On the Shoulders of Giants* (1965)
   ch. 9. Cf. Coleridge 212:4, Newton 493:19

Eric Berne 1910–70

American psychiatrist

10 Games people play: the psychology of human
relationships.
   Title of book (1964)

11 Human life [as] . . . a process of filling in time until the
arrival of death, or Santa Claus, with very little
choice, if any, of what kind of business one is going to
transact during the long wait, is a commonplace but
not the final answer.
   Games People Play (1964) ch. 18

Wendell Berry 1934–

American poet and novelist

12 We stare dumb
Upon the fulcrum dust, across which death
Lifts up our love.
   'Elegy' (1964)

13 I come into the peace of wild things
who do not tax their lives with forethought
of grief. I come into the presence of still water.
And I feel above me the day-blind stars
waiting with their light.
   'The Peace of Wild Things' (1968)

14 Our hair
turns white with our ripening
as though to fly away in some
coming wind, bearing the seed
of what we know.
   'Ripening' (1980)

15 Radiances know him. Grown lighter
than breath, he is set free
in our remembering. Grown brighter
than vision, he goes dark
into the life of the hill
that holds his peace.
   'Three Elegiac Poems' (1969)

John Berryman 1914–72

American poet

16   People will take balls,
Balls will be lost always, little boy,
And no one buys a ball back.
   'The Ball Poem' (1948)

17 We must travel in the direction of our fear.
   'A Point of Age' (1942)

18 Life, friends, is boring. We must not say so . . .
And moreover my mother taught me as a boy
(repeatedly) 'Ever to confess you're bored
means you have no

Inner Resources.' I conclude now I have no
inner resources, because I am heavy bored.
   77 Dream Songs (1964) no. 14

19 I seldom go to films. They are too exciting,
said the Honourable Possum.
   77 Dream Songs (1964) no. 53

Charles Best

English poet

1 Look how the pale Queen of the silent night
Doth cause the Ocean to attend upon her,
And he, as long as she is in his sight,
With his full tide is ready her to honour.
    'Of the Moon' (1602) in N. Ault (ed.) *Elizabethan Lyrics
    from the Original Texts* (1925)

Theobald von Bethmann Hollweg
1856–1921

Chancellor of Germany, 1909–17

2 Just for a word 'neutrality'—a word which in wartime
has so often been disregarded—just for a scrap of
paper, Great Britain is going to make war on a kindred
nation who desires nothing better than to be friends
with her.
    Summary of a report by Sir E. Goschen to Sir Edward Grey
    in *British Documents on Origins of the War 1898–1914*
    (1926) vol. 11, p. 351. See *The Diary of Edward Goschen
    1900–1914* (1980) Appendix B for a discussion of the
    contentious origins of this statement

Sir John Betjeman 1906–84

English poet

3 He sipped at a weak hock and seltzer
As he gazed at the London skies
Through the Nottingham lace of the curtains
Or was it his bees-winged eyes?

He rose, and he put down *The Yellow Book*.
He staggered—and, terrible-eyed,
He brushed past the palms on the staircase
And was helped to a hansom outside.
    'The Arrest of Oscar Wilde at the Cadogan Hotel' (1937)

4 And girls in slacks remember Dad,
And oafish louts remember Mum,
And sleepless children's hearts are glad,
And Christmas-morning bells say 'Come!'
Even to shining ones who dwell
Safe in the Dorchester Hotel.

And is it true? And is it true,
This most tremendous tale of all,
Seen in a stained-glass window's hue,
A Baby in an ox's stall?
The Maker of the stars and sea
Become a Child on earth for me?
    'Christmas' (1954)

5 Oh! Chintzy, Chintzy cheeriness,
Half dead and half alive!
    'Death in Leamington' (1931)

6 Spirits of well-shot woodcock, partridge, snipe
Flutter and bear him up the Norfolk sky.
    'Death of King George V' (1937)

7 Old men in country houses hear clocks ticking
Over thick carpets with a deadened force.
    'Death of King George V' (1937)

8 Old men who never cheated, never doubted,
Communicated monthly, sit and stare
At the new suburb stretched beyond the run-way
Where a young man lands hatless from the air.
    'Death of King George V' (1937)

9 Whist upon whist upon whist upon whist drive, in
    Institute, Legion and Social Club.
Horny hands that hold the aces which this morning
    held the plough.
    'Dorset' (1937)

10 Oh shall I see the Thames again?
The prow-promoted gems again,
As beefy ATS
Without their hats
Come shooting through the bridge?
And 'cheerioh' or 'cheeri-bye'
Across the waste of waters die
And low the mists of evening lie
And lightly skims the midge.
    'Henley-on-Thames' (1945)

11 Phone for the fish-knives, Norman
As Cook is a little unnerved;
You kiddies have crumpled the serviettes
And I must have things daintily served.
    'How to get on in Society' (1954)

12 Milk and then just as it comes dear?
I'm afraid the preserve's full of stones;
Beg pardon, I'm soiling the doileys
With afternoon tea-cakes and scones.
    'How to get on in Society' (1954)

13 In the Garden City Café with its murals on the wall
Before a talk on 'Sex and Civics' I meditated on the
    Fall.
    'Huxley Hall' (1954)

14 The Church's Restoration
In eighteen-eighty-three
Has left for contemplation
Not what there used to be.
    'Hymn' (1931)

15 Think of what our Nation stands for,
Books from Boots' and country lanes,
Free speech, free passes, class distinction,
Democracy and proper drains.
Lord, put beneath Thy special care
One-eighty-nine Cadogan Square.
    'In Westminster Abbey' (1940)

16 In the licorice fields at Pontefract
My love and I did meet
And many a burdened licorice bush
Was blooming round our feet;
Red hair she had and golden skin,
Her sulky lips were shaped for sin,
Her sturdy legs were flannel-slack'd,
The strongest legs in Pontefract.
    'The Licorice Fields at Pontefract' (1954)

1 Belbroughton Road is bonny, and pinkly bursts the
　　spray
　Of prunus and forsythia across the public way,
　For a full spring-tide of blossom seethed and departed
　　hence,
　Leaving land-locked pools of jonquils by sunny garden
　　fence.

　And a constant sound of flushing runneth from
　　windows where
　The toothbrush too is airing in this new North Oxford
　　air.
　　　'May-Day Song for North Oxford' (1945)

2 Gaily into Ruislip Gardens
　Runs the red electric train,
　With a thousand Ta's and Pardon's
　Daintily alights Elaine;
　Hurries down the concrete station
　With a frown of concentration,
　Out into the outskirt's edges
　Where a few surviving hedges
　Keep alive our lost Elysium—rural Middlesex again.
　　　'Middlesex' (1954)

3 Pam, I adore you, Pam, you great big mountainous
　　sports girl,
　Whizzing them over the net, full of the strength of
　　five:
　That old Malvernian brother, you zephyr and khaki
　　shorts girl,
　Although he's playing for Woking,
　Can't stand up to your wonderful backhand drive.
　　　'Pot Pourri from a Surrey Garden' (1940)

4 The gas was on in the Institute,
　The flare was up in the gymn,
　A man was running a mineral line,
　A lass was singing a hymn,
　When Captain Webb the Dawley man,
　Captain Webb from Dawley,
　Came swimming along in the old canal
　That carries the bricks to Lewley.
　　　'A Shropshire Lad' (1940)

5 Come, friendly bombs, and fall on Slough!
　It isn't fit for humans now,
　There isn't grass to graze a cow.
　Swarm over, Death!
　　　'Slough' (1937)

6 Miss J. Hunter Dunn, Miss J. Hunter Dunn,
　Furnish'd and burnish'd by Aldershot sun,
　What strenuous singles we played after tea,
　We in the tournament—you against me.

　Love-thirty, love-forty, oh! weakness of joy,
　The speed of a swallow, the grace of a boy,
　With carefullest carelessness, gaily you won,
　I am weak from your loveliness, Joan Hunter Dunn.

　Miss Joan Hunter Dunn, Miss Joan Hunter Dunn,
　How mad I am, sad I am, glad that you won.
　The warm-handled racket is back in its press,
　But my shock-headed victor, she loves me no less.
　　　'A Subaltern's Love-Song' (1945)

7 By roads 'not adopted', by woodlanded ways,
　She drove to the club in the late summer haze,
　Into nine-o'clock Camberley, heavy with bells
　And mushroomy, pine-woody, evergreen smells.

　Miss Joan Hunter Dunn, Miss Joan Hunter Dunn,
　I can hear from the car-park the dance has begun.
　Oh! full Surrey twilight! importunate band!
　Oh! strongly adorable tennis-girl's hand!
　　　'A Subaltern's Love-Song' (1945)

8 The dread of beatings! Dread of being late!
　And, greatest dread of all, the dread of games!
　　　Summoned by Bells (1960) ch. 7

9 There was sun enough for lazing upon beaches,
　There was fun enough for far into the night.
　But I'm dying now and done for,
　What on earth was all the fun for?
　For God's sake keep that sunlight out of sight.
　　　'Sun and Fun' (1954)

10 Broad of Church and 'broad of Mind',
　Broad before and broad behind,
　A keen ecclesiologist,
　A rather dirty Wykehamist.
　　　'The Wykehamist' (1931)

11 Ghastly good taste, or a depressing story of the rise
　and fall of English architecture.
　　　Title of book (1933)

Aneurin Bevan 1897–1960
British Labour politician

12 This island is made mainly of coal and surrounded by
　fish. Only an organizing genius could produce
　a shortage of coal and fish at the same time.
　　　Speech at Blackpool 24 May 1945, in *Daily Herald* 25 May
　　　1945

13 No amount of cajolery, and no attempts at ethical or
　social seduction, can eradicate from my heart a deep
　burning hatred for the Tory Party . . . So far as I am
　concerned they are lower than vermin.
　　　Speech at Manchester, 4 July 1948, in *The Times* 5 July
　　　1948

14 The language of priorities is the religion of Socialism.
　　　Speech at Labour Party Conference in Blackpool, 8 June
　　　1949, in *Report of the 48th Annual Conference* (1949) p. 172

15 Why read the crystal when he can read the book?
　　　Referring to Robert Boothby during a debate on the Sterling
　　　Exchange Rate, *Hansard* 29 September 1949, col. 319

16 [Winston Churchill] does not talk the language of the
　20th century but that of the 18th. He is still fighting
　Blenheim all over again. His only answer to a difficult
　situation is send a gun-boat.
　　　Speech at Labour Party Conference, Scarborough, 2 October
　　　1951, in *Daily Herald* 3 October 1951

17 I am not going to spend any time whatsoever in
　attacking the Foreign Secretary . . . If we complain
　about the tune, there is no reason to attack the
　monkey when the organ grinder is present.
　　　During a debate on the Suez crisis, *Hansard* 16 May 1957,
　　　col. 680

1 If you carry this resolution you will send Britain's
Foreign Secretary naked into the conference chamber.
> Speech at Labour Party Conference in Brighton, 3 October
> 1957, against a motion proposing unilateral nuclear
> disarmament by the UK, in *Daily Herald* 4 October 1957

2 I stuffed their mouths with gold.
> On his handling of the consultants during the establishment
> of the National Health Service, in Brian Abel-Smith *The
> Hospitals 1800–1948* (1964) ch. 29

3 Listening to a speech by Chamberlain is like paying
a visit to Woolworth's: everything in its place and
nothing above sixpence.
> In Michael Foot *Aneurin Bevan* (1962) vol. 1, ch. 8

4 I know that the right kind of leader for the Labour
Party is a desiccated calculating machine who must
not in any way permit himself to be swayed by
indignation. If he sees suffering, privation or injustice
he must not allow it to move him, for that would be
evidence of the lack of proper education or of absence
of self-control. He must speak in calm and objective
accents and talk about a dying child in the same way
as he would about the pieces inside an internal
combustion engine.
> In Michael Foot *Aneurin Bevan* (1973) vol. 2, ch. 11

5 Damn it all, you can't have the crown of thorns *and*
the thirty pieces of silver.
> In Michael Foot *Aneurin Bevan* (1973) vol. 2, ch. 13

6 We know what happens to people who stay in the
middle of the road. They get run down.
> In *Observer* 6 December 1953

7 I read the newspapers avidly. It is my one form of
continuous fiction.
> In *The Times* 29 March 1960

William Henry Beveridge (1st Baron Beveridge) 1879–1963
British economist

8 Ignorance is an evil weed, which dictators may
cultivate among their dupes, but which no democracy
can afford among its citizens.
> *Full Employment in a Free Society* (1944) pt. 7

9 The object of government in peace and in war is not
the glory of rulers or of races, but the happiness of the
common man.
> *Social Insurance and Allied Services* (1942) pt. 7

10 Want is one only of five giants on the road of
reconstruction . . . the others are Disease, Ignorance,
Squalor and Idleness.
> *Social Insurance and Allied Services* (1942) pt. 7

11 The state is or can be master of money, but in a free
society it is master of very little else.
> *Voluntary Action* (1948) ch. 12

Ernest Bevin 1881–1951
British Labour politician and trade unionist

12 The most conservative man in this world is the British
Trade Unionist when you want to change him.
> Speech, 8 September 1927, in *Report of Proceedings of the
> Trades Union Congress* (1927) p. 298

13 I hope you will carry no resolution of an emergency
character telling a man with a conscience like
Lansbury what he ought to do . . . It is placing the
Executive in an absolutely wrong position to be taking
your conscience round from body to body to be told
what you ought to do with it.
> *Labour Party Conference Report* (1935)

14 There never has been a war yet which, if the facts had
been put calmly before the ordinary folk, could not
have been prevented . . . The common man, I think, is
the great protection against war.
> Speech, *Hansard* 23 November 1945, col. 786

15 My [foreign] policy is to be able to take a ticket at
Victoria Station and go anywhere I damn well please.
> In *Spectator* 20 April 1951, p. 514

16 If you open that Pandora's Box, you never know what
Trojan 'orses will jump out.
> On the Council of Europe, in Sir Roderick Barclay *Ernest
> Bevin and the Foreign Office* (1975) ch. 3

17 I didn't ought never to have done it. It was you,
Willie, what put me up to it.
> To Lord Strang, after officially recognizing Communist
> China, in C. Parrott *Serpent and Nightingale* (1977) ch. 3

The Bible (Authorized Version, 1611)

18 Upon the setting of that bright Occidental Star, Queen
Elizabeth of most happy memory.
> The Epistle Dedicatory

19 The appearance of Your Majesty, as of the Sun in his
strength.
> The Epistle Dedicatory

Old Testament: Genesis

20 In the beginning God created the heaven and the
earth. And the earth was without form, and void;
and darkness was upon the face of the deep. And
the Spirit of God moved upon the face of the waters.
And God said, Let there be light: and there was light.
> Genesis ch. 1, v. 1

21 And the evening and the morning were the first day.
> Genesis ch. 1, v. 5

22 And God saw that it was good.
> Genesis ch. 1, v. 10

23 And God made two great lights; the greater light to
rule the day, and the lesser light to rule the night:
he made the stars also.
> Genesis ch. 1, v. 16

24 And God said, Let us make man in our image, after
our likeness: and let them have dominion over the
fish of the sea, and over the fowl of the air, and
over the cattle, and over all the earth and over
every creeping thing that creepeth upon the earth.
> Genesis ch. 1, v. 26

25 Male and female created he them.
> Genesis ch. 1, v. 27

26 Be fruitful, and multiply, and replenish the earth, and
subdue it.
> Genesis ch. 1, v. 28

1 And the Lord God formed man of the dust of the ground, and breathed into his nostrils the breath of life; and man became a living soul.
And the Lord God planted a garden eastward in Eden.
Genesis ch. 2, v. 7

2 And out of the ground made the Lord God to grow every tree that is pleasant to the sight, and good for food; the tree of life also in the midst of the garden, and the tree of knowledge of good and evil.
Genesis ch. 2, v. 9

3 But of the tree of the knowledge of good and evil, thou shalt not eat of it: for in the day that thou eatest thereof thou shalt surely die.
Genesis ch. 2, v. 17

4 It is not good that the man should be alone; I will make him an help meet for him.
Genesis ch. 2, v. 18

5 And the Lord God caused a deep sleep to fall upon Adam, and he slept: and he took one of his ribs, and closed up the flesh instead thereof;
And the rib, which the Lord God had taken from man, made he a woman.
Genesis ch. 2, v. 21

6 This is now bone of my bones, and flesh of my flesh: she shall be called Woman, because she was taken out of Man.
Genesis ch. 2, v. 23

7 Therefore shall a man leave his father and his mother, and shall cleave unto his wife: and they shall be one flesh.
Genesis ch. 2, v. 24

8 Now the serpent was more subtil than any beast of the field.
Genesis ch. 3, v. 1

9 Ye shall be as gods, knowing good and evil.
Genesis ch. 3, v. 5

10 And they sewed fig leaves together, and made themselves aprons.
And they heard the voice of the Lord God walking in the garden in the cool of the day.
Genesis ch. 3, v. 7 ('and made themselves breeches' in the Geneva Bible, 1560, known for that reason as the 'Breeches Bible')

11 The woman whom thou gavest to be with me, she gave me of the tree, and I did eat.
Genesis ch. 3, v. 12

12 What is this that thou hast done?
Genesis ch. 3, v. 13

13 The serpent beguiled me, and I did eat.
Genesis ch. 3, v. 13

14 It shall bruise thy head, and thou shalt bruise his heel.
Genesis ch. 3, v. 15

15 In sorrow thou shalt bring forth children.
Genesis ch. 3, v. 16

16 In the sweat of thy face shalt thou eat bread.
Genesis ch. 3, v. 19

17 For dust thou art, and unto dust shalt thou return.
Genesis ch. 3, v. 19

18 Am I my brother's keeper?
Genesis ch. 4, v. 9

19 The voice of thy brother's blood crieth unto me from the ground.
Genesis ch. 4, v. 10

20 My punishment is greater than I can bear.
Genesis ch. 4, v. 13

21 And the Lord set a mark upon Cain.
Genesis ch. 4, v. 15

22 And Cain went out from the presence of the Lord, and dwelt in the land of Nod, on the east of Eden.
Genesis ch. 4, v. 16

23 And Enoch walked with God: and he was not; for God took him.
Genesis ch. 5, v. 24

24 And all the days of Methuselah were nine hundred sixty and nine years: and he died.
Genesis ch. 5, v. 27

25 There were giants in the earth in those days; and also after that, when the sons of God came in unto the daughters of men, and they bare children to them, the same became mighty men which were of old, men of renown.
Genesis ch. 6, v. 4

26 There went in two and two unto Noah into the Ark, the male and the female.
Genesis ch. 7, v. 9

27 But the dove found no rest for the sole of her foot.
Genesis ch. 8, v. 9

28 For the imagination of man's heart is evil from his youth.
Genesis ch. 8, v. 21

29 While the earth remaineth, seedtime and harvest, and cold and heat, and summer and winter, and day and night shall not cease.
Genesis ch. 8, v. 22

30 At the hand of every man's brother will I require the life of man.
Genesis ch. 9, v. 5

31 Whoso sheddeth man's blood, by man shall his blood be shed.
Genesis ch. 9, v. 6

32 I do set my bow in the cloud, and it shall be for a token of a covenant between me and the earth. And it shall come to pass, when I bring a cloud over the earth, that the bow shall be seen in the cloud.
Genesis ch. 9, v. 13

33 Even as Nimrod the mighty hunter before the Lord.
Genesis ch. 10, v. 9

34 Let there be no strife, I pray thee, between thee and me . . . for we be brethren.
Genesis ch. 13, v. 8

35 An horror of great darkness fell upon him.
Genesis ch. 15, v. 12

36 Thou shalt be buried in a good old age.
Genesis ch. 15, v. 15

37 His [Ishmael's] hand will be against every man, and every man's hand against him.
Genesis ch. 16, v. 12

1 Now Abraham and Sarah were old and well stricken in age; and it ceased to be with Sarah after the manner of women.
Genesis ch. 18, v. 11

2 Shall not the Judge of all the earth do right.
Genesis ch. 18, v. 25

3 But his wife looked back from behind him, and she became a pillar of salt.
Genesis ch. 19, v. 26

4 Take now thy son, thine only son Isaac, whom thou lovest.
Genesis ch. 22, v. 2

5 My son, God will provide himself a lamb.
Genesis ch. 22, v. 8

6 Behold behind him a ram caught in a thicket by his horns.
Genesis ch. 22, v. 13

7 Esau selleth his birthright for a mess of potage.
Genesis ch. 25 (chapter heading in Geneva Bible, 1560). Cf. Proverbs 78:35

8 Esau was a cunning hunter, a man of the field; and Jacob was a plain man, dwelling in tents.
Genesis ch. 25, v. 27

9 And he sold his birthright unto Jacob.
Genesis ch. 25, v. 33

10 Behold, Esau my brother is a hairy man, and I am a smooth man.
Genesis ch. 27, v. 11

11 The voice is Jacob's voice, but the hands are the hands of Esau.
Genesis ch. 27, v. 22

12 Thy brother came with subtilty, and hath taken away thy blessing.
Genesis ch. 27, v. 35

13 And he dreamed, and behold a ladder set up on the earth, and the top of it reached to heaven: and behold the angels of God ascending and descending on it.
Genesis ch. 28, v. 12

14 Surely the Lord is in this place; and I knew it not.
Genesis ch. 28, v. 16

15 This is none other but the house of God, and this is the gate of heaven.
Genesis ch. 28, v. 17

16 And Jacob served seven years for Rachel; and they seemed unto him but a few days, for the love he had to her.
Genesis ch. 29, v. 20

17 The Lord watch between me and thee, when we are absent one from another.
Genesis ch. 31, v. 49

18 I will not let thee go, except thou bless me.
Genesis ch. 32, v. 26

19 For I have seen God face to face, and my life is preserved.
Genesis ch. 32, v. 30

20 Now Israel loved Joseph more than all his children, because he was the son of his old age; and he made him a coat of many colours.
Genesis ch. 37, v. 3

21 Behold, your sheaves stood round about, and made obeisance to my sheaf.
Genesis ch. 37, v. 7

22 Behold, this dreamer cometh.
Genesis ch. 37, v. 19

23 Some evil beast hath devoured him.
Genesis ch. 37, v. 20

24 And she caught him by his garment, saying, Lie with me; and he left his garment in her hand, and fled.
Genesis ch. 39, v. 12

25 And the lean and the ill favoured kine did eat up the first seven fat kine.
Genesis ch. 41, v. 20

26 And the thin ears devoured the seven good ears.
Genesis ch. 41, v. 24

27 Jacob saw that there was corn in Egypt.
Genesis ch. 42, v. 1

28 Ye are spies; to see the nakedness of the land ye are come.
Genesis ch. 42, v. 9

29 My son shall not go down with you; for his brother is dead, and he is left alone: if mischief befall him by the way in which ye go, then shall ye bring down my grey hairs with sorrow to the grave.
Genesis ch. 42, v. 38

30 Ye shall eat the fat of the land.
Genesis ch. 45, v. 18

31 See that ye fall not out by the way.
Genesis ch. 45, v. 24

32 Few and evil have the days of the years of my life been.
Genesis ch. 47, v. 9

33 Unstable as water, thou shalt not excel.
Genesis ch. 49, v. 4

Exodus

34 She took for him an ark of bulrushes, and daubed it with slime.
Exodus ch. 2, v. 3

35 Who made thee a prince and a judge over us?
Exodus ch. 2, v. 14

36 I have been a stranger in a strange land.
Exodus ch. 2, v. 22. See Exodus ch. 18, v. 3

37 Behold, the bush burned with fire, and the bush was not consumed.
Exodus ch. 3, v. 2

38 Put off thy shoes from off thy feet, for the place whereon thou standest is holy ground.
Exodus ch. 3, v. 5

39 And Moses hid his face; for he was afraid to look upon God.
Exodus ch. 3, v. 6

40 A land flowing with milk and honey.
Exodus ch. 3, v. 8

41 I AM THAT I AM.
Exodus ch. 3, v. 14

42 The Lord God of your fathers, the God of Abraham, the God of Isaac, and the God of Jacob.
Exodus ch. 3, v. 15

1 But I am slow of speech, and of a slow tongue.
Exodus ch. 4, v. 10

2 I know not the Lord, neither will I let Israel go.
Exodus ch. 5, v. 2

3 And I will harden Pharaoh's heart, and multiply my signs and my wonders in the land of Egypt.
Exodus ch. 7, v. 3

4 Aaron's rod swallowed up their rods.
And he hardened Pharaoh's heart, that he hearkened not.
Exodus ch. 7, v. 12

5 Let my people go.
Exodus ch. 7, v. 16

6 A boil breaking forth with blains.
Exodus ch. 9, v. 10

7 Stretch out thine hand toward heaven, that there may be darkness over the land of Egypt, even darkness which may be felt.
Exodus ch. 10, v. 21

8 Your lamb shall be without blemish.
Exodus ch. 12, v. 5

9 And they shall eat the flesh in that night, roast with fire, and unleavened bread; and with bitter herbs they shall eat it.
Eat not of it raw, nor sodden at all with water, but roast with fire; his head with his legs, and with the purtenance thereof.
Exodus ch. 12, v. 8

10 With your loins girded, your shoes on your feet, and your staff in your hand; and ye shall eat it in haste; it is the Lord's passover.
For I will pass through the land of Egypt this night, and will smite all the firstborn in the land of Egypt, both man and beast.
Exodus ch. 12, v. 11

11 And Pharaoh rose up in the night, he, and all his servants, and all the Egyptians; and there was a great cry in Egypt; for there was not a house where there was not one dead.
Exodus ch. 12, v. 30

12 And they spoiled the Egyptians.
Exodus ch. 12, v. 36

13 And the Lord went before them by day in a pillar of a cloud, to lead them the way; and by night in a pillar of fire, to give them light.
Exodus ch. 13, v. 21

14 The Lord is a man of war.
Exodus ch. 15, v. 3

15 Would to God we had died by the hand of the Lord in the land of Egypt, when we sat by the flesh pots, and when we did eat bread to the full.
Exodus ch. 16, v. 3

16 And God spake all these words, saying,
I am the Lord thy God, which have brought thee out of the land of Egypt, out of the house of bondage.
Thou shalt have no other gods before me.
Thou shalt not make unto thee any graven image, or any likeness of any thing that is in heaven above, or that is in the earth beneath, or that is in the water under the earth:
Thou shalt not bow down thyself to them, nor serve them: for I the Lord thy God am a jealous God, visiting the iniquity of the fathers upon the children unto the third and fourth generation of them that hate me;
And showing mercy unto thousands of them that love me, and keep my commandments.
Thou shalt not take the name of the Lord thy God in vain; for the Lord will not hold him guiltless that taketh his name in vain.
Remember the sabbath day, to keep it holy.
Six days shalt thou labour, and do all thy work:
But the seventh day is the sabbath of the Lord thy God: in it thou shalt not do any work, thou, nor thy son, nor thy daughter, thy manservant, nor thy maidservant, nor thy cattle, nor thy stranger that is within thy gates:
For in six days the Lord made heaven and earth, the sea, and all that in them is, and rested the seventh day: wherefore the Lord blest the sabbath day, and hallowed it.
Honour thy father and thy mother: that thy days may be long upon the land which the Lord thy God giveth thee.
Thou shalt not kill.
Thou shalt not commit adultery.
Thou shalt not steal.
Thou shalt not bear false witness against thy neighbour.
Thou shalt not covet thy neighbour's house, thou shalt not covet thy neighbour's wife, nor his manservant, nor his maidservant, nor his ox, nor his ass, nor any thing that is thy neighbour's.
Exodus ch. 20, v. 1

17 Life for life,
Eye for eye, tooth for tooth, hand for hand, foot for foot,
Burning for burning, wound for wound, stripe for stripe.
Exodus ch. 21, v. 23

18 And thou shalt put in the breastplate of judgement the Urim and the Thummim.
Exodus ch. 28, v. 30 (sacred symbols worn on the breastplate of the high priest)

19 These be thy gods, O Israel.
Exodus ch. 32, v. 4

20 And the people sat down to eat and to drink, and rose up to play.
Exodus ch. 32, v. 6

21 I will not go up in the midst of thee; for thou art a stiffnecked people: lest I consume thee in the way.
Exodus ch. 33, v. 3

22 There shall no man see me and live.
Exodus ch. 33, v. 20

Leviticus

1 And the swine, though he divide the hoof, and be cloven-footed, yet he cheweth not the cud; he is unclean to you.
Leviticus ch. 11, v. 7

2 Let him go for a scapegoat into the wilderness.
Leviticus ch. 16, v. 10

3 Thou shalt love thy neighbour as thyself.
Leviticus ch. 19, v. 18. See St Matthew ch. 19, v. 19

Numbers

4 The Lord bless thee, and keep thee:
The Lord make his face shine upon thee, and be gracious unto thee:
The Lord lift up his countenance upon thee, and give thee peace.
Numbers ch. 6, v. 24

5 These are the names of the men which Moses sent to spy out the land.
Numbers ch. 13, v. 16

6 And there we saw the giants, the sons of Anak, which come of the giants: and we were in our own sight as grasshoppers, and so we were in their sight.
Numbers ch. 13, v. 33

7 And Israel smote him with the edge of the sword, and possessed his land.
Numbers ch. 21, v. 24

8 He whom thou blessest is blessed, and he whom thou cursest is cursed.
Numbers ch. 22, v. 6

9 God is not a man, that he should lie.
Numbers ch. 23, v. 19

10 What hath God wrought!
Numbers ch. 23, v. 23 (quoted by Samuel Morse in the first electric telegraph message, 24 May 1844)

11 I called thee to curse mine enemies, and, behold, thou hast altogether blessed them these three times.
Numbers ch. 24, v. 10

12 Be sure your sin will find you out.
Numbers ch. 32, v. 23

Deuteronomy

13 I call heaven and earth to witness against you this day.
Deuteronomy ch. 4, v. 26

14 Remember that thou wast a servant in the land of Egypt, and that the Lord thy God brought thee out thence through a mighty hand and by a stretched out arm.
Deuteronomy ch. 5, v. 15

15 Hear, O Israel: The Lord our God is one Lord.
Deuteronomy ch. 6, v. 4

16 For the Lord thy God is a jealous God.
Deuteronomy ch. 6, v. 15. Cf. Exodus 72:16

17 If there arise among you a prophet, or a dreamer of dreams . . . Thou shalt not hearken.
Deuteronomy ch. 13, v. 1

18 If thy brother, the son of thy mother, or thy son, or thy daughter, or the wife of thy bosom, or thy friend, which is as thine own soul, entice thee secretly . . . Thou shalt not consent.
Deuteronomy ch. 13, v. 6

19 The secret things belong unto the Lord our God.
Deuteronomy ch. 29, v. 29

20 I have set before you life and death, blessing and cursing: therefore choose life that both thou and thy seed may live.
Deuteronomy ch. 30, v. 19

21 He found him in a desert land, and in the waste howling wilderness; he led him about, he instructed him, he kept him as the apple of his eye.
Deuteronomy ch. 32, v. 10

22 For they are a very froward generation, children in whom is no faith.
Deuteronomy ch. 32, v. 20

23 I will heap mischiefs upon them; I will spend mine arrows upon them.
Deuteronomy ch. 32, v. 23

24 The eternal God is thy refuge, and underneath are the everlasting arms.
Deuteronomy ch. 33, v. 27

25 No man knoweth of his [Moses's] sepulchre unto this day.
Deuteronomy ch. 34, v. 6

Joshua

26 As I was with Moses, so I will be with thee: I will not fail thee, nor forsake thee.
Joshua ch. 1, v. 5

27 Be strong and of a good courage; be not afraid, neither be thou dismayed: for the Lord thy God is with thee, whithersoever thou goest.
Joshua ch. 1, v. 9

28 This line of scarlet thread.
Joshua ch. 2, v. 18

29 All the Israelites passed over on dry ground.
Joshua ch. 3, v. 17

30 When the people heard the sound of the trumpet, and the people shouted with a great shout, that the wall fell down flat, so that the people went up into the city.
Joshua ch. 6, v. 20

31 Let them live; but let them be hewers of wood and drawers of water unto all the congregation.
Joshua ch. 9, v. 21

32 Sun, stand thou still upon Gibeon; and thou, Moon, in the valley of Ajalon.
Joshua ch. 10, v. 12

33 I am going the way of all the earth.
Joshua ch. 23, v. 14

Judges

34 He delivered them into the hands of spoilers.
Judges ch. 2, v. 14

1 Then Jael Heber's wife took a nail of the tent, and took an hammer in her hand, and went softly unto him, and smote the nail into his temples, and fastened it into the ground: for he was fast asleep and weary.
Judges ch. 4, v. 21

2 I arose a mother in Israel.
Judges ch. 5, v. 7

3 The stars in their courses fought against Sisera.
Judges ch. 5, v. 20

4 He asked water, and she gave him milk; she brought forth butter in a lordly dish.
Judges ch. 5, v. 25

5 At her feet he bowed, he fell, he lay down.
Judges ch. 5, v. 27

6 The mother of Sisera looked out at a window, and cried through the lattice, Why is his chariot so long in coming? why tarry the wheels of his chariots?
Judges ch. 5, v. 28

7 The Lord is with thee, thou mighty man of valour.
Judges ch. 6, v. 12

8 The Spirit of the Lord came upon Gideon, and he blew a trumpet.
Judges ch. 6, v. 34

9 The host of Midian was beneath him in the valley.
Judges ch. 7, v. 8

10 Is not the gleaning of the grapes of Ephraim better than the vintage of Abi-ezer?
Judges ch. 8, v. 2

11 Faint, yet pursuing.
Judges ch. 8, v. 4

12 Let fire come out of the bramble and devour the cedars of Lebanon.
Judges ch. 9, v. 15

13 Then said they unto him, Say now Shibboleth: and he said Sibboleth: for he could not frame to pronounce it right. Then they took him, and slew him.
Judges ch. 12, v. 6

14 Out of the eater came forth meat, and out of the strong came forth sweetness.
Judges ch. 14, v. 14

15 If ye had not plowed with my heifer, ye had not found out my riddle.
Judges ch. 14, v. 18

16 He smote them hip and thigh.
Judges ch. 15, v. 8

17 With the jawbone of an ass, heaps upon heaps, with the jaw of an ass have I slain a thousand men.
Judges ch. 15, v. 16

18 The Philistines be upon thee, Samson.
Judges ch. 16, v. 9

19 He wist not that the Lord was departed from him.
Judges ch. 16, v. 20

20 He did grind in the prison house.
Judges ch. 16, v. 21

21 The dead which he slew at his death were more than they which he slew in his life.
Judges ch. 16, v. 30

22 In those days there was no king in Israel, but every man did that which was right in his own eyes.
Judges ch. 17, v. 6

23 From Dan even to Beer-sheba.
Judges ch. 20, v. 1

24 The people arose as one man.
Judges ch. 20, v. 8

Ruth

25 Intreat me not to leave thee, or to return from following after thee: for whither thou goest, I will go; and where thou lodgest, I will lodge: thy people shall be my people, and thy God my God:
Where thou diest, will I die, and there will I be buried: the Lord do so to me, and more also, if ought but death part thee and me.
Ruth ch. 1, v. 16

I Samuel

26 All the increase of thy house shall die in the flower of their age.
I Samuel ch. 2, v. 33

27 The Lord called Samuel: and he answered, Here am I.
I Samuel ch. 3, v. 4

28 Speak, Lord; for thy servant heareth.
I Samuel ch. 3, v. 9

29 The ears of every one that heareth it shall tingle.
I Samuel ch. 3, v. 11

30 Quit yourselves like men, and fight.
I Samuel ch. 4, v. 9

31 He fell from off the seat backward by the side of the gate, and his neck brake.
I Samuel ch. 4, v. 18

32 And she named the child I-chabod, saying, The glory is departed from Israel.
I Samuel ch. 4, v. 21

33 Is Saul also among the prophets?
I Samuel ch. 10, v. 11

34 God save the king.
I Samuel ch. 10, v. 24

35 A man after his own heart.
I Samuel ch. 13, v. 14

36 I did but taste a little honey with the end of the rod that was in mine hand, and, lo, I must die.
I Samuel ch. 14, v. 43

37 To obey is better than sacrifice, and to hearken than the fat of rams.
For rebellion is as the sin of witchcraft.
I Samuel ch. 15, v. 22

38 For the Lord seeth not as man seeth: for man looketh on the outward appearance, but the Lord looketh on the heart.
I Samuel ch. 16, v. 7

39 Now he was ruddy, and withal of a beautiful countenance, and goodly to look to.
I Samuel ch. 16, v. 12

40 I know thy pride, and the naughtiness of thine heart.
I Samuel ch. 17, v. 28

1 Let no man's heart fail because of him.
I Samuel ch. 17, v. 32

2 Go, and the Lord be with thee.
I Samuel ch. 17, v. 37

3 And he took his staff in his hand and chose him five smooth stones out of the brook.
I Samuel ch. 17, v. 40

4 Am I a dog, that thou comest to me with staves?
I Samuel ch. 17, v. 43

5 Saul hath slain his thousands, and David his ten thousands.
I Samuel ch. 18, v. 7

6 And Saul said, God hath delivered him into mine hand.
I Samuel ch. 23, v. 7

7 Behold, I have played the fool, and have erred exceedingly.
I Samuel ch. 26, v. 21

II Samuel

8 The beauty of Israel is slain upon thy high places: how are the mighty fallen!
Tell it not in Gath, publish it not in the streets of Askelon; lest the daughters of the Philistines rejoice, lest the daughters of the uncircumcised triumph.
Ye mountains of Gilboa, let there be no dew, neither let there be rain, upon you, nor fields of offerings: for there the shield of the mighty is vilely cast away.
II Samuel ch. 1, v. 19

9 Saul and Jonathan were lovely and pleasant in their lives, and in their death they were not divided: they were swifter than eagles, they were stronger than lions.
Ye daughters of Israel, weep over Saul, who clothed you in scarlet, with other delights, who put on ornaments of gold upon your apparel.
How are the mighty fallen in the midst of the battle! O Jonathan, thou wast slain in thine high places.
I am distressed for thee, my brother Jonathan: very pleasant hast thou been unto me: thy love to me was wonderful, passing the love of women.
How are the mighty fallen, and the weapons of war perished!
II Samuel ch. 1, v. 23

10 And David danced before the Lord with all his might.
II Samuel ch. 6, v. 14

11 The poor man had nothing, save one little ewe lamb.
II Samuel ch. 12, v. 3

12 Thou art the man.
II Samuel ch. 12, v. 7

13 While the child was yet alive, I fasted and wept . . . But now he is dead, wherefore should I fast? can I bring him back again? I shall go to him but he shall not return to me.
II Samuel ch. 12, v. 22

14 For we needs must die, and are as water spilt on the ground, which cannot be gathered up again; neither doth God respect any person.
II Samuel ch. 14, v. 14

15 Come out, come out, thou bloody man, and thou man of Belial.
II Samuel ch. 16, v. 7

16 And when Ahithophel saw that his counsel was not followed, he saddled his ass, and arose, and gat him home to his house, to his city, and put his household in order, and hanged himself.
II Samuel ch. 17, v. 23

17 And the king was much moved, and went up to the chamber over the gate, and wept: and as he went, thus he said, O my son Absalom, my son, my son Absalom! would God I had died for thee, O Absalom, my son, my son!
II Samuel ch. 18, v. 33

18 By my God have I leaped over a wall.
II Samuel ch. 22, v. 30

19 David . . . the sweet psalmist of Israel.
II Samuel ch. 23, v. 1

20 Went in jeopardy of their lives.
II Samuel ch. 23, v. 17

I Kings

21 And Zadok the priest took an horn of oil out of the tabernacle, and anointed Solomon. And they blew the trumpet; and all the people said, God save king Solomon.
I Kings ch. 1, v. 39

22 Then will I cut off Israel out of the land which I have given them; and this house, which I have hallowed for my name, will I cast out of my sight; and Israel shall be a proverb and a byword among all people.
I Kings ch. 9, v. 7

23 And when the queen of Sheba had seen all Solomon's wisdom . . . there was no more spirit in her.
I Kings ch. 10, v. 4

24 Behold, the half was not told me.
I Kings ch. 10, v. 7

25 Once in three years came the navy of Tharshish, bringing gold, and silver, ivory, and apes, and peacocks.
I Kings ch. 10, v. 22

26 But king Solomon loved many strange women.
I Kings ch. 11, v. 1

27 My little finger shall be thicker than my father's loins.
I Kings ch. 12, v. 10

28 My father hath chastised you with whips, but I will chastise you with scorpions.
I Kings ch. 12, v. 11

29 To your tents, O Israel: now see to thine own house, David.
I Kings ch. 12, v. 16

30 He slept with his fathers.
I Kings ch. 14, v. 20

31 He went and dwelt by the brook Cherith, that is before Jordan.
And the ravens brought him bread and flesh in the morning, and bread and flesh in the evening; and he drank of the brook.
I Kings ch. 17, v. 5

32 An handful of meal in a barrel, and a little oil in a cruse.
I Kings ch. 17, v. 12

1 How long halt ye between two opinions?
I Kings ch. 18, v. 21

2 He is talking, or he is pursuing, or he is in a journey, or peradventure he sleepeth, and must be awaked.
I Kings ch. 18, v. 27

3 There is a sound of abundance of rain.
I Kings ch. 18, v. 41

4 There ariseth a little cloud out of the sea, like a man's hand.
I Kings ch. 18, v. 44

5 He girded up his loins, and ran before Ahab.
I Kings ch. 18, v. 46

6 He himself went a day's journey into the wilderness, and came and sat down under a juniper tree.
I Kings ch. 19, v. 4

7 But the Lord was not in the wind: and after the wind an earthquake; but the Lord was not in the earthquake:
And after the earthquake a fire: but the Lord was not in the fire: and after the fire a still small voice.
I Kings ch. 19, v. 11

8 Elijah passed by him, and cast his mantle upon him.
I Kings ch. 19, v. 19

9 Let not him that girdeth on his harness boast himself as he that putteth it off.
I Kings ch. 20, v. 11

10 Naboth the Jezreelite had a vineyard, which was in Jezreel, hard by the palace of Ahab King of Samaria.
And Ahab spake unto Naboth, saying, Give me thy vineyard, that I may have it for a garden of herbs, because it is near unto my house.
I Kings ch. 21, v. 1

11 Hast thou found me, O mine enemy?
I Kings ch. 21, v. 20

12 I saw all Israel scattered upon the hills, as sheep that have not a shepherd.
I Kings ch. 22, v. 17

13 Feed him with bread of affliction and with water of affliction, until I come in peace.
And Micaiah said, If thou return at all in peace, the Lord hath not spoken by me.
I Kings ch. 22, v. 27

14 And a certain man drew a bow at a venture, and smote the king of Israel between the joints of the harness.
I Kings ch. 22, v. 34

II Kings

15 Elijah went up by a whirlwind into heaven.
And Elisha saw it, and he cried, My father, my father, the chariot of Israel, and the horsemen thereof.
II Kings ch. 2, v. 11

16 The spirit of Elijah doth rest on Elisha.
II Kings ch. 2, v. 15

17 Go up, thou bald head.
II Kings ch. 2, v. 23

18 Is it well with the child? And she answered, It is well.
II Kings ch. 4, v. 26

19 There is death in the pot.
II Kings ch. 4, v. 40

20 He shall know that there is a prophet in Israel.
II Kings ch. 5, v. 8

21 Are not Abana and Pharpar, rivers of Damascus, better than all the waters of Israel?
II Kings ch. 5, v. 12

22 I bow myself in the house of Rimmon.
II Kings ch. 5, v. 18

23 Whence comest thou, Gehazi?
II Kings ch. 5, v. 25

24 Is thy servant a dog, that he should do this great thing?
II Kings ch. 8, v. 13

25 Is it peace? And Jehu said, What hast thou to do with peace? turn thee behind me.
II Kings ch. 9, v. 18

26 The driving is like the driving of Jehu, the son of Nimshi; for he driveth furiously.
II Kings ch. 9, v. 20

27 She painted her face, and tired her head, and looked out at a window.
II Kings ch. 9, v. 30

28 Had Zimri peace, who slew his master?
II Kings ch. 9, v. 31

29 Who is on my side? who?
II Kings ch. 9, v. 32

30 They found no more of her than the skull, and the feet, and the palms of her hands.
II Kings ch. 9, v. 35

31 Thou trustest upon the staff of this bruised reed, even upon Egypt, on which if a man lean, it will go into his hand, and pierce it.
II Kings ch. 18, v. 21

I Chronicles

32 For we are strangers before thee, and sojourners, as were all our fathers: our days on the earth are as a shadow, and there is none abiding.
I Chronicles ch. 29, v. 15

33 He died in a good old age, full of days, riches, and honour.
I Chronicles ch. 29, v. 28

Nehemiah

34 Every one with one of his hands wrought in the work, and with the other hand held a weapon.
Nehemiah ch. 4, v. 17

Esther

35 And if I perish, I perish.
Esther ch. 4, v. 16

36 Thus shall it be done to the man whom the king delighteth to honour.
Esther ch. 6, v. 9

Job

37 And the Lord said unto Satan, Whence comest thou? Then Satan answered the Lord, and said, From going to and fro in the earth, and from walking up and down in it.
Job ch. 1, v. 7

1 Doth Job fear God for naught?
Job ch. 1, v. 9

2 The Lord gave, and the Lord hath taken away; blessed be the name of the Lord.
Job ch. 1, v. 21

3 All that a man hath will he give for his life.
Job ch. 2, v. 4

4 And he took him a potsherd to scrape himself withal.
Job ch. 2, v. 8

5 Curse God, and die.
Job ch. 2, v. 9

6 Let the day perish wherein I was born, and the night in which it was said, There is a man child conceived.
Job ch. 3, v. 3

7 For now should I have lain still and been quiet, I should have slept: then had I been at rest,
With kings and counsellors of the earth, which built desolate places for themselves.
Job ch. 3, v. 13

8 There the wicked cease from troubling, and there the weary be at rest.
Job ch. 3, v. 17

9 Wherefore is light given to him that is in misery, and life unto the bitter in soul?
Job ch. 3, v. 20

10 Then a spirit passed before my face; the hair of my flesh stood up.
Job ch. 4, v. 15

11 Shall mortal man be more just than God? shall a man be more pure than his maker?
Job ch. 4, v. 17

12 Man is born unto trouble, as the sparks fly upward.
Job ch. 5, v. 7

13 My days are swifter than a weaver's shuttle.
Job ch. 7, v. 6

14 He shall return no more to his house, neither shall his place know him any more.
Job ch. 7, v. 10

15 Let me alone, that I may take comfort a little,
Before I go whence I shall not return, even to the land of darkness and the shadow of death.
Job ch. 10, v. 20

16 A land . . . where the light is as darkness.
Job ch. 10, v. 22

17 Canst thou by searching find out God?
Job ch. 11, v. 7

18 No doubt but ye are the people, and wisdom shall die with you.
Job ch. 12, v. 2

19 With the ancient is wisdom; and in length of days understanding.
Job ch. 12, v. 12

20 Though he slay me, yet will I trust in him: but I will maintain mine own ways before him.
Job ch. 13, v. 15

21 Man that is born of a woman is of few days, and full of trouble.
He cometh forth like a flower, and is cut down: he fleeth also as a shadow, and continueth not.
Job ch. 14, v. 1. Cf. Book of Common Prayer 124:3

22 Miserable comforters are ye all.
Job ch. 16, v. 2

23 I also could speak as ye do: if your soul were in my soul's stead.
Job ch. 16, v. 4

24 I am escaped with the skin of my teeth.
Job ch. 19, v. 20

25 I know that my redeemer liveth, and that he shall stand at the latter day upon the earth:
And though after my skin worms destroy this body, yet in my flesh shall I see God.
Job ch. 19, v. 25

26 Ye should say, Why persecute we him, seeing the root of the matter is found in me?
Job ch. 19, v. 28

27 But where shall wisdom be found? and where is the place of understanding?
Job ch. 28, v. 12

28 The price of wisdom is above rubies.
Job ch. 28, v. 18

29 I was eyes to the blind, and feet was I to the lame.
Job ch. 29, v. 15

30 For I know that thou wilt bring me to death, and to the house appointed for all living.
Job ch. 30, v. 23

31 I am a brother to dragons, and a companion to owls.
Job ch. 30, v. 29

32 Great men are not always wise.
Job ch. 32, v. 9

33 Who is this that darkeneth counsel by words without knowledge?
Job ch. 38, v. 2

34 Where wast thou when I laid the foundations of the earth? declare, if thou hast understanding.
Job ch. 38, v. 4

35 When the morning stars sang together, and all the sons of God shouted for joy.
Job ch. 38, v. 7

36 Hath the rain a father? or who hath begotten the drops of dew?
Job ch. 38, v. 28

37 Canst thou bind the sweet influences of Pleiades, or loose the bands of Orion?
Job ch. 38, v. 31

38 He paweth in the valley, and rejoiceth in his strength: he goeth on to meet the armed men.
Job ch. 39, v. 21

39 He swalloweth the ground with fierceness and rage: neither believeth he that it is the sound of the trumpet.
He saith among the trumpets, Ha, ha; and he smelleth the battle afar off, the thunder of the captains, and the shouting.
Job ch. 39, v. 24

1 Behold now behemoth, which I made with thee; he eateth grass as an ox.
Job ch. 40, v. 15

2 He is the chief of the ways of God: he that made him can make his sword to approach unto him.
Job ch. 40, v. 19

3 The shady trees cover him with their shadow; the willows of the brook compass him about.
Behold, he drinketh up a river, and hasteth not.
Job ch. 40, v. 22

4 Canst thou draw out leviathan with an hook?
Job ch. 41, v. 1

5 I have heard of thee by the hearing of the ear: but now mine eye seeth thee.
Job ch. 42, v. 5

6 So the Lord blessed the latter end of Job more than his beginning.
Job ch. 42, v. 12

Proverbs

7 For whom the Lord loveth he correcteth.
Proverbs ch. 3, v. 12

8 Length of days is in her right hand; and in her left hand riches and honour.
Proverbs ch. 3, v. 16

9 Her ways are ways of pleasantness, and all her paths are peace.
Proverbs ch. 3, v. 17

10 Wisdom is the principal thing; therefore get wisdom: and with all thy getting get understanding.
Proverbs ch. 4, v. 7

11 The path of the just is as the shining light, that shineth more and more unto the perfect day.
Proverbs ch. 4, v. 18

12 For the lips of a strange woman drop as an honeycomb, and her mouth is smoother than oil:
But her end is bitter as wormwood, sharp as a two-edged sword.
Her feet go down to death; her steps take hold on hell.
Proverbs ch. 5, v. 3

13 Go to the ant thou sluggard; consider her ways, and be wise.
Proverbs ch. 6, v. 6

14 How long wilt thou sleep, O sluggard? When wilt thou arise out of thy sleep?
Yet a little sleep, a little slumber, a little folding of the hands to sleep:
So shall thy poverty come as one that travelleth, and thy want as an armed man.
Proverbs ch. 6, v. 9. See Proverbs ch. 24, v. 33

15 Can a man take fire in his bosom, and his clothes not be burned?
Proverbs ch. 6, v. 27

16 Come, let us take our fill of love until the morning: let us solace ourselves with loves.
For the goodman is not at home, he is gone a long journey.
Proverbs ch. 7, v. 18

17 He goeth after her straightway, as an ox goeth to the slaughter.
Proverbs ch. 7, v. 22

18 Wisdom hath builded her house, she hath hewn out her seven pillars.
Proverbs ch. 9, v. 1

19 Stolen waters are sweet, and bread eaten in secret is pleasant.
Proverbs ch. 9, v. 17

20 A wise son maketh a glad father: but a foolish son is the heaviness of his mother.
Proverbs ch. 10, v. 1

21 The destruction of the poor is their poverty.
Proverbs ch. 10, v. 15

22 He that is surety for a stranger shall smart for it.
Proverbs ch. 11, v. 15

23 As a jewel of gold in a swine's snout, so is a fair woman which is without discretion.
Proverbs ch. 11, v. 22

24 A virtuous woman is a crown to her husband.
Proverbs ch. 12, v. 4

25 A righteous man regardeth the life of his beast: but the tender mercies of the wicked are cruel.
Proverbs ch. 12, v. 10

26 Hope deferred maketh the heart sick: but when the desire cometh, it is a tree of life.
Proverbs ch. 13, v. 12

27 The way of transgressors is hard.
Proverbs ch. 13, v. 15

28 The desire accomplished is sweet to the soul.
Proverbs ch. 13, v. 19

29 He that spareth his rod hateth his son.
Proverbs ch. 13, v. 24

30 Even in laughter the heart is sorrowful.
Proverbs ch. 14, v. 13

31 In all labour there is profit.
Proverbs ch. 14, v. 23

32 Righteousness exalteth a nation.
Proverbs ch. 14, v. 34

33 A soft answer turneth away wrath.
Proverbs ch. 15, v. 1

34 A merry heart maketh a cheerful countenance.
Proverbs ch. 15, v. 13

35 Better is a dinner of herbs where love is, than a stalled ox and hatred therewith.
Proverbs ch. 15, v. 17; 'Better is a mess of pottage with love, than a fat ox with evil will' in Matthew's Bible (1535)

36 A word spoken in due season, how good is it!
Proverbs ch. 15, v. 23

37 Pride goeth before destruction, and an haughty spirit before a fall.
Proverbs ch. 16, v. 18

38 He that is slow to anger is better than the mighty; and he that ruleth his spirit than he that taketh a city.
Proverbs ch. 16, v. 32

39 He that repeateth a matter separateth very friends.
Proverbs ch. 17, v. 9

40 A friend loveth at all times, and a brother is born for adversity.
Proverbs ch. 17, v. 17

1 A merry heart doeth good like a medicine.
Proverbs ch. 17, v. 22

2 A wounded spirit who can bear?
Proverbs ch. 18, v. 14

3 There is a friend that sticketh closer than a brother.
Proverbs ch. 18, v. 24

4 Wine is a mocker, strong drink is raging.
Proverbs ch. 20, v. 1

5 Every fool will be meddling.
Proverbs ch. 20, v. 3

6 Even a child is known by his doings.
Proverbs ch. 20, v. 11

7 The hearing ear, and the seeing eye, the Lord hath made even both of them.
Proverbs ch. 20, v. 12

8 It is naught, it is naught, saith the buyer: but when he is gone his way, then he boasteth.
Proverbs ch. 20, v. 14

9 It is better to dwell in a corner of the housetop, than with a brawling woman in a wide house.
Proverbs ch. 21, v. 9

10 A good name is rather to be chosen than great riches.
Proverbs ch. 22, v. 1

11 Train up a child in the way he should go: and when he is old, he will not depart from it.
Proverbs ch. 22, v. 6

12 Remove not the ancient landmark, which thy fathers have set.
Proverbs ch. 22, v. 28

13 Look not thou upon the wine when it is red, when it giveth his colour in the cup . . . At the last it biteth like a serpent, and stingeth like an adder.
Proverbs ch. 23, v. 31

14 The heart of kings is unsearchable.
Proverbs ch. 25, v. 3

15 A word fitly spoken is like apples of gold in pictures of silver.
Proverbs ch. 25, v. 11

16 Whoso boasteth himself of a false gift is like clouds and wind without rain.
Proverbs ch. 25, v. 14

17 Withdraw thy foot from thy neighbour's house; lest he be weary of thee, and so hate thee.
Proverbs ch. 25, v. 17

18 If thine enemy be hungry, give him bread to eat; and if he be thirsty, give him water to drink.
For thou shalt heap coals of fire upon his head, and the Lord shall reward thee.
Proverbs ch. 25, v. 21

19 As cold waters to a thirsty soul, so is good news from a far country.
Proverbs ch. 25, v. 25

20 Answer not a fool according to his folly, lest thou also be like unto him.
Answer a fool according to his folly, lest he be wise in his own conceit.
Proverbs ch. 26, v. 4

21 As a dog returneth to his vomit, so a fool returneth to his folly.
Proverbs ch. 26, v. 11

22 Seest thou a man wise in his own conceit? There is more hope of a fool than of him.
Proverbs ch. 26, v. 12

23 The sluggard is wiser in his own conceit than seven men that can render a reason.
Proverbs ch. 26, v. 16

24 Boast not thyself of to morrow; for thou knowest not what a day may bring forth.
Proverbs ch. 27, v. 1

25 Open rebuke is better than secret love.
Proverbs ch. 27, v. 5

26 Faithful are the wounds of a friend.
Proverbs ch. 27, v. 6

27 A continual dropping in a very rainy day and a contentious woman are alike.
Proverbs ch. 27, v. 15

28 The wicked flee when no man pursueth: but the righteous are bold as a lion.
Proverbs ch. 28, v. 1

29 He that maketh haste to be rich shall not be innocent.
Proverbs ch. 28, v. 20

30 A fool uttereth all his mind.
Proverbs ch. 29, v. 11

31 Where there is no vision, the people perish.
Proverbs ch. 29, v. 18

32 Give me neither poverty nor riches; feed me with food convenient for me.
Proverbs ch. 30, v. 8

33 There be three things which are too wonderful for me, yea, four which I know not:
The way of an eagle in the air; the way of a serpent upon a rock; the way of a ship in the midst of the sea; and the way of a man with a maid.
Proverbs ch. 30, v. 18

34 Give strong drink unto him that is ready to perish, and wine unto those that be of heavy hearts.
Proverbs ch. 31, v. 6

35 Who can find a virtuous woman? for her price is far above rubies.
Proverbs ch. 31, v. 10

Ecclesiastes

36 Vanity of vanities, saith the Preacher, vanity of vanities; all is vanity.
What profit hath a man of all his labour which he taketh under the sun?
One generation passeth away, and another generation cometh.
Ecclesiastes ch. 1, v. 2

37 All the rivers run into the sea; yet the sea is not full.
Ecclesiastes ch. 1, v. 7

1 All things are full of labour; man cannot utter it: the eye is not satisfied with seeing, nor the ear filled with hearing.

The thing that hath been, it is that which shall be; and that which is done is that which shall be done: and there is no new thing under the sun.
Ecclesiastes ch. 1, v. 8

2 All is vanity and vexation of spirit.
Ecclesiastes ch. 1, v. 14

3 He that increaseth knowledge increaseth sorrow.
Ecclesiastes ch. 1, v. 18

4 Wisdom excelleth folly, as far as light excelleth darkness.
Ecclesiastes ch. 2, v. 13

5 To every thing there is a season, and a time to every purpose under the heaven:

A time to be born, and a time to die; a time to plant, and a time to pluck up that which is planted;

A time to kill, and a time to heal; a time to break down, and a time to build up;

A time to weep, and a time to laugh; a time to mourn, and a time to dance;

A time to cast away stones, and a time to gather stones together; a time to embrace, and a time to refrain from embracing;

A time to get, and a time to lose; a time to keep, and a time to cast away;

A time to rend, and a time to sew; a time to keep silence, and a time to speak;

A time to love, and a time to hate; a time of war, and a time of peace.
Ecclesiastes ch. 3, v. 1

6 For that which befalleth the sons of men befalleth beasts; even one thing befalleth them: as the one dieth, so dieth the other; yea, they have all one breath; so that a man hath no preeminence above a beast: for all is vanity.
Ecclesiastes ch. 3, v. 19

7 Wherefore I praised the dead which are already dead more than the living which are yet alive.
Ecclesiastes ch. 4, v. 2

8 A threefold cord is not quickly broken.
Ecclesiastes ch. 4, v. 12

9 God is in heaven, and thou upon earth: therefore let thy words be few.
Ecclesiastes ch. 5, v. 2

10 The sleep of a labouring man is sweet.
Ecclesiastes ch. 5, v. 12

11 As the crackling of thorns under a pot, so is the laughter of a fool.
Ecclesiastes ch. 7, v. 6

12 Better is the end of a thing than the beginning thereof.
Ecclesiastes ch. 7, v. 8

13 Say not thou, What is the cause that the former days were better than these? for thou dost not enquire wisely concerning this.
Ecclesiastes ch. 7, v. 10

14 In the day of prosperity be joyful, but in the day of adversity consider.
Ecclesiastes ch. 7, v. 14

15 God hath made man upright; but they have sought out many inventions.
Ecclesiastes ch. 7, v. 29

16 There is no man that hath power over the spirit to retain the spirit; neither hath he power in the day of death; there is no discharge in that war.
Ecclesiastes ch. 8, v. 8

17 A man hath no better thing under the sun, than to eat, and to drink, and to be merry.
Ecclesiastes ch. 8, v. 15. Cf. Isaiah 83:7, St Luke 94:23, I Corinthians 101:9

18 A living dog is better than a dead lion.
Ecclesiastes ch. 9, v. 4

19 Go thy way, eat thy bread with joy, and drink thy wine with a merry heart; for God now accepteth thy works.
Ecclesiastes ch. 9, v. 7

20 Whatsoever thy hand findeth to do, do it with thy might; for there is no work, nor device, nor knowledge, nor wisdom, in the grave, whither thou goest.
Ecclesiastes ch. 9, v. 10

21 The race is not to the swift, nor the battle to the strong.
Ecclesiastes ch. 9, v. 11

22 He that diggeth a pit shall fall into it.
Ecclesiastes ch. 10, v. 8

23 Woe to thee, O land, when thy king is a child, and thy princes eat in the morning!
Ecclesiastes ch. 10, v. 16

24 Wine maketh merry: but money answereth all things.
Ecclesiastes ch. 10, v. 19

25 Cast thy bread upon the waters: for thou shalt find it after many days.
Ecclesiastes ch. 11, v. 1

26 In the place where the tree falleth, there it shall be.
Ecclesiastes ch. 11, v. 3

27 He that observeth the wind shall not sow; and he that regardeth the clouds shall not reap.
Ecclesiastes ch. 11, v. 4

28 In the morning sow thy seed, and in the evening withhold not thine hand.
Ecclesiastes ch. 11, v. 6

29 Truly the light is sweet, and a pleasant thing it is for the eyes to behold the sun.
Ecclesiastes ch. 11, v. 7

30 Rejoice, O young man, in thy youth; and let thy heart cheer thee in the days of thy youth.
Ecclesiastes ch. 11, v. 9

1 Remember now thy Creator in the days of thy youth, while the evil days come not, nor the years draw nigh, when thou shalt say, I have no pleasure in them;

While the sun, or the light, or the moon, or the stars, be not darkened, nor the clouds return after the rain:

In the day when the keepers of the house shall tremble, and the strong men shall bow themselves, and the grinders cease because they are few, and those that look out of the windows be darkened,

And the doors shall be shut in the streets, when the sound of the grinding is low, and he shall rise up at the voice of the bird, and all the daughters of music shall be brought low;

Also when they shall be afraid of that which is high, and fears shall be in the way, and the almond tree shall flourish, and the grasshopper shall be a burden, and desire shall fail: because man goeth to his long home, and the mourners go about the streets:

Or ever the silver cord be loosed, or the golden bowl be broken, or the pitcher be broken at the fountain, or the wheel broken at the cistern.

Then shall the dust return to the earth as it was: and the spirit shall return unto God who gave it.
Ecclesiastes ch. 12, v. 1

2 The words of the wise are as goads.
Ecclesiastes ch. 12, v. 11

3 Of making many books there is no end; and much study is a weariness of the flesh.
Ecclesiastes ch. 12, v. 12

4 Fear God, and keep his commandments: for this is the whole duty of man.

For God shall bring every work into judgement, with every secret thing, whether it be good, or whether it be evil.
Ecclesiastes ch. 12, v. 13

Song of Solomon

5 The song of songs, which is Solomon's.

Let him kiss me with the kisses of his mouth: for thy love is better than wine.
Song of Solomon ch. 1, v. 1

6 I am black, but comely, O ye daughters of Jerusalem, as the tents of Kedar, as the curtains of Solomon.
Song of Solomon ch. 1, v. 5

7 A bundle of myrrh is my wellbeloved unto me; he shall lie all night betwixt my breasts.
Song of Solomon ch. 1, v. 13

8 I am the rose of Sharon, and the lily of the valleys.
Song of Solomon ch. 2, v. 1

9 Rise up, my love, my fair one, and come away.

For, lo, the winter is past, the rain is over and gone;

The flowers appear on the earth; the time of the singing of birds is come, and the voice of the turtle is heard in our land.
Song of Solomon ch. 2, v. 10

10 Take us the foxes, the little foxes, that spoil the vines.
Song of Solomon ch. 2, v. 15

11 My beloved is mine, and I am his: he feedeth among the lilies.

Until the day break, and the shadows flee away.
Song of Solomon ch. 2, v. 16

12 By night on my bed I sought him whom my soul loveth.
Song of Solomon ch. 3, v. 1

13 Behold, thou art fair, my love; behold, thou art fair; thou hast doves' eyes within thy locks: thy hair is as a flock of goats, that appear from mount Gilead.

Thy teeth are like a flock of sheep that are even shorn, which came up from the washing; whereof every one bear twins, and none is barren among them.

Thy lips are like a thread of scarlet, and thy speech is comely: thy temples are like a piece of a pomegranate within thy locks.

Thy neck is like the tower of David builded for an armoury, whereon there hang a thousand bucklers, all shields of mighty men.

Thy two breasts are like two young roes that are twins, which feed among the lilies.
Song of Solomon ch. 4, v. 1

14 Thou art all fair, my love; there is no spot in thee.
Song of Solomon ch. 4, v. 7

15 A garden inclosed is my sister, my spouse; a spring shut up, a fountain sealed.
Song of Solomon ch. 4, v. 12

16 Awake, O north wind; and come, thou south; blow upon my garden, that the spices thereof may flow out. Let my beloved come into his garden, and eat his pleasant fruits.
Song of Solomon ch. 4, v. 16

17 I sleep, but my heart waketh: it is the voice of my beloved that knocketh, saying, Open to me, my sister, my love, my dove, my undefiled.
Song of Solomon ch. 5, v. 2

18 The watchmen that went about the city found me, they smote me, they wounded me; the keepers of the walls took away my veil from me.

I charge you, O daughters of Jerusalem, if ye find my beloved, that ye tell him, that I am sick of love.

What is thy beloved more than another beloved, O thou fairest among women?
Song of Solomon ch. 5, v. 7

19 My beloved is white and ruddy, the chiefest among ten thousand.
Song of Solomon ch. 5, v. 10

20 His hands are as gold rings set with the beryl: his belly is as bright ivory overlaid with sapphires.

His legs are as pillars of marble, set upon sockets of fine gold: his countenance is as Lebanon, excellent as the cedars.

His mouth is most sweet: yea, he is altogether lovely. This is my beloved, and this is my friend, O daughters of Jerusalem.
Song of Solomon ch. 5, v. 14

21 Who is she that looketh forth as the morning, fair as the moon, clear as the sun, and terrible as an army with banners?
Song of Solomon ch. 6, v. 10

22 Return, return, O Shulamite; return, return, that we may look upon thee.
Song of Solomon ch. 6, v. 13

1 How beautiful are thy feet with shoes, O prince's daughter!
Song of Solomon ch. 7, v. 1

2 Thy navel is like a round goblet, which wanteth not liquor: thy belly is like an heap of wheat set about with lilies.
Song of Solomon ch. 7, v. 2

3 Thy neck is as a tower of ivory; thine eyes like the fishpools in Heshbon, by the gate of Bath-rabbim: thy nose is as the tower of Lebanon which looketh toward Damascus.
Song of Solomon ch. 7, v. 4

4 Like the best wine, for my beloved, that goeth down sweetly, causing the lips of those that are asleep to speak.
Song of Solomon ch. 7, v. 9

5 Set me as a seal upon thine heart, as a seal upon thine arm: for love is strong as death; jealousy is cruel as the grave.
Song of Solomon ch. 8, v. 6

6 Many waters cannot quench love, neither can the floods drown it: if a man would give all the substance of his house for love, it would utterly be contemned.
Song of Solomon ch. 8, v. 7

7 Make haste, my beloved, and be thou like to a roe or to a young hart upon the mountains of spices.
Song of Solomon ch. 8, v. 14

Isaiah

8 The daughter of Zion is left as a cottage in a vineyard, as a lodge in a garden of cucumbers, as a besieged city.
Isaiah ch. 1, v. 8

9 Bring no more vain oblations; incense is an abomination unto me; the new moons and sabbaths, the calling of assemblies, I cannot away with.
Isaiah ch. 1, v. 13

10 Though your sins be as scarlet, they shall be as white as snow.
Isaiah ch. 1, v. 18

11 They shall beat their swords into plowshares, and their spears into pruninghooks: nation shall not lift up sword against nation, neither shall they learn war any more.
Isaiah ch. 2, v. 4. See also Micah ch. 4, v. 3, Joel ch. 3, v. 10

12 What mean ye that ye beat my people to pieces, and grind the faces of the poor?
Isaiah ch. 3, v. 15

13 My well-beloved hath a vineyard in a very fruitful hill.
Isaiah ch. 5, v. 1

14 And he looked that it should bring forth grapes, and it brought forth wild grapes.
Isaiah ch. 5, v. 2

15 And he looked for judgement, but behold oppression; for righteousness, but behold a cry.
Isaiah ch. 5, v. 7

16 Woe unto them that join house to house, that lay field to field, till there be no place.
Isaiah ch. 5, v. 8

17 Woe unto them that call evil good, and good evil.
Isaiah ch. 5, v. 20

18 For all this his anger is not turned away, but his hand is stretched out still.
Isaiah ch. 5, v. 25

19 In the year that king Uzziah died I saw also the Lord sitting upon a throne, high and lifted up, and his train filled the temple.
Above it stood the seraphims: each one had six wings; with twain he covered his face, and with twain he covered his feet, and with twain he did fly.
And one cried unto another, and said, Holy, holy, holy, is the Lord of hosts: the whole earth is full of his glory.
Isaiah ch. 6, v. 1

20 Then said I, Woe is me! for I am undone; because I am a man of unclean lips, and I dwell in the midst of a people of unclean lips.
Isaiah ch. 6, v. 5

21 Then flew one of the seraphims unto me, having a live coal in his hand, which he had taken with the tongs from off the altar.
And he laid it upon my mouth, and said, Lo, this hath touched thy lips.
Isaiah ch. 6, v. 6

22 Whom shall I send, and who will go for us? Then said I, Here am I; send me.
Isaiah ch. 6, v. 8

23 Then said I, Lord, how long?
Isaiah ch. 6, v. 11

24 Behold, a virgin shall conceive, and bear a son, and shall call his name Immanuel.
Butter and honey shall he eat, that he may know to refuse the evil, and choose the good.
Isaiah ch. 7, v. 14

25 Sanctify the Lord of hosts himself; and let him be your fear, and let him be your dread.
And he shall be for a sanctuary; but for a stone of stumbling and for a rock of offence to both the houses of Israel.
Isaiah ch. 8, v. 13

26 The people that walked in darkness have seen a great light: they that dwell in the land of the shadow of death, upon them hath the light shined.
Thou hast multiplied the nation, and not increased the joy: they joy before thee according to the joy in harvest, and as men rejoice when they divide the spoil.
Isaiah ch. 9, v. 2. Cf. Scottish Metrical Psalms 561:11

27 For unto us a child is born, unto us a son is given: and the government shall be upon his shoulder: and his name shall be called Wonderful, Counsellor, The mighty God, The everlasting Father, The Prince of Peace.
Of the increase of his government and peace there shall be no end.
Isaiah ch. 9, v. 6

28 The zeal of the Lord of hosts will perform this.
Isaiah ch. 9, v. 7

1 And there shall come forth a rod out of the stem of
Jesse, and a branch shall grow out of his roots:
And the spirit of the Lord shall rest upon him, the
spirit of wisdom and understanding, the spirit of
counsel and might, the spirit of knowledge and of
the fear of the Lord.
Isaiah ch. 11, v. 1

2 The wolf also shall dwell with the lamb, and the
leopard shall lie down with the kid; and the calf and
the young lion and the fatling together; and a little
child shall lead them.
Isaiah ch. 11, v. 6

3 And the lion shall eat straw like the ox.
And the sucking child shall play on the hole of the
asp, and the weaned child shall put his hand on the
cockatrice' den.
They shall not hurt nor destroy in all my holy
mountain: for the earth shall be full of the
knowledge of the Lord, as the waters cover the sea.
Isaiah ch. 11, v. 7

4 And the wild beasts of the islands shall cry in their
desolate houses, and dragons in their pleasant
palaces.
Isaiah ch. 13, v. 22

5 How art thou fallen from heaven, O Lucifer, son of the
morning!
Isaiah ch. 14, v. 12

6 Watchman, what of the night? Watchman, what of
the night?
The watchman said, The morning cometh, and also
the night.
Isaiah ch. 21, v. 11

7 Let us eat and drink; for to morrow we shall die.
*Isaiah ch. 22, v. 13. Cf. Ecclesiastes 80:17, St Luke 94:23,
I Corinthians 101:9*

8 In this mountain shall the Lord of hosts make unto all
people a feast of fat things, a feast of wine on the
lees, of fat things full of marrow, of wine on the lees
well refined.
Isaiah ch. 25, v. 6

9 He will swallow up death in victory; and the Lord God
will wipe away tears from off all faces.
Isaiah ch. 25, v. 8

10 We have as it were brought forth wind.
Isaiah ch. 26, v. 18

11 For precept must be upon precept, precept upon
precept; line upon line, line upon line; here a little,
and there a little.
Isaiah ch. 28, v. 10

12 We have made a covenant with death, and with hell
are we at agreement.
Isaiah ch. 28, v. 15

13 Speak unto us smooth things, prophesy deceits.
Isaiah ch. 30, v. 10

14 In quietness and in confidence shall be your strength.
Isaiah ch. 30, v. 15

15 The bread of adversity, and the waters of affliction.
Isaiah ch. 30, v. 20

16 This is the way, walk ye in it.
Isaiah ch. 30, v. 21

17 And a man shall be as an hiding place from the wind,
and a covert from the tempest; as rivers of water in
a dry place, as the shadow of a great rock in a
weary land.
Isaiah ch. 32, v. 2

18 And thorns shall come up in her palaces, nettles and
brambles in the fortresses thereof: and it shall be an
habitation of dragons, and a court for owls.
Isaiah ch. 34, v. 13

19 The wilderness and the solitary place shall be glad for
them; and the desert shall rejoice, and blossom as
the rose.
Isaiah ch. 35, v. 1

20 Strengthen ye the weak hands, and confirm the feeble
knees.
Isaiah ch. 35, v. 3

21 Then shall the lame man leap as an hart, and the
tongue of the dumb sing: for in the wilderness shall
waters break out, and streams in the desert.
Isaiah ch. 35, v. 6

22 They shall obtain joy and gladness, and sorrow and
sighing shall flee away.
Isaiah ch. 35, v. 10

23 Set thine house in order: for thou shalt die, and not
live.
Isaiah ch. 38, v. 1

24 I shall go softly all my years in the bitterness of my
soul.
Isaiah ch. 38, v. 15

25 Comfort ye, comfort ye my people, saith your God.
Speak ye comfortably to Jerusalem, and cry unto her,
that her warfare is accomplished.
Isaiah ch. 40, v. 1

26 The voice of him that crieth in the wilderness, Prepare
ye the way of the Lord, make straight in the desert
a highway for our God.
Every valley shall be exalted, and every mountain and
hill shall be made low: and the crooked shall be
made straight, and the rough places plain:
And the glory of the Lord shall be revealed, and all
flesh shall see it together: for the mouth of the Lord
hath spoken it.
Isaiah ch. 40, v. 3. Cf. St Matthew 88:13

27 The voice said, Cry. And he said, What shall I cry? All
flesh is grass, and all the goodliness thereof is as the
flower of the field:
The grass withereth, the flower fadeth: because the
spirit of the Lord bloweth upon it: surely the people
is grass.
Isaiah ch. 40, v. 6. Cf. I Peter 105:9

28 He shall feed his flock like a shepherd: he shall gather
the lambs with his arm, and carry them in his
bosom, and shall gently lead those that are with
young.
Isaiah ch. 40, v. 11

29 The nations are as a drop of a bucket, and are counted
as the small dust of the balance: behold, he taketh
up the isles as a very little thing.
Isaiah ch. 40, v. 15

30 Have ye not known? have ye not heard? hath it not
been told you from the beginning?
Isaiah ch. 40, v. 21

1 But they that wait upon the Lord shall renew their strength: they shall mount up with wings as eagles; they shall run, and not be weary; and they shall walk, and not faint.
Isaiah ch. 40, v. 31

2 A bruised reed shall he not break, and the smoking flax shall he not quench.
Isaiah ch. 42, v. 3

3 Woe unto him that striveth with his maker! Let the potsherd strive with the potsherds of the earth. Shall the clay say to him that fashioneth it, What makest thou?
Isaiah ch. 45, v. 9

4 I have chosen thee in the furnace of affliction.
Isaiah ch. 48, v. 10

5 O that thou hadst hearkened to my commandments! then had thy peace been as a river, and thy righteousness as the waves of the sea.
Isaiah ch. 48, v. 18

6 There is no peace, saith the Lord, unto the wicked.
Isaiah ch. 48, v. 22

7 Can a woman forget her sucking child, that she should not have compassion on the son of her womb? yea, they may forget, yet will I not forget thee.
Isaiah ch. 49, v. 15

8 How beautiful upon the mountains are the feet of him that bringeth good tidings, that publisheth peace; that bringeth good tidings of good, that publisheth salvation; that saith unto Zion, Thy God reigneth!
Isaiah ch. 52, v. 7

9 For they shall see eye to eye, when the Lord shall bring again Zion.
Break forth into joy, sing together, ye waste places of Jerusalem: for the Lord hath comforted his people, he hath redeemed Jerusalem.
Isaiah ch. 52, v. 8

10 Who hath believed our report? and to whom is the arm of the Lord revealed?
Isaiah ch. 53, v. 1

11 He hath no form nor comeliness; and when we shall see him there is no beauty that we should desire him.
He is despised and rejected of men; a man of sorrows, and acquainted with grief: and we hid as it were our faces from him; he was despised, and we esteemed him not.
Surely he hath borne our griefs, and carried our sorrows.
Isaiah ch. 53, v. 2

12 But he was wounded for our transgressions, he was bruised for our iniquities: the chastisement of our peace was upon him; and with his stripes we are healed.
All we like sheep have gone astray; we have turned every one to his own way; and the Lord hath laid on him the iniquity of us all.
He was oppressed, and he was afflicted, yet he opened not his mouth: he is brought as a lamb to the slaughter, and as a sheep before her shearers is dumb, so he openeth not his mouth.
Isaiah ch. 53, v. 5

13 He was cut off out of the land of the living.
Isaiah ch. 53, v. 8

14 He was numbered with the transgressors; and he bare the sin of many, and made intercession for the transgressors.
Isaiah ch. 53, v. 12

15 Ho, every one that thirsteth, come ye to the waters, and he that hath no money; come ye, buy, and eat; yea, come, buy wine and milk without money and without price.
Wherefore do ye spend money for that which is not bread? and your labour for that which satisfieth not?
Isaiah ch. 55, v. 1

16 Seek ye the Lord while he may be found, call ye upon him while he is near.
Isaiah ch. 55, v. 6

17 For my thoughts are not your thoughts, neither are your ways my ways, saith the Lord.
Isaiah ch. 55, v. 8

18 Instead of the thorn shall come up the fir tree, and instead of the brier shall come up the myrtle tree.
Isaiah ch. 55, v. 13

19 I will give them an everlasting name, that shall not be cut off.
Isaiah ch. 56, v. 5

20 The righteous perisheth, and no man layeth it to heart.
Isaiah ch. 57, v. 1

21 Peace to him that is far off, and to him that is near.
Isaiah ch. 57, v. 19

22 Is not this the fast that I have chosen? to loose the bands of wickedness, to undo the heavy burdens, and to let the oppressed go free, and that ye break every yoke?
Isaiah ch. 58, v. 6

23 Then shall thy light break forth as the morning, and thine health shall spring forth speedily.
Isaiah ch. 58, v. 8

24 They make haste to shed innocent blood.
Isaiah ch. 59, v. 7

25 Arise, shine; for thy light is come, and the glory of the Lord is risen upon thee.
Isaiah ch. 60, v. 1

26 The Spirit of the Lord God is upon me . . . To bind up the brokenhearted, to proclaim liberty to the captives, and the opening of the prison to them that are bound;
To proclaim the acceptable year of the Lord, and the day of vengeance of our God; to comfort all that mourn.
Isaiah ch. 61, v. 1

27 To give unto them beauty for ashes, the oil of joy for mourning, the garment of praise for the spirit of heaviness.
Isaiah ch. 61, v. 3

28 All our righteousnesses are as filthy rags; and we all do fade as a leaf.
Isaiah ch. 64, v. 6

1 Stand by thyself, come not near to me; for I am holier
  than thou.
  Isaiah ch. 65, v. 5

2 For, behold, I create new heavens and a new earth.
  Isaiah ch. 65, v. 17

Jeremiah

3 Can a maid forget her ornaments, or a bride her
  attire?
  Jeremiah ch. 2, v. 32

4 They were as fed horses in the morning: every one
  neighed after his neighbour's wife.
  Jeremiah ch. 5, v. 8

5 This people hath a revolting and a rebellious heart.
  Jeremiah ch. 5, v. 23

6 The prophets prophesy falsely, and the priests bear
  rule by their means; and my people love to have it
  so: and what will ye do in the end thereof?
  Jeremiah ch. 5, v. 31

7 They have healed also the hurt of the daughter of my
  people slightly, saying, Peace, peace; when there is
  no peace.
  Jeremiah ch. 6, v. 14

8 The harvest is past, the summer is ended, and we are
  not saved.
  Jeremiah ch. 8, v. 20

9 Is there no balm in Gilead?
  Jeremiah ch. 8, v. 22

10 Can the Ethiopian change his skin, or the leopard his
  spots?
  Jeremiah ch. 13, v. 23

11 Woe is me, my mother, that thou hast borne me a
  man of strife and a man of contention to the whole
  earth!
  Jeremiah ch. 15, v. 10

12 The heart is deceitful above all things, and desperately
  wicked.
  Jeremiah ch. 17, v. 9

13 As the partridge sitteth on eggs, and hatcheth them
  not; so he that getteth riches, and not by right,
  shall leave them in the midst of his days.
  Jeremiah ch. 17, v. 11

14 Behold, I will make thee a terror to thyself, and to all
  thy friends.
  Jeremiah ch. 20, v. 4

Lamentations

15 How doth the city sit solitary, that was full of people!
  Lamentations ch. 1, v. 1

16 Is it nothing to you, all ye that pass by? behold, and
  see if there be any sorrow like unto my sorrow.
  Lamentations ch. 1, v. 12

17 And I said, My strength and my hope is perished from
  the Lord:
  Remembering mine affliction and my misery, the
  wormwood and the gall.
  Lamentations ch. 3, v. 18

18 It is good for a man that he bear the yoke in his
  youth.
  Lamentations ch. 3, v. 27

19 He giveth his cheek to him that smiteth him.
  Lamentations ch. 3, v. 30

20 O Lord, thou hast seen my wrong: judge thou my
  cause.
  Lamentations ch. 4, v. 59

Ezekiel

21 As is the mother, so is her daughter.
  Ezekiel ch. 16, v. 44

22 The fathers have eaten sour grapes, and the children's
  teeth are set on edge.
  Ezekiel ch. 18, v. 2

23 When the wicked man turneth away from his
  wickedness that he hath committed, and doeth that
  which is lawful and right, he shall save his soul
  alive.
  Ezekiel ch. 18, v. 27

24 The king of Babylon stood at the parting of the ways.
  Ezekiel ch. 21, v. 21

25 The hand of the Lord was upon me, and carried me
  out in the spirit of the Lord, and set me down in the
  midst of the valley which was full of bones.
  Ezekiel ch. 37, v. 1

26 Can these bones live?
  Ezekiel ch. 37, v. 3

27 Again he said unto me, Prophesy upon these bones,
  and say unto them, O ye dry bones, hear the word
  of the Lord.
  Ezekiel ch. 37, v. 4

Daniel

28 To you it is commanded, O peoples, nations, and
  languages,
  That at what time ye hear the sound of the cornet,
  flute, harp, sackbut, psaltery, dulcimer, and all
  kinds of music, ye fall down and worship the golden
  image that Nebuchadnezzar the king hath set up:
  And whoso falleth not down and worshippeth shall
  the same hour be cast into the midst of a burning
  fiery furnace.
  Daniel ch. 3, v. 4

29 Shadrach, Meshach, and Abed-nego, ye servants of
  the most high God, come forth and come hither.
  Daniel ch. 3, v. 26

30 In the same hour came forth fingers of a man's hand,
  and wrote over against the candlestick upon the
  plaister of the wall of the king's palace.
  Daniel ch. 5, v. 5

31 And this is the writing that was written, MENE, MENE,
  TEKEL, UPHARSIN.
  This is the interpretation of the thing: MENE; God hath
  numbered thy kingdom, and finished it.
  TEKEL; Thou art weighed in the balances and art
  found wanting.
  PERES; Thy kingdom is divided, and given to the Medes
  and Persians.
  Daniel ch. 5, v. 25

32 Now, O king, establish the decree, and sign the
  writing, that it be not changed, according to the
  law of the Medes and Persians, which altereth not.
  Daniel ch. 6, v. 8

1 The Ancient of days did sit, whose garment was white as snow, and the hair of his head like the pure wool: his throne was like the fiery flame, and his wheels as burning fire.

A fiery stream issued and came forth from behind him: thousand thousands ministered unto him, and ten thousand times ten thousand stood before him: the judgement was set, and the books were opened.
Daniel ch. 7, v. 9

2 O Daniel, a man greatly beloved.
Daniel ch. 10, v. 11

3 Many shall run to and fro, and knowledge shall be increased.
Daniel ch. 12, v. 4

Hosea

4 They have sown the wind, and they shall reap the whirlwind.
Hosea ch. 8, v. 7

5 I drew them . . . with bands of love.
Hosea ch. 11, v. 4

Joel

6 That which the palmerworm hath left hath the locust eaten.
Joel ch. 1, v. 4

7 I will restore to you the years that the locust hath eaten, the cankerworm, and the caterpillar, and the palmerworm, my great army which I sent among you.
Joel ch. 2, v. 25

8 And it shall come to pass afterward, that I will pour out my spirit upon all flesh; and your sons and your daughters shall prophesy, your old men shall dream dreams, your young men shall see visions.
Joel ch. 2, v. 28

9 Multitudes, multitudes in the valley of decision: for the day of the Lord is near in the valley of decision.
Joel ch. 3, v. 14

Amos

10 Can two walk together, except they be agreed?
Amos ch. 3, v. 3

11 Shall there be evil in a city, and the Lord hath not done it?
Amos ch. 3, v. 6

12 I have overthrown some of you, as God overthrew Sodom and Gomorrah, and ye were as a firebrand plucked out of the burning.
Amos ch. 4, v. 11

Micah

13 But thou, Bethlehem Ephratah, though thou be little among the thousands of Judah, yet out of thee shall he come forth unto me that is to be ruler in Israel.
Micah ch. 5, v. 2

14 What doth the Lord require of thee, but to do justly, and to love mercy, and to walk humbly with thy God?
Micah ch. 6, v. 8

Nahum

15 Woe to the bloody city! it is all full of lies and robbery; the prey departeth not.
Nahum ch. 3, v. 1

Habakkuk

16 Write the vision, and make it plain upon tables, that he may run that readeth it.
Habakkuk ch. 2, v. 2

Zephaniah

17 Woe to her that is filthy and polluted, to the oppressing city!
Zephaniah ch. 3, v. 1

Haggai

18 Ye have sown much, and bring in little; ye eat but ye have not enough . . . and he that earneth wages earneth wages to put it into a bag with holes.
Haggai ch. 1, v. 6

Malachi

19 But unto you that fear my name shall the Sun of righteousness arise with healing in his wings.
Malachi ch. 4, v. 2

Apocrypha

20 The first wrote, Wine is the strongest. The second wrote, The king is strongest. The third wrote, Women are strongest: but above all things Truth beareth away the victory.
I Esdras ch. 3, v. 10

21 Great is Truth, and mighty above all things.
I Esdras ch. 4, v. 41. Cf. Vulgate 108:18

22 Nourish thy children, O thou good nurse; stablish their feet.
II Esdras ch. 2, v. 25

23 For the world has lost his youth, and the times begin to wax old.
II Esdras ch. 14, v. 10

24 I shall light a candle of understanding in thine heart, which shall not be put out.
II Esdras ch. 14, v. 25

25 The ear of jealousy heareth all things.
Wisdom of Solomon ch. 1, v. 10

26 Let us crown ourselves with rosebuds, before they be withered.
Wisdom of Solomon ch. 2, v. 8

27 Through envy of the devil came death into the world.
Wisdom of Solomon ch. 2, v. 24

28 But the souls of the righteous are in the hand of God, and there shall no torment touch them.

In the sight of the unwise they seemed to die: and their departure is taken for misery,

And their going from us to be utter destruction: but they are in peace.

For though they be punished in the sight of men, yet is their hope full of immortality.

And having been a little chastised, they shall be greatly rewarded: for God proved them, and found them worthy for himself.
Wisdom of Solomon ch. 3, v. 1

1 And in the time of their visitation they shall shine, and run to and fro like sparks among the stubble.
Wisdom of Solomon ch. 3, v. 7

2 He, being made perfect in a short time, fulfilled a long time.
Wisdom of Solomon ch. 4, v. 13

3 We fools accounted his life madness, and his end to be without honour:
How is he numbered among the children of God, and his lot is among the saints!
Wisdom of Solomon ch. 5, v. 4

4 Even so we in like manner, as soon as we were born, began to draw to our end.
Wisdom of Solomon ch. 5, v. 13

5 For the hope of the ungodly . . . passeth away as the remembrance of a guest that tarrieth but a day.
Wisdom of Solomon ch. 5, v. 14

6 And love is the keeping of her laws; and the giving heed unto her laws is the assurance of incorruption.
Wisdom of Solomon ch. 6, v. 18

7 For the same things uttered in Hebrew, and translated into another tongue, have not the same force in them: and not only these things, but the law itself, and the prophets, and the rest of the books, have no small difference, when they are spoken in their own language.
Ecclesiasticus: The Prologue

8 For the Lord is full of compassion and mercy, long-suffering, and very pitiful, and forgiveth sins, and saveth in time of affliction.
Ecclesiasticus ch. 2, v. 11

9 We will fall into the hands of the Lord, and not into the hands of men: for as his majesty is, so is his mercy.
Ecclesiasticus ch. 2, v. 18

10 Be not curious in unnecessary matters: for more things are shewed unto thee than men understand.
Ecclesiasticus ch. 3, v. 23

11 Be not ignorant of any thing in a great matter or a small.
Ecclesiasticus ch. 5, v. 15

12 A faithful friend is the medicine of life.
Ecclesiasticus ch. 6, v. 16

13 Laugh no man to scorn in the bitterness of his soul.
Ecclesiasticus ch. 7, v. 11

14 Miss not the discourse of the elders.
Ecclesiasticus ch. 8, v. 9

15 Open not thine heart to every man.
Ecclesiasticus ch. 8, v. 19

16 Forsake not an old friend; for the new is not comparable to him; a new friend is as new wine; when it is old, thou shalt drink it with pleasure.
Ecclesiasticus ch. 9, v. 10

17 Many kings have sat down upon the ground; and one that was never thought of hath worn the crown.
Ecclesiasticus ch. 11, v. 5

18 Judge none blessed before his death.
Ecclesiasticus ch. 11, v. 28

19 He that toucheth pitch shall be defiled therewith.
Ecclesiasticus ch. 13, v. 1

20 For how agree the kettle and the earthen pot together?
Ecclesiasticus ch. 13, v. 2

21 When a rich man is fallen, he hath many helpers: he speaketh things not to be spoken, and yet men justify him: the poor man slipped, and yet they rebuked him too; he spake wisely, and could have no place.
Ecclesiasticus ch. 14, v. 22

22 When thou hast enough, remember the time of hunger.
Ecclesiasticus ch. 18, v. 25

23 Be not made a beggar by banqueting upon borrowing.
Ecclesiasticus ch. 18, v. 33

24 He that contemneth small things shall fall by little and little.
Ecclesiasticus ch. 19, v. 1

25 Neither [give] a wicked woman liberty to gad abroad.
Ecclesiasticus ch. 25, v. 25

26 A merchant shall hardly keep himself from doing wrong.
Ecclesiasticus ch. 26, v. 29

27 Many have fallen by the edge of the sword: but not so many as have fallen by the tongue.
Ecclesiasticus ch. 28, v. 18

28 And weigh thy words in a balance, and make a door and bar for thy mouth.
Ecclesiasticus ch. 28, v. 25

29 Envy and wrath shorten the life.
Ecclesiasticus ch. 30, v. 24

30 Leave off first for manners' sake.
Ecclesiasticus ch. 31, v. 17

31 Wine is as good as life to a man, if it be drunk moderately: what life is then to a man that is without wine? for it was made to make men glad.
Ecclesiasticus ch. 31, v. 27

32 Leave not a stain in thine honour.
Ecclesiasticus ch. 33, v. 22

33 Honour a physician with the honour due unto him for the uses which ye may have of him: for the Lord hath created him.
Ecclesiasticus ch. 38, v. 1

34 He that sinneth before his Maker, let him fall into the hand of the physician.
Ecclesiasticus ch. 38, v. 15

35 The wisdom of a learned man cometh by opportunity of leisure: and he that hath little business shall become wise.
Ecclesiasticus ch. 38, v. 24

36 How can he get wisdom . . . whose talk is of bullocks?
Ecclesiasticus ch. 38, v. 25

37 Let us now praise famous men, and our fathers that begat us.
Ecclesiasticus ch. 44, v. 1

38 Such as did bear rule in their kingdoms.
Ecclesiasticus ch. 44, v. 3

1 Such as found out musical tunes, and recited verses in
  writing:
  Rich men furnished with ability, living peaceably in
  their habitations.
  Ecclesiasticus ch. 44, v. 5

2 There be of them, that have left a name behind them.
  Ecclesiasticus ch. 44, v. 8

3 And some there be, which have no memorial . . . and
  are become as though they had never been born . . .
  But these were merciful men, whose righteousness
  hath not been forgotten . . .
  Their seed shall remain for ever, and their glory shall
  not be blotted out.
  Their bodies are buried in peace; but their name liveth
  for evermore.
  Ecclesiasticus ch. 44, v. 9

4 As the flower of roses in the spring of the year, as lilies
  by the rivers of waters, and as the branches of the
  frankincense tree in the time of summer.
  Ecclesiasticus ch. 50, v. 8

5 Get learning with a great sum of money, and get
  much gold by her.
  Ecclesiasticus ch. 51, v. 28

6 It is a foolish thing to make a long prologue, and to be
  short in the story itself.
  II Maccabees ch. 2, v. 32

7 When he was at the last gasp.
  II Maccabees ch. 7, v. 9

New Testament: St Matthew

8 There came wise men from the east to Jerusalem,
  Saying, Where is he that is born King of the Jews? for
  we have seen his star in the east, and are come to
  worship him.
  St Matthew ch. 2, v. 1

9 They presented unto him gifts; gold, and frankincense,
  and myrrh.
  St Matthew ch. 2, v. 11

10 They departed into their own country another way.
   St Matthew ch. 2, v. 12

11 In Rama was there a voice heard, lamentation, and
   weeping, and great mourning, Rachel weeping for
   her children, and would not be comforted, because
   they are not.
   St Matthew ch. 2, v. 18. See Jeremiah ch. 31, v. 15

12 Repent ye: for the kingdom of heaven is at hand.
   St Matthew ch. 3, v. 2

13 The voice of one crying in the wilderness, Prepare ye
   the way of the Lord, make his paths straight.
   St Matthew ch. 3, v. 3. Cf. Isaiah 83:26

14 John had his raiment of camel's hair, and a leathern
   girdle about his loins; and his meat was locusts and
   wild honey.
   St Matthew ch. 3, v. 4

15 O generation of vipers, who hath warned you to flee
   from the wrath to come?
   St Matthew ch. 3, v. 7

16 And now also the axe is laid unto the root of the trees.
   St Matthew ch. 3, v. 10

17 This is my beloved Son, in whom I am well pleased.
   St Matthew ch. 3, v. 17

18 Man shall not live by bread alone, but by every word
   that proceedeth out of the mouth of God.
   St Matthew ch. 4, v. 4. See Deuteronomy ch. 8, v. 3

19 Thou shalt not tempt the Lord thy God.
   St Matthew ch. 4, v. 7. See Deuteronomy ch. 6, v. 16

20 The devil taketh him up into an exceeding high
   mountain, and sheweth him all the kingdoms of the
   world, and the glory of them.
   St Matthew ch. 4, v. 8

21 Angels came and ministered unto him.
   St Matthew ch. 4, v. 11

22 Follow me, and I will make you fishers of men.
   St Matthew ch. 4, v. 19

23 Blessed are the poor in spirit: for theirs is the kingdom
   of heaven.
   Blessed are they that mourn: for they shall be
   comforted.
   Blessed are the meek: for they shall inherit the earth.
   Blessed are they which do hunger and thirst after
   righteousness: for they shall be filled.
   Blessed are the merciful: for they shall obtain mercy.
   Blessed are the pure in heart: for they shall see God.
   Blessed are the peacemakers: for they shall be called
   the children of God.
   St Matthew ch. 5, v. 3

24 Ye are the salt of the earth: but if the salt have lost
   his savour, wherewith shall it be salted?
   St Matthew ch. 5, v. 13

25 Ye are the light of the world. A city that is set on an
   hill cannot be hid.
   St Matthew ch. 5, v. 14

26 Let your light so shine before men, that they may see
   your good works.
   St Matthew ch. 5, v. 16

27 Think not that I am come to destroy the law, or the
   prophets: I am come not to destroy, but to fulfil.
   St Matthew ch. 5, v. 17

28 Except your righteousness shall exceed the
   righteousness of the scribes and Pharisees, ye shall
   in no case enter into the kingdom of heaven.
   St Matthew ch. 5, v. 20

29 Whosoever shall say, Thou fool, shall be in danger of
   hell fire.
   St Matthew ch. 5, v. 22

30 Till thou hast paid the uttermost farthing.
   St Matthew ch. 5, v. 26

31 Swear not at all; neither by heaven; for it is God's
   throne:
   Nor by the earth; for it is his footstool.
   St Matthew ch. 5, v. 34

32 Resist not evil: but whosoever shall smite thee on thy
   right cheek, turn to him the other also.
   St Matthew ch. 5, v. 39

33 Whosoever shall compel thee to go a mile, go with
   him twain.
   St Matthew ch. 5, v. 41

34 He maketh his sun to rise on the evil and on the good,
   and sendeth rain on the just and on the unjust.
   St Matthew ch. 5, v. 45

1 For if ye love them which love you, what reward have ye? do not even the publicans the same?
St Matthew ch. 5, v. 46

2 Be ye therefore perfect, even as your Father which is in heaven is perfect.
St Matthew ch. 5, v. 48

3 When thou doest alms, let not thy left hand know what thy right hand doeth.
That thine alms may be in secret: and thy Father which seeth in secret himself shall reward you openly.
St Matthew ch. 6, v. 3

4 Use not vain repetitions, as the heathen do: for they think that they shall be heard for their much speaking.
St Matthew ch. 6, v. 7

5 After this manner therefore pray ye: Our Father which art in heaven, Hallowed be thy name.
Thy kingdom come. Thy will be done in earth, as it is in heaven.
Give us this day our daily bread.
And forgive us our debts, as we forgive our debtors.
And lead us not into temptation, but deliver us from evil: For thine is the kingdom, and the power, and the glory, for ever. Amen.
St Matthew ch. 6, v. 9. See St Luke ch. 11, v. 2

6 Lay not up for yourselves treasures upon earth, where moth and rust doth corrupt, and where thieves break through and steal:
But lay up for yourselves treasures in heaven.
St Matthew ch. 6, v. 19

7 Where your treasure is, there will your heart be also.
St Matthew ch. 6, v. 21

8 No man can serve two masters . . . Ye cannot serve God and mammon.
St Matthew ch. 6, v. 24

9 Is not the life more than meat, and the body than raiment?
Behold the fowls of the air: for they sow not, neither do they reap, nor gather into barns.
St Matthew ch. 6, v. 25

10 Which of you by taking thought can add one cubit unto his stature?
St Matthew ch. 6, v. 27

11 Consider the lilies of the field, how they grow; they toil not, neither do they spin:
And yet I say unto you, That even Solomon in all his glory was not arrayed like one of these.
St Matthew ch. 6, v. 28

12 Seek ye first the kingdom of God, and his righteousness; and all these things shall be added unto you.
St Matthew ch. 6, v. 33

13 Take therefore no thought for the morrow: for the morrow shall take thought for the things of itself. Sufficient unto the day is the evil thereof.
St Matthew ch. 6, v. 34

14 Judge not, that ye be not judged.
St Matthew ch. 7, v. 1

15 Why beholdest thou the mote that is in thy brother's eye, but considerest not the beam that is in thine own eye?
St Matthew ch. 7, v. 3

16 Neither cast ye your pearls before swine.
St Matthew ch. 7, v. 6

17 Ask, and it shall be given you; seek, and ye shall find; knock, and it shall be opened unto you.
St Matthew ch. 7, v. 7

18 Every one that asketh receiveth; and he that seeketh findeth.
St Matthew ch. 7, v. 8

19 Or what man is there of you, whom if his son ask bread, will he give him a stone?
St Matthew ch. 7, v. 9

20 Therefore all things whatsoever ye would that men should do to you, do ye even so to them: for this is the law and the prophets.
St Matthew ch. 7, v. 12

21 Wide is the gate, and broad is the way, that leadeth to destruction, and many there be that go in thereat.
St Matthew ch. 7, v. 13

22 Strait is the gate, and narrow is the way, which leadeth unto life, and few there be that find it.
St Matthew ch. 7, v. 14

23 Beware of false prophets, which come to you in sheep's clothing, but inwardly they are ravening wolves.
St Matthew ch. 7, v. 15

24 Do men gather grapes of thorns, or figs of thistles?
St Matthew ch. 7, v. 16

25 By their fruits ye shall know them.
St Matthew ch. 7, v. 20

26 The winds blew, and beat upon that house; and it fell not: for it was founded upon a rock.
St Matthew ch. 7, v. 25

27 Every one that heareth these sayings of mine, and doeth them not, shall be likened unto a foolish man, which built his house upon the sand:
And the rain descended, and the floods came, and the winds blew, and beat upon that house; and it fell: and great was the fall of it.
St Matthew ch. 7, v. 27

28 For he taught them as one having authority, and not as the scribes.
St Matthew ch. 7, v. 29

29 Lord I am not worthy that thou shouldest come under my roof.
St Matthew ch. 8, v. 8

30 I am a man under authority, having soldiers under me: and I say to this man, Go, and he goeth; and to another, Come, and he cometh; and to my servant, Do this, and he doeth it.
St Matthew ch. 8, v. 9

31 I have not found so great faith, no, not in Israel.
St Matthew ch. 8, v. 10

32 But the children of the kingdom shall be cast out into outer darkness: there shall be weeping and gnashing of teeth.
St Matthew ch. 8, v. 12

1 The foxes have holes, and the birds of the air have nests; but the Son of man hath not where to lay his head.
St Matthew ch. 8, v. 20

2 Let the dead bury their dead.
St Matthew ch. 8, v. 22

3 The whole herd of swine ran violently down a steep place into the sea, and perished in the waters.
St Matthew ch. 8, v. 32

4 He saw a man, named Matthew, sitting at the receipt of custom: and he saith unto him, Follow me. And he arose and followed him.
St Matthew ch. 9, v. 9

5 Why eateth your Master with publicans and sinners?
St Matthew ch. 9, v. 11

6 They that be whole need not a physician, but they that are sick.
St Matthew ch. 9, v. 12

7 I am not come to call the righteous, but sinners to repentance.
St Matthew ch. 9, v. 13

8 Neither do men put new wine into old bottles.
St Matthew ch. 9, v. 17

9 Thy faith hath made thee whole.
St Matthew ch. 9, v. 22

10 The maid is not dead, but sleepeth.
St Matthew ch. 9, v. 24

11 He casteth out devils through the prince of the devils.
St Matthew ch. 9, v. 34

12 The harvest truly is plenteous, but the labourers are few.
St Matthew ch. 9, v. 37

13 Go rather to the lost sheep of the house of Israel.
St Matthew ch. 10, v. 6

14 Freely ye have received, freely give.
St Matthew ch. 10, v. 8

15 When ye depart out of that house or city, shake off the dust of your feet.
St Matthew ch. 10, v. 14

16 Be ye therefore wise as serpents, and harmless as doves.
St Matthew ch. 10, v. 16

17 The disciple is not above his master, nor the servant above his lord.
St Matthew ch. 10, v. 24

18 The very hairs of your head are all numbered.
St Matthew ch. 10, v. 30

19 Fear ye not therefore, ye are of more value than many sparrows.
St Matthew ch. 10, v. 31

20 I came not to send peace, but a sword.
St Matthew ch. 10, v. 34

21 A man's foes shall be they of his own household.
St Matthew ch. 10, v. 36

22 He that findeth his life shall lose it: and he that loseth his life for my sake shall find it.
St Matthew ch. 10, v. 39

23 Whosoever shall give to drink unto one of these little ones a cup of cold water only in the name of a disciple, verily I say unto you, he shall in no wise lose his reward.
St Matthew ch. 10, v. 42

24 Art thou he that should come, or do we look for another?
St Matthew ch. 11, v. 3

25 What went ye out into the wilderness to see? A reed shaken with the wind?
But what went ye out for to see? A man clothed in soft raiment? . . .
But what went ye out for to see? A prophet? yea, I say unto you, and more than a prophet.
St Matthew ch. 11, v. 7

26 We have piped unto you, and ye have not danced; we have mourned unto you, and ye have not lamented.
St Matthew ch. 11, v. 17

27 Wisdom is justified of her children.
St Matthew ch. 11, v. 19

28 Come unto me, all ye that labour and are heavy laden, and I will give you rest.
Take my yoke upon you, and learn of me; for I am meek and lowly in heart: and ye shall find rest unto your souls.
For my yoke is easy, and my burden is light.
St Matthew ch. 11, v. 28

29 He that is not with me is against me.
St Matthew ch. 12, v. 30 and St Luke ch. 11, v. 23

30 The blasphemy against the Holy Ghost shall not be forgiven unto men.
St Matthew ch. 12, v. 31

31 The tree is known by his fruit.
St Matthew ch. 12, v. 33

32 Out of the abundance of the heart the mouth speaketh.
St Matthew ch. 12, v. 34

33 Every idle word that men shall speak, they shall give account thereof in the day of judgement.
St Matthew ch. 12, v. 36

34 An evil and adulterous generation seeketh after a sign.
St Matthew ch. 12, v. 39

35 Behold, a greater than Solomon is here.
St Matthew ch. 12, v. 42

36 When the unclean spirit is gone out of a man, he walketh through dry places, seeking rest, and findeth none.
Then he saith, I will return into my house from whence I came out; and when he is come, he findeth it empty, swept, and garnished.
St Matthew ch. 12, v. 43

37 Then goeth he, and taketh with himself seven other spirits more wicked than himself, and they enter in and dwell there: and the last state of that man is worse than the first.
St Matthew ch. 12, v. 45

38 Behold my mother and my brethren!
St Matthew ch. 12, v. 49

1 Behold, a sower went forth to sow;
And when he sowed, some seeds fell by the wayside, and the fowls came and devoured them up:
Some fell upon stony places, where they had not much earth: and forthwith they sprung up, because they had no deepness of earth:
And when the sun was up, they were scorched; and because they had no root, they withered away.
And some fell among thorns; and the thorns sprang up and choked them:
But other fell into good ground, and brought forth fruit, some an hundredfold, some sixtyfold, some thirtyfold.
St Matthew ch. 13, v. 3

2 He also that received the seed among the thorns is he that heareth the word; and the care of this world, and the deceitfulness of riches, choke the word, and he becometh unfruitful.
St Matthew ch. 13, v. 22

3 The kingdom of heaven is like to a grain of mustard seed, which a man took, and sowed in his field:
Which indeed is the least of all seeds: but when it is grown, it is the greatest among herbs, and becometh a tree, so that the birds of the air come and lodge in the branches thereof.
St Matthew ch. 13, v. 31

4 The kingdom of heaven is like unto a merchant man, seeking goodly pearls:
Who, when he had found one pearl of great price, went and sold all that he had, and bought it.
St Matthew ch. 13, v. 45

5 A prophet is not without honour, save in his own country, and in his own house.
St Matthew ch. 13, v. 57

6 In the fourth watch of the night Jesus went unto them, walking on the sea.
St Matthew ch. 14, v. 25

7 Be of good cheer; it is I; be not afraid.
St Matthew ch. 14, v. 27

8 O thou of little faith, wherefore didst thou doubt?
St Matthew ch. 14, v. 31

9 Not that which goeth into the mouth defileth a man; but that which cometh out of the mouth, this defileth a man.
St Matthew ch. 15, v. 11

10 They be blind leaders of the blind. And if the blind lead the blind, both shall fall into the ditch.
St Matthew ch. 15, v. 14

11 Truth, Lord: yet the dogs eat of the crumbs which fall from their masters' table.
St Matthew ch. 15, v. 27

12 When it is evening, ye say, It will be fair weather: for the sky is red.
St Matthew ch. 16, v. 2

13 Ye can discern the face of the sky; but can ye not discern the signs of the times?
St Matthew ch. 16, v. 3

14 Thou art Peter, and upon this rock I will build my church; and the gates of hell shall not prevail against it.
St Matthew ch. 16, v. 18

15 Get thee behind me, Satan.
St Matthew ch. 16, v. 23

16 If ye have faith as a grain of mustard seed, ye shall say unto this mountain, Remove hence to yonder place; and it shall remove.
St Matthew ch. 17, v. 20

17 Except ye be converted, and become as little children, ye shall not enter into the kingdom of heaven.
St Matthew ch. 18, v. 3

18 Whoso shall receive one such little child in my name receiveth me.
But whoso shall offend one of these little ones which believe in me, it were better for him that a millstone were hanged abut his neck, and that he were drowned in the depth of the sea.
St Matthew ch. 18, v. 5. See also St Luke ch. 17, v. 2

19 If thine eye offend thee, pluck it out, and cast it from thee: it is better for thee to enter into life with one eye, rather than having two eyes to be cast into hell fire.
St Matthew ch. 18, v. 9

20 For where two or three are gathered together in my name, there am I in the midst of them.
St Matthew ch. 18, v. 20

21 Lord, how oft shall my brother sin against me, and I forgive him? till seven times?
Jesus saith unto him I say not unto thee, Until seven times: but Until seventy times seven.
St Matthew ch. 18, v. 21

22 What therefore God hath joined together, let not man put asunder.
St Matthew ch. 19, v. 6

23 If thou wilt be perfect, go and sell that thou hast, and give to the poor, and thou shalt have treasure in heaven.
St Matthew ch. 19, v. 21

24 He went away sorrowful: for he had great possessions.
St Matthew ch. 19, v. 22

25 It is easier for a camel to go through the eye of a needle, than for a rich man to enter into the kingdom of God.
St Matthew ch. 19, v. 24. See also St Luke ch. 18, v. 24

26 With men this is impossible; but with God all things are possible.
St Matthew ch. 19, v. 26

27 But many that are first shall be last; and the last shall be first.
St Matthew ch. 19, v. 30

28 These last have wrought but one hour, and thou hast made them equal unto us, which have borne the burden and heat of the day.
St Matthew ch. 20, v. 12

29 I will give unto this last, even as unto thee.
Is it not lawful for me to do what I will with mine own?
St Matthew ch. 20, v. 14

30 It is written, My house shall be called the house of prayer; but ye have made it a den of thieves.
St Matthew ch. 21, v. 13. See Isaiah ch. 56, v. 7

1 For many are called, but few are chosen.
St Matthew ch. 22, v. 14

2 Render therefore unto Caesar the things which are Caesar's; and unto God the things that are God's.
St Matthew ch. 22, v. 21

3 For in the resurrection they neither marry, nor are given in marriage.
St Matthew ch. 22, v. 30

4 They make broad their phylacteries, and enlarge the borders of their garments,
And love the uppermost rooms at feasts, and the chief seats in the synagogues.
St Matthew ch. 23, v. 5

5 Woe unto you, scribes and Pharisees, hypocrites! for ye pay tithe of mint and anise and cummin, and have omitted the weightier matters of the law, judgement, mercy, and faith: these ought ye to have done, and not to leave the other undone.
Ye blind guides, which strain at a gnat, and swallow a camel.
St Matthew ch. 23, v. 23

6 Ye are like unto whited sepulchres, which indeed appear beautiful outward, but are within full of dead men's bones, and of all uncleanness.
St Matthew ch. 23, v. 27

7 O Jerusalem, Jerusalem, thou that killest the prophets, and stonest them which are sent unto thee, how often would I have gathered thy children together, even as a hen gathereth her chickens under her wings, and ye would not!
St Matthew ch. 23, v. 37

8 Ye shall hear of wars and rumours of wars: see that ye be not troubled: for all these things must come to pass but the end is not yet.
St Matthew ch. 24, v. 6

9 For nation shall rise against nation, and kingdom against kingdom.
St Matthew ch. 24, v. 7

10 When ye therefore shall see the abomination of desolation, spoken of by Daniel the prophet, stand in the holy place.
St Matthew ch. 24, v. 15. See Daniel ch. 12, v. 11

11 Wheresoever the carcase is, there will the eagles be gathered together.
St Matthew ch. 24, v. 28

12 Heaven and earth shall pass away, but my words shall not pass away.
St Matthew ch. 24, v. 35

13 For as in the days that were before the flood they were eating and drinking, marrying and giving in marriage, until the day that Noe entered into the ark,
And knew not until the flood came, and took them all away; so shall also the coming of the Son of Man be.
St Matthew ch. 24, v. 38

14 One shall be taken, and the other left.
St Matthew ch. 24, v. 40

15 Watch therefore: for ye know not what hour your Lord doth come.
St Matthew ch. 24, v. 42

16 Well done, thou good and faithful servant: thou hast been faithful over a few things, I will make thee a ruler over many things: enter thou into the joy of thy lord.
St Matthew ch. 25, v. 21

17 Lord, I knew thee that thou art an hard man, reaping where thou hast not sown, and gathering where thou hast not strawed.
St Matthew ch. 25, v. 24

18 Unto every one that hath shall be given, and he shall have abundance: but from him that hath not shall be taken away even that which he hath.
St Matthew ch. 25, v. 29

19 And he shall set the sheep on his right hand, but the goats on the left.
St Matthew ch. 25, v. 33

20 For I was an hungred, and ye gave me meat: I was thirsty and ye gave me drink: I was a stranger, and ye took me in:
Naked, and ye clothed me: I was sick, and ye visited me: I was in prison, and ye came unto me.
St Matthew ch. 25, v. 35

21 Inasmuch as ye have done it unto one of the least of these my brethren, ye have done it unto me.
St Matthew ch. 25, v. 40

22 There came unto him a woman having an alabaster box of very precious ointment, and poured it on his head, as he sat at meat.
But when his disciples saw it, they had indignation saying, To what purpose is this waste?
For this ointment might have been sold for much, and given to the poor.
St Matthew ch. 26, v. 7. See also St John ch. 12, v. 5

23 What will ye give me, and I will deliver him unto you? And they covenanted with him for thirty pieces of silver.
St Matthew ch. 26, v. 15

24 It had been good for that man if he had not been born.
St Matthew ch. 26, v. 24

25 Jesus took bread, and blessed it, and brake it, and gave it to the disciples, and said, Take, eat; this is my body.
St Matthew ch. 26, v. 26

26 This night, before the cock crow, thou shalt deny me thrice.
St Matthew ch. 26, v. 34

27 Though I should die with thee, yet will I not deny thee.
St Matthew ch. 26, v. 35

28 If it be possible, let this cup pass from me.
St Matthew ch. 26, v. 39

29 What, could ye not watch with me one hour?
St Matthew ch. 26, v. 40

30 Watch and pray, that ye enter not into temptation: the spirit indeed is willing but the flesh is weak.
St Matthew ch. 26, v. 41

31 Friend, wherefore art thou come?
St Matthew ch. 26, v. 50

1 All they that take the sword shall perish with the
sword.
St Matthew ch. 26, v. 52

2 Thy speech bewrayeth thee.
Then began he to curse and to swear, saying, I know
not the man. And immediately the cock crew.
St Matthew ch. 26, v. 73

3 He took water, and washed his hands before the
multitude, saying, I am innocent of the blood of this
just person: see ye to it.
St Matthew ch. 27, v. 24

4 He saved others; himself he cannot save.
St Matthew ch. 27, v. 42

5 Eli, Eli, lama sabachthani? . . . My God, my God, why
hast thou forsaken me?
St Matthew ch. 27, v. 46. Cf. Book of Common Prayer
125:9

6 And, lo, I am with you alway, even unto the end of
the world.
St Matthew ch. 28, v. 20

St Mark

7 The sabbath was made for man, and not man for the
sabbath.
St Mark ch. 2, v. 27

8 If a house be divided against itself, that house cannot
stand.
St Mark ch. 3, v. 25

9 He that hath ears to hear, let him hear.
St Mark ch. 4, v. 9

10 With what measure ye mete, it shall be measured to
you.
St Mark ch. 4, v. 24

11 My name is Legion: for we are many.
St Mark ch. 5, v. 9

12 Jesus, immediately knowing in himself that virtue had
gone out of him, turned him about in the press, and
said, Who touched my clothes?
St Mark ch. 5, v. 30

13 I see men as trees, walking.
St Mark ch. 8, v. 24

14 For what shall it profit a man, if he shall gain the
whole world, and lose his own soul?
St Mark ch. 8, v. 36. See also St Matthew ch. 16, v. 26

15 Lord, I believe; help thou mine unbelief.
St Mark ch. 9, v. 24

16 Suffer the little children to come unto me, and forbid
them not: for of such is the kingdom of God.
St Mark ch. 10, v. 14

17 Beware of the scribes, which love to go in long
clothing, and love salutations in the marketplaces,
And the chief seats in the synagogues, and the
uppermost rooms at feasts:
Which devour widows' houses, and for a pretence
make long prayers.
St Mark ch. 12, v. 38

18 And there came a certain poor widow, and she threw
in two mites.
St Mark ch. 12, v. 42

19 Watch ye therefore: for ye know not when the master
of the house cometh . . . Lest coming suddenly he
find you sleeping.
St Mark ch. 13, v. 35

20 Go ye into all the world, and preach the gospel to
every creature.
St Mark ch. 16, v. 15

St Luke

21 Hail, thou that art highly favoured, the Lord is with
thee: blessed art thou among women.
St Luke ch. 1, v. 28

22 And Mary said,
My soul doth magnify the Lord,
And my spirit hath rejoiced in God my Saviour.
For he hath regarded the low estate of his
handmaiden: for, behold, from henceforth all
generations shall call me blessed.
St Luke ch. 1, v. 46 ('Tell out my soul, the greatness of the
Lord' in *New English Bible*). Cf. Vulgate 108:9

23 He hath shewed strength with his arm; he hath
scattered the proud in the imagination of their
hearts.
He hath put down the mighty from their seats, and
exalted them of low degree.
He hath filled the hungry with good things; and the
rich he hath sent empty away.
St Luke ch. 1, v. 51. Cf. Vulgate 108:10

24 To give light to them that sit in darkness and in the
shadow of death, to guide our feet into the way of
peace.
St Luke ch. 1, v. 79

25 And it came to pass in those days, that there went out
a decree from Caesar Augustus, that all the world
should be taxed.
St Luke ch. 2, v. 1

26 She brought forth her firstborn son, and wrapped him
in swaddling clothes, and laid him in a manger;
because there was no room for them in the inn.
And there were in the same country shepherds
abiding in the field, keeping watch over their flock
by night.
And, lo, the angel of the Lord came upon them, and
the glory of the Lord shone round about them: and
they were sore afraid.
St Luke ch. 2, v. 7

27 Behold, I bring you good tidings of great joy.
St Luke ch. 2, v. 10

28 Glory to God in the highest, and on earth peace, good
will toward men.
St Luke ch. 2, v. 14

29 Lord, now lettest thou thy servant depart in peace,
according to thy word.
St Luke ch. 2, v. 29. Cf. Vulgate 108:11

30 Wist ye not that I must be about my Father's
business?
St Luke ch. 2, v. 49

31 Jesus increased in wisdom and stature, and in favour
with God and man.
St Luke ch. 2, v. 52

1 And the devil, taking him up into a high mountain, shewed unto him all the kingdoms of the world in a moment of time.
St Luke ch. 4, v. 5

2 Physician, heal thyself.
St Luke ch. 4, v. 23

3 Master, we have toiled all the night, and have taken nothing: nevertheless at thy word I will let down the net.
St Luke ch. 5, v. 5

4 No man . . . having drunk old wine straightway desireth new: for he saith, The old is better.
St Luke ch. 5, v. 39

5 Woe unto you, when all men shall speak well of you!
St Luke ch. 6, v. 26

6 Love your enemies, do good to them which hate you.
St Luke ch. 6, v. 27

7 Give, and it shall be given unto you; good measure, pressed down, and shaken together, and running over, shall men give into your bosom.
St Luke ch. 6, v. 38

8 Her sins, which are many, are forgiven; for she loved much.
St Luke ch. 7, v. 47

9 No man, having put his hand to the plough, and looking back, is fit for the kingdom of God.
St Luke ch. 9, v. 62

10 For the labourer is worthy of his hire.
St Luke ch. 10, v. 7

11 I beheld Satan as lightning fall from heaven.
St Luke ch. 10, v. 18

12 Blessed are the eyes which see the things which ye see:
For I tell you, that many prophets and kings have desired to see those things which ye see, and have not seen them; and to hear those things which ye hear, and have not heard them.
St Luke ch. 10, v. 23

13 A certain man went down from Jerusalem to Jericho, and fell among thieves.
St Luke ch. 10, v. 30

14 He passed by on the other side.
St Luke ch. 10, v. 31

15 He took out two pence, and gave them to the host, and said unto him, Take care of him; and whatsoever thou spend more, when I come again, I will repay thee.
St Luke ch. 10, v. 35

16 Go, and do thou likewise.
St Luke ch. 10, v. 37

17 But Martha was cumbered about much serving, and came to him, and said, Lord, dost thou not care that my sister hath left me to serve alone? bid her therefore that she help me.
St Luke ch. 10, v. 40

18 But one thing is needful: and Mary hath chosen that good part, which shall not be taken away from her.
St Luke ch. 10, v. 42

19 When a strong man armed keepeth his palace, his goods are in peace. But when a stronger than he shall come upon him, and overcome him, he taketh from him all his armour wherein he trusted, and divideth his spoils.
St Luke ch. 11, v. 21

20 No man, when he hath lighted a candle, putteth it in a secret place, neither under a bushel, but on a candlestick, that they which come in may see the light.
St Luke ch. 11, v. 33

21 Woe unto you, lawyers! for ye have taken away the key of knowledge.
St Luke ch. 11, v. 52

22 Are not five sparrows sold for two farthings, and not one of them is forgotten before God?
St Luke ch. 12, v. 6. See also St Matthew ch. 10, v. 29

23 Soul, thou hast much goods laid up for many years; take thine ease, eat, drink, and be merry.
St Luke ch. 12, v. 19. Cf. Ecclesiastes 80:17, Isaiah 83:7, I Corinthians 101:9

24 Thou fool, this night thy soul shall be required of thee.
St Luke ch. 12, v. 20

25 Let your loins be girded about, and your lights burning.
St Luke ch. 12, v. 35

26 When thou art bidden of any man to a wedding, sit not down in the highest room; lest a more honourable man than thou be bidden of him;
And he that bade thee and him come and say to thee, Give this man place; and thou begin with shame to take the lowest room.
St Luke ch. 14, v. 8

27 Friend, go up higher.
St Luke ch. 14, v. 10

28 For whosoever exalteth himself shall be abased; and he that humbleth himself shall be exalted.
St Luke ch. 14, v. 11. See also St Matthew ch. 23, v. 12

29 They all with one consent began to make excuse . . . I pray thee have me excused.
St Luke ch. 14, v. 18

30 I have married a wife, and therefore I cannot come.
St Luke ch. 14, v. 20

31 Go out quickly into the streets and lanes of the city, and bring in hither the poor, and the maimed, and the halt, and the blind.
St Luke ch. 14, v. 21

32 Go out into the highways and hedges, and compel them to come in.
St Luke ch. 14, v. 23

33 For which of you, intending to build a tower, sitteth not down first, and counteth the cost, whether he have sufficient to finish it?
St Luke ch. 14, v. 28

34 Leave the ninety and nine in the wilderness.
St Luke ch. 15, v. 4

35 Rejoice with me; for I have found my sheep which was lost.
St Luke ch. 15, v. 6

1 Joy shall be in heaven over one sinner that repenteth, more than over ninety and nine just persons, which need no repentance.
St Luke ch. 15, v. 7

2 The younger son gathered all together, and took his journey into a far country, and there wasted his substance with riotous living.
St Luke ch. 15, v. 13

3 He would fain have filled his belly with the husks that the swine did eat: and no man gave unto him.
And when he came to himself, he said, How many hired servants of my father's have bread enough and to spare, and I perish with hunger!
I will arise and go to my father, and will say unto him, Father, I have sinned against heaven, and before thee,
And am no more worthy to be called thy son: make me as one of thy hired servants.
St Luke ch. 15, v. 16

4 Bring hither the fatted calf, and kill it.
St Luke ch. 15, v. 23

5 This my son was dead, and is alive again; he was lost, and is found.
St Luke ch. 15, v. 24

6 And the Lord commended the unjust steward, because he had done wisely: for the children of this world are in their generation wiser than the children of light.
St Luke ch. 16, v. 8

7 Make to yourselves friends of the mammon of unrighteousness; that, when ye fail, they may receive you into everlasting habitations.
St Luke ch. 16, v. 9

8 He that is faithful in that which is least is faithful also in much.
St Luke ch. 16, v. 10

9 There was a certain rich man, which was clothed in purple and fine linen, and fared sumptuously every day:
And there was a certain beggar named Lazarus, which was laid at his gate, full of sores,
And desiring to be fed with the crumbs which fell from the rich man's table: moreover the dogs licked his sores.
And it came to pass that the beggar died, and was carried by the angels into Abraham's bosom.
St Luke ch. 16, v. 19

10 Between us and you there is a great gulf fixed.
St Luke ch. 16, v. 26

11 The kingdom of God is within you.
St Luke ch. 17, v. 21

12 Remember Lot's wife.
St Luke ch. 17, v. 32

13 Men ought always to pray, and not to faint.
St Luke ch. 18, v. 1

14 God, I thank thee, that I am not as other men are.
St Luke ch. 18, v. 11

15 God be merciful to me a sinner.
St Luke ch. 18, v. 13

16 Out of thine own mouth will I judge thee, thou wicked servant. Thou knewest that I was an austere man.
St Luke ch. 19, v. 22

17 If these should hold their peace, the stones would immediately cry out.
St Luke ch. 19, v. 40

18 If thou hadst known, even thou, at least in this thy day, the things which belong unto thy peace! but now they are hid from thine eyes.
St Luke ch. 19, v. 42

19 And when they heard it, they said, God forbid.
St Luke ch. 20, v. 16

20 He shall show you a large upper room furnished.
St Luke ch. 22, v. 12

21 I am among you as he that serveth.
St Luke ch. 22, v. 27

22 Nevertheless, not my will, but thine, be done.
St Luke ch. 22, v. 42

23 And the Lord turned, and looked upon Peter.
St Luke ch. 22, v. 61

24 For if they do these things in a green tree, what shall be done in the dry?
St Luke ch. 23, v. 31

25 Father, forgive them: for they know not what they do.
St Luke ch. 23, v. 34

26 Lord, remember me when thou comest into thy kingdom.
St Luke ch. 23, v. 42

27 To day shalt thou be with me in paradise.
St Luke ch. 23, v. 43

28 Father, into thy hands I commend my spirit.
St Luke ch. 23, v. 46. Cf. Book of Common Prayer 126:7

29 He was a good man, and a just.
St Luke ch. 23, v. 50

30 Why seek ye the living among the dead?
St Luke ch. 24, v. 5

31 Their words seemed to them as idle tales.
St Luke ch. 24, v. 11

32 Did not our heart burn within us, while he talked with us by the way?
St Luke ch. 24, v. 32

33 He was known of them in breaking of bread.
St Luke ch. 24, v. 35

34 They gave him a piece of a broiled fish, and of an honeycomb.
St Luke ch. 24, v. 42

St John

35 In the beginning was the Word, and the Word was with God, and the Word was God.
St John ch. 1, v. 1

36 All things were made by him; and without him was not any thing made that was made.
St John ch. 1, v. 3

37 And the light shineth in darkness; and the darkness comprehended it not.
St John ch. 1, v. 5

1 There was a man sent from God, whose name was John.
St John ch. 1, v. 6

2 He was not that Light, but was sent to bear witness of that Light.
That was the true Light, which lighteth every man that cometh into the world.
St John ch. 1, v. 8

3 He was in the world, and the world was made by him, and the world knew him not.
He came unto his own, and his own received him not.
St John ch. 1, v. 10

4 And the Word was made flesh, and dwelt among us, (and we beheld his glory, the glory as of the only begotten of the Father), full of grace and truth.
St John ch. 1, v. 14

5 No man hath seen God at any time.
St John ch. 1, v. 18. See also I John ch. 4, v. 12

6 I baptize with water: but there standeth one among you, whom ye know not;
He it is, who coming after me is preferred before me, whose shoe's latchet I am not worthy to unloose.
St John ch. 1, v. 26

7 Behold the Lamb of God, which taketh away the sin of the world.
St John ch. 1, v. 29

8 Can there any good thing come out of Nazareth?
St John ch. 1, v. 46

9 Behold an Israelite indeed, in whom is no guile!
St John ch. 1, v. 47

10 Woman, what have I to do with thee? mine hour is not yet come.
St John ch. 2, v. 4

11 Every man at the beginning doth set forth good wine; and when men have well drunk, then that which is worse: but thou hast kept the good wine until now.
St John ch. 2, v. 10

12 When he had made a scourge of small cords, he drove them all out of the temple.
St John ch. 2, v. 15

13 Verily, verily, I say unto thee, Except a man be born again, he cannot see the kingdom of God.
St John ch. 3, v. 3

14 The wind bloweth where it listeth, and thou hearest the sound thereof, but canst not tell whence it cometh, and whither it goeth.
St John ch. 3, v. 8

15 God so loved the world, that he gave his only begotten Son, that whosoever believeth in him should not perish, but have everlasting life.
St John ch. 3, v. 16

16 Men loved darkness rather than light, because their deeds were evil.
St John ch. 3, v. 19

17 God is a Spirit: and they that worship him must worship him in spirit and in truth.
St John ch. 4, v. 24

18 Except ye see signs and wonders, ye will not believe.
St John ch. 4, v. 48

19 Rise, take up thy bed, and walk.
St John ch. 5, v. 8

20 He was a burning and a shining light.
St John ch. 5, v. 35

21 Search the scriptures; for in them ye think ye have eternal life: and they are which testify of me.
St John ch. 5, v. 39

22 There is a lad here, which hath five barley loaves, and two small fishes: but what are they among so many?
St John ch. 6, v. 9

23 Gather up the fragments that remain, that nothing be lost.
St John ch. 6, v. 12

24 Verily, verily, I say unto you . . . my Father giveth you the true bread from heaven.
For the bread of God is he which cometh down from heaven, and giveth life to the world.
St John ch. 6, v. 32

25 I am the bread of life: he that cometh to me shall never hunger; and he that believeth on me shall never thirst.
St John ch. 6, v. 35

26 Him that cometh to me I will in no wise cast out.
St John ch. 6, v. 37

27 Verily, verily, I say unto you, He that believeth on me hath everlasting life.
St John ch. 6, v. 47

28 It is the spirit that quickeneth.
St John ch. 6, v. 63

29 And the scribes and the Pharisees brought unto him a woman taken in adultery.
St John ch. 8, v. 3

30 He that is without sin among you, let him first cast a stone at her.
St John ch. 8, v. 7

31 Neither do I condemn thee: go, and sin no more.
St John ch. 8, v. 11

32 And ye shall know the truth, and the truth shall make you free.
St John ch. 8, v. 32

33 Ye are of your father the devil, and the lusts of your father ye will do. He was a murderer from the beginning, and abode not in the truth, because there is no truth in him. When he speaketh a lie, he speaketh of his own: for he is a liar, and the father of it.
St John ch. 8, v. 44

34 The night cometh, when no man can work.
St John ch. 9, v. 4

35 He is of age; ask him: he shall speak for himself.
St John ch. 9, v. 21

36 One thing I know, that, whereas I was blind, now I see.
St John ch. 9, v. 25

37 I am the door.
St John ch. 10, v. 9

38 I am the good shepherd: the good shepherd giveth his life for the sheep.
St John ch. 10, v. 11

1 The hireling fleeth, because he is an hireling, and
   careth not for the sheep.
   St John ch. 10, v. 13

2 Other sheep I have, which are not of this fold.
   St John ch. 10, v. 16

3 Though ye believe not me, believe the works.
   St John ch. 10, v. 38

4 I am the resurrection, and the life.
   St John ch. 11, v. 25

5 Jesus wept.
   St John ch. 11, v. 35

6 Ye know nothing at all,
   Nor consider that it is expedient for us, that one man
   should die for the people, and that the whole nation
   perish not.
   St John ch. 11, v. 49

7 The poor always ye have with you.
   St John ch. 12, v. 8

8 Lord, dost thou wash my feet?
   St John ch. 13, v. 6

9 That thou doest, do quickly.
   St John ch. 13, v. 27

10 Let not your heart be troubled: ye believe in God,
   believe also in me.
   St John ch. 14, v. 1

11 In my Father's house are many mansions . . . I go to
   prepare a place for you.
   St John ch. 14, v. 2

12 I am the way, the truth, and the life: no man cometh
   unto the Father, but by me.
   St John ch. 14, v. 6

13 Have I been so long time with you, and yet hast thou
   not known me, Philip?
   St John ch. 14, v. 9

14 Judas saith unto him, not Iscariot.
   St John ch. 14, v. 22

15 Peace I leave with you, my peace I give unto you: not
   as the world giveth, give I unto you.
   St John ch. 14, v. 27

16 Greater love hath no man than this, that a man lay
   down his life for his friends.
   St John ch. 15, v. 13

17 Ye have not chosen me, but I have chosen you.
   St John ch. 15, v. 16

18 It is expedient for you that I go away: for if I go not
   away, the Comforter will not come unto you.
   St John ch. 16, v. 7

19 I have yet many things to say unto you, but ye
   cannot bear them now.
   St John ch. 16, v. 12

20 A little while, and ye shall not see me: and again, a
   little while, and ye shall see me, because I go to the
   Father.
   St John ch. 16, v. 16

21 In the world ye shall have tribulation: but be of good
   cheer; I have overcome the world.
   St John ch. 16, v. 33

22 While I was with them in the world, I kept them in
   thy name: those that thou gavest me I have kept,
   and none of them is lost but the son of perdition.
   St John ch. 17, v. 12

23 Put up thy sword into the sheath.
   St John ch. 18, v. 11

24 Pilate saith unto him, What is truth?
   St John ch. 18, v. 38

25 Now Barabbas was a robber.
   St John ch. 18, v. 40

26 What I have written I have written.
   St John ch. 19, v. 22

27 Woman, behold thy son! . . .
   Behold thy mother!
   St John ch. 19, v. 26

28 I thirst.
   St John ch. 19, v. 28

29 It is finished.
   St John ch. 19, v. 30. Cf. Vulgate 108:15

30 The first day of the week cometh Mary Magdalene
   early, when it was yet dark, unto the sepulchre,
   and seeth the stone taken away from the sepulchre.
   St John ch. 20, v. 1

31 So they ran both together: and the other disciple did
   outrun Peter, and came first to the sepulchre.
   St John ch. 20, v. 4

32 They have taken away my Lord, and I know not
   where they have laid him.
   St John ch. 20, v. 13

33 Jesus saith unto her, Woman, why weepest thou?
   whom seekest thou? She supposing him to be the
   gardener saith unto him, Sir, if thou have borne
   him hence, tell me where thou hast laid him, and I
   will take him away.
   St John ch. 20, v. 15

34 Touch me not.
   St John ch. 20, v. 17. Cf. Vulgate 108:16

35 Except I shall see in his hands the print of the nails,
   and put my finger into the print of the nails, and
   thrust my hand into his side, I will not believe.
   St John ch. 20, v. 25

36 Be not faithless, but believing.
   St John ch. 20, v. 27

37 Thomas answered and said unto him, My Lord and
   my God.
   St John ch. 20, v. 28

38 Thomas, because thou hast seen me, thou hast
   believed: blessed are they that have not seen, and
   yet have believed.
   St John ch. 20, v. 29

39 Simon Peter saith unto them, I go a fishing.
   St John ch. 21, v. 3

40 Simon, son of Jonas, lovest thou me more than these?
   . . . Feed my lambs.
   St John ch. 21, v. 15

41 Feed my sheep.
   St John ch. 21, v. 16

1 Lord, thou knowest all things; thou knowest that I love thee.
St John ch. 21, v. 17

2 When thou wast young, thou girdedst thyself, and walkedst whither thou wouldest: but when thou shalt be old, thou shalt stretch forth thy hands, and another shall gird thee, and carry thee whither thou wouldest not.
St John ch. 21, v. 18

3 Peter, turning about, seeth the disciple whom Jesus loved following; which also leaned on his breast at supper, and said Lord, which is he that betrayeth thee?
St John ch. 21, v. 20

4 What shall this man do?
Jesus saith unto him, If I will that he tarry till I come, what is that to thee?
St John ch. 21, v. 21

Acts of the Apostles

5 Ye men of Galilee, why stand ye gazing up into heaven?
Acts of the Apostles ch. 1, v. 11

6 And suddenly there came a sound from heaven as of a rushing mighty wind, and it filled all the house where they were sitting.
And there appeared unto them cloven tongues like as of fire.
Acts of the Apostles ch. 2, v. 2

7 Parthians, and Medes, and Elamites, and the dwellers in Mesopotamia, and in Judaea, and Cappadocia, in Pontus, and Asia,
Phrygia, and Pamphylia, in Egypt, and in the parts of Libya about Cyrene, and strangers of Rome, Jews and proselytes,
Cretes and Arabians, we do hear them speak in our tongues the wonderful works of God.
Acts of the Apostles ch. 2, v. 9

8 And all that believed were together, and had all things common.
Acts of the Apostles ch. 2, v. 44

9 Silver and gold have I none; but such as I have give I thee.
Acts of the Apostles ch. 3, v. 6

10 Walking, and leaping, and praising God.
Acts of the Apostles ch. 3, v. 8

11 It is not reason that we should leave the word of God, and serve tables.
Acts of the Apostles ch. 6, v. 2

12 The witnesses laid down their clothes at a young man's feet, whose name was Saul.
Acts of the Apostles ch. 7, v. 58

13 Saul was consenting unto his death.
Acts of the Apostles ch. 8, v. 1

14 Thy money perish with thee, because thou hast thought that the gift of God may be purchased with money.
Acts of the Apostles ch. 8, v. 20

15 Saul, Saul, why persecutest thou me?
Acts of the Apostles ch. 9, v. 4

16 It is hard for thee to kick against the pricks.
Acts of the Apostles ch. 9, v. 5

17 The street which is called Straight.
Acts of the Apostles ch. 9, v. 11

18 Dorcas: this woman was full of good works.
Acts of the Apostles ch. 9, v. 36

19 He fell into a trance,
And saw heaven opened, and a certain vessel descending unto him, as it had been a great sheet knit at the four corners, and let down to the earth:
Wherein were all manner of four-footed beasts of the earth, and wild beasts, and creeping things, and fowls of the air.
Acts of the Apostles ch. 10, v. 10

20 What God hath cleansed, that call not thou common.
Acts of the Apostles ch. 10, v. 15

21 God is no respecter of persons.
Acts of the Apostles ch. 10, v. 34. See also Romans ch. 2, v. 11

22 He was eaten of worms, and gave up the ghost.
Acts of the Apostles ch. 12, v. 23

23 The gods are come down to us in the likeness of men.
Acts of the Apostles ch. 14, v. 11

24 We also are men of like passions with you.
Acts of the Apostles ch. 14, v. 15

25 Come over into Macedonia, and help us.
Acts of the Apostles ch. 16, v. 9

26 What must I do to be saved?
Acts of the Apostles ch. 16, v. 30

27 The Jews which believed not, moved with envy, took unto them certain lewd fellows of the baser sort, and gathered a company, and set all the city on an uproar.
Acts of the Apostles ch. 17, v. 5

28 Those that have turned the world upside down are come hither also;
Whom Jason hath received: and these all do contrary to the decrees of Caesar, saying that there is another king, one Jesus.
Acts of the Apostles ch. 17, v. 6

29 What will this babbler say?
Acts of the Apostles ch. 17, v. 18

30 For all the Athenians and strangers which were there spent their time in nothing else, but either to tell, or to hear some new thing.
Acts of the Apostles ch. 17, v. 21

31 Ye men of Athens, I perceive that in all things ye are too superstitious.
For as I passed by, and beheld your devotions, I found an altar with this inscription, TO THE UNKNOWN GOD. Whom therefore ye ignorantly worship, him declare I unto you.
Acts of the Apostles ch. 17, v. 22

32 God that made the world and all things therein, seeing that he is Lord of Heaven and earth, dwelleth not in temples made with hands.
Acts of the Apostles ch. 17, v. 24

33 For in him we live, and move, and have our being.
Acts of the Apostles ch. 17, v. 28

1 We have not so much as heard whether there be any Holy Ghost.
Acts of the Apostles ch. 19, v. 2

2 All with one voice about the space of two hours cried out, Great is Diana of the Ephesians.
Acts of the Apostles ch. 19, v. 34

3 I go bound in the spirit unto Jerusalem.
Acts of the Apostles ch. 20, v. 22

4 It is more blessed to give than to receive.
Acts of the Apostles ch. 20, v. 35

5 But Paul said, I am a man which am a Jew of Tarsus, a city in Cilicia, a citizen of no mean city.
Acts of the Apostles ch. 21, v. 39

6 And the chief captain answered, With a great sum obtained I this freedom. And Paul said, But I was free born.
Acts of the Apostles ch. 22, v. 28

7 A conscience void of offence toward God, and toward men.
Acts of the Apostles ch. 24, v. 16

8 I appeal unto Caesar.
Acts of the Apostles ch. 25, v. 11

9 Hast thou appealed unto Caesar? unto Caesar shalt thou go.
Acts of the Apostles ch. 25, v. 12

10 Paul, thou art beside thyself; much learning doth make thee mad.
Acts of the Apostles ch. 26, v. 24

11 For this thing was not done in a corner.
Acts of the Apostles ch. 26, v. 26

12 Almost thou persuadest me to be a Christian.
Acts of the Apostles ch. 26, v. 28

13 I would to God, that not only thou, but also all that hear me this day, were both almost, and altogether such as I am, except these bonds.
Acts of the Apostles ch. 26, v. 29

Romans

14 Without ceasing I make mention of you always in my prayers.
Romans ch. 1, v. 9

15 I am debtor both to the Greeks, and to the Barbarians; both to the wise, and to the unwise.
Romans ch. 1, v. 14

16 The just shall live by faith.
Romans ch. 1, v. 17

17 Worshipped and served the creature more than the Creator.
Romans ch. 1, v. 25

18 Patient continuance in well doing.
Romans ch. 2, v. 7

19 A law unto themselves.
Romans ch. 2, v. 14

20 Let God be true, but every man a liar.
Romans ch. 3, v. 4

21 Let us do evil, that good may come.
Romans ch. 3, v. 8

22 For all have sinned, and come short of the glory of God.
Romans ch. 3, v. 23

23 For where no law is, there is no transgression.
Romans ch. 4, v. 15

24 Who against hope believed in hope, that he might become the father of many nations.
Romans ch. 4, v. 18 (on Abraham)

25 Hope maketh not ashamed; because the love of God is shed abroad in our hearts by the Holy Ghost which is given unto us.
Romans ch. 5, v. 5

26 Where sin abounded, grace did much more abound.
Romans ch. 5, v. 20

27 Shall we continue in sin, that grace may abound? God forbid. How shall we, that are dead to sin, live any longer in sin?
Romans ch. 6, v. 1

28 We also should walk in newness of life.
Romans ch. 6, v. 4

29 Christ being raised from the dead dieth no more; death hath no more dominion over him.
For in that he died, he died unto sin once: but in that he liveth, he liveth unto God.
Romans ch. 6, v. 9

30 The wages of sin is death.
Romans ch. 6, v. 23

31 Is the law sin? God forbid. Nay, I had not known sin, but by the law.
Romans ch. 7, v. 7

32 For the good that I would I do not: but the evil which I would not, that I do.
Romans ch. 7, v. 19. Cf. Ovid 502:24

33 O wretched man that I am! who shall deliver me from the body of this death?
Romans ch. 7, v. 24

34 They that are after the flesh do mind the things of the flesh; but they that are after the Spirit the things of the Spirit.
For to be carnally minded is death.
Romans ch. 8, v. 5

35 For ye have not received the spirit of bondage again to fear; but ye have received the Spirit of adoption, whereby we cry, Abba, Father.
Romans ch. 8, v. 15

36 We are the children of God:
And if the children, then heirs; heirs of God, and joint-heirs with Christ.
Romans ch. 8, v. 16

37 For we know that the whole creation groaneth and travaileth in pain together until now.
Romans ch. 8, v. 22

38 All things work together for good to them that love God.
Romans ch. 8, v. 28

39 If God be for us, who can be against us?
Romans ch. 8, v. 31

1 For I am persuaded, that neither death, nor life, nor angels, nor principalities, nor powers, nor things present, nor things to come,

Nor height, nor depth, nor any other creature, shall be able to separate us from the love of God, which is in Christ Jesus our Lord.
Romans ch. 8, v. 38

2 Shall the thing formed say to him that formed it, Why hast thou made me thus?

Hath not the potter power over the clay, of the same lump to make one vessel unto honour, and another unto dishonour?
Romans ch. 9, v. 20

3 I beseech you therefore, brethren, by the mercies of God, that ye present your bodies a living sacrifice, holy, acceptable unto God.
Romans ch. 12, v. 1

4 Rejoice with them that do rejoice, and weep with them that weep.
Romans ch. 12, v. 15

5 Mind not high things, but condescend to men of low estate. Be not wise in your own conceits.
Romans ch. 12, v. 16

6 Vengeance is mine; I will repay, saith the Lord.
Romans ch. 12, v. 19

7 Be not overcome of evil, but overcome evil with good.
Romans ch. 12, v. 21

8 Let every soul be subject unto the higher powers . . . the powers that be are ordained of God.
Romans ch. 13, v. 1

9 Render therefore to all their dues: tribute to whom tribute is due; custom to whom custom; fear to whom fear; honour to whom honour.

Owe no man anything, but to love one another: for he that loveth another hath fulfilled the law.
Romans ch. 13, v. 7

10 Now it is high time to awake out of sleep: for now is our salvation nearer than when we believed.

The night is far spent, the day is at hand: let us therefore cast off the works of darkness, and let us put on the armour of light.
Romans ch. 13, v. 11

11 Make not provision for the flesh, to fulfil the lusts thereof.
Romans ch. 13, v. 14

12 Doubtful disputations.
Romans ch. 14, v. 1

13 Let every man be fully persuaded in his own mind.
Romans ch. 14, v. 5

14 Salute one another with an holy kiss.
Romans ch. 16, v. 16

I Corinthians

15 The foolishness of preaching to save them that believe.
I Corinthians ch. 1, v. 21

16 God hath chosen the foolish things of the world to confound the wise; and God hath chosen the weak things of the world to confound the things which are mighty.
I Corinthians ch. 1, v. 27

17 I have planted, Apollos watered; but God gave the increase.
I Corinthians ch. 3, v. 6

18 Stewards of the mysteries of God.
I Corinthians ch. 4, v. 1

19 We are made a spectacle unto the world, and to angels.
I Corinthians ch. 4, v. 9

20 Absent in body, but present in spirit.
I Corinthians ch. 5, v. 3

21 Know ye not that a little leaven leaveneth the whole lump?
I Corinthians ch. 5, v. 6

22 Christ our passover is sacrificed for us:

Therefore let us keep the feast, not with the old leaven, neither with the leaven of malice and wickedness; but with the unleavened bread of sincerity and truth.
I Corinthians ch. 5, v. 7

23 Your body is the temple of the Holy Ghost.
I Corinthians ch. 6, v. 19

24 It is better to marry than to burn.
I Corinthians ch. 7, v. 9

25 The unbelieving husband is sanctified by the wife.
I Corinthians ch. 7, v. 14

26 The fashion of this world passeth away.
I Corinthians ch. 7, v. 31

27 Knowledge puffeth up, but charity edifieth.
I Corinthians ch. 8, v. 1

28 Who goeth a warfare any time at his own charges? who planteth a vineyard, and eateth not of the fruit thereof?
I Corinthians ch. 9, v. 7

29 I am made all things to all men.
I Corinthians ch. 9, v. 22

30 Know ye not that they which run in a race run all, but one receiveth the prize?
I Corinthians ch. 9, v. 24

31 Now they do it to obtain a corruptible crown; but we an incorruptible.

I therefore so run, not as uncertainly; so fight I, not as one that beateth the air.

But I keep under my body, and bring it into subjection; lest that by any means, when I have preached to others, I myself should be a castaway.
I Corinthians ch. 9, v. 25

32 All things are lawful for me, but all things are not expedient.
I Corinthians ch. 10, v. 23

33 For the earth is the Lord's and the fulness thereof.
I Corinthians ch. 10, v. 26. Cf. Book of Common Prayer 125:16

34 Doth not even nature itself teach you, that if a man have long hair, it is a shame unto him?

But if a woman have long hair, it is a glory to her.
I Corinthians ch. 11, v. 14

35 Now there are diversities of gifts, but the same Spirit.
I Corinthians ch. 12, v. 4

1 Though I speak with the tongues of men and of
angels, and have not charity, I am become as
sounding brass, or a tinkling cymbal.
And though I have the gift of prophecy, and
understand all mysteries, and all knowledge; and
though I have all faith; so that I could remove
mountains; and have not charity, I am nothing.
And though I bestow all my goods to feed the poor,
and though I give my body to be burned, and have
not charity, it profiteth me nothing.
Charity suffereth long, and is kind; charity envieth
not; charity vaunteth not itself, is not puffed up,
Doth not behave itself unseemly, seeketh not her own,
is not easily provoked, thinketh no evil;
Rejoiceth not in iniquity, but rejoiceth in the truth;
Beareth all things, believeth all things, hopeth all
things, endureth all things.
Charity never faileth: but whether there be
prophecies, they shall fail; whether there be
tongues; they shall cease; whether there be
knowledge, it shall vanish away.
For we know in part, and we prophesy in part.
But when that which is perfect is come, then that
which is in part shall be done away.
When I was a child, I spake as a child, I understood as
a child, I thought as a child: but when I became a
man, I put away childish things.
For now we see through a glass, darkly; but then face
to face: now I know in part; but then shall I know
even as also I am known.
And now abideth faith, hope, charity, these three; but
the greatest of these is charity.
I Corinthians ch. 13, v. 1

2 If the trumpet give an uncertain sound, who shall
prepare himself to the battle?
I Corinthians ch. 14, v. 8

3 Let all things be done decently and in order.
I Corinthians ch. 14, v. 40

4 Last of all he was seen of me also, as of one born out
of due time.
For I am the least of the apostles, that am not meet to
be called an apostle, because I persecuted the
church of God.
But by the grace of God I am what I am.
I Corinthians ch. 15, v. 8

5 I laboured more abundantly than they all: yet not I,
but the grace of God which was with me.
I Corinthians ch. 15, v. 10

6 If in this life only we have hope in Christ, we are of all
men most miserable.
I Corinthians ch. 15, v. 19

7 But now is Christ risen from the dead, and become the
first fruits of them that slept.
For since by man came death, by man came also the
resurrection of the dead.
For as in Adam all die, even so in Christ shall all be
made alive.
I Corinthians ch. 15, v. 20

8 The last enemy that shall be destroyed is death.
I Corinthians ch. 15, v. 26

9 If after the manner of men I have fought with beasts
at Ephesus, what advantageth it me, if the dead rise
not? let us eat and drink; for to morrow we die.
I Corinthians ch. 15, v. 32. Cf. Ecclesiastes 80:17, Isaiah
83:7, St Luke 94:23

10 Evil communications corrupt good manners.
I Corinthians ch. 15, v. 33

11 One star differeth from another star in glory.
I Corinthians ch. 15, v. 41

12 So also is the resurrection of the dead. It is sown in
corruption; it is raised in incorruption.
I Corinthians ch. 15, v. 42

13 The first man is of the earth, earthy.
I Corinthians ch. 15, v. 47

14 Behold, I shew you a mystery; We shall not all sleep,
but we shall all be changed,
In a moment, in the twinkling of an eye, at the last
trump; for the trumpet shall sound, and the dead
shall be raised incorruptible, and we shall be
changed.
For this corruptible must put on incorruption, and this
mortal must put on immortality.
I Corinthians ch. 15, v. 51

15 O death, where is thy sting? O grave, where is thy
victory?
I Corinthians ch. 15, v. 55

II Corinthians

16 Our sufficiency is of God;
Who also hath made us able ministers of the new
testament; not of the letter, but of the spirit: for the
letter killeth, but the spirit giveth life.
II Corinthians ch. 3, v. 5

17 We have this treasure in earthen vessels.
II Corinthians ch. 4, v. 7

18 We know that if our earthly house of this tabernacle
were dissolved, we have a building of God, an house
not made with hands, eternal in the heavens.
II Corinthians ch. 5, v. 1

19 For he saith, I have found thee in a time accepted, and
in the day of salvation have I succoured thee:
behold, now is the accepted time; behold, now is
the day of salvation.
II Corinthians ch. 6, v. 2

20 As having nothing, and yet possessing all things.
II Corinthians ch. 6, v. 10

21 God loveth a cheerful giver.
II Corinthians ch. 9, v. 7

22 For ye suffer fools gladly, seeing ye yourselves are
wise.
II Corinthians ch. 9, v. 19

23 Are they Hebrews? so am I. Are they Israelites? so am
I. Are they the seed of Abraham? so am I.
Are they ministers of Christ? (I speak as a fool) I am
more.
II Corinthians ch. 11, v. 22

1 Of the Jews five times received I forty stripes save one.
Thrice was I beaten with rods, once was I stoned, thrice I suffered shipwreck, a night and a day have I been in the deep;
In journeyings often, in perils of waters, in perils of robbers, in perils by mine own countrymen, in perils by the heathen, in perils of the city, in perils in the wilderness, in perils in the sea, in perils among false brethren;
In weariness and painfulness, in watchings often, in hunger and thirst, in fastings often, in cold and nakedness.
Beside those things that are without, that which cometh upon me daily, the care of all the churches.
II Corinthians ch. 11, v. 24

2 There was given to me a thorn in the flesh, the messenger of Satan to buffet me.
II Corinthians ch. 12, v. 7

3 My strength is made perfect in weakness.
II Corinthians ch. 12, v. 9

Galatians

4 The right hands of fellowship.
Galatians ch. 2, v. 9

5 It is written, that Abraham had two sons, the one by a bondmaid, the other by a freewoman.
But he who was of the bondwoman was born after the flesh; but he of the freewoman was by promise.
Which things are an allegory.
Galatians ch. 4, v. 22

6 Ye are fallen from grace.
Galatians ch. 5, v. 4

7 But the fruit of the Spirit is love, joy, peace, longsuffering, gentleness, goodness, faith,
Meekness, temperance.
Galatians ch. 5, v. 22

8 Be not deceived; God is not mocked: for whatsoever a man soweth, that shall he also reap.
Galatians ch. 6, v. 7

9 Let us not be weary in well doing: for in due season we shall reap, if we faint not.
Galatians ch. 6, v. 9. See also II Thessalonians ch. 3, v. 13

10 Ye see how large a letter I have written unto you with mine own hand.
Galatians ch. 6, v. 11

Ephesians

11 [Christ] came and preached peace to you which were afar off, and to them that were nigh.
Ephesians ch. 2, v. 17

12 Unto me, who am less than the least of all saints, is this grace given, that I should preach among the Gentiles the unsearchable riches of Christ.
Ephesians ch. 3, v. 8

13 I bow my knees unto the Father of our Lord Jesus Christ,
Of whom the whole family in heaven and earth is named,
That he would grant you, according to the riches of his glory, to be strengthened with might by his Spirit in the inner man.
Ephesians ch. 3, v. 14

14 The love of Christ, which passeth knowledge.
Ephesians ch. 3, v. 19

15 Now unto him that is able to do exceeding abundantly above all that we ask or think, according to the power that worketh in us,
Unto him be glory in the church by Christ Jesus throughout all ages, world without end. Amen.
Ephesians ch. 3, v. 20

16 I therefore, the prisoner of the Lord, beseech you that ye walk worthy of the vocation wherewith ye are called.
Ephesians ch. 4, v. 1

17 He gave some, apostles; and some, prophets; and some, evangelists; and some, pastors and teachers;
For the perfecting of the saints, for the work of the ministry, for the edifying of the body of Christ:
Till we all come in the unity of the faith, and of the knowledge of the Son of God, unto a perfect man, unto the measure of the stature of the fulness of Christ:
That we henceforth be no more children, tossed to and fro, and carried about with every wind of doctrine, by the sleight of men, and cunning craftiness, whereby they lie in wait to deceive.
Ephesians ch. 4, v. 11

18 We are members one of another.
Ephesians ch. 4, v. 25

19 Be ye angry and sin not: let not the sun go down upon your wrath.
Ephesians ch. 4, v. 26

20 Fornication, and all uncleanness, or covetousness, let it not be once named among you, as becometh saints;
Neither filthiness, nor foolish talking, nor jesting, which are not convenient.
Ephesians ch. 5, v. 3

21 Let no man deceive you with vain words: for because of these things cometh the wrath of God upon the children of disobedience.
Ephesians ch. 5, v. 6

22 See then that ye walk circumspectly, not as fools, but as wise,
Redeeming the time, because the days are evil.
Ephesians ch. 5, v. 15

23 Be not drunk with wine, wherein is excess; but be filled with the Spirit;
Speaking to yourselves in psalms and hymns and spiritual songs, singing and making melody in your heart to the Lord.
Ephesians ch. 5, v. 18

24 Ye fathers, provoke not your children to wrath.
Ephesians ch. 6, v. 4

25 Not with eyeservice, as menpleasers.
Ephesians ch. 6, v. 6

26 Put on the whole armour of God.
Ephesians ch. 6, v. 11

1 For we wrestle not against flesh and blood, but against principalities, against powers, against the rulers of the darkness of this world, against spiritual wickedness in high places.
Wherefore take unto you the whole armour of God, that ye may be able to withstand in the evil day, and having done all, to stand.
Stand therefore, having your loins girt about with truth, and having on the breastplate of righteousness;
And your feet shod with the preparation of the gospel of peace;
Above all, taking the shield of faith, wherewith ye shall be able to quench all the fiery darts of the wicked.
Ephesians ch. 6, v. 12

Philippians

2 For me to live is Christ, and to die is gain.
Philippians ch. 1, v. 21

3 Having a desire to depart, and to be with Christ; which is far better.
Philippians ch. 1, v. 23

4 Let this mind be in you, which was also in Christ Jesus:
Who, being in the form of God, thought it not robbery to be equal with God:
But made himself of no reputation, and took upon him the form of a servant and was made in the likeness of men.
Philippians ch. 2, v. 5

5 God hath also highly exalted him, and given him a name which is above every name:
That at the name of Jesus every knee should bow, of things in heaven, and things in earth, and things under the earth.
Philippians ch. 2, v. 9

6 Work out your own salvation with fear and trembling.
Philippians ch. 2, v. 12

7 If any other man thinketh that he hath whereof he might trust in the flesh, I more:
Circumcised the eighth day, of the stock of Israel, of the tribe of Benjamin, an Hebrew of the Hebrews; as touching the law, a Pharisee.
Philippians ch. 3, v. 4

8 But what things were gain to me, those I counted loss for Christ.
Philippians ch. 3, v. 7

9 Forgetting those things which are behind, and reaching forth unto those things which are before,
I press toward the mark.
Philippians ch. 3, v. 13

10 Whose God is their belly, and whose glory is in their shame.
Philippians ch. 3, v. 19

11 Rejoice in the Lord alway: and again I say, Rejoice.
Philippians ch. 4, v. 4

12 The peace of God, which passeth all understanding, shall keep your hearts and minds through Christ Jesus.
Philippians ch. 4, v. 7

13 Whatsoever things are true, whatsoever things are honest, whatsoever things are just, whatsoever things are pure, whatsoever things are lovely, whatsoever things are of good report; if there be any virtue and if there be any praise, think on these things.
Philippians ch. 4, v. 8

14 I can do all things through Christ which strengtheneth me.
Philippians ch. 4, v. 13

Colossians

15 Set your affection on things above, not on things on the earth.
Colossians ch. 3, v. 2

16 Ye have put off the old man with his deeds:
And have put on the new man, which is renewed in knowledge after the image of him that created him:
Where there is neither Greek nor Jew, circumcision nor uncircumcision, Barbarian, Scythian, bond nor free: but Christ is all, and in all.
Colossians ch. 3, v. 9

17 Husbands, love your wives, and be not bitter against them.
Colossians ch. 3, v. 19

18 Let your speech be alway with grace, seasoned with salt.
Colossians ch. 4, v. 6

I Thessalonians

19 We give thanks to God always for you all, making mention of you in our prayers;
Remembering without ceasing your work of faith and labour of love, and patience of hope in our Lord Jesus Christ.
I Thessalonians ch. 1, v. 2

20 Study to be quiet, and to do your own business.
I Thessalonians ch. 4, v. 11

21 But let us, who are of the day, be sober, putting on the breastplate of faith and love; and for an helmet, the hope of salvation.
I Thessalonians ch. 5, v. 8

22 Rejoice evermore. Pray without ceasing. In everything give thanks.
I Thessalonians ch. 5, v. 16

23 Prove all things; hold fast that which is good.
1 Thessalonians ch. 5, v. 21

II Thessalonians

24 If any would not work, neither should he eat.
II Thessalonians ch. 3, v. 10

I Timothy

25 Sinners; of whom I am chief.
I Timothy ch. 1, v. 15

26 A bishop then must be blameless, the husband of one wife, vigilant, sober, of good behaviour, given to hospitality, apt to teach;
Not given to wine, no striker, not greedy of filthy lucre; but patient, not a brawler, not covetous.
I Timothy ch. 3, v. 2

1 Refuse profane and old wives' fables, and exercise
  thyself rather unto godliness.
   I Timothy ch. 4, v. 7

2 For we brought nothing into this world, and it is
  certain we can carry nothing out.
   I Timothy ch. 6, v. 7

3 The love of money is the root of all evil.
   I Timothy ch. 6, v. 10

4 Fight the good fight of faith, lay hold on eternal life.
   I Timothy ch. 6, v. 12

II Timothy

5 For God hath not given us the spirit of fear; but of
  power, and of love, and of a sound mind.
   II Timothy ch. 1, v. 7

6 Hold fast the form of sound words.
   II Timothy ch. 1, v. 13

7 Be instant in season, out of season.
   II Timothy ch. 4, v. 2

8 I have fought a good fight, I have finished my course,
  I have kept the faith.
   II Timothy ch. 4, v. 7

Titus

9 Unto the pure all things are pure.
   Titus ch. 1, v. 15

Hebrews

10 God, who at sundry times and in divers manners
  spake in time past unto the fathers by the prophets,
  Hath in these last days spoken unto us by his Son,
  whom he hath appointed heir of all things, by
  whom he also made the worlds:
  Who being the brightness of his glory, and the express
  image of his person, and upholding all things by the
  word of his power, when he had by himself purged
  our sins, sat down on the right hand of the Majesty
  on high.
   Hebrews ch. 1, v. 1

11 Without shedding of blood is no remission.
   Hebrews ch. 9, v. 22

12 It is a fearful thing to fall into the hands of the living
  God.
   Hebrews ch. 10, v. 31

13 Faith is the substance of things hoped for, the evidence
  of things not seen.
   Hebrews ch. 11, v. 1

14 For he looked for a city which hath foundations,
  whose maker and builder is God.
   Hebrews ch. 11, v. 10

15 These all died in faith, not having received the
  promises, but having seen them afar off, and were
  persuaded of them, and embraced them, and
  confessed that they were strangers and pilgrims on
  the earth.
   Hebrews ch. 11, v. 13

16 Of whom the world was not worthy.
   Hebrews ch. 11, v. 38

17 Wherefore seeing we also are compassed about with so
  great a cloud of witnesses, let us lay aside every
  weight, and the sin which doth so easily beset us,
  and let us run with patience the race that is set
  before us,
  Looking unto Jesus the author and finisher of our
  faith; who for the joy that was set before him
  endured the cross, despising the shame, and is set
  down at the right hand of God.
   Hebrews ch. 12, v. 1

18 Whom the Lord loveth he chasteneth.
   Hebrews ch. 12, v. 6

19 The spirits of just men made perfect.
   Hebrews ch. 12, v. 23

20 Let brotherly love continue.
  Be not forgetful to entertain strangers: for thereby
  some have entertained angels unawares.
   Hebrews ch. 13, v. 1

21 Jesus Christ the same yesterday, and to day, and for
  ever.
   Hebrews ch. 13, v. 8

22 For here have we no continuing city, but we seek one
  to come.
   Hebrews ch. 13, v. 14

23 To do good and to communicate forget not.
   Hebrews ch. 13, v. 16

James

24 Let patience have her perfect work.
   James ch. 1, v. 4

25 Blessed is the man that endureth temptation: for when
  he is tried, he shall receive the crown of life.
   James ch. 1, v. 12

26 Every good gift and every perfect gift is from above,
  and cometh down from the Father of lights, with
  whom is no variableness, neither shadow of
  turning.
   James ch. 1, v. 17

27 Be swift to hear, slow to speak, slow to wrath:
  For the wrath of man worketh not the righteousness
  of God.
  Wherefore lay apart all filthiness and superfluity of
  naughtiness, and receive with meekness the
  engrafted word, which is able to save your souls,
  But be ye doers of the word, and not hearers only,
  deceiving your own selves.
  For if any be a hearer of the word, and not a doer, he
  is like unto a man beholding his natural face in a
  glass:
  For he beholdeth himself, and goeth his way, and
  straightway forgetteth what manner of man he was.
   James ch. 1, v. 19

28 If any man among you seem to be religious, and
  bridleth not his tongue, but deceiveth his own
  heart, this man's religion is vain.
  Pure religion and undefiled before God and the Father
  is this, To visit the fatherless and widows in their
  affliction, and to keep himself unspotted from the
  world.
   James ch. 1, v. 26

29 Faith without works is dead.
   James ch. 2, v. 20

1 How great a matter a little fire kindleth.
James ch. 3, v. 5

2 The tongue can no man tame; it is an unruly evil.
James ch. 3, v. 8

3 Doth a fountain send forth at the same place sweet water and bitter?
James ch. 3, v. 11

4 For what is your life? It is even a vapour, that appeareth for a little time, and then vanisheth away.
James ch. 4, v. 14

5 Ye have heard of the patience of Job.
James ch. 5, v. 11

6 Let your yea be yea; and your nay, nay.
James ch. 5, v. 12

7 The effectual fervent prayer of a righteous man availeth much.
James ch. 5, v. 16

I Peter

8 Jesus Christ: Whom having not seen, ye love; in whom, though now ye see him not, yet believing, ye rejoice with joy unspeakable and full of glory.
I Peter ch. 1, v. 7

9 All flesh is as grass, and all the glory of man as the flower of grass. The grass withereth, and the flower thereof falleth away.
I Peter ch. 1, v. 24. Cf. Isaiah 83:26

10 As newborn babes, desire the sincere milk of the word, that ye may grow thereby:
If so be ye have tasted that the Lord is gracious.
I Peter ch. 2, v. 2. Cf. Vulgate 108:17

11 But ye are a chosen generation, a royal priesthood, an holy nation, a peculiar people.
I Peter ch. 2, v. 9

12 Abstain from fleshly lusts, which war against the soul.
I Peter ch. 2, v. 11

13 Honour all men. Love the brotherhood. Fear God. Honour the king.
I Peter ch. 2, v. 17

14 For what glory is it, if, when ye be buffeted for your faults, ye shall take it patiently? but if, when ye do well, and suffer for it, ye take it patiently, this is acceptable with God.
I Peter ch. 2, v. 20

15 Ye were as sheep going astray; but are now returned unto the Shepherd and Bishop of your souls.
I Peter ch. 2, v. 25

16 The ornament of a meek and quiet spirit.
I Peter ch. 3, v. 4

17 Giving honour unto the wife, as unto the weaker vessel.
I Peter ch. 3, v. 7

18 Not rendering evil for evil, or railing for railing: but contrariwise blessing.
I Peter ch. 3, v. 9

19 The end of all things is at hand.
I Peter ch. 4, v. 7

20 Charity shall cover the multitude of sins.
I Peter ch. 4, v. 8

21 Be sober, be vigilant; because your adversary the devil, as a roaring lion, walketh about, seeking whom he may devour.
I Peter ch. 5, v. 8

II Peter

22 And the day star arise in your hearts.
II Peter ch. 1, v. 19

23 They are not afraid to speak evil of dignities.
II Peter ch. 2, v. 10

24 The dog is turned to his own vomit again.
II Peter ch. 2, v. 22

I John

25 If we say that we have no sin, we deceive ourselves, and the truth is not in us.
I John ch. 1, v. 8

26 But whoso hath this world's good, and seeth his brother have need, and shutteth up his bowels of compassion from him, how dwelleth the love of God in him?
I John ch. 3, v. 17

27 He that loveth not knoweth not God; for God is love.
I John ch. 4, v. 8

28 There is no fear in love; but perfect love casteth out fear.
I John ch. 4, v. 18

29 If a man say, I love God, and hateth his brother, he is a liar: for he that loveth not his brother whom he hath seen, how can he love God whom he hath not seen?
I John ch. 4, v. 20

III John

30 He that doeth good is of God: but he that doeth evil hath not seen God.
III John v. 11

Revelation

31 John to the seven churches which are in Asia: Grace be unto you, and peace, from him which is, and which was, and which is to come.
Revelation ch. 1, v. 4

32 Behold, he cometh with clouds; and every eye shall see him, and they also which pierced him: and all kindreds of the earth shall wail because of him. Even so, Amen.
I am Alpha and Omega, the beginning and the ending, saith the Lord.
Revelation ch. 1, v. 7

33 I was in the Spirit on the Lord's day, and heard behind me a great voice as of a trumpet.
Revelation ch. 1, v. 10

34 What thou seest, write in a book, and send it unto the seven churches which are in Asia.
Revelation ch. 1, v. 11

35 Being turned, I saw seven golden candlesticks.
Revelation ch. 1, v. 12

1 His head and his hairs were white like wool, as white as snow; and his eyes were as a flame of fire;
And his feet like unto fine brass, as if they burned in a furnace; and his voice as the sound of many waters.
And he had in his right hand seven stars: and out of his mouth went a sharp two-edged sword: and his countenance was as the sun shineth in his strength.
And when I saw him, I fell at his feet as dead.
Revelation ch. 1, v. 14

2 I am he that liveth, and was dead; and, behold, I am alive for evermore, Amen; and have the keys of hell and of death.
Revelation ch. 1, v. 18

3 I have somewhat against thee, because thou hast left thy first love.
Revelation ch. 2, v. 4

4 Be thou faithful unto death, and I will give thee a crown of life.
Revelation ch. 2, v. 10

5 I will not blot out his name out of the book of life.
Revelation ch. 3, v. 5

6 I will write upon him my new name.
Revelation ch. 3, v. 12

7 I know thy works, that thou art neither cold nor hot: I would thou wert cold or hot.
So then because thou art lukewarm, and neither cold nor hot, I will spew thee out of my mouth.
Revelation ch. 3, v. 15

8 Behold, I stand at the door, and knock.
Revelation ch. 3, v. 20

9 And he that sat was to look upon like a jasper and a sardine stone: and there was a rainbow round about the throne, in sight like unto an emerald.
Revelation ch. 4, v. 3

10 And before the throne there was a sea of glass like unto crystal: and in the midst of the throne, and round about the throne, were four beasts full of eyes before and behind.
Revelation ch. 4, v. 6

11 They were full of eyes within: and they rest not day and night, saying, Holy, holy, holy, Lord God Almighty, which was, and is, and is to come.
Revelation ch. 4, v. 8

12 Thou hast created all things, and for thy pleasure they are and were created.
Revelation ch. 4, v. 11

13 Who is worthy to open the book, and to loose the seals thereof?
Revelation ch. 5, v. 2

14 The four beasts and four and twenty elders fell down before the Lamb, having every one of them harps, and golden vials full of odours, which are the prayers of saints.
Revelation ch. 5, v. 8

15 He went forth conquering, and to conquer.
Revelation ch. 6, v. 2

16 And I looked, and behold a pale horse: and his name that sat on him was Death.
Revelation ch. 6, v. 8

17 The kings of the earth, and the great men, and the rich men, and the chief captains, and the mighty men, and every bondman, and every free man, hid themselves in the dens and in the rocks of the mountains;
And said to the mountains and rocks, Fall on us, and hide us from the face of him that sitteth upon the throne, and from the wrath of the Lamb:
For the great day of his wrath is come; and who shall be able to stand?
Revelation ch. 6, v. 15

18 A great multitude, which no man could number, of all nations, and kindreds, and people, and tongues, stood before the throne, and before the Lamb.
Revelation ch. 7, v. 9

19 And all the angels stood round about the throne, and about the elders and the four beasts, and fell before the throne on their faces, and worshipped God.
Revelation ch. 7, v. 11

20 And one of the elders answered, saying unto me, What are these which are arrayed in white robes? and whence came they?
Revelation ch. 7, v. 13

21 These are they which came out of great tribulation, and have washed their robes, and made them white in the blood of the Lamb.
Revelation ch. 7, v. 14

22 They shall hunger no more, neither thirst any more; neither shall the sun light on them, nor any heat.
Revelation ch. 7, v. 16

23 God shall wipe away all tears from their eyes.
Revelation ch. 7, v. 17

24 And when he had opened the seventh seal, there was silence in heaven about the space of half an hour.
Revelation ch. 8, v. 1

25 And the name of the star is called Wormwood.
Revelation ch. 8, v. 11

26 And in those days shall men seek death, and shall not find it; and shall desire to die, and death shall flee from them.
Revelation ch. 9, v. 6

27 And there were stings in their tails.
Revelation ch. 9, v. 10

28 It was in my mouth sweet as honey: and as soon as I had eaten it, my belly was bitter.
Revelation ch. 10, v. 10

29 And there appeared a great wonder in heaven; a woman clothed with the sun, and the moon under her feet, and upon her head a crown of twelve stars.
Revelation ch. 12, v. 1

30 And there was war in heaven: Michael and his angels fought against the dragon; and the dragon fought and his angels.
Revelation ch. 12, v. 7

31 Who is like unto the beast? who is able to make war with him?
Revelation ch. 13, v. 4

32 And that no man might buy or sell, save he that had the mark, or the name of the beast, or the number of his name.
Revelation ch. 13, v. 17

1 Let him that hath understanding count the number of the beast: for it is the number of a man; and his number is Six hundred threescore and six.
Revelation ch. 13, v. 18

2 And I heard a voice from heaven, as the voice of many waters, and as the voice of a great thunder: and I heard the voice of harpers harping with their harps:
And they sung as it were a new song . . . and no man could learn that song but the hundred and forty and four thousand, which were redeemed from the earth.
Revelation ch. 14, v. 2

3 Babylon is fallen, is fallen, that great city.
Revelation ch. 14, v. 8

4 And the smoke of their torment ascendeth up for ever and ever: and they have no rest day or night, who worship the beast and his image.
Revelation ch. 14, v. 11

5 Blessed are the dead which die in the Lord from henceforth: Yea, saith the Spirit, that they may rest from their labours; and their works do follow them.
Revelation ch. 14, v. 13

6 And I saw as it were a sea of glass mingled with fire.
Revelation ch. 15, v. 2

7 Behold, I come as a thief.
Revelation ch. 16, v. 15

8 And he gathered them together into a place called in the Hebrew tongue Armageddon.
Revelation ch. 16, v. 16

9 I will shew unto thee the judgement of the great whore that sitteth upon many waters.
Revelation ch. 17, v. 1

10 And upon her forehead was a name written, MYSTERY, BABYLON THE GREAT, THE MOTHER OF HARLOTS AND ABOMINATIONS OF THE EARTH.
Revelation ch. 17, v. 5

11 And a mighty angel took up a stone like a great millstone, and cast it into the sea, saying, Thus with violence shall that great city Babylon be thrown down, and shall be found no more at all.
Revelation ch. 18, v. 21

12 And I saw heaven opened, and behold a white horse; and he that sat upon him was called Faithful and True.
Revelation ch. 19, v. 11

13 And he hath on his vesture and on his thigh a name written, KING OF KINGS, AND LORD OF LORDS.
Revelation ch. 19, v. 16

14 And he laid hold on the dragon, that old serpent, which is the Devil, and Satan, and bound him a thousand years.
Revelation ch. 20, v. 2

15 And I saw a great white throne.
Revelation ch. 20, v. 11

16 And the sea gave up the dead which were in it; and death and hell delivered up the dead which were in them: and they were judged every man according to their works.
Revelation ch. 20, v. 13

17 And I saw a new heaven and a new earth: for the first heaven and the first earth were passed away; and there was no more sea.
And I John saw the holy city, new Jerusalem, coming down from God out of heaven, prepared as a bride adorned for her husband.
Revelation ch. 21, v. 1

18 And God shall wipe away all tears from their eyes; and there shall be no more death, neither sorrow, nor crying, neither shall there be any more pain: for the former things are passed away.
And he that sat upon the throne said, Behold, I make all things new. And he said unto me, Write: for these words are true and faithful.
Revelation ch. 21, v. 4

19 I will give unto him that is athirst of the fountain of the water of life freely.
Revelation ch. 21, v. 6

20 The street of the city was pure gold.
Revelation ch. 21, v. 21

21 And the gates of it shall not be shut at all by day: for there shall be no night there.
Revelation ch. 21, v. 25

22 And he shewed me a pure river of water of life, clear as crystal, proceeding out of the throne of God and of the Lamb.
Revelation ch. 22, v. 1

23 And the leaves of the tree were for the healing of the nations.
Revelation ch. 22, v. 2

24 And, behold, I come quickly.
Revelation ch. 22, v. 12

25 For without are dogs, and sorcerers, and whoremongers, and murderers, and idolaters, and whosoever loveth and maketh a lie.
Revelation ch. 22, v. 15

26 Amen. Even so, come, Lord Jesus.
Revelation ch. 22, v. 20

Vulgate

27 *Dominus illuminatio mea, et salus mea, quem timebo?*
The Lord is the source of my light and my safety, so whom shall I fear?
Psalm 26, v. 1. Cf. Book of Common Prayer 125:24

28 *Asperges me hyssopo, et mundabor; lavabis me, et super nivem dealbabor.*
You will sprinkle me with hyssop, and I shall be made clean; you will wash me and I shall be made whiter than snow.
Psalm 50, v. 9 (Psalm 51, v. 7 in the Authorized Version). Cf. Book of Common Prayer 128:5

29 *Cantate Domino canticum novum, quia mirabilia fecit.*
Sing to the Lord a new song, because he has done marvellous things.
Psalm 97, v. 1 (Psalm 98, v. 1 in the Authorized Version). Cf. Book of Common Prayer 131:13

30 *Jubilate Deo, omnis terra; servite Domino in laetitia.*
Sing joyfully to God, all the earth; serve the Lord with gladness.
Psalm 99, v. 2 (Psalm 100, v. 2 in the Authorized Version). Cf. Book of Common Prayer 131:17

1 *Beatus vir qui timet Dominum, in mandatis ejus volet nimis!*

Happy is the man who fears the Lord, who is only too willing to follow his orders.
Psalm 111, v. 1 (Psalm 112, v. 1 in the Authorized Version)

2 *Non nobis, Domine, non nobis; sed nomini tuo da gloriam.*

Not unto us, Lord, not unto us; but to thy name give glory.
Psalm 113 (second part), v. 1 (Psalm 115, v. 1 in the Authorized Version). Cf. Book of Common Prayer PRBK9717

3 *Laudate Dominum, omnes gentes; laudate eum, omnes populi.*

Praise the Lord, all nations; praise him, all people.
Psalm 116, v. 1 (Psalm 117, v. 1 in the Authorized Version)

4 *Nisi Dominus aedificaverit domum, in vanum laboraverunt qui aedificant eam.*
Nisi Dominus custodierit civitatem, frustra vigilat qui custodit eam.

Unless the Lord has built the house, its builders have laboured in vain. Unless the Lord guards the city, the watchman watches in vain.
Psalm 126, v. 1 (Psalm 127, v. 1 in the Authorized Version; contracted to 'Nisi Dominus frustra' for the motto of the city of Edinburgh). Cf. Book of Common Prayer 134:6

5 *De profundis clamavi ad te, Domine; Domine, exaudi vocem meam.*

Up from the depths I have cried to thee, Lord; Lord, hear my voice.
Psalm 129, v. 1 (Psalm 130, v. 1 in the Authorized Version). Cf. Book of Common Prayer 134:11

6 *Vanitas vanitatum, dixit Ecclesiastes; vanitas vanitatum, et omnia vanitas.*

Vanity of vanities, said the preacher; vanity of vanities, and everything is vanity.
Ecclesiastes ch. 1, v. 2. Cf. Ecclesiastes 79:36

7 *Rorate, coeli, desuper, et nubes pluant Justum; aperiatur terra, et germinet Salvatorem.*

Drop down dew, heavens, from above, and let the clouds rain down righteousness; let the earth be opened, and a saviour spring to life.
Isaiah ch. 45, v. 8

8 *Benedicite, omnia opera Domini, Domino; laudate et superexaltate eum in secula.*

Bless the Lord, all the works of the Lord; praise him and exalt him above all things for ever.
Daniel ch. 3, v. 57. Cf. Book of Common Prayer 118:15

9 *Magnificat anima mea Dominum; Et exsultavit spiritus meus in Deo salutari meo.*

My soul doth magnify the Lord: and my spirit hath rejoiced in God my Saviour.
St Luke ch. 1, v. 46. Cf. St Luke 93:22

10 *Esurientes implevit bonis, et divites dimisit inanes.*

He hath filled the hungry with good things: and the rich he hath sent empty away.
St Luke ch. 1, v. 53. Cf. St Luke 93:23

11 *Nunc dimittis servum tuum, Domine, secundum verbum tuum in pace.*

Lord, now lettest thou thy servant depart in peace: according to thy word.
St Luke ch. 2, v. 29. Cf. St Luke 93:29

12 *Pax Vobis.*

Peace be unto you.
St Luke ch. 24, v. 36

13 *Quo vadis?*

Where are you going?
St John ch. 16, v. 5

14 *Ecce homo.*

Behold the man.
St John ch. 19, v. 5

15 *Consummatum est.*

It is achieved.
St John ch. 19, v. 30. Cf. St John 97:29

16 *Noli me tangere.*

Do not touch me.
St John ch. 20, v. 17. Cf. St John 97:34

17 *Sicut modo geniti infantes, rationabile, sine dolo lac concupiscite.*

After the fashion of newborn babes, desire the sincere milk of the word.
I Peter ch. 2, v. 2. Cf. I Peter 105:10

18 *Magna est veritas, et praevalet.*

Great is truth, and it prevails.
III Esdras ch. 4, v. 41. Cf. Apocrypha 86:21

See also BOOK OF COMMON PRAYER (Psalms)

Isaac Bickerstaffe 1733–c.1808
Irish playwright

19 Perhaps it was right to dissemble your love,
But—why did you kick me downstairs?
'An Expostulation' (1789)

20 There was a jolly miller once,
Lived on the river Dee;
He worked and sang from morn till night;
No lark more blithe than he.
Love in a Village (a comic opera with music by Thomas Arne, 1762) act 1, sc. 2

21 And ah! this the burthen of his song,
For ever used to be,
I care for nobody, not I,
If no one cares for me.
Love in a Village (1762) act 1, sc. 2

E. H. Bickersteth 1825–1906
English clergyman

22 Peace, perfect peace, in this dark world of sin?
The Blood of Jesus whispers peace within.
Songs in the House of Pilgrimage (1875) 'Peace, perfect peace'

Georges Bidault 1899–1983

French politician; Prime Minister, 1946, 1949–50

1 The weak have one weapon: the errors of those who think they are strong.

In *Observer* 15 July 1962 'Sayings of the Week'

Ambrose Bierce 1842–c.1914

American writer

2 ACQUAINTANCE, *n.* A person whom we know well enough to borrow from, but not well enough to lend to. A degree of friendship called slight when its object is poor or obscure, and intimate when he is rich or famous.

The Cynic's Word Book (1906) p. 12

3 ALLIANCE, *n.* In international politics, the union of two thieves who have their hands so deeply inserted in each other's pocket that they cannot separately plunder a third.

The Cynic's Word Book (1906) p. 16

4 APPLAUSE, *n.* The echo of a platitude.

The Cynic's Word Book (1906) p. 19

5 AUCTIONEER, *n.* The man who proclaims with a hammer that he has picked a pocket with his tongue.

The Cynic's Word Book (1906) p. 24

6 BATTLE, *n.* A method of untying with the teeth a political knot that would not yield to the tongue.

The Cynic's Word Book (1906) p. 30

7 CALAMITY, *n.* . . . . Calamities are of two kinds: misfortune to ourselves, and good fortune to others.

The Cynic's Word Book (1906) p. 41

8 CONSERVATIVE, *n.* A statesman who is enamoured of existing evils, as distinguished from the Liberal, who wishes to replace them with others.

The Cynic's Word Book (1906) p. 56

9 DESTINY, *n.* A tyrant's authority for crime and a fool's excuse for failure.

The Enlarged Devil's Dictionary (1967) p. 64

10 FUTURE, *n.* That period of time in which our affairs prosper, our friends are true, and our happiness is assured.

The Cynic's Word Book (1906) p. 129

11 HISTORY, *n.* An account, mostly false, of events, mostly unimportant, which are brought about by rulers, mostly knaves, and soldiers, mostly fools.

The Cynic's Word Book (1906) p. 161

12 PATIENCE, *n.* A minor form of despair, disguised as a virtue.

The Devil's Dictionary (1911) p. 248

13 PEACE, *n.* In international affairs, a period of cheating between two periods of fighting.

The Devil's Dictionary (1911) p. 248

14 PREJUDICE, *n.* A vagrant opinion without visible means of support.

The Devil's Dictionary (1911) p. 264

15 SAINT, *n.* A dead sinner revised and edited.

The Devil's Dictionary (1911) p. 306

Roger Bigod, Earl of Norfolk 1245–1306

Marshal of England, 1270–1301

16 By God, O King, I will neither go nor hang!

Replying to King Edward I's 'By God, earl, you shall either go or hang', 24 February 1297, when requiring the barons to invade France through Gascony while he himself took command in Flanders; in Harry Rothwell (ed.) *The Chronicle of Walter of Guisbrough* Camden Society Series 3, vol. 89 (1957) p. 291

Josh Billings (Henry Wheeler Shaw) 1818–85

American humorist

17 Love iz like the meazles; we kant have it bad but onst, and the latter in life we hav it the tuffer it goes with us.

Josh Billings' Wit and Humour (1874) p. 146

18 Natur never makes enny blunders. When she makes a phool she means it.

Josh Billings' Wit and Humour (1874) p. 174

19 'Vote early and vote often' is the Politishun's golden rule.

Josh Billings' Wit and Humour (1874) p. 180

Laurence Binyon 1869–1943

English poet

20 They shall grow not old, as we that are left grow old.
Age shall not weary them, nor the years condemn.
At the going down of the sun and in the morning
We will remember them.

'For the Fallen' (1914)

21 Now is the time for the burning of the leaves.

'The Ruins' (1942)

Nigel Birch (Baron Rhyl) 1906–81

British Conservative politician

22 My God! They've shot our fox!

On hearing of the resignation of Hugh Dalton, Chancellor of the Exchequer in the Labour Government, 13 November 1947; in Harold Macmillan *Tides of Fortune* (1969) ch. 3

Earl of Birkenhead

See F. E. SMITH

Augustine Birrell 1850–1933

British essayist

23 That great dust-heap called 'history'.

Obiter Dicta (1884) 'Carlyle'

Elizabeth Bishop 1911–79

American poet

24 The state with the prettiest name,
the state that floats in brackish water,
held together by mangrave roots.

'Florida' (1946)

1 This iceberg cuts its facets from within.
Like jewelry from a grave
it saves itself perpetually and adorns
only itself.
> 'The Imaginary Iceberg' (1946)

2 Topography displays no favourites; North's as near as
West.
More delicate than the historians' are the
map-makers' colours.
> 'The Map' (1946)

3 The armoured cars of dreams, contrived to let us do
so many a dangerous thing.
> 'Sleeping Standing Up' (1946)

Prince Otto von Bismarck 1815–98

German statesman

4 *Die Politik ist die Lehre vom Möglichen.*

Politics is the art of the possible.
> In conversation with Meyer von Waldeck, 11 August 1867,
> in H. Amelung *Bismarck-Worte* (1918) p. 19

5 *Die Vermittlung des Friedens denke ich mir nicht so, dass
wir nun bei divergierenden Ansichten den Schiedsrichter
spielen . . . mehr die eines ehrlichen Maklers, der das
Geschäft wirklich zu Stande bringen will.*

I do not regard the procuring of peace as a matter in
which we should play the role of arbiter between
different opinions . . . more that of an honest broker
who really wants to press the business forward.
> Speech to the Reichstag, 19 February 1878, in Ludwig
> Hahn (ed.) *Fürst Bismarck. Sein politisches Leben und Wirken*
> vol. 3 (1881) p. 90

6 *Legt eine möglichst starke militärische Kraft . . . in die
Hand des Königs von Preussen, dann wird er die Politik
machen können, die Ihr wünscht; mit Reden und
Schützenfesten und Liedern macht sie sich nicht, sie macht
sich nur durch Blut und Eisen.*

Place in the hands of the King of Prussia the strongest
possible military power, then he will be able to carry
out the policy you wish; this policy cannot succeed
through speeches, and shooting-matches, and songs;
it can only be carried out through blood and iron.
> Speech in the Prussian House of Deputies, 28 January
> 1886, in *Fürst Bismarck als Redner. Vollständige Sammlung
> der parliamentarischen Reden* (1885–91) vol. 15, p. 157. In a
> speech on 30 September 1862, Bismarck had used the form
> '*Eisen und Blut* [Iron and blood]'. See *Fürst Bismarck. Sein
> politisches Leben und Wirken* (1878) vol. 4, p. 66

7 Herr Ballen, the great shipping magnate, told me that
he had heard Bismarck say towards the end of his life,
'If there is ever another war in Europe, it will come
out of some damned silly thing in the Balkans.'
> In *Hansard* 16 August 1945, col. 84

8 A lath of wood painted to look like iron.
> Describing Lord Salisbury; attributed, but vigorously denied
> by Sidney Whitman in *Personal Reminiscences of Prince
> Bismarck* (1902) ch. 14

Valentine Blacker 1728–1823

Anglo-Indian soldier

9 Put your trust in God, my boys, and keep your powder
dry.
> 'Oliver's Advice' in E. Hayes *Ballads of Ireland* (1856) vol. 1,
> p. 192 (often attributed to Oliver Cromwell himself)

Sir William Blackstone 1723–80

English jurist

10 Man was formed for society.
> *Commentaries on the Laws of England* (1765) introduction,
> sect. 2. Cf. Aristotle 25:15

11 The king never dies.
> *Commentaries on the Laws of England* (1765) bk. 1, ch. 7

12 The royal navy of England hath ever been its greatest
defence and ornament; it is its ancient and natural
strength; the floating bulwark of the island.
> *Commentaries on the Laws of England* (1765) bk. 1, ch. 13

13 That the king can do no wrong, is a necessary and
fundamental principle of the English constitution.
> *Commentaries on the Laws of England* (1765) bk. 3, ch. 17

14 It is better that ten guilty persons escape than one
innocent suffer.
> *Commentaries on the Laws of England* (1765) bk. 4, ch. 27

Robert Blair 1699–1746

Scottish poet

15 Oft, in the lone church-yard at night I've seen,
The schoolboy with a satchel in his hand,
Whistling aloud to keep his courage up . . .
Sudden he starts! and hears, or thinks he hears,
The sound of something purring at his heels;
Full fast he flies, and dares not look behind him,
Till out of breath, he overtakes his fellows.
> *The Grave* (1743) l. 57. Cf. Coleridge 211:14

Eubie Blake (James Hubert Blake) 1883–1983

American ragtime pianist

16 If I'd known I was gonna live this long, I'd have taken
better care of myself.
> On reaching the age of 100, in *Observer* 13 February 1983
> 'Sayings of the Week'

William Blake 1757–1827

English poet

17 When Sir Joshua Reynolds died
All Nature was degraded:
The King dropped a tear into the Queen's ear;
And all his pictures faded.
> Annotations to The Works of Sir Joshua Reynolds p. cix
> 'When Sir Joshua Reynolds died' (c.1808)

18 To see a world in a grain of sand
And a heaven in a wild flower
Hold infinity in the palm of your hand
And eternity in an hour.
> 'Auguries of Innocence' (c.1803) l. 1

1 A robin red breast in a cage
Puts all Heaven in a rage.
'Auguries of Innocence' (c.1803) l. 5

2 A dog starved at his master's gate
Predicts the ruin of the State
A horse misused upon the road
Calls to Heaven for human blood
Each outcry of the hunted hare
A fibre from the brain does tear
A skylark wounded in the wing
A cherubim does cease to sing.
'Auguries of Innocence' (c.1803) l. 9

3 The bat that flits at close of eve
Has left the brain that won't believe.
'Auguries of Innocence' (c.1803) l. 25

4 He who shall hurt the little wren
Shall never be beloved by men
He who the ox to wrath has moved
Shall never be by woman loved.
'Auguries of Innocence' (c.1803) l. 29

5 The caterpillar on the leaf
Repeats to thee thy mother's grief
Kill not the moth nor butterfly
For the Last Judgement draweth nigh.
'Auguries of Innocence' (c.1803) l. 37

6 A truth that's told with bad intent
Beats all the lies you can invent
It is right it should be so
Man was made for joy and woe
And when this we rightly know
Thro' the world we safely go
Joy and woe are woven fine
A clothing for the soul divine.
'Auguries of Innocence' (c.1803) l. 53

7 The bleat the bark bellow and roar
Are waves that beat on heavens shore.
'Auguries of Innocence' (c.1803) l. 71

8 The strongest poison ever known
Came from Caesar's laurel crown.
'Auguries of Innocence' (c.1803) l. 97

9 The whore and gambler by the State
Licensed build that nation's fate
The harlot's cry from street to street
Shall weave old England's winding sheet.
'Auguries of Innocence' (c.1803) l. 113

10 God appears and God is Light
To those poor souls who dwell in night
But does a human form display
To those who dwell in realms of day.
'Auguries of Innocence' (c.1803) l. 129

11 Does the eagle know what is in the pit?
Or wilt thou go ask the mole:
Can wisdom be put in a silver rod?
Or love in a golden bowl?
The Book of Thel (1789) plate i 'Thel's Motto'

12   Everything that lives,
Lives not alone, nor for itself.
The Book of Thel (1789) plate 3, l. 26

13 The Vision of Christ that thou dost see
Is my vision's greatest enemy
Thine has a great hook nose like thine
Mine has a snub nose like to mine.
The Everlasting Gospel (c.1818) (a) l. 1

14 Both read the Bible day and night
But thou read'st black where I read white.
The Everlasting Gospel (c.1818) (a) l. 13

15 Was Jesus gentle or did he
Give any marks of gentility
When twelve years old he ran away
And left his parents in dismay.
The Everlasting Gospel (c.1818) (b) l. 1

16 Was Jesus humble or did he
Give any proofs of humility
Boast of high things with humble tone
And give with charity a stone.
The Everlasting Gospel (c.1818) (d) l. 1

17 Humility is only doubt
And does the sun and moon blot out
Rooting over with thorns and stems
The buried soul and all its gems
This life's dim windows of the soul
Distorts the heavens from pole to pole
And leads you to believe a lie
When you see with not through the eye.
The Everlasting Gospel (c.1818) (d) l. 99

18 Was Jesus chaste or did he
Give any lessons of chastity
The morning blushed fiery red
Mary was found in adulterous bed.
The Everlasting Gospel (c.1818) (e) l. 1

19 Jesus was sitting in Moses chair
They brought the trembling woman there
Moses commands she be stoned to death
What was the sound of Jesus breath
He laid His hand on Moses Law
The ancient Heavens in silent awe
Writ with curses from pole to pole
All away began to roll.
The Everlasting Gospel (c.1818) (e) l. 7

20 I am sure this Jesus will not do
Either for Englishman or Jew.
The Everlasting Gospel (c.1818) (f) l. 1

21 Did Jesus teach doubt or did he
Give any lessons of philosophy
Charge visionaries with deceiving
Or call men wise for not believing.
The Everlasting Gospel (c.1818) (h) l. 1

22 Mutual Forgiveness of each vice,
Such are the Gates of Paradise.
For the Sexes: The Gates of Paradise 'Mutual Forgiveness of each Vice' [prologue]

23 Truly, my Satan, thou art but a dunce,
And dost not know the garment from the man;
Every harlot was a virgin once,
Nor can'st thou ever change Kate into Nan.

Tho' thou art worshipped by the names divine
Of Jesus and Jehovah, thou art still
The Son of Morn in weary Night's decline,
The lost traveller's dream under the hill.
For the Sexes: The Gates of Paradise 'To the Accuser who is The God of This World' [epilogue]

1 I must create a system, or be enslaved by another
man's.
I will not reason and compare: my business is to
create.

Jerusalem (1815) 'Chapter 1' (plate 10, l. 20)

2   Near mournful
Ever weeping Paddington.

Jerusalem (1815) 'Chapter 1' (plate 12, l. 27)

3 The fields from Islington to Marybone,
To Primrose Hill and Saint John's Wood
Were builded over with pillars of gold;
And there Jerusalem's pillars stood.

Jerusalem (1815) 'To the Jews' (plate 27, l. 1) "The fields
from Islington to Marybone"

4 Pancras and Kentish-town repose
Among her golden pillars high
Among her golden arches which
Shine upon the starry sky.

Jerusalem (1815) 'To the Jews' (plate 27, l. 9) "The fields
from Islington to Marybone"

5 For a tear is an intellectual thing;
And a sigh is the sword of an Angel King
And the bitter groan of the martyr's woe
Is an arrow from the Almighty's bow!

Jerusalem (1815) 'To the Deists' (plate 52, l. 25) "I saw a
Monk of Charlemaine"

6 He who would do good to another, must do it in
minute particulars
General good is the plea of the scoundrel, hypocrite
and flatterer:
For Art and Science cannot exist but in minutely
organized particulars.

Jerusalem (1815) 'Chapter 3' (plate 55, l. 60)

7 I give you the end of a golden string;
Only wind it into a ball:
It will lead you in at Heaven's gate,
Built in Jerusalem's wall.

Jerusalem (1815) 'To the Christians' (plate 77) "I give you
the end of a golden string"

8 England! awake! awake! awake!
Jerusalem thy sister calls!
Why wilt thou sleep the sleep of death,
And close her from thy ancient walls?

Jerusalem (1815) 'To the Christians' (plate 77) "England!
awake! ... "

9 And now the time returns again:
Our souls exult, and London's towers,
Receive the Lamb of God to dwell
In England's green and pleasant bowers.

Jerusalem (1815) 'To the Christians' (plate 77)

10 I care not whether a man is good or evil; all that I
care
Is whether he is a wise man or a fool. Go! put off
holiness
And put on Intellect.

Jerusalem (1815) 'Chapter 4' (plate 91, l. 54)

11   May God us keep
From Single vision and Newton's sleep!

'Letter to Thomas Butts, 22 November 1802'

12 O why was I born with a different face?
Why was I not born like the rest of my race?

'Letter to Thomas Butts, 16 August 1803'

13 Without contraries is no progression. Attraction and
repulsion, reason and energy, love and hate, are
necessary to human existence.

The Marriage of Heaven and Hell (1790–3) 'The Argument'

14 Energy is Eternal Delight.

The Marriage of Heaven and Hell (1790–3) 'The voice of the
Devil'

15 The reason Milton wrote in fetters when he wrote of
Angels and God, and at liberty when of Devils and
Hell, is because he was a true Poet, and of the Devil's
party without knowing it.

The Marriage of Heaven and Hell (1790–3) 'The voice of the
Devil' (note)

16 The road of excess leads to the palace of wisdom.

The Marriage of Heaven and Hell (1790–3) 'Proverbs of Hell'

17 Prudence is a rich, ugly, old maid courted by
Incapacity.

The Marriage of Heaven and Hell (1790–3) 'Proverbs of Hell'

18 He who desires but acts not, breeds pestilence.

The Marriage of Heaven and Hell (1790–3) 'Proverbs of Hell'

19 A fool sees not the same tree that a wise man sees.

The Marriage of Heaven and Hell (1790–3) 'Proverbs of Hell'

20 Eternity is in love with the productions of time.

The Marriage of Heaven and Hell (1790–3) 'Proverbs of Hell'

21 Bring out number weight and measure in a year of
dearth.

The Marriage of Heaven and Hell (1790–3) 'Proverbs of Hell'

22 If the fool would persist in his folly he would become
wise.

The Marriage of Heaven and Hell (1790–3) 'Proverbs of Hell'

23 Prisons are built with stones of Law, brothels with
bricks of Religion.

The Marriage of Heaven and Hell (1790–3) 'Proverbs of Hell'

24 The pride of the peacock is the glory of God.
The lust of the goat is the bounty of God.
The wrath of the lion is the wisdom of God.
The nakedness of woman is the work of God.

The Marriage of Heaven and Hell (1790–3) 'Proverbs of Hell'

25 The tygers of wrath are wiser than the horses of
instruction.

The Marriage of Heaven and Hell (1790–3) 'Proverbs of Hell'

26 Damn braces: Bless relaxes.

The Marriage of Heaven and Hell (1790–3) 'Proverbs of Hell'

27 Exuberance is beauty.

The Marriage of Heaven and Hell (1790–3) 'Proverbs of Hell'

28 Sooner murder an infant in its cradle than nurse
unacted desires.

The Marriage of Heaven and Hell (1790–3) 'Proverbs of Hell'

29 Truth can never be told so as to be understood, and
not be believed.

The Marriage of Heaven and Hell (1790–3) 'Proverbs of Hell'

30 How do you know but every bird that cuts the airy
way
Is an immense world of delight, closed by your senses
five?

The Marriage of Heaven and Hell (1790–3) 'A Memorable
Fancy' plate 7

1 Then I asked: 'Does a firm persuasion that a thing
is so, make it so?'
    He replied: 'All Poets believe that it does, and in
ages of imagination this firm persuasion removed
mountains; but many are not capable of a firm
persuasion of anything.'
    The Marriage of Heaven and Hell (1790–3) 'A Memorable
    Fancy' plates 12–13

2 If the doors of perception were cleansed everything
would appear to man as it is, infinite.
    The Marriage of Heaven and Hell (1790–3) 'A Memorable
    Fancy' plate 14

3 I was in a printing house in Hell, and saw the method
in which knowledge is transmitted from generation to
generation.
    The Marriage of Heaven and Hell (1790–3) 'A Memorable
    Fancy' plates 15–17

4 And did those feet in ancient time
Walk upon England's mountains green?
And was the holy Lamb of God
On England's pleasant pastures seen?

And did the Countenance Divine
Shine forth upon our clouded hills?
And was Jerusalem builded here
Among these dark Satanic mills?

Bring me my bow of burning gold:
Bring me my arrows of desire:
Bring me my spear: O clouds, unfold!
Bring me my chariot of fire.

I will not cease from mental fight,
Nor shall my sword sleep in my hand,
Till we have built Jerusalem,
In England's green and pleasant land.
    Milton (1804–10) preface 'And did those feet in ancient
    time'

5 Mock on mock on Voltaire Rousseau
Mock on mock on tis all in vain
You throw the sand against the wind
And the wind blows it back again.
    MS Note-Book p. 7

6 The atoms of Democritus
And Newtons particles of light
Are sands upon the Red sea shore
Where Israel's tents do shine so bright.
    MS Note-Book p. 7

7 He has observed the golden rule
Till he's become the golden fool.
    MS Note-Book p. 30

8 To forgive enemies H— does pretend
Who never in his life forgave a friend.
    MS Note-Book p. 34

9 The errors of a wise man make your rule
Rather than the perfections of a fool.
    MS Note-Book p. 42

10 Great things are done when men and mountains meet
This is not done by jostling in the street.
    MS Note-Book p. 43

11 He who binds to himself a joy
Doth the winged life destroy
But he who kisses the joy as it flies
Lives in Eternity's sunrise.
    MS Note-Book p. 99 'Several Questions Answered'—"He
    who binds to himself a joy"

12 What is it men in women do require
The lineaments of gratified desire
What is it women do in men require
The lineaments of gratified desire.
    MS Note-Book p. 99 'Several Questions Answered'—"What
    is it men in women do require"

13 The sword sung on the barren heath
The sickle in the fruitful field
The sword he sung a song of death,
But could not make the sickle yield.
    MS Note-Book p. 105

14 Abstinence sows sand all over
The ruddy limbs and flaming hair
But Desire gratified
Plants fruits of life and beauty there.
    MS Note-Book p. 105

15 Never pain to tell thy love
Love that never told can be
For the gentle wind does move
Silently, invisibly.
    MS Note-Book p. 115

16 Piping down the valleys wild
Piping songs of pleasant glee
On a cloud I saw a child.
And he laughing said to me.

Pipe a song about a Lamb;
So I piped with merry cheer,
Piper pipe that song again—
So I piped, he wept to hear.
    Songs of Innocence (1789) introduction

17 When my mother died I was very young,
And my father sold me while yet my tongue
Could scarcely cry weep weep weep weep.
So your chimneys I sweep and in soot I sleep.
    Songs of Innocence (1789) 'The Chimney Sweeper'

18 To Mercy Pity Peace and Love,
All pray in their distress.
    Songs of Innocence (1789) 'The Divine Image'

19 For Mercy has a human heart
Pity a human face:
And Love, the human form divine,
And Peace, the human dress.
    Songs of Innocence (1789) 'The Divine Image'

20 Then cherish pity, lest you drive an angel from your
door.
    Songs of Innocence (1789) 'Holy Thursday'

21 Little Lamb who made thee
Dost thou know who made thee
Gave thee life and bid thee feed.
By the stream and o'er the mead;
Gave thee clothing of delight,
Softest clothing woolly bright;
Gave thee such a tender voice,
Making all the vales rejoice!
    Songs of Innocence (1789) 'The Lamb'

1 My mother bore me in the southern wild,
And I am black, but O! my soul is white;
White as an angel is the English child:
But I am black as if bereaved of light.
Songs of Innocence (1789) 'The Little Black Boy'

2 When the voices of children are heard on the green
And laughing is heard on the hill.
Songs of Innocence (1789) 'Nurse's Song'

3 Can I see another's woe,
And not be in sorrow too.
Can I see another's grief,
And not seek for kind relief.
Songs of Innocence (1789) 'On Another's Sorrow'

4 Hear the voice of the Bard!
Who present, past, and future, sees.
Songs of Experience (1794) introduction

5 Ah, Sun-flower! weary of time,
Who countest the steps of the Sun;
Seeking after that sweet golden clime
Where the traveller's journey is done:

Where the Youth pined away with desire,
And the pale Virgin shrouded in snow:
Arise from their graves and aspire,
Where my Sun-flower wishes to go.
Songs of Experience (1794) 'Ah, Sun-flower!'

6 Love seeketh not itself to please,
Nor for itself hath any care;
But for another gives its ease,
And builds a Heaven in Hell's despair.
Songs of Experience (1794) 'The Clod and the Pebble'

7 Love seeketh only Self to please,
To bind another to its delight,
Joys in another's loss of ease,
And builds a Hell in Heaven's despite.
Songs of Experience (1794) 'The Clod and the Pebble'

8 My mother groaned! my father wept.
Into the dangerous world I leapt:
Helpless, naked, piping loud;
Like a fiend hid in a cloud.
Songs of Experience (1794) 'Infant Sorrow'

9 Children of the future age,
Reading this indignant page:
Know that in a former time
Love! sweet love! was thought a crime.
Songs of Experience (1794) 'A Little Girl Lost'

10 Then the Parson might preach, and drink, and sing.
And we'd be as happy as birds in the spring:
And modest dame Lurch, who is always at church,
Would not have bandy children nor fasting nor birch.
Songs of Experience (1794) 'The Little Vagabond'

11 I was angry with my friend;
I told my wrath, my wrath did end.
I was angry with my foe:
I told it not, my wrath did grow.
Songs of Experience (1794) 'A Poison Tree'

12 O Rose, thou art sick!
The invisible worm
That flies in the night,
In the howling storm:

Has found out thy bed
Of crimson joy:
And his dark secret love
Does thy life destroy.
Songs of Experience (1794) 'The Sick Rose'

13 Tyger Tyger, burning bright,
In the forests of the night;
What immortal hand or eye,
Could frame thy fearful symmetry?
Songs of Experience (1794) 'The Tiger'

14 What the hand dare seize the fire?

And what shoulder, and what art,
Could twist the sinews of thy heart?
And when thy heart began to beat,
What dread hand? and what dread feet?
Songs of Experience (1794) 'The Tiger'

15 When the stars threw down their spears
And watered heaven with their tears:
Did he smile his work to see?
Did he who made the Lamb make thee?
Songs of Experience (1794) 'The Tiger'

16 Cruelty has a human heart,
And Jealousy a human face;
Terror the human form divine,
And Secrecy the human dress.
'A Divine Image'; etched but not included in *Songs of Experience* (1794)

17 Vision or Imagination is a Representation of what
Eternally Exists, Really and Unchangeably.
A Vision of the Last Judgement (1810) in *MS Note-Book* p. 68

18 What it will be questioned when the sun rises do you
not see a round disc of fire somewhat like a guinea O
no no I see an innumerable company of the heavenly
host crying Holy, Holy, Holy is the Lord God
Almighty.
A Vision of the Last Judgement (1810) in *MS Note-Book* p. 95

Susanna Blamire 1747–94

English poet

19 I've gotten a rock, I've gotten a reel,
I've gotten a wee bit spinning-wheel;
An' by the whirling rim I've found
How the weary, weary warl goes round.
'I've Gotten a Rock, I've Gotten a Reel' (c.1790) l. 1

20 Should we miss but a tree where we used to be
playing,
Or find the wood cut where we sauntered a-Maying,—
If the yew-seat's away, or the ivy's a-wanting,
We hate the fine lawn and the new-fashioned
planting.
Each thing called improvement seems blackened with
crimes,
If it tears up one record of blissful old times.
'When Home We Return' (c.1790) l. 7

Lesley Blanch 1907–

British writer

1 She was an Amazon. Her whole life was spent riding at breakneck speed towards the wilder shores of love.
   The Wilder Shores of Love (1954) pt. 2, ch. 1

Karen Blixen

See ISAK DINESEN

Philip Paul Bliss 1838–76

American evangelist

2 Hold the fort, for I am coming.
   Gospel Hymns and Sacred Songs (1875) no. 14 (suggested by a flag message from General W. T. Sherman near Atlanta, October 1864)

Alexander Blok 1880–1921

Russian poet

3 Когда в листве сырой и ржавой
  Рябины заалеет гроздь, —
  Когда плач рукой костлявой
  Бобьет в ладонь последний гвоздь ...

  Тогда — просторно и далеко
  Смотрю сквозь кровь предсмертных слез,
  И вижу: по реке широкой
  Ко мне плывет в челне Христос.

  When rowan leaves are dank and rusting
  And rowan berries red as blood,
  When in my palm the hangman's thrusting
  The final nail with bony thud ...

  Then, through the blood and weeping, stretches
  My dying sight to space remote;
  I see upon the river's reaches
  Christ sailing to me in a boat.
     'Autumn Love' (1907) (translated by Maurice Bowra)

4 Все это было, было, было,
  Свершился дней круговорот.
  Какая ложь, какая сила
  Тебя, прошедшее, вернет?

  All that is finished, finished, finished;
  The circle of our days is done.
  And what illusion, and what power,
  Recalls you, Past, when you have gone?
     'Russia' (1908) (translated by Jon Stallworthy and Peter France)

5 Испепеляющие годы!
  Безумья ль б вас, надежды ль весть?
  От дней войны, от дней свободы —
  Кровавый отсвет в лицах есть.

  What message, years of conflagration,
  have you: madness or hope? On thin cheeks strained by war and liberation
  bloody reflections still remain.
     'Those Born in Years of Stagnation' (1914) (translated by Jon Stallworthy and Peter France)

6 Гуляет ветер, порхает снег.
  Идут двенадцать человек.

  Винтовок черные ремни,
  Кругом — огни, огни, огни.

  The wind plays up; snow flutters down.
  Twelve men are marching through the town.

  Their rifle-butts on black slings sway.
  Lights left, right, left, wink all the way.
     'The Twelve' (1918) (translated by Jon Stallworthy and Peter France)

7 В зубах — цигарка, примят картуз,
  На спину б надо бубновый туз!

  Caps tilted, fag drooping, every one looks like a jailbird on the run.
     'The Twelve' (1918) (translated by Jon Stallworthy and Peter France)

8 Товарищи, винтовку держи, не трусь!
  Пальнем-ка пулей в Святую Русь —
  В кондовую,
  В избяную
  В толстозадую!
  Эх, эх, без креста!

  Grip your gun like a man, brother!
  Let's have a crack at Holy Russia,
  Mother
  Russia
  with her big, fat arse!
  Freedom, freedom! Down with the cross!
     'The Twelve' (1918)

9 Так идут державным шагом —
  Позади — голодный пес,
  Впереди — с кровавым флагом,
  И за вьюгой невидим,
  И от пули невредим,
  Нежной поступью надвьюжной,
  Снежной россыпью жемчужной,
  В белом венчике из роз —
  Впереди — Иисус Христос.

  So they march with sovereign tread
  Behind them limps the hungry dog,
  and wrapped in wild snow at their head
  carrying a blood-red flag—
  soft-footed where the blizzard swirls,
  invulnerable where bullets crossed—
  crowned with a crown of snowflake pearls,
  a flowery diadem of frost,
  ahead of them goes Jesus Christ.
     'The Twelve' (1918) (translated by Jon Stallworthy and Peter France)

Gebhard Lebrecht Blücher 1742–1819

Prussian field marshal

10 *Was für Plunder!*

   What rubbish!
      Of London, as seen from the Monument in June 1814; in Evelyn Princess Blücher *Memoirs of Prince Blücher* (1932) p. 33 (often misquoted '*Was für plündern* [What a place to plunder]!')

Edmund Blunden 1896–1974

English poet

1 All things they have in common being so poor,
And their one fear, Death's shadow at the door.
'Almswomen' (1920)

2 I am for the woods against the world,
But are the woods for me?
'The Kiss' (1931)

3 Dance on this ball-floor thin and wan,
Use him as though you love him;
Court him, elude him, reel and pass,
And let him hate you through the glass.
'Midnight Skaters' (1925)

4 I have been young, and now am not too old;
And I have seen the righteous forsaken,
His health, his honour and his quality taken.
This is not what we were formerly told.
'Report on Experience' (1929)

5 This was my country and it may be yet,
But something flew between me and the sun.
'The Resignation' (1928)

Wilfrid Scawen Blunt 1840–1922

English poet

6 To the Grafton Gallery to look at . . . the
Post-Impressionist pictures sent over from Paris . . .
The drawing is on the level of that of an untaught
child of seven or eight years old, the sense of colour
that of a tea-tray painter, the method that of
a schoolboy who wipes his fingers on a slate after
spitting on them . . . These are not works of art at all,
unless throwing a handful of mud against a wall may
be called one. They are the works of idleness and
impotent stupidity, a pornographic show.
My Diaries (1920) 15 November 1910

Robert Bly 1926–

American poet

7 Terror just before death,
Shoulders torn, shot
From helicopters, the boy
Tortured with the telephone generator,
'I felt sorry for him
And blew his head off with a shotgun.'
These instants become crystals,
Particles
The grass cannot dissolve. Our own gaiety
Will end up
In Asia, and in your cup you will look down
And see
Black Starfighters.
We were the ones we intended to bomb!
'Driving Through Minnesota During the Hanoi Bombings'
(1968)

8 Alive, we are like a sleek black water beetle.
Skating across still water in any direction
We choose, and soon to be swallowed
Suddenly from beneath.
'Night' (1962)

Ronald Blythe 1922–

English writer

9 As for the British churchman, he goes to church as he
goes to the bathroom, with the minimum of fuss and
with no explanation if he can help it.
The Age of Illusion (1963) ch. 12

10 An industrial worker would sooner have a £5 note but
a countryman must have praise.
Akenfield (1969) ch. 5

John Ernest Bode 1816–74

English clergyman

11 O let me hear thee speaking
In accents clear and still,
Above the storms of passion,
The murmurs of self-will;
O speak to reassure me,
To hasten or control;
O speak, and make me listen,
Thou Guardian of my soul.
'O Jesus, I have promised' (1869 hymn); written for the
confirmation of Bode's three children

Boethius AD c.476–524

Roman statesman and philosopher

12 *Nam in omni adversitate fortunae infelicissimum est genus
infortunii, fuisse felicem.*

For in every ill-turn of fortune the most unhappy sort
of unfortunate man is the one who has been happy.
De Consolatione Philosophiae bk. 2, prose 4

Louise Bogan 1897–1970

American poet

13 Women have no wilderness in them,
They are provident instead,
Content in the tight hot cell of their hearts
To eat dusty bread.
'Women' (1923)

John B. Bogart 1848–1921

American journalist

14 When a dog bites a man, that is not news, because it
happens so often. But if a man bites a dog, that is
news.
In F. M. O'Brien *The Story of the* [New York] *Sun* (1918)
ch. 10 (often attributed to Charles A. Dana)

Niels Bohr 1885–1962

Danish physicist

1 One of the favourite maxims of my father was the distinction between the two sorts of truths, profound truths recognized by the fact that the opposite is also a profound truth, in contrast to trivialities where opposites are obviously absurd.
In S. Rozental *Niels Bohr* (1967) p. 328

Nicolas Boileau 1636–1711

French critic and poet

2 *Enfin Malherbe vint, et, le premier en France,*
Fit sentir dans les vers une juste cadence.
At last came Malherbe, and he was the first in France to give poetry a proper flow.
L'Art poétique (1674) canto 1, l. 131

3 *Un sot trouve toujours un plus sot qui l'admire.*
A fool can always find a greater fool to admire him.
L'Art poétique (1674) canto 1, l. 232

4 *Qu'en un lieu, qu'en un jour, un seul fait accompli*
Tienne jusqu'à la fin le théâtre rempli.
Let a single completed action, all in one place, all in one day, keep the theatre packed to the end of your play.
L'Art poétique (1674) canto 3, l. 45

5 *Si j'écris quatre mots, j'en effacerai trois.*
Of every four words I write, I strike out three.
Satire (2). *A M. Molière* (1665)

Alan Bold 1943–

Scottish poet

6 Scotland, land of the omnipotent No.
'A Memory of Death' (1969)

Henry St John, 1st Viscount Bolingbroke 1678–1751

English statesman

7 They make truth serve as a stalking-horse to error.
Letters on the Study and Use of History (1752) No. 4, pt. 1

8 They [Thucydides and Xenophon] maintained the dignity of history.
Letters on the Study and Use of History (1752) No. 5, pt. 2

9 Nations, like men, have their infancy.
On the Study of History letter 5, in *Works* (1809) vol. 3, p. 414

10 Truth lies within a little and certain compass, but error is immense.
Reflections upon Exile (1716)

11 What a world is this, and how does fortune banter us!
Letter to Jonathan Swift, 3 August 1714, in Harold Williams (ed.) *Correspondence of Jonathan Swift* (1963) vol. 2, p. 101

12 The great mistake is that of looking upon men as virtuous, or thinking that they can be made so by laws.
Comment (*c*.1728), in Joseph Spence *Observations, Anecdotes, and Characters* (1820, ed. J. M. Osborn, 1966) Anecdote 882

13 The greatest art of a politician is to render vice serviceable to the cause of virtue.
Comment (*c*.1728), in Joseph Spence *Observations, Anecdotes, and Characters* (1820, ed. J. M. Osborn, 1966) Anecdote 882

Robert Bolt 1924–

English playwright

14 Morality's *not* practical. Morality's a gesture. A complicated gesture learned from books.
A Man for All Seasons (1960) act 2. Cf. Whittington 733:11

15 It profits a man nothing to give his soul for the whole world . . . But for Wales—!
A Man for All Seasons (1960) act 2

Edmund Bolton *c*.1575–*c*.1633

English poet

16 The withered primrose by the mourning river,
The faded summer's sun from weeping fountains,
The light-blown bubble vanished for ever,
The molten snow upon the naked mountains,
Are emblems that the treasures we up-lay
Soon wither, vanish, fade, and melt away.
'A Palinode' (1600)

Carrie Jacobs Bond 1862–1946

American songwriter

17 When you come to the end of a perfect day,
And you sit alone with your thought,
While the chimes ring out with a carol gay
For the joy that the day has brought,
Do you think what the end of a perfect day
Can mean to a tired heart,
When the sun goes down with a flaming ray,
And the dear friends have to part?
'A Perfect Day' (1910 song)

Sir David Bone 1874–1959

Scottish naval officer and writer

18 It's 'Damn you, Jack—I'm all right!' with you chaps.
Brassbounder (1910) ch. 3

Dietrich Bonhoeffer 1906–45

German Lutheran theologian and martyr

1 *Es ist der Vorzug und das Wesen der Starken, dass sie die grossen Entscheidungsfragen stellen und zu ihnen klar Stellung nehmen können. Die Schwachen müssen sich immer zwischen Alternativen entscheiden, die nicht die ihren sind.*

It is the nature, and the advantage, of strong people that they can bring out the crucial questions and form a clear opinion about them. The weak always have to decide between alternatives that are not their own.

Widerstand und Ergebung (Resistance and Submission, 1951) 'Ein paar Gedanken über Verschiedenes'

2 *Jesus nur 'für andere da ist' . . . Gott in Menschengestalt! . . . nicht die griechische Gott-Menschgestalt des 'Menschen an sich', sondern 'der Mensch für andere', darum der Gekreuzigte.*

Jesus is there only for others . . . God in human form! not . . . in the Greek divine-human form of 'man in himself', but 'the man for others', and therefore the crucified.

Widerstand und Ergebung (Resistance and Submission, 1951) 'Entwurf einer Arbeit'

The Book of Common Prayer 1662

3 It hath been the wisdom of the Church of England, ever since the first compiling of her Publick Liturgy, to keep the mean between the two extremes, of too much stiffness in refusing, and of too much easiness in admitting any variation from it.
The Preface

4 There was never any thing by the wit of man so well devised, or so sure established, which in continuance of time hath not been corrupted.
The Preface Concerning the Service of the Church

5 Dearly beloved brethren, the Scripture moveth us in sundry places to acknowledge and confess our manifold sins and wickedness; and that we should not dissemble nor cloke them before the face of Almighty God our heavenly Father; but confess them with an humble, lowly, penitent, and obedient heart.
Morning Prayer Sentences of the Scriptures

6 I pray and beseech you, as many as are here present, to accompany me with a pure heart, and humble voice, unto the throne of the heavenly grace.
Morning Prayer Sentences of the Scriptures

7 We have erred, and strayed from thy ways like lost sheep. We have followed too much the devices and desires of our own hearts.
Morning Prayer General Confession

8 We have left undone those things which we ought to have done; And we have done those things which we ought not to have done; And there is no health in us.
Morning Prayer General Confession

9 Restore thou them that are penitent; According to thy promises declared unto mankind in Christ Jesu our Lord. And grant, O most merciful Father, for his sake; That we may hereafter live a godly, righteous, and sober life.
Morning Prayer General Confession

10 And forgive us our trespasses, As we forgive them that trespass against us.
Morning Prayer The Lord's Prayer. Cf. St Matthew 89:5, Missal 477:3

11 Glory be to the Father, and to the Son: and to the Holy Ghost; As it was in the beginning, is now, and ever shall be: world without end. Amen.
Morning Prayer Gloria. Cf. Missal 476:15

12 We praise thee, O God: we acknowledge thee to be the Lord.
All the earth doth worship thee: the Father everlasting.
To thee all Angels cry aloud: the Heavens, and all the Powers therein.
To thee Cherubin, and Seraphin: continually do cry, Holy, Holy, Holy: Lord God of Sabaoth;
Heaven and earth are full of the Majesty: of thy Glory.
The glorious company of the Apostles: praise thee.
The goodly fellowship of the Prophets: praise thee.
The noble army of Martyrs: praise thee.
Morning Prayer Te Deum. Cf. Anonymous 22:17

13 When thou hadst overcome the sharpness of death: thou didst open the Kingdom of Heaven to all believers.
Morning Prayer Te Deum. Cf. Anonymous 22:17

14 Day by day: we magnify thee;
And we worship thy Name: ever world without end.
Vouchsafe, O Lord: to keep us this day without sin.
O Lord, have mercy upon us: have mercy upon us.
O Lord, let thy mercy lighten upon us: as our trust is in thee.
O Lord, in thee have I trusted: let me never be confounded.
Morning Prayer Te Deum. Cf. Anonymous 22:17

15 O all ye Works of the Lord, bless ye the Lord.
Morning Prayer Benedicite

16 O ye Waters that be above the Firmament, bless ye the Lord.
Morning Prayer Benedicite

17 O ye Showers, and Dew, bless ye the Lord: praise him, and magnify him for ever.
O ye Winds of God, bless ye the Lord: praise him, and magnify him for ever.
Morning Prayer Benedicite

18 O ye Dews, and Frosts, bless ye the Lord: praise him, and magnify him for ever.
O ye Frost and Cold, bless ye the Lord: praise him and magnify him for ever.
O ye Ice and Snow, bless ye the Lord: praise him and magnify him for ever.
O ye Nights, and Days, bless ye the Lord: praise him, and magnify him for ever.
Morning Prayer Benedicite

19 O let the Earth bless the Lord: yea, let it praise him, and magnify him for ever.
Morning Prayer Benedicite

20 O all ye Green Things upon the Earth, bless ye the Lord: praise him, and magnify him for ever.
Morning Prayer Benedicite

21 O ye Whales, and all that move in the Waters, bless ye the Lord: praise him, and magnify him for ever.
Morning Prayer Benedicite

1 I believe in God the Father Almighty, Maker of heaven and earth:
And in Jesus Christ his only Son our Lord, Who was conceived by the Holy Ghost, Born of the Virgin Mary, Suffered under Pontius Pilate, Was crucified, dead, and buried, He descended into hell; The third day he rose again from the dead, He ascended into heaven, And sitteth on the right hand of God the Father Almighty; From thence he shall come to judge the quick and the dead.
I believe in the Holy Ghost; The holy Catholic Church; The Communion of Saints; The Forgiveness of sins; The Resurrection of the body, And the life everlasting. Amen.
Morning Prayer The Apostles' Creed. Cf. Missal 476:21, Book of Common Prayer 121:19

2 Give peace in our time, O Lord.
Morning Prayer Versicle

3 O God, who art the author of peace and lover of concord, in knowledge of whom standeth our eternal life, whose service is perfect freedom; Defend us thy humble servants in all assaults of our enemies.
Morning Prayer The Second Collect, for Peace

4 Grant that this day we fall into no sin, neither run into any kind of danger.
Morning Prayer The Third Collect, for Grace

5 In Quires and Places where they sing, here followeth the Anthem.
Morning Prayer rubric following Third Collect

6 Endue her plenteously with heavenly gifts; grant her in health and wealth long to live.
Morning Prayer Prayer for the Queen's Majesty

7 Almighty God, the fountain of all goodness.
Morning Prayer Prayer for the Royal Family

8 Almighty and everlasting God, who alone workest great marvels; Send down upon our Bishops, and Curates, and all Congregations committed to their charge, the healthful Spirit of thy grace; and that they may truly please thee, pour upon them the continual dew of thy blessing.
Morning Prayer Prayer for the Clergy and People

9 Almighty God, who hast given us grace at this time with one accord to make our common supplications unto thee; and dost promise, that when two or three are gathered together in thy Name thou wilt grant their requests: Fulfil now, O Lord, the desires and petitions of thy servants, as may be most expedient for them.
Morning Prayer Prayer of St Chrysostom

10 O God, from whom all holy desires, all good counsels, and all just works do proceed; Give unto thy servants that peace which the world cannot give.
Evening Prayer Second Collect

11 Lighten our darkness, we beseech thee, O Lord; and by thy great mercy defend us from all perils and dangers of this night.
Evening Prayer Third Collect

12 Whosoever will be saved: before all things it is necessary that he hold the Catholic Faith.
At Morning Prayer Athanasian Creed 'Quicunque vult'

13 And the Catholic Faith is this: That we worship one God in Trinity, and Trinity in Unity;
Neither confounding the Persons: nor dividing the Substance.
At Morning Prayer Athanasian Creed 'Quicunque vult'

14 There are not three incomprehensibles, nor three uncreated: but one uncreated, and one incomprehensible.
At Morning Prayer Athanasian Creed 'Quicunque vult'

15 Perfect God, and perfect Man: of a reasonable soul and human flesh subsisting;
Equal to the Father, as touching his Godhead: and inferior to the Father, as touching his Manhood.
At Morning Prayer Athanasian Creed 'Quicunque vult'

16 Have mercy upon us miserable sinners.
The Litany

17 From all evil and mischief; from sin, from the crafts and assaults of the devil; from thy wrath, and from everlasting damnation,
Good Lord, deliver us.
From all blindness of heart; from pride, vain-glory, and hypocrisy; from envy, hatred, and malice, and from all uncharitableness,
Good Lord, deliver us.
From fornication, and all other deadly sin; and from all the deceits of the world, the flesh, and the devil,
Good Lord, deliver us.
From lightning and tempest; from plague, pestilence, and famine; from battle and murder, and from sudden death,
Good Lord, deliver us.
The Litany

18 By thine Agony and bloody Sweat; by thy Cross and Passion; by thy precious Death and Burial; by thy glorious Resurrection and Ascension; and by the coming of the Holy Ghost,
Good Lord, deliver us.
In all time of our tribulation; in all time of our wealth; in the hour of death, and in the day of judgement,
Good Lord, deliver us.
The Litany

19 That it may please thee to illuminate all Bishops, Priests, and Deacons, with true knowledge and understanding of thy Word; and that both by their preaching and living they may set it forth, and show it accordingly;
We beseech thee to hear us, good Lord.
The Litany

20 That it may please thee to strengthen such as do stand; and to comfort and help the weak-hearted; and to raise up them that fall; and finally to beat down Satan under our feet;
We beseech thee to hear us, good Lord.
The Litany

1 That it may please thee to preserve all that travel by
land or by water, all women labouring of child, all
sick persons, and young children; and to shew thy
pity upon all prisoners and captives;
We beseech thee to hear us, good Lord.
That it may please thee to defend, and provide for, the
fatherless children, and widows, and all that are
desolate and oppressed;
We beseech thee to hear us, good Lord.
The Litany

2 That it may please thee to give and preserve to our
use the kindly fruits of the earth, so as in due time
we may enjoy them;
We beseech thee to hear us, good Lord.
The Litany

3 O God, merciful Father, that despisest not the sighing
of a contrite heart, not the desire of such as be
sorrowful; Mercifully assist our prayers that we make
before thee in all our troubles and adversities,
whensoever they oppress us.
The Litany

4 O God, whose nature and property is ever to have
mercy and to forgive, receive our humble petitions;
and though we be tied and bound with the chain of
our sins, yet let the pitifulness of thy great mercy loose
us; for the honour of Jesus Christ, our Mediator and
Advocate.
Prayers . . . upon Several Occasions A prayer

5 O God, the Creator and Preserver of all mankind, we
humbly beseech thee for all sorts and conditions of
men.
Prayers . . . upon Several Occasions 'Collect or Prayer for all
Conditions of Men'

6 We pray for the good estate of the Catholick Church;
that it may be so guided and governed by thy good
Spirit, that all who profess and call themselves
Christians may be led into the way of truth.
Prayers . . . upon Several Occasions 'Collect or Prayer for all
Conditions of Men'

7 We commend to thy fatherly goodness all those, who
are any ways afflicted, or distressed, in mind, body, or
estate; that it may please thee to comfort and relieve
them, according to their several necessities, giving
them patience under their sufferings, and a happy
issue out of all their afflictions.
Prayers . . . upon Several Occasions 'Collect or Prayer for all
Conditions of Men'

8 We bless thee for our creation, preservation, and all
the blessings of this life; but above all, for thine
inestimable love in the redemption of the world by our
Lord Jesus Christ; for the means of grace, and for the
hope of glory.
Thanksgivings General Thanksgiving

9 O God our heavenly Father, who by thy gracious
providence dost cause the former and the latter rain to
descend upon the earth, that it may bring forth fruit
for the use of man; We give thee humble thanks that
it hath pleased thee, in our great necessity, to send us
at the last a joyful rain upon thine inheritance, and to
refresh it when it was dry.
Thanksgivings For Rain

10 Almighty God, give us grace that we may cast away
the works of darkness, and put upon us the armour of
light, now in the time of this mortal life, in which thy
Son Jesus Christ came to visit us in great humility.
Collects The first Sunday in Advent

11 Blessed Lord, who hast caused all holy Scriptures to be
written for our learning; Grant that we may in such
wise hear them, read, mark, learn, and inwardly
digest them, that by patience, and comfort of thy holy
Word, we may embrace, and ever hold fast the blessed
hope of everlasting life.
Collects The second Sunday in Advent

12 That whereas, through our sins and wickedness, we
are sore let and hindered in running the race that is
set before us, thy bountiful grace and mercy may
speedily help and deliver us.
Collects The fourth Sunday in Advent

13 O Lord, we beseech thee mercifully to receive the
prayers of thy people which call upon thee; and grant
that they may both perceive and know what things
they ought to do, and also may have grace and power
faithfully to fulfil the same.
Collects The first Sunday after the Epiphany

14 O God, who knowest us to be set in the midst of so
many and great dangers, that by reason of the frailty
of our nature we cannot always stand upright; Grant
to us such strength and protection, as may support us
in all dangers, and carry us through all temptations.
Collects The fourth Sunday after the Epiphany

15 Almighty God, who seest that we have no power of
ourselves to help ourselves; Keep us both outwardly in
our bodies, and inwardly in our souls; that we may be
defended from all adversities which may happen to the
body, and from all evil thoughts which may assault
and hurt the soul.
Collects The second Sunday in Lent

16 We humbly beseech thee, that, as by thy special grace
preventing us thou dost put into our minds good
desires, so by thy continued help we may bring the
same to good effect.
Collects Easter-Day

17 Grant us so to put away the leaven of malice and
wickedness, that we may alway serve thee in pureness
of living and truth.
Collects The first Sunday after Easter

18 O Almighty God, who alone canst order the unruly
wills and affections of sinful men; Grant unto thy
people, that they may love the thing which thou
commandest, and desire that which thou dost
promise; that so, among the sundry and manifold
changes of the world, our hearts may surely there be
fixed, where true joys are to be found.
Collects The fourth Sunday after Easter

19 We beseech thee, leave us not comfortless; but send to
us thine Holy Ghost to comfort us, and exalt us unto
the same place whither our Saviour Christ is gone
before.
Collects Sunday after Ascension Day

20 God, who as at this time didst teach the hearts of thy
faithful people, by the sending to them the light of thy
Holy Spirit; Grant us by the same Spirit to have a
right judgement in all things.
Collects Whit-Sunday

1 Because through the weakness of our mortal nature we can do no good thing without thee, grant us the help of thy grace, that in keeping of thy commandments we may please thee, both in will and deed.
Collects The first Sunday after Trinity

2 O God, the protector of all that trust in thee, without whom nothing is strong, nothing is holy; Increase and multiply upon us thy mercy; that, thou being our ruler and guide, we may so pass through things temporal, that we finally lose not the things eternal.
Collects The fourth Sunday after Trinity

3 Grant, O Lord, we beseech thee, that the course of this world may be so peaceably ordered by thy governance, that thy Church may joyfully serve thee in all godly quietness.
Collects The fifth Sunday after Trinity

4 O God, who hast prepared for them that love thee such good things as pass man's understanding; Pour into our hearts such love toward thee, that we, loving thee above all things, may obtain thy promises, which exceed all that we can desire.
Collects The sixth Sunday after Trinity

5 Lord of all power and might, who art the author and giver of all good things; Graft in our hearts the love of thy Name, increase in us true religion, nourish us with all goodness, and of thy great mercy keep us in the same.
Collects The seventh Sunday after Trinity

6 Pour down upon us the abundance of thy mercy; forgiving us those things whereof our conscience is afraid.
Collects The twelfth Sunday after Trinity

7 O God, forasmuch as without thee we are not able to please thee; Mercifully grant, that thy Holy Spirit may in all things direct and rule our hearts.
Collects The nineteenth Sunday after Trinity

8 Grant, we beseech thee, merciful Lord, to thy faithful people pardon and peace, that they may be cleansed from all their sins, and serve thee with a quiet mind.
Collects The one and twentieth Sunday after Trinity

9 Lord, we beseech thee to keep thy household the Church in continual godliness.
Collects The two and twentieth Sunday after Trinity

10 Grant that those things which we ask faithfully we may obtain effectually.
Collects The three and twentieth Sunday after Trinity

11 Stir up, we beseech thee, O Lord, the wills of thy faithful people; that they, plenteously bringing forth the fruit of good works, may of thee be plenteously rewarded.
Collects The five and twentieth Sunday after Trinity

12 Give us grace, that, being not like children carried away with every blast of vain doctrine, we may be established in the truth of thy holy Gospel.
Collects St Mark's Day

13 O Almighty God, who hast knit together thine elect in one communion and fellowship, in the mystical body of thy Son Christ our Lord; Grant us grace so to follow thy blessed Saints in all virtuous and godly living, that we may come to those unspeakable joys, which thou hast prepared for them that unfeignedly love thee.
Collects All Saints' Day

14 So many as intend to be partakers of the holy Communion shall signify their names to the Curate, at least some time the day before.
And if any of those be an open and notorious evil liver, or have done any wrong to his neighbours by word or deed, so that the Congregation be thereby offended; the Curate, having knowledge thereof, shall call him and advertise him, that in any wise he presume not to come to the Lord's Table, until he have openly declared himself to have truly repented and amended his former naughty life.
Holy Communion introductory rubric

15 The Table, at the Communion-time having a fair white linen cloth upon it, shall stand in the Body of the Church, or in the Chancel.
Holy Communion introductory rubric

16 Almighty God, unto whom all hearts be open, all desires known, and from whom no secrets are hid; Cleanse the thoughts of our hearts by the inspiration of thy Holy Spirit, that we may perfectly love thee, and worthily magnify thy holy Name.
Holy Communion The Collect

17 Incline our hearts to keep this law.
Holy Communion The Ten Commandments (response)

18 Thou shalt do no murder.
Holy Communion The Ten Commandments. Cf. Exodus 72:16

19 I believe in one God the Father Almighty, Maker of heaven and earth, And of all things visible and invisible:
And in one Lord Jesus Christ, the only-begotten Son of God, Begotten of his Father before all worlds, God of God, Light of Light, Very God of very God, Begotten, not made, Being of one substance with the Father, By whom all things were made.
Holy Communion Nicene Creed. Cf. Missal 476:21, Book of Common Prayer 119:1

20 And I believe in the Holy Ghost, the Lord and giver of life, Who proceedeth from the Father and the Son, Who with the Father and the Son together is worshipped and glorified, Who spake by the Prophets. And I believe one Catholick and Apostolick Church.
Holy Communion Nicene Creed. Cf. Missal 476:21

21 Let us pray for the whole state of Christ's Church militant here in earth.
Holy Communion Prayer for the Church Militant

22 We humbly beseech thee most mercifully to accept our alms and oblations, and to receive these our prayers, which we offer unto thy Divine Majesty; beseeching thee to inspire continually the universal Church with the spirit of truth, unity, and concord: And grant, that all they that do confess thy holy Name may agree in the truth of thy holy Word, and live in unity, and godly love.
Holy Communion Prayer for the Church Militant

1 Grant unto her [the Queen's] whole Council, and to all that are put in authority under her, that they may truly and indifferently minister justice.
Holy Communion Prayer for the Church Militant

2 Give grace, O heavenly Father, to all Bishops and Curates, that they may both by their life and doctrine set forth thy true and lively Word.
Holy Communion Prayer for the Church Militant

3 We most humbly beseech thee of thy goodness, O Lord, to comfort and succour all them, who in this transitory life are in trouble, sorrow, need, sickness, or any other adversity. And we also bless thy holy Name for all thy servants departed this life in thy faith and fear.
Holy Communion Prayer for the Church Militant

4 Because it is requisite, that no man should come to the holy Communion, but with a full trust in God's mercy, and with a quiet conscience; therefore if there be any of you, who by this means cannot quiet his own conscience herein, but requireth further comfort or counsel, let him come to me, or to some other discreet and learned Minister of God's Word, and open his grief.
Holy Communion First Exhortation

5 Ye that do truly and earnestly repent you of your sins, and are in love and charity with your neighbours, and intend to lead a new life, following the commandments of God, and walking from henceforth in his holy ways; Draw near with faith, and take this holy Sacrament to your comfort; and make your humble confession to Almighty God, meekly kneeling upon your knees.
Holy Communion The Invitation

6 We do earnestly repent, And are heartily sorry for these our misdoings; The remembrance of them is grievous unto us; The burden of them is intolerable.
Holy Communion General Confession

7 Hear what comfortable words our Saviour Christ saith unto all that truly turn to him.
Holy Communion Comfortable Words (preamble)

8 Lift up your hearts.
Holy Communion versicles and responses. Cf. Missal 476:24

9 It is meet and right so to do.
Holy Communion versicles and responses

10 It is very meet, right, and our bounden duty, that we should at all times, and in all places, give thanks unto thee, O Lord, Holy Father, Almighty, Everlasting God.
Therefore with Angels and Archangels, and with all the company of heaven, we laud and magnify thy glorious Name; evermore praising thee, and saying, Holy, holy, holy, Lord God of hosts, heaven and earth are full of thy glory: Glory be to thee, O Lord most High.
Holy Communion Hymn of Praise. Cf. Revelation 106:11, Missal 477:1

11 Almighty God, our heavenly Father, who of thy tender mercy didst give thine only Son Jesus Christ to suffer death upon the cross for our redemption; who made there (by his one oblation of himself once offered) a full, perfect, and sufficient sacrifice, oblation, and satisfaction, for the sins of the whole world.
Holy Communion Prayer of Consecration

12 Who, in the same night that he was betrayed, took Bread; and, when he had given thanks, he brake it, and gave it to his disciples, saying, Take, eat, this is my Body which is given for you: Do this in remembrance of me. Likewise after supper he took the Cup; and, when he had given thanks, he gave it to them, saying, Drink ye all of this; for this is my Blood of the New Testament, which is shed for you and for many for the remission of sins: Do this, as oft as ye shall drink it, in remembrance of me.
Holy Communion Prayer of Consecration

13 Although we be unworthy, through our manifold sins, to offer unto thee any sacrifice, yet we beseech thee to accept this our bounden duty and service; not weighing our merits, but pardoning our offences.
Holy Communion First Prayer of Oblation

14 We are very members incorporate in the mystical body of thy Son, which is the blessed company of all faithful people; and are also heirs through hope of thy everlasting kingdom.
Holy Communion Second (alternative) Prayer of Oblation. The *Alternative Service Book* Post-Communion prayer reads: 'Father of all, We give you thanks and praise, that when we were still far off you met us in your Son and brought us home. Dying and living, he declared your love, gave us grace, and opened the gate of glory.'

15 The blessing of God Almighty, the Father, the Son, and the Holy Ghost, be amongst you and remain with you always.
Holy Communion The Blessing

16 Assist us mercifully, O Lord, in these our supplications and prayers, and dispose the way of thy servants towards the attainment of everlasting salvation; that, among all the changes and chances of this mortal life, they may ever be defended by thy most gracious and ready help.
Holy Communion Collects after the Offertory

17 Prevent us, O Lord, in all our doings with thy most gracious favour, and further us with thy continual help; that in all our works, begun, continued, and ended in thee, we may glorify thy holy Name.
Holy Communion Collects after the Offertory

18 Those things, which for our unworthiness we dare not, and for our blindness we cannot ask, vouchsafe to give us, for the worthiness of thy Son Jesus Christ our Lord.
Holy Communion Collects after the Offertory

19 It is expedient that Baptism be administered in the vulgar tongue.
Public Baptism of Infants introductory rubric

20 O merciful God, grant that the old Adam in this Child may be so buried, that the new man may be raised up in him.
Public Baptism of Infants Invocation of blessing on the child

1 Humbly we beseech thee to grant, that he, being dead unto sin, and living unto righteousness, and being buried with Christ in his death, may crucify the old man, and utterly abolish the whole body of sin.
Public Baptism of Infants Thanksgiving

2 And as for you, who have now by Baptism put on Christ, it is your part and duty also, being made the children of God and of the light, by faith in Jesus Christ, to walk answerably to your Christian calling, and as becometh the children of light.
Baptism of Such as are of Riper Years Priest's final address

3 QUESTION: Who gave you this Name?
ANSWER: My Godfathers and Godmothers in my Baptism; wherein I was made a member of Christ, the child of God, and an inheritor of the kingdom of heaven.
Catechism

4 I should renounce the devil and all his works, the pomps and vanity of this wicked world, and all the sinful lusts of the flesh.
Catechism

5 QUESTION: What dost thou chiefly learn by these Commandments?
ANSWER: I learn two things: my duty towards God, and my duty to my Neighbour.
Catechism

6 My duty towards my Neighbour, is to love him as myself, and to do to all men, as I would they should do unto me.
Catechism

7 To submit myself to all my governors, teachers, spiritual pastors and masters.
Catechism

8 To keep my hands from picking and stealing, and my tongue from evil-speaking, lying, and slandering.
Catechism

9 Not to covet nor desire other men's goods; but to learn and labour truly to get mine own living, and to do my duty in that state of life, unto which it shall please God to call me.
Catechism

10 QUESTION: How many Sacraments hath Christ ordained in his Church?
ANSWER: Two only, as generally necessary to salvation, that is to say, Baptism, and the Supper of the Lord.
QUESTION: What meanest thou by this word Sacrament?
ANSWER: I mean an outward and visible sign of an inward and spiritual grace.

11 Our help is in the name of the Lord;
Who hath made heaven and earth.
Order of Confirmation

12 Lord, hear our prayers.
And let our cry come unto thee.
Order of Confirmation

13 Defend, O Lord, this thy Child [*or* this thy Servant] with thy heavenly grace, that he may continue thine for ever; and daily increase in thy holy Spirit more and more, until he come unto thy everlasting kingdom.
Order of Confirmation

14 If any of you know cause, or just impediment, why these two persons should not be joined together in holy Matrimony, ye are to declare it. This is the first [*second*, or *third*] time of asking.
Solemnization of Matrimony The Banns

15 Dearly beloved, we are gathered together here in the sight of God, and in the face of this congregation, to join together this Man and this Woman in holy Matrimony.
Solemnization of Matrimony Exhortation

16 Which holy estate Christ adorned and beautified with his presence, and first miracle that he wrought, in Cana of Galilee; and is commended of Saint Paul to be honourable among all men: and therefore not by any to be enterprised, nor taken in hand, unadvisedly, lightly, or wantonly, to satisfy men's carnal lusts and appetites, like brute beasts that have no understanding.
Solemnization of Matrimony Exhortation

17 First, It was ordained for the procreation of children, to be brought up in the fear and nurture of the Lord, and to the praise of his holy Name.
Solemnization of Matrimony Exhortation

18 If any man can shew any just cause, why they may not lawfully be joined together, let him now speak, or else hereafter for ever hold his peace.
Solemnization of Matrimony Exhortation

19 Wilt thou have this Woman to thy wedded wife, to live together after God's ordinance in the holy estate of Matrimony? Wilt thou love her, comfort her, honour, and keep her in sickness and in health; and, forsaking all other, keep thee only unto her, so long as ye both shall live?
Solemnization of Matrimony Betrothal

20 I N. take thee M. to my wedded husband, to have and to hold from this day forward, for better for worse, for richer for poorer, in sickness and in health, to love, cherish, and to obey, till death us do part, according to God's holy ordinance; and thereto I give thee my troth.
Solemnization of Matrimony Betrothal (the man having used the words 'I plight thee my troth' and not having promised 'to obey')

21 With this Ring I thee wed, with my body I thee worship, and with all my worldly goods I thee endow.
Solemnization of Matrimony Wedding. ('All that I am I give to you, and all that I have I share with you' in Alternative Service Book)

22 Those whom God hath joined together let no man put asunder.
Solemnization of Matrimony Wedding. Cf. St Matthew 91:22

23 Forasmuch as M. and N. have consented together in holy wedlock, and have witnessed the same before God and this company, and thereto have given and pledged their troth either to other, and have declared the same by giving and receiving of a Ring, and by joining of hands; I pronounce that they be Man and Wife together.
Solemnization of Matrimony Minister's Declaration

24 Peace be to this house, and to all that dwell in it.
The Visitation of the Sick

1 Unto God's gracious mercy and protection we commit thee.

The Visitation of the Sick

2 The Office ensuing is not to be used for any that die unbaptized, or excommunicate, or have laid violent hands upon themselves.

The Burial of the Dead introductory rubric

3 Man that is born of a woman hath but a short time to live, and is full of misery.

The Burial of the Dead First Anthem. Cf. Job 77:21

4 In the midst of life we are in death.

The Burial of the Dead First Anthem

5 Forasmuch as it hath pleased Almighty God of his great mercy to take unto himself the soul of our dear brother here departed, we therefore commit his body to the ground; earth to earth, ashes to ashes, dust to dust; in sure and certain hope of the Resurrection to eternal life, through our Lord Jesus Christ; who shall change our vile body, that it may be like unto his glorious body, according to the mighty working, whereby he is able to subdue all things to himself.

The Burial of the Dead Interment

6 Blessed is the man that hath not walked in the counsel of the ungodly, nor stood in the way of sinners: and hath not sat in the seat of the scornful.

Psalm 1, v. 1

7 Why do the heathen so furiously rage together: and why do the people imagine a vain thing?

Psalm 2, v. 1

8 Let us break their bonds asunder: and cast away their cords from us.

Psalm 2, v. 3

9 The Lord shall have them in derision.

Psalm 2, v. 4

10 Thou shalt bruise them with a rod of iron: and break them in pieces like a potter's vessel.

Psalm 2, v. 9

11 Kiss the Son, lest he be angry, and so ye perish from the right way: if his wrath be kindled, (yea, but a little,) blessed are all they that put their trust in him.

Psalm 2, v. 12

12 Stand in awe, and sin not: commune with your own heart, and in your chamber, and be still.

Psalm 4, v. 4

13 Lord, lift thou up: the light of thy countenance upon us.

Psalm 4, v. 7

14 I will lay me down in peace, and take my rest.

Psalm 4, v. 9

15 The Lord will abhor both the bloodthirsty and deceitful man.

Psalm 5, v. 6

16 Make thy way plain before my face.

Psalm 5, v. 8

17 Let them perish through their own imaginations.

Psalm 5, v. 11

18 I am weary of my groaning; every night wash I my bed: and water my couch with my tears.

Psalm 6, v. 6

19 Away from me, all ye that work vanity.

Psalm 6, v. 8

20 Out of the mouth of very babes and sucklings hast thou ordained strength, because of thine enemies: that thou mightest still the enemy, and the avenger.

For I will consider thy heavens, even the works of thy fingers: the moon and the stars, which thou hast ordained.

What is man, that thou art mindful of him: and the son of man, that thou visitest him?

Thou madest him lower than the angels: to crown him with glory and worship.

Psalm 8, v. 2

21 Up, Lord, and let not man have the upper hand.

Psalm 9, v. 19

22 He that said in his heart, Tush, I shall never be cast down: there shall no harm happen unto me.

Psalm 10, v. 6

23 Upon the ungodly he shall rain snares, fire and brimstone, storm and tempest: this shall be their portion to drink.

Psalm 11, v. 7

24 Help me, Lord, for there is not one godly man left: for the faithful are minished from among the children of men.

They talk of vanity every one with his neighbour: they do but flatter with their lips, and dissemble in their double heart.

Psalm 12, v. 1

25 How long wilt thou forget me, O Lord, for ever: how long wilt thou hide thy face from me?

Psalm 13, v. 1

26 The fool hath said in his heart: There is no God.

They are corrupt, and become abominable in their doings: there is none that doeth good, no not one.

Psalm 14, v. 1

27 They are all gone out of the way, they are altogether become abominable.

Psalm 14, v. 4

28 Lord, who shall dwell in thy tabernacle: or who shall rest upon thy holy hill?

Even he, that leadeth an uncorrupt life: and doeth the thing which is right, and speaketh the truth from his heart.

He that hath used no deceit in his tongue, nor done evil to his neighbour: and hath not slandered his neighbour.

Psalm 15, v. 1

29 He that sweareth unto his neighbour, and disappointeth him not: though it were to his own hindrance.

He that hath not given his money upon usury: nor taken reward against the innocent.

Whoso doeth these things: shall never fall.

Psalm 15, v. 5

30 The lot is fallen unto me in a fair ground: yea, I have a goodly heritage.

Psalm 16, v. 7 ('The lines are fallen unto me in pleasant places' in the Authorized Version of the Bible, v. 6)

31 Thou shalt not leave my soul in hell: neither shalt thou suffer thy Holy One to see corruption.

Psalm 16, v. 11

1 He rode upon the cherubims, and did fly: he came
flying upon the wings of the wind.
Psalm 18, v. 10

2 At the brightness of his presence his clouds removed:
hailstones, and coals of fire.
Psalm 18, v. 12

3 With the help of my God I shall leap over the wall.
Psalm 18, v. 29

4 The heavens declare the glory of God: and the
firmament sheweth his handy-work.
One day telleth another: and one night certifieth
another.
There is neither speech nor language: but their voices
are heard among them.
Their sound is gone out into all lands: and their words
into the ends of the world.
In them hath he set a tabernacle for the sun: which
cometh forth as a bridegroom out of his chamber,
and rejoiceth as a giant to run his course.
Psalm 19, v. 1

5 The law of the Lord is an undefiled law, converting
the soul: the testimony of the Lord is sure, and
giveth wisdom unto the simple.
The statutes of the Lord are right, and rejoice the
heart: the commandment of the Lord is pure, and
giveth light unto the eyes.
The fear of the Lord is clean, and endureth for ever:
the judgements of the Lord are true, and righteous
altogether.
More to be desired are they than gold, yea, than much
fine gold: sweeter also than honey, and the
honey-comb.
Psalm 19, v. 7

6 Who can tell how oft he offendeth: O cleanse thou me
from my secret faults.
Keep thy servant also from presumptuous sins, lest
they get the dominion over me: so shall I be
undefiled, and innocent from the great offence.
Let the words of my mouth, and the meditation of my
heart: be alway acceptable in thy sight,
O Lord: my strength, and my redeemer.
Psalm 19, v. 12

7 Some put their trust in chariots, and some in horses:
but we will remember the Name of the Lord our
God.
Psalm 20, v. 7

8 They intended mischief against thee: and imagined
such a device as they are not able to perform.
Psalm 21, v. 11

9 My God, my God, look upon me; why hast thou
forsaken me: and art so far from my health, and
from the words of my complaint?
O my God, I cry in the day-time, but thou hearest
not: and in the night-season also I take no rest.
Psalm 22, v. 1

10 But as for me, I am a worm, and no man: a very
scorn of men, and the out-cast of the people.
All they that see me laugh me to scorn: they shoot
out their lips, and shake their heads, saying,
He trusted in God, that he would deliver him: let him
deliver him, if he will have him.
Psalm 22, v. 6

11 Many oxen are come about me: fat bulls of Basan
close me in on every side.
Psalm 22, v. 12

12 I am poured out like water, and all my bones are out
of joint: my heart also in the midst of my body is
even like melting wax.
Psalm 22, v. 14

13 They pierced my hands and my feet; I may tell all my
bones: they stand staring and looking upon me.
They part my garments among them: and cast lots
upon my vesture.
Psalm 22, v. 17

14 The Lord is my shepherd: therefore can I lack nothing.
He shall feed me in a green pasture: and lead me forth
beside the waters of comfort.
Psalm 23, v. 1. Cf. Scottish Metrical Psalms 561:8

15 Yea, though I walk through the valley of the shadow
of death, I will fear no evil: for thou art with me;
thy rod and thy staff comfort me.
Thou shalt prepare a table before me against them
that trouble me: thou hast anointed my head with
oil, and my cup shall be full.
But thy loving-kindness and mercy shall follow me all
the days of my life: and I will dwell in the house of
the Lord for ever.
Psalm 23, v. 4. Cf. Scottish Metrical Psalms 561:8

16 The earth is the Lord's, and all that therein is: the
compass of the world, and they that dwell therein.
Psalm 24, v. 1

17 Lift up your heads, O ye gates, and be ye lift up, ye
everlasting doors: and the King of glory shall come
in.
Who is the King of glory: it is the Lord strong and
mighty, even the Lord mighty in battle.
Psalm 24, v. 7

18 Even the Lord of hosts, he is the King of glory.
Psalm 24, v. 10

19 O remember not the sins and offences of my youth.
Psalm 25, v. 6

20 Deliver Israel, O God: out of all his troubles.
Psalm 25, v. 21

21 Examine me, O Lord, ꓺnd prove me: try out my reins
and my heart.
Psalm 26, v. 2

22 I will wash my hands in innocency, O Lord: and so
will I go to thine altar;
That I may shew the voice of thanksgiving: and tell of
all thy wondrous works.
Psalm 26, v. 6

23 My foot standeth right: I will praise the Lord in the
congregation.
Psalm 26, v. 12

24 The Lord is my light, and my salvation; whom then
shall I fear: the Lord is the strength of my life; of
whom then shall I be afraid?
Psalm 27, v. 1. Cf. Vulgate 107:27

25 Teach me thy way, O Lord: and lead me in the right
way, because of mine enemies.
Psalm 27, v. 13

1 I should utterly have fainted: but that I believe verily to see the goodness of the Lord in the land of the living.
Psalm 27, v. 15

2 The voice of the Lord breaketh the cedar-trees: yea, the Lord breaketh the cedars of Libanus.
He maketh them also to skip like a calf: Libanus also, and Sirion, like a young unicorn.
Psalm 29, v. 5

3 The voice of the Lord maketh the hinds to bring forth young, and discovereth the thick bushes.
Psalm 29, v. 8

4 The Lord shall give strength unto his people: the Lord shall give his people the blessing of peace.
Psalm 29, v. 10

5 Sing praises unto the Lord, O ye saints of his: and give thanks unto him for a remembrance of his holiness.
For his wrath endureth but the twinkling of an eye, and in his pleasure is life: heaviness may endure for a night, but joy cometh in the morning.
Psalm 30, v. 4

6 Then cried I unto thee, O Lord: and gat me to my Lord right humbly.
Psalm 30, v. 8

7 Into thy hands I commend my spirit.
Psalm 31, v. 6. Cf. St John 95:28

8 Blessed is the man unto whom the Lord imputeth no sin: and in whose spirit there is no guile.
For while I held my tongue: my bones consumed away through my daily complaining.
Psalm 32, v. 2

9 For this shall every one that is godly make his prayer unto thee, in a time when thou mayest be found: but in the great water-floods they shall not come nigh him.
Psalm 32, v. 7

10 I will inform thee, and teach thee in the way wherein thou shalt go: and I will guide thee with mine eye.
Be ye not like to horse and mule, which have no understanding: whose mouths must be held with bit and bridle, lest they fall upon thee.
Great plagues remain for the ungodly: but whoso putteth his trust in the Lord, mercy embraceth him on every side.
Psalm 32, v. 9

11 Sing unto the Lord a new song: sing praises lustily unto him with a good courage.
Psalm 33, v. 3

12 A horse is counted but a vain thing to save a man: neither shall he deliver any man by his great strength.
Psalm 33, v. 16

13 O taste and see, how gracious the Lord is: blessed is the man that trusteth in him.
Psalm 34, v. 8

14 The lions do lack, and suffer hunger: but they who seek the Lord shall want no manner of thing that is good.
Psalm 34, v. 10

15 What man is he that lusteth to live: and would fain see good days?
Keep thy tongue from evil: and thy lips, that they speak no guile.
Eschew evil, and do good: seek peace, and ensue it.
Psalm 34, v. 12

16 They rewarded me evil for good: to the great discomfort of my soul.
Psalm 35, v. 12

17 O deliver my soul from the calamities which they bring on me, and my darling from the lions.
Psalm 35, v. 17

18 Fret not thyself because of the ungodly.
Psalm 37, v. 1

19 The meek-spirited shall possess the earth: and shall be refreshed in the multitude of peace.
Psalm 37, v. 11

20 I have been young, and now am old: and yet saw I never the righteous forsaken, nor his seed begging their bread.
Psalm 37, v. 25

21 I myself have seen the ungodly in great power: and flourishing like a green bay-tree.
I went by, and lo, he was gone: I sought him, but his place could no where be found.
Keep innocency, and take heed unto the thing that is right: for that shall bring a man peace at the last.
Psalm 37, v. 36

22 I held my tongue, and spake nothing: I kept silence, yea, even from good words; but it was pain and grief to me.
My heart was hot within me, and while I was thus musing the fire kindled: and at the last I spake with my tongue;
Lord, let me know mine end, and the number of my days: that I may be certified how long I have to live.
Psalm 39, v. 3

23 For man walketh in a vain shadow, and disquieteth himself in vain: he heapeth up riches, and cannot tell who shall gather them.
Psalm 39, v. 7

24 I waited patiently for the Lord: and he inclined unto me, and heard my calling.
He brought me also out of the horrible pit, out of the mire and clay: and set my feet upon the rock, and ordered my goings.
Psalm 40, v. 1

25 Sacrifice, and meat-offering, thou wouldest not: but mine ears hast thou opened.
Burnt-offerings, and sacrifice for sin, hast thou not required: then said I, Lo, I come.
In the volume of the book it is written of me, that I should fulfil thy will, O my God.
Psalm 40, v. 8

26 Thou art my helper and redeemer: make no long tarrying, O my God.
Psalm 40, v. 21

27 Blessed is he that considereth the poor and needy: the Lord shall deliver him in the time of trouble.
Psalm 41, v. 1

1 Yea, even mine own familiar friend, whom I trusted: who did also eat of my bread, hath laid great wait for me.

Psalm 41, v. 9 ('hath lifted up his heel against me' in the Authorized Version of the Bible)

2 Like as the hart desireth the water-brooks: so longeth my soul after thee, O God.

My soul is a thirst for God, yea, even for the living God.

Psalm 42, v. 1 ('As the hart panteth after the water brooks, so panteth my soul after thee, O God. My soul thirsteth for God, the living God' in the Authorized Version of the Bible)

3 Why art thou so full of heaviness, O my soul: and why art thou so disquieted within me?

Psalm 42, v. 6

4 My God, my soul is vexed within me: therefore will I remember thee concerning the land of Jordan, and the little hill of Hermon.

One deep calleth another, because of the noise of the water-pipes: all thy waves and storms are gone over me.

Psalm 42, v. 8

5 I will say unto the God of my strength, Why hast thou forgotten me: why go I thus heavily, while the enemy oppresseth me?

My bones are smitten asunder as with a sword: while mine enemies that trouble me cast me in the teeth;

Namely, while they say daily unto me: Where is now thy God?

Psalm 42, v. 11

6 Give sentence with me, O God, and defend my cause against the ungodly people: O deliver me from the deceitful and wicked man.

Psalm 43, v. 1

7 O send out thy light and thy truth, that they may lead me: and bring me unto thy holy hill, and to thy dwelling.

And that I may go unto the altar of God, even unto the God of my joy and gladness: and upon the harp will I give thanks unto thee, O God, my God.

Psalm 43, v. 3

8 O put thy trust in God: for I will yet give him thanks, which is the help of my countenance, and my God.

Psalm 43, v. 6

9 We have heard with our ears, O God, our fathers have told us: what thou hast done in their time of old.

Psalm 44, v. 1

10 My heart is inditing of a good matter: I speak of the things which I have made unto the King.

My tongue is the pen: of a ready writer.

Psalm 45, v. 1

11 Thou hast loved righteousness, and hated iniquity: wherefore God, even thy God, hath anointed thee with the oil of gladness above thy fellows.

Psalm 45, v. 8

12 Kings' daughters were among thy honourable women: upon thy right hand did stand the queen in a vesture of gold, wrought about with divers colours.

Psalm 45, v. 10

13 The King's daughter is all glorious within: her clothing is of wrought gold.

She shall be brought unto the King in raiment of needlework: the virgins that be her fellows shall bear her company, and shall be brought unto thee.

Psalm 45, v. 14

14 Instead of thy fathers thou shalt have children: whom thou mayest make princes in all lands.

Psalm 45, v. 17

15 God is our hope and strength: a very present help in trouble. Therefore will we not fear, though the earth be moved: and though the hills be carried into the midst of the sea.

Psalm 46, v. 1

16 God is in the midst of her, therefore shall she not be removed: God shall help her, and that right early.

The heathen make much ado, and the kingdoms are moved: but God hath shewed his voice, and the earth shall melt away.

The Lord of hosts is with us: the God of Jacob is our refuge.

Psalm 46, v. 5

17 He maketh wars to cease in all the world: he breaketh the bow, and knappeth the spear in sunder, and burneth the chariots in the fire.

Be still then, and know that I am God: I will be exalted among the heathen, and I will be exalted in the earth.

Psalm 46, v. 9

18 O clap your hands together, all ye people: O sing unto God with the voice of melody.

Psalm 47, v. 1

19 He shall subdue the people under us: and the nations under our feet.

Psalm 47, v. 3

20 God is gone up with a merry noise: and the Lord with the sound of the trump.

Psalm 47, v. 5

21 For lo, the kings of the earth: are gathered, and gone by together.

They marvelled to see such things: they were astonished, and suddenly cast down.

Psalm 48, v. 3

22 Thou shalt break the ships of the sea: through the east-wind.

Psalm 48, v. 6

23 Walk about Sion, and go round about her: and tell the towers thereof.

Mark well her bulwarks, set up her houses: that ye may tell them that come after.

Psalm 48, v. 11

24 Wise men also die, and perish together: as well as the ignorant and foolish, and leave their riches for other.

And yet they think that their houses shall continue for ever: and that their dwelling-places shall endure from one generation to another; and call the lands after their own names.

Nevertheless, man will not abide in honour: seeing he may be compared unto the beasts that perish; this is the way of them.

Psalm 49, v. 10

1 They lie in the hell like sheep, death gnaweth upon them, and the righteous shall have domination over them in the morning: their beauty shall consume in the sepulchre out of their dwelling.
   Psalm 49, v. 14

2 All the beasts of the forest are mine: and so are the cattle upon a thousand hills.
   Psalm 50, v. 10

3 Thinkest thou that I will eat bulls' flesh: and drink the blood of goats?
   Psalm 50, v. 13

4 Wash me throughly from my wickedness: and cleanse me from my sin.
   For I acknowledge my faults: and my sin is ever before me.
   Against thee only have I sinned, and done this evil in thy sight.
   Psalm 51, v. 2

5 Behold, I was shapen in wickedness: and in sin hath my mother conceived me.
   But lo, thou requirest truth in the inward parts: and shalt make me to understand wisdom secretly.
   Thou shalt purge me with hyssop, and I shall be clean: thou shalt wash me, and I shall be whiter than snow.
   Thou shalt make me hear of joy and gladness: that the bones which thou hast broken may rejoice.
   Psalm 51, v. 5. Cf. Vulgate 107:28

6 Make me a clean heart, O God: and renew a right spirit within me.
   Cast me not away from thy presence: and take not thy holy Spirit from me.
   O give me the comfort of thy help again: and stablish me with thy free Spirit.
   Psalm 51, v. 10

7 Deliver me from blood-guiltiness, O God.
   Psalm 51, v. 14

8 Thou shalt open my lips, O Lord: and my mouth shall shew thy praise.
   For thou desirest no sacrifice, else would I give it thee: but thou delightest not in burnt-offerings.
   The sacrifice of God is a troubled spirit: a broken and contrite heart, O God, shalt thou not despise.
   O be favourable and gracious unto Sion: build thou the walls of Jerusalem.
   Psalm 51, v. 15

9 Then shall they offer young bullocks upon thine altar.
   Psalm 51, v. 19

10 O that I had wings like a dove: for then would I flee away, and be at rest.
   Psalm 55, v. 6

11 It was even thou, my companion: my guide, and mine own familiar friend.
   We took sweet counsel together: and walked in the house of God as friends.
   Psalm 55, v. 14

12 The words of his mouth were softer than butter, having war in his heart: his words were smoother than oil, and yet they be very swords.
   Psalm 55, v. 22

13 Thou tellest my flittings; put my tears into thy bottle: are not these things noted in thy book?
   Psalm 56, v. 8

14 Under the shadow of thy wings shall be my refuge, until this tyranny be over-past.
   Psalm 57, v. 1

15 God shall send forth his mercy and truth: my soul is among lions.
   And I lie even among the children of men, that are set on fire: whose teeth are spears and arrows, and their tongue a sharp sword.
   Set up thyself, O God, above the heavens: and thy glory above all the earth.
   They have laid a net for my feet, and pressed down my soul: they have digged a pit before me, and are fallen into the midst of it themselves.
   Psalm 57, v. 4

16 Awake up, my glory; awake, lute and harp: I myself will awake right early.
   Psalm 57, v. 9

17 They are as venomous as the poison of a serpent: even like the deaf adder that stoppeth her ears;
   Which refuseth to hear the voice of the charmer: charm he never so wisely.
   Psalm 58, v. 4

18 Gilead is mine, and Manasses is mine: Ephraim also is the strength of my head; Judah is my law-giver;
   Moab is my wash-pot; over Edom will I cast out my shoe: Philistia, be thou glad of me.
   Psalm 60, v. 7

19 Their delight is in lies; they give good words with their mouth, but curse with their heart.
   Psalm 62, v. 4

20 As for the children of men, they are but vanity: the children of men are deceitful upon the weights, they are altogether lighter than vanity itself.
   O trust not in wrong and robbery, give not yourselves unto vanity: if riches increase, set not your heart upon them.
   God spake once, and twice I have also heard the same: that power belongeth unto God;
   And that thou, Lord, art merciful: for thou rewardest every man according to his work.
   Psalm 62, v. 9

21 My soul thirsteth for thee, my flesh also longeth after thee: in a barren and dry land where no water is.
   Psalm 63, v. 2

22 These also that seek the hurt of my soul: they shall go under the earth.
   Let them fall upon the edge of the sword: that they may be a portion for foxes.
   Psalm 63, v. 10

23 Thou, O God, art praised in Sion: and unto thee shall the vow be performed in Jerusalem.
   Thou that hearest the prayer: unto thee shall all flesh come.
   Psalm 65, v. 1

1 Thou that art the hope of all the ends of the earth,
   and of them that remain in the broad sea.
   Who in his strength setteth fast the mountains: and is
   girded about with power.
   Who stilleth the raging of the sea: and the noise of his
   waves, and the madness of the people.
   Psalm 65, v. 5

2 Thou visitest the earth, and blessest it: thou makest it
   very plenteous.
   Psalm 65, v. 9

3 Thou waterest her furrows, thou sendest rain into the
   little valleys thereof: thou makest it soft with the
   drops of rain, and blessest the increase of it.
   Thou crownest the year with thy goodness: and thy
   clouds drop fatness.
   They shall drop upon the dwellings of the wilderness:
   and the little hills shall rejoice on every side.
   The folds shall be full of sheep: the valleys also shall
   stand so thick with corn, that they shall laugh and
   sing.
   Psalm 65, v. 11

4 God be merciful unto us, and bless us: and shew us
   the light of his countenance, and be merciful unto
   us;
   That thy way may be known upon earth: thy saving
   health among all nations.
   Let the people praise thee, O God: yea, let all the
   people praise thee.
   Psalm 67, v. 1

5 Then shall the earth bring forth her increase: and
   God, even our own God, shall give us his blessing.
   Psalm 67, v. 6

6 Let God arise, and let his enemies be scattered: let
   them also that hate him flee before him.
   Psalm 68, v. 1

7 O sing unto God, and sing praises unto his name:
   magnify him that rideth upon the heavens, as it
   were upon an horse; praise him in his name JAH,
   and rejoice before him.
   He is a Father of the fatherless, and defendeth the
   cause of the widows: even God in his holy
   habitation.
   He is the God that maketh men to be of one mind in
   an house, and bringeth the prisoners out of
   captivity: but letteth the runagates continue in
   scarceness.
   O God, when thou wentest forth before the people:
   when thou wentest through the wilderness,
   The earth shook, and the heavens dropped at the
   presence of God.
   Psalm 68, v. 4

8 The Lord gave the word: great was the company of
   the preachers.
   Kings with their armies did flee, and were discomfited:
   and they of the household divided the spoil.
   Though ye have lien among the pots, yet shall ye be
   as the wings of a dove: that is covered with silver
   wings, and her feathers like gold.
   Psalm 68, v. 11

9 Why hop ye so, ye high hills? this is God's hill, in
   which it pleaseth him to dwell.
   Psalm 68, v. 16

10 Thou art gone up on high, thou hast led captivity
   captive, and received gifts for men.
   Psalm 68, v. 18

11 The zeal of thine house hath even eaten me.
   Psalm 69, v. 9

12 Thy rebuke hath broken my heart; I am full of
   heaviness: I looked for some to have pity on me, but
   there was no man, neither found I any to comfort
   me.
   They gave me gall to eat: and when I was thirsty they
   gave me vinegar to drink.
   Psalm 69, v. 21

13 Let their habitation be void: and no man to dwell in
   their tents.
   Psalm 69, v. 26

14 Let them be wiped out of the book of the living: and
   not be written among the righteous.
   Psalm 69, v. 29

15 Let them be ashamed and confounded that seek after
   my soul: let them be turned backward and put to
   confusion that wish me evil.
   Let them for their reward be soon brought to shame:
   that cry over me, There, there.
   Psalm 70, v. 2

16 I am become as it were a monster unto many: but my
   sure trust is in thee.
   Psalm 71, v. 6

17 Cast me not away in the time of age: forsake me not
   when my strength faileth me.
   Psalm 71, v. 8

18 Give the King thy judgements, O God: and thy
   righteousness unto the King's son.
   Psalm 72, v. 1

19 The mountains also shall bring peace: and the little
   hills righteousness unto the people.
   Psalm 72, v. 3

20 His dominion shall be also from the one sea to the
   other: and from the flood unto the world's end.
   They that dwell in the wilderness shall kneel before
   him: his enemies shall lick the dust.
   The Kings of Tharsis and of the isles shall give
   presents: the kings of Arabia and Saba shall bring
   gifts.
   All kings shall fall down before him: all nations shall
   do him service.
   Psalm 72, v. 8

21 He shall live, and unto him shall be given of the gold
   of Arabia.
   Psalm 72, v. 15

1 Therefore fall the people unto them: and thereout suck they no small advantage.
Tush, say they, how should God perceive it: is there knowledge in the most High?
Psalm 73, v. 10

2 Then thought I to understand this: but it was too hard for me.
Until I went into the sanctuary of God: then understood I the end of these men.
Psalm 73, v. 15

3 O deliver not the soul of thy turtle-dove unto the multitude of the enemies: and forget not the congregation of the poor for ever.
Psalm 74, v. 20

4 The earth is weak, and all the inhabiters thereof: I bear up the pillars of it.
Psalm 75, v. 4

5 For promotion cometh neither from the east, nor from the west: nor yet from the south.
And why? God is the Judge: he putteth down one, and setteth up another.
Psalm 75, v. 7

6 In Jewry is God known: his Name is great in Israel.
At Salem is his tabernacle: and his dwelling in Sion.
Psalm 76, v. 1

7 I have considered the days of old: and the years that are past.
Psalm 77, v. 5

8 Hear my law, O my people: incline your ears unto the words of my mouth.
I will open my mouth in a parable: I will declare hard sentences of old;
Which we have heard and known: and such as our fathers have told us.
Psalm 78, v. 1

9 Not to be as their forefathers, a faithless and stubborn generation: a generation that set not their heart aright, and whose spirit cleaveth not stedfastly unto God.
Psalm 78, v. 9

10 He divided the sea, and let them go through: he made the waters to stand on an heap.
Psalm 78, v. 14

11 He rained down manna also upon them for to eat: and gave them food from heaven.
So man did eat angels' food: for he sent them meat enough.
Psalm 78, v. 25

12 So the Lord awaked as one out of sleep: and like a giant refreshed with wine.
Psalm 78, v. 66

13 Turn us again, O God: shew the light of thy countenance, and we shall be whole.
Psalm 80, v. 3

14 Sing we merrily unto God our strength: make a cheerful noise unto the God of Jacob.
Take the psalm, bring hither the tabret: the merry harp with the lute.
Blow up the trumpet in the new-moon: even in the time appointed, and upon our solemn feast-day.
Psalm 81, v. 1

15 I have said, Ye are gods: and ye are all children of the most Highest.
But ye shall die like men: and fall like one of the princes.
Psalm 82, v. 6

16 O how amiable are thy dwellings: thou Lord of hosts!
My soul hath a desire and longing to enter into the courts of the Lord: my heart and my flesh rejoice in the living God.
Yea, the sparrow hath found her an house, and the swallow a nest where she may lay her young: even thy altars, O Lord of hosts, my King and my God.
Psalm 84, v. 1

17 Blessed is the man whose strength is in thee: in whose heart are thy ways.
Who going through the vale of misery use it for a well: and the pools are filled with water.
They will go from strength to strength: and unto the God of gods appeareth every one of them in Sion.
Psalm 84, v. 5

18 For one day in thy courts: is better than a thousand.
I had rather be a door-keeper in the house of my God: than to dwell in the tents of ungodliness.
Psalm 84, v. 10

19 Wilt thou not turn again, and quicken us: that thy people may rejoice in thee?
Psalm 85, v. 6

20 Mercy and truth are met together: righteousness and peace have kissed each other.
Truth shall flourish out of the earth: and righteousness hath looked down from heaven.
Psalm 85, v. 10

21 Very excellent things are spoken of thee: thou city of God.
Psalm 87, v. 2

22 Lord, thou hast been our refuge: from one generation to another.
Before the mountains were brought forth, or ever the earth and the world were made: thou art God from everlasting, and world without end.
Psalm 90, v. 1

23 For a thousand years in thy sight are but as yesterday: seeing that is past as a watch in the night.
As soon as thou scatterest them they are even as a sleep: and fade away suddenly like the grass.
In the morning it is green, and groweth up: but in the evening it is cut down, dried up, and withered.
Psalm 90, v. 4

1 The days of our age are threescore years and ten; and though men be so strong that they come to fourscore years: yet is their strength then but labour and sorrow; so soon passeth it away, and we are gone.
Psalm 90, v. 10

2 So teach us to number our days: that we may apply our hearts unto wisdom.
Psalm 90, v. 12

3 For he shall deliver thee from the snare of the hunter: and from the noisome pestilence.
He shall defend thee under his wings, and thou shalt be safe under his feathers: his faithfulness and truth shall be thy shield and buckler.
Thou shalt not be afraid for any terror by night: nor for the arrow that flieth by day;
For the pestilence that walketh in darkness: nor for the sickness that destroyeth in the noon-day.
A thousand shall fall beside thee, and ten thousand at thy right hand: but it shall not come nigh thee.
Psalm 91, v. 3

4 For thou, Lord, art my hope: thou hast set thine house of defence very high.
There shall no evil happen unto thee: neither shall any plague come nigh thy dwelling.
For he shall give his angels charge over thee: to keep thee in all thy ways.
They shall bear thee in their hands: that thou hurt not thy foot against a stone.
Thou shalt go upon the lion and adder: the young lion and the dragon shalt thou tread under thy feet.
Psalm 91, v. 9

5 With long life will I satisfy him: and shew him my salvation.
Psalm 91, v. 16

6 The Lord is King, and hath put on glorious apparel: the Lord hath put on his apparel, and girded himself with strength.
He hath made the round world so sure: that it cannot be moved.
Psalm 93, v. 1

7 The floods are risen, O Lord, the floods have lift up their voice: the floods lift up their waves.
The waves of the sea are mighty, and rage horribly: but yet the Lord, who dwelleth on high, is mightier.
Thy testimonies, O Lord, are very sure: holiness becometh thine house for ever.
Psalm 93, v. 4

8 He that planted the ear, shall he not hear? or he that made the eye, shall he not see?
Psalm 94, v. 9

9 O come, let us sing unto the Lord: let us heartily rejoice in the strength of our salvation.
Let us come before his presence with thanksgiving: and shew ourselves glad in him with psalms.
Psalm 95, v. 1

10 In his hand are all the corners of the earth: and the strength of the hills is his also.
The sea is his, and he made it: and his hands prepared the dry land.
O come, let us worship and fall down: and kneel before the Lord our Maker.
For he is the Lord our God: and we are the people of his pasture, and the sheep of his hand.
To-day if ye will hear his voice, harden not your hearts: as in the provocation, and as in the day of temptation in the wilderness;
When your fathers tempted me: proved me, and saw my works.
Forty years long was I grieved with this generation, and said: It is a people that do err in their hearts, for they have not known my ways;
Unto whom I sware in my wrath: that they should not enter into my rest.
Psalm 95, v. 4

11 Ascribe unto the Lord the honour due unto his Name: bring presents, and come into his courts.
O worship the Lord in the beauty of holiness: let the whole earth stand in awe of him.
Psalm 96, v. 8

12 The Lord is King, the earth may be glad thereof: yea, the multitude of the isles may be glad thereof.
Psalm 97, v. 1

13 O sing unto the Lord a new song: for he hath done marvellous things.
With his own right hand, and with his holy arm: hath he gotten himself the victory.
Psalm 98, v. 1. Cf. Vulgate 107:29

14 Praise the Lord upon the harp: sing to the harp with a psalm of thanksgiving.
With trumpets also, and shawms: O shew yourselves joyful before the Lord the King.
Psalm 98, v. 6

15 With righteousness shall he judge the world: and the people with equity.
Psalm 98, v. 10

16 The Lord is King, be the people never so impatient: he sitteth between the cherubims, be the earth never so unquiet.
Psalm 99, v. 1

17 O be joyful in the Lord, all ye lands: serve the Lord with gladness, and come before his presence with a song.
Be ye sure that the Lord he is God: it is he that hath made us, and not we ourselves; we are his people, and the sheep of his pasture.
Psalm 100, v. 1. Cf. Vulgate 107:30

18 I am become like a pelican in the wilderness: and like an owl that is in the desert.
I have watched, and am even as it were a sparrow: that sitteth alone upon the house-top.
Psalm 102, v. 6

1 Thou, Lord, in the beginning hast laid the foundation of the earth: and the heavens are the work of thy hands.

They shall perish, but thou shalt endure: they all shall wax old as doth a garment;

And as a vesture shalt thou change them, and they shall be changed: but thou art the same, and thy years shall not fail.

Psalm 102, v. 25

2 Praise the Lord, O my soul: and forget not all his benefits.

Psalm 103, v. 2

3 Who satisfieth thy mouth with good things: making thee young and lusty as an eagle.

Psalm 103, v. 5

4 The Lord is full of compassion and mercy: long-suffering, and of great goodness.

He will not alway be chiding: neither keepeth he his anger for ever.

Psalm 103, v. 8

5 For look how high the heaven is in comparison of the earth: so great is his mercy also toward them that fear him.

Look how wide also the east is from the west: so far hath he set our sins from us.

Yea, like as a father pitieth his own children: even so is the Lord merciful unto them that fear him.

For he knoweth whereof we are made: he remembereth that we are but dust.

The days of man are but as grass: for he flourisheth as a flower of a field.

For as soon as the wind goeth over it, it is gone: and the place thereof shall know it no more.

Psalm 103, v. 11

6 Who layeth the beams of his chambers in the waters: and maketh the clouds his chariot, and walketh upon the wings of the wind.

He maketh his angels spirits: and his ministers a flaming fire.

He laid the foundations of the earth: that it never should move at any time.

Thou coveredst it with the deep like as with a garment: the waters stand in the hills.

Psalm 104, v. 3

7 Thou hast set them their bounds which they shall not pass: neither turn again to cover the earth.

He sendeth the springs into the rivers: which run among the hills.

All beasts of the field drink thereof: and the wild asses quench their thirst.

Beside them shall the fowls of the air have their habitation: and sing among the branches.

Psalm 104, v. 9

8 He bringeth forth grass for the cattle: and green herb for the service of men;

That he may bring food out of the earth, and wine that maketh glad the heart of man: and oil to make him a cheerful countenance, and bread to strengthen man's heart.

The trees of the Lord also are full of sap: even the cedars of Libanus which he hath planted.

Psalm 104, v. 14

9 The high hills are a refuge for the wild goats: and so are the stony rocks for the conies.

He appointed the moon for certain seasons: and the sun knoweth his going down.

Thou makest darkness that it may be night: wherein all the beasts of the forest do move.

The lions roaring after their prey: do seek their meat from God.

The sun ariseth, and they get them away together: and lay them down in their dens.

Man goeth forth to his work, and to his labour: until the evening.

O Lord, how manifold are thy works, in wisdom hast thou made them all; the earth is full of thy riches.

So is the great and wide sea also: wherein are creeping things innumerable, both small and great beasts.

There go the ships, and there is that Leviathan: whom thou hast made to take his pastime therein.

These wait all upon thee: that thou mayest give them meat in due season.

Psalm 104, v. 18

10 The earth shall tremble at the look of him: if he do but touch the hills, they shall smoke.

Psalm 104, v. 32

11 He had sent a man before them: even Joseph, who was sold to be a bond-servant;

Whose feet they hurt in the stocks: the iron entered into his soul.

Psalm 105, v. 17

12 The king sent, and delivered him: the prince of the people let him go free.

He made him lord also of his house: and ruler of all his substance;

That he might inform his princes after his will: and teach his senators wisdom.

Psalm 105, v. 20

13 Yea, they thought scorn of that pleasant land: and gave no credence to his word;

But murmured in their tents: and hearkened not unto the voice of the Lord.

Psalm 106, v. 24

14 Thus were they stained with their own works: and went a whoring with their own inventions.

Psalm 106, v. 38

15 O that men would therefore praise the Lord for his goodness: and declare the wonders that he doeth for the children of men!

For he satisfieth the empty soul: and filleth the hungry soul with goodness.

Such as sit in darkness, and in the shadow of death: being fast bound in misery and iron;

Because they rebelled against the words of the Lord: and lightly regarded the counsel of the most Highest.

Psalm 107, v. 8

16 Their soul abhorred all manner of meat: and they were even hard at death's door.

Psalm 107, v. 18

1 They that go down to the sea in ships: and occupy their business in great waters;

These men see the works of the Lord: and his wonders in the deep.

Psalm 107, v. 23

2 They reel to and fro, and stagger like a drunken man: and are at their wit's end.

So when they cry unto the Lord in their trouble: he delivereth them out of their distress.

For he maketh the storm to cease: so that the waves thereof are still.

Then are they glad, because they are at rest: and so he bringeth them unto the heaven where they would be.

Psalm 107, v. 27

3 The Lord said unto my Lord: Sit thou on my right hand, until I make thine enemies thy footstool.

Psalm 110, v. 1

4 Thou art a Priest for ever after the order of Melchisedech.

Psalm 110, v. 4

5 The fear of the Lord is the beginning of wisdom: a good understanding have all they that do thereafter; the praise of it endureth for ever.

Psalm 111, v. 10

6 A good man is merciful, and lendeth: and will guide his words with discretion.

For he shall never be moved: and the righteous shall be had in everlasting remembrance.

Psalm 112, v. 5

7 He maketh the barren woman to keep house: and to be a joyful mother of children.

Psalm 113, v. 8

8 When Israel came out of Egypt: and the house of Jacob from among the strange people,

Judah was his sanctuary: and Israel his dominion.

The sea saw that, and fled: Jordan was driven back.

The mountains skipped like rams: and the little hills like young sheep.

Psalm 114, v. 1

9 Not unto us, O Lord, not unto us, but unto thy Name give the praise.

Psalm 115, v. 1. Cf. Vulgate 108:2

10 They have mouths, and speak not: eyes have they, and see not.

They have ears, and hear not: noses have they, and smell not.

They have hands, and handle not: feet have they, and walk not: neither speak they through their throat.

Psalm 115, v. 5

11 The snares of death compassed me round about: and the pains of hell gat hold upon me.

Psalm 116, v. 3

12 And why? thou hast delivered my soul from death: mine eyes from tears, and my feet from falling.

Psalm 116, v. 8

13 I said in my haste, All men are liars.

Psalm 116, v. 10

14 I will pay my vows now in the presence of all his people: right dear in the sight of the Lord is the death of his saints.

Psalm 116, v. 13

15 The right hand of the Lord hath the pre-eminence: the right hand of the Lord bringeth mighty things to pass.

Psalm 118, v. 16

16 The same stone which the builders refused: is become the head-stone in the corner.

This is the Lord's doing: and it is marvellous in our eyes.

This is the day which the Lord hath made: we will rejoice and be glad in it.

Psalm 118, v. 22

17 Blessed be he that cometh in the Name of the Lord: we have wished you good luck, ye that are of the house of the Lord.

Psalm 118, v. 26

18 Wherewithal shall a young man cleanse his way: even by ruling himself after thy word.

Psalm 119, v. 9

19 The law of thy mouth is dearer unto me: than thousands of gold and silver.

Psalm 119, v. 72

20 Thy word is a lantern unto my feet: and a light unto my paths.

Psalm 119, v. 105

21 Woe is me that I am constrained to dwell with Mesech: and to have my habitation among the tents of Kedar.

Psalm 120, v. 4

22 I labour for peace, but when I speak unto them therof: they make them ready to battle.

Psalm 120, v. 6

23 I will lift up mine eyes unto the hills: from whence cometh my help.

My help cometh even from the Lord: who hath made heaven and earth.

He will not suffer thy foot to be moved: and he that keepeth thee will not sleep.

Behold, he that keepeth Israel: shall neither slumber nor sleep.

The Lord himself is thy keeper: the Lord is thy defence upon thy right hand;

So that the sun shall not burn thee by day: neither the moon by night.

Psalm 121, v. 1. Cf. Scottish Metrical Psalms 561:10

24 The Lord shall preserve thy going out, and thy coming in: from this time forth for evermore.

Psalm 121, v. 8

25 I was glad when they said unto me: We will go into the house of the Lord.

Our feet shall stand in thy gates: O Jerusalem.

Jerusalem is built as a city: that is at unity in itself.

For thither the tribes go up, even the tribes of the Lord.

Psalm 122, v. 1

26 O pray for the peace of Jerusalem: they shall prosper that love thee.

Peace be within thy walls: and plenteousness with thy palaces.

For my brethren and companions' sakes: I will wish thee prosperity.

Psalm 122, v. 6

1 If the Lord himself had not been on our side, now may Israel say: if the Lord himself had not been on our side, when men rose up against us;
They had swallowed us up quick: when they were so wrathfully displeased at us.
Psalm 124, v. 1

2 Our soul is escaped even as a bird out of the snare of the fowler: the snare is broken, and we are delivered.
Our help standeth in the Name of the Lord: who hath made heaven and earth.
Psalm 124, v. 6. Cf. Book of Common Prayer 123:11

3 The hills stand about Jerusalem: even so standeth the Lord round about his people, from this time forth for evermore.
Psalm 125, v. 2

4 When the Lord turned again the captivity of Sion: then were we like unto them that dream.
Then was our mouth filled with laughter: and our tongue with joy.
Psalm 126, v. 1

5 Turn our captivity, O Lord: as the rivers in the south.
They that sow in tears: shall reap in joy.
He that now goeth on his way weeping, and beareth forth good seed: shall doubtless come again with joy, and bring his sheaves with him.
Psalm 126, v. 5

6 Except the Lord build the house: their labour is but lost that build it.
Except the Lord keep the city: the watchman waketh but in vain.
Psalm 127, v. 1. Cf. Vulgate 108:4

7 Like as the arrows in the hand of the giant: even so are the young children.
Happy is the man that hath his quiver full of them: they shall not be ashamed when they speak with their enemies in the gate.
Psalm 127, v. 5

8 Thy wife shall be as the fruitful vine: upon the walls of thine house.
Thy children like the olive-branches: round about thy table.
Psalm 128, v. 3

9 Many a time have they fought against me from my youth up: may Israel now say.
Psalm 129, v. 1

10 But they have not prevailed against me.
The plowers plowed upon my back: and made long furrows.
Psalm 129, v. 2

11 Out of the deep have I called unto thee, O Lord: Lord, hear my voice.
O let thine ears consider well: the voice of my complaint.
If thou, Lord, wilt be extreme to mark what is done amiss: O Lord, who may abide it?
Psalm 130, v. 1. Cf. Vulgate 108:5

12 My soul fleeth unto the Lord: before the morning watch, I say, before the morning watch.
Psalm 130, v. 6

13 Lord, I am not high-minded: I have no proud looks.
I do not exercise myself in great matters: which are too high for me.
Psalm 131, v. 1

14 Behold, how good and joyful a thing it is: brethren, to dwell together in unity!
Psalm 133, v. 1

15 He smote divers nations: and slew mighty kings;
Sehon king of the Amorites, and Og the king of Basan: and all the kingdoms of Canaan;
And gave their land to be an heritage: even an heritage unto Israel his people.
Psalm 135, v. 10

16 O give thanks unto the Lord, for he is gracious: and his mercy endureth for ever.
Psalm 136, v. 1

17 By the waters of Babylon we sat down and wept: when we remembered thee, O Sion.
As for our harps, we hanged them up: upon the trees that are therein.
For they that led us away captive required of us then a song, and melody, in our heaviness: Sing us one of the songs of Sion.
How shall we sing the Lord's song: in a strange land?
If I forget thee, O Jerusalem: let my right hand forget her cunning.
If I do not remember thee, let my tongue cleave to the roof of my mouth: yea, if I prefer not Jerusalem in my mirth.
Psalm 137, v. 1

18 O Lord, thou hast searched me out, and known me: thou knowest my down-sitting, and mine up-rising; thou understandest my thoughts long before.
Psalm 139, v. 1

19 Such knowledge is too wonderful and excellent for me: I cannot attain unto it.
Whither shall I go then from thy Spirit: or whither shall I go then from thy presence?
If I climb up into the heaven, thou art there: if I go down to hell, thou art there also.
If I take the wings of the morning: and remain in the uttermost parts of the sea;
Even there also shall thy hand lead me: and thy right hand shall hold me.
If I say, Peradventure the darkness shall cover me: then shall my night be turned to day.
Yea, the darkness is no darkness with thee, but the night is as clear as the day: the darkness and light to thee are both alike.
Psalm 139, v. 5

20 I will give thanks unto thee, for I am fearfully and wonderfully made.
Psalm 139, v. 13

21 Thine eyes did see my substance, yet being imperfect: and in thy book were all my members written;
Which day by day were fashioned: when as yet there were none of them.
Psalm 139, v. 15

22 Try me, O God, and seek the ground of my heart: prove me, and examine my thoughts.
Psalm 139, v. 23

1 Let the lifting up of my hands be an evening sacrifice. Set a watch, O Lord, before my mouth: and keep the door of my lips.
   Psalm 141, v. 2

2 Let the ungodly fall into their own nets together: and let me ever escape them.
   Psalm 141, v. 11

3 Enter not into judgement with thy servant: for in thy sight shall no man living be justified.
   Psalm 143, v. 2

4 Save me, and deliver me from the hand of strange children: whose mouth talketh of vanity, and their right hand is a right hand of iniquity.
   That our sons may grow up as the young plants: and that our daughters may be as the polished corners of the temple.
   Psalm 144, v. 11

5 That our sheep may bring forth thousands and ten thousands in our streets.
   That our oxen may be strong to labour, that there be no decay: no leading into captivity, and no complaining in our streets.
   Psalm 144, v. 13

6 The Lord upholdeth all such as fall: and lifteth up all those that are down.
   Psalm 145, v. 14

7 Thou givest them their meat in due season.
   Thou openest thine hand: and fillest all things living with plenteousness.
   Psalm 145, v. 15

8 O put not your trust in princes, nor in any child of man: for there is no help in them.
   Psalm 146, v. 2

9 The Lord looseth men out of prison: the Lord giveth sight to the blind.
   Psalm 146, v. 7

10 The Lord careth for the strangers; he defendeth the fatherless and widow: as for the way of the ungodly, he turneth it upside down.
   Psalm 146, v. 9

11 A joyful and pleasant thing it is to be thankful.
   The Lord doth build up Jerusalem: and gather together the out-casts of Israel.
   He healeth those that are broken in heart: and giveth medicine to heal their sickness.
   He telleth the number of the stars: and calleth them all by their names.
   Psalm 147, v. 1

12 He hath no pleasure in the strength of an horse: neither delighteth he in any man's legs.
   Psalm 147, v. 10

13 He giveth snow like wool: and scattereth the hoar-frost like ashes.
   He casteth forth his ice like morsels: who is able to abide his frost?
   Psalm 147, v. 16

14 Praise the Lord upon earth: ye dragons, and all deeps;
   Fire and hail, snow and vapours: wind and storm, fulfilling his word.
   Psalm 148, v. 7

15 Young men and maidens, old men and children, praise the Name of the Lord: for his Name only is excellent, and his praise above heaven and earth.
   Psalm 148, v. 12

16 Let the saints be joyful with glory: let them rejoice in their beds.
   Let the praises of God be in their mouth: and a two-edged sword in their hands;
   To be avenged of the heathen: and to rebuke the people;
   To bind their kings in chains: and their nobles with links of iron.
   Psalm 149, v. 5

17 Praise him upon the well-tuned cymbals: praise him upon the loud cymbals.
   Let every thing that hath breath: praise the Lord.
   Psalm 150, v. 5

18 Be pleased to receive into thy Almighty and most gracious protection the persons of us thy servants, and the Fleet in which we serve.
   Forms of Prayer to be Used at Sea First Prayer

19 That we may be ... a security for such as pass on the seas upon their lawful occasions.
   Forms of Prayer to be Used at Sea First Prayer

20 We therefore commit his body to the deep, to be turned into corruption, looking for the resurrection of the body (when the Sea shall give up her dead).
   Forms of Prayer to be Used at Sea At the Burial of their Dead at Sea

21 Come, Holy Ghost, our souls inspire,
   And lighten with celestial fire.
   Thou the anointing Spirit art,
   Who dost thy seven-fold gifts impart.

   Thy blessed Unction from above,
   Is comfort, life, and fire of love.
   Enable with perpetual light
   The dulness of our blinded sight.

   Anoint and cheer our soilèd face
   With the abundance of thy grace.
   Keep far our foes, give peace at home:
   Where thou art guide, no ill can come.
   Ordering of Priests 'Veni, Creator Spiritus' (translation from the c.9th century original by Bishop John Cosin, 1627)

22 Holy Scripture containeth all things necessary to salvation.
   Articles of Religion (1562) no. 6

23 Man is very far gone from original righteousness.
   Articles of Religion (1562) no. 9

24 It is a thing plainly repugnant to the Word of God, and the custom of the Primitive Church, to have publick Prayer in the Church, or to minister the Sacraments in a tongue not understanded of the people.
   Articles of Religion (1562) no. 24

25 The sacrifices of Masses, in the which it was commonly said, that the Priest did offer Christ for the quick and the dead, to have remission of pain or guilt, were blasphemous fables, and dangerous deceits.
   Articles of Religion (1562) no. 31

26 The Bishop of Rome hath no jurisdiction in this Realm of England.
   Articles of Religion (1562) no. 37

1 It is lawful for Christian men, at the commandment of the Magistrate, to wear weapons, and serve in the wars.

Articles of Religion (1562) no. 37

2 The Riches and Goods of Christians are not common, as touching the right, title, and possession of the same, as certain Anabaptists do falsely boast.

Articles of Religion (1562) no. 38

3 A Man may not marry his Mother.

A Table of Kindred and Affinity

John Wilkes Booth 1838–65

American assassin

4 *Sic semper tyrannis!* The South is avenged.

Having shot President Lincoln, 14 April 1865 ('*Sic semper tyrannis* [Thus always to tyrants]'—motto of the State of Virginia). *See New York Times* 15 April 1865 (the second part of the statement possibly apocryphal)

General William Booth 1829 1912

Founder of the Salvation Army, 1878

5 The Submerged Tenth.

In Darkest England (1890) pt. 1, title of ch. 2, in which Booth defines them as 'three million men, women, and children, a vast despairing multitude in a condition nominally free, but really enslaved'

Frances Boothby fl. 1670

English playwright

6 I'm hither come, but what d'ye think to say?
A woman's pen presents you with a play:
Who smiling told me I'd be sure to see
That once confirmed, the house would empty be.

Marcelia (1670) prologue

James H. Boren 1925–

American bureaucrat

7 Guidelines for bureaucrats: (1) When in charge, ponder. (2) When in trouble, delegate. (3) When in doubt, mumble.

In New York Times 8 November 1970, p. 45

Jorge Luis Borges 1899–1986

Argentinian writer

8 On those remote pages [of the *Celestial Emporium of Benevolent Knowledge*] it is written that animals are divided into (a) those that belong to the Emperor, (b) embalmed ones, (c) those that are trained, (d) suckling pigs, (e) mermaids, (f) fabulous ones, (g) stray dogs, (h) those that are included in this classification, (i) those that tremble as if they were mad, (j) innumerable ones, (k) those drawn with a very fine camel's hair brush, (l) others, (m) those that have just broken a flower vase, (n) those that resemble flies from a distance.

Other Inquisitions (1966) p. 108

9 *El original es infiel a la traducción.*

The original is unfaithful to the translation.

On Henley's translation, in *Sobre el 'Vathek' de William Beckford*; in *Obras Completas* (1974) p. 730

10 *Para uno de esos gnósticos, el visible universo era una ilusión ó (mas precisamente) un sofisma. Los espejos y la paternidad son abominables porque lo multiplican y lo divulgan.*

For one of those gnostics, the visible universe was an illusion or, more precisely, a sophism. Mirrors and fatherhood are abominable because they multiply it and extend it.

Tlön, Uqbar, Orbis, Tertius (1941) in *Obras Completas* (1974) p. 431

11 The Falklands thing was a fight between two bald men over a comb.

In *Time* 14 February 1983

Cesare Borgia 1476–1507

Italian statesman

12 *Aut Caesar, aut nihil.*

Caesar or nothing.

Motto inscribed on his sword. *See* John Leslie Garner *Caesar Borgia* (1912) p. 309

George Borrow 1803–81

English writer

13 There are no countries in the world less known by the British than these selfsame British Islands.

Lavengro (1851) preface

14 There's night and day, brother, both sweet things; sun, moon, and stars, brother, all sweet things: there's likewise a wind on the heath. Life is very sweet, brother; who would wish to die?

Lavengro (1851) ch. 25

15 Let no one sneer at the bruisers of England—what were the gladiators of Rome, or the bull-fighters of Spain, in its palmiest days, compared to England's bruisers?

Lavengro (1851) ch. 26

16 A losing trade, I assure you, sir: literature is a drug.

Lavengro (1851) ch. 30

17 Youth will be served, every dog has his day, and mine has been a fine one.

Lavengro (1851) ch. 92

18 Fear God, and take your own part.

The Romany Rye (1857) ch. 16

Pierre Bosquet 1810–61

French general

19 *C'est magnifique, mais ce n'est pas la guerre.*

It is magnificent, but it is not war.

On the charge of the Light Brigade at Balaclava, 25 October 1854, in Cecil Woodham-Smith *The Reason Why* (1953) ch. 12

John Collins Bossidy 1860–1928

1 And this is good old Boston,
The home of the bean and the cod,
Where the Lowells talk to the Cabots
And the Cabots talk only to God.

> Verse spoken at Holy Cross College alumni dinner in
> Boston, Massachusetts, 1910, in *Springfield Sunday
> Republican* 14 December 1924

Jacques-Bénigne Bossuet 1627–1704

French preacher

2 *L'Angleterre, ah, la perfide Angleterre, que le rempart de
ses mers rendait inaccessible aux Romains, la foi du
Sauveur y est abordée.*

England, ah, faithless England, which the protection
afforded by its seas rendered inaccessible to the
Romans, the faith of the Saviour spread even there.

> First sermon on the feast of the Circumcision, in *Oeuvres de
> Bossuet* (1816) vol. 11, p. 469. Cf. Ximénèz 750:12

James Boswell 1740–95

Scottish lawyer; biographer of Samuel Johnson

3 We may be in some degree whatever character we
choose.

> *Boswell's London Journal* (ed. F. A. Pottle, 1950)
> 21 November 1762

4 I think there is a blossom about me of something more
distinguished than the generality of mankind.

> *Boswell's London Journal* (ed. F. A. Pottle, 1950) 20 January
> 1763

5 I am, I flatter myself, completely a citizen of the world.
In my travels through Holland, Germany, Switzerland,
Italy, Corsica, France, I never felt myself from home.

> *Journal of a Tour to the Hebrides* (ed. F. A. Pottle, 1936)
> 14 August 1773

6 We [Boswell and Johnson] are both *Tories*; both
convinced of the utility of monarchical power, and
both lovers of that reverence and affection for a
sovereign which constitute loyalty, a principle which I
take to be absolutely extinguished in Britain.

> *Journal of a Tour to the Hebrides* (ed. F. A. Pottle, 1936)
> 13 September 1773

7 A page of my Journal is like a cake of portable soup. A
little may be diffused into a considerable portion.

> *Journal of a Tour to the Hebrides* (ed. F. A. Pottle, 1936)
> 13 September 1773

8 I have never yet exerted ambition in rising in the
state. But sure I am, no man has made his way better
to the best company.

> *Journal of a Tour to the Hebrides* (ed. F. A. Pottle, 1936)
> 16 September 1773

9 JOHNSON: Well, we had a good talk.
BOSWELL: Yes, Sir; you tossed and gored several
persons.

> *The Life of Samuel Johnson* (1934 ed.) vol. 2, p. 66 (Summer
> 1768)

10 A man, indeed, is not genteel when he gets drunk;
but most vices may be committed very genteelly: a
man may debauch his friend's wife genteelly: he may
cheat at cards genteelly.

> *The Life of Samuel Johnson* (1934 ed.) vol. 2, p. 340 (6 April
> 1775)

Gordon Bottomley 1874–1948

English poet

11 Your worship is your furnaces,
Which, like old idols, lost obscenes,
Have molten bowels; your vision is
Machines for making more machines.

> 'To Ironfounders and Others' (1912)

Horatio Bottomley 1860–1933

British newspaper proprietor and financier

12 No, reaping.

> Reply to a prison visitor who asked if he were sewing, in S.
> T. Felstead *Horatio Bottomley* (1936) ch. 16

13 Gentlemen: I have not had your advantages. What
poor education I have received has been gained in the
University of Life.

> Speech at the Oxford Union, 2 December 1920, in Beverley
> Nichols 25 (1926) ch. 7

Dion Boucicault (Dionysius Lardner Boursiquot) 1820–90

Irish playwright

14 Men talk of killing time, while time quietly kills them.

> *London Assurance* (1841) act 2, sc. 1. Cf. Sitwell 648:18

Antoine Boulay de la Meurthe 1761–1840

French statesman

15 *C'est pire qu'un crime, c'est une faute.*

It is worse than a crime, it is a blunder.

> On hearing of the execution of the Duc d'Enghien, 1804, in
> C.-A. Sainte-Beuve *Nouveaux Lundis* (1870) vol. 12, p. 52

Sir Harold Edwin Boulton 1859–1935

British songwriter

16 When Adam and Eve were dispossessed
Of the garden hard by Heaven,
They planted another one down in the west,
'Twas Devon, glorious Devon!

> 'Glorious Devon' (1902)

17 Speed, bonnie boat, like a bird on the wing,
'Onward,' the sailors cry;
Carry the lad that's born to be king,
Over the sea to Skye.

> 'Skye Boat Song' (1908)

Matthew Boulton 1728–1809

British engineer

1 I sell here, Sir, what all the world desires to have—POWER.

> Speaking to Boswell of his engineering works, in James Boswell *Life of Samuel Johnson* (1934 ed.) vol. 2, p. 459 (22 March 1776)

F. W. Bourdillon 1852–1921

English poet

2 The night has a thousand eyes,
And the day but one;
Yet the light of the bright world dies,
With the dying sun.

The mind has a thousand eyes,
And the heart but one;
Yet the light of a whole life dies,
When love is done.

> *Among the Flowers* (1878) 'Light'. Cf. Lyly 433:11

Lord Bowen 1835–94

English judge

3 When I hear of an 'equity' in a case like this, I am reminded of a blind man in a dark room—looking for a black hat—which isn't there.

> In John Alderson Foote *Pie-Powder* (1911) p. 25

4 The rain, it raineth on the just
And also on the unjust fella:
But chiefly on the just, because
The unjust steals the just's umbrella.

> In Walter Sichel *Sands of Time* (1923) ch. 4

E. E. Bowen 1836–1901

English schoolmaster

5 Forty years on, when afar and asunder
Parted are those who are singing to-day.

> 'Forty Years On' (Harrow School Song, published 1886)

6 Follow up! Follow up! Follow up! Follow up! Follow up!
Till the field ring again and again,
With the tramp of the twenty-two men,
Follow up!

> 'Forty Years On' (Harrow School Song, published 1886)

Elizabeth Bowen 1899–1973

Anglo-Irish novelist

7 The innocent are so few that two of them seldom meet—when they do, their victims lie strewn around.

> *The Death of the Heart* (1938) pt. 1, ch. 8

8 It is about five o'clock in an evening that the first hour of spring strikes—autumn arrives in the early morning, but spring at the close of a winter day.

> *The Death of the Heart* (1938) pt. 2, ch. 1

9 Some people are moulded by their admirations, others by their hostilities.

> *The Death of the Heart* (1938) pt. 2, ch. 2

10 There is no end to the violations committed by children on children, quietly talking alone.

> *The House in Paris* (1935) pt. 1, ch. 2

11 Fate is not an eagle, it creeps like a rat.

> *The House in Paris* (1935) pt. 2, ch. 2

12 Jealousy is no more than feeling alone against smiling enemies.

> *The House in Paris* (1935) pt. 2, ch. 8

13 It is not only our fate but our business to lose innocence, and once we have lost that, it is futile to attempt a picnic in Eden.

> 'Out of a Book' in *Orion III* (ed. Rosamund Lehmann et al, 1946)

14 A high altar on the move.

> Describing Edith Sitwell, in V. Glendinning *Edith Sitwell* (1981) ch. 25

David Bowie (*David Jones*) 1947–

English rock musician

15 Ground control to Major Tom.

> 'Space Oddity' (1969 song)

William Lisle Bowles 1762–1850

English clergyman and poet

16 The cause of Freedom is the cause of God!

> *A Poetical Address to the Right Honourable Edmund Burke* (1791) l. 78

Sir Maurice Bowra 1898–1971

English scholar and literary critic

17 I'm a man more dined against than dining.

> In John Betjeman *Summoned by Bells* (1960) ch. 9. Cf. *King Lear* 596:1

18 My dear fellow, buggers can't be choosers.

> On being told he should not marry anyone as plain as his fiancée, in Hugh Lloyd-Jones *Maurice Bowra: a Celebration* (1974) p. 150 (possibly apocryphal)

Charles Brackett 1892–1969 *and* Billy Wilder 1906–

American screenwriters

19 NINOTCHKA: Why should you carry other people's bags?
PORTER: Well, that's my business, Madame.
NINOTCHKA: That's no business. That's social injustice.
PORTER: That depends on the tip.

> *Ninotchka* (1939 film, with Walter Reisch)

20 JOE GILLIS: You used to be in pictures. You used to be big.
NORMA DESMOND: I am big. It's the pictures that got small.

> *Sunset Boulevard* (1950 film, with D. M. Marshman Jr.)

E. E. Bradford 1860–1944

English clergyman and poet

1 I walked with Will through bracken turning brown,
Pale yellow, orange, dun and golden-red.
'God made the country and man made the town—
And woman made Society,' he said.

'Society'. Cf. Cowper 223:18

John Bradford c.1510–55

English Protestant martyr

2 But for the grace of God there goes John Bradford.

On seeing a group of criminals being led to their execution,
in *Dictionary of National Biography* (1917–) p. 1067 (usually
quoted 'There but for the grace of God go I')

F. H. Bradley 1846–1924

English philosopher

3 Metaphysics is the finding of bad reasons for what we
believe upon instinct; but to find these reasons is no
less an instinct.

Appearance and Reality (1893) preface

4 The world is the best of all possible worlds, and
everything in it is a necessary evil.

Appearance and Reality (1893) preface

5 Where everything is bad it must be good to know the
worst.

Appearance and Reality (1893) preface

6 That the glory of this world . . . is appearance leaves
the world more glorious, if we feel it is a show of some
fuller splendour; but the sensuous curtain is a
deception . . . if it hides some colourless movement of
atoms, some . . . unearthly ballet of bloodless
categories.

Principles of Logic (1883) bk. 3, pt. 2, ch. 4

Omar Bradley 1893–1981

American general

7 We have grasped the mystery of the atom and rejected
the Sermon on the Mount.

Speech on Armistice Day, 1948, in *Collected Writings*
(1967) vol. 1, p. 588

8 The world has achieved brilliance without wisdom,
power without conscience. Ours is a world of nuclear
giants and ethical infants.

Speech on Armistice Day, 1948, in *Collected Writings*
(1967) vol. 1, p. 589

John Bradshaw 1602–59

English judge at the trial of Charles I

9 Rebellion to tyrants is obedience to God.

Supposititious epitaph. See Henry S. Randall *Life of Thomas
Jefferson* (1865) vol. 3, appendix 4, p. 585

Anne Bradstreet c.1612–72

English-born first poet of the New World

10 I am obnoxious to each carping tongue,
Who says my hand a needle better fits,
A poet's pen, all scorn, I should thus wrong;
For such despite they cast on female wits:
If what I do prove well, it won't advance,
They'll say it's stolne, or else, it was by chance.

'The Prologue' (1650)

11 Let Greeks be Greeks, and Women what they are,
Men have precedency, and still excel.

'The Prologue' (1650)

12 This mean and unrefinèd stuff of mine,
Will make your glistering gold but more to shine.

'The Prologue' (1650)

Ernest Bramah (*Ernest Bramah Smith*) 1868–1942

English writer

13 It is a mark of insincerity of purpose to spend one's
time in looking for the sacred Emperor in the low-class
tea-shops.

The Wallet of Kai Lung (1900) p. 6

14 In his countenance this person read an expression of
no-encouragement towards his venture.

The Wallet of Kai Lung (1900) p. 224

15 The whole narrative is permeated with the odour of
joss-sticks and honourable high-mindedness.

The Wallet of Kai Lung (1900) p. 330

James Bramston c.1694–1744

English clergyman and poet

16 What's not destroyed by Time's devouring hand?
Where's Troy, and where's the Maypole in the
Strand?

The Art of Politics (1729) l. 71

Georges Braque 1882–1963

French painter

17 L'Art est fait pour troubler, la Science rassure.

Art is meant to disturb, science reassures.

Le Jour et la nuit: Cahiers 1917–52 p. 11. Cf. Murdoch
488:8

18 La vérité existe; on n'invente que le mensonge.

Truth exists; only lies are invented.

Le Jour et la nuit: Cahiers 1917–52 p. 20

Richard Brathwaite c.1588–1673

English poet

19 To Banbury came I, O profane one!
Where I saw a Puritane-one
Hanging of his cat on Monday
For killing of a mouse on Sunday.

Barnabee's Journal (1638) pt. 1, st. 4

John W. Bratton and James B. Kennedy
British songwriters

1 If you go down in the woods today
You're sure of a big surprise
If you go down in the woods today
You'd better go in disguise
For every Bear that ever there was
Will gather there for certain because,
Today's the day the Teddy Bears have their Picnic.
 'The Teddy Bear's Picnic' (1932 song)

Bertolt Brecht 1898–1956
German playwright

2 *Der aufhaltsame Aufstieg des Arturo Ui.*

The resistible rise of Arturo Ui.
 Title of play (1941)

3 *Und der Haifisch, der hat Zähne*
 Und die trägt er im Gesicht
 Und Macheath, der hat ein Messer
 Doch das Messer sieht man nicht.

Oh, the shark has pretty teeth, dear,
And he shows them pearly white.
Just a jack-knife has Macheath, dear
And he keeps it out of sight.
 Die Dreigroschenoper (1928) prologue

4 *Erst kommt das Fressen, dann kommt die Moral.*

Food comes first, then morals.
 Die Dreigroschenoper (1928) act 2, sc. 3

5 *Was ist ein Einbruch in eine Bank gegen die Gründung einer Bank?*

What is robbing a bank compared with founding a bank?
 Die Dreigroschenoper (1928) act 3, sc. 3

6 ANDREA: *Unglücklich das Land, das keine Helden hat!* ...
 GALILEI: *Nein. Unglücklich das Land, das Helden nötig hat.*

ANDREA: Unhappy the land that has no heroes! ...
GALILEO: No. Unhappy the land that needs heroes.
 Leben des Galilei (1939) sc. 13

7 *Man merkts, hier ist zu lang kein Krieg gewesen. Wo soll da Moral herkommen, frag ich? Frieden, das ist nur Schlamperei, erst der Krieg schafft Ordnung.*

One observes, they have gone too long without a war here. Where is morality to come from in such a case, I ask? Peace is nothing but slovenliness, only war creates order.
 Mutter Courage (1939) sc. 1

8 *Weil ich ihm nicht trau, sind wir befreundet.*

Because I don't trust him, we are friends.
 Mutter Courage (1939) sc. 3

9 *Die schönsten Plän sind schon zuschanden geworden durch die Kleinlichkeit von denen, wo sie ausführen sollten, denn die Kaiser selber können ja nix machen.*

The finest plans are always ruined by the littleness of those who ought to carry them out, for the Emperors can actually do nothing.
 Mutter Courage (1939) sc. 6

10 *Der Krieg findet immer einen Ausweg.*

War always finds a way.
 Mutter Courage (1939) sc. 6

11 *Sagen Sie mir nicht, dass Friede ausgebrochen ist, wo ich eben neue Vorräte eingekauft hab.*

Don't tell me peace has broken out, when I've just bought some new supplies.
 Mutter Courage (1939) sc. 8

Gerald Brenan 1894–
British travel writer and novelist

12 Those who have some means think that the most important thing in the world is love. The poor know that it is money.
 Thoughts in a Dry Season (1978) p. 22. Cf. Baldwin 48:4

13 Religions are kept alive by heresies, which are really sudden explosions of faith. Dead religions do not produce them.
 Thoughts in a Dry Season (1978) p. 45

Jane Brereton (*née Hughes*) 1685–1740
English poet

14 The picture, placed the busts between,
Adds to the thought much strength:
Wisdom and Wit are little seen,
But Folly's at full length.
 'On Mr Nash's Picture at Full Length, between the Busts of Sir Isaac Newton and Mr Pope' (1744)

Nicholas Breton c.1545–1626
English writer and poet

15 We rise with the lark and go to bed with the lamb.
 The Court and Country (1618) para. 8

16 I wish my deadly foe, no worse
Than want of friends, and empty purse.
 'A Farewell to Town' (1577)

17 Come little babe, come silly soul,
Thy father's shame, thy mother's grief,
Born as I doubt to all our dole,
And to thy self unhappy chief.
 'A Sweet Lullaby' (1597)

Aristide Briand 1862–1932

French statesman

1 *Les hautes parties contractantes déclarent solennellement
... qu'elles condamnent le recours à la guerre ... et y
renoncent en tant qu'instrument de politique nationale
dans leurs relations mutuelles ... le règlement ou la
solution de tous les différends ou conflits—de quelque
nature ou de quelque origine qu'ils puissent être—qui
pourront surgir entre elles ne devra jamais être cherché
que par des moyens pacifiques.*

The high contracting powers solemnly declare ... that
they condemn recourse to war and renounce it ... as
an instrument of their national policy towards each
other ... The settlement or the solution of all disputes
or conflicts of whatever nature or of whatever origin
they may be which may arise ... shall never be
sought by either side except by pacific means.

Draft, 20 June 1927, later incorporated into the Kellogg
Pact, 1928, in *Le Temps* 13 April 1928

Robert Bridges 1844–1930

English poet

2 All my hope on God is founded;
He doth still my trust renew,
Me through change and chance he guideth,
Only good and only true.
God unknown,
He alone
Calls my heart to be his own.

'All my hope on God is founded' (1899 hymn)

3 When men were all asleep the snow came flying,
In large white flakes falling on the city brown,
Stealthily and perpetually settling and loosely lying,
Hushing the latest traffic of the drowsy town.

'London Snow' (1890)

4 All night it fell, and when full inches seven
It lay in the depth of its uncompacted lightness,
The clouds blew off from a high and frosty heaven;
And all woke earlier for the unaccustomed brightness
Of the winter dawning, the strange unheavenly glare.

'London Snow' (1890)

5 So sweet love seemed that April morn,
When first we kissed beside the thorn,
So strangely sweet, it was not strange
We thought that love could never change.

But I can tell—let truth be told—
That love will change in growing old;
Though day by day is nought to see,
So delicate his motions be.

'So sweet love seemed' (1894)

John Bright 1811–89

English Liberal politician and reformer

6 The angel of death has been abroad throughout the
land; you may almost hear the beating of his wings.

On the effects of the war in the Crimea, in *Hansard*,
23 February 1855, col. 1761

7 I am for 'Peace, retrenchment, and reform', the
watchword of the great Liberal party 30 years ago.

Speech at Birmingham, 28 April 1859, in *The Times*
29 April 1859; the phrase quoted may be found in Samuel
Warren's novel *Ten Thousand a Year* (1841) bk. 7, ch. 1

8 My opinion is that the Northern States will manage
somehow to muddle through.

Said during the American Civil War, in Justin McCarthy
Reminiscences (1899) vol. 1, ch. 5

9 England is the mother of Parliaments.

Speech at Birmingham, 18 January 1865, in *The Times*
19 January 1865

10 The right hon Gentleman ... has retired into what
may be called his political Cave of Adullam—and he
has called about him every one that was in distress
and every one that was discontented.

Referring to Robert Lowe, leader of the dissident Whigs
opposed to the Reform Bill of 1866; in *Hansard*, 13 March
1866, col. 219. *See* I Samuel ch. 22

11 This party of two is like the Scotch terrier that was so
covered with hair that you could not tell which was
the head and which was the tail.

Speech, *Hansard* 13 March 1866, col. 220

12 Force is not a remedy.

Speech to the Birmingham Junior Liberal Club,
16 November 1880, in *The Times* 17 November 1880

13 The knowledge of the ancient languages is mainly a
luxury.

Letter in *Pall Mall Gazette* 30 November 1886

Anthelme Brillat-Savarin 1755–1826

French jurist and gourmet

14 *Dis-moi ce que tu manges, je te dirai ce que tu es.*

Tell me what you eat and I will tell you what you are.

Physiologie du Goût (1825) 'Aphorismes pour servir de
prolégomènes' no. 4. Cf. Feuerbach 281:12

Alexander Brome 1620–66

English poet

15 I have been in love, and in debt, and in drink,
This many and many a year.

Songs and Other Poems (2nd ed., 1664) pt. 1 'The Mad
Lover'

16 Come, blessed peace, we once again implore,
And let our pains be less, or power more.

Songs and Other Poems (1661) 'The Riddle' (written 1644)

Jacob Bronowski 1908–74

Polish-born mathematician and humanist

17 The world can only be grasped by action, not by
contemplation ... The hand is the cutting edge of the
mind.

The Ascent of Man (1973) ch. 3

18 The essence of science: ask an impertinent question,
and you are on the way to a pertinent answer.

The Ascent of Man (1973) ch. 4

1 The wish to hurt, the momentary intoxication with pain, is the loophole through which the pervert climbs into the minds of ordinary men.

The Face of Violence (1954) ch. 5

Charlotte Brontë 1816–55

English novelist

2 We wove a web in childhood,
A web of sunny air;
We dug a spring in infancy
Of water pure and fair;
We sowed in youth a mustard seed,
We cut an almond rod;
We are now grown up to riper age—
Are they withered in the sod?

'We wove a web in childhood' (written 1835)

3 Conventionality is not morality. Self-righteousness is not religion. To attack the first is not to assail the last. To pluck the mask from the face of the Pharisee, is not to lift an impious hand to the Crown of Thorns.

Jane Eyre (2nd ed., 1848) preface

4 Women are supposed to be very calm generally: but women feel just as men feel; they need exercise for their faculties, and a field for their efforts as much as their brothers do; they suffer from too rigid a restraint, too absolute a stagnation, precisely as men would suffer ... it is thoughtless to condemn them, or laugh at them, if they seek to do more than custom has pronounced necessary for their sex.

Jane Eyre (1847) ch. 12

5 As his curate, his comrade, all would be right ... There would be recesses in my mind which would be only mine, to which he never came; and sentiments growing there, fresh and sheltered, which his austerity could never blight, nor his measured warrior-march trample down. But as his wife ... forced to keep the fire of my nature continually low, to compel it to burn inwardly and never utter a cry ... *this* would be unendurable.

Jane Eyre (1847) ch. 34

6 Reader, I married him.

Jane Eyre (1847) ch. 38

7 Of late years an abundant shower of curates has fallen upon the North of England.

Shirley (1849) ch. 1

8 Be a governess! Better be a slave at once!

Shirley (1849) ch. 13

9 It is rustic all through. It is moorish, and wild, and knotty as a root of heath.

On the setting of Emily Brontë's *Wuthering Heights*, in her own preface to the 1850 edition

10 You are not to suppose any of the characters in *Shirley* intended as literal portraits ... We only suffer reality to *suggest*, never to *dictate*.

Letter to Ellen Nussey, 16 November 1849, in Elizabeth Gaskell *The Life of Charlotte Bronte* (1857) ch. 18

Emily Brontë 1818–48

English novelist and poet

11 The night is darkening round me,
The wild winds coldly blow;
But a tyrant spell has bound me
And I cannot, cannot go ...

Clouds beyond clouds above me,
Wastes beyond wastes below;
But nothing drear can move me;
I will not, cannot go.

'The night is darkening round me' (written 1837)

12 No coward soul is mine,
No trembler in the world's storm-troubled sphere:
I see Heaven's glories shine,
And faith shines equal, arming me from fear.

'No coward soul is mine' (1846)

13 Though earth and moon were gone
And suns and universes ceased to be
And thou wert left alone
Every existence would exist in thee.

'No coward soul is mine' (1846)

14 Oh! dreadful is the check—intense the agony—
When the ear begins to hear, and the eye begins to see;
When the pulse begins to throb, the brain to think again;
The soul to feel the flesh, and the flesh to feel the chain.

'The Prisoner' (1846)

15 Cold in the earth—and fifteen wild Decembers,
From those brown hills, have melted into spring.

'Remembrance' (1846)

16 Sweet Love of youth, forgive, if I forget thee,
While the world's tide is bearing me along;
Other desires and other hopes beset me,
Hopes which obscure, but cannot do thee wrong!

'Remembrance' (1846)

17 But when the days of golden dreams had perished,
And even Despair was powerless to destroy,
Then did I learn how existence could be cherished,
Strengthened, and fed without the aid of joy.

'Remembrance' (1846)

18 If all else perished, and he remained, I should still continue to be; and if all else remained, and he were annihilated, the universe would turn to a mighty stranger: I should not seem a part of it. My love for Linton is like the foliage in the woods; time will change it, I'm well aware, as winter changes the trees—My love for Heathcliff resembles the eternal rocks beneath:—a source of little visible delight, but necessary.

Wuthering Heights (1847) ch. 9

19 I lingered round them, under that benign sky: watched the moths fluttering among the heath and hare-bells; listened to the soft wind breathing through the grass; and wondered how any one could ever imagine unquiet slumbers for the sleepers in that quiet earth.

Wuthering Heights (1847) *ad fin.*

Patrick Brontë 1777–1861

Perpetual curate of Haworth, Yorkshire from 1820

1 No quailing, Mrs Gaskell! no drawing back!
   Apropos her undertaking to write the life of Charlotte
   Brontë; letter from Mrs Gaskell to Ellen Nussey, 24 July
   1855, in J. A. V. Chapple and A. Pollard (eds.) *The Letters
   of Mrs Gaskell* (1966) no. 257

Henry Brooke 1703–83

Irish poet and playwright

2 For righteous monarchs,
   Justly to judge, with their own eyes should see;
   To rule o'er freemen, should themselves be free.
   Earl of Essex (performed 1750, published 1761) act 1

Rupert Brooke 1887–1915

English poet

3 Blow out, you bugles, over the rich Dead!
   There's none of these so lonely and poor of old,
   But, dying, has made us rarer gifts than gold.
   These laid the world away; poured out the red
   Sweet wine of youth; gave up the years to be
   Of work and joy, and that unhoped serene,
   That men call age; and those that would have been,
   Their sons, they gave, their immortality.
   'The Dead' (1914)

4 Honour has come back, as a king, to earth,
   And paid his subjects with a royal wage;
   And Nobleness walks in our ways again;
   And we have come into our heritage.
   'The Dead' (1914)

5 ... The cool kindliness of sheets, that soon
   Smooth away trouble; and the rough male kiss
   Of blankets.
   'The Great Lover' (1914)

6 Fish say, they have their stream and pond;
   But is there anything beyond?
   'Heaven' (1915)

7 One may not doubt that, somehow, good
   Shall come of water and of mud;
   And sure, the reverent eye must see
   A purpose in liquidity.
   'Heaven' (1915)

8 Fat caterpillars drift around,
   And Paradisal grubs are found;
   Unfading moths, immortal flies,
   And the worm that never dies.
   And in that Heaven of all their wish,
   There shall be no more land, say fish.
   'Heaven' (1915)

9 Just now the lilac is in bloom,
   All before my little room.
   'The Old Vicarage, Grantchester' (1915)

10 Unkempt about those hedges blows
   An English unofficial rose.
   'The Old Vicarage, Grantchester' (1915)

11 Curates, long dust, will come and go
   On lissom, clerical, printless toe;
   And oft between the boughs is seen
   The sly shade of a Rural Dean.
   'The Old Vicarage, Grantchester' (1915)

12 God! I will pack, and take a train,
   And get me to England once again!
   For England's the one land, I know,
   Where men with Splendid Hearts may go.
   'The Old Vicarage, Grantchester' (1915)

13 For Cambridge people rarely smile,
   Being urban, squat, and packed with guile.
   'The Old Vicarage, Grantchester' (1915)

14 They love the Good; they worship Truth;
   They laugh uproariously in youth;
   (And when they get to feeling old,
   They up and shoot themselves, I'm told).
   'The Old Vicarage, Grantchester' (1915)

15 Stands the Church clock at ten to three?
   And is there honey still for tea?
   'The Old Vicarage, Grantchester' (1915)

16 Now, God be thanked Who has matched us with His
      hour,
   And caught our youth, and wakened us from sleeping,
   With hand made sure, clear eye, and sharpened
      power,
   To turn, as swimmers into cleanness leaping.
   'Peace' (1914)

17 Naught broken save this body, lost but breath;
   Nothing to shake the laughing heart's long peace
      there
   But only agony, and that has ending;
   And the worst friend and enemy is but Death.
   'Peace' (1914)

18 If I should die, think only this of me:
   That there's some corner of a foreign field
   That is for ever England. There shall be
   In that rich earth a richer dust concealed;
   A dust whom England bore, shaped, made aware,
   Gave, once, her flowers to love, her ways to roam,
   A body of England's, breathing English air,
   Washed by the rivers, blest by suns of home.

   And think, this heart, all evil shed away,
   A pulse in the eternal mind, no less
   Gives somewhere back the thoughts by England given;
   Her sights and sounds; dreams happy as her day;
   And laughter, learnt of friends; and gentleness,
   In hearts at peace, under an English heaven.
   'The Soldier' (1914)

Anita Brookner 1938–

British novelist and art historian

19 What is the most potent myth of all? ... The tortoise
   and the hare ... the hare is always convinced of his
   own superiority; he simply does not recognize the
   tortoise as a worthy adversary. That is why the hare
   wins.
   Hotel du Lac (1984) ch. 2

20 Good women always think it is their fault when
   someone else is being offensive. Bad women never take
   the blame for anything.
   Hotel du Lac (1984) ch. 7

1 They were reasonable people, and no one was to be hurt, not even with words.
   Hotel du Lac (1984) ch. 9

2 They were privileged children ... they would always expect to be greeted with smiles.
   Lewis Percy (1989) ch. 9

3 Dr Weiss, at forty, knew that her life had been ruined by literature.
   A Start in Life (1981) ch. 1

Phillips Brooks 1835–93

American clergyman

4 O little town of Bethlehem,
   How still we see thee lie!
   Above thy deep and dreamless sleep
   The silent stars go by.
   Yet in thy dark streets shineth
   The everlasting light;
   The hopes and fears of all the years
   Are met in thee to-night.
   'O Little town of Bethlehem' (1868 hymn)

Thomas Brooks 1608–80

English Puritan divine

5 For (*magna est veritas et praevalebit*) great is truth, and shall prevail.
   The Crown and Glory of Christianity (1662) p. 407.
   Cf. Vulgate 108:18

Robert Barnabas Brough 1828–60

English satirical writer

6 My Lord Tomnoddy is thirty-four;
   The Earl can last but a few years more.
   My Lord in the Peers will take his place:
   Her Majesty's councils his words will grace.
   Office he'll hold and patronage sway;
   Fortunes and lives he will vote away;
   And what are his qualifications?—ONE!
   He's the Earl of Fitzdotterel's eldest son.
   Songs of the Governing Classes (1855) 'My Lord Tomnoddy'

Lord Brougham (Henry Peter, Baron Brougham and Vaux) 1778–1868

Scottish lawyer and politician; Lord Chancellor

7 In my mind, he was guilty of no error—he was chargeable with no exaggeration—he was betrayed by his fancy into no metaphor, who once said, that all we see about us, King, Lords, and Commons, the whole machinery of the State, all the apparatus of the system, and its varied workings, end in simply bringing twelve good men into a box.
   Hansard 7 February 1828, col. 131

8 Look out, gentlemen, the schoolmaster is abroad!
   Hansard 29 January 1828, col. 58

9 Education makes a people easy to lead, but difficult to drive; easy to govern, but impossible to enslave.
   Attributed

Heywood Broun 1888–1939

American journalist

10 Just as every conviction begins as a whim so does every emancipator serve his apprenticeship as a crank. A fanatic is a great leader who is just entering the room.
   New York World 6 February 1928, p. 11

H. Rap Brown (Hubert Geroid Brown) 1943–

American Black Power leader

11 I say violence is necessary. It is as American as cherry pie.
   Speech at Washington, 27 July 1967, in *Washington Post* 28 July 1967, p. A7

John Brown 1715–66

English clergyman and writer

12 I have seen some extracts from Johnson's Preface to his 'Shakespeare' ... No feeling nor pathos in him! Altogether upon the high horse, and blustering about Imperial Tragedy!
   Letter to Garrick, 27 October 1765, in *The Private Correspondence of David Garrick* (1831) vol. 1, p. 204

John Brown 1800–59

American abolitionist

13 Now, if it is deemed necessary that I should forfeit my life for the furtherance of the ends of justice, and mingle my blood further with the blood of my children, and with the blood of millions in this slave country whose rights are disregarded by wicked, cruel, and unjust enactments, I say let it be done.
   Last speech to the court, 2 November 1859, in *The Life, Trial and Execution of Captain John Brown* (1859) p. 95

14 I, John Brown, am now quite certain that the crimes of this guilty land will never be purged away but with blood.
   Written on the day of his execution, 2 December 1859, in R. J. Hinton *John Brown and His Men* (1894) ch. 12

Lew Brown (Louis Brownstein) 1893–1958

American songwriter

15 Life is just a bowl of cherries.
   Title of song (1931)

Thomas Brown 1663–1704

English satirist

16 A little before you made a leap into the dark.
   Letters from the Dead to the Living (1702) 'Answer to Mr Joseph Haines'. Cf. Hobbes 340:14

1 I do not love thee, Dr Fell.
The reason why I cannot tell;
But this I know, and know full well,
I do not love thee, Dr Fell.
> Written while an undergraduate at Christ Church, Oxford,
> of which Dr Fell was Dean; in A. L. Hayward (ed.)
> *Amusements Serious and Comical by Tom Brown* (1927)
> p. xiii. Cf. Martial 449:12

T. E. Brown 1830–97

English schoolmaster and poet

2 A garden is a lovesome thing, God wot!
> 'My Garden' (1893)

3 O blackbird, what a boy you are!
How you do go it!
> 'Vespers' (1900)

Cecil Browne 1932–

American businessman

4 But not so odd
As those who choose
A Jewish God,
But spurn the Jews.
> Reply to verse by William Norman Ewer. Cf. Ewer 279:11

Sir Thomas Browne 1605–82

English writer and physician

5 Oblivion is a kind of Annihilation.
> *Christian Morals* (1716) pt. 1, sect. 21

6 He who discommendeth others obliquely commendeth
himself.
> *Christian Morals* (1716) pt. 1, sect. 34

7 As for that famous network of Vulcan, which enclosed
Mars and Venus, and caused that unextinguishable
laugh in heaven, since the gods themselves could not
discern it, we shall not pry into it.
> *The Garden of Cyrus* (1658) ch. 2

8 Life itself is but the shadow of death, and souls
departed but the shadows of the living: all things fall
under this name. The sun itself is but the dark
simulacrum, and light but the shadow of God.
> *The Garden of Cyrus* (1658) ch. 4

9 Flat and flexible truths are beat out by every hammer;
but Vulcan and his whole forge sweat to work out
Achilles his armour.
> *The Garden of Cyrus* (1658) ch. 5

10 The quincunx of heaven runs low, and 'tis time to
close the five ports of knowledge.
> *The Garden of Cyrus* (1658) ch. 5

11 All things began in order, so shall they end, and so
shall they begin again; according to the ordainer of
order and mystical mathematics of the city of heaven.
> *The Garden of Cyrus* (1658) ch. 5

12 Nor will the sweetest delight of gardens afford much
comfort in sleep; wherein the dullness of that sense
shakes hands with delectable odours; and though in
the bed of Cleopatra, can hardly with any delight raise
up the ghost of a rose.
> *The Garden of Cyrus* (1658) ch. 5

13 Though Somnus in Homer be sent to rouse up
Agamemnon, I find no such effects in these drowsy
approaches of sleep. To keep our eyes open longer
were but to act our Antipodes. The huntsmen are up
in America, and they are already past their first sleep
in Persia. But who can be drowsy at that hour which
freed us from everlasting sleep? or have slumbering
thoughts at that time, when sleep itself must end, and
as some conjecture all shall awake again?
> *The Garden of Cyrus* (1658) ch. 5

14 Old mortality, the ruins of forgotten times.
> *Hydriotaphia* (Urn Burial, 1658) Epistle Dedicatory

15 With rich flames and hired tears they solemnized their
obsequies.
> *Hydriotaphia* (Urn Burial, 1658) ch. 3

16 Men have lost their reason in nothing so much as
their religion, wherein stones and clouts make
martyrs.
> *Hydriotaphia* (Urn Burial, 1658) ch. 4

17 Were the happiness of the next world as closely
apprehended as the felicities of this, it were a
martyrdom to live.
> *Hydriotaphia* (Urn Burial, 1658) ch. 4

18 The long habit of living indisposeth us for dying.
> *Hydriotaphia* (Urn Burial, 1658) ch. 5

19 What song the Syrens sang, or what name Achilles
assumed when he hid himself among women, though
puzzling questions, are not beyond all conjecture.
> *Hydriotaphia* (Urn Burial, 1658) ch. 5

20 But to subsist in bones, and be but pyramidally extant,
is a fallacy in duration.
> *Hydriotaphia* (Urn Burial, 1658) ch. 5

21 Generations pass while some trees stand, and old
families last not three oaks.
> *Hydriotaphia* (Urn Burial, 1658) ch. 5

22 To be nameless in worthy deeds exceeds an infamous
history.
> *Hydriotaphia* (Urn Burial, 1658) ch. 5

23 The iniquity of oblivion blindly scattereth her poppy,
and deals with the memory of men without distinction
to merit perpetuity.
> *Hydriotaphia* (Urn Burial, 1658) ch. 5

24 The night of time far surpasseth the day, and who
knows when was the equinox?
> *Hydriotaphia* (Urn Burial, 1658) ch. 5

25 Diurnity is a dream and folly of expectation.
> *Hydriotaphia* (Urn Burial, 1658) ch. 5

26 Man is a noble animal, splendid in ashes, and
pompous in the grave.
> *Hydriotaphia* (Urn Burial, 1658) ch. 5

27 Ready to be any thing, in the ecstasy of being ever.
> *Hydriotaphia* (Urn Burial, 1658) ch. 5

28 At my devotion I love to use the civility of my knee,
my hat, and hand.
> *Religio Medici* (1643) pt. 1, sect. 3

29 Many from ... an inconsiderate zeal unto truth, have
too rashly charged the troops of error, and remain as
trophies unto the enemies of truth.
> *Religio Medici* (1643) pt. 1, sect. 6

1 A man may be in as just possession of truth as of a
city, and yet be forced to surrender.
   Religio Medici (1643) pt. 1, sect. 6

2 As for those wingy mysteries in divinity and airy
subtleties in religion, which have unhinged the brains
of better heads, they never stretched the *pia mater* of
mine; methinks there be not impossibilities enough in
religion for an active faith.
   Religio Medici (1643) pt. 1, sect. 9

3 I love to lose myself in a mystery, to pursue my reason
to an *O altitudo*!
   Religio Medici (1643) pt. 1, sect. 9

4 Who can speak of eternity without a solecism, or
think thereof without an ecstasy? Time we may
comprehend, 'tis but five days elder than ourselves.
   Religio Medici (1643) pt. 1, sect. 11

5 I have often admired the mystical way of Pythagoras,
and the secret magic of numbers.
   Religio Medici (1643) pt. 1, sect. 12

6 We carry within us the wonders we seek without us:
there is all Africa and her prodigies in us.
   Religio Medici (1643) pt. 1, sect. 15

7 All things are artificial, for nature is the art of God.
   Religio Medici (1643) pt. 1, sect. 16

8 Obstinacy in a bad cause, is but constancy in a good.
   Religio Medici (1643) pt. 1, sect. 25

9 Persecution is a bad and indirect way to plant religion.
   Religio Medici (1643) pt. 1, sect. 25

10 Not wrung from speculations and subtleties, but from
common sense, and observation; not picked from the
leaves of any author, but bred among the weeds and
tares of mine own brain.
   Religio Medici (1643) pt. 1, sect. 36

11 I am not so much afraid of death, as ashamed thereof;
'tis the very disgrace and ignominy of our natures,
that in a moment can so disfigure us that our nearest
friends, wife, and children, stand afraid and start at
us.
   Religio Medici (1643) pt. 1, sect. 40

12 Certainly there is no happiness within this circle of
flesh, nor is it in the optics of these eyes to behold
felicity; the first day of our Jubilee is death.
   Religio Medici (1643) pt. 1, sect. 44

13 He forgets that he can die who complains of misery,
we are in the power of no calamity, while death is in
our own.
   Religio Medici (1643) pt. 1, sect. 44

14 All places, all airs make unto me one country: I am in
England, everywhere, and under any meridian.
   Religio Medici (1643) pt. 2, sect. 1

15 If there be any among those common objects of hatred
I do condemn and laugh at, it is that great enemy of
reason, virtue and religion, the multitude, that
numerous piece of monstrosity, which taken asunder
seem men, and the reasonable creatures of God; but
confused together, make but one great beast, and a
monstrosity more prodigious than Hydra.
   Religio Medici (1643) pt. 2, sect. 1

16 This trivial and vulgar way of coition; it is the
foolishest act a wise man commits in all his life, nor is
there any thing that will more deject his cooled
imagination, when he shall consider what an odd and
unworthy piece of folly he hath committed.
   Religio Medici (1643) pt. 2, sect. 9

17 Sure there is music even in the beauty, and the silent
note which Cupid strikes, far sweeter than the sound
of an instrument. For there is music wherever there is
a harmony, order or proportion; and thus far we may
maintain the music of the spheres; for those
well-ordered motions, and regular paces, though they
give no sound unto the ear, yet to the understanding
they strike a note most full of harmony.
   Religio Medici (1643) pt. 2, sect. 9

18 We all labour against our own cure, for death is the
cure of all diseases.
   Religio Medici (1643) pt. 2, sect. 9

19 For the world, I count it not an inn, but an hospital,
and a place, not to live, but to die in.
   Religio Medici (1643) pt. 2, sect. 11

20 There is surely a piece of divinity in us, something
that was before the elements, and owes no homage
unto the sun.
   Religio Medici (1643) pt. 2, sect. 11

21 We term sleep a death, and yet it is waking that kills
us, and destroys those spirits which are the house of
life.
   Religio Medici (1643) pt. 2, sect. 12

22 Half our days we pass in the shadow of the earth; and
the brother of death exacteth a third part of our lives.
   S. Wilkin (ed.) *Sir Thomas Browne's Works* (1835) vol. 4,
   p. 355 'On Dreams'

23 That children dream not in the first half year, that
men dream not in some countries, are to me sick
men's dreams, dreams out of the ivory gate, and
visions before midnight.
   S. Wilkin (ed.) *Sir Thomas Browne's Works* (1835) vol. 4,
   p. 359 'On Dreams'

William Browne *c.*1590–1643

English poet

24 Underneath this sable hearse
Lies the subject of all verse;
Sidney's sister, Pembroke's mother,
Death, ere thou hast slain another,
Fair and learn'd, and good as she,
Time shall throw a dart at thee.
   'Epitaph on the Countess Dowager of Pembroke' (1623)

Sir William Browne 1692–1774

English physician and writer

25 The King to Oxford sent a troop of horse,
For Tories own no argument but force:
With equal skill to Cambridge books he sent,
For Whigs admit no force but argument.
   Reply to Trapp's epigram, in J. Nichols *Literary Anecdotes*
   vol. 3 (1812) p. 330. Cf. Trapp 702:3

Elizabeth Barrett Browning 1806–61

English poet

1 The works of women are symbolical.
We sew, sew, prick our fingers, dull our sight,
Producing what? A pair of slippers, sir,
To put on when you're weary.
  Aurora Leigh (1857) bk. 1, l. 456

2   Near all the birds
Will sing at dawn,—and yet we do not take
The chaffering swallow for the holy lark.
  Aurora Leigh (1857) bk. 1, l. 951

3 God answers sharp and sudden on some prayers,
And thrusts the thing we have prayed for in our face,
A gauntlet with a gift in't.
  Aurora Leigh (1857) bk. 2, l. 952

4 I think it frets the saints in heaven to see
How many desolate creatures on the earth
Have learnt the simple dues of fellowship
And social comfort, in a hospital.
  Aurora Leigh (1857) bk. 3, l. 1121

5 Nay, if there's room for poets in this world
A little overgrown (I think there is)
Their sole work is to represent the age,
Their age, not Charlemagne's.
  Aurora Leigh (1857) bk. 5, l. 200

6   King Arthur's self
Was commonplace to Lady Guenever;
And Camelot to minstrels seemed as flat
As Fleet Street to our poets.
  Aurora Leigh (1857) bk. 5, l. 210

7 Since when was genius found respectable?
  Aurora Leigh (1857) bk. 6, l. 275

8 The devil's most devilish when respectable.
  Aurora Leigh (1857) bk. 7, l. 105

9 Earth's crammed with heaven,
And every common bush afire with God:
But only he who sees, takes off his shoes;
The rest sit round it, and pluck blackberries,
And daub their natural faces unaware
More and more, from the first similitude.
  Aurora Leigh (1857) bk. 7, l. 821

10 And kings crept out again to feel the sun.
  'Crowned and Buried' (1844) st. 11

11 Do ye hear the children weeping, O my brothers,
Ere the sorrow comes with years?
  'The Cry of the Children' (1844) st. 1

12 And lips say, 'God be pitiful,'
Who ne'er said, 'God be praised.'
  'The Cry of the Human' (1844) st. 1

13 I tell you, hopeless grief is passionless.
  'Grief' (1844)

14   Deep-hearted man, express
Grief for thy dead in silence like to death;
Most like a monumental statue set
In everlasting watch and moveless woe,
Till itself crumble to the dust beneath.
Touch it: the marble eyelids are not wet—
If it could weep, it could arise and go.
  'Grief' (1844)

15 Or from Browning some 'Pomegranate', which, if cut
   deep down the middle,
Shows a heart within blood-tinctured, of a veined
   humanity.
  'Lady Geraldine's Courtship' (1844) st. 41

16 'Yes,' I answered you last night;
'No,' this morning, sir, I say.
Colours seen by candle-light
Will not look the same by day.
  'The Lady's Yes' (1844)

17 What was he doing, the great god Pan,
Down in the reeds by the river?
Spreading ruin and scattering ban,
Splashing and paddling with hoofs of a goat,
And breaking the golden lilies afloat
With the dragon-fly on the river.
  'A Musical Instrument' (1862)

18   Straightway I was 'ware,
So weeping, how a mystic shape did move
Behind me, and drew me backward by the hair
And a voice said in mastery while I strove . . .
'Guess now who holds thee?'—'Death', I said. But,
   there,
The silver answer rang . . . 'Not Death, but Love.'
  Sonnets from the Portuguese (1850) no. 1

19   For frequent tears have run
The colours from my life.
  Sonnets from the Portuguese (1850) no. 8

20 How do I love thee? Let me count the ways.
  Sonnets from the Portuguese (1850) no. 43

21 I love thee with the breath,
Smiles, tears, of all my life!—and if God choose,
I shall but love thee better after death.
  Sonnets from the Portuguese (1850) no. 43

22 Thou large-brained woman and large-hearted man.
  'To George Sand—A Desire' (1844)

23 And the rolling anapaestic
Curled like vapour over shrines!
  'Wine of Cyprus' (1844) st. 10

Sir Frederick Browning 1896–1965

British soldier

24 I think we might be going a bridge too far.
  Expressing reservations about the Arnhem 'Market Garden'
  operation to Field Marshal Montgomery on 10 September
  1944, in R. E. Urquhart *Arnhem* (1958) p. 4

Robert Browning 1812–89

English poet

25 Burrow awhile and build, broad on the roots of things.
  'Abt Vogler' (1864) st. 2

26 On the earth the broken arcs; in the heaven, a perfect
round.
  'Abt Vogler' (1864) st. 9

1 The high that proved too high, the heroic for earth too
  hard,
  The passion that left the ground to lose itself in the
  sky,
  Are music sent up to God by the lover and the bard;
  Enough that he heard it once: we shall hear it
  by-and-by.
  'Abt Vogler' (1864) st. 10

2 . . . I feel for the common chord again . . .
  The C Major of this life.
  'Abt Vogler' (1864) st. 12

3 Ah, but a man's reach should exceed his grasp,
  Or what's a heaven for?
  'Andrea del Sarto' (1855) l. 97

4 Re-coin thyself and give it them to spend,—
  It all comes to the same thing at the end,
  Since mine thou wast, mine art, and mine shalt be.
  'Any Wife to Any Husband' (1855) st. 16

5 But, thanks to wine-lees and democracy,
  We've still our stage where truth calls spade a spade!
  Aristophanes' Apology (1875) l. 409

6 One who never turned his back but marched breast
  forward,
  Never doubted clouds would break,
  Never dreamed, though right were worsted, wrong
  would triumph,
  Held we fall to rise, are baffled to fight better,
  Sleep to wake.
  Asolando (1889) 'Epilogue'

7 Greet the unseen with a cheer!
  Asolando (1889) 'Epilogue'

8 I find earth not grey but rosy,
  Heaven not grim but fair of hue.
  Do I stoop? I pluck a posy.
  Do I stand and stare? All's blue.
  'At the Mermaid' (1876) st. 12

9 There spoke up a brisk little somebody,
  Critic and whippersnapper, in a rage
  To set things right.
  Balaustion's Adventure (1871) l. 306

10   Don't you know,
  I promised, if you'd watch a dinner out,
  We'd see truth dawn together?—truth that peeps
  Over the glasses' edge when dinner's done,
  And body gets its sop and holds its noise
  And leaves soul free a little.
  'Bishop Blougram's Apology' (1855) l. 15

11 Just when we are safest, there's a sunset-touch,
  A fancy from a flower-bell, some one's death,
  A chorus-ending from Euripides,—
  And that's enough for fifty hopes and fears
  As old and new at once as nature's self,
  To rap and knock and enter in our soul,
  Take hands and dance there, a fantastic ring,
  Round the ancient idol, on his base again,—
  The grand Perhaps!
  'Bishop Blougram's Apology' (1855) l. 182

12 All we have gained then by our unbelief
  Is a life of doubt diversified by faith,
  For one of faith diversified by doubt:
  We called the chess-board white,—we call it black.
  'Bishop Blougram's Apology' (1855) l. 209

13 Our interest's on the dangerous edge of things.
  The honest thief, the tender murderer,
  The superstitious atheist, demirep
  That loves and saves her soul in new French books—
  We watch while these in equilibrium keep
  The giddy line midway.
  'Bishop Blougram's Apology' (1855) l. 395

14 You, for example, clever to a fault,
  The rough and ready man who write apace,
  Read somewhat seldomer, think perhaps even less.
  'Bishop Blougram's Apology' (1855) l. 420

15 No, when the fight begins within himself,
  A man's worth something.
  'Bishop Blougram's Apology' (1855) l. 693

16 He said true things, but called them by wrong names.
  'Bishop Blougram's Apology' (1855) l. 996

17 And have I not Saint Praxed's ear to pray
  Horses for ye, and brown Greek manuscripts,
  And mistresses with great smooth marbly limbs?
  —That's if ye carve my epitaph aright.
  'The Bishop Orders his Tomb' (1845) l. 73

18 And then how I shall lie through centuries,
  And hear the blessed mutter of the mass,
  And see God made and eaten all day long,
  And feel the steady candle-flame, and taste
  Good strong thick stupefying incense-smoke!
  'The Bishop Orders his Tomb' (1845) l. 80

19 I was so young, I loved him so, I had
  No mother, God forgot me, and I fell.
  A Blot in the 'Scutcheon (1843) act 1, sc. 3, l. 237

20 Boot, saddle, to horse, and away!
  'Boot and Saddle' (1842)

21 How well I know what I mean to do
  When the long dark autumn-evenings come.
  'By the Fireside' (1855) st. 1

22 I shall be found by the fire, suppose,
  O'er a great wise book as beseemeth age,
  While the shutters flap as the cross-wind blows
  And I turn the page, and I turn the page,
  Not verse now, only prose!
  'By the Fireside' (1855) st. 2

23   I will speak now,
  No longer watch you as you sit
  Reading by fire-light, that great brow
  And the spirit-small hand propping it,
  Mutely.
  'By the Fireside' (1855) st. 23

24 When earth breaks up and heaven expands,
  How will the change strike me and you
  In the house not made with hands?
  'By the Fireside' (1855) st. 27. Cf. II Corinthians 101:18

25 Oh, the little more, and how much it is!
  And the little less, and what worlds away!
  'By the Fireside' (1855) st. 39

26 If two lives join, there is oft a scar,
  They are one and one, with a shadowy third;
  One near one is too far.
  'By the Fireside' (1855) st. 46

1 And it is good to cheat the pair, and gibe,
Letting the rank tongue blossom into speech.

Setebos, Setebos, and Setebos!
'Thinketh, He dwelleth i' the cold o' the moon.
'Thinketh He made it, with the sun to match,
But not the stars; the stars came otherwise.
  'Caliban upon Setebos' (1864) l. 22

2 'Let twenty pass, and stone the twenty-first,
Loving not, hating not, just choosing so.
  'Caliban upon Setebos' (1864) l. 102

3 Dauntless the slug-horn to my lips I set,
And blew. 'Childe Roland to the Dark Tower came.'
  'Childe Roland to the Dark Tower Came' (1855) st. 34.
  Cf. *King Lear* 596:17

4 In the natural fog of the good man's mind.
  'Christmas-Eve' (1850) l. 226

5 The raree-show of Peter's successor.
  'Christmas-Eve' (1850) l. 1242

6 For the preacher's merit or demerit,
It were to be wished the flaws were fewer
In the earthen vessel, holding treasure
Which lies as safe in a golden ewer;
But the main thing is, does it hold good measure?
Heaven soon sets right all other matters!
  'Christmas-Eve' (1850) l. 1311

7 And I have written three books on the soul,
Proving absurd all written hitherto,
And putting us to ignorance again.
  'Cleon' (1855) l. 57

8 What is he buzzing in my ears?
'Now that I come to die,
Do I view the world as a vale of tears?'
Ah, reverend sir, not I!
  'Confessions' (1864) st. 1

9 We loved, sir—used to meet:
How sad and bad and mad it was—
But then, how it was sweet!
  'Confessions' (1864) st. 9

10 Stung by the splendour of a sudden thought.
  'A Death in the Desert' (1864) l. 59

11 For I say, this is death and the sole death,
When a man's loss comes to him from his gain,
Darkness from light, from knowledge ignorance,
And lack of love from love made manifest.
  'A Death in the Desert' (1864) l. 482

12 ... Progress, man's distinctive mark alone,
Not God's, and not the beasts': God is, they are,
Man partly is and wholly hopes to be.
  'A Death in the Desert' (1864) l. 586

13 With the beanflowers' boon,
And the blackbird's tune,
And May, and June!
  'De Gustibus' (1855) pt. 1, l. 11

14 Italy, my Italy!
Queen Mary's saying serves for me—
(When fortune's malice
Lost her—Calais—)
Open my heart and you will see
Graved inside of it, 'Italy'.
  'De Gustibus' (1855) pt. 2, l. 39

15 Reads verse and thinks she understands.
  'Dîs Aliter Visum' (1864) st. 4

16 Sure of the Fortieth spare Arm-chair
When gout and glory seat me there.
  'Dîs Aliter Visum' (1864) st. 12

17   'Tis well averred,
A scientific faith's absurd.
  'Easter-Day' (1850) l. 123

18   At last awake
From life, that insane dream we take
For waking now.
  'Easter-Day' (1850) l. 479

19 Karshish, the picker-up of learning's crumbs,
The not-incurious in God's handiwork.
  'An Epistle ... of Karshish' (1855)

20 Beautiful Evelyn Hope is dead!
  'Evelyn Hope' (1855)

21 You will wake, and remember, and understand.
  'Evelyn Hope' (1855)

22 So absolutely good is truth, truth never hurts
The teller.
  Fifine at the Fair (1872) st. 32

23 I must learn Spanish, one of these days,
Only for that slow sweet name's sake.
  'The Flower's Name' (1845)

24 If you get simple beauty and naught else,
You get about the best thing God invents.
  'Fra Lippo Lippi' (1855) l. 217

25   This world's no blot for us,
Nor blank; it means intensely, and means good:
To find its meaning is my meat and drink.
  'Fra Lippo Lippi' (1855) l. 313

26 Our low life was the level's and the night's;
He's for the morning.
  'A Grammarian's Funeral' (1855) l. 23

27 This is our master, famous calm and dead,
Borne on our shoulders.
  'A Grammarian's Funeral' (1855) l. 27

28 Yea, but we found him bald too, eyes like lead,
Accents uncertain:
'Time to taste life,' another would have said,
'Up with the curtain!'
  'A Grammarian's Funeral' (1855) l. 53

29 Yea, this in him was the peculiar grace
(Hearten our chorus!)
That before living he'd learn how to live—
No end to learning.
  'A Grammarian's Funeral' (1855) l. 75

30 He said, 'What's time? Leave Now for dogs and apes!
Man has Forever.'
  'A Grammarian's Funeral' (1855) l. 83

1 That low man seeks a little thing to do,
Sees it and does it:
This high man, with a great thing to pursue,
Dies ere he knows it.
That low man goes on adding one to one,
His hundred's soon hit:
This high man, aiming at a million,
Misses an unit.
That, has the world here—should he need the next,
Let the world mind him!
This, throws himself on God, and unperplexed
Seeking shall find him.
'A Grammarian's Funeral' (1855) l. 113

2 Lofty designs must close in like effects:
Loftily lying,
Leave him—still loftier than the world suspects,
Living and dying.
'A Grammarian's Funeral' (1855) l. 145

3 The Lord will have mercy on Jacob yet,
And again in his border see Israel set.
'Holy-Cross Day' (1855) st. 13

4 We withstood Christ then? Be mindful how
At least we withstand Barabbas now!
'Holy-Cross Day' (1855) st. 18

5 Oh, to be in England
Now that April's there,
And whoever wakes in England
Sees, some morning, unaware,
That the lowest boughs and the brushwood sheaf
Round the elm-tree bole are in tiny leaf,
While the chaffinch sings on the orchard bough
In England—now!
'Home-Thoughts, from Abroad' (1845)

6 That's the wise thrush; he sings each song twice over,
Lest you should think he never could recapture
The first fine careless rapture!
'Home-Thoughts, from Abroad' (1845)

7 Nobly, nobly Cape Saint Vincent to the North-west
died away;
Sunset ran, one glorious blood-red, reeking into Cadiz
Bay.
'Home-Thoughts, from the Sea' (1845)

8 'Here and here did England help me: how can I help
England?'—say,
Whoso turns as I, this evening, turn to God to praise
and pray,
While Jove's planet rises yonder, silent over Africa.
'Home-Thoughts, from the Sea' (1845)

9   'With this same key
Shakespeare unlocked his heart,' once more!
Did Shakespeare? If so, the less Shakespeare he!
'House' (1876). Cf. Wordsworth 747:17

10 I sprang to the stirrup, and Joris, and he;
I galloped, Dirck galloped, we galloped all three.
'How they brought the Good News from Ghent to Aix'
(1845) l. 1

11 A man can have but one life and one death,
One heaven, one hell.
'In a Balcony' (1855) l. 13

12   I count life just a stuff
To try the soul's strength on, educe the man.
'In a Balcony' (1855) l. 651

13 The moth's kiss, first!
Kiss me as if you made believe
You were not sure, this eve,
How my face, your flower, had pursed
Its petals up . . .
The bee's kiss, now!
Kiss me as if you entered gay
My heart at some noonday.
'In a Gondola' (1842) l. 49

14 'You're wounded!' 'Nay,' the soldier's pride
Touched to the quick, he said:
'I'm killed, Sire!' And his chief beside,
Smiling the boy fell dead.
'Incident of the French Camp' (1842) st. 5

15 Ignorance is not innocence but sin.
The Inn Album (1875) canto 5

16 The swallow has set her six young on the rail,
And looks sea-ward.
'James Lee's Wife' (1864) pt. 3, st. 1

17 Oh, good gigantic smile o' the brown old earth,
This autumn morning!
'James Lee's Wife' (1864) pt. 7, st. 1

18 Good, to forgive;
Best, to forget!
Living, we fret;
Dying, we live.
La Saisiaz (1878) prologue

19 I said—Then, dearest, since 'tis so,
Since now at length my fate I know,
Since nothing all my love avails,
Since all, my life seemed meant for, fails,
Since this was written and needs must be—
My whole heart rises up to bless
Your name in pride and thankfulness!
Take back the hope you gave,—I claim
Only a memory of the same.
'The Last Ride Together' (1855) st. 1

20 Who knows but the world may end tonight?
'The Last Ride Together' (1855) st. 2

21   My soul
Smoothed itself out, a long-cramped scroll
Freshening and fluttering in the wind.
'The Last Ride Together' (1855) st. 4

22 Had I said that, had I done this,
So might I gain, so might I miss.
Might she have loved me? just as well
She might have hated, who can tell!
'The Last Ride Together' (1855) st. 4

23 Look at the end of work, contrast
The petty done, the undone vast,
This present of theirs with the hopeful past!
'The Last Ride Together' (1855) st. 5

24 'Tis an awkward thing to play with souls,
And matter enough to save one's own.
'A Light Woman' (1855) st. 12

25 Just for a handful of silver he left us,
Just for a riband to stick in his coat.
'The Lost Leader' (1845) (of Wordsworth)

1 We that had loved him so, followed him, honoured
   him,
   Lived in his mild and magnificent eye,
   Learned his great language, caught his clear accents,
   Made him our pattern to live and to die!
   Shakespeare was of us, Milton was for us,
   Burns, Shelley, were with us—they watch from their
   graves!
   'The Lost Leader' (1845)

2 Never glad confident morning again!
   'The Lost Leader' (1845)

3 All's over, then: does truth sound bitter
   As one at first believes?
   'The Lost Mistress' (1845)

4 Oppression makes the wise man mad.
   Luria (1846) act 4, l. 16

5 Kentish Sir Byng stood for his King,
   Bidding the crop-headed Parliament swing:
   And, pressing a troop unable to stoop
   And see the rogues flourish and honest folk droop,
   Marched them along, fifty-score strong,
   Great-hearted gentlemen, singing this song.

   God for King Charles! Pym and such carles
   To the Devil that prompts 'em their treasonous parles!
   'Marching Along' (1842)

6 And find a poor devil has ended his cares
   At the foot of your rotten-runged rat-riddled stairs?
   Do I carry the moon in my pocket?
   'Master Hugues of Saxe-Gotha' (1855) st. 29

7 A tap at the pane, the quick sharp scratch
   And blue spurt of a lighted match,
   And a voice less loud, through its joys and fears,
   Than the two hearts beating each to each!
   'Meeting at Night' (1845)

8 Ah, did you once see Shelley plain,
   And did he stop and speak to you
   And did you speak to him again?
   How strange it seems, and new!
   'Memorabilia' (1855)

9   There's a real love of a lie,
   Liars find ready-made for lies they make
   As hand for glove, or tongue for sugar-plum.
   'Mr Sludge, "The Medium"' (1864) l. 694

10 There's a more hateful form of foolery—
   The social sage's, Solomon of saloons
   And philosophic diner-out.
   'Mr Sludge, "The Medium"' (1864) l. 773

11 That's my last Duchess painted on the wall,
   Looking as if she were alive.
   'My Last Duchess' (1842) l. 1

12   She had
   A heart—how shall I say?—too soon made glad,
   Too easily impressed; she liked whate'er
   She looked on, and her looks went everywhere.
   'My Last Duchess' (1842) l. 21

13 Never the time and the place
   And the loved one all together!
   'Never the Time and the Place' (1883)

14 A lion who dies of an ass's kick,
   The wronged great soul of an ancient Master.
   'Old Pictures in Florence' (1855) st. 6

15   What's come to perfection perishes.
   Things learned on earth, we shall practise in heaven:
   Works done least rapidly, Art most cherishes.
   'Old Pictures in Florence' (1855) st. 17

16 Dante, who loved well because he hated,
   Hated wickedness that hinders loving.
   'One Word More' (1855) st. 5

17 God be thanked, the meanest of his creatures
   Boasts two soul-sides, one to face the world with,
   One to show a woman when he loves her!
   'One Word More' (1855) st. 17

18   God is the perfect poet,
   Who in his person acts his own creations.
   Paracelsus (1835) pt. 2, l. 648

19 Measure your mind's height by the shade it casts!
   Paracelsus (1835) pt. 3, l. 821

20 I give the fight up: let there be an end,
   A privacy, an obscure nook for me.
   I want to be forgotten even by God.
   Paracelsus (1835) pt. 5, l. 363

21 Round the cape of a sudden came the sea,
   And the sun looked over the mountain's rim:
   And straight was a path of gold for him,
   And the need of a world of men for me.
   'Parting at Morning' (1849)

22 It was roses, roses, all the way.
   'The Patriot' (1855)

23 The air broke into a mist with bells.
   'The Patriot' (1855)

24 Sun-treader, life and light be thine for ever!
   Pauline (1833) l. 151 (of Shelley)

25 Ah, thought which saddens while it soothes!
   'Pictor Ignotus' (1845)

26 Rats!
   They fought the dogs and killed the cats,
   And bit the babies in the cradles,
   And ate the cheeses out of the vats,
   And licked the soup from the cooks' own ladles,
   Split open the kegs of salted sprats,
   Made nests inside men's Sunday hats,
   And even spoiled the women's chats
   By drowning their speaking
   With shrieking and squeaking
   In fifty different sharps and flats.
   'The Pied Piper of Hamelin' (1842) st. 2

27 So munch on, crunch on, take your nuncheon,
   Breakfast, supper, dinner, luncheon!
   'The Pied Piper of Hamelin' (1842) st. 7

28 The year's at the spring
   And day's at the morn;
   Morning's at seven;
   The hill-side's dew-pearled;
   The lark's on the wing;
   The snail's on the thorn:
   God's in his heaven—
   All's right with the world!
   Pippa Passes (1841) pt. 1, l. 221

29 You'll look at least on love's remains,
   A grave's one violet:
   Your look?—that pays a thousand pains.
   What's death? You'll love me yet!
   Pippa Passes (1841) pt. 3, l. 312

1 All service ranks the same with God—
With God, whose puppets, best and worst,
Are we: there is no last nor first.
Pippa Passes (1841) epilogue

2 Stand still, true poet that you are!
I know you; let me try and draw you.
Some night you'll fail us: when afar
You rise, remember one man saw you,
Knew you, and named a star!
'Popularity' (1855) st. 1

3   All her hair
In one long yellow string I wound
Three times her little throat around,
And strangled her. No pain felt she;
I am quite sure she felt no pain.
'Porphyria's Lover' (1842) l. 38

4 Fear death?—to feel the fog in my throat,
The mist in my face.
'Prospice' (1864)

5 I was ever a fighter, so—one fight more,
The best and the last!
I would hate that death bandaged my eyes, and
forbore,
And bade me creep past.
No! let me taste the whole of it, fare like my peers
The heroes of old,
Bear the brunt, in a minute pay glad life's arrears
Of pain, darkness and cold.
'Prospice' (1864)

6 Grow old along with me!
The best is yet to be,
The last of life, for which the first was made:
Our times are in His hand
Who saith, 'A whole I planned,
Youth shows but half; trust God: see all nor be
afraid!'
'Rabbi Ben Ezra' (1864) st. 1

7 Shall life succeed in that it seems to fail:
What I aspired to be,
And was not, comforts me:
A brute I might have been, but would not sink i' the
scale.
'Rabbi Ben Ezra' (1864) st. 7

8 For note, when evening shuts,
A certain moment cuts
The deed off, calls the glory from the grey.
'Rabbi Ben Ezra' (1864) st. 16

9 Fancies that broke through language and escaped.
'Rabbi Ben Ezra' (1864) st. 25

10 Fool! All that is, at all,
Lasts ever, past recall;
Earth changes, but thy soul and God stand sure.
'Rabbi Ben Ezra' (1864) st. 27

11 Time's wheel runs back or stops: potter and clay
endure.
'Rabbi Ben Ezra' (1864) st. 27

12 He fixed thee 'mid this dance
Of plastic circumstance.
'Rabbi Ben Ezra' (1864) st. 28

13 My times be in Thy hand!
Perfect the cup as planned!
Let age approve of youth, and death complete the
same!
'Rabbi Ben Ezra' (1864) st. 32

14   Youth means love,
Vows can't change nature, priests are only men.
The Ring and the Book (1868–9) bk. 1, l. 1056

15 O lyric Love, half-angel and half-bird
And all a wonder and a wild desire.
The Ring and the Book (1868–9) bk. 1, l. 1391

16   So, Pietro craved an heir,
(The story always old and always new).
The Ring and the Book (1868–9) bk. 2, l. 213

17   Go practise if you please
With men and women: leave a child alone
For Christ's particular love's sake!
The Ring and the Book (1868–9) bk. 3, l. 88

18 In the great right of an excessive wrong.
The Ring and the Book (1868–9) bk. 3, l. 1055

19   Through such souls alone
God stooping shows sufficient of His light
For us i' the dark to rise by. And I rise.
The Ring and the Book (1868–9) bk. 7, l. 1843

20 Faultless to a fault.
The Ring and the Book (1868–9) bk. 9, l. 1175

21 Why comes temptation but for man to meet
And master and make crouch beneath his foot,
And so be pedestalled in triumph?
The Ring and the Book (1868–9) bk. 10, l. 1184

22 White shall not neutralize the black, nor good
Compensate bad in man, absolve him so:
Life's business being just the terrible choice.
The Ring and the Book (1868–9) bk. 10, l. 1235

23   There's a new tribunal now
Higher than God's,—the educated man's!
The Ring and the Book (1868–9) bk. 10, l. 1975

24 Into that sad obscure sequestered state
Where God unmakes but to remake the soul
He else made first in vain; which must not be.
The Ring and the Book (1868–9) bk. 10, l. 2129

25   It is the glory and good of Art,
That Art remains the one way possible
Of speaking truth, to mouths like mine, at least.
The Ring and the Book (1868–9) bk. 12, l. 838

26 'Tis not what man Does which exalts him, but what
man Would do!
'Saul' (1855) st. 18

27 I want to know a butcher paints,
A baker rhymes for his pursuit,
Candlestick-maker much acquaints
His soul with song, or, haply mute,
Blows out his brains upon the flute!
'Shop' (1876) st. 21

28 There's a great text in Galatians,
Once you trip on it, entails
Twenty-nine distinct damnations,
One sure, if another fails.
'Soliloquy of the Spanish Cloister' (1842) st. 7

1 Sidney's self, the starry paladin.
  Sordello (1840) bk. 1, l. 69

2 Still more labyrinthine buds the rose.
  Sordello (1840) bk. 1, l. 476

3   A touch divine—
  And the scaled eyeball owns the mystic rod;
  Visibly through his garden walketh God.
  Sordello (1840) bk. 1, l. 502

4   Any nose
  May ravage with impunity a rose.
  Sordello (1840) bk. 6, l. 881

5 The glory dropped from their youth and love,
  And both perceived they had dreamed a dream.
  'The Statue and the Bust' (1855) l. 152

6 The soldier-saints, who row on row,
  Burn upward each to his point of bliss.
  'The Statue and the Bust' (1855) l. 222

7 And the sin I impute to each frustrate ghost
  Is—the unlit lamp and the ungirt loin,
  Though the end in sight was a vice, I say.
  'The Statue and the Bust' (1863 revision) l. 246

8 Oh Galuppi, Baldassaro, this is very sad to find!
  I can hardly misconceive you; it would prove me deaf
    and blind;
  But although I take your meaning, 'tis with such a
    heavy mind!
  'A Toccata of Galuppi's' (1855) st. 1

9 Hark, the dominant's persistence till it must be
    answered to!
  'A Toccata of Galuppi's' (1855) st. 8

10 What of soul was left, I wonder, when the kissing had
    to stop?
  'A Toccata of Galuppi's' (1855) st. 14

11 Dear dead women, with such hair, too—what's
    become of all the gold
  Used to hang and brush their bosoms? I feel chilly and
    grown old.
  'A Toccata of Galuppi's' (1855) st. 15

12 Grand rough old Martin Luther
  Bloomed fables—flowers on furze,
  The better the uncouther:
  Do roses stick like burrs?
  'The Twins' (1855)

13 I would that you were all to me,
  You that are just so much, no more.
  'Two in the Campagna' (1855) st. 8

14   I pluck the rose
  And love it more than tongue can speak—
  Then the good minute goes.
  'Two in the Campagna' (1855) st. 10

15   Only I discern—
  Infinite passion, and the pain
  Of finite hearts that yearn.
  'Two in the Campagna' (1855) st. 12

16 Let's contend no more, Love,
  Strive nor weep:
  All be as before, Love,
  —Only sleep!
  'A Woman's Last Word' (1855) st. 1

17 I knew you once: but in Paradise,
  If we meet, I will pass nor turn my face.
  'The Worst of It' (1864) st. 19

18 Ay, dead! and were yourself alive, good Fitz,
  How to return your thanks would pass my wits.
  Kicking you seems the common lot of curs—
  While more appropriate greeting lends you grace:
  Surely to spit there glorifies your face—
  Spitting from lips once sanctified by Hers.
  Rejoinder to Edward Fitzgerald, who had 'thanked God my
  wife was dead', in *Athenaeum* 13 July 1889. Cf. Fitzgerald
  284:18

Robert Bruce 1554–1631
Scottish minister and Laird of Kinnaird

19 Now, God be with you, my children: I have
  breakfasted with you and shall sup with my Lord Jesus
  Christ this night.
  In Robert Fleming *The Fulfilling of the Scripture* (3rd ed.,
  1693) p. 372

Beau Brummell (George Bryan Brummell) 1778–1840
English dandy

20 Who's your fat friend?
  Referring to the Prince of Wales, in Capt. Jesse *Life of George
  Brummell* (1844) vol. 1, p. 273

21 [Brummell] used to say that, whether it was summer
  or winter, he always liked to have the morning
  well-aired before he got up.
  Charles Macfarlane *Reminiscences of a Literary Life* (1917)
  ch. 27

22 No perfumes, but very fine linen, plenty of it, and
  country washing.
  In *Memoirs of Harriette Wilson* (1825) vol. 1, p. 42

William Jennings Bryan 1860–1925
American Democratic politician

23 The humblest citizen of all the land, when clad in the
  armour of a righteous cause, is stronger than all the
  hosts of error.
  Speech at the Democratic National Convention, Chicago,
  1896, in *The First Battle. A Story of the Campaign of 1896*
  (1896) vol. 1, ch. 10

24 You shall not press down upon the brow of labour this
  crown of thorns, you shall not crucify mankind upon
  a cross of gold.
  Speech at the Democratic National Convention, Chicago,
  1896, in *The First Battle. A Story of the Campaign of 1896*
  (1896) vol. 1, ch. 10

Martin Buber 1878–1965
Austrian-born religious philosopher and Zionist

25 *Der Mensch wird am Du zum Ich.*
  Through the Thou a person becomes I.
  Ich und Du (1923) in *Werke* (1962) vol. 1, p. 97

John Buchan (1st Baron Tweedsmuir)
1875–1940

Scottish novelist; Governor-General of Canada, 1935–40

1 'Back to Glasgow to do some work for the cause,'
I said lightly. 'Just so,' he said, with a grin. 'It's a great
life if you don't weaken.'
  Mr Standfast (1919) ch. 5

2 An atheist is a man who has no invisible means of
support.
  In H. E. Fosdick *On Being a Real Person* (1943) ch. 10

Robert Buchanan 1841–1901

Scottish man of letters

3   She just wore
Enough for modesty—no more.
  'White Rose and Red' (1873) pt. 1, sect. 5, l. 60

4 The sweet post-prandial cigar.
  'De Berny' (1874)

Frank Buchman 1878–1961

*American evangelist; founder of the Moral Re-Armament
movement*

5 I thank heaven for a man like Adolf Hitler, who built
a front line of defence against the anti-Christ of
Communism.
  New York World-Telegram 26 August 1936

6 Suppose everybody cared enough, everybody shared
enough, wouldn't everybody have enough? There is
enough in the world for everyone's need, but not
enough for everyone's greed.
  Remaking the World (1947) p. 56

Gene Buck (Edward Eugene Buck)
1885–1957 *and Herman Ruby* 1891–1959

7 That Shakespearian rag,—
Most intelligent, very elegant.
  'That Shakespearian Rag' (1912 song). Cf. Eliot 273:5

George Villiers, 2nd Duke of Buckingham
1628–87

English courtier and writer

8 The world is made up for the most part of fools and
knaves, both irreconcilable foes to truth.
  The Dramatic Works (1715) vol. 2 'To Mr Clifford On his
  Humane Reason'

9 What a devil is the plot good for, but to bring in fine
things?
  The Rehearsal (1672) act 3, sc. 1

10 Ay, now the plot thickens very much upon us.
  The Rehearsal (1672) act 3, sc. 2

John Sheffield, 1st Duke of Buckingham
and Normanby 1648–1721

English poet and politician

11 Learn to write well, or not to write at all.
  'An Essay upon Satire' (1689) *ad fin.*

H. J. Buckoll 1803–71

English clergyman; master at Rugby School from 1826

12 Lord, dismiss us with Thy blessing,
Thanks for mercies past receive.
Pardon all, their faults confessing;
Time that's lost may all retrieve.
  Psalms and Hymns for the Use of Rugby School Chapel (1850)
  'Lord, Dismiss us with Thy Blessing'

J. B. Buckstone 1802–79

English comedian and playwright

13 On such an occasion as this,
All time and nonsense scorning,
Nothing shall come amiss,
And we won't go home till morning.
  Billy Taylor (performed 1829) act 1, sc. 2

Eustace Budgell 1686–1737

English writer

14 What Cato did, and Addison approved,
Cannot be wrong.
  Lines found on his desk after he, too, had taken his own
  life, in Colley Cibber *Lives of the Poets* (1753) vol. 5 'Life of
  Eustace Budgell'

Comte de Buffon (George-Louis Leclerc)
1707–88

French naturalist

15 *Ces choses sont hors de l'homme, le style est l'homme
même.*
These things [subject matter] are external to the man;
style is the man.
  Discours sur le style (address given to the Académie
  Française, 25 August 1753)

16 *Le génie n'est qu'une plus grande aptitude à la patience.*
Genius is only a greater aptitude for patience.
  In Hérault de Séchelles *Voyage à Montbar* (1803) p. 15

Arthur Buller 1874–1944

British botanist and mycologist

17 There was a young lady named Bright,
Whose speed was far faster than light;
She set out one day
In a relative way
And returned on the previous night.
  'Relativity' in *Punch* 19 December 1923

Ivor Bulmer-Thomas 1905–

British Conservative politician

1 If he ever went to school without any boots it was because he was too big for them.
  Referring to Harold Wilson in a speech at the Conservative Party Conference, in *Manchester Guardian* 13 October 1949

Prince Bernhard von Bülow 1849–1929

Chancellor of Germany, 1900–9

2 *Mit einem Worte: wir wollen niemand in den Schatten stellen, aber wir verlangen auch unseren Platz an der Sonne.*

In a word, we desire to throw no one into the shade [in East Asia], but we also demand our own place in the sun.
  Reichstag, 6 December 1897, in *Graf Bülows Reden* (1903) p. 8. Cf. Wilhelm II 736:18

Edward George Bulwer-Lytton (1st Baron Lytton) 1803–73

British novelist and politician

3 Here Stanley meets,—how Stanley scorns, the glance!
The brilliant chief, irregularly great,
Frank, haughty, rash,—the Rupert of Debate!
  On Edward Stanley, 14th Earl of Derby, in *The New Timon* (1846) pt. 1, sect. 3, l. 202. Cf. Disraeli 246:17

4 Out-babying Wordsworth and out-glittering Keats.
  On Tennyson, in *The New Timon* (1846) pt. 2, sect. 1, l. 62

5 Beneath the rule of men entirely great
The pen is mightier than the sword.
  Richelieu (1839) act 2, sc. 2, l. 307. Cf. Burton 164:22

6 There is no man so friendless but what he can find a friend sincere enough to tell him disagreeable truths.
  What will he do with it? (1857) vol. 1, bk. 3, ch. 15

Edward Robert Bulwer, Earl of Lytton

See OWEN MEREDITH

Alfred 'Poet' Bunn c.1796–1860

English theatrical manager and librettist

7 I dreamed that I dwelt in marble halls
With vassals and serfs at my side.
  The Bohemian Girl (1843) act 2 'The Gipsy Girl's Dream'

Basil Bunting 1900–85

English poet

8 Praise the green earth. Chance has appointed her home, workshop, larder, middenpit.
Her lousy skin scabbed here and there by cities provides us with name and nation.
  'Attis: or, Something Missing' (1931) pt. 1

9 Brag, sweet tenor bull,
descant on Rawthey's madrigal,
each pebble its part
for the fells' late spring.
Dance tiptoe, bull,
black against may.
Ridiculous and lovely
chase hurdling shadows
morning into noon.
  'Briggflatts' (1965) pt. 1

10   Our doom
is, to be sifted by the wind,
heaped up, smoothed down like silly sands.
We are less permanent than thought.
  'Villon' (1925) pt. 1

Luis Buñuel 1900–83

Spanish film director

11 *Le charme discret de la bourgeoisie.*
The discreet charm of the bourgeoisie.
  Title of film (1972)

12 *Grâce à Dieu, je suis toujours athée.*
Thanks to God, I am still an atheist.
  In *Le Monde* 16 December 1959

John Bunyan 1628–88

English writer and Nonconformist preacher

Page references are to the World's Classics edition

13 As I walked through the wilderness of this world.
  The Pilgrim's Progress (1678) pt. 1, opening words

14 The name of the slough was Despond.
  The Pilgrim's Progress (1678) pt. 1, p. 12

15 CHRISTIAN: Gentlemen, Whence came you, and whither do you go?
  FORMALIST AND HYPOCRISY: We were born in the land of Vainglory, and we are going for praise to Mount Sion.
  The Pilgrim's Progress (1678) pt. 1, p. 33

16 It is an hard matter for a man to go down into the valley of Humiliation . . . and to catch no slip by the way.
  The Pilgrim's Progress (1678) pt. 1, p. 46

17 A foul Fiend coming over the field to meet him; his name is Apollyon.
  The Pilgrim's Progress (1678) pt. 1, p. 46

18 It beareth the name of Vanity-Fair, because the town where 'tis kept, is lighter than vanity.
  The Pilgrim's Progress (1678) pt. 1, p. 72. Cf. Book of Common Prayer 128:20

19 Hanging is too good for him, said Mr Cruelty.
  The Pilgrim's Progress (1678) pt. 1, p. 79

20 Yet my great-grandfather was but a water-man, looking one way, and rowing another: and I got most of my estate by the same occupation.
  The Pilgrim's Progress (1678) pt. 1, p. 81. Cf. Burton 164:17

1 They are for religion when in rags and contempt; but I am for him when he walks in his golden slippers, in the sunshine and with applause.
The Pilgrim's Progress (1678) pt. 1, p. 83

2 Now Giant Despair had a wife, and her name was Diffidence.
The Pilgrim's Progress (1678) pt. 1, p. 93

3 A grievous crab-tree cudgel.
The Pilgrim's Progress (1678) pt. 1, p. 93

4 They came to the Delectable Mountains.
The Pilgrim's Progress (1678) pt. 1, p. 97

5 Sleep is sweet to the labouring man.
The Pilgrim's Progress (1678) pt. 1, p. 111. Cf. Ecclesiastes 80:10

6 Then I saw that there was a way to Hell, even from the gates of heaven.
The Pilgrim's Progress (1678) pt. 1, p. 133

7 So I awoke, and behold it was a dream.
The Pilgrim's Progress (1678) pt. 1, p. 133

8 A man that could look no way but downwards, with a muckrake in his hand.
The Pilgrim's Progress (1684) pt. 2, p. 164. Cf. Roosevelt 546:11

9 One leak will sink a ship, and one sin will destroy a sinner.
The Pilgrim's Progress (1684) pt. 2, p. 168

10 He that is down needs fear no fall,
He that is low no pride.
He that is humble ever shall
Have God to be his guide.
The Pilgrim's Progress (1684) pt. 2, p. 197 'Shepherd Boy's Song'

11 A very zealous man ... difficulties, lions, or Vanity-Fair, he feared not at all: 'twas only sin, death, and Hell that was to him a terror.
The Pilgrim's Progress (1684) pt. 2, p. 211 (of Mr Fearing)

12 A man there was, tho' some did count him mad, The more he cast away, the more he had.
The Pilgrim's Progress (1684) pt. 2, p. 219

13 Mercy ... laboured much for the poor ... an ornament to her profession.
The Pilgrim's Progress (1684) pt. 2, p. 231

14 Who would true valour see,
Let him come hither;
One here will constant be,
Come wind, come weather.
There's no discouragement
Shall make him once relent
His first avowed intent
To be a pilgrim.

Who so beset him round
With dismal stories,
Do but themselves confound—
His strength the more is.
The Pilgrim's Progress (1684) pt. 2, p. 247

15 The last words of Mr Despondency were, Farewell night, welcome day. His daughter went through the river singing, but none could understand what she said.
The Pilgrim's Progress (1684) pt. 2, p. 259

16 I am going to my Fathers, and tho' with great difficulty I am got hither, yet now I do not repent me of all the trouble I have been at to arrive where I am. My sword, I give to him that shall succeed me in my pilgrimage, and my courage and skill to him that can get it. My marks and scars I carry with me, to be a witness for me, that I have fought his battles, who will now be my rewarder ... So he passed over, and the trumpets sounded for him on the other side.
The Pilgrim's Progress (1684) pt. 2, p. 259 (Mr Valiant-for-Truth)

17 I have formerly lived by hearsay and faith, but now I go where I shall live by sight, and shall be with Him in whose company I delight myself.
The Pilgrim's Progress (1684) pt. 2, p. 261 (Mr Standfast)

Samuel Dickinson Burchard 1812–91
American Presbyterian minister

18 We are Republicans and don't propose to leave our party and identify ourselves with the party whose antecedents are rum, Romanism, and rebellion.
Speech at the Fifth Avenue Hotel, New York, 29 October 1884, in *New York World* 30 October 1884

Anthony Burgess 1917–
English novelist and critic

19 A clockwork orange.
Title of novel (1962)

20 It was the afternoon of my eighty-first birthday, and I was in bed with my catamite when Ali announced that the archbishop had come to see me.
Earthly Powers (1980) p. 7

21 He said it was artificial respiration, but now I find I am to have his child.
Inside Mr Enderby (1963) pt. 1, ch. 4

Gelett Burgess 1866–1951
American humorist and illustrator

22 I never saw a Purple Cow,
I never hope to see one;
But I can tell you, anyhow,
I'd rather see than be one!
The Burgess Nonsense Book (1914) 'The Purple Cow'

23 Ah, yes! I wrote the 'Purple Cow'—
I'm sorry, now, I wrote it!
But I can tell you anyhow,
I'll kill you if you quote it!
The Burgess Nonsense Book (1914) 'Confessional'

John William Burgon 1813–88
English clergyman; Dean of Chichester from 1876

24 Match me such marvel, save in Eastern clime,—
A rose-red city—'half as old as Time'!
Petra (1845) l. 131. Cf. Rogers 544:13

Sir John Burgoyne 1722–92

English general and playwright

1 You have only, when before your glass, to keep pronouncing to yourself nimini-pimini—the lips cannot fail of taking their plie.
The Heiress (1786) act 3, sc. 2

Edmund Burke 1729–97

Irish-born Whig politician and man of letters

2 The conduct of a losing party never appears right: at least it never can possess the only infallible criterion of wisdom to vulgar judgements—success.
Letter to a Member of the National Assembly (1791) p. 7

3 Those who have been once intoxicated with power, and have derived any kind of emolument from it, even though but for one year, can never willingly abandon it.
Letter to a Member of the National Assembly (1791) p. 12

4 Tyrants seldom want pretexts.
Letter to a Member of the National Assembly (1791) p. 25

5 You can never plan the future by the past.
Letter to a Member of the National Assembly (1791) p. 73

6 To innovate is not to reform.
A Letter to a Noble Lord (1796) p. 20

7 The king, and his faithful subjects, the lords and commons of this realm,—the triple cord, which no man can break.
A Letter to a Noble Lord (1796) p. 54. Cf. Ecclesiastes 80:8

8 I know many have been taught to think that moderation, in a case like this, is a sort of treason.
Letter to the Sheriffs of Bristol (1777) p. 30

9 Between craft and credulity, the voice of reason is stifled.
Letter to the Sheriffs of Bristol (1777) p. 34

10 Liberty too must be limited in order to be possessed.
Letter to the Sheriffs of Bristol (1777) p. 55

11 Nothing in progression can rest on its original plan. We may as well think of rocking a grown man in the cradle of an infant.
Letter to the Sheriffs of Bristol (1777) p. 59

12 Among a people generally corrupt, liberty cannot long exist.
Letter to the Sheriffs of Bristol (1777) p. 71

13 There is, however, a limit at which forbearance ceases to be a virtue.
Observations on a late Publication on the Present State of the Nation (2nd ed., 1769) p. 3

14 It is a general popular error to imagine the loudest complainers for the public to be the most anxious for its welfare.
Observations on a late Publication on the Present State of the Nation (2nd ed., 1769) p. 63

15 It is the nature of all greatness not to be exact; and great trade will always be attended with considerable abuses.
On American Taxation (1775) p. 26

16 Falsehood has a perennial spring.
On American Taxation (1775) p. 30

17 To tax and to please, no more than to love and to be wise, is not given to men.
On American Taxation (1775) p. 49

18 I have in general no very exalted opinion of the virtue of paper government.
On Conciliation with America (1775) p. 4

19 The concessions of the weak are the concessions of fear.
On Conciliation with America (1775) p. 7

20 When we speak of the commerce with our colonies, fiction lags after truth; invention is unfruitful, and imagination cold and barren.
On Conciliation with America (1775) p. 12

21 The use of force alone is but *temporary*. It may subdue for a moment; but it does not remove the necessity of subduing again; and a nation is not governed, which is perpetually to be conquered.
On Conciliation with America (1775) p. 14

22 Nothing less will content me, than *whole America*.
On Conciliation with America (1775) p. 15

23 Abstract liberty, like other mere abstractions, is not to be found.
On Conciliation with America (1775) p. 16

24 All Protestantism, even the most cold and passive, is a sort of dissent. But the religion most prevalent in our northern colonies is a refinement on the principle of resistance; it is the dissidence of dissent, and the Protestantism of the Protestant religion.
On Conciliation with America (1775) p. 18

25 I do not know the method of drawing up an indictment against an whole people.
On Conciliation with America (1775) p. 28

26 It is not, what a lawyer tells me I *may* do; but what humanity, reason, and justice, tells me I ought to do.
On Conciliation with America (1775) p. 31

27 Freedom and not servitude is the cure of anarchy; as religion, and not atheism, is the true remedy for superstition.
On Conciliation with America (1775) p. 40

28 Instead of a standing revenue, you will have therefore a perpetual quarrel.
On Conciliation with America (1775) p. 57

29 Parties must ever exist in a free country.
On Conciliation with America (1775) p. 59

30 Slavery they can have anywhere. It is a weed that grows in every soil.
On Conciliation with America (1775) p. 61

31 Deny them this participation of freedom, and you break that sole bond, which originally made, and must still preserve the unity of the empire.
On Conciliation with America (1775) p. 61

32 It is the love of the people; it is their attachment to their government, from the sense of the deep stake they have in such a glorious institution, which gives you your army and your navy, and infuses into both that liberal obedience, without which your army would be a base rabble, and your navy nothing but rotten timber.
On Conciliation with America (1775) p. 61

1 Magnanimity in politics is not seldom the truest
wisdom; and a great empire and little minds go ill
together.
On Conciliation with America (1775) p. 62

2 By adverting to the dignity of this high calling, our
ancestors have turned a savage wilderness into a
glorious empire: and have made the most extensive,
and the only honourable conquests; not by destroying,
but by promoting the wealth, the number, the
happiness of the human race.
On Conciliation with America (1775) p. 62

3 No passion so effectually robs the mind of all its
powers of acting and reasoning as fear.
On the Sublime and Beautiful (1757) pt. 2, sect. 2

4 Custom reconciles us to everything.
On the Sublime and Beautiful (1757) pt. 4, sect. 18

5 I flatter myself that I love a manly, moral, regulated
liberty as well as any gentleman.
Reflections on the Revolution in France (1790) p. 7

6 Whenever our neighbour's house is on fire, it cannot
be amiss for the engines to play a little on our own.
Reflections on the Revolution in France (1790) p. 10

7 A state without the means of some change is without
the means of its conservation.
Reflections on the Revolution in France (1790) p. 29

8 Make the Revolution a parent of settlement, and not a
nursery of future revolutions.
Reflections on the Revolution in France (1790) p. 38

9 People will not look forward to posterity, who never
look backward to their ancestors.
Reflections on the Revolution in France (1790) p. 47

10 Those who attempt to level never equalize.
Reflections on the Revolution in France (1790) p. 72

11 Whatever each man can separately do, without
trespassing upon others, he has a right to do for
himself; and he has a right to a fair portion of all
which society, with all its combinations of skill and
force, can do in his favour.
Reflections on the Revolution in France (1790) p. 87

12 Government is a contrivance of human wisdom to
provide for human *wants*. Men have a right that these
wants should be provided for by this wisdom.
Reflections on the Revolution in France (1790) p. 88

13 The age of chivalry is gone. — That of sophisters,
economists, and calculators, has succeeded; and the
glory of Europe is extinguished for ever.
Reflections on the Revolution in France (1790) p. 113

14 The unbought grace of life, the cheap defence of
nations, the nurse of manly sentiment and heroic
enterprise is gone! It is gone, that sensibility of
principle, that chastity of honour, which felt a stain
like a wound, which inspired courage whilst it
mitigated ferocity, which ennobled whatever it
touched, and under which vice itself lost half its evil,
by losing all its grossness.
Reflections on the Revolution in France (1790) p. 113

15 This barbarous philosophy, which is the offspring of
cold hearts and muddy understandings.
Reflections on the Revolution in France (1790) p. 115

16 In the groves of *their* academy, at the end of every
vista, you see nothing but the gallows.
Reflections on the Revolution in France (1790) p. 115.
Cf. Horace 348:19

17 Kings will be tyrants from policy when subjects are
rebels from principle.
Reflections on the Revolution in France (1790) p. 116

18 Learning will be cast into the mire, and trodden down
under the hoofs of a swinish multitude.
Reflections on the Revolution in France (1790) p. 117

19 Man is by his constitution a religious animal; atheism
is against not only our reason, but our instincts.
Reflections on the Revolution in France (1790) p. 135.
Cf. Aristotle 25:15

20 A perfect democracy is therefore the most shameless
thing in the world.
Reflections on the Revolution in France (1790) p. 139

21 Society is indeed a contract ... it becomes a
partnership not only between those who are living,
but between those who are living, those who are dead,
and those who are to be born.
Reflections on the Revolution in France (1790) p. 113

22 Nobility is a graceful ornament to the civil order. It is
the Corinthian capital of polished society.
Reflections on the Revolution in France (1790) p. 205

23 Superstition is the religion of feeble minds.
Reflections on the Revolution in France (1790) p. 234

24 He that wrestles with us strengthens our nerves, and
sharpens our skill. Our antagonist is our helper.
Reflections on the Revolution in France (1790) p. 246

25 Our patience will achieve more than our force.
Reflections on the Revolution in France (1790) p. 249

26 By hating vices too much, they come to love men too
little.
Reflections on the Revolution in France (1790) p. 251

27 We begin our public affections in our families. No cold
relation is a zealous citizen.
Reflections on the Revolution in France (1790) p. 286

28 Good order is the foundation of all good things.
Reflections on the Revolution in France (1790) p. 351

29 Every politician ought to sacrifice to the graces; and to
join compliance with reason.
Reflections on the Revolution in France (1790) p. 352

30 The greater the power, the more dangerous the abuse.
Speech on the Middlesex Election, 7 February 1771, in
The Speeches (1854) p. 357

31 Your representative owes you, not his industry only,
but his judgement; and he betrays, instead of serving
you, if he sacrifices it to your opinion.
Speech, 3 November 1774, in *Speeches at his Arrival at
Bristol* (1774) p. 14

32 Individuals pass like shadows; but the commonwealth
is fixed and stable.
Speech, Hansard 11 February 1780, col. 48

33 The people are the masters.
Speech, Hansard 11 February 1780, col. 67

34 Bad laws are the worst sort of tyranny.
Speech at Bristol, previous to the Late Election (1780)

1 Every other conqueror of every other description has left some monument, either of state or beneficence, behind him. Were we to be driven out of India this day, nothing would remain to tell that it had been possessed, during the inglorious period of our dominion, by anything better than the orang-outang or the tiger.

> Speech on Fox's East India Bill, *Hansard* 1 December 1783, col. 1333

2 Your governor [Warren Hastings] stimulates a rapacious and licentious soldiery to the personal search of women, lest these unhappy creatures should avail themselves of the protection of their sex to secure any supply for their necessities.

> Speech on Fox's East India Bill, *Hansard* 1 December 1783, col. 1350

3 The people never give up their liberties but under some delusion.

> Speech at County Meeting of Buckinghamshire, 1784, attributed in E. Latham *Famous Sayings* (1904), with 'except' substituted for 'but'

4 Religious persecution may shield itself under the guise of a mistaken and over-zealous piety.

> Speech, 18 February 1788, in E. A. Bond (ed.) *Speeches . . . in the Trial of Warren Hastings* (1859) vol. 1, p. 104

5 An event has happened, upon which it is difficult to speak, and impossible to be silent.

> Speech, 5 May 1789, in E. A. Bond (ed.) *Speeches . . . in the Trial of Warren Hastings* (1859) vol. 2, p. 109

6 At last dying in the last dyke of prevarication.

> Speech, 7 May 1789, in E. A. Bond (ed.) *Speeches . . . in the Trial of Warren Hastings* (1859) vol. 2, p. 179

7 Old religious factions are volcanoes burnt out.

> Speech on the Petition of the Unitarians, 11 May 1792, in *The Works* vol. 5 (1812). Cf. Disraeli 247:20

8 Dangers by being despised grow great.

> Speech on the Petition of the Unitarians, 11 May 1792, in *The Works* vol. 5 (1812)

9 There is but one law for all, namely, that law which governs all law—the law of our Creator, the law of humanity, justice, equity, the law of nature and of nations.

> Speech, 28 May 1794, in E. A. Bond (ed.) *Speeches . . . in the Trial of Warren Hastings* (1859) vol. 4, p. 377

10 And having looked to government for bread, on the very first scarcity they will turn and bite the hand that fed them.

> *Thoughts and Details on Scarcity* (1800) p. 31

11 To complain of the age we live in, to murmur at the present possessors of power, to lament the past, to conceive extravagant hopes of the future, are the common dispositions of the greatest part of mankind.

> *Thoughts on the Cause of the Present Discontents* (1770) p. 4

12 I am not one of those who think that the people are never in the wrong. They have been so, frequently and outrageously, both in other countries and in this. But I do say, that in all disputes between them and their rulers, the presumption is at least upon a par in favour of the people.

> *Thoughts on the Cause of the Present Discontents* (1770) p. 7

13 The power of the crown, almost dead and rotten as Prerogative, has grown up anew, with much more strength, and far less odium, under the name of Influence.

> *Thoughts on the Cause of the Present Discontents* (1770) p. 10

14 We must soften into a credulity below the milkiness of infancy to think all men virtuous. We must be tainted with a malignity truly diabolical, to believe all the world to be equally wicked and corrupt.

> *Thoughts on the Cause of the Present Discontents* (1770) p. 30

15 When bad men combine, the good must associate; else they will fall, one by one, an unpitied sacrifice in a contemptible struggle.

> *Thoughts on the Cause of the Present Discontents* (1770) p. 71

16 Of this stamp is the cant of *Not men, but measures*; a sort of charm by which many people get loose from every honourable engagement.

> *Thoughts on the Cause of the Present Discontents* (1770) p. 75

17 It is therefore our business carefully to cultivate in our minds, to rear to the most perfect vigour and maturity, every sort of generous and honest feeling that belongs to our nature. To bring the dispositions that are lovely in private life into the service and conduct of the commonwealth; so to be patriots, as not to forget we are gentlemen.

> *Thoughts on the Cause of the Present Discontents* (1770) p. 77

18 Laws, like houses, lean on one another.

> *A Tract on the Popery Laws* (planned *c*.1765) ch. 3, pt. 1 in *The Works* vol. 5 (1812)

19 In all forms of Government the people is the true legislator.

> *A Tract on the Popery Laws* ch. 3, pt. 1 in *The Works* vol. 5 (1812)

20 All men that are ruined are ruined on the side of their natural propensities.

> *Two Letters on the Proposals for Peace with the Regicide Directory* (9th ed., 1796) p. 69

21 Example is the school of mankind, and they will learn at no other.

> *Two Letters on the Proposals for Peace with the Regicide Directory* (9th ed., 1796) p. 125

22 Never, no never, did Nature say one thing and Wisdom say another.

> *Third Letter . . . on the Proposals for Peace with the Regicide Directory* (1797) p. 30

23 Well is it known that ambition can creep as well as soar.

> *Third Letter . . . on the Proposals for Peace with the Regicide Directory* (1797) p. 38

24 People crushed by law have no hopes but from power. If laws are their enemies, they will be enemies to laws; and those, who have much to hope and nothing to lose, will always be dangerous, more or less.

> Letter to Charles James Fox, 8 October 1777, in *The Correspondence of Edmund Burke* vol. 3 (1961)

25 The silent touches of time.

> Letter to William Smith, 29 January 1795, in *The Correspondence of Edmund Burke* vol. 8 (1969)

26 Somebody has said, that a king may make a nobleman but he cannot make a gentleman.

> Letter to William Smith, 29 January 1795, in *The Correspondence of Edmund Burke* vol. 8 (1969)

1 His virtues were his arts.
> Inscription on the pedestal of the statue of the Marquis of
> Rockingham in Wentworth Park

2 Not merely a chip of the old 'block', but the old block itself.
> On the younger Pitt's maiden Speech, February 1781, in
> N. W. Wraxall *Historical Memoirs of My Own Time*
> (1904 ed.) pt. 2, p. 377

3 The cold neutrality of an impartial judge.
> J. P. Brissot *To his Constituents* (1794) 'Translator's Preface'
> (written by Burke)

4 It is necessary only for the good man to do nothing for evil to triumph.
> Attributed (in a number of forms) to Burke, but not found
> in his writings. Cf. Burke 159:15

Johnny Burke 1908–64
American songwriter

5 Every time it rains, it rains
Pennies from heaven.
Don't you know each cloud contains
Pennies from heaven?
> 'Pennies from Heaven' (1936 song)

6 Like Webster's Dictionary, we're Morocco bound.
> *The Road to Morocco* (1942 film) title song

Lord Burleigh
See WILLIAM CECIL

Fanny Burney (Mme d'Arblay) 1752–1840
English novelist and diarist

7 A little alarm now and then keeps life from stagnation.
> *Camilla* (1796) bk. 3, ch. 11

8 There is nothing upon the face of the earth so insipid as a medium. Give me love or hate! a friend that will go to jail for me, or an enemy that will run me through the body!
> *Camilla* (1796) bk. 3, ch. 12

9 It's a delightful thing to think of perfection; but it's vastly more amusing to talk of errors and absurdities.
> *Camilla* (1796) bk. 3, ch. 12

10 Vice is detestable; I banish all its appearances from my coteries; and I would banish its reality, too, were I sure I should then have any thing but empty chairs in my drawing-room.
> *Camilla* (1796) bk. 5, ch. 6

11 The cure of a romantic first flame is a better surety to subsequent discretion, than all the exhortations of all the fathers, and mothers, and guardians, and maiden aunts in the universe.
> *Camilla* (1796) bk. 5, ch. 6

12 O, we all acknowledge our faults, now; 'tis the mode of the day: but the acknowledgement passes for current payment; and therefore we never amend them.
> *Camilla* (1796) bk. 6, ch. 2

13 No man is in love when he marries. He may have loved before; I have even heard he has sometimes loved after: but at the time never. There is something in the formalities of the matrimonial preparations that drive away all the little cupidons.
> *Camilla* (1796) bk. 6, ch. 10

14 Travelling is the ruin of all happiness! There's no looking at a building here after seeing Italy.
> *Cecilia* (1782) bk. 4, ch. 2

15 'True, very true, ma'am,' said he, yawning, 'one really lives no where; one does but vegetate, and wish it all at an end.'
> *Cecilia* (1782) bk. 7, ch. 5

16 'The whole of this unfortunate business,' said Dr Lyster, 'has been the result of PRIDE AND PREJUDICE.'
> *Cecilia* (1782) bk. 10, ch. 10

17 'Do you come to the play without knowing what it is?' 'O yes, Sir, yes, very frequently; I have no time to read play-bills; one merely comes to meet one's friends, and show that one's alive.'
> *Evelina* (1778) Letter 20

18 The freedom with which Dr Johnson condemns whatever he disapproves is astonishing.
> *Diary and Letters of Madame D'Arblay* (1842) pt. 2, p. 50
> (23 August 1778)

19 The delusive seduction of martial music.
> In Joyce Hemlow et al. (eds.) *Journals and Letters of Fanny
> Burney* vol. 5 (1975) 'Paris Journal'

20 Such a set of tittle tattle, prittle prattle visitants! Oh dear! I am so sick of the ceremony and fuss of these fall lall people! So much dressing—chit chat—complimentary nonsense—In short, a country town is my detestation.
> *Journal* 17 July 1768 in *Early Journals and Letters of Fanny
> Burney* (ed. L. E. Troide, 1988) vol. 1

21 O! how short a time does it take to put an end to a woman's liberty!
> *Journal* 20 July 1768 in *Early Journals and Letters of Fanny
> Burney* (ed. L. E. Troide, 1988) vol. 1 (referring to a
> wedding)

John Burns 1858–1943
British Liberal politician

22 The Thames is liquid history.
> To an American who had compared the Thames
> disparagingly with the Mississippi, in *Daily Mail* 25 January
> 1943

Robert Burns 1759–96
Scottish poet

23 O thou! whatever title suit thee,
Auld Hornie, Satan, Nick, or Clootie.
> 'Address to the Deil' (1786)

1 Ye high, exalted, virtuous dames,
  Tied up in godly laces,
  Before ye gie poor Frailty names,
  Suppose a change o' cases:
  A dear-lov'd lad, convenience snug,
  A treach'rous inclination—
  But, let me whisper in your lug,
  Ye're aiblins nae temptation.

  Then gently scan your brother man,
  Still gentler sister woman;
  Tho' they may gang a kennin wrang,
  To step aside is human.
     'Address to the Unco Guid' (1787); *aiblins* perhaps

2 Ae fond kiss, and then we sever;
  Ae farewell, and then for ever!
     'Ae fond Kiss' (1792)

3 Flow gently, sweet Afton, among thy green braes,
  Flow gently, I'll sing thee a song in thy praise.
  My Mary's asleep by thy murmuring stream,
  Flow gently, sweet Afton, disturb not her dream.
     'Afton Water' (1792)

4 Should auld acquaintance be forgot
  And never brought to mind?
     'Auld Lang Syne' (1796)

5 We'll tak a cup o' kindness yet,
  For auld lang syne.
     'Auld Lang Syne' (1796)

6 And there's a hand, my trusty fiere!
  And gie's a hand o'thine!
     'Auld Lang Syne' (1796)

7 Freedom and Whisky gang thegither!
     'The Author's Earnest Cry and Prayer' (1786) l. 185

8 Ay waukin, Oh,
  Waukin still and weary:
  Sleep I can get nane,
  For thinking on my dearie.
     'Ay Waukin O' (1790)

9 Ye banks and braes o' bonny Doon,
  How can ye bloom sae fresh and fair;
  How can ye chant, ye little birds,
  And I sae weary fu' o' care!
     'The Banks o' Doon' (1792)

10 Thou minds me o' departed joys,
   Departed, never to return.
      'The Banks o' Doon' (1792)

11 And my fause luver stole my rose,
   But ah! he left the thorn wi' me.
      'The Banks o' Doon' (1792)

12 O saw ye bonnie Lesley,
   As she gaed o'er the border?
   She's gane, like Alexander,
   To spread her conquests farther.

   To see her is to love her,
   And love but her for ever;
   For Nature made her what she is
   And never made anither!
      'Bonnie Lesley' (1798)

13 Gin a body meet a body
   Comin thro' the rye,
   Gin a body kiss a body
   Need a body cry?
      'Comin thro' the rye' (1796)

14 Contented wi' little and cantie wi' mair,
   Whene'er I forgather wi' Sorrow and Care,
   I gie them a skelp, as they're creeping alang,
   Wi' a cog o' gude swats and an auld Scotish sang.
      'Contented wi' little' (1796)

15 Th' expectant wee-things, toddlin', stacher through
   To meet their Dad, wi' flichterin' noise an' glee.
      'The Cotter's Saturday Night' (1786) st. 3

16 They never sought in vain that sought the Lord
   aright.
      'The Cotter's Saturday Night' (1786) st. 6

17 The healsome porritch, chief of Scotia's food.
      'The Cotter's Saturday Night' (1786) st. 11

18 The sire turns o'er, wi' patriarchal grace,
   The big ha'-Bible, ance his father's pride.
      'The Cotter's Saturday Night' (1786) st. 12

19 From scenes like these old Scotia's grandeur springs,
   That makes her lov'd at home, revered abroad:
   Princes and Lords are but the breath of kings,
   'An honest man's the noblest work of God.'
      'The Cotter's Saturday Night' (1786) st. 19. Cf. Pope
      522:20

20 I wasna fou, but just had plenty.
      'Death and Dr Hornbook' (1787) st. 3

21 On ev'ry hand it will allow'd be,
   He's just—nae better than he shou'd be.
      'A Dedication to G[avin] H[amilton]' (1786) l. 25

22 There's threesome reels, there's foursome reels,
   There's hornpipes and strathspeys, man,
   But the best dance e'er cam to the land
   Was, the deil's awa wi' th'Exciseman.
      'The Deil's awa wi' th'Exciseman' (1792)

23 Perhaps it may turn out a sang;
   Perhaps, turn out a sermon.
      'Epistle to a Young Friend' (1786) st. 1

24 I waive the quantum o' the sin;
   The hazard of concealing;
   But och! it hardens a' within,
   And petrifies the feeling!
      'Epistle to a Young Friend' (1786) st. 6

25 An atheist-laugh's a poor exchange
   For Deity offended!
      'Epistle to a Young Friend' (1786) st. 9

26 Gie me ae spark o' Nature's fire,
   That's a' the learning I desire.
      'Epistle to J. L[aprai]k' (1786) st. 13

27 For thus the royal mandate ran,
   When first the human race began,
   'The social, friendly, honest man,
   Whate'er he be,
   'Tis he fulfils great Nature's plan,
   And none but he.'
      'To the same [John Lapraik]' st. 15

28 The rank is but the guinea's stamp,
   The man's the gowd for a' that!
      'For a' that and a' that' (1790)

29 A man's a man for a' that.
      'For a' that and a' that' (1790)

1 Green grow the rashes, O,
  Green grow the rashes, O;
  The sweetest hours that e'er I spend,
  Are spent among the lasses, O.
      'Green Grow the Rashes' (1787)

2 Auld nature swears, the lovely dears
  Her noblest work she classes, O;
  Her prentice han' she tried on man,
  An' then she made the lasses, O.
      'Green Grow the Rashes' (1787)

3 O, gie me the lass that has acres o' charms,
  O, gie me the lass wi' the weel-stockit farms.
      'Hey for a Lass wi' a Tocher' (1799)

4 Here, some are thinkin' on their sins,
  An' some upo' their claes.
      'The Holy Fair' (1786) st. 10

5 Leeze me on drink! it gi'es us mair
  Than either school or college.
      'The Holy Fair' (1786) st. 19

6 There's some are fou o' love divine;
  There's some are fou o' brandy.
      'The Holy Fair' (1786) st. 27

7 O L--d thou kens what zeal I bear,
  When drinkers drink, and swearers swear,
  And singin' there, and dancin' here,
  Wi' great an' sma';
  For I am keepet by thy fear,
  Free frae them a'.

  But yet—O L--d—confess I must—
  At times I'm fash'd wi' fleshly lust . . .

  O L--d—yestreen—thou kens—wi' Meg—
  Thy pardon I sincerely beg!
  O may 't ne'er be a living plague,
  To my dishonour!
  And I'll ne'er lift a lawless leg
  Again upon her.
      'Holy Willie's Prayer' (1785)

8 There's death in the cup—so beware!
      'Inscription on a Goblet' (published 1834)

9 It was a' for our rightfu' King
  We left fair Scotland's strand.
      'It was a' for our Rightfu' King' (1796)

10 John Anderson my jo, John,
   When we were first acquent,
   Your locks were like the raven,
   Your bonny brow was brent.
       'John Anderson my Jo' (1790)

11 I once was a maid, tho' I cannot tell when,
   And still my delight is in proper young men.
       'The Jolly Beggars' (1799) l. 57, also known as 'Love and Liberty—A Cantata'

12 Partly wi' LOVE o'ercome sae sair,
   And partly she was drunk.
       'The Jolly Beggars' (1799) l. 183

13 A fig for those by law protected!
   LIBERTY's a glorious feast!
   Courts for cowards were erected,
   Churches built to please the PRIEST.
       'The Jolly Beggars' (1799) l. 254

14 Life is all a VARIORUM,
   We regard not how it goes;
   Let them cant about DECORUM,
   Who have characters to lose.
       'The Jolly Beggars' (1799) l. 270

15 Some have meat and cannot eat,
   Some cannot eat that want it:
   But we have meat and we can eat,
   Sae let the Lord be thankit.
       'The Kirkudbright Grace' (1790), also known as 'The Selkirk Grace'

16 I've seen sae mony changefu' years,
   On earth I am a stranger grown:
   I wander in the ways of men,
   Alike unknowing and unknown.
       'Lament for James, Earl of Glencairn' (1793)

17 May coward shame distain his name,
   The wretch that dares not die!
       'McPherson's Farewell' (1788)

18   Nature's law,
   That man was made to mourn!
       'Man was made to Mourn' (1786) st. 4

19 Man's inhumanity to man
   Makes countless thousands mourn!
       'Man was made to Mourn' (1786) st. 7

20 O Death! the poor man's dearest friend,
   The kindest and the best!
       'Man was made to Mourn' (1786) st. 11

21 Go fetch to me a pint o' wine,
   An' fill it in a silver tassie.
       'My Bonnie Mary' (1790)

22 My heart's in the Highlands, my heart is not here;
   My heart's in the Highlands a-chasing the deer;
   Chasing the wild deer, and following the roe,
   My heart's in the Highlands, wherever I go.
       'My Heart's in the Highlands' (1790)

23 Farewell to the Highlands, farewell to the North;
   The birth-place of valour, the country of worth.
       'My Heart's in the Highlands' (1790)

24 The minister kiss'd the fiddler's wife,
   An' could na preach for thinkin' o't.
       'My Love She's but a Lassie yet' (1790)

25 The wan moon sets behind the white wave,
   And time is setting with me, Oh.
       'Open the door to me, Oh' (1793)

26 O whistle, an' I'll come to you, my lad:
   O whistle, an' I'll come to you, my lad:
   Tho' father and mither should baith gae mad,
   O whistle, and I'll come to you, my lad.
       'O Whistle, an' I'll come to you, my Lad' (1788). Cf. Fletcher 287:22

27 O, my Luve's like a red, red rose
   That's newly sprung in June;
   O my Luve's like the melodie
   That's sweetly play'd in tune.
       'A Red Red Rose' (1796) (derived from various folk-songs)

1 Scots, wha hae wi' Wallace bled,
Scots, wham Bruce has aften led,
Welcome to your gory bed,—
Or to victorie.

Now's the day, and now's the hour;
See the front o' battle lour;
See approach proud Edward's power,
Chains and slaverie.
'Robert Bruce's March to Bannockburn' (1799) (also
known as 'Scots, Wha Hae')

2 Liberty's in every blow!
Let us do—or die!!!
'Robert Bruce's March to Bannockburn' (1799)

3 Good Lord, what is man! for as simple he looks,
Do but try to develop his hooks and his crooks,
With his depths and his shallows, his good and his
evil,
All in all he's a problem must puzzle the devil.
'Sketch' inscribed to Charles James Fox (1800)

4 His ancient, trusty, drouthy crony,
Tam lo'ed him like a vera brither;
They had been fou for weeks thegither.
'Tam o' Shanter' (1791) l. 42

5 Kings may be blest, but Tam was glorious,
O'er a' the ills o' life victorious!
'Tam o' Shanter' (1791) l. 57

6 But pleasures are like poppies spread,
You seize the flow'r, its bloom is shed;
Or like the snow falls in the river,
A moment white—then melts for ever.
'Tam o' Shanter' (1791) l. 59

7 Nae man can tether time or tide.
'Tam o' Shanter' (1791) l. 67

8 Inspiring, bold John Barleycorn,
What dangers thou canst make us scorn!
Wi' tippenny, we fear nae evil;
Wi' usquebae, we'll face the devil!
'Tam o' Shanter' (1791) l. 105

9 As Tammie glowr'd, amaz'd, and curious,
The mirth and fun grew fast and furious.
'Tam o' Shanter' (1791) l. 143

10 Tam tint his reason a' thegither,
And roars out—'Weel done, Cutty-sark!'
'Tam o' Shanter' (1791) l. 185

11 Ah Tam! ah Tam! thou'll get thy fairin'!
In hell they'll roast thee like a herrin!
'Tam o' Shanter' (1791) l. 201

12 A man may drink and no be drunk;
A man may fight and no be slain;
A man may kiss a bonnie lass,
And aye be welcome back again.
'There was a Lass' (1788)

13 Fair fa' your honest, sonsie face,
Great chieftain o' the puddin'-race!
Aboon them a' ye tak your place,
Painch, tripe, or thairm:
Weel are ye wordy o' a grace
As lang's my arm.
'To a Haggis' (1787)

14 O wad some Pow'r the giftie gie us
To see oursels as others see us!
It wad frae mony a blunder free us,
And foolish notion.
'To a Louse' (1786)

15 Wee, sleekit, cow'rin', tim'rous beastie,
O what a panic's in thy breastie!
Thou need na start awa sae hasty,
Wi' bickering brattle!
I wad be laith to rin an' chase thee,
Wi' murd'ring pattle!
'To a Mouse' (1786)

16 I'm truly sorry Man's dominion
Has broken Nature's social union,
An' justifies that ill opinion
Which makes thee startle,
At me, thy poor, earth-born companion,
An' fellow-mortal!
'To a Mouse' (1786)

17 The best laid schemes o' mice an' men
Gang aft a-gley.
'To a Mouse' (1786)

18 Come, Firm Resolve, take thou the van,
Thou stalk o' carl-hemp in man!
And let us mind, faint heart ne'er wan
A lady fair;
Wha does the utmost that he can,
Will whyles do mair.
'To Dr Blacklock' (1800)

19 Just now I've taen the fit o' rhyme,
My barmie noddle's working prime.
'To J. S[mith]' (1786) st. 4

20 Some rhyme a neebor's name to lash;
Some rhyme (vain thought!) for needfu' cash;
Some rhyme to court the countra clash,
An' raise a din;
For me, an aim I never fash;
I rhyme for fun.
'To J. S[mith]' (1786) st. 5

21 An' fareweel dear, deluding woman,
The joy of joys!
'To J. S[mith]' (1786) st. 14

22 Their sighan', cantan', grace-proud faces,
Their three-mile prayers, and half-mile graces.
'To the Rev. John M'Math' (1808)

23 We labour soon, we labour late,
To feed the titled knave, man;
And a' the comfort we're to get,
Is that ayont the grave, man.
'The Tree of Liberty' (1838)

24 His lockèd, lettered, braw brass collar,
Shew'd him the gentleman and scholar.
'The Twa Dogs' (1786) l. 13

25 An' there began a lang digression
About the lords o' the creation.
'The Twa Dogs' (1786) l. 45

26 Rejoiced they were na men, but dogs.
'The Twa Dogs' (1786) l. 236

1 All in this mottie, misty clime,
I backward mus'd on wasted time,
How I had spent my youthfu' prime
An' done nae-thing,
But stringing blethers up to rhyme
For fools to sing.
'The Vision' (1785)

2 What can a young lassie, what shall a young lassie,
What can a young lassie do wi' an auld man?
'What can a Young Lassie do wi' an Auld Man' (1792)

3 It is the moon, I ken her horn,
That's blinkin in the lift sae hie;
She shines sae bright to wyle us hame,
But by my sooth she'll wait a wee!
'Willie Brew'd a Peck o' Maut' (1790)

4 Don't let the awkward squad fire over me.
Said shortly before his death, in A. Cunningham *The Works of Robert Burns; with his Life* vol. 1 (1834) p. 344

William S. Burroughs 1914–

American novelist

5 The face of 'evil' is always the face of total need.
The Naked Lunch (1959) introduction

6 What we on earth call God is a little tribal God who has made an awful mess.
Paris Review Fall 1965

Sir Fred Burrows 1887–1973

British public servant; President of the National Union of Railwaymen, 1942–4

7 Unlike my predecessors I have devoted more of my life to shunting and hooting than to hunting and shooting.
Speech as last Governor of undivided Bengal (1946–7). See *Daily Telegraph* 24 April 1973, obituary notice

Benjamin Hapgood Burt 1880–1950

American songwriter

8 One evening in October, when I was one-third sober,
An' taking home a 'load' with manly pride;
My poor feet began to stutter, so I lay down in the gutter,
And a pig came up an' lay down by my side;
Then we sang 'It's all fair weather when good fellows get together,'
Till a lady passing by was heard to say:
'You can tell a man who "boozes" by the company he chooses'
And the pig got up and slowly walked away.
'The Pig Got Up and Slowly Walked Away' (1933 song)

9 When you're all dressed up and no place to go.
Title of song (1913)

Nat Burton

10 There'll be bluebirds over the white cliffs of Dover,
Tomorrow, just you wait and see.
'The White Cliffs of Dover' (1941 song)

Sir Richard Burton 1821–90

English explorer, anthropologist, and translator

11 Don't be frightened; I am recalled. Pay, pack, and follow at convenience.
Note to his wife, 19 August 1871, on being replaced as British Consul to Damascus; in Isabel Burton *Life of Captain Sir Richard F. Burton* (1893) vol. 1, ch. 21

Robert Burton 1577–1640

English clergyman and scholar

12 All my joys to this are folly,
Naught so sweet as Melancholy.
The Anatomy of Melancholy (1621–51) 'The Author's Abstract of Melancholy'

13 I write of melancholy, by being busy to avoid melancholy.
The Anatomy of Melancholy (1621–51) 'Democritus to the Reader' (p. 20, Everyman ed., 1932)

14 They lard their lean books with the fat of others' works.
The Anatomy of Melancholy (1621–51) 'Democritus to the Reader' (p. 23, Everyman ed., 1932)

15 A loose, plain, rude writer . . . I call a spade a spade.
The Anatomy of Melancholy (1621–51) 'Democritus to the Reader' (p. 31, Everyman ed., 1932)

16 I had not time to lick it into form, as she [a bear] doth her young ones.
The Anatomy of Melancholy (1621–51) 'Democritus to the Reader' (p. 31, Everyman ed., 1932)

17 Like watermen, that row one way and look another.
The Anatomy of Melancholy (1621–51) 'Democritus to the Reader' (p. 55, Everyman ed., 1932). Cf. Bunyan 155:20

18 Him that makes shoes go barefoot himself.
The Anatomy of Melancholy (1621–51) 'Democritus to the Reader' (p. 66, Everyman ed., 1932)

19 All poets are mad.
The Anatomy of Melancholy (1621–51) 'Democritus to the Reader' (p. 112, Everyman ed., 1932). Cf. Wordsworth 747:11

20 What, if a dear year come or dearth, or some loss?
And were it not that they are loath to lay out money on a rope, they would be hanged forthwith, and sometimes die to save charges.
The Anatomy of Melancholy (1621–51) pt. 1, sect. 2, member 3, subsect. 12

21 I may not here omit those two main plagues, and common dotages of human kind, wine and women, which have infatuated and besotted myriads of people. They go commonly together.
The Anatomy of Melancholy (1621–51) pt. 1, sect. 2, member 3, subsect. 13

22 *Hinc quam sit calamus saevior ense patet.*
From this it is clear how much the pen is worse than the sword.
The Anatomy of Melancholy (1621–51) pt. 1, sect. 2, member 4, subsect. 4. Cf. Bulwer-Lytton 155:5

23 See one promontory (said Socrates of old), one mountain, one sea, one river, and see all.
The Anatomy of Melancholy (1621–51) pt. 1, sect. 2, member 4, subsect. 7

1 One was never married, and that's his hell: another is, and that's his plague.
> *The Anatomy of Melancholy* (1621–51) pt. 1, sect. 2, member 4, subsect. 7

2 The gods are well pleased when they see great men contending with adversity.
> *The Anatomy of Melancholy* (1621–51) pt. 2, sect. 3, member 1, subsect. 1

3 Every thing, saith Epictetus, hath two handles, the one to be held by, the other not.
> *The Anatomy of Melancholy* (1621–51) pt. 2, sect. 3, member 3, subsect. 1

4 Who cannot give good counsel? 'tis cheap, it costs them nothing.
> *The Anatomy of Melancholy* (1621–51) pt. 2, sect. 3, member 3, subsect. 1

5 What is a ship but a prison?
> *The Anatomy of Melancholy* (1621–51) pt. 2, sect. 3, member 4, subsect. 1. Cf. Johnson 371:23

6 All places are distant from Heaven alike.
> *The Anatomy of Melancholy* (1621–51) pt. 2, sect. 3, member 4, subsect. 1

7 'Let me not live,' saith Aretine's Antonia, 'if I had not rather hear thy discourse than see a play!'
> *The Anatomy of Melancholy* (1621–51) pt. 3, sect. 1, member 1, subsect. 1

8 To enlarge or illustrate this power and effect of love is to set a candle in the sun.
> *The Anatomy of Melancholy* (1621–51) pt. 3, sect. 2, member 1, subsect. 2. Cf. Sidney 646:11, Young 754:11

9 No cord nor cable can so forcibly draw, or hold so fast, as love can do with a twined thread.
> *The Anatomy of Melancholy* (1621–51) pt. 3, sect. 2, member 1, subsect. 2

10 To these crocodile's tears they will add sobs, fiery sighs, and sorrowful countenance, pale colour, leanness.
> *The Anatomy of Melancholy* (1621–51) pt. 3, sect. 2, member 2, subsect. 4

11 Diogenes struck the father when the son swore.
> *The Anatomy of Melancholy* (1621–51) pt. 3, sect. 2, member 2, subsect. 5

12 England is a paradise for women, and hell for horses: Italy a paradise for horses, hell for women, as the diverb goes.
> *The Anatomy of Melancholy* (1621–51) pt. 3, sect. 3, member 1, subsect. 2. Cf. Florio 288:5

13 One religion is as true as another.
> *The Anatomy of Melancholy* (1621–51) pt. 3, sect. 4, member 2, subsect. 1

14 Be not solitary, be not idle.
> *The Anatomy of Melancholy* (1621–51) *ad fin.*

Hermann Busenbaum 1600–68

German theologian

15 *Cum finis est licitus, etiam media sunt licita.*
The end justifies the means.
> *Medulla Theologiae Moralis* (1650); literally 'When the end is allowed, the means also are allowed'

George Bush 1924–

41st President of the USA

16 Read my lips: no new taxes.
> Campaign pledge on taxation, in *New York Times* 19 August 1988

Comte de Bussy-Rabutin 1618–93

French soldier and poet

17 *L'amour vient de l'aveuglement,*
L'amitié de la connaissance.
Love comes from blindness,
Friendship from knowledge.
> *Histoire Amoureuse des Gaules: Maximes d'Amour* (1665) pt. 1

18 *L'absence est à l'amour ce qu'est au feu le vent;*
Il éteint le petit, il allume le grand.
Absence is to love what wind is to fire;
It extinguishes the small, it kindles the great.
> *Histoire Amoureuse des Gaules: Maximes d'Amour* (1665) pt. 2. Cf. Francis 292:10, La Rochefoucauld 410:19

19 *Comme vous savez, Dieu est d'ordinaire pour les gros escadrons contre les petits.*
As you know, God is usually on the side of the big squadrons against the small.
> Letter to the Comte de Limoges, 18 October 1677, in *Lettres de . . . Comte de Bussy* (1697) vol. 4. Cf. Anouilh 23:2, Tacitus 678:5, Voltaire 716:20

Joseph Butler 1692–1752

English bishop and theologian

20 It has come, I know not how, to be taken for granted, by many persons, that Christianity is not so much as a subject of inquiry; but that it is, now at length, discovered to be fictitious.
> *The Analogy of Religion* (1736) 'Advertisement'

21 But to us, probability is the very guide of life.
> *The Analogy of Religion* (1736) 'Introduction'

22 Things and actions are what they are, and the consequences of them will be what they will be: why then should we desire to be deceived?
> *Fifteen Sermons preached at the Rolls Chapel* (1726) no. 7

Nicholas Murray Butler 1862–1947

President of Columbia University, 1901–45

23 An expert is one who knows more and more about less and less.
> Commencement address at Columbia University (attributed)

Samuel ('Hudibras') Butler 1612–80

English poet

24 He'd run in debt by disputation,
And pay with ratiocination.
> *Hudibras* pt. 1 (1663), canto 1, l. 77

25 For rhetoric he could not ope
His mouth, but out there flew a trope.
> *Hudibras* pt. 1 (1663), canto 1, l. 81

1 For all a rhetorician's rules
   Teach nothing but to name his tools.
   Hudibras pt. 1 (1663), canto 1, l. 89

2 A Babylonish dialect
   Which learned pedants much affect.
   Hudibras pt. 1 (1663), canto 1, l. 93

3 What ever sceptic could inquire for;
   For every why he had a wherefore.
   Hudibras pt. 1 (1663), canto 1, l. 131

4 He knew what's what, and that's as high
   As metaphysic wit can fly.
   Hudibras pt. 1 (1663), canto 1, l. 149

5 Such as take lodgings in a head
   That's to be let unfurnished.
   Hudibras pt. 1 (1663), canto 1, l. 159

6 And still be doing, never done:
   As if Religion were intended
   For nothing else but to be mended.
   Hudibras pt. 1 (1663), canto 1, l. 202

7 Compound for sins, they are inclined to,
   By damning those they have no mind to.
   Hudibras pt. 1 (1663), canto 1, l. 213

8 The trenchant blade, Toledo trusty,
   For want of fighting was grown rusty,
   And eat into it self, for lack
   Of some body to hew and hack.
   Hudibras pt. 1 (1663), canto 1, l. 357

9 For rhyme the rudder is of verses,
   With which like ships they steer their courses.
   Hudibras pt. 1 (1663), canto 1, l. 457

10 Great actions are not always true sons
   Of great and mighty resolutions.
   Hudibras pt. 1 (1663), canto 1, l. 877

11 Cleric before, and Lay behind;
   A lawless linsy-woolsy brother,
   Half of one order, half another.
   Hudibras pt. 1 (1663), canto 3, l. 1226

12 Learning, that cobweb of the brain,
   Profane, erroneous, and vain.
   Hudibras pt. 1 (1663), canto 3, l. 1339

13 She that with poetry is won,
   Is but a desk to write upon.
   Hudibras pt. 2 (1664), canto 1, l. 591

14 Love is a boy, by poets styled,
   Then spare the rod, and spoil the child.
   Hudibras pt. 2 (1664), canto 1, l. 843

15 Oaths are but words, and words but wind.
   Hudibras pt. 2 (1664), canto 2, l. 107

16 Doubtless the pleasure is as great
   Of being cheated, as to cheat.
   As lookers-on feel most delight,
   That least perceive a juggler's sleight;
   And still the less they understand,
   The more th' admire his sleight of hand.
   Hudibras pt. 2 (1664), canto 3, l. 1

17 What makes all doctrines plain and clear?
   About two hundred pounds a year.
   And that which was proved true before,
   Prove false again? Two hundred more.
   Hudibras pt. 3 (1680), canto 1, l. 1277

18 He that complies against his will,
   Is of his own opinion still.
   Hudibras pt. 3 (1680), canto 3, l. 547

19 For Justice, though she's painted blind,
   Is to the weaker side inclined.
   Hudibras pt. 3 (1680), canto 3, l. 709

20 For money has a power above
   The stars and fate, to manage love.
   Hudibras pt. 3 (1680) 'The Lady's Answer to the Knight'
   l. 131

21 All love at first, like generous wine,
   Ferments and frets, until 'tis fine;
   But when 'tis settled on the lee,
   And from th' impurer matter free,
   Becomes the richer still, the older,
   And proves the pleasanter, the colder.
   Genuine Remains (1759) 'Miscellaneous Thoughts'

22 The law can take a purse in open court,
   Whilst it condemns a less delinquent for't.
   Genuine Remains (1759) 'Miscellaneous Thoughts'

Samuel Butler 1835–1902

English novelist and sometime sheep farmer

23 It has been said that though God cannot alter the
   past, historians can; it is perhaps because they can be
   useful to Him in this respect that He tolerates their
   existence.
   Erewhon Revisited (1901) ch. 14. Cf. Agathon 5:15

24 Adversity, if a man is set down to it by degrees, is
   more supportable with equanimity by most people
   than any great prosperity arrived at in a single
   lifetime.
   The Way of All Flesh (1903) ch. 5

25 All animals, except man, know that the principal
   business of life is to enjoy it.
   The Way of All Flesh (1903) ch. 19

26 The advantage of doing one's praising for oneself is
   that one can lay it on so thick and exactly in the right
   places.
   The Way of All Flesh (1903) ch. 34

27 Young as he was, his instinct told him that the best
   liar is he who makes the smallest amount of lying go
   the longest way.
   The Way of All Flesh (1903) ch. 39

28 'Tis better to have loved and lost than never to have
   lost at all.
   The Way of All Flesh (1903) ch. 67. Cf. Tennyson 683:12

29 It was very good of God to let Carlyle and Mrs Carlyle
   marry one another and so make only two people
   miserable instead of four.
   *Letters between Samuel Butler and Miss E. M. A. Savage
   1871–1885* (1935) 21 November 1884

30 Life is one long process of getting tired.
   Notebooks (1912) ch. 1

31 All progress is based upon a universal innate desire on
   the part of every organism to live beyond its income.
   Notebooks (1912) ch. 1

32 The history of art is the history of revivals.
   Notebooks (1912) ch. 8

1 Our ideas. They are for the most part like bad
sixpences and we spend our lives in trying to pass
them on one another.
   Notebooks (1912) ch. 14

2 An apology for the Devil: It must be remembered that
we have only heard one side of the case. God has
written all the books.
   Notebooks (1912) ch. 14

3 A definition is the enclosing a wilderness of idea within
a wall of words.
   Notebooks (1912) ch. 14

4 To live is like to love — all reason is against it, and all
healthy instinct for it.
   Notebooks (1912) ch. 14

5 The public buys its opinions as it buys its meat, or
takes in its milk, on the principle that it is cheaper to
do this than to keep a cow. So it is, but the milk is
more likely to be watered.
   Notebooks (1912) ch. 17

6 The three most important things a man has are,
briefly, his private parts, his money, and his religious
opinions.
   Further Extracts from Notebooks (1934) p. 93

7 Jesus! with all thy faults I love thee still.
   Further Extracts from Notebooks (1934) p. 117

8 Conscience is thoroughly well-bred and soon leaves off
talking to those who do not wish to hear it.
   Further Extracts from Notebooks (1934) p. 279

9 Life is like playing a violin solo in public and learning
the instrument as one goes on.
   Speech at the Somerville Club, 27 February 1895, in R. A.
   Streatfield *Essays on Life, Art and Science* (1904) p. 69

10 Yet meet we shall, and part, and meet again
Where dead men meet, on lips of living men.
   'Not on sad Stygian shore' (1904)

11 Dusty, cobweb-covered, maimed, and set at naught,
Beauty crieth in an attic, and no man regardeth.
O God! O Montreal!
   'Psalm of Montreal', in *Spectator* 18 May 1878

William Butler 1535–1618

12 Doubtless God could have made a better berry, but
doubtless God never did.
   On the strawberry, in Izaak Walton *The Compleat Angler*
   (3rd ed., 1661) pt. 1, ch. 5

John Byrom 1692–1763

English poet

13 I am content, I do not care,
Wag as it will the world for me.
   'Careless Content' (1773)

14 Christians, awake! Salute the happy morn,
Whereon the Saviour of the world was born.
   Hymn (c.1750)

15 Some say, that Signor Bononcini,
Compared to Handel's a mere ninny;
Others aver, that to him Handel
Is scarcely fit to hold a candle.
Strange! that such high dispute should be
'Twixt Tweedledum and Tweedledee.
   'On the Feuds between Handel and Bononcini' (1727)

16 Stones towards the earth descend;
Rivers to the ocean roll;
Ev'ry motion has some end;—
What is thine, beloved soul?
   'The Soul's Tendency towards its True Centre' (1773)

17 God bless the King, I mean the Faith's Defender;
God bless—no harm in blessing—the Pretender;
But who Pretender is, or who is King,
God bless us all—that's quite another thing.
   'To an Officer in the Army, Extempore, Intended to allay
   the Violence of Party-Spirit' (1773)

Lord Byron (George Gordon, 6th Baron Byron) 1788–1824

English poet

18 Proud Wellington, with eagle beak so curled,
That nose, the hook where he suspends the world!
   'The Age of Bronze' (1823) st. 13

19 For what were all these country patriots born?
To hunt, and vote, and raise the price of corn?
   'The Age of Bronze' (1823) st. 14

20 Year after year they voted cent per cent
Blood, sweat, and tear-wrung millions—why? for
rent!
   'The Age of Bronze' (1823) st. 14

21 Did'st ever see a gondola? . . .
It glides along the water looking blackly,
Just like a coffin clapt in a canoe.
   Beppo (1818) st. 19

22 In short, he was a perfect cavaliero,
And to his very valet seemed a hero.
   Beppo (1818) st. 33. Cf. Cornuel 219:10

23 His heart was one of those which most enamour us,
Wax to receive, and marble to retain.
   Beppo (1818) st. 34

24 Our cloudy climate, and our chilly women.
   Beppo (1818) st. 49

25 A pretty woman as was ever seen,
Fresh as the Angel o'er a new inn door.
   Beppo (1818) st. 57

26 Where the virgins are soft as the roses they twine,
And all, save the spirit of man, is divine.
   The Bride of Abydos (1813) canto 1, st. 1

27 Such was Zuleika, such around her shone
The nameless charms unmarked by her alone—
The light of love, the purity of grace,
The mind, the Music breathing from her face,
The heart whose softness harmonized the whole,
And oh! that eye was in itself a Soul!
   The Bride of Abydos (1813) canto 1, st. 6

1   I have looked out
In the vast desolate night in search of him;
And when I saw gigantic shadows in
The umbrage of the walls of Eden, chequered
By the far-flashing of the cherubs' swords,
I watched for what I thought his coming: for
With fear rose longing in my heart to know
What 'twas which shook us all—but nothing came.
           Cain (1821) act 1, sc. 1, l. 266

2 The laughing dames in whom he did delight,
Whose large blue eyes, fair locks, and snowy hands,
Might shake the saintship of an anchorite.
           Childe Harold's Pilgrimage (1812–18) canto 1, st. 11

3 Adieu, adieu! my native shore
Fades o'er the waters blue.
           Childe Harold's Pilgrimage (1812–18) canto 1, st. 13

4 Lo! where the Giant on the mountain stands,
His blood-red tresses deep'ning in the sun,
With death-shot glowing in his fiery hands,
And eye that scorcheth all it glares upon.
           Childe Harold's Pilgrimage (1812–18) canto 1, st. 39

5 Here all were noble, save Nobility.
           Childe Harold's Pilgrimage (1812–18) canto 1, st. 85

6 Cold is the heart, fair Greece! that looks on thee,
Nor feels as lovers o'er the dust they loved;
Dull is the eye that will not weep to see
Thy walls defaced, thy mouldering shrines removed
By British hands.
           Childe Harold's Pilgrimage (1812–18) canto 2, st. 15

7 None are so desolate but something dear,
Dearer than self, possesses or possessed
A thought, and claims the homage of a tear.
           Childe Harold's Pilgrimage (1812–18) canto 2, st. 24

8 Dark Sappho! could not verse immortal save
That breast imbued with such immortal fire?
Could she not live who life eternal gave?
           Childe Harold's Pilgrimage (1812–18) canto 2, st. 39

9 Fair Greece! sad relic of departed worth!
Immortal, though no more! though fallen, great!
           Childe Harold's Pilgrimage (1812–18) canto 2, st. 73

10 Hereditary bondsmen! know ye not
Who would be free themselves must strike the blow?
           Childe Harold's Pilgrimage (1812–18) canto 2, st. 76

11 What is the worst of woes that wait on age?
What stamps the wrinkle deeper on the brow?
To view each loved one blotted from life's page,
And be alone on earth, as I am now.
           Childe Harold's Pilgrimage (1812–18) canto 2, st. 98

12 Once more upon the waters! yet once more!
And the waves bound beneath me as a steed
That knows his rider.
           Childe Harold's Pilgrimage (1812–18) canto 3, st. 2

13 The wandering outlaw of his own dark mind.
           Childe Harold's Pilgrimage (1812–18) canto 3, st. 3

14   Years steal
Fire from the mind as vigour from the limb;
And life's enchanted cup but sparkles near the brim.
           Childe Harold's Pilgrimage (1812–18) canto 3, st. 8

15 There was a sound of revelry by night,
And Belgium's capital had gathered then
Her beauty and her chivalry, and bright
The lamps that shone o'er fair women and brave men;
A thousand hearts beat happily; and when
Music arose with its voluptuous swell,
Soft eyes looked love to eyes which spake again,
And all went merry as a marriage bell;

But hush! hark! a deep sound strikes like a rising
   knell!
           Childe Harold's Pilgrimage (1812–18) canto 3, st. 11

16 On with the dance! let joy be unconfined;
No sleep till morn, when Youth and Pleasure meet
To chase the glowing Hours with flying feet.
           Childe Harold's Pilgrimage (1812–18) canto 3, st. 12

17 Where rose the mountains, there to him were friends;
Where rolled the ocean, thereon was his home;
Where a blue sky, and glowing clime, extends,
He had the passion and the power to roam.
           Childe Harold's Pilgrimage (1812–18) canto 3, st. 13

18 The very knowledge that he lived in vain,
That all was over on this side the tomb,
Had made Despair a smilingness assume.
           Childe Harold's Pilgrimage (1812–18) canto 3, st. 16

19 He rushed into the field, and, foremost fighting, fell.
           Childe Harold's Pilgrimage (1812–18) canto 3, st. 23

20 The earth is covered thick with other clay,
Which her own clay shall cover, heaped and pent,
Rider and horse,—friend, foe,—in one red burial
   blent!
           Childe Harold's Pilgrimage (1812–18) canto 3, st. 28

21   But life will suit
Itself to Sorrow's most detested fruit,
Like to the apples on the Dead Sea's shore,
All ashes to the taste.
           Childe Harold's Pilgrimage (1812–18) canto 3, st. 34

22 Quiet to quick bosoms is a hell.
           Childe Harold's Pilgrimage (1812–18) canto 3, st. 42

23 To fly from, need not be to hate, mankind.
           Childe Harold's Pilgrimage (1812–18) canto 3, st. 69

24 I live not in myself, but I become
Portion of that around me; and to me,
High mountains are a feeling, but the hum
Of human cities torture.
           Childe Harold's Pilgrimage (1812–18) canto 3, st. 72

25 His love was passion's essence:—as a tree
On fire by lightning, with ethereal flame
Kindled he was, and blasted.
           Childe Harold's Pilgrimage (1812–18) canto 3, st. 78

26 Sapping a solemn creed with solemn sneer.
           Childe Harold's Pilgrimage (1812–18) canto 3, st. 107 (of
           Edward Gibbon)

27 I have not loved the world, nor the world me;
I have not flattered its rank breath, nor bowed
To its idolatries a patient knee.
           Childe Harold's Pilgrimage (1812–18) canto 3, st. 113

28   I stood
Among them, but not of them; in a shroud
Of thoughts which were not their thoughts.
           Childe Harold's Pilgrimage (1812–18) canto 3, st. 113

1 The moon is up, and yet it is not night;
Sunset divides the sky with her—a sea
Of glory streams along the Alpine height
Of blue Friuli's mountains; Heaven is free
From clouds, but of all colours seems to be
Melted to one vast Iris of the West,
Where the day joins the past eternity.
Childe Harold's Pilgrimage (1812–18) canto 4, st. 27

2 Italia! oh Italia! thou who hast
The fatal gift of beauty.
Childe Harold's Pilgrimage (1812–18) canto 4, st. 42

3 Oh Rome! my country! city of the soul!
Childe Harold's Pilgrimage (1812–18) canto 4, st. 78

4 Alas! our young affections run to waste,
Or water but the desert.
Childe Harold's Pilgrimage (1812–18) canto 4, st. 120

5 Of its own beauty is the mind diseased.
Childe Harold's Pilgrimage (1812–18) canto 4, st. 122

6 Time, the avenger! unto thee I lift
My hands, and eyes, and heart, and crave of thee a gift.
Childe Harold's Pilgrimage (1812–18) canto 4, st. 130

7 But I have lived, and have not lived in vain:
My mind may lose its force, my blood its fire,
And my frame perish even in conquering pain;
But there is that within me which shall tire
Torture and Time, and breathe when I expire.
Childe Harold's Pilgrimage (1812–18) canto 4, st. 137

8 *There* were his young barbarians all at play,
There was their Dacian mother— he, their sire,
Butchered to make a Roman holiday.
Childe Harold's Pilgrimage (1812–18) canto 4, st. 141

9 A ruin—yet what ruin! from its mass
Walls, palaces, half-cities, have been reared.
Childe Harold's Pilgrimage (1812–18) canto 4, st. 143

10 While stands the Coliseum, Rome shall stand;
When falls the Coliseum, Rome shall fall;
And when Rome falls—the World.
Childe Harold's Pilgrimage (1812–18) canto 4, st. 145

11 The Lord of the unerring bow,
The God of life, and poesy, and light.
Childe Harold's Pilgrimage (1812–18) canto 4, st. 161

12 Oh! that the desert were my dwelling-place,
With one fair spirit for my minister,
That I might all forget the human race,
And, hating no one, love but only her!
Childe Harold's Pilgrimage (1812–18) canto 4, st. 177

13 There is a pleasure in the pathless woods,
There is a rapture on the lonely shore,
There is society, where none intrudes,
By the deep sea, and music in its roar:
I love not man the less, but nature more,
From these our interviews, in which I steal
From all I may be, or have been before,
To mingle with the universe, and feel
What I can ne'er express, yet cannot all conceal.
Childe Harold's Pilgrimage (1812–18) canto 4, st. 178

14 Roll on, thou deep and dark blue Ocean—roll!
Ten thousand fleets sweep over thee in vain;
Man marks the earth with ruin—his control
Stops with the shore.
Childe Harold's Pilgrimage (1812–18) canto 4, st. 179

15 When, for a moment, like a drop of rain,
He sinks into thy depths with bubbling groan,
Without a grave, unknelled, uncoffined, and unknown.
Childe Harold's Pilgrimage (1812–18) canto 4, st. 179

16 Dark-heaving;—boundless, endless, and sublime—
The image of eternity.
Childe Harold's Pilgrimage (1812–18) canto 4, st. 183 (of the sea)

17 The glory and the nothing of a name.
'Churchill's Grave' (1816)

18 Such hath it been—shall be—beneath the sun
The many still must labour for the one.
The Corsair (1814) canto 1, st. 8

19 There was a laughing devil in his sneer,
That raised emotions both of rage and fear;
And where his frown of hatred darkly fell,
Hope withering fled, and Mercy sighed farewell!
The Corsair (1814) canto 1, st. 9

20 Deep in my soul that tender secret dwells,
Lonely and lost to light for evermore,
Save when to thine my heart responsive swells,
Then trembles into silence as before.
The Corsair (1814) canto 1, st. 14 'Medora's Song'

21 The spirit burning but unbent,
May writhe, rebel—the weak alone repent!
The Corsair (1814) canto 2, st. 10

22 Oh! too convincing—dangerously dear—
In woman's eye the unanswerable tear!
The Corsair (1814) canto 2, st. 15

23 And she for him had given
Her all on earth, and more than all in heaven!
The Corsair (1814) canto 3, st. 17

24 He left a Corsair's name to other times,
Linked with one virtue, and a thousand crimes.
The Corsair (1814) canto 3, st. 24

25 Slow sinks, more lovely ere his race be run,
Along Morea's hills the setting sun;
Not, as in northern climes, obscurely bright,
But one unclouded blaze of living light.
'The Curse of Minerva' (1812) l. 1 and *The Corsair* (1814) canto 3, st. 1

26 A land of meanness, sophistry, and mist.
'The Curse of Minerva' (1812) l. 138 (of Scotland)

27 Each breeze from foggy mount and marshy plain
Dilutes with drivel every drizzly brain,
Till, burst at length, each wat'ry head o'erflows,
Foul as their soil, and frigid as their snows.
'The Curse of Minerva' (1812) l. 139 (of Scotland)

28 The Assyrian came down like the wolf on the fold,
And his cohorts were gleaming in purple and gold;
And the sheen of their spears was like stars on the sea,
When the blue wave rolls nightly on deep Galilee.
'The Destruction of Sennacherib' (1815) st. 1

29 For the Angel of Death spread his wings on the blast,
And breathed in the face of the foe as he passed.
'The Destruction of Sennacherib' (1815) st. 3

1 And Coleridge, too, has lately taken wing,
But, like a hawk encumbered with his hood,
Explaining metaphysics to the nation—
I wish he would explain his explanation.
Don Juan (1819–24) canto 1, dedication st. 2

2 The intellectual eunuch Castlereagh.
Don Juan (1819–24) canto 1, dedication st. 11

3 My way is to begin with the beginning.
Don Juan (1819–24) canto 1, st. 7

4 But—Oh! ye lords of ladies intellectual,
Inform us truly, have they not hen-pecked you all?
Don Juan (1819–24) canto 1, st. 22

5 Married, charming, chaste, and twenty-three.
Don Juan (1819–24) canto 1, st. 59

6 What men call gallantry, and gods adultery,
Is much more common where the climate's sultry.
Don Juan (1819–24) canto 1, st. 63

7 Christians have burnt each other, quite persuaded
That all the Apostles would have done as they did.
Don Juan (1819–24) canto 1, st. 83

8 He thought about himself, and the whole earth,
Of man the wonderful, and of the stars,
And how the deuce they ever could have birth;
And then he thought of earthquakes, and of wars,
How many miles the moon might have in girth,
Of air-balloons, and of the many bars
To perfect knowledge of the boundless skies;
And then he thought of Donna Julia's eyes.
Don Juan (1819–24) canto 1, st. 92

9 'Twas strange that one so young should thus concern
His brain about the action of the sky;
If *you* think 'twas philosophy that this did,
I can't help thinking puberty assisted.
Don Juan (1819–24) canto 1, st. 93

10 A little still she strove, and much repented,
And whispering 'I will ne'er consent'—consented.
Don Juan (1819–24) canto 1, st. 117

11 Sweet is revenge—especially to women.
Don Juan (1819–24) canto 1, st. 124.

12 Pleasure's a sin, and sometimes sin's a pleasure.
Don Juan (1819–24) canto 1, st. 133

13 Man's love is of man's life a thing apart,
'Tis woman's whole existence.
Don Juan (1819–24) canto 1, st. 194

14 A panoramic view of hell's in training,
After the style of Virgil and of Homer,
So that my name of Epic's no misnomer.
Don Juan (1819–24) canto 1, st. 200

15 So for a good old-gentlemanly vice,
I think I must take up with avarice.
Don Juan (1819–24) canto 1, st. 216

16 There's nought, no doubt, so much the spirit calms
As rum and true religion.
Don Juan (1819–24) canto 2, st. 34

17 A solitary shriek, the bubbling cry
Of some strong swimmer in his agony.
Don Juan (1819–24) canto 2, st. 53

18 Let us have wine and women, mirth and laughter,
Sermons and soda-water the day after.
Don Juan (1819–24) canto 2, st. 178

19 Man, being reasonable, must get drunk;
The best of life is but intoxication:
Glory, the grape, love, gold, in these are sunk
The hopes of all men, and of every nation.
Don Juan (1819–24) canto 2, st. 179

20 They looked up to the sky, whose floating glow
Spread like a rosy ocean, vast and bright;
They gazed upon the glittering sea below,
Whence the broad moon rose circling into sight;
They heard the wave's splash, and the wind so low,
And saw each other's dark eyes darting light
Into each other—and, beholding this,
Their lips drew near, and clung into a kiss.
Don Juan (1819–24) canto 2, st. 185

21 And thus they form a group that's quite antique,
Half naked, loving, natural, and Greek.
Don Juan (1819–24) canto 2, st. 194

22 Alas! the love of women! it is known
To be a lovely and a fearful thing!
Don Juan (1819–24) canto 2, st. 199

23 In her first passion woman loves her lover,
In all the others all she loves is love.
Don Juan (1819–24) canto 3, st. 3

24 'Tis melancholy, and a fearful sign
Of human frailty, folly, also crime,
That love and marriage rarely can combine,
Although they both are born in the same clime;
Marriage from love, like vinegar from wine—
A sad, sour, sober beverage—by time
Is sharpened from its high celestial flavour,
Down to a very homely household savour.
Don Juan (1819–24) canto 3, st. 5

25 Think you, if Laura had been Petrarch's wife,
He would have written sonnets all his life?
Don Juan (1819–24) canto 3, st. 8

26 All tragedies are finished by a death,
All comedies are ended by a marriage;
The future states of both are left to faith.
Don Juan (1819–24) canto 3, st. 9

27 Dreading that climax of all human ills,
The inflammation of his weekly bills.
Don Juan (1819–24) canto 3, st. 35

28 ... He was the mildest mannered man
That ever scuttled ship or cut a throat,
With such true breeding of a gentleman,
You never could divine his real thought.
Don Juan (1819–24) canto 3, st. 41

29 But Shakespeare also says, 'tis very silly
'To gild refinèd gold, or paint the lily.'
Don Juan (1819–24) canto 3, st. 76. Cf. *King John*
594:9

30 The isles of Greece, the isles of Greece!
Where burning Sappho loved and sung,
Where grew the arts of war and peace,
Where Delos rose, and Phoebus sprung!
Eternal summer gilds them yet,
But all, except their sun, is set!
Don Juan (1819–24) canto 3, st. 86 (1)

1 The mountains look on Marathon—
And Marathon looks on the sea;
And musing there an hour alone,
I dreamed that Greece might still be free.
Don Juan (1819–24) canto 3, st. 86 (3)

2 For what is left the poet here?
For Greeks a blush—for Greece a tear.
Don Juan (1819–24) canto 3, st. 86 (6)

3 Milton's the prince of poets—so we say;
A little heavy, but no less divine.
Don Juan (1819–24) canto 3, st. 91

4 A drowsy frowzy poem, called the 'Excursion',
Writ in a manner which is my aversion.
Don Juan (1819–24) canto 3, st. 94

5 We learn from Horace, Homer sometimes sleeps;
We feel without him: Wordsworth sometimes wakes.
Don Juan (1819–24) canto 3, st. 98. Cf. Horace 347:17

6 Ave Maria! 'tis the hour of prayer!
Ave Maria! 'tis the hour of love!
Don Juan (1819–24) canto 3, st. 103

7 Now my sere fancy 'falls into the yellow
Leaf,' and imagination droops her pinion,
And the sad truth which hovers o'er my desk
Turns what was once romantic to burlesque.
Don Juan (1819–24) canto 4, st. 3. Cf. *Macbeth* 604:21

8 And if I laugh at any mortal thing,
'Tis that I may not weep.
Don Juan (1819–24) canto 4, st. 4

9 'Whom the gods love die young' was said of yore.
And many deaths do they escape by this.
Don Juan (1819–24) canto 4, st. 12. Cf. Menander 457:2

10   I've stood upon Achilles' tomb,
And heard Troy doubted; time will doubt of Rome.
Don Juan (1819–24) canto 4, st. 101

11 When amatory poets sing their loves
In liquid lines mellifluously bland,
And pair their rhymes as Venus yokes her doves.
They little think what mischief is in hand.
Don Juan (1819–24) canto 5, st. 1

12 And is this blood, then, formed but to be shed?
Can every element our elements mar?
And air—earth—water—fire live—and we dead?
We, whose minds comprehend all things?
Don Juan (1819–24) canto 5, st. 39

13 ... That all-softening, overpowering knell,
The tocsin of the soul—the dinner bell.
Don Juan (1819–24) canto 5, st. 49

14 Why don't they knead two virtuous souls for life
Into that moral centaur, man and wife?
Don Juan (1819–24) canto 5, st. 158

15 There is a tide in the affairs of women,
Which, taken at the flood, leads—God knows where.
Don Juan (1819–24) canto 6, st. 2. Cf. *Julius Caesar* 593:12

16 A lady of a 'certain age', which means
Certainly aged.
Don Juan (1819–24) canto 6, st. 69

17 'Let there be light!' said God, and there was light!'
'Let there be blood!' says man, and there's a sea!
Don Juan (1819–24) canto 7, st. 41

18 That water-land of Dutchmen and of ditches.
Don Juan (1819–24) canto 10, st. 63

19 When Bishop Berkeley said 'there was no matter',
And proved it—'twas no matter what he said.
Don Juan (1819–24) canto 11, st. 1

20 And, after all, what is a lie? 'Tis but
The truth in masquerade.
Don Juan (1819–24) canto 11, st. 37

21 'Tis strange the mind, that very fiery particle,
Should let itself be snuffed out by an article.
Don Juan (1819–24) canto 11, st. 60 (on Keats 'who was killed off by one critique')

22 For talk six times with the same single lady,
And you may get the wedding dresses ready.
Don Juan (1819–24) canto 12, st. 59

23   Merely innocent flirtation,
Not quite adultery, but adulteration.
Don Juan (1819–24) canto 12, st. 63

24 Now hatred is by far the longest pleasure;
Men love in haste, but they detest at leisure.
Don Juan (1819–24) canto 13, st. 4. Cf. Congreve 215:25

25 Cervantes smiled Spain's chivalry away.
Don Juan (1819–24) canto 13, st. 11

26 The English winter—ending in July,
To recommence in August.
Don Juan (1819–24) canto 13, st. 42

27 Society is now one polished horde,
Formed of two mighty tribes, the *Bores* and *Bored*.
Don Juan (1819–24) canto 13, st. 95

28 Of all the horrid, hideous notes of woe,
Sadder than owl-songs or the midnight blast,
Is that portentous phrase, 'I told you so.'
Don Juan (1819–24) canto 14, st. 50

29 'Tis strange—but true; for truth is always strange;
Stranger than fiction.
Don Juan (1819–24) canto 14, st. 101

30 All present life is but an Interjection,
An 'Oh!' or 'Ah!' of joy or misery,
Or a 'Ha! ha!' or 'Bah!'—a yawn, or 'Pooh!'
Of which perhaps the latter is most true.
Don Juan (1819–24) canto 15, st. 1

31 A lovely being, scarcely formed or moulded,
A rose with all its sweetest leaves yet folded.
Don Juan (1819–24) canto 15, st. 43

32 'Tis wonderful what fable will not do!
'Tis said it makes reality more bearable:
But what's reality? Who has its clue?
Philosophy? No; she too much rejects.
Religion? Yes; but which of all her sects?
Don Juan (1819–24) canto 15, st. 89

33 Between two worlds life hovers like a star,
'Twixt night and morn, upon the horizon's verge.
How little do we know that which we are!
How less what we may be!
Don Juan (1819–24) canto 15, st. 99

1 The worlds beyond this world's perplexing waste
Had more of her existence for in her
There was a depth of feeling to embrace
Thoughts, boundless, deep, but silent too as space.
Don Juan (1819–24) canto 16, st. 48

2   The mind can make
Substance, and people planets of its own
With beings brighter than have been, and give
A breath to forms which can outlive all flesh.
'The Dream' (1816) st. 1

3   I'll publish, right or wrong:
Fools are my theme, let satire be my song.
English Bards and Scotch Reviewers (1809) l. 5

4 A man must serve his time to every trade
Save censure—critics all are ready made.
Take hackneyed jokes from Miller, got by rote,
With just enough of learning to misquote.
English Bards and Scotch Reviewers (1809) l. 63

5 Each country Book-club bows the knee to Baal,
And, hurling lawful Genius from the throne,
Erects a shrine and idol of its own.
English Bards and Scotch Reviewers (1809) l. 138

6 Who, both by precept and example, shows
That prose is verse, and verse is merely prose,
Convincing all by demonstration plain,
Poetic souls delight in prose insane;
And Christmas stories tortured into rhyme,
Contain the essence of the true sublime.
English Bards and Scotch Reviewers (1809) l. 241 (of
Wordsworth)

7 Be warm, but pure; be amorous, but be chaste.
English Bards and Scotch Reviewers (1809) l. 306

8 The petrifactions of a plodding brain.
English Bards and Scotch Reviewers (1809) l. 416

9 Then let Ausonia, skilled in every art
To soften manners, but corrupt the heart,
Pour her exotic follies o'er the town,
To sanction Vice, and hunt Decorum down.
English Bards and Scotch Reviewers (1809) l. 618

10 Lords too are bards, such things at times befall,
And 'tis some praise in peers to write at all.
English Bards and Scotch Reviewers (1809) l. 719

11 Let simple Wordsworth chime his childish verse,
And brother Coleridge lull the babe at nurse.
English Bards and Scotch Reviewers (1809) l. 917

12 And glory, like the phoenix midst her fires,
Exhales her odours, blazes, and expires.
English Bards and Scotch Reviewers (1809) l. 959

13 Dusky like night, but night with all her stars,
Or cavern sparkling with its native spars;
With eyes that were a language and a spell,
A form like Aphrodite's in her shell,
With all her loves around her on the deep,
Voluptuous as the first approach of sleep.
'The Island' (1823) canto 2, st. 7

14 Beside the jutting rock the few appeared,
Like the last remnant of the red-deer's herd;
Their eyes were feverish, and their aspect worn,
But still the hunter's blood was on their horn,
A little stream came tumbling from the height,
And straggling into ocean as it might,
Its bounding crystal frolicked in the ray,
And gushed from cliff to crag with saltless spray . . .
To this young spring they rushed,—all feelings first
Absorbed in passion's and in nature's thirst,—
Drank as they do who drink their last, and threw
Their arms aside to revel in its dew;
Cooled their scorched throats, and washed the gory
  stains
From wounds whose only bandage might be chains.
'The Island' (1823) canto 3, st. 3

15 Friendship is Love without his wings!
'L'Amitié est l'amour sans ailes' (written 1806, published
1831)

16 Sorrow is knowledge: they who know the most
Must mourn the deepest o'er the fatal truth,
The Tree of Knowledge is not that of Life.
Manfred (1817) act 1, sc. 1, l. 10

17 How beautiful is all this visible world!
How glorious in its action and itself!
But we, who name ourselves its sovereigns, we,
Half dust, half deity, alike unfit
To sink or soar, with our mixed essence make
A conflict of its elements, and breathe
The breath of degradation and of pride.
Manfred (1817) act 1, sc. 2, l. 37

18 I linger yet with nature, for the night
Hath been to me a more familiar face
Than that of man; and in her starry shade
Of dim and solitary loveliness
I learned the language of another world.
Manfred (1817) act 3, sc. 4, l. 2

19 Old man! 'tis not so difficult to die.
Manfred (2nd ed., 1819) act 3, sc. 4, l. 151

20   You have deeply ventured;
But all must do so who would greatly win.
Marino Faliero (1821) act 1, sc. 2

21 'Tis done—but yesterday a King!
And armed with Kings to strive—
And now thou art a nameless thing:
So abject—yet alive!
'Ode to Napoleon Bonaparte' (1814) st. 1

22 The arbiter of others' fate
A suppliant for his own!
'Ode to Napoleon Bonaparte' (1814) st. 5

23 The Cincinnatus of the West.
'Ode to Napoleon Bonaparte' (1814) st. 19 (of George
Washington)

24 It is not in the storm nor in the strife
We feel benumbed, and wish to be no more,
But in the after-silence on the shore,
When all is lost, except a little life.
'On hearing that Lady Byron was ill' (written 1816)

1 My days are in the yellow leaf;
  The flowers and fruits of love are gone;
  The worm, the canker, and the grief
  Are mine alone!
    'On This Day I Complete my Thirty-Sixth Year' (1824). Cf.
    Macbeth 604:21

2 My hair is grey, but not with years,
  Nor grew it white
  In a single night,
  As men's have grown from sudden fears.
    The Prisoner of Chillon (1816) st. 1

3 She walks in beauty, like the night
  Of cloudless climes and starry skies;
  And all that's best of dark and bright
  Meet in her aspect and her eyes:
  Thus mellowed to that tender light
  Which heaven to gaudy day denies.
    'She Walks in Beauty' (1815) st. 1

4 Born in the garret, in the kitchen bred,
  Promoted thence to deck her mistress' head.
    'A Sketch from Private Life' (1816)

5 Eternal spirit of the chainless mind!
  Brightest in dungeons, Liberty! thou art.
    'Sonnet on Chillon' (1816)

6 So, we'll go no more a-roving
  So late into the night,
  Though the heart be still as loving,
  And the moon be still as bright.
    'So we'll go no more a-roving' (written 1817)

7 There's not a joy the world can give like that it takes
  away.
    'Stanzas for Music' (1816)

8 Oh, talk not to me of a name great in story;
  The days of our youth are the days of our glory;
  And the myrtle and ivy of sweet two-and-twenty
  Are worth all your laurels, though ever so plenty.
    'Stanzas Written on the Road between Florence and Pisa,
    November 1821'

9 I knew it was love, and I felt it was glory.
    'Stanzas Written on the Road between Florence and Pisa,
    November 1821'

10 I am ashes where once I was fire.
    'To the Countess of Blessington' (written 1823)

11 Still I can't contradict, what has so oft been said,
   'Though women are angels, yet wedlock's the devil.'
    'To Eliza' (1806)

12 And when we think we lead, we are most led.
    The Two Foscari (1821) act 2, sc. 1, l. 361

13 The angels all were singing out of tune,
   And hoarse with having little else to do,
   Excepting to wind up the sun and moon,
   Or curb a runaway young star or two.
    The Vision of Judgement (1822) st. 2

14 And when the gorgeous coffin was laid low,
   It seemed the mockery of hell to fold
   The rottenness of eighty years in gold.
    The Vision of Judgement (1822) st. 10 (on the burial of
    George III)

15 In whom his qualities are reigning still,
   Except that household virtue, most uncommon,
   Of constancy to a bad, ugly woman.
    The Vision of Judgement (1822) st. 12

16 As he drew near, he gazed upon the gate
   Ne'er to be entered more by him or Sin,
   With such a glance of supernatural hate,
   As made Saint Peter wish himself within;
   He pattered with his keys at a great rate,
   And sweated through his apostolic skin:
   Of course his perspiration was but ichor,
   Or some such other spiritual liquor.
    The Vision of Judgement (1822) st. 25

17 Yet still between his Darkness and his Brightness
   There passed a mutual glance of great politeness.
    The Vision of Judgement (1822) st. 35

18   Satan met his ancient friend
   With more hauteur, as might an old Castilian
   Poor noble meet a mushroom rich civilian.
    The Vision of Judgement (1822) st. 36

19 And when the tumult dwindled to a calm,
   I left him practising the hundredth psalm.
    The Vision of Judgement (1822) st. 106

20 When we two parted
   In silence and tears,
   Half broken-hearted
   To sever for years,
   Pale grew thy cheek and cold,
   Colder thy kiss.
    'When we two parted' (1816)

21 If I should meet thee
   After long years,
   How should I greet thee?—
   With silence and tears.
    'When we two parted' (1816)

22 The man is mad, Sir, mad, frightful as a Mandrake,
   and lean as a rutting Stag, and all about a bitch not
   worth a Bank token.
    Of the Revd Robert Bland in a letter to John Cam
    Hobhouse, 16 November 1811; in L. A. Marchand (ed.)
    Byron's Letters and Journals vol. 2 (1973)

23 My Princess of Parallelograms.
    Of Annabella Milbanke, a keen amateur mathematician, in
    a letter to Lady Melbourne, 18 October 1812; in L. A.
    Marchand (ed.) Byron's Letters and Journals vol. 2 (1973).
    Byron explains: 'Her proceedings are quite rectangular, or
    rather we are two parallel lines prolonged to infinity side by
    side but never to meet'

24 We have progressively improved into a less spiritual
   species of tenderness—but the seal is not yet fixed
   though the wax is preparing for the impression.
    Of his relationship with Lady Frances Webster, in a letter to
    Lady Melbourne, 14 October 1813; in L. A. Marchand (ed.)
    Byron's Letters and Journals vol. 3 (1974)

25 I by no means rank poetry high in the scale of
   intelligence—this may look like affectation—but it is
   my real opinion—it is the lava of the imagination
   whose eruption prevents an earthquake.
    Letter to Annabella Milbanke, 29 November 1813, in L. A.
    Marchand (ed.) Byron's Letters and Journals vol. 3 (1974)

26 I prefer the talents of action—of war—of the
   senate—or even of science—to all the speculations of
   those mere dreamers of another existence.
    Letter to Annabella Milbanke, 29 November 1813, in L. A.
    Marchand (ed.) Byron's Letters and Journals vol. 3 (1974)

1 What is hope? nothing but the paint on the face of Existence; the least touch of truth rubs it off, and then we see what a hollow-cheeked harlot we have got hold of.
> Letter to Thomas Moore, 28 October 1815, in L. A. Marchand (ed.) *Byron's Letters and Journals* vol. 4 (1975)

2 Like other parties of the kind, it was first silent, then talky, then argumentative, then disputatious, then unintelligible, then altogethery, then inarticulate, and then drunk.
> Letter to Thomas Moore, 31 October 1815, in L. A. Marchand (ed.) *Byron's Letters and Journals* vol. 4 (1975)

3 Wordsworth—stupendous genius! damned fool! These poets run about their ponds though they cannot fish.
> Fragment of a letter to James Hogg, recorded in the diary of Henry Crabb Robinson, 1 December 1816; in L. A. Marchand (ed.) *Byron's Letters and Journals* vol. 5 (1976) p. 13

4 Love in this part of the world is no sinecure.
> Letter to John Murray from Venice, 27 December 1816, in L. A. Marchand (ed.) *Byron's Letters and Journals* vol. 5 (1976)

5 I hate things all *fiction* . . . there should always be some foundation of fact for the most airy fabric and pure invention is but the talent of a liar.
> Letter to John Murray from Venice, 2 April 1817; in L. A. Marchand (ed.) *Byron's Letters and Journals* vol. 5 (1976)

6 Is it not *life*, is it not *the thing*?—Could any man have written it—who has not lived in the world?—and tooled in a post-chaise? in a hackney coach? in a gondola? Against a wall? in a court carriage? in a *vis-à-vis*?—on a table?—and under it?
> Of *Don Juan*, in a letter to Douglas Kinnaird, 26 October 1819; in L. A. Marchand (ed.) *Byron's Letters and Journals* vol. 6 (1978)

7 The reading or non-reading a book—will never keep down a single petticoat.
> Letter to Richard Hoppner, 29 October 1819, in L. A. Marchand (ed.) *Byron's Letters and Journals* vol. 6 (1978)

8 Such writing is a sort of mental masturbation—he is always f—gg—g his *imagination*.—I don't mean that he is indecent but viciously soliciting his own ideas into a state which is neither poetry nor any thing else but a Bedlam vision produced by raw pork and opium.
> Of Keats, in a letter to John Murray, 9 November 1820; in L. A. Marchand (ed.) *Byron's Letters and Journals* vol. 7 (1979)

9 I awoke one morning and found myself famous.
> On the instantaneous success of *Childe Harold*, in Thomas Moore *Letters and Journals of Lord Byron* (1830) vol. 1, p. 346

10 You should have a softer pillow than my heart.
> To his wife, who had rested her head on his breast, in E. C. Mayne (ed.) *The Life and Letters of Anne Isabella, Lady Noel Byron* (1929) ch. 11

James Branch Cabell 1879–1958

American novelist and essayist

11 A man possesses nothing certainly save a brief loan of his own body.
> *Jurgen* (1919) ch. 20

12 The optimist proclaims that we live in the best of all possible worlds; and the pessimist fears this is true.
> *The Silver Stallion* (1926) bk. 4, ch. 26

Augustus Caesar

See AUGUSTUS

Irving Caesar 1895–

American songwriter

13 Picture you upon my knee,
Just tea for two and two for tea.
> 'Tea for Two' (1925 song)

Julius Caesar 100–44 BC

Roman general and statesman

14 *Gallia est omnis divisa in partes tres.*
Gaul as a whole is divided into three parts.
> *De Bello Gallico* bk. 1, sect. 1

15 *Fere libenter homines id quod volunt credunt.*
Men are nearly always willing to believe what they wish.
> *De Bello Gallico* bk. 3, sect. 18

16 Caesar's wife must be above suspicion.
> Oral tradition, based on Plutarch *Parallel Lives* 'Julius Caesar' ch. 10, sect. 9

17 Caesar, when he first went into Gaul, made no scruple to profess 'That he had rather be first in a village than second at Rome'.
> Francis Bacon *The Advancement of Learning* pt. 2, ch. 23, sect. 36 (based on Plutarch *Parallel Lives* 'Julius Caesar' ch. 11)

18 Καίσαρα φέρεις καὶ τὴν Καίσαρος τύχην συμπλέουσαν.
Thou hast Caesar and his fortune with thee.
> Plutarch *Parallel Lives* 'Julius Caesar' ch. 38, sect. 3 (translated by T. North, 1579; literally 'You are carrying Caesar, and his fortune is in the same boat')

19 The die is cast.
> At the crossing of the Rubicon, in Suetonius *Lives of the Caesars* 'Divus Julius' sect. 32 (often quoted in Latin 'Iacta alea est' but originally spoken in Greek). See Plutarch *Parallel Lives* 'Pompey' ch. 60, sect. 2

20 *Veni, vidi, vici.*
I came, I saw, I conquered.
> Inscription displayed in Caesar's Pontic triumph, according to Suetonius *Lives of the Caesars* 'Divus Julius' sect. 37; or, according to Plutarch *Parallel Lives* 'Julius Caesar' ch. 50, sect. 2, written in a letter by Caesar, announcing the victory of Zela which concluded the Pontic campaign

21 *Et tu, Brute?*
You too, Brutus?
> Traditional rendering of Suetonius *Lives of the Caesars* 'Divus Julius' sect. 82: 'Some have written that when Marcus Brutus rushed at him, he said in Greek, "You too, my child [καὶ σύ, τέκνον]?" ' Cf. *Julius Caesar* 591:13

John Cage 1912–

American composer, pianist, and writer

22
>   I have nothing to say
>   and I am saying it   and that is
> poetry.
> 'Lecture on nothing' (1961)

James M. Cain 1892–1977
American novelist

1 The postman always rings twice.
  Title of novel (1934)

Sir Joseph Cairns 1920–
British industrialist and politician

2 The betrayal of Ulster, the cynical and entirely
  undemocratic banishment of its properly elected
  Parliament and a relegation to the status of a fuzzy
  wuzzy colony is, I hope, a last betrayal contemplated
  by Downing Street because it is the last that Ulster will
  countenance.
  Speech on retiring as Lord Mayor of Belfast, 31 May 1972,
  in *Daily Telegraph* 1 June 1972

Pedro Calderón de La Barca 1600–81
Spanish dramatist and poet

3 . . . *Aun en sueños*
  no se pierde el hacer bien.

  Even in dreams good works are not wasted.
  La Vida es Sueño (1636) 'Segunda Jornada' l. 2146

4 *¿Qué es la vida? Un frenesí.*
  ¿Qué es la vida? Una ilusión,
  una sombra, una ficción,
  y el mayor bien es pequeño;
  que toda la vida es sueño,
  y los sueños, sueños son.

  What is life? a frenzy. What is life? An illusion, a
  shadow, a fiction. And the greatest good is of slight
  worth, as all life is a dream, and dreams are dreams.
  La Vida es Sueño (1636) 'Segunda Jornada' l. 2183. Cf.
  Montaigne 481:10

Caligula (Gaius Julius Caesar Germanicus)
AD 12–41
Roman emperor from AD 37

5 *Utinam populus Romanus unam cervicem haberet!*
  Would that the Roman people had but one neck!
  In Suetonius *Lives of the Caesars* 'Gaius Caligula' sect. 30

6 *Ita feri ut se mori sentiat.*
  Strike him so that he can feel that he is dying.
  In Suetonius *Lives of the Caesars* 'Gaius Caligula' sect. 30

Callimachus c.305–c.240 BC
Hellenistic poet and scholar

7 μισῶ καὶ περίφοιτον ἐρώμενον, οὐδ' ἀπὸ κρήνης πίνω·
  σικχαίνω πάντα τὰ δημόσια.

  I abhor, too, the roaming lover, nor do I drink from
  every well; I loathe all things held in common.
  In R. Pfeiffer (ed.) *Callimachus* (1949–53) Epigram 28

8 μέγα βιβλίον ἴσον τῷ μεγάλῳ κακῷ.
  A great book is like great evil.
  In R. Pfeiffer (ed.) *Callimachus* (1949–53) Fragment 465
  (proverbially contracted 'Great book, great evil')

Charles Alexandre de Calonne
1734–1802

9 *Madame, si c'est possible, c'est fait; impossible? cela se
  fera.*

  Madam, if a thing is possible, consider it done; the
  impossible? that will be done.
  In J. Michelet *Histoire de la Révolution Française* (1847)
  vol. 1, pt. 2, sect. 8; better known as the US Armed Forces'
  slogan: 'The difficult we do immediately; the impossible
  takes a little longer.' Cf. Nansen 489:8

C. S. Calverley (born Blayds) 1831–84
English writer

10 The farmer's daughter hath soft brown hair;
  (*Butter and eggs and a pound of cheese*)
  And I met with a ballad, I can't say where,
  Which wholly consisted of lines like these.
  'Ballad' (1872)

11 And this song is considered a perfect gem,
  And as to the meaning, it's what you please.
  'Ballad' (1872)

12 O Beer! O Hodgson, Guinness, Allsopp, Bass!
  Names that should be on every infant's tongue!
  'Beer' (1861)

13 Life is with such all beer and skittles;
  They are not difficult to please
  About their victuals.
  'Contentment' (1872)

14 For king-like rolls the Rhine,
  And the scenery's divine,
  And the victuals and the wine
  Rather good.
  'Dover to Munich' (1861)

15 For I've read in many a novel that, unless they've
  souls that grovel,
  Folks *prefer* in fact a hovel to your dreary marble halls.
  'In the Gloaming' (1872). Cf. Bunn 155:7

16 How Eugene Aram, though a thief, a liar, and a
  murderer,
  Yet, being intellectual, was amongst the noblest of
  mankind.
  'Of Reading' (1861)

Italo Calvino 1923–85
Italian novelist and short-story writer

17 *Lo sguardo dei cani che non capiscono e non sanno che
  possono aver ragione a non capire.*

  The gaze of dogs who don't understand and who don't
  know that they may be right not to understand.
  Il Barone Rampante (1957) ch. 10

18 *I rivoluzionari sono più formalisti dei conservatori.*

  Revolutionaries are more formalistic than
  conservatives.
  Il Barone Rampante (1957) ch. 28

Pierre, Baron de Cambronne 1770–1842

French general

1 *La Garde meurt, mais ne se rend pas.*

The Guards die but do not surrender.

> Attributed to Cambronne when called upon to surrender at Waterloo, 1815, but later denied by him. See H. Houssaye *La Garde meurt et ne se rend pas* (1907)

Lord Camden (*Charles Pratt, 1st Earl Camden*) 1714–94

British Whig politician; Lord Chancellor, 1766–70

2 Taxation and representation are inseparable . . . whatever is a man's own, is absolutely his own; no man hath a right to take it from him without his consent either expressed by himself or representative; whoever attempts to do it, attempts an injury; whoever does it, commits a robbery; he throws down and destroys the distinction between liberty and slavery.

> Speech in the House of Lords, on the taxation of Americans by the British parliament; *Hansard* 10 February 1766, col. 177. Cf. Otis 502:7

William Camden 1551–1623

English antiquary and historian

3 A gentleman falling off his horse brake his neck . . . A good friend made this good epitaph . . .

My friend, judge not me,
Thou seest I judge not thee.
Betwixt the stirrup and the ground
Mercy I asked, mercy I found.

> *Remains Concerning Britain* (1605) 'Epitaphs'

Jane Montgomery Campbell 1817–78

English hymn-writer

4 We plough the fields, and scatter
The good seed on the land,
But it is fed and watered
By God's almighty hand;
He sends the snow in winter,
The warmth to swell the grain,
The breezes and the sunshine,
And soft refreshing rain.

> 'We plough the fields, and scatter' (1861 hymn); translated from the German of Matthias Claudius (1740–1815)

Mrs Patrick Campbell (*Beatrice Stella Tanner*) 1865–1940

English actress

5 It doesn't matter what you do in the bedroom as long as you don't do it in the street and frighten the horses.

> In Daphne Fielding *The Duchess of Jermyn Street* (1964) ch. 2

6 The deep, deep peace of the double-bed after the hurly-burly of the chaise-longue.

> On her recent marriage, in Alexander Woollcott *While Rome Burns* (1934) 'The First Mrs Tanqueray'

Roy Campbell 1901–57

South African poet

7   Giraffes!—a People
Who live between the earth and skies,
Each in his lone religious steeple,
Keeping a light-house with his eyes.

> 'Dreaming Spires' (1946)

8 You praise the firm restraint with which they write—
I'm with you there, of course:
They use the snaffle and the curb all right,
But where's the bloody horse?

> 'On Some South African Novelists' (1930)

Thomas Campbell 1777–1844

Scottish poet

9 There was silence deep as death,
And the boldest held his breath
For a time.

> 'Battle of the Baltic' (1809)

10 Let us think of them that sleep,
Full many a fathom deep,
By thy wild and stormy steep,
Elsinore!

> 'Battle of the Baltic' (1809)

11 O leave this barren spot to me!
Spare, woodman, spare the beechen tree.

> 'The Beech-Tree's Petition' (1800). Cf. Morris 485:8

12 To-morrow let us do or die!

> 'Gertrude of Wyoming' (1809) pt. 3, st. 37

13 On the green banks of Shannon, when Sheelah was nigh,
No blithe Irish lad was so happy as I;
No harp like my own could so cheerily play,
And wherever I went was my poor dog Tray.

> 'The Harper' (1799)

14 Better be courted and jilted
Than never be courted at all.

> 'The Jilted Nymph' (1843)

15 A chieftain to the Highlands bound
Cries, 'Boatman, do not tarry!
And I'll give thee a silver pound
To row us o'er the ferry.'

> 'Lord Ullin's Daughter' (1809)

16 'Tis distance lends enchantment to the view,
And robes the mountain in its azure hue.

> *Pleasures of Hope* (1799) pt. 1, l. 7

17 Hope, for a season, bade the world farewell,
And Freedom shrieked—as Kosciusko fell!

> *Pleasures of Hope* (1799) pt. 1, l. 381

18 What millions died—that Caesar might be great!

> *Pleasures of Hope* (1799) pt. 2, l. 174

19 What though my wingèd hours of bliss have been,
Like angel-visits, few and far between?

> *Pleasures of Hope* (1799) pt. 2, l. 375

20 An original something, fair maid, you would win me
To write—but how shall I begin?
For I fear I have nothing original in me—
Excepting Original Sin.

> 'To a Young Lady, Who Asked Me to Write Something Original for Her Album' (1843)

1 With thunders from her native oak
She quells the floods below.
'Ye Mariners of England' (1801)

2 Now Barabbas was a publisher.

Attributed, in Samuel Smiles *A Publisher and his Friends:
Memoir and Correspondence of the late John Murray* vol. 1,
ch. 14; also attributed, wrongly, to Byron. See *Notes and
Queries* 11th series, vol. 2, 30 July 1910, p. 92

Thomas Campion 1567–1620

English poet and musician

3 My sweetest Lesbia let us live and love,
And though the sager sort our deeds reprove,
Let us not weigh them: Heav'n's great lamps do dive
Into their west, and straight again revive,
But soon as once set is our little light,
Then must we sleep one ever-during night.
A Book of Airs (1601) no. 1 'My sweetest Lesbia'
(translation of Catullus *Carmina* no. 5). Cf. Catullus
185:15

4 When timely death my life and fortune ends,
Let not my hearse be vexed with mourning friends
But let all lovers, rich in triumph, come
And with sweet pastimes grace my happy tomb.
And, Lesbia, close up thou my little light,
And crown with love my ever-during night.
A Book of Airs (1601) no. 1 'My sweetest Lesbia'

5 When to her lute Corinna sings,
Her voice revives the leaden strings,
And both in highest notes appear,
As any challenged echo clear.
But when she doth of mourning speak,
Ev'n with her sighs the strings do break.
A Book of Airs (1601) no. 6

6 Follow your Saint, follow with accents sweet;
Haste you, sad notes, fall at her flying feet.
A Book of Airs (1601) no. 10

7 Good thoughts his only friends,
His wealth a well-spent age,
The earth his sober inn
And quiet pilgrimage.
A Book of Airs (1601) no. 18

8 Rose-cheeked Laura, come;
Sing thou smoothly with thy beauty's
Silent music, either other
Sweetly gracing.
'Rose-cheeked Laura' (1602)

9 Kind are her answers,
But her performance keeps no day;
Breaks time, as dancers
From their own music when they stray.
The Third Book of Airs (1617) no. 7

Albert Camus 1913–60

French novelist, playwright, and essayist

10 *Intellectuel = celui qui se dédouble.*
An intellectual is someone whose mind watches itself.
Carnets, 1935–42 (1962) p. 41

11 *La politique et le sort des hommes sont formés par des
hommes sans idéal et sans grandeur. Ceux qui ont une
grandeur en eux ne font pas de politique.*
Politics and the fate of mankind are formed by men
without ideals and without greatness. Those who have
greatness within them do not go in for politics.
Carnets, 1935–42 (1962) p. 99

12 *Vous savez ce qu'est le charme: une manière de s'entendre
répondre oui sans avoir posé aucune question claire.*
You know what charm is: a way of getting the
answer yes without having asked any clear question.
La Chute (1956) p. 62

13 *Nous sommes tous des cas exceptionnels. Nous voulons
tous faire appel de quelque chose! Chacun exige d'être
innocent, à tout prix, même si, pour cela, il faut accuser le
genre humain et le ciel.*
We are all special cases. We all want to appeal against
something! Everyone insists on his innocence, at all
costs, even if it means accusing the rest of the human
race and heaven.
La Chute (1956) p. 95

14 *Nous nous confions rarement à ceux qui sont meilleurs que
nous.*
We seldom confide in those who are better than
ourselves.
La Chute (1956) p. 97

15 *Je vais vous dire un grand secret, mon cher. N'attendez pas
le jugement dernier. Il a lieu tous les jours.*
I'll tell you a great secret, my friend. Don't wait for
the last judgement. It happens every day.
La Chute (1956) p. 129

16 *Aujourd'hui, maman est morte. Ou peut-être hier, je ne
sais pas.*
Mother died today. Or perhaps it was yesterday, I
don't know.
L'Étranger (1944) p. 9

17 *Qu'est-ce qu'un homme révolté ? Un homme qui dit non.*
What is a rebel? A man who says no.
L'Homme révolté (1951) p. 25

18 *Toutes les révolutions modernes ont abouti à un
renforcement de l'État.*
All modern revolutions have ended in a reinforcement
of the State.
L'Homme révolté (1951) p. 221

19 *Tout révolutionnaire finit en oppresseur ou en hérétique.*
Every revolutionary ends as an oppressor or a heretic.
L'Homme révolté (1951) p. 306

20 *Sisyphe, prolétaire des dieux, impuissant et révolté,
connaît toute l'entendue de sa misérable condition: c'est à
elle qu'il pense pendant sa descente. La clairvoyance qui
devait faire son tourment consomme du même coup sa
victoire. Il n'est pas de destin que ne se surmonte par le
mépris.*
Sisyphus, proletarian of the gods, powerless and
rebellious, knows the whole extent of his wretched
condition; it is what he thinks of during his descent.
The lucidity that was to constitute his torture at the
same time crowns his victory. There is no fate that
cannot be surmounted by scorn.
Le Mythe de Sisyphe (1942) p. 165 (translated by Justin
O'Brien)

1 *La lutte elle-même vers les sommets suffit à remplir un cœur d'homme. Il faut imaginer Sisyphe heureux.*

The struggle itself towards the heights is enough to fill a human heart. One must imagine that Sisyphus is happy.

    Le Mythe de Sisyphe (1942) p. 168

Elias Canetti 1905–

Bulgarian-born writer and novelist

2 *Alles was man vergessen hat, schreit im Traum um Hilfe.*

All the things one has forgotten scream for help in dreams.

    Die Provinz der Menschen (1973) p. 269

George Canning 1770–1827

British Tory politician; Prime Minister, 1827

3 In matters of commerce the fault of the Dutch
Is offering too little and asking too much.
The French are with equal advantage content,
So we clap on Dutch bottoms just twenty per cent.

    Dispatch, in cipher, to the English ambassador at the Hague, 31 January 1826; in Sir Harry Poland *Mr Canning's Rhyming 'Dispatch' to Sir Charles Bagot* (1905)

4 A steady patriot of the world alone,
The friend of every country but his own.

    On the Jacobin, in 'New Morality' (1821) l. 113. Cf. Disraeli 247:26, Overbury 502:10

5 And finds, with keen discriminating sight,
Black's not so black;—nor white so very white.

    'New Morality' (1821) l. 199

6 Give me the avowed, erect and manly foe;
Firm I can meet, perhaps return the blow;
But of all plagues, good Heaven, thy wrath can send,
Save me, oh, save me, from the candid friend.

    'New Morality' (1821) l. 207

7 Pitt is to Addington
As London is to Paddington.

    'The Oracle' (*c.*1803)

8 Man, only—rash, refined, presumptuous man,
Starts from his rank, and mars creation's plan.

    'The Progress of Man' (1799) l. 55

9 Whene'er with haggard eyes I view
This Dungeon, that I'm rotting in,
I think of those Companions true
Who studied with me at the U-
-NIVERSITY OF GOTTINGEN,-
-NIVERSITY OF GOTTINGEN.

    'Song'

10 Away with the cant of 'Measures not men'!—the idle supposition that it is the harness and not the horses that draw the chariot along. If the comparison must be made, if the distinction must be taken, men are everything, measures comparatively nothing.

    Speech on the Army estimates, 8 December 1802, in *Speeches of . . . Canning* (1828) vol. 2, p. 61. The phrase 'measures not men' may be found as early as 1742 (in a letter from Chesterfield to Dr Chevenix, 6 March); also in Goldsmith *The Good Natured Man* (1768) act 2, sc. 1: 'Measures not men, have always been my mark'

11 I called the New World into existence, to redress the balance of the Old.

    Speech on the affairs of Portugal, in *Hansard* 12 December 1826, col. 397

12 You well know how soon one of these stupendous masses, now reposing on their shadows in perfect stillness, would upon any call of patriotism or of necessity, assume the likeness of an animated thing, instinct with life and motion: how soon it would ruffle, as it were its swelling plumage, how quickly it would put forth all its beauty and its bravery, collect its scattered elements of strength and waken its dormant thunder . . . Such is England herself; while apparently passive and motionless, she silently concentrates the power to be put forth on an adequate occasion.

    Speech at Plymouth, 12 December 1823, on the men-of-war lying at anchor in the harbour; in R. W. Seton-Watson *Britain in Europe 1789–1914* (1945) p. 85

Hughie Cannon 1877–1912

American songwriter

13 Won't you come home Bill Bailey, won't you come home?

    'Bill Bailey, Won't You Please Come Home' (1902 song)

Truman Capote 1924–84

American writer and novelist

14 Other voices, other rooms.

    Title of novel (1948)

Al Capp (*Alfred Gerard Caplin*) 1907–79

American cartoonist

15 A product of the untalented, sold by the unprincipled to the utterly bewildered.

    On abstract art, in *National Observer* 1 July 1963. Cf. Zappa 755:9

Francesco Caracciolo 1752–99

Neapolitan diplomat

16 *Il y a en Angleterre soixante sectes religieuses différentes, et une seule sauce.*

In England there are sixty different religions, and only one sauce.

    Attributed. See *Notes and Queries* December 1968

Ethna Carbery (*Anna MacManus*) 1866–1902

Irish poet

17 Oh, Kathaleen Ní Houlihan, your road's a thorny way,
And 'tis a faithful soul would walk the flints with you for aye,
Would walk the sharp and cruel flints until his locks grew grey.

    'The Passing of the Gael' (1902)

Richard Carew 1555–1620
English poet

1 Will you have all in all for prose and verse? Take the miracle of our age, Sir Philip Sidney.

> In William Camden *Remains concerning Britain* (1614) 'The Excellency of the English Tongue'

Thomas Carew c.1595–1640
English poet and courtier

2 He that loves a rosy cheek,
Or a coral lip admires,
Or, from star-like eyes, doth seek
Fuel to maintain his fires;
As old Time makes these decay,
So his flames must waste away.

> 'Disdain Returned' (1640)

3 The Muses' garden with pedantic weeds
O'erspread, was purged by thee; the lazy seeds
Of servile imitation thrown away,
And fresh invention planted.

> 'An Elegy upon the Death of Dr John Donne' (1640)

4 Here lies a king, that ruled as he thought fit
The universal monarchy of wit.

> 'An Elegy upon the Death of Dr John Donne' (1640)

5 The purest soul that e'er was sent
Into a clayey tenement.

> 'Epitaph On the Lady Mary Villiers' (1640)

6 Know, Celia (since thou art so proud),
'Twas I that gave thee thy renown.
Thou had'st in the forgotten crowd
Of common beauties lived unknown,
Had not my verse extolled thy name,
And with it imped the wings of fame.

> 'Ingrateful Beauty Threatened' (1640)

7 Good to the poor, to kindred dear,
To servants kind, to friendship clear,
To nothing but herself severe.

> 'Inscription on the Tomb of Lady Mary Wentworth' (1640)

8 So though a virgin, yet a bride
To every Grace, she justified
A chaste polygamy, and died.

> 'Inscription on the Tomb of Lady Mary Wentworth' (1640)

9 Give me more love or more disdain;
The torrid or the frozen zone:
Bring equal ease unto my pain;
The temperate affords me none.

> 'Mediocrity in Love Rejected' (1640)

10 Though a stranger to this place,
Bewail in theirs thine own hard case:
For thou perhaps at thy return
Mayst find thy darling in an urn.

> 'On the Lady Mary Villiers' (1640)

11 Ask me no more where Jove bestows,
When June is past, the fading rose;
For in your beauty's orient deep
These flowers, as in their causes, sleep.

> 'A Song' (1640)

12 Ask me no more whither doth haste
The nightingale when May is past;
For in your sweet dividing throat
She winters and keeps warm her note.

> 'A Song' (1640)

13 Ask me no more if east or west
The Phoenix builds her spicy nest;
For unto you at last she flies,
And in your fragrant bosom dies.

> 'A Song' (1640)

14 When thou, poor excommunicate
From all the joys of love, shalt see
The full reward and glorious fate
Which my strong faith shall purchase me,
Then curse thine own inconstancy.

> 'To My Inconstant Mistress' (1640)

George Carey 1935–
Archbishop of Canterbury from 1991

15 I see it as an elderly lady, who mutters away to herself in a corner, ignored most of the time.

> On the Church of England, in *Readers Digest* (British ed.) March 1991, p. 41

Henry Carey c.1687–1743
English comic playwright and songwriter

16 Let your little verses flow
Gently, sweetly, row by row;
Let the verse the subject fit,
Little subject, little wit.

> 'Namby-Pamby: or, A Panegyric on the New Versification' (1725)

17 As an actor does his part,
So the nurses get by heart
Namby-pamby's little rhymes,
Little jingle, little chimes.

> 'Namby-Pamby' (1725)

18 Of all the girls that are so smart
There's none like pretty Sally,
She is the darling of my heart,
And she lives in our alley.

> 'Sally in our Alley' (1729)

Jane Carlyle (née Welsh) 1801–66
Wife of Thomas Carlyle

19 I am not at all the sort of person you and I took me for.

> Letter to Thomas Carlyle, 7 May 1822, in C. R. Sanders et al. (eds.) *Collected Letters of Thomas and Jane Welsh Carlyle* (1970) vol. 2

Thomas Carlyle 1795–1881
Scottish historian and political philosopher

20 A witty statesman said, you might prove anything by figures.

> *Chartism* (1839) ch. 2

1 Surely of all 'rights of man', this right of the ignorant man to be guided by the wiser, to be, gently or forcibly, held in the true course by him, is the indisputablest.
   Chartism (1839) ch. 6

2 In epochs when cash payment has become the sole nexus of man to man.
   Chartism (1839) ch. 6

3 The 'golden-calf of self-love.'
   Critical and Miscellaneous Essays (1838) 'Burns'

4 The foul sluggard's comfort: 'It will last my time.'
   Critical and Miscellaneous Essays (1838) 'Count Cagliostro. Flight Last'

5 Thou wretched fraction, wilt thou be the ninth part even of a tailor?
   Critical and Miscellaneous Essays (1838) 'Francia'

6 What is all knowledge too but recorded experience, and a product of history; of which, therefore, reasoning and belief, no less than action and passion, are essential materials?
   Critical and Miscellaneous Essays (1838) 'On History'

7 History is the essence of innumerable biographies.
   Critical and Miscellaneous Essays (1838) 'On History'

8 A well-written Life is almost as rare as a well-spent one.
   Critical and Miscellaneous Essays (1838) 'Jean Paul Friedrich Richter'

9 There is no life of a man, faithfully recorded, but is a heroic poem of its sort, rhymed or unrhymed.
   Critical and Miscellaneous Essays (1838) 'Sir Walter Scott'

10 Under all speech that is good for anything there lies a silence that is better. Silence is deep as Eternity; speech is shallow as Time.
   Critical and Miscellaneous Essays (1838) 'Sir Walter Scott'

11 To the very last he [Napoleon] had a kind of idea; that, namely, of *La carrière ouverte aux talents*, The tools to him that can handle them.
   Critical and Miscellaneous Essays (1838) 'Sir Walter Scott' (*La carrière ...* Career open to the talents)

12 It can be said of him, when he departed, he took a man's life along with him.
   Critical and Miscellaneous Essays (1838) 'Sir Walter Scott'

13 This idle habit of 'accounting for the moral sense' ... The moral sense, thank God, is a thing you will never 'account for' ... By no greatest happiness principle, greatest nobleness principle, or any principle whatever, will you make that in the least clearer than it already is.
   Critical and Miscellaneous Essays (1838) 'Shooting Niagara: and After?'

14 It is the Age of Machinery, in every outward and inward sense of that word.
   Critical and Miscellaneous Essays (1838) 'Signs of the Times'

15 The Bible-Society ... is found, on inquiry, to be ... a machine for converting the Heathen.
   Critical and Miscellaneous Essays (1838) 'Signs of the Times'

16 Thought, he [Dr Cabanis] is inclined to hold, is still secreted by the brain; but then Poetry and Religion (and it is really worth knowing) are 'a product of the smaller intestines'!
   Critical and Miscellaneous Essays (1838) 'Signs of the Times'

17 The three great elements of modern civilization, Gunpowder, Printing, and the Protestant Religion.
   Critical and Miscellaneous Essays (1838) 'The State of German Literature'. Cf. Bacon 45:21

18 'Genius' (which means transcendent capacity of taking trouble, first of all).
   History of Frederick the Great (1858–65) bk. 4, ch. 3. Cf. Buffon 154:16

19 A whiff of grapeshot.
   History of the French Revolution (1837) vol. 1, bk. 5, ch. 3

20 History a distillation of rumour.
   History of the French Revolution (1837) vol. 1, bk. 7, ch. 5

21 The difference between Orthodoxy or My-doxy and Heterodoxy or Thy-doxy.
   History of the French Revolution (1837) vol. 2, bk. 4, ch. 2

22 The seagreen Incorruptible.
   Describing Robespierre, in *History of the French Revolution* (1837) vol. 2, bk. 4, ch. 4

23 France was long a despotism tempered by epigrams.
   History of the French Revolution (1837) vol. 3, bk. 7, ch. 7

24 Aristocracy of the Moneybag.
   History of the French Revolution (1837) vol. 3, bk. 7, ch. 7

25 Worship is transcendent wonder.
   On Heroes, Hero-Worship, and the Heroic (1841) 'The Hero as Divinity'

26 I hope we English will long maintain our *grand talent pour le silence*.
   On Heroes, Hero-Worship, and the Heroic (1841) 'The Hero as King'

27 In books lies the *soul* of the whole Past Time; the articulate audible voice of the Past, when the body and material substance of it has altogether vanished like a dream.
   On Heroes, Hero-Worship, and the Heroic (1841) 'The Hero as Man of Letters'

28 The true University of these days is a collection of books.
   On Heroes, Hero-Worship, and the Heroic (1841) 'The Hero as Man of Letters'

29 Adversity is sometimes hard upon a man; but for one man who can stand prosperity, there are a hundred that will stand adversity.
   On Heroes, Hero-Worship, and the Heroic (1841) 'The Hero as Man of Letters'

30 Maid-servants, I hear people complaining, are getting instructed in the 'ologies'.
   Inaugural Address at Edinburgh, 2 April 1866, on being installed as Rector of the University

31 A Parliament speaking through reporters to Buncombe and the twenty-seven millions mostly fools.
   Latter-Day Pamphlets (1850) 'Parliaments'. Cf. Walker 717:15

32 The Dismal Science.
   On political economy, in *Latter-Day Pamphlets* (1850) 'The Present Time'

1 Little other than a redtape talking-machine, and unhappy bag of parliamentary eloquence.

> Describing himself, in *Latter-Day Pamphlets* (1850) 'The Present Time'

2 Transcendental moonshine.

> *The Life of John Sterling* (1851) pt. 1, ch. 15 (on the influence of a romantic imagination in motivating Sterling to enter the priesthood)

3 Captains of industry.

> *Past and Present* (1843) bk. 4, ch. 4 (title)

4 He who first shortened the labour of copyists by device of *Movable Types* was disbanding hired armies, and cashiering most Kings and Senates, and creating a whole new democratic world: he had invented the art of printing.

> *Sartor Resartus* (1834) bk. 1, ch. 5

5 Man is a tool-using animal . . . Without tools he is nothing, with tools he is all.

> *Sartor Resartus* (1834) bk. 1, ch. 5

6 Whoso has sixpence is sovereign (to the length of sixpence) over all men; commands cooks to feed him, philosophers to teach him, kings to mount guard over him,—to the length of sixpence.

> *Sartor Resartus* (1834) bk. 1, ch. 5

7 Language is called the garment of thought: however, it should rather be, language is the flesh-garment, the body, of thought.

> *Sartor Resartus* (1834) bk. 1, ch. 11

8 The end of man is an action and not a thought, though it were the noblest.

> *Sartor Resartus* (1834) bk. 2, ch. 6

9 The everlasting No.

> *Sartor Resartus* (1834) bk. 2, ch. 7 (title)

10 Man's unhappiness, as I construe, comes of his greatness; it is because there is an Infinite in him, which with all his cunning he cannot quite bury under the Finite.

> *Sartor Resartus* (1834) bk. 2, ch. 9

11 Be no longer a chaos, but a world, or even worldkin. Produce! Produce! Were it but the pitifullest infinitesimal fraction of a product, produce it in God's name! 'Tis the utmost thou hast in thee: out with it, then.

> *Sartor Resartus* (1834) bk. 2, ch. 9

12 Does it not stand on record that the English Queen Elizabeth, receiving a deputation of eighteen tailors, address them with a 'Good morning, gentlemen both!'

> *Sartor Resartus* (1834) bk. 3, ch. 11, quoting an imaginary work by Diogenes Teufelsdröctch

13 A good book is the purest essence of a human soul.

> Speech in support of the London Library, 24 June 1840, in F. Harrison *Carlyle and the London Library* (1907) p. 66

14 'Gad! she'd better!'

> On hearing that Margaret Fuller 'accept[ed] the universe', in William James *Varieties of Religious Experience* (1902) lecture 2, p. 41

15 Macaulay is well for a while, but one wouldn't *live* under Niagara.

> In R. M. Milnes *Notebook* (1838) p. 157

16 Cobden is an inspired bagman, who believes in a calico millenium.

> In T. W. Reid *Life, Letters and Friendships of Richard Monckton* (1890) vol. 1, ch. 10

17 If Jesus Christ were to come to-day, people would not even crucify him. They would ask him to dinner, and hear what he had to say, and make fun of it.

> In D. A. Wilson *Carlyle at his Zenith* (1927) p. 238

Andrew Carnegie 1835–1919

American industrialist and philanthropist

18 The man who dies . . . rich dies disgraced.

> *North American Review* June 1889 'Wealth'

Dale Carnegie 1888–1955

American writer and lecturer

19 How to win friends and influence people.

> Title of book (1936)

Julia A. Carney 1823–1908

20 Little drops of water,
Little grains of sand,
Make the mighty ocean
And the beauteous land.

> 'Little Things' (1845)

Joseph Edwards Carpenter 1813–85

English poet and songwriter

21 What are the wild waves saying
Sister, the whole day long,
That ever amid our playing,
I hear but their low lone song?

> 'What are the Wild Waves Saying?' (1850 song)

J. L. Carr 1912–

English novelist

22 *You* have not had thirty years' experience . . . *You* have had one year's experience 30 times.

> *The Harpole Report* (1972) p. 128

Lewis Carroll (Charles Lutwidge Dodgson) 1832–98

English writer and logician

23 'What is the use of a book', thought Alice, 'without pictures or conversations?'

> *Alice's Adventures in Wonderland* (1865) ch. 1

24 'Curiouser and curiouser!' cried Alice.

> *Alice's Adventures in Wonderland* (1865) ch. 2

25 How doth the little crocodile
Improve his shining tail,
And pour the waters of the Nile
On every golden scale!

> *Alice's Adventures in Wonderland* (1865) ch. 2. Cf. Watts 722:12

1 How cheerfully he seems to grin,
How neatly spreads his claws,
And welcomes little fishes in
With gently smiling jaws!
Alice's Adventures in Wonderland (1865) ch. 2

2 'I'll be judge, I'll be jury,' said cunning old Fury;
'I'll try the whole cause, and condemn you to death.'
Alice's Adventures in Wonderland (1865) ch. 3

3 'You are old, Father William,' the young man said,
'And your hair has become very white;
And yet you incessantly stand on your head—
Do you think, at your age, it is right?'
Alice's Adventures in Wonderland (1865) ch. 5. Cf. Southey 657:13

4 'I have answered three questions, and that is enough,'
Said his father; 'don't give yourself airs!
Do you think I can listen all day to such stuff?
Be off, or I'll kick you downstairs!'
Alice's Adventures in Wonderland (1865) ch. 5. Cf. Bickerstaffe 108:19

5 Speak roughly to your little boy,
And beat him when he sneezes;
He only does it to annoy,
Because he knows it teases.
Alice's Adventures in Wonderland (1865) ch. 6

6 'Then you should say what you mean,' the March Hare went on. 'I do,' Alice hastily replied; 'at least—at least I mean what I say—that's the same thing, you know.' 'Not the same thing a bit!' said the Hatter. 'Why, you might just as well say that "I see what I eat" is the same thing as "I eat what I see!" '
Alice's Adventures in Wonderland (1865) ch. 7

7 Twinkle, twinkle, little bat!
How I wonder what you're at!
Up above the world you fly!
Like a teatray in the sky.
Alice's Adventures in Wonderland (1865) ch. 7. Cf. Taylor 679:14

8 'Take some more tea,' the March Hare said to Alice, very earnestly. 'I've had nothing yet,' Alice replied in an offended tone, 'so I can't take more.' 'You mean you can't take *less*,' said the Hatter: 'it's very easy to take *more* than nothing.'
Alice's Adventures in Wonderland (1865) ch. 7

9 Everything's got a moral, if you can only find it.
Alice's Adventures in Wonderland (1865) ch. 9

10 Take care of the sense, and the sounds will take care of themselves.
Alice's Adventures in Wonderland (1865) ch. 9. Cf. Lowndes 431:1

11 'That's nothing to what I could say if I chose,' the Duchess replied.
Alice's Adventures in Wonderland (1865) ch. 9

12 'That's the reason they're called lessons,' the Gryphon remarked: 'because they lessen from day to day.'
Alice's Adventures in Wonderland (1865) ch. 9

13 'Will you walk a little faster?' said a whiting to a snail,
'There's a porpoise close behind us, and he's treading on my tail.'
Alice's Adventures in Wonderland (1865) ch. 10

14 Will you, won't you, will you, won't you, will you join the dance?
Alice's Adventures in Wonderland (1865) ch. 10

15 'Where shall I begin, please your Majesty?' he asked. 'Begin at the beginning,' the King said, gravely, 'and go on till you come to the end: then stop.'
Alice's Adventures in Wonderland (1865) ch. 12

16 'That's not a regular rule: you invented it just now.' 'It's the oldest rule in the book,' said the King. 'Then it ought to be Number One,' said Alice.
Alice's Adventures in Wonderland (1865) ch. 12

17 No! No! Sentence first—verdict afterwards.
Alice's Adventures in Wonderland (1865) ch. 12

18 'Twas brillig, and the slithy toves
Did gyre and gimble in the wabe;
All mimsy were the borogoves,
And the mome raths outgrabe.

'Beware the Jabberwock, my son!
The jaws that bite, the claws that catch!'
Through the Looking-Glass (1872) ch. 1

19 And as in uffish thought he stood,
The Jabberwock, with eyes of flame,
Came whiffling through the tulgey wood,
And burbled as it came!

One, two! One, two! And through and through
The vorpal blade went snicker-snack!
He left it dead, and with its head
He went galumphing back.

'And hast thou slain the Jabberwock?
Come to my arms, my beamish boy!
O frabjous day! Callooh! Callay!'
He chortled in his joy.
Through the Looking-Glass (1872) ch. 1

20 Curtsey while you're thinking what to say. It saves time.
Through the Looking-Glass (1872) ch. 2

21 Now, *here*, you see, it takes all the running *you* can do, to keep in the same place. If you want to get somewhere else, you must run at least twice as fast as that!
Through the Looking-Glass (1872) ch. 2

22 Speak in French when you can't think of the English for a thing.
Through the Looking-Glass (1872) ch. 2

23 If you think we're wax-works, you ought to pay, you know. Wax-works weren't made to be looked at for nothing. Nohow!
Through the Looking-Glass (1872) ch. 4

24 'Contrariwise,' continued Tweedledee, 'if it was so, it might be; and if it were so, it would be: but as it isn't, it ain't. That's logic.'
Through the Looking-Glass (1872) ch. 4

1 The Walrus and the Carpenter
Were walking close at hand;
They wept like anything to see
Such quantities of sand:
'If this were only cleared away,'
They said, 'it would be grand!'

'If seven maids with seven mops
Swept it for half a year,
Do you suppose,' the Walrus said,
'That they could get it clear?'
'I doubt it,' said the Carpenter,
And shed a bitter tear.
Through the Looking-Glass (1872) ch. 4

2 'The time has come,' the Walrus said,
'To talk of many things:
Of shoes—and ships—and sealing wax—
Of cabbages—and kings—
And why the sea is boiling hot—
And whether pigs have wings.'
Through the Looking-Glass (1872) ch. 4

3 But answer came there none—
And this was scarcely odd because
They'd eaten every one.
Through the Looking-Glass (1872) ch. 4. Cf. Scott
559:7

4 'You know,' he said very gravely, 'it's one of the most
serious things that can possibly happen to one in a
battle—to get one's head cut off.'
Through the Looking-Glass (1872) ch. 4

5 The rule is, jam to-morrow and jam yesterday—but
never jam today.
Through the Looking-Glass (1872) ch. 5

6 'It's a poor sort of memory that only works
backwards,' the Queen remarked.
Through the Looking-Glass (1872) ch. 5

7 Consider anything, only don't cry!
Through the Looking-Glass (1872) ch. 5

8 Why, sometimes I've believed as many as six
impossible things before breakfast.
Through the Looking-Glass (1872) ch. 5

9 With a name like yours, you might be any shape,
almost.
Through the Looking-Glass (1872) ch. 6

10 They gave it me,—for an un-birthday present.
Through the Looking-Glass (1872) ch. 6

11 'There's glory for you!' 'I don't know what you mean
by "glory",' Alice said. 'I meant, "there's a nice
knock-down argument for you!"' ' But "glory"
doesn't mean "a nice knock-down argument",' Alice
objected. 'When *I* use a word,' Humpty Dumpty said
in a rather scornful tone, 'it means just what I choose
it to mean—neither more nor less.'
Through the Looking-Glass (1872) ch. 6

12 'The question is,' said Humpty Dumpty, 'which is to
be master—that's all.'
Through the Looking-Glass (1872) ch. 6

13 You see it's like a portmanteau—there are two
meanings packed up into one word.
Through the Looking-Glass (1872) ch. 6

14 '*I* can repeat poetry as well as other folk if it comes to
that—' 'Oh, it needn't come to that!' Alice hastily
said.
Through the Looking-Glass (1872) ch. 6

15 The little fishes of the sea,
They sent an answer back to me.

The little fishes' answer was
'We cannot do it, Sir, because—'
Through the Looking-Glass (1872) ch. 6

16 He's an Anglo-Saxon Messenger—and those are
Anglo-Saxon attitudes.
Through the Looking-Glass (1872) ch. 7

17 The other Messenger's called Hatta. I must have *two*
you know—to come and go. One to come, and one to
go.
Through the Looking-Glass (1872) ch. 7

18 'There's nothing like eating hay when you're faint' . . .
'I didn't say there was nothing *better*,' the King
replied, 'I said there was nothing *like* it.'
Through the Looking-Glass (1872) ch. 7

19 'I'm sure nobody walks much faster than I do!' 'He
can't do that,' said the King, 'or else he'd have been
here first.'
Through the Looking-Glass (1872) ch. 7

20 It's as large as life, and twice as natural!
Through the Looking-Glass (1872) ch. 7

21 I'll tell thee everything I can:
There's little to relate.
I saw an aged, aged man,
A-sitting on a gate.
Through the Looking-Glass (1872) ch. 8

22 He said, 'I look for butterflies
That sleep among the wheat:
I make them into mutton-pies,
And sell them in the street.'
Through the Looking-Glass (1872) ch. 8

23 Or madly squeeze a right-hand foot
Into a left-hand shoe.
Through the Looking-Glass (1872) ch. 8

24 No admittance till the week after next!
Through the Looking-Glass (1872) ch. 9

25 It isn't etiquette to cut any one you've been
introduced to. Remove the joint.
Through the Looking-Glass (1872) ch. 9

26 Un-dish-cover the fish, or dishcover the riddle.
Through the Looking-Glass (1872) ch. 9

27 What I tell you three times is true.
The Hunting of the Snark (1876) 'Fit the First: The Landing'

28 He would answer to 'Hi!' or to any loud cry,
Such as 'Fry me!' or 'Fritter-my-wig!'
The Hunting of the Snark (1876) 'Fit the First: The Landing'

1 His intimate friends called him 'Candle-ends',
   And his enemies, 'Toasted-cheese'.
   The Hunting of the Snark (1876) 'Fit the First: The Landing'

2 'What's the good of *Mercator's* North Poles and
      Equators,
   Tropics, Zones and Meridian lines?'
   So the Bellman would cry: and the crew would reply,
   'They are merely conventional signs!'
   The Hunting of the Snark (1876) 'Fit the Second: The
   Bellman's Speech'

3 But the principal failing occurred in the sailing,
   And the Bellman, perplexed and distressed,
   Said he *had* hoped, at least, when the wind blew due
      East,
   That the ship would *not* travel due West!
   The Hunting of the Snark (1876) 'Fit the Second: The
   Bellman's Speech'

4 But oh, beamish nephew, beware of the day,
   If your Snark be a Boojum! For then
   You will softly and suddenly vanish away,
   And never be met with again!
   The Hunting of the Snark (1876) 'Fit the Third: The Baker's
   Tale'

5 They sought it with thimbles, they sought it with
      care;
   They pursued it with forks and hope;
   They threatened its life with a railway-share;
   They charmed it with smiles and soap.
   The Hunting of the Snark (1876) 'Fit the Fifth: The Beaver's
   Lesson'

6 I never loved a dear Gazelle—
   Nor anything that cost me much:
   High prices profit those who sell,
   But why should I be fond of such?
   Phantasmagoria (1869) 'Theme with Variations'. Cf. Moore
   483:14

7 He thought he saw an Elephant,
   That practised on a fife:
   He looked again, and found it was
   A letter from his wife.
   'At length I realize,' he said,
   'The bitterness of life!'
   Sylvie and Bruno (1889) ch. 5

8 He thought he saw a Rattlesnake
   That questioned him in Greek,
   He looked again and found it was
   The Middle of Next Week.
   'The one thing I regret,' he said,
   'Is that it cannot speak!'
   Sylvie and Bruno (1889) ch. 6

William Herbert Carruth 1859–1924

9 Some call it evolution,
   And others call it God.
   'Each In His Own Tongue' (1908)

Edward Carson (Baron Carson) 1854–1935
British lawyer and politician

10 My only great qualification for being put at the head
   of the Navy is that I am very much at sea.
   In Ian Colvin *Life of Lord Carson* (1936) vol. 3, ch. 23

Henry Carter d. 1806

11 From distant climes, o'er widespread seas we come,
   Though not with much *éclat* or beat of drum;
   True patriots we; for be it understood,
   We left our country for our country's good.
   No private views disgraced our generous zeal,
   What urged our travels was our country's weal;
   And none will doubt but that our emigration
   Has proved most useful to the British nation.
   Prologue, written for, but not recited at, the opening of the
   Playhouse, Sydney, New South Wales, 16 January 1796,
   when the actors were principally convicts. See A. W. Jose
   and H. J. Carter (eds.) *The Australian Encyclopaedia* (1927)
   p. 139. Previously attributed to George Barrington
   (b. 1755). Cf. Fitzgeffrey 283:9

Sydney Carter 1915–
English folk-song writer

12 It's God they ought to crucify
   Instead of you and me,
   I said to the carpenter
   A-hanging on the tree.
   'Friday Morning' (1967)

13 I danced in the morning
   When the world was begun
   And I danced in the moon
   And the stars and the sun
   And I came down from heaven
   And I danced on the earth—
   At Bethlehem I had my birth.
   Dance then wherever you may be,
   I am the Lord of the Dance, said he,
   And I'll lead you all, wherever you may be
   And I'll lead you all in the dance, said he.
   'Lord of the Dance' (1967)

John Cartwright 1740–1824
English political reformer

14 One man shall have one vote.
   The People's Barrier Against Undue Influence (1780) ch. 1
   'Principles, maxims, and primary rules of politics' no. 68

Ted Castle (Baron Castle of Islington) 1907–79
British journalist

15 In place of strife.
   Title of Labour Government White Paper, 17 January
   1969; suggested by Castle to his wife, Barbara Castle, then
   Secretary of State for Employment. See Barbara Castle
   Diaries (1984) 15 January 1969

Fidel Castro 1926–
Cuban revolutionary

1 *La historia me absolverá.*

History will absolve me.
  Title of pamphlet (1953)

Edward Caswall 1814–78
English hymn-writer

2 Jesu, the very thought of Thee
With sweetness fills the breast.
  'Jesu, the very thought of thee' (1849 hymn); translation
  of '*Jesu dulcis memoria, dans vera cordis gaudia*', usually
  attributed to St Bernard (1090–1153)

3 My God, I love Thee; not because
I hope for heaven thereby.
  'My God, I Love Thee' (1849 hymn); translation of '*O deus
  ego amo te, nec amo te ut salves me*'; usually attributed to
  St Francis Xavier (1506–52)

4 See, amid the winter's snow,
Born for us on earth below,
See, the Lamb of God appears,
Promised from eternal years!

Hail, thou ever-blessèd morn!
Hail, redemption's happy dawn!
Sing through all Jerusalem:
Christ is born in Bethlehem!
  'See, amid the winter's snow' (1858 hymn)

5 When morning gilds the skies.
  Title of hymn (1854)

A Catechism of Christian Doctrine
1898
Popularly known as the 'Penny Catechism'

6 Who made you? God made me.
Why did God make you? God made me to know Him,
love him, and serve Him in this world, and to be
happy with Him for ever in the next.

Catherine the Great 1729–96
Empress of Russia from 1762

7 *Moi, je serai autocrate: c'est mon métier. Et le bon Dieu
me pardonnera: c'est son métier.*

I shall be an autocrat: that's my trade. And the good
Lord will forgive me: that's his.
  Attributed. Cf. Heine 331:4

Cato the Elder (or 'the Censor')
234–149 BC
Roman statesman, orator, and writer

8 *Delenda est Carthago.*

Carthage must be destroyed.
  In Pliny the Elder *Naturalis Historia* bk. 15, ch. 74

9 *Rem tene; verba sequentur.*

Grasp the subject, the words will follow.
  In Caius Julius Victor *Ars Rhetorica* 'De inventione'

Catullus c.84–c.54 BC
Roman poet

10 *Cui dono lepidum novum libellum
Arido modo pumice expolitum?*

To whom shall I give my nice new little book polished
dry with pumice?
  Carmina no. 1

11   *Namque tu solebas
Meas esse aliquid putare nugas.*

For you used to think my trifles were worth
something.
  Carmina no. 1

12 *Plus uno maneat perenne saeclo.*

May it live and last for more than a century.
  Carmina no. 1

13 *Lugete, O Veneres Cupidinesque,
Et quantum est hominum venustiorum.
Passer mortuus est meae puellae,
Passer, deliciae meae puellae.*

Mourn, you powers of Charm and Desire, and all you
who are endowed with charm. My lady's sparrow is
dead, the sparrow which was my lady's darling.
  Carmina no. 3

14 *Qui nunc it per iter tenebricosum
Illuc, unde negant redire quemquam.*

Now he goes along the darksome road, thither whence
they say no one returns.
  Carmina no. 4

15 *Vivamus, mea Lesbia, atque amemus,
Rumoresque senum severiorum
Omnes unius aestimemus assis.
Soles occidere et redire possunt:
Nobis cum semel occidit brevis lux
Nox est perpetua una dormienda.*

Let us live, my Lesbia, and let us love, and let us
reckon all the murmurs of more censorious old men as
worth one farthing. Suns can set and come again: for
us, when once our brief light has set, one everlasting
night is to be slept.
  Carmina no. 5. Cf. Campion 177:3

1 *Da mi basia mille, deinde centum,*
Dein mille altera, dein secunda centum,
Deinde usque altera mille, deinde centum.

Give me a thousand kisses, then a hundred, then
another thousand, then a second hundred, then yet
another thousand, then a hundred.
Carmina no. 5

2 *Miser Catulle, desinas ineptire,*
Et quod vides perisse perditum ducas.

Poor Catullus, drop your silly fancies, and what you
see is lost let it be lost.
Carmina no. 8

3 *Paene insularum, Sirmio, insularumque*
Ocelle . . .
O quid solutis est beatius curis?
Cum mens onus reponit, ac peregrino
Labore fessi venimus larem ad nostrum,
Desideratoque acquiescimus lecto.
Hoc est quod unum est pro laboribus tantis.
Salve O venusta Sirmio atque hero gaude;
Gaudete vosque O Lydiae lacus undae;
Ridete quidquid est domi cachinnorum.

Sirmio, bright eye of peninsulas and islands . . . Ah,
what is more blessed than to put cares away, when
the mind lays by its burden, and tired with labour of
far travel we have come to our own home and rest on
the couch we have longed for? This it is which alone
is worth all these toils. Hail, sweet Sirmio, and make
cheer for your master. Rejoice ye too, waters of the
Lydian lake, and laugh out aloud all the laughter you
have at your command.
Carmina no. 31

4 *Nam risu inepto res ineptior nulla est.*

For there is nothing sillier than a silly laugh.
Carmina no. 39. Cf. Congreve 215:1

5 *Iam ver egelidos refert tepores.*

Now Spring restores balmy warmth.
Carmina no. 46

6 *Gratias tibi maximas Catullus*
Agit pessimus omnium poeta,
Tanto pessimus omnium poeta,
Quanto tu optimus omnium's patronum.

Catullus gives you warmest thanks,
And he the worst of poets ranks;
As much the worst of bards confessed,
As you of advocates the best.
Carmina no. 49 (letter of thanks to Cicero, translated by Sir
William Marris)

7 *Ille mi par esse deo videtur,*
Ille, si fas est, superare divos,
Qui sedens adversus identidem te
Spectat et audit
Dulce ridentem, misero quod omnis
Eripit sensus mihi.

Like a god he seems to me, above the gods, if so may
be, who sitting often close to you may see and hear
you sweetly laughing, which snatches away all the
senses from poor me.
Carmina no. 51 (a translation of Sappho). Cf. Sappho
556:1

8 *Caeli, Lesbia nostra, Lesbia illa,*
Illa Lesbia, quam Catullus unam
Plus quam se atque suos amavit omnes,
Nunc in quadriviis et angiportis
Glubit magnanimos Remi nepotes.

O Caelius, our Lesbia, that Lesbia whom Catullus once
loved uniquely, more than himself and more than all
his own, now at the crossroads and in the alleyways
has it off with the high-minded descendants of Remus.
Carmina no. 58

9 *Ut flos in saeptis secretus nascitur hortis,*
Ignotus pecori, nullo contusus aratro,
Quem mulcent aurae, firmat sol, educat imber;
Multi illum pueri, multae optavere puellae.

As a flower grows concealed in an enclosed garden,
unknown to the cattle, bruised by no plough, and
which the breezes caress, the sun makes strong, and
the rain brings out; many boys and many girls long
for it.
Carmina no. 62

10 *Sed mulier cupido quod dicit amanti,*
In vento et rapida scribere oportet aqua.

But what a woman says to her lusting lover it is best
to write in wind and swift-flowing water.
Carmina no. 70

11 *Desine de quoquam quicquam bene velle mereri,*
Aut aliquem fieri posse putare pium.

Give up wanting to deserve any thanks from anyone,
or thinking that anybody can be grateful.
Carmina no. 73

12 *Siqua recordanti benefacta priora voluptas*
Est homini.

If a man can take any pleasure in recalling the
thought of kindnesses done.
Carmina no. 76

13 *Difficile est longum subito deponere amorem.*

It is difficult suddenly to lay aside a long-cherished
love.
Carmina no. 76

14 *Si vitam puriter egi.*

If I have led a pure life.
Carmina no. 76

15 *O di, reddite mi hoc pro pietate mea.*

O gods, grant me this in return for my piety.
Carmina no. 76

16 *Chommoda dicebat, si quando commoda vellet*
Dicere, et insidias Arrius hinsidias.

Arrius, if he wanted to say 'amenities' used to say
'hamenities', and for 'intrigue' 'hintrigue'.
Carmina no. 84

17 *Odi et amo: quare id faciam, fortasse requiris.*
Nescio, sed fieri sentio et excrucior.

I hate and I love: why I do so you may well ask. I do
not know, but I feel it happen and am in agony.
Carmina no. 85

1 *Multas per gentes et multa per aequora vectus*
Advenio has miseras, frater, ad inferias,
Ut te postremo donarem munere mortis
Et mutam nequiquam alloquerer cinerem.
Quandoquidem fortuna mihi tete abstulit ipsum,
Heu miser indigne frater adempte mihi,
Nunc tamen interea haec prisco quae more parentum
Tradita sunt tristi munere ad inferias,
Accipe fraterno multum manantia fletu,
Atque in perpetuum, frater, ave atque vale.

By many lands and over many a wave
I come, my brother, to your piteous grave,
To bring you the last offering in death
And o'er dumb dust expend an idle breath;
For fate has torn your living self from me,
And snatched you, brother, O, how cruelly!
Yet take these gifts, brought as our fathers bade
For sorrow's tribute to the passing shade;
A brother's tears have wet them o'er and o'er;
And so, my brother, hail, and farewell evermore!
    Carmina no. 101 (translated by Sir William Marris)

2 *At non effugies meos iambos.*

But you shall not escape my iambics.
    R. A. B. Mynors (ed.) *Catulli Carmina* (1958) Fragment 3

Charles Causley 1917–
English poet and schoolmaster

3 Timothy Winters comes to school
With eyes as wide as a football-pool,
Ears like bombs and teeth like splinters:
A blitz of a boy is Timothy Winters.
    'Timothy Winters' (1957)

Constantine Cavafy 1863–1933
Greek poet

4 Σὰ βγεῖς στὸν πηγαιμὸ γιὰ τὴν Ἰθάκη,
Νὰ εὔχεσαι νᾶναι μακρὺς ὁ δρόμος

When you set out for Ithaka
ask that your way be long.
    'Ithaka' (1911) (translated by E. Keeley and P. Sherrard)

5 Πάντα στὸν νοῦ σου νἄχεις τὴν Ἰθάκη.
Τὸ φθάσιμον ἐκεῖ εἶν' ὁ προορισμός σου

Have Ithaka always in your mind.
Your arrival there is what you are destined for.
    'Ithaka' (1911)

6 Ἡ Ἰθάκη σ' ἔδωσε τ' ὡραῖο ταξεῖδι.
Χωρὶς αὐτὴν δὲν θἄβγαινες στὸν δρόμο.
Ἄλλα δὲν ἔχει νὰ σὲ δώσει πιά.

Ithaka gave you the splendid journey.
Without her you would not have set out.
She hasn't anything else to give you.
    'Ithaka' (1911)

7 Τί περιμένουμε στὴν ἀγορὰ συναθροισμένοι;
Εἶναι οἱ βάρβαροι νά φθάσουν σήμερα.

What are we waiting for, gathered in the
    market-place?
The barbarians are to arrive today.
    'Waiting for the Barbarians' (1904) (translated by E. Keeley
    and P. Sherrard)

8 Καὶ τώρα τί θὰ γένουμε χωρὶς βαρβάρους;
Οἱ ἄνθρωποι αὐτοὶ ἦσαν μιὰ κάποια λύσις.

And now, what will become of us without the
    barbarians?
Those people were a kind of solution.
    'Waiting for the Barbarians' (1904)

9 Καινούριους τόπους δὲν θὰ βρεῖς, δὲν θἄβρεις ἄλλες
    θάλασσες,
Ἡ πόλις θὰ σὲ ἀκολουθεῖ.

New places you will not find, you will not find another
    sea
The city will follow you.
    'The Town' (1911) (translated by E. Keeley and
    P. Sherrard)

Edith Cavell 1865–1915
*English nurse, executed by the Germans for assisting in
the escape of British soldiers from occupied Belgium*

10 Standing, as I do, in view of God and eternity, I realize
that patriotism is not enough. I must have no hatred
or bitterness towards anyone.
    On the eve of her execution, in *The Times* 23 October 1915

Margaret Cavendish (Duchess of Newcastle) *c.*1624–74
English woman of letters

11 Greek, Latin poets, I could never read,
Nor their historians, but our English Speed;
I could not steal their wit, nor plots out take;
All my plays' plots, my own poor brain did make.
    Plays (1662) 'To the Readers'

12 Marriage is the grave or tomb of wit.
    Plays (1662) 'Nature's Three Daughters' pt. 2, act 5, sc. 20

13 If Nature had not befriended us with beauty, and
other good graces, to help us to insinuate our selves
into men's affections, we should have been more
enslaved than any other of Nature's creatures she
hath made.
    Sociable Letters (1664) p. 27

14 But for the most part, women are not educated as
they should be, I mean those of quality; oft their
education is only to dance, sing, and fiddle, to write
complimental letters, to read romances, to speak some
languages that is not their native . . . their parents
take more care of their feet than their head, more of
their words than their reason.
    Sociable Letters (1664) p. 50

Count Cavour (Camillo Benso di Cavour) 1810–61
Italian statesman

15 *Noi siamo pronti a proclamare nell'Italia questo gran*
principio: Libera Chiesa in libero Stato.

We are ready to proclaim throughout Italy this great
principle: a free church in a free state.
    Speech, 27 March 1861, in William de la Rive
    Reminiscences of the Life and Character of Count Cavour
    (1862) ch. 13

William Caxton c.1421–91

First English printer

1 The worshipful father and first founder and embellisher of ornate eloquence in our English, I mean Master Geoffrey Chaucer.

Caxton's edition (c.1478) of Chaucer's translation of Boethius *De Consolacione Philosophie* epilogue

2 It is notoriously known through the universal world that there be nine worthy and the best that ever were. That is to wit three paynims, three Jews, and three Christian men. As for the paynims they were . . . the first Hector of Troy . . . the second Alexander the Great; and the third Julius Caesar . . . As for the three Jews . . . the first was Duke Joshua . . . the second David, King of Jerusalem; and the third Judas Maccabaeus . . . And sith the said Incarnation . . . was first the noble Arthur . . . The second was Charlemagne or Charles the Great . . . and the third and last was Godfrey of Bouillon.

Sir Thomas Malory *Le Morte D'Arthur* (1485) prologue

3 I, according to my copy, have done set it in imprint, to the intent that noble men may see and learn the noble acts of chivalry, the gentle and virtuous deeds that some knights used in those days.

Sir Thomas Malory *Le Morte D'Arthur* (1485) prologue

William Cecil (1st Lord Burghley)
1520–98

English courtier and politician

4 What! all this for a song?

To Queen Elizabeth, on being ordered to make a gratuity of £100 to Spenser in return for some poems; in Edmund Spenser *The Faerie Queene* (1751) 'The Life of Mr Edmund Spenser' by Thomas Birch

Susannah Centlivre c.1669–1723

English actress and playwright

5 For he or she, who drags the marriage chain,
And finds in spouse occasion to complain,
Should hide their frailties with a lover's care,
And let th'ill-judging world conclude 'em fair;
Better th'offence ne'er reach the offender's ear.
For they who sin with caution, whilst concealed,
Grow impudently careless, when revealed.

The Artifice (1722) act 5, sc. 3

6 Nothing to be done without a bribe I find, in love as well as law.

The Perjured Husband (1700) act 3, sc. 2

7 The carping malice of the vulgar world; who think it a proof of sense to dislike every thing that is writ by Women.

The Platonic Lady (1707) dedication

Cervantes (Miguel de Cervantes Saavedra)
1547–1616

Spanish novelist

8 *El Caballero de la Triste Figura.*
The Knight of the Doleful Countenance.

Don Quixote (1605) pt. 1, ch. 19

9 *La mejor salsa del mundo es el hambre.*
Hunger is the best sauce in the world.

Don Quixote (1605) pt. 2, ch. 5

10 *El pan comido y la compañía deshecha.*
With the bread eaten up, up breaks the company.

Don Quixote (1605) pt. 2, ch. 7

11 *No todos podemos ser frailes, y muchos son los caminos por donde lleva Dios a los suyos al cielo: religión es la caballería.*
We cannot all be friars, and many are the ways by which God leads his own to eternal life.
Knight-errantry *is* religion.

Don Quixote (1605) pt. 2, ch. 8 (to Sancho, on his asking whether, to get to heaven, we ought not all to become monks)

12 *Es un entreverado loco, lleno de lúcidos intervalos.*
He's a muddle-headed fool, with frequent lucid intervals.

Don Quixote (1605) pt. 2, ch. 18 (Don Lorenzo of Don Quixote)

13 *Dos linajes solos hay en el mundo, como decía una abuela mía, que son el tener y el no tener.*
There are only two families in the world, as a grandmother of mine used to say: the haves and the have-nots.

Don Quixote (1605) pt. 2, ch. 20

14 *Digo, paciencia y barajar.*
What I say is, patience, and shuffle the cards.

Don Quixote (1605) pt. 2, ch. 23

15 *La diligencia es madre de la buena ventura y la pereza, su contrario, jamás llegó al término que pide un buen deseo.*
Diligence is the mother of good fortune, and idleness, its opposite, never led to good intention's goal.

Don Quixote (1605) pt. 2, ch. 43

16 *Bien haya el que inventó el sueño, capa que cubre todos los humanos pensamientos, manjar que quita la hambre, agua que ahuyenta la sed, fuego que calienta el frío, frío que templa el ardor, y, finalmente, moneda general con que todas las cosas se compran, balanza y peso que iguala al pastor con el rey y al simple con el discreto.*
Blessings on him who invented sleep, the mantle that covers all human thoughts, the food that satisfies hunger, the drink that slakes thirst, the fire that warms cold, the cold that moderates heat, and, lastly, the common currency that buys all things, the balance and weight that equalizes the shepherd and the king, the simpleton and the sage.

Don Quixote (1605) pt. 2, ch. 68

17 *Los buenos pintores imitan la naturaleza, pero los malos la vomitan.*
Good painters imitate nature, bad ones spew it up.

El Licenciado Vidriera in *Novelas Ejemplares* (1613)

18 *Puesto ya el pie en el estribo.*
With one foot already in the stirrup.

Apprehending his own, imminent death: *Los Trabajos de Persiles y Sigismunda* (1617) preface

John Chalkhill c.1600–42

English poet

1 Oh, the gallant fisher's life,
It is the best of any
'Tis full of pleasure, void of strife,
And 'tis beloved of many.
  'Piscator's Song', in Izaak Walton *The Compleat Angler*
  (1653–76)

Joseph Chamberlain 1836–1914

British Liberal politician

2 In politics, there is no use looking beyond the next
fortnight.
  In A. J. Balfour *Chapters of Autobiography* (1930) ch. 16,
  letter from Balfour to 3rd Marquess of Salisbury, 24 March
  1886

3 Provided that the City of London remains, as it is at
present, the clearing-house of the world, any other
nation may be its workshop.
  Speech at the Guildhall, 19 January 1904, in *The Times*
  20 January 1904

4 The day of small nations has long passed away. The
day of Empires has come.
  Speech at Birmingham, 12 May 1904, in *The Times* 13 May
  1904

5 We are not downhearted. The only trouble is we
cannot understand what is happening to our
neighbours.
  Speech at Smethwick, 18 January 1906 (referring to a
  constituency which had remained unaffected by an
  electoral landslide) in *The Times* 19 January 1906

Neville Chamberlain 1869–1940

British Conservative politician; Prime Minister, 1937–40

6 In war, whichever side may call itself the victor, there
are no winners, but all are losers.
  Speech at Kettering, 3 July 1938, in *The Times* 4 July 1938

7 How horrible, fantastic, incredible it is that we should
be digging trenches and trying on gas-masks here
because of a quarrel in a far away country between
people of whom we know nothing.
  On Germany's annexation of the Sudetenland; radio
  broadcast, 27 September 1938, in *The Times* 28 September
  1938

8 This is the second time in our history that there has
come back from Germany to Downing Street peace
with honour. I believe it is peace for our time.
  Speech from 10 Downing Street, 30 September 1938, in
  The Times 1 October 1938. Cf. Disraeli 247:27, Russell
  552:2

9 Whatever may be the reason—whether it was that
Hitler thought he might get away with what he had
got without fighting for it, or whether it was that after
all the preparations were not sufficiently
complete—however, one thing is certain—he missed
the bus.
  Speech at Central Hall, Westminster, 4 April 1940, in *The
  Times* 5 April 1940

Haddon Chambers 1860–1921

English playwright

10 The long arm of coincidence.
  Captain Swift (1888) act 2

Nicolas-Sébastien Chamfort 1741–94

French writer

11 *Vivre est une maladie dont le sommeil nous soulage toutes
les 16 heures. C'est un palliatif. La mort est le remède.*
  Living is an illness to which sleep provides relief every
  sixteen hours. It's a palliative. The remedy is death.
  Maximes et Pensées (1796) ch. 2

12 *Des qualités trop supérieures rendent souvent un homme
moins propre à la société. On ne va pas au marché avec des
lingots; on y va avec de l'argent ou de la petite monnaie.*
  Qualities too elevated often unfit a man for society. We
  don't take ingots with us to market; we take silver or
  small change.
  Maximes et Pensées (1796) ch. 3

13 *L'amour, tel qu'il existe dans la société, n'est que
l'échange de deux fantaisies et le contact de deux
épidermes.*
  Love, in the form in which it exists in society, is
  nothing but the exchange of two fantasies and the
  superficial contact of two bodies.
  Maximes et Pensées (1796) ch. 6

14 *Je dirais volontiers des métaphysiciens ce que Scaliger
disait des Basques, on dit qu'ils s'entendent, mais je n'en
crois rien.*
  I am tempted to say of metaphysicians what Scaliger
  used to say of the Basques: they are said to
  understand one another, but I don't believe a word of
  it.
  Maximes et Pensées (1796) ch. 7

15 *Les pauvres sont les nègres de l'Europe.*
  The poor are Europe's blacks.
  Maximes et Pensées (1796) ch. 8

16 *Sois mon frère, ou je te tue.*
  Be my brother, or I kill you.
  His interpretation of '*Fraternité ou la mort* [Fraternity or
  death]', in P. R. Anguis (ed.) *Oeuvres Complètes* (1824)
  vol. 1 'Notice Historique sur la Vie et les Écrits de
  Chamfort'. Cf. Anonymous 21:1

John Chandler 1806–76

English clergyman

17 Conquering kings their titles take
From the foes they captive make:
Jesu, by a nobler deed,
From the thousands He hath freed.
  Hymn (1837); translation from a Latin original: '*Victis sibi
  cognomina sumant tyranni gentibus . . .* '

Raymond Chandler 1888–1959

American writer of detective fiction

1 It was about eleven o'clock in the morning, mid October, with the sun not shining and a look of hard wet rain in the clearness of the foothills. I was wearing my powder-blue suit, with dark blue shirt, tie and display handkerchief, black brogues, black wool socks with dark blue clocks on them. I was neat, clean, shaved and sober, and I didn't care who knew it.

The Big Sleep (1939) ch. 1

2 It was a blonde. A blonde to make a bishop kick a hole in a stained glass window.

Farewell, My Lovely (1940) ch. 13

3 A big hard-boiled city with no more personality than a paper cup.

The Little Sister (1949) ch. 26 (Los Angeles)

4 I let go of her wrists, closed the door with my elbow and slid past her. It was like the first time. 'You ought to carry insurance on those,' I said.

The Little Sister (1949) ch. 34

5 Down these mean streets a man must go who is not himself mean, who is neither tarnished nor afraid.

Atlantic Monthly December 1944 'The Simple Art of Murder'

6 If my books had been any worse, I should not have been invited to Hollywood, and if they had been any better, I should not have come.

Letter to Charles W. Morton, 12 December 1945, in Dorothy Gardiner and Katherine S. Walker *Raymond Chandler Speaking* (1962) p. 126

7 Would you convey my compliments to the purist who reads your proofs and tell him or her that I write in a sort of broken-down patois which is something like the way a Swiss waiter talks, and that when I split an infinitive, God damn it, I split it so it will stay split.

Letter to Edward Weeks, 18 January 1947, in F. MacShane *Life of Raymond Chandler* (1976) ch. 7

Coco Chanel (Gabrielle Bonheur) 1883–1971

French couturière

8 You ask if they were happy. This is not a characteristic of a European. To be contented—that's for the cows.

In A. Madsen *Coco Chanel* (1990) ch. 35

Charlie Chaplin (Sir Charles Spencer Chaplin) 1889–1977

English film actor and director

9 All I need to make a comedy is a park, a policeman and a pretty girl.

My Autobiography (1964) ch. 10

Arthur Chapman 1873–1935

American poet

10 Out where the handclasp's a little stronger,
Out where the smile dwells a little longer,
That's where the West begins.

Out Where the West Begins (1916) p. 1

George Chapman c.1559–1634

English scholar, poet, and playwright

11   I know an Englishman,
Being flattered, is a lamb; threatened, a lion.

Alphonsus, Emperor of Germany (1654) act 1

12 Man is a torch borne in the wind; a dream
But of a shadow, summed with all his substance.

Bussy D'Ambois (1607–8) act 1, sc. 1

13 Who to himself is law, no law doth need,
Offends no law, and is a king indeed.

Bussy D'Ambois (1607–8) act 2, sc. 1

14   Oh my fame,
Live in despite of murder! Take thy wings
And haste thee where the grey eyed Morn perfumes
Her rosy chariot with Sabaean spices!
Fly, where the Evening from th'Iberian vales
Takes on her swarthy shoulders Hecate,
Crowned with a grove of oaks; fly where men feel
The burning axletree, and those that suffer
Beneath the chariot of the snowy Bear.

Bussy D'Ambois (1607–8) act 5, sc. 3

15 There is no danger to a man, that knows
What life and death is; there's not any law,
Exceeds his knowledge; neither is it lawful
That he should stoop to any other law,
He goes before them, and commands them all,
That to himself is a law rational.

The Conspiracy of Charles, Duke of Byron (1608) act 3, sc. 3

16 O incredulity! the wit of fools,
That slovenly will spit on all things fair,
The coward's castle, and the sluggard's cradle.

'De Guiana' l. 82, verses prefixed to Lawrence Keymis *A Relation of the Second Voyage to Guiana* (1596)

17 Come, come, dear Night, Love's mart of kisses,
Sweet close of his ambitious line,
The fruitful summer of his blisses,
Love's glory doth in darkness shine.
O come, soft rest of cares, come Night,
Come naked Virtue's only tire,
The reapèd harvest of the light,
Bound up in sheaves of sacred fire.

Hero and Leander (1598)

18 We have watered our houses in Helicon.

May-Day (1611) act 3, sc. 3; occasionally misread 'We have watered our horses in Helicon'. See A. H. Holaday (ed.) *The Plays of George Chapman: The Comedies* (1970) p. 383

19 For one heat, all know, doth drive out another,
One passion doth expel another still.

Monsieur D'Olive (1606) act 5, sc. 1

20 I am ashamed the law is such an ass.

Revenge for Honour (1654) act 3, sc. 2. Cf. Dickens 242:29

1 They're only truly great who are truly good.

> *Revenge for Honour* (1654) act 5, sc. 2, last line

2 A poem, whose subject is not truth, but things like truth.

> *The Revenge of Bussy D'Ambois* (1613) dedication

3 Danger, the spur of all great minds.

> *The Revenge of Bussy D'Ambois* (1613) act 5, sc. 1

4 And let a scholar all Earth's volumes carry,
He will be but a walking dictionary.

> *The Tears of Peace* (1609) l. 530

Charles I 1600–49

King of England, Scotland, and Ireland from 1625

5 Never make a defence or apology before you be accused.

> Letter to Lord Wentworth, 3 September 1636, in Sir Charles Petrie (ed.) *Letters of King Charles I* (1935)

6 I see all the birds are flown.

> In the House of Commons, 4 January 1642, after attempting to arrest the Five Members: *Hansard Parliamentary History to the year 1803* vol. 2 (1807) col. 1010

7 Sweet-heart, now they will cut off thy father's head. Mark, child, what I say: they will cut off my head, and perhaps make thee a king. But mark what I say: you must not be a king, so long as your brothers Charles and James do live.

> Said to Prince Henry, in *Reliquiae Sacrae Carolinae* (1650) p. 337

8 You manifestly wrong even the poorest ploughman, if you demand not his free consent.

> The King's Reasons for declining the jurisdiction of the High Court of Justice, 21 January 1649, in S. R. Gardiner *Constitutional Documents of the Puritan Revolution* (1906 ed.) p. 375

9 As to the King, the laws of the land will clearly instruct you for that ... For the people; and truly I desire their liberty and freedom, as much as any body: but I must tell you, that their liberty and freedom consists in having the government of those laws, by which their life and their goods may be most their own; 'tis not for having share in government [sirs] that is nothing pertaining to 'em. A subject and a sovereign are clean different things ... If I would have given way to an arbitrary way, for to have all laws changed according to the power of the sword, I needed not to have come here; and therefore I tell you (and I pray God it be not laid to your charge) that I am the martyr of the people.

> Speech on the scaffold, 30 January 1649. See J. Rushworth *Historical Collections* pt. 4, vol. 2 (1701) p. 1429

10 I die a Christian, according to the profession of the Church of England, as I found it left me by my father.

> In J. Rushworth *Historical Collections* pt. 4, vol. 2 (1701) p. 1430

Charles II 1630–85

King of England, Scotland and Ireland from 1660

11 It is upon the navy under the good Providence of God that the safety, honour, and welfare of this realm do chiefly depend.

> 'Articles of War' preamble, in Sir Geoffrey Callender *The Naval Side of British History* (1952) pt. 1, ch. 8

12 This is very true: for my words are my own, and my actions are my ministers'.

> Reply to Lord Rochester's epitaph on him, in *Thomas Hearne: Remarks and Collections* (1885–1921) 17 November 1706. Cf. Rochester 543:5

13 Better than a play.

> On the debates in the House of Lords on Lord Ross's Divorce Bill, 1670; in A. Bryant *King Charles II* (1931) p. 209

14 He [Charles II] said once to myself, he was no atheist, but he could not think God would make a man miserable only for taking a little pleasure out of the way.

> Bishop Gilbert Burnet *History of My Own Time* (1724) vol. 1, bk. 2, p. 93

15 He [Lauderdale] told me, the king spoke to him to let that [Presbytery] go, for it was not a religion for gentlemen.

> Bishop Gilbert Burnet *History of My Own Time* (1724) vol. 1, bk. 2, p. 107

16 His nonsense suits their nonsense.

> Said of Woolly, afterwards Bishop of Clonfert ('a very honest man, but a very great blockhead') who had gone from house to house trying to persuade Nonconformists to go to church; in Bishop Gilbert Burnet *History of My Own Time* (1724) vol. 1, bk. 2, p. 258

17 Let not poor Nelly starve.

> Of Nell Gwyn, his mistress, in Bishop Gilbert Burnet *History of My Own Time* (1724) vol. 1, bk. 3, p. 609

18 Never *in* the way, and never *out* of the way.

> Of Lord Godolphin, who had been raised as page to the king, in *Dictionary of National Biography* (1917–) vol. 8, p. 43

19 I am sure no man in England will take away my life to make you King.

> To his brother James, in William King *Political & Literary Anecdotes* (1818) p. 62

20 He had been, he said, an unconscionable time dying; but he hoped that they would excuse it.

> Lord Macaulay *History of England* (1849) vol. 1, ch. 4

Charles V 1500–58

Holy Roman Emperor, 1519–56; King of Spain from 1516

21 To God I speak Spanish, to women Italian, to men French, and to my horse—German.

> Attributed. See Lord Chesterfield *Letters to his Son* (ed. Dobrée, 1932) vol. 4, p. 1497

Prince Charles (*Charles Philip Arthur George, Prince of Wales*) 1948–

Heir apparent to the British throne

1 A monstrous carbuncle on the face of a much-loved and elegant friend.

On the proposed extension to the National Gallery, London; speech to the Royal Institute of British Architects, 30 May 1984, in *The Times* 31 May 1984. Cf. Spencer 658:25

Pierre Charron 1541–1603

French philosopher and theologian

2 *La vraie science et le vrai étude de l'homme, c'est l'homme.*

The true science and study of man is man.

De la Sagesse (1601) bk. 1, preface. Cf. Pope 522:9

Salmon Portland Chase 1808–73

American lawyer and politician

3 The Constitution, in all its provisions, looks to an indestructible Union composed of indestructible States.

Decision in Texas v. White, 1868, in *Cases Argued and Decided in the Supreme Court of the United States* (1926) bk. 19, p. 237

François-René Chateaubriand (*Vicomte de Chateaubriand*) 1768–1848

French writer and diplomat

4 *L'écrivain original n'est pas celui qui n'imite personne, mais celui que personne ne peut imiter.*

The original writer is not he who refrains from imitating others, but he who can be imitated by none.

Le Génie du Christianisme (1802) pt. 2, bk. 1, ch. 3

Geoffrey Chaucer *c.*1343–1400

English poet

Line references are to *The Riverside Chaucer* (ed. F. N. Robinson, 1987)

5 Ful craftier to pley she was
Than Athalus, that made the game
First of the ches, so was his name.

The Book of the Duchess l. 662

6 Whan that Aprill with his shoures soote
The droghte of March hath perced to the roote.

The Canterbury Tales 'The General Prologue' l. 1

7 And smale foweles maken melodye,
That slepen al the nyght with open ye
(So priketh hem nature in hir corages),
Thanne longen folk to goon on pilgrimages.

The Canterbury Tales 'The General Prologue' l. 9

8   He loved chivalrie,
Trouthe and honour, fredom and curteisie.

The Canterbury Tales 'The General Prologue' l. 45

9 He was a verray, parfit gentil knyght.

The Canterbury Tales 'The General Prologue' l. 72

10 He was as fressh as is the month of May.

The Canterbury Tales 'The General Prologue' l. 92

11 He koude songes make and wel endite.

The Canterbury Tales 'The General Prologue' l. 95

12 Curteis he was, lowely, and servysable,
And carf biforn his fader at the table.

The Canterbury Tales 'The General Prologue' l. 99

13 Hire gretteste ooth was but by Seinte Loy.

The Canterbury Tales 'The General Prologue' l. 120

14 Ful weel she soong the service dyvyne,
Entuned in hir nose ful semely;
And Frenssh she spak ful faire and fetisly,
After the scole of Stratford atte Bowe,
For Frenssh of Parys was to hire unknowe.

The Canterbury Tales 'The General Prologue' l. 122

15 She wolde wepe, if that she saugh a mous
Kaught in a trappe, if it were deed or bledde.
Of smale houndes hadde she that she fedde
With rosted flessh, or milk and wastel-breed.
But soore wepte she if oon of hem were deed.

The Canterbury Tales 'The General Prologue' l. 144

16 Of smal coral aboute hire arm she bar
A peire of bedes, gauded al with grene,
And theron heng a brooch of gold ful sheene,
On which ther was first write a crowned A,
And after *Amor vincit omnia*.

The Canterbury Tales 'The General Prologue' l. 158. Cf. Virgil 715:8

17 He yaf nat of that text a pulled hen,
That seith that hunters ben nat hooly men.

The Canterbury Tales 'The General Prologue' l. 177

18 Somwhat he lipsed, for his wantownesse,
To make his Englissh sweete upon his tonge.

The Canterbury Tales 'The General Prologue' l. 264

19 A Clerk there was of Oxenford also,
That unto logyk hadde longe ygo.
As leene was his hors as is a rake,
And he was nat right fat, I undertake,
But looked holwe, and therto sobrely.

The Canterbury Tales 'The General Prologue' l. 285

20 For hym was levere have at his beddes heed
Twenty bookes, clad in blak or reed,
Of Aristotle and his philosophie
Than robes riche, or fithele, or gay sautrie.
But al be that he was a philosophre,
Yet hadde he but litel gold in cofre.

The Canterbury Tales 'The General Prologue' l. 293

21 And gladly wolde he lerne and gladly teche.

The Canterbury Tales 'The General Prologue' l. 308

22 Nowher so bisy a man as he ther nas,
And yet he semed bisier than he was.

The Canterbury Tales 'The General Prologue' l. 321

23 For he was Epicurus owene sone.

The Canterbury Tales 'The General Prologue' l. 336

24 It snewed in his hous of mete and drynke.

The Canterbury Tales 'The General Prologue' l. 345

25 Housbondes at chirche dore she hadde fyve,
Withouten oother compaignye in youthe—
But thereof nedeth nat to speke as nowthe.

The Canterbury Tales 'The General Prologue' l. 460

1 This noble ensample to his sheep he yaf,
That first he wroghte, and afterward he taughte.
The Canterbury Tales 'The General Prologue' l. 496

2 If gold ruste, what shall iren do?
The Canterbury Tales 'The General Prologue' l. 500

3 But Cristes loore and his apostels twelve
He taughte; but first he folwed it hymselve.
The Canterbury Tales 'The General Prologue' l. 527

4 His nosethirles blake were and wyde.
A swerd and a bokeler bar he by his syde.
His mouth as greet was as a greet forneys.
He was a janglere and a goliardeys,
And that was moost of synne and harlotries.
The Canterbury Tales 'The General Prologue' l. 557

5 A Somonour was ther with us in that place,
That hadde a fyr-reed cherubynnes face,
For saucefleem he was, with eyen narwe.
As hoot he was and lecherous as a sparwe.
The Canterbury Tales 'The General Prologue' l. 623

6 Wel loved he garleek, oynons, and eek lekes,
And for to drynken strong wyn, reed as blood.
The Canterbury Tales 'The General Prologue' l. 634

7 His walet, biforn him in his lappe,
Bretful of pardoun, comen from Rome al hoot.
The Canterbury Tales 'The General Prologue' l. 686

8 He hadde a croys of latoun ful of stones,
And in a glas he hadde pigges bones.
But with thise relikes, whan that he fond
A povre person dwellynge upon lond,
Upon a day he gat hym moore moneye
Than that the person gat in monthes tweye;
And thus, with feyned flaterye and japes,
He made the person and the peple his apes.
The Canterbury Tales 'The General Prologue' l. 699

9 O stormy peple! Unsad and evere untrewe!
The Canterbury Tales 'The Clerk's Tale' l. 995

10 Grisilde is deed, and eek hire pacience,
And bothe atones buryed in Ytaille;
For which I crie in open audience
No wedded man so hardy be t'assaille
His wyves pacience in trust to fynde
Grisildis, for in certein he shal faille.
The Canterbury Tales 'The Clerk's Tale. Lenvoy de Chaucer'
l. 1177

11 Ye archewyves, stondeth at defense,
Syn ye be strong as is a greet camaille;
Ne suffreth nat that men yow doon offense.
And sklendre wyves, fieble as in bataille,
Beth egre as is a tygre yond in Ynde;
Ay clappeth as a mille, I yow consaille.
The Canterbury Tales 'The Clerk's Tale: Lenvoy de Chaucer'
l. 1195

12 Be ay of chiere as light as leef on lynde,
And lat hym care, and wepe, and wrynge, and
waille!
The Canterbury Tales 'The Clerk's Tale: Lenvoy de Chaucer'
l. 1211

13 For o thyng, sires, saufly dar I seye,
That freendes everych oother moot obeye,
If they wol longe holden compaignye.
Love wol nat been constreyned by maistrye.
When maistrie comth, the God of Love anon
Beteth his wynges, and farewel, he is gon!
Love is a thyng as any spirit free.
Wommen, of kynde, desiren libertee,
And nat to been constreyned as a thral;
And so doon men, if I sooth seyen shal.
The Canterbury Tales 'The Franklin's Tale' l. 761

14 Til that the brighte sonne loste his hewe;
For th'orisonte hath reft the sonne his lyght—
This is as muche to seye as it was nyght.
The Canterbury Tales 'The Franklin's Tale' l. 1016

15 Trouthe is the hyeste thyng that man may kepe.
The Canterbury Tales 'The Franklin's Tale' l. 1479

16 The carl spak oo thing, but he thoghte another.
The Canterbury Tales 'The Friar's Tale' l. 1568

17 And therefore, at the kynges court, my brother,
Ech man for hymself, ther is noon oother.
The Canterbury Tales 'The Knight's Tale' l. 1181

18 And whan a beest is deed he hath no peyne;
But man after his deeth moot wepe and pleyne.
The Canterbury Tales 'The Knight's Tale' l. 1319

19 The bisy larke, messager of day.
The Canterbury Tales 'The Knight's Tale' l. 1491

20 For pitee renneth soone in gentil herte.
The Canterbury Tales 'The Knight's Tale' l. 1761

21 The smylere with the knyf under the cloke.
The Canterbury Tales 'The Knight's Tale' l. 1999

22 Up roos the sonne, and up roos Emelye.
The Canterbury Tales 'The Knight's Tale' l. 2273

23 What is this world? what asketh men to have?
Now with his love, now in his colde grave.
The Canterbury Tales 'The Knight's Tale' l. 2777

24 She is mirour of alle curteisye.
The Canterbury Tales 'The Man of Law's Tale' l. 166

25 Have ye nat seyn somtyme a pale face,
Among a prees, of hym that hath be lad
Toward his deeth, wher as hym gat no grace,
And swich a colour in his face hath had
Men myghte knowe his fact that was bistad
Amonges alle the faces in that route?
The Canterbury Tales 'The Man of Law's Tale' l. 645

26 Lat take a cat, and fostre hym wel with milk
And tendre flessh, and make his couche of silk,
And lay hym seen a mous go by the wal,
Anon he weyveth milk and flessh and al,
And every deyntee that is in that hous,
Swich appetit hath he to ete a mous.
The Canterbury Tales 'The Manciple's Tale' l. 175

27 Kepe wel they tonge, and thenk upon the crowe.
The Canterbury Tales 'The Manciple's Tale' l. 362

28 And what is bettre than wisedoom? Womman. And
what is bettre than a good womman? Nothyng.
The Canterbury Tales 'The Tale of Melibee' l. 1107

29 She was a prymerole, a piggesnye,
For any lord to leggen in his bedde,
Or yet for any good yeman to wedde.
The Canterbury Tales 'The Miller's Tale' l. 3268

1 Derk was the nyght as pich, or as the cole,
And at the wyndow out she putte hir hole,
And Absolon, hym fil no bet be wers,
But with his mouth he kiste hir naked ers
Ful savourly, er he were war of this.
Abak he stirte, and thoughte it was amys,
For wel he wiste a womman hath no berd,
He felte a thyng al rough and long yherd,
And seyde, 'Fy! allas! what have I to do?'
'Tehee!' quod she, and clapte the wyndow to.
The Canterbury Tales 'The Miller's Tale' l. 3730

2 For certein, whan that Fortune list to flee,
Ther may no man the cours of hire withholde.
The Canterbury Tales 'The Monk's Tale' l. 1995

3 Ful wys is he that kan hymselven knowe!
The Canterbury Tales 'The Monk's Tale' l. 2139

4 Redeth the grete poete of Ytaille
That highte Dant, for he kan al devyse
Fro point to point; nat o word wol he faille.
The Canterbury Tales 'The Monk's Tale' l. 2460

5 His coomb was redder than the fyn coral,
And batailled as it were a castel wal;
His byle was blak, and as the jeet it shoon;
Lyk asure were his legges and his toon;
His nayles whitter than the lylye flour,
And lyk the burned gold was his colour,
This gentil cok hadde in his governaunce
Sevene hennes for to doon al his plesaunce,
Whiche were his sustres and his paramours,
And wonder lyk to hym, as of colours;
Of whiche the faireste hewed on hir throte
Was cleped fair damoysele Pertelote.
The Canterbury Tales 'The Nun's Priest's Tale' l. 2859

6 Mordre wol out; that se we day by day.
The Canterbury Tales 'The Nun's Priest's Tale' l. 3052

7 Whan that the month in which the world bigan,
That highte March, whan God first maked man.
The Canterbury Tales 'The Nun's Priest's Tale' l. 3187

8 And on a Friday fil al this meschaunce.
The Canterbury Tales 'The Nun's Priest's Tale' l. 3341

9 Thanne peyne I me to strecche forth the nekke,
And est and west upon the peple I bekke.
The Canterbury Tales 'The Pardoner's Prologue' l. 395

10 O wombe! O bely! O stynkyng cod
Fulfilled of dong and of corrupcioun!
The Canterbury Tales 'The Pardoner's Tale' l. 534

11 What, carl, with sory grace!
The Canterbury Tales 'The Pardoner's Tale' l. 717

12 And lightly as it comth, so wol we spende.
The Canterbury Tales 'The Pardoner's Tale' l. 781

13 Yet in oure asshen olde is fyr yreke.
The Canterbury Tales 'The Reeve's Prologue' l. 3882

14 The gretteste clerkes been noght wisest men.
The Canterbury Tales 'The Reeve's Tale' l. 4054

15 So was hir joly whistle wel ywet.
The Canterbury Tales 'The Reeve's Tale' l. 4155

16 Thou lookest as thou woldest fynde an hare,
For evere upon the ground I se thee stare.
The Canterbury Tales 'Prologue to Sir Thopas' l. 696

17 He hadde a semely nose.
The Canterbury Tales 'Sir Thopas' l. 729

18 'By God,' quod he, 'for pleynly, at a word,
Thy drasty rymyng is nat worth a toord!'
The Canterbury Tales 'Sir Thopas' l. 929

19 Experience, though noon auctoritee
Were in this world, is right ynogh for me
To speke of wo that is in mariage.
The Canterbury Tales 'The Wife of Bath's Prologue' l. 1

20 Yblessed be god that I have wedded fyve!
Welcome the sixte, whan that evere he shal.
For sothe, I wol nat kepe me chaast in al.
Whan myn housbonde is fro the world ygon,
Som Cristen man shall wedde me anon.
The Canterbury Tales 'The Wife of Bath's Prologue' l. 44

21 And after wyn on Venus moste I thynke,
For al so siker as cold engendreth hayl,
A likerous mouth moste han a likerous tayl.
The Canterbury Tales 'The Wife of Bath's Prologue' l. 464

22 But—Lord Crist!—what that it remembreth me
Upon my yowthe, and on my jolitee,
It tikleth me aboute myn herte roote.
Unto this day it dooth myn herte boote
That I have had my world as in my time.
The Canterbury Tales 'The Wife of Bath's Prologue' l. 469

23 And for to se, and eek for to be seye
Of lusty folk.
The Canterbury Tales 'The Wife of Bath's Prologue' l. 552

24 But yet I hadde alwey a coltes tooth.
Gat-tothed I was, and that bicam me weel.
The Canterbury Tales 'The Wife of Bath's Prologue' l. 602

25 Of which mayde anon, maugree hir heed,
By verray force, he rafte hire maydenhed.
The Canterbury Tales 'The Wife of Bath's Tale' l. 887

26 'My lige lady, generally,' quod he,
'Wommen desiren to have sovereynetee
As wel over hir housbond as hir love.'
The Canterbury Tales 'The Wife of Bath's Tale' l. 1037

27 That he is gentil that dooth gentil dedis.
The Canterbury Tales 'The Wife of Bath's Tale' l. 1170

28   Venus clerk Ovide,
That hath ysowen wonder wide
The grete god of Loves name.
The House of Fame l. 1487

29 A thousand tymes have I herd men telle
That ther ys joy in hevene and peyne in helle,
And I acorde wel that it ys so;
But, natheles, yet wot I wel also
That ther nis noon dwellyng in this contree
That eyther hath in hevene or helle ybe,
Ne may of hit noon other weyes witen
But as he hath herd seyd or founde it writen;
For by assay ther may no man it preve.
But God forbede but men shulde leve
Wel more thing then men han seen with ye!
Men shal not wenen every thing a lye
But yf himself yt seeth, or elles dooth;
For, God wot, thing is never the lasse sooth,
Thogh every wight ne may it nat ysee.
Bernard the monk ne saugh nat all, pardee!
The Legend of Good Women 'The Prologue' l. 1

1 And as for me, though that I konne but lyte,
On bokes for to rede I me delyte,
And to hem yive I feyth and ful credence,
And in myn herte have hem in reverence
So hertely, that ther is game noon
That fro my bokes maketh me to goon,
But yt be seldom on the holyday,
Save, certeynly, whan that the month of May
Is comen, and that I here the foules synge,
And that the floures gynnen for to sprynge,
Farewel my bok and my devocioun!
The Legend of Good Women 'The Prologue' l. 29

2   Of al the floures in the mede,
Thanne love I most thise floures white and rede,
Swiche as men callen daysyes in our toun.
The Legend of Good Women 'The Prologue' l. 41

3 That wel by reson men it calle may
The 'dayesye,' or elles the 'ye of day,'
The emperice and flour of floures alle.
I pray to God that faire mote she falle,
And alle that loven floures, for hire sake!
The Legend of Good Women 'The Prologue' l. 183

4 And she was fayr as is the rose in May.
The Legend of Good Women 'Cleopatra' l. 613

5 That lyf so short, the craft so long to lerne,
Th'assay so hard, so sharp the conquerynge.
The Parliament of Fowls l. 1. Cf. Hippocrates 339:6

6 Thou shalt make castels thanne in Spayne
And dreme of joye, all but in vayne.
The Romaunt of the Rose l. 2573

7 O blynde world, O blynde entencioun!
How often falleth al the effect contraire
Of surquidrie and foul presumpcioun;
For kaught is proud, and kaught is debonaire.
This Troilus is clomben on the staire,
And litel weneth that he moot descenden;
But alday faileth thing that fooles wenden.
Troilus and Criseyde bk. 1, l. 211

8 For evere it was, and evere it shal byfalle,
That Love is he that alle thing may bynde,
For may no man fordon the lawe of kynde.
Troilus and Criseyde bk. 1, l. 236

9 For it is seyd, 'Man maketh ofte a yerde
With which the maker is hymself ybeten
In sondry manere.'
Troilus and Criseyde bk. 1, l. 740

10 But love a womman that she woot it nought,
And she wol quyte it that thow shalt nat fele;
Unknowe, unkist, and lost, that is unsought.
Troilus and Criseyde bk. 1, l. 807

11 O wynd, O wynd, the weder gynneth clere.
Troilus and Criseyde bk. 2, l. 2

12 Ye knowe ek that in forme of speche is chaunge
Withinne a thousand yeer, and wordes tho
That hadden pris, now wonder nyce and straunge
Us thinketh hem, and yet thei spake hem so.
Troilus and Criseyde bk. 2, l. 22

13 So longe mote ye lyve, and alle proude,
Til crowes feet be growe under youre yë.
Troilus and Criseyde bk. 2, l. 402

14 And we shall speek of the somwhat, I trowe,
Whan thow art gon, to don thyn eris glowe!
Troilus and Criseyde bk. 2, l. 1021

15 God loveth, and to love wol nought werne,
And in this world no lyves creature
Withouten love is worth, or may endure.
Troilus and Criseyde bk. 3, l. 12

16 It is nought good a slepyng hound to wake.
Troilus and Criseyde bk. 3, l. 764

17 For I have seyn of a ful misty morwe
Folowen ful ofte a myrie someris day.
Troilus and Criseyde bk. 3, l. 1060

18 Right as an aspes leef she gan to quake.
Troilus and Criseyde bk. 3, l. 1200

19 And as the newe abaysed nyghtyngale,
That stynteth first whan she bygynneth to synge.
Troilus and Criseyde bk. 3, l. 1233

20 For of fortunes sharpe adversitee
The worst kynde of infortune is this,
A man to han ben in prosperitee,
And it remembren, whan it passed is.
Troilus and Criseyde bk. 3, l. 1625. Cf. Boethius 116:12,
Dante 230:11

21 Oon ere it herde, at tother out it wente.
Troilus and Criseyde bk. 4, l. 434

22 But manly sette the world on six and sevene;
And if thow deye a martyr, go to hevene!
Troilus and Criseyde bk. 4, l. 622

23 For tyme ylost may nought recovered be.
Troilus and Criseyde bk. 4, l. 1283

24 Ye, farc wel al the snow of ferne yere!
Troilus and Criseyde bk. 5, l. 1176

25 Ek gret effect men write in place lite;
Th' entente is al, and nat the lettres space.
Troilus and Criseyde bk. 5, l. 1629

26 Go, litel bok, go, litel myn tragedye,
Ther God thi makere yet, er that he dye,
So sende myght to make in som comedye!
But litel bok, no makyng thow n'envie,
But subgit be to alle poesye;
And kis the steppes, where as thow seest pace
Virgile, Ovide, Omer, Lucan, and Stace.
And for ther is so gret diversite
In Englissh and in writyng of oure tonge,
So prey I God that non myswrite the,
Ne the mysmetre for defaute of tonge;
And red wherso thow be, or elles songe,
That thow be understonde, God I biseche!
Troilus and Criseyde bk. 5, l. 1786

1 And whan that he was slayn in this manere,
His lighte goost ful blisfully is went
Up to the holughnesse of the eighthe spere,
In convers letyng everich element;
And ther he saugh, with ful avysement
The erratik sterres, herkenyng armonye
With sownes ful of hevenyssh melodie.
And doun from thennes faste he gan avyse
This litel spot of erthe, that with the se
Embraced is, and fully gan despise
This wrecched world, and held al vanite
To respect of the pleyn felicite
That is in hevene above.
  Troilus and Criseyde bk. 5, l. 1807

2 O yonge, fresshe folkes, he or she,
In which that love up groweth with youre age,
Repeyreth hom fro worldly vanyte,
And of youre herte up casteth the visage
To thilke God that after his ymage
Yow made, and thynketh al nys but a faire,
This world that passeth soone as floures faire.
And loveth hym the which that right for love
Upon a crois, our soules for to beye,
First start, and roos, and sit in hevene above;
For he nyl falsen no wight, dar I seye,
That wol his herte al holly on hym leye.
And syn he best to love is, and most meke,
What nedeth feynede loves for to seke?
Lo here, of payens corsed olde rites!
Lo here, what alle hire goddes may availle!
Lo here, thise wrecched worldes appetites!
Lo here, the fyn and guerdoun for travaille
Of Jove, Appollo, of Mars, of swich rascaille!
  Troilus and Criseyde bk. 5, l. 1835

3 O moral Gower, this book I directe
To the.
  Troilus and Criseyde bk. 5, l. 1856

4 Flee fro the prees, and dwelle with sothfastnesse.
  'Truth: Balade de Bon Conseyle' l. 1

5 Forth, pilgrim, forth! Forth, beste, out of thy stal!
Know thy contree, look up, thank God of al;
Hold the heye wey, and lat thy gost thee lede,
And trowth thee shal delivere, it is no drede.
  'Truth: Balade de Bon Conseyle' l. 18

Anton Chekhov 1860–1904
Russian playwright and short-story writer

6 Если против какой-нибудь болезни предлагается очень много средств, то это значит, что болезнь неизлечима.

If a lot of cures are suggested for a disease, it means that the disease is incurable.
  The Cherry Orchard (1904) act 1 (translated by Elisaveta Fen)

7 Какая там гордость, есть ли в ней смысл, если человек физиологически устроен неважно, если в своем громадном большинстве он груб, неумен, глубоко несчастлив?

Where's the sense in being proud when you consider that Man, as a species, is not very well constructed physiologically, and in the vast majority of cases is coarse, stupid, and profoundly unhappy, too?
  The Cherry Orchard (1904) act 2 (translated by Elisaveta Fen)

8 Господи, ты дал нам громадные леса, необъятные поля, глубочайшие горизонты, и, живя тут, мы сами должны бы по-настоящему быть великанами.

The Lord God has given us vast forests, immense fields, wide horizons; surely we ought to be giants, living in such a country as this.
  The Cherry Orchard (1904) act 2 (translated by Elisaveta Fen)

9 Чтобы начать жить в настоящем, надо сначала искупить наше прошлое, покончить с ним, а искупить его можно только страданием, только необычайным, непрырывным трудом.

To begin to live in the present, we must first atone for our past and be finished with it, and we can only atone for it by suffering, by extraordinary, unceasing exertion.
  The Cherry Orchard (1904) act 2 (translated by Elisaveta Fen)

10 Все прекрасно на этом свете, все, кроме того, что мы сами мыслим и делаем, когда забываем о высших целях бытия, о своем человеческом достоинстве.

[Gurov reflected that] . . . everything in the world was really beautiful, everything but our own thoughts and actions when we lose sight of the higher aims of existence and our dignity as human beings.
  The Lady with the Little Dog ch. 2 (translated by David Magarshak)

11 МЕДВЕДЕНКО: Отчего вы всегда ходите в черном?
  МАША: Это траур по моей жизни.

MEDVEDENKO: Why do you wear black all the time?
  MASHA: I'm in mourning for my life, I'm unhappy.
  The Seagull (1896) act 1

12 НИНА: В вашей пьесе трудно играть. В ней нет живых лиц.
  ТРЕПЛЕВ: Живые лица! Надо изображать жизнь не такою, как она есть, и не такою, как должна быть, а такою, как она представляется в мечтах.

NINA: Your play's hard to act, there are no living people in it.
  TREPLEV: Living people! We should show life neither as it is nor as it ought to be, but as we see it in our dreams.
  The Seagull (1896) act 1

13 Женщины не прощают неуспеха.

Women can't forgive failure.
  The Seagull (1896) act 2

1 Я — чайка. Нет, не то . . . Помните, вы
подстрелили чайку? Случайно пришел человек,
увидел и от нечего делать погубил . . . Сюжет для
рассказа.

I'm a seagull. No, that's wrong. Remember you shot a
seagull? A man happened to come along, saw it and
killed it, just to pass the time. A plot for a short story.

The Seagull (1896) act 4

2 Человек должен трудиться, работать в поте
лица, кто бы он ни был, и в этом одном
заключается смысл и цель его жизни, его счастье,
его восторги.

Man must work by the sweat of his brow whatever his
class, and that should make up the whole meaning
and purpose of his life and happiness and
contentment.

The Three Sisters (1901) act 1 (translated by Elisaveta Fen)

3 Счастлив тот, кто не замечает, лето теперь или
зима.

People who don't even notice whether it's summer or
winter are lucky!

The Three Sisters (1901) act 2 (translated by Elisaveta Fen)

4 Жизнь наша еще не закончена. Будем жить . . . еще
немного, и мы узнаем, зачем мы живем, зачем
страдаем.

Life isn't finished for us yet! We're going to live! . . .
Maybe, if we wait a little longer, we shall find out why
we live, why we suffer.

The Three Sisters (1901) act 4 (translated by Elisaveta Fen)

5 Человек одарен разумом и творческою силой,
чтобы преумножать то, что ему дано, но до сих
пор он не творил, а разрушал. Лесов всё меньше и
меньше, реки сохнут, дичь перевелась, климат
испорчен, и с каждым днем земля становится
всё беднее и безобразнее.

Man has been endowed with reason, with the power
to create, so that he can add to what he's been given.
But up to now he hasn't been a creator, only a
destroyer. Forests keep disappearing, rivers dry up,
wild life's become extinct, the climate's ruined and the
land grows poorer and uglier every day.

Uncle Vanya (1897) act 1

6 Женщина может быть другом мужчины лишь в той
последовательности: сначала приятель, потом
любовница, а затем уж друг.

A woman can become a man's friend only in the
following stages—first an acquaintance, next a
mistress, and only then a friend.

Uncle Vanya (1897) act 2

7 Когда женщина некрасива, то ей говорят: «У вас
прекрасные глаза, у вас прекрасные волосы.»

When a woman isn't beautiful, people always say,
'You have lovely eyes, you have lovely hair.'

Uncle Vanya (1897) act 3

8 Субъективность ужасная вещь. Она нехороша уже
и тем, что выдает бедного автора с руками и
ногами.

Subjectivity is a terrible thing. It is bad in this alone,
that it reveals the author's hands and feet.

Letter to Alexander Chekhov, April 1883, in L. S. Friedland
(ed.) *Anton Chekhov: Letters on the Short Story* . . . (1964)

9 Литератор должен быть так же объективен, как
химик; он должен отрешиться от житейской
субъективности и знать, что навозные кучи в
пейзаже играют очень почтенную роль, а злые
страсти так же присущи жизни, как и добрые.

A writer must be as objective as a chemist: he must
abandon the subjective line; he must know that
dung-heaps play a very reasonable part in a
landscape, and that evil passions are as inherent in life
as good ones.

Letter to M. V. Kiselev, 14 January 1887, in L. S. Friedland
(ed.) *Anton Chekhov: Letters on the Short Story* . . . (1964)

10 Медицина — моя законная жена, а литература —
любовница. Когда надоедает одна, я ночую у
другой.

Medicine is my lawful wife and literature is my
mistress. When I get tired of one I spend the night
with the other.

Letter to A. S. Suvorin, 11 September 1888, in L. S.
Friedland (ed.) *Anton Chekhov: Letters on the Short Story* . . .
(1964)

11 Моя святая святых — это человеческое тело,
здоровье, ум, талант, вдохновение, любовь и
абсолютнейшая свобода, свобода от силы и лжи,
в чем бы последние две ни выражались.

My holy of holies is the human body, health,
intelligence, talent, inspiration, love and the most
absolute freedom—freedom from violence and lying,
whatever the forms they may take.

Letter to A. N. Pleshcheyev, 4 October 1888, in L. S.
Friedland (ed.) *Anton Chekhov: Letters on the Short Story* . . .
(1964)

12 Краткость — сестра таланта.

Brevity is the sister of talent.

Letter to Alexander Chekhov, 11 April 1889, in L. S.
Friedland (ed.) *Anton Chekhov: Letters on the Short Story* . . .
(1964)

13 В «Анне Карениной» и в «Онегине» не решен ни
один вопрос, но они Вас вполне
удовлетворяют, потому только, что все
вопросы подставлены в них правильно. Суд
обязан ставить правильно вопросы, а решают
пусть присяжные, каждый на свой вкус.

In *Anna Karenina* and *Onegin* not a single problem is
solved, but they satisfy you completely just because all
their problems are correctly presented. The court is
obliged to submit the case fairly, but let the jury do
the deciding, each according to its own judgement.

Letter to Alexei Suvorin, 27 October 1888, in L. Hellman
(ed.) *Selected Letters of Anton Chekhov* (1955, translated by
S. Lederer)

Lord Chesterfield (*Philip Dormer Stanhope, 4th Earl of Chesterfield*) 1694–1773

English writer and politician

14 Unlike my subject will I frame my song,
It shall be witty and it sha'n't be long.

Epigram on 'Long' Sir Thomas Robinson in the *Dictionary of
National Biography* (1917–) vol. 17, p. 51

1 In scandal, as in robbery, the receiver is always thought as bad as the thief.

Advice to his Son (1775) 'Rules for Conversation: Private Scandal'

2 In matters of religion and matrimony I never give any advice; because I will not have anybody's torments in this world or the next laid to my charge.

Letters to Arthur Charles Stanhope, Esq. (1817) 12 October 1765

3 Religion is by no means a proper subject of conversation in a mixed company.

Letters . . . to his Godson and Successor (1890) Letter 142

4 Cunning is the dark sanctuary of incapacity.

Letters . . . to his Godson and Successor (1890) 'Letter . . . to be delivered after his own death'

5 In my opinion, parsons are very like men, and neither the better nor the worse for wearing a black gown.

Letters to his Son (1774) 5 April 1746

6 The knowledge of the world is only to be acquired in the world, and not in a closet.

Letters to his Son (1774) 4 October 1746

7 An injury is much sooner forgotten than an insult.

Letters to his Son (1774) 9 October 1746

8 Courts and camps are the only places to learn the world in.

Letters to his Son (1774) 2 October 1747

9 Take the tone of the company that you are in.

Letters to his Son (1774) 16 October 1747

10 Do as you would be done by is the surest method that I know of pleasing.

Letters to his Son (1774) 16 October 1747

11 I recommend to you to take care of minutes: for hours will take care of themselves.

Letters to his Son (1774) 6 November 1747. Cf. Lowndes 431:1

12 Advice is seldom welcome; and those who want it the most always like it the least.

Letters to his Son (1774) 29 January 1748

13 Wear your learning, like your watch in a private pocket: and do not merely pull it out and strike it, merely to show that you have one.

Letters to his Son (1774) 22 February 1748

14 Speak of the moderns without contempt, and of the ancients without idolatry.

Letters to his Son (1774) 27 February 1748

15 In my mind, there is nothing so illiberal and so ill-bred, as audible laughter.

Letters to his Son (1774) 9 March 1748. Cf. Catullus 186:3, Congreve 215:1

16 Women, then, are only children of a larger growth.

Letters to his Son (1774) 5 September 1748. Cf. Dryden 260:1

17 It must be owned, that the Graces do not seem to be natives of Great Britain; and I doubt, the best of us here have more of rough than polished diamond.

Letters to his Son (1774) 18 November 1748

18 Idleness is only the refuge of weak minds.

Letters to his Son (1774) 20 July 1749

19 Putting moral virtues at the highest, and religion at the lowest, religion must still be allowed to be a collateral security, at least, to virtue; and every prudent man will sooner trust to two securities than to one.

Letters to his Son (1774) 8 January 1750

20 It is commonly said, and more particularly by Lord Shaftesbury, that ridicule is the best test of truth.

Letters to his Son (1774) 6 February 1752. Cf. Shaftesbury 563:21, 563:22

21 Knowledge may give weight, but accomplishments give lustre, and many more people see than weigh.

Maxims, in *Letters to his Son* (3rd ed., 1774) vol. 4, p. 304

22 The chapter of knowledge is a very short, but the chapter of accidents is a very long one.

Letter to Solomon Dayrolles, 16 February 1753, in M. Maty (ed.) *Miscellaneous Works* vol. 2 (1778) no. 79

23 I . . . could not help reflecting in my way upon the singular ill-luck of this my dear country, which, as long as ever I remember it, and as far back as I have read, has always been governed by the only two or three people, out of two or three millions, totally incapable of governing, and unfit to be trusted.

M. Maty (ed.) *Miscellaneous Works* vol. 2 (1778) 'Miscellaneous Pieces' no. 45 (first published in *The World* 7 October 1756)

24 Tyrawley and I have been dead these two years; but we don't choose to have it known.

In James Boswell *Life of Samuel Johnson* (1934 ed.) vol. 2, p. 211 (3 April 1773)

25 The pleasure is momentary, the position ridiculous, and the expense damnable.

On sex (attributed)

26 Give Dayrolles a chair.

Last words (Dayrolles being his godson), in W. H. Craig *Life of Lord Chesterfield* (1907) p. 343

G. K. Chesterton 1874–1936

English essayist, novelist, and poet

27 I tell you naught for your comfort,
Yea, naught for your desire,
Save that the sky grows darker yet
And the sea rises higher.

The Ballad of the White Horse (1911) bk. 1, p. 18

28 For the great Gaels of Ireland
Are the men that God made mad,
For all their wars are merry,
And all their songs are sad.

The Ballad of the White Horse (1911) bk. 2, p. 35

29 The thing on the blind side of the heart,
On the wrong side of the door,
The green plant groweth, menacing
Almighty lovers in the Spring;
There is always a forgotten thing,
And love is not secure.

The Ballad of the White Horse (1911) bk. 3, p. 52

30 Fools! For I also had my hour;
One far fierce hour and sweet:
There was a shout about my ears,
And palms before my feet.

'The Donkey' (1900)

1 They died to save their country and they only saved the world.
'English Graves' (1922)

2 Why do you rush through the fields in trains,
Guessing so much and so much.
Why do you flash through the flowery meads,
Fat-head poet that nobody reads;
And why do you know such a frightful lot
About people in gloves and such?
'The Fat White Woman Speaks' (1933); an answer to Frances Cornford. Cf. Cornford 219:4

3 From all that terror teaches,
From lies of tongue and pen,
From all the easy speeches
That comfort cruel men,
From sale and profanation
Of honour and the sword,
From sleep and from damnation,
Deliver us, good Lord!
'A Hymn' (1915)

4 Strong gongs groaning as the guns boom far,
Don John of Austria is going to the war.
'Lepanto' (1915)

5 Before the Roman came to Rye or out to Severn strode,
The rolling English drunkard made the rolling English road.
A reeling road, a rolling road, that rambles round the shire,
And after him the parson ran, the sexton and the squire;
A merry road, a mazy road, and such as we did tread
The night we went to Birmingham by way of Beachy Head.
'The Rolling English Road' (1914)

6 For there is good news yet to hear and fine things to be seen,
Before we go to Paradise by way of Kensal Green.
'The Rolling English Road' (1914)

7 Smile at us, pay us, pass us; but do not quite forget.
For we are the people of England, that never have spoken yet.
'The Secret People' (1915)

8 We only know the last sad squires ride slowly towards the sea,
And a new people takes the land: and still it is not we.
'The Secret People' (1915)

9 And I dream of the days when work was scrappy,
And rare in our pockets the mark of the mint,
When we were angry and poor and happy,
And proud of seeing our names in print.
'A Song of Defeat' (1915)

10 They haven't got no noses,
The fallen sons of Eve.
'The Song of Quoodle' (1914)

11 And goodness only knowses
The Noselessness of Man.
'The Song of Quoodle' (1914)

12 And Noah he often said to his wife when he sat down to dine,
'I don't care where the water goes if it doesn't get into the wine.'
'Wine and Water' (1914)

13 An adventure is only an inconvenience rightly considered. An inconvenience is only an adventure wrongly considered.
All Things Considered (1908) 'On Running after one's Hat'

14 Literature is a luxury; fiction is a necessity.
The Defendant (1901) 'A Defence of Penny Dreadfuls'

15 The rich are the scum of the earth in every country.
The Flying Inn (1914) ch. 15

16 Bigotry may be roughly defined as the anger of men who have no opinions.
Heretics (1905) ch. 20

17 Thieves respect property. They merely wish the property to become their property that they may more perfectly respect it.
The Man who was Thursday (1908) ch. 4

18 Democracy means government by the uneducated, while aristocracy means government by the badly educated.
New York Times 1 February 1931, pt. 5, p. 1

19 Tradition means giving votes to the most obscure of all classes, our ancestors. It is the democracy of the dead.
Orthodoxy (1908) ch. 4

20 Democrats object to men being disqualified by the accident of birth; tradition objects to their being disqualified by the accident of death.
Orthodoxy (1908) ch. 4

21 All conservatism is based upon the idea that if you leave things alone you leave them as they are. But you do not. If you leave a thing alone you leave it to a torrent of change.
Orthodoxy (1908) ch. 7

22 He could not think up to the height of his own towering style.
The Victorian Age in Literature (1912) ch. 3 (Tennyson)

23 The Christian ideal has not been tried and found wanting. It has been found difficult; and left untried.
What's Wrong with the World (1910) pt. 1 'The Unfinished Temple'

24 The prime truth of woman, the universal mother . . . that if a thing is worth doing, it is worth doing badly.
What's Wrong with the World (1910) pt. 4 'Folly and Female Education'

Erskine Childers 1870–1922
Anglo-Irish writer and political activist

25 The riddle of the sands.
Title of novel (1903)

26 Come closer, boys. It will be easier for you.
To the firing squad at his execution, in Burke Wilkinson *The Zeal of the Convert* (1976) ch. 26

William Chillingworth 1602–44
English scholar

27 The Bible and the Bible only is the religion of Protestants.
The Religion of Protestants (1637)

28 I once knew a man out of courtesy help a lame dog over a stile, and he for requital bit his fingers.
The Religion of Protestants (1637)

Charles Chilton 1914–

See JOAN LITTLEWOOD

Thomas O. Chisholm 1866–1960

1 Great is thy faithfulness! Great is thy faithfulness!
  Morning by morning new mercies I see;
  All I have needed thy hand has provided.
  Great is thy faithfulness, Lord, unto me.
    'Great is thy faithfulness' (hymn)

Rufus Choate 1799–1859

American lawyer and politician

2 Its constitution the glittering and sounding generalities
  of natural right which make up the Declaration of
  Independence.
    Letter to the Maine Whig State Central Committee,
    9 August 1856, in S. G. Brown *The Works of Rufus Choate
    with a Memoir of his Life* (1862) vol. 1, p. 215. Cf. Emerson
    277:16

Noam Chomsky 1928–

American linguistics scholar

3 The notion 'grammatical' cannot be identified with
  'meaningful' or 'significant' in any semantic sense.
  Sentences (1) and (2) are equally nonsensical, but . . .
  only the former is grammatical.
    (1) Colourless green ideas sleep furiously.
    (2) Furiously sleep ideas green colourless.
    Syntactic Structures (1957) ch. 2

4 The empiricist view is so deep-seated in our way of
  looking at the human mind that it almost has the
  character of a superstition.
    Radio discussion, in *Listener* 30 May 1968

5 As soon as questions of will or decision or reason or
  choice of action arise, human science is at a loss.
    Television interview, in *Listener* 6 April 1978

Dame Agatha Christie (*née Miller*)
1890–1976

English writer of detective fiction

6 I learned . . . that one can never go back, that one
  should not ever try to go back—that the essence of life
  is going forward. Life is really a One Way Street.
    At Bertram's Hotel (1965) ch. 20

7 War settles *nothing* . . . to *win* a war is as disastrous as
  to lose one!
    An Autobiography (1977) pt. 10

8 He [Hercule Poirot] tapped his forehead. 'These little
  grey cells. It is "up to them".'
    The Mysterious Affair at Styles (1920) ch. 10

9 Trust the train, Mademoiselle, for it is *le bon Dieu* who
  drives it.
    The Mystery of the Blue Train (1928) ch. 36

Chuang-tzu (*or Zhuangzi*) c.369–286 BC

Chinese philosopher

10 I do not know whether I was then a man dreaming I
   was a butterfly, or whether I am now a butterfly
   dreaming I am a man.
    Chuang Tzu (1889) ch. 2 (translated by H. A. Giles)

Mary, Lady Chudleigh (*née Leigh*)
1656–1710

English poet

11 'Tis hard we should be by the men despised,
   Yet kept from knowing what would make us prized;
   Debarred from knowledge, banished from the schools,
   And with the utmost industry bred fools.
    The Ladies Defence (1701)

12 Wife and Servant are the same,
   But only differ in the name.
    Poems (1703) 'To the Ladies'

13 Then shun, oh! shun that wretched state
   And all the fawning flatterers hate:
   Value yourselves, and men despise
   You must be proud if you'll be wise.
    Poems (1703) 'To the Ladies' (on marriage)

Charles Churchill 1731–64

English poet

14 Though by whim, envy, or resentment led,
   They damn those authors whom they never read.
    The Candidate (1764) l. 57

15 The only difference, after all their rout,
   Is, that the one is in, the other out.
    The Conference (1763) l. 165

16 The danger chiefly lies in acting well;
   No crime's so great as daring to excel.
    An Epistle to William Hogarth (1763) l. 51

17   Be England what she will,
   With all her faults, she is my country still.
    The Farewell (1764) l. 27. Cf. Cowper 223:20

18 It can't be Nature, for it is not sense.
    The Farewell (1764) l. 200

19 England—a happy land we know,
   Where follies naturally grow.
    The Ghost (1763) bk. 1, l. 111

20 And adepts in the speaking trade
   Keep a cough by them ready made.
    The Ghost (1763) bk. 2, l. 545

21 Just to the windward of the law.
    The Ghost (1763) bk. 3, l. 56

22 . . . He for subscribers baits his hook,
   And takes your cash; but where's the book?
   No matter where; wise fear, you know,
   Forbids the robbing of a foe;
   But what, to serve our private ends,
   Forbids the cheating of our friends?
    The Ghost (1763) bk. 3, l. 801 (satirizing Samuel Johnson)

23 A joke's a very serious thing.
    The Ghost (1763) bk. 4, l. 1386

1 Happy, thrice happy now the savage race,
  Since Europe took their gold, and gave them grace!
  Pastors she sends to help them in their need,
  Some who can't write, with others who can't read.
  Gotham (1764) bk. 1, l. 67

2 Our vices, with more zeal than holy prayers,
  She teaches them, and in return takes theirs.
  Gotham (1764) bk. 1, l. 73

3 Old-age, a second child, by Nature cursed
  With more and greater evils than the first,
  Weak, sickly, full of pains; in ev'ry breath
  Railing at life, and yet afraid of death.
  Gotham (1764) bk. 1, l. 215

4 Keep up appearances; there lies the test;
  The world will give thee credit for the rest.
  Outward be fair, however foul within;
  Sin if thou wilt, but then in secret sin.
  Night (1761) l. 311

5 Stay out all night, but take especial care
  That Prudence bring thee back to early prayer
  As one with watching and with study faint,
  Reel in a drunkard, and reel out a saint.
  Night (1761) l. 321

6 Grave without thought, and without feeling gay.
  The Prophecy of Famine (1763) l. 60 (on pretentious poets)

7 Me . . . no Muse of heav'nly birth inspires,
  No judgement tempers when rash genius fires,
  Who boast no merit but mere knack of rhyme,
  Short gleams of sense, and satire out of time.
  The Prophecy of Famine (1763) l. 79

8 Apt Alliteration's artful aid.
  The Prophecy of Famine (1763) l. 86

9 He sickened at all triumphs but his own.
  The Rosciad (1761) l. 64 (of Thomas Franklin, Professor of
  Greek at Cambridge University)

10 To mischief trained, e'en from his mother's womb,
  Grown old in fraud, tho' yet in manhood's bloom.
  Adopting arts, by which gay villains rise,
  And reach the heights, which honest men despise;
  Mute at the bar, and in the senate loud,
  Dull 'mongst the dullest, proudest of the proud;
  A pert, prim prater of the northern race,
  Guilt in his heart, and famine in his face.
  The Rosciad (1761) l. 69 (of Alexander Wedderburn, later
  Lord Loughborough)

11 Ne'er blushed unless, in spreading .e's snares,
  She blundered on some virtue unawares.
  The Rosciad (1761) l. 137

12 So much they talked, so very little said.
  The Rosciad (1761) l. 550

13 Learned without sense, and venerably dull.
  The Rosciad (1761) l. 592 (of Arthur Murphy)

14 But, spite of all the criticizing elves,
  Those who would make us feel, must feel themselves.
  The Rosciad (1761) l. 961

15 The two extremes appear like man and wife,
  Coupled together for the sake of strife.
  The Rosciad (1761) l. 1005

16 Where he falls short, 'tis Nature's fault alone;
  Where he succeeds, the merit's all his own.
  The Rosciad (1761) l. 1025 (of the actor, Thomas Sheridan)

Lord Randolph Churchill 1849–94
British Conservative politician

17 For the purposes of recreation he [Gladstone] has
  selected the felling of trees, and we may usefully
  remark that his amusements, like his politics, are
  essentially destructive . . . The forest laments in order
  that Mr Gladstone may perspire.
  Speech on Financial Reform, delivered in Blackpool,
  24 January 1884, in F. Banfield (ed.) *Life and Speeches of
  Lord Randolph Churchill* (1884)

18 He [Gladstone] told them that he would give them and
  all other subjects of the Queen much legislation, great
  prosperity, and universal peace, and he has given
  them nothing but chips. Chips to the faithful allies in
  Afghanistan, chips to the trusting native races of
  South Africa, chips to the Egyptian fellah, chips to the
  British farmer, chips to the manufacturer and the
  artisan, chips to the agricultural labourer, chips to the
  House of Commons itself.
  Speech on Financial Reform, delivered in Blackpool,
  24 January 1884, in F. Banfield (ed.) *Life and Speeches of
  Lord Randolph Churchill* (1884)

19 Ulster will fight; Ulster will be right.
  Public letter, 7 May 1886, in R. F. Foster *Lord Randolph
  Churchill* (1981) p. 258

20 An old man in a hurry.
  On Gladstone, in an address to the electors of South
  Paddington, 19 June 1886; in W. S. Churchill *Lord
  Randolph Churchill* (1906) vol. 2, p. 491

21 I decided some time ago that if the G.O.M. [Gladstone]
  went for Home Rule, the Orange card would be the
  one to play. Please God it may turn out the ace of
  trumps and not the two.
  Letter to Lord Justice FitzGibbon, 16 February 1834, in
  Robert Rhodes James *Lord Randolph Churchill* (1959) ch. 8
  (*G.O.M.* Grand Old Man)

22 All great men make mistakes. Napoleon forgot
  Blücher, I forgot Goschen.
  In *Leaves from the Notebooks of Lady Dorothy Nevill* (1907)
  p. 21

Sir Winston Churchill 1874–1965
*British Conservative politician; Prime Minister, 1940–5,
1951–5*

23 A labour contract into which men enter voluntarily
  for a limited and for a brief period, under which they
  are paid wages which they consider adequate, under
  which they are not bought or sold and from which
  they can obtain relief . . . on payment of £17.10s, the
  cost of their passage, may not be a healthy or proper
  contract, but it cannot in the opinion of His Majesty's
  Government be classified as slavery in the extreme
  acceptance of the word without some risk of
  terminological inexactitude.
  Speech, *Hansard* 22 February 1906, col. 555

24 He [Lord Charles Beresford] is one of those orators of
  whom it was well said, 'Before they get up, they do
  not know what they are going to say; when they are
  speaking, they do not know what they are saying;
  and when they have sat down, they do not know
  what they have said.'
  Speech, *Hansard* 20 December 1912, col. 1893

1 Business carried on as usual during alterations on the map of Europe.

Speech at Guildhall, 9 November 1914, *Complete Speeches* (1974) vol. 3, p. 2341 (on the self-adopted 'motto' of the British people)

2 The whole map of Europe has been changed ... but as the deluge subsides and the waters fall short we see the dreary steeples of Fermanagh and Tyrone emerging once again.

Speech, *Hansard* 16 February 1922, col. 1270

3 I remember, when I was a child, being taken to the celebrated Barnum's circus, which contained an exhibition of freaks and monstrosities, but the exhibit on the programme which I most desired to see was the one described as 'The Boneless Wonder'. My parents judged that that spectacle would be too revolting and demoralizing for my youthful eyes, and I have waited 50 years to see the boneless wonder sitting on the Treasury Bench.

Speech, *Hansard* 28 January 1931, col. 1021 (referring to Ramsay Macdonald)

4 So they [the Government] go on in strange paradox, decided only to be undecided, resolved to be irresolute, adamant for drift, solid for fluidity, all-powerful to be impotent.

Speech, *Hansard* 12 November 1936, col. 1107

5 Dictators ride to and fro upon tigers which they dare not dismount. And the tigers are getting hungry.

Letter, 11 November 1937, in *Step by Step* (1939) p. 186. See *Concise Oxford Dictionary of Proverbs* under 'rides'

6 The utmost he [Neville Chamberlain] has been able to gain for Czechoslovakia and in the matters which were in dispute has been that the German dictator, instead of snatching his victuals from the table, has been content to have them served to him course by course.

Speech, *Hansard* 5 October 1938, col. 361

7 I cannot forecast to you the action of Russia. It is a riddle wrapped in a mystery inside an enigma.

Radio broadcast, 1 October 1939, in *Into Battle* (1941) p. 131

8 I have nothing to offer but blood, toil, tears and sweat.

Speech, *Hansard* 13 May 1940, col. 1502

9 What is our policy? ... to wage war against a monstrous tyranny, never surpassed in the dark, lamentable catalogue of human crime.

Speech, *Hansard* 13 May 1940, col. 1502

10 What is our aim? ... Victory, victory at all costs, victory in spite of all terror; victory, however long and hard the road may be; for without victory, there is no survival.

Speech, *Hansard* 13 May 1940, col. 1502

11 We shall not flag or fail. We shall go on to the end. We shall fight in France, we shall fight on the seas and oceans, we shall fight with growing confidence and growing strength in the air, we shall defend our island, whatever the cost may be. We shall fight on the beaches, we shall fight on the landing grounds, we shall fight in the fields and in the streets, we shall fight in the hills; we shall never surrender.

Speech, *Hansard* 4 June 1940, col. 796

12 Let us therefore brace ourselves to our duty, and so bear ourselves that, if the British Commonwealth and its Empire lasts for a thousand years, men will still say, 'This was their finest hour.'

Speech, *Hansard* 18 June 1940, col. 60

13 Never in the field of human conflict was so much owed by so many to so few.

Speech, *Hansard* 20 August 1940, col. 1166 (on the skill and courage of British airmen)

14 No one can guarantee success in war, but only deserve it.

Letter to Lord Wavell, 26 November 1940, in *The Second World War* vol. 2 (1949) ch. 27. Cf. Addison 3:16

15 Here is the answer which I will give to President Roosevelt ... Give us the tools and we will finish the job.

Radio broadcast, 9 February 1941, in *Complete Speeches* (1974) vol. 6, p. 6350

16 When I warned them [the French Government] that Britain would fight on alone whatever they did, their generals told their Prime Minister and his divided Cabinet, 'In three weeks England will have her neck wrung like a chicken.' Some chicken! Some neck!

Speech to Canadian Parliament, 30 December 1941, in *Complete Speeches* (1974) vol. 6, p. 6544

17 Now this is not the end. It is not even the beginning of the end. But it is, perhaps, the end of the beginning.

Speech at the Mansion House, London, 10 November 1942, in *The End of the Beginning* (1943) p. 214 (on the Battle of Egypt)

18 We make this wide encircling movement in the Mediterranean, having for its primary object the recovery of the command of that vital sea, but also having for its object the exposure of the under-belly of the Axis, especially Italy, to heavy attack.

Speech, *Hansard* 11 November 1942, col. 28 (often misquoted 'the soft under-belly of the Axis')

19 National compulsory insurance for all classes for all purposes from the cradle to the grave.

Radio broadcast, 21 March 1943, in *Complete Speeches* (1974) vol. 7, p. 6760

20 There is no finer investment for any community than putting milk into babies.

Radio broadcast, 21 March 1943, in *Complete Speeches* (1974) vol. 7, p. 6761

21 The empires of the future are the empires of the mind.

Speech at Harvard, 6 September 1943, in *Onwards to Victory* (1944) p. 238

22 From Stettin in the Baltic to Trieste in the Adriatic an iron curtain has descended across the Continent.

Speech at Westminster College, Fulton, Missouri, 5 March 1946, in *Complete Speeches* (1974) vol. 7, p. 7290. The expression 'iron curtain' previously had been applied by others to the Soviet Union or her sphere of influence, e.g. Ethel Snowden *Through Bolshevik Russia* (1920), Dr Goebbels *Das Reich* (25 February 1945), and by Churchill himself in a cable to President Truman (4 June 1945)

23 No one pretends that democracy is perfect or all-wise. Indeed, it has been said that democracy is the worst form of Government except all those other forms that have been tried from time to time.

Speech, *Hansard* 11 November 1947, col. 206

1 To jaw-jaw is always better than to war-war.

Speech at White House, 26 June 1954, in *New York Times* 27 June 1954, p. 1

2 Mr Gladstone read Homer for fun, which I thought served him right.

My Early Life (1930) ch. 2

3 In war: resolution. In defeat: defiance. In victory: magnanimity. In peace: goodwill.

The Second World War vol. 1 (1948) epigraph, which according to Sir Edward Marsh in *A Number of People* (1939) p. 152, occurred to Churchill shortly after the conclusion of the First World War

4 The loyalties which centre upon number one are enormous. If he trips he must be sustained. If he makes mistakes they must be covered. If he sleeps he must not be wantonly disturbed. If he is no good he must be pole-axed. But this last extreme process cannot be carried out every day; and certainly not in the days just after he has been chosen.

The Second World War vol. 2 (1949) ch. 1

5 I did not suffer from any desire to be relieved of my responsibilities. All I wanted was compliance with my wishes after reasonable discussion.

The Second World War vol. 4 (1951) ch. 5

6 Jellicoe was the only man on either side who could lose the war in an afternoon.

The World Crisis (1927) pt. 1, ch. 5

7 The ability to foretell what is going to happen tomorrow, next week, next month, and next year. And to have the ability afterwards to explain why it didn't happen.

Describing the qualifications desirable in a prospective politician, in B. Adler *Churchill Wit* (1965) p. 4

8 The Prime Minister has nothing to hide from the President of the United States

On stepping from his bath in the presence of a startled President Roosevelt, as recalled by Roosevelt's son in *Churchill* (BBC television series presented by Martin Gilbert, 1992) pt. 3

9 This is the sort of English up with which I will not put.

In Ernest Gowers *Plain Words* (1948) 'Troubles with Prepositions'

10 Don't talk to me about naval tradition. It's nothing but rum, sodomy, and the lash.

In Sir Peter Gretton *Former Naval Person* (1968) ch. 1

11 A sheep in sheep's clothing.

On Clement Attlee, in Lord Home *The Way the Wind Blows* (1976) ch. 6. Cf. Gosse 312:16

12 Take away that pudding — it has no theme.

In Lord Home *The Way the Wind Blows* (1976) ch. 16

13 In defeat unbeatable: in victory unbearable.

Of Viscount Montgomery, in Edward Marsh *Ambrosia and Small Beer* (1964) ch. 5

14 The candle in that great turnip has gone out.

Of Stanley Baldwin, in *Harold Nicolson: Diaries and Letters 1945–62* (1968) Diary 17 August 1950

15 I have taken more out of alcohol than alcohol has taken out of me.

In Quentin Reynolds *By Quentin Reynolds* (1964) ch. 11

Count Galeazzo Ciano 1903–44

Italian fascist politician; son-in-law of Mussolini

16 *La vittoria trova cento padri, e nessuno vuole riconoscere l'insuccesso.*

Victory has a hundred fathers, but defeat is an orphan.

Diary (1946) vol. 2, 9 September 1942 (literally 'no-one wants to recognise defeat as his own')

Colley Cibber 1671–1757

English playwright

17 Whilst thus I sing, I am a King,
Altho' a poor blind boy.

'The Blind Boy' (1734)

18 Oh! how many torments lie in the small circle of a wedding-ring!

The Double Gallant (1707) act 1, sc. 2

19 One had as good be out of the world, as out of the fashion.

Love's Last Shift (1696) act 2

20 Off with his head—so much for Buckingham.

Richard III (1700) act 4 (adapted from Shakespeare). Cf. *Richard III* 622:2

21 Perish the thought!

Richard III (1700) act 5 (adapted from Shakespeare)

22 Conscience avaunt, Richard's himself again:
Hark! the shrill trumpet sounds, to horse, away,
My soul's in arms, and eager for the fray.

Richard III (1700) act 5 (adapted from Shakespeare)

23 Stolen sweets are best.

The Rival Fools (1709) act 1, sc. 1

Cicero (Marcus Tullius Cicero) 106–43 BC

Roman orator and statesman

24 *Dicit enim tamquam in Platonis πολιτεία, non tamquam in Romuli faece sententiam.*

For he delivers his opinions as though he were living in Plato's Republic rather than among the dregs of Romulus.

Ad Atticum bk. 2, letter 1, sect. 8 (of M. Porcius Cato, the Younger)

25 *Sed nescio quo modo nihil tam absurde dici potest quod non dicatur ab aliquo philosophorum.*

There is nothing so absurd but some philosopher has said it.

De Divinatione bk. 2, ch. 119

26 *Vulgo enim dicitur: Iucundi acti labores.*

For it is commonly said: completed labours are pleasant.

De Finibus bk. 2, ch. 105

27 *Salus populi suprema est lex.*

The good of the people is the chief law.

De Legibus bk. 3, ch. 8

28 *'Ipse dixit.' 'Ipse' autem erat Pythagoras.*

'He himself said', and this 'himself' was Pythagoras.

De Natura Deorum bk. 1, ch. 10

1 *Summum bonum.*

The highest good.

De Officiis bk. 1, ch. 5

2 *Cedant arma togae, concedant laurea laudi.*

Let war yield to peace, laurels to paeans.

De Officiis bk. 1, ch. 77

3 *Numquam se minus otiosum esse quam cum otiosus, nec minus solum quam cum solus esset.*

Never less idle than when wholly idle, nor less alone than when wholly alone.

De Officiis bk. 3, ch. 1

4 *Mens cuiusque is est quisque.*

The spirit is the true self.

De Republica bk. 6, ch. 26

5 *Quousque tandem abutere, Catilina, patientia nostra?*

How long will you abuse our patience, Catiline?

In Catilinam Speech 1, ch. 1

6 *O tempora, O mores!*

Oh, the times! Oh, the manners!

In Catilinam Speech 1, ch. 1

7 *Abiit, excessit, evasit, erupit.*

He departed, he withdrew, he strode off, he broke forth.

In Catilinam Speech 2, ch. 1

8 *Civis Romanus sum.*

I am a Roman citizen.

In Verrem Speech 5, ch. 147

9 *Quod di omen avertant.*

May the gods avert this omen.

Third Philippic ch. 35

10 *Nervos belli, pecuniam infinitam.*

The sinews of war, unlimited money.

Fifth Philippic ch. 5

11 *Silent enim leges inter arma.*

Laws are silent in time of war.

Pro Milone ch. 11

12 *Cui bono?*

To whose profit?

Pro Roscio Amerino ch. 84 and Pro Milone ch. 12, sect. 32, quoting L. Cassius Longinus Ravilla

13 *Id quod est praestantissimum maximeque optabile omnibus sanis et bonis et beatis, cum dignitate otium.*

The thing which is the most outstanding and chiefly to be desired by all healthy and good and well-off persons, is leisure with honour.

Pro Sestio ch. 98

14 *Errare mehercule malo cum Platone . . . quam cum istis vera sentire.*

I would rather be wrong, by God, with Plato . . . than be correct with those men.

Tusculanae Disputationes bk. 1, ch. 39 (on Pythagoreans)

15 *O fortunatam natam me consule Romam!*

O happy Rome, born when I was consul!

In Juvenal Satires poem 10, l. 122

John Clare 1793–1864
English poet

16 When badgers fight and everyone's a foe.

'Badger' (written c.1836)

17 He could not die when the trees were green,
For he loved the time too well.

'The Dying Child'

18 My life hath been one chain of contradictions,
Madhouses, prisons, whore-shops.

'Child Harold' (written 1841) l. 146

19 They took me from my wife, and to save trouble
I wed again, and made the error double.

'Child Harold' (written 1841) l. 152

20 Here let the Muse Oblivion's curtain draw,
And let man think—for God hath often saw
Things here too dirty for the light of day;
For in a madhouse there exists no law
Now stagnant grows my too refinèd clay;
I envy birds their wings to fly away.

'Child Harold' (written 1841) l. 157

21 Pale death, the grand physician, cures all pain;
The dead rest well who lived for joys in vain.

'Child Harold' (written 1841) l. 215

22 When words refuse before the crowd
My Mary's name to give,
The muse in silence sings aloud:
And there my love will live.

'Child Harold' (written 1841) l. 513

23 Hopeless hope hopes on and meets no end,
Wastes without springs and homes without a friend.

'Child Harold' (written 1841) l. 1018

24 A quiet, pilfering, unprotected race.

'The Gipsy Camp' (1841)

25 I am—yet what I am, none cares or knows;
My friends forsake me like a memory lost:
I am the self-consumer of my woes.

'I Am' (1848)

26 I long for scenes where man hath never trod
A place where woman never smiled or wept
There to abide with my Creator God
And sleep as I in childhood sweetly slept,
Untroubling and untroubled where I lie
The grass below, above, the vaulted sky.

'I Am' (1848)

27 The present is the funeral of the past,
And man the living sepulchre of life.

'The present is the funeral of the past' (written 1845)

28 Summers pleasures they are gone like to visions every one
And the cloudy days of autumn and of winter cometh on
I tried to call them back but unbidden they are gone
Far away from heart and eye and for ever far away.

'Remembrances'

Edward Hyde, Earl of Clarendon 1609–74
English statesman and historian

1 Without question, when he first drew the sword, he threw away the scabbard.
> *The History of the Rebellion* (1703, ed. W. D. Macray, 1888) vol. 3, bk. 7, sect. 84 (of Hampden)

2 He had a head to contrive, a tongue to persuade, and a hand to execute any mischief.
> *The History of the Rebellion* (1703, ed. W. D. Macray, 1888) vol. 3, bk. 7, sect. 84 (of Hampden). Cf. Gibbon 302:5

3 He . . . would, with a shrill and sad accent, ingeminate the word *Peace, Peace*.
> *The History of the Rebellion* (1703, ed. W. D. Macray, 1888) vol. 3, bk. 7, sect. 233 (of Falkland)

4 So enamoured on peace that he would have been glad the King should have bought it at any price.
> *The History of the Rebellion* (1703, ed. W. D. Macray, 1888) vol. 3, bk. 7, sect. 233 (of Falkland)

5 He will be looked upon by posterity as a brave bad man.
> *The History of the Rebellion* (1703, ed. W. D. Macray, 1888) vol. 6, bk. 15, *ad fin.* (of Cromwell)

Claribel (Mrs Charlotte Alington Barnard) 1840–69
English writer of ballads

6 I cannot sing the old songs
I sang long years ago,
For heart and voice would fail me,
And foolish tears would flow.
> 'The Old Songs' (1865)

Kenneth Clark (Baron Clark) 1903–83
English art historian

7 Medieval marriages were entirely a matter of property, and, as everyone knows, marriage without love means love without marriage.
> *Civilisation* (1969) ch. 3

8 It's a curious fact that the all-male religions have produced no religious imagery—in most cases have positively forbidden it. The great religious art of the world is deeply involved with the female principle.
> *Civilisation* (1969) ch. 7

9 Perrault's façade [of the Louvre] reflects the triumph of an authoritarian state . . . the work not of craftsmen, but of wonderfully gifted civil servants.
> *Civilisation* (1969) ch. 9

Arthur C. Clarke 1917–
English science fiction writer

10 If an elderly but distinguished scientist says that something is possible he is almost certainly right, but if he says that it is impossible he is very probably wrong.
> In *New Yorker* 9 August 1969

Grant Clarke 1891–1931 *and Edgar Leslie* 1885–1976

11 He'd have to get under, get out and get under
And fix up his automobile.
> *He'd Have to Get Under—Get Out and Get Under* (1913 song)

James Stanier Clarke c.1765–1834
Chaplain and private English secretary to Prince Leopold of Coburg

12 Perhaps when you again appear in print you may choose to dedicate your volumes to Prince Leopold: any historical romance, illustrative of the history of the august House of Coburg, would just now be very interesting.
> Letter to Jane Austen, 27 March 1816, in R. W. Chapman (ed.) *Jane Austen's Letters* (1952)

John Clarke d. 1658

13 He that would thrive
Must rise at five;
He that hath thriven
May lie till seven.
> *Paraemiologia Anglo-Latina* (1639) 'Diligentia'

14 Home is home, though it be never so homely.
> *Paraemiologia Anglo-Latina* (1639) 'Domi vivere'

Appius Claudius Caecus fl. 312–279 BC
Roman censor, orator, and prose writer

15 *Faber est suae quisque fortunae.*
Each man is the smith of his own fortune.
> In Sallust *Ad Caesarem Senem de Re Publica Oratio* ch. 1, sect. 2

Karl von Clausewitz 1780–1831
Prussian soldier and military theorist

16 *Der Krieg ist nichts als eine Fortsetzung des politischen Verkehrs mit Einmischung anderer Mittel.*
War is nothing but a continuation of politics with the admixture of other means.
> *Vom Kriege* (1832–4) bk. 8, ch. 6, sect. B (commonly rendered 'War is the continuation of politics by other means')

Henry Clay 1777–1852
American politician

17 If you wish to avoid foreign collision, you had better abandon the ocean.
> Speech in the House of Representatives, 22 January 1812, in C. Colton *The Life, Correspondence and Speeches of Henry Clay* (1864) vol. 5, p. 44

18 The gentleman [Josiah Quincy] can not have forgotten his own sentiment, uttered even on the floor of this House, 'peaceably if we can, forcibly if we must'.
> Speech in Congress, 8 January 1813, in C. Colton (ed.) *The Works of Henry Clay* (1904) vol. 1, p. 197. Cf. Quincy 534:12

1 The arts of power and its minions are the same in all countries and in all ages. It marks a victim; denounces it; and excites the public odium and the public hatred, to conceal its own abuses and encroachments.

> Speech in the Senate, 14 March 1834, in C. Colton (ed.) *The Works of Henry Clay* (1904) vol. 5, p. 627

2 I had rather be right than be President.

> To Senator Preston of South Carolina, 1839. See S. W. McCall *Life of Thomas Brackett Reed* (1914) ch. 14

Eldridge Cleaver 1935–

American political activist

3 What we're saying today is that you're either part of the solution or you're part of the problem.

> Speech in San Francisco, 1968, in R. Scheer *Eldridge Cleaver, Post Prison Writings and Speeches* (1969) p. 32

John Cleland 1710–89

English writer

4 Truth! stark naked truth, is the word.

> *Memoirs of a Woman of Pleasure* a.k.a. *Fanny Hill* (1749) vol. 1

Georges Clemenceau 1841–1929

French politician; Prime Minister of France, 1906–9, 1917–20

5 *La guerre, c'est une chose trop grave pour la confier à des militaires.*

War is too serious a matter to entrust to military men.

> Attributed to Clemenceau, e.g. in Hampden Jackson *Clemenceau and the Third Republic* (1946) p. 228, but also to Briand and Talleyrand

6 *Politique intérieure, je fais la guerre; politique extérieure, je fais la guerre. Je fais toujours la guerre.*

My home policy: I wage war; my foreign policy: I wage war. All the time I wage war.

> Speech to French Chamber of Deputies, 8 March 1918, in *Discours de Guerre* (1968) p. 172

7 *Il est plus facile de faire la guerre que la paix.*

It is easier to make war than to make peace.

> Speech at Verdun, 20 July 1919, in *Discours de Paix* (1938) p. 122

8 *Que voulez vous que je fasse entre deux hommes dont un se croit Napoléon et l'autre Jésus Christ?*

What do you expect when I'm between two men of whom one [Lloyd George] thinks he is Napoleon and the other [Woodrow Wilson] thinks he is Jesus Christ?

> To André Tardieu, on being asked why he always gave in to Lloyd George at the Paris Peace Conference, 1918; in James Lees-Milne *Harold Nicolson* (1980) vol. 1, ch. 7, letter from Nicolson to his wife, 20 May 1919

Clement XIII 1693–1769

Pope, 1758–69

9 *Sint ut sunt aut non sint.*

Let them be as they are or not be at all.

> Replying to a request for changes in the constitutions of the Society of Jesus, in J. A. M. Crétineau-Joly *Clément XIV et les Jésuites* (1847) p. 370 n.

Grover Cleveland 1837–1908

22nd and 24th President of the USA

10 I have considered the pension list of the republic a roll of honour.

> Veto of Dependent Pension Bill, 5 July 1888, in *A Compilation of the Messages and Papers of the Presidents* vol. 11 (1897) p. 5269

11 The lessons of paternalism ought to be unlearned and the better lesson taught that, while the people should patriotically and cheerfully support their government, its functions do not include the support of the people.

> Inaugural Address, 4 March 1893, in *New York Times* 5 March 1893

Harlan Cleveland 1918–

American government official

12 The revolution of rising expectations.

> Phrase coined, 1950. See Arthur Schlesinger *A Thousand Days* (1965) ch. 16

John Cleveland 1613–58

English poet

13 Here lies wise and valiant dust,
Huddled up, 'twixt fit and just:
Strafford, who was hurried hence
'Twixt treason and convenience.
He spent his time here in a mist,
A Papist, yet a Calvinist . . .
Riddles lie here, or in a word,
Here lies blood; and let it lie
Speechless still, and never cry.

> 'Epitaph on the Earl of Strafford' (1647)

14 Had Cain been Scot, God would have changed his doom
Nor forced him wander, but confined him home.

> 'The Rebel Scot' (1647)

Lord Clive (Robert, Baron Clive of Plassey) 1725–74

British general; Governor of Bengal

15 I feel that I am reserved for some end or other.

> When his pistol twice failed to fire, while attempting to take his own life, in G. R. Gleig *The Life of Robert, First Lord Clive* (1848) ch. 1

16 By God, Mr Chairman, at this moment I stand astonished at my own moderation!

> Reply during Parliamentary cross-examination, 1773, in G. R. Gleig *The Life of Robert, First Lord Clive* (1848) ch. 29

Arthur Hugh Clough 1819–61

English poet

17 Rome, believe me, my friend, is like its own Monte Testaceo,
Merely a marvellous mass of broken and castaway wine-pots.

> *Amours de Voyage* (1858) canto 1, pt. 2

18 The horrible pleasure of pleasing inferior people.

> *Amours de Voyage* (1858) canto 1, pt. 11

1 Am I prepared to lay down my life for the British
   female?
   Really, who knows? . . .
   Ah, for a child in the street I could strike; for the
     full-blown lady—
   Somehow, Eustace, alas! I have not felt the vocation.
     Amours de Voyage (1858) canto 2, pt. 4

2 I do not like being moved: for the will is excited; and
   action
   Is a most dangerous thing: I tremble for something
     factitious,
   Some malpractice of heart and illegitimate process;
   We are so prone to these things with our terrible
     notions of duty.
     Amours de Voyage (1858) canto 2, pt. 11

3 But for his funeral train which the bridegroom sees in
   the distance,
   Would he so joyfully, think you, fall in with the
     marriage-procession?
     Amours de Voyage (1858) canto 3, pt. 6

4 Allah is great, no doubt, and Juxtaposition his
   prophet.
     Amours de Voyage (1858) canto 3, pt. 6

5 Mild monastic faces in quiet collegiate cloisters.
     Amours de Voyage (1858) canto 3, pt. 9

6 Whither depart the souls of the brave that die in the
   battle,
   Die in the lost, lost fight, for the cause that perishes
     with them?
     Amours de Voyage (1858) canto 5, pt. 6

7 Sesquipedalian blackguard.
     The Bothie of Tober-na-Vuolich (1848) pt. 2, l. 223

8 Good, too, Logic, of course; in itself, but not in fine
   weather.
     The Bothie of Tober-na-Vuolich (1848) pt. 2, l. 249

9 Grace is given of God, but knowledge is bought in the
   market.
     The Bothie of Tober-na-Vuolich (1848) pt. 4, l. 159

10 Afloat. We move: Delicious! Ah,
    What else is like the gondola?
     Dipsychus (1865) sc. 5

11 This world is bad enough may-be;
    We do not comprehend it;
    But in one fact can all agree
    God won't, and we can't mend it.
     Dipsychus (1865) sc. 5

12 I drive through the street, and I care not a d—mn;
    The people they stare, and they ask who I am;
    And if I should chance to run over a cad,
    I can pay for the damage if ever so bad.
    So pleasant it is to have money, heigh ho!
    So pleasant it is to have money.
     Dipsychus (1865) sc. 5

13 They may talk as they please about what they call
    pelf,
    And how one ought never to think of one's self,
    And how pleasures of thought surpass eating and
     drinking—
    My pleasure of thought is the pleasure of thinking
    How pleasant it is to have money, heigh ho!
    How pleasant it is to have money.
     Dipsychus (1865) sc. 5

14 'There is no God,' the wicked saith,
    'And truly it's a blessing,
    For what he might have done with us
    It's better only guessing.'
     Dipsychus (1865) sc. 6

15 And almost every one when age,
    Disease, or sorrows strike him,
    Inclines to think there is a God,
    Or something very like Him.
     Dipsychus (1865) sc. 6

16 Thou shalt have one God only; who
    Would be at the expense of two?
     'The Latest Decalogue' (1862)

17 Thou shalt not kill; but need'st not strive
    Officiously to keep alive.
     'The Latest Decalogue' (1862)

18 Do not adultery commit;
    Advantage rarely comes of it.
     'The Latest Decalogue' (1862)

19 Thou shalt not steal; an empty feat,
    When it's so lucrative to cheat.
     'The Latest Decalogue' (1862)

20 Thou shalt not covet; but tradition
    Approves all forms of competition.
     'The Latest Decalogue' (1862)

21 'Tis better to have fought and lost,
    Than never to have fought at all.
     'Peschiera' (1854). Cf. Tennyson 683:12

22 As ships, becalmed at eve, that lay
    With canvas drooping, side by side,
    Two towers of sail at dawn of day
    Are scarce long leagues apart descried.
     'Qua Curam Ventus' (1849)

23 Say not the struggle naught availeth,
    The labour and the wounds are vain,
    The enemy faints not, nor faileth,
    And as things have been, things remain.
     'Say not the struggle naught availeth' (1855)

24 If hopes were dupes, fears may be liars.
     'Say not the struggle naught availeth' (1855)

25 In front the sun climbs slow, how slowly,
    But westward, look, the land is bright.
     'Say not the struggle naught availeth' (1855)

26 What shall we do without you? Think where we are.
    Carlyle has led us all out into the desert, and he has
    left us there.
     Parting words to Ralph Waldo Emerson, 15 July 1848, in
     E. E. Hale *James Russell Lowell and his Friends* (1889) ch. 9

William Cobbett 1762–1835

English political reformer and radical journalist

27 Resolve to free yourselves from the slavery of the tea
    and coffee and other slop-kettle.
     Advice to Young Men (1829) letter 1, sect. 31

28 Nouns of number, or multitude, such as Mob,
    Parliament, Rabble, House of Commons, Regiment,
    Court of King's Bench, Den of Thieves, and the like.
     English Grammar (1817) letter 17 'Syntax as Relating to
     Pronouns'

1 From a very early age, I had imbibed the opinion, that it was every man's duty to do all that lay in his power to leave his country as good as he had found it.
Political Register 22 December 1832

2 But what is to be the fate of the great wen of all? The monster, called ... 'the metropolis of the empire'?
Rural Rides: The Kentish Journal in Cobbett's Weekly Political Register 5 January 1822, vol. 40, col. 1609 (of London)

Alison Cockburn (née Rutherford) 1713–94
Scottish poet and songwriter

3 I've seen the smiling of Fortune beguiling,
I've felt all its favours and found its decay;
Sweet was its blessing, kind its caressing,
But now it is fled, fled far, far away.
'The Flowers of the Forest' (1765)

4 O fickle Fortune, why this cruel sporting?
Why thus torment us poor sons of day?
Nae mair your smiles can cheer me, nae mair your frowns can fear me,
For the flowers of the forest are a' wade away.
'The Flowers of the Forest' (1765); *wade* weeded (often quoted 'For the flowers of the forest are withered away'). Cf. Elliot 275:9

Claud Cockburn 1904–81
British writer and journalist

5 Small earthquake in Chile. Not many dead.
The words with which Cockburn claims to have won a competition at *The Times* for the dullest headline; in *In Time of Trouble* (1956) ch. 10

Jean Cocteau 1889–1963
French playwright and film director

6 La poésie est une religion sans espoir.
Poetry is a religion with no hope.
Journal d'un inconnu (1953) 'De l'invisibilité'

7 L'Histoire est un alliage de réel et de mensonge. Le réel de l'Histoire devient un mensonge. L'irréel de la fable devient vérité.
History is a combination of reality and lies. The reality of History becomes a lie. The unreality of the fable becomes the truth.
Journal d'un inconnu (1953) 'De la prééminence des fables'

8 Vivre est une chute horizontale.
Life is a horizontal fall.
Opium (1930) p. 37

9 Victor Hugo était un fou qui se croyait Victor Hugo.
Victor Hugo was a madman who thought he was Victor Hugo.
Opium (1930) p. 77

10 Le tact dans l'audace c'est de savoir jusqu'où on peut aller trop loin.
Being tactful in audacity is knowing how far one can go too far.
Le Rappel à l'ordre (1926) 'Le Coq et l'Arlequin' p. 2

11 Le pire drame pour un poète, c'est d'être admiré par malentendu.
The worst tragedy for a poet is to be admired through being misunderstood.
Le Rappel à l'ordre (1926) 'Le Coq et l'Arlequin' p. 20

12 S'il faut choisir un crucifié, la foule sauve toujours Barabbas.
If it has to choose who is to be crucified, the crowd will always save Barabbas.
Le Rappel à l'ordre (1926) 'Le Coq et l'Arlequin' p. 39

George M. Cohan 1878–1942
American songwriter, playwright and producer

13 I'm a Yankee Doodle Dandy,
A Yankee Doodle, do or die;
A real live nephew of my Uncle Sam's,
Born on the fourth of July.
I've got a Yankee Doodle sweetheart,
She's my Yankee Doodle joy.
Yankee Doodle came to London,
Just to ride the ponies;
I am the Yankee Doodle Boy.
'Yankee Doodle Boy' (1904 song). Cf. Anonymous 20:1

Sir Aston Cokayne 1608–84
English poet

14 Sydney, whom we yet admire
Lighting our little torches at his fire.
Funeral Elegies, no. 1 'On the Death of my very good Friend Mr Michael Drayton' (1658)

Desmond Coke 1879–1931
English writer and schoolmaster

15 His blade struck the water a full second before any other: the lad had started well. Nor did he flag as the race wore on ... as the boats began to near the winning-post, his oar was dipping into the water nearly *twice* as often as any other.
Sandford of Merton (1903) ch. 12 (often quoted 'All rowed fast, but none so fast as stroke')

Sir Edward Coke 1552–1634
English jurist

16 How long soever it hath continued, if it be against reason, it is of no force in law.
The First Part of the Institutes of the Laws of England (1628) bk. 1, ch. 10, sect. 80, p. 62 recto

17 Reason is the life of the law, nay the common law itself is nothing else but reason ... The law, which is the perfection of reason.
The First Part of the Institutes of the Laws of England (1628) bk. 2, ch. 6, sect. 138, p. 97 verso

18 The gladsome light of Jurisprudence.
The First Part of the Institutes of the Laws of England (1628) 'Epilogus' ad fin.

1 For a man's house is his castle, *et domus sua cuique est tutissimum refugium* [and each man's home is his safest refuge].
  The Third Part of the Institutes of the Laws of England (1628) ch. 73, p. 162

2 Six hours in sleep, in law's grave study six,
  Four spend in prayer, the rest on Nature fix.
  Translation of a quotation from Justinian *The Pandects* (or *Digest*) bk. 2, ch. 4 'De in Jus Vocando'. Cf. Jones 378:2

3 They [corporations] cannot commit treason, nor be outlawed, nor excommunicate, for they have no souls.
  The Reports of Sir Edward Coke (1658) vol. 5, pt. 10 'The case of Sutton's Hospital' p. 32 verso

4 Magna Charta is such a fellow, that he will have no sovereign.
  On the Lords' Amendment to the Petition of Right, 17 May 1628, in J. Rushworth *Historical Collections* (1659) vol. 1, p. 562

Hartley Coleridge 1796–1849
English poet; eldest son of Samuel Taylor Coleridge

5 But what is Freedom? Rightly understood,
  A universal licence to be good.
  'Liberty' (1833)

6 She is not fair to outward view
  As many maidens be;
  Her loveliness I never knew
  Until she smiled on me.
  Oh! then I saw her eye was bright,
  A well of love, a spring of light.
  'She is not fair' (1833)

John Duke, 1st Baron Coleridge 1820–94
English jurist

7 I speak not of this college or of that, but of the University as a whole; and, gentlemen, what a *whole* Oxford is!
  In G. Russell *Collections & Recollections* (1903 ed.) ch. 29

Mary Coleridge 1861–1907
English poet, novelist, and essayist

8 Egypt's might is tumbled down
  Down a-down the deeps of thought;
  Greece is fallen and Troy town,
  Glorious Rome hath lost her crown,
  Venice' pride is nought.

  But the dreams their children dreamed
  Fleeting, unsubstantial, vain
  Shadowy as the shadows seemed
  Airy nothing, as they deemed,
  These remain.
  'Egypt's might is tumbled down' (1908)

Samuel Taylor Coleridge 1772–1834
English poet, critic, and philosopher

9 Behold! her bosom and half her side—
  A sight to dream of, not to tell!
  'Christabel' (1816) pt. 1, l. 252

10 Alas! they had been friends in youth;
   But whispering tongues can poison truth;
   And constancy lives in realms above;
   And life is thorny; and youth is vain;
   And to be wroth with one we love
   Doth work like madness in the brain.
   'Christabel' (1816) pt. 2, l. 408

11 A little child, a limber elf,
   Singing, dancing to itself,
   A fairy thing with red round cheeks,
   That always finds, and never seeks,
   Makes such a vision to the sight
   As fills a father's eyes with light.
   'Christabel' (1816) pt. 2, conclusion, l. 656

12 I see them all so excellently fair,
   I see, not feel, how beautiful they are!
   'Dejection: an Ode' (1802) st. 2

13 I may not hope from outward forms to win
   The passion and the life, whose fountains are within.
   'Dejection: an Ode' (1802) st. 3

14 O Lady! we receive but what we give,
   And in our life alone does Nature live.
   'Dejection: an Ode' (1802) st. 4

15 Ah! from the soul itself must issue forth
   A light, a glory, a fair luminous cloud
   Enveloping the Earth—
   And from the soul itself must there be sent
   A sweet and potent voice, of its own birth,
   Of all sweet sounds the life and element!
   'Dejection: an Ode' (1802) st. 4

16 For hope grew round me, like the twining vine,
   And fruits, and foliage, not my own, seemed mine.
   'Dejection: an Ode' (1802) st. 6

17 But oh! each visitation
   Suspends what nature gave me at my birth,
   My shaping spirit of imagination.
   'Dejection: an Ode' (1802) st. 6. Cf. Coleridge 212:2

18 And the Devil did grin, for his darling sin
   Is pride that apes humility.
   'The Devil's Thoughts' (1799)

19 Oh! the one life within us and abroad,
   Which meets all motion and becomes its soul,
   A light in sound, a sound-like power in light,
   Rhythm in all thought, and joyance everywhere.
   'The Eolian Harp' (1796) l. 26

20 And what if all animated nature
   Be but organic harps diversely framed,
   That tremble into thought, as o'er them sweeps,
   Plastic and vast, one intellectual breeze,
   At once the soul of each, and god of all?
   'The Eolian Harp' (1796) l. 44

21 What is an Epigram? a dwarfish whole,
   Its body brevity, and wit its soul.
   'Epigram' (1809)

22 O, lift one thought in prayer for S. T. C.;
   That he who many a year with toil of breath
   Found death in life, may here find life in death.
   'Epitaph for Himself' (1834)

1 Ere sin could blight or sorrow fade,
   Death came with friendly care:
   The opening bud to Heaven conveyed
   And bade it blossom there.
      'Epitaph on an Infant' (1794)

2 Forth from his dark and lonely hiding-place
   (Portentous sight!) the owlet Atheism,
   Sailing on obscene wings athwart the noon,
   Drops his blue-fringèd lids, and holds them close,
   And hooting at the glorious sun in Heaven,
   Cries out, 'Where is it?'
      'Fears in Solitude' (1798)

3 The frost performs its secret ministry,
   Unhelped by any wind.
      'Frost at Midnight' (1798) l. 1

4   Sea, and hill, and wood,
   With all the numberless goings-on of life,
   Inaudible as dreams!
      'Frost at Midnight' (1798) l. 11

5 Only that film, which fluttered on the grate,
   Still flutters there, the sole unquiet thing.
      'Frost at Midnight' (1798) l. 15

6   Whether the eave-drops fall
   Heard only in the trances of the blast,
   Or if the secret ministry of frost
   Shall hang them up in silent icicles,
   Quietly shining to the quiet moon.
      'Frost at Midnight' (1798) l. 70

7 O struggling with the darkness all the night,
   And visited all night by troops of stars.
      'Hymn before Sunrise, in the Vale of Chamouni' (1809)
      l. 30

8 On awaking he . . . instantly and eagerly wrote down
   the lines that are here preserved. At this moment he
   was unfortunately called out by a person on business
   from Porlock.
      'Kubla Khan' (1816) preliminary note

9 In Xanadu did Kubla Khan
   A stately pleasure-dome decree:
   Where Alph, the sacred river, ran
   Through caverns measureless to man
   Down to a sunless sea.
   So twice five miles of fertile ground
   With walls and towers were girdled round.
      'Kubla Khan' (1816)

10 A savage place! as holy and enchanted
   As e'er beneath a waning moon was haunted
   By woman wailing for her demon-lover!
   And from this chasm, with ceaseless turmoil seething,
   As if this earth in fast thick pants were breathing,
   A mighty fountain momently was forced.
      'Kubla Khan' (1816)

11 It was a miracle of rare device,
   A sunny pleasure-dome with caves of ice.
      'Kubla Khan' (1816)

12 And 'mid this tumult Kubla heard from far
   Ancestral voices prophesying war!
      'Kubla Khan' (1816)

13 A damsel with a dulcimer
   In a vision once I saw:
   It was an Abyssinian maid,
   And on her dulcimer she played,
   Singing of Mount Abora.
      'Kubla Khan' (1816)

14 And all who heard should see them there,
   And all should cry, Beware! Beware!
   His flashing eyes, his floating hair!
   Weave a circle round him thrice,
   And close your eyes with holy dread,
   For he on honey-dew hath fed,
   And drunk the milk of Paradise.
      'Kubla Khan' (1816)

15 All thoughts, all passions, all delights,
   Whatever stirs this mortal frame,
   All are but ministers of Love,
   And feed his sacred flame.
      'Love' (1800)

16 With Donne, whose muse on dromedary trots,
   Wreathe iron pokers into true-love knots.
   Rhyme's sturdy cripple, fancy's maze and clue,
   Wit's forge and fire-blast, meaning's press and screw.
      'On Donne's Poetry' (1818)

17 But still the heart doth need a language, still
   Doth the old instinct bring back the old names.
      The Piccolomini (1800) act 2, sc. 4 (translated from the
      German of Friedrich von Schiller)

18 It is an ancient Mariner,
   And he stoppeth one of three.
   'By thy long grey beard and glittering eye,
   Now wherefore stopp'st thou me?'
      'The Rime of the Ancient Mariner' (1798) pt. 1

19 He holds him with his glittering eye—
   The Wedding-Guest stood still,
   And listens like a three years' child:
   The Mariner hath his will.
   The Wedding-Guest sat on a stone:
   He cannot choose but hear;
   And thus spake on that ancient man,
   The bright-eyed Mariner.
      'The Rime of the Ancient Mariner' (1798) pt. 1

20 The Wedding-Guest here beat his breast,
   For he heard the loud bassoon.
      'The Rime of the Ancient Mariner' (1798) pt. 1

21 And ice, mast-high, came floating by,
   As green as emerald.
      'The Rime of the Ancient Mariner' (1798) pt. 1

22 'God save thee, ancient Mariner!
   From the fiends that plague thee thus!—
   Why look'st thou so?'—With my cross-bow
   I shot the Albatross.
      'The Rime of the Ancient Mariner' (1798) pt. 1

23 Nor dim nor red, like God's own head,
   The glorious Sun uprist.
      'The Rime of the Ancient Mariner' (1798) pt. 2

24 We were the first that ever burst
   Into that silent sea.
      'The Rime of the Ancient Mariner' (1798) pt. 2

25 As idle as a painted ship
   Upon a painted ocean.
      'The Rime of the Ancient Mariner' (1798) pt. 2

1 Water, water, everywhere,
 And all the boards did shrink;
 Water, water, everywhere,
 Nor any drop to drink.
 The very deep did rot: O Christ!
 That ever this should be!
 Yes, slimy things did crawl with legs
 Upon the slimy sea.
  'The Rime of the Ancient Mariner' (1798) pt. 2

2 *Her* lips were red, *her* looks were free,
 Her locks were yellow as gold:
 Her skin was white as leprosy,
 The Night-mare LIFE-IN-DEATH was she,
 Who thicks man's blood with cold.
  'The Rime of the Ancient Mariner' (1798) pt. 3

3 The Sun's rim dips; the stars rush out;
 At one stride comes the dark.
  'The Rime of the Ancient Mariner' (1798) pt. 3

4 We listened and looked sideways up!
  'The Rime of the Ancient Mariner' (1798) pt. 3

5 The hornèd Moon, with one bright star
 Within the nether tip.
  'The Rime of the Ancient Mariner' (1798) pt. 3

6 I fear thee, ancient Mariner!
 I fear thy skinny hand!
 And thou art long, and lank, and brown,
 As is the ribbed sea-sand.
  'The Rime of the Ancient Mariner' (1798) pt. 4

7 Alone, alone, all, all alone,
 Alone on a wide wide sea!
 And never a saint took pity on
 My soul in agony.
  'The Rime of the Ancient Mariner' (1798) pt. 4

8 And a thousand thousand slimy things
 Lived on; and so did I.
  'The Rime of the Ancient Mariner' (1798) pt. 4

9 A spring of love gushed from my heart,
 And I blessed them unaware.
  'The Rime of the Ancient Mariner' (1798) pt. 4

10 Oh Sleep! it is a gentle thing,
 Beloved from pole to pole,
 To Mary Queen the praise be given!
 She sent the gentle sleep from Heaven,
 That slid into my soul.
  'The Rime of the Ancient Mariner' (1798) pt. 5

11 Sure I had drunken in my dreams,
 And still my body drank.
  'The Rime of the Ancient Mariner' (1798) pt. 5

12 We were a ghastly crew.
  'The Rime of the Ancient Mariner' (1798) pt. 5

13 It ceased; yet still the sails made on
 A pleasant noise till noon,
 A noise like of a hidden brook
 In the leafy month of June,
 That to the sleeping woods all night
 Singeth a quiet tune.
  'The Rime of the Ancient Mariner' (1798) pt. 5

14 Like one, that on a lonesome road
 Doth walk in fear and dread,
 And having once turned round walks on,
 And turns no more his head;
 Because he knows, a frightful fiend
 Doth close behind him tread.
  'The Rime of the Ancient Mariner' (1798) pt. 6

15 No voice; but oh! the silence sank
 Like music on my heart.
  'The Rime of the Ancient Mariner' (1798) pt. 6

16 I pass, like night, from land to land;
 I have strange power of speech.
  'The Rime of the Ancient Mariner' (1798) pt. 7

17 He prayeth well, who loveth well
 Both man and bird and beast.
 He prayeth best, who loveth best
 All things both great and small.
  'The Rime of the Ancient Mariner' (1798) pt. 7

18 He went like one that hath been stunned,
 And is of sense forlorn:
 A sadder and a wiser man,
 He rose the morrow morn.
  'The Rime of the Ancient Mariner' (1798) pt. 7

19 So for the mother's sake the child was dear,
 And dearer was the mother for the child.
  'Sonnet to a Friend Who Asked How I Felt When the Nurse
  First Presented My Infant to Me' (1797)

20 Well, they are gone, and here must I remain,
 This lime-tree bower my prison!
  'This Lime-Tree Bower my Prison' (1800) l. 1

21   When the last rook
 Beat its straight path along the dusky air.
  'This Lime-Tree Bower my Prison' (1800) l. 68

22 'Alas!' said she, 'we ne'er can be
 Made happy by compulsion!'
  'The Three Graves' (1809) pt. 4, st. 12

23 Lingering he raised his latch at eve,
 Though tired in heart and limb:
 He loved no other place, and yet
 Home was no home to him.
  'The Three Graves' (1798) pt. 4, st. 16

24 Work without hope draws nectar in a sieve,
 And hope without an object cannot live.
  'Work without Hope' (1828)

25 Like some poor nigh-related guest,
 That may not rudely be dismist;
 Yet hath outstayed his welcome while,
 And tells the jest without the smile.
  'Youth and Age' (1834)

26 He who begins by loving Christianity better than
 Truth will proceed by loving his own sect or church
 better than Christianity, and end by loving himself
 better than all.
  Aids to Reflection (1825) 'Moral and Religious Aphorisms'
  no. 25

27 Until you understand a writer's ignorance, presume
 yourself ignorant of his understanding.
  Biographia Literaria (1817) ch. 12

1 The primary imagination I hold to be the living Power and prime Agent of all human Perception, and as a repetition in the finite mind of the eternal act of creation in the infinite I AM.
Biographia Literaria (1817) ch. 13

2 That willing suspension of disbelief for the moment, which constitutes poetic faith.
Biographia Literaria (1817) ch. 14

3 Our *myriad-minded* Shakespeare.
Footnote. Ἀνὴρ μυριόνους, a phrase which I have borrowed from a Greek monk, who applies it to a Patriarch of Constantinople.
Biographia Literaria (1817) ch. 15

4 The dwarf sees farther than the giant, when he has the giant's shoulder to mount on.
The Friend (1818) vol. 2 'On the Principles of Political Knowledge'. Cf. Bernard 66:9, Newton 493:19

5 Iago's soliloquy— the motive-hunting of motiveless malignity.
The Literary Remains of Samuel Taylor Coleridge (1836) bk. 2 'Notes on the Tragedies of Shakespeare: Othello'

6 Reviewers are usually people who would have been poets, historians, biographers, &c., if they could; they have tried their talents at one or at the other, and have failed; therefore they turn critics.
Seven Lectures on Shakespeare and Milton (delivered 1811–12, published 1856) Lecture 1

7 You abuse snuff! Perhaps it is the final cause of the human nose.
Table Talk (1835) 4 January 1823

8 To see him act, is like reading Shakespeare by flashes of lightning.
Table Talk (1835) 27 April 1823 (on Edmund Kean)

9 Prose = words in their best order;—poetry = the *best* words in the best order.
Table Talk (1835) 12 July 1827

10 The man's desire is for the woman; but the woman's desire is rarely other than for the desire of the man.
Table Talk (1835) 23 July 1827

11 Poetry is certainly something more than good sense, but it must be good sense at all events; just as a palace is more than a house, but it must be a house, at least.
Table Talk (1835) 9 May 1830

12 Swift was *anima Rabelaisii habitans in sicco*—the soul of Rabelais dwelling in a dry place.
Table Talk (1835) 15 June 1830

13 In politics, what begins in fear usually ends in folly.
Table Talk (1835) 5 October 1830

14 If men could learn from history, what lessons it might teach us! But passion and party blind our eyes, and the light which experience gives is a lantern on the stern, which shines only on the waves behind us!
Table Talk (1835) 18 December 1831

15 That passage is what I call the sublime dashed to pieces by cutting too close with the fiery four-in-hand round the corner of nonsense.
Table Talk (1835) 20 January 1834 (on lines excluded from his own poem *Limbo*, written 1817)

16 Shakespeare . . . is of no age—nor of any religion, or party or profession. The body and substance of his works came out of the unfathomable depths of his own oceanic mind.
Table Talk (1835) 15 March 1834

17 Bygone images and scenes of early life have stolen into my mind, like breezes blown from the spice-islands of Youth and Hope—those twin realities of this phantom world!
Table Talk (1835) 10 July 1834

18 Summer has set in with its usual severity.
In Alfred Ainger (ed.) *Letters of Charles Lamb* (1888) vol. 2, letter to Vincent Novello, 9 May 1826

Colette (Sidonie-Gabrielle Colette)
1873–1954
French novelist

19 *Le monde des émotions qu'on nomme, à la légère, physiques.*
The world of the emotions that are so lightly called physical.
Le Blé en herbe (1923) p. 161

20 *Son enfance, son adolescence lui avaient appris la patience, l'espoir, le silence, le maniement aisé des armes et des vertus des prisonniers.*
Her childhood, then her adolescence, had taught her patience, hope, silence and the easy manipulation of the weapons and virtues of all prisoners.
Chéri (1920) pt. 2 (translated by Janet Flanner, 1930, p. 138)

21 *Allons acheter des cartes à jouer, du bon vin, des marques de bridge, des aiguilles à tricoter, tous les bibelots qu'il faut pour boucher un grand trou, tout ce qu'il faut pour déguiser le monstre—la vieille femme.*
Let's buy a pack of cards, good wine, bridge scores, knitting needles, all the paraphernalia needed to fill an enormous void, everything needed to hide that horror—the old woman.
Chéri (1920) pt. 2 (translated by Janet Flanner, 1930, p. 207)

22 *Si on voulait être sincère, on avouerait qu'il y a l'amour bien nourri, et l'amour mal nourri. Et le reste c'est de la littérature.*
If we want to be sincere, we must admit that there is a well-nourished love and an ill-nourished love. And the rest is literature.
La Fin de Chéri (1926) p. 139 (translated by Viola Gerard Garvin)

Mary Collier *c.*1690–*c.*1762
English washerwoman and poet

23 Though we all day with care our work attend,
Such is our fate, we know not when 'twill end.
When evening's come, you homeward take your way;
We, till our work is done, are forced to stay.
The Woman's Labour (1739) p. 14

1 So the industrious bees do hourly strive
To bring their loads of honey to the hive;
Their sordid owners always reap the gains,
And poorly recompense their toils and pains.
  The Woman's Labour (1739) p. 17

2 The greatest heroes that the world can know,
To *women* their original must owe.
  'The Three Wise Sentences, from the First Book of Esdras'
  (1740) l. 132

William Collingbourne d. 1484

English landowner; conspirator against Richard III

3 The Cat, the Rat, and Lovell our dog
Rule all England under a hog.
  Referring to Sir William Catesby (d. 1485), Sir Richard
  Ratcliffe (d. 1485), Lord Lovell (1454–c.1487), whose crest
  was a dog, and King Richard III, whose emblem was a wild
  boar. Collingbourne was executed on Tower Hill. See
  Robert Fabyan *The Concordance of Chronicles* (ed. H. Ellis,
  1811) p. 672

Admiral Collingwood (Cuthbert, Baron Collingwood) 1748–1810

English naval commander

4 Now, gentlemen, let us do something today which the
world may talk of hereafter.
  Before the Battle of Trafalgar, 21 October 1805, in G. L.
  Newnham Collingwood (ed.) *A Selection from the
  Correspondence of Lord Collingwood* (1828) vol. 1, p. 168

R. G. Collingwood 1889–1943

English philosopher and archaeologist

5 Perfect freedom is reserved for the man who lives by
his own work and in that work does what he wants to
do.
  Speculum Mentis (1924) p. 25. Cf. Gill 306:26

Charles Collins

English songwriter

6 Any old iron, any old iron,
Any any old old iron?
You look neat
Talk about a treat,
You look dapper from your napper to your feet.
Dressed in style, brand new tile,
And your father's old green tie on,
But I wouldn't give you tuppence for your old watch
  chain;
Old iron, old iron?
  'Any Old Iron' (1911 song, with E. A. Sheppard and Fred
  Terry); the second line often sung 'Any any any old iron?'

7 My old man said, 'Follow the van,
Don't dilly-dally on the way!'
Off went the cart with the home packed in it,
I walked behind with my old cock linnet.
But I dillied and dallied, dallied and dillied,
Lost the van and don't know where to roam.
You can't trust the 'specials' like the old time 'coppers'
When you can't find your way home.
  'Don't Dilly-Dally on the Way' (1919 song, with Fred
  Leigh); popularized by Marie Lloyd

John Churton Collins 1848–1908

English lecturer and critic

8 To ask advice is in nine cases out of ten to tout for
flattery.
  In L. C. Collins *Life of John Churton Collins* (1912) p. 316

Michael Collins 1890–1922

Irish revolutionary

9 Think—what I have got for Ireland? Something which
she has wanted these past seven hundred years. Will
anyone be satisfied at the bargain? Will anyone? I tell
you this—early this morning I signed my death
warrant. I thought at the time how odd, how
ridiculous—a bullet may just as well have done the
job five years ago.
  Letter, 6 December 1921, in T. R. Dwyer *Michael Collins and
  the Treaty* (1981) ch. 4

William Collins 1721–59

English poet

10 To fair Fidele's grassy tomb
Soft maids and village hinds shall bring
Each opening sweet of earliest bloom,
And rifle all the breathing spring.
  'Dirge' (1744); occasionally included in 18th-century
  performances of Shakespeare's *Cymbeline*

11 Now air is hushed, save where the weak-eyed bat,
With short shrill shriek flits by on leathern wing,
Or where the beetle winds
His small but sullen horn,
As oft he rises 'midst the twilight path,
Against the pilgrim borne in heedless hum.
  'Ode to Evening' (1747)

12 How sleep the brave, who sink to rest,
By all their country's wishes blest!
  'Ode Written in the Year 1746' (1748)

13 By fairy hands their knell is rung,
By forms unseen their dirge is sung.
  'Ode Written in the Year 1746' (1748)

14 With eyes up-raised, as one inspired,
Pale Melancholy sate retired,
And from her wild sequestered seat,
In notes by distance made more sweet,
Poured thro' the mellow horn her pensive soul.
  'The Passions, an Ode for Music' (1747)

15 Love of peace, and lonely musing,
In hollow murmurs died away.
  'The Passions, an Ode for Music' (1747)

16 Too nicely Jonson knew the critic's part,
Nature in him was almost lost in Art.
  'Verses addressed to Sir Thomas Hanmer' (1743)

George Colman, the Elder 1732–94 *and* David Garrick 1717–79

English playwrights

17 Love and a cottage! Eh, Fanny! Ah, give me
indifference and a coach and six!
  The Clandestine Marriage (1766) act 1

George Colman, the Younger 1762–1836
English playwright

1 Oh, London is a fine town,
A very famous city,
Where all the streets are paved with gold,
And all the maidens pretty.
The Heir at Law (performed 1797, published 1808) act 1,
sc. 2

2 Says he, 'I am a handsome man, but I'm a gay
deceiver.'
Love Laughs at Locksmiths (1808) act 2

3 My father was an eminent button maker ... but I had
a soul above buttons ... I panted for a liberal
profession.
New Hay at the Old Market (1795) sc. 1

4 Johnson's style was grand and Gibbon's elegant; the
stateliness of the former was sometimes pedantic, and
the polish of the latter was occasionally finical.
Johnson marched to kettle-drums and trumpets;
Gibbon moved to flute and hautboys: Johnson hewed
passages through the Alps, while Gibbon levelled
walks through parks and gardens.
Random Records (1830) vol. 1, p. 122

5 As the lone Angler, patient man,
At Mewry-Water, or the Banne,
Leaves off, against his placid wish,
Impaling worms to torture fish.
The Lady of the Wreck (1813) canto 2, st. 18

6 And, on the label of the stuff,
He wrote this verse;
Which one would think was clear enough,
And terse:—
When taken,
To be well shaken.
'The Newcastle Apothecary' (1797)

Charles Caleb Colton c.1780–1832
English clergyman and writer

7 When you have nothing to say, say nothing.
Lacon (1820) vol. 1, no. 183

8 Examinations are formidable even to the best
prepared, for the greatest fool may ask more than the
wisest man can answer.
Lacon (1820) vol. 1, no. 322

9 If you would be known, and not know, vegetate in a
village; if you would know, and not be known, live in
a city.
Lacon (1820) vol. 1, no. 334

10 Man is an embodied paradox, a bundle of
contradictions.
Lacon (1820) vol. 1, no. 408

Betty Comden 1919– and
Adolph Green 1915–

11 New York, New York,—a helluva town,
The Bronx is up but the Battery's down,
And people ride in a hole in the ground:
New York, New York, — It's a helluva town.
New York, New York (1945 song); music by Leonard
Bernstein

12 The party's over, it's time to call it a day.
'The Party's Over' (1956); music by Jule Styne

Dame Ivy Compton-Burnett 1884–1969
English novelist

13 Time has too much credit ... It is not a great healer.
It is an indifferent and perfunctory one. Sometimes it
does not heal at all. And sometimes when it seems to,
no healing has been necessary.
Darkness and Day (1951) ch. 7

14 Well, of course, people are only human ... But it
really does not seem much for them to be.
A Family and a Fortune (1939) ch. 2

15 People don't resent having nothing nearly as much as
too little.
A Family and a Fortune (1939) ch. 4

16 'The more we ask, the more we have. And, it is fair
enough: asking is not always easy.'
'And it is said to be hard to accept ... So no wonder
we have so little.'
The Mighty and their Fall (1961) ch. 6

17 There are different kinds of wrong. The people sinned
against are not always the best.
The Mighty and their Fall (1961) ch. 7

18 We must use words as they are used or stand aside
from life.
Mother and Son (1955) ch. 9

19 My point is that it [wickedness] is not punished, and
that is why it is natural to be guilty of it. When it is
likely to be punished, most of us avoid it.
In *Orion* (1945) 'A Conversation between I.
Compton-Burnett and M. Jourdain'

Auguste Comte 1798–1857
French philosopher

20 M. Comte used to reproach his early English admirers
with maintaining the 'conspiracy of silence'
concerning his later performances.
J. S. Mill *Auguste Comte and Positivism* (1865) p. 199

Prince de Condé (the Great Condé)
1621–86
French general

21 *Silence! Voilà l'ennemi!*
Hush! Here comes the enemy!
As Bourdaloue mounted the pulpit at St Sulpice, in P. M.
Lauras *Bourdaloue: sa vie et ses oeuvres* (1881) vol. 2, p. 72

William Congreve 1670–1729
English playwright

22 It is the business of a comic poet to paint the vices and
follies of human kind.
The Double Dealer (1694) epistle dedicatory

23 Retired to their tea and scandal, according to their
ancient custom.
The Double Dealer (1694) act 1, sc. 1

1 There is nothing more unbecoming a man of quality than to laugh; Jesu, 'tis such a vulgar expression of the passion!
The Double Dealer (1694) act 1, sc. 4. Cf. Catullus 186:4

2 Tho' marriage makes man and wife one flesh, it leaves 'em still two fools.
The Double Dealer (1694) act 2, sc. 3

3 She lays it on with a trowel.
The Double Dealer (1694) act 3, sc. 10

4 See how love and murder will out.
The Double Dealer (1694) act 4, sc. 6

5 No mask like open truth to cover lies,
As to go naked is the best disguise.
The Double Dealer (1694) act 5, sc. 6

6 I am always of the opinion with the learned, if they speak first.
Incognita (1692)

7 Has he not a rogue's face? . . . a hanging-look to me . . . has a damned Tyburn-face, without the benefit o' the Clergy.
Love for Love (1695) act 2, sc. 7

8 I came upstairs into the world; for I was born in a cellar.
Love for Love (1695) act 2, sc. 7

9 I know that's a secret, for it's whispered every where.
Love for Love (1695) act 3, sc. 3

10 He that first cries out stop thief, is often he that has stolen the treasure.
Love for Love (1695) act 3, sc. 14

11 Women are like tricks by slight of hand,
Which, to admire, we should not understand.
Love for Love (1695) act 4, sc. 21

12 A branch of one of your antediluvian families, fellows that the flood could not wash away.
Love for Love (1695) act 5, sc. 2

13 To find a young fellow that is neither a wit in his own eye, nor a fool in the eye of the world, is a very hard task.
Love for Love (1695) act 5, sc. 2

14 Aye, 'tis well enough for a servant to be bred at an University. But the education is a little too pedantic for a gentleman.
Love for Love (1695) act 5, sc. 3

15 Nay, for my part I always despised Mr Tattle of all things; nothing but his being my husband could have made me like him less.
Love for Love (1695) act 5, sc. 11

16 Music has charms to sooth a savage breast.
The Mourning Bride (1697) act 1, sc. 1

17 Heaven has no rage, like love to hatred turned,
Nor Hell a fury, like a woman scorned.
The Mourning Bride (1697) act 3, sc. 8

18   Is he then dead?
What, dead at last, quite, quite for ever dead!
The Mourning Bride (1697) act 5, sc. 11

19 In my conscience I believe the baggage loves me, for she never speaks well of me herself, nor suffers any body else to rail at me.
The Old Bachelor (1693) act 1, sc. 1

20 Man was by Nature Woman's cully made:
We never are, but by ourselves, betrayed.
The Old Bachelor (1693) act 3, sc. 1

21 Bilbo's the word, and slaughter will ensue.
The Old Bachelor (1693) act 3, sc. 7

22 If this be not love, it is madness, and then it is pardonable.
The Old Bachelor (1693) act 3, sc. 10

23 Eternity was in that moment.
The Old Bachelor (1693) act 4, sc. 7

24 Now am I slap-dash down in the mouth.
The Old Bachelor (1693) act 4, sc. 9

25 SHARPER: Thus grief still treads upon the heels of pleasure:
Married in haste, we may repent at leisure.
SETTER: Some by experience find those words mis-placed:
At leisure married, they repent in haste.
The Old Bachelor (1693) act 5, sc. 1

26 I could find it in my heart to marry thee, purely to be rid of thee.
The Old Bachelor (1693) act 5, sc. 10

27 Courtship to marriage, as a very witty prologue to a very dull play.
The Old Bachelor (1693) act 5, sc. 10

28 They come together like the Coroner's Inquest, to sit upon the murdered reputations of the week.
The Way of the World (1700) act 1, sc. 1

29 Ay, ay, I have experience: I have a wife, and so forth.
The Way of the World (1700) act 1, sc. 3

30 I always take blushing either for a sign of guilt, or of ill breeding.
The Way of the World (1700) act 1, sc. 9

31 Say what you will, 'tis better to be left than never to have been loved.
The Way of the World (1700) act 2, sc. 1. Cf. Tennyson 683:12

32 Here she comes i' faith full sail, with her fan spread and streamers out, and a shoal of fools for tenders.
The Way of the World (1700) act 2, sc. 4

33 WITWOUD: Madam, do you pin up your hair with all your letters?
MILLAMANT: Only with those in verse, Mr Witwoud. I never pin up my hair with prose.
The Way of the World (1700) act 2, sc. 4

34 Beauty is the lover's gift.
The Way of the World (1700) act 2, sc. 4

35 A little disdain is not amiss; a little scorn is alluring.
The Way of the World (1700) act 3, sc. 5

36 O, nothing is more alluring than a levee from a couch in some confusion.
The Way of the World (1700) act 4, sc. 1

1 Don't let us be familiar or fond, nor kiss before folks, like my Lady Fadler and Sir Francis: nor go to Hyde-Park together the first Sunday in a new chariot, to provoke eyes and whispers, and then never be seen there together again; as if we were proud of one another the first week, and ashamed of one another ever after . . . Let us be very strange and well-bred: Let us be as strange as if we had been married a great while, and as well-bred as if we were not married at all.
   The Way of the World (1700) act 4, sc. 5

2 These articles subscribed, if I continue to endure you a little longer, I may by degrees dwindle into a wife.
   The Way of the World (1700) act 4, sc. 5

3 I hope you do not think me prone to any iteration of nuptials.
   The Way of the World (1700) act 4, sc. 12

4 Careless she is with artful care,
   Affecting to seem unaffected.
   'Amoret'

5 Music alone with sudden charms can bind
   The wand'ring sense, and calm the troubled mind.
   'Hymn to Harmony'

6 Would I were free from this restraint,
   Or else had hopes to win her;
   Would she could make of me a saint,
   Or I of her a sinner.
   'Pious Selinda Goes to Prayers' (song)

7 For 'tis some virtue, virtue to commend.
   'To Sir Godfrey Kneller'

James M. Connell 1852–1929

Irish socialist songwriter

8 The people's flag is deepest red;
   It shrouded oft our martyred dead,
   And ere their limbs grew stiff and cold,
   Their heart's blood dyed its every fold.
   Then raise the scarlet standard high!
   Within its shade we'll live or die.
   Tho' cowards flinch and traitors sneer,
   We'll keep the red flag flying here.
   'The Red Flag' (1889) in H. E. Piggott *Songs that made History* (1937) ch. 6

Billy Connolly 1942–

Scottish comedian

9 Marriage is a wonderful invention; but, then again, so is a bicycle repair kit.
   In Duncan Campbell *Billy Connolly* (1976) p. 92

Cyril Connolly 1903–74

English writer

10 I ask very little. Some fragments of Pamphilides, a Choctaw blood-mask, the prose of Scaliger the Elder, a painting by Fuseli, an occasional visit to the all-in wrestling, or to my meretrix; a cook who can produce a passable 'poulet à la Khmer', a Pong vase. Simple tastes, you will agree, and it is my simple habit to indulge them.
   The Condemned Playground 'Told in Gath', a parody of Aldous Huxley

11 Whom the gods wish to destroy they first call promising.
   Enemies of Promise (1938) ch. 13

12 There is no more sombre enemy of good art than the pram in the hall.
   Enemies of Promise (1938) ch. 14

13 The Mandarin style . . . is beloved by literary pundits, by those who would make the written word as unlike as possible to the spoken one. It is the style of those writers whose tendency is to make their language convey more than they mean or more than they feel, it is the style of most artists and all humbugs.
   Enemies of Promise (1938) ch. 20

14 It is closing time in the gardens of the West and from now on an artist will be judged only by the resonance of his solitude or the quality of his despair.
   Horizon December 1949–January 1950, p. 362

15 Life is a maze in which we take the wrong turning before we have learnt to walk.
   The Unquiet Grave (1944) pt. 1

16 Civilization is an active deposit which is formed by the combustion of the Present with the Past.
   The Unquiet Grave (1944) pt. 2

17 Imprisoned in every fat man a thin one is wildly signalling to be let out.
   The Unquiet Grave (1944) pt. 2. Cf. Orwell 499:23

18 The true index of a man's character is the health of his wife.
   The Unquiet Grave (1944) pt. 2

19 We are all serving a life-sentence in the dungeon of self.
   The Unquiet Grave (1944) pt. 2

20 Peeling off the kilometres to the tune of 'Blue Skies', sizzling down the long black liquid reaches of Nationale Sept, the plane trees going sha-sha-sha through the open window, the windscreen yellowing with crushed midges, she with the Michelin beside me, a handkerchief binding her hair.
   The Unquiet Grave (1944) pt. 3

21 Our memories are card-indexes consulted, and then put back in disorder by authorities whom we do not control.
   The Unquiet Grave (1944) pt. 3

22 Destroy him as you will, the bourgeois always bounces up—execute him, expropriate him, starve him out *en masse*, and he reappears in your children.
   In *Observer* 7 March 1937

23 Perfect fear casteth out love.
   In *Observer* 1 December 1974; obituary notice by Philip Toynbee, to whom Connolly addressed the remark during the Blitz

James Connolly 1868–1916

Irish labour leader; executed after the Easter Rising, 1916

24 The worker is the slave of capitalist society, the female worker is the slave of that slave.
   The Re-conquest of Ireland (1915) p. 38

Joseph Conrad (Teodor Josef Konrad Korzeniowski) 1857–1924

Polish-born English novelist

1 In plucking the fruit of memory one runs the risk of spoiling its bloom.
   The Arrow of Gold (1924 Uniform Edition) p. viii

2 The conquest of the earth, which mostly means the taking it away from those who have a different complexion or slightly flatter noses than ourselves, is not a pretty thing when you look into it.
   Heart of Darkness (1902) ch. 1

3 We live, as we dream — alone.
   Heart of Darkness (1902) ch. 1

4 Exterminate all the brutes!
   Heart of Darkness (1902) ch. 2

5 The horror! The horror!
   Heart of Darkness (1902) ch. 3

6 Mistah Kurtz—he dead.
   Heart of Darkness (1902) ch. 3

7 A man that is born falls into a dream like a man who falls into the sea. If he tries to climb out into the air as inexperienced people endeavour to do, he drowns . . . to the destructive element submit yourself, and with the exertions of your hands and feet in the water make the deep, deep sea keep you up.
   Lord Jim (1900) ch. 20

8 You shall judge of a man by his foes as well as by his friends.
   Lord Jim (1900) ch. 34

9 My task which I am trying to achieve is by the power of the written word, to make you hear, to make you feel—it is, before all, to make you *see*. That—and no more, and it is everything.
   The Nigger of the Narcissus (1897) preface

10 Action is consolatory. It is the enemy of thought and the friend of flattering illusions.
   Nostromo (1904) pt. 1, ch. 6

11 It's only those who do nothing that make no mistakes, I suppose.
   Outcast of the Islands (1896) pt. 3, ch. 2

12 The terrorist and the policeman both come from the same basket.
   The Secret Agent (1907) ch. 4

13 All ambitions are lawful except those which climb upwards on the miseries or credulities of mankind.
   Some Reminiscences (1912) preface

14 Only in men's imagination does every truth find an effective and undeniable existence. Imagination, not invention, is the supreme master of art, as of life.
   Some Reminiscences (1912) ch. 1

15 The scrupulous and the just, the noble, humane, and devoted natures; the unselfish and the intelligent may begin a movement—but it passes away from them. They are not the leaders of a revolution. They are its victims.
   Under Western Eyes (1911) pt. 2, ch. 3

16 A belief in a supernatural source of evil is not necessary; men alone are quite capable of every wickedness.
   Under Western Eyes (1911) pt. 2, ch. 4

17 I remember my youth and the feeling that will never come back any more—the feeling that I could last for ever, outlast the sea, the earth, and all men; the deceitful feeling that lures us on to joys, to perils, to love, to vain effort—to death; the triumphant conviction of strength, the heat of life in the handful of dust, the glow in the heart that with every year grows dim, grows cold, grows small, and expires—and expires, too soon, too soon—before life itself.
   Youth (1902) p. 41

18 The *whole* of the truth lies in the presentation; therefore the expression should be studied in the interest of veracity. This is the only morality of *art* apart from *subject*.
   Letter to Sir Hugh Clifford, 9 October 1899, in G. Jean-Aubrey (ed.) *Joseph Conrad: Life and Letters* (1927)

Shirley Conran (née Pearce) 1932–

English writer

19 Life is too short to stuff a mushroom.
   Superwoman (1975) p. 15

Henry Constable 1562–1613

English poet

20 I did not know that thou wert dead before;
   I did not feel the grief I did sustain;
   The greater stroke astonisheth the more;
   Astonishment takes from us sense of pain.
   I stood amazed when others' tears begun,
   And now begin to weep when they have done.
   'To Sir Philip Sidney's Soul' (1595)

21 When thee (O holy sacrificial Lamb)
   In severed signs I white and liquid see:
   As on thy body slain I think on thee,
   Which pale by shedding of thy blood became;
   And when again I do behold the same
   Veiled in white to be received of me,
   Thou seemest in thy sindon wrapped to be
   Like to a corse, whose monument I am.
   'To the Blessed Sacrament' (first published 1815)

John Constable 1776–1837

English painter

22 The sound of water escaping from mill-dams, etc., willows, old rotten planks, slimy posts, and brickwork . . . those scenes made me a painter and I am grateful.
   Letter to John Fisher, 23 October 1821, in C. R. Leslie *Memoirs of the Life of John Constable* (1843) ch. 5

23 There is nothing ugly; *I never saw an ugly thing in my life*: for let the form of an object be what it may,—light, shade, and perspective will always make it beautiful.
   In C. R. Leslie *Memoirs of the Life of John Constable* (1843) ch. 17

24 In Claude's landscape all is lovely—all amiable—all is amenity and repose;—the calm sunshine of the heart.
   Lecture, 2 June 1836, in C. R. Leslie *Memoirs of the Life of John Constable* (1843) ch. 18

Benjamin Constant (Henri Benjamin Constant de Rebecque) 1767–1834

French novelist, political philosopher, and politician

1 *L'art pour l'art, sans but, car tout but dénature l'art. Mais l'art atteint au but qu'il n'a pas.*

Art for art's sake, with no purpose, for any purpose perverts art. But art achieves a purpose which is not its own.

Journal intime 11 February 1804, in *Revue Internationale* 10 January 1887 p. 96 (describing a conversation with Crabb Robinson about the latter's work on Kant's aesthetics). Cf. Cousin 220:6

Constantine the Great AD c.288–337

Roman emperor from AD 306

2 *In hoc signo vinces.*

In this sign shalt thou conquer.

Traditional form of Constantine's vision (AD 312), reported in Greek—τούτῳ νίκα [By this, conquer]—in Eusebius *Life of Constantine* bk. 1, ch. 28

A. J. Cook 1885–1931

English labour leader; Secretary of the Miners' Federation of Great Britain, 1924–31

3 Not a penny off the pay, not a second on the day.

Speech at York, 3 April 1926, in *The Times* 5 April 1926 (often quoted with 'minute' substituted for 'second')

Dan Cook

American sports editor

4 The opera ain't over 'til the fat lady sings.

In *Washington Post* 3 June 1978. See *Concise Oxford Dictionary of Proverbs* under 'opera'

Eliza Cook 1818–89

English poet

5 Better build schoolrooms for 'the boy', Than cells and gibbets for 'the man'.

'A Song for the Ragged Schools' (1853)

Calvin Coolidge 1872–1933

30th President of the USA

6 Civilization and profits go hand in hand.

Speech in New York, 27 November 1920, in *New York Times* 28 November 1920, p. 20

7 The chief business of the American people is business.

Speech in Washington, 17 January 1925, in *New York Times* 18 January 1925, p. 19

8 They hired the money, didn't they?

On the subject of war debts incurred by England and others, in John H. McKee *Coolidge: Wit and Wisdom* (1933) p. 118

Duff Cooper (1st Viscount Norwich) 1890–1954

British Conservative politician, diplomat, and writer

9 Your two stout lovers frowning at one another across the hearth rug, while your small, but perfectly formed one kept the party in a roar.

Letter to Lady Diana Manners, later his wife, October 1914; in Artemis Cooper *Durable Fire* (1983) p. 17

Wendy Cope 1945–

English poet

10 It's nice to meet serious people
And hear them explain their views:
Your concern for the rights of women
Is especially welcome news.
I'm sure you'd never exploit one;
I expect you'd rather be dead;
I'm thoroughly convinced of it—
Now can we go to bed?

'From June to December' (1986)

Richard Corbet 1582–1635

English poet and prelate; chaplain to James I

11 Farewell, rewards and Fairies,
Good housewives now may say,
For now foul sluts in dairies
Do fare as well as they.

'The Fairies' Farewell'

12 Who of late for cleanliness,
Finds sixpence in her shoe?

'The Fairies' Farewell'

13 By which we note the Fairies
Were of the old profession;
Their songs were Ave Marys,
Their dances were procession.

'The Fairies' Farewell'

14 I wish thee all thy mother's graces,
Thy father's fortunes, and his places.
I wish thee friends, and one at Court,
Not to build on, but support;
To keep thee, not in doing many
Oppressions, but from suffering any.

'To his Son, Vincent Corbet'

Pierre Corneille 1606–84

French playwright

15 *A vaincre sans péril, on triomphe sans gloire.*

When there is no peril in the fight, there is no glory in the triumph.

Le Cid (1637) act 2, sc. 2

16 *Faites votre devoir et laissez faire aux dieux.*

Do your duty, and leave the outcome to the Gods.

Horace (1640) act 2, sc. 8

17 *Un premier mouvement ne fut jamais un crime.*

A first impulse was never a crime.

Horace (1640) act 5, sc. 3. Cf. Montrond 482:2

Bernard Cornfeld 1927–
American businessman

1 Do you sincerely want to be rich?
> Cornfeld's stock question to salesmen. See Charles Raw et al. *Do You Sincerely Want to be Rich?* (1971) p. 67

Frances Cornford (*née Darwin*)
1886–1960
English poet; wife of Francis M. Cornford

2 Whoso maintains that I am humbled now
(Who wait the Awful Day) is still a liar;
I hope to meet my Maker brow to brow
And find my own the higher.
> 'Epitaph for a Reviewer' (1954)

3 How long ago Hector took off his plume,
Not wanting that his little son should cry,
Then kissed his sad Andromache goodbye—
And now we three in Euston waiting-room.
> 'Parting in Wartime' (1948)

4 O fat white woman whom nobody loves,
Why do you walk through the fields in gloves,
When the grass is soft as the breast of doves
And shivering-sweet to the touch?
O why do you walk through the fields in gloves,
Missing so much and so much?
> 'To a Fat Lady seen from the Train' (1910). Cf. Chesterton 199:2

5 A young Apollo, golden-haired,
Stands dreaming on the verge of strife,
Magnificently unprepared
For the long littleness of life.
> 'Youth' (1910) (of Rupert Brooke)

Francis M. Cornford 1874–1943

6 University printing presses exist, and are subsidised by the Government for the purpose of producing books which no one can read; and they are true to their high calling.
> *Microcosmographia Academica* (1908) ch. 5

7 Every public action, which is not customary, either is wrong, or, if it is right, is a dangerous precedent. It follows that nothing should ever be done for the first time.
> *Microcosmographia Academica* (1908) ch. 7

8 The Principle of Unripe Time is that people should not do at the present moment what they think right at that moment, because the moment at which they think it right has not yet arrived ... Time, by the way, is like the medlar; it has a trick of going rotten before it is ripe.
> *Microcosmographia Academica* (1908) ch. 7

9 Another sport which wastes unlimited time is comma-hunting. Once start a comma and the whole pack will be off, full cry, especially if they have had a literary training ... But comma-hunting is so exciting as to be a little dangerous. When attention is entirely concentrated on punctuation, there is some fear that the conduct of business may suffer, and a proposal get through without being properly obstructed on its demerits. It is therefore wise, when a kill has been made, to move at once for adjournment.
> *Microcosmographia Academica* (1908) ch. 8

Mme Cornuel 1605–94
French society hostess

10 *Il n'y a point de héros pour son valet de chambre.*
No man is a hero to his valet.
> In *Lettres de Mlle Aïssé à Madame C* (1787) Letter 13 'De Paris, 1728'

Coronation Service

11 We present you with this Book, the most valuable thing that this world affords. Here is wisdom; this is the royal Law; these are the lively Oracles of God.
> The Presenting of the Holy Bible. See L. G. Wickham Legge *English Coronation Records* (1901) p. 334

Correggio (*Antonio Allegri Correggio*)
c.1489–1534
Italian painter

12 *Son pittore ancor io!*
I, too, am a painter!
> On seeing Raphael's *St Cecilia* at Bologna, c.1525, in L. Pungileoni *Memorie Istoriche de ... Correggio* (1817) vol. 1, p. 61

William Cory (*born Johnson*) 1823–92
English poet; assistant master at Eton College, 1845–72

13 Jolly boating weather,
And a hay harvest breeze,
Blade on the feather,
Shade off the trees
Swing, swing together
With your body between your knees.
> 'Eton Boating Song' in *Eton Scrap Book* (1865). See E. Parker *Floreat* (1923) p. 109

14 Nothing in life shall sever
The chain that is round us now.
> 'Eton Boating Song' in *Eton Scrap Book* (1865). See E. Parker *Floreat* (1923) p. 109

15 They told me, Heraclitus, they told me you were dead,
They brought me bitter news to hear and bitter tears to shed.
I wept as I remembered how often you and I
Had tired the sun with talking and sent him down the sky.
> 'Heraclitus' (1858); translation of Callimachus 'Epigram 2' in R. Pfeiffer (ed.) *Callimachus* (1949–53)

1 You promise heavens free from strife,
Pure truth, and perfect change of will;
But sweet, sweet is this human life,
So sweet, I fain would breathe it still;
Your chilly stars I can forgo,
This warm kind world is all I know.
'Mimnermus in Church' (1858)

2 All beauteous things for which we live
By laws of space and time decay.
But Oh, the very reason why
I clasp them, is because they die.
'Mimnermus in Church' (1858)

Charles Cotton 1630–87

English poet

3 The shadows now so long do grow,
That brambles like tall cedars show,
Molehills seem mountains, and the ant
Appears a monstrous elephant.
'Evening Quatrains' (1689) st. 3

Baron Pierre de Coubertin 1863–1937

French sportsman and educationist

4 *L'important dans la vie ce n'est point le triomphe mais le
combat; l'essentiel ce n'est pas d'avoir vaincu mais de
s'être bien battu.*

The important thing in life is not the victory but the
contest; the essential thing is not to have won but to
have fought well.
Speech at a government banquet in London, 24 July 1908,
in T. A. Cook *Fourth Olympiad* (1909) p. 793

Émile Coué 1857–1926

French psychologist

5 *Tous les jours, à tous points de vue, je vais de mieux en
mieux.*

Every day, in every way, I am getting better and
better.
To be said 15 to 20 times, morning and evening, in *De la
suggestion et de ses applications* (1915) p. 17

Victor Cousin 1792–1867

French philosopher

6 *Il faut de la religion pour la religion, de la morale pour la
morale, comme de l'art pour l'art ... le beau ne peut être
la voie ni de l'utile, ni du bien, ni du saint; il ne conduit
qu'à lui-même.*

We must have religion for religion's sake, morality for
morality's sake, as with art for art's sake ... the
beautiful cannot be the way to what is useful, or to
what is good, or to what is holy; it leads only to itself.
Du Vrai, du beau, et du bien [Sorbonne lecture, 1818] (1853)
pt. 2, p. 197. Cf. Constant 218:1

Thomas Coventry (1st Baron Coventry) 1578–1640

English judge

7 The dominion of the sea, as it is an ancient and
undoubted right of the crown of England, so it is the
best security of the land ... The wooden walls are the
best walls of this kingdom.
Speech to the Judges, 17 June 1635, in J. Rushworth
Historical Collections (1680) vol. 2, p. 297 (*wooden walls*
ships). See Herodotus *Histories* bk. 7, ch. 141–3

Noël Coward 1899–1973

English playwright, actor, and composer

8 Dance, dance, dance, little lady!
Leave tomorrow behind.
'Dance, Little Lady' (1928 song)

9 Don't let's be beastly to the Germans
When our Victory is ultimately won.
'Don't Let's Be Beastly to the Germans' (1943 song)

10 There's sand in the porridge and sand in the bed,
And if this is pleasure we'd rather be dead.
'The English Lido' (1928)

11 I believe that since my life began
The most I've had is just
A talent to amuse.
Heigho, if love were all!
'If Love Were All' (1929 song)

12 I'll see you again,
Whenever spring breaks through again.
'I'll See You Again' (1929 song)

13 Mad about the boy,
It's pretty funny but I'm mad about the boy.
He has a gay appeal
That makes me feel
There may be something sad about the boy.
'Mad about the Boy' (1932 song)

14 Mad dogs and Englishmen
Go out in the midday sun.
The Japanese don't care to,
The Chinese wouldn't dare to,
The Hindus and Argentines sleep firmly from twelve to
one,
But Englishmen detest a siesta.
In the Philippines, there are lovely screens
To protect you from the glare;
In the Malay states, they have hats like plates
Which the Britishers won't wear.
At twelve noon, the natives swoon,
And no further work is done;
But mad dogs and Englishmen go out in the midday
sun.
'Mad Dogs and Englishmen' (1931 song)

15 Don't put your daughter on the stage, Mrs
Worthington,
Don't put your daughter on the stage.
'Mrs Worthington' (1935 song)

16 Poor little rich girl
You're a bewitched girl,
Better beware!
'Poor Little Rich Girl' (1925 song)

1 Someday I'll find you,
  Moonlight behind you,
  True to the dream I am dreaming.
  'Someday I'll Find You' (1930 song)

2 The Stately Homes of England,
  How beautiful they stand,
  To prove the upper classes
  Have still the upper hand.
  'The Stately Homes of England' (1938 song). Cf. Hemans
  331:11

3 Very flat, Norfolk.
  Private Lives (1930) act 1

4 Extraordinary how potent cheap music is.
  Private Lives (1930) act 1

5 Certain women should be struck regularly, like gongs.
  Private Lives (1930) act 3

6 Two wise acres and a cow.
  Describing the Sitwells, in John Pearson *Façades* (1978)
  ch. 10. Cf. Anonymous 19:1

Abraham Cowley 1618–67

English poet and essayist

7 The thirsty earth soaks up the rain,
  And drinks, and gapes for drink again.
  The plants suck in the earth, and are
  With constant drinking fresh and fair.
  'Drinking' (1656)

8 Fill all the glasses there, for why
  Should every creature drink but I,
  Why, man of morals, tell me why?
  'Drinking' (1656)

9 God the first garden made, and the first city Cain.
  Essays, in Verse and Prose (1668) 'The Garden'. Cf. Cowper
  223:18

10 Hence, ye profane; I hate ye all;
   Both the great vulgar, and the small.
   Essays, in Verse and Prose (1668) 'Of Greatness' (translation
   of Horace *Odes* bk. 3, no. 1). Cf. Horace 349:22

11 This only grant me, that my means may lie
   Too low for envy, for contempt too high.
   Essays, in Verse and Prose (1668) 'Of Myself'

12 Acquaintance I would have, but when't depends
   Not on the number, but the choice of friends.
   Essays, in Verse and Prose (1668) 'Of Myself'

13 Love in her sunny eyes does basking play;
   Love walks the pleasant mazes of her hair;
   Love does on both her lips for ever stray;
   And sows and reaps a thousand kisses there.
   In all her outward parts Love's always seen;
   But, oh, he never went within.
   The Mistress: or . . . Love Verses (1647) 'The Change'

14 The world's a scene of changes, and to be
   Constant, in Nature were inconstancy.
   The Mistress: or . . . Love Verses (1647) 'Inconstancy'

15 Lukewarmness I account a sin
   As great in love as in religion.
   The Mistress: or . . . Love Verses 'The Request'

16 Well then; I now do plainly see
   This busy world and I shall ne'er agree;
   The very honey of all earthly joy
   Does of all meats the soonest cloy,
   And they (methinks) deserve my pity,
   Who for it can endure the stings,
   The crowd, and buzz, and murmurings
   Of this great hive, the city.
   The Mistress: or . . . Love Verses (1647) 'The Wish'

17 Nothing so soon the drooping spirits can raise
   As praises from the men, whom all men praise.
   'Ode upon a Copy of Verses of My Lord Broghill's' (1663)

18 Poet and Saint! to thee alone are given
   The two most sacred names of earth and Heaven.
   'On the Death of Mr Crashaw' (1656)

19 Hail, Bard triumphant! and some care bestow
   On us, the Poets Militant below!
   'On the Death of Mr Crashaw' (1656)

20 Ye fields of Cambridge, our dear Cambridge, say,
   Have ye not seen us walking every day?
   Was there a tree about which did not know
   The love betwixt us two?
   'On the Death of Mr William Hervey' (1656)

21 Life is an incurable disease.
   'To Dr Scarborough' (1656) st. 6

Hannah Cowley (*née Parkhouse*)
1743–1809

English playwright

22 Five minutes! Zounds! I have been five minutes too
   late all my life-time!
   The Belle's Stratagem (1780) act 1, sc. 1

23 Vanity, like murder, will out.
   The Belle's Stratagem (1780) act 1, sc. 4

24 But what is woman?—only one of Nature's agreeable
   blunders.
   Who's the Dupe? (1779) act 2

William Cowper 1731–1800

English poet

25 No voice divine the storm allayed,
   No light propitious shone;
   When snatched from all effectual aid,
   We perished, each alone:
   But I beneath a rougher sea,
   And whelmed in deeper gulfs than he.
   'The Castaway' (written 1799) l. 61

26 Grief is itself a med'cine.
   'Charity' (1782) l. 159

27 He found it inconvenient to be poor.
   'Charity' (1782) l. 189 (of a burglar)

28 Spare the poet for his subject sake.
   'Charity' (1782) l. 636

29 'Tis hard if all is false that I advance
   A fool must now and then be right, by chance.
   'Conversation' (1782) l. 95

1 A tale should be judicious, clear, succinct;
The language plain, and incidents well linked;
Tell not as new what ev'ry body knows,
And new or old, still hasten to a close.
'Conversation' (1782) l. 235

2 The pipe with solemn interposing puff,
Makes half a sentence at a time enough;
The dozing sages drop the drowsy strain,
Then pause, and puff—and speak, and pause again.
'Conversation' (1782) l. 245

3 Pernicious weed! whose scent the fair annoys,
Unfriendly to society's chief joys.
'Conversation' (1782) l. 251 (on tobacco)

4 His wit invites you by his looks to come,
But when you knock it never is at home.
'Conversation' (1782) l. 303

5 . . . Thousands, careless of the damning sin,
Kiss the book's outside who ne'er look within.
'Expostulation' (1782) l. 388 (on oath-taking)

6 The man that hails you Tom or Jack,
And proves by thumps upon your back
How he esteems your merit,
Is such a friend, that one had need
Be very much his friend indeed
To pardon or to bear it.
'Friendship' (1782) l. 169

7 Damned below Judas; more abhorred than he was.
'Hatred and vengeance, my eternal portion' (written
c.1774)

8 Man disavows, and Deity disowns me.
'Hatred and vengeance, my eternal portion' (written
c.1774)

9 Men deal with life, as children with their play,
Who first misuse, then cast their toys away.
'Hope' (1782) l. 127

10 Could he with reason murmur at his case,
Himself sole author of his own disgrace?
'Hope' (1782) l. 316

11 And differing judgements serve but to declare
That truth lies somewhere, if we knew but where.
'Hope' (1782) l. 423

12 John Gilpin was a citizen
Of credit and renown,
A train-band captain eke was he
Of famous London town.
'John Gilpin' (1785) l. 1

13 My sister and my sister's child,
Myself and children three,
Will fill the chaise; so you must ride
On horseback after we.
'John Gilpin' (1785) l. 13

14 O'erjoy'd was he to find
That, though on pleasure she was bent,
She had a frugal mind.
'John Gilpin' (1785) l. 30

15 Beware of desperate steps. The darkest day
(Live till tomorrow) will have passed away.
'The Needless Alarm' (written c.1790) l. 132

16 No dancing bear was so genteel,
Or half so dégagé.
'Of Himself' (written 1752)

17 God moves in a mysterious way
His wonders to perform;
He plants his footsteps in the sea,
And rides upon the storm . . .

Blind unbelief is sure to err,
And scan his work in vain;
God is his own interpreter,
And he will make it plain.
Olney Hymns (1779) 'Light Shining out of Darkness'

18 Ye fearful saints fresh courage take,
The clouds ye so much dread
Are big with mercy, and shall break
In blessings on your head.
Olney Hymns (1779) 'Light Shining out of Darkness'

19 Behind a frowning providence
He hides a smiling face.
Olney Hymns (1779) 'Light Shining out of Darkness'

20 Hark, my soul! it is the Lord;
'Tis thy Saviour, hear his word;
Jesus speaks, and speaks to thee;
'Say, poor sinner, lov'st thou me?'
Olney Hymns (1779) 'Lovest Thou Me?'

21 There is a fountain filled with blood
Drawn from Emmanuel's veins,
And sinners, plunged beneath that flood,
Lose all their guilty stains.
Olney Hymns (1779) 'Praise for the Fountain Opened'

22 Oh! for a closer walk with God,
A calm and heav'nly frame;
A light to shine upon the road
That leads me to the Lamb!
Olney Hymns (1779) 'Walking with God'

23 My dog! what remedy remains,
Since, teach you all I can,
I see you, after all my pains,
So much resemble man!
'On a Spaniel called Beau, killing a young bird' (written
1793)

24 Toll for the brave—
The brave! that are no more:
All sunk beneath the wave,
Fast by their native shore.
'On the Loss of the Royal George' (written 1782)

25 Oh, fond attempt to give a deathless lot
To names ignoble, born to be forgot!
'On Observing Some Names of Little Note Recorded in the
Biographia Britannica' (1782)

26 Thy morning bounties ere I left my home,
The biscuit, or confectionary plum.
'On the Receipt of My Mother's Picture out of Norfolk'
(1798) l. 60

27 Me howling winds drive devious, tempest-tossed,
Sails ripped, seams op'ning wide, and compass lost.
'On the Receipt of My Mother's Picture out of Norfolk'
(1798) l. 102

28 I shall not ask Jean Jacques Rousseau,
If birds confabulate or no.
'Pairing Time Anticipated' (1795)

29 The poplars are felled, farewell to the shade
And the whispering sound of the cool colonnade.
'The Poplar-Field' (written 1784)

1 Oh, laugh or mourn with me the rueful jest,
A cassocked huntsman and a fiddling priest!
'The Progress of Error' (1782) l. 110

2 Himself a wand'rer from the narrow way,
His silly sheep, what wonder if they stray?
'The Progress of Error' (1782) l. 118

3 Remorse, the fatal egg by pleasure laid.
'The Progress of Error' (1782) l. 239

4 As creeping ivy clings to wood or stone,
And hides the ruin that it feeds upon,
So sophistry, cleaves close to, and protects
Sin's rotten trunk, concealing its defects.
'The Progress of Error' (1782) l. 285

5 How much a dunce that has been sent to roam
Excels a dunce that has been kept at home.
'The Progress of Error' (1782) l. 415

6 Thou god of our idolatry, the press . . .
Thou fountain, at which drink the good and wise;
Thou ever-bubbling spring of endless lies;
Like Eden's dread probationary tree,
Knowledge of good and evil is from thee.
'The Progress of Error' (1782) l. 461

7 Laugh at all you trembled at before.
'The Progress of Error' (1782) l. 592

8 The disencumbered Atlas of the state.
'Retirement' (1782) l. 394 (of the statesman)

9 He likes the country, but in truth must own,
Most likes it, when he studies it in town.
'Retirement' (1782) l. 573

10   Philologists, who chase
A panting syllable through time and space,
Start it at home, and hunt it in the dark,
To Gaul, to Greece, and into Noah's ark.
'Retirement' (1782) l. 691

11 'Till authors hear at length, one gen'ral cry,
Tickle and entertain us, or we die.
The loud demand from year to year the same,
Beggars invention and makes fancy lame.
'Retirement' (1782) l. 707

12 Admirals extolled for standing still,
Or doing nothing with a deal of skill.
'Table Talk' (1782) l. 192

13 Freedom has a thousand charms to show,
That slaves, howe'er contented, never know.
'Table Talk' (1782) l. 260

14 Stamps God's own name upon a lie just made,
To turn a penny in the way of trade.
'Table Talk' (1782) l. 420 (Perjury)

15 But he (his musical finesse was such,
So nice his ear, so delicate his touch)
Made poetry a mere mechanic art,
And ev'ry warbler has his tune by heart.
'Table Talk' (1782) l. 652 (on Pope)

16 Thus first necessity invented stools,
Convenience next suggested elbow-chairs,
And luxury the accomplished sofa last.
The Task (1785) bk. 1 'The Sofa' l. 86

17 The nurse sleeps sweetly, hired to watch the sick,
Whom, snoring, she disturbs.
The Task (1785) bk. 1 'The Sofa' l. 89

18 God made the country, and man made the town.
The Task (1785) bk. 1 'The Sofa' l. 749. Cf. Bradford 139:1, Cowley 221:9

19 Slaves cannot breathe in England, if their lungs
Receive our air, that moment they are free;
They touch our country, and their shackles fall.
The Task (1785) bk. 2 'The Timepiece' l. 40. Cf. Anonymous 17:5

20 England, with all thy faults, I love thee still—
My country!
The Task (1785) bk. 2 'The Timepiece' l. 206. Cf. Churchill 200:17

21 There is a pleasure in poetic pains
Which only poets know.
The Task (1785) bk. 2 'The Timepiece' l. 285

22 Variety's the very spice of life,
That gives it all its flavour.
The Task (1785) bk. 2 'The Timepiece' l. 606

23 I was a stricken deer, that left the herd
Long since.
The Task (1785) bk. 3 'The Garden' l. 108. Cf. Hamlet 576:20

24   Charge
His mind with meanings that he never had.
The Task (1785) bk. 3 'The Garden' l. 148

25 Great contest follows, and much learned dust
Involves the combatants.
The Task (1785) bk. 3 'The Garden' l. 161

26 Defend me, therefore, common sense, say I,
From reveries so airy, from the toil
Of dropping buckets into empty wells,
And growing old in drawing nothing up!
The Task (1785) bk. 3 'The Garden' l. 187

27   Newton, childlike sage!
Sagacious reader of the works of God.
The Task (1785) bk. 3 'The Garden' l. 252

28   Detested sport,
That owes its pleasures to another's pain.
The Task (1785) bk. 3 'The Garden' l. 326 (of hunting)

29 Studious of laborious ease.
The Task (1785) bk. 3 'The Garden' l. 361

30 To combat may be glorious, and success
Perhaps may crown us; but to fly is safe.
The Task (1785) bk. 3 'The Garden' l. 686

31 Now stir the fire, and close the shutters fast,
Let fall the curtains, wheel the sofa round,
And, while the bubbling and loud-hissing urn
Throws up a steamy column, and the cups,
That cheer but not inebriate, wait on each,
So let us welcome peaceful evening in.
The Task (1785) bk. 4 'The Winter Evening' l. 34. Cf. Berkeley 65:8

32 'Tis pleasant through the loopholes of retreat
To peep at such a world; to see the stir
Of the great Babel, and not feel the crowd.
The Task (1785) bk. 4 'The Winter Evening' l. 88

33 I crown thee king of intimate delights,
Fire-side enjoyments, home-born happiness.
The Task (1785) bk. 4 'The Winter Evening' l. 139

34 A Roman meal . . .
. . . a radish and an egg.
The Task (1785) bk. 4 'The Winter Evening' l. 168

1 The slope of faces, from the floor to th' roof,
(As if one master-spring controlled them all),
Relaxed into a universal grin.
The Task (1785) bk. 4 'The Winter Evening' l. 202 (of the theatre)

2 Shaggy, and lean, and shrewd, with pointed ears
And tail cropped short, half lurcher and half cur.
The Task (1785) bk. 5 'The Winter Morning Walk' l. 45

3 But war's a game, which, were their subjects wise,
Kings would not play at.
The Task (1785) bk. 5 'The Winter Morning Walk' l. 187

4   Knowledge dwells
In heads replete with thoughts of other men;
Wisdom in minds attentive to their own.
The Task (1785) bk. 6 'The Winter Walk at Noon' l. 89

5 Knowledge is proud that he has learned so much;
Wisdom is humble that he knows no more.
The Task (1785) bk. 6 'The Winter Walk at Noon' l. 96

6 Nature is but a name for an effect,
Whose cause is God.
The Task (1785) bk. 6 'The Winter Walk at Noon' l. 223

7 A cheap but wholesome salad from the brook.
The Task (1785) bk. 6 'The Winter Walk at Noon' l. 304

8 I would not enter on my list of friends
(Tho' graced with polished manners and fine sense,
Yet wanting sensibility) the man
Who needlessly sets foot upon a worm.
The Task (1785) bk. 6 'The Winter Walk at Noon' l. 560

9 Public schools 'tis public folly feeds.
'Tirocinium' (1785) l. 250

10 The parson knows enough who knows a duke.
'Tirocinium' (1785) l. 403

11   As a priest,
A piece of mere church furniture at best.
'Tirocinium' (1785) l. 425

12   Tenants of life's middle state,
Securely placed between the small and great.
'Tirocinium' (1785) l. 807

13 He has no hope that never had a fear.
'Truth' (1782) l. 298

14 But what is man in his own proud esteem?
Hear him, himself the poet and the theme;
A monarch clothed with majesty and awe,
His mind his kingdom and his will his law.
'Truth' (1782) l. 403

15 I am monarch of all I survey,
My right there is none to dispute;
From the centre all round to the sea
I am lord of the foul and the brute.
O solitude where are the charms
That sages have seen in thy face?
Better dwell in the midst of alarms,
Than reign in this horrible place.
'Verses Supposed to be Written by Alexander Selkirk' (1782)

16 Oh! I could thresh his old jacket till I made his pension jingle in his pockets.
On Johnson's inadequate treatment of *Paradise Lost*, in a letter to the Revd William Unwin, 31 October 1779; J. King and C. Ryskamp (eds.) *Letters and Prose Writings of William Cowper* vol. 1 (1979) p. 308

17 Our severest winter, commonly called the spring.
Letter to the Revd William Unwin, 8 June 1783, in J. King and C. Ryskamp (eds.) *Letters and Prose Writings of William Cowper* vol. 2 (1981) p. 139

18 Mr Grenville squeezed me by the hand again, kissed the ladies, and withdrew. He kissed likewise the maid in the kitchen, and seemed upon the whole a most loving, kissing, kind-hearted gentleman.
Letter to the Revd John Newton, 29 March 1784, in J. King and C. Ryskamp (eds.) *Letters and Prose Writings of William Cowper* vol. 2 (1981) p. 229

George Crabbe 1754–1832

English poet

19 'What is a church?'—Our honest sexton tells,
''Tis a tall building, with a tower and bells.'
The Borough (1810) Letter 2 'The Church' l. 11

20 Virtues neglected then, adored become,
And graces slighted, blossom on the tomb.
The Borough (1810) Letter 2 'The Church' l. 133

21 Ye Lilies male! think (as your tea you sip,
While the Town small-talk flows from lip to lip;
Intrigues half-gathered, conversation-scraps,
Kitchen-cabals, and nursery-mishaps,)
If the vast world may not some scene produce,
Some state where your small talents might have use.
The Borough (1810) Letter 3 'The Vicar' l. 69

22 Habit with him was all the test of truth,
'It must be right: I've done it from my youth.'
The Borough (1810) Letter 3 'The Vicar' l. 138

23 There anchoring, Peter chose from man to hide,
There hang his head, and view the lazy tide
In its hot slimy channel slowly glide;
Where the small eels that left the deeper way
For the warm shore, within the shallows play;
Where gaping mussels, left upon the mud,
Slope their slow passage to the fallen flood;—
Here dull and hopeless he'd lie down and trace
How sidelong crabs had scrawled their crooked race ...
He nursed the feelings these dull scenes produce,
And loved to stop beside the opening sluice;
Where the small stream, confined in narrow bound,
Ran with a dull, unvaried, sad'ning sound;
Where all presented to the eye or ear,
Oppressed the soul! with misery, grief, and fear.
The Borough (1810) Letter 22 'Peter Grimes' l. 185

24 Lo! the poor toper whose untutored sense,
Sees bliss in ale, and can with wine dispense;
Whose head proud fancy never taught to steer,
Beyond the muddy ecstasies of beer.
'Inebriety' (in imitation of Pope, 1775) pt. 1, l. 132. Cf. Pope 522:2

25 With awe, around these silent walks I tread;
These are the lasting mansions of the dead.
'The Library' (1808) l. 105

26 Lo! all in silence, all in order stand,
And mighty folios first, a lordly band;
Then quartos their well-ordered ranks maintain,
And light octavos fill a spacious plain;
See yonder, ranged in more frequented rows,
A humbler band of duodecimos.
'The Library' (1808) l. 128

1 Fashion, though Folly's child, and guide of fools,
Rules e'en the wisest, and in learning rules.
'The Library' (1808) l. 167

2 Coldly profane and impiously gay.
'The Library' (1808) l. 265

3 The murmuring poor, who will not fast in peace.
'The Newspaper' (1785) l. 158

4 A master passion is the love of news.
'The Newspaper' (1785) l. 279

5 Our farmers round, well pleased with constant gain,
Like other farmers, flourish and complain.
'The Parish Register' (1807) pt. 1, l. 273

6 That all was wrong because not all was right.
Tales (1812) 'The Convert' l. 313

7 He tried the luxury of doing good.
Tales of the Hall (1819) 'Boys at School' l. 139

8 'The game,' said he, 'is never lost till won.'
Tales of the Hall (1819) 'Gretna Green' l. 334

9 The face the index of a feeling mind.
Tales of the Hall (1819) 'Lady Barbara' l. 124

10 Secrets with girls, like loaded guns with boys,
Are never valued till they make a noise.
Tales of the Hall (1819) 'The Maid's Story' l. 84

11 Yes, thus the Muses sing of happy swains,
Because the Muses never knew their pains:
They boast their peasants' pipes, but peasants now
Resign their pipes and plod behind the plough.
The Village (1783) bk. 1, l. 21

12 I grant indeed that fields and flocks have charms,
For him that gazes or for him that farms.
The Village (1783) bk. 1, l. 39

13   I paint the cot,
As truth will paint it, and as bards will not.
The Village (1783) bk. 1, l. 53

14 Where Plenty smiles—alas! she smiles for few,
And those who taste not, yet behold her store,
Are as the slaves that dig the golden ore,
The wealth around them makes them doubly poor.
The Village (1783) bk. 1, l. 136

15 The cold charities of man to man.
The Village (1783) bk. 1, l. 245

16 A potent quack, long versed in human ills,
Who first insults the victim whom he kills;
Whose murd'rous hand a drowsy bench protect,
And whose most tender mercy is neglect.
The Village (1783) bk. 1, l. 282

Hart Crane 1899–1932

American poet

17 The bell-rope that gathers God at dawn
Dispatches me as though I dropped down the knell
Of a spent day—to wander the cathedral lawn
From pit to crucifix, feet chill on steps from hell.
'The Broken Tower' (1933)

18 Stars scribble on our eyes the frosty sagas,
The gleaming cantos of unvanquished space.
'Cape Hatteras' (1930)

19 Cowslip and shad-blow, flaked like tethered foam
Around bared teeth of stallions, bloomed that spring
When first I read thy lines, rife as the loam
Of prairies, yet like breakers cliffward leaping!
... My hand
in yours,
Walt Whitman —
so—
'Cape Hatteras' (1930)

20 We have seen
The moon in lonely alleys make
A grail of laughter of an empty ash can.
'Chaplinesque' (1926)

21 The apple on its bough is her desire,—
Shining suspension, mimic of the sun.
'Garden Abstract' (1926)

22 Ah, madame! truly it's not right
When one isn't the real Gioconda,
To adapt her methods and deportment
For snaring the poor world in a blue funk.
'Locutions des Pierrots' (1933)

23 So the 20th Century—so whizzed the Limited—roared
by and left three men, still hungry on the tracks,
ploddingly watching the tail lights widen and
converge, slipping gimleted and neatly out of sight.
'The River' (1930)

24 O Sleepless as the river under thee,
Vaulting the sea, the prairies' dreaming sod,
Unto us lowliest sometime sweep, descend
And of the curveship lend a myth to God.
'To Brooklyn Bridge' (1930)

25 How many dawns, chill from his rippling rest
The seagull's wings shall dip and pivot him,
Shedding white rings of tumult, building high
Over the chained bay waters Liberty—

Then, with inviolate curve, forsake our eyes
As apparitional as sails that cross
Some page of figures to be filed away;
—Till elevators drop us from our day.
'To Brooklyn Bridge' (1927)

26 You who desired so much—in vain to ask—
Yet fed your hunger like an endless task,
Dared dignify the labor, bless the quest—
Achieved that stillness ultimately best,

Being, of all, least sought for: Emily, hear!
'To Emily Dickinson' (1927)

Stephen Crane 1871–1900

American writer

27 The red badge of courage.
Title of novel (1895)

Thomas Cranmer 1489–1556

Anglican prelate and martyr; Archbishop of Canterbury from 1553

28 This was the hand that wrote it [his recantation],
therefore it shall suffer first punishment.
At the stake, 21 March 1556, in John Richard Green A
Short History of the English People (1874) ch. 7, sect. 2

Richard Crashaw c.1612–49

English poet

1 Lord, what is man? Why should he cost thee
So dear? What had his ruin lost thee?
Lord, what is man, that thou hast overbought
So much a thing of nought?
    'Caritas Nimia, or The Dear Bargain' (1648)

2 *Nympha pudica Deum vidit, et erubuit.*
The conscious water saw its God, and blushed.
    Epigrammata Sacra (1634) 'Aquae in vinum versae'
    (Dryden's translation; literally 'the chaste nymph saw ... ').
    See *Notes and Queries* 4th series (1869) vol. 4, p. 244

3 Love's passives are his activ'st part.
The wounded is the wounding heart.
    'The Flaming Heart upon the Book of Saint Teresa' (1652)
    l. 73

4 By all the eagle in thee, all the dove.
    'The Flaming Heart upon the Book of Saint Teresa' (1652)
    l. 95

5 Love, thou art absolute sole Lord
Of life and death.
    'Hymn to the Name and Honour of the Admirable Saint
    Teresa' (1652) l. 1

6 Gloomy night embraced the place
Where the noble Infant lay.
The Babe looked up and showed his face;
In spite of darkness, it was day.
It was Thy day, sweet! and did rise
Not from the East, but from thine eyes.
    'Hymn of the Nativity' (1652)

7 Poor World (said I) what wilt thou do
To entertain this starry stranger?
Is this the best thou canst bestow?
A cold, and not too cleanly, manger?
Contend, ye powers of heav'n and earth
To fit a bed for this huge birth.
    'Hymn of the Nativity' (1652)

8 Welcome, all wonders in one sight!
Eternity shut in a span.
    'Hymn of the Nativity' (1652)

9 Lo here a little volume, but large book.
    'On a Prayer book' (1646)

10 It is love's great artillery
Which here contracts itself and comes to lie
Close couched in your white bosom.
    'On a Prayer book' (1646)

11 I would be married, but I'd have no wife,
I would be married to a single life.
    'On Marriage' (1646)

12 Two walking baths; two weeping motions;
Portable, and compendious oceans.
    'Saint Mary Magdalene, or The Weeper' (1652) st. 19

13 All is Caesar's; and what odds
So long as Caesar's self is God's?
    Steps to the Temple (1646) 'Mark 12'

14 And when life's sweet fable ends,
Soul and body part like friends;
No quarrels, murmurs, no delay;
A kiss, a sigh, and so away.
    'Temperance' (1652)

15 Whoe'er she be,
That not impossible she
That shall command my heart and me;

Where'er she lie,
Locked up from mortal eye,
In shady leaves of destiny.
    'Wishes to His (Supposed) Mistress' (1646)

Julia Crawford fl. 1835

16 Kathleen Mavourneen! the grey dawn is breaking,
The horn of the hunter is heard on the hill;
The lark from her light wing the bright dew is
    shaking;
Kathleen Mavourneen! what, slumbering still?
Oh! hast thou forgotten how soon we must sever?
Oh! hast thou forgotten this day we must part?
It may be for years, and it may be for ever,
Oh! why art thou silent, thou voice of my heart?
    'Kathleen Mavourneen' in *Metropolitan Magazine*, London
    (1835)

James Creelman 1901–41 *and*
Ruth Rose

17 Oh no, it wasn't the aeroplanes. It was Beauty killed
the Beast.
    King Kong (1933 film) final words

Mandell Creighton 1843–1901

English prelate

18 No people do so much harm as those who go about
doing good.
    In *The Life and Letters of Mandell Creighton* by his wife
    (1904) vol. 2, p. 503

Sir Ranulphe Crewe 1558–1646

English judge

19 And yet time hath his revolution; there must be a
period and an end to all temporal things, *finis rerum*,
an end of names and dignities and whatsoever is
terrene; and why not of De Vere? Where is Bohun,
where's Mowbray, where's Mortimer? Nay, which is
more and most of all, where is Plantagenet? They are
entombed in the urns and sepulchres of mortality. And
yet let the name and dignity of De Vere stand so long
as it pleaseth God.
    Speech in Oxford Peerage Case, 1625. See *Dictionary of
    National Biography* (1917–) vol. 5, p. 82

Francis Crick 1916–

British molecular biologist

20 Almost all aspects of life are engineered at the
molecular level, and without understanding molecules
we can only have a very sketchy understanding of life
itself.
    What Mad Pursuit (1988) ch. 5

Quentin Crisp 1908–

English writer

1 There was no need to do any housework at all. After the first four years the dirt doesn't get any worse.
The Naked Civil Servant (1968) ch. 15

2 An autobiography is an obituary in serial form with the last instalment missing.
The Naked Civil Servant (1968) ch. 29

Julian Critchley 1930–

British Conservative politician and journalist

3 The only safe pleasure for a parliamentarian is a bag of boiled sweets.
Listener 10 June 1982

Richmal Crompton (Richmal Crompton Lamburn) 1890–1969

English author of books for children

4 I'll thcream and thcream and thcream till I'm thick.
Still—William (1925) ch. 8 (Violet Elizabeth)

Oliver Cromwell 1599–1658

English soldier, politician, and general; Lord Protector from 1653

5 A few honest men are better than numbers.
Letter to Sir William Spring, September 1643, in Thomas Carlyle *Oliver Cromwell's Letters and Speeches* (2nd ed., 1846)

6 I would rather have a plain russet-coated captain that knows what he fights for, and loves what he knows, than that which you call 'a gentleman' and is nothing else.
Letter to Sir William Spring, September 1643, in Thomas Carlyle *Oliver Cromwell's Letters and Speeches* (2nd ed., 1846)

7 Cruel necessity.
On the execution of Charles I, in Joseph Spence *Anecdotes* (1820) p. 286

8 I beseech you, in the bowels of Christ, think it possible you may be mistaken.
Letter to the General Assembly of the Kirk of Scotland, 3 August 1650, in Thomas Carlyle *Oliver Cromwell's Letters and Speeches* (1845)

9 The dimensions of this mercy are above my thoughts. It is, for aught I know, a crowning mercy.
Letter to William Lenthall, Speaker of the Parliament of England, 4 September 1651, in Thomas Carlyle *Oliver Cromwell's Letters and Speeches* (1845)

10 You have sat too long here for any good you have been doing. Depart, I say, and let us have done with you. In the name of God, go!
Addressing the Rump Parliament, 20 April 1653 (oral tradition; quoted by Leo Amery, *Hansard* 7 May 1940, col. 1150). See Bulstrode Whitelock *Memorials of the English Affairs* (1732 ed.) p. 529

11 Take away that fool's bauble, the mace.
At the dismissal of the Rump Parliament, 20 April 1653, in Bulstrode Whitelock *Memorials of the English Affairs* (1732 ed.) p. 529 (often quoted 'Take away these baubles')

12 It's a maxim not to be despised, 'Though peace be made, yet it's interest that keeps peace.'
Speech to Parliament, 4 September 1654, in Thomas Carlyle *Oliver Cromwell's Letters and Speeches* (1845)

13 Necessity hath no law. Feigned necessities, imaginary necessities . . . are the greatest cozenage that men can put upon the Providence of God, and make pretences to break known rules by.
Speech to Parliament, 12 September 1654, in Thomas Carlyle *Oliver Cromwell's Letters and Speeches* (1845). Cf. Publilius Syrus 531:4

14 Your poor army, those poor contemptible men, came up hither.
Speech to Parliament, 21 April 1657, in Thomas Carlyle *Oliver Cromwell's Letters and Speeches* (1845). Cf. Anonymous 13:7

15 You have accounted yourselves happy on being environed with a great ditch from all the world besides.
Speech to Parliament, 25 January 1658, in Thomas Carlyle *Oliver Cromwell's Letters and Speeches* (1845)

16 Mr Lely, I desire you would use all your skill to paint my picture truly like me, and not flatter me at all; but remark all these roughnesses, pimples, warts, and everything as you see me; otherwise I will never pay a farthing for it.
In Horace Walpole *Anecdotes of Painting in England* vol. 3 (1763) ch. 1 (commonly quoted 'warts and all')

17 My design is to make what haste I can to be gone.
Last words, in John Morley *Oliver Cromwell* (1900) bk. 5, ch. 10

Bing Crosby 1903–77

American singer and film actor

18 Where the blue of the night
Meets the gold of the day,
Someone waits for me.
'Where the Blue of the Night meets the Gold of the Day' (1931 song, with Roy Turk and Fred Ahlert)

Douglas Cross

American songwriter

19 I left my heart in San Francisco
High on a hill it calls to me.
To be where little cable cars climb half-way to the stars,
The morning fog may chill the air—
I don't care!
'I Left My Heart in San Francisco' (1954 song)

Richard Assheton, Viscount Cross 1823–1914

British Conservative politician

20 I hear a smile.
When the House of Lords laughed at his speech in favour of Spiritual Peers, in G. W. E. Russell *Collections and Recollections* (1898) ch. 29

Richard Crossman 1907–74

British Labour politician

1 The Civil Service is profoundly deferential — 'Yes,
Minister! No, Minister! If you wish it, Minister!'
Diaries of a Cabinet Minister vol. 1 (1975) 22 October 1964

Samuel Crossman 1624–83

English clergyman

2 My song is love unknown,
My saviour's love for me,
Love to the loveless shown,
That they might lovely be.
O, who am I,
That for my sake
My Lord should take
Frail flesh and die?
'My song is love unknown' (1664); set to music as a hymn
from 1868, and by John Ireland in 1919

Aleister Crowley 1875–1947

English diabolist

3 Do what thou wilt shall be the whole of the Law.
Book of the Law (1909) l. 40. Cf. Rabelais 534:19

Richard Cumberland 1631–1718

English divine

4 It is better to wear out than to rust out.
In George Horne *The Duty of Contending for the Faith* (1786)
p. 21 n.

e. e. cummings (Edward Estlin Cummings) 1894–1962

American poet

5 anyone lived in a pretty how town
(with up so floating many bells down)
spring summer autumn winter
he sang his didn't he danced his did.
50 Poems (1949) no. 29

6 'next to of course god america i
love you land of the pilgrims' and so forth oh
say can you see by the dawn's early my
country 'tis of centuries come and go
and are no more what of it we should worry
in every language even deafanddumb
thy sons acclaim your glorious name by gorry
by jingo by gee by gosh by gum
why talk of beauty what could be more beautiful than these heroic happy dead
who rushed like lions to the roaring slaughter
they did not stop to think they died instead
then shall the voices of liberty be mute?

He spoke. And drank rapidly a glass of water.
is 5 (1926) p. 62

7 Humanity i love you because
when you're hard up you pawn your
intelligence to buy a drink.
'La Guerre' no. 2 (1925)

8 o to be a metope
now that triglyph's here.
'Memorabilia' (1926). Cf. Browning 150:5

9 a politician is an arse upon
which everyone has sat except a man.
1 × 1 (1944) no. 10

10 plato told

him: he couldn't
believe it (jesus

told him; he
wouldn't believe
it) lao

tsze
certainly told
him, and general
(yes

mam)
sherman.
1 × 1 (1944) no. 13

11 pity this busy monster, manunkind,
not. Progress is a comfortable disease.
1 × 1 (1944) no. 14

12 We doctors know
a hopeless case if—listen: there's a hell
of a good universe next door; let's go.
1 × 1 (1944) no. 14

13 when god decided to invent
everything he took one
breath bigger than a circustent
and everything began

when man determined to destroy
himself he picked the was
of shall and finding only why
smashed it into because.
1 × 1 (1944) no. 26

14 Buffalo Bill's
defunct
who used to
ride a watersmooth-silver
stallion
and break onetwothreefourfive pigeons-
justlikethat
Jesus
he was a handsome man
and what i want to know is
how do you like your blueeyed boy
Mister Death.
'Portraits' no. 8 (1923)

15 (i do not know what it is about you that closes
and opens; only something in me understands
the voice of your eyes is deeper than all noses)
nobody, not even the rain, has such small hands.
'somewhere I have never travelled' (1931)

16 i like my body when it is with your
body. It is so quite new a thing.
Muscles better and nerves more.
i like your body. i like what it does,
i like its hows.
'Sonnets–Actualities' no. 8 (1925)

17 the Cambridge ladies who live in furnished souls
are unbeautiful and have comfortable minds.
'Sonnets–Realities' no. 1 (1923)

William Thomas Cummings 1903–45

American priest

1 There are no atheists in the foxholes.
   In Carlos P. Romulo *I Saw the Fall of the Philippines* (1943)
   ch. 15

Allan Cunningham 1784–1842

Scottish poet

2 A wet sheet and a flowing sea,
   A wind that follows fast
   And fills the white and rustling sail
   And bends the gallant mast.
   'A Wet Sheet and a Flowing Sea' (1825)

3 It's hame and it's hame, hame fain wad I be,
   O, hame, hame, hame to my ain countree!
   'It's hame and It's hame', in James Hogg *Jacobite Relics of
   Scotland* (1819) vol. 1, p. 134. In his notes, vol. 1, p. 294,
   he says he took it from R. H. Cromek's *Remains of Nithsdale
   and Galloway Song* (1810) and supposes that it owed much
   to Cunningham

John Philpot Curran 1750–1817

Irish judge

4 The condition upon which God hath given liberty to
   man is eternal vigilance; which condition if he break,
   servitude is at once the consequence of his crime, and
   the punishment of his guilt.
   Speech on the right of election of the Lord Mayor of Dublin,
   10 July 1790, in Thomas Davis (ed.) *Speeches* (1845) p. 94

5 Like the silver plate on a coffin.
   Describing Sir Robert Peel's smile; quoted by Daniel
   O'Connell, *Hansard* 26 February 1835, col. 397

Michael Curtiz 1888–1962

Hungarian-born American film director

6 Bring on the empty horses!
   Said while directing the 1936 film *The Charge of the Light
   Brigade*, in David Niven *Bring on the Empty Horses* (1975)
   ch. 6

Lord Curzon (1st Marquess Curzon of Kedleston) 1859–1925

*British Conservative politician; Viceroy of India
1898–1905*

7 Gentlemen do not take soup at luncheon.
   In E. L. Woodward *Short Journey* (1942) ch. 7

St Cyprian c. AD 200–258

Latin Christian writer and martyr; Bishop of Carthage

8 *Habere non potest Deum patrem qui ecclesiam non habet
   matrem.*
   He cannot have God for his father who has not the
   church for his mother.
   De Ecclesiae Catholicae Unitate sect. 6. Cf. St Augustine
   37:4

9 *Fratres nostros non esse lugendos arcessitione dominica de
   saeculo liberatos, cum sciamus non amitti sed praemitti.*
   Our brethren who have been freed from the world by
   the summons of the Lord should not be mourned,
   since we know that they are not lost but sent before.
   De Mortalite ch. 20 (ed. M. L. Hannam, 1933)

10 *Nemine salus esse nisi in Ecclesia potest.*
   There cannot be salvation for any, except in the
   Church.
   Epistle Ad Pomponium, De Virginibus sect. 4. Cf. Augustine
   37:4, Cyprian 229:8

Samuel Daniel 1563–1619

English poet and playwright

11 And look, how Thames, enriched with many a
   flood . . .
   Glides on, with pomp of waters, unwithstood,
   Unto the ocean.
   The Civil Wars (1595) bk. 2, st. 7

12 A place there is, where proudly raised there stands
   A huge aspiring rock, neighbouring the skies,
   Whose surly brow imperiously commands
   The sea his bounds, that at his proud feet lies;
   And spurns the waves, that in rebellious bands
   Assault his empire, and against him rise;
   Under whose craggy government there was
   A niggard narrow way for men to pass.
   The Civil Wars (1595) bk. 2, st. 48 (on Richard II's being
   taken into custody)

13 Custom that is before all law, Nature that is above
   all art.
   A Defence of Rhyme (1603)

14 Men do not weigh the stalk for that it was,
   When once they find her flower, her glory, pass.
   Delia (1592) Sonnet 32

15 Fresh shalt thou see in me the wounds thou madest,
   Though spent thy flame, in me the heat remaining;
   I that have loved thee thus before thou fadest,
   My faith shall wax, when thou art in thy waning.
   The world shall find this miracle in me,
   That fire can burn when all the matter's spent.
   Delia (1592) Sonnet 33

16 Care-charmer Sleep, son of the sable Night,
   Brother to Death, in silent darkness born:
   Relieve my languish, and restore the light,
   With dark forgetting of my care return,
   And let the day be time enough to mourn
   The shipwreck of my ill adventured youth:
   Let waking eyes suffice to wail their scorn,
   Without the torment of the night's untruth.
   Delia (1592) Sonnet 54

17 Fond man, Musophilus, that thus dost spend
   In an ungrateful art thy dearest days,
   Tiring thy wits and toiling to no end,
   But to attain that idle smoke of praise.
   Musophilus (1599) l. 1

18 . . . If I may attain but to redeem
   My name from dissolution and the grave,
   I shall have done enough, and better deem
   T'have lived to be, than to have died to have.
   Musophilus (1599) l. 29

1 Soul of the world, knowledge, without thee
What hath the earth that truly glorious is?
Why should our pride make such a stir to be,
To be forgot?
Musophilus (1599) l. 195

2 And who, in time, knows whither we may vent
The treasure of our tongue, to what strange shores
This gain of our best glory shall be sent,
T'enrich unknowing nations with our stores?
What worlds in th'yet unformed Occident
May come refined with th'accents that are ours?
Musophilus (1599) l. 957

3   But years hath done this wrong,
To make me write too much, and live too long.
Philotas (1605) 'To the Prince' (dedication) l. 108

4   Princes in this case
Do hate the traitor, though they love the treason.
The Tragedy of Cleopatra (1594) act 4, sc. 1. Cf. Dryden
260:27

Dante Alighieri 1265–1321
Italian poet

5 *Nel mezzo del cammin di nostra vita.*

Midway along the path of our life.
Divina Commedia 'Inferno' canto 1, l. 1

6 PER ME SI VA NELLA CITTÀ DOLENTE,
PER ME SI VA NELL' ETERNO DOLORE,
PER ME SI VA TRA LA PERDUTA GENTE . . .

LASCIATE OGNI SPERANZA VOI CH'ENTRATE!

Through me is the way to the sorrowful city. Through
me is the way to eternal suffering. Through me is the
way to join the lost people . . . Abandon all hope, you
who enter!
Divina Commedia 'Inferno' canto 3, l. 1 (inscription at the
entrance to Hell)

7 *Non ragioniam di lor, ma guarda, e passa.*

Let us not speak of them, but look, and pass on.
Divina Commedia 'Inferno' canto 3, l. 51

8 *Il gran rifiuto.*

The great refusal.
Divina Commedia 'Inferno' canto 3, l. 60

9 *Onorate l'altissimo poeta.*

Honour the greatest poet.
Divina Commedia 'Inferno' canto 4, l. 80

10 *Il maestro di color che sanno.*

The master of those who know.
Divina Commedia 'Inferno' canto 4, l. 131 (of Aristotle)

11 . . . *Nessun maggior dolore,*
Che ricordarsi del tempo felice
Nella miseria.

There is no greater pain than to remember a happy
time when one is in misery.
Divina Commedia 'Inferno' canto 5, l. 121. Cf. Boethius
116:12

12 *Noi leggiavamo un giorno per diletto*
Di Lancialotto, come amor lo strinse:
Soli eravamo, e sanza alcun sospetto.

One day, we were reading for pleasure about Lancelot,
and how love constrained him: we were alone and
completely unsuspecting.
Divina Commedia 'Inferno' canto 5, l. 127

13 *Galeotto fu il libro e chi lo scrisse:*
Quel giorno più non vi leggemmo avante.

A Galeotto [a pander] was the book and writer too:
that day we did not read any more.
Divina Commedia 'Inferno' canto 5, l. 137

14 *Siete voi qui, ser Brunetto?*

Are *you* here, Advocate Brunetto?
Divina Commedia 'Inferno' canto 15, l. 30 (of Brunetto
Latini, an old and respected friend of Dante, encountered in
hell with other 'Sodomites')

15 *La cara e buona imagine paterna.*

The dear and kindly paternal image.
Divina Commedia 'Inferno' canto 15, l. 83

16 *Considerate la vostra semenza:*
Fatti non foste a viver come bruti,
Ma per seguir virtute e conoscenza.

Consider your origins: you were not made to live as
brutes, but to follow virtue and knowledge.
Divina Commedia 'Inferno' canto 26, l. 118

17 *E quindi uscimmo a riveder le stelle.*

Thence we came forth to see the stars again.
Divina Commedia 'Inferno' canto 34, l. 139

18 *Puro e disposto a salire alle stelle.*

Pure and ready to mount to the stars.
Divina Commedia 'Purgatorio' canto 33, l. 145

19 *E'n la sua volontade è nostra pace.*

In His will is our peace.
Divina Commedia 'Paradiso' canto 3, l. 85

20 *Tu proverai sì come sa di sale*
Lo pane altrui, e com'è duro calle
Lo scendere e'l salir per l'altrui scale.

You shall find out how salt is the taste of another
man's bread, and how hard is the way up and down
another man's stairs.
Divina Commedia 'Paradiso' canto 17, l. 58

21 *L'amor che muove il sole e l'altre stelle.*

The love that moves the sun and the other stars.
Divina Commedia 'Paradiso' canto 33, l. 145

Georges Jacques Danton 1759–94
French revolutionary

22 *De l'audace, et encore de l'audace, et toujours de l'audace!*

Boldness, and again boldness, and always boldness!
Speech to the Legislative Committee of General Defence,
2 September 1792, in *Le Moniteur* 4 September 1792.
Cf. Bacon 42:29

23 Thou wilt show my head to the people: it is worth
showing.
To his executioner, 5 April 1794, in Thomas Carlyle *History
of the French Revolution* (1837) vol. 3, bk. 6, ch. 2

Joe Darion 1917–

American songwriter

1 Dream the impossible dream.
  'The Quest' (1965 song)

George Darley 1795–1846

Irish-born poet

2 O blest unfabled Incense Tree,
  That burns in glorious Araby.
  'Nepenthe' (1835) l. 147

Clarence Darrow 1857–1938

American lawyer

3 I do not pretend to know where many ignorant men
  are sure — that is all that agnosticism means.
  Speech at the trial of John Thomas Scopes, 15 July 1925, in
  The World's Most Famous Court Trial (1925) ch. 4

Charles Darwin 1809–82

English natural historian

4 The highest possible stage in moral culture is when we
  recognize that we ought to control our thoughts.
  The Descent of Man (1871) ch. 4

5 A hairy quadruped, furnished with a tail and pointed
  ears, probably arboreal in its habits.
  The Descent of Man (1871) ch. 21 (on man's probable
  ancestors)

6 Man with all his noble qualities . . . still bears in his
  bodily frame the indelible stamp of his lowly origin.
  The Descent of Man (1871) closing words

7 I have called this principle, by which each slight
  variation, if useful, is preserved, by the term of
  Natural Selection.
  On the Origin of Species (1859) ch. 3

8 We will now discuss in a little more detail the Struggle
  for Existence.
  On the Origin of Species (1859) ch. 3

9 The expression often used by Mr Herbert Spencer of
  the Survival of the Fittest is more accurate [than
  'Struggle for Existence'], and is sometimes equally
  convenient.
  On the Origin of Species (1869 ed.) ch. 3. Cf. Spencer
  658:17

10 From the war of nature, from famine and death, the
   most exalted object which we are capable of
   conceiving, namely, the production of the higher
   animals, directly follows.
   On the Origin of Species (1859) ch. 3

11 What a book a devil's chaplain might write on the
   clumsy, wasteful, blundering, low, and horridly cruel
   works of nature!
   Letter to J. D. Hooker, 13 July 1856, in *Correspondence of
   Charles Darwin* vol. 6 (1990)

12 Animals, whom we have made our slaves, we do not
   like to consider our equal.
   Notebook B (1837–8) in P. H. Barrett et al. (eds.) *Charles
   Darwin's Notebooks 1836–1844* (1987) p. 228

Erasmus Darwin 1731–1802

English physician; grandfather of Charles Darwin

13 A fool . . . is a man who never tried an experiment in
   his life.
   In F. V. Barry (ed.) *Maria Edgeworth: Chosen Letters* (1931)
   To Sophy Ruxton, 9 March 1792

14 No, Sir, because I have time to think before I speak,
   and don't ask impertinent questions.
   When asked if he found his stammering very inconvenient,
   in 'Reminiscences of My Father's Everyday Life', an
   appendix by Francis Darwin to his edition of Charles
   Darwin *Autobiography* (1877)

Sir Francis Darwin 1848–1925

English botanist; son of Charles Darwin

15 In science the credit goes to the man who convinces
   the world, not to the man to whom the idea first
   occurs.
   Eugenics Review April 1914 'Francis Galton'

Charles D'Avenant 1656–1714

English playwright and political economist

16 Custom, that unwritten law,
   By which the people keep even kings in awe.
   Circe (1677) act 2, sc. 3

Sir William D'Avenant 1606–68

English playwright and poet

17 In every grave make room, make room!
   The world's at an end, and we come, we come.
   The Law against Lovers (1673) act 3, sc. 1 'Viola's Song'

18 Had laws not been, we never had been blamed;
   For not to know we sin is innocence.
   'The Philosopher's Disquisition directed to the Dying
   Christian' (1672) st. 76

19 For I must go where lazy Peace
   Will hide her drowsy head;
   And, for the sport of kings, increase
   The number of the dead.
   'The Soldier Going to the Field' (1673)

20 The lark now leaves his wat'ry nest
   And, climbing, shakes his dewy wings.
   'Song: The Lark' (1638)

John Davidson 1857–1909

English poet

21 A runnable stag, a kingly crop.
   'A Runnable Stag' (1906)

22 In anguish we uplift
   A new unhallowed song:
   The race is to the swift,
   The battle to the strong.
   'War Song' (1899) st. 1

23 And blood in torrents pour
   In vain—always in vain,
   For war breeds war again.
   'War Song' (1899) st. 7

Sir John Davies 1569–1626
English poet

1 Wedlock, indeed, hath oft compared been
To public feasts where meet a public rout,
Where they that are without would fain go in
And they that are within would fain go out.
'A Contention Betwixt a Wife, a Widow, and a Maid for
Precedence' (1608) l. 193

2 Skill comes so slow, and life so fast doth fly,
We learn so little and forget so much.
'Nosce Teipsum' (1599) st. 19

3 For this, the wisest of all moral men
Said *he knew nought, but that he nought did know*;
And the great mocking master mocked not then,
When he said, *Truth was buried deep below.*
'Nosce Teipsum' (1599) st. 20. Cf. Milton 473:21, Socrates
654:10

4 I know my life's a pain and but a span,
I know my sense is mocked in every thing;
And to conclude, I know myself a man,
Which is a proud and yet a wretched thing.
'Nosce Teipsum' (1599) st. 45

5 This wondrous miracle did Love devise,
For dancing is love's proper exercise.
'Orchestra, or a Poem of Dancing' (1596) st. 18

6 What makes the vine about the elm to dance
With turnings, windings, and embracements round?
What makes the lodestone to the north advance
His subtle point, as if from thence he found
His chief attractive virtue to redound?
Kind nature first doth cause all things to love;
Love makes them dance, and in just order move.
'Orchestra, or a Poem of Dancing' (1596) st. 56

7 Since all the world's great fortune and affairs
Forward and backward rapt and whirlèd are,
According to the music of the spheres;
And Chance herself her nimble feet upbears
On a round slippery wheel, that rolleth aye.
And turns all states with her imperious sway;

Learn then to dance, you that are princes born,
And lawful lords of earthly creatures all;
Imitate them, and thereof take no scorn,
(For this new art to them is natural)
And imitate the stars celestial.
For when pale death your vital twist shall sever,
Your better parts must dance with them forever.
'Orchestra, or a Poem of Dancing' (1596) st 60

Scrope Davies c.1783–1852
English conversationalist

8 Babylon in all its desolation is a sight not so awful as
that of the human mind in ruins.
Letter to Thomas Raikes, May 1835, in *A Portion of the
Journal kept by Thomas Raikes* (1856) vol. 2, p. 113.
Addison, in *The Spectator* no. 421 (3 July 1712), also
remarked of 'a distracted person' that 'Babylon in ruins is
not so melancholy a spectacle'. Cf. Doyle 256:10

W. H. Davies 1871–1940
Welsh poet

9 And hear the pleasant cuckoo, loud and long—
The simple bird that thinks two notes a song.
'April's Charms' (1916)

10 A rainbow and a cuckoo's song
May never come together again;
May never come
This side the tomb.
'A Great Time' (1914)

11 It was the Rainbow gave thee birth,
And left thee all her lovely hues.
'Kingfisher' (1910)

12 What is this life if, full of care,
We have no time to stand and stare.
'Leisure' (1911)

13 Come, lovely Morning, rich in frost
On iron, wood and glass . . .

Come, rich and lovely Winter's Eve,
That seldom handles gold;
And spread your silver sunsets out,
In glittering fold on fold.
'Silver Hours' (1932)

14 Sweet Stay-at-Home, sweet Well-content,
Thou knowest of no strange continent:
Thou hast not felt thy bosom keep
A gentle motion with the deep;
Thou hast not sailed in Indian seas,
Where scent comes forth in every breeze.
'Sweet Stay-At-Home' (1913)

Sammy Davis Jnr. 1925–90
American entertainer

15 Being a star has made it possible for me to get insulted
in places where the average Negro could never *hope* to
go and get insulted.
In *Yes I Can* (1965) pt. 3, ch. 23

Thomas Davis 1814–45
Irish poet and politician

16 Come in the evening, or come in the morning,
Come when you're looked for, or come without
warning.
'The Welcome' (1846)

Richard Dawkins
English biologist

17 [Natural selection] has no vision, no foresight, no
sight at all. If it can be said to play the role of
watchmaker in nature, it is the *blind* watchmaker.
The Blind Watchmaker (1986) ch. 1. Cf. Paley 505:5

18 However many ways there may be of being alive, it is
certain that there are vastly more ways of being dead.
The Blind Watchmaker (1986) ch. 1

19 The essence of life is statistical improbability on a
colossal scale.
The Blind Watchmaker (1986) ch. 11

1 They are in you and in me; they created us, body and mind; and their preservation is the ultimate rationale for our existence ... they go by the name of genes, and we are their survival machines.

> The Selfish Gene (1976) ch. 2

Lord Dawson of Penn (Bertrand Edward Dawson, Viscount Dawson of Penn) 1864–1945

Physician to King George V

2 The King's life is moving peacefully towards its close.

> Bulletin, drafted on a menu card at Buckingham Palace on the eve of the king's death, 20 January 1936, in Kenneth Rose *King George V* (1983) ch. 10

C. Day-Lewis 1904–72

Anglo-Irish poet and critic

3   Hurry! We burn
For Rome so near us, for the phoenix moment
When we have thrown off this traveller's trance,
And mother-naked and ageless-ancient
Wake in her warm nest of renaissance.

> 'Flight to Italy' (1953)

4 Do not expect again a phoenix hour,
The triple-towered sky, the dove complaining,
Sudden the rain of gold and heart's first ease
Traced under trees by the eldritch light of sundown.

> 'From Feathers to Iron' (1935)

5 Tempt me no more; for I
Have known the lightning's hour,
The poet's inward pride,
The certainty of power.

> The Magnetic Mountain (1933) pt. 3, no. 24

6 You that love England, who have an ear for her music,
The slow movement of clouds in benediction,
Clear arias of light thrilling over her uplands,
Over the chords of summer sustained peacefully.

> The Magnetic Mountain (1933) pt. 4, no. 32

7 It is the logic of our times,
No subject for immortal verse—
That we who lived by honest dreams
Defend the bad against the worse.

> 'Where are the War Poets?' (1943)

Percy Dearmer 1867–1936

English clergyman

8 Jesu, good above all other,
Gentle Child of gentle Mother,
In a stable born our Brother,
Give us grace to persevere.

> 'Jesu, good above all other' (1906 hymn)

Simone de Beauvoir 1908–86

French novelist and feminist

9 *Ce n'est pas en donnant la vie, c'est en risquant sa vie que l'homme s'élève au-dessus de l'animal; c'est pourquoi dans l'humanité la supériorité est accordée non au sexe qui engendre mais à celui qui tue.*

It is not in giving life but in risking life that man is raised above the animal; that is why superiority has been accorded to humanity not to the sex that brings forth but to that which kills.

> Le deuxième sexe (1949) vol. 1, pt. 2, ch. 1

10 *On ne naît pas femme: on le devient.*

One is not born a woman: one becomes one.

> Le deuxième sexe (1949) vol. 2, pt. 1, ch. 1

Edward de Bono 1933–

British writer and physician

11 Some people are aware of another sort of thinking which ... leads to those simple ideas that are obvious only after they have been thought of ... the term 'lateral thinking' has been coined to describe this other sort of thinking; 'vertical thinking' is used to denote the conventional logical process.

> The Use of Lateral Thinking (1967) foreword

Eugene Victor Debs 1855–1926

Founder of the Socialist party of America

12 When great changes occur in history, when great principles are involved, as a rule the majority are wrong. The minority are right.

> Speech at his trial for sedition in Cleveland, Ohio, 11 September 1918; in *Speeches* (1928) p. 66

13 While there is a lower class, I am in it; while there is a criminal element, I am of it; while there is a soul in prison, I am not free.

> Speech at his trial for sedition in Cleveland, Ohio, 14 September 1918; in *Liberator* November 1918, p. 12

Stephen Decatur 1779–1820

American naval officer

14 Our country! In her intercourse with foreign nations, may she always be in the right; but our country, right or wrong.

> Decatur's toast at Norfolk, Virginia, April 1816, in A. S. Mackenzie *Life of Stephen Decatur* (1846) ch. 14

Daniel Defoe 1660–1731

English novelist and journalist

15 We must distinguish between a man of polite learning and a mere scholar: the first is a gentleman and what a gentleman should be; the last is a mere book-case, a bundle of letters, a head stuffed with the jargon of languages, a man that understands every body but is understood by no body.

> The Complete English Gentleman (written 1728–9) ch. 5

16 Pleasure is a *thief* to business.

> The Complete English Tradesman (1725) vol. 1, ch. 9

1 The soul is placed in the body like a rough diamond, and must be polished, or the lustre of it will never appear.
   An Essay Upon Projects (1697) 'Of Academies: An Academy for Women'

2 Why then should women be denied the benefits of instruction? If knowledge and understanding had been useless additions to the sex, God almighty would never have given them capacities.
   An Essay Upon Projects (1697) 'Of Academies: An Academy for Women'

3 Vice came in always at the door of necessity, not at the door of inclination.
   Moll Flanders (1721, ed. G. A. Starr, 1971) p. 128

4 As covetousness is the root of all evil, so poverty is the worst of all snares.
   Moll Flanders (1721, ed. G. A. Starr, 1971) p. 188

5 Give me not poverty lest I steal.
   Review vol. 8, no. 75 (15 September 1711); later incorporated into *Moll Flanders* (1721)

6 He told me ... that mine was the middle state, or what might be called the upper station of low life, which he had found by long experience was the best state in the world, the most suited to human happiness.
   Robinson Crusoe (1719, ed. J. D. Crowley, 1972) p. 4

7 I never saw them afterwards, or any sign of them, except three of their hats, one cap, and two shoes that were not fellows.
   Robinson Crusoe (1719, ed. J. D. Crowley, 1972) p. 46 (on his shipmates)

8 I smiled to myself at the sight of this money. 'O drug!' said I aloud, 'what art thou good for? Thou art not worth to me, no, not the taking off of the ground; one of those knives is worth all this heap; I have no manner of use for thee, e'en remain where thou art, and go to the bottom as a creature whose life is not worth saving.' However, upon second thoughts I took it away.
   Robinson Crusoe (1719, ed. J. D. Crowley, 1972) p. 57

9 It happened one day, about noon, going towards my boat, I was exceedingly surprised with the print of a man's naked foot on the shore, which was very plain to be seen in the sand. I stood like one thunderstruck, or as if I had seen an apparition.
   Robinson Crusoe (1719, ed. J. D. Crowley, 1972) p. 153

10 My man Friday.
   Robinson Crusoe (1719, ed. J. D. Crowley, 1972) p. 207

11 My island was now peopled, and I thought my self very rich in subjects; and it was a merry reflection which I frequently made, how like a king I looked.
   Robinson Crusoe (1719, ed. J. D. Crowley, 1972) p. 241

12 In trouble to be troubled
   Is to have your trouble doubled.
   The Farther Adventures of Robinson Crusoe (1719, ed. G. Aitken, 1895) p. 108

13 Necessity makes an honest man a knave.
   The Serious Reflections of Robinson Crusoe (1720) ch. 2

14 The best of men cannot suspend their fate:
   The good die early, and the bad die late.
   'Character of the late Dr S. Annesley' (1697)

15 We loved the doctrine for the teacher's sake.
   'Character of the late Dr S. Annesley' (1697)

16 Actions receive their tincture from the times,
   And as they change are virtues made or crimes.
   A Hymn to the Pillory (1703) l. 29

17 Nature has left this tincture in the blood,
   That all men would be tyrants if they could.
   The History of the Kentish Petition (1712–13) addenda, l. 11

18 Fools out of favour grudge at knaves in place.
   The True-Born Englishman (1701) introduction, l. 7

19 Wherever God erects a house of prayer,
   The Devil always builds a chapel there;
   And 'twill be found, upon examination,
   The latter has the largest congregation.
   The True-Born Englishman (1701) pt. 1, l. 1. Cf. Bancroft 51:12, Luther 432:12

20 In their religion they are so uneven,
   That each one goes his own by-way to heaven.
   The True-Born Englishman (1701) pt. 1, l. 104

21 From this amphibious ill-born mob began
   That vain, ill-natured thing, an Englishman.
   The True-Born Englishman (1701) pt. 1, l. 132

22 Your Roman-Saxon-Danish-Norman English.
   The True-Born Englishman (1701) pt. 1, l. 139

23 His lazy, long, lascivious reign.
   The True-Born Englishman (1701) pt. 1, l. 236 (of Charles II)

24 Great families of yesterday we show,
   And lords whose parents were the Lord knows who.
   The True-Born Englishman (1701) pt. 1, l. 374

25 And of all plagues with which mankind are curst,
   Ecclesiastic tyranny's the worst.
   The True-Born Englishman (1701) pt. 2, l. 299

26 When kings the sword of justice first lay down,
   They are no kings, though they possess the crown.
   Titles are shadows, crowns are empty things,
   The good of subjects is the end of kings.
   The True-Born Englishman (1701) pt. 2, l. 313

Edgar Degas 1834–1917
French artist

27 *L'art, c'est le vice. On ne l'épouse pas légitimement, on le viole.*
   Art is vice. You don't marry it legitimately, you rape it.
   In Paul Lafond *Degas* (1918) p. 140

Charles de Gaulle 1890–1970
French general; President of France, 1959–69

28 *La France a perdu une bataille! Mais la France n'a pas perdu la guerre!*
   France has lost a battle. But France has not lost the war!
   Proclamation, 18 June 1940, in *Discours, messages et déclarations du Général de Gaulle* (1941) p. 15

1 *Puisque ceux qui avaient le devoir de manier l'épée de la France l'ont laissée tomber brisée, moi, j'ai ramassé le tronçon du glaive.*

Since they whose duty it was to wield the sword of France have let it fall shattered to the ground, I have taken up the broken blade.

Speech, 13 July 1940, in *Discours et Messages* (1942) p. 12

2 *Je vous ai compris.*

I have understood you.

Speech at Algiers, 4 June 1958, in *Discours et Messages* vol. 3 (1970) p. 15

3 *Oui, c'est l'Europe, depuis l'Atlantique jusqu'à l'Oural, c'est l'Europe, c'est toute l'Europe, qui décidera du destin du monde.*

Yes, it is Europe, from the Atlantic to the Urals, it is Europe, it is the whole of Europe, that will decide the fate of the world.

Speech to the people of Strasbourg, 23 November 1959, in *Le Monde* 24 November 1959, p. 4

4 *Les traités, voyez-vous, sont comme les jeunes filles et comme les roses: ça dure ce que ça dure.*

Treaties, you see, are like girls and roses: they last while they last.

Speech at Elysée Palace, 2 July 1963, in André Passeron *De Gaulle parle 1962–6* (1966) p. 340

5 *Vive Le Québec Libre.*

Long Live Free Quebec.

Speech in Montreal, 24 July 1967, in *Discours et messages* (1970) p. 192

6 *L'auctorité ne vas pas sans prestige, ni le prestige sans l'éloignement.*

Authority doesn't work without prestige, or prestige without distance.

Le Fil de l'épée (1932) 'Du caractère' sect. 2

7 *L'épée est l'axe du monde et la grandeur ne se divise pas.*

The sword is the axis of the world and its power is absolute.

Vers l'armée de métier (1934) 'Comment?' Commandement 3

8 Politics are too serious a matter to be left to the politicians.

Replying to Clement Attlee's remark that 'De Gaulle is a very good soldier and a very bad politician', in Attlee *A Prime Minister Remembers* (1961) ch. 4

9 *Ce que nous pensons de la mort n'a d'importance que pour ce que la mort nous fait penser de la vie.*

What we think about death only matters for what death makes us think about life.

In A. Malraux *Les Chênes qu'on abat* (1971) p. 68

10 *Comment voulez-vous gouverner un pays qui a deux cent quarante-six variétés de fromage?*

How can you govern a country which has 246 varieties of cheese?

In Ernest Mignon *Les Mots du Général* (1962) p. 57

11 *Comme un homme politique ne croit jamais ce qu'il dit, il est tout étonné quand il est cru sur parole.*

Since a politician never believes what he says, he is quite surprised to be taken at his word.

In Ernest Mignon *Les Mots du Général* (1962) p. 67

12 *Et maintenant elle est comme les autres.*

And now she is like everyone else.

On the death of his daughter, who had been born with Down's Syndrome (attributed)

Thomas Dekker 1570–1641

English playwright

13 That great fishpond (the sea).

The Honest Whore (1604) pt. 1, act 1, sc. 2

14   The best of men
That e'er wore earth about him, was a sufferer,
A soft, meek, patient, humble, tranquil spirit,
The first true gentleman that ever breathed.

The Honest Whore (1604) pt. 1, act 1, sc. 2

15 Art thou poor, yet hast thou golden slumbers?
O sweet content!
Art thou rich, yet is thy mind perplexed?
O, punishment!
Dost thou laugh to see how fools are vexed
To add to golden numbers, golden numbers?
O, sweet content, O, sweet, O, sweet content!
Work apace, apace, apace, apace;
Honest labour bears a lovely face;
Then hey nonny, nonny; hey nonny, nonny.

Patient Grissil (1603) act 1, sc. 1

16 Canst drink the waters of the crispèd spring?
O sweet content!
Swim'st thou in wealth, yet sink'st in thine own tears?
O punishment!

Patient Grissil (1603) act 1, sc. 1

17 Golden slumbers kiss your eyes,
Smiles awake you when you rise:
Sleep, pretty wantons, do not cry,
And I will sing a lullaby:
Rock them, rock them, lullaby.

Patient Grissil (1603) act 4, sc. 2

18 Prince I am not, yet I am nobly born.

The Shoemaker's Holiday (1600) sc. 7

Walter de la Mare 1873–1956

English poet and novelist

19 Ann, Ann!
Come! quick as you can!
There's a fish that *talks*
In the frying-pan.

'Alas, Alack' (1913)

20 Oh, no man knows
Through what wild centuries
Roves back the rose.

'All That's Past' (1912)

21 He is crazed with the spell of far Arabia,
They have stolen his wits away.

'Arabia' (1912)

22 Thy clouds—how oft have I
Watched their bright towers of silence steal
Into infinity.

'England' (1906)

1 Here lies a most beautiful lady,
Light of step and heart was she;
I think she was the most beautiful lady
That ever was in the West Country.
But beauty vanishes; beauty passes;
However rare—rare it be;
And when I crumble, who will remember
This lady of the West Country?
   'Epitaph' (1912)

2 Look thy last on all things lovely,
Every hour. Let no night
Seal thy sense in deathly slumber
Till to delight
Thou have paid thy utmost blessing;
Since that all things thou wouldst praise
Beauty took from those who loved them
In other days.
   'Fare Well' (1918)

3 A face peered. All the grey night
In chaos of vacancy shone;
Nought but vast Sorrow was there —
The sweet cheat gone.
   'The Ghost' (1918)

4 Hi! handsome hunting man
Fire your little gun.
Bang! Now the animal
Is dead and dumb and done.
Nevermore to peep again, creep again, leap again,
Eat or sleep or drink again, Oh, what fun!
   'Hi!' (1930)

5 Three jolly gentlemen,
In coats of red,
Rode their horses
Up to bed.
   'The Huntsmen' (1913)

6 'Is there anybody there?' said the Traveller,
Knocking on the moonlit door;
And his horse in the silence champed the grasses
Of the forest's ferny floor.
   'The Listeners' (1912)

7 'Tell them I came, and no one answered,
That I kept my word,' he said.
   'The Listeners' (1912)

8 Ay, they heard his foot upon the stirrup,
And the sound of iron on stone,
And how the silence surged softly backward,
When the plunging hoofs were gone.
   'The Listeners' (1912)

9 What is the world, O soldiers?
It is I:
I, this incessant snow,
This northern sky;
Soldiers, this solitude
Through which we go
Is I.
   'Napoleon' (1906)

10 Softly along the road of evening,
In a twilight dim with rose,
Wrinkled with age, and drenched with dew,
Old Nod, the shepherd, goes.
   'Nod' (1912)

11 Slowly, silently, now the moon
Walks the night in her silver shoon.
   'Silver' (1913)

12 Behind the blinds I sit and watch
The people passing—passing by;
And not a single one can see
My tiny watching eye.
   'The Window' (1913)

Shelagh Delaney 1939–

English playwright

13 Women never have young minds. They are born three
thousand years old.
   A Taste of Honey (1959) act 1, sc. 2

Walter de Leon and Paul M. Jones

14 It's a funny old world—a man's lucky if he gets out of
it alive.
   You're Telling Me (1934 film); spoken by W. C. Fields

Jack Dempsey 1895–1983

American boxer

15 Honey, I just forgot to duck.
   To his wife, on losing the World Heavyweight title,
   23 September 1926, in J. and B. P. Dempsey *Dempsey*
   (1977) p. 202. After a failed attempt on his life in 1981,
   Ronald Reagan quipped to his wife 'Honey, I forgot to duck'

Sir John Denham 1615–69

English poet

16 Thames, the most loved of all the Ocean's sons,
By his old sire, to his embraces runs,
Hasting to pay his tribute to the Sea,
Like mortal life to meet eternity.
   'Cooper's Hill' (1642)

17 O could I flow like thee, and make thy stream
My great example, as it is my theme!
Though deep, yet clear, though gentle, yet not dull,
Strong without rage, without o'erflowing full.
   'Cooper's Hill' (1642)

18 Youth, what man's age is like to be doth show;
We may our ends by our beginnings know.
   'Of Prudence' (1668) l. 225

19 Old Mother Wit, and Nature gave
Shakespeare and Fletcher all they have;
In Spenser, and in Jonson, Art,
Of slower Nature got the start.
   'On Mr Abraham Cowley' (1667)

20 Such is our pride, our folly, or our fate,
That few, but such as cannot write, translate.
   'To Richard Fanshaw' (1648)

Lord Denman (Thomas, 1st Baron Denman) 1779–1854

English politician and lawyer; Lord Chief Justice, 1832–50

1 If it is possible that such a practice as that which has taken place in the present instance should be allowed to pass without a remedy . . . trial by jury itself, instead of being a security to persons who are accused, will be a delusion, a mockery, and a snare.

Speech in the House of Lords, 4 September 1844; in E. W. Cox (ed.) *Reports of Cases in Criminal Law* (1846) vol. 1, p. 519

John Dennis 1657–1734

English critic, poet, and playwright

2 A man who could make so vile a pun would not scruple to pick a pocket.

The Gentleman's Magazine (1781) p. 324 (editorial note)

3 The great design of art is to restore the decays that happened to human nature by the fall, by restoring order.

The Grounds of Criticism in Poetry (1704) ch. 2

4 Damn them! They will not let my play run, but they steal my thunder!

On hearing his new thunder effects used at a performance of *Macbeth*, following the withdrawal of one of his own plays after only a short run; in William S. Walsh *A Handy-Book of Literary Curiosities* (1893) p. 1052

Nigel Dennis 1912–

English novelist

5 I am a well-to-do, revered and powerful figure. That Establishment which we call England has taken me in: I am become her Fortieth Article. I sit upon her Boards, I dominate her stage, her museums, her dances and her costumes; I have an honoured voice in her elected House. To her — and her alone — I bend the knee, and in return for my homage she is gently blind to my small failings, asking only that I indulge them privately.

Cards of Identity (1955) pt. 2, p. 230

Thomas De Quincey 1785–1859

English essayist and critic

6 The burden of the incommunicable.

Confessions of an English Opium Eater (1856 ed.) pt. 1

7 So, then, Oxford Street, stony-hearted stepmother, thou that listenest to the sighs of orphans, and drinkest the tears of children, at length I was dismissed from thee.

Confessions of an English Opium Eater (1822, ed. 1856) pt. 1

8 It was a Sunday afternoon, wet and cheerless: and a duller spectacle this earth of ours has not to show than a rainy Sunday in London.

Confessions of an English Opium Eater (1822, ed. 1856) pt. 2

9 Thou hast the keys of Paradise, oh just, subtle, and mighty opium!

Confessions of an English Opium Eater (1822, ed. 1856) pt. 2

10 Everlasting farewells! and again, and yet again reverberated—everlasting farewells!

Confessions of an English Opium Eater (1822, ed. 1856) pt. 3

11 Murder considered as one of the fine arts.

Blackwood's Magazine February 1827 (essay title)

12 If once a man indulges himself in murder, very soon he comes to think little of robbing; and from robbing he comes next to drinking and sabbath-breaking, and from that to incivility and procrastination.

'On Murder Considered as One of the Fine Arts' (Supplementary Paper) in *Blackwood's Magazine* November 1839

13 There is first the literature of *knowledge*, and secondly, the literature of *power*.

Review of the *Works of Pope* (1847 ed.) in *North British Review* August 1848, vol. 9, p. 301

14 Books, we are told, propose to *instruct* or to *amuse*. Indeed! . . . The true antithesis to knowledge, in this case, is not *pleasure*, but *power*. All that is literature seeks to communicate power; all that is not literature, to communicate knowledge.

Letters to a Young Man whose Education has been Neglected no. 3, in the *London Magazine* January–July 1823; De Quincey adds that he is indebted for this distinction to 'many years' conversation with Mr Wordsworth'

Edward Stanley, 14th Earl of Derby 1799–1869

British Conservative politician; Prime Minister, 1852, 1858–9, 1866–8

15 The duty of an Opposition [is] very simple . . . to oppose everything, and propose nothing.

Quoting 'Mr Tierney, a great Whig authority', in *Hansard* 4 June 1841, col. 1188

16 Meddle and muddle.

Summarizing Earl Russell's foreign policy, in Speech on the Address, *Hansard* (Lords) 4 February 1864, col. 28

René Descartes 1596–1650

French philosopher and mathematician

17 *Le bon sens est la chose du monde la mieux partagée, car chacun pense en être bien pourvu.*

Common sense is the best distributed commodity in the world, for every man is convinced that he is well supplied with it.

Le Discours de la méthode (1637) pt. 1

18 *Cogito, ergo sum.*

I think, therefore I am.

Le Discours de la méthode (1637) pt. 4

19 *Repugnare ut detur vacuum sive in quo nulla plane sit res.*

It is contrary to reason to say that there is a vacuum or space in which there is absolutely nothing.

Principia Philosophiae (1644) pt. 2, sect. 16 (translated by E. S. Haldane and G. R. T. Ross)

Camille Desmoulins 1760–94

French revolutionary

1 My age is that of the *bon Sansculotte Jésus*; an age fatal to Revolutionists.

> Reply given at his trial, in Thomas Carlyle *History of the French Revolution* (1837) bk. 6, ch. 2

Philippe Néricault Destouches 1680–1754

French playwright

2 *Les absents ont toujours tort.*

The absent are always in the wrong.

> *L'Obstacle imprévu* (1717) act 1, sc. 6

Edward De Vere, Earl of Oxford

See OXFORD

Robert Devereux, Earl of Essex

See ESSEX

Bernard De Voto 1897–1955

American writer

3 The proper union of gin and vermouth is a great and sudden glory; it is one of the happiest marriages on earth, and one of the shortest lived.

> *Harper's Magazine* December 1949, p. 70

Peter De Vries 1910–

American novelist

4 It is the final proof of God's omnipotence that he need not exist in order to save us.

> *The Mackerel Plaza* (1958) ch. 1

5 The value of marriage is not that adults produce children but that children produce adults.

> *The Tunnel of Love* (1954) ch. 8

Sir James Dewar 1842–1923

Scottish physicist

6 Minds are like parachutes. They only function when they are open.

> Attributed

Lord Dewar (Baron Dewar) 1864–1930

British industrialist

7 [There are] only two classes of pedestrians in these days of reckless motor traffic—the quick, and the dead.

> In George Robey *Looking Back on Life* (1933) ch. 28

George Dewey 1837–1917

American naval officer

8 You may fire when you are ready, Gridley.

> To the captain of his flagship at Manila, 1 May 1898, in *Autobiography* (1913) ch. 15

Sergei Diaghilev 1872–1929

Russian ballet impresario

9 *Étonne-moi.*

Astonish me.

> To Jean Cocteau, in Wallace Fowlie (ed.) *Journals of Jean Cocteau* (1956) ch. 1

Porfirio Diaz 1830–1915

President of Mexico, 1877–80, 1884–1911

10 Poor Mexico, so far from God and so close to the United States.

> Attributed

Charles Dibdin 1745–1814

English songwriter and playwright

11 Did you ever hear of Captain Wattle?
He was all for love, and a little for the bottle.

> 'Captain Wattle and Miss Roe' (1797)

12 For a soldier I listed, to grow great in fame,
And be shot at for sixpence a-day.

> 'Charity' (1791)

13 In every mess I finds a friend,
In every port a wife.

> 'Jack in his Element' (1790)

14 But the standing toast that pleased the most
Was—The wind that blows, the ship that goes,
And the lass that loves a sailor!

> 'The Lass that Loves a Sailor' (1811)

15 What argufies sniv'ling and piping your eye?

> 'Poor Jack' (1789)

16 Here, a sheer hulk, lies poor Tom Bowling,
The darling of our crew.

> 'Tom Bowling' (1790)

17 Faithful, below, he did his duty;
But now he's gone aloft.

> 'Tom Bowling' (1790)

Thomas Dibdin 1771–1841

English songwriter

18 Oh! what a snug little Island,
A right little, tight little Island!

> 'The Snug Little Island' (1833)

Charles Dickens 1812–70

English novelist

Barnaby Rudge

19 Something will come of this. I hope it mayn't be human gore.

> *Barnaby Rudge* (1841) ch. 4 (Simon Tappertit)

20 There are strings . . . in the human heart that had better not be wibrated.

> *Barnaby Rudge* (1841) ch. 22 (Mr Tappertit)

Bleak House

1 Jarndyce and Jarndyce still drags its dreary length before the Court, perennially hopeless.
Bleak House (1853) ch. 1

2 This is a London particular . . . A fog, miss.
Bleak House (1853) ch. 3

3 The wind's in the east . . . I am always conscious of an uncomfortable sensation now and then when the wind is blowing in the east.
Bleak House (1853) ch. 6 (Mr Jarndyce)

4 'Not to put too fine a point upon it'—a favourite apology for plain-speaking with Mr Snagsby.
Bleak House (1853) ch. 11

5 He wos wery good to me, he wos!
Bleak House (1853) ch. 11 (Jo)

6 He is celebrated, almost everywhere, for his Deportment.
Bleak House (1853) ch. 14 (Caddy)

7 What is peace? Is it war? No. Is it strife? No.
Bleak House (1853) ch. 19 (Mr Chadband)

8 You are a human boy, my young friend. A human boy. O glorious to be a human boy! . . .
O running stream of sparkling joy
To be a soaring human boy!
Bleak House (1853) ch. 19 (Mr Chadband)

9 Jobling, there *are* chords in the human mind.
Bleak House (1853) ch. 20 (Mr Guppy)

10 'It is,' says Chadband, 'the ray of rays, the sun of suns, the moon of moons, the star of stars. It is the light of Terewth.'
Bleak House (1853) ch. 25

11 Lo, the city is barren, I have seen but an eel.
Bleak House (1853) ch. 25 (Mr Chadband)

12 It's my old girl that advises. She has the head. But I never own to it before her. Discipline must be maintained.
Bleak House (1853) ch. 27 (Mr Bagnet)

13 The one great principle of the English law is, to make business for itself.
Bleak House (1853) ch. 39

14 Dead, your Majesty, Dead, my lords and gentlemen. Dead, Right Reverends and Wrong Reverends of every Order. Dead, men and women, born with heavenly compassion in your hearts. And dying thus around us, every day.
Bleak House (1853) ch. 47 (on the death of Jo)

15 I call them the Wards in Jarndyce. They are caged up with all the others. With Hope, Joy, Youth, Peace, Rest, Life, Dust, Ashes, Waste, Want, Ruin, Despair, Madness, Death, Cunning, Folly, Words, Wigs, Rags, Sheepskin, Plunder, Precedent, Jargon, Gammon, and Spinach!
Bleak House (1853) ch. 60 (Miss Flite's birds)

The Chimes

16 O let us love our occupations,
Bless the squire and his relations,
Live upon our daily rations,
And always know our proper stations.
The Chimes (1844) 'The Second Quarter'

A Christmas Carol

17 'Bah,' said Scrooge. 'Humbug!'
A Christmas Carol (1843) stave 1

18 'God bless us every one!' said Tiny Tim, the last of all.
A Christmas Carol (1843) stave 3

19 It *was* a turkey! He could never have stood upon his legs, that bird. He would have snapped 'em off short in a minute, like sticks of sealing-wax.
A Christmas Carol (1843) stave 5

David Copperfield

20 I am a lone lorn creetur . . . and everythink goes contrairy with me.
David Copperfield (1850) ch. 3 (Mrs Gummidge)

21 I'd better go into the house, and die and be a riddance!
David Copperfield (1850) ch. 3 (Mrs Gummidge)

22 She's been thinking of the old 'un!
David Copperfield (1850) ch. 3 (Mr Peggotty of Mrs Gummidge)

23 Barkis is willin'.
David Copperfield (1850) ch. 5

24 I live on broken wittles—and I sleep on the coals.
David Copperfield (1850) ch. 5 (The Waiter)

25 When a man says he's willin' . . . it's as much as to say, that a man's waitin' for an answer.
David Copperfield (1850) ch. 8 (Mr Barkis)

26 Experientia does it—as papa used to say.
David Copperfield (1850) ch. 11 (Mrs Micawber). See Tacitus *The Histories* bk. 5, ch. 6: '*Experientia docuit* [experience has taught]' commonly quoted '*Experientia docet* [experience teaches]'

27 I have known him come home to supper with a flood of tears, and a declaration that nothing was now left but a jail; and go to bed making a calculation of the expense of putting bow-windows to the house, 'in case anything turned up,' which was his favourite expression.
David Copperfield (1850) ch. 11 (of Mr Micawber)

28 Annual income twenty pounds, annual expenditure nineteen nineteen six, result happiness. Annual income twenty pounds, annual expenditure twenty pounds ought and six, result misery.
David Copperfield (1850) ch. 12 (Mr Micawber)

29 We live in a numble abode.
David Copperfield (1850) ch. 16 (Uriah Heep)

30 We are so very 'umble.
David Copperfield (1850) ch. 17 (Uriah Heep)

31 'Orses and dorgs is some men's fancy. They're wittles and drink to me—lodging, wife, and children—reading, writing and 'rithmetic—snuff, tobacker, and sleep.
David Copperfield (1850) ch. 19 (The Gentleman on the Canterbury coach)

32 I only ask for information.
David Copperfield (1850) ch. 20 (Miss Rosa Dartle)

33 It was as true . . . as taxes is. And nothing's truer than them.
David Copperfield (1850) ch. 21 (Mr Barkis). Cf. Franklin 293:3

1 What a world of gammon and spinnage it is, though, ain't it!
   David Copperfield (1850) ch. 22 (Miss Mowcher)

2 Other things are all very well in their way, but give me Blood!
   David Copperfield (1850) ch. 25 (Mr Waterbrook)

3 I assure you she's the dearest girl.
   David Copperfield (1850) ch. 27 (Traddles)

4 Accidents will occur in the best-regulated families.
   David Copperfield (1850) ch. 28 (Mr Micawber). Cf. North 496:17

5 He told me, only the other day, that it was provided for. That was Mr Micawber's expression, 'Provided for.'
   David Copperfield (1850) ch. 28 (Traddles)

6 'People can't die, along the coast,' said Mr Peggotty, 'except when the tide's pretty nigh out. They can't be born, unless it's pretty nigh in—not properly born, till flood. He's a going out with the tide.'
   David Copperfield (1850) ch. 30

7 Mrs Crupp had indignantly assured him that there wasn't room to swing a cat there; but, as Mr Dick justly observed to me, sitting down on the foot of the bed, nursing his leg, 'You know, Trotwood, I don't want to swing a cat. I never do swing a cat. Therefore, what does that signify to *me!*'
   David Copperfield (1850) ch. 35

8 It's only my child-wife.
   David Copperfield (1850) ch. 44 (of Dora)

9 Circumstances beyond my individual control.
   David Copperfield (1850) ch. 49 (Mr Micawber)

10 I'm Gormed—and I can't say no fairer than that!
    David Copperfield (1850) ch. 63 (Mr Peggotty)

Dombey and Son

11 He's tough, ma'am, tough is J.B. Tough, and devilish sly!
    Dombey and Son (1848) ch. 7 (Major Bagstock)

12 Papa! What's money?
    Dombey and Son (1848) ch. 8 (Paul Dombey)

13 There was no light nonsense about Miss Blimber . . . she was dry and sandy with working in the graves of deceased languages. None of your live languages for Miss Blimber. They must be dead—stone dead—and then Miss Blimber dug them up like a Ghoul.
    Dombey and Son (1848) ch. 11

14 As to Mr Feeder, B.A., Doctor Blimber's assistant, he was a kind of human barrel-organ, with a little list of tunes at which he was continually working, over and over again, without any variation.
    Dombey and Son (1848) ch. 11

15 If I could have known Cicero, and been his friend, and talked with him in his retirement at Tusculum (beau-ti-ful Tusculum), I could have died contented.
    Dombey and Son (1848) ch. 11 (Mrs Blimber)

16 In the Proverbs of Solomon you will find the following words, 'May we never want a friend in need, nor a bottle to give him!' When found, make a note of.
    Dombey and Son (1848) ch. 15 (Captain Cuttle)

17 What the waves were always saying.
    Dombey and Son (1848) title of ch. 16

18 Cows are my passion.
    Dombey and Son (1848) ch. 21 (Mrs Skewton)

19 It's of no consequence.
    Dombey and Son (1848) ch. 22 (Mr Toots)

20 The bearings of this observation lays in the application of it.
    Dombey and Son (1848) ch. 23 (Bunsby)

21 Say, like those wicked Turks, there is no What's-his-name but Thingummy, and What-you-may-call-it is his prophet!
    Dombey and Son (1848) ch. 27 (Mrs Skewton)

22 I positively adore Miss Dombey;—I—I am perfectly sore with loving her.
    Dombey and Son (1848) ch. 30 (Mr Toots)

23 If you could see my legs when I take my boots off, you'd form some idea of what unrequited affection is.
    Dombey and Son (1848) ch. 48 (Mr Toots)

Edwin Drood

24 Stranger, pause and ask thyself the question, Canst thou do likewise? If not, with a blush retire.
    Edwin Drood (1870) ch. 4

25 'Dear me,' said Mr Grewgious, peeping in, 'it's like looking down the throat of Old Time.'
    Edwin Drood (1870) ch. 9

Great Expectations

26 Your sister is given to government.
    Great Expectations (1861) ch. 7 (Joe Gargery)

27 'He calls the knaves, Jacks, this boy,' said Estella with disdain, before our first game was out.
    Great Expectations (1861) ch. 8

28 In the little world in which children have their existence, whosoever brings them up, there is nothing so finely perceived and so finely felt, as injustice.
    Great Expectations (1861) ch. 8

29 I had cherished a profound conviction that her bringing me up by hand, gave her no right to bring me up by jerks.
    Great Expectations (1861) ch. 8

30 It is a most miserable thing to feel ashamed of home.
    Great Expectations (1861) ch. 14

31 On the Rampage, Pip, and off the Rampage, Pip; such is Life!
    Great Expectations (1861) ch. 15 (Joe Gargery)

Hard Times

32 Now, what I want is, Facts . . . Facts alone are wanted in life.
    Hard Times (1854) bk. 1, ch. 1 (Mr Gradgrind)

33 Ah, Rachael, aw a muddle! Fro' first to last, a muddle!
    Hard Times (1854) bk. 3, ch. 6 (Stephen Blackpool)

34 People mutht be amuthed. They can't be alwayth a learning, nor yet they can't be alwayth a working, they an't made for it.
    Hard Times (1854) bk. 3, ch. 8 (Mr Sleary)

Little Dorrit

1 Whatever was required to be done, the Circumlocution Office was beforehand with all the public departments in the art of perceiving—HOW NOT TO DO IT.
   Little Dorrit (1857) bk. 1, ch. 10

2 Look here. Upon my soul you mustn't come into the place saying you want to know, you know.
   Little Dorrit (1857) bk. 1, ch. 10 (Barnacle Junior)

3 There's milestones on the Dover Road!
   Little Dorrit (1857) bk. 1, ch. 23 (Mr F.'s Aunt)

4 I revere the memory of Mr F. as an estimable man and most indulgent husband, only necessary to mention Asparagus and it appeared or to hint at any little delicate thing to drink and it came like magic in a pint bottle it was not ecstasy but it was comfort.
   Little Dorrit (1857) bk. 1, ch. 24 (Flora Finching)

5 As to marriage on the part of a man, my dear, Society requires that he should retrieve his fortunes by marriage. Society requires that he should gain by marriage. Society requires that he should found a handsome establishment by marriage. Society does not see, otherwise, what he has to do with marriage.
   Little Dorrit (1857) bk. 1, ch. 33 (Mrs Merdle)

6 Father is rather vulgar, my dear. The word Papa, besides, gives a pretty form to the lips. Papa, potatoes, poultry, prunes, and prism, are all very good words for the lips: especially prunes and prism.
   Little Dorrit (1857) bk. 2, ch. 5 (Mrs General)

7 Once a gentleman, and always a gentleman.
   Little Dorrit (1857) bk. 2, ch. 28 (Rigaud)

Martin Chuzzlewit

8 Any man may be in good spirits and good temper when he's well dressed. There an't much credit in that.
   Martin Chuzzlewit (1844) ch. 5 (Mark Tapley)

9 Affection beaming in one eye, and calculation shining out of the other.
   Martin Chuzzlewit (1844) ch. 8 (Mrs Todgers)

10 Charity and Mercy. Not unholy names, I hope?
   Martin Chuzzlewit (1844) ch. 9 (Mr Pecksniff)

11 Let us be moral. Let us contemplate existence.
   Martin Chuzzlewit (1844) ch. 9 (Mr Pecksniff)

12 Here's the rule for bargains: 'Do other men, for they would do you.' That's the true business precept.
   Martin Chuzzlewit (1844) ch. 11 (Jonas Chuzzlewit)

13 'Mrs Harris,' I says, 'leave the bottle on the chimley-piece, and don't ask me to take none, but let me put my lips to it when I am so dispoged.'
   Martin Chuzzlewit (1844) ch. 19 (Mrs Gamp)

14 Some people . . . may be Rooshans, and others may be Prooshans; they are born so, and will please themselves. Them which is of other naturs thinks different.
   Martin Chuzzlewit (1844) ch. 19 (Mrs Gamp)

15 Therefore I *do* require it, which I makes confession, to be brought reg'lar and draw'd mild.
   Martin Chuzzlewit (1844) ch. 25 (Mrs Gamp on her 'half a pint of porter')

16 She's the sort of woman . . . one would almost feel disposed to bury for nothing: and do it neatly, too!
   Martin Chuzzlewit (1844) ch. 25 (Mould)

17 He'd make a lovely corpse.
   Martin Chuzzlewit (1844) ch. 25 (Mrs Gamp)

18 All the wickedness of the world is print to him.
   Martin Chuzzlewit (1844) ch. 26 (Mrs Gamp)

19 'Sairey,' says Mrs Harris, 'sech is life. Vich likeways is the hend of all things!'
   Martin Chuzzlewit (1844) ch. 29 (Mrs Gamp)

20 We never knows wot's hidden in each other's hearts; and if we had glass winders there, we'd need keep the shutters up, some on us, I do assure you!
   Martin Chuzzlewit (1844) ch. 29 (Mrs Gamp)

21 Our fellow-countryman is a model of a man, quite fresh from Natur's mould! . . . Rough he may be. So air our Barrs. Wild he may be. So air our Buffalers. But he is the child of Natur', and a child of Freedom; and his boastful answer to the Despot and the Tyrant is, that his bright home is in the Settin Sun.
   Martin Chuzzlewit (1844) ch. 34 (Pogram)

22 'Mind and matter,' said the lady in the wig, 'glide swift into the vortex of immensity. Howls the sublime, and softly sleeps the calm Ideal, in the whispering chambers of Imagination.'
   Martin Chuzzlewit (1844) ch. 34

23 'The Ankworks package . . . I wish it was in Jonadge's belly, I do,' cried Mrs Gamp; appearing to confound the prophet with the whale in this miraculous aspiration.
   Martin Chuzzlewit (1844) ch. 40

24 And what a Life Young Bailey's was!
   Martin Chuzzlewit (1844) ch. 49 (Poll Sweedlepiper)

25 'Who deniges of it?' Mrs Gamp enquired.
   Martin Chuzzlewit (1844) ch. 49

26 His 'owls was organs.
   Martin Chuzzlewit (1844) ch. 49 (Mrs Gamp)

27 No, Betsey! Drink fair, wotever you do!
   Martin Chuzzlewit (1844) ch. 49 (Mrs Gamp)

28 The words she spoke of Mrs Harris, lambs could not forgive . . . nor worms forget.
   Martin Chuzzlewit (1844) ch. 49 (Mrs Gamp)

29 Farewell! Be the proud bride of a ducal coronet, and forget me! . . . Unalterably, never yours, Augustus.
   Martin Chuzzlewit (1844) ch. 54 (Augustus Moddle)

Nicholas Nickleby

30 United Metropolitan Improved Hot Muffin and Crumpet Baking and Punctual Delivery Company.
   Nicholas Nickleby (1839) ch. 2

31 EDUCATION.—At Mr Wackford Squeers's Academy, Dotheboys Hall, at the delightful village of Dotheboys, near Greta Bridge in Yorkshire, Youth are boarded, clothed, booked, furnished with pocket-money, provided with all necessaries, instructed in all languages living and dead, mathematics, orthography, geometry, astronomy, trigonometry, the use of the globes, algebra, single stick (if required), writing, arithmetic, fortification, and every other branch of classical literature. Terms, twenty guineas per annum. No extras, no vacations, and diet unparalleled.
   Nicholas Nickleby (1839) ch. 3

1 He had but one eye, and the popular prejudice runs in favour of two.
   Nicholas Nickleby (1839) ch. 4 (Mr Squeers)

2 Serve it right for being so dear.
   Nicholas Nickleby (1839) ch. 5 (Mr Squeers)

3 Here's richness!
   Nicholas Nickleby (1839) ch. 5 (Mr Squeers)

4 Subdue your appetites my dears, and you've conquered human natur.
   Nicholas Nickleby (1839) ch. 5 (Mr Squeers)

5 C-l-e-a-n, clean, verb active, to make bright, to scour. W-i-n, win, d-e-r, der, winder, a casement. When the boy knows this out of the book, he goes and does it.
   Nicholas Nickleby (1839) ch. 8 (Mr Squeers)

6 As she frequently remarked when she made any such mistake, it would be all the same a hundred years hence.
   Nicholas Nickleby (1839) ch. 9 (Mrs Squeers)

7 There are only two styles of portrait painting; the serious and the smirk.
   Nicholas Nickleby (1839) ch. 10 (Miss La Creevy)

8 Sir, My pa requests me to write to you, the doctors considering it doubtful whether he will ever recuvver the use of his legs which prevents his holding a pen.
   Nicholas Nickleby (1839) ch. 15 (Fanny Squeers)

9 'It's very easy to talk,' said Mrs Mantalini. 'Not so easy when one is eating a demnition egg,' replied Mr Mantalini; 'for the yolk runs down the waistcoat, and yolk of egg does not match any waistcoat but a yellow waistcoat, demmit.'
   Nicholas Nickleby (1839) ch. 17

10 Language was not powerful enough to describe the infant phenomenon.
   Nicholas Nickleby (1839) ch. 23

11 The unities, sir . . . are a completeness—a kind of universal dovetailedness with regard to place and time.
   Nicholas Nickleby (1839) ch. 24 (Mr Curdle)

12 She's the only sylph I ever saw, who could stand upon one leg, and play the tambourine on her other knee, like a sylph.
   Nicholas Nickleby (1839) ch. 25 (Mr Crummles)

13 Bring in the bottled lightning, a clean tumbler, and a corkscrew.
   Nicholas Nickleby (1839) ch. 49 (The Gentleman in the Small-clothes)

14 All is gas and gaiters.
   Nicholas Nickleby (1839) ch. 49 (The Gentleman in the Small-clothes)

15 My life is one demd horrid grind!
   Nicholas Nickleby (1839) ch. 64 (Mr Mantalini)

16 He has gone to the demnition bow-wows.
   Nicholas Nickleby (1839) ch. 64 (Mr Mantalini)

The Old Curiosity Shop

17 What is the odds so long as the fire of soul is kindled at the taper of conwiviality, and the wing of friendship never moults a feather!
   The Old Curiosity Shop (1841) ch. 2 (Dick Swiveller)

18 Fan the sinking flame of hilarity with the wing of friendship; and pass the rosy wine.
   The Old Curiosity Shop (1841) ch. 7 (Dick Swiveller)

19 Codlin's the friend, not Short.
   The Old Curiosity Shop (1841) ch. 19 (Codlin)

20 If I know'd a donkey wot wouldn't go
   To see Mrs Jarley's waxwork show,
   Do you think I'd acknowledge him,
   Oh no no!
   The Old Curiosity Shop (1841) ch. 27 (Codlin)

21 I never nursed a dear Gazelle, to glad me with its soft black eye, but when it came to know me well, and love me, it was sure to marry a market-gardener.
   The Old Curiosity Shop (1841) ch. 56 (Dick Swiveller). Cf. Moore 483:14

22 It was a maxim with Foxey—our revered father, gentlemen—'Always suspect everybody.'
   The Old Curiosity Shop (1841) ch. 66 (Sampson Brass)

Oliver Twist

23 Please, sir, I want some more.
   Oliver Twist (1838) ch. 2 (Oliver)

24 Known by the *sobriquet* of 'The artful Dodger.'
   Oliver Twist (1838) ch. 8

25 There is a passion for hunting something deeply implanted in the human breast.
   Oliver Twist (1838) ch. 10

26 I only know two sorts of boys. Mealy boys, and beef-faced boys.
   Oliver Twist (1838) ch. 14 (Mr Grimwig)

27 Oh, Mrs Corney, what a prospect this opens! What a opportunity for a jining of hearts and house-keepings!
   Oliver Twist (1838) ch. 27 (Bumble)

28 This ain't the shop for justice.
   Oliver Twist (1838) ch. 43 (The Artful Dodger)

29 'If the law supposes that,' said Mr Bumble . . . 'the law is a ass—a idiot.'
   Oliver Twist (1838) ch. 51 (Bumble). Cf. Chapman 190:20

30 Strike them all dead! What right have they to butcher me?
   Oliver Twist (1838) ch. 52 (Fagin)

Our Mutual Friend

31 A literary man—*with* a wooden leg.
   Our Mutual Friend (1865) bk. 1, ch. 5 (Mr Boffin, of Silas Wegg)

32 Professionally he declines and falls, and as a friend he drops into poetry.
   Our Mutual Friend (1865) bk. 1, ch. 5 (Mr Boffin, on Silas Wegg)

33 Meaty jelly, too, especially when a little salt, which is the case when there's ham, is mellering to the organ.
   Our Mutual Friend (1865) bk. 1, ch. 5 (Silas Wegg)

34 There is in the Englishman a combination of qualities, a modesty, an independence, a responsibility, a repose, combined with an absence of everything calculated to call a blush into the cheek of a young person, which one would seek in vain among the Nations of the Earth.
   Our Mutual Friend (1865) bk. 1, ch. 11 (Mr Podsnap)

1 A slap-up gal in a bang-up chariot.
Our Mutual Friend (1865) bk. 2, ch. 8

2 He'd be sharper than a serpent's tooth, if he wasn't as dull as ditch water.
Our Mutual Friend (1865) bk. 3, ch. 10 (Fanny Cleaver)

3 I want to be something so much worthier than the doll in the doll's house.
Our Mutual Friend (1865) bk. 4, ch. 5 (Bella)

Pickwick Papers

4 Heads, heads, take care of your heads . . . Five children—mother—tall lady, eating sandwiches—forgot the arch—crash—knock—children look round—mother's head off—sandwich in her hand—no mouth to put it in—head of a family off—shocking, shocking!
Pickwick Papers (1837) ch. 2 (Jingle)

5 'I was ruminating,' said Mr Pickwick, 'on the strange mutability of human affairs.' 'Ah, I see—in at the palace door one day, out at the window the next. Philosopher, sir?' 'An observer of human nature, sir,' said Mr Pickwick.
Pickwick Papers (1837) ch. 2

6 Kent, sir—everybody knows Kent—apples, cherries, hops, and women.
Pickwick Papers (1837) ch. 2 (Jingle)

7 I wants to make your flesh creep.
Pickwick Papers (1837) ch. 8 (The Fat Boy)

8 'It's always best on these occasions to do what the mob do.' 'But suppose there are two mobs?' suggested Mr Snodgrass. 'Shout with the largest,' replied Mr Pickwick.
Pickwick Papers (1837) ch. 13

9 Can I unmoved see thee dying
On a log,
Expiring frog!
Pickwick Papers (1837) ch. 15 (Mrs Leo Hunter)

10 Battledore and shuttlecock's a wery good game, vhen you an't the shuttlecock and two lawyers the battledores, in which case it gets too excitin' to be pleasant.
Pickwick Papers (1837) ch. 20 (Mr Weller)

11 The wictim o' connubiality, as Blue Beard's domestic chaplain said, with a tear of pity, ven he buried him.
Pickwick Papers (1837) ch. 20 (Mr Weller)

12 It's a wery remarkable circumstance . . . that poverty and oysters always seem to go together.
Pickwick Papers (1837) ch. 22 (Sam Weller)

13 It's over, and can't be helped, and that's one consolation, as they always says in Turkey, ven they cuts the wrong man's head off.
Pickwick Papers (1837) ch. 23 (Sam Weller)

14 Dumb as a drum vith a hole in it, sir.
Pickwick Papers (1837) ch. 25 (Sam Weller)

15 Ven you're a married man, Samivel, you'll understand a good many things as you don't understand now; but vether it's worth while goin' through so much to learn so little, as the charity-boy said ven he got to the end of the alphabet, is a matter o' taste.
Pickwick Papers (1837) ch. 27 (Mr Weller)

16 'Eccentricities of genius, Sam,' said Mr Pickwick.
Pickwick Papers (1837) ch. 30

17 A double glass o' the inwariable.
Pickwick Papers (1837) ch. 33 (Mr Weller)

18 It's my opinion, sir, that this meeting is drunk, sir!
Pickwick Papers (1837) ch. 33 (Mr Stiggins)

19 'Do you spell it with a "V" or a "W"?' inquired the judge. 'That depends upon the taste and fancy of the speller, my Lord,' replied Sam [Weller].
Pickwick Papers (1837) ch. 34

20 'Little to do, and plenty to get, I suppose?' said Sergeant Buzfuz, with jocularity. 'Oh, quite enough to get, sir, as the soldier said ven they ordered him three hundred and fifty lashes,' replied Sam. 'You must not tell us what the soldier, or any other man, said, sir,' interposed the judge; 'it's not evidence.'
Pickwick Papers (1837) ch. 34

21 'Yes, I have a pair of eyes,' replied Sam, 'and that's just it. If they wos a pair o' patent double million magnifyin' gas microscopes of hextra power, p'raps I might be able to see through a flight o' stairs and a deal door; but bein' only eyes, you see my wision's limited.'
Pickwick Papers (1837) ch. 34

22 A good uniform must work its way with the women, sooner or later.
Pickwick Papers (1837) ch. 37 (The Gentleman in Blue)

23 'And a bird-cage, sir,' says Sam. 'Veels vithin veels, a prison in a prison.'
Pickwick Papers (1837) ch. 40

24 'It would make anyone go to sleep, that bedstead would, whether they wanted to or not.' 'I should think,' said Sam . . . 'poppies was nothing to it.'
Pickwick Papers (1837) ch. 41

25 The have-his-carcase, next to the perpetual motion, is vun of the blessedest things as wos ever made.
Pickwick Papers (1837) ch. 43 (Sam Weller)

26 Anythin' for a quiet life, as the man said wen he took the sitivation at the lighthouse.
Pickwick Papers (1837) ch. 43 (Sam Weller). Cf. Middleton 459:12

27 'Never . . . see . . . a dead postboy, did you?' inquired Sam . . . 'No,' rejoined Bob, 'I never did.' 'No!' rejoined Sam triumphantly. 'Nor never vill; and there's another thing that no man never see, and that's a dead donkey.'
Pickwick Papers (1837) ch. 51

28 ''Cos a coachman's a privileged indiwidual,' replied Mr Weller, looking fixedly at his son. ''Cos a coachman may do vithout suspicion wot other men may not; 'cos a coachman may be on the wery amicablest terms with eighty mile o' females, and yet nobody think that he ever means to marry any vun among them.'
Pickwick Papers (1837) ch. 52

Sketches by Boz

29 Minerva House . . . where some twenty girls . . . acquired a smattering of everything, and a knowledge of nothing.
Sketches by Boz (1839) Tales, ch. 3 'Sentiment'

A Tale of Two Cities

1 It was the best of times, it was the worst of times, it was the age of wisdom, it was the age of foolishness, it was the epoch of belief, it was the epoch of incredulity, it was the season of Light, it was the season of Darkness, it was the spring of hope, it was the winter of despair, we had everything before us, we had nothing before us, we were all going direct to Heaven, we were all going direct the other way.
   A Tale of Two Cities (1859) bk. 1, ch. 1

2 I pass my whole life, miss, in turning an immense pecuniary Mangle.
   A Tale of Two Cities (1859) bk. 1, ch. 4 (Mr Lorry)

3 A likely thing . . . If it was ever intended that I should go across salt water, do you suppose Providence would have cast my lot in an island?
   A Tale of Two Cities (1859) bk. 1, ch. 4 (Miss Pross)

4 If you must go flopping yourself down, flop in favour of your husband and child, and not in opposition to 'em.
   A Tale of Two Cities (1859) bk. 2, ch. 1 (Jerry Cruncher)

5 'It is possible—that it may not come, during our lives . . . We shall not see the triumph.' 'We shall have helped it,' returned madame.
   A Tale of Two Cities (1859) bk. 2, ch. 16 (Monsieur and Madame Defarge)

6 There might be medical doctors . . . a cocking their medical eyes.
   A Tale of Two Cities (1859) bk. 3, ch. 9 (Jerry Cruncher)

7 It is a far, far better thing that I do, than I have ever done; it is a far, far better rest that I go to, than I have ever known.
   A Tale of Two Cities (1859) bk. 3, ch. 15 (Sydney Carton's thoughts on the scaffold)

8 My faith in the people governing is, on the whole, infinitesimal; my faith in The People governed is, on the whole, illimitable.
   Speech at Birmingham and Midland Institute, 27 September 1869, in K. J. Fielding (ed.) *Speeches of Charles Dickens* (1960)

Emily Dickinson 1830–86

American poet

9 After great pain, a formal feeling comes—
   The Nerves sit ceremonious, like Tombs—
   The stiff Heart questions was it He, that bore,
   And Yesterday, or Centuries before?
   'After great pain, a formal feeling comes' (1862)

10 This is the Hour of Lead—
   Remembered, if outlived,
   As Freezing persons, recollect the Snow—
   First—Chill—then Stupor—then the letting go.
   'After great pain, a formal feeling comes' (1862)

11 Because I could not stop for Death—
   He kindly stopped for me—
   The Carriage held but just Ourselves—
   And Immortality.
   'Because I could not stop for Death' (c.1863)

12 Since then—'tis Centuries—and yet
   Feels shorter than the Day
   I first surmised the Horses Heads
   Were toward Eternity.
   'Because I could not stop for Death' (c.1863)

13 The Bustle in a House
   The Morning after Death
   Is solemnest of industries
   Enacted upon Earth—

   The Sweeping up the Heart
   And putting Love away
   We shall not want to use again
   Until Eternity.
   'The Bustle in a House' (c.1866)

14 What fortitude the Soul contains,
   That it can so endure
   The accent of a coming Foot—
   The opening of a Door
   'Elysium is as far as to' (c.1882)

15 There interposed a Fly—

   With Blue—uncertain stumbling Buzz—
   Between the light—and me—
   And then the Windows failed—and then
   I could not see to see.
   'I heard a Fly buzz—when I died' (c.1862)

16 My life closed twice before its close;
   It yet remains to see
   If Immortality unveil
   A third event to me,

   So huge, so hopeless to conceive
   As these that twice befel.
   Parting is all we know of heaven,
   And all we need of hell.
   'My life closed twice before its close'

17 The Soul selects her own Society—
   Then—shuts the Door—
   To her divine Majority—
   Present no more.
   'The Soul selects her own Society' (c.1862)

18 I've known her—from an ample nation—
   Choose One—
   Then—close the Valves of her attention—
   Like Stone.
   'The Soul selects her own Society' (c.1862)

19 Success is counted sweetest
   By those who ne'er succeed.
   To comprehend a nectar
   Requires sorest need.
   'Success is counted sweetest' (1859)

20 There's a certain Slant of light,
   Winter Afternoons—
   That oppresses like the Heft
   Of Cathedral Tunes—

   Heavenly Hurt, it gives us—
   We can find no scar,
   But internal difference,
   Where the Meanings, are.
   'There's a certain Slant of light' (c.1861)

1 They shut me up in prose—
As when a little girl
They put me in the closet—
Because they liked me 'still'.
>'They shut me up in prose' (c.1862)

2 This is my letter to the world
That never wrote to me—
The simple news that Nature told,
With tender majesty.

Her message is committed
To hands I cannot see—
For love of her—sweet-countrymen—
Judge tenderly—of me.
>'This is my letter to the world' (c.1862)

3 This quiet Dust was Gentlemen and Ladies
And Lads and Girls—
Was laughter and ability and Sighing
And Frocks and Curls.
>'This quiet Dust was Gentlemen and Ladies' (c.1864)

4 What Soft—Cherubic Creatures—
These Gentlewomen are—
One would as soon assault a Plush—
Or violate a Star—

Such Dimity Convictions—
A Horror so refined
Of freckled Human Nature—
Of Deity—ashamed.
>'What Soft—Cherubic Creatures' (c.1862)

5 Friday I tasted life. It was a vast morsel. A Circus
passed the house—still I feel the red in my mind
though the drums are out. The Lawn is full of south
and the odors tangle, and I hear to-day for the first
time the river in the tree.
>Letter to Mrs J. G. Holland, May 1866, in T. H. Johnson
>(ed.) *The Letters of Emily Dickinson* vol. 2 (1958) p. 452

Goldsworthy Lowes Dickinson
1862–1932
English historian and essayist

6 Dissatisfaction with the world in which we live and
determination to realize one that shall be better, are
the prevailing characteristics of the modern spirit.
>*The Greek View of Life* (1898) ch. 5

John Dickinson 1732–1808
American politician

7 We have counted the cost of this contest, and find
nothing so dreadful as voluntary slavery ... Our cause
is just, our union is perfect.
>Declaration of reasons for taking up arms against England,
>presented to Congress, 8 July 1775, in C. J. Stillé *The Life
>and Times of John Dickinson* (1891) ch. 5

8 Then join hand in hand, brave Americans all,—
By uniting we stand, by dividing we fall.
>'The Liberty Song' (1768), in *The Writings of John Dickinson*
>vol. 1 (1895) p. 421

Paul Dickson 1939–
American writer

9 Rowe's Rule: the odds are five to six that the light at
the end of the tunnel is the headlight of an oncoming
train.
>*Washingtonian* November 1978. Cf. Lowell 430:19

Denis Diderot 1713–84
French philosopher and man of letters

10 *Il y a deux sortes de lois, les unes d'une équité, d'une
généralité absolues, d'autres bizarres, qui ne doivent leur
sanction qu'à l'aveuglement ou la nécessité des
circonstances. Celles-ci ne couvrent le coupable qui les
enfreint, que d'une ignominie passagère, ignominie que le
temps reverse sur les juges et sur les nations, pour y rester
à jamais.*

There are two sorts of laws, those of absolute equity
and universality, and the bizarre ones which owe their
autonomy only to blindness or to the force of
circumstance. The latter merely cover the man who is
breaking them with a passing disgrace, which time
then transfers to the judges and the nations, on whom
it remains forever.
>*Oeuvres romanesques* (ed. H. Bénac, revised L. Perol, 1981)
>p. 401 (translated by Peter France)

11 *Le premier serment que se firent deux êtres de chair, ce fut
au pied d'un rocher qui tombait en poussière; ils
attestèrent de leur constance un ciel qui n'est pas un
instant le même; tout passait en eux et autour d'eux, et
ils croyaient leurs cœurs affranchis de vicissitudes. O
enfants!*

The first vows sworn by two creatures of flesh and
blood were made at the foot of a rock that was
crumbling to dust; they called as witness to their
constancy a heaven which never stays the same for
one moment; everything within them and around
them was changing, and they thought their hearts
were exempt from vicissitudes. Children!
>*Oeuvres romanesques* (ed. H. Bénac, revised L. Perol, 1981)
>p. 632 (translated by Peter France)

12 *L'esprit de l'escalier.*

Staircase wit.
>The witty riposte one thinks of only when one has left the
>drawing-room and is already on the way downstairs, in
>*Paradoxe sur le Comédien* (written 1773–8, published 1830)

13 *Voyez-vous cet œuf. C'est avec cela qu'on renverse toutes
les écoles de théologie, et tous les temples de la terre.*

See this egg. It is with this that all the schools of
theology and all the temples of the earth are to be
overturned.
>*Le Rêve de d'Alembert* (written 1769, published 1830) pt. 1

Joan Didion 1934–
American writer

14 Was there ever in anyone's life span a point free in
time, devoid of memory, a night when choice was any
more than the sum of all the choices gone before?
>*Run River* (1963) ch. 4

1 When we start deceiving ourselves into thinking not that we want something or need something, not that it is a pragmatic necessity for us to have it, but that it is a *moral imperative* that we have it, then is when we join the fashionable madmen, and then is when the thin whine of hysteria is heard in the land, and then is when we are in bad trouble.

Slouching towards Bethlehem (1968) 'On Morality'

Wentworth Dillon, 4th Earl of Roscommon c.1633–1685

Irish poet and critic

2 But words once spoke can never be recalled.

Art of Poetry (1680) l. 438. Cf. Horace 348:12

3 Choose an author as you choose a friend.

Essay on Translated Verse (1684) l. 96

4 Immodest words admit of no defence,
For want of decency is want of sense.

Essay on Translated Verse (1684) l. 113

5 The multitude is always in the wrong.

Essay on Translated Verse (1684) l. 183

Ernest Dimnet

French priest, writer, and lecturer

6 Architecture, of all the arts, is the one which acts the most slowly, but the most surely, on the soul.

What We Live By (1932) pt. 2, ch. 12

Isak Dinesen (Karen Blixen) 1885–1962

Danish novelist and short-story writer

7 A herd of elephant . . . pacing along as if they had an appointment at the end of the world.

Out of Africa (1937) pt. 1, ch. 1

8 The giraffe, in their queer, inimitable, vegetative gracefulness . . . a family of rare, long-stemmed, speckled gigantic flowers slowly advancing.

Out of Africa (1937) pt. 1, ch. 1

9 The true aristocracy and the true proletariat of the world are both in understanding with tragedy. To them it is the fundamental principle of God, and the key, the minor key, to existence. They differ in this way from the bourgeoisie of all classes, who deny tragedy, who will not tolerate it, and to whom the word tragedy means in itself unpleasantness.

Out of Africa (1937) pt. 5, ch. 1

10 What is man, when you come to think upon him, but a minutely set, ingenious machine for turning, with infinite artfulness, the red wine of Shiraz into urine?

Seven Gothic Tales (1934) 'The Dreamers'

Diogenes c.400–c.325 BC

Greek Cynic philosopher

11 ὡς δ' ἐκεῖνος . . . προσειπὼν αὐτὸν ἠρώτησεν εἴ τινος τυγχάνει δεόμενος . . . "μικρόν", εἶπεν, "ἀπὸ τοῦ ἡλίου μετάστηθι."

Alexander . . . asked him if he lacked anything. 'Yes,' said he, 'that I do: that you stand out of my sun a little.'

Plutarch *Parallel Lives* 'Alexander' ch. 14, sect. 4 (translated by T. North, 1579)

Dionysius of Halicarnassus fl. 30–7 BC

Greek historian, resident in Rome from 30 BC

12 ἱστορία φιλοσοφία ἐστὶν ἐκ παραδειγμάτων.

History is philosophy from examples.

Ars Rhetorica ch. 11, sect. 2

Benjamin Disraeli (1st Earl of Beaconsfield) 1804–81

British Conservative politician and novelist; Prime Minister, 1868, 1874–80

13 In the 'Town' yesterday, I am told 'some one asked Disraeli, in offering himself for Marylebone, on what he intended *to stand*. "On my head," was the reply.'

Lord Beaconsfield's Correspondence with his Sister 1832–1852 (1886) 8 April 1833

14 Though I sit down now, the time will come when you will hear me.

Maiden speech in the House of Commons, *Hansard* 7 December 1837, col. 807

15 The Continent will [not] suffer England to be the workshop of the world.

Speech, *Hansard* 15 March 1838, col. 940

16 Thus you have a starving population, an absentee aristocracy, and an alien Church, and in addition the weakest executive in the world. That is the Irish Question.

Speech, *Hansard* 16 February 1844, col. 1016

17 The noble Lord is the Prince Rupert of Parliamentary discussion.

Speech, *Hansard* 24 April 1844, col. 248 (of Lord Stanley). Cf. Bulwer-Lytton 155:3

18 The right hon. Gentleman caught the Whigs bathing, and walked away with their clothes.

Speech, *Hansard* 28 February 1845, col. 154 (on Sir Robert Peel's abandoning protection in favour of free trade, traditionally the policy of the [Whig] Opposition)

19 Protection is not a principle, but an expedient.

Speech, *Hansard* 17 March 1845, col. 1023

20 A Conservative Government is an organized hypocrisy.

Speech, *Hansard* 17 March 1845, col. 1028. Bagehot, quoting Disraeli in *The English Constitution* (1867) 'The House of Lords', elaborated on the theme with the words 'so much did the ideas of its "head" differ from the sensations of its "tail"'

21 He traces the steam-engine always back to the tea-kettle.

Speech, *Hansard* 11 April 1845, col. 558 (of Sir Robert Peel)

1 Justice is truth in action.
   Speech, Hansard 11 February 1851, col. 412

2 I read this morning an awful, though monotonous, manifesto in the great organ of public opinion, which always makes me tremble: Olympian bolts; and yet I could not help fancying amid their rumbling terrors I heard the plaintive treble of the Treasury Bench.
   Speech, Hansard 13 February 1851, col. 602

3 He has to learn that petulance is not sarcasm, and that insolence is not invective.
   Speech, Hansard 16 December 1852, col. 1653 (of Sir Charles Wood)

4 England does not love coalitions.
   Speech, Hansard 16 December 1852, col. 1666

5 Finality is not the language of politics.
   Speech, Hansard 28 February 1859, col. 998

6 It is, I say, in the noble Lord's power to come to some really cordial understanding ... between this country and France ... and to put an end to these bloated armaments which only involve states in financial embarrassment.
   Speech, Hansard 8 May 1862, col. 1425

7 He seems to think that posterity is a pack-horse, always ready to be loaded.
   Speech, 3 June 1862 (attributed)

8 Colonies do not cease to be colonies because they are independent.
   Speech, Hansard 5 February 1863, col. 81

9 You are not going, I hope, to leave the destinies of the British Empire to prigs and pedants.
   Speech, Hansard 5 February 1863, col. 96

10 I hold that the characteristic of the present age is craving credulity.
   Speech at Oxford, 25 November 1864, in The Times 26 November 1864

11 Man, my Lord, is a being born to believe.
   Speech at Oxford, 25 November 1864, in The Times 26 November 1864

12 Party is organized opinion.
   Speech at Oxford, 25 November 1864, in The Times 26 November 1864

13 Is man an ape or an angel? Now I am on the side of the angels.
   Speech at Oxford, 25 November 1864, in The Times 26 November 1864

14 Assassination has never changed the history of the world.
   Speech, Hansard 1 May 1865, col. 1246

15 I had to prepare the mind of the country, and ... to educate our party.
   Speech at Edinburgh, 29 October 1867, in The Times 30 October 1867

16 Change is inevitable in a progressive country. Change is constant.
   Speech at Edinburgh, 29 October 1867, in The Times 30 October 1867

17 There can be no economy where there is no efficiency.
   Address to his Constituents, 1 October 1868, in The Times 3 October 1868

18 We have legalized confiscation, consecrated sacrilege, and condoned high treason.
   Speech, Hansard 27 February 1871, col. 1007

19 I believe that without party Parliamentary government is impossible.
   Speech at Manchester, 3 April 1872, in The Times 4 April 1872

20 You behold a range of exhausted volcanoes.
   Speaking of the Treasury Bench at Manchester, 3 April 1872, in The Times 4 April 1872. Cf. Burke 159:7

21 Increased means and increased leisure are the two civilizers of man.
   Speech at Manchester, 3 April 1872, in The Times 4 April 1872

22 A University should be a place of light, of liberty, and of learning.
   Speech, Hansard 11 March 1873, col. 1814

23 An author who speaks about his own books is almost as bad as a mother who talks about her own children.
   At a banquet given in Glasgow on his installation as Lord Rector, 19 November 1873, in The Times 20 November 1873

24 Upon the education of the people of this country the fate of this country depends.
   Speech, Hansard 15 June 1874, col. 1618

25 He is a great master of gibes and flouts and jeers.
   Speech, Hansard 5 August 1874, col. 1358 (of the Marquess of Salisbury)

26 Cosmopolitan critics, men who are the friends of every country save their own.
   Speech at Guildhall, 9 November 1877, in The Times 10 November 1877. Cf. Canning 178:4, Overbury 502:10 !

27 Lord Salisbury and myself have brought you back peace   but a peace I hope with honour.
   Speech on returning from the Congress of Berlin, 16 July 1878, in The Times 17 July 1878. Cf. Chamberlain 189:8, Russell 552:2

28 A series of congratulatory regrets.
   Describing Lord Harrington's Resolution on the Berlin Treaty at a banquet, Knightsbridge, 27 July 1878; in The Times 29 July 1878

29 A sophistical rhetorician, inebriated with the exuberance of his own verbosity.
   Of Gladstone, in The Times 29 July 1878

30 I admit that there is gossip ... But the government of the world is carried on by sovereigns and statesmen, and not by anonymous paragraph writers ... or by the hare-brained chatter of irresponsible frivolity.
   Speech at Guildhall, London, 9 November 1878, in The Times 11 November 1878

31 One of the greatest of Romans, when asked what were his politics, replied, Imperium et Libertas. That would not make a bad programme for a British Ministry.
   Speech at Mansion House, London, 10 November 1879, paraphrasing Tacitus Agricola ch. 3. See Winston Churchill Divi Britannici (1675) p. 349 and Notes and Queries (8th series) vol. 10, p. 453

32 The key of India is London.
   Speech, Hansard 4 March 1881, col. 299

33 These wretched colonies will all be independent, too, in a few years, and are a millstone round our necks.
   Letter to Lord Malmesbury, 13 August 1852, in W. Monypenny and G. Buckle Life of Benjamin Disraeli vol. 3 (1914) ch. 12

1 No Government can be long secure without a formidable Opposition.
Coningsby (1844) bk. 2, ch. 1

2 A government of statesmen or of clerks? Of Humbug or Humdrum?
Coningsby (1844) bk. 2, ch. 4

3 Conservatism discards Prescription, shrinks from Principle, disavows Progress; having rejected all respect for antiquity, it offers no redress for the present, and makes no preparation for the future.
Coningsby (1844) bk. 2, ch. 5

4 'A sound Conservative government,' said Taper, musingly. 'I understand: Tory men and Whig measures.'
Coningsby (1844) bk. 2, ch. 6

5 Youth is a blunder; Manhood a struggle; Old Age a regret.
Coningsby (1844) bk. 3, ch. 1

6 It seems to me a barren thing this Conservatism—an unhappy cross-breed, the mule of politics that engenders nothing.
Coningsby (1844) bk. 3, ch. 5

7 The depositary of power is always unpopular.
Coningsby (1844) bk. 4, ch. 13

8 Where can we find faith in a nation of sectaries?
Coningsby (1844) bk. 4, ch. 13

9 Man is only truly great when he acts from the passions.
Coningsby (1844) bk. 4, ch. 13

10 Read no history: nothing but biography, for that is life without theory.
Contarini Fleming (1832) pt. 1, ch. 23. Cf. Emerson 276:28

11 The practice of politics in the East may be defined by one word—dissimulation.
Contarini Fleming (1832) pt. 5, ch. 10

12 His Christianity was muscular.
Endymion (1880) ch. 14

13 Said Waldershare, 'Sensible men are all of the same religion.' 'And pray what is that?' ... 'Sensible men never tell.'
Endymion (1880) ch. 81. Cf. Shaftesbury 563:20

14 The sweet simplicity of the three per cents.
Endymion (1880) ch. 91. Cf. Stowell 670:11

15 I believe they went out, like all good things, with the Stuarts.
Endymion (1880) ch. 99

16 Time is the great physician.
Henrietta Temple (1837) bk. 6, ch. 9

17 They mean well; their feelings are strong, but their hearts are in the right place.
The Infernal Marriage (1834) pt. 1, 1 (of the Furies)

18 The blue ribbon of the turf.
Lord George Bentinck (1852) ch. 26 (of the Derby)

19 Every day when he looked into the glass, and gave the last touch to his consummate toilette, he offered his grateful thanks to Providence that his family was not unworthy of him.
Lothair (1870) ch. 1

20 A Protestant, if he wants aid or advice on any matter, can only go to his solicitor.
Lothair (1870) ch. 27

21 London: a nation, not a city.
Lothair (1870) ch. 27

22 The gondola of London.
Lothair (1870) ch. 27 (a hansom cab)

23 When a man fell into his anecdotage it was a sign for him to retire from the world.
Lothair (1870) ch. 28

24 You know who the critics are? The men who have failed in literature and art.
Lothair (1870) ch. 35. Cf. Coleridge 212:6

25 To do nothing and get something, formed a boy's ideal of a manly career.
Sybil (1845) bk. 1, ch. 5

26 'Two nations; between whom there is no intercourse and no sympathy; who are as ignorant of each other's habits, thoughts, and feelings, as if they were dwellers in different zones, or inhabitants of different planets; who are formed by a different breeding, are fed by a different food, are ordered by different manners, and are not governed by the same laws.' 'You speak of—' said Egremont, hesitatingly, 'THE RICH AND THE POOR.'
Sybil (1845) bk. 2, ch. 5. Cf. Foster 291:7

27 Mr Kremlin himself was distinguished for ignorance, for he had only one idea,—and that was wrong.
Sybil (1845) bk. 4, ch. 5. Cf. Johnson 373:10

28 I was told that the Privileged and the People formed Two Nations.
Sybil (1845) bk. 4, ch. 8

29 The Youth of a Nation are the trustees of Posterity.
Sybil (1845) bk. 6, ch. 13

30 That fatal drollery called a representative government.
Tancred (1847) bk. 2, ch. 13

31 A majority is always the best repartee.
Tancred (1847) bk. 2, ch. 14

32 The East is a career.
Tancred (1847) bk. 2, ch. 14

33 London is a modern Babylon.
Tancred (1847) bk. 5, ch. 5

34 Experience is the child of Thought, and Thought is the child of Action. We cannot learn men from books.
Vivian Grey (1826) bk. 5, ch. 1

35 I repeat ... that all power is a trust—that we are accountable for its exercise—that, from the people, and for the people, all springs, and all must exist.
Vivian Grey (1826) bk. 6, ch. 7

36 All Paradise opens! Let me die eating ortolans to the sound of soft music!
The Young Duke (1831) bk. 1, ch. 10

37 'The age of chivalry is past,' said May Dacre. 'Bores have succeeded to dragons.'
The Young Duke (1831) bk. 2, ch. 5

38 We came here for fame.
To John Bright, in the House of Commons, in Robert Blake *Disraeli* (1966) ch. 4

39 The school of Manchester.
Describing the free trade politics of Cobden and Bright, in Robert Blake *Disraeli* (1966) ch. 10

1 I will not go down to posterity talking bad grammar.
  While correcting proofs of his last Parliamentary speech,
  31 March 1881, in Robert Blake *Disraeli* (1966) ch. 32

2 Take away that emblem of mortality.
  On being offered an air cushion to sit on, 1881, in Robert
  Blake *Disraeli* (1966) ch. 32

3 Damn your principles! Stick to your party.
  Attributed to Disraeli and believed to have been said to
  Edward Bulwer-Lytton, in E. Latham *Famous Sayings and
  their Authors* (1904) p. 11

4 I never deny; I never contradict; I sometimes forget.
  Said to Lord Esher of his relations with Queen Victoria, in
  Elizabeth Longford *Victoria R. I* (1964) ch. 27

5 Protection is not only dead, but damned.
  In W. Monypenny and G. Buckle *Life of Benjamin Disraeli*
  vol. 3 (1914) ch. 8

6 Pray remember, Mr Dean, no dogma, no Dean.
  In W. Monypenny and G. Buckle *Life of Benjamin Disraeli*
  vol. 4 (1916) ch. 10

7 I have climbed to the top of the greasy pole.
  On becoming Prime Minister, in W. Monypenny and G.
  Buckle *Life of Benjamin Disraeli* vol. 4 (1916) ch. 16

8 I am dead; dead, but in the Elysian fields.
  To a peer, on his elevation to the House of Lords, in W.
  Monypenny and G. Buckle *Life of Benjamin Disraeli* vol. 5
  (1920) ch. 13

9 When I want to read a novel, I write one.
  In W. Monypenny and G. Buckle *Life of Benjamin Disraeli*
  vol. 6 (1920) ch. 17. Cf. Punch 531:24

10 Never complain and never explain.
  In J. Morley *Life of William Ewart Gladstone* (1903) vol. 1,
  p. 123. Cf. Fisher 283:5, Hubbard 353:9

11 Everyone likes flattery; and when you come to Royalty
  you should lay it on with a trowel.
  To Matthew Arnold, in G. W. E. Russell *Collections and
  Recollections* (1898) ch. 23

12 Coffee house babble.
  On the Bulgarian Atrocities, 1876, in R. W. Seton-Watson
  Britain in Europe 1789–1914 (1955) p. 515

13 There are three kinds of lies: lies, damned lies and
  statistics.
  Attributed to Disraeli in Mark Twain *Autobiography* (1924)
  vol. 1, p. 246

14 No it is better not. She would only ask me to take a
  message to Albert.
  On his death-bed, declining a proposed visit from Queen
  Victoria, in Robert Blake *Disraeli* (1966) ch. 32

Isaac D'Israeli 1766–1848

British literary historian; father of Benjamin Disraeli

15 It is a wretched taste to be gratified with mediocrity
  when the excellent lies before us.
  Curiosities of Literature. Second Series (1823) 'Quotation'

16 He wreathed the rod of criticism with roses.
  Curiosities of Literature (9th ed., 1834) vol. 1, p. 20 (of
  Pierre Bayle)

17 There is an art of reading, as well as an art of
  thinking, and an art of writing.
  The Literary Character (1795) ch. 11

William Chatterton Dix 1837–98

English clergyman

18 Alleluia! sing to Jesus,
  His the sceptre, his the throne;
  Alleluia! his the triumph,
  His the victory alone:
  Hark! the songs of peaceful Zion
  Thunder like a mighty flood;
  Jesus, out of every nation,
  Hath redeemed us by his blood.
  'Alleluia! sing to Jesus' (1867 hymn)

19 As with gladness men of old
  Did the guiding star behold,
  As with joy they hailed its light,
  Leading onward, beaming bright,
  So, most gracious Lord, may we
  Evermore be led to thee.
  'As with gladness men of old' (1861 hymn)

Henry Austin Dobson 1840–1921

English poet, biographer, and essayist

20 All passes. Art alone
  Enduring stays to us;
  The Bust outlasts the throne,—
  The Coin, Tiberius.
  'Ars Victrix' (1876); translation of Théophile Gautier's
  'L'Art': *Toute passe.—L'art robuste / Seul à l'éternité, / Le
  Buste / Servit à la cité*

21 Fame is a food that dead men eat,—
  I have no stomach for such meat.
  'Fame is a Food' (1906)

22 The ladies of St James's!
  They're painted to the eyes;
  Their white it stays for ever,
  Their red it never dies:
  But Phyllida, my Phyllida!
  Her colour comes and goes;
  It trembles to a lily, —
  It wavers to a rose.
  'The Ladies of St James's' (1883)

23 Time goes, you say? Ah no!
  Alas, Time stays, *we* go.
  'The Paradox of Time' (1877)

Ken Dodd 1931–

British comedian

24 Freud's theory was that when a joke opens a window
  and all those bats and bogeymen fly out, you get a
  marvellous feeling of relief and elation. The trouble
  with Freud is that he never had to play the old
  Glasgow Empire on a Saturday night after Rangers
  and Celtic had both lost.
  Guardian 30 April 1991, p. 19 (quoted in many, usually
  much contracted, forms since the mid-1960s)

Philip Doddridge 1702–51

English Nonconformist divine

1 Ye servants of the Lord,
  Each in his office wait,
  Observant of his heavenly word
  And watchful at his gate.
    Hymns (1755) 'The active Christian'

2 My thoughts with ecstasy unknown,
  While from his grave they view his throne,
  Through mine own sepulchre can see
  A paradise reserved for me.
    Hymns (1755) 'Meditations on the Sepulchre in the Garden'

3 O God of Bethel, by whose hand
  Thy people still are fed,
  Who through this weary pilgrimage
  Hast all our fathers led.
    Hymns (1755) 'O God of Bethel'

Bubb Dodington (*1st Baron Melcombe*) 1691–1762

English politician

4 Love thy country, wish it well,
  Not with too intense a care,
  'Tis enough, that when it fell,
  Thou its ruin didst not share.
    'Ode' (written 1761) in Joseph Spence *Anecdotes* (1820)
    p. 358

Aelius Donatus

4th-century Latin grammarian

5 *Pereant, inquit, qui ante nos nostra dixerunt.*
  Confound those who have said our remarks before us.
    In St Jerome *Commentary on Ecclesiastes* bk 1; J.-P. Migne
    Patrologiae Latinae vol. 23, col. 1019. Cf. Terence
    690:11

J. P. Donleavy 1926–

Irish-American novelist

6 When you don't have any money, the problem is food.
  When you have money, it's sex. When you have both
  it's health.
    The Ginger Man (1955) ch. 5

John Donne 1572–1631

English poet and divine

Verse dates are those of composition

7 And new philosophy calls all in doubt,
  The element of fire is quite put out;
  The sun is lost, and th'earth, and no man's wit
  Can well direct him, where to look for it.
    An Anatomy of the World: The First Anniversary (1611)
    l. 205

8 She, she is dead; she's dead; when thou know'st this,
  Thou know'st how dry a cinder this world is.
    An Anatomy of the World: The First Anniversary (1611)
    l. 427

9 Love built on beauty, soon as beauty, dies.
    Elegies 'The Anagram' (*c.*1595)

10 No spring, nor summer beauty hath such grace,
   As I have seen in one autumnal face.
    Elegies 'The Autumnal' (*c.*1600)

11 Whoever loves, if he do not propose
   The right true end of love, he's one that goes
   To sea for nothing but to make him sick.
    Elegies 'Love's Progress' (*c.*1600)

12 ... The straight Hellespont between
   The Sestos and Abydos of her breasts.
    Elegies 'Love's Progress' (*c.*1600)

13 By our first strange and fatal interview,
   By all desires which thereof did ensue.
    Elegies 'On His Mistress' (*c.*1600)

14 Nurse, O my love is slain; I saw him go
   O'er the white Alps, alone; I saw him, I,
   Assailed, fight, taken, stabbed, bleed, fall, and die
    Elegies 'On His Mistress' (*c.*1600)

15   We easily know
   By this these angels from an evil sprite,
   They set our hairs, but these our flesh upright.
    Elegies 'To His Mistress Going to Bed' (*c.*1595)

16 Licence my roving hands, and let them go,
   Behind, before, above, between, below.
   O my America, my new found land,
   My kingdom, safeliest when with one man manned.
    Elegies 'To His Mistress Going to Bed' (*c.*1595)

17 Hail, Bishop Valentine, whose day this is,
   All the air is thy Diocese.
    'An Epithalamion ... on the Lady Elizabeth and Count
    Palatine being Married on St Valentine's Day' (1613)

18 The household bird, with the red stomacher.
    'An Epithalamion ... on the Lady Elizabeth and Count
    Palatine ... ' (1613)

19 Clothed in her virgin white integrity.
    'A Funeral Elegy' (1610) l. 75

20 At the round earth's imagined corners, blow
   Your trumpets, angels, and arise, arise
   From death, you numberless infinities
   Of souls, and to your scattered bodies go.
    Holy Sonnets (1609) no. 4 (ed. J. Carey, 1990)

21 All whom war, dearth, age, agues, tyrannies,
   Despair, law, chance, hath slain.
    Holy Sonnets (1609) no. 4 (ed. J. Carey, 1990)

22 Death be not proud, though some have called thee
   Mighty and dreadful, for thou art not so,
   For, those, whom thou think'st, thou dost overthrow,
   Die not, poor death, nor yet canst thou kill me.
    Holy Sonnets (1609) no. 6 (ed. J. Carey, 1990)

23 One short sleep past, we wake eternally,
   And death shall be no more; Death thou shalt die.
    Holy Sonnets (1609) no. 6 (ed. J. Carey, 1990)

24 Batter my heart, three-personed God; for, you
   As yet but knock, breathe, shine, and seek to mend.
    Holy Sonnets (after 1609) no. 10 (ed. J. Carey, 1990)

25 Take me to you, imprison me, for I
   Except you enthral me, never shall be free,
   Nor ever chaste, except you ravish me.
    Holy Sonnets (after 1609) no. 10 (ed. J. Carey, 1990)

1 I am a little world made cunningly
   Of elements, and an angelic sprite.
       Holy Sonnets (after 1609) no. 15 (ed. J. Carey, 1990)

2 What if this present were the world's last night?
       Holy Sonnets (after 1609) no. 19 (ed. J. Carey, 1990)

3   As thou
   Art jealous, Lord, so I am jealous now,
   Thou lov'st not, till from loving more, thou free
   My soul; who ever gives, takes liberty:
   O, if thou car'st not whom I love
   Alas, thou lov'st not me.
       'A Hymn to Christ, at the Author's last going into
       Germany' (1619)

4 Seal then this bill of my divorce to all.
       'A Hymn to Christ, at the Author's last going into
       Germany' (1619)

5 To see God only, I go out of sight:
   And to 'scape stormy days, I choose
   An everlasting night.
       'A Hymn to Christ, at the Author's last going into
       Germany' (1619)

6 Since I am coming to that holy room,
   Where, with thy choir of saints for evermore,
   I shall be made thy music; as I come
   I tune the instrument here at the door,
   And what I must do then, think now before.
       'Hymn to God my God, in my Sickness' (1623)

7 Wilt thou forgive that sin where I begun,
   Which is my sin, though it were done before?
   Wilt thou forgive those sins, through which I run
   And do them still: though still I do deplore?
   When thou hast done, thou hast not done,
   For, I have more.

   Wilt thou forgive that sin by which I have won
   Others to sin? and, made my sin their door?
   Wilt thou forgive that sin which I did shun
   A year, or two: but wallowed in, a score?
   When thou has done, thou hast not done,
   For I have more.
       'A Hymn to God the Father' (1623)

8 Immensity cloistered in thy dear womb,
   Now leaves his well-beloved imprisonment.
       La Corona (1609) 'Nativity'

9 Think then, my soul, that death is but a groom,
   Which brings a taper to the outward room.
       Of the Progress of the Soul: The Second Anniversary (1612)
       l. 85

10   Her pure and eloquent blood
   Spoke in her cheeks, and so distinctly wrought,
   That one might almost say, her body thought.
       Of the Progress of the Soul: The Second Anniversary (1612)
       l. 244

11 I sing the progress of a deathless soul.
       'The Progress of the Soul' (1601) st. 1

12 Great Destiny the commissary of God.
       'The Progress of the Soul' (1601) st. 4

13 So, of a lone unhaunted place possessed,
   Did this soul's second inn, built by the guest,
   This living buried man, this quiet mandrake, rest.
       'The Progress of the Soul' (1601) st. 16

14 Nature's great masterpiece, an elephant,
   The only harmless great thing.
       'The Progress of the Soul' (1601) st. 39

15   On a huge hill,
   Cragged, and steep, Truth stands, and he that will
   Reach her, about must, and about must go.
       Satire no. 3 (1594–5) l. 79

16 Twice or thrice had I loved thee,
   Before I knew thy face or name;
   So in a voice, so in a shapeless flame,
   Angels affect us oft, and worshipped be.
       Songs and Sonnets 'Air and Angels'

17   Just such disparity
   As is 'twixt air and angels' purity,
   'Twixt women's love, and men's will ever be.
       Songs and Sonnets 'Air and Angels'

18 All other things, to their destruction draw,
   Only our love hath no decay;
   This, no tomorrow hath, nor yesterday,
   Running it never runs from us away,
   But truly keeps his first, last, everlasting day.
       Songs and Sonnets 'The Anniversary'

19 Come live with me, and be my love,
   And we will some new pleasures prove
   Of golden sands, and crystal brooks,
   With silken lines, and silver hooks.
       Songs and Sonnets 'The Bait' Cf. Marlowe 447:17, Ralegh
       535:11

20 A naked thinking heart, that makes no show,
   Is to a woman, but a kind of ghost.
       Songs and Sonnets 'The Blossom' l. 27

21 For God's sake hold your tongue, and let me love.
       Songs and Sonnets 'The Canonization'

22 Dear love, for nothing less than thee
   Would I have broke this happy dream,
   It was a theme
   For reason, much too strong for fantasy,
   Therefore thou waked'st me wisely; yet
   My dream thou brok'st not, but continued'st it.
       Songs and Sonnets 'The Dream' ('Dear love, for nothing less
       than thee')

23 So, if I dream I have you, I have you,
   For, all our joys are but fantastical.
       Songs and Sonnets 'The Dream' ('Image of her whom I love')

24 Where, like a pillow on a bed,
   A pregnant bank swelled up, to rest
   The violet's reclining head,
   Sat we two, one another's best.
       Songs and Sonnets 'The Ecstasy'

25 But O alas, so long, so far
   Our bodies why do we forbear?
   They're ours, though they're not we, we are
   The intelligencies, they the sphere.
       Songs and Sonnets 'The Ecstasy'

26 So must pure lovers' souls descend
   T'affections, and to faculties,
   Which sense may reach and apprehend,
   Else a great prince in prison lies.
       Songs and Sonnets 'The Ecstasy'

1 So, so, break off this last lamenting kiss,
 Which sucks two souls, and vapours both away,
 Turn thou ghost that way, and let me turn this,
 And let our selves benight our happiest day.
 We asked none leave to love; nor will we owe
 Any, so cheap a death, as saying, Go.
  Songs and Sonnets 'The Expiration'

2 Oh wrangling schools, that search what fire
 Shall burn this world, had none the wit
 Unto this knowledge to aspire,
 That this her fever might be it?
  Songs and Sonnets 'A Fever'

3 Whoever comes to shroud me, do not harm
 Nor question much
 That subtle wreath of hair, which crowns my arm;
 The mystery, the sign you must not touch,
 For 'tis my outward soul,
 Viceroy to that, which then to heaven being gone,
 Will leave this to control,
 And keep these limbs, her provinces, from dissolution.
  Songs and Sonnets 'The Funeral'

4 I wonder by my troth, what thou, and I
 Did, till we loved, were we not weaned till then?
 But sucked on country pleasures, childishly?
 Or snorted we in the seven sleepers den?
  Songs and Sonnets 'The Good-Morrow'

5 And now good morrow to our waking souls,
 Which watch not one another out of fear.
  Songs and Sonnets 'The Good-Morrow'

6 Stand still, and I will read to thee
 A lecture, love, in love's philosophy.
  Songs and Sonnets 'A Lecture in the Shadow'

7 Love is a growing or full constant light;
 And his first minute, after noon, is night.
  Songs and Sonnets 'A Lecture in the Shadow'

8 When I died last, and, dear, I die
 As often as from thee I go,
 Though it be but an hour ago,
 And lovers' hours be full eternity.
  Songs and Sonnets 'The Legacy'

9 If yet I have not all thy love,
 Dear, I shall never have it all.
  Songs and Sonnets 'Lovers' Infiniteness'

10 I long to talk with some old lover's ghost,
 Who died before the god of love was born.
  Songs and Sonnets 'Love's Deity'

11 'Tis the year's midnight, and it is the day's.
  Songs and Sonnets 'A Nocturnal upon St Lucy's Day'

12 The world's whole sap is sunk:
 The general balm th'hydroptic earth hath drunk.
  Songs and Sonnets 'A Nocturnal upon St Lucy's Day'

13 When my grave is broke up again
 Some second guest to entertain,
 (For graves have learnt that woman-head
 To be to more than one a bed)
 And he that digs it, spies
 A bracelet of bright hair about the bone,
 Will he not let us alone?
  Songs and Sonnets 'The Relic'

14 Go, and catch a falling star,
 Get with child a mandrake root,
 Tell me, where all past years are,
 Or who cleft the Devil's foot.
  Songs and Sonnets 'Song: Go and catch a falling star'

15 Sweetest love, I do not go,
 For weariness of thee,
 Nor in hope the world can show
 A fitter love for me;
 But since that I
 Must die at last, 'tis best,
 To use my self in jest
 Thus by feigned deaths to die.
  Songs and Sonnets 'Song: Sweetest love, I do not go'

16 Busy old fool, unruly sun,
 Why dost thou thus,
 Through windows, and through curtains call on us?
 Must to thy motions lovers' seasons run?
  Songs and Sonnets 'The Sun Rising'

17 Love, all alike, no season knows, nor clime,
 Nor hours, days, months, which are the rags of time.
  Songs and Sonnets 'The Sun Rising'

18 This bed thy centre is, these walls thy sphere.
  Songs and Sonnets 'The Sun Rising'

19 I am two fools, I know,
 For loving, and for saying so
 In whining poetry.
  Songs and Sonnets 'The Triple Fool'

20 I have done one braver thing
 Than all the Worthies did,
 And yet a braver thence doth spring,
 Which is, to keep that hid.
  Songs and Sonnets 'The Undertaking'

21 As virtuous men pass mildly away,
 And whisper to their souls, to go,
 Whilst some of their sad friends do say,
 The breath goes now, and some say, no:

 So let us melt, and make no noise,
 No tear-floods, nor sigh-tempests move,
 'Twere profanation of our joys
 To tell the laity our love.
  Songs and Sonnets 'A Valediction: forbidding mourning'

22 Thy firmness makes my circle just,
 And makes me end, where I begun.
  Songs and Sonnets 'A Valediction: forbidding mourning'

23   O more than moon,
 Draw not up seas to drown me in thy sphere,
 Weep me not dead, in thine arms, but forbear
 To teach the sea what it may do too soon.
  Songs and Sonnets 'A Valediction: of Weeping'

24 Sir, more than kisses, letters mingle souls.
  'To Sir Henry Wotton' (1597–8)

25 And seeing the snail, which everywhere doth roam,
 Carrying his own house still, still is at home,
 Follow (for he is easy paced) this snail,
 Be thine own palace, or the world's thy gaol.
  'To Sir Henry Wotton' (1597–8)

26 We have a winding sheet in our mother's womb,
 which grows with us from our conception, and we
 come into the world, wound up in that winding sheet,
 for we come to seek a grave.
  Death's Duel (1632)

1 That which we call life, is but *hebdomada mortium*, a week of death, seven days, seven periods of our life spent in dying, a dying seven times over; and there is an end.

Death's Duel (1632)

2 There we leave you, in that blessed dependancy, to hang upon him that hangs upon the Cross, there bathe in his tears, there suck at his wounds, and lie down in peace in his grave, till he vouchsafe you a resurrection, and an ascension into that Kingdom, which he hath prepared for you, with the inestimable price of his incorruptible blood. Amen.

Death's Duel (1632)

3 My God, my God, thou art a direct God, may I not say a literal God, a God that wouldst be understood literally and according to the plain sense of all that thou sayest? But thou art also … a figurative, a metaphorical God too.

Devotions upon Emergent Occasions (1624) 'Expostulation XIX'

4 But I do nothing upon my self, and yet I am mine own *Executioner*.

Devotions upon Emergent Occasions (1624) 'Meditation XII'

5 No man is an Island, entire of it self; every man is a piece of the Continent, a part of the main; if a clod be washed away by the sea, Europe is the less, as well as if a promontory were, as well as if a manor of thy friends or of thine own were; any man's death diminishes me, because I am involved in Mankind; And therefore never send to know for whom the bell tolls; it tolls for thee.

Devotions upon Emergent Occasions (1624) 'Meditation XVII'

6 From this I testify her holy cheerfulness, and religious alacrity, (one of the best evidences of a good conscience), that as she came to this place, God's house of Prayer … she ever hastened her family, and her company hither, with that cheerful provocation, For God's sake let's go, For God's sake let's be there at the Confession.

A Sermon of Commemoration of the Lady Danvers [mother of George Herbert] (1627)

7 [Death] comes equally to us all, and makes us all equal when it comes. The ashes of an Oak in the Chimney, are no epitaph of that Oak, to tell me how high or how large that was; It tells me not what flocks it sheltered while it stood, nor what men it hurt when it fell. The dust of great persons' graves is speechless too, it says nothing, it distinguishes nothing: As soon the dust of a wretch whom thou wouldest not, as of a Prince whom thou couldest not look upon, will trouble thine eyes, if the wind blow it thither; and when a whirlwind hath blown the dust of the Churchyard into the Church, and the man sweeps out the dust of the Church into the Churchyard, who will undertake to sift those dusts again, and to pronounce, This is the Patrician, this is the noble flower, and this the yeomanly, this the Plebeian bran.

LXXX Sermons (1640) 8 March 1621/2

8 A day that hath no *pridie*, nor *postridie*, yesterday doth not usher it in, nor tomorrow shall not drive it out. *Methusalem*, with all his hundreds of years, was but a mushroom of a night's growth, to this day, And all the four Monarchies, with all their thousands of years, and all the powerful Kings and all the beautiful Queens of this world, were but as a bed of flowers, some gathered at six, some at seven, some at eight, All in one Morning, in respect of this Day.

LXXX Sermons (1640) 30 April 1626 'Eternity'

9 I throw myself down in my Chamber, and I call in, and invite God, and his Angels thither, and when they are there, I neglect God and his Angels, for the noise of a fly, for the rattling of a coach, for the whining of a door.

LXXX Sermons (1640) 12 December 1626 'At the Funeral of Sir William Cokayne'

10 A memory of yesterday's pleasures, a fear of tomorrow's dangers, a straw under my knee, a noise in mine ear, a light in mine eye, an anything, a nothing, a fancy, a chimera in my brain, troubles me in my prayer. So certainly is there nothing, nothing in spiritual things, perfect in this world.

LXXX Sermons (1640) 12 December 1626 'At the Funeral of Sir William Cokayne'

11 There is nothing that God hath established in a constant course of nature, and which therefore is done every day, but would seem a Miracle, and exercise our admiration, if it were done but once.

LXXX Sermons (1640) Easter Day, 25 March 1627

12 Man is but earth; 'Tis true; but earth is the centre. That man who dwells upon himself, who is always conversant in himself, rests in his true centre.

LXXX Sermons (1640) Christmas Day, 1627

13 Poor intricated soul! Riddling, perplexed, labyrinthical soul!

LXXX Sermons (1640) 25 January 1628/9

14 They shall awake as Jacob did, and say as Jacob said, *Surely the Lord is in this place*, and *this is no other but the house of God, and the gate of heaven*, And into that gate they shall enter, and in that house they shall dwell, where there shall be no Cloud nor Sun, no darkness nor dazzling, but one equal light, no noise nor silence, but one equal music, no fears nor hopes, but one equal possession, no foes nor friends, but one equal communion and identity, no ends nor beginnings, but one equal eternity.

XXVI Sermons (1660) 29 February 1627/8

15 John Donne, Anne Donne, Un-done.

In a letter to his wife, on being dismissed from the service of his father-in-law, Sir George More; in Izaak Walton *The Life of Dr Donne* (first printed in *LXXX Sermons*, 1640)

Sir Reginald Dorman-Smith 1899–1977

British politician; Minister of Agriculture and Fisheries, 1939–40

1 Let 'Dig for Victory' be the motto of every one with a garden and of every able-bodied man and woman capable of digging an allotment in their spare time.

Radio broadcast, 3 October 1939, in *The Times* 4 October 1939

Fedor Dostoevsky 1821–81

Russian novelist

2 Уничтожьте в человечестве веру в свое бессмертие, в нем тотчас же иссякнет не только любовь, но и всякая живая сила, чтобы продолжать мировую жизнь.

If you were to destroy in mankind the belief in immortality, not only love but every living force maintaining the life of the world would at once be dried up.

The Brothers Karamazov (1879–80) bk. 2, ch. 6

3 Ужасно то, что красота есть не только страшная, но и таинственная вещь. Тут дьявол с богом борется, а поле битвы — сердца людей.

The awful thing is that beauty is mysterious as well as terrible. God and devil are fighting there, and the battlefield is the heart of man.

The Brothers Karamazov (1879–80) bk. 3, ch. 3

4 Если дьявол не существует, и, стало быть, создал его человек, то создал он его по своему образу и подобию.

If the devil doesn't exist, but man has created him, he has created him in his own image and likeness.

The Brothers Karamazov (1879–80) bk. 5, ch. 4

5 Слишком дорого оценили гармонию, не по карману нашему вовсе столько платить за вход. А потому свой билет на вход спешу возвратить обратно ... Не бога я не принимаю, Алеша, я только билет ему почтительнейше возвращаю.

Too high a price is asked for harmony; it's beyond our means to pay so much to enter. And so I hasten to give back my entrance ticket ... It's not God that I don't accept, Alyosha, only I most respectfully return Him the ticket.

The Brothers Karamazov (1879–80) bk. 5, ch. 4

6 Представь, что это ты сам возводишь здание судьбы человеческой с целью в финале осчастливить людей, дать им, наконец, мир и покой, но для этого необходимо и неминуемо предстояло бы замучить всего лишь одно только крохотное созданьице ... и на неотомщенных слезках его основать это здание, согласился ли бы ты быть архитектором на этих условиях?

Imagine that you are creating a fabric of human destiny with the object of making men happy in the end, giving them peace and rest at last, but that it was essential and inevitable to torture to death only one tiny creature ... and to found that edifice on its unavenged tears, would you consent to be the architect on those conditions?

The Brothers Karamazov (1879–80) bk. 5, ch. 4

7 Нет заботы беспрерывнее и мучительнее для человека, как, оставшись свободным, сыскать поскорее того, пред кем преклониться.

So long as man remains free he strives for nothing so incessantly and so painfully as to find someone to worship.

The Brothers Karamazov (1879–80) bk. 5, ch. 5

8 Не принимает род людской пророков своих и избивает их, но любят люди мучеников своих и чтят тех, коих замучили.

Men reject their prophets and slay them, but they love their martyrs and honour those whom they have slain.

The Brothers Karamazov (1879–80) bk. 6, ch. 3

9 Все люди как-то разделяются на «обыкновенных» и «необыкновенных». Обыкновенные должны жить в послушании и не имеют права переступать закона, потому что они ... обыкновенные. А необыкновенные имеют право делать всякие преступления и всячески переступать закон, собственно потому, что они необыкновенные.

All people seem to be divided into 'ordinary' and 'extraordinary'. The ordinary people must lead a life of strict obedience and have no right to transgress the law because ... they are ordinary. Whereas the extraordinary people have the right to commit any crime they like and transgress the law in any way just because they happen to be extraordinary.

Crime and Punishment (1866) pt. 3, ch. 5 (translated by David Magarshak)

10 Сломать что надо, раз навсегда, да и только: и страдание взять на себя! ... Свобода и власть, а главное власть! Надо всею дрожащею тварью и над всем муравейником!

We have to break with what must be broken with once and for all ... and we have to take the suffering upon ourselves ... Freedom and power—power above all. Power over all the tumbling vermin and over all the ant-hill!

Crime and Punishment (1866) pt. 4, ch. 4 (translated by David Magarshak)

11 Власть дается только тому, кто посмеет наклониться и взять ее ... Стоит только посметь!

Power is given only to him who dares to stoop and take it ... one must have the courage to dare.

Crime and Punishment (1866) pt. 5, ch. 4 (translated by David Magarshak)

12 Я захотел ... убить для себя ... а там стал ли бы я чьим-нибудь благодетелем или всю жизнь, как паук, ловил бы всех в паутину и из всех живые соки высасывал, мне, в ту минуту, все равно должно было быть!

I wanted to murder, for my own satisfaction ... At that moment I did not care a damn whether I would become the benefactor of someone, or would spend the rest of my life like a spider catching them all in my web and sucking the living juices out of them.

Crime and Punishment (1866) pt. 5, ch. 4 (translated by David Magarshak)

1 Деньги есть чеканенная свобода, а потому для человека, лишенного совершенно свободы, они дороже вдесятеро. Если они только брякают у него в кармане, он уже вполовину утешен, хотя бы и не мог их тратить.

Money is coined liberty, and so it is ten times dearer to a man who is deprived of freedom. If money is jingling in his pocket, he is half consoled, even though he cannot spend it.

   House of the Dead (1862) pt. 1, ch. 1 (translated by Constance Garnett)

2 Если б захотели вполне раздавить, уничтожать человека, наказать его самым ужасным наказанием, так что самый страшный убийца содрогнулся бы от этого наказания и пугался его заранее, то стоило бы только придать работе характер совершенной, полнейшей безполезности и бессмыслицы.

To crush, to annihilate a man utterly, to inflict on him the most terrible punishment so that the most ferocious murderer would shudder at it beforehand, one need only give him work of an absolutely, completely useless and irrational character.

   House of the Dead (1862) pt. 1, ch. 1 (translated by Constance Garnett)

3 В Петербурге, самом отвлеченном и умышленном городе на всем земном шаре.

Petersburg, the most abstract and premeditated city on earth.

   Notes from Underground (1864) pt. 1, ch. 2 (translated by Andrew R. McAndrew)

4 В отчаянии-то и бывают самые жгучие наслаждения, особенно когда уж очень сильно сознаешь безвыходность своего положения.

In despair there are the most intense enjoyments, especially when one is very acutely conscious of the hopelessness of one's position.

   Notes from Underground (1864) pt. 1, ch. 2 (translated by Andrew R. McAndrew)

5 Человек надо — одного только *самостоятельного* хотенья, чего бы эта самостоятельность ни стоила и к чему бы ни привела.

What man wants is simply *independent* choice, whatever that independence may cost and wherever it may lead.

   Notes from Underground (1864) pt. 1, ch. 7 (translated by Constance Garnett)

6 Слишком сознавать — это болезнь, настоящая, полная болезнь.

To be conscious is an illness—a real thorough-going illness.

   Notes from Underground (1864) pt. 1, ch. 2 (translated by Constance Garnett)

Lord Alfred Douglas 1870–1945

Poet and intimate of Oscar Wilde

7 I am the Love that dare not speak its name.
   'Two Loves' (1896)

Gavin Douglas c.1475–1522

Scottish poet and prelate

8 And all small fowlys singis on the spray:
Welcum the lord of lycht and lamp of day.
   Eneados (1553) bk. 12, prologue l. 251

James Douglas, 4th Earl of Morton c.1516–81

Scottish courtier

9 Here lies he who neither feared nor flattered any flesh.
   Of John Knox, said as he was buried, 26 November 1572, in George R. Preedy *The Life of John Knox* (1940) ch. 7

Keith Douglas 1920–44

English poet

10 If at times my eyes are lenses
through which the brain explores
constellations of feeling
my ears yielding like swinging doors
admit princes to the corridors
into the mind, do not envy me.
I have a beast on my back.
   'Bête Noire' (1944)

11 And all my endeavours are unlucky explorers
come back, abandoning the expedition;
the specimens, the lilies of ambition
still spring in their climate, still unpicked:
but time, time is all I lacked
to find them, as the great collectors before me.
   'On Return from Egypt, 1943–4' (1946)

12 Remember me when I am dead
And simplify me when I'm dead.
   'Simplify me when I'm Dead' (1941)

13 But she would weep to see today
how on his skin the swart flies move;
the dust upon the paper eye
and the burst stomach like a cave.
For here the lover and killer are mingled
who had one body and one heart.
And death, who had the soldier singled
has done the lover mortal hurt.
   'Vergissmeinnicht, 1943'

Norman Douglas 1868–1952

Scottish-born novelist and essayist

14 To find a friend one must close one eye. To keep him—two.
   Almanac (1941) p. 77

15 Many a man who thinks to found a home discovers that he has merely opened a tavern for his friends.
   South Wind (1917) ch. 20

Sir Alec Douglas-Home 1903–

See LORD HOME

Lorenzo Dow 1777–1834

American divine

1 You will be damned if you do—And you will be
damned if you don't.

> *Reflections on the Love of God* (1836) ch. 6 (on 'the doctrine
> of Particular Election')

Ernest Dowson 1867–1900

English poet

2 I have forgot much, Cynara! gone with the wind,
Flung roses, roses, riotously, with the throng,
Dancing, to put thy pale, lost lilies out of mind;
But I was desolate and sick of an old passion,
Yea, all the time, because the dance was long:
I have been faithful to thee, Cynara! in my fashion.

> 'Non Sum Qualis Eram' (1896) (also known as 'Cynara').
> Cf. Horace 350:11

3 They are not long, the weeping and the laughter,
Love and desire and hate:
I think they have no portion in us after
We pass the gate.
They are not long, the days of wine and roses:
Out of a misty dream
Our path emerges for a while, then closes
Within a dream.

> 'Vitae Summa Brevis' (1896)

Sir Arthur Conan Doyle 1859–1930

Scottish-born writer of detective fiction

4 Singularity is almost invariably a clue. The more
featureless and commonplace a crime is, the more
difficult is it to bring it home.

> *The Adventures of Sherlock Holmes* (1892) 'The Boscombe
> Valley Mystery'

5 It is my belief, Watson, founded upon my experience,
that the lowest and vilest alleys in London do not
present a more dreadful record of sin than does the
smiling and beautiful countryside.

> *The Adventures of Sherlock Holmes* (1892) 'The Copper
> Beeches'

6 A man should keep his little brain attic stocked with
all the furniture that he is likely to use, and the rest
he can put away in the lumber room of his library,
where he can get it if he wants it.

> *The Adventures of Sherlock Holmes* (1892) 'The Five Orange
> Pips'

7 It is quite a three-pipe problem, and I beg that you
won't speak to me for fifty minutes.

> *The Adventures of Sherlock Holmes* (1892) 'The Red-Headed
> League'

8 You see, but you do not observe.

> *The Adventures of Sherlock Holmes* (1892) 'Scandal in
> Bohemia'

9 Matilda Briggs . . . was a ship which is associated with
the giant rat of Sumatra, a story for which the world
is not yet prepared.

> *The Case-Book of Sherlock Homes* (1927) 'The Sussex
> Vampire'

10 Of all ruins that of a noble mind is the most
deplorable.

> *His Last Bow* (1917) 'The Dying Detective'. Cf. Davies
> 232:8

11 Good old Watson! You are the one fixed point in a
changing age.

> *His Last Bow* (1917) title story

12 'Excellent,' I cried. 'Elementary,' said he.

> *The Memoirs of Sherlock Holmes* (1894) 'The Crooked Man'.
> 'Elementary, my dear Watson' is not found in any book by
> Conan Doyle, although a review of the film *The Return of
> Sherlock Holmes* in *New York Times* 19 October 1929, p. 22,
> states: 'In the final scene Dr Watson is there with his
> "Amazing, Holmes", and Holmes comes forth with his
> "Elementary, my dear Watson, elementary" '

13 Ex-Professor Moriarty of mathematical celebrity . . . is
the Napoleon of crime, Watson.

> *The Memoirs of Sherlock Holmes* (1894) 'The Final Problem'

14 'Is there any other point to which you would wish to
draw my attention?'
'To the curious incident of the dog in the night-time.'
'The dog did nothing in the night-time.'
'That was the curious incident,' remarked Sherlock
Holmes.

> *The Memoirs of Sherlock Holmes* (1894) 'Silver Blaze'

15 I didn't think there was a soul in England who didn't
know Godfrey Staunton, the back three-quarter,
Cambridge, Blackheath, and five Internationals. Good
Lord! Mr Holmes where *have* you lived.

> *The Return of Sherlock Holmes* (1905) 'The Missing
> Three-Quarter'

16 You live in a different world to me, Mr Overton, a
sweeter and a healthier one. My ramifications stretch
out into many sections of society, but never, I am
happy to say, into amateur sport, which is the best
and soundest thing in England.

> *The Return of Sherlock Holmes* (1905) 'The Missing
> Three-Quarter'

17 Detection is, or ought to be, an exact science, and
should be treated in the same cold and unemotional
manner. You have attempted to tinge it with
romanticism, which produces much the same effect as
if you worked a love-story or an elopement into the
fifth proposition of Euclid.

> *The Sign of Four* (1890) ch. 1

18 How often have I said to you that when you have
eliminated the impossible, whatever remains, *however
improbable*, must be the truth?

> *The Sign of Four* (1890) ch. 6

19 You know my methods. Apply them.

> *The Sign of Four* (1890) ch. 6

20 It is the unofficial force—the Baker Street irregulars.

> *The Sign of Four* (1890) ch. 8

21 London, that great cesspool into which all the
loungers and idlers of the Empire are irresistibly
drained.

> *A Study in Scarlet* (1888) ch. 1

22 It is a capital mistake to theorize before you have all
the evidence. It biases the judgement.

> *A Study in Scarlet* (1888) ch. 3

23 Where there is no imagination there is no horror.

> *A Study in Scarlet* (1888) ch. 5

1 The vocabulary of 'Bradshaw' is nervous and terse, but limited. The selection of words would hardly lend itself to the sending of general messages.
  The Valley of Fear (1915) ch. 1

2 Mediocrity knows nothing higher than itself, but talent instantly recognizes genius.
  The Valley of Fear (1915) ch. 1

3 What of the bow?
The bow was made in England,
Of true wood, of yew wood,
The wood of English bows.
  The White Company (1891) 'Song of the Bow'

Sir Francis Doyle 1810–88
English verse-writer

4 Last night, among his fellow roughs,
He jested, quaffed, and swore.
  'The Private of the Buffs' (1866)

5 His creed no parson ever knew,
For this was still his 'simple plan',
To have with clergymen to do
As little as a Christian can.
  'The Unobtrusive Christian' (1866)

Margaret Drabble 1939–
English novelist

6 England's not a bad country ... It's just a mean, cold, ugly, divided, tired, clapped-out, post-imperial, post-industrial slag-heap covered in polystyrene hamburger cartons.
  A Natural Curiosity (1989) p. 308

7 Affluence was, quite simply, a question of texture ... The threadbare carpets of infancy, the coconut matting, the ill-laid linoleum, the utility furniture ... had all spoken of a life too near the bones of subsistence, too little padded, too severely worn.
  The Needle's Eye (1972) pt. 1

8 Perhaps the rare and simple pleasure of being seen for what one is compensates for the misery of being it.
  A Summer Bird-Cage (1963) ch. 7

Sir Francis Drake c.1540–96
English sailor and explorer

9 There must be a beginning of any great matter, but the continuing unto the end until it be thoroughly finished yields the true glory.
  Dispatch to Sir Francis Walsingham, 17 May 1587, in *Navy Records Society* vol. 11 (1898) p. 134

10 The singeing of the King of Spain's Beard.
  On the expedition to Cadiz, 1587, in Francis Bacon *Considerations touching a War with Spain* (1629)

11 I must have the gentleman to haul and draw with the mariner, and the mariner with the gentleman ... I would know him, that would refuse to set his hand to a rope, but I know there is not any such here.
  In J. S. Corbett *Drake and the Tudor Navy* (1898) vol. 1, ch. 9

12 There is plenty of time to win this game, and to thrash the Spaniards too.
  Attributed, in *Dictionary of National Biography* (1917–) vol. 5, p. 1342

Joseph Rodman Drake 1795–1820
American poet

13 Forever float that standard sheet!
Where breathes the foe but falls before us,
With Freedom's soil beneath our feet,
And Freedom's banner streaming o'er us?
  'The American Flag' in *New York Evening Post*, 29 May 1819 (also attributed to Fitz-Greene Halleck)

Milton Drake et al.

14 Mares eat oats
And does eat oats
And little lambs eat ivy.
  'Mairzy Doats' (1943 song)

Michael Drayton 1563–1631
English poet

15 Ill news hath wings, and with the wind doth go,
Comfort's a cripple and comes ever slow.
  The Barons' Wars (1603) canto 2, st. 28

16 The mind is free, whate'er afflict the man,
A King's a King, do Fortune what she can.
  The Barons' Wars (1603) canto 5, st. 36

17 Thus when we fondly flatter our desires,
Our best conceits do prove the greatest liars.
  The Barons' Wars (1603) canto 6, st. 94

18 Let peevish worldlings prate of right and wrong;
Leave plaints and pleas to whom they do belong;
Let old men speak of chances and events,
And lawyers talk of titles and descents;
Leave fond reports to such as stories tell,
And covenants to those that buy and sell:
Love, my sweet Tudor, that becomes thee best;
And to our good success refer the rest.
  England's Heroical Epistles (1597) 'Queen Katharine to Owen Tudor'

19 All men to some one quality incline:
Only to love is naturally mine.
  England's Heroical Epistles (1597) 'Owen Tudor to Queen Katharine'

20 Love, in a humour, played the prodigal,
And bade my senses to a solemn feast;
Yet more to grace the company withal,
Invites my heart to be the chiefest guest.
No other drink would serve this glutton's turn
But precious tears distilling from mine eyne,
Which with my sighs this epicure doth burn,
Quaffing carouses in this costly wine.
  Idea (1619) Sonnet 7

1 Since there's no help, come let us kiss and part,
Nay, I have done: you get no more of me,
And I am glad, yea glad with all my heart,
That thus so cleanly, I myself can free,
Shake hands for ever, cancel all our vows,
And when we meet at any time again,
Be it not seen in either of our brows,
That we one jot of former love retain;
Now at the last gasp of Love's latest breath,
When his pulse failing, Passion speechless lies,
When Faith is kneeling by his bed of death,
And Innocence is closing up his eyes,
Now if thou wouldst, when all have given him over,
From death to life, thou might'st him yet recover.
  Idea (1619) Sonnet 61

2 That shire which we the Heart of England well may
call.
  Poly-Olbion (1612–22) Song 13, l. 2 (of Warwickshire)

3 But when the bowels of the earth were sought,
And men her golden entrails did espy,
This mischief then into the world was brought,
This framed the mint which coined our misery.

Then lofty pines were by ambition hewn,
And men sea-monsters swam the brackish flood
In wainscot tubs to seek out worlds unknown,
For certain ill to leave assurèd good . . .

The city-builder then entrenched his towers,
And walled his wealth within the fencèd town,
Which afterward in bloody stormy stours
Kindled that flame which burnt his bulwarks down.

And thus began th'exordium of our woes,
The fatal dumb-show of our misery;
Here sprang the tree on which our mischief grows,
The dreary subject of world's tragedy.
  The Shepherd's Garland (1593) Eclogue 8

4 For that fine madness still he did retain
Which rightly should possess a poet's brain.
  'To Henry Reynolds, of Poets and Poesy' (1627) l. 109 (on
  Marlowe)

5 Next these, learn'd Jonson, in this list I bring,
Who had drunk deep of the Pierian spring.
  'To Henry Reynolds, of Poets and Poesy' (1627) l. 129. Cf.
  Pope 521:8

6 I pray thee leave, love me no more,
Call home the heart you gave me,
I but in vain the saint adore,
That can, but will not, save me.
  'To His Coy Love' (1619)

7 These poor half-kisses kill me quite.
  'To His Coy Love' (1619)

8 Fair stood the wind for France
When we our sails advance,
Nor now to prove our chance
Longer will tarry.
  To the Cambro-Britons (1619) 'Agincourt'

William Drennan 1754–1820
Irish writer of patriotic verse

9 Nor one feeling of vengeance presume to defile
The cause, or the men, of the Emerald Isle.
  Erin (1795) st. 3

John Drinkwater 1882–1937
English poet and playwright

10 In the corridors under there is nothing but sleep.
And stiller than ever on orchard boughs they keep
Tryst with the moon, and deep is the silence, deep
On moon-washed apples of wonder.
  'Moonlit Apples' (1917)

Thomas Drummond 1797–1840
*British government official; Under-secretary of State for
Ireland, 1835–40*

11 Property has its duties as well as its rights.
  Letter to the Earl of Donoughmore, 22 May 1838, in
  R. Barry O'Brien *Thomas Drummond . . . Life and Letters*
  (1889) p. 284

William Drummond of Hawthornden
1585–1649
Scottish poet

12 Only the echoes which he made relent,
Ring from their marble caves repent, repent.
  'For the Baptist' (1623)

13 Phoebus, arise,
And paint the sable skies,
With azure, white, and red.
  'Song: Phoebus, arise' (1614)

14   A morn
Of bright carnations did o'erspread her face.
  'Sonnet: Alexis here she stayed' (1614)

15 I long to kiss the image of my death.
  'Sonnet: Sleep, Silence Child' (1614)

John Dryden 1631–1700
English poet, critic, and playwright

16 In pious times, ere priestcraft did begin,
Before polygamy was made a sin.
  Absalom and Achitophel (1681) pt. 1, l. 1

17 Then Israel's monarch, after Heaven's own
heart,
His vigorous warmth did, variously, impart
To wives and slaves: and, wide as his command,
Scattered his Maker's image through the land.
  Absalom and Achitophel (1681) pt. 1, l. 7

18 Whate'er he did was done with so much ease,
In him alone, 'twas natural to please.
  Absalom and Achitophel (1681) pt. 1, l. 27

19 Plots, true or false, are necessary things,
To raise up commonwealths and ruin kings.
  Absalom and Achitophel (1681) pt. 1, l. 83

1 Of these the false Achitophel was first,
A name to all succeeding ages curst.
For close designs and crooked counsels fit,
Sagacious, bold, and turbulent of wit,
Restless, unfixed in principles and place,
In power unpleased, impatient of disgrace;
A fiery soul, which working out its way,
Fretted the pigmy body to decay:
And o'er informed the tenement of clay.
A daring pilot in extremity;
Pleased with the danger, when the waves went high
He sought the storms; but for a calm unfit,
Would steer too nigh the sands to boast his wit.
Great wits are sure to madness near allied,
And thin partitions do their bounds divide.
Absalom and Achitophel (1681) pt. 1, l. 150

2 Why should he, with wealth and honour blest,
Refuse his age the needful hours of rest?
Punish a body which he could not please;
Bankrupt of life, yet prodigal of ease?
And all to leave what with his toil he won
To that unfeathered two-legged thing, a son.
Absalom and Achitophel (1681) pt. 1, l. 165

3 In friendship false, implacable in hate:
Resolved to ruin or to rule the state.
Absalom and Achitophel (1681) pt. 1, l. 173

4 The people's prayer, the glad diviner's theme,
The young men's vision and the old men's dream!
Absalom and Achitophel (1681) pt. 1, l. 238

5 All empire is no more than power in trust.
Absalom and Achitophel (1681) pt. 1, l. 411

6 Better one suffer, than a nation grieve.
Absalom and Achitophel (1681) pt. 1, l. 416

7 But far more numerous was the herd of such
Who think too little and who talk too much.
Absalom and Achitophel (1681) pt. 1, l. 533

8 A man so various that he seemed to be
Not one, but all mankind's epitome.
Stiff in opinions, always in the wrong;
Was everything by starts, and nothing long:
But, in the course of one revolving moon,
Was chemist, fiddler, statesman, and buffoon.
Absalom and Achitophel (1681) pt. 1, l. 545

9 In squandering wealth was his peculiar art:
Nothing went unrewarded, but desert.
Beggared by fools, whom still he found too late:
He had his jest, and they had his estate.
Absalom and Achitophel (1681) pt. 1, l. 559

10 Youth, beauty, graceful action seldom fail:
But common interest always will prevail:
And pity never ceases to be shown
To him, who makes the people's wrongs his own.
Absalom and Achitophel (1681) pt. 1, l. 723

11 For who can be secure of private right,
If sovereign sway may be dissolved by might?
Nor is the people's judgement always true:
The most may err as grossly as the few.
Absalom and Achitophel (1681) pt. 1, l. 779

12 Never was patriot yet, but was a fool.
Absalom and Achitophel (1681) pt. 1, l. 968

13 Beware the fury of a patient man.
Absalom and Achitophel (1681) pt. 1, l. 1005

14 Doeg, though without knowing how or why,
Made still a blund'ring kind of melody;
Spurred boldly on, and dashed through thick and thin,
Through sense and nonsense, never out nor in;
Free from all meaning, whether good or bad,
And in one word, heroically mad.
Absalom and Achitophel (1681) pt. 2, l. 412

15 Rhyme is the rock on which thou art to wreck.
Absalom and Achitophel (1681) pt. 2, l. 486

16 Happy, happy, happy, pair!
None but the brave,
None but the brave,
None but the brave deserves the fair.
Alexander's Feast (1697) l. 4

17 With ravished ears
The monarch hears,
Assumes the god,
Affects to nod,
And seems to shake the spheres.
Alexander's Feast (1697) l. 42

18 Drinking is the soldier's pleasure;
Rich the treasure;
Sweet the pleasure;
Sweet is pleasure after pain.
Alexander's Feast (1697) l. 57

19 Fallen from his high estate,
And welt'ring in his blood:
Deserted at his utmost need
By those his former bounty fed;
On the bare earth exposed he lies,
With not a friend to close his eyes.
Alexander's Feast (1697) l. 78

20 Revolving in his altered soul
The various turns of chance below.
Alexander's Feast (1697) l. 85

21 War, he sung, is toil and trouble;
Honour but an empty bubble.
Never ending, still beginning,
Fighting still, and still destroying,
If the world be worth thy winning,
Think, oh think, it worth enjoying.
Alexander's Feast (1697) l. 97

22 Sighed and looked, and sighed again.
Alexander's Feast (1697) l. 120

23 Let old Timotheus yield the prize,
Or both divide the crown:
He raised a mortal to the skies;
She drew an angel down.
Alexander's Feast (1697) l. 177 (of 'Divine Cecilia')

24 Errors, like straws, upon the surface flow;
He who would search for pearls must dive below.
All for Love (1678) prologue

25 My love's a noble madness.
All for Love (1678) act 2, sc. 1

26   Give, you gods,
Give to your boy, your Caesar,
The rattle of a globe to play withal,
This gewgaw world, and put him cheaply off:
I'll not be pleased with less than Cleopatra.
All for Love (1678) act 2, sc. 1

1 Men are but children of a larger growth;
Our appetites as apt to change as theirs,
And full as craving too, and full as vain.
All for Love (1678) act 4, sc. 1. Cf. Chesterfield 198:16

2 Welcome, thou kind deceiver!
Thou best of thieves; who, with an easy key,
Dost open life, and, unperceived by us,
Even steal us from ourselves.
All for Love (1678) act 5, sc. 1 (of Love)

3 By viewing nature, nature's handmaid art,
Makes mighty things from small beginnings grow:
Thus fishes first to shipping did impart,
Their tail the rudder, and their head the prow.
Annus Mirabilis (1667) st. 155

4 An horrid stillness first invades the ear,
And in that silence we the tempest fear.
Astraea Redux (1660) l. 7

5 Death, in itself, is nothing; but we fear,
To be we know not what, we know not where.
Aureng-Zebe (1675) act 4, sc. 1

6 None would live past years again,
Yet all hope pleasure in what yet remain;
And, from the dregs of life, think to receive,
What the first sprightly running could not give.
Aureng-Zebe (1675) act 4, sc. 1

7 Refined himself to soul, to curb the sense
And made almost a sin of abstinence.
'The Character of a Good Parson' (1700) l. 10

8 I am as free as nature first made man,
Ere the base laws of servitude began,
When wild in woods the noble savage ran.
The Conquest of Granada (1670) pt. 1, act 1, sc. 1

9 Forgiveness to the injured does belong;
But they ne'er pardon, who have done the wrong.
The Conquest of Granada (1670) pt. 2, act 1, sc. 2

10 Thou strong seducer, opportunity!
The Conquest of Granada (1670) pt. 2, act 4, sc. 3

11 Bold knaves thrive without one grain of sense,
But good men starve for want of impudence.
Constantine the Great (1684) epilogue

12 He trudged along unknowing what he sought,
And whistled as he went, for want of thought.
Cymon and Iphigenia (1700) l. 84

13 She hugged the offender, and forgave the offence.
Cymon and Iphigenia (1700) l. 367. Cf. Augustine 37:8,
Dryden 260:27

14 Of seeming arms to make a short essay,
Then hasten to be drunk, the business of the day.
Cymon and Iphigenia (1700) l. 407

15 His colours laid so thick on every place,
As only showed the paint, but hid the face.
Epistle 'To my honoured friend Sir Robert Howard' (1660)
l. 75

16 Better to hunt in fields, for health unbought,
Than fee the doctor for a nauseous draught.
The wise, for cure, on exercise depend;
God never made his work, for man to mend.
Epistle 'To my honoured kinsman John Driden' (1700) l. 92

17 Even victors are by victories undone.
Epistle 'To my honoured kinsman John Driden' (1700)
l. 164

18 For he was great, ere fortune made him so.
Heroic Stanzas (1659, on the death of Oliver Cromwell) st. 6

19 And doomed to death, though fated not to die.
The Hind and the Panther (1687) pt. 1, l. 8

20 For truth has such a face and such a mien
As to be loved needs only to be seen.
The Hind and the Panther (1687) pt. 1, l. 33

21 My manhood, long misled by wandering fires,
Followed false lights; and when their glimpse was
gone
My pride struck out new sparkles of her own . . .
Good life be now my task: my doubts are done;
(What more could fright my faith than Three in One?)
The Hind and the Panther (1687) pt. 1, l. 72

22 Reason to rule, but mercy to forgive:
The first is law, the last prerogative.
The Hind and the Panther (1687) pt. 1, l. 261

23 Either be wholly slaves or wholly free.
The Hind and the Panther (1687) pt. 2, l. 285

24 Much malice mingled with a little wit
Perhaps may censure this mysterious writ.
The Hind and the Panther (1687) pt. 3, l. 1

25 For present joys are more to flesh and blood
Than a dull prospect of a distant good.
The Hind and the Panther (1687) pt. 3, l. 364

26 By education most have been misled;
So they believe, because they so were bred.
The priest continues what the nurse began,
And thus the child imposes on the man.
The Hind and the Panther (1687) pt. 3, l. 389

27 T'abhor the makers, and their laws approve,
Is to hate traitors and the treason love.
The Hind and the Panther (1687) pt. 3, l. 706. Cf. Augustine
37:8, Dryden 260:13

28 For those whom God to ruin has designed,
He fits for fate, and first destroys their mind.
The Hind and the Panther (1687) pt. 3, l. 1093. Cf.
Anonymous 21:15, Duport 264:8

29 And love's the noblest frailty of the mind.
The Indian Emperor (1665) act 2, sc. 2. Cf. Shadwell
563:14 l

30 Repentance is the virtue of weak minds.
The Indian Emperor (1665) act 3, sc. 1

31 For all the happiness mankind can gain
Is not in pleasure, but in rest from pain.
The Indian Emperor (1665) act 4, sc. 1

32 That fairy kind of writing which depends only upon
the force of imagination.
King Arthur (1691) dedication

33 War is the trade of kings.
King Arthur (1691) act 2, sc. 2

34 Fairest Isle, all isles excelling,
Seat of pleasures, and of loves;
Venus here will choose her dwelling,
And forsake her Cyprian groves.
King Arthur (1691) act 5 'Song of Venus'

35 Ovid, the soft philosopher of love.
Love Triumphant (1694) act 2, sc. 1

36 Thou tyrant, tyrant Jealousy,
Thou tyrant of the mind!
Love Triumphant (1694) act 3, sc. 1 'Song of Jealousy'

1 All human things are subject to decay,
And, when fate summons, monarchs must obey.
MacFlecknoe (1682) l. 1

2 The rest to some faint meaning make pretence,
But Shadwell never deviates into sense.
Some beams of wit on other souls may fall,
Strike through and make a lucid interval;
But Shadwell's genuine night admits no ray,
His rising fogs prevail upon the day.
MacFlecknoe (1682) l. 19

3 Thy genius calls thee not to purchase fame
In keen iambics, but mild anagram:
Leave writing plays, and choose for thy command
Some peaceful province in Acrostic Land.
There thou mayest wings display and altars raise,
And torture one poor word ten thousand ways.
MacFlecknoe (1682) l. 203

4 I am resolved to grow fat and look young till forty,
and then slip out of the world with the first wrinkle
and the reputation of five-and-twenty.
The Maiden Queen (1668) act 3, sc. 1

5 I am to be married within these three days; married
past redemption.
Marriage à la Mode (1672) act 1, sc. 1

6 We loathe our manna, and we long for quails.
The Medal (1682) l. 131

7 But treason is not owned when 'tis descried;
Successful crimes alone are justified.
The Medal (1682) l. 207

8 Whatever is, is in its causes just.
Oedipus (with Nathaniel Lee, 1679) act 3, sc. 1

9 But love's a malady without a cure.
Palamon and Arcite (1700) bk. 2, l. 110

10 Fool, not to know that love endures no tie,
And Jove but laughs at lovers' perjury.
Palamon and Arcite (1700) bk. 2, l. 148. Cf. Ovid 502:14

11 And Antony, who lost the world for love.
Palamon and Arcite (1700) bk. 2, l. 607

12 Repentance is but want of power to sin.
Palamon and Arcite (1700) bk. 3, l. 813

13 Since every man who lives is born to die,
And none can boast sincere felicity,
With equal mind, what happens, let us bear,
Nor joy nor grieve too much for things beyond our
care.
Like pilgrims to th'appointed place we tend;
The world's an inn, and death the journey's end.
Palamon and Arcite (1700) bk. 3, l. 883

14 A virgin-widow, and a *mourning bride*.
Palamon and Arcite (1700) bk. 3, l. 927

15 But 'tis the talent of our English nation,
Still to be plotting some new reformation.
'The Prologue at Oxford, 1680' (prologue to Nathaniel Lee
Sophonisba, 2nd ed., 1681)

16 So poetry, which is in Oxford made
An art, in London only is a trade.
'Prologue to the University of Oxon . . . at the Acting of *The
Silent Woman*' (1673)

17 And this unpolished rugged verse I chose
As fittest for discourse and nearest prose.
Religio Laici (1682) l. 453

18 I strongly wish for what I faintly hope:
Like the day-dreams of melancholy men,
I think and think on things impossible,
Yet love to wander in that golden maze.
The Rival Ladies (1664) act 3, sc. 1

19 A very merry, dancing, drinking,
Laughing, quaffing, and unthinking time.
The Secular Masque (1700) l. 39

20 Joy ruled the day, and Love the night.
The Secular Masque (1700) l. 81

21 All, all of a piece throughout;
Thy chase had a beast in view;
Thy wars brought nothing about;
Thy lovers were all untrue.
'Tis well an old age is out,
And time to begin a new.
The Secular Masque (1700) l. 92

22 For secrets are edged tools,
And must be kept from children and from fools.
Sir Martin Mar-All (1667) act 2, sc. 2

23 From harmony, from heavenly harmony
This universal frame began:
From harmony to harmony
Through all the compass of the notes it ran,
The diapason closing full in Man.
A Song for St Cecilia's Day (1687) st. 1

24 What passion cannot Music raise and quell?
A Song for St Cecilia's Day (1687) st. 2

25 The soft complaining flute.
A Song for St Cecilia's Day (1687) st. 4

26 The trumpet shall be heard on high,
The dead shall live, the living die,
And Music shall untune the sky.
A Song for St Cecilia's Day (1687) 'Grand Chorus'

27   There is a pleasure sure,
In being mad, which none but madmen know!
The Spanish Friar (1681) act 1, sc. 1

28 And, dying, bless the hand that gave the blow.
The Spanish Friar (1681) act 2, sc. 2

29 Mute and magnificent, without a tear.
Threnodia Augustalis (1685) st. 2

30 Freedom which in no other land will thrive,
Freedom an English subject's sole prerogative.
Threnodia Augustalis (1685) st. 10

31   Wit will shine
Through the harsh cadence of a rugged line.
'To the Memory of Mr Oldham' (1684)

32 Thou youngest virgin-daughter of the skies,
Made in the last promotion of the blest.
'To the pious Memory of . . . Mrs Anne Killigrew'
(1686) l. 1

33 And he, who servilely creeps after sense,
Is safe, but ne'er will reach an excellence.
Tyrannic Love (1669) prologue

34 All delays are dangerous in war.
Tyrannic Love (1669) act 1, sc. 1

35 Pains of love be sweeter far
Than all other pleasures are.
Tyrannic Love (1669) act 4, sc. 1

1 Happy the man, and happy he alone,
  He, who can call to-day his own:
  He who, secure within, can say,
  To-morrow do thy worst, for I have lived to-day.
  Translation of Horace *Odes* bk. 3, no. 29. Cf. Smith
  653:19 |

2 Not Heaven itself upon the past has power;
  But what has been, has been, and I have had my
  hour.
  Translation of Horace *Odes* bk. 3, no. 29

3 I can enjoy her while she's kind;
  But when she dances in the wind,
  And shakes the wings, and will not stay,
  I puff the prostitute away.
  Translation of Horace *Odes* bk. 3, no. 29 (of Fortune)

4 Look round the habitable world! how few
  Know their own good; or knowing it, pursue.
  Translation of Juvenal *Satires* no. 10

5 To see and be seen, in heaps they run;
  Some to undo, and some to be undone.
  Translation of Ovid *The Art of Love* bk. 1, l. 109

6 She knows her man, and when you rant and swear,
  Can draw you to her *with a single hair.*
  Translation of Persius *Satires* no. 5, l. 246

7 Arms, and the man I sing, who, forced by fate,
  And haughty Juno's unrelenting hate,
  Expelled and exiled, left the Trojan shore.
  Translation of Virgil *Aeneid* (*Aeneis*, 1697) bk. 1, l. 1.
  Cf. Virgil 711:18

8 We must beat the iron while it is hot, but we may
  polish it at leisure.
  Aeneis (1697) dedication

9 Every age has a kind of universal genius, which
  inclines those that live in it to some particular studies.
  An Essay of Dramatic Poesy (1668)

10 A thing well said will be wit in all languages.
  An Essay of Dramatic Poesy (1668)

11 He was the man who of all modern, and perhaps
  ancient poets, had the largest and most comprehensive
  soul . . . He was naturally learn'd; he needed not the
  spectacles of books to read Nature: he looked inwards,
  and found her there . . . He is many times flat, insipid;
  his comic wit degenerating into clenches, his serious
  swelling into bombast. But he is always great.
  An Essay of Dramatic Poesy (1668) on Shakespeare

12 He invades authors like a monarch; and what would
  be theft in other poets, is only victory in him.
  An Essay of Dramatic Poesy (1668) on Ben Jonson

13 If by the people you understand the multitude, the *hoi
  polloi*, 'tis no matter what they think; they are
  sometimes in the right, sometimes in the wrong: their
  judgement is a mere lottery.
  An Essay of Dramatic Poesy (1668)

14 [Shakespeare] is the very Janus of poets; he wears
  almost everywhere two faces; and you have scarce
  begun to admire the one, ere you despise the other.
  Essay on the Dramatic Poetry of the Last Age (1672)

15 What judgement I had increases rather than
  diminishes; and thoughts, such as they are, come
  crowding in so fast upon me, that my only difficulty is
  to choose or reject; to run them into verse or to give
  them the other harmony of prose.
  Fables Ancient and Modern (1700) preface

16 'Tis sufficient to say [of Chaucer], according to the
  proverb, that here is God's plenty.
  Fables Ancient and Modern (1700) preface

17 [Chaucer] is a perpetual fountain of good sense.
  Fables Ancient and Modern (1700) preface

18 One of our late great poets is sunk in his reputation,
  because he could never forgive any conceit which
  came in his way; but swept like a drag-net, great and
  small. There was plenty enough, but the dishes were
  ill-sorted; whole pyramids of sweetmeats, for boys and
  women; but little of solid meat for men.
  Fables Ancient and Modern (1700) preface (on Abraham
  Cowley)

19 Sure the poet . . . spewed up a good lump of clotted
  nonsense at once.
  Notes and Observations on the Empress of Morocco [by
  Elkanah Settle] (1674) 'The First Act'

20 How easy it is to call rogue and villain, and that
  wittily! But how hard to make a man appear a fool, a
  blockhead, or a knave, without using any of those
  opprobrious terms! To spare the grossness of the
  names, and to do the thing yet more severely, is to
  draw a full face, and to make the nose and cheeks
  stand out, and yet not to employ any depth of
  shadowing.
  Of Satire (1693)

21 A man may be capable, as Jack Ketch's wife said of his
  servant, of a plain piece of work, a bare hanging; but
  to make a malefactor die sweetly was only belonging
  to her husband.
  Of Satire (1693)

Alexander Dubček 1921–
*Czechoslovak politician; First Secretary of the
Czechoslovak Communist Party, 1968*

22 *Ve službách lidu dělali takovou politiku, aby socialismus
  neztrácel svou lidskou tvář.*

  In the service of the people we followed such a policy
  that socialism would not lose its human face.
  In *Rudé Právo* 19 July 1968. A resolution by the party
  group in the Ministry of Foreign Affairs, 1968, referred to
  Czechoslovakian foreign policy acquiring 'its own defined
  face'; in *Rudé Právo* 14 March 1968

Joachim Du Bellay 1522–60
French poet

23 *France, mère des arts, des armes et des lois.*

  France, mother of arts, of warfare, and of laws.
  Les Regrets (1558) Sonnet no. 9

262

1 *Heureux qui comme Ulysse a fait un beau voyage*
Ou comme celui-là qui conquit la toison,
Et puis est retourné, plein d'usage et raison,
Vivre entre ses parents le reste de son âge!

Happy he who like Ulysses has made a great journey,
or like that man who won the Fleece and then came
home, full of experience and good sense, to live the
rest of his time among his family!
    Les Regrets (1558) Sonnet no. 31

2 *Plus que le marbre dur me plaît l'ardoise fine,*
Plus mon Loire Gaulois, que le Tibre Latin,
Plus mon petit Lyré, que le mont Palatin,
Et plus que l'air marin la douceur angevine.

I love thin slate more than hard marble, my Gallic
Loire more than the Latin Tiber, my little Liré more
than the Palatine Hill, and more than the sea air the
sweetness of Anjou.
    Les Regrets (1558) Sonnet no. 31

W. E. B. Du Bois 1868–1963

American social reformer and political activist

3 One thing alone I charge you. As you live, believe in
life! Always human beings will live and progress to
greater, broader and fuller life. The only possible death
is to lose belief in this truth simply because the great
end comes slowly, because time is long.
    Last message, written 26 June, 1957, and read at his
    funeral, 1963, in *Journal of Negro History* April 1964

4 The problem of the twentieth century is the problem of
the colour line—the relation of the darker to the
lighter races of men in Asia and Africa, in America
and the islands of the sea.
    The Souls of Black Folk (1905) ch. 2

5 Herein lies the tragedy of the age: not that men are
poor . . . not that men are wicked . . . but that men
know so little of men.
    The Souls of Black Folk (1905) ch. 12

Stephen Duck 1705–56

English poet and clergyman

6 Let those who feast at ease on dainty fare,
Pity the reapers, who their feasts prepare.
    'The Thresher's Labour' (1730)

7 Like Sisyphus, our work is never done;
Continually rolls back the restless stone.
    'The Thresher's Labour' (1730)

Mme Du Deffand (Marie de Vichy-Chamrond) 1697–1780

French literary hostess

8 *La distance n'y fait rien; il n'y a que le premier pas qui
coûte.*

The distance is nothing; it is only the first step that is
difficult.
    Commenting on the legend that St Denis, carrying his head
    in his hands, walked two leagues: letter to Jean Le Rond
    d'Alembert, 7 July 1763, in Gaston Maugras *Trois mois à la
    cour de Frédéric* (1886) p. 28

George Duffield 1818–88

American Presbyterian minister

9 Stand up!—stand up for Jesus!
Ye soldiers of the Cross.
    'Stand Up, Stand Up for Jesus' (1858 hymn); the opening
    line inspired by the dying words of the American evangelist,
    Dudley Atkins Tyng, to Duffield: 'Tell them to stand up for
    Jesus'

Georges Duhamel 1884–1966

French novelist

10 *Je respecte trop l'idée de Dieu pour la rendre responsable
d'un monde aussi absurde.*

I have too much respect for the idea of God to make it
responsible for such an absurd world.
    Le désert de Bièvres (1937) in *Chronique des Pasquier* (1948)
    vol. 5, p. 249

John Foster Dulles 1888–1959

American international lawyer and politician

11 You have to take chances for peace, just as you must
take chances in war. Some say that we were brought
to the verge of war. Of course we were brought to the
verge of war. The ability to get to the verge without
getting into the war is the necessary art. If you cannot
master it, you inevitably get into war. If you try to
run away from it, if you are scared to go to the brink,
you are lost. We've had to look it square in the face
— on the question of enlarging the Korean war, on
the question of getting into the Indochina war, on the
question of Formosa. We walked to the brink and we
looked it in the face.
    In *Life* 16 January 1956

Alexandre Dumas ('Dumas père') 1802–70

French novelist and playwright

12 *Cherchons la femme.*

Let us look for the woman.
    Les Mohicans de Paris (1854–5) *passim*; attributed to Joseph
    Fouché (1763–1820) in the form '*Cherchez la femme*'

13 *Tous pour un, un pour tous.*

All for one, one for all.
    Les Trois Mousquetaires (1844) ch. 9.

Dame Daphne Du Maurier 1907–89

English novelist

14 Last night I dreamt I went to Manderley again.
    Rebecca (1938) ch. 1

Charles François du Périer Dumouriez
1739–1823
French general

1 *Les courtisans qui l'entourent n'ont rien oublié et n'ont rien appris.*

The courtiers who surround him have forgotten nothing and learnt nothing.

> Of Louis XVIII, at the time of the Declaration of Verona, September 1795, in *Examen impartial d'un Écrit intitulé Déclaration de Louis XVIII* (1795) p. 40; quoted by Napoleon in his Declaration to the French on his return from Elba

Paul Lawrence Dunbar 1872–1906
American poet

2 I know why the caged bird sings!
> 'Sympathy' st. 3 (adopted by Maya Angelou as the title of her autobiography, 1969). Cf. Webster 726:9

William Dunbar *c*.1465–*c*.1513
Scottish poet and priest

3 I that in heill wes and gladnes
Am trublit now with gret seiknes
And feblit with infirmitie:
Timor mortis conturbat me.
> 'Lament for the Makaris' (*makaris* makers, i.e. poets)

4 All love is lost but upon God alone.
> 'The Merle and the Nightingale' st. 2

Isadora Duncan 1878–1927
American dancer

5 *Adieu, mes amis. Je vais à la gloire.*

Farewell, my friends. I go to glory.
> Last words before her scarf caught in a car wheel, breaking her neck; in Mary Desti *Isadora Duncan's End* (1929) ch. 25

Ian Dunlop 1925–
British art historian

6 The shock of the new: seven historic exhibitions of modern art.
> Title of book (1972)

John Dunning (Baron Ashburton) 1731–83
English lawyer and politician

7 The influence of the Crown has increased, is increasing, and ought to be diminished.
> Resolution passed in the House of Commons, 6 April 1780, in *Parliamentary History of England* (T. C. Hansard, 1814) vol. 21, col. 347

James Duport 1606–79
English Hellenist

8 *Quem Jupiter vult perdere, dementat prius.*

Whom God would destroy He first sends mad.
> *Homeri Gnomologia* (1660) p. 282. Cf. Anonymous 21:15

Richard Duppa 1770–1831
English artist and writer

9 In language, the ignorant have prescribed laws to the learned.
> *Maxims* (1830) no. 252

Ray Durem 1915–63
American poet

10 Some of my best friends are white boys.
when I meet 'em
I treat 'em
just the same as if they was people.
> 'Broadminded' (written 1951)

Leo Durocher 1906–91
American baseball coach

11 I called off his players' names as they came marching up the steps behind him . . . All nice guys. They'll finish last. Nice guys. Finish last.
> Casual remark at a practice ground in the presence of a number of journalists, July 1946: in *Nice Guys Finish Last* (as the remark generally is quoted, 1975) pt. 1, p. 14

Ian Dury 1942–
British rock singer and songwriter

12 Sex and drugs and rock and roll.
> Title of song (1977)

13 I could be the catalyst that sparks the revolution.
I could be an inmate in a long term institution
I could lean to wild extremes I could do or die,
I could yawn and be withdrawn and watch them gallop by,
What a waste, what a waste, what a waste, what a waste.
> 'What a Waste' (1978 song)

Sir Edward Dyer d. 1607
English poet

14 Silence augmenteth grief, writing increaseth rage,
Staled are my thoughts, which loved and lost, the wonder of our age,
Yet quickened now with fire, though dead with frost ere now,
Enraged I write, I know not what: dead, quick, I know not how.
> 'Elegy on the Death of Sir Philip Sidney' (1593) (previously attributed to Fulke Greville, 1554–1628)

15 My mind to me a kingdom is.
Such perfect joy therein I find
That it excels all other bliss
That world affords or grows by kind.
Though much I want which most would have,
Yet still my mind forbids to crave.
> 'In praise of a contented mind' (1588). Attributed

1 Some have too much, yet still do crave;
I little have, and seek no more.
They are but poor, though much they have,
And I am rich with little store.
They poor, I rich; they beg, I give;
They lack, I leave; they pine, I live.
    'In praise of a contented mind' (1588)

John Dyer 1700–58

Welsh clergyman and poet

2 The care of sheep, the labours of the loom,
And arts of trade, I sing.
    The Fleece (1757) bk. 1, l. 1

3   The younger hands
Ply at the easy work of winding yarn
On swiftly-circling engines, and their notes
Warble together as a choir of larks:
Such joy arises in the mind employed.
    The Fleece (1757) bk. 3, l. 281

4   Industry,
Which dignifies the artist, lifts the swain,
And the straw cottage to a palace turns.
    The Fleece (1757) bk. 3, l. 332

5 While, ever and anon, there falls
Huge heaps of hoary, mouldered walls.
    Grongar Hill (1726) l. 82

6 But transient is the smile of fate:
A little rule, a little sway,
A sunbeam in a winter's day,
Is all the proud and mighty have
Between the cradle and the grave.
    Grongar Hill (1726) l. 88

7 The town and village, dome and farm,
Each give each a double charm,
As pearls upon an Ethiop's arm.
    Grongar Hill (1726) l. 111

8   The pilgrim oft
At dead of night, mid his orison hears
Aghast the voice of Time, disparting tow'rs.
    The Ruins of Rome (1740) l. 38

John Dyer

English poet

9 And he that will this health deny,
Down among the dead men let him lie.
    'Down among the Dead Men' (c.1700)

Bob Dylan (*Robert Zimmerman*) 1941–

American singer and songwriter

10 I ain't lookin' to block you up,
Shock or knock or lock you up,
Analyze you, categorize you,
Finalize you or advertise you.
    'All I Really Want To Do' (1964 song)

11 How many roads must a man walk down
Before you can call him a man? . . .
The answer, my friend, is blowin' in the wind,
The answer is blowin' in the wind.
    'Blowin' in the Wind' (1962 song)

12 Praise be to Nero's Neptune
The Titanic sails at dawn
And everybody's shouting
'Which Side Are You On?'
And Ezra Pound and T. S. Eliot
Fighting in the captain's tower
While calypso singers laugh at them
And fishermen hold flowers.
    'Desolation Row' (1965 song)

13 I ain't sayin' you treated me unkind
You could have done better but I don't mind
You just kinda wasted my precious time
But don't think twice, it's all right.
    'Don't Think Twice, It's All Right' (1963 song)

14 The motorcycle black madonna
Two-wheeled gypsy queen.
    'Gates of Eden' (1965 song)

15 I saw ten thousand talkers whose tongues were all
    broken,
I saw guns and sharp swords, in the hands of young
    children . . .
And it's a hard rain's a gonna fall.
    'A Hard Rain's A Gonna Fall' (1963 song)

16 Money doesn't talk, it swears.
    'It's Alright, Ma (I'm Only Bleeding)' (1965 song)

17 She knows there's no success like failure
And that failure's no success at all.
    'Love Minus Zero / No Limit' (1965 song)

18 Hey! Mr Tambourine Man, play a song for me.
I'm not sleepy and there is no place I'm going to.
    'Mr Tambourine Man' (1965 song)

19 Ah, but I was so much older then,
I'm younger than that now.
    'My Back Pages' (1964 song)

20 Señor, señor, do you know where we're headin'?
Lincoln County Road or Armageddon?
    'Señor (Tale of Yankee Power)' (1978 song)

21 All that foreign oil controlling American soil.
    'Slow Train' (1979 song)

22 Don't follow leaders
Watch the parkin' meters.
    'Subterranean Homesick Blues' (1965 song)

23 Come mothers and fathers,
Throughout the land
And don't criticize
What you can't understand.
Your sons and your daughters
Are beyond your command
Your old road is
Rapidly agin'
Please get out of the new one
If you can't lend your hand
For the times they are a-changin'!
    'The Times They Are A-Changing' (1964 song)

24 But I can't think for you
You'll have to decide,
Whether Judas Iscariot
Had God on his side.
    'With God on our Side' (1963 song)

Abba Eban 1915–

Israeli diplomat

1 History teaches us that men and nations behave
wisely once they have exhausted all other alternatives.
  Speech in London, 16 December 1970, in *The Times*
  17 December 1970

Sir Arthur Eddington 1882–1944

British astrophysicist

2 Let us draw an arrow arbitrarily. If as we follow the
arrow we find more and more of the random element
in the world, then the arrow is pointing towards the
future; if the random element decreases the arrow
points towards the past . . . I shall use the phrase
'time's arrow' to express this one-way property of time
which has no analogue in space.
  The Nature of the Physical World (1928) ch. 4

3 If someone points out to you that your pet theory of
the universe is in disagreement with Maxwell's
equations—then so much the worse for Maxwell's
equations. If it is found to be contradicted by
observation—well, these experimentalists do bungle
things sometimes. But if your theory is found to be
against the second law of thermodynamics I can give
you no hope; there is nothing for it but to collapse in
deepest humiliation.
  The Nature of the Physical World (1928) ch. 14

4 I am standing on the threshold about to enter a room.
It is a complicated business. In the first place I must
shove against an atmosphere pressing with a force of
fourteen pounds on every square inch of my body. I
must make sure of landing on a plank travelling at
twenty miles a second round the sun—a fraction of a
second too early or too late, the plank would be miles
away. I must do this whilst hanging from a round
planet, head outward into space, and with a wind of
aether blowing at no one knows how many miles a
second through every interstice of my body.
  The Nature of the Physical World (1928) ch. 15

5 I ask you to look both ways. For the road to a
knowledge of the stars leads through the atom; and
important knowledge of the atom has been reached
through the stars.
  Stars and Atoms (1928) Lecture 1

6 Science is one thing, wisdom is another. Science is an
edged tool, with which men play like children, and cut
their own fingers.
  Attributed in Robert L. Weber *More Random Walks in
  Science* (1982) p. 48

Sir Anthony Eden (Earl of Avon)
1897–1977

British Conservative politician; Prime Minister, 1955–7

7 We are in an armed conflict; that is the phrase I have
used. There has been no declaration of war.
  Speech, *Hansard* 1 November 1956, col. 1641 (on the Suez
  crisis)

Marriott Edgar 1880–1951

8 There's a famous seaside place called Blackpool,
That's noted for fresh air and fun,
And Mr and Mrs Ramsbottom
Went there with young Albert, their son.
  'The Lion and Albert' (1932)

Maria Edgeworth 1768–1849

Anglo-Irish novelist

9 Well! some people talk of morality, and some of
religion, but give me a little snug property.
  The Absentee (1812) ch. 2

10 To be sure a love match was the only thing for
happiness, where the parties could any way afford it.
  Castle Rackrent (1800) 'Continuation of Memoirs'

11 Come when you're called;
And do as you're bid;
Shut the door after you;
And you'll never be chid.
  The Contrast (1804) ch. 1

12 Business was his aversion; pleasure was his business.
  The Contrast (1804) ch. 2

13 What a misfortune it is to be born a woman! . . . Why
seek for knowledge, which can prove only that our
wretchedness is irremediable? If a ray of light break in
upon us, it is but to make darkness more visible; to
show us the new limits, the Gothic structure, the
impenetrable barriers of our prison.
  Leonora (1806) Letter 1

14 Possessed, as are all the fair daughters of Eve, of an
hereditary propensity, transmitted to them
undiminished through succeeding generations, to be
'soon moved with the slightest touch of blame'; very
little precept and practice will confirm them in the
habit, and instruct them in all the maxims, of
self-justification.
  Letters for Literary Ladies (1795) 'An Essay on the Noble
  Science of Self-Justification'

15 Man is to be held only by the *slightest* chains, with the
idea that he can break them at pleasure, he submits to
them in sport.
  Letters for Literary Ladies (1795) 'Letters of Julia and
  Caroline' no. 1

Thomas Alva Edison 1847–1931

American inventor

16 Genius is one per cent inspiration, ninety-nine per
cent perspiration.
  Said *c*.1903, in *Harper's Monthly Magazine* September 1932.
  Cf. Buffon 154:16

James Edmeston 1791–1867

English architect and hymn-writer

17 Lead us, Heavenly Father, lead us
O'er the world's tempestuous sea;
Guard us, guide us, keep us, feed us,
For we have no help but Thee;
Yet possessing every blessing,
If our God our Father be.
  'Lead us, heavenly Father, lead us' (1821)

John Maxwell Edmonds 1875–1958

English classicist

1 When you go home, tell them of us and say,
'For your tomorrows these gave their today.'
Inscriptions Suggested for War Memorials (1919)

Edward III 1312–77

King of England from 1327

2 Also say to them, that they suffre hym this day to
wynne his spurres, for if god be pleased, I woll this
journey be his, and the honoure therof.
Speaking of the Black Prince at Crécy, 1345 (commonly
quoted 'Let the boy win his spurs'), in *The Chronicle of
Froissart* (translated by Sir John Bourchier, Lord Berners,
1523–5) ch. 130

Edward VII 1841–1910

King of the United Kingdom from 1901

3 I thought everyone must know that a *short* jacket is
always worn with a silk hat at a private view in the
morning.
To Sir Frederick Ponsonby, who had proposed
accompanying him in a tail-coat; in Sir Philip Magnus
Edward VII (1964) ch. 19

Edward VIII (Duke of Windsor) 1894–1972

King of the United Kingdom, 1936

4 These works brought all these people here. Something
should be done to get them at work again.
Speaking at the derelict Dowlais Iron and Steel Works,
18 November 1936, in *Western Mail* 19 November 1936
(generally quoted 'Something must be done')

5 At long last I am able to say a few words of my own
... you must believe me when I tell you that I have
found it impossible to carry the heavy burden of
responsibility and to discharge my duties as King as I
would wish to do without the help and support of the
woman I love.
Radio broadcast following his abdication, 11 December
1936, in *The Times* 12 December 1936

6 The thing that impresses me most about America is
the way parents obey their children.
Look 5 March 1957

Jonathan Edwards 1703–58

American theologian

7 Of all Insects no one is more wonderful than the spider
especially with Respect to their sagacity and admirable
way of working ... I ... once saw a very large spider
to my surprise swimming in the air ... and others
have assured me that they often have seen spiders fly,
the appearance is truly very pretty and pleasing.
*The Flying Spider—Observations by Jonathan Edwards when a
boy* 'Of Insects' in *Andover Review* vol. 13 (1890) p. 5

8 The bodies of those that made such a noise and
tumult when alive, when dead, lie as quietly among
the graves of their neighbours as any others.
Sermon on procrastination (*Miscellaneous Discourses*) in
Works (1834) vol. 2, p. 241

Oliver Edwards 1711–91

English lawyer

9 I have tried too in my time to be a philosopher; but, I
don't know how, cheerfulness was always breaking in.
In James Boswell *Life of Samuel Johnson* (1934 ed.) vol. 3,
p. 305 (17 April 1778)

10 For my part now, I consider supper as a turnpike
through which one must pass, in order to get to bed.
In James Boswell *Life of Samuel Johnson* (1934 ed.) vol. 3,
p. 306 (17 April 1778). Boswell notes: 'I am not absolutely
sure but this was my own suggestion, though it is truly in
the character of Edwards'

Richard Edwards c.1523–66

English poet and playwright

11 In going to my naked bed, as one that would have
slept,
I heard a wife sing to her child, that long before had
wept.
She sighed sore, and sang full sweet, to bring the babe
to rest,
That would not cease, but cried still in sucking at her
breast.
She was full weary of her watch and grieved with her
child,
She rocked it, and rated it, till that on her it smiled.
Then did she say, 'Now have I found this proverb true
to prove:
The falling out of faithful friends, renewing is of love.'
The Paradise of Dainty Devices (1576) 'Amantium Irae'

Sarah Egerton 1670–1723

English poet

12 From the first dawn of life unto the grave,
Poor womankind's in every state a slave.
'The Emulation' (1703)

13 We will our rights in learning's world maintain;
Wit's empire now shall know a female reign.
'The Emulation' (1703)

John Ehrlichman 1925–

Presidential assistant to Richard Nixon

14 I think we ought to let him hang there. Let him twist
slowly, slowly in the wind.
Speaking of Patrick Gray (regarding his nomination as
director of the FBI) in a telephone conversation with John
Dean; in *Washington Post* 27 July 1973, p. A27

Albert Einstein 1879–1955

German-born theoretical physicist; originator of the theory of relativity

1 *Raffiniert ist der Herrgott, aber boshaft ist er nicht.*

God is subtle but he is not malicious.

Remark made at Princeton University, May 1921, in R. W. Clark *Einstein* (1973) ch. 14

2 *Jedenfalls bin ich überzeugt, dass der nicht würfelt.*

At any rate, I am convinced that *He* [God] does not play dice.

Letter to Max Born, 4 December 1926; in *Einstein und Born Briefwechsel* (1969) p. 130 (often quoted: '*Gott würfelt nicht* [God does not play dice]')

3 If my theory of relativity is proven correct, Germany will claim me as a German and France will declare that I am a citizen of the world. Should my theory prove untrue, France will say that I am a German and Germany will declare that I am a Jew.

Address at the Sorbonne, Paris, possibly early December 1929, in *New York Times* 16 February 1930

4 The unleashed power of the atom has changed everything save our modes of thinking and we thus drift toward unparalleled catastrophe.

Telegram to prominent Americans, 24 May 1946, in *New York Times* 25 May 1946

5 If *A* is a success in life, then *A* equals *x* plus *y* plus *z*. Work is *x*; *y* is play; and *z* is keeping your mouth shut.

In *Observer* 15 January 1950

6 Science without religion is lame, religion without science is blind.

Science, Philosophy and Religion: a Symposium (1941) ch. 13

7 Equations are more important to me, because politics is for the present, but an equation is something for eternity.

In Stephen Hawking *A Brief History of Time* (1988) p. 178. See also C. P. Snow 'Einstein' in M. Goldsmith et al. (eds.) *Einstein* (1980) p. 17

8 Nationalism is an infantile sickness. It is the measles of the human race.

In Helen Dukas and Banesh Hoffman *Albert Einstein, the Human Side* (1979) p. 38

9 I never think of the future. It comes soon enough.

In an interview, given on the *Belgenland*, December 1930

Dwight D. Eisenhower 1890–1969

34th President of the USA

10 Every gun that is made, every warship launched, every rocket fired signifies, in the final sense, a theft from those who hunger and are not fed, those who are cold and are not clothed. This world in arms is not spending money alone. It is spending the sweat of its labourers, the genius of its scientists, the hopes of its children.

Speech in Washington, 16 April 1953, in *Public Papers of Presidents 1953* (1960) p. 182

11 You have broader considerations that might follow what you might call the 'falling domino' principle. You have a row of dominoes set up. You knock over the first one, and what will happen to the last one is that it will go over very quickly. So you have the beginning of a disintegration that would have the most profound influences.

Speech at press conference, 7 April 1954, in *Public Papers of Presidents 1954* (1960) p. 383

12 I think that people want peace so much that one of these days governments had better get out of the way and let them have it.

Broadcast discussion, 31 August 1959, in *Public Papers of Presidents 1959* (1960) p. 625

Sir Edward Elgar 1857–1934

English composer

13 To my friends pictured within.

Enigma Variations (1899) dedication

14 There is music in the air

In R. J. Buckley *Sir Edward Elgar* (1905) ch. 4

George Eliot (Mary Ann Evans) 1819–80

English novelist

15 Our deeds determine us, as much as we determine our deeds; and until we know what has been or will be the peculiar combination of outward with inward facts, which constitute a man's critical actions, it will be better not to think ourselves wise about his character.

Adam Bede (1859) ch. 29

16 A maggot must be born i' the rotten cheese to like it.

Adam Bede (1859) ch. 32

17 He was like a cock who thought the sun had risen to hear him crow.

Adam Bede (1859) ch. 33

18 Deep, unspeakable suffering may well be called a baptism, a regeneration, the initiation into a new state.

Adam Bede (1859) ch. 42

19 We hand folks over to God's mercy, and show none ourselves.

Adam Bede (1859) ch. 42

20 The mother's yearning, that completest type of the life in another life which is the essence of real human love, feels the presence of the cherished child even in the debased, degraded man.

Adam Bede (1859) ch. 43

21 Gossip is a sort of smoke that comes from the dirty tobacco-pipes of those who diffuse it: it proves nothing but the bad taste of the smoker.

Daniel Deronda (1876) bk. 2, ch. 13

22 A difference of taste in jokes is a great strain on the affections.

Daniel Deronda (1876) bk. 2, ch. 15

23 There is a great deal of unmapped country within us which would have to be taken into account in an explanation of our gusts and storms.

Daniel Deronda (1876) bk. 3, ch. 24

1 Friendships begin with liking or gratitude—roots that can be pulled up.
  Daniel Deronda (1876) bk. 4, ch. 32

2 Half the sorrows of women would be averted if they could repress the speech they know to be useless; nay, the speech they have resolved not to make.
  Felix Holt (1866) ch. 2

3 There is no private life which has not been determined by a wider public life.
  Felix Holt (1866) ch. 3

4 An election is coming. Universal peace is declared, and the foxes have a sincere interest in prolonging the lives of the poultry.
  Felix Holt (1866) ch. 5

5 A little daily embroidery had been a constant element in Mrs Transome's life; that soothing occupation of taking stitches to produce what neither she nor any one else wanted, was then the resource of many a well-born and unhappy woman.
  Felix Holt (1866) ch. 7

6 Speech is often barren; but silence also does not necessarily brood over a full nest. Your still fowl, blinking at you without remark, may all the while be sitting on one addled egg; and when it takes to cackling will have nothing to announce but that addled delusion.
  Felix Holt (1866) ch. 15

7 A woman can hardly ever choose . . . she is dependent on what happens to her. She must take meaner things, because only meaner things are within her reach.
  Felix Holt (1866) ch. 27

8 There's many a one who would be idle if hunger didn't pinch him; but the stomach sets us to work.
  Felix Holt (1866) ch. 30

9 'Abroad', that large home of ruined reputations.
  Felix Holt (1866) epilogue

10 Debasing the moral currency.
  The Impressions of Theophrastus Such (1879) essay title

11 Many Theresas have been born who found for themselves no epic life wherein there was a constant unfolding of far-resonant action; perhaps only a life of mistakes, the offspring of a certain spiritual grandeur ill-matched with the meanness of opportunity; perhaps a tragic failure which found no sacred poet and sank unwept into oblivion.
  Middlemarch (1871–2) Prelude

12 A woman dictates before marriage in order that she may have an appetite for submission afterwards.
  Middlemarch (1871–2) bk. 1, ch. 9

13 He said he should prefer not to know the sources of the Nile, and that there should be some unknown regions preserved as hunting-grounds for the poetic imagination.
  Middlemarch (1871–2) bk. 1, ch. 9

14 Among all forms of mistake, prophecy is the most gratuitous.
  Middlemarch (1871–2) bk. 1, ch. 10

15 Plain women he regarded as he did the other severe facts of life, to be faced with philosophy and investigated by science.
  Middlemarch (1871–2) bk. 1, ch. 11

16 Any one watching keenly the stealthy convergence of human lots, sees a slow preparation of effects from one life on another, which tells like a calculated irony on the indifference or the frozen stare with which we look at our unintroduced neighbour.
  Middlemarch (1871–2) bk. 1, ch. 11

17 If we had a keen vision and feeling of all ordinary human life, it would be like hearing the grass grow and the squirrel's heart beat, and we should die of that roar which lies on the other side of silence.
  Middlemarch (1871–2) bk. 2, ch. 20

18 We do not expect people to be deeply moved by what is not unusual. That element of tragedy which lies in the very fact of frequency, has not yet wrought itself into the coarse emotion of mankind.
  Middlemarch (1871–2) bk. 2, ch. 20

19 A woman, let her be as good as she may, has got to put up with the life her husband makes for her.
  Middlemarch (1871–2) bk. 3, ch. 25

20 It is an uneasy lot at best, to be what we call highly taught and yet not to enjoy: to be present at this great spectacle of life and never to be liberated from a small hungry shivering self.
  Middlemarch (1871–2) bk. 3, ch. 29

21 A man is seldom ashamed of feeling that he cannot love a woman so well when he sees a certain greatness in her: nature having intended greatness for men.
  Middlemarch (1871–2) bk. 4, ch. 39

22 Anger and jealousy can no more bear to lose sight of their objects than love.
  The Mill on the Floss (1860) bk. 1, ch. 10

23 The dead level of provincial existence.
  The Mill on the Floss (1860) bk. 5, ch. 3

24 The happiest women, like the happiest nations, have no history.
  The Mill on the Floss (1860) bk. 6, ch. 3. Cf. Montesquieu 481:17

25 I should like to know what is the proper function of women, if it is not to make reasons for husbands to stay at home, and still stronger reasons for bachelors to go out.
  The Mill on the Floss (1860) bk. 6, ch. 6

26 'Character' says Novalis, in one of his questionable aphorisms—'character is destiny.'
  The Mill on the Floss (1860) bk. 6, ch. 6. Cf. Novalis 497:3

27 In every parting there is an image of death.
  Scenes of Clerical Life (1858) 'Amos Barton' ch. 10

28 Errors look so very ugly in persons of small means—one feels they are taking quite a liberty in going astray; whereas people of fortune may naturally indulge in a few delinquencies.
  Scenes of Clerical Life (1858) 'Janet's Repentance' ch. 25

29 Oh may I join the choir invisible
  Of those immortal dead who live again
  In minds made better by their presence.
  'Oh May I Join the Choir Invisible' (1867)

1 Life is too precious to be spent in this weaving and
unweaving of false impressions, and it is better to live
quietly under some degree of misrepresentation than
to attempt to remove it by the uncertain process of
letter-writing.

> Letter to Mrs Peter Taylor, 8 June 1856, in G. S. Haight
> (ed.) *The George Eliot Letters* vol. 2 (1954) p. 254

2 If art does not enlarge men's sympathies, it does
nothing morally.

> Letter to Charles Bray, 5 July 1859, in G. S. Haight (ed.)
> *The George Eliot Letters* vol. 3 (1954) p. 111

3 The idea of God, so far as it has been a high spiritual
influence, is the ideal of a goodness entirely human.

> Letter to the Hon. Mrs H. F. Ponsonby, 10 December 1874,
> in G. S. Haight (ed.) *The George Eliot Letters* vol. 6 (1956)
> p. 98

4 She, stirred somewhat beyond her wont, and taking as
her text the three words which have been used so
often as the inspiring trumpet-calls of men—the words
God, Immortality, Duty—pronounced, with terrible
earnestness, how inconceivable was the *first*, how
unbelievable the *second*, and yet how peremptory and
absolute the third. Never, perhaps, have sterner
accents affirmed the sovereignty of impersonal and
unrecompensing Law.

> F. W. H. Myers 'George Eliot', in *Century Magazine*
> November 1881

T. S. Eliot (*Thomas Stearns Eliot*)
1888–1965

Anglo-American poet, critic, and playwright

5 Because I do not hope to turn again
Because I do not hope
Because I do not hope to turn.

> *Ash-Wednesday* (1930) pt. 1

6 Because these wings are no longer wings to fly
But merely vans to beat the air
The air which is now thoroughly small and dry
Smaller and dryer than the will
Teach us to care and not to care
Teach us to sit still.

> *Ash-Wednesday* (1930) pt. 1

7 Lady, three white leopards sat under a juniper-tree
In the cool of the day.

> *Ash-Wednesday* (1930) pt. 2

8 You've missed the point completely, Julia:
There *were* no tigers. *That* was the point.

> *The Cocktail Party* (1950) act 1, sc. 1

9 What is hell?
Hell is oneself,
Hell is alone, the other figures in it
Merely projections. There is nothing to escape from
And nothing to escape to. One is always alone.

> *The Cocktail Party* (1950) act 1, sc. 3. Cf. Sartre 556:11

10 Where are the eagles and the trumpets?

Buried beneath some snow-deep Alps.
Over buttered scones and crumpets
Weeping, weeping multitudes
Droop in a hundred A.B.C.'s.

> 'Cooking Egg' (1920)

11 Success is relative:
It is what we can make of the mess we have made of
things.

> *The Family Reunion* (1939) pt. 2, sc. 3

12 Round and round the circle
Completing the charm
So the knot be unknotted
The cross be uncrossed
The crooked be made straight
And the curse be ended.

> *The Family Reunion* (1939) pt. 2, sc. 3

13 Time present and time past
Are both perhaps present in time future,
And time future contained in time past.

> *Four Quartets* 'Burnt Norton' (1936) pt. 1

14 Footfalls echo in the memory
Down the passage which we did not take
Towards the door we never opened
Into the rose-garden. My words echo
Thus, in your mind.

> *Four Quartets* 'Burnt Norton' (1936) pt. 1

15   Human kind
Cannot bear very much reality.

> *Four Quartets* 'Burnt Norton' (1936) pt. 1.

16 At the still point of the turning world. Neither flesh
nor fleshless;
Neither from nor towards; at the still point, there the
dance is,
But neither arrest nor movement.

> *Four Quartets* 'Burnt Norton' (1936) pt. 2

17   Words strain,
Crack and sometimes break, under the burden,
Under the tension, slip, slide, perish,
Decay with imprecision, will not stay in place,
Will not stay still.

> *Four Quartets* 'Burnt Norton' (1936) pt. 5

18 In my beginning is my end.

> *Four Quartets* 'East Coker' (1940) pt. 1. Cf. Mary Stuart
> 452:17

19 That was a way of putting it—not very satisfactory:
A periphrastic study in a worn-out poetical fashion,
Leaving one still with the intolerable wrestle
With words and meanings. The poetry does not
matter.

> *Four Quartets* 'East Coker' (1940) pt. 2

20 The houses are all gone under the sea.
The dancers are all gone under the hill.

> *Four Quartets* 'East Coker' (1940) pt. 2

21 O dark dark dark. They all go into the dark,
The vacant interstellar spaces, the vacant into the
vacant.

> *Four Quartets* 'East Coker' (1940) pt. 3

22 The wounded surgeon plies the steel
That questions the distempered part;
Beneath the bleeding hands we feel
The sharp compassion of the healer's art
Resolving the enigma of the fever chart.

> *Four Quartets* 'East Coker' (1940) pt. 4

1   Each venture
Is a new beginning, a raid on the inarticulate
With shabby equipment always deteriorating
In the general mess of imprecision of feeling.
 Four Quartets 'East Coker' (1940) pt. 5

2 I do not know much about gods; but I think that the
   river
Is a strong brown god—sullen, untamed and
   intractable.
 Four Quartets 'The Dry Salvages' (1941) pt. 1

3 And what the dead had no speech for, when living,
They can tell you, being dead: the communication
Of the dead is tongued with fire beyond the language
   of the living.
 Four Quartets 'Little Gidding' (1942) pt. 1

4 Ash on an old man's sleeve
Is all the ash the burnt roses leave.
Dust in the air suspended
Marks the place where a story ended.
Dust inbreathed was a house—
The wall, the wainscot and the mouse.
The death of hope and despair,
This is the death of air.
 Four Quartets 'Little Gidding' (1942) pt. 2

5 Since our concern was speech, and speech impelled us
To purify the dialect of the tribe
And urge the mind to aftersight and foresight.
 Four Quartets 'Little Gidding' (1942) pt. 2

6 We shall not cease from exploration
And the end of all our exploring
Will be to arrive where we started
And know the place for the first time.
 Four Quartets 'Little Gidding' (1942) pt. 5

7 What we call the beginning is often the end
And to make an end is to make a beginning.
The end is where we start from.
 Four Quartets 'Little Gidding' (1942) pt. 5

8 A people without history
Is not redeemed from time, for history is a pattern
Of timeless moments. So, while the light fails
On a winter's afternoon, in a secluded chapel
History is now and England.
 Four Quartets 'Little Gidding' (1942) pt. 5

9 A condition of complete simplicity
(Costing not less than everything)
And all shall be well and
All manner of thing shall be well
When the tongues of flame are in-folded
Into the crowned knot of fire
And the fire and the rose are one.
 Four Quartets 'Little Gidding' (1942) pt. 5. Cf. Julian of
   Norwich 382:10

10 Here I am, an old man in a dry month
Being read to by a boy, waiting for rain.
 'Gerontion' (1920)

11 After such knowledge, what forgiveness? Think now
History has many cunning passages, contrived
   corridors
And issues, deceives with whispering ambitions,
Guides us by vanities.
 'Gerontion' (1920)

12 Tenants of the house,
Thoughts of a dry brain in a dry season.
 'Gerontion' (1920)

13 The hippopotamus's day
Is passed in sleep; at night he hunts;
God works in a mysterious way—
The Church can feed and sleep at once.
 'The Hippopotamus' (1919)

14 We are the hollow men
We are the stuffed men
Leaning together
Headpiece filled with straw. Alas!
 'The Hollow Men' (1925)

15 *Here we go round the prickly pear*
Prickly pear prickly pear
Here we go round the prickly pear
At five o'clock in the morning.

Between the idea
And the reality
Between the motion
And the act
Falls the Shadow.
 'The Hollow Men' (1925)

16 This is the way the world ends
Not with a bang but a whimper.
 'The Hollow Men' (1925)

17 A cold coming we had of it,
Just the worst time of the year
For a journey, and such a long journey:
The ways deep and the weather sharp,
The very dead of winter.
 'Journey of the Magi' (1927). Cf. Andrewes 11:13

18 But set down
This set down
This: were we led all that way for
Birth or Death? There was a Birth, certainly,
We had evidence and no doubt. I had seen birth and
   death
But had thought they were different; this Birth was
Hard and bitter agony for us, like Death, our death.
We returned to our places, these Kingdoms,
But no longer at ease here, in the old dispensation,
With an alien people clutching their gods.
I should be glad of another death.
 'Journey of the Magi' (1927)

19 Stand on the highest pavement of the stair—
Lean on a garden urn—
Weave, weave the sunlight in your hair.
 'La Figlia Che Piange' (1917)

20 Sometimes these cogitations still amaze
The troubled midnight and the noon's repose.
 'La Figlia Che Piange' (1917)

21 Let us go then, you and I,
When the evening is spread out against the sky
Like a patient etherized upon a table.
 'The Love Song of J. Alfred Prufrock' (1917)

1 In the room the women come and go
Talking of Michelangelo.

The yellow fog that rubs its back upon the
window-panes.
The yellow smoke that rubs its muzzle on the
window-panes.
Licked its tongue into the corners of the evening.
'The Love Song of J. Alfred Prufrock' (1917)

2 I have measured out my life with coffee spoons.
'The Love Song of J. Alfred Prufrock' (1917)

3 I should have been a pair of ragged claws
Scuttling across the floors of silent seas.
'The Love Song of J. Alfred Prufrock' (1917)

4 I have seen the moment of my greatness flicker,
And I have seen the eternal Footman hold my coat,
and snicker,
And in short, I was afraid.
'The Love Song of J. Alfred Prufrock' (1917)

5 No! I am not Prince Hamlet, nor was meant to be;
Am an attendant lord, one that will do
To swell a progress, start a scene or two,
Advise the prince.
'The Love Song of J. Alfred Prufrock' (1917)

6 I grow old ... I grow old ...
I shall wear the bottoms of my trousers rolled.

Shall I part my hair behind? Do I dare to eat a peach?
I shall wear white flannel trousers, and walk upon the
beach.
I have heard the mermaids singing, each to each.

I do not think that they will sing to me.
'The Love Song of J. Alfred Prufrock' (1917)

7 I am aware of the damp souls of housemaids
Sprouting despondently at area gates.
'Morning at the Window' (1917)

8 Polyphiloprogenitive
The sapient sutlers of the Lord
Drift across window-panes
In the beginning was the Word.
'Mr Eliot's Sunday Morning Service' (1919)

9 Yet we have gone on living,
Living and partly living.
Murder in the Cathedral (1935) pt. 1

10 The last temptation is the greatest treason:
To do the right deed for the wrong reason.
Murder in the Cathedral (1935) pt. 1

11 Clear the air! clean the sky! wash the wind! take the
stone from stone, take the skin from the arm, take the
muscle from bone, and wash them.
Murder in the Cathedral (1935) pt. 2

12 Macavity, Macavity, there's no one like Macavity,
There never was a Cat of such deceitfulness and
suavity.
He always has an alibi, and one or two to spare:
At whatever time the deed took place — MACAVITY
WASN'T THERE!
Old Possum's Book of Practical Cats (1939) 'Macavity: the
Mystery Cat'

13 The winter evening settles down
With smell of steaks in passageways.
Six o'clock.
The burnt-out ends of smoky days.
'Preludes' (1917)

14 Every street lamp that I pass
Beats like a fatalistic drum,
And through the spaces of the dark
Midnight shakes the memory
As a madman shakes a dead geranium.
'Rhapsody on a Windy Night' (1917)

15 Where is the Life we have lost in living?
Where is the wisdom we have lost in knowledge?
Where is the knowledge we have lost in information?
The Rock (1934) pt. 1

16 And the wind shall say: 'Here were decent godless
people:
Their only monument the asphalt road
And a thousand lost golf balls.'
The Rock (1934) pt. 1

17 Birth, and copulation, and death.
That's all the facts when you come to brass tacks:
Birth, and copulation, and death.
I've been born, and once is enough.
Sweeney Agonistes (1932) 'Fragment of an Agon'

18 Any man has to, needs to, wants to
Once in a lifetime, do a girl in.
Sweeney Agonistes (1932) 'Fragment of an Agon'

19 I gotta use words when I talk to you.
Sweeney Agonistes (1932) 'Fragment of an Agon'

20 The host with someone indistinct
Converses at the door apart,
The nightingales are singing near
The Convent of the Sacred Heart,

And sang within the bloody wood
When Agamemnon cried aloud
And let their liquid siftings fall
To stain the stiff dishonoured shroud.
'Sweeney among the Nightingales' (1919)

21 April is the cruellest month, breeding
Lilacs out of the dead land, mixing
Memory and desire, stirring
Dull roots with spring rain.
Winter kept us warm, covering
Earth in forgetful snow, feeding
A little life with dried tubers.
The Waste Land (1922) pt. 1

22 I read, much of the night, and go south in the winter.
The Waste Land (1922) pt. 1

23 And I will show you something different from either
Your shadow at morning striding behind you
Or your shadow at evening rising to meet you;
I will show you fear in a handful of dust.
The Waste Land (1922) pt. 1. Cf. Conrad 217:17

24 Madame Sosostris, famous clairvoyante,
Had a bad cold, nevertheless
Is known to be the wisest woman in Europe,
With a wicked pack of cards.
The Waste Land (1922) pt. 1

1   Unreal City,
Under the brown fog of a winter dawn,
A crowd flowed over London Bridge, so many,
I had not thought death had undone so many.
Sighs, short and infrequent, were exhaled,
And each man fixed his eyes before his feet
Flowed up the hill and down King William Street,
To where Saint Mary Woolnoth kept the hours
With a dead sound on the final stroke of nine.
The Waste Land (1922) pt. 1

2 The Chair she sat in, like a burnished throne,
Glowed on the marble.
The Waste Land (1922) pt. 2. Cf. *Antony and Cleopatra* 565:5

3 And still she cried, and still the world pursues,
'Jug Jug' to dirty ears.
The Waste Land (1922) pt. 2. Cf. Lyly 433:10

4 I think we are in rats' alley
Where the dead men lost their bones.
The Waste Land (1922) pt. 2

5 o o o o that Shakespeherian Rag—
It's so elegant
So intelligent.
The Waste Land (1922) pt. 2. Cf. Buck 154:7

6 Hurry up please it's time.
The Waste Land (1922) pt. 2

7 But at my back from time to time I hear
The sound of horns and motors, which shall bring
Sweeney to Mrs Porter in the spring.
O the moon shone bright on Mrs Porter
And on her daughter
They wash their feet in soda water.
The Waste Land (1922) pt. 3. Cf. Marvell 451:3

8 At the violet hour, when the eyes and back
Turn upward from the desk, when the human engine waits
Like a taxi throbbing waiting,
I, Tiresias, though blind, throbbing between two lives,
Old man with wrinkled female breasts, can see
At the violet hour, the evening hour that strives
Homeward, and brings the sailor home from sea,
The typist home at teatime, clears her breakfast, lights
Her stove, and lays out food in tins.
The Waste Land (1922) pt. 3

9 I Tiresias, old man with wrinkled dugs
Perceived the scene, and foretold the rest—
I too awaited the expected guest.
He, the young man carbuncular, arrives,
A small house agent's clerk, with one bold stare,
One of the low on whom assurance sits
As a silk hat on a Bradford millionaire.
The Waste Land (1922) pt. 3

10 When lovely woman stoops to folly and
Paces about her room again, alone,
She smoothes her hair with automatic hand,
And puts a record on the gramophone.
The Waste Land (1922) pt. 3. Cf. Goldsmith 311:33

11 Phlebas the Phoenician, a fortnight dead,
Forgot the cry of gulls, and the deep sea swell
And the profit and loss.
The Waste Land (1922) pt. 4

12 Who is the third who walks always beside you?
When I count, there are only you and I together
But when I look ahead up the white road
There is always another one walking beside you.
The Waste Land (1922) pt. 5

13 A woman drew her long black hair out tight
And fiddled whisper music on those strings
And bats with baby faces in the violet light
Whistled.
The Waste Land (1922) pt. 5

14 These fragments I have shored against my ruins.
The Waste Land (1922) pt. 5

15 Webster was much possessed by death
And saw the skull beneath the skin;
And breastless creatures underground
Leaned backward with a lipless grin.
'Whispers of Immortality' (1919)

16 Grishkin is nice: her Russian eye
Is underlined for emphasis;
Uncorseted, her friendly bust
Gives promise of pneumatic bliss.
'Whispers of Immortality' (1919)

17 The only way of expressing emotion in the form of art
is by finding an 'objective correlative'; in other words,
a set of objects, a situation, a chain of events which
shall be the formula of that *particular* emotion; such
that when the external facts, which must terminate in
sensory experience, are given, the emotion is
immediately evoked.
The Sacred Wood (1920) 'Hamlet and his Problems'

18 Immature poets imitate; mature poets steal.
The Sacred Wood (1920) 'Philip Massinger'

19 Someone said: 'The dead writers are remote from us
because we *know* so much more than they did.'
Precisely, and they are that which we know.
The Sacred Wood (1920) 'Tradition and Individual Talent'

20 Poetry is not a turning loose of emotion, but an escape
from emotion; it is not the expression of personality
but an escape from personality.
The Sacred Wood (1920) 'Tradition and Individual Talent'

21 We know too much and are convinced of too little.
Our literature is a substitute for religion, and so is our
religion.
Selected Essays (1932) 'A Dialogue on Dramatic Poetry'
(1928)

22 In the seventeenth century a dissociation of sensibility
set in, from which we have never recovered; and this
dissociation, as is natural, was due to the influence of
the two most powerful poets of the century, Milton
and Dryden.
Selected Essays (1932) 'The Metaphysical Poets' (1921)

23 Poets in our civilization, as it exists at present, must
be *difficult*.
Selected Essays (1932) 'The Metaphysical Poets' (1921)

24 To me ... [*The Waste Land*] was only the relief of a
personal and wholly insignificant grouse against life; it
is just a piece of rhythmical grumbling.
The Waste Land (ed. Valerie Eliot, 1971) epigraph

Elizabeth I 1533–1603

Queen of England and Ireland from 1558

1 I am your anointed Queen. I will never be by violence constrained to do anything. I thank God that I am endued with such qualities that if I were turned out of the Realm in my petticoat, I were able to live in any place in Christome.

> Speech to Members of Parliament, 5 November 1566, in J. E. Neale *Elizabeth I and her Parliaments 1559–1581* (1953) pt. 3, ch. 1

2 As for me, I assure you I find no great cause I should be fond to live. I take no such pleasure in it that I should much wish it, nor conceive such terror in death that I should greatly fear it . . . I have had good experience and trial of this world. I know what it is to be a subject, what to be a Sovereign, what to have good neighbours, and sometimes meet evil-willers.

> Speech to a Parliamentary deputation at Richmond, 12 November 1586, in Sir John Neale *Elizabeth I and her Parliaments 1584–1601* (1957) p. 118, from a report 'which the Queen herself heavily amended in her own hand'. The traditional version concludes: 'In trust I have found treason'.

3 I know I have the body of a weak and feeble woman, but I have the heart and stomach of a king, and of a king of England too; and think foul scorn that Parma or Spain, or any prince of Europe, should dare to invade the borders of my realm.

> Speech to the troops at Tilbury on the approach of the Armada, 1588, in Lord Somers *A Third Collection of Scarce and Valuable Tracts* (1751) p. 196

4 Though God hath raised me high, yet this I count the glory of my crown: that I have reigned with your loves.

> The Golden Speech, 1601, in *The Journals of All the Parliaments . . . Collected by Sir Simonds D'Ewes* (1682) p. 659

5 My Lord, I had forgot the fart.

> To Edward de Vere, Earl of Oxford, on his return from seven years self-imposed exile, occasioned by the acute embarrassment to himself of breaking wind in the presence of the Queen; in John Aubrey *Brief Lives* 'Edward de Vere'

6 Like strawberry wives, that laid two or three great strawberries at the mouth of their pot, and all the rest were little ones.

> Describing the tactics of the Commission of Sales, in their dealings with her, in Francis Bacon *Apophthegms New and Old* (1625) no. 54

7 I think that, at the worst, God has not yet ordained that England shall perish.

> In F. Chamberlin *Sayings of Queen Elizabeth* (1923)

8 I will make you shorter by the head.

> To the leaders of her Council, who were opposing her course towards Mary Queen of Scots, in F. Chamberlin *Sayings of Queen Elizabeth* (1923)

9 My lord, we make use of you, not for your bad legs, but for your good head.

> To William Cecil, who suffered from gout, in F. Chamberlin *Sayings of Queen Elizabeth* (1923)

10 I do entreat heaven daily for your longer life, else will my people and myself stand in need of cordials too. My comfort hath been in my people's happiness and their happiness in thy discretion.

> To William Cecil on his death-bed, in F. Chamberlin *Sayings of Queen Elizabeth* (1923)

11 'Twas God the word that spake it,
He took the bread and brake it;
And what the word did make it;
That I believe, and take it.

> Answer on being asked her opinion of Christ's presence in the Sacrament, in S. Clarke *The Marrow of Ecclesiastical History* (1675) pt. 2, bk. 1 'The Life of Queen Elizabeth' p. 94

12 If thy heart fails thee, climb not at all.

> Lines after Sir Walter Ralegh, written on a window-pane; in Thomas Fuller *Worthies of England* vol. 1, p. 419. Cf. Ralegh 536:2

13 Must! Is *must* a word to be addressed to princes? Little man, little man! thy father, if he had been alive, durst not have used that word.

> To Robert Cecil, on his saying she must go to bed, in J. R. Green *A Short History of the English People* (1874) ch. 7. *Dodd's Church History of England* vol. 3 (ed. M. A. Tierney, 1840) p. 72 adds: 'but thou knowest I must die, and that maketh thee so presumptuous'

14 Madam I may not call you; mistress I am ashamed to call you; and so I know not what to call you; but howsoever, I thank you.

> To the wife of the Archbishop of Canterbury, the Queen disapproving of marriage among the clergy, in Sir John Harington *A Brief View of the State of the Church of England* (1653) p. 4

15 God may pardon you, but I never can.

> To the dying Countess of Nottingham, in David Hume *The History of England under the House of Tudor* (1759) vol. 2, ch. 7

16 The queen of Scots is this day leichter of a fair son, and I am but a barren stock.

> To her ladies, in Sir James Melville *Memoirs of His Own Life* (1827 ed.) p. 159

17 The daughter of debate, that eke discord doth sow.

> On Mary Queen of Scots in George Puttenham (ed.) *The Art of English Poesie* (1589) bk. 3, ch. 20

18 I would not open windows into men's souls.

> Oral tradition, in J. B. Black *Reign of Elizabeth 1558–1603* (1936) p. 19 (the words very possibly originating in a letter drafted by Bacon). See J. Spedding (ed.) *Works of Francis Bacon* (1862) vol. 8, p. 98

19 All my possessions for a moment of time.

> Last words (attributed, but almost certainly apocryphal)

Elizabeth II 1926–

Queen of the United Kingdom from 1952

20 I declare before you all that my whole life, whether it be long or short, shall be devoted to your service and the service of our great Imperial family to which we all belong.

> Broadcast speech, as Princess Elizabeth, to the Commonwealth from Cape Town, 21 April 1947, in *The Times* 22 April 1947

1 I think everybody really will concede that on this, of all days, I should begin my speech with the words 'My husband and I'.

> Speech at Guildhall, London, on her 25th wedding anniversary, in *The Times* 21 November 1972

Queen Elizabeth, the Queen Mother
1900–

Queen Consort of George VI

2 I'm glad we've been bombed. It makes me feel I can look the East End in the face.

> To a London policeman, 13 September 1940, in John Wheeler-Bennett *King George VI* (1958) pt. 3, ch. 6

3 How small and selfish is sorrow. But it bangs one about until one is senseless.

> Letter to Edith Sitwell, shortly after the death of George VI, in Victoria Glendinning *Edith Sitwell* (1983) ch. 25

4 The Princesses would never leave without me and I couldn't leave without the King, and the King will never leave.

> On the suggestion that the royal family be evacuated during the Blitz, in Penelope Mortimer *Queen Elizabeth* (1986) ch. 25

Alf Ellerton

5 Belgium put the kibosh on the Kaiser.

> Title of song (1914)

John Ellerton 1826–93

English clergyman

6 The day Thou gavest, Lord, is ended,
The darkness falls at Thy behest.
To Thee our morning hymns ascended,
Thy praise shall sanctify our rest.

> Hymn (1870), the first line borrowed from an earlier, anonymous hymn

7 This is the day of prayer:
Let earth to Heaven draw near;
Lift up our hearts to seek Thee there,
Come down to meet us here.

> 'This is the day of light' (1867 hymn)

Emily Elizabeth Steele Elliot 1836–97

English hymn-writer

8 Thou didst leave thy throne
And thy kingly crown
When thou camest to earth for me,
But in Bethlehem's home
Was there found no room
For thy holy nativity:
O come to my heart, Lord Jesus!
There is room in my heart for thee.

> 'Thou didst leave thy throne and thy kingly crown' (1870 hymn)

Jane Elliot 1727–1805

Scottish poet

9 I've heard them lilting, at the ewe milking.
Lasses a' lilting, before dawn of day;
But now they are moaning, on ilka green loaning;
The flowers of the forest are a' wede away.

> 'The Flowers of the Forest' (1769) the most popular version of the traditional lament for Flodden. Cf. Cockburn 208:4

Charlotte Elliott 1789–1871

English hymn-writer

10 Just as I am, without one plea
But that Thy blood was shed for me,
And that Thou bidd'st me come to Thee,
O Lamb of God, I come!

> *Invalid's Hymn Book* (1834) 'Just as I am'

11 'Christian! seek not yet repose,'
Hear thy guardian angel say;
Thou art in the midst of foes—
'Watch and pray.'

> *Morning and Evening Hymns* (1836) 'Christian! seek not yet repose'

Ebenezer Elliott 1781–1849

English poet known as the 'Corn Law Rhymer'

12 What is a communist? One who hath yearnings
For equal division of unequal earnings.

> 'Epigram' (1850)

13 When wilt thou save the people?
Oh, God of Mercy! when?
The people, Lord, the people!
Not thrones and crowns, but men!

> 'The People's Anthem' (1850)

George Ellis 1753–1815

English poet and journalist

14 Snowy, Flowy, Blowy,
Showery, Flowery, Bowery,
Hoppy, Croppy, Droppy,
Breezy, Sneezy, Freezy.

> 'The Twelve Months'

Havelock Ellis (Henry Havelock Ellis)
1859–1939

English sexologist

15 What we call 'progress' is the exchange of one nuisance for another nuisance.

> *Impressions and Comments* (1914) 31 July 1912

16 All civilization has from time to time become a thin crust over a volcano of revolution.

> *Little Essays of Love and Virtue* (1922) ch. 7

Friar Elstow

1 With thanks to God we know the way to heaven, to be as ready by water as by land, and therefore we care not which way we go.

> When threatened with drowning by Henry VIII, in John Stow *The Annals of England* (1615) p. 543. Cf. Gilbert 303:12

Paul Éluard 1895–1952

French poet

2 *L'espoir ne fait pas de poussière.*

Hope raises no dust.

> 'Ailleurs, ici, partout' (1946)

3 *Adieu tristesse*
Bonjour tristesse
Tu es inscrite dans les lignes du plafond.

Farewell sadness
Good-day sadness
You are inscribed in the lines of the ceiling.

> 'À peine défigurée' (1932)

4 *Ce qui a été compris n'existe plus.*

What has been understood no longer exists.

> 'Le Miroir d'un Moment' (1926)

Ralph Waldo Emerson 1803–82

American philosopher and poet

5 If the red slayer think he slays,
Or if the slain think he is slain,
They know not well the subtle ways
I keep, and pass, and turn again.

> 'Brahma' (1867)

6 I am the doubter and the doubt,
And I the hymn the Brahmin sings.

> 'Brahma' (1867)

7 By the rude bridge that arched the flood,
Their flag to April's breeze unfurled,
Here once the embattled farmers stood,
And fired the shot heard round the world.

> 'Concord Hymn' (1837)

8 Good-bye, proud world! I'm going home:
Thou art not my friend, and I'm not thine.

> 'Good-bye' (1847)

9 Things are in the saddle,
And ride mankind.

> 'Ode' Inscribed to W. H. Channing (1847)

10 I like a church; I like a cowl;
I love a prophet of the soul;
And on my heart monastic aisles
Fall like sweet strains, or pensive smiles;
Yet not for all his faith can see,
Would I that cowlèd churchman be.

> 'The Problem' (1847)

11 He builded better than he knew;—
The conscious stone to beauty grew.

> 'The Problem' (1847)

12 The frolic architecture of the snow.

> 'The Snowstorm' (1847)

13 Wilt thou seal up the avenues of ill?
Pay every debt, as if God wrote the bill.

> 'Suum Cuique' (1867)

14 So nigh is grandeur to our dust,
So near is God to man,
When Duty whispers low, *Thou must,*
The youth replies, *I can.*

> 'Voluntaries' no. 3 (1867)

15 Make yourself necessary to someone.

> *The Conduct of Life* (1860) 'Considerations by the way'

16 All sensible people are selfish, and nature is tugging at every contract to make the terms of it fair.

> *The Conduct of Life* (1860) 'Considerations by the way'

17 Art is a jealous mistress.

> *The Conduct of Life* (1860) 'Wealth'

18 The louder he talked of his honour, the faster we counted our spoons.

> *The Conduct of Life* (1860) 'Worship'. Cf. Johnson 372:9, Shaw 637·16

19 I feel in regard to this aged England ... that she sees a little better on a cloudy day, and that, in storm of battle and calamity, she has a secret vigour and a pulse like a cannon.

> Speech at Manchester, November 1847 in *English Traits* (1883 ed.) p. 295

20 Beauty will not come at the call of a legislature ... It will come, as always, unannounced, and spring up between the feet of brave and earnest men.

> *Essays* (1841) 'Art'

21 Conversation is a game of circles. In conversation we pluck up the *termini* which bound the common of silence on every side.

> *Essays* (1841) 'Circles'

22 People wish to be settled: only as far as they are unsettled is there any hope for them.

> *Essays* (1841) 'Circles'

23 Thou art to me a delicious torment.

> *Essays* (1841) 'Friendship'

24 A friend is a person with whom I may be sincere. Before him I may think aloud.

> *Essays* (1841) 'Friendship'

25 The only reward of virtue is virtue; the only way to have a friend is to be one.

> *Essays* (1841) 'Friendship'

26 We need books of this tart cathartic virtue, more than books of political science or of private economy.

> On Plutarch's *Lives*, in *Essays* (1841) 'Heroism'

27 It was a high counsel that I once heard given to a young person, 'Always do what you are afraid to do.'

> *Essays* (1841) 'Heroism'

28 There is properly no history; only biography.

> *Essays* (1841) 'History'. Cf. Disraeli 248:10

29 The faith that stands on authority is not faith.

> *Essays* (1841) 'The Over-Soul'

30 In skating over thin ice, our safety is in our speed.

> *Essays* (1841) 'Prudence'

31 Whoso would be a man must be a nonconformist.

> *Essays* (1841) 'Self-Reliance'

1 It is easy in the world to live after the world's opinion;
it is easy in solitude to live after our own.
  Essays (1841) 'Self-Reliance'

2 A foolish consistency is the hobgoblin of little minds,
adored by little statesmen and philosophers and
divines. With consistency a great soul has simply
nothing to do.
  Essays (1841) 'Self-Reliance'

3 Is it so bad, then, to be misunderstood? Pythagoras
was misunderstood, and Socrates, and Jesus, and
Luther, and Copernicus, and Galileo, and Newton, and
every pure and wise spirit that ever took flesh. To be
great is to be misunderstood.
  Essays (1841) 'Self-Reliance'

4 To fill the hour—that is happiness.
  Essays. Second Series (1844) 'Experience'

5 The years teach much which the days never know.
  Essays. Second Series (1844) 'Experience'

6 Men are conservatives when they are least vigorous,
or when they are most luxurious. They are
conservatives after dinner.
  Essays. Second Series (1844) 'New England Reformers'

7 Every man is wanted, and no man is wanted much.
  Essays. Second Series (1844) 'Nominalist and Realist'

8 Language is fossil poetry.
  Essays. Second Series (1844) 'The Poet'

9 What is a weed? A plant whose virtues have not been
discovered.
  Fortune of the Republic (1878) p. 3

10 Old age brings along with its uglinesses the comfort
that you will soon be out of it,—which ought to be a
substantial relief to such discontented pendulums as
we are. To be out of the war, out of debt, out of the
drouth, out of the blues, out of the dentist's hands,
out of the second thoughts, mortifications, and
remorses that inflict such twinges and shooting
pains,—out of the next winter, and the high prices,
and company below your ambition,—surely these are
soothing hints.
  Journal, 1864, in Linda Allardt et al. (eds.) *Journals and
  Miscellaneous Notebooks of Ralph Waldo Emerson* vol. 15,
  1860–6 (1982) p. 428

11 Is not marriage an open question, when it is alleged,
from the beginning of the world, that such as are in
the institution wish to get out; and such as are out
wish to get in.
  Representative Men (1850) 'Montaigne'

12 Every hero becomes a bore at last.
  Representative Men (1850) 'Uses of Great Men'

13 Hitch your wagon to a star.
  Society and Solitude (1870) 'Civilization'

14 We boil at different degrees.
  Society and Solitude (1870) 'Eloquence'

15 America is a country of young men.
  Society and Solitude (1870) 'Old Age'

16 Glittering generalities! They are blazing ubiquities.
  On Rufus Choate (attributed). Cf. Choate 200:2

17 If a man write a better book, preach a better sermon,
or make a better mouse-trap than his neighbour, tho'
he build his house in the woods, the world will make
a beaten path to his door.
  Attributed to Emerson in Sarah S. B. Yule *Borrowings*
  (1889). Mrs Yule states in *The Docket* February 1912 that
  she copied this in her handbook from a lecture delivered by
  Emerson; the quotation was the occasion of a long
  controversy owing to Elbert Hubbard's claim to its
  authorship

Sir William Empson 1906–84
English poet and literary critic

18 Waiting for the end, boys, waiting for the end.
  'Just a smack at Auden' (1940)

19 It is this deep blankness is the real thing strange.
The more things happen to you the more you can't
Tell or remember even what they were.

The contradictions cover such a range.
The talk would talk and go so far about.
You don't want madhouse and the whole thing there.
  'Let it Go' (1955)

20 Slowly the poison the whole blood stream fills.
It is not the effort nor the failure tires.
The waste remains, the waste remains and kills.
  'Missing Dates' (1935)

21 Seven types of ambiguity.
  Title of book (1930)

Friedrich Engels 1820–95
*German socialist; founder, with Karl Marx, of modern
Communism*

22 *Der Staat wird nicht 'abgeschafft', er stirbt ab.*
The State is not 'abolished', *it withers away.*
  Anti-Dühring (1878) pt. 3, ch. 2

23 Naturally, the workers are perfectly free; the
manufacturer does not force them to take his
materials and his cards, but he says to them ... 'If
you don't like to be frizzled in my frying-pan, you can
take a walk into the fire'.
  The Condition of the Working Class in England in 1844 (1892)
  ch. 7
  See also KARL MARX and FRIEDRICH ENGELS

Thomas Dunn English 1819–1902
American physician, lawyer, and writer

24 Oh! don't you remember sweet Alice, Ben Bolt,
Sweet Alice, whose hair was so brown,
Who wept with delight when you gave her a smile,
And trembled with fear at your frown?
  'Ben Bolt' (1885)

Ennius 239–169 BC
Roman writer

25 *O Tite tute Tati tibi tanta tyranne tulisti!*
O tyrant Titus Tatius, what a lot you brought upon
yourself!
  Annals bk. 1 (l. 104 in O. Skutsch (ed.) *Annals of Q. Ennius*,
  1985)

1 *Moribus antiquis res stat Romana virisque.*

The Roman state survives by its ancient customs and its manhood.
> *Annals* bk. 5 (l. 156 in O. Skutsch (ed.) *Annals of Q. Ennius*, 1985)

2 *Unus homo nobis cunctando restituit rem.*

One man by delaying put the state to rights for us.
> *Annals* bk. 12 (l. 363 in O. Skutsch (ed.) *Annals of Q. Ennius*, 1985); referring to the Roman general Fabius Cunctator ('The Delayer')

3 *At tuba terribili sonitu taratantara dixit.*

And the trumpet in terrible tones went taratantara.
> *Annals* (l. 451 in O. Skutsch (ed.) *Annals of Q. Ennius*, 1985)

'Ephelia'
17th-century poet

4 And yet I love this false, this worthless man,
With all the passion that a woman can;
Dote on his imperfections, though I spy
Nothing to love; I love, and know not why.
> *Female Poems* (1679) 'To one that asked me why I loved J.G.'

Sir Jacob Epstein 1880–1959
British sculptor

5 Why don't they stick to murder and leave art to us?
> On hearing that his statue of Lazarus in New College chapel, Oxford, kept Khrushchev awake at night (attributed)

Julius J. Epstein 1909– et al.

6 Of all the gin joints in all the towns in all the world, she walks into mine.
> *Casablanca* (1942 film)

7 If she can stand it, I can. Play it!
> *Casablanca* (1942 film). Spoken by Humphrey Bogart and usually misquoted 'Play it again, Sam'; earlier in the film Ingrid Bergman says, 'Play it, Sam. Play *As Time Goes By*'. Cf. Hupfeld 357:2

8 Here's looking at you, kid.
> *Casablanca* (1942 film)

9 Major Strasser has been shot. Round up the usual suspects.
> *Casablanca* (1942 film)

Olaudah Equiano c.1745–c.1797
African writer and former slave

10 We are . . . a nation of dancers, singers and poets.
> *Narrative of the Life of Olaudah Equiano* (1789) ch. 1 (the Ibo people)

11 When I recovered a little I found some black people about me . . . I asked them if we were not to be eaten by those white men with horrible looks, red faces, and loose hair.
> *Narrative of the Life of Olaudah Equiano* (1789) ch. 3

Erasmus (Desiderius Erasmus)
c.1469–1536
Dutch Christian humanist

12 *In regione caecorum rex est luscus.*

In the country of the blind the one-eyed man is king.
> *Adages* bk. 3, century 4, no. 96

Susan Ertz 1894–1985
American writer

13 Someone has somewhere commented on the fact that millions long for immortality who don't know what to do with themselves on a rainy Sunday afternoon.
> *Anger in the Sky* (1943) p. 137

Robert Devereux, 2nd Earl of Essex
1566–1601
English soldier and courtier, executed for treason

14 Reasons are not like garments, the worse for wearing.
> Letter to Lord Willoughby, 4 January 1599, in *Notes and Queries* 10th Series, vol. 2 (1904) p. 23

Henri Estienne 1531–98
French printer and publisher

15 *Si jeunesse savait; si vieillesse pouvait.*

If youth knew; if age could.
> *Les Prémices* (1594) bk. 4, epigram 4

Sir George Etherege (or Etheredge)
c.1635–91
English playwright

16 I walk within the purlieus of the Law.
> *Love in a Tub* (1664) act 1, sc. 3

17 When love grows diseased, the best thing we can do is put it to a violent death; I cannot endure the torture of a lingering and consumptive passion.
> *The Man of Mode* (1676) act 2, sc. 2

18 Writing, Madam, 's a mechanic part of wit! A gentleman should never go beyond a song or a billet.
> *The Man of Mode* (1676) act 4, sc. 1

19 Fear not, though love and beauty fail,
My reason shall my heart direct:
Your kindness now will then prevail,
And passion turn into respect:
Chloris, at worst, you'll in the end
But change your Lover for a friend.
> *New Academy of Compliments* (1671) 'Chloris, 'tis not in your power'

Euclid fl. c.300 BC
Greek mathematician

20 ὅπερ ἔδει δεῖξαι.

Which was to be proved.
> *Elementa* bk. 1, proposition 5 and *passim* (usually quoted in Latin: 'Quod erat demonstrandum')

1 γραμμὴ δὲ μῆκος ἀπλατές.

A line is length without breadth.
Elementa bk. 1, definition 2

2 μὴ εἶναι βασιλικὴν ἀτραπὸν ἐπὶ γεωμετρίαν.

There is no 'royal road' to geometry.
Addressed to Ptolemy I, in Proclus *Commentary on the First Book of Euclid's Elementa* prologue, pt. 2

Euripides c.485–c.406 BC

Greek playwright

3 ἡ γλῶσσ᾽ ὀμώμοχ᾽, ἡ δὲ φρὴν ἀνώμοτος.

My tongue swore, but my mind's unsworn.
Hippolytus l. 612 (Hippolytus lamenting his breaking of an oath)

Abel Evans 1679–1737

English poet and divine

4 Under this stone, Reader, survey
Dead Sir John Vanbrugh's house of clay.
Lie heavy on him, Earth! for he
Laid many heavy loads on thee!
'Epitaph on Sir John Vanbrugh, Architect of Blenheim Palace'

John Evelyn 1620–1706

English diarist

5 This knight was indeed a valiant Gent: but not a little given to romance, when he spake of himself.
E. S. de Beer (ed.) *Diary of John Evelyn* (1955) vol. 3, p. 40 (6 September 1651)

6 Mulberry Garden, now the only place of refreshment about the town for persons of the best quality to be exceedingly cheated at.
E. S. de Beer (ed.) *Diary of John Evelyn* (1955) vol. 3, p. 96 (10 May 1654)

7 That miracle of a youth, Mr Christopher Wren.
E. S. de Beer (ed.) *Diary of John Evelyn* (1955) vol. 3, p. 106 (11 July 1654)

8 I saw Hamlet Prince of Denmark played, but now the old play began to disgust this refined age.
E. S. de Beer (ed.) *Diary of John Evelyn* (1955) vol. 3, p. 304 (26 November 1661)

David Everett 1769–1813

American lawyer and writer

9 You'd scarce expect one of my age
To speak in public on the stage;
And if I chance to fall below
Demosthenes or Cicero,
Don't view me with a critic's eye,
But pass my imperfections by.
Large streams from little fountains flow,
Tall oaks from little acorns grow.
'Lines Written for a School Declamation' (aged 7)

Viscount Eversley

See CHARLES SHAW-LEFEVRE

William Norman Ewer 1885–1976

British writer

10 I gave my life for freedom — This I know:
For those who bade me fight had told me so.
'Five Souls' (1917)

11 How odd
Of God
To choose
The Jews.
In *Week-End Book* (1924) p. 117. Cf. Browne 145:4

F. W. Faber 1814–63

English priest

12 My God, how wonderful Thou art!
Thy Majesty how bright!
Oratory Hymns (1854) 'The Eternal Father'

13 The music of the Gospel leads us home.
Oratory Hymns (1854) 'The Pilgrims of the Night'

14 There's a wideness in God's mercy
Like the wideness of the sea.
Oratory Hymns (1854) 'Souls of men, why will ye scatter'

Robert Fabyan d. 1513

English chronicler

15 Finally he paid the debt of nature.
The New Chronicles of England and France (1516) vol. 1, ch. 41

16 King Henry [I] being in Normandy, after some writers, fell from or with his horse, whereof he caught his death; but Ranulphe says he took a surfeit by eating of a lamprey, and thereof died.
The New Chronicles of England and France (1516) vol. 1, ch. 229

17 The Duke of Clarence ... then being a prisoner in the Tower, was secretly put to death and drowned in a barrel of Malmesey wine within the said Tower.
The New Chronicles of England and France (1516) vol. 2 '1478' ('malvesye' for 'malmesey' in early editions)

Clifton Fadiman 1904–

American critic

18 Milk's leap toward immortality.
Any Number Can Play (1957) p. 105 (of cheese)

19 The mama of dada.
Party of One (1955) p. 90 (of Gertrude Stein)

Lucius Cary (2nd Viscount Falkland) 1610–43

English royalist politician

20 When it is not necessary to change, it is necessary not to change.
Discourses of Infallibility (1660) 'A Speech concerning Episcopacy' delivered in 1641

Sir Richard Fanshawe 1605–66

English diplomat and translator

1 Ten years the world upon him falsely smiled,
Sheathing in fawning looks the deadly knife
Long aimed at his head; that so beguiled
It more securely might bereave his life:
Then threw him to a scaffold from a throne.
Much doctrine lies under this little stone.
> *The Faithful Shepherd* (1647) 'The Fall' (translation of G. B. Guarini's *Il pastor fido*, 1589)

2 White Peace (the beautiful'st of things)
Seems here her everlasting rest
To fix, and spreads her downy wings over the nest.
> *The Faithful Shepherd* (1648) 'An Ode, upon occasion of His Majesty's Proclamation in the Year 1630'

Michael Faraday 1791–1867

English physicist and chemist

3 Tyndall, I must remain plain Michael Faraday to the last; and let me now tell you, that if I accepted the honour which the Royal Society desires to confer upon me, I would not answer for the integrity of my intellect for a single year.
> On being offered the Presidency of the Royal Society, in J. Tyndall *Faraday as a Discoverer* (1868) 'Illustrations of Character'

Eleanor Farjeon 1881–1965

English writer for children

4 Morning has broken
Like the first morning,
Blackbird has spoken
Like the first bird.
Praise for the singing!
Praise for the morning!
Praise for them, springing
Fresh from the Lord!
> *Children's Bells* (1957) 'A Morning Song (for the First Day of Spring)'

Edward Farmer c.1809–76

English poet

5 I have no pain, dear mother, now;
But oh! I am so dry:
Just moisten poor Jim's lips once more;
And, mother, do not cry!
> 'The Collier's Dying Child' Cf. Anonymous 14:15

Farouk 1920–65

King of Egypt, 1936–52

6 The whole world is in revolt. Soon there will be only five Kings left—the King of England, the King of Spades, the King of Clubs, the King of Hearts and the King of Diamonds.
> In Lord Boyd-Orr *As I Recall* (1966) ch. 21 (addressed to the author at a conference in Cairo, 1948)

George Farquhar 1678–1707

Irish playwright

7 Sir, you shall taste my *Anno Domini*.
> *The Beaux' Stratagem* (1707) act 1, sc. 1

8 I have fed purely upon ale; I have eat my ale, drank my ale, and I always sleep upon ale.
> *The Beaux' Stratagem* (1707) act 1, sc. 1

9 My Lady Bountiful.
> *The Beaux' Stratagem* (1707) act 1, sc. 1

10 There is no scandal like rags, nor any crime so shameful as poverty.
> *The Beaux' Stratagem* (1707) act 1, sc. 1

11 There's some diversion in a talking blockhead; and since a woman must wear chains, I would have the pleasure of hearing 'em rattle a little.
> *The Beaux' Stratagem* (1707) act 2, sc. 2

12 No woman can be a beauty without a fortune.
> *The Beaux' Stratagem* (1707) act 2, sc. 2

13 I believe they talked of me, for they laughed consumedly.
> *The Beaux' Stratagem* (1707) act 3, sc. 1

14 'Twas for the good of my country that I should be abroad.—Anything for the good of one's country—I'm a Roman for that.
> *The Beaux' Stratagem* (1707) act 3, sc. 2

15 AIMWELL: Then you understand Latin, Mr Bonniface?
BONNIFACE: Not I, Sir, as the saying is, but he talks it so very fast that I'm sure it must be good.
> *The Beaux' Stratagem* (1707) act 3, sc. 2

16 Spare all I have, and take my life.
> *The Beaux' Stratagem* (1707) act 5, sc. 2

17 I hate all that don't love me, and slight all that do.
> *The Constant Couple* (1699) act 1, sc. 2

18 Grant me some wild expressions, Heavens, or I shall burst— ... Words, words or I shall burst.
> *The Constant Couple* (1699) act 5, sc. 3

19 Charming women can true converts make,
We love the precepts for the teacher's sake.
> *The Constant Couple* (1699) act 5, sc. 3. Cf. Defoe 234:15

20 Crimes, like virtues, are their own rewards.
> *The Inconstant* (1702) act 4, sc. 2

21 Money is the sinews of love, as of war.
> *Love and a Bottle* (1698) act 2, sc. 1. Cf. Cicero 204:10

22 Poetry's a mere drug, Sir.
> *Love and a Bottle* (1698) act 3, sc. 2. Cf. Lowell 429:14

23 Hanging and marriage, you know, go by Destiny.
> *The Recruiting Officer* (1706) act 3, sc. 2

24 I could be mighty foolish, and fancy my self mighty witty; Reason still keeps its throne, but it nods a little, that's all.
> *The Recruiting Officer* (1706) act 3, sc. 2

25 I'm privileged to be very impertinent, being an Oxonian.
> *Sir Harry Wildair* (1701) act 2, sc. 1

26 A lady, if undressed at Church, looks silly,
One cannot be devout in dishabilly.
> *The Stage Coach* (1704) prologue

David Glasgow Farragut 1801–70

American admiral

1 Damn the torpedoes! Full speed ahead.
> At the battle of Mobile Bay, 5 August 1864 (*torpedoes* mines). See A. T. Mahan *Great Commanders: Admiral Farragut* (1892) ch. 10

William Faulkner 1897–1962

American novelist

2 He [the writer] must teach himself that the basest of all things is to be afraid and, teaching himself that, forget it forever, leaving no room in his workshop for anything but the old verities and truths of the heart, the old universal truths lacking which any story is ephemeral and doomed—love and honor and pity and pride and compassion and sacrifice.
> Nobel Prize speech, 1950, in *Les Prix Nobel en 1950* (1951) p. 71

3 I believe man will not merely endure, he will prevail. He is immortal, not because he, alone among creatures, has an inexhaustible voice but because he has a soul, a spirit capable of compassion and sacrifice and endurance.
> Nobel Prize speech, 1950, in *Les Prix Nobel en 1950* (1951) p. 71

4 The writer's only responsibility is to his art. He will be completely ruthless if he is a good one. He has a dream. It anguishes him so much he must get rid of it. He has no peace until then. Everything goes by the board . . . If a writer has to rob his mother, he will not hesitate; the *Ode on a Grecian Urn* is worth any number of old ladies.
> In *Paris Review* Spring 1956, p. 30

5 A man shouldn't fool with booze until he's fifty; then he's a damn fool if he doesn't.
> In James M. Webb and A. Wigfall Green *William Faulkner of Oxford* (1965) p. 110

Guy Fawkes 1570–1606

Conspirator in the Gunpowder Plot, 1605

6 A desperate disease requires a dangerous remedy.
> 6 November 1605. See *Dictionary of National Biography* (1917–) vol. 6, p. 1132. Cf. *Hamlet* 577:27

James Fenton 1949–

English poet

7 It is not what they built. It is what they knocked down.
It is not the houses. It is the spaces between the houses.
It is not the streets that exist. It is the streets that no longer exist.
> *German Requiem* (1981) p. 1

Edna Ferber 1887–1968

American writer

8 Being an old maid is like death by drowning, a really delightful sensation after you cease to struggle.
> In R. E. Drennan *Wit's End* (1973)

Ferdinand I 1503–64

Holy Roman Emperor from 1558

9 *Fiat justitia et pereat mundus.*
Let justice be done, though the world perish.
> Motto. *See* Johannes Manlius *Locorum Communium Collectanea* (1563) vol. 2 'De Lege: Octatum Praeceptum'. Cf. Watson 722:8

Robert Fergusson 1750–74

Scottish poet

10 For thof ye had as wise a snout on
As Shakespeare or Sir Isaac Newton,
Your judgement fouk woud hae a doubt on,
I'll tak my aith,
Till they could see ye wi' a suit on
O' gude Braid Claith.
> 'Braid Claith' (1773)

11 The Lawyers may revere that tree
Where thieves so oft have swung,
Since, by the Law's most wise decree,
Her thieves are never hung.
> 'Epigram on a Lawyer's desiring one of the Tribe to look with respect to a Gibbet' (1779)

Ludwig Feuerbach 1804–72

German philosopher

12 *Der Mensch ist, was er isst.*
Man is what he eats.
> In Jacob Moleschott *Lehre der Nahrungsmittel: Für das Volk* (1850) 'Advertisement'. Cf. Brillat-Savarin 141:14

Eugene Field 1850–95

American poet and journalist

13 But I, when I undress me
Each night, upon my knees,
Will ask the Lord to bless me,
With apple pie and cheese.
> 'Apple Pie and Cheese' (1889)

14 Wynken, Blynken, and Nod one night
Sailed off in a wooden shoe—
Sailed on a river of crystal light,
Into a sea of dew.
> 'Wynken, Blynken, and Nod' (1889)

15 He played the King as though under momentary apprehension that someone else was about to play the ace.
> Writing of Creston Clarke as King Lear, in a review attributed to Field, in the *Denver Tribune* c.1880

Henry Fielding 1707–54

English novelist and playwright

16 It hath been often said, that it is not death, but dying, which is terrible.
> *Amelia* (1751) bk. 3, ch. 4

17 One fool at least in every married couple.
> *Amelia* (1751) bk. 9, ch. 4

1 The dusky night rides down the sky,
And ushers in the morn;
The hounds all join in glorious cry,
The huntsman winds his horn:
And a-hunting we will go.
    Don Quixote in England (1733) act 2, sc. 5 'A-Hunting We
    Will Go'

2 Oh! The roast beef of England,
And old England's roast beef.
    The Grub Street Opera (1731) act 3, sc. 3

3 He in a few minutes ravished this fair creature, or at
least would have ravished her, if she had not, by a
timely compliance, prevented him.
    Jonathan Wild (1743) bk. 3, ch. 7

4 To whom nothing is given, of him can nothing be
required.
    Joseph Andrews (1742) bk. 2, ch. 8

5 I describe not men, but manners; not an individual,
but a species.
    Joseph Andrews (1742) bk. 3, ch. 1

6 Public schools are the nurseries of all vice and
immorality.
    Joseph Andrews (1742) bk. 3, ch. 5

7 Love and scandal are the best sweeteners of tea.
    Love in Several Masques (1728) act 4, sc. 11

8 Necessity is a bad recommendation to favours . . .
which as seldom fall to those who really want them,
as to those who really deserve them.
    The Modern Husband (1732) act 2, sc. 5

9 Map me no maps, sir, my head is a map, a map of the
whole world.
    Rape upon Rape (1730) act 2, sc. 5

10 When I mention religion, I mean the Christian
religion; and not only the Christian religion, but the
Protestant religion; and not only the Protestant
religion but the Church of England.
    Tom Jones (1749) bk. 3, ch. 3

11 Thwackum was for doing justice, and leaving mercy
to heaven.
    Tom Jones (1749) bk. 3, ch. 10

12 What is commonly called love, namely the desire of
satisfying a voracious appetite with a certain quantity
of delicate white human flesh.
    Tom Jones (1749) bk. 6, ch. 1

13 O! more than Gothic ignorance.
    Tom Jones (1749) bk. 7, ch. 3

14 His designs were strictly honourable, as the phrase is;
that is, to rob a lady of her fortune by way of
marriage.
    Tom Jones (1749) bk. 11, ch. 4

15 That monstrous animal, a husband and wife.
    Tom Jones (1749) bk. 15, ch. 9

16 All Nature wears one universal grin.
    Tom Thumb the Great (1731) act 1, sc. 1

17 When I'm not thanked at all, I'm thanked enough,
I've done my duty, and I've done no more.
    Tom Thumb the Great (1731) act 1, sc. 3

Dorothy Fields 1905–74

American songwriter

18 A fine romance with no kisses.
A fine romance, my friend, this is.
    'A Fine Romance' (1936 song); music by Jerome Kern

19 Grab your coat, and get your hat,
Leave your worry on the doorstep,
Just direct your feet
To the sunny side of the street.
    'On the Sunny Side of the Street' (1930 song)

W. C. Fields (William Claude Dukenfield) 1880–1946

American humorist

20 Never give a sucker an even break.
    Title of a W. C. Fields film (1941); the catch-phrase
    (Fields's own) is said to have originated in the musical
    comedy *Poppy* (1923)

21 Some weasel took the cork out of my lunch.
    You Can't Cheat an Honest Man (1939 film)

22 It ain't a fit night out for man or beast.
    Adopted by Fields but claimed by him not to be original.
    See Letter, 8 February 1944, in *W. C. Fields by Himself*
    (1974) pt. 2

23 Hell, I never vote *for* anybody. I always vote *against*.
    In Robert Lewis Taylor *W. C. Fields* (1950) p. 228.
    Cf. Adams 2:5
    See also LEO ROSTEN

Harry Julian Fink et al.

24 Go ahead, make my day.
    Dirty Harry (1971 film); spoken by Clint Eastwood

Ronald Firbank 1886–1926

English novelist

25 'O! help me, heaven,' she prayed, 'to be decorative
and to do right!'
    The Flower Beneath the Foot (1923) ch. 2

26 I remember the average curate at home as something
between a eunuch and a snigger.
    The Flower Beneath the Foot (1923) ch. 4

27 There was a pause—just long enough for an angel to
pass, flying slowly.
    Vainglory (1915) ch. 6

28 All millionaires love a baked apple.
    Vainglory (1915) ch. 13

29 'I know of no joy,' she airily began, 'greater than a
cool white dress after the sweetness of confession.'
    Valmouth (1919) ch. 4

L'Abbé Edgeworth de Firmont 1745–1807

Irish-born confessor to Louis XVI

30 *Fils de Saint Louis, montez au ciel.*
Son of Saint Louis, ascend to heaven.
    To Louis XVI as he mounted the steps of the guillotine,
    1793 (attributed)

H. A. L. Fisher 1856–1940

English historian

1 Men wiser and more learned than I have discerned in history a plot, a rhythm, a predetermined pattern. These harmonies are concealed from me. I can see only one emergency following upon another as wave follows upon wave, only one great fact with respect to which, since it is unique, there can be no generalizations, only one safe rule for the historian: that he should recognize in the development of human destinies the play of the contingent and the unforeseen.
A History of Europe (1935) p. vii

2 Purity of race does not exist. Europe is a continent of energetic mongrels.
A History of Europe (1935) ch. 1

John Arbuthnot Fisher (Baron Fisher) 1841–1920

British Admiral

3 The best scale for an experiment is 12 inches to a foot.
Memories (1919) p. 276

4 Sack the lot!
Letter to *The Times*, 2 September 1919 (on overmanning and overspending within government departments)

5 Never contradict
Never explain
Never apologize.
Letter to *The Times*, 5 September 1919. Cf. Disraeli 249:10, Hubbard 353:9

6 Yours till Hell freezes.
Attributed to Fisher, but not original. See F. Ponsonby *Reflections of Three Reigns* (1951) p. 131: 'Once an officer in India wrote to me and ended his letter "Yours till Hell freezes". I used this forcible expression in a letter to Fisher, and he adopted it'

Marve Fisher

American songwriter

7 I like Chopin and Bizet, and the voice of Doris Day,
Gershwin songs and old forgotten carols.
But the music that excels is the sound of oil wells
As they slurp, slurp, slurp into the barrels.

My little home will be quaint as an old parasol,
Instead of fitted carpets I'll have money wall to wall.
I want an old-fashioned house
With an old-fashioned fence
And an old-fashioned millionaire.
'An Old-Fashioned Girl' (1954 song)

Albert H. Fitz

8 You are my honey, honeysuckle, I am the bee.
'The Honeysuckle and the Bee' (1901 song)

Charles Fitzgeffrey c.1575–1638

English poet

9 And bold and hard adventures t' undertake,
Leaving his country for his country's sake.
Sir Francis Drake (1596) st. 213

Edward Fitzgerald 1809–83

English scholar and poet

10 Awake! for Morning in the bowl of night
Has flung the stone that puts the stars to flight:
And Lo! the Hunter of the East has caught
The Sultan's turret in a noose of light.
The Rubáiyát of Omar Khayyám (1859) st. 1

11 And look—a thousand blossoms with the day
Woke—and a thousand scattered into clay.
The Rubáiyát of Omar Khayyám (1859) st. 8

12 Each morn a thousand roses brings, you say;
Yes, but where leaves the rose of yesterday?
The Rubáiyát of Omar Khayyám (4th ed., 1879) st. 9

13 Here with a loaf of bread beneath the bough,
A flask of wine, a book of verse—and Thou
Beside me singing in the wilderness—
And wilderness is paradise enow.
The Rubáiyát of Omar Khayyám (1859) st. 11; 'A book of verses underneath the bough, / A jug of wine, a loaf of bread—and Thou / Beside me singing in the wilderness— / Oh, wilderness were paradise enow!' in 4th ed. (1879) st. 12

14 Ah, take the cash in hand and waive the rest;
Oh, the brave music of a *distant* drum!
The Rubáiyát of Omar Khayyám (1859) st. 12; 'Ah, take the cash and let the credit go, / Nor heed the rumble of a distant drum!' in 4th ed. (1879) st. 13

15 Think, in this battered caravanserai
Whose doorways are alternate night and day,
How sultan after sultan with his pomp
Abode his hour or two, and went his way.
The Rubáiyát of Omar Khayyám (1859) st. 15; 'Think, in this battered caravanserai / Whose portals are alternate night and day, / How sultan after sultan with his pomp / Abode his destined hour, and went his way.' in 4th ed. (1879) st. 17

16 I sometimes think that never blows so red
The rose as where some buried Caesar bled.
The Rubáiyát of Omar Khayyám (1859) st. 18

17 Ah, my beloved, fill the cup that clears
To-day of past regrets and future fears:
To-morrow! —Why, to-morrow I may be
Myself with yesterday's seven thousand years.
The Rubáiyát of Omar Khayyám (1859) st. 20

18 Ah, make the most of what we yet may spend,
Before we too into the dust descend;
Dust into dust, and under dust, to lie,
Sans wine, sans song, sans singer, and—sans End!
The Rubáiyát of Omar Khayyám (1859) st. 23

1 Oh, come with old Khayyám, and leave the wise
  To talk; one thing is certain, that life flies;
  One thing is certain, and the rest is lies;
  The flower that once hath blown for ever dies.
> *The Rubáiyát of Omar Khayyám* (1859) st. 26; 'Oh threats of
> Hell and hopes of Paradise! / One thing at least is
> certain—*This* life flies; / One thing is certain and the rest is
> lies; / The flower that once has blown for ever dies.' in 4th
> ed. (1879) st. 63

2 With them the seed of wisdom did I sow,
  And with mine own hand wrought to make it grow;
  And this was all the harvest that I reaped—
  'I came like water, and like wind I go'.
> *The Rubáiyát of Omar Khayyám* (1859) st. 28

3 Ah, fill the cup:—what boots it to repeat
  How time is slipping underneath our feet:
  Unborn TO-MORROW, and dead YESTERDAY,
  Why fret about them if TO-DAY be sweet!
> *The Rubáiyát of Omar Khayyám* (1859) st. 37

4 The grape that can with logic absolute
  The two-and-seventy jarring sects confute
> *The Rubáiyát of Omar Khayyám* (1859) st. 43

5 For in and out, above, about, below,
  'Tis nothing but a magic shadow-show,
  Played in a box whose candle is the sun,
  Round which we phantom figures come and go.
> *The Rubáiyát of Omar Khayyám* (1859) st. 46

6 Strange, is it not? that of the myriads who
  Before us passed the door of darkness through,
  Not one returns to tell us of the road,
  Which to discover we must travel too.
> *The Rubáiyát of Omar Khayyám* (4th ed., 1879) st. 64

7 'Tis all a chequer-board of nights and days
  Where Destiny with Men for pieces plays:
  Hither and thither moves, and mates, and slays,
  And one by one back in the closet lays.
> *The Rubáiyát of Omar Khayyám* (1859) st. 49; 'But helpless
> pieces of the game he plays / Upon this chequer-board of
> nights and days; / Hither and thither moves, and checks,
> and slays, / And one by one back in the closet lays.' in 4th
> ed. (1879) st. 69

8 The ball no question makes of Ayes and Noes,
  But here or there as strikes the player goes;
  And he that tossed you down into the field,
  He knows about it all—HE knows—HE knows!
> *The Rubáiyát of Omar Khayyám* (4th ed., 1879) st. 70

9 The moving finger writes; and, having writ,
  Moves on: nor all thy piety nor wit
  Shall lure it back to cancel half a line,
  Nor all thy tears wash out a word of it.
> *The Rubáiyát of Omar Khayyám* (1859) st. 51; 'all your
> tears' in 4th ed. (1879) st. 71

10 And that inverted bowl we call The Sky,
   Whereunder crawling cooped we live and die,
   Lift not thy hands to *It* for help—for It
   Rolls impotently on as Thou or I.
> *The Rubáiyát of Omar Khayyám* (1859) st. 52; ' . . . they call
> the Sky . . . / As impotently moves as you or I.' in 4th ed.
> (1879) st. 72

11 Drink! for you know not whence you came, nor why:
   Drink! for you know not why you go, nor where.
> *The Rubáiyát of Omar Khayyám* (4th ed., 1879) st. 74

12 After a momentary silence spake
   Some vessel of a more ungainly make;
   'They sneer at me for leaning all awry;
   What! did the hand then of the potter shake?'
> *The Rubáiyát of Omar Khayyám* (4th ed., 1879) st. 86

13 'Who *is* the potter, pray, and who the pot?'
> *The Rubáiyát of Omar Khayyám* (1859) st. 60

14 Then said another—'Surely not in vain
   My substance from the common earth was ta'en,
   That He who subtly wrought me into shape,
   Should stamp me back to common earth again.'
> *The Rubáiyát of Omar Khayyám* (1859) st. 61

15 Indeed the idols I have loved so long
   Have done my credit in this world much wrong:
   Have drowned my glory in a shallow cup
   And sold my reputation for a song.
> *The Rubáiyát of Omar Khayyám* (4th ed., 1879) st. 93

16 Alas, that spring should vanish with the rose!
   That youth's sweet-scented manuscript should close!
   The nightingale that in the branches sang,
   Ah, whence, and whither flown again, who knows!
> *The Rubáiyát of Omar Khayyám* (1859) st. 72

17 And when Thyself with shining foot shall pass
   Among the guests star-scattered on the grass,
   And in thy joyous errand reach the spot
   Where I made one—turn down an empty glass!
> *The Rubáiyát of Omar Khayyám* (1859) st. 75; 'And when
> like her, O Saki, you shall pass . . . / And in your joyous
> errand reach the spot.' in 4th ed. (1879) st. 101

18 Mrs Browning's death is rather a relief to me, I must
   say: no more Aurora Leighs, thank God! A woman of
   real genius, I know; but what is the upshot of it all?
   She and her sex had better mind the kitchen and their
   children; and perhaps the poor: except in such things
   as little novels, they only devote themselves to what
   men do much better, leaving that which men do
   worse or not at all.
> Letter to W. H. Thompson, 15 July 1861, in A. M. and
> A. B. Terhune (eds.) *Letters of Edward Fitzgerald* (1980)
> vol. 2, p. 407. Cf. Browning 153:18

19 Taste is the feminine of genius.
> Letter to J. R. Lowell, October 1877, in A. M. and A. B.
> Terhune (eds.) *Letters of Edward Fitzgerald* (1980) vol. 4,
> p. 79

F. Scott Fitzgerald 1896–1940

American novelist

20 Let me tell you about the very rich. They are different
   from you and me.
> *All the Sad Young Men* (1926) 'Rich Boy', to which Ernest
> Hemingway replied, 'Yes, they have more money'; in
> *Esquire* August 1936 'The Snows of Kilimanjaro'

21 The beautiful and damned.
> Title of novel (1922)

22 No grand idea was ever born in a conference, but a lot
   of foolish ideas have died there.
> Edmund Wilson (ed.) *The Crack-Up* (1945) 'Note-Books E'

23 Show me a hero and I will write you a tragedy.
> Edmund Wilson (ed.) *The Crack-Up* (1945) 'Note-Books E'

1 In his blue gardens, men and girls came and went like moths among the whisperings and the champagne and the stars.

The Great Gatsby (1925) ch. 3

2 Her voice is full of money.

The Great Gatsby (1925) ch. 7

3 They were careless people, Tom and Daisy—they smashed up things and creatures and then retreated back into their money or their vast carelessness, or whatever it was that kept them together, and let other people clean up the mess they had made.

The Great Gatsby (1925) ch. 9

4 Gatsby believed in the green light, the orgastic future that year by year recedes before us. It eluded us then, but that's no matter ... So we beat on, boats against the current, borne back ceaselessly into the past.

The Great Gatsby (1925) ch. 9

5 In a real dark night of the soul it is always three o'clock in the morning.

'Handle with Care' in *Esquire* March 1936, 'Dark night of the soul' being a translation of the Spanish title of a work by St John of the Cross, known in English as *The Ascent of Mount Carmel* (1578–80)

6 There are no second acts in American lives.

Edmund Wilson (ed.) *The Last Tycoon* (1941) 'Hollywood, etc.'

Robert Fitzsimmons 1862–1917

New Zealand boxer

7 The bigger they are, the further they have to fall.

Prior to a fight, in *Brooklyn Daily Eagle* 11 August 1900 (similar forms found in proverbs since the 15th century)

Bud Flanagan 1896–1968

British comedian

8 Underneath the Arches,
I dream my dreams away,
Underneath the Arches,
On cobble-stones I lay.

'Underneath the Arches' (1932 song)

Michael Flanders 1922–75 and Donald Swann 1923–

English songwriters

9 Have Some Madeira, M'dear.

Title of song (c.1956)

10 Mud! Mud! Glorious mud!
Nothing quite like it for cooling the blood.
So, follow me, follow,
Down to the hollow,
And there let us wallow
In glorious mud.

'The Hippopotamus' (1952)

11 Ma's out, Pa's out—let's talk rude:
Pee, po, belly, bum, drawers.

'P**, P*, B****, B**, D******' (c.1956)

12 Eating people is wrong!

'The Reluctant Cannibal' (1956 song); adopted as the title of a novel (1959) by Malcolm Bradbury

13 The English, the English, the English are best!
I wouldn't give tuppence for all of the rest!

'Song of Patriotic Prejudice' (c.1963 song)

14 That monarch of the road,
Observer of the Highway Code,
That big six-wheeler
Scarlet-painted
London Transport
Diesel-engined
Ninety-seven horse power
Omnibus!

'A Transport of Delight' (c.1956 song)

Thomas Flatman 1637–88

English poet

15 There's an experienced rebel, Time,
And in his squadrons Poverty;
There's Age that brings along with him
A terrible artillery:
And if against all these thou keep'st thy crown,
Th'usurper Death will make thee lay it down.

'The Defiance' (1686)

Gustave Flaubert 1821–80

French novelist

16 *La parole humaine est comme un chaudron fêlé où nous battons des mélodies à faire danser les ours, quand on voudrait attendrir les étoiles.*

Human speech is like a cracked kettle on which we tap crude rhythms for bears to dance to, while we long to make music that will melt the stars.

Madame Bovary (1857) pt. 1, ch. 12 (translated by F. Steegmuller)

17 *De temps à autre, dans les villes, j'ouvre un journal. Il me semble que nous allons rondement. Nous dansons non pas sur un volcan, mais sur la planche d'une latrine, qui m'a l'air passablement pourrie.*

From time to time, in the towns, I open a newspaper. Things seem to be going at a dizzy rate. We are dancing not on a volcano, but on the rotten seat of a latrine.

Letter to Louis Bouilhet, 14 November 1850, in M. Nadeau (ed.) *Correspondence 1846–51* (1964) (translated by F. Steegmuller)

18 *La prose est née d'hier; voilà ce qu'il faut se dire. Le vers est la forme par excellence des littératures anciennes. Toutes les combinaisons prosodiques ont été faites; mais celles de la prose, tant s'en fait.*

Prose was born yesterday—this is what we must tell ourselves. Poetry is pre-eminently the medium of past literatures. All the metrical combinations have been tried but nothing like this can be said of prose.

Letter to Louise Colet, 24 April 1852, in M. Nadeau (ed.) *Correspondence 1852* (1964)

19 *On peut calculer la valeur d'un homme d'après le nombre de ses ennemis et l'importance d'une oeuvre du mal qu'on en dit.*

You can calculate the worth of a man by the number of his enemies, and the importance of a work of art by the harm that is spoken of it.

Letter to Louise Colet, 14 June 1853, in M. Nadeau (ed.) *Correspondence 1853–56* (1964)

1 *Tout ce qu'on invente est vrai, soi-en sûre. La poésie est une chose aussi précise que la géométrie.*

Everything you invent is true: you can be sure of that. Poetry is a subject as precise as geometry.

Letter to Louise Colet, 14 August 1853, in M. Nadeau (ed.) *Correspondence 1853–56* (1964)

2 *Le style c'est la vie! C'est le sang même de la pensée! Boileau était une petite rivière, étroite, peu profonde, mais admirablement limpide et bien encaissée. C'est pourquoi cette onde ne se tarit pas.*

Style is life! It is the very life-blood of thought! Boileau was a little river, narrow, not very deep, but beautifully clear and well embanked. That's why his waters never run dry.

Letter to Louise Colet, 7 September 1853, in M. Nadeau (ed.) *Correspondence 1853–56* (1964)

3 *L'artiste doit être dans son oeuvre comme Dieu dans la création, invisible et tout-puissant; qu'on le sente partout, mais qu'on ne le voie pas.*

The artist must be in his work as God is in creation, invisible and all-powerful; one must sense him everywhere but never see him.

Letter to Mademoiselle Leroyer de Chantepie, 18 March 1857, in M. Nadeau (ed.) *Correspondence 1857–64* (1965)

4 *Les livres ne se font pas comme les enfants, mais comme les pyramides . . . et ça ne sert à rien! et ça reste dans le désert! . . . Les chacals pissent au bas et les bourgeois montent dessus.*

Books are made not like children but like pyramids . . . and they're just as useless! and they stay in the desert! . . . Jackals piss at their foot and the bourgeois climb up on them.

Letter to Ernest Feydeau, November/December 1857, in M. Nadeau (ed.) *Correspondence 1857–64* (1965)

5 *La vie humaine est une triste boutique, décidément, une chose laide, lourde et compliquée. L'art n'a point d'autre but pour les gens d'esprit que d'en escamoter le fardeau et l'amertume.*

Human life is a sad show, undoubtedly: ugly, heavy and complex. Art has no other end, for people of feeling, than to conjure away the burden and bitterness.

Letter to Amelie Bosquet, July 1864, in M. Nadeau (ed.) *Correspondence 1857–64* (1965)

James Elroy Flecker 1884–1915
English poet

6 Noon strikes on England, noon on Oxford town,
Beauty she was statue cold—there's blood upon her gown.
'The Dying Patriot' (1913)

7 West of these out to seas colder than the Hebrides I must go
Where the fleet of stars is anchored and the young Star captains glow.
'The Dying Patriot' (1913)

8 The dragon-green, the luminous, the dark, the serpent-haunted sea.
'The Gates of Damascus' (1913)

9 We who with songs beguile your pilgrimage
And swear that beauty lives though lilies die,
We poets of the proud old lineage
Who sing to find your hearts, we know not why,—
What shall we tell you? Tales, marvellous tales
Of ships and stars and isles where good men rest.
The Golden Journey to Samarkand (1913) 'Prologue'

10 When the great markets by the sea shut fast
All that calm Sunday that goes on and on:
When even lovers find their peace at last,
And earth is but a star, that once had shone.
The Golden Journey to Samarkand (1913) 'Prologue'

11 For lust of knowing what should not be known,
We take the Golden Road to Samarkand.
The Golden Journey to Samarkand (1913) pt. 1, 'Epilogue'

12 I have seen old ships sail like swans asleep
Beyond the village which men still call Tyre,
With leaden age o'ercargoed, dipping deep
For Famagusta and the hidden sun
That rings black Cyprus with a lake of fire.
'Old Ships' (1915)

13 It was so old a ship—who knows, who knows?
—And yet so beautiful, I watched in vain
To see the mast burst open with a rose,
And the whole deck put on its leaves again.
'Old Ships' (1915)

14 A ship, an isle, a sickle moon—
With few but with how splendid stars
The mirrors of the sea are strewn
Between their silver bars!
'A Ship, an Isle, and a Sickle Moon' (1913)

15 O friend unseen, unborn, unknown,
Student of our sweet English tongue,
Read out my words at night, alone:
I was a poet, I was young.
'To a Poet a Thousand Years Hence' (1910)

16 And some to Meccah turn to pray, and I toward thy bed, Yasmin.
'Yasmin' (1913)

Richard Flecknoe d. c.1678
Irish poet

17 Still-born Silence! thou that art
Floodgate of the deeper heart.
'Invocation of Silence' (1653)

Ian Fleming 1908–64
English thriller writer

18 A medium Vodka dry Martini—with a slice of lemon peel. Shaken and not stirred.
Dr No (1958) ch. 14

Marjory Fleming 1803–11
English child writer

19 A direful death indeed they had
That would put any parent mad
But she was more than usual calm
She did not give a singel dam.
Journals, Letters and Verses (ed. A. Esdaile, 1934) p. 29

1 The most devilish thing is 8 times 8 and 7 times 7 it is what nature itselfe cant endure.
Journals, Letters and Verses (ed. A. Esdaile, 1934) p. 47

2 To-day I pronunced a word which should never come out of a lady's lips it was that I called John a Impudent Bitch.
Journals, Letters and Verses (ed. A. Esdaile, 1934) p. 51

3 I am going to turn over a new life and am going to be a very good girl and be obedient to Isa Keith, here there is planty of goosaberys which makes my teath watter.
Journals, Letters and Verses (ed. A. Esdaile, 1934) p. 76

4 I hope I will be religious again but as for reganing my charecter I despare for it.
Journals, Letters and Verses (ed. A. Esdaile, 1934) p. 80

5 An annibabtist is a thing I am not a member of.
Journals, Letters and Verses (ed. A. Esdaile, 1934) p. 99

6 Sentiment is what I am not acquainted with.
Journals, Letters and Verses (ed. A. Esdaile, 1934) p. 99

7 My dear Isa, I now sit down on my botom to answer all your kind and beloved letters which you was so good as to write to me.
Journals, Letters and Verses (ed. A. Esdaile, 1934) Letter to Isabella, p. 157

8 O lovely O most charming pug
Thy graceful air and heavenly mug . . .
His noses cast is of the roman
He is a very pretty weoman
I could not get a rhyme for roman
And was obliged to call it weoman.
'Sonnet'

Robert, Marquis de Flers 1872–1927 *and* Arman de Caillavet 1869–1915

French playwrights

9 *Démocratie est le nom que nous donnons au peuple toutes les fois que nous avons besoin de lui.*
Democracy is the name we give the people whenever we need them.
L'habit vert act 1, sc. 12, in *La petite illustration série théâtre* 31 May 1913

Andrew Fletcher of Saltoun 1655–1716

Scottish patriot and anti-Unionist

10 I knew a very wise man so much of Sir Chr—'s sentiment, that he believed if a man were permitted to make all the ballads, he need not care who should make the laws of a nation.
'An Account of a Conversation concerning a Right Regulation of Government for the Good of Mankind. In a Letter to the Marquis of Montrose' (1704) in *Political Works* (1732) pt. 7

John Fletcher 1579–1625

English playwright

11 Best while you have it use your breath,
There is no drinking after death.
The Bloody Brother, or *Rollo Duke of Normandy* (with Ben Jonson and others, performed c.1616) act 2, sc. 2 'Song'

12 And he that will go to bed sober,
Falls with the leaf still in October.
The Bloody Brother act 2, sc. 2 'Song'

13 Three merry boys, and three merry boys,
And three merry boys are we,
As ever did sing in a hempen string
Under the Gallows-Tree.
The Bloody Brother act 3, sc. 2

14 Come, we are stark naught all, bad's the best of us.
The Bloody Brother act 4, sc. 2

15 Death hath so many doors to let out life.
The Custom of the Country (with Massinger) act 2, sc. 2. Cf. Massinger 453:16, Seneca 563:2

16 Our acts our angels are, or good or ill,
Our fatal shadows that walk by us still.
The Honest Man's Fortune epilogue

17 Nothing's so dainty sweet, as lovely melancholy.
The Nice Valour (with Middleton) act 3, sc. 3, 'Song'

18 Are you at ease now? Is your heart at rest?
Now you have got a shadow, an umbrella
To keep the scorching world's opinion
From your fair credit.
Rule a Wife and Have a Wife (performed 1624) act 3, sc. 1

19 Daisies smell-less, yet most quaint,
And sweet thyme true,
Primrose first born child of Ver,
Merry Springtime's Harbinger.
Two Noble Kinsmen (with Shakespeare) act 1, sc. 1

20 Care-charming Sleep, thou easer of all woes,
Brother to Death.
Valentinian (performed c.1610–14) act 5, sc. 7 'Song'

21 Come sing now, sing; for I know ye sing well,
I see ye have a singing face.
The Wild-Goose Chase (performed 1621) act 2, sc. 2

22 Whistle and she'll come to you.
Wit Without Money act 4, sc. 4. Cf. Burns 162:26

23 Charity and beating begins at home.
Wit Without Money act 5, sc. 2

See also FRANCIS BEAUMONT *and* JOHN FLETCHER, SHAKESPEARE *Henry VIII*

Phineas Fletcher 1582–1650

English clergyman and poet

24 Drop, drop, slow tears,
And bathe those beauteous feet,
Which brought from Heaven
The news and Prince of Peace.
Poetical Miscellanies (1633) 'An Hymn'

25 In your deep floods
Drown all my faults and fears;
Not let His eye
See sin, but through my tears.
Poetical Miscellanies (1633) 'An Hymn'

26 Love's tongue is in the eyes.
Piscatory Eclogues (1633) no. 5, st. 13

27 Poorly (poor man) he lived; poorly (poor man) he died.
The Purple Island (1633) canto 1, st. 19

1 His little son into his bosom creeps,
  The lively picture of his father's face.
  The Purple Island (1633) canto 12, st. 6

2 Love is like linen often changed, the sweeter.
  Sicelides (performed 1614) act 3, sc. 5

3 The coward's weapon, poison.
  Sicelides (performed 1614) act 5, sc. 3

Jean-Pierre Claris de Florian 1755–94
French writer and poet

4 *Plaisir d'amour ne dure qu'un moment,*
  Chagrin d'amour dure toute la vie.
  Love's pleasure lasts but a moment; love's sorrow lasts
  all through life.
  Célestine (1784) Cf. Malory 443:7

John Florio c.1553–1625
English lexicographer; translator of Montaigne's essays

5 England is the paradise of women, the purgatory of
  men, and the hell of horses.
  Second Frutes (1591) ch. 12

Ferdinand Foch 1851–1929
French Marshal

6 *Mon centre cède, ma droite recule, situation excellente,*
  j'attaque.
  My centre is giving way, my right is retreating,
  situation excellent, I am attacking.
  Message sent during the first Battle of the Marne,
  September 1914, in R. Recouly *Foch* (1919) ch. 6

7 *Ce n'est pas un traité de paix, c'est un armistice de vingt*
  ans.
  This is not a peace treaty, it is an armistice for twenty
  years.
  At the signing of the Treaty of Versailles, 1919, in Paul
  Reynaud *Mémoires* (1963) vol. 2, p. 457

J. Foley 1906–1970
British songwriter

8 Old soldiers never die,
  They simply fade away.
  'Old Soldiers Never Die' (1920 song); copyrighted by Foley
  but possibly a 'folk-song' from the First World War

José da Fonseca and Pedro Carolino
fl. 1855

9 The walls have hearsay.
  O Novo Guia da Conversação em Português e Inglês (1855)
  'Idiotisms and Proverbs'; selections from this book were
  first published in England by James Millington as *English as*
  she is spoke: or a Jest in sober earnest (1883)

10 *Por dinheiro baila o perro.*
  Nothing some money nothing of Swiss.
  O Novo Guia da Conversação em Português e Inglês (1855)
  'Idiotisms and Proverbs'. A literal translation of the
  Portuguese proverb would be 'The dog dances for money':
  it is suspected that the *Novo Guia* was prepared with the
  help of a French–English dictionary. Cf. Racine 535:6

Michael Foot 1913–
British Labour politician

11 A speech from Ernest Bevin on a major occasion had
  all the horrific fascination of a public execution. If the
  mind was left immune, eyes and ears and emotions
  were riveted.
  Aneurin Bevan (1962) vol. 1, ch. 13

12 Think of it! A second Chamber selected by the Whips.
  A seraglio of eunuchs.
  Speech, *Hansard* 3 February 1969, col. 88

13 It is not necessary that every time he rises he should
  give his famous imitation of a semi-house-trained
  polecat.
  Speech, *Hansard* 2 March 1978, col. 668 (of Norman
  Tebbit)

Samuel Foote 1720–77
English actor and playwright

14 Born in a cellar . . . and living in a garret.
  The Author (1757) act 2

15 So she went into the garden to cut a cabbage-leaf to
  make an apple-pie; and at the same time a great
  she-bear coming up the street, pops its head into the
  shop. 'What! no soap?' So he died, and she very
  imprudently married the barber; and there were
  present the Picninnies, and the Joblillies, and the
  Garyulies, and the grand Panjandrum himself, with
  the little round button at top; and they all fell to
  playing the game of catch as catch can, till the gun
  powder ran out at the heels of their boots.
  Nonsense composed to test the vaunted memory of the
  actor Charles Macklin, in Maria Edgeworth *Harry and Lucy*
  (1825) vol. 2, p. 152. See *Quarterly Review* (1854) vol. 95,
  p. 516

16 Between the muse and the magistrate there is a
  natural confederacy; what the last cannot punish the
  first often corrects.
  Letter to the Lord Chamberlain, 1775, in Simon Trefman
  Sam Foote, Comedian (1973) p. 261

17 He is not only dull in himself, but the cause of
  dullness in others.
  On a dull law lord, in James Boswell *Life of Samuel Johnson*
  (1934 ed.) vol. 4, p. 178 (1783). Cf. *Henry IV* 582:14

18 God's revenge against vanity.
  To David Garrick, who had asked him what he thought of a
  heavy shower of rain falling on the day of the Shakespeare
  Jubilee, organized by and chiefly starring Garrick himself;
  in W. Cooke *Memoirs of Samuel Foote* (1805) vol. 2, p. 86

Miss C. F. Forbes 1817–1911
English writer

19 The sense of being well-dressed gives a feeling of
  inward tranquillity which religion is powerless to
  bestow.
  In R. W. Emerson *Letters and Social Aims* (1876) p. 79

Gerald Ford 1909–

38th President of the USA

1 I am a Ford, not a Lincoln.

> On taking the vice-presidential oath, 6 December 1973, in *Washington Post* 7 December 1973

2 Our long national nightmare is over. Our Constitution works; our great Republic is a Government of laws and not of men.

> On being sworn in as President, 9 August 1974; in G. J. Lankevich *Gerald R. Ford* (1977)

3 If the Government is big enough to give you everything you want, it is big enough to take away everything you have.

> In John F. Parker *If Elected* (1960) p. 193

Henry Ford 1863–1947

American car manufacturer

4 History is more or less bunk. It's tradition. We don't want tradition. We want to live in the present and the only history that is worth a tinker's damn is the history we make today.

> In *Chicago Tribune* 25 May 1916 (interview with Charles N. Wheeler)

5 Any colour—so long as it's black.

> On the choice of colour for the Model T Ford, in Allan Nevins *Ford* (1957) vol. 2, ch. 15

6 What we call evil is simply ignorance bumping its head in the dark.

> In *Observer* 16 March 1930

John Ford 1586–after 1639

English playwright

7 Tempt not the stars, young man, thou canst not play
With the severity of fate.

> *The Broken Heart* (1633) act 1, sc. 3

8 I am . . . a mushroom
On whom the dew of heaven drops now and then.

> *The Broken Heart* (1633) act 1, sc. 3

9 The joys of marriage are the heaven on earth,
Life's paradise, great princess, the soul's quiet,
Sinews of concord, earthly immortality,
Eternity of pleasures; no restoratives
Like to a constant woman.

> *The Broken Heart* (1633) act 2, sc. 2

10   There's not a hair
Sticks on my head but, like a leaden plummet,
It sinks me to the grave: I must creep thither;
The journey is not long.

> *The Broken Heart* (1633) act 4, sc. 2

11 He hath shook hands with time.

> *The Broken Heart* (1633) act 5, sc. 2

12   Tell us, pray, what devil
This melancholy is, which can transform
Men into monsters.

> *The Lady's Trial* (1639) act 3, sc. 1

13   I have spent
Many a silent night in sighs and groans,
Run over all my thoughts, despised my fate,
Reasoned against the reasons of my love,
Done all that smoothed-cheek Virtue could advise,
But found all bootless: 'tis my destiny
That you must either love, or I must die.

> *'Tis Pity She's a Whore* (1633) act 1, sc. 2

14 Brother, even by our mother's dust, I charge you,
Do not betray me to your mirth or hate.

> *'Tis Pity She's a Whore* (1633) act 1, sc. 2

15   Why, I hold fate
Clasped in my fist, and could command the course
Of time's eternal motion, hadst thou been
One thought more steady than an ebbing sea.

> *'Tis Pity She's a Whore* (1633) act 5, sc. 4

Lena Guilbert Ford 1870–1916

16 Keep the Home-fires burning,
While your hearts are yearning,
Though your lads are far away
They dream of Home.
There's a silver lining
Through the dark cloud shining;
Turn the dark cloud inside out,
Till the boys come Home.

> 'Till the Boys Come Home!' (1914 song); music by Ivor Novello

Carl Foreman 1914–

American film director and screenwriter

17 Madness! Madness!

> *The Bridge on the River Kwai* (1957 film of the novel by Pierre Boulle) *ad fin.*

Howell Forgy 1908–83

American naval chaplain

18 Praise the Lord and pass the ammunition.

> At Pearl Harbor, 7 December 1941, as Forgy moved along a line of sailors passing ammunition by hand to the deck; in *New York Times* 1 November 1942 (later the title of a song by Frank Loesser, 1942)

E. M. Forster 1879–1970

English novelist

19 American women shoot the hippopotamus with eyebrows made of platinum.

> *Abinger Harvest* (1936) 'Mickey and Minnie'. Cf. Belloc 60:23

20 [Public schoolboys] go forth into a world that is not entirely composed of public-school men or even of Anglo-Saxons, but of men who are as various as the sands of the sea; into a world of whose richness and subtlety they have no conception. They go forth into it with well-developed bodies, fairly developed minds, and undeveloped hearts.

> *Abinger Harvest* (1936) 'Notes on English Character'

1 It is not that the Englishman can't feel—it is that he is afraid to feel. He has been taught at his public school that feeling is bad form. He must not express great joy or sorrow, or even open his mouth too wide when he talks—his pipe might fall out if he did.
Abinger Harvest (1936) 'Notes on English Character'

2 Yes—oh dear yes—the novel tells a story.
Aspects of the Novel (1927) ch. 2

3 For me the whole intricate question of method resolves itself not into formulae but into the power of the writer to bounce the reader into accepting what he says.
Aspects of the Novel (1927) ch. 4

4 We may divide [fictional] characters into flat and round ... The test of a round character is whether it is capable of surprising in a convincing way. If it never surprises, it is flat. If it does not convince, it is flat pretending to be round.
Aspects of the Novel (1927) ch. 4

5 Beauty [is that] at which a novelist should never aim, though he fails if he does not achieve it.
Aspects of the Novel (1927) ch. 5

6 A dogged attempt to cover the universe with mud, an inverted Victorianism, an attempt to make crossness and dirt succeed where sweetness and light failed.
Aspects of the Novel (1927) ch. 6 (of James Joyce's *Ulysses*)

7 Death is nothing if one can approach it as such. I was just a tiny night-light, suffocated in its own wax, and on the point of expiring.
Philip Gardner (ed.) *E. M. Forster: Commonplace Book* (1985) p. 231

8 Railway termini. They are our gates to the glorious and the unknown. Through them we pass out into adventure and sunshine, to them, alas! we return.
Howards End (1910) ch. 2

9 To trust people is a luxury in which only the wealthy can indulge; the poor cannot afford it.
Howards End (1910) ch. 5

10 She felt that those who prepared for all the emergencies of life beforehand may equip themselves at the expense of joy.
Howards End (1910) ch. 7

11 The poor cannot always reach those whom they want to love, and they can hardly ever escape from those whom they no longer love.
Howards End (1910) ch. 7

12 Certainly London fascinates ... It lies beyond everything: Nature, with all her cruelty, comes nearer to us than do those crowds of men.
Howards End (1910) ch. 13

13 Personal relations are the important thing for ever and ever, and not this outer life of telegrams and anger.
Howards End (1910) ch. 19

14 Only connect! ... Only connect the prose and the passion, and both will be exalted, and human love will be seen at its height.
Howards End (1910) ch. 22

15 Death destroys a man: the idea of death saves him.
Howards End (1910) ch. 27

16 Of all means to regeneration Remorse is surely the most wasteful. It cuts away healthy tissue with the poisoned. It is a knife that probes far deeper than the evil.
Howards End (1910) ch. 41

17 It's the worst thing that can ever happen to you in all your life, and you've got to mind it ... They'll come saying, 'Bear up—trust to time.' No, no; they're wrong. Mind it.
The Longest Journey (1907) ch. 5

18 There is much good luck in the world, but it is luck. We are none of us safe. We are children, playing or quarrelling on the line.
The Longest Journey (1907) ch. 12

19 Very notable was his distinction between coarseness and vulgarity (coarseness, revealing something; vulgarity, concealing something).
The Longest Journey (1907) ch. 26

20 The so-called white races are really pinko-grey.
A Passage to India (1924) ch. 7

21 Nothing in India is identifiable, the mere asking of a question causes it to disappear or to merge in something else.
A Passage to India (1924) ch. 8

22 Hope, politeness, the blowing of a nose, the squeak of a boot, all produce 'boum'.
A Passage to India (1924) ch. 14

23 Most of life is so dull that there is nothing to be said about it, and the books and talk that would describe it as interesting are obliged to exaggerate, in the hope of justifying their own existence.
A Passage to India (1924) ch. 14

24 Pathos, piety, courage—they exist, but are identical, and so is filth. Everything exists, nothing has value.
A Passage to India (1924) ch. 14

25 Where there is officialism every human relationship suffers.
A Passage to India (1924) ch. 24

26 Like all gossip—it's merely one of those half-alive things that try to crowd out real life.
A Passage to India (1924) ch. 31

27 God si [is] Love. Is this the final message of India?
A Passage to India (1924) ch. 33

28 Think before you speak is criticism's motto; speak before you think creation's.
Two Cheers for Democracy (1951) 'Raison d'être of Criticism'

29 If I had to choose between betraying my country and betraying my friend, I hope I should have the guts to betray my country.
Two Cheers for Democracy (1951) 'What I Believe'

30 So Two cheers for Democracy: one because it admits variety and two because it permits criticism. Two cheers are quite enough: there is no occasion to give three. Only Love the Beloved Republic deserves that.
Two Cheers for Democracy (1951) 'What I Believe' ('Love, the beloved republic' borrowed from Swinburne's poem 'Hertha')

Venantius Fortunatus AD c.530–c.610

Poet and priest; Bishop of Poitiers from AD 599

1 *Pange, lingua, gloriosi*
Proelium certaminis.

Sing, my tongue, of the battle in the glorious struggle.
'Pange lingua gloriosi' (Passiontide hymn: 'Sing, my
tongue, the glorious battle')

2 *Vexilla regis prodeunt,*
Fulget crucis mysterium;
Qua vita mortem pertulit,
Et morte vitam protulit.

The banners of the king advance, the mystery of the
cross shines bright; where his life went through with
death, and from death brought forth life.
'Vexilla Regis' (hymn: 'The royal banners forward go')

3 *Regnavit a ligno Deus.*

God reigned from the wood.
'Vexilla Regis'

Harry Emerson Fosdick 1878–1969

American Baptist minister

4 I renounce war for its consequences, for the lies it lives
on and propagates, for the undying hatred it arouses,
for the dictatorships it puts in the place of democracy,
for the starvation that stalks after it.
*Armistice Day Sermon in New York, 1933, in The Secret of
Victorious Living (1934) p. 97*

Charles Foster 1828–1904

American politician

5 Isn't this a billion dollar country?
At the 51st Congress, responding to a Democratic gibe
about a 'million dollar Congress', also attributed to Thomas
B. Reed, who reported the exchange in *North American
Review* March 1892, vol. 154, p. 319

Sir George Foster 1847–1931

Canadian politician

6 In these somewhat troublesome days when the great
Mother Empire stands splendidly isolated in Europe.
In *Official Report of the Debates of the House of Commons of
the Dominion of Canada* (1896) vol. 41, col. 176 (for
16 January 1896). On 22 January 1896, *The Times* referred
to this speech under the heading 'Splendid Isolation'

John Foster 1770–1843

English Baptist minister

7 But the two classes [the educated and the uneducated]
so beheld in contrast, might they not seem to belong
to two different nations?
Essay on the Evils of Popular Ignorance (1820) p. 277. Cf.
Disraeli DISR0094

8 An idea cannot well be accompanied by a stronger
kind of interest than the earnest wish to escape
from it.
Essays (1805) 'On the Aversion of Men of Taste to
Evangelical Religion'

9 They [the wealthy] are in a religious diving-bell;
religion is not circumambient, but a little is conveyed
down into the worldly depth, where they breathe by a
sort of artificial inlet—a tube.
Journal Item 420 in Life and Correspondence (1846)

10 Is not the pleasure of feeling and exhibiting *power* over
other beings, a principal part of the gratification of
cruelty?
Journal Item 772 in Life and Correspondence (1846)

Stephen Collins Foster 1826–64

American songwriter

11 Beautiful dreamer, wake unto me,
Starlight and dewdrop are waiting for thee.
'Beautiful Dreamer' (1864 song)

12 Gwine to run all night!
Gwine to run all day!
I'll bet my money on de bobtail nag—
Somebody bet on de bay.
'De Camptown Races' (1850) chorus

13 I dream of Jeanie with the light brown hair,
Floating, like a vapour, on the soft summer air.
'Jeanie with the Light Brown Hair' (1854)

14 Way down upon the Swanee River,
Far, far, away,
There's where my heart is turning ever;
There's where the old folks stay.
'The Old Folks at Home' (1851)

15 All the world is sad and dreary
Everywhere I roam,
Oh! darkies, how my heart grows weary,
Far from the old folks at home.
'The Old Folks at Home' (1851) chorus

Charles Fourier 1772–1837

French social theorist

16 *L'extension des privilèges des femmes est le principe
général de tous progrès sociaux.*

The extension of women's rights is the basic principle
of all social progress.
Théorie des Quatre Mouvements (1808) vol. 2, ch. 4

Charles James Fox 1749–1806

English Whig politician

17 He [Pitt the Younger] was uniformly of an opinion
which, though not a popular one, he was ready to
aver, that the right of governing was not property but
a trust.
On Pitt's scheme of Parliamentary Reform, 1785, in J. L.
Hammond *Charles James Fox* (1903) ch. 4

18 How much the greatest event it is that ever happened
in the world! and how much the best!
On the fall of the Bastille; letter to Richard Fitzpatrick,
30 July 1789, in Lord John Russell *Life and Times of C. J.
Fox* vol. 2 (1859) p. 361

19 I die happy.
Last words, in Lord John Russell *Life and Times of C. J. Fox*
vol. 3 (1860) ch. 69

George Fox 1624–91

English founder of the Society of Friends (Quakers)

1 I saw also that there was an ocean of darkness and death, but an infinite ocean of light and love, which flowed over the ocean of darkness.
> *Journal* 1647 (ed. J. L. Nickalls, 1952, p. 19)

2 I told them I lived in the virtue of that life and power that took away the occasion of all wars.
> On being offered a captaincy in the army of the Commonwealth, against the forces of the King, in *Journal* 1651 (ed. J. L. Nickalls, 1952, p. 65)

3 Walk cheerfully over the world, answering that of God in every one.
> *Journal* 1656 (ed. J. L. Nickalls, 1952, p. 263)

4 Be still and cool in thy own mind and spirit from thy own thoughts, and then thou wilt feel the principle of God to turn thy mind to the Lord God.
> *Journal* 1658 (ed. J. L. Nickalls, 1952, p. 346)

5 All bloody principles and practices, we, as to our own particulars, do utterly deny, with all outward wars and strife and fightings with outward weapons, for any end or under any pretence whatsoever. And this is our testimony to the whole world.
> *Journal* 1661 (ed. J. L. Nickalls, 1952, p. 399)

Henry Fox

See 1ST LORD HOLLAND

Anatole France (Jacques-Anatole-François Thibault) 1844–1924

French novelist and man of letters

6 *Dans tout État policé, la richesse est chose sacrée; dans les démocraties elle est la seule chose sacrée.*

In every well-governed state, wealth is a sacred thing; in democracies it is the only sacred thing.
> *L'Île des pingouins* (1908) pt. 6, ch. 2

7 *Ils [les pauvres] y doivent travailler devant la majestueuse égalité des lois, qui interdit au riche comme au pauvre de coucher sous les ponts, de mendier dans les rues et de voler du pain.*

They [the poor] have to labour in the face of the majestic equality of the law, which forbids the rich as well as the poor to sleep under bridges, to beg in the streets, and to steal bread.
> *Le Lys rouge* (1894) ch. 7

8 *Le bon critique est celui qui raconte les aventures de son âme au milieu des chefs-d'œuvre.*

The good critic is he who relates the adventures of his soul in the midst of masterpieces.
> *La Vie littéraire* (1888) dedicatory letter

Francis I 1494–1547

King of France from 1515

9 *De toutes choses ne m'est demeuré que l'honneur et la vie qui est saulve.*

Of all I had, only honour and life have been spared.
> Letter to his mother following his defeat at Pavia, 1525, in *Collection des Documents Inédits sur l'Histoire de France* (1847) vol. 1, p. 129 (usually quoted '*Tout est perdu fors l'honneur* [All is lost save honour]')

St Francis de Sales 1567–1622

Bishop of Geneva; leader of the Counter-Reformation

10 *Ce sont les grans feux qui s'enflamment au vent, mais les petits s'esteignent si on ne les y porte a couvert.*

Big fires flare up in a wind, but little ones are blown out unless they are carried in under cover.
> *Introduction à la vie dévote* (1609) pt. 3, ch. 34. Cf. Bussy-Rabutin 165:18, La Rochefoucauld 410:19

11 *Quantum ore dixerimus, sane cor cordi loquitur, lingua non nisi aures pulsat.*

It has been well said, that heart speaks to heart, whereas language only speaks to the ears.
> Latin translation of a letter to the Archbishop of Bourges, 5 October 1604, which John Henry Newman paraphrased for his motto as '*cor ad cor loquitur* [heart speaks to heart]'. See *Oeuvres de Saint François de Sales* (1834) vol. 3, p. 29

St Francis of Assisi
1181–1226

Founder of the Franciscan Order

12 Lord, make me an instrument of Your peace!
Where there is hatred let me sow love;
Where there is injury, pardon;
Where there is doubt, faith;
Where there is despair, hope;
Where there is darkness, light;
Where there is sadness, joy.

O divine Master, grant that I may not so much seek
To be consoled as to console;
To be understood as to understand;
To be loved as to love.
For it is in giving that we receive;
It is in pardoning that we are pardoned;
And it is in dying that we are born to eternal life.
> 'Prayer of St Francis' (attributed)

Benjamin Franklin 1706–90

American politician, inventor, and scientist

13 Remember that time is money.
> *Advice to a Young Tradesman* (1748)

14 Some are weather-wise, some are otherwise.
> *Poor Richard's Almanac* (1735) February

15 Necessity never made a good bargain.
> *Poor Richard's Almanac* (1735) April

16 At twenty years of age, the will reigns; at thirty, the wit; and at forty, the judgement.
> *Poor Richard's Almanac* (1741) June

17 He that lives upon hope will die fasting.
> *Poor Richard's Almanac* (1758) preface

18 A little neglect may breed mischief . . . for want of a nail, the shoe was lost; for want of a shoe the horse was lost; and for want of a horse the rider was lost.
> *Poor Richard's Almanac* (1758) preface

19 Here Skugg
Lies snug
As a bug
In a rug.
> Letter to Georgiana Shipley on the death of her squirrel, 26 September 1772, in W. B. Willcox (ed.) *Papers of Benjamin Franklin* vol. 19 (1975) p. 302 (*skugg* squirrel)

1 We must indeed all hang together, or, most assuredly, we shall all hang separately.

> At the Signing of the Declaration of Independence, 4 July 1776 (possibly not original). See P. M. Zall *Ben Franklin* (1980) p. 154

2 There never was a good war, or a bad peace.

> Letter to Josiah Quincy, 11 September 1783, in *Works* (1882) vol. 10, p. 11

3 In this world nothing can be said to be certain, except death and taxes.

> Letter to Jean Baptiste Le Roy, 13 November 1789, in *Works of Benjamin Franklin* (1817) ch. 6. See Daniel Defoe *History of the Devil* (1726) bk. 2, ch. 6: 'Things as certain as death and taxes, can be more firmly believed'

4 Man is a tool-making animal.

> In James Boswell *Life of Samuel Johnson* (1934 ed.) vol. 3, p. 245 (7 April 1778)

5 What is the use of a new-born child?

> When asked what was the use of a new invention, in J. Parton *Life and Times of Benjamin Franklin* (1864) pt. 4, ch. 17

6
> The body of
> Benjamin Franklin, printer,
> (Like the cover of an old book,
> Its contents worn out,
> And stripped of its lettering and gilding)
> Lies here, food for worms!
> Yet the work itself shall not be lost,
> For it will, as he believed, appear once more
> In a new
> And more beautiful edition,
> Corrected and amended
> By its Author!

> Epitaph for himself (1728). Cf. Turgot 705:13

Oliver Franks (Baron Franks) 1905–

British philosopher and administrator

7 The Pentagon, that immense monument to modern man's subservience to the desk.

> In *Observer* 30 November 1952

8 A secret in the Oxford sense: you may tell it to only one person at a time.

> In *Sunday Telegraph* 30 January 1977

Sir James George Frazer 1854–1941

Scottish anthropologist

9 The awe and dread with which the untutored savage contemplates his mother-in-law are amongst the most familiar facts of anthropology.

> *The Golden Bough* (2nd ed., 1900) vol. 1, p. 288

Frederick the Great 1712–86

King of Prussia from 1740

10 *Chassez les préjugés par la porte, ils rentreront par la fenêtre.*

> Drive out prejudices through the door, and they will return through the window.

> Letter to Voltaire, 19 March 1771, in *Oeuvres Complètes* (1790) vol. 12

11 My people and I have come to an agreement which satisfies us both. They are to say what they please, and I am to do what I please.

> His interpretation of benevolent despotism (attributed)

12 *Ihr Racker, wollt ihr ewig leben?*

> Rascals, would you live for ever?

> To hesitant Guards at Kolin, 18 June 1757 (attributed)

E. A. Freeman 1823–92

English historian

13 History is past politics, and politics is present history.

> *Methods of Historical Study* (1886) p. 44

14 A saying which fell from myself in one of the debates in Congregation on the Modern Language Statute has been quoted in several places . . . 'chatter about Shelley' . . . I mentioned that I had lately read a review of a book about Shelley in which the critic . . . praised or blamed the author . . . for his 'treatment of the Harriet problem'.

> 'Literature and Language' in *Contemporary Review* October 1887 (commonly telescoped as 'chatter about Harriet')

John Freeth c.1731–1808

English poet

15 The loss of America what can repay?
New colonies seek for at Botany Bay.

> 'Botany Bay' in *New London Magazine* (1786)

John Hookham Frere 1769–1846

English poet

16 The feathered race with pinions skim the air—
Not so the mackerel, and still less the bear!

> 'The Progress of Man' (1798) canto 1, l. 34

17 Ah! who has seen the mailed lobster rise,
Clap her broad wings, and soaring claim the skies?

> 'The Progress of Man' (1798) canto 1, l. 44

Sigmund Freud 1856–1939

Austrian psychiatrist; originator of psychoanalysis

18 We are so made, that we can only derive intense enjoyment from a contrast, and only very little from a state of things.

> *Civilization and its Discontents* (1930) ch. 2

19 Anatomy is destiny.

> *Collected Writings* (1924) vol. 5, p. 210

20 The interpretation of dreams is the royal road to a knowledge of the unconscious activities of the mind.

> *The Interpretation of Dreams* (2nd ed., 1909) ch. 7, sect. E (often quoted 'Dreams are the royal road to the unconscious')

21 Analogies decide nothing, that is true, but they can make one feel more at home.

> *New Introductory Lectures on Psychoanalysis* (1933) ch. 31

22 'Itzig, where are you riding to?' 'Don't ask me, ask the horse.'

> Letter to Wilhelm Fliess, 7 July 1898, in *Origins of Psychoanalysis* (1950) p. 275

1 The great question that has never been answered and which I have not yet been able to answer, despite my thirty years of research into the feminine soul, is 'What does a woman want?'
  Letter to Marie Bonaparte, in Ernest Jones *Sigmund Freud: Life and Work* (1955) vol. 2, pt. 3, ch. 16

2 All that matters is love and work.
  Attributed

Betty Friedan 1921–
American feminist

3 The problem that has no name.
  The Feminine Mystique (1963) ch. 14 (being the fact that American women are kept from growing to their full human capacities)

Max Frisch 1911–
Swiss novelist and playwright

4 *Technik ... Kniff, die Welt so einzurichten, dass wir sie nicht erleben müssen.*

  Technology ... the knack of so arranging the world that we need not experience it.
  Homo Faber (1957) pt. 2

Charles Frohman 1860–1915
American theatrical manager

5 Why fear death? It is the most beautiful adventure in life.
  Last words before drowning in the *Lusitania*, 7 May 1915; in I. F. Marcosson and D. Frohman *Charles Frohman* (1916) ch. 19. Cf. Barrie 54:8

Erich Fromm 1900–80
American philosopher and psychologist

6 Man's main task in life is to give birth to himself, to become what he potentially is. The most important product of his effort is his own personality.
  Man for Himself (1947) ch. 4

7 In the nineteenth century the problem was that *God is dead*; in the twentieth century the problem is that *man is dead*. In the nineteenth century inhumanity meant cruelty; in the twentieth century it means schizoid self-alienation. The danger of the past was that men became slaves. The danger of the future is that men may become robots.
  The Sane Society (1955) ch. 9

Robert Frost 1874–1963
American poet

8 I have been one acquainted with the night.
  'Acquainted with the Night' (1928)

9   Often you must have seen them
  Loaded with ice a sunny winter morning
  After a rain. They click upon themselves
  As the breeze rises, and turn many-coloured
  As the stir cracks and crazes their enamel.
  Soon the sun's warmth makes them shed crystal shells
  Shattering and avalanching on the snow crust—
  Such heaps of broken glass to sweep away
  You'd think the inner dome of heaven had fallen.
  'Birches' (1916)

10 ... Life is too much like a pathless wood
  Where your face burns and tickles with the cobwebs
  Broken across it, and one eye is weeping
  From a twig's having lashed across it open.
  'Birches' (1916)

11 I'd like to get away from earth awhile
  And then come back to it and begin over.
  May no fate wilfully misunderstand me
  And half grant what I wish and snatch me away
  Not to return. Earth's the right place for love:
  I don't know where it's likely to go better.
  'Birches' (1916)

12 Most of the change we think we see in life
  Is due to truths being in and out of favour.
  'The Black Cottage' (1914)

13 Forgive, O Lord, my little jokes on Thee
  And I'll forgive Thy great big one on me.
  'Cluster of Faith' (1962)

14 And nothing to look backward to with pride,
  And nothing to look forward to with hope.
  'The Death of the Hired Man' (1914)

15 'Home is the place where, when you have to go there,
  They have to take you in.'
  'I should have called it
  Something you somehow haven't to deserve.'
  'The Death of the Hired Man' (1914)

16 They cannot scare me with their empty spaces
  Between stars—on stars where no human race is.
  I have it in me so much nearer home
  To scare myself with my own desert places.
  'Desert Places' (1936)

17 Some say the world will end in fire,
  Some say in ice.
  From what I've tasted of desire
  I hold with those who favour fire.
  But if it had to perish twice,
  I think I know enough of hate
  To say that for destruction ice
  Is also great
  And would suffice.
  'Fire and Ice' (1923)

18 The land was ours before we were the land's.
  She was our land more than a hundred years
  Before we were her people.
  'The Gift Outright' (1942)

19 Happiness makes up in height for what it lacks in length.
  Title of poem (1942)

...nt
Where the spender ...nks it went.
...ly was ever meant
To remember ... I spent
...he did with every cent.
'... arithm ...of Accounting' (1936)

... an epitaph to be my story
... a short one ready for my own.
...uld have written of me on my stone:
I had a lover's quarrel with the world.
'The Lesson for Today' (1942)

3 Something there is that doesn't love a wall,
That sends the frozen-ground-swell under it.
'Mending Wall' (1914)

4 My apple trees will never get across
And eat the cones under his pines, I tell him.
He only says, 'Good fences make good neighbours.'
'Mending Wall' (1914)

5 Before I built a wall I'd ask to know
What I was walling in or walling out,
And to whom I was like to give offence.
'Mending Wall' (1914)

6 The water comes ashore,
And the people look at the sea.
They cannot look out far.
They cannot look in deep.
But when was that ever a bar
To any watch they keep?
'Neither Out Far Nor In Deep' (1928)

7 I'm going out to clean the pasture spring;
I'll only stop to rake the leaves away
(And wait to watch the water clear, I may):
I shan't be gone long.—You come too.
'The Pasture' (1914)

8 I never dared be radical when young
For fear it would make me conservative when old.
'Precaution' (1936)

9 I shall be telling this with a sigh
Somewhere ages and ages hence:
Two roads diverged in a wood, and I—
I took the one less travelled by,
And that has made all the difference.
'The Road Not Taken' (1916)

10 We dance round in a ring and suppose,
But the Secret sits in the middle and knows.
'The Secret Sits' (1942)

11 I've broken Anne of gathering bouquets.
It's not fair to the child. It can't be helped though:
Pressed into service means pressed out of shape.
'The Self-Seeker' (1914)

12 Len says one steady pull more ought to do it.
He says the best way out is always through.
'A Servant to Servants' (1914)

13 The woods are lovely, dark and deep.
But I have promises to keep,
And miles to go before I sleep,
And miles to go before I sleep.
'Stopping by Woods on a Snowy Evening' (1923)

14 It should be of the pleasure of a poem itself to tell how
it can. The figure a poem makes. It begins in delight
and ends in wisdom. The figure is the same as for
love:
Collected Poems (1939) 'The Figure a Poem Makes'

15 No tears in the writer, no tears in the reader. No
surprise for the writer, no surprise for the reader.
Collected Poems (1939) 'The Figure a Poem Makes'

16 Like a piece of ice on a hot stove the poem must ride
on its own melting. A poem may be worked over once
it is in being, but may not be worried into being.
Collected Poems (1939) 'The Figure a Poem Makes'

17 I'd as soon write free verse as play tennis with the net
down.
In Edward Lathem Interviews with Robert Frost (1966)
p. 203

18 Poetry is a way of taking life by the throat.
In Elizabeth S. Sergeant Robert Frost (1960) ch. 18

19 Poetry is what is lost in translation. It is also what is
lost in interpretation.
In Louis Untermeyer Robert Frost (1964) p. 18

Christopher Fry 1907–
English playwright

20 The dark is light enough.
Title of play (1954)

21   What after all
Is a halo? It's only one more thing to keep clean.
The Lady's not for Burning (1949) act 1

22 What is official
Is incontestable. It undercuts
The problematical world and sells us life
At a discount.
The Lady's not for Burning (1949) act 1

23 Where in this small-talking world can I find
A longitude with no platitude?
The Lady's not for Burning (1949) act 3

24   The best
Thing we can do is to make wherever we're lost in
Look as much like home as we can.
The Lady's not for Burning (1949) act 3

25   I hope
I've done nothing so monosyllabic as to cheat,
A spade is never so merely a spade as the word
Spade would imply.
Venus Observed (1950) act 2, sc. 1

Roger Fry 1866–1934
English art critic

26 Art is significant deformity.
In Virginia Woolf Roger Fry (1940) ch. 8

R. Buckminster Fuller 1895–1983
American designer and architect

27 Either war is obsolete or men are.
In New Yorker 8 January 1966, p. 93

1 God, to me, it seems,
is a verb
not a noun,
proper or improper.
No More Secondhand God (1963) p. 28 (untitled poem written in 1940). Cf. Hugo 354:13

2 Now there is one outstandingly important fact regarding Spaceship Earth, and that is that no instruction book came with it.
Operating Manual for Spaceship Earth (1969) ch. 4

Sam Fuller

American film director

3 When you're in the battlefield, survival is all there is. Death is the only great emotion.
In *Guardian* 26 February 1991

Thomas Fuller 1608–61

English preacher and historian

4 But our captain counts the Image of God nevertheless his image, cut in ebony as if done in ivory.
The Holy State and the Profane State (1642) bk. 2 'The Good Sea-Captain'

5 Know most of the rooms of thy native country before thou goest over the threshold thereof.
The Holy State and the Profane State bk. 3 'Of Travelling'

6 Anger is one of the sinews of the soul.
The Holy State and the Profane State bk. 3 'Of Anger'

7 Light (God's eldest daughter) is a principal beauty in building.
The Holy State and the Profane State bk. 3 'Of Building'

8 He was one of a lean body and visage, as if his eager soul, biting for anger at the clog of his body, desired to fret a passage through it.
The Holy State and the Profane State bk. 5 'Life of the Duke of Alva'

Thomas Fuller 1654–1734

English writer and physician

9 We are all Adam's children but silk makes the difference.
Gnomologia (1732) no. 5425

Alfred Funke b. 1869

German writer

10 *Gott strafe England!*
God punish England!
Schwert und Myrte (1914) p. 78

Sir David Maxwell Fyfe 1900–67

See LORD KILMUIR

Rose Fyleman 1877–1957

English writer for children

11 There are fairies at the bottom of our garden!
Fairies and Chimneys (1918) 'The Fairies' (first published in *Punch* 23 May 1917)

Zsa Zsa Gabor (Sari Gabor) 1919–

Hungarian-born film actress

12 A man in love is incomplete until he has married. Then he's finished.
In *Newsweek* 28 March 1960, p. 89

Thomas Gainsborough 1727–88

English painter

13 Recollect that painting and punctuality mix like oil and vinegar, and that genius and regularity are utter enemies, and must be to the end of time.
Letter to the Hon. Edward Stratford, 1 May 1772, in Mary Woodall (ed.) *The Letters of Thomas Gainsborough* (1961)

14 We are all going to Heaven, and Vandyke is of the company.
Attributed last words, in William B. Boulton *Thomas Gainsborough* (1905) ch. 9

Thomas Gaisford 1779–1855

English classicist; Dean of Christ Church, Oxford, from 1831

15 Nor can I do better, in conclusion, than impress upon you the study of Greek literature, which not only elevates above the vulgar herd, but leads not infrequently to positions of considerable emolument.
Christmas Day Sermon in the Cathedral, Oxford, in W. Tuckwell *Reminiscences of Oxford* (2nd ed., 1907) p. 124

Hugh Gaitskell 1906–63

British Labour politician

16 There are some of us ... who will fight and fight and fight again to save the Party we love.
Speech at Labour Party Conference, 5 October 1960, in *Report of 59th Annual Conference* p. 201

17 It means the end of a thousand years of history.
On a European federation; Speech at Labour Party Conference, 3 October 1962, in *Report of 61st Annual Conference* p. 159

Gaius (or Caius) AD c.110–c.180

Roman jurist

18 *Damnosa hereditas.*
Ruinous inheritance.
The Institutes bk. 2, ch. 163

J. K. Galbraith 1908–

American economist

19 These are the days when men of all social disciplines and all political faiths seek the comfortable and the accepted; when the man of controversy is looked upon as a disturbing influence; when originality is taken to be a mark of instability; and when, in minor modification of the scriptural parable, the bland lead the bland.
The Affluent Society (1958) ch. 1, sect. 3

1 It is a far, far better thing to have a firm anchor in nonsense than to put out on the troubled seas of thought.
    The Affluent Society (1958) ch. 11, sect. 4

2 The greater the wealth, the thicker will be the dirt.
    The Affluent Society (1958) ch. 18, sect. 2

3 Politics is not the art of the possible. It consists in choosing between the disastrous and the unpalatable.
    Letter to President Kennedy, 2 March 1962, in *Ambassador's Journal* (1969) p. 312. Cf. Bismarck 110:4

Galileo Galilei 1564–1642
Italian astronomer and physicist

4 *Eppur si muove.*

But it does move.
    Attributed to Galileo after his recantation, that the earth moves around the sun, in 1632. See Baretti *Italian Library* (1757) p. 52 for possibly the earliest appearance of the phrase

John Galsworthy 1867–1933
English novelist

5 He was afflicted by the thought that where Beauty was, nothing ever ran quite straight, which, no doubt, was why so many people looked on it as immoral.
    In Chancery (1920) pt. 1, ch. 13

6 A man of action forced into a state of thought is unhappy until he can get out of it.
    Maid in Waiting (1931) ch. 3

John Galt 1779–1839
Scottish writer

7 From the lone shieling of the misty island
Mountains divide us, and the waste of seas—
Yet still the blood is strong, the heart is Highland,
And we in dreams behold the Hebrides!
Fair these broad meads, these hoary woods are grand;
But we are exiles from our fathers' land.
    'Canadian Boat Song' translated from the Gaelic in *Blackwoods Edinburgh Magazine* September 1829 'Noctes Ambrosianae' no. 46 (attributed to Galt)

Mahatma Gandhi (*Mohandas Karamchand Gandhi*) 1869–1948
Indian statesman

8 What difference does it make to the dead, the orphans and the homeless, whether the mad destruction is wrought under the name of totalitarianism or the holy name of liberty or democracy?
    Non-Violence in Peace and War (1942) vol. 1, ch. 142

9 The moment the slave resolves that he will no longer be a slave, his fetters fall. He frees himself and shows the way to others. Freedom and slavery are mental states.
    Non-Violence in Peace and War (1949) vol. 2, ch. 5

10 Non-violence is the first article of my faith. It is also the last article of my creed.
    Speech at Shahi Bag, 18 March 1922, on a charge of sedition, in *Young India* 23 March 1922

Greta Garbo (*Greta Lovisa Gustafsson*) 1905–90
Swedish film actress

11 I want to be alone.
    Grand Hotel (1932 film), the phrase already being associated with Garbo

Federico García Lorca 1899–1936
Spanish poet and playwright

12 *A las cinco de la tarde.*
Eran las cinco en punto de la tarde.
Un niño trajo la blanca sábana
a las cinco de la tarde.

At five in the afternoon.
It was exactly five in the afternoon.
A boy brought the white sheet
at five in the afternoon.
    Llanto por Ignacio Sánchez Mejías (1935) 'La Cogida y la muerte'

13 *Verde que te quiero verde.*
Verde viento. Verdes ramas.
El barco sobre la mar
y el caballo en la montaña.

Green how I love you green.
Green wind.
Green boughs.
The ship on the sea
and the horse on the mountain.
    Romance sonámbulo (1924–7)

Richard Gardiner b. c.1533
English writer

14 Sowe Carrets in your Gardens, and humbly praise God for them, as for a singular and great blessing.
    Profitable Instructions for the Manuring, Sowing and Planting of Kitchen Gardens (1599)

Ed Gardner 1901–63
American radio comedian

15 Opera is when a guy gets stabbed in the back and, instead of bleeding, he sings.
    In *Duffy's Tavern* (US radio programme, 1940s)

James A. Garfield 1831–81
20th President of the USA

16 Fellow-citizens: God reigns, and the Government at Washington lives!
    Speech on the assassination of President Lincoln, 1865. See *Death of President Garfield* (1881) p. 24

Giuseppe Garibaldi 1807–82

Italian patriot and military leader

1 *Soldati, io esco da Roma. Chi vuole continuare la guerra
contro lo straniero venga con me. Non posso offrirgli né
onori né stipendi; gli offro fame, sete, marcie forzate,
battaglie e morte. Chi ama la patria mi segua.*

Men, I'm getting out of Rome. Anyone who wants to
carry on the war against the outsiders, come with me.
I can offer you neither honours nor wages; I offer you
hunger, thirst, forced marches, battles and death.
Anyone who loves his country, follow me.
> In Giuseppe Guerzoni *Garibaldi* (1882) vol. 1, p. 331 (not a
> verbatim record)

John Nance Garner 1868–1967

American politician

2 The vice-presidency isn't worth a pitcher of warm piss.
> In O. C. Fisher *Cactus Jack* (1978) ch. 11

David Garrick 1717–79

English actor-manager

3 Farewell, great painter of mankind!
Who reached the noblest point of art,
Whose pictured morals charm the mind
And through the eye correct the heart.
> Epitaph on Hogarth's monument in Chiswick churchyard
> (1772)

4 Heart of oak are our ships,
Heart of oak are our men:
We always are ready;
Steady, boys, steady;
We'll fight and we'll conquer again and again.
> *Harlequin's Invasion* (1759) 'Heart of Oak' (song)

5 Here lies Nolly Goldsmith, for shortness called Noll,
Who wrote like an angel, but talked like poor Poll.
> 'Impromptu Epitaph' (written 1773/4). Cf. Goldsmith
> 311:3, Johnson 375:17

6 A fellow-feeling makes one wond'rous kind.
> 'An Occasional Prologue on Quitting the Theatre' 10 June
> 1776

7 Are these the choice dishes the Doctor has sent us?
Is this the great poet whose works so content us?
This Goldsmith's fine feast, who has written fine
books?
Heaven sends us good meat, but the Devil sends cooks.
> 'On Doctor Goldsmith's Characteristical Cookery' (1777)

8 Prologues precede the piece—in mournful verse;
As undertakers—walk before the hearse.
> Prologue to Arthur Murphy's *The Apprentice* (1756)

9 I've that within—for which there are no plaisters.
> Prologue to Oliver Goldsmith's *She Stoops to Conquer* (1773)

10 Kitty, a fair, but frozen maid,
Kindled a flame I still deplore.
> 'A Riddle' (1762)

See also GEORGE COLMAN and DAVID GARRICK

William Lloyd Garrison 1805–79

American anti-slavery campaigner

11 I am in earnest—I will not equivocate—I will not
excuse—I will not retreat a single inch—and I will be
heard!
> *The Liberator* 1 January 1831 'Salutatory Address'

12 Our country is the world—our countrymen are all
mankind.
> *The Liberator* 15 December 1837 'Prospectus'

13 The compact which exists between the North and the
South is 'a covenant with death and an agreement
with hell'.
> Resolution adopted by the Massachusetts Anti-Slavery
> Society, 27 January 1843, in Archibald H. Grimke *William
> Lloyd Garrison: The Abolitionist* (1891) ch. 16. Cf. Isaiah
> 83:12

Sir Samuel Garth 1661–1719

English poet and physician

14 Hard was their lodging, homely was their food;
For all their luxury was doing good.
> 'Claremont' (1715) l. 148

15 A barren superfluity of words.
> *The Dispensary* (1699) canto 2, l. 82

George Gascoigne c.1534–77

English soldier and poet

16 The common speech is, spend and God will send.
But what sends he? a bottle and a bag,
A staff, a wallet and a woeful end,
For such as list in bravery so to brag.
> '*Magnum vectigal parsimonia* [Thrift makes a good income]'
> (1573)

17 I not deny but some men have good hap,
To climb aloft by scales of courtly grace,
And win the world with liberality:
Yet he that yerks old angels out apace,
And hath no new to purchase dignity,
When orders fall, may chance to lack his grace.
For haggard hawks mislike an empty hand.
> '*Magnum vectigal parsimonia*' (1573) (*yerks* flings, *angels*
> coins)

18 The carrion crow, that loathsome beast,
Which cries against the rain,
Both for her hue and for the rest,
The Devil resembleth plain:
And as with guns we kill the crow,
For spoiling our relief,
The Devil so must we overthrow,
With gunshot of belief.
> 'Gascoigne's Good Morrow' (1573)

19 As busy brains must beat on tickle toys,
As rash invention breeds a raw device,
So sudden falls do hinder hasty joys;
And as swift baits do fleetest fish entice,
So haste makes waste, and therefore now I say,
No haste but good, where wisdom makes the way.
> 'No haste but good' (1573)

Elizabeth Gaskell 1810–65

English novelist

1 A man ... is *so* in the way in the house!
  Cranford (1853) ch. 1

2 Economy was always 'elegant', and money-spending always 'vulgar' and ostentatious— a sort of sour-grapeism, which made us very peaceful and satisfied.
  Cranford (1853) ch. 1

3 Bombazine would have shown a deeper sense of her loss.
  Cranford (1853) ch. 7

4 I'll not listen to reason ... Reason always means what someone else has got to say.
  Cranford (1853) ch. 14

5 We donnot want dainties, we want belly-fulls; we donnot want gimcrack coats and waistcoats, we want warm clothes; and so that we get 'em, we'd not quarrel wi' what they're made on.
  Mary Barton (1848) ch. 16

6 That kind of patriotism which consists in hating all other nations.
  Sylvia's Lovers (1863) ch. 1

Alan Gaunt 1935–

7 We pray for peace,
  But not the easy peace
  Built on complacency
  And not the truth of God.
  'We pray for peace' (hymn)

Gavarni (Guillaume Sulpice Chevalier) 1804–66

French lithographer

8 *Les enfants terribles.*
  The little terrors.
  Title of a series of prints (1842)

John Gay 1685–1732

English poet and playwright

9 O ruddier than the cherry,
  O sweeter than the berry.
  Acis and Galatea (performed 1718, published 1732) pt. 2

10 How, like a moth, the simple maid
  Still plays about the flame!
  The Beggar's Opera (1728) act 1, sc. 4, air 4

11 Our Polly is a sad slut! nor heeds what we have taught her.
  I wonder any man alive will ever rear a daughter!
  The Beggar's Opera (1728) act 1, sc. 8, air 7

12 Do you think your mother and I should have lived comfortably so long together, if ever we had been married?
  The Beggar's Opera (1728) act 1, sc. 8

13 Can Love be controlled by advice?
  The Beggar's Opera (1728) act 1, sc. 8, air 8

14 POLLY: Then all my sorrows are at an end.
  MRS PEACHUM: A mighty likely speech, in troth, for a wench who is just married!
  The Beggar's Opera (1728) act 1, sc. 8

15 Money, wife, is the true fuller's earth for reputations, there is not a spot or a stain but what it can take out.
  The Beggar's Opera (1728) act 1, sc. 9

16 The comfortable estate of widowhood, is the only hope that keeps up a wife's spirits.
  The Beggar's Opera (1728) act 1, sc. 10

17 If with me you'd fondly stray.
  Over the hills and far away.
  The Beggar's Opera (1728) act 1, sc. 13, air 16

18 We retrench the superfluities of mankind.
  The Beggar's Opera (1728) act 2, sc. 1

19 Fill ev'ry glass, for wine inspires us,
  And fires us
  With courage, love and joy.
  Women and wine should life employ.
  Is there ought else on earth desirous?
  The Beggar's Opera (1728) act 2, sc. 1, air 19

20 If the heart of a man is deprest with cares,
  The mist is dispelled when a woman appears.
  The Beggar's Opera (1728) act 2, sc. 3, air 21

21 I must have women. There is nothing unbends the mind like them.
  The Beggar's Opera (1728) act 2, sc. 3

22 Youth's the season made for joys;
  Love is then our duty.
  The Beggar's Opera (1728) act 2, sc. 4, air 22

23 To cheat a man is nothing; but the woman must have fine parts indeed who cheats a woman!
  The Beggar's Opera (1728) act 2, sc. 4

24 I am ready, my dear Lucy, to give you satisfaction—if you think there is any in marriage?
  The Beggar's Opera (1728) act 2, sc. 9

25 In one respect indeed, our employment may be reckoned dishonest, because, like great Statesmen, we encourage those who betray their friends.
  The Beggar's Opera (1728) act 2, sc. 10

26 How happy could I be with either,
  Were t'other dear charmer away!
  The Beggar's Opera (1728) act 2, sc. 13, air 35

27 She who has never loved, has never lived.
  The Captives (1724) act 2, sc. 2

28 She who trifles with all
  Is less likely to fall
  Than she who but trifles with one.
  'The Coquet Mother and the Coquet Daughter' (1727)

29 Behold the victim of Parthenia's pride!
  He saw, he sighed, he loved, was scorned and died.
  Dione (1720) act 1, sc. 1

30 A woman's friendship ever ends in love.
  Dione (1720) act 4, sc. 6

31 Whence is thy learning? Hath thy toil
  O'er books consumed the midnight oil?
  Fables (1727) introduction, l. 15. Cf. Quarles 533:17

32 Envy's a sharper spur than pay,
  No author ever spared a brother,
  Wits are gamecocks to one another.
  Fables (1727) 'The Elephant and the Bookseller' l. 74

1 And when a lady's in the case,
You know, all other things give place.
  Fables (1727) 'The Hare and Many Friends' l. 41

2 Those who in quarrels interpose,
Must often wipe a bloody nose.
  Fables (1727) 'The Mastiffs' l. 1

3 Where yet was ever found a mother,
Who'd give her booby for another?
  Fables (1727) 'The Mother, the Nurse, and the Fairy' l. 33

4 An open foe may prove a curse,
But a pretended friend is worse.
  Fables (1727) 'The Shepherd's Dog and the Wolf' l. 33

5 I know you lawyers can, with ease,
Twist words and meanings as you please;
That language, by your skill made pliant,
Will bend to favour ev'ry client.
  Fables (1738) 'The Dog and the Fox' l. 1

6 Studious of elegance and ease,
Myself alone I seek to please.
  Fables (1738) 'The Man, the Cat, the Dog, and the Fly'
  l. 127

7 That politician tops his part,
Who readily can lie with art.
  Fables (1738) 'The Squire and his Cur' l. 27

8 Give me, kind heaven, a private station,
A mind serene for contemplation.
  Fables (1738) 'The Vulture, the Sparrow, and Other Birds'
  l. 69

9 Behold the bright original appear.
  'A Letter to a Lady' (1714) l. 85

10 Praising all alike, is praising none.
  'A Letter to a Lady' (1714) l. 114

11 Life is a jest; and all things show it.
I thought so once; but now I know it.
  'My Own Epitaph' (1720)

12 Whether we can afford it or no, we must have
superfluities.
  'Polly' (1729) act 1, sc. 1

13 No, sir, tho' I was born and bred in England, I can
dare to be poor, which is the only thing now-a-days
men are ashamed of.
  'Polly' (1729) act 1, sc. 11

14 An inconstant woman, tho' she has no chance to be
very happy, can never be very unhappy.
  'Polly' (1729) act 1, sc. 14

15 All in the Downs the fleet was moored,
The streamers waving in the wind,
When black-eyed Susan came aboard.
  'Sweet William's Farewell to Black-Eyed Susan' (1720)

16 They'll tell thee, sailors, when away,
In ev'ry port a mistress find.
  'Sweet William's Farewell to Black-Eyed Susan' (1720)

17 Adieu, she cries! and waved her lily hand.
  'Sweet William's Farewell to Black-Eyed Susan' (1720)

18 A miss for pleasure, and a wife for breed.
  'The Toilette' (1716)

Noel Gay (*Richard Moxon Armitage*)
1898–1954
British songwriter

19 I'm leaning on a lamp-post at the corner of the street,
In case a certain little lady comes by.
  'Leaning on a Lamp-Post' (1937); sung by George Formby
  in the film *Father Knew Best*

Sir Eric Geddes 1875–1937
British politician and administrator

20 The Germans, if this Government is returned, are
going to pay every penny; they are going to be
squeezed as a lemon is squeezed—until the pips
squeak.
  Speech at Cambridge, 10 December 1918, in *Cambridge
  Daily News* 11 December 1918

Bob Geldof 1954– *and Midge Ure* 1953–
Irish rock musician; Scottish rock musician

21 Do they know it's Christmas?
  Title of song (1984)

George I 1660–1727
King of Great Britain and Ireland from 1714

22 I hate all Boets and Bainters.
  In John Campbell *Lives of the Chief Justices* (1849) 'Lord
  Mansfield'

George II 1683–1760
King of Great Britain and Ireland from 1727

23 *Non, j'aurai des maîtresses.*
No, I shall have mistresses.
  When Queen Caroline, on her deathbed, urged him to
  marry again; in John Hervey *Memoirs of the Reign of George
  II* (1848) vol. 2. The Queen replied, '*Ah! mon dieu! cela
  n'empêche pas* [Oh, my God! That won't make any
  difference]'

24 We are come for your good, for all your goods.
  Speech at Portsmouth, probably 1716, in Joseph Spence
  Anecdotes (ed. J. M. Osborn, 1966) no. 903

25 Mad, is he? Then I hope he will *bite* some of my other
generals.
  Replying to the Duke of Newcastle, who had complained
  that General Wolfe was a madman, in Henry Beckles
  Willson *Life and Letters of James Wolfe* (1909) ch. 17

George III 1738–1820
King of Great Britain and Ireland from 1760

26 Born and educated in this country, I glory in the
name of Briton.
  The King's Speech on Opening the Session in *Hansard*
  18 November 1760, col. 942

27 Was there ever such stuff as great part of
Shakespeare? Only one must not say so! But what
think you?—what?—Is there not sad stuff?
what?—what?
  To Fanny Burney, in *Diary and Letters of Madame d'Arblay*
  vol. 2 (1842) Diary, 19 December 1785

George IV 1762–1830

King of Great Britain and Ireland from 1820

1 Harris, I am not well; pray get me a glass of brandy.

On first seeing Caroline of Brunswick, his future wife; in Earl of Malmesbury *Diaries and Correspondence* (1844) vol. 3, 5 April 1795

George V 1865–1936

King of Great Britain and Ireland from 1910

2 I venture to allude to the impression which seemed generally to prevail among their brethren across the seas, that the Old Country must wake up if she intends to maintain her old position of pre-eminence in her Colonial trade against foreign competitors.

Speech at Guildhall, 5 December 1901, in Harold Nicolson *King George V* (1952) p. 73 (the speech was reprinted in 1911 with the title 'Wake up, England')

3 I have many times asked myself whether there can be more potent advocates of peace upon earth through the years to come than this massed multitude of silent witnesses to the desolation of war.

Message read at Terlincthun Cemetery, Boulogne, 13 May 1922, in *The Times* 15 May 1922

4 I said to your predecessor: 'You know what they're all saying, no more coals to Newcastle, no more Hoares to Paris.' The fellow didn't even laugh.

In conversation with Anthony Eden, 23 December 1935, following Samuel Hoare's resignation as Foreign Secretary on 18 December 1935; in Earl of Avon *Facing the Dictators* (1962) pt. 2, ch. 1

5 After I am dead, the boy will ruin himself in twelve months.

On his son, the future King Edward VIII, in Keith Middlemas and John Barnes *Baldwin* (1969) ch. 34

6 Bugger Bognor.

Comment made either in 1929, when it was proposed that the town be named Bognor Regis on account of the king's convalescence there after a serious illness; or on his deathbed in 1936, when someone remarked 'Cheer up, your Majesty, you will soon be at Bognor again.' See Kenneth Rose *King George V* (1983) ch. 9

7 How's the Empire?

To his private secretary on the morning of his death, probably prompted by an article in *The Times*, which he held open at the imperial and foreign page. See Kenneth Rose *King George V* (1983) ch. 10

George VI 1895–1952

King of Great Britain and Northern Ireland from 1936

8 Abroad is bloody.

In W. H. Auden *A Certain World* (1970) 'Royalty'. Cf. Mitford 478:8

9 Personally I feel happier now that we have no allies to be polite to and to pamper.

To Queen Mary, 27 June 1940, in John Wheeler-Bennett *King George VI* (1958) pt. 3, ch. 6

Daniel George (Daniel George Bunting)

English writer

10 O Freedom, what liberties are taken in thy name!

The Perpetual Pessimist (1963) p. 58. Cf. Roland 545:7

David Lloyd George

See LLOYD GEORGE

Ira Gershwin 1896–1983

American songwriter

11 A foggy day in London Town
Had me low and had me down.
I viewed the morning with alarm,
The British Museum had lost its charm.
How long, I wondered, could this thing last?
But the age of miracles hadn't passed,
For, suddenly, I saw you there
And through foggy London town the sun was shining everywhere.

Damsel in Distress (1937) 'A Foggy Day' (music by George Gershwin)

12 Holding hands at midnight
'Neath a starry sky,
Nice work if you can get it,
And you can get it if you try.

Damsel in Distress (1937) 'Nice Work If You Can Get It' (music by George Gershwin)

13 You've made my life so glamorous,
You can't blame me for feeling amorous.

Funny Face (1927) ''S Wonderful' (music by George Gershwin)

14 Embrace me, my sweet embraceable you!
Embrace me, you irreplaceable you!
Just one look at you, my heart grew tipsy in me;
You and you alone bring out the gypsy in me!

Girl Crazy (1930) 'Embraceable you' (music by George Gershwin)

15 In time the Rockies may crumble,
Gibraltar may tumble,
They're only made of clay,
But our love is here to stay.

The Goldwyn Follies (1938) 'Love is Here to Stay' (music by George Gershwin)

16 The way you wear your hat,
The way you sip your tea,
The mem'ry of all that—
No, no! They can't take that away from me!

Shall We Dance? (1937) 'They Can't Take That Away from Me' (music by George Gershwin)

Giuseppe Giacosa 1847–1906 *and* Luigi Illica 1857–1919

Italian librettists

17 Che gelida manina.
Your tiny hand is frozen.

La Bohème (1896) act 1; music by Puccini (Rodolfo to Mimi)

Edward Gibbon 1737–94

English historian

18 The various modes of worship, which prevailed in the Roman world, were all considered by the people as equally true; by the philosopher, as equally false; and by the magistrate, as equally useful. And thus toleration produced not only mutual indulgence, but even religious concord.

The Decline and Fall of the Roman Empire (1776–88) ch. 2

1 The principles of a free constitution are irrecoverably lost, when the legislative power is nominated by the executive.
The Decline and Fall of the Roman Empire (1776–88) ch. 3

2 History ... is, indeed, little more than the register of the crimes, follies, and misfortunes of mankind.
The Decline and Fall of the Roman Empire (1776–88) ch. 3. Cf. Voltaire 716:12

3 In every age and country, the wiser, or at least the stronger, of the two sexes, has usurped the powers of the state, and confined the other to the cares and pleasures of domestic life.
The Decline and Fall of the Roman Empire (1776–88) ch. 6

4 Corruption, the most infallible symptom of constitutional liberty.
The Decline and Fall of the Roman Empire (1776–88) ch. 21

5 In every deed of mischief he had a heart to resolve, a head to contrive, and a hand to execute.
The Decline and Fall of the Roman Empire (1776–88) ch. 48 (of Comenus). Cf. Clarendon 205:2

6 Our sympathy is cold to the relation of distant misery.
The Decline and Fall of the Roman Empire (1776–88) ch. 49

7 Persuasion is the resource of the feeble; and the feeble can seldom persuade.
The Decline and Fall of the Roman Empire (1776–88) ch. 68

8 All that is human must retrograde if it does not advance.
The Decline and Fall of the Roman Empire (1776–88) ch. 71

9 The satirist may laugh, the philosopher may preach, but Reason herself will respect the prejudices and habits which have been consecrated by the experience of mankind.
Memoirs of My Life (1796) ch. 1

10 To the University of Oxford I acknowledge no obligation; and she will as cheerfully renounce me for a son, as I am willing to disclaim her for a mother. I spent fourteen months at Magdalen College: they proved the fourteen months the most idle and unprofitable of my whole life.
Memoirs of My Life (1796) ch. 3

11 Their dull and deep potations excused the brisk intemperance of youth.
Memoirs of My Life (1796) ch. 3 (on the dons at Oxford)

12 Dr — well remembered that he had a salary to receive, and only forgot that he had a duty to perform.
Memoirs of My Life (1796) ch. 3

13 It was here that I suspended my religious inquiries (aged 17).
Memoirs of My Life (1796) ch. 4

14 I saw and loved.
Memoirs of My Life (1796) ch. 4

15 I sighed as a lover, I obeyed as a son.
Memoirs of My Life (1796) ch. 4 n.

16 Crowds without company, and dissipation without pleasure.
Memoirs of My Life (1796) ch. 5

17 The captain of the Hampshire grenadiers ... has not been useless to the historian of the Roman empire.
Memoirs of My Life (1796) ch. 5 (of his own army service)

18 It was at Rome, on the fifteenth of October, 1764, as I sat musing amidst the ruins of the Capitol, while the barefoot friars were singing vespers in the Temple of Jupiter, that the idea of writing the decline and fall of the city first started to my mind.
Memoirs of My Life (1796) ch. 6 n.

19 I will not dissemble the first emotions of joy on the recovery of my freedom, and, perhaps, the establishment of my fame. But my pride was soon humbled, and a sober melancholy was spread over my mind, by the idea that I had taken an everlasting leave of an old and agreeable companion, and that whatsoever might be the future date of my History, the life of the historian must be short and precarious.
Memoirs of My Life (1796) ch. 8 (on the completion of *The Decline and Fall of the Roman Empire*)

20 My English text is chaste, and all licentious passages are left in the obscurity of a learned language.
Memoirs of My Life (1796) ch. 8 (parodied as 'decent obscurity' in the *Anti-Jacobin*, 1797–8)

21 The abbreviation of time, and the failure of hope, will always tinge with a browner shade the evening of life.
Memoirs of My Life (1796) ch. 8

Orlando Gibbons 1583–1625

English organist and composer

22 The silver swan, who, living had no note,
When death approached unlocked her silent throat.
The First Set of Madrigals and Motets of Five Parts (1612) 'The Silver Swan'

Stella Gibbons 1902–89

English novelist

23 Every year, in the fulness o' summer, when the sukebind hangs heavy from the wains ... 'tes the same. And when the spring comes her hour is upon her again. 'Tes the hand of Nature and we women cannot escape it.
Cold Comfort Farm (1932) ch. 5

24 Something nasty in the woodshed.
Cold Comfort Farm (1932) ch. 10

25 By god, D. H. Lawrence was right when he had said there must be a dumb, dark, dull, bitter belly-tension between a man and a woman, and how else could this be achieved save in the long monotony of marriage?
Cold Comfort Farm (1932) ch. 20

Wolcott Gibbs 1902–58

American critic

26 Backward ran sentences until reeled the mind.
New Yorker 28 November 1936 'Time ... Fortune ... Life ... Luce' (satirizing the style of *Time* magazine)

Kahlil Gibran 1883–1931
Syrian writer and painter

1 Are you a politician who says to himself: 'I will use my country for my own benefit'? . . . Or are you a devoted patriot, who whispers in the ear of his inner self: 'I love to serve my country as a faithful servant.'
> *The New Frontier* (1931), translated by Anthony R. Ferris in *The Voice of the Master* (1958) p. 34. Cf. Kennedy 394:2

2 Your children are not your children.
They are the sons and daughters of Life's longing for itself.
They came through you but not from you
And though they are with you yet they belong not to you.
You may give them your love but not your thoughts,
For they have their own thoughts.
You may house their bodies but not their souls,
For their souls dwell in the house of tomorrow, which you cannot visit, not even in your dreams.
You may strive to be like them, but seek not to make them like you,
For life goes not backward nor tarries with yesterday.
You are the bows from which your children as living arrows are sent forth.
> *The Prophet* (1923) 'On Children'

3 Work is love made visible. And if you cannot work with love but only with distaste, it is better that you should leave your work and sit at the gate of the temple and take alms of those who work with joy.
> *The Prophet* (1923) 'On Work'

4 An exaggeration is a truth that has lost its temper.
> *Sand and Foam* (1926) p. 59

Wilfrid Wilson Gibson 1878–1962
English poet

5 But we, how shall we turn to little things
And listen to the birds and winds and streams
Made holy by their dreams,
Nor feel the heart-break in the heart of things?
> 'Lament' (1918)

André Gide 1869–1951
French novelist and critic

6 M'est avis . . . que le profit n'est pas toujours ce qui mène l'homme; qu'il y a des actions désintéressées . . . Par désintéressé j'entends: gratuit. Et que le mal, ce que l'on appelle: le mal, peut être aussi gratuit que le bien.

I believe . . . that profit is not always what motivates man; that there are disinterested actions . . . By *disinterested* I mean: gratuitous. And that evil acts, what people call evil, can be as gratuitous as good acts.
> *Les Caves du Vatican* (1914) bk. 4, ch. 7

7 Transporter le drame sur le plan moral, c'était pourtant l'effort du Christianisme.

The whole effect of Christianity was to transfer the drama onto the moral plane.
> *Les Faux Monnayeurs* (1925) pt. 1, ch. 13 (translated by Dorothy Bussy)

8 Le grand secret de Stendhal, sa grande malice, c'est d'écrire toute de suite . . . pensée émue.

The great secret of Stendhal, his great shrewdness, consisted in writing *at once* . . . thought charged with emotion.
> *Journal* (1939) vol. 3, 3 September 1937 (translated by Justin O'Brien)

9 Hugo—hélas!

Hugo—alas!
> When asked who was the greatest 19th-century poet, in Claude Martin *La Maturité d'André Gide* (1977) p. 502

Thomas Gilbart fl. *c.*1583
English poet

10 Shall silence shroud such sin
As Satan seems to show
Even in his imps, in these our days
That all men might it know?

No, no, it cannot be.
> 'A declaration of the death of John Lewes' (1583)

11 And when the fire did compass him
About on every side,
The people looked he then would speak,
And therefore loud they cried:

'Now call on Christ to save thy soul;
Now trust in Christ his death.'
But all in vain; no words he spake,
But thus yields up his breath.

Oh, woeful state, oh danger deep,
That he was drownèd in!
Oh grant us, God, for Christ his sake,
We fall not in such sin.
> 'A declaration of the death of John Lewes' (1583)

Sir Humphrey Gilbert *c.*1537–83
English explorer

12 We are as near to heaven by sea as by land!
> In Richard Hakluyt *Third and Last Volume of the Voyages . . . of the English Nation* (1600) p. 159. Cf. Elstow 276:1

W. S. Gilbert (Sir William Schwenck Gilbert) 1836–1911
English writer of comic and satirical verse

13 Then they began to sing
That extremely lovely thing,
'Scherzando! ma non troppo ppp.'
> The '*Bab*' *Ballads* (1869) 'Story of Prince Agib'

14 That celebrated,
Cultivated,
Underrated
Nobleman,
The Duke of Plaza Toro!
> *The Gondoliers* (1889) act 1

15 Of that there is no manner of doubt—
No probable, possible shadow of doubt—
No possible doubt whatever.
> *The Gondoliers* (1889) act 1

1 All shall equal be.
The Earl, the Marquis, and the Dook,
The Groom, the Butler, and the Cook,
The Aristocrat who banks with Coutts,
The Aristocrat who cleans the boots.
The Gondoliers (1889) act 1

2 But the privilege and pleasure
That we treasure beyond measure
Is to run on little errands for the Ministers of State.
The Gondoliers (1889) act 2

3 Take a pair of sparkling eyes,
Hidden, ever and anon,
In a merciful eclipse.
The Gondoliers (1889) act 2

4 Ambassadors cropped up like hay,
Prime Ministers and such as they
Grew like asparagus in May,
And dukes were three a penny.
The Gondoliers (1889) act 2

5 When every one is somebodee,
Then no one's anybody.
The Gondoliers (1889) act 2

6 Bow, bow, ye lower middle classes!
Bow, bow, ye tradesmen, bow, ye masses.
Iolanthe (1882) act 1

7 The Law is the true embodiment
Of everything that's excellent.
It has no kind of fault or flaw,
And I, my Lords, embody the Law.
Iolanthe (1882) act 1

8 Spurn not the nobly born
With love affected,
Nor treat with virtuous scorn
The well-connected.
Iolanthe (1882) act 1

9 Hearts just as pure and fair
May beat in Belgrave Square
As in the lowly air
Of Seven Dials.
Iolanthe (1882) act 1

10 I often think it's comical
How Nature always does contrive
That every boy and every gal,
That's born into the world alive,
Is either a little Liberal,
Or else a little Conservative!
Iolanthe (1882) act 2

11 When in that House MPs divide,
If they've a brain and cerebellum too,
They have to leave that brain outside,
And vote just as their leaders tell 'em to.
Iolanthe (1882) act 2

12 The prospect of a lot
Of dull MPs in close proximity,
All thinking for themselves is what
No man can face with equanimity.
Iolanthe (1882) act 2

13 The House of Peers, throughout the war,
Did nothing in particular,
And did it very well.
Iolanthe (1882) act 2

14 When you're lying awake with a dismal headache,
and repose is taboo'd by anxiety,
I conceive you may use any language you choose to
indulge in, without impropriety.
Iolanthe (1882) act 2

15 For you dream you are crossing the Channel, and
tossing about in a steamer from Harwich—
Which is something between a large bathing machine
and a very small second class carriage.
Iolanthe (1882) act 2

16 And bound on that journey you find your attorney
(who started that morning from Devon);
He's a bit undersized, and you don't feel surprised
when he tells you he's only eleven.
Iolanthe (1882) act 2

17 In your shirt and your socks (the black silk with gold
clocks), crossing Salisbury Plain on a bicycle.
Iolanthe (1882) act 2

18 The shares are a penny, and ever so many are taken
by Rothschild and Baring,
And just as a few are allotted to you, you awake with
a shudder despairing.
Iolanthe (1882) act 2

19 A wandering minstrel I—
A thing of shreds and patches.
Of ballads, songs and snatches,
And dreamy lullaby!
The Mikado (1885) act 1. Cf. *Hamlet* 577:17

20 I can trace my ancestry back to a protoplasmal
primordial atomic globule. Consequently, my family
pride is something in-conceivable. I can't help it. I
was born sneering.
The Mikado (1885) act 1

21 As some day it may happen that a victim must be
found,
I've got a little list—I've got a little list
Of society offenders who might well be under ground
And who never would be missed—who never would
be missed!
The Mikado (1885) act 1

22 The idiot who praises, with enthusiastic tone,
All centuries but this, and every country but his own.
The Mikado (1885) act 1. Cf. Canning 178:4, Disraeli
247:26, Overbury 502:10

23 Three little maids from school are we,
Pert as a schoolgirl well can be,
Filled to the brim with girlish glee.
The Mikado (1885) act 1

24 Life is a joke that's just begun.
The Mikado (1885) act 1

25 Three little maids who, all unwary,
Come from a ladies' seminary.
The Mikado (1885) act 1

26 Modified rapture!
The Mikado (1885) act 1

27 Awaiting the sensation of a short, sharp shock,
From a cheap and chippy chopper on a big black
block.
The Mikado (1885) act 1

28 Here's a how-de-doo!
The Mikado (1885) act 2

1 Here's a state of things!
   The Mikado (1885) act 2

2 Matrimonial devotion
   Doesn't seem to suit her notion.
   The Mikado (1885) act 2

3 My object all sublime
   I shall achieve in time—
   To let the punishment fit the crime—
   The punishment fit the crime.
   The Mikado (1885) act 2

4 The music-hall singer attends a series
   Of masses and fugues and 'ops'
   By Bach, interwoven
   With Spohr and Beethoven,
   At classical Monday Pops.
   The Mikado (1885) act 2

5 The billiard sharp whom any one catches,
   His doom's extremely hard—
   He's made to dwell—
   In a dungeon cell
   On a spot that's always barred.
   And there he plays extravagant matches
   In fitless finger-stalls
   On a cloth untrue
   With a twisted cue
   And elliptical billiard balls.
   The Mikado (1885) act 2

6 I have a left shoulder-blade that is a miracle of
   loveliness. People come miles to see it. My right elbow
   has a fascination that few can resist.
   The Mikado (1885) act 2

7 Something lingering, with boiling oil in it, I fancy.
   The Mikado (1885) act 2

8 Merely corroborative detail, intended to give artistic
   verisimilitude to an otherwise bald and unconvincing
   narrative.
   The Mikado (1885) act 2

9 The flowers that bloom in the spring,
   Tra la,
   Have nothing to do with the case.
   The Mikado (1885) act 2

10 I've got to take under my wing,
   Tra la,
   A most unattractive old thing,
   Tra la,
   With a caricature of a face.
   The Mikado (1885) act 2

11 On a tree by a river a little tom-tit
   Sang 'Willow, titwillow, titwillow!'
   And I said to him, 'Dicky-bird, why do you sit
   Singing Willow, titwillow, titwillow?'
   The Mikado (1885) act 2

12 'Is it weakness of intellect, birdie?' I cried,
   'Or a rather tough worm in your little inside?'
   With a shake of his poor little head he replied,
   'Oh, willow, titwillow, titwillow!'
   The Mikado (1885) act 2

13 He sobbed and he sighed, and a gurgle he gave,
   Then he plunged himself into the billowy wave,
   And an echo arose from the suicide's grave—
   'Oh willow, titwillow, titwillow!'
   The Mikado (1885) act 2

14 There's a fascination frantic
   In a ruin that's romantic;
   Do you think you are sufficiently decayed?
   The Mikado (1885) act 2

15 If you're anxious for to shine in the high aesthetic line
   as a man of culture rare.
   Patience (1881) act 1

16 You must lie upon the daisies and discourse in novel
   phrases of your complicated state of mind,
   The meaning doesn't matter if it's only idle chatter of
   a transcendental kind.
   Patience (1881) act 1

17 Then a sentimental passion of a vegetable fashion
   must excite your languid spleen,
   An attachment à la Plato for a bashful young potato,
   or a not too French French bean!
   Though the Philistines may jostle, you will rank as an
   apostle in the high aesthetic band,
   If you walk down Piccadilly with a poppy or a lily in
   your medieval hand.
   Patience (1881) act 1

18 While this magnetic,
   Peripatetic
   Lover, he lived to learn,
   By no endeavour
   Can magnet ever
   Attract a Silver Churn!
   Patience (1881) act 2

19 'High diddle diddle'
   Will rank as an idyll,
   If I pronounce it chaste!
   Patience (1881) act 2

20 Francesca di Rimini, mimini, piminy,
   Je-ne-sais-quoi young man!
   Patience (1881) act 2

21 A greenery-yallery, Grosvenor Gallery,
   Foot-in-the-grave young man!
   Patience (1881) act 2

22 I'm called Little Buttercup—dear Little Buttercup,
   Though I could never tell why.
   HMS Pinafore (1878) act 1

23 What, never?
   No, never!
   What, *never*?
   Hardly ever!
   HMS Pinafore (1878) act 1

24 Though 'Bother it' I may
   Occasionally say,
   I never use a big, big D—
   HMS Pinafore (1878) act 1

25 And so do his sisters, and his cousins and his aunts!
   His sisters and his cousins,
   Whom he reckons up by dozens,
   And his aunts!
   HMS Pinafore (1878) act 1

26 When I was a lad I served a term
   As office boy to an Attorney's firm.
   I cleaned the windows and I swept the floor,
   And I polished up the handle of the big front door.
   I polished up that handle so carefullee
   That now I am the Ruler of the Queen's Navee!
   HMS Pinafore (1878) act 1

1 I always voted at my party's call,
And I never thought of thinking for myself at all.
HMS Pinafore (1878) act 1

2 Stick close to your desks and never go to sea,
And you all may be Rulers of the Queen's Navee!
HMS Pinafore (1878) act 1

3 Things are seldom what they seem,
Skim milk masquerades as cream.
HMS Pinafore (1878) act 2

4 He is an Englishman!
For he himself has said it,
And it's greatly to his credit,
That he is an Englishman!
HMS Pinafore (1878) act 2

5 For he might have been a Roosian,
A French, or Turk, or Proosian,
Or perhaps Ital-ian!
But in spite of all temptations
To belong to other nations,
He remains an Englishman!
HMS Pinafore (1878) act 2

6 The other, upper crust,
A regular patrician.
HMS Pinafore (1878) act 2

7 It is, it is a glorious thing
To be a Pirate King.
The Pirates of Penzance (1879) act 1

8 The question is, had he not been
A thing of beauty,
Would she be swayed by quite as keen
A sense of duty?
The Pirates of Penzance (1879) act 1

9 I'm very good at integral and differential calculus,
I know the scientific names of beings animalculous;
In short, in matters vegetable, animal, and mineral,
I am the very model of a modern Major-General.
The Pirates of Penzance (1879) act 1

10 About binomial theorem I'm teeming with a lot of news,
With many cheerful facts about the square on the hypotenuse.
The Pirates of Penzance (1879) act 1

11 When constabulary duty's to be done,
A policeman's lot is not a happy one.
The Pirates of Penzance (1879) act 2

12 They are no members of the common throng;
They are all noblemen who have gone wrong!
The Pirates of Penzance (1879) act 2

13 No Englishman unmoved that statement hears,
Because, with all our faults, we love our House of Peers.
The Pirates of Penzance (1879) act 2

14 To everybody's prejudice I know a thing or two;
I can tell a woman's age in half a minute—and I do!
Princess Ida (1884) act 1

15 Man is Nature's sole mistake!
Princess Ida (1884) act 2

16 You must stir it and stump it,
And blow your own trumpet,
Or trust me, you haven't a chance.
Ruddigore (1887) act 1

17 He combines the manners of a Marquis with the morals of a Methodist.
Ruddigore (1887) act 1

18 If a man can't forge his own will, whose will can he forge?
Ruddigore (1887) act 2

19 Some word that teems with hidden meaning—like Basingstoke.
Ruddigore (1887) act 2

20 This particularly rapid, unintelligible patter
Isn't generally heard, and if it is it doesn't matter.
Ruddigore (1887) act 2

21 I was a pale young curate then.
The Sorcerer (1877) act 1

22 So I fell in love with a rich attorney's
Elderly ugly daughter.
Trial by Jury (1875)

23 She may very well pass for forty-three
In the dusk with a light behind her!
Trial by Jury (1875)

24 It's a song of a merryman, moping mum,
Whose soul was sad, and whose glance was glum,
Who sipped no sup, and who craved no crumb,
As he sighed for the love of a ladye.
The Yeoman of the Guard (1888) act 1

25 'Tis ever thus with simple folk—an accepted wit has but to say 'Pass the mustard', and they roar their ribs out!
The Yeoman of the Guard (1888) act 2

Eric Gill 1882–1940
English sculptor, engraver, and typographer

26 That state is a state of slavery in which a man does what he likes to do in his spare time and in his working time that which is required of him.
Art-nonsense and Other Essays (1929) 'Slavery and Freedom'. Cf. Collingwood 213:5

Allen Ginsberg 1926–
American poet and novelist

27 What if someone gave a war & Nobody came?
Life would ring the bells of Ecstasy and Forever be Itself again.
'Graffiti' (1972). Cf. Sandburg 555:9

28 I saw the best minds of my generation destroyed by madness, starving hysterical naked,
dragging themselves through the negro streets at dawn looking for an angry fix,
angelheaded hipsters burning for the ancient heavenly connection to the starry dynamo in the machinery of the night.
Howl (1956) p. 9

29 What peaches and what penumbras! Whole families shopping at night! Aisles full of husbands! Wives in the avocados, babies in the tomatoes!—and you, Garcia Lorca what were you doing down by the watermelons?
'A Supermarket in California' (1956)

George Gipp d. 1920

American footballer

1 Win just one for the Gipper.

Catch-phrase later associated with Ronald Reagan, who
uttered the immortal words in the 1940 film *Knute Rockne,
All American*. See Knut Rockne 'Gipp the Great' in *Collier's*
22 November 1930

Jean Giraudoux 1882–1944

French playwright

2 *Dès que la guerre est déclarée, impossible de tenir les
poètes. La rime, c'est encore le meilleur tambour.*

As soon as war is declared it will be impossible to hold
the poets back. Rhyme is still the most effective drum.

La Guerre de Troie n'aura pas lieu (1935) act 2, sc. 4
(translated by Christopher Fry as *Tiger at the Gates*, 1955)

3 *Nous savons tous ici que le droit est la plus puissante des
écoles de l'imagination. Jamais poète n'a interprété la
nature aussi librement qu'un juriste la réalité.*

All of us here know there's no better way of exercising
the imagination than the study of law. No poet ever
interpreted nature as freely as a lawyer interprets the
truth.

La Guerre de Troie n'aura pas lieu (1935) act 2, sc. 5

W. E. Gladstone 1809–98

*British Liberal politician; Prime Minister, 1868–74,
1880–5, 1886, 1892–4*

4 This is the negation of God erected into a system of
Government.

*A Letter to the Earl of Aberdeen on the State Prosecutions of the
Neapolitan Government* (1851) p. 9 n.

5 Finance is, as it were, the stomach of the country,
from which all the other organs take their tone.

Article on finance, 1858, in H. C. G. Matthew *Gladstone
1809–1874* (1986) ch. 5

6 You cannot fight against the future. Time is on our
side.

Speech on the Reform Bill, in *Hansard* 27 April 1866,
col. 152

7 My mission is to pacify Ireland.

On receiving news that he was to form his first cabinet, 1st
December 1868, in H. C. G. Matthew *Gladstone 1809–1874*
(1986) ch. 5

8 Swimming for his life, a man does not see much of the
country through which the river winds.

Diary, 31 December 1868 in M. R. D. Foot and H. C. G.
Matthew (eds.) *The Gladstone Diaries* vol. 6 (1978)

9 We have been borne down in a torrent of gin and
beer.

Letter to his brother, 6 February 1874, in John Morley *Life
of William Ewart Gladstone* (1903) vol. 2, ch. 14

10 Let the Turks now carry away their abuses in the only
possible manner, namely by carrying off themselves
... one and all, bag and baggage, shall I hope clear
out from the province they have desolated and
profaned.

Bulgarian Horrors and the Question of the East (1876) p. 61

11 Our first site in Egypt, be it by larceny or be it by
emption, will be the almost certain egg of a North
African Empire, that will grow and grow until another
Victoria and another Albert, titles of the Lake-sources
of the White Nile, come within our borders; and till
we finally join hands across the Equator with Natal
and Cape Town, to say nothing of the Transvaal and
the Orange River on the south, or of Abyssinia or
Zanzibar to be swallowed by way of *viaticum* on our
journey.

Aggression on Egypt and Freedom in the East (1884) p. 16

12 The resources of civilization against its enemies are
not yet exhausted.

Speech at Leeds, 7 October 1881, on the Land League, in
H. W. Lucy (ed.) *Speeches of ... Gladstone* (1885) p. 57

13 Ideal perfection is not the true basis of English
legislation. We look at the attainable; we look at the
practical, and we have too much English sense to be
drawn away by those sanguine delineations of what
might possibly be attained in Utopia, from a path
which promises to enable us to effect great good for
the people of England.

Speech on the Reform Bill, in *Hansard* 28 February 1884,
col. 123

14 It is perfectly true that these gentlemen wish to march
through rapine to disintegration and dismemberment
of the Empire, and, I am sorry to say, even to the
placing of different parts of the Empire in direct
hostility one with the other.

On the Irish Land League in a speech at Knowsley,
27 October 1881, in *The Times*, 28 October 1881

15 I would tell them of my own intention to keep my
counsel ... and I will venture to recommend them, as
an old Parliamentary hand, to do the same.

Speech, *Hansard* 21 January 1886, col. 112

16 This, if I understand it, is one of those golden
moments of our history, one of those opportunities
which may come and may go, but which rarely
returns.

Speech on the Second Reading of the Home Rule Bill, in
Hansard 7 June 1886, col. 1237

17 I will venture to say, that upon the one great class of
subjects, the largest and the most weighty of them all,
where the leading and determining considerations that
ought to lead to a conclusion are truth, justice, and
humanity—upon these, gentlemen, all the world over,
I will back the masses against the classes.

Speech in Liverpool, 28 June 1886, in *The Times* 29 June
1886

18 What that Sicilian mule was to me, I have been to the
Queen.

Memorandum on relations with Queen Victoria, 20 March
1894, in *Autobiographical Memoranda 1868–94* (1981)
p. 100

19 We are bound to lose Ireland in consequence of years
of cruelty, stupidity and misgovernment and I would
rather lose her as a friend than as a foe.

In Margot Asquith *More Memories* (1933) ch. 8

20 It is not a Life at all. It is a Reticence, in three
volumes.

On J. W. Cross's *Life of George Eliot*; in E. F. Benson *As We
Were* (1930) ch. 6

1 I absorb the vapour and return it as a flood.

> On public speaking, in Lord Riddell *Some Things That Matter* (1927 ed.) p. 69

Hannah Glasse fl. 1747

English cook

2 Take your hare when it is cased.

> *The Art of Cookery Made Plain and Easy* (1747) ch. 1 (*cased* skinned). The proverbial 'First catch your hare' dates from *c*.1300

William Henry, 1st Duke of Gloucester 1743–1805

3 Another damned, thick, square book! Always scribble, scribble, scribble! Eh! Mr Gibbon?

> In Henry Best *Personal and Literary Memorials* (1829) p. 68 (also attributed to the Duke of Cumberland and King George III). See D. M. Low *Edward Gibbon* (1937) p. 315

Jean-Luc Godard 1930–

French film director

4 *La photographie, c'est la vérité. Le cinéma: la vérité vingt-quatre fois par seconde.*

Photography is truth. The cinema is truth 24 times per second.

> *Le Petit Soldat* (1960 film)

5 'Movies should have a beginning, a middle and an end,' harrumphed French film maker Georges Franju ... 'Certainly,' replied Jean-Luc Godard. 'But not necessarily in that order.'

> *Time* 14 September 1981

A. D. Godley 1856–1925

English classicist

6 Great and good is the typical Don, and of evil and
> wrong the foe,
Good, and great, I'm a Don myself, and therefore I
> ought to know.

> 'The Megalopsychiad' (1904)

7 What is this that roareth thus?
Can it be a Motor Bus?
Yes, the smell and hideous hum
Indicat Motorem Bum!...
How shall wretches live like us
Cincti Bis Motoribus?
Domine, defende nos
Contra hos Motores Bos!

> Letter to C. R. L. Fletcher, 10 January 1914, in *Reliquiae* (1926) vol. 1, p. 292

Sidney Godolphin 1610–43

English poet

8 Or love me less, or love me more
And play not with my liberty;
Either take all, or all restore,
Bind me at least, or set me free.

> 'Song'

William Godwin 1756–1836

English philosopher and novelist; husband of Mary Wollstonecraft and father of Mary Shelley

9 Perfectibility is one of the most unequivocal characteristics of the human species.

> *An Enquiry concerning the Principles of Political Justice* (1793) bk. 1, ch. 2

10 The illustrious bishop of Cambrai was of more worth than his chambermaid, and there are few of us that would hesitate to pronounce, if his palace were in flames, and the life of only one of them could be preserved, which of the two ought to be preferred.

> *An Enquiry concerning the Principles of Political Justice* (1793) bk. 2, ch. 2

11 Love of our country is another of those specious illusions, which have been invented by impostors in order to render the multitude the blind instruments of their crooked designs.

> *An Enquiry concerning the Principles of Political Justice* (1793) bk. 5, ch. 16

12 It is a most mistaken way of teaching men to feel they are brothers, by imbuing their mind with perpetual hatred.

> *An Enquiry concerning the Principles of Political Justice* (1793) bk. 5, ch. 18 (on the subject of war)

13 What ... can be more shameless than for society to make an example of those whom she has goaded to the breach of order, instead of amending her own institutions which, by straining order into tyranny, produced the mischief?

> *An Enquiry concerning the Principles of Political Justice* (1793) bk. 7, ch. 3 (on the penal laws)

Joseph Goebbels 1897–1945

German Nazi leader

14 *Ohne Butter werden wir fertig, aber nicht beispielsweise ohne Kanonen. Wenn wir einmal überfallen werden, dann können wir uns nicht mit Butter, sondern nur mit Kanonen verteidigen.*

We can manage without butter but not, for example, without guns. If we are attacked we can only defend ourselves with guns not with butter.

> Speech in Berlin, 17 January 1936, in *Deutsche Allgemeine Zeitung* 18 January 1936. Cf. Goering 308:15

Hermann Goering 1893–1946

German Nazi leader

15 We have no butter ... but I ask you—would you rather have butter or guns? ... preparedness makes us powerful. Butter merely makes us fat.

> Speech at Hamburg, 1936, in W. Frischauer *Goering* (1951) ch. 10. Cf. Goebbels 308:14

16 I herewith commission you to carry out all preparations with regard to ... a *total solution* of the Jewish question in those territories of Europe which are under German influence.

> Instructions to Heydrich, 31 July 1941, in W. L. Shirer *The Rise and Fall of the Third Reich* (1962) bk. 5, ch. 27

Johann Wolfgang von Goethe 1749–1832

German poet, novelist and playwright

1 *Es irrt der Mensch, so lang er strebt.*

Man will err while yet he strives.
> *Faust* pt. 1 (1808) 'Prolog im Himmel'

2 *Zwei Seelen wohnen, ach! in meiner Brust.*

Two souls dwell, alas! in my breast.
> *Faust* pt. 1 (1808) 'Vor dem Thor'

3 *Ich bin der Geist der stets verneint.*

I am the spirit that always denies.
> *Faust* pt. 1 (1808) 'Studierzimmer'

4 *Entbehren sollst Du! sollst entbehren!*
Das ist der ewige Gesang.

Deny yourself! You must deny yourself!
That is the song that never ends.
> *Faust* pt. 1 (1808) 'Studierzimmer'

5 *Grau, teurer Freund, ist alle Theorie*
Und grün des Lebens goldner Baum.

All theory, dear friend, is grey, but the golden tree of
actual life springs ever green.
> *Faust* pt. 1 (1808) 'Studierzimmer'

6 *Meine Ruh' ist hin,*
Mein Herz ist schwer.

My peace is gone,
My heart is heavy.
> *Faust* pt. 1 (1808) 'Gretchen am Spinnrad'

7 *Die Tat ist alles, nichts der Ruhm.*

The deed is all, the glory nothing.
> *Faust* pt. 2 (1832) 'Hochgebirg'

8 *Das Ewig-Weibliche zieht uns hinan.*

Eternal Woman draws us upward.
> *Faust* pt. 2 (1832) 'Hochgebirg' *ad fin.*

9 *Du musst herrschen und gewinnen,*
Oder dienen und verlieren,
Leiden oder triumphieren
Amboss oder Hammer sein.

You must be master and win, or serve and lose, grieve
or triumph, be the anvil or the hammer.
> *Der Gross-Cophta* (1791) act 2

10 *Wenn es eine Freude ist das Gute zu geniessen, so ist es*
eine grössere das Bessere zu empfinden, und in der Kunst
ist das Beste gut genug.

Since it is a joy to have the benefit of what is good, it
is a greater one to experience what is better, and in
art the best is good enough.
> *Italienische Reise* (1816–17) 3 March 1787

11 *Der Aberglaube ist die Poesie des Lebens.*

Superstition is the poetry of life.
> *Maximen und Reflexionen* (1819) 'Literatur und Sprache'
> no. 908

12 *Es bildet ein Talent sich in der Stille,*
Sich ein Charakter in dem Strom der Welt.

Talent develops in quiet places, character in the full
current of human life.
> *Torquato Tasso* (1790) act 1, sc. 2

13 *Die Wahlverwandtschaften.*

Elective affinities.
> Title of novel (1809)

14 *Über allen Gipfeln*
Ist Ruh'.

Over all the mountain tops is peace.
> *Wanderers Nachtlied* (1821)

15 *Wer nie sein Brot mit Tränen ass,*
Wer nie die kummervollen Nächte
Auf seinem Bette weinend sass,
Der kennt euch nicht, ihr himmlischen Mächte.

Who never ate his bread in sorrow,
Who never spent the darksome hours
Weeping and watching for the morrow
He knows ye not, ye heavenly powers.
> *Wilhelm Meisters Lehrjahre* (1795–6) bk. 2, ch. 13
> (translated by Carlyle)

16 *Kennst du das Land, wo die Zitronen blühn?*
Im dunkeln Laub die Gold-Orangen glühn,
Ein sanfter Wind vom blauen Himmel weht,
Die Myrte still und hoch der Lorbeer steht—
Kennst du es wohl?
Dahin! Dahin
Möcht ich mit dir, o mein Geliebter, ziehn!

Know you the land where the lemon-trees bloom? In
the dark foliage the gold oranges glow; a soft wind
hovers from the sky, the myrtle is still and the laurel
stands tall—do you know it well? There, there, I
would go, O my beloved, with thee!
> *Wilhelm Meisters Lehrjahre* (1795–6) bk. 3, ch. 1

17 *Ohne Hast, aber ohne Rast.*

Without haste, but without rest.
> *Zahme Xenien* (with Schiller, 1796) sect. 2, no. 6, l. 281

18 *Im übrigen aber ist es zuletzt die grösste Kunst, sich zu*
beschränken und zu isolieren.

For the rest of it, the last and greatest art is to limit
and isolate oneself.
> J. P. Eckermann *Gespräche mit Goethe* (1836–48) 20 April
> 1825

19 *Ich kenne mich auch nicht und Gott soll mich auch davor*
behüten.

I do not know myself, and God forbid that I should.
> J. P. Eckermann *Gespräche mit Goethe* (1836–48) 10 April
> 1829. Cf. Anonymous 21:13

20 *Mehr Licht!*

More light!
> Attributed dying words (actually '*Macht doch den zweiten*
> *Fensterladen auch auf, damit mehr Licht hereinkomme* [Open
> the second shutter, so that more light can come in]')

Nikolai Gogol 1809–52

Russian writer

21 Забирайте же с собою в путь, выходя из мягких
юношеских лет в суровое ожесточающее
мужество, забирайте с собою все человеческие
движения, не оставляйте их на дороге, не
подымете потом!

As you pass from the tender years of youth into harsh
and embittered manhood, make sure you take with
you on your journey all the human emotions! Don't
leave them on the road, for you will not pick them up
afterwards!
> *Dead Souls* (1842) pt. 1, ch. 6 (translated by David
> Magarshak)

1 Определено мне чудной властью идти об руку с
моими странными героями, озирать всю
громаднонесущуюся жизнь, озирать ее сквозь
видный миру смех и незримые, неведомые ему
слезы!

I am destined by the mysterious powers to walk hand
in hand with my strange heroes, viewing life in all its
immensity as it rushes past me, viewing it through
laughter seen by the world and tears unseen and
unknown by it.
> *Dead Souls* (1842) pt. 1, ch. 7 (translated by David
> Magarshak)

2 И ты, Русь, что бойкая необгонимая тройка
несешься? . . . Летит мимо всё, что ни есть на
земле и, косясь, просторониваются и дают ей
дорогу народы и государства.

[Are not] you too, Russia, speeding along like a
spirited *troika* that nothing can overtake? . . .
Everything on earth is flying past, and looking
askance, other nations and states draw aside and
make way.
> *Dead Souls* (1842) pt. 1, ch. 11 (translated by David
> Magarshak)

Isaac Goldberg 1887–1938

3 Diplomacy is to do and say
The nastiest thing in the nicest way.
> *The Reflex* October 1927, p. 77

Emma Goldman 1869–1940
American anarchist

4 Anarchism, then, really, stands for the liberation of
the human mind from the dominion of religion; the
liberation of the human body from the dominion of
property; liberation from the shackles and restraints of
government.
> *Anarchism and Other Essays* (1910) p. 68

Oliver Goldsmith 1730–74
Anglo-Irish writer, poet, and playwright

5 Sweet Auburn, loveliest village of the plain,
Where health and plenty cheered the labouring swain.
> *The Deserted Village* (1770) l. 1

6 Ill fares the land, to hast'ning ills a prey,
Where wealth accumulates, and men decay;
Princes and lords may flourish, or may fade;
A breath can make them, as a breath has made;
But a bold peasantry, their country's pride,
When once destroyed, can never be supplied.
A time there was, ere England's griefs began,
When every rood of ground maintained its man;
For him light labour spread her wholesome store,
Just gave what life required, but gave no more;
His best companions, innocence and health;
And his best riches, ignorance of wealth.
> *The Deserted Village* (1770) l. 51

7 How happy he who crowns in shades like these,
A youth of labour with an age of ease.
> *The Deserted Village* (1770) l. 99

8 The watchdog's voice that bayed the whisp'ring wind,
And the loud laugh that spoke the vacant mind.
> *The Deserted Village* (1770) l. 121. Cf. Chesterfield
> 198:15

9 A man he was to all the country dear,
And passing rich with forty pounds a year;
Remote from towns he ran his godly race,
Nor e'er had changed nor wished to change his place.
> *The Deserted Village* (1770) l. 141

10 He chid their wand'rings, but relieved their pain.
> *The Deserted Village* (1770) l. 150

11 Truth from his lips prevailed with double sway,
And fools, who came to scoff, remained to pray.
> *The Deserted Village* (1770) l. 179

12 A man severe he was, and stern to view;
I knew him well, and every truant knew;
Well had the boding tremblers learned to trace
The day's disasters in his morning face;
Full well they laughed with counterfeited glee,
At all his jokes, for many a joke had he.
> *The Deserted Village* (1770) l. 197

13 The village all declared how much he knew;
'Twas certain he could write and cypher too.
> *The Deserted Village* (1770) l. 207

14 In arguing too, the parson owned his skill,
For e'en though vanquished, he could argue still;
While words of learned length, and thund'ring sound
Amazed the gazing rustics ranged around,
And still they gazed, and still the wonder grew,
That one small head could carry all he knew.
> *The Deserted Village* (1770) l. 211

15 The white-washed wall, the nicely sanded floor,
The varnished clock that clicked behind the door;
The chest contrived a double debt to pay,
A bed at night, a chest of drawers by day.
> *The Deserted Village* (1770) l. 227

16   How wide the limits stand
Between a splendid and a happy land.
> *The Deserted Village* (1770) l. 267

17 In all the silent manliness of grief.
> *The Deserted Village* (1770) l. 384

18 I see the rural virtues leave the land.
> *The Deserted Village* (1770) l. 398

19 Thou source of all my bliss, and all my woe,
That found'st me poor at first, and keep'st me so.
> *The Deserted Village* (1770) l. 413 (on poetry)

20 Man wants but little here below,
Nor wants that little long.
> 'Edwin and Angelina, or the Hermit' (1766). Cf. Young
> 754:21

21 The doctor found, when she was dead,—
Her last disorder mortal.
> 'Elegy on Mrs Mary Blaize' (1759)

22 The naked every day he clad,
When he put on his clothes.
> 'Elegy on the Death of a Mad Dog' (1766)

23 The dog, to gain some private ends,
Went mad and bit the man.
> 'Elegy on the Death of a Mad Dog' (1766)

1 The man recovered of the bite,
  The dog it was that died.
  'Elegy on the Death of a Mad Dog' (1766)

2 Brutes never meet in bloody fray,
  Nor cut each other's throats, for pay.
  'Logicians Refuted' (1759) l. 39 (attribution uncertain)

3 Our Garrick's a salad; for in him we see
  Oil, vinegar, sugar, and saltness agree.
  Retaliation (1774) l. 11. Cf. Garrick 298:5

4 Who, too deep for his hearers, still went on refining,
  And thought of convincing, while they thought of
    dining;
  Though equal to all things, for all things unfit,
  Too nice for a statesman, too proud for a wit.
  Retaliation (1774) l. 29 (of Edmund Burke)

5 Here lies David Garrick, describe me, who can,
  An abridgement of all that was pleasant in man.
  Retaliation (1774) l. 93

6 On the stage he was natural, simple, affecting;
  'Twas only that when he was off he was acting.
  Retaliation (1774) l. 101 (of Garrick)

7 When they talked of their Raphaels, Correggios, and
    stuff,
  He shifted his trumpet, and only took snuff.
  Retaliation (1774) l. 145 (of Reynolds)

8 Where'er I roam, whatever realms to see,
  My heart untravelled fondly turns to thee;
  Still to my brother turns with ceaseless pain,
  And drags at each remove a lengthening chain.
  The Traveller (1764) l. 7

9 Such is the patriot's boast, where'er we roam,
  His first, best country ever is, at home.
  The Traveller (1764) l. 73

10 Pride in their port, defiance in their eye,
   I see the lords of human kind pass by.
   The Traveller (1764) l. 327

11 Laws grind the poor, and rich men rule the law.
   The Traveller (1764) l. 386

12 How small, of all that human hearts endure,
   That part which laws or kings can cause or cure!
   The Traveller (1764) l. 429

13 The true use of speech is not so much to express our
   wants as to conceal them.
   The Bee no. 3 (20 October 1759) 'On the Use of Language'

14 This same philosophy is a good horse in the stable, but
   an arrant jade on a journey.
   The Good-Natured Man (1768) act 1

15 We must touch his weaknesses with a delicate hand.
   There are some faults so nearly allied to excellence,
   that we can scarce weed out the fault without
   eradicating the virtue.
   The Good-Natured Man (1768) act 1

16 All his faults are such that one loves him still the
   better for them.
   The Good-Natured Man (1768) act 1

17 Friendship is a disinterested commerce between
   equals; love, an abject intercourse between tyrants
   and slaves.
   The Good-Natured Man (1768) act 1

18 Silence is become his mother tongue.
   The Good-Natured Man (1768) act 2

19 You, that are going to be married, think things can
   never be done too fast; but we, that are old, and know
   what we are about, must elope methodically, madam.
   The Good-Natured Man (1768) act 2

20 Let schoolmasters puzzle their brain,
   With grammar, and nonsense, and learning,
   Good liquor, I stoutly maintain,
   Gives genius a better discerning.
   She Stoops to Conquer (1773) act 1, sc. 1 'Song'

21 Is it one of my well-looking days, child? Am I in face
   to-day?
   She Stoops to Conquer (1773) act 1

22 The very pink of perfection.
   She Stoops to Conquer (1773) act 1

23 I'll be with you in the squeezing of a lemon.
   She Stoops to Conquer (1773) act 1

24 It's a damned long, dark, boggy, dirty, dangerous
   way.
   She Stoops to Conquer (1773) act 1

25 This is Liberty-Hall, gentlemen.
   She Stoops to Conquer (1773) act 2

26 The first blow is half the battle.
   She Stoops to Conquer (1773) act 2

27 Was there ever such a cross-grained brute?
   She Stoops to Conquer (1773) act 3

28 I was ever of opinion, that the honest man who
   married and brought up a large family, did more
   service than he who continued single and only talked
   of population.
   The Vicar of Wakefield (1766) ch. 1

29 I . . . chose my wife, as she did her wedding gown, not
   for a fine glossy surface, but such qualities as would
   wear well.
   The Vicar of Wakefield (1766) ch. 1

30 All our adventures were by the fire-side, and all our
   migrations from the blue bed to the brown.
   The Vicar of Wakefield (1766) ch. 1

31 The virtue which requires to be ever guarded is scarce
   worth the sentinel.
   The Vicar of Wakefield (1766) ch. 5

32 It seemed to me pretty plain, that they had more of
   love than matrimony in them.
   The Vicar of Wakefield (1766) ch. 16

33 When lovely woman stoops to folly
   And finds too late that men betray,
   What charm can soothe her melancholy,
   What art can wash her guilt away?
   The Vicar of Wakefield (1766) ch. 29

34 There is no arguing with Johnson; for when his pistol
   misses fire, he knocks you down with the butt end of
   it.
   In James Boswell Life of Samuel Johnson (1934 ed.) vol. 2,
   p. 100 (26 October 1769)

35 As I take my shoes from the shoemaker, and my coat
   from the tailor, so I take my religion from the priest.
   In James Boswell Life of Samuel Johnson (1934 ed.) vol. 2,
   p. 214 (9 April 1773)

Barry Goldwater 1909–

American politician

1 I would remind you that extremism in the defence of liberty is no vice! And let me remind you also that moderation in the pursuit of justice is no virtue!
> Accepting the presidential nomination, 16 July 1964, in *New York Times* 17 July 1964, p. 1

Sam Goldwyn (*Samuel Goldfish*) 1882–1974

American film producer

2 Gentlemen, include me out.
> On resigning from the Motion Picture Producers and Distributors of America, October 1933, in Michael Freedland *The Goldwyn Touch* (1986) ch. 10

3 A verbal contract isn't worth the paper it is written on.
> In Alva Johnston *The Great Goldwyn* (1937) ch. 1

4 That's the way with these directors, they're always biting the hand that lays the golden egg.
> In Alva Johnston *The Great Goldwyn* (1937) ch. 1

5 Pictures are for entertainment, messages should be delivered by Western Union.
> In Arthur Marx *Goldwyn* (1976) ch. 15

6 Any man who goes to a psychiatrist should have his head examined.
> In Norman Zierold *Moguls* (1969) ch. 3

7 Why should people go out and pay to see bad movies when they can stay at home and see bad television for nothing?
> In *Observer* 9 September 1956

Ivan Goncharov 1812–91

Russian novelist

8 Вся тревога разрешалась вздохом и замирала в апатии или в дремоте.

All his anxiety resolved itself into a sigh and dissolved into apathy and drowsiness.
> *Obolomov* (1859) pt. 1, ch. 1 (translated by David Magarshak)

9 В жизни моей ведь никогда не загоралось никакого, не спасительного, не разрушительного огня? . . . жизнь моя началась с погасания.

The trouble is that no devastating or redeeming fires have ever burnt in my life . . . My life began by flickering out.
> *Obolomov* (1859) pt. 2, ch. 4 (translated by David Magarshak)

10 Ты свое уменье затерял еще в детстве, в Обломовке . . . Началось с неуменья надевать чулки и кончилось неуменьем жить.

You lost your ability for doing things in childhood, in Oblomovka . . . It all began with your inability to put on your socks and ended by your inability to live.
> *Obolomov* (1859) pt. 4, ch. 2 (translated by David Magarshak)

Barnabe Googe 1540–94

English poet

11 Fair face show friends
When riches do abound:
Come time of proof,
Farewell, they must away.
Believe me well,
They are not to be found,
If God but send
Thee once a lowering day.
Gold never starts
Aside, but in distress
Finds ways enough
To ease thine heaviness.
> 'Of Money' (1563)

Adam Lindsay Gordon 1833–70

Australian poet

12 Life is mostly froth and bubble,
Two things stand like stone,
Kindness in another's trouble,
Courage in your own.
> *Ye Wearie Wayfarer* (1866) 'Fytte 8'

Mack Gordon 1904–59

American songwriter

13 Pardon me boy is that the Chattanooga Choo-choo,
Track twenty nine,
Boy you can gimme a shine.
I can afford to board a Chattanooga Choo-choo,
I've got my fare and just a trifle to spare.
You leave the Pennsylvania station 'bout a quarter to four,
Read a magazine and then you're in Baltimore,
Dinner in the diner nothing could be finer
Than to have your ham'n eggs in Carolina.
> 'Chattanooga Choo-choo' (1941 song)

Stuart Gorrell 1902–63

American songwriter

14 Georgia, Georgia, no peace I find,
Just an old sweet song keeps Georgia on my mind.
> 'Georgia on my Mind' (1930 song); music by Hoagy Carmichael

George Joachim, 1st Lord Goschen 1831–1907

British politician

15 I have the courage of my opinions, but I have not the temerity to give a political blank cheque to Lord Salisbury.
> Speech, *Hansard* 19 February 1884, col. 1420

Sir Edmund Gosse 1849–1928

English poet and man of letters

16 A sheep in sheep's clothing.
> Of the 'woolly-bearded poet' Sturge Moore, in F. Greenslet *Under the Bridge* (1943) ch. 10. Cf. Churchill 203:11

Edward Meyrick Goulburn 1818–97

Dean of Norwich, 1866–89

1 Let the scintillations of your wit be like the coruscations of summer lightning, lambent but innocuous.

   Sermon at Rugby School, in W. Tuckwell *Reminiscences of Oxford* (2nd ed., 1907) p. 272

John Gower c.1330–1408

English poet

2 It hath and schal ben evermor
That love is maister wher he wile.

   Confessio Amantis (1386–90) prologue, l. 34

Sir Ernest Gowers 1880–1966

British public servant

3 It is not easy nowadays to remember anything so contrary to all appearances as that officials are the servants of the public; and the official must try not to foster the illusion that it is the other way round.

   Plain Words (1948) ch. 3

4 We are all esquires now, and we are none of us gentlemen any more.

   In H. W. Fowler *A Dictionary of Modern English Usage* (2nd ed., 1965) p. 223

Goya (Francisco José de Goya y Lucientes) 1746–1828

Spanish painter

5 El sueño de la razón produce monstruos.
The dream of reason produces monsters.

   Los Caprichos (1799) plate 43 (title)

Clementina Stirling Graham 1782–1877

Scottish writer

6 The best way to get the better of temptation is just to yield to it.

   Mystifications (1859) 'Soirée at Mrs Russel's'

D. M. Graham 1911–

7 That this House will in no circumstances fight for its King and Country.

   Motion worded by Graham for a debate at the Oxford Union, of which he was Librarian, 9 February 1933 (passed by 275 votes to 153)

Harry Graham 1874–1936

British writer and journalist

8 Weep not for little Léonie
Abducted by a French Marquis!
Though loss of honour was a wrench
Just think how it's improved her French.

   More Ruthless Rhymes for Heartless Homes (1930) 'Compensation'

9 O'er the rugged mountain's brow
Clara threw the twins she nursed,
And remarked, 'I wonder now
Which will reach the bottom first?'

   Ruthless Rhymes for Heartless Homes (1899) 'Calculating Clara'

10 Aunt Jane observed, the second time
She tumbled off a bus,
'The step is short from the Sublime
To the Ridiculous.'

   Ruthless Rhymes for Heartless Homes (1899) 'Equanimity'. Cf. Napoleon 489:16

11 'There's been an accident,' they said,
'Your servant's cut in half; he's dead!'
'Indeed!' said Mr Jones, 'and please,
Send me the half that's got my keys.'

   Ruthless Rhymes for Heartless Homes (1899) 'Mr Jones' (attributed to 'G.W.')

12 Billy, in one of his nice new sashes,
Fell in the fire and was burnt to ashes;
Now, although the room grows chilly,
I haven't the heart to poke poor Billy.

   Ruthless Rhymes for Heartless Homes (1899) 'Tender-Heartedness'

James Graham, 1st Marquess of Montrose 1612–50

Scottish royalist general and poet

13 Great, Good and Just, could I but rate
My grief to thy too rigid fate!

   'Epitaph on King Charles I'

14 Let them bestow on every airth a limb;
Then open all my veins, that I may swim
To thee, my Maker! in that crimson lake;
Then place my parboiled head upon a stake—
Scatter my ashes—strew them in the air;—
Lord! since thou know'st where all these atoms are,
I'm hopeful thou'lt recover once my dust,
And confident thou'lt raise me with the just.

   'Lines written on the Window of his Jail the Night before his Execution'

15 He either fears his fate too much,
Or his deserts are small,
That puts it not unto the touch
To win or lose it all.

   'My Dear and Only Love' (written c.1642)

16 But if thou wilt be constant then,
And faithful of thy word,
I'll make thee glorious by my pen,
And famous by my sword.

   'My Dear and Only Love' (written c.1642)

Kenneth Grahame 1859–1932

Scottish-born writer

17 The curate faced the laurels—hesitatingly. But Aunt Maria flung herself on him. 'O Mr Hodgitts!' I heard her cry, 'you are brave! for my sake do not be rash!' He was not rash.

   The Golden Age (1895) 'The Burglars'

1 Monkeys . . . very sensibly refrain from speech, lest they should be set to earn their livings.

   The Golden Age (1895) 'Lusisti Satis'

2 There is *nothing*—absolutely nothing—half so much worth doing as simply messing about in boats.

   The Wind in the Willows (1908) ch. 1

3 The poetry of motion! The *real* way to travel! The *only* way to travel! Here today—in next week tomorrow! Villages skipped, towns and cities jumped—always somebody else's horizon!

   The Wind in the Willows (1908) ch. 2. Cf. Kaufman and Anthony 385:16

James Grainger *c.*1721–66

English physician and man of letters

4 What is fame? an empty bubble; Gold? a transient, shining trouble.

   'Solitude' (1755) l. 96

5   Knock off the chains Of heart-debasing slavery; give to man, Of every colour and of every clime, Freedom, which stamps him image of his God.

   The Sugar Cane (1764) bk. 4

Sir Robert Grant 1785–1838

British lawyer and politician

6 O worship the King, all-glorious above; O gratefully sing his power and his love: Our Shield and Defender, the Ancient of Days, Pavilioned in splendour, and girded with praise.

   'O worship the King, all glorious above' (1833 hymn)

Ulysses S. Grant 1822–85

18th President of the USA

7 No terms except unconditional and immediate surrender can be accepted. I propose to move immediately upon your works.

   To Simon Bolivar Buckner, under siege at Fort Donelson, 16 February 1862; in P. C. Headley *The Life and Campaigns of General U. S. Grant* (1869) ch. 6

8 I purpose to fight it out on this line, if it takes all summer.

   Dispatch to Washington, from head-quarters in the field, 11 May 1864, in P. C. Headley *The Life and Campaigns of General U. S. Grant* (1869) ch. 23

9 Let us have peace.

   Letter to General Joseph R. Hawkey, 29 May 1868, accepting the presidential nomination, in P. C. Headley *The Life and Campaigns of General U. S. Grant* (1869) ch. 29

10 I know no method to secure the repeal of bad or obnoxious laws so effective as their stringent execution.

   Inaugural Address, 4 March 1869, in P. C. Headley *The Life and Campaigns of General U. S. Grant* (1869) ch. 29

11 Let no guilty man escape, if it can be avoided . . . No personal consideration should stand in the way of performing a public duty.

   Endorsement of a letter relating to the Whiskey Ring, 29 July 1875, in E. P. Oberholtzer *History of the United States Since the Civil War* (1937) vol. 3, ch. 19

George Granville, Baron Lansdowne
1666–1735

English poet and playwright

12 Bright as the day, and like the morning, fair, Such Cloe is . . . and common as the air.

   'Cloe' (1712)

13 Of all pains, the greatest pain Is to love, and love in vain.

   'The happiest mortals once were we'

14 Cowards in scarlet pass for men of war.

   The She Gallants (1696) act 5

15 I'll be this abject thing no more; Love, give me back my heart again.

   'Song for Myra' (1712)

John Woodcock Graves 1795–1886

British huntsman and songwriter

16 D'ye ken John Peel with his coat so grey? D'ye ken John Peel at the break of the day? D'ye ken John Peel when he's far far away With his hounds and his horn in the morning? 'Twas the sound of his horn called me from my bed, And the cry of his hounds has me oft-times led; For Peel's view-hollo would waken the dead, Or a fox from his lair in the morning.

   'John Peel' (1820)

Robert Graves 1895–1985

English poet

17 Children are dumb to say how hot the day is, How hot the scent is of the summer rose.

   'The Cool Web' (1927)

18 There's a cool web of language winds us in, Retreat from too much joy or too much fear.

   'The Cool Web' (1927)

19 Counting the beats, Counting the slow heart beats, The bleeding to death of time in slow heart beats, Wakeful they lie.

   'Counting the Beats' (1951)

20 His eyes are quickened so with grief, He can watch a grass or leaf Every instant grow; he can Clearly through a flint wall see, Or watch the startled spirit flee From the throat of a dead man.

   'Lost Love' (1921)

21 Truth-loving Persians do not dwell upon The trivial skirmish fought near Marathon.

   'The Persian Version' (1945)

22 As you are woman, so be lovely: As you are lovely, so be various, Merciful as constant, constant as various, So be mine, as I yours for ever.

   'Pygmalion to Galatea' (1927)

1 Far away is close at hand
  Close joined is far away,
  Love shall come at your command
  Yet will not stay.
    'Song of Contrariety' (1923)

2 To evoke posterity
  Is to weep on your own grave,
  Ventriloquizing for the unborn.
    'To Evoke Posterity' (1938)

3 Goodbye to all that.
    Title of autobiography (1929)

John Chipman Gray 1839–1915
American lawyer

4 Dirt is only matter out of place; and what is a blot on
  the escutcheon of the Common Law may be a jewel in
  the crown of the Social Republic.
    Restraints on the Alienation of Property (2nd ed., 1895)
    preface

Patrick, 6th Lord Gray d. 1612

5 A dead woman bites not.
    Oral tradition, Gray being said to have pressed hard for the
    execution of Mary Queen of Scots in 1587, with the words
    'Mortua non mordet [Being dead, she will bite no more]'; in
    A. Darcy's 1625 translation of William Camden's *Annals of
    the Reign of Queen Elizabeth* (1615) vol. 1, p. 196. See *Oxford
    Dictionary of English Proverbs*

Thomas Gray 1716–71
English poet

6 Ruin seize thee, ruthless King!
  Confusion on thy banners wait,
  Tho' fanned by Conquest's crimson wing
  They mock the air with idle state.
    The Bard (1757) l. 1

7 Loose his beard, and hoary hair
  Streamed, like a meteor, to the troubled air.
    The Bard (1757) l. 19. Cf. Milton 468:22

8 Weave the warp, and weave the woof,
  The winding-sheet of Edward's race.
  Give ample room, and verge enough
  The characters of hell to trace.
    The Bard (1757) l. 49

9 Fair laughs the morn, and soft the zephyr blows,
  While proudly riding o'er the azure realm
  In gallant trim the gilded vessel goes;
  Youth on the prow, and Pleasure at the helm;
  Regardless of the sweeping whirlwind's sway,
  That, hushed in grim repose, expects his evening prey.
    'The Bard' (1757) l. 71

10 The curfew tolls the knell of parting day,
   The lowing herd wind slowly o'er the lea,
   The ploughman homeward plods his weary way,
   And leaves the world to darkness and to me.

   Now fades the glimmering landscape on the sight,
   And all the air a solemn stillness holds,
   Save where the beetle wheels his droning flight,
   And drowsy tinklings lull the distant folds.
    Elegy Written in a Country Churchyard (1751) l. 1

11 Save that from yonder ivy-mantled tow'r,
   The moping owl does to the moon complain.
    Elegy Written in a Country Churchyard (1751) l. 9

12 Beneath those rugged elms, that yew-tree's shade,
   Where heaves the turf in many a mouldering heap,
   Each in his narrow cell for ever laid,
   The rude forefathers of the hamlet sleep.

   The breezy call of incense-breathing Morn,
   The swallow twitt'ring from the straw-built shed,
   The cock's shrill clarion, or the echoing horn,
   No more shall rouse them from their lowly bed.
    Elegy Written in a Country Churchyard (1751) l. 13

13 Let not ambition mock their useful toil,
   Their homely joys, and destiny obscure;
   Nor grandeur hear with a disdainful smile,
   The short and simple annals of the poor.

   The boast of heraldry, the pomp of pow'r,
   And all that beauty, all that wealth e'er gave,
   Awaits alike th' inevitable hour,
   The paths of glory lead but to the grave.
    Elegy Written in a Country Churchyard (1751) l. 29

14 Can storied urn or animated bust
   Back to its mansion call the fleeting breath?
   Can honour's voice provoke the silent dust,
   Or flatt'ry soothe the dull cold ear of death?
    Elegy Written in a Country Churchyard (1751) l. 41

15 Full many a gem of purest ray serene,
   The dark unfathomed caves of ocean bear:
   Full many a flower is born to blush unseen,
   And waste its sweetness on the desert air.

   Some village-Hampden, that with dauntless breast
   The little tyrant of his fields withstood,
   Some mute inglorious Milton here may rest,
   Some Cromwell guiltless of his country's blood.
    Elegy Written in a Country Churchyard (1751) l. 53

16 Their lot forbad: nor circumscribed alone
   Their growing virtues, but their crimes confined;
   Forbad to wade through slaughter to a throne,
   And shut the gates of mercy on mankind.
    Elegy Written in a Country Churchyard (1751) l. 65

17 Far from the madding crowd's ignoble strife,
   Their sober wishes never learned to stray;
   Along the cool sequestered vale of life
   They kept the noiseless tenor of their way.
    Elegy Written in a Country Churchyard (1751) l. 73

18 For who to dumb Forgetfulness a prey,
   This pleasing anxious being e'er resigned,
   Left the warm precincts of the cheerful day,
   Nor cast one longing ling'ring look behind?
    Elegy Written in a Country Churchyard (1751) l. 85

19 Mindful of th' unhonoured dead
    Elegy Written in a Country Churchyard (1751) l. 93

20 Here rests his head upon the lap of Earth
   A youth to fortune and to fame unknown.
   Fair Science frowned not on his humble birth,
   And Melancholy marked him for her own.
    Elegy Written in a Country Churchyard (1751) l. 117

21 Ye distant spires, ye antique towers,
   That crown the wat'ry glade.
    Ode on a Distant Prospect of Eton College (1747) l. 1

1 Still as they run they look behind,
   They hear a voice in every wind,
   And snatch a fearful joy.
   Ode on a Distant Prospect of Eton College (1747) l. 38

2 Alas, regardless of their doom,
   The little victims play!
   No sense have they of ills to come,
   Nor care beyond to-day.
   Ode on a Distant Prospect of Eton College (1747) l. 51

3 To each his suff'rings, all are men,
   Condemned alike to groan;
   The tender for another's pain,
   Th' unfeeling for his own.

   Yet ah! why should they know their fate?
   Since sorrow never comes too late,
   And happiness too swiftly flies.
   Thought would destroy their paradise.
   No more; where ignorance is bliss,
   'Tis folly to be wise.
   Ode on a Distant Prospect of Eton College (1747) l. 91

4 Not all that tempts your wand'ring eyes
   And heedless hearts, is lawful prize;
   Nor all, that glisters, gold.
   'Ode on the Death of a Favourite Cat' (1748)

5 The Attic warbler pours her throat,
   Responsive to the cuckoo's note,
   The untaught harmony of spring.
   'Ode on the Spring' (1748) l. 5

6 . . . Far from the sun and summer-gale,
   In thy green lap was Nature's darling laid.
   The Progress of Poesy (1757) l. 83 (of Shakespeare)

7 Nor second he, that rode sublime
   Upon the seraph-wings of ecstasy,
   The secrets of th' abyss to spy.
   He passed the flaming bounds of place and time:
   The living throne, the sapphire-blaze,
   Where angels tremble, while they gaze,
   He saw; but blasted with excess of light,
   Closed his eyes in endless night.
   The Progress of Poesy (1757) l. 95 (of Milton)

8 Thoughts, that breathe, and words, that burn.
   The Progress of Poesy (1757) l. 110

9 Beyond the limits of a vulgar fate,
   Beneath the good how far—but far above the great.
   The Progress of Poesy (1757) l. 122

10 Too poor for a bribe, and too proud to importune,
   He had not the method of making a fortune.
   'Sketch of his own Character' (written 1761)

11 The language of the age is never the language of
   poetry, except among the French, whose verse, where
   the thought or image does not support it, differs in
   nothing from prose.
   Letter to Richard West, 8 April 1742, in H. W. Starr (ed.)
   Correspondence of Thomas Gray (1971) vol. 1

12 It has been usual to catch a mouse or two (for form's
   sake) in public once a year.
   On refusing the Laureateship, in a letter to William Mason,
   19 December 1757; in H. W. Starr (ed.) *Correspondence of
   Thomas Gray* (1971) vol. 2

13 I shall be but a shrimp of an author.
   Letter to Horace Walpole, 25 February 1768, in H. W.
   Starr (ed.) *Correspondence of Thomas Gray* (1971) vol. 3

14 Any fool may write a most valuable book by chance, if
   he will only tell us what he heard and saw with
   veracity.
   Letter to Horace Walpole, 25 February 1768, in H. W.
   Starr (ed.) *Correspondence of Thomas Gray* (1971) vol. 3

Horace Greeley 1811–72
American founder and editor of the New York Tribune

15 Go West, young man, and grow up with the country.
   Hints toward Reforms (1850). Cf. Soule 656:19

Hannah Green (Joanne Greenberg)
American novelist

16 I never promised you a rose garden.
   Title of novel (1964)

Matthew Green 1696–1737
English poet

17 They politics like ours profess,
   The greater prey upon the less.
   The Grotto (1732) l. 69

18 Fling but a stone, the giant dies.
   Laugh and be well.
   The Spleen (1737) l. 92

19 By happy alchemy of mind
   They turn to pleasure all they find.
   The Spleen (1737) l. 610

Graham Greene 1904–91
English novelist

20 Catholics and Communists have committed great
   crimes, but at least they have not stood aside, like an
   established society, and been indifferent. I would
   rather have blood on my hands than water like Pilate.
   The Comedians (1966) pt. 3, ch. 4

21 He gave her a bright fake smile; so much of life was a
   putting-off of unhappiness for another time. Nothing
   was ever lost by delay.
   The Heart of the Matter (1948) bk. 1, pt. 1, ch. 1

22 Against the beautiful and the clever and the
   successful, one can wage a pitiless war, but not
   against the unattractive.
   The Heart of the Matter (1948) bk. 1, pt. 1, ch. 2

23 They had been corrupted by money, and he had been
   corrupted by sentiment. Sentiment was the more
   dangerous, because you couldn't name its price. A
   man open to bribes was to be relied upon below a
   certain figure, but sentiment might uncoil in the heart
   at a name, a photograph, even a smell remembered.
   The Heart of the Matter (1948) bk. 1, pt. 1, ch. 2

24 Here you could love human beings nearly as God
   loved them, knowing the worst; you didn't love a
   pose, a pretty dress, a sentiment artfully assumed.
   The Heart of the Matter (1948) bk. 1, pt. 1, ch. 5

25 He felt the loyalty we all feel to unhappiness—the
   sense that that is where we really belong.
   The Heart of the Matter (1948) bk. 2, pt. 2, ch. 1

1 Any victim demands allegiance.
The Heart of the Matter (1948) bk. 3, pt. 1, ch. 1

2 His hilarity was like a scream from a crevasse.
The Heart of the Matter (1948) bk. 3, pt. 1, ch. 1

3 There is always one moment in childhood when the door opens and lets the future in.
The Power and the Glory (1940) pt. 1, ch. 1

4 Innocence always calls mutely for protection, when we would be so much wiser to guard ourselves against it: innocence is like a dumb leper who has lost his bell, wandering the world meaning no harm.
The Quiet American (1955) pt. 1, ch. 3

5 If only it were possible to love without injury—fidelity isn't enough ... The hurt is in the act of possession: we are too small in mind and body to possess another person without pride or to be possessed without humiliation.
The Quiet American (1955) pt. 2, ch. 3

6 [I wanted] to discover what lies behind the dark, thick leaf of the aspidistra that guards ... the vulnerable gap between the lace curtains.
On early attempts to experience life outside his own social class, in Norman Sherry *Life of Graham Greene 1904–39* (1989) ch. 39

Robert Greene *c.*1560–92
English poet and playwright

7 Hangs in the uncertain balance of proud time.
Friar Bacon and Friar Bungay (1594) act 3, sc. 1

8 Deceiving world, that with alluring toys
Hast made my life the subject of thy scorn,
And scornest now to lend thy fading joys,
To length my life, whom friends have left forlorn,
How well are they that die ere they be born;
And never see thy sleights, which few men shun
Till unawares they helpless are undone.
The Groatsworth of Wit (1592) 'Deceiving World'

9 Ah! were she pitiful as she is fair,
Or but as mild as she is seeming so.
Pandosto. The Triumph of Time (1694 ed.)

10 'Men, when they lust, can many fancies feign,'
Said Phillis. This not Coridon denied,
That lust had lies. 'But love,' quoth he, 'says truth.'
Perimedes (1588) 'Phillis kept sheep'

11 Ah! what is love! It is a pretty thing,
As sweet unto a shepherd as a king,
And sweeter too;
For kings have cares that wait upon a crown,
And cares can make the sweetest love to frown.
Ah then, ah then,
If country loves such sweet desires do gain,
What lady would not love a shepherd swain?
'The Shepherd's Wife's Song' (1590)

Germaine Greer 1939–
Australian feminist

12 Security is when everything is settled, when nothing can happen to you; security is the denial of life.
The Female Eunuch (1970) 'Security'

13 The stereotype is the Eternal Feminine. She is the Sexual Object sought by all men, and by all women. She is of neither sex, for she has herself no sex at all. Her value is solely attested by the demand she excites in others. All she must contribute is her existence. She need achieve nothing, for she is the reward of achievement.
The Female Eunuch (1970) 'The Stereotype'

14 You can now see the Female Eunuch the world over ... spreading herself wherever blue jeans and Coca-Cola may go. Wherever you see nail varnish, lipstick, brassieres, and high heels, the Eunuch has set up her camp.
The Female Eunuch (20th anniversary ed., 1991) foreword

15 I didn't fight to get women out from behind the vacuum cleaner to get them onto the board of Hoover.
In *Guardian* 27 October 1986

16 Human beings have an inalienable right to invent themselves; when that right is pre-empted it is called brain-washing.
The Times 1 February 1986

Gregory the Great AD *c.*540–604
Pope from 590

17 *Non Angli sed Angeli.*
Not Angles but Angels.
Oral tradition. See Bede *Historia Ecclesiastica* bk. 2, sect. 1: 'Responsum est, quod Angli vocarentur. At ille: "Bene," inquit; "nam et angelicam habent faciem, et tales angelorum in caelis decet esse coheredes"' [They answered that they were called Angles. "It is well," he said, "for they have the faces of angels, and such should be the co-heirs of the angels of heaven"]'

Gregory VII *c.*1020–85
Pope from 1073

18 *Dilexi iustitiam et odi iniquitatem, propterea morior in exilio.*
I have loved justice and hated iniquity: therefore I die in exile.
Last words, in J. W. Bowden *The Life and Pontificate of Gregory VII* (1840) vol. 2, bk. 3, ch. 20

Stephen Grellet 1773–1855
French missionary

19 I expect to pass through this world but once; any good thing therefore that I can do, or any kindness that I can show to any fellow-creature, let me do it now; let me not defer or neglect it, for I shall not pass this way again.
Attributed. See John o' London *Treasure Trove* (1925) p. 48 for some of the many claimants to authorship

Joyce Grenfell (née Phipps) 1910–79

English comedy actress and writer

1 Stately as a galleon, I sail across the floor,
  Doing the Military Two-step, as in the days of yore . . .

  So gay the band,
  So giddy the sight,
  Full evening dress is a must,
  But the zest goes out of a beautiful waltz
  When you dance it bust to bust.
      'Stately as a Galleon' (1978 song)

Julian Grenfell 1888–1915

English soldier and poet

2 The naked earth is warm with Spring,
  And with green grass and bursting trees
  Leans to the sun's kiss glorying,
  And quivers in the sunny breeze;

  And Life is Colour and Warmth and Light
  And a striving evermore for these;
  And he is dead, who will not fight;
  And who dies fighting has increase.

  The fighting man shall from the sun
  Take warmth, and life from the glowing earth.
  Speed with the light-foot winds to run,
  And with the trees to newer birth.
      'Into Battle' in *The Times* 28 May 1915

Frances Greville (née Macartney) c.1724–89

Irish poet; wife of Fulke Greville (1717–c.1805)

3 Far as distress the soul can wound
  'Tis pain in each degree;
  Bliss goes but to a certain bound,
  Beyond is agony.
      'A Prayer for Indifference' (1759)

4 Half-pleased, contented will I be,
  Contented, half to please.
      'A Prayer for Indifference' (1759)

Fulke Greville (1st Baron Brooke) 1554–1628

English poet, writer, and politician

5 He that lets his Cynthia lie,
  Naked on a bed of play,
  To say prayers ere she die,
  Teacheth time to run away.
  Let no love-desiring heart,
  In the stars go seek his fate,
  Love is only Nature's art,
  Wonder hinders love and hate.
  None can well behold with eyes,
  But what underneath him lies.
      Caelica (1633) 'All my senses, like beacon's flame'

6 Man torn with love, with inward furies blasted,
  Drowned with despair, with fleshly lustings shaken,
  Cannot for this with heaven be distasted;
  Love, fury, lustings out of man are taken.

  Then man, endure thyself, those clouds will vanish;
  Life is a top which whipping Sorrow driveth;
  Wisdom must bear what our flesh cannot banish,
  The humble lead, the stubborn bootless striveth.
      Caelica (1633) 'The earth with thunder torn, with fire blasted'

7 When as man's life, the light of human lust,
  In socket of his earthly lantern burns,
  That all this glory unto ashes must,
  And generation to corruption turns;
  Then fond desires that only fear their end,
  Do vainly wish for life, but to amend.

  But when this life is from the body fled,
  To see itself in that eternal glass,
  Where time doth end, and thoughts accuse the dead,
  Where all to come, is one with all that was;
  Then living men ask how he left his breath,
  That while he lived never thought of death.
      Caelica (1633) 'When as man's life, the light of human lust'

8 O wearisome condition of humanity!
  Born under one law, to another bound;
  Vainly begot, and yet forbidden vanity;
  Created sick, commanded to be sound.
      Mustapha (1609) act 5, sc. 4

9 The mind of man is this world's true dimension,
  And knowledge is the measure of the mind;
  And as the mind in her vast comprehension
  Contains more worlds than all the world can find,
  So knowledge doth itself far more extend
  Than all the minds of men can comprehend.
      A Treaty of Human Learning (1633) st. 1

Sir Edward Grey (Viscount Grey of Fallodon) 1862–1933

British Liberal politician

10 The lamps are going out all over Europe; we shall not
   see them lit again in our lifetime.
      25 Years (1925) vol. 2, ch. 18 (on the eve of the First World War)

Mervyn Griffith-Jones 1909–79

British lawyer

11 Is it a book you would even wish your wife or your
   servants to read?
      Of D. H. Lawrence's *Lady Chatterley's Lover*, while appearing for the prosecution at the Central Criminal Court, Old Bailey, 20 October 1960; in *The Times* 21 October 1960

Nicholas Grimald 1519–62

English poet

12 Of all the heavenly gifts that mortal men commend,
   What trusty treasure in the world can countervail a
   friend?
      'Of Friendship' (1557)

George Grossmith 1847–1912
English actor, singer, and writer

1 You should see me dance the Polka,
  You should see me cover the ground,
  You should see my coat-tails flying,
  As I jump my partner round;
  When the band commences playing,
  My feet begin to go,
  For a rollicking romping Polka,
  Is the jolliest fun I know.
    'See me Dance the Polka' (c.1887 song)

George and Weedon Grossmith 1847–1912, 1854–1919
English writers

2 What's the good of a home if you are never in it?
    The Diary of a Nobody (1894) ch. 1

3 I ... recognized her as a woman who used to work years ago for my old aunt at Clapham. It only shows how small the world is.
    The Diary of a Nobody (1894) ch. 2

4 He suggested we should play 'Cutlets', a game we never heard of. He sat on a chair, and asked Carrie to sit on his lap, an invitation which dear Carrie rightly declined.
    The Diary of a Nobody (1894) ch. 7

5 I left the room with silent dignity, but caught my foot in the mat.
    The Diary of a Nobody (1894) ch. 12

6 I am a poor man, but I would gladly give ten shillings to find out who sent me the insulting Christmas card I received this morning.
    The Diary of a Nobody (1894) ch. 13

Philip Guedalla 1889–1944
British historian and biographer

7 Any stigma, as the old saying is, will serve to beat a dogma.
    Masters and Men (1923) 'Ministers of State'

8 The little ships, the unforgotten Homeric catalogue of *Mary Jane* and *Peggy IV*, of *Folkestone Belle*, *Boy Billy*, and *Ethel Maud*, of *Lady Haig* and *Skylark* ... the little ships of England brought the Army home.
    Mr Churchill (1941) ch. 7 (on the evacuation of Dunkirk)

9 The cheerful clatter of Sir James Barrie's cans as he went round with the milk of human kindness.
    Supers and Supermen (1920) 'Some Critics'

10 The work of Henry James has always seemed divisible by a simple dynastic arrangement into three reigns: James I, James II, and the Old Pretender.
    Supers and Supermen (1920) 'Some Critics'

11 History repeats itself. Historians repeat each other.
    Supers and Supermen (1920) 'Some Historians'

Hervé Guibert 1955–91
French writer

12 An illness in stages, a very long flight of steps that led assuredly to death, but whose every step represented a unique apprenticeship. It was a disease that gave death time to live and its victims time to die, time to discover time, and in the end to discover life.
    To the Friend who did not Save my Life (1991) ch. 61 (translated by Linda Coverdale)

Texas Guinan (Mary Louise Cecilia Guinan) 1884–1933
American actress

13 Fifty million Frenchmen can't be wrong.
    In *New York World–Telegram* 21 March 1931, p. 25, which asserts that Guinan used the phrase at least six or seven years previously; also attributed to Jack Osterman and Mae West, it was the title of a 1927 song by Billy Rose and Willie Raskin, and of a 1931 film

Nubar Gulbenkian 1896–1972
British industrialist and philanthropist

14 The best number for a dinner party is two—myself and a dam' good head waiter.
    In *Daily Telegraph* 14 January 1965

Nikolai Gumilev 1886–1921
Russian poet

15 Прекрасно в нас влюбленное вино
  И добрый хлеб, что в печь для нас садится,
  И женщина, которою дано,
  Сперва измучившись, нам насладиться.

  Fine is the wine that is in love with us, and the goodly bread that goes into the oven for our sake, and the woman whom we enjoy, after she has tormented us to the full.
    'Sixth Sense' (1921) (translated by Dmitri Obolensky)

16   наша свобода
  Только оттуда бьющий свет.

  Our freedom is but a light that breaks through from another world.
    'The Tram that Lost its Way' (1921) (translated by Dmitri Obolensky)

Dorothy Frances Gurney 1858–1932
English poet

17 The kiss of the sun for pardon,
  The song of the birds for mirth,
  One is nearer God's Heart in a garden
  Than anywhere else on earth.
    'God's Garden' (1913)

Ivor Gurney 1890–1937

English poet

1 I paid the prices of life
Standing where Rome immortal heard October's strife,
A war poet whose right of honour cuts falsehood like
a knife.
'Poem for End' (*c.*1922–5)

2 War told me truth: I have Severn's right of maker,
As of Cotswold: war told me: I was elect, I was born
fit
To praise the three hundred feet depth of every acre
Between Tewkesbury and Stroudway, Side and Wales
Gate.
'While I Write' (*c.*1922–5)

John Hampden Gurney 1802–62

English clergyman

3 Ye holy angels bright,
Who wait at God's right hand,
Or through the realms of light
Fly at your Lord's command,
Assist our song,
Or else the theme
Too high doth seem
For mortal tongue.
'Ye holy angels bright' (1838 hymn); based on a poem by
Richard Baxter (1615–91)

4 My soul, bear thou thy part,
Triumph in God above,
And with a well-tuned heart
Sing thou the songs of love.
'Ye holy angels bright' (1838 hymn)

Woody Guthrie (*Woodrow Wilson Guthrie*) 1912–67

American folksinger and songwriter

5 This land is your land, this land is my land,
From California to the New York Island.
From the redwood forest to the Gulf Stream waters
This land was made for you and me.
'This Land is Your Land' (1956 song)

Nell Gwyn 1650–87

English actress and courtesan

6 Pray, good people, be civil. I am the Protestant whore.
At Oxford, during the Popish Terror, 1681; in B. Bevan
Nell Gwyn (1969) ch. 13

Alan Hackney

British novelist

7 Miles of cornfields, and ballet in the evening.
Russia, as described in *Private Life* (1958) ch. 11 (later
filmed as *I'm All Right Jack*, 1959)

Hadrian AD 76–138

Roman emperor from 117

8 *Animula vagula blandula,*
Hospes comesque corporis,
Quae nunc abibis in loca
Pallidula rigida nudula,
Nec ut soles dabis iocos!

Ah! gentle, fleeting, wav'ring sprite,
Friend and associate of this clay!
To what unknown region borne,
Wilt thou now wing thy distant flight?
No more with wonted humour gay,
But pallid, cheerless, and forlorn.
In J. W. Duff (ed.) *Minor Latin Poets* (1934) p. 445
(translated by Byron as 'Adrian's Address to His Soul When
Dying')

Rider Haggard (*Sir Henry Rider Haggard*) 1856–1925

English writer

9 She who must be obeyed.
She (1887) ch. 6 and *passim*

C. F. S. Hahnemann 1755–1843

German physician; founder of homeopathy

10 *Similia similibus curantur.*

Like cures like.
Motto of homeopathic medicine, although not found in this
form in Hahnemann's writings. His use of '*Similia similibus*'
occurs in C. W. Hufeland *Journal der practischen Arzneykunde
und Wundarzneykunst* (1796) vol. 2, p. 433. '*Similia
similibus curantur*' appears as an anonymous side-note in
Paracelsus *Opera Omnia* (*c.*1490–1541, ed. 1658) vol. 1,
p. 196

Earl Haig (*1st Earl Haig of Bemersyde*) 1861–1928

Commander of British armies in France, 1915–18

11 A very weak-minded fellow I am afraid, and, like the
feather pillow, bears the marks of the last person who
has sat on him!
Describing the 17th Earl of Derby in a letter to Lady Haig,
14 January 1918; in R. Blake *Private Papers of Douglas Haig*
(1952) ch. 16

12 Every position must be held to the last man: there
must be no retirement. With our backs to the wall,
and believing in the justice of our cause, each one of
us must fight on to the end.
Order to British troops, 12 April 1918, in A. Duff Cooper
Haig (1936) vol. 2, ch. 23

Lord Hailsham (*Quintin Hogg, Baron Hailsham*) 1907–

British Conservative politician

13 Conservatives do not believe that the political struggle
is the most important thing in life . . . The simplest of
them prefer fox-hunting—the wisest religion.
The Case for Conservatism (1947) pt. 1, p. 10

1 A great party is not to be brought down because of a
scandal by a woman of easy virtue and a proved liar.
   In a BBC television interview on the Profumo affair, in *The
   Times* 14 June 1963

J. B. S. Haldane 1892–1964
Scottish mathematical biologist

2 Now, my own suspicion is that the universe is not
only queerer than we suppose, but queerer than we
can suppose . . . I suspect that there are more things in
heaven and earth than are dreamed of, or can be
dreamed of, in any philosophy.
   Possible Worlds and Other Essays (1927) 'Possible Worlds'.
   Cf. *Hamlet* 574:4

3 The Creator, if He exists, has a special preference for
beetles.
   On observing that there 'are 400,000 species of beetle on
   this planet, but only 8,000 species of mammals; report of
   lecture, 7 April 1951, in *Journal of the British Interplanetary
   Society* (1951) vol. 10, p. 156

H. R. Haldeman 1929–
Presidential assistant to Richard Nixon

4 Once the toothpaste is out of the tube, it is awfully
hard to get it back in.
   To John Dean on the Watergate affair, 8 April 1973, in
   *Hearings Before the Select Committee on Presidential Campaign
   Activities of US Senate: Watergate and Related Activities*
   (1973) vol. 4, p. 1399

Edward Everett Hale 1822–1909
American clergyman

5 'Do you pray for the senators, Dr Hale?' 'No, I look at
the senators and I pray for the country.'
   Van Wyck Brooks *New England Indian Summer* (1940)
   p. 418 n.

Sir Matthew Hale 1609–76
English judge

6 Christianity is part of the laws of England.
   Sir William Blackstone's summary of Hale's words (Taylor's
   case, 1676) in *Commentaries* (1769) vol. 4, p. 59. See
   Holdsworth's *History of English Law* (1937 ed.) vol. 8,
   p. 403 where the origin of the expression is traced to Sir
   John Prisot (d. 1460)

Nathan Hale 1755–76
American revolutionary

7 I only regret that I have but one life to lose for my
country.
   Prior to his execution by the British for spying,
   22 September 1776, in Henry Phelps Johnston *Nathan Hale,
   1776* (1914) ch. 7. Cf. Addison 3:21

Sarah Josepha Hale 1788–1879
American writer

8 Mary had a little lamb,
Its fleece was white as snow,
And everywhere that Mary went
The lamb was sure to go.
   Poems for Our Children (1830) 'Mary's Little Lamb'

T. C. Haliburton ('Sam Slick') 1796–1865
Canadian humorist

9 I want you to see Peel, Stanley, Graham, Shiel,
Russell, Macaulay, Old Joe, and so on. These men are
all upper crust here.
   The Attaché or Sam Slick in England (1843–4) ch. 24

George Savile, 1st Marquess of Halifax ('the Trimmer') 1633–95
English politician and essayist

10 Love is a passion that hath friends in the garrison.
   Advice to a Daughter (1688) 'Behaviour and Conversation'

11 The best way to suppose what may come, is to
remember what is past.
   Political, Moral, and Miscellaneous Thoughts and Reflections
   (1750) 'Miscellaneous: Experience'

12 Anger is never without an argument, but seldom with
a good one.
   Political, Moral, and Miscellaneous Thoughts and Reflections
   (1750) 'Of Anger'

13 Most men make little other use of their speech than to
give evidence against their own understanding.
   Political, Moral, and Miscellaneous Thoughts and Reflections
   (1750) 'Of Folly and Fools'

14 There is . . . no fundamental, but that *every supreme
power must be arbitrary.*
   Political, Moral, and Miscellaneous Thoughts and Reflections
   (1750) 'Of Fundamentals'

15 Malice is of a low stature, but it hath very long arms.
   Political, Moral, and Miscellaneous Thoughts and Reflections
   (1750) 'Of Malice and Envy'

16 When the people contend for their liberty, they seldom
get anything by their victory but new masters.
   Political, Moral, and Miscellaneous Thoughts and Reflections
   (1750) 'Of Prerogative, Power and Liberty'

17 Power is so apt to be insolent and Liberty to be saucy,
that they are very seldom upon good terms.
   Political, Moral, and Miscellaneous Thoughts and Reflections
   (1750) 'Of Prerogative, Power and Liberty'

18 Men are not hanged for stealing horses, but that
horses may not be stolen.
   Political, Moral, and Miscellaneous Thoughts and Reflections
   (1750) 'Of Punishment'

19 To the question, What shall we do to be saved in this
World? there is no other answer but this, Look to
your Moat.
   A Rough Draft of a New Model at Sea (1694) p. 4

1 Lord Rochester was made Lord president: which being a post superior in rank, but much inferior both in advantage and credit to that he held formerly, drew a jest from Lord Halifax . . . he had heard of many kicked down stairs, but never of any that was kicked up stairs before.

> Gilbert Burnet *History of My Own Time* (written 1683–6) vol. 1 (1724) p. 592

Joseph Hall 1574–1656

English bishop

2 I first adventure, follow me who list
And be the second English satirist.
> *Virgidemiae* (1597) prologue

3 Perfection is the child of Time.
> *Works* (1625) p. 670

Radclyffe Hall (*Marguerite Radclyffe Hall*) 1883–1943

English novelist

4 You're neither unnatural, nor abominable, nor mad; you're as much a part of what people call nature as anyone else; only you're unexplained as yet—you've not got your niche in creation.
> *The Well of Loneliness* (1928) bk. 2, ch. 20, sect. 3

Fitz-Greene Halleck 1790–1867

American poet

5 They love their land because it is their own,
And scorn to give aught other reason why;
Would shake hands with a king upon his throne,
And think it kindness to his Majesty.
> 'Connecticut' (1847)

6 Green be the turf above thee,
Friend of my better days!
None knew thee but to love thee,
Nor named thee but to praise.
> 'On the Death of Joseph Rodman Drake' (1820)

Friedrich Halm (*Baron von Münch-Bellinghausen*) 1806–71

German playwright

7 *Mein Herz ich will dich fragen:*
Was ist denn Liebe? Sag'!—
'Zwei Seelen und ein Gedanke,
Zwei Herzen und ein Schlag!'

What love is, if thou wouldst be taught,
Thy heart must teach alone—
Two souls with but a single thought,
Two hearts that beat as one.
> *Der Sohn der Wildnis* (1842) act 2 *ad fin.* (translated by Maria Lovell as *Ingomar the Barbarian*, 1854)

Margaret Halsey 1910–

American writer

8 The English never smash in a face. They merely refrain from asking it to dinner.
> *With Malice Toward Some* (1938) pt. 3, p. 208

W. F. ('Bull') Halsey 1882–1959

American admiral

9 The Third Fleet's sunken and damaged ships have been salvaged and are retiring at high speed toward the enemy.
> Report, 14 October 1944, on hearing claims that the Japanese had virtually annihilated the US fleet, in E. B. Potter *Bull Halsey* (1985) ch. 17

Alex Hamilton 1936–

British journalist

10 Those who stand for nothing fall for anything.
> 'Born Old' (radio broadcast), in *Listener* 9 November 1978

Alexander Hamilton c.1755–1804

American politician

11 A national debt, if it is not excessive, will be to us a national blessing.
> Letter to Robert Morris, 30 April 1781, in John C. Hamilton (ed.) *Works of Alexander Hamilton* vol. 1 (1850) p. 257

Sir William Hamilton 1788–1856

Scottish metaphysician

12 Truth, like a torch, the more it's shook it shines.
> *Discussions on Philosophy* (1852) title page (epigram)

13 On earth there is nothing great but man; in man there is nothing great but mind.
> *Lectures on Metaphysics and Logic* (ed. Mamsel and Veitch, 1859) vol. 1, p. 24. Attributed in a Latin form to Favorinus in Pico di Mirandola (1463–94) *Disputationes Adversus Astrologiam Divinatricem* (ed. E. Garin, 1946) bk. 3, ch. 27

Oscar Hammerstein II 1895–1960

American songwriter

14 You are the promised kiss of springtime that makes the lonely winter seem long.
You are the breathless hush of evening that trembles on the brink of a lovely song.
> 'All the Things You Are' (1940 song)

15 The last time I saw Paris
Her heart was warm and gay,
I heard the laughter of her heart in ev'ry street café.
> *Lady Be Good* (1941) 'The Last Time I saw Paris' (music by Jerome Kern)

16 The corn is as high as an elephant's eye,
An' it looks like it's climbin' clear up to the sky.
> *Oklahoma!* (1943) 'Oh, What a Beautiful Mornin' ' (music by Richard Rodgers)

17 Fish got to swim and birds got to fly
I got to love one man till I die,
Can't help lovin' dat man of mine.
> *Showboat* (1927) 'Can't Help Lovin' Dat Man of Mine' (music by Jerome Kern)

18 Ol' man river, dat ol' man river,
He must know sumpin', but don't say nothin',
He jus' keeps rollin',
He jus' keeps rollin' along.
> *Showboat* (1927) 'Ol' Man River' (music by Jerome Kern)

1 I'm as corny as Kansas in August,
  High as a flag on the Fourth of July!
    South Pacific (1949) 'A Wonderful Guy' (music by Richard
    Rodgers)

2 You've got to be taught to be afraid
  Of people whose eyes are oddly made,
  Of people whose skin is a different shade.
  You've got to be carefully taught.

  You've got to be taught before it's too late,
  Before you are six or seven or eight,
  To hate all the people your relatives hate.
  You've got to be carefully taught.
    South Pacific (1949) 'You've Got to be Carefully Taught'
    (music by Richard Rodgers)

Christopher Hampton 1946–

English playwright

3 A definition of capitalism . . . the process whereby
  American girls turn into American women.
    Savages (1974) sc. 16

Learned Hand 1872–1961

American judge

4 A self-made man may prefer a self-made name.
    On Samuel Goldfish changing his name to Samuel
    Goldwyn, in Bosley Crowther *Lion's Share* (1957) ch. 7

Minnie Hanff 1880–1942

5 High o'er the fence leaps Sunny Jim
  'Force' is the food that raises him.
    Advertising slogan for breakfast cereal (1903)

Kate Hankey 1834–1911

English evangelist

6 Tell me the old, old story
  Of unseen things above,
  Of Jesus and his glory,
  Of Jesus and his love.
    'Tell me the old, old story' (1867 hymn)

Brian Hanrahan 1949–

British journalist

7 I counted them all out and I counted them all back.
    On the number of British aeroplanes (which he was not
    permitted to disclose) joining the raid on Port Stanley in the
    Falkland Islands; BBC broadcast report, 1 May 1982, in
    Battle for the Falklands (1982) p. 21

Edmond Haraucourt 1856–1941

French poet

8 *Partir c'est mourir un peu,*
  C'est mourir à ce qu'on aime:
  On laisse un peu de soi-même
  En toute heure et dans tout lieu.

  To go away is to die a little, it is to die to that which
  one loves: everywhere and always, one leaves behind
  a part of oneself.
    Seul (1891) 'Rondel de l'Adieu'

Otto Harbach 1873–1963

American songwriter

9 They asked me how I knew
  My true love was true.
  I of course replied
  'Something here inside
  Cannot be denied' . . .
  Now laughing friends deride tears I cannot hide,
  So I smile and say 'When a lovely flame dies,
  Smoke gets in your eyes.'
    'Smoke Gets in your Eyes' (1933 song); music by Jerome
    Kern

E. Y. ('Yip') Harburg 1898–1981

American songwriter

10 Brother can you spare a dime?
    Title of song (1932)

11 Wanna cry, wanna croon.
  Wanna laugh like a loon.
  It's that Old Devil Moon in your eyes.
    Finian's Rainbow (1946) 'Old Devil Moon' (music by Burton
    Lane)

12 Say, it's only a paper moon,
  Sailing over a cardboard sea.
    'It's Only a Paper Moon' (1933 song, with Billy Rose);
    music by Harold Arlen

13 Somewhere over the rainbow
  Way up high,
  There's a land that I heard of
  Once in a lullaby.
    The Wizard of Oz (1939) 'Over the Rainbow' (music by
    Harold Arlen)

Sir William Harcourt 1827–1904

British Liberal politician

14 We are all socialists now.
    During the passage of the 1894 budget, which equalized
    death duties on real and personal property (attributed). See
    Hubert Bland 'The Outlook' in G. B. Shaw (ed.) *Fabian
    Essays in Socialism* (1889)

Keir Hardie 1856–1915

Scottish Labour politician

15 From his childhood onward this boy [the future
  Edward VIII] will be surrounded by sycophants and
  flatterers by the score—[*Cries of* 'Oh, oh!']—and will
  be taught to believe himself as of a superior creation.
  [*Cries of* 'Oh, oh!'] A line will be drawn between him
  and the people whom he is to be called upon some day
  to reign over. In due course, following the precedent
  which has already been set, he will be sent on a tour
  round the world, and probably rumours of a
  morganatic alliance will follow—[*Loud cries of* 'Oh,
  oh!' *and* 'Order!']—and the end of it all will be that
  the country will be called upon to pay the bill. [*Cries of*
  Divide!]
    Speech, *Hansard* 28 June 1894, col. 463

D. W. Harding 1906–
British psychologist and critic

1 Regulated hatred.
   Title of an article on the novels of Jane Austen, in *Scrutiny*
   March 1940

Warren G. Harding 1865–1923
29th President of the USA

2 America's present need is not heroics, but healing; not
   nostrums but normalcy; not revolution, but
   restoration.
   Speech at Boston, 14 May 1920, in Frederick E.
   Schortemeier *Rededicating America* (1920) ch. 17

Philip Yorke, Earl of Hardwicke
1690–1764
English judge

3 His doubts are better than most people's certainties.
   Of *Dirleton's Doubts*, in James Boswell *Life of Samuel Johnson*
   (1934 ed.) vol. 3, p. 205

Godfrey Harold Hardy 1877–1947
English mathematician

4 Beauty is the first test: there is no permanent place in
   the world for ugly mathematics.
   A Mathematician's Apology (1940) p. 25

Thomas Hardy 1840–1928
English novelist and poet

5 A local thing called Christianity.
   The Dynasts (1904) pt. 1, act 1, sc. 6

6 War makes rattling good history; but Peace is poor
   reading.
   The Dynasts (1904) pt. 1, act 2, sc. 5

7 It is hard for a woman to define her feelings in
   language which is chiefly made by men to express
   theirs.
   Far from the Madding Crowd (1874) ch. 81. Cf. Austen 39:6

8 A lover without indiscretion is no lover at all.
   The Hand of Ethelberta (1876) ch. 20

9 Done because we are too menny.
   Jude the Obscure (1896) pt. 6, ch. 2

10 Her occasional pretty and picturesque use of dialect
   words—those terrible marks of the beast to the truly
   genteel.
   The Mayor of Casterbridge (1886) ch. 20

11 She whose youth had seemed to teach that happiness
   was but the occasional episode in a general drama of
   pain.
   The Mayor of Casterbridge (1886) ch. 45, closing words

12 It was at present a place perfectly accordant with
   man's nature—neither ghastly, hateful, nor ugly:
   neither commonplace, unmeaning, nor tame; but, like
   man, slighted and enduring; and withal singularly
   colossal and mysterious in its swarthy monotony. As
   with some persons who have long lived a past,
   solitude seemed to look out of its countenance. It had
   a lonely face, suggesting tragical possibilities.
   The Return of the Native (1878) bk. 1, ch. 1 (Egdon Heath)

13 Human beings, in their generous endeavour to
   construct a hypothesis that shall not degrade a First
   Cause, have always hesitated to conceive a dominant
   power of a lower moral quality than their own.
   The Return of the Native (1878) bk. 6, ch. 1

14 A novel is an impression, not an argument.
   Tess of the D'Urbervilles (5th ed., 1892) preface

15 Why it was that upon this beautiful feminine tissue,
   sensitive as gosssamer, and practically blank as snow
   as yet, there should have been traced such a coarse
   pattern as it was doomed to receive; why so often the
   coarse appropriates the finer thus, the wrong man the
   woman, the wrong woman the man, many thousand
   years of analytical philosophy have failed to explain to
   our sense of order.
   Tess of the D'Urbervilles (1891) ch. 11

16 She had been made to break an accepted social law,
   but no law known to the environment in which she
   fancied herself such an anomaly.
   Tess of the D'Urbervilles (1891) ch. 14

17 The two forces were at work here as everywhere, the
   inherent will to enjoy, and the circumstantial will
   against enjoyment.
   Tess of the D'Urbervilles (1891) ch. 43

18 'Justice' was done, and the President of the Immortals
   (in Aeschylean phrase) had ended his sport with Tess.
   Tess of the D'Urbervilles (1891) ch. 59

19 Good, but not religious-good.
   Under the Greenwood Tree (1872) ch. 2

20 It was one of those sequestered spots outside the gates
   of the world ... where, from time to time, dramas of a
   grandeur and unity truly Sophoclean are enacted in
   the real, by virtue of the concentrated passions and
   closely knit interdependence of the lives therein.
   The Woodlanders (1887) ch. 1

21 The business of the poet and novelist is to show the
   sorriness underlying the grandest things, and the
   grandeur underlying the sorriest things.
   Notebook entry for 19 April 1885, in Florence Hardy *The
   Early Life of Thomas Hardy 1840–91* (1928) ch. 13

22 When the Present has latched its postern behind my
     tremulous stay,
   And the May month flaps its glad green leaves like
     wings,
   Delicate-filmed as new-spun silk, will the neighbours
     say,
   'He was a man who used to notice such things'?
   'Afterwards' (1917)

1 The bower we shrined to Tennyson,
  Gentlemen,
Is roof-wrecked; damps there drip upon
Sagged seats, the creeper-nails are rust,
The spider is sole denizen;
Even she who voiced those rhymes is dust,
Gentlemen!
  'An Ancient to Ancients' (1922)

2 'Peace upon earth!' was said. We sing it,
And pay a million priests to bring it.
After two thousand years of mass
We've got as far as poison-gas.
  'Christmas: 1924' (1928)

3 In a solitude of the sea
Deep from human vanity,
And the Pride of Life that planned her, stilly couches
  she.

Steel chambers, late the pyres
Of her salamandrine fires,
Cold currents thrid, and turn to rhythmic tidal lyres.

Over the mirrors meant
To glass the opulent
The sea-worm crawls—grotesque, slimed, dumb,
  indifferent.
  'Convergence of the Twain' (1914)

4 The Immanent Will that stirs and urges everything.
  'Convergence of the Twain' (1914)

5 At once a voice outburst among
The bleak twigs overhead
In a full-hearted evensong
Of joy illimited;
An aged thrush, frail, gaunt, and small,
In blast-beruffled plume,
Had chosen thus to fling his soul
Upon the growing gloom.

So little cause for carollings
Of such ecstatic sound
Was written on terrestrial things
Afar or nigh around,
That I could think there trembled through
His happy good-night air
Some blessed Hope, whereof he knew
And I was unaware.
  'The Darkling Thrush' (1902)

6 If way to the Better there be, it exacts a full look at the
  worst.
  'De Profundis' (1902)

7 Well, World, you have kept faith with me,
Kept faith with me;
Upon the whole you have proved to be
Much as you said you were.
  'He Never Expected Much' (1928)

8 I am the family face;
Flesh perishes, I live on,
Projecting trait and trace
Through time to times anon,
And leaping from place to place
Over oblivion.
  'Heredity' (1917)

9 I look into my glass,
And viewing wasting skin,
And say, 'Would God it came to pass
My heart had shrunk as thin!'

For then, I, undistrest,
By hearts grown cold to me,
Could lonely wait my endless rest
With equanimity.

But Time, to make me grieve,
Part steals, lets part abide;
And shakes this fragile frame at eve
With throbbings of noontide.
  'I look into my glass' (1898)

10 Only a man harrowing clods
In a slow silent walk
With an old horse that stumbles and nods
Half asleep as they stalk.

Only thin smoke without flame
From the heaps of couch-grass;
Yet this will go onward the same
Though Dynasties pass.

Yonder a maid and her wight
Come whispering by:
War's annals will cloud into night
Ere their story die.
  'In Time of "The Breaking of Nations"' (1917)

11 Let me enjoy the earth no less
Because the all-enacting Might
That fashioned forth its loveliness
Had other aims than my delight.
  'Let me Enjoy' (1909)

12 Yes; quaint and curious war is!
You shoot a fellow down
You'd treat if met where any bar is,
Or help to half-a-crown.
  'The Man he Killed' (1909)

13 What of the faith and fire within us
Men who march away
Ere the barn-cocks say
Night is growing grey,
To hazards whence no tears can win us;
What of the faith and fire within us
Men who march away?
  'Men Who March Away' (1914)

14 In the third-class seat sat the journeying boy
And the roof-lamp's oily flame
Played down on his listless form and face,
Bewrapt past knowing to what he was going,
Or whence he came.
  'Midnight on the Great Western' (1917)

15 Woman much missed, how you call to me, call to me,
Saying that now you are not as you were
When you had changed from the one who was all to
  me,
But as at first, when our day was fair.
  'The Voice' (1914)

1 This is the weather the cuckoo likes,
   And so do I;
   When showers betumble the chestnut spikes,
   And nestlings fly:
   And the little brown nightingale bills his best,
   And they sit outside at 'The Travellers' Rest',
   And maids come forth sprig-muslin drest,
   And citizens dream of the south and west,
   And so do I.
      'Weathers' (1922)

2 And meadow rivulets overflow,
   And drops on gate-bars hang in a row,
   And rooks in families homeward go,
   And so do I.
      'Weathers' (1922)

3 When I set out for Lyonnesse,
   A hundred miles away,
   The rime was on the spray,
   And starlight lit my lonesomeness
   When I set out for Lyonnesse
   A hundred miles away.
      'When I set out for Lyonnesse' (1914)

Julius Hare 1795–1855 *and* Augustus Hare 1792–1834

English writers and clergymen

4 The ancients dreaded death: the Christian can only fear dying.
   Guesses at Truth (1827) Series 1, p. 8

5 Half the failures in life arise from pulling in one's horse as he is leaping.
   Guesses at Truth (1827) Series 1, p. 137

6 Truth, when witty, is the wittiest of all things.
   Guesses at Truth (3rd ed., 1847) Series 1, p. 339

Maurice Evan Hare 1886–1967

English limerick writer

7 There once was an old man who said, 'Damn!
   It is borne in upon me I am
   An engine that moves
   In determinate grooves,
   I'm not even a bus, I'm a tram.'
      'Limerick' (1905)

W. F. Hargreaves 1846–1919

British songwriter

8 I'm Burlington Bertie
   I rise at ten thirty and saunter along like a toff,
   I walk down the Strand with my gloves on my hand,
   Then I walk down again with them off.
      'Burlington Bertie from Bow' (1915 song)

9 I acted so tragic the house rose like magic,
   The audience yelled 'You're sublime.'
   They made me a present of Mornington Crescent
   They threw it a brick at a time.
      'The Night I Appeared as Macbeth' (1922 song)

John Harington d. 1582

English poet

10 There was a battle fought of late,
   Yet was the slaughter small;
   The strife was, whether I should write,
   Or send nothing at all.
   Of one side were the captains' names
   Short Time and Little Skill;
   One fought alone against them both,
   Whose name was Great Good-will.
   Short Time enforced me in a strait,
   And bade me hold my hand;
   Small Skill also withstood desire
   My writing to withstand.
   But Great Good-will, in show though small,
   To write encouraged me,
   And to the battle held on still,
   No common thing to see.
      'To his mother' (written 1540)

Sir John Harington 1561–1612

English writer and courtier

11   When I make a feast,
   I would my guests should praise it, not the cooks.
      Epigrams (1618) bk. 1, no. 5

12 Treason doth never prosper, what's the reason?
   For if it prosper, none dare call it treason.
      Epigrams (1618) bk. 4, no. 5

Lord Harlech (David Ormsby Gore) 1918–85

British Ambassador to Washington, 1961–5

13 Britain will be honoured by historians more for the way she disposed of an empire than for the way in which she acquired it.
      In *New York Times* 28 October 1962, sect. 4, p. 11

Harold II c.1019–66

King of England, 1066

14 He will give him seven feet of English ground, or as much more as he may be taller than other men.
      His offer to Harald Sigurdson, invading England; *King Harald's Saga* sect. 91, in Snorri Sturluson *Heimskringla* (c.1260, first translated by Samuel Laing as *History of the Norse Kings*, 1844)

Jimmy Harper, Will E. Haines, and Tommy Connor

15 The biggest aspidistra in the world.
      Title of song (1938); popularized by Gracie Fields

Joel Chandler Harris 1848–1908

American writer

16 W'en folks git ole en strucken wid de palsy, dey mus speck ter be laff'd at.
      Nights with Uncle Remus (1883) ch. 23

1 Hit look lak sparrer-grass, hit feel like sparrer-grass, hit tas'e lak sparrer-grass, en I bless ef 'taint sparrer-grass.
   Nights with Uncle Remus (1883) ch. 27

2 All by my own-alone self.
   Nights with Uncle Remus (1883) ch. 36

3 We er sorter po'ly, Sis Tempy, I'm 'blige ter you. You know w'at de jay-bird say ter der squinch-owl! 'I'm sickly but sassy.'
   Nights with Uncle Remus (1883) ch. 50

4 Bred en bawn in a brier-patch!
   Uncle Remus and His Legends of the Old Plantation (1881) 'How Mr Rabbit was too Sharp for Mr Fox'

5 Lounjun 'roun' en suffer'n'.
   Uncle Remus and His Legends of the Old Plantation (1881) 'Mr Wolf tackles Old Man Tarrypin'

6 Tar-baby ain't sayin' nuthin', en Brer Fox, he lay low.
   Uncle Remus and His Legends of the Old Plantation (1881) 'The Wonderful Tar-Baby Story'

7 Licker talks mighty loud w'en it git loose fum de jug.
   Uncle Remus: His Songs and His Sayings (1880) 'Plantation Proverbs'

8 Hongry rooster don't cackle w'en he fine a wum.
   Uncle Remus: His Songs and His Sayings (1880) 'Plantation Proverbs'

9 Oh, whar shill we go w'en de great day comes,
Wid de blowin' er de trumpits en de bangin' er de drums?
How many po' sinners'll be kotched out late
En fine no latch ter de golden gate?
   Uncle Remus: His Songs and His Sayings (1880) 'Revival Hymn'

Josephine Hart

10 Damaged people are dangerous. They know they can survive.
   Damage (1991) ch. 12

Lorenz Hart 1895–1943

American songwriter

11 When love congeals
It soon reveals
The faint aroma of performing seals,
The double crossing of a pair of heels.
I wish I were in love again!
   Babes in Arms (1937) 'I Wish I Were in Love Again' (music by Richard Rodgers)

12 I get too hungry for dinner at eight.
I like the theatre, but never come late.
I never bother with people I hate.
That's why the lady is a tramp.
   Babes in Arms (1937) 'The Lady is a Tramp' (music by Richard Rodgers)

13 In a mountain greenery
Where God paints the scenery—
Just two crazy people together.
   'Mountain Greenery' (1926 song); music by Richard Rodgers

14 I'm wild again
Beguiled again
A simpering, whimpering child again,
Bewitched, bothered, and bewildered am I.
   Pal Joey (1941) 'Bewitched' (music by Richard Rodgers)

15 Thou swell! Thou witty!
Thou sweet! Thou grand!
Wouldst kiss me pretty?
Wouldst hold my hand?
   'Thou Swell' (1927 song); music by Richard Rodgers

Bret Harte 1836–1902

American poet

16 And on that grave where English oak and holly
And laurel wreaths entwine
Deem it not all a too presumptuous folly,—
This spray of Western pine!
   'Dickens in Camp' (1870)

17 Which I wish to remark,
And my language is plain,
That for ways that are dark
And for tricks that are vain,
The heathen Chinee is peculiar,
Which the same I would rise to explain.
   The Heathen Chinee: Plain Language from Truthful James (1870)

18 Thar ain't no sense
In gittin' riled!
   'Jim' (1870)

19 If, of all words of tongue and pen,
The saddest are, 'It might have been,'
More sad are these we daily see:
'It is, but hadn't ought to be!'
   'Mrs Judge Jenkins' (1867). Cf. Whittier 733:8

20 I reside at Table Mountain, and my name is Truthful James;
I am not up to small deceit, or any sinful games.
   'The Society upon the Stanislaus' (1868) st. 1

21 And he smiled a kind of sickly smile, and curled up on the floor,
And the subsequent proceedings interested him no more.
   'The Society upon the Stanislaus' (1868) st. 7

L. P. Hartley 1895–1972

English novelist

22 The past is a foreign country: they do things differently there.
   The Go-Between (1953) prologue. Cf. Morley 484:19

F. W. Harvey b. 1888

English poet

23 From troubles of the world
I turn to ducks
Beautiful comical things.
   'Ducks' (1919)

Minnie Louise Haskins 1875–1957
English teacher and writer

1 And I said to the man who stood at the gate of the
year: 'Give me a light that I may tread safely into the
unknown.'
  And he replied:
'Go out into the darkness and put your hand into
the Hand of God. That shall be to you better than light
and safer than a known way.'
> *Desert* (1908) 'God Knows' (quoted by King George VI in
> his Christmas broadcast, 25 December 1939)

Edwin Hatch 1835–89
English clergyman and scholar

2 Breathe on me, Breath of God,
Fill me with life anew,
That I may love what thou dost love,
And do what thou wouldst do.
> 'Breathe on me, Breath of God' (1878 hymn)

Stephen Hawes d. c.1523
English poet

3 The end of joy and all prosperity
Is death at last, thorough his course and might;
After the day there cometh the dark night;
For though the day be never so long,
At last the bells ringeth to evensong.
> *The Pastime of Pleasure* (1509) ch. 42, st. 10

R. S. Hawker 1803–75
English clergyman and poet

4 And have they fixed the where and when?
And shall Trelawny die?
Here's twenty thousand Cornish men
Will know the reason why!
> 'The Song of the Western Men' (the last three lines having
> been in existence since the imprisonment by James II, in
> 1688, of the seven Bishops, including Trelawny, Bishop of
> Bristol)

Stephen Hawking 1942–
English theoretical physicist

5 Each equation . . . in the book would halve the sales.
> *A Brief History of Time* (1988) p. vi

6 In effect, we have redefined the task of science to be
the discovery of laws that will enable us to predict
events up to the limits set by the uncertainty principle.
> *A Brief History of Time* (1988) ch. 11

7 If we find the answer to that [why it is that we and
the universe exist], it would be the ultimate triumph
of human reason—for then we would know the mind
of God.
> *A Brief History of Time* (1988) ch. 11

Nathaniel Hawthorne 1804–64
American novelist

8 Dr Johnson's morality was as English an article as a
beefsteak.
> *Our Old Home* (1863) 'Lichfield and Uttoxeter'

Ian Hay (John Hay Beith) 1876–1952
Scottish novelist and playwright

9 What do you mean, funny? Funny-peculiar or funny
ha-ha?
> *The Housemaster* (1938) act 3

J. Milton Hayes 1884–1940
British writer

10 There's a one-eyed yellow idol to the north of
Khatmandu,
There's a little marble cross below the town,
There's a broken-hearted woman tends the grave of
Mad Carew,
And the Yellow God forever gazes down.
> *The Green Eye of the Yellow God* (1911)

Eliza Haywood c.1693–1756
English actress, playwright, and novelist

11 One has no sooner left off one's bib and apron, than
people cry—'Miss will soon be married!'—and this
man, and that man, is presently picked out for a
husband. Mighty ridiculous! they want to deprive us
of all the pleasures of life, just when one begins to
have a relish for them.
> *The History of Miss Betty Thoughtless* (1751) p. 452 in
> Pandora ed., 1986

William Hazlitt 1778–1830
English essayist

12 His sayings are generally like women's letters; all the
pith is in the postscript.
> On Charles Lamb in *Conversations of James Northcote*
> (1826–7)

13 He talked on for ever; and you wished him to talk on
for ever.
> *Lectures on the English Poets* (1818) 'On the Living Poets'
> (Coleridge)

14 So have I loitered my life away, reading books, looking
at pictures, going to plays, hearing, thinking, writing
on what pleased me best. I have wanted only one
thing to make me happy, but wanting that have
wanted everything.
> *Literary Remains* (1836) 'My First Acquaintance with Poets'

15 The dupe of friendship, and the fool of love; have I not
reason to hate and to despise myself? Indeed I do; and
chiefly for not having hated and despised the world
enough.
> *The Plain Speaker* (1826) 'On the Pleasure of Hating'

16 The love of liberty is the love of others; the love of
power is the love of ourselves.
> *Political Essays* (1819) 'The Times Newspaper'

1 There is nothing good to be had in the country, or if there is, they will not let you have it.
The Round Table (1817) 'Observations on Mr Wordsworth's Poem *The Excursion*'

2 The art of pleasing consists in being pleased.
The Round Table (1817) 'On Manner'

3 But of all footmen the lowest class is *literary footmen*.
Sketches and Essays (1839) 'Footmen'

4 A nickname is the heaviest stone that the devil can throw at a man.
Sketches and Essays (1839) 'Nicknames'

5 The greatest offence against virtue is to speak ill of it.
Sketches and Essays (1839) 'On Cant and Hypocrisy'

6 There is an unseemly exposure of the mind, as well as of the body.
Sketches and Essays (1839) 'On Disagreeable People'

7 Rules and models destroy genius and art.
Sketches and Essays (1839) 'On Taste'

8 Death cancels everything but truth; and strips a man of everything but genius and virtue. It is a sort of natural canonization.
The Spirit of the Age (1825) 'Lord Byron'

9 The present is an age of talkers, and not of doers; and the reason is, that the world is growing old. We are so far advanced in the Arts and Sciences, that we live in retrospect, and dote on past achievement.
The Spirit of the Age (1825) 'Mr Coleridge'

10 He writes as fast as they can read, and he does not write himself down ... His worst is better than any other person's best ... His works (taken together) are almost like a new edition of human nature. This is indeed to be an author!
The Spirit of the Age (1825) 'Sir Walter Scott'

11 Mr Wordsworth's genius is a pure emanation of the Spirit of the Age. Had he lived in any other period of the world, he would never have been heard of.
The Spirit of the Age (1825) 'Mr Wordsworth'

12 You will hear more good things on the outside of a stagecoach from London to Oxford than if you were to pass a twelvemonth with the undergraduates, or heads of colleges, of that famous university.
Table Talk vol. 1 (1821) 'The Ignorance of the Learned'

13 We can scarcely hate any one that we know.
Table Talk vol. 2 (1822) 'On Criticism'

14 Give me the clear blue sky over my head, and the green turf beneath my feet, a winding road before me, and a three hours' march to dinner—and then to thinking! It is hard if I cannot start some game on these lone heaths.
Table Talk vol. 2 (1822) 'On Going a Journey'

15 Well, I've had a happy life.
Last words, in W. C. Hazlitt *Memoirs of William Hazlitt* (1867)

Denis Healey 1917–

British Labour politician

16 Like being savaged by a dead sheep.
On being criticized by Sir Geoffrey Howe in the House of Commons, *Hansard* 14 June 1978, col. 1027

Seamus Heaney 1939–

Irish poet

17 All agog at the plasterer on his ladder
Skimming our gable and writing our name there
With his trowel point, letter by strange letter.
'Alphabets' (1987)

18 Between my finger and my thumb
The squat pen rests.
I'll dig with it.
'Digging' (1966)

19 Don't be surprised
If I demur, for, be advised
My passport's green.
No glass of ours was ever raised
To toast *The Queen*.
Open Letter (Field Day pamphlet no. 2, 1983) p. 9, rebuking the editors of *The Penguin Book of Contemporary British Poetry* for including him among its authors

20 Who would connive
in civilised outrage
yet understand the exact
and tribal, intimate revenge.
'Punishment' (1975)

21   The famous
Northern reticence, the tight gag of place
And times: yes, yes. Of the 'wee six' I sing
Where to be saved you only must save face
And whatever you say, you say nothing.
'Whatever You Say Say Nothing' (1975)

22 Is there a life before death? That's chalked up
In Ballymurphy. Competence with pain,
Coherent miseries, a bite and sup,
We hug our little destiny again.
'Whatever You Say Say Nothing' (1975)

Edward Heath 1916–

British Conservative politician; Prime Minister, 1970–4

23 The unpleasant and unacceptable face of capitalism.
Hansard 15 May 1973, col. 1243 (on the Lonrho affair)

John Heath-Stubbs 1918–

English poet

24 I am coming to think now that all I have loved were shadows
Strayed up from a dead world, through a gap in a raped tomb.
'Address Not Known' (1954)

25 The sun will not haver in its course for the lack of you,
Nor the flowers fail in colour, nor the bird stint in its song.
Only the heart that wanted somehow to have opened up
Finds the frost in the day's air, and the nights which appear too long.
'Address Not Known' (1954)

1 Venerable Mother Toothache
Climb down from the white battlements,
Stop twisting in your yellow fingers
The fourfold rope of nerves;
And tomorrow I will give you a tot of whisky
To hold in your cupped hands,
A garland of anise flowers,
And three cloves like nails.
   'A Charm Against the Toothache' (1954)

Reginald Heber 1783–1826

English clergyman; Bishop of Calcutta from 1823

2 Brightest and best of the sons of the morning,
Dawn on our darkness and lend us thine aid;
Star of the east, the horizon adorning,
Guide where our infant Redeemer is laid.
   'Brightest and best of the sons of the morning' (1827
   hymn)

3 From Greenland's icy mountains,
From India's coral strand,
Where Afric's sunny fountains
Roll down their golden sand.
   'From Greenland's icy mountains' (1821 hymn)

4 What though the spicy breezes
Blow soft o'er Ceylon's isle;
Though every prospect pleases,
And only man is vile:
In vain with lavish kindness
The gifts of God are strown;
The heathen in his blindness
Bows down to wood and stone.
   'From Greenland's icy mountains' (1821 hymn); Heber
   later altered 'Ceylon's isle' to 'Java's isle'. Cf. Kipling
   398:19

5 Holy, Holy, Holy! Lord God Almighty!
Early in the morning our song shall rise to thee:
Holy, Holy, Holy! merciful and mighty!
God in Three Persons, blessèd Trinity!

Holy, Holy, Holy! all the saints adore thee,
Casting down their golden crowns around the glassy
   sea,
Cherubim and Seraphim falling down before thee,
Which wert, and art, and evermore shalt be.
   'Holy, Holy, Holy! Lord God Almighty!' (1826 hymn)

G. W. F. Hegel 1770–1831

German idealist philosopher

6 Poetry is the universal art of the spirit which has
become free in itself and which is not tied down for its
realization to external sensuous material; instead, it
launches out exclusively in the inner space and the
inner time of ideas and feelings.
   Introduction to Aesthetics (1842, translated by T. M. Knox,
   1979) p. 89

7 What experience and history teach is this—that
nations and governments have never learned anything
from history, or acted upon any lessons they might
have drawn from it.
   Lectures on the Philosophy of World History: Introduction
   (1830, translated by H. B. Nisbet, 1975) introduction

8 Only in the state does man have a rational existence
... Man owes his entire existence to the state, and has
his being within it alone. Whatever worth and
spiritual reality he possesses are his solely by virtue of
the state.
   Lectures on the Philosophy of World History: Introduction
   (1830, translated by H. B. Nisbet, 1975) p. 94

9 In history, we are concerned with what has been and
what is; in philosophy, however, we are concerned
not with what belongs exclusively to the past or to the
future, but with that which *is*, both now and
eternally—in short, with reason.
   Lectures on the Philosophy of World History: Introduction
   (1830, translated by H. B. Nisbet, 1975) p. 171

10 When philosophy paints its grey on grey, then has a
shape of life grown old. By philosophy's grey on grey
it cannot be rejuvenated but only understood. The owl
of Minerva spreads its wings only with the falling of
the dusk.
   Philosophy of Right (1821, translated by T. M. Knox, 1952)
   p. 13

11 Civil society has the right and duty of superintending
and influencing education, inasmuch as education
bears upon the child's capacity to become a member of
society. Society's right here is paramount over the
arbitrary and contingent preferences of parents.
   Philosophy of Right (1821, translated by T. M. Knox, 1952)
   sect. 239

12 Thus to be independent of public opinion is the first
formal condition of achieving anything great or
rational whether in life or in science. Great
achievement is assured, however, of subsequent
recognition and grateful acceptance by public opinion,
which in due course will make it one of its own
prejudices.
   Philosophy of Right (1821, translated by T. M. Knox, 1952)
   sect. 318

Heinrich Heine 1797–1856

German poet

13   *Dort, wo man Bücher*
Verbrennt, verbrennt man auch am Ende Menschen.
Wherever books will be burned, men also, in the end,
are burned.
   Almansor (1823) l. 245

14 *Auf Flügeln des Gesanges.*
On wings of song.
   Title of song (1823)

15 *Ich weiss nicht, was soll es bedeuten,*
Dass ich so traurig bin;
Ein Märchen aus alten Zeiten,
Das kommt mir nicht aus dem Sinn.
I know not why I am so sad; I cannot get out of my
head a fairy-tale of olden times.
   'Die Lorelei' (1826–31)

16 *Es ist eine alte Geschichte,*
Doch bleibt sie immer neu.
It is so old a story,
Yet somehow always new.
   Lyrisches Intermezzo (1823) no. 39 (translated by Hal
   Draper)

1 *Sie hatten sich beide so herzlich lieb,*
Spitzbübin war sie, er war ein Dieb.

They loved each other beyond belief—
She was a strumpet, he was a thief.
   Neue Gedichte (1852) 'Ein Weib' (translated by Louis
   Untermeyer, 1938)

2 *Hört ihr das Glöckchen klingeln? Kniet nieder—Man*
bringt die Sakramente einem sterbenden Gotte.

Do you hear the little bell tinkle? Kneel down. They
are bringing the sacraments to a dying god.
   Zur Geschichte der Religion und Philosophie in Deutschland
   (1834) bk. 2 *ad fin.*

3 *Dieses merkt Euch, Ihr stolzen Männer der Tat. Ihr seid*
nichts als unbewusste Handlanger der Gedankenmänner
... Maximilian Robespierre war nichts als die Hand von
Jean Jacques Rousseau, die blutige Hand, die aus dem
Schosse der Zeit den Leib hervorzog, dessen Seele Rousseau
geschaffen.

Note this, you proud men of action. You are nothing
but the unconscious hodmen of the men of ideas ...
Maximilien Robespierre was nothing but the hand of
Jean Jacques Rousseau, the bloody hand that drew
from the womb of time the body whose soul Rousseau
had created.
   Zur Geschichte der Religion und Philosophie in Deutschland
   (1834) bk. 3, para. 3

4 *Dieu me pardonnera, c'est son métier.*

God will pardon me, it is His trade.
   On his deathbed, in Alfred Meissner *Heinrich Heine.*
   Erinnerungen (1856) ch. 5. Cf. Catherine 185:7

Werner Heisenberg 1901–76
German mathematical physicist

5 *Ein Fachmann ist ein Mann, der einige der gröbsten*
Fehler kennt, die man in dem betreffenden Fach machen
kann und der sie deshalb zu vermeiden versteht.

An expert is someone who knows some of the worst
mistakes that can be made in his subject and who
manages to avoid them.
   Der Teil und das Ganze (1969) ch. 17 (translated by A. J.
   Pomerans as *Physics and Beyond*, 1971)

Joseph Heller 1923–
American novelist

6 There was only one catch and that was Catch-22,
which specified that a concern for one's own safety in
the face of dangers that were real and immediate was
the process of a rational mind ... Orr would be crazy
to fly more missions and sane if he didn't, but if he
was sane he had to fly them. If he flew them he was
crazy and didn't have to; but if he didn't want to he
was sane and had to.
   Catch-22 (1961) ch. 5

7 Some men are born mediocre, some men achieve
mediocrity, and some men have mediocrity thrust
upon them. With Major Major it had been all three.
   Catch-22 (1961) ch. 9. Cf. *Twelfth Night* 630:4

Lillian Hellman 1905–84
American playwright

8 I cannot and will not cut my conscience to fit this
year's fashions.
   Letter to John S. Wood, 19 May 1952, in *US Congress*
   Committee Hearing on Un-American Activities (1952) pt. 8,
   p. 3546

Helvétius (Claude Arien Helvétius) 1715–71
French philosopher

9 *L'éducation nous faisait ce que nous sommes.*
Education made us what we are.
   De l'esprit (1758) 'Discours 3' ch. 30

Felicia Hemans (neé Browne) 1793–1835
English poet

10 The boy stood on the burning deck
Whence all but he had fled;
The flame that lit the battle's wreck
Shone round him o'er the dead.
   'Casabianca' (1849)

11 The stately homes of England,
How beautiful they stand!
Amidst their tall ancestral trees,
O'er all the pleasant land.
   'The Homes of England' (1849)

John Heming 1556–1630 *and* Henry Condell d. 1627
Joint editors of the First Folio

12 Well! it is now public, and you will stand for your
privileges we know: to read, and censure. Do so, but
buy it first. That doth best commend a book, the
stationer says.
   First Folio Shakespeare (1623) preface

13 Who, as he was a happy imitator of Nature, was a
most gentle expresser of it. His mind and hand went
together: And what he thought, he uttered with that
easiness, that we have scarce received from him a
blot.
   First Folio Shakespeare (1623) preface. Cf. Jonson 380:9,
   Pope 523:5

Ernest Hemingway 1899–1961
American novelist

14 Where do the noses go? I always wondered where the
noses would go.
   For Whom the Bell Tolls (1940) ch. 7

15 But did thee feel the earth move?
   For Whom the Bell Tolls (1940) ch. 13

16 Paris is a movable feast.
   A Movable Feast (1964) epigraph

17 The sun also rises.
   Title of novel (1926)

1 Grace under pressure.

When asked what he meant by 'guts' in an interview with Dorothy Parker; in *New Yorker* 30 November 1929

2 Switzerland is a small, steep country, much more up and down than sideways, and is all stuck over with large brown hotels built on the cuckoo clock style of architecture.

Toronto Star Weekly 4 March 1922

See also F. SCOTT FITZGERALD

Jimi Hendrix (James Marshall Hendrix) 1942–70

American rock musician

3 Purple haze is in my brain
Lately things don't seem the same.
'Purple Haze' (1967 song)

4 A musician, if he's a messenger, is like a child who hasn't been handled too many times by man, hasn't had too many fingerprints across his brain.
In *Life Magazine* (1969)

Arthur W. D. Henley

5 Nobody loves a fairy when she's forty.
Title of song (1934)

W. E. Henley 1849–1903

English poet and playwright

6 Out of the night that covers me,
Black as the Pit from pole to pole,
I thank whatever gods may be
For my unconquerable soul.

In the fell clutch of circumstance,
I have not winced nor cried aloud:
Under the bludgeonings of chance
My head is bloody, but unbowed.
'Invictus. In Memoriam R.T.H.B.' (1888)

7 It matters not how strait the gate,
How charged with punishments the scroll,
I am the master of my fate:
I am the captain of my soul.
'Invictus. In Memoriam R.T.H.B.' (1888)

8 So be my passing!
My task accomplished and the long day done,
My wages taken, and in my heart
Some late lark singing,
Let me be gathered to the quiet west,
The sundown splendid and serene,
Death.
'Margaritae Sororis' (1888)

9 What have I done for you,
England, my England?
'Pro Rege Nostro' (1900). Cf. Macdonell 437:14

Henri IV (of Navarre) 1553–1610

King of France from 1589

10 *Je veux qu'il n'y ait si pauvre paysan en mon royaume qu'il n'ait tous les dimanches sa poule au pot.*

I want there to be no peasant in my kingdom so poor that he is unable to have a chicken in his pot every Sunday.
In Hardouin de Péréfixe *Histoire de Henry le Grand* (1681)

11 *Pends-toi, brave Crillon; nous avons combattu à Arques et tu n'y étais pas.*

Hang yourself, brave Crillon; we fought at Arques and you were not there.
Traditional form given by Voltaire to a letter from Henri to Crillon, 20 September 1597, in *Lettres missives de Henri IV, Collection des documents inédits de l'histoire de France* vol. 4 (1847) p. 848. Henri's actual words were: 'Brave Crillon, pendez-vous de n'avoir été ici près de moi lundi dernier à la plus belle occasion qui se soit jamais vue et qui peut-être se verra jamais [My good man, Crillon, hang yourself for not having been at my side last Monday at the greatest event that's ever been seen and perhaps ever will be seen]'

12 *Paris vaut bien une messe.*

Paris is well worth a mass.
Attributed to Henri IV; alternatively to his minister Sully, in conversation with Henri

13 The wisest fool in Christendom.
Of James I of England; attributed both to Henri IV and Sully (French original not known)

Henry II 1133–89

King of England from 1154

14 Will no one rid me of this turbulent priest?
Of Thomas Becket, Archbishop of Canterbury, murdered in Canterbury Cathedral, December 1170. Oral tradition, conflating a number of variant forms, including G. Lyttelton *History of the Life of King Henry the Second* (1769) pt. 4, p. 353: 'so many cowardly and ungrateful men in his court, none of whom would revenge him of the injuries he sustained from one turbulent priest'

Henry VIII 1491–1547

King of England from 1509

15 The King found her [Anne of Cleves] so different from her picture . . . that . . . he swore they had brought him a Flanders mare.
Tobias Smollett *A Complete History of England* (3rd ed., 1759) vol. 6, p. 68

16 This man hath the right sow by the ear.
Of Thomas Cranmer, June 1529, in *Acts and Monuments of John Foxe* ['Fox's Book of Martyrs', 1570] vol. 8, p. 7 (1877 ed.). See J. J. Scarisbrick *Henry VIII* (1968) p. 255

Matthew Henry 1662–1714

English divine

17 The better day, the worse deed.
An Exposition on the Old and New Testament (1710) Genesis ch. 3, v. 6, gloss 2

18 He rolls it under his tongue as a sweet morsel.
An Exposition on the Old and New Testament (1710) Psalm 36, v. 2, gloss 1

1 They that die by famine die by inches.
>An Exposition on the Old and New Testament (1710) Psalm 59, v. 15, gloss 5 (referring incorrectly to v. 13)

O. Henry (William Sydney Porter)
1862–1910
American short-story writer

2 Life is made up of sobs, sniffles, and smiles, with sniffles predominating.
>Four Million (1906) 'Gift of the Magi'

3 It was beautiful and simple as all truly great swindles are.
>Gentle Grafter (1908) 'Octopus Marooned'

4 Turn up the lights; I don't want to go home in the dark.
>Last words, quoting 1907 song by Harry Williams, in Charles Alphonso Smith O. Henry Biography (1916) ch. 9

Patrick Henry 1736–99
American statesman

5 Caesar had his Brutus—Charles the First, his Cromwell—and George the Third—('Treason,' cried the Speaker) . . . *may profit by their example. If this be treason, make the most of it.*
>Speech in the Virginia assembly, May 1765, in William Wirt Patrick Henry (1818) sect. 2, p. 65

6 I am not a Virginian, but an American.
>In [John Adams's] Notes of Debates in the Continental Congress, Philadelphia, 6 September 1774; in L. H. Butterfield (ed.) Diary and Autobiography of John Adams (1961) vol. 2, p. 125

7 I know not what course others may take; but as for me, give me liberty, or give me death!
>Speech in Virginia Convention, 23 March 1775, in William Wirt Patrick Henry (1818) sect. 4, p. 123

Philip Henry 1631–96
English clergyman

8 All this, and heaven too!
>In Matthew Henry Life of Mr Philip Henry (1698) ch. 5

Joseph Henshaw 1603–79
English divine; Bishop of Peterborough from 1663

9 One doth but breakfast here, another dines, he that liveth longest doth but sup; we must all go to bed in another world.
>Horae Succisivae (1631) pt. 1, p. 80

Heraclitus c.540–c.480 BC
Greek philosopher

10 πάντα χωρεῖ, οὐδὲν μένει.
Everything flows and nothing stays.
>In Plato Cratylus 402a

11 δὶς ἐς τὸν αὐτὸν ποταμὸν οὐκ ἂν ἐμβαίης.
You can't step twice into the same river.
>In Plato Cratylus 402a

12 ἦθος ἀνθρώπῳ δαίμων.
A man's character is his fate.
>On the Universe fragment 121 (translated by W. H. S. Jones). Cf. Eliot 269:26, Novalis 497:3

13 ὁδὸς ἄνω κάτω μία καὶ ὡυτή
The road up and the road down are one and the same.
>In H. Diels and W. Kranz Die Fragmente der Vorsokratiker (7th ed., 1954) fragment 60

A. P. Herbert (Sir Alan Patrick Herbert)
1890–1971
English writer and humorist

14 Don't let's go to the dogs tonight,
For mother will be there.
>'Don't Let's Go to the Dogs Tonight' (1926)

15 Don't tell my mother I'm living in sin,
Don't let the old folks know.
>'Don't Tell My Mother I'm Living in Sin' (1925)

16 The Farmer will never be happy again;
He carries his heart in his boots;
For either the rain is destroying his grain
Or the drought is destroying his roots.
>'The Farmer' (1922)

17 As my poor father used to say
In 1863,
Once people start on all this Art
Goodbye, moralitee!
>'Lines for a Worthy Person' (1930)

18 Other people's babies—
That's my life!
Mother to dozens,
And nobody's wife.
>'Other People's Babies' (1930)

19 This high official, all allow,
Is grossly overpaid;
There wasn't any Board, and now
There isn't any Trade.
>'The President of the Board of Trade' (1922)

20 Nothing is wasted, nothing is in vain:
The seas roll over but the rocks remain.
>Tough at the Top (operetta c.1949)

21 Holy deadlock.
>Title of novel (1934)

22 People must not do things for fun. We are not here for fun. There is no reference to fun in any Act of Parliament.
>Uncommon Law (1935) 'Is it a Free Country?'

23 The critical period in matrimony is breakfast-time.
>Uncommon Law (1935) 'Is Marriage Lawful?'

24 'Was the cow crossed?'
'No, your worship, it was an open cow.'
>Uncommon Law (1935) 'The Negotiable Cow' (in which an attempt is made to write a cheque on a cow)

1 The Common Law of England has been laboriously
built about a mythical figure—the figure of 'The
Reasonable Man'.
   Uncommon Law (1935) 'The Reasonable Man'

Lord Herbert of Cherbury 1583–1648

English philosopher and poet; brother of George Herbert

2 Now that the April of your youth adorns
The garden of your face.
   'Ditty: Now that the April' (1665)

George Herbert 1593–1633

English poet and clergyman

3 Whereas my birth and spirit rather took
The way that takes the town;
Thou didst betray me to a lingering book,
And wrap me in a gown.
   'Affliction (1)' (1633) l. 37

4 Now I am here, what thou wilt do with me
None of my books will show:
I read, and sigh, and wish I were a tree;
For then I should grow
To fruit or shade: at least some bird would trust
Her household to me, and I should be just.
   'Affliction (1)' (1633) l. 55

5 Ah, my dear God! though I am clean forgot,
Let me not love Thee, if I love Thee not.
   'Affliction (1)' (1633) l. 65

6 Love is that liquor sweet and most divine,
Which my God feels as blood; but I, as wine.
   'The Agonie' (1633) l. 17

7 Let all the world in ev'ry corner sing
My God and King.
The heavens are not too high,
His praise may thither fly;
The earth is not too low,
His praises there may grow.
Let all the world in ev'ry corner sing
My God and King.
The Church with psalms must shout,
No door can keep them out:
But above all, the heart
Must bear the longest part.
   'Antiphon: Let all the world in ev'ry corner sing' (1633)

8 Hearken unto a Verser, who may chance
Rhyme thee to good, and make a bait of pleasure.
A verse may find him, who a sermon flies,
And turn delight into a sacrifice.
   'The Church Porch' (1633) st. 1

9 O England! full of sin, but most of sloth;
Spit out thy phlegm, and fill thy breast with glory.
   'The Church Porch' (1633) st. 16

10 Judge not the preacher, for he is thy Judge:
If thou mislike him, thou conceiv'st him not.
God calleth preaching folly. Do not grudge
To pick out treasures from an earthen pot.
The worst speaks something good: if all want sense,
God takes a text, and preacheth patience.
   'The Church Porch' (1633) st. 72

11 I struck the board, and cried, 'No more.
I will abroad.'
What? shall I ever sigh and pine?
My lines and life are free; free as the road,
Loose as the wind, as large as store.
Shall I be still in suit?
Have I no harvest but a thorn
To let me blood, and not restore
What I have lost with cordial fruit?
Sure there was wine
Before my sighs did dry it; there was corn
Before my tears did drown it;
Is the year only lost to me?
Have I no bays to crown it?
   'The Collar' (1633)

12 Away; take heed:
I will abroad.
Call in thy death's-head there: tie up thy fears.
He that forbears
To suit and serve his need,
Deserves his load.
But as I raved and grew more fierce and wild
At every word,
Methought I heard one calling, 'Child';
And I replied, 'My Lord.'
   'The Collar' (1633)

13 O that thou shouldst give dust a tongue
To cry to thee,
And then not hear it crying!
   'Denial' (1633) l. 16

14 Love is swift of foot;
Love's a man of war,
And can shoot,
And can hit from far.
   'Discipline' (1633)

15 I got me flowers to strew Thy way;
I got me boughs off many a tree:
But Thou wast up by break of day,
And brought'st Thy sweets along with Thee.
   'Easter' (1633)

16 Teach me, my God and King,
In all things Thee to see,
And what I do in any thing
To do it as for Thee.
   'The Elixir' (1633)

17 A man that looks on glass,
On it may stay his eye;
Or if he pleaseth, through it pass,
And then the heaven espy.
   'The Elixir' (1633)

18 A servant with this clause
Makes drudgery divine:
Who sweeps a room as for Thy laws
Makes that and th' action fine.
   'The Elixir' (1633)

1 Oh that I were an orange-tree,
That busy plant!
Then I should ever laden be,
And never want
Some fruit for Him that dressed me.
    'Employment: He that is weary, let him sit' (1633)

2 Who would have thought my shrivelled heart
Could have recovered greenness?
    'The Flower' (1633)

3 And now in age I bud again,
After so many deaths I live and write;
I once more smell the dew and rain,
And relish versing: O my only Light,
It cannot be
That I am he
On whom Thy tempests fell all night.
    'The Flower' (1633)

4 Lovely enchanting language, sugar-cane,
Honey of roses!
    'The Forerunners' (1633)

5 Death is still working like a mole,
And digs my grave at each remove.
    'Grace' (1633)

6 Who says that fictions only and false hair
Become a verse? Is there in truth no beauty?
Is all good structure in a winding stair?
May no lines pass, except they do their duty
Not to a true, but painted chair?
    'Jordan (1)' (1633)

7 I made a posy while the day ran by:
Here will I smell my remnant out, and tie
My life within this band.
But Time did beckon to the flowers, and they
By noon most cunningly did steal away,
And withered in my hand.
    'Life' (1633)

8 Love bade me welcome: yet my soul drew back,
Guilty of dust and sin.
But quick-eyed Love, observing me grow slack
From my first entrance in,
Drew nearer to me, sweetly questioning,
If I lacked any thing.
    'Love: Love bade me welcome' (1633)

9 'You must sit down,' says Love, 'and taste my meat.'
So I did sit and eat.
    'Love: Love bade me welcome' (1633)

10 For us the winds do blow,
The earth doth rest, heaven move, and fountains flow.
Nothing we see, but means our good,
As our delight or as our treasure:
The whole is either our cupboard of food,
Or cabinet of pleasure.
    'Man' (1633)

11 Oh mighty love! Man is one world, and hath
Another to attend him.
    'Man' (1633)

12 When boys go first to bed,
They step into their voluntary graves.
    'Mortification' (1633)

13 Exalted manna, gladness of the best,
Heaven in ordinary, man well drest,
The Milky Way, the bird of Paradise,
Church-bells beyond the stars heard, the soul's blood,
The land of spices; something understood.
    'Prayer: Prayer the Church's banquet' (1633)

14 When God at first made man,
Having a glass of blessings standing by;
Let us (said he) pour on him all we can:
Let the world's riches, which dispersed lie,
Contract into a span.
    'The Pulley' (1633)

15 He would adore my gifts instead of Me,
And rest in Nature, not the God of Nature:
So both should losers be.
    'The Pulley' (1633)

16 Yet let him keep the rest,
But keep them with repining restlessness:
Let him be rich and weary, that at least,
If goodness lead him not, yet weariness
May toss him to My breast.
    'The Pulley' (1633)

17 But who does hawk at eagles with a dove?
    'The Sacrifice' (1633) l. 91

18 Man stole the fruit, but I must climb the tree.
    'The Sacrifice' (1633) l. 202

19 Lord, with what care Thou hast begirt us round!
Parents first season us: then schoolmasters
Deliver us to laws; they send us bound
To rules of reason, holy messengers,
Pulpits and Sundays, sorrow dogging sin,
Afflictions sorted, anguish of all sizes,
Fine nets and stratagems to catch us in,
Bibles laid open, millions of surprises.
    'Sin: Lord, with what care Thou hast begirt us round!'
    (1633)

20 Yet all these fences and their whole array
One cunning bosom—sin blows quite away.
    'Sin: Lord, with what care Thou hast begirt us round!'
    (1633)

21 Grasp not at much, for fear thou losest all.
    'The Size' (1633)

22 The God of love my Shepherd is,
And He that doth me feed:
While He is mine, and I am His,
What can I want or need?
    'The 23rd Psalm' (1633). Cf. Book of Common Prayer
    125:14

23 Lord, make me coy and tender to offend:
In friendship, first I think, if that agree
Which I intend,
Unto my friend's intent and end.
I would not use a friend, as I use Thee.
    'Unkindness' (1633)

24 My friend may spit upon my curious floor:
Would he have gold? I lend it instantly;
But let the poor,
And Thou within them, starve at door.
I cannot use a friend, as I use Thee.
    'Unkindness' (1633)

1 Sweet day, so cool, so calm, so bright,
  The bridal of the earth and sky,
  The dew shall weep thy fall to-night;
  For thou must die.

  Sweet rose, whose hue angry and brave
  Bids the rash gazer wipe his eye:
  Thy root is ever in its grave,
  And thou must die.

  Sweet spring, full of sweet days and roses,
  A box where sweets compacted lie;
  My music shows ye have your closes,
  And all must die.
    'Virtue' (1633)

2 Only a sweet and virtuous soul,
  Like seasoned timber, never gives;
  But though the whole world turn to coal,
  Then chiefly lives.
    'Virtue' (1633)

3 He that makes a good war makes a good peace.
    Outlandish Proverbs (1640) no. 420

4 He that lives in hope danceth without music.
    Outlandish Proverbs (1640) no. 1006

Robert Herrick 1591–1674

English poet and clergyman

5 Here a little child I stand,
  Heaving up my either hand;
  Cold as paddocks though they be,
  Here I lift them up to Thee,
  For a benison to fall
  On our meat, and on us all. Amen.
    'Another Grace for a Child' (1647)

6 I sing of brooks, of blossoms, birds, and bowers:
  Of April, May, of June, and July-flowers.
  I sing of May-poles, Hock-carts, wassails, wakes,
  Of bride-grooms, brides, and of their bridal-cakes.
    'The Argument of his Book' from *Hesperides* (1648)

7 And once more yet (ere I am laid out dead)
  Knock at a star with my exalted head.
    'The Bad Season Makes the Poet Sad' (1648)

8 Cherry-ripe, ripe, ripe, I cry,
  Full and fair ones; come and buy:
  If so be, you ask me where
  They do grow? I answer, there,
  Where my Julia's lips do smile;
  There's the land, or cherry-isle.
    'Cherry-Ripe' (1648)

9 Get up, get up for shame, the blooming morn
  Upon her wings presents the god unshorn.
    'Corinna's Going a-Maying' (1648)

10 Get up, sweet Slug-a-bed, and see
   The dew bespangling herb and tree.
    'Corinna's Going a-Maying' (1648)

11 So when or you or I are made
   A fable, song, or fleeting shade;
   All love, all liking, all delight
   Lies drowned with us in endless night.
   Then while time serves, and we are but decaying;
   Come, my Corinna, come, let's go a-Maying.
    'Corinna's Going a-Maying' (1648)

12 A sweet disorder in the dress
   Kindles in clothes a wantonness:
   A lawn about the shoulders thrown
   Into a fine distraction . . .
   A careless shoe-string, in whose tie
   I see a wild civility:
   Do more bewitch me, than when Art
   Is too precise in every part.
    'Delight in Disorder' (1648)

13 It is the end that crowns us, not the fight.
    'The End' (1648)

14 In prayer the lips ne'er act the winning part,
   Without the sweet concurrence of the heart.
    'The Heart' (1647)

15 When the artless doctor sees
   No one hope, but of his fees,
   And his skill runs on the lees;
   Sweet Spirit, comfort me!

   When his potion and his pill,
   Has, or none, or little skill,
   Meet for nothing, but to kill;
   Sweet Spirit, comfort me!
    'His Litany to the Holy Spirit' (1647)

16 Only a little more
   I have to write,
   Then I'll give o'er,
   And bid the world Good-night.
    'His Poetry his Pillar' (1648)

17 Love is a circle that doth restless move
   In the same sweet eternity of love.
    'Love What It Is' (1648)

18 Her eyes the glow-worm lend thee,
   The shooting-stars attend thee;
   And the elves also,
   Whose little eyes glow,
   Like the sparks of fire, befriend thee.
    'The Night-Piece, to Julia' (1648)

19 Night makes no difference 'twixt the Priest and Clerk;
   Joan as my Lady is as good i' th' dark.
    'No Difference i' th' Dark' (1648)

20 Made us nobly wild, not mad.
    'An Ode for him [Ben Jonson]' (1648)

21 And yet each verse of thine
   Out-did the meat, out-did the frolic wine.
    'An Ode for him [Ben Jonson]' (1648)

22 Fain would I kiss my Julia's dainty leg,
   Which is as white and hairless as an egg.
    'On Julia's Legs' (1648)

23 Praise they that will times past, I joy to see
   My self now live: this age best pleaseth me.
    'The Present Time Best Pleaseth' (1648)

24 But, for Man's fault, then was the thorn,
   Without the fragrant rose-bud, born;
   But ne'er the rose without the thorn.
    'The Rose' (1647)

25 A little saint best fits a little shrine,
   A little prop best fits a little vine,
   As my small cruse best fits my little wine.
    'A Ternary of Littles, upon a Pipkin of Jelly sent to a Lady'
    (1648)

1 For my Embalming (Sweetest) there will be
No Spices wanting, when I'm laid by thee.
'To Anthea: Now is the Time' (1648)

2 Bid me to live, and I will live
Thy Protestant to be:
Or bid me love, and I will give
A loving heart to thee.
'To Anthea, Who May Command Him Anything' (1648)

3 Bid me despair, and I'll despair,
Under that cypress tree:
Or bid me die, and I will dare
E'en Death, to die for thee.

Thou art my life, my love, my heart,
The very eyes of me:
And hast command of every part,
To live and die for thee.
'To Anthea, Who May Command Him Anything' (1648)

4 Fair daffodils, we weep to see
You haste away so soon:
As yet the early-rising sun
Has not attained his noon.
Stay, stay,
Until the hasting day
Has run
But to the even-song;
And, having prayed together, we
Will go with you along.

We have short time to stay, as you,
We have as short a Spring;
As quick a growth to meet decay,
As you or any thing.
'To Daffodils' (1648)

5 If any thing delight me for to print
My book, 'tis this; that Thou, my God, art in't.
'To God' (1647)

6 He loves his bonds, who when the first are broke,
Submits his neck unto a second yoke.
'To Love' (1648)

7 Gather ye rosebuds while ye may,
Old Time is still a-flying:
And this same flower that smiles to-day,
To-morrow will be dying.
'To the Virgins, to Make Much of Time' (1648)

8 Then be not coy, but use your time;
And while ye may, go marry:
For having lost but once your prime,
You may for ever tarry.
'To the Virgins, to Make Much of Time' (1648)

9 Whenas in silks my Julia goes,
Then, then (methinks) how sweetly flows
That liquefaction of her clothes.
Next, when I cast mine eyes and see
That brave vibration each way free;
O how that glittering taketh me!
'Upon Julia's Clothes' (1648)

10 So smooth, so sweet, so silvery is thy voice,
As, could they hear, the damned would make no
noise,
But listen to thee (walking in thy chamber)
Melting melodious words, to lutes of amber.
'Upon Julia's Voice' (1648)

11 To work a wonder, God would have her shown,
At once, a bud, and yet a rose full-blown.
'The Virgin Mary' (1647)

Lord Hervey (John, Baron Hervey of Ickworth) 1696–1743
English politician and writer

12 Whoever would lie usefully should lie seldom.
Memoirs of the Reign of George II (ed. J. W. Croker, 1848) vol. 1, ch. 19

13 I am fit for nothing but to carry candles and set chairs all my life.
Letter to Sir Robert Walpole, 1737, in *Memoirs of the Reign of George II* (ed. J. W. Croker, 1848) vol. 2, ch. 40

Hesiod c.700 BC
Greek poet

14 πλέον ἥμισυ παντός.

The half is greater than the whole.
Works and Days l. 40

Hermann Hesse 1877–1962
German novelist and poet

15 *Wenn wir einen Menschen hassen, so hassen wir in seinem Bild etwas, was in uns selber sitzt. Was nicht in uns selber ist, das regt uns nicht auf.*

If you hate a person, you hate something in him that is part of yourself. What isn't part of ourselves doesn't disturb us.
Demian (1919) ch. 6

16 *Auf Kosten der Intensität also erreicht er [der Bürger] Erhaltung und Sicherheit, statt Gottbesessenheit erntet er Gewissensruhe, statt Lust Behagen, statt Freiheit Bequemlichkeit, statt tödlicher Glut eine angenehme Temperatur.*

The bourgeois prefers comfort to pleasure, convenience to liberty, and a pleasant temperature to the deathly inner consuming fire.
Der Steppenwolf (1927) 'Tractat vom Steppenwolf'

Gordon Hewart (Viscount Hewart) 1870–1943
British lawyer and politician

17 A long line of cases shows that it is not merely of some importance, but is of fundamental importance that justice should not only be done, but should manifestly and undoubtedly be seen to be done.
Rex v Sussex Justices, 9 November 1923, in *Law Reports King's Bench Division* (1924) vol. 1, p. 259

Du Bose Heyward 1885–1940

American songwriter

1 It ain't necessarily so,
  It ain't necessarily so,
  De t'ings dat yo' li'ble
  To read in de Bible
  It ain't necessarily so.
> *Porgy and Bess* (1935) 'It ain't necessarily so' (with Ira Gershwin; music by George Gershwin)

2 Summer time an' the livin' is easy,
  Fish are jumpin' an' the cotton is high.
  Oh, yo' daddy's rich, and yo' ma' is good-lookin',
  So hush, little baby, don' yo' cry.
> *Porgy and Bess* (1935) 'Summertime' (with Ira Gershwin; music by George Gershwin)

3 Woman may born you, love you, an' mourn you,
  But a woman is a sometime thing.
> *Porgy and Bess* (1935) 'A Woman is a Sometime Thing' (with Ira Gershwin; music by George Gershwin)

John Heywood *c*.1497–*c*.1580

English playwright

4 All a green willow, willow;
  All a green willow is my garland.
> 'The Green Willow'. Cf. *Othello* 617:22

5 I hear no noise mine ease to break,
  Thy butt'ry door I hear not creak.
  Thy kitchen cumbreth not by heat,
  Thy cooks chop neither herbs nor meat.
  I never heard thy fire once spark,
  I never heard thy dog once bark.
  I never heard once in thy house
  So much as one peep of one mouse.
  I never heard thy cat once mew.
  These praises are not small nor few.
> 'A quiet neighbour' (1556)

Thomas Heywood *c*.1574–1641

English playwright

6 Seven cities warred for Homer, being dead,
  Who, living, had no roof to shroud his head.
> 'The Hierarchy of the Blessed Angels' (1635). Cf. Anonymous 17:19

J. R. Hicks (Sir John Hicks) 1904–

British economist

7 The best of all monopoly profits is a quiet life.
> *Econometrica* (1935) 'The Theory of Monopoly'

Aaron Hill 1685–1750

English poet and playwright

8 Tender-handed stroke a nettle,
  And it stings you for your pains;
  Grasp it like a man of mettle,
  And it soft as silk remains.
> 'Verses Written on a Window in Scotland'

Geoffrey Hill 1932–

English poet

9   Poetry
  Unearths from among the speechless dead

  Lazarus mystified, common man
  Of death. The lily rears its gouged face
  From the provided loam.
> 'History as Poetry' (1968)

10 She kept the siege. And every day
   We watched her brooding over death
   Like a strong bird above its prey.
   The room filled with the kettle's breath.

   Damp curtains glued against the pane
   Sealed time away. Her body froze
   As if to freeze us all, and chain
   Creation to a stunned repose.
> 'In Memory of Jane Fraser' (1959)

11 I love my work and my children. God
   Is distant, difficult. Things happen.
   Too near the ancient troughs of blood
   Innocence is no earthly weapon.
> 'Ovid in the Third Reich' (1968)

Joe Hill (Joel Hägglund) 1879–1915

American labour leader and songwriter

12 You will eat, bye and bye,
   In that glorious land above the sky;
   Work and pray, live on hay,
   You'll get pie in the sky when you die.
> 'Preacher and the Slave' in *Songs of the Workers* (Industrial Workers of the World, 1911)

13 I will die like a true-blue rebel. Don't waste any time in mourning—organize.
> Farewell telegram to Bill Haywood, 18 November 1915, prior to his death by firing squad, in *Salt Lake* (Utah) *Tribune* 19 November 1915

Pattie S. Hill 1868–1946

American educationist

14 Happy birthday to you.
> Title of song (1935); music by Mildred J. Hill

Rowland Hill 1744–1833

English clergyman

15 He did not see any reason why the devil should have all the good tunes.
> In E. W. Broome *The Rev. Rowland Hill* (1881) ch. 7

Sir Edmund Hillary 1919–

New Zealand mountaineer

16 Well, we knocked the bastard off!
> On conquering Mount Everest, in *Nothing Venture, Nothing Win* (1975) ch. 10. Cf. Mallory 443:2

Fred Hillebrand 1893–

17 Home James, and don't spare the horses.
> Title of song (1934)

Hillel 'The Elder' c.60 BC–AD c.9

Rabbi

1 A name made great is a name destroyed.

Pirqe Aboth ch. 1, no. 14, in C. Taylor (ed.) *Sayings of the Jewish Fathers* (1877)

2 If I am not for myself who is for me; and being for my own self what am I? If not now when?

Pirqe Aboth ch. 1, no. 15, in C. Taylor (ed.) *Sayings of the Jewish Fathers* (1877)

Lady Hillingdon 1857–1940

3 I am happy now that Charles calls on my bedchamber less frequently than of old. As it is, I now endure but two calls a week and when I hear his steps outside my door I lie down on my bed, close my eyes, open my legs, and think of England.

Journal 1912, in J. Gathorne-Hardy *The Rise and Fall of the British Nanny* (1972) ch. 3

James Hilton 1900–54

English novelist

4 Nothing really wrong with him—only anno domini, but that's the most fatal complaint of all, in the end.

Goodbye, Mr Chips (1934) ch. 1

Hippocleides

6th-century Athenian aristocrat

5 οὐ φροντὶς Ἱπποκλείδῃ.

Hippocleides doesn't care.

On being told that he had ruined his marriage chances with the daughter of a tyrant, concluding a dance by standing on his head and gesticulating with his legs; in Herodotus *Histories* bk. 6, sect. 129

Hippocrates c.460–357 BC

Greek physician

6 ὁ βίος βραχύς, ἡ δὲ τέχνη μακρή.

Life is short, the art long.

Aphorisms sect. 1, para. 1 (translated by W. H. S. Jones) and often quoted 'Ars longa, vita brevis'. See Seneca *De Brevitate Vitae* sect. 1. Cf. Chaucer 195:5

7 Χρόνος ἐστὶν ἐν ᾧ καιρός, καὶ καιρὸς ἐν ᾧ χρόνος οὐ πολύς.

Time is that wherein there is opportunity, and opportunity is that wherein there is no great time.

Precepts ch. 1 (translated by W. II. S. Jones, 1923)

8 ἄκεσις χρόνῳ, ἔστι δὲ ἡνίκα καὶ καιρῷ.

Healing is a matter of time, but it is sometimes also a matter of opportunity.

Precepts ch. 1 (translated by W. H. S. Jones, 1923)

Alfred Hitchcock 1899–1980

British-born film director

9 Television has brought back murder into the home—where it belongs.

In *Observer* 19 December 1965

Adolf Hitler 1889–1945

German dictator

10 *Die Nacht der langen Messer.*

The night of the long knives.

Phrase given to the massacre of Ernst Roehm and his associates by Hitler on 29–30 June 1934, though taken from an early Nazi marching song. See S. H. Roberts *The House Hitler Built* (1937) pt. 2, ch. 3. The phrase was subsequently associated with Harold Macmillan's Cabinet dismissals of 13 July 1962

11 *Ich gehe mit traumwandlerischer Sicherheit den Weg, den mich die Vorsehung gehen heisst.*

I go the way that Providence dictates with the assurance of a sleepwalker.

Speech in Munich, 15 March 1936, in Max Domarus (ed.) *Hitler: Reden und Proklamationen 1932–1945* (1962) p. 606

12 *Es ist die letzte territoriale Forderung, die ich Europa zu stellen habe, aber es ist die Forderung, von der ich nicht abgehe, und die ich, so Gott will, erfüllen werde.*

It is the last territorial claim which I have to make in Europe, but it is the claim from which I will not recede and which, God-willing, I will make good.

On the Sudetenland, in Speech at Berlin Sportpalast, 26 September 1938; in Max Domarus (ed.) *Hitler: Reden und Proklamationen 1932–1945* (1962) p. 927

13 *In bezug auf das sudetendeutsche Problem ist meine Geduld jetzt zu Ende!*

With regard to the problem of the Sudeten Germans, my patience is now at an end!

Speech at Berlin Sportpalast, 26 September 1938, in Max Domarus (ed.) *Hitler: Reden und Proklamationen 1932–1945* (1962) p. 932

14 *Die breite Masse eines Volkes ... fällt einer grossen Lüge leichter zum Opfer als einer kleinen.*

The broad mass of a nation ... will more easily fall victim to a big lie than to a small one.

Mein Kampf (1925) vol. 1, ch. 10

15 *Brennt Paris?*

Is Paris burning?

25 August 1944, in Larry Collins and Dominique Lapierre *Is Paris Burning?* (1965) ch. 5

Thomas Hobbes 1588–1679

English philosopher

16 Laughter is nothing else but sudden glory arising from some sudden conception of some eminency in ourselves, by comparison with the infirmity of others, or with our own formerly.

Human Nature (1650) ch. 9, sect. 13

17 True and False are attributes of speech, not of things. And where speech is not, there is neither Truth nor Falsehood.

Leviathan (1651) pt. 1, ch. 4

18 In Geometry (which is the only science that it hath pleased God hitherto to bestow on mankind) men begin at settling the significations of their words; which ... they call Definitions.

Leviathan (1651) pt. 1, ch. 4

1 Words are wise men's counters, they do but reckon by them: but they are the money of fools, that value them by the authority of an Aristotle, a Cicero, or a Thomas, or any other doctor whatsoever, if but a man.
Leviathan (1651) pt. 1, ch. 4

2 The power of a man, to take it universally, is his present means, to obtain some future apparent good; and is either original or instrumental.
Leviathan (1651) pt. 1, ch. 10

3 I put for a general inclination of all mankind, a perpetual and restless desire of power after power, that ceaseth only in death.
Leviathan (1651) pt. 1, ch. 11

4 They that approve a private opinion, call it opinion; but they that mislike it, heresy: and yet heresy signifies no more than private opinion.
Leviathan (1651) pt. 1, ch. 11

5 During the time men live without a common power to keep them all in awe, they are in that condition which is called war; and such a war as is of every man against every man.
Leviathan (1651) pt. 1, ch. 13

6 For as the nature of foul weather, lieth not in a shower or two of rain; but in an inclination thereto of many days together: so the nature of war consisteth not in actual fighting, but in the known disposition thereto during all the time there is no assurance to the contrary.
Leviathan (1651) pt. 1, ch. 13

7 No arts; no letters; no society; and which is worst of all, continual fear and danger of violent death; and the life of man, solitary, poor, nasty, brutish, and short.
Leviathan (1651) pt. 1, ch. 13

8 Force, and fraud, are in war the two cardinal virtues.
Leviathan (1651) pt. 1, ch. 13

9 They that are discontented under *monarchy*, call it *tyranny*; and they that are displeased with *aristocracy*, call it *oligarchy*: so also, they which find themselves grieved under a *democracy*, call it *anarchy*, which signifies the want of government; and yet I think no man believes, that want of government, is any new kind of government.
Leviathan (1651) pt. 2, ch. 19

10 Whereas some have attributed the dominion [of the family] to the man only, as being of the more excellent sex; they misreckon in it. For there is not always that difference of strength, or prudence between the man and the woman, as that the right can be determined without war.
Leviathan (1651) pt. 2, ch. 20

11 For it is with the mysteries of our religion, as with wholesome pills for the sick, which swallowed whole, have the virtue to cure; but chewed, are for the most part cast up again without effect.
Leviathan (1651) pt. 3, ch. 32

12 The papacy is not other than the ghost of the deceased Roman Empire, sitting crowned upon the grave thereof.
Leviathan (1651) pt. 4, ch. 47

13 The praise of ancient authors proceeds not from the reverence of the dead, but from the competition, and mutual envy of the living.
Leviathan (1651) 'A Review and Conclusion'

14 I am about to take my last voyage, a great leap in the dark.
Last words. See John Watkins *Anecdotes of Men of Learning* (1808) p. 276

John Cam Hobhouse (Baron Broughton)
1786–1869

English politician

15 When I invented the phrase 'His Majesty's Opposition' [Canning] paid me a compliment on the fortunate hit.
Recollections of a Long Life (1865) vol. 2, ch. 12

Ralph Hodgson 1871–1962

English poet

16 'Twould ring the bells of Heaven
The wildest peal for years,
If Parson lost his senses
And people came to theirs,
And he and they together
Knelt down with angry prayers
For tamed and shabby tigers
And dancing dogs and bears,
And wretched, blind, pit ponies,
And little hunted hares.
'Bells of Heaven' (1917)

17 Reason has moons, but moons not hers,
Lie mirrored on her sea,
Confounding her astronomers,
But, O! delighting me.
'Reason Has Moons' (1917)

18 When stately ships are twirled and spun
Like whipping tops and help there's none
And mighty ships ten thousand ton
Go down like lumps of lead.
'Song of Honour' (1917)

19 Time, you old gipsy man,
Will you not stay,
Put up your caravan
Just for one day?
'Time, You Old Gipsy Man' (1917)

Eric Hoffer 1902–83

American philosopher

20 When people are free to do as they please, they usually imitate each other. Originality is deliberate and forced, and partakes of the nature of a protest.
Passionate State of Mind (1955) p. 21

August Heinrich Hoffman (Hoffman von Fallersleben) 1798–1874

German poet

21 *Deutschland über alles.*
Germany above all.
Title of poem (1841)

Heinrich Hoffmann 1809–94

German writer for children

1 Augustus was a chubby lad;
Fat ruddy cheeks Augustus had:
And everybody saw with joy
The plump and hearty, healthy boy.
He ate and drank as he was told,
And never let his soup get cold.
But one day, one cold winter's day,
He screamed out, 'Take the soup away!
O take the nasty soup away!
I won't have any soup today.'
> *Struwwelpeter* (1848) 'Augustus'

2 Let me see if Philip can
Be a little gentleman;
Let me see, if he is able
To sit still for once at table.
> *Struwwelpeter* (1848) 'Fidgety Philip'

3 But fidgety Phil,
He won't sit still;
He wriggles
And giggles,
And then, I declare,
Swings backwards and forwards,
And tilts up his chair,
Just like any rocking-horse—
'Philip! I am getting cross!'
> *Struwwelpeter* (1848) 'Fidgety Philip'

4 Look at little Johnny there,
Little Johnny Head-In-Air!
> *Struwwelpeter* (1848) 'Johnny Head-In-Air'

5 Silly little Johnny, look,
You have lost your writing-book!
> *Struwwelpeter* (1848) 'Johnny Head-In-Air'

6 The door flew open, in he ran,
The great, long, red-legged scissor-man.
> *Struwwelpeter* (1848) 'The Little Suck-a-Thumb'

7 Snip! Snap! Snip! They go so fast.
That both his thumbs are off at last.
> *Struwwelpeter* (1848) 'The Little Suck-a-Thumb'

8 He finds it hard, without a pair
Of spectacles, to shoot the hare.
The hare sits snug in leaves and grass,
And laughs to see the green man pass.
> *Struwwelpeter* (1848) 'The Man Who Went Out Shooting'

9 And now she's trying all she can,
To shoot the sleepy, green-coat man.
> *Struwwelpeter* (1848) 'The Man Who Went Out Shooting'

10 The hare's own child, the little hare.
> *Struwwelpeter* (1848) 'The Man Who Went Out Shooting'

11 Anything to me is sweeter
Than to see Shock-headed Peter.
> *Struwwelpeter* (1848) 'Shock-Headed Peter' (title poem)

Max Hoffman 1869–1927

German soldier

12 LUDENDORFF: The English soldiers fight like lions.
HOFFMAN: True. But don't we know that they are lions led by donkeys.
> During the First World War, in Alan Clark *The Donkeys* (1961) epigraph (from Falkenhayn's *Memoirs*)

Gerard Hoffnung 1925–59

English humorist

13 Standing among savage scenery, the hotel offers stupendous revelations. There is a French widow in every bedroom, affording delightful prospects.
> Supposedly quoting a letter from a Tyrolean landlord; in speech at the Oxford Union, 4 December 1958

Lancelot Hogben 1895–1975

English scientist

14 This is not the age of pamphleteers. It is the age of the engineers. The spark-gap is mightier than the pen. Democracy will not be salvaged by men who talk fluently, debate forcefully and quote aptly.
> *Science for the Citizen* (1938) epilogue

James Hogg 1770–1835

Scottish poet

15 Cock up your beaver, and cock it fu' sprush;
We'll over the Border and gi'e them a brush;
There's somebody there we'll teach better behaviour.
Hey, Johnnie lad, cock up your beaver!
> 'Cock Up Your Beaver' in *Jacobite Relics of Scotland* Second Series (1821) p. 127

16 Where the pools are bright and deep
Where the gray trout lies asleep,
Up the river and o'er the lea
That's the way for Billy and me.
> 'A Boy's Song' (1838)

17 God bless our lord the king!
God save our lord the king!
God save the king!
Make him victorious,
Happy, and glorious,
Long to reign over us:
God save the king!
> 'The King's Anthem' in *Jacobite Relics of Scotland* Second Series (1821) p. 50. Cf. Anonymous 13:18

18 We'll o'er the water, we'll o'er the sea,
We'll o'er the water to Charlie;
Come weel, come wo, we'll gather and go,
And live or die wi' Charlie.
> 'O'er the Water to Charlie' in *Jacobite Relics of Scotland* Second Series (1821) p. 76

Paul Henri, Baron d'Holbach 1723–89

French philosopher

19 *L'art n'est que la Nature agissante à l'aide des instruments qu'elle a faits.*
Art is only Nature operating with the aid of the instruments she has made.
> *Système de la Nature* (1780 ed.) pt. 1, ch. 1

20 *Si l'ignorance de la nature donna la naissance aux dieux, la connaissance de la nature est faite pour les détruire.*
If ignorance of nature gave birth to the Gods, knowledge of nature is destined to destroy them.
> *Système de la Nature* (1770) pt. 2, ch. 1

Billie Holiday (Eleanor Fagan) 1915–59

American singer

1 Them that's got shall get,
Them that's not shall lose,
So the Bible said,
And it still is news;
Mama may have, papa may have,
But God bless the child that's got his own!
That's got his own.
'God Bless the Child' (1941 song, with Arthur Herzog Jnr)

2 Mom and Pop were just a couple of kids when they
got married. He was eighteen, she was sixteen, and I
was three.
Lady Sings the Blues (1958) opening words

Henry Fox, 1st Lord Holland 1705–74

English Whig politician

3 If Mr Selwyn calls again, shew him up: if I am alive I
shall be delighted to see him; and if I am dead he
would like to see me.
During his last illness, in J. H. Jesse *George Selwyn and his
Contemporaries* (1844) vol. 3, p. 50

Henry Scott Holland 1847–1918

English theologian and preacher

4 Death is nothing at all; it does not count. I have only
slipped away into the next room.
Sermon preached on Whitsunday 1910, in *Facts of the
Faith* (1919) 'The King of Terrors'

Stanley Holloway 1890–1982

English actor and singer

5 Sam, Sam, pick up tha' musket.
'Pick Up Tha' Musket' (1930 recorded monologue)

John H. Holmes 1879–1964

American Unitarian minister

6 This, now, is the judgement of our scientific age—the
third reaction of man upon the universe! This
universe is not hostile, nor yet is it friendly. It is
simply indifferent.
The Sensible Man's View of Religion (1932) ch. 4

Oliver Wendell Holmes 1809–94

American physician, poet, and essayist

7 The axis of the earth sticks out visibly through the
centre of each and every town or city.
The Autocrat of the Breakfast-Table (1858) ch. 6

8 It is the province of knowledge to speak and it is the
privilege of wisdom to listen.
The Poet at the Breakfast Table (1872) ch. 10

9 His humid front the cive, anheling, wipes.
And dreams of erring on ventiferous ripes.
'Aestivation' (1858)

10 Depart,—be off,—excede,—evade,—erump!
'Aestivation' (1858). Cf. Cicero 204:7

11 Sweet is the scene where genial friendship plays
The pleasing game of interchanging praise.
'An After-Dinner Poem' (1848)

12 Fate tried to conceal him by naming him Smith.
'The Boys' (1858) (of Samuel Francis Smith)

13 A general flavour of mild decay.
'The Deacon's Masterpiece' (1858)

14 Lean, hungry, savage anti-everythings.
'A Modest Request' (1848)

15 Wisdom has taught us to be calm and meek,
To take one blow, and turn the other cheek;
It is not written what a man shall do
If the rude caitiff smite the other too!
'Non-Resistance' (1861)

16 And, when you stick on conversation's burrs,
Don't strew your pathway with those dreadful urs.
'A Rhymed Lesson' (1848)

17 Man wants but little drink below,
But wants that little strong.
'A Song of other Days' (1848). Cf. Goldsmith 310:20

18 Blank cheques of intellectual bankruptcy.
Definition of catch-phrases

John Home 1722–1808

Scottish playwright

19 My name is Norval; on the Grampian hills
My father feeds his flocks; a frugal swain,
Whose constant cares were to increase his store
And keep his only son, myself, at home.
Douglas (1756) act 2, sc. 1

20 Like Douglas conquer, or like Douglas die.
Douglas (1756) act 5

Lord Home (14th Earl of Home, formerly Sir Alec Douglas-Home) 1903–

British Conservative politician; Prime Minister, 1963–4

21 As far as the fourteenth earl is concerned, I suppose
Mr Wilson, when you come to think of it, is the
fourteenth Mr Wilson.
Replying to Harold Wilson's remark (on Home's leading the
Conservatives to victory in the 1963 election) that 'the
whole [democratic] process has ground to a halt with a
fourteenth Earl'; in *Daily Telegraph* 22 October 1963

Homer

Greek poet of the 8th century BC

22 μῆνιν ἄειδε, θεά, Πηληϊάδεω Ἀχιλῆος
οὐλομένην, ἣ μυρί' Ἀχαιοῖς ἄλγε' ἔθηκε.
Achilles' cursed anger sing, O goddess, that son of
Peleus, which started a myriad sufferings for the
Achaeans.
The Iliad bk. 1, l. 1 ('Achilles' wrath, to Greece the direful
spring / Of woes unnumbered, heavenly goddess, sing' in
Pope's translation)

23 ἔπεα πτερόεντα.
Winged words.
The Iliad bk. 1, l. 201

1 Ἦ καὶ κυανέῃσιν ἐπ' ὀφρύσι νεῦσε Κρονίων.
ἀμβρόσιαι δ' ἄρα χαῖται ἐπερρώσαντο ἄνακτος
κρατὸς ἀπ' ἀθανάτοιο. μέγαν δ' ἐλέλιξεν Ὄλυμπον.

The son of Kronos [Zeus] spoke, and nodded with his
darkish brows, and immortal locks fell forward from
the lord's deathless head, and he made great Olympus
tremble.

The Iliad bk. 1, l. 528

2 οὐ νέμεσις Τρῶας καὶ ἐϋκνήμιδας Ἀχαιοὺς
τοιῇδ' ἀμφὶ γυναικὶ πολὺν χρόνον ἄλγεα πάσχειν·
αἰνῶς ἀθανάτῃσι θεῇς εἰς ὦπα ἔοικεν.

It is no cause for anger that the Trojans and the
well-greaved Achaeans have suffered for so long over
such a woman: she is wondrously like the immortal
goddesses to look upon.

The Iliad bk. 3, l. 156 (of Helen)

3 Ἀτρεΐδη, ποῖόν σε ἔπος φύγεν ἕρκος ὀδόντων;

Son of Atreus, what manner of speech has escaped the
barrier of your teeth?

The Iliad bk. 4, l. 350

4 οἵη περ φύλλων γενεή, τοίη δὲ καὶ ἀνδρῶν.

Like that of leaves is a generation of men.

The Iliad bk. 6, l. 146

5 αἰὲν ἀριστεύειν καὶ ὑπείροχον ἔμμεναι ἄλλων.

Always to be best, and to be distinguished above the
rest.

The Iliad bk. 6, l. 208

6 δακρυόεν γελάσασα.

Smiling through her tears.

The Iliad bk. 6, l. 484

7 ἐχθρὸς γάρ μοι κεῖνος ὁμῶς Ἀΐδαο πύλῃσιν
ὅς χ' ἕτερον μὲν κεύθῃ ἐνὶ φρεσίν, ἄλλο δὲ εἴπῃ.

Hateful to me as the gates of Hades is that man who
hides one thing in his heart and speaks another.

The Iliad bk. 9, l. 312

8 εἷς οἰωνὸς ἄριστος, ἀμύνεσθαι περὶ πάτρης.

This is the one best omen, to fight in defence of one's
country.

The Iliad bk. 12, l. 243

9 κεῖτο μέγας μεγαλωστί, λελασμένος ἱπποσυνάων.

He lay great and greatly fallen, forgetful of his
horsemanship.

The Iliad bk. 16, l. 776

10 θεῶν ἐν γούνασι κεῖται.

It lies in the lap of the gods.

The Iliad bk. 17, l. 514 and elsewhere

11 ἄνδρα μοι ἔννεπε, Μοῦσα, πολύτροπον, ὃς μάλα πολλὰ
πλάγχθη, ἐπεὶ Τροίης ἱερὸν πτολίεθρον ἔπερσε,
πολλῶν δ' ἀνθρώπων ἴδεν ἄστεα καὶ νόον ἔγνω.

Tell me, Muse, of the man of many devices, who
wandered far and wide after he had sacked Troy's
sacred city, and saw the towns of many men and
knew their mind.

The Odyssey bk. 1, l. 1 (of Odysseus)

12 ῥοδοδάκτυλος Ἠώς.

Rosy-fingered dawn.

The Odyssey bk. 2, l. 1 and *passim*

13 βουλοίμην κ' ἐπάρουρος ἐὼν θητευέμεν ἄλλῳ
ἀνδρὶ παρ' ἀκλήρῳ, ᾧ μὴ βίοτος πολὺς εἴη,
ἢ πᾶσιν νεκύεσσι καταφθιμένοισιν ἀνάσσειν.

I would rather be tied to the soil as another man's
serf, even a poor man's, who hadn't much to live on
himself, than be King of all these the dead and
destroyed.

The Odyssey bk. 11, l. 489

Arthur Honegger 1892–1955

Swiss composer

14 *La première qualité d'un compositeur, c'est d'être mort.*

The first requirement for a composer is to be dead.

Je suis compositeur (1951) p. 16

Thomas Hood 1799–1845

English poet and humorist

15 Take her up tenderly,
Lift her with care;
Fashioned so slenderly,
Young, and so fair!

'The Bridge of Sighs' (1844)

16 Mad from life's history,
Glad to death's mystery,
Swift to be hurled—
Anywhere, anywhere,
Out of the world!

'The Bridge of Sighs' (1844)

17 Ben Battle was a soldier bold,
And used to war's alarms:
But a cannon-ball took off his legs,
So he laid down his arms!

'Faithless Nelly Gray' (1826)

18 For here I leave my second leg,
And the Forty-second Foot!

'Faithless Nelly Gray' (1826)

19 The love that loves a scarlet coat
Should be more uniform.

'Faithless Nelly Gray' (1826)

20 His death, which happened in his berth,
At forty-odd befell:
They went and told the sexton, and
The sexton tolled the bell.

'Faithless Sally Brown' (1826)

21 I remember, I remember,
The house where I was born,
The little window where the sun
Came peeping in at morn.

'I Remember' (1826)

22 What is a modern poet's fate?
To write his thoughts upon a slate;
The critic spits on what is done,
Gives it a wipe—and all is gone.

'A Joke', in Hallam Tennyson *Alfred Lord Tennyson* (1897)
vol. 2, ch. 3 (not found in Hood's *Complete Works*)

23 But evil is wrought by want of thought,
As well as want of heart!

'The Lady's Dream' (1844)

24 Home-made dishes that drive one from home.

Miss Kilmansegg and her Precious Leg (1841–3) 'Her Misery'

1 No sun—no moon!
No morn—no noon
No dawn—no dusk—no proper time of day.
'No!' (1844)

2 No warmth, no cheerfulness, no healthful ease,
No comfortable feel in any member—
No shade, no shine, no butterflies, no bees,
No fruits, no flowers, no leaves, no birds,—
November!
'No!' (1844)

3 I saw old Autumn in the misty morn
Stand shadowless like Silence, listening
To silence.
'Ode: Autumn' (1823)

4 The bird forlorn,
That singeth with her breast against a thorn.
'The Plea of the Midsummer Fairies' (1827) st. 30

5 When Eve upon the first of Men
The apple pressed with specious cant,
Oh! what a thousand pities then
That Adam was not Adamant!
'A Reflection' (1842)

6 She stood breast high amid the corn,
Clasped by the golden light of morn,
Like the sweetheart of the sun,
Who many a glowing kiss had won.
'Ruth' (1827). Cf. Keats 389:15

7 With fingers weary and worn,
With eyelids heavy and red,
A woman sat, in unwomanly rags,
Plying her needle and thread—
Stitch! stitch! stitch!
In poverty, hunger, and dirt.
And still with a voice of dolorous pitch
She sang the 'Song of the Shirt'.
'The Song of the Shirt' (1843)

8 O! men with sisters dear,
O! men with mothers and wives!
It is not linen you're wearing out,
But human creatures' lives!
'The Song of the Shirt' (1843)

9 Oh! God! that bread should be so dear,
And flesh and blood so cheap!
'The Song of the Shirt' (1843)

10 The sedate, sober, silent, serious, sad-coloured sect.
Comic Annual (1839) 'The Doves and the Crows' (of Quakers)

11 'Extremes meet', as the whiting said with its tail in its mouth.
Comic Annual (1839) 'The Doves and the Crows'

12 Holland . . . lies so low they're only saved by being dammed.
Up the Rhine (1840) 'Letter from Martha Penny to Rebecca Page'

Richard Hooker c.1554–1600

English theologian

13 He that goeth about to persuade a multitude, that they are not so well governed as they ought to be, shall never want attentive and favourable hearers.
Of the Laws of Ecclesiastical Polity (1593) bk. 1, ch. 1, sect. 1

14 Of Law there can be no less acknowledged, than that her seat is the bosom of God, her voice the harmony of the world: all things in heaven and earth do her homage, the very least as feeling her care, and the greatest as not exempted from her power.
Of the Laws of Ecclesiastical Polity (1593) bk. 1, ch. 16, sect. 8

15 Alteration though it be from worse to better hath in it inconveniences, and those weighty.
Of the Laws of Ecclesiastical Polity (1593) bk. 4, ch. 14, sect. 1. Cf. Johnson 367:19

Ellen Sturgis Hooper 1816–41

American poet

16 I slept, and dreamed that life was beauty;
I woke, and found that life was duty.
'Beauty and Duty' (1840)

Herbert Hoover 1874–1964

31st President of the USA

17 Our country has deliberately undertaken a great social and economic experiment, noble in motive and far-reaching in purpose.
On the Eighteenth Amendment enacting Prohibition, in a letter to Senator W. H. Borah, 23 February 1928; in Claudius O. Johnson Borah of Idaho (1936) ch. 21

18 The American system of rugged individualism.
Speech in New York City, 22 October 1928, in New Day (1928) p. 154

19 The grass will grow in the streets of a hundred cities, a thousand towns.
Speech, 31 October 1932, in State Papers of Herbert Hoover (1934) vol. 2, p. 418 (on proposals 'to reduce the protective tariff to a competitive tariff for revenue')

20 Older men declare war. But it is youth who must fight and die.
Speech at the Republican National Convention, Chicago, 27 June 1944, in Addresses upon the American Road (1946) p. 254

Anthony Hope (Sir Anthony Hope Hawkins) 1863–1933

English novelist

21 Economy is going without something you do want in case you should, some day, want something you probably won't want.
The Dolly Dialogues (1894) no. 12

22 'You oughtn't to yield to temptation.' 'Well, somebody must, or the thing becomes absurd,' said I.
The Dolly Dialogues (1894) no. 14

23 Bourgeois . . . is an epithet which the riff-raff apply to what is respectable, and the aristocracy to what is decent.
The Dolly Dialogues (1894) no. 17

24 His foe was folly and his weapon wit.
Inscription on W. S. Gilbert's memorial on the Victoria Embankment, London, 1915

25 Oh, for an hour of Herod!
At the first night of J. M. Barrie's Peter Pan in 1904, in Denis Mackail The Story of JMB (1941) ch. 17

Bob Hope 1903–

American comedian

1 A bank is a place that will lend you money if you can
prove that you don't need it.
   In Alan Harrington *Life in the Crystal Palace* (1959) 'The
   Tyranny of Forms'

Francis Hope 1938–74

British journalist and poet

2 And scribbled lines like fallen hopes
On backs of tattered envelopes.
   'Instead of a Poet' (1965)

Laurence Hope (Adela Florence Nicolson)
1865–1904

Anglo-Indian poet

3 Pale hands I loved beside the Shalimar,
Where are you now? Who lies beneath your spell? . . .
Pale hands, pink tipped, like lotus buds that float
On those cool waters where we used to dwell,
I would have rather felt you round my throat
Crushing out life; than waving me farewell!
   The Garden of Kama (1901) 'Kashmiri Song'

4 Less than the dust, beneath thy Chariot wheel,
Less than the rust, that never stained thy Sword,
Less than the trust thou hast in me, Oh, Lord,
Even less than these!
Less than the weed, that grows beside thy door,
Less than the speed, of hours, spent far from thee,
Less than the need thou hast in life of me.
Even less am I.
   The Garden of Kama (1901) 'Less than the Dust'

Gerard Manley Hopkins 1844–89

English poet and priest

5 Ten or twelve, only ten or twelve
Strokes of havoc únselve
The sweet especial scene,
Rural scene, a rural scene,
Sweet especial rural scene.
   'Binsey Poplars' (written 1879)

6 Wild air, world-mothering air,
Nestling me everywhere.
   'The Blessed Virgin Compared to the Air We Breathe'
   (written 1883)

7 Not, I'll not, carrion comfort, Despair, not feast on
thee;
Not untwist—slack they may be—these last strands of
man
In me or, most weary, cry *I can no more.* I can;
Can something, hope, wish day come, not choose not
to be.
   'Carrion Comfort' (written 1885)

8   That night, that year
Of now done darkness I wretch lay wrestling with (my
God!) my God.
   'Carrion Comfort' (written 1885)

9 Towery city and branchy between towers;
Cuckoo-echoing, bell-swarmèd, lark-charmèd,
rook-racked, river-rounded.
   'Duns Scotus's Oxford' (written 1879)

10 The world is charged with the grandeur of God.
It will flame out like shining from shook foil . . .
Generations have trod, have trod, have trod;
And all is seared with trade; bleared, smeared with
toil;
And wears man's smudge and shares man's smell: the
soil
Is bare now, nor can foot feel, being shod.
   'God's Grandeur' (written 1877)

11   Because the Holy Ghost over the bent
World broods with warm breast and with ah! bright
wings.
   'God's Grandeur' (written 1877)

12 Elected Silence, sing to me
And beat upon my whorlèd ear,
Pipe me to pastures still and be
The music that I care to hear.
   'The Habit of Perfection' (written 1866)

13 Palate, the hutch of tasty lust,
Desire not to be rinsed with wine:
The can must be so sweet, the crust
So fresh that come in fasts divine!
   'The Habit of Perfection' (written 1866)

14 I have desired to go
Where springs not fail,
To fields where flies no sharp and sided hail
And a few lilies blow.
And I have asked to be
Where no storms come,
Where the green swell is in the havens dumb,
And out of the swing of the sea.
   'Heaven-Haven' (written 1864)

15 What would the world be, once bereft
Of wet and wildness? Let them be left,
O let them be left, wildness and wet;
Long live the weeds and the wilderness yet.
   'Inversnaid' (written 1881)

16 No worst, there is none. Pitched past pitch of grief,
More pangs will, schooled at forepangs, wilder wring.
Comforter, where, where is your comforting?
   'No worst, there is none' (written 1885)

17 O the mind, mind has mountains; cliffs of fall
Frightful, sheer, no-man-fathomed. Hold them cheap
May who ne'er hung there.
   'No worst, there is none' (written 1885)

18   Here! creep,
Wretch, under a comfort serves in a whirlwind: all
Life death does end and each day dies with sleep.
   'No worst, there is none' (written 1885)

19 Glory be to God for dappled things.
   'Pied Beauty' (written 1877)

20 All things counter, original, spare, strange;
Whatever is fickle, freckled (who knows how?)
With swift, slow; sweet, sour; adazzle, dim;
He fathers-forth whose beauty is past change:
Praise him.
   'Pied Beauty' (written 1877)

1 The glassy peartree leaves and blooms, they brush
  The descending blue; that blue is all in a rush
  With richness.
  'Spring' (written 1877)

2 Márgarét, áre you gríeving
  Over Goldengrove unleaving?
  'Spring and Fall: to a young child' (written 1880)

3 Áh! ás the heart grows older
  It will come to such sights colder
  By and by, not spare a sigh
  Though worlds of wanwood leafmeal lie;
  And yet you *will* weep and know why.
  'Spring and Fall: to a young child' (written 1880)

4 It ís the blight man was born for,
  It is Margaret you mourn for.
  'Spring and Fall: to a young child' (written 1880)

5 Look at the stars! look, look up at the skies!
  O look at all the fire-folk sitting in the air!
  The bright boroughs, the circle citadels there!
  'The Starlight Night' (written 1877)

6 Ah well! it is all a purchase, all is a prize.
  Buy then! bid then!—What?— Prayer, patience, alms, vows.
  Look, look: a May-mess, like on orchard boughs!
  Look! March-bloom, like on mealed-with-yellow sallows!
  These are indeed the barn; withindoors house
  The shocks. This piece-bright paling shuts the spouse
  Christ home, Christ and his mother and all his hallows.
  'The Starlight Night' (written 1877)

7 I am all at once what Christ is, since he was what I am, and
  This Jack, joke, poor potsherd, patch, matchwood, immortal diamond,
  Is immortal diamond.
  'That Nature is a Heraclitean Fire' (written 1888)

8 Thou art indeed just, Lord, if I contend
  With thee; but, sir, so what I plead is just.
  Why do sinners' ways prosper? and why must
  Disappointment all I endeavour end?
  'Thou art indeed just, Lord' (written 1889)

9 Birds build—but not I build; no, but strain,
  Time's eunuch, and not breed one work that wakes.
  Mine, O thou lord of life, send my roots rain.
  'Thou art indeed just, Lord' (written 1889)

10 I caught this morning morning's minion, kingdom of daylight's dauphin, dapple-dawn-drawn Falcon.
  'The Windhover' (written 1877)

11   My heart in hiding
  Stirred for a bird,—the achieve of, the mastery of the thing!
  'The Windhover' (written 1877)

12   I did say yes
  O at lightning and lashed rod;
  Thou heardst me truer than tongue confess
  Thy terror, O Christ, O God.
  'The Wreck of the Deutschland' (written 1876) pt. 1, st. 2

13 How a lush-kept plush-capped sloe
  Will, mouthed to flesh-burst,
  Gush!—flush the man, the being with it, sour or sweet,
  Brim, in a flash, full!
  'The Wreck of the Deutschland' (written 1876) pt. 1, st. 8

14 Time has three dimensions and one positive pitch or direction. It is therefore not so much like any river or any sea as like the Sea of Galilee, which has the Jordan running through it and giving a current to the whole.
  'Creation and Redemption The Great Sacrifice' (written 1881), in Christopher Devlin (ed.) *The Sermons and Devotional Writings of Gerard Manley Hopkins* (1959) ch. 8

15 Crystal sincerity hath found no shelter but in a fool's cap.
  Floris in Italy (written 1864) prose scene; in H. House and G. Storey (eds.) *The Journals and Papers of Gerard Manley Hopkins* (1959) p. 42

16 To lift up the hands in prayer gives God glory, but a man with a dungfork in his hand, a woman with a slop-pail, give him glory too. He is so great that all things give him glory if you mean they should.
  G. Roberts (ed.) *Gerard Manley Hopkins. Selected Prose* (1980) 'The Principle or Foundation' (1882) ad fin.

17 I am surprised you should say fancy and aesthetic tastes have led me to my present state of mind; these would be better satisfied in the Church of England, for bad taste is always meeting one in the accessories of Catholicism.
  On his adoption of the Catholic faith, in a letter to his father, 16 October 1866; in G. Roberts (ed.) *Gerard Manley Hopkins. Selected Prose* (1980)

18 I can scarcely fancy myself to ask a superior to publish a volume of my verses and I own that humanly there is very little likelihood of that ever coming to pass. And to be sure if I chose to look at things on one side and not the other I could of course regret this bitterly. But there is more peace and it is the holier lot to be unknown than to be known.
  Letter to Richard Watson Dixon, 29 October 1881, in C. C. Abbott (ed.) *The Correspondence of Gerard Manley Hopkins and Richard Watson Dixon* (1935)

19 The fine pleasure is not to do a thing but to feel that you could . . . If I could but get on, if I could but produce a work I should not mind its being buried, silenced, and going no further; but it kills me to be time's eunuch and never to beget.
  Letter to Robert Bridges, 1 September 1885, in C. C. Abbott (ed.) *The Correspondence of Gerard Manley Hopkins and Robert Bridges* (1935)

Joseph Hopkinson 1770–1842
American politician

20 Hail, Columbia! happy land!
  Hail, ye heroes! heaven-born band!
  'Hail, Columbia!' in *Porcupine's Gazette* 20 April 1798

Horace (Quintus Horatius Flaccus) 65–8 BC

Roman poet

1   Ut turpiter atrum
Desinat in piscem mulier formosa superne.

So that what is a beautiful woman on top ends in a
black and ugly fish.
  Ars Poetica l. 3

2   'Pictoribus atque poetis
Quidlibet audendi semper fuit aequa potestas.'
Scimus, et hanc veniam petimusque damusque vicissim.

'Painters and poets alike have always had licence to
dare anything.' We know that, and we both claim and
permit others this indulgence.
  Ars Poetica l. 9

3 Inceptis gravibus plerumque et magna professis
Purpureus, late qui splendeat, unus et alter
Adsuitur pannus.

Works of serious purpose and grand promises often
have a purple patch or two stitched on, to shine far
and wide.
  Ars Poetica l. 14

4   Brevis esse laboro,
Obscurus fio.

I strive to be brief, and I become obscure.
  Ars Poetica l. 25

5 Dixeris egregie notum si callida verbum
Reddiderit iunctura novum.

You will have written exceptionally well if, by skilful
arrangement of your words, you have made an
ordinary one seem original.
  Ars Poetica l. 47

6 Multa renascentur quae iam cecidere, cadentque
Quae nunc sunt in honore vocabula, si volet usus,
Quem penes arbitrium est et ius et norma loquendi.

Many terms which have now dropped out of favour
will be revived, and those that are at present
respectable will drop out, if usage so choose, with
whom lies the decision, the judgement, and the rule of
speech.
  Ars Poetica l. 70

7 Grammatici certant et adhuc sub iudice lis est.

Scholars dispute, and the case is still before the courts.
  Ars Poetica l. 78

8 Proicit ampullas et sesquipedalia verba.

He throws aside his paint-pots and his words a foot
and a half long.
  Ars Poetica l. 97

9   Si vis me flere, dolendum est
Primum ipsi tibi.

If you want me to weep, you must first feel grief
yourself.
  Ars Poetica l. 102

10 Difficile est proprie communia dicere.

It is hard to utter common notions in an individual
way.
  Ars Poetica l. 128

11 Parturient montes, nascetur ridiculus mus.

Mountains will go into labour, and a silly little mouse
will be born.
  Ars Poetica l. 139

12 Non fumum ex fulgore, sed ex fumo dare lucem
Cogitat.

His thinking does not produce smoke after the flame,
but light after smoke.
  Ars Poetica l. 143

13 Semper ad eventum festinat et in medias res
Non secus ac notas auditorem rapit.

He always hurries to the main event and whisks his
audience into the middle of things as though they
knew already.
  Ars Poetica l. 148

14 Difficilis, querulus, laudator temporis acti
Se puero, castigator censorque minorum.

Tiresome, complaining, a praiser of past times, when
he was a boy, a castigator and censor of the young
generation.
  Ars Poetica l. 173

15 Omne tulit punctum qui miscuit utile dulci,
Lectorem delectando pariterque monendo.

He has gained every point who has mixed profit with
pleasure, by delighting the reader at the same time as
instructing him.
  Ars Poetica l. 343

16 Verum ubi plura nitent in carmine, non ego paucis
Offendar maculis.

When many beauties grace a poem, I shall not take
offence at a few faults.
  Ars Poetica l. 351

17 Indignor quandoque bonus dormitat Homerus.

I'm aggrieved when sometimes even excellent Homer
nods.
  Ars Poetica l. 359

18 Ut pictura poesis.

A poem is like a painting.
  Ars Poetica l. 361

19   Mediocribus esse poetis
Non homines, non di, non concessere columnae.

Not gods, nor men, nor even booksellers have put up
with poets being second-rate.
  Ars Poetica l. 372

20 Nullius addictus iurare in verba magistri,
Quo me cumque rapit tempestas, deferor hospes.

Not bound to swear allegiance to any master,
wherever the wind takes me I travel as a visitor.
  Epistles bk. 1, no. 1, l. 14. *Nullius in verba* is the motto of
  the Royal Society

21 Condicio dulcis sine pulvere palmae.

The happy state of winning the palm without the dust
of racing.
  Epistles bk. 1, no. 1, l. 51

22 Si possis recte, si non, quocumque modo rem.

If possible honestly, if not, somehow, make money.
  Epistles bk. 1, no. 1, l. 66

1 *Olim quod vulpes aegroto cauta leoni*
Respondit referam: 'quia me vestigia terrent,
Omnia te adversum spectantia, nulla retrorsum.'

Let me remind you what the wary fox said once upon a time to the sick lion: 'Because those footprints scare me, all directed your way, none coming back.'

Epistles bk. 1, no. 1, l. 73 (explaining why he did not follow popular opinion)

2 *Quidquid delirant reges plectuntur Achivi.*

Whatever madness their kings commit, the Greeks take the beating.

Epistles bk. 1, no. 2, l. 14

3 *Nos numerus sumus et fruges consumere nati.*

We are just statistics, born to consume resources.

Epistles bk. 1, no. 2, l. 27

4 *Dimidium facti qui coepit habet: sapere aude.*

To have begun is half the job: be bold and be sensible.

Epistles bk. 1, no. 2, l. 40

5 *Ira furor brevis est.*

Anger is a short madness.

Epistles bk. 1, no. 2, l. 62

6 *Omnem crede diem tibi diluxisse supremum.*
Grata superveniet quae non sperabitur hora.
Me pinguem et nitidum bene curata cute vises
Cum ridere voles Epicuri de grege porcum.

Believe each day that has dawned is your last. Some hour to which you have not been looking forward will prove lovely. As for me, if you want a good laugh, you will come and find me fat and sleek, in excellent condition, one of Epicurus's herd of pigs.

Epistles bk. 1, no. 4, l. 13

7 *Nil admirari prope res est una, Numici,*
Solaque quae possit facere et servare beatum.

To marvel at nothing is just about the one and only thing, Numicius, that can make a man happy and keep him that way.

Epistles bk. 1, no. 6, l. 1

8 *Naturam expelles furca, tamen usque recurret.*

You may drive out nature with a pitchfork, yet she'll be constantly running back.

Epistles bk. 1, no. 10, l. 24

9 *Caelum non animum mutant qui trans mare currunt.*
Strenua nos exercet inertia: navibus atque
Quadrigis petimus bene vivere. Quod petis hic est,
Est Ulubris, animus si te non deficit aequus.

They change their clime, not their frame of mind, who rush across the sea. We strain at achieving nothing: we seek happiness in boats and carriage rides. What you seek is here, at Ulubrae, so long as peace of mind does not desert you.

Epistles bk. 1, no. 11, l. 27

10 *Concordia discors.*

Discordant harmony.

Epistles bk. 1, no. 12, l. 19

11 *Principibus placuisse viris non ultima laus est.*
Non cuivis homini contingit adire Corinthum.

It is not the least praise to have pleased leading men. Not everyone is lucky enough to get to Corinth.

Epistles bk. 1, no. 17, l. 35

12 *Et semel emissum volat irrevocabile verbum.*

And once sent out a word takes wing beyond recall.

Epistles bk. 1, no. 18, l. 71

13 *Nam tua res agitur, paries cum proximus ardet.*

For it is your business, when the wall next door catches fire.

Epistles bk. 1, no. 18, l. 84

14 *Fallentis semita vitae.*

The pathway of a life unnoticed.

Epistles bk. 1, no. 18, l. 103

15 *Nulla placere diu nec vivere carmina possunt*
Quae scribuntur aquae potoribus.

No verse can give pleasure for long, nor last, that is written by drinkers of water.

Epistles bk. 1, no. 19, l. 2

16 *O imitatores, servum pecus.*

O imitators, you slavish herd.

Epistles bk. 1, no. 19, l. 19

17 *Scribimus indocti doctique poemata passim.*

Skilled or unskilled, we all scribble poems.

Epistles bk. 2, no. 1, l. 117. Cf. Pope 523:3

18 *Si foret in terris, rideret Democritus.*

If he were on earth, Democritus would laugh at the sight.

Epistles bk. 2, no. 1, l. 194

19 *Atque inter silvas Academi quaerere verum.*

And seek for truth in the groves of Academe.

Epistles bk. 2, no. 2, l. 45

20 *Multa fero, ut placem genus irritabile vatum.*

I have to put up with a lot, to please the touchy breed of poets.

Epistles bk. 2, no. 2, l. 102

21 *Quid te exempta iuvat spinis de pluribus una?*
Vivere si recte nescis, decede peritis.
Lusisti satis, edisti satis atque bibisti:
Tempus abire tibi est.

What pleasure does it give to be rid of one thorn out of many? If you don't know how to live right, give way to those who are expert at it. You have had enough fun, eaten and drunk enough: it is time for you to go.

Epistles bk. 2, no. 2, l. 212

22 *Beatus ille, qui procul negotiis,*
Ut prisca gens mortalium,
Paterna rura bubus exercet suis,
Solutus omni faenore.

Happy the man who, far away from business, like the race of men of old, tills his ancestral fields with his own oxen, unbound by any interest to pay.

Epodes epode 2, l. 1

23 *Indocilis pauperiem pati.*

Untaught to bear poverty.

Odes bk. 1, no. 1, l. 18

24 *Quodsi me lyricis vatibus inseres,*
Sublimi feriam sidera vertice.

And if you include me among the lyric poets, I'll hold my head so high it'll strike the stars.

Odes bk. 1, no. 1, l. 35

1 *Animae dimidium meae.*

Half my own soul.
> *Odes* bk. 1, no. 3, l. 8 (of Virgil)

2 *Illi robur et aes triplex*
Circa pectus erat, qui fragilem truci
Commisit pelago ratem
Primus.

Oak was round his breast, and triple bronze, who first
launched his frail boat on the rough sea.
> *Odes* bk. 1, no. 3, l. 9

3 *Pallida Mors aequo pulsat pede pauperum tabernas*
Regumque turris.

Pale Death breaks into the cottages of the poor as into
the castles of kings.
> *Odes* bk. 1, no. 4, l. 13

4 *Vitae summa brevis spem nos vetat incohare longam.*

Life's short span forbids us to enter on far-reaching
hopes.
> *Odes* bk. 1, no. 4, l. 15

5 *Nil desperandum.*

Never despair.
> *Odes* bk. 1, no. 7, l. 27

6 *Cras ingens iterabimus aequor.*

Tomorrow we shall sail again on the vast ocean.
> *Odes* bk. 1, no. 7, l. 32

7 *Quid sit futurum cras fuge quaerere et*
Quem Fors dierum cumque dabit lucro
Appone.

Drop the question what tomorrow may bring, and
count as profit every day that Fate allows you.
> *Odes* bk. 1, no. 9, l. 13

8 *Tu ne quaesieris, scire nefas, quem mihi, quem tibi*
Finem di dederint.

Do not try to find out—we're forbidden to
know—what end the gods may bestow on me or you.
> *Odes* bk. 1, no. 11, l. 1

9 *Dum loquimur, fugerit invida*
Aetas: carpe diem, quam minimum credula postero.

While we're talking, envious time is fleeing: seize the
day, put no trust in the future.
> *Odes* bk. 1, no. 11, l. 7

10 *Felices ter et amplius*
Quos irrupta tenet copula nec malis
Divulsus querimoniis
Suprema citius solvet amor die.

Thrice blessed (and more) are they whom an
unbroken bond holds and whose love, never strained
by nasty quarrels, will not slip until their dying day.
> *Odes* bk. 1, no. 13, l. 17

11 *Integer vitae scelerisque purus.*

Wholesome of life and free of crimes.
> *Odes* bk. 1, no. 22, l. 1

12 *Dulce ridentem Lalagen amabo,*
Dulce loquentem.

I will go on loving Lalage, who laughs so sweetly and
talks so sweetly.
> *Odes* bk. 1, no. 22, l. 23

13 *Parcus deorum cultor et infrequens.*

A grudging and irregular worshipper of the gods.
> *Odes* bk. 1, no. 34, l. 1

14 *Nunc est bibendum, nunc pede libero*
Pulsanda tellus.

Now for drinking, now the Earth must shake beneath
a lively foot.
> *Odes* bk. 1, no. 37, l. 1

15 *Persicos odi, puer, apparatus.*

I hate all that Persian gear, boy.
> *Odes* bk. 1, no. 38, l. 1

16 *Mitte sectari, rosa quo locorum*
Sera moretur.

Stop looking for the place where a late rose may yet
linger.
> *Odes* bk. 1, no. 38, l. 3

17 *Aequam memento rebus in arduis*
Servare mentem.

When the going gets rough, remember to keep calm.
> *Odes* bk. 2, no. 3, l. 1

18 *Auream quisquis mediocritatem*
Diligit.

Someone who loves the golden mean.
> *Odes* bk. 2, no. 10, l. 5

19 *Eheu fugaces, Postume, Postume,*
Labuntur anni.

Ah me, Postumus, Postumus, the fleeting years are
slipping by.
> *Odes* bk. 2, no. 14, l. 1

20 *Nihil est ab omni*
Parte beatum.

Nothing is an unmixed blessing.
> *Odes* bk. 2, no. 16, l. 27

21 *Credite posteri.*

Believe me, you who come after me!
> *Odes* bk. 2, no. 19, l. 2

22 *Odi profanum vulgus et arceo;*
Favete linguis; carmina non prius
Auditu Musarum sacerdos
Virginibus puerisque canto.

I hate the common herd and keep them off. Hush your
tongues; as a priest of the Muses, I sing songs never
heard before to virgin girls and boys.
> *Odes* bk. 3, no. 1, l. 1

23 *Omne capax movet urna nomen.*

The enormous tombola shakes up everyone's name.
> *Odes* bk. 3, no. 1, l. 16

24 *Post equitem sedet atra Cura.*

Black Care sits behind the horseman.
> *Odes* bk. 3, no. 1, l. 40

25 *Dulce et decorum est pro patria mori.*

Lovely and honourable it is to die for one's country.
> *Odes* bk. 3, no. 2, l. 13. (referred to as 'The old Lie' by
> Wilfred Owen)

1 *Iustum et tenacem propositi virum*
Non civium ardor prava iubentium,
Non vultus instantis tyranni
Mente quatit solida.

The just man having a firm grasp of his intentions, neither the heated passions of his fellow men ordaining something awful, nor a tyrant staring him in the face, will shake in his convictions.
Odes bk. 3, no. 3, l. 1

2 *Si fractus illabatur orbis,*
Impavidum ferient ruinae.

If the world should break and fall on him, its ruins would strike him unafraid.
Odes bk. 3, no. 3, l. 7

3   *Opaco*
Pelion imposuisse Olympo.

To pile Pelion on top of shady Olympus.
Odes bk. 3, no. 4, l. 52

4 *Vis consili expers mole ruit sua.*

Force, unaided by judgement, collapses through its own weight.
Odes bk. 3, no. 4, l. 65

5 *Damnosa quid non imminuit dies?*
Aetas parentum peior avis tulit
Nos nequiores, mox daturos
Progeniem vitiosiorem.

What do the ravages of time not injure? Our parents' age (worse than our grandparents') has produced us, more worthless still, who will soon give rise to a yet more vicious generation.
Odes bk. 3, no. 6, l. 45

6 *Splendide mendax et in omne virgo*
Nobilis aevum.

Gloriously deceitful and a virgin renowned for ever.
Odes bk. 3, no. 11, l. 35 (of the Danaid Hypermestra)

7 *Magnas inter opes inops.*

A beggar amidst great riches.
Odes bk. 3, no. 16, l. 28

8 *Fumum et opes strepitumque Romae.*

The smoke and wealth and din of Rome.
Odes bk. 3, no. 29, l. 12

9 *Exegi monumentum aere perennius.*

I have erected a monument more lasting than bronze.
Odes bk. 3, no. 30, l. 1

10 *Non omnis moriar.*

I shall not altogether die.
Odes bk. 3, no. 30, l. 6

11 *Non sum qualis eram bonae*
Sub regno Cinarae.

I am not as I was when good Cinara was my queen.
Odes bk. 4, no. 1, l. 3

12 *Quod spiro et placeo, si placeo, tuum est.*

That I make poetry and give pleasure (if I give pleasure) are because of you.
Odes bk. 4, no. 3, l. 24

13 *Merses profundo: pulchrior evenit.*

Plunge it in deep water: it comes up more beautiful.
Odes bk. 4, no. 4, l. 65

14   *Occidit, occidit*
Spes omnis et fortuna nostri
Nominis Hasdrubale interempto.

All our hope is fallen, fallen, and the luck of our name lost with Hasdrubal.
Odes bk. 4, no. 4, l. 70

15 *Diffugere nives, redeunt iam gramina campis*
Arboribusque comae.

The snows have dispersed, now grass returns to the fields and leaves to the trees.
Odes bk. 4, no. 7, l. 1

16 *Immortalia ne speres, monet annus et almum*
Quae rapit hora diem.

The year and the hour which robs us of the fair day warn us not to hope for things to last for ever.
Odes bk. 4, no. 7, l. 7

17 *Dignum laude virum Musa vetat mori.*

The man worthy of praise the Muse forbids to die.
Odes bk. 4, no. 8, l. 28

18 *Vixere fortes ante Agamemnona*
Multi; sed omnes illacrimabiles
Urgentur ignotique longa
Nocte, carent quia vate sacro.

Many brave men lived before Agamemnon's time; but they are all, unmourned and unknown, covered by the long night, because they lack their sacred poet.
Odes bk. 4, no. 9, l. 25

19 *Non possidentem multa vocaveris*
Recte beatum: rectius occupat
Nomen beati, qui deorum
Muneribus sapienter uti
Duramque callet pauperiem pati
Peiusque leto flagitium timet.

It is not he who has many possessions that you should call blessed: he more rightly deserves that name who knows how to use the gods' gifts wisely and to endure harsh poverty, and who fears dishonour more than death.
Odes bk. 4, no. 9, l. 45

20 *Misce stultitiam consiliis brevem:*
Dulce est desipere in loco.

Mix a little foolishness with your prudence: it's good to be silly at the right moment.
Odes bk. 4, no. 12, l. 27

21 *Qui fit, Maecenas, ut nemo, quam sibi sortem*
Seu ratio dederit seu fors obiecerit, illa
Contentus vivat, laudet diversa sequentis?

How is it, Maecenas, that no one lives contented with his lot, whether he has planned it for himself or fate has flung him into it, but yet he praises those who follow different paths?
Satires bk. 1, no. 1, l. 1

22 *. . . Mutato nomine de te*
Fabula narratur.

Change the name and it's about you, that story.
Satires bk. 1, no. 1, l. 69

23 *Est modus in rebus.*

There is moderation in everything.
Satires bk. 1, no. 1, l. 106

1 *Hoc genus omne.*

All that tribe.

   Satires bk. 1, no. 2, l. 2

2 ... *Ab ovo*
Usque ad mala.

From the egg right through to the apples.

   Satires bk. 1, no. 3, l. 6 (i.e. from the start to the finish of a
   meal)

3 *Etiam disiecti membra poetae.*

Even though broken up, the limbs of a poet.

   Satires bk. 1, no. 4, l. 62 (of Ennius)

4 ... *Ad unguem*
Factus homo.

An accomplished man to his finger-tips.

   Satires bk. 1, no. 5, l. 32

5 ... *Credat Iudaeus Apella,*
Non ego.

Let Apella the Jew believe it; I shan't.

   Satires bk. 1, no. 5, l. 100

6 *In silvam ... ligna feras insanius.*

It's insane to carry timber to the forest.

   Satires bk. 1, no. 10, l. 34

7 *Solventur risu tabulae, tu missus abibis.*

The case will be dismissed with a laugh. You will get
off scot-free.

   Satires bk. 2, no. 1, l. 86 (translated by H. R. Fairclough)

8 *Par nobile fratrum.*

A noble pair of brothers.

   Satires bk. 2, no. 3, l. 243 (i.e. notorious villains)

9 *Hoc erat in votis: modus agri non ita magnus,*
Hortus ubi et tecto vicinus iugis aquae fons
Et paulum silvae super his foret.

This was among my prayers: a piece of land not so
very large, where a garden should be and a spring of
ever-flowing water near the house, and a bit of
woodland as well as these.

   Satires bk. 2, no. 6, l. 1

10 *O noctes cenaeque deum!*

O nights and feasts divine!

   Satires bk. 2, no. 6, l. 65

11 *Responsare cupidinibus, contemnere honores*
Fortis, et in se ipso totus, teres, atque rotundus.

Strong enough to answer back to desires, to despise
honours, and a whole man in himself, polished and
well-rounded.

   Satires bk. 2, no. 7, l. 85

Samuel Horsley 1733–1806

English bishop

12 In this country ... the individual subject ... 'has
nothing to do with the laws but to obey them.'

   Hansard (Lords) 13 November 1795, col. 268 (defending a
   maxim he had used earlier in committee)

A. E. Housman 1859–1936

English poet

13 Oh who is that young sinner with the handcuffs on
      his wrists?
   And what has he been after that they groan and
      shake their fists?
   And wherefore is he wearing such
      a conscience-stricken air?
   Oh they're taking him to prison for the colour of his
      hair.

   Collected Poems (1939) 'Additional Poems' no. 18

14 Mud's sister, not himself, adorns my legs.

   Fragment of a Greek Tragedy (Bromsgrovian vol. 2, no. 5,
   1883)

15 The Grizzly Bear is huge and wild;
   He has devoured the infant child.
   The infant child is not aware
   He has been eaten by the bear.

   'Infant Innocence' (1938)

16 Pass me the can, lad; there's an end of May.

   Last Poems (1922) no. 9

17 May will be fine next year as like as not:
   Oh, ay, but then we shall be twenty-four.

   Last Poems (1922) no. 9

18 The troubles of our proud and angry dust
   Are from eternity, and shall not fail.
   Bear them we can, and if we can we must.
   Shoulder the sky, my lad, and drink your ale.

   Last Poems (1922) no. 9

19 But men at whiles are sober
   And think by fits and starts,
   And if they think, they fasten
   Their hands upon their hearts.

   Last Poems (1922) no. 10

20 And how am I to face the odds
   Of man's bedevilment and God's?
   I, a stranger and afraid
   In a world I never made.

   Last Poems (1922) no. 12

21 The candles burn their sockets,
   The blinds let through the day,
   The young man feels his pockets
   And wonders what's to pay.

   Last Poems (1922) no. 21

22 These, in the day when heaven was falling,
   The hour when earth's foundations fled,
   Followed their mercenary calling
   And took their wages and are dead.

   Their shoulders held the sky suspended;
   They stood, and earth's foundations stay;
   What God abandoned, these defended,
   And saved the sum of things for pay.

   Last Poems (1922) no. 37 'Epitaph on an Army of
   Mercenaries'

1 For nature, heartless, witless nature,
Will neither care nor know
What stranger's feet may find the meadow
And trespass there and go,
Nor ask amid the dews of morning
If they are mine or no.
Last Poems (1922) no. 40

2 The rainy Pleiads wester,
Orion plunges prone,
The stroke of midnight ceases,
And I lie down alone.
More Poems (1936) no. 11

3 Life, to be sure, is nothing much to lose;
But young men think it is, and we were young.
More Poems (1936) no. 36

4 Good-night. Ensured release
Imperishable peace,
Have these for yours,
While earth's foundations stand
And sky and sea and land
And heaven endures.
More Poems (1936) no. 48 'Alta Quies'

5 Loveliest of trees, the cherry now
Is hung with bloom along the bough,
And stands about the woodland ride
Wearing white for Eastertide.
A Shropshire Lad (1896) no. 2

6 And since to look at things in bloom
Fifty springs are little room,
About the woodlands I will go
To see the cherry hung with snow.
A Shropshire Lad (1896) no. 2

7 Clay lies still, but blood's a rover;
Breath's a ware that will not keep.
Up, lad: when the journey's over
There'll be time enough to sleep.
A Shropshire Lad (1896) no. 4

8 And naked to the hangman's noose
The morning clocks will ring
A neck God made for other use
Than strangling in a string.
A Shropshire Lad (1896) no. 9

9 When I was one-and-twenty
I heard a wise man say,
'Give crowns and pounds and guineas
But not your heart away;
Give pearls away and rubies,
But keep your fancy free.'
But I was one-and-twenty,
No use to talk to me.
A Shropshire Lad (1896) no. 13

10 In summertime on Bredon
The bells they sound so clear;
Round both the shires they ring them
In steeples far and near,
A happy noise to hear.

Here of a Sunday morning
My love and I would lie,
And see the coloured counties,
And hear the larks so high
About us in the sky.
A Shropshire Lad (1896) no. 21

11 The lads in their hundreds to Ludlow come in for the fair,
There's men from the barn and the forge and the mill and the fold,
The lads for the girls and the lads for the liquor are there,
And there with the rest are the lads that will never be old.
A Shropshire Lad (1896) no. 23

12 On Wenlock Edge the wood's in trouble;
His forest fleece the Wrekin heaves;
The wind it plies the saplings double,
And thick on Severn snow the leaves.
A Shropshire Lad (1896) no. 31

13 The gale, it plies the saplings double,
It blows so hard, 'twill soon be gone:
To-day the Roman and his trouble
Are ashes under Uricon.
A Shropshire Lad (1896) no. 31

14 From far, from eve and morning
And yon twelve-winded sky,
The stuff of life to knit me
Blew hither: here am I.
A Shropshire Lad (1896) no. 32

15 Into my heart an air that kills
From yon far country blows:
What are those blue remembered hills,
What spires, what farms are those?

That is the land of lost content,
I see it shining plain,
The happy highways where I went
And cannot come again.
A Shropshire Lad (1896) no. 40

16 And bound for the same bourn as I,
On every road I wandered by,
Trod beside me, close and dear,
The beautiful and death-struck year.
A Shropshire Lad (1896) no. 41

17 Clunton and Clunbury,
Clungunford and Clun,
Are the quietest places
Under the sun.
A Shropshire Lad (1896) no. 50 (epigraph)

18 By brooks too broad for leaping
The lightfoot boys are laid;
The rose-lipt girls are sleeping
In fields where roses fade.
A Shropshire Lad (1896) no. 54

19 Say, for what were hop-yards meant,
Or why was Burton built on Trent?
Oh many a peer of England brews
Livelier liquor than the Muse,
And malt does more than Milton can
To justify God's ways to man.
Ale, man, ale's the stuff to drink
For fellows whom it hurts to think.
A Shropshire Lad (1896) no. 62. Cf. Milton 467:21

20 I tell the tale that I heard told.
Mithridates, he died old.
A Shropshire Lad (1896) no. 62

1 This great College, of this ancient University, has seen
some strange sights. It has seen Wordsworth drunk
and Porson sober. And here am I, a better poet than
Porson, and a better scholar than Wordsworth,
betwixt and between.
      Speech at Trinity College, Cambridge, in G. K. Chesterton
      Autobiography (1936) ch. 12

Julia Ward Howe 1819–1910

American Unitarian lay preacher

2 Mine eyes have seen the glory of the coming of the
Lord:
He is trampling out the vintage where the grapes of
  wrath are stored;
He hath loosed the fateful lightning of his terrible swift
  sword:
His truth is marching on.
      'Battle Hymn of the Republic' (1862)

James Howell c.1593–1666

Anglo-Welsh man of letters

3 Some hold translations not unlike to be
The wrong side of a Turkey tapestry.
      Familiar Letters (1645–55) bk. 1, no. 6

4 One hair of a woman can draw more than a hundred
pair of oxen.
      Familiar Letters (1645–55) bk. 2, no. 4

Frankie Howerd (*Francis Alex Howard*) 1922–92

British comedian

5 Such cruel glasses.
      Of Robin Day in *That Was The Week That Was* (BBC
      television series, from 1963)

Mary Howitt (*née Botham*) 1799–1888

English writer for children

6 Buttercups and daisies,
Oh, the pretty flowers;
Coming ere the springtime,
To tell of sunny hours.
      'Buttercups and Daisies' (1838)

7 'Will you walk into my parlour?' said a spider to a fly:
'Tis the prettiest little parlour that ever you did spy.'
      'The Spider and the Fly' (1834)

Edmond Hoyle 1672–1769

English writer on card-games

8 When in doubt, win the trick.
      Hoyle's Games Improved (ed. Charles Jones, 1790)
      'Twenty-four Short Rules for Learners' (though attributed
      to Hoyle, this may well have been an editorial addition by
      Jones, since it is not found in earlier editions)

Elbert Hubbard 1859–1915

American writer

9 Never explain—your friends do not need it and your
enemies will not believe you anyway.
      The Motto Book (1907) p. 31. Cf. Wodehouse 740:18

10 Life is just one damned thing after another.
      Philistine December 1909, p. 32 (often attributed to Frank
      Ward O'Malley)

11 Editor: a person employed by a newspaper, whose
business it is to separate the wheat from the chaff, and
to see that the chaff is printed.
      The Roycroft Dictionary (1914) p. 46

Frank McKinney ('Kin') Hubbard 1868–1930

American humorist

12 Classic music is th'kind that we keep thinkin'll turn
into a tune.
      Comments of Abe Martin and His Neighbors (1923)

13 It's no disgrace t'be poor, but it might as well be.
      Short Furrows (1911) p. 42

L. Ron Hubbard 1911–86

American Scientologist and science fiction writer

14 If you really want to make a million . . . the quickest
way is to start your own religion.
      Speaking to the Eastern Science Fiction Association at
      Newark, New Jersey, in 1947; in B. Corydon and L. Ron
      Hubbard Jr. *L. Ron Hubbard* (1987) ch. 3 (Ronald Edward
      DeWolf, formerly L. Ron Hubbard Jr., has now dissociated
      himself from this book and this quotation.)

Howard Hughes Jr. 1905–76

American industrialist, aviator and film producer

15 That man's ears make him look like a taxi-cab with
both doors open.
      Of Clark Gable, in Charles Higham and Joel Greenberg
      Celluloid Muse (1969) p. 156

Jimmy Hughes and Frank Lake

16 They say there's a troopship just leaving Bombay,
Bound for Old Blighty shore,
Heavily laden with time expired men,
Bound for the land they adore.
There's many an airman just finishing his time,
There's many a twirp signing on,
You'll get no promotion this side of the ocean,
So cheer up, my lads, Bless 'em all!
Bless 'em all! Bless 'em all! The long and the short
  and the tall.
      'Bless 'Em All' (1940 song)

Langston Hughes 1902–67

American writer and poet

1 I, too, sing America.

I am the darker brother.
They send me to eat in the kitchen
When company comes.
But I laugh,
And eat well,
And grow strong.
Tomorrow
I'll sit at the table
When company comes
Nobody'll dare
Say to me,
'Eat in the kitchen'
Then.

Besides, they'll see how
beautiful I am
And be ashamed,—

I, too, am America.
    'I, Too' in *Survey Graphic* March 1925

2 'It's powerful,' he said.
    'What?'
    'That one drop of Negro blood—because just *one*
drop of black blood makes a man coloured. *One* drop—
you are a Negro!'
    Simple Takes a Wife (1953) p. 85

Ted Hughes 1930–

English poet

3 Daylong this tomcat lies stretched flat
As an old rough mat, no mouth and no eyes,
Continual wars and wives are what
Have tattered his ears and battered his head.
    'Esther's Tomcat' (1960)

4 It took the whole of Creation
To produce my foot, my each feather:
Now I hold Creation in my foot.
    'Hawk Roosting' (1960)

5   I saw the horses:
Huge in the dense grey—ten together—
Megalith-still. They breathed, making no move,
With draped manes and tilted hind-hooves,
Making no sound.
I passed: not one snorted or jerked its head.
Grey silent fragments
Of a grey silent world.

I listened in emptiness on the moor-ridge.
The curlew's tear turned its edge on the silence.
Slowly detail leafed from the darkness. Then the sun
Orange, red, red erupted
Silently, and splitting to its core tore and flung cloud,
Shook the gulf open, showed blue,
And the big planets hanging.
    'The Horses' (1957)

6 Minute after minute, aeon after aeon,
Nothing lets up or develops.
And this is neither a bad variant nor a tryout.
This is where the staring angels go through.
This is where all the stars bow down.
    'Pibroch' (1967)

7 No, the serpent did not
Seduce Eve to the apple.
All that's simply
Corruption of the facts.

Adam ate the apple.
Eve ate Adam.
The serpent ate Eve.
This is the dark intestine.

The serpent, meanwhile,
Sleeps his meal off in Paradise—
Smiling to hear
God's querulous calling.
    'Theology' (1967)

8 Grape is my mulatto mother
In this frozen whited country. Her veined interior
Hangs hot open for me to re-enter
The blood-coloured glasshouse against which the
    stone world
Thins to a dew and steams off.
    'Wino' (1967)

Thomas Hughes 1822–96

English lawyer, politician, and writer

9 Tom and his younger brothers as they grew up, went
on playing with the village boys without the idea of
equality or inequality (except in wrestling, running,
and climbing) ever entering their heads, as it doesn't
till it's put there by Jack Nastys or fine ladies' maids.
    Tom Brown's Schooldays (1857) pt. 1, ch. 3

10 'I don't care a straw for Greek particles, or the
digamma, no more does his mother. What is he sent
to school for? . . . If he'll only turn out a brave,
helpful, truth-telling Englishman, and a gentleman,
and a Christian, that's all I want,' thought the Squire.
    Tom Brown's Schooldays (1857) pt. 1, ch. 4

11 He never wants anything but what's right and fair;
only when you come to settle what's right and fair,
it's everything that he wants and nothing that you
want. And that's his idea of a compromise. Give me
the Brown compromise when I'm on his side.
    Tom Brown's Schooldays (1857) pt. 2, ch. 2

12 It's more than a game. It's an institution.
    Tom Brown's Schooldays (1857) pt. 2, ch. 7 (of cricket)

Victor Hugo 1802–85

French poet, novelist, and playwright

13 *Le mot, c'est le Verbe, et le Verbe, c'est Dieu.*

The word is the Verb, and the Verb is God.
    Contemplations (1856) bk. 1, no. 8

14 *Souffrons, mais souffrons sur les cimes.*

If suffer we must, let's suffer on the heights.
    Contemplations (1856) bk. 5, no. 26 'Les Malheureux'

15 *On résiste à l'invasion des armées; on ne résiste pas à
l'invasion des idées.*

A stand can be made against invasion by an army; no
stand can be made against invasion by an idea.
    Histoire d'un Crime (written 1851–2, published 1877) pt. 5,
    sect. 10

1 *La symétrie, c'est l'ennui, et l'ennui est le fond même du deuil. Le désespoir bâille.*

Symmetry is tedious, and tedium is the very basis of mourning. Despair yawns.

Les Misérables (1862) vol. 2, bk. 4, ch. 1

2 *Jésus a pleuré, Voltaire a souri; c'est de cette larme divine et de ce sourire humain qu'est faite la douceur de la civilisation actuelle.* (Applaudissements prolongés.)

Jesus wept; Voltaire smiled. Of that divine tear and of that human smile the sweetness of present civilisation is composed. (*Hearty applause.*)

Transcript of centenary oration on Voltaire, 30 May 1878, *Centenaire de Voltaire* (1878)

David Hume 1711–76

Scottish philosopher

3 Custom, then, is the great guide of human life.

An Enquiry Concerning Human Understanding (1748) sect. 5, pt. 1

4 If we take in our hand any volume; of divinity or school metaphysics, for instance; let us ask, *Does it contain any abstract reasoning concerning quantity or number? No. Does it contain any experimental reasoning, concerning matter of fact and existence? No.* Commit it then to the flames: for it can contain nothing but sophistry and illusion.

An Enquiry Concerning Human Understanding (1748) sect. 12, pt. 3

5 Their credulity increases his impudence: and his impudence overpowers their credulity.

An Enquiry Concerning Human Understanding (1748) 'Of Miracles' pt. 2 (of religious enthusiasts)

6 We soon learn that there is nothing mysterious or supernatural in the case, but that all proceeds from the usual propensity of mankind towards the marvellous, and that, though this inclination may at intervals receive a check from sense and learning, it can never be thoroughly extirpated from human nature.

An Enquiry Concerning Human Understanding (1748) 'Of Miracles' pt. 2

7 The Christian religion not only was at first attended with miracles, but even at this day cannot be believed by any reasonable person without one. Mere reason is insufficient to convince us of its veracity: and whoever is moved by faith to assent to it, is conscious of a continued miracle in his own person, which subverts all the principles of his understanding, and gives him a determination to believe what is most contrary to custom and experience.

An Enquiry Concerning Human Understanding (1748) 'Of Miracles' pt. 2

8 Avarice, the spur of industry, is so obstinate a passion, and works its way through so many real dangers and difficulties, that it is not likely to be scared by an imaginary danger, which is so small that it scarcely admits of calculation.

Essays: Moral and Political (1741–2) 'Of Civil Liberty'

9 Money . . . is none of the wheels of trade: it is the oil which renders the motion of the wheels more smooth and easy.

Essays: Moral and Political (1741–2) 'Of Money'

10 How many frivolous quarrels and disgusts are there, which people of common prudence endeavour to forget, when they lie under the necessity of passing their lives together; but which would soon inflame into the most deadly hatred, were they pursued to the utmost, under the prospect of an easy separation?

Essays: Moral and Political (1741–2) 'Of Polygamy and Divorces'

11 It cannot reasonably be doubted, but a little miss, dressed in a new gown for a dancing-school ball, receives as complete enjoyment as the greatest orator, who triumphs in the splendour of his eloquence, while he governs the passions and resolutions of a numerous assembly.

Essays: Moral and Political (1741–2) 'The Sceptic'

12 Should it be said, that, by living under the dominion of a prince, which one might leave, every individual has given a tacit assent to his authority . . . We may as well assert, that a man by remaining in a vessel, freely consents to the dominion of the master; though he was carried on board while asleep, and must leap into the ocean, and perish, the moment he leaves her.

Essays, Moral, Political, and Literary (ed. T. H. Green and T. H. Grose, 1875) 'Of the Original Contract' (1748)

13 In all ages of the world, priests have been enemies of liberty.

Essays, Moral, Political, and Literary (ed. T. H. Green and T. H. Grose, 1875) 'Of the Parties of Great Britain' (1741–2)

14 The heart of man is made to reconcile the most glaring contradictions.

Essays, Moral, Political, and Literary (ed. T. H. Green and T. H. Grose, 1875) 'Of the Parties of Great Britain' (1741–2)

15 In all matters of opinion and science . . . the difference between men is . . . oftener found to lie in generals than in particulars; and to be less in reality than in appearance. An explanation of the terms commonly ends the controversy, and the disputants are surprised to find that they had been quarrelling, while at bottom they agreed in their judgement.

Essays, Moral, Political, and Literary (ed. T. H. Green and T. H. Grose, 1875) 'Of the Standard of Taste' (1757)

16 Beauty is no quality in things themselves. It exists merely in the mind which contemplates them.

Essays, Moral, Political, and Literary (ed. T. H. Green and T. H. Grose, 1875) 'Of the Standard of Taste' (1757)

17 Opposing one species of superstition to another, set them a quarrelling; while we ourselves, during their fury and contention, happily make our escape into the calm, though obscure, regions of philosophy.

Four Dissertations (1757) 'The Natural History of Religion' sect. 15

18 Never literary attempt was more unfortunate than my Treatise of Human Nature. It fell *dead-born from the press.*

My Own Life (1777) ch. 1

19 Poets . . . though liars by profession, always endeavour to give an air of truth to their fictions.

A Treatise upon Human Nature (1739) bk. 1, pt. 3

20 Reason is, and ought only to be the slave of the passions, and can never pretend to any other office than to serve and obey them.

A Treatise upon Human Nature (1739) bk. 2, pt. 3

1 It is not contrary to reason to prefer the destruction of the whole world to the scratching of my finger.
   A Treatise upon Human Nature (1739) bk. 2, pt. 3

2 In every system of morality, which I have hitherto met with, I have always remarked, that the author proceeds for some time in the ordinary way of reasoning, and establishes the being of a god, or makes observations concerning human affairs; when of a sudden I am surprized to find that instead of the usual copulations of proposition, *is* and *is not*, I meet with no proposition that is not connected with an *ought* or an *ought not*. This change is imperceptible; but it is, however, of the last consequence.
   A Treatise upon Human Nature (1739) bk. 3, pt. 1

Hubert Humphrey 1911–78

American Democratic politician

3 Here we are the way politics ought to be in America, the politics of happiness, the politics of purpose and the politics of joy.
   Speech in Washington, 27 April 1968, in *New York Times* 28 April 1968, p. 66

Leigh Hunt 1784–1859

English poet and essayist

4 Abou Ben Adhem (may his tribe increase!)
   Awoke one night from a deep dream of peace,
   And saw, within the moonlight in his room,
   Making it rich, and like a lily in bloom,
   An angel writing in a book of gold:—
   Exceeding peace had made Ben Adhem bold,
   And to the presence in the room he said,
   'What writest thou?'—The vision raised its head,
   And with a look made of all sweet accord,
   Answered, 'The names of those who love the Lord.'
   'Abou Ben Adhem' (1838)

5 ... I pray thee then,
   Write me as one that loves his fellow-men.
   'Abou Ben Adhem' (1838)

6 You strange, astonished-looking, angle-faced,
   Dreary-mouthed, gaping wretches of the sea.
   'The Fish, the Man, and the Spirit' (1836)

7 'By God!' said Francis, 'rightly done!' and he rose from where he sat:
   'No love,' quoth he, 'but vanity, sets love a task like that.'
   'The Glove and the Lions' (1836)

8 The laughing queen that caught the world's great hands.
   'The Nile' (1818); referring to Cleopatra

9 Jenny kissed me when we met,
   Jumping from the chair she sat in;
   Time, you thief, who love to get
   Sweets into your list, put that in:
   Say I'm weary, say I'm sad,
   Say that health and wealth have missed me,
   Say I'm growing old, but add,
   Jenny kissed me.
   'Rondeau' (1838)

10 Stolen sweets are always sweeter,
   Stolen kisses much completer,
   Stolen looks are nice in chapels,
   Stolen, stolen, be your apples.
   'Song of Fairies Robbing an Orchard' (1830)

11 And all the scene, in short—sky, earth, and sea,
   Breathes like a bright-eyed face, that laughs out openly.
   'Tis nature, full of spirits, waked and springing:—
   The birds to the delicious time are singing,
   Darting with freaks and snatches up and down,
   Where the light woods go seaward from the town.
   'The Story of Rimini' (1816) canto 1, l. 18

12 The two divinest things this world has got,
   A lovely woman in a rural spot!
   'The Story of Rimini' (1816) canto 3, l. 257

13 His forehead was prodigious—a great piece of placid marble; and his fine eyes, in which all the activity of his mind seemed to concentrate, moved under it with a sprightly ease, as if it was pastime to them to carry all that thought.
   Autobiography (1850) ch. 16 (of S. T. Coleridge)

14 Never lay yourself open to what is called conviction: you might as well open your waist-coat to receive a knock-down blow.
   The Examiner 6 March 1808 'Rules for the Conduct of Newspaper Editors'

15 A playful moderation in politics is just as absurd as a remonstrative whisper to a mob.
   The Examiner 6 March 1808 'Rules for the Conduct of Newspaper Editors'

16 A mere gossiping entertainment: a few child's squalls, a few mumbled amens, and a few mumbled cakes, and a few smirks accompanied by a few fees.
   On the christening of his godson, in a letter to Marianne Kent, February 1806; in T. L. Hunt *Correspondence of Leigh Hunt* (1862) vol. 1

17 A pleasure so exquisite as almost to amount to pain.
   Letter to Alexander Ireland, 2 June 1848, on receiving 'a glorious batch of *Examiners*', in T. L. Hunt *Correspondence of Leigh Hunt* (1862) vol. 2, p. 122

18 It is the entire man that writes and thinks, and not merely the head. His leg has often as much to do with it as his head—the state of his calves, his vitals and his nerves.
   Stories in Verse (1855) preface

19 Poetry, in the most comprehensive application of the term, I take to be the flower of any kind of experience, rooted in truth, and issuing forth into beauty.
   The Story of Rimini (1832 ed.) preface

20 The pretension is nothing; the performance every thing. A good apple is better than an insipid peach.
   The Story of Rimini (1832 ed.) preface

Anne Hunter 1742–1821

Scottish poet

21 My mother bids me bind my hair
   With bands of rosy hue,
   Tie up my sleeves with ribbons rare,
   And lace my bodice blue.
   'A Pastoral Song' (1794)

William Hunter 1718–83

Scottish obstetrician

1 Some physiologists will have it that the stomach is a
mill;—others, that it is a fermenting vat;—others
again that it is a stew-pan;—but in my view of the
matter, it is neither a mill, a fermenting vat, nor a
stew-pan—but a *stomach*, gentlemen, a *stomach*.
  MS note from his lectures, in J. A. Paris *A Treatise on Diet*
  (1824) epigraph

Herman Hupfeld 1894–1951

American songwriter

2 You must remember this, a kiss is still a kiss,
A sigh is just a sigh;
The fundamental things apply,
As time goes by.
  'As Time Goes By' (1931 song). Cf. Epstein 278:7

John Huss c.1372–1415

Bohemian preacher and reformer

3 *O sancta simplicitas!*

O holy simplicity!
  At the stake, seeing an aged peasant bringing a bundle of
  twigs to throw on the pile; in J. W. Zincgreff and J. L.
  Weidner *Apophthegmata* (Amsterdam, 1653) pt. 3, p. 383.
  Cf. Jerome 365:11

Saddam Hussein 1937–

President of Iraq from 1979

4 The mother of battles.
  Popular interpretation of his description of the approaching
  Gulf War, given in a speech in Baghdad, 6 January 1991;
  The Times, 7 January 1991, reported that Saddam had no
  intention of relinquishing Kuwait and was ready for the
  'mother of all wars'

Francis Hutcheson 1694–1746

Scottish philosopher

5 Wisdom denotes the pursuing of the best ends by the
best means.
  An Inquiry into the Original of our Ideas of Beauty and Virtue
  (1725) Treatise 1, sect. 5, subsect. 16

6 That action is best, which procures the greatest
happiness for the greatest numbers.
  An Inquiry into the Original of our Ideas of Beauty and Virtue
  (1725) Treatise 2, sect. 3, subsect. 8. Cf. Bentham
  64:4

Aldous Huxley 1894–1963

English novelist

7 Christlike in my behaviour,
Like every good believer,
I imitate the Saviour,
And cultivate a beaver.
  Antic Hay (1923) ch. 4

8 There are few who would not rather be taken in
adultery than in provincialism.
  Antic Hay (1923) ch. 10

9 Official dignity tends to increase in inverse ratio to the
importance of the country in which the office is held.
  Beyond the Mexique Bay (1934) p. 34

10 The sexophones wailed like melodious cats under the
moon.
  Brave New World (1932) ch. 5

11 The proper study of mankind is books.
  Crome Yellow (1921) ch. 28. Cf. Pope 522:9

12 Too much consistency is as bad for the mind as it is
for the body. Consistency is contrary to nature,
contrary to life. The only completely consistent people
are the dead.
  Do What You Will (1929) 'Wordsworth in the Tropics'

13 The end cannot justify the means, for the simple and
obvious reason that the means employed determine
the nature of the ends produced.
  Ends and Means (1937) ch. 1

14 So long as men worship the Caesars and Napoleons,
Caesars and Napoleons will duly arise and make them
miserable.
  Ends and Means (1937) ch. 8

15 Chastity—the most unnatural of all the sexual
perversions.
  Eyeless in Gaza (1936) ch. 27

16 I can sympathize with people's pains, but not with
their pleasures. There is something curiously boring
about somebody else's happiness.
  Limbo (1920) 'Cynthia'

17 Several excuses are always less convincing than one.
  Point Counter Point (1928) ch. 1

18 Brought up in an epoch when ladies apparently rolled
along on wheels, Mr Quarles was peculiarly
susceptible to calves.
  Point Counter Point (1928) ch. 20

19 A million million spermatozoa,
All of them alive:
Out of their cataclysm but one poor Noah
Dare hope to survive.
And among that billion minus one
Might have chanced to be
Shakespeare, another Newton, a new Donne—
But the One was Me.
  'Fifth Philosopher's Song' (1920)

20 Ragtime . . . but when the wearied Band
Swoons to a waltz, I take her hand,
And there we sit in peaceful calm,
Quietly sweating palm to palm.
  'Frascati's' (1920)

21 Beauty for some provides escape,
Who gain a happiness in eyeing
The gorgeous buttocks of the ape
Or Autumn sunsets exquisitely dying.
  'Ninth Philosopher's Song' (1920)

22 Then brim the bowl with atrabilious liquor!
We'll pledge our Empire vast across the flood:
For Blood, as all men know, than Water's thicker,
But Water's wider, thank the Lord, than Blood.
  'Ninth Philosopher's Song' (1920)

Sir Julian Huxley 1887–1975

English biologist

1 Operationally, God is beginning to resemble not a ruler but the last fading smile of a cosmic Cheshire cat.

Religion without Revelation (1957 ed.) ch. 3

T. H. Huxley 1825–95

English biologist

2 Every variety of philosophical and theological opinion was represented there [the Metaphysical Society], and expressed itself with entire openness; most of my colleagues were *-ists* of one sort or another; and, however kind and friendly they might be, I, the man without a rag of a label to cover himself with, could not fail to have some of the uneasy feelings which must have beset the historical fox when, after leaving the trap in which his tail remained, he presented himself to his normally elongated companions. So I took thought, and invented what I conceived to be the appropriate title of 'agnostic'.

Collected Essays (1893–4) 'Agnosticism'

3 The great tragedy of Science—the slaying of a beautiful hypothesis by an ugly fact.

Collected Essays (1893–4) 'Biogenesis and Abiogenesis'

4 Science is nothing but trained and organized common sense, differing from the latter only as a veteran may differ from a raw recruit: and its methods differ from those of common sense only as far as the guardsman's cut and thrust differ from the manner in which a savage wields his club.

Collected Essays (1893–4) 'The Method of Zadig'

5 If some great Power would agree to make me always think what is true and do what is right, on condition of being turned into a sort of clock and wound up every morning before I got out of bed, I should instantly close with the offer.

Collected Essays (1893–4) 'On Descartes' *Discourse on Method*' (written 1870)

6 If a little knowledge is dangerous, where is the man who has so much as to be out of danger?

Collected Essays vol. 3 (1895) 'On Elementary Instruction in Physiology' (written 1877)

7 The chess-board is the world; the pieces are the phenomena of the universe; the rules of the game are what we call the laws of Nature. The player on the other side is hidden from us. We know that his play is always fair, just, and patient. But also we know, to our cost, that he never overlooks a mistake, or makes the smallest allowance for ignorance.

Lay Sermons, Addresses, and Reviews (1870) 'A Liberal Education'

8 Some experience of popular lecturing had convinced me that the necessity of making things plain to uninstructed people was one of the very best means of clearing up the obscure corners in one's own mind.

Man's Place in Nature (1894 ed.) preface

9 It is the customary fate of new truths to begin as heresies and to end as superstitions.

Science and Culture and Other Essays (1881) 'The Coming of Age of the Origin of Species'

10 Irrationally held truths may be more harmful than reasoned errors.

Science and Culture and Other Essays (1881) 'The Coming of Age of the Origin of Species'

11 Logical consequences are the scarecrows of fools and the beacons of wise men.

Science and Culture and Other Essays (1881) 'On the Hypothesis that Animals are Automata'

12 I asserted—and I repeat—that a man has no reason to be ashamed of having an ape for his grandfather. If there were an ancestor whom I should feel shame in recalling it would rather be a *man*—a man of restless and versatile intellect—who, not content with an equivocal success in his own sphere of activity, plunges into scientific questions with which he has no real acquaintance, only to obscure them by an aimless rhetoric, and distract the attention of his hearers from the real point at issue by eloquent digressions and skilled appeals to religious prejudice.

Replying to Bishop Samuel Wilberforce in the debate on Darwin's theory of evolution at a meeting of the British Association in Oxford, 30 June 1860. See letter from J. R. Green to Professor Boyd Dawkins in Leonard Huxley (ed.) *Life and Letters of Thomas Henry Huxley* (1900). In a letter to Francis Darwin, Huxley agreed that this account was fair if not wholly accurate: there is no reliable verbatim transcript

13 I am too much of a sceptic to deny the possibility of anything.

Letter to Herbert Spencer, 22 March 1886, in Leonard Huxley *Life and Letters of Thomas Henry Huxley* (1900) vol. 2, ch. 8

Edward Hyde

See EARL OF CLARENDON

Dolores Ibarruri ('La Pasionaria') 1895–1989

Spanish Communist leader

14 *Il vaut mieux mourir debout que de vivre à genoux!*

It is better to die on your feet than to live on your knees.

Speech in Paris, 3 September 1936, in *L'Humanité* 4 September 1936 (also attributed to Emiliano Zapata)

15 *No pasarán.*

They shall not pass.

Radio broadcast, Madrid, 19 July 1936, in *Speeches and Articles 1936–38* (1938) p. 7. Cf. Anonymous 20:10

Henrik Ibsen 1828–1906

Norwegian playwright

16 *Luftslotter, — de er så nemme at ty ind i, de. Og nemme at bygge også.*

Castles in the air—they are so easy to take refuge in. And easy to build, too.

The Master Builder (1892) act 3

1 *Flertallet har aldrig retten på sin side. Aldrig, siger jeg!
Det er en af disse samfundsløgnere, som en fri, tænkende
mand må gøre oprør imod. Hvem er det, som udgør
flertallet af beboerne i et land? Er det de kloge folk, eller er
'det dè dumme? Jeg tænker, vi får være enige om, at
dumme mennesker er tilstede i en ganske forskrækkelig
overvældende majoritet rundt omkring på den hele vide
jord. Men det kan da vel, for fanden, aldrig i evighed være
ret, at de dumme skal herske over de kloge!*

The majority never has right on its side. Never I say!
That is one of the social lies that a free, thinking man
is bound to rebel against. Who makes up the majority
in any given country? Is it the wise men or the fools?
I think we must agree that the fools are in a terrible
overwhelming majority, all the wide world over. But,
damn it, it can surely never be right that the stupid
should rule over the clever!
An Enemy of the People (1882) act 4

2 *En skulde aldrig ha' sine bedste buxer på, når en er ude og
strider for frihed og sandhed.*

You should never have your best trousers on when
you go out to fight for freedom and truth.
An Enemy of the People (1882) act 5

3 *Sagen er den, ser I, at den stærkeste mand i verden, det er
han, som står mest alene.*

The thing is, you see, that the strongest man in the
world is the man who stands most alone.
An Enemy of the People (1882) act 5

4 *Mor, gi' mig solen.*

Mother, give me the sun.
Ghosts (1881) act 3

5 *Men, gud sig forbarme,—sligt noget gør man da ikke!*

But good God, people don't do such things!
Hedda Gabler (1890) act 4

6 *Hvad skal manden være? Sig selv, det er mit korte svar.*

What ought a man to be? Well, my short answer is
'himself'.
Peer Gynt (1867) act 4

7 *Tar De livsløgnen fra et gennemsnitsmenneske, så tar De
lykken fra ham med det samme.*

Take the life-lie away from the average man and
straight away you take away his happiness.
The Wild Duck (1884) act 5

St Ignatius Loyola 1491–1556

Spanish theologian, founder of the Jesuits

8 Teach us, good Lord, to serve Thee as Thou
deservest:
To give and not to count the cost;
To fight and not to heed the wounds;
To toil and not to seek for rest;
To labour and not to ask for any reward
Save that of knowing that we do Thy will.
'Prayer for Generosity' (1548)

Francis Iles (*Anthony Berkeley Cox*)
1893–1970

English crime writer

9 It was not until several weeks after he had decided to
murder his wife that Dr Bickleigh took any active steps
in the matter. Murder is a serious business.
Malice Aforethought (1931) p. 7

Ivan Illich 1926–

American sociologist

10 In a consumer society there are inevitably two kinds of
slaves: the prisoners of addiction and the prisoners of
envy.
Tools for Conviviality (1973) ch. 3

Charles Inge 1868–1957

11 This very remarkable man
Commends a most practical plan:
You can do what you want
If you don't think you can't,
So don't think you can't think you can.
'On Monsieur Coué' (1928). Cf. Coué 220:5

William Ralph Inge 1860–1954

English writer; Dean of St. Paul's, 1911–34

12 The enemies of Freedom do not argue; they shout and
they shoot.
End of an Age (1948) ch. 4

13 The effect of boredom on a large scale in history is
underestimated. It is a main cause of revolutions, and
would soon bring to an end all the static Utopias and
the farmyard civilization of the Fabians.
End of an Age (1948) ch. 6

14 To become a popular religion, it is only necessary for
a superstition to enslave a philosophy.
Idea of Progress (Romanes Lecture delivered at Oxford,
27 May 1920) p. 9

15 Many people believe that they are attracted by God, or
by Nature, when they are only repelled by man.
More Lay Thoughts of a Dean (1931) pt. 4, ch. 1

16 It takes in reality only one to make a quarrel. It is
useless for the sheep to pass resolutions in favour of
vegetarianism, while the wolf remains of a different
opinion.
Outspoken Essays: First Series (1919) 'Patriotism'

17 The nations which have put mankind and posterity
most in their debt have been small states—Israel,
Athens, Florence, Elizabethan England.
Outspoken Essays: Second Series (1922) 'State, visible and
invisible'

18 A man may build himself a throne of bayonets, but he
cannot sit on it.
Philosophy of Plotinus (1923) vol. 2, Lecture 22 (quoted by
Boris Yeltsin at the time of the failed military coup in
Russia, August 1991)

1 The aim of education is the knowledge not of facts but of values.
'The Training of the Reason' in A. C. Benson (ed.) *Cambridge Essays on Education* (1917) ch. 2

Jean Ingelow 1820–97

English poet

2 Play uppe, play uppe, O Boston bells!
Play all your changes, all your swells.
'The High Tide on the Coast of Lincolnshire, 1571' (1863)

3 Play uppe 'The Brides of Enderby'.
'The High Tide on the Coast of Lincolnshire, 1571' (1863)

4 'Cusha! Cusha! Cusha!' calling
E'er the early dews were falling,
Farre away I heard her song.
'The High Tide on the Coast of Lincolnshire, 1571' (1863)

5 Come uppe, Whitefoot, come uppe Lightfoot,
Come uppe Jetty, rise and follow,
Jetty, to the milking shed.
'The High Tide on the Coast of Lincolnshire, 1571' (1863)

6 But each will mourn her own (she saith)
And sweeter woman ne'er drew breath
Than my sonne's wife, Elizabeth.
'The High Tide on the Coast of Lincolnshire, 1571' (1863)

Robert G. Ingersoll 1833–99

American agnostic

7 An honest God is the noblest work of man.
The Gods (1876) pt. 1, p. 2. Cf. Pope 522:20

8 In nature there are neither rewards nor punishments—there are consequences.
Some Reasons Why (1881) pt. 8 'The New Testament'

J. A. D. Ingres 1780–1867

French painter

9 *Le dessin est la probité de l'art.*
Drawing is the true test of art.
Pensées d'Ingres (1922) p. 70

Eugène Ionesco 1912–

French playwright

10 *C'est une chose anormale de vivre.*
Living is abnormal.
Le Rhinocéros (1959) act 1

11 *Tu ne prévois les événements que lorsqu'ils sont déjà arrivés.*
You can only predict things after they have happened.
Le Rhinocéros (1959) act 3

12 *Un fonctionnaire ne plaisante pas.*
A civil servant doesn't make jokes.
Tueur sans gages (The Killer, 1958) act 1

Weldon J. Irvine

13 Young, gifted and black.
Title of song (1969)

Washington Irving 1783–1859

American writer

14 A woman's whole life is a history of the affections.
The Sketch Book (1820) 'The Broken Heart'

15 A tart temper never mellows with age, and a sharp tongue is the only edged tool that grows keener with constant use.
The Sketch Book (1820) 'Rip Van Winkle'

16 They who drink beer will think beer
The Sketch Book (1820) 'Stratford-on-Avon'

17 There is a certain relief in change, even though it be from bad to worse . . . it is often a comfort to shift one's position and be bruised in a new place.
Tales of a Traveller (1824) 'To the Reader'

18 The almighty dollar, that great object of universal devotion.
Wolfert's Roost (1855) 'The Creole Village'

Anne Ingram (née Howard), Viscountess Irwin c.1696–1764

English poet

19 A female mind like a rude fallow lies;
No seed is sown, but weeds spontaneous rise.
As well might we expect, in winter, spring,
As land untilled a fruitful crop should bring.
'An Epistle to Mr Pope. Occasioned by his Characters of Women' in the *Gentleman's Magazine* (1736)

20 Untaught the noble end of glorious truth,
Bred to deceive even from their earliest youth.
'An Epistle to Mr Pope. Occasioned by his Characters of Women' in the *Gentleman's Magazine* (1736)

Christopher Isherwood 1904–86

English novelist

21 The common cormorant (or shag)
Lays eggs inside a paper bag,
You follow the idea, no doubt?
It's to keep the lightning out.

But what these unobservant birds
Have never thought of, is that herds
Of wandering bears might come with buns
And steal the bags to hold the crumbs.
'The Common Cormorant' (written c.1925)

22 I am a camera with its shutter open, quite passive, recording, not thinking.
Goodbye to Berlin (1939) 'Berlin Diary' Autumn 1930

Sir Alec Issigonis 1906–88

British engineer

23 A camel is a horse designed by a committee.
On his dislike of working in teams, in *Guardian* 14 January 1991 'Notes and Queries' (attributed)

Andrew Jackson 1767–1845

7th President of the USA

1 Each public officer who takes an oath to support the constitution swears that he will support it as he understands it, and not as it is understood by others.

> Presidential message vetoing the bill to re-charter the Bank of the United States, 10 July 1832, in H. S. Commager (ed.) *Documents of American History* vol. 1 (1963) p. 272

2 Our Federal Union: it must be preserved.

> Toast given on the Jefferson Birthday Celebration, 13 April 1830; in Thomas Hart Benton *Thirty Years' View* (1856) vol. 1

3 You are uneasy; you never sailed with *me* before, I see.

> In James Parton *Life of Jackson* (1860) vol. 3, ch. 35

Holbrook Jackson 1874–1948

English writer and critic

4 Pedantry is the dotage of knowledge.

> *Anatomy of Bibliomania* (1930) vol. 1, p. 150

5 As soon as an idea is accepted it is time to reject it.

> *Platitudes in the Making* (1911) p. 13

Joe Jacobs 1896–1940

American boxing manager

6 We was robbed!

> After Jack Sharkey beat Max Schmeling (of whom Jacobs was manager) in the heavyweight title fight, 21 June 1932; in Peter Heller *In This Corner* (1975) p. 44

7 I should of stood in bed.

> After leaving his sick-bed in October 1935 to attend the World Baseball Series in Detroit, and betting on the losers, in John Lardner *Strong Cigars* (1951) p. 61

Jacopone da Todi c.1230–1306

Franciscan lay brother

8 *Stabat Mater dolorosa,*
Iuxta crucem lacrimosa,
Dum pendebat filius.

At the cross her station keeping,
Stood the mournful Mother weeping,
Where he hung, the dying Lord.

> 'Stabat Mater dolorosa', ascribed also to Pope Innocent III and others (translation based on that of E. Caswall in *Lyra Catholica*, 1849)

Mick Jagger 1943– *and* Keith Richard 1943–

English rock musicians

9 Get off of my cloud.

> Title of song (1966)

10 Mother needs something today to calm her down,
And though she's not really ill,
There's a little yellow pill:
She goes running for the shelter
Of a mother's little helper,
And it helps her on her way,
Gets her through her busy day.

> 'Mother's Little Helper' (1966 song)

11 I can't get no satisfaction
I can't get no girl reaction.

> '(I Can't Get No) Satisfaction' (1965 song)

12 Ev'rywhere I hear the sound of marching, charging feet, boy,
'Cause summer's here and the time is right for fighting in the street, boy.
But what can a poor boy do
Except to sing for a rock 'n' roll band,
'Cause in sleepy London town
There's just no place for a street fighting man!

> 'Street Fighting Man' (1968 song)

13 Please allow me to introduce myself
I'm a man of wealth and taste
I've been around for a long, long year
Stole many a man's soul and faith
And I was round when Jesus Christ
Had his moments of doubt and pain
Made damn sure that Pilate
Washed his hands and sealed his fate
Pleased to meet you, hope you guess my name
But what's puzzling you
Is the nature of my game.

> 'Sympathy for the Devil' (1968 song)

14 I watched with glee while your kings and queens
Fought for ten decades for the gods they made
I shouted out 'Who killed the Kennedys?'
When after all, it was you and me.

> 'Sympathy for the Devil' (1968 song)

Richard Jago 1715–81

English poet

15 With leaden foot time creeps along
While Delia is away.

> 'Absence'

James I (James VI of Scotland) 1566–1625

King of Scotland from 1567 and of England from 1603

16 A branch of the sin of drunkenness, which is the root of all sins.

> *A Counterblast to Tobacco* (1604)

17 A custom loathsome to the eye, hateful to the nose, harmful to the brain, dangerous to the lungs, and in the black, stinking fume thereof, nearest resembling the horrible Stygian smoke of the pit that is bottomless.

> *A Counterblast to Tobacco* (1604)

18 Herein is not only a great vanity, but a great contempt of God's good gifts, that the sweetness of man's breath, being a good gift of God, should be wilfully corrupted by this stinking smoke.

> *A Counterblast to Tobacco* (1604)

1 The state of monarchy is the supremest thing upon earth; for kings are not only God's lieutenants upon earth, and sit upon God's throne, but even by God himself they are called gods.
> Speech to Parliament, 21 March 1610, in *Works* (1616) p. 529

2 The king is truly *parens patriae*, the polite father of his people.
> Speech to Parliament, 21 March 1610, in *Works* (1616) p. 529

3 That which concerns the mystery of the king's power is not lawful to be disputed; for that is to wade into the weakness of Princes and to take away the mystical reverence, that belongs unto them that sit in the throne of God.
> 'A Speech in the Star Chamber' [speech to the judges] 20 June 1616, in *Works* (1616) p. 557

4 No bishop, no King.
> To a deputation of Presbyterians from the Church of Scotland, seeking religious tolerance in England, in W. Barlow *Sum and Substance of the Conference* (1604) p. 82

5 I will govern according to the common weal, but not according to the common will.
> December, 1621, in J. R. Green *History of the English People* vol. 3 (1879) bk. 7, ch. 4

6 Dr Donne's verses are like the peace of God; they pass all understanding.
> Remark recorded by Archdeacon Plume (1630–1704)

7 You cannot name any example in any heathen author but I will better it in Scripture.
> 'Crumms Fal'n From King James's Table' no. 10, in E. F. Rimbault (ed.) *Miscellaneous Works of Sir Thomas Overbury* (1856) p. 257

James V 1512–42

King of Scotland from 1513

8 It came with a lass, and it will pass with a lass.
> Of the crown of Scotland, on learning of the birth of Mary Queen of Scots, December 1542; in Robert Lindsay of Pitscottie (c.1500–65) *History of Scotland* (1728) p. 176

Henry James 1843–1916

American novelist

9 The ever-importunate murmur, 'Dramatize it, dramatize it!'
> *The Altar of the Dead* (1909 ed.) preface

10 The Story is just the spoiled child of art.
> *The Ambassadors* (1909 ed.) preface

11 The terrible *fluidity of self-revelation*.
> *The Ambassadors* (1909 ed.) preface

12 Live all you can; it's a mistake not to. It doesn't so much matter what you do in particular, so long as you have your life. If you haven't had that, what *have* you had?
> *The Ambassadors* (1903) bk. 5, ch. 11

13 The deep well of unconscious cerebration.
> *The American* (1909 ed.) preface

14 The balloon of experience is in fact of course tied to the earth, and under that necessity we swing, thanks to a rope of remarkable length, in the more or less commodious car of the imagination; but it is by the rope we know where we are, and from the moment that cable is cut we are at large and unrelated.
> *The American* (1909 ed.) preface

15 The historian, essentially, wants more documents than he can really use; the dramatist only wants more liberties than he can really take.
> *The Aspern Papers* (1909 ed.) preface

16 Most English talk is a quadrille in a sentry-box.
> *The Awkward Age* (1899) bk. 5, ch. 19

17 Vereker's secret, my dear man—the general intention of his books: the string the pearls were strung on, the buried treasure, the figure in the carpet.
> *The Figure in the Carpet* (1896) ch. 11

18 It takes a great deal of history to produce a little literature.
> *Hawthorne* (1879) ch. 1

19 One might enumerate the items of high civilization, as it exists in other countries, which are absent from the texture of American life, until it should become a wonder to know what was left. No State, in the European sense of the word, and indeed barely a specific national name. No sovereign, no court, no personal loyalty, no aristocracy, no church, no clergy, no army, no diplomatic service, no country gentlemen, no palaces, no castles, nor manors, nor old country houses, nor parsonages, nor thatched cottages, nor ivied ruins; no cathedrals nor abbeys, nor little Norman churches; no great universities nor public schools—no Oxford, nor Eton, nor Harrow; no literature, no novels, no museums, no pictures, no political society, no sporting class—no Epsom nor Ascot! ... The natural remark in the almost lurid light of such an indictment, would be that if these things are left out, everything is left out.
> *Hawthorne* (1879) ch. 2

20 He was imperfect, unfinished, inartistic; he was worse than provincial—he was parochial.
> *Hawthorne* (1879) ch. 4 (of H. D. Thoreau)

21 The black and merciless things that are behind the great possessions.
> *The Ivory Tower* (1917) notes p. 287

22 Don't let anyone persuade you ... that Form *is* [not] substance to that degree that there is absolutely no substance without it. Form alone *takes*, and holds and preserves, substance.
> Letter to Hugh Walpole, 19 May 1912, in Leon Edel (ed.) *Letters* vol. 4 (1984) p. 619

23 I could come back to America ... to die—but never, never to live.
> Letter to Mrs William James, 1 April 1913, in Leon Edel (ed.) *Letters* vol. 4 (1984) p. 657

24 Cats and monkeys—monkeys and cats—all human life is there!
> *The Madonna of the Future* (1879) vol. 1, p. 59 ('All human life is there' became the slogan of the *News of the World* from the late 1950s)

1 We work in the dark—we do what we can—we give what we have. Our doubt is our passion and our passion is our task. The rest is the madness of art.
'The Middle Years' (short story, 1893)

2 Tennyson was not Tennysonian.
The Middle Years (1917 autobiography) ch. 6

3 Experience is never limited, and it is never complete; it is an immense sensibility, a kind of huge spider-web of the finest silken threads suspended in the chamber of consciousness, and catching every air-borne particle in its tissue.
Partial Portraits (1888) 'The Art of Fiction'

4 What is character but the determination of incident? What is incident but the illustration of character?
Partial Portraits (1888) 'The Art of Fiction'

5 The house of fiction has in short not one window, but a million ... but they are, singly or together, as nothing without the posted presence of the watcher.
The Portrait of a Lady (1908 ed.) preface

6 The note I wanted; that of the strange and sinister embroidered on the very type of the normal and easy.
Prefaces (1909) 'The Altar of the Dead'

7 Life being all inclusion and confusion, and art being all discrimination and selection.
The Spoils of Poynton (1909 ed.) preface

8 The fatal futility of Fact.
The Spoils of Poynton (1909 ed.) preface

9 We were alone with the quiet day, and his little heart, dispossessed, had stopped.
The Turn of the Screw (1898) p. 169

10 Of course, of course.
On hearing that Rupert Brooke had died on a Greek island, in C. Hassall *Rupert Brooke* (1964) ch. 14

11 Summer afternoon—summer afternoon ... the two most beautiful words in the English language.
In Edith Wharton *A Backward Glance* (1934) ch. 10

12 So here it is at last, the distinguished thing!
On experiencing his first stroke, in Edith Wharton *A Backward Glance* (1934) ch. 14

William James 1842–1910

American philosopher; brother of Henry James

13 Man, biologically considered, and whatever else he may be into the bargain, is simply the most formidable of all the beasts of prey, and, indeed, the only one that preys systematically on its own species.
Atlantic Monthly December 1904, p. 845

14 The moral flabbiness born of the exclusive worship of the bitch-goddess *success*. That—with the squalid cash interpretation put on the word success—is our national disease.
Letter to H. G. Wells, 11 September 1906, in *Letters* (1920) vol. 2

15 Real culture lives by sympathies and admirations, not by dislikes and disdains—under all misleading wrappings it pounces unerringly upon the human core.
McClure's Magazine February 1908, p. 422

16 There is no more miserable human being than one in whom nothing is habitual but indecision.
The Principles of Psychology (1890) vol. 1, ch. 4

17 The art of being wise is the art of knowing what to overlook.
The Principles of Psychology (1890) vol. 2, ch. 22

18 There is no worse lie than a truth misunderstood by those who hear it.
The Varieties of Religious Experience (1902) p. 355

19 Hogamus, higamus
Man is polygamous
Higamus, hogamus
Woman monogamous.
In *Oxford Book of Marriage* (1990) p. 195

Randall Jarrell 1914–65

American poet

20 In bombers named for girls, we burned
The cities we had learned about in school—
Till our lives wore out; our bodies lay among
The people we had killed and never seen.
When we lasted long enough they gave us medals;
When we died they said, 'Our casualties were low.'
'Losses' (1963)

21 To Americans, English manners are far more frightening than none at all.
Pictures from an Institution (1954) pt. 1, ch. 4

22 It is better to entertain an idea than to take it home to live with you for the rest of your life.
Pictures from an Institution (1954) pt. 1, ch. 4

Douglas Jay 1907–

British Labour politician

23 Fair shares for all, is Labour's call.
Change and Fortune (1980) ch. 7 (slogan devised for the North Battersea by-election, 1946)

24 In the case of nutrition and health, just as in the case of education, the gentleman in Whitehall really does know better what is good for people than the people know themselves.
The Socialist Case (1939) ch. 30

Jean Paul

See JOHANN PAUL FRIEDRICH RICHTER

Sir James Jeans 1877–1946

English astronomer, physicist, and mathematician

25 Taking a very gloomy view of the future of the human race, let us suppose that it can only expect to survive for two thousand million years longer, a period about equal to the past age of the earth. Then, regarded as a being destined to live for three-score years and ten, humanity, although it has been born in a house seventy years old, is itself only three days old.
Eos (1928) p. 12

26 Life exists in the universe only because the carbon atom possesses certain exceptional properties.
The Mysterious Universe (1930) ch. 1

27 From the intrinsic evidence of his creation, the Great Architect of the Universe now begins to appear as a pure mathematician.
The Mysterious Universe (1930) ch. 5

Thomas Jefferson 1743–1826

3rd President of the USA

1 When in the course of human events, it becomes necessary for one people to dissolve the political bonds which have connected them with another, and to assume among the powers of the earth the separate and equal station to which the laws of nature and of Nature's God entitle them, a decent respect to the opinions of mankind requires that they should declare the causes which impel them to the separation.

> American Declaration of Independence, 4 July 1776 (preamble)

2 We hold these truths to be sacred and undeniable; that all men are created equal and independent, that from that equal creation they derive rights inherent and inalienable, among which are the preservation of life, and liberty, and the pursuit of happiness.

> 'Rough Draft' of the American Declaration of Independence, in J. P. Boyd et al. *Papers of Thomas Jefferson* vol. 1 (1950) p. 423. Cf. Anonymous 19:7

3 All, too, will bear in mind this sacred principle, that though the will of the majority is in all cases to prevail, that will to be rightful must be reasonable; that the minority possess their equal rights, which equal law must protect, and to violate would be oppression.

> *The Speech* [First Inaugural Address] . . . on the 4th of March, 1801

4 Would the honest patriot, in the full tide of successful experiment, abandon a government which has so far kept us free and firm?

> *The Speech* [First Inaugural Address] . . . on the 4th of March, 1801

5 Peace, commerce, and honest friendship with all nations—entangling alliances with none.

> *The Speech* [First Inaugural Address] . . . on the 4th of March, 1801

6 Freedom of religion; freedom of the press, and freedom of person under the protection of *habeas corpus*, and trial by juries impartially selected. These principles form the bright constellation which has gone before us, and guided our steps through an age of revolution and reformation.

> *The Speech* [First Inaugural Address] . . . on the 4th of March, 1801

7 Experience declares that man is the only animal which devours its own kind, for I can apply no milder term to the governments of Europe, and to the general prey of the rich on the poor.

> Letter to Colonel Edward Carrington, 16 January 1787, in *Papers of Thomas Jefferson* vol. 11 (1955) p. 49

8 A little rebellion now and then is a good thing.

> Letter to James Madison, 30 January 1787, in *Papers of Thomas Jefferson* vol. 11 (1955) p. 93

9 The tree of liberty must be refreshed from time to time with the blood of patriots and tyrants. It is its natural manure.

> Letter to W. S. Smith, 13 November 1787, in *Papers of Thomas Jefferson* vol. 12 (1955) p. 356

10 Whenever a man has cast a longing eye on them [official positions], a rottenness begins in his conduct.

> Letter to Tench Coxe, 21 May 1799, in P. L. Ford (ed.) *Writings of Thomas Jefferson* vol. 7 (1896) p. 381

11 If the principle were to prevail, of a common law [i.e. a single government] being in force in the U.S. . . . it would become the most corrupt government on the earth.

> Letter to Gideon Granger, 13 August 1800, in P. L. Ford (ed.) *Writings of Thomas Jefferson* vol. 7 (1896) p. 451

12 If a due participation of office is a matter of right, how are vacancies to be obtained? Those by death are few; by resignation none.

> Letter to E. Shipman and others, 12 July 1801 (usually quoted: 'Few die and none resign'), in P. L. Ford (ed.) *Writings of Thomas Jefferson* vol. 8 (1897) p. 70

13 I agree with you that there is a natural aristocracy among men. The grounds of this are virtue and talents.

> Letter to John Adams, 28 October 1813, in P. L. Ford (ed.) *Writings of Thomas Jefferson* vol. 9 (1898) p. 425

14 If a nation expects to be ignorant and free, in a state of civilization, it expects what never was and never will be.

> Letter to Colonel Charles Yancey, 6 January 1816, in P. L. Ford (ed.) *Writings of Thomas Jefferson* vol. 10 (1899) p. 4

15 I know no safe depository of the ultimate powers of the society but the people themselves; and if we think them not enlightened enough to exercise their control with a wholesome discretion, the remedy is not to take it from them, but to inform their discretion by education.

> Letter to William Charles Jarvis, 28 September 1820, in P. L. Ford (ed.) *Writings of Thomas Jefferson* vol. 10 (1899) p. 161

16 To attain all this [universal republicanism], however, rivers of blood must yet flow, and years of desolation pass over; yet the object is worth rivers of blood, and years of desolation.

> Letter to John Adams, 4 September 1823, in P. L. Ford *Writings of Thomas Jefferson* vol. 10 (1899) p. 270. Cf. Powell 528:10, Virgil 713:10

17 Millions of innocent men, women, and children, since the introduction of Christianity, have been burnt, tortured, fined, imprisoned; yet we have not advanced one inch towards uniformity [of opinion]. What has been the effect of coercion? To make one half the world fools, and the other half hypocrites.

> *Notes on the State of Virginia* (1781–5) Query 17

18 Indeed I tremble for my country when I reflect that God is just.

> *Notes on the State of Virginia* (1781–5) Query 18

19 No duty the Executive had to perform was so trying as to put the right man in the right place.

> In J. B. MacMaster *History of the People of the United States* (1883–1913) vol. 2, ch. 13, p. 586

20 We have the wolf by the ears; and we can neither hold him, nor safely let him go. Justice is in one scale, and self-preservation in the other.

> On slavery in a letter to John Holmes, 22 April 1820; in A. A. Lipscome and A. E. Berg (eds) *Writings of Thomas Jefferson* (1903) vol. 15

21 When a man assumes a public trust, he should consider himself as public property.

> To Baron von Humboldt, 1807, in B. L. Rayner *Life of Jefferson* (1834) p. 356

Francis, Lord Jeffrey 1773–1850

Scottish critic

1 This will never do.

On Wordsworth's *The Excursion* (1814) in *Edinburgh Review* November 1814

David Jenkins 1925–

English theologian; Bishop of Durham from 1984

2 JOHN MORTIMER: You said you were going to lie low like Brer Rabbit.
BISHOP OF DURHAM: That was misinterpreted. I only meant that I was going away for the weekend.

Interview in *Observer* 12 May 1985

3 The withdrawal of an imported, elderly American to leave a reconciling opportunity for some local product is surely neither dishonourable nor improper.

Referring to Ian MacGregor, Chairman of the National Coal Board, in *The Times* 22 September 1984. Cf. MacGregor 438:3

4 I am not clear that God manoeuvres physical things ... After all, a conjuring trick with bones only proves that it is as clever as a conjuring trick with bones ... A resuscitated corpse might be a resuscitated corpse and might be the sign of something, but there is still the question of what it is the symbol of.

Of the Resurrection, in 'Poles Apart' (BBC radio, 4 October 1984)

Roy Jenkins (Baron Jenkins of Hillhead) 1920–

British politician; co-founder of the Social Democratic Party, 1981

5 The politics of the left and centre of this country are frozen in an out-of-date mould which is bad for the political and economic health of Britain and increasingly inhibiting for those who live within the mould. Can it be broken?

Speech to Parliamentary Press Gallery, 9 June 1980, in *The Times* 10 June 1980

Paul Jennings 1918–89

English writer

6 Resistentialism is concerned with what Things think about men.

Even Oddlier (1952) 'Developments in Resistentialism'

7 In this concept of Activated Sludge, two perfectly opposite forces are held in perfect equilibrium.

Oddly Enough (1950) 'Activated Sludge'

Soame Jenyns 1704–87

English politician and writer

8 Omnipotence cannot work contradictions; it can only effect all possible things.

A Free Enquiry into the Nature and Origin of Evil (1757) Letter 1

9 Those who profess outrageous zeal for the liberty and prosperity of their country, and at the same time infringe her laws, affront her religion and debauch her people, are but despicable quacks.

A Free Enquiry into the Nature and Origin of Evil (1757) Letter 5

10 Thousands are collected from the idle and the extravagant for seeing dogs, horses, men and monkeys perform feats of activity, and, in some places, for the privilege only of seeing one another.

Works (1790) vol. 2 'Thoughts on the National Debt'

St Jerome c. AD 342–420

Christian monk and scholar; translator of the original Bible texts into Latin (the Vulgate)

11 *Venerationi mihi semper fuit non verbosa rusticitas, sed sancta simplicitas.*

I have revered always not crude verbosity, but holy simplicity.

Letter 'Ad Pammachium' in *Patrologiae Latinae* vol. 22 (1864) col. 579

12 Hooly writ is the scripture of puples, for it is maad, that alle puplis schulden knowe it.

Attributed, in J. Forshall and F. Madden (eds.) *The Holy Bible ... in the Earliest English Versions* (1850) vol. 1 'The Prologue' [probably by John Purvey, c.1353–c.1428] ch. 15

Jerome K. Jerome 1859–1927

English writer

13 It is impossible to enjoy idling thoroughly unless one has plenty of work to do.

Idle Thoughts of an Idle Fellow (1886) 'On Being Idle'

14 The passing of the third floor back.

Title of story (1907) and play (1910)

15 I want a house that has got over all its troubles; I don't want to spend the rest of my life bringing up a young and inexperienced house.

They and I (1909) ch. 11

16 But there, everything has its drawbacks, as the man said when his mother-in-law died, and they came down upon him for the funeral expenses.

Three Men in a Boat (1889) ch. 3

William Jerome 1865–1932

American songwriter

17 Any old place I can hang my hat is home sweet home to me.

Title of song (1901)

Douglas Jerrold 1803–57

English playwright and journalist

18 Religion's in the heart, not in the knees.

The Devil's Ducat (1830) act 1, sc. 2

19 The best thing I know between France and England is—the sea.

The Wit and Opinions of Douglas Jerrold (1859) 'The Anglo-French Alliance'

1 Earth is here so kind, that just tickle her with a hoe
and she laughs with a harvest.
The Wit and Opinions of Douglas Jerrold (1859) 'A Land of
Plenty' (Australia)

2 Love's like the measles—all the worse when it comes
late in life.
The Wit and Opinions of Douglas Jerrold (1859) 'Love'

3 Some people are so fond of ill-luck that they run
half-way to meet it.
The Wit and Opinions of Douglas Jerrold (1859) 'Meeting
Troubles Half-way'

4 We love peace, as we abhor pusillanimity; but not
peace at any price. There is a peace more destructive
of the manhood of living man than war is destructive
of his material body. Chains are worse than bayonets.
The Wit and Opinions of Douglas Jerrold (1859) 'Peace'

5 If an earthquake were to engulf England to-morrow,
the English would manage to meet and dine
somewhere among the rubbish, just to celebrate the
event.
In Blanchard Jerrold *The Life and Remains of Douglas Jerrold*
(1859) ch. 14

W. Stanley Jevons 1835–82
English economist

6 All classes of society are trades unionists at heart, and
differ chiefly in the boldness, ability, and secrecy with
which they pursue their respective interests.
The State in Relation to Labour (1882) p. vi

John Jewel 1522–71
English bishop

7 In old time we had treen chalices and golden priests,
but now we have treen priests and golden chalices.
Certain Sermons Preached Before the Queen's Majesty (1609)
p. 176

C. E. M. Joad 1891–1953
English philosopher

8 It all depends what you mean by . . .
Answering questions on 'The Brains Trust' (formerly 'Any
Questions'), BBC radio (1941–8)

9 My life is spent in a perpetual alternation between two
rhythms, the rhythm of attracting people for fear
I may be lonely, and the rhythm of trying to get rid of
them because I know that I am bored.
In *Observer* 12 December 1948, p. 2

John XXIII (Angelo Giuseppe Roncalli)
1881–1963
Pope from 1958

10 If civil authorities legislate for or allow anything that
is contrary to that order and therefore contrary to the
will of God, neither the laws made or the
authorizations granted can be binding on the
consciences of the citizens, since God has more right to
be obeyed than man.
Pacem in Terris (1963) p. 142

11 The social progress, order, security and peace of each
country are necessarily connected with the social
progress, order, security and peace of all other
countries.
Pacem in Terris (1963) p. 150

12 [In the universal *Declaration of Human Rights*
(December, 1948)] in most solemn form, the dignity of
a person is acknowledged to all human beings; and as
a consequence there is proclaimed, as a fundamental
right, the right of free movement in search for truth
and in the attainment of moral good and of justice,
and also the right to a dignified life.
Pacem in Terris (1963) p. 152

St John of the Cross 1542–91
Spanish mystic and poet

13 *Muero porque no muero.*
I die because I do not die.
'Coplas del alma que pena por ver a Dios' (*c*.1578). The
same words occur in St Teresa of Ávila 'Versos nacidos del
fuego del amor de Dios' (*c*.1571–3)

14 *Con un no saber sabiendo.*
With a knowing ignorance.
'Coplas hechas sobre un éxtasis de alta contemplación'

John of Salisbury c.1115–80
English ecclesiastical scholar; supporter of Thomas Becket

15 *Siquidem uita breuis, sensus hebes, neglegentiae torpor,
inutilis occupatio, nos paucula scire permittunt, et eadem
iugiter excutit et auellit ab animo fraudatrix scientiae,
inimica et infida semper memoriae nouerca, obliuio.*
The brevity of our life, the dullness of our senses, the
torpor of our indifference, the futility of our
occupation, suffer us to know but little: and that little
is soon shaken and then torn from the mind by that
traitor to learning, that hostile and faithless
stepmother to memory, oblivion.
Prologue to the Policraticus (ed. C. C. I. Webb, 1909) vol. 1,
p. 12, l. 13 (translated by Helen Waddell)

Linton Kwesi Johnson b. 1952
Anglo-Jamaican poet

16 Brothers and sisters rocking,
a dread beat pulsing fire, burning.
'Dread Beat an Blood' (1975)

17 Cold lights hurting, breaking, hurting;
fire in the head and a dread beat bleeding, beating
fire: dread.
'Dread Beat an Blood' (1975)

Lionel Johnson 1867–1902
English poet

18 The saddest of all Kings
Crowned, and again discrowned.
'By the Statue of King Charles I at Charing Cross' (1895)

19 Alone he rides, alone,
The fair and fatal king.
'By the Statue of King Charles I at Charing Cross' (1895)

1 There Shelley dreamed his white Platonic dreams.
'Oxford' (1897).

2   In her ears the chime
Of full, sad bells brings back her old springtide.
'Oxford' (1897)

3 I know you: solitary griefs,
Desolate passions, aching hours.
'The Precept of Silence' (1895)

Lyndon Baines Johnson 1908–73
36th President of the USA

4 I am a free man, an American, a United States
Senator, and a Democrat, in that order.
Texas Quarterly Winter 1958

5 All I have I would have given gladly not to be standing
here today.
First speech to Congress as President, 27 November 1963,
following the assassination of J. F. Kennedy, in *Public Papers
of . . . Lyndon B. Johnson 1963–64* vol. 1, p. 8

6 We have talked long enough in this country about
equal rights. We have talked for a hundred years or
more. It is time now to write the next chapter, and to
write it in the books of law.
Speech to Congress, 27 November 1963, in *Public Papers of
. . . Lyndon B. Johnson 1963–64* vol. 1, p. 9

7 We hope that the world will not narrow into
a neighbourhood before it has broadened into
a brotherhood.
Speech at the lighting of the Nation's Christmas Tree,
22 December 1963, in *Public Papers of . . . Lyndon B.
Johnson 1963–64* vol. 1, item 65

8 In your time we have the opportunity to move not
only toward the rich society and the powerful society,
but upward to the Great Society.
Speech at University of Michigan, 22 May 1964, in *Public
Papers of . . . Lyndon B. Johnson 1963–64* vol. 1, p. 704

9 We Americans know, although others appear to
forget, the risks of spreading conflict. We still seek no
wider war.
Speech on radio and television, 4 August 1964, in *Public
Papers of . . . Lyndon B. Johnson 1963–64* vol. 2, p. 927

10 We are not about to send American boys 9 or 10,000
miles away from home to do what Asian boys ought
to be doing for themselves.
Speech at Akron University, 21 October 1964, in *Public
Papers of . . . Lyndon B. Johnson 1963–64* vol. 2, p. 1391.
Cf. Roosevelt 546:1

11 I don't want loyalty. I want *loyalty*. I want him to kiss
my ass in Macy's window at high noon and tell me it
smells like roses. I want his pecker in my pocket.
In David Halberstam *The Best and the Brightest* (1972)
ch. 20 (discussing a prospective assistant)

12 Better to have him inside the tent pissing out, than
outside pissing in.
In David Halberstam *The Best and the Brightest* (1972)
ch. 20 (of J. Edgar Hoover)

13 So dumb he can't fart and chew gum at the same
time.
In Richard Reeves *A Ford, not a Lincoln* (1975) ch. 2 (of
Gerald Ford)

Paul Johnson 1928–
British journalist

14 Tories, in short, are atrophied Englishmen, lacking
certain moral and intellectual reflexes. They are
recognizable, homely—even, on occasions,
endearing—but liable to turn very nasty at short
notice.
New Statesman 18 October 1958 'Rule Like Pigs'

Philander Chase Johnson 1866–1939

15 Cheer up! the worst is yet to come!
Everybody's Magazine May 1920

Philip Johnson 1906–
American architect

16 Architecture is the art of how to waste space.
New York Times 27 December 1964, p. 9

Samuel Johnson 1709–84
English poet, critic, and lexicographer

17 In all pointed sentences, some degree of accuracy must
be sacrificed to conciseness.
'The Bravery of the English Common Soldier' in *The British
Magazine* January 1760 (Yale ed., vol. 10, p. 281)

18 Liberty is, to the lowest rank of every nation, little
more than the choice of working or starving.
'The Bravery of the English Common Soldier' in *The British
Magazine* January 1760 (Yale ed., vol. 10, p. 283)

19 Change is not made without inconvenience, even from
worse to better.
A Dictionary of the English Language (1755) preface.
Cf. Hooker 344:15

20 I am not yet so lost in lexicography as to forget that
words are the daughters of earth, and that things are
the sons of heaven. Language is only the instrument
of science, and words are but the signs of ideas: I
wish, however, that the instrument might be less apt
to decay, and that signs might be permanent, like the
things which they denote.
A Dictionary of the English Language (1755) preface.
Cf. Madden 441:14

21 Every quotation contributes something to the stability
or enlargement of the language.
A Dictionary of the English Language (1755) preface (on
citations of usage in a dictionary)

22 But these were the dreams of a poet doomed at last to
wake a lexicographer.
A Dictionary of the English Language (1755) preface

23 If the changes we fear be thus irresistible, what
remains but to acquiesce with silence, as in the other
insurmountable distresses of humanity? It remains
that we retard what we cannot repel, that we palliate
what we cannot cure.
A Dictionary of the English Language (1755) preface

24 *Dull.* To make dictionaries is dull work.
A Dictionary of the English Language (1755) 'dull' (8th
definition)

25 *Excise.* A hateful tax levied upon commodities.
A Dictionary of the English Language (1755)

1 *Lexicographer*. A writer of dictionaries, a harmless drudge.
   A Dictionary of the English Language (1755)

2 *Network*. Anything reticulated or decussated at equal distances, with interstices between the intersections.
   A Dictionary of the English Language (1755)

3 *Oats*. A grain, which in England is generally given to horses, but in Scotland supports the people.
   A Dictionary of the English Language (1755)

4 *Patron*. Commonly a wretch who supports with insolence, and is paid with flattery.
   A Dictionary of the English Language (1755)

5 *Pension*. Pay given to a state hireling for treason to his country.
   A Dictionary of the English Language (1755)

6 The only end of writing is to enable the readers better to enjoy life, or better to endure it.
   A Free Enquiry (1757, ed. D. Greene, 1984)

7 When two Englishmen meet, their first talk is of the weather.
   The Idler no. 11 (24 June 1758)

8 Among the calamities of war may be jointly numbered the diminution of the love of truth, by the falsehoods which interest dictates and credulity encourages.
   The Idler no. 30 (11 November 1758); possibly the source, in essence, of 'When war is declared, Truth is the first casualty', epigraph to Arthur Ponsonby's *Falsehood in Wartime* (1928). In this form, it has been attributed also to Hiram Johnson, speaking in the US Senate, 1918, but is not recorded in his speech

9 Promise, large promise, is the soul of an advertisement.
   The Idler no. 40 (20 January 1759)

10 Nothing is more hopeless than a scheme of merriment.
   The Idler no. 58 (26 May 1759)

11 I directed them to bring a bundle [of hay] into the room, and slept upon it in my riding coat. Mr Boswell, being more delicate, laid himself sheets with hay over and under him, and lay in linen like a gentleman.
   A Journey to the Western Islands of Scotland (1775) 'Glenelg'

12 A Scotchman must be a very sturdy moralist, who does not love Scotland better than truth.
   A Journey to the Western Islands of Scotland (1775) 'Ostig in Sky'

13 At seventy-seven it is time to be in earnest.
   A Journey to the Western Islands of Scotland (1775) 'Col'

14 Whatever withdraws us from the power of our senses; whatever makes the past, the distant, or the future predominate over the present, advances us in the dignity of thinking beings.
   A Journey to the Western Islands of Scotland (1775) 'Inch Kenneth'

15 Grief is a species of idleness.
   Letter to Mrs Thrale, 17 March 1773, in R. W. Chapman (ed.) *Letters of Samuel Johnson* (1952) vol. 1

16 He is gone, and we are going.
   Letter to Mrs Thrale on the death of her son, Harry, 25 March 1776, in R. W. Chapman (ed.) *Letters of Samuel Johnson* (1952) vol. 3

17 The black dog I hope always to resist, and in time to drive, though I am deprived of almost all those that used to help me . . . When I rise my breakfast is solitary, the black dog waits to share it, from breakfast to dinner he continues barking, except that Dr Brocklesby for a little keeps him at a distance . . . Night comes at last, and some hours of restlessness and confusion bring me again to a day of solitude. What shall exclude the black dog from a habitation like this?
   Letter to Mrs Thrale, 28 June 1783, in R. W. Chapman (ed.) *Letters of Samuel Johnson* (1952) vol. 3 (on his attacks of melancholia; more recently associated with Winston Churchill, who used the phrase 'black dog' when alluding to his own periodic bouts of depression)

18 A hardened and shameless tea-drinker, who has for twenty years diluted his meals with only the infusion of this fascinating plant; whose kettle has scarcely time to cool; who with tea amuses the evening, with tea solaces the midnight, and with tea welcomes the morning.
   Review in the *Literary Magazine* vol. 2, no. 13 (1757)

19 About things on which the public thinks long it commonly attains to think right.
   Lives of the English Poets (1779–81) 'Addison'

20 Whoever wishes to attain an English style, familiar but not coarse, and elegant but not ostentatious, must give his days and nights to the volumes of Addison.
   Lives of the English Poets (1779–81) 'Addison'

21 The great source of pleasure is variety. Uniformity must tire at last, though it be uniformity of excellence. We love to expect; and, when expectation is disappointed or gratified, we want to be again expecting.
   Lives of the English Poets (1779–81) 'Butler'

22 A man, doubtful of his dinner, or trembling at a creditor, is not much disposed to abstracted meditation, or remote enquiries.
   Lives of the English Poets (1779–81) 'Collins'

23 The true genius is a mind of large general powers, accidentally determined to some particular direction.
   Lives of the English Poets (1779–81) 'Cowley'

24 Language is the dress of thought.
   Lives of the English Poets (1779–81) 'Cowley'. Cf. Pope 521:12, Wesley 729:5

25 The father of English criticism.
   Lives of the English Poets (1779–81) 'Dryden'

26 This play . . . was first offered to Cibber and his brethren at Drury-Lane, and rejected; it being then carried to Rich had the effect, as was ludicrously said, of making Gay *rich*, and Rich *gay*.
   Lives of the English Poets (1779–81) 'John Gay' (of Gay's *The Beggar's Opera*)

27 In the character of his Elegy I rejoice to concur with the common reader; for by the common sense of readers uncorrupted with literary prejudices . . . must be finally decided all claim to poetical honours.
   Lives of the English Poets (1779–81) 'Gray'

28 An exotic and irrational entertainment, which has been always combated, and always has prevailed.
   Lives of the English Poets (1779–81) 'Hughes' (of Italian opera)

1 We are perpetually moralists, but we are geometricians only by chance. Our intercourse with intellectual nature is necessary; our speculations upon matter are voluntary and at leisure.
Lives of the English Poets (1779–81) 'Milton'

2 An acrimonious and surly republican.
Lives of the English Poets (1779–81) 'Milton'

3 I am disappointed by that stroke of death, which has eclipsed the gaiety of nations and impoverished the public stock of harmless pleasure.
Lives of the English Poets (1779–81) 'Edmund Smith' (on the death of Garrick)

4 He washed himself with oriental scrupulosity.
Lives of the English Poets (1779–81) 'Swift'

5 Friendship is not always the sequel of obligation.
Lives of the English Poets (1779–81) 'James Thomson'

6 Nothing can please many, and please long, but just representations of general nature.
Plays of William Shakespeare . . . (1765) preface (Yale ed., p. 61)

7 He that tries to recommend him [Shakespeare] by select quotations, will succeed like the pedant in Hierocles, who, when he offered his house to sale, carried a brick in his pocket as a specimen.
Plays of William Shakespeare . . . (1765) preface (Yale ed., p. 62)

8 Love is only one of many passions.
Plays of William Shakespeare . . . (1765) preface (Yale ed., p. 63)

9 Shakespeare has united the powers of exciting laughter and sorrow not only in one mind but in one composition . . . That this is a practice contrary to the rules of criticism will be readily allowed; but there is always an appeal open from criticism to nature.
Plays of William Shakespeare . . . (1765) preface (Yale ed., p. 67)

10 A quibble is to Shakespeare, what luminous vapours are to the traveller; he follows it at all adventures, it is sure to lead him out of his way and sure to engulf him in the mire.
Plays of William Shakespeare . . . (1765) preface (Yale ed., p. 74)

11 It must be at last confessed, that as we owe everything to him [Shakespeare], he owes something to us; that, if much of our praise is paid by perception and judgement, much is likewise given by custom and veneration. We fix our eyes upon his graces, and turn them from his deformities, and endure in him what we should in another loathe or despise.
Plays of William Shakespeare . . . (1765) preface (Yale ed., p. 91)

12 I have always suspected that the reading is right, which requires many words to prove it wrong; and the emendation wrong, that cannot without so much labour appear to be right.
Plays of William Shakespeare . . . (1765) preface (Yale ed., p. 108)

13 Notes are often necessary, but they are necessary evils.
Plays of William Shakespeare . . . (1765) preface (Yale ed., p. 111)

14 This world where much is to be done and little to be known.
Prayers and Meditations (1785) no. 170 'Against inquisitive and perplexing Thoughts' 12 August 1784

15 There are minds so impatient of inferiority, that their gratitude is a species of revenge, and they return benefits, not because recompense is a pleasure, but because obligation is a pain.
The Rambler no. 87 (15 January 1751)

16 No place affords a more striking conviction of the vanity of human hopes, than a public library.
The Rambler no. 106 (23 March 1751)

17 I have laboured to refine our language to grammatical purity, and to clear it from colloquial barbarisms, licentious idioms, and irregular combinations.
The Rambler no. 208 (14 March 1752)

18 Ye who listen with credulity to the whispers of fancy, and pursue with eagerness the phantoms of hope; who expect that age will perform the promises of youth, and that the deficiencies of the present day will be supplied by the morrow; attend to the history of Rasselas prince of Abyssinia.
Rasselas (1759) ch. 1

19 The business of a poet, said Imlac, is to examine, not the individual, but the species; to remark general properties and appearances: he does not number the streaks of the tulip, or describe the different shades in the verdure of the forest.
Rasselas (1759) ch. 10

20 He [the poet] must write as the interpreter of nature, and the legislator of mankind, and consider himself as presiding over the thoughts and manners of future generations; as a being superior to time and place.
Rasselas (1759) ch. 10. Cf. Shelley 644:8

21 Human life is everywhere a state in which much is to be endured, and little to be enjoyed.
Rasselas (1759) ch. 11

22 Marriage has many pains, but celibacy has no pleasures.
Rasselas (1759) ch. 26

23 Example is always more efficacious than precept.
Rasselas (1759) ch. 30

24 It [the Pyramids] seems to have been erected only in compliance with that hunger of imagination which preys incessantly upon life, and must be always appeased by some employment . . . I consider this mighty structure as a monument of the insufficiency of human enjoyments.
Rasselas (1759) ch. 32

25 Integrity without knowledge is weak and useless, and knowledge without integrity is dangerous and dreadful.
Rasselas (1759) ch. 41

26 There is perhaps no class of men, to whom the precept given by the Apostle to his converts against too great confidence in their understandings, may be more properly inculcated, than those who are dedicated to the profession of literature.
Sermons (1788) no. 8

1 In this state of temporary honour, a proud man is too willing to exert his prerogative; and too ready to forget that he is dictating to those, who may one day dictate to him.

Sermons (1788) no. 8 (on schoolmasters)

2 He [God] will not leave his promises unfulfilled, nor his threats unexecuted . . . Neither can he want power to execute his purposes; he who spoke, and the world was made, can speak again, and it will perish.

Sermons (1788) no. 10

3 How is it that we hear the loudest yelps for liberty among the drivers of negroes?

Taxation No Tyranny (1775) (Yale ed., vol. 10, p. 454)

4 A generous and elevated mind is distinguished by nothing more certainly than an eminent degree of curiosity.

Dedication of his English translation of Fr. J. Lobo's *Voyage to Abyssinia* (1735), signed 'the editor' but attributed to Johnson in James Boswell *Life of Samuel Johnson* (1791) vol. 1, p. 89 (1734)

5 Unmoved though witlings sneer and rivals rail; Studious to please, yet not ashamed to fail.

Irene (1749) prologue

6 There Poetry shall tune her sacred voice, And wake from ignorance the Western World.

Irene (1749) act 4, sc. 1, l. 122 (Demetrius forecasting the Renaissance)

7 Here falling houses thunder on your head, And here a female atheist talks you dead.

London (1738) l. 17

8 Of all the griefs that harrass the distressed, Sure the most bitter is a scornful jest; Fate never wounds more deep the gen'rous heart, Than when a blockhead's insult points the dart.

London (1738) l. 166

9 This mournful truth is ev'rywhere confessed, Slow rises worth, by poverty depressed.

London (1738) l. 176

10 Condemned to hope's delusive mine, As on we toil from day to day, By sudden blasts, or slow decline, Our social comforts drop away.

'On the Death of Dr Robert Levet' (1783)

11 When learning's triumph o'er her barb'rous foes First reared the stage, immortal Shakespeare rose; Each change of many-coloured life he drew, Exhausted worlds, and then imagined new.

'Prologue spoken at the Opening of the Theatre in Drury Lane' (1747)

12 The stage but echoes back the public voice. The drama's laws the drama's patrons give, For we that live to please, must please to live.

'Prologue spoken at the Opening of the Theatre in Drury Lane' (1747)

13 How small of all that human hearts endure, That part which laws or kings can cause or cure. Still to ourselves in every place consigned, Our own felicity we make or find.

Lines added to Oliver Goldsmith's *The Traveller* (1764) l. 429. Cf. Goldsmith 311:12

14 Let observation with extensive view, Survey mankind, from China to Peru.

The Vanity of Human Wishes (1749) l. 1

15 Deign on the passing world to turn thine eyes, And pause awhile from letters, to be wise; There mark what ills the scholar's life assail, Toil, envy, want, the patron, and the jail.

The Vanity of Human Wishes (1749) l. 157

16 A frame of adamant, a soul of fire, No dangers fright him, and no labours tire.

The Vanity of Human Wishes (1749) l. 193 (of Charles XII of Sweden)

17 His fall was destined to a barren strand, A petty fortress, and a dubious hand; He left the name, at which the world grew pale, To point a moral, or adorn a tale.

The Vanity of Human Wishes (1749) l. 219 (of Charles XII of Sweden)

18 Enlarge my life with multitude of days, In health, in sickness, thus the suppliant prays; Hides from himself his state, and shuns to know, That life protracted is protracted woe. Time hovers o'er, impatient to destroy, And shuts up all the passages of joy.

The Vanity of Human Wishes (1749) l. 255

19 Superfluous lags the vet'ran on the stage.

The Vanity of Human Wishes (1749) l. 308

20 In life's last scene what prodigies surprise, Fears of the brave, and follies of the wise? From Marlb'rough's eyes the streams of dotage flow, And Swift expires a driv'ler and a show.

The Vanity of Human Wishes (1749) l. 315

21 Must helpless man, in ignorance sedate, Roll darkling down the torrent of his fate?

The Vanity of Human Wishes (1749) l. 345

22 Still raise for good the supplicating voice, But leave to heaven the measure and the choice.

The Vanity of Human Wishes (1749) l. 351

23 A lawyer has no business with the justice or injustice of the cause which he undertakes, unless his client asks his opinion, and then he is bound to give it honestly. The justice or injustice of the cause is to be decided by the judge.

In James Boswell *Journal of a Tour to the Hebrides* (1785) 15 August 1773

24 Let him go abroad to a distant country; let him go to some place where he is *not* known. Don't let him go to the devil where he is known!

In . . . *Tour to the Hebrides* (1785) 18 August 1773 (Boswell having asked if someone should commit suicide to avoid certain disgrace)

25 I have, all my life long, been lying till noon; yet I tell all young men, and tell them with great sincerity, that nobody who does not rise early will ever do any good.

In . . . *Tour to the Hebrides* (1785) 14 September 1773

26 I inherited a vile melancholy from my father, which has made me mad all my life, at least not sober.

In . . . *Tour to the Hebrides* (1785) 16 September 1773

27 I am always sorry when any language is lost, because languages are the pedigree of nations.

In . . . *Tour to the Hebrides* (1785) 18 September 1773

28 I do not much like to see a Whig in any dress; but I hate to see a Whig in a parson's gown.

In . . . *Tour to the Hebrides* (1785) 24 September 1773

1 A cucumber should be well sliced, and dressed with pepper and vinegar, and then thrown out, as good for nothing.

   In ... *Tour to the Hebrides* (1785) 5 October 1773

2 I am sorry I have not learned to play at cards. It is very useful in life: it generates kindness and consolidates society.

   In ... *Tour to the Hebrides* (1785) 21 November 1773

The Life of Samuel Johnson (1791) by James Boswell (references are to G. B. Hill's edition, 1934, revised by L. F. Powell, 1964)

3 [JOHNSON:] I had no notion that I was wrong or irreverent to my tutor.
   [BOSWELL:] That, Sir, was great fortitude of mind.
   [JOHNSON:] No, Sir; stark insensibility.

   Boswell *Life* vol. 1, p. 60 (31 October 1728)

4 Sir, we are a nest of singing birds.

   Boswell *Life* vol. 1, p. 75 (1730) of Pembroke College, Oxford

5 He was a vicious man, but very kind to me. If you call a dog *Hervey*, I shall love him.

   Boswell *Life* vol. 1, p. 106 (1737)

6 My old friend, Mrs Carter, could make a pudding, as well as translate Epictetus.

   Boswell *Life* vol. 1, p. 122, n. 4 (Spring 1738)

7 Tom Birch is as brisk as a bee in conversation; but no sooner does he take a pen in his hand, than it becomes a torpedo to him, and benumbs all his faculties.

   Boswell *Life* vol. 1, p. 159 (1743)

8 I'll come no more behind your scenes, David; for the silk stockings and white bosoms of your actresses excite my amorous propensities.

   Boswell *Life* vol. 1, p. 201 (1750). John Wilkes (Appendix G, p. 539) recalls the remark [to Garrick] in the form: 'the silk stockings and white bosoms of your actresses do make my genitals to quiver'

9 A man may write at any time, if he will set himself doggedly to it.

   Boswell *Life* vol. 1, p. 203 (March 1750)

10 Thy body is all vice, and thy mind all virtue.

   Boswell *Life* vol. 1, p. 250 (March 1752) to Beauclerk

11 I had done all that I could; and no man is well pleased to have his all neglected, be it ever so little.

   Boswell *Life* vol. 1, p. 261 (7 February 1755) letter to Lord Chesterfield

12 The shepherd in Virgil grew at last acquainted with Love, and found him a native of the rocks.

   Boswell *Life* vol. 1, p. 262 (7 February 1755) letter to Lord Chesterfield

13 Is not a Patron, my Lord, one who looks with unconcern on a man struggling for life in the water, and, when he has reached ground, encumbers him with help? The notice which you have been pleased to take of my labours, had it been early, had been kind; but it has been delayed till I am indifferent, and cannot enjoy it; till I am solitary, and cannot impart it; till I am known, and do not want it.

   Boswell *Life* vol. 1, p. 262 (7 February 1755) letter to Lord Chesterfield

14 A fly, Sir, may sting a stately horse and make him wince; but one is but an insect, and the other is a horse still.

   Boswell *Life* vol. 1, p. 263, n. 3 (1754)

15 This man [Lord Chesterfield] I thought had been a Lord among wits; but, I find, he is only a wit among Lords.

   Boswell *Life* vol. 1, p. 266 (1754)

16 They [the *Letters* of Lord Chesterfield] teach the morals of a whore, and the manners of a dancing master.

   Boswell *Life* vol. 1, p. 266 (1754)

17 There are two things which I am confident I can do very well: one is an introduction to any literary work, stating what it is to contain, and how it should be executed in the most perfect manner; the other is a conclusion, shewing from various causes why the execution has not been equal to what the author promised to himself and to the public.

   Boswell *Life* vol. 1, p. 292 (1755)

18 Ignorance, madam, pure ignorance.

   Boswell *Life* vol. 1, p. 293 (1755) on being asked why he had defined *pastern* as the 'knee' of a horse

19 Dictionaries are like watches, the worst is better than none, and the best cannot be expected to go quite true.

   Boswell *Life* vol. 1, p. 293, n. 3, letter to Francesco Sastres, 21 August 1784

20 I have protracted my work till most of those whom I wished to please have sunk into the grave; and success and miscarriage are empty sounds.

   Boswell *Life* vol. 1, p. 297 (1755)

21 If a man does not make new acquaintance as he advances through life, he will soon find himself left alone. A man, Sir, should keep his friendship in constant repair.

   Boswell *Life* vol. 1, p. 300 (1755)

22 The worst of Warburton is, that he has a rage for saying something, when there's nothing to be said.

   Boswell *Life* vol. 1, p. 329 (1758)

23 No man will be a sailor who has contrivance enough to get himself into a jail; for being in a ship is being in a jail, with the chance of being drowned ... A man in a jail has more room, better food, and commonly better company.

   Boswell *Life* vol. 1, p. 348 (16 March 1759). Cf. Burton 165:5

24 No, Sir, I am not a botanist; and (alluding, no doubt, to his near sightedness) should I wish to become a botanist, I must first turn myself into a reptile.

   Boswell *Life* vol. 1, p. 377 n. 2 (20 July 1762)

25 [BOSWELL:] I do indeed come from Scotland, but I cannot help it ...
   [JOHNSON:] That, Sir, I find, is what a very great many of your countrymen cannot help.

   Boswell *Life* vol. 1, p. 392 (16 May 1763)

26 The notion of liberty amuses the people of England, and helps to keep off the *taedium vitae*. When a butcher tells you that *his heart bleeds for his country* he has, in fact, no uneasy feeling.

   Boswell *Life* vol. 1, p. 394 (16 May 1763)

1 Yes, Sir, many men, many women, and many children.

> Boswell *Life* vol. 1, p. 396 (24 May 1763) on Dr Blair's asking whether any man of a modern age could have written *Ossian*

2 I did not think he ought to be shut up. His infirmities were not noxious to society. He insisted on people praying with him; and I'd as lief pray with Kit Smart as any one else. Another charge was, that he did not love clean linen; and I have no passion for it.

> Boswell *Life* vol. 1, p. 397 (24 May 1763)

3 You *may* abuse a tragedy, though you cannot write one. You may scold a carpenter who has made you a bad table, though you cannot make a table. It is not your trade to make tables.

> Boswell *Life* vol. 1, p. 409 (25 June 1763) on literary criticism

4 I am afraid he has not been in the inside of a church for many years; but he never passes a church without pulling off his hat. This shows that he has good principles.

> Boswell *Life* vol. 1, p. 418 (1 July 1763) of Dr John Campbell

5 The richest author that ever grazed the common of literature.

> Boswell *Life* vol. 1, p. 418 n. 1 (1 July 1763) of Dr John Campbell

6 Great abilities are not requisite for an historian . . . imagination is not required in any high degree.

> Boswell *Life* vol. 1, p. 424 (6 July 1763)

7 Norway, too, has noble wild prospects; and Lapland is remarkable for prodigious noble wild prospects. But, Sir, let me tell you, the noblest prospect which a Scotchman ever sees, is the high road that leads him to England!

> Boswell *Life* vol. 1, p. 425 (6 July 1763)

8 A man ought to read just as inclination leads him; for what he reads as a task will do him little good.

> Boswell *Life* vol. 1, p. 428 (14 July 1763)

9 But if he does really think that there is no distinction between virtue and vice, why, Sir, when he leaves our houses, let us count our spoons.

> Boswell *Life* vol. 1, p. 432 (14 July 1763)

10 All the arguments which are brought to represent poverty as no evil, show it to be evidently a great evil. You never find people labouring to convince you that you may live very happily upon a plentiful fortune.

> Boswell *Life* vol. 1, p. 441 (20 July 1763)

11 Truth, Sir, is a cow, that will yield such people [sceptics] no more milk, and so they are gone to milk the bull.

> Boswell *Life* vol. 1, p. 444 (21 July 1763)

12 Young men have more virtue than old men; they have more generous sentiments in every respect.

> Boswell *Life* vol. 1, p. 445 (21 July 1763)

13 In my early years I read very hard. It is a sad reflection, but a true one, that I knew almost as much at eighteen as I do now.

> Boswell *Life* vol. 1, p. 445 (21 July 1763)

14 Your levellers wish to level *down* as far as themselves; but they cannot bear levelling *up* to themselves.

> Boswell *Life* vol. 1, p. 448 (21 July 1763)

15 It is no matter what you teach them [children] first, any more than what leg you shall put into your breeches first.

> Boswell *Life* vol. 1, p. 452 (26 July 1763)

16 Why, Sir, Sherry is dull, naturally dull; but it must have taken him a great deal of pains to become what we now see him. Such an excess of stupidity, Sir, is not in Nature.

> Boswell *Life* vol. 1, p. 453 (28 July 1763) of Thomas Sheridan

17 It is burning a farthing candle at Dover, to shew light at Calais.

> Boswell *Life* vol. 1, p. 454 (28 July 1763) on Thomas Sheridan's influence on the English language. Cf. Young 754:11

18 A woman's preaching is like a dog's walking on his hinder legs. It is not done well; but you are surprised to find it done at all.

> Boswell *Life* vol. 1, p. 463 (31 July 1763)

19 I look upon it, that he who does not mind his belly will hardly mind anything else.

> Boswell *Life* vol. 1, p. 467 (5 August 1763)

20 We could not have had a better dinner had there been a *Synod of Cooks*.

> Boswell *Life* vol. 1, p. 470 (5 August 1763)

21 Don't, Sir, accustom yourself to use big words for little matters. It would *not* be *terrible*, though I *were* to be detained some time here.

> Boswell *Life* vol. 1, p. 471 (6 August 1763) when Boswell said it would be 'terrible' if Johnson should not be able to return speedily from Harwich

22 I refute it *thus*.

> Boswell *Life* vol. 1, p. 471 (6 August 1763). Boswell observed of Bishop Berkeley's theory of the non-existence of matter that though they were satisfied it was not true, they were unable to refute it. Johnson struck his foot against a large stone, till he rebounded from it, with these words

23 Sir John, Sir, is a very unclubbable man.

> Boswell *Life* vol. 1, p. 480 n. 1 (Spring 1764) of Sir John Hawkins

24 That all who are happy, are equally happy, is not true. A peasant and a philosopher may be equally *satisfied*, but not equally *happy*. Happiness consists in the multiplicity of agreeable consciousness.

> Boswell *Life* vol. 2, p. 9 (February 1766)

25 It is our first duty to serve society, and, after we have done that, we may attend wholly to the salvation of our own souls. A youthful passion for abstracted devotion should not be encouraged.

> Boswell *Life* vol. 2, p. 10 (February 1766)

26 Our tastes greatly alter. The lad does not care for the child's rattle, and the old man does not care for the young man's whore.

> Boswell *Life* vol. 2, p. 14 (Spring 1766)

27 It was not for me to bandy civilities with my Sovereign.

> Boswell *Life* vol. 2, p. 35 (February 1767)

28 There was as great a difference between them as between a man who knew how a watch was made, and a man who could tell the hour by looking on the dial-plate.

> Boswell *Life* vol. 2, p. 49 (Spring 1768)

1 I love Robertson, and I won't talk of his book.
  Boswell *Life* vol. 2, p. 53 (Spring 1768) of William
  Robertson's *History of Scotland*

2 Let me smile with the wise, and feed with the rich.
  Boswell *Life* vol. 2, p. 79 (6 October 1769); responding to a
  line from Garrick's *Florizel and Perdita* act 2, sc. 1: 'They
  smile with the simple, and feed with the poor'

3 We *know* our will is free, and *there's* an end on't.
  Boswell *Life* vol. 2, p. 82 (16 October 1769)

4 In the description of night in Macbeth, the beetle and
  the bat detract from the general idea of
  darkness,—inspissated gloom.
  Boswell *Life* vol. 2, p. 90 (16 October 1769)

5 I do not know, Sir, that the fellow is an infidel; but if
  he be an infidel, he is an infidel as a dog is an infidel;
  that is to say, he has never thought upon the subject.
  Boswell *Life* vol. 2, p. 95 (19 October 1769) of Samuel Foote

6 [BOSWELL:] So, Sir, you laugh at schemes of political
  improvement.
  [JOHNSON:] Why, Sir, most schemes of political
  improvement are very laughable things.
  Boswell *Life* vol. 2, p. 102 (26 October 1769)

7 It matters not how a man dies, but how he lives. The
  act of dying is not of importance, it lasts so short a
  time.
  Boswell *Life* vol. 2, p. 106 (26 October 1769)

8 Burton's *Anatomy of Melancholy*, he said, was the only
  book that ever took him out of bed two hours sooner
  than he wished to rise.
  Boswell *Life* vol. 2, p. 121 (1770)

9 Want of tenderness, he always alleged, was want of
  parts, and was no less a proof of stupidity than
  depravity.
  Boswell *Life* vol. 2, p. 122 (1770)

10 That fellow seems to me to possess but one idea, and
   that is a wrong one.
   Boswell *Life* vol. 2, p. 126 (1770) of 'a dull tiresome fellow,
   whom he chanced to meet'

11 Johnson observed, that 'he did not care to speak ill of
   any man behind his back, but he believed the
   gentleman was an *attorney*.'
   Boswell *Life* vol. 2, p. 126 (1770)

12 The triumph of hope over experience.
   Boswell *Life* vol. 2, p. 128 (1770) of a man who remarried
   immediately after the death of a wife with whom he had
   been unhappy

13 Every man has a lurking wish to appear considerable
   in his native place.
   Boswell *Life* vol. 2, p. 141, letter to Sir Joshua Reynolds,
   17 July 1771

14 It is so far from being natural for a man and woman
   to live in a state of marriage, that we find all the
   motives which they have for remaining in that
   connection, and the restraints which civilized society
   imposes to prevent separation, are hardly sufficient to
   keep them together.
   Boswell *Life* vol. 2, p. 165 (31 March 1772)

15 Nobody can write the life of a man, but those who
   have eat and drunk and lived in social intercourse
   with him.
   Boswell *Life* vol. 2, p. 166 (31 March 1772)

16 I would not give half a guinea to live under one form
   of government rather than another. It is of no
   moment to the happiness of an individual.
   Boswell *Life* vol. 2, p. 170 (31 March 1772)

17 If a sovereign oppresses his people to a great degree,
   they will rise and cut off his head. There is a remedy
   in human nature against tyranny, that will keep us
   safe under every form of government.
   Boswell *Life* vol. 2, p. 170 (31 March 1772)

18 A man who is good enough to go to heaven, is good
   enough to be a clergyman.
   Boswell *Life* vol. 2, p. 171 (5 April 1772)

19 Why, Sir, if you were to read Richardson for the story,
   your impatience would be so much fretted that you
   would hang yourself.
   Boswell *Life* vol. 2, p. 175 (6 April 1772)

20 He has, indeed, done it very well; but it is a foolish
   thing well done.
   Boswell *Life* vol. 2, p. 210 (3 April 1773); on Goldsmith's
   apology in the *London Chronicle* for physically assaulting
   Thomas Evans, who had published a damaging open letter
   to Goldsmith in the *London Packet* 24 March 1773

21 All intellectual improvement arises from leisure.
   Boswell *Life* vol. 2, p. 219 (13 April 1773)

22 [ELPHINSTON:] What, have you not read it through?
   [JOHNSON:] No, Sir, do *you* read books *through*?
   Boswell *Life* vol. 2, p. 226 (19 April 1773)

23 Read over your compositions, and where ever you
   meet with a passage which you think is particularly
   fine, strike it out.
   Boswell *Life* vol. 2, p. 237 (30 April 1773) quoting a college
   tutor

24 I hope I shall never be deterred from detecting what I
   think a cheat, by the menaces of a ruffian ['Ossian'].
   Boswell *Life* vol. 2, p. 298, letter to James Macpherson,
   20 January 1775

25 There are few ways in which a man can be more
   innocently employed than in getting money.
   Boswell *Life* vol. 2, p. 323 (27 March 1775)

26 He was dull in a new way, and that made many
   people think him *great*.
   Boswell *Life* vol. 2, p. 327 (28 March 1775) of Thomas
   Gray

27 I never think I have hit hard, unless it rebounds.
   Boswell *Life* vol. 2, p. 335 (2 April 1775)

28 Fleet-street has a very animated appearance; but I
   think the full tide of human existence is at
   Charing-Cross.
   Boswell *Life* vol. 2, p. 337 (2 April 1775)

29 George the First knew nothing, and desired to know
   nothing; did nothing, and desired to do nothing; and
   the only good thing that is told of him is, that he
   wished to restore the crown to its hereditary
   successor.
   Boswell *Life* vol. 2, p. 342 (6 April 1775)

30 It is wonderful, when a calculation is made, how little
   the mind is actually employed in the discharge of any
   profession.
   Boswell *Life* vol. 2, p. 344 (6 April 1775)

1 The greatest part of a writer's time is spent in reading, in order to write: a man will turn over half a library to make one book.
Boswell *Life* vol. 2, p. 344 (6 April 1775)

2 Patriotism is the last refuge of a scoundrel.
Boswell *Life* vol. 2, p. 348 (7 April 1775)

3 Their [the Scots'] learning is like bread in a besieged town: every man gets a little, but no man gets a full meal.
Boswell *Life* vol. 2, p. 363 (18 April 1775)

4 Knowledge is of two kinds. We know a subject ourselves, or we know where we can find information upon it.
Boswell *Life* vol. 2, p. 365 (18 April 1775)

5 Politics are now nothing more than means of rising in the world.
Boswell *Life* vol. 2, p. 369 (18 April 1775)

6 Players, Sir! I look upon them as no better than creatures set upon tables and joint-stools to make faces and produce laughter, like dancing dogs.
Boswell *Life* vol. 2, p. 404 (1775)

7 In lapidary inscriptions a man is not upon oath.
Boswell *Life* vol. 2, p. 407 (1775)

8 There is now less flogging in our great schools than formerly, but then less is learned there; so that what the boys get at one end they lose at the other.
Boswell *Life* vol. 2, p. 407 (1775)

9 Nothing odd will do long. *Tristram Shandy* did not last.
Boswell *Life* vol. 2, p. 449 (20 March 1776)

10 There is nothing which has yet been contrived by man, by which so much happiness is produced as by a good tavern or inn.
Boswell *Life* vol. 2, p. 452 (21 March 1776)

11 Marriages would in general be as happy, and often more so, if they were all made by the Lord Chancellor, upon a due consideration of characters and circumstances, without the parties having any choice in the matter.
Boswell *Life* vol. 2, p. 461 (22 March 1776)

12 Fine clothes are good only as they supply the want of other means of procuring respect.
Boswell *Life* vol. 2, p. 475 (27 March 1776)

13 If a madman were to come into this room with a stick in his hand, no doubt we should pity the state of his mind; but our primary consideration would be to take care of ourselves. We should knock him down first, and pity him afterwards.
Boswell *Life* vol. 3, p. 11 (3 April 1776)

14 We would all be idle if we could.
Boswell *Life* vol. 3, p. 13 (3 April 1776)

15 No man but a blockhead ever wrote, except for money.
Boswell *Life* vol. 3, p. 19 (5 April 1776)

16 It is better that some should be unhappy than that none should be happy, which would be the case in a general state of equality.
Boswell *Life* vol. 3, p. 26 (7 April 1776)

17 A man who has not been in Italy, is always conscious of an inferiority, from his not having seen what it is expected a man should see.
Boswell *Life* vol. 3, p. 36 (11 April 1776)

18 [BOSWELL:] Sir, what is poetry?
[JOHNSON:] Why Sir, it is much easier to say what it is not. We all *know* what light is; but it is not easy to *tell* what it is.
Boswell *Life* vol. 3, p. 38 (12 April 1776)

19 Every man of any education would rather be called a rascal, than accused of deficiency in *the graces*.
Boswell *Life* vol. 3, p. 54 (May 1776)

20 Sir, you have but two topics, yourself and me. I am sick of both.
Boswell *Life* vol. 3, p. 57 (May 1776)

21 *Olivarii Goldsmith,*
Poetae, Physici, Historici,
Qui nullum fere scribendi genus
Non tetigit,
Nullum quod tetigit non ornavit.

To Oliver Goldsmith, A Poet, Naturalist, and Historian, who left scarcely any style of writing untouched, and touched none that he did not adorn.
Boswell *Life* vol. 3, p. 82 (22 June 1776) epitaph on Goldsmith

22 If I had no duties, and no reference to futurity, I would spend my life in driving briskly in a post-chaise with a pretty woman.
Boswell *Life* vol. 3, p. 162 (19 September 1777)

23 Depend upon it, Sir, when a man knows he is to be hanged in a fortnight, it concentrates his mind wonderfully.
Boswell *Life* vol. 3, p. 167 (19 September 1777) on the execution of Dr Dodd

24 When a man is tired of London, he is tired of life; for there is in London all that life can afford.
Boswell *Life* vol. 3, p. 178 (20 September 1777)

25 All argument is against it [ghosts]; but all belief is for it.
Boswell *Life* vol. 3, p. 230 (31 March 1778)

26 John Wesley's conversation is good, but he is never at leisure. He is always obliged to go at a certain hour. This is very disagreeable to a man who loves to fold his legs and have out his talk, as I do.
Boswell *Life* vol. 3, p. 230 (31 March 1778)

27 Though we cannot out-vote them we will out-argue them.
Boswell *Life* vol. 3, p. 234 (3 April 1778) on the practical value of speeches in the House of Commons

28 Every man thinks meanly of himself for not having been a soldier, or not having been at sea.
Boswell *Life* vol. 3, p. 265 (10 April 1778)

29 A mere antiquarian is a rugged being.
Boswell *Life* vol. 3, p. 278 (April 1778) letter to Boswell, 23 April 1778

30 Johnson had said that he could repeat a complete chapter of 'The Natural History of Iceland', from the Danish of Horrebow, the whole of which was exactly thus:—'CHAP. LXXII. *Concerning snakes*. There are no snakes to be met with throughout the whole island.'
Boswell *Life* vol. 3, p. 279 (13 April 1778)

31 The more contracted that power is, the more easily it is destroyed. A country governed by a despot is an inverted cone.
Boswell *Life* vol. 3, p. 283 (14 April 1778)

1 So it is in travelling; a man must carry knowledge with him, if he would bring home knowledge.
    Boswell *Life* vol. 3, p. 302 (17 April 1778)

2 Sir, the insolence of wealth will creep out.
    Boswell *Life* vol. 3, p. 316 (18 April 1778)

3 All censure of a man's self is oblique praise. It is in order to shew how much he can spare.
    Boswell *Life* vol. 3, p. 323 (25 April 1778)

4 I have always said, the first Whig was the Devil.
    Boswell *Life* vol. 3, p. 326 (28 April 1778)

5 It is thus that mutual cowardice keeps us in peace. Were one half of mankind brave and one half cowards, the brave would be always beating the cowards. Were all brave, they would lead a very uneasy life; all would be continually fighting: but being all cowards, we go on very well.
    Boswell *Life* vol. 3, p. 326 (28 April 1778)

6 Were it not for imagination, Sir, a man would be as happy in the arms of a chambermaid as of a Duchess.
    Boswell *Life* vol. 3, p. 341 (9 May 1778)

7 Claret is the liquor for boys; port, for men; but he who aspires to be a hero (smiling) must drink brandy.
    Boswell *Life* vol. 3, p. 381 (7 April 1779)

8 A man who exposes himself when he is intoxicated, has not the art of getting drunk.
    Boswell *Life* vol. 3, p. 389 (24 April 1779)

9 Remember that all tricks are either knavish or childish.
    Boswell *Life* vol. 3, p. 396, letter to Boswell, 9 September 1779

10 Worth seeing, yes; but not worth going to see.
    Boswell *Life* vol. 3, p. 410 (12 October 1779) on the Giant's Causeway

11 If you are idle, be not solitary; if you are solitary, be not idle.
    Boswell *Life* vol. 3, p. 415, letter to Boswell, 27 October 1779. Cf. Burton 165:14

12 Among the anfractuosities of the human mind, I know not if it may not be one, that there is a superstitious reluctance to sit for a picture.
    Boswell *Life* vol. 4, p. 4 (1780)

13 Every man has a right to utter what he thinks truth, and every other man has a right to knock him down for it. Martyrdom is the test.
    Boswell *Life* vol. 4, p. 12 (1780)

14 They are forced plants, raised in a hot-bed; and they are poor plants; they are but cucumbers after all.
    Boswell *Life* vol. 4, p. 13 (1780) of Thomas Gray's *Odes*

15 A Frenchman must be always talking, whether he knows anything of the matter or not; an Englishman is content to say nothing, when he has nothing to say.
    Boswell *Life* vol. 4, p. 15 (1780)

16 Sir, your wife, under pretence of keeping a bawdy-house, is a receiver of stolen goods.
    Boswell *Life* vol. 4, p. 26 (1780) during an exchange of coarse raillery customary among people travelling upon the Thames

17 No man was more foolish when he had not a pen in his hand, or more wise when he had.
    Boswell *Life* vol. 4, p. 29 (1780) of Oliver Goldsmith. Cf. Garrick 298:5

18 Depend upon it, said he, that if a man talks of his misfortunes there is something in them that is not disagreeable to him; for where there is nothing but pure misery, there never is any recourse to the mention of it.
    Boswell *Life* vol. 4, p. 31 (1780)

19 I believe that is true. The dogs don't know how to write trifles with dignity.
    Boswell *Life* vol. 4, p. 34, n. 5 (1781) to Fowke, who had observed that in writing biography Johnson infinitely exceeded his contemporaries

20 Mrs Montagu has dropt me. Now, Sir, there are people whom one should like very well to drop, but would not wish to be dropped by.
    Boswell *Life* vol. 4, p. 73 (March 1781)

21 This merriment of parsons is mighty offensive.
    Boswell *Life* vol. 4, p. 76 (March 1781)

22 Mr Long's character is very *short*. It is nothing. He fills a chair. He is a man of genteel appearance, and that is all.
    Boswell *Life* vol. 4, p. 81 (1 April 1781) of Mr Dudley Long

23 We are not here to sell a parcel of boilers and vats, but the potentiality of growing rich, beyond the dreams of avarice.
    Boswell *Life* vol. 4, p. 87 (6 April 1781) at the sale of Thrale's brewery. Cf. Moore 482:7

24 Classical quotation is the *parole* of literary men all over the world.
    Boswell *Life* vol. 4, p. 102 (8 May 1781)

25 Why, that is, because, dearest, you're a dunce.
    Boswell *Life* vol. 4, p. 109 (May 1781) to Miss Monckton, later Lady Corke, who said that Sterne's writings affected her

26 Sir, I have two very cogent reasons for not printing any list of subscribers;—one, that I have lost all the names,—the other, that I have spent all the money.
    Boswell *Life* vol. 4, p. 111 (May 1781)

27 Always, Sir, set a high value on spontaneous kindness. He whose inclination prompts him to cultivate your friendship of his own accord, will love you more than one whom you have been at pains to attach to you.
    Boswell *Life* vol. 4, p. 115 (May 1781)

28 A wise Tory and a wise Whig, I believe, will agree. Their principles are the same, though their modes of thinking are different.
    Boswell *Life* vol. 4, p. 117 (May 1781) written statement given to Boswell

29 Officious, innocent, sincere,
    Of every friendless name the friend.

    Yet still he fills affection's eye,
    Obscurely wise, and coarsely kind.
    Boswell *Life* vol. 4, p. 137 (20 January 1782) on the death of Mr Levett

30 Then, with no throbs of fiery pain,
    No cold gradations of decay,
    Death broke at once the vital chain,
    And freed his soul the nearest way.
    Boswell *Life* vol. 4, p. 139 (20 January 1782) on the death of Mr Levett

1 Resolve not to be poor: whatever you have, spend less. Poverty is a great enemy to human happiness; it certainly destroys liberty, and it makes some virtues impracticable, and others extremely difficult.
> Boswell *Life* vol. 4, p. 157, letter to Boswell, 7 December 1782

2 I hate a fellow whom pride, or cowardice, or laziness drives into a corner, and who does nothing when he is there but sit and *growl*; let him come out as I do, and *bark*.
> Boswell *Life* vol. 4, p. 161, n. 3 (10 October 1782) of Jeremiah Markland

3 How few of his friends' houses would a man choose to be at when he is sick.
> Boswell *Life* vol. 4, p. 181 (1783)

4 There is a wicked inclination in most people to suppose an old man decayed in his intellects. If a young or middle-aged man, when leaving a company, docs not recollect where he laid his hat, it is nothing; but if the same inattention is discovered in an old man, people will shrug up their shoulders, and say, 'His memory is going.'
> Boswell *Life* vol. 4, p. 181 (1783)

5 A man might write such stuff for ever, if he would *abandon* his mind to it.
> Boswell *Life* vol. 4, p. 183 (1783) of Ossian

6 Sir, there is no settling the point of precedency between a louse and a flea.
> Boswell *Life* vol. 4, p. 192 (1783) on the relative merits of two minor poets

7 When I observed he was a fine cat, saying, 'Why yes, Sir, but I have had cats whom I liked better than this'; and then as if perceiving Hodge to be out of countenance, adding, 'but he is a very fine cat, a very fine cat indeed.'
> Boswell *Life* vol. 4, p. 197 (1783)

8 My dear friend, clear your *mind* of cant . . . You may *talk* in this manner; it is a mode of talking in Society: but don't *think* foolishly.
> Boswell *Life* vol. 4, p. 221 (15 May 1783)

9 As I know more of mankind I expect less of them, and am ready now to call a man *a good man*, upon easier terms than I was formerly.
> Boswell *Life* vol. 4, p. 239 (September 1783)

10 If a man were to go by chance at the same time with Burke under a shed, to shun a shower, he would say—'this is an extraordinary man.'
> On Edmund Burke, in Boswell *Life* vol. 4, p. 275 (15 May 1784)

11 It is as bad as bad can be: it is ill-fed, ill-killed, ill-kept, and ill-drest.
> Boswell *Life* vol. 4, p. 284 (3 June 1784) on the roast mutton he had been served at an inn

12 [JOHNSON:] As I cannot be sure that I have fulfilled the conditions on which salvation is granted, I am afraid I may be one of those who shall be damned (looking dismally).
> [DR ADAMS:] What do you mean by damned?
> [JOHNSON:] (passionately and loudly) Sent to Hell, Sir, and punished everlastingly.
> Boswell *Life* vol. 4, p. 299 (12 June 1784)

13 Milton, Madam, was a genius that could cut a Colossus from a rock; but could not carve heads upon cherry-stones.
> Boswell *Life* vol. 4, p. 305 (13 June 1784) to Hannah More, who had expressed a wonder that the poet who had written *Paradise Lost* should write such poor sonnets

14 It might as well be said 'Who drives fat oxen should himself be fat.'
> Boswell *Life* vol. 4, p. 313 (June 1784) parodying Henry Brooke. Cf. Brooke 143:2

15 Sir, I have found you an argument; but I am not obliged to find you an understanding.
> Boswell *Life* vol. 4, p. 313 (June 1784)

16 No man is a hypocrite in his pleasures.
> Boswell *Life* vol. 4, p. 316 (June 1784). Cf. Pope 520:28

17 Talking of the Comedy of 'The Rehearsal,' he said, 'It has not wit enough to keep it sweet.' This was easy;—he therefore caught himself, and pronounced a more rounded sentence; 'It has not vitality enough to preserve it from putrefaction.'
> Boswell *Life* vol. 4, p. 320 (June 1784)

18 Who can run the race with Death?
> Boswell *Life* vol. 4, p. 360, letter to Dr Burney, 2 August 1784

19 Sir, I look upon every day to be lost, in which I do not make a new acquaintance.
> Boswell *Life* vol. 4, p. 374 (November 1784)

20 I will be conquered; I will not capitulate.
> Boswell *Life* vol. 4, p. 374 (November 1784) on his illness

21 Long-expected one-and-twenty,
Ling'ring year, at length is flown;
Pride and pleasure, pomp and plenty,
Great [Sir John], are now your own.
> Boswell *Life* vol. 4, p. 413 (December 1784)

22 An odd thought strikes me:—we shall receive no letters in the grave.
> Boswell *Life* vol. 4, p. 413 (December 1784)

23 Madam, before you flatter a man so grossly to his face, you should consider whether or not your flattery is worth his having.
> Remark to Hannah More, in Charlotte Barrett (ed.) *Diary and Letters of Madame D'Arblay* [Fanny Burney] (1842) vol. 1, pt. 2, p. 55 (August 1778)

24 Every man has, some time in his life, an ambition to be a wag.
> In Joyce Hemlow (ed.) *Journals and Letters of Fanny Burney* vol. 1 (1972) p. 182

25 Love is the wisdom of the fool and the folly of the wise.
> In William Cooke *Life of Samuel Foote* (1805) vol. 2, p. 154

26 As with my hat upon my head
I walked along the Strand,
I there did meet another man
With his hat in his hand.
> In *European Magazine* January 1785 'Anecdotes by George Steevens'

27 Of music Dr Johnson used to say that it was the only sensual pleasure without vice.
> In *European Magazine* (1795) p. 82

1 Fly fishing may be a very pleasant amusement; but angling or float fishing I can only compare to a stick and a string, with a worm at one end and a fool at the other.

> Attributed, in Hawker *Instructions to Young Sportsmen* (1859) p. 197, though not found in Johnson's works. See *Notes and Queries* 11 December 1915. The remark has also been attributed to Jonathan Swift, in *The Indicator* 27 October 1819, p. 44

2 I dogmatise and am contradicted, and in this conflict of opinions and sentiments I find delight.

> On his conversation in taverns, in John Hawkins *Life of Samuel Johnson* (1787) p. 87

3 Corneille is to Shakespeare . . . as a clipped hedge is to a forest.

> In Hester Lynch Piozzi *Anecdotes of . . . Johnson* (1786) p. 59

4 If the man who turnips cries,
Cry not when his father dies,
'Tis a proof that he had rather
Have a turnip than his father.

> Burlesque of Lope de Vega's lines '*Si a quien los leones vence* [He who can conquer a lion . . .]', in Hester Lynch Piozzi *Anecdotes of . . . Johnson* (1786) p. 67

5 Dear Bathurst (said he to me one day) was a man to my very heart's content: he hated a fool, and he hated a rogue, and he hated a whig; he was a very good hater.

> Hester Lynch Piozzi *Anecdotes of . . . Johnson* (1786) p. 83

6 One day at Streatham . . . a young gentleman called to him suddenly, and I suppose he thought disrespectfully, in these words: 'Mr Johnson, would you advise me to marry?' 'I would advise no man to marry, Sir,' returns for answer in a very angry tone Dr Johnson, 'who is not likely to propagate understanding.'

> Hester Lynch Piozzi *Anecdotes of . . . Johnson* (1786) p. 97

7 [Goldsmith] seeming to repine at the success of Beattie's Essay on Truth—'Here's such a stir (said he) about a fellow that has written one book, and I have written many.' Ah, Doctor (says his friend [Johnson]), there go two-and-forty sixpences you know to one guinea.

> Hester Lynch Piozzi *Anecdotes of . . . Johnson* (1786) p. 179

8 It is very strange, and very melancholy, that the paucity of human pleasures should persuade us ever to call hunting one of them.

> In Hester Lynch Piozzi *Anecdotes of . . . Johnson* (1786) p. 206

9 Was there ever yet anything written by mere man that was wished longer by its readers, excepting *Don Quixote*, *Robinson Crusoe*, and the *Pilgrim's Progress*?

> In Hester Lynch Piozzi *Anecdotes of . . . Johnson* (1786) p. 281

10 Abstinence is as easy to me, as temperance would be difficult.

> In William Roberts (ed.) *Memoirs of the Life and Correspondence of Mrs Hannah More* (1834) vol. 1, p. 251

11 What is written without effort is in general read without pleasure.

> In William Seward *Biographia* (1799) p. 260

12 Difficult do you call it, Sir? I wish it were impossible.

> On the performance of a celebrated violinist, in William Seward *Supplement to the Anecdotes of Distinguished Persons* (1797) p. 267

13 *Iam moriturus.*

I who am about to die.

> To Francesco Sastres, shortly before his death on 13 December 1784, in Sir John Hawkins *Life of Samuel Johnson* (1787) p. 591. Cf. Anonymous 22:2

Samuel Johnson 1822–82

American nonconformist minister

14 City of God, how broad and far
Outspread thy walls sublime!
The true thy chartered freemen are
Of every age and clime.

> 'City of God, how broad and far' (1864)

John Benn Johnstone 1803–91

English playwright

15 I want you to assist me in forcing her on board the lugger; once there, I'll frighten her into marriage.

> *The Gipsy Farmer* (performed 1845); since quoted 'Once aboard the lugger and the maid is mine'

Hanns Johst 1890–1978

German playwright

16 *Wenn ich Kultur höre . . . entsichere ich meinen Browning!*

Whenever I hear the word culture . . . I release the safety-catch of my Browning!

> *Schlageter* (1933) act 1, sc. 1 (often attributed to Hermann Goering, and quoted, 'Whenever I hear the word culture, I reach for my pistol!')

Al Jolson (Asa Yoelson) 1886–1950

American singer

17 You think that's noise—you ain't heard nuttin' yet!

> In a café, prior to an encore, the applause for his previous rendering having been obliterated by the din from a neighbouring building site; in Martin Abramson *The Real Story of Al Jolson* (1950) p. 12 (later the title of a Jolson song, 1919, in the form 'You Ain't Heard Nothing Yet')

Henry Arthur Jones 1851–1929 *and* Henry Herman 1832–94

English playwrights

18 O God! Put back Thy universe and give me yesterday.

> *The Silver King* (1907) act 2, sc. 4

John Paul Jones 1747–92

American admiral

19 I have not yet begun to fight.

> As his ship was sinking, 23 September 1779, having been asked whether he had lowered his flag; in Mrs Reginald De Koven *Life and Letters of John Paul Jones* (1914) vol. 1, p. 455

LeRoi Jones

See IMAMU AMIRI BARAKA

Sir William Jones 1746–94

English jurist

1 My opinion is, that power should always be distrusted, in whatever hands it is placed.
> Letter to Lord Althorpe, 5 October 1782, in Lord Teignmouth *Life of Sir W. Jones* (1835) vol. 1

2 Seven hours to law, to soothing slumber seven, Ten to the world allot, and *all* to Heaven.
> Lines in substitution for Sir Edward Coke's lines 'Six hours in sleep . . . ', in Lord Teignmouth *Life of Sir W. Jones* (1835) vol. 2. Cf. Coke 209:2

Erica Jong 1942–

American novelist

3 The zipless fuck is absolutely pure. It is free of ulterior motives. There is no power game. The man is not 'taking' and the woman is not 'giving' . . . The zipless fuck is the purest thing there is. And it is rarer than the unicorn.
> *Fear of Flying* (1973) ch. 1

Ben Jonson c.1573–1637

English playwright and poet

4 Fortune, that favours fools.
> *The Alchemist* (1610) prologue

5 The children of perdition are oft-times Made instruments even of the greatest works.
> *The Alchemist* (1610) act 3, sc. 1

6 　　　　　We will eat our mullets, Soused in high-country wines, sup pheasants' eggs, And have our cockles boiled in silver shells; Our shrimps to swim again, as when they lived, In a rare butter made of dolphins' milk, Whose cream does look like opals.
> *The Alchemist* (1610) act 4, sc. 1

7 　　　　　If I have outstripped An old man's gravity, or strict canon, think What a young wife and a good brain may do: Stretch age's truth sometimes, and crack it too.
> *The Alchemist* (1610) act 5, sc. 2

8 Leave thy exercise of widow-hunting once, this drawing after an old reverend smock by the splay-foot!
> *Bartholomew Fair* (1614) act 1, sc. 3

9 The very womb and bed of enormity.
> *Bartholomew Fair* (1614) act 2, sc. 1 (of Ursula, the 'pig-woman')

10 The lungs of the tobacconist are rotted, the liver spotted, the brain smoked like the backside of the pig-woman's booth here, and the whole body within, black as her pan you saw e'en now without.
> *Bartholomew Fair* (1614) act 2, sc. 1

11 Neither do thou lust after that tawney weed tobacco.
> *Bartholomew Fair* (1614) act 2, sc. 6

12 PEOPLE: The Voice of Cato is the voice of Rome.
CATO: The voice of Rome is the consent of heaven!
> *Catiline his Conspiracy* (1611) act 3, sc. 1

13 　　　　　Where it concerns himself, Who's angry at a slander makes it true.
> *Catiline his Conspiracy* (1611) act 3, sc. 1

14 Slow, slow, fresh fount, keep time with my salt tears: Yet, slower, yet; O faintly, gentle springs: List to the heavy part the music bears, Woe weeps out her division, when she sings.
> *Cynthia's Revels* (1600) act 1, sc. 1

15 　　　　　So they be ill men, If they spake worse, 'twere better: for of such To be dispraised, is the most perfect praise.
> *Cynthia's Revels* (1600) act 3, sc. 2

16 Queen and huntress, chaste and fair, Now the sun is laid to sleep, Seated in thy silver chair, State in wonted manner keep: Hesperus entreats thy light, Goddess, excellently bright.
> *Cynthia's Revels* (1600) act 5, sc. 3

17 This is Mab, the Mistress-Fairy That doth nightly rob the dairy.
> *The Entertainment at Althorpe* (1603)

18 Still to be neat, still to be drest, As you were going to a feast; Still to be powdered, still perfumed, Lady, it is to be presumed, Though art's hid causes are not found, All is not sweet, all is not sound.

Give me a look, give me a face, That makes simplicity a grace; Robes loosely flowing, hair as free: Such sweet neglect more taketh me, Than all the adulteries of art; They strike mine eyes, but not my heart.
> *Epicene* (1609) act 1, sc. 1

19 I do honour the very flea of his dog.
> *Every Man in His Humour* (1598) act 4, sc. 2

20 　　　　　Well, I will scourge those apes, And to these courteous eyes oppose a mirror, As large as is the stage whereon we act; Where they shall see the time's deformity Anatomised in every nerve, and sinew, With constant courage, and contempt of fear.
> *Every Man out of His Humour* (1600) Induction

21 　　　　　My strict hand Was made to seize on vice, and with a gripe Squeeze out the humour of such spongy souls, As lick up every idle vanity.
> *Every Man out of His Humour* (1600) Induction

22 　　　　　Blind Fortune still Bestows her gifts on such as cannot use them.
> *Every Man out of His Humour* (1599) act 2, sc. 2

23 Ramp up my genius, be not retrograde; But boldly nominate a spade a spade.
> *The Poetaster* (1601) act 5, sc. 1

24 Detraction is but baseness' varlet; And apes are apes, though clothed in scarlet.
> *The Poetaster* (1601) act 5, sc. 1

25 　　　　　Tell proud Jove, Between his power and thine there is no odds: 'Twas only fear first in the world made gods.
> *Sejanus* (1603) act 2, sc. 2

1 Riches, the dumb god that giv'st all men tongues,
  That canst do nought, and yet mak'st men do all
     things;
  The price of souls; even hell, with thee to boot,
  Is made worth heaven! Thou art virtue, fame,
  Honour, and all things else.
     Volpone (1606) act 1, sc. 1

2   I glory
  More in the cunning purchase of my wealth
  Than in the glad possession.
     Volpone (1606) act 1, sc. 1

3   Give 'em words;
  Pour oil into their ears, and send them hence.
     Volpone (1606) act 1, sc. 4

4   What a rare punishment
  Is avarice to itself!
     Volpone (1606) act 1, sc. 4

5 Whilst others have been at the balloo, I have been at
  my book, and am now past the craggy paths of study,
  and come to the flowery plains of honour and
  reputation.
     Volpone (1606) act 2, sc. 1

6 Calumnies are answered best with silence.
     Volpone (1605) act 2, sc. 2

7   Almost
  All the wise world is little else in nature
  But parasites or sub-parasites.
     Volpone (1606) act 3, sc. 1

8 Suns, that set, may rise again;
  But if once we lose this light,
  'Tis with us perpetual night.
     Volpone (1605) act 3, sc. 5. Cf. Catullus 185:15

9 Our drink shall be prepared gold and amber;
  Which we will take, until my roof whirl around
  With the *vertigo*: and my dwarf shall dance.
     Volpone (1605) act 3, sc. 5

10 Come, my Celia, let us prove,
  While we can, the sports of love.
     Volpone (1605) act 3, sc. 5. Cf. Catullus 185:15

11   Honour! tut, a breath,
  There's no such thing in nature; a mere term
  Invented to awe fools.
     Volpone (1606) act 3, sc. 7

12 You have a gift, sir, (thank your education),
  Will never let you want, while there are men,
  And malice, to breed causes.
     Volpone (1605) act 5, sc. 1 (to a lawyer)

13   Mischiefs feed
  Like beasts, till they be fat, and then they bleed.
     Volpone (1605) act 5, sc. 8

14 And it is not always face,
  Clothes, or fortune gives the grace,
  Or the feature, or the youth;
  But the language, and the truth,
  With the ardour and the passion,
  Gives the lover weight and fashion.
     'A Celebration of Charis' (1640) no. 1 'His Excuse for
     Loving'

15 Or scorn, or pity on me take,
  I must the true relation make:
  I am undone tonight;
  Love in a subtle dream disguised
  Hath bought my heart and me surprised,
  Whom never yet he durst attempt awake;
  Nor will he tell me for whose sake
  He did me the delight,
  Or spite,
  But leaves me to inquire,
  In all my wild desire
  Of sleep again, who was his aid;
  And sleep so guilty and afraid
  As, since, he dares not come within my sight.
     'The Dream' (1640)

16 The voice so sweet, the words so fair,
  As some soft chime had stroked the air;
  And though the sound were parted thence,
  Still left an echo in the sense.
     'Eupheme' (1640) no. 4 'The Mind'

17 Rest in soft peace, and, asked, say here doth lie
  Ben Jonson his best piece of poetry.
     'On My First Son' (1616)

18 This figure that thou here seest put,
  It was for gentle Shakespeare cut,
  Wherein the graver had a strife
  With Nature, to out-do the life:
  O could he but have drawn his wit
  As well in brass, as he has hit
  His face; the print would then surpass
  All that was ever writ in brass.
  But since he cannot, reader, look
  Not on his picture, but his book.
     On the Portrait of Shakespeare, from *First Folio Shakespeare*
     (1623) 'To the Reader'

19 Follow a shadow, it still flies you;
  Seem to fly it, it will pursue:
  So court a mistress, she denies you;
  Let her alone, she will court you.
  Say, are not women truly then
  Styled but the shadows of us men?
     'That Women are but Men's Shadows' (1616)

20 Drink to me only with thine eyes,
  And I will pledge with mine;
  Or leave a kiss but in the cup,
  And I'll not look for wine.
     'To Celia' (1616)

21 It is not growing like a tree
  In bulk, doth make men better be;
  Or standing long an oak, three hundred year,
  To fall a log at last, dry, bald, and sere:
  A lily of a day
  Is fairer far, in May,
  Although it fall and die that night;
  It was the plant and flower of light.
  In small proportions we just beauty see,
  And in short measures life may perfect be.
     'To the Immortal Memory . . . of . . . Sir Lucius Carey and
     Sir H. Morison' (1640)

1   Soul of the Age!
The applause, delight, the wonder of our stage!
'To the Memory of My Beloved, the Author, Mr William Shakespeare' (1623)

2   How far thou didst our Lyly outshine,
Or sporting Kyd, or Marlowe's mighty line.
'To the Memory of . . . Shakespeare' (1623)

3 Thou hadst small Latin, and less Greek.
'To the Memory of . . . Shakespeare' (1623)

4 He was not of an age, but for all time!
'To the Memory of . . . Shakespeare' (1623)

5 Sweet Swan of Avon! What a sight it were
To see thee in our waters yet appear,
And make those flights upon the banks of Thames
That so did take Eliza, and our James!
'To the Memory of . . . Shakespeare' (1623)

6 Thou art not, Penshurst, built to envious show
Of touch or marble, nor canst boast a row
Of polished pillars, or a roof of gold;
Thou hast no lantern whereof tales are told,
Or stair, or courts; but standst an ancient pile,
And these grudged at, art reverenced the while.
'To Penshurst' (1616) l. 1

7 The blushing apricot and woolly peach
Hang on thy walls, that every child may reach.
'To Penshurst' (1616) l. 43

8 Donne, for not keeping of accent, deserved hanging
. . . Shakespeare wanted art.
In *Conversations with William Drummond of Hawthornden* (written 1619) no. 3

9 The players have often mentioned it as an honour to Shakespeare that in his writing, whatsoever he penned, he never blotted out a line. My answer hath been 'Would he had blotted a thousand' . . . But he redeemed his vices with his virtues. There was ever more in him to be praised than to be pardoned.
Timber, or Discoveries made upon Men and Matter (1641) l. 658 'De Shakespeare Nostrati'. Cf. Heming 331:13, Pope 523:5

10 The fear of every man that heard him was, lest he should make an end.
Timber, or Discoveries made upon Men and Matter (1641) l. 906 'Dominus Verulamius' (on Francis Bacon)

11 Talking and eloquence are not the same: to speak, and to speak well, are two things.
Timber, or Discoveries made upon Men and Matter (1641) l. 1882 'Praecept[a] Element[aria]'

Janis Joplin 1943–70

American singer

12 Fourteen heart attacks and he had to die in my week. In MY week.
When ex-President Eisenhower's death prevented her photograph appearing on the cover of *Newsweek*, in *New Musical Express* 12 April 1969

Thomas Jordan *c.*1612–85

English poet and playwright

13 They plucked communion tables down
And broke our painted glasses;
They threw our altars to the ground
And tumbled down the crosses.
They set up Cromwell and his heir—
The Lord and Lady Claypole—
Because they hated Common Prayer,
The organ and the maypole.
'How the War began' (1664)

John Jortin 1698–1770

English ecclesiastical historian

14 *Palmam qui meruit, ferat.*
Let him who has won it bear the palm.
Lusus Poetici (3rd ed., 1748) 'Ad Ventos' (adopted by Lord Nelson as his motto)

Sir Keith Joseph (Baron Joseph) 1918–

British Conservative politician

15 Problems reproduce themselves from generation to generation . . . I refer to this as a 'cycle of deprivation'.
Speech in London to the Pre-School Playgroups Association, 29 June 1972, in *The Times* 30 June 1972

16 We [the Conservative Party] found it hard to avoid the feeling that somehow the lean and tight-lipped mufflered men in the 1930s dole queue were at least partly our fault.
Reflection occasioned in 1945 by the national euphoria on the outcome of the Second World War, in Peter Jenkins *Mrs Thatcher's Revolution* (1987) p. 63

Benjamin Jowett 1817–93

English classicist; Master of Balliol College, Oxford, from 1870

17 One man is as good as another until he has written a book.
In Evelyn Abbott and Lewis Campbell (eds.) *Life and Letters of Benjamin Jowett* (1897) vol. 1, p. 248

18 Nowhere probably is there more true feeling, and nowhere worse taste, than in a churchyard.
In Evelyn Abbott and Lewis Campbell (eds.) *Letters of Benjamin Jowett* (1899) ch. 6

19 The lie in the soul is a true lie.
Introduction to his translation (1871) of Plato's *Republic* bk. 2

James Joyce 1882–1941

Irish novelist

20 His soul swooned slowly as he heard the snow falling faintly through the universe and faintly falling, like the descent of their last end, upon all the living and the dead.
Dubliners (1914) 'The Dead'

21 riverrun, past Eve and Adam's, from swerve of shore to bend of bay, brings us by a commodious vicus of recirculation back to Howth Castle and Environs.
Finnegans Wake (1939) pt. 1, p. 3

1 That ideal reader suffering from an ideal insomnia.
  Finnegans Wake (1939) pt. 1, p. 120

2 The flushpots of Euston and the hanging garments of
  Marylebone.
  Finnegans Wake (1939) pt. 1, p. 192

3   O
                       tell me all about
              Anna Livia! I want to hear all
  about Anna Livia. Well, you know Anna Livia? Yes,
  of course, we all know Anna Livia. Tell me all. Tell me
  now.
  Finnegans Wake (1939) pt. 1, p. 196

4 Tell me, tell me, tell me, elm! Night night! Telmetale
  of stem or stone. Beside the rivering waters of
  hitherandthithering waters of. Night!
  Finnegans Wake (1939) pt. 1, p. 216

5 All moanday, tearsday, wailsday, thumpsday,
  frightday, shatterday till the fear of the Law.
  Finnegans Wake (1939) pt. 2, p. 301

6 Three quarks for Muster Mark!
  Finnegans Wake (1939) pt. 2, p. 383

7 The Gracehoper was always jigging ajog, hoppy on
  akkant of his joyicity.
  Finnegans Wake (1939) pt. 3, p. 414

8 If I seen him bearing down on me now under
  whitespread wings like he'd come from Arkangels,
  I sink I'd die down over his feet, humbly dumbly, only
  to washup.
  Finnegans Wake (1939) pt. 4, p. 627

9 Once upon a time and a very good time it was there
  was a moocow coming down along the road and this
  moocow that was down along the road met a nicens
  little boy named baby tuckoo.
  A Portrait of the Artist as a Young Man (1916) ch. 1

10 When the soul of a man is born in this country, there
   are nets flung at it to hold it back from flight. You talk
   to me of nationality, language, religion. I shall try to
   fly by those nets.
   A Portrait of the Artist as a Young Man (1916) ch. 5

11 Ireland is the old sow that eats her farrow.
   A Portrait of the Artist as a Young Man (1916) ch. 5

12 Pity is the feeling which arrests the mind in the
   presence of whatsoever is grave and constant in
   human sufferings and unites it with the human
   sufferer. Terror is the feeling which arrests the mind in
   the presence of whatsoever is grave and constant in
   human sufferings and unites it with the secret cause.
   A Portrait of the Artist as a Young Man (1916) ch. 5

13 The artist, like the God of the creation, remains within
   or behind or beyond or above his handiwork, invisible,
   refined out of existence, indifferent, paring his
   fingernails.
   A Portrait of the Artist as a Young Man (1916) ch. 5

14 I will not serve that in which I no longer believe
   whether it call itself my home, my fatherland or my
   church: and I will try to express myself in some mode
   of life or art as freely as I can and as wholly as I can,
   using for my defence the only arms I allow myself to
   use, silence, exile, and cunning.
   A Portrait of the Artist as a Young Man (1916) ch. 5

15 Welcome, O life! I go to encounter for the millionth
   time the reality of experience and to forge in the
   smithy of my soul the uncreated conscience of my race
   . . . Old father, old artificer, stand me now and ever in
   good stead.
   A Portrait of the Artist as a Young Man (1916) ch. 5

16 By an epiphany he meant a sudden spiritual
   manifestation, whether in vulgarity of speech or of
   gesture or in a memorable phase of the mind itself. He
   believed that it was for the man of letters to recover
   these epiphanies with extreme care, seeing that they
   themselves are the most delicate and evanescent of
   moments.
   Stephen Hero (1944) ch. 25 (part of a first draft of *A Portrait
   of the Artist as a Young Man*)

17 Stately, plump Buck Mulligan came from the
   stairhead, bearing a bowl of lather on which a mirror
   and a razor lay crossed. A yellow dressinggown,
   ungirdled, was sustained gently behind him on the
   mild morning air. He held the bowl aloft and intoned:
   —Introibo ad altare Dei.
   Ulysses (1922) p. 1

18 The snotgreen sea. The scrotumtightening sea.
   Ulysses (1922) p. 5

19 It is a symbol of Irish art. The cracked lookingglass of
   a servant.
   Ulysses (1922) p. 7

20 When I makes tea I makes tea, as old mother Grogan
   said. And when I makes water I makes water . . .
   *Begob, ma'am, says Mrs Cahill, God send you don't make
   them in the one pot.*
   Ulysses (1922) p. 12

21 I fear those big words, Stephen said, which make us so
   unhappy.
   Ulysses (1922) p. 31

22 History, Stephen said, is a nightmare from which I am
   trying to awake.
   Ulysses (1922) p. 34

23 Lawn Tennyson, gentleman poet.
   Ulysses (1922) p. 50

24 Mr Leopold Bloom ate with relish the inner organs of
   beasts and fowls. He liked thick giblet soup, nutty
   gizzards, a stuffed roast heart, liverslices fried with
   crustcrumbs, fried hencod's roes. Most of all he liked
   grilled mutton kidneys which gave to his palate a fine
   tang of faintly scented urine.
   Ulysses (1922) p. 53

25 He . . . saw the dark tangled curls of his bush floating,
   floating hair of the stream around the limp father of
   thousands, a languid floating flower.
   Ulysses (1922) p. 83

26 Come forth, Lazarus! And he came fifth and lost the
   job.
   Ulysses (1922) p. 102

27 Plenty to see and hear and feel yet. Feel live warm
   beings near you. They aren't going to get me this
   innings. Warm beds: warm full blooded life.
   Ulysses (1922) p. 102

1 She used to say Ben Dollard had a base barreltone voice.
Ulysses (1922) p. 147

2 A man of genius makes no mistakes. His errors are volitional and are the portals of discovery.
Ulysses (1922) p. 182

3 But it's no use, says he. Force, hatred, history, all that. That's not life for men and women, insult and hatred. And everybody knows that it's the very opposite of that that is really life.
Ulysses (1922) p. 317

4 And they beheld Him, even Him, ben Bloom Elijah, amid clouds of angels ascend to the glory of the brightness at an angle of forty-five degrees over Donohoe's in Little Green Street like a shot off a shovel.
Ulysses (1922) p. 330

5 Greater love than this, he said, no man hath that a man lay down his wife for his friend. Go thou and do likewise. Thus, or words to that effect, saith Zarathustra, sometime regius professor of French letters to the university of Oxtail.
Ulysses (1922) p. 375

6 The heaventree of stars hung with humid nightblue fruit.
Ulysses (1922) p. 651

7 He kissed me under the Moorish wall and I thought well as well him as another and then I asked him with my eyes to ask again yes and then he asked me would I yes to say yes my mountain flower and first I put my arms around him yes and drew him down to me so he could feel my breasts all perfume yes and his heart was going like mad and yes I said yes I will Yes.
Ulysses (1922) p. 732

Jack Judge 1878–1938 *and* Harry Williams 1874–1924

British songwriters

8 It's a long way to Tipperary,
It's a long way to go;
It's a long way to Tipperary,
To the sweetest girl I know!
Goodbye, Piccadilly,
Farewell, Leicester Square,
It's a long, long way to Tipperary,
But my heart's right there!
'It's a Long Way to Tipperary' (1912 song)

Julian the Apostate AD *c*.332–363

Roman emperor from AD 360

9 *Vicisti, Galilaee.*

You have won, Galilean.
Supposed dying words, though in fact a late embellishment of Theodoret *Ecclesiastical History* (AD *c*.450) bk. 3, ch. 25

Julian of Norwich 1343–after 1416

English anchoress

10 Sin is behovely, but all shall be well and all shall be well and all manner of thing shall be well.
Revelations of Divine Love (the long text) ch. 27, Revelation 13

11 Wouldest thou wit thy Lord's meaning in this thing? Wit it well: Love was his meaning. Who shewed it thee? Love. What shewed He thee? Love. Wherefore shewed it He? for Love . . . Thus was I learned that Love is our Lord's meaning.
Revelations of Divine Love (the long text) ch. 86, Revelation 16

Carl Gustav Jung 1875–1961

Swiss psychologist

12 *Eine gewissermassen oberflächliche Schicht des Unbewussten ist zweifellos persönlich. Wir nennen sie das persönliche Unbewusste. Dieses ruht aber auf einer tieferen Schicht, welche nicht mehr persönlicher Erfahrung und Erwerbung entstammt, sondern angeboren ist. Diese tiefere Schicht ist das sogenannte kollektive Unbewusste . . . Die Inhalte des persönlichen Unbewussten sind in der Hauptsache die sogenannten gefühlsbetonten Komplexe . . . Die Inhalte des kollektiven Unbewussten dagegen sind die sogenannten* Archetypen.

A more or less superficial layer of the unconscious is undoubtedly personal. I call it the *personal unconscious*. But this personal unconscious rests upon a deeper layer, which does not derive from personal experience and is not a personal acquisition but is inborn. This deeper layer I call the *collective unconscious* . . . The contents of the personal unconscious are chiefly the *feeling-toned complexes* . . . The contents of the collective unconscious, on the other hand, are known as *archetypes*.
Eranos Jahrbuch (1934) p. 180

13 *Ein Mensch, der nicht durch die Hölle seiner Leidenschaften gegangen ist, hat sie auch nie überwunden.*

A man who has not passed through the inferno of his passions has never overcome them.
Erinnerungen, Träume, Gedanken (1962) ch. 9

14 *Soweit wir zu erkennen vermögen, ist es der einzige Sinn der menschlichen Existenz, ein Licht anzuzünden in der Finsternis des blossen Seins.*

As far as we can discern, the sole purpose of human existence is to kindle a light in the darkness of mere being.
Erinnerungen, Träume, Gedanken (1962) ch. 11

15 *Jede Form von Süchtigkeit ist von übel, gleichgültig, ob es sich um Alkohol oder Morphium oder Idealismus handelt.*

Every form of addiction is bad, no matter whether the narcotic be alcohol or morphine or idealism.
Erinnerungen, Träume, Gedanken (1962) ch. 12

1 *Wo die Liebe herrscht, da gibt es keinen Machtwillen, und wo die Macht den Vorrang hat, da fehlt die Liebe. Das eine ist der Schatten des andern.*

Where love rules, there is no will to power, and where power predominates, love is lacking. The one is the shadow of the other.

Gesammelte Werke vol. 7 (1964) 'Über die Psychologie des Unbewussten' (1917)

2 *Alles, was wir an den Kindern ändern wollen, sollten wir zunächst wohl aufmerksam prüfen, ob es nicht etwas sei, was besser an uns zu ändern wäre.*

If there is anything that we wish to change in the child, we should first examine it and see whether it is not something that could better be changed in ourselves.

Gesammelte Werke vol. 17 (1972) 'Vom Werden der Persönlichkeit' (1932)

'Junius'

18th-century pseudonymous writer

3 The liberty of the press is the *Palladium* of all the civil, political, and religious rights of an Englishman.

The Letters of Junius (1772 ed.) 'Dedication to the English Nation'

4 The right of election is the very essence of the constitution.

Public Advertiser 24 April 1769, Letter 11

5 Is this the wisdom of a great minister? or is it the ominous vibration of a pendulum?

Public Advertiser 30 May 1769, Letter 12

6 There is a holy mistaken zeal in politics as well as in religion. By persuading others, we convince ourselves.

Public Advertiser 19 December 1769, Letter 35

7 However distinguished by rank or property, in the rights of freedom we are all equal.

Public Advertiser 19 March 1770, Letter 37

8 The injustice done to an individual is sometimes of service to the public.

Public Advertiser 14 November 1770, Letter 41

9 As for Mr Wedderburne, there is something about him, which even treachery cannot trust.

Public Advertiser 22 June 1771, Letter 49

Sir John Junor 1919–

10 Pass the sick bag, Alice.

Referring to a canteen lady at the old *Express* building in Fleet Street, who conveyed plates of egg and chips to journalists at their desks; in *Guardian* 'Notes and Queries' (1991)

11 Such a graceful exit. And then he had to go and do this on the doorstep.

On Harold Wilson's 'Lavender List' (the honours list he drew up on resigning the British premiership in 1976); in *Observer* 23 January 1990

Justinian AD 483–565

Roman emperor from AD 527

12 Justice is the constant and perpetual wish to render to every one his due.

Institutes bk. 1, ch. 1, para. 1

Juvenal AD c.60–c.130

Roman satirist

13 *Difficile est saturam non scribere.*
It's hard not to write satire.
Satires no. 1, l. 30

14 *Probitas laudatur et alget.*
Honesty is praised and left to shiver.
Satires no. 1, l. 74 (translation by G. G. Ramsay)

15 *Si natura negat, facit indignatio versum.*
Even if nature says no, indignation makes me write verse.
Satires no. 1, l. 79

16 *Quidquid agunt homines, votum timor ira voluptas Gaudia discursus nostri farrago libelli est.*
Everything mankind does, their hope, fear, rage, pleasure, joys, business, are the hotch-potch of my little book.
Satires no. 1, l. 85

17 *Quis tulerit Gracchos de seditione querentes?*
Who would put up with the Gracchi complaining about subversion?
Satires no. 2, l. 24

18 *Nemo repente fuit turpissimus.*
No one ever suddenly became depraved.
Satires no. 2, l. 83

19 *Iam pridem Syrus in Tiberim defluxit Orontes Et linguam et mores.*
The Syrian Orontes has now for long been pouring into the Tiber, with its own language and ways of behaving.
Satires no. 3, l. 62

20 *Grammaticus, rhetor, geometres, pictor, aliptes, Augur, schoenobates, medicus, magus, omnia novit Graeculus esuriens: in caelum iusseris ibit.*
Scholar, public speaker, geometrician, painter, physical training instructor, diviner of the future, rope-dancer, doctor, magician, the hungry little Greek can do everything: send him to—heaven (and he'll go there).
Satires no. 3, l. 76

21 *Nil habet infelix paupertas durius in se Quam quod ridiculos homines facit.*
The misfortunes of poverty carry with them nothing harder to bear than that it makes men ridiculous.
Satires no. 3, l. 152

22 *Haud facile emergunt quorum virtutibus obstat Res angusta domi.*
They do not easily rise out of obscurity whose talents obstruct at home.
Satires no. 3, l. 164

23 *... Omnia Romae Cum pretio.*
Everything in Rome has its price.
Satires no. 3, l. 183

24 *Rara avis in terris nigroque simillima cycno.*
A rare bird on this earth, like nothing so much as a black swan.
Satires no. 6, l. 165

1 *Hoc volo, sic iubeo, sit pro ratione voluntas.*

I will have this done, so I order it done; let my will
replace reasoned judgement.

Satires no. 6, l. 223

2 *'Pone seram, cohibe.' Sed quis custodiet ipsos
Custodes? Cauta est et ab illis incipit uxor.*

'Bolt her in, keep her indoors.' But who is to guard
the guards themselves? Your wife is prudent and
begins with them.

Satires no. 6, l. 347

3   *Tenet insanabile multos
Scribendi cacoethes et aegro in corde senescit.*

Many suffer from the incurable disease of writing, and
it becomes chronic in their sick minds.

Satires no. 7, l. 51

4 *Summum crede nefas animam praeferre pudori
Et propter vitam vivendi perdere causas.*

Count it the greatest sin to prefer mere existence to
honour, and for the sake of life to lose the reasons for
living.

Satires no. 8, l. 83

5 *Cantabit vacuus coram latrone viator.*

Travel light and you can sing in the robber's face.

Satires no. 10, l. 22

6 *. . . Verbosa et grandis epistula venit
A Capreis.*

A huge wordy letter came from Capri.

On the Emperor Tiberius's letter to the Senate, which
caused the downfall of Sejanus in AD 31; in Satires no. 10,
l. 71

7 *. . . Duas tantum res anxius optat,
Panem et circenses.*

Only two things does he [the modern citizen]
anxiously wish for—bread and the big match.

Satires no. 10, l. 80 (usually quoted 'bread and circuses')

8 *Expende Hannibalem: quot libras in duce summo
Invenies?*

Weigh Hannibal: how many pounds will you find in
that great general?

Satires no. 10, l. 147

9 *. . . I, demens, et saevas curre per Alpes
Ut pueris placeas et declamatio fias.*

Off you go, madman, and hurry across the horrible
Alps, duly to delight schoolboys and become a subject
for practising speech-making.

Satires no. 10, l. 166 (on Hannibal)

10   *Mors sola fatetur
Quantula sint hominum corpuscula.*

Death alone reveals how small are men's poor bodies.

Satires no. 10, l. 172 (on Hannibal)

11 *Orandum est ut sit mens sana in corpore sano.*

You should pray to have a sound mind in a sound
body.

Satires no. 10, l. 356

12 *. . . Prima est haec ultio, quod se
Iudice nemo nocens absolvitur.*

This is the first of punishments, that no guilty man is
acquitted if judged by himself.

Satires no. 13, l. 2

13   *Quippe minuti
Semper et infirmi est animi exiguique voluptas
Ultio.*

Indeed, revenge is always the pleasure of a paltry,
feeble, tiny mind.

Satires no. 13, l. 189

14 *Maxima debetur puero reverentia, siquid
Turpe paras, nec tu pueri contempseris annos.*

A child is owed the greatest respect; if you ever have
something disgraceful in mind, don't ignore your son's
tender years.

Satires no. 14, l. 47

Franz Kafka 1883–1924

Czech novelist

15 *Jemand musste Josef K. verleumdet haben, denn ohne dass
er etwas Böses getan hätte, wurde er eines Morgens
verhaftet.*

Someone must have traduced Joseph K., for without
having done anything wrong he was arrested one fine
morning.

The Trial (1925) ch. 1

16 *Sie können einwenden, dass es ja überhaupt kein Verfahren
ist. Sie haben sehr recht, denn es ist ja nur ein Verfahren,
wenn ich es als solches anerkenne.*

You may object that it is not a trial at all; you are
quite right, for it is only a trial if I recognize it as such.

The Trial (1925) ch. 2

17 *Es ist oft besser, in Ketten als frei zu sein.*

It's often better to be in chains than to be free.

The Trial (1925) ch. 8

18 *Als Gregor Samsa eines Morgens aus unruhigen Träumen
erwachte, fand er sich in seinem Bett zu einem
ungeheueren Ungeziefer verwandelt.*

When Gregor Samsa awoke one morning from uneasy
dreams he found himself transformed in his bed into
a gigantic insect.

The Metamorphosis (1915) ch. 1

Gus Kahn 1886–1941 and
Raymond B. Egan 1890–1952

American songwriters

19 There's nothing surer,
The rich get rich and the poor get children.
In the meantime, in between time,
Ain't we got fun.

'Ain't We Got Fun' (1921 song)

Nicholas Kaldor 1908–86

British economist

20 There is no need for the economist to prove . . . that as
a result of the adoption of a certain measure nobody is
going to suffer. In order to establish his case, it is quite
sufficient for him to show that even if all those who
suffer as a result are fully compensated for their loss,
the rest of the community will still be better off than
before.

'Welfare Propositions of Economics' in Economic Journal
September 1939

Bert Kalmar 1884–1947 *et al.*

1 Remember, you're fighting for this woman's honour
. . . which is probably more than she ever did.
Duck Soup (1933 film); spoken by Groucho Marx

2 If you can't leave in a taxi you can leave in a huff. If
that's too soon, you can leave in a minute and a huff.
Duck Soup (1933 film); spoken by Groucho Marx

Henry Home, Lord Kames
1696–1782
Scottish judge and landowner

3 Avoid as much as possible abstract and general terms
. . . Images, which are the life of poetry, cannot be
raised in any perfection but by introducing particular
objects.
Elements of Criticism (1762) vol. 1, ch. 4

Immanuel Kant 1724–1804
German philosopher

4 *Zwei Dinge erfüllen das Gemüt mit immer neuer und
zunehmender Bewunderung und Ehrfurcht, je öfter und
anhaltender sich das Nachdenken damit beschäftigt: der
bestirnte Himmel über mir, und das moralische Gesetz in
mir.*

Two things fill the mind with ever new and increasing
wonder and awe, the more often and the more
seriously reflection concentrates upon them: the starry
heaven above me and the moral law within me.
Critique of Practical Reason (1788) p. 2

5 *Es ist überall nichts in der Welt, ja überhaupt auch ausser
derselben zu denken möglich, was ohne Einschränkung für
gut könnte gehalten werden, als allein guter Wille.*

Nothing in the world—indeed nothing even beyond
the world—can possibly be conceived which could be
called good without qualification except a *good will*.
Foundation of the Metaphysics of Morals (1785) sect. 1

6 *Ich soll niemals anders verfahren, als so, dass ich auch
wollen könne, meine Maxime solle ein allgemeines Gesetz
werden.*

I am never to act otherwise than so that I could also
will that my maxim should become a universal law.
Fundamental Principles of the Metaphysics of Ethics (1785)
sect. 1 (translated by T. K. Abbott)

7 *Endlich giebt es einen Imperativ, der, ohne irgend eine
andere durch ein gewisses Verhalten zu erreichende Absicht
als Bedingung zum Grunde zu legen, dieses Verhalten
unmittelbar gebietet. Dieser Imperativ ist categorisch . . .
Dieser Imperativ mag der der Sittlichkeit heissen.*

Finally, there is an imperative which commands a
certain conduct immediately, without having as its
condition any other purpose to be attained by it. This
imperative is Categorical . . . This imperative may be
called that of Morality.
Fundamental Principles of the Metaphysics of Ethics (1785)
sect. 2 (translated by T. K. Abbott)

8 *Wer den Zweck will, will (so fern die Vernunft auf seine
Handlungen entscheidenden Einfluss hat), auch das dazu
unentbehrlich nothwendige Mittel, das in seiner Gewalt
ist.*

Whoever wills the end, wills also (so far as reason
decides his conduct) the means in his power which are
indispensably necessary thereto.
Fundamental Principles of the Metaphysics of Ethics (1785)
sect. 2 (translated by T. K. Abbott)

9 *Glückseligkeit ist nicht ein Ideal der Vernunft, sondern der
Einbildungstraft.*

Happiness is not an ideal of reason but of imagination.
Fundamental Principles of the Metaphysics of Ethics (1785)
sect. 2 (translated by T. K. Abbott)

10 *Handle so, dass du die Menschheit, so wohl in deiner
Person, als in der Person eines jeden andern, jederzeit
zugleich als Zweck, niemals bloss als Mittel brauchest.*

So act as to treat humanity, whether in thine own
person or in that of any other, in every case as an end
withal, never as means only.
Fundamental Principles of the Metaphysics of Ethics (1785)
sect. 2 (translation by T. K. Abbott)

11 *Aus so krummem Holze, als woraus der Mensch gemacht
ist, kann nichts ganz gerades gezimmert werden.*

Out of the crooked timber of humanity no straight
thing can ever be made.
Idee zu einer allgemeinen Geschichte in weltbürgerlicher Absicht
(1784) proposition 6

Alphonse Karr 1808–90
French novelist and journalist

12 *Si l'on veut abolir la peine de mort en ce cas, que MM les
assassins commencent.*

In that case, if we are to abolish the death penalty, let
the murderers take the first step.
Les Guêpes January 1849 (6th series, 1859) p. 304

13 *Plus ça change, plus c'est la même chose.*

The more things change, the more they are the same.
Les Guêpes January 1849 (6th series, 1859) p. 305

George S. Kaufman 1889–1961
American playwright

14 Satire is what closes Saturday night.
In Scott Meredith *George S. Kaufman and his Friends* (1974)
ch. 6

Gerald Kaufman 1930–
British Labour politician

15 The longest suicide note in history.
On the Labour Party's *New Hope for Britain* (1983), in
Denis Healey *The Time of My Life* (1989) ch. 23

Paul Kaufman and Mike Anthony
American songwriters

16 Poetry in motion.
Title of song (1960). Cf. Grahame 314:3

Christoph Kaufmann 1753–95

German man of letters

1 *Sturm und Drang.*

Storm and stress.

Title suggested by Kaufmann for a romantic drama of the American War of Independence by the German playwright, F. M. Klinger (1775), and thereafter given to a period of literary ferment which prevailed in Germany during the latter part of the 18th century

Patrick Kavanagh 1905–67

Irish poet

2 Cassiopeia was over
Cassidy's hanging hill,
I looked and three whin bushes rode across
The horizon — the Three Wise Kings.
'A Christmas Childhood' (1947)

3 Clay is the word and clay is the flesh
Where the potato-gatherers like mechanized
  scarecrows move
Along the side-fall of the hill—Maguire and his men.
'The Great Hunger' (1947)

4 That was how his life happened.
No mad hooves galloping in the sky,
But the weak, washy way of true tragedy—
A sick horse nosing around the meadow for a clean
  place to die.
'The Great Hunger' (1947)

5 I hate what every poet hates in spite
Of all the solemn talk of contemplation.
Oh, Alexander Selkirk knew the plight
Of being king and government and nation.
A road, a mile of kingdom, I am king
Of banks and stones and every blooming thing.
'Inniskeen Road: July Evening' (1936). Cf. Cowper
224:15

John Keats 1795–1821

English poet

6 . . . Other spirits there are standing apart
Upon the forehead of the age to come.
'Addressed to [Haydon]' (1817)

7 Bards of Passion and of Mirth,
Ye have left your souls on earth!
Have ye souls in heaven too,
Double-lived in regions new?
'Bards of Passion and of Mirth' (1820)

8 Where the nightingale doth sing
Not a senseless, trancèd thing,
But divine melodious truth.
'Bards of Passion and of Mirth' (1820)

9 Bright star, would I were steadfast as thou art—
Not in lone splendour hung aloft the night,
And watching, with eternal lids apart,
Like nature's patient, sleepless Eremite,
The moving waters at their priestlike task
Of pure ablution round earth's human shores.
'Bright star, would I were steadfast as thou art' (written
1819)

10 Still, still to hear her tender-taken breath,
And so live ever—or else swoon to death.
'Bright star, would I were steadfast as thou art' (written
1819)

11 The day is gone, and all its sweets are gone!
Sweet voice, sweet lips, soft hand, and softer breast.
'The day is gone, and all its sweets are gone' (written
1819)

12 The imagination of a boy is healthy, and the mature
imagination of a man is healthy; but there is a space
of life between, in which the soul is in a ferment, the
character undecided, the way of life uncertain, the
ambition thick-sighted: thence proceeds mawkishness.
Endymion (1818) preface

13 A thing of beauty is a joy for ever:
Its loveliness increases; it will never
Pass into nothingness; but still will keep
A bower quiet for us, and a sleep
Full of sweet dreams, and health, and quiet breathing.
Endymion (1818) bk. 1, l. 1

14   The grandeur of the dooms
We have imagined for the mighty dead.
Endymion (1818) bk. 1, l. 20

15 They alway must be with us, or we die.
Endymion (1818) bk. 1, l. 33

16   Who, of men, can tell
That flowers would bloom, or that green fruit would
  swell
To melting pulp, that fish would have bright mail,
The earth its dower of river, wood, and vale,
The meadows runnels, runnels pebble-stones,
The seed its harvest, or the lute its tones,
Tones ravishment, or ravishment its sweet,
If human souls did never kiss and greet?
Endymion (1818) bk. 1, l. 835

17   Here is wine,
Alive with sparkles—never, I aver,
Since Ariadne was a vintager,
So cool a purple.
Endymion (1818) bk. 2, l. 441

18 To Sorrow,
I bade good-morrow,
And thought to leave her far away behind;
But cheerly, cheerly,
She loves me dearly;
She is so constant to me, and so kind.
Endymion (1818) bk. 4, l. 173

19   Their smiles,
Wan as primroses gathered at midnight
By chilly fingered spring.
Endymion (1818) bk. 4, l. 969

20 St Agnes' Eve—Ah, bitter chill it was!
The owl, for all his feathers, was a-cold;
The hare limped trembling through the frozen grass,
And silent was the flock in woolly fold.
'The Eve of St Agnes' (1820) st. 1

21 The sculptured dead, on each side, seem to freeze,
Emprison'd in black, purgatorial rails.
'The Eve of St Agnes' (1820) st. 2

22 The silver, snarling trumpets 'gan to chide.
'The Eve of St Agnes' (1820) st. 4

1 And soft adorings from their loves receive
Upon the honeyed middle of the night.
   'The Eve of St Agnes' (1820) st. 6

2 The music, yearning like a God in pain.
   'The Eve of St Agnes' (1820) st. 7

3 A poor, weak, palsy-stricken, churchyard thing.
   'The Eve of St Agnes' (1820) st. 18

4 Out went the taper as she hurried in;
Its little smoke, in pallid moonshine, died.
   'The Eve of St Agnes' (1820) st. 23

5 A casement high and triple-arched there was,
All garlanded with carven imag'ries
Of fruits, and flowers, and bunches of knot-grass,
And diamonded with panes of quaint device,
Innumerable of stains and splendid dyes,
As are the tiger-moth's deep-damasked wings.
   'The Eve of St Agnes' (1820) st. 24

6   By degrees
Her rich attire creeps rustling to her knees.
   'The Eve of St Agnes' (1820) st. 26

7 Trembling in her soft and chilly nest.
   'The Eve of St Agnes' (1820) st. 27

8 As though a rose should shut, and be a bud again.
   'The Eve of St Agnes' (1820) st. 27

9 And still she slept an azure-lidded sleep,
In blanchèd linen, smooth, and lavendered,
While he from forth the closet brought a heap
Of candied apple, quince, and plum, and gourd;
With jellies soother than the creamy curd,
And lucent syrops, tinct with cinnamon;
Manna and dates, in argosy transferred
From Fez; and spiced dainties, every one,
From silken Samarcand to cedared Lebanon.
   'The Eve of St Agnes' (1820) st. 30

10 He played an ancient ditty, long since mute,
In Provence called, 'La belle dame sans mercy.'
   'The Eve of St Agnes' (1820) st. 33

11 And the long carpets rose along the gusty floor.
   'The Eve of St Agnes' (1820) st. 40

12 And they are gone: aye, ages long ago
These lovers fled away into the storm.
   'The Eve of St Agnes' (1820) st. 42

13 The Beadsman, after thousand aves told,
For aye unsought for slept among his ashes cold.
   'The Eve of St Agnes' (1820) st. 42

14 Fanatics have their dreams, wherewith they weave
A paradise for a sect.
   'The Fall of Hyperion' (written 1819) l. 1

15 'None can usurp this height,' returned that shade,
'But those to whom the miseries of the world
Are misery, and will not let them rest.'
   'The Fall of Hyperion' (written1819) l. 147

16 The poet and the dreamer are distinct,
Diverse, sheer opposite, antipodes.
The one pours out a balm upon the world,
The other vexes it.
   'The Fall of Hyperion' (written 1819) l. 199

17 Ever let the fancy roam,
Pleasure never is at home.
   'Fancy' (1820) l. 1

18 O sweet Fancy! let her loose;
Summer's joys are spoilt by use.
   'Fancy' (1820) l. 9

19 Where's the cheek that doth not fade,
Too much gazed at? Where's the maid
Whose lip mature is ever new?
   'Fancy' (1820) l. 69

20   Where's the face
One would meet in every place?
   'Fancy' (1820) l. 73

21 Four seasons fill the measure of the year;
There are four seasons in the mind of man.
   'The Human Seasons' (1819)

22 Deep in the shady sadness of a vale
Far sunken from the healthy breath of morn,
Far from the fiery noon, and eve's one star,
Sat grey-haired Saturn, quiet as a stone.
   'Hyperion: A Fragment' (1820) bk. 1, l. 1

23   No stir of air was there,
Not so much life as on a summer's day
Robs not one light seed from the feathered grass,
But where the dead leaf fell, there did it rest.
   'Hyperion: A Fragment' (1820) bk. 1, l. 7

24   The Naiad 'mid her reeds
Pressed her cold finger closer to her lips.
   'Hyperion: A Fragment' (1820) bk. 1, l. 13

25 That large utterance of the early gods!
   'Hyperion: A Fragment' (1820) bk. 1, l. 51

26 O aching time! O moments big as years!
   'Hyperion: A Fragment' (1820) bk. 1, l. 64

27 As when, upon a trancèd summer-night,
Those green-robed senators of mighty woods,
Tall oaks, branch-charmèd by the earnest stars,
Dream, and so dream all night without a stir.
   'Hyperion: A Fragment' (1820) bk. 1, l. 72

28   Sometimes eagle's wings,
Unseen before by gods or wondering men,
Darkened the place.
   'Hyperion: A Fragment' (1820) bk. 1, l. 182

29 And still they were the same bright, patient stars.
   'Hyperion: A Fragment' (1820) bk. 1, l. 353

30 Knowledge enormous makes a god of me.
   'Hyperion: A Fragment' (1820) bk. 3, l. 113

31 I had a dove and the sweet dove died;
And I have thought it died of grieving:
O, what could it grieve for? Its feet were tied,
With a silken thread of my own hand's weaving.
   'I had a dove and the sweet dove died' (written 1818)

32 In drear nighted December
Too happy, happy tree
Thy branches ne'er remember
Their green felicity.
   'In drear nighted December' (written 1817)

33 But were there ever any
Writhed not of passèd joy:
To know the change and feel it
When there is none to heal it
Nor numbed sense to steel it
Was never said in rhyme.
   'In drear nighted December' (written 1817)

1 Why were they proud? again we ask aloud,
Why in the name of Glory were they proud?
'Isabella; or, The Pot of Basil' (1820) st. 16

2 So the two brothers and their murdered man
Rode past fair Florence.
'Isabella; or, The Pot of Basil' (1820) st. 27

3 And she forgot the stars, the moon, and sun,
And she forgot the blue above the trees,
And she forgot the dells where waters run,
And she forgot the chilly autumn breeze;
She had no knowledge when the day was done,
And the new morn she saw not: but in peace
Hung over her sweet Basil evermore,
And moistened it with tears unto the core.
'Isabella; or, The Pot of Basil' (1820) st. 53

4   'For cruel 'tis,' said she,
'To steal my Basil-pot away from me.'
'Isabella; or, The Pot of Basil' (1820) st. 62

5   And then there crept
A little noiseless noise among the leaves,
Born of the very sigh that silence heaves.
'I stood tip-toe upon a little hill' (1817) l. 10

6 Here are sweet peas, on tip-toe for a flight.
'I stood tip-toe upon a little hill' (1817) l. 57

7 Oh, what can ail thee knight at arms
Alone and palely loitering?
The sedge has withered from the lake
And no birds sing!
'La belle dame sans merci' (1820) st. 1

8 I see a lily on thy brow
With anguish moist and fever dew,
And on thy cheeks a fading rose
Fast withereth too.
'La belle dame sans merci' (1820) st. 3

9 I met a lady in the meads
Full beautiful, a faery's child
Her hair was long, her foot was light
And her eyes were wild.
'La belle dame sans merci' (1820) st. 4

10 She looked at me as she did love
And made sweet moan.
'La belle dame sans merci' (1820) st. 5

11 I set her on my pacing steed
And nothing else saw all day long
For sidelong would she bend and sing
A faery's song.
'La belle dame sans merci' (1820) st. 6

12 . . . La belle dame sans merci
Thee hath in thrall.
'La belle dame sans merci' (1820) st. 10

13 I saw their starved lips in the gloam
With horrid warning gapèd wide
And I awoke and found me here
On the cold hill's side.
'La belle dame sans merci' (1820) st. 11

14 She was a gordian shape of dazzling hue,
Vermilion-spotted, golden, green, and blue;
Striped like a zebra, freckled like a pard,
Eyed like a peacock, and all crimson barred.
'Lamia' (1820) pt. 1, l. 47

15 Real are the dreams of Gods, and smoothly pass
Their pleasures in a long immortal dream.
'Lamia' (1820) pt. 1, l. 127

16 Love in a hut, with water and a crust,
Is—Love, forgive us!—cinders, ashes, dust;
Love in a palace is perhaps at last
More grievous torment than a hermit's fast.
'Lamia' (1820) pt. 2, l. 1

17 That purple-linèd palace of sweet sin.
'Lamia' (1820) pt. 2, l. 31

18 In pale contented sort of discontent.
'Lamia' (1820) pt. 2, l. 135

19   Do not all charms fly
At the mere touch of cold philosophy?
There was an awful rainbow once in heaven:
We know her woof, her texture; she is given
In the dull catalogue of common things.
Philosophy will clip an Angel's wings.
'Lamia' (1820) pt. 2, l. 229

20 Souls of poets dead and gone,
What Elysium have ye known,
Happy field or mossy cavern,
Choicer than the Mermaid Tavern?
Have ye tippled drink more fine
Than mine host's Canary wine?
'Lines on the Mermaid Tavern' (1820)

21 . . . Pledging with contented smack
The Mermaid in the Zodiac.
'Lines on the Mermaid Tavern' (1820)

22 Rich in the simple worship of a day.
'Mother of Hermes! and still youthful Maia!' (written 1818)

23 Thou still unravished bride of quietness,
Thou foster-child of silence and slow time.
'Ode on a Grecian Urn' (1820) st. 1

24 What men or gods are these? What maidens loth?
What mad pursuit? What struggle to escape?
What pipes and timbrels? What wild ecstasy?
'Ode on a Grecian Urn' (1820) st. 1

25 Heard melodies are sweet, but those unheard
Are sweeter; therefore, ye soft pipes, play on;
Not to the sensual ear, but, more endeared,
Pipe to the spirit ditties of no tone.
'Ode on a Grecian Urn' (1820) st. 2

26 For ever wilt thou love, and she be fair!
'Ode on a Grecian Urn' (1820) st. 2

27 For ever piping songs for ever new.
'Ode on a Grecian Urn' (1820) st. 3

28 For ever warm and still to be enjoyed,
For ever panting, and for ever young;
All breathing human passion far above,
That leaves a heart high-sorrowful and cloyed,
A burning forehead, and a parching tongue.
'Ode on a Grecian Urn' (1820) st. 3

29 Who are these coming to the sacrifice?
To what green altar, O mysterious priest,
Lead'st thou that heifer lowing at the skies,
And all her silken flanks with garlands dressed?
What little town by river or sea shore,
Or mountain-built with peaceful citadel,
Is emptied of this folk, this pious morn?
'Ode on a Grecian Urn' (1820) st. 4

1 O Attic shape! Fair attitude!
  'Ode on a Grecian Urn' (1820) st. 5

2 Thou, silent form, dost tease us out of thought
  As doth eternity: Cold Pastoral!
  'Ode on a Grecian Urn' (1820) st. 5

3 'Beauty is truth, truth beauty,'—that is all
  Ye know on earth, and all ye need to know.
  'Ode on a Grecian Urn' (1820) st. 5

4 No, no, go not to Lethe, neither twist
  Wolf's-bane, tight-rooted, for its poisonous wine.
  'Ode on Melancholy' (1820) st. 1

5 Nor let the beetle, nor the death-moth be
  Your mournful Psyche.
  'Ode on Melancholy' (1820) st. 1

6 But when the melancholy fit shall fall
  Sudden from heaven like a weeping cloud,
  That fosters the droop-headed flowers all,
  And hides the green hill in an April shroud;
  Then glut thy sorrow on a morning rose,
  Or on the rainbow of the salt sand-wave,
  Or on the wealth of globèd peonies;
  Or if thy mistress some rich anger shows,
  Emprison her soft hand, and let her rave,
  And feed deep, deep upon her peerless eyes.
  'Ode on Melancholy' (1820) st. 2

7 She dwells with Beauty—Beauty that must die;
  And Joy, whose hand is ever at his lips
  Bidding adieu; and aching Pleasure nigh,
  Turning to poison while the bee-mouth sips:
  Ay, in the very temple of Delight
  Veiled Melancholy has her sovran shrine,
  Though seen of none save him whose strenuous
      tongue
  Can burst Joy's grape against his palate fine;
  His soul shall taste the sadness of her might,
  And be among her cloudy trophies hung.
  'Ode on Melancholy' (1820) st. 3

8 My heart aches, and a drowsy numbness pains
  My sense, as though of hemlock I had drunk,
  Or emptied some dull opiate to the drains
  One minute past, and Lethe-wards had sunk:
  'Tis not through envy of thy happy lot,
  But being too happy in thine happiness,—
  That thou, light-wingèd Dryad of the trees,
  In some melodious plot
  Of beechen green, and shadows numberless,
  Singest of summer in full-throated ease.
  'Ode to a Nightingale' (1820) st. 1

9 O, for a draught of vintage! that hath been
  Cooled a long age in the deep-delvèd earth,
  Tasting of Flora and the country green,
  Dance, and Provençal song, and sunburnt mirth!
  O for a beaker full of the warm South,
  Full of the true, the blushful Hippocrene,
  With beaded bubbles winking at the brim,
  And purple-stainèd mouth;
  That I might drink, and leave the world unseen,
  And with thee fade away into the forest dim.
  'Ode to a Nightingale' (1820) st. 2

10 Fade far away, dissolve, and quite forget
   What thou among the leaves hast never known,
   The weariness, the fever, and the fret
   Here, where men sit and hear each other groan;
   Where palsy shakes a few, sad, last grey hairs,
   Where youth grows pale, and spectre-thin, and dies;
   Where but to think is to be full of sorrow
   And leaden-eyed despairs.
   'Ode to a Nightingale' (1820) st. 3

11 Away! away! for I will fly to thee,
   Not charioted by Bacchus and his pards,
   But on the viewless wings of Poesy,
   Though the dull brain perplexes and retards:
   Already with thee! tender is the night.
   'Ode to a Nightingale' (1820) st. 4

12 I cannot see what flowers are at my feet,
   Nor what soft incense hangs upon the boughs.
   'Ode to a Nightingale' (1820) st. 5

13 Fast fading violets covered up in leaves;
   And mid-May's eldest child,
   The coming musk-rose, full of dewy wine,
   The murmurous haunt of flies on summer eves.
   'Ode to a Nightingale' (1820) st. 5

14 Darkling I listen; and, for many a time
   I have been half in love with easeful Death,
   Called him soft names in many a musèd rhyme,
   To take into the air my quiet breath;
   Now more than ever seems it rich to die,
   To cease upon the midnight with no pain.
   'Ode to a Nightingale' (1820) st. 6

15 Thou wast not born for death, immortal bird!
   No hungry generations tread thee down;
   The voice I hear this passing night was heard
   In ancient days by emperor and clown:
   Perhaps the self-same song that found a path
   Through the sad heart of Ruth, when, sick for home,
   She stood in tears amid the alien corn;
   The same that oft-times hath
   Charmed magic casements, opening on the foam
   Of perilous seas, in faery lands forlorn.
   'Ode to a Nightingale' (1820) st. 7

16 Forlorn! the very word is like a bell
   To toll me back from thee to my sole self!
   Adieu! the fancy cannot cheat so well
   As she is famed to do, deceiving elf.
   'Ode to a Nightingale' (1820) st. 8

17 Was it a vision, or a waking dream?
   Fled is that music:—do I wake or sleep?
   'Ode to a Nightingale' (1820) st. 8

18 'Mid hushed, cool-rooted flowers, fragrant-eyed,
   Blue, silver-white, and budded Tyrian.
   'Ode to Psyche' (1820) st. 1

19 Nor virgin-choir to make delicious moan
   Upon the midnight hours.
   'Ode to Psyche' (1820) st. 2

20 Yes, I will be thy priest, and build a fane
   In some untrodden region of my mind,
   Where branchèd thoughts, new grown with pleasant
       pain,
   Instead of pines shall murmur in the wind.
   'Ode to Psyche' (1820) st. 4

1 A bright torch, and a casement ope at night,
  To let the warm Love in!
    'Ode to Psyche' (1820) st. 4

2 Much have I travelled in the realms of gold,
  And many goodly states and kingdoms seen.
    'On First Looking into Chapman's Homer' (1817)

3 Then felt I like some watcher of the skies
  When a new planet swims into his ken;
  Or like stout Cortez when with eagle eyes
  He stared at the Pacific—and all his men
  Looked at each other with a wild surmise—
  Silent, upon a peak in Darien.
    'On First Looking into Chapman's Homer' (1817)

4   Mortality
  Weighs heavily on me like unwilling sleep.
    'On Seeing the Elgin Marbles' (1817)

5 The poetry of earth is never dead:
  When all the birds are faint with the hot sun,
  And hide in cooling trees, a voice will run
  From hedge to hedge about the new-mown mead.
    'On the Grasshopper and Cricket' (1817)

6 It keeps eternal whisperings around
  Desolate shores,—and with its mighty swell
  Gluts twice ten thousand Caverns.
    'On the Sea' (1817)

7 Yet the sweet converse of an innocent mind,
  Whose words are images of thoughts refined,
  Is my soul's pleasure; and it sure must be
  Almost the highest bliss of human-kind,
  When to thy haunts two kindred spirits flee.
    'O Solitude! if I must with thee dwell' (1817)

8 O fret not after knowledge—I have none,
  And yet my song comes native with the warmth.
  O fret not after knowledge—I have none,
  And yet the Evening listens.
    'O thou whose face hath felt the winter's wind' (written 1818)

9 Dry your eyes—O dry your eyes
  For I was taught in Paradise
  To ease my breast of melodies.
    'Shed no tear—O shed no tear' (written 1819)

10 Stop and consider! life is but a day;
  A fragile dew-drop on its perilous way
  From a tree's summit; a poor Indian's sleep
  While his boat hastens to the monstrous steep
  Of Montmorenci.
    'Sleep and Poetry' (1817) l. 85

11 O for ten years, that I may overwhelm
  Myself in poesy; so I may do the deed
  That my own soul has to itself decreed.
    'Sleep and Poetry' (1817) l. 96

12 They swayed about upon a rocking horse,
  And thought it Pegasus.
    'Sleep and Poetry' (1817) l. 186

13 And they shall be accounted poet kings
  Who simply tell the most heart-easing things.
    'Sleep and Poetry' (1817) l. 267

14 O soft embalmer of the still midnight,
  Shutting, with careful fingers and benign
  Our gloom-pleased eyes.
    'Sonnet to Sleep' (written 1819)

15 Turn the key deftly in the oilèd wards,
  And seal the hushèd casket of my soul.
    'Sonnet to Sleep' (written 1819)

16 This living hand, now warm and capable
  Of earnest grasping, would, if it were cold
  And in the icy silence of the tomb,
  So haunt thy days and chill thy dreaming nights
  That thou wouldst wish thine own heart dry of blood
  So in my veins red life might stream again,
  And thus be conscience-calmed—see here it is
  I hold it towards you.
    'This living hand, now warm and capable' (written 1819)

17 Season of mists and mellow fruitfulness,
  Close bosom-friend of the maturing sun;
  Conspiring with him how to load and bless
  With fruit the vines that round the thatch-eaves run.
    'To Autumn' (1820) st. 1

18 Who hath not seen thee oft amid thy store?
  Sometimes whoever seeks abroad may find
  Thee sitting careless on a granary floor,
  Thy hair soft-lifted by the winnowing wind;
  Or on a half-reaped furrow sound asleep,
  Drowsed with the fume of poppies while thy hook
  Spares the next swath and all its twinèd flowers.
    'To Autumn' (1820) st. 2

19 Where are the songs of Spring? Ay, where are they?
  Think not of them, thou hast thy music too.
    'To Autumn' (1820) st. 3

20 Then in a wailful choir the small gnats mourn
  Among the river sallows, borne aloft
  Or sinking as the light wind lives or dies.
    'To Autumn' (1820) st. 3

21 The red-breast whistles from a garden-croft;
  And gathering swallows twitter in the skies.
    'To Autumn' (1820) st. 3

22 Oh Chatterton! how very sad thy fate!
  Dear child of sorrow! son of misery!
  How soon the film of death obscured that eye,
  Whence genius wildly flashed.
    'To Chatterton' (written 1815)

23 Sweet are the pleasures that to verse belong,
  And doubly sweet a brotherhood in song.
    'To George Felton Mathew' (1817)

24 Aye on the shores of darkness there is light,
  And precipices show untrodden green,
  There is a budding morrow in midnight,
  There is a triple sight in blindness keen.
    'To Homer' (written 1818)

25   It is a flaw
  In happiness, to see beyond our bourn—
  It forces us in summer skies to mourn:
  It spoils the singing of the nightingale.
    'To J. H. Reynolds, Esq.' (written 1818)

26 Glory and loveliness have passed away.
    'To Leigh Hunt, Esq.' (1817)

27 To one who has been long in city pent,
  'Tis very sweet to look into the fair
  And open face of heaven.
    'To one who has been long in city pent' (1817)

28 When I have fears that I may cease to be
  Before my pen has gleaned my teeming brain.
    'When I have fears that I may cease to be' (written 1818)

1 When I behold, upon the night's starred face
Huge cloudy symbols of a high romance.
   'When I have fears that I may cease to be' (written 1818)

2   Then on the shore
Of the wide world I stand alone and think
Till love and fame to nothingness do sink.
   'When I have fears that I may cease to be' (written 1818)

3 Woman! when I behold thee flippant, vain,
Inconstant, childish, proud, and full of fancies.
   'Woman! when I behold thee flippant, vain' (1817)

4 A long poem is a test of invention which I take to be
the polar star of poetry, as fancy is the sails, and
imagination the rudder.
   Letter to Benjamin Bailey, 8 October 1817, in H. E. Rollins
   (ed.) *Letters of John Keats* (1958) vol. 1

5 I am certain of nothing but the holiness of the heart's
affections and the truth of imagination—what the
imagination seizes as beauty must be truth—whether
it existed before or not.
   Letter to Benjamin Bailey, 22 November 1817, in H. E.
   Rollins (ed.) *Letters of John Keats* (1958) vol. 1. Cf. Keats
   389:3

6 I have never yet been able to perceive how anything
can be known for truth by consecutive
reasoning—and yet it must be.
   Letter to Benjamin Bailey, 22 November 1817, in H. E.
   Rollins (ed.) *Letters of John Keats* (1958) vol. 1

7 O for a life of sensations rather than of thoughts!
   Letter to Benjamin Bailey, 22 November 1817, in H. E.
   Rollins (ed.) *Letters of John Keats* (1958) vol. 1

8 A man should have the fine point of his soul taken off
to become fit for this world.
   Letter to J. H. Reynolds, 22 November 1817, in H. E.
   Rollins (ed.) *Letters of John Keats* (1958) vol. 1

9 The excellence of every art is its intensity, capable of
making all disagreeables evaporate, from their being in
close relationship with beauty and truth.
   Letter to George and Thomas Keats, 21 December 1817, in
   H. E. Rollins (ed.) *Letters of John Keats* (1958) vol. 1

10 Negative Capability, that is when man is capable of
being in uncertainties, mysteries, doubts, without any
irritable reaching after fact and reason—Coleridge, for
instance, would let go by a fine isolated verisimilitude
caught from the penetralium of mystery, from being
incapable of remaining content with half knowledge.
   Letter to George and Thomas Keats, 21 December 1817, in
   H. E. Rollins (ed.) *Letters of John Keats* (1958) vol. 1

11 There is nothing stable in the world—uproar's your
only music.
   Letter to George and Thomas Keats, 13 January 1818, in
   H. E. Rollins (ed.) *Letters of John Keats* (1958) vol. 1

12 For the sake of a few fine imaginative or domestic
passages, are we to be bullied into a certain
philosophy engendered in the whims of an egotist?
   Letter to J. H. Reynolds, 3 February 1818, in H. E. Rollins
   (ed.) *Letters of John Keats* (1958) vol. 1 (on the overbearing
   influence of Wordsworth upon his contemporaries)

13 We hate poetry that has a palpable design upon
us—and if we do not agree, seems to put its hand in
its breeches pocket. Poetry should be great and
unobtrusive, a thing which enters into one's soul, and
does not startle it or amaze it with itself, but with its
subject.
   Letter to J. H. Reynolds, 3 February 1818, in H. E. Rollins
   (ed.) *Letters of John Keats* (1958) vol. 1

14 Poetry should surprise by a fine excess, and not by
singularity—it should strike the reader as a wording of
his own highest thoughts, and appear almost a
remembrance.
   Letter to John Taylor, 27 February 1818, in H. E. Rollins
   (ed.) *Letters of John Keats* (1958) vol. 1

15 Its [poetry's] touches of beauty should never be half
way, thereby making the reader breathless, instead of
content . . . If poetry comes not as naturally as the
leaves to a tree it had better not come at all.
   Letter to John Taylor, 27 February 1818, in H. E. Rollins
   (ed.) *Letters of John Keats* (1958) vol. 1

16 Scenery is fine—but human nature is finer.
   Letter to Benjamin Bailey, 13 March 1818, in H. E. Rollins
   (ed.) *Letters of John Keats* (1958) vol. 1

17 It is impossible to live in a country which is
continually under hatches . . . Rain! Rain! Rain!
   Letter to J. H. Reynolds from Devon, 10 April 1818, in H.
   E. Rollins (ed.) *Letters of John Keats* (1958) vol. 1

18 Axioms in philosophy are not axioms until they are
proved upon our pulses: We read fine things, but
never feel them to the full until we have gone the
same steps as the author.
   Letter to J. H. Reynolds, 3 May 1818, in H. E. Rollins (ed.)
   Letters of John Keats (1958) vol. 1

19 I am in that temper that if I were under water I would
scarcely kick to come to the top.
   Letter to Benjamin Bailey, 25 May 1818, in H. E. Rollins
   (ed.) *Letters of John Keats* (1958) vol. 1

20 I do think better of womankind than to suppose they
care whether Mister John Keats five feet high likes
them or not.
   Letter to Benjamin Bailey, 18 July 1818, in H. E. Rollins
   (ed.) *Letters of John Keats* (1958) vol. 1

21 There is an awful warmth about my heart like a load
of immortality.
   Letter to J. H. Reynolds, 22 September 1818, in H. E.
   Rollins (ed.) *Letters of John Keats* (1958) vol. 1

22 In Endymion, I leaped headlong into the sea, and
thereby have become better acquainted with the
soundings, the quicksands, and the rocks, than if I
had stayed upon the green shore, and piped a silly
pipe, and took tea and comfortable advice.
   Letter to James Hessey, 8 October 1818, in H. E. Rollins
   (ed.) *Letters of John Keats* (1958) vol. 1

23 As to the poetical character itself, (I mean that sort of
which, if I am any thing, I am a member; that sort
distinguished from the Wordsworthian or egotistical
sublime; which is a thing *per se* and stands alone) it is
not itself—it has no self . . . It has as much delight in
conceiving an Iago as an Imogen.
   Letter to Richard Woodhouse, 27 October 1818, in H. E.
   Rollins (ed.) *Letters of John Keats* (1958) vol. 1

1 A poet is the most unpoetical of any thing in existence, because he has no identity; he is continually in for—and filling some other body.
> Letter to Richard Woodhouse, 27 October 1818, in H. E. Rollins (ed.) *Letters of John Keats* (1958) vol. 1

2 The roaring of the wind is my wife and the stars through the window pane are my children.
> Letter to George and Georgiana Keats, 24 October 1818, in H. E. Rollins (ed.) *Letters of John Keats* (1958) vol. 1

3 A man's life of any worth is a continual allegory.
> Letter to George and Georgiana Keats, 19 February 1819, in H. E. Rollins (ed.) *Letters of John Keats* (1958) vol. 2

4 I have come to this resolution—never to write for the sake of writing, or making a poem, but from running over with any little knowledge or experience which many years of reflection may perhaps give me—otherwise I shall be dumb.
> Letter to B. R. Haydon, 8 March 1819, in H. E. Rollins (ed.) *Letters of John Keats* (1958) vol. 2

5 It is true that in the height of enthusiasm I have been cheated into some fine passages but that is nothing.
> Letter to B. R. Haydon, 8 March 1819, in H. E. Rollins (ed.) *Letters of John Keats* (1958) vol. 2

6 I go among the fields and catch a glimpse of a stoat or a fieldmouse peeping out of the withered grass—The creature hath a purpose and its eyes are bright with it—I go amongst the buildings of a city and I see a man hurrying along—to what? The Creature has a purpose and his eyes are bright with it.
> Letter to George and Georgiana Keats, 19 March 1819, in H. E. Rollins (ed.) *Letters of John Keats* (1958) vol. 2

7 Call the world if you please 'The vale of soul-making'.
> Letter to George and Georgiana Keats, 21 April 1819, in H. E. Rollins (ed.) *Letters of John Keats* (1958) vol. 2

8 I have met with women whom I really think would like to be married to a poem and to be given away by a novel.
> Letter to Fanny Brawne, 8 July 1819, in H. E. Rollins (ed.) *Letters of John Keats* (1958) vol. 2

9 I have two luxuries to brood over in my walks, your loveliness and the hour of my death. O that I could have possession of them both in the same minute.
> Letter to Fanny Brawne, 25 July 1819, in H. E. Rollins (ed.) *Letters of John Keats* (1958) vol. 2

10 I am convinced more and more day by day that fine writing is next to fine doing the top thing in the world.
> Letter to J. H. Reynolds, 24 August 1819, in H. E. Rollins (ed.) *Letters of John Keats* (1958) vol. 2

11 All clean and comfortable I sit down to write.
> Letter to George and Georgiana Keats, 17 September 1819, in H. E. Rollins (ed.) *Letters of John Keats* (1958) vol. 2

12 The only means of strengthening one's intellect is to make up one's mind about nothing—to let the mind be a thoroughfare for all thoughts. Not a select party.
> Letter to George and Georgiana Keats, 24 September 1819, in H. E. Rollins (ed.) *Letters of John Keats* (1958) vol. 2

13 'If I should die,' said I to myself, 'I have left no immortal work behind me—nothing to make my friends proud of my memory—but I have loved the principle of beauty in all things, and if I had had time I would have made myself remembered.'
> Letter to Fanny Brawne, *c.*February 1820, in H. E. Rollins (ed.) *Letters of John Keats* (1958) vol. 2

14 I wish you could invent some means to make me at all happy without you. Every hour I am more and more concentrated in you; every thing else tastes like chaff in my mouth.
> Letter to Fanny Brawne, August 1820, in H. E. Rollins (ed.) *Letters of John Keats* (1958) vol. 2

15 You I am sure will forgive me for sincerely remarking that you might curb your magnanimity and be more of an artist, and 'load every rift' of your subject with ore.
> Letter to Shelley, August 1820, in H. E. Rollins (ed.) *Letters of John Keats* (1958) vol. 2 (echoing Edmund Spenser *The Faerie Queen* (1596) bk. 2, canto 7, st. 28, l. 5: 'And with rich metal loaded every rift')

16 I shall soon be laid in the quiet grave—thank God for the quiet grave—O! I can feel the cold earth upon me—the daisies growing over me—O for this quiet—it will be my first.
> In a letter from Joseph Severn to John Taylor, 6 March 1821, in H. E. Rollins (ed.) *Letters of John Keats* (1958) vol. 2

17 Here lies one whose name was writ in water.
> Epitaph for himself, in Richard Monckton Milnes *Life, Letters and Literary Remains of John Keats* (1848) vol. 2, p. 91. Cf. *Henry VIII* 589:9

John Keble 1792–1866
English clergyman; leader of the Oxford Movement

18 Blessed are the pure in heart,
For they shall see our God,
The secret of the Lord is theirs,
Their soul is Christ's abode.
> *The Christian Year* (1827) 'Blessed are the pure in heart'

19 New every morning is the love
Our wakening and uprising prove;
Through sleep and darkness safely brought,
Restored to life, and power, and thought.
> *The Christian Year* (1827) 'Morning'

20 The trivial round, the common task,
Would furnish all we ought to ask;
Room to deny ourselves; a road
To bring us, daily, nearer God.
> *The Christian Year* (1827) 'Morning'

21 There is a book, who runs may read,
Which heavenly truth imparts,
And all the lore its scholars need,
Pure eyes and Christian hearts.
> *The Christian Year* (1827) 'Septuagesima'

22 The voice that breathed o'er Eden,
That earliest wedding-day,
The primal marriage blessing,
It hath not passed away.
> 'Holy Matrimony' (1857 hymn)

23 If the Church of England were to fail, it would be found in my parish.
> In D. Newsome *The Parting of Friends* (1966) ch. 8, pt. 3

George Keith, 5th Earl Marischal
1553–1623
Scottish politician

1 They haif said: Quhat say they? Lat thame say.
  Motto of the Earls Marischal of Scotland, inscribed at Marischal College; a similarly defiant motto in Greek has been found engraved in remains from classical antiquity

Frank B. Kellogg
See ARISTIDE BRIAND

Hugh Kelly 1739–77
Irish playwright

2 Of all the stages in a woman's life, none is so dangerous as the period between her acknowledgment of a passion for a man, and the day set apart for her nuptials.
  Memoirs of a Magdalen (1767, ed. 1782) p. 15

3 Your people of refined sentiments are the most troublesome creatures in the world to deal with.
  False Delicacy (performed 1768) act 5, sc. 1

Thomas Kelly 1769–1855
Irish clergyman and hymn-writer

4 The head that once was crowned with thorns
  Is crowned with glory now;
  A royal diadem adorns
  The mighty Victor's brow.
  'The head that once was crowned with thorns' (1820 hymn)

Thomas à Kempis
See THOMAS

Thomas Ken 1637–1711
English divine; Bishop of Bath and Wells, 1684–91, and formerly chaplain to Charles II

5 Awake, my soul, and with the sun
  Thy daily stage of duty run.
  Shake off dull sloth, and joyful rise
  To pay thy morning sacrifice.
  'Morning Hymn' in Winchester College *Manual of Prayers* (1695) but already in use by 1674

6 Redeem thy mis-spent time that's past,
  And live this day as if thy last.
  'Morning Hymn' (1709 ed.) v. 2

7 All praise to thee, my God, this night,
  For all the blessings of the light;
  Keep me, O keep me, King of Kings,
  Beneath thy own almighty wings.
  'Evening Hymn' in Winchester College *Manual of Prayers* (1695) but already in use by 1674 (the first line later changed to 'Glory to thee, my God this night')

8 Teach me to live, that I may dread
  The grave as little as my bed.
  'Evening Hymn' (1695) v. 3

Jimmy Kennedy and Michael Carr
British songwriters

9 We're gonna hang out the washing on the Siegfried Line.
  Title of song (1939)

John F. Kennedy 1917–63
35th President of the USA

10 Don't buy a single vote more than necessary. I'll be damned if I'm going to pay for a landslide.
  Telegraphed message from his father, read at a Gridiron dinner in Washington, 15 March 1958, and almost certainly JFK's invention; in J. F. Cutler *Honey Fitz* (1962) p. 306

11 We stand today on the edge of a new frontier . . . But the New Frontier of which I speak is not a set of promises — it is a set of challenges. It sums up not what I intend to offer the American people, but what I intend to ask of them.
  Speech accepting the Democratic nomination in Los Angeles, 15 July 1960, in *Vital Speeches* 1 August 1960, p. 611

12 Let the word go forth from this time and place, to friend and foe alike, that the torch has been passed to a new generation of Americans—born in this century, tempered by war, disciplined by a hard and bitter peace, proud of our ancient heritage—and unwilling to witness or permit the slow undoing of those human rights to which this nation has always been committed, and to which we are committed today at home and around the world.
  Let every nation know, whether it wishes us well or ill, that we shall pay any price, bear any burden, meet any hardship, support any friend, oppose any foe to assure the survival and the success of liberty.
  Inaugural address, 20 January 1961, in *Vital Speeches* 1 February 1961, p. 226

13 If a free society cannot help the many who are poor, it cannot save the few who are rich.
  Inaugural address, 20 January 1961, in *Vital Speeches* 1 February 1961, p. 226

14 Let us never negotiate out of fear. But let us never fear to negotiate.
  Inaugural address, 20 January 1961, in *Vital Speeches* 1 February 1961, p. 227

15 All this will not be finished in the first 100 days. Nor will it be finished in the first 1,000 days, nor in the life of this Administration, nor even perhaps in our lifetime on this planet. But let us begin.
  Inaugural address, 20 January 1961, in *Vital Speeches* 1 February 1961, p. 227

1 Now the trumpet summons us again—not as a call to bear arms, though arms we need—not as a call to battle, though embattled we are—but a call to bear the burden of a long twilight struggle, year in and year out, 'rejoicing in hope, patient in tribulation'—a struggle against the common enemies of man: tyranny, poverty, disease and war itself.
  Inaugural address, 20 January 1961, in *Vital Speeches* 1 February 1961, p. 227

2 And so, my fellow Americans: ask not what your country can do for you—ask what you can do for your country. My fellow citizens of the world: ask not what America will do for you, but what together we can do for the freedom of man.
  Inaugural address, 20 January 1961, in *Vital Speeches* 1 February 1961, p. 227. Oliver Wendell Holmes Jr., speaking at Keene, New Hampshire, 30 May 1884 said: 'We pause to . . . recall what our country has done for each of us and to ask ourselves what we can do for our country in return'. Cf. Gibran 303:1

3 Mankind must put an end to war or war will put an end to mankind.
  Speech to United Nations General Assembly, 25 September 1961, in *New York Times* 26 September 1961, p. 14

4 Those who make peaceful revolution impossible will make violent revolution inevitable.
  Speech at the White House, 13 March 1962, in *Vital Speeches* 1 April 1962, p. 356

5 No one has been barred on account of his race from fighting or dying for America—there are no 'white' or 'coloured' signs on the foxholes or graveyards of battle.
  Message to Congress on proposed Civil Rights Bill, 19 June 1963, in *New York Times* 20 June 1963, p. 16

6 *Ich bin ein Berliner.*
  I am a Berliner.
  Speech in West Berlin, 26 June 1963, in *New York Times* 27 June 1963, p. 12 (*ein Berliner* being the name given in Germany to a doughnut, and the occasion, therefore, of much hilarity). Cf. Cicero 204:8

7 When power leads man toward arrogance, poetry reminds him of his limitations. When power narrows the areas of man's concern, poetry reminds him of the richness and diversity of his existence. When power corrupts, poetry cleanses. For art establishes the basic human truths which must serve as the touchstone of our judgement.
  Speech at Amherst College, Mass., 26 October 1963, in *New York Times* 27 October 1963, p. 87

8 In free society art is not a weapon . . . Artists are not engineers of the soul.
  Speech at Amherst College, Mass., 26 October 1963, in *New York Times* 27 October 1963, p. 87

9 It was involuntary. They sank my boat.
  On being asked how he became a war hero, in Arthur M. Schlesinger Jr. *A Thousand Days* (1965) ch. 4

Joseph P. Kennedy 1888–1969
American financier and diplomat; father of J. F. Kennedy

10 When the going gets tough, the tough get going.
  In J. H. Cutler *Honey Fitz* (1962) p. 291 (also attributed to Knute Rockne)

Lady Caroline Keppel b. 1735
English poet

11 What's this dull town to me?
  Robin's not near.
  He whom I wished to see,
  Wished for to hear;
  Where's all the joy and mirth
  Made life a heaven on earth?
  O! they're all fled with thee,
  Robin Adair.
    'Robin Adair' (*c.*1750)

Jack Kerouac 1922–69
Amerian novelist

12 The beat generation.
  Phrase coined in the course of a conversation; in *Playboy* June 1959, p. 32

William Kethe d. 1594
Scottish Calvinist

13 All people that on earth do dwell,
  Sing to the Lord with cheerful voice;
  Him serve with fear, his praise forth tell,
  Come ye before him, and rejoice.

  The Lord, ye know, is God indeed;
  Without our aid he did us make;
  We are his folk, he doth us feed,
  And for his sheep he doth us take.

  O enter then his gates with praise,
  Approach with joy his courts unto;
  Praise, laud, and bless his name always,
  For it is seemly so to do.

  for why? the Lord our God is good;
  His mercy is for ever sure;
  His truth at all times firmly stood,
  And shall from age to age endure.
    'All people that on earth do dwell' in *Fourscore and Seven Psalms of David* (Geneva, 1561; later known as the Geneva Psalter)

Ralph Kettell 1563–1643
President of Trinity College, Oxford, from 1599

14 Here is Hey for Garsington! and Hey for Cuddesdon! and Hey Hockley! but here's nobody cries, Hey for God Almighty!
  Sermon at Garsington Revel, in Oliver Lawson Dick (ed.) *Aubrey's Brief Lives* (1949) 'Ralph Kettell'

Francis Scott Key 1779–1843
American lawyer and verse-writer

15 'Tis the star-spangled banner; O long may it wave O'er the land of the free, and the home of the brave!
  'The Star-Spangled Banner' (1814)

John Maynard Keynes (1st Baron Keynes)
1883–1946
English economist

1 I work for a Government I despise for ends I think criminal.
>Letter to Duncan Grant, 15 December 1917, in *British Library Add. MSS 57931* fo. 119

2 He felt about France what Pericles felt of Athens—unique value in her, nothing else mattering; but his theory of politics was Bismarck's. He had one illusion—France; and one disillusion—mankind, including Frenchmen, and his colleagues not least.
>*The Economic Consequences of the Peace* (1919) ch. 3 (of Clemenceau)

3 Like Odysseus, the President looked wiser when he was seated.
>*The Economic Consequences of the Peace* (1919) ch. 3 (of Woodrow Wilson)

4 Lenin was right. There is no subtler, no surer means of overturning the existing basis of society than to debauch the currency. The process engages all the hidden forces of economic law on the side of destruction, and does it in a manner which not one man in a million is able to diagnose.
>*The Economic Consequences of the Peace* (1919) ch. 6

5 I do not know which makes a man more conservative—to know nothing but the present, or nothing but the past.
>*The End of Laissez-Faire* (1926) pt. 1

6 The important thing for Government is not to do things which individuals are doing already, and to do them a little better or a little worse; but to do those things which at present are not done at all.
>*The End of Laissez-Faire* (1926) pt. 4

7 This extraordinary figure of our time, this syren, this goat-footed bard, this half-human visitor to our age from the hag-ridden magic and enchanted woods of Celtic antiquity.
>*Essays in Biography* (1933) 'Mr Lloyd George'

8 We take it as a fundamental psychological rule of any modern community that, when its real income is increased, it will not increase its consumption by an equal *absolute* amount.
>*General Theory* (1936) bk. 3, ch. 8

9 If the Treasury were to fill old bottles with banknotes, bury them at suitable depths in disused coalmines which are then filled up to the surface with town rubbish, and leave it to private enterprise on well-tried principles of *laissez-faire* to dig the notes up again (the right to do so being obtained, of course, by tendering for leases of the note-bearing territory) there need be no more unemployment and, with the help of the repercussions, the real income of the community, and its capital wealth also, would probably become a good deal greater than it actually is. It would, indeed, be more sensible to build houses and the like; but as there are political and practical difficulties in the way of this, the above would be better than nothing.
>*General Theory* (1936) bk. 3, ch. 10

10 The ideas of economists and political philosophers, both when they are right and when they are wrong, are more powerful than is commonly understood ... Practical men, who believe themselves to be quite exempt from any intellectual influences, are usually the slaves of some defunct economist. Madmen in authority, who hear voices in the air, are distilling their frenzy from some academic scribbler of a few years back.
>*General Theory* (1947 ed.) ch. 24

11 *In the long run* we are all dead.
>*A Tract on Monetary Reform* (1923) ch. 3

12 I evidently knew more about economics than my examiners.
>Explaining why he performed badly in the Civil Service examinations, in Sir Roy Harrod *Life of John Maynard Keynes* (1951) ch. 3

John Neville Keynes 1852–1949
English economist; father of J. M. Keynes

13 A *positive science* may be defined as a body of systematized knowledge concerning what is; a *normative* or *regular science* a body of systematized knowledge relating to criteria of what ought to be, and concerned therefore with the ideal as distinguished from the actual.
>*The Scope and Method of Political Economy* (4th ed., 1917) ch. 2, p. 34

Nikita Khrushchev 1894–1971
Soviet statesman; Premier, 1958–64

14 If anyone believes that our smiles involve abandonment of the teaching of Marx, Engels and Lenin he deceives himself. Those who wait for that must wait until a shrimp learns to whistle.
>Speech in Moscow, 17 September 1955, in *New York Times* 18 September 1955, p. 19

15 We say this not only for the socialist states, who are more akin to us. We base ourselves on the idea that we must peacefully co-exist. About the capitalist States, it doesn't depend on you whether or not we exist. If you don't like us, don't accept our invitations and don't invite us to come to see you. Whether you like it or not, history is on our side. We will bury you.
>Speech to Western diplomats at reception in Moscow for Polish leader Mr Gomulka, 18 November 1956, in *The Times* 19 November 1956

16 Anyone who believes that the worker can be lulled by fine revolutionary phrases is mistaken ... If no concern is shown for the growth of material and spiritual riches, the people will listen today, they will listen tomorrow, and then they may say: 'Why do you promise us everything for the future? You are talking, so to speak, about life beyond the grave. The priest has already told us about this.'
>Speech at World Youth Forum, 19 September 1964, in *Pravda* 22 September 1964

17 If one cannot catch the bird of paradise, better take a wet hen.
>In *Time* 6 January 1958

1 If you start throwing hedgehogs under me, I shall throw a couple of porcupines under you.
   In *New York Times* 7 November 1963

Joyce Kilmer 1886–1918

American poet

2 I think that I shall never see
   A poem lovely as a tree.
   'Trees' (1914)

3 Poems are made by fools like me,
   But only God can make a tree.
   'Trees' (1914)

Lord Kilmuir (Sir David Maxwell Fyfe) 1900–67

British Conservative politician and lawyer

4 Loyalty is the Tory's secret weapon.
   In Anthony Sampson *Anatomy of Britain* (1962) ch. 6. Cf. Anonymous 16:18

Francis Kilvert 1840–79

English clergyman and diarist

5 Of all noxious animals, too, the most noxious is a tourist. And of all tourists the most vulgar, ill-bred, offensive and loathsome is the British tourist.
   W. Plomer (ed.) *Selections from the Diary of the Rev. Francis Kilvert* (1938–40) 5 April 1870

6 The Vicar of St Ives says the smell of fish there is sometimes so terrific as to stop the church clock.
   W. Plomer (ed.) *Selections from the Diary* . . . 21 July 1870

7 It is a fine thing to be out on the hills alone. A man can hardly be a beast or a fool alone on a great mountain.
   W. Plomer (ed.) *Selections from the Diary* . . . 29 May 1871

8 An angel satyr walks these hills.
   W. Plomer (ed.) *Selections from the Diary* . . . 20 June 1871 (on 'the Black Mountain' in Wales)

Benjamin Franklin King 1857–94

American poet

9 Nothing to do but work,
   Nothing to eat but food,
   Nothing to wear but clothes
   To keep one from going nude.

   Nothing to breathe but air,
   Quick as a flash 't is gone;
   Nowhere to fall but off,
   Nowhere to stand but on.
   'The Pessimist'

10 Nowhere to go but out,
   Nowhere to come but back.
   'The Pessimist'

Henry King 1592–1669

English poet; Bishop of Chichester from 1642

11 Sleep on (my Love!) in thy cold bed
   Never to be disquieted.
   My last Good-night! Thou wilt not wake
   Till I thy fate shall overtake:
   Till age, or grief, or sickness must
   Marry my body to that dust
   It so much loves; and fill the room
   My heart keeps empty in thy tomb.
   Stay for me there: I will not fail
   To meet thee in that hollow vale.
   And think not much of my delay;
   I am already on the way,
   And follow thee with all the speed
   Desire can make, or sorrows breed.
   'An Exequy' (1657) l. 81 (written for his wife Anne, d. 1624)

12 But hark! My pulse, like a soft drum
   Beats my approach, tells thee I come;
   And, slow howe'er my marches be,
   I shall at last sit down by thee.
   The thought of this bids me go on,
   And wait my dissolution
   With hope and comfort. Dear! (forgive
   The crime) I am content to live
   Divided, with but half a heart,
   Till we shall meet and never part.
   'An Exequy' (1657) l. 111

13 We that did nothing study but the way
   To love each other, with which thoughts the day
   Rose with delight to us, and with them set,
   Must learn the hateful art, how to forget.
   'The Surrender' (1657)

Martin Luther King 1929–68

American civil rights leader

14 I want to be the white man's brother, not his brother-in-law.
   In *New York Journal-American* 10 September 1962, p. 1

15 Injustice anywhere is a threat to justice everywhere.
   Letter from Birmingham Jail, Alabama, 16 April 1963, in *Atlantic Monthly* August 1963, p. 78

16 The Negro's great stumbling block in the stride toward freedom is not the White Citizens Councillor or the Ku Klux Klanner but the white moderate who is more devoted to order than to justice; who prefers a negative peace which is the absence of tension to a positive peace which is the presence of justice.
   Letter from Birmingham Jail, Alabama, 16 April 1963, in *Atlantic Monthly* August 1963, p. 81

17 I submit to you that if a man hasn't discovered something he will die for, he isn't fit to live.
   Speech in Detroit, 23 June 1963, in James Bishop *The Days of Martin Luther King* (1971) ch. 4

1 I have a dream that one day on the red hills of
Georgia the sons of former slaves and the sons of
former slave owners will be able to sit down together
at the table of brotherhood . . .
    I have a dream that my four little children will one
day live in a nation where they will not be judged by
the colour of their skin but by the content of their
character.

> Speech at Civil Rights March in Washington,
> 28 August 1963, in *New York Times* 29 August 1963,
> p. 21

2 We must learn to live together as brothers or perish
together as fools.

> Speech at St Louis, 22 March 1964, in *St Louis
> Post-Dispatch* 23 March 1964

3 The means by which we live have outdistanced the
ends for which we live. Our scientific power has
outrun our spiritual power. We have guided missiles
and misguided men.

> *Strength to Love* (1963) ch. 7

4 A riot is at bottom the language of the unheard.

> *Where Do We Go From Here?* (1967) ch. 4

5 I just want to do God's will. And he's allowed me to
go up to the mountain. And I've looked over, and
I've seen the promised land . . . So I'm happy tonight.
I'm not worried about anything. I'm not fearing any
man.

> Speech in Memphis, 3 April 1968 (the day before
> his assassination), in *New York Times* 4 April 1968,
> p. 24

Stoddard King 1889–1933

British songwriter

6 There's a long, long trail awinding
Into the land of my dreams,
Where the nightingales are singing
And a white moon beams;
There's a long, long night of waiting
Until my dreams all come true,
Till the day when I'll be going down
That long, long trail with you.

> 'There's a Long, Long Trail' (1913 song)

Charles Kingsley 1819–75

English writer and clergyman

7 Airly Beacon, Airly Beacon;
Oh the pleasant sight to see
Shires and towns from Airly Beacon,
While my love climbed up to me!

> 'Airly Beacon' (1858)

8 Airly Beacon, Airly Beacon;
Oh the weary haunt for me,
All alone on Airly Beacon,
With his baby on my knee!

> 'Airly Beacon' (1858)

9 Be good, sweet maid, and let who will be clever;
Do noble things, not dream them, all day long:
And so make life, death, and that vast for-ever
One grand, sweet song.

> 'A Farewell' (1858)

10 What we can we will be,
Honest Englishmen.
Do the work that's nearest,
Though it's dull at whiles,
Helping, when we meet them,
Lame dogs over stiles.

> 'The Invitation. To Tom Hughes' (1856)

11 'Tis the hard grey weather
Breeds hard English men.

> 'Ode to the North-East Wind' (1858)

12 Come; and strong within us
Stir the Vikings' blood;
Bracing brain and sinew;
Blow, thou wind of God!

> 'Ode to the North-East Wind' (1858)

13 'O Mary, go and call the cattle home,
And call the cattle home,
And call the cattle home,
Across the sands of Dee.'
The western wind was wild and dank with foam,
And all alone went she.

> 'The Sands of Dee' (1858)

14 The western tide crept up along the sand,
And o'er and o'er the sand,
And round and round the sand,
As far as eye could see.
The rolling mist came down and hid the land:
And never home came she.

> 'The Sands of Dee' (1858)

15 Three fishers went sailing away to the west,
Away to the west as the sun went down;
Each thought on the woman who loved him the best,
And the children stood watching them out of the
town.

> 'The Three Fishers' (1858)

16 For men must work, and women must weep,
And there's little to earn, and many to keep,
Though the harbour bar be moaning.

> 'The Three Fishers' (1858)

17 When all the world is young, lad,
And all the trees are green;
And every goose a swan, lad,
And every lass a queen;
Then hey for boot and horse, lad,
And round the world away:
Young blood must have its course, lad,
And every dog his day.

> 'Young and Old' (from *The Water Babies*, 1863)

18 To be discontented with the divine discontent, and to
be ashamed with the noble shame, is the very germ
and first upgrowth of all virtue.

> *Health and Education* (1874) p. 20

1 We have used the Bible as if it was a constable's handbook—an opium-dose for keeping beasts of burden patient while they are being overloaded.
  Letters to the Chartists no. 2. Cf. Marx 452:2

2 As thorough an Englishman as ever coveted his neighbour's goods.
  The Water Babies (1863) ch. 4

3 Eustace is a man no longer; he is become a thing, a tool, a Jesuit.
  Westward Ho! (1855) ch. 23

4 Truth, for its own sake, had never been a virtue with the Roman clergy.
  Reviewing J. A. Froude's *History of England*, in *Macmillan's Magazine* January 1864

Hugh Kingsmill (Hugh Kingsmill Lunn)
1889–1949
English man of letters

5 What still alive at twenty-two,
  A clean upstanding chap like you?
  Sure, if your throat 'tis hard to slit,
  Slit your girl's, and swing for it.

  Like enough, you won't be glad,
  When they come to hang you, lad:
  But bacon's not the only thing
  That's cured by hanging from a string.
  'Two Poems, after A. E. Housman' (1933) no. 1

6 'Tis Summer Time on Bredon,
  And now the farmers swear:
  The cattle rise and listen
  In valleys far and near,
  And blush at what they hear.

  But when the mists in autumn
  On Bredon top are thick,
  And happy hymns of farmers
  Go up from fold and rick,
  The cattle then are sick.
  'Two Poems, after A. E. Housman' (1933) no. 2

7 God's apology for relations.
  On friends, in Michael Holroyd *The Best of Hugh Kingsmill* (1970) introduction

8 Society is based on the assumption that everyone is alike and no one is alive.
  In Michael Holroyd *Hugh Kingsmill* (1964) ch. 16

Neil Kinnock 1942–
British Labour politician

9 I warn you not to be ordinary, I warn you not to be young, I warn you not to fall ill, and I warn you not to grow old.
  On the prospect of a Conservative re-election, in speech at Bridgend, 7 June 1983; in *Guardian* 8 June 1983

10 It's a pity others had to leave theirs on the ground at Goose Green to prove it.
  Referring to servicemen in the Falklands War, when replying to a heckler who said that Mrs Thatcher 'showed guts'; television interview, 6 June 1983, in *Guardian* 7 June 1983, p. 2

Rudyard Kipling 1865–1936
English writer and poet

11 When you've shouted 'Rule Britannia', when you've sung 'God save the Queen'—
  When you've finished killing Kruger with your mouth—
  Will you kindly drop a shilling in my little tambourine
  For a gentleman in *Kharki* ordered South?
  He's an absent-minded beggar and his weaknesses are great—
  But we and Paul must take him as we find him—
  He is out on active service, wiping something off a slate—
  And he's left a lot o' little things behind him!
  'The Absent-Minded Beggar' (1899) st. 1

12 England's on the anvil—hear the hammers ring—
  Clanging from the Severn to the Tyne!
  Never was a blacksmith like our Norman King—
  England's being hammered, hammered, hammered into line!
  'The Anvil' (1927)

13 Oh, East is East, and West is West, and never the twain shall meet,
  Till Earth and Sky stand presently at God's great Judgement Seat;
  But there is neither East nor West, Border, nor Breed, nor Birth,
  When two strong men stand face to face, tho' they come from the ends of earth!
  'The Ballad of East and West' (1892)

14 And the talk slid north, and the talk slid south,
  With the sliding puffs from the hookah-mouth.
  Four things greater than all things are,—
  Women and Horses and Power and War.
  'The Ballad of the King's Jest' (1892)

15 Foot—foot—foot—foot—sloggin' over Africa—
  (Boots—boots—boots—boots—movin' up and down again!)
  'Boots' (1903)

16 If any question why we died,
  Tell them, because our fathers lied.
  'Common Form' (1919)

17 We know that the tail must wag the dog, for the horse is drawn by the cart;
  But the Devil whoops, as he whooped of old: 'It's clever, but is it Art?'
  'The Conundrum of the Workshops' (1892)

18 For they're hangin' Danny Deever, you can hear the Dead March play,
  The regiment's in 'ollow square—they're hangin' him to-day;
  They've taken of his buttons off an' cut his stripes away,
  An' they're hangin' Danny Deever in the mornin'.
  'Danny Deever' (1892)

19 The 'eathen in 'is blindness bows down to wood an' stone;
  'E don't obey no orders unless they is 'is own;
  'E keeps 'is side-arms awful: 'e leaves 'em all about,
  An' then comes up the Regiment an' pokes the 'eathen out.
  'The 'Eathen' (1896). Cf. Heber 330:4

1 The 'eathen in 'is blindness must end where 'e
    began.
    But the backbone of the Army is the
    non-commissioned man!
    'The 'Eathen' (1896)

2 Winds of the World, give answer! They are
    whimpering to and fro—
    And what should they know of England who only
    England know?—
    The poor little street-bred people that vapour and
    fume and brag.
    'The English Flag' (1892)

3 The female of the species is more deadly than the
    male.
    'The Female of the Species' (1919)

4 There is but one task for all—
    For each one life to give.
    What stands if freedom fall?
    Who dies if England live?
    For All We Have and Are (1914) p. 2

5 So 'ere's *to* you, Fuzzy-Wuzzy, at your 'ome in the
    Soudan;
    You're a pore benighted 'eathen but a first-class
    fightin' man;
    An' 'ere's *to* you, Fuzzy-Wuzzy, with your 'ayrick 'ead
    of 'air—
    You big black boundin' beggar—for you broke a
    British square!
    'Fuzzy-Wuzzy' (1892)

6 We're poor little lambs who've lost our way,
    Baa! Baa! Baa!
    We're little black sheep who've gone astray,
    Baa-aa-aa!
    Gentlemen-rankers out on the spree,
    Damned from here to Eternity,
    God ha' mercy on such as we,
    Baa! Yah! Bah!
    'Gentlemen-Rankers' (1892)

7 Our England is a garden, and such gardens are not
    made
    By singing:—'Oh, how beautiful!' and sitting in the
    shade,
    While better men than we go out and start their
    working lives
    At grubbing weeds from gravel paths with broken
    dinner-knives.
    'The Glory of the Garden' (1911)

8 As it will be in the future, it was at the birth of Man—
    There are only four things certain since Social
    Progress began:—
    That the Dog returns to his Vomit and the Sow
    returns to her Mire,
    And the burnt Fool's bandaged finger goes wabbling
    back to the Fire.
    'The Gods of the Copybook Headings' (1927)

9 The uniform 'e wore
    Was nothin' much before,
    An' rather less than 'arf o' that be'ind.
    'Gunga Din' (1892)

10 Though I've belted you and flayed you,
    By the livin' Gawd that made you,
    You're a better man than I am, Gunga Din!
    'Gunga Din' (1892)

11 There are nine and sixty ways of constructing tribal
    lays,
    And—every—single—one—of—them—is—right!
    'In the Neolithic Age' (1893)

12 But I consort with long-haired things
    In velvet collar-rolls,
    Who talk about the Aims of Art,
    And 'theories' and 'goals',
    And moo and coo with women-folk
    About their blessed souls.
    'In Partibus' (1909)

13 Then ye returned to your trinkets; then ye contented
    your souls
    With the flannelled fools at the wicket or the muddied
    oafs at the goals.
    'The Islanders' (1903)

14 I've taken my fun where I've found it,
    An' now I must pay for my fun,
    For the more you 'ave known o' the others
    The less will you settle to one.
    'The Ladies' (1896)

15 When you get to a man in the case,
    They're like as a row of pins—
    For the Colonel's Lady an' Judy O'Grady
    Are sisters under their skins!
    'The Ladies' (1896)

16 And Ye take mine honour from me if Ye take away
    the sea!
    'The Last Chantey' (1896)

17 There be triple ways to take, of the eagle or the
    snake,
    Or the way of a man with a maid;
    But the sweetest way to me is a ship's upon the sea
    In the heel of the North-East Trade.
    'L'Envoi' (*Barrack-Room Ballads*, 1892). Cf. Proverbs 79:33

18 Down to Gehenna or up to the Throne,
    He travels the fastest who travels alone.
    'L'Envoi' (*The Story of the Gadsbys*, 1890)

19 The Liner she's a lady, an' she never looks nor
    'eeds—
    The Man-o'-War's 'er 'usband, an' 'e gives 'er all she
    needs;
    But, oh, the little cargo boats that sail the wet seas
    roun',
    They're just the same as you an' me a-plyin' up and
    down!
    'The Liner She's a Lady' (1896)

20 It's north you may run to the rime-ringed sun,
    Or south to the blind Horn's hate;
    Or east all the way into Mississippi Bay,
    Or west to the Golden Gate.
    'The Long Trail' (1918)

1 By the old Moulmein Pagoda, lookin' eastward to the
   sea,
   There's a Burma girl a-settin', and I know she thinks
   o' me;
   For the wind is in the palm-trees, an' the temple-bells
   they say:
   'Come you back, you British soldier; come you back to
   Mandalay!'
   Come you back to Mandalay,
   Where the old flotilla lay:
   Can't you 'ear their paddles chunkin' from Rangoon
   to Mandalay?
   On the road to Mandalay,
   Where the flyin'-fishes play,
   An' the dawn comes up like thunder outer China
   'crost the Bay!
   'Mandalay' (1892)

2 An' I seed her first a-smokin' of a whackin' white
   cheroot,
   An' a-wastin' Christian kisses on an 'eathen idol's
   foot.
   'Mandalay' (1892)

3 Ship me somewheres east of Suez, where the best is
   like the worst,
   Where there aren't no Ten Commandments an' a man
   can raise a thirst.
   'Mandalay' (1892)

4 And the end of the fight is a tombstone white, with
   the name of the late deceased,
   And the epitaph drear: 'A fool lies here who tried to
   hustle the East.'
   The Naulahka (1892) ch. 5

5 A Nation spoke to a Nation,
   A Throne sent word to a Throne:
   'Daughter am I in my mother's house,
   But mistress in my own.
   The gates are mine to open,
   As the gates are mine to close,
   And I abide by my Mother's House.'
   Said our Lady of the Snows.
   'Our Lady of the Snows' (1898)

6 The toad beneath the harrow knows
   Exactly where each tooth-point goes;
   The butterfly upon the road
   Preaches contentment to that toad.
   'Pagett, MP' (1886)

7 There is sorrow enough in the natural way
   From men and women to fill our day;
   But when we are certain of sorrow in store,
   Why do we always arrange for more?
   Brothers and Sisters, I bid you beware
   Of giving your heart to a dog to tear.
   'The Power of the Dog' (1909)

8 What is a woman that you forsake her,
   And the hearth-fire and the home-acre,
   To go with the old grey Widow-maker?
   Puck of Pook's Hill (1906) 'Harp Song of the Dane
   Women'

9 Five and twenty ponies,
   Trotting through the dark—
   Brandy for the Parson,
   'Baccy for the Clerk;
   Laces for a lady, letters for a spy,
   Watch the wall, my darling, while the Gentlemen go
   by!
   Puck of Pook's Hill (1906) 'A Smuggler's Song'

10 Of all the trees that grow so fair,
    Old England to adorn,
    Greater are none beneath the Sun,
    Than Oak, and Ash, and Thorn.
    Puck of Pook's Hill (1906) 'A Tree Song'

11 The tumult and the shouting dies—
    The captains and the kings depart—
    Still stands Thine ancient Sacrifice,
    An humble and a contrite heart.
    Lord God of Hosts, be with us yet,
    Lest we forget—lest we forget!
    'Recessional' (1897). Cf. Job 77:39

12 Far-called our navies melt away—
    On dune and headland sinks the fire—
    Lo, all our pomp of yesterday
    Is one with Nineveh, and Tyre!
    'Recessional' (1897)

13 If, drunk with sight of power, we loose
    Wild tongues that have not Thee in awe—
    Such boasting as the Gentiles use,
    Or lesser breeds without the Law.
    'Recessional' (1897)

14 If you can keep your head when all about you
    Are losing theirs and blaming it on you;
    If you can trust yourself when all men doubt you,
    But make allowance for their doubting too;
    If you can wait and not be tired by waiting,
    Or being lied about, don't deal in lies,
    Or being hated, don't give way to hating,
    And yet don't look too good, nor talk too wise;
    If you can dream—and not make dreams your master;
    If you can think—and not make thoughts your aim,
    If you can meet with triumph and disaster
    And treat those two imposters just the same...
    Rewards and Fairies (1910) 'If—'

15 If you can talk with crowds and keep your virtue,
    Or walk with Kings—nor lose the common touch,
    If neither foes nor loving friends can hurt you,
    If all men count with you, but none too much;
    If you can fill the unforgiving minute
    With sixty seconds' worth of distance run,
    Yours is the Earth and everything that's in it,
    And—which is more—you'll be a Man, my son!
    Rewards and Fairies (1910) 'If—'

16 One man in a thousand, Solomon says,
    Will stick more close than a brother.
    Rewards and Fairies (1910) 'The Thousandth Man'. Cf.
    Proverbs BIBLE5414

17 They shut the road through the woods
    Seventy years ago.
    Weather and rain have undone it again,
    And now you would never know
    There was once a road through the woods.
    Rewards and Fairies (1910) 'The Way through the Woods'

1 Who hath desired the Sea?—the sight of salt water
  unbounded—
The heave and the halt and the hurl and the crash of
  the comber wind-hounded?
The sleek-barrelled swell before storm, grey, foamless,
  enormous, and growing—
Stark calm on the lap of the Line or the crazy-eyed
  hurricane blowing.
  'The Sea and the Hills' (1903)

2 We have fed our sea for a thousand years
And she calls us, still unfed,
Though there's never a wave of all her waves
But marks our English dead:
We have strawed our best to the weed's unrest
To the shark and sheering gull.
If blood be the price of admiralty,
Lord God, we ha' paid in full!
  'The Song of the Dead' (1896)

3 And here the sea-fogs lap and cling
And here, each warning each,
The sheep-bells and the ship-bells ring
Along the hidden beach.
  'Sussex' (1903)

4 For the sin ye do by two and two ye must pay for one
  by one!
  'Tomlinson' (1892)

5 Then it's Tommy this, an' Tommy that, an' 'Tommy
  'ow's yer soul?'
But it's 'Thin red line of 'eroes' when the drums begin
  to roll.
  'Tommy' (1892)

6 For it's Tommy this, an' Tommy that, an' 'Chuck him
  out, the brute!'
But it's 'Saviour of 'is country' when the guns begin
  to shoot.
  'Tommy' (1892)

7 A fool there was and he made his prayer
(Even as you and I!)
To a rag and a bone and a hank of hair
(We called her the woman who did not care)
But the fool he called her his lady fair—
(Even as you and I!)
  'The Vampire' st. 1

8 It is always a temptation to a rich and lazy nation,
To puff and look important and to say:-
'Though we know we should defeat you, we have not
  the time to meet you,
We will therefore pay you cash to go away.'

And that is called paying the Dane-geld;
But we've proved it again and again,
That if once you have paid him the Dane-geld
You never get rid of the Dane.
  'What Dane-geld means' (1911)

9 And only the Master shall praise us, and only the
  Master shall blame;
And no one shall work for money, and no one shall
  work for fame,
But each for the joy of the working, and each, in his
  separate star,
Shall draw the Thing as he sees It for the God of
  Things as They are!
  'When Earth's Last Picture is Painted' (1896)

10 When 'Omer smote 'is bloomin' lyre,
He'd 'eard men sing by land an' sea;
An' what he thought 'e might require,
'E went an' took—the same as me!
  'When 'Omer smote 'is bloomin' lyre' (1896)

11 Take up the White Man's burden—
Send forth the best ye breed—
Go, bind your sons to exile
To serve your captives' need.
  'The White Man's Burden' (1899)

12 When you're wounded and left on Afghanistan's
  plains
And the women come out to cut up what remains
Just roll to your rifle and blow out your brains
An' go to your Gawd like a soldier.
  'The Young British Soldier' (1892)

13 What the horses o' Kansas think to-day, the horses of
America will think tomorrow; an' I tell *you* that when
the horses of America rise in their might, the day o'
the Oppressor is ended.
  The Day's Work (1898) 'A Walking Delegate'

14 Lalun is a member of the most ancient profession in
the world.
  In Black and White (1888) 'On the City Wall'

15 'We be one blood, thou and I', Mowgli answered. 'I
take my life from thee to-night. My kill shall be thy
kill if ever thou art hungry, O Kaa.'
  The Jungle Book (1894) 'Kaa's Hunting'

16 Brother, thy tail hangs down behind!
  The Jungle Book (1894) 'Road Song of the Bandar-Log'

17 Yes, weekly from Southampton,
Great steamers, white and gold,
Go rolling down to Rio
(Roll down—roll down to Rio!).
  Just So Stories (1902) 'The Beginning of the Armadilloes'

18 He walked by himself, and all places were alike to
him.
  Just So Stories (1902) 'The Cat that Walked by Himself'

19 And he went back through the Wet Wild Woods,
waving his wild tail and walking by his wild lone. But
he never told anybody.
  Just So Stories (1902) 'The Cat that Walked by Himself'

20 One Elephant—a new Elephant—an Elephant's
Child—who was full of 'satiable curtiosity.
  Just So Stories (1902) 'The Elephant's Child'

21 Then the Elephant's Child put his head down close to
the Crocodile's musky, tusky mouth, and the Crocodile
caught him by his little nose . . . 'Led go! You are
hurtig be!'
  Just So Stories (1902) 'The Elephant's Child'

22 I keep six honest serving-men
(They taught me all I knew);
Their names are What and Why and When
And How and Where and Who.
  Just So Stories (1902) 'The Elephant's Child'

23 The cure for this ill is not to sit still,
Or frowst with a book by the fire;
But to take a large hoe and a shovel also,
And dig till you gently perspire.
  Just So Stories (1902) 'How the Camel got his Hump'

1 You must *not* forget the suspenders, Best Beloved.
   Just So Stories (1902) 'How the Whale got his Throat'

2 And the small 'Stute Fish said in a small 'stute voice,
   'Noble and generous Cetacean, have you ever tasted
   Man?' 'No,' said the Whale. 'What is it like?' 'Nice,'
   said the small 'Stute Fish. 'Nice but nubbly.'
   Just So Stories (1902) 'How the Whale got his Throat'

3 He had his Mummy's leave to paddle, or else he would
   never have done it, because he was a man of
   infinite-resource-and-sagacity.
   Just So Stories (1902) 'How the Whale got his Throat'

4 Little Friend of all the World.
   Kim (1901) ch. 1 (Kim's nickname)

5 The mad all are in God's keeping.
   Kim (1901) ch. 2

6 The man who would be king.
   Title of story (1888)

7 Every one is more or less mad on one point.
   Plain Tales from the Hills (1888) 'On the Strength of a
   Likeness'

8 Take my word for it, the silliest woman can manage a
   clever man; but it takes a very clever woman to
   manage a fool.
   Plain Tales from the Hills (1888) 'Three and—an Extra'

9 Now this is the Law of the Jungle—as old and as true
   as the sky;
   And the Wolf that shall keep it may prosper, but the
   Wolf that shall break it must die.
   The Second Jungle Book (1895) 'The Law of the Jungle'

10 Mr Raymond Martin, beyond question, was born in a
    gutter, and bred in a Board-School, where they played
    marbles. He was further (I give the barest handful
    from great store) a Flopshus Cad, an Outrageous
    Stinker, a Jelly-bellied Flag-flapper . . . and several
    other things which it is not seemly to put down.
    Stalky & Co. (1899) p. 214

11 Being kissed by a man who *didn't* wax his moustache
    was—like eating an egg without salt.
    The Story of the Gadsbys (1889) 'Poor Dear Mamma'

12 'Tisn't beauty, so to speak, nor good talk necessarily.
    It's just It. Some women'll stay in a man's memory if
    they once walked down a street.
    Traffics and Discoveries (1904) 'Mrs Bathurst'

13 Power without responsibility: the prerogative of the
    harlot throughout the ages.
    Summing up Max Aitken (Lord Beaverbrook)'s political
    standpoint *vis-à-vis* the *Daily Express*, the latter having said
    in conversation with Kipling: 'What I want is power. Kiss
    'em one day and kick 'em the next'; in *Kipling Journal*
    vol. 38, no. 180, December 1971, p. 6. Stanley Baldwin,
    Kipling's cousin, subsequently obtained permission to use
    the phrase in a speech in London on 18 March 1931

Henry Kissinger 1923–

American politician

14 Power is the great aphrodisiac.
    In *New York Times* 19 January 1971, p. 12

15 We are the President's men.
    In M. and B. Kalb *Kissinger* (1974) ch. 7

Fred Kitchen 1872–1950

British writer

16 Meredith, we're in!
    Catch-phrase originating in *The Bailiff* (1907 stage sketch).
    See J. P. Gallagher *Fred Karno* (1971) ch. 9, p. 90

Lord Kitchener 1850–1916

British soldier and statesman

17 You are ordered abroad as a soldier of the King to help
    our French comrades against the invasion of a
    common enemy . . . In this new experience you may
    find temptations both in wine and women. You must
    entirely resist both temptations, and, while treating all
    women with perfect courtesy, you should avoid any
    intimacy. Do your duty bravely. Fear God. Honour the
    King.
    Message to soldiers of the British Expeditionary Force
    (1914), in *The Times* 19 August 1914

18 I don't mind your being killed, but I object to your
    being taken prisoner.
    To the Prince of Wales (later King Edward VIII) on his
    asking to be allowed to the Front during the First World
    War, in *Journals and Letters of Reginald Viscount Esher* vol. 3
    (1938) p. 198 (18 December 1914)

Paul Klee 1879–1940

Swiss painter

19 *Kunst gibt nicht das Sichtbare wieder, sondern macht
    sichtbar.*

    Art does not reproduce the visible; rather, it makes
    visible.
    Inward Vision (1958) 'Creative Credo' (1920)

20 *Eine aktive Linie, die sich frei ergeht, ein Spaziergang um
    seiner selbst willen, ohne Ziel. Das agens ist ein Punkt, der
    sich verschiebt.*

    An active line on a walk, moving freely without a
    goal. A walk for walk's sake. The agent is a point that
    shifts position.
    Pedagogical Sketchbook (1925) p. 6

Friedrich Klopstock 1724–1803

German poet

21 God and I both knew what it meant once; now God
    alone knows.
    In C. Lombroso *The Man of Genius* (1891) pt. 1, ch. 2 (also
    attributed to Browning, apropos *Sordello*, in the form 'When
    it was written, God and Robert Browning knew what it
    meant; now only God knows')

Charles Knight and Kenneth Lyle

British songwriters

22 When there's trouble brewing,
    When there's something doing,
    Are we downhearted?
    No! Let 'em all come!
    'Here we are! Here we are again!!' (1914 song)

Frank H. Knight 1885–1973
American economist

1 Costs merely register competing attractions.
> *Risk, Uncertainty and Profit* (1921) p. 159

Mary Knowles (*née Morris*) 1733–1807
English Quaker

2 He gets at the substance of a book directly; he tears out the heart of it.
> On Samuel Johnson, in James Boswell *The Life of Samuel Johnson* (1934 ed.) vol. 3, p. 284 (15 April 1778)

John Knox c.1505–72
Scottish Protestant reformer

3 *Un homme avec Dieu est toujours dans la majorité.*
A man with God is always in the majority.
> Inscription on the Reformation Monument, Geneva

4 The First Blast of the Trumpet Against the Monstrous Regiment of Women.
> Title of Pamphlet (1558)

Ronald Knox 1888–1957
English writer and Roman Catholic priest

5 When suave politeness, tempering bigot zeal,
Corrected *I believe* to *One does feel.*
> 'Absolute and Abitofhell' (1913)

6 After all, what was a paradox but a statement of the obvious so as to make it sound untrue?
> *A Spiritual Aeneid* (1918) p. 120

7 The tumult and the shouting dies,
The captains and the kings depart,
And we are left with large supplies
Of cold blancmange and rhubarb tart.
> 'After the Party' in L. E. Eyres (ed.) *In Three Tongues* (1959) p. 130. Cf. Kipling 400:11

8 Hail him like Etonians, without a single word,
Absolutely silent and indefinitely bored.
> 'Magister Reformator' (1906)

9 O God, for as much as without Thee
We are not enabled to doubt Thee,
Help us all by Thy grace
To convince the whole race
It knows nothing whatever about Thee.
> In Langford Reed *Complete Limerick Book* (1924)

10 There once was a man who said, 'God
Must think it exceedingly odd
If he finds that this tree
Continues to be
When there's no one about in the Quad.'
> In Langford Reed *Complete Limerick Book* (1924), to which came the anonymous reply: 'Dear Sir, / Your astonishment's odd: / I am always about in the Quad. / And that's why the tree / Will continue to be, / Since observed by / Yours faithfully, / God.'

11 Evangelical vicar, in want of a portable, second-hand font, would dispose, for the same, of a portrait, in frame, of the Bishop, elect, of Vermont.
> Advertisement placed in a newspaper, in W. S. Baring-Gould *The Lure of the Limerick* (1968) pt. 1, ch. 1, n. 5

12 The baby doesn't understand English and the Devil knows Latin.
> On being asked to perform a baptism in English, in Evelyn Waugh *Ronald Knox* (1959) pt. 1, ch. 5

13 A loud noise at one end and no sense of responsibility at the other.
> Definition of a baby (attributed)

Vicesimus Knox 1752–1821
English writer

14 That learning belongs not to the female character, and that the female mind is not capable of a degree of improvement equal to that of the other sex, are narrow and unphilosophical prejudices.
> *Essays Moral and Literary* (1782) no. 142

15 All sensible people agree in thinking that large seminaries of young ladies, though managed with all the vigilance and caution which human abilities can exert, are in danger of great corruption.
> *Liberal Education* (1780) sect. 27 'On the literary education of women'

16 Can anything be more absurd than keeping women in a state of ignorance, and yet so vehemently to insist on their resisting temptation?
> In Mary Wollstonecraft *A Vindication of the Rights of Woman* (1792) ch. 7

Ted Koehler
American songwriter

17 Stormy weather,
Since my man and I ain't together.
> 'Stormy Weather' (1933 song); music by Harold Arlen

Arthur Koestler 1905–83
Hungarian-born writer

18 One may not regard the world as a sort of metaphysical brothel for emotions.
> *Darkness at Noon* (1940) 'The Second Hearing' pt. 7

19 The definition of the individual was: a multitude of one million divided by one million.
> *Darkness at Noon* (1940) 'The Grammatical Fiction' pt. 2

20 Behaviourism is indeed a kind of flat-earth view of the mind . . . it has substituted for the erstwhile anthropomorphic view of the rat, a ratomorphic view of man.
> *The Ghost in the Machine* (1967) ch. 1

21 God seems to have left the receiver off the hook, and time is running out.
> *The Ghost in the Machine* (1967) ch. 18

22 A writer's ambition should be . . . to trade a hundred contemporary readers for ten readers in ten years' time and for one reader in a hundred years.
> In *New York Times Book Review* 1 April 1951, p. 24

Jiddu Krishnamurti d. 1986

Indian spiritual philosopher

1 Truth is a pathless land, and you cannot approach it
by any path whatsoever, by any religion, by any sect.
Speech in Holland, 3 August 1929, in Lilly Heber
Krishnamurti (1931) ch. 2

2 Religion is the frozen thought of men out of which
they build temples.
In *Observer* 22 April 1928 'Sayings of the Week'

Kris Kristofferson 1936–

American actor

3 Freedom's just another word for nothin' left to lose,
Nothin' ain't worth nothin', but it's free.
'Me and Bobby McGee' (1969 song, with Fred Foster)

Jeremy Joe Kronsberg

American screenwriter

4 Every which way but loose.
Title of film (1978); starring Clint Eastwood

Paul Kruger 1825–1904

South African soldier and statesman

5 A bill of indemnity . . . for raid by Dr Jameson and the
British South Africa Company's troops. The amount
falls under two heads—first, material damage, total of
claim, £677,938 3*s*. 3*d*.—second, moral or
intellectual damage, total of claim, £1,000,000.
Telegram from the South African Republic, communicated
to the House of Commons by Joseph Chamberlain; in
Hansard 18 February 1897, col. 726

Joseph Wood Krutch 1893–1970

American critic and naturalist

6 The most serious charge which can be brought
against New England is not Puritanism but February.
The Twelve Seasons (1949) 'February'

Stanley Kubrick 1928–

American film director

7 The great nations have always acted like gangsters,
and the small nations like prostitutes.
In *Guardian* 5 June 1963

Satish Kumar 1937–

Indian writer

8 Lead me from death to life, from falsehood to truth.
Lead me from despair to hope, from fear to trust.
Lead me from hate to love, from war to peace.
Let peace fill our heart, our world, our universe.
'Prayer for Peace' (1981); adapted from the Upanishads

Milan Kundera 1929–

Czech novelist

9 The unbearable lightness of being.
Title of novel (1984)

Thomas Kyd 1558–94

English playwright

10 What outcries pluck me from my naked bed?
The Spanish Tragedy (1592) act 2, sc. 5, l. 1

11 Oh eyes, no eyes, but fountains fraught with tears;
Oh life, no life, but lively form of death;
Oh world, no world, but mass of public wrongs.
The Spanish Tragedy (1592) act 3, sc. 2, l. 1

12 Thus must we toil in other men's extremes,
That know not how to remedy our own.
The Spanish Tragedy (1592) act 3, sc. 6, l. 1

13 I am never better than when I am mad. Then
methinks I am a brave fellow; then I do wonders. But
reason abuseth me, and there's the torment, there's
the hell.
The Spanish Tragedy (1592) act 3, sc. 7, The Fourth Addition
(1602 ed.) l. 164

14 My son—and what's a son? A thing begot
Within a pair of minutes, thereabout,
A lump bred up in darkness.
The Spanish Tragedy (1592) act 3, sc. 11, The Third Addition
(1602 ed.) l. 5

15   Duly twice a morning
Would I be sprinkling it with fountain water.
At last it grew, and grew, and bore, and bore,
Till at the length
It grew a gallows and did bear our son,
It bore thy fruit and mine: O wicked, wicked plant.
The Spanish Tragedy (1592) act 3, sc. 12, The Fourth
Addition (1602 ed.) l. 66

16 For what's a play without a woman in it?
The Spanish Tragedy (1592) act 4, sc. 1, l. 97

Henry Labouchere 1831–1912

British politician

17 He [Labouchere] did not object to the old man always
having a card up his sleeve, but he did object to his
insinuating that the Almighty had placed it there.
On Gladstone's 'frequent appeals to a higher power', in Earl
Curzon *Modern Parliamentary Eloquence* (1913) p. 25. A. L.
Thorold quotes Labouchere from a private letter in *The Life
of Henry Labouchere* (1913) ch. 15: 'Who cannot refrain
from perpetually bringing an ace down his sleeve, even
when he has only to play fair to win the trick'

Jean de la Bruyère 1645–96

French satiric moralist

18 *Le commencement et le déclin de l'amour se font sentir par
l'embarras où l'on est de se trouver seuls.*

The onset and the waning of love make themselves felt
in the uneasiness experienced at being alone together.
Les Caractères ou les moeurs de ce siècle (1688) 'Du Coeur'

1 *Le peuple n'a guère d'esprit et les grands n'ont point d'âme
... faut-il opter, je ne balance pas, je veux être peuple.*

The people have little intelligence, the great no heart
... if I had to choose I should have no hesitation: I
would be of the people.

Les Caractères ou les moeurs de ce siècle (1688) 'Des Grands'

2 *Il n'y a pour l'homme que trois événements: naître, vivre
et mourir. Il ne se sent pas naître, il souffre à mourir, et il
oublie de vivre.*

Man has but three events in his life: to be born, to
live, and to die. He is not conscious of his birth, he
suffers at his death and he forgets to live.

Les Caractères ou les moeurs de ce siècle (1688) 'De l'homme'

3 *Entre le bon sens et le bon goût il y a la différence de la
cause et son effet.*

Between good sense and good taste there is the same
difference as between cause and effect.

Les Caractères ou les moeurs de ce siècle (1688) 'Des
Jugements'

4 *Tout est dit et l'on vient trop tard depuis plus de sept mille
ans qu'il y a des hommes et qui pensent.*

Everything has been said, and we are more than seven
thousand years of human thought too late.

Les Caractères ou les moeurs de ce siècle (1688) 'Des Ouvrages
de l'esprit'

5 *C'est un métier que de faire un livre, comme de faire une
pendule: il faut plus que de l'esprit pour être auteur.*

Making a book is a craft, as is making a clock; it takes
more than wit to become an author.

Les Caractères ou les moeurs de ce siècle (1688) 'Des Ouvrages
de l'esprit'

Nivelle de la Chaussée 1692–1754

French playwright

6 *Quand tout le monde a tort, tout le monde a raison.*

When everyone is wrong, everyone is right.

La Gouvernante (1747) act 1, sc. 3

James Lackington 1746–1815

English bookseller

7 At last, by singing and repeating enthusiastic amorous
hymns, and ignorantly applying particular texts of
scripture, I got my imagination to the proper pitch,
and thus was I born again in an instant.

Memoirs (1792 ed.) Letter 6

Jean de la Fontaine 1621–95

French poet

8 *Aide-toi, le ciel t'aidera.*

Help yourself, and heaven will help you.

Fables bk. 6 (1668) 'Le Chartier Embourbé'

9 *Je plie et ne romps pas.*

I bend and I break not.

Fables bk. 1 (1668) 'Le Chêne et le Roseau'

10 *C'est double plaisir de tromper le trompeur.*

It is doubly pleasing to trick the trickster.

Fables bk. 2 (1668) 'Le Coq et le Renard'

11 *La raison du plus fort est toujours la meilleure.*

The reason of the strongest is always the best.

Fables bk. 1 (1668) 'Le Loup et l'Agneau'

12 *Il connaît l'univers et ne se connaît pas.*

He knows the universe and does not know himself.

Fables bk. 8 (1678–9) 'Démocrite et les Abdéritains'

13 *La mort ne surprend point le sage,
Il est toujours prêt à partir.*

Death never takes the wise man by surprise; he is
always ready to go.

Fables bk. 8 (1678–9) 'La Mort et le Mourant'. Cf.
Montaigne 480:14

14 *Certain renard voulut, dit-on, se faire loup. Hé! qui peu
dire que pour le métier de mouton jamais aucun loup ne
soupire?*

A certain fox, it is said, wanted to become a wolf. Ah!
who can say why no wolf has ever craved the life of a
sheep?

Fables Choisies (1693 ed.) bk. 7, no. 9

Jules Laforgue 1860–87

French poet

15 *Ah! que la vie est quotidienne.*

Oh, what a day-to-day business life is.

Complainte sur certains ennuis (1885)

Fiorello La Guardia 1882–1947

American politician

16 When I make a mistake, it's a beaut!

On the appointment of Herbert O'Brien as a judge in 1936,
in William Manners *Patience and Fortitude* (1976) p. 219

R. D. Laing 1927–89

Scottish psychiatrist

17 The divided self.

Title of book (1960) on schizophrenia

18 The brotherhood of man is evoked by particular men
according to their circumstances ... In the name of
our freedom and our brotherhood we are prepared to
blow up the other half of mankind and to be blown up
in turn.

The Politics of Experience (1967) ch. 4

19 Madness need not be all breakdown. It may also be
break-through.

The Politics of Experience (1967) ch. 6

20 True guilt is guilt at the obligation one owes to oneself
to be oneself. False guilt is guilt felt at not being what
other people feel one ought to be or assume that
one is.

Self and Others (1961) ch. 10

Alphonse de Lamartine 1790–1869

French poet

21 *Un être seul vous manque, et tout est dépeuplé.*

Only one being is wanting, and your whole world is
bereft of people.

'L'Isolement' (1820)

1 *Ô temps! suspend ton vol, et vous, heures propices!*
Suspendez votre cours.

O Time! arrest your flight, and you, propitious hours,
stay your course.
   Le Lac (1820) st. 6

Lady Caroline Lamb 1785–1828

Wife of William Lamb, 2nd Viscount Melbourne

2 Mad, bad, and dangerous to know.
   Writing of Byron in her journal after their first meeting at a
   ball in March 1812; in Elizabeth Jenkins *Lady Caroline Lamb*
   (1932) ch. 6

Charles Lamb 1775–1834

English writer

3 I know that a sweet child is the sweetest thing in
nature . . . but the prettier the kind of a thing is, the
more desirable it is that it should be pretty of its kind.
   Essays of Elia (1823) 'A Bachelor's Complaint of the
   Behaviour of Married People'

4 If the husband be a man with whom you have lived
on a friendly footing before marriage,—if you did not
come in on the wife's side,—if you did not sneak into
the house in her train, but were an old friend in first
habits of intimacy before their courtship was so much
as thought on,—look about you . . . Every long
friendship, every old authentic intimacy, must be
brought into their office to be new stamped with their
currency, as a sovereign Prince calls in the good old
money that was coined in some reign before he was
born or thought of, to be new marked and minted
with the stamp of his authority, before he will let it
pass current in the world.
   Essays of Elia (1823) 'A Bachelor's Complaint of the
   Behaviour of Married People'

5 Ceremony is an invention to take off the uneasy
feeling which we derive from knowing ourselves to be
less the object of love and esteem with a
fellow-creature than some other person is. It
endeavours to make up, by superior attentions in little
points, for that invidious preference which it is forced
to deny in the greater.
   Essays of Elia (1823) 'A Bachelor's Complaint of the
   Behaviour of Married People'

6 I have no ear.
   Essays of Elia (1823) 'A Chapter on Ears'

7 Sentimentally I am disposed to harmony. But
organically I am incapable of a tune.
   Essays of Elia (1823) 'A Chapter on Ears'

8 Presents, I often say, endear Absents.
   Essays of Elia (1823) 'A Dissertation upon Roast Pig'

9 She unbent her mind afterwards—over a book.
   Essays of Elia (1823) 'Mrs Battle's Opinions on Whist'

10 A votary of the desk—a notched and cropt
scrivener—one that sucks his substance, as certain
sick people are said to do, through a quill.
   Essays of Elia (1823) 'Oxford in the Vacation'

11 The uncommunicating muteness of fishes.
   Essays of Elia (1823) 'A Quakers' Meeting'

12 The human species, according to the best theory I can
form of it, is composed of two distinct races, *the men
who borrow*, and *the men who lend*.
   Essays of Elia (1823) 'The Two Races of Men'

13 Your *borrowers of books*—those mutilators of
collections, spoilers of the symmetry of shelves, and
creators of odd volumes.
   Essays of Elia (1823) 'The Two Races of Men'

14 Not many sounds in life, and I include all urban and
all rural sounds, exceed in interest a knock at the
door.
   Essays of Elia (1823) 'Valentine's Day'

15 Credulity is the man's weakness, but the child's
strength.
   Essays of Elia (1823) 'Witches, and Other Night-Fears'

16 How sickness enlarges the dimensions of a man's self
to himself.
   Last Essays of Elia (1833) 'The Convalescent'

17 Books think for me.
   Last Essays of Elia (1833) 'Detached Thoughts on Books
   and Reading'

18 Things in books' clothing.
   Last Essays of Elia (1833) 'Detached Thoughts on Books
   and Reading'

19 A poor relation—is the most irrelevant thing in
nature.
   Last Essays of Elia (1833) 'Poor Relations'

20 [A pun] is a pistol let off at the ear; not a feather to
tickle the intellect.
   Last Essays of Elia (1833) 'Popular Fallacies' no. 9

21 I have something more to do than feel.
   On the death of his mother, at his sister Mary's hands;
   letter to S. T. Coleridge, 27 September 1796, in E. W. Marrs
   (ed.) *Letters of Charles and Mary Lamb* vol. 1 (1975)

22 Cultivate simplicity, Coleridge.
   Letter to S. T. Coleridge, 8 November 1796, in E. W. Marrs
   (ed.) *Letters of Charles and Mary Lamb* vol. 1 (1975)

23 The man must have a rare recipe for melancholy, who
can be dull in Fleet Street.
   Letter to Thomas Manning, 15 February 1802, in E. W.
   Marrs (ed.) *Letters of Charles and Mary Lamb* vol. 2 (1976)

24 Nursed amid her noise, her crowds, her beloved
smoke—what have I been doing all my life, if I have
not lent out my heart with usury to such scenes?
   Of London; letter to Thomas Manning, 15 February 1802,
   in E. W. Marrs (ed.) *Letters of Charles and Mary Lamb* vol. 2
   (1976)

25 Nothing puzzles me more than time and space; and
yet nothing troubles me less, as I never think about
them.
   Letter to Thomas Manning, 2 January 1810, in E. W.
   Marrs (ed.) *Letters of Charles and Mary Lamb* vol. 3 (1978)

26 Anything awful makes me laugh.
   Letter to Robert Southey, 9 August 1815, in E. W. Marrs
   (ed.) *Letters of Charles and Mary Lamb* vol. 3 (1978)

27 This very night I am going to leave off tobacco! Surely
there must be some other world in which this
unconquerable purpose shall be realized.
   Letter to Thomas Manning, 26 December 1815, in E. W.
   Marrs (ed.) *Letters of Charles and Mary Lamb* vol. 3 (1978)

28 An Archangel a little damaged.
   Of Coleridge; letter to Wordsworth, 26 April 1816, in E. W.
   Marrs (ed.) *Letters of Charles and Mary Lamb* vol. 3 (1978)

1 The rogue gives you Love Powders, and then a strong horse drench to bring 'em off your stomach that they mayn't hurt you.

Of Coleridge; letter to Wordsworth, 23 September 1816, in E. W. Marrs (ed.) *Letters of Charles and Mary Lamb* vol. 3 (1978)

2 Fanny Kelly's divine plain face.

Letter to Mary Wordsworth, 18 February 1818, in Henry H. Harper (ed.) *Letters of Charles Lamb* (1905) vol. 4

3 Who first invented work—and tied the free
And holy-day rejoicing spirit down
To the ever-haunting importunity
Of business?

Letter to Bernard Barton, 11 September 1822, in Henry H. Harper (ed.) *Letters of Charles Lamb* (1905) vol. 4

4 The greatest pleasure I know, is to do a good action by stealth, and to have it found out by accident.

'Table Talk by the late Elia' in *The Athenaeum* 4 January 1834

5 For thy sake, Tobacco, I
Would do any thing but die.

'A Farewell to Tobacco' l. 122

6   Gone before
To that unknown and silent shore.

'Hester' (1803) st. 7

7 I have had playmates, I have had companions,
In my days of childhood, in my joyful school-days,—
All, all are gone, the old familiar faces.

'The Old Familiar Faces'

8 A child's a plaything for an hour.

'Parental Recollections' (1809); often attributed to Lamb's sister Mary

9 If ever I marry a wife,
I'll marry a landlord's daughter,
For then I may sit in the bar,
And drink cold brandy and water.

'Written in a copy of *Coelebs in Search of a Wife*'

10 If dirt were trumps, what hands you would hold!

In Leigh Hunt *Lord Byron and his Contemporaries* (1828) p. 299

11 I do not [know the lady]; but damn her at a venture.

In E. V. Lucas *Charles Lamb* (1905) vol. 1, p. 320 n.

12 The last breath he drew in he wished might be through a pipe and exhaled in a pun.

In *Diaries of William Charles Macready 1833–1851* (ed. W. Toynbee, 1912) 9 January 1834

13 I toiled after it, sir, as some men toil after virtue.

On being asked 'how he had acquired his power of smoking at such a rate', in Thomas Noon Talfourd *Memoirs of Charles Lamb* (1892) p. 262

Constant Lambert 1905–51

English composer

14 The whole trouble with a folk song is that once you have played it through there is nothing much you can do except play it over again and play it rather louder.

Music Ho! (1934) ch. 3

15 The average English critic is a don *manqué*, hopelessly parochial when not exaggeratedly teutonophile, over whose desk must surely hang the motto (presumably in Gothic lettering) 'Above all no enthusiasm'.

Opera December 1950. Cf. Talleyrand 678:8

John George Lambton (1st Earl of Durham) 1792–1840

English Whig politician

16 £40,000 a year a moderate income—such a one as a man *might jog on with*.

In Sir Herbert Maxwell (ed.) *The Creevey Papers* (1903) vol. 2, p. 32, from a letter from Mr Creevey to Miss Elizabeth Ord, 13 September 1821

George Lamming b. 1927

Barbados-born novelist and poet

17 In the castle of my skin.

Title of novel (1953)

Giuseppe di Lampedusa 1896–1957

18 *Se vogliamo che tutto rimanga come è, bisogna che tutto cambi.*

If we want things to stay as they are, things will have to change.

The Leopard (1957) p. 33

Sir Osbert Lancaster 1908–86

English writer and cartoonist

19 Nymphs and tribal deities of excessive female physique and alarming size balanced precariously on broken pediments, threatening the passer-by with a shower of stone fruit.

Pillar to Post (1938) 'Edwardian Baroque'

20 Fan-vaulting . . . from an aesthetic standpoint frequently belongs to the 'Last-supper-carved-on-a-peach-stone' class of masterpiece.

Pillar to Post (1938) 'Perpendicular'

21 All over the country the latest and most scientific methods of mass-production are being utilized to turn out a stream of old oak beams, leaded window-panes and small discs of bottle-glass, all structural devices which our ancestors lost no time in abandoning as soon as an increase in wealth and knowledge enabled them to do so.

Pillar to Post (1938) 'Stockbroker's Tudor'

Bert Lance 1931–

American government official

22 If it ain't broke, don't fix it.

In *Nation's Business* May 1977, p. 27

Letitia Elizabeth Landon (L. E. L.) 1802–38

English writer

23 Few, save the poor, feel for the poor.

'The Poor'

Walter Savage Landor 1775–1864
English poet

1 Death stands above me, whispering low
I know not what into my ear;
Of his strange language all I know
Is, there is not a word of fear.
'Death stands above me' (1853)

2 I strove with none; for none was worth my strife;
Nature I loved, and, next to Nature, Art.
'Dying Speech of an Old Philosopher' (1853)

3 Ireland never was contented . . .
Say you so? You are demented.
Ireland was contented when
All could use the sword and pen,
And when Tara rose so high
That her turrets split the sky,
And about her courts were seen
Liveried Angels robed in green,
Wearing, by St Patrick's bounty,
Emeralds big as half a county.
'Ireland never was contented' (1853)

4 Ah, what avails the sceptred race!
Ah, what the form divine!
'Rose Aylmer' (1806)

5 Past ruined Ilion Helen lives,
Alcestis rises from the shades;
Verse calls them forth; 'tis verse that gives
Immortal youth to mortal maids.
'To Ianthe' (1831)

6 There is delight in singing, tho' none hear
Beside the singer.
'To Robert Browning' (1846)

7 Thee gentle Spenser fondly led;
But me he mostly sent to bed.
'To Wordsworth: Those Who Have Laid the Harp Aside' (1846)

8 George the First was always reckoned
Vile, but viler George the Second;
And what mortal ever heard
Any good of George the Third?
When from earth the Fourth descended
God be praised the Georges ended!
Epigram in *The Atlas*, 28 April 1855. See *Notes & Queries* 3 May 1902, p. 354, for an earlier version

9 There are no fields of amaranth on this side of the grave.
Imaginary Conversations 'Aesop and Rhodope' in *Works of Walter Savage Landor* (1846) vol. 2

10 Prose on certain occasions can bear a great deal of poetry: on the other hand, poetry sinks and swoons under a moderate weight of prose.
Imaginary Conversations 'Archdeacon Hare and Walter Landor' in *The Last Fruit off an Old Tree* (1853)

11 States, like men, have their growth, their manhood, their decrepitude, their decay.
Imaginary Conversations 'Pollio and Calvus' in *Works of Walter Savage Landor* (1876) vol. 2, p. 441

12 Clear writers, like clear fountains, do not seem so deep as they are; the turbid look the most profound.
Imaginary Conversations (1824) 'Southey and Porson'

13 Fleas know not whether they are upon the body of a giant or upon one of ordinary size.
Imaginary Conversations (1824) 'Southey and Porson'

Andrew Lang 1844–1912
Scottish man of letters

14 St Andrews by the Northern sea,
A haunted town it is to me!
'Almae Matres' (1884)

15 If the wild bowler thinks he bowls,
Or if the batsman thinks he's bowled,
They know not, poor misguided souls,
They too shall perish unconsoled.
I am the batsman and the bat,
I am the bowler and the ball,
The umpire, the pavilion cat,
The roller, pitch, and stumps, and all.
'Brahma'. Cf. Emerson 276:5

16 They hear like ocean on a western beach
The surge and thunder of the Odyssey.
'The Odyssey' (1881)

Julia Lang 1921–
British broadcaster

17 Are you sitting comfortably?
Listen with Mother (BBC radio programme for children, 1950–82)

Susanne Langer 1895–1985
American philosopher

18 Art is the objectification of feeling, and the subjectification of nature.
Mind (1967) vol. 1, pt. 2, ch. 4

William Langland c.1330–c.1400
English poet

19 In a somer seson, whan softe was the sonne.
The Vision of Piers Plowman B text (ed. A. V. C. Schmidt, 1987) prologue l. 1

20 Ac on a May morwenynge on Malverne hilles
Me bifel a ferly, of Fairye me thoghte.
The Vision of Piers Plowman B text (ed. A. V. C. Schmidt, 1987) prologue l. 5 ('Ac on a May mornyng on Maluerne hulles / Me biful for to slepe, for werynesse of-walked' in C text (ed. D. Pearsall, 1978) prologue l. 6)

21 A faire feeld ful of folk fond I ther bitwene—
Of alle manere of men, the meene and the riche,
Werchynge and wandrynge as the world asketh.
The Vision of Piers Plowman B text (ed. A. V. C. Schmidt, 1987) prologue l. 17

22 A gloton of wordes.
The Vision of Piers Plowman B text (ed. A. V. C. Schmidt, 1987) prologue l. 139

23 Whan alle tresors arn tried, Truthe is the beste.
The Vision of Piers Plowman B text (ed. A. V. C. Schmidt, 1987) Passus 1, l. 135

1 Brewesters and baksters, bochiers and cokes—
For thise are men on this molde that moost harm
wercheth
To the povere peple.
> *The Vision of Piers Plowman* B text (ed. A. V. C. Schmidt,
> 1987) Passus 3, l. 79 ('As bakeres and breweres, bocheres
> and cokes; / For thyse men don most harm to the mene
> peple' in C text (ed. D. Pearsall, 1978) Passus 3, l. 80)

2 For if hevene be on this erthe, and ese to any soule,
It is in cloistre or in scole.
> *The Vision of Piers Plowman* B text (ed. A. V. C. Schmidt,
> 1987) Passus 10, l. 297

3 Suffraunce is a soverayn vertue, and a swift
vengeaunce.
Who suffreth moore than God?
> *The Vision of Piers Plowman* B text (ed. A. V. C. Schmidt,
> 1987) Passus 11, l. 378

4 Grammer, the ground of al.
> *The Vision of Piers Plowman* B text (ed. A. V. C. Schmidt,
> 1987) Passus 15, l. 370

5 Innocence is next God, and nyght and day it crieth
'Vengeaunce! Vengeaunce! Forgyve be it nevere
That shente us and shedde oure blood!
> *The Vision of Piers Plowman* B text (ed. A. V. C. Schmidt,
> 1987) Passus 17, l. 289

6 'After sharpest shoures,' quath Pees 'most shene is the
sonne;
Is no weder warmer than after watry cloudes.'
> *The Vision of Piers Plowman* B text (ed. A. V. C. Schmidt,
> 1987) Passus 18, l. 411 (*Pees* Peace)

7 Forthi be noght abasshed to bide and to be nedy,
Since he that wroghte al the world was wilfulliche
nedy.
> *The Vision of Piers Plowman* B text (ed. A. V. C. Schmidt,
> 1987) Passus 20, l. 48

Stephen Langton d. 1228
Archbishop of Canterbury

8 *Veni, Sancte Spiritus,*
Et emitte coelitus
Lucis tuae radium.

Come, Holy Spirit, and send out from heaven the
beam of your light.
> The 'Golden Sequence' for Whit Sunday (also attributed to
> several others, notably Pope Innocent III)

9 *Lava quod est sordidum,*
Riga quod est aridum,
Sana quod est saucium.
Flecte quod est rigidum,
Fove quod est frigidum,
Rege quod est devium.

Wash what is dirty, water what is dry, heal what is
wounded. Bend what is stiff, warm what is cold, guide
what goes off the road.
> The 'Golden Sequence' for Whit Sunday

Lao-tsu c.604–c.531 BC
Chinese philosopher; founder of Taoism

10 Heaven and Earth are not ruthful;
To them the Ten Thousand Things are but as straw
dogs.
> *Tao-Té-Ching* ch. 5 (translated by Arthur Waley in *The Way
> and its Power*, 1934). (*Ten thousand Things* all life forms;
> *straw dogs* sacrificial tokens)

Ring Lardner 1885–1933
American writer

11 Are you lost daddy I arsked tenderly.
Shut up he explained.
> *The Young Immigrunts* (1920) ch. 10

Philip Larkin 1922–1985
English poet

12 Sexual intercourse began
In nineteen sixty-three
(Which was rather late for me) —
Between the end of the *Chatterley* ban
And the Beatles' first LP.
> 'Annus Mirabilis' (1974)

13 Time has transfigured them into
Untruth. The stone fidelity
They hardly meant has come to be
Their final blazon, and to prove
Our almost-instinct almost true:
What will survive of us is love.
> 'An Arundel Tomb' (1964)

14 Hatless, I take off
My cycle-clips in awkward reverence.
> 'Church Going' (1955)

15 A serious house on serious earth it is,
In whose blent air all our compulsions meet,
Are recognised, and robed as destinies.
> 'Church Going' (1955)

16 What are days for?
Days are where we live.
They come, they wake us
Time and time over.
They are to be happy in:
Where can we live but days?
> 'Days' (1964)

17 Life is first boredom, then fear.
Whether or not we use it, it goes,
And leaves what something hidden from us chose,
And age, and then the only end of age.
> 'Dockery & Son' (1964)

18 Rather than words comes the thought of high
windows:
The sun-comprehending glass,
And beyond it, the deep blue air, that shows
Nothing, and is nowhere, and is endless.
> 'High Windows' (1974)

19 Next year we are to bring the soldiers home
For lack of money, and it is all right.
Places they guarded, or kept orderly,
Must guard themselves, and keep themselves orderly.
> 'Homage to a Government' (1974)

1 Next year we shall be living in a country
That brought its soldiers home for lack of money.
The statues will be standing in the same
Tree-muffled squares, and look nearly the same.
Our children will not know it's a different country.
All we can hope to leave them now is money.
'Homage to a Government' (1974)

2 Nothing, like something, happens anywhere.
'I Remember, I Remember' (1955)

3 Never such innocence,
Never before or since,
As changed itself to past
Without a word—the men
Leaving the gardens tidy,
The thousands of marriages
Lasting a little while longer:
Never such innocence again.
'MCMXIV' (1964)

4 Perhaps being old is having lighted rooms
Inside your head, and people in them, acting.
People you know, yet can't quite name.
'The Old Fools' (1974)

5 Don't read too much now: the dude
Who lets the girl down before
The hero arrives, the chap
Who's yellow and keeps the store,
Seem far too familiar. Get stewed:
Books are a load of crap.
'Study of Reading Habits' (1964)

6 They fuck you up, your mum and dad.
They may not mean to, but they do.
They fill you with the faults they had
And add some extra, just for you.
'This Be The Verse' (1974)

7 Man hands on misery to man.
It deepens like a coastal shelf.
Get out as early as you can,
And don't have any kids yourself.
'This Be The Verse' (1974)

8 Why should I let the toad *work*
Squat on my life?
Can't I use my wit as a pitchfork
And drive the brute off?

Six days of the week it soils
With its sickening poison—
Just for paying a few bills!
That's out of proportion.
'Toads' (1955)

9 Give me your arm, old toad;
Help me down Cemetery Road.
'Toads Revisited' (1964)

10 I thought of London spread out in the sun,
Its postal districts packed like squares of wheat.
'The Whitsun Weddings' (1964)

11 A beginning, a muddle, and an end.
New Fiction no. 15, January 1978 (on the 'classic formula' for a novel)

12 Deprivation is for me what daffodils were for Wordsworth.
Required Writing (1983) p. 47

Duc de la Rochefoucauld 1613–80
French moralist

13 *Nous avons tous assez de force pour supporter les maux d'autrui.*

We are all strong enough to bear the misfortunes of others.
Maximes (1678) no. 19

14 *Il est plus honteux de se défier de ses amis que d'en être trompé.*

It is more shameful to doubt one's friends than to be duped by them.
Maximes (1678) no. 84

15 *Il y a de bons mariages, mais il n'y en a point de délicieux.*

There are good marriages, but no delightful ones.
Maximes (1678) no. 113

16 *L'hypocrisie est un hommage que le vice rend à la vertu.*

Hypocrisy is a tribute which vice pays to virtue.
Maximes (1678) no. 218

17 *C'est une grande habileté que de savoir cacher son habileté.*

The height of cleverness is to be able to conceal it.
Maximes (1678) no. 245

18 *Il n'y a guère d'homme assez habile pour connaître tout le mal qu'il fait.*

There is scarcely a single man sufficiently aware to know all the evil he does.
Maximes (1678) no. 269

19 *L'absence diminue les médiocres passions, et augmente les grandes, comme le vent éteint les bougies, et allume le feu.*

Absence diminishes commonplace passions and increases great ones, as the wind extinguishes candles and kindles fire.
Maximes (1678) no. 276. Cf. Bussy-Rabutin 165:18, Francis de Sales 292:10

20 *La reconnaissance de la plupart des hommes n'est qu'une secrète envie de recevoir de plus grands bienfaits.*

In most of mankind gratitude is merely a secret hope for greater favours.
Maximes (1678) no. 298

21 *L'accent du pays où l'on est né demeure dans l'esprit et dans le coeur comme dans le langage.*

The accent of one's birthplace lingers in the mind and in the heart as it does in one's speech.
Maximes (1678) no. 342

22 *Dans l'adversité de nos meilleurs amis, nous trouvons toujours quelque chose qui ne nous déplaît pas.*

In the misfortune of our best friends, we always find something which is not displeasing to us.
Réflexions ou Maximes Morales (1665) maxim 99

23 *On n'est jamais si malheureux qu'on croit, ni si heureux qu'on espère.*

One is never as unhappy as one thinks, nor as happy as one hopes.
Sentences et Maximes de Morale (Dutch edition, 1664) maxim 128

Duc de la Rochefoucauld-Liancourt
1747–1827

French social reformer

1 LOUIS XVI: *C'est une grande révolte.*
LA ROCHEFOUCAULD-LIANCOURT: *Non, Sire, c'est une grande révolution.*

LOUIS XVI: It is a big revolt.
LA ROCHEFOUCAULD-LIANCOURT: No, Sir, a big revolution.
> On a report reaching Versailles of the Fall of the Bastille, 1789, in F. Dreyfus *La Rochefoucauld-Liancourt* (1903) ch. 2, sect. 3

Hugh Latimer *c.*1485–1555

English Protestant martyr

2 *Gutta cavat lapidem, non vi sed saepe cadendo.*

The drop of rain maketh a hole in the stone, not by violence, but by oft falling.
> *The Second Sermon preached before the King's Majesty* (19 April 1549). Cf. Ovid 502:19

3 Be of good comfort Master Ridley, and play the man. We shall this day light such a candle by God's grace in England, as (I trust) shall never be put out.
> Prior to being burned for heresy, 16 October 1555, in John Foxe *Actes and Monuments* (1570 ed.) p. 1937

William Laud 1573–1645

Archbishop of Canterbury from 1633; executed for treason

4 Lord I am coming as fast as I can, I know I must pass through the shadow of death, before I can come to see thee; But it is but *Umbra Mortis*, a mere shadow of death, a little darkness upon nature; but thou by thy merits and passion, hast broke through the jaws of death; the Lord receive my soul, and have mercy upon me, and bless this kingdom with peace and plenty, and with brotherly love and charity, that there may not be this effusion of Christian blood amongst them, for Jesus Christ his sake, if it be thy will.
> Prayer at the scaffold, in Peter Heylin *Cyprianus Anglicus* (1668) p. 537

Sir Harry Lauder (Hugh MacLennan)
1870–1950

Scottish music-hall entertainer

5 Keep right on to the end of the road,
Keep right on to the end.
Tho' the way be long, let your heart be strong,
Keep right on round the bend.
Tho' you're tired and weary,
Still journey on
Till you come to your happy abode,
Where all you love you've been dreaming of
Will be there at the end of the road.
> 'The End of the Road' (1924 song)

6 I love a lassie, a bonnie, bonnie lassie,
She's as pure as the lily in the dell.
She's as sweet as the heather, the bonnie bloomin' heather—
Mary, ma Scotch Bluebell.
> 'I Love a Lassie' (1905 song)

7 Roamin' in the gloamin',
On the bonnie banks o' Clyde.
Roamin' in the gloamin'
Wae my lassie by my side.
> 'Roamin' in the Gloamin'' (1911 song)
> *See also* R. F. MORRISON

Stan Laurel (Arthur Stanley Jefferson)
1890–1965

American film comedian, born in Britain

8 Another nice mess you've gotten me into.
> *Another Fine Mess* (1930 film) and many other Laurel and Hardy films; spoken by Oliver Hardy

William L. Laurence 1888–1977

American journalist

9 At first it was a giant column that soon took the shape of a supramundane mushroom.
> On the first atomic explosion in New Mexico, 16 July 1945, in *New York Times* 26 September 1945

James Laver 1899–1975

British fashion writer

10 The same costume will be
Indecent . . . 10 years before its time
Shameless . . . 5 years before its time
Outré (daring) 1 year before its time
Smart
Dowdy . . . 1 year after its time
Hideous . . . 10 years after its time
Ridiculous . . . 20 years after its time
Amusing . . . 30 years after its time
Quaint . . . 50 years after its time
Charming . . . 70 years after its time
Romantic . . . 100 years after its time
Beautiful . . . 150 years after its time
> *Taste and Fashion* (1937) ch. 18

D. H. Lawrence 1885–1930

English novelist and poet

11 To the Puritan all things are impure, as somebody says.
> *Etruscan Places* (1932) 'Cerveteri'

12 Ours is essentially a tragic age, so we refuse to take it tragically.
> *Lady Chatterley's Lover* (1928) ch. 1

13 And here lies the vast importance of the novel, properly handled. It can inform and lead into new places the flow of our sympathetic consciousness and it can lead our sympathy away in recoil from things gone dead.
> *Lady Chatterley's Lover* (1928) ch. 9

1 John Thomas says good-night to Lady Jane, a little
droopingly, but with a hopeful heart.
Lady Chatterley's Lover (1928) ch. 19

2 The English . . . are paralysed by fear. That is what
thwarts and distorts the Anglo-Saxon existence . . .
Nothing could be more lovely and fearless than
Chaucer. But already Shakespeare is morbid with fear,
fear of consequences. That is the strange phenomenon
of the English Renaissance: this mystic terror of the
consequences, the consequences of action.
Phoenix (1936) 'An Introduction to these Paintings'

3 If you try to nail anything down in the novel, either it
kills the novel, or the novel gets up and walks away
with the nail.
Phoenix (1936) 'Morality and the Novel'

4 Morality in the novel is the trembling instability of the
balance. When the novelist puts his thumb in the
scale, to pull down the balance to his own
predilection, that is immorality.
Phoenix (1936) 'Morality and the Novel'

5 Pornography is the attempt to insult sex, to do dirt on
it.
Phoenix (1936) 'Pornography and Obscenity' ch. 3

6 In life . . . no new thing has ever arisen, or can arise,
save out of the impulse of the male upon the female,
the female upon the male. The interaction of the male
and female spirit begot the wheel, the plough, and the
first utterance that was made on the face of the earth.
Phoenix (1936) 'Study of Thomas Hardy' ch. 7

7 The novel is the one bright book of life.
Phoenix (1936) 'Why the novel matters'

8 Never trust the artist. Trust the tale. The proper
function of a critic is to save the tale from the artist
who created it.
Studies in Classic American Literature (1923) ch. 1

9 Be a good animal, true to your instincts.
The White Peacock (1911) pt. 2, ch. 2

10 Don't you find it a beautiful clean thought, a world
empty of people, just uninterrupted grass, and a hare
sitting up?
Women in Love (1920) ch. 11

11 Is it the secret of the long-nosed Etruscans?
The long-nosed, sensitive-footed, subtly-smiling
Etruscans
Who made so little noise outside the cypress groves?
'Cypresses' (1923)

12 Don't be sucked in by the su-superior,
don't swallow the culture bait,
don't drink, don't drink and get beerier and beerier,
do learn to discriminate.
'Don'ts' (1929)

13 Along the avenue of cypresses
All in their scarlet cloaks, and surplices
Of linen go the chanting choristers,
The priests in gold and black, the villagers.
'Giorno dei Morti' (1917)

14 How beastly the bourgeois is
Especially the male of the species.
'How Beastly the Bourgeois Is' (1929)

15 . . . While we think of it, and talk of it
Let us leave it alone, physically, keep apart.
For while we have sex in the mind, we truly have
none in the body.
'Leave Sex Alone' (1929)

16 Men! The only animal in the world to fear!
'Mountain Lion' (1923)

17 So now it is vain for the singer to burst into clamour
With the great black piano appassionato. The glamour
Of childish days is upon me, my manhood is cast
Down in the flood of remembrance, I weep like a child
for the past.
'Piano' (1918)

18 I never saw a wild thing
Sorry for itself.
'Self-Pity' (1929)

19 Now it is autumn and the falling fruit
And the long journey towards oblivion . . .
Have you built your ship of death, O have you?
O build your ship of death, for you will need it.
'Ship of Death' (1932)

20 A snake came to my water-trough
On a hot, hot day, and I in pyjamas for the heat,
To drink there.
'Snake' (1923)

21 And I thought of the albatross,
And I wished he would come back, my snake.
For he seemed to me again like a king,
Like a king in exile, uncrowned in the underworld,
Now due to be crowned again.
And so, I missed my chance with one of the lords
Of life.
And I have something to expiate:
A pettiness.
'Snake' (1923)

22 Not I, not I, but the wind that blows through me!
A fine wind is blowing the new direction of Time.
'Song of a Man who has Come Through' (1917)

23 When I read Shakespeare I am struck with wonder
That such trivial people should muse and thunder
In such lovely language.
'When I Read Shakespeare' (1929)

24 Curse the blasted, jelly-boned swines, the slimy, the
belly-wriggling invertebrates, the miserable sodding
rotters, the flaming sods, the snivelling, dribbling,
dithering, palsied, pulse-less lot that make up England
today. They've got white of egg in their veins, and
their spunk is that watery it's a marvel they can
breed. They *can* nothing but frog-spawn—the
gibberers! God, how I hate them!
Letter to Edward Garnett, 3 July 1912, in H. T. Moore (ed.)
Collected Letters of D. H. Lawrence (1962) vol. 1

25 Tragedy ought really to be a great kick at misery.
Letter to A. W. McLeod, 6 October 1912, in H. T. Moore
(ed.) *Collected Letters of D. H. Lawrence* (1962) vol. 1

26 I like to write when I feel spiteful; it's like having
a good sneeze.
Letter to Lady Cynthia Asquith, c.25 November 1913, in
H. T. Moore (ed.) *Collected Letters of D. H. Lawrence* (1962)
vol. 1

27 The dead don't die. They look on and help.
Letter to J. Middleton Murry, 2 February 1923, in H. T.
Moore (ed.) *Collected Letters of D. H. Lawrence* (1962) vol. 2

1 I want to go south, where there is no autumn, where the cold doesn't crouch over one like a snow-leopard waiting to pounce. The heart of the North is dead, and the fingers of cold are corpse fingers.

Letter to J. Middleton Murry, 3 October 1924, in H. T. Moore (ed.) *Collected Letters of D. H. Lawrence* (1962) vol. 2

2 I'd like to write an essay on [Arnold] Bennett—sort of pig in clover.

Letter to Aldous Huxley, 27 March 1928, in H. T. Moore (ed.) *Collected Letters of D. H. Lawrence* (1962) vol. 2

3 My God, what a clumsy *olla putrida* James Joyce is! Nothing but old fags and cabbage-stumps of quotations from the Bible and the rest, stewed in the juice of deliberate, journalistic dirty-mindedness.

Letter to Aldous and Maria Huxley, 15 August 1928, in H. T. Moore (ed.) *Collected Letters of D. H. Lawrence* (1962) vol. 2

T. E. Lawrence 1888–1935

English soldier and writer

4 Many men would take the death-sentence without a whimper to escape the life-sentence which fate carries in her other hand.

The Mint (1955) pt. 1, ch. 4

5 The trumpets came out brazenly with the last post. We all swallowed our spittle, chokingly, while our eyes smarted against our wills. A man hates to be moved to folly by a noise.

The Mint (1955) pt. 3, ch. 9

6 I loved you, so I drew these tides of men into my
　　hands and wrote my will across the sky in stars
To earn you freedom, the seven pillared worthy house,
　　that your eyes might be shining for me
When we came.

The Seven Pillars of Wisdom (1926) dedication. Cf. Proverbs 78:18

Emma Lazarus 1849–87

American poet

7 Give me your tired, your poor,
Your huddled masses yearning to breathe free,
The wretched refuse of your teeming shore,
Send these, the homeless, tempest-tossed, to me:
I lift my lamp beside the golden door.

'The New Colossus' (1883); inscription on the Statue of Liberty, New York

Sir Edmund Leach 1910–

English anthropologist

8 Far from being the basis of the good society, the family, with its narrow privacy and tawdry secrets, is the source of all our discontents.

BBC Reith Lectures, 1967, in *Listener* 30 November 1967

Stephen Leacock 1869–1944

Canadian humorist

9 I am what is called a *professor emeritus* — from the Latin *e*, 'out', and *meritus*, 'so he ought to be'.

Here are my Lectures (1938) ch. 14

10 The landlady of a boarding-house is a parallelogram—that is, an oblong figure, which cannot be described, but which is equal to anything.

Literary Lapses (1910) 'Boarding-House Geometry'

11 There are no handles to a horse, but the 1910 model has a string to each side of its face for turning its head when there is anything you want it to see.

Literary Lapses (1910) 'Reflections on Riding'

12 A sportsman is a man who, every now and then, simply has to get out and kill something. Not that he's cruel. He wouldn't hurt a fly. It's not big enough.

My Remarkable Uncle (1942) p. 73

13 Lord Ronald said nothing; he flung himself from the room, flung himself upon his horse and rode madly off in all directions.

Nonsense Novels (1911) 'Gertrude the Governess'

14 A decision of the courts decided that the game of golf may be played on Sunday, not being a game within the view of the law, but being a form of moral effort.

Over the Footlights (1923) 'Why I Refuse to Play Golf'

Mary Leapor 1722–46

English poet and sometime cook-maid

15 In spite of all romantic poets sing,
This gold, my dearest, is an useful thing.

'Mira to Octavia'

16 Woman, a pleasing but a short-lived flower,
Too soft for business and too weak for power:
A wife in bondage, or neglected maid:
Despised, if ugly; if she's fair, betrayed.

'An Essay on Woman'

Edward Lear 1812–88

English artist and writer of humorous verse

17 Who, or why, or which, or what,
Is the Akond of Swat?

'The Akond of Swat' (1888)

18 There was an Old Man with a beard,
Who said, 'It is just as I feared!—
Two Owls and a Hen,
Four Larks and a Wren,
Have all built their nests in my beard!'

A Book of Nonsense (1846)

19 On the coast of Coromandel
Where the early pumpkins blow,
In the middle of the woods,
Lived the Yonghy-Bonghy-Bó.
Two old chairs, and half a candle;—
One old jug without a handle,—
These were all his worldly goods.

'The Courtship of the Yonghy-Bonghy-Bó' (1871)

20 When awful darkness and silence reign
Over the great Gromboolian plain,
Through the long, long wintry nights,
When the angry breakers roar
As they beat on the rocky shore;—
When storm-clouds brood on the towering heights
Of the Hills of the Chankly Bore.

'The Dong with a Luminous Nose' (1871)

1 And those who watch at that midnight hour
From Hall or Terrace or lofty Tower,
Cry as the wild light passes along,—
'The Dong!—the Dong!
The wandering Dong through the forest goes!
The Dong!—the Dong!
The Dong with a Luminous Nose!'
'The Dong with a Luminous Nose' (1871)

2 O My agèd Uncle Arly!
Sitting on a heap of Barley
Thro' the silent hours of night,—
Close beside a leafy thicket;—
On his nose there was a Cricket,—
In his hat a Railway-Ticket;—
(But his shoes were far too tight.)
'Incidents in the Life of my Uncle Arly' (1871)

3 Far and few, far and few,
Are the lands where the Jumblies live;
Their heads are green, and their hands are blue,
And they went to sea in a Sieve.
'The Jumblies' (1871)

4 They called aloud 'Our Sieve ain't big,
But we don't care a button! We don't care a fig!'
'The Jumblies' (1871)

5 And they brought an Owl, and a useful Cart,
And a pound of Rice, and a Cranberry Tart,
And a hive of silvery Bees.
And they brought a Pig, and some green Jack-daws,
And a lovely Monkey with lollipop paws, and forty
bottles of Ring-Bo-Ree,
And no end of Stilton Cheese.
'The Jumblies' (1871)

6 Nasticreechia Krorluppia.
More Nonsense (1872) 'Nonsense Botany'

7 There was an old person of Ware,
Who rode on the back of a bear:
When they asked,—'Does it trot?'—
He said, 'Certainly not!
He's a Moppsikon Floppsikon bear.'
More Nonsense (1872) 'One Hundred Nonsense Pictures and
Rhymes'

8 There was an old man of Thermopylae,
Who never did anything properly;
But they said, 'If you choose
To boil eggs in your shoes,
You shall never remain in Thermopylae.'
More Nonsense (1872) 'One Hundred Nonsense Pictures and
Rhymes'

9 Till Mrs Discobbolos said
'Oh! W! X! Y! Z!
It has just come into my head—
Suppose we should happen to fall!!!!
Darling Mr Discobbolos?'
'Mr and Mrs Discobbolos' (1871)

10 'How pleasant to know Mr Lear!'
Who has written such volumes of stuff!
Some think him ill-tempered and queer,
But a few think him pleasant enough.
Nonsense Songs (1871) preface

11 He has many friends, laymen and clerical.
Old Foss is the name of his cat:
His body is perfectly spherical,
He weareth a runcible hat.
Nonsense Songs (1871) preface

12 The Owl and the Pussy-Cat went to sea
In a beautiful pea-green boat.
They took some honey, and plenty of money,
Wrapped up in a five-pound note.
The Owl looked up to the Stars above
And sang to a small guitar,
'Oh lovely Pussy! O Pussy, my love,
What a beautiful Pussy you are.'
'The Owl and the Pussy-Cat' (1871)

13 Pussy said to the Owl, 'You elegant fowl!
How charmingly sweet you sing!
O let us be married! too long we have tarried:
But what shall we do for a ring?'
They sailed away for a year and a day,
To the land where the Bong-tree grows,
And there in a wood a Piggy-wig stood
With a ring at the end of his nose.
'The Owl and the Pussy-Cat' (1871)

14 'Dear Pig, are you willing to sell for one shilling
Your ring?' Said the Piggy, 'I will.'
'The Owl and the Pussy-Cat' (1871)

15 They dined on mince, and slices of quince,
Which they ate with a runcible spoon;
And hand in hand, on the edge of the sand,
They danced by the light of the moon.
'The Owl and the Pussy-Cat' (1871)

16 The Pobble who has no toes
Had once as many as we;
When they said, 'Some day you may lose them all';—
He replied,—'Fish fiddle de-dee!'
His Aunt Jobiska made him drink
Lavender water tinged with pink,
For she said, 'The world in general knows
There's nothing so good for a Pobble's toes!'
'The Pobble Who Has No Toes' (1871)

17 When boats or ships came near him
He tinkledy-binkledy-winkled a bell.
'The Pobble Who Has No Toes' (1871)

18 He has gone to fish, for his Aunt Jobiska's
Runcible Cat with crimson whiskers!
'The Pobble Who Has No Toes' (1871)

19 'But the longer I live on this Crumpetty Tree
The plainer than ever it seems to me
That very few people come this way
And that life on the whole is far from gay!'
Said the Quangle-Wangle Quee.
'The Quangle-Wangle's Hat' (1871)

20 And what can we expect if we haven't any dinner,
But to lose our teeth and eyelashes and keep on
growing thinner?
'The Two Old Bachelors' (1871)

Timothy Leary 1920–
American psychologist

1 If you take the game of life seriously, if you take your nervous system seriously, if you take your sense organs seriously, if you take the energy process seriously, you must turn on, tune in and drop out.
   Lecture, June 1966, in *The Politics of Ecstasy* (1968) ch. 21

Mary Elizabeth Lease 1853–1933
American writer and lecturer

2 Kansas had better stop raising corn and begin raising hell.
   In E. J. James et al. *Notable American Women 1607–1950* (1971) vol. 2, p. 381

F. R. Leavis 1895–1978
English literary critic

3 The common pursuit.
   Title of book (1952)

4 The few really great—the major novelists ... are significant in terms of the human awareness they promote; awareness of the possibilities of life.
   The Great Tradition (1948) ch. 1

5 He [Rupert Brooke] energized the Garden-Suburb ethos with a certain original talent and the vigour of a prolonged adolescence ... rather like Keats's vulgarity with a Public School accent.
   New Bearings in English Poetry (1932) ch. 2

6 The Sitwells belong to the history of publicity rather than of poetry.
   New Bearings in English Poetry (1932) ch. 2

7 Self-contempt, well-grounded.
   On the foundation of T. S. Eliot's work, in *Times Literary Supplement* 21 October 1988, p. 1177 (quoted by Christopher Ricks in a BBC radio talk)

Fran Lebowitz 1946–
American writer

8 There is no such thing as inner peace. There is only nervousness or death.
   Metropolitan Life (1978) p. 6

9 Life is something to do when you can't get to sleep.
   Metropolitan Life (1978) p. 101

Stanislaw Lec 1909–66
Polish writer

10 Is it progress if a cannibal uses knife and fork?
   Unkempt Thoughts (1962) p. 78

John le Carré (David John Moore Cornwell) 1931–
English thriller writer

11 The spy who came in from the cold.
   Title of novel (1963)

Le Corbusier (Charles-Édouard Jeanneret) 1887–1965
French architect

12 *Une maison est une machine-à-habiter.*
   A house is a machine for living in.
   Vers une architecture (1923) p. ix. Cf. Tolstoy 701:1

13 This frightful word [function] was born under other skies than those I have loved—those where the sun reigns supreme.
   In Stephen Gardiner *Le Corbusier* (1974) introduction

Alexandre Auguste Ledru-Rollin 1807–74
French politician

14 *Eh! je suis leur chef, il fallait bien les suivre.*
   Ah well! I am their leader, I really had to follow them!
   In E. de Mirecourt *Les Contemporains* vol. 14 (1857) 'Ledru-Rollin'

Gypsy Rose Lee (Rose Louise Hovick) 1914–70
American striptease artiste

15 God is love, but get it in writing.
   Attributed

Harper Lee 1926–
American novelist

16 Shoot all the bluejays you want, if you can hit 'em, but remember it's a sin to kill a mockingbird.
   To Kill a Mockingbird (1960) ch. 10

Henry Lee ('Light-Horse Harry') 1756–1818
American soldier and politician

17 A citizen, first in war, first in peace, and first in the hearts of his countrymen.
   Funeral Oration on the death of General Washington (1800) p. 14

Laurie Lee 1914–
English writer

18 I was set down from the carrier's cart at the age of three; and there with a sense of bewilderment and terror my life in the village began.
   Cider with Rosie (1959) p. 9

19 Such a morning it is when love
leans through geranium windows
and calls with a cockerel's tongue.

When red-haired girls scamper like roses
over the rain-green grass,
and the sun drips honey.
   'Day of these Days' (1947)

Nathaniel Lee c.1653–92

English playwright

1 When the sun sets, shadows, that showed at noon
But small, appear most long and terrible.
  Oedipus (with John Dryden, 1679) act 4, sc. 1

2 He speaks the kindest words, and looks such things,
Vows with so much passion, swears with so much
grace.
That 'tis a kind of heaven to be deluded by him.
  The Rival Queens (1677) act 1

3 'Tis beauty calls and glory leads the way.
  The Rival Queens (1677) act 1

4 Then he will talk, Good Gods,
How he will talk.
  The Rival Queens (1677) act 3

5 When Greeks joined Greeks, then was the tug of war!
  The Rival Queens (1677) act 4, sc. 2

6 Philip fought men, but Alexander women.
  The Rival Queens (1677) act 4, sc. 2

7 Man, false man, smiling, destructive man.
  Theodosius (1680) act 3, sc. 2

Robert E. Lee 1807–70

American Confederate general

8 It is well that war is so terrible. We should grow too
fond of it.
  After the battle of Fredericksburg, December 1862
(attributed)

Richard Le Gallienne 1866–1947

English poet

9 The cry of the Little Peoples goes up to God in vain,
For the world is given over to the cruel sons of Cain.
  'The Cry of the Little Peoples' (1899)

Ernest Lehman 1920–

American screenwriter

10 Sweet smell of success.
  Title of book and film (1957)

Tom Lehrer 1928–

American humorist

11 Plagiarize! Let no one else's work evade your eyes,
Remember why the good Lord made your eyes.
  'Lobachevski' (1953 song)

12 Life is like a sewer. What you get out of it depends on
what you put into it.
  'We Will All Go Together When We Go' (preamble), in *An
Evening Wasted with Tom Lehrer* (1953 record album)

Gottfried Wilhelm Leibniz 1646–1716

German philosopher

13 *C'est Dieu qui est la dernière raison des choses, et la
connaissance de Dieu n'est pas moins la principe des
sciences, que son essence et sa volonté sont les principes
des êtres.*
  It is God who is the ultimate reason of things, and the
knowledge of God is no less the beginning of science
than his essence and will are the beginning of beings.
  *Letter on a General Principle Useful in Explaining the Laws of
Nature* (1687) in *Leibniz: Philosophical Papers and Letters*
(translated by L. E. Loemker, 1969) p. 353

14 *Mais la connaissance des vérités nécessaires et éternelles
est ce qui nous distingue des simples animaux et nous fait
avoir la Raison et les sciences, en nous élevant à la
connaissance de nous-mêmes et de Dieu. Et c'est ce qu'on
appelle en nous Âme Raisonnable, ou Esprit.*
  It is the knowledge of necessary and eternal truths
which distinguishes us from mere animals, and gives
us *Reason* and the sciences, raising us to knowledge of
ourselves and of God. It is this in us which we call the
rational soul or *Mind.*
  The Monadology (1714) sect. 29 (translated by R. Latta)

15 *Nihil est sine ratione.*
  There is nothing without a reason.
  Studies in Physics and the Nature of Body (1671) in *Leibniz:
Philosophical Papers and Letters* (translated by L. E. Loemker,
1969) p. 142

16 *Eadem sunt quorum unum potest substitui alteri salva
veritate.*
  Two things are identical if one can be substituted for
the other without affecting the truth.
  'Table de définitions' (1704) in L. Coutourat (ed.) *Opuscules
et fragments inédits de Leibniz* (1903)

17 *Deus enim vult quae optima item harmonicota intelligit
eaque velut seligit ex numero omnium possibilium infinito.*
  God wills the things which he understands to be the
best and most harmonious and selects them, as it
were, from an infinite number of all possibilities.
  Letter to Magnus Wedderkopf, 1671, in *Leibniz:
Philosophical Papers and Letters* (translated by L. E. Loemker,
1969) p. 146

18 *Nous voudrions que la Nature n'allât pas plus loin, qu'elle
fût finie, comme notre esprit: mais ce n'est point connaître
la grandeur et la majesté de l'Auteur des choses.*
  We should like Nature to go no further; we should
like it to be finite, like our mind; but this is to ignore
the greatness and majesty of the Author of things.
  Letter to S. Clarke, 1715, translated by M. Morris and
G. H. R. Parkinson in *Leibniz: Philosophical Writings* (1973)

Fred W. Leigh d. 1924

British songwriter

19 Here's the very note,
This is what he wrote—
'Can't get away to marry you today,
My wife won't let me!'
  'Waiting at the Church (My Wife Won't Let Me)' (1906
song)

1 Why am I always the bridesmaid,
Never the blushing bride?

    'Why Am I Always the Bridesmaid?' (1917 song, with Charles Collins and Lily Morris)

Henry Sambrooke Leigh 1837–83

English writer

2 The rapturous, wild, and ineffable pleasure
Of drinking at somebody else's expense.

    Carols of Cockayne (1869) 'Stanzas to an Intoxicated Fly'

Curtis E. LeMay 1906–90

US air-force officer

3 They've got to draw in their horns and stop their aggression, or we're going to bomb them back into the Stone Age.

    On the North Vietnamese, in *Mission with LeMay* (1965) p. 565

Lenin (Vladimir Ilich Ulyanov) 1870–1924

Russian revolutionary

4 Communism is Soviet power plus the electrification of the whole country.

    Report to 8th Congress, 1920, in *Collected Works* (ed. 5) vol. 42, p. 30

5 Imperialism is the monopoly stage of capitalism.

    Imperialism as the Last Stage of Capitalism (1916) ch. 7 'Briefest possible definition of imperialism'

6 No, Democracy is *not* identical with majority rule. Democracy is a *State* which recognizes the subjection of the minority to the majority, that is, an organization for the systematic use of *force* by one class against the other, by one part of the population against another.

    State and Revolution (1919) ch. 4

7 While the State exists, there can be no freedom. When there is freedom there will be no State.

    State and Revolution (1919) ch. 5

8 What is to be done?

    Title of pamphlet (1902); originally the title of a novel (1863) by N. G. Chernyshevsky

9 Who? Whom?

    Definition of political science, meaning 'Who will outstrip whom?'; in, e.g., *Polnoe Sobranie Sochinenii* vol. 44 (1970) p. 161 (17 October 1921)

10 A good man fallen among Fabians.

    Of George Bernard Shaw, in Arthur Ransome *Six Weeks in Russia in 1919* (1919) 'Notes of Conversations with Lenin'

11 Liberty is precious—so precious that it must be rationed.

    In Sidney and Beatrice Webb *Soviet Communism* (1936) p. 1036

John Lennon 1940–80

English pop singer and songwriter

12 Imagine there's no heaven,
It's easy if you try,
No hell below us,
Above us only sky,
Imagine all the people
Living for today.

    'Imagine' (1971 song)

13 We're more popular than Jesus now; I don't know which will go first—rock 'n' roll or Christianity.

    Interview in *Evening Standard* 4 March 1966 (of The Beatles)

14 Will the people in the cheaper seats clap your hands? All the rest of you, if you'll just rattle your jewellery.

    At Royal Variety Performance, 4 November 1963, in R. Colman *John Winston Lennon* (1984) pt. 1, ch. 11

John Lennon 1940–1980 *and* Paul McCartney 1942–

English pop singers and songwriters

15 Back in the USSR.

    Title of song (1968)

16 For I don't care too much for money,
For money can't buy me love.

    'Can't Buy Me Love' (1964 song)

17 I heard the news today, oh boy.
Four thousand holes in Blackburn Lancashire.
And though the holes were rather small,
They had to count them all.
Now they know how many holes it takes to fill the Albert Hall.
I'd love to turn you on.

    'A Day in the Life' (1967 song)

18 Eleanor Rigby picks up the rice in the church where a wedding has been,
Lives in a dream.
Waits at the window, wearing the face that she keeps in a jar by the door,
Who is it for?
All the lonely people, where do they all come from?

    'Eleanor Rigby' (1966 song)

19 Give peace a chance.

    Title of song (1969)

20 It's been a hard day's night,
And I've been working like a dog.

    'A Hard Day's Night' (1964 song)

21 *Michelle ma belle,*
Sont les mots qui vont bien ensemble, tres bien ensemble.

My beautiful Michelle, these are the words which go together so well.

    'Michelle' (1965 song)

1 Strawberry fields forever.
  Title of song (1967)

2 She's got a ticket to ride, but she don't care.
  'Ticket to Ride' (1965 song)

3 Will you still need me, will you still feed me,
  When I'm sixty four?
  'When I'm Sixty Four' (1967 song)

4 Oh I get by with a little help from my friends,
  Mm, I get high with a little help from my friends.
  'With a Little Help From My Friends' (1967 song)

Dan Leno (George Galvin)
1860–1904

English entertainer

5 Ah! what is man? Wherefore does he why? Whence
  did he whence? Whither is he withering?
  Dan Leno Hys Booke (1901) ch. 1

William Lenthall 1591–1662

Speaker of the House of Commons

6 I have neither eye to see, nor tongue to speak here,
  but as the House is pleased to direct me.
  To Charles I, 4 January 1642, on being asked if he had
  seen any of the five MPs whom the King had ordered to be
  arrested; in John Rushworth *Historical Collections. The Third
  Part* vol. 2 (1692) p. 478

Leonardo da Vinci 1452–1519

Italian painter and designer

7 Life well spent is long.
  Edward McCurdy (ed. and trans.) *Leonardo da Vinci's
  Notebooks* (1906) bk. 1, p. 65

8 Whoever in discussion adduces authority uses not
  intellect but rather memory.
  Edward McCurdy (ed. and trans.) *Leonardo da Vinci's
  Notebooks* (1906) bk. 1, p. 54

9 Iron rusts from disuse; stagnant water loses its purity
  and in cold weather becomes frozen; even so does
  inaction sap the vigour of the mind.
  Edward McCurdy (ed. and trans.) *Leonardo da Vinci's
  Notebooks* (1906) bk. 1, p. 86

10 Human subtlety . . . will never devise an invention
  more beautiful, more simple or more direct than does
  Nature, because in her inventions nothing is lacking,
  and nothing is superfluous.
  Edward McCurdy (ed. and trans.) *Leonardo da Vinci's
  Notebooks* (1906) bk. 1, p. 171

11 Every man at three years old is half his height.
  Irma A. Richter (ed.) *Selections from the Notebooks of
  Leonardo da Vinci* (World's Classics, 1952) p. 149

12 The poet ranks far below the painter in the
  representation of visible things, and far below the
  musician in that of invisible things.
  Irma A. Richter (ed.) *Selections from the Notebooks of
  Leonardo da Vinci* (World's Classics, 1952) p. 198

Mikhail Lermontov 1814–41

Russian novelist and poet

13 Самые счастливые люди — невежды, а слава —
  удача, и чтоб добиться ее, надо только быть
  ловким.
  Happy people are ignoramuses and glory is nothing
  else but success, and to achieve it one only has to be
  cunning.
  A Hero of our Time (1840) 'Bella' (translated by Philip
  Longworth)

14 Любовь дикарки немногим лучше любви знатной
  барыни; невежество и простосердечие одной так
  же надоедает, как и кокетство другой.
  The love of savages isn't much better than the love of
  noble ladies; ignorance and simple-heartedness can be
  as tiresome as coquetry.
  A Hero of our Time (1840) 'Bella' (translated by Philip
  Longworth)

15 Из двух друзей всегда один раб другого.
  Of two close friends, one is always the slave of the
  other.
  A Hero of our Time (1840) 'Princess Mary' (translated by
  Philip Longworth)

16 С тех пор как я живу и действую, судьба как-то
  всегда приводила меня к развязке чужих драм,
  как будто без меня никто не мог бы ни умереть,
  ни прийти в отчаяние! Я был необходимое лицо
  пятого акта.
  Ever since I lived and entered into action, fate has
  somehow led me to the climax of other people's
  dramas, as if no one could die, no one could despair
  without me. I have always been the essential
  character of the fifth act.
  A Hero of our Time (1840) 'Princess Mary' (translated by
  Philip Longworth)

17 Я — как человек, зевая на бале, который не едет
  спать только потому, что еще нет его кареты.
  I am like a man yawning at a ball; the only reason he
  does not go home to bed is that his carriage has not
  arrived yet.
  A Hero of our Time (1840) 'Princess Mary' (translated by
  Philip Longworth)

18 Что страсти? — ведь рано иль поздно их сладкий
  недуг
  Исчезнет при слове рассудка;
  И жизнь, как посмотришь с холодным вниманьем
  вокруг, —
  Такая пустая и глупая шутка.
  What is passion? That sickness so sweet, either early
  or late,
  Will vanish at reason's protesting;
  And life, if you ever, attentive and cool, contemplate,
  Is but empty and meaningless jesting.
  'I'm lonely and sad' (1840) (translated by C. M. Bowra)

1 Нет, я не Байрон, я другой,
Еще неведомый избранник,
Как он гонимый миром странник,
Но только с русскою душой.

No, I'm not Byron, it's my role
To be an undiscovered wonder,
Like him, a persecuted wand'rer,
But furnished with a Russian soul.

'No, I'm not Byron' (1832) (translated by Alan Myers)

Alan Jay Lerner 1918–86

American songwriter

2 We met at nine.
We met at eight.
I was on time.
No, you were late.
Ah yes! I remember it well.

Gigi (1958) 'I Remember it Well' (music by Frederick
Loewe)

3 Why can't a woman be more like a man?
Men are so honest, so thoroughly square;
Eternally noble, historically fair;
Who, when you win, will always give your back a pat.
Why can't a woman be like that?

My Fair Lady (1956) 'A Hymn to Him' (music by Frederick
Loewe)

4 I've grown accustomed to the trace
Of something in the air;
Accustomed to her face.

My Fair Lady (1956) 'I've Grown Accustomed to her Face'
(music by Frederick Loewe)

5 The rain in Spain stays mainly in the plain.

My Fair Lady (1956) 'The Rain in Spain' (music by
Frederick Loewe)

6 In Hertford, Hereford, and Hampshire,
Hurricanes hardly happen.

My Fair Lady (1956) 'The Rain in Spain' (music by
Frederick Loewe)

7 Oozing charm from every pore,
He oiled his way around the floor.

My Fair Lady (1956) 'You Did It' (music by Frederick
Loewe)

Doris Lessing 1919–

English writer

8 When old settlers say 'One has to understand the
country,' what they mean is, 'You have to get used to
our ideas about the native.'

The Grass is Singing (1950) ch. 1

9 Pleasure resorts are like film stars and royalty . . .
embarrassed by the figures they cut in the fantasies of
people who have never met them.

The Habit of Loving (1957) ch. 17

10 What of October, that ambiguous month, the month
of tension, the unendurable month?

Martha Quest (1952) pt. 4, sect. 1

11 What is charm then? The free giving of a grace, the
spending of something given by nature in her role of
spendthrift . . . something extra, superfluous,
unnecessary, essentially a power thrown away.

Particularly Cats (1967) ch. 9

G. E. Lessing 1729–81

German playwright and critic

12 *Gestern liebt' ich,*
Heute leid' ich,
Morgen sterb' ich:
Dennoch denk' ich
Heut und morgen
Gern an gestern.

Yesterday I loved, today I suffer, tomorrow I die: but
I still think fondly, today and tomorrow, of yesterday.

'Lied aus dem Spanischen' (1780)

13 *Ein einziger dankbarer Gedanke gen Himmel ist das*
vollkommenste Gebet.

One single grateful thought raised to heaven is the
most perfect prayer.

Minna von Barnhelm (1767) act 2, sc. 7

14 *Wenn Gott in seiner Rechten alle Wahrheit und in seiner*
Linken den einzigen, immer regen Trieb nach Wahrheit,
obgleich mit dem Zusatz, mich immer und ewig zu irren,
verschlossen hielte und spräche zu mir: Wähle! ich fiele
ihm mit Demut in seine Linke und sagte: Vater, gieb! Die
reine Wahrheit ist ja doch nur für Dich allein.

If God were to hold out enclosed in His right hand all
Truth, and in His left hand just the active search for
Truth, though with the condition that I should always
err therein, and He should say to me: Choose!
I should humbly take His left hand and say: Father!
Give me this one; absolute Truth belongs to Thee
alone.

Eine Duplik (1778) pt. 1

Winifred Mary Letts 1882–1972

English writer

15 I saw the spires of Oxford
As I was passing by,
The grey spires of Oxford
Against a pearl-grey sky;
My heart was with the Oxford men
Who went abroad to die.

'The Spires of Oxford' (1916)

Ros Levenstein

British advertising copywriter

16 I'm only here for the beer.

Slogan for Double Diamond beer, 1971 onwards

Ada Leverson 1865–1936

English novelist

17 He seemed at ease and to have the look of the last
gentleman in Europe.

Letters to the Sphinx (1930) p. 34 (of Oscar Wilde)

18 You don't know a woman until you have had a letter
from her.

Tenterhooks (1912) ch. 7

19 'No hurry, no hurry,' said Sir James, with that air of
self-denial that conveys the urgent necessity of intense
speed.

The Twelfth Hour (1907) ch. 2

1 Before he left, Aunt William pressed a sovereign into his hand, as if it were conscience money. He, on his side, took it as though it were a doctor's fee, and both ignored the transaction.

> *The Twelfth Hour* (1907) ch. 4

Bernard Levin 1928–

British journalist

2 Paul Getty . . . had always been vastly, immeasurably wealthy, and yet went about looking like a man who cannot quite remember whether he remembered to turn the gas off before leaving home.

> *The Pendulum Years* (1970) ch. 1

3 In every age of transition men are never so firmly bound to one way of life as when they are about to abandon it, so that fanaticism and intolerance reach their most intense forms just before tolerance and mutual acceptance come to be the natural order of things.

> *The Pendulum Years* (1970) ch. 4

4 Between them, then, Walrus and Carpenter, they divided up the Sixties.

> Of the Harolds, Macmillan and Wilson, in *The Pendulum Years* (1970) ch. 12

5 The Stag at Bay with the mentality of a fox at large.

> Of Harold Macmillan, in *The Pendulum Years* (1970) ch. 12

6 Whom the mad would destroy, they first make gods.

> Of Mao Tse-tung in 1967; Levin quoting himself in *The Times* 21 September 1987. Cf. Duport 264:8

Duc de Lévis 1764–1830

French soldier and writer

7 *Noblesse oblige.*

Nobility has its obligations.

> *Maximes et Réflexions* (1812 ed.) 'Morale: Maximes et Préceptes' no. 73

8 *Gouverner, c'est choisir.*

To govern is to choose.

> *Maximes et Réflexions* (1812 ed.) 'Politique: Maximes de Politique' no. 19

Claude Lévi-Strauss 1908–

French social anthropologist

9 *La langue est une raison humaine qui a ses raisons, et que l'homme ne connaît pas.*

Language is a form of human reason, and has its reasons which are unknown to man.

> *La Pensée sauvage* (1962) ch. 9. Cf. Pascal 507:17

G. H. Lewes 1817–78

English man of letters; common-law husband of George Eliot

10 Murder, like talent, seems occasionally to run in families.

> *The Physiology of Common Life* (1859) ch. 12

11 The pen, in our age, weighs heavier in the social scale than the sword of a Norman Baron.

> *Ranthorpe* (1847) epilogue

12 Many a genius has been slow of growth. Oaks that flourish for a thousand years do not spring up into beauty like a reed.

> *The Spanish Drama* (1846) ch. 2

C. S. Lewis 1898–1963

English literary scholar

13 We have trained them [men] to think of the Future as a promised land which favoured heroes attain—not as something which everyone reaches at the rate of sixty minutes an hour, whatever he does, whoever he is.

> *The Screwtape Letters* (1942) no. 25

14 She's the sort of woman who lives for others—you can always tell the others by their hunted expression.

> *The Screwtape Letters* (1942) no. 26

15 This extraordinary pride in being exempt from temptation that you have not yet risen to the level of! Eunuchs boasting of their chastity!

> 'Unreal Estates' in Kingsley Amis and Robert Conquest (eds.) *Spectrum IV* (1965)

16 Leavis demands moral earnestness; I prefer morality . . . I mean I'd sooner live among people who don't cheat at cards than among people who are earnest about not cheating at cards.

> 'Unreal Estates' in Kingsley Amis and Robert Conquest (eds.) *Spectrum IV* (1965)

17 Courage is not simply *one* of the virtues but the form of every virtue at the testing point.

> In Cyril Connolly *The Unquiet Grave* (1944) ch. 3

Esther Lewis (later Clark) fl. 1747–89

English poet

18 Are simple women only fit
To dress, to darn, to flower, or knit,
To mind the distaff, or the spit?
Why are the needle and the pen
Thought incompatible by men?

> 'A Mirror for Detractors' (1754) l. 146

Sir George Cornewall Lewis 1806–63

British Liberal politician and writer

19 Life would be tolerable but for its amusements.

> In *The Times* 18 September 1872, p. 4

John Spedan Lewis 1885–1963

English shopkeeper and industrial reformer

20 Never knowingly undersold.

> Motto (from *c.*1920) of the John Lewis Partnership, in *Partnership for All* (1948) ch. 29

Sam M. Lewis 1885–1959 *and* Joe Young 1889–1939

American songwriters

21 How 'ya gonna keep 'em down on the farm (after they've seen Paree)?

> Title of song (1919)

1 Mammy, Mammy, look at me. Don't you know me?
I'm your little baby.
'My Mammy' (1918 song); sung by Al Jolson

Sinclair Lewis 1885–1951

American novelist

2 Our American professors like their literature clear and
cold and pure and very dead.
The American Fear of Literature (Nobel Prize Address,
12 December 1930), in H. Frenz *Literature 1901–1967*
(1969) p. 285

3 To George F. Babbitt, as to most prosperous citizens of
Zenith, his motor car was poetry and tragedy, love
and heroism. The office was his pirate ship but the car
his perilous excursion ashore.
Babbitt (1922) ch. 3

4 In other countries, art and literature are left to a lot of
shabby bums living in attics and feeding on booze and
spaghetti, but in America the successful writer or
picture-painter is indistinguishable from any other
decent business man.
Babbitt (1922) ch. 14

5 She did her work with the thoroughness of a mind
which reveres details and never quite understands
them.
Babbitt (1922) ch. 18

6 It can't happen here.
Title of novel (1935)

Wyndham Lewis (Percy Wyndham Lewis) 1882–1957

British novelist, painter, and critic

7 Those prosperous mountebanks who alternately
imitate and mock at and traduce those figures they at
once admire and hate.
The Apes of God (1930) pt. 3 (definition of the title)

8 Gertrude Stein's prose-song [*Three Lives*, 1909] is
a cold, black suet-pudding . . . Cut it at any point, it is
the same thing . . . all fat, without nerve.
Time and Western Man (1927) pt. 1, ch. 13

9 Angels in jumpers.
Describing the figures in Stanley Spencer's paintings
(attributed)

Robert Ley 1890–1945

German Nazi; head of the Labour Front from 1933

10 Kraft durch Freude.
Strength through joy.
German Labour Front slogan from 1933

George Leybourne d. 1884

English songwriter

11 He'd fly through the air with the greatest of ease,
A daring young man on the flying trapeze.
'The Flying Trapeze' (1868 song)

Liberace (Wladziu Valentino Liberace) 1919–87

American showman

12 When the reviews are bad I tell my staff that they can
join me as I cry all the way to the bank.
Autobiography (1973) ch. 2 (a joke coined in the
mid-1950s). See *Collier's* 17 September 1954

Georg Christoph Lichtenberg 1742–99

German scientist and drama critic

13 *Die Zeitungsschreiber haben sich ein hölzernes Capellchen
erbaut, das sie auch den Tempel des Ruhms nennen,
worinn sie den ganzen Tag Vorträte anschlagen und
abnehmen und ein Gehämmer machen, dass man sein
eignes Wort nicht hört.*

The journalists have constructed for themselves a little
wooden chapel, which they also call the Temple of
Fame, in which they put up and take down portraits
all day long and make such a hammering you can't
hear yourself speak.
In A. Leitzmann *Georg Christoph Lichtenberg Aphorismen*
(1904) p. 108

Charles-Joseph, Prince de Ligne 1735–1814

Belgian soldier

14 *Le congrès ne marche pas, il danse.*
The Congress makes no progress; it dances.
In Auguste de la Garde-Chambonas *Souvenirs du Congrès de
Vienne* (1820) ch. 1

Beatrice Lillie 1894–1989

British comedienne

15 Never darken my Dior again!
To a waiter who had spilled soup down her neck, in *Every
Other Inch a Lady* (1973) ch. 14

George Lillo 1693–1739

Flemish-born playwright

16 There's sure no passion in the human soul,
But finds its food in music.
The Fatal Curiosity (1736) act 1, sc. 2

Abraham Lincoln 1809–65

16th President of the USA

17 To give victory to the right, not bloody bullets, but
peaceful ballots only, are necessary.
Speech, 18 May 1858, in R. P. Basler (ed.) *Collected Works
of Abraham Lincoln* (1953) vol. 2, p. 454 (usually quoted
'The ballot is stronger than the bullet')

18 'A house divided against itself cannot stand.' I believe
this government cannot endure permanently, half
slave and half free.
Speech, 16 June 1858, in R. P. Basler (ed.) *Collected Works
. . .* (1953) vol. 2, p. 461. Cf. St Mark 93:8

1 What is conservatism? Is it not adherence to the old and tried, against the new and untried?

Speech, 27 February 1860, in R. P. Basler (ed.) *Collected Works . . .* (1953) vol. 3, p. 537

2 Let us have faith that right makes might, and in that faith, let us, to the end, dare to do our duty as we understand it.

Speech, 27 February 1860, in R. P. Basler (ed.) *Collected Works . . .* (1953) vol. 3, p. 550

3 I take the official oath to-day with no mental reservations, and with no purpose to construe the Constitution or laws by any hypercritical rules.

First Inaugural Address, 4 March 1861, in R. P. Basler (ed.) *Collected Works . . .* (1953) vol. 4, p. 264

4 This country, with its institutions, belongs to the people who inhabit it. Whenever they shall grow weary of the existing government, they can exercise their constitutional right of amending it, or their revolutionary right to dismember or overthrow it.

First Inaugural Address, 4 March 1861, in R. P. Basler (ed.) *Collected Works . . .* (1953) vol. 4, p. 269

5 Fellow citizens, we cannot escape history . . . No personal significance or insignificance can spare one or another of us. The fiery trial through which we pass will light us down in honour or dishonour to the last generation.

Annual Message to Congress, 1 December 1862, in R. P. Basler (ed.) *Collected Works . . .* (1953) vol. 5, p. 537

6 In giving freedom to the slave, we assure freedom to the free—honourable alike in what we give and what we preserve. We shall nobly save, or meanly lose, the last, best hope of earth.

Annual Message to Congress, 1 December 1862, in R. P. Basler (ed.) *Collected Works . . .* (1953) vol. 5, p. 537

7 It is not best to swap horses when crossing streams.

Reply to National Union League, 9 June 1864, in R. P. Basler (ed.) *Collected Works . . .* (1953) vol. 7, p. 384

8 Fondly do we hope, fervently do we pray, that this mighty scourge of war may speedily pass away. Yet, if God wills that it continue until all the wealth piled by the bond-man's two hundred and fifty years of unrequited toil shall be sunk, and until every drop of blood drawn with the lash shall be paid by another drawn with the sword, as was said three thousand years ago, so still it must be said, 'The judgements of the Lord are true and righteous altogether.'

Second Inaugural Address, 4 March 1865, in R. P. Basler (ed.) *Collected Works . . .* (1953) vol. 8, p. 333

9 With malice toward none; with charity for all; with firmness in the right, as God gives us to see the right, let us strive on to finish the work we are in: to bind up the nation's wounds; to care for him who shall have borne the battle, and for his widow and his orphan, to do all which may achieve and cherish a just and lasting peace among ourselves, and with all nations.

Second Inaugural Address, 4 March 1865, in R. P. Basler (ed.) *Collected Works . . .* (1953) vol. 8, p. 333

10 Fourscore and seven years ago our fathers brought forth upon this continent a new nation, conceived in liberty, and dedicated to the proposition that all men are created equal . . . In a larger sense we cannot dedicate, we cannot consecrate, we cannot hallow this ground. The brave men, living and these dead, who struggled here, have consecrated it far above our power to add or detract. The world will little note, nor long remember, what we say here, but it can never forget what they did here. It is for us, the living, rather to be dedicated here to the unfinished work which they who fought here have thus far so nobly advanced . . . we here highly resolve that the dead shall not have died in vain, that this nation, under God, shall have a new birth of freedom; and that government of the people, by the people, and for the people, shall not perish from the earth.

Address at the Dedication of the National Cemetery at Gettysburg, 19 November 1863, in R. P. Basler (ed.) *Collected Works . . .* (1953) vol. 7, p. 23, as reported the following day; the Lincoln Memorial inscription reads 'by the people, for the people'

11 I think the necessity of being *ready* increases. Look to it.

The whole of a letter to Governor Andrew Curtin of Pennsylvania, 8 April 1861, in R. P. Basler (ed.) *Collected Works . . .* (1953) vol. 4, p. 324

12 My paramount object in this struggle is to save the Union . . . If I could save the Union without freeing any slave, I would do it; and if I could save it by freeing all the slaves, I would do it; and if I could save it by freeing some and leaving others alone, I would also do that . . . I have here stated my purpose according to my views of official duty and I intend no modification of my oft-expressed personal wish that all men everywhere could be free.

Letter to Horace Greeley, 22 August 1862, in R. P. Basler (ed.) *Collected Works . . .* (1953) vol. 5, p. 388

13 I claim not to have controlled events, but confess plainly that events have controlled me.

Letter to A. G. Hodges, 4 April 1864, in R. P. Basler (ed.) *Collected Works . . .* (1953) vol. 7, p. 282

14 You may fool all the people some of the time; you can even fool some of the people all the time; but you can't fool all of the people all the time.

In Alexander K. McClure *Lincoln's Yarns and Stories* (1904); also attributed to Phineas Barnum

15 The Lord prefers common-looking people. That is why he makes so many of them.

Attributed. See James Morgan *Our Presidents* (1928) ch. 6

16 People who like this sort of thing will find this the sort of thing they like.

Judgement of a book, in G. W. E. Russell *Collections and Recollections* (1898) ch. 30

17 So you're the little woman who wrote the book that made this great war!

On meeting Harriet Beecher Stowe, author of *Uncle Tom's Cabin* (1852); in Carl Sandburg *Abraham Lincoln: The War Years* (1936) vol. 2, ch. 39

18 As President, I have no eyes but constitutional eyes; I cannot see you.

Reply to the South Carolina Commissioners (attributed). Cf. Lenthall 418:6

R. M. Lindner 1914–56

American novelist

1 Rebel without a cause.
  Title of book (1944) and film (1955) starring James Dean

Vachel Lindsay 1879–1931

American poet

2 Then I saw the Congo, creeping through the black,
  Cutting through the forest with a golden track.
  'The Congo' pt. 1 (1914)

3 Booth led boldly with his big bass drum—
  (Are you washed in the blood of the Lamb?)
  'General William Booth Enters into Heaven' (1913). Cf.
  Revelation 106:21

4 Booth died blind and still by faith he trod,
  Eyes still dazzled by the ways of God.
  'General William Booth Enters into Heaven' (1913)

Eric Linklater 1899–1974

Scottish novelist

5 'There won't be any revolution in America,' said
  Isadore. Nikitin agreed. 'The people are all too clean.
  They spend all their time changing their shirts and
  washing themselves. You can't feel fierce and
  revolutionary in a bathroom.'
  Juan in America (1931) bk. 5, pt. 3

Art Linkletter 1912–

American broadcaster and humorist

6 The four stages of man are infancy, childhood,
  adolescence and obsolescence.
  A Child's Garden of Misinformation (1965) ch. 8

George Linley 1798–1865

English songwriter

7 Among our ancient mountains,
  And from our lovely vales,
  Oh, let the prayer re-echo:
  'God bless the Prince of Wales!'
  'God Bless the Prince of Wales' (1862 song); translated
  from the Welsh original by J. C. Hughes (1837–87)

Walter Lippmann 1889–1974

American journalist

8 Mr Coolidge's genius for inactivity is developed to
  a very high point. It is far from being an indolent
  activity. It is a grim, determined, alert inactivity which
  keeps Mr Coolidge occupied constantly. Nobody has
  ever worked harder at inactivity, with such force of
  character, with such unremitting attention to detail,
  with such conscientious devotion to the task.
  Men of Destiny (1927) p. 12

Richard Littledale 1833–90

English clergyman

9 Come down, O Love divine,
  Seek thou this soul of mine,
  And visit it with thine own ardour glowing;
  O Comforter, draw near,
  Within my heart appear,
  And kindle it, thy holy flame bestowing.

  O let it freely burn,
  Till earthly passion turn
  To dust and ashes in its heat consuming;
  And let thy glorious light
  Shine ever on my sight,
  And clothe me round, the while my path illuming.

  Let holy charity
  Mine outward vesture be,
  And lowliness become mine inner clothing;
  True lowliness of heart,
  Which takes the humbler part,
  And o'er its own shortcomings weeps with loathing.
  'Come down, O Love divine' (1867 hymn); translation of
  'Discendi, Amor santo' by Bianco da Siena (c.1350–1434)

Joan Littlewood 1914– and Charles Chilton 1914–

10 Oh what a lovely war.
   Title of stage show (1963)

Maxim Litvinov 1876–1951

Soviet diplomat

11 Peace is indivisible.
   Note to the Allies, 25 February 1920, in A. U. Pope *Maxim
   Litvinoff* (1943) p. 234

Livy (Titus Livius) 59 BC–AD 17

Roman historian

12 *Vae victis.*
   Down with the defeated!
   Cry (already proverbial) of the Gallic King, Brennus, on
   capturing Rome (390 BC), in *Ab Urbe Condita* bk. 5, ch. 48,
   sect. 9

13 *Pugna magna victi sumus.*
   We were defeated in a great battle.
   The announcement of disaster for the Romans in
   Hannibal's ambush at Lake Trasimene (217 BC), in *Ab Urbe
   Condita* bk. 22, ch. 7, sect. 8

Richard Llewellyn (Richard Llewellyn Lloyd) 1907–83

Welsh novelist and playwright

14 How green was my valley.
   Title of book (1939)

Robert Lloyd

English poet

1 Turn parson, Colman, that's the way to thrive;
Your parsons are the happiest men alive.
 'The Law-Student' (1762)

2 Alone from Jargon born to rescue Law,
From precedent, grave hum, and formal saw!
To strip chicanery of its vain pretence,
And marry Common Law to Common Sense!
 'The Law-Student' (1762); on Lord Mansfield, Lord Chief
 Justice, 1756–88

3 True Genius, like Armida's wand,
Can raise the spring from barren land.
While all the art of Imitation,
Is pilf'ring from the first creation.
 'Shakespeare' (1762)

David Lloyd George (1st Earl Lloyd George of Dwyfor) 1863–1945

British Liberal politician; Prime Minister, 1916–22

4 The leal and trusty mastiff which is to watch over our
interests, but which runs away at the first snarl of the
trade unions ... A mastiff? It is the right hon.
Gentleman's poodle.
 On the House of Lords and Lord Balfour respectively, in
 Hansard 26 June 1907, col. 1429

5 A fully-equipped duke costs as much to keep up as
two Dreadnoughts; and dukes are just as great
a terror and they last longer.
 Speech at Newcastle, 9 October 1909, in *The Times*
 11 October 1909

6 The great peaks of honour we had forgotten—Duty,
Patriotism, and—clad in glittering white—the great
pinnacle of Sacrifice, pointing like a rugged finger to
Heaven.
 Speech at Queen's Hall, London, 19 September 1914, in
 The Times 20 September 1914

7 At eleven o'clock this morning came to an end the
cruellest and most terrible war that has ever scourged
mankind. I hope we may say that thus, this fateful
morning, came to an end all wars.
 Speech, *Hansard* 11 November 1918, col. 2463. Cf. Wells
 727:23

8 What is our task? To make Britain a fit country for
heroes to live in.
 Speech at Wolverhampton, 23 November 1918, in *The
 Times* 25 November 1918

9 M. Clemenceau ... is one of the greatest living
orators, but he knows that the finest eloquence is that
which gets things done and the worst is that which
delays them.
 Speech at Paris Peace Conference, 18 January 1919, in *The
 Times* 20 January 1919

10 A politician was a person with whose politics you did
not agree. When you did agree, he was a statesman.
 Speech at Central Hall, Westminster, 2 July 1935, in *The
 Times* 3 July 1935

11 Negotiating with de Valera ... is like trying to pick up
mercury with a fork.
 In M. J. MacManus *Eamon de Valera* (1944) ch. 6 (to which
 de Valera replied, 'Why doesn't he use a spoon?')

12 The world is becoming like a lunatic asylum run by
lunatics.
 In *Observer* 8 January 1933. Cf. Rowland 549:11

13 Sufficient conscience to bother him, but not sufficient
to keep him straight.
 Of Ramsay MacDonald, in A. J. Sylvester *Life with Lloyd
 George* (1975) p. 216

John Locke 1632–1704

English philosopher

14 New opinions are always suspected, and usually
opposed, without any other reason but because they
are not already common.
 An Essay concerning Human Understanding (1690)
 'Dedicatory Epistle'

15 The commonwealth of learning is not at this time
without master-builders, whose mighty designs, in
advancing the sciences, will leave lasting monuments
to the admiration of posterity ... in an age that
produces such masters as the great Huygenius and the
incomparable Mr Newton ... 'tis ambition enough to
be employed as an under-labourer in clearing ground
a little, and removing some of the rubbish that lies in
the way of knowledge.
 An Essay concerning Human Understanding (1690) 'Epistle to
 the Reader'

16 General propositions are seldom mentioned in the huts
of Indians: much less are they to be found in the
thoughts of children.
 An Essay concerning Human Understanding (1690) bk. 1,
 ch. 2, sect. 11

17 Nature never makes excellent things for mean or no
uses.
 An Essay concerning Human Understanding (1690) bk. 2,
 ch. 1, sect. 15

18 No man's knowledge here can go beyond his
experience.
 An Essay concerning Human Understanding (1690) bk. 2,
 ch. 1, sect. 19

19 It is one thing to show a man that he is in error, and
another to put him in possession of truth.
 An Essay concerning Human Understanding (1690) bk. 4,
 ch. 7, sect. 11

20 There are very few lovers of truth, for truth-sake, even
among those who persuade themselves that they are
so. How a man may know, whether he be so, in
earnest, is worth enquiry; and I think, there is this
one unerring mark of it, viz. the not entertaining any
proposition with greater assurance than the proofs it is
built on will warrant. Whoever goes beyond this
measure of assent, it is plain, receives not truth in the
love of it, loves not truth for truth-sake, but for some
other by-end.
 An Essay concerning Human Understanding (1690) bk. 4,
 ch. 19, sect. 1

21 Reason is natural revelation, whereby the eternal
Father of light, and fountain of all knowledge
communicates to mankind that portion of truth which
he has laid within the reach of their natural faculties.
 An Essay concerning Human Understanding (1690) bk. 4,
 ch. 19, sect. 4

1 Crooked things may be as stiff and unflexible as straight: and men may be as positive in error as in truth.

An Essay concerning Human Understanding (1690) bk. 4, ch. 19, sect. 11

2 All men are liable to error; and most men are, in many points, by passion or interest, under temptation to it.

An Essay concerning Human Understanding (1690) bk. 4, ch. 20, sect. 17

3 Whatsoever . . . [man] removes out of the state that nature hath provided and left it in, he hath mixed his labour with, and joined to it something that is his own, and thereby makes it his property.

Second Treatise of Civil Government (1690) ch. 5, sect. 27

4 [That] ill deserves the name of confinement which hedges us in only from bogs and precipices. So that, however it may be mistaken, the end of law is, not to abolish or restrain, but to preserve and enlarge freedom.

Second Treatise of Civil Government (1690) ch. 6, sect. 57

5 Man . . . hath by nature a power . . . to preserve his property—that is, his life, liberty, and estate—against the injuries and attempts of other men.

Second Treatise of Civil Government (1690) ch. 7, sect. 87

6 Man being . . . by nature all free, equal, and independent, no one can be put out of this estate, and subjected to the political power of another, without his own consent.

Second Treatise of Civil Government (1690) ch. 8, sect. 95

7 The great and chief end, therefore, of men's uniting into commonwealths, and putting themselves under government, is the preservation of their property.

Second Treatise of Civil Government (1690) ch. 9, sect. 124

8 The only way by which any one divests himself of his natural liberty and puts on the bonds of civil society is by agreeing with other men to join and unite into a community.

Second Treatise of Civil Government (1690) ch. 8, sect. 95

9 This power to act according to discretion for the public good, without the prescription of the law, and sometimes even against it, is that which is called prerogative.

Second Treatise of Civil Government (1690) ch. 14, sect. 160

10 The rod, which is the only instrument of government that tutors generally know, or ever think of, is the most unfit of any to be used in education.

Some Thoughts Concerning Education (5th ed., 1705) sect. 47

11 You would think him a very foolish fellow, that should not value a virtuous, or a wise man, infinitely before a great scholar.

Some Thoughts Concerning Education (5th ed., 1705) sect. 147

Frederick Locker-Lampson 1821–95

English writer of light verse

12 The world's as ugly, ay, as sin,
And almost as delightful.
'The Jester's Plea' (1868)

13 And many are afraid of God—
And more of Mrs Grundy.
'The Jester's Plea' (1868)

14 Some men are good for righting wrongs,—
And some for writing verses.
'The Jester's Plea' (1868)

John Gibson Lockhart 1794–1854

Scottish writer and critic

15 It is a better and a wiser thing to be a starved apothecary than a starved poet; so back to the shop Mr John, back to 'plasters, pills, and ointment boxes.'
Reviewing Keats's *Endymion* in *Blackwood's Edinburgh Magazine* August 1818

16 Barring drink and the girls, I ne'er heard of a sin:
Many worse, better few, than bright, broken Maginn.
'Epitaph for William Maginn (1794–1842)', in *William Maginn Miscellanies* (1885) vol. 1, p. xviii

17 Here lies that peerless paper peer Lord Peter,
Who broke the laws of God and man and metre.
Epitaph for Patrick ('Peter'), Lord Robertson, in *The Journal of Sir Walter Scott* (1890) vol. 1, p. 259, n. 2

David Lodge 1935–

English novelist

18 Literature is mostly about having sex and not much about having children. Life is the other way round.
The British Museum is Falling Down (1965) ch. 4

19 Four times, under our educational rules, the human pack is shuffled and cut—at eleven-plus, sixteen-plus, eighteen-plus and twenty-plus—and happy is he who comes top of the deck on each occasion, but especially the last. This is called Finals, the very name of which implies that nothing of importance can happen after it.
Changing Places (1975) ch. 1

20 He understood . . . Walt Whitman who laid end to end words never seen in each other's company before outside of a dictionary, and Herman Melville who split the atom of the traditional novel in the effort to make whaling a universal metaphor.
Changing Places (1975) ch. 5

21 I gave up screwing around a long time ago. I came to the conclusion that sex is a sublimation of the work instinct.
Small World (1984) pt. 1, ch. 2

22 Morris read through the letter. Was it a shade too fulsome? No, that was another law of academic life: *it is impossible to be excessive in flattery of one's peers.*
Small World (1984) pt. 3, ch. 1

Thomas Lodge 1558–1625

English man of letters

23 Love in my bosom like a bee
Doth suck his sweet;
Now with his wings he plays with me,
Now with his feet.
Within mine eyes he makes his nest,
His bed amidst my tender breast;
My kisses are his daily feast,
And yet he robs me of my rest.
Ah, wanton, will ye?
'Love in my bosom like a bee' (1590)

1 Love guards the roses of thy lips
And flies about them like a bee;
If I approach he forward skips,
And if I kiss he stingeth me.

Love in thine eyes doth build his bower,
And sleeps within their pretty shine;
And if I look the boy will lour,
And from their orbs shoots shafts divine.
   'Love guards the roses of thy lips' (1593)

Frank Loesser 1910–69

American songwriter

2 See what the boys in the back room will have
And tell them I'm having the same.
   'Boys in the Back Room' (1939 song)

3 Isn't it grand! Isn't it fine! Look at the cut, the style,
the line!
The suit of clothes is altogether, but altogether it's
altogether
The most remarkable suit of clothes that I have ever
seen.
   'The King's New Clothes' (1952 song); from the film *Hans Christian Andersen*

Friedrich von Logau 1604–55

German epigrammatist

4 *Gottes Mühlen mahlen langsam, mahlen aber trefflich klein;*
Ob aus Langmut Er sich säumet, bringt mit Schärf' Er alles ein.
Though the mills of God grind slowly, yet they grind
exceeding small;
Though with patience He stands waiting, with
exactness grinds He all.
   Sinnegedichte (1654) 'Desz Dritten Tausend, Andres Hundert' no. 24 (translated by Longfellow). Von Logau's first line is itself a translation of an anonymous verse in Sextus Empiricus *Adversus Mathematicos* bk. 1, sect. 287

Jack London 1876–1916

American novelist

5 The call of the wild.
   Title of novel (1903)

Huey Long 1893–1935

American politician; sometime lawyer and travelling salesman

6 I can go Mr Wilson one better; I was born barefoot.
   Answering his opponent's supporters, who said their candidate had gone barefoot as a boy; in T. Harry Williams *Huey Long* (1969) p. 250

7 Oh hell, say that I am *sui generis* and let it go at that.
   To journalists attempting to analyse his political personality, in T. Harry Williams *Huey Long* (1969) p. 414

8 Bible's the greatest book ever written. But I sure don't need anybody I can buy for six bits and a chew of tobacco to explain it to me. When I need preachers I buy 'em cheap.
   In T. Harry Williams *Huey Long* (1969) p. 592

9 The time has come for all good men to rise above principle.
   Attributed

Henry Wadsworth Longfellow 1807–82

American poet

10 I shot an arrow into the air,
It fell to earth, I knew not where.
   'The Arrow and the Song' (1845)

11 Thou, too, sail on, O Ship of State!
Sail on, O Union, strong and great!
Humanity with all its fears,
With all the hopes of future years,
Is hanging breathless on thy fate!
   'The Building of the Ship' (1849)

12 Ye are better than all the ballads
That ever were sung or said;
For ye are living poems,
And all the rest are dead.
   'Children' (1849)

13 Between the dark and the daylight,
When the night is beginning to lower,
Comes a pause in the day's occupations,
That is known as the Children's Hour.
   'The Children's Hour' (1859)

14 The cares that infest the day
Shall fold their tents, like the Arabs,
And as silently steal away.
   'The Day is Done' (1844)

15 If you would hit the mark, you must aim a little above
it;
Every arrow that flies feels the attraction of earth.
   'Elegiac Verse' (1880)

16 This is the forest primeval.
   Evangeline (1847) introduction

17 Sorrow and silence are strong, and patient endurance
is godlike.
   Evangeline (1847) pt. 2, l. 60

18 The shades of night were falling fast,
As through an Alpine village passed
A youth, who bore, 'mid snow and ice,
A banner with the strange device,
Excelsior!
   'Excelsior' (1841)

19 'Try not the Pass!' the old man said;
'Dark lowers the tempest overhead.'
   'Excelsior' (1841)

20 A traveller, by the faithful hound,
Half-buried in the snow was found.
   'Excelsior' (1841)

21   Giotto's tower,
The lily of Florence blossoming in stone.
   'Giotto's Tower' (1866)

22 I like that ancient Saxon phrase, which calls
The burial-ground God's-Acre!
   'God's-Acre' (1841)

23 The holiest of all holidays are those
Kept by ourselves in silence and apart;
The secret anniversaries of the heart.
   'Holidays' (1877)

1 The heights by great men reached and kept
Were not attained by sudden flight,
But they, while their companions slept,
Were toiling upward in the night.
'The Ladder of Saint Augustine' (1850)

2 Standing, with reluctant feet,
Where the brook and river meet,
Womanhood and childhood fleet!
'Maidenhood' (1841)

3 The men that women marry,
And why they marry them, will always be
A marvel and a mystery to the world.
Michael Angelo (1883) pt. 1, sect. 5

4 I remember the black wharves and the slips,
And the sea-rides tossing free;
And Spanish sailors with bearded lips,
And the beauty and mystery of the ships,
And the magic of the sea.
And the voice of that wayward song
Is singing and saying still:
'A boy's will is the wind's will'
And the thoughts of youth are long, long thoughts.'
'My Lost Youth' (1858)

5 *Emigravit* is the inscription on the tombstone where he lies;
Dead he is not, but departed,—for the artist never dies.
'Nuremberg' (1844) (on Albrecht Dürer)

6 Not in the clamour of the crowded street,
Not in the shouts and plaudits of the throng,
But in ourselves, are triumph and defeat.
'The Poets' (1876)

7 Tell me not, in mournful numbers,
Life is but an empty dream!
For the soul is dead that slumbers,
And things are not what they seem.
Life is real! Life is earnest!
And the grave is not its goal;
Dust thou art, to dust returnest,
Was not spoken of the soul.
'A Psalm of Life' (1838). Cf. Genesis 70:17

8 Art is long, and Time is fleeting,
And our hearts, though stout and brave,
Still, like muffled drums, are beating
Funeral marches to the grave.
'A Psalm of Life' (1838). Cf. Hippocrates 339:6

9 Trust no Future, howe'er pleasant!
Let the dead Past bury its dead!
Act,—act in the living Present!
Heart within, and God o'erhead!
'A Psalm of Life' (1838). Cf. St Matthew 90:2

10 Lives of great men all remind us
We can make our lives sublime,
And, departing, leave behind us
Footprints on the sands of time.
'A Psalm of Life' (1838)

11 Let us, then, be up and doing,
With a heart for any fate;
Still achieving, still pursuing,
Learn to labour and to wait.
'A Psalm of Life' (1838)

12 There is no flock, however watched and tended,
But one dead lamb is there!
There is no fireside, howsoe'er defended,
But has one vacant chair!
'A Psalm of Life' (1838)

13 A Lady with a Lamp shall stand
In the great history of the land,
A noble type of good,
Heroic womanhood.
'Santa Filomena' (1857) (on Florence Nightingale)

14 The forests, with their myriad tongues,
Shouted of liberty;
And the Blast of the Desert cried aloud,
With a voice so wild and free,
That he started in his sleep and smiled
At their tempestuous glee.
'The Slave's Dream' (1842)

15 By the shore of Gitche Gumee,
By the shining Big-Sea-Water,
Stood the wigwam of Nokomis,
Daughter of the Moon, Nokomis.
Dark behind it rose the forest,
Rose the black and gloomy pine-trees,
Rose the firs with cones upon them;
Bright before it beat the water,
Beat the clear and sunny water,
Beat the shining Big-Sea-Water.
The Song of Hiawatha (1855) 'Hiawatha's Childhood'

16 From the waterfall he named her,
Minnehaha, Laughing Water.
The Song of Hiawatha (1855) 'Hiawatha and Mudjekeewis'

17 Onaway! Awake, beloved!
The Song of Hiawatha (1855) 'Hiawatha's Wedding-feast'

18 He is dead, the sweet musician!
He the sweetest of all singers!
He has gone from us for ever,
He has moved a little nearer
To the Master of all music,
To the Master of all singing!
O my brother, Chibiabos!
The Song of Hiawatha (1855) 'Hiawatha's Lamentation'

19 Listen, my children, and you shall hear
Of the midnight ride of Paul Revere,
On the eighteenth of April in Seventy-five.
Tales of a Wayside Inn pt. 1 (1863) 'The Landlord's Tale: Paul Revere's Ride'

20 A hurry of hoofs in a village street,
A shape in the moonlight, a bulk in the dark,
And beneath, from the pebbles, in passing, a spark
Struck out from a steed flying fearless and fleet:
That was all! And yet, through the gloom and the light,
The fate of a nation was riding that night.
Tales of a Wayside Inn pt. 1 (1863) 'The Landlord's Tale: Paul Revere's Ride'

1 Ships that pass in the night, and speak each other in
passing;
Only a signal shown and a distant voice in the
darkness;
So on the ocean of life we pass and speak one another,
Only a look and a voice; then darkness again and
a silence.
Tales of a Wayside Inn pt. 3 (1874) 'The Theologian's Tale:
Elizabeth' pt. 4

2 Under a spreading chestnut tree
The village smithy stands;
The smith, a mighty man is he,
With large and sinewy hands;
And the muscles of his brawny arms
Are strong as iron bands.
'The Village Blacksmith' (1839)

3 It was the schooner Hesperus,
That sailed the wintry sea;
And the skipper had taken his little daughter,
To bear him company.
'The Wreck of the Hesperus' (1839)

4 But the father answered never a word,
A frozen corpse was he.
'The Wreck of the Hesperus' (1839)

5 There was a little girl
Who had a little curl
Right in the middle of her forehead,
When she was good
She was very, very good,
But when she was bad she was horrid.
Composed for, and sung to, his second daughter while a
babe in arms, c.1850. See B. R. Tucker-Macchetta *The
Home Life of Henry W. Longfellow* (1882) ch. 5; also E. W.
Longfellow *Random Memories* (1922) p. 15

6 The square root of half a number of bees, and also
eight-ninths of the whole, alighted on the jasmines,
and a female buzzed responsive to the hum of the male
inclosed at night in a water-lily. O, beautiful damsel,
tell me the number of bees.
Kavanagh (1849) ch. 4
See also FRIEDRICH VON LOGAU

Longinus on the Sublime
Greek literary treatise of unknown authorship and date

7 ὕψος μεγαλοφροσύνης ἀπήχημα.
Sublimity is the echo of a noble mind.
Sect. 9

Anita Loos 1893–1981
American writer

8 So this gentleman said a girl with brains ought to do
something with them besides think.
Gentlemen Prefer Blondes (1925) ch. 1

9 She said she always believed in the old addage, 'Leave
them while you're looking good.'
Gentlemen Prefer Blondes (1925) ch. 1

10 Fun is fun but no girl wants to laugh all of the time.
Gentlemen Prefer Blondes (1925) ch. 4

11 So then Dr Froyd said that all I needed was to cultivate
a few inhibitions and get some sleep.
Gentlemen Prefer Blondes (1925) ch. 5

Frederico García Lorca
See GARCÍA LORCA

Konrad Lorenz 1903–89
Austro-German zoologist

12 Überhaupt ist es für den Forscher ein guter Morgensport,
täglich vor dem Frühstück eine Lieblingshypothese
einzustampfen—das erhält jung.
It is a good morning exercise for a research scientist to
discard a pet hypothesis every day before breakfast. It
keeps him young.
Das Sogenannte Böse (1963; translated by Marjorie Latzke as
On Aggression, 1966) ch. 2

Louis XIV (the 'Sun King') 1638–1715
King of France from 1643

13 L'État c'est moi.
I am the State.
Before the Parlement de Paris, 13 April 1655, in J. A.
Dulaure *Histoire de Paris* (1834) vol. 6, p. 298 (probably
apocryphal)

14 J'ai failli attendre.
I was nearly kept waiting.
Attribution queried, among others, by E. Fournier in
L'Esprit dans l'Histoire (1857) ch. 48

15 Toutes les fois que je donne une place vacante, je fais cent
mécontents et un ingrat.
Every time I create an appointment, I create a hundred
malcontents and one ingrate.
In Voltaire *Siècle de Louis XIV* (1768 ed.) vol. 2, ch. 26

16 Il n'y a plus de Pyrénées.
The Pyrenees are no more.
On the accession of his grandson to the throne of Spain,
1700 (attributed to Louis by Voltaire in *Siècle de Louis XIV*
(1753) ch. 26, but to the Spanish Ambassador to France in
the *Mercure Galant* (Paris) November 1700, p. 237)

Louis XVIII 1755–1824
King of France from 1814; titular king from 1795

17 Rappelez-vous bien qu'il n'est aucun de vous qui n'ait dans
sa giberne le bâton de maréchal du duc de Reggio; c'est à
vous à l'en faire sortir.
Remember that there is not one of you who does not
carry in his cartridge-pouch the marshal's baton of
the duke of Reggio; it is up to you to bring it forth.
Speech to Saint-Cyr cadets, 9 August 1819, in *Moniteur
Universel* 10 August 1819

18 L'exactitude est la politesse des rois.
Punctuality is the politeness of kings.
In *Souvenirs de J. Lafitte* (1844) bk. 1, ch. 3 (attributed)

Richard Lovelace 1618–58
English poet

19 Lucasta that bright northern star.
'Amyntor from Beyond the Sea to Alexis' (1649)

20 Forbear, thou great good husband, little ant.
'The Ant' (1660)

1 When Love with unconfinèd wings
  Hovers within my gates;
  And my divine Althea brings
  To whisper at the grates:
  When I lie tangled in her hair,
  And fettered to her eye;
  The Gods, that wanton in the air
  Know no such liberty.
    'To Althea, From Prison' (1649)

2 When flowing cups run swiftly round
  With no allaying Thames.
    'To Althea, From Prison' (1649)

3 When thirsty grief in wine we steep,
  When healths and draughts go free,
  Fishes, that tipple in the deep,
  Know no such liberty.
    'To Althea, From Prison' (1649)

4 Stone walls do not a prison make,
  Nor iron bars a cage;
  Minds innocent and quiet take
  That for an hermitage;
  If I have freedom in my love,
  And in my soul am free;
  Angels alone, that soar above,
  Enjoy such liberty.
    'To Althea, From Prison' (1649)

5 If to be absent were to be
  Away from thee;
  Or that when I am gone,
  You or I were alone;
  Then my Lucasta might I crave
  Pity from blust'ring wind, or swallowing wave.
    'To Lucasta, Going Beyond the Seas' (1649)

6 Tell me not, Sweet, I am unkind,
  That from the nunnery
  Of thy chaste breast, and quiet mind,
  To war and arms I fly.
  True; a new mistress now I chase,
  The first foe in the field;
  And with a stronger faith embrace
  A sword, a horse, a shield.
  Yet this inconstancy is such,
  As you too shall adore;
  I could not love thee, Dear, so much,
  Loved I not honour more.
    'To Lucasta, Going to the Wars' (1649)

Samuel Lover 1797–1868
Irish writer

7 When once the itch of literature comes over a man,
  nothing can cure it but the scratching of a pen.
    Handy Andy (1842) ch. 36

Sir David Low 1891–1963
British political cartoonist

8 Colonel Blimp.
    Cartoon creation, proponent of reactionary establishment
    opinions

9 I have never met anyone who wasn't against war.
  Even Hitler and Mussolini were, according to
  themselves.
    New York Times Magazine 10 February 1946

Robert Lowe, Viscount Sherbrooke
1811–92
British Liberal politician

10 I believe it will be absolutely necessary that you should
   prevail on our future masters to learn their letters.
    Speech, *Hansard* 15 July 1867, col. 1549, on the passing of
    the Reform Bill, popularized as 'We must educate our
    masters'

11 The Chancellor of the Exchequer is a man whose
   duties make him more or less of a taxing machine. He
   is intrusted with a certain amount of misery which it
   is his duty to distribute as fairly as he can.
    Speech, *Hansard* 11 April 1870, col. 1639

Amy Lowell 1874–1925
American poet

12 And the softness of my body will be guarded by
   embrace
   By each button, hook, and lace.
   For the man who should loose me is dead,
   Fighting with the Duke in Flanders,
   In a pattern called a war.
   Christ! What are patterns for?
    'Patterns' (1916)

13 I [Death] was astonished to see him in Baghdad, for
   I had an appointment with him tonight in Samarra.
    Sheppy (1933) act 3

14 All books are either dreams or swords,
   You can cut, or you can drug, with words.
    'Sword Blades and Poppy Seed' (1914). Cf. Farquhar
    280:22

James Russell Lowell 1819–91
American poet

15 An' you've gut to git up airly
   Ef you want to take in God.
    The Biglow Papers (First Series, 1848) no. 1 'A Letter'

16 It ain't by princerples nor men
   My preudunt course is steadied,—
   I scent wich pays the best, an' then
   Go into it baldheaded.
    The Biglow Papers (First Series, 1848) no. 6 'The Pious
    Editor's Creed'

17 We've a war, an' a debt, an' a flag; an' ef this
   Ain't to be inderpendunt, why, wut on airth is?
    The Biglow Papers (Second Series, 1867) no. 4 'A Message of
    Jeff. Davis in Secret Session'

18 There comes Poe with his raven like Barnaby Rudge,
   Three-fifths of him genius, and two-fifths sheer fudge.
    'A Fable for Critics' (1848) l. 1215. Cf. Poe 518:8

19 No man is born into the world, whose work
   Is not born with him; there is always work,
   And tools to work withal, for those who will:
   And blessèd are the horny hands of toil!
    'A Glance Behind the Curtain' (1844)

1 These pearls of thought in Persian gulfs were bred,
Each softly lucent as a rounded moon;
The diver Omar plucked them from their bed,
Fitzgerald strung them on an English thread.
'In a Copy of Omar Khayyám'

2 Before Man made us citizens, great Nature made us
men.
'On the Capture of Fugitive Slaves' (1854)

3 Once to every man and nation comes the moment to
decide,
In the strife of Truth with Falsehood, for the good or
evil side.
'The Present Crisis' (1845)

4 Truth forever on the scaffold, Wrong forever on the
throne,—
Yet that scaffold sways the future, and, behind the
dim unknown,
Standeth God within the shadow, keeping watch
above his own.
'The Present Crisis' (1845)

5 New occasions teach new duties: Time makes ancient
good uncouth;
They must upward still, and onward, who would keep
abreast of Truth.
'The Present Crisis' (1845)

6 May is a pious fraud of the almanac.
'Under the Willows' (1869) l. 21

7 There is no good in arguing with the inevitable. The
only argument available with an east wind is to put
on your overcoat.
Democracy and other Addresses (1887) 'Democracy'

Robert Lowell 1917–77

American poet

8 It's amazing
the day is still here
like lightning on an open field,
terra firma and transient
swimming on variation,
fresh as when man first broke
like the crocus all over the earth.
'The Day' (1977)

9 My eyes have seen what my hand did.
'Dolphin' (1973)

10 Terrible that old life of decency
without unseemly intimacy
or quarrels, when the unemancipated woman
still had her Freudian papa and maids!
'During Fever' (1959)

11 The aquarium is gone. Everywhere,
giant finned cars nose forward like fish;
a savage servility
slides by on grease.
'For the Union Dead' (1964)

12 Their monument sticks like a fishbone
in the city's throat.
'For the Union Dead' (1964)

13 These are the tranquillized *Fifties*,
and I am forty. Ought I to regret my seed-time?
'Memories of West Street and Lepke' (1956)

14 At forty-five,
What next, what next?
At every corner,
I meet my Father,
my age, still alive.
'Middle Age' (1964)

15 I saw the spiders marching through the air,
Swimming from tree to tree that mildewed day
In latter August when the hay
Came creaking to the barn.
'Mr Edwards and the Spider' (1950)

16   This is death.
To die and know it. This is the Black Widow, death.
'Mr Edwards and the Spider' (1950)

17 After fifty
the clock can't stop,
each saving breath
takes something.
'Our Afterlife I' (1977)

18 The Lord survives the rainbow of His will.
'The Quaker Graveyard in Nantucket' (1950)

19 We feel the machine slipping from our hands
As if someone else were steering;
If we see light at the end of the tunnel,
It's the light of the oncoming train.
'Since 1939' (1977). Cf. Dickson 245:9

20 My mind's not right.

A car radio bleats,
'Love, O careless Love . . .' I hear
my ill-spirit sob in each blood cell,
as if my hand were at its throat . . .
I myself am hell,
nobody's here.
'Skunk Hour' (1959) st. 5

21 But I suppose even God was born
too late to trust the old religion—
all those settings out
that never left the ground,
beginning in wisdom, dying in doubt.
'Tenth Muse' (1964)

22 Pity the planet, all joy gone
from this sweet volcanic cone;
peace to our children when they fall
in small war on the heels of small war—until the end
of time
to police the earth, a ghost
orbiting forever lost
in our monotonous sublime.
'Waking Early Sunday Morning' (1965)

23 Folly comes from something—
the present, yes,
we are in it,
it's the infection
of things gone.
'We Took Our Paradise' (1977)

24 Who asks for me, the Shelley of my age,
must lay his heart out for my bed and board.
'Words for Hart Crane' (1959)

William Lowndes 1652–1724

English politician

1 Take care of the pence, and the pounds will take care of themselves.

> In Lord Chesterfield *Letters to his Son* (1774) 5 February 1750 ('*for the pounds . . .* ' in an earlier letter, 6 November 1747)

L. S. Lowry 1887–1976

English painter

2 I'm a simple man, and I use simple materials.

> In Mervyn Levy *Paintings of L. S. Lowry* (1975) p. 11

Malcolm Lowry 1909–57

English novelist

3 How alike are the groans of love to those of the dying.

> *Under the Volcano* (1947) ch. 12

Lucan (Marcus Annaeus Lucanus) AD 39–65

Roman poet

4   *Quis iustius induit arma*
Scire nefas, magno se iudice quisque tuetur:
Victrix causa deis placuit, sed victa Catoni.

It is not granted to know which man took up arms with more right on his side. Each pleads his cause before a great judge: the winning cause pleased the gods, but the losing one pleased Cato.

> *Pharsalia* bk. 1, l. 126

5 *Stat magni nominis umbra.*

There stands the ghost of a great name.

> *Pharsalia* bk. 1, l. 135 (of Pompey)

6 *Nil actum credens, dum quid superesset agendum.*

Thinking nothing done while anything remained to be done.

> *Pharsalia* bk. 2, l. 657

7   *Coniunx*
Est mihi, sunt nati: dedimus tot pignora fatis.

I have a wife, I have sons: we have given so many hostages to the fates.

> *Pharsalia* bk. 6, l. 661. Cf. Bacon 44:3

8 *Jupiter est quodcumque vides, quocumque moveris.*

Jupiter is whatever you see, whichever way you move.

> *Pharsalia* bk. 9, l. 580

George Lucas 1944–

American film director and producer

9 The Empire strikes back.

> Title of film (1980)

10 Man your ships, and may the force be with you.

> *Star Wars* (1977 film)

Lucilius (Gaius Lucilius) c.180–102 BC

Latin poet

11 *Maior erat natu; non omnia possumus omnes.*

He was greater in years; we cannot all do everything.

> In Macrobius *Saturnalia* bk. 6, ch. 1, sect. 35. Cf. Virgil 715:6

Lucretius (Titus Lucretius Carus) c.94–55 BC

Roman poet

12 *Ergo vivida vis animi pervicit, et extra*
Processit longe flammantia moenia mundi
Atque omne immensum peragravit, mente animoque.

So the vital strength of his spirit won through, and he made his way far outside the flaming walls of the world and ranged over the measureless whole, both in mind and spirit.

> *De Rerum Natura* bk. 1, l. 72 (on Epicurus)

13 *Tantum religio potuit suadere malorum.*

So much wrong could religion induce.

> *De Rerum Natura* bk. 1, l. 101

14 . . . *Nil posse creari*
De nilo.

Nothing can be created out of nothing.

> *De Rerum Natura* bk. 1, l. 155

15 *Suave, mari magno turbantibus aequora ventis,*
E terra magnum alterius spectare laborem;
Non quia vexari quemquamst iucunda voluptas,
Sed quibus ipse malis careas quia cernere suave est.
Suave etiam belli certamina magna tueri
Per campos instructa tua sine parte pericli.
Sed nil dulcius est, bene quam munita tenere
Edita doctrina sapientum templa serena,
Despicere unde queas alios passimque videre
Errare atque viam palantis quaerere vitae,
Certare ingenio, contendere nobilitate,
Noctes atque dies niti praestante labore
Ad summas emergere opes rerumque potiri.

Lovely it is, when the winds are churning up the waves on the great sea, to gaze out from the land on the great efforts of someone else; not because it's an enjoyable pleasure that somebody is in difficulties, but because it's lovely to realize what troubles you are yourself spared. Lovely also to witness great battle-plans of war, carried out across the plains, without your having any share in the danger. But nothing is sweeter than to occupy the quiet precincts that are well protected by the teachings of the wise, from where you can look down on others and see them wandering all over the place, getting lost and striving as they seek the way in life, striving by their wits, pitting their noble birth, by night and by day struggling by superior efforts to rise to power at the top and gain possession of all things.

> *De Rerum Natura* bk. 2, l. 1

1 *Augescunt aliae gentes, aliae minuuntur,*
   Inque brevi spatio mutantur saecla animantum
   Et quasi cursores vitai lampada tradunt.

   Some races increase, others are reduced, and in a
   short while the generations of living creatures are
   changed and like runners relay the torch of life.
   De Rerum Natura bk. 2, l. 7

2 *Nil igitur mors est ad nos neque pertinet hilum,*
   Quandoquidem natura animi mortalis habetur.

   Death therefore is nothing to us nor does it concern us
   a scrap, seeing that the nature of the spirit we possess
   is something mortal.
   De Rerum Natura bk. 3, l. 830

3 *Scire licet nobis nil esse in morte timendum*
   Nec miserum fieri qui non est posse neque hilum
   Differre an nullo fuerit iam tempore natus,
   Mortalem vitam mors cum immortalis ademit.

   We can know there is nothing to be feared in death,
   that one who is not cannot be made unhappy, and
   that it matters not a scrap whether one might ever
   have been born at all, when death that is immortal
   has taken over one's mortal life.
   De Rerum Natura bk. 3, l. 866

4 *Cur non ut plenus vitae conviva recedis*
   Aequo animoque capis securam, stulte, quietem?

   Why not, like a banqueter fed full of life, withdraw
   with contentment and rest in peace, you fool?
   De Rerum Natura bk. 3, l. 938

5 *Vitaque mancipio, nulli datur, omnibus usu.*

   And life is given to none freehold, but it is leasehold
   for all.
   De Rerum Natura bk. 3, l. 971

6   *Medio de fonte leporum*
   Surgit amari aliquid quod in ipsis floribus angat.

   From the midst of the fountain of delights rises
   something bitter that chokes them all amongst the
   flowers.
   De Rerum Natura bk. 4, l. 1133

Fray Luis de León *c.1527–91*

Spanish poet and religious writer

7 *Que descansada vida*
   la del que huye el mundanal ruido,
   y sigue la escondida
   senda, por donde han ido
   los pocos sabios que en el mundo han sido!

   What a relaxed life is that which flees the worldly
   clamour, and follows the hidden path down which
   have gone the few wise men there have been in the
   world!
   'Vida Retirada'

8 *Dicebamus hesterno die . . .*

   We were saying yesterday . . .
   On resuming a lecture at Salamanca University in 1577,
   after five years' imprisonment (attributed, among others, by
   A. F. G. Bell in *Luis de León* (1925) ch. 8)

Martin Luther *1483–1546*

German Protestant theologian

9 *Esto peccator et pecca fortiter, sed fortius fide et gaude in*
   Christo.

   Be a sinner and sin strongly, but more strongly have
   faith and rejoice in Christ.
   Letter to Melanchthon, 1521, in *Epistolae* (Jena, 1556)
   vol. 1, folio 345 verso

10 *Hier stehe ich. Ich kann nicht anders. Gott helfe mir.*
    Amen.

    Here stand I. I can do no other. God help me. Amen.
    Speech at the Diet of Worms, 18 April 1521 (attributed)

11 *Wenn ich gewusst hätte, dass so viel Teufel auf mich*
    gezielet hätten, als Ziegel auf den Dächern waren zu
    Worms, wäre ich dennoch eingeritten.

    If I had heard that as many devils would set on me in
    Worms as there are tiles on the roofs, I should none
    the less have ridden there.
    To the Princes of Saxony, 21 August 1524, in *Sämmtliche*
    Schriften vol. 16 (1745) ch. 10, sect. 1, no. 763:15

12 For, where God built a church, there the devil would
    also build a chapel . . . In such sort is the devil always
    God's ape.
    Colloquia Mensalia (1566) ch. 2 (translated by H. Bell as
    Martin Luther's Divine Discourses, 1652). Cf. Bancroft
    51:12, Becon 58:6

13 *Eine feste Burg ist unser Gott,*
    Ein gute Wehr und Waffen.

    A safe stronghold our God is still,
    A trusty shield and weapon.
    'Eine feste Burg ist unser Gott' (1529); translated by
    Thomas Carlyle

14 *Das alleine das trawen und gleuben des hertzens machet*
    beide Gott und abeGott.

    The confidence and faith of the heart alone make both
    God and an idol.
    Large Catechism (1529) 'The First Commandment'

15 *Wo rauff du nu . . . dein hertz hengest und verlessest, das*
    ist eygentlich dein Gott.

    Whatever your heart clings to and confides in, that is
    really your God.
    Large Catechism (1529) 'The First Commandment'

16 *Darum gibt unser Herr Gott gemeiniglich Reichtum den*
    grossen Eseln, denen er sonst nichts gönnt.

    So our Lord God commonly gives riches to those gross
    asses to whom He vouchsafes nothing else.
    Tischreden oder Colloquia (collected by J. Aurifaber, 1566)
    ch. 4

17 *Wer nicht liebt Wein, Weib und Gesang,*
    Der bleibt ein Narr sein Leben lang.

    Who loves not woman, wine, and song
    Remains a fool his whole life long.
    Attributed (later inscribed in the Luther room in the
    Wartburg, but with no proof of authorship)

Rosa Luxemburg 1871–1919

German revolutionary

1 Freiheit ist immer nur Freiheit des anders Denkenden.

Freedom is always and exclusively freedom for the one who thinks differently.

Die Russische Revolution (1918) sect. 4

John Lydgate c.1370–c.1451

English poet

2 Sithe off oure language he was the lodesterre.

The Fall of Princes (1431–8) prologue l. 252 (of Chaucer)

3 Sithe he off Inglissh in makyng was the beste,
Preie onto God to yiue his soule good reste.

The Fall of Princes (1431–8) prologue l. 356

4 Comparisouns doon offte gret greuaunce.

The Fall of Princes (1431–8) bk. 3, l. 2188

5 Woord is but wynd; leff woord and tak the dede.

Secrets of Old Philosophers l. 1224

6 Love is mor than gold or gret richesse.

The Story of Thebes pt. 3, l. 2716

John Lyly c.1554–1606

English poet and playwright

7 CAMPASPE: Were women never so fair, men would be false.
APELLES: Were women never so false, men would be fond.

Campaspe (1584) act 3, sc. 3

8 Cupid and my Campaspe played
At cards for kisses, Cupid paid.

Campaspe (1584) act 3, sc. 5

9 At last he set her both his eyes;
She won, and Cupid blind did rise.
O Love! has she done this to thee?
What shall, alas! become of me?

Campaspe (1584) act 3, sc. 5

10 What bird so sings, yet so does wail?
O 'tis the ravished nightingale.
Jug, jug, jug, jug, tereu, she cries,
And still her woes at midnight rise.

Campaspe (1584) act 5, sc. 1

11 Night hath a thousand eyes.

The Maydes Metamorphosis (1600) act 3, sc. 1

12 O cruel Love, on thee I lay
My curse, which shall strike blind the day:
Never may sleep with velvet hand
Charm thine eyes with sacred wand …
The bed thou liest on be despair;
Thy sleep, fond dreams; thy dreams, long care;
Hope (like thy fool) at thy bed's head
Mock thee, till madness strike thee dead.

Sappho and Phao (written c.1582)

13 If all the earth were paper white
And all the sea were ink
'Twere not enough for me to write
As my poor heart doth think.

'If all the earth were paper white' in R. Warwick Bond (ed.) *The Complete Works* (1902) vol. 3, p. 452

Baron Lyndhurst 1772–1863

English politician and lawyer; three times Lord Chancellor

14 Campbell has added another terror to death.

On Lord Campbell's *Lives of the Lord Chancellors* being written without the consent of heirs or executors, in E. Bowen-Rowlands *Seventy-Two Years At the Bar* (1924) ch. 10. Cf. Arbuthnot 24:10, Tree 702:7, Wetherell 729:22

Lysander d. 395 BC

Spartan naval commander

15 τοὺς μὲν παῖδας ἀστραγάλοις, τοὺς δὲ ἄνδρας ὅρκοις ἐξαπατᾶν.

Deceive boys with toys, but men with oaths.

In Plutarch *Parallel Lives* 'Lysander' ch. 8

Henry Francis Lyte 1793–1847

Perpetual curate of Lower Brixham, Devon, from 1823

16 Abide with me: fast falls the eventide;
The darkness deepens; Lord, with me abide:
When other helpers fail, and comforts flee,
Help of the helpless, O abide with me.
Swift to its close ebbs out life's little day;
Earth's joys grow dim, its glories pass away;
Change and decay in all around I see;
O Thou, who changest not, abide with me.

'Abide with Me' (probably written in 1847). See St Luke ch. 24, v. 29: 'Abide with us: for it is toward evening, and the day is far spent'

17 Praise my soul, the King of heaven;
To his feet thy tribute bring.
Ransomed, healed, restored, forgiven,
Who like me his praise should sing? …
Praise the everlasting King!

Praise him for his grace and favour
To our fathers in distress;
Praise him still the same for ever,
Slow to chide, and swift to bless …

Father-like, he tends and spares us;
Well our feeble frame he knows …
Praise him! Praise him!
Widely as his mercy flows.

'Praise, my soul, the King of heaven' (1834 hymn)

George Lyttelton (1st Baron Lyttelton) 1709–73

English politician and man of letters

18 Seek to be good, but aim not to be great;
A woman's noblest station is retreat.

'Advice to a Lady' (1773)

E. R. Bulwer, 1st Earl of Lytton

See OWEN MEREDITH

Alexander McArthur and H. Kingsley Long

1 Battles and sex are the only free diversions in slum life. Couple them with drink, which costs money, and you have the three principal outlets for that escape complex which is for ever working in the tenement dweller's subconscious mind.

No Mean City (1935) ch. 4

Douglas MacArthur 1880–1964

American general

2 In war, indeed, there can be no substitute for victory.

Congressional Record 19 April 1951, vol. 97, pt. 3, p. 4125

3 I came through and I shall return.

On reaching Australia, 20 March 1942, having broken through Japanese lines en route from Corregidor; in *New York Times* 21 March 1942, p. 1

Rose Macaulay 1881–1958

English novelist

4 Gentlemen know that fresh *air* should be kept in its proper place—out of doors—and that, God having given us indoors and out-of-doors, we should not attempt to do away with this distinction.

Crewe Train (1926) pt. 1, ch. 5

5 'What does a lovely maid with rhyming, pray?' 'It makes no differ, being a maid,' Julian told him ... 'It makes no differ. Men or women, if we crave to write verse, we must write it, and write it the best we can.'

They Were Defeated (1932) pt. 3, sect. 5

6 'Take my camel, dear,' said my aunt Dot, as she climbed down from this animal on her return from High Mass.

The Towers of Trebizond (1956) p. 9

Thomas Babington, 1st Baron Macaulay 1800–59

English politician and historian

7 In order that he might rob a neighbour whom he had promised to defend, black men fought on the coast of Coromandel, and red men scalped each other by the Great Lakes of North America.

Biographical Essays (1857) 'Frederic the Great'

8 The object of oratory alone is not truth, but persuasion.

'Essay on Athenian Orators' in *Knight's Quarterly Magazine* August 1824

9 The business of everybody is the business of nobody.

Essays Contributed to the Edinburgh Review (1843) vol. 1 'Hallam'

10 The gallery in which the reporters sit has become a fourth estate of the realm.

Essays Contributed to the Edinburgh Review (1843) vol. 1 'Hallam'

11 He knew that the essence of war is violence, and that moderation in war is imbecility.

Essays Contributed to the Edinburgh Review (1843) vol. 1 'John Hampden'

12 The Life of Johnson is assuredly a great, a very great work. Homer is not more decidedly the first of heroic poets, Shakespeare is not more decidedly the first of dramatists, Demosthenes is not more decidedly the first of orators, than Boswell is the first of biographers.

Essays Contributed to the Edinburgh Review (1843) vol. 1 'Samuel Johnson'

13 They knew luxury; they knew beggary; but they never knew comfort.

Essays Contributed to the Edinburgh Review (1843) vol. 1 'Samuel Johnson' (of writers struggling to make a living in Johnson's day)

14 The gigantic body, the huge massy face, seamed with the scars of disease, the brown coat, the black worsted stockings, the grey wig with the scorched foretop, the dirty hands, the nails bitten and pared to the quick.

Essays Contributed to the Edinburgh Review (1843) vol. 1 'Samuel Johnson'

15 Out of his surname they have coined an epithet for a knave, and out of his Christian name a synonym for the Devil.

Essays Contributed to the Edinburgh Review (1843) vol. 1 'Machiavelli'

16 As civilization advances, poetry almost necessarily declines.

Essays Contributed to the Edinburgh Review (1843) vol. 1 'Milton'

17 Many politicians of our time are in the habit of laying it down as a self-evident proposition, that no people ought to be free till they are fit to use their freedom. The maxim is worthy of the fool in the old story, who resolved not to go into the water till he had learnt to swim. If men are to wait for liberty till they become wise and good in slavery, they may indeed wait for ever.

Essays Contributed to the Edinburgh Review (1843) vol. 1 'Milton'

18 On the rich and the eloquent, on nobles and priests, they [the Puritans] looked down with contempt: for they esteemed themselves rich in a more precious treasure, and eloquent in a more sublime language, nobles by the right of an earlier creation, and priests by the imposition of a mightier hand.

Essays Contributed to the Edinburgh Review (1843) vol. 1 'Milton'

19 We know no spectacle so ridiculous as the British public in one of its periodical fits of morality.

Essays Contributed to the Edinburgh Review (1843) vol. 1 'Moore's *Life of Lord Byron*'

20 From the poetry of Lord Byron they drew a system of ethics, compounded of misanthropy and voluptuousness, a system in which the two great commandments were, to hate your neighbour, and to love your neighbour's wife.

Essays Contributed to the Edinburgh Review (1843) vol. 1 'Moore's *Life of Lord Byron*'

21 We have heard it said that five per cent is the natural interest of money.

Essays Contributed to the Edinburgh Review (1843) vol. 1 'Southey's Colloquies'

1 With the dead there is no rivalry. In the dead there is no change. Plato is never sullen. Cervantes is never petulant. Demosthenes never comes unseasonably. Dante never stays too long. No difference of political opinion can alienate Cicero. No heresy can excite the horror of Bossuet.

Essays Contributed to the Edinburgh Review (1843) vol. 2 'Lord Bacon'

2 An acre in Middlesex is better than a principality in Utopia.

Essays Contributed to the Edinburgh Review (1843) vol. 2 'Lord Bacon'

3 The rising hope [i.e. Gladstone] of those stern and unbending Tories.

Essays Contributed to the Edinburgh Review (1843) vol. 2 'Gladstone on Church and State'

4 The highest intellects, like the tops of mountains, are the first to catch and to reflect the dawn.

Essays Contributed to the Edinburgh Review (1843) vol. 2 'Sir James Mackintosh'

5 The history of England is emphatically the history of progress.

Essays Contributed to the Edinburgh Review (1843) vol. 2 'Sir James Mackintosh'

6 Biographers, translators, editors, all, in short, who employ themselves in illustrating the lives or writings of others, are peculiarly exposed to the *Lues Boswelliana*, or disease of admiration.

Essays Contributed to the Edinburgh Review (1843) vol. 2 'William Pitt, Earl of Chatham'

7 The conformation of his mind was such that whatever was little seemed to him great, and whatever was great seemed to him little.

Essays Contributed to the Edinburgh Review (1843) vol. 2 'Horace Walpole'

8 The reluctant obedience of distant provinces generally costs more than it [the territory] is worth.

Essays Contributed to the Edinburgh Review (1843) vol. 2 'The War of Succession in Spain'

9 Every schoolboy knows who imprisoned Montezuma, and who strangled Atahualpa.

Essays Contributed to the Edinburgh Review (1843) vol. 3 'Lord Clive'

10 The Chief Justice was rich, quiet, and infamous.

Essays Contributed to the Edinburgh Review (1843) vol. 3 'Warren Hastings'

11 That temple of silence and reconciliation where the enmities of twenty generations lie buried.

Essays Contributed to the Edinburgh Review (1843) vol. 3 'Warren Hastings' (of Westminster Abbey)

12 She [the Roman Catholic Church] may still exist in undiminished vigour when some traveller from New Zealand shall, in the midst of a vast solitude, take his stand on a broken arch of London Bridge to sketch the ruins of St Paul's.

Essays Contributed to the Edinburgh Review (1843) vol. 3 'Von Ranke'. Cf. Walpole 719:16

13 She [the Church of Rome] thoroughly understands what no other church has ever understood, how to deal with enthusiasts.

Essays Contributed to the Edinburgh Review (1843) vol. 3 'Von Ranke'

14 A rake among scholars, and a scholar among rakes.

Essays Contributed to the Edinburgh Review (1850) 'The Life and Writings of Addison' (of Richard Steele)

15 I shall cheerfully bear the reproach of having descended below the dignity of history.

History of England vol. 1 (1849) ch. 1

16 Thus our democracy was, from an early period, the most aristocratic, and our aristocracy the most democratic in the world.

History of England vol. 1 (1849) ch. 1

17 Persecution produced its natural effect on them [Puritans and Calvinists]. It found them a sect; it made them a faction.

History of England vol. 1 (1849) ch. 1

18 It was a crime in a child to read by the bedside of a sick parent one of those beautiful collects which had soothed the griefs of forty generations of Christians.

History of England vol. 1 (1849) ch. 2

19 The Puritan hated bear-baiting, not because it gave pain to the bear, but because it gave pleasure to the spectators.

History of England vol. 1 (1849) ch. 2

20 We must at present do our best to form a class who may be interpreters between us and the millions whom we govern; a class of persons, Indian in blood and colour, but English in taste, in opinions, in morals, and in intellect.

Minute, as Member of Supreme Council of India, 2 February 1835, in W. Nassan Lees *Indian Musalmàns* (1871) p. 102

21 The English Bible, a book which, if everything else in our language should perish, would alone suffice to show the whole extent of its beauty and power.

T. F. Ellis (ed.) *Miscellaneous Writings of Lord Macaulay* (1860) 'John Dryden' (1828)

22 His imagination resembled the wings of an ostrich. It enabled him to run, though not to soar.

T. F. Ellis (ed.) *Miscellaneous Writings of Lord Macaulay* (1860) 'John Dryden' (1828)

23 This province of literature [history] is a debatable line. It lies on the confines of two distinct territories. It is under the jurisdiction of two hostile powers; and like other districts similarly situated it is ill-defined, ill-cultivated, and ill-regulated. Instead of being equally shared between its two rulers, the Reason and the Imagination, it falls alternately under the sole and absolute dominion of each. It is sometimes fiction. It is sometimes theory.

T. F. Ellis (ed.) *Miscellaneous Writings of Lord Macaulay* (1860) vol. 1 'History' (1828)

24 Knowledge advances by steps, and not by leaps.

T. F. Ellis (ed.) *Miscellaneous Writings of Lord Macaulay* (1860) vol. 1 'History' (1828)

25 Thank you, madam, the agony is abated.

Aged four, having had hot coffee spilt over his legs; in G. O. Trevelyan *Life and Letters of Lord Macaulay* (1876) ch. 1

26 We were regaled by a dogfight . . . How odd that people of sense should find any pleasure in being accompanied by a beast who is always spoiling conversation.

In G. O. Trevelyan *Life and Letters of Macaulay* (1876) ch. 14

1 The rugged miners poured to war from Mendip's
sunless caves.
'The Armada' (1833)

2 Till Belvoir's lordly terraces the sign to Lincoln sent,
And Lincoln sped the message on o'er the wide vale of
Trent;
Till Skiddaw saw the fire that burned on Gaunt's
embattled pile,
And the red glare on Skiddaw roused the burghers of
Carlisle.
'The Armada' (1833)

3 Obadiah Bind-their-kings-in-chains-and-their-nobles-
with-links-of-iron.
'The Battle of Naseby' (1824) fictitious author's name. Cf.
Book of Common Prayer 135:16

4 Oh, wherefore come ye forth in triumph from the
north,
With your hands, and your feet, and your raiment all
red?
And wherefore doth your rout send forth a joyous
shout?
And whence be the grapes of the wine-press which ye
tread?
'The Battle of Naseby' (1824)

5 And the Man of Blood was there, with his long
essenced hair,
And Astley, and Sir Marmaduke, and Rupert of the
Rhine.
'The Battle of Naseby' (1824)

6 To my true king I offered free from stain
Courage and faith; vain faith, and courage vain.
'A Jacobite's Epitaph' (1845)

7 By those white cliffs I never more must see,
By that dear language which I spake like thee,
Forget all feuds, and shed one English tear
O'er English dust. A broken heart lies here.
'A Jacobite's Epitaph' (1845)

8 Let no man stop to plunder,
But slay, and slay, and slay;
The Gods who live for ever
Are on our side to-day.
Lays of Ancient Rome (1842) 'The Battle of Lake Regillus'
st. 35

9 Lars Porsena of Clusium
By the nine gods he swore
That the great house of Tarquin
Should suffer wrong no more.
By the Nine Gods he swore it,
And named a trysting day,
And bade his messengers ride forth,
East and west and south and north,
To summon his array.
Lays of Ancient Rome (1842) 'Horatius' st. 1

10 Then out spake brave Horatius,
The Captain of the Gate:
'To every man upon this earth
Death cometh soon or late.
And how can man die better
Than facing fearful odds,
For the ashes of his fathers,
And the temples of his Gods?'
Lays of Ancient Rome (1842) 'Horatius' st. 27

11 Now who will stand on either hand,
And keep the bridge with me?
Lays of Ancient Rome (1842) 'Horatius' st. 29

12 Then none was for a party;
Then all were for the state;
Then the great man helped the poor,
And the poor man loved the great:
Then lands were fairly portioned;
Then spoils were fairly sold:
The Romans were like brothers
In the brave days of old.
Lays of Ancient Rome (1842) 'Horatius' st. 32

13 Was none who would be foremost
To lead such dire attack;
But those behind cried 'Forward!'
And those before cried 'Back!'
Lays of Ancient Rome (1842) 'Horatius' st. 50

14 Oh, Tiber! father Tiber
To whom the Romans pray,
A Roman's life, a Roman's arms,
Take thou in charge this day!
Lays of Ancient Rome (1842) 'Horatius' st. 59

15 And even the ranks of Tuscany
Could scarce forbear to cheer.
Lays of Ancient Rome (1842) 'Horatius' st. 60

16 With weeping and with laughter
Still is the story told,
How well Horatius kept the bridge
In the brave days of old.
Lays of Ancient Rome (1842) 'Horatius' st. 70

Anthony McAuliffe 1898–1975
American general

17 Nuts!
Replying to the German demand for surrender at Bastogne,
Belgium, 22 December 1944; in New York Times
28 December 1944, p. 4

Joseph McCarthy 1908–57
American politician and anti-Communist agitator

18 McCarthyism is Americanism with its sleeves rolled.
Speech in Wisconsin, 1952, in Richard Rovere Senator Joe
McCarthy (1973) p. 8

Mary McCarthy 1912–89
American novelist

19 The immense popularity of American movies abroad
demonstrates that Europe is the unfinished negative of
which America is the proof.
On the Contrary (1961) 'America the Beautiful'

20 If someone tells you he is going to make a 'realistic
decision', you immediately understand that he has
resolved to do something bad.
On the Contrary (1961) 'American Realist Playwrights'

21 In violence, we forget who we are.
On the Contrary (1961) 'Characters in Fiction'

22 There are no new truths, but only truths that have
not been recognized by those who have perceived
them without noticing.
On the Contrary (1961) 'Vita Activa'

1 Every word she writes is a lie, including 'and' and
'the'.

> Quoting herself on Lillian Hellman in *New York Times*
> 16 February 1980, p. 12

George B. McClellan 1826–85

American soldier and politician

2 All quiet along the Potomac.

> Said at the time of the American Civil War (attributed).
> Cf. Beers 59:22

David McCord 1897–

3 By and by
God caught his eye.

> 'Remainders' (1935); epitaph for a waiter

Horace McCoy 1897–1955

American novelist

4 They shoot horses don't they.

> Title of novel (1935)

John McCrae 1872–1918

Canadian poet and military physician

5 In Flanders fields the poppies blow
Between the crosses, row on row,
That mark our place; and in the sky
The larks, still bravely singing, fly
Scarce heard amid the guns below.

> 'In Flanders Fields' (1915)

6 To you from failing hands we throw
The torch; be yours to hold it high.
If ye break faith with us who die
We shall not sleep, though poppies grow.

> 'In Flanders Fields' (1915)

Hugh MacDiarmid (Christopher Murray Grieve) 1892–1978

Scottish poet and nationalist

7 I'll ha'e nae hauf-way hoose, but aye be whaur
Extremes meet—it's the only way I ken
To dodge the curst conceit o' bein' richt
That damns the vast majority o' men.

> *A Drunk Man Looks at the Thistle* (1926) p. 6

8 He's no a man ava',
And lacks a proper pride,
Gin less than a' the world
Can ser' him for a bride!

> *A Drunk Man Looks at the Thistle* (1926) p. 36

George MacDonald 1824–1905

Scottish writer and poet

9 Where did you come from, baby dear?
Out of the everywhere into here.

> *At the Back of the North Wind* (1871) ch. 33 'Song'

10 Here lie I, Martin Elginbrodde:
Hae mercy o' my soul, Lord God;
As I wad do, were I Lord God,
And ye were Martin Elginbrodde.

> *David Elginbrod* (1863) bk. 1, ch. 13

11 They all were looking for a king
To slay their foes, and lift them high;
Thou cam'st, a little baby thing,
That made a woman cry.

> 'That Holy Thing' (1883)

Ramsay MacDonald 1866–1937

British Labour politician; Prime Minister, 1924, 1931–5

12 We hear war called murder. It is not: it is suicide.

> In *Observer* 4 May 1930

13 Tomorrow every Duchess in London will be wanting
to kiss me!

> After forming the National Government, 25 August 1931;
> in Viscount Snowden *An Autobiography* (1934) vol. 2,
> p. 957

A. G. MacDonell 1889–1941

Scottish writer

14 England, their England.

> Title of novel (1933). Cf. Henley 332:9

Ian McEwan 1948–

English novelist

15 Shakespeare would have grasped wave functions,
Donne would have understood complementarity and
relative time. They would have been excited. What
richness! They would have plundered this new science
for their imagery. And they would have educated their
audiences too. But you 'arts' people, you're not only
ignorant of these magnificent things, you're rather
proud of knowing nothing.

> *The Child in Time* (1987) ch. 2

William McGonagall c.1825–1902

Scottish writer of doggerel

16 Alas! Lord and Lady Dalhousie are dead, and buried at
last,
Which causes many people to feel a little downcast.

> 'The Death of Lord and Lady Dalhousie'

17 Beautiful Railway Bridge of the Silv'ry Tay!
Alas, I am very sorry to say
That ninety lives have been taken away
On the last Sabbath day of 1879,
Which will be remembered for a very long time.

> 'The Tay Bridge Disaster'

Roger McGough 1937–

English poet

1 You will put on a dress of guilt
and shoes with broken high ideals.
'Comeclose and Sleepnow' (1967)

2 Let me die a youngman's death
Not a clean & in-between-
The-sheets, holy-water death,
Not a famous-last-words
Peaceful out-of-breath death.
'Let Me Die a Youngman's Death' (1967)

Sir Ian MacGregor 1912–

*British industrialist; Chairman of the National Coal
Board, 1983–6*

3 People are now discovering the price of
insubordination and insurrection. And boy, are we
going to make it stick!
During the coal-miners' strike, in *Sunday Telegraph*
10 March 1985. Cf. Jenkins 365:3

Jimmy McGregor

Scottish singer and songwriter

4 Oh, he's football crazy, he's football mad
And the football it has robbed him o' the wee bit sense
he had.
And it would take a dozen skivvies, his clothes to
wash and scrub,
Since our Jock became a member of that terrible
football club.
'Football Crazy' (1960 song)

Niccolò Machiavelli 1469–1527

Florentine statesman and political philosopher

5 *E seppure qualche volta è necessario nascondere con le
parole una cosa, bisogna farlo in modo o che non appaia, o
apparendo, sia parata e prestala difesa.*

And if, to be sure, sometimes you need to conceal a
fact with words, do it in such a way that it does not
become known, or, if it does become known, that you
have a ready and quick defence.
'Advice to Raffaello Girolami when he went as Ambassador
to the Emperor' (October 1522) in *Machiavelli: The Chief
Works and Others* (translated by Allan Gilbert, 1965)

6 *È necessario a chi dispone una republica, ed ordina
leggi in quella, prassuppoie tutti gli nomini rei, e che li
abbiano sempre a usare la malignità dello animo loro,
qualunque volta ne abbiano libera occasione.*

It is necessary for him who lays out a state and
arranges laws for it to presuppose that all men are evil
and that they are always going to act according to the
wickedness of their spirits whenever they have free
scope.
Discorsi Supra la Prima Deca di Tito Livio (written 1513–17)
bk. 1, ch. 3 (translated by Allan Gilbert)

7 *Gli nomini si debbano o vezzeggiate o peguere; perchè si
vendiciano delle leggieri offese, delle gravi non possono.*

Men should be either treated generously or destroyed,
because they take revenge for slight injuries—for
heavy ones they cannot.
Il Principe (written 1513) ch. 3 (translated by Allan Gilbert)

8 *Nasce da questo una disputa: s'egli è meglio essere amato
che temuto, o è converso. Rispondesi che si voiebbe essere
l'uno e l'altro; ma perchè egli è difficile accozzarli insieme,
è molto più sicuro essere temuto che amato, quando si
abbia a mancare dell'uno de'due.*

This leads to a debate: is it better to be loved than
feared, or the reverse? The answer is that it is
desirable to be both, but because it is difficult to join
them together, it is much safer for a prince to be
feared than loved, if he is to fail in one of the two.
Il Principe (written 1513) ch. 8 (translated by Allan Gilbert)

9 *E non sia alcuno che repugni a questa mia opinione con
quello proverbio trito, che chi fonda in sul popolo, fonda in
sul fango.*

Let no one oppose this belief of mine with that
well-worn proverb: 'He who builds on the people
builds on mud.'
Il Principe (written 1513) ch. 9 (translated by Allan Gilbert)

10 *Uno principe necessitato sapere bene usare la bestia, debbe
di quelle pigliare la golpe e il lione; perchè il lione non si
defende da'lupi. Bisogna, adunque, essere golpe a conoscere
e' lacci, e lione a sbigottire e' lupi.*

Since, then, a prince is necessitated to play the animal
well, he chooses among the beasts the fox and the
lion, because the lion does not protect himself from
traps; the fox does not protect himself from wolves.
The prince must be a fox, therefore, to recognize the
traps and a lion to frighten the wolves.
Il Principe (written 1513) ch. 18 (translated by Allan
Gilbert)

11 *Qualunque volta alle universalità degli nomini non si toglie
nè roba nè onore, vivono contenti.*

So long as the great majority of men are not deprived
of either property or honour, they are satisfied.
Il Principe (written 1513) ch. 19 (translated by Allan
Gilbert)

12 *Non ci è altro modo a guardarsi dalle adulazioni, se non
che gli nomini intendino che non ti offendino a dirti el
vero; ma quando ciascuno può dirti el vero, ti manca la
reverenzia.*

There is no other way for securing yourself against
flatteries except that men understand that they do not
offend you by telling you the truth; but when
everybody can tell you the truth, you fail to get
respect.
Il Principe (written 1513) ch. 23 (translated by Allan
Gilbert)

Fritz Machlup 1902–83

Austrian economist

13 Let us remember the unfortunate econometrician who,
in one of the major functions of his system, had to use
a proxy for risk and a dummy for sex.
In *Journal of Political Economy* July/August 1974, p. 892

Claude McKay 1890–1948
American poet and novelist

1 If we must die, let it not be like hogs
Hunted and penned in an inglorious spot,
While round us bark the mad and hungry dogs,
Making their mock at our accursed lot.
'If We Must Die' (1953)

Sir Compton Mackenzie 1883–1972
English novelist

2 Prostitution. Selling one's body to keep one's soul: this
is the meaning of the sins that were forgiven to the
woman because she loved much: one might say of
most marriages that they were selling one's soul to
keep one's body.
The Adventures of Sylvia Scarlett (1918) bk. 2, ch. 5

3 Women do not find it difficult nowadays to behave like
men, but they often find it extremely difficult to
behave like gentlemen.
Literature in My Time (1933) ch. 22

4 You are offered a piece of bread and butter that feels
like a damp handkerchief and sometimes, when
cucumber is added to it, like a wet one.
Vestal Fire (1927) bk. 1, ch. 3

Sir James Mackintosh 1765–1832
Scottish philosopher and historian

5 Men are never so good or so bad as their opinions.
Dissertation on the Progress of Ethical Philosophy (1830)
sect. 6 'Jeremy Bentham'

6 The Commons, faithful to their system, remained in
a wise and masterly inactivity.
Vindiciae Gallicae (1791) sect. 1

Alexander Maclaren 1826–1910
Scottish divine

7 'The Church is an anvil which has worn out many
hammers', and the story of the first collision is, in
essentials, the story of all.
Expositions of Holy Scripture: Acts of the Apostles (1907)
ch. 4

Don McLean 1945–
American songwriter

8 I can't remember if I cried
When I read about his widowed bride.
Something touched me deep inside
The day the music died.

So, bye, bye, Miss American Pie,
Drove my Chevy to the levee
But the levee was dry.
Them good old boys was drinkin' whiskey and rye
Singin' 'This'll be the day that I die.'
'American Pie' (1972 song, on the death of Buddy Holly)

Archibald MacLeish 1892–1982
American poet, later public official

9 A Poem should be palpable and mute
As a globed fruit

Dumb
As old medallions to the thumb

Silent as the sleeve-worn stone
Of casement ledges where the moss has grown—
A poem should be wordless
As the flight of birds.
'Ars Poetica' (1926)

10 A poem should not mean
But be.
'Ars Poetica' (1926)

Murdoch McLennan fl. 1715
Scottish poet

11 There's some say that we wan, some say that they
wan,
Some say that nane wan at a', man;
But one thing I'm sure, that at Sheriffmuir
A battle there was which I saw, man:
And we ran, and they ran, and they ran, and we ran,
And we ran; and they ran awa', man!
'Sheriffmuir' in J. Woodfall Ebsworth (ed.) *Roxburghe Ballads*
vol. 6 (1889). In James Hogg *The Jacobite Relics of Scotland*
(1821) vol. 2, the last line reads: 'But Florence ran fastest
of a', man' (Florence being the Marquis of Huntley's horse)

Fiona McLeod (William Sharp) 1855–1905
Scottish writer

12 My heart is a lonely hunter that hunts on a lonely
hill.
'The Lonely Hunter' (1896) st. 6 (reworked by Carson
McCullers as 'The heart is a lonely hunter' for the title of a
novel, 1940)

Marshall McLuhan 1911–80
Canadian communications scholar

13 The new electronic interdependence recreates the
world in the image of a global village.
The Gutenberg Galaxy (1962) p. 31

14 The medium is the message.
Understanding Media (1964) ch. 1 (title)

15 The name of a man is a numbing blow from which he
never recovers.
Understanding Media (1964) ch. 2

16 The car has become an article of dress without which
we feel uncertain, unclad and incomplete in the urban
compound.
Understanding Media (1964) ch. 22

Comte de Macmahon 1808–93

French military commander; President of the Third Republic, 1873–9

1 *J'y suis, j'y reste.*

Here I am, and here I stay.

> At the taking of the Malakoff fortress during the Crimean War, 8 September 1855. See G. Hanotaux *Histoire de la France Contemporaine* (1903–8) vol. 2, ch. 1, sect. 1

Harold Macmillan (1st Earl of Stockton) 1894–1986

British Conservative politician; Prime Minister, 1957–63

2 There ain't gonna be no war.

> At a London press conference, 24 July 1955, following the Geneva summit; in *News Chronicle* 25 July 1955

3 Let us be frank about it: most of our people have never had it so good.

> Speech at Bedford, 20 July 1957, in *The Times* 22 July 1957 ('You Never Had It So Good' was the Democratic Party slogan during the 1952 US election campaign)

4 I thought the best thing to do was to settle up these little local difficulties, and then turn to the wider vision of the Commonwealth.

> Statement at London airport on leaving for a Commonwealth tour, 7 January 1958, following the resignation of the Chancellor of the Exchequer and others; in *The Times* 8 January 1958

5 The wind of change is blowing through this continent, and, whether we like it or not, this growth of [African] national consciousness is a political fact.

> Speech at Cape Town, 3 February 1960, in *Pointing the Way* (1972) p. 475

6 First of all the Georgian silver goes, and then all that nice furniture that used to be in the saloon. Then the Canalettos go.

> Speech on privatization to the Tory Reform Group, 8 November 1985, in *The Times* 9 November 1985

7 Forever poised between a cliché and an indiscretion.

> In *Newsweek* 30 April 1956 (on the life of a Foreign Secretary)

8 He [Aneurin Bevan] enjoys prophesying the imminent fall of the capitalist system and is prepared to play a part, any part, in its burial, except that of mute.

> In Michael Foot *Aneurin Bevan* (1962) pt. 1, ch. 5

9 I was determined that no British government should be brought down by the action of two tarts.

> Comment on the Profumo affair, July 1963, in Anthony Sampson *Macmillan* (1967) p. 243

10 There are three bodies no sensible man directly challenges: the Roman Catholic Church, the Brigade of Guards and the National Union of Mineworkers.

> In *Observer* 22 February 1981. Cf. Baldwin 48:12

Leonard MacNally 1752–1820

Irish poet and playwright

11 This lass so neat, with smiles so sweet,
Has won my right good-will,
I'd crowns resign to call thee mine,
Sweet lass of Richmond Hill.

> 'The Lass of Richmond Hill' (also attributed to W. Upton in *The Oxford Song Book* (1916), and to W. Hudson in S. Baring-Gould *English Minstrelsie* (1895) vol. 3, p. 54)

Louis MacNeice 1907–63

British poet, born in Belfast

12 Better authentic mammon than a bogus god.

> *Autumn Journal* (1939) p. 49

13 It's no go the merrygoround, it's no go the rickshaw,
All we want is a limousine and a ticket for the peepshow.

> 'Bagpipe Music' (1938)

14 It's no go the picture palace, it's no go the stadium,
It's no go the country cot with a pot of pink geraniums,
It's no go the Government grants, it's no go the elections,
Sit on your arse for fifty years and hang your hat on a pension.

> 'Bagpipe Music' (1938)

15 It's no go my honey love, it's no go my poppet;
Work your hands from day to day, the winds will blow the profit.
The glass is falling hour by hour, the glass will fall for ever,
But if you break the bloody glass you won't hold up the weather.

> 'Bagpipe Music' (1938)

16 And under the totem poles—the ancient terror—
Between the enormous fluted Ionic columns
There seeps from heavily jowled or hawk-like foreign faces
The guttural sorrow of the refugees.

> 'The British Museum Reading Room' (1941)

17 Crumbling between the fingers, under the feet,
Crumbling behind the eyes,
Their world gives way and dies
And something twangs and breaks at the end of the street.

> 'Débâcle' (1941)

18 So they were married—to be the more together—
And found they were never again so much together,
Divided by the morning tea,
By the evening paper,
By children and tradesmen's bills.

> 'Les Sylphides' (1941)

19 Time was away and somewhere else,
There were two glasses and two chairs
And two people with the one pulse
(Somebody stopped the moving stairs):
Time was away and somewhere else.

> 'Meeting Point' (1941)

1 I am not yet born; O fill me
With strength against those who would freeze my
humanity, would dragoon me into a lethal automaton,
would make me a cog in a machine, a thing with
one face, a thing, and against all those
who would dissipate my entirety, would
blow me like thistledown hither and
thither or hither and thither
like water held in the
hands would spill me.
Let them not make me a stone and let them not spill
me,
Otherwise kill me.
'Prayer Before Birth' (1944)

2 World is crazier and more of it than we think,
Incorrigibly plural. I peel and portion
A tangerine and spit the pips and feel
The drunkenness of things being various.
'Snow' (1935)

3 Down the road someone is practising scales,
The notes like little fishes vanish with a wink of tails,
Man's heart expands to tinker with his car
For this is Sunday morning, Fate's great bazaar.
'Sunday Morning' (1935)

4 The sunlight on the garden
Hardens and grows cold,
We cannot cage the minute
Within its net of gold,
When all is told
We cannot beg for pardon.
'Sunlight on the Garden' (1938)

5 Our freedom as free lances
Advances towards its end;
The earth compels, upon it
Sonnets and birds descend;
And soon, my friend,
We shall have no time for dances.
'Sunlight on the Garden' (1938)

6 By a high star our course is set,
Our end is Life. Put out to sea.
'Thalassa' (1964)

Geoffrey Madan 1895–1947

English bibliophile

7 King George, passing slowly in a closed car, looking
like a big, rather worn *penny* in the window.
Geoffrey Madan's Notebooks (1981) p. 66 (of George V)

8 The great tragedy of the classical languages is to have
been born twins.
Geoffrey Madan's Notebooks (1981) p. 67

9 Peers: a kind of eye-shade or smoked glass, to protect
us from the full glare of Royalty.
Geoffrey Madan's Notebooks (1981) p. 70

10 Don's room, like the nest of a foolish bird.
Geoffrey Madan's Notebooks (1981) p. 70

11 Conservative ideal of freedom and progress: everyone
to have an unfettered opportunity of remaining
exactly where they are.
Geoffrey Madan's Notebooks (1981) p. 70

12 The dust of exploded beliefs may make a fine sunset.
Livre sans nom: Twelve Reflections (privately printed 1934)
no. 12

Salvador de Madariaga 1886–1978

Spanish writer and diplomat

13 Since, in the main, it is not armaments that cause
wars but wars (or the fears thereof) that cause
armaments, it follows that every nation will at every
moment strive to keep its armament in an efficient
state as required by its fear, otherwise styled security.
Morning Without Noon (1974) pt. 1, ch. 9

Samuel Madden 1686–1765

Irish poet

14 Words are men's daughters, but God's sons are things.
Boulter's Monument (1745) l. 377. Cf. Johnson 367:20

James Madison 1751–1836

4th President of the USA

15 Liberty is to faction what air is to fire, an ailment
without which it instantly expires. But it could not be
less folly to abolish liberty, which is essential to
political life, because it nourishes faction than it would
be to wish the annihilation of air, which is essential to
animal life, because it imparts to fire its destructive
agency.
The Federalist (1787) no. 10

16 The diversity in the faculties of men, from which the
rights of property originate, is not less an insuperable
obstacle to a uniformity of interests. The protection of
these faculties is the first object of government. From
the protection of different and unequal faculties of
acquiring property, the possession of different degrees
and kinds of property immediately results.
The Federalist (1787) no. 10

Maurice Maeterlinck 1862–1949

Belgian poet, playwright, and essayist

17 *Il n'y a pas de morts.*
There are no dead.
L'Oiseau bleu (1909) act 4

William Connor Magee 1821–91

English prelate

18 It would be better that England should be free than
that England should be compulsorily sober.
Speech on the Intoxicating Liquor Bill in *Hansard* (House of
Lords) 2 May 1872, col. 86

Magna Carta

Political charter signed by King John at Runnymede,
1215

19 *Quod Anglicana ecclesia libera sit.*
That the English Church shall be free.
Clause 1

1 *Nullius liber homo capiatur, vel imprisonetur, aut*
  dissaisiatur, aut utlagetur, aut exuletur, aut aliquo modo
  destruator, nec super eum ibimus, nec super eum
  mittemus, nisi per legale judicium parium suorum vel per
  legem terrae.

  No free man shall be taken or imprisoned or
  dispossessed, or outlawed or exiled, or in any way
  destroyed, nor will we go upon him, nor will we send
  against him except by the lawful judgement of his
  peers or by the law of the land.
    Clause 39

2 *Nulli vendemus, nulli negabimus aut differemus, rectum*
  aut justitiam.

  To no man will we sell, or deny, or delay, right or
  justice.
    Clause 40

Alfred T. Mahan 1840–1914

American naval officer and historian

3 Those far distant, storm-beaten ships, upon which the
  Grand Army never looked, stood between it and the
  dominion of the world.
    The Influence of Sea Power upon the French Revolution and
    Empire 1793–1812 (1892) vol. 2, ch. 15

Gustav Mahler 1860–1911

Austrian composer

4 Fortissimo at last!
    On seeing Niagara Falls, in K. Blaukopf *Gustav Mahler*
    (1973) ch. 8

Derek Mahon 1941–

Irish poet

5 'I am just going outside and may be some time.'
  The others nod, pretending not to know.
  At the heart of the ridiculous, the sublime.
    Antarctica (1985) title poem. Cf. Oates 497:9

Norman Mailer 1923–

American novelist and essayist

6 Sentimentality is the emotional promiscuity of those
  who have no sentiment.
    Cannibals and Christians (1966) p. 51

7 The horror of the Twentieth Century was the size of
  each event, and the paucity of its reverberation.
    A Fire on the Moon (1970) pt. 1, ch. 2

8 So we think of Marilyn who was every man's love
  affair with America, Marilyn Monroe who was blonde
  and beautiful and had a sweet little rinky-dink of
  a voice and all the cleanliness of all the clean
  American backyards.
    Marilyn (1973) p. 15

9 Ultimately a hero is a man who would argue with the
  Gods, and so awakens devils to contest his vision.
    The Presidential Papers (1976) Special Preface to the 1st
    Berkeley Edition

10 Hip is the sophistication of the wise primitive in
   a giant jungle.
    Voices of Dissent (1959) 'The White Negro'

Sir Henry Maine 1822–88

English jurist

11 The movement of the progressive societies has hitherto
   been a movement *from Status to Contract.*
    Ancient Law (1861) ch. 5

12 So great is the ascendancy of the Law of Actions in
   the infancy of Courts of Justice, that substantive law
   has at first the look of being gradually secreted in the
   interstices of procedure; and the early lawyer can only
   see the law through the envelope of its technical
   forms.
    Dissertations on Early Law and Custom (1883) ch. 11

13 Except the blind forces of Nature, nothing moves in
   this world which is not Greek in its origin.
    Village Communities (3rd ed., 1876) p. 238

Josephe de Maistre 1753–1821

French writer and diplomat

14 *Toute nation a le gouvernement qu'elle mérite.*

   Every country has the government it deserves.
    Lettres et Opuscules Inédits (1851) vol. 1, letter 53
    (15 August 1811)

Bernard Malamud 1914–86

American novelist and short-story writer

15 The past exudes legend: one can't make pure clay of
   time's mud. There is no life that can be recaptured
   wholly; as it was. Which is to say that all biography is
   ultimately fiction.
    Dubin's Lives (1979) p. 20

Stéphane Mallarmé 1842–98

French poet

16 *La chair est triste, hélas! et j'ai lu tous les livres.*

   The flesh, alas, is wearied; and I have read all the
   books there are.
    'Brise Marin' (1887)

17 *Prélude à l'après-midi d'un faune.*

   Prelude to the afternoon of a fawn.
    Title of poem (c.1865)

18 *Le vierge, le vivace et le bel aujourd'hui.*

   That virgin, vital, fine day: today.
    Plusieurs Sonnets (1881) no. 1

19 *Un coup de dés jamais n'abolira le hasard.*

   A throw of the dice will never eliminate chance.
    Title of poem (1897)

David Mallet (or Malloch) c.1705–65

Scottish poet

20 O grant me, Heaven, a middle state,
   Neither too humble nor too great;
   More than enough, for nature's ends,
   With something left to treat my friends.
    'Imitation of Horace'. Cf. Horace 351:9

1 And thrice he called on Margaret's name,
And thrice he wept full sore:
Then laid his cheek to her cold grave.
And word spake never more.
   'William and Margaret' l. 65

George Leigh Mallory 1886–1924

British mountaineer

2 Because it's there.
   On being asked why he wanted to climb Mount Everest, in
   New York Times 18 March 1923

Sir Thomas Malory d. 1471

English writer

3 Whoso pulleth out this sword of this stone and anvil is
rightwise King born of all England.
   Le Morte D'Arthur (finished 1470, printed by Caxton 1485)
   bk. 1, ch. 4

4 Me repenteth, said Merlin; because of the death of that
lady thou shalt strike a stroke most dolorous that ever
man struck, except the stroke of our Lord, for thou
shalt hurt the truest knight and the man of most
worship that now liveth, and through that stroke
three kingdoms shall be in great poverty, misery and
wretchedness twelve years, and the knight shall not be
whole of that wound for many years.
   Le Morte D'Arthur (1485) bk. 2, ch. 8

5 Ah, my little son, thou hast murdered thy mother!
And therefore I suppose thou that art a murderer so
young, thou art full likely to be a manly man in thine
age ... When he is christened let call him Tristram,
that is as much to say as a sorrowful birth.
   Le Morte D'Arthur (1485) bk. 8, ch. 1

6 Meanwhile came Sir Palomides, the good knight,
following the questing beast that had in shape like
a serpent's head and a body like a leopard, buttocked
like a lion and footed like a hart. And in his body there
was such a noise as it had been twenty couple of
hounds questing, and such noise that beast made
wheresomever he went.
   Le Morte D'Arthur (1485) bk. 9, ch. 12 (*questing* yelping)

7 God defend me, said Dinadan, for the joy of love is too
short, and the sorrow thereof, and what cometh
thereof, dureth over long.
   Le Morte D'Arthur (1485) bk. 10, ch. 56

8 Fair lord, salute me to my lord, Sir Launcelot, my
father, and as soon as ye see him, bid him remember
of this unstable world.
   Le Morte D'Arthur (1485) bk. 17, ch. 22

9 Thus endeth the story of the Sangreal, that was briefly
drawn out of French into English, the which is a story
chronicled for one of the truest and the holiest that is
in this world.
   Le Morte D'Arthur (1485) bk. 17, ch. 23

10 Therefore all ye that be lovers call unto your
remembrance the month of May, like as did Queen
Guenevere, for whom I make here a little mention,
that while she lived she was a true lover, and therefore
she had a good end.
   Le Morte D'Arthur (1485) bk. 18, ch. 25

11 Through this man and me hath all this war been
wrought, and the death of the most noblest knights of
the world; for through our love that we have loved
together is my most noble lord slain.
   Le Morte D'Arthur (1485) bk. 21, ch. 9

12 Wherefore, madam, I pray you kiss me and never no
more. Nay, said the queen, that shall I never do, but
abstain you from such works: and they departed. But
there was never so hard an hearted man but he would
have wept to see the dolour that they made.
   Le Morte D'Arthur (1485) bk. 21, ch. 10

13 Said Sir Ector ... Sir Launcelot ... thou wert never
matched of earthly knight's hand; and thou wert the
courteoust knight that ever bare shield; and thou wert
the truest friend to thy lover that ever bestrad horse;
and thou wert the truest lover of a sinful man that
ever loved woman; and thou wert the kindest man
that ever struck with sword; and thou wert the
goodliest person that ever came among press of
knights; and thou wert the meekest man and the
gentlest that ever ate in hall among ladies; and thou
wert the sternest knight to thy mortal foe that ever
put spear in the rest.
   Le Morte D'Arthur (1485) bk. 21, ch. 13

André Malraux 1901–76

French novelist, essayist, and art critic

14 *La Condition humaine.*

The human condition.
   Title of book (1933)

15 *Il n'y a pas cinquante manières de combattre, il n'y en a
qu'une, c'est d'être vainqueur. Ni la révolution ni la guerre
ne consistent à se plaire à soi-même.*

There are not fifty ways of fighting, there's only one,
and that's to win. Neither revolution nor war consists
in doing what one pleases.
   L'Espoir (1937) pt. 2, sect. 2, ch. 12

16 *L'homme sait que le monde n'est pas à l'échelle humaine;
et il voudrait qu'il le fût.*

Man knows that the world is not made on a human
scale; and he wishes that it were.
   Les Noyers d'Altenburg (1945) pt. 2, ch. 3

17 *L'art est un anti-destin.*

Art is a revolt against fate.
   Les Voix du silence (1951) pt. 4, ch. 7

Thomas Robert Malthus 1766–1834

English political economist

18 Population, when unchecked, increases in
a geometrical ratio. Subsistence only increases in an
arithmetical ratio.
   Essay on the Principle of Population (1798) ch. 1

19 The perpetual struggle for room and food.
   Essay on the Principle of Population (1798) ch. 3

Lord Mancroft (Baron Mancroft) 1914–
British Conservative politician

1 Cricket—a game which the English, not being
a spiritual people, have invented in order to give
themselves some conception of eternity.
   Bees in Some Bonnets (1979) p. 185

W. R. Mandale

2 Up and down the City Road,
In and out the Eagle,
That's the way the money goes—
Pop goes the weasel!
   'Pop Goes the Weasel' (1853 song); also attributed to
   Charles Twiggs

Winnie Mandela 1934–
South African political activist

3 With that stick of matches, with our necklace, we
shall liberate this country.
   Speech in black townships, 14 April 1986, in *Guardian*
   15 April 1986

Osip Mandelstam 1892–1938
Russian poet

4 Это век волну колышет
Человеческой тоской,
И в траве гадюка дышит
Мерой века золотой.

И еще набухнут почки,
Брызнет зелени побег,
Но разбит твой позвоночник,
Мой прекрасный жалкий век.
И с бессмысленной улыбкой
Вспять глядишь, жесток и слаб,
Словно зверь, когда-то гибкий,
На следы своих не лап.

The age is rocking the wave
with human grief
to a golden beat, and an adder
is breathing in time with it in the grass.

The buds will go on swelling,
the rush of green will explode,
but your spine has been shattered,
my splendid derelict, my age.
Cruel and feeble, you'll look back
with the smile of a half-wit:
an animal that could run once,
staring at its own tracks.
   'The Age' (1923) (translated by C. M. Bowra)

5 Я изучил науку расставанья
В простоволосых жалобах ночных.

I've studied all the lore of separation
From grievances bare-headed in the night.
   'Tristia' (1919) (translated by C. M. Bowra)

6 Нам только в битвах выпадает жребий
А им дано гадая умереть.

Only in war our fate has consummation,
And divination too will perish them.
   'Tristia' (1919) (translated by C. M. Bowra)

7 Быть может, прежде губ уже родился шопот.

Perhaps my whisper was already born before my lips.
   Selected Poems (1973, translated by D. McDuff) 'Poems
   Published Posthumously' (written 1934)

Manilius (Marcus Manilius)
1st-century Latin poet

8 *Eripuitque Jovi fulmen viresque tonandi,*
et sonitum ventis concessit, nubibus ignem.

And snatched from Jove the lightning shaft and power
to thunder, and attributed the noise to the winds, the
flame to the clouds.
   Astronomica bk. 1, l. 104 (of human intelligence)

Joseph L. Mankiewicz 1909–
American screenwriter, producer, and director

9 Fasten your seat-belts, it's going to be a bumpy night.
   All About Eve (1950 film); spoken by Bette Davis

Mrs Manley 1663–1724
English novelist and playwright

10 No time like the present.
   The Lost Lover (1696) act 4, sc. 1

Horace Mann 1796–1859
American educationist

11 The object of punishment is, prevention from evil; it
never can be made impulsive to good.
   Lectures and Reports on Education (1867 ed.) Lecture 7

12 Lost, yesterday, somewhere between Sunrise and
Sunset, two golden hours, each set with sixty diamond
minutes. No reward is offered, for they are gone
forever.
   'Lost, Two Golden Hours'

Thomas Mann 1875–1955
German novelist

13 *Unsere Fähigkeit zum Ekel ist, wie ich anmerken möchte,*
desto grösser, je lebhafter unsere Begierde ist, das heisst:
je inbrünstiger wir eigentlich der Welt und ihren
Darbietungen anhangen.

Our capacity for disgust, let me observe, is in
proportion to our desires; that is in proportion to the
intensity of our attachment to the things of this world.
   The Confessions of Felix Krull (1954) pt. 1, ch. 5 (translated
   by Denver Lindley)

1 *Die Zeit hat in Wirklichkeit keine Einschnitte, es gibt kein Gewitter oder Drommetengetön beim Beginn eines neuen Monats oder Jahres, und selbst bei dem eines neuen Säkulums sind es nur wir Menschen, die schiessen und läuten.*

Time has no divisions to mark its passage, there is never a thunderstorm or blare of trumpets to announce the beginning of a new month or year. Even when a new century begins it is only we mortals who ring bells and fire off pistols.
The Magic Mountain (1924) ch. 4, sect. 4 (translated by H. T. Lowe-Porter)

2 *Warten heisst: Voraneilen, heisst: Zeit und Gegenwart nicht als Geschenk, sondern nur als Hindernis empfinden, ihren Eigenwert verneinen und vernichten und sie im Geist überspringen. Warten, sagt man, sei langweilig. Es ist jedoch ebensowohl oder sogar eigentlich kurzweilig, indem es Zeitmengen verschlingt, ohne sie um ihrer selbst willen zu leben und auszunutzen.*

And waiting means hurrying on ahead, it means regarding time and the present moment not as a boon, but an obstruction; it means making their actual content null and void, by mentally overleaping them. Waiting we say is long. We might just as well—or more accurately—say it is short, since it consumes whole spaces of time without our living them or making any use of them as such.
The Magic Mountain (1924) ch. 5, sect. 5 (translated by H. T. Lowe-Porter)

3 *Wir kommen aus dem Dunkel und gehen ins Dunkel, dazwischen liegen Erlebnisse; aber Anfang und Ende, Geburt und Tod, werden von uns nicht erlebt, sie haben keinen subjektiven Charakter, sie fallen als Vorgänge ganz ins Gebiet des Objektiven, so ist es damit.*

We come out of the dark and go into the dark again, and in between lie the experiences of our life. But the beginning and end, birth and death, we do not experience; they have no subjective character, they fall entirely in the category of objective events, and that's that.
The Magic Mountain (1924) ch. 6, sect. 8 (translated by H. T. Lowe-Porter)

4 *Unser Sterben ist mehr eine Angelegenheit der Weiterlebenden als unserer selbst.*

A man's dying is more the survivors' affair than his own.
The Magic Mountain (1924) ch. 6, sect. 8 (translated by H. T. Lowe-Porter)

5 *Die Zeit ist das Element der Erzählung, wie sie das Element des Lebens ist,—unlösbar damit verbunden, wie mit den Körpern im Raum. Sie ist auch das Element der Musik, als welche die Zeit misst und gliedert, sie kurzweilig und kostbar auf einmal macht.*

For time is the medium of narration, as it is the medium of life. Both are inextricably bound up with it, as are bodies in space. Similarly, time is the medium of music; music divides, measures, articulates time, and can shorten it, yet enhance its value, both at once.
The Magic Mountain (1924) ch. 7, sect. 1 (translated by H. T. Lowe-Porter)

Lord John Manners, 7th Duke of Rutland
1818–1906
English Tory politician and writer

6 Let wealth and commerce, laws and learning die,
But leave us still our old nobility!
England's Trust (1841) pt. 3, l. 227

Katherine Mansfield (Kathleen Mansfield Beauchamp) 1888–1923
New Zealand-born short-story writer

7 I hate the sort of licence that English people give themselves . . . to spread over and flop and roll about. I feel as fastidious as though I wrote with acid.
Letter to John Middleton Murray, 19 May 1913, in V. O. Sullivan and M. Scott (eds.) *Collected Letters* (1984) vol. 1

8 E. M. Forster never gets any further than warming the teapot. He's a rare fine hand at that. Feel this teapot. Is it not beautifully warm? Yes, but there ain't going to be no tea.
Journal (1927) p. 69 (May 1917)

9 Whenever I prepare for a journey I prepare as though for death. Should I never return, all is in order.
Journal (1927) p. 224 (29 January 1922)

William Murray, 1st Lord Mansfield
1705–93
Scottish lawyer and politician

10 The constitution does not allow reasons of state to influence our judgements: God forbid it should! We must not regard political consequences; however formidable soever they might be: if rebellion was the certain consequence, we are bound to say '*fiat justitia, ruat caelum*'.
Rex v. Wilkes, 8 June 1768, in *The English Reports* (1909) vol. 98, p. 347. Cf. Watson 722:8

11 Consider what you think justice requires, and decide accordingly. But never give your reasons; for your judgement will probably be right, but your reasons will certainly be wrong.
Advice to a newly appointed colonial governor ignorant in the law, in John Lord Campbell *The Lives of the Chief Justices of England* (1849) vol. 2, ch. 40

Richard Mant 1776–1848
Irish divine and ecclesiastical historian

12 Bright the vision that delighted
Once the sight of Judah's seer;
Sweet the countless tongues united
To entrance the prophet's ear.
'Bright the vision that delighted' (1837 hymn)

Mao Tse-tung 1893–1976
Chinese statesman; de facto leader of the Communist Party

13 Politics is war without bloodshed while war is politics with bloodshed.
Lecture, 1938, in *Selected Works* (1965) vol. 2, p. 153

1 Every Communist must grasp the truth, 'Political power grows out of the barrel of a gun'.
> Speech, 6 November 1938, in *Selected Works* (1965) vol. 2, p. 224

2 The atom bomb is a paper tiger which the United States reactionaries use to scare people. It looks terrible, but in fact it isn't ... All reactionaries are paper tigers.
> Interview, 1946, in *Selected Works* (1961) vol. 4, p. 100

3 Letting a hundred flowers blossom and a hundred schools of thought contend is the policy for promoting progress in the arts and the sciences and a flourishing socialist culture in our land.
> Speech in Peking, 27 February 1957, in *Quotations of Chairman Mao* (1966) p. 302

William Learned Marcy 1786–1857
American politician

4 The politicians of New York ... see nothing wrong in the rule, that to the victor belong the spoils of the enemy.
> Speech to the Senate, 25 January 1832, in James Parton *Life of Andrew Jackson* (1860) vol. 3, ch. 29

Miriam Margolyes
English actress

5 Life, if you're fat, is a minefield—you have to pick your way, otherwise you blow up.
> In *Observer* 9 June 1991

Marie-Antoinette 1755–93
Queen consort of Louis XVI

6 Qu'ils mangent de la brioche.

Let them eat cake.
> On being told that her people had no bread. In *Confessions* (1740) Rousseau refers to a similar remark being a well-known saying; in *Relation d'un Voyage à Bruxelles et à Coblentz en 1791* (1823) p. 59, Louis XVIII attributes 'Que ne mangent-ils de la croûte de pâté? [Why don't they eat pastry?]' to Marie-Thérèse (1638–83), wife of Louis XIV

Edwin Markham 1852–1940
American poet

7 Bowed by the weight of centuries he leans
Upon his hoe and gazes on the ground,
The emptiness of ages in his face,
And on his back the burden of the world.
Who made him dead to rapture and despair,
A thing that grieves not and that never hopes,
Stolid and stunned, a brother to the ox?
> 'The Man with the Hoe' (1899)

Johnny Marks 1909–85
American songwriter

8 Rudolph, the Red-Nosed Reindeer
Had a very shiny nose,
And if you ever saw it,
You would even say it glows.
> 'Rudolph, the Red-Nosed Reindeer' (1949 song)

Sarah, 1st Duchess of Marlborough
1660–1744

9 The Duke returned from the wars today and did pleasure me in his top-boots.
> Oral tradition, attributed in various forms. See, among others, I. Butler *Rule of Three* (1967) ch. 7

10 If I were young and handsome as I was, instead of old and faded as I am, and you could lay the empire of the world at my feet, you should never share the heart and hand that once belonged to John, Duke of Marlborough.
> Refusing an offer of marriage from the Duke of Somerset, in W. S. Churchill *Marlborough: His Life and Times* vol. 4 (1938) ch. 39

Bob Marley 1945–81
Jamaican reggae musician and songwriter

11 Get up, stand up
Stand up for your rights
Get up, stand up
Never give up the fight.
> 'Get up, Stand up' (1973 song)

12 I shot the sheriff
But I swear it was in self-defence
I shot the sheriff
And they say it is a capital offence.
> 'I Shot the Sheriff' (1974 song)

Christopher Marlowe 1564–93
English playwright and poet

13 Sweet Analytics, 'tis thou hast ravished me.
> *Doctor Faustus* (1604) act 1, sc. 1

14 I'll have them fly to India for gold,
Ransack the ocean for orient pearl.
> *Doctor Faustus* (1604) act 1, sc. 1

15 Why, this is hell, nor am I out of it:
Thinkst thou that I who saw the face of God,
And tasted the eternal joys of heaven,
Am not tormented with ten thousand hells
In being deprived of everlasting bliss!
> *Doctor Faustus* (1604) act 1, sc. 3

16 Hell hath no limits nor is circumscribed
In one self place, where we are is Hell,
And to be short, when all the world dissolves,
And every creature shall be purified,
All places shall be hell that are not heaven.
> *Doctor Faustus* (1604) act 2, sc. 1

17 Was this the face that launched a thousand ships,
And burnt the topless towers of Ilium?
Sweet Helen, make me immortal with a kiss!
Her lips suck forth my soul: see, where it flies!
Come Helen, come give me my soul again.
Here will I dwell, for heaven be in these lips,
And all is dross that is not Helena.
> *Doctor Faustus* (1604) act 5, sc. 1

1 Now hast thou but one bare hour to live,
  And then thou must be damned perpetually.
  Stand still, you ever-moving spheres of heaven,
  That time may cease, and midnight never come.
  Fair nature's eye, rise, rise again and make
  Perpetual day; or let this hour be but
  A year, a month, a week, a natural day,
  That Faustus may repent and save his soul.
  O lente lente currite noctis equi.
  The stars move still, time runs, the clock will strike,
  The devil will come, and Faustus must be damned.
  O I'll leap up to my God: who pulls me down?
  See, see, where Christ's blood streams in the
    firmament.
  One drop would save my soul, half a drop, ah my
    Christ.
    Doctor Faustus (1604) act 5, sc. 2

2 You stars that reigned at my nativity,
  Whose influence hath allotted death and hell,
  Now draw up Faustus like a foggy mist,
  Into the entrails of yon labouring cloud,
  That when you vomit forth into the air,
  My limbs may issue from your smoky mouths,
  So that my soul may but ascend to heaven.
    Doctor Faustus (1604) act 5, sc. 2

3 Ah, Pythagoras' metempsychosis, were that true,
  This soul should fly from me, and I be changed
  Unto some brutish beast.
    Doctor Faustus (1604) act 5, sc. 2

4 O soul, be changed into little water drops,
  And fall into the ocean, ne'er be found:
  My God, my God, look not so fierce on me.
    Doctor Faustus (1604) act 5, sc. 2

5 Cut is the branch that might have grown full straight,
  And burnèd is Apollo's laurel bough,
  That sometime grew within this learned man.
    Doctor Faustus (1604) epilogue

6 My men, like satyrs grazing on the lawns,
  Shall with their goat feet dance an antic hay.
    Edward II (1593) act 1, sc. 1

7 Stand still you watches of the element;
  All times and seasons, rest you at a stay,
  That Edward may be still fair England's king.
    Edward II (1593) act 5, sc. 1

8 Base Fortune, now I see, that in thy wheel
  There is a point, to which when men aspire,
  They tumble headlong down: that point I touched,
  And, seeing there was no place to mount up higher,
  Why should I grieve at my declining fall?
    Edward II (1593) act 5, sc. 6

9 His body was as straight as Circe's wand;
  Jove might have sipped out nectar from his hand.
  Even as delicious meat is to the taste,
  So was his neck in touching, and surpassed
  The white of Pelops' shoulder. I could tell ye
  How smooth his breast was, and how white his belly,
  And whose immortal fingers did imprint
  That heavenly path, with many a curious dint,
  That runs along his back.
    Hero and Leander (1598) First Sestiad, l. 61

10 It lies not in our power to love, or hate,
  For will in us is over-ruled by fate.
  When two are stripped, long ere the course begin,
  We wish that one should lose, the other win;
  And one especially do we affect
  Of two gold ingots, like in each respect.
  The reason no man knows; let it suffice,
  What we behold is censured by our eyes.
  Where both deliberate, the love is slight;
  Who ever loved that loved not at first sight?
    Hero and Leander (1598) First Sestiad, l. 167. Cf. *As You Like It* 569:15

11 And as she wept, her tears to pearl he turned,
  And wound them on his arm, and for her mourned.
    Hero and Leander (1598) First Sestiad, l. 375

12 I count religion but a childish toy,
  And hold there is no sin but ignorance.
    The Jew of Malta (c.1592) prologue

13 Thus methinks should men of judgement frame
  Their means of traffic from the vulgar trade,
  And, as their wealth increaseth, so enclose
  Infinite riches in a little room.
    The Jew of Malta (c.1592) act 1, sc. 1

14 As for myself, I walk abroad o' nights
  And kill sick people groaning under walls:
  Sometimes I go about and poison wells.
    The Jew of Malta (c.1592) act 2, sc. 3

15 BARNARDINE: Thou hast committed—
  BARABAS: Fornication? But that was in another
    country: and besides, the wench is dead.
    The Jew of Malta (c.1592) act 4, sc. 1

16 That like I best, that flies beyond my reach.
    The Massacre at Paris act 1, sc. 2

17 Come live with me, and be my love,
  And we will all the pleasures prove,
  That valleys, groves, hills and fields,
  Woods or steepy mountain yields.
    'The Passionate Shepherd to his Love'. Cf. Donne 251:19, Ralegh 535:11

18 By shallow rivers, to whose falls,
  Melodious birds sing madrigals.
    'The Passionate Shepherd to his Love'

19 From jigging veins of rhyming mother-wits,
  And such conceits as clownage keeps in pay,
  We'll lead you to the stately tents of war.
    Tamburlaine the Great (1590) pt. 1, prologue

20 With milk-white harts upon an ivory sled
  Thou shalt be drawn amidst the frozen pools,
  And scale the icy mountains' lofty tops,
  Which with thy beauty will be soon resolved.
    Tamburlaine the Great (1590) pt. 1, act 1, sc. 2

21 Our swords shall play the orators for us.
    Tamburlaine the Great (1590) pt. 1, act 1, sc. 2

22 His looks do menace heaven and dare the Gods.
  His fiery eyes are fixed upon the earth.
    Tamburlaine the Great (1590) pt. 1, act 1, sc. 2

23 Accurst be he that first invented war.
    Tamburlaine the Great (1590) pt. 1, act 2, sc. 4

24 Is it not passing fair to be a king,
  And ride in triumph through Persepolis?
    Tamburlaine the Great (1590) pt. 1, act 2, sc. 5

1 Nature that framed us of four elements,
Warring within our breasts for regiment,
Doth teach us all to have aspiring minds:
Our souls, whose faculties can comprehend
The wondrous architecture of the world:
And measure every wand'ring planet's course,
Still climbing after knowledge infinite,
And always moving as the restless spheres,
Wills us to wear ourselves and never rest,
Until we reach the ripest fruit of all,
That perfect bliss and sole felicity,
The sweet fruition of an earthly crown.
   Tamburlaine the Great (1590) pt. 1, act 2, sc. 7

2 Virtue is the fount whence honour springs.
   Tamburlaine the Great (1590) pt. 1, act 4, sc. 4

3 What is beauty saith my sufferings, then?
If all the pens that ever poets held
Had fed the feeling of their masters' thoughts,
And every sweetness that inspired their hearts,
Their minds, and muses on admired themes:
If all the heavenly quintessence they still
From their immortal flowers of Poesy,
Wherein as in a mirror we perceive
The highest reaches of a human wit;
If these had made one poem's period,
And all combined in beauty's worthiness,
Yet should there hover in their restless heads
One thought, one grace, one wonder at the least,
Which into words no virtue can digest.
   Tamburlaine the Great (1590) pt. 1, act 5, sc. 1

4 And every warrior that is rapt with love
Of fame, of valour, and of victory,
Must needs have beauty beat on his conceits.
   Tamburlaine the Great (1590) pt. 1, act 5, sc. 1

5 Ah fair Zenocrate, divine Zenocrate,
Fair is too foul an epithet for thee.
   Tamburlaine the Great (1590) pt. 1, act 5, sc. 5

6 Now walk the angels on the walls of heaven,
As sentinels to warn th' immortal souls,
To entertain divine Zenocrate.
   Tamburlaine the Great (1590) pt. 2, act 2, sc. 4

7 Yet let me kiss my Lord before I die,
And let me die with kissing of my Lord.
   Tamburlaine the Great (1590) pt. 2, act 2, sc. 4

8 More childish valorous than manly wise.
   Tamburlaine the Great (1590) pt. 2, act 4, sc. 1

9 Holla, ye pampered jades of Asia!
What, can ye draw but twenty miles a day . . . ?
   Tamburlaine the Great (1590) pt. 2, act 4, sc. 3

Don Marquis 1878–1937

American poet and journalist

10 procrastination is the
art of keeping
up with yesterday.
   archy and mehitabel (1927) 'certain maxims of archy'

11 an optimist is a guy
that has never had
much experience.
   archy and mehitabel (1927) 'certain maxims of archy'

12 but wotthehell
archy wotthehell
it s cheerio
my deario that
pulls a lady through.
   archy and mehitabel (1927) 'cheerio, my deario'

13 I have got you out here
in the great open spaces
where cats are cats.
   archy and mehitabel (1927) 'mehitabel has an adventure'

14 but wotthehell archy wotthehell
jamais triste archy jamais triste
that is my motto.
   archy and mehitabel (1927) 'mehitabel sees paris'

15 but wotthehell wotthehell
oh i should worry and fret
death and I will coquette
there s a dance in the old dame yet
toujours gai toujours gai.
   archy and mehitabel (1927) 'the song of mehitabel'

16 boss there is always
a comforting thought
in time of trouble when
it is not our trouble.
   archy does his part (1935) 'comforting thoughts'

17 honesty is a good
thing but
it is not profitable to
its possessor
unless it is
kept under control.
   archys life of mehitabel (1933) 'archygrams'

18 did you ever
notice that when
a politician
does get an idea
he usually
gets it all wrong.
   archys life of mehitabel (1933) 'archygrams'

19 now and then
there is a person born
who is so unlucky
that he runs into accidents
which started to happen
to somebody else.
   archys life of mehitabel (1933) 'archy says'

20 Writing a book of poetry is like dropping a rose petal
down the Grand Canyon and waiting for the echo.
   In E. Anthony *O Rare Don Marquis* (1962) p. 146

21 The art of newspaper paragraphing is to stroke
a platitude until it purrs like an epigram.
   In E. Anthony *O Rare Don Marquis* (1962) p. 354

John Marriot 1780–1825
English clergyman

1 Thou, whose eternal Word
  Chaos and darkness heard,
  And took their flight,
  Hear us, we humbly pray,
  And, where the Gospel-day
  Sheds not its glorious ray,
  Let there be light!
    'Thou, whose eternal Word' (hymn written *c*.1813);
    'almighty' substituted for 'eternal' from 1861

Frederick Marryat 1792–1848
English naval captain and novelist

2 There's no getting blood out of a turnip.
    Japhet, in Search of a Father (1836) ch. 4

3 As savage as a bear with a sore head.
    The King's Own (1830) vol. 2, ch. 6

4 If you please, ma'am, it was a very little one.
    Mr Midshipman Easy (1836) ch. 3 (the nurse, excusing her
    illegitimate baby)

5 All zeal . . . all zeal, Mr Easy.
    Mr Midshipman Easy (1836) ch. 9

Arthur Marshall 1910–89
British journalist and former schoolmaster

6 Oh My! Bertha's got a bang on the boko. Keep a stiff
  upper lip, Bertha dear. What, knocked a tooth out?
  Never mind, dear, laugh it off, laugh it off; it's all part
  of life's rich pageant.
    The Games Mistress (recorded monologue, 1937)

Thomas R. Marshall 1854–1925
American politician

7 What this country needs is a really good 5-cent cigar.
    In *New York Tribune* 4 January 1920, pt. 7, p. 1

John Marston 1576–1634
English poet

8 Foul canker of fair virtuous action,
  Vile blaster of the freshest blooms on earth,
  Envy's abhorrèd child, Detraction,
  I here expose, to thy all-tainting breath,
  The issue of my brain: snarl, rail, bark, bite,
  Know that my spirit scorns Detraction's spite.
    The Scourge of Villainy (1598) 'To Detraction I present my
    Poesy'

9 My mind disdains the dungy muddy scum
  Of abject thoughts and Envy's raging hate.
    The Scourge of Villainy (1598) 'To Detraction I present my
    Poesy'

10 'A man, a man!' 'Peace, Cynic, yon is one:
   A complete soul of all perfection.'
   'What, mean'st thou him that walks all
       open-breasted,
   Drawn through the ear, with ribands, plumy-crested;
   He that doth snort in fat-fed luxury,
   And gapes for some grinding monopoly;
   He that in effeminate invention,
   In beastly source of all pollution,
   In riot, lust, and fleshly seeming sweetness,
   Sleeps sound, secure, under the shade of greatness?
    Satire VII (1598)

Martial AD *c*.40–*c*.104
Spanish-born Latin epigrammatist

11 *Non est, crede mihi, sapientis dicere 'Vivam':*
   Sera nimis vita est crastina: vive hodie.
   Believe me, wise men don't say 'I shall live to do that',
   tomorrow's life's too late; live today.
    Epigrammata bk. 1, no. 15

12 *Non amo te, Sabidi, nec possum dicere quare:*
   Hoc tantum possum dicere, non amo te.
   I don't love you, Sabidius, and I can't tell you why;
   all I can tell you is this, that I don't love you.
    Epigrammata bk. 1, no. 32. Cf. Brown 145:1

13 *Laudant illa sed ista legunt.*
   They praise those works, but read these.
    Epigrammata bk. 4, no. 49

14   *Bonosque*
   Soles effugere atque abire sentit,
   Qui nobis pereunt et imputantur.
   Each of us feels the good days speed and depart, and
   they're lost to us and counted against us.
    Epigrammata bk. 5, no. 20

15 *Non est vivere, sed valere vita est.*
   Life's not just being alive, but being well.
    Epigrammata bk. 6, no. 70

16 *Difficilis facilis, iucundus acerbus es idem:*
   Nec tecum possum vivere nec sine te.
   Difficult or easy, pleasant or bitter, you are the same
   you: I cannot live with you—or without you.
    Epigrammata bk. 12, no. 46(47)

17 *Rus in urbe.*
   Country in the town.
    Epigrammata bk. 12, no. 57

Andrew Marvell 1621–78
English poet

18 Where the remote Bermudas ride
   In the ocean's bosom unespied.
    'Bermudas' (*c*.1653)

19 He hangs in shades the orange bright,
   Like golden lamps in a green night.
    'Bermudas' (*c*.1653)

20 And makes the hollow seas, that roar,
   Proclaim the ambergris on shore.
   He cast (of which we rather boast)
   The gospel's pearl upon our coast.
    'Bermudas' (*c*.1653)

1 Oh let our voice his praise exalt,
  Till it arrive at heaven's vault:
  Which thence (perhaps) rebounding, may
  Echo beyond the Mexique Bay.
  'Bermudas' (c.1653)

2 My love is of a birth as rare
  As 'tis for object strange and high:
  It was begotten by Despair
  Upon Impossibility.

  Magnanimous Despair alone
  Could show me so divine a thing,
  Where feeble Hope could ne'er have flown
  But vainly flapped its tinsel wing.
  'The Definition of Love' (1681)

3 As lines (so loves) oblique may well
  Themselves in every angle greet:
  But ours so truly parallel,
  Though infinite, can never meet.

  Therefore the love which us doth bind,
  But Fate so enviously debars,
  Is the conjunction of the mind,
  And opposition of the stars.
  'The Definition of Love' (1681)

4 Choosing each stone, and poising every weight,
  Trying the measures of the breadth and height;
  Here pulling down, and there erecting new,
  Founding a firm state by proportions true.
  'The First Anniversary of the Government under His
  Highness the Lord Protector, 1655' l. 245

5 How vainly men themselves amaze
  To win the palm, the oak, or bays,
  And their uncessant labours see
  Crowned from some single herb or tree,
  Whose short and narrow vergèd shade
  Does prudently their toils upbraid,
  While all flowers and all trees do close
  To weave the garlands of repose.
  'The Garden' (1681) st. 1

6 Fair Quiet, have I found thee here,
  And Innocence, thy sister dear!
  'The Garden' (1681) st. 2

7 Society is all but rude,
  To this delicious solitude.
  'The Garden' (1681) st. 2

8 The gods, that mortal beauty chase,
  Still in a tree did end their race.
  Apollo hunted Daphne so,
  Only that she might laurel grow.
  And Pan did after Syrinx speed,
  Not as a nymph, but for a reed.
  'The Garden' (1681) st. 4

9 What wondrous life is this I lead!
  Ripe apples drop about my head;
  The luscious clusters of the vine
  Upon my mouth do crush their wine;
  The nectarine, and curious peach,
  Into my hands themselves do reach;
  Stumbling on melons, as I pass,
  Ensnared with flowers, I fall on grass.
  'The Garden' (1681) st. 5

10 Meanwhile the mind, from pleasure less,
   Withdraws into its happiness.
   'The Garden' (1681) st. 6

11 Annihilating all that's made
   To a green thought in a green shade.
   'The Garden' (1681) st. 6

12 Here at the fountain's sliding foot,
   Or at some fruit-tree's mossy root,
   Casting the body's vest aside,
   My soul into the boughs does glide.
   'The Garden' (1681) st. 7

13 Such was that happy garden-state,
   While man there walked without a mate.
   'The Garden' (1681) st. 8

14 But 'twas beyond a mortal's share
   To wander solitary there:
   Two paradises 'twere in one
   To live in paradise alone.
   'The Garden' (1681) st. 8

15 *He* nothing common did or mean
   Upon that memorable scene:
   But with his keener eye
   The axe's edge did try:
   Nor called the gods with vulgar spite
   To vindicate his helpless right,
   But bowed his comely head,
   Down as upon a bed.
   'An Horatian Ode upon Cromwell's Return from Ireland'
   (written 1650) l. 57 (on the execution of Charles I)

16 And now the Irish are ashamed
   To see themselves in one year tamed:
   So much one man can do,
   That does both act and know.
   'An Horatian Ode upon Cromwell's Return from Ireland'
   (written 1650) l. 73

17 Ye living lamps, by whose dear light
   The nightingale does sit so late,
   And studying all the summer night,
   Her matchless songs does meditate;

   Ye country comets, that portend
   No war, nor prince's funeral,
   Shining unto no higher end
   Then to presage the grass's fall.
   'The Mower to the Glow-worms' (1681)

18 It is a wondrous thing, how fleet
   'Twas on those little silver feet.
   With what a pretty skipping grace,
   It oft would challenge me the race:
   And when 't had left me far away,
   'Twould stay, and run again, and stay.
   For it was nimbler much than hinds;
   And trod, as on the foúr winds.
   'The Nymph Complaining for the Death of her Fawn'
   (1681) l. 63

19 I have a garden of my own
   But so with roses overgrown,
   And lilies, that you would it guess
   To be a little wilderness.
   'The Nymph Complaining for the Death of her Fawn'
   (1681) l. 71

20 Had it lived long, it would have been
   Lilies without, roses within.
   'The Nymph Complaining for the Death of her Fawn'
   (1681) l. 91

1 For though the whole world cannot show such
   another,
   Yet we'd better by far have him than his brother.
   'The Statue in Stocks-Market' (1689) (on Charles II)

2 Had we but world enough, and time,
   This coyness, lady, were no crime.
   We would sit down, and think which way
   To walk, and pass our long love's day.
   Thou by the Indian Ganges' side
   Shouldst rubies find: I by the tide
   Of Humber would complain. I would
   Love you ten years before the flood:
   And you should, if you please, refuse
   Till the conversion of the Jews.
   My vegetable love should grow
   Vaster than empires, and more slow.
   'To His Coy Mistress' (1681) l. 1

3 But at my back I always hear
   Time's wingèd chariot hurrying near:
   And yonder all before us lie
   Deserts of vast eternity.
   Thy beauty shall no more be found;
   Nor, in thy marble vault, shall sound
   My echoing song: then worms shall try
   That long preserved virginity:
   And your quaint honour turn to dust;
   And into ashes all my lust.
   The grave's a fine and private place,
   But none, I think, do there embrace.
   'To His Coy Mistress' (1681) l. 21

4 Let us roll all our strength, and all
   Our sweetness, up into one ball:
   And tear our pleasures with rough strife,
   Thorough the iron gates of life.
   Thus, though we cannot make our sun
   Stand still, yet we will make him run.
   'To His Coy Mistress' (1681) l. 41

5 He is translation's thief that addeth more,
   As much as he that taketh from the store
   Of the first author.
   'To His Worthy Friend Dr Witty' (1651)

6 What need of all this marble crust
   T'impark the wanton mote of dust.
   'Upon Appleton House' (1681) st. 3

7 A stately frontispiece of poor
   Adorns without the open door:
   Nor less the rooms within commends
   Daily new furniture of friends.
   The House was built upon the place
   Only as for a mark of grace;
   And for an inn to entertain
   Its lord a while, but not remain.
   'Upon Appleton House' (1681) st. 9

8 Oh thou, that dear and happy isle
   The garden of the world ere while,
   Thou paradise of four seas,
   Which heaven planted us to please,
   But, to exclude the world, did guard
   With watery if not flaming sword;
   What luckless apple did we taste,
   To make us mortal, and thee waste?
   'Upon Appleton House' (1681) st. 41

9 For he did, with his utmost skill,
   Ambition weed, but conscience till—
   Conscience, that heaven-nursèd plant,
   Which most our earthy gardens want.
   A prickling leaf it bears, and such
   As that which shrinks at every touch;
   But flowers eternal, and divine,
   That in the crowns of saints do shine.
   'Upon Appleton House' (1681) st. 45

10 And now to the abyss I pass
   Of that unfathomable grass,
   Where men like grasshoppers appear,
   But grasshoppers are giants there:
   They, in their squeaking laugh, contemn
   Us as we walk more low than them:
   And, from the precipices tall
   Of the green spires, to us do call.
   'Upon Appleton House' (1681) st. 47

11 Unhappy birds! what does it boot
   To build below the grass's root,
   When lowness is unsafe as height,
   And chance o'ertakes, what 'scapeth spite?
   'Upon Appleton House' (1681) st. 52

12 'Tis not what once it was, the world,
   But a rude heap together hurled.
   'Upon Appleton House' (1681) st. 96

13 But now the salmon-fishers moist
   Their leathern boats begin to hoist;
   And, like Antipodes in shoes,
   Have shod their heads in their canoes.
   How tortoise-like, but not so slow,
   These rational amphibii go!
   'Upon Appleton House' (1681) st. 97

Holt Marvell
English songwriter

14 A cigarette that bears a lipstick's traces,
   An airline ticket to romantic places;
   And still my heart has wings
   These foolish things
   Remind me of you.
   'These Foolish Things Remind Me of You' (1935 song)

Chico Marx 1891–1961
American film comedian

15 I wasn't kissing her, I was just whispering in her
   mouth.
   On being discovered by his wife with a chorus girl, in
   Groucho Marx and Richard J. Anobile *Marx Brothers
   Scrapbook* (1973) ch. 24

Groucho Marx 1895–1977
American film comedian

16 PLEASE ACCEPT MY RESIGNATION. I DON'T WANT TO
   BELONG TO ANY CLUB THAT WILL ACCEPT ME AS A MEMBER.
   Groucho and Me (1959) ch. 26

17 Either he's dead, or my watch has stopped.
   In *A Day at the Races* (1937 film; script by Robert Pirosh,
   George Seaton, and George Oppenheimer)

1 I never forget a face, but in your case I'll be glad to make an exception.

    In Leo Rosten *People I have Loved, Known or Admired* (1970) 'Groucho'

Karl Marx 1818–83

German political philosopher; founder of modern Communism

2 Religion . . . is the opium of the people.

    A Contribution to the Critique of Hegel's Philosophy of Right (1843–4) introduction. Cf. Kingsley 398:1

3 Mankind always sets itself only such problems as it can solve; since, looking at the matter more closely, it will always be found that the task itself arises only when the material conditions for its solution already exist or are at least in the process of formation.

    A Contribution to the Critique of Political Economy (1859) preface (translated by D. McLellan)

4 It is not the consciousness of men that determines their being, but, on the contrary, their social being that determines their consciousness.

    A Contribution to the Critique of Political Economy (1859) preface (translated by D. McLellan)

5 From each according to his abilities, to each according to his needs.

    Critique of the Gotha Programme (written 1875, but of earlier origin). See Morelly *Code de la nature* (1755) pt. 4, p. 190, and J. J. L. Blanc *Organisation du travail* (1839) p. 126 (who, in quoting Saint-Simon, rejects the notion) for possible sources. Cf. Bakunin 47:23

6 And even when a society has got upon the right track for the discovery of the natural laws of its movement—and it is the ultimate aim of this work, to lay bare the economic law of motion of modern society—it can neither clear by bold leaps, nor remove by legal enactments, the obstacles offered by the successive phases of its normal development. But it can shorten and lessen the birth-pangs.

    Das Kapital (1st German ed., 1867) preface (25 July 1865)

7 Hegel says somewhere that all great events and personalities in world history reappear in one fashion or another. He forgot to add: the first time as tragedy, the second as farce.

    The Eighteenth Brumaire of Louis Bonaparte (1852) sect. 1. Cf. Hegel 330:7

8 The philosophers have only interpreted the world in various ways; the point is to change it.

    Theses on Feuerbach (written 1845, published 1888) no. 11

9 What I did that was new was to prove . . . that the class struggle necessarily leads to the dictatorship of the proletariat.

    Letter to Georg Weydemeyer 5 March 1852. The phrase 'dictatorship of the proletariat' had been used earlier in the Constitution of the World Society of Revolutionary Communists (1850), signed by Marx and others. Marx claimed that the phrase had been coined by Auguste Blanqui (1805–81), but it has not been found in this form in Blanqui's work. See D. Fernbach (ed.) *Karl Marx: The Revolutions of 1848: Political Writings* (1973) vol. 1, p. 24

10 All I know is that I am not a Marxist.

    Attributed in a letter from Friedrich Engels to Conrad Schmidt, 5 August 1890; in Karl Marx and Friedrich Engels *Correspondence* (1934) p. 472

Karl Marx 1818–83 *and* Friedrich Engels 1820–95

Co-founders of modern Communism

11 A spectre is haunting Europe—the spectre of Communism.

    The Communist Manifesto (1848) opening words

12 The history of all hitherto existing society is the history of class struggles.

    The Communist Manifesto (1848) pt. 1

13 In place of the old bourgeois society, with its classes and class antagonists, we shall have an association, in which the free development of each is the free development of all.

    The Communist Manifesto (1848) pt. 2

14 The proletarians have nothing to lose but their chains. They have a world to win. WORKING MEN OF ALL COUNTRIES, UNITE!

    The Communist Manifesto (1848) *ad fin.* (from the 1888 translation by Samuel Moore, edited by Engels and commonly rendered 'Workers of the world, unite!'). See D. Fernbach (ed.) *Karl Marx: The Revolutions of 1848: Political Writings* (1973) vol. 1, p. 62

Queen Mary 1867–1953

Queen Consort of George V

15 All *this* thrown away for *that*.

    On returning home to Marlborough House, London after the abdication of her son, King Edward VIII, December 1936; in David Duff *George and Elizabeth* (1983) ch. 10

16 I do not think you have ever realised the shock, which the attitude you took up caused your family and the whole nation. It seemed inconceivable to those who had made such sacrifices during the war that you, as their King, refused a lesser sacrifice.

    Letter to the Duke of Windsor, July 1938, in J. Pope-Hennessy *Queen Mary* (1959) ch. 7

Mary, Queen of Scots 1542–87

Queen of Scotland, 1542–67

17 *En ma fin git mon commencement.*

In my end is my beginning.

    Motto embroidered with an emblem of her mother, Mary of Guise, and quoted in a letter from William Drummond of Hawthornden to Ben Jonson in 1619. See F. de Zulueta *Embroideries by Mary Stuart and Elizabeth Talbot* (1923) p. 5. Cf. Eliot 270:18

Mary Tudor (Mary I) 1516–58
Queen of England from 1553

1 When I am dead and opened, you shall find 'Calais' lying in my heart.
   Holinshed's Chronicles vol. 4 (1808) p. 137

John Masefield 1878–1967
English poet

2 Quinquireme of Nineveh from distant Ophir
   Rowing home to haven in sunny Palestine,
   With a cargo of ivory,
   And apes and peacocks,
   Sandalwood, cedarwood, and sweet white wine.
   'Cargoes' (1903). Cf. I Kings 75:25

3 Dirty British coaster with a salt-caked smoke stack,
   Butting through the Channel in the mad March days,
   With a cargo of Tyne coal,
   Road-rails, pig lead,
   Firewood, ironware, and cheap tin trays.
   'Cargoes' (1903)

4 In the dark womb where I began
   My mother's life made me a man.
   Through all the months of human birth
   Her beauty fed my common earth.
   I cannot see, nor breathe, nor stir,
   But through the death of some of her.
   'C. L. M.' (1910)

5 Jane brought the bowl of stewing gin
   And poured the egg and lemon in,
   And whisked it up and served it out
   While bawdy questions went about.
   Jack chucked her chin, and Jim accost her
   With bits out of the 'Maid of Gloster'.
   And fifteen arms went round her waist.
   (And then men ask, Are Barmaids Chaste?)
   'The Everlasting Mercy' (1911) st. 26

6 The corn that makes the holy bread
   By which the soul of man is fed,
   The holy bread, the food unpriced,
   Thy everlasting mercy, Christ.
   'The Everlasting Mercy' (1911) st. 86

7 I must go down to the sea again, to the lonely sea and the sky,
   And all I ask is a tall ship and a star to steer her by,
   And the wheel's kick and the wind's song and the white sail's shaking,
   And a grey mist on the sea's face and a grey dawn breaking.
   'Sea Fever' ('I must down to the seas' in the original of 1902, possibly a misprint)

8 I must go down to the sea again, for the call of the running tide
   Is a wild call and a clear call that may not be denied.
   'Sea Fever' (1902)

9 I must go down to the sea again, to the vagrant gypsy life,
   To the gull's way and the whale's way where the wind's like a whetted knife;
   And all I ask is a merry yarn from a laughing fellow-rover,
   And quiet sleep and a sweet dream when the long trick's over.
   'Sea Fever' (1902)

10 Death opens unknown doors. It is most grand to die.
   Pompey The Great (1910) act 2

Donald Mason 1913–
American naval officer

11 Sighted sub, sank same.
   Radio message, 28 January 1942, on sinking a Japanese submarine in the Atlantic region (the first US naval success in the war); in *New York Times* 27 February 1942

Philip Massinger 1583–1640
English playwright

12 Ambition, in a private man a vice,
   Is in a prince the virtue.
   The Bashful Lover (licensed 1636, published 1655) act 1, sc. 2

13   Pray enter
   You are learned Europeans and we worse
   Than ignorant Americans.
   The City Madam (licensed 1632, published 1658) act 3, sc. 3

14   Greatness, with private men
   Esteemed a blessing, is to me a curse;
   And we, whom, for our high births, they conclude
   The only freemen, are the only slaves.
   Happy the golden mean!
   The Great Duke of Florence (licensed 1627, printed 1635) act 1, sc. 1. Cf. Horace 351:9

15 Oh that thou hadst like others been all words,
   And no performance.
   The Parliament of Love (1624) act 4, sc. 2

16 Death has a thousand doors to let out life:
   I shall find one.
   A Very Woman (licensed 1634, published 1655) act 5, sc. 4. Cf. Fletcher 287:15, Seneca 563:2, Webster 725:22

Sir James Mathew 1830–1908
Irish judge

17 In England, justice is open to all—like the Ritz Hotel.
   In R. E. Megarry *Miscellany-at-Law* (1955) p. 254. Cf. Anonymous 13:14

Henri Matisse 1869–1954

French painter

1 *Ce que je rêve, c'est un art d'équilibre, de pureté, de tranquillité, sans sujet inquiétant ou préoccupant, qui soit ... un lénifiant, un calmant cérébral, quelque chose d'analogue à un bon fauteuil qui le délasse de ses fatigues physiques.*

What I dream of is an art of balance, of purity and serenity devoid of troubling or depressing subject matter ... a soothing, calming influence on the mind, rather like a good armchair which provides relaxation from physical fatigue.

Notes d'un peintre (1908), in Dominique Fourcade *Écrits et propos sur l'art* (1972) p. 30

W. Somerset Maugham 1874–1965

English novelist

2 Hypocrisy is the most difficult and nerve-racking vice that any man can pursue; it needs an unceasing vigilance and a rare detachment of spirit. It cannot, like adultery or gluttony, be practised at spare moments; it is a whole-time job.

Cakes and Ale (1930) ch. 1

3 From the earliest times the old have rubbed it into the young that they are wiser than they, and before the young had discovered what nonsense this was they were old too, and it profited them to carry on the imposture.

Cakes and Ale (1930) ch. 11

4 Poor Henry [James], he's spending eternity wandering round and round a stately park and the fence is just too high for him to peep over and they're having tea just too far away for him to hear what the countess is saying.

Cakes and Ale (1930) ch. 11

5 You can't learn too soon that the most useful thing about a principle is that it can always be sacrificed to expediency.

The Circle (1921) act 3

6 A woman will always sacrifice herself if you give her the opportunity. It is her favourite form of self-indulgence.

The Circle (1921) act 3

7 Impropriety is the soul of wit.

The Moon and Sixpence (1919) ch. 4

8 It is not true that suffering ennobles the character; happiness does that sometimes, but suffering, for the most part, makes men petty and vindictive.

The Moon and Sixpence (1919) ch. 17

9 A woman can forgive a man for the harm he does her, but she can never forgive him for the sacrifices he makes on her account.

The Moon and Sixpence (1919) ch. 41

10 Like all weak men he laid an exaggerated stress on not changing one's mind.

Of Human Bondage (1915) ch. 39

11 People ask you for criticism, but they only want praise.

Of Human Bondage (1915) ch. 50

12 Money is like a sixth sense without which you cannot make a complete use of the other five.

Of Human Bondage (1915) ch. 51

13 Few misfortunes can befall a boy which bring worse consequences than to have a really affectionate mother.

A Writer's Notebook (1949) p. 27 (written in 1896)

Bill Mauldin 1921–

American cartoonist

14 I feel like a fugitive from th' law of averages.

Cartoon caption in *Up Front* (1945)

James Maxton 1885–1946

British Labour politician

15 All I say is, if you cannot ride two horses you have no right in the circus.

Opposing disaffiliation of the Scottish Independent Labour Party from the Labour Party, in *Daily Herald* 12 January 1931 (often quoted ' ... no right in the bloody circus')

Vladimir Mayakovsky 1893–1930

Russian poet

16 Парадом развернув
моих страниц войска
А прохожу
по строчечному фронту.
Стихи стоят
свинцово-тяжело,
готовые и к смерти
и к бессмертной славе.

Deploying in a parade
the armies of my pages,
I pass in review
the front of my lines.
Verses stand
lead-heavily,
ready for death
and for immortal fame.

'At the Top of my Voice' (1929–30) (translated by C. M. Bowra)

17 Хотите —
... буду безукоризненно нежный,
не мужчина, а — облако в штанах!

If you wish—
... I'll be irreproachably tender;
not a man, but—a cloud in trousers!

'The Cloud in Trousers' (1915) (translated by Samuel Charteris)

1 Глухо.
Вселенная спит,
положив на лапу
с клещами звезд огромное ухо.

Not a sound. The universe sleeps, resting a huge ear
on its paw with mites of stars.
'The Cloud in Trousers' (1915) (translated by Samuel
Charteris)

2 Говоря по-нашему, рифма — бочка.
Бочка с динамитом. Строчка — фитиль.
Строчка додымит, взрывается строчка,
и город на воздух строфой летит.

In our language rhyme is a barrel. A barrel of
dynamite. The line is a fuse. The line smoulders to the
end and explodes; and the town is blown sky-high in
a stanza.
'Conversation with an Inspector of Taxes about Poetry'
(1926) (translated by Dmitri Obolensky)

3 Долг наш — реветь медногорлой сиреной
в тумане мещанья, у бурь в кипеньи.
Поэт всегда должник вселенной,
платящий на горе проценты и пени.

Our duty is to blare like brazen-throated horns in the
fog of philistinism and in seething storms. The poet is
always indebted to the universe, paying interest and
fines on sorrow.
'Conversation with an Inspector of Taxes about Poetry'
(1926) (translated by Dmitri Obolensky)

4 Я хочу
быть понят моей страной
а не буду понят, —
Что ж,
по родной стране
пройду стороной
как проходит
косой дождь.

I want to be understood by my country, and if I am
not—never mind, I will pass over my native land
sideways, as a slanted rain passes.
'Homewards' (1926) (translated by Lily Feiler)

5 Нам
любовь
гудит про то,
что опять
в работу пущен
сердца
выстывший мотор.

To us love says humming that the heart's stalled
motor has begun working again.
'Letter from Paris to Comrade Kostorov on the Nature of
Love' (1928) (translated by Samuel Charteris)

6 Бейте в площади бунтов топот!
Выше, гордых голов гряда!
Мы разливом второго потопа
перемоем миров города.

Tramp squares with rebellious treading!
Up heads! As proud peaks be seen!
In the second flood we are spreading
Every city on earth will be clean.
'Our March' (1917) (translated by C. M. Bowra)

7 Наша земля
Воздух — наш.
Нашу звезд алмазные копи.
И мы никогда,
никогда!
никому,
никому не позволим!
землю нашу ядрами рвать,
воздух наш раздирать остриями отточенных
копий.

Ours is the land.
The air—ours.
Ours the diamond mines of stars.
And we will never,
never!
Allow anyone,
anyone!
To ravage our land with shells,
to tear our air with sharpened spear points.
'Revolution: a Poet's Chronicle' (1917) (translated by C. M.
Bowra)

8 любовная лодка разбилась о быт
С тобой мы в расчете и не к чему перечень
взаимных болей бед и обид.

The love boat has crashed against the everyday. You
and I, we are quits, and there is no point in listing
mutual pains, sorrows, and hurts.
From an unfinished poem found among Mayakovsky's
papers, a variant of which he quoted in his suicide letter
12 April 1930

Jonathan Mayhew 1720–66
American divine

9 Rulers have no authority from God to do mischief.
*A Discourse Concerning Unlimited Submission and
Non-Resistance to the Higher Powers* (1750) p. 26

10 As soon as the prince sets himself up above the law,
he loses the king in the tyrant; he does to all intents
and purpose unking himself . . . And in such cases,
has no more right to be obeyed, than any inferior
officer who acts beyond his commission.
*A Discourse Concerning Unlimited Submission and
Non-Resistance to the Higher Powers* (1750) p. 45 n.

Margaret Mead 1901–78
American anthropologist

11 The knowledge that the personalities of the two sexes
are socially produced is congenial to every programme
that looks forward towards a planned order of society.
It is a two-edged sword.
Sex and Temperament in Three Primitive Societies (1935) pt. 4
'Conclusion'

Shepherd Mead 1914–
American advertising executive

12 How to succeed in business without really trying.
Title of book (1952)

Hughes Mearns 1875–1965

American writer

1 As I was walking up the stair
I met a man who wasn't there.
He wasn't there again today.
I wish, I wish he'd stay away.

> Lines written for *The Psycho-ed*, an amateur play, in
> Philadelphia, 1910 (set to music in 1939 as 'The Little
> Man Who Wasn't There')

Cosimo de' Medici 1389–1464

Italian statesman and patron of the arts

2 We read that we ought to forgive our enemies; but we
do not read that we ought to forgive our friends.

> In Francis Bacon *Apophthegms* (1625) no. 206 (speaking of
> what Bacon refers to as 'perfidious friends')

Lorenzo de' Medici 1449–92

Italian statesman and poet

3 *Quanto è bella giovinezza*
Che si fugge tuttavia!
Chi vuol esser lieto sia:
Di doman non ci è certezza.

How beautiful is youth, that is always slipping away!
Whoever wants to be happy, let him be so: of
tomorrow there's no knowing.

> 'Trionfo di Bacco e di Arianna'

Dame Nellie Melba (Helen Porter Mitchell)1861–1931

Australian operatic soprano

4 Sing 'em muck! It's all they can understand!

> Advice to Dame Clara Butt, prior to her departure for
> Australia, in W. H. Ponder *Clara Butt* (1928) ch. 12

William Lamb, 2nd Lord Melbourne 1779–1848

British Whig politician; Prime Minister 1834, 1835–41

5 Now, is it to lower the price of corn, or isn't it? It is
not much matter which we say, but mind, we must
all say *the same.*

> Attributed, in Walter Bagehot *The English Constitution*
> (1867) ch. 1, p. 16 n.

6 God help the Minister that meddles with art!

> In Lord David Cecil *Lord M* (1954) ch. 3

7 What I want is men who will support me when I am
in the wrong.

> Replying to a politician who said 'I will support you as long
> as you are in the right', in Lord David Cecil *Lord M* (1954)
> ch. 4

8 Damn it! Another Bishop dead! I believe they die to
vex me.

> Attributed, in Lord David Cecil *Lord M* (1954) ch. 4

9 I have always thought complaints of ill-usage
contemptible, whether from a seduced disappointed
girl or a turned-out Prime Minister.

> On being dismissed by William IV, in V. Dickinson (ed.)
> *Miss Eden's Letters* (1919) letter from Emily Eden to Mrs
> Lister, 23 November 1834

10 What all the wise men promised has not happened,
and what all the d—d fools said would happen has
come to pass.

> Of the Catholic Emancipation Act (1829), in H. Dunckley
> *Lord Melbourne* (1890) ch. 9

11 Things have come to a pretty pass when religion is
allowed to invade the sphere of private life.

> On hearing an evangelical sermon, in G. W. E. Russell
> *Collections and Recollections* (1898) ch. 6

Herman Melville 1819–91

American novelist and poet

12 That Calvinistic sense of innate depravity and original
sin from whose visitations, in some shape or other, no
deeply thinking mind is always and wholly free.

> *Hawthorne and His Mosses* (1850)

13 Genius, all over the world, stands hand in hand, and
one shock of recognition runs the whole circle round.

> *Hawthorne and His Mosses* (1850)

14 Call me Ishmael.

> *Moby Dick* (1851) ch. 1

15 Delight,—top-gallant delight is to him, who
acknowledges no law or lord, but the Lord his God,
and is only a patriot to heaven.

> *Moby Dick* (1851) ch. 9

16 But when a man's religion becomes really frantic;
when it is a positive torment to him; and, in fine,
makes this earth of ours an uncomfortable inn to
lodge in; then I think it high time to take that
individual aside and argue the point with him.

> *Moby Dick* (1851) ch. 17

17 A whaleship was my Yale College and my Harvard.

> *Moby Dick* (1851) ch. 24

18 This it is, that forever keeps God's true princes of the
Empire from the world's hustings; and leaves the
highest honours that this air can give, to those men
who become famous more through their infinite
inferiority to the choice hidden handful of the Divine
Inert, than through their undoubted superiority over
the dead level of the mass.

> *Moby Dick* (1851) ch. 33

19 Aye, toil as we may, we all sleep at last on the field.
Sleep? Aye, and rust amid greenness; as last year's
scythes flung down, and left in the half-cut swaths.

> *Moby Dick* (1851) ch. 132

20 Towards thee I roll, thou all-destroying but
unconquering whale . . . from hell's heart I stab at
thee.

> *Moby Dick* (1851) ch. 135

Gilles Ménage 1613–92

French scholar

1 *Comme nous nous entretenions de ce qui pouvait rendre heureux, je lui dis;* Sanitas sanitatum, et omnia sanitas.

While we were discussing what could make one happy, I said to him: *Sanitas sanitatum et omnia sanitas.*

From a conversation with Jean-Louis Guez de Balzac (1594–1654), in *Ménagiana* (1693) p. 166 (*sanitas* health). Cf. Vulgate 108:6

Menander 342–*c*.292 BC

Greek comic playwright

2 ὃν οἱ θεοὶ φιλοῦσιν ἀποθνῄσκει νέος.

Whom the gods love dies young.

Dis Exapaton fragment 4, in F. H. Sandbach (ed.) *Menandri Reliquiae Selectae* (1990)

3 ζῶμεν γὰρ οὐχ ὡς θέλομεν, ἀλλ' ὡς δυνάμεθα.

We live, not as we wish to, but as we can.

The Lady of Andros in *Menander: the Principal Fragments* (translated by F. G. Allinson, 1951) p. 316

H. L. Mencken 1880–1956

American journalist and literary critic

4 He [Calvin Coolidge] slept more than any other President, whether by day or by night. Nero fiddled, but Coolidge only snored.

American Mercury April 1933

5 The saddest life is that of a political aspirant under democracy. His failure is ignominious and his success is disgraceful.

Baltimore Evening Sun 9 December 1929

6 Love is the delusion that one woman differs from another.

Chrestomathy (1949) ch. 30. Cf. Shaw 637:3

7 Puritanism. The haunting fear that someone, somewhere, may be happy.

Chrestomathy (1949) ch. 30

8 Democracy is the theory that the common people know what they want, and deserve to get it good and hard.

A Little Book in C major (1916) p. 19

9 Conscience: the inner voice which warns us that someone may be looking.

A Little Book in C major (1916) p. 42

10 It is now quite lawful for a Catholic woman to avoid pregnancy by a resort to mathematics, though she is still forbidden to resort to physics and chemistry.

Notebooks (1956) 'Minority Report'

David Mercer 1928–80

English playwright

11 A suitable case for treatment.

Title of television play (1962); later filmed as *Morgan–A Suitable Case for Treatment* (1966)

Johnny Mercer 1909–76

American songwriter

12 You've got to ac-cent-tchu-ate the positive
Elim-my-nate the negative
Latch on to the affirmative
Don't mess with Mister In-between.

'Ac-cent-tchu-ate the Positive' (1944 song)

13 Jeepers Creepers—where you get them peepers?

'Jeepers Creepers' (1938 song); sung to a horse of the same name by Louis Armstrong in the film *Going Places* (1939)

14 We're drinking my friend,
To the end of a brief episode,
Make it one for my baby
And one more for the road.

'One For My Baby' (1943 song)

15 That old black magic.

Title of song (1942)

George Meredith 1828–1909

English novelist and poet

16 Thoughts of heroes were as good as warming-pans.

Beauchamp's Career (1876) ch. 4

17 A witty woman is a treasure; a witty beauty is a power.

Diana of the Crossways (1885) ch. 1

18 'Tis Ireland gives England her soldiers, her generals too.

Diana of the Crossways (1885) ch. 2

19 She was a lady of incisive features bound in stale parchment.

Diana of the Crossways (1885) ch. 14

20 There is nothing the body suffers the soul may not profit by.

Diana of the Crossways (1885) ch. 43

21 A Phoebus Apollo turned fasting friar.

The Egoist (1879) ch. 2

22 A dainty rogue in porcelain.

The Egoist (1879) ch. 5

23 Cynicism is intellectual dandyism without the coxcomb's feathers.

The Egoist (1879) ch. 7

24 In ... the Book of Egoism it is written: Possession without obligation to the object possessed approaches felicity.

The Egoist (1879) ch. 14

25 None of your dam punctilio.

One of Our Conquerors (1891) ch. 1

26 I expect that Woman will be the last thing civilized by Man.

The Ordeal of Richard Feverel (1859) ch. 1

27 In action Wisdom goes by majorities.

The Ordeal of Richard Feverel (1859) ch. 1

28 Who rises from prayer a better man, his prayer is answered.

The Ordeal of Richard Feverel (1859) ch. 12

29 The sun is coming down to earth, and walks the fields and the waters. The sun is coming down to earth, and the fields and the waters shout to him golden shouts.

The Ordeal of Richard Feverel (1859) ch. 19

1 Kissing don't last: cookery do!
   The Ordeal of Richard Feverel (1859) ch. 28

2 Speech is the small change of silence.
   The Ordeal of Richard Feverel (1859) ch. 34

3 Much benevolence of the passive order may be traced
   to a disinclination to inflict pain upon oneself.
   Vittoria (1866) ch. 42

4 The lark ascending.
   Title of poem (1881)

5 She whom I love is hard to catch and conquer,
   Hard, but O the glory of the winning were she
   won!
   'Love in the Valley' st. 2

6 On a starred night Prince Lucifer uprose.
   Tired of his dark dominion swung the fiend . . .
   He reached a middle height, and at the stars,
   Which are the brain of heaven, he looked, and
   sank
   Around the ancient track marched, rank on rank,
   The army of unalterable law.
   'Lucifer in Starlight' (1883)

7 'I play for Seasons; not Eternities!'
   Says Nature.
   Modern Love (1862) st. 13

8   In tragic life, God wot,
   No villain need be! Passions spin the plot:
   We are betrayed by what is false within.
   Modern Love (1862) st. 43

9 Ah, what a dusty answer gets the soul
   When hot for certainties in this our life!
   Modern Love (1862) st. 50

Owen Meredith (*Edward Robert Bulwer Lytton, 1st Earl of Lytton*)
1831–91

English poet and statesman; Viceroy of India, 1876–80

10 Genius does what it must, and Talent does what it
   can.
   'Last Words of a Sensitive Second-Rate Poet' (1868)

11 We may live without poetry, music and art;
   We may live without conscience, and live without
   heart;
   We may live without friends; we may live without
   books;
   But civilized man cannot live without cooks.

   He may live without books,—what is knowledge but
   grieving?
   He may live without hope,—what is hope but
   deceiving?
   He may live without love,—what is passion but
   pining?
   But where is the man that can live without dining?
   Lucile (1860) pt. 1, canto 2, sect. 24

James Merrill 1926–

American poet

12 The good grey guardians of art
   Patrol the halls on spongy shoes,
   Impartially protective, though
   Perhaps suspicious of Toulouse.
   Here dozes one against the wall,
   Disposed upon a funeral chair.
   A Degas dancer pirouettes
   Upon the parting of his hair.
   'Museum Piece' (1950)

13 Free me, I pray, to go in search of joys
   Unembroidered by your high, soft voice,
   Along that stony path the senses pave.
   'The Thousand and Second Night' (1973)

Dixon Lanier Merritt 1879–1972

14 Oh, a wondrous bird is the pelican!
   His beak holds more than his belican.
   He takes in his beak
   Food enough for a week.
   But I'll be darned if I know how the helican.
   In *Nashville Banner* 22 April 1913

Jean Meslier c.1664–1733

French priest

15 *Il me souvient à ce sujet d'un souhait que faisait autrefois un homme, qui n'avait ni science ni étude . . . Il souhaitait, disait-il . . . que tous les grands de la terre et que tous les nobles fussent pendus et étranglés avec les boyaux des prêtres. Pour ce qui est de moi . . . je souhaitais d'avoir les bras et la force d'Hercule pour purger le monde de tout vice et de toute iniquité, et pour avoir le plaisir d'assommer tous ces monstres d'erreurs et d'iniquité qui font gémir si pitoyablement tous les peuples de la terre.*

   I remember, on this matter, the wish made once by an ignorant, uneducated man . . . He said he wished . . . that all the great men in the world and all the nobility could be hanged, and strangled with the guts of priests. For myself . . . I wish I could have the strength of Hercules to purge the world of all vice and sin, and to have the pleasure of destroying all those monsters of error and sin [priests] who make all the peoples of the world groan so pitiably.
   Testament (ed. R. Charles, 1864) vol. 1, ch. 2 (often quoted '*Je voudrais . . . que le dernier des rois fût étranglé avec les boyaux du dernier prêtre* [I should like . . . the last of the kings to be strangled with the guts of the last priest]' or, in Diderot's version, '*Et des boyaux du dernier prêtre / Serrons le cou du dernier roi* [And [with] the guts of the last priest / Let's shake the neck of the last king]')

Methodist Service Book 1975

16 I am no longer my own, but yours. Put me to what
   you will, rank me with whom you will; put me to
   doing, put me to suffering; let me be employed for you
   or laid aside for you, exalted for you or brought low
   for you; let me be full, let me be empty; let me have
   all things, let me have nothing.
   The Covenant Prayer (based on the words of Richard
   Alleine in the First Covenant Service, 1782)

Prince Metternich 1773–1859

Austrian statesman

1 Religion, morality, legislation, economics, politics, administration, all seem to have become a common good and accessible to everyone. Science appears intuitive, experience has no value for the presumptuous; faith means nothing to him, and he substitutes for it the pretence of a personal conviction.

'Profession de foi' in *Aus Metternich's Nachgelassenen Papieren* (ed. A. von Klinkowström, 1880) vol. 3, p. 404

2 The word 'freedom' means for me not a point of departure but a genuine point of arrival. The point of departure is defined by the word 'order'. Freedom cannot exist without the concept of order.

Mein Politisches Testament in *Aus Metternich's Nachgelassenen Papieren* (ed. A. von Klinkowström, 1880) vol. 7, p. 636

3 I feel obliged to call to the supporters of the social uprising: Citizens of a dream-world, nothing is altered. On 14 March 1848, there was merely one man fewer.

Of his own downfall, in *Aus Metternich's Nachgelassenen Papieren* (ed. A. von Klinkowström, 1880) vol. 8, p. 233

4 *Der Kaiser ist Alles, Wien ist nichts!*

The Emperor is everything, Vienna is nothing.

Letter to Count Bombelles, 5 June 1848, in *Aus Metternich's Nachgelassenen Papieren* (ed. A. von Klinkowström, 1880) vol. 8, p. 426

5 The greatest gift of any statesman rests not in knowing what concessions to make, but recognising when to make them.

Concessionen und Nichtconcessionen (1852) in *Aus Metternich's Nachgelassenen Papieren* (ed. A. von Klinkowström, 1880) vol. 8, p. 562

6 *L'erreur n'a jamais approché de mon esprit.*

Error has never approached my spirit.

Addressed to Guizot in 1848, in François Pierre G. Guizot *Mémoires* (1858–67) vol. 4, p. 21

7 Italy is a geographical expression.

Discussing the Italian question with Palmerston in 1847; in *Mémoires, Documents, etc. de Metternich publiés par son fils* (1883) vol. 7, p. 415

Charlotte Mew 1869–1928

English poet

8 She sleeps up in the attic there
Alone, poor maid. 'Tis but a stair
Betwixt us. Oh! my God! the down,
The soft young down of her, the brown,
The brown of her—her eyes, her hair, her hair!

'The Farmer's Bride' (1916)

Sir Anthony Meyer 1920–

British Conservative politician

9 I question the right of that great Moloch, national sovereignty, to burn its children to save its pride.

Speaking against the Falklands War, 1982; in *Listener* 27 September 1990, p. 31

William Julius Mickle 1735–88

Scottish poet

10 For there's nae luck about the house,
There's nae luck at a',
There's little pleasure in the house
When our gudeman's awa.

'The Mariner's Wife' (1769)

Thomas Middleton c.1580–1627

English playwright

11 Anything for a quiet life.

Title of play (written c.1620, possibly with John Webster). Cf. Dickens 243:26

12   I never heard
Of any true affection, but 'twas nipt
With care.

Blurt, Master-Constable (1602) act 3, sc. 1

13 I could not get the ring without the finger.

The Changeling (with William Rowley, c.1622) act 3, sc. 4

14 Y'are the deed's creature.

The Changeling (with William Rowley, c.1622) act 3, sc. 4

15 O come not near me sir; I shall defile you.
I that am of your blood was taken from you
For your better health. Look no more upon't,
But cast it to the ground regardlessly;
Let the common sewer take it from distinction.
Beneath the stars, upon yon meteor
Ever hung my fate, 'mongst things corruptible;
I ne'er could pluck it from him. My loathing
Was prophet to the rest, but ne'er believed.

The Changeling (with William Rowley, c.1622) act 5, sc. 3

16 My study's ornament, thou shell of death,
Once the bright face of my betrothèd lady.

The Revenger's Tragedy (1607) act 1, sc. 1 (previously attributed to Cyril Tourneur, c.1575–1626)

17   I was begot
After some gluttonous dinner—some stirring dish
Was my first father; when deep healths went round
And ladies cheeks were painted red with wine,
Their tongues as short and nimble as their heels
Uttering words sweet and thick; and when they rose
Were merrily disposed to fall again.

The Revenger's Tragedy (1607) act 1, sc. 2

18 Oh think upon the pleasure of the palace,
Securèd ease and state; the stirring meats
Ready to move out of the dishes
That e'en now quicken when they're eaten;
Banquets abroad by torchlight, Musics, sports,
Bare-headed vassals that had ne'er the fortune
To keep on their own hats, but let horns wear 'em;
Nine coaches waiting—hurry, hurry, hurry.

The Revenger's Tragedy (1607) act 2, sc. 1

19 Now 'tis full sea abed over the world,
There's juggling of all sides. Some that were maids
E'en at sunset are now perhaps i' the toll-book;
This woman in immodest thin apparel
Lets in her friend by water, here a dame
Cunning, nails leather hinges to a door
To avoid proclamation.

The Revenger's Tragedy (1607) act 2, sc. 2

1 Does the silk-worm expend her yellow labours
For thee? for thee does she undo herself?
   The Revenger's Tragedy (1607) act 3, sc. 5

2 There's no hate lost between us.
   The Witch (written 1609–16) act 4, sc. 3

George Mikes 1912–

Hungarian-born writer

3 On the Continent people have good food; in England
people have good table manners.
   How to be an Alien (1946) p. 10

4 Continental people have sex life; the English have
hot-water bottles.
   How to be an Alien (1946) p. 25

5 An Englishman, even if he is alone, forms an orderly
queue of one.
   How to be an Alien (1946) p. 44

John Stuart Mill 1806–73

English philosopher and economist

6 As often as a study is cultivated by narrow minds,
they will draw from it narrow conclusions.
   Auguste Comte and Positivism (1865) pt. 1, p. 82

7 Ask yourself whether you are happy, and you cease to
be so.
   Autobiography (1873) ch. 5

8 No great improvements in the lot of mankind are
possible, until a great change takes place in the
fundamental constitution of their modes of thought.
   Autobiography (1873) ch. 7

9 The Conservatives . . . being by the law of their
existence the stupidest party.
   Considerations on Representative Government (1861) ch. 7 n.

10 When society requires to be rebuilt, there is no use in
attempting to rebuild it on the old plan.
   Dissertations and Discussions vol. 1 (1859) 'Essay on
   Coleridge'

11 If we may be excused the antithesis, we should say
that eloquence is *heard*, poetry is *overheard*.
   Dissertations and Discussions vol. 1 (1859) 'Thoughts on
   Poetry and its Varieties'

12 Detention by the State of the unearned increment of
rent.
   Dissertations and Discussions vol. 4 (1875) 'The Right of
   Property in Land'

13 I will call no being good, who is not what I mean
when I apply that epithet to my fellow-creatures; and
if such a being can sentence me to hell for not so
calling him, to hell I will go.
   Examination of Sir William Hamilton's Philosophy (1865)
   ch. 7

14 The sole end for which mankind are warranted,
individually or collectively, in interfering with the
liberty of action of any of their number, is
self-protection.
   On Liberty (1859) ch. 1

15 The only purpose for which power can be rightfully
exercised over any member of a civilized community,
against his will, is to prevent harm to others. His own
good, either physical or moral, is not a sufficient
warrant.
   On Liberty (1859) ch. 1

16 If all mankind minus one were of one opinion, and
only one person were of the contrary opinion,
mankind would be no more justified in silencing that
one person, than he, if he had the power, would be
justified in silencing mankind.
   On Liberty (1859) ch. 2

17 A party of order or stability, and a party of progress or
reform, are both necessary elements of a healthy state
of political life.
   On Liberty (1859) ch. 2

18 The liberty of the individual must be thus far limited;
he must not make himself a nuisance to other people.
   On Liberty (1859) ch. 3

19 Liberty consists in doing what one desires.
   On Liberty (1859) ch. 5

20 A State which dwarfs its men, in order that they may
be more docile instruments in its hands even for
beneficial purposes, will find that with small men no
great thing can really be accomplished.
   On Liberty (1859) ch. 5

21 The great majority of those who speak of perfectibility
as a dream, do so because they feel that it is one
which would afford them no pleasure if it were
realized.
   Speech on Perfectibility (1828) in *Autobiography* (ed. Harold
   J. Laski, 1924) p. 290

22 The principle which regulates the existing social
relations between the two sexes—the legal
subordination of one sex to the other—is wrong in
itself, and now one of the chief hindrances to human
improvement.
   The Subjection of Women (1869) ch. 1

23 Laws and systems of polity always begin by
recognising the relations they find already existing
between individuals. They convert what was a mere
physical fact into a legal right, give it the sanction of
society, and principally aim at the substitution of
public and organised means of asserting and
protecting these rights, instead of the irregular and
lawless conflict of physical strength.
   The Subjection of Women (1869) ch. 1

24 Everyone who desires power, desires it most over those
who are nearest to him, with whom his life is passed,
with whom he has most concerns in common, and in
whom any independence of his authority is oftenest
likely to interfere with his individual preferences.
   The Subjection of Women (1869) ch. 1

25 What is now called the nature of women is an
eminently artificial thing—the result of forced
repression in some directions, unnatural stimulation in
others.
   The Subjection of Women (1869) ch. 1

26 No slave is a slave to the same lengths, and in so full
a sense of the word, as a wife is.
   The Subjection of Women (1869) ch. 2

1 The laws of most countries are far worse than the people who execute them, and many of them are only able to remain laws by being seldom or never carried into effect. If married life were all that it might be expected to be, looking to the laws alone, society would be a hell upon earth.
   The Subjection of Women (1869) ch. 2

2 The true virtue of human beings is fitness to live together as equals; claiming nothing for themselves but what they as freely concede to everyone else; regarding command of any kind as an exceptional necessity, and in all cases a temporary one.
   The Subjection of Women (1869) ch. 2

3 The most important thing women have to do is to stir up the zeal of women themselves.
   Letter to Alexander Bain, 14 July 1869, in Hugh S. R. Elliot (ed.) *Letters of John Stuart Mill* vol. 2 (1910)

4 Were there but a few hearts and intellects like hers this earth would already become the hoped-for heaven.
   Epitaph (1859) inscribed on the tomb of his wife, Harriet, at the cemetery of St Véran, near Avignon. See M. St J. Packe *Life of John Stuart Mill* (1954) bk. 7, ch. 3

Edna St Vincent Millay 1892–1950
American poet

5 Childhood is not from birth to a certain age and at a certain age
The child is grown, and puts away childish things.
Childhood is the kingdom where nobody dies.
Nobody that matters, that is.
   'Childhood is the Kingdom where Nobody dies' (1934). Cf. I Corinthians 101:1

6 Down, down, down into the darkness of the grave
Gently they go, the beautiful, the tender, the kind;
Quietly they go, the intelligent, the witty, the brave.
I know. But I do not approve. And I am not resigned.
   'Dirge Without Music' (1928)

7 My candle burns at both ends;
It will not last the night;
But ah, my foes, and oh, my friends—
It gives a lovely light.
   A Few Figs From Thistles (1920) 'First Fig'

8 Safe upon solid rock the ugly houses stand:
Come and see my shining palace built upon the sand!
   A Few Figs From Thistles (1920) 'Second Fig'

9 I only know that summer sang in me
A little while, that in me sings no more.
   The Harp-Weaver and Other Poems (1923) sonnet 19

10 Death devours all lovely things;
Lesbia with her sparrow
Shares the darkness—presently
Every bed is narrow.
   'Passer Mortuus Est' (1921). Cf. Catullus 185:13

11 After all, my erstwhile dear,
My no longer cherished,
Need we say it was not love,
Now that love is perished?
   'Passer Mortuus Est' (1921)

Alice Duer Miller 1874–1942
American writer

12 I am American bred,
I have seen much to hate here—much to forgive,
But in a world where England is finished and dead,
I do not wish to live.
   The White Cliffs (1940) p. 70

Arthur Miller 1915–
American playwright

13 A suicide kills two people, Maggie, that's what it's for!
   After the Fall (1964) act 2

14 All organization is and must be grounded on the idea of exclusion and prohibition just as two objects cannot occupy the same space.
   The Crucible (1952) act 1

15 The world is an oyster, but you don't crack it open on a mattress.
   Death of a Salesman (1949) act 1

16 Willy Loman never made a lot of money. His name was never in the paper. He's not the finest character that ever lived. But he's a human being, and a terrible thing is happening to him. So attention must be paid.
   Death of a Salesman (1949) act 1

17 For a salesman, there is no rock bottom to the life. He don't put a bolt to a nut, he don't tell you the law or give you medicine. He's a man way out there in the blue, riding on a smile and a shoeshine. And when they start not smiling back—that's an earthquake. And then you get yourself a couple of spots on your hat, and you're finished. Nobody dast blame this man. A salesman is got to dream, boy. It comes with the territory.
   Death of a Salesman (1949) 'Requiem'

18 The car, the furniture, the wife, the children—everything has to be disposable. Because you see the main thing today is—shopping.
   The Price (1968) act 1

19 This is Red Hook, not Sicily . . . This is the gullet of New York swallowing the tonnage of the world.
   A View from the Bridge (1955) act 1

20 The structure of a play is always the story of how the birds came home to roost.
   'Shadows of the Gods' in *Harper's Magazine* August 1958

21 A good newspaper, I suppose, is a nation talking to itself.
   In *Observer* 26 November 1961

22 A theatre where no-one is allowed to walk out and everyone is forced to applause.
   Describing Eastern Europe in *Omnibus* (BBC TV) 30 October 1987; in *Independent* 31 October 1987

Henry Miller 1891–1980
American novelist

23 Even before the music begins there is that bored look on people's faces. A polite form of self-imposed torture, the concert.
   Tropic of Cancer (1934) p. 84

1 Every man with a bellyful of the classics is an enemy
to the human race.
Tropic of Cancer (1934) p. 280

Jonathan Miller 1934–

English writer and director

2 In fact, I'm not really a *Jew*. Just Jew-*ish*. Not the
whole hog, you know.
Beyond the Fringe (1960 review) 'Real Class'

William Miller 1810–72

Scottish writer of children's verse

3 Wee Willie Winkie rins through the town,
Up stairs and down stairs in his nicht-gown,
Tirling at the window, crying at the lock,
Are the weans in their bed, for it's now ten o'clock?
'Willie Winkie' (1841)

Spike Milligan (Terence Alan Milligan) 1918–

Irish comedian

4 You silly twisted boy.
The Goon Show (BBC radio series) 'The Dreaded Batter
Pudding Hurler' 12 October 1954

5 Money couldn't buy friends but you got a better class
of enemy.
Puckoon (1963) ch. 6

A. J. Mills, Fred Godfrey, and Bennett Scott

British songwriters

6 Take me back to dear old Blighty,
Put me on the train to London Town.
'Take me back to dear old Blighty' (1916 song)

Henry Hart Milman 1791–1868

English clergyman

7 Ride on! ride on in majesty!
The wingèd squadrons of the sky
Look down with sad and wond'ring eyes
To see the approaching sacrifice.
'Ride on! ride on in majesty!' (1827 hymn)

A. A. Milne 1882–1956

English writer for children

8 The more he looked inside the more Piglet wasn't
there.
The House at Pooh Corner (1928) ch. 1

9 'I don't *want* him,' said Rabbit. 'But it's always useful
to know where a friend-and-relation *is*, whether you
want him or whether you don't.'
The House at Pooh Corner (1928) ch. 3

10 He respects Owl, because you can't help respecting
anybody who can spell TUESDAY, even if he doesn't
spell it right; but spelling isn't everything. There are
days when spelling Tuesday simply doesn't count.
The House at Pooh Corner (1928) ch. 5

11 Pooh began to feel a little more comfortable, because
when you are a Bear of Very Little Brain, and you
Think of Things, you find sometimes that a Thing
which seemed very Thingish inside you is quite
different when it gets out into the open and has other
people looking at it.
The House at Pooh Corner (1928) ch. 6

12 They're changing guard at Buckingham Palace—
Christopher Robin went down with Alice.
Alice is marrying one of the guard.
'A soldier's life is terrible hard,'
Says Alice.
When We Were Very Young (1924) 'Buckingham Palace'

13 James James
Morrison Morrison
Weatherby George Dupree
Took great
Care of his Mother,
Though he was only three.
James James
Said to his Mother,
'Mother,' he said, said he;
'You must never go down to the end of the town, if
you don't go down with me.'
When We Were Very Young (1924) 'Disobedience'

14 There once was a Dormouse who lived in a bed
Of delphiniums (blue) and geraniums (red),
And all the day long he'd a wonderful view
Of geraniums (red) and delphiniums (blue).
When We Were Very Young (1924) 'The Dormouse and the
Doctor'

15 The King asked
The Queen, and
The Queen asked
The Dairymaid:
'Could we have some butter for
The Royal slice of bread?'
When We Were Very Young (1924) 'The King's Breakfast'

16 And some of the bigger bears try to pretend
That they came round the corner to look for a friend;
And they try to pretend that nobody cares
Whether you walk on the lines or squares.

But only the sillies believe their talk;
It's ever so portant how you walk.
And it's ever so jolly to call out, 'Bears,
Just watch me walking in all the squares!'
When We Were Very Young (1924) 'Lines and Squares'

17 *What* is the matter with Mary Jane?
She's perfectly well and she hasn't a pain,
And it's lovely rice pudding for dinner again!
What *is* the matter with Mary Jane?
When We Were Very Young (1924) 'Rice Pudding'

18 Little Boy kneels at the foot of the bed,
Droops on the little hands little gold head.
Hush! Hush! Whisper who dares!
Christopher Robin is saying his prayers.
When We Were Very Young (1924) 'Vespers'

19 Isn't it funny
How a bear likes honey?
Buzz! Buzz! Buzz!
I wonder why he does?
Winnie-the-Pooh (1926) ch. 1

1 How sweet to be a Cloud
Floating in the Blue!
It makes him very proud
To be a little cloud.
  Winnie-the-Pooh (1926) ch. 1

2 Pooh woke up suddenly with a sinking feeling. He had
had that sinking feeling before, and he knew what it
meant. *He was hungry.*
  Winnie-the-Pooh (1926) ch. 5

3 Cottleston, Cottleston, Cottleston Pie.
A fly can't bird, but a bird can fly.
Ask me a riddle and I reply:
'Cottleston, Cottleston, Cottleston Pie.'
  Winnie-the-Pooh (1926) ch. 6

4 Time for a little something.
  Winnie-the-Pooh (1926) ch. 6

5 My spelling is Wobbly. It's good spelling but it
Wobbles, and the letters get in the wrong places.
  Winnie-the-Pooh (1926) ch. 6

6 Owl hasn't exactly got Brain, but he Knows Things.
  Winnie-the-Pooh (1926) ch. 9

Alfred, 1st Viscount Milner 1854–1925
British colonial administrator

7 If we believe a thing to be bad, and if we have a right
to prevent it, it is our duty to try to prevent it and to
damn the consequences.
  Speech in Glasgow, 26 November 1909, in *The Times*
  27 November 1909

John Milton 1608–74
English poet

8 Such sweet compulsion doth in music lie.
  'Arcades' (1645) l. 68

9 Blest pair of Sirens, pledges of heaven's joy,
Sphere-born harmonious sisters, Voice, and Verse.
  'At a Solemn Music' (1645)

10 Where the bright seraphim in burning row
Their loud uplifted angel trumpets blow.
  'At a Solemn Music' (1645)

11 Before the starry threshold of Jove's Court
My mansion is.
  Comus (1637) l. 1

12 Above the smoke and stir of this dim spot,
Which men call earth.
  Comus (1637) l. 5

13 Yet some there be that by due steps aspire
To lay their just hands on that golden key
That opes the palace of eternity.
  Comus (1637) l. 12

14 That like to rich and various gems inlay
The unadornèd bosom of the deep.
  Comus (1637) l. 22

15 An old and haughty nation proud in arms.
  Comus (1637) l. 33

16 And the gilded car of day
His glowing axle doth allay
In the steep Atlantic stream.
  Comus (1637) l. 95

17 What hath night to do with sleep?
  Comus (1637) l. 122

18 Come, knit hands, and beat the ground,
In a light fantastic round.
  Comus (1637) l. 143

19 ... When the grey-hooded Even
Like a sad votarist in palmer's weed
Rose from the hindmost wheels of Phoebus' wain.
  Comus (1637) l. 188

20   O thievish Night
Why shouldst thou, but for some felonious end,
In thy dark lantern thus close up the stars,
That Nature hung in heaven, and filled their lamps
With everlasting oil, to give due light
To the misled and lonely traveller?
  Comus (1637) l. 195

21 Was I deceived, or did a sable cloud
Turn forth her silver lining on the night?
  Comus (1637) l. 221

22 Sweet Echo, sweetest nymph that liv'st unseen
Within thy airy shell
By slow Meander's margent green,
And in the violet-embroidered vale.
  Comus (1637) l. 230

23 Can any mortal mixture of earth's mould
Breathe such divine enchanting ravishment?
  Comus (1637) l. 244

24 Such sober certainty of waking bliss
I never heard till now.
  Comus (1637) l. 263

25 ... Shepherd, I take thy word,
And trust thy honest-offered courtesy,
Which oft is sooner found in lowly sheds
With smoky rafters, than in tap'stry halls
And courts of princes.
  Comus (1637) l. 321

26 With thy long levelled rule of streaming light.
  Comus (1637) l. 340

27 Virtue could see to do what Virtue would
By her own radiant light, though sun and moon
Were in the flat sea sunk. And Wisdom's self
Oft seeks to sweet retirèd solitude,
Where with her best nurse Contemplation,
She plumes her feathers, and lets grow her wings
That in the various bustle of resort
Were all to-ruffled, and sometimes impaired.
He that has light within his own clear breast
May sit i' the centre, and enjoy bright day,
But he that hides a dark soul, and foul thoughts
Benighted walks under the midday sun;
Himself is his own dungeon.
  Comus (1637) l. 373

28 Yet where an equal poise of hope and fear
Does arbitrate the event, my nature is
That I incline to hope, rather than fear,
And gladly banish squint suspicion.
  Comus (1637) l. 410

29 'Tis chastity, my brother, chastity:
She that has that, is clad in complete steel.
  Comus (1637) l. 420

1 How charming is divine philosophy!
 Not harsh and crabbèd, as dull fools suppose,
 But musical as is Apollo's lute,
 And a perpetual feast of nectared sweets,
 Where no crude surfeit reigns.
  Comus (1637) l. 475

2 What the sage poets taught by th' heavenly Muse,
 Storied of old in high immortal verse
 Of dire chimeras and enchanted isles,
 And rifted rocks whose entrance leads to hell,
 For such there be, but unbelief is blind.
  Comus (1637) l. 515

3 And filled the air with barbarous dissonance.
  Comus (1637) l. 550

4   I was all ear,
 And took in strains that might create a soul
 Under the ribs of death.
  Comus (1637) l. 560

5   Against the threats
 Of malice or of sorcery, or that power
 Which erring men call chance, this I hold firm,
 Virtue may be assailed, but never hurt,
 Surprised by unjust force, but not enthralled.
  Comus (1637) l. 586

6 O foolishness of men! that lend their ears
 To those budge doctors of the Stoic fur,
 And fetch their precepts from the Cynic tub,
 Praising the lean and sallow Abstinence.
  Comus (1637) l. 706

7 Beauty is Nature's coin, must not be hoarded,
 But must be current, and the good thereof
 Consists in mutual and partaken bliss.
  Comus (1637) l. 739

8 Beauty is Nature's brag, and must be shown
 In courts, at feasts, and high solemnities
 Where most may wonder at the workmanship;
 It is for homely features to keep home,
 They had their name thence; coarse complexions
 And cheeks of sorry grain will serve to ply
 The sampler, and to tease the housewife's wool.
 What need a vermeil-tinctured lip for that,
 Love-darting eyes, or tresses like the morn?
  Comus (1637) l. 745

9 Obtruding false rules pranked in reason's garb.
  Comus (1637) l. 759

10 Sabrina fair,
 Listen where thou art sitting
 Under the glassy, cool, translucent wave,
 In twisted braids of lilies knitting
 The loose train of thy amber-dropping hair.
  Comus (1637) l. 859 'Song'

11 Thus I set my printless feet
 O'er the cowslip's velvet head,
 That bends not as I tread.
  Comus (1637) l. 897

12 Love Virtue, she alone is free,
 She can teach ye how to climb
 Higher than the sphery chime;
 Or, if Virtue feeble were,
 Heaven itself would stoop to her.
  Comus (1637) l. 1019

13 Hence, vain deluding joys,
 The brood of folly without father bred.
  'Il Penseroso' (1645) l. 1

14 As thick and numberless
 As the gay motes that people the sunbeams.
  'Il Penseroso' (1645) l. 7

15 Hail, divinest Melancholy,
 Whose saintly visage is too bright
 To hit the sense of human sight;
 And therefore to our weaker view,
 O'erlaid with black staid wisdom's hue.
  'Il Penseroso' (1645) l. 12

16 Come, pensive nun, devout and pure,
 Sober, steadfast, and demure.
  'Il Penseroso' (1645) l. 31

17 And join with thee calm Peace, and Quiet,
 Spare Fast, that oft with gods doth diet
  'Il Penseroso' (1645) l. 45

18 And add to these retirèd Leisure,
 That in trim gardens takes his pleasure.
  'Il Penseroso' (1645) l. 49

19 Sweet bird that shunn'st the noise of folly,
 Most musical, most melancholy!
  'Il Penseroso' (1645) l. 61

20 And missing thee, I walk unseen
 On the dry smooth-shaven green,
 To behold the wandering moon,
 Riding near her highest noon,
 Like one that had been led astray
 Through the heaven's wide pathless way;
 And oft, as if her head she bowed,
 Stooping through a fleecy cloud.
  'Il Penseroso' (1645) l. 65

21 Oft on a plat of rising ground,
 I hear the far-off curfew sound
 Over some wide-watered shore,
 Swinging slow with sullen roar.
  'Il Penseroso' (1645) l. 73

22 Where glowing embers through the room
 Teach light to counterfeit a gloom,
 Far from all resort of mirth,
 Save the cricket on the hearth.
  'Il Penseroso' (1645) l. 79

23 Or bid the soul of Orpheus sing
 Such notes as warbled to the string,
 Drew iron tears down Pluto's cheek.
  'Il Penseroso' (1645) l. 105

24 Where more is meant than meets the ear.
  'Il Penseroso' (1645) l. 120

25 Hide me from day's garish eye,
 While the bee with honied thigh,
 That at her flowery work doth sing,
 And the waters murmuring
 And such consort as they keep,
 Entice the dewy-feathered Sleep.
  'Il Penseroso' (1645) l. 141

26 But let my due feet never fail
 To walk the studious cloister's pale.
  'Il Penseroso' (1645) l. 155

1 And love the high embowèd roof,
With antique pillars' massy proof,
And storied windows richly dight,
Casting a dim religious light.
There let the pealing organ blow
To the full-voiced quire below,
In service high, and anthems clear,
As may with sweetness, through mine ear,
Dissolve me into ecstasies,
And bring all heaven before mine eyes.
    'Il Penseroso' (1645) l. 157

2 Till old experience do attain
To something like prophetic strain.
    'Il Penseroso' (1645) l. 173

3 Hence, loathèd Melancholy,
Of Cerberus, and blackest Midnight born,
In Stygian cave forlorn
'Mongst horrid shapes, and shrieks, and sights unholy.
    'L'Allegro' (1645) l. 1

4 So buxom, blithe, and debonair.
    'L'Allegro' (1645) l. 24 (of Euphrosyne [Mirth], one of the
    three Graces)

5 Haste thee nymph, and bring with thee
Jest and youthful jollity,
Quips and cranks, and wanton wiles,
Nods, and becks, and wreathèd smiles.
    'L'Allegro' (1645) l. 25

6 Sport that wrinkled Care derides,
And Laughter holding both his sides.
Come, and trip it as ye go
On the light fantastic toe,
And in thy right hand lead with thee,
The mountain nymph, sweet Liberty.
    'L'Allegro' (1645) l. 31

7 Mirth, admit me of thy crew
To live with her, and live with thee,
In unreprovèd pleasures free.
    'L'Allegro' (1645) l. 38

8 While the cock with lively din
Scatters the rear of darkness thin,
And to the stack, or the barn door,
Stoutly struts his dames before.
    'L'Allegro' (1645) l. 49

9 Right against the eastern gate,
Where the great sun begins his state.
    'L'Allegro' (1645) l. 59

10 While the ploughman near at hand,
Whistles o'er the furrowed land,
And the milkmaid singeth blithe,
And the mower whets his scythe,
And every shepherd tells his tale
Under the hawthorn in the dale.
    'L'Allegro' (1645) l. 63

11 Meadows trim with daisies pied,
Shallow brooks, and rivers wide,
Towers, and battlements it sees
Bosomed high in tufted trees,
Where perhaps some beauty lies,
The cynosure of neighbouring eyes.
    'L'Allegro' (1645) l. 75

12 Of herbs, and other country messes,
Which the neat-handed Phyllis dresses.
    'L'Allegro' (1645) l. 85

13 And the jocund rebecks sound
To many a youth, and many a maid,
Dancing in the chequered shade;
And young and old come forth to play
On a sunshine holiday.
    'L'Allegro' (1645) l. 94

14 Then to the spicy nut-brown ale.
    'L'Allegro' (1645) l. 100

15 Towered cities please us then,
And the busy hum of men.
    'L'Allegro' (1645) l. 117

16 With store of ladies, whose bright eyes
Rain influence, and judge the prize
Of wit or arms.
    'L'Allegro' (1645) l. 121

17 There let Hymen oft appear
In saffron robe, with taper clear,
And pomp, and feast, and revelry,
With masque, and antique pageantry:
Such sights as youthful poets dream
On summer eves by haunted stream.
Then to the well-trod stage anon,
If Jonson's learnèd sock be on,
Or sweetest Shakespeare fancy's child,
Warble his native wood-notes wild,
And ever against eating cares,
Lap me in soft Lydian airs,
Married to immortal verse
Such as the meeting soul may pierce
In notes, with many a winding bout
Of linkèd sweetness long drawn out.
    'L'Allegro' (1645) l. 125

18 Such strains as would have won the ear
Of Pluto, to have quite set free
His half-regained Eurydice.
    'L'Allegro' (1645) l. 148

19 Let us with a gladsome mind
Praise the Lord, for he is kind,
For his mercies ay endure,
Ever faithful, ever sure.
    'Let us with a gladsome mind' (1645); paraphrase of
    Psalm 136

20 Yet once more, O ye laurels, and once more
Ye myrtles brown, with ivy never sere,
I come to pluck your berries harsh and crude,
And with forced fingers rude
Shatter your leaves before the mellowing year.
Bitter constraint, and sad occasion dear,
Compels me to disturb your season due;
For Lycidas is dead, dead ere his prime,
Young Lycidas, and hath not left his peer:
Who would not sing for Lycidas? he knew
Himself to sing, and build the lofty rhyme.
He must not float upon his watery bier
Unwept, and welter to the parching wind,
Without the meed of some melodious tear.
    'Lycidas' (1638) l. 1

21 Hence with denial vain, and coy excuse.
    'Lycidas' (1638) l. 18

22 For we were nursed upon the self-same hill.
    'Lycidas' (1638) l. 23

1 But O the heavy change, now thou art gone,
Now thou art gone, and never must return!
'Lycidas' (1638) l. 37

2   The woods, and desert caves,
With wild thyme and the gadding vine o'ergrown.
'Lycidas' (1638) l. 39

3 Where were ye nymphs, when the remorseless deep
Closed o'er the head of your loved Lycidas?
'Lycidas' (1638) l. 50

4 Alas! What boots it with uncessant care
To tend the homely slighted shepherd's trade,
And strictly meditate the thankless muse;
Were it not better done as others use,
To sport with Amaryllis in the shade,
Or with the tangles of Neaera's hair?
Fame is the spur that the clear spirit doth raise
(That last infirmity of noble mind)
To scorn delights, and live laborious days;
But the fair guerdon when we hope to find,
And think to burst out into sudden blaze,
Comes the blind Fury with th' abhorrèd shears,
And slits the thin-spun life.
'Lycidas' (1638) l. 64

5 Fame is no plant that grows on mortal soil.
'Lycidas' (1638) l. 78

6 It was that fatal and perfidious bark
Built in th' eclipse, and rigged with curses dark,
That sunk so low that sacred head of thine.
'Lycidas' (1638) l. 100

7 Last came, and last did go,
The pilot of the Galilean lake,
Two massy keys he bore of metals twain
(The golden opes, the iron shuts amain).
'Lycidas' (1638) l. 108

8 Enow of such as for their bellies' sake,
Creep and intrude, and climb into the fold!
Of other care they little reck'ning make,
Than how to scramble at the shearers' feast,
And shove away the worthy bidden guest.
Blind mouths! that scarce themselves know how to
hold
A sheep-hook, or have learned aught else the least
That to the faithful herdman's art belongs!
'Lycidas' (1638) l. 114

9 And when they list, their lean and flashy songs
Grate on their scrannel pipes of wretched straw,
The hungry sheep look up, and are not fed,
But swoll'n with wind, and the rank mist they draw,
Rot inwardly, and foul contagion spread;
Besides what the grim wolf with privy paw
Daily devours apace, and nothing said;
But that two-handed engine at the door
Stands ready to smite once, and smite no more.
'Lycidas' (1638) l. 123

10 Return, Alpheus, the dread voice is past
That shrunk thy streams; return Sicilian muse.
'Lycidas' (1638) l. 132

11 Bring the rathe primrose that forsaken dies,
The tufted crow-toe, and pale jessamine,
The white pink, and the pansy freaked with jet,
The glowing violet,
The musk-rose, and the well-attired woodbine,
With cowslips wan that hang the pensive head,
And every flower that sad embroidery wears:
Bid amaranthus all his beauty shed,
And daffodillies fill their cups with tears,
To strew the laureate hearse where Lycid lies.
'Lycidas' (1638) l. 142

12 Whether beyond the stormy Hebrides,
Where thou perhaps under the whelming tide
Visit'st the bottom of the monstrous world;
Or whether thou, to our moist vows denied,
Sleep'st by the fable of Bellerus old,
Where the great vision of the guarded mount
Looks toward Namancos and Bayona's hold;
Look homeward angel now, and melt with ruth.
'Lycidas' (1638) l. 156

13 For Lycidas your sorrow is not dead,
Sunk though he be beneath the watery floor;
So sinks the day-star in the ocean bed,
And yet anon repairs his drooping head,
And tricks his beams, and with new spangled ore,
Flames in the forehead of the morning sky:
So Lycidas sunk low, but mounted high,
Through the dear might of Him that walked the
waves.
'Lycidas' (1638) l. 166

14 There entertain him all the saints above,
In solemn troops, and sweet societies
That sing, and singing in their glory move,
And wipe the tears for ever from his eyes.
'Lycidas' (1638) l. 178

15 Thus sang the uncouth swain to th' oaks and rills,
While the still morn went out with sandals grey,
He touched the tender stops of various quills,
With eager thought warbling his Doric lay.
'Lycidas' (1638) l. 186

16 At last he rose, and twitched his mantle blue:
Tomorrow to fresh woods, and pastures new.
'Lycidas' (1638) l. 192

17 What needs my Shakespeare for his honoured bones,
The labour of an age in pilèd stones,
Or that his hallowed relics should be hid
Under a star-ypointing pyramid?
'On Shakespeare' (1632)

18 O fairest flower no sooner blown but blasted,
Soft silken primrose fading timelessly.
'On the Death of a Fair Infant Dying of a Cough' (1673)
st. 1

19 For what can war, but endless war still breed?
'On the Lord General Fairfax at the Siege of Colchester'
(written 1648)

20 This is the month, and this the happy morn
Wherein the son of heaven's eternal king,
Of wedded maid, and virgin mother born,
Our great redemption from above did bring;
For so the holy sages once did sing,
That he our deadly forfeit should release,
And with his father work us a perpetual peace.
'On the Morning of Christ's Nativity' (1645) st. 1

1 The star-led wizards haste with odours sweet.
  'On the Morning of Christ's Nativity' (1645) st. 4

2 It was the winter wild,
  While the heaven-born-child
  All meanly wrapped in the rude manger lies;
  Nature in awe to him
  Had doffed her gaudy trim,
  With her great master so to sympathize.
  'On the Morning of Christ's Nativity' (1645) 'The Hymn'
  st. 1

3 No war, or battle's sound
  Was heard the world around,
  The idle spear and shield were high up hung.
  'On the Morning of Christ's Nativity' (1645) 'The Hymn'
  st. 4

4 The stars with deep amaze
  Stand fixed in steadfast gaze,
  Bending one way their precious influence,
  And will not take their flight
  For all the morning light,
  Or Lucifer that often warned them thence;
  But in their glimmering orbs did glow,
  Until their Lord himself bespake, and bid them go.
  'On the Morning of Christ's Nativity' (1645) 'The Hymn'
  st. 6

5 Perhaps their loves, or else their sheep,
  Was all that did their silly thoughts so busy keep.
  'On the Morning of Christ's Nativity' (1645) 'The Hymn'
  st. 8

6 The helmèd cherubim
  And sworded seraphim
  Are seen in glittering ranks with wings displayed.
  'On the Morning of Christ's Nativity' (1645) 'The Hymn'
  st. 11

7 Ring out, ye crystal spheres,
  Once bless our human ears
  (If ye have power to touch our senses so),
  And let your silver chime
  Move in melodious time;
  And let the base of heaven's deep organ blow,
  And with your ninefold harmony
  Make up full consort to the angelic symphony.
  'On the Morning of Christ's Nativity' (1645) 'The Hymn'
  st. 13

8 For if such holy song
  Enwrap our fancy long,
  Time will run back, and fetch the age of gold,
  And speckled vanity
  Will sicken soon and die.
  'On the Morning of Christ's Nativity' (1645) 'The Hymn'
  st. 14

9 And hell itself will pass away,
  And leave her dolorous mansions to the peering day.
  'On the Morning of Christ's Nativity' (1645) 'The Hymn'
  st. 14

10 Swinges the scaly horror of his folded tail.
  'On the Morning of Christ's Nativity' (1645) 'The Hymn'
  st. 18

11 The oracles are dumb,
  No voice or hideous hum
  Runs through the archèd roof in words deceiving.
  Apollo from his shrine
  Can no more divine,
  With hollow shriek the steep of Delphos leaving.
  'On the Morning of Christ's Nativity' (1645) 'The Hymn'
  st. 19

12 So when the sun in bed,
  Curtained with cloudy red,
  Pillows his chin upon an orient wave.
  'On the Morning of Christ's Nativity' (1645) 'The Hymn'
  st. 26

13 But see the virgin blest,
  Hath laid her babe to rest.
  Time is our tedious song should here have ending.
  'On the Morning of Christ's Nativity' (1645) 'The Hymn'
  st. 27

14 New *Presbyter* is but old *Priest* writ large.
  'On the New Forcers of Conscience under the Long
  Parliament' (1646)

15 Fly envious Time, till thou run out thy race,
  Call on the lazy leaden-stepping hours.
  'On Time' (1645)

16 Showed him his room where he must lodge that night,
  Pulled off his boots, and took away the light:
  If any ask for him, it shall be said,
  Hobson has supped, and's newly gone to bed.
  'On the University Carrier' (1645)

17 Rhyme being no necessary adjunct or true ornament
  of poem or good verse, in longer works especially, but
  the invention of a barbarous age, to set off wretched
  matter and lame metre.
  Paradise Lost (1667) 'The Verse' (preface, added 1668)

18 The troublesome and modern bondage of rhyming.
  Paradise Lost (1667) 'The Verse' (preface, added 1668)

19 Of man's first disobedience, and the fruit
  Of that forbidden tree, whose mortal taste
  Brought death into the world, and all our woe,
  With loss of Eden.
  Paradise Lost (1667) bk. 1, l. 1

20 Things unattempted yet in prose or rhyme.
  Paradise Lost (1667) bk. 1, l. 16

21   What in me is dark
  Illumine, what is low raise and support;
  That to the height of this great argument
  I may assert eternal providence,
  And justify the ways of God to men.
  Paradise Lost (1667) bk. 1, l. 22

22 The infernal serpent; he it was, whose guile
  Stirred up with envy and revenge, deceived
  The mother of mankind.
  Paradise Lost (1667) bk. 1, l. 34

23   Him the almighty power
  Hurled headlong flaming from the ethereal sky
  With hideous ruin and combustion down
  To bottomless perdition, there to dwell
  In adamantine chains and penal fire,
  Who durst defy the omnipotent to arms.
  Paradise Lost (1667) bk. 1, l. 44

1 A dungeon horrible, on all sides round
As one great furnace flamed, yet from those flames
No light, but rather darkness visible
Served only to discover sights of woe,
Regions of sorrow, doleful shades, where peace
And rest can never dwell, hope never comes
That comes to all.
Paradise Lost (1667) bk. 1, l. 61

2 ... But O how fallen! how changed
From him, who in the happy realms of light
Clothed with transcendent brightness didst outshine
Myriads though bright.
Paradise Lost (1667) bk. 1, l. 84

3 United thoughts and counsels, equal hope
And hazard in the glorious enterprise.
Paradise Lost (1667) bk. 1, l. 88

4   Yet not for those,
Nor what the potent victor in his rage
Can else inflict, do I repent or change,
Though changed in outward lustre; that fixed mind
And high disdain, from sense of injured merit.
Paradise Lost (1667) bk. 1, l. 94

5 ... What though the field be lost?
All is not lost; the unconquerable will,
And study of revenge, immortal hate,
And courage never to submit or yield:
And what is else not to be overcome?
Paradise Lost (1667) bk. 1, l. 105

6 Vaunting aloud, but racked with deep despair.
Paradise Lost (1667) bk. 1, l. 126

7 Fallen cherub, to be weak is miserable,
Doing or suffering: but of this be sure,
To do aught good never will be our task,
But ever to do ill our sole delight.
Paradise Lost (1667) bk. 1, l. 157

8 And out of good still to find means of evil.
Paradise Lost (1667) bk. 1, l. 165

9 What reinforcement we may gain from hope;
If not, what resolution from despair.
Paradise Lost (1667) bk. 1, l. 190

10   The will
And high permission of all-ruling heaven
Left him at large to his own dark designs,
That with reiterated crimes he might
Heap on himself damnation.
Paradise Lost (1667) bk. 1, l. 211

11 Is this the region, this the soil, the clime,
Said then the lost archangel, this the seat
That we must change for heaven, this mournful
   gloom
For that celestial light?
Paradise Lost (1667) bk. 1, l. 242

12   Farewell, happy fields
Where joy for ever dwells: hail horrors, hail
Infernal world, and thou profoundest hell
Receive thy new possessor: one who brings
A mind not to be changed by place or time.
The mind is its own place, and in itself
Can make a heaven of hell, a hell of heaven.
Paradise Lost (1667) bk. 1, l. 249

13 Here we may reign secure, and in my choice
To reign is worth ambition though in hell:
Better to reign in hell, than serve in heaven.
Paradise Lost (1667) bk. 1, l. 261

14 His spear, to equal which the tallest pine
Hewn on Norwegian hills, to be the mast
Of some great admiral, were but a wand,
He walked with to support uneasy steps
Over the burning marl.
Paradise Lost (1667) bk. 1, l. 292

15 Thick as autumnal leaves that strew the brooks
In Vallombrosa, where the Etrurian shades
High overarched imbower.
Paradise Lost (1667) bk. 1, l. 302

16 First Moloch, horrid king besmeared with blood
Of human sacrifice, and parents' tears.
Paradise Lost (1667) bk. 1, l. 392

17   For spirits when they please
Can either sex assume, or both; so soft
And uncompounded is their essence pure.
Paradise Lost (1667) bk. 1, l. 423

18   But in what shape they choose,
Dilated or condensed, bright or obscure,
Can execute their aery purposes.
Paradise Lost (1667) bk. 1, l. 428

19 Astarte, queen of heaven, with crescent horns.
Paradise Lost (1667) bk. 1, l. 439

20   Thammuz came next behind,
Whose annual wound in Lebanon allured
The Syrian damsels to lament his fate
In amorous ditties all a summer's day,
While smooth Adonis from his native rock
Ran purple to the sea.
Paradise Lost (1667) bk. 1, l. 446

21   And when night
Darkens the streets, then wander forth the sons
Of Belial, flown with insolence and wine.
Paradise Lost (1667) bk. 1, l. 500

22 The imperial ensign, which full high advanced
Shone like a meteor streaming to the wind.
Paradise Lost (1667) bk. 1, l. 536

23 Sonorous metal blowing martial sounds:
At which the universal host upsent
A shout that tore hell's concave, and beyond
Frighted the reign of Chaos and old Night.
Paradise Lost (1667) bk. 1, l. 540

24   Anon they move
In perfect phalanx to the Dorian mode
Of flutes and soft recorders.
Paradise Lost (1667) bk. 1, l. 549

25 ... That small infantry
Warred on by cranes.
Paradise Lost (1667) bk. 1, l. 575 (the Pygmies)

1   What resounds
In fable or romance of Uther's son
Begirt with British and Armoric knights;
And all who since, baptized or infidel,
Jousted in Aspramont or Montalban,
Damasco, or Marocco, or Trebisond,
Or whom Biserta sent from Afric shore
When Charlemain with all his peerage fell
By Fontarabia.
     Paradise Lost (1667) bk. 1, l. 579

2 . . . As when the sun new risen
Looks through the horizontal misty air
Shorn of his beams, or from behind the moon
In dim eclipse disastrous twilight sheds
On half the nations, and with fear of change
Perplexes monarchs.
     Paradise Lost (1667) bk. 1, l. 594

3   Who overcomes
By force, hath overcome but half his foe.
     Paradise Lost (1667) bk. 1, l. 648

4   Mammon led them on,
Mammon, the least erected spirit that fell
From heaven, for even in heaven his looks and
    thoughts
Were always downward bent, admiring more
The riches of heaven's pavement, trodden gold,
Than aught divine or holy else enjoyed
In vision beatific.
     Paradise Lost (1667) bk. 1, l. 678

5   Let none admire
That riches grow in hell; that soil may best
Deserve the precious bane.
     Paradise Lost (1667) bk. 1, l. 690

6 Anon out of the earth a fabric huge
Rose like an exhalation.
     Paradise Lost (1667) bk. 1, l. 710

7   From morn
To noon he fell, from noon to dewy eve,
A summer's day; and with the setting sun
Dropped from the zenith like a falling star.
     Paradise Lost (1667) bk. 1, l. 742

8   Nor aught availed him now
To have built in heaven high towers; nor did he scape
By all his engines, but was headlong sent
With his industrious crew to build in hell.
     Paradise Lost (1667) bk. 1, l. 748

9 . . . Pandemonium, the high capital
Of Satan and his peers.
     Paradise Lost (1667) bk. 1, l. 756

10 High on a throne of royal state, which far
Outshone the wealth of Ormuz and of Ind,
Or where the gorgeous East with richest hand
Showers on her kings barbaric pearl and gold,
Satan exalted sat, by merit raised
To that bad eminence; and from despair
Thus high uplifted beyond hope.
     Paradise Lost (1667) bk. 2, l. 1

11 . . . The strongest and the fiercest spirit
That fought in heaven; now fiercer by despair:
His trust was with the eternal to be deemed
Equal in strength, and rather than be less
Cared not to be at all.
     Paradise Lost (1667) bk. 2, l. 44

12 My sentence is for open war: of wiles
More unexpert, I boast not.
     Paradise Lost (1667) bk. 2, l. 51

13 Belial, in act more graceful and humane;
A fairer person lost not heaven; he seemed
For dignity composed and high exploit:
But all was false and hollow; though his tongue
Dropped manna, and could make the worse appear
The better reason.
     Paradise Lost (1667) bk. 2, l. 109. Cf. Aristophanes 25:3

14   For who would lose,
Though full of pain, this intellectual being,
Those thoughts that wander through eternity,
To perish rather, swallowed up and lost
In the wide womb of uncreated night,
Devoid of sense and motion?
     Paradise Lost (1667) bk. 2, l. 146

15 There to converse with everlasting groans,
Unrespited, unpitied, unreprieved,
Ages of hopeless end.
     Paradise Lost (1667) bk. 2, l. 184

16 Thus Belial with words clothed in reason's garb
Counselled ignoble ease, and peaceful sloth,
Not peace.
     Paradise Lost (1667) bk. 2, l. 226

17 Our torments also may in length of time
Become our elements.
     Paradise Lost (1667) bk. 2, l. 274

18   With grave
Aspect he rose, and in his rising seemed
A pillar of state; deep on his front engraven
Deliberation sat and public care;
And princely counsel in his face yet shone,
Majestic though in ruin.
     Paradise Lost (1667) bk. 2, l. 300

19   To sit in darkness here
Hatching vain empires.
     Paradise Lost (1667) bk. 2, l. 377

20 . . . Who shall tempt with wandering feet
The dark unbottomed infinite abyss
And through the palpable obscure find out
His uncouth way.
     Paradise Lost (1667) bk. 2, l. 404

21   Long is the way
And hard, that out of hell leads up to light.
     Paradise Lost (1667) bk. 2, l. 432

22 O shame to men! Devil with devil damned
Firm concord holds, men only disagree
Of creatures rational.
     Paradise Lost (1667) bk. 2, l. 496

23   In discourse more sweet
(For eloquence the soul, song charms the sense,)
Others apart sat on a hill retired,
In thoughts more elevate, and reasoned high
Of providence, foreknowledge, will and fate,
Fixed fate, free will, foreknowledge absolute,
And found no end, in wandering mazes lost.
     Paradise Lost (1667) bk. 2, l. 555

1 Of good and evil much they argued then,
Of happiness and final misery,
Passion and apathy, and glory and shame,
Vain wisdom all, and false philosophy.
Paradise Lost (1667) bk. 2, l. 562

2   The parching air
Burns frore, and cold performs the effect of fire.
Paradise Lost (1667) bk. 2, l. 594

3   Feel by turns the bitter change
Of fierce extremes, extremes by change more fierce.
Paradise Lost (1667) bk. 2, l. 598

4 O'er many a frozen, many a fiery alp,
Rocks, caves, lakes, fens, bogs, dens, and shades of
    death,
A universe of death, which God by curse
Created evil, for evil only good,
Where all life dies, death lives, and nature breeds,
Perverse, all monstrous, all prodigious things,
Abominable, inutterable, and worse
Than fables yet have feigned, or fear conceived,
Gorgons and Hydras, and Chimeras dire.
Paradise Lost (1667) bk. 2, l. 620

5   The other shape,
If shape it might be called that shape had none
Distinguishable in member, joint, or limb,
Or substance might be called that shadow seemed,
For each seemed either; black it stood as night,
Fierce as ten Furies, terrible as hell,
And shook a dreadful dart; what seemed his head
The likeness of a kingly crown had on.
Paradise Lost (1667) bk. 2, l. 666

6 Whence and what art thou, execrable shape?
Paradise Lost (1667) bk. 2, l. 681

7 Incensed with indignation Satan stood
Unterrified, and like a comet burned
That fires the length of Ophiuchus huge
In the Arctic sky, and from his horrid hair
Shakes pestilence and war.
Paradise Lost (1667) bk. 2, l. 707

8 ... Their fatal hands
No second stroke intend.
Paradise Lost (1667) bk. 2, l. 712

9   I fled, and cried out Death!
Hell trembled at the hideous name, and sighed
From all her caves, and back resounded Death.
Paradise Lost (1667) bk. 2, l. 787

10   On a sudden open fly
With impetuous recoil and jarring sound
The infernal doors, and on their hinges grate
Harsh thunder.
Paradise Lost (1667) bk. 2, l. 879

11   Chaos umpire sits,
And by decision more embroils the fray
By which he reigns; next him high arbiter
Chance governs all.
Paradise Lost (1667) bk. 2, l. 907

12 Sable-vested Night, eldest of things.
Paradise Lost (1667) bk. 2, l. 962

13 With ruin upon ruin, rout on rout,
Confusion worse confounded.
Paradise Lost (1667) bk. 2, l. 995

14 So he with difficulty and labour hard
Moved on, with difficulty and labour he.
Paradise Lost (1667) bk. 2, l. 1021

15 Hail, holy Light, offspring of heaven first-born,
Or of the eternal co-eternal beam
May I express thee unblamed? since God is light,
And never but in unapproachèd light
Dwelt from eternity, dwelt then in thee,
Bright effluence of bright essence increate.
Or hear'st thou rather pure ethereal stream,
Whose fountain who shall tell?
Paradise Lost (1667) bk. 3, l. 1

16 Then feed on thoughts that voluntary move
Harmonious numbers, as the wakeful bird
Sings darkling, and in shadiest covert hid,
Tunes her nocturnal note. Thus with the year
Seasons return, but not to me returns
Day, or the sweet approach of ev'n or morn,
Or sight of vernal bloom, or summer's rose,
Or flocks, or herds, or human face divine;
But cloud instead, and ever-during dark
Surrounds me, from the cheerful ways of men
Cut off, and for the book of knowledge fair
Presented with a universal blank
Of Nature's works to me expunged and razed,
And wisdom at one entrance quite shut out.
Paradise Lost (1667) bk. 3, l. 37

17 Die he or justice must.
Paradise Lost (1667) bk. 3, l. 210. Cf. Andrewes 11:11

18 Dark with excessive bright.
Paradise Lost (1667) bk. 3, l. 380

19 So on this windy sea of land, the fiend
Walked up and down alone bent on his prey.
Paradise Lost (1667) bk. 3, l. 440

20 Into a limbo large and broad, since called
The Paradise of Fools, to few unknown.
Paradise Lost (1667) bk. 3, l. 495

21 For neither man nor angel can discern
Hypocrisy, the only evil that walks
Invisible, except to God alone.
Paradise Lost (1667) bk. 3, l. 682

22   At whose sight all the stars
Hide their diminished heads.
Paradise Lost (1667) bk. 4, l. 34

23 Warring in heaven against heaven's matchless king.
Paradise Lost (1667) bk. 4, l. 41

24   A grateful mind
By owing owes not, but still pays, at once
Indebted and discharged.
Paradise Lost (1667) bk. 4, l. 55

25 Me miserable! which way shall I fly
Infinite wrath, and infinite despair?
Which way I fly is hell; myself am hell;
And in the lowest deep a lower deep
Still threatening to devour me opens wide,
To which the hell I suffer seems a heaven.
Paradise Lost (1667) bk. 4, l. 73

26 So farewell hope, and with hope farewell fear,
Farewell remorse! All good to me is lost;
Evil, be thou my good.
Paradise Lost (1667) bk. 4, l. 108

1 So clomb this first grand thief into God's fold:
So since into his church lewd hirelings climb.
Thence up he flew, and on the tree of life,
The middle tree and highest there that grew,
Sat like a cormorant.
    Paradise Lost (1667) bk. 4, l. 192

2 Groves whose rich trees wept odorous gums and balm,
Others whose fruit burnished with golden rind
Hung amiable, Hesperian fables true,
If true, here only.
    Paradise Lost (1667) bk. 4, l. 248

3 Flowers of all hue, and without thorn the rose.
    Paradise Lost (1667) bk. 4, l. 256

4   Not that fair field
Of Enna, where Proserpine gathering flowers
Herself a fairer flower by gloomy Dis
Was gathered, which cost Ceres all that pain.
    Paradise Lost (1667) bk. 4, l. 268

5 For contemplation he and valour formed,
For softness she and sweet attractive grace,
He for God only, she for God in him:
His fair large front and eye sublime declared
Absolute rule.
    Paradise Lost (1667) bk. 4, l. 297

6 And by her yielded, by him best received,
Yielded with coy submission, modest pride,
And sweet reluctant amorous delay.
    Paradise Lost (1667) bk. 4, l. 309

7 Adam, the goodliest man of men since born
His sons, the fairest of her daughters Eve.
    Paradise Lost (1667) bk. 4, l. 323

8   The unwieldy elephant
To make them mirth used all his might, and wreathed
His lithe proboscis.
    Paradise Lost (1667) bk. 4, l. 345

9   These two
Emparadised in one another's arms
The happier Eden, shall enjoy their fill
Of bliss on bliss.
    Paradise Lost (1667) bk. 4, l. 505

10 Now came still evening on, and twilight grey
Had in her sober livery all things clad;
Silence accompanied, for beast and bird,
They to their grassy couch, these to their nests
Were slunk, all but the wakeful nightingale;
She all night long her amorous descant sung;
Silence was pleased: now glowed the firmament
With living sapphires: Hesperus that led
The starry host, rode brightest, till the moon
Rising in clouded majesty, at length
Apparent queen unveiled her peerless light,
And o'er the dark her silver mantle threw.
    Paradise Lost (1667) bk. 4, l. 598

11 God is thy law, thou mine: to know no more
Is woman's happiest knowledge and her praise.
With thee conversing I forget all time.
    Paradise Lost (1667) bk. 4, l. 637

12   Sweet the coming on
Of grateful evening mild, then silent night
With this her solemn bird and this fair moon,
And these the gems of heaven, her starry train.
    Paradise Lost (1667) bk. 4, l. 646

13 Millions of spiritual creatures walk the earth
Unseen, both when we wake, and when we sleep.
    Paradise Lost (1667) bk. 4, l. 677

14   Into their inmost bower
Handed they went; and eased the putting off
These troublesome disguises which we wear,
Strait side by side were laid, nor turned I ween
Adam from his fair spouse, nor Eve the rites
Mysterious of connubial love refused:
Whatever hypocrites austerely talk
Of purity and place and innocence,
Defaming as impure what God declares
Pure, and commands to some, leaves free to all.
    Paradise Lost (1667) bk. 4, l. 738

15 Hail, wedded love, mysterious law, true source
Of human offspring, sole propriety
In Paradise of all things common else.
    Paradise Lost (1667) bk. 4, l. 750

16   Sleep on
Blest pair; and O yet happiest if ye seek
No happier state, and know to know no more.
    Paradise Lost (1667) bk. 4, l. 773

17   Him there they found
Squat like a toad, close at the ear of Eve.
    Paradise Lost (1667) bk. 4, l. 799

18 But wherefore thou alone? Wherefore with thee
Came not all hell broke loose?
    Paradise Lost (1667) bk. 4, l. 917

19 Then when I am thy captive talk of chains,
Proud limitary cherub.
    Paradise Lost (1667) bk. 4, l. 970

20   His sleep
Was airy light from pure digestion bred.
    Paradise Lost (1667) bk. 5, l. 3

21 My fairest, my espoused, my latest found,
Heaven's last best gift, my ever new delight.
    Paradise Lost (1667) bk. 5, l. 18

22 Best image of myself and dearer half.
    Paradise Lost (1667) bk. 5, l. 95

23 On earth join all ye creatures to extol
Him first, him last, him midst, and without end.
    Paradise Lost (1667) bk. 5, l. 164

24 So saying, with dispatchful looks in haste
She turns, on hospitable thoughts intent.
    Paradise Lost (1667) bk. 5, l. 331

25   Nor jealousy
Was understood, the injured lover's hell.
    Paradise Lost (1667) bk. 5, l. 449

26   Freely we serve,
Because we freely love, as in our will
To love or not; in this we stand or fall.
    Paradise Lost (1667) bk. 5, l. 538

27   What if earth
Be but the shadow of heaven, and things therein
Each to other like, more than on earth is thought?
    Paradise Lost (1667) bk. 5, l. 574

28 Hear all ye angels, progeny of light,
Thrones, dominations, princedoms, virtues, powers.
    Paradise Lost (1667) bk. 5, l. 600

1 All seemed well pleased, all seemed, but were not all.
Paradise Lost (1667) bk. 5, l. 617

2 Mystical dance, which yonder starry sphere
Of planets and of fixed in all her wheels
Resembles nearest, mazes intricate,
Eccentric intervolved, yet regular
Then most, when most irregular they seem,
And in their motions harmony divine
So smoothes her charming tones, that God's own ear
Listens delighted.
Paradise Lost (1667) bk. 5, l. 620

3 Satan, so call him now, his former name
Is heard no more in heaven.
Paradise Lost (1667) bk. 5, l. 658

4 Servant of God, well done, well hast thou fought
The better fight, who single has maintained
Against revolted multitudes the cause
Of truth, in word mightier than they in arms.
Paradise Lost (1667) bk. 6, l. 29

5 Headlong themselves they threw
Down from the verge of heaven, eternal wrath
Burnt after them to the bottomless pit.
Paradise Lost (1667) bk. 6, l. 864

6 Standing on earth, not rapt above the pole,
More safe I sing with mortal voice, unchanged
To hoarse or mute, though fall'n on evil days,
On evil days though fallen, and evil tongues.
Paradise Lost (1667) bk. 7, l. 23

7 Still govern thou my song,
Urania, and fit audience find, though few.
But drive far off the barbarous dissonance
Of Bacchus and his revellers.
Paradise Lost (1667) bk. 7, l. 30

8 Necessity and chance
Approach not me, and what I will is fate.
Paradise Lost (1667) bk. 7, l. 172

9 There Leviathan
Hugest of living creatures, on the deep
Stretched like a promontory sleeps or swims,
And seems a moving land, and at his gills
Draws in, and at his trunk spouts out a sea.
Paradise Lost (1667) bk. 7, l. 412

10 The planets in their stations listening stood,
While the bright pomp ascended jubilant.
Open, ye everlasting gates, they sung,
Open, ye heavens, your living doors; let in
The great creator from his work returned
Magnificent, his six days' work, a world.
Paradise Lost (1667) bk. 7, l. 563

11 He his fabric of the heavens
Hath left to their disputes, perhaps to move
His laughter at their quaint opinions wide
Hereafter, when they come to model heaven
And calculate the stars, how they will wield
The mighty frame, how build, unbuild, contrive
To save appearances, how gird the sphere
With centric and eccentric scribbled o'er,
Cycle and epicycle, orb in orb.
Paradise Lost (1667) bk. 8, l. 76

12 Heaven is for thee too high
To know what passes there; be lowly wise:
Think only what concerns thee and thy being.
Paradise Lost (1667) bk. 8, l. 172

13 Tell me, how may I know him, how adore,
From whom I have that thus I move and live,
And feel that I am happier than I know?
Paradise Lost (1667) bk. 8, l. 280

14 In solitude
What happiness? who can enjoy alone,
Or all enjoying, what contentment find?
Paradise Lost (1667) bk. 8, l. 364

15 So absolute she seems
And in herself complete, so well to know
Her own, that what she wills to do or say
Seems wisest, virtuousest, discreetest, best.
Paradise Lost (1667) bk. 8, l. 547

16 Oft-times nothing profits more
Than self esteem, grounded on just and right
Well managed.
Paradise Lost (1667) bk. 8, l. 571

17 . . . My celestial patroness, who deigns
Her nightly visitation unimplored,
And dictates to me slumbering, or inspires
Easy my unpremeditated verse:
Since first this subject for heroic song
Pleased me long choosing, and beginning late.
Paradise Lost (1667) bk. 9, l. 21

18 . . . Unless an age too late, or cold
Climate, or years damp my intended wing.
Paradise Lost (1667) bk. 9, l. 44

19 The serpent subtlest beast of all the field.
Paradise Lost (1667) bk. 9, l. 86

20 For solitude sometimes is best society,
And short retirement urges sweet return.
Paradise Lost (1667) bk. 9, l. 249

21 As one who long in populous city pent,
Where houses thick and sewers annoy the air,
Forth issuing on a summer's morn to breathe
Among the pleasant villages and farms
Adjoined, from each thing met conceives delight.
Paradise Lost (1667) bk. 9, l. 445

22 She fair, divinely fair, fit love for gods.
Paradise Lost (1667) bk. 9, l. 489

23 God so commanded, and left that command
Sole daughter of his voice; the rest, we live
Law to our selves, our reason is our law.
Paradise Lost (1667) bk. 9, l. 652

24 Her rash hand in evil hour
Forth reaching to the fruit, she plucked, she ate:
Earth felt the wound, and Nature from her seat
Sighing through all her works gave signs of woe
That all was lost.
Paradise Lost (1667) bk. 9, l. 780

25 O fairest of creation, last and best
Of all God's works, creature in whom excelled
Whatever can to sight or thought be formed,
Holy, divine, good, amiable or sweet!
Paradise Lost (1667) bk. 9, l. 896

26 For with thee
Certain my resolution is to die;
How can I live without thee, how forgo
Thy sweet converse and love so dearly joined,
To live again in these wild woods forlorn?
Paradise Lost (1667) bk. 9, l. 906

1   Flesh of flesh,
Bone of my bone thou art, and from thy state
Mine never shall be parted, bliss or woe.
Paradise Lost (1667) bk. 9, l. 914

2   What thou art is mine;
Our state cannot be severed, we are one,
One flesh; to lose thee were to lose my self.
Paradise Lost (1667) bk. 9, l. 957

3 ... Yet I shall temper so
Justice with mercy.
Paradise Lost (1667) bk. 10, l. 77

4   He hears
On all sides, from innumerable tongues
A dismal universal hiss, the sound
Of public scorn.
Paradise Lost (1667) bk. 10, l. 506

5   O why did God,
Creator wise, that peopled highest heaven
With spirits masculine, create at last
This novelty on earth, this fair defect
Of nature?
Paradise Lost (1667) bk. 10, l. 888

6 Demoniac frenzy, moping melancholy
And moon-struck madness.
Paradise Lost (1667) bk. 11, l. 485

7 Henceforth I fly not death, nor would prolong
Life much, bent rather how I may be quit
Fairest and easiest of this cumbrous charge,
Which I must keep till my appointed day
Of rendering up, and patiently attend
My dissolution.
Paradise Lost (1667) bk. 11, l. 547

8 Nor love thy life, nor hate; but what thou liv'st
Live well, how long or short permit to heaven.
Paradise Lost (1667) bk. 11, l. 553

9 ... The evening star,
Love's harbinger.
Paradise Lost (1667) bk. 11, l. 588

10   For now I see
Peace to corrupt no less than war to waste.
Paradise Lost (1667) bk. 11, l. 783

11 O goodness infinite, goodness immense!
That all this good of evil shall produce,
And evil turn to good; more wonderful
Than that which by creation first brought forth
Light out of darkness! full of doubt I stand,
Whether I should repent me now of sin
By me done and occasioned, or rejoice
Much more, that much more good thereof shall
   spring.
Paradise Lost (1667) bk. 12, l. 469

12   Only add
Deeds to thy knowledge answerable, add faith,
Add virtue, patience, temperance, add love,
By name to come called Charity, the soul
Of all the rest: then wilt thou not be loath
To leave this Paradise, but shalt possess
A paradise within thee, happier far.
Paradise Lost (1667) bk. 12, l. 581

13 In me is no delay; with thee to go,
Is to stay here; without thee here to stay,
Is to go hence unwilling; thou to me
Art all things under heaven, all places thou,
Who for my wilful crime art banished hence.
Paradise Lost (1667) bk. 12, l. 615

14 They looking back, all the eastern side beheld
Of Paradise, so late their happy seat,
Waved over by that flaming brand, the gate
With dreadful faces thronged and fiery arms:
Some natural tears they dropped, but wiped them
   soon;
The world was all before them, where to choose
Their place of rest, and Providence their guide:
They hand in hand, with wandering steps and slow,
Through Eden took their solitary way.
Paradise Lost (1667) bk. 12, l. 641

15 Skilled to retire, and in retiring draw
Hearts after them tangled in amorous nets.
Paradise Regained (1671) bk. 2, l. 161

16 Of whom to be dispraised were no small praise.
Paradise Regained (1671) bk. 3, l. 56

17 But on occasion's forelock watchful wait.
Paradise Regained (1671) bk. 3, l. 173

18 He who seeking asses found a kingdom.
Paradise Regained (1671) bk. 3, l. 242 (of Saul). See Samuel
ch. 9, v. 3

19 ... The childhood shows the man,
As morning shows the day. Be famous then
By wisdom; as thy empire must extend,
So let extend thy mind o'er all the world.
Paradise Regained (1671) bk. 4, l. 220

20 Athens, the eye of Greece, mother of arts
And eloquence, native to famous wits
Or hospitable, in her sweet recess,
City or suburban, studious walks and shades;
See there the olive grove of Academe,
Plato's retirement, where the Attic bird
Trills her thick-warbled notes the summer long.
Paradise Regained (1671) bk. 4, l. 240

21 The first and wisest of them all professed
To know this only, that he nothing knew.
Paradise Regained (1671) bk. 4, l. 293. Cf. Davies 232:3,
Socrates 654:10

22   Who reads
Incessantly, and to his reading brings not
A spirit and judgement equal or superior
(And what he brings, what needs he elsewhere seek?)
Uncertain and unsettled still remains,
Deep-versed in books and shallow in himself.
Paradise Regained (1671) bk. 4, l. 322

23 In them is plainest taught, and easiest learnt,
What makes a nation happy, and keeps it so.
Paradise Regained (1671) bk. 4, l. 361 (of the prophets)

24 But headlong joy is ever on the wing.
'The Passion' (1645) st. 1

25 Ask for this great deliverer now, and find him
Eyeless in Gaza at the mill with slaves.
Samson Agonistes (1671) l. 40

1 O dark, dark, dark, amid the blaze of noon,
Irrecoverably dark, total eclipse
Without all hope of day!
Samson Agonistes (1671) l. 80

2 The sun to me is dark
And silent as the moon,
When she deserts the night
Hid in her vacant interlunar cave.
Samson Agonistes (1671) l. 86

3 To live a life half dead, a living death.
Samson Agonistes (1671) l. 100

4 Ran on embattled armies clad in iron,
And, weaponless himself,
Made arms ridiculous.
Samson Agonistes (1671) l. 129

5   Wisest men
Have erred, and by bad women been deceived;
And shall again, pretend they ne'er so wise.
Samson Agonistes (1671) l. 210

6 Just are the ways of God,
And justifiable to men;
Unless there be who think not God at all.
Samson Agonistes (1671) l. 293

7 . . . Of such doctrine never was there school,
But the heart of the fool,
And no man therein doctor but himself.
Samson Agonistes (1671) l. 297

8 But what availed this temperance, not complete
Against another object more enticing?
What boots it at one gate to make defence,
And at another to let in the foe?
Samson Agonistes (1671) l. 558

9   That grounded maxim
So rife and celebrated in the mouths
Of wisest men; that to the public good
Private respects must yield.
Samson Agonistes (1671) l. 865

10 Yet beauty, though injurious, hath strange power,
After offence returning, to regain
Love once possessed.
Samson Agonistes (1671) l. 1003

11 Love-quarrels oft in pleasing concord end.
Samson Agonistes (1671) l. 1008

12 Lords are lordliest in their wine.
Samson Agonistes (1671) l. 1418

13 For evil news rides post, while good news baits.
Samson Agonistes (1671) l. 1538

14 And as an evening dragon came,
Assailant on the perchèd roosts,
And nests in order ranged
Of tame villatic fowl.
Samson Agonistes (1671) l. 1692

15 Like that self-begotten bird
In the Arabian woods embossed,
That no second knows nor third,
And lay erewhile a holocaust.
Samson Agonistes (1671) l. 1699

16 And though her body die, her fame survives,
A secular bird ages of lives.
Samson Agonistes (1671) l. 1706

17   Samson hath quit himself
Like Samson, and heroically hath finished
A life heroic.
Samson Agonistes (1671) l. 1709

18 Nothing is here for tears, nothing to wail
Or knock the breast, no weakness, no contempt,
Dispraise, or blame, nothing but well and fair,
And what may quiet us in a death so noble.
Samson Agonistes (1671) l. 1721

19 All is best, though we oft doubt,
What the unsearchable dispose
Of highest wisdom brings about,
And ever best found in the close.
Samson Agonistes (1671) l. 1745

20 His servants he, with new acquist
Of true experience from this great event
With peace and consolation hath dismissed,
And calm of mind, all passion spent.
Samson Agonistes (1671) l. 1755

21 How soon hath time the subtle thief of youth,
Stol'n on his wing my three and twentieth year!
Sonnet 7 'How soon hath time' (1645)

22 I did but prompt the age to quit their clogs
By the known rules of ancient liberty,
When straight a barbarous noise environs me
Of owls and cuckoos, asses, apes, and dogs.
Sonnet 12 'I did but prompt the age' (1673)

23 Licence they mean when they cry liberty;
For who loves that, must first be wise and good.
Sonnet 12 'I did but prompt the age' (1673)

24 When I consider how my light is spent,
E're half my days, in this dark world and wide,
And that one talent which is death to hide
Lodged with me useless . . .
Doth God exact day-labour, light denied,
I fondly ask; but patience to prevent
That murmur, soon replies, God doth not need
Either man's work or his own gifts, who best
Bear his mild yoke, they serve him best, his state
Is kingly. Thousands at his bidding speed
And post o'er land and ocean without rest:
They also serve who only stand and wait.
Sonnet 16 'When I consider how my light is spent' (1673)

25 Today deep thoughts resolve with me to drench
In mirth, that after no repenting draws.
Sonnet 18 'Cyriack, whose grandsire on the royal bench'
(1673)

26 Methought I saw my late espousèd saint
Brought to me like Alcestis from the grave.
Sonnet 19 'Methought I saw my late espousèd saint' (1673)

27 But oh as to embrace me she inclined
I waked, she fled, and day brought back my night.
Sonnet 19 'Methought I saw my late espousèd saint' (1673)

28 Cromwell, our chief of men.
'To the Lord General Cromwell' (written 1652)

29 . . . Peace hath her victories
No less renowned than war.
'To the Lord General Cromwell' (written 1652)

30 He who would not be frustrate of his hope to write
well hereafter in laudable things, ought himself to be a
true poem.
An Apology for Smectymnuus (1642) introduction, p. 16

1 His words . . . like so many nimble and airy servitors trip about him at command.
An Apology for Smectymnuus (1642) sect. 12, p. 55

2 For this is not the liberty which we can hope, that no grievance ever should arise in the Commonwealth, that let no man in this world expect; but when complaints are freely heard, deeply considered, and speedily reformed, then is the utmost bound of civil liberty attained that wise men look for.
Areopagitica (1644) p. 1

3 Books are not absolutely dead things, but do contain a potency of life in them to be as active as that soul was whose progeny they are; nay they do preserve as in a vial the purest efficacy and extraction of that living intellect that bred them.
Areopagitica (1644) p. 4

4 As good almost kill a man as kill a good book: who kills a man kills a reasonable creature, God's image; but he who destroys a good book, kills reason itself, kills the image of God, as it were in the eye.
Areopagitica (1644) p. 4

5 A good book is the precious life-blood of a master spirit, embalmed and treasured up on purpose to a life beyond life.
Areopagitica (1644) p. 4

6 It was from out the rind of one apple tasted that the knowledge of good and evil as two twins cleaving together leaped forth into the world. And perhaps this is that doom that Adam fell into of knowing good and evil, that is to say, of knowing good by evil.
Areopagitica (1644) p. 12

7 He that can apprehend and consider vice with all her baits and seeming pleasures, and yet abstain, and yet distinguish, and yet prefer that which is truly better, he is the true warfaring Christian. I cannot praise a fugitive and cloistered virtue, unexercised and unbreathed, that never sallies out and sees her adversary, but slinks out of the race, where that immortal garland is to be run for, not without dust and heat. Assuredly we bring not innocence into the world, we bring impurity much rather: that which purifies us is trial, and trial is by what is contrary.
Areopagitica (1644) p. 12

8 If we think to regulate printing, thereby to rectify manners, we must regulate all recreations and pastimes, all that is delightful to man . . . It will ask more than the work of twenty licensers to examine all the lutes, the violins, and the guitars in every house; they must not be suffered to prattle as they do, but must be licensed what they may say. And who shall silence all the airs and madrigals, that whisper softness in chambers?
Areopagitica (1644) p. 16

9 From that time ever since, the sad friends of Truth, such as durst appear, imitating the careful search that Isis made for the mangled body of Osiris, went up and down gathering up limb by limb still as they could find them. We have not yet found them all, Lords and Commons, nor ever shall do, till her Master's second coming; He shall bring together every joint and member, and shall mould them into an immortal feature of loveliness and perfection.
Areopagitica (1644) p. 29

10 To be still searching what we know not, by what we know, still closing up truth to truth as we find it (for all her body is homogeneal and proportional), this is the golden rule in theology as well as in arithmetic, and makes up the best harmony in a church.
Areopagitica (1644) p. 30

11 God is decreeing to begin some new and great period in his Church, even to the reforming of Reformation itself. What does he then but reveal Himself to his servants, and as his manner is, first to his Englishmen?
Areopagitica (1644) p. 31

12 Behold now this vast city; a city of refuge, the mansion-house of liberty, encompassed and surrounded with his protection.
Areopagitica (1644) p. 31 (of London)

13 Where there is much desire to learn, there of necessity will be much arguing, much writing, many opinions; for opinion in good men is but knowledge in the making.
Areopagitica (1644) p. 31

14 Methinks I see in my mind a noble and puissant nation rousing herself like a strong man after sleep, and shaking her invincible locks. Methinks I see her as an eagle mewing her mighty youth, and kindling her undazzled eyes at the full midday beam.
Areopagitica (1644) p. 34

15 Give me the liberty to know, to utter, and to argue freely according to conscience, above all liberties.
Areopagitica (1644) p. 34

16 Though all the winds of doctrine were let loose to play upon the earth, so Truth be in the field, we do injuriously by licensing and prohibiting to misdoubt her strength. Let her and Falsehood grapple; who ever knew Truth put to the worse, in a free and open encounter?
Areopagitica (1644) p. 35

17 Let not England forget her precedence of teaching nations how to live.
The Doctrine and Discipline of Divorce (1643) 'To the Parliament of England'

18 I owe no light or leading received from any man in the discovery of this truth.
The Judgement of Martin Bucer (1644), 'this truth' being Milton's *Doctrine and Discipline of Divorce* (1643)

19 I call therefore a complete and generous education that which fits a man to perform justly, skilfully and magnanimously all the offices both private and public of peace and war.
Of Education (1644)

20 Ornate rhetoric taught out of the rule of Plato . . . To which poetry would be made subsequent, or indeed rather precedent, as being less subtle and fine, but more simple, sensuous and passionate.
Of Education (1644)

1 In those vernal seasons of the year, when the air is calm and pleasant, it were an injury and sullenness against nature not to go out, and see her riches, and partake in her rejoicing with heaven and earth.
Of Education (1644) 'Their Exercise'

2 What I have spoken, is the language of that which is not called amiss *The good old Cause.*
The Ready and Easy Way to Establish a Free Commonwealth (2nd ed., 1660) p. 106

3 But because about the manner and order of this government, whether it ought to be Presbyterial, or Prelatical, such endless question, or rather uproar is arisen in this land, as may be justly termed, what the fever is to the physicians, the eternal reproach of our divines.
The Reason of Church Government (1642) preface

4 This manner of writing [prose] wherein knowing myself inferior to myself . . . I have the use, as I may account it, but of my left hand.
The Reason of Church Government (1642) bk. 2, introduction

5 By labour and intent study (which I take to be my portion in this life) joined with the strong propensity of nature, I might perhaps leave something so written to aftertimes, as they should not willingly let it die.
The Reason of Church Government (1642) bk. 2, introduction

6 The land had once enfranchised herself from this impertinent yoke of prelaty, under whose inquisitorious and tyrannical duncery no free and splendid wit can flourish.
The Reason of Church Government (1642) bk. 2, introduction

7 Beholding the bright countenance of truth in the quiet and still air of delightful studies.
The Reason of Church Government (1642) bk. 2, introduction

8 None can love freedom heartily, but good men; the rest love not freedom, but licence.
The Tenure of Kings and Magistrates (1649)

9 No man who knows aught, can be so stupid to deny that all men naturally were born free.
The Tenure of Kings and Magistrates (1649)

Comte de Mirabeau 1749–91
French revolutionary

10 *La guerre est l'industrie nationale de la Prusse.*
War is the national industry of Prussia.
Attributed to Mirabeau by Albert Sorel (1842–1906), based on Mirabeau's introduction to *De la monarchie prussienne sous Frédéric le Grand* (1788)

The Missal
Texts used in the service of the Mass throughout the year

11 *Asperges me, Domine, hyssopo, et mundabor.*
Sprinkle me with hyssop, O Lord, and I shall be cleansed.
Anthem at Sprinkling the Holy Water. Cf. Book of Common Prayer 128:5

12 *Dominus vobiscum.*
Et cum spiritu tuo.
The Lord be with you.
And with thy spirit.
The Ordinary of the Mass

13 *In Nomine Patris, et Filii, et Spiritus Sancti.*
In the Name of the Father, and of the Son, and of the Holy Ghost.
The Ordinary of the Mass

14 *Introibo ad altare Dei.*
I will go unto the altar of God.
The Ordinary of the Mass. Cf. Book of Common Prayer 127:7

15 *Gloria Patri, et Filio, et Spiritui Sancto. Sicut erat in principio, et nunc, et semper, et in saecula saeculorum.*
Glory be to the Father, and to the Son, and to the Holy Ghost. As it was in the beginning, is now, and ever shall be, world without end.
The Ordinary of the Mass 'The Doxology'. Cf. Book of Common Prayer 118:11

16 *Confiteor Deo omnipotenti . . . quia peccavi nimis cogitatione, verbo, et opere, mea culpa, mea culpa, mea maxima culpa.*
I confess to almighty God . . . that I have sinned exceedingly in thought, word, and deed, through my fault, through my fault, through my most grievous fault.
The Ordinary of the Mass

17 *Kyrie eleison . . . Christe eleison.*
Lord, have mercy upon us . . . Christ, have mercy upon us.
The Ordinary of the Mass

18 *Gloria in excelsis Deo, et in terra pax hominibus bonae voluntatis. Laudamus te, benedicimus te, adoramus te, glorificamus te.*
Glory be to God on high, and on earth peace to men of good will. We praise thee, we bless thee, we adore thee, we glorify thee.
The Ordinary of the Mass. Cf. St Luke 93:28

19 *Oremus.*
Let us pray.
The Ordinary of the Mass

20 *Deo gratias.*
Thanks be to God.
The Ordinary of the Mass

21 *Credo in unum Deum, Patrem omnipotentem, factorem coeli et terrae, visibilium omnium et invisibilium.*
I believe in one God, the Father almighty, maker of heaven and earth, and of all things visible and invisible.
The Ordinary of the Mass 'The Nicene Creed'. Cf. Book of Common Prayer 119:1, 121:19

22 *Deum de Deo, lumen de lumine, Deum verum de Deo vero.*
God of God, light of light; true God of true God.
The Ordinary of the Mass 'The Nicene Creed'

23 *Et incarnatus est de Spiritu Sancto, ex Maria Virgine;* ET HOMO FACTUS EST.
And became incarnate by the Holy Ghost, of the Virgin Mary; AND WAS MADE MAN.
The Ordinary of the Mass 'The Nicene Creed'

24 *Sursum corda.*
Lift up your hearts.
The Ordinary of the Mass. Cf. Book of Common Prayer 122:8

1 *Dignum et justum est.*

It is right and fitting.

The Ordinary of the Mass. Cf. Book of Common Prayer 122:9

2 *Sanctus, sanctus, sanctus, Dominus Deus Sabaoth. Pleni sunt coeli et terra gloria tua. Hosanna in excelsis. Benedictus qui venit in nomine Domini.*

Holy, holy, holy, Lord God of Hosts. Heaven and earth are full of thy glory. Hosanna in the highest. Blessed is he that cometh in the name of the Lord.

The Ordinary of the Mass. Cf. Book of Common Prayer 122:10

3 *Pater noster, qui es in coelis, sanctificetur nomen tuum; adveniat regnum tuum; fiat voluntas tua sicut in coelo, et in terra ... sed libera nos a malo.*

Our Father, who art in heaven, hallowed be thy name; thy kingdom come; thy will be done on earth, as it is in heaven ... but deliver us from evil.

The Ordinary of the Mass. Cf. St Matthew 89:5

4 *Pax Domini sit semper vobiscum.*

The peace of the Lord be always with you.

The Ordinary of the Mass

5 *Agnus Dei, qui tollis peccata mundi, miserere nobis. Agnus Dei, qui tollis peccata mundi, dona nobis pacem.*

Lamb of God, who takest away the sins of the world, have mercy on us. Lamb of God, who takest away the sins of the world, give us peace.

The Ordinary of the Mass

6 *Domine, non sum dignus ut intres sub tectum meum; sed tantum dic verbo, et sanabitur anima mea.*

Lord, I am not worthy that thou shouldst enter under my roof; but say only the word, and my soul shall be healed.

The Ordinary of the Mass. Cf. St Matthew 89:29

7 *Ite missa est.*

Go, you are dismissed.

The Ordinary of the Mass (commonly interpreted as 'Go, the Mass is ended')

8 *In principio erat Verbum, et Verbum erat apud Deum, et Deus erat Verbum.*

In the beginning was the Word, and the Word was with God, and the Word was God.

The Ordinary of the Mass. Cf. St John 95:35

9 VERBUM CARO FACTUM EST.

THE WORD WAS MADE FLESH.

The Ordinary of the Mass. Cf. St John 96:4

10 *Requiem aeternam dona eis, Domine: et lux perpetua luceat eis.*

Grant them eternal rest, O Lord; and let perpetual light shine on them.

Order of Mass for the Dead

11 *Dies irae, dies illa,*
Solvet saeclum in favilla,
Teste David cum Sibylla.

That day, the day of wrath, will turn the universe to ashes, as David foretells (and the Sibyl too).

Order of Mass for the Dead 'Sequentia' (commonly known as Dies Irae) l. 1 (attributed to Thomas of Celano, c.1190–1260)

12 *Tuba mirum spargens sonum*
Per sepulcra regionum,
Coget omnes ante thronum.
Mors stupebit et natura,
Cum resurget creatura
Iudicanti responsura.
Liber scriptus proferetur,
In quo totum continetur
Unde mundus iudicetur.

The trumpet will fling out a wonderful sound through the tombs of all regions, it will drive everyone before the throne. Death will be aghast and so will nature, when creation rises again to make answer to the judge. The written book will be brought forth, in which everything is included whereby the world will be judged.

Order of Mass for the Dead 'Sequentia' l. 7

13 *Rex tremendae maiestatis,*
Qui salvandos salvas gratis,
Salva me, fons pietatis!

O King of tremendous majesty, who freely saves those who should be saved, save me, O source of pity!

Order of Mass for the Dead 'Sequentia' l. 22

14 *Inter oves locum praesta*
Et ab haedis me sequestra
Statuens in parte dextra.

Among the sheep set me a place and separate me from the goats, standing me on the right-hand side.

Order of Mass for the Dead 'Sequentia' l. 43

15 *Requiescant in pace.*

May they rest in peace.

Order of Mass for the Dead

16 *O felix culpa, quae talem ac tantum meruit habere Redemptorem.*

O happy fault, which has earned such a mighty Redeemer.

'Exsultet' on Holy Saturday

Adrian Mitchell 1932–

English poet, novelist, and playwright

17 Most people ignore most poetry
because
most poetry ignores most people.

Poems (1964) p. 8

Joni Mitchell (Roberta Joan Anderson) 1945–

Canadian singer and songwriter

18 They paved paradise
And put up a parking lot,
With a pink hotel,
A boutique, and a swinging hot spot.

'Big Yellow Taxi' (1970 song)

19 I've looked at life from both sides now,
From win and lose and still somehow
It's life's illusions I recall;
I really don't know life at all.

'Both Sides Now' (1967 song)

1 We are stardust,
We are golden,
And we got to get ourselves
Back to the garden.
'Woodstock' (1969 song)

Margaret Mitchell 1900–49

American novelist

2 Death and taxes and childbirth! There's never any convenient time for any of them.
Gone with the Wind (1936) ch. 38. Cf. Franklin 293:3

3 I wish I could care what you do or where you go but I can't . . . My dear, I don't give a damn.
Gone with the Wind (1936) ch. 57 (Rhett Butler to Scarlett). 'Frankly, my dear, I don't give a damn!' in the 1939 screen version by Sidney Howard

4 After all, tomorrow is another day.
Gone with the Wind (1936) ad fin.

Nancy Mitford 1904–73

English writer

5 'Always be civil to the girls, you never know who they may marry' is an aphorism which has saved many an English spinster from being treated like an Indian widow.
Love in a Cold Climate (1949) pt. 1, ch. 2

6 An aristocracy in a republic is like a chicken whose head has been cut off: it may run about in a lively way, but in fact it is dead.
Noblesse Oblige (1956) 'The English Aristocracy'

7 Wooing, so tiring.
The Pursuit of Love (1945) ch. 4

8 Frogs . . . are slightly better than Huns or Wops, but abroad is unutterably bloody and foreigners are fiends.
The Pursuit of Love (1945) ch. 15. Cf. George VI 301:8

François Mitterrand 1916–

French socialist politician; President of France from 1981

9 You, Attali, are a mere chapter. I am the entire volume.
To his adviser, Jacques Attali, in *Observer* 'Sayings of the Year' (29 December 1991)

Wilson Mizner 1876–1933

American playwright

10 Be nice to people on your way up because you'll meet 'em on your way down.
In Alva Johnston *The Legendary Mizners* (1953) ch. 4

11 If you steal from one author, it's plagiarism; if you steal from many, it's research.
In Alva Johnston *The Legendary Mizners* (1953) ch. 4

12 A trip through a sewer in a glass-bottomed boat.
Of Hollywood, in Alva Johnston *The Legendary Mizners* (1953) ch. 4 (reworked by Mayor Jimmy Walker into 'A reformer is a guy who rides through a sewer in a glass-bottomed boat')

Molière (Jean-Baptiste Poquelin) 1622–73

French comic playwright

13 *Présentez toujours le devant au monde.*
Always present your front to the world.
L'Avare (1669) act 3, sc. 1

14 *Il faut manger pour vivre et non pas vivre pour manger.*
One should eat to live, and not live to eat.
L'Avare (1669) act 3, sc. 1

15 *Tout ce qui n'est point prose est vers; et tout ce qui n'est point vers est prose.*
All that is not prose is verse; and all that is not verse is prose.
Le Bourgeois Gentilhomme (1671) act 2, sc. 4

16 M. JOURDAIN: *Quoi? quand je dis: 'Nicole, apportez-moi mes pantoufles, et me donnez mon bonnet de nuit', c'est de la prose?*
MAÎTRE DE PHILOSOPHIE: *Oui, Monsieur.*
M. JOURDAIN: *Par ma foi! il y a plus de quarante ans que je dis de la prose sans que j'en susse rien.*

M. JOURDAIN: What? when I say: 'Nicole, bring me my slippers, and give me my night-cap,' is that prose?
PHILOSOPHY TEACHER: Yes, Sir.
M. JOURDAIN: Good heavens! For more than forty years I have been speaking prose without knowing it.
Le Bourgeois Gentilhomme (1671) act 2, sc. 4

17 *Ah, la belle chose que de savoir quelque chose.*
Ah, it's a lovely thing, to know a thing or two.
Le Bourgeois Gentilhomme (1671) act 2, sc. 4

18 *C'est une étrange entreprise que celle de faire rire les honnêtes gens.*
It's an odd job, making decent people laugh.
La Critique de l'école des femmes (1663) sc. 6

19 *Je voudrais bien savoir si la grande règle de toutes les règles n'est pas de plaire.*
I shouldn't be surprised if the greatest rule of all weren't to give pleasure.
La Critique de l'école des femmes (1663) sc. 6

20 *On ne meurt qu'une fois, et c'est pour si longtemps!*
One dies only once, and it's for such a long time!
Le Dépit amoureux (performed 1656, published 1662) act 5, sc. 3

21 *Qui vit sans tabac n'est pas digne de vivre.*
He who lives without tobacco is not worthy to live.
Don Juan (performed 1665) act 1, sc. 1

22 *Je vis de bonne soupe et non de beau langage.*
It's good food and not fine words that keeps me alive.
Les Femmes savantes (1672) act 2, sc. 7

23 *Guenille, si l'on veut: ma guenille m'est chère.*
Rags and tatters, if you like: I am fond of my rags and tatters.
Les Femmes savantes (1672) act 2, sc. 7

1 *Un sot savant est sot plus qu'un sot ignorant.*

A knowledgeable fool is a greater fool than an ignorant fool.
Les Femmes savantes (1672) act 4, sc. 3

2 *Les livres cadrent mal avec le mariage.*

Reading and marriage don't go well together.
Les Femmes savantes (1672) act 5, sc. 3

3 GÉRONTE: *Il me semble que vous les placez autrement qu'ils ne sont: que le coeur est du côté gauche, et le foie du côté droit.*

SGANARELLE: *Oui, cela était autrefois ainsi, mais nous avons changé tout cela, et nous faisons maintenant la médecine d'une méthode toute nouvelle.*

GÉRONTE: It seems to me you are locating them wrongly: the heart is on the left and the liver is on the right.
SGANARELLE: Yes, in the old days that was so, but we have changed all that, and we now practise medicine by a completely new method.
Le Médecin malgré lui (1667) act 2, sc. 4

4 *Il faut, parmi le monde, une vertu traitable.*

What's needed in this world is an accommodating sort of virtue.
Le Misanthrope (1666) act 1, sc. 1

5 *Et c'est une folie à nulle autre seconde,*
De vouloir se mêler de corriger le monde.

Of all human follies there's none could be greater
Than trying to render our fellow-men better.
Le Misanthrope (1666) act 1, sc. 1

6 *On doit se regarder soi-même, un fort long temps,*
Avant que de songer à condamner les gens.

One should look long and carefully at oneself before one considers judging others.
Le Misanthrope (1666) act 3, sc. 4

7 *C'est un homme expéditif, qui aime à dépêcher ses malades; et quand on a à mourir, cela se fait avec lui le plus vite du monde.*

He's an expeditious man, who likes to hurry his patients along; and when you have to die, he sees to that quicker than anyone.
Monsieur de Pourceaugnac (1670) act 1, sc. 5

8 *Ils commencent ici par faire pendre un homme et puis ils lui font son procès.*

Here [in Paris] they hang a man first, and try him afterwards.
Monsieur de Pourceaugnac (1670) act 1, sc. 5

9 *Les gens de qualité savent tout sans avoir jamais rien appris.*

People of quality know everything without ever having been taught anything.
Les Précieuses ridicules (1660) sc. 9

10 *Assassiner c'est le plus court chemin.*

Assassination is the quickest way.
Le Sicilien (1668) sc. 12

11 *Ah, pour être dévot, je n'en suis pas moins homme.*

I am not the less human for being devout.
Le Tartuffe (performed 1664, published 1669) act 3, sc. 3

12 *Le ciel défend, de vrai, certains contentements,*
Mais on trouve avec lui des accommodements.

God, it is true, does some delights condemn,
But 'tis not hard to come to terms with Him.
Le Tartuffe (1669) act 4, sc. 5

13 *Le scandale du monde est ce qui fait l'offense,*
Et ce n'est pas pécher que pécher en silence.

It is public scandal that constitutes offence, and to sin in secret is not to sin at all.
Le Tartuffe (1669) act 4, sc. 5

14 *L'homme est, je vous l'avoue, un méchant animal.*

Man, I can assure you, is a nasty creature.
Le Tartuffe (1669) act 5, sc. 6

15 *Il m'est permis de reprendre mon bien où je le trouve.*

It is permitted me to take good fortune where I find it.
In J. L. Le Gallois *La Vie de Molière* (1704) p. 14

Mary Mollineux (née Southworth) 1651–95

English Quaker and poet

16 How sweet is harmless solitude!
What can its joys control?
Tumults and noise may not intrude,
To interrupt the soul.
'Solitude' (1670)

Helmuth von Moltke 1800–91

Prussian military commander

17 *Der ewige Friede ist ein Traum, und nicht einmal ein schöner, und der Krieg ein Glied in Gottes Weltordnung ... Ohne den Krieg würde die Welt in Materialismus versumpfen.*

Everlasting peace is a dream, and not even a pleasant one; and war is a necessary part of God's arrangement of the world ... Without war the world would deteriorate into materialism.
Letter to Dr J. K. Bluntschli, 11 December 1880 (translated by Mary Herms), in *Helmuth von Moltke as a Correspondent* (1893)

William Cosmo Monkhouse 1840–1901

English poet and critic

18 There once was an old man of Lyme
Who married three wives at a time,
When asked 'Why a third?'
He replied, 'One's absurd!
And bigamy, Sir, is a crime!'
Nonsense Rhymes (1902)

Duke of Monmouth 1649–85

Illegitimate son of Charles II; leader of the failed Monmouth rebellion against James II

19 Do not hack me as you did my Lord Russell.
Words addressed to his executioner, in T. B. Macaulay *History of England* vol. 1 (1849) ch. 5

John Samuel Bewley Monsell 1811–75
Irish-born clergyman

1 Fight the good fight with all thy might,
Christ is thy strength and Christ thy right;
Lay hold on life, and it shall be
Thy joy and crown eternally.

Run the straight race through God's good grace,
Lift up thine eyes and seek his face;
Life with its way before us lies,
Christ is the path and Christ the prize.
'Fight the good fight with all thy might' (1863 hymn)

2 O worship the Lord in the beauty of holiness,
Bow down before him, his glory proclaim;
With gold of obedience and incense of lowliness,
Kneel and adore him: the Lord is his name.
'O worship the Lord in the beauty of holiness' (1863 hymn)

Lady Mary Wortley Montagu 1689–1762
English writer

3 But the fruit that can fall without shaking,
Indeed is too mellow for me.
'Answered, for Lord William Hamilton' in J. Dodsley (ed.)
A Collection of Poems vol. 6 (1758) p. 231

4 Let this great maxim be my virtue's guide:
In part she is to blame, who has been tried,
He comes too near, that comes to be denied.
The Plain Dealer (27 April 1724) 'The Resolve'

5 And we meet with champagne and a chicken at last.
Six Town Eclogues (1747) 'The Lover' l. 25

6 As Ovid has sweetly in parable told,
We harden like trees, and like rivers grow cold.
Six Town Eclogues (1747) 'The Lover' l. 47

7 In chains and darkness, wherefore should I stay,
And mourn in prison, while I keep the key?
'Verses on Self-Murder' in *The London Magazine* (1749)

8 This world consists of men, women, and Herveys.
Attributed by Lord Wharncliffe in *Letters and Works of Lady Mary Wortley Montagu* (1837) vol. 1, p. 67 ('Herveys' being a reference to John Hervey, Baron Hervey of Ickworth, 1696–1743)

9 General notions are generally wrong.
Letter to her husband Edward Wortley Montagu, 28 March 1710, in Robert Halsband (ed.) *Complete Letters of Lady Mary Wortley Montagu* vol. 1 (1965)

10 Civility costs nothing and buys everything.
Letter to her daughter Mary, Countess of Bute, 30 May 1756, in Robert Halsband (ed.) *Complete Letters of Lady Mary Wortley Montagu* vol. 3 (1967)

11 People wish their enemies dead—but I do not; I say give them the gout, give them the stone!
In W. S. Lewis et al. (eds.) *Horace Walpole's Correspondence* vol. 35 (1973) p. 489

C. E. Montague 1867–1928
British writer

12 War hath no fury like a non-combatant.
Disenchantment (1922) ch. 16

Montaigne (Michel Eyquem de Montaigne) 1533–92
French moralist and essayist

13 *Pour juger des choses grandes et hautes, il faut une âme de même, autrement nous leur attribuons le vice qui est le nôtre.*
To make judgements about great and lofty things, a soul of the same stature is needed; otherwise we ascribe to them that vice which is our own.
Essais (1580, ed. M. Rat, 1958) bk. 1, ch. 14

14 *Il faut être toujours botté et prêt à partir.*
One should always have one's boots on, and be ready to leave.
Essais (1580, ed. M. Rat, 1958) bk. 1, ch. 20.
Cf. La Fontaine 405:13

15 *Je veux . . . que la mort me trouve plantant mes choux, mais nonchalant d'elle, et encore plus de mon jardin imparfait.*
I want death to find me planting my cabbages, but caring little for it, and even less about the imperfections of my garden.
Essais (1580, ed. M. Rat, 1958) bk. 1, ch. 20

16 *Le continuel ouvrage de votre vie, c'est bâtir la mort.*
The ceaseless labour of your life is to build the house of death.
Essais (1580, ed. M. Rat, 1958) bk. 1, ch. 20

17 *L'utilité du vivre n'est pas en l'espace, elle est en l'usage; tel a vécu longtemps qui a peu vécu . . . Il gît en votre volonté, non au nombre des ans, que vous ayez assez vécu.*
The value of life lies not in the length of days but in the use you make of them; he has lived for a long time who has little lived. Whether you have lived enough depends not on the number of your years but on your will.
Essais (1580, ed. M. Rat, 1958) bk. 1, ch. 20

18 *Il faut noter, que les jeux d'enfants ne sont pas jeux, et les faut juger en eux comme leurs plus sérieuses actions.*
It should be noted that children at play are not playing about; their games should be seen as their most serious-minded activity.
Essais (1580, ed. M. Rat, 1958) bk. 1, ch. 23

19 *Si on me presse de dire pourquoi je l'aimais, je sens que cela ne se peut s'exprimer, qu'en répondant: 'Parce que c'était lui; parce que c'était moi.'*
If I am pressed to say why I loved him, I feel it can only be explained by replying: 'Because it was he; because it was me.'
Essais (1580, ed. M. Rat, 1958) bk. 1, ch. 28 (of his friend Étienne de la Boétie)

20 *Il n'y a guère moins de tourment au gouvernement d'une famille que d'un état entier . . . et, pour être les occupations domestiques moins importantes, elles n'en sont pas moins importunes.*
There is scarcely any less bother in the running of a family than in that of an entire state. And domestic business is no less importunate for being less important.
Essais (1580, ed. M. Rat, 1958) bk. 1, ch. 39

1 *Il se faut réserver une arrière boutique toute nôtre, toute franche, en laquelle nous établissons nôtre vraie liberté et principale retraite et solitude.*

A man should keep for himself a little back shop, all his own, quite unadulterated, in which he establishes his true freedom and chief place of seclusion and solitude.

    Essais (1580, ed. M. Rat, 1958) bk. 1, ch. 39

2 *La plus grande chose du monde, c'est de savoir être à soi.*

The greatest thing in the world is to know how to be oneself.

    Essais (1580, ed. M. Rat, 1958) bk. 1, ch. 39

3 *La gloire et le repos sont choses qui ne peuvent loger en même gîte.*

Fame and tranquillity can never be bedfellows.

    Essais (1580, ed. M. Rat, 1958) bk. 1, ch. 39

4 *Mon métier et mon art c'est vivre.*

Living is my job and my art.

    Essais (1580, ed. M. Rat, 1958) bk. 2, ch. 6

5 *La vertu refuse la facilité pour compagne ... Elle demande un chemin âpre et épineux.*

Virtue shuns ease as a companion ... It demands a rough and thorny path.

    Essais (1580, ed. M. Rat, 1958) bk. 2, ch. 11

6 *Notre religion est faite pour extirper les vices; elle les couvre, les nourrit, les incite.*

Our religion is made so as to wipe out vices; it covers them up, nourishes them, incites them.

    Essais (1580, ed. M. Rat, 1958) bk. 2, ch. 12

7 *Quand je me joue à ma chatte, qui sait si elle passe son temps de moi plus que je ne fais d'elle?*

When I play with my cat, who knows whether she isn't amusing herself with me more than I am with her?

    Essais (1580, ed. M. Rat, 1958) bk. 2, ch. 12

8 *Que sais-je?*

What do I know?

    Essais (1580, ed. M. Rat, 1958) bk. 2, ch. 12 (on the position of the sceptic)

9 *L'homme est bien insensé. Il ne saurait forger un ciron, et forge des dieux à douzaines.*

Man is quite insane. He wouldn't know how to create a maggot, and he creates gods by the dozen.

    Essais (1580, ed. M. Rat, 1958) bk. 2, ch. 12

10 *Ceux qui ont apparié notre vie à un songe, ont eu de la raison, à l'aventure plus qu'ils ne pensaient ... Nous veillons dormants, et veillants dormons.*

Those who have likened our life to a dream were more right, by chance, than they realised. We are awake while sleeping, and waking sleep.

    Essais (1580, ed. M. Rat, 1958) bk. 2, ch. 12

11 *Quelqu'un pourrait dire de moi que j'ai seulement fait ici un amas de fleurs étrangères, n'y ayant fourni du mien que le filet à les lier.*

It could be said of me that in this book I have only made up a bunch of other men's flowers, providing of my own only the string that ties them together.

    Essais (1580, ed. M. Rat, 1958) bk. 3, ch. 12

Eugenio Montale 1896–1981

Italian poet

12 *Felicità raggiunta, si cammina*
per te sul fil di lama.
Agli occhi sei barlume che vacilla
al piede, teso ghiaccio che s'incrina;
e dunque non ti tocchi chi piu t'ama.

Happiness, for you we walk on a knife edge. To the eyes you are a flickering light, to the feet, thin ice that cracks; and so may no one touch you who loves you.

    'Felicità raggiunta' (1925)

Montesquieu (Charles-Louis de Secondat) 1689–1755

French political philosopher

13 *Il faut pleurer les hommes à leur naissance, et non pas à leur mort.*

Men should be bewailed at their birth, and not at their death.

    Lettres Persones (1721) no. 40 (translated by J. Ozell, 1722)

14 *Si les triangles faisoient un Dieu, ils lui donneroient trois côtés.*

If the triangles were to make a God they would give him three sides.

    Lettres Persones (1721) no. 59 (translated by J. Ozell, 1722)

15 *Les grands seigneurs ont des plaisirs, le peuple a de la joie.*

Great lords have their pleasures, but the people have fun.

    Pensées et fragments inédits ... vol. 2 (1901) no. 992

16 *Les Anglais sont occupés; ils n'ont pas le temps d'être polis.*

The English are busy; they don't have time to be polite.

    Pensées et fragments inédits ... vol. 2 (1901) no. 1428

17 Happy the people whose annals are blank in history-books!

    Attributed to Montesquieu by Thomas Carlyle in *History of Frederick the Great* bk. 16, ch. 1. Cf. Eliot 269:24

Bernard Law Montgomery (Viscount Montgomery of Alamein) 1887–1976

British field marshal

18 Rule 1, on page 1 of the book of war, is: 'Do not march on Moscow' ... [Rule 2] is: 'Do not go fighting with your land armies in China.'

    Hansard (Lords) 30 May 1962, col. 227

19 I have heard some say ... [homosexual] practices are allowed in France and in other NATO countries. We are not French, and we are not other nationals. We are British, thank God!

    Speaking on the 2nd reading of the Sexual Offences Bill, in *Hansard* (Lords) 24 May 1965, col. 648

Robert Montgomery 1807–55

English clergyman and poet

20 The solitary monk who shook the world.

    Luther: a Poem (1842) ch. 3 'Man's Need and God's Supply'

1 And thou, vast ocean! on whose awful face
Time's iron feet can print no ruin-trace.
  The Omnipresence of the Deity (1830 ed.) pt. 1, l. 105

Casimir, Comte de Montrond 1768–1843

French diplomat

2 *Défiez-vous des premiers mouvements parce qu'ils sont bons.*

Have no truck with first impulses for they are always generous ones.
  Attributed, in Comte J. d'Estourmel *Derniers Souvenirs* (1860) p. 319 (where the alternative attribution to Talleyrand is denied). Cf. Corneille 218:17

3 *S'il vous arrive quelque chose d'heureux, ne manquez pas d'aller le dire à vos amis, afin de leur faire de la peine.*

If something pleasant happens to you, don't forget to tell it to your friends, to make them feel bad.
  Attributed, in Comte J. d'Estourmel *Derniers Souvenirs* (1860) p. 319

Marquess of Montrose

See JAMES GRAHAM

Percy Montrose

American songwriter

4 In a cavern, in a canyon,
Excavating for a mine,
Dwelt a miner, Forty-niner,
And his daughter, Clementine.
Oh, my darling, oh my darling, oh my darling
  Clementine!
Thou art lost and gone for ever, dreadful sorry,
  Clementine.
  'Clementine' (1884 song)

Clement C. Moore 1779–1863

American writer

5 'Twas the night before Christmas, when all through the house
Not a creature was stirring, not even a mouse;
The stockings were hung by the chimney with care,
In hopes that St Nicholas soon would be there.
  'A Visit from St Nicholas' (December 1823)

Edward Moore 1712–57

English playwright

6 This is adding insult to injuries.
  The Foundling (1748) act 5, sc. 5

7 I am rich beyond the dreams of avarice.
  The Gamester (1753) act 2, sc. 2. Cf. Johnson 375:23

George Moore 1852–1933

Anglo-Irish novelist

8 All reformers are bachelors.
  The Bending of the Bough (1900) act 1

9 A man travels the world in search of what he needs and returns home to find it.
  The Brook Kerith (1916) ch. 11

10 Art must be parochial in the beginning to become cosmopolitan in the end.
  Hail and Farewell: Ave (1911) p. 3

11 The lot of critics is to be remembered by what they failed to understand.
  Impressions and Opinions (1891) 'Balzac'

Marianne Moore 1887–1972

American poet

12   O to be a dragon,
a symbol of the power of Heaven—of silkworm
size or immense; at times invisible.
Felicitous phenomenon!
  'O To Be a Dragon' (1959)

13 I, too, dislike it: there are things that are important beyond all this fiddle.
  Reading it, however, with a perfect contempt for it, one discovers in it, after all, a place for the genuine.
  'Poetry' (1935)

14 Nor till the poets among us can be
'literalists of
the imagination'—above
insolence and triviality and can present
for inspection, imaginary gardens with real toads in
  them, shall we have
it.
  'Poetry' (1935)

15 My father used to say,
'Superior people never make long visits,
have to be shown Longfellow's grave
or the glass flowers at Harvard.'
  'Silence' (1935)

16 Nor was he insincere in saying, 'Make my house your inn.'
Inns are not residences.
  'Silence' (1935)

Sturge Moore 1870–1944

English poet and engraver

17 Then, cleaving the grass, gazelles appear
(The gentler dolphins of kindlier waves)
With sensitive heads alert of ear;
Frail crowds that a delicate hearing saves.
  'The Gazelles' (1904)

Thomas Moore 1779–1852

Irish musician and songwriter

18 Yet, who can help loving the land that has taught us
Six hundred and eighty-five ways to dress eggs?
  The Fudge Family in Paris (1818) Letter 8, l. 64

19 For you know, dear—I may, without vanity, hint—
Though an angel should write, still 'tis *devils* must print.
  The Fudges in England (1835) Letter 3, l. 64

1 Believe me, if all those endearing young charms,
Which I gaze on so fondly today,
Were to change by tomorrow, and fleet in my arms,
Like fairy gifts fading away!
Thou wouldst still be adored as this moment thou art,
Let thy loveliness fade as it will,
And around the dear ruin each wish of my heart
Would entwine itself verdantly still.
  Irish Melodies (1807) 'Believe me, if all those endearing
  young charms'

2 No, the heart that has truly loved never forgets,
But as truly loves on to the close,
As the sun-flower turns on her god, when he sets,
The same look which she turned when he rose.
  Irish Melodies (1807) 'Believe me, if all those endearing
  young charms'

3 'Twas from Kathleen's eyes he flew,
Eyes of most unholy blue!
  Irish Melodies (1807) 'By that Lake'

4 You may break, you may shatter the vase, if you will,
But the scent of the roses will hang round it still.
  Irish Melodies (1807) 'Farewell!—but whenever'

5 The harp that once through Tara's halls
The soul of music shed,
Now hangs as mute on Tara's walls
As if that soul were fled.—
So sleeps the pride of former days,
So glory's thrill is o'er;
And hearts, that once beat high for praise,
Now feel that pulse no more.
  Irish Melodies (1807) 'The harp that once through Tara's
  halls'

6 No, there's nothing half so sweet in life
As love's young dream.
  Irish Melodies (1807) 'Love's Young Dream'

7 The Minstrel Boy to the war is gone,
In the ranks of death you'll find him;
His father's sword he has girded on,
And his wild harp slung behind him.
  Irish Melodies (1807) 'The Minstrel Boy'

8 Oh! blame not the bard, if he fly to the bowers,
Where Pleasure lies, carelessly smiling at Fame.
  Irish Melodies (1807) 'Oh! blame not the bard'

9 Oh! breathe not his name, let it sleep in the shade,
Where cold and unhonoured his relics are laid.
  Irish Melodies (1807) 'Oh! breathe not his name'

10 Rich and rare were the gems she wore,
And a bright gold ring on her wand she bore.
  Irish Melodies (1807) 'Rich and rare were the gems she
  wore'

11 My only books
Were woman's looks,
And folly's all they've taught me.
  Irish Melodies (1807) 'The time I've lost in wooing'

12 'Tis the last rose of summer
Left blooming alone;
All her lovely companions
Are faded and gone.
  Irish Melodies (1807) ''Tis the last rose of summer'

13 Then awake! the heavens look bright, my dear;
'Tis never too late for delight, my dear;
And the best of all ways
To lengthen our days
Is to steal a few hours from the night, my dear!
  Irish Melodies (1807) 'The young May moon'

14 Oh! ever thus, from childhood's hour,
I've seen my fondest hopes decay;
I never loved a tree or flower,
But 'twas the first to fade away.
I never nursed a dear gazelle,
To glad me with its soft black eye,
But when it came to know me well,
And love me, it was sure to die!
  Lalla Rookh (1817) 'The Fire-Worshippers' pt. 1, l. 279

15 Like Dead Sea fruits, that tempt the eye,
But turn to ashes on the lips!
  Lalla Rookh (1817) 'The Fire-Worshippers' pt. 2, l. 484

16 But Faith, fanatic Faith, once wedded fast
To some dear falsehood, hugs it to the last.
  Lalla Rookh (1817) 'The Veiled Prophet' pt. 3, l. 356

17 Oft, in the stilly night,
Ere Slumber's chain has bound me,
Fond Memory brings the light
Of other days around me.
  National Airs (1815) 'Oft in the Stilly Night'

Thomas Osbert Mordaunt 1730–1809

18 Sound, sound the clarion, fill the fife,
Throughout the sensual world proclaim,
One crowded hour of glorious life
Is worth an age without a name.
  'A Poem, said to be written by Major Mordaunt during the
  last German War', in *The Bee, or Literary Weekly
  Intelligencer* 12 October 1791

Hannah More 1745–1833

English writer of tracts

19 For you'll ne'er mend your fortunes, nor help the just
  cause,
By breaking of windows, or breaking of laws.
  'An Address to the Meeting in Spa Fields' (1817) in
  H. Thompson *Life of Hannah More* (1838) appendix, no. 7

20 Small habits, well pursued betimes,
May reach the dignity of crimes.
  Florio (1786) pt. 1, l. 77

21 He liked those literary cooks
Who skim the cream of others' books;
And ruin half an author's graces
By plucking bon-mots from their places.
  Florio (1786) pt. 1, l. 123

22   Did not God
Sometimes withhold in mercy what we ask,
We should be ruined at our own request.
  Moses in the Bulrushes (1782) pt. 1, l. 35

1 Whether we consider the manual industry of the poor, or the intellectual exertions of the superior classes, we shall find that diligent occupation, if not criminally perverted from its purposes, is at once the instrument of virtue and the secret of happiness. Man cannot be safely trusted with a life of leisure.

Christian Morals (1813) vol. 2, ch. 23

2 The prevailing manners of an age depend more than we are aware, or are willing to allow, on the conduct of the women; this is one of the principal hinges on which the great machine of human society turns.

Essays on Various Subjects . . . for Young Ladies (1777) 'On Dissipation'

3 How much it is to be regretted, that the British ladies should ever sit down contented to polish, when they are able to reform; to entertain, when they might instruct; and to dazzle for an hour, when they are candidates for eternity!

Essays on Various Subjects . . . for Young Ladies (1777) 'On Dissipation'

4 It is humbling to reflect, that in those countries in which the fondness for the mere persons of women is carried to the highest excess, they are slaves; and that their moral and intellectual degradation increases in direct proportion to the adoration which is paid to mere external charms.

Strictures on the Modern System of Female Education (1799) vol. 1, ch. 1

Sir Thomas More 1478–1535

English scholar and saint; Lord Chancellor of England, 1529–32

5 *Oves inquam vestrae, quae tam mites esse, tamque exiguo solent ali, nunc (uti fertur) tam edaces atque indomitae esse coeperunt ut homines devorent ipsos.*

Your sheep, that were wont to be so meek and tame, and so small eaters, now, as I hear say, be become so great devourers, and so wild, that they eat up and swallow down the very men themselves.

Utopia (1516) bk. 1 (following the marginal précis 'The Disaster Produced by Standing Military Garrisons')

6 After his head was upon the block, [he] lift it up again, and gently drew his beard aside, and said, *This hath not offended the king.*

Francis Bacon *Apophthegms New and Old* (1625) no. 22

7 Son Roper, I may tell thee I have no cause to be proud thereof [the King having entertained him at Chelsea], for if my head could wish him a castle in France it should not fail to go.

In William Roper *Life of Sir Thomas More* (Everyman ed., 1963) p. 12

8 We may not look at our pleasure to go to heaven in feather-beds; it is not the way.

In William Roper *Life of Sir Thomas More* p. 14

9 If the parties will at my hands call for justice, then, all were it my father stood on the one side, and the Devil on the other, his cause being good, the Devil should have right.

In William Roper *Life of Sir Thomas More* p. 21

10 In good faith, I rejoiced, son, that I had given the devil a foul fall, and that with those Lords I had gone so far, as without great shame I could never go back again.

In William Roper *Life of Sir Thomas More* p. 34

11 'By god's body, master More, *Indignatio principis mors est* [The anger of the sovereign is death].' 'Is that all, my Lord?' quoth he [to the Duke of Norfolk]. 'Then in good faith is there no more difference between your grace and me, but that I shall die to-day, and you to-morrow.'

In William Roper *Life of Sir Thomas More* p. 35

12 Son Roper, I thank our Lord the field is won.

In William Roper *Life of Sir Thomas More* p. 36

13 Is not this house [the Tower of London] as nigh heaven as my own?

In William Roper *Life of Sir Thomas More* p. 41

14 I pray you, master Lieutenant, see me safe up, and my coming down let me shift for my self.

On mounting the scaffold, in William Roper *Life of Sir Thomas More* p. 50

15 Pluck up thy spirits, man, and be not afraid to do thine office; my neck is very short; take heed therefore thou strike not awry, for saving of thine honesty.

Words addressed to the executioner, in William Roper *Life of Sir Thomas More* p. 50

16 I cumber you good Margaret much, but I would be sorry, if it should be any longer than tomorrow, for it is S. Thomas even and the vtas of Saint Peter and therefore tomorrow long I to go to God, it were a day very meet and convenient for me. I never liked your manner toward me better than when you kissed me last for I love when daughterly love and dear charity hath no leisure to look to worldly courtesy. Fare well my dear child and pray for me, and I shall for you and all your friends that we may merrily meet in heaven.

Last letter to his daughter Margaret Roper, 5 July 1535, on the eve of his execution, in E. F. Rogers (ed.) *Correspondence of Sir Thomas More* (1947)

Thomas Morell 1703–84

English librettist

17 See, the conquering hero comes!
Sound the trumpets, beat the drums!

Judas Maccabeus (1747) 'A chorus of youths' and *Joshua* (1748) pt. 3 (to music by Handel)

Robin Morgan 1941–

American feminist

18 Sisterhood is powerful.

Title of book (1970)

Christopher Morley 1890–1957

American writer

19 Life is a foreign language: all men mispronounce it.

Thunder on the Left (1925) ch. 14. Cf. Hartley 327:22

Lord Morley (John, 1st Viscount Morley of Blackburn)1838–1923
British Liberal politician and writer

1 The golden Gospel of Silence is effectively compressed in thirty fine volumes.

> *Critical Miscellanies* (1886) 'Carlyle' (on Carlyle's *History of Frederick the Great* (1858–65), Carlyle having written of his subject as 'that strong, silent man')

2 You have not converted a man, because you have silenced him.

> *On Compromise* (1874) ch. 5

Countess Morphy (Marcelle Azra Forbes)
fl. 1930–50

3 The tragedy of English cooking is that 'plain' cooking cannot be entrusted to 'plain' cooks.

> *English Recipes* (1935) p. 17

Charles Morris 1745–1838
English songwriter

4 But a house is much more to my mind than a tree, And for groves, O! a good grove of chimneys for me.

> 'Country and Town' (1840)

Desmond Morris 1928–
English anthropologist

5 The city is not a concrete jungle, it is a human zoo.

> *The Human Zoo* (1969) introduction

6 There are one hundred and ninety-three living species of monkeys and apes. One hundred and ninety-two of them are covered with hair. The exception is a naked ape self-named *Homo sapiens*.

> *The Naked Ape* (1967) introduction

7 Life is like a very short visit to a toyshop between birth and death.

> In *Sunday Express* 3 November 1991

George Pope Morris 1802–64
American poet

8 Woodman, spare that tree!
Touch not a single bough!
In youth it sheltered me,
And I'll protect it now.

> 'Woodman, Spare That Tree' (1830). Cf. Campbell 176:11

William Morris 1834–96
English writer, artist, and designer

9 What is this, the sound and rumour? What is this that all men hear,
Like the wind in hollow valleys when the storm is drawing near,
Like the rolling on of ocean in the eventide of fear?
'Tis the people marching on.

> *Chants for Socialists* (1885) 'The March of the Workers'

10 Nor for my words shall ye forget your tears,
Or hope again for aught that I can say,
The idle singer of an empty day.

> *The Earthly Paradise* (1868–70) 'An Apology'

11 Dreamer of dreams, born out of my due time,
Why should I strive to set the crooked straight?
Let it suffice me that my murmuring rhyme
Beats with light wing against the ivory gate,
Telling a tale not too importunate
To those who in the sleepy region stay,
Lulled by the singer of an empty day.

> *The Earthly Paradise* (1868–70) 'An Apology'

12 Forget six counties overhung with smoke,
Forget the snorting steam and piston stroke,
Forget the spreading of the hideous town;
Think rather of the pack-horse on the down,
And dream of London, small and white and clean,
The clear Thames bordered by its gardens green.

> *The Earthly Paradise* (1868–70) 'Prologue: The Wanderers' l. 1

13 Had she come all the way for this,
To part at last without a kiss?
Yea, had she borne the dirt and rain
That her own eyes might see him slain
Beside the haystack in the floods?

> 'The Haystack in the Floods' (1858) l. 1

14 And ever she sung from noon to noon,
'Two red roses across the moon.'

> 'Two Red Roses across the Moon' (1858)

15 Fellowship is heaven, and lack of fellowship is hell: fellowship is life, and lack of fellowship is death: and the deeds that ye do upon the earth, it is for fellowship's sake that ye do them.

> *A Dream of John Ball* (1888) ch. 4

16 Have nothing in your houses that you do not know to be useful, or believe to be beautiful.

> *Hopes and Fears for Art* (1882) 'Making the Best of It'

17 The reward of labour is life.

> *News from Nowhere* (1891) ch. 15

Herbert Morrison (Baron Morrison of Lambeth) 1888–1965
British Labour politician

18 Work is the call. Work at war speed. Good-night—and go to it.

> Broadcast as Minister of Supply, 22 May 1940, in *Daily Herald* 23 May 1940

Jim Morrison 1943–71
American rock singer and songwriter

19 C'mon, baby, light my fire.

> 'Light My Fire' (1967 song, with Robby Krieger)

20 Five to one, baby, one in five,
No one here gets out alive ...
They got the guns but we got the numbers
Gonna win, yeah, we're taking over.

> 'Five to One' (1968 song)

1 What have they done to the earth?
What have they done to our fair sister?
Ravaged and plundered and ripped her and did her,
Stuck her with knives in the side of the dawn,
And tied her with fences and dragged her down.
I hear a very gentle sound,
With your ear down to the ground:
WE WANT THE WORLD AND WE WANT IT NOW!
'When the Music's Over' (1967 song)

R. F. Morrison

2 Just a wee deoch-an-doris,
Just a wee yin, that's a'.
Just a wee deoch-an-doris,
Before we gang awa'.
There's a wee wifie waitin',
In a wee but-an-ben;
If you can say
'It's a braw bricht moonlicht nicht',
Ye're a' richt, ye ken.
'Just a Wee Deoch-an-Doris' (1911 song); popularized by Harry Lauder

Dwight Morrow 1873–1931

American lawyer, banker, and diplomat

3 The world is divided into people who do things and people who get the credit. Try, if you can, to belong to the first class. There's far less competition.
Letter to his son, in Harold Nicolson *Dwight Morrow* (1935) ch. 3

John Mortimer 1923–

English novelist, barrister, and playwright

4 The law seems like a sort of maze through which a client must be led to safety, a collection of reefs, rocks, and underwater hazards through which he or she must be piloted.
Clinging to the Wreckage (1982) ch. 7

5 They do you a decent death on the hunting-field.
Paradise Postponed (1985) ch. 18

6 At school I never minded the lessons. I just resented having to work terribly hard at playing.
A Voyage Round My Father (1971) act 1

7 No brilliance is needed in the law. Nothing but common sense, and relatively clean finger nails.
A Voyage Round My Father (1971) act 1

8 The virtue of much literature is that it is dangerous and may do you extreme harm.
Foreword to C. H. Rolph *Books in the Dock* (1969)

9 [Irritable judges] suffer from a bad case of premature adjudication.
In *Listener* 22 January 1987, p. 8

10 Champagne socialist.
Description of himself (attributed)

J. B. Morton ('Beachcomber') 1893–1975

British journalist

11 One disadvantage of being a hog is that at any moment some blundering fool may try to make a silk purse out of your wife's ear.
By the Way (1931) p. 282

12 Hush, hush,
Nobody cares!
Christopher Robin
Has
Fallen
Down-
Stairs.
By the Way (1931) p. 367

13 The man with the false nose had gone to that bourne from which no hollingsworth returns.
Gallimaufry (1936) 'Another True Story'

14 The Doctor is said also to have invented an extraordinary weapon which will make war less brutal. It is described as a very powerful liquid which rots braces at a distance of a mile.
Gallimaufry (1936) 'Bracerot'

15 Dr Strabismus (Whom God Preserve) of Utrecht has patented a new invention. It is an illuminated trouser-clip for bicyclists who are using main roads at night.
Morton's Folly (1933) p. 99

Rogers Morton 1914–79

American public relations officer

16 I'm not going to rearrange the furniture on the deck of the Titanic.
Having lost five of the last six primaries as President Ford's campaign manager, in *Washington Post* 16 May 1976, p. C8

Thomas Morton c.1764–1838

English playwright

17 Approbation from Sir Hubert Stanley is praise indeed.
A Cure for the Heartache (1797) act 5, sc. 2

18 I eat well, and I drink well, and I sleep well—but that's all.
A Roland for an Oliver (1819) act 1, sc. 1

19 Always ding, dinging Dame Grundy into my ears—what will Mrs Grundy zay? What will Mrs Grundy think?
Speed the Plough (1798) act 1, sc. 1

Sir Oswald Mosley 1896–1980

English Fascist leader

20 I am not, and never have been, a man of the right. My position was on the left and is now in the centre of politics.
Letter to *The Times* 26 April 1968

Andrew Motion 1952–

English poet

1 I'll always arrive like this,
  having no death to mourn,
  but rather the life we share
  nowhere beyond your room,
  our love repeating itself
  like snow I watch tonight,
  which spins against my window
  then vanishes into the dark.
  'Anniversaries: The Fourth' (1978)

2 Each sudden gust of light explains itself
  as flames, but neither they, nor even

  bombs redoubled on the hills tonight
  can quite include me in their fear.
  What does remains invisible, is lost
  in curt societies whose deaths become
  revenge by morning, and whose homes
  are nothing more than all they pity most.
  'Leaving Belfast' (1978)

John Lothrop Motley 1814–77

American historian

3 As long as he lived, he was the guiding-star of a
  whole brave nation, and when he died the little
  children cried in the streets.
  Of William of Orange in *The Rise of the Dutch Republic*
  (1856) pt. 6, ch. 7. Cf. Auden 34:10

4 Give us the luxuries of life, and we will dispense with
  its necessities.
  In Oliver Wendell Holmes *Autocrat of the Breakfast-Table*
  (1857–8) ch. 6

Peter Anthony Motteux 1660–1718

English translator

5 The devil was sick, the devil a monk would be;
  The devil was well, and the devil a monk he'd be.
  Translation of Rabelais *Gargantua and Pantagruel* (1693)
  bk. 4 (1708 ed.) ch. 24 (variant of a medieval Latin
  proverb)

Louis Mountbatten (Earl Mountbatten of Burma) 1900–79

British sailor, soldier, and statesman

6 The nuclear arms race has no military purpose. Wars
  cannot be fought with nuclear weapons. Their
  existence only adds to our perils.
  Speech at Strasbourg, 11 May 1979, in P. Ziegler
  Mountbatten (1985) ch. 52

Robert Mugabe 1924–

African politician; Prime Minister of Zimbabwe, 1980–7

7 Cricket civilizes people and creates good gentlemen.
  I want everyone to play cricket in Zimbabwe; I want
  ours to be a nation of gentlemen.
  In *Sunday Times* 26 February 1984

Malcolm Muggeridge 1903–90

British journalist

8 To succeed pre-eminently in English public life it is
  necessary to conform either to the popular image of a
  bookie or of a clergyman; Churchill being a perfect
  example of the former, Halifax of the latter.
  The Infernal Grove (1973) ch. 1

9 An orgy looks particularly alluring seen through the
  mists of righteous indignation.
  The Most of Malcolm Muggeridge (1966) 'Dolce Vita in a Cold
  Climate'

10 Good taste and humour . . . are a contradiction in
   terms, like a chaste whore.
   Time 14 September 1953

11 The orgasm has replaced the Cross as the focus of
   longing and the image of fulfilment.
   Tread Softly (1966) p. 46

12 He was not only a bore; he bored for England.
   Tread Softly (1966) p. 147 (of Sir Anthony Eden)

Edwin Muir 1887–1959

Scottish poet

13 And without fear the lawless roads
   Ran wrong through all the land.
   Journeys and Places (1937) 'Hölderlin's Journey'

Frank Muir 1920–

English writer and broadcaster

14 The thinking man's crumpet.
   Description of Joan Bakewell (attributed)

Herbert J. Muller 1905–

15 Few have heard of Fra Luca Pacioli, the inventor of
   double-entry book-keeping; but he has probably had
   much more influence on human life than has Dante or
   Michelangelo.
   Uses of the Past (1957) ch. 8

Wilhelm Müller 1794–1827

German poet

16 *Vom Abendrot zum Morgenlicht*
   Ward mancher Kopf zum Greise.
   Wer glaubt's? Und meiner ward es nicht
   Auf dieser ganzen Reise.

   Between dusk and dawn many a head has turned
   white. Who can believe it? And mine has not changed
   on all this long journey.
   Die Winterreise (1823) bk. 2 'Der greise Kopf'

Ethel Watts Mumford et al. 1878–1940

17 In the midst of life we are in debt.
   Altogether New Cynic's Calendar (1907). Cf. Book of
   Common Prayer 124:4

Lewis Mumford 1895–

American sociologist

1 Every generation revolts against its fathers and makes friends with its grandfathers.
  The Brown Decades (1931) p. 3

2 Our national flower is the concrete cloverleaf.
  Quote Magazine 8 October 1961

Iris Murdoch 1919–

English novelist

3 Dora Greenfield left her husband because she was afraid of him. She decided six months later to return to him for the same reason.
  The Bell (1958) Ch. 1

4 Only in our virtues are we original, because virtue is difficult ... Vices are general, virtues are particular.
  Nuns and Soldiers (1980) ch. 1

5 One doesn't have to get anywhere in a marriage. It's not a public conveyance.
  A Severed Head (1961) ch. 3

6 Freedom is not choosing; that is merely the move that we make when all is already lost. Freedom is knowing and understanding and respecting things quite other than ourselves.
  'The Sublime and the Beautiful Revisited' in *Yale Review* 49 (1959) p. 270

7 Love is the extremely difficult realisation that something other than oneself is real. Love, and so art and morals, is the discovery of reality.
  'The Sublime and the Good' in *Chicago Review* 13 (1959) p. 51

8 Anything that consoles is fake.
  In R. Harries *Prayer and the Pursuit of Happiness* (1985) p. 113. Cf. Braque 139:17

9 We live in a fantasy world, a world of illusion. The great task in life is to find reality.
  In *The Times* 15 April 1983 'Profile'

C. W. Murphy and Will Letters

10 Has anybody here seen Kelly?
   Kelly from the Isle of Man?
   'Has Anybody Here Seen Kelly?' (1909 song)

Fred Murray

American songwriter

11 Ginger, you're balmy!
   Title of song (1910)

Ed Murrow 1908–65

American broadcaster and journalist

12 He [Winston Churchill] mobilized the English language and sent it into battle to steady his fellow countrymen and hearten those Europeans upon whom the long dark night of tyranny had descended.
   Broadcast, 30 November 1954, in *In Search of Light* (1967) p. 276

13 Anyone who isn't confused doesn't really understand the situation.
   On the Vietnam War, in Walter Bryan *The Improbable Irish* (1969) ch. 1

Alfred de Musset 1810–57

French poet and playwright

14 *Je haïs comme la mort l'état de plagiaire;*
   Mon verre n'est pas grand mais je bois dans mon verre.
   I hate like death the situation of the plagiarist; the glass I drink from is not large, but at least it is my own.
   La Coupe et les lèvres (1832) in *Poésies Complètes* (1957) p. 155

15 *Malgré moi l'infini me tourmente.*
   I can't help it, the idea of the infinite torments me.
   'L'Espoir en Dieu' (1838)

16 *Le seul bien qui me reste au monde*
   Est d'avoir quelquefois pleuré.
   The only good thing left to me is that I have sometimes wept.
   'Tristesse' (1841)

17 *Je suis venu trop tard dans un monde trop vieux.*
   I have come too late into a world too old.
   Rollo (1833)

Benito Mussolini 1883–1945

Italian Fascist dictator

18 *Voglio partire in perfetto orario ... D'ora innanzi ogni cosa deve camminare alla perfezione.*
   We must leave exactly on time ... From now on everything must function to perfection.
   To a station-master, in Giorgio Pini *Mussolini* (1939) vol. 2, ch. 6, p. 251. See HRH Infanta Eulalia of Spain *Courts and Countries after the War* (1925) ch. 13: 'The first benefit of Benito Mussolini's direction in Italy begins to be felt when one crosses the Italian Frontier and hears "*Il treno arriva all'orario* [the train is arriving on time]" '

A. J. Muste 1885–1967

American pacifist

19 There is no way to peace. Peace is the way.
   In *New York Times* 16 November 1967, p. 46

Vladimir Nabokov 1899–1977

Russian novelist

20 Her exotic daydreams do not prevent her from being small-town bourgeois at heart, clinging to conventional ideas or committing this or that conventional violation of the conventional, adultery being a most conventional way to rise above the conventional.
   Lectures on Literature (1980) 'Madame Bovary'

21 Lolita, light of my life, fire of my loins. My sin, my soul. Lo-lee-ta: the tip of the tongue taking a trip of three steps down the palate to tap, at three, on the teeth. Lo. Lee. Ta.
   Lolita (1955) ch. 1

1 Life is a great surprise. I do not see why death should
not be an even greater one.
  Pale Fire (1962) p. 225. Cf. Barrie BARRIE0010

2 The cradle rocks above an abyss, and common sense
tells us that our existence is but a brief crack of light
between two eternities of darkness.
  Speak, Memory (1951) ch. 1

3 I think like a genius, I write like a distinguished
author, and I speak like a child.
  Strong Opinions (1973) foreword

4 A work of art has no importance whatever to society.
It is only important to the individual, and only the
individual reader is important to me.
  Strong Opinions (1973) p. 33

Ralph Nader 1934–

American consumer protectionist

5 Unsafe at any speed.
  Title of book (1965)

Sarojini Naidu 1879–1949

Indian politician

6 If only Bapu [Gandhi] knew the cost of setting him up
in poverty!
  In A. Campbell-Johnson *Mission with Mountbatten* (1951)
  ch. 12

Ian Nairn 1930–

British architect

7 If what is called development is allowed to multiply at
the present rate, then by the end of the century Great
Britain will consist of isolated oases of preserved
monuments in a desert of wire, concrete roads, cosy
plots and bungalows ... Upon this new Britain the
Review bestows a name in the hope that it will
stick—SUBTOPIA.
  Architectural Review June 1955, p. 365

Fridtjof Nansen 1861–1930

Norwegian polar explorer

8 Never stop because you are afraid—you are never so
likely to be wrong. Never keep a line of retreat: it is
a wretched invention. The difficult is what takes a little
time; the impossible is what takes a little longer.
  In *Listener* 14 December 1939, p. 1153. Cf. Calonne
  175:9

Napoléon I 1769–1821

Emperor of France, 1804–15

9 *C'est un fossé qui sera franchi lorsqu'on aura l'audace de
le tenter.*
  It [the Channel] is a mere ditch, and will be crossed as
  soon as someone has the courage to attempt it.
    Letter to Consul Cambacérès, 16 November 1803, in
    Correspondance de Napoléon Ier (1858–69) vol. 9

10 *Un prince qui, la première année de son regne, passe pour
être si bon, est un prince dont on se moque à la seconde.*
  A prince who gets a reputation for good nature in the
  first year of his reign, is laughed at in the second.
    Letter to the King of Holland, 4 April 1807, in
    Correspondance de Napoléon Ier (1858–69) vol. 15

11 *La religion est une importante affaire dans une institution
publique de demoiselles. Elle est, quoi qu'on en puisse dire,
le plus sûr garant pour les mères et pour les maris.
Élevez-vous des croyants et ne pas des raisonneuses.*
  Religion is an all-important matter in a public school
  for girls. Whatever people say, it is the mother's
  safeguard, and the husband's. What we ask of
  education is not that girls should think, but that they
  should believe.
    'Note sur L'Établissement D'Écouen' 15 May 1807, in
    Correspondance de Napoléon Ier (1858–69) vol. 15

12 *A la guerre, les trois quarts sont des affaires morales, la
balance des forces réelles n'est que pour un autre quart.*
  In war, three-quarters turns on personal character
  and relations; the balance of manpower and materials
  counts only for the remaining quarter.
    'Observations sur les affaires d'Espagne, Saint-Cloud, 27
    août 1808' in *Correspondance de Napoléon Ier* (1858–69)
    vol. 17

13 *Il y a des grands intérêts attachés à ce que font les
souverains, au lieu qu'aucun intérêt n'est attaché à ce que
fait la grande duchesse.*
  It is a matter of great interest what sovereigns are
  doing; but as to what Grand Duchesses are
  doing—Who cares?
    Lettres inédits de Napoléon I (1897) vol. 2, p. 915
    (17 December 1811)

14 *Rien n'est plus contraire à l'organisation de l'esprit, de la
mémoire et de l'imagination ... Le nouveau système de
poids et mesures sera un sujet d'embarras et de difficultés
pour plusieurs générations ... C'est tourmenter le peuple
par des vétilles!!!*
  Nothing is more contrary to the organization of the
  mind, of the memory, and of the imagination ... The
  new system of weights and measures will be a
  stumbling block and the source of difficulties for
  several generations ... It's just tormenting the people
  with trivia!!!
    On the introduction of the metric system, in *Mémoires* ...
    écrits à Ste-Hélène (1823–5) bk. 4, ch. 21, pt. 4

15 *On supporte moins impatiemment des choses fâcheuses
d'un homme qui est dans votre sens, que d'un homme qui
se montre d'une opinion opposée.*
  It is easier to put up with unpleasantness from a man
  of one's own way of thinking than from one who
  takes an entirely different point of view.
    Letter to J. Finckenstein, 14 April 1807, in *Mémoires et
    Correspondance politique et militaire du Roi Joseph* (1854)
    vol. 3

16 *Du sublime au ridicule il n'y a qu'un pas.*
  There is only one step from the sublime to the
  ridiculous.
    To De Pradt, Polish ambassador, after the retreat from
    Moscow in 1812; in D. G. De Pradt *Histoire de l'Ambassade
    dans le grand-duché de Varsovie en 1812* (1815) p. 215. Cf.
    Paine 504:9

1 *Soldats, songez que, du haut de ces pyramides, quarante siècles vous contemplent.*

Think of it, soldiers; from the summit of these pyramids, forty centuries look down upon you.

> Speech to the Army of Egypt on 21 July 1798, before the Battle of the Pyramids in Gaspard Gourgaud *Mémoires* (1823) vol. 2 'Égypte—Bataille des Pyramides'

2 *Quant au courage moral, il avait trouvé fort rare, disait-il, celui de deux heures après minuit; c'est-à-dire le courage de l'improviste.*

As to moral courage, I have very rarely met with two o'clock in the morning courage: I mean instantaneous courage.

> In E. A. de Las Cases *Mémorial de Ste-Hélène* (1823) vol. 1, pt. 2, 4–5 December 1815

3 An army marches on its stomach.

> Attributed, but probably condensed from a long passage in E. A. de Las Cases *Mémorial de Ste-Hélène* (1823) vol. 4, 14 November 1816. See *Windsor Magazine* 1904, p. 268. Also attributed to Frederick the Great, in *Notes and Queries* 10 March 1866, p. 196

4 *La carrière ouverte aux talents.*

The career open to the talents.

> In Barry E. O'Meara *Napoleon in Exile* (1822) vol. 1, p. 103

5 *L'Angleterre est une nation de boutiquiers.*

England is a nation of shopkeepers.

> In Barry E. O'Meara *Napoleon in Exile* (1822) vol. 2, p. 81. Cf. Adams 3:9, Smith 651:1

6 As though he had 200,000 men.

> When asked how to deal with the Pope, in J. M. Robinson *Cardinal Consalvi* (1987) p. 65. Cf. Stalin 662:5

7 Not tonight, Josephine.

> Attributed, but probably apocryphal. R. H. Horne *The History of Napoleon* (1841) vol. 2, ch. 8 describes the circumstances in which the affront may have occurred

Ogden Nash 1902–71

American humorist

8 The turtle lives 'twixt plated decks
Which practically conceal its sex.
I think it clever of the turtle
In such a fix to be so fertile.
> 'Autres Bêtes, Autres Moeurs' (1931)

9 The camel has a single hump;
The dromedary, two;
Or else the other way around,
I'm never sure. Are you?
> 'The Camel' (1936)

10 The cow is of the bovine ilk;
One end is moo, the other, milk.
> 'The Cow' (1931)

11 One would be in less danger
From the wiles of the stranger
If one's own kin and kith
Were more fun to be with.
> 'Family Court' (1931)

12 Professional men, they have no cares;
Whatever happens, they get theirs.
> 'I Yield to My Learned Brother' (1935)

13 Beneath this slab
John Brown is stowed.
He watched the ads,
And not the road.
> 'Lather as You Go' (1942)

14 I have a bone to pick with Fate.
Come here and tell me, girlie,
Do you think my mind is maturing late,
Or simply rotted early?
> 'Lines on Facing Forty' (1942)

15 The Ostrich roams the great Sahara.
Its mouth is wide, its neck is narra.
It has such long and lofty legs,
I'm glad it sits to lay its eggs.
> 'The Ostrich' (1957)

16 He tells you when you've got on too much lipstick,
And helps you with your girdle when your hips stick.
> 'The Perfect Husband' (1949)

17 Any kiddie in school can love like a fool,
But hating, my boy, is an art.
> 'Plea for Less Malice Toward None' (1933)

18 Candy
Is dandy
But liquor
Is quicker.
> 'Reflections on Ice-breaking' (1931)

19 I test my bath before I sit,
And I'm always moved to wonderment
That what chills the finger not a bit
Is so frigid upon the fundament.
> 'Samson Agonistes' (1942)

20 I think that I shall never see
A billboard lovely as a tree.
Perhaps, unless the billboards fall,
I'll never see a tree at all.
> 'Song of the Open Road' (1933). Cf. Kilmer 396:2

21 Sure, deck your lower limbs in pants;
Yours are the limbs, my sweeting.
You look divine as you advance—
Have you seen yourself retreating?
> 'What's the Use?' (1940)

Thomas Nashe 1567–1601

English pamphleteer and playwright

22 O, tis a precious apothegmatical Pedant, who will find matter enough to dilate a whole day of the first invention of *Fy, fa, fum, I smell the blood of an English-man.*

> *Have with you to Saffron-walden* (1596) F3 recto

23 Fair summer droops, droop men and beasts therefore:
So fair a summer look for never more.
All good things vanish, less than in a day,
Peace, plenty, pleasure, suddenly decay.
Go not yet away, bright soul of the sad year;
The earth is hell when thou leav'st to appear.

> *Summer's Last Will and Testament* (1600) l. 105

1 Beauty is but a flower
 Which wrinkles will devour;
 Brightness falls from the air;
 Queens have died young and fair;
 Dust hath closed Helen's eye.
 I am sick, I must die.
 Lord have mercy on us.
   Summer's Last Will and Testament (1600) l. 1588

2 From winter, plague and pestilence, good lord, deliver
 us!
   Summer's Last Will and Testament (1600) l. 1878

James Ball Naylor 1860–1945

3 King David and King Solomon
 Led merry, merry lives,
 With many, many lady friends,
 And many, many wives;
 But when old age crept over them—
 With many, many qualms!—
 King Solomon wrote the Proverbs
 And King David wrote the Psalms.
   'King David and King Solomon' (1935)

John Mason Neale 1818–66

English clergyman

4 All glory, laud, and honour
 To thee, Redeemer, King,
 To whom the lips of children
 Made sweet hosannas ring.
   'All glory, laud, and honour' (1851 hymn)

5 Jerusalem the golden,
 With milk and honey blessed,
 Beneath thy contemplation
 Sink heart and voice oppressed.
 I know not, O I know not
 What joys await us there,
 What radiancy of glory,
 What light beyond compare.
   'Jerusalem the golden' (1858 hymn); translated from the
   Latin of St Bernard of Cluny (b. *c*.1100)

Jawaharlal Nehru 1889–1964

Indian statesman

6 The light has gone out of our lives and there is
 darkness everywhere.
   Broadcast, 30 January 1948, following Gandhi's
   assassination; in Richard J. Walsh *Nehru on Gandhi* (1948)
   ch. 6

7 Democracy and socialism are means to an end, not
 the end itself.
   'Basic Approach'; written for private circulation and
   reprinted in Vincent Shean *Nehru: the Years of Power*
   (1960)

8 Normally speaking, it may be said that the forces of
 a capitalist society, if left unchecked, tend to make the
 rich richer and the poor poorer and thus increase the
 gap between them.
   'Basic Approach' in Vincent Shean *Nehru . . .* (1960)

Horatio, Lord Nelson 1758–1805

British admiral

9 It is my turn now; and if I come back, it is yours.
   Exercising his privilege, as second lieutenant, to board a
   prize ship before the Master, in Robert Southey *Life of
   Nelson* (1813) ch. 1

10 You must consider every man your enemy who speaks
 ill of your king: and . . . you must hate a Frenchman
 as you hate the devil.
   In Robert Southey *Life of Nelson* (1813) ch. 3

11 Before this time to-morrow I shall have gained a
 peerage, or Westminster Abbey.
   Before the battle of the Nile, in Robert Southey *Life of Nelson*
   (1813) ch. 5

12 I have only one eye,—I have a right to be blind
 sometimes . . . I really do not see the signal!
   At the battle of Copenhagen, in Robert Southey *Life of
   Nelson* (1813) ch. 7

13 In honour I gained them, and in honour I will die
 with them.
   When asked to cover the stars on his uniform, in Robert
   Southey *Life of Nelson* (1813) ch. 9

14 I believe my arrival was most welcome, not only to
 the Commander of the Fleet but almost to every
 individual in it; and when I came to explain to them
 the 'Nelson touch', it was like an electric shock. Some
 shed tears, all approved—'It was new—it was
 singular—it was simple!'
   Letter to Lady Hamilton, 1 October 1805, in Robert
   Southey *Life of Nelson* (1813) ch. 9

15 May the Great God, whom I worship, grant to my
 Country and for the benefit of Europe in general a
 great and glorious victory; and may no misconduct in
 anyone tarnish it; and may humanity after Victory be
 the predominant feature of the British Fleet. For
 myself, individually, I commit my life to Him who
 made me, and may His blessing light upon my
 endeavours for serving my Country faithfully. To Him
 I resign myself and the just cause which is entrusted
 to me to defend. Amen. Amen. Amen.
   Diary entry, on the eve of the battle of Trafalgar,
   21 October 1805, in Sir Nicholas Harris Nicolas (ed.)
   Dispatches and Letters of . . . Nelson (1846) vol. 7, p. 139

16 England expects that every man will do his duty.
   At the battle of Trafalgar, in Robert Southey *Life of Nelson*
   (1813) ch. 9

17 This is too warm work, Hardy, to last long.
   At the battle of Trafalgar, in Robert Southey *Life of Nelson*
   (1813) ch. 9

18 Thank God, I have done my duty.
   At the battle of Trafalgar, in Robert Southey *Life of Nelson*
   (1813) ch. 9

19 Kiss me, Hardy.
   At the battle of Trafalgar, in Robert Southey *Life of Nelson*
   (1813) ch. 9

Nero (Nero Claudius Caesar) AD 37–68

Roman emperor from AD 54

20 *Qualis artifex pereo!*
 What an artist dies with me!
   In Suetonius *Lives of the Caesars* 'Nero' sect. 49

Gérard de Nerval 1808–55

French poet

1 *Dieu est mort! le ciel est vide—*
Pleurez! enfants, vous n'avez plus de père.

God is dead! Heaven is empty—Weep, children, you
no longer have a father.

> Les Chimères (1854) 'Le Christ aux Oliviers' epigraph
> (summarizing a passage in Jean Paul's *Blumen-Frucht-und*
> *Dornstücke* (1796–7) in which God's children are referred to
> as 'orphans')

2 *Je suis le ténébreux,—le veuf,—l'inconsolé,*
Le prince d'Aquitaine à la tour abolie:
Ma seule étoile est morte, et mon luth constellé
Porte le soleil noir de la mélancolie.

I am the darkly shaded, the bereaved, the inconsolate,
the prince of Aquitaine, with the blasted tower. My
only *star* is dead, and my star-strewn lute carries on it
the black *sun of melancholy.*

> Les Chimères (1854) 'El Desdichado'

3 *En quoi un homard est-il plus ridicule qu'un chien . . . ou*
[que] toute autre bête dont on se fait suivre? J'ai le goût
des homards, qui sont tranquilles, sérieux, savent les
secrets de la mer, n'aboient pas et n'avalent pas la monade
des gens comme les chiens, si antipathiques à Goethe,
lequel pourtant n'était pas fou.

Why should a lobster be any more ridiculous than a
dog . . . or any other animal that one chooses to take
for a walk? I have a liking for lobsters. They are
peaceful, serious creatures. They know the secrets of
the sea, they don't bark, and they don't gnaw upon
one's monadic privacy like dogs do. And Goethe had
an aversion to dogs, and he wasn't mad.

> Justifying his walking a lobster on a lead in the gardens of
> the Palais Royal; in T. Gautier *Portraits et Souvenirs*
> *Littéraires* (1875), translated by Richard Holmes in
> T. Gautier *My Phantoms* (1976) p. 149

Otto Neurath 1882–1945

German philosopher

4 We are like sailors who must rebuild their ship on the
open sea, never able to dismantle it in dry-dock and to
reconstruct it there out of the best materials.

> 'Protocol Sentences', in A. J. Ayer (ed.) *Logical Positivism*
> (1959)

Allan Nevins 1890–1971

American historian

5 The former Allies had blundered in the past by offering
Germany too little, and offering even that too late,
until finally Nazi Germany had become a menace to all
mankind.

> In *Current History* (New York) May 1935, p. 178

Sir Henry Newbolt 1862–1938

English lawyer, poet, and man of letters

6 'Take my drum to England, hang et by the shore,
Strike et when your powder's runnin' low;
If the Dons sight Devon, I'll quit the port o' Heaven,
An' drum them up the Channel as we drummed them
  long ago.'

> 'Drake's Drum' (1897)

7 Drake he's in his hammock till the great Armadas
  come.
(Capten, art tha sleepin' there below?)
Slung atween the round shot, listenin' for the drum,
An' dreamin' arl the time o' Plymouth Hoe.
Call him on the deep sea, call him up the Sound,
Call him when ye sail to meet the foe;
Where the old trade's plyin' an' the old flag flyin'
They shall find him ware an' wakin', as they found
  him long ago!

> 'Drake's Drum' (1897)

8 Now the sunset breezes shiver,
And she's fading down the river,
But in England's song for ever
She's the Fighting Téméraire.

> 'The Fighting Téméraire' (1897)

9 There's a breathless hush in the Close to-night—
Ten to make and the match to win—
A bumping pitch and a blinding light,
An hour to play and the last man in.
And it's not for the sake of a ribboned coat,
Or the selfish hope of a season's fame,
But his Captain's hand on his shoulder smote—
'Play up! play up! and play the game!'

> 'Vitaï Lampada' (1897)

Anthony Newley 1931– *and Leslie Bricusse* 1931–

10 Stop the world, I want to get off.

> Title of musical (1961)

John Henry Newman 1801–90

English theologian and leader of the Oxford Movement;
later Cardinal

11 It is very difficult to get up resentment towards
persons whom one has never seen.

> *Apologia pro Vita Sua* (1864) 'Mr Kingsley's Method of
> Disputation'

12 There is such a thing as legitimate warfare: war has
its laws; there are things which may fairly be done,
and things which may not be done . . . He has
attempted (as I may call it) to *poison the wells.*

> *Apologia pro Vita Sua* (1864) 'Mr Kingsley's Method of
> Disputation'

13 I will vanquish, not my Accuser, but my judges.

> *Apologia pro Vita Sua* (1864) 'True Mode of meeting Mr
> Kingsley'

14 Two and two only supreme and luminously
self-evident beings, myself and my Creator.

> *Apologia pro Vita Sua* (1864) 'History of My Religious
> Opinions to the Year 1833'

15 It would be a gain to the country were it vastly more
superstitious, more bigoted, more gloomy, more fierce
in its religion than at present it shows itself to be.

> *Apologia pro Vita Sua* (1864) 'History of My Religious
> Opinions from 1833 to 1839'

1 From the age of fifteen, dogma has been the fundamental principle of my religion: I know no other religion; I cannot enter into the idea of any other sort of religion; religion, as a mere sentiment, is to me a dream and a mockery.

Apologia pro Vita Sua (1864) 'History of My Religious Opinions from 1833 to 1839'

2 This is what the Church is said to want, not party men, but sensible, temperate, sober, well-judging persons, to guide it through the channel of no-meaning, between the Scylla and Charybdis of Aye and No.

Apologia pro Vita Sua (1864) 'History of My Religious Opinions from 1833 to 1839'

3 Ten thousand difficulties do not make one doubt.

Apologia pro Vita Sua (1864) 'Position of my Mind since 1845'

4 The all-corroding, all-dissolving scepticism of the intellect in religious enquiries.

Apologia pro Vita Sua (1864) 'Position of my Mind since 1845'

5 It is almost a definition of a gentleman to say that he is one who never inflicts pain.

The Idea of a University (1852) 'Knowledge and Religious Duty'

6 She [the Catholic Church] holds that it were better for sun and moon to drop from heaven, for the earth to fail, and for all the many millions who are upon it to die of starvation in extremest agony, as far as temporal affliction goes, than that one soul, I will not say, should be lost, but should commit one single venial sin, should tell one wilful untruth . . . or steal one poor farthing without excuse.

Lectures on Anglican Difficulties (1852) Lecture 8

7 If I am obliged to bring religion into after-dinner toasts (which indeed does not seem quite the thing) I shall drink—to the Pope, if you please—still, to Conscience first, and to the Pope afterwards.

A Letter Addressed to the Duke of Norfolk . . . (1875) sect. 5

8 And this is all that is known, and more than all—yet nothing to what the angels know—of the life of a servant of God, who sinned and repented, and did penance and washed out his sins, and became a Saint, and reigns with Christ in heaven.

Lives of the English Saints (1844–5) 'The Legend of Saint Bettelin'; though attributed to Newman, 'and more than all' may have been added by J. A. Froude (1818–94)

9 It is as absurd to argue men, as to torture them, into believing.

'The Usurpations of Reason' (1831) in *Oxford University Sermons* (1843) no. 4

10 When men understand what each other mean, they see, for the most part, that controversy is either superfluous or hopeless.

'Faith and Reason, contrasted as Habits of Mind' (Epiphany, 1839) in *Oxford University Sermons* (1843) no. 10

11 May He support us all the day long, till the shades lengthen, and the evening comes, and the busy world is hushed, and the fever of life is over, and our work is done! Then in His mercy may He give us a safe lodging, and a holy rest, and peace at the last.

'Wisdom and Innocence' (19 February 1843) in *Sermons Bearing on Subjects of the Day* (1843) no. 20

12 Firmly I believe and truly
God is Three, and God is One;
And I next acknowledge duly
Manhood taken by the Son.

The Dream of Gerontius (1865)

13 Praise to the Holiest in the height,
And in the depth be praise;
In all his words most wonderful,
Most sure in all His ways.

The Dream of Gerontius (1865)

14 Lead, kindly Light, amid the encircling gloom,
Lead thou me on;
The night is dark, and I am far from home,
Lead thou me on.
Keep Thou my feet; I do not ask to see
The distant scene; one step enough for me.

'Lead, kindly Light' (1834)

15 I loved the garish day, and spite of fears,
Pride ruled my will: remember not past years.

'Lead, kindly Light' (1834). Cf. Milton 464:25

16 *We can believe what we choose. We are answerable for what we choose to believe.*

Letter to Mrs William Froude, 27 June 1848, in C. S. Dessain (ed.) *Letters and Diaries of John Henry Newman* vol. 12 (1962)

17 *Ex umbris et imaginibus in veritatem.*

From shadows and types to the reality.

Motto on his memorial tablet, in Owen Chadwick *Newman* (1983) p. 78

Huey Newton 1942–
American political activist

18 I suggested [in 1966] that we use the panther as our symbol and call our political vehicle the Black Panther Party. The panther is a fierce animal, but he will not attack until he is backed into a corner; then he will strike out.

Revolutionary Suicide (1973) ch. 16

Sir Isaac Newton 1642–1727
English mathematician and physicist

19 If I have seen further it is by standing on the shoulders of giants.

Letter to Robert Hooke, 5 February 1676, in H. W. Turnbull (ed.) *Correspondence of Isaac Newton* vol. 1 (1959) p. 416. Cf. Bernard 66:9, Coleridge 212:4

20 Philosophy is such an impertinently litigious lady that a man has as good be engaged in law suits as have to do with her.

Letter to Edmond Halley, 20 June 1686, in H. W. Turnbull (ed.) *Correspondence of Isaac Newton* vol. 2 (1960) p. 437

21 Whence is it that Nature does nothing in vain: and whence arises all that order and beauty which we see in the world? . . . does it not appear from phenomena that there is a Being incorporeal, living, intelligent, omnipresent, who in infinite space, as it were in his Sensory, sees the things themselves intimately, and thoroughly perceives them, and comprehends them wholly.

Opticks (1730 ed.) bk. 3, pt. 1, question 28

1 The changing of bodies into light, and light into bodies, is very conformable to the course of Nature, which seems delighted with transmutations.

Opticks (1730 ed.) bk. 3, pt. 1, question 30

2 *Corpus omne perseverare in statu suo quiescendi vel movendi uniformiter in directum, nisi quatenus illud a viribus impressis cogitur statum suum mutare.*

Every body continues in its state of rest, or of uniform motion in a right line, unless it is compelled to change that state by forces impressed upon it.

Principia Mathematica (1687) Laws of Motion 1 (translated by Andrew Motte, 1729)

3 *Mutationem motus proportionalem esse vi motrici impressae et fieri secundum lineam rectam qua vis illa imprimitur.*

The alteration of motion is ever proportional to the motive force impressed; and is made in the direction of the right line in which that force is impressed.

Principia Mathematica (1687) Laws of Motion 2 (translated by Andrew Motte, 1729)

4 *Actioni contrarium semper et aequalem esse reactionem: sive corporum duorum actiones in se mutuo semper esse aequales et in partes contrarias dirigi.*

To every action there is always opposed an equal reaction: or, the mutual actions of two bodies upon each other are always equal, and directed to contrary parts.

Principia Mathematica (1687) Laws of Motion 3 (translated by Andrew Motte, 1729)

5 *Hypotheses non fingo.*

I do not feign hypotheses.

Principia Mathematica (1713 ed.) 'Scholium Generale'

6 O Diamond! Diamond! thou little knowest the mischief done!

To a dog, who knocked over a candle which set fire to some papers and thereby 'destroyed the almost finished labours of some years'; in Thomas Maude *Wensley-Dale . . . a Poem* (1772) st. 23 n. (probably apocryphal). *See* D. Gjertsen *The Newton Handbook* (1986) p. 177

7 I don't know what I may seem to the world, but as to myself, I seem to have been only like a boy playing on the sea-shore and diverting myself in now and then finding a smoother pebble or a prettier shell than ordinary, whilst the great ocean of truth lay all undiscovered before me.

In Joseph Spence *Anecdotes* (ed. J. Osborn, 1966) no. 1259

John Newton 1725–1807

English clergyman

8 Amazing grace! how sweet the sound
That saved a wretch like me!
I once was lost, but now am found,
Was blind, but now I see.

Olney Hymns (1779) 'Amazing grace'

9 Glorious things of thee are spoken,
Zion, city of our God!

Olney Hymns (1779) 'Glorious things of thee are spoken'

10 How sweet the name of Jesus sounds
In a believer's ear!
It soothes his sorrows, heals his wounds,
And drives away his fear.

It makes the wounded spirit whole,
And calms the troubled breast;
'Tis manna to the hungry soul,
And to the weary rest.

Olney Hymns (1779) 'How sweet the name of Jesus sounds'

Nicholas I 1796–1855

Russian emperor from 1825

11 Turkey is a dying man. We may endeavour to keep him alive, but we shall not succeed. He will, he must die.

In F. Max Müller (ed.) *Memoirs of Baron Stockmar* (translated by G. A. M. Müller, 1873) vol. 2, p. 107

12 Russia has two generals in whom she can confide—Generals Janvier [January] and Février [February].

Attributed. See *Punch* 10 March 1855

Nicias c.470–413 BC

Athenian politician and general

13 ἄνδρες γὰρ πόλις, καὶ οὐ τείχη οὐδὲ νῆες ἀνδρῶν κεναί

For a city consists in men, and not in walls nor in ships empty of men.

Speech to the defeated Athenian army at Syracuse, 413 BC, in Thucydides *History of the Peloponnesian Wars* bk. 7, sect. 77

Sir Harold Nicolson 1886–1968

English diplomat, politician, and writer

14 Ponderous and uncertain is that relation between pressure and resistance which constitutes the balance of power. The arch of peace is morticed by no iron tendons . . . One night a handful of dust will patter from the vaulting: the bats will squeak and wheel in sudden panic: nor can the fragile fingers of man then stay the rush and rumble of destruction.

Public Faces (1932) ch. 6

15 We shall have to walk and live a Woolworth life hereafter.

Anticipating the aftermath of the Second World War, in *Diaries and Letters 1939–45* (1967) 4 June 1941

16 I am haunted by mental decay such as I saw creeping over Ramsay MacDonald. A gradual dimming of the lights.

In *Diaries and Letters 1945–62* (1968) 28 April 1947

17 For seventeen years he did nothing at all but kill animals and stick in stamps.

Of King George V, in *Diaries and Letters 1945–62* (1968) 17 August 1949

Reinhold Niebuhr 1892–1971

American theologian

1 Man's capacity for justice makes democracy possible, but man's inclination to injustice makes democracy necessary.

Children of Light and Children of Darkness (1944) foreword

Martin Niemöller 1892–1984

German theologian

2 When Hitler attacked the Jews I was not a Jew, therefore, I was not concerned. And when Hitler attacked the Catholics, I was not a Catholic, and therefore, I was not concerned. And when Hitler attacked the unions and the industrialists, I was not a member of the unions and I was not concerned. Then, Hitler attacked me and the Protestant church—and there was nobody left to be concerned.

In *Congressional Record* 14 October 1968, p. 31636 (often quoted in the form 'In Germany they came first for the Communists, and I didn't speak up because I wasn't a Communist . . . ' and so on)

Friedrich Nietzsche 1844–1900

German philosopher and writer

3 *Ich lehre euch den Übermenschen. Der Mensch ist Etwas, das überwunden werden soll.*

I teach you the superman. Man is something to be surpassed.

Also Sprach Zarathustra (1883) prologue, sect. 3

4 *Du gehst zu Frauen? Vergiss die Peitsche nicht!*

You are going to women? Do not forget the whip!

Also Sprach Zarathustra (1883) bk. 1 'Von Alten und jungen Weiblein'

5 *Auf Andere warte ich . . . auf Höhere, Stärkere, Sieghaftere, Wohlgemutere, Solche, die rechtwinklig gebaut sind an Leib und Seele: lachende Löwen müssen kommen.*

For others do I wait . . . for higher ones, stronger ones, more triumphant ones, merrier ones, for such as are built squarely in body and soul: laughing lions must come.

Also Sprach Zarathustra (1883) bk. 4 'Die Begrüssung'

6 *Das Erbarmen Gottes mit der einzigen Not, die alle Paradiese an sich haben, kennt keine Grenzen: er schuf alsbald noch andere Tiere. Erster Fehlgriff Gottes: der Mensch fand die Tiere nicht unterhaltend,—er herrschte über sie, er wollte nicht einmal 'Tier' sein.*

[Man found a solitary existence tedious.] There are no limits to God's compassion with Paradises over their one universally felt want: he immediately created other animals besides. God's first blunder: Man didn't find the animals amusing,—he dominated them, and didn't even want to be an 'animal'.

Der Antichrist (1888) aphorism 48

7 *Das Weib war der zweite Fehlgriff Gottes.*

Woman was God's second blunder.

Der Antichrist (1888) aphorism 48

8 *Wie ich den Philosophen verstehe, als einen furchtbaren Explosionsstoff, vor dem Alles in Gefahr ist.*

What I understand by 'philosopher': a terrible explosive in the presence of which everything is in danger.

Ecce Homo (1908) 'Die Unzeitgemässen' sect. 3

9 *Gott ist tot: aber so wie die Art der Menschen ist, wird es vielleicht noch Jahrtausende lang Höhlen geben, in denen man seinen Schatten zeigt.*

God is dead: but considering the state the species Man is in, there will perhaps be caves, for ages yet, in which his shadow will be shown.

Die fröhliche Wissenschaft (1882) bk. 3, sect. 108

10 *Moralität ist Heerden-Instinkt in Einzelnen.*

Morality is the herd-instinct in the individual.

Die fröhliche Wissenschaft (1882) bk. 3, sect. 116

11 *Der christliche Entschluss, die Welt hässlich und schlecht zu finden, hat die Welt hässlich und schlecht gemacht.*

The Christian resolution to find the world ugly and bad has made the world ugly and bad.

Die fröhliche Wissenschaft (1882) bk. 3, sect. 130

12 *Glaubt es mir!—das Geheimniss, um die grösste Fruchtbarkeit und den grössten Genuss vom Dasein einzuernten, heisst: gefährlich leben!*

Believe me! The secret of reaping the greatest fruitfulness and the greatest enjoyment from life is *to live dangerously!*

Die fröhliche Wissenschaft (1882) bk. 4, sect. 283

13 *Wer mit Ungeheuern kämpft, mag zusehn, dass er nicht dabei zum Ungeheuer wird. Und wenn du lange in einen Abgrund blickst, blickt der Abgrund auch in dich hinein.*

He who fights with monsters might take care lest he thereby become a monster. And if you gaze for long into an abyss, the abyss gazes also into you.

Jenseits von Gut und Böse (1886) ch. 4, no. 146

14 *Der Gedanke an den Selbstmord ist ein starkes Trostmittel: mit ihm kommt man gut über manche böse Nacht hinweg.*

The thought of suicide is a great source of comfort: with it a calm passage is to be made across many a bad night.

Jenseits von Gut und Böse (1886) ch. 4, no. 157

15 *Herren-Moral und Sklaven-Moral.*

Master-morality and slave-morality.

Jenseits von Gut und Böse (1886) ch. 9, no. 260

16 *Der Witz ist das Epigramm auf den Tod eines Gefühls.*

Wit is the epitaph of an emotion.

Menschliches, Allzumenschliches (1867–80) vol. 2, sect. 1, no. 202

17 *Auf dem Grunde aller dieser vornehmen Rassen ist das Raubtier, die prachtvolle nach Beute und Sieg lüstern schweifende blonde Bestie nicht zu verkennen.*

At the base of all these aristocratic races the predator is not to be mistaken, the splendorous *blond beast,* avidly rampant for plunder and victory.

Zur Genealogie der Moral (1887) 1st treatise, no. 11

Florence Nightingale 1820–1910
English nurse

1 No *man*, not even a doctor, ever gives any other definition of what a nurse should be than this—'devoted and obedient.' This definition would do just as well for a porter. It might even do for a horse. It would not do for a policeman.
Notes on Nursing (1860) p. 200

2 Too kind, too kind.
On the Order of Merit being brought to her at her home, 5 December 1907; in E. Cook *Life of Florence Nightingale* (1913) vol. 2, pt. 7, ch. 9

Richard Milhous Nixon 1913–
37th President of the USA

3 The great silent majority.
Broadcast, 3 November 1969 in *New York Times* 4 November 1969, p. 16

4 There can be no whitewash at the White House.
Television speech on Watergate, 30 April 1973, in *New York Times* 1 May 1973, p. 31

5 I made my mistakes, but in all my years of public life, I have never profited, never profited from public service. I've earned every cent. And in all of my years in public life I have never obstructed justice . . .
I welcome this kind of examination because people have got to know whether or not their President is a crook. Well, I'm not a crook.
Speech at press conference, 17 November 1973, in *New York Times* 18 November 1973, p. 62

6 This country needs good farmers, good businessmen, good plumbers, good carpenters.
Farewell address at White House, 9 August 1974, in *New York Times* 10 August 1974, p. 4

7 When the President does it, that means that it is not illegal.
In David Frost *I Gave Them a Sword* (1978) ch. 8

8 I brought myself down. I gave them a sword. And they stuck it in.
Television interview, 19 May 1977, in David Frost *I Gave Them a Sword* (1978) ch. 10

Caroline Maria Noel 1817–77
English hymn-writer

9 At the name of Jesus
Every knee shall bow,
Every tongue confess him
King of glory now;
'Tis the Father's pleasure
We should call him Lord,
Who from the beginning
Was the mighty word.
'At the name of Jesus' (1861 hymn)

Thomas Noel 1799–1861
English poet

10 Rattle his bones over the stones;
He's only a pauper, whom nobody owns!
'The Pauper's Drive' (1841)

Charles Howard, 11th Duke of Norfolk 1746–1815

11 I cannot be a good Catholic; I cannot go to heaven; and if a man is to go to the devil, he may as well go thither from the House of Lords as from any other place on earth.
In Henry Best *Personal and Literary Memorials* (1829) ch. 18

Christopher North (Professor John Wilson) 1785–1854
Scottish literary critic

12 Minds like ours, my dear James, must always be above national prejudices, and in all companies it gives me true pleasure to declare, that, as a people, the English are very little indeed inferior to the Scotch.
Blackwood's Magazine (October 1826) 'Noctes Ambrosianae' no. 20

13 His Majesty's dominions, on which the sun never sets.
Blackwood's Magazine (April 1829) 'Noctes Ambrosianae' no. 42

14 Laws were made to be broken.
Blackwood's Magazine (May 1830) 'Noctes Ambrosianae' no. 49

15 Insultin the sun, and quarrellin wi' the equawtor.
Blackwood's Magazine (May 1830) 'Noctes Ambrosianae' no. 49

16 Animosities are mortal, but the Humanities live for ever.
Blackwood's Magazine (August 1834) 'Noctes Ambrosianae' no. 67

17 Such accidents will happen in the best-regulated families.
Blackwood's Magazine (August 1834) 'Noctes Ambrosianae' no. 67. Cf. Dickens 240:4

18 I cannot sit still, James, and hear you abuse the shopocracy.
Blackwood's Magazine (February 1835) 'Noctes Ambrosianae' no. 71

Lord Northcliffe (Alfred Charles William Harmsworth, 1st Viscount Northcliffe) 1865–1922
British newspaper proprietor

19 The power of the press is very great, but not so great as the power of suppress.
Office message, *Daily Mail* 1918, in Reginald Rose and Geoffrey Harmsworth *Northcliffe* (1959) ch. 22

20 When I want a peerage, I shall buy it like an honest man.
In Tom Driberg *Swaff* (1974) ch. 2

Caroline Norton (née Sheridan) 1808–77

English poet and songwriter

1 For death and life, in ceaseless strife,
Beat wild on this world's shore,
And all our calm is in that balm—
Not lost but gone before.
  'Not Lost but Gone Before'. Cf. Cyprian 229:9

Jack Norworth 1879–1959

American songwriter

2 Oh, shine on, shine on, harvest moon
Up in the sky.
I ain't had no lovin'
Since April, January, June, or July.
  'Shine On, Harvest Moon' (1908 song)

Novalis (Friedrich von Hardenberg) 1772–1801

German poet and novelist

3 *Oft fühl ich jetzt ... [und] je tiefer ich einsehe, dass
Schicksal und Gemüt Namen eines Begriffes sind.*

I often feel, and ever more deeply I realize, that fate
and character are the same conception.
  Heinrich von Ofterdingen (1802) bk. 2 (often quoted
  'Character is destiny' or 'Character is fate'). Cf. Eliot
  269:26, Heraclitus 333:12

4 *Ein Gott-betrunkener Mensch.*

A God-intoxicated man.
  Of Spinoza (attributed)

Alfred Noyes 1880–1958

English poet

5 The landlord's black-eyed daughter,
Bess, the landlord's daughter,
Plaiting a dark red love-knot into her long black hair.
  'The Highwayman' (1907)

6 Look for me by moonlight;
Watch for me by moonlight;
I'll come to thee by moonlight, though hell should bar
  the way!
  'The Highwayman' (1907)

Bill Nye (Edgar Wilson Nye)

American humorist

7 I have been told that Wagner's music is better than it
sounds.
  In Mark Twain *Autobiography* (1924) vol. 1, p. 338

Charles Edward Oakley 1832–65

English clergyman

8 Hills of the North, rejoice:
Rivers and mountain-spring,
Hark to the advent voice!
Valley and lowland, sing!

Though absent long, your Lord is nigh,
He judgement brings, and victory.
  'Hills of the North, rejoice' (1870 hymn)

Captain Lawrence Oates 1880–1912

English polar explorer

9 I am just going outside and may be some time.
  Last words, in *Scott's Last Expedition* (1913) ch. 20 (Scott's
  diary entry, 16–17 March 1912)

Edna O'Brien 1936–

Irish novelist and short-story writer

10 August is a wicked month.
  Title of novel (1965)

Flann O'Brien (Brian O'Nolan or O Nuallain) 1911–66

Irish novelist and journalist

11 The conclusion of your syllogism, I said lightly, is
fallacious, being based upon licensed premises.
  At Swim-Two-Birds (1939) ch. 1

12 A pint of plain is your only man.
  At Swim-Two-Birds (1939) 'The Workman's Friend'

13 It is not that I half knew my mother. I knew half of
her: the lower half—her lap, legs, feet, her hands and
wrists as she bent forward.
  The Hard Life (1961) p. 11

Sean O'Casey 1880–1964

Irish playwright

14 I killin' meself workin', an' he shruttin' about from
mornin' till night like a paycock!
  Juno and the Paycock (1925) act 1

15 He's an oul' butty o' mine—oh, he's a darlin' man,
a daarlin' man.
  Juno and the Paycock (1925) act 1

16 The whole worl's in a state o' chassis!
  Juno and the Paycock (1925) act 1

17 The Polis as Polis, in this city, is Null an' Void!
  Juno and the Paycock (1925) act 3

18 There's no reason to bring religion into it. I think we
ought to have as great a regard for religion as we can,
so as to keep it out of as many things as possible.
  The Plough and the Stars (1926) act 1

19 It's my rule never to lose me temper till it would be
dethrimental to keep it.
  The Plough and the Stars (1926) act 2

20 English literature's performing flea.
  Of P. G. Wodehouse, in P. G. Wodehouse *Performing Flea*
  (1953) p. 217

William of Occam c.1285–1349

English Franciscan friar and philosopher

1 *Entia non sunt multiplicanda praeter necessitatem.*

No more things should be presumed to exist than are absolutely necessary.

> 'Occam's Razor', an ancient philosophical principle often attributed to Occam but earlier in origin; not found in this form in his writings, although he frequently used similar expressions, e.g. *'Pluralitas non est ponenda sine necessitate* [Plurality should not be assumed unnecessarily]' in *Quodlibeta* (c.1324) no. 5, question 1, art. 2. See J. C. Way (ed.) *Opera Theologica* (1980) vol. 9, p. 476

Adolph S. Ochs 1858–1935

American newspaper proprietor

2 All the news that's fit to print.
> Motto of the *New York Times*, from 1896

David Ogilvy 1911–

British-born advertising executive

3 The consumer isn't a moron; she is your wife.
> *Confessions of an Advertising Man* (1963) ch. 5

James Ogilvy, 1st Earl of Seafield 1664–1730

Lord Chancellor of Scotland

4 Now there's ane end of ane old song.
> As he signed the engrossed exemplification of the Act of Union, 1706, in *The Lockhart Papers* (1817) vol. 1, p. 223

John O'Hara 1905–70

American writer

5 An artist is his own fault.
> *The Portable F. Scott Fitzgerald* (1945) introduction

Theodore O'Hara 1820–67

American poet

6 Sons of the dark and bloody ground.
> 'The Bivouac of the Dead' (1847) st. 1

Patrick O'Keefe 1872–1934

American advertising agent

7 Say it with flowers.
> Slogan for the Society of American Florists, in *Florists' Exchange* 15 December 1917, p. 1268

John O'Keeffe 1747–1833

Irish playwright

8 Amo, amas, I love a lass,
As a cedar tall and slender;
Sweet cowslip's grace
Is her nom'native case,
And she's of the feminine gender.
> *The Agreeable Surprise* (1781) act 2, sc. 2

9 Fat, fair and forty were all the toasts of the young men.
> *The Irish Mimic* (1795) sc. 2

Dennis O'Kelly c.1720–87

Irish racehorse-owner

10 Eclipse first, the rest nowhere.
> Comment at Epsom, 3 May 1769, in *Annals of Sporting* vol. 2 (1822) p. 271. *Dictionary of National Biography* gives the occasion as the Queen's Plate at Winchester, 1769

William Oldys 1696–1761

English antiquary

11 Busy, curious, thirsty fly,
Gently drink, and drink as I;
Freely welcome to my cup.
> 'The Fly' (1732)

Frederick Scott Oliver 1864–1934

Scottish writer

12 A wise politician will never grudge a genuflexion or a rapture if it is expected of him by prevalent opinion.
> *The Endless Adventure* (1930) vol. 1, pt. 1, ch. 20

Laurence Olivier (Baron Olivier of Brighton) 1907–89

English actor and director

13 The tragedy of a man who could not make up his mind.
> Introduction to his 1948 screen adaptation of *Hamlet*

14 Shakespeare—the nearest thing in incarnation to the eye of God.
> In *Kenneth Harris Talking To . . .* (1971) 'Sir Laurence Olivier'

15 Acting is a masochistic form of exhibitionism. It is not quite the occupation of an adult.
> In *Time* 3 July 1978, p. 33

16 Can a muse of fire exist under a ceiling of commerce?
> Appealing on behalf of the Rose Theatre remains; in *The Times* 12 July 1989, p. 24. Cf. *Henry V* 584:16

Frank Ward O'Malley

See ELBERT HUBBARD

Eugene O'Neill 1888–1953

American playwright

17 For de little stealin' dey gits you in jail soon or late. For de big stealin' dey makes you Emperor and puts you in de Hall o' Fame when you croaks.
> *The Emperor Jones* (1921) sc. 1. Cf. Veblen 709:16

18 The iceman cometh.
> Title of play (1946)

19 A long day's journey into night.
> Title of play (written 1940–1)

20 Life is perhaps most wisely regarded as a bad dream between two awakenings, and every day is a life in miniature.
> *Marco Millions* (1928) act 2, sc. 2

1 The sea hates a coward!
  Mourning becomes Electra (1931) pt. 2, act 4

2 The only living life is in the past and future ... the present is an interlude ... strange interlude in which we call on past and future to bear witness we are living.
  Strange Interlude (1928) pt. 2, act 8

Yoko Ono 1933–

Japanese poet and songwriter

3 Woman is the nigger of the world.
  Remark made in a 1968 interview for *Nova* magazine and adopted by John Lennon as the title of a song (1972). See J. Robertson *Art and Music of John Lennon* (1990) ch. 11

Brian O'Nolan

See FLANN O'BRIEN

John Opie 1761–1807

English painter

4 I mix them with my brains, sir.
  On being asked with what he mixed his colours, in Samuel Smiles *Self-Help* (1859) ch. 4

J. Robert Oppenheimer 1904–67

American physicist

5 In some sort of crude sense which no vulgarity, no humour, no overstatement can quite extinguish, the physicists have known sin; and this is a knowledge which they cannot lose.
  Open Mind (1955) ch. 5 (lecture, 1947)

Susie Orbach 1946–

American psychotherapist

6 Fat is a feminist issue.
  Title of book (1978)

Roy Orbison and Joe Melsom

7 Only the lonely (know the way I feel).
  Title of song (1960)

Baroness Orczy (Mrs Montague Barstow) 1865–1947

Hungarian-born novelist

8 We seek him here, we seek him there,
  Those Frenchies seek him everywhere.
  Is he in heaven?—Is he in hell?
  That demmed, elusive Pimpernel?
  The Scarlet Pimpernel (1905) ch. 12

Meta Orred

19th-century writer and poet

9 In the gloaming, Oh my darling!
  When the lights are dim and low,
  And the quiet shadows falling
  Softly come and softly go.
  'In the Gloaming' (1877 song)

José Ortega y Gasset 1883–1955

Spanish writer and philosopher

10 *Yo soy yo y mi circunstancia, y si no la salvo a ella no me salvo yo.*
  I am I plus my surroundings, and if I do not preserve the latter I do not preserve myself.
  Meditaciones del Quijote (1914) in *Obras Completas* (1946) vol. 1, p. 322

11 *La civilización no es otra cosa que el ensayo de reducir la fuerza a ultima ratio.*
  Civilization is nothing more than the effort to reduce the use of force to the last resort.
  La Rebelión de las Masas (1930) in *Obras Completas* (1947) vol. 4, p. 191

Joe Orton 1933–67

English playwright

12 I'd the upbringing a nun would envy ... Until I was fifteen I was more familiar with Africa than my own body.
  Entertaining Mr Sloane (1964) act 1

13 KATH: Can he be present at the birth of his child? ...
  ED: It's all any reasonable child can expect if the dad is present at the conception.
  Entertaining Mr Sloane (1964) act 3

14 Every luxury was lavished on you—atheism, breast-feeding, circumcision.
  Loot (1967) act 1

15 Policemen, like red squirrels, must be protected.
  Loot (1967) act 1

16 Reading isn't an occupation we encourage among police officers. We try to keep the paper work down to a minimum.
  Loot (1967) act 2

17 You were born with your legs apart. They'll send you to the grave in a Y-shaped coffin.
  What the Butler Saw (1969) act 1

George Orwell (Eric Blair) 1903–50

English novelist

18 Man is the only creature that consumes without producing.
  Animal Farm (1945) ch. 1

19 Four legs good, two legs bad.
  Animal Farm (1945) ch. 3

20 All animals are equal but some animals are more equal than others.
  Animal Farm (1945) ch. 10

21 Good prose is like a window-pane.
  Collected Essays (1968) vol. 1 'Why I Write'

22 At 50, everyone has the face he deserves.
  Last words in his notebook, 17 April 1949, in *Collected Essays, Journalism and Letters ...* (1968) vol. 4, p. 515

23 I'm fat, but I'm thin inside. Has it ever struck you that there's a thin man inside every fat man, just as they say there's a statue inside every block of stone?
  Coming up For Air (1939) pt. 1, ch. 3. Cf. Connolly 10:15

1 He was an embittered atheist (the sort of atheist who does not so much disbelieve in God as personally dislike Him), and took a sort of pleasure in thinking that human affairs would never improve.
Down and Out in Paris and London (1933) ch. 30

2 Down here it was still the England I had known in my childhood: the railway cuttings smothered in wild flowers . . . the red buses, the blue policemen—all sleeping the deep, deep sleep of England, from which I sometimes fear that we shall never wake till we are jerked out of it by the roar of bombs.
Homage to Catalonia (1938) ch. 14

3 Whatever is funny is subversive, every joke is ultimately a custard pie . . . A dirty joke is a sort of mental rebellion.
Horizon September 1941 'The Art of Donald McGill'

4 Most revolutionaries are potential Tories, because they imagine that everything can be put right by altering the *shape* of society; once that change is effected, as it sometimes is, they see no need for any other.
Inside the Whale (1940) 'Charles Dickens'

5 Keep the aspidistra flying.
Title of novel (1936)

6 England . . . resembles a family, a rather stuffy Victorian family, with not many black sheep in it but with all its cupboards bursting with skeletons. It has rich relations who have to be kowtowed to and poor relations who are horribly sat upon, and there is a deep conspiracy of silence about the source of the family income. It is a family in which the young are generally thwarted and most of the power is in the hands of irresponsible uncles and bed-ridden aunts. Still, it is a family. It has its private language and its common memories, and at the approach of an enemy it closes its ranks. A family with the wrong members in control.
The Lion and the Unicorn (1941) pt. 1 'England Your England'

7 Probably the battle of Waterloo *was* won on the playing-fields of Eton, but the opening battles of all subsequent wars have been lost there.
The Lion and the Unicorn (1941) pt. 1 'England Your England'. Cf. Wellington 727:7

8 It was a bright cold day in April, and the clocks were striking thirteen.
Nineteen Eighty-Four (1949) pt. 1, ch. 1

9 BIG BROTHER IS WATCHING YOU.
Nineteen Eighty-Four (1949) pt. 1, ch. 1

10 War is peace. Freedom is slavery. Ignorance is strength.
Nineteen Eighty-Four (1949) pt. 1, ch. 1

11 Who controls the past controls the future: who controls the present controls the past.
Nineteen Eighty-Four (1949) pt. 1, ch. 3

12 Don't you see that the whole aim of Newspeak is to narrow the range of thought? In the end we shall make thoughtcrime literally impossible, because there will be no words in which to express it.
Nineteen Eighty-Four (1949) pt. 1, ch. 5

13 Freedom is the freedom to say that two plus two make four. If that is granted, all else follows.
Nineteen Eighty-Four (1949) pt. 1, ch. 7

14 Syme was not only dead, he was abolished, an un-person.
Nineteen Eighty-Four (1949) pt. 2, ch. 5

15 *Doublethink* means the power of holding two contradictory beliefs in one's mind simultaneously, and accepting both of them.
Nineteen Eighty-Four (1949) pt. 2, ch. 9

16 Power is not a means, it is an end. One does not establish a dictatorship in order to safeguard a revolution; one makes the revolution in order to establish the dictatorship.
Nineteen Eighty-Four (1949) pt. 3, ch. 3

17 If you want a picture of the future, imagine a boot stamping on a human face—for ever.
Nineteen Eighty-Four (1949) pt. 3, ch. 3

18 The quickest way of ending a war is to lose it.
Polemic May 1946 'Second Thoughts on James Burnham'

19 A person of bourgeois origin goes through life with some expectation of getting what he wants, within reasonable limits. Hence the fact that in times of stress 'educated' people tend to come to the front.
The Road to Wigan Pier (1937) ch. 3

20 In a Lancashire cotton-town you could probably go for months on end without once hearing an 'educated' accent, whereas there can hardly be a town in the South of England where you could throw a brick without hitting the niece of a bishop.
The Road to Wigan Pier (1937) ch. 7

21 The typical Socialist is . . . a prim little man with a white-collar job, usually a secret teetotaller and often with vegetarian leanings, with a history of Nonconformity behind him, and, above all, with a social position which he has no intention of forfeiting.
The Road to Wigan Pier (1937) ch. 11

22 To the ordinary working man, the sort you would meet in any pub on Saturday night, Socialism does not mean much more than better wages and shorter hours and nobody bossing you about.
The Road to Wigan Pier (1937) ch. 11

23 The high-water mark, so to speak, of Socialist literature is W. H. Auden, a sort of gutless Kipling.
The Road to Wigan Pier (1937) ch. 11

24 We of the sinking middle class . . . may sink without further struggles into the working class where we belong, and probably when we get there it will not be so dreadful as we feared, for, after all, we have nothing to lose but our aitches.
The Road to Wigan Pier (1937) ch. 13

25 Serious sport has nothing to do with fair play. It is bound up with hatred, jealousy, boastfulness, and disregard of all the rules.
Shooting an Elephant (1950) 'I Write as I Please'

26 In our time, political speech and writing are largely the defence of the indefensible.
Shooting an Elephant (1950) 'Politics and the English Language'

1 The great enemy of clear language is insincerity. When there is a gap between one's real and one's declared aims, one turns as it were instinctively to long words and exhausted idioms, like a cuttlefish squirting out ink.
Shooting an Elephant (1950) 'Politics and the English Language'

2 Political language ... is designed to make lies sound truthful and murder respectable, and to give an appearance of solidity to pure wind.
Shooting an Elephant (1950) 'Politics and the English Language'

3 Saints should always be judged guilty until they are proved innocent.
Shooting an Elephant (1950) 'Reflections on Gandhi'

4 Advertising is the rattling of a stick inside a swill bucket.
Attributed

Dorothy Osborne 1627–95
Wife of Sir William Temple from 1654

5 About six or seven o'clock, I walk out into a common that lies hard by the house, where a great many young wenches keep sheep and cows and sit in the shade singing of ballads ... I talk to them, and find they want nothing to make them the happiest people in the world, but the knowledge that they are so.
Letters of Dorothy Osborne to William Temple (ed. G. C. Moore Smith, 1928) 2 June 1653

6 All letters, methinks, should be free and easy as one's discourse, not studied as an oration, nor made up of hard words like a charm.
Letters of Dorothy Osborne to William Temple (ed. G. C. Moore Smith, 1928) September 1653

7 Dr Taylor ... says there is a great advantage to be gained in resigning up one's will to the command of another, because the same action which in itself is wholly indifferent if done upon our own choice, becomes an act of duty and religion if done in obedience to the command of any person whom nature, the laws, or our selves have given a power over us.
Letters of Dorothy Osborne to William Temple (ed. G. C. Moore Smith, 1928) 19 February 1654

John Osborne 1929–
English playwright

8 Don't clap too hard—it's a very old building.
The Entertainer (1957) no. 7

9 Thank God we're normal,
Yes, this is our finest shower!
The Entertainer (1957) no. 7

10 But I have a go, lady, don't I? I 'ave a go. I do.
The Entertainer (1957) no. 7

11 I'm dead behind these eyes. I'm dead, just like the whole inert, shoddy lot out there. It doesn't matter because I don't feel a thing, and neither do they.
The Entertainer (1957) no. 8

12 Oh heavens, how I long for a little ordinary human enthusiasm. Just enthusiasm—that's all. I want to hear a warm, thrilling voice cry out Hallelujah! Hallelujah! I'm alive!
Look Back in Anger (1956) act 1

13 His knowledge of life and ordinary human beings is so hazy, he really deserves some sort of decoration for it—a medal inscribed 'For Vaguery in the Field'.
Look Back in Anger (1956) act 1

14 Slamming their doors, stamping their high heels, banging their irons and saucepans—the eternal flaming racket of the female.
Look Back in Anger (1956) act 1

15 I don't think one 'comes down' from Jimmy's university. According to him, it's not even red brick, but white tile.
Look Back in Anger (1956) act 2, sc. 1

16 Reason and Progress, the old firm, is selling out! Everyone get out while the going's good. Those forgotten shares you had in the old traditions, the old beliefs are going up—up and up and up.
Look Back in Anger (1956) act 2, sc. 1

17 They spend their time mostly looking forward to the past.
Look Back in Anger (1956) act 2, sc. 1

18 There aren't any good, brave causes left. If the big bang does come, and we all get killed off, it won't be in aid of the old-fashioned, grand design. It'll just be for the Brave New-nothing-very-much-thank-you. About as pointless and inglorious as stepping in front of a bus.
Look Back in Anger (1956) act 3, sc. 1

19 She's like the old line about justice—not only must be done, but must be seen to be done.
Time Present (1968) act 1

20 This is a letter of hate. It is for you my countrymen, I mean those men of my country who have defiled it. The men with manic fingers leading the sightless, feeble, betrayed body of my country to its death ... damn you England.
Tribune 18 August 1961

21 Monarchy is the gold filling in the mouth of decay.
In Bernard Levin *The Pendulum Years* (1976) ch. 19

Arthur O'Shaughnessy 1844–81
English poet

22 We are the music makers,
We are the dreamers of dreams ...
We are the movers and shakers
Of the world for ever, it seems.
'Ode' (1874)

23 For each age is a dream that is dying,
Or one that is coming to birth.
'Ode' (1874)

Sir William Osler 1849–1919
Canadian-born physician

24 That man can interrogate as well as observe nature, was a lesson slowly learned in his evolution.
Aphorisms from his Bedside Teachings (1961) p. 62

1 One finger in the throat and one in the rectum makes a good diagnostician.
   Aphorisms from his Bedside Teachings (1961) p. 104

2 The natural man has only two primal passions, to get and beget.
   Science and Immortality (1904) ch. 2

3 The desire to take medicine is perhaps the greatest feature which distinguishes man from animals.
   In H. Cushing *Life of Sir William Osler* (1925) vol. 1, ch. 14

John L. O'Sullivan 1813–95
American journalist and diplomat

4 Understood as a central consolidated power, managing and directing the various general interests of the society, all government is evil, and the parent of evil ... The best government is that which governs least.
   United States Magazine and Democratic Review (1837) introduction

5 A spirit of hostile interference against us ... checking the fulfilment of our manifest destiny to overspread the continent allotted by Providence for the free development of our yearly multiplying millions.
   On opposition to the annexation of Texas, in *United States Magazine and Democratic Review* (1845) vol. 17 p. 5

6 A torchlight procession marching down your throat.
   Describing certain kinds of whisky, in G. W. E. Russell *Collections and Recollections* (1898) ch. 19

James Otis 1725–83
American politician

7 Taxation without representation is tyranny.
   Watchword (*c*.1761) of the American Revolution. See *Dictionary of American Biography* vol. 14, p. 102

Thomas Otway 1652–85
English playwright

8 No praying, it spoils business.
   Venice Preserved (1682) act 2, l. 87

Peter Demianovich Ouspensky 1878–1947
Russian-born journalist and philosopher

9 Truths that become old become decrepit and unreliable; sometimes they may be kept going artificially for a certain time, but there is no life in them.
   A New Model of the Universe (2nd ed., 1934) preface

Sir Thomas Overbury 1581–1613
English poet and courtier

10 He disdains all things above his reach, and preferreth all countries before his own.
   Miscellaneous Works (1632) 'An Affected Traveller'. Cf. Canning 178:4, Disraeli 247:26, Gilbert 304:22

Ovid (Publius Ovidius Naso) 43 BC–AD *c*.17
Roman poet

11 *Procul omen abesto!*
   Far be that fate from us!
   Amores bk. 1, no. 14, l. 41

12 *Procul hinc, procul este, severae!*
   Far hence, keep far from me, you grim women!
   Amores bk. 2, no. 1, l. 3

13 *Spectatum veniunt, veniunt spectentur ut ipsae.*
   The women come to see the show, they come to make a show themselves.
   Ars Amatoria bk. 1, l. 99

14 *Iuppiter ex alto periuria ridet amantum.*
   Jupiter from on high laughs at lovers' perjuries.
   Ars Amatoria bk. 1, l. 633

15 *Expedit esse deos, et, ut expedit, esse putemus.*
   It is convenient that there be gods, and, as it is convenient, let us believe that there are.
   Ars Amatoria bk. 1, l. 637

16 *Forsitan et nostrum nomen miscebitur istis.*
   Perhaps my name too will be linked with theirs.
   Ars Amatoria bk. 3, l. 339

17 *Adde quod ingenuas didicisse fideliter artes*
   Emollit mores nec sinit esse feros.
   Add the fact that to have conscientiously studied the liberal arts refines behaviour and does not allow it to be savage.
   Epistulae Ex Ponto bk. 2, no. 9, l. 47

18 *Ut desint vires, tamen est laudanda voluntas.*
   Though the strength is lacking, yet the willingness is commendable.
   Epistulae Ex Ponto bk. 3, no. 4, l. 79

19 *Gutta cavat lapidem, consumitur anulus usu.*
   Dripping water hollows out a stone, a ring is worn away by use.
   Epistulae Ex Ponto bk. 4, no. 10, l. 5. Cf. Latimer 411:2

20 *Chaos, rudis indigestaque moles.*
   Chaos, a rough and unordered mass.
   Metamorphoses bk. 1, l. 7

21 *Medio tutissimus ibis.*
   You will go most safely by the middle way.
   Metamorphoses bk. 2, l. 137

22 *Inopem me copia fecit.*
   Plenty has made me poor.
   Metamorphoses bk. 3, l. 466

23 *Ipse docet quid agam; fas est et ab hoste doceri.*
   He himself teaches what I should do; it is right to be taught by the enemy.
   Metamorphoses bk. 4, l. 428

24 *Video meliora, proboque;*
   Deteriora sequor.
   I see the better things, and approve; I follow the worse.
   Metamorphoses bk. 7, l. 20

1 *Tempus edax rerum.*

Time the devourer of everything.
   Metamorphoses bk. 15, l. 234

2 *Iamque opus exegi, quod nec Iovis ira, nec ignis,*
   Nec poterit ferrum, nec edax abolere vetustas.

And now I have finished the work, which neither the
wrath of Jove, nor fire, nor the sword, nor devouring
age shall be able to destroy.
   Metamorphoses bk. 15, l. 871

3 *Principiis obsta; sero medicina paratur*
   Cum mala per longas convaluere moras.

Stop it at the start, it's late for medicine to be prepared
when disease has grown strong through long delays.
   Remedia Amoris l. 91

4 *Qui finem quaeris amoris,*
   Cedet amor rebus; res age, tutus eris.

You who seek an end of love, love will yield to
business: be busy, and you will be safe.
   Remedia Amoris l. 143

5 *Teque, rebellatrix, tandem, Germania, magni*
   Triste caput pedibus supposuisse ducis!

How you, rebellious Germany, laid your wretched
head beneath the feet of the great general.
   Tristia bk. 3, no. 12, l. 47

6 *Sponte sua carmen numeros veniebat ad aptos,*
   Et quod temptabam dicere versus erat.

Of its own accord my song would come in the right
rhythms, and what I was trying to say was poetry.
   Tristia bk. 4, no. 10, l. 25

7 *Vergilium vidi tantum.*

I have just seen Virgil.
   Tristia bk. 4, no. 10, l. 51

John Owen *c.*1563–1622

Epigrammatist

8 God and the doctor we alike adore
But only when in danger, not before;
The danger o'er, both are alike requited,
God is forgotten, and the Doctor slighted.
   Epigrams. Cf. Quarles 533:13

Robert Owen 1771–1858

Welsh-born socialist and philanthropist

9 All the world is queer save thee and me, and even
thou art a little queer.
   To his partner W. Allen, on severing business relations at
   New Lanark, 1828 (attributed)

Wilfred Owen 1893–1918

English poet

10 My subject is War, and the pity of War.
The Poetry is in the pity.
   Preface (written 1918) in *Poems* (1963)

11 All a poet can do today is warn.
   Preface (written 1918) in *Poems* (1963)

12 What passing-bells for these who die as cattle?
Only the monstrous anger of the guns.
Only the stuttering rifles' rapid rattle
Can patter out their hasty orisons.
No mockeries now for them; no prayers nor bells,
Nor any voice of mourning save the choirs,—
The shrill, demented choirs of wailing shells;
And bugles calling for them from sad shires.
   'Anthem for Doomed Youth' (written 1917)

13 The pallor of girls' brows shall be their pall;
Their flowers the tenderness of patient minds,
And each slow dusk a drawing-down of blinds.
   'Anthem for Doomed Youth' (written 1917)

14 Move him into the sun—
Gently its touch awoke him once,
At home, whispering of fields half-sown.
   'Futility' (written 1918)

15 Red lips are not so red
As the stained stones kissed by the English dead.
   'Greater Love' (written 1917)

16 Oh, Death was never enemy of ours!
We laughed at him, we leagued with him, old chum.
No soldier's paid to kick against His powers.
   'The Next War' (1917)

17 So secretly, like wrongs hushed-up, they went.
They were not ours:
We never heard to which front these were sent.
   'The Send-Off' (written 1918)

18 It seemed that out of battle I escaped
Down some profound dull tunnel, long since scooped
Through granites which titanic wars had groined.
   'Strange Meeting' (written 1918)

19 'Strange friend,' I said, 'here is no cause to mourn.'
'None,' said that other, 'save the undone years,
The hopelessness. Whatever hope is yours,
Was my life also.'
   'Strange Meeting' (written 1918)

20 I am the enemy you killed, my friend.
I knew you in this dark: for you so frowned
Yesterday through me as you jabbed and killed . . .
Let us sleep now.
   'Strange Meeting' (written 1918)

Count Oxenstierna 1583–1654

Swedish statesman

21 *Vet du icke, min son, med husu liten wishet verlden*
   regeras?

Dost thou not know, my son, with how little wisdom
the world is governed?
   Letter to his son, 1648, in J. F. af Lundblad *Svensk Plutark*
   (1826) pt. 2, p. 95. John Selden, in *Table Talk* (1689) 'Pope'
   no. 2, quotes 'a certain Pope' (possibly Julius III) saying
   'Thou little thinkest what *a little foolery governs the whole*
   world!'

Edward de Vere, 17th Earl of Oxford
1550–1604
English poet

1 The labouring man, that tills the fertile soil,
And reaps the harvest fruit, hath not in deed
The gain, but pain; and if for all his toil
He gets the straw, the lord will have the seed.
   'The labouring man, that tills the fertile soil' (1573) st. 1

2 So he that takes the pain to pen the book
Reaps not the gifts of goodly golden Muse;
But those gain that who on the work shall look,
And from the sour the sweet by skill doth choose.
For he that beats the bush the bird not gets,
But who sits still and holdeth fast the nets.
   'The labouring man, that tills the fertile soil' (1573) st. 6

Vance Packard 1914–
American writer and journalist

3 The hidden persuaders.
   Title of a study of the advertising industry (1957)

William Tyler Page 1868–1942

4 I believe in the United States of America as
a government of the people, by the people, for the
people, whose just powers are derived from the
consent of the governed; a democracy in a republic;
a sovereign Nation of many sovereign States; a perfect
Union, one and inseparable, established upon those
principles of freedom, equality, justice, and humanity
for which American patriots sacrificed their lives and
fortunes. I therefore believe it is my duty to my
country to love it, to support its Constitution, to obey
its laws, to respect its flag, and to defend it against all
enemies.
   American's Creed (prize-winning competition entry, 1918) in
   Congressional Record vol. 56, p. 286. Cf. Lincoln 422:10

Marcel Pagnol 1895–1974
French playwright and film-maker

5 L'honneur, c'est comme les allumettes: ça ne sert qu'une
fois.
   Honour is like a match, you can only use it once.
   Marius (1946) act 4, sc. 5

6 Les coupables, il vaut mieux les choisir que les chercher.
   It's better to choose the culprits than to seek them
   out.
   Topaze (1930) act 1

Thomas Paine 1737–1809
English political theorist

7 It is necessary to the happiness of man that he be
mentally faithful to himself. Infidelity does not consist
in believing, or in disbelieving, it consists in professing
to believe what one does not believe.
   The Age of Reason pt. 1 (1794) p. 2

8 Any system of religion that has any thing in it that
shocks the mind of a child cannot be a true system.
   The Age of Reason pt. 1 (1794) p. 39

9 The sublime and the ridiculous are often so nearly
related, that it is difficult to class them separately. One
step above the sublime, makes the ridiculous; and one
step above the ridiculous, makes the sublime again.
   The Age of Reason pt. 2 (1795) p. 20

10 Government, even in its best state, is but a necessary
evil; in its worst state, an intolerable one.
   Government, like dress, is the badge of lost innocence;
   the palaces of kings are built upon the ruins of the
   bowers of paradise.
   Common Sense (1776) ch. 1

11 As to religion, I hold it to be the indispensable duty of
government to protect all conscientious professors
thereof, and I know of no other business which
government hath to do therewith.
   Common Sense (1776) ch. 4

12 These are the times that try men's souls. The summer
soldier and the sunshine patriot will, in this crisis,
shrink from the service of their country; but he that
stands it *now*, deserves the love and thanks of men
and women.
   The Crisis (December 1776) introduction

13 As he rose like a rocket, he fell like the stick.
   On Edmund Burke losing the debate on the French
   Revolution to Charles James Fox, in the House of
   Commons; in *Letter to the Addressers on the late Proclamation*
   (1792) p. 4

14 The religion of humanity.
   Letter . . . on the Invasion of England (1804)

15 [Edmund Burke] is not affected by the reality of
distress touching his heart, but by the showy
resemblance of it striking his imagination. He pities
the plumage, but forgets the dying bird.
   The Rights of Man (1791, ed. P. S. Foner, 1945) p. 260 (on
   Burke's *Reflections on the Revolution in France*, 1790)

16 Lay then the axe to the root, and teach governments
humanity. It is their sanguinary punishments which
corrupt mankind.
   The Rights of Man (1791, ed. P. S. Foner, 1945) p. 266

17 [In France] All that class of equivocal generation,
which in some countries is called *aristocracy*, and in
others *nobility*, is done away, and the peer is exalted
into MAN.
   The Rights of Man (1791, ed. P. S. Foner, 1945) p. 286

18 Titles are but nick-names, and every nick-name is a
title.
   The Rights of Man (1791, ed. P. S. Foner, 1945) p. 286

19 Persecution is not an original feature of *any* religion;
but it is always the strongly marked feature of all
law-religions, or religions established by law.
   The Rights of Man (1791, ed. P. S. Foner, 1945) p. 293

20 All hereditary government is in its nature tyranny . . .
To inherit a government, is to inherit the people, as if
they were flocks and herds.
   The Rights of Man pt. 2 (1792, ed. P. S. Foner, 1945)
   p. 364

21 When, in countries that are called civilized, we see age
going to the workhouse and youth to the gallows,
something must be wrong in the system of
government.
   The Rights of Man pt. 2 (1792, ed. P. S. Foner, 1945)
   p. 404

1 My country is the world, and my religion is to do good.

> *The Rights of Man* pt. 2 (1792, ed. P. S. Foner, 1945) p. 414

2 I do not believe that any two men, on what are called doctrinal points, think alike who think at all. It is only those who have not thought that appear to agree.

> *The Rights of Man* pt. 2 (1792, ed. P. S. Foner, 1945) p. 452

3 A share in two revolutions is living to some purpose.

> In Eric Foner *Tom Paine and Revolutionary America* (1976) ch. 7

José de Palafox 1780–1847

Spanish general

4 *Guerra a cuchillo.*

War to the knife.

> On 4 August 1808, at the siege of Saragossa, the French general Verdier sent a one-word suggestion: 'Capitulation'. Palafox replied 'Guerra y cuchillo [War and the knife]', later reported as above. It subsequently appeared, at the behest of Palafox himself, on survivors' medals. *See* José Gòmez de Arteche y Moro *Guerra de la Independencia* (1875) vol. 2, ch. 4.

William Paley 1743–1805

English theologian and philosopher

5 Suppose I had found a *watch* upon the ground, and it should be enquired how the watch happened to be in that place . . . the inference, we think, is inevitable; that the watch must have had a maker, that there must have existed, at some time and at some place or other, an artificer or artificers, who formed it for the purpose which we find it actually to answer; who comprehended its construction, and designed its use.

> *Natural Theology* (1802) ch. 1

6 Who can refute a sneer?

> *Principles of Moral and Political Philosophy* (1785) bk. 5, ch. 9

Lord Palmerston (Henry John Temple, 3rd Viscount Palmerston) 1784–1865

British politician; Prime Minister, 1855–8, 1859–65

7 We have no eternal allies and we have no perpetual enemies. Our interests are eternal and perpetual, and those interests it is our duty to follow.

> Speech, *Hansard* 1 March 1848, col. 122

8 I therefore fearlessly challenge the verdict which this House . . . is to give . . . whether, as the Roman, in days of old, held himself free from indignity, when he could say *Civis Romanus sum*; so also a British subject, in whatever land he may be, shall feel confident that the watchful eye and the strong arm of England will protect him against injustice and wrong.

> Speech in the Don Pacifico debate, *Hansard* 25 June 1850, col. 444. Cf. Cicero 204:8

9 You may call it combination, you may call it the accidental and fortuitous concurrence of atoms.

> On a projected Palmerston–Disraeli coalition, in *Hansard* 5 March 1857, col. 1934

10 We do not want Egypt any more than any rational man with an estate in the north of England and a residence in the south, would have wished to possess the inns on the north road. All he could want would have been that the inns should be well kept, always accessible, and furnishing him, when he came, with mutton chops and post horses.

> Letter to Earl Cowley, 25 November 1859, in Hon. Evelyn Ashley *Life of . . . Viscount Palmerston 1846–65* (1876) vol. 2, ch. 4

11 What is merit? The opinion one man entertains of another.

> In T. Carlyle *Shooting Niagara: and After?* (1867) ch. 8

12 The function of a government is to calm, rather than to excite agitation.

> In P. Guedella *Gladstone and Palmerston* (1928) p. 281

13 Lord Palmerston, with characteristic levity had once said that only three men in Europe had ever understood [the Schleswig-Holstein question], and of these the Prince Consort was dead, a Danish statesman (unnamed) was in an asylum, and he himself had forgotten it.

> In R. W. Seton-Watson *Britain in Europe 1789–1914* (1937) ch. 11

14 Yes we have. Humbug.

> On being told there was no English word equivalent to *sensibilité* (attributed)

15 Die, my dear Doctor, that's the last thing I shall do!

> Last words, in E. Latham *Famous Sayings and their Authors* (1904) p. 12

Norman Panama 1914– and Melvin Frank 1913–88

American screenwriters

16 The pellet with the poison's in the vessel with the pestle. The chalice from the palace has the brew that is true.

> *The Court Jester* (1955 film); spoken by Danny Kaye

Dame Christabel Pankhurst 1880–1958

English suffragette; daughter of Emmeline Pankhurst

17 Never lose your temper with the Press or the public is a major rule of political life.

> *Unshackled* (1959) ch. 5

18 We are here to claim our right as women, not only to be free, but to fight for freedom. That it is our right as well as our duty.

> *Votes for Women* 31 March 1911

Emmeline Pankhurst 1858–1928

English suffragette leader; founder of the Women's Social and Political Union, 1903

19 There is something that Governments care far more for than human life, and that is the security of property, and so it is through property that we shall strike the enemy . . . I say to the Government: You have not dared to take the leaders of Ulster for their incitement to rebellion. Take me if you dare.

> Speech at Albert Hall, 17 October 1912, in *My Own Story* (1914) p. 265

1 The argument of the broken window pane is the most
valuable argument in modern politics.
> In George Dangerfield *The Strange Death of Liberal England*
> (1936) pt. 2, ch. 3, sect. 4

Mitchell Parish

2 When the deep purple falls over sleepy garden walls,
And the stars begin to flicker in the sky,
Thru' the mist of a memory you wander back to me,
Breathing my name with a sigh.
> 'Deep Purple' (1939); words added to music (1934) by
> Peter de Rose

Charlie Parker 1920–55

American jazz saxophonist

3 Music is your own experience, your thoughts, your
wisdom. If you don't live it, it won't come out of your
horn.
> In Nat Shapiro and Nat Hentoff *Hear Me Talkin' to Ya*
> (1955) p. 358

Dorothy Parker 1893–1967

American critic and humorist

4 Scratch a lover, and find a foe.
> 'Ballade of a Great Weariness' (1937)

5 Oh, life is a glorious cycle of song,
A medley of extemporanea;
And love is a thing that can never go wrong;
And I am Marie of Roumania.
> 'Comment' (1937)

6 Woman lives but in her lord;
Count to ten, and man is bored.
With this the gist and sum of it,
What earthly good can come of it?
> 'General Review of the Sex Situation' (1937)

7 Four be the things I'd been better without:
Love, curiosity, freckles, and doubt.
> 'Inventory' (1937)

8 Men seldom make passes
At girls who wear glasses.
> 'News Item' (1937)

9 Why is it no one ever sent me yet
One perfect limousine, do you suppose?
Ah no, it's always just my luck to get
One perfect rose.
> 'One Perfect Rose' (1937)

10 If, with the literate, I am
Impelled to try an epigram,
I never seek to take the credit;
We all assume that Oscar said it.
> 'A Pig's-Eye View of Literature' (1937)

11 Guns aren't lawful;
Nooses give;
Gas smells awful;
You might as well live.
> 'Résumé' (1937)

12 By the time you say you're his,
Shivering and sighing
And he vows his passion is
Infinite, undying—
Lady, make a note of this:
One of you is lying.
> 'Unfortunate Coincidence' (1937)

13 And I'll stay off Verlaine too; he was always chasing
Rimbauds.
> *Here Lies* (1939) 'The Little Hours'

14 Sorrow is tranquillity remembered in emotion.
> *Here Lies* (1939) 'Sentiment'. Cf. Wordsworth 748:19

15 How do they know?
> On being told that Calvin Coolidge had died, in Malcolm
> Cowley *Writers at Work* 1st Series (1958) p. 65

16 As artists they're rot, but as providers they're oil
wells; they gush.
> On lady novelists, in Malcolm Cowley *Writers at Work* 1st
> Series (1958) p. 69

17 Hollywood money isn't money. It's congealed snow,
melts in your hand, and there you are.
> In Malcolm Cowley *Writers at Work* 1st Series (1958) p. 81

18 *House Beautiful* is play lousy.
> *New Yorker* review (1933), in Phyllis Hartnoll *Plays and
> Players* (1984) p. 89

19 Brevity is the soul of lingerie, as the Petticoat said to
the Chemise.
> Caption written for *Vogue* (1916) in John Keats *You Might
> as well Live* (1970) p. 32. Cf. *Hamlet* 574:11

20 You can lead a horticulture, but you can't make her
think.
> In John Keats *You Might as well Live* (1970) p. 46

21 It serves me right for putting all my eggs in one
bastard.
> On her abortion, in John Keats *You Might as well Live*
> (1970) pt. 2, ch. 3

22 There's a hell of a distance between wise-cracking and
wit. Wit has truth in it; wise-cracking is simply
callisthenics with words.
> In *Paris Review* Summer 1956, p. 81

23 She ran the whole gamut of the emotions from A to B.
> Of Katherine Hepburn at a Broadway first night (attributed)

24 Excuse My Dust.
> Suggested epitaph for herself (1925), in Alexander
> Woollcott *While Rome Burns* (1934) 'Our Mrs Parker'

Martin Parker d. c.1656

English balladmonger

25 You gentlemen of England
Who live at home at ease,
How little do you think
On the dangers of the seas.
> 'The Valiant Sailors'. See J. O. Halliwell (ed.) *Early Naval
> Ballads* (Percy Society, 1841) p. 34

26 But all's to no end, for the times will not mend
Till the King enjoys his own again.
> 'Upon Defacing of Whitehall' (1671)

Ross Parker 1914–74 and Hugh Charles 1907–

British songwriters

1 There'll always be an England
While there's a country lane,
Wherever there's a cottage small
Beside a field of grain.
   'There'll always be an England' (1939 song)

C. Northcote Parkinson 1909–

English writer

2 Expenditure rises to meet income.
   The Law and the Profits (1960) ch. 1

3 Work expands so as to fill the time available for its completion.
   Parkinson's Law (1958) ch. 1

4 Time spent on any item of the agenda will be in inverse proportion to the sum involved.
   Parkinson's Law (1958) ch. 3

5 The man who is denied the opportunity of taking decisions of importance begins to regard as important the decisions he is allowed to take.
   Parkinson's Law (1958) ch. 10

6 Men enter local politics solely as a result of being unhappily married.
   Parkinson's Law (1958) ch. 10

Charles Stewart Parnell 1846–91

Irish nationalist leader

7 No man has a right to fix the boundary of the march of a nation; no man has a right to say to his country—thus far shalt thou go and no further.
   Speech at Cork, 21 January 1885, in *The Times* 22 January 1885

Blaise Pascal 1623–62

French mathematician, physicist, and moralist

8 *Je n'ai fait celle-ci plus longue que parce que je n'ai pas eu le loisir de la faire plus courte.*
   I have made this [letter] longer than usual, only because I have not had the time to make it shorter.
   Lettres Provinciales (1657) no. 16

9 *La dernière chose qu'on trouve en faisant un ouvrage, est de savoir celle qu'il faut mettre la première.*
   The last thing one knows in constructing a work is what to put first.
   Pensées (1670, ed. L. Brunschvicg, 1909) sect. 1, no. 19

10 *Quand on voit le style naturel, on est tout étonné et ravi, car on s'attendait de voir un auteur, et on trouve un homme.*
   When we see a natural style, we are quite surprised and delighted, for we expected to see an author and we find a man.
   Pensées (1670, ed. L. Brunschvicg, 1909) sect. 1, no. 29

11 *Quelle vanité que la peinture, qui attire l'admiration par la ressemblance des choses dont on n'admire point les originaux.*
   How vain painting is, exciting admiration by its resemblance to things of which we do not admire the originals.
   Pensées (1670, ed. L. Brunschvicg, 1909) sect. 2, no. 134

12 *Tout le malheur des hommes vient d'une seule chose, qui est de ne savoir pas demeurer en repos dans une chambre.*
   All the misfortunes of men derive from one single thing, which is their inability to be at ease in a room.
   Pensées (1670, ed. L. Brunschvicg, 1909) sect. 2, no. 139

13 *Le nez de Cléopâtre: s'il eût été plus court, toute la face de la terre aurait changé.*
   Had Cleopatra's nose been shorter, the whole face of the world would have changed.
   Pensées (1670, ed. L. Brunschvicg, 1909) sect. 2, no. 162

14 *Le silence éternel de ces espaces infinis m'effraie.*
   The eternal silence of these infinite spaces [the heavens] terrifies me.
   Pensées (1670, ed. L. Brunschvicg, 1909) sect. 2, no. 206

15 *Le dernier acte est sanglant, quelque belle que soit la comédie en tout le reste.*
   The last act is bloody, however charming the rest of the play may be.
   Pensées (1670, ed. L. Brunschvicg, 1909) sect. 3, no. 210

16 *On mourra seul.*
   We shall die alone.
   Pensées (1670, ed. L. Brunschvicg, 1909) sect. 3, no. 211

17 *Le coeur a ses raisons que la raison ne connaît point.*
   The heart has its reasons which reason knows nothing of.
   Pensées (1670, ed. L. Brunschvicg, 1909) sect. 4, no. 277

18 *L'homme n'est qu'un roseau, le plus faible de la nature; mais c'est un roseau pensant.*
   Man is only a reed, the weakest thing in nature; but he is a thinking reed.
   Pensées (1670, ed. L. Brunschvicg, 1909) sect. 6, no. 347

19 *L'éloquence continue ennuie.*
   Continual eloquence is tedious.
   Pensées (1670, ed. L. Brunschvicg, 1909) sect. 6, no. 355

20 *Le moi est haïssable.*
   The *self* is hateful.
   Pensées (1670, ed. L. Brunschvicg, 1909) sect. 7, no. 455

21 *Console-toi, tu ne me chercherais pas si tu ne m'avais trouvé.*
   Comfort yourself, you would not seek me if you had not found me.
   Pensées (1670, ed. L. Brunschvicg, 1909) sect. 7, no. 553

1 FEU. *Dieu d'Abraham, Dieu d'Isaac, Dieu de Jacob, non des philosophes et savants. Certitude. Certitude. Sentiment. Joie. Paix.*

FIRE. God of Abraham, God of Isaac, God of Jacob, not of the philosophers and scholars. Certainty. Certainty. Feeling. Joy. Peace.

> On a paper, dated 23 November 1654, stitched into the lining of his coat and found after his death

Boris Pasternak 1890–1960
Russian novelist and poet

2 Человек рождается жить, а не готовиться к жизни.

Man is born to live, not to prepare for life.

> *Doctor Zhivago* (1958) pt. 2, ch. 9, sect. 14 (translated by Max Hayward and Manya Harari)

3 Но любят все, не замечая небывалости чувства.

Most people experience love, without noticing that there is anything remarkable about it.

> *Doctor Zhivago* (1958) pt. 2, ch. 13, sect. 10 (translated by Max Hayward and Manya Harari)

4 Я не люблю правых, не падавших, не оступавшихся. Их добродетель мертва и малоценна. Красота жизни не открывалась им.

I don't like people who have never fallen or stumbled. Their virtue is lifeless and it isn't of much value. Life hasn't revealed its beauty to them.

> *Doctor Zhivago* (1958) pt. 2, ch. 13, sect. 12 (translated by Max Hayward and Manya Harari)

5 Всё бытовое опрокинуто и разрушено. Осталась одна небытовая, неприложенная сила голой, до нитки обобранной душевности, для которой ничего не изменилось потому, что она во все времена зябла, дрожала и тянулась к ближащей рядом, такой же обнаженной и одинокой.

The whole human way of life has been destroyed and ruined. All that's left is the bare, shivering human soul, stripped to the last shred, the naked force of the human psyche for which nothing has changed because it was always cold and shivering and reaching out to its nearest neighbour, as cold and lonely as itself.

> *Doctor Zhivago* (1958) pt. 2, ch. 13, sect. 13 (translated by Max Hayward and Manya Harari)

6 Искусство всегда служит красоте, а красота есть счастье обладания формой, форма же есть органический ключ существования, формой должно владеть все живущее, чтобы существовать.

Art always serves beauty, and beauty is the joy of possessing form, and form is the key to organic life since no living thing can exist without it.

> *Doctor Zhivago* (1958) pt. 2, ch. 14, sect. 14 (translated by Max Hayward and Manya Harari)

7 Однажды Лариса Федоровна ушла из дому и больше не возвращалась . . . она умерла или пропала неизвестно где, забытая под каким-нибудь безымянным номером из впоследствии запропастившихся списков.

One day Lara went out and did not come back . . . She died or vanished somewhere, forgotten as a nameless number on a list which was afterwards mislaid.

> *Doctor Zhivago* (1958) pt. 2, ch. 15, sect. 17 (translated by Max Hayward and Manya Harari)

8 Но продуман распорядок действий,
И неотвратим конец пути.
Я один, все тонет в фарисействе.
Жизнь прожить — не поле перейти.

Yet the order of the acts is planned
And the end of the way inescapable,
I am alone; all drowns in the Pharisees' hypocrisy.
To live your life is not as simple as to cross a field.

> *Doctor Zhivago* (1958) 'Zhivago's Poems: Hamlet'

9 Как у дюжей скотиницы работа,
Дело у весны кипит в руках.

Work seethes in the hands of spring,
That strapping dairymaid.

> *Doctor Zhivago* (1958) 'Zhivago's Poems: March'

10 Как затопляет камыши
Волненье после шторма,
Ушли на дно его души
Ее черты и формы.

В года мытарств, во времена
Немыслимого быта
Она волной судьбы со дна
Была к нему прибита.

As after a storm
The surf floods over the reeds,
So in his heart
Her image is submerged.

In the years of trial,
When life was inconceivable,
From the bottom of the sea the tide of destiny
Washed her up to him.

> *Doctor Zhivago* (1958) 'Zhivago's Poems: Parting'

11 Сестра моя — жизнь и сегодня в разливе
Расшиблась весенним дождем обо всех.

My sister life's in flood today, she's broken / her waves over us all in the spring rain.

> 'My Sister Life' (1922) (translated by J. M. Cohen)

12 Мы в будущем, твержу я им, как все, кто жил в эти дни. А если из калек,
То все равно: телегою проекта
Нас переехал новый человек.

In time to come, I tell them, we'll be equal / to any living now. If cripples, then / no matter; we shall just have been run over / by 'New Man' in the wagon of his 'Plan'.

> 'When I Grow Weary' (1932) (translated by J. M. Cohen)

1 Как будто внутренность собора —
Простор земли, и чрез окно
Далекий отголосок хора
Мне слышать иногда дано.

Природа, мир, тайник вселенной,
Я службу долгую твою,
Объятый дрожью сокровенной
В слезах от счастья отстою.

The whole wide world is a cathedral;
I stand inside, the air is calm,
And from afar at times there reaches
My ear the echo of a psalm.

World, Nature, Universe's Essence,
With secret trembling, to the end,
I will thy long and moving service
In tears of happiness attend.

'When It Clears Up' (1958) (translated by Lydia Pasternak Slater)

Louis Pasteur 1822–95

French chemist and bacteriologist

2 *Dans les champs de l'observation le hasard ne favorise que les esprits préparés.*

Where observation is concerned, chance favours only the prepared mind.

Address given on the inauguration of the Faculty of Science, University of Lille, 7 December 1854; in R. Vallery-Radot *La Vie de Pasteur* (1900) ch. 4

3 *Il n'existe pas de sciences appliquées, mais seulement des applications de la science.*

There are no such things as applied sciences, only applications of science.

Address, 11 September 1872, in *Comptes rendus des travaux du Congrès viticole et séricicole de Lyon, 9–14 septembre 1872* p. 49

Walter Pater 1839–94

English essayist and critic

4 Hers is the head upon which all 'the ends of the world are come', and the eyelids are a little weary.

Of the *Mona Lisa* in *Studies in the History of the Renaissance* (1873) 'Leonardo da Vinci'. Cf. Book of Common Prayer 129:1

5 She is older than the rocks among which she sits; like the vampire, she has been dead many times, and learned the secrets of the grave.

Studies in the History of the Renaissance (1873) 'Leonardo da Vinci' (of the *Mona Lisa*)

6 All art constantly aspires towards the condition of music.

Studies in the History of the Renaissance (1873) 'The School of Giorgione'

7 A counted number of pulses is given to us only of a variegated, dramatic life. How may we see in them all that is to be seen in them by the finest senses? How can we pass most swiftly from point to point, and be present always at the focus where the greatest number of vital forces unite in their purest energy? To burn always with this hard, gemlike flame, to maintain this ecstasy, is success in life.

Studies in the History of the Renaissance (1873) 'Conclusion'

8 Not to discriminate every moment some passionate attitude in those about us, and in the brilliance of their gifts some tragic dividing of forces on their ways is, on this short day of frost and sun, to sleep before evening.

Studies in the History of the Renaissance (1873) 'Conclusion'

'Banjo' Paterson (Andrew Barton Paterson) 1864–1941

Australian poet

9 Once a jolly swagman camped by a billabong,
Under the shade of a coolibah tree;
And he sang as he watched and waited till his 'Billy' boiled:
'You'll come a-waltzing, Matilda, with me.'

'Waltzing Matilda' (1903 song)

Coventry Patmore 1823–96

English poet

10 Kind souls, you wonder why, love you,
When you, you wonder why, love none.
We love, Fool, for the good we do,
Not that which unto us is done!

The Angel in the House (1854–62) bk. 1, canto 6, 'A Riddle Solved'

11 Ah, none but I discerned her looks,
When in the throng she passed me by,
For love is like a ghost, and brooks
Only the chosen seer's eye.

The Angel in the House (1854–62) bk. 2, canto 3, 'The County Ball'

12 'I saw you take his kiss!' ''Tis true.'
'O modesty!' ''Twas strictly kept:
He thought me asleep; at least, I knew
He thought I thought he thought I slept.'

The Angel in the House (1854–62) bk. 2, canto 8, 'The Kiss'

13 Some dish more sharply spiced than this
Milk-soup men call domestic bliss.

'Olympus' l. 15

14 He that but once too nearly hears
The music of forfended spheres
Is thenceforth lonely, and for all
His days as one who treads the Wall
Of China, and, on this hand, sees
Cities and their civilities
And, on the other, lions.

The Victories of Love bk. 1 (1860) 'From Mrs Graham'

Alan Paton 1903–

South African writer

15 Cry, the beloved country.

Title of novel (1948)

Mark Pattison 1813–84

English educationist

1 In research the horizon recedes as we advance, and is no nearer at sixty than it was at twenty. As the power of endurance weakens with age, the urgency of the pursuit grows more intense . . . And research is always incomplete.
  Isaac Casaubon (1875) ch. 10

Leslie Paul 1905–85

Irish writer

2 Angry young man.
  Title of book (1951); the phrase subsequently associated with John Osborne's play *Look Back in Anger* (1956)

James Payn 1830–98

English writer

3 I had never had a piece of toast
  Particularly long and wide,
  But fell upon the sanded floor,
  And always on the buttered side.
  Chambers's Journal 2 February 1884. Cf. Moore 483:14

J. H. Payne 1791–1852

American actor, playwright, and songwriter

4 Mid pleasures and palaces though we may roam,
  Be it ever so humble, there's no place like home;
  A charm from the skies seems to hallow us there,
  Which, seek through the world, is ne'er met with elsewhere.
  Home, home, sweet, sweet home!
  There's no place like home! there's no place like home!
  Clari, or, The Maid of Milan (1823 opera) 'Home, Sweet Home'

Thomas Love Peacock 1785–1866

English novelist and poet

5 Ancient sculpture is the true school of modesty. But where the Greeks had modesty, we have cant; where they had poetry, we have cant; where they had patriotism, we have cant; where they had anything that exalts, delights, or adorns humanity, we have nothing but cant, cant, cant.
  Crotchet Castle (1831) ch. 7

6 The march of mind has marched in through my back parlour shutters, and out with my silver spoons, in the dead of night. The policeman, who was sent down to examine, says my house has been broken open on the most scientific principles.
  Crotchet Castle (1831) ch. 17

7 A Sympathizer would seem to imply a certain degree of benevolent feeling. Nothing of the kind. It signifies a ready-made accomplice in any species of political villainy.
  Gryll Grange (1861) ch. 1

8 Marriage may often be a stormy lake, but celibacy is almost always a muddy horsepond.
  Melincourt (1817) ch. 7

9 Laughter is pleasant, but the exertion is too much for me.
  Nightmare Abbey (1818) ch. 5

10 Sir, I have quarrelled with my wife; and a man who has quarrelled with his wife is absolved from all duty to his country.
  Nightmare Abbey (1818) ch. 11

11 Long night succeeds thy little day
  Oh blighted blossom! can it be,
  That this grey stone and grassy clay
  Have closed our anxious care of thee?
  Epitaph on his daughter Margaret, who died at the age of three, in H. Cole (ed.) *Works of Peacock* (1875) p. xxxviii

12 But though first love's impassioned blindness
  Has passed away in colder light,
  I still have thought of you with kindness,
  And shall do, till our last good-night.
  The ever-rolling silent hours
  Will bring a time we shall not know,
  When our young days of gathering flowers
  Will be an hundred years ago.
  'Love and Age' (1860)

Norman Vincent Peale 1898–

American religious broadcaster and writer

13 The power of positive thinking.
  Title of book (1952)

Hesketh Pearson 1887–1964

English actor and biographer

14 Misquotation is, in fact, the pride and privilege of the learned. A widely-read man never quotes accurately, for the rather obvious reason that he has read too widely.
  Common Misquotations (1934) introduction

15 There is no stronger craving in the world than that of the rich for titles, except perhaps that of the titled for riches.
  The Pilgrim Daughters (1961) ch. 6

Pedro I (Pedro IV of Portugal) 1798–1834

First emperor of Brazil, 1822–31

16 *Como é para o bem de todos e a felicidade geral da nação, estou pronto. Diga ao povo que fico.*

  As it is for the good of all and the general happiness of the nation, I am ready and willing. Tell the people I'm staying.
  Letter to D. João VI, 9 January 1822, in response to a popular delegation, and in defiance of a decree from Lisbon requiring his return (commonly rendered 'Fico [I'm staying]'). See R. J. Barman *Brazil* (1988) p. 268

Sir Robert Peel 1788–1850

British Conservative politician; Prime Minister, 1834–5, 1841–6

1 I may be a Tory. I may be an illiberal—but . . . Tory as I am, I have the further satisfaction of knowing that there is not a single law connected with my name which has not had as its object some mitigation of the severity of the criminal law; some prevention of abuse in the exercise of it; or some security for its impartial administration.

   Speech, *Hansard* 1 May 1827, col. 411

George Peele c.1556–96

English playwright and poet

2 Fair and fair, and twice so fair,
   As fair as any may be;
   The fairest shepherd on our green,
   A love for any lady.

   The Arraignment of Paris (1584) act 1, sc. 5 'Song of Oenone and Paris'

3 What thing is love for (well I wot) love is a thing.
   It is a prick, it is a sting,
   It is a pretty, pretty thing;
   It is a fire, it is a coal
   Whose flame creeps in at every hole.

   The Hunting of Cupid (c.1591)

4 When as the rye reach to the chin,
   And chopcherry, chopcherry ripe within,
   Strawberries swimming in the cream,
   And schoolboys playing in the stream,
   Then O, then O, then O, my true love said,
   Till that time come again,
   She could not live a maid.

   The Old Wive's Tale (1595) l. 75 'Song'

5 His golden locks time hath to silver turned;
   O time too swift, O swiftness never ceasing!
   His youth 'gainst time and age hath ever spurned
   But spurned in vain; youth waneth by increasing:
   Beauty, strength, youth, are flowers but fading seen;
   Duty, faith, love, are roots, and ever green.

   His helmet now shall make a hive for bees,
   And, lovers' sonnets turned to holy psalms,
   A man-at-arms must now serve on his knees,
   And feed on prayers, which are age his alms:
   But though from court to cottage he depart,
   His saint is sure of his unspotted heart . . .

   Goddess, allow this aged man his right,
   To be your beadsman now that was your knight.

   Polyhymnia (1590) *ad fin.* 'Sonnet'

Charles Péguy 1873–1914

French poet and essayist

6 *Qui ne gueule pas la vérité, quand il sait la vérité, se fait le complice des menteurs et des faussaires.*
   He who does not bellow the truth when he knows the truth makes himself the accomplice of liars and forgers.

   Basic Verities (1943) 'Lettre du Provincial' 21 December 1899

7 *La tyrannie est toujours mieux organisée que la liberté.*
   Tyranny is always better organised than freedom.

   Basic Verities (1943) 'War and Peace'. Cf. Baez 46:8

8 *Le pécheur est au coeur même de chrétienté . . . Nul n'est aussi compétent que le pécheur en matiere de chrétienté. Nul, si ce n'est le saint.*
   The sinner is at the heart of Christianity . . . No one is as competent as the sinner in matters of Christianity. No one, except a saint.

   Basic Verities (1943) 'Un Nouveau théologien . . . ' (1911)

William Herbert, 1st Earl of Pembroke c.1501–70

9 Out ye whores, to work, to work, ye whores, go spin.

   In Andrew Clark (ed.) '*Brief Lives*' . . . *by John Aubrey* (1898) vol. 1 'William Herbert, 1st Earl of Pembroke' (commonly quoted 'Go spin, you jades, go spin')

Henry Herbert, 2nd Earl of Pembroke c.1534–1601

10 A parliament can do any thing but make a man a woman, and a woman a man.

   Quoted by his son, the 4th Earl, in a speech on 11 April 1648, proving himself Chancellor of Oxford; in *Harleian Miscellany* (1745) vol. 5, p. 106

Henry Herbert, 10th Earl of Pembroke 1734–94

11 Dr Johnson's sayings would not appear so extraordinary, were it not for his bow-wow way.

   In James Boswell *Life of Samuel Johnson* (1934 ed.) vol. 2, p. 326 n. (27 March 1775)

Vladimir Peniakoff 1897–1951

Belgian soldier and writer

12 A message came on the wireless for me. It said: 'SPREAD ALARM AND DESPONDENCY'. So the time had come, I thought, Eighth Army was taking the offensive. The date was, I think, May 18th, 1942.

   Private Army (1950) pt. 2, ch. 5. The phrase 'reports calculated to create unnecessary alarm or despondency' derives from the Army Act of 1879

William Penn 1644–1718

English Quaker; founder of Pennsylvania

13 No pain, no palm; no thorns, no throne; no gall, no glory; no cross, no crown.

   No Cross, No Crown (1669 pamphlet)

14 It is a reproach to religion and government to suffer so much poverty and excess.

   Some Fruits of Solitude (1693) pt. 1, no. 52

15 Men are generally more careful of the breed of their horses and dogs than of their children.

   Some Fruits of Solitude (1693) pt. 1, no. 85

16 The taking of a bribe or gratuity, should be punished with as severe penalties as the defrauding of the State.

   Some Fruits of Solitude (1693) pt. 1, no. 384

Roger Penrose 1931–

British mathematician and theoretical physicist

1 Consciousness . . . is the phenomenon whereby the universe's very existence is made known.
   The Emperor's New Mind (1989) ch. 10 'Conclusion'

Samuel Pepys 1633–1703

English diarist

2 Strange the difference of men's talk!
   Diary 4 January 1660

3 And so to bed.
   Diary 20 April 1660

4 I went out to Charing Cross, to see Major-general Harrison hanged, drawn, and quartered; which was done there, he looking as cheerful as any man could do in that condition.
   Diary 13 October 1660

5 A good honest and painful sermon.
   Diary 17 March 1661

6 If ever I was foxed it was now.
   Diary 23 April 1661

7 But methought it lessened my esteem of a king, that he should not be able to command the rain.
   Diary 19 July 1662

8 I see it is impossible for the King to have things done as cheap as other men.
   Diary 21 July 1662

9 But Lord! to see the absurd nature of Englishmen, that cannot forbear laughing and jeering at everything that looks strange.
   Diary 27 November 1662

10 My wife, who, poor wretch, is troubled with her lonely life.
   Diary 19 December 1662

11 A woman sober, and no high flyer, as he calls it.
   Diary 27 May 1663

12 Most of their discourse was about hunting, in a dialect I understand very little.
   Diary 22 November 1663

13 While we were talking came by several poor creatures carried by, by constables, for being at a conventicle . . . I would to God they would either conform, or be more wise, and not be catched!
   Diary 7 August 1664

14 Pretty witty Nell.
   Diary 3 April 1665 (of Nell Gwynne)

15 Strange to see how a good dinner and feasting reconciles everybody.
   Diary 9 November 1665

16 Strange to say what delight we married people have to see these poor fools decoyed into our condition.
   Diary 25 December 1665

17 Music and women I cannot but give way to, whatever my business is.
   Diary 9 March 1666

18 But it is pretty to see what money will do.
   Diary 21 March 1667

19 This day my wife made it appear to me that my late entertainment this week cost me above £12, an expense which I am almost ashamed of, though it is but once in a great while, and is the end for which, in the most part, we live, to have such a merry day once or twice in a man's life.
   Diary 6 March 1669

20 And so I betake myself to that course, which is almost as much as to see myself go into my grave—for which, and all the discomforts that will accompany my being blind, the good God prepare me!
   Diary 31 May 1669 *ad fin.*

S. J. Perelman 1904–79

American humorist

21 Crazy like a fox.
   Title of book (1944)

Pericles c.495–429 BC

Athenian statesman

22 φιλοκαλοῦμεν γὰρ μετ' εὐτελείας καὶ φιλοσοφοῦμεν ἄνευ μαλακίας.

   Our love of what is beautiful does not lead to extravagance; our love of the things of the mind does not make us soft.
   Funeral Oration, Athens, 430 BC, in Thucydides *History of the Peloponnesian War* bk. 2, ch. 40, sect. 1 (translated by Rex Warner)

23 ἀνδρῶν γὰρ ἐπιφανῶν πᾶσα γῆ τάφος.

   For famous men have the whole earth as their memorial.
   In Thucydides *History of the Peloponnesian War* bk. 2, ch. 43, sect. 3 (translated by Rex Warner)

24 τῆς τε γὰρ ὑπαρχούσης φύσεως μὴ χείροσι γενέσθαι ὑμῖν μεγάλη ἡ δόξα καὶ ἧς ἂν ἐπ' ἐλάχιστον ἀρετῆς πέρι ἢ ψόγου ἐν τοῖς ἄρσεσι κλέος ᾖ.

   Your great glory is not to be inferior to what God has made you, and the greatest glory of a woman is to be least talked about by men, whether they are praising you or criticizing you.
   In Thucydides *History of the Peloponnesian War* bk. 2, ch. 45, sect. 2 (translated by Rex Warner)

Charles Perrault 1628–1703

French poet and critic

25 'Anne, ma sœur Anne, ne vois-tu rien venir?' Et la sœur Anne lui répondit, 'Je ne vois rien que le soleil qui poudroye, et l'herbe qui verdoye.'

   'Anne, sister Anne, do you see nothing coming?' And her sister Anne replied, 'I see nothing but the sun showing up the dust, and the grass looking green.'
   Histoires et contes du temps passé (1697) 'La barbe bleue'

Edward Perronet 1726–92

English clergyman

1 All hail the power of Jesus' Name;
   Let Angels prostrate fall;
   Bring forth the royal diadem
   To crown Him Lord of all.
   'All hail the power of Jesus' Name' (1780 hymn)

Jimmy Perry

British songwriter

2 Who do you think you are kidding, Mister Hitler?
   If you think we're on the run?
   We are the boys who will stop your little game
   We are the boys who will make you think again.
   'Who do you think you are kidding, Mister Hitler' (theme song of *Dad's Army*, BBC television, 1968–77)

Persius (Aulus Persius Flaccus) AD 34–62

Roman poet

3 *Nec te quaesiveris extra.*
   And don't consult anyone's opinions but your own.
   Satires no. 1, l. 7

4 *Virtutem videant intabescantque relicta.*
   Let them recognize virtue and rot for having lost it.
   Satires no. 3, l. 38

5 *Venienti occurrite morbo.*
   Confront disease at its onset.
   Satires no. 3, l. 64. Cf. Ovid 503:3

6 *Tecum habita: noris quam sit tibi curta supellex.*
   Live with yourself: get to know how poorly furnished you are.
   Satires no. 4, l. 52

Henri Philippe Pétain 1856–1951

French marshal

7 To write one's memoirs is to speak ill of everybody except oneself.
   In *Observer* 26 May 1946

Ted Persons

8 Things ain't what they used to be.
   Title of song (1941)

Laurence Peter 1919–

Canadian writer

9 In a hierarchy every employee tends to rise to his level of incompetence.
   The Peter Principle (1969) ch. 1

Petrarch (Francesco Petrarca) 1304–74

Italian poet

10 *E del mio vaneggiar vergogna è 'l frutto*
    e 'l pentersi, e 'l conoscer chiaramente
    che quanto piace al mondo è breve sogno.
    And the fruit of my vanity is shame, and repentance, and the clear knowledge that whatever the world finds pleasing, is but a brief dream.
    'Voi ch'ascoltate in rime sparse il suono' (*c*.1352)

Petronius (Petronius Arbiter) d. AD 65

Roman satirist

11 *Canis ingens, catena vinctus, in pariete erat pictus superque quadrata littera scriptum 'Cave canem.'*
    A huge dog, tied by a chain, was painted on the wall and over it was written in capital letters 'Beware of the dog.'
    Satyricon 'Cena Trimalchionis' ch. 29, sect. 1

12 *Abiit ad plures.*
    He's gone to join the majority [the dead].
    Satyricon 'Cena Trimalchionis' ch. 42, sect. 5

13 *Nam Sibyllam quidem Cumis ego ipse oculis meis vidi in ampulla pendere, et cum illi pueri dicerent: Σίβυλλα, τί θέλεις; respondebat illa: ἀποθανεῖν θέλω.*
    'I saw the Sibyl at Cumae'
    (One said) 'with mine own eye.
    She hung in a cage, and read her rune
    To all the passers-by.
    Said the boys, "What wouldst thou, Sibyl?"
    She answered, "I would die." '
    Satyricon 'Cena Trimalchionis' ch. 48, sect. 8 (translated by D. G. Rossetti)

14 *Horatii curiosa felicitas.*
    Horace's careful felicity.
    Satyricon ch. 118, sect. 5

15 *Foeda est in coitu et brevis voluptas*
    Et taedet Veneris statim peractae.
    Delight of lust is gross and brief
    And weariness treads on desire.
    In A. Baehrens *Poetae Latini Minores* (1882) vol. 4, no. 101 (translated by Helen Waddell)

Pheidippides (or Philippides) d. 490 BC

Athenian runner

16 χαίρετε, νικῶμεν.
    Greetings, we win!
    Dying words, having run back to Athens from Marathon with news of victory over the Persians; in Lucian bk. 3, ch. 64 'Pro Lapsu inter salutandum' para. 3

Edward John Phelps 1822–1900

American lawyer and diplomat

17 The man who makes no mistakes does not usually make anything.
    Speech at the Mansion House, London, 24 January 1889; in *The Times* 25 January 1889, p. 10

Kim Philby (Harold Adrian Russell Philby) 1912–88

British intelligence officer and Soviet spy

1 To betray, you must first belong.

In *Sunday Times* 17 December 1967, p. 2

John Woodward ('Jack') Philip 1840–1900

American naval captain in the Spanish–American war

2 Don't cheer, men; those poor devils are dying.

At the Battle of Santiago, 4 July 1898; in *Dictionary of American Biography* vol. 14 (1934) 'John Woodward Philip'

Ambrose Philips c.1675–1749

English poet

3 The flowers anew, returning seasons bring;
But beauty faded has no second spring.

The First Pastoral (1708) 'Lobbin' l. 47

4 There solid billows of enormous size,
Alps of green ice, in wild disorder rise.

'A Winter-Piece' in *The Tatler* (7 May 1709)

5 The stag in limpid currents with surprise,
Sees crystal branches on his forehead rise.

'A Winter-Piece' in *The Tatler* (7 May 1709)

Morgan Phillips 1902–63

British Labour politician

6 The Labour Party owes more to Methodism than to Marxism.

In James Callaghan *Time and Chance* (1987) ch. 1

Stephen Phillips 1864–1915

English poet

7 Behold me now
A man not old, but mellow, like good wine.
Not over-jealous, yet an eager husband.

Ulysses (1902) act 3, sc. 2

Eden Phillpotts 1862–1960

English writer

8 Now old man's talk o' the days behind me;
My darter's youngest darter to mind me;
A little dreamin', a little dyin',
A little lew corner of airth to lie in.

'Gaffer's Song' (1942)

Pablo Picasso 1881–1973

Spanish painter

9 We all know that Art is not truth. Art is a lie that makes us realize truth.

In Dore Ashton *Picasso on Art* (1972) 'Two statements by Picasso'

10 God is really only another artist. He invented the giraffe, the elephant, and the cat. He has no real style. He just goes on trying other things.

In F. Gilot and C. Lake *Life With Picasso* (1964) pt. 1

11 Every positive value has its price in negative terms . . . The genius of Einstein leads to Hiroshima.

In F. Gilot and C. Lake *Life With Picasso* (1964) pt. 2

12 I paint objects as I think them, not as I see them.

In John Golding *Cubism* (1959) p. 60

Pindar 518–438 BC

Greek lyric poet

13 Ἄριστον μὲν ὕδωρ, ὁ δὲ χρυσὸς αἰθόμενον πῦρ
ἅτε διαπρέπει νυκτὶ μεγάνορος ἔξοχα πλούτου.

Water is best. But gold shines like fire blazing in the night, supreme of lordly wealth.

Olympian Odes bk. 1, l. 1

14 . . . πολλά μοι ὑπ᾽ ἀγκῶνος ὠκέα βέλη
ἔνδον ἐντὶ φαρέτρας
φωνᾶντα συνετοῖσιν· ἐς δὲ τὸ πᾶν ἑρμηνέων
χατίζει. σοφὸς ὁ πολλὰ εἰδὼς φυᾷ· μαθόντες δὲ λάβροι
παγγλωσσίᾳ, κόρακες ὥς, ἄκραντα γαρύετον
Διὸς πρὸς ὄρνιχα θεῖον.

I have many swift arrows in my quiver which speak to the wise, but for the crowd they need interpreters. The skilled poet is one who knows much through natural gift, but those who have learned their art chatter turbulently, like ravens, vainly, against the divine bird of Zeus.

Olympian Odes bk. 2, l. 83

15 μή, φίλα ψυχά, βίον ἀθάνατον
σπεῦδε, τὰν δ᾽ ἔμπρακτον ἄντλει μαχανάν.

My soul, do not seek immortal life, but exhaust the realm of the possible.

Pythian Odes bk. 3, l. 109

16 ἐπάμεροι· τί δέ τις; τί δ᾽ οὔ τις; σκιᾶς ὄναρ
ἄνθρωπος. ἀλλ᾽ ὅταν αἴγλα διόσδοτος ἔλθῃ,
λαμπρὸν φέγγος ἔπεστιν ἀνδρῶν καὶ μείλιχος αἰών.

Creatures of a day, what is a man? What is he not? Mankind is a dream of a shadow. But when a god-given brightness comes, a radiant light rests on men, and a gentle life.

Pythian Odes bk. 8, l. 135

Harold Pinter 1930–

English playwright

17 Them bastards at the monastery let me down again.

The Caretaker (1960) act 1

18 I said to this monk, here, I said, look here, mister . . . you haven't got a pair of shoes, have you, a pair of shoes, I said, enough to help me on my way. Look at these, they're nearly out, I said, they're no good to me. I heard you got a stock of shoes here. Piss off, he said to me.

The Caretaker (1960) act 1

19 If only I could get down to Sidcup! I've been waiting for the weather to break. He's got my papers, this man I left them with, it's got it all down there, I could prove everything.

The Caretaker (1960) act 1

1 Apart from the known and the unknown, what else is there?

The Homecoming (1965) act 2, sc. 1

2 The weasel under the cocktail cabinet.

On being asked what his plays were about, in J. Russell Taylor *Anger and After* (1962) p. 231

Luigi Pirandello 1867–1936

Italian playwright and novelist

3 *Sei personaggi in cerca d'autore.*

Six characters in search of an author.

Title of play (1921)

Robert M. Pirsig 1928–

American writer

4 That's the classical mind at work, runs fine inside but looks dingy on the surface.

Zen and the Art of Motorcycle Maintenance (1974) pt. 3, ch. 26

William Pitt, Earl of Chatham 1708–78

British Whig politician; Prime Minister, 1766–8

5 The atrocious crime of being a young man . . . I shall neither attempt to palliate nor deny.

Speech, *Hansard* 2 March 1741, col. 115

6 The poorest man may in his cottage bid defiance to all the forces of the Crown. It may be frail—its roof may shake—the wind may blow through it—the storm may enter—the rain may enter—but the King of England cannot enter!

Speech, *c.* March 1763, in Lord Brougham *Historical Sketches of Statesmen in the Time of George III* First Series (1845) vol. 1, p. 53

7 Confidence is a plant of slow growth in an aged bosom: youth is the season of credulity.

Speech, *Hansard* 14 January 1766, col. 97

8 Unlimited power is apt to corrupt the minds of those who possess it.

Speech, *Hansard* (House of Lords) 9 January 1770, col. 665. Cf. Acton 1:10

9 There is something behind the throne greater than the King himself.

Speech, *Hansard* (House of Lords) 2 March 1770, col. 843

10 We have a Calvinistic creed, a Popish liturgy, and an Arminian clergy.

Speech, the House of Lords, 19 May 1772. See Basil Williams *Life of William Pitt Earl of Chatham* (1913) vol. 2, ch. 24

11 You cannot conquer America.

Speech, *Hansard* (House of Lords) 18 November 1777, col. 363

12 I invoke the genius of the Constitution!

Speech, *Hansard* (House of Lords) 18 November 1777, col. 369

13 The parks are the lungs of London.

In *Hansard* 30 June 1808, col. 1124 (quoted by William Windham)

14 Our watchword is security.

Attributed

William Pitt 1759–1806

British Tory politician; Prime Minister, 1783–1801, 1804–6

15 Necessity is the plea for every infringement of human freedom: it is the argument of tyrants; it is the creed of slaves.

Speech, *Hansard* 18 November 1783, col. 1209

16 We must recollect . . . what it is we have at stake, what it is we have to contend for. It is for our property, it is for our liberty, it is for our independence, nay, for our existence as a nation; it is for our character, it is for our very name as Englishmen, it is for everything dear and valuable to man on this side of the grave.

On the rupture of the Peace of Amiens and the resumption of war with Napoleon, in *Speeches of the Rt. Hon. William Pitt* (1806) vol. 4, p. 262 (22 July 1803)

17 England has saved herself by her exertions, and will, as I trust, save Europe by her example.

Replying to a toast in which he had been described as the saviour of his country in the wars with France, in R. Coupland *War Speeches of William Pitt* (1915) p. 35

18 Roll up that map; it will not be wanted these ten years.

Of a map of Europe, on hearing of Napoleon's victory at Austerlitz, December 1805; in Earl Stanhope *Life of the Rt. Hon. William Pitt* vol. 4 (1862) ch. 43

19 Oh, my country! how I leave my country!

Last words, in Earl Stanhope *Life of the Rt. Hon. William Pitt* vol. 3 (1879) ch. 43 ('How I love my country' in the 1st ed., vol. 4 (1862) ch. 43). G. Rose *Diaries and Correspondence* (1860) vol. 2, p. 233, 23 January 1806, cites 'My country! oh, my country!', whereas oral tradition reports 'I think I could eat one of Bellamy's veal pies'

Pius VII 1742–1823

Pope from 1800

20 We are prepared to go to the gates of Hell—but no further.

Attempting to reach an agreement with Napoleon, *c.*1800–1, in J. M. Robinson *Cardinal Consalvi* (1987) p. 66

Max Planck 1858–1947
German physicist

1 A new scientific truth does not triumph by
convincing its opponents and making them see the
light, but rather because its opponents eventually
die, and a new generation grows up that is familiar
with it.
> *A Scientific Autobiography* (1949) p. 33 (translated by
> F. Gaynor)

Sylvia Plath 1932–63
American poet

2 A living doll, everywhere you look.
It can sew, it can cook,
It can talk, talk, talk.

It works, there is nothing wrong with it.
You have a hole, it's a poultice.
You have an eye, it's an image.
My boy, it's your last resort.
Will you marry it, marry it, marry it.
> 'The Applicant' (1966)

3 Is there no way out of the mind?
> 'Apprehensions' (1971)

4 I have always been scared of *you*,
With your Luftwaffe, your gobbledygoo.
And your neat moustache
And your Aryan eye, bright blue.
Panzer-man, panzer-man, O You—
> 'Daddy' (1963)

5 Every woman adores a Fascist,
The boot in the face, the brute
Brute heart of a brute like you.
> 'Daddy' (1963)

6 Dying,
Is an art, like everything else.
> 'Lady Lazarus' (1963)

7 Love set you going like a fat gold watch.
The midwife slapped your footsoles, and your
 bald cry
Took its place among the elements.
> 'Morning Song' (1965)

8 Widow. The word consumes itself.
> 'Widow' (1971)

Plato 429–347 BC
Greek philosopher

9 Σωκράτη φησὶν ἀδικεῖν τούς τε νέους διαφθείροντα καὶ
θεοὺς οὓς ἡ πόλις νομίζει οὐ νομίζοντα, ἕτερα δὲ δαιμόνια
καινά.

Socrates, he says, breaks the law by corrupting young
men and not recognizing the gods that the city
recognizes, but some other new deities.
> *Apologia* 24b

10 ἆρα τὸ ὅσιον, ὅτι ὅσιόν ἐστιν, φιλεῖται ὑπὸ τῶν θεῶν, ἢ
ὅτι φιλεῖται, ὅσιόν ἐστιν;

Is that which is holy loved by the gods because it is
holy, or is it holy because it is loved by the gods?
> *Euthyphro* 10

11 ὁ Σώκρατες, ἔφη, οὐ καταγνώσομαι σοῦ ὅπερ ἄλλων
καταγιγνώσκω, ὅτι μοι χαλεπαίνουσι καὶ καταρῶνται,
ἐπειδὰν αὐτοῖς παραγγέλλω πίνειν τὸ φάρμακον
ἀναγκαζόντων τῶν ἀρχόντων. σὲ δὲ ἐγὼ καὶ ἄλλως
ἔγνωκα ἐν τούτῳ τῷ χρόνῳ γενναιότατον καὶ πρᾳότατον
καὶ ἄριστον ἄνδρα ὄντα τῶν πώποτε δεῦρο ἀφικομένων,
καὶ δὴ καὶ νῦν εὖ οἶδ' ὅτι οὐκ ἐμοὶ χαλεπαίνεις,
γιγνώσκεις γὰρ τοὺς αἰτίους, ἀλλὰ ἐκείνοις.

Socrates, I shall not accuse you as I accuse others, of
getting angry and cursing me when I tell them to
drink the poison imposed by the authorities. I know
you on the contrary in your time here to be the
noblest and gentlest and best man of all who ever
came here; and now I am sure you are not angry
with me, for you know who are responsible, but with
them.
> *Phaedo* 116c (spoken by Socrates' jailer)

12 Ἥδε ἡ τελευτή, ὦ Ἐχέκρατες, τοῦ ἑταίρου ἡμῖν ἐγένετο,
ἀνδρός, ὡς ἡμεῖς φαῖμεν ἄν, τῶν τότε ὧν ἐπειράθημεν
ἀρίστου καὶ ἄλλως φρονιμωτάτου καὶ δικαιοτάτου.

This was the end, Echekrates, of our friend; a man of
whom we may say that of all whom we met at that
time he was the wisest and justest and best.
> *Phaedo* 118a (on the death of Socrates)

13 φημὶ γὰρ ἐγὼ εἶναι τὸ δίκαιον οὐκ ἄλλο τι ἢ τὸ τοῦ
κρείττονος ξυμφέρον.

What I say is that 'just' or 'right' means nothing but
what is in the interest of the stronger party.
> Spoken by Thrasymachus in *The Republic* bk. 1, 338c
> (translated by F. M. Cornford)

14 οὐ γὰρ περὶ τοῦ ἐπιτυχόντος ὁ λόγος, ἀλλὰ περὶ τοῦ
ὄντινα τρόπον χρὴ ζῆν.

For our discussion is about no ordinary matter, but on
the right way to conduct our lives.
> *The Republic* bk. 1, 352d

15 Καὶ τοῖς γιγνωσκομένοις τοίνυν μὴ μόνον τὸ
γιγνώσκεσθαι φάναι ὑπὸ τοῦ ἀγαθοῦ παρεῖναι, ἀλλὰ καὶ
τὸ εἶναί τε καὶ τὴν οὐσίαν ὑπ' ἐκείνου αὐτοῖς προσεῖναι,
οὐκ οὐσίας ὄντος τοῦ ἀγαθοῦ, ἀλλ' ἔτι ἐπέκεινα τῆς
οὐσίας πρεσβείᾳ καὶ καὶ δυνάμει ὑπερέχοντος.

And so with the objects of knowledge: these derive
from the Good not only their power of being known,
but their very being and reality; and Goodness is not
the same thing as being, but even beyond being,
surpassing it in dignity and power.
> *The Republic* bk. 6, 509b (translated by
> F. M. Cornford)

16 αἰτία ἑλομένου· θεὸς ἀναίτιος.

The blame is his who chooses: God is blameless.
> *The Republic* bk. 10, 617e

1 ἀλλ᾽ ἂν ἐμοὶ πειθώμεθα, νομίζοντες ἀθάνατον ψυχὴν καὶ δυνατὴν πάντα μὲν κακὰ ἀνέχεσθαι, πάντα δὲ ἀγαθά, τῆς ἄνω ὁδοῦ ἀεὶ ἑξόμεθα καὶ δικαιοσύνην μετὰ φρονήσεως παντὶ τρόπῳ ἐπιτηδεύσομεν, ἵνα καὶ ἡμῖν αὐτοῖς φίλοι ὦμεν καὶ τοῖς θεοῖς, αὐτοῦ τε μένοντες ἐνθάδε, καὶ ἐπειδὰν τὰ ἆθλα αὐτῆς κομιζώμεθα.

But if we are guided by me we shall believe that the soul is immortal and capable of enduring all extremes of good and evil, and so we shall hold ever to the upward way and pursue righteousness with wisdom always and ever, that we may be dear to ourselves and to the gods both during our sojourn here and when we receive our reward.

The Republic bk. 10, 621c

2 Ἀλλ᾽ οὔτ᾽ ἀπολέσθαι τὰ κακὰ δυνατόν, ὦ Θεόδωρε— ὑπεναντίον γάρ τι τῷ ἀγαθῷ ἀεὶ εἶναι ἀνάγκη—οὔτ᾽ ἐν θεοῖς αὐτὰ ἱδρῦσθαι, τὴν δὲ θνητὴν φύσιν καὶ τόνδε τὸν τόπον περιπολεῖ ἐξ ἀνάγκης. διὸ καὶ πειρᾶσθαι χρὴ ἐνθένδε ἐκεῖσε φεύγειν ὅτι τάχιστα· φυγὴ δὲ ὁμοίωσις θεῷ κατὰ τὸ δυνατόν· ὁμοίωσις δὲ δίκαιον καὶ ὅσιον μετὰ φρονήσεως γενέσθαι.

Evils, Theodorus, can never pass away, for there must always remain something which is antagonistic to good. Having no place among the gods in heaven, of necessity they hover around the mortal nature and this earthly sphere. Wherefore we ought to fly away from earth to heaven as quickly as we can; and to fly away is to become like God, as far as this is possible; and to become like him is to become holy, just, and wise.

Theaetetus 176a (translated by Benjamin Jowett)

Plautus *c.*250–184 BC

Roman comic playwright

3 *Lupus est homo homini, non homo, quom qualis sit non novit.*

A man is a wolf rather than a man to another man, when he hasn't yet found out what he's like.

Asinaria l. 495 (often quoted 'Homo homini lupus [A man is a wolf to another man]')

4 *Dictum sapienti sat est.*

A sentence is enough for a sensible man.

Persa l. 729 (proverbially: 'Verbum sapienti sat est [A word is enough for the wise]')

5 LABRAX: *Immo edepol una littera plus sum quam medicus.*
GRIPUS: *Tum tu Mendicus es?*
LABRAX: *Tetigisti acu.*

LABRAX: One letter more than a medical man, that's what I am.
GRIPUS: Then you're a mendicant?
LABRAX: You've hit the point.

Rudens l. 1305

Pliny the Elder AD 23–79

Roman statesman and scholar

6 *Bruta fulmina.*

Harmless thunderbolts.

Historia Naturalis bk. 2, sect. 113

7 *Semper aliquid novi Africam adferre.*

Africa always brings [us] something new.

Historia Naturalis bk. 8, sect. 42 (often quoted 'Ex Africa semper aliquid novi [Always something new out of Africa]')

8 *Optimumque est, ut volgo dixere, aliena insania frui.*

And the best plan is, as the popular saying was, to profit by the folly of others.

Historia Naturalis bk. 18, sect. 31

9 *Addito salis grano.*

With the addition of a grain of salt.

Historia Naturalis bk. 23, sect. 149 (commonly quoted 'Cum grano salis [With a grain of salt]')

William Plomer 1903–73

British poet

10 Out of that bungled, unwise war
An alp of unforgiveness grew.

'The Boer War' (1960)

11 A family portrait not too stale to record
Of a pleasant old buffer, nephew to a lord,
Who believed that the bank was mightier than the sword,
And that an umbrella might pacify barbarians abroad:
Just like an old liberal
Between the wars.

'Father and Son: 1939' (1945)

12 With first-rate sherry flowing into second-rate whores,
And third-rate conversation without one single pause:
Just like a young couple
Between the wars.

'Father and Son: 1939' (1945)

13 On a sofa upholstered in panther skin
Mona did researches in original sin.

'Mews Flat Mona' (1960)

14 A rose-red sissy half as old as time.

'Playboy of the Demi-World: 1938' (1945). Cf. Burgon 156:24

Plutarch AD *c.*46–*c.*120

Greek philosopher and biographer

15 ὁ γὰρ ὅρκῳ παρακρουόμενος τὸν μὲν ἐχθρὸν ὁμολογεῖ δεδιέναι, τοῦ δὲ θεοῦ καταφρονεῖν.

He who cheats with an oath acknowledges that he is afraid of his enemy, but that he thinks little of God.

Parallel Lives 'Lysander' ch. 8. Cf. Lysander 433:15

16 λέγεται γὰρ ὡς, ἀμφοτέρους τινός ἱμοῦ διαβάλλοντος πρὸς αὐτόν, εἴποι, μὴ δεδιέναι τοὺς παχεῖς τούτους καὶ κομήτας, ἀλλὰ τοὺς ὠχροὺς καὶ λεπτοὺς ἐκείνους.

For we are told that when a certain man was accusing both of them to him, he [Caesar] said that he had no fear of those fat and long-haired fellows, but rather of those pale and thin ones.

Parallel Lives 'Anthony' sect. 11. Cf. Julius Caesar 590:6

Edgar Allan Poe 1809–49

American writer

17 This maiden she lived with no other thought
Than to love and be loved by me.

'Annabel Lee' (1849)

1 I was a child and she was a child,
In this kingdom by the sea;
But we loved with a love which was more than love—
I and my Annabel Lee.
'Annabel Lee' (1849)

2 And so, all the night-tide, I lie down by the side
Of my darling, my darling, my life and my bride
In her sepulchre there by the sea,
In her tomb by the side of the sea.
'Annabel Lee' (1849)

3 Keeping time, time, time,
In a sort of Runic rhyme,
To the tintinnabulation that so musically wells
From the bells, bells, bells, bells.
'The Bells' (1849) st. 1

4 All that we see or seem
Is but a dream within a dream.
'A Dream within a Dream' (1849)

5 The fever called 'Living'
Is conquered at last.
'For Annie' (1849)

6 Once upon a midnight dreary, while I pondered, weak and weary,
Over many a quaint and curious volume of forgotten lore,
While I nodded, nearly napping, suddenly there came a tapping,
As of some one gently rapping, rapping at my chamber door.
'The Raven' (1845) st. 1

7 Eagerly I wished the morrow,—vainly had I sought to borrow
From my books surcease of sorrow—sorrow for the lost Lenore—
For the rare and radiant maiden whom the angels name Lenore—
Nameless here for evermore.
'The Raven' (1845) st. 2

8 Take thy beak from out my heart, and take thy form from off my door!
Quoth the Raven, 'Nevermore'.
'The Raven' (1845) st. 17

9 Helen, thy beauty is to me
Like those Nicean barks of yore,
That gently, o'er a perfumed sea,
The weary, wayworn wanderer bore
To his own native shore.

On desperate seas long wont to roam,
Thy hyacinth hair, thy classic face,
Thy Naiad airs have brought me home,
To the glory that was Greece
And the grandeur that was Rome.
'To Helen' (1831)

Henri Poincaré 1854–1912
French mathematician and philosopher of science

10 Science is built up of facts, as a house is built of stones; but an accumulation of facts is no more a science than a heap of stones is a house.
Science and Hypothesis (1905) ch. 9

John Pomfret 1667–1702
English clergyman

11 We live and learn, but not the wiser grow.
'Reason' (1700) l. 112

Madame de Pompadour (Antoinette Poisson, Marquise de Pompadour) 1721–64
Favourite of Louis XV of France

12 *Après nous le déluge.*
After us the deluge.
In Madame du Hausset *Mémoires* (1824) p. 19

Georges Pompidou 1911–74
French politician; President of France from 1969

13 A statesman is a politician who places himself at the service of the nation. A politician is a statesman who places the nation at his service.
In *Observer* 30 December 1973 'Sayings of the Year'

Alexander Pope 1688–1744
English poet

14 Poetic Justice, with her lifted scale,
Where, in nice balance, truth with gold she weighs,
And solid pudding against empty praise.
The Dunciad (1742) bk. 1, l. 52

15 While pensive poets painful vigils keep,
Sleepless themselves, to give their readers sleep.
The Dunciad (1742) bk. 1, l. 93

16 Or where the pictures for the page atone,
And Quarles is saved by beauties not his own.
The Dunciad (1742) bk. 1, l. 139

17 Gentle Dullness ever loves a joke.
The Dunciad (1742) bk. 2, l. 34

18 A brain of feathers, and a heart of lead.
The Dunciad (1742) bk. 2, l. 44

19 How little, mark! that portion of the ball,
Where, faint at best, the beams of science fall.
The Dunciad (1742) bk. 3, l. 83

20 All crowd, who foremost shall be damned to Fame.
The Dunciad (1742) bk. 3, l. 158

21 Flow Welsted, flow! like thine inspirer, Beer,
Tho' stale, not ripe; tho' thin, yet never clear;
So sweetly mawkish, and so smoothly dull;
Heady, not strong; o'erflowing tho' not full.
The Dunciad (1742) bk. 3, l. 169

22 Proceed, great days! 'till learning fly the shore,
'Till birch shall blush with noble blood no more,
'Till Thames see Eton's sons for ever play,
'Till Westminster's whole year be holiday,
'Till Isis' elders reel, their pupils' sport,
And Alma mater lie dissolved in port!
The Dunciad (1742) bk. 3, l. 333

23 None need a guide, by sure attraction led,
And strong impulsive gravity of head.
The Dunciad (1742) bk. 4, l. 75

1 A wit with dunces, and a dunce with wits.
The Dunciad (1742) bk. 4, l. 90

2 Whate'er the talents, or howe'er designed,
We hang one jingling padlock on the mind.
The Dunciad (1742) bk. 4, l. 161

3 The Right Divine of Kings to govern wrong.
The Dunciad (1742) bk. 4, l. 187

4 For thee explain a thing till all men doubt it,
And write about it, Goddess, and about it.
The Dunciad (1742) bk. 4, l. 251

5 With the same cement, ever sure to bind,
We bring to one dead level ev'ry mind.
Then take him to develop, if you can,
And hew the block off, and get out the man.
The Dunciad (1742) bk. 4, l. 267

6 Isles of fragrance, lily-silver'd vales.
The Dunciad (1742) bk. 4, l. 303

7 Love-whisp'ring woods, and lute-resounding waves.
The Dunciad (1742) bk. 4, l. 306

8   She marked thee there,
Stretched on the rack of a too easy chair,
And heard thy everlasting yawn confess
The pains and penalties of idleness.
The Dunciad (1742) bk. 4, l. 341

9 Thy truffles, Perigord! thy hams, Bayonne!
The Dunciad (1742) bk. 4, l. 558

10 See skulking Truth to her old cavern fled,
Mountains of casuistry heaped o'er her head!
Philosophy, that leaned on Heav'n before,
Shrinks to her second cause, and is no more.
Physic of Metaphysic begs defence,
And Metaphysic calls for aid on Sense!
The Dunciad (1742) bk. 4, l. 641

11 Religion blushing veils her sacred fires,
And unawares Morality expires.
The Dunciad (1742) bk. 4, l. 649

12 Lo! thy dread empire, Chaos! is restored;
Light dies before thy uncreating word:
Thy hand, great Anarch! lets the curtain fall;
And universal darkness buries all.
The Dunciad (1742) bk. 4, l. 653

13 Vital spark of heav'nly flame!
Quit, oh quit this mortal frame:
Trembling, hoping, ling'ring, flying,
Oh the pain, the bliss of dying!
'The Dying Christian to his Soul' (1730). Cf. Hadrian 320:8

14 What beck'ning ghost, along the moonlight shade
Invites my step, and points to yonder glade?
'Elegy to the Memory of an Unfortunate Lady' (1717) l. 1

15 Is it, in heav'n, a crime to love too well?
'Elegy to the Memory of an Unfortunate Lady' (1717) l. 6

16 Is there no bright reversion in the sky,
For those who greatly think, or bravely die?
'Elegy to the Memory of an Unfortunate Lady' (1717) l. 9

17 Ambition first sprung from your blest abodes;
The glorious fault of angels and of gods.
'Elegy to the Memory of an Unfortunate Lady' (1717) l. 13

18 On all the line a sudden vengeance waits,
And frequent hearses shall besiege your gates.
'Elegy to the Memory of an Unfortunate Lady' (1717) l. 37

19 Oh happy state! when souls each other draw,
When love is liberty, and nature, law:
All then is full, possessing, and possessed,
No craving void left aching in the breast.
'Eloisa to Abelard' (1717) l. 91

20 Of all affliction taught a lover yet,
'Tis sure the hardest science to forget!
How shall I lose the sin, yet keep the sense,
And love th'offender, yet detest th'offence?
'Eloisa to Abelard' (1717) l. 189. Cf. Augustine 37:8

21 How happy is the blameless Vestal's lot!
The world forgetting, by the world forgot.
'Eloisa to Abelard' (1717) l. 207

22 You beat your pate, and fancy wit will come:
Knock as you please, there's nobody at home.
'Epigram: You beat your pate' (1732)

23 I am his Highness' dog at Kew;
Pray, tell me sir, whose dog are you?
'Epigram Engraved on the Collar of a Dog which I gave to his Royal Highness' (1738)

24 Sir, I admit your gen'ral rule
That every poet is a fool:
But you yourself may serve to show it,
That every fool is not a poet.
'Epigram from the French' (1732)

25 Shut, shut the door, good John! fatigued I said,
Tie up the knocker, say I'm sick, I'm dead,
The dog-star rages!
'An Epistle to Dr Arbuthnot' (1735) l. 1

26 You think this cruel? take it for a rule,
No creature smarts so little as a fool.
Let peals of laughter, Codrus! round thee break,
Thou unconcerned canst hear the mighty crack.
Pit, box, and gall'ry in convulsions hurled,
Thou stand'st unshook amidst a bursting world.
'An Epistle to Dr Arbuthnot' (1735) l. 83. Cf. Addison 4:5, Horace 350:1

27 Destroy his fib, or sophistry; in vain,
The creature's at his dirty work again.
'An Epistle to Dr Arbuthnot' (1735) l. 91

28 As yet a child, nor yet a fool to fame,
I lisped in numbers, for the numbers came.
'An Epistle to Dr Arbuthnot' (1735) l. 127. Cf. Ovid 503:6

29 The Muse but served to ease some friend, not wife,
To help me through this long disease, my life.
'An Epistle to Dr Arbuthnot' (1735) l. 131. Cf. Ovid 503:16

30 Pretty! in amber to observe the forms
Of hairs, or straws, or dirt, or grubs, or worms;
The things, we know, are neither rich nor rare,
But wonder how the devil they got there?
'An Epistle to Dr Arbuthnot' (1735) l. 169

31 And he, whose fustian's so sublimely bad,
It is not poetry, but prose run mad.
'An Epistle to Dr Arbuthnot' (1735) l. 187

32 Damn with faint praise, assent with civil leer,
And without sneering, teach the rest to sneer;
Willing to wound, and yet afraid to strike,
Just hint a fault, and hesitate dislike.
'An Epistle to Dr Arbuthnot' (1735) l. 201 (of Addison). Cf. Wycherley 750:8

1 But still the great have kindness in reserve,
He helped to bury whom he helped to starve.
　　'An Epistle to Dr Arbuthnot' (1735) l. 247 (of a noble
　　patron)

2 Let Sporus tremble—'What? that thing of silk,
Sporus, that mere white curd of ass's milk?
Satire or sense, alas! can Sporus feel?
Who breaks a butterfly upon a wheel?'
　　'An Epistle to Dr Arbuthnot' (1735) l. 305 (of Lord Hervey)

3 Yet let me flap this bug with gilded wings,
This painted child of dirt that stinks and stings.
　　'An Epistle to Dr Arbuthnot' (1735) l. 309 (of Lord Hervey)

4 Eternal smiles his emptiness betray,
As shallow streams run dimpling all the way.
　　'An Epistle to Dr Arbuthnot' (1735) l. 315 (of Lord Hervey)

5 And he himself one vile antithesis.
　　'An Epistle to Dr Arbuthnot' (1735) l. 325 (of Lord Hervey)

6 A cherub's face, a reptile all the rest.
　　'An Epistle to Dr Arbuthnot' (1735) l. 331 (of Lord Hervey)

7 Unlearn'd, he knew no schoolman's subtle art,
No language, but the language of the heart.
　　'An Epistle to Dr Arbuthnot' (1735) l. 398 (of his own
　　father)

8 A very heathen in the carnal part,
Yet still a sad, good Christian at her heart.
　　Epistles to Several Persons 'To a Lady' (1735) l. 67

9 Chaste to her husband, frank to all beside,
A teeming mistress, but a barren bride.
　　Epistles to Several Persons 'To a Lady' (1735) l. 71

10 Virtue she finds too painful an endeavour,
Content to dwell in decencies for ever.
　　Epistles to Several Persons 'To a Lady' (1735) l. 163

11 Still round and round the ghosts of Beauty glide,
And haunt the places where their honour died.
See how the world its veterans rewards!
A youth of frolics, an old age of cards.
　　Epistles to Several Persons 'To a Lady' (1735) l. 241

12 And mistress of herself, though china fall.
　　Epistles to Several Persons 'To a Lady' (1735) l. 268

13 Woman's at best a contradiction still.
　　Epistles to Several Persons 'To a Lady' (1735) l. 270

14 Who shall decide, when doctors disagree,
And soundest casuists doubt, like you and me?
　　Epistles to Several Persons 'To Lord Bathurst' (1733) l. 1

15 But thousands die, without or this or that,
Die, and endow a college, or a cat.
　　Epistles to Several Persons 'To Lord Bathurst' (1733) l. 97

16 The ruling passion, be it what it will,
The ruling passion conquers reason still.
　　Epistles to Several Persons 'To Lord Bathurst' (1733) l. 155.
　　Cf. Pope 520:28

17 Who sees pale Mammon pine amidst his store,
Sees but a backward steward for the poor;
This year a reservoir, to keep and spare,
The next a fountain, spouting through his heir,
In lavish streams to quench a country's thirst,
And men and dogs shall drink him 'till they burst.
　　Epistles to Several Persons 'To Lord Bathurst' (1733) l. 173

18 In the worst inn's worst room, with mat half-hung,
The floors of plaister, and the walls of dung,
On once a flock-bed, but repaired with straw,
With tape-tied curtains, never meant to draw,
The George and Garter dangling from that bed
Where tawdry yellow strove with dirty red,
Great Villiers lies.
　　Epistles to Several Persons 'To Lord Bathurst' (1733) l. 299

19 Consult the genius of the place in all.
　　Epistles to Several Persons 'To Lord Burlington' (1731) l. 57

20 Still follow sense, of ev'ry art the soul,
Parts answering parts shall slide into a whole.
　　Epistles to Several Persons 'To Lord Burlington' (1731) l. 65

21 To rest, the cushion and soft Dean invite,
Who never mentions Hell to ears polite.
　　Epistles to Several Persons 'To Lord Burlington' (1731)
　　l. 149

22 Another age shall see the golden ear
Imbrown the slope, and nod on the parterre,
Deep harvests bury all his pride has planned,
And laughing Ceres re-assume the land.
　　Epistles to Several Persons 'To Lord Burlington' (1731)
　　l. 173

23 'Tis use alone that sanctifies expense,
And splendour borrows all her rays from sense.
　　Epistles to Several Persons 'To Lord Burlington' (1731)
　　l. 179

24 To observations which ourselves we make,
We grow more partial for th' observer's sake.
　　Epistles to Several Persons 'To Lord Cobham' (1734) l. 11

25 Like following life thro' creatures you dissect,
You lose it in the moment you detect.
　　Epistles to Several Persons 'To Lord Cobham' (1734) l. 39

26 'Tis from high life high characters are drawn;
A saint in crape is twice a saint in lawn.
　　Epistles to Several Persons 'To Lord Cobham' (1734) l. 87

27 'Tis education forms the common mind,
Just as the twig is bent, the tree's inclined.
　　Epistles to Several Persons 'To Lord Cobham' (1734) l. 101

28 Search then the Ruling Passion: There, alone,
The wild are constant, and the cunning known;
The fool consistent, and the false sincere.
　　Epistles to Several Persons 'To Lord Cobham' (1734) l. 174.
　　Cf. Pope 520:16

29 Odious! in woollen! 'twould a saint provoke!
　　Epistles to Several Persons 'To Lord Cobham' (1734) l. 242

30 One would not, sure, be frightful when one's dead—
And—Betty—give this cheek a little red.
　　Epistles to Several Persons 'To Lord Cobham' (1734) l. 246

31 Old politicians chew on wisdom past,
And totter on in business to the last.
　　Epistles to Several Persons 'To Lord Cobham' (1734) l. 248

32 Statesman, yet friend to Truth! of soul sincere,
In action faithful, and in honour clear;
Who broke no promise, served no private end,
Who gained no title, and who lost no friend.
　　Epistles to Several Persons 'To Mr Addison' (1720) l. 67

1 She went, to plain-work, and to purling brooks,
Old-fashioned halls, dull aunts, and croaking rooks:
She went from op'ra, park, assembly, play,
To morning-walks, and prayers three hours a day;
To pass her time 'twixt reading and Bohea,
To muse, and spill her solitary tea,
Or o'er cold coffee trifle with the spoon,
Court the slow clock, and dine exact at noon.
'Epistle to Miss Blount, on her leaving the Town, after the Coronation [of King George I, 1715]' (1717)

2 Nature, and Nature's laws lay hid in night.
God said, *Let Newton be!* and all was light.
'Epitaph: Intended for Sir Isaac Newton' (1730). Cf. Squire 661:18

3 Of manners gentle, of affections mild;
In wit, a man; simplicity, a child;
With native humour temp'ring virtuous rage,
Formed to delight at once and lash the age.
'Epitaph: On Mr Gay in Westminster Abbey' (1733)

4 Some are bewildered in the maze of schools,
And some made coxcombs Nature meant but fools.
An Essay on Criticism (1711) l. 26

5 Some have at first for wits, then poets passed,
Turned critics next, and proved plain fools at last.
An Essay on Criticism (1711) l. 36

6 First follow Nature, and your judgement frame
By her just standard, which is still the same:
Unerring Nature, still divinely bright,
One clear, unchanged, and universal light,
Life, force and beauty must to all impart,
At once the source and end and test of art.
An Essay on Criticism (1711) l. 68

7 Great wits may sometimes gloriously offend,
And rise to faults true critics dare not mend.
From vulgar bounds with brave disorder part
And snatch a grace beyond the reach of art.
An Essay on Criticism (1711) l. 152. Cf. Addison 5:1

8 A little learning is a dangerous thing;
Drink deep, or taste not the Pierian spring:
There shallow draughts intoxicate the brain,
And drinking largely sobers us again.
An Essay on Criticism (1711) l. 215. Cf. Drayton 258:5

9 Hills peep o'er hills, and Alps on Alps arise!
An Essay on Criticism (1711) l. 232

10 Whoever thinks a faultless piece to see,
Thinks what ne'er was, nor is, nor e'er shall be.
An Essay on Criticism (1711) l. 253

11 Poets like painters, thus unskilled to trace
The naked nature and the living grace,
With gold and jewels cover ev'ry part,
And hide with ornaments their want of art.
True wit is Nature to advantage dressed,
What oft was thought, but ne'er so well expressed.
An Essay on Criticism (1711) l. 293

12 Expression is the dress of thought.
An Essay on Criticism (1711) l. 318. Cf. Wesley 729:5

13   As some to church repair,
Not for the doctrine, but the music there.
An Essay on Criticism (1711) l. 342

14 And ten low words oft creep in one dull line.
An Essay on Criticism (1711) l. 347

15 Then, at the last and only couplet fraught
With some unmeaning thing they call a thought,
A needless Alexandrine ends the song,
That, like a wounded snake, drags its slow length along.
An Essay on Criticism (1711) l. 354

16 True ease in writing comes from art, not chance,
As those move easiest who have learned to dance.
'Tis not enough no harshness gives offence,
The sound must seem an echo to the sense.
An Essay on Criticism (1711) l. 362

17 But when loud surges lash the sounding shore,
The hoarse, rough verse should like the torrent roar.
When Ajax strives, some rock's vast weight to throw,
The line too labours, and the words move slow.
An Essay on Criticism (1711) l. 368

18 Yet let not each gay turn thy rapture move,
For fools admire, but men of sense approve.
An Essay on Criticism (1711) l. 390

19 What woeful stuff this madrigal would be,
In some starved hackney sonneteer, or me?
But let a Lord once own the happy lines,
How the wit brightens! how the style refines!
An Essay on Criticism (1711) l. 418

20 Some praise at morning what they blame at night;
But always think the last opinion right.
An Essay on Criticism (1711) l. 430

21 To err is human; to forgive, divine.
An Essay on Criticism (1711) l. 525

22 All seems infected that th'infected spy,
As all looks yellow to the jaundiced eye.
An Essay on Criticism (1711) l. 558

23 Men must be taught as if you taught them not,
And things unknown proposed as things forgot.
An Essay on Criticism (1711) l. 574

24 The bookful blockhead, ignorantly read,
With loads of learned lumber in his head.
An Essay on Criticism (1711) l. 612

25 For fools rush in where angels fear to tread.
An Essay on Criticism (1711) l. 625

26 Awake, my St John! leave all meaner things
To low ambition, and the pride of kings.
Let us (since Life can little more supply
Than just to look about us and to die)
Expatiate free o'er all this scene of man;
A mighty maze! but not without a plan.
An Essay on Man Epistle 1 (1733) l. 1

27 Eye Nature's walks, shoot Folly as it flies,
And catch the Manners living as they rise.
Laugh where we must, be candid where we can;
But vindicate the ways of God to man.
An Essay on Man Epistle 1 (1733) l. 13. Cf. Milton 467:21

28 Observe how system into system runs,
What other planets circle other suns.
An Essay on Man Epistle 1 (1733) l. 25

29 Who sees with equal eye, as God of all,
A hero perish, or a sparrow fall,
Atoms or systems into ruin hurled,
And now a bubble burst, and now a world.
An Essay on Man Epistle 1 (1733) l. 87

1 Hope springs eternal in the human breast:
Man never Is, but always To be blest.
An Essay on Man Epistle 1 (1733) l. 95

2 Lo! the poor Indian, whose untutored mind
Sees God in clouds, or hears him in the wind;
His soul proud Science never taught to stray
Far as the solar walk, or milky way;
Yet simple Nature to his hope has giv'n,
Behind the cloud-topped hill, an humbler heav'n.
An Essay on Man Epistle 1 (1733) l. 99

3 But thinks, admitted to that equal sky,
His faithful dog shall bear him company.
An Essay on Man Epistle 1 (1733) l. 111

4 Pride still is aiming at the blest abodes,
Men would be angels, angels would be gods.
An Essay on Man Epistle 1 (1733) l. 125

5 Why has not man a microscopic eye?
For this plain reason, man is not a fly.
An Essay on Man Epistle 1 (1733) l. 193

6 The spider's touch, how exquisitely fine!
Feels at each thread, and lives along the line.
An Essay on Man Epistle 1 (1733) l. 217

7 All are but parts of one stupendous whole,
Whose body, Nature is, and God the soul.
An Essay on Man Epistle 1 (1733) l. 267

8 All nature is but art, unknown to thee;
All chance, direction, which thou canst not see;
All discord, harmony, not understood;
All partial evil, universal good:
And, spite of Pride, in erring Reason's spite,
One truth is clear, 'Whatever IS, is RIGHT.'
An Essay on Man Epistle 1 (1733) l. 289

9 Know then thyself, presume not God to scan;
The proper study of mankind is man.
Placed on this isthmus of a middle state,
A being darkly wise, and rudely great:
With too much knowledge for the sceptic side,
With too much weakness for the stoic's pride,
He hangs between; in doubt to act or rest,
In doubt to deem himself a god, or beast;
In doubt his mind or body to prefer,
Born but to die, and reas'ning but to err;
Alike in ignorance, his reason such,
Whether he thinks too little, or too much.
An Essay on Man Epistle 2 (1733) l. 1. Cf. Charron
192:2

10 Created half to rise, and half to fall;
Great lord of all things, yet a prey to all;
Sole judge of truth, in endless error hurled;
The glory, jest, and riddle of the world!
An Essay on Man Epistle 2 (1733) l. 15

11 Go, teach Eternal Wisdom how to rule—
Then drop into thyself, and be a fool!
An Essay on Man Epistle 2 (1733) l. 29

12 Fixed like a plant on his peculiar spot,
To draw nutrition, propagate, and rot.
An Essay on Man Epistle 2 (1733) l. 63

13 Vice is a monster of so frightful mien,
As, to be hated, needs but to be seen;
Yet seen too oft, familiar with her face,
We first endure, then pity, then embrace.
An Essay on Man Epistle 2 (1733) l. 217

14 The learn'd is happy nature to explore,
The fool is happy that he knows no more.
An Essay on Man Epistle 2 (1733) l. 263

15 Behold the child, by Nature's kindly law
Pleased with a rattle, tickled with a straw.
An Essay on Man Epistle 2 (1733) l. 275

16 Scarfs, garters, gold, amuse his riper stage;
And beads and pray'r-books are the toys of age:
Pleased with this bauble still, as that before;
Till tired he sleeps, and life's poor play is o'er!
An Essay on Man Epistle 2 (1733) l. 279

17 For forms of government let fools contest;
Whate'er is best administered is best:
An Essay on Man Epistle 3 (1733) l. 303

18 Thus God and nature linked the gen'ral frame,
And bade self-love and social be the same.
An Essay on Man Epistle 3 (1733) l. 317. See also *An Essay
on Man* Epistle 4 (1734) l. 396

19 Oh Happiness! our being's end and aim!
Good, pleasure, ease, content! whate'er thy name:
That something still which prompts th' eternal sigh,
For which we bear to live, or dare to die.
An Essay on Man Epistle 4 (1734) l. 1

20 A wit's a feather, and a chief a rod;
An honest man's the noblest work of God.
An Essay on Man Epistle 4 (1734) l. 247

21 If parts allure thee, think how Bacon shined,
The wisest, brightest, meanest of mankind:
Or ravished with the whistling of a name,
See Cromwell, damned to everlasting fame!
An Essay on Man Epistle 4 (1734) l. 281

22 Slave to no sect, who takes no private road,
But looks thro' Nature, up to Nature's God.
An Essay on Man Epistle 4 (1734) l. 331

23 All our knowledge is, ourselves to know.
An Essay on Man Epistle 4 (1734) l. 398

24 For I, who hold sage Homer's rule the best,
Welcome the coming, speed the going guest.
Imitations of Horace Horace bk. 2, Satire 2 (1734) l. 159
('speed the parting guest' in Pope's translation of *The
Odyssey* (1725–6) bk. 15, l. 84)

25 Our Gen'rals now, retired to their estates,
Hang their old trophies o'er the garden gates,
In life's cool ev'ning satiate of applause.
Imitations of Horace Horace bk. 1, Epistle 1 (1738) l. 7

26 Not to go back, is somewhat to advance,
And men must walk at least before they dance.
Imitations of Horace Horace bk. 1, Epistle 1 (1738) l. 53

27 Get place and wealth, if possible, with grace;
If not, by any means get wealth and place.
Imitations of Horace Horace bk. 1, Epistle 1 (1738) l. 103

28 Not to admire, is all the art I know,
To make men happy, and to keep them so.
Imitations of Horace Horace bk. 1, Epistle 6 (1738) l. 1

29 The worst of madmen is a saint run mad.
Imitations of Horace Horace bk. 1, Epistle 6 (1738) l. 27

30 Shakespeare (whom you and ev'ry play-house bill
Style the divine, the matchless, what you will)
For gain, not glory, winged his roving flight,
And grew immortal in his own despite.
Imitations of Horace Horace bk. 2, Epistle 1 (1737) l. 69

1 Who now reads Cowley? if he pleases yet,
His moral pleases, not his pointed wit.
Imitations of Horace Horace bk. 2, Epistle 1 (1737) l. 75

2   The people's voice is odd,
It is, and it is not, the voice of God.
Imitations of Horace Horace bk. 2, Epistle 1 (1737) l. 89.
Cf. Alcuin 8:2

3 But those who cannot write, and those who can,
All rhyme, and scrawl, and scribble, to a man.
Imitations of Horace Horace bk. 2, Epistle 1 (1737) l. 187.
Cf. Horace 348:17

4 Waller was smooth; but Dryden taught to join
The varying verse, the full-resounding line,
The long majestic march, and energy divine.
Imitations of Horace Horace bk. 2, Epistle 1 (1737) l. 267

5 Ev'n copious Dryden, wanted, or forgot,
The last and greatest art, the art to blot.
Imitations of Horace Horace bk. 2, Epistle 1 (1737) l. 280.
Cf. Heming 331:13, Jonson 380:9

6 There still remains, to mortify a wit,
The many-headed monster of the pit.
Imitations of Horace Horace bk. 2, Epistle 1 (1737) l. 304

7 Let humble Allen, with an awkward shame,
Do good by stealth, and blush to find it fame.
Imitations of Horace Epilogue to the Satires (1738)
Dialogue 1, l. 135

8 Ask you what provocation I have had?
The strong antipathy of good to bad.
Imitations of Horace Epilogue to the Satires (1738)
Dialogue 2, l. 197

9 Yes, I am proud; I must be proud to see
Men not afraid of God, afraid of me.
Imitations of Horace Epilogue to the Satires (1738)
Dialogue 2, l. 208

10 Ye gods! annihilate but space and time,
And make two lovers happy.
Martinus Scriblerus . . . or The Art of Sinking in Poetry ch. 11
(Miscellanies, 1727); possibly quoting another poet

11 Happy the man, whose wish and care
A few paternal acres bound,
Content to breathe his native air,
In his own ground.
'Ode on Solitude' (written *c.*1700, aged about twelve)

12 Thus let me live, unseen, unknown;
Thus unlamented let me die;
Steal from the world, and not a stone
Tell where I lie.
'Ode on Solitude' (written *c.*1700)

13 Where'er you walk, cool gales shall fan the glade,
Trees, where you sit, shall crowd into a shade:
Where'er you tread, the blushing flow'rs shall rise,
And all things flourish where you turn your eyes.
Pastorals (1709) 'Summer' l. 73

14 To wake the soul by tender strokes of art,
To raise the genius, and to mend the heart;
To make mankind, in conscious virtue bold,
Live o'er each scene, and be what they behold:
For this the Tragic Muse first trod the stage.
Prologue to Addison's *Cato* (1713) l. 1

15 What dire offence from am'rous causes springs,
What mighty contests rise from trivial things.
The Rape of the Lock (1714) canto 1, l. 1

16 Now lap-dogs give themselves the rousing shake,
And sleepless lovers, just at twelve, awake.
The Rape of the Lock (1714) canto 1, l. 15

17 With varying vanities, from ev'ry part,
They shift the moving toyshop of their heart.
The Rape of the Lock (1714) canto 1, l. 99

18 Here files of pins extend their shining rows,
Puffs, powders, patches, bibles, billet-doux.
The Rape of the Lock (1714) canto 1, l. 137

19 Bright as the sun, her eyes the gazers strike,
And, like the sun, they shine on all alike.
The Rape of the Lock (1714) canto 2, l. 13

20 If to her share some female errors fall,
Look on her face, and you'll forget 'em all.
The Rape of the Lock (1714) canto 2, l. 17

21 Fair tresses man's imperial race insnare,
And beauty draws us with a single hair.
The Rape of the Lock (1714) canto 2, l. 27

22 Belinda smiled, and all the world was gay.
The Rape of the Lock (1714) canto 2, l. 52

23 Whether the nymph shall break Diana's law,
Or some frail china jar receive a flaw,
Or stain her honour, or her new brocade,
Forget her pray'rs, or miss a masquerade.
The Rape of the Lock (1714) canto 2, l. 105

24 Here thou, great Anna! whom three realms obey,
Dost sometimes counsel take—and sometimes tea.
The Rape of the Lock (1714) canto 3, l. 7

25 At ev'ry word a reputation dies.
The Rape of the Lock (1714) canto 3, l. 16

26 The hungry judges soon the sentence sign,
And wretches hang that jury-men may dine.
The Rape of the Lock (1714) canto 3, l. 21

27 Let spades be trumps! she said, and trumps they were.
The Rape of the Lock (1714) canto 3, l. 46

28 Coffee, (which makes the politician wise,
And see thro' all things with his half-shut eyes).
The Rape of the Lock (1714) canto 3, l. 117

29 Not louder shrieks to pitying heav'n are cast,
When husbands or when lapdogs breathe their last.
The Rape of the Lock (1714) canto 3, l. 157

30 Sir Plume, of amber snuff-box justly vain,
And the nice conduct of a clouded cane.
The Rape of the Lock (1714) canto 4, l. 123

31 Beauties in vain their pretty eyes may roll;
Charms strike the sight, but merit wins the soul.
The Rape of the Lock (1714) canto 5, l. 33

32 Teach me to feel another's woe;
To hide the fault I see;
That mercy I to others show,
That mercy show to me.
'The Universal Prayer' (1738)

33 Here hills and vales, the woodland and the plain,
Here earth and water seem to strive again;
Not chaos-like together crushed and bruised,
But, as the world, harmoniously confused:
Where order in variety we see,
And where, though all things differ, all agree.
'Windsor Forest' (1711) l. 11

1 Party-spirit, which at best is but the madness of many for the gain of a few.

> Letter to Edward Blount, 27 August 1714, in G. Sherburn (ed.) *Correspondence of Alexander Pope* (1956) vol. 1, p. 247

2 How often are we to die before we go quite off this stage? In every friend we lose a part of ourselves, and the best part.

> Letter to Jonathan Swift, 5 December 1732, in G. Sherburn (ed.) *Correspondence of Alexander Pope* (1956) vol. 3, p. 335

3 To endeavour to work upon the vulgar with fine sense, is like attempting to hew blocks with a razor.

> *Miscellanies* (1727) vol. 2 'Thoughts on Various Subjects'

4 A man should never be ashamed to own he has been in the wrong, which is but saying, in other words, that he is wiser to-day than he was yesterday.

> *Miscellanies* (1727) vol. 2 'Thoughts on Various Subjects'

5 It is with narrow-souled people as with narrow-necked bottles. the less they have in them, the more noise they make in pouring it out.

> *Miscellanies* (1727) vol. 2 'Thoughts on Various Subjects'

6 When men grow virtuous in their old age, they only make a sacrifice to God of the devil's leavings.

> *Miscellanies* (1727) vol. 2 'Thoughts on Various Subjects'

7 The most positive men are the most credulous.

> *Miscellanies* (1727) vol. 2 'Thoughts on Various Subjects'

8 All gardening is landscape-painting.

> In Joseph Spence *Anecdotes* (ed. J. Osborn, 1966) no. 606

9 Here am I, dying of a hundred good symptoms.

> To George, Lord Lyttelton, 15 May 1744, in Joseph Spence *Anecdotes* (ed. J. Osborn, 1966) no. 637

Sir Karl Popper 1902–

Austrian-born philosopher

10 I shall certainly admit a system as empirical or scientific only if it is capable of being *tested* by experience. These considerations suggest that not the *verifiability* but the *falsifiability* of a system is to be taken as a criterion of demarcation ... *It must be possible for an empirical scientific system to be refuted by experience.*

> *The Logic of Scientific Discovery* (1934) ch. 1, sect. 6

11 We may become the makers of our fate when we have ceased to pose as its prophets.

> *The Open Society and its Enemies* (1945) introduction

12 We must plan for freedom, and not only for security, if for no other reason than that only freedom can make security secure.

> *The Open Society and its Enemies* (1945) vol. 2, ch. 21

13 There is no history of mankind, there are only many histories of all kinds of aspects of human life. And one of these is the history of political power. This is elevated into the history of the world.

> *The Open Society and its Enemies* (1945) vol. 2, ch. 25

14 Piecemeal social engineering resembles physical engineering in regarding the *ends* as beyond the province of technology.

> *The Poverty of Historicism* (1957) pt. 3, sect. 21

15 Science must begin with myths, and with the criticism of myths.

> 'The Philosophy of Science' in C. A. Mace (ed.) *British Philosophy in the Mid-Century* (1957)

16 On the pre-scientific level we hate the very idea that we may be mistaken. So we cling dogmatically to our conjectures, as long as possible. On the scientific level, we systematically search for our mistakes ... Thus on the pre-scientific level, we are often ourselves destroyed, eliminated, with our false theories; we perish with our false theories. On the scientific level, we systematically try to eliminate our false theories—we try to let our false theories die in our stead.

> In B. Magee (ed.) *Modern British Philosophy* (1971) 'Conversation with Karl Popper'

17 But spectacles have a *function*, and they function only when you put them on, to look through them *at the world*. It is the same with language. That is to say, one shouldn't waste one's life in spectacle-cleaning or in talking about language, or in trying to get a clear view of our language, or of 'our conceptual scheme'. The fundamental thing about human languages is that they can and should be used to describe something; and this something is, somehow, the world.

> In B. Magee (ed.) *Modern British Philosophy* (1971) 'Discussion among Karl Popper, Peter Strawson and Geoffrey Warnock'

Cole Porter 1891–1964

American songwriter

18 In olden days a glimpse of stocking
Was looked on as something shocking
Now, heaven knows,
Anything goes.

> *Anything Goes* (1934) title song

19 I get no kick from champagne,
Mere alcohol doesn't thrill me at all,
So tell me why should it be true
That I get a kick out of you?

> *Anything Goes* (1934) 'I Get a Kick Out of You'

20 You're the top! You're the Coliseum,
You're the top! You're the Louvre Museum,
You're a melody
From a symphony by Strauss,
You're a Bendel bonnet,
A Shakespeare sonnet,
You're Mickey Mouse!

> *Anything Goes* (1934) 'You're the Top'

21 When they begin the Beguine
It brings back the sound of music so tender,
It brings back a night of tropical splendour,
It brings back a memory ever green.

> 'Begin the Beguine' (1935 song)

22 When you're near there's such an air of spring about it;
I can hear a lark somewhere begin to sing about it;
There's no love song finer,
But how strange the change from major to minor
Every time we say goodbye.

> 'Every Time We Say Goodbye' (1944 song)

23 Night and day, you are the one,
Only you beneath the moon and under the sun.

> *Gay Divorce* (1932) 'Night and Day'

1 So goodbye dear, and Amen,
Here's hoping we meet now and then,
It was great fun,
But it was just one of those things.
'Just One of Those Things' (1935 song)

2 Birds do it, bees do it,
Even educated fleas do it.
Let's do it, let's fall in love.
'Let's Do It' (1954 song; words added to the 1928
original)

3 Miss Otis regrets (she's unable to lunch today).
Title of song (1934)

4 My heart belongs to Daddy.
Title of song (1938)

5 Have you heard it's in the stars,
Next July we collide with Mars?
Well, did you evah! What a swell party this is.
'Well, Did You Evah?' (1940 song; revived for the film
High Society, 1956)

Beilby Porteus 1731–1808
English poet and prelate

6 . . . One murder made a villain,
Millions a hero.
Death (1759) l. 154. Cf. Rostand 548:1

7 War its thousands slays, Peace its ten thousands.
Death (1759) l. 179

8   Teach him how to live,
And, oh! still harder lesson! how to die.
Death (1759) l. 319

Francis Pott 1832–1909
English clergyman

9 The strife is o'er, the battle done;
Now is the Victor's triumph won;
O let the song of praise be sung:
Alleluia!
'The strife is o'er, the battle done' (1861 hymn);
translation of 'Finita iam sunt praelia'
(c.1695)

Beatrix Potter 1866–1943
English writer for children

10 In the time of swords and periwigs and full-
skirted coats with flowered lappets—when gentlemen wore ruffles, and gold-laced waistcoats of
paduasoy and taffeta—there lived a tailor in
Gloucester.
The Tailor of Gloucester (1903) p. 9

11 I am worn to a ravelling . . . I am undone and worn to
a thread-paper, for I have NO MORE TWIST.
The Tailor of Gloucester (1903) p. 22

12 It is said that the effect of eating too much lettuce is
'soporific'.
The Tale of the Flopsy Bunnies (1909) p. 9

13 Don't go into Mr McGregor's garden: your father had
an accident there, he was put into a pie by Mrs
McGregor.
The Tale of Peter Rabbit (1902) p. 10

Henry Codman Potter
1835–1908
Bishop of New York from 1887

14 We have exchanged the Washingtonian dignity for the
Jeffersonian simplicity, which was, in truth, only
another name for the Jacksonian vulgarity.
Bishop Potter's Address (1890) p. 12 (30 April 1889)

Stephen Potter 1900–69
British writer

15 A good general rule is to state that the bouquet is
better than the taste, and vice versa.
One-Upmanship (1952) ch. 14 (on wine-tasting)

16 How to be one up—how to make the other man feel
that something has gone wrong, however slightly.
Lifemanship (1950) p. 14

17 Each of us can, by ploy or gambit, most naturally gain
the advantage.
Lifemanship (1950) p. 15

18 'Yes, but not in the South', with slight adjustments,
will do for any argument about any place, if not about
any person.
Lifemanship (1950) p. 43

19 If you have nothing to say, or, rather, something
extremely stupid and obvious, say it, but in a
'plonking' tone of voice—i.e. roundly, but hollowly
and dogmatically.
Lifemanship (1950) p. 43

20 In Newstatesmanship . . . definite pros and cons are
barred: and they are difficult, anyway, because
pro-ing and conning is never the best way of going
one better.
Lifemanship (1950) p. 73

21 The theory and practice of gamesmanship or
The art of winning games without actually
cheating.
Title of book (1947)

Eugène Pottier 1816–87

French politician

1 *Debout! les damnés de la terre!*
Debout! les forçats de la faim!
La raison tonne en son cratère,
C'est l'éruption de la fin . . .
Nous ne sommes rien, soyons tout!
C'est la lutte finale
Groupons-nous, et, demain,
L'Internationale
Sera le genre humain.

On your feet, you damned souls of the earth! On your feet, inmates of hunger's prison! Reason is rumbling in its crater, and its final eruption is on its way . . . We are nothing, let us be everything! This is the final conflict: let us form up and, tomorrow, the International will encompass the human race.

'L'Internationale' in H. E. Piggot *Songs that made History* (1937) ch. 6

Ezra Pound 1885–1972

American poet

2 Winter is icummen in,
Lhude sing Goddamm,
Raineth drop and staineth slop,
And how the wind doth ramm!
Sing: Goddamm.

'Ancient Music' (1917). Cf. Anonymous 18:6

3 With *Usura*
With usura hath no man a house of good stone
each block cut smooth and well fitting.

Cantos (1954) no. 45

4 Usura slayeth the child in the womb
It stayeth the young man's courting
It hath brought palsey to bed, lyeth
between the young bride and her bridegroom
CONTRA NATURAM
They have brought whores for Eleusis
Corpses are set to banquet
at behest of usura.

Cantos (1954) no. 45

5 Tching prayed on the mountain and
wrote MAKE IT NEW
on his bath tub.
Day by day make it new
cut underbrush,
pile the logs
keep it growing.

Cantos (1954) no. 53

6 Bah! I have sung women in three cities,
But it is all the same;
And I will sing of the sun.

'Cino' (1908)

7 Hang it all, Robert Browning,
There can be but the one 'Sordello'.

Draft of XXX Cantos (1930) no. 2

8 In the gloom, the gold gathers the light against it.

Draft of XXX Cantos (1930) no. 11

9 And even I can remember
A day when the historians left blanks in their
writings,
I mean for things they didn't know.

Draft of XXX Cantos (1930) no. 13

10 And she is dying piece-meal
of a sort of emotional anaemia.

And round about there is a rabble
of the filthy, sturdy, unkillable infants of the very
poor.

'The Garden' (1916)

11 For three years, out of key with his time,
He strove to resuscitate the dead art
Of poetry; to maintain 'the sublime'
In the old sense. Wrong from the start—

No, hardly, but seeing he had been born
In a half-savage country, out of date;
Bent resolutely on wringing lilies from the acorns;
Capaneus; trout for factitious bait.

Hugh Selwyn Mauberley (1920) 'E. P. Ode pour l'élection de son sépulcre' pt. 1

12 His true Penelope was Flaubert,
He fished by obstinate isles;
Observed the elegance of Circe's hair
Rather than the mottoes on sundials.

Hugh Selwyn Mauberley (1920) 'E. P. Ode . . . ' pt. 1

13 The age demanded an image
Of its accelerated grimace,
Something for the modern stage,
Not, at any rate, an Attic grace;
Not, not certainly, the obscure reveries
Of the inward gaze;
Better mendacities
Than the classics in paraphrase!

Hugh Selwyn Mauberley (1920) 'E. P. Ode . . . ' pt. 2

14 The tea-rose tea-gown, etc.
Supplants the mousseline of Cos,
The pianola 'replaces'
Sappho's barbitos.

Christ follows Dionysus,
Phallic and ambrosial
Made way for macerations;
Caliban casts out Ariel.

All things are a flowing,
Sage Heracleitus says;
But a tawdry cheapness
Shall outlast our days.

Even the Christian beauty
Defects—after Samothrace;
We see τὸ καλόν
Decreed in the market place.

Hugh Selwyn Mauberley (1920) 'E. P. Ode . . . ' pt. 3

15 O bright Apollo,
τίν' ἄνδρα, τίν' ἥρωα, τίνα θεόν,
What god, man, or hero
Shall I place a tin wreath upon!

Hugh Selwyn Mauberley (1920) 'E. P. Ode . . . ' pt. 3

1 Some quick to arm,
some for adventure,
some from fear of weakness,
some from fear of censure,
some for love of slaughter, in imagination,
learning later . . .
some in fear, learning love of slaughter;

Died some, pro patria,
non 'dulce' non 'et decor' . . .
walked eye-deep in hell
believing in old men's lies, the unbelieving
came home, home to a lie.
  Hugh Selwyn Mauberley (1920) 'E. P. *Ode* . . . ' pt. 4

2 hysterias, trench confessions,
laughter out of dead bellies.
  Hugh Selwyn Mauberley (1920) 'E. P. *Ode* . . . ' pt. 4

3 There died a myriad,
And of the best, among them,
For an old bitch gone in the teeth,
For a botched civilization,

Charm, smiling at the good mouth,
Quick eyes gone under earth's lid,

For two gross of broken statues,
For a few thousand battered books.
  Hugh Selwyn Mauberley (1920) 'E. P. *Ode* . . . ' pt. 5

4 The tip's a good one, as for literature
It gives no man a sinecure.

And no one knows, at sight, a masterpiece.
And give up verse, my boy,
There's nothing in it.
  Hugh Selwyn Mauberley (1920) 'Mr Nixon'

5 The apparition of these faces in the crowd;
Petals on a wet, black bough.
  'In a Station of the Metro' (1916)

6 O woe, woe,
People are born and die,
We also shall be dead pretty soon
Therefore let us act as if we were dead already.
  Mr Housman's Message (1911)

7 The ant's a centaur in his dragon world.
Pull down thy vanity, it is not man
Made courage, or made order, or made grace,
Pull down thy vanity, I say pull down.
Learn of the green world what can be thy place
In scaled invention or true artistry,
Pull down thy vanity,
Paquin pull down!
The green casque has outdone your elegance.
  Pisan Cantos (1948) no. 81

8 Pull down thy vanity
Thou art a beaten dog beneath the hail,
A swollen magpie in a fitful sun,
Half black half white
Nor knowst'ou wing from tail
Pull down thy vanity,
Paquin, pull down!
The green casque has outdone your elegance.
  Pisan Cantos (1948) no. 81

9 Haie! Haie!
These were the swift to harry;
These were the keen-scented;
These were the souls of blood.

Slow on the leash,
pallid the leash-men!
  'The Return' (1912)

10 The leaves fall early this autumn, in wind.
The paired butterflies are already yellow with August
Over the grass in the West garden;
They hurt me. I grow older.
If you are coming down through the narrows of the
    river Kiang,
Please let me know beforehand,
And I will come out to meet you
As far as Cho-fu-sa.
  'The River Merchant's Wife' (1915); from the Chinese of
  Rihaku

11 He hath not heart for harping, nor in ring-having
Nor winsomeness to wife, nor world's delight
Nor any whit else save the wave's slash,
Yet longing comes upon him to fare forth on the
    water.
Bosque takes blossom, cometh beauty of berries,
Fields to fairness, land fares brisker,
All this admonisheth man eager of mood,
The heart turns to travel so that he then thinks
On flood-ways to be far departing.
Cuckoo calleth with gloomy crying,
He singeth summerward, bodeth sorrow,
The bitter heart's blood.
  'The Seafarer' (1912); from the Anglo-Saxon original

12 I had over-prepared the event,
that much was ominous.
With middle-ageing care
I had laid out just the right books.
I had almost turned down the pages.
  'Villanelle: the psychological hour' (1916)

13 The author's conviction on this day of New Year is
that music begins to atrophy when it departs too far
from the dance; that poetry begins to atrophy when it
gets too far from music.
  The ABC of Reading (1934) 'Warning'

14 Any general statement is like a cheque drawn on
a bank. Its value depends on what is there to meet it.
  The ABC of Reading (1934) ch. 1

15 Literature is news that STAYS news.
  The ABC of Reading (1934) ch. 2

16 Real education must ultimately be limited to one who
INSISTS on knowing, the rest is mere sheep-herding.
  The ABC of Reading (1934) ch. 8

17 Great literature is simply language charged with
meaning to the utmost possible degree.
  How To Read (1931) pt. 2

18 Artists are the antennae of the race, but the
bullet-headed many will never learn to trust their
great artists.
  Literary Essays (1954)'Henry James'

19 Poetry must be *as well written as prose*.
  Letter to Harriet Monroe, January 1915, in D. D. Paige
  (ed.) *Selected Letters of Ezra Pound* (1950) p. 48

1 Objectivity and again objectivity, and expression: no hindside-before-ness, no straddled adjectives (as 'addled mosses dank'), no Tennysonianness of speech; nothing—nothing that you couldn't, in some circumstance, in the stress of some emotion, actually say.
   Letter to Harriet Monroe, January 1915, in D. D. Paige (ed.) *Selected Letters of Ezra Pound* (1950) p. 48

Anthony Powell 1905–

English novelist

2 He fell in love with himself at first sight and it is a passion to which he has always remained faithful.
   The Acceptance World (1955) ch. 1

3 Dinner at the Huntercombes' possessed 'only two dramatic features—the wine was a farce and the food a tragedy'.
   The Acceptance World (1955) ch. 4

4 Books do furnish a room.
   Title of novel (1971). Cf. Smith 653:10

5 Parents—especially step-parents—are sometimes a bit of a disappointment to their children. They don't fufil the promise of their early years.
   A Buyer's Market (1952) ch. 2

6 A dance to the music of time.
   Title of novel sequence (1951–75), after *Le 4 stagioni che ballano al suono del tempo* (title given by Giovanni Pietro Bellori to a painting by Nicolas Poussin)

7 He's so wet you could shoot snipe off him.
   A Question of Upbringing (1951) ch. 1

8 Growing old is like being increasingly penalized for a crime you haven't committed.
   Temporary Kings (1973) ch. 1

Enoch Powell 1912–

British Conservative politician

9 History is littered with the wars which everybody knew would never happen.
   Speech to the Conservative Party Conference, 19 October 1967, in *The Times* 20 October 1967

10 As I look ahead, I am filled with foreboding. Like the Roman, I seem to see 'the River Tiber foaming with much blood'.
   Speech at the Annual Meeting of the West Midlands Area Conservative Political Centre, Birmingham, 20 April 1968, in *Observer* 21 April 1968. Cf. Virgil 713:10

Sir John Powell 1645–1713

English judge

11 Let us consider the reason of the case. For nothing is law that is not reason.
   Lord Raymond's *Reports* (1765) vol. 2, p. 911

John O'Connor Power b. 1846

Irish lawyer and politician

12 The mules of politics: without pride of ancestry, or hope of posterity.
   Of the Liberal Unionists, in H. H. Asquith *Memories and Reflections* (1928) vol. 1, ch. 16

Winthrop Mackworth Praed 1802–39

English writer of humorous verse

13 Of science and logic he chatters
   As fine and as fast as he can;
   Though I am no judge of such matters,
   I'm sure he's a talented man.
   'The Talented Man'

Keith Preston 1884–1927

American poet

14 Of all the literary scenes
   Saddest this sight to me:
   The graves of little magazines
   Who died to make verse free.
   'The Liberators'

Jacques Prévert 1900–77

French poet and screenwriter

15 *C'est tellement simple, l'amour.*
   Love is so simple.
   Les Enfants du Paradis (1945 film)

16 *Notre Père qui êtes aux cieux*
   Restez-y
   Et nous nous resterons sur la terre
   Qui est quelquefois si jolie.
   Our Father which art in heaven
   Stay there
   And we will stay on earth
   Which is sometimes so pretty.
   'Pater Noster' (1949)

Richard Price 1723–91

English nonconformist minister

17 Now, methinks, I see the ardour for liberty catching and spreading; a general amendment beginning in human affairs; the dominion of kings changed for the dominion of laws, and the dominion of priests giving way to the dominion of reason and conscience.
   A Discourse on the Love of our Country (1790) p. 49

J. B. Priestley 1894–1984

English novelist, playwright, and critic

18 To say that these men paid their shillings to watch twenty-two hirelings kick a ball is merely to say that a violin is wood and catgut, that *Hamlet* is so much paper and ink. For a shilling the Bruddersford United AFC offered you Conflict and Art.
   Good Companions (1929) bk. 1, ch. 1

19 I can't help feeling wary when I hear anything said about the masses. First you take their faces from 'em by calling 'em the masses and then you accuse 'em of not having any faces.
   Saturn Over the Water (1961) ch. 2

1 This little steamer, like all her brave and battered sisters, is immortal. She'll go sailing proudly down the years in the epic of Dunkirk. And our great-grand-children, when they learn how we began this war by snatching glory out of defeat, and then swept on to victory, may also learn how the little holiday steamers made an excursion to hell and came back glorious.

> Radio broadcast, 5 June 1940, in *Listener* 13 June 1940

2 God can stand being told by Professor Ayer and Marghanita Laski that He doesn't exist.

> In *Listener* 1 July 1965, p. 12

Joseph Priestley 1733–1804

English nonconformist minister

3 Every man, when he comes to be sensible of his natural rights, and to feel his own importance, will consider himself as fully equal to any other person whatever.

> *An Essay on the First Principles of Government* (1768) pt. 1

Matthew Prior 1664–1721

English poet

4 I court others in verse: but I love thee in prose:
And they have my whimsies, but thou hast my heart.
> 'A Better Answer' (1718)

5 Be to her virtues very kind;
Be to her faults a little blind;
Let all her ways be unconfined;
And clap your padlock—on her mind.
> 'An English Padlock' (1705) l. 79

6 Nobles and heralds, by your leave,
Here lies what once was Matthew Prior,
The son of Adam and of Eve,
Can Stuart or Nassau go higher?
> 'Epitaph' (1702)

7 For the idiom of words very little she heeded,
Provided the matter she drove at succeeded,
She took and gave languages just as she needed.
> 'Jinny the Just' (after 1700)

8 Venus, take my votive glass;
Since I am not what I was,
What from this day I shall be,
Venus, let me never see.
> 'The Lady who Offers her Looking-Glass to Venus' (1718)

9 The merchant, to secure his treasure,
Conveys it in a borrowed name:
Euphelia serves to grace my measure;
But Chloe is my real flame.
> 'An Ode' (1709)

10 He ranged his tropes, and preached up patience;
Backed his opinion with quotations.
> 'Paulo Purganti and his Wife' (1709) l. 138

11 Cured yesterday of my disease,
I died last night of my physician.
> 'The Remedy Worse than the Disease' (1727)

12 What is a King?—a man condemned to bear
The public burden of the nation's care.
> *Solomon* (1718) bk. 3, l. 275

13 For, as our different ages move,
'Tis so ordained (would Fate but mend it!)
That I shall be past making love,
When she begins to comprehend it.
> 'To a Child of Quality of Five Years Old' (1704)

14 From ignorance our comfort flows,
The only wretched are the wise.
> 'To the Hon. Charles Montague' (1692) st. 9. Cf. Gray 316:3

15 No, no; for my virginity,
When I lose that, says Rose, I'll die:
Behind the elms last night, cried Dick,
Rose, were you not extremely sick?
> 'A True Maid' (1718)

16 They never taste who always drink;
They always talk, who never think.
> 'Upon this Passage in Scaligerana' (1740)

V. S. Pritchett 1900–

English writer and critic

17 The principle of procrastinated rape is said to be the ruling one in all the great best-sellers.
> *The Living Novel* (1946) 'Clarissa'

18 What Chekhov saw in our failure to communicate was something positive and precious: the private silence in which we live, and which enables us to endure our own solitude. We live, as his characters do, beyond any tale we happen to enact.
> *Myth Makers* (1979) 'Chekhov, a doctor'

19 The detective novel is the art-for-art's-sake of our yawning Philistinism, the classic example of a specialized form of art removed from contact with the life it pretends to build on.
> *New Statesman* 16 June 1951 'Books in General'

Adelaide Ann Procter 1825–64

English writer of popular verse

20 Seated one day at the organ,
I was weary and ill at ease,
And my fingers wandered idly
Over the noisy keys.
> 'A Lost Chord' (1858)

21 But I struck one chord of music,
Like the sound of a great Amen.
> 'A Lost Chord' (1858)

Propertius c.50–after 16 BC

Roman poet

22 *Navita de ventis, de tauris narrat arator,*
Enumerat miles vulnera, pastor oves.

The seaman tells stories of winds, the ploughman of bulls; the soldier details his wounds, the shepherd his sheep.
> *Elegies* bk. 2, no. 1, l. 43

1 *Quod si deficiant vires, audacia certe*
Laus erit: in magnis et voluisse sat est.

Even if strength fail, boldness at least will deserve praise: in great endeavours even to have had the will is enough.
Elegies bk. 2, no. 10, l. 5

2 *Cedite Romani scriptores, cedite Grai!*
Nescioquid maius nascitur Iliade.

Make way, you Roman writers, make way, Greeks! Something greater than the Iliad is born.
Elegies bk. 2, no. 34, l. 65 (of Virgil's *Aeneid*)

Protagoras b. c.485 BC
Greek sophist

3 Πάντων χρημάτων ἄνθρωπον μέτρον εἶναι.

[That] man is the measure of all things.
In Plato *Theaetetus* 160d

Pierre-Joseph Proudhon 1809–65
French social reformer

4 *La propriété c'est le vol.*

Property is theft.
Qu'est-ce que la propriété? (1840) ch. 1

Marcel Proust 1871–1922
French novelist

Textual translations are those of C. K. Scott-Moncrieff and S. Hudson, revised by T. Kilmartin, 1981

5 *A la recherche du temps perdu.*

In search of lost time.
Title of novel (1913–27, translated by C. K. Scott-Moncrieff and S. Hudson, 1922–31, as 'Remembrance of things past')

6 *Longtemps, je me suis couché de bonne heure.*

For a long time I used to go to bed early.
Du côté de chez Swann (Swann's Way, 1913) vol. 1, p. 1

7 *Et tout d'un coup le souvenir m'est apparu. Ce goût c'était celui du petit morceau de madeleine que le dimanche matin à Combray ... ma tante Léonie m'offrait après l'avoir trempé dans son infusion de thé ou de tilleul.*

And suddenly the memory revealed itself. The taste was that of the little piece of madeleine which on Sunday mornings at Combray ... my aunt Léonie used to give me, dipping it first in her own cup of tea or tisane.
Du côté de chez Swann (Swann's Way, 1913) vol. 1, p. 61

8 *Et il ne fut plus question de Swann chez les Verdurin.*

After which there was no more talk of Swann at the Verdurins'.
Du côté de chez Swann (Swann's Way, 1913) vol. 2, p. 99

9 *Dire que j'ai gâché des années de ma vie, que j'ai voulu mourir, que j'ai eu mon plus grand amour, pour une femme qui ne me plaisait pas, qui n'était pas mon genre!*

To think that I've wasted years of my life, that I've longed to die, that I've experienced my greatest love for a woman who didn't appeal to me, who wasn't even my type!
Du côté de chez Swann (Swann's Way, 1913) vol. 2, p. 228

10 *On devient moral dès qu'on est malheureux.*

One becomes moral as soon as one is unhappy.
A l'ombre des jeunes filles en fleurs (Within a Budding Grove, 1918) vol. 1, p. 290

11 *Tout ce que nous connaissons de grand nous vient des nerveux. Ce sont eux et non pas d'autres qui ont fondé les religions et composé les chefs-d'œuvre. Jamais le monde ne saura tout ce qu'il leur doit et surtout ce qu'eux ont souffert pour le lui donner.*

Everything we think of as great has come to us from neurotics. It is they and they alone who found religions and create great works of art. The world will never realise how much it owes to them and what they have suffered in order to bestow their gifts on it.
Le Côté de Guermantes (Guermantes Way, 1921) vol. 1, p. 418

12 *Il n'y a rien comme le désir pour empêcher les choses qu'on dit d'avoir aucune ressemblance avec ce qu'on a dans la pensée.*

There is nothing like desire for preventing the things one says from bearing any resemblance to what one has in one's mind.
Le Côté de Guermantes (Guermantes Way, 1921) vol. 2, p. 60

13 *Un artiste n'a pas besoin d'exprimer directement sa pensée dans son ouvrage pour que celui-ci en reflète la qualité; on a même pu dire que la louange la plus haute de Dieu est dans la négation de l'athée qui trouve la Création assez parfaite pour se passer d'un créateur.*

An artist has no need to express his thought directly in his work for the latter to reflect its quality; it has even been said that the highest praise of God consists in the denial of Him by the atheist who finds creation so perfect that it can dispense with a creator.
Le Côté de Guermantes (Guermantes Way, 1921) vol. 2, p. 147

14 *Du reste, continua Mme de Cambremer, j'ai horreur des couchers de soleil, c'est romantique, c'est opéra.*

'Anyhow,' Mme de Cambremer went on, 'I have a horror of sunsets, they're so romantic, so operatic.'
Sodome et Gomorrhe (Cities of the Plain, 1922) vol. 1, p. 296

15 *Une de ces dépêches dont M. de Guermantes avait spirituellement fixé le modèle: 'Impossible venir, mensonge suit'.*

One of those telegrams of which M. de Guermantes had wittily fixed the formula: 'Cannot come, lie follows'.
Le Temps retrouvé (Time Regained, 1926) ch. 1, p. 7. Cf. Beresford 65:4

16 *Les vrais paradis sont les paradis qu'on a perdus.*

The true paradises are the paradises that we have lost.
Le Temps retrouvé (Time Regained, 1926) ch. 3, p. 215

17 *Le bonheur seul est salutaire pour le corps, mais c'est le chagrin qui développe les forces de l'esprit.*

For if unhappiness develops the forces of the mind, happiness alone is salutary to the body.
Le Temps retrouvé (Time Regained, 1926) ch. 3, p. 259

Publilius Syrus

Writer of Latin mimes in the 1st century BC

1 *Formosa facies muta commendatio est.*

A beautiful face is a mute recommendation.

Sententiae no. 199, in J. and A. Duff *Minor Latin Poets* (Loeb ed., 1934); translated by Thomas Tenison in *Baconiana* (1679) 'Ornamenta Rationalia' no. 12

2 *Inopi beneficium bis dat qui dat celeriter.*

He gives the poor man twice as much good who gives quickly.

Sententiae no. 274, in J. and A. Duff *Minor Latin Poets* (proverbially '*Bis dat qui cito dat* [He gives twice who gives soon]')

3 *Iudex damnatur ubi nocens absolvitur.*

The judge is condemned when the guilty party is acquitted.

Sententiae no. 296, in J. and A. Duff *Minor Latin Poets*

4 *Necessitas dat legem non ipsa accipit.*

Necessity gives the law without itself acknowledging one.

Sententiae no. 444, in J. and A. Duff *Minor Latin Poets* (proverbially '*Necessitas non habet legem* [Necessity has no law]')

John Pudney 1909–77

English poet and writer

5 Do not despair
For Johnny-head-in-air;
He sleeps as sound
As Johnny underground.
Fetch out no shroud
For Johnny-in-the-cloud;
And keep your tears
For him in after years.
Better by far
For Johnny-the-bright-star,
To keep your head,
And see his children fed.

'For Johnny' (1942)

William Pulteney, Earl of Bath 1684–1764

6 For Sir Ph—p well knows
That innuendos
Will serve him no longer in verse or in prose,
Since twelve honest men have decided the cause,
And were judges of fact, tho' not judges of laws.

'The Honest Jury' (1729) st. 3 (on Sir Philip Yorke's unsuccessful prosecution of *The Craftsman*, 1729)

Punch 1841–1992

English humorous weekly periodical

7 Advice to persons about to marry.—'Don't.'
vol. 8, p. 1 (1845)

8 You pays your money and you takes your choice.
vol. 10, p. 17 (1846)

9 The Half-Way House to Rome, Oxford.
vol. 16, p. 36 (1849)

10 What is better than presence of mind in a railway accident? Absence of body.
vol. 16, p. 231 (1849)

11 Never do to-day what you can put off till to-morrow.
vol. 17, p. 241 (1849)

12 Who's 'im, Bill?
A stranger!
'Eave 'arf a brick at 'im.
vol. 26, p. 82 (1854)

13 What is Matter?—Never mind.
What is Mind?—No matter.
vol. 29, p. 19 (1855)

14 It ain't the 'unting as 'urts 'im, it's the 'ammer, 'ammer, 'ammer along the 'ard 'igh road.
vol. 30, p. 218 (1856)

15 Mun, a had na' been the-erre abune two hours when—*bang*—went saxpence!!!
vol. 54, p. 235 (1868)

16 Cats is 'dogs' and rabbits is 'dogs' and so's Parrats, but this 'ere 'Tortis' is a insect, and there ain't no charge for it.
vol. 56, p. 96 (1869)

17 Nothink for nothink 'ere, and precious little for sixpence.
vol. 57, p. 152 (1869)

18 Sure, the next train has gone ten minutes ago.
vol. 60, p. 206 (1871)

19 It appears the Americans have taken umbrage.
The deuce they have!
Whereabouts is that?
vol. 63, p. 189 (1872)

20 Go directly—see what she's doing, and tell her she mustn't.
vol. 63, p. 202 (1872)

21 There was one poor tiger that hadn't *got* a Christian.
vol. 68, p. 143 (1875)

22 There was an old owl lived in an oak
The more he heard, the less he spoke;
The less he spoke, the more he heard
O, if men were all like that wise bird!
vol. 68, p. 155 (1875)

23 It's worse than wicked, my dear, it's vulgar.
Almanac (1876)

24 I never read books—I *write* them.
vol. 74, p. 210 (1878). Cf. Disraeli 249:9

25 I am not hungry; but thank goodness, I am greedy.
vol. 75, p. 290 (1878)

26 BISHOP: Who is it that sees and hears all we do, and before whom even I am but as a crushed worm?
PAGE: The Missus, my Lord.
vol. 79, p. 63 (1880)

27 Ah whiles hae ma doobts aboot the meenister.
vol. 79, p. 275 (1880)

1 What sort of a doctor is he?
Oh, well, I don't know very much about his ability;
but he's got a very good bedside manner!
vol. 86, p. 121 (1884)

2 I used your soap two years ago; since then I have
used no other.
vol. 86, p. 197 (1884)

3 Don't look at me, Sir, with—ah—in that tone of
voice.
vol. 87, p. 38 (1884)

4 WIFE OF TWO YEARS' STANDING: Oh yes! I'm sure
he's not so fond of me as at first. He's away so
much, neglects me dreadfully, and he's so cross
when he comes home. What *shall* I do?
WIDOW: Feed the brute!
vol. 89, p. 206 (1885)

5 Nearly all our best men are dead! Carlyle, Tennyson,
Browning, George Eliot!—I'm not feeling very well
myself.
vol. 104, p. 210 (1893)

6 Botticelli isn't a wine, you Juggins! Botticelli's a
cheese!
vol. 106, p. 270 (1894)

7 I'm afraid you've got a bad egg, Mr Jones.
Oh no, my Lord, I assure you! Parts of it are
excellent!
vol. 109, p. 222 (1895)

8 Look here, Steward, if this is coffee, I want tea; but if
this is tea, then I wish for coffee.
vol. 123, p. 44 (1902)

9 Sometimes I sits and thinks, and then again I just sits.
vol. 131, p. 297 (1906)

Alexander Pushkin 1799–1837

Russian poet

10   в присутствии луны
Как легкий бег саней с подругой быстр и волен,
Когда под соболем, согрета и свежа,
Она вам руку жмет, пылая и дрожа!

How smoothly, rapidly, and freely the sleigh glides in
the moonlight when you are with a friend and when,
warm and fresh beneath her sable fur, flushed and
trembling, she squeezes your hand.
'Autumn' (1833) st. 2 (translated by Dmitri Obolensky)

11 Мчатся тучи, вьются тучи;
Невидимкою луна
Освещает снег летучий;
Мутно небо, ночь мутна.

Storm-clouds whirl and storm-clouds scurry;
From behind them pale moonlight
Flickers where the snowflakes hurry.
Dark the sky and dark the night.
'Devils' (1830) (translated by C. M. Bowra)

12   Рукой пристрастной
Прими собранье пестрых глав . . .
Ума холодных наблюдений
И сердца горестных замет.

              Look with favour
Upon the chapters in your hand . . .
The mind's reflections coldly noted,
The bitter insights of the heart.
Eugene Onegin (1833) 'Dedication' (translated by Babette
Deutsch)

13 Что знал он тверже всех наук,
Что было для него измлада . . .
Была наука страсти нежной.

From early youth his dedication
Was to a single occupation . . .
The science of the tender passion.
Eugene Onegin (1833) ch. 1, st. 8 (translated by Babette
Deutsch)

14 Быть можно дельным человеком
И думать о красе ногтей:
К чему бесплодно спорить с веком?
Обычай деспот меж людей.

A man of sense, I am conceding,
Can pay attention to his nails;
Why should one quarrel with good breeding?
With some folk, custom's rule prevails.
Eugene Onegin (1833) ch. 1, st. 25 (translated by Babette
Deutsch)

15 Чем меньше женщину мы любим,
Тем легче нравимся мы ей,
И тем ее вернее губим
Средь обольстительных сетей.

A woman's love for us increases
The less we love her, sooth to say—
She stoops, she falls, her struggling ceases;
Caught fast, she cannot get away.
Eugene Onegin (1833) ch. 4, st. 1 (translated by Babette
Deutsch)

16 Уж небо осенью дышало,
Уж реже солнышко блистало,
Короче становился день,
Лесов таинственная сень
С печальным шумом обнажалась,
Ложился на поля туман,
Гусей крикливых караван
Тянулся к югу: приближалась
Довольно скучная пора;
Стоял ноябрь уж у двора.

The sky breathed autumn, sombre, shrouded;
Shorter and shorter grew the days;
Sad murmurs filled the woodland ways
As the dark coverts were denuded;
Now southward swept the caravan
Of the wild geese, a noisy clan;
And mists above the meadows brooded;
A tedious season they await
Who hear November at the gate.
Eugene Onegin (1833) ch. 4, st. 40 (translated by Babette
Deutsch)

1 Москва ... как много в этом звуке
Для сердца русского слилось!

Moscow: those syllables can start
A tumult in the Russian heart.

Eugene Onegin (1833) ch. 7, st. 36 (translated by Babette Deutsch)

2 Пора, мой друг, пора! покоя сердце просит —
Летят за днями дни, и каждый час уносит
Частичку бытия, а мы с тобой вдвоем
Предполагаем жить ... И глядь — как раз —
умрем.

It's time, my dear, it's time! The heart demands its quittance—
As day flies after day and each bears off its pittance
Withdrawn from living's store and meanwhile you and I
Draw up our plans to live ... And then, why then, we'll die.

'It's Time' (1834) (translated by Alan Myers)

3 ... Лишь божественный глагол
До слуха чуткого коснется,
Душа поэта встрепенется,
Как пробудившийся орел.

No sooner does the divine word touch his keen hearing than the poet's soul starts like an eagle that has been roused.

'The Poet' (1827) (translated by Dmitri Obolensky)

4 У лукоморья дуб зеленый;
Златая цепь на дубе том.

A green oak grows by a curving shore;
And round that oak hangs a golden chain.

Ruslan and Lyudmila (1820) 'Prologue' (translated by Elisaveta Fen)

5 Когда для смертного умолкнет шумный день
И на немые стогны града
Полупрозрачная наляжет ночи тень
И сон, дневных трудов награда,
В то время для меня влачатся в тишине
Часы томительного бденья.

When trade and traffic and all the noise of town
Is dimmed, and on the streets and squares
The filmy curtain of the night sinks down
With sleep, the recompense of cares,
To me the darkness brings not sleep nor rest.

'Remembrances' (1828) (translated by R. M. Hewitt)

Israel Putnam 1718–90
American general

6 Men, you are all marksmen—don't one of you fire until you see the white of their eyes.

At Bunker Hill, 1775, in R. Frothingham *History of the Siege of Boston* (1873) ch. 5 n. (also attributed to William Prescott, 1726–95)

Mario Puzo 1920–
American novelist

7 I'll make him an offer he can't refuse.

The Godfather (1969) ch. 1

8 A lawyer with his briefcase can steal more than a hundred men with guns.

The Godfather (1969) ch. 1

Barbara Pym 1913–80
English novelist

9 Yes, it seems suitable that things like that should go on in London ... It is better taste somehow that a man should be unfaithful to his wife away from home.

Jane and Prudence (1953) ch. 7

10 She experienced all the cosiness and irritation which can come from living with thoroughly nice people with whom one has nothing in common.

Less than Angels (1955) ch. 23

11 What is the future of my kind of writing? ... Perhaps in retirement ... a quieter, narrower kind of life can be worked out and adopted. Bounded by English literature and the Anglican Church and small pleasures like sewing and choosing dress material for this uncertain summer.

Diary, 6 March 1972, in Hazel Holt and Hilary Pym (eds.) *A Very Private Life* (1985) p. 373 (on having a novel rejected)

Pyrrhus 319–272 BC
King of Epirus from 306 BC

12 ἂν ἔτι μίαν μάχην 'Ρωμαίους νικήσωμεν, ἀπολούμεθα παντελῶς.

One more such victory and we are lost.

On defeating the Romans at Asculum, 279 BC, in Plutarch *Parallel Lives* 'Pyrrhus' ch. 21, sect. 9

Francis Quarles 1592–1644
English poet

13 Our God and soldiers we alike adore
Ev'n at the brink of danger; not before:
After deliverance, both alike requited,
Our God's forgotten, and our soldiers slighted.

Divine Fancies (1632) 'Of Common Devotion'. Cf. Owen 503:8

14 I wish thee as much pleasure in the reading, as I had in the writing.

Emblems (1635) 'To the Reader'

15 The heart is a small thing, but desireth great matters. It is not sufficient for a kite's dinner, yet the whole world is not sufficient for it.

Emblems (1635) bk. 1, no. 12 'Hugo de Anima'

16 My soul, sit thou a patient looker-on;
Judge not the play before the play is done:
Her plot hath many changes; every day
Speaks a new scene; the last act crowns the play.

Emblems (1635) bk. 1, no. 15 'Respice Finem'

17 We spend our midday sweat, our midnight oil;
We tire the night in thought, the day in toil.

Emblems (1635) bk. 2, no. 2, l. 33

18 Be wisely worldly, be not worldly wise.

Emblems (1635) bk. 2, no. 2, l. 46

19 Man is Heaven's masterpiece.

Emblems (1635) bk. 2, no. 6, epigram 6

1 Thou art my way; I wander, if thou fly;
   Thou art my light; if hid, how blind am I!
   Thou art my life; if thou withdraw, I die.
   Emblems (1643) bk. 3, no. 7

2 He teaches to deny that faintly prays.
   A Feast for Worms (1620) sect. 7, Meditation 7, l. 2

3 Man is man's A.B.C. There is none that can
   Read God aright, unless he first spell Man.
   Hieroglyphics of the Life of Man (1638) no. 1, l. 1

4 He that begins to live, begins to die.
   Hieroglyphics of the Life of Man (1638) no. 1, epigram 1

5 Physicians of all men are most happy; what good
   success soever they have, the world proclaimeth, and
   what faults they commit, the earth covereth.
   Hieroglyphics of the Life of Man (1638) no. 4

6 We'll cry both arts and learning down,
   And hey! then up go we!
   The Shepherd's Oracles (1646) Eclogue 11 'Song of
   Anarchus'

Peter Quennell 1905–

English writer

7 An elderly fallen angel travelling incognito.
   The Sign of the Fish (1960) ch. 2 (of André Gide)

François Quesnay 1694–1774

French political economist

8 *Vous ne connaissez qu'une seule règle du commerce; c'est
   (pour me servir de vos propres termes) de laisser passer et
   de laisser faire tous les acheteurs et tous les vendeurs
   quelconques.*

   You recognize but one rule of commerce; that is (to
   avail myself of your own terms) to allow free passage
   and freedom of action to all buyers and sellers
   whoever they may be.
   *Letter from M. Alpha to de Quesnay, 1767, in L. Salleron
   François Quesnay et la Physiocratie* (1958) vol. 2, p. 940, but
   not found in de Quesnay's writings. Cf. Anonymous 20:15,
   D'Argenson 24:18

Sir Arthur Quiller-Couch ('Q') 1863–1944

English writer and critic

9 The best is the best, though a hundred judges have
   declared it so.
   Oxford Book of English Verse (1900) preface

10 Simple this tale!—but delicately perfumed
   As the sweet roadside honeysuckle. That's why,
   Difficult though its metre was to tackle,
   I'm glad I wrote it.
   'Lady Jane. Sapphics'

11 O pastoral heart of England! like a psalm
   Of green days telling with a quiet beat.
   'Ode upon Eckington Bridge' (1896)

Josiah Quincy 1772–1864

American Federalist politician

12 As it will be the right of all, so it will be the duty of
   some, definitely to prepare for a separation, amicably if
   they can, violently if they must.
   Abridgement of Debates of Congress vol. 4, p. 327 (14 January
   1811). Cf. Clay 205:18

W. V. O. Quine 1908–

American philosopher

13 On the doctrinal side, I do not see that we are farther
   along today than where [David] Hume left us. The
   Humean predicament is the human predicament.
   Ontological Relativity and Other Essays (1969) ch. 3

14 It is the tension between the scientist's laws and his
   own attempted breaches of them that powers the
   engines of science and makes it forge ahead.
   Quiddities (1987) p. 8 'Anomaly'

15 Students of the heavens are separable into
   astronomers and astrologers as readily as are the
   minor domestic ruminants into sheep and goats, but
   the separation of philosophers into sages and cranks
   seems to be more sensitive to frames of reference.
   Theories and Things (1981) ch. 23

Quintilian AD c.35–c.96

Roman rhetorician

16 *Satura quidem tota nostra est.*
   Verse satire indeed is entirely our own.
   Institutio Oratoria bk. 10, ch. 1, sect. 93 (meaning Roman
   as opposed to Greek)

François Rabelais c.1494–c.1553

French humanist, satirist, and physician

17 *L'appétit vient en mangeant.*
   The appetite grows by eating.
   Gargantua (1534) bk. 1, ch. 5

18 *Natura vacuum abhorret.*
   Nature abhors a vacuum.
   Gargantua (1534) bk. 1, ch. 5 (quoting, in Latin, an article
   of ancient wisdom)

19 *Fay ce que vouldras.*
   Do what you like.
   Gargantua (1534) bk. 1, ch. 57

20 *Quaestio subtilissima, utrum chimera in vacuo bombinans
   possit comedere secundas intentiones.*
   A most subtle question: whether a chimera buzzing in
   a vacuum can devour second intentions.
   Pantagruel bk. 2, ch. 7

21 *Je vais quérir un grand peut-être . . . Tirez le rideau, la
   farce est jouée.*
   I am going to seek a great perhaps . . . Bring down the
   curtain, the farce is played out.
   Attributed last words. See Jean Fleury *Rabelais et ses oeuvres*
   (1877) vol. 1, ch. 3, pt. 15, where it is said that none of his
   contemporaries authenticated the remarks, which have
   become part of the 'Rabelaisian legend'

Jean Racine 1639–99
French tragedian

1 *Je l'ai trop aimé pour ne le point haïr!*

   I have loved him too much not to feel any hatred for him.
   Andromaque (1667) act 2, sc. 1

2 *C'était pendant l'horreur d'une profonde nuit.*

   It was during the horror of a deep night.
   Athalie (1691) act 2, sc. 5

3 *Elle flotte, elle hésite; en un mot, elle est femme.*

   She floats, she hesitates; in a word, she's a woman.
   Athalie (1691) act 3, sc. 3

4 *Ce n'est plus une ardeur dans mes veines cachée:*
   C'est Vénus tout entière à sa proie attachée.

   It's no longer a burning within my veins: it's Venus entire latched onto her prey.
   Phèdre (1677) act 1, sc. 3

5 *Tous les jours se levaient clairs et sereins pour eux.*

   Every day dawned clear and untroubled for them.
   Phèdre (1677) act 4, sc. 6

6 *Point d'argent, point de Suisse, et ma porte était close.*

   No money, no service, and my door stayed shut.
   Les Plaideurs (1668) act 1, sc. 1

7 *Sans argent l'honneur n'est qu'une maladie.*

   Honour, without money, is just a disease.
   Les Plaideurs (1668) act 1, sc. 1

James Rado 1939– and
Gerome Ragni 1942–
American songwriters

8 When the moon is in the seventh house,
   And Jupiter aligns with Mars . . .
   This is the dawning of the age of Aquarius.
   Hair (1967) 'Aquarius'

John Rae 1931–
English writer

9 War is, after all, the universal perversion . . . war stories, the pornography of war.
   The Custard Boys (1960) ch. 13

Thomas Rainborowe d. 1648
English soldier and parliamentarian

10 The poorest he that is in England hath a life to live as the greatest he.
   During the Army debates at Putney, 29 October 1647, in C. H. Firth (ed.) *The Clarke Papers* vol. 1, Camden Society, New Series 49 (1891) p. 301

Sir Walter Ralegh c.1552–1618
English explorer and courtier

11 If all the world and love were young,
   And truth in every shepherd's tongue,
   These pretty pleasures might me move
   To live with thee, and be thy love.
   'Answer to Marlow' Cf. Donne 251:19, Marlowe 447:17

12 Desire himself runs out of breath,
   And getting, doth but gain his death;
   Desire, nor reason hath, nor rest,
   And blind doth seldom choose the best;
   Desire attained is not desire,
   But as the cinders of the fire.
   'Conceit begotten by the Eyes' (1602)

13 Now what is love? I pray thee, tell.
   It is that fountain and that well,
   Where pleasure and repentance dwell.
   It is perhaps that saucing bell,
   That tolls all in to heaven or hell:
   And this is love, as I hear tell.
   'A Description of Love'

14 A maze wherein affection finds no end,
   A ranging cloud that runs before the wind,
   A substance like the shadow of the sun,
   A goal of grief for which the wisest run.
   'Farewell false love' (1588)

15 Go, Soul, the body's guest,
   Upon a thankless arrant;
   Fear not to touch the best;
   The truth shall be thy warrant:
   Go, since I needs must die,
   And give the world the lie.

   Say to the court, it glows
   And shines like rotten wood;
   Say to the church, it shows
   What's good, and doth no good:
   If church and court reply,
   Then give them both the lie.
   'The Lie' (1608)

16 Tell zeal it wants devotion;
   Tell love it is but lust;
   Tell time it metes but motion;
   Tell flesh it is but dust:
   And wish them not reply,
   For thou must give the lie.
   'The Lie' (1608)

17 We die in earnest, that's no jest.
   'On the Life of Man'

18 Give me my scallop-shell of quiet,
   My staff of faith to walk upon,
   My scrip of joy, immortal diet,
   My bottle of salvation,
   My gown of glory, hope's true gage,
   And thus I'll take my pilgrimage.
   'The Passionate Man's Pilgrimage' (1604)

19 Our passions are most like to floods and streams;
   The shallow murmur, but the deep are dumb.
   'Sir Walter Ralegh to the Queen' (1655)

1 As you came from the holy land
Of Walsinghame,
Met you not with my true love
By the way as you came?

How shall I know your true love,
That have met many one
As I went to the holy land,
That have come, that have gone?
'Walsinghame'

2 Fain would I climb, yet fear I to fall.
Line written on a window-pane, in Thomas Fuller *History of the Worthies of England* (1662) 'Devonshire' p. 261. Cf. Elizabeth I 274:12

3 Even such is Time, which takes in trust
Our youth, our joys, and all we have,
And pays us but with age and dust;
Who in the dark and silent grave,
When we have wandered all our ways,
Shuts up the story of our days:
And from which earth, and grave, and dust,
The Lord shall raise me up, I trust.
Written the night before his death, and found in his Bible in the Gate-house at Westminster. See V. B. Heltzel 'Ralegh's "Even such is time" ' in *Huntingdon Library Bulletin* no. 10 (October 1936)

4 [History] hath triumphed over time, which besides it, nothing but eternity hath triumphed over.
The History of the World (1614) preface

5 Whosoever, in writing a modern history, shall follow truth too near the heels, it may happily strike out his teeth.
The History of the World (1614) preface

6 O eloquent, just, and mighty Death! ... thou hast drawn together all the farstretched greatness, all the pride, cruelty, and ambition of man, and covered it all over with these two narrow words, *Hic jacet* [Here lies].
The History of the World (1614) bk. 5, ch. 6

7 'Tis a sharp remedy, but a sure one for all ills.
On feeling the edge of the axe prior to his execution, in D. Hume *History of Great Britain* (1754) vol. 1, ch. 4

8 So the heart be right, it is no matter which way the head lies.
At his execution, on being asked which way he preferred to lay his head, in W. Stebbing *Sir Walter Raleigh* (1891) ch. 30

9 I have a long journey to take, and must bid the company farewell.
Parting words, in E. Thompson *Sir Walter Raleigh* (1935) ch. 26

Sir Walter Raleigh 1861–1922

English lecturer and critic

10 In examinations those who do not wish to know ask questions of those who cannot tell.
Laughter from a Cloud (1923) 'Some Thoughts on Examinations'

11 We could not lead a pleasant life,
And 'twould be finished soon,
If peas were eaten with the knife,
And gravy with the spoon.
Eat slowly: only men in rags
And gluttons old in sin
Mistake themselves for carpet bags
And tumble victuals in.
'Stans Puer ad Mensam' (1923)

12 I wish I loved the Human Race;
I wish I loved its silly face;
I wish I liked the way it walks;
I wish I liked the way it talks;
And when I'm introduced to one
I wish I thought *What Jolly Fun!*
'Wishes of an Elderly Man' (1923)

Srinivasa Ramanujan 1887–1920

Indian mathematician

13 No, it is a very interesting number; it is the smallest number expressible as a sum of two cubes in two different ways.
Replying to G. H. Hardy's suggestion that a certain cab—number 1729—was 'dull'; in *Proceedings of the London Mathematical Society* 26 May 1921, p. 57 (the two ways being $1^3 + 12^3$ and $9^3 + 10^3$)

John Crowe Ransom 1888–1974

American poet and critic

14 Here lies a lady of beauty and high degree.
Of chills and fever she died, of fever and chills,
The delight of her husband, her aunts, an infant of three,
And of medicos marvelling sweetly on her ills.
'Here Lies a Lady' (1924)

15 Two evils, monstrous either one apart,
Possessed me, and were long and loath at going:
A cry of Absence, Absence, in the heart,
And in the wood the furious winter blowing.
'Winter Remembered' (1945)

Arthur Ransome 1884–1967

English writer

16 BETTER DROWNED THAN DUFFERS IF NOT DUFFERS WONT DROWN. 'Does that mean Yes?' asked Roger. 'I think so.'
Swallows and Amazons (1930) ch. 1

Frederic Raphael 1931–

British novelist and screenwriter

17 Your idea of fidelity is not having more than one man in bed at the same time.
Darling (1965) ch. 18

18 City of perspiring dreams.
The Glittering Prizes (1976) ch. 3 (of Cambridge). Cf. Arnold 28:25, Smith 651:13

1 I come from suburbia ... and I don't ever want to go back. It's the one place in the world that's further away than anywhere else.

The Glittering Prizes (1976) 'A Sex Life' pt. 1, sect. 3

Terence Rattigan 1911–77
English playwright

2 Do you know what 'le vice Anglais'—the English vice—really is? Not flagellation, not pederasty—whatever the French believe it to be. It's our refusal to admit our emotions. We think they demean us, I suppose.

In Praise of Love (1973) act 2

3 You can be in the Horseguards and still be common, dear.

Separate Tables (1954) 'Table Number Seven' sc. 1

Gwen Raverat 1885–1957
English wood-engraver

4 Ladies were ladies in those days; they did not do things themselves.

Period Piece (1952) ch. 5

Irving Ravetch and Harriet Frank
American screenwriters

5 The long hot summer.

Title of film (1958) based on stories by William Faulkner. 'The Long Summer' is the title of bk. 3 of Faulkner's *The Hamlet* (1940)

Sir Herbert Read 1893–1968
English art historian

6 Do not judge this movement kindly. It is not just another amusing stunt. It is defiant—the desperate act of men too profoundly convinced of the rottenness of our civilization to want to save a shred of its respectability.

International Surrealist Exhibition Catalogue, New Burlington Galleries, London, 11 June–4 July 1936, introduction

7 Art is ... pattern informed by sensibility.

The Meaning of Art (1955) ch. 1

Charles Reade 1814–84
English novelist and playwright

8 *Courage, mon ami, le diable est mort!*

Take courage, my friend, the devil is dead!

The Cloister and the Hearth (1861) ch. 24, and *passim*

9 Sow an act, and you reap a habit. Sow a habit and you reap a character. Sow a character, and you reap a destiny.

Attributed. See *Notes and Queries* (9th Series) vol. 12, 17 October 1903, p. 309

Ronald Reagan 1911–
40th President of the USA

10 Politics is supposed to be the second oldest profession. I have come to realize that it bears a very close resemblance to the first.

At a conference in Los Angeles, 2 March 1977; in Bill Adler *Reagan Wit* (1981) ch. 5

11 You can tell a lot about a fellow's character by his way of eating jellybeans.

In *New York Times* 15 January 1981

12 So in your discussions of the nuclear freeze proposals, I urge you to beware the temptation of pride—the temptation blithely to declare yourselves above it all and label both sides equally at fault, to ignore the facts of history and the aggressive impulses of an evil empire.

Speech to the National Association of Evangelicals, 8 March 1983; in *New York Times* 9 March 1983

13 We are especially not going to tolerate these attacks from outlaw states run by the strangest collection of misfits, Looney Tunes, and squalid criminals since the advent of the Third Reich.

Speech following the hijack of a US plane, 8 July 1985, in *New York Times* 9 July 1985

14 This mad dog of the Middle East.

Of Col. Gadaffi of Libya, 9 April 1986; in *New York Times* 10 April 1986, p. A 22

Erell Reaves

15 Lady of Spain, I adore you.
Right from the night I first saw you,
My heart has been yearning for you,
What else could any heart do?

'Lady of Spain' (1913 song)

Henry Reed 1914–86
English poet and playwright

16 As we get older we do not get any younger.
Seasons return, and today I am fifty-five,
And this time last year I was fifty-four,
And this time next year I shall be sixty-two.

'Chard Whitlow (Mr Eliot's Sunday Evening Postscript)' (1946)

17 It is, we believe,
Idle to hope that the simple stirrup-pump
Can extinguish hell.

'Chard Whitlow . . . ' (1946)

18 Today we have naming of parts. Yesterday,
We had daily cleaning. And tomorrow morning,
We shall have what to do after firing. But today,
Today we have naming of parts. Japonica
Glistens like coral in all of the neighbour gardens,
And today we have naming of parts.

'Lessons of the War: 1, Naming of Parts' (1946)

1 They call it easing the Spring: it is perfectly easy
If you have any strength in your thumb: like the bolt,
And the breech, and the cocking-piece, and the point
   of balance,
Which in our case we have not got; and the almond
   blossom
Silent in all of the gardens and the bees going
   backwards and forwards,
For today we have naming of parts.
  'Lessons of the War: 1, Naming of Parts' (1946)

2 And the various holds and rolls and throws and
   breakfalls
Somehow or other I always seemed to put
In the wrong place. And as for war, my wars
Were global from the start.
  'Lessons of the War: 3, Unarmed Combat' (1946)

3 I think it may justly be said that English women in
general are very common diatonic little numbers.
  Emily Butler (unpublished radio play, 1958)

4 Henry has always led what could be called a sedentary
life, if only he'd ever got as far as actually sitting up.
  Not a Drum was Heard: The War Memoirs of General Gland
  (unpublished radio play, 1959)

5 In a civil war, a general must know—and I'm afraid
it's a thing rather of instinct than of practice—he
must know exactly when to move over to the other
side.
  Not a Drum was Heard: The War Memoirs of General Gland
  (unpublished radio play, 1959)

6 GLAND: I would say it's somehow redolent, and full of
   vitality.
  HILDA: Well, I would say it's got about as much life
   in it as a potted shrimp.
  GLAND: Well, I think we're probably both trying to
   say the same thing in different words.
  The Primal Scene, as it were (1958 radio play) in *Hilda Tablet
  and Others* (1971) p. 162

7 And the sooner the tea's out of the way, the sooner
we can get out the gin, eh?
  Private Life of Hilda Tablet (1954 radio play) in *Hilda Tablet
  and Others* (1971) p. 60

8 Of course we've all *dreamed* of reviving the *castrati*; but
it's needed Hilda to take the first practical steps
towards making them a reality . . . She's drawn up
a list of well-known singers who she thinks would
benefit . . . It's only a question of getting them to
agree.
  Private Life of Hilda Tablet (1954 radio play) in *Hilda Tablet
  and Others* (1971) p. 72

9 Modest? My word, no . . . He was an all-the-lights-on
man.
  A Very Great Man Indeed (1953 radio play) in *Hilda Tablet
  and Others* (1971) p. 23

10 I have known her pass the whole evening without
mentioning a single book, or *in fact anything
unpleasant*, at all.
  A Very Great Man Indeed (1953 radio play) in *Hilda Tablet
  and Others* (1971) p. 45

John Reed 1887–1920
American journalist and revolutionary

11 Ten days that shook the world.
  Title of book (1919)

Joseph Reed 1741–85
American Revolutionary politician

12 I am not worth purchasing, but such as I am, the
King of Great Britain is not rich enough to do it.
  Replying to an offer from Governor George Johnstone of
  £10,000, and any office in the Colonies in the King's gift, if
  he were able successfully to promote a Union between the
  UK and the US. See W. B. Read *Life and Correspondence of
  Joseph Reed* (1847) vol. 1, ch. 18

Max Reger 1873–1916
German composer

13 *Ich sitze in dem kleinsten Zimmer in meinem Hause. Ich
habe Ihre Kritik vor mir. Im nächsten Augenblick wird sie
hinter mir sein.*

I am sitting in the smallest room of my house. I have
your review before me. In a moment it will be behind
me.
  Responding to a savage review by Rudolph Louis in
  Münchener Neueste Nachrichten, 7 February 1906; in Nicolas
  Slonimsky *Lexicon of Musical Invective* (1953) p. 139

Charles A. Reich 1928–
American jurist

14 The greening of America.
  Title of book (1970)

Keith Reid 1946–
English pop singer and songwriter

15 Her face, at first . . . just ghostly
Turned a whiter shade of pale.
  'A Whiter Shade of Pale' (1967 song)

Erich Maria Remarque 1898–1970
German novelist

16 All quiet on the western front.
  English title of *Im Westen nichts Neues* (1929 novel). Cf.
  Beers 59:22, McClellan 437:2

Jules Renard 1864–1910
French novelist and playwright

17 *Les bourgeois, ce sont les autres.*

The bourgeois are other people.
  Journal, 28 January 1890, in *Oeuvres Complètes* (1925–7)
  vol. 5, p. 65

Montague John Rendall 1862–1950
Member of the first BBC Board of Governors

18 Nation shall speak peace unto nation.
  Motto of the BBC. Cf. Isaiah 82:11

Jean Renoir 1894–1979
French film director

19 Is it possible to succeed without any act of betrayal?
  My Life and My Films (1974) 'Nana'

Pierre Auguste Renoir 1841–1919
French painter

1 I paint with my prick.

Much quoted, but possibly an inversion of 'It's with my brush that I make love', in A. André *Renoir* (1919) p. 10

2 *C'étaient des fous, mais ils avaient cette petite flamme qui ne s'éteint pas.*

They were madmen; but they had in them that little flame which is not to be snuffed out.

On the men of the French Commune, in Jean Renoir *Renoir, My Father* (translated by R. and D. Weaver, 1962) ch. 12

Frederic Reynolds 1764–1841
English playwright

3 It is better to have written a damned play, than no play at all—it snatches a man from obscurity.

The Dramatist (1789) act 1, sc. 1

Sir Joshua Reynolds 1723–92
English painter

4 Few have been taught to any purpose who have not been their own teachers.

Discourses on Art (ed. R. Wark, 1975) no. 2 (11 December 1769)

5 If you have great talents, industry will improve them: if you have but moderate abilities, industry will supply their deficiency.

Discourses on Art (ed. R. Wark, 1975) no. 2 (11 December 1769)

6 A mere copier of nature can never produce anything great.

Discourses on Art (ed. R. Wark, 1975) no. 3 (14 December 1770)

7 Could we teach taste or genius by rules, they would be no longer taste and genius.

Discourses on Art (ed. R. Wark, 1975) no. 3 (14 December 1770)

8 The whole beauty and grandeur of the art consists . . . in being able to get above all singular forms, local customs, particularities, and details of every kind.

Discourses on Art (ed. R. Wark, 1975) no. 3 (14 December 1770)

9 The value and rank of every art is in proportion to the mental labour employed in it, or the mental pleasure produced by it.

Discourses on Art (ed. R. Wark, 1975) no. 4 (10 December 1771)

10 Genius . . . is the child of imitation.

Discourses on Art (ed. R. Wark, 1975) no. 6 (10 December 1774)

11 The mind is but a barren soil; a soil which is soon exhausted, and will produce no crop, or only one, unless it be continually fertilized and enriched with foreign matter.

Discourses on Art (ed. R. Wark, 1975) no. 6 (10 December 1774)

12 Art in its perfection is not ostentatious; it lies hid, and works its effect, itself unseen.

Discourses on Art (ed. R. Wark, 1975) no. 6 (10 December 1774)

13 It is the very same taste which relishes a demonstration in geometry, that is pleased with the resemblance of a picture to an original, and touched with the harmony of music.

Discourses on Art (ed. R. Wark, 1975) no. 7 (10 December 1776)

14 I should desire that the last words which I should pronounce in this Academy, and from this place, might be the name of—Michael Angelo.

Discourses on Art (ed. R. Wark, 1975) no. 15 (10 December 1790)

Malvina Reynolds 1900–78
American songwriter

15 Little boxes on the hillside . . .
And they're all made out of ticky-tacky
And they all look just the same.

'Little Boxes' (1962 song); on the tract houses in the hills to the south of San Francisco

Cecil Rhodes 1853–1902
South African statesman

16 Ask any man what nationality he would prefer to be, and ninety-nine out of a hundred will tell you that they would prefer to be Englishmen.

In Gordon Le Sueur *Cecil Rhodes* (1913) p. 40

17 So little done, so much to do.

Said on the day of his death, in Lewis Michell *Life of Rhodes* (1910) vol. 2, ch. 39

Jean Rhys (Ella Gwendolen Rees Williams) c.1890–1979
British novelist and short-story writer

18 We can't all be happy, we can't all be rich, we can't all be lucky—and it would be so much less fun if we were . . . Some must cry so that others may be able to laugh the more heartily.

Good Morning, Midnight (1939) pt. 1

19 The perpetual hunger to be beautiful and that thirst to be loved which is the real curse of Eve.

The Left Bank (1927) 'Illusion'

20 Only the hopeless are starkly sincere and . . . only the unhappy can either give or take sympathy.

The Left Bank (1927) 'In the Rue de l'Arrivée'

21 The feeling of Sunday is the same everywhere, heavy, melancholy, standing still. Like when they say 'As it was in the beginning, is now, and ever shall be, world without end.'

Voyage in the Dark (1934) ch. 4, pt. 1

22 A doormat in a world of boots.

Describing herself; in *Guardian* 6 December 1990, p. 24

David Ricardo 1772–1823
British economist

23 Rent is that portion of the earth, which is paid to the landlord for the use of the original and indestructible powers of the soil.

On the Principles of Political Economy and Taxation (1817) ch. 2

Grantland Rice 1880–1954

American sports writer

1 For when the One Great Scorer comes to mark against
your name,
He writes—not that you won or lost—but how you
played the Game.
'Alumnus Football' (1941)

2 All wars are planned by old men
In council rooms apart.
'The Two Sides of War' (1955)

3 Outlined against a blue-grey October sky, the Four
Horsemen rode again. In dramatic lore they were
known as Famine, Pestilence, Destruction, and Death.
These are only aliases. Their real names are
Stuhldreher, Miller, Crowley, and Layden. They
formed the crest of the South Bend cyclone before
which another fighting Army football team was swept
over the precipice.
Report of football match between US Military Academy at
West Point NY and University of Notre Dame, in *New York
Tribune* 19 October 1924

Sir Stephen Rice 1637–1715

Irish lawyer

4 I will drive a coach and six horses through the Act of
Settlement.
In W. King *State of the Protestants of Ireland* (1672) ch. 3,
sect. 8, p. 6

Tim Rice 1944–

English songwriter

5 Prove to me that you're no fool
Walk across my swimming pool.
Jesus Christ Superstar (1970) 'Herod's Song'; music by
Andrew Lloyd Webber

Mandy Rice-Davies 1944–

English courtesan

6 He would, wouldn't he?
At the trial of Stephen Ward, 29 June 1963, on being told
that Lord Astor claimed that her allegations, concerning
himself and his house parties at Cliveden, were untrue; in
Guardian 1 July 1963

Frank Richards (Charles Hamilton)
1876–1961

English writer for boys

7 The fat greedy owl of the Remove.
'Billy Bunter' in the *Magnet* (1909) vol. 3, no. 72 'The
Greyfriars Photographer'

I. A. Richards 1893–1979

English literary critic

8 It [poetry] is capable of saving us; it is a perfectly
possible means of overcoming chaos.
Science and Poetry (1926) ch. 7

Samuel Richardson 1689–1761

English novelist

9 I have known a bird actually starve itself, and die with
grief, at its being caught and caged—But never did I
meet with a lady who was so silly . . . And yet we
must all own that it is more difficult to catch a bird
than a lady.
Clarissa (1747–8) Letter 170

10 Mine is the most plotting heart in the world.
Clarissa (1747–8) Letter 171

11 I love to write to the moment.
Clarissa (1747–8) Letter 224

12 What, my Lord, is ancestry? I live to my own heart.
History of Sir Charles Grandison (1754) vol. 3,
Letter 26

13 A feeling heart is a blessing that no one, who has it,
would be without; and it is a moral security of
innocence; since the heart that is able to partake of
the distress of another, cannot wilfully give it.
History of Sir Charles Grandison (1754) vol. 3,
Letter 32

14 This world, if we can enjoy it with innocent
cheerfulness, and be serviceable to our
fellow-creatures, is not to be despised, even by a
Philosopher.
History of Sir Charles Grandison (1754) vol. 5,
Letter 37

15 His spurious brat, Tom Jones.
Of Fielding's novel; letter to Thomas Edwards, 21 February
1752, in J. Carroll (ed.) *Selected Letters* (1964) p. 196

Hans Richter 1843–1916

German conductor

16 Up with your damned nonsense will I put twice, or
perhaps once, but sometimes always, by God, never.
Attributed

Johann Paul Friedrich Richter
('Jean Paul') 1763–1825

German novelist

17 Providence has given to the French the empire of the
land, to the English that of the sea, and to the
Germans that of—the air!
In Thomas Carlyle 'Jean Paul Friedrich Richter' in
Edinburgh Review no. 91 (1827)

George Ridding 1828–1904

Bishop of Southwell from 1884

18 I feel a feeling which I feel you all feel.
Sermon in the London Mission, 1885; in G. W. E. Russell
Collections and Recollections (1898) ch. 29

Rainer Maria Rilke 1875–1926
German poet

1 *Kunst-Werke sind von einer unendlichen Einsamkeit und
mit nichts so wenig erreichbar als mit Kritik. Nur Liebe
kann sie erfassen und halten und kann gerecht sein gegen
sie.*

Works of art are of an infinite solitariness, and
nothing is less likely to bring us near to them than
criticism. Only love can apprehend and hold them,
and can be just towards them.
   Briefe an einen jungen Dichter (1929) 23 April 1903
   (translated by Reginald Snell)

2 *Wer hat uns also umgedreht, dass wir,
was wir auch tun, in jener Haltung sind
von einem, welcher fortgeht? Wie er auf
dem letzten Hügel, der ihm ganz sein Tal
noch einmal zeigt, sich wendet, anhält, weilt—,
so leben wir und nehmen immer Abschied.*

Who's turned us around like this, so that we always,
do what we may, retain the attitude
of someone who's departing? Just as he,
on the last hill, that shows him all his valley
for the last time, will turn and stop and linger,
we live our lives, for ever taking leave.
   Duineser Elegien (translated by J. B. Leishman and Stephen
   Spender, 1948) no. 8

3 *Ich halte für die höchste Aufgabe einer Verbindung zweier
Menschen diese: dass einer dem andern seine Einsamkeit
bewache.*

I hold this to be the highest task for a bond between
two people: that each protects the solitude of the
other.
   Letter to Paula Modersohn-Becker, 12 February 1902, in
   Gesammelte Briefe (1904) vol. 1, p. 204

Arthur Rimbaud 1854–91
French poet

4 *Plus douce qu'aux enfants la chair des pommes surettes,
L'eau verte pénétra ma coque de sapin.*

Sweeter than the flesh of tart apples to children, the
green water penetrates my wooden hull.
   'Le Bâteau ivre' (1883)

5 *. . . Je me suis baigné dans le Poème
De la Mer, infusé d'astres, et lactescent,
Dévorant les azurs verts.*

I have bathed in the Poem of the Sea, steeped in stars,
and milky, devouring the green azures.
   'Le Bâteau ivre' (1883)

6 *J'ai vu le soleil bas, taché d'horreurs mystiques
Illuminant de longs figements violets,
Pareils à des acteurs de drames très-antiques.*

I have seen the sun set, stained with mystic horrors,
illuminating the long violet [blood-] clots, just like
actors in very ancient plays.
   'Le Bâteau ivre' (1883)

7 *Je regrette l'Europe aux anciens parapets!*

I pine for Europe of the ancient parapets!
   'Le Bâteau ivre' (1883)

8 *Je m'en allais, les poings dans mes poches crevées;
Mon paletot aussi devenait idéal.*

I was walking along, hands in holey pockets; my
overcoat also was entering the realms of the ideal.
   'Ma Bohème' (1870)

9 *Ô saisons, ô châteaux!
Quelle âme est sans défauts?
Ô saisons, ô châteaux,
J'ai fait la magique étude
Du bonheur, que nul n'élude.*

O seasons, O castles! What soul is without fault? I
have made the magic study of good fortune which not
one eludes.
   'Ô saisons, ô châteaux' (1872)

10 *A noir, E blanc, I rouge, U vert, O bleu: voyelles,
Je dirais quelque jour vos naissances latentes . . .
I, pourpres, sang craché, rire des lèvres belles
Dans la colère ou les ivresses pénitentes.*

A black, E white, I red, U green, O blue: vowels, some
day I will tell of the births that may be yours. I,
purples, coughed-up blood, laughter of beautiful lips in
anger or penitent drunkennesses.
   'Voyelles' (1870)

Hal Riney 1932–
American advertising executive

11 It's morning again in America.
   Slogan for Ronald Reagan's election campaign, 1984; in
   Newsweek 6 August 1984

César Ritz 1850–1918
Swiss hotel proprietor

12 *Le client n'a jamais tort.*

The customer is never wrong.
   In R. Nevill and C. E. Jerningham *Piccadilly to Pall Mall*
   (1908) p. 94

Antoine de Rivarol 1753–1801
French man of letters

13 *Ce qui n'est pas clair n'est pas français.*

What is not clear is not French.
   Discours sur l'Universalité de la Langue Française (1784)

Joan Riviere b. 1883

14 Civilization and its discontents.
   Title given to her translation of Sigmund Freud's *Das
   Unbehagen in der Kultur* (1930)

Lord Robbins (Lionel Charles Robbins) 1898–1984
British economist

15 Economics is the science which studies human
behaviour as a relationship between ends and scarce
means which have alternative uses.
   Essay on the Nature and Significance of Economic Science
   (1932) ch. 1, sect. 3

Maximilien Robespierre 1758–94

French revolutionary

1 *Je ne suis pas ni le courtisan, ni le modérateur, ni le tribun, ni le défenseur du peuple, je sais peuple moi-même.*

I am no courtesan, nor moderator, nor Tribune, nor defender of the people: I am myself the people.

Speech at the Jacobin Club, 27 April 1792; in G. Laurent (ed.) *Le Défenseur de la Constitution* (1939) p. 39

2 *La volonté générale gouverne la société comme la volonté particulière gouverne chaque individu isolé.*

The general will rules in society as the private will governs each separate individual.

Lettres à ses commettans (2nd series) 5 January 1793

3 *Toute loi qui viole les droits imprescriptibles de l'homme, est essentiellement injuste et tyrannique; elle n'est point une loi.*

Any law which violates the inalienable rights of man is essentially unjust and tyrannical; it is not a law at all.

Déclaration des droits de l'homme 24 April 1793, article 6; this article, in slightly different form, is recorded as having figured in Robespierre's *Projet* of 21 April 1793

4 *Toute institution qui ne suppose pas le peuple bon, et le magistrat corruptible, est vicieuse.*

Any institution which does not suppose the people good, and the magistrate corruptible, is evil.

Déclaration des droits de l'homme 24 April 1793, article 25

5 *L'immoralité est la base du despotisme comme la vertu est l'essence de la République.*

Wickedness is the root of despotism as virtue is the essence of the Republic.

In the Convention, 7 May 1794; in C. Vellay (ed.) *Discours et Rapports de Robespierre* (1908) p. 354

6 *Il faut une volonté une.*

One single will is necessary.

Private note, in S. A. Berville and J. F. Barrière *Papiers inédits trouvés chez Robespierre* vol. 2 (1828) no. 44

Leo Robin 1900–

American songwriter

7 A kiss on the hand may be quite continental,
But diamonds are a girl's best friend . . .

Men grow cold as girls grow old
And we all lose our charms in the end.
But square cut or pear shape,
These rocks won't lose their shape,
Diamonds are a girl's best friend.

'Diamonds are a Girl's Best Friend' from the 1949 film *Gentlemen Prefer Blondes* (music by Jule Styne)

8 Thanks for the memory.

Title of song (with Ralph Rainger, 1937)

Edwin Arlington Robinson 1869–1935

American poet

9 I shall have more to say when I am dead.

'John Brown' (1920)

10 Miniver loved the Medici,
Albeit he had never seen one;
He would have sinned incessantly
Could he have been one.

'Miniver Cheevy' (1910)

11 So on we worked, and waited for the light,
And went without meat, and cursed the bread;
And Richard Cory, one calm summer night,
Went home and put a bullet through his head.

'Richard Cory' (1897)

12 The world is not a 'prison house', but a kind of kindergarten, where millions of bewildered infants are trying to spell God with the wrong blocks.

Literature in the Making (1917) p. 266

Joan Robinson (née Maurice) 1903–

British economist

13 Current experience suggests that socialism is not a stage beyond capitalism but a substitute for it—a means by which the nations which did not share in the Industrial Revolution can imitate its technical achievements; a means to achieve rapid accumulation under a different set of rules of the game.

Collected Economic Papers vol. 2 (1960) 'Marx, Marshall and Keynes' (1955)

John Robinson 1919–83

English theologian; Bishop of Woolwich, 1959–69

14 Honest to God.

Title of book (1963)

15 I think Lawrence tried to portray this [sex] relation as in a real sense an act of holy communion. For him flesh was sacramental of the spirit.

As defence witness in the case against Penguin Books for publishing *Lady Chatterley's Lover*; in *The Times* 28 October 1960

Mary Robinson (née Darby) 1758–1800

English poet

16 Pavement slippery, people sneezing,
Lords in ermine, beggars freezing;
Titled gluttons dainties carving,
Genius in a garret starving.

'January, 1795'

Sir Boyle Roche 1743–1807

Irish politician

17 Mr Speaker, I smell a rat; I see him forming in the air and darkening the sky; but I'll nip him in the bud.

Attributed

John Wilmot, Earl of Rochester 1647–80

English poet

18 Tell me no more of constancy,
that frivolous pretence,
Of cold age, narrow jealousy,
disease and want of sense.

'Against Constancy' (1676)

1 Then bring my bath, and strew my bed,
as each kind night returns,
I'll change a mistress till I'm dead,
and fate change me for worms.
'Against Constancy' (1676)

2 Kindness only can persuade;
It gilds the lover's servile chain
And makes the slave grow pleased and vain.
'Give me leave to rail at you' (1680)

3   'Is there then no more?'
She cries. 'All this to love and rapture's due;
Must we not pay a debt to pleasure too?'
'The Imperfect Enjoyment' (1680)

4 May'st thou ne'er piss, who didst refuse to spend
When all my joys did on false thee depend.
'The Imperfect Enjoyment' (1680)

5 Here lies a great and mighty king
Whose promise none relies on;
He never said a foolish thing,
Nor ever did a wise one.
'The King's Epitaph' (an alternative first line reads: 'Here
lies our sovereign lord the King'); in C. E. Doble et al.
Thomas Hearne: Remarks and Collections (1885–1921)
17 November 1706. Cf. Charles II 191:12

6 Love . . .
That cordial drop heaven in our cup has thrown
To make the nauseous draught of life go down.
'A Letter from Artemisia in the Town to Chloe in the
Country' (1679)

7 All my past life is mine no more:
The flying hours are gone
Like transitory dreams given o'er,
Whose images are kept in store
By memory alone.
'Love and Life' (1680)

8 An age in her embraces passed
Would seem a winter's day,
Where life and light with envious haste
Are torn and snatched away.
'The Mistress: A Song' (1691)

9 Kind jealous doubts, tormenting fears,
And anxious cares, when past,
Prove our hearts' treasure fixed and dear,
And make us blest at last.
'The Mistress: A Song' (1691)

10 . . . Natural freedoms are but just:
There's something generous in mere lust.
'A Ramble in St James' Park' (1680)

11 Reason, an *ignis fatuus* of the mind,
Which leaves the light of nature, sense, behind.
'A Satire against Mankind' (1679) l. 11

12 Then Old Age, and Experience, hand in hand,
Lead him to Death, and make him understand,
After a search so painful, and so long
That all his life he has been in the wrong.
Huddled in dirt the reasoning engine lies,
Who was so proud, so witty and so wise.
'A Satire against Mankind' (1679) l. 25

13 Wretched *Man* is still in arms for fear;
For fear he arms, and is of arms afraid,
By fear, to fear, successively betrayed
Base fear.
'A Satire against Mankind' (1679) l. 141

14 For all men would be cowards if they durst.
'A Satire against Mankind' (1679) l. 158

15 A merry monarch, scandalous and poor.
'A Satire on King Charles II' (1697)

16 Love a woman? You're an ass!
'Tis a most insipid passion
To choose out for your happiness
The silliest part of God's creation.
'Song' (1680)

17 Ancient person, for whom I
All the flattering youth defy,
Long be it ere thou grow old,
Aching, shaking, crazy, cold;
But still continue as thou art,
Ancient person of my heart.
'A Song of a Young Lady to her Ancient Lover'
(1691)

18 Nothing, thou elder brother even to shade!
Thou hadst a being ere the world was made,
And, well fixed, art alone of ending not afraid.

Ere time and place were, time and place were not;
Where primitive nothing something straight begot;
Then all proceeded from the great united what.
'Upon Nothing' (1680)

19 Matter, the wickedest offspring of thy race,
By form assisted, flew from thy embrace,
And rebel light obscured thy reverend dusky face.

With form and matter, time and place did join;
Body, thy foe, with these did leagues combine,
To spoil thy peaceful realm, and ruin all thy line.
'Upon Nothing' (1680)

John D. Rockefeller 1839–1937
American industrialist and philanthropist

20 The growth of a large business is merely a survival of
the fittest . . . The American beauty rose can be
produced in the splendour and fragrance which bring
cheer to its beholder only by sacrificing the early buds
which grow up around it.
In W. J. Ghent *Our Benevolent Feudalism* (1902) p. 29
('American Beauty Rose' became the title of a 1950 song
by Hal David and others). Cf. Darwin 231:9, Spencer
658:17

Gene Roddenberry 1921–91
American film producer

21 These are the voyages of the starship *Enterprise*. Its
five-year mission . . . to boldly go where no man has
gone before.
Star Trek (television series, from 1966)

22 Beam us up, Mr Scott.
Star Trek 'Gamesters of Triskelion' (usually quoted 'Beam
me up, Scotty')

Richard Rodgers 1902–79

American composer and songwriter

1 The sweetest sounds I'll ever hear
Are still inside my head.
The kindest words I'll ever know
Are waiting to be said.
The most entrancing sight of all
Is yet for me to see.
And the dearest love in all the world
Is waiting somewhere for me.
  No Strings (1962) 'The Sweetest Sounds'

See also OSCAR HAMMERSTEIN II

Theodore Roethke 1908–63

American poet

2 Thought does not crush to stone.
The great sledge drops in vain.
Truth never is undone;
Its shafts remain.
  'The Adamant' (1941)

3 I can hear, underground, that sucking and sobbing,
In my veins, in my bones I feel it,—
The small waters seeping upward,
The tight grains parting at last.
  'Cuttings Later' (1948)

4 I have known the inexorable sadness of pencils,
Neat in their boxes, dolour of pad and paper-weight,
All the misery of manilla folders and mucilage,
Desolation in immaculate public places.
  'Dolour' (1948)

5 I remember the neckcurls, limp and damp, as tendrils;
And her quick look, a sidelong pickerel smile;
And how, once startled into talk, the light syllables
    leaped for her,
And she balanced in the delight of her thought.
  'Elegy for Jane' (1953)

6 In a dark wood I saw—
I saw my several selves
Come running from the leaves,
Lewd, tiny, careless lives
That scuttled under stones,
Or broke, but would not go.
  'The Exorcism' (1958)

7 To know that light falls and fills, often without our
    knowing,
As an opaque vase fills to the brim from a quick
    pouring,
Fills and trembles at the edge yet does not flow over,
Still holding and feeding the stem of the contained
    flower.
  'A Field of Light' (1948)

8 I gave her kisses back, and woke a ghost.
O what lewd music crept into our ears!
The body and the soul know how to play
In that dark world where gods have lost thir way.
  'Four for Sir John Davies' (1953) no. 2

9 My secrets cry aloud.
I have no need for tongue.
My heart keeps open house,
My doors are widely flung,
An epic of the eyes
My love with no disguise.
  'Open House' (1941)

10   O who can be
Both moth and flame? The weak moth blundering by.
Whom do we love? I thought I knew the truth;
Of grief I died, but no one knew my death.
  'The Sequel' (1964)

Samuel Rogers 1763–1855

English poet

11 Think nothing done while aught remains to do.
  'Human Life' (1819) l. 49. Cf. Lucan 431:6

12 But there are moments which he calls his own,
Then, never less alone than when alone,
Those whom he loved so long and sees no more,
Loved and still loves—not dead—but gone before,
He gathers round him.
  'Human Life' (1819) l. 755

13 By many a temple half as old as Time.
  Italy (1838 ed.) epilogue. Cf. Burgon 156:24

14 Go—you may call it madness, folly;
You shall not chase my gloom away.
There's such a charm in melancholy,
I would not, if I could, be gay.
  'To —, 1814'

15 It doesn't much signify whom one marries, for one is
sure to find next morning that it was someone else.
  In Alexander Dyce (ed.) *Table Talk of Samuel Rogers* (1860)

Thorold Rogers 1823–90

English economic historian

16 See, ladling butter from alternate tubs
Stubbs butters Freeman, Freeman butters Stubbs.
  In W. H. Hutton (ed.) *Letters of William Stubbs* (1904)
  p. 149

Will Rogers 1879–1935

American actor and humorist

17 There is only one thing that can kill the movies, and
that is education.
  Autobiography of Will Rogers (1949) ch. 6

18 The more you read and observe about this Politics
thing, you got to admit that each party is worse than
the other.
  The Illiterate Digest (1924) 'Breaking into the Writing Game'

19 Income Tax has made more Liars out of the American
people than Golf.
  The Illiterate Digest (1924) 'Helping the Girls with their
  Income Taxes'

20 Everything is funny as long as it is happening to
Somebody Else.
  The Illiterate Digest (1924) 'Warning to Jokers: lay off the
  prince'

1 Communism is like prohibition, it's a good idea but it won't work.
> *Weekly Articles* (1981) vol. 3, p. 93 (first published 1927)

2 Well, all I know is what I read in the papers.
> *New York Times* 30 September 1923

3 You know everybody is ignorant, only on different subjects.
> *New York Times* 31 August 1924

4 You can't say civilization don't advance, however, for in every war they kill you in a new way.
> *New York Times* 23 December 1929

5 Half our life is spent trying to find something to do with the time we have rushed through life trying to save.
> Letter in *New York Times* 29 April 1930

6 Coolidge is a better example of evolution than either Bryan or Darrow, for he knows when not to talk, which is the biggest asset the monkey possesses over the human.
> In *Saturday Review* 25 August 1962 'A Rogers Thesaurus'

Mme Roland (*Marie-Jeanne Philipon*) 1754–93
French revolutionary

7 Ô liberté! Ô liberté! que de crimes on commet en ton nom!

O liberty! O liberty! what crimes are committed in thy name!
> In A. de Lamartine *Histoire des Girondins* (1847) bk. 51, ch. 8

Frederick William Rolfe ('*Baron Corvo*') 1860–1913
English novelist

8 'There is no Holiness here,' George interrupted, in that cold, white, candent voice which was more caustic than silver nitrate and more thrilling than a scream.
> *Hadrian VII* (1904) ch. 21

9 Pray for the repose of His soul. He was so tired.
> *Hadrian VII* (1904) ch. 24

Richard Rolle de Hampole *c*.1290–1349
English mystic

10 When Adam dalfe and Eve spane
Go spire if thou may spede,
Where was than the pride of man
That now merres his mede?
> In G. G. Perry *Religious Pieces* (Early English Text Society, Original Series no. 26, revised ed. 1914). Taken in altered form by John Ball as the text of his revolutionary sermon on the outbreak of the Peasants' Revolt, 1381: 'When Adam delved and Eve span, who was then the gentleman?' See J. R. Green *A Short History of the English People* (1874) ch. 5, sect. 4

Pierre de Ronsard 1524–85
French poet

11 *Mignonne, allons voir si la rose,*
Qui, ce matin, avait déclose
Sa robe de pourpre au soleil,
A point perdu, cette vêprée,
Les plis de sa robe pourprée
Et son teint au vôtre pareil.

See, Mignonne, hath not the rose
That this morning did unclose
Her purple mantle to the light,
Lost, before the day be dead,
The glory of her raiment red,
Her colour, bright as yours is bright?
> *Odes, à Cassandre* (1555) bk. 1, no. 17 (translated by Andrew Lang)

12 *Quand vous serez bien vieille, au soir, à la chandelle,*
Assise auprès du feu, dévidant et filant,
Direz, chantant mes vers, en vous émerveillant,
Ronsard me célébrait du temps que j'étais belle.

When you are very old, and sit in the candle-light at evening spinning by the fire, you will say, as you murmur my verses, a wonder in your eyes, 'Ronsard sang of me in the days when I was fair.'
> *Sonnets pour Hélène* (1578) bk. 2, no. 42

Eleanor Roosevelt 1884–1962
American humanitarian and diplomat

13 No one can make you feel inferior without your consent.
> In *Catholic Digest* August 1960, p. 102

Franklin D. Roosevelt 1882–1945
32nd President of the USA

14 These unhappy times call for the building of plans that ... build from the bottom up and not from the top down, that put their faith once more in the forgotten man at the bottom of the economic pyramid.
> Radio address, 7 April 1932, in *Public Papers* (1938) vol. 1, p. 625

15 I pledge you, I pledge myself, to a new deal for the American people.
> Speech to the Democratic Convention in Chicago, 2 July 1932, accepting the presidential nomination; in *Public Papers* (1938) vol. 1, p. 647

16 The only thing we have to fear is fear itself.
> Inaugural address, 4 March 1933, in *Public Papers* (1938) vol. 2, p. 11

17 In the field of world policy I would dedicate this Nation to the policy of the good neighbour.
> Inaugural address, 4 March 1933, in *Public Papers* (1938) vol. 2, p. 14

18 I have seen war ... I hate war.
> Speech at Chautauqua, NY, 14 August 1936, in *Public Papers* (1938) vol. 5, p. 289

19 I see one-third of a nation ill-housed, ill-clad, ill-nourished.
> Second inaugural address, 20 January 1937, in *Public Papers* (1941) vol. 6, p. 5

1 I have said this before, but I shall say it again and again and again: Your boys are not going to be sent into any foreign wars.

Speech in Boston, 30 October 1940, in *Public Papers* (1941) vol. 9, p. 517. Cf. Johnson 367:10

2 We have the men—the skill—the wealth—and above all, the will ... We must be the great arsenal of democracy.

'Fireside Chat' radio broadcast, 29 December 1940, in *Public Papers* (1941) vol. 9, p. 643

3 We look forward to a world founded upon four essential human freedoms. The first is freedom of speech and expression—everywhere in the world. The second is freedom of every person to worship God in his own way—everywhere in the world. The third is freedom from want ... everywhere in the world. The fourth is freedom from fear ... anywhere in the world.

Message to Congress, 6 January 1941, in *Public Papers* (1941) vol. 9, p. 672

4 Yesterday, December 7, 1941—a date which will live in infamy—the United States of America was suddenly and deliberately attacked by naval and air forces of the Empire of Japan.

Address to Congress, 8 December 1941, in *Public Papers* (1950) vol. 10, p. 514

5 Books can not be killed by fire. People die, but books never die. No man and no force can abolish memory ... In this war, we know, books are weapons. And it is a part of your dedication always to make them weapons for man's freedom.

'Message to the Booksellers of America' 6 May 1942, in *Publisher's Weekly* 9 May 1942

6 It is fun to be in the same decade with you.

Cabled reply to Winston Churchill, acknowledging congratulations on his 60th birthday, in W. S. Churchill *The Hinge of Fate* (1950) ch. 4

7 The work, my friend, is peace. More than an end of this war—an end to the beginnings of all wars.

Undelivered address for Jefferson Day, 13 April 1945 (the day after Roosevelt died) in *Public Papers* (1950) vol. 13, p. 615

Theodore Roosevelt 1858–1919

26th President of the USA

8 I wish to preach, not the doctrine of ignoble ease, but the doctrine of the strenuous life.

Speech to the Hamilton Club, Chicago, 10 April 1899, in *Works* (Memorial edition, 1923–6), vol. 15

9 There is a homely old adage which runs: 'Speak softly and carry a big stick; you will go far.' If the American nation will speak softly, and yet build and keep at a pitch of the highest training a thoroughly efficient navy, the Monroe Doctrine will go far.

Speech in Chicago, 3 April 1903, in *New York Times* 4 April 1903

10 A man who is good enough to shed his blood for the country is good enough to be given a square deal afterwards. More than that no man is entitled to, and less than that no man shall have.

Speech at the Lincoln Monument, Springfield, Illinois, 4 June 1903, in *Addresses and Presidential Messages 1902–4* (1904)

11 The men with the muck-rakes are often indispensable to the well-being of society; but only if they know when to stop raking the muck.

Speech in Washington, 14 April 1906, in *Works* (Memorial edition, 1923–6) vol. 18. Cf. Bunyan 156:8

12 There is no room in this country for hyphenated Americanism ... The one absolutely certain way of bringing this nation to ruin, of preventing all possibility of its continuing to be a nation at all, would be to permit it to become a tangle of squabbling nationalities.

Speech in New York, 12 October 1915, in *Works* (Memorial edition, 1923–6) vol. 20

13 Foolish fanatics ... the men who form the lunatic fringe in all reform movements.

Autobiography (1913) ch. 7

14 I am as strong as a bull moose and you can use me to the limit.

Letter to Mark Hanna, 27 June 1900, in *Works* (Memorial edition, 1923–6) vol. 23. 'Bull Moose' subsequently became the popular name of the Progressive Party

Lord Rosebery (5th Earl of Rosebery)
1847–1929

British Liberal politician; Prime Minister, 1894–5

15 Imperialism, sane Imperialism, as distinguished from what I may call wild-cat Imperialism, is nothing but this—a larger patriotism.

Speech, City of London Liberal Club, 5 May 1899, in *Daily News* 6 May 1899, p. 4

16 It is beginning to be hinted that we are a nation of amateurs.

Rectorial Address at Glasgow University, 16 November 1900, in *The Times* 17 November 1900

17 I must plough my furrow alone.

Speech on remaining outside the Liberal Party leadership, 19 July 1901, in *The Times* 20 July 1901

18 Men who sit still with the fly-blown phylacteries bound round their obsolete policy.

On certain members of the Liberal Party; speech at Chesterfield, 16 December 1901, in *The Times* 17 December 1901, p. 10

Ethel Rosenberg 1916–53 *and* Julius Rosenberg 1918–53

Husband and wife; convicted of spying for the Russians

19 We are innocent ... To forsake this truth is to pay too high a price even for the priceless gift of life.

Petition for executive clemency, filed 9 January 1953, in Ethel Rosenberg *Death House Letters* (1953) p. 149

20 We are the first victims of American Fascism.

Letter from Julius to Emanuel Bloch before the Rosenbergs' execution, 19 June 1953; in *Testament of Ethel and Julius Rosenberg* (1954) p. 187

Alan S. C. Ross 1907–80

British linguistics scholar

1 There are, it is true, still a few minor points of life which may serve to demarcate the upper class, but they are only minor ones ... when drunk, gentlemen often become amorous or maudlin or vomit in public, but they never become truculent.
  'U and Non-U. An essay in sociological linguistics' (1954) in Nancy Mitford (ed.) *Noblesse Oblige* (1956)

Christina Rossetti 1830–94

English poet; sister of D. G. Rossetti

2 Because the birthday of my life
  Is come, my love is come to me.
  'A Birthday' (1862)

3 Come to me in the silence of the night;
  Come in the speaking silence of a dream;
  Come with soft rounded cheeks and eyes as bright
  As sunlight on a stream;
  Come back in tears,
  O memory, hope, love of finished years.
  'Echo' (1862)

4 In the bleak mid-winter
  Frosty wind made moan,
  Earth stood hard as iron,
  Water like a stone;
  Snow had fallen, snow on snow,
  Snow on snow,
  In the bleak mid-winter,
  Long ago.
  'Mid-Winter' (1875)

5 The hope I dreamed of was a dream,
  Was but a dream; and now I wake,
  Exceeding comfortless, and worn, and old,
  For a dream's sake.
  'Mirage' (1862)

6 Oh roses for the flush of youth,
  And laurel for the perfect prime;
  But pluck an ivy branch for me
  Grown old before my time.
  'Oh roses for the flush of youth' (1862)

7 Remember me when I am gone away,
  Gone far away into the silent land.
  'Remember' (1862)

8 Better by far you should forget and smile
  Than that you should remember and be sad.
  'Remember' (1862)

9 O Earth, lie heavily upon her eyes;
  Seal her sweet eyes weary of watching, Earth.
  'Rest' (1862)

10 Silence more musical than any song.
  'Rest' (1862)

11 Does the road wind up-hill all the way?
  Yes, to the very end.
  Will the day's journey take the whole long day?
  From morn to night, my friend.
  'Up-Hill' (1862)

12 When I am dead, my dearest,
  Sing no sad songs for me;
  Plant thou no roses at my head,
  Nor shady cypress tree:
  Be the green grass above me
  With showers and dewdrops wet;
  And if thou wilt, remember,
  And if thou wilt, forget.
  'When I am dead' (1862)

Dante Gabriel Rossetti 1828–82

English poet and painter

13 Like the sweet apple which reddens upon the topmost bough,
  A-top on the topmost twig,—which the pluckers forgot, somehow,—
  Forgot it not, nay, but got it not, for none could get it till now.
  'Beauty: A Combination from Sappho' (1861). Cf. Sappho 556:2

14 The blessed damozel leaned out
  From the gold bar of Heaven;
  Her eyes were deeper than the depth
  Of waters stilled at even;
  She had three lilies in her hand,
  And the stars in her hair were seven.
  'The Blessed Damozel' (1870) st. 1

15 Her hair that lay along her back
  Was yellow like ripe corn.
  'The Blessed Damozel' (1870) st. 2

16 As low as where this earth
  Spins like a fretful midge.
  'The Blessed Damozel' (1870) st. 6

17 And the souls mounting up to God
  Went by her like thin flames.
  'The Blessed Damozel' (1870) st. 7

18 'We two,' she said, 'will seek the groves
  Where the lady Mary is,
  With her five handmaidens, whose names
  Are five sweet symphonies,
  Cecily, Gertrude, Magdalen,
  Margaret and Rosalys.'
  'The Blessed Damozel' (1870) st. 18

19 A sonnet is a moment's monument,—
  Memorial from the Soul's eternity
  To one dead deathless hour.
  The House of Life (1881) pt. 1, introduction

20 'Tis visible silence, still as the hour-glass.
  The House of Life (1881) pt. 1 'Silent Noon'

21 Deep in the sun-searched growths the dragon-fly
  Hangs like a blue thread loosened from the sky:—
  So this winged hour is dropt to us from above.
  Oh! clasp we to our hearts, for deathless dower,
  This close-companioned inarticulate hour
  When twofold silence was the song of love.
  The House of Life (1881) pt. 1 'Silent Noon'

22 Lo! as that youth's eyes burned at thine, so went
  Thy spell through him, and left his straight neck bent
  And round his heart one strangling golden hair.
  The House of Life (1881) pt. 2 'Body's Beauty'

1 They die not,—for their life was death,—but cease;
   And round their narrow lips the mould falls close.
   The House of Life (1881) pt. 2 'The Choice' pt. 1

2 I do not see them here; but after death
   God knows I know the faces I shall see,
   Each one a murdered self, with low last breath.
   'I am thyself,—what hast thou done to me?'
   'And I—and I—thyself,' (lo! each one saith,)
   'And thou thyself to all eternity!'
   The House of Life (1881) pt. 2 'Lost Days'

3 Give honour unto Luke Evangelist;
   For he it was (the aged legends say)
   Who first taught Art to fold her hands and pray.
   The House of Life (1881) pt. 2 'Old and New Art'

4 When vain desire at last and vain regret
   Go hand in hand to death, and all is vain,
   What shall assuage the unforgotten pain
   And teach the unforgetful to forget?
   The House of Life (1881) pt. 2 'The One Hope'

5 Look in my face; my name is Might-have-been;
   I am also called No-more, Too-late, Farewell.
   The House of Life (1881) pt. 2 'A Superscription'

6 Sleepless with cold commemorative eyes.
   The House of Life (1881) pt. 2 'A Superscription'

7 Unto the man of yearning thought
   And aspiration, to do nought
   Is in itself almost an act.
   'Soothsay' (1881) st. 10

8 I have been here before,
   But when or how I cannot tell:
   I know the grass beyond the door,
   The sweet keen smell,
   The sighing sound, the lights around the shore.
   'Sudden Light' (1870)

Gioacchino Rossini 1792–1868

Italian composer

9 *Monsieur Wagner a de beaux moments, mais de mauvais quart d'heures.*

   Wagner has lovely moments but awful quarters of an hour.
   To Emile Naumann, April 1867, in E. Naumann *Italienische Tondichter* (1883) vol. 4, p. 541

Edmond Rostand 1868–1918

French playwright

10 ... *Un grand nez est proprement l'indice*
    D'un homme affable, bon, courtois, spirituel,
    Libéral, courageux, tel que je suis.

    A large nose is in fact the sign of an affable man, good, courteous, witty, liberal, courageous, such as I am.
    Cyrano de Bergerac (1897) act 1, sc. 1

11 *Il y a malgré vous quelque chose*
    Que j'emporte, et ce soir, quand j'entrerai chez Dieu,
    Mon salut balaiera largement le seuil bleu,
    Quelque chose que sans un pli, sans une tache,
    J'emporte malgré vous ... et c'est ... Mon panache!

    There is, in spite of you, something which I shall take with me. And tonight, when I go into God's house, my bow will make a wide sweep across the blue threshold. Something which, with not a crease, not a mark, I'm taking away in spite of you ... and it's ... My panache!
    Cyrano de Bergerac (1897) act 5, sc. 4

12 *Le seul rêve intéresse,*
    Vivre sans rêve, qu'est-ce?

    The dream, alone, is of interest. What is life, without a dream?
    La Princesse Lointaine (1895) act 1, sc. 4

Jean Rostand 1894–1977

French biologist

13 *On tue un homme, on est un assassin. On tue des millions d'hommes, on est conquérant. On les tue tous, on est un dieu.*

    Kill a man, and you are an assassin. Kill millions of men, and you are a conqueror. Kill everyone, and you are a god.
    Pensées d'un biologiste (1939) p. 116. Cf. Porteus 525:6, Young 754:10

Leo Rosten 1908–

American writer and social scientist

14 Any man who hates dogs and babies can't be all bad.
    Of W. C. Fields, and often attributed to him, in speech at Masquers' Club dinner, 16 February 1939. See letter in *Times Literary Supplement* 24 January 1975, p. 85

Philip Roth 1933–

American novelist

15 A Jewish man with parents alive is a fifteen-year-old boy, and will remain a fifteen-year-old boy until *they* die!
    Portnoy's Complaint (1967) p. 111

16 Doctor, my doctor, what do you say, LET'S PUT THE ID BACK IN YID!
    Portnoy's Complaint (1967) p. 124

Claude-Joseph Rouget de Lisle 1760–1836

French soldier

17 *Allons, enfants de la patrie,*
    Le jour de gloire est arrivé ...
    Aux armes, citoyens!
    Formez vos battaillons!

    Come, children of our country, the day of glory has arrived ... To arms, citizens! Form your battalions!
    'La Marseillaise' (25 April 1792)

Charles Roupell
Official referee of the British High Court of Justice

1 To play billiards well is a sign of an ill-spent youth.
Attributed, in D. Duncan *Life of Herbert Spencer* (1908) ch. 20

Jean-Jacques Rousseau 1712–78
French philosopher and novelist

2 *L'homme est né libre, et partout il est dans les fers.*
Man was born free, and everywhere he is in chains.
Du Contrat social (1762) ch. 1

3 *Laisse, mon ami, ces vains moralistes et rentre au fond de ton âme: c'est là que tu retrouveras toujours la source de ce feu sacré qui nous embrasa tant de fois de l'amour des sublimes vertus; c'est là que tu verras ce simulacre éternel du vrai beau dont la contemplation nous anime d'un saint enthousiasme.*

Leave those vain moralists, my friend, and return to the depth of your soul: that is where you will always rediscover the source of the sacred fire which so often inflamed us with love of the sublime virtues; that is where you will see the eternal image of true beauty, the contemplation of which inspires us with a holy enthusiasm.
La Nouvelle Héloïse (1761, ed. M. Launay, 1967) pt. 2, letter 11

Martin Joseph Routh 1755–1854
English classicist

4 You will find it a very good practice always to verify your references, sir!
In John William Burgon *Lives of Twelve Good Men* (1888 ed.) vol. 1, p. 73

Nicholas Rowe 1674–1718
English playwright

5 Is this that haughty, gallant, gay Lothario?
The Fair Penitent (1703) act 5, sc. 1

6 Like Helen, in the night when Troy was sacked,
Spectatress of the mischief which she made.
The Fair Penitent (1703) act 5, sc. 1

7 Death is the privilege of human nature,
And life without it were not worth our taking.
The Fair Penitent (1703) act 5, sc. 1

Helen Rowland 1875–1950
American writer

8 A husband is what is left of a lover, after the nerve has been extracted.
A Guide to Men (1922) p. 19

9 Somehow a bachelor never quite gets over the idea that he is a thing of beauty and a boy forever.
A Guide to Men (1922) p. 25. Cf. Keats 386:13

10 The follies which a man regrets most, in his life, are those which he didn't commit when he had the opportunity.
A Guide to Men (1922) p. 25

Richard Rowland c.1881–1947
American film producer

11 The lunatics have taken charge of the asylum.
On the take-over of United Artists by Charles Chaplin, Mary Pickford, Douglas Fairbanks and D. W. Griffith, in Terry Ramsaye *A Million and One Nights* (1926) vol. 2, ch. 79. Cf. Lloyd George 424:12

Maude Royden 1876–1956
English religious writer

12 The Church should go forward along the path of progress and be no longer satisfied only to represent the Conservative Party at prayer.
Address at Queen's Hall, London, 16 July 1917, in *The Times* 17 July 1917

Naomi Royde-Smith c.1875–1964
English novelist and playwright

13 I know two things about the horse
And one of them is rather coarse.
Weekend Book (1928) p. 231

Matthew Roydon fl. 1580–1622
English poet

14 A sweet attractive kind of grace,
A full assurance given by looks,
Continual comfort in a face,
The lineaments of Gospel books;
I trow that countenance cannot lie,
Whose thoughts are legible in the eye.
'An Elegy . . . for his Astrophill [Sir Philip Sidney]' (1593) st. 18

15 Was never eye, did see that face,
Was never ear, did hear that tongue,
Was never mind, did mind his grace,
That ever thought the travel long—
But eyes, and ears, and ev'ry thought,
Were with his sweet perfections caught.
'An Elegy . . . for his Astrophill' (1593) st. 19

Paul Alfred Rubens 1875–1917
English songwriter

16 Oh! we don't want to lose you but we think you ought to go
For your King and your Country both need you so;
We shall want you and miss you but with all our might and main
We shall cheer you, thank you, kiss you
When you come back again.
'Your King and Country Want You' (1914 song)

Richard Rumbold c.1622–85
English republican conspirator

17 I never could believe that Providence had sent a few men into the world, ready booted and spurred to ride, and millions ready saddled and bridled to be ridden.
On the scaffold, in T. B. Macaulay *History of England* vol. 1 (1849) ch. 1

Damon Runyon 1884–1946

American writer

1 Guys and dolls.
   Title of book (1931)

2 I do see her in tough joints more than somewhat.
   Collier's 22 May 1930, 'Social Error'

3 'You are snatching a hard guy when you snatch
   Bookie Bob. A very hard guy, indeed. In fact,' I say, 'I
   hear the softest thing about him is his front teeth.'
   Collier's 26 September 1931, 'The Snatching of Bookie Bob'

4 I always claim the mission workers came out too early
   to catch any sinners on this part of Broadway. At
   such an hour the sinners are still in bed resting up
   from their sinning of the night before, so they will be
   in good shape for more sinning a little later on.
   Collier's 28 January 1933, 'The Idyll of Miss Sarah Brown'

5 I long ago come to the conclusion that all life is 6 to 5
   against.
   Collier's 8 September 1934, 'A Nice Price'

6 'My boy,' he says, 'always try to rub up against
   money, for if you rub up against money long enough,
   some of it may rub off on you.'
   Cosmopolitan August 1929, 'A Very Honourable Guy'

Dean Rusk 1909–

US politician; Secretary of State, 1961–9

7 We're eyeball to eyeball, and I think the other fellow
   just blinked.
   On the Cuban missile crisis, 24 October 1962, in *Saturday
   Evening Post* 8 December 1962

John Ruskin 1819–1900

English art and social critic

8 You hear of me, among others, as a respectable
   architectural man-milliner; and you send for me, that
   I may tell you the leading fashion.
   The Crown of Wild Olive (1866) Lecture 2 'Traffic'

9 Thackeray settled like a meat-fly on whatever one had
   got for dinner, and made one sick of it.
   Fors Clavigera (1871–84) Letter 31, 1 July 1873

10 I have seen, and heard, much of Cockney impudence
   before now; but never expected to hear a coxcomb ask
   two hundred guineas for flinging a pot of paint in the
   public's face.
   Fors Clavigera (1871–84) Letter 79, 18 June 1877, on
   Whistler's *Nocturne in Black and Gold.* Cf. Whistler 730:23

11 No person who is not a great sculptor or painter can
   be an architect. If he is not a sculptor or painter, he
   can only be a *builder.*
   Lectures on Architecture and Painting (1854) Lectures 1 and
   2 (addenda)

12 Life without industry is guilt, and industry without art
   is brutality.
   Lectures on Art (1870) Lecture 3 'The Relation of Art to
   Morals' sect. 95

13 What is poetry? . . . The suggestion, by the
   imagination, of noble grounds for the noble emotions.
   Modern Painters (1856) vol. 3, pt. 4, ch. 1

14 All violent feelings . . . produce in us a falseness in all
   our impressions of external things, which I would
   generally characterize as the 'Pathetic Fallacy'.
   Modern Painters (1856) vol. 3, pt. 4, ch. 12

15 Mountains are the beginning and the end of all
   natural scenery.
   Modern Painters (1856) vol. 4, pt. 5, ch. 20

16 There was a rocky valley between Buxton and
   Bakewell . . . You enterprised a railroad . . . you
   blasted its rocks away . . . And now, every fool in
   Buxton can be at Bakewell in half-an-hour, and every
   fool in Bakewell at Buxton.
   Praeterita vol. 3 (1889) 'Joanna's Cave'

17 All books are divisible into two classes, the books of
   the hour, and the books of all time.
   Sesame and Lilies (1865) p. 16 'Of Kings' Treasuries'

18 Be sure that you go to the author to get at his
   meaning, not to find yours.
   Sesame and Lilies (1865) p. 24 'Of Kings' Treasuries'

19 Which of us . . . is to do the hard and dirty work for
   the rest—and for what pay? Who is to do the pleasant
   and clean work, and for what pay?
   Sesame and Lilies (1865) p. 69 n. 'Of Kings' Treasuries'

20 We call ourselves a rich nation, and we are filthy and
   foolish enough to thumb each other's books out of
   circulating libraries!
   Sesame and Lilies (1865) p. 77 'Of Kings' Treasuries'

21 I believe the right question to ask, respecting all
   ornament, is simply this: Was it done with
   enjoyment—was the carver happy while he was about
   it?
   Seven Lamps of Architecture (1849) 'The Lamp of Life'
   sect. 24

22 Better the rudest work that tells a story or records a
   fact, than the richest without meaning.
   Seven Lamps of Architecture (1849) 'The Lamp of Memory'
   sect. 7

23 When we build, let us think that we build for ever.
   Seven Lamps of Architecture (1849) 'The Lamp of Memory'
   sect. 10

24 Remember that the most beautiful things in the world
   are the most useless; peacocks and lilies for instance.
   Stones of Venice vol. 1 (1851) ch. 2, sect. 17

25 Labour without joy is base. Labour without sorrow is
   base. Sorrow without labour is base. Joy without
   labour is base.
   Time and Tide (1867) Letter 5

26 Your honesty is *not* to be based either on religion or
   policy. Both your religion and policy must be based on
   it.
   Time and Tide (1867) Letter 8

27 The first duty of a State is to see that every child born
   therein shall be well housed, clothed, fed and
   educated, till it attain years of discretion.
   Time and Tide (1867) Letter 13

28 Fine art is that in which the hand, the head, and the
   heart of man go together.
   The Two Paths (1859) Lecture 2

29 Not only is there but one way of *doing* things rightly,
   but there is only one way of *seeing* them, and that is,
   seeing the whole of them.
   The Two Paths (1859) Lecture 2

1 Nobody cares much at heart about Titian; only there
   is a strange undercurrent of everlasting murmur about
   his name, which means the deep consent of all great
   men that he is greater than they.
   The Two Paths (1859) Lecture 2

2 It ought to be quite as natural and straightforward a
   matter for a labourer to take his pension from his
   parish, because he has deserved well of his parish, as
   for a man in higher rank to take his pension from his
   country, because he has deserved well of his country.
   Unto this Last (1862) preface, p. xviii

3 The force of the guinea you have in your pocket
   depends wholly on the default of a guinea in your
   neighbour's pocket. If he did not want it, it would be
   of no use to you.
   Unto this Last (1862) Essay 2, p. 40

4 Soldiers of the ploughshare as well as soldiers of the
   sword.
   Unto this Last (1862) Essay 3, p. 102

5 Government and co-operation are in all things the
   laws of life; anarchy and competition the laws of
   death.
   Unto this Last (1862) Essay 3, p. 102

6 Whereas it has long been known and declared that
   the poor have no right to the property of the rich, I
   wish it also to be known and declared that the rich
   have no right to the property of the poor.
   Unto this Last (1862) Essay 3, p. 103

7 There is no wealth but life.
   Unto this Last (1862) Essay 4, p. 156

Bertrand Russell (3rd Earl Russell)
1872–1970

British philosopher and mathematician

8 Men who are unhappy, like men who sleep badly, are
   always proud of the fact.
   The Conquest of Happiness (1930) ch. 1

9 Boredom is . . . a vital problem for the moralist, since
   half the sins of mankind are caused by the fear of it.
   The Conquest of Happiness (1930) ch. 4

10 One of the symptoms of approaching nervous
   breakdown is the belief that one's work is terribly
   important, and that to take a holiday would bring all
   kinds of disaster.
   The Conquest of Happiness (1930) ch. 5

11 One should as a rule respect public opinion in so far as
   is necessary to avoid starvation and to keep out of
   prison, but anything that goes beyond this is
   voluntary submission to an unnecessary tyranny.
   The Conquest of Happiness (1930) ch. 9

12 A sense of duty is useful in work, but offensive in
   personal relations. People wish to be liked, not to be
   endured with patient resignation.
   The Conquest of Happiness (1930) ch. 10

13 Of all forms of caution, caution in love is perhaps the
   most fatal to true happiness.
   The Conquest of Happiness (1930) ch. 12

14 To be able to fill leisure intelligently is the last product
   of civilization.
   The Conquest of Happiness (1930) ch. 14

15 Work is of two kinds: first, altering the position of
   matter at or near the earth's surface relatively to other
   such matter; second, telling other people to do so. The
   first kind is unpleasant and ill paid; the second is
   pleasant and highly paid.
   In Praise of Idleness and Other Essays (1986) title essay
   (1932)

16 To fear love is to fear life, and those who fear life are
   already three parts dead.
   Marriage and Morals (1929) ch. 19

17 Mathematics may be defined as the subject in which
   we never know what we are talking about, nor
   whether what we are saying is true.
   Mysticism and Logic (1918) ch. 4

18 The law of causality, I believe, like much that passes
   muster among philosophers, is a relic of a bygone age,
   surviving, like the monarchy, only because it is
   erroneously supposed to do no harm.
   Mysticism and Logic (1918) ch. 9

19 Only on the firm foundation of unyielding despair, can
   the soul's habitation henceforth be safely built.
   Philosophical Essays (1910) no. 2

20 Mathematics, rightly viewed, possesses not only truth,
   but supreme beauty—a beauty cold and austere, like
   that of sculpture.
   Philosophical Essays (1910) no. 4

21 Every man, wherever he goes, is encompassed by
   a cloud of comforting convictions, which move with
   him like flies on a summer day.
   Sceptical Essays (1928) 'Dreams and Facts'

22 The infliction of cruelty with a good conscience is
   a delight to moralists. That is why they invented Hell.
   Sceptical Essays (1928) 'On the Value of Scepticism'

23 It is obvious that 'obscenity' is not a term capable of
   exact legal definition; in the practice of the Courts, it
   means 'anything that shocks the magistrate'.
   Sceptical Essays (1928) 'The Recrudescence of Puritanism'

24 Next to enjoying ourselves, the next greatest pleasure
   consists in preventing others from enjoying
   themselves, or, more generally, in the acquisition of
   power.
   Sceptical Essays (1928) 'The Recrudescence of Puritanism'

25 Fear is the main source of superstition, and one of the
   main sources of cruelty.
   Unpopular Essays (1950) 'An Outline of Intellectual
   Rubbish'

26 The linguistic philosophy, which cares only about
   language, and not about the world, is like the boy
   who preferred the clock without the pendulum
   because, although it no longer told the time, it went
   more easily than before and at a more exhilarating
   pace.
   Foreword to Ernest Gellner *Words and Things* (1959)

Dora Russell 1894–1986

English feminist

27 We want better reasons for having children than not
   knowing how to prevent them
   Hypatia (1925) ch. 4

George William Russell

See Æ.

Lord John Russell 1792–1878

British Whig politician; Prime Minister 1846–52, 1865–6

1 It is impossible that the whisper of a faction should prevail against the voice of a nation.

> Reply to an Address from a meeting of 150,000 persons at Birmingham on the defeat of the second Reform Bill, October 1831, in S. Walpole *Life of Lord John Russell* (1889) vol. 1, ch. 7

2 If peace cannot be maintained with honour, it is no longer peace.

> Speech at Greenock, 19 September 1853, in *The Times* 21 September 1853, p. 7. Cf. Chamberlain 189:8

3 Among the defects of the Bill, which were numerous, one provision was conspicuous by its presence and another by its absence.

> Speech to the electors of the City of London, April 1859, in *The Times* 9 April 1859, p. 9

4 A proverb is one man's wit and all men's wisdom.

> In R. J. Mackintosh *Sir James Mackintosh* (1835) vol. 2, ch. 7

Sir William Howard Russell 1820–1907

British journalist; war correspondent of The Times

5 They dashed on towards that thin red line tipped with steel.

> Of the Russians charging the British, in *The British Expedition to the Crimea* (1877) p. 156. Russell's original dispatch to *The Times*, 14 November 1854, reads 'That thin red streak tipped with a line of steel'

Ernest Rutherford (Baron Rutherford of Nelson) 1871–1937

British physicist

6 All science is either physics or stamp collecting.

> In J. B. Birks *Rutherford at Manchester* (1962) p. 108

7 We haven't got the money, so we've got to think!

> In *Bulletin of the Institute of Physics* (1962) vol. 13, p. 102 (as recalled by R. V. Jones)

Gilbert Ryle 1900–76

English philosopher

8 A myth is, of course, not a fairy story. It is the presentation of facts belonging to one category in the idioms appropriate to another. To explode a myth is accordingly not to deny the facts but to re-allocate them.

> *The Concept of Mind* (1949) introduction

9 Philosophy is the replacement of category-habits by category-disciplines.

> *The Concept of Mind* (1949) introduction

10 The dogma of the Ghost in the Machine.

> *The Concept of Mind* (1949) ch. 1 (on the mental-conduct concepts of Descartes)

Rafael Sabatini 1875–1950

Italian novelist

11 He was born with a gift of laughter and a sense that the world was mad. And that was all his patrimony.

> *Scaramouche* (1921) bk. 1, ch. 1

Thomas Sackville, 1st Earl of Dorset 1536–1608

12 The wrathful winter, 'proaching on apace,
With blustering blasts had all ybared the treen,
And old Saturnus, with his frosty face,
With chilling cold had pierced the tender green . . .

And sorrowing I to see the summer flowers,
The lively green, the lusty leas, forlorn,
The sturdy trees so shattered with the showers,
The fields so fade that flourished so beforn,
It taught me well all earthly things be born
To die the death, for nought long time may last;
The summer's beauty yields to winter's blast.

> *The Mirror for Magistrates* (1563) st. 1

13 Whence come I am, the dreary destiny
And luckless lot for to bemoan of those
Whom Fortune, in this maze of misery,
Of wretched chance most woeful mirrors chose;
That when thou seest how lightly they did lose
Their pomp, their power, and that they thought most sure,
Thou mayst soon deem no earthly joy may dure.

> *The Mirror for Magistrates* (1563) st. 16

14 Crookbacked he was, tooth-shaken, and blear-eyed,
Went on three feet, and sometime crept on four,
With old lame bones that rattled by his side,
His scalp all pilled and he will eld forlore;
His withered fist still knocking at Death's door,
Fumbling and drivelling as he draws his breath;
For brief, the shape and messenger of Death.

> *The Mirror for Magistrates* (1563) st. 48 (on Old Age)

Victoria ('Vita') Sackville-West 1892–1962

English writer and gardener; wife of Harold Nicolson

15 The greater cats with golden eyes
Stare out between the bars.
Deserts are there, and different skies,
And night with different stars.

> *The King's Daughter* (1929) pt. 2, no. 1

16 The country habit has me by the heart,
For he's bewitched for ever who has seen,
Not with his eyes but with his vision, Spring
Flow down the woods and stipple leaves with sun.

> *The Land* (1926) 'Winter'

Françoise Sagan 1935–

French novelist

17 *Rien n'est plus affreux que le rire pour la jalousie.*
To jealousy, nothing is more frightful than laughter.

> *La Chamade* (1965) ch. 9

Charles-Augustin Sainte-Beuve
1804–69

1 *Et Vigny plus secret,*
Comme en sa tour d'ivoire, avant midi rentrait.

And Vigny more discreet, as if in his ivory tower,
returned before noon.
Les Pensées d'Août, à M. Villemain (1837) p. 152

Antoine de Saint-Exupéry 1900–44
French novelist

2 *Les grandes personnes ne comprennent jamais rien toutes*
seules, et c'est fatigant, pour les enfants, de toujours et
toujours leur donner des explications.

Grown-ups never understand anything for themselves,
and it is tiresome for children to be always and forever
explaining things to them.
Le Petit Prince (1943) ch. 1

3 *On ne voit bien qu'avec le cœur. L'essentiel est invisible*
pour les yeux.

It is only with the heart that one can see rightly;
what is essential is invisible to the eye.
Le Petit Prince (1943) ch. 21

4 *L'expérience nous montre qu'aimer ce n'est point nous*
regarder l'un l'autre mais regarder ensemble dans la même
direction.

Experience shows us that love does not consist in
gazing at each other but in looking together in the
same direction.
Terre des Hommes (translated as 'Wind, Sand and Stars',
1939) ch. 8

Saki (Hector Hugh Munro) 1870–1916
Scottish writer

5 It is one of the consolations of middle-aged reformers
that the good they inculcate must live after them if it
is to live at all.
Beasts and Super-Beasts (1914) 'The Byzantine Omelette'

6 Waldo is one of those people who would be
enormously improved by death.
Beasts and Super-Beasts (1914) 'The Feast of Nemesis'

7 The people of Crete unfortunately make more history
than they can consume locally.
Chronicles of Clovis (1911) 'The Jesting of Arlington
Stringham'

8 All decent people live beyond their incomes nowadays,
and those who aren't respectable live beyond other
peoples'.
Chronicles of Clovis (1911) 'The Match-Maker'

9 The cook was a good cook, as cooks go; and as good
cooks go, she went.
Reginald (1904) 'Reginald on Besetting Sins'

10 I always say beauty is only sin deep.
Reginald (1904) 'Reginald's Choir Treat'

11 Good gracious, you've got to educate him first. You
can't expect a boy to be vicious till he's been to a good
school.
Reginald in Russia (1910) 'The Baker's Dozen'

12 Addresses are given to us to conceal our whereabouts.
Reginald in Russia (1910) 'Cross Currents'

13 A little inaccuracy sometimes saves tons of
explanation.
The Square Egg (1924) 'Clovis on the Alleged Romance of
Business'

14 Children with Hyacinth's temperament don't know
better as they grow older; they merely know more.
Toys of Peace and Other Papers (1919) 'Hyacinth'

15 We all know that Prime Ministers are wedded to the
truth, but like other married couples they sometimes
live apart.
The Unbearable Bassington (1912) ch. 13

J. D. Salinger 1919
American novelist and short-story writer

16 Sex is something I really don't understand too hot.
You never know *where* the hell you are. I keep making
up these sex rules for myself, and then I break them
right away.
The Catcher in the Rye (1951) ch. 9

17 Take most people, they're crazy about cars. They
worry if they get a little scratch on them, and they're
always talking about how many miles they get to
a gallon . . . I don't even like *old* cars. I mean they
don't even interest me. I'd rather have a goddam
horse. A horse is at least *human*, for God's sake.
The Catcher in the Rye (1951) ch. 17

18 I keep picturing all these little kids playing some game
in this big field of rye and all . . . I mean if they're
running and they don't look where they're going
I have to come out from somewhere and catch them.
That's all I'd do all day. I'd just be the catcher in the
rye.
The Catcher in the Rye (1951) ch. 22

Lord Salisbury (3rd Marquess of Salisbury) 1830–1903
*British Conservative politician; Prime Minister 1855–6,
1886–92, 1895–1902*

19 English policy is to float lazily downstream,
occasionally putting out a diplomatic boathook to
avoid collisions.
*Letter to Lord Lytton, 9 March 1877, in Lady G. Cecil
Cecil Life of Robert Marquis of Salisbury (1921–32) vol. 1,
p. 130*

1 A great deal of misapprehension arises from the popular use of maps on a small scale. As with such maps you are able to put a thumb on India and a finger on Russia, some persons at once think that the political situation is alarming and that India must be looked to. If the noble Lord would use a larger map—say one on the scale of the Ordnance Map of England—he would find that the distance between Russia and British India is not to be measured by the finger and thumb, but by a rule.

Speech, *Hansard* 11 June 1877, col. 1565

2 No lesson seems to be so deeply inculcated by the experience of life as that you never should trust experts. If you believe the doctors, nothing is wholesome: if you believe the theologians, nothing is innocent: if you believe the soldiers, nothing is safe. They all require to have their strong wine diluted by a very large admixture of insipid common sense.

Letter to Lord Lytton, 15 June 1877; in Lady Gwendolen Cecil *Life of Robert, Marquis of Salisbury* (1921–32) vol. 2, ch. 4

3 The agonies of a man who has to finish a difficult negotiation, and at the same time to entertain four royalties at a country house can be better imagined than described.

Letter to Lord Lyons, 5 June 1878; in Lady Gwendolen Cecil *Life of Robert, Marquis of Salisbury* (1921–32) vol. 2, p. 275

4 What with deafness, ignorance of French, and Bismarck's extraordinary mode of speech, Beaconsfield has the dimmest idea of what is going on—understands everything crossways—and imagines a perpetual conspiracy.

Letter to Lady Salisbury from the Congress of Berlin, 23 June 1878; in Lady Gwendolen Cecil *Life of Robert, Marquis of Salisbury* (1921–32) vol. 2, p. 287

5 We are part of the community of Europe and we must do our duty as such.

Speech at Caernarvon, 10 April 1888, in *The Times* 11 April 1888

6 Where property is in question I am guilty ... of erecting individual liberty as an idol, and of resenting all attempts to destroy or fetter it; but when you pass from liberty to life, in no well-governed State, in no State governed according to the principles of common humanity, are the claims of mere liberty allowed to endanger the lives of the citizens.

Speech, *Hansard* (Lords) 29 July 1897, col. 1436

7 Horny-handed sons of toil.

Quarterly Review October 1873, p. 543 (later popularized in the US by Denis Kearney, 1847–1907). Cf. Lowell 429:1

8 I rank myself no higher in the scheme of things than a policeman—whose utility would disappear if there were no criminals.

Comparing his role in the Conservative Party with that of Gladstone, in Lady Gwendolen Cecil *Biographical Studies ... of Robert, Third Marquess of Salisbury* (1962) p. 84

9 By office boys for office boys.

Of the *Daily Mail*, in H. Hamilton Fyfe *Northcliffe, an Intimate Biography* (1930) ch. 4

Lord Salisbury (5th Marquess of Salisbury) 1893–1972

British Conservative politician

10 Too clever by half.

Of Iain Macleod, Colonial Secretary, 'in his relationship to the white communities of Africa'; in *Hansard* (Lords) 7 March 1961, col. 307

Sallust (Gaius Sallustius Crispus) 86–35 BC

Roman historian

11 *Alieni appetens, sui profusus.*

Greedy for the property of others, extravagant with his own.

Catiline ch. 5

12 *Quieta movere magna merces videbatur.*

To stir up undisputed matters seemed a great reward in itself.

Catiline ch. 21

13 *Esse quam videri bonus malebat.*

He preferred to be rather than to seem good.

Catiline ch. 54 (of Cato)

14 *Urbem venalem et mature perituram, si emptorem invenerit.*

A venal city ripe to perish, if a buyer can be found.

Jugurtha ch. 35 (of Rome)

15 *Punica fide.*

With Carthaginian trustworthiness.

Jugurtha ch. 108, sect. 3 (meaning treachery)

Anthony Sampson 1926–

British journalist

16 Members [of civil service orders] rise from CMG (known sometimes in Whitehall as 'Call Me God') to the KCMG ('Kindly Call Me God') to—for a select few governors and super-ambassadors—the GCMG ('God Calls Me God').

Anatomy of Britain (1962) ch. 18

Lord Samuel (1st Viscount Samuel) 1870–1963

British Liberal politician

17 A library is thought in cold storage.

A Book of Quotations (1947) p. 10

18 Without doubt the greatest injury of all was done by basing morals on myth. For, sooner or later, myth is recognized for what it is, and disappears. Then morality loses the foundation on which it has been built.

Romanes Lecture (1947) p. 14

Paul A. Samuelson 1915–

American economist

1 The consumer, so it is said, is the king ... each is a voter who uses his money as votes to get the things done that he wants done.
Economics (8th ed., 1970) p. 55

Carl Sandburg 1878–1967

American poet

2 Hog Butcher for the World,
Tool Maker, Stacker of Wheat,
Player with Railroads and the Nation's Freight Handler;
Stormy, husky, brawling,
City of the Big Shoulders.
'Chicago' (1916)

3 When Abraham Lincoln was shovelled into the tombs, he forgot the copperheads and the assassin ...
in the dust, in the cool tombs.
'Cool Tombs' (1918)

4 The fog comes
on little cat feet.
It sits looking
over harbour and city
on silent haunches
and then moves on.
'Fog' (1916)

5 Pile the bodies high at Austerlitz and Waterloo.
Shovel them under and let me work—
I am the grass; I cover all.
'Grass' (1918)

6 Why is there always a secret singing
When a lawyer cashes in?
Why does a hearse horse snicker
Hauling a lawyer away?
'The Lawyers Know Too Much' (1920)

7 I tell you the past is a bucket of ashes.
'Prairie' (1918)

8 I am an idealist. I don't know where I'm going but I'm on the way.
Incidentals (1907) p. 8

9 Little girl ... Sometime they'll give a war and nobody will come.
The People, Yes (1936). 'Suppose They Gave a War and No One Came?' was the title of a piece by Charlotte Keyes in *McCall's* October 1966; 'Suppose They Gave a War and Nobody Came?' was the title of a 1970 film. Cf. Ginsberg 306:27

10 Poetry is the opening and closing of a door, leaving those who look through to guess about what is seen during a moment.
Atlantic Monthly March 1923 'Poetry Considered'

11 Poetry is the achievement of the synthesis of hyacinths and biscuits.
Atlantic Monthly March 1923 'Poetry Considered'

12 Slang is a language that rolls up its sleeves, spits on its hands and goes to work.
In *New York Times* 13 February 1959, p. 21

Henry 'Red' Sanders

13 Sure, winning isn't everything. It's the only thing.
In *Sports Illustrated* 26 December 1955 (often attributed to Vince Lombardi)

Martha Sansom (*née Fowke*) 1690–1736

English poet

14 Foolish eyes, thy streams give over,
Wine, not water, binds the lover:
At the table then be shining,
Gay coquette, and all designing.
'Song' (written c.1726)

George Santayana 1863–1952

Spanish-born philosopher and critic

15 Fanaticism consists in redoubling your effort when you have forgotten your aim.
The Life of Reason (1905) vol. 1, Introduction

16 Those who cannot remember the past are condemned to repeat it.
The Life of Reason (1905) vol. 1, ch. 12

17 It takes patience to appreciate domestic bliss; volatile spirits prefer unhappiness.
The Life of Reason (1905) vol. 2, ch. 2

18 An artist is a dreamer consenting to dream of the actual world.
The Life of Reason (1905) vol. 4, ch. 3

19 Music is essentially useless, as life is: but both have an ideal extension which lends utility to its conditions.
The Life of Reason (1905) vol. 4, ch. 4

20 The truth is cruel, but it can be loved, and it makes free those who have loved it.
Little Essays (1920) 'Ideal Immortality'

21 There is no cure for birth and death save to enjoy the interval.
Soliloquies in England (1922) 'War Shrines'

'Sapper' (*Herman Cyril McNeile*) 1888–1937

British novelist

22 Hugh pulled out his cigarette-case. 'Turkish this side Virginia that.'
Bull-dog Drummond (1920) ch. 8

Sappho

Greek lyric poet of the late 7th century BC

1 φαίνεταί μοι κῆνος ἴσος θέοισιν
ἔμμεν' ὤνηρ, ὄττις ἐνάντιός τοι
ἰσδάνει καὶ πλάσιον ἆδυ φωνεί-
σας ὐπακούει.

καὶ γελαίσας ἰμέροεν, τό μ' ἦ μὰν
καρδίαν ἐν στήθεσιν ἐπτόαισεν,
ὠς γὰρ ἔς σ' ἴδω βρόχε', ὤς με φώναι-
σ' οὐδ' ἒν ἔτ' εἴκει,

ἀλλ' ἄκαν μὲν γλῶσσα πέπαγε, λέπτον
δ' αὔτικα χρῶι πῦρ ὐπαδεδρόμηκεν,
ὀππάτεσσι δ' οὐδ' ἒν ὄρημμ', ἐπιρρόμ-
βεισι δ' ἄκουαι,

κὰδ δέ μ' ἴδρως κακχέεται, τρόμος δὲ
παῖσαν ἄγρει, χλωροτέρα δὲ ποίας
ἔμμι, τεθνάκην δ' ὀλίγω 'πιδεύης
φαίνομ' ἔμ' αὔται.

That man seems to me on a par with the gods who
sits in your company and listens to you so close to
him speaking sweetly and laughing sexily, such a
thing makes my heart flutter in my breast, for when I
see you even for a moment, then power to speak
another word fails me, instead my tongue freezes into
silence, and at once a gentle fire has caught
throughout my flesh, and I see nothing with my eyes,
and there's a drumming in my ears, and sweat pours
down me, and trembling seizes all of me, and I become
paler than grass, and I seem to fail almost to the point
of death in my very self.

D. L. Page (ed.) *Lyrica Graeca Selecta* (1968) no. 199

2 οἶον τὸ γλυκύμαλον ἐρεύθεται ἄκρῳ ἐπ' ὔσδῳ,
ἄκρον ἐπ' ἀκροτάτῳ, λελάθοντο δὲ μαλοδρόπηες,
οὐ μὰν ἐκλελάθοντ', ἀλλ' οὐκ ἐδύναντ' ἐπίκεσθαι.

Just as the sweet-apple reddens on the high branch,
high on the highest, and the apple-pickers missed it,
or rather did not miss it out, but could not reach it.

D. L. Page (ed.) *Lyrica Graeca Selecta* (1968) no. 224
(describing a girl before her marriage). Cf. Rossetti 547:13

John Singer Sargent 1856–1925

American painter

3 Every time I paint a portrait I lose a friend.

In N. Bentley and E. Esar *Treasury of Humorous Quotations*
(1951)

Leslie Sarony 1897–1985

British songwriter

4 Ain't it grand to be blooming well dead?

Title of song (1932)

Nathalie Sarraute 1902–

French novelist

5 Radio and television . . . have succeeded in lifting the
manufacture of banality out of the sphere of
handicraft and placed it in that of a major industry.

Times Literary Supplement 10 June 1960, p. 371

Jean-Paul Sartre 1905–80

French philosopher, novelist, playwright, and critic

6 *Quand les riches se font la guerre ce sont les pauvres qui
meurent.*

When the rich wage war it's the poor who die.

Le Diable et le bon Dieu (1951) act 1, tableau 1

7 *L'écrivain doit donc refuser de se laisser transformer en
institution.*

A writer must refuse, therefore, to allow himself to be
transformed into an institution.

Refusing the Nobel Prize at Stockholm, 22 October 1964;
in M. Contat and M. Rybalka (eds.) *Les Écrits de Sartre*
(1970) p. 403

8 *L'existence précède et commande l'essence.*

Existence precedes and rules essence.

L'Être et le néant (1943) pt. 4, ch. 1

9 *Je suis condamné à être libre.*

I am condemned to be free.

L'Être et le néant (1943) pt. 4, ch. 1

10 *L'homme est une passion inutile.*

Man is a useless passion.

L'Être et le néant (1943) pt. 4, ch. 2

11 *Alors, c'est ça l'Enfer. Je n'aurais jamais cru . . . Vous
vous rappelez: le soufre, le bûcher, le gril . . . Ah! quelle
plaisanterie. Pas besoin de gril, l'Enfer, c'est les Autres.*

So that's what Hell is: I'd never have believed it . . .
Do you remember, brimstone, the stake, the gridiron?
. . . What a joke! No need of a gridiron, Hell is other
people.

Huis Clos (1944) sc. 5. Cf. Eliot 270:9

12 *Comme tous les songe-creux, je confondis le
désenchantement avec la vérité.*

Like all dreamers, I mistook disenchantment for truth.

Les Mots (1964) 'Écrire'

13 *Je confondis les choses avec leurs noms: c'est croire.*

I confused things with their names: that is belief.

Les Mots (1964) 'Écrire'

14 *Il n'y a pas de bon père, c'est la règle; qu'on n'en tienne
pas grief aux hommes mais au lien de paternité qui est
pourri. Faire des enfants, rien de mieux; en avoir, quelle
iniquité!*

There is no good father, that's the rule. Don't lay the
blame on men but on the bond of paternity, which is
rotten. To beget children, nothing better; to *have*
them, what iniquity!

Les Mots (1964) 'Lire'

15 *Les bons pauvres ne savent pas que leur office est d'exercer
notre générosité.*

The poor don't know that their function in life is to
exercise our generosity.

Les Mots (1964) 'Lire'

16 *Elle ne croyait à rien; seul, son scepticisme l'empêchait
d'être athée.*

She believed in nothing; only her scepticism kept her
from being an atheist.

Les Mots (1964) 'Lire'

17 *La vie humaine commence de l'autre côté du désespoir.*

Human life begins on the far side of despair.

Les Mouches (1943) act 3, sc. 2

1 *Ma pensée, c'est moi: voilà pourquoi je ne peux pas m'arrêter. J'existe par ce que je pense . . . et je ne peux pas m'empêcher de penser.*

My thought is me: that's why I can't stop. I exist by what I think . . . and I can't prevent myself from thinking.

   La Nausée (1938) 'Lundi'

2 *Je déteste les victimes quand elles respectent leurs bourreaux.*

I hate victims who respect their executioners.

   Les Séquestrés d'Altona (1960) act 1, sc. 1

3 *Je me méfie des incommunicables, c'est la source de toute violence.*

I distrust the incommunicable: it is the source of all violence.

   'Qu'est-ce que la littérature?' in *Les Temps Modernes* July 1947, p. 106

Siegfried Sassoon 1886–1967

English poet

4 If I were fierce, and bald, and short of breath,
I'd live with scarlet Majors at the Base,
And speed glum heroes up the line to death.
   'Base Details' (1918)

5 I'd like to see a Tank come down the stalls,
Lurching to rag-time tunes, or 'Home, sweet Home',—
And there'd be no more jokes in Music-halls
To mock the riddled corpses round Bapaume.
   'Blighters' (1917)

6 Does it matter?—losing your sight? . . .
There's such splendid work for the blind;
And people will always be kind,
As you sit on the terrace remembering
And turning your face to the light.
   'Does it Matter?' (1918)

7 Soldiers are citizens of death's grey land,
Drawing no dividend from time's tomorrows.
   'Dreamers' (1918)

8 Why do you lie with your legs ungainly huddled,
And one arm bent across your sullen cold
Exhausted face? . . .
You are too young to fall asleep for ever;
And when you sleep you remind me of the dead.
   'The Dug-Out' (1919)

9 Everyone suddenly burst out singing;
And I was filled with such delight
As prisoned birds must find in freedom.
   'Everyone Sang' (1919)

10 The song was wordless; the singing will never be done.
   'Everyone Sang' (1919)

11 'Good-morning; good morning!' the General said
When we met him last week on our way to the line.
Now the soldiers he smiled at are most of 'em dead,
And we're cursing his staff for incompetent swine.
'He's a cheery old card,' grunted Harry to Jack
As they slogged up to Arras with rifle and pack.

But he did for them both by his plan of attack.
   'The General' (1918)

12 Splendid to eat and sleep and choose a wife,
Safe with his wound, a citizen of life.
He hobbled blithely through the garden gate,
And thought: 'Thank God they had to amputate!'
   'The One-Legged Man' (1917)

13 Here was the world's worst wound. And here with pride
'Their name liveth for ever' the Gateway claims.
Was ever an immolation so belied
As these intolerably nameless names?
   'On Passing the New Menin Gate' (1928)

George Savile

See 1st MARQUESS OF HALIFAX

Dorothy L. Sayers 1893–1957

English writer of detective fiction

14 A society in which consumption has to be artificially stimulated in order to keep production going is a society founded on trash and waste, and such a society is a house built upon sand.
   Creed or Chaos? (1947) ch. 6

15 I admit it is better fun to punt than to be punted, and that a desire to have all the fun is nine-tenths of the law of chivalry.
   Gaudy Night (1935) ch. 14

Al Scalpone

16 The family that prays together stays together.
   Motto devised for the Roman Catholic Family Rosary Crusade, 1947

Hugh Scanlon (Baron Scanlon) 1913–

British trades-union leader

17 Of course liberty is not licence. Liberty in my view is conforming to majority opinion.
   Television interview, 9 August 1977, in *Listener* 11 August 1977

Arthur Scargill 1938–

British trades-union leader

18 Parliament itself would not exist in its present form had people not defied the law.
   Evidence to House of Commons Select Committee on Employment, 2 April 1980, in *House of Commons Paper no. 462 of Session 1979–80* p. 55

Friedrich von Schelling 1775–1854

German philosopher

19 *Architektur ist überhaupt die erstarrte Musik.*

Architecture in general is frozen music

   Philosophie der Kunst (1809) in *Werke* (1916) vol. 2, p. 34

Friedrich von Schiller 1759–1805

German playwright and poet

1 *Freude, schöner Götterfunken,*
Tochter aus Elysium,
Wir betreten feuertrunken,
Himmlische, dein Heiligtum.
Deine Zauber binden wieder,
Was die Mode streng geteilt,
Alle Menschen werden Brüder
Wo dein sanfter Flügel weilt.

Joy, beautiful radiance of the gods, daughter of
Elysium, we set foot in your heavenly shrine dazzled
by your brilliance. Your charms re-unite what
common use has harshly divided: all men become
brothers under your tender wing.
   'An die Freude' (1785)

2 *Die Sonne geht in meinem Staat nicht unter.*

The sun does not set in my dominions.
   Don Carlos (1787) act 1, sc. 6 (Philip II)

3 *Mit der Dummheit kämpfen Götter selbst vergebens.*

With stupidity the gods themselves struggle in vain.
   Die Jungfrau von Orleans (1801) act 3, sc. 6

4 *Die Weltgeschichte ist das Weltgericht.*

The world's history is the world's judgement.
   'Resignation' (1786) st. 19

Moritz Schlick

German philosopher

5 The meaning of a proposition is the method of its
verification.
   Philosophical Review (1936) vol. 45, p. 341

Artur Schnabel 1882–1951

Austrian-born pianist

6 I know two kinds of audiences only—one coughing,
and one not coughing.
   My Life and Music (1961) pt. 2, ch. 10

7 The notes I handle no better than many pianists. But
the pauses between the notes—ah, that is where the
art resides!
   In *Chicago Daily News* 11 June 1958

8 Too easy for children, and too difficult for artists.
   Of Mozart's sonatas, in Nat Shapiro (ed.) *Encyclopaedia of
   Quotations about Music* (1978) p. 58. In *My Life and Music*
   (1961) p. 122, Schnabel says: 'Children are given Mozart
   because of the small *quantity* of the notes; grown-ups avoid
   Mozart because of the great *quality* of the notes'

Budd Schulberg 1914–

American screenwriter

9 I could have had class. I could have been a contender.
   On the Waterfront (1954 film); spoken by Marlon Brando

Diane B. Schulder 1937–

American lawyer

10 Law is a reflection and a source of prejudice. It both
enforces and suggests forms of bias.
   In Robin Morgan *Sisterhood is Powerful* (1970) p. 139

E. F. Schumacher 1911–77

German-born economist

11 Call a thing immoral or ugly, soul-destroying or
a degradation of man, a peril to the peace of the world
or to the well-being of future generations: as long as
you have not shown it to be 'uneconomic' you have
not really questioned its right to exist, grow, and
prosper.
   Small is Beautiful (1973) pt. 1, ch. 3

J. A. Schumpeter 1883–1950

American economist

12 The cold metal of economic theory is in Marx's pages
immersed in such a wealth of steaming phrases as to
acquire a temperature not naturally its own.
   Capitalism, Socialism and Democracy (1942) p. 21

Carl Schurz 1829–1906

American soldier and politician

13 My country, right or wrong; if right, to be kept right;
and if wrong, to be set right!
   Speech, US Senate, 29 February 1872, in *Congressional
   Globe* vol. 45, p. 1287. Cf. Decatur 233:14

Albert Schweitzer 1875–1965

Franco-German missionary

14 *Am Abend des dritten Tages, als wir bei Sonnenuntergang*
gerade durch eine Herde Nilpferde hindurchfuhren, stand
urplötzlich, von mir nicht geahnt und nicht gesucht, das
Wort 'Ehrfurcht vor dem Leben' vor mir.

Late on the third day, at the very moment when, at
sunset, we were making our way through a herd of
hippopotamuses, there flashed upon my mind,
unforeseen and unsought, the phrase, 'Reverence for
Life'.
   Aus meinem Leben und Denken (1933) ch. 13

15 *Die Wahrheit hat keine Stunde. Ihre Zeit ist immer und*
gerade dann wenn sie am unzeitgemässesten scheint.

Truth has no special time of its own. Its hour is now
—always, and indeed then most truly when it seems
most unsuitable to actual circumstances.
   Zwischen Wasser und Urwald (On the Edge of the Primeval
   Forest, 1922) ch. 11

Kurt Schwitters 1887–1948

German painter

16 *Ich bin Maler, ich nagle meine Bilder.*

I am a painter and I nail my pictures together.
   In R. Hausmann *Am Anfang war Dada* (1972) p. 63

Alexander Scott *c.*1525–*c.*1584

Scottish poet

1 Love is ane fervent fire,
Kindled without desire,
Short pleasure, long displeasure;
Repentance is the hire;
And pure treasure without measure.
Love is ane fervent fire.
   'Lo, What it is to Love' (*c.*1568)

C. P. Scott 1846–1932

British journalist; editor of the Manchester Guardian,
1872–1929

2 A newspaper is of necessity something of a monopoly,
and its first duty is to shun the temptations of
monopoly. Its primary office is the gathering of news.
At the peril of its soul it must see that the supply is
not tainted. Neither in what it gives, nor in what it
does not give, nor in the mode of presentation must
the unclouded face of truth suffer wrong. Comment is
free, but facts are sacred.
   Manchester Guardian 5 May 1921

Robert Falcon Scott 1868–1912

English polar explorer

3 Great God! this is an awful place.
   Of the South Pole; Journal, 17 January 1912, in *Scott's Last*
   Expedition (1913) vol. 1, ch. 18

4 For God's sake look after our people.
   Last journal entry, 29 March 1912, in *Scott's Last*
   Expedition (1913) vol. 1, ch. 20

5 Make the boy interested in natural history if you can;
it is better than games.
   Last letter to his wife, in *Scott's Last Expedition* (1913)
   vol. 1, ch. 20

6 Had we lived, I should have had a tale to tell of the
hardihood, endurance, and courage of my companions
which would have stirred the heart of every
Englishman. These rough notes and our dead bodies
must tell the tale.
   'Message to the Public' in late editions of *The Times*
   11 February 1913, and those of the following day; in
   Scott's Last Expedition (1913) vol. 1, ch. 20

Sir Walter Scott 1771–1832

Scottish novelist and poet

7 The valiant Knight of Triermain
Rung forth his challenge-blast again,
But answer came there none.
   The Bridal of Triermain (1813) canto 3, st. 10

8 To the Lords of Convention 'twas Claver'se who spoke,
'Ere the King's crown shall fall there are crowns to be
   broke;
So let each cavalier who loves honour and me,
Come follow the bonnet of Bonny Dundee.
Come fill up my cup, come fill up my can,
Come saddle your horses, and call up your men;
Come open the West Port, and let me gang free,
And it's room for the bonnets of Bonny Dundee!'
   The Doom of Devorgoil (1830) act 2, sc. 2 'Bonny Dundee'.
   Cf. Scott 560:3

9 His ready speech flowed fair and free,
In phrase of gentlest courtesy;
Yet seemed that tone, and gesture bland,
Less used to sue than to command.
   The Lady of the Lake (1810) canto 1, st. 21

10 He is gone on the mountain,
He is lost to the forest,
Like a summer-dried fountain,
When our need was the sorest.
   The Lady of the Lake (1810) canto 3, st. 16

11 Respect was mingled with surprise,
And the stern joy which warriors feel
In foemen worthy of their steel.
   The Lady of the Lake (1810) canto 5, st. 10

12 Vengeance, deep-brooding o'er the slain,
Had locked the source of softer woe;
And burning pride and high disdain
Forbade the rising tear to flow.
   The Lay of the Last Minstrel (1805) canto 1, st. 9

13 If thou would'st view fair Melrose aright,
Go visit it by the pale moonlight;
For the gay beams of lightsome day
Gild, but to flout, the ruins grey.
   The Lay of the Last Minstrel (1805) canto 2, st. 1

14   For ne'er
Was flattery lost on poet's ear:
A simple race! they waste their toil
For the vain tribute of a smile.
   The Lay of the Last Minstrel (1805) canto 4, *ad fin.*

15 It is the secret sympathy,
The silver link, the silken tie,
Which heart to heart, and mind to mind,
In body and in soul can bind.
   The Lay of the Last Minstrel (1805) canto 5, st. 13

16 Breathes there the man, with soul so dead,
Who never to himself hath said,
This is my own, my native land!
Whose heart hath ne'er within him burned,
As home his footsteps he hath turned
From wandering on a foreign strand!
   The Lay of the Last Minstrel (1805) canto 6, st. 1

17 Despite those titles, power, and pelf,
The wretch, concentred all in self,
Living, shall forfeit fair renown,
And, doubly dying, shall go down
To the vile dust, from whence he sprung,
Unwept, unhonoured, and unsung.

O Caledonia! stern and wild,
Meet nurse for a poetic child!
Land of brown heath and shaggy wood,
Land of the mountain and the flood,
Land of my sires! what mortal hand
Can e'er untie the filial band
That knits me to thy rugged strand!
   The Lay of the Last Minstrel (1805) canto 6, st. 1

18 O! many a shaft, at random sent,
Finds mark the archer little meant!
And many a word, at random spoken,
May soothe or wound a heart that's broken.
   The Lord of the Isles (1813) canto 5, st. 18

19 Had'st thou but lived, though stripped of power,
A watchman on the lonely tower,
   Marmion (1808) introduction to canto 1, st. 9

1 Now is the stately column broke,
  The beacon-light is quenched in smoke,
  The trumpet's silver sound is still,
  The warder silent on the hill!
    Marmion (1808) introduction to canto 1, st. 8

2 And come he slow, or come he fast,
  It is but Death who comes at last.
    Marmion (1808) canto 2, st. 30

3 O, young Lochinvar is come out of the west,
  Through all the wide Border his steed was the best.
    Marmion (1808) canto 5, st. 12 ('Lochinvar' st. 1)

4 So faithful in love, and so dauntless in war,
  There never was knight like the young Lochinvar.
    Marmion (1808) canto 5, st. 12 ('Lochinvar' st. 1)

5 For a laggard in love, and a dastard in war,
  Was to wed the fair Ellen of brave Lochinvar.
    Marmion (1808) canto 5, st. 12 ('Lochinvar' st. 2)

6 O come ye in peace here, or come ye in war,
  Or to dance at our bridal, young Lord Lochinvar?
    Marmion (1808) canto 5, st. 12 ('Lochinvar' st. 3)

7 And now I am come, with this lost love of mine,
  To lead but one measure, drink one cup of wine.
    Marmion (1808) canto 5, st. 12 ('Lochinvar' st. 4)

8 O what a tangled web we weave,
  When first we practise to deceive!
    Marmion (1808) canto 6, st. 17

9 O Woman! in our hours of ease,
  Uncertain, coy, and hard to please,
  And variable as the shade
  By the light quivering aspen made;
  When pain and anguish wring the brow,
  A ministering angel thou!
    Marmion (1808) canto 6, st. 30

10 The stubborn spear-men still made good
   Their dark impenetrable wood,
   Each stepping where his comrade stood,
   The instant that he fell.
    Marmion (1808) canto 6, st. 34

11 Still from the sire the son shall hear
   Of the stern strife, and carnage drear,
   Of Flodden's fatal field,
   Where shivered was fair Scotland's spear,
   And broken was her shield!
    Marmion (1808) canto 6, st. 34

12 O, Brignal banks are wild and fair,
   And Greta woods are green,
   And you may gather garlands there
   Would grace a summer queen.
    Rokeby (1813) canto 3, st. 16

13 It's no fish ye're buying—it's men's lives.
    The Antiquary (1816) ch. 11

14 Widowed wife, and married maid,
   Betrothed, betrayer, and betrayed!
    The Betrothed (1825) ch. 15

15 Vacant heart and hand, and eye,—
   Easy live and quiet die.
    The Bride of Lammermoor (1819) ch. 2

16 I live by twa trades . . . fiddle, sir, and spade; filling
   the world, and emptying of it.
    The Bride of Lammermoor (1819) ch. 24

17 Touch not the cat but a glove.
    The Fair Maid of Perth (1828) ch. 34 (*but* without)

18 It's ill taking the breeks aff a wild Highlandman.
    The Fortunes of Nigel (1822) ch. 5

19 Gin by pailfuls, wine in rivers,
   Dash the window-glass to shivers!
   For three wild lads were we, brave boys,
   And three wild lads were we;
   Thou on the land, and I on the sand,
   And Jack on the gallows-tree!
    Guy Mannering (1815) ch. 34

20 The hour is come, but not the man.
    The Heart of Midlothian (1818) ch. 4, title

21 The passive resistance of the Tolbooth-gate.
    The Heart of Midlothian (1818) ch. 6

22 Proud Maisie is in the wood,
   Walking so early,
   Sweet Robin sits in the bush,
   Singing so rarely.
    The Heart of Midlothian (1818) ch. 40

23 'Pax vobiscum [Peace be with you]' will answer all
   queries.
    Ivanhoe (1819) ch. 26

24 His morning walk was beneath the elms in the
   churchyard; 'for death,' he said, 'had been his
   next-door neighbour for so many years, that he had
   no apology for dropping the acquaintance.'
    A Legend of Montrose (1819) introduction

25 March, march, Ettrick and Teviotdale,
   Why the deil dinna ye march forward in order?
   March, march, Eskdale and Liddesdale,
   All the Blue Bonnets are bound for the Border.
    The Monastery (1820) ch. 25

26 Ah! County Guy, the hour is nigh,
   The sun has left the lea,
   The orange flower perfumes the bower,
   The breeze is on the sea.
    Quentin Durward (1823) ch. 4

27 And it's ill speaking between a fou man and a fasting.
    Redgauntlet (1824) letter 11 'Wandering Willie's Tale'

28 The ae half of the warld thinks the tither daft.
    Redgauntlet (1824) 'Journal of Darsie Latimer' ch. 7

29 But with the morning cool repentance came.
    Rob Roy (1817) ch. 12

30 Come fill up my cup, come fill up my cann,
   Come saddle my horses, and call up my man;
   Come open your gates, and let me gae free,
   I daurna stay langer in bonny Dundee.
    Rob Roy (1817) ch. 23. Cf. Scott 559:8

31 There's a gude time coming.
    Rob Roy (1817) ch. 32

32 The play-bill, which is said to have announced the
   tragedy of Hamlet, the character of the Prince of
   Denmark being left out.
    The Talisman (1825) introduction (commonly alluded to as
    'Hamlet without the Prince'). See W. J. Parke *Musical
    Memories* (1830) vol. 1, p. 97 for a similar anecdote from
    1787

33 Rouse the lion from his lair.
    The Talisman (1825) ch. 6

1 The Big Bow-Wow strain I can do myself like any now
  going; but the exquisite touch, which renders
  ordinary commonplace things and characters
  interesting, from the truth of the description and the
  sentiment, is denied to me.
    On Jane Austen, in W. E. K. Anderson (ed.) *Journals of Sir
    Walter Scott* (1972) 14 March 1826. Cf. Pembroke 511:11

2 I would like to be there, were it but to see how the cat
  jumps.
    In W. E. K. Anderson (ed.) *Journals of Sir Walter Scott*
    (1972) 7 October 1826

3 The blockheads talk of my being like
  Shakespeare—not fit to tie his brogues.
    In W. E. K. Anderson (ed.) *Journals of Sir Walter Scott*
    (1972) 11 December 1826

4 Too many flowers . . . too little fruit.
    Describing the work of Felicia Hemans; letter to Joanna
    Baillie, 18 July 1823, in *Letters* (Centenary ed.) vol. 8

5 Their factions have been so long envenomed and
  having so little ground to fight their battle in that they
  [the Irish] are like people fighting with daggers in a
  hogshead.
    Letter to Joanna Baillie, 12 October 1825, in H. J. C.
    Grierson (ed.) *Letters of Sir Walter Scott* vol. 9 (1935)

6 All men who have turned out worth anything have
  had the chief hand in their own education.
    Letter to J. G. Lockhart, *c*.16 June 1830, in H. J. C.
    Grierson (ed.) *Letters of Sir Walter Scott* vol. 11 (1936)

7 We shall never learn to feel and respect our real
  calling and destiny, unless we have taught ourselves
  to consider every thing as moonshine, compared with
  the education of the heart.
    To J. G. Lockhart, August 1825, in Lockhart's *Life of Sir
    Walter Scott* vol. 6 (1837) ch. 2

Scottish Metrical Psalms 1650

8 The Lord's my shepherd, I'll not want.
  He makes me down to lie
  In pastures green: he leadeth me
  the quiet waters by.
  My soul he doth restore again;
  and me to walk doth make
  Within the paths of righteousness,
  ev'n for his own name's sake.

  Yea, though I walk in death's dark vale,
  yet will I fear none ill:
  For thou art with me; and thy rod
  and staff me comfort still.
  My table thou hast furnished
  in presence of my foes;
  My head thou dost with oil anoint,
  and my cup overflows.
    Psalm 23, v. 1. Cf. Book of Common Prayer 125:14

9 How lovely is thy dwelling-place,
  O Lord of hosts, to me!
  The tabernacles of thy grace
  how pleasant, Lord, they be!
    Psalm 84, v. 1. Cf. Book of Common Prayer 130:16

10 I to the hills will lift mine eyes
   from whence doth come mine aid.
   My safety cometh from the Lord,
   who heav'n and earth hath made.
    Psalm 121, v. 1. Cf. Book of Common Prayer 133:23

11 The race that long in darkness pined
   have seen a glorious light.
    Paraphrase 19. Cf. Isaiah 82:26

Edmund Hamilton Sears 1810–76

American minister

12 It came upon the midnight clear,
   That glorious song of old,
   From Angels bending near the earth
   To touch their harps of gold;
   'Peace on the earth, good will to man
   From Heaven's all gracious King.'
   The world in solemn stillness lay
   To hear the angels sing.
    The Christian Register (1850) 'That Glorious Song of Old'

Sir Charles Sedley c.1639–1701

English playwright and poet

13 Ah, Chloris! that I now could sit
   As unconcerned as when
   Your infant beauty could beget
   No pleasure, nor no pain!
    'Child and Maiden' (1668)

14 Love still has something of the sea
   From whence his mother rose.
    'Love still has something'

15 Phyllis, without frown or smile,
   Sat and knotted all the while.
    'Phyllis Knotting' (1694)

16 Phyllis is my only joy,
   Faithless as the winds or seas;
   Sometimes coming, sometimes coy,
   Yet she never fails to please.
    'Song'

17 She deceiving,
   I believing,
   What need lovers wish for more?
    'Song'

Alan Seeger 1888–1916

American poet

18 I have a rendezvous with Death
   At some disputed barricade.
    'I Have a Rendezvous with Death' (1916)

Pete Seeger 1919–

American folk singer and songwriter

19 Where have all the flowers gone?
    Title of song (1961)

Sir John Seeley 1834–95

English historian

1 We [the English] seem, as it were, to have conquered and peopled half the world in a fit of absence of mind.
   The Expansion of England (1883) Lecture 1

John Selden 1584–1654

English historian and antiquary

2 *Scrutamini scripturas* [Let us look at the scriptures]. These two words have undone the world.
   Table Talk (1689) 'Bible Scripture'. Cf. St John 96:21

3 Old friends are best. King James used to call for his old shoes; they were easiest for his feet.
   Table Talk (1689) 'Friends'

4 'Tis not the drinking that is to be blamed, but the excess.
   Table Talk (1689) 'Humility'

5 Ignorance of the law excuses no man; not that all men know the law, but because 'tis an excuse every man will plead, and no man can tell how to confute him.
   Table Talk (1689) 'Law'

6 Take a straw and throw it up into the air, you shall see by that which way the wind is.
   Table Talk (1689) 'Libels'

7 Marriage is nothing but a civil contract.
   Table Talk (1689) 'Marriage'

8 A king is a thing men have made for their own sakes, for quietness' sake. Just as in a family one man is appointed to buy the meat.
   Table Talk (1689) 'Of a King'

9 There never was a merry world since the fairies left off dancing, and the Parson left conjuring.
   Table Talk (1689) 'Parson'

10 There is not anything in the world so much abused as this sentence, *Salus populi suprema lex esto.*
   Table Talk (1689) 'People'. Cf. Cicero 203:27

11 Pleasure is nothing else but the intermission of pain.
   Table Talk (1689) 'Pleasure'

12 Syllables govern the world.
   Table Talk (1689) 'Power: State'

13 Preachers say, Do as I say, not as I do.
   Table Talk (1689) 'Preaching'

Arthur Seldon 1916–

British economist

14 Government of the busy by the bossy for the bully.
   Capitalism (1990) p. 111 (subheading on over-government)

W. C. Sellar 1898–1951 *and* R. J. Yeatman 1898–1968

British writers

15 For every person who wants to teach there are approximately thirty who don't want to learn—much.
   And Now All This (1932) introduction

16 History is not what you thought. *It is what you can remember.*
   1066 and All That (1930) 'Compulsory Preface'

17 The Roman Conquest was, however, a *Good Thing*, since the Britons were only natives at the time.
   1066 and All That (1930) ch. 1

18 Edward III had very good manners ... and made the memorable epitaph: 'Honi soie qui mal y pense' ('Honey, your silk stocking's hanging down').
   1066 and All That (1930) ch. 24. Cf. Anonymous 20:9

19 The cruel Queen died and a post-mortem examination revealed the word 'CALLOUS' engraved on her heart.
   1066 and All That (1930) ch. 32. Cf. Mary Tudor 453:1

20 The Cavaliers (Wrong but Wromantic) and the Roundheads (Right but Repulsive).
   1066 and All That (1930) ch. 35

21 The Rump Parliament—so called because it had been sitting for such a long time.
   1066 and All That (1930) ch. 35

22 Charles II was always very merry and was therefore not so much a king as a Monarch.
   1066 and All That (1930) ch. 36

23 The National Debt is a very Good Thing and it would be dangerous to pay it off, for fear of Political Economy.
   1066 and All That (1930) ch. 38

24 Napoleon's armies always used to march on their stomachs shouting: 'Vive l'Intérieur!'
   1066 and All That (1930) ch. 48. Cf. Napoleon 490:3

25 Most memorable ... was the discovery (made by all the rich men in England at once) that women and children could work twenty-five hours a day in factories without many of them dying or becoming excessively deformed. This was known as the Industrial Revelation.
   1066 and All That (1930) ch. 49

26 Gladstone ... spent his declining years trying to guess the answer to the Irish Question; unfortunately whenever he was getting warm, the Irish secretly changed the Question.
   1066 and All That (1930) ch. 57

27 AMERICA was thus clearly top nation, and History came to a .
   1066 and All That (1930) ch. 62

Seneca ('the Younger') *c.*4 BC–AD 65

Roman philosopher and poet

28 *Ignoranti, quem portum petat, nullus suus ventus est.*
   If one does not know to which port one is sailing, no wind is favourable.
   Epistulae Morales no. 71, sect. 3

29 *Homines dum docent discunt.*
   Even while they teach, men learn.
   Epistulae Morales no. 7, sect. 8

1 *Nil melius aeterna lex fecit, quam quod unum introitum nobis ad vitam dedit, exitus multos.*

Eternal law has arranged nothing better than this, that it has given us one way in to life, but many ways out.

Epistulae Morales no. 70, sect. 14

2 *Eripere vitam nemo non homini potest,*
At nemo mortem; mille ad hanc aditus patent.

Anyone can stop a man's life, but no one his death; a thousand doors open on to it.

Phoenissae l. 152

3 *Illi mors gravis incubat*
Qui notus nimis omnibus
Ignotus moritur sibi.

On him does death lie heavily who, but too well known to all, dies to himself unknown.

Thyestes chorus 2 (translated by F. J. Miller)

Robert W. Service 1874–1958

Canadian poet

4 A promise made is a debt unpaid, and the trail has its own stern code.

'The Cremation of Sam McGee' (1907)

5 Ah! the clock is always slow;
It is later than you think.

'It Is Later Than You Think' (1921)

6 This is the law of the Yukon, that only the Strong shall thrive;
That surely the Weak shall perish, and only the Fit survive.

'The Law of the Yukon' (1907)

7 When we, the Workers, all demand: 'What are WE fighting for?' . . .
Then, then we'll end that stupid crime, that devil's madness—War.

'Michael' (1921)

8 Back of the bar, in a solo game, sat Dangerous Dan McGrew,
And watching his luck was his light-o'-love, the lady that's known as Lou.

'The Shooting of Dan McGrew' (1907)

William Seward 1801–72

American politician

9 I know, and all the world knows, that revolutions never go backward.

Speech at Rochester, 25 October 1858, in *The Irrepressible Conflict* (1858)

Edward Sexby d. 1658

English conspirator

10 Killing no murder briefly discourst in three questions.

Title of pamphlet (an apology for tyrannicide, 1657)

Anne Sexton 1928–74

American poet

11 In a dream you are never eighty.

'Old' (1962)

James Seymour and Rian James

12 You're going out a youngster but you've *got* to come back a star.

42nd Street (1933 film)

Thomas Shadwell c.1642–92

English playwright

13 Words may be false and full of art,
Sighs are the natural language of the heart.

Psyche (1675) act 3

14 And wit's the noblest frailty of the mind.

A True Widow (1679) act 2, sc. 1. Cf. Dryden 260:29

15 The haste of a fool is the slowest thing in the world.

A True Widow (1679) act 3, sc. 1

16 Every man loves what he is good at.

A True Widow (1679) act 5, sc. 1

17 Instantly, in the twinkling of a bed-staff.

The Virtuoso (1676) act 1, sc. 1

Peter Shaffer 1926–

English playwright

18 All my wife has ever taken from the Mediterranean—from that whole vast intuitive culture—are four bottles of Chianti to make into lamps.

Equus (1973) act 1, sc. 18

19 The Normal is the good smile in a child's eyes—all right. It is also the dead stare in a million adults. It both sustains and kills—like a God. It is the Ordinary made beautiful; it is also the Average made lethal.

Equus (1983 ed.) act 1, sc. 19

1st Earl of Shaftesbury 1621–83

English statesman

20 'People differ in their discourse and profession about these matters, but men of sense are really but of one religion.' . . . 'Pray, my lord, what religion is that which men of sense agree in?' 'Madam,' says the earl immediately, 'men of sense never tell it.'

Bishop Gilbert Burnet *History of My Own Time* vol. 1 (1724) bk. 2, ch. 1 n.

3rd Earl of Shaftesbury 1671–1713

English statesman and philosopher

21 How comes it to pass, then, that we appear such cowards in reasoning, and are so afraid to stand the test of ridicule?

A Letter Concerning Enthusiasm (1708) sect. 2

22 Truth, 'tis supposed, may bear all lights: and one of those in which things are to be viewed, in order to [attain] a thorough recognition is that by which we discern whatever is liable to ridicule in any subject.

Sensus Communis: an essay on the freedom of wit and humour (1709) pt. 1, sect. 1. Cf. Christ. 6:11 109:40

William Shakespeare 1564–1616

English playwright

The line number is given without brackets where the scene is all verse up to the quotation and the line number is certain, and in square brackets where prose makes it variable. All references are to the Oxford Standard Authors edition in one volume

All's Well that Ends Well

1　　　　　It were all one
That I should love a bright particular star
And think to wed it, he is so above me.
All's Well that Ends Well (1603–4) act 1, sc. 1, l. [97]

2 The hind that would be mated with the lion
Must die of love.
All's Well that Ends Well (1603–4) act 1, sc. 1, l. [103]

3 Your virginity, your old virginity, is like one of our French withered pears; it looks ill, it eats drily.
All's Well that Ends Well (1603–4) act 1, sc. 1, l. [176]

4 Our remedies oft in ourselves do lie
Which we ascribe to heaven. The fated sky
Gives us free scope, only doth backward pull
Our slow designs when we ourselves are dull.
All's Well that Ends Well (1603–4) act 1, sc. 1, l. [232]

5 It is like a barber's chair that fits all buttocks.
All's Well that Ends Well (1603–4) act 2, sc. 2, l. [18]

6 A young man married is a man that's marred.
All's Well that Ends Well (1603–4) act 2, sc. 3, l. [315]

7 I know a man that had this trick of melancholy sold a goodly manor for a song.
All's Well that Ends Well (1603–4) act 3, sc. 2, l. [8]

8 The web of our life is of a mingled yarn, good and ill together: our virtues would be proud if our faults whipped them not; and our crimes would despair if they were not cherished by our own virtues.
All's Well that Ends Well (1603–4) act 4, sc. 3, l. [83]

9　　　　　Simply the thing I am
Shall make me live.
All's Well that Ends Well (1603–4) act 4, sc. 3, l. 333

10 The flowery way that leads to the broad gate and the great fire.
All's Well that Ends Well (1603–4) act 4, sc. 5, l. [58].
Cf. Macbeth 602:10

11 ... Praising what is lost
Makes the remembrance dear.
All's Well that Ends Well (1603–4) act 5, sc. 3, l. 19

Antony and Cleopatra

12 The triple pillar of the world transformed
Into a strumpet's fool.
Antony and Cleopatra (1606–7) act 1, sc. 1, l. 12

13 CLEOPATRA: If it be love indeed, tell me how much.
ANTONY: There's beggary in the love that can be reckoned.
CLEOPATRA: I'll set a bourn how far to be beloved.
ANTONY: Then must thou needs find out new heaven, new earth.
Antony and Cleopatra (1606–7) act 1, sc. 1, l. 14

14 Let Rome in Tiber melt, and the wide arch
Of the ranged empire fall. Here is my space.
Kingdoms are clay; our dungy earth alike
Feeds beast as man; the nobleness of life
Is to do thus; when such a mutual pair
And such a twain can do't.
Antony and Cleopatra (1606–7) act 1, sc. 1, l. 33

15 O excellent! I love long life better than figs.
Antony and Cleopatra (1606–7) act 1, sc. 2, l. [34]

16　　　　　On the sudden
A Roman thought hath struck him.
Antony and Cleopatra (1606–7) act 1, sc. 2, l. [90]

17 The nature of bad news infects the teller.
Antony and Cleopatra (1606–7) act 1, sc. 2, l. [103]

18 There's a great spirit gone!
Antony and Cleopatra (1606–7) act 1, sc. 2, l. [131]

19 I have seen her die twenty times upon far poorer moment. I do think there is mettle in death which commits some loving act upon her, she hath such a celerity in dying.
Antony and Cleopatra (1606–7) act 1, sc. 2, l. [150]

20 O sir! you had then left unseen a wonderful piece of work which not to have been blessed withal would have discredited your travel.
Antony and Cleopatra (1606–7) act 1, sc. 2, l. [164]

21 Indeed the tears live in an onion that should water this sorrow.
Antony and Cleopatra (1606–7) act 1, sc. 2, l. [181]

22　　　　　If you find him sad,
Say I am dancing; if in mirth, report
That I am sudden sick.
Antony and Cleopatra (1606–7) act 1, sc. 3, l. 3

23 CHARMIAN: In each thing give him way, cross him in nothing.
CLEOPATRA: Thou teachest like a fool; the way to lose him.
Antony and Cleopatra (1606–7) act 1, sc. 3, l. 9

24 In time we hate that which we often fear.
Antony and Cleopatra (1606–7) act 1, sc. 3, l. 12

25 Eternity was in our lips and eyes,
Bliss in our brows bent.
Antony and Cleopatra (1606–7) act 1, sc. 3, l. 35

26 O! my oblivion is a very Antony,
And I am all forgotten.
Antony and Cleopatra (1606–7) act 1, sc. 3, l. 90

27 It hath been taught us from the primal state
That he which is was wished until he were,
And the ebbed man, ne'er loved till ne'er worth love,
Comes deared by being lacked. This common body,
Like to a vagabond flag upon the stream,
Goes to, and back, lackeying the varying tide,
To rot itself with motion.
Antony and Cleopatra (1606–7) act 1, sc. 4, l. 41

28 Give me to drink mandragora ...
That I might sleep out this great gap of time
My Antony is away.
Antony and Cleopatra (1606–7) act 1, sc. 5, l. 4

1 O happy horse, to bear the weight of Antony!
   Do bravely, horse, for wot'st thou whom thou mov'st?
   The demi-Atlas of this earth, the arm
   And burgonet of men. He's speaking now,
   Or murmuring 'Where's my serpent of old Nile?'
   Antony and Cleopatra (1606–7) act 1, sc. 5, l. 21

2   Think on me,
   That am with Phoebus' amorous pinches black,
   And wrinkled deep in time?
   Antony and Cleopatra (1606–7) act 1, sc. 5, l. 27

3   My salad days,
   When I was green in judgment, cold in blood,
   To say as I said then!
   Antony and Cleopatra (1606–7) act 1, sc. 5, l. 73

4 I do not much dislike the matter, but
   The manner of his speech.
   Antony and Cleopatra (1606–7) act 2, sc. 2, l. 117

5 The barge she sat in, like a burnished throne,
   Burned on the water; the poop was beaten gold,
   Purple the sails, and so perfumed, that
   The winds were love-sick with them, the oars were
      silver,
   Which to the tune of flutes kept stroke, and made
   The water which they beat to follow faster,
   As amorous of their strokes. For her own person,
   It beggared all description; she did lie
   In her pavilion,—cloth-of-gold of tissue,—
   O'er-picturing that Venus where we see
   The fancy outwork nature; on each side her
   Stood pretty-dimpled boys, like smiling Cupids,
   With divers-coloured fans, whose wind did seem
   To glow the delicate cheeks which they did cool,
   And what they undid did.
   Antony and Cleopatra (1606–7) act 2, sc. 2, l. [199]

6 Her gentlewomen, like the Nereides,
   So many mermaids, tended her i' the eyes,
   And made their bends adornings; at the helm
   A seeming mermaid steers; the silken tackle
   Swell with the touches of those flower-soft hands,
   That yarely frame the office. From the barge
   A strange invisible perfume hits the sense
   Of the adjacent wharfs. The city cast
   Her people out upon her, and Antony,
   Enthroned i' the market-place, did sit alone,
   Whistling to the air; which, but for vacancy,
   Had gone to gaze on Cleopatra too
   And made a gap in nature.
   Antony and Cleopatra (1606–7) act 2, sc. 2, l. [214]

7   I saw her once
   Hop forty paces through the public street;
   And having lost her breath, she spoke, and panted
   That she did make defect perfection,
   And, breathless, power breathe forth.
   Antony and Cleopatra (1606–7) act 2, sc. 2, l. [236]

8 Age cannot wither her, nor custom stale
   Her infinite variety; other women cloy
   The appetites they feed, but she makes hungry
   Where most she satisfies; for vilest things
   Become themselves in her, that the holy priests
   Bless her when she is riggish.
   Antony and Cleopatra (1606–7) act 2, sc. 2, l. [243]

9 I have not kept the square, but that to come
   Shall all be done by the rule.
   Antony and Cleopatra (1606–7) act 2, sc. 3, l. 6

10 I' the east my pleasure lies.
    Antony and Cleopatra (1606–7) act 2, sc. 3, l. 40

11 Give me some music—music, moody food
    Of us that trade in love.
    Antony and Cleopatra (1606–7) act 2, sc. 5, l. 1

12 Give me mine angle; we'll to the river: there—
    My music playing far off—I will betray
    Tawny-finned fishes; my bended hook shall pierce
    Their slimy jaws; and, as I draw them up,
    I'll think them every one an Antony,
    And say, 'Ah, ha!' you're caught.
    Antony and Cleopatra (1606–7) act 2, sc. 5, l. 10

13 I laughed him out of patience; and that night
    I laughed him into patience: and next morn,
    Ere the ninth hour, I drunk him to his bed.
    Antony and Cleopatra (1606–7) act 2, sc. 5, l. 19

14 I will praise any man that will praise me.
    Antony and Cleopatra (1606–7) act 2, sc. 6, l. [88]

15 LEPIDUS: What manner o' thing is your crocodile?
    ANTONY: It is shaped, sir, like itself, and it is as broad
    as it hath breadth; it is just so high as it is, and
    moves with its own organs; it lives by that which
    nourisheth it; and the elements once out of it, it
    transmigrates.
    Antony and Cleopatra (1606–7) act 2, sc. 7, l. [47]

16   Egypt, thou knew'st too well
    My heart was to thy rudder tied by th' strings,
    And thou shouldst tow me after.
    Antony and Cleopatra (1606–7) act 3, sc. 9, l. 56

17   He wears the rose
    Of youth upon him.
    Antony and Cleopatra (1606–7) act 3, sc. 11, l. 20

18 Against the blown rose may they stop their nose,
    That kneeled unto the buds.
    Antony and Cleopatra (1606–7) act 3, sc. 11, l. 39

19   Yet he that can endure
    To follow with allegiance a fall'n lord,
    Does conquer him that did his master conquer,
    And earns a place i' the story.
    Antony and Cleopatra (1606–7) act 3, sc. 11, l. 43

20 I found you as a morsel, cold upon
    Dead Caesar's trencher.
    Antony and Cleopatra (1606–7) act 3, sc. 11, l. 116

21 To let a fellow that will take rewards
    And say 'God quit you!' be familiar with
    My playfellow, your hand; this kingly seal
    And plighter of high hearts.
    Antony and Cleopatra (1606–7) act 3, sc. 11, l. 123

22 Let's have one other gaudy night: call to me
    All my sad captains; fill our bowls once more;
    Let's mock the midnight bell.
    Antony and Cleopatra (1606–7) act 3, sc. 11, l. 182

23   Since my lord
    Is Antony again, I will be Cleopatra.
    Antony and Cleopatra (1606–7) act 3, sc. 11, l. 185

24 To business that we love we rise betime,
    And go to 't with delight
    Antony and Cleopatra (1606–7) act 4, sc. 4, l. 20

1   O! my fortunes have
Corrupted honest men.
Antony and Cleopatra (1606–7) act 4, sc. 5, l. 16

2 CLEOPATRA: Lord of lords!
O infinite virtue! com'st thou smiling from
The world's great snare uncaught?
ANTONY: My nightingale,
We have beat them to their beds.
Antony and Cleopatra (1606–7) act 4, sc. 8, l. 16

3 O sovereign mistress of true melancholy,
The poisonous damp of night disponge upon me,
That life, a very rebel to my will,
May hang no longer on me.
Antony and Cleopatra (1606–7) act 4, sc. 9, l. 12

4   The hearts
That spanieled me at heels, to whom I gave
Their wishes, do discandy, melt their sweets
On blossoming Caesar.
Antony and Cleopatra (1606–7) act 4, sc. 10, l. 33

5 The soul and body rive not more in parting
Than greatness going off.
Antony and Cleopatra (1606–7) act 4, sc. 11, l. 5

6 Sometimes we see a cloud that's dragonish;
A vapour sometime like a bear or lion,
A towered citadel, a pendant rock,
A forked mountain, or blue promontory
With trees upon 't, that nod unto the world
And mock our eyes with air: thou hast seen these
    signs;
They are black vesper's pageants.
Antony and Cleopatra (1606–7) act 4, sc. 12, l. 2

7 That which is now a horse, even with a thought
The rack dislimns, and makes it indistinct,
As water is in water.
Antony and Cleopatra (1606–7) act 4, sc. 12, l. 9

8 Unarm, Eros; the long day's task is done,
And we must sleep.
Antony and Cleopatra (1606–7) act 4, sc. 12, l. 35

9 Lie down, and stray no further. Now all labour
Mars what it does; yea, very force entangles
Itself with strength . . .
           Stay for me:
Where souls do couch on flowers, we'll hand in hand,
And with our sprightly port make the ghosts gaze;
Dido and her Aeneas shall want troops,
And all the haunt be ours.
Antony and Cleopatra (1606–7) act 4, sc. 12, l. 47

10   I will be
A bridegroom in my death, and run into 't
As to a lover's bed.
Antony and Cleopatra (1606–7) act 4, sc. 12, l. 99

11 All strange and terrible events are welcome,
But comforts we despise.
Antony and Cleopatra (1606–7) act 4, sc. 13, l. 3

12 ANTONY: Not Caesar's valour hath o'erthrown
      Antony
But Antony's hath triumphed on itself.
CLEOPATRA: So it should be, that none but Antony
Should conquer Antony.
Antony and Cleopatra (1606–7) act 4, sc. 13, l. 14

13 I am dying, Egypt, dying; only
I here importune death awhile, until
Of many thousand kisses the poor last
I lay upon thy lips.
Antony and Cleopatra (1606–7) act 4, sc. 13, l. 18

14 The miserable change now at my end
Lament nor sorrow at; but please your thoughts
In feeding them with those my former fortunes
Wherein I lived, the greatest prince o' the world,
The noblest; and do now not basely die,
Not cowardly put off my helmet to
My countryman; a Roman by a Roman
Valiantly vanquished.
Antony and Cleopatra (1606–7) act 4, sc. 13, l. 51

15 Hast thou no care of me? shall I abide
In this dull world, which in thy absence is
No better than a sty? O! see my women,
The crown o' the earth doth melt. My lord!
O! withered is the garland of the war,
The soldier's pole is fall'n; young boys and girls
Are level now with men; the odds is gone,
And there is nothing left remarkable
Beneath the visiting moon.
Antony and Cleopatra (1606–7) act 4, sc. 13, l. 60

16 No more, but e'en a woman and commanded
By such poor passion as the maid that milks
And does the meanest chares.
Antony and Cleopatra (1606–7) act 4, sc. 13, l. 73

17   What's brave, what's noble,
Let's do it after the high Roman fashion,
And make death proud to take us.
Antony and Cleopatra (1606–7) act 4, sc. 13, l. 86

18   A rarer spirit never
Did steer humanity; but you, gods, will give us
Some faults to make us men.
Antony and Cleopatra (1606–7) act 5, sc. 1, l. 31

19 My desolation does begin to make
A better life. 'Tis paltry to be Caesar;
Not being Fortune, he's but Fortune's knave,
A minister of her will; and it is great
To do that thing that ends all other deeds,
Which shackles accidents, and bolts up change,
Which sleeps, and never palates more the dug,
The beggar's nurse and Caesar's.
Antony and Cleopatra (1606–7) act 5, sc. 2, l. 1

20 His legs bestrid the ocean; his reared arm
Crested the world; his voice was propertied
As all the tuned spheres, and that to friends;
But when he meant to quail and shake the orb,
He was as rattling thunder. For his bounty,
There was no winter in 't; an autumn was
That grew the more by reaping; his delights
Were dolphin-like, they showed his back above
The element they lived in; in his livery
Walked crowns and crownets, realms and islands were
As plates dropped from his pocket.
Antony and Cleopatra (1606–7) act 5, sc. 2, l. 82

21 He words me, girls, he words me, that I should not
Be noble to myself.
Antony and Cleopatra (1606–7) act 5, sc. 2, l. 190

22 Finish, good lady; the bright day is done,
And we are for the dark.
Antony and Cleopatra (1606–7) act 5, sc. 2, l. 192

1   Antony
Shall be brought drunken forth, and I shall see
Some squeaking Cleopatra boy my greatness
I' the posture of a whore.
Antony and Cleopatra (1606–7) act 5, sc. 2, l. 217

2 My resolution's placed, and I have nothing
Of woman in me; now from head to foot
I am marble-constant, now the fleeting moon
No planet is of mine.
Antony and Cleopatra (1606–7) act 5, sc. 2, l. 237

3 His biting is immortal; those that do die of it do
seldom or never recover.
Antony and Cleopatra (1606–7) act 5, sc. 2, l. [246]

4 A very honest woman, but something given to lie.
Antony and Cleopatra (1606–7) act 5, sc. 2, l. [251]

5 I wish you all joy of the worm.
Antony and Cleopatra (1606–7) act 5, sc. 2, l. [260]

6 I know that a woman is a dish for the gods, if the
devil dress her not.
Antony and Cleopatra (1606–7) act 5, sc. 2, l. [274]

7 Give me my robe, put on my crown; I have
Immortal longings in me.
Antony and Cleopatra (1606–7) act 5, sc. 2, l. [282]

8   Husband, I come:
Now to that name my courage prove my title!
I am fire and air; my other elements
I give to baser life.
Antony and Cleopatra (1606–7) act 5, sc. 2, l. [289]

9 If thou and nature can so gently part,
The stroke of death is as a lover's pinch,
Which hurts, and is desired.
Antony and Cleopatra (1606–7) act 5, sc. 2, l. [296]

10 If thus thou vanishest, thou tell'st the world
It is not worth leave-taking.
Antony and Cleopatra (1606–7) act 5, sc. 2, l. [299]

11 CLEOPATRA: If she first meet the curlèd Antony,
He'll make demand of her, and spend that kiss
Which is my heaven to have. Come, thou mortal
  wretch,
With thy sharp teeth this knot intrinsicate
Of life at once untie; poor venomous fool,
Be angry, and dispatch. O! couldst thou speak,
That I might hear thee call great Caesar ass
Unpolicied.
CHARMIAN: O eastern star!
CLEOPATRA: Peace! peace!
  Dost thou not see my baby at my breast,
  That sucks the nurse asleep?
Antony and Cleopatra (1606–7) act 5, sc. 2, l. [303]

12 Now boast thee, death, in thy possession lies
A lass unparalleled.
Antony and Cleopatra (1606–7) act 5, sc. 2, l. [317]

13   She looks like sleep,
As she would catch a second Antony
In her strong toil of grace.
Antony and Cleopatra (1606–7) act 5, sc. 2, l. [347]

14 She hath pursued conclusions infinite
Of easy ways to die.
Antony and Cleopatra (1606–7) act 5, sc. 2, l. [356]

15 She shall be buried by her Antony:
No grave upon the earth shall clip in it
A pair so famous.
Antony and Cleopatra (1606–7) act 5, sc. 2, l. [359]

As You Like It

16 Fleet the time carelessly, as they did in the golden
world.
As You Like It (1599) act 1, sc. 1, l. [126]

17 Let us sit and mock the good housewife Fortune from
her wheel, that her gifts may henceforth be bestowed
equally.
As You Like It (1599) act 1, sc. 2, l. [35]

18 How now, wit! whither wander you?
As You Like It (1599) act 1, sc. 2, l. [60]

19 Sir, you have wrestled well, and overthrown
More than your enemies.
As You Like It (1599) act 1, sc. 2, l. [271]

20 Hereafter, in a better world than this,
I shall desire more love and knowledge of you.
As You Like It (1599) act 1, sc. 2, l. [301]

21 Thus must I from the smoke into the smother;
From tyrant duke unto a tyrant brother.
As You Like It (1599) act 1, sc. 2, l. [304]

22 O, how full of briers is this working-day world!
As You Like It (1599) act 1, sc. 3, l. [12]

23 We'll have a swashing and a martial outside,
As many other mannish cowards have
That do outface it with their semblances.
As You Like It (1599) act 1, sc. 3, l. [123]

24 Hath not old custom made this life more sweet
Than that of painted pomp? Are not these woods
More free from peril than the envious court?
Here feel we but the penalty of Adam,
The seasons' difference; as, the icy fang
And churlish chiding of the winter's wind,
Which, when it bites and blows upon my body,
Even till I shrink with cold, I smile and say,
'This is no flattery.'
As You Like It (1599) act 2, sc. 1, l. 2

25 Sweet are the uses of adversity,
Which like the toad, ugly and venomous,
Wears yet a precious jewel in his head;
And this our life, exempt from public haunt,
Finds tongues in trees, books in the running brooks,
Sermons in stones, and good in everything.
As You Like It (1599) act 2, sc. 1, l. 12

26   The big round tears
Coursed one another down his innocent nose,
In piteous chase.
As You Like It (1599) act 2, sc. 1, l. 38

27 Unregarded age in corners thrown.
As You Like It (1599) act 2, sc. 3, l. 42

28 Therefore my age is as a lusty winter,
Frosty, but kindly.
As You Like It (1599) act 2, sc. 3, l. 52

1 O good old man! how well in thee appears
The constant service of the antique world,
When service sweat for duty, not for meed!
Thou art not for the fashion of these times,
Where none will sweat but for promotion,
And having that, do choke their service up
Even with the having.
As You Like It (1599) act 2, sc. 3, l. 56

2 Ay, now am I in Arden; the more fool I. When I was
at home I was in a better place; but travellers must be
content.
As You Like It (1599) act 2, sc. 4, l. [16]

3 In thy youth thou wast as true a lover
As ever sighed upon a midnight pillow.
As You Like It (1599) act 2, sc. 4, l. [26]

4 If thou remember'st not the slightest folly
That ever love did make thee run into,
Thou hast not loved.
As You Like It (1599) act 2, sc. 4, l. [34]

5 We that are true lovers run into strange capers.
As You Like It (1599) act 2, sc. 4, l. [53]

6 Thou speakest wiser than thou art ware of.
As You Like It (1599) act 2, sc. 4, l. [57]

7 I shall ne'er be ware of mine own wit till I break my
shins against it.
As You Like It (1599) act 2, sc. 4, l. [59]

8 Under the greenwood tree
Who loves to lie with me,
And turn his merry note
Unto the sweet bird's throat,
Come hither, come hither, come hither:
Here shall he see
No enemy
But winter and rough weather.
As You Like It (1599) act 2, sc. 5, l. 1

9 I can suck melancholy out of a song as a weasel sucks
eggs.
As You Like It (1599) act 2, sc. 5, l. [12]

10 Who doth ambition shun
And loves to live i' the sun,
Seeking the food he eats,
And pleased with what he gets.
As You Like It (1599) act 2, sc. 5, l. [38]

11 I'll go to sleep if I can; if I cannot, I'll rail against all
the first-born of Egypt.
As You Like It (1599) act 2, sc. 5, l. [60]

12 And so, from hour to hour, we ripe and ripe,
And then from hour to hour, we rot and rot:
And thereby hangs a tale.
As You Like It (1599) act 2, sc. 7, l. 26

13 My lungs began to crow like chanticleer,
That fools should be so deep-contemplative,
And I did laugh sans intermission
An hour by his dial. O noble fool!
A worthy fool! Motley's the only wear.
As You Like It (1599) act 2, sc. 7, l. 30

14 O worthy fool! One that hath been a courtier,
And says, if ladies be but young and fair,
They have the gift to know it: and in his brain,—
Which is as dry as the remainder biscuit
After a voyage,—he hath strange places crammed
With observation, the which he vents
In mangled forms.
As You Like It (1599) act 2, sc. 7, l. 36

15   I must have liberty
Withal, as large a charter as the wind,
To blow on whom I please.
As You Like It (1599) act 2, sc. 7, l. 47

16 All the world's a stage,
And all the men and women merely players:
They have their exits and their entrances;
And one man in his time plays many parts,
His acts being seven ages. At first the infant,
Mewling and puking in the nurse's arms.
And then the whining schoolboy, with his satchel,
And shining morning face, creeping like snail
Unwillingly to school. And then the lover,
Sighing like furnace, with a woful ballad
Made to his mistress' eyebrow. Then a soldier,
Full of strange oaths, and bearded like the pard,
Jealous in honour, sudden and quick in quarrel,
Seeking the bubble reputation
Even in the cannon's mouth. And then the justice,
In fair round belly with good capon lined,
With eyes severe, and beard of formal cut,
Full of wise saws and modern instances;
And so he plays his part. The sixth age shifts
Into the lean and slippered pantaloon,
With spectacles on nose and pouch on side,
His youthful hose well saved a world too wide
For his shrunk shank; and his big manly voice,
Turning again towards childish treble, pipes
And whistles in his sound. Last scene of all,
That ends this strange eventful history,
Is second childishness, and mere oblivion,
Sans teeth, sans eyes, sans taste, sans everything.
As You Like It (1599) act 2, sc. 7, l. 139

17 Blow, blow, thou winter wind,
Thou art not so unkind
As man's ingratitude:
Thy tooth is not so keen,
Because thou art not seen,
Although thy breath be rude.
Heigh-ho! sing, heigh-ho! unto the green holly:
Most friendship is feigning, most loving mere folly.
Then heigh-ho! the holly!
This life is most jolly.

Freeze, freeze, thou bitter sky,
That dost not bite so nigh
As benefits forgot:
Though thou the waters warp,
Thy sting is not so sharp
As friend remembered not.
As You Like It (1599) act 2, sc. 7, l. 174

18 Run, run, Orlando: carve on every tree
The fair, the chaste, and unexpressive she.
As You Like It (1599) act 3, sc. 2, l. 9

19 He that wants money, means, and content is without
three good friends.
As You Like It (1599) act 3, sc. 2, l. [25]

1 I earn that I eat, get that I wear, owe no man hate, envy no man's happiness, glad of other men's good, content with my harm.
As You Like It (1599) act 3, sc. 2, l. [78]

2 From the east to western Ind,
No jewel is like Rosalind.
As You Like It (1599) act 3, sc. 2, l. [94]

3 Let us make an honourable retreat; though not with bag and baggage, yet with scrip and scrippage.
As You Like It (1599) act 3, sc. 2, l. [170]

4 O wonderful, wonderful, and most wonderful wonderful! and yet again wonderful, and after that, out of all whooping!
As You Like It (1599) act 3, sc. 2, l. [202]

5 It is as easy to count atomies as to resolve the propositions of a lover.
As You Like It (1599) act 3, sc. 2, l. [246]

6 Do you not know I am a woman? when I think, I must speak.
As You Like It (1599) act 3, sc. 2, l. [265]

7 I do desire we may be better strangers.
As You Like It (1599) act 3, sc. 2, l. [276]

8 JAQUES: I do not like her name.
ORLANDO: There was no thought of pleasing you when she was christened.
As You Like It (1599) act 3, sc. 2, l. [283]

9 ROSALIND: Time travels in divers paces with divers persons . . .
ORLANDO: Who stays it still withal?
ROSALIND: With lawyers in the vacation; for they sleep between term and term.
As You Like It (1599) act 3, sc. 2, l. [328]

10 There were none principal; they were all like one another as half-pence are; every one fault seeming monstrous till his fellow fault came to match it.
As You Like It (1599) act 3, sc. 2, l. [376] (of women's offences)

11 Truly, I would the gods had made thee poetical.
As You Like It (1599) act 3, sc. 3, l. [16]

12 I am not a slut, though I thank the gods I am foul.
As You Like It (1599) act 3, sc. 3, l. [40]

13   Down on your knees,
And thank heaven, fasting, for a good man's love.
As You Like It (1599) act 3, sc. 5, l. 57

14 I pray you, do not fall in love with me,
For I am falser than vows made in wine.
As You Like It (1599) act 3, sc. 5, l. [72]

15 Dead shepherd, now I find thy saw of might:
'Who ever loved that loved not at first sight?'
As You Like It (1599) act 3, sc. 5, l. [81]. Cf. Marlowe 447:10

16 Come, woo me, woo me; for now I am in a holiday humour, and like enough to consent.
As You Like It (1599) act 4, sc. 1, l. [70]

17 You were better speak first, and when you were gravelled for lack of matter, you might take occasion to kiss.
As You Like It (1599) act 4, sc. 1, l. [74]

18 Men are April when they woo, December when they wed: maids are May when they are maids, but the sky changes when they are wives.
As You Like It (1599) act 4, sc. 1, l. [153]

19 The horn, the horn, the lusty horn
Is not a thing to laugh to scorn.
As You Like It (1599) act 4, sc. 2, l. [17]

20 Oh! how bitter a thing it is to look into happiness through another man's eyes.
As You Like It (1599) act 5, sc. 2, l. [48]

21 PHOEBE: Good shepherd, tell this youth what 'tis to love.
SILVIUS: It is to be all made of sighs and tears . . .
It is to be all made of faith and service . . .
It is to be all made of fantasy,
All made of passion, and all made of wishes;
All adoration, duty, and observance;
All humbleness, all patience, and impatience;
All purity, all trial, all obeisance.
As You Like It (1599) act 5, sc. 2, l. [90]

22 'Tis like the howling of Irish wolves against the moon.
As You Like It (1599) act 5, sc. 2, l. [120]

23 It was a lover and his lass,
With a hey, and a ho, and a hey nonino,
That o'er the green cornfield did pass,
In the spring time, the only pretty ring time,
When birds do sing, hey ding a ding, ding;
Sweet lovers love the spring.
As You Like It (1599) act 5, sc. 3, l. [18]

24 Here comes a pair of very strange beasts, which in all tongues are called fools.
As You Like It (1599) act 5, sc. 4, l. [36]

25 A poor virgin, sir, an ill-favoured thing, sir, but mine own: a poor humour of mine, sir, to take that that no man else will. Rich honesty dwells like a miser, sir, in a poor house, as your pearl in your foul oyster.
As You Like It (1599) act 5, sc. 4, l. [60]

26 The retort courteous . . . the quip modest . . . the reply churlish . . . the reproof valiant . . . the countercheck quarrelsome . . . the lie circumstantial . . . the lie direct.
As You Like It (1599) act 5, sc. 4, l. [96] (of the degrees of a lie)

27 Your 'if' is the only peace-maker; much virtue in 'if'.
As You Like It (1599) act 5, sc. 4, l. [108]

28 He uses his folly like a stalking-horse, and under the presentation of that he shoots his wit.
As You Like It (1599) act 5, sc. 4, l. [112]

29 If it be true that 'good wine needs no bush', 'tis true that a good play needs no epilogue.
As You Like It (1599) act 5, sc. 4, epilogue l. [3]

The Comedy of Errors

30 I to the world am like a drop of water
That in the ocean seeks another drop,
Who, falling there to find his fellow forth,
Unseen, inquisitive, confounds himself.
The Comedy of Errors (1593) act 1, sc. 2, l. 35

1 They brought one Pinch, a hungry, lean-faced villain,
   A mere anatomy, a mountebank,
   A threadbare juggler, and a fortune-teller,
   A needy, hollow-eyed, sharp-looking wretch,
   A living-dead man.
     The Comedy of Errors (1594) act 5, sc. 1, l. 238

Coriolanus

2 He's a very dog to the commonalty.
     Coriolanus (1608) act 1, sc. 1, l. [29]

3 The kingly crownèd head, the vigilant eye,
   The counsellor heart, the arm our soldier,
   Our steed the leg, the tongue our trumpeter.
     Coriolanus (1608) act 1, sc. 1, l. [121]

4 What's the matter, you dissentious rogues,
   That, rubbing the poor itch of your opinion,
   Make yourselves scabs?
     Coriolanus (1608) act 1, sc. 1, l. [170]

5   He that depends
   Upon your favours swims with fins of lead,
   And hews down oaks with rushes.
     Coriolanus (1608) act 1, sc. 1, l. 179

6   They threw their caps
   As they would hang them on the horns o' the moon,
   Shouting their emulation.
     Coriolanus (1608) act 1, sc. 1, l. [218]

7 I am known to be . . . one that loves a cup of hot wine
   with not a drop of allaying Tiber in't.
     Coriolanus (1608) act 2, sc. 1, l. [52]

8   Bid them wash their faces,
   And keep their teeth clean.
     Coriolanus (1608) act 2, sc. 1, l. [65]

9 My gracious silence, hail!
     Coriolanus (1608) act 2, sc. 1, l. [194]

10   Custom calls me to 't:
   What custom wills, in all things should we do't,
   The dust on antique time would lie unswept,
   And mountainous error be too highly heaped
   For truth to o'erpeer.
     Coriolanus (1608) act 2, sc. 3, l. [124]

11 Hear you this Triton of the minnows? mark you
   His absolute 'shall'?
     Coriolanus (1608) act 3, sc. 1, l. 88

12 What is the city but the people?
     Coriolanus (1608) act 3, sc. 1, l. 198

13 You common cry of curs! whose breath I hate
   As reek o' the rotten fens, whose loves I prize
   As the dead carcases of unburied men
   That do corrupt my air,—I banish you.
     Coriolanus (1608) act 3, sc. 3, l. 118

14   Would you have me
   False to my nature? Rather say I play
   The man I am.
     Coriolanus (1608) act 3, sc. 2, l. 14

15   Despising,
   For you, the city, thus I turn my back:
   There is a world elsewhere.
     Coriolanus (1608) act 3, sc. 3, l. 131

16   The beast
   With many heads butts me away.
     Coriolanus (1608) act 4, sc. 1, l. 1

17 Thou hast a grim appearance, and thy face
   Bears a command in't; though thy tackle's torn,
   Thou show'st a noble vessel. What's thy name?
     Coriolanus (1608) act 4, sc. 5, l. [66]

18 Let me have war, say I; it exceeds peace as far as day
   does night; it's spritely, waking, audible, and full of
   vent. Peace is a very apoplexy, lethargy: mulled, deaf,
   sleepy, insensible; a getter of more bastard children
   than war's a destroyer of men.
     Coriolanus (1608) act 4, sc. 5, l. [237]

19   I think he'll be to Rome
   As is the osprey to the fish, who takes it
   By sovereignty of nature.
     Coriolanus (1608) act 4, sc. 7, l. 33

20   I'll never
   Be such a gosling to obey instinct, but stand
   As if a man were author of himself
   And knew no other kin.
     Coriolanus (1608) act 5, sc. 3, l. 34

21   Like a dull actor now,
   I have forgot my part, and I am out,
   Even to a full disgrace.
     Coriolanus (1608) act 5, sc. 3, l. 40

22   O! a kiss
   Long as my exile, sweet as my revenge!
   Now, by the jealous queen of heaven, that kiss
   I carried from thee, dear, and my true lip
   Hath virgined it e'er since.
     Coriolanus (1608) act 5, sc. 3, l. 44

23   Chaste as the icicle
   That's curdied by the frost from purest snow,
   And hangs on Dian's temple.
     Coriolanus (1608) act 5, sc. 3, l. 65

24   The god of soldiers,
   With the consent of supreme Jove, inform
   Thy thoughts with nobleness; that thou mayst prove
   To shame unvulnerable, and stick i' the wars
   Like a great sea-mark, standing every flaw,
   And saving those that eye thee!
     Coriolanus (1608) act 5, sc. 3, l. 70

25   Thou hast never in thy life
   Showed thy dear mother any courtesy;
   When she—poor hen! fond of no second brood—
   Has clucked thee to the wars, and safely home,
   Loaden with honour.
     Coriolanus (1608) act 5, sc. 3, l. 160

26   O mother, mother!
   What have you done? Behold, the heavens do ope,
   The gods look down, and this unnatural scene
   They laugh at.
     Coriolanus (1608) act 5, sc. 3, l. 182

27 If you have writ your annals true, 'tis there,
   That, like an eagle in a dove-cote, I
   Fluttered your Volscians in Corioli:
   Alone I did it.
     Coriolanus (1608) act 5, sc. 5, l. 114

Cymbeline

28 If she be furnished with a mind so rare,
   She is alone the Arabian bird, and I
   Have lost the wager. Boldness be my friend!
   Arm me, audacity.
     Cymbeline (1609–10) act 1, sc. 6, l. 16

1   Cytherea,
How bravely thou becom'st thy bed! fresh lily,
And whiter than the sheets! That I might touch!
But kiss: one kiss! Rubies unparagoned,
How dearly they do't! 'Tis her breathing that
Perfumes the chamber thus; the flame of the taper
Bows toward her, and would under-peep her lids
To see the enclosed lights, now canopied
Under these windows, white and azure laced
With blue of heaven's own tinct.
Cymbeline (1609–10) act 2, sc. 2, l. 14

2   On her left breast
A mole cinque-spotted, like the crimson drops
I' the bottom of a cowslip.
Cymbeline (1609–10) act 2, sc. 2, l. 37

3 Hark! hark! the lark at heaven's gate sings,
And Phoebus 'gins arise,
His steeds to water at those springs
On chaliced flowers that lies;
And winking Mary-buds begin
To ope their golden eyes:
With everything that pretty is,
My lady sweet, arise!
Cymbeline (1609–10) act 2, sc. 3, l. [22]

4 Is there no way for men to be, but women
Must be half-workers?
Cymbeline (1609–10) act 2, sc. 5, l. 1

5   I thought her
As chaste as unsunned snow.
Cymbeline (1609–10) act 2, sc. 5, l. 12

6 The natural bravery of your isle, which stands
As Neptune's park, ribbed and paled in
With rocks unscalable, and roaring waters.
Cymbeline (1609–10) act 3, sc. 1, l. 18

7 O, for a horse with wings!
Cymbeline (1609–10) act 3, sc. 2, l. [49]

8   What should we speak of
When we are old as you? when we shall hear
The rain and wind beat dark December, how,
In this our pinching cave, shall we discourse
The freezing hours away? We have seen nothing.
Cymbeline (1609–10) act 3, sc. 3, l. 35

9 How hard it is to hide the sparks of nature!
Cymbeline (1609 10) act 3, sc. 3, l. 79

10   Some jay of Italy,
Whose mother was her painting, hath betrayed him:
Poor I am stale, a garment out of fashion.
Cymbeline (1609–10) act 3, sc. 4, l. [51]

11 Hath Britain all the sun that shines?
Cymbeline (1609–10) act 3, sc. 4, l. [139]

12   Weariness
Can snore upon the flint when resty sloth
Finds the down pillow hard.
Cymbeline (1609–10) act 3, sc. 6, l. 33

13 Great griefs, I see, medicine the less.
Cymbeline (1609–10) act 4, sc. 2, l. 243

14   Though mean and mighty rotting
Together, have one dust, yet reverence—
That angel of the world—doth make distinction
Of place 'tween high and low.
Cymbeline (1609–10) act 4, sc. 2, l. 246

15 Thersites' body is as good as Ajax'
When neither are alive.
Cymbeline (1609–10) act 4, sc. 2, l. 252

16 Fear no more the heat o' the sun,
Nor the furious winter's rages;
Thou thy worldly task hast done,
Home art gone and ta'en thy wages:
Golden lads and girls all must,
As chimney-sweepers, come to dust.

Fear no more the frown o' the great,
Thou art past the tyrant's stroke:
Care no more to clothe and eat;
To thee the reed is as the oak:
The sceptre, learning, physic, must
All follow this, and come to dust.

Fear no more the lightning flash,
Nor the all-dreaded thunder-stone;
Fear not slander, censure rash;
Thou hast finished joy and moan:
All lovers young, all lovers must
Consign to thee, and come to dust.

No exorciser harm thee!
Nor no witchcraft charm thee!
Ghost unlaid forbear thee!
Nothing ill come near thee!
Quiet consummation have:
And renowned be thy grave!
Cymbeline (1609–10) act 4, sc. 2, l. 258

17 Every good servant does not all commands.
Cymbeline (1609–10) act 5, sc. 1, l. 6

18 He that sleeps feels not the toothache.
Cymbeline (1609–10) act 5, sc. 4, l. [176]

19 He spake of her as Dian had hot dreams,
And she alone were cold.
Cymbeline (1609–10) act 5, sc. 5, l. 181

20   Hang there like fruit, my soul,
Till the tree die.
Cymbeline (1609–10) act 5, sc. 5, l. 263

Hamlet

21 You come most carefully upon your hour.
Hamlet (1601) act 1, sc. 1, l. 6

22 For this relief much thanks; 'tis bitter cold
And I am sick at heart.
Hamlet (1601) act 1, sc. 1, l. 8

23 Not a mouse stirring.
Hamlet (1601) act 1, sc. 1, l. 10

24 Look, where it comes again!
Hamlet (1601) act 1, sc. 1, l. 40

25 But in the gross and scope of my opinion,
This bodes some strange eruption to our state.
Hamlet (1601) act 1, sc. 1, l. 68

26 In the most high and palmy state of Rome,
A little ere the mightiest Julius fell,
The graves stood tenantless and the sheeted dead
Did squeak and gibber in the Roman streets.
Hamlet (1601) act 1, sc. 1, l. 113

27 I'll cross it, though it blast me.
Hamlet (1601) act 1, sc. 1, l. 127

1 And then it started like a guilty thing
Upon a fearful summons.
Hamlet (1601) act 1, sc. 1, l. 148

2 It faded on the crowing of the cock.
Some say that ever 'gainst that season comes
Wherein our Saviour's birth is celebrated,
The bird of dawning singeth all night long;
And then, they say, no spirit can walk abroad;
The nights are wholesome; then no planets strike,
No fairy takes, nor witch hath power to charm,
So hallowed and so gracious is the time.
Hamlet (1601) act 1, sc. 1, l. 157

3 But, look, the morn, in russet mantle clad,
Walks o'er the dew of yon high eastern hill.
Hamlet (1601) act 1, sc. 1, l. 166

4 Though yet of Hamlet our dear brother's death
The memory be green . . .
Therefore our sometime sister, now our queen, . . .
Have we, as 'twere with a defeated joy,
With one auspicious and one dropping eye,
With mirth in funeral and with dirge in marriage,
In equal scale weighing delight and dole,
Taken to wife.
Hamlet (1601) act 1, sc. 2, l. 1

5 The head is not more native to the heart,
The hand more instrumental to the brain,
Than is the throne of Denmark to thy father.
Hamlet (1601) act 1, sc. 2, l. 47

6 A little more than kin, and less than kind.
Hamlet (1601) act 1, sc. 2, l. 65

7 Not so, my lord; I am too much i' the sun.
Hamlet (1601) act 1, sc. 2, l. 67

8 Good Hamlet, cast thy nighted colour off,
And let thine eye look like a friend on Denmark.
Hamlet (1601) act 1, sc. 2, l. 68

9 QUEEN: Thou know'st 'tis common; all that live must
    die,
    Passing through nature to eternity.
HAMLET: Ay, madam, it is common.
Hamlet (1601) act 1, sc. 2, l. 72

10 Seems, madam! Nay, it is; I know not 'seems'.
'Tis not alone my inky cloak, good mother,
Nor customary suits of solemn black,
Nor windy suspiration of forced breath,
No, nor the fruitful river in the eye,
Nor the dejected 'haviour of the visage,
Together with all forms, modes, shows of grief,
That can denote me truly; these indeed seem,
For they are actions that a man might play:
But I have that within which passeth show;
These but the trappings and the suits of woe.
Hamlet (1601) act 1, sc. 2, l. 76

11   But to persever
In obstinate condolement is a course
Of impious stubbornness; 'tis unmanly grief;
It shows a will most incorrect to heaven,
A heart unfortified, a mind impatient.
Hamlet (1601) act 1, sc. 2, l. 92

12 O! that this too too solid flesh would melt,
Thaw, and resolve itself into a dew;
Or that the Everlasting had not fixed
His canon 'gainst self-slaughter! O God! O God!
How weary, stale, flat, and unprofitable
Seem to me all the uses of this world.
Fie on't! O fie! 'tis an unweeded garden,
That grows to seed; things rank and gross in nature
Possess it merely. That it should come to this!
But two months dead: nay, not so much, not two:
So excellent a king; that was, to this,
Hyperion to a satyr: so loving to my mother,
That he might not beteem the winds of heaven
Visit her face too roughly. Heaven and earth!
Must I remember? Why, she would hang on him,
As if increase of appetite had grown
By what it fed on; and yet, within a month,
Let me not think on't: Frailty, thy name is woman!
A little month; or ere those shoes were old
With which she followed my poor father's body,
Like Niobe, all tears; why she, even she,—
O God! a beast, that wants discourse of reason,
Would have mourned longer,—married with mine
    uncle,
My father's brother, but no more like my father
Than I to Hercules.
Hamlet (1601) act 1, sc. 2, l. 129

13 It is not, nor it cannot come to good;
But break, my heart, for I must hold my tongue!
Hamlet (1601) act 1, sc. 2, l. 158

14 A truant disposition, good my lord.
Hamlet (1601) act 1, sc. 2, l. 169

15 We'll teach you to drink deep ere you depart.
Hamlet (1601) act 1, sc. 2, l. 175

16 Thrift, thrift, Horatio! the funeral baked meats
Did coldly furnish forth the marriage tables.
Would I had met my dearest foe in heaven
Ere I had ever seen that day, Horatio!
Hamlet (1601) act 1, sc. 2, l. 180

17 He was a man, take him for all in all,
I shall not look upon his like again.
Hamlet (1601) act 1, sc. 2, l. 187

18 In the dead vast and middle of the night.
Hamlet (1601) act 1, sc. 2, l. 198

19 These hands are not more like.
Hamlet (1601) act 1, sc. 2, l. 212

20 But answer made it none.
Hamlet (1601) act 1, sc. 2, l. 215

21 A countenance more in sorrow than in anger.
Hamlet (1601) act 1, sc. 2, l. 231

22 Give it an understanding, but no tongue.
Hamlet (1601) act 1, sc. 2, l. 249

23   All is not well;
I doubt some foul play.
Hamlet (1601) act 1, sc. 2, l. 254

24   Foul deeds will rise,
Though all the earth o'erwhelm them, to men's eyes.
Hamlet (1601) act 1, sc. 2, l. 256

1 And keep you in the rear of your affection,
Out of the shot and danger of desire.
The chariest maid is prodigal enough
If she unmask her beauty to the moon.
Hamlet (1601) act 1, sc. 3, l. 34

2 Do not, as some ungracious pastors do,
Show me the steep and thorny way to heaven,
Whiles, like a puffed and reckless libertine,
Himself the primrose path of dalliance treads,
And recks not his own rede.
Hamlet (1601) act 1, sc. 3, l. 47

3   Give thy thoughts no tongue,
Nor any unproportioned thought his act.
Be thou familiar, but by no means vulgar;
The friends thou hast, and their adoption tried,
Grapple them to thy soul with hoops of steel.
Hamlet (1601) act 1, sc. 3, l. 59

4 Give every man thine ear, but few thy voice;
Take each man's censure, but reserve thy judgment.
Costly thy habit as thy purse can buy,
But not expressed in fancy; rich, not gaudy;
For the apparel oft proclaims the man ...
Neither a borrower, nor a lender be;
For loan oft loses both itself and friend,
And borrowing dulls the edge of husbandry,
This above all: to thine own self be true,
And it must follow, as the night the day,
Thou canst not then be false to any man.
Hamlet (1601) act 1, sc. 3, l. 68

5   You speak like a green girl,
Unsifted in such perilous circumstance.
Hamlet (1601) act 1, sc. 3, l. 101

6 Ay, springes to catch woodcocks.
Hamlet (1601) act 1, sc. 3, l. 115

7 HAMLET: The air bites shrewdly; it is very cold.
HORATIO: It is a nipping and an eager air.
Hamlet (1601) act 1, sc. 4, l. 1

8 But to my mind,—though I am native here,
And to the manner born,—it is a custom
More honoured in the breach than the observance.
Hamlet (1601) act 1, sc. 4, l. 14

9 Angels and ministers of grace defend us!
Be thou a spirit of health or goblin damned,
Bring with thee airs from heaven or blasts from hell,
Be thy intents wicked or charitable,
Thou com'st in such a questionable shape
That I will speak to thee: I'll call thee Hamlet,
King, father; royal Dane, O! answer me:
Let me not burst in ignorance ...
                What may this mean,
That thou, dead corse again in complete steel
Revisit'st thus the glimpses of the moon,
Making night hideous; and we fools of nature
So horridly to shake our disposition
With thoughts beyond the reaches of our souls?
Hamlet (1601) act 1, sc. 4, l. 39

10 I do not set my life at a pin's fee;
And for my soul, what can it do to that,
Being a thing immortal as itself?
Hamlet (1601) act 1, sc. 4, l. 65

11   Unhand me, gentlemen,
By heaven! I'll make a ghost of him that lets me.
Hamlet (1601) act 1, sc. 4, l. 84

12 Something is rotten in the state of Denmark.
Hamlet (1601) act 1, sc. 4, l. 90

13 I am thy father's spirit;
Doomed for a certain term to walk the night.
Hamlet (1601) act 1, sc. 5, l. 9

14   But that I am forbid
To tell the secrets of my prison-house,
I could a tale unfold whose lightest word
Would harrow up thy soul, freeze thy young blood,
Make thy two eyes, like stars, start from their spheres,
Thy knotted and combinèd locks to part,
And each particular hair to stand on end,
Like quills upon the fretful porpentine:
But this eternal blazon must not be
To ears of flesh and blood. List, list, O, list!
Hamlet (1601) act 1, sc. 5, l. 13

15 Revenge his foul and most unnatural murder.
Hamlet (1601) act 1, sc. 5, l. 25

16 Murder most foul, as in the best it is;
But this most foul, strange, and unnatural.
Hamlet (1601) act 1, sc. 5, l. 27

17 And duller shouldst thou be than the fat weed
That rots itself in ease on Lethe wharf,
Wouldst thou not stir in this.
Hamlet (1601) act 1, sc. 5, l. 32

18   O my prophetic soul!
My uncle!
Hamlet (1601) act 1, sc. 5, l. 40

19 But, soft! methinks I scent the morning air.
Hamlet (1601) act 1, sc. 5, l. 58

20 Thus was I, sleeping, by a brother's hand,
Of life, of crown, of queen, at once dispatched;
Cut off even in the blossoms of my sin,
Unhouseled, disappointed, unaneled,
No reckoning made, but sent to my account
With all my imperfections on my head:
O, horrible! O, horrible! most horrible!
If thou hast nature in thee, bear it not.
Hamlet (1601) act 1, sc. 5, l. 74

21 The glow-worm shows the matin to be near,
And 'gins to pale his uneffectual fire.
Hamlet (1601) act 1, sc. 5, l. 89

22   Remember thee!
Ay, thou poor ghost, while memory holds a seat
In this distracted globe. Remember thee!
Yea, from the table of my memory
I'll wipe away all trivial fond records,
All saws of books, all forms, all pressures past,
That youth and observation copied there.
Hamlet (1601) act 1, sc. 5, l. 95

23 O most pernicious woman!
O villain, villain, smiling, damnèd villain!
My tables,—meet it is I set it down,
That one may smile, and smile, and be a villain;
At least I'm sure it may be so in Denmark.
Hamlet (1601) act 1, sc. 5, l. 105

1 HAMLET: There's ne'er a villain dwelling in all
    Denmark,
    But he's an arrant knave.
    HORATIO: There needs no ghost, my lord, come from
    the grave,
    To tell us this.
    Hamlet (1601) act 1, sc. 5, l. 123

2 These are but wild and whirling words, my lord.
    Hamlet (1601) act 1, sc. 5, l. 133

3 Well said, old mole! canst work i' the earth so fast?
    Hamlet (1601) act 1, sc. 5, l. 162

4 There are more things in heaven and earth, Horatio,
    Than are dreamt of in your philosophy.
    Hamlet (1601) act 1, sc. 5, l. 166

5 To put an antic disposition on.
    Hamlet (1601) act 1, sc. 5, l. 172

6 Rest, rest, perturbèd spirit.
    Hamlet (1601) act 1, sc. 5, l. 182

7 The time is out of joint; O cursèd spite,
    That ever I was born to set it right!
    Hamlet (1601) act 1, sc. 5, l. 188

8 By indirections find directions out.
    Hamlet (1601) act 2, sc. 1, l. 66

9 Lord Hamlet, with his doublet all unbraced;
    No hat upon his head; his stockings fouled,
    Ungartered, and down-gyvèd to his ancle.
    Hamlet (1601) act 2, sc. 1, l. 78

10 This is the very ecstasy of love.
    Hamlet (1601) act 2, sc. 1, l. 101

11 Brevity is the soul of wit.
    Hamlet (1601) act 2, sc. 2, l. 90

12   To define true madness,
    What is't but to be nothing else but mad?
    Hamlet (1601) act 2, sc. 2, l. 93

13 More matter with less art.
    Hamlet (1601) act 2, sc. 2, l. 95

14 That's an ill phrase, a vile phrase; 'beautified' is a vile
    phrase.
    Hamlet (1601) act 2, sc. 2, l. [110]

15 Doubt thou the stars are fire;
    Doubt that the sun doth move;
    Doubt truth to be a liar;
    But never doubt I love.
    Hamlet (1601) act 2, sc. 2, l. [115]

16 Lord Hamlet is a prince, out of thy star.
    Hamlet (1601) act 2, sc. 2, l. [141]

17 And he, repulsèd,—a short tale to make,—
    Fell into a sadness, then into a fast,
    Thence to a watch, thence into a weakness,
    Thence to a lightness; and by this declension
    Into the madness wherein now he raves,
    And all we wail for.
    Hamlet (1601) act 2, sc. 2, l. [146]

18 POLONIUS: Do you know me, my lord?
    HAMLET: Excellent well; you are a fishmonger.
    Hamlet (1601) act 2, sc. 2, l. [173]

19 Ay, sir; to be honest, as this world goes, is to be one
    man picked out of ten thousand.
    Hamlet (1601) act 2, sc. 2, l. [179]

20 Still harping on my daughter.
    Hamlet (1601) act 2, sc. 2, l. [190]

21 POLONIUS: What do you read, my lord?
    HAMLET: Words, words, words.
    Hamlet (1601) act 2, sc. 2, l. [195]

22 The satirical rogue says here that old men have grey
    beards, that their faces are wrinkled, their eyes
    purging thick amber and plum-tree gum, and that
    they have a plentiful lack of wit, together with most
    weak hams: all of which, sir, though I most potently
    and powerfully believe, yet I hold it not honesty to
    have it thus set down.
    Hamlet (1601) act 2, sc. 2, l. [201]

23 Though this be madness, yet there is method in't.
    Hamlet (1601) act 2, sc. 2, l. [211]

24 POLONIUS: My honourable lord, I will most humbly
    take my leave of you.
    HAMLET: You cannot, sir, take from me any thing
    that I will more willingly part withal; except my
    life, except my life, except my life.
    Hamlet (1601) act 2, sc. 2, l. [221]

25 GUILDENSTERN: On Fortune's cap we are not the very
    button.
    HAMLET: Nor the soles of her shoe?
    ROSENCRANTZ: Neither, my lord.
    HAMLET: Then you live about her waist, or in the
    middle of her favours?
    GUILDENSTERN: Faith, her privates, we.
    HAMLET: In the secret parts of Fortune? O! most true;
    she is a strumpet. What news?
    ROSENCRANTZ: None, my lord, but that the world's
    grown honest.
    HAMLET: Then is doomsday near.
    Hamlet (1601) act 2, sc. 2, l. [237]

26 There is nothing either good or bad, but thinking
    makes it so.
    Hamlet (1601) act 2, sc. 2, l. [259]

27 O God! I could be bounded in a nut-shell, and count
    myself a king of infinite space, were it not that I have
    bad dreams.
    Hamlet (1601) act 2, sc. 2, l. [263]

28 It goes so heavily with my disposition that this goodly
    frame, the earth, seems to me a sterile promontory;
    this most excellent canopy, the air, look you, this
    brave o'erhanging firmament, this majestical roof
    fretted with golden fire, why, it appears no other thing
    to me but a foul and pestilent congregation of
    vapours. What a piece of work is a man! How noble
    in reason! how infinite in faculty! in form, in moving,
    how express and admirable! in action how like an
    angel! in apprehension how like a god! the beauty of
    the world! the paragon of animals! And yet, to me,
    what is this quintessence of dust? man delights not
    me; no, nor woman neither, though, by your smiling,
    you seem to say so.
    Hamlet (1601) act 2, sc. 2, l. [316]

29 He that plays the king shall be welcome; his majesty
    shall have tribute of me.
    Hamlet (1601) act 2, sc. 2, l. [341]

30 There is something in this more than natural, if
    philosophy could find it out.
    Hamlet (1601) act 2, sc. 2, l. [392]

1 I am but mad north-north-west; when the wind is
southerly, I know a hawk from a handsaw.
Hamlet (1601) act 2, sc. 2, l. [405]

2 The best actors in the world, either for tragedy,
comedy, history, pastoral, pastoral-comical,
historical-pastoral, tragical-historical,
tragical-comical-historical-pastoral, scene individable,
or poem unlimited.
Hamlet (1601) act 2, sc. 2, l. [424]

3 One fair daughter and no more,
The which he loved passing well.
Hamlet (1601) act 2, sc. 2, l. [435]

4 Come, give us a taste of your quality.
Hamlet (1601) act 2, sc. 2, l. [460]

5 The play, I remember, pleased not the million; 'twas
caviare to the general.
Hamlet (1601) act 2, sc. 2, l. [465]

6 Good my lord, will you see the players well bestowed?
Do you hear, let them be well used; for they are the
abstracts and brief chronicles of the time: after your
death you were better have a bad epitaph than their ill
report while you live.
Hamlet (1601) act 2, sc. 2, l. [553]

7 Use every man after his desert, and who should 'scape
whipping?
Hamlet (1601) act 2, sc. 2, l. [561]

8 O, what a rogue and peasant slave am I:
Is it not monstrous that this player here,
But in a fiction, in a dream of passion,
Could force his soul so to his own conceit
That from her working all his visage wanned,
Tears in his eyes, distraction in 's aspect,
A broken voice, and his whole function suiting
With forms to his conceit? and all for nothing!
For Hecuba!
What's Hecuba to him or he to Hecuba
That he should weep for her?
Hamlet (1601) act 2, sc. 2, l. [584]

9   He would drown the stage with tears,
And cleave the general ear with horrid speech,
Make mad the guilty, and appal the free,
Confound the ignorant, and amaze, indeed,
The very faculties of eyes and ears.
Hamlet (1601) act 2, sc. 2, l. [596]

10   I,
A dull and muddy-mettled rascal, peak,
Like John-a-dreams, unpregnant of my cause,
And can say nothing.
Hamlet (1601) act 2, sc. 2, l. [601]

11   Am I a coward?
Who calls me villain? breaks my pate across?
Plucks off my beard and blows it in my face?
Tweaks me by the nose? gives me the lie i' the throat,
As deep as to the lungs?
Hamlet (1601) act 2, sc. 2, l. [606]

12 But I am pigeon-livered, and lack gall
To make oppression bitter, or ere this
I should have fatted all the region kites
With this slave's offal. Bloody, bawdy villain!
Remorseless, treacherous, lecherous, kindless villain!
Hamlet (1601) act 2, sc. 2, l. [612]

13   I have heard,
That guilty creatures sitting at a play
Have by the very cunning of the scene
Been struck so to the soul that presently
They have proclaimed their malefactions;
For murder, though it have no tongue, will speak
With most miraculous organ.
Hamlet (1601) act 2, sc. 2, l. [625]

14   The play's the thing
Wherein I'll catch the conscience of the king.
Hamlet (1601) act 2, sc. 2, l. [641]

15 'Tis too much proved—that with devotion's visage
And pious action, we do sugar o'er
The devil himself.
Hamlet (1601) act 3, sc. 1, l. 47

16 To be, or not to be: that is the question:
Whether 'tis nobler in the mind to suffer
The slings and arrows of outrageous fortune,
Or to take arms against a sea of troubles,
And by opposing end them? To die: to sleep;
No more; and, by a sleep to say we end
The heart-ache and the thousand natural shocks
That flesh is heir to, 'tis a consummation
Devoutly to be wished. To die, to sleep;
To sleep: perchance to dream: ay, there's the rub;
For in that sleep of death what dreams may come
When we have shuffled off this mortal coil,
Must give us pause. There's the respect
That makes calamity of so long life;
For who would bear the whips and scorns of time,
The oppressor's wrong, the proud man's contumely,
The pangs of disprized love, the law's delay,
The insolence of office, and the spurns
That patient merit of the unworthy takes,
When he himself might his quietus make
With a bare bodkin? Who would fardels bear,
To grunt and sweat under a weary life,
But that the dread of something after death,
The undiscovered country from whose bourn
No traveller returns, puzzles the will,
And makes us rather bear those ills we have,
Than fly to others that we know not of?
Thus conscience doth make cowards of us all;
And thus the native hue of resolution
Is sicklied o'er with the pale cast of thought,
And enterprises of great pith and moment
With this regard their currents turn awry,
And lose the name of action.
Hamlet (1601) act 3, sc. 1, l. 56

17   Nymph, in thy orisons
Be all my sins remembered.
Hamlet (1601) act 3, sc. 1, l. 89

18 Get thee to a nunnery: why wouldst thou be a breeder
of sinners? I am myself indifferent honest; but yet I
could accuse me of such things that it were better my
mother had not borne me. I am very proud,
revengeful, ambitious; with more offences at my beck
than I have thoughts to put them in, imagination to
give them shape, or time to act them in. What should
such fellows as I do crawling between heaven and
earth? We are arrant knaves, all; believe none of us.
Hamlet (1601) act 3, sc. 1, l. [131]

1 Be thou as chaste as ice, as pure as snow, thou shalt
not escape calumny. Get thee to a nunnery, go;
farewell.
  Hamlet (1601) act 3, sc. 1, l. [142]

2 I have heard of your paintings too, well enough. God
hath given you one face and you make yourselves
another.
  Hamlet (1601) act 3, sc. 1, l. [150]

3 I say, we will have no more marriages.
  Hamlet (1601) act 3, sc. 1, l. [156]

4 O! what a noble mind is here o'erthrown:
The courtier's, soldier's, scholar's, eye, tongue, sword;
The expectancy and rose of the fair state,
The glass of fashion, and the mould of form,
The observed of all observers, quite, quite, down!
And I, of ladies most deject and wretched,
That sucked the honey of his music vows,
Now see that noble and most sovereign reason,
Like sweet bells jangled, out of tune and harsh;
That unmatched form and figure of blown youth,
Blasted with ecstasy: O! woe is me,
To have seen what I have seen, see what I see!
  Hamlet (1601) act 3, sc. 1, l. [159]

5 Speak the speech, I pray you, as I pronounced it to
you, trippingly on the tongue; but if you mouth it, as
many of your players do, I had as lief the town-crier
spoke my lines. Nor do not saw the air too much with
your hand, thus; but use all gently: for in the very
torrent, tempest, and—as I may say—whirlwind of
passion, you must acquire and beget a temperance,
that may give it smoothness. O! it offends me to the
soul to hear a robustious periwig-pated fellow tear a
passion to tatters, to very rags, to split the ears of the
groundlings, who for the most part are capable of
nothing but inexplicable dumb-shows and noise: I
would have such a fellow whipped for o'erdoing
Termagant; it out-herods Herod: pray you, avoid it.
  Hamlet (1601) act 3, sc. 2, l. 1

6 Be not too tame neither, but let your own discretion
be your tutor: suit the action to the word, the word to
the action; with this special observance, that you
o'erstep not the modesty of nature; for anything so
overdone is from the purpose of playing, whose end,
both at the first and now, was and is, to hold, as
'twere, the mirror up to nature; to show virtue her
own feature, scorn her own image, and the very age
and body of the time his form and pressure. Now, this
overdone, or come tardy off, though it make the
unskilful laugh, cannot but make the judicious grieve;
the censure of which one must in your allowance
o'erweigh a whole theatre of others. O! there be
players that I have seen play, and heard others praise,
and that highly, not to speak it profanely, that,
neither having the accent of Christians nor the gait of
Christian, pagan, nor man, have so strutted and
bellowed that I have thought some of nature's
journeymen had made men and not made them well,
they imitated humanity so abominably.
  Hamlet (1601) act 3, sc. 2, l. [19]

7   Give me that man
That is not passion's slave, and I will wear him
In my heart's core, ay, in my heart of heart,
As I do thee.
  Hamlet (1601) act 3, sc. 2, l. [76]

8 It is a damnèd ghost we have seen,
And my imaginations are as foul
As Vulcan's stithy.
  Hamlet (1601) act 3, sc. 2, l. [87]

9 The chameleon's dish: I eat the air,
promise-crammed; you cannot feed capons so.
  Hamlet (1601) act 3, sc. 2, l. [98]

10 Here's metal more attractive.
  Hamlet (1601) act 3, sc. 2, l. [117]

11 That's a fair thought to lie between maids' legs.
  Hamlet (1601) act 3, sc. 2, l. [126]

12 Die two months ago, and not forgotten yet? Then
there's hope a great man's memory may outlive his
life half a year; but, by'r lady, he must build churches
then.
  Hamlet (1601) act 3, sc. 2, l. [140]

13 For, O! for, O! the hobby-horse is forgot.
  Hamlet (1601) act 3, sc. 2, l. [145]

14 Marry, this is miching mallecho; it means mischief.
  Hamlet (1601) act 3, sc. 2, l. [148]

15 OPHELIA: 'Tis brief, my lord.
HAMLET: As woman's love.
  Hamlet (1601) act 3, sc. 2, l. [165]

16 The lady doth protest too much, methinks.
  Hamlet (1601) act 3, sc. 2, l. [242]

17 HAMLET: No, no, they do but jest, poison in jest; no
offence i' the world.
KING: What do you call the play?
HAMLET: The Mouse-trap.
  Hamlet (1601) act 3, sc. 2, l. [247]

18 We that have free souls, it touches us not: let the
galled jade wince, our withers are unwrung.
  Hamlet (1601) act 3, sc. 2, l. [255]

19 What! frighted with false fire?
  Hamlet (1601) act 3, sc. 2, l. [282]

20 Why, let the stricken deer go weep,
The hart ungallèd play;
For some must watch, while some must sleep:
So runs the world away.
  Hamlet (1601) act 3, sc. 2, l. [287]

21 The proverb is something musty.
  Hamlet (1601) act 3, sc. 2, l. [366]

22 You would play upon me; you would seem to know
my stops; you would pluck out the heart of my
mystery; you would sound me from my lowest note to
the top of my compass.
  Hamlet (1601) act 3, sc. 2, l. [387]

23 Do you think I am easier to be played on than a pipe?
Call me what instrument you will, though you can
fret me, you cannot play upon me.
  Hamlet (1601) act 3, sc. 2, l. [393]

24 They fool me to the top of my bent.
  Hamlet (1601) act 3, sc. 2, l. [408]

25 'Tis now the very witching time of night,
When churchyards yawn and hell itself breathes out
Contagion to this world: now could I drink hot blood,
And do such bitter business as the day
Would quake to look on.
  Hamlet (1601) act 3, sc. 2, l. [413]

1 Let me be cruel, not unnatural;
   I will speak daggers to her, but use none.
   Hamlet (1601) act 3, sc. 2, l. [420]

2 O! my offence is rank, it smells to heaven.
   Hamlet (1601) act 3, sc. 3, l. 36

3 Now might I do it pat, now he is praying.
   Hamlet (1601) act 3, sc. 3, l. 73

4 He took my father grossly, full of bread,
   With all his crimes broad blown, as flush as May;
   And how his audit stands who knows save heaven?
   Hamlet (1601) act 3, sc. 3, l. 80

5 My words fly up, my thoughts remain below:
   Words without thoughts never to heaven go.
   Hamlet (1601) act 3, sc. 3, l. 97

6 You go not, till I set you up a glass
   Where you may see the inmost part of you.
   Hamlet (1601) act 3, sc. 4, l. 19

7 How now! a rat? Dead, for a ducat, dead!
   Hamlet (1601) act 3, sc. 4, l. 23

8 A bloody deed! almost as bad, good mother,
   As kill a king, and marry with his brother.
   Hamlet (1601) act 3, sc. 4, l. 28

9 Thou wretched, rash, intruding fool, farewell!
   I took thee for thy better.
   Hamlet (1601) act 3, sc. 4, l. 31

10   Ay me! what act,
   That roars so loud, and thunders in the index?
   Hamlet (1601) act 3, sc. 4, l. 51

11 Look here, upon this picture, and on this.
   Hamlet (1601) act 3, sc. 4, l. 53

12 Could you on this fair mountain leave to feed,
   And batten on this moor?
   Hamlet (1601) act 3, sc. 4, l. 66

13 You cannot call it love, for at your age
   The hey-day in the blood is tame, it's humble,
   And waits upon the judgment.
   Hamlet (1601) act 3, sc. 4, l. 68

14   Speak no more;
   Thou turn'st mine eyes into my very soul.
   Hamlet (1601) act 3, sc. 4, l. 88

15   Nay, but to live
   In the rank sweat of an enseamèd bed,
   Stewed in corruption, honeying and making love
   Over the nasty sty.
   Hamlet (1601) act 3, sc. 4, l. 91

16 A cut-purse of the empire and the rule,
   That from a shelf the precious diadem stole,
   And put it in his pocket!
   Hamlet (1601) act 3, sc. 4, l. 99

17 A king of shreds and patches.
   Hamlet (1601) act 3, sc. 4, l. 102

18   Mother, for love of grace,
   Lay not that flattering unction to your soul.
   Hamlet (1601) act 3, sc. 4, l. 142

19   Confess yourself to heaven;
   Repent what's past; avoid what is to come.
   Hamlet (1601) act 3, sc. 4, l. 149

20 For in the fatness of these pursy times,
   Virtue itself of vice must pardon beg.
   Hamlet (1601) act 3, sc. 4, l. 153

21 QUEEN: O Hamlet! thou hast cleft my heart in twain.
   HAMLET: O! throw away the worser part of it,
      And live the purer with the other half.
   Hamlet (1601) act 3, sc. 4, l. 156

22 Assume a virtue, if you have it not.
   That monster, custom, who all sense doth eat,
   Of habits devil, is angel yet in this.
   Hamlet (1601) act 3, sc. 4, l. 160

23 I must be cruel only to be kind.
   Hamlet (1601) act 3, sc. 4, l. 178

24 For 'tis the sport to have the enginer
   Hoist with his own petar: and it shall go hard
   But I will delve one yard below their mines,
   And blow them at the moon.
   Hamlet (1601) act 3, sc. 4, l. 206

25 I'll lug the guts into the neighbour room.
   Hamlet (1601) act 3, sc. 4, l. 212

26   Indeed this counsellor
   Is now most still, most secret, and most grave,
   Who was in life a foolish prating knave.
   Hamlet (1601) act 3, sc. 4, l. 213

27   Diseases desperate grown,
   By desperate appliances are relieved,
   Or not at all.
   Hamlet (1601) act 4, sc. 2, l. 9

28 A certain convocation of politic worms are e'en at
   him. Your worm is your only emperor for diet.
   Hamlet (1601) act 4, sc. 2, l. [21]

29 A man may fish with the worm that hath eat of a
   king, and eat of the fish that hath fed of that worm.
   Hamlet (1601) act 4, sc. 2, l. [29]

30 We go to gain a little patch of ground,
   That hath in it no profit but the name.
   Hamlet (1601) act 4, sc. 4, l. 18

31 How all occasions do inform against me,
   And spur my dull revenge! What is a man,
   If his chief good and market of his time
   Be but to sleep and feed? a beast, no more.
   Sure he that made us with such large discourse,
   Looking before and after, gave us not
   That capability and god-like reason
   To fust in us unused.
   Hamlet (1601) act 4, sc. 4, l. 32

32   Some craven scruple
   Of thinking too precisely on the event.
   Hamlet (1601) act 4, sc. 4, l. 40

33   Rightly to be great
   Is not to stir without great argument,
   But greatly to find quarrel in a straw
   When honour's at the stake.
   Hamlet (1601) act 4, sc. 4, l. 53

34 How should I your true love know
   From another one?
   By his cockle hat and staff,
   And his sandal shoon.
   Hamlet (1601) act 4, sc. 5, l. [23]

35 He is dead and gone, lady,
   He is dead and gone,
   At his head a grass-green turf;
   At his heels a stone.
   Hamlet (1601) act 4, sc. 5, l. [29]

1 Lord! we know what we are, but know not what we
may be.
Hamlet (1601) act 4, sc. 5, l. [43]

2 Come, my coach! Good-night, ladies; good-night,
sweet ladies; good-night, good-night.
Hamlet (1601) act 4, sc. 5, l. [72]

3 When sorrows come, they come not single spies,
But in battalions.
Hamlet (1601) act 4, sc. 5, l. [78]

4   We have done but greenly
In hugger-mugger to inter him.
Hamlet (1601) act 4, sc. 5, l. [83]

5 There's such divinity doth hedge a king,
That treason can but peep to what it would.
Hamlet (1601) act 4, sc. 5, l. [123]

6 They bore him barefaced on the bier;
Hey non nonny, nonny, hey nonny;
And in his grave rained many a tear.
Hamlet (1601) act 4, sc. 5, l. [163]

7 There's rosemary, that's for remembrance; pray, love,
remember: and there is pansies, that's for thoughts.
Hamlet (1601) act 4, sc. 5, l. [174]

8 There's fennel for you, and columbines; there's rue for
you; and here's some for me; we may call it herb of
grace o' Sundays. O! you must wear your rue with a
difference. There's a daisy; I would give you some
violets, but they withered all when my father died.
They say he made a good end,— For bonny sweet
Robin is all my joy.
Hamlet (1601) act 4, sc. 5, l. [179]

9 His means of death, his obscure burial,
No trophy, sword, nor hatchment o'er his bones,
No noble rite nor formal ostentation.
Hamlet (1601) act 4, sc. 5, l. [213]

10 And where the offence is let the great axe fall.
Hamlet (1601) act 4, sc. 5, l. [218]

11 A very riband in the cap of youth,
Yet needful too; for youth no less becomes
The light and careless livery that it wears
Than settled age his sables and his weeds,
Importing health and graveness.
Hamlet (1601) act 4, sc. 7, l. 77

12 No place, indeed should murder sanctuarize.
Hamlet (1601) act 4, sc. 7, l. 127

13 There is a willow grows aslant a brook,
That shows his hoar leaves in the glassy stream;
There with fantastic garlands did she come,
Of crow-flowers, nettles, daisies, and long purples,
That liberal shepherds give a grosser name,
But our cold maids do dead men's fingers call them:
There, on the pendent boughs her coronet weeds
Clambering to hang, an envious sliver broke,
When down her weedy trophies and herself
Fell in the weeping brook. Her clothes spread wide,
And, mermaid-like, awhile they bore her up;
Which time she chanted snatches of old tunes,
As one incapable of her own distress.
Hamlet (1601) act 4, sc. 7, l. 167

14 Too much of water hast thou, poor Ophelia,
And therefore I forbid my tears; but yet
It is our trick, nature her custom holds,
Let shame say what it will.
Hamlet (1601) act 4, sc. 7, l. 186

15 Is she to be buried in Christian burial that wilfully
seeks her own salvation?
Hamlet (1601) act 5, sc. 1, l. 1

16 There is no ancient gentlemen but gardeners, ditchers
and grave-makers; they hold up Adam's profession.
Hamlet (1601) act 5, sc. 1, l. [32]

17 FIRST CLOWN: What is he that builds stronger than
either the mason, the shipwright, or the carpenter?
SECOND CLOWN: The gallows-maker; for that frame
outlives a thousand tenants.
Hamlet (1601) act 5, sc. 1, l. [44]

18 Cudgel thy brains no more about it, for your dull ass
will not mend his pace with beating.
Hamlet (1601) act 5, sc. 1, l. [61]

19 The houses that he makes last till doomsday.
Hamlet (1601) act 5, sc. 1, l. [64]

20 This might be the pate of a politician . . . one that
would circumvent God, might it not?
Hamlet (1601) act 5, sc. 1, l. [84]

21 How absolute the knave is! we must speak by the
card, or equivocation will undo us.
Hamlet (1601) act 5, sc. 1, l. [147]

22 The age is grown so picked that the toe of the peasant
comes so near the heel of the courtier, he galls his
kibe.
Hamlet (1601) act 5, sc. 1, l. [150]

23 Alas, poor Yorick. I knew him, Horatio; a fellow of
infinite jest, of most excellent fancy.
Hamlet (1601) act 5, sc. 1, l. [201]

24 To what base uses we may return, Horatio!
Hamlet (1601) act 5, sc. 1, l. [222]

25 Imperious Caesar, dead, and turned to clay,
Might stop a hole to keep the wind away.
Hamlet (1601) act 5, sc. 1, l. [235]

26   Lay her i' the earth;
And from her fair and unpolluted flesh
May violets spring! I tell thee, churlish priest,
A ministering angel shall my sister be,
When thou liest howling.
Hamlet (1601) act 5, sc. 1, l. [260]

27 Sweets to the sweet: farewell!
Hamlet (1601) act 5, sc. 1, l. [265]

28 I thought thy bride-bed to have decked, sweet maid,
And not have strewed thy grave.
Hamlet (1601) act 5, sc. 1, l. [267]

29 I loved Ophelia: forty thousand brothers
Could not, with all their quantity of love,
Make up my sum.
Hamlet (1601) act 5, sc. 1, l. [291]

30 There's a divinity that shapes our ends,
Rough-hew them how we will.
Hamlet (1601) act 5, sc. 2, l. 10

1 I once did hold it, as our statists do,
A baseness to write fair, and laboured much
How to forget that learning; but, sir, now
It did me yeoman's service.
Hamlet (1601) act 5, sc. 2, l. 33

2 Not a whit, we defy augury; there's a special
providence in the fall of a sparrow. If it be now, 'tis
not to come; if it be not to come, it will be now; if it
be not now, yet it will come: the readiness is all.
Hamlet (1601) act 5, sc. 2, l. [232]

3 I have shot mine arrow o'er the house,
And hurt my brother.
Hamlet (1601) act 5, sc. 2, l. [257]

4 Now the king drinks to Hamlet!
Hamlet (1601) act 5, sc. 2, l. [292]

5 A hit, a very palpable hit.
Hamlet (1601) act 5, sc. 2, l. [295]

6 Why, as a woodcock to mine own springe, Osric;
I am justly killed with my own treachery.
Hamlet (1601) act 5, sc. 2, l. [320]

7 The point envenomed too!—
Then, venom, to thy work.
Hamlet (1601) act 5, sc. 2, l. [335]

8   This fell sergeant, death,
Is swift in his arrest.
Hamlet (1601) act 5, sc. 2, l. [350]

9   Report me and my cause aright
To the unsatisfied.
Hamlet (1601) act 5, sc. 2, l. [353]

10 I am more an antique Roman than a Dane.
Hamlet (1601) act 5, sc. 2, l. [355]

11 If thou didst ever hold me in thy heart,
Absent thee from felicity awhile,
And in this harsh world draw thy breath in pain,
To tell my story.
Hamlet (1601) act 5, sc. 2, l. [360]

12 The potent poison quite o'ercrows my spirit.
Hamlet (1601) act 5, sc. 2, l. [367]

13 The rest is silence.
Hamlet (1601) act 5, sc. 2, l. [372]

14 Now cracks a noble heart. Good-night, sweet prince,
And flights of angels sing thee to thy rest!
Hamlet (1601) act 5, sc. 2, l. [373]

15 The ears are senseless that should give us hearing,
To tell him his commandment is fulfilled,
That Rosencrantz and Guildenstern are dead.
Hamlet (1601) act 5, sc. 2, l. [383]

16   Let four captains
Bear Hamlet, like a soldier, to the stage;
For he was likely, had he been put on,
To have proved most royally.
Hamlet (1601) act 5, sc. 2, l. [409]

Henry IV, Part 1

17 So shaken as we are, so wan with care.
Henry IV, Part 1 (1597) act 1, sc. 1, l. 1

18 Let us be Diana's foresters, gentlemen of the shade,
minions of the moon.
Henry IV, Part 1 (1597) act 1, sc. 2, l. [28]

19 FALSTAFF: And is not my hostess of the tavern a most
sweet wench?
PRINCE: As the honey of Hybla, my old lad of the
castle.
Henry IV, Part 1 (1597) act 1, sc. 2, l. [44]

20 What, in thy quips and thy quiddities?
Henry IV, Part 1 (1597) act 1, sc. 2, l. [50]

21 Shall there be gallows standing in England when thou
art king, and resolution thus fobbed as it is with the
rusty curb of old father antick, the law?
Henry IV, Part 1 (1597) act 1, sc. 2, l. [66]

22 Thou hast the most unsavoury similes.
Henry IV, Part 1 (1597) act 1, sc. 2, l. [89]

23 I would to God thou and I knew where a commodity
of good names were to be bought.
Henry IV, Part 1 (1597) act 1, sc. 2, l. [92]

24 O! thou hast damnable iteration, and art, indeed, able
to corrupt a saint.
Henry IV, Part 1 (1597) act 1, sc. 2, l. [101]

25 Now am I, if a man should speak truly, little better
than one of the wicked.
Henry IV, Part 1 (1597) act 1, sc. 2, l. [105]

26 I'll be damned for never a king's son in Christendom.
Henry IV, Part 1 (1597) act 1, sc. 2, l. [108]

27 Why, Hal, 'tis my vocation, Hal; 'tis no sin for a man
to labour in his vocation.
Henry IV, Part 1 (1597) act 1, sc. 2, l. [116] (referring to
stealing)

28 If he fight longer than he sees reason, I'll forswear
arms.
Henry IV, Part 1 (1597) act 1, sc. 2, l. [206]

29 If all the year were playing holidays,
To sport would be as tedious as to work;
But when they seldom come, they wished for come.
Henry IV, Part 1 (1597) act 1, sc. 2, l. [226]

30 And as the soldiers bore dead bodies by,
He called them untaught knaves, unmannerly,
To bring a slovenly, unhandsome corpse
Betwixt the wind and his nobility.
With many holiday and lady terms
He questioned me.
Henry IV, Part 1 (1597) act 1, sc. 3, l. 42

31 So pestered with a popinjay.
Henry IV, Part 1 (1597) act 1, sc. 3, l. 50

32   It was great pity, so it was,
This villainous saltpetre should be digged
Out of the bowels of the harmless earth,
Which many a good tall fellow had destroyed
So cowardly; and but for these vile guns,
He would himself have been a soldier.
Henry IV, Part 1 (1597) act 1, sc. 3, l. 59

33 To put down Richard, that sweet lovely rose,
And plant this thorn, this canker, Bolingbroke.
Henry IV, Part 1 (1597) act 1, sc. 3, l. 175

34   O! the blood more stirs
To rouse a lion than to start a hare.
Henry IV, Part 1 (1597) act 1, sc. 3, l. [197]

1 By heaven methinks it were an easy leap
To pluck bright honour from the pale-faced moon,
Or dive into the bottom of the deep,
Where fathom-line could never touch the ground,
And pluck up drownèd honour by the locks.
Henry IV, Part 1 (1597) act 1, sc. 3, l. 201

2 Why, what a candy deal of courtesy
This fawning greyhound then did proffer me!
Henry IV, Part 1 (1597) act 1, sc. 3, l. 251

3 I know a trick worth two of that.
Henry IV, Part 1 (1597) act 2, sc. 1, l. [40]

4 We have the receipt of fern-seed, we walk invisible.
Henry IV, Part 1 (1597) act 2, sc. 1, l. [95]

5 I am bewitched with the rogue's company. If the
rascal have not given me medicines to make me love
him, I'll be hanged.
Henry IV, Part 1 (1597) act 2, sc. 2, l. [19]

6 Go hang thyself in thine own heir-apparent garters!
Henry IV, Part 1 (1597) act 2, sc. 2, l. [49]

7 On, bacons, on!
Henry IV, Part 1 (1597) act 2, sc. 2, l. [99]

8 It would be argument for a week, laughter for a
month, and a good jest for ever.
Henry IV, Part 1 (1597) act 2, sc. 2, l. [104]

9   Falstaff sweats to death
And lards the lean earth as he walks along.
Henry IV, Part 1 (1597) act 2, sc. 2, l. [119]

10 Out of this nettle, danger, we pluck this flower, safety.
Henry IV, Part 1 (1597) act 2, sc. 3, l. [11]

11 A good plot, good friends, and full of expectation; an
excellent plot, very good friends.
Henry IV, Part 1 (1597) act 2, sc. 3, l. [21]

12 Away, you trifler! Love! I love thee not,
I care not for thee, Kate: this is no world
To play with mammets and to tilt with lips:
We must have bloody noses and cracked crowns.
Henry IV, Part 1 (1597) act 2, sc. 3, l. [95]

13   Constant you are,
But yet a woman: and for secrecy,
No lady closer; for I well believe
Thou wilt not utter what thou dost not know.
Henry IV, Part 1 (1597) act 2, sc. 3, l. [113]

14 I am not yet of Percy's mind, the Hotspur of the
North; he that kills me some six or seven dozen of
Scots at a breakfast, washes his hands, and says to his
wife, 'Fie upon this quiet life! I want work.'
Henry IV, Part 1 (1597) act 2, sc. 4, l. [116]

15 There live not three good men unhanged in England,
and one of them is fat and grows old.
Henry IV, Part 1 (1597) act 2, sc. 4, l. [146]

16 Call you that backing of your friends? A plague upon
such backing! give me them that will face me.
Henry IV, Part 1 (1597) act 2, sc. 4, l. [168]

17 A plague of all cowards, still say I.
Henry IV, Part 1 (1597) act 2, sc. 4, l. [175]

18 I am a Jew else; an Ebrew Jew.
Henry IV, Part 1 (1597) act 2, sc. 4, l. [201]

19 Nay that's past praying for: I have peppered two of
them: two I am sure I have paid, two rogues in
buckram suits. I tell thee what, Hal, if I tell thee a lie,
spit in my face, call me horse. Thou knowest my old
ward; here I lay, and thus I bore my point. Four
rogues in buckram let drive at me,—
Henry IV, Part 1 (1597) act 2, sc. 4, l. [214]

20 O monstrous! eleven buckram men grown out of two.
Henry IV, Part 1 (1597) act 2, sc. 4, l. [247]

21 These lies are like the father that begets them; gross
as a mountain, open, palpable.
Henry IV, Part 1 (1597) act 2, sc. 4, l. [253]

22 Give you a reason on compulsion! if reasons were as
plentiful as blackberries I would give no man a reason
upon compulsion, I.
Henry IV, Part 1 (1597) act 2, sc. 4, l. [267]

23 Mark now, how a plain tale shall put you down.
Henry IV, Part 1 (1597) act 2, sc. 4, l. [285]

24 What a slave art thou, to hack thy sword as thou hast
done, and then say it was in fight!
Henry IV, Part 1 (1597) act 2, sc. 4, l. [292]

25 Instinct is a great matter, I was a coward on instinct.
Henry IV, Part 1 (1597) act 2, sc. 4, l. [304]

26 What doth gravity out of his bed at midnight?
Henry IV, Part 1 (1597) act 2, sc. 4, l. [328]

27 A plague of sighing and grief! it blows a man up like a
bladder.
Henry IV, Part 1 (1597) act 2, sc. 4, l. [370]

28 I will do it in King Cambyses' vein.
Henry IV, Part 1 (1597) act 2, sc. 4, l. [430]

29 Shall the blessed sun of heaven prove a micher and
eat blackberries? a question not to be asked.
Henry IV, Part 1 (1597) act 2, sc. 4, l. [454]

30 There is a devil haunts thee in the likeness of a fat old
man; a tun of man is thy companion.
Henry IV, Part 1 (1597) act 2, sc. 4, l. [498]

31 That roasted Manningtree ox with the pudding in his
belly, that reverend vice, that grey iniquity, that father
ruffian, that vanity in years.
Henry IV, Part 1 (1597) act 2, sc. 4, l. [504]

32 If sack and sugar be a fault, God help the wicked!
Henry IV, Part 1 (1597) act 2, sc. 4, l. [524]

33 No, my good lord; banish Peto, banish Bardolph,
banish Poins; but for sweet Jack Falstaff, kind Jack
Falstaff, true Jack Falstaff, valiant Jack Falstaff, and
therefore more valiant, being, as he is, old Jack
Falstaff, banish not him thy Harry's company, banish
not him thy Harry's company: banish plump Jack and
banish all the world.
Henry IV, Part 1 (1597) act 2, sc. 4, l. [528]

34 Play out the play.
Henry IV, Part 1 (1597) act 2, sc. 4, l. [539]

35 O monstrous! but one half-pennyworth of bread to
this intolerable deal of sack!
Henry IV, Part 1 (1597) act 2, sc. 4, l. [598]

1 GLENDOWER: At my nativity
  The front of heaven was full of fiery shapes,
  Of burning cressets; and at my birth
  The frame and huge foundation of the earth
  Shaked like a coward.
HOTSPUR: Why, so it would have done at the same
  season, if your mother's cat had but kittened.
  Henry IV, Part 1 (1597) act 3, sc. 1, l. 13

2 And all the courses of my life do show
  I am not in the roll of common men.
  Henry IV, Part 1 (1597) act 3, sc. 1, l. [42]

3 GLENDOWER: I can call spirits from the vasty deep.
HOTSPUR: Why, so can I, or so can any man;
  But will they come when you do call for them?
  Henry IV, Part 1 (1597) act 3, sc. 1, l. [53]

4 I had rather be a kitten and cry mew
  Than one of these same metre ballad-mongers.
  Henry IV, Part 1 (1597) act 3, sc. 1, l. [128]

5 That would set my teeth nothing on edge,
  Nothing so much as mincing poetry:
  'Tis like the forced gait of a shuffling nag.
  Henry IV, Part 1 (1597) act 3, sc. 1, l. [132]

6 And such a deal of skimble-skamble stuff
  As puts me from my faith.
  Henry IV, Part 1 (1597) act 3, sc. 1, l. [153]

7   O! he's as tedious
  As a tired horse, a railing wife;
  Worse than a smoky house. I had rather live
  With cheese and garlic in a windmill, far,
  Than feed on cates and have him talk to me
  In any summer-house in Christendom.
  Henry IV, Part 1 (1597) act 3, sc. 1, l. [158]

8 I understand thy kisses, and thou mine,
  And that's a feeling disputation.
  Henry IV, Part 1 (1597) act 3, sc. 1, l. [204]

9   Thy tongue
  Makes Welsh as sweet as ditties highly penned,
  Sung by a fair queen in a summer's bower,
  With ravishing division, to her lute.
  Henry IV, Part 1 (1597) act 3, sc. 1, l. [207]

10 Now I perceive the devil understands Welsh.
  Henry IV, Part 1 (1597) act 3, sc. 1, l. [233]

11 You swear like a comfit-maker's wife.
  Henry IV, Part 1 (1597) act 3, sc. 1, l. [252]

12 Swear me, Kate, like a lady as thou art,
  A good mouth-filling oath.
  Henry IV, Part 1 (1597) act 3, sc. 1, l. [257]

13 The skipping king, he ambled up and down
  With shallow jesters and rash bavin wits.
  Henry IV, Part 1 (1597) act 3, sc. 2, l. 60

14 Being daily swallowed by men's eyes,
  They surfeited with honey and began
  To loathe the taste of sweetness, whereof a little
  More than a little is by much too much.
  So, when he had occasion to be seen,
  He was but as the cuckoo is in June,
  Heard, not regarded.
  Henry IV, Part 1 (1597) act 3, sc. 2, l. 70

15 My near'st and dearest enemy.
  Henry IV, Part 1 (1597) act 3, sc. 2, l. 123

16 Well, I'll repent, and that suddenly, while I am in
  some liking; I shall be out of heart shortly, and then I
  shall have no strength to repent.
  Henry IV, Part 1 (1597) act 3, sc. 3, l. [5]

17 Company, villanous company, hath been the spoil of
  me.
  Henry IV, Part 1 (1597) act 3, sc. 3, l. [10]

18 Thou knowest in the state of innocency Adam fell;
  and what should poor Jack Falstaff do in the days of
  villany. Thou seest I have more flesh than another
  man, and therefore more frailty.
  Henry IV, Part 1 (1597) act 3, sc. 3, l. [184]

19   Where is his son,
  That nimble-footed madcap Prince of Wales,
  And his comrades, that daffed the world aside,
  And bid it pass?
  Henry IV, Part 1 (1597) act 4, sc. 1, l. 94

20 I saw young Harry, with his beaver on,
  His cushes on his thighs, gallantly armed,
  Rise from the ground like feathered Mercury,
  And vaulted with such ease into his seat,
  As if an angel dropped down from the clouds,
  To turn and wind a fiery Pegasus,
  And witch the world with noble horsemanship.
  Henry IV, Part 1 (1597) act 4, sc. 1, l. 104

21 Doomsday is near; die all, die merrily.
  Henry IV, Part 1 (1597) act 4, sc. 1, l. 134

22 I have misused the king's press damnably.
  Henry IV, Part 1 (1597) act 4, sc. 2, l. [13]

23 The cankers of a calm world and a long peace.
  Henry IV, Part 1 (1597) act 4, sc. 2, l. [32]

24 I am as vigilant as a cat to steal cream.
  Henry IV, Part 1 (1597) act 4, sc. 2, l. [64]

25 Tut, tut; good enough to toss; food for powder, food
  for powder; they'll fill a pit as well as better: tush,
  man, mortal men, mortal men.
  Henry IV, Part 1 (1597) act 4, sc. 2, l. [72]

26 Greatness knows itself.
  Henry IV, Part 1 (1597) act 4, sc. 3, l. 74

27 For mine own part, I could be well content
  To entertain the lag-end of my life
  With quiet hours.
  Henry IV, Part 1 (1597) act 5, sc. 1, l. 23

28 Rebellion lay in his way, and he found it.
  Henry IV, Part 1 (1597) act 5, sc. 1, l. 28

29 I do not think a braver gentleman,
  More active-valiant or more valiant-young,
  More daring or more bold, is now alive
  To grace this latter age with noble deeds.
  For my part, I may speak it to my shame,
  I have a truant been to chivalry.
  Henry IV, Part 1 (1597) act 5, sc. 1, l. 89

30 FALSTAFF: I would it were bed-time, Hal, and all well.
PRINCE: Why, thou owest God a death.
  Henry IV, Part 1 (1597) act 5, sc. 1, l. [125]. Cf. *Henry IV,
  Part 2* 583·19

1 Honour pricks me on. Yea, but how if honour prick me off when I come on? how then? Can honour set-to a leg? No. Or an arm? No. Or take away the grief of a wound? No. Honour hath no skill in surgery, then? No. What is honour? A word. What is that word, honour? Air. A trim reckoning! Who hath it? He that died o' Wednesday. Doth he feel it? No. Doth he hear it? No. It is insensible then? Yea, to the dead. But will it not live with the living? No. Why? Detraction will not suffer it. Therefore I'll none of it: honour is a mere scutcheon: and so ends my catechism.
  Henry IV, Part 1 (1597) act 5, sc. 1, l. [131]

2 O gentlemen! the time of life is short;
To spend that shortness basely were too long.
  Henry IV, Part 1 (1597) act 5, sc. 2, l. 81

3 Now, *Esperance!* Percy! and set on.
  Henry IV, Part 1 (1597) act 5, sc. 2, l. 96

4 I like not such grinning honour as Sir Walter hath: give me life; which if I can save, so; if not, honour comes unlooked for, and there's an end.
  Henry IV, Part 1 (1597) act 5, sc. 3, l. [61]

5 Two stars keep not their motion in one sphere.
  Henry IV, Part 1 (1597) act 5, sc. 4, l. 65

6 But thought's the slave of life, and life time's fool;
And time, that takes survey of all the world,
Must have a stop.
  Henry IV, Part 1 (1597) act 5, sc. 4, l. [81]

7   Fare thee well, great heart!
Ill-weaved ambition, how much art thou shrunk!
When that this body did contain a spirit,
A kingdom for it was too small a bound;
But now two paces of the vilest earth
Is room enough: this earth, that bears thee dead,
Bears not alive so stout a gentleman.
  Henry IV, Part 1 (1597) act 5, sc. 4, l. [87]

8 Thy ignominy sleep with thee in the grave,
But not remembered in thy epitaph!
What! old acquaintance! could not all this flesh
Keep in a little life? Poor Jack, farewell!
I could have better spared a better man.
  Henry IV, Part 1 (1597) act 5, sc. 4, l. [100]

9 Lord, Lord, how this world is given to lying! I grant you I was down and out of breath; and so was he; but we rose both at an instant, and fought a long hour by Shrewsbury clock.
  Henry IV, Part 1 (1597) act 5, sc. 4, l. [148]

10 For my part, if a lie may do thee grace,
I'll gild it with the happiest terms I have.
  Henry IV, Part 1 (1597) act 5, sc. 4, l. [161]

11 I'll purge, and leave sack, and live cleanly, as a nobleman should do.
  Henry IV, Part 1 (1597) act 5, sc. 4, l. [168]

Henry IV, Part 2

12   Rumour is a pipe
Blown by surmises, jealousies, conjectures,
And of so easy and so plain a stop
That the blunt monster with uncounted heads,
The still-discordant wavering multitude,
Can play upon it.
  Henry IV, Part 2 (1597) induction, l. 15

13 Yet the first bringer of unwelcome news
Hath but a losing office, and his tongue
Sounds ever after as a sullen bell,
Remembered knolling a departed friend.
  Henry IV, Part 2 (1597) act 1, sc. 1, l. 100

14 The brain of this foolish-compounded clay, man, is not able to invent anything that tends to laughter, more than I invent or is invented on me: I am not only witty in myself, but the cause that wit is in other men. I do here walk before thee like a sow that hath overwhelmed all her litter but one.
  Henry IV, Part 2 (1597) act 1, sc. 2, l. [7]

15 A rascally yea-forsooth knave.
  Henry IV, Part 2 (1597) act 1, sc. 2, l. [40]

16 Your lordship, though not clean past your youth, hath yet some smack of age in you, some relish of the saltness of time.
  Henry IV, Part 2 (1597) act 1, sc. 2, l. [111]

17 This apoplexy is, as I take it, a kind of lethargy, an't please your lordship; a kind of sleeping in the blood, a whoreson tingling.
  Henry IV, Part 2 (1597) act 1, sc. 2, l. [127]

18 It is the disease of not listening, the malady of not marking, that I am troubled withal.
  Henry IV, Part 2 (1597) act 1, sc. 2, l. [139]

19 I am as poor as Job, my lord, but not so patient.
  Henry IV, Part 2 (1597) act 1, sc. 2, l. [145]

20 Have you not a moist eye, a dry hand, a yellow cheek, a white beard, a decreasing leg, an increasing belly? Is not your voice broken, your wind short, your chin double, your wit single, and every part about you blasted with antiquity, and will you yet call yourself young? Fie, fie, fie, Sir John!
  Henry IV, Part 2 (1597) act 1, sc. 2, l. [206]

21 My lord, I was born about three of the clock in the afternoon, with a white head, and something of a round belly. For my voice, I have lost it with hollaing, and singing of anthems.
  Henry IV, Part 2 (1597) act 1, sc. 2, l. [213]

22 CHIEF JUSTICE: God send the prince a better companion!
FALSTAFF: God send the companion a better prince! I cannot rid my hands of him.
  Henry IV, Part 2 (1597) act 1, sc. 2, l. [227]

23 It was always yet the trick of our English nation, if they have a good thing, to make it too common.
  Henry IV, Part 2 (1597) act 1, sc. 2, l. [244]

24 I would to God my name were not so terrible to the enemy as it is: I were better to be eaten to death with rust than to be scoured to nothing with perpetual motion.
  Henry IV, Part 2 (1597) act 1, sc. 2, l. [247]

25 I can get no remedy against this consumption of the purse: borrowing only lingers and lingers it out, but the disease is incurable.
  Henry IV, Part 2 (1597) act 1, sc. 2, l. [268]

1 When we mean to build,
We first survey the plot, then draw the model;
And when we see the figure of the house,
Then we must rate the cost of the erection;
Which if we find outweighs ability,
What do we then but draw anew the model
In fewer offices, or at last desist
To build at all?
  Henry IV, Part 2 (1597) act 1, sc. 3, l. [41]

2 A hundred mark is a long one for a poor lone woman
to bear; and I have borne, and borne, and borne; and
have been fubbed off, and fubbed off, and fubbed off,
from this day to that day, that it is a shame to be
thought on.
  Henry IV, Part 2 (1597) act 2, sc. 1, l. [36]

3 Away, you scullion! you rampallion! you fustilarian!
I'll tickle your catastrophe.
  Henry IV, Part 2 (1597) act 2, sc. 1, l. [67]

4 Thou didst swear to me upon a parcel-gilt goblet,
sitting in my Dolphin-chamber, at the round table, by
a sea-coal fire, upon Wednesday in Wheeson week.
  Henry IV, Part 2 (1597) act 2, sc. 1, l. [97]

5 Doth it not show vilely in me to desire small beer?
  Henry IV, Part 2 (1597) act 2, sc. 2, l. [7]

6 Let the end try the man.
  Henry IV, Part 2 (1597) act 2, sc. 2, l. [52]

7   He was indeed the glass
Wherein the noble youth did dress themselves.
  Henry IV, Part 2 (1597) act 2, sc. 3, l. 21

8   Shall pack-horses,
And hollow pampered jades of Asia,
Which cannot go but thirty miles a day,
Compare with Caesars, and with Cannibals,
And Trojan Greeks? nay, rather damn them with
King Cerberus; and let the welkin roar.
  Henry IV, Part 2 (1597) act 2, sc. 4, l. [176]. Cf. Marlowe
  448:9

9 Thou whoreson little tidy Bartholomew boar-pig,
when wilt thou leave fighting o' days, and foining o'
nights, and begin to patch up thine old body for
heaven?
  Henry IV, Part 2 (1597) act 2, sc. 4, l. [249]

10 Is it not strange that desire should so many years
outlive performance?
  Henry IV, Part 2 (1597) act 2, sc. 4, l. [283]

11   O sleep! O gentle sleep!
Nature's soft nurse, how have I frighted thee,
That thou no more wilt weigh mine eyelids down
And steep my senses in forgetfulness?
Why rather, sleep, liest thou in smoky cribs,
Upon uneasy pallets stretching thee,
And hushed with buzzing night-flies to thy slumber,
Than in the perfumed chambers of the great,
Under the canopies of costly state,
And lulled with sound of sweetest melody?
  Henry IV, Part 2 (1597) act 3, sc. 1, l. 5

12 Uneasy lies the head that wears a crown
  Henry IV, Part 2 (1597) act 3, sc. 1, l. 31

13 O God! that one might read the book of fate,
And see the revolution of the times
Make mountains level, and the continent,—
Weary of solid firmness,—melt itself
Into the sea!
  Henry IV, Part 2 (1597) act 3, sc. 1, l. 45

14   O! if this were seen,
The happiest youth, viewing his progress through,
What perils past, what crosses to ensue,
Would shut the book, and sit him down and die.
  Henry IV, Part 2 (1597) act 3, sc. 1, l. 54

15 There is a history in all men's lives,
Figuring the nature of the times deceased,
The which observed, a man may prophesy,
With a near aim, of the main chance of things
As yet not come to life, which in their seeds
And weak beginnings lie intreasurèd.
  Henry IV, Part 2 (1597) act 3, sc. 1, l. 80

16 A soldier is better accommodated than with a wife.
  Henry IV, Part 2 (1597) act 3, sc. 2, l. [73]

17 Most forcible Feeble.
  Henry IV, Part 2 (1597) act 3, sc. 2, l. [181]

18 We have heard the chimes at midnight.
  Henry IV, Part 2 (1597) act 3, sc. 2, l. [231]

19 I care not; a man can die but once; we owe God a
death.
  Henry IV, Part 2 (1597) act 3, sc. 2, l. [253]. Cf. *Henry IV,
  Part 1* 581:30

20 He that dies this year is quit for the next.
  Henry IV, Part 2 (1597) act 3, sc. 2, l. [257]

21 Lord, Lord! how subject we old men are to this vice of
lying.
  Henry IV, Part 2 (1597) act 3, sc. 2, l. [329]

22 When a' was naked, he was, for all the world, like a
forked radish, with a head fantastically carved upon it
with a knife.
  Henry IV, Part 2 (1597) act 3, sc. 2, l. [335]

23 Talks as familiarly of John a Gaunt as if he had been
sworn brother to him.
  Henry IV, Part 2 (1597) act 3, sc. 2, l. [348]

24 Against ill chances men are ever merry,
But heaviness foreruns the good event.
  Henry IV, Part 2 (1597) act 4, sc. 2, l. 81

25 That I may justly say with the hook-nosed fellow of
Rome, 'I came, saw, and overcame.'
  Henry IV, Part 2 (1597) act 4, sc. 3, l. [44]. Cf. *Julius Caesar*
  174:20

26 A man cannot make him laugh; but that's no marvel;
he drinks no wine.
  Henry IV, Part 2 (1597) act 4, sc. 3, l. [95]

27 Skill in the weapon is nothing without sack, for that
sets it a-work; and learning, a mere hoard of gold
kept by a devil till sack commences it and sets it in
act and use.
  Henry IV, Part 2 (1597) act 4, sc. 3, l. [120]

28 If I had a thousand sons, the first human principle I
would teach them should be, to forswear thin
potations.
  Henry IV, Part 2 (1597) act 4, sc. 3, l. [133]

1 O polished perturbation! golden care!
   That keep'st the ports of slumber open wide
   To many a watchful night! Sleep with it now!
   Yet not so sound, and half so deeply sweet
   As he whose brow with homely biggin bound
   Snores out the watch of night.
      Henry IV, Part 2 (1597) act 4, sc. 5, l. 22

2 This sleep is sound indeed; this is a sleep
   That from this golden rigol hath divorced
   So many English kings.
      Henry IV, Part 2 (1597) act 4, sc. 5, l. 34

3 Thy wish was father, Harry, to that thought.
      Henry IV, Part 2 (1597) act 4, sc. 5, l. 91

4   Commit
   The oldest sins the newest kind of ways.
      Henry IV, Part 2 (1597) act 4, sc. 5, l. 124

5 It hath been prophesied to me many years
   I should not die but in Jerusalem,
   Which vainly I supposed the Holy Land.
   But bear me to that chamber; there I'll lie:
   In that Jerusalem shall Harry die.
      Henry IV, Part 2 (1597) act 4, sc. 5, l. 235

6 Any pretty little tiny kickshaws, tell William
   Cook.
      Henry IV, Part 2 (1597) act 5, sc. 1, l. [29]

7 This is the English, not the Turkish court;
   Not Amurath an Amurath succeeds,
   But Harry, Harry.
      Henry IV, Part 2 (1597) act 5, sc. 2, l. 47

8 Sorrow so royally in you appears,
   That I will deeply put the fashion on.
      Henry IV, Part 2 (1597) act 5, sc. 2, l. 51

9 My father is gone wild into his grave.
      Henry IV, Part 2 (1597) act 5, sc. 2, l. 123

10 'Tis merry in hall when beards wag all.
      Henry IV, Part 2 (1597) act 5, sc. 3, l. [35]

11 A foutra for the world, and worldlings base!
   I speak of Africa and golden joys.
      Henry IV, Part 2 (1597) act 5, sc. 3, l. [100]

12 I know thee not, old man: fall to thy prayers;
   How ill white hairs become a fool and jester!
   I have long dreamed of such a kind of man,
   So surfeit-swelled, so old, and so profane.
      Henry IV, Part 2 (1597) act 5, sc. 5, l. [52]

13 Make less thy body hence, and more thy grace;
   Leave gourmandising; know the grave doth
      gape
   For thee thrice wider than for other men.
      Henry IV, Part 2 (1597) act 5, sc. 5, l. [57]

14 Presume not that I am the thing I was.
      Henry IV, Part 2 (1597) act 5, sc. 5, l. [61]

15 Falstaff shall die of a sweat, unless already a' be killed
   with your hard opinions.
      Henry IV, Part 2 (1597) act 5, sc. 5, epilogue, l. [32]

Henry V

16 O! for a Muse of fire, that would ascend
   The brightest heaven of invention;
   A kingdom for a stage, princes to act
   And monarchs to behold the swelling scene.
      Henry V (1599) chorus, l. 1

17   Can this cockpit hold
   The vasty fields of France? or may we cram
   Within this wooden O the very casques
   That did affright the air at Agincourt?
      Henry V (1599) chorus, l. 11

18 Consideration like an angel came,
   And whipped the offending Adam out of him.
      Henry V (1599) act 1, sc. 1, l. 28

19   When he speaks,
   The air, a chartered libertine, is still.
      Henry V (1599) act 1, sc. 1, l. 47

20 O noble English! that could entertain
   With half their forces the full pride of France,
   And let another half stand laughing by,
   All out of work, and cold for action.
      Henry V (1599) act 1, sc. 2, l. 111

21 And make your chronicle as rich with praise
   As is the owse and bottom of the sea
   With sunken wrack and sumless treasuries.
      Henry V (1599) act 1, sc. 2, l. 163

22   For so work the honey-bees,
   Creatures that by a rule in nature teach
   The act of order to a peopled kingdom.
   They have a king and officers of sorts;
   Where some, like magistrates, correct at home,
   Others, like merchants, venture trade abroad,
   Others, like soldiers, armèd in their stings,
   Make boot upon the summer's velvet buds;
   Which pillage they with merry march bring home
   To the tent-royal of their emperor:
   Who, busied in his majesty, surveys
   The singing masons building roofs of gold,
   The civil citizens kneading up the honey,
   The poor mechanic porters crowding in
   Their heavy burdens at his narrow gate,
   The sad-eyed justice, with his surly hum,
   Delivering o'er to executors pale
   The lazy yawning drone.
      Henry V (1599) act 1, sc. 2, l. 187

23 His present and your pains we thank you for:
   When we have matched our rackets to these
      balls,
   We will in France, by God's grace, play a set
   Shall strike his father's crown into the hazard.
      Henry V (1599) act 1, sc. 2, l. 260

1 Now all the youth of England are on fire,
And silken dalliance in the wardrobe lies;
Now thrive the armourers, and honour's thought
Reigns solely in the breast of every man:
They sell the pasture now to buy the horse,
Following the mirror of all Christian kings,
With wingèd heels, as English Mercuries.
For now sits Expectation in the air
And hides a sword from hilts unto the point
With crowns imperial, crowns and coronets,
Promised to Harry and his followers.
Henry V (1599) act 2, chorus, l. 1

2 O England! model to thy inward greatness,
Like little body with a mighty heart,
What might'st thou do, that honour would thee do,
Were all thy children kind and natural!
But see thy fault!
Henry V (1599) act 2, chorus, l. 16

3 I dare not fight; but I will wink and hold out mine
iron.
Henry V (1599) act 2, sc. 1, l. [7]

4 Would I were with him, wheresome'er he is, either in
heaven or in hell.
Henry V (1599) act 2, sc. 3, l. [7]

5 He's in Arthur's bosom, if ever man went to Arthur's
bosom. A' made a finer end, and went away an it had
been any christom child; a' parted even just between
twelve and one, even at the turning o' the tide: for
after I saw him fumble with the sheets and play with
flowers and smile upon his fingers' ends, I knew there
was but one way; for his nose was as sharp as a pen,
and a' babbled of green fields.
Henry V (1599) act 2, sc. 3, l. [9]

6   Trust none;
For oaths are straws, men's faiths are wafer-cakes,
And hold-fast is the only dog, my duck.
Henry V (1599) act 2, sc. 3, l. [53]

7 Once more unto the breach, dear friends, once more;
Or close the wall up with our English dead!
In peace there's nothing so becomes a man
As modest stillness and humility:
But when the blast of war blows in our ears,
Then imitate the action of the tiger;
Stiffen the sinews, summon up the blood,
Disguise fair nature with hard-favoured rage;
Then lend the eye a terrible aspect.
Henry V (1599) act 3, sc. 1, l. 1

8   On, on you noblest English!
Whose blood is fet from fathers of war-proof;
Fathers that, like so many Alexanders,
Have in these parts from morn till even fought,
And sheathed their swords for lack of argument.
Henry V (1599) act 3, sc. 1, l. 17

9   And you, good yeomen,
Whose limbs were made in England, show us here
The mettle of your pasture.
Henry V (1599) act 3, sc. 1, l. [25]

10 I see you stand like greyhounds in the slips,
Straining upon the start. The game's afoot:
Follow your spirit; and, upon this charge
Cry 'God for Harry! England and Saint George!'
Henry V (1599) act 3, sc. 1, l. 31

11 Would I were in an alehouse in London! I would give
all my fame for a pot of ale, and safety.
Henry V (1599) act 3, sc. 2, l. [13]

12 Men of few words are the best men.
Henry V (1599) act 3, sc. 2, l. [40]

13 Give them great meals of beef and iron and steel, they
will eat like wolves and fight like devils.
Henry V (1599) act 3, sc. 7, l. [166]

14 Now entertain conjecture of a time
When creeping murmur and the poring dark
Fills the wide vessel of the universe.
From camp to camp, through the foul womb of night,
The hum of either army stilly sounds,
That the fixed sentinels almost receive
The secret whispers of each other's watch.
Fire answers fire, and through their paly flames
Each battle sees the other's umbered face:
Steed threatens steed, in high and boastful neighs
Piercing the night's dull ear; and from the tents
The armourers, accomplishing the knights,
With busy hammers closing rivets up,
Give dreadful note of preparation.
Henry V (1599) act 4, chorus, l. 1

15 The royal captain of this ruined band.
Henry V (1599) act 4, chorus, l. 29

16 A largess universal, like the sun
His liberal eye doth give to every one,
Thawing cold fear.
Henry V (1599) act 4, chorus, l. 43

17 A little touch of Harry in the night.
Henry V (1599) act 4, chorus, l. 47

18   Yet sit and see;
Minding true things by what their mockeries be.
Henry V (1599) act 4, chorus, l. 52

19 Gloucester, 'tis true that we are in great danger;
The greater therefore should our courage be.
Henry V (1599) act 4, sc. 1, l. 1

20 Thus may we gather honey from the weed,
And make a moral of the devil himself.
Henry V (1599) act 4, sc. 1, l. 11

21 Discuss unto me; art thou officer?
Or art thou base, common and popular?
Henry V (1599) act 4, sc. 1, l. 37

22 The king's a bawcock, and a heart of gold,
A lad of life, an imp of fame,
Of parents good, of fist most valiant:
I kiss his dirty shoe, and from my heart-string
I love the lovely bully.
Henry V (1599) act 4, sc. 1, l. [44]

1 If you would take the pains but to examine the wars
of Pompey the Great, you shall find, I warrant you,
that there is no tiddle-taddle nor pibble-pabble in
Pompey's camp.
Henry V (1599) act 4, sc. 1, l. [69]

2 Though it appear a little out of fashion,
There is much care and valour in this Welshman.
Henry V (1599) act 4, sc. 1, l. [86]

3 I think the king is but a man, as I am: the violet
smells to him as it doth to me.
Henry V (1599) act 4, sc. 1, l. [106]

4 I am afeard there are few die well that die in a battle;
for how can they charitably dispose of any thing when
blood is their argument?
Henry V (1599) act 4, sc. 1, l. [149]

5 Every subject's duty is the king's; but every subject's
soul is his own.
Henry V (1599) act 4, sc. 1, l. [189]

6 Upon the king! let us our lives, our souls,
Our debts, our careful wives,
Our children, and our sins lay on the king!
We must bear all. O hard condition!
Henry V (1599) act 4, sc. 1, l. [250]

7   What infinite heart's ease
Must kings neglect, that private men enjoy!
And what have kings that privates have not too,
Save ceremony, save general ceremony?
Henry V (1599) act 4, sc. 1, l. [256]

8 'Tis not the balm, the sceptre and the ball,
The sword, the mace, the crown imperial,
The intertissued robe of gold and pearl,
The farcèd title running 'fore the king,
The throne he sits on, nor the tide of pomp
That beats upon the high shore of this world,
No, not all these, thrice-gorgeous ceremony,
Not all these, laid in bed majestical,
Can sleep so soundly as the wretched slave,
Who with a body filled and vacant mind
Gets him to rest, crammed with distressful bread;
Never sees horrid night, the child of hell,
But, like a lackey, from the rise to set
Sweats in the eye of Phoebus, and all night
Sleeps in Elysium.
Henry V (1599) act 4, sc. 1, l. [280]

9 O God of battles! steel my soldiers' hearts;
Possess them not with fear; take from them now
The sense of reckoning, if the opposèd numbers
Pluck their hearts from them.
Henry V (1599) act 4, sc. 1, l. [309]

10 If we are marked to die, we are enow
To do our country loss; and if to live,
The fewer men, the greater share of honour.
Henry V (1599) act 4, sc. 3, l. 20

11 He which hath no stomach to this fight,
Let him depart; his passport shall be made,
And crowns for convoy put into his purse:
We would not die in that man's company
That fears his fellowship to die with us.
This day is called the feast of Crispian:
He that outlives this day and comes safe home,
Will stand a tip-toe when this day is named,
And rouse him at the name of Crispian.
He that shall live this day, and see old age,
Will yearly on the vigil feast his neighbours,
And say, 'To-morrow is Saint Crispian:'
Then will he strip his sleeve and show his scars,
And say, 'These wounds I had on Crispin's day.'
Old men forget: yet all shall be forgot,
But he'll remember with advantages
What feats he did that day. Then shall our names,
Familiar in his mouth as household words,
Harry the King, Bedford and Exeter,
Warwick and Talbot, Salisbury and Gloucester,
Be in their flowing cups freshly remembered.
This story shall the good man teach his son;
And Crispin Crispian shall ne'er go by,
From this day to the ending of the world,
But we in it shall be rememberèd;
We few, we happy few, we band of brothers;
For he to-day that sheds his blood with me
Shall be my brother; be he ne'er so vile
This day shall gentle his condition:
And gentlemen in England, now a-bed
Shall think themselves accursed they were not here,
And hold their manhoods cheap whiles any speaks
That fought with us upon Saint Crispin's day.
Henry V (1599) act 4, sc. 3, l. 35

12 Thou damned and luxurious mountain goat.
Henry V (1599) act 4, sc. 4, l. [20]

13   But now behold,
In the quick forge and working-house of thought,
How London doth pour out her citizens.
Henry V (1599) act 5, chorus, l. 22

14 Not for Cadwallader and all his goats.
Henry V (1599) act 5, sc. 1, l. [29]

15 By this leek, I will most horribly revenge.
Henry V (1599) act 5, sc. 1, l. [49]

16   Let it not disgrace me
If I demand before this royal view,
What rub or what impediment there is,
Why that the naked, poor, and mangled Peace,
Dear nurse of arts, plenties, and joyful births,
Should not in this best garden of the world,
Our fertile France, put up her lovely visage?
Henry V (1599) act 5, sc. 2, l. 31

17   Her fallow leas
The darnel, hemlock and rank fumitory
Doth root upon, while that the coulter rusts
That should deracinate such savagery;
The even mead, that erst brought sweetly forth
The freckled cowslip, burnet, and green clover,
Wanting the scythe, all uncorrected, rank,
Conceives by idleness, and nothing teems
But hateful docks, rough thistles, kecksies, burs,
Losing both beauty and utility.
Henry V (1599) act 5, sc. 2, l. 44

1 For these fellows of infinite tongue, that can rhyme
themselves into ladies' favours, they do always reason
themselves out again.
Henry V (1599) act 5, sc. 2, l. [162]

2 Shall not thou and I, between Saint Denis and Saint
George, compound a boy, half-French, half-English,
that shall go to Constantinople and take the Turk by
the beard?
Henry V (1599) act 5, sc. 2, l. [218]

3 God, the best maker of all marriages,
Combine your hearts in one.
Henry V (1599) act 5, sc. 2, l. [387]

4 Thus far, with rough and all-unable pen,
Our bending author hath pursued the story,
In little room confining mighty men,
Mangling by starts the full course of their glory.
Small time, but in that small most greatly lived
This star of England. Fortune made his sword,
By which the world's best garden he achieved,
And of it made his son imperial lord.
Henry V (1599) epilogue

Henry VI, Part 1

5 Hung be the heavens with black, yield day to night!
Henry VI, Part 1 (1592) act 1, sc. 1, l. 1

6 Expect Saint Martin's summer, halcyon days.
Henry VI, Part 1 (1592) act 1, sc. 2, l. 131

7   Unbidden guests
Are often welcomest when they are gone.
Henry VI, Part 1 (1592) act 2, sc. 2, l. 55

8 But in these nice sharp quillets of the law,
Good faith, I am no wiser than a daw.
Henry VI, Part 1 (1592) act 2, sc. 4, l. 17

9 PLANTAGENET: Let him that is a true-born gentleman,
And stands upon the honour of his birth,
If he suppose that I have pleaded truth,
From off this brier pluck a white rose with me.
SOMERSET: Let him that is no coward nor no flatterer,
But dare maintain the party of the truth,
Pluck a red rose from off this thorn with me.
Henry VI, Part 1 (1592) act 2, sc. 4, l. 27

10 Delays have dangerous ends.
Henry VI, Part 1 (1592) act 3, sc. 2, l. 33

11 I owe him little duty and less love.
Henry VI, Part 1 (1592) act 4, sc. 4, l. 34

12 So doth the swan her downy cygnets save,
Keeping them prisoners underneath her wings.
Henry VI, Part 1 (1592) act 5, sc. 3, l. 56

13 She's beautiful and therefore to be wooed;
She is a woman, therefore to be won.
Henry VI, Part 1 (1592) act 5, sc. 3, l. 78. Cf. *Titus
Andronicus* 626:22

Henry VI, Part 2

14 Put forth thy hand, reach at the glorious gold.
Henry VI, Part 2 (1592) act 1, sc. 2, l. 11

15 Is this the fashion of the court of England?
Is this the government of Britain's isle,
And this the royalty of Albion's king?
Henry VI, Part 2 (1592) act 1, sc. 3, l. [46]

16 She bears a duke's revenues on her back,
And in her heart she scorns our poverty.
Henry VI, Part 2 (1592) act 1, sc. 3, l. [83]

17 Could I come near your beauty with my nails
I'd set my ten commandments in your face.
Henry VI, Part 2 (1592) act 1, sc. 3, l. [144]

18 What stronger breastplate than a heart untainted!
Thrice is he armed that hath his quarrel just,
And he but naked, though locked up in steel,
Whose conscience with injustice is corrupted.
Henry VI, Part 2 (1592) act 3, sc. 2, l. 232

19 Forbear to judge, for we are sinners all.
Close up his eyes, and draw the curtain close;
And let us all to meditation.
Henry VI, Part 2 (1592) act 3, sc. 3, l. 31

20 The gaudy, blabbing, and remorseful day
Is crept into the bosom of the sea.
Henry VI, Part 2 (1592) act 4, sc. 1, l. 1

21 True nobility is exempt from fear:
More can I bear than you dare execute.
Henry VI, Part 2 (1592) act 4, sc. 1, l. 129

22 I say it was never merry world in England since
gentlemen came up.
Henry VI, Part 2 (1592) act 4, sc. 2, l. [10]

23 CADE: There shall be in England seven halfpenny
loaves sold for a penny; the three-hooped pot shall
have ten hoops; and I will make it felony to drink
small beer. All the realm shall be in common, and
in Cheapside shall my palfrey go to grass. And
when I am king,—as king I will be,— ... there
shall be no money; all shall eat and drink on my
score; and I will apparel them all in one livery, that
they may agree like brothers, and worship me their
lord.
DICK: The first thing we do, let's kill all the lawyers.
Henry VI, Part 2 (1592) act 4, sc. 2, l. [73]

24 Is not this a lamentable thing, that of the skin of an
innocent lamb should be made parchment? that
parchment, being scribbled o'er, should undo a man?
Henry VI, Part 2 (1592) act 4, sc. 2, l. [88]

25 And Adam was a gardener.
Henry VI, Part 2 (1592) act 4, sc. 2, l. [146]

26 Thou hast most traitorously corrupted the youth of
the realm in erecting a grammar school: and whereas,
before, our forefathers had no other books but the
score and the tally, thou hast caused printing to be
used; and, contrary to the king, his crown and
dignity, thou hast built a paper-mill.
Henry VI, Part 2 (1592) act 4, sc. 7, l. [35]

27 Away with him! away with him! he speaks Latin.
Henry VI, Part 2 (1592) act 4, sc. 7, l. [62]

Henry VI, Part 3

28 O tiger's heart wrapped in a woman's hide!
Henry VI, Part 3 (1592) act 1, sc. 4, l. 137

29 This battle fares like to the morning's war,
When dying clouds contend with growing light,
What time the shepherd, blowing of his nails,
Can neither call it perfect day nor night.
Henry VI, Part 3 (1592) act 1, sc. 5, l. 1

1 O God! methinks it were a happy life,
  To be no better than a homely swain;
  To sit upon a hill, as I do now,
  To carve out dials, quaintly, point by point,
  Thereby to see the minutes how they run,
  How many make the hour full complete;
  How many hours bring about the day;
  How many days will finish up the year;
  How many years a mortal man may live.
  Henry VI, Part 3 (1592) act 1, sc. 5, l. 21

2 Gives not the hawthorn bush a sweeter shade
  To shepherds, looking on their silly sheep,
  Than doth a rich embroidered canopy
  To kings that fear their subjects' treachery?
  Henry VI, Part 3 (1592) act 1, sc. 5, l. 42

3 Why, I can smile, and murder whiles I smile,
  And cry 'Content!' to that which grieves my heart,
  And wet my cheeks with artificial tears,
  And frame my face to all occasions.
  I'll drown more sailors than the mermaid shall;
  I'll slay more gazers than the basilisk;
  I'll play the orator as well as Nestor,
  Deceive more slyly than Ulysses could,
  And, like a Sinon, take another Troy.
  I can add colours to the chameleon,
  Change shapes with Proteus for advantages,
  And set the murderous Machiavel to school.
  Can I do this, and cannot get a crown?
  Tut, were it farther off, I'll pluck it down.
  Henry VI, Part 3 (1592) act 3, sc. 2, l. 182

4 Peace! impudent and shameless Warwick, peace;
  Proud setter up and puller down of kings.
  Henry VI, Part 3 (1592) act 3, sc. 3, l. 156

5 A little fire is quickly trodden out,
  Which, being suffered, rivers cannot quench.
  Henry VI, Part 3 (1592) act 4, sc. 8, l. 7

6 Lo! now my glory smeared in dust and blood;
  My parks, my walks, my manors that I had,
  Even now forsake me; and, of all my lands
  Is nothing left me but my body's length.
  Why, what is pomp, rule, reign, but earth and dust?
  And, live we how we can, yet die we must.
  Henry VI, Part 3 (1592) act 5, sc. 2, l. 23

7 Suspicion always haunts the guilty mind;
  The thief doth fear each bush an officer.
  Henry VI, Part 3 (1592) act 5, sc. 6, l. 11

8 Down, down to hell; and say I sent thee thither.
  Henry VI, Part 3 (1592) act 5, sc. 6, l. 67

Henry VIII

9 Heat not a furnace for your foe so hot
  That it do singe yourself.
  Henry VIII (1613) act 1, sc. 1, l. 140

10 If I chance to talk a little wild, forgive me;
   I had it from my father.
   Henry VIII (1613) act 1, sc. 4, l. 26

11 Go with me, like good angels, to my end;
   And, as the long divorce of steel falls on me,
   Make of your prayers one sweet sacrifice,
   And lift my soul to heaven.
   Henry VIII (1613) act 2, sc. 1, l. 75

12 CHAMBERLAIN: It seems the marriage with his
                 brother's wife
   Has crept too near his conscience.
   SUFFOLK: No; his conscience
   Has crept too near another lady.
   Henry VIII (1613) act 2, sc. 2, l. [17]

13   Heaven will one day open
   The king's eyes, that so long have slept upon
   This bold bad man.
   Henry VIII (1613) act 2, sc. 2, l. [42]. Cf. Spenser
   659:23

14   I would not be a queen
   For all the world
   Henry VIII (1613) act 2, sc. 2, l. 45

15 Orpheus with his lute made trees,
   And the mountain-tops that freeze,
   Bow themselves when he did sing.
   Henry VIII (1613) act 3, sc. 1, l. 3

16 In sweet music is such art,
   Killing care and grief of heart
   Fall asleep, or hearing die.
   Henry VIII (1613) act 3, sc. 1, l. 12

17 A spleeny Lutheran.
   Henry VIII (1613) act 3, sc. 2, l. 100

18   I shall fall
   Like a bright exhalation in the evening,
   And no man see me more.
   Henry VIII (1613) act 3, sc. 2, l. 226

19 Farewell! a long farewell, to all my greatness!
   This is the state of man: to-day he puts forth
   The tender leaves of hope; to-morrow blossoms,
   And bears his blushing honours thick upon him;
   The third day comes a frost, a killing frost;
   And, when he thinks, good easy man, full surely
   His greatness is a-ripening, nips his root,
   And then he falls, as I do. I have ventured,
   Like little wanton boys that swim on bladders,
   This many summers in a sea of glory,
   But far beyond my depth: my high-blown pride
   At length broke under me, and now has left me
   Weary and old with service, to the mercy
   Of a rude stream that must for ever hide me.
   Vain pomp and glory of this world, I hate ye:
   I feel my heart new opened. O how wretched
   Is that poor man that hangs on princes' favours!
   There is, betwixt that smile we would aspire to,
   That sweet aspect of princes, and their ruin,
   More pangs and fears than wars or women have;
   And when he falls, he falls like Lucifer,
   Never to hope again.
   Henry VIII (1613) act 3, sc. 2, l. 352

20 A peace above all earthly dignities,
   A still and quiet conscience.
   Henry VIII (1613) act 3, sc. 2, l. 380

21 A load would sink a navy.
   Henry VIII (1613) act 3, sc. 2, l. 384

1 Cromwell, I charge thee, fling away ambition:
By that sin fell the angels; how can man then,
The image of his Maker, hope to win by't?
Love thyself last: cherish those hearts that hate thee;
Corruption wins not more than honesty.
Still in thy right hand carry gentle peace,
To silence envious tongues: be just, and fear not.
Let all the ends thou aim'st at be thy country's,
Thy God's, and truth's: then if thou fall'st, O
    Cromwell!
Thou fall'st a blessed martyr.
Henry VIII (1613) act 3, sc. 2, l. 441

2 Had I but served my God with half the zeal
I served my king, he would not in mine age
Have left me naked to mine enemies.
Henry VIII (1613) act 3, sc. 2, l. 456

3 She had all the royal makings of a queen.
Henry VIII (1613) act 4, sc. 1, l. 87

4 An old man, broken with the storms of state
Is come to lay his weary bones among ye;
Give him a little earth for charity.
Henry VIII (1613) act 4, sc. 2, l. 21

5 He gave his honours to the world again,
His blessed part to Heaven, and slept in peace.
Henry VIII (1613) act 4, sc. 2, l. 29

6 So may he rest; his faults lie gently on him!
Henry VIII (1613) act 4, sc. 2, l. 31

7   He was a man
Of an unbounded stomach.
Henry VIII (1613) act 4, sc. 2, l. 33

8 His promises were, as he then was, mighty;
But his performance, as he is now, nothing.
Henry VIII (1613) act 4, sc. 2, l. 41

9 Men's evil manners live in brass; their virtues
We write in water.
Henry VIII (1613) act 4, sc. 2, l. 45

10 He was a scholar, and a ripe and good one;
Exceeding wise, fair-spoken, and persuading:
Lofty and sour to them that loved him not;
But, to those men that sought him, sweet as summer.
Henry VIII (1613) act 4, sc. 2, l. 51

11 Those twins of learning that he raised in you,
Ipswich and Oxford!
Henry VIII (1613) act 4, sc. 2, l. 58

12 After my death I wish no other herald,
No other speaker of my living actions,
To keep mine honour from corruption,
Than such an honest chronicler as Griffith.
Henry VIII (1613) act 4, sc. 2, l. 69

13   I had thought
They had parted so much honesty among 'em,—
At least, good manners,—as not thus to suffer
A man of his place, and so near our favour,
To dance attendance on their lordships' pleasures,
And at the door too, like a post with packets.
Henry VIII (1613) act 5, sc. 2, l. 26

14   'Tis a cruelty
To load a falling man.
Henry VIII (1613) act 5, sc. 2, l. 74

15 In her days every man shall eat in safety
Under his own vine what he plants; and sing
The merry songs of peace to all his neighbours.
Henry VIII (1613) act 5, sc. 5, l. 34

16   Those about her
From her shall read the perfect ways of honour.
Henry VIII (1613) act 5, sc. 5, l. 37

17 Nor shall this peace sleep with her; but as when
The bird of wonder dies, the maiden phoenix,
Her ashes new-create another heir
As great in admiration as herself.
Henry VIII (1613) act 5, sc. 5, l. 40

18 Some come to take their ease
And sleep an act or two.
Henry VIII (1613) act 5, epilogue, l. 2

Julius Caesar

19 Hence! home, you idle creatures, get you home:
Is this a holiday?
Julius Caesar (1599) act 1, sc. 1, l. 1

20 You blocks, you stones, you worse than senseless
    things!
O you hard hearts, you cruel men of Rome,
Knew you not Pompey?
Julius Caesar (1599) act 1, sc. 1, l. [39]

21 CAESAR: Who is it in the press that calls on me?
    I hear a tongue, shriller than all the music,
    Cry 'Caesar'. Speak; Caesar is turned to hear.
SOOTHSAYER: Beware the ides of March.
Julius Caesar (1599) act 1, sc. 2, l. 15

22 He is a dreamer; let us leave him: pass.
Julius Caesar (1599) act 1, sc. 2, l. 24

23 I am not gamesome: I do lack some part
Of that quick spirit that is in Antony.
Julius Caesar (1599) act 1, sc. 2, l. 28

24 Brutus, I do observe you now of late:
I have not from your eyes that gentleness
And show of love as I was wont to have:
You bear too stubborn and too strange a hand
Over your friend that loves you.
Julius Caesar (1599) act 1, sc. 2, l. 32

25   Poor Brutus, with himself at war,
Forgets the shows of love to other men.
Julius Caesar (1599) act 1, sc. 2, l. 46

26 Set honour in one eye and death i' the other,
And I will look on both indifferently.
Julius Caesar (1599) act 1, sc. 2, l. 86

27 Well, honour is the subject of my story.
I cannot tell what you and other men
Think of this life: but, for my single self,
I had as lief not be as live to be
In awe of such a thing as I myself.
Julius Caesar (1599) act 1, sc. 2, l. 92

28 I was born free as Caesar; so were you:
We both have fed as well, and we can both
Endure the winter's cold as well as he
Julius Caesar (1599) act 1, sc. 2, l. 97

1 He had a fever when he was in Spain,
And when the fit was on him, I did mark
How he did shake; 'tis true, this god did shake;
His coward lips did from their colour fly,
And that same eye whose bend doth awe the world
Did lose his lustre.
  Julius Caesar (1599) act 1, sc. 2, l. 119

2   Ye gods, it doth amaze me,
A man of such a feeble temper should
So get the start of the majestic world,
And bear the palm alone.
  Julius Caesar (1599) act 1, sc. 2, l. 128

3 Why, man, he doth bestride the narrow world
Like a Colossus; and we petty men
Walk under his huge legs, and peep about
To find ourselves dishonourable graves.
Men at some time are masters of their fates:
The fault, dear Brutus, is not in our stars,
But in ourselves, that we are underlings.
  Julius Caesar (1599) act 1, sc. 2, l. 134

4 'Brutus' will start a spirit as soon as 'Caesar'.
Now in the names of all the gods at once,
Upon what meat doth this our Caesar feed,
That he is grown so great?
  Julius Caesar (1599) act 1, sc. 2, l. 146

5 When could they say, till now, that talked of Rome,
That her wide walls encompassed but one man?
Now is it Rome indeed and room enough,
When there is in it but one only man.
  Julius Caesar (1599) act 1, sc. 2, l. 153

6 Let me have men about me that are fat;
Sleek-headed men and such as sleep o' nights;
Yond' Cassius has a lean and hungry look;
He thinks too much: such men are dangerous.
  Julius Caesar (1599) act 1, sc. 2, l. 191

7 Would he were fatter! but I fear him not:
Yet if my name were liable to fear,
I do not know the man I should avoid
So soon as that spare Cassius. He reads much;
He is a great observer, and he looks
Quite through the deeds of men; he loves no plays,
As thou dost, Antony; he hears no music;
Seldom he smiles, and smiles in such a sort
As if he mocked himself, and scorned his spirit,
That could be moved to smile at anything.
Such men as he be never at heart's ease,
Whiles they behold a greater than themselves,
And therefore are they very dangerous.
I rather tell thee what is to be feared
Than what I fear, for always I am Caesar.
  Julius Caesar (1599) act 1, sc. 2, l. 197

8 'Tis very like: he hath the falling sickness.
  Julius Caesar (1599) act 1, sc. 2, l. [255]

9 CASSIUS: Did Cicero say any thing?
CASCA: Ay, he spoke Greek.
CASSIUS: To what effect?
CASCA: Nay, an I tell you that, I'll ne'er look you i'
  the face again; but those that understood him
  smiled at one another and shook their heads; but,
  for mine own part, it was Greek to me.
  Julius Caesar (1599) act 1, sc. 2, l. [282]

10   Yesterday the bird of night did sit,
Even at noon-day, upon the market-place,
Hooting and shrieking.
  Julius Caesar (1599) act 1, sc. 3, l. 26

11 Cassius from bondage will deliver Cassius.
  Julius Caesar (1599) act 1, sc. 3, l. 90

12 Nor stony tower, nor walls of beaten brass,
Nor airless dungeon, nor strong links of iron,
Can be retentive to the strength of spirit;
But life, being weary of these worldly bars,
Never lacks power to dismiss itself.
  Julius Caesar (1599) act 1, sc. 3, l. 93

13 It is the bright day that brings forth the adder;
And that craves wary walking.
  Julius Caesar (1599) act 2, sc. 1, l. 14

14   'Tis a common proof,
That lowliness is young ambition's ladder,
Whereto the climber-upward turns his face;
But when he once attains the upmost round,
He then unto the ladder turns his back,
Looks in the clouds, scorning the base degrees
By which he did ascend.
  Julius Caesar (1599) act 2, sc. 1, l. 21

15 Between the acting of a dreadful thing
And the first motion, all the interim is
Like a phantasma, or a hideous dream:
The genius and the mortal instruments
Are then in council; and the state of man,
Like to a little kingdom, suffers then
The nature of an insurrection.
  Julius Caesar (1599) act 2, sc. 1, l. 63

16   O conspiracy!
Sham'st thou to show thy dangerous brow by night,
When evils are most free?
  Julius Caesar (1599) act 2, sc. 1, l. 77

17 Let us be sacrificers, but not butchers, Caius.
  Julius Caesar (1599) act 2, sc. 1, l. 166

18 Let's carve him as a dish fit for the gods,
Not hew him as a carcass fit for hounds.
  Julius Caesar (1599) act 2, sc. 1, l. 173

19 For he is superstitious grown of late,
Quite from the main opinion he held once
Of fantasy, of dreams, and ceremonies.
  Julius Caesar (1599) act 2, sc. 1, l. 195

20 But when I tell him he hates flatterers,
He says he does, being then most flattered.
  Julius Caesar (1599) act 2, sc. 1, l. 207

21 Enjoy the honey-heavy dew of slumber.
  Julius Caesar (1599) act 2, sc. 1, l. 230

22   What! is Brutus sick,
And will he steal out of his wholesome bed
To dare the vile contagion of the night?
  Julius Caesar (1599) act 2, sc. 1, l. 263

1   That great vow
Which did incorporate and make us one.
Julius Caesar (1599) act 2, sc. 1, l. 272

2 PORTIA: Dwell I but in the suburbs
Of your good pleasure? If it be no more,
Portia is Brutus' harlot, not his wife.
BRUTUS: You are my true and honourable wife,
As dear to me as are the ruddy drops
That visit my sad heart.
Julius Caesar (1599) act 2, sc. 1, l. 285

3 I grant I am a woman, but, withal,
A woman that Lord Brutus took to wife;
I grant I am a woman, but, withal,
A woman well-reputed, Cato's daughter.
Think you I am no stronger than my sex,
Being so fathered and so husbanded?
Julius Caesar (1599) act 2, sc. 1, l. 292

4 Nor heaven nor earth have been at peace to-night.
Julius Caesar (1599) act 2, sc. 2, l. 1

5 CALPHURNIA: When beggars die, there are no comets
    seen;
The heavens themselves blaze forth the death of
    princes.
CAESAR: Cowards die many times before their deaths;
The valiant never taste of death but once.
Of all the wonders that I yet have heard,
It seems to me most strange that men should fear;
Seeing that death, a necessary end,
Will come when it will come.
Julius Caesar (1599) act 2, sc. 2, l. 30

6   Danger knows full well
That Caesar is more dangerous than he:
We are two lions littered in one day,
And I the elder and more terrible.
Julius Caesar (1599) act 2, sc. 2, l. 44

7 The cause is in my will: I will not come.
Julius Caesar (1599) act 2, sc. 2, l. 71

8 See! Antony, that revels long o' nights,
Is notwithstanding up.
Julius Caesar (1599) act 2, sc. 2, l. 116

9 O constancy! be strong upon my side;
Set a huge mountain 'tween my heart and tongue;
I have a man's mind, but a woman's might.
How hard it is for women to keep counsel!
Julius Caesar (1599) act 2, sc. 4, l. 6

10 CAESAR: The ides of March are come.
SOOTHSAYER: Ay, Caesar; but not gone.
Julius Caesar (1599) act 3, sc. 1, l. 1

11   Be not fond,
To think that Caesar bears such rebel blood
That will be thawed from the true quality
With that which melted fools; I mean sweet words,
Low-crooked curtsies, and base spaniel fawning.
Thy brother by decree is banishèd:
If thou dost bend and pray and fawn for him,
I spurn thee like a cur out of my way.
Julius Caesar (1599) act 3, sc. 1, l. 39

12 If I could pray to move, prayers would move me;
But I am constant as the northern star,
Of whose true-fixed and resting quality
There is no fellow in the firmament.
The skies are painted with unnumbered sparks,
They are all fire and every one doth shine,
But there's but one in all doth hold his place:
So, in the world; 'tis furnished well with men,
And men are flesh and blood, and apprehensive;
Yet in the number I do know but one
That unassailable holds on his rank,
Unshaked of motion: and that I am he.
Julius Caesar (1599) act 3, sc. 1, l. 59

13 *Et tu, Brute?* Then fall, Caesar!
Julius Caesar (1599) act 3, sc. 1, l. 77. Cf. Caesar
174:21

14 Ambition's debt is paid.
Julius Caesar (1599) act 3, sc. 1, l. 83

15 That we shall die, we know; 'tis but the time
And drawing days out, that men stand upon.
Julius Caesar (1599) act 3, sc. 1, l. 99

16 He that cuts off twenty years of life
Cuts off so many years of fearing death.
Julius Caesar (1599) act 3, sc. 1, l. 101

17 CASSIUS: How many ages hence
Shall this our lofty scene be acted o'er,
In states unborn, and accents yet unknown!
BRUTUS: How many times shall Caesar bleed in sport.
Julius Caesar (1599) act 3, sc. 1, l. 111

18 O mighty Caesar! dost thou lie so low?
Are all thy conquests, glories, triumphs, spoils,
Shrunk to this little measure?
Julius Caesar (1599) act 3, sc. 1, l. 148

19   Your swords, made rich
With the most noble blood of all this world.
Julius Caesar (1599) act 3, sc. 1, l. 155

20   Live a thousand years,
I shall not find myself so apt to die:
No place will please me so, no mean of death,
As here by Caesar, and by you cut off,
The choice and master spirits of this age.
Julius Caesar (1599) act 3, sc. 1, l. 159

21 Had I as many eyes as thou hast wounds,
Weeping as fast as they stream forth thy blood,
It would become me better than to close
In terms of friendship with thine enemies.
Julius Caesar (1599) act 3, sc. 1, l. 200

22 The enemies of Caesar shall say this;
Then, in a friend, it is cold modesty.
Julius Caesar (1599) act 3, sc. 1, l. 212

23 O! pardon me, thou bleeding piece of earth,
That I am meek and gentle with these butchers;
Thou art the ruins of the noblest man
That ever livèd in the tide of times.
Julius Caesar (1599) act 3, sc. 1, l. 254

24   Caesar's spirit, ranging for revenge,
With Ate by his side, come hot from hell,
Shall in these confines, with a monarch's voice
Cry, 'Havoc!' and let slip the dogs of war;
That this foul deed shall smell above the earth
With carrion men, groaning for burial.
Julius Caesar (1599) act 3, sc. 1, l. 270

1 Passion, I see, is catching.

  Julius Caesar (1599) act 3, sc. 1, l. 283

2 Not that I loved Caesar less, but that I loved Rome
  more.

  Julius Caesar (1599) act 3, sc. 2, l. [22]

3 As he was valiant, I honour him: but, as he was
  ambitious, I slew him.

  Julius Caesar (1599) act 3, sc. 2, l. [27]

4 Who is here so base that would be a bondman? If
  any, speak; for him have I offended. Who is here so
  rude that would not be a Roman? If any, speak; for
  him have I offended. Who is here so vile that will not
  love his country? If any, speak; for him have I
  offended. I pause for a reply.

  Julius Caesar (1599) act 3, sc. 2, l. [31]

5 Friends, Romans, countrymen, lend me your ears;
  I come to bury Caesar, not to praise him.
  The evil that men do lives after them,
  The good is oft interrèd with their bones;
  So let it be with Caesar. The noble Brutus
  Hath told you Caesar was ambitious;
  If it were so, it was a grievous fault;
  And grievously hath Caesar answered it.
  Here, under leave of Brutus and the rest,—
  For Brutus is an honourable man;
  So are they all, all honourable men,—
  Come I to speak in Caesar's funeral.

  Julius Caesar (1599) act 3, sc. 2, l. [79]

6 He was my friend, faithful and just to me:
  But Brutus says he was ambitious;
  And Brutus is an honourable man.

  Julius Caesar (1599) act 3, sc. 2, l. [91]

7 When that the poor have cried, Caesar hath wept;
  Ambition should be made of sterner stuff.

  Julius Caesar (1599) act 3, sc. 2, l. [97]

8   On the Lupercal
  I thrice presented him a kingly crown
  Which he did thrice refuse: was this ambition?

  Julius Caesar (1599) act 3, sc. 2, l. [101]

9 You all did love him once, not without cause.

  Julius Caesar (1599) act 3, sc. 2, l. [108]

10 O judgement! thou art fled to brutish beasts,
   And men have lost their reason.

  Julius Caesar (1599) act 3, sc. 2, l. [110]

11 But yesterday the word of Caesar might
   Have stood against the world; now lies he there,
   And none so poor to do him reverence.

  Julius Caesar (1599) act 3, sc. 2, l. [124]

12 You are not wood, you are not stones, but men;
   And, being men, hearing the will of Caesar,
   It will inflame you, it will make you mad.

  Julius Caesar (1599) act 3, sc. 2, l. [148]

13 If you have tears, prepare to shed them now.
   You all do know this mantle: I remember
   The first time ever Caesar put it on;
   'Twas on a summer's evening, in his tent,
   That day he overcame the Nervii.

  Julius Caesar (1599) act 3, sc. 2, l. [174]

14 This was the most unkindest cut of all;
   For when the noble Caesar saw him stab,
   Ingratitude, more strong than traitors' arms,
   Quite vanquished him: then burst his mighty heart;
   And, in his mantle muffling up his face,
   Even at the base of Pompey's statua,
   Which all the while ran blood, great Caesar fell.
   O! what a fall was there, my countrymen;
   Then I, and you, and all of us fell down,
   Whilst bloody treason flourished over us.
   O! now you weep, and I perceive you feel
   The dint of pity; these are gracious drops.

  Julius Caesar (1599) act 3, sc. 2, l. [188]

15 I come not, friends, to steal away your hearts:
   I am no orator, as Brutus is;
   But, as you know me all, a plain, blunt man,
   That love my friend.

  Julius Caesar (1599) act 3, sc. 2, l. [220]

16 For I have neither wit, nor words, nor worth,
   Action, nor utterance, nor power of speech,
   To stir men's blood; I only speak right on;
   I tell you that which you yourselves do know.

  Julius Caesar (1599) act 3, sc. 2, l. [225]

17   But were I Brutus,
   And Brutus Antony, there were an Antony
   Would ruffle up your spirits, and put a tongue
   In every wound of Caesar, that should move
   The stones of Rome to rise and mutiny.

  Julius Caesar (1599) act 3, sc. 2, l. [230]

18   He hath left you all his walks,
   His private arbours, and new-planted orchards,
   On this side Tiber; he hath left them you,
   And to your heirs for ever; common pleasures,
   To walk abroad, and recreate yourselves.

  Julius Caesar (1599) act 3, sc. 2, l. [252]

19 Here was a Caesar! when comes such another?

  Julius Caesar (1599) act 3, sc. 2, l. [257]

20 Now let it work; mischief, thou art afoot,
   Take thou what course thou wilt!

  Julius Caesar (1599) act 3, sc. 2, l. [265]

21   Fortune is merry,
   And in this mood will give us anything.

  Julius Caesar (1599) act 3, sc. 2, l. [271]

22 Tear him for his bad verses, tear him for his bad
   verses.

  Julius Caesar (1599) act 3, sc. 3, l. [34]

23 He shall not live; look, with a spot I damn him.

  Julius Caesar (1599) act 4, sc. 1, l. 6

24 This is a slight unmeritable man,
   Meet to be sent on errands.

  Julius Caesar (1599) act 4, sc. 1, l. 12

25 When love begins to sicken and decay,
   It useth an enforcèd ceremony.
   There are no tricks in plain and simple faith.

  Julius Caesar (1599) act 4, sc. 2, l. 20

26 Let me tell you, Cassius, you yourself
   Are much condemned to have an itching palm.

  Julius Caesar (1599) act 4, sc. 3, l. 7

27   Shall we now
   Contaminate our fingers with base bribes?

  Julius Caesar (1599) act 4, sc. 3, l. 23

1 I had rather be a dog, and bay the moon,
Than such a Roman.
Julius Caesar (1599) act 4, sc. 3, l. 27

2 Away, slight man!
Julius Caesar (1599) act 4, sc. 3, l. 37

3 You wrong me every way; you wrong me, Brutus;
I said an elder soldier, not a better:
Did I say 'better'?
Julius Caesar (1599) act 4, sc. 3, l. 55

4 Do not presume too much upon my love;
I may do that I shall be sorry for.
Julius Caesar (1599) act 4, sc. 3, l. 63

5 There is no terror, Cassius, in your threats;
For I am armed so strong in honesty
That they pass by me as the idle wind,
Which I respect not.
Julius Caesar (1599) act 4, sc. 3, l. 66

6 By heaven, I had rather coin my heart,
And drop my blood for drachmas, than to wring
From the hard hands of peasants their vile trash
By any indirection.
Julius Caesar (1599) act 4, sc. 3, l. 72

7 A friend should bear his friend's infirmities,
But Brutus makes mine greater than they are.
Julius Caesar (1599) act 4, sc. 3, l. 85

8 Cassius is aweary of the world;
Hated by one he loves; braved by his brother;
Checked like a bondman; all his faults observed,
Set in a note-book, learned, and conned by rote,
To cast into my teeth.
Julius Caesar (1599) act 4, sc. 3, l. 94

9 O Cassius! you are yokèd with a lamb
That carries anger as the flint bears fire;
Who, much enforcèd, shows a hasty spark,
And straight is cold again.
Julius Caesar (1599) act 4, sc. 3, l. 109

10 O Cassius! I am sick of many griefs.
Julius Caesar (1599) act 4, sc. 3, l. 143

11 Good reasons must, of force, give place to better.
Julius Caesar (1599) act 4, sc. 3, l. 202

12 The enemy increaseth every day;
We, at the height, are ready to decline.
There is a tide in the affairs of men,
Which, taken at the flood, leads on to fortune;
Omitted, all the voyage of their life
Is bound in shallows and in miseries.
On such a full sea are we now afloat,
And we must take the current when it serves,
Or lose our ventures.
Julius Caesar (1599) act 4, sc. 3, l. 215

13 The deep of night is crept upon our talk,
And nature must obey necessity.
Julius Caesar (1599) act 4, sc. 3, l. 225

14 But for your words, they rob the Hybla bees,
And leave them honeyless.
Julius Caesar (1599) act 5, sc. 1, l. 34

15 If we do meet again, why, we shall smile!
If not, why then, this parting was well made.
Julius Caesar (1599) act 5, sc. 1, l. 118

16   O! that a man might know
The end of this day's business, ere it come;
But it sufficeth that the day will end,
And then the end is known.
Julius Caesar (1599) act 5, sc. 1, l. 123

17 This day I breathèd first: time is come round,
And where I did begin, there shall I end;
My life is run his compass.
Julius Caesar (1599) act 5, sc. 3, l. 23

18 O hateful error, melancholy's child!
Why dost thou show, to the apt thoughts of men,
The things that are not?
Julius Caesar (1599) act 5, sc. 3, l. 67

19 O Julius Caesar! thou art mighty yet!
Thy spirit walks abroad, and turns our swords
In our own proper entrails.
Julius Caesar (1599) act 5, sc. 3, l. 94

20   I had rather have
Such men my friends than enemies.
Julius Caesar (1599) act 5, sc. 4, l. 28

21 Thou seest the world, Volumnius, how it goes;
Our enemies have beat us to the pit:
It is more worthy to leap in ourselves,
Than tarry till they push us.
Julius Caesar (1599) act 5, sc. 5, l. 22

22 Thou art a fellow of a good respect;
Thy life hath had some smatch of honour in it.
Hold then my sword, and turn away thy face,
While I do run upon it.
Julius Caesar (1599) act 5, sc. 5, l. 45

23 This was the noblest Roman of them all;
All the conspirators save only he
Did that they did in envy of great Caesar;
He, only, in a general honest thought
And common good to all, made one of them.
His life was gentle, and the elements
So mixed in him that Nature might stand up
And say to all the world, 'This was a man!'
Julius Caesar (1599) act 5, sc. 5, l. 68

King John

24   Hadst thou rather be a Faulconbridge
And like thy brother, to enjoy thy land,
Or the reputed son of Coeur-de-Lion,
Lord of thy presence and no land beside.
King John (1591–8) act 1, sc. 1, l. 134

25 And if his name be George, I'll call him Peter;
For new-made honour doth forget men's names.
King John (1591–8) act 1, sc. 1, l. 186

26 Sweet, sweet, sweet poison for the age's tooth.
King John (1591–8) act 1, sc. 1, l. 213

27 Courage mounteth with occasion.
King John (1591–8) act 2, sc. 1, l. 82

28 Saint George, that swinged the dragon and e'er since
Sits on his horse back at mine hostess' door.
King John (1591–8) act 2, sc. 1, l. 288

29 Mad world! mad kings! mad composition!
King John (1591–8) act 2, sc. 1, l. 561

30 That smooth-faced gentleman, tickling Commodity,
Commodity, the bias of the world.
King John (1591–8) act 2, sc. 1, l. 573

1 Well, whiles I am a beggar, I will rail,
   And say there is no sin, but to be rich;
   And, being rich, my virtue then shall be,
   To say there is no vice, but beggary.
   King John (1591–8) act 2, sc. 1, l. 593

2 Old Time the clock-setter, that bald sexton, Time.
   King John (1591–8) act 3, sc. 1, l. 324

3 Bell, book, and candle shall not drive me back,
   When gold and silver becks me to come on.
   King John (1591–8) act 3, sc. 3, l. 12

4 Grief fills the room up of my absent child,
   Lies in his bed, walks up and down with me,
   Puts on his pretty looks, repeats his words,
   Remembers me of all his gracious parts,
   Stuffs out his vacant garments with his form:
   Then have I reason to be fond of grief.
   King John (1591–8) act 3, sc. 4, l. 93

5 Life is as tedious as a twice-told tale,
   Vexing the dull ear of a drowsy man.
   King John (1591–8) act 3, sc. 4, l. 108

6 Heat me these irons hot.
   King John (1591–8) act 4, sc. 1, l. 1

7 Methinks nobody should be sad but I:
   Yet I remember, when I was in France,
   Young gentlemen would be as sad as night,
   Only for wantonness.
   King John (1591–8) act 4, sc. 1, l. 13

8   Will you put out mine eyes?
   These eyes that never did nor never shall
   So much as frown on you?
   King John (1591–8) act 4, sc. 1, l. 56

9 ... To be possessed with double pomp,
   To guard a title that was rich before,
   To gild refinèd gold, to paint the lily,
   To throw a perfume on the violet,
   To smooth the ice, or add another hue
   Unto the rainbow, or with taper light
   To seek the beauteous eye of heaven to garnish,
   Is wasteful and ridiculous excess.
   King John (1591–8) act 4, sc. 2, l. 9

10 The spirit of the time shall teach me speed.
    King John (1591–8) act 4, sc. 2, l. 176

11 Another lean unwashed artificer
    Cuts off his tale and talks of Arthur's death.
    King John (1591–8) act 4, sc. 2, l. 201

12 How oft the sight of means to do ill deeds
    Makes ill deeds done!
    King John (1591–8) act 4, sc. 2, l. 219

13 Heaven take my soul, and England keep my bones!
    King John (1591–8) act 4, sc. 3, l. 10

14 Whate'er you think, good words, I think, were best.
    King John (1591–8) act 4, sc. 3, l. 28

15 ... None of you will bid the winter come
    To thrust his icy fingers in my maw;
    Nor let my kingdom's rivers take their course
    Through my burned bosom; nor entreat the north
    To make his bleak winds kiss my parchèd lips
    And comfort me with cold. I do not ask you much:
    I beg cold comfort; and you are so strait
    And so ingrateful you deny me that.
    King John (1591–8) act 5, sc. 7, l. 36

16 This England never did, nor never shall,
    Lie at the proud foot of a conqueror,
    But when it first did help to wound itself.
    Now these her princes are come home again,
    Come the three corners of the world in arms,
    And we shall shock them: nought shall make us rue,
    If England to itself do rest but true.
    King John (1591–8) act 5, sc. 7, l. 112

King Lear

17 Meantime we shall express our darker purpose.
    King Lear (1605–6) act 1, sc. 1, l. 36

18 Nothing will come of nothing: speak again.
    King Lear (1605 6) act 1, sc. 1, l. [92]

19 LEAR: So young, and so untender?
    CORDELIA: So young, my lord, and true.
    LEAR: Let it be so; thy truth then be thy dower:
       For, by the sacred radiance of the sun,
       The mysteries of Hecate and the night,
       By all the operation of the orbs
       From whom we do exist and cease to be,
       Here I disclaim all my paternal care,
       Propinquity and property of blood,
       And as a stranger to my heart and me
       Hold thee from this for ever.
    King Lear (1605–6) act 1, sc. 1, l. [108]

20 Come not between the dragon and his wrath.
    King Lear (1605–6) act 1, sc. 1, l. [124]

21   I want that glib and oily art
    To speak and purpose not; since what I well intend,
    I'll do't before I speak.
    King Lear (1605–6) act 1, sc. 1, l. [227]

22 It is no vicious blot nor other foulness,
    No unchaste action, or dishonoured step,
    That hath deprived me of your grace and favour,
    But even for want of that for which I am richer,
    A still-soliciting eye, and such a tongue
    That I am glad I have not, though not to have it
    Hath lost me in your liking.
    King Lear (1605–6) act 1, sc. 1, l. [230]

23   Love is not love
    When it is mingled with regards that stand
    Aloof from the entire point.
    King Lear (1605–6) act 1, sc. 1, l. [241]

24 Fairest Cordelia, that art most rich, being poor;
    Most choice, forsaken; and most loved, despised!
    King Lear (1605–6) act 1, sc. 1, l. [253]

25 'Tis the infirmity of his age; yet he hath ever but
    slenderly known himself.
    King Lear (1605–6) act 1, sc. 1, l. 293

26   Why bastard? wherefore base?
    When my dimensions are as well compact,
    My mind as generous, and my shape as true,
    As honest madam's issue? Why brand they us
    With base? with baseness? bastardy? base, base?
    Who in the lusty stealth of nature take
    More composition and fierce quality
    Than doth, within a dull, stale, tired bed,
    Go to the creating a whole tribe of fops,
    Got 'tween asleep and wake?
    King Lear (1605–6) act 1, sc. 2, l. 6

1 I grow, I prosper;
Now, gods, stand up for bastards!
King Lear (1605–6) act 1, sc. 2, l. 21

2 This is the excellent foppery of the world, that, when
we are sick in fortune,—often the surfeit of our own
behaviour,— we make guilty of our own disasters the
sun, the moon, and the stars; as if we were villains by
necessity, fools by heavenly compulsion, knaves,
thieves, and treachers by spherical predominance,
drunkards, liars, and adulterers by an enforced
obedience of planetary influence; and all that we are
evil in, by a divine thrusting on: an admirable evasion
of whoremaster man, to lay his goatish disposition to
the charge of a star! My father compounded with my
mother under the dragon's tail, and my nativity was
under *ursa major*; so that it follows I am rough and
lecherous. 'Sfoot! I should have been that I am had
the maidenliest star in the firmament twinkled on my
bastardizing.
King Lear (1605–6) act 1, sc. 2, l. [132]

3 Pat he comes, like the catastrophe of the old comedy;
my cue is villanous melancholy, with a sigh like Tom
o' Bedlam.
King Lear (1605–6) act 1, sc. 2, l. [150]

4 LEAR: Dost thou know me, fellow?
KENT: No, sir; but you have that in your countenance
which I would fain call master.
LEAR: What's that?
KENT: Authority.
King Lear (1605–6) act 1, sc. 4, l. [28]

5 Not so young, sir, to love a woman for singing, nor so
old to dote on her for any thing.
King Lear (1605–6) act 1, sc. 4, l. [40]

6 Have more than thou showest,
Speak less than thou knowest,
Lend less than thou owest.
King Lear (1605–6) act 1, sc. 4, l. [132]

7 LEAR: Dost thou call me fool, boy?
FOOL: All thy other titles thou hast given away; that
thou wast born with.
King Lear (1605–6) act 1, sc. 4, l. [163]

8 Who is it that can tell me who I am?
King Lear (1605–6) act 1, sc. 4, l. 230

9 Ingratitude, thou marble-hearted fiend,
More hideous, when thou show'st thee in a child,
Than the sea-monster.
King Lear (1605–6) act 1, sc. 4, l. [283]

10 How sharper than a serpent's tooth it is
To have a thankless child!
King Lear (1605–6) act 1, sc. 4, l. [312]

11 O! let me not be mad, not mad, sweet heaven;
Keep me in temper; I would not be mad!
King Lear (1605–6) act 1, sc. 5, l. [51]

12 Thou whoreson zed! thou unnecessary letter!
King Lear (1605–6) act 2, sc. 2, l. [68]

13 Goose, if I had you upon Sarum plain,
I'd drive ye cackling home to Camelot.
King Lear (1605–6) act 2, sc. 2, l. [88]

14   Down, thou climbing sorrow!
Thy element's below.
King Lear (1605–6) act 2, sc. 4, l. [57]

15   O, sir! you are old;
Nature in you stands on the very verge
Of her confine.
King Lear (1605–6) act 2, sc. 4, l. [148]

16 O reason not the need! Our basest beggars
Are in the poorest thing superfluous.
Allow not nature more than nature needs,
Man's life is cheap as beast's.
King Lear (1605–6) act 2, sc. 4, l. 264

17 You see me here, you gods, a poor old man,
As full of grief as age; wretched in both!
King Lear (1605–6) act 2, sc. 4, l. [275]

18 Touch me with noble anger,
And let not women's weapons, water-drops,
Stain my man's cheeks! No, you unnatural hags,
I will have such revenges on you both
That all the world shall—I will do such things,—
What they are yet I know not,—but they shall be
The terrors of the earth. You think I'll weep;
No, I'll not weep:
I have full cause of weeping, but this heart
Shall break into a hundred thousand flaws
Or ere I'll weep. O fool! I shall go mad.
King Lear (1605–6) act 2, sc. 4, l. [279]

19 Contending with the fretful elements;
Bids the wind blow the earth into the sea,
Or swell the curlèd waters 'bove the main,
That things might change or cease.
King Lear (1605–6) act 3, sc. 1, l. 4

20 Blow, winds, and crack your cheeks! rage! blow!
You cataracts and hurricanoes, spout
Till you have drenched our steeples, drowned the
cocks!
You sulphurous and thought-executing fires,
Vaunt-couriers to oak-cleaving thunderbolts,
Singe my white head! And thou, all-shaking thunder,
Strike flat the thick rotundity o' the world!
Crack nature's moulds, all germens spill at once
That make ingrateful man!
King Lear (1605–6) act 3, sc. 2, l. 1

21 Rumble thy bellyful! Spit, fire! Spout, rain!
Nor rain, wind, thunder, fire, are my daughters:
I tax not you, you elements, with unkindness;
I never gave you kingdom, called you children,
You owe me no subscription: then, let fall
Your horrible pleasure; here I stand, your slave,
A poor, infirm, weak, and despised old man.
King Lear (1605–6) act 3, sc. 2, l. 14

22 There was never yet fair woman but she made mouths
in a glass.
King Lear (1605–6) act 3, sc. 2, l. [35]

23 No, I will be the pattern of all patience; I will say
nothing.
King Lear (1605–6) act 3, sc. 2, l. [37]

24 Marry, here's grace and a cod-piece; that's a wise
man and a fool.
King Lear (1605–6) act 3, sc. 2, l. [40]

25   Things that love night
Love not such nights as these.
King Lear (1605–6) act 3, sc. 2, l. [42]

1   Close pent-up guilts,
Rive your concealing continents, and cry
These dreadful summoners grace. I am a man
More sinned against than sinning.
King Lear (1605–6) act 3, sc. 2, l. [57]

2 The art of our necessities is strange,
That can make vile things precious.
King Lear (1605–6) act 3, sc. 2, l. [70]

3 He that has a little tiny wit,
With hey, ho, the wind and the rain,
Must make content with his fortunes fit,
Though the rain it raineth every day.
King Lear (1605–6) act 3, sc. 2, l. [74]

4   When the mind's free,
The body's delicate.
King Lear (1605–6) act 3, sc. 4, l. 11

5 O! that way madness lies; let me shun that.
King Lear (1605–6) act 3, sc. 4, l. 21

6 Poor naked wretches, wheresoe'er you are,
That bide the pelting of this pitiless storm,
How shall your houseless heads and unfed sides,
Your looped and windowed raggedness, defend you
From seasons such as these?
King Lear (1605–6) act 3, sc. 4, l. 28

7   Take physic, pomp;
Expose thyself to feel what wretches feel.
King Lear (1605–6) act 3, sc. 4, l. 33

8 Pillicock sat on Pillicock-hill:
Halloo, halloo, loo, loo!
King Lear (1605–6) act 3, sc. 4, l. [75]

9 A serving-man, proud in heart and mind: that curled
my hair, wore gloves in my cap, served the lust of my
mistress's heart, and did the act of darkness with her;
swore as many oaths as I spake words, and broke
them in the sweet face of heaven; one that slept in the
contriving of lust, and waked to do it. Wine loved I
deeply, dice dearly, and in woman out-paramoured
the Turk.
King Lear (1605–6) act 3, sc. 4, l. [84]

10 Keep thy foot out of brothels, thy hand out of plackets,
thy pen from lenders' books, and defy the foul fiend.
King Lear (1605–6) act 3, sc. 4, l. [96]

11 Thou art the thing itself; unaccommodated man is no
more but such a poor, bare, forked animal as thou art.
Off, off, you lendings! Come; unbutton here.
King Lear (1605–6) act 3, sc. 4, l. [109]

12 'Tis a naughty night to swim in.
King Lear (1605–6) act 3, sc. 4, l. [113]

13 This is the foul fiend Flibbertigibbet: he begins at
curfew, and walks till the first cock; he gives the web
and the pin, squints the eye, and makes the harelip;
mildews the white wheat, and hurts the poor
creatures of earth.
King Lear (1605–6) act 3, sc. 4, l. [118]

14 The green mantle of the standing pool.
King Lear (1605–6) act 3, sc. 4, l. [136]

15 The prince of darkness is a gentleman.
King Lear (1605–6) act 3, sc. 4, l. [148]

16 Poor Tom's a-cold.
King Lear (1605–6) act 3, sc. 4, l. [151]

17 Child Roland to the dark tower came,
His word was still, Fie, foh, and fum,
I smell the blood of a British man.
King Lear (1605–6) act 3, sc. 4, l. [185]. Cf. Nashe
490:22

18 He's mad that trusts in the tameness of a wolf, a
horse's health, a boy's love, or a whore's oath.
King Lear (1605–6) act 3, sc. 6, l. [20]

19   The little dogs and all,
Tray, Blanch, and Sweet-heart, see, they bark at me.
King Lear (1605–6) act 3, sc. 6, l. [65]

20 By the kind gods, 'tis most ignobly done
To pluck me by the beard.
King Lear (1605–6) act 3, sc. 7, l. [35]

21 I am tied to the stake, and I must stand the course.
King Lear (1605–6) act 3, sc. 7, l. [54]

22 CORNWALL: Out, vile jelly!
Where is thy lustre now?
GLOUCESTER: All dark and comfortless.
King Lear (1605–6) act 3, sc. 7, l. [83]

23 Yet better thus, and known to be contemned,
Than still contemned and flattered. To be worst,
The lowest and most dejected thing of fortune,
Stands still in esperance, lives not in fear:
The lamentable change is from the best;
The worst returns to laughter.
King Lear (1605–6) act 4, sc. 1, l. 1

24 I have no way, and therefore want no eyes;
I stumbled when I saw.
King Lear (1605–6) act 4, sc. 1, l. 18

25 Might I but live to see thee in my touch,
I'd say I had eyes again.
King Lear (1605–6) act 4, sc. 1, l. 23

26   The worst is not,
So long as we can say, 'This is the worst.'
King Lear (1605–6) act 4, sc. 1, l. 27

27 As flies to wanton boys, are we to the gods;
They kill us for their sport.
King Lear (1605–6) act 4, sc. 1, l. 36

28 You are not worth the dust which the rude wind
Blows in your face.
King Lear (1605–6) act 4, sc. 2, l. 30

29 Wisdom and goodness to the vile seem vile;
Filths savour but themselves.
King Lear (1605–6) act 4, sc. 2, l. 38

30   It is the stars,
The stars above us, govern our conditions.
King Lear (1605–6) act 4, sc. 3, l. [34]

31   He was met even now
As mad as the vexed sea; singing aloud;
Crowned with rank fumitor and furrow weeds,
With burdocks, hemlock, nettles, cuckoo-flowers,
Darnel, and all the idle weeds that grow
In our sustaining corn.
King Lear (1605–6) act 4, sc. 4, l. 1

1   How fearful
And dizzy 'tis to cast one's eyes so low!
The crows and choughs that wing the midway air
Show scarce so gross as beetles; half-way down
Hangs one that gathers samphire, dreadful trade!
Methinks he seems no bigger than his head.
The fishermen that walk upon the beach
Appear like mice, and yond tall anchoring bark
Diminished to her cock, her cock a buoy
Almost too small for sight. The murmuring surge,
That on the unnumbered idle pebbles chafes,
Cannot be heard so high.
   King Lear (1605–6) act 4, sc. 6, l. 12

2 They told me I was every thing; 'tis a lie, I am not
ague-proof.
   King Lear (1605–6) act 4, sc. 6, l. [107]

3 GLOUCESTER: Is't not the king?
LEAR: Ay, every inch a king.
   King Lear (1605–6) act 4, sc. 6, l. [110]

4   Die: die for adultery! No:
The wren goes to't, and the small gilded fly
Does lecher in my sight.
Let copulation thrive.
   King Lear (1605–6) act 4, sc. 6, l. [114]

5 LEAR: The fitchew nor the soiled horse goes to't
With a more riotous appetite.
Down from the waist they are Centaurs,
Though women all above:
But to the girdle do the Gods inherit,
Beneath is all the fiends':
There's hell, there's darkness, there is the
   sulphurous pit,
Burning, scalding, stench, consumption; fie, fie, fie!
   pah, pah! Give me an ounce of civet, good
   apothecary, to sweeten my imagination; there's
   money for thee.
GLOUCESTER: O! let me kiss that hand!
LEAR: Let me wipe it first; it smells of mortality.
GLOUCESTER: O ruined piece of nature! This great
   world
Should so wear out to nought.
   King Lear (1605–6) act 4, sc. 6, l. [125]

6 A man may see how this world goes with no eyes.
Look with thine ears: see how yond justice rails upon
yond simple thief. Hark, in thine ear: change places;
and, handy-dandy, which is the justice, which is the
thief?
   King Lear (1605–6) act 4, sc. 6, l. [154]

7 There thou mightst behold the great image of
   authority. A dog's obeyed in office.
Thou rascal beadle, hold thy bloody hand!
Why dost thou lash that whore? Strip thine own
   back;
Thou hotly lust'st to use her in that kind
For which thou whipp'st her.
   King Lear (1605–6) act 4, sc. 6, l. 157

8   Plate sin with gold,
And the strong lance of justice hurtless breaks;
Arm it in rags, a pigmy's straw doth pierce it.
   King Lear (1605–6) act 4, sc. 6, l. [170]

9   Get thee glass eyes;
And, like a scurvy politician, seem
To see the things thou dost not.
   King Lear (1605–6) act 4, sc. 6, l. [175]

10 I know thee well enough; thy name is Gloucester:
Thou must be patient; we came crying hither:
Thou know'st the first time that we smell the air
We waul and cry.
   King Lear (1605–6) act 4, sc. 6, l. [182]

11 When we are born we cry that we are come
To this great stage of fools.
   King Lear (1605–6) act 4, sc. 6, l. [187]

12   Mine enemy's dog,
Though he had bit me, should have stood that night
Against my fire.
   King Lear (1605–6) act 4, sc. 7, l. 36

13 Thou art a soul in bliss; but I am bound
Upon a wheel of fire, that mine own tears
Do scald like molten lead.
   King Lear (1605–6) act 4, sc. 7, l. 46

14 I am a very foolish, fond old man,
Fourscore and upward, not an hour more or less;
And, to deal plainly,
I fear I am not in my perfect mind.
   King Lear (1605–6) act 4, sc. 7, l. 60

15   Men must endure
Their going hence, even as their coming hither:
Ripeness is all.
   King Lear (1605–6) act 5, sc. 2, l. 9

16   Come, let's away to prison;
We two alone will sing like birds i' the cage:
When thou dost ask me blessing, I'll kneel down,
And ask of thee forgiveness: and we'll live,
And pray, and sing, and tell old tales, and laugh
At gilded butterflies, and hear poor rogues
Talk of court news; and we'll talk with them too,
Who loses and who wins; who's in, who's out;
And take upon 's the mystery of things,
As if we were God's spies; and we'll wear out,
In a walled prison, packs and sets of great ones
That ebb and flow by the moon.
   King Lear (1605–6) act 5, sc. 3, l. 8. Cf. Webster 726:9

17 Upon such sacrifices, my Cordelia,
The gods themselves throw incense.
   King Lear (1605–6) act 5, sc. 3, l. 20

18 The gods are just, and of our pleasant vices
Make instruments to plague us.
   King Lear (1605–6) act 5, sc. 3, l. [172]

19 The wheel is come full circle.
   King Lear (1605–6) act 5, sc. 3, l. [176]

20 His flawed heart,—
Alack! too weak the conflict to support;
'Twixt two extremes of passion, joy and grief,
Burst smilingly.
   King Lear (1605–6) act 5, sc. 3, l. [198]

21 Howl, howl, howl, howl! O! you are men of stones:
Had I your tongue and eyes, I'd use them so
That heaven's vaults should crack. She's gone for
   ever!
   King Lear (1605–6) act 5, sc. 3, l. [259]

1   KENT: Is this the promised end?
EDGAR: Or image of that horror?
ALBION: Fall and cease?
   King Lear (1605–6) act 5, sc. 3, l. [265]

2   Her voice was ever soft,
Gentle and low, an excellent thing in woman.
   King Lear (1605–6) act 5, sc. 3, l. [274]

3   And my poor fool is hanged! No, no, no life!
Why should a dog, a horse, a rat, have life,
And thou no breath at all? Thou'lt come no more,
Never, never, nèver, never, never!
Pray you, undo this button.
   King Lear (1605–6) act 5, sc. 3, l. [307]

4   Vex not his ghost: O! let him pass; he hates him
That would upon the rack of this tough world
Stretch him out longer.
   King Lear (1605–6) act 5, sc. 3, l. [314]

5   The weight of this sad time we must obey,
Speak what we feel; not what we ought to say.
The oldest hath borne most: we that are young,
Shall never see so much, nor live so long.
   King Lear (1605–6) act 5, sc. 3, l. [325]

Love's Labour's Lost

6   Let fame, that all hunt after in their lives,
Live registered upon our brazen tombs,
And then grace us in the disgrace of death;
When, spite of cormorant devouring Time,
The endeavour of this present breath may buy
That honour which shall bate his scythe's keen edge,
And make us heirs of all eternity.
   Love's Labour's Lost (1595) act 1, sc. 1, l. 1

7   Study is like the heaven's glorious sun,
That will not be deep-searched with saucy looks;
Small have continual plodders ever won,
Save base authority from others' books.
These earthly godfathers of Heaven's lights
That give a name to every fixèd star,
Have no more profit of their shining nights
Than those that walk and wot not what they are.
   Love's Labour's Lost (1595) act 1, sc. 1, l. 84

8   At Christmas I no more desire a rose
Than wish a snow in May's new-fangled mirth;
But like of each thing that in season grows.
   Love's Labour's Lost (1595) act 1, sc. 1, l. 105

9   Assist me some extemporal god of rime, for I am sure I
shall turn sonneter. Devise, wit; write, pen; for I am
for whole volumes in folio.
   Love's Labour's Lost (1595) act 1, sc. 2, l. [192]

10   Beauty is bought by judgement of the eye,
Not uttered by base sale of chapmen's tongues.
   Love's Labour's Lost (1595) act 2, sc. 1, l. 15

11   Your wit's too hot, it speeds too fast, 'twill tire.
   Love's Labour's Lost (1595) act 2, sc. 1, l. [119]

12   Warble, child; make passionate my sense of hearing.
   Love's Labour's Lost (1595) act 3, sc. 1, l. 1

13   This wimpled, whining, purblind, wayward boy,
This senior-junior, giant-dwarf, Dan Cupid;
Regent of love rhymes, lord of folded arms,
The anointed sovereign of sighs and groans,
Liege of all loiterers and malecontents,
Dread prince of plackets, king of codpieces,
Sole imperator and great general
Of trotting 'paritors: O my little heart!
   Love's Labour's Lost (1595) act 3, sc. 1, l. [189]

14   A wightly wanton with a velvet brow,
With two pitch balls stuck in her face for eyes;
Ay, and, by heaven, one that will do the deed
Though Argus were her eunuch and her guard:
And I to sigh for her! to watch for her!
To pray for her!
   Love's Labour's Lost (1595) act 3, sc. 1, l. [206]

15   He hath not fed of the dainties that are bred in a
book; he hath not eat paper, as it were; he hath not
drunk ink.
   Love's Labour's Lost (1595) act 4, sc. 2, l. [25]

16   Old Mantuan! old Mantuan! Who understandeth thee
not, loves thee not.
   Love's Labour's Lost (1595) act 4, sc. 2, l. [102]

17   Here are only numbers ratified; but, for the elegancy,
facility, and golden cadence of poesy, *caret*. Ovidius
Naso was the man: and why, indeed, Naso, but for
smelling out the odoriferous flowers of fancy, the jerks
of invention?
   Love's Labour's Lost (1595) act 4, sc. 2, l. [126]

18   Did not the heavenly rhetoric of thine eye,
'Gainst whom the world cannot hold argument,
Persuade my heart to this false perjury?
Vows for thee broke deserve not punishment.
   Love's Labour's Lost (1595) act 4, sc. 3, l. [60]

19   From women's eyes this doctrine I derive:
They are the ground, the books, the academes,
From whence doth spring the true Promethean fire.
   Love's Labour's Lost (1595) act 4, sc. 3, l. [302]. Cf. *Love's
Labour's Lost* 599 : 1

20   But love, first learnèd in a lady's eyes,
Lives not alone immurèd in the brain,
But, with the motion of all elements,
Courses as swift as thought in every power,
And gives to every power a double power,
Above their functions and their offices.
It adds a precious seeing to the eye;
A lover's eyes will gaze an eagle blind;
A lover's ears will hear the lowest sound,
When the suspicious head of theft is stopped:
Love's feeling is more soft and sensible
Than are the tender horns of cockled snails:
Love's tongue proves dainty Baccus gross in taste.
For valour, is not love a Hercules,
Still climbing trees in the Hesperides?
Subtle as Sphinx; as sweet and musical
As bright Apollo's lute, strung with his hair;
And when Love speaks, the voice of all the gods
Makes heaven drowsy with the harmony.
Never durst poet touch a pen to write
Until his ink were tempered with Love's sighs.
   Love's Labour's Lost (1595) act 4, sc. 3, l. [327]

1 From women's eyes this doctrine I derive:
They sparkle still the right Promethean fire;
They are the books, the arts, the academes,
That show, contain, and nourish all the world.
Love's Labour's Lost (1595) act 4, sc. 3, l. [350]. Cf. *Love's Labour's Lost* 598:19

2 He draweth out the thread of his verbosity finer than
the staple of his argument.
Love's Labour's Lost (1595) act 5, sc. 1, l. [18]

3 Bone? *bone*, for *bene*: Priscian a little scratched; 'twill
serve.
Love's Labour's Lost (1595) act 5, sc. 1, l. [31]

4 MOTH: They have been at a great feast of languages,
and stolen the scraps.
COSTARD: O! they have lived long on the alms-basket
of words. I marvel thy master hath not eaten thee
for a word; for thou art not so long by the head as
honorificabilitudinitatibus: thou art easier swallowed
than a flap-dragon.
Love's Labour's Lost (1595) act 5, sc. 1, l. [39]

5 The posteriors of this day; which the rude multitude
call the afternoon.
Love's Labour's Lost (1595) act 5, sc. 1, l. [96]

6   Had she been light, like you,
Of such a merry, nimble, stirring spirit,
She might ha' been a grandam ere she died;
And so may you; for a light heart lives long.
Love's Labour's Lost (1595) act 5, sc. 2, l. 15

7 Taffeta phrases, silken terms precise,
Three-piled hyperboles, spruce affectation,
Figures pedantical; these summer flies
Have blown me full of maggot ostentation:
I do forswear them.
Love's Labour's Lost (1595) act 5, sc. 2, l. 407

8 Henceforth my wooing mind shall be expressed
In russet yeas and honest kersey noes:
And, to begin, wench,—so God help me, la!—
My love to thee is sound, sans crack or flaw.
Love's Labour's Lost (1595) act 5, sc. 2, l. 413

9 A jest's prosperity lies in the ear
Of him that hears it, never in the tongue
Of him that makes it.
Love's Labour's Lost (1595) act 5, sc. 2, l. [869]

10 When daisies pied and violets blue
And lady-smocks all silver-white
And cuckoo-buds of yellow hue
Do paint the meadows with delight,
The cuckoo then, on every tree,
Mocks married men; for thus sings he,
Cuckoo;
Cuckoo, cuckoo; O, word of fear,
Unpleasing to a married ear!
Love's Labour's Lost (1595) act 5, sc. 2, l. [902]

11 When icicles hang by the wall,
And Dick the shepherd, blows his nail,
And Tom bears logs into the hall,
And milk comes frozen home in pail,
When blood is nipped and ways be foul,
Then nightly sings the staring owl,
Tu-who;
Tu-whit, tu-who—a merry note,
While greasy Joan doth keel the pot.

When all aloud the wind doth blow,
And coughing drowns the parson's saw;
And birds sit brooding in the snow,
And Marion's nose looks red and raw,
When roasted crabs hiss in the bowl.
Love's Labour's Lost (1595) act 5, sc. 2, l. [920]

12 The words of Mercury are harsh after the songs of
Apollo. You, that way: we, this way.
Love's Labour's Lost (1595) act 5, sc. 2, l. [938]

Macbeth

13 FIRST WITCH: When shall we three meet again
   In thunder, lightning, or in rain?
SECOND WITCH: When the hurly-burly's done,
   When the battle's lost and won.
THIRD WITCH: That will be ere the set of sun.
FIRST WITCH: Where the place?
SECOND WITCH: Upon the heath.
THIRD WITCH: There to meet with Macbeth.
FIRST WITCH: I come, Graymalkin!
SECOND WITCH: Paddock calls.
THIRD WITCH: Anon!
ALL: Fair is foul, and foul is fair:
   Hover through the fog and filthy air.
Macbeth (1606) act 1, sc. 1, l. 1

14 What bloody man is that?
Macbeth (1606) act 1, sc. 2, l. 1

15 Brave Macbeth,— well he deserves that name,—
Disdaining fortune, with his brandished steel,
Which smoked with bloody execution,
Like valour's minion carved out his passage
Till he faced the slave;
Which ne'er shook hands, nor bade farewell to
   him,
Till he unseamed him from the nave to the chaps,
And fixed his head upon our battlements.
Macbeth (1606) act 1, sc. 2, l. 16

16   They
Doubly redoubled strokes upon the foe:
Except they meant to bathe in reeking wounds,
Or memorize another Golgotha,
I cannot tell.
Macbeth (1606) act 1, sc. 2, l. 38

17 . . . Bellona's bridegroom, lapped in proof,
Confronted him with self-comparisons,
Point against point, rebellious arm 'gainst arm,
Curbing his lavish spirit.
Macbeth (1606) act 1, sc. 2, l. 55

1 A sailor's wife had chestnuts in her lap,
  And munched, and munched, and munched: 'Give
    me,' quoth I:
  'Aroint thee, witch!' the rump-fed ronyon cries.
  Her husband's to Aleppo gone, master o' the Tiger:
  But in a sieve I'll thither sail,
  And, like a rat without a tail,
  I'll do, I'll do, and I'll do.
    Macbeth (1606) act 1, sc. 3, l. 4

2 Sleep shall neither night nor day
  Hang upon his pent-house lid.
  He shall live a man forbid.
  Weary se'nnights nine times nine
  Shall he dwindle, peak, and pine:
  Though his bark cannot be lost,
  Yet it shall be tempest-tost.
    Macbeth (1606) act 1, sc. 3, l. 19

3 THIRD WITCH: A drum! a drum!
  Macbeth doth come.
  ALL: The weird sisters, hand in hand,
  Posters of the sea and land,
  Thus do go about, about.
    Macbeth (1606) act 1, sc. 3, l. 30

4 So foul and fair a day I have not seen.
    Macbeth (1606) act 1, sc. 3, l. 38

5   What are these,
  So withered, and so wild in their attire,
  That look not like th' inhabitants o' the earth,
  And yet are on 't?
    Macbeth (1606) act 1, sc. 3, l. 39

6 If you can look into the seeds of time,
  And say which grain will grow and which will not,
  Speak then to me, who neither beg nor fear
  Your favours nor your hate.
    Macbeth (1606) act 1, sc. 3, l. 58

7   Say, from whence
  You owe this strange intelligence? or why
  Upon this blasted heath you stop our way
  With such prophetic greeting?
    Macbeth (1606) act 1, sc. 3, l. 72

8 Were such things here as we do speak about?
  Or have we eaten on the insane root
  That takes the reason prisoner?
    Macbeth (1606) act 1, sc. 3, l. 83

9 What! can the devil speak true?
    Macbeth (1606) act 1, sc. 3, l. 107

10 Oftentimes, to win us to our harm,
  The instruments of darkness tell us truths;
  Win us with honest trifles, to betray's
  In deepest consequence.
    Macbeth (1606) act 1, sc. 3, l. 123

11   Two truths are told,
  As happy prologues to the swelling act
  Of the imperial theme.
    Macbeth (1606) act 1, sc. 3, l. 127

12 This supernatural soliciting
  Cannot be ill, cannot be good; if ill,
  Why hath it given me earnest of success,
  Commencing in a truth? I am Thane of Cawdor:
  If good, why do I yield to that suggestion
  Whose horrid image doth unfix my hair
  And make my seated heart knock at my ribs,
  Against the use of nature? Present fears
  Are less than horrible imaginings;
  My thought, whose murder yet is but fantastical,
  Shakes so my single state of man that function
  Is smothered in surmise, and nothing is
  But what is not.
    Macbeth (1606) act 1, sc. 3, l. 130

13   Come what come may,
  Time and the hour runs through the roughest day.
    Macbeth (1606) act 1, sc. 3, l. 146

14 MALCOLM: Nothing in his life
  Became him like the leaving it: he died
  As one that had been studied in his death
  To throw away the dearest thing he owed
  As 'twere a careless trifle.
  DUNCAN: There's no art
  To find the mind's construction in the face;
  He was a gentleman on whom I built
  An absolute trust.
    Macbeth (1606) act 1, sc. 4, l. 7

15 Glamis thou art, and Cawdor; and shalt be
  What thou art promised. Yet I do fear thy nature;
  It is too full o' the milk of human kindness
  To catch the nearest way; thou wouldst be great,
  Art not without ambition; but without
  The illness should attend it; what thou wouldst
    highly,
  That thou wouldst holily; wouldst not play false,
  And yet wouldst wrongly win.
    Macbeth (1606) act 1, sc. 5, l. [16]

16   The raven himself is hoarse
  That croaks the fatal entrance of Duncan
  Under my battlements. Come, you spirits
  That tend on mortal thoughts! unsex me here,
  And fill me from the crown to the toe top full
  Of direst cruelty; make thick my blood,
  Stop up the access and passage to remorse,
  That no compunctious visitings of nature
  Shake my fell purpose, nor keep peace between
  The effect and it! Come to my woman's breasts,
  And take my milk for gall, you murdering ministers,
  Wherever in your sightless substances
  You wait on nature's mischief! Come, thick night,
  And pall thee in the dunnest smoke of hell,
  That my keen knife see not the wound it makes,
  Nor heaven peep through the blanket of the dark,
  To cry 'Hold, hold!'
    Macbeth (1606) act 1, sc. 5, l. [38]

17 Your face, my thane, is as a book where men
  May read strange matters. To beguile the time,
  Look like the time; bear welcome in your eye,
  Your hand, your tongue: look like the innocent
    flower,
  But be the serpent under't.
    Macbeth (1606) act 1, sc. 5, l. [63]

1 DUNCAN: This castle hath a pleasant seat; the air
Nimbly and sweetly recommends itself
Unto our gentle senses.
BANQUO: This guest of summer,
The temple-haunting martlet, does approve
By his loved mansionry that the heaven's breath
Smells wooingly here: no jutty, frieze,
Buttress, nor coign of vantage, but this bird
Hath made his pendent bed and procreant cradle:
Where they most breed and haunt, I have
observed,
The air is delicate.
Macbeth (1606) act 1, sc. 6, l. 1

2 If it were done when 'tis done, then 'twere well
It were done quickly: if the assassination
Could trammel up the consequence, and catch
With his surcease success; that but this blow
Might be the be-all and the end-all here,
But here, upon this bank and shoal of time,
We'd jump the life to come. But in these cases
We still have judgement here; that we but teach
Bloody instructions, which, being taught, return,
To plague the inventor; this even-handed justice
Commends the ingredients of our poisoned chalice
To our own lips.
Macbeth (1606) act 1, sc. 7, l. 1

3 Besides, this Duncan
Hath borne his faculties so meek, hath been
So clear in his great office, that his virtues
Will plead like angels trumpet-tongued, against
The deep damnation of his taking-off;
And pity, like a naked new-born babe,
Striding the blast, or heaven's cherubim, horsed
Upon the sightless couriers of the air,
Shall blow the horrid deed in every eye,
That tears shall drown the wind. I have no spur
To prick the sides of my intent, but only
Vaulting ambition, which o'erleaps itself,
And falls on the other.
Macbeth (1606) act 1, sc. 7, l. 16

4 We will proceed no further in this business:
He hath honoured me of late; and I have bought
Golden opinions from all sorts of people.
Macbeth (1606) act 1, sc. 7, l. 31

5 Was the hope drunk,
Wherein you dressed yourself? hath it slept since,
And wakes it now, to look so green and pale
At what it did so freely? From this time
Such I account thy love. Art thou afeard
To be the same in thine own act and valour
As thou art in desire? Wouldst thou have that
Which thou esteem'st the ornament of life,
And live a coward in thine own esteem,
Letting 'I dare not' wait upon 'I would,'
Like the poor cat i' the adage?
Macbeth (1606) act 1, sc. 7, l. 35

6 I dare do all that may become a man,
Who dares do more is none.
Macbeth (1606) act 1, sc. 7, l. 46

7 LADY MACBETH: I have given suck, and know
How tender 'tis to love the babe that milks me:
I would, while it was smiling in my face,
Have plucked my nipple from his boneless gums,
And dash'd the brains out, had I so sworn as you
Have done to this.
MACBETH: If we should fail,—
LADY MACBETH: We fail!
But screw your courage to the sticking-place,
And we'll not fail.
Macbeth (1606) act 1, sc. 7, l. 54

8 Bring forth men-children only;
For thy undaunted mettle should compose
Nothing but males.
Macbeth (1606) act 1, sc. 7, l. 72

9 False face must hide what the false heart doth know.
Macbeth (1606) act 1, sc. 7, l. 82

10 There's husbandry in heaven;
Their candles are all out.
Macbeth (1606) act 2, sc. 1, l. 4

11 A heavy summons lies like lead upon me,
And yet I would not sleep.
Macbeth (1606) act 2, sc. 1, l. 6

12 Is this a dagger which I see before me,
The handle toward my hand? Come, let me clutch
thee:
I have thee not, and yet I see thee still.
Art thou not, fatal vision, sensible
To feeling as to sight? or art thou but
A dagger of the mind, a false creation,
Proceeding from the heat-oppressed brain?
Macbeth (1606) act 2, sc. 1, l. 33

13 Now o'er the one half-world
Nature seems dead, and wicked dreams abuse
The curtained sleep; witchcraft celebrates
Pale Hecate's offerings; and withered murder,
Alarumed by his sentinel, the wolf,
Whose howl's his watch, thus with his stealthy pace,
With Tarquin's ravishing strides, toward his design
Moves like a ghost. Thou sure and firm-set earth,
Hear not my steps, which way they walk, for fear
The very stones prate of my whereabout,
And take the present horror from the time,
Which now suits with it. Whiles I threat he lives:
Words to the heat of deeds too cold breath gives.
I go, and it is done; the bell invites me.
Hear it not, Duncan; for it is a knell
That summons thee to heaven or to hell.
Macbeth (1606) act 2, sc. 1, l. 49

14 That which hath made them drunk hath made me
bold,
What hath quenched them hath given me fire.
Macbeth (1606) act 2, sc. 2, l. 1

15 It was the owl that shrieked, the fatal bellman,
Which gives the stern'st good-night.
Macbeth (1606) act 2, sc. 2, l. 4

16 The attempt and not the deed,
Confounds us.
Macbeth (1606) act 2, sc. 2, l. 12

17 Had he not resembled
My father as he slept I had done't.
Macbeth (1606) act 2, sc. 2, l. 14

1 . . . Wherefore could not I pronounce 'Amen'?
   I had most need of blessing, and 'Amen'
   Stuck in my throat.
   Macbeth (1606) act 2, sc. 2, l. 32

2 Methought I heard a voice cry, 'Sleep no more!
   Macbeth does murder sleep,' the innocent sleep,
   Sleep that knits up the ravelled sleave of care,
   The death of each day's life, sore labour's bath,
   Balm of hurt minds, great nature's second course,
   Chief nourisher in life's feast.
   Macbeth (1606) act 2, sc. 2, l. 36

3 Glamis hath murdered sleep, and therefore Cawdor
   Shall sleep no more, Macbeth shall sleep no more!
   Macbeth (1606) act 2, sc. 2, l. 43

4 MACBETH: I am afraid to think what I have done;
      Look on't again I dare not.
   LADY MACBETH: Infirm of purpose!
      Give me the daggers. The sleeping and the dead
      Are but as pictures; 'tis the eye of childhood
      That fears a painted devil. If he do bleed
      I'll gild the faces of the grooms withal;
      For it must seem their guilt.
   Macbeth (1606) act 2, sc. 2, l. 52

5   Whence is that knocking?
   How is't with me, when every noise appals me?
   Macbeth (1606) act 2, sc. 2, l. 58

6 Will all great Neptune's ocean wash this blood
   Clean from my hand? No, this my hand will rather
   The multitudinous seas incarnadine,
   Making the green one red.
   Macbeth (1606) act 2, sc. 2, l. 61

7 A little water clears us of this deed.
   Macbeth (1606) act 2, sc. 2, l. 68

8 Here's a knocking, indeed! If a man were porter of
   hell-gate he should have old turning the key. Knock,
   knock, knock! Who's there i' the name of Beelzebub?
   Here's a farmer that hanged himself on the
   expectation of plenty.
   Macbeth (1606) act 2, sc. 3, l. 1

9 Who's there i' the other devil's name! Faith, here's an
   equivocator, that could swear in both the scales
   against either scale; who committed treason enough
   for God's sake, yet could not equivocate to heaven: O!
   come in, equivocator.
   Macbeth (1606) act 2, sc. 3, l. [9]

10 This place is too cold for hell. I'll devil-porter it no
   further: I had thought to have let in some of all
   professions, that go the primrose way to the
   everlasting bonfire.
   Macbeth (1606) act 2, sc. 3, l. [19]. Cf. *All's Well That
   Ends Well* 564:10

11 PORTER: Drink, sir, is a great provoker of three things.
   MACDUFF: What three things does drink especially
      provoke?
   PORTER: Marry, sir, nose-painting, sleep, and urine.
      Lechery, sir, it provokes, and unprovokes; it
      provokes the desire, but it takes away the
      performance.
   Macbeth (1606) act 2, sc. 3, l. [28]

12 The labour we delight in physics pain.
   Macbeth (1606) act 2, sc. 3, l. [56]

13 The night has been unruly: where we lay
   Our chimneys were blown down; and, as they say,
   Lamentings heard i' the air; strange screams of death,
   And prophesying with accents terrible
   Of dire combustion and confused events
   New-hatched to the woeful time. The obscure bird
   Clamoured the live-long night: some say the earth
   Was feverous and did shake.
   Macbeth (1606) act 2, sc. 3, l. [60]

14 Confusion now hath made his masterpiece!
   Most sacrilegious murder hath broke ope
   The Lord's anointed temple, and stole thence
   The life o' the building!
   Macbeth (1606) act 2, sc. 3, l. [72]

15 Shake off this downy sleep, death's counterfeit,
   And look on death itself! up, up, and see
   The great doom's image!
   Macbeth (1606) act 2, sc. 3, l. [83]

16 MACDUFF: Our royal master's murdered!
   LADY MACBETH: Woe, alas!
      What! in our house?
   Macbeth (1606) act 2, sc. 3, l. [95]

17 Had I but died an hour before this chance,
   I had lived a blessed time; for, from this instant,
   There's nothing serious in mortality:
   All is but toys; renown and grace is dead,
   The wine of life is drawn, and the mere lees
   Is left this vault to brag of.
   Macbeth (1606) act 2, sc. 3, l. [98]

18 Who can be wise, amazed, temperate, and furious,
   Loyal and neutral, in a moment? No man.
   Macbeth (1606) act 2, sc. 3, l. [115]

19   Where we are,
   There's daggers in men's smiles: the near in blood,
   The nearer bloody.
   Macbeth (1606) act 2, sc. 3, l. [146]

20 A falcon, towering in her pride of place,
   Was by a mousing owl hawked at and killed.
   Macbeth (1606) act 2, sc. 4, l. 12

21 Thou hast it now: King, Cawdor, Glamis, all,
   As the weird women promised; and, I fear,
   Thou play'dst most foully for't.
   Macbeth (1606) act 3, sc. 1, l. 1

22 BANQUO: Go not my horse the better,
      I must become a borrower of the night
      For a dark hour or twain.
   MACBETH: Fail not our feast.
   Macbeth (1606) act 3, sc. 1, l. 26

23   To be thus is nothing;
   But to be safely thus.
   Macbeth (1606) act 3, sc. 1, l. 48

24 FIRST MURDERER: We are men, my liege.
   MACBETH: Ay, in the catalogue ye go for men,
      As hounds and greyhounds, mongrels, spaniels,
         curs,
      Shoughs, water-rugs, and demi-wolves are clipt
      All by the name of dogs.
   Macbeth (1606) act 3, sc. 1, l. 90

1 SECOND MURDERER: I am one, my liege,
   Whom the vile blows and buffets of the world
   Have so incensed, that I am reckless what
   I do to spite the world.
   FIRST MURDERER: I another,
   So weary with disasters, tugged with fortune,
   That I would set my life on any chance,
   To mend it or be rid on't.
   Macbeth (1606) act 3, sc. 1, l. 108

2 Leave no rubs nor botches in the work.
   Macbeth (1606) act 3, sc. 1, l. 134

3 LADY MACBETH: Things without all remedy
   Should be without regard: what's done is done.
   MACBETH: We have scotched the snake, not killed it:
   She'll close and be herself, whilst our poor malice
   Remains in danger of her former tooth.
   But let the frame of things disjoint, both the worlds
      suffer,
   Ere we will eat our meal in fear, and sleep
   In the affliction of these terrible dreams
   That shake us nightly. Better be with the dead,
   Whom we, to gain our peace, have sent to peace,
   Than on the torture of the mind to lie
   In restless ecstasy. Duncan is in his grave;
   After life's fitful fever he sleeps well;
   Treason has done his worst: nor steel, nor poison,
   Malice domestic, foreign levy, nothing,
   Can touch him further.
   Macbeth (1606) act 3, sc. 2, l. 11

4   Ere the bat hath flown
   His cloistered flight, ere, to black Hecate's summons
   The shard-borne beetle with his drowsy hums
   Hath rung night's yawning peal, there shall be done
   A deed of dreadful note.
   Macbeth (1606) act 3, sc. 2, l. 40

5 Be innocent of the knowledge, dearest chuck,
   Till thou applaud the deed. Come, seeling night,
   Scarf up the tender eye of pitiful day,
   And with thy bloody and invisible hand,
   Cancel and tear to pieces that great bond
   Which keeps me pale! Light thickens, and the crow
   Makes wing to the rooky wood;
   Good things of day begin to droop and drowse,
   Whiles night's black agents to their preys do rouse.
   Macbeth (1606) act 3, sc. 2, l. 45

6 The west yet glimmers with some streaks of day:
   Now spurs the lated traveller apace
   To gain the timely inn.
   Macbeth (1606) act 3, sc. 3, l. 5

7 Ourself will mingle with society
   And play the humble host.
   Macbeth (1606) act 3, sc. 4, l. 3

8 ... Now I am cabined, cribbed, confined, bound in
   To saucy doubts and fears.
   Macbeth (1606) act 3, sc. 4, l. 24

9 Now good digestion wait on appetite,
   And health on both!
   Macbeth (1606) act 3, sc. 4, l. 38

10 Thou canst not say I did it: never shake
   Thy gory locks at me.
   Macbeth (1606) act 3, sc. 4, l. 50

11 What man dare, I dare;
   Approach thou like the rugged Russian bear,
   The armed rhinoceros or the Hyrcan tiger,
   Take any shape but that, and my firm nerves
   Shall never tremble.
   Macbeth (1606) act 3, sc. 4, l. 99

12 Stand not upon the order of your going.
   Macbeth (1606) act 3, sc. 4, l. 119

13 MACBETH: It will have blood, they say; blood will
      have blood:
   Stones have been known to move and trees to speak;
   Augurs and understood relations have
   By maggot-pies and choughs and rooks brought forth
   The secret'st man of blood. What is the night?
   LADY MACBETH: Almost at odds with morning, which
      is which.
   Macbeth (1606) act 3, sc. 4, l. 122

14   I am in blood
   Stepped in so far that, should I wade no more,
   Returning were as tedious as go o'er.
   Macbeth (1606) act 3, sc. 4, l. 136

15 You lack the season of all natures, sleep.
   Macbeth (1606) act 3, sc. 4, l. 141

16   Security
   Is mortals' chiefest enemy.
   Macbeth (1606) act 3, sc. 5, l. 32

17 Round about the cauldron go;
   In the poisoned entrails throw.
   Toad, that under cold stone
   Days and nights hast thirty-one
   Sweltered venom sleeping got,
   Boil thou first i' the charmèd pot.
   Double, double toil and trouble;
   Fire burn and cauldron bubble.
   Macbeth (1606) act 4, sc. 1, l. 4

18 Eye of newt, and toe of frog,
   Wool of bat, and tongue of dog,
   Adder's fork, and blind-worm's sting,
   Lizard's leg, and howlet's wing,
   For a charm of powerful trouble,
   Like a hell-broth boil and bubble.
   Macbeth (1606) act 4, sc. 1, l. 14

19 Liver of blaspheming Jew,
   Gall of goat, and slips of yew
   Slivered in the moon's eclipse,
   Nose of Turk, and Tartar's lips,
   Finger of birth-strangled babe
   Ditch-delivered by a drab,
   Make the gruel thick and slab.
   Macbeth (1606) act 4, sc. 1, l. 26

20 SECOND WITCH: By the pricking of my thumbs,
   Something wicked this way comes.
   Open, locks,
   Whoever knocks.
   MACBETH: How now, you secret, black, and midnight
      hags!
   What is't you do?
   WITCHES: A deed without a name.
   Macbeth (1606) act 4, sc. 1, l. 44

21 Be bloody, bold, and resolute; laugh to scorn
   The power of man, for none of woman born
   Shall harm Macbeth.
   Macbeth (1606) act 4, sc. 1, l. 79

1 But yet, I'll make assurance double sure,
And take a bond of fate.
Macbeth (1606) act 4, sc. 1, l. 83

2 Macbeth shall never vanquished be until
Great Birnam wood to high Dunsinane hill
Shall come against him.
Macbeth (1606) act 4, sc. 1, l. 92

3 His flight was madness: when our actions do not,
Our fears do make us traitors.
Macbeth (1606) act 4, sc. 2, l. 3

4   He loves us not;
He wants the natural touch, for the poor wren,
The most diminutive of birds, will fight—
Her young ones in her nest—against the owl.
Macbeth (1606) act 4, sc. 2, l. 8

5 SON: And must they all be hanged that swear and lie?
LADY MACDUFF: Every one.
SON: Who must hang them?
LADY MACDUFF: Why, the honest men.
SON: Then the liars and swearers are fools, for there
are liars and swearers enow to beat the honest men
and hang up them.
Macbeth (1606) act 4, sc. 2, l. [51]

6 Angels are bright still, though the brightest fell.
Macbeth (1606) act 4, sc. 3, l. 22

7 Stands Scotland where it did?
Macbeth (1606) act 4, sc. 3, l. 164

8 What! man; ne'er pull your hat upon your brows;
Give sorrow words: the grief that does not speak
Whispers the o'er-fraught heart, and bids it break.
Macbeth (1606) act 4, sc. 3, l. 208

9 MALCOLM: Let's make us medicine of our great
revenge,
To cure this deadly grief.
MACDUFF: He has no children. All my pretty ones?
Did you say all? O hell-kite! All?
What! all my pretty chickens and their dam,
At one fell swoop?
Macbeth (1606) act 4, sc. 3, l. 216

10 MALCOLM: Dispute it like a man.
MACDUFF: I shall do so;
But I must also feel it as a man.
Macbeth (1606) act 4, sc. 3, l. 219

11 DOCTOR: You see her eyes are open.
GENTLEWOMAN: Ay, but their sense is shut.
Macbeth (1606) act 5, sc. 1, l. [27]

12 Out, damned spot! out, I say! Onc; two: why then,
'tis time to do't. Hell is murky! Fie, my lord, fie! a
soldier, and afeard? What need we fear who knows it,
when none can call our power to account? Yet who
would have thought the old man to have had so much
blood in him?
Macbeth (1606) act 5, sc. 1, l. [38]

13 The Thane of Fife had a wife: where is she now?
What! will these hands ne'er be clean? No more o'
that, my lord, no more o' that: you mar all with this
starting.
Macbeth (1606) act 5, sc. 1, l. [46]

14 Here's the smell of the blood still: all the perfumes of
Arabia will not sweeten this little hand.
Macbeth (1606) act 5, sc. 1, l. [55]

15 I would not have such a heart in my bosom for the
dignity of the whole body.
Macbeth (1606) act 5, sc. 1, l. [60]

16 What's done cannot be undone.
Macbeth (1606) act 5, sc. 1, l. [74]

17 Foul whisperings are abroad. Unnatural deeds
Do breed unnatural troubles; infected minds
To their deaf pillows will discharge their secrets;
More needs she the divine than the physician.
Macbeth (1606) act 5, sc. 1, l. [78]

18 Those he commands move only in command,
Nothing in love; now does he feel his title
Hang loose about him, like a giant's robe
Upon a dwarfish thief.
Macbeth (1606) act 5, sc. 2, l. 19

19 Bring me no more reports; let them fly all:
Till Birnam wood remove to Dunsinane
I cannot taint with fear.
Macbeth (1606) act 5, sc. 3, l. 1

20 The devil damn thee black, thou cream-faced loon!
Where gott'st thou that goose look?
Macbeth (1606) act 5, sc. 3, l. 11

21 I have lived long enough: my way of life
Is fall'n into the sear, the yellow leaf;
And that which should accompany old age,
As honour, love, obedience, troops of friends,
I must not look to have; but, in their stead,
Curses, not loud but deep, mouth-honour, breath,
Which the poor heart would fain deny, and dare not.
Macbeth (1606) act 5, sc. 3, l. 22

22 MACBETH: Canst thou not minister to a mind diseased,
Pluck from the memory a rooted sorrow,
Raze out the written troubles of the brain,
And with some sweet oblivious antidote
Cleanse the stuffed bosom of that perilous stuff
Which weighs upon the heart?
DOCTOR: Therein the patient
Must minister to himself.
MACBETH: Throw physic to the dogs; I'll none of it.
Macbeth (1606) act 5, sc. 3, l. 37

23 Hang out our banners on the outward walls;
The cry is still, 'They come'; our castle's strength
Will laugh a siege to scorn.
Macbeth (1606) act 5, sc. 5, l. 1

24 I have almost forgot the taste of fears.
The time has been my senses would have cooled
To hear a night-shriek, and my fell of hair
Would at a dismal treatise rouse and stir
As life were in't. I have supped full with horrors;
Direness, familiar to my slaughterous thoughts,
Cannot once start me.
Macbeth (1606) act 5, sc. 5, l. 9

1 She should have died hereafter;
  There would have been a time for such a word,
  To-morrow, and to-morrow, and to-morrow,
  Creeps in this petty pace from day to day,
  To the last syllable of recorded time;
  And all our yesterdays have lighted fools
  The way to dusty death. Out, out, brief candle!
  Life's but a walking shadow, a poor player,
  That struts and frets his hour upon the stage,
  And then is heard no more; it is a tale
  Told by an idiot, full of sound and fury,
  Signifying nothing.
    Macbeth (1606) act 5, sc. 5, l. 16

2 If that which he avouches does appear,
  There is nor flying hence, nor tarrying here.
  I 'gin to be aweary of the sun,
  And wish the estate o' the world were now undone.
  Ring the alarum-bell! Blow, wind! come, wrack!
  At least we'll die with harness on our back.
    Macbeth (1606) act 5, sc. 5, l. 47

3 MACBETH: I bear a charmèd life, which must not yield
    To one of woman born.
  MACDUFF: Despair thy charm;
    And let the angel who thou still hast served
    Tell thee, Macduff was from his mother's womb
    Untimely ripped.
    Macbeth (1606) act 5, sc. 7, l. 41

4   Lay on, Macduff;
  And damned be him that first cries, 'Hold, enough!'
    Macbeth (1606) act 5, sc. 7, l. 62

5 SIWARD: Had he his hurts before?
  ROSS: Ay, on the front.
  SIWARD: Why, then, God's soldier be he!
    Had I as many sons as I have hairs,
    I would not wish them to a fairer death.
    Macbeth (1606) act 5, sc. 7, l. 75

Measure for Measure

6 Heaven doth with us as we with torches do,
  Not light them for themselves; for if our virtues
  Did not go forth of us, 'twere all alike
  As if we had them not.
    Measure for Measure (1604) act 1, sc. 1, l. 32

7   Now, as fond fathers,
  Having bound up the threat'ning twigs of birch,
  Only to stick it in their children's sight
  For terror, not to use, in time the rod
  Becomes more mocked than feared; so our decrees,
  Dead to infliction, to themselves are dead,
  And liberty plucks justice by the nose;
  The baby beats the nurse, and quite athwart
  Goes all decorum.
    Measure for Measure (1604) act 1, sc. 3, l. 23

8 I hold you as a thing enskyed and sainted;
  By your renouncement an immortal spirit,
  And to be talked with in sincerity,
  As with a saint.
    Measure for Measure (1604) act 1, sc. 4, l. 34

9 Your brother and his lover have embraced:
  As those that feed grow full, as blossoming time
  That from the seedness the bare fallow brings
  To teeming foison, even so her plenteous womb
  Expresseth his full tilth and husbandry.
    Measure for Measure (1604) act 1, sc. 4, l. 40

10   A man whose blood
  Is very snow-broth; one who never feels
  The wanton stings and motions of the sense,
  But doth rebate and blunt his natural edge
  With profits of the mind, study and fast.
    Measure for Measure (1604) act 1, sc. 4, l. 57

11 We must not make a scarecrow of the law,
  Setting it up to fear the birds of prey,
  And let it keep one shape, till custom make it
  Their perch and not their terror.
    Measure for Measure (1604) act 2, sc. 1, l. 1

12 'Tis one thing to be tempted, Escalus,
  Another thing to fall. I not deny,
  The jury, passing on the prisoner's life,
  May in the sworn twelve have a thief or two
  Guiltier than him they try.
    Measure for Measure (1604) act 2, sc. 1, l. 17

13 This will last out a night in Russia,
  When nights are longest there.
    Measure for Measure (1604) act 2, sc. 1, l. [144]

14 There is a vice that most I do abhor,
  And most desire should meet the blow of justice,
  For which I would not plead, but that I must;
  For which I must not plead, but that I am
  At war 'twixt will and will not.
    Measure for Measure (1604) act 2, sc. 2, l. 29

15 Condemn the fault and not the actor of it?
    Measure for Measure (1604) act 2, sc. 2, l. 37

16 No ceremony that to great ones 'longs,
  Not the king's crown, nor the deputed sword,
  The marshal's truncheon, nor the judge's robe,
  Become them with one half so good a grace
  As mercy does.
    Measure for Measure (1604) act 2, sc. 2, l. 59

17   O! it is excellent
  To have a giant's strength, but it is tyrannous
  To use it like a giant.
    Measure for Measure (1604) act 2, sc. 2, l. 107

18   Man, proud man,
  Drest in a little brief authority,
  Most ignorant of what he's most assured,
  His glassy essence, like an angry ape,
  Plays such fantastic tricks before high heaven,
  As make the angels weep.
    Measure for Measure (1604) act 2, sc. 2, l. 117

19 Great men may jest with saints; 'tis wit in
    them,
  But in the less foul profanation.
    Measure for Measure (1604) act 2, sc. 2, l. 127

1 That in the captain's but a choleric word,
Which in the soldier is flat blasphemy.
Measure for Measure (1604) act 2, sc. 2, l. 130

2   Is this her fault or mine?
The tempter or the tempted, who sins most?
Measure for Measure (1604) act 2, sc. 2, l. 162

3 O cunning enemy, that, to catch a saint,
With saints dost bait thy hook! Most dangerous
Is that temptation that doth goad us on
To sin in loving virtue; never could the strumpet,
With all her double vigour, art and nature,
Once stir my temper; but this virtuous maid
Subdues me quite. Ever till now
When men were fond, I smiled and wondered how.
Measure for Measure (1604) act 2, sc. 2, l. 180

4 Might there not be a charity in sin
To save this brother's life?
Measure for Measure (1604) act 2, sc. 4, l. 64

5 Thus wisdom wishes to appear most bright
When it doth tax itself.
Measure for Measure (1604) act 2, sc. 4, l. 78

6 CLAUDIO: The miserable have no other medicine
  But only hope:
  I have hope to live, and am prepared to die.
DUKE: Be absolute for death; either death or life
  Shall thereby be the sweeter. Reason thus with life:
  If I do lose thee, I do lose a thing
  That none but fools would keep: a breath thou art
  Servile to all the skyey influences,
  That dost this habitation, where thou keep'st,
  Hourly afflict. Merely, thou art death's fool;
  For him thou labour'st by thy flight to shun,
  And yet run'st toward him still.
Measure for Measure (1604) act 3, sc. 1, l. 2

7   If thou art rich, thou'rt poor;
For, like an ass whose back with ingots bows,
Thou bear'st thy heavy riches but a journey,
And death unloads thee.
Measure for Measure (1604) act 3, sc. 1, l. 25

8   Thou hast nor youth nor age;
But, as it were, an after-dinner's sleep,
Dreaming on both; for all thy blessed youth
Becomes as aged, and doth beg the alms
Of palsied eld.
Measure for Measure (1604) act 3, sc. 1, l. 32

9   Dar'st thou die?
The sense of death is most in apprehension,
And the poor beetle, that we tread upon,
In corporal sufferance finds a pang as great
As when a giant dies.
Measure for Measure (1604) act 3, sc. 1, l. 75

10   If I must die,
I will encounter darkness as a bride,
And hug it in mine arms.
Measure for Measure (1604) act 3, sc. 1, l. 81

11 CLAUDIO: Death is a fearful thing.
ISABELLA: And shamed life a hateful.
CLAUDIO: Ay, but to die, and go we know not where;
  To lie in cold obstruction and to rot;
  This sensible warm motion to become
  A kneaded clod; and the delighted spirit
  To bathe in fiery floods or to reside
  In thrilling region of thick-ribbèd ice;
  To be imprisoned in the viewless winds,
  And blown with restless violence round about
  The pendant world; or to be worse than worst
  Of those that lawless and incertain thoughts
  Imagine howling: 'tis too horrible!
  The weariest and most loathèd worldly life
  That age, ache, penury, and imprisonment
  Can lay on nature, is a paradise
  To what we fear of death.
Measure for Measure (1604) act 3, sc. 1, l. 114

12 The hand that hath made you fair hath made you good.
Measure for Measure (1604) act 3, sc. 1, l. [182]

13 Virtue is bold, and goodness never fearful.
Measure for Measure (1604) act 3, sc. 1, l. [214]

14 There, at the moated grange, resides this dejected Mariana.
Measure for Measure (1604) act 3, sc. 1, l. [279]

15 When he makes water his urine is congealed ice.
Measure for Measure (1604) act 3, sc. 2, l. [119]

16 A very superficial, ignorant, unweighing fellow.
Measure for Measure (1604) act 3, sc. 2, l. [151]

17 Take, O take those lips away,
That so sweetly were forsworn;
And those eyes, the break of day,
Lights that do mislead the morn:
But my kisses bring again, bring again;
Seals of love, but sealed in vain, sealed in vain.
Measure for Measure (1604) act 4, sc. 1, l. 1

18 ... Though music oft hath such a charm
To make bad good, and good provoke to harm.
Measure for Measure (1604) act 4, sc. 1, l. 16

19 Every true man's apparel fits your thief.
Measure for Measure (1604) act 4, sc. 2, l. [46]

20 A man that apprehends death no more dreadfully but
as a drunken sleep; careless, reckless, and fearless of
what's past, present, or to come; insensible of
mortality, and desperately mortal.
Measure for Measure (1604) act 4, sc. 2, l. [148]

21 O! death's a great disguiser.
Measure for Measure (1604) act 4, sc. 2, l. [185]

22 The old fantastical Duke of dark corners.
Measure for Measure (1604) act 4, sc. 3, l. 156

23 I am a kind of burr; I shall stick.
Measure for Measure (1604) act 4, sc. 3, l. [193]

24   Let the devil
Be sometime honoured for his burning throne.
Measure for Measure (1604) act 5, sc. 1, l. [289]

25 Haste still pays haste, and leisure answers leisure;
Like doth quit like, and Measure still for Measure.
Measure for Measure (1604) act 5, sc. 1, l. [411]

1 They say best men are moulded out of faults,
 And, for the most, become much more the better
 For being a little bad: so may my husband.
  Measure for Measure (1604) act 5, sc. 1, l. [440]

The Merchant of Venice

2 ANTONIO: In sooth I know not why I am so sad:
 It wearies me; you say it wearies you;
 But how I caught it, found it, or came by it,
 What stuff 'tis made of, whereof it is born,
 I am to learn;
 And such a want-wit sadness makes of me,
 That I have much ado to know myself.
 SALARINO: Your mind is tossing on the ocean;
 There, where your argosies with portly sail,—
 Like signiors and rich burghers on the flood,
 Or, as it were, the pageants of the sea,—
 Do overpeer the petty traffickers,
 That curtsy to them, do them reverence,
 As they fly by them with their woven wings.
  The Merchant of Venice (1596–8) act 1, sc. 1, l. 1

3 You have too much respect upon the world:
 They lose it that do buy it with much care.
  The Merchant of Venice (1596–8) act 1, sc. 1, l. 74

4 I hold the world but as the world, Gratiano;
 A stage where every man must play a part,
 And mine a sad one.
  The Merchant of Venice (1596–8) act 1, sc. 1, l. 77

5 Why should a man, whose blood is warm within,
 Sit like his grandsire cut in alabaster?
  The Merchant of Venice (1596–8) act 1, sc. 1, l. 83

6 There are a sort of men whose visages
 Do cream and mantle like a standing pond,
 And do a wilful stillness entertain,
 With purpose to be dressed in an opinion
 Of wisdom, gravity, profound conceit;
 As who should say, 'I am Sir Oracle,
 And when I ope my lips let no dog bark!'
 O, my Antonio, I do know of these,
 That therefore only are reputed wise,
 For saying nothing.
  The Merchant of Venice (1596–8) act 1, sc. 1, l. 88

7   Fish not, with this melancholy bait,
 For this fool gudgeon, this opinion.
  The Merchant of Venice (1596–8) act 1, sc. 1, l. 101

8   Silence is only commendable
 In a neat's tongue dried and a maid not vendible.
  The Merchant of Venice (1596–8) act 1, sc. 1, l. 111

9 My purse, my person, my extremest means
 Lie all unlocked to your occasions.
  The Merchant of Venice (1596–8) act 1, sc. 1, l. [139]

10 In Belmont is a lady richly left,
 And she is fair, and fairer than the word,
 Of wondrous virtues; sometimes from her eyes
 I did receive fair speechless messages.
  The Merchant of Venice (1596–8) act 1, sc. 1, l. [162]

11 They are as sick that surfeit with too much, as they
 that starve with nothing. It is no mean happiness,
 therefore, to be seated in the mean: superfluity comes
 sooner by white hairs, but competency lives longer.
  The Merchant of Venice (1596–8) act 1, sc. 1, l. [9]

12 If to do were as easy as to know what were good to
 do, chapels had been churches, and poor men's
 cottages princes' palaces. It is a good divine that
 follows his own instructions; I can easier teach twenty
 what were good to be done, than be one of the twenty
 to follow mine own teaching.
  The Merchant of Venice (1596–8) act 1, sc. 2, l. [13]

13 God made him, and therefore let him pass for a man.
  The Merchant of Venice (1596–8) act 1, sc. 2, l. [59]

14 If I should marry him, I should marry twenty
 husbands.
  The Merchant of Venice (1596–8) act 1, sc. 2, l. [66]

15 I think he bought his doublet in Italy, his round hose
 in France, his bonnet in Germany, and his behaviour
 everywhere.
  The Merchant of Venice (1596–8) act 1, sc. 2, l. [78]

16 I will do anything, Nerissa, ere I will be married to a
 sponge.
  The Merchant of Venice (1596–8) act 1, sc. 2, l. [105]

17 There is not one among them but I dote on his very
 absence.
  The Merchant of Venice (1596–8) act 1, sc. 2, l. [117]

18 Ships are but boards, sailors but men; there be
 land-rats and water-rats, land-thieves and
 water-thieves.
  The Merchant of Venice (1596–8) act 1, sc. 3, l. [22]

19 I will buy with you, sell with you, talk with you, walk
 with you, and so following; but I will not eat with
 you, drink with you, nor pray with you. What news
 on the Rialto?
  The Merchant of Venice (1596–8) act 1, sc. 3, l. [36]

20 How like a fawning publican he looks!
 I hate him for he is a Christian;
 But more for that in low simplicity
 He lends out money gratis, and brings down
 The rate of usance here with us in Venice.
 If I can catch him once upon the hip,
 I will feed fat the ancient grudge I bear him.
 He hates our sacred nation, and he rails,
 Even there where merchants most do congregate,
 On me, my bargains, and my well-won thrift,
 Which he calls interest.
  The Merchant of Venice (1596–8) act 1, sc. 3, l. [42]

21 The devil can cite Scripture for his purpose.
 An evil soul, producing holy witness,
 Is like a villain with a smiling cheek,
 A goodly apple rotten at the heart.
 O, what a goodly outside falsehood hath!
  The Merchant of Venice (1596–8) act 1, sc. 3, l. [99]

22 Signior Antonio, many a time and oft
 In the Rialto you have rated me
 About my moneys and my usances:
 Still have I borne it with a patient shrug,
 For sufferance is the badge of all our tribe.
 You call me misbeliever, cut-throat dog,
 And spit upon my Jewish gaberdine,
 And all for use of that which is mine own.
  The Merchant of Venice (1596–8) act 1, sc. 3, l. [107]

1 Shall I bend low, and in a bondman's key,
With bated breath, and whispering humbleness,
Say this:—
'Fair sir, you spat on me Wednesday last;
You spurned me such a day; another time
You called me dog; and for these courtesies
I'll lend you thus much moneys?'
The Merchant of Venice (1596–8) act 1, sc. 3, l. [124]

2 O father Abram! what these Christians are,
Whose own hard dealing teaches them suspect
The thoughts of others!
The Merchant of Venice (1596–8) act 1, sc. 3, l. [161]

3 ANTONIO: This Hebrew will turn Christian, he grows
kind.
BASSANIO: I like not fair terms and a villain's mind.
The Merchant of Venice (1596–8) act 1, sc. 3, l. [179]

4 Mislike me not for my complexion,
The shadowed livery of the burnished sun,
To whom I am a neighbour and near bred.
The Merchant of Venice (1596–8) act 2, sc. 1, l. 1

5 My conscience says, 'Launcelot, budge not.' 'Budge,'
says the fiend. 'Budge not,' says my conscience.
'Conscience,' say I, 'you counsel well;' 'fiend,' say I,
'you counsel well.'
The Merchant of Venice (1596–8) act 2, sc. 2, l. [19]

6 The boy was the very staff of my age, my very prop.
The Merchant of Venice (1596–8) act 2, sc. 2, l. [71]

7 It is a wise father that knows his own child.
The Merchant of Venice (1596–8) act 2, sc. 2, l. [83]

8 Truth will come to light; murder cannot be hid long.
The Merchant of Venice (1596–8) act 2, sc. 2, l. [86]

9 There is some ill a-brewing towards my rest.
For I did dream of money-bags to-night.
The Merchant of Venice (1596–8) act 2, sc. 5, l. 17

10 Let not the sound of shallow foppery enter
My sober house.
The Merchant of Venice (1596–8) act 2, sc. 5, l. [35]

11 Love is blind, and lovers cannot see
The pretty follies that themselves commit.
The Merchant of Venice (1596–8) act 2, sc. 6, l. 36

12 What! must I hold a candle to my shames?
The Merchant of Venice (1596–8) act 2, sc. 6, l. 41

13   Men that hazard all
Do it in hope of fair advantages:
A golden mind stoops not to shows of dross.
The Merchant of Venice (1596–8) act 2, sc. 7, l. 18

14 Had you been as wise as bold,
Young in limbs, in judgement old,
Your answer had not been inscrolled.
The Merchant of Venice (1596–8) act 2, sc. 7, l. 70

15 My daughter! O my ducats! O my daughter!
Fled with a Christian! O my Christian ducats!
Justice! the law! my ducats, and my daughter!
The Merchant of Venice (1596–8) act 2, sc. 8, l. 15

16 What many men desire! that 'many' may be meant
By the fool multitude, that choose by show,
Not learning more than the fond eye doth teach;
Which pries not to the interior; but, like the martlet,
Builds in the weather on the outward wall,
Even in the force and road of casualty.
I will not choose what many men desire,
Because I will not jump with common spirits
And rank me with the barbarous multitude.
The Merchant of Venice (1596–8) act 2, sc. 9, l. 25

17 The portrait of a blinking idiot.
The Merchant of Venice (1596–8) act 2, sc. 9, l. 54

18 The fire seven times tried this:
Seven times tried that judgement is
That did never choose amiss.
Some there be that shadows kiss;
Such have but a shadow's bliss.
The Merchant of Venice (1596–8) act 2, sc. 9, l. 63

19 Thus hath the candle singed the moth.
O, these deliberate fools!
The Merchant of Venice (1596–8) act 2, sc. 9, l. 79

20 The Goodwins, I think they call the place; a very
dangerous flat, and fatal, where the carcasses of many
a tall ship lie buried, as they say, if my gossip Report
be an honest woman of her word.
The Merchant of Venice (1596–8) act 3, sc. 1, l. [4]

21 Let him look to his bond.
The Merchant of Venice (1596–8) act 3, sc. 1, l. [51]

22 Hath not a Jew eyes? hath not a Jew hands, organs,
dimensions, senses, affections, passions? fed with the
same food, hurt with the same weapons, subject to the
same diseases, healed by the same means, warmed
and cooled by the same winter and summer, as a
Christian is? If you prick us, do we not bleed? if you
tickle us, do we not laugh? if you poison us, do we
not die? and if you wrong us, shall we not revenge? If
we are like you in the rest, we will resemble you in
that.
The Merchant of Venice (1596–8) act 3, sc. 1, l. 63

23 The villany you teach me I will execute, and it shall
go hard but I will better the instruction.
The Merchant of Venice (1596–8) act 3, sc. 1, l. [76]

24   He makes a swan-like end,
Fading in music.
The Merchant of Venice (1596–8) act 3, sc. 2, l. 44

25 Tell me where is fancy bred.
Or in the heart or in the head?
How begot, how nourishèd ... ?

It is engendered in the eyes,
With gazing fed; and fancy dies
In the cradle where it lies.
The Merchant of Venice (1596–8) act 3, sc. 2, l. 63

26 So may the outward shows be least themselves:
The world is still deceived with ornament.
In law, what plea so tainted and corrupt
But, being seasoned with a gracious voice,
Obscures the show of evil? In religion,
What damnèd error, but some sober brow
Will bless it and approve it with a text,
Hiding the grossness with fair ornament?
There is no vice so simple but assumes
Some mark of virtue on his outward parts.
The Merchant of Venice (1596–8) act 3, sc. 2, l. 73

1 Ornament is but the guilèd shore
To a most dangerous sea; the beauteous scarf
Veiling an Indian beauty; in a word,
The seeming truth which cunning times put on
To entrap the wisest.
The Merchant of Venice (1596–8) act 3, sc. 2,
l. 97

2 You see me, Lord Bassanio, where I stand,
Such as I am: though for myself alone
I would not be ambitious in my wish,
To wish myself much better; yet, for you
I would be trebled twenty times myself;
A thousand times more fair, ten thousand times
More rich;
That only to stand high in your account,
I might in virtues, beauties, livings, friends,
Exceed account: but the full sum of me
Is sum of nothing; which, to term in gross,
Is an unlessoned girl, unschooled, unpractised;
Happy in this, she is not yet so old
But she may learn; happier than this,
She is not bred so dull but she can learn.
The Merchant of Venice (1596–8) act 3, sc. 2, l. 149

3 Here are a few of the unpleasant'st words
That ever blotted paper!
The Merchant of Venice (1596–8) act 3, sc. 2, l. 252

4 I will have my bond.
The Merchant of Venice (1596–8) act 3, sc. 3, l. 17

5 How every fool can play upon the word!
The Merchant of Venice (1596–8) act 3, sc. 5, l. [48]

6 Wilt thou show the whole wealth of thy wit in an
instant? I pray thee, understand a plain man in his
plain meaning.
The Merchant of Venice (1596–8) act 3, sc. 5, l. [62]

7 You'll ask me, why I rather choose to have
A weight of carrion flesh than to receive
Three thousand ducats: I'll not answer that:
But say it is my humour: is it answered?
The Merchant of Venice (1596–8) act 4, sc. 1, l. 40

8 Some men there are love not a gaping pig;
Some, that are mad if they behold a cat;
And others, when the bagpipe sings i' the nose,
Cannot contain their urine.
The Merchant of Venice (1596–8) act 4, sc. 1, l. 47

9 I am not bound to please thee with my answer.
The Merchant of Venice (1596–8) act 4, sc. 1, l. 65

10 What judgement shall I dread, doing no wrong?
The Merchant of Venice (1596–8) act 4, sc. 1, l. 89

11 I am a tainted wether of the flock,
Meetest for death: the weakest kind of fruit
Drops earliest to the ground.
The Merchant of Venice (1596–8) act 4, sc. 1,
l. 114

00 I never knew so young a body with so old a head.
The Merchant of Venice (1596–8) act 4, sc. 1,
l. [163]

13 The quality of mercy is not strained,
It droppeth as the gentle rain from heaven
Upon the place beneath: it is twice blessed;
It blesseth him that gives and him that takes:
'Tis mightiest in the mightiest: it becomes
The thronèd monarch better than his crown;
His sceptre shows the force of temporal power,
The attribute to awe and majesty,
Wherein doth sit the dread and fear of kings;
But mercy is above this sceptred sway,
It is enthronèd in the hearts of kings,
It is an attribute to God himself,
And earthly power doth then show likest God's
When mercy seasons justice. Therefore, Jew,
Though justice be thy plea, consider this,
That in the course of justice none of us
Should see salvation: we do pray for mercy,
And that same prayer doth teach us all to render
The deeds of mercy.
The Merchant of Venice (1596–8) act 4, sc. 1, l. [182]

14 My deeds upon my head! I crave the law.
The Merchant of Venice (1596–8) act 4, sc. 1, l. [206]

15 Wrest once the law to your authority:
To do a great right, do a little wrong.
The Merchant of Venice (1596–8) act 4, sc. 1, l. [215]

16 A Daniel come to judgement! yea, a Daniel!
The Merchant of Venice (1596–8) act 4, sc. 1, l. [223]

17 An oath, an oath, I have an oath in heaven:
Shall I lay perjury upon my soul?
No, not for Venice.
The Merchant of Venice (1596–8) act 4, sc. 1, l. [228]

18 The court awards it, and the law doth give it.
The Merchant of Venice (1596–8) act 4, sc. 1, l. [301]

19   Thyself shalt see the act;
For, as thou urgest justice, be assured
Thou shalt have justice, more than thou desir'st.
The Merchant of Venice (1596–8) act 4, sc. 1, l. [315]

20 Nay, take my life and all; pardon not that:
You take my house when you do take the prop
That doth sustain my house; you take my life
When you do take the means whereby I live.
The Merchant of Venice (1596–8) act 4, sc. 1, l. [375]

21 He is well paid that is well satisfied.
The Merchant of Venice (1596–8) act 4, sc. 1, l. [416]

22 I see, sir, you are liberal in offers:
You taught me first to beg, and now methinks
You teach me how a beggar should be answered.
The Merchant of Venice (1596–8) act 4, sc. 1, l. [439]

23 The moon shines bright: in such a night as this,
When the sweet wind did gently kiss the trees
And they did make no noise, in such a night
Troilus methinks mounted the Troyan walls,
And sighed his soul toward the Grecian tents,
Where Cressid lay that night.
The Merchant of Venice (1596–8) act 5, sc. 1, l. 1

24   In such a night
Stood Dido with a willow in her hand
Upon the wild sea-banks, and waft her love
To come again to Carthage.
The Merchant of Venice (1596–8) act 5, sc. 1, l. 9

1 How sweet the moonlight sleeps upon this bank!
Here will we sit, and let the sounds of music
Creep in our ears; soft stillness and the night
Become the touches of sweet harmony.
Sit, Jessica: look, how the floor of heaven
Is thick inlaid with patines of bright gold:
There's not the smallest orb which thou behold'st
But in this motion like an angel sings
Still quiring to the young-eyed cherubins;
Such harmony is in immortal souls;
But, whilst this muddy vesture of decay
Doth grossly close it in, we cannot hear it.
The Merchant of Venice (1596–8) act 5, sc. 1, l. 54

2 I am never merry when I hear sweet music.
The Merchant of Venice (1596–8) act 5, sc. 1, l. 69

3 The man that hath no music in himself,
Nor is not moved with concord of sweet sounds,
Is fit for treasons, stratagems, and spoils;
The motions of his spirit are dull as night,
And his affections dark as Erebus:
Let no such man be trusted.
The Merchant of Venice (1596–8) act 5, sc. 1, l. 79

4 PORTIA: How far that little candle throws his beams!
So shines a good deed in a naughty world.
NERISSA: When the moon shone, we did not see the
candle.
PORTIA: So doth the greater glory dim the less:
A substitute shines brightly as a king
Until a king be by, and then his state
Empties itself, as doth an inland brook
Into the main of waters.
The Merchant of Venice (1596–8) act 5, sc. 1, l. 90

5 The crow doth sing as sweetly as the lark
When neither is attended, and I think
The nightingale, if she should sing by day,
When every goose is cackling, would be thought
No better a musician than the wren.
How many things by season seasoned are
To their right praise and true perfection!
The Merchant of Venice (1596–8) act 5, sc. 1, l. 102

6 This night methinks is but the daylight sick.
The Merchant of Venice (1596–8) act 5, sc. 1, l. 124

7 Let me give light, but let me not be light:
For a light wife doth make a heavy husband.
The Merchant of Venice (1596–8) act 5, sc. 1, l. 129

8 These blessed candles of the night.
The Merchant of Venice (1596–8) act 5, sc. 1, l. 220

The Merry Wives of Windsor

9 I will make a Star-Chamber matter of it.
The Merry Wives of Windsor (1597) act 1, sc. 1, l. 1

10 She has brown hair, and speaks small like a woman.
The Merry Wives of Windsor (1597) act 1, sc. 1, l. [48]

11 'Convey,' the wise it call. 'Steal!' foh! a fico for the
phrase!
The Merry Wives of Windsor (1597) act 1, sc. 3, l. [30]

12 Here will be an old abusing of God's patience, and the
king's English.
The Merry Wives of Windsor (1597) act 1, sc. 4, l. [5]

13 We burn daylight.
The Merry Wives of Windsor (1597) act 2, sc. 1, l. [54]

14 Why, then the world's mine oyster,
Which I with sword will open.
The Merry Wives of Windsor (1597) act 2, sc. 2, l. 2

15 FALSTAFF: Of what quality was your love, then?
FORD: Like a fair house built upon another man's
ground; so that I have lost my edifice by mistaking
the place where I erected it.
The Merry Wives of Windsor (1597) act 2, sc. 2, l. [228]

16 He capers, he dances, he has eyes of youth, he writes
verses, he speaks holiday, he smells April and May.
The Merry Wives of Windsor (1597) act 3, sc. 2, l. [71]

17 O, what a world of vile ill-favoured faults
Looks handsome in three hundred pounds a year!
The Merry Wives of Windsor (1597) act 3, sc. 4, l. [32]

18 You may know by my size that I have a kind of
alacrity in sinking.
The Merry Wives of Windsor (1597) act 3, sc. 5, l. [12]

19 There is divinity in odd numbers, either in nativity,
chance or death.
The Merry Wives of Windsor (1597) act 5, sc. 1, l. 3

A Midsummer Night's Dream

20   Question your desires;
Know of your youth, examine well your blood,
Whether, if you yield not to your father's choice,
You can endure the livery of a nun,
For aye to be in shady cloister mewed,
To live a barren sister all your life,
Chanting faint hymns to the cold fruitless moon,
Thrice blessèd they that master so their blood,
To undergo such maiden pilgrimage;
But earthlier happy is the rose distilled,
Than that which withering on the virgin thorn
Grows, lives, and dies, in single blessedness.
A Midsummer Night's Dream (1595–6) act 1, sc. 1, l. 67

21 Ay me! for aught that ever I could read,
Could ever hear by tale or history,
The course of true love never did run smooth.
A Midsummer Night's Dream (1595–6) act 1, sc. 1, l. 132

22 O hell! to choose love by another's eye.
A Midsummer Night's Dream (1595–6) act 1, sc. 1, l. 140

23   If there were a sympathy in choice,
War, death, or sickness did lay siege to it,
Making it momentany as a sound,
Swift as a shadow, short as any dream,
Brief as the lightning in the collied night,
That, in a spleen, unfolds both heaven and earth,
And ere a man hath power to say, 'Behold!'
The jaws of darkness do devour it up:
So quick bright things come to confusion.
A Midsummer Night's Dream (1595–6) act 1, sc. 1, l. 141

24 Your eyes are lodestars! and your tongue's sweet air
More tuneable than lark to shepherd's ear,
When wheat is green, when hawthorn buds appear.
A Midsummer Night's Dream (1595–6) act 1, sc. 1, l. 183

1 How happy some o'er other some can be!
Through Athens I am thought as fair as she;
But what of that? Demetrius thinks not so;
He will not know what all but he do know;
And as he errs, doting on Helen's eyes,
So I, admiring of his qualities,
Things base and vile, holding no quantity,
Love can transpose to form and dignity.
Love looks not with the eyes, but with the mind,
And therefore is winged Cupid painted blind.
     A Midsummer Night's Dream (1595–6) act 1, sc. 1, l. 226

2 The most lamentable comedy, and most cruel death of
Pyramus and Thisby.
     A Midsummer Night's Dream (1595–6) act 1, sc. 2, l. [11]

3 Masters, spread yourselves.
     A Midsummer Night's Dream (1595–6) act 1, sc. 2, l. [16]

4 If I do it, let the audience look to their eyes.
     A Midsummer Night's Dream (1595–6) act 1, sc. 2, l. [28]

5 I could play Ercles rarely, or a part to tear a cat in, to
make all split.
     A Midsummer Night's Dream (1595–6) act 1, sc. 2, l. [31]

6 This is Ercles' vein, a tyrant's vein.
     A Midsummer Night's Dream (1595–6) act 1, sc. 2, l. [43]

7 Nay, faith, let me not play a woman; I have a beard
coming.
     A Midsummer Night's Dream (1595–6) act 1, sc. 2, l. [50]

8 I will roar you as gently as any sucking dove; I will
roar you as 'twere any nightingale.
     A Midsummer Night's Dream (1595–6) act 1, sc. 2, l. [85]

9 Pyramus is a sweet-faced man; a proper man, as one
shall see in a summer's day.
     A Midsummer Night's Dream (1595–6) act 1, sc. 2, l. [89]

10 Hold, or cut bow-strings.
     A Midsummer Night's Dream (1595–6) act 1, sc. 2, l. [115]

11 PUCK: How now, spirit! whither wander you?
FAIRY: Over hill, over dale,
    Thorough bush, thorough brier,
    Over park, over pale,
    Thorough flood, thorough fire,
    I do wander everywhere,
    Swifter than the moone's sphere;
    And I serve the fairy queen,
    To dew her orbs upon the green:
    The cowslips tall her pensioners be;
    In their gold coats spots you see;
    Those be rubies, fairy favours,
    In those freckles live their savours:
    I must go seek some dew-drops here,
    And hang a pearl in every cowslip's ear.
     A Midsummer Night's Dream (1595–6) act 2, sc. 1, l. 1

12 The wisest aunt, telling the saddest tale,
Sometime for three-foot stool mistaketh me;
Then slip I from her bum, down topples she,
And 'tailor' cries, and falls into a cough;
And then the whole quire hold their hips and loff.
     A Midsummer Night's Dream (1595–6) act 2, sc. 1, l. 51

13 Ill met by moonlight, proud Titania.
     A Midsummer Night's Dream (1595–6) act 2, sc. 1, l. 60

14 The fold stands empty in the drownèd field,
And crows are fatted with the murrion flock;
The nine men's morris is filled up with mud.
     A Midsummer Night's Dream (1595–6) act 2, sc. 1, l. 96

15 Therefore the moon, the governess of floods,
Pale in her anger, washes all the air,
That rheumatic diseases do abound:
And thorough this distemperature we see
The seasons alter: hoary-headed frosts
Fall in the fresh lap of the crimson rose.
     A Midsummer Night's Dream (1595–6) act 2, sc. 1, l. 103

16 Since once I sat upon a promontory,
And heard a mermaid on a dolphin's back
Uttering such dulcet and harmonious breath,
That the rude sea grew civil at her song,
And certain stars shot madly from their spheres,
To hear the sea-maid's music.
     A Midsummer Night's Dream (1595–6) act 2, sc. 1, l. 149

17 But I might see young Cupid's fiery shaft
Quenched in the chaste beams of the wat'ry moon,
And the imperial votaress passed on,
In maiden meditation, fancy-free.
Yet marked I where the bolt of Cupid fell:
It fell upon a little western flower,
Before milk-white, now purple with love's wound,
And maidens call it, Love-in-idleness.
     A Midsummer Night's Dream (1595–6) act 2, sc. 1, l. 161

18 I'll put a girdle round about the earth
In forty minutes.
     A Midsummer Night's Dream (1595–6) act 2, sc. 1, l. 175

19 I know a bank whereon the wild thyme blows,
Where oxlips and the nodding violet grows
Quite over-canopied with luscious woodbine,
With sweet musk-roses, and with eglantine:
There sleeps Titania some time of the night,
Lulled in these flowers with dances and delight;
And there the snake throws her enamelled skin,
Weed wide enough to wrap a fairy in.
     A Midsummer Night's Dream (1595–6) act 2, sc. 1, l. 249

20 You spotted snakes with double tongue,
Thorny hedge-hogs, be not seen;
Newts, and blind-worms, do no wrong;
Come not near our fairy queen.
     A Midsummer Night's Dream (1595–6) act 2, sc. 2, l. 9

21 Weaving spiders come not here;
Hence you long-legged spinners, hence!
Beetles black, approach not near;
Worm nor snail, do no offence.
     A Midsummer Night's Dream (1595–6) act 2, sc. 2, l. 20

22 God shield us!—a lion among ladies, is a most
dreadful thing; for there is not a more fearful
wild-fowl than your lion living.
     A Midsummer Night's Dream (1595–6) act 3, sc. 1, l. [32]

23 Look in the almanack; find out moonshine, find out
moonshine.
     A Midsummer Night's Dream (1595–6) act 3, sc. 1, l. [55]

24 What hempen home-spuns have we swaggering here,
So near the cradle of the fairy queen?
     A Midsummer Night's Dream (1595–6) act 3, sc. 1, l. [82]

25 Bless thee, Bottom! bless thee! thou art translated.
     A Midsummer Night's Dream (1595–6) act 3, sc. 1, l. [124]

26 What angel wakes me from my flowery bed?
     A Midsummer Night's Dream (1595–6) act 3, sc. 1, l. [135]

27 Out of this wood do not desire to go.
     A Midsummer Night's Dream (1595–6) act 3, sc. 1, l. [159]

1 As wild geese that the creeping fowler eye,
Or russet-pated choughs, many in sort,
Rising and cawing at the gun's report,
Sever themselves, and madly sweep the sky;
So, at his sight, away his fellows fly.
A Midsummer Night's Dream (1595–6) act 3, sc. 2, l. 20

2 Lord, what fools these mortals be!
A Midsummer Night's Dream (1595–6) act 3, sc. 2, l. 115

3   So we grew together,
Like to a double cherry, seeming parted,
But yet an union in partition;
Two lovely berries moulded on one stem;
So, with two seeming bodies, but one heart.
A Midsummer Night's Dream (1595–6) act 3, sc. 2, l. 208

4 Ay, do, persever, counterfeit sad looks,
Make mouths upon me when I turn my back.
A Midsummer Night's Dream (1595–6) act 3, sc. 2, l. 237

5 O! when she's angry she is keen and shrewd.
She was a vixen when she went to school:
And though she be but little, she is fierce.
A Midsummer Night's Dream (1595–6) act 3, sc. 2, l. 323

6 ... Night's swift dragons cut the clouds full fast,
And yonder shines Aurora's harbinger;
At whose approach, ghosts, wandering here and
there,
Troop home to churchyards.
A Midsummer Night's Dream (1595–6) act 3, sc. 2, l. 379

7 Cupid is a knavish lad,
Thus to make poor females mad.
A Midsummer Night's Dream (1595–6) act 3, sc. 2, l. 440

8 Jack shall have Jill;
Nought shall go ill;
The man shall have his mare again,
And all shall be well.
A Midsummer Night's Dream (1595–6) act 3, sc. 2, l. 461

9 I must to the barber's, monsieur, for methinks I am
marvellous hairy about the face.
A Midsummer Night's Dream (1595–6) act 4, sc. 1, l. [25]

10 I have a reasonable good ear in music: let us have the
tongs and the bones.
A Midsummer Night's Dream (1595–6) act 4, sc. 1, l. [32]

11 Methinks I have a great desire to a bottle of hay: good
hay, sweet hay, hath no fellow.
A Midsummer Night's Dream (1595–6) act 4, sc. 1, l. [37]

12 I pray you, let none of your people stir me: I have an
exposition of sleep come upon me.
A Midsummer Night's Dream (1595–6) act 4, sc. 1, l. [43]

13 My Oberon! what visions have I seen!
Methought I was enamoured of an ass.
A Midsummer Night's Dream (1595–6) act 4, sc. 1, l. [82]

14 I was with Hercules and Cadmus once,
When in a wood of Crete they bayed the bear
With hounds of Sparta: never did I hear ...
So musical a discord, such sweet thunder.
A Midsummer Night's Dream (1595–6) act 4, sc. 1, l. [118]

15 I have had a dream, past the wit of man to say what
dream it was.
A Midsummer Night's Dream (1595–6) act 4, sc. 1, l. [211]

16 The eye of man hath not heard, the ear of man hath
not seen, man's hand is not able to taste, his tongue
to conceive, nor his heart to report, what my dream
was.
A Midsummer Night's Dream (1595–6) act 4, sc. 1, l. [218]

17 The lunatic, the lover, and the poet,
Are of imagination all compact:
One sees more devils than vast hell can hold,
That is, the madman; the lover, all as frantic,
Sees Helen's beauty in a brow of Egypt:
The poet's eye, in a fine frenzy rolling,
Doth glance from heaven to earth, from earth to
heaven;
And, as imagination bodies forth
The forms of things unknown, the poet's pen
Turns them to shapes, and gives to airy nothing
A local habitation and a name.
Such tricks hath strong imagination,
That, if it would but apprehend some joy,
It comprehends some bringer of that joy;
Or in the night, imagining some fear,
How easy is a bush supposed a bear!
A Midsummer Night's Dream (1595–6) act 5, sc. 1, l. 7

18 What revels are in hand? Is there no play,
To ease the anguish of a torturing hour?
A Midsummer Night's Dream (1595–6) act 5, sc. 1, l. 36

19 *A tedious brief scene of young Pyramus*
And his love Thisbe: very tragical mirth.
Merry and tragical! tedious and brief!
That is, hot ice and wondrous strange snow.
A Midsummer Night's Dream (1595–6) act 5, sc. 1, l. 56

20 For never anything can be amiss,
When simpleness and duty tender it.
A Midsummer Night's Dream (1595–6) act 5, sc. 1, l. 82

21 Out of this silence yet I picked a welcome;
And in the modesty of fearful duty
I read as much as from the rattling tongue
Of saucy and audacious eloquence.
A Midsummer Night's Dream (1595–6) act 5, sc. 1, l. 100

22 If we offend, it is with our good will.
That you should think, we come not to offend,
But with good will. To show our simple skill,
That is the true beginning of our end.
Consider then we come but in despite.
We do not come as minding to content you,
Our true intent is. All for your delight,
We are not here.
A Midsummer Night's Dream (1595–6) act 5, sc. 1, l. [108]

23 Whereat, with blade, with bloody blameful blade,
He bravely broached his boiling bloody breast.
A Midsummer Night's Dream (1595–6) act 5, sc. 1, l. [148]

24 I see a voice: now will I to the chink,
To spy an I can hear my Thisby's face.
A Midsummer Night's Dream (1595–6) act 5, sc. 1, l. [195]

25 The best in this kind are but shadows, and the worst
are no worse, if imagination amend them.
A Midsummer Night's Dream (1595–6) act 5, sc. 1, l. [215]

26 The iron tongue of midnight hath told twelve;
Lovers, to bed; 'tis almost fairy time.
A Midsummer Night's Dream (1595–6) act 5, sc. 1, l. [372]

1 Now the hungry lion roars,
And the wolf behowls the moon;
Whilst the heavy ploughman snores,
All with weary task fordone.
A Midsummer Night's Dream (1595–6) act 5, sc. 2, l. 1

2   Not a mouse
Shall disturb this hallowed house:
I am sent with broom before,
To sweep the dust behind the door.
A Midsummer Night's Dream (1595–6) act 5, sc. 2, l. 17

3 If we shadows have offended,
Think but this, and all is mended,
That you have but slumbered here
While these visions did appear.
A Midsummer Night's Dream (1595–6) act 5, sc. 2, l. 54

Much Ado About Nothing

4 A victory is twice itself when the achiever brings
home full numbers.
Much Ado About Nothing (1598–9) act 1, sc. 1, l. [8]

5 He hath indeed better bettered expectation than you
must expect of me to tell you how.
Much Ado About Nothing (1598–9) act 1, sc. 1, l. [15]

6 How much better is it to weep at joy than to joy at
weeping.
Much Ado About Nothing (1598–9) act 1, sc. 1, l. [27]

7 He is a very valiant trencher-man.
Much Ado About Nothing (1598–9) act 1, sc. 1, l. [52]

8 I see, lady, the gentleman is not in your books.
Much Ado About Nothing (1598–9) act 1, sc. 1, l. [79]

9 BEATRICE: I wonder that you will still be talking,
Signior Benedick: nobody marks you.
BENEDICK: What! my dear Lady Disdain, are you yet
living?
Much Ado About Nothing (1598–9) act 1, sc. 1, l. [121]

10 Shall I never see a bachelor of three-score again?
Much Ado About Nothing (1598–9) act 1, sc. 1, l. [209]

11 In time the savage bull doth bear the yoke.
Much Ado About Nothing (1598–9) act 1, sc. 1, l. [271]

12 Lord! I could not endure a husband with a beard on
his face: I had rather lie in the woollen.
Much Ado About Nothing (1598–9) act 2, sc. 1, l. [31]

13 Would it not grieve a woman to be over-mastered
with a piece of valiant dust? to make an account of
her life to a clod of wayward marl?
Much Ado About Nothing (1598–9) act 2, sc. 1, l. [64]

14 I have a good eye, uncle: I can see a church by
daylight.
Much Ado About Nothing (1598–9) act 2, sc. 1, l. [86]

15 Speak low, if you speak love.
Much Ado About Nothing (1598–9) act 2, sc. 1, l. [104]

16 Friendship is constant in all other things
Save in the office and affairs of love.
Much Ado About Nothing (1598–9) act 2, sc. 1, l. [184]

17 She speaks poniards, and every word stabs: if her
breath were as terrible as her terminations, there were
no living near her; she would infect to the north star.
Much Ado About Nothing (1598–9) act 2, sc. 1, l. [257]

18 I will go on the slightest errand now to the Antipodes
that you can devise to send me on; I will fetch you a
toothpicker now from the furthest inch of Asia; bring
you the length of Prester John's foot; fetch you a hair
off the Great Cham's beard; do you any embassage to
the Pigmies, rather than hold three words' conference
with this harpy.
Much Ado About Nothing (1598–9) act 2, sc. 1, l. [274]

19 Speak, cousin, or, if you cannot, stop his mouth with
a kiss.
Much Ado About Nothing (1598–9) act 2, sc. 1, l. [322]

20 DON PEDRO: Out of question, you were born in a
merry hour.
BEATRICE: No, sure, my lord, my mother cried; but
then there was a star danced, and under that was I
born.
Much Ado About Nothing (1598–9) act 2, sc. 1, l. [348]

21 She is never sad but when she sleeps; and not ever
sad then, for I have heard my daughter say, she hath
often dreamed of unhappiness and waked herself with
laughing.
Much Ado About Nothing (1598–9) act 2, sc. 1, l. [360]

22 I have known, when he would have walked ten miles
afoot to see a good armour; and now will he lie ten
nights awake, carving the fashion of a new doublet.
Much Ado About Nothing (1598–9) act 2, sc. 3, l. [16]

23 Is it not strange, that sheeps' guts should hale souls
out of men's bodies?
Much Ado About Nothing (1598–9) act 2, sc. 3, l. [62]

24 Sigh no more, ladies, sigh no more,
Men were deceivers ever;
One foot in sea, and one on shore,
To one thing constant never.
Much Ado About Nothing (1598–9) act 2, sc. 3, l. [65]

25 Sits the wind in that corner?
Much Ado About Nothing (1598–9) act 2, sc. 3, l. [108]

26 Doth not the appetite alter? A man loves the meat in
his youth that he cannot endure in his age.
Much Ado About Nothing (1598–9) act 2, sc. 3, l. [258]

27 The world must be peopled. When I said I would die a
bachelor, I did not think I should live till I were
married.
Much Ado About Nothing (1598–9) act 2, sc. 3, l. [262]

28   Now begin;
For look where Beatrice, like a lapwing, runs
Close by the ground, to hear our counsel.
Much Ado About Nothing (1598–9) act 3, sc. 1, l. 23

29 Disdain and scorn ride sparkling in her eyes.
Much Ado About Nothing (1598–9) act 3, sc. 1, l. 51

30 Contempt, farewell! and maiden pride, adieu!
No glory lives behind the back of such.
And, Benedick, love on; I will requite thee,
Taming my wild heart to thy loving hand.
Much Ado About Nothing (1598–9) act 3, sc. 1, l. 109

31 He hath a heart as sound as a bell, and his tongue is
the clapper; for what his heart thinks his tongue
speaks.
Much Ado About Nothing (1598–9) act 3, sc. 2, l. [12]

32 Well, every one can master a grief but he that has it.
Much Ado About Nothing (1598–9) act 3, sc. 2, l. [28]

1 The barber's man hath been seen with him; and the
old ornament of his cheek hath already stuffed
tennis-balls.
Much Ado About Nothing (1598–9) act 3, sc. 2, l. [45]

2 To be a well-favoured man is the gift of fortune; but
to write and read comes by nature.
Much Ado About Nothing (1598–9) act 3, sc. 3, l. [14]

3 The most peaceable way for you, if you do take a
thief, is, to let him show himself what he is and steal
out of your company.
Much Ado About Nothing (1598–9) act 3, sc. 3, l. [61]

4 I thank God, I am as honest as any man living, that is
an old man and no honester than I.
Much Ado About Nothing (1598–9) act 3, sc. 5, l. [15]

5 Comparisons are odorous.
Much Ado About Nothing (1598–9) act 3, sc. 5, l. [18]

6 A good old man, sir; he will be talking: as they say,
'when the age is in, the wit is out.'
Much Ado About Nothing (1598–9) act 3, sc. 5, l. [36]

7 Well, God's a good man.
Much Ado About Nothing (1598–9) act 3, sc. 5, l. [39]

8 O! what men dare do! what men may do! what men
daily do, not knowing what they do!
Much Ado About Nothing (1598–9) act 4, sc. 1, l. [19]

9 BEATRICE: You have stayed me in a happy hour. I
was about to protest I loved you.
BENEDICK: And do it with all thy heart.
BEATRICE: I love you with so much of my heart that
none is left to protest.
Much Ado About Nothing (1598–9) act 4, sc. 1, l. [283]

10 O God, that I were a man! I would eat his heart in the
market-place.
Much Ado About Nothing (1598–9) act 4, sc. 1, l. [311]

11 Flat burglary as ever was committed.
Much Ado About Nothing (1598–9) act 4, sc. 2, l. [54]

12 Patch grief with proverbs.
Much Ado About Nothing (1598–9) act 5, sc. 1, l. 17

13   There was never yet philosopher
That could endure the toothache patiently.
Much Ado About Nothing (1598–9) act 5, sc. 1, l. 35

14 In a false quarrel there is no true valour.
Much Ado About Nothing (1598–9) act 5, sc. 1, l. [121]

15 What though care killed a cat, thou hast mettle
enough in thee to kill care.
Much Ado About Nothing (1598–9) act 5, sc. 1, l. [135]

16 No, I was not born under a rhyming planet.
Much Ado About Nothing (1598–9) act 5, sc. 2, l. [40]

17 Good morrow, masters: put your torches out,
The wolves have preyed; and look, the gentle day,
Before the wheels of Phoebus, round about
Dapples the drowsy east with spots of grey.
Much Ado About Nothing (1598–9) act 5, sc. 3, l. 24

Othello

18   'Tis the curse of service,
Preferment goes by letter and affection,
Not by the old gradation, where each second
Stood heir to the first.
Othello (1602–4) act 1, sc. 1, l. 35

19   You shall mark
Many a duteous and knee-crooking knave,
That, doting on his own obsequious bondage,
Wears out his time, much like his master's ass,
For nought but provender.
Othello (1602–4) act 1, sc. 1, l. 44

20 In following him, I follow but myself.
Othello (1602–4) act 1, sc. 1, l. 58

21 But I will wear my heart upon my sleeve
For daws to peck at: I am not what I am.
Othello (1602–4) act 1, sc. 1, l. 64

22 Even now, now, very now, an old black ram
Is tupping your white ewe.
Othello (1602–4) act 1, sc. 1, l. 88

23 'Zounds! sir, you are one of those that will not serve
God if the devil bid you.
Othello (1602–4) act 1, sc. 1, l. 108

24 Your daughter and the Moor are now making the
beast with two backs.
Othello (1602–4) act 1, sc. 1, l. [117]

25 Though I do hate him as I do hell-pains,
Yet, for necessity of present life,
I must show out a flag and sign of love,
Which is indeed but sign.
Othello (1602–4) act 1, sc. 1, l. [155]

26 Though in the trade of war I have slain men,
Yet do I hold it very stuff o' the conscience
To do no contrived murder: I lack iniquity
Sometimes to do me service.
Othello (1602–4) act 1, sc. 2, l. 1

27 Keep up your bright swords, for the dew will rust
them.
Othello (1602–4) act 1, sc. 2, l. 59

28 I'll refer me to all things of sense,
Whether a maid so tender, fair, and happy,
So opposite to marriage that she shunned
The wealthy curlèd darlings of our nation,
Would ever have, to incur a general mock,
Run from her guardage to the sooty bosom
Of such a thing as thou.
Othello (1602–4) act 1, sc. 2, l. 64

29   My particular grief
Is of so flood-gate and o'bearing nature
That it engluts and swallows other sorrows
And it is still itself.
Othello (1602–4) act 1, sc. 3, l. 55

30   Rude am I in my speech,
And little blessed with the soft phrase of peace.
Othello (1602–4) act 1, sc. 3, l. 81

31 OTHELLO: I will a round unvarnished tale deliver
Of my whole course of love; what drugs, what
charms,
What conjuration, and what mighty magic,
For such proceeding I am charged withal,
I won his daughter.
BRABANTIO: A maiden never bold;
Of spirit so still and quiet, that her motion
Blushed at herself.
Othello (1602–4) act 1, sc. 3, l. 90

1 Her father loved me; oft invited me;
  Still questioned me the story of my life
From year to year, the battles, sieges, fortunes
That I have passed.
I ran it through, even from my boyish days
To the very moment that he bade me tell it;
Wherein I spake of most disastrous chances,
Of moving accidents by flood and field,
Of hair-breadth 'scapes i' the imminent deadly breach,
Of being taken by the insolent foe
And sold to slavery, of my redemption thence
And portance in my travel's history;
Wherein of antres vast and deserts idle,
Rough quarries, rocks and hills whose heads touch
  heaven,
It was my hint to speak, such was the process;
And of the Cannibals that each other eat,
The Anthropophagi, and men whose heads
Do grow beneath their shoulders. This to hear
Would Desdemona seriously incline.
   Othello (1602–4) act 1, sc. 3, l. 128

2   My story being done,
She gave me for my pains a world of sighs:
She swore, in faith, 'twas strange, 'twas passing
  strange;
'Twas pitiful, 'twas wondrous pitiful.
   Othello (1602–4) act 1, sc. 3, l. 158

3 She loved me for the dangers I had passed,
And I loved her that she did pity them.
   Othello (1602–4) act 1, sc. 3, l. 167

4 I do perceive here a divided duty.
   Othello (1602–4) act 1, sc. 3, l. 181

5 The robbed that smiles steals something from the thief.
   Othello (1602–4) act 1, sc. 3, l. 208

6 But words are words; I never yet did hear
That the bruised heart was piercèd through the ear.
   Othello (1602–4) act 1, sc. 3, l. 218

7 The tyrant custom, most grave senators,
Hath made the flinty and steel couch of war
My thrice-driven bed of down.
   Othello (1602–4) act 1, sc. 3, l. [230]

8   If I be left behind,
A moth of peace, and he go to the war,
The rites for which I love him are bereft me,
And I a heavy interim shall support
By his dear absence. Let me go with him.
   Othello (1602–4) act 1, sc. 3, l. [257]

9 RODERIGO: I will incontinently drown myself.
IAGO: Well, if thou dost, I shall never love thee after.
  Why, thou silly gentleman!
RODERIGO: It is silliness to live when to live is
  torment; and then have we a prescription to die
  when death is our physician.
   Othello (1602–4) act 1, sc. 3, l. [307]

10 Virtue! a fig! 'tis in ourselves that we are thus, or
thus. Our bodies are our gardens, to the which our
wills are gardeners.
   Othello (1602–4) act 1, sc. 3, l. [323]

11 There are many events in the womb of time which
will be delivered.
   Othello (1602–4) act 1, sc. 3, l. [377]

12 He hath a person and a smooth dispose
Framed to make women false.
The Moor is of a free and open nature,
That thinks men honest that but seem to be so.
   Othello (1602–4) act 1, sc. 3, l. [403]

13 I have't; it is engendered; hell and night
Must bring this monstrous birth to the world's light.
   Othello (1602–4) act 1, sc. 3, l. [409]

14 Our great captain's captain.
   Othello (1602–4) act 2, sc. 1, l. 74

15   You are pictures out of doors,
Bells in your parlours, wild cats in your kitchens,
Saints in your injuries, devils being offended,
Players in your housewifery, and housewives in your
  beds.
   Othello (1602–4) act 2, sc. 1, l. 109

16   Do not put me to't,
For I am nothing if not critical.
   Othello (1602–4) act 2, sc. 1, l. 118

17 I am not merry, but I do beguile
The thing I am by seeming otherwise.
   Othello (1602–4) act 2, sc. 1, l. 122

18 To suckle fools and chronicle small beer.
   Othello (1602–4) act 2, sc. 1, l. 163

19 With as little a web as this will I ensnare as great a fly
as Cassio.
   Othello (1602–4) act 2, sc. 1, l. [169]

20   If it were now to die,
'Twere now to be most happy.
   Othello (1602–4) act 2, sc. 1, l. [192]

21 A slipper and subtle knave, a finder-out of occasions,
that has an eye can stamp and counterfeit advantages,
though true advantage never present itself; a devilish
knave! Besides, the knave is handsome, young, and
hath all those requisites in him that folly and green
minds look after; a pestilent complete knave! and the
woman hath found him already.
   Othello (1602–4) act 2, sc. 1, l. [247]

22 Make the Moor thank me, love me, and reward me
For making him egregiously an ass
And practising upon his peace and quiet
Even to madness.
   Othello (1602–4) act 2, sc. 1, l. [320]

23 I have very poor and unhappy brains for drinking: I
could well wish courtesy would invent some other
custom of entertainment.
   Othello (1602–4) act 2, sc. 3, l. [34]

24 CASSIO: 'Fore God, an excellent song.
IAGO: I learned it in England, where indeed they are
  most potent in potting; your Dane, your German,
  and your swag-bellied Hollander,—drink, ho!—are
  nothing to your English.
   Othello (1602–4) act 2, sc. 3, l. [78]

25 'Tis pride that pulls the country down.
   Othello (1602–4) act 2, sc. 3, l. [99]

1 Silence that dreadful bell! it frights the isle
From her propriety.
   Othello (1602–4) act 2, sc. 3, l. [177]

2 But men are men; the best sometimes forget.
   Othello (1602–4) act 2, sc. 3, l. [243]

3 Thy honesty and love doth mince this matter.
   Othello (1602–4) act 2, sc. 3, l. [249]

4 O! I have lost my reputation. I have lost the immortal
part of myself, and what remains is bestial.
   Othello (1602–4) act 2, sc. 3, l. [264]

5 O thou invisible spirit of wine! if thou hast no name to
be known by, let us call thee devil!
   Othello (1602–4) act 2, sc. 3, l. [285]

6 O God! that men should put an enemy in their
mouths to steal away their brains; that we should,
with joy, pleasance, revel, and applause, transform
ourselves into beasts.
   Othello (1602–4) act 2, sc. 3, l. [293]

7 Come, come; good wine is a good familiar creature if
it be well used; exclaim no more against it.
   Othello (1602–4) act 2, sc. 3, l. [315]

8 How poor are they that have not patience!
What wound did ever heal but by degrees?
   Othello (1602–4) act 2, sc. 3, l. [379]

9 O! thereby hangs a tail.
   Othello (1602–4) act 3, sc. 1, l. [8]

10 Excellent wretch! Perdition catch my soul
But I do love thee! and when I love thee not,
Chaos is come again.
   Othello (1602–4) act 3, sc. 3, l. 90

11 By heaven, he echoes me,
As if there were some monster in his thought
Too hideous to be shown.
   Othello (1602–4) act 3, sc. 3, l. 106

12 Good name in man and woman, dear my lord,
Is the immediate jewel of their souls;
Who steals my purse steals trash; 'tis something,
   nothing;
'Twas mine, 'tis his, and has been slave to thousands;
But he that filches from me my good name
Robs me of that which not enriches him,
And makes me poor indeed.
   Othello (1602–4) act 3, sc. 1, l. 155

13   O! beware, my lord, of jealousy;
It is the green-eyed monster which doth mock
The meat it feeds on.
   Othello (1602–4) act 3, sc. 1, l. 165

14 In Venice they do let heaven see the pranks
They dare not show their husbands; their best
   conscience
Is not to leave't undone, but keep't unknown.
   Othello (1602–4) act 3, sc. 1, l. 202

15 Not to affect many proposèd matches
Of her own clime, complexion, and degree,
Whereto, we see, in all things nature tends;
Foh! one may smell in such, a will most rank,
Foul disposition, thoughts unnatural.
   Othello (1602–4) act 3, sc. 3, l. 229

16   If I do prove her haggard,
Though that her jesses were my dear heart-strings,
I'd whistle her off and let her down the wind,
To prey at fortune. Haply, for I am black,
And have not those soft parts of conversation
That chamberers have, or, for I am declined
Into the vale of years—yet that's not much—
She's gone, I am abused; and my relief
Must be to loathe her. O curse of marriage!
That we can call these delicate creatures ours,
And not their appetites. I had rather be a toad,
And live upon the vapour of a dungeon,
Than keep a corner in the thing I love
For others' uses.
   Othello (1602–4) act 3, sc. 3, l. 260

17 If she be false, O! then heaven mocks itself.
I'll not believe it.
   Othello (1602–4) act 3, sc. 3, l. 278

18   Trifles light as air
Are to the jealous confirmations strong
As proofs of holy writ.
   Othello (1602–4) act 3, sc. 3, l. 323

19   Not poppy, nor mandragora,
Nor all the drowsy syrups of the world,
Shall ever medicine thee to that sweet sleep
Which thou owedst yesterday.
   Othello (1602–4) act 3, sc. 3, l. 331

20 I had been happy, if the general camp,
Pioneers and all, had tasted her sweet body,
So I had nothing known. O! now, for ever
Farewell the tranquil mind; farewell content!
Farewell the plumèd troop and the big wars
That make ambition virtue! O, farewell!
Farewell the neighing steed and the shrill trump,
The spirit-stirring drum, the ear-piercing fife,
The royal banner, and all quality,
Pride, pomp, and circumstance of glorious war!
And, O you mortal engines, whose rude throats
The immortal Jove's dread clamours counterfeit,
Farewell! Othello's occupation's gone!
   Othello (1602–4) act 3, sc. 3, l. 346

21   O wretched fool!
That liv'st to make thine honesty a vice.
O monstrous world! Take note, take note, O world!
To be direct and honest is not safe.
   Othello (1602–4) act 3, sc. 3, l. 376

22 This denoted a foregone conclusion.
   Othello (1602–4) act 3, sc. 3, l. 429

23   Like to the Pontick sea,
Whose icy current and compulsive course
Ne'er feels retiring ebb, but keeps due on
To the Propontic and the Hellespont,
Even so my bloody thoughts, with violent pace,
Shall ne'er look back, ne'er ebb to humble love,
Till that a capable and wide revenge
Swallow them up.
   Othello (1602–4) act 3, sc. 3, l. 454

1 For here's a young and sweating devil here,
That commonly rebels. 'Tis a good hand,
A frank one.
  Othello (1602–4) act 3, sc. 4, l. 43

2 That handkerchief
Did an Egyptian to my mother give.
  Othello (1602–4) act 3, sc. 4, l. 56

3 'Tis true; there's magic in the web of it;
A sibyl, that had numbered in the world
The sun to course two hundred compasses,
In her prophetic fury sewed the work;
The worms were hallowed that did breed the silk,
And it was dyed in mummy which the skilful
Conserved of maidens' hearts.
  Othello (1602–4) act 3, sc. 4, l. 70

4 Jealous souls will not be answered so;
They are not ever jealous for the cause,
But jealous for they are jealous.
  Othello (1602–4) act 3, sc. 4, l. 158

5 What! keep a week away? seven days and nights?
Eight score eight hours? and lovers' absent hours,
More tedious than the dial eight score times?
O, weary reckoning!
  Othello (1602–4) act 3, sc. 4, l. 172

6   O! it comes o'er my memory,
As doth the raven o'er the infected house,
Boding to all.
  Othello (1602–4) act 4, sc. 1, l. 20

7 Work on,
My medicine, work! Thus credulous fools are caught.
  Othello (1602–4) act 4, sc. 1, l. 45

8 'Tis the strumpet's plague
To beguile many and be beguiled by one.
  Othello (1602–4) act 4, sc. 1, l. 97

9 My heart is turned to stone; I strike it, and it hurts my
hand. O! the world hath not a sweeter creature; she
might lie by an emperor's side and command him
tasks.
  Othello (1602–4) act 4, sc. 1, l. [190]

10 An admirable musician! O, she will sing the
savageness out of a bear.
  Othello (1602–4) act 4, sc. 1, l. [197]

11 But yet the pity of it, Iago! O! Iago, the pity of it,
Iago!
  Othello (1602–4) act 4, sc. 1, l. [205]

12 O well-painted passion!
  Othello (1602–4) act 4, sc. 1, l. [268]

13   Is this the noble nature
Whom passion could not shake? whose solid virtue
The shot of accident nor dart of chance
Could neither graze nor pierce?
  Othello (1602–4) act 4, sc. 1, l. [277]

14 Your mystery, your mystery; nay, dispatch.
  Othello (1602–4) act 4, sc. 2, l. 29

15   Had it pleased heaven
To try me with affliction, had he rained
All kinds of sores, and shames, on my bare head,
Steeped me in poverty to the very lips,
Given to captivity me and my utmost hopes,
I should have found in some part of my soul
A drop of patience; but, alas! to make me
The fixèd figure for the time of scorn
To point his slow and moving finger at;
Yet could I bear that too; well, very well.
But there, where I have garnered up my heart,
Where either I must live or bear no life,
The fountain from the which my current runs
Or else dries up; to be discarded thence!
Or keep it as a cistern for foul toads
To knot and gender in! Turn thy complexion there,
Patience, thou young and rose-lipped cherubin;
Ay, there, look grim as hell!
  Othello (1602–4) act 4, sc. 2, l. 46

16   O thou weed!
Who art so lovely fair and smell'st so sweet
That the sense aches at thee, would thou hadst ne'er
been born!
  Othello (1602–4) act 4, sc. 2, l. 66

17 Heaven stops the nose at it and the moon winks.
  Othello (1602–4) act 4, sc. 2, l. 76

18   I cry you mercy, then;
I took you for that cunning whore of Venice
That married with Othello. You, mistress,
That have the office opposite to Saint Peter,
And keep the gate of hell!
  Othello (1602–4) act 4, sc. 2, l. 87

19 Those that do teach young babes
Do it with gentle means and easy tasks;
He might have chid me so; for, in good faith,
I am a child to chiding.
  Othello (1602–4) act 4, sc. 2, l. 111

20   Unkindness may do much;
And his unkindness may defeat my life,
But never taint my love.
  Othello (1602–4) act 4, sc. 2, l. 159

21   My love doth so approve him,
That even his stubbornness, his checks and frowns . . .

Have grace and favour in them.
  Othello (1602–4) act 4, sc. 3, l. 19

22 The poor soul sat sighing by a sycamore tree,
Sing all a green willow;
Her hand on her bosom, her head on her knee,
Sing willow, willow, willow:
The fresh streams ran by her, and murmured her
moans;
Sing willow, willow, willow:
Her salt tears fell from her, and softened the stones;—
Sing willow, willow, willow:
Sing all a green willow must be my garland.
  Othello (1602–4) act 4, sc. 3, l. [41]. Cf. Heywood
  338:4

23 DESDEMONA: Mine eyes do itch;
Doth that bode weeping?
EMILIA: 'Tis neither here nor there.
  Othello (1602–4) act 4, sc. 3, l. [59]

1 Who would not make her husband a cuckold to make
  him a monarch?
    Othello (1602–4) act 4, sc. 3, l. [76]

2   Let husbands know
Their wives have sense like them. They see, and smell,
And have their palates both for sweet and sour,
As husbands have.
    Othello (1602–4) act 4, sc. 3, l. 93

3 He hath a daily beauty in his life.
  That makes me ugly.
    Othello (1602–4) act 5, sc. 1, l. 19

4   This is the night
That either makes me or fordoes me quite.
    Othello (1602–4) act 5, sc. 1, l. 128

5 It is the cause, it is the cause, my soul;
Let me not name it to you, you chaste stars!
It is the cause. Yet I'll not shed her blood,
Nor scar that whiter skin of hers than snow,
And smooth as monumental alabaster.
Yet she must die, else she'll betray more men.
Put out the light, and then put out the light:
If I quench thee, thou flaming minister,
I can again thy former light restore,
Should I repent me; but once put out thy light,
Thou cunning'st pattern of excelling nature,
I know not where is that Promethean heat
That can thy light relume. When I have plucked the
  rose,
I cannot give it vital growth again,
It needs must wither: I'll smell it on the tree.
O balmy breath, that dost almost persuade
Justice to break her sword! One more, one more.
Be thus when thou art dead, and I will kill thee,
And love thee after. One more, and this the last:
So sweet was ne'er so fatal. I must weep,
But they are cruel tears; this sorrow's heavenly,
It strikes where it doth love.
    Othello (1602–4) act 5, sc. 2, l. 1

6 Alas! why gnaw you so your nether lip?
Some bloody passion shakes your very frame;
These are portents, but yet, I hope, I hope
They do not point on me.
    Othello (1602–4) act 5, sc. 2, l. 43

7 Kill me to-morrow; let me live to-night!
    Othello (1602–4) act 5, sc. 2, l. 80

8 It is the very error of the moon;
She comes more near the earth than she was wont,
And makes men mad.
    Othello (1602–4) act 5, sc. 2, l. 107

9   Murder's out of tune,
And sweet revenge grows harsh.
    Othello (1602–4) act 5, sc. 2, l. 113

10 OTHELLO: She's like a liar gone to burning hell;
    'Twas I that killed her.
  EMILIA: O! the more angel she,
    And you the blacker devil.
    Othello (1602–4) act 5, sc. 2, l. 127

11   Nay, had she been true,
If heaven would make me such another world
Of one entire and perfect chrysolite,
I'd not have sold her for it.
    Othello (1602–4) act 5, sc. 2, l. 141

12   May his pernicious soul
Rot half a grain a day! he lies to the heart:
She was too fond of her most filthy bargain.
    Othello (1602–4) act 5, sc. 2, l. 153

13 Thou hast not half the power to do me harm
As I have to be hurt.
    Othello (1602–4) act 5, sc. 2, l. 160

14   Are there no stones in heaven
But what serve for the thunder?
    Othello (1602–4) act 5, sc. 2, l. 232

15   I will play the swan,
And die in music.
    Othello (1602–4) act 5, sc. 2, l. 245

16 Who can control his fate?
    Othello (1602–4) act 5, sc. 2, l. 264

17 Be not afraid, though you do see me weaponed;
Here is my journey's end, here is my butt,
And very sea-mark of my utmost sail.
    Othello (1602–4) act 5, sc. 2, l. 265

18   O ill-starred wench!
Pale as thy smock! when we shall meet at compt,
This look of thine will hurl my soul from heaven,
And fiends will snatch at it. Cold, cold, my girl!
Even like thy chastity.
O! cursèd, cursèd slave. Whip me, ye devils,
From the possession of this heavenly sight!
Blow me about in winds! roast me in sulphur!
Wash me in steep-down gulfs of liquid fire!
O Desdemona! Desdemona! dead!
    Othello (1602–4) act 5, sc. 2, l. 271

19 An honourable murderer, if you will;
For nought did I in hate, but all in honour.
    Othello (1602–4) act 5, sc. 2, l. 293

20 I have done the state some service, and they know 't;
No more of that. I pray you, in your letters,
When you shall these unlucky deeds relate,
Speak of me as I am; nothing extenuate,
Nor set down aught in malice: then, must you speak
Of one that loved not wisely but too well;
Of one not easily jealous, but, being wrought,
Perplexed in the extreme; of one whose hand,
Like the base Indian, threw a pearl away
Richer than all his tribe; of one whose subdued eyes
Albeit unusèd to the melting mood,
Drop tears as fast as the Arabian trees
Their med'cinable gum. Set you down this;
And say besides, that in Aleppo once,
Where a malignant and a turbaned Turk
Beat a Venetian and traduced the state,
I took by the throat the circumcised dog,
And smote him thus.
    Othello (1602–4) act 5, sc. 2, l. 338

21 GRATIANO: All that's spoke is marred.
  OTHELLO: I kissed thee ere I killed thee, no way but
    this,
    Killing myself to die upon a kiss.
    Othello (1602–4) act 5, sc. 2, l. 356

Pericles

22 See where she comes apparelled like the spring.
    Pericles (1606–8) act 1, sc. 1, l. 12

23 Few love to hear the sins they love to act.
    Pericles (1606–8) act 1, sc. 1, l. 92

1 THIRD FISHERMAN: Master, I marvel how the fishes
live in the sea.
FIRST FISHERMAN: Why, as men do a-land: the great
ones eat up the little ones.
Pericles (1606–8) act 2, sc. 1, l. 26. Cf. Sidney 646:10

2   O you gods!
Why do you make us love your goodly gifts,
And snatch them straight away?
Pericles (1606–8) act 3, sc. 1, l. 22

3 A terrible childbed hast thou had, my dear,
No light, no fire. Th' unfriendly elements
Forgot thee utterly, nor have I time
To give thee hallowed to thy grave, but straight
Must cast thee, scarcely coffined, in the ooze,
Where, for a monument upon thy bones
And aye-remaining lamps, the belching whale
And humming water must o'erwhelm thy corpse,
Lying with simple shells.
Pericles (1606–8) act 3, sc. 1, l. 56

4 This world to me is but a ceaseless storm
Whirring me from my friends.
Pericles (1606–8) act 4, sc. 1, l. 19

5 Give me a gash, put me to present pain,
Lest this great sea of joys rushing upon me
O'erbear the shores of my mortality
And drown me in their sweetness!
Pericles (1606–8) act 5, sc. 1, l. 193

Richard II

6 Old John of Gaunt, time-honoured Lancaster.
Richard II (1595) act 1, sc. 1, l. 1

7 The purest treasure mortal times afford
Is spotless reputation; that away,
Men are but gilded loam or painted clay.
A jewel in a ten-times-barred-up chest
Is a bold spirit in a loyal breast.
Mine honour is my life; both grow in one;
Take honour from me, and my life is done.
Richard II (1595) act 1, sc. 1, l. 177

8 We were not born to sue, but to command.
Richard II (1595) act 1, sc. 1, l. 196

9 The language I have learned these forty years,
My native English, now I must forego;
And now my tongue's use is to me no more
Than an unstringèd viol or a harp.
Richard II (1595) act 1, sc. 3, l. 159

10 How long a time lies in one little word!
Four lagging winters and four wanton springs
End in a word; such is the breath of kings.
Richard II (1595) act 1, sc. 3, l. 213

11 Things sweet to taste prove in digestion sour.
Richard II (1595) act 1, sc. 3, l. 236

12 Must I not serve a long apprenticehood
To foreign passages, and in the end,
Having my freedom, boast of nothing else
But that I was a journeyman to grief?
Richard II (1595) act 1, sc. 3, l. 271

13 All places that the eye of heaven visits
Are to a wise man ports and happy havens.
Teach thy necessity to reason thus;
There is no virtue like necessity.
Richard II (1595) act 1, sc. 3, l. 278

14 O! who can hold a fire in his hand
By thinking on the frosty Caucasus?
Or cloy the hungry edge of appetite,
By bare imagination of a feast?
Or wallow naked in December snow
By thinking on fantastic summer's heat?
O, no! the apprehension of the good
Gives but the greater feeling to the worse.
Richard II (1595) act 1, sc. 3, l. 294

15   They say the tongues of dying men
Enforce attention, like deep harmony.
Richard II (1595) act 2, sc. 1, l. 5

16 More are men's ends marked than their lives before:
The setting sun, and music at the close,
As the last taste of sweets, is sweetest last,
Writ in remembrance more than things long past.
Richard II (1595) act 2, sc. 1, l. 11

17 His rash fierce blaze of riot cannot last,
For violent fires soon burn out themselves;
Small showers last long, but sudden storms are short;
He tires betimes that spurs too fast betimes.
Richard II (1595) act 2, sc. 1, l. 33

18 This royal throne of kings, this sceptered isle,
This earth of majesty, this seat of Mars,
This other Eden, demi-paradise,
This fortress built by Nature for herself
Against infection and the hand of war,
This happy breed of men, this little world,
This precious stone set in the silver sea,
Which serves it in the office of a wall,
Or as a moat defensive to a house,
Against the envy of less happier lands,
This blessèd plot, this earth, this realm, this England,
This nurse, this teeming womb of royal kings,
Feared by their breed and famous by their birth,
Renownèd for their deeds as far from home,—
For Christian service and true chivalry,—
As is the sepulchre in stubborn Jewry
Of the world's ransom, blessèd Mary's Son:
This land of such dear souls, this dear, dear land,
Dear for her reputation through the world,
Is now leased out,—I die pronouncing it,—
Like to a tenement or pelting farm:
England, bound in with the triumphant sea,
Whose rocky shore beats back the envious siege
Of watery Neptune, is now bound in with shame,
With inky blots, and rotten parchment bonds:
That England, that was wont to conquer others,
Hath made a shameful conquest of itself.
Richard II (1595) act 2, sc. 1, l. 40

19 I am a stranger here in Gloucestershire:
These high wild hills and rough uneven ways
Draw out our miles and make them wearisome.
Richard II (1595) act 2, sc. 3, l. 2

20 I count myself in nothing else so happy
As in a soul remembering my good friends.
Richard II (1595) act 2, sc. 3, l. 46

21 Grace me no grace, nor uncle me no uncle.
Richard II (1595) act 2, sc. 3, l. 87

22 The caterpillars of the commonwealth.
Richard II (1595) act 2, sc. 3, l. 166

1 Things past redress are now with me past care.
Richard II (1595) act 2, sc. 3, l. 171

2 Eating the bitter bread of banishment.
Richard II (1595) act 3, sc. 1, l. 21

3 Not all the water in the rough rude sea
Can wash the balm from an anointed king;
The breath of worldly men cannot depose
The deputy elected by the Lord.
For every man that Bolingbroke hath pressed
To lift shrewd steel against our golden crown,
God for his Richard hath in heavenly pay
A glorious angel; then, if angels fight,
Weak men must fall, for heaven still guards the right.
Richard II (1595) act 3, sc. 2, l. 54

4 O! call back yesterday, bid time return.
Richard II (1595) act 3, sc. 2, l. 69

5 Is not the king's name twenty thousand names?
Arm, arm, my name! A puny subject strikes
At thy great glory.
Richard II (1595) act 3, sc. 2, l. 85

6 The worst is death, and death will have his day.
Richard II (1595) act 3, sc. 2, l. 103

7   Of comfort no man speak:
Let's talk of graves, of worms, and epitaphs;
Make dust our paper, and with rainy eyes
Write sorrow on the bosom of the earth.
Let's choose executors, and talk of wills.
Richard II (1595) act 3, sc. 2, l. 144

8 For God's sake, let us sit upon the ground
And tell sad stories of the death of kings:
How some have been deposed, some slain in war,
Some haunted by the ghosts they have deposed,
Some poisoned by their wives, some sleeping killed;
All murdered: for within the hollow crown
That rounds the mortal temples of a king
Keeps Death his court, and there the antick sits,
Scoffing his state and grinning at his pomp;
Allowing him a breath, a little scene,
To monarchize, be feared, and kill with looks,
Infusing him with self and vain conceit
As if this flesh which walls about our life
Were brass impregnable; and humoured thus
Comes at the last, and with a little pin
Bores through his castle wall, and farewell king!
Richard II (1595) act 3, sc. 2, l. 155

9 See, see, King Richard doth himself appear,
As doth the blushing discontented sun
From out the fiery portal of the east.
Richard II (1595) act 3, sc. 3, l. 62

10 The purple testament of bleeding war.
Richard II (1595) act 3, sc. 3, l. 94

11   O! that I were as great
As is my grief, or lesser than my name,
Or that I could forget what I have been,
Or not remember what I must be now.
Richard II (1595) act 3, sc. 3, l. 136

12 What must the king do now? Must he submit?
The king shall do it: must he be deposed?
The king shall be contented: must he lose
The name of king? o' God's name, let it go.
I'll give my jewels for a set of beads,
My gorgeous palace for a hermitage,
My gay apparel for an almsman's gown,
My figured goblets for a dish of wood,
My sceptre for a palmer's walking staff,
My subjects for a pair of carved saints,
And my large kingdom for a little grave,
A little little grave, an obscure grave;
Or I'll be buried in the king's highway,
Some way of common trade, where subjects' feet
May hourly trample on their sovereign's head;
For on my heart they tread now whilst I live;
And buried once, why not upon my head?
Richard II (1595) act 3, sc. 3, l. 143

13 Shall we play the wantons with our woes,
And make some pretty match with shedding tears?
Richard II (1595) act 3, sc. 3, l. 164

14 Go, bind thou up yon dangling apricocks,
Which, like unruly children, make their sire
Stoop with oppression of their prodigal weight.
Richard II (1595) act 3, sc. 4, l. 29

15 Old Adam's likeness, set to dress this garden.
Richard II (1595) act 3, sc. 4, l. 73

16 Here did she fall a tear; here, in this place,
I'll set a bank of rue, sour herb of grace;
Rue, even for ruth, here shortly shall be seen,
In the remembrance of a weeping queen.
Richard II (1595) act 3, sc. 4, l. 104

17 Peace shall go sleep with Turks and infidels,
And in this seat of peace tumultuous wars
Shall kin with kin and kind with kind confound;
Disorder, horror, fear and mutiny
Shall here inhabit, and this land be called
The field of Golgotha and dead men's skulls.
Richard II (1595) act 4, sc. 1, l. 139

18 God save the king! Will no man say, amen?
Am I both priest and clerk? Well then, amen.
Richard II (1595) act 4, sc. 1, l. 172

19 Give me the crown. Here, cousin, seize the crown;
Here cousin,
On this side my hand and on that side thine.
Now is this golden crown like a deep well
That owes two buckets filling one another;
The emptier ever dancing in the air,
The other down, unseen, and full of water:
That bucket down and full of tears am I,
Drinking my griefs, whilst you mount up on high.
Richard II (1595) act 4, sc. 1, l. 181

20 You may my glories and my state depose,
But not my griefs; still am I king of those.
Richard II (1595) act 4, sc. 1, l. 192

21 Now mark me how I will undo myself.
Richard II (1595) act 4, sc. 1, l. 203

22 With mine own tears I wash away my balm,
With mine own hands I give away my crown.
Richard II (1595) act 4, sc. 1, l. 207

1 Mine eyes are full of tears, I cannot see:
And yet salt water blinds them not so much
But they can see a sort of traitors here.
Nay, if I turn my eyes upon myself,
I find myself a traitor with the rest.
Richard II (1595) act 4, sc. 1, l. 244

2 A brittle glory shineth in this face:
As brittle as the glory is the face.
Richard II (1595) act 4, sc. 1, l. 287

3   This is the way
To Julius Caesar's ill-erected tower.
Richard II (1595) act 5, sc. 1, l. 1

4   I am sworn brother, sweet,
To grim Necessity, and he and I
Will keep a league till death.
Richard II (1595) act 5, sc. 1, l. 20

5 In winter's tedious nights sit by the fire
With good old folks, and let them tell thee tales
Of woeful ages, long ago betid;
And ere thou bid good night, to quit their grief,
Tell thou the lamentable tale of me,
And send the hearers weeping to their beds.
Richard II (1595) act 5, sc. 1, l. 40

6 That were some love but little policy.
Richard II (1595) act 5, sc. 1, l. 84

7 As in a theatre, the eyes of men,
After a well-graced actor leaves the stage,
Are idly bent on him that enters next,
Thinking his prattle to be tedious;
Even so, or with much more contempt, men's eyes
Did scowl on Richard.
Richard II (1595) act 5, sc. 2, l. 23

8   Who are the violets now
That strew the green lap of the new come spring?
Richard II (1595) act 5, sc. 2, l. 46

9 He prays but faintly and would be denied.
Richard II (1595) act 5, sc. 3, l. 103

10 I have been studying how I may compare
This prison where I live unto the world.
Richard II (1595) act 5, sc. 5, l. 1

11   How sour sweet music is,
When time is broke, and no proportion kept!
So is it in the music of men's lives.
Richard II (1595) act 5, sc. 5, l. 42

12 I wasted time, and now doth time waste me.
Richard II (1595) act 5, sc. 5, l. 49

13 Mount, mount, my soul! thy seat is up on high,
Whilst my gross flesh sinks downwards here to die.
Richard II (1595) act 5, sc. 5, l. 112

Richard III

14 Now is the winter of our discontent
Made glorious summer by this sun of York.
Richard III (1591) act 1, sc. 1, l. 1

15 Grim-visaged war hath smoothed his wrinkled front;
And now, instead of mounting barbèd steeds,
To fright the souls of fearful adversaries,—
He capers nimbly in a lady's chamber
To the lascivious pleasing of a lute.
But I, that am not shaped for sportive tricks,
Nor made to court an amorous looking-glass;
I, that am rudely stamped, and want love's majesty
To strut before a wanton ambling nymph;
I, that am curtailed of this fair proportion,
Cheated of feature by dissembling nature,
Deformed, unfinished, sent before my time
Into this breathing world, scarce half made up,
And that so lamely and unfashionable
That dogs bark at me, as I halt by them;
Why, I, in this weak piping time of peace,
Have no delight to pass away the time.
Richard III (1591) act 1, sc. 1, l. 9

16 And therefore, since I cannot prove a lover,
To entertain these fair well-spoken days,
I am determinèd to prove a villain,
And hate the idle pleasures of these days.
Richard III (1591) act 1, sc. 1, l. 28

17 No beast so fierce but knows some touch of pity.
Richard III (1591) act 1, sc. 2, l. 71

18 Teach not thy lip such scorn, for it was made
For kissing, lady, not for such contempt.
Richard III (1591) act 1, sc. 2, l. 172

19 Was ever woman in this humour wooed?
Was ever woman in this humour won?
I'll have her, but I will not keep her long.
Richard III (1591) act 1, sc. 2, l. 229

20 Cannot a plain man live and think no harm,
But that his simple truth must be abused
By silken, sly, insinuating Jacks?
Richard III (1591) act 1, sc. 3, l. 51

21 Since every Jack became a gentleman
There's many a gentle person made a Jack.
Richard III (1591) act 1, sc. 3, l. 72

22 And thus I clothe my naked villany
With odd old ends stol'n forth of holy writ,
And seem a saint when most I play the devil.
Richard III (1591) act 1, sc. 3, l. 336

23 Lord, Lord! methought what pain it was to drown:
What dreadful noise of water in mine ears!
What sights of ugly death within mine eyes!
Methought I saw a thousand fearful wracks;
A thousand men that fishes gnawed upon;
Wedges of gold, great anchors, heaps of pearl,
Inestimable stones, unvalued jewels,
All scattered in the bottom of the sea.
Some lay in dead men's skulls; and in those holes
Where eyes did once inhabit, there were crept
As 'twere in scorn of eyes, reflecting gems,
That wooed the slimy bottom of the deep,
And mocked the dead bones that lay scattered by.
Richard III (1591) act 1, sc. 4, l. 21

24 Clarence is come,—false, fleeting, perjured Clarence.
Richard III (1591) act 1, sc. 4, l. 55

25 Woe to the land that's governed by a child!
Richard III (1591) act 2, sc. 3, l. 11. Cf. Ecclesiastes 00.23.

1 So wise so young, they say, do never live long.
Richard III (1591) act 3, sc. 1, l. 79

2 Talk'st thou to me of 'ifs'? Thou art a traitor:
Off with his head!
Richard III (1591) act 3, sc. 4, l. 74

3 I am not in the giving vein to-day.
Richard III (1591) act 4, sc. 2, l. 115

4 The sons of Edward sleep in Abraham's bosom.
Richard III (1591) act 4, sc. 3, l. 38

5 Thou cam'st on earth to make the earth my hell.
A grievous burden was thy birth to me;
Tetchy and wayward was thy infancy,
Thy school-days frightful, desperate, wild and furious;
Thy prime of manhood daring, bold, and venturous;
Thy age confirmed, proud, subtle, sly, and bloody,
More mild, but yet more harmful, kind in hatred;
What comfortable hour canst thou name
That ever graced me in thy company?
Richard III (1591) act 4, sc. 4, l. 167

6 An honest tale speeds best being plainly told.
Richard III (1591) act 4, sc. 4, l. 359

7 Harp not on that string.
Richard III (1591) act 4, sc. 4, l. 365

8 True hope is swift, and flies with swallow's wings;
Kings it makes gods, and meaner creatures kings.
Richard III (1591) act 5, sc. 2, l. 23

9 The king's name is a tower of strength.
Richard III (1591) act 5, sc. 3, l. 12

10 Give me another horse! bind up my wounds!
Have mercy, Jesu! Soft! I did but dream.
O coward conscience, how dost thou afflict me!
Richard III (1591) act 5, sc. 3, l. 178

11 My conscience hath a thousand several tongues,
And every tongue brings in a several tale,
And every tale condemns me for a villain.
Richard III (1591) act 5, sc. 3, l. 194

12 I shall despair. There is no creature loves me;
And if I die, no soul will pity me:
Nay, wherefore should they, since that I myself
Find in myself no pity to myself?
Richard III (1591) act 5, sc. 3, l. 201

13 By the apostle Paul, shadows to-night
Have struck more terror to the soul of Richard
Than can the substance of ten thousand soldiers.
Richard III (1591) act 5, sc. 3, l. 217

14 Conscience is but a word that cowards use,
Devised at first to keep the strong in awe.
Richard III (1591) act 5, sc. 3, l. 310

15 A horse! a horse! my kingdom for a horse!
Richard III (1591) act 5, sc. 4, l. 7

16 Slave! I have set my life upon a cast,
And I will stand the hazard of the die.
Richard III (1591) act 5, sc. 4, l. 9

Romeo and Juliet

17 From forth the fatal loins of these two foes
A pair of star-crossed lovers take their life.
Romeo and Juliet (1595) prologue

18 The fearful passage of their death-marked love,
And the continuance of their parents' rage,
Which, but their children's end, nought could remove,
Is now the two hours' traffick of our stage.
Romeo and Juliet (1595) prologue

19   'Tis not hard, I think,
For men so old as we to keep the peace.
Romeo and Juliet (1595) act 1, sc. 2, l. 2

20 PARIS: Younger than she are happy mothers made.
CAPULET: And too soon marred are those so early
made.
Romeo and Juliet (1595) act 1, sc. 2, l. 12

21 O! then, I see, Queen Mab hath been with you ...
She is the fairies' midwife, and she comes
In shape no bigger than an agate-stone
On the forefinger of an alderman,
Drawn with a team of little atomies
Athwart men's noses as they lie asleep.
Romeo and Juliet (1595) act 1, sc. 4, l. 53

22 This is the hag, when maids lie on their backs,
That presses them and learns them first to bear,
Making them women of good carriage.
Romeo and Juliet (1595) act 1, sc. 4, l. 93

23 You and I are past our dancing days.
Romeo and Juliet (1595) act 1, sc. 5, l. [35]

24 O! she doth teach the torches to burn bright.
It seems she hangs upon the cheek of night
Like a rich jewel in an Ethiop's ear;
Beauty too rich for use, for earth too dear.
Romeo and Juliet (1595) act 1, sc. 5, l. [48]

25   Gentlemen, prepare not to be gone;
We have a trifling foolish banquet towards.
Romeo and Juliet (1595) act 1, sc. 5, l. [125]

26 My only love sprung from my only hate!
Too early seen unknown, and known too late!
Romeo and Juliet (1595) act 1, sc. 5, l. [142]

27 He jests at scars, that never felt a wound.
But, soft! what light through yonder window breaks?
It is the east, and Juliet is the sun.
Romeo and Juliet (1595) act 2, sc. 2, l. 1

28 See! how she leans her cheek upon her hand:
O! that I were a glove upon that hand,
That I might touch that cheek.
Romeo and Juliet (1595) act 2, sc. 2, l. 23

29 O Romeo, Romeo! wherefore art thou Romeo?
Romeo and Juliet (1595) act 2, sc. 2, l. 33

30 What's in a name? that which we call a rose
By any other name would smell as sweet.
Romeo and Juliet (1595) act 2, sc. 2, l. 43

31 With love's light wings did I o'er-perch these walls;
For stony limits cannot hold love out,
And what love can do that dares love attempt.
Romeo and Juliet (1595) act 2, sc. 2, l. 66

32 Thou know'st the mask of night is on my face,
Else would a maiden blush bepaint my cheek
For that which thou hast heard me speak tonight.
Romeo and Juliet (1595) act 2, sc. 2, l. 85

33 Fain would I dwell on form, fain, fain deny
What I have spoke: but farewell compliment!
Romeo and Juliet (1595) act 2, sc. 2, l. 88

1   At lovers' perjuries,
They say, Jove laughs. O gentle Romeo!
If thou dost love, pronounce it faithfully:
Or if thou think'st I am too quickly won,
I'll frown and be perverse and say thee nay,
So thou wilt woo.
Romeo and Juliet (1595) act 2, sc. 2, l. 92

2 O! swear not by the moon, the inconstant moon,
That monthly changes in her circled orb,
Lest that thy love prove likewise variable.
Romeo and Juliet (1595) act 2, sc. 2, l. 109

3 It is too rash, too unadvised, too sudden;
Too like the lightning, which doth cease to be
Ere one can say it lightens. Sweet, good-night!
This bud of love, by summer's ripening breath,
May prove a beauteous flower when next we meet.
Romeo and Juliet (1595) act 2, sc. 2, l. 118

4 My bounty is as boundless as the sea,
My love as deep; the more I give to thee,
The more I have, for both are infinite.
Romeo and Juliet (1595) act 2, sc. 2, l. 133

5 Love goes toward love, as schoolboys from their
books;
But love from love, toward school with heavy looks.
Romeo and Juliet (1595) act 2, sc. 2, l. 156

6 JULIET: O! for a falconer's voice,
To lure this tassel-gentle back again.
Bondage is hoarse, and may not speak aloud,
Else would I tear the cave where Echo lies,
And make her airy tongue more hoarse than mine,
With repetition of my Romeo's name.
ROMEO: It is my soul that calls upon my name:
How silver-sweet sound lovers' tongues by night,
Like softest music to attending ears!
Romeo and Juliet (1595) act 2, sc. 2, l. 158

7 JULIET: 'Tis almost morning; I would have thee gone;
And yet no further than a wanton's bird,
Who lets it hop a little from her hand,
Like a poor prisoner in his twisted gyves,
And with a silk thread plucks it back again,
So loving-jealous of his liberty.
ROMEO: I would I were thy bird.
JULIET: Sweet, so would I:
Yet I should kill thee with much cherishing.
Good-night, good-night! parting is such sweet sorrow
That I shall say good-night till it be morrow.
Romeo and Juliet (1595) act 2, sc. 2, l. 176

8 O flesh, flesh, how art thou fishified!
Romeo and Juliet (1595) act 2, sc. 4, l. [41]

9 I am the very pink of courtesy.
Romeo and Juliet (1595) act 2, sc. 4, l. [63]

10 A gentleman, nurse, that loves to hear himself talk,
and will speak more in a minute than he will stand to
in a month.
Romeo and Juliet (1595) act 2, sc. 4, l. [156]

11   O! so light a foot
Will ne'er wear out the everlasting flint.
Romeo and Juliet (1595) act 2, sc. 6, l. 16

12 Thy head is as full of quarrels as an egg is full of meat.
Romeo and Juliet (1595) act 3, sc. 1, l. [23]

13 No, 'tis not so deep as a well, nor so wide as a church
door; but 'tis enough, 'twill serve.
Romeo and Juliet (1595) act 3, sc. 1, l. [100]

14 A plague o' both your houses!
Romeo and Juliet (1595) act 3, sc. 1, l. [112]

15 O! I am Fortune's fool.
Romeo and Juliet (1595) act 3, sc. 1, l. [142]

16 Gallop apace, you fiery-footed steeds,
Towards Phoebus' lodging; such a waggoner
As Phaethon would whip you to the west,
And bring in cloudy night immediately.
Spread thy close curtain, love-performing night!
That runaway's eyes may wink, and Romeo
Leap to these arms, untalked of and unseen!
Lovers can see to do their amorous rites
By their own beauties; or, if love be blind,
It best agrees with night. Come, civil night,
Thou sober-suited matron, all in black.
Romeo and Juliet (1595) act 3, sc. 2, l. 1

17 Come, night! come, Romeo! come, thou day in night!
For thou wilt lie upon the wings of night,
Whiter than new snow on a raven's back.
Come, gentle night; come, loving, black-browed night,
Give me my Romeo: and, when he shall die,
Take him and cut him out in little stars,
And he will make the face of heaven so fine
That all the world will be in love with night,
And pay no worship to the garish sun.
Romeo and Juliet (1595) act 3, sc. 2, l. 17

18 Romeo, come forth; come forth, thou fearful man:
Affliction is enamoured of thy parts,
And thou art wedded to calamity.
Romeo and Juliet (1595) act 3, sc. 3, l. 1

19 Thou cutt'st my head off with a golden axe,
And smil'st upon the stroke that murders me.
Romeo and Juliet (1595) act 3, sc. 3, l. 22

20 Adversity's sweet milk, philosophy.
Romeo and Juliet (1595) act 3, sc. 3, l. 54

21 O Lord, I could have stayed here all the night
To hear good counsel. O, what learning is!
Romeo and Juliet (1595) act 3, sc. 3, l. 159

22 Wilt thou be gone? it is not yet near day:
It was the nightingale, and not the lark,
That pierced the fearful hollow of thine ear.
Romeo and Juliet (1595) act 3, sc. 5, l. 1

23 Night's candles are burnt out, and jocund day
Stands tiptoe on the misty mountain tops.
Romeo and Juliet (1595) act 3, sc. 5, l. 9

24 I have more care to stay than will to go.
Romeo and Juliet (1595) act 3, sc. 5, l. 23

25 Thank me no thankings, nor proud me no prouds.
Romeo and Juliet (1595) act 3, sc. 5, l. 153

26 Is there no pity sitting in the clouds,
That sees into the bottom of my grief?
Romeo and Juliet (1595) act 3, sc. 5, l. 198

27 Romeo's a dishclout to him.
Romeo and Juliet (1595) act 3, sc. 5, l. 221

28 Farewell! God knows when we shall meet again.
I have a faint cold fear thrills through my veins,
That almost freezes up the heat of life.
Romeo and Juliet (1595) act 4, sc. 3, l. 14

1   Out, alas! she's cold;
Her blood is settled, and her joints are stiff;
Life and these lips have long been separated:
Death lies on her like an untimely frost
Upon the sweetest flower of all the field.
    Romeo and Juliet (1595) act 4, sc. 5, l. 25

2 My bosom's lord sits lightly on his throne;
And all this day an unaccustomed spirit
Lifts me above the ground with cheerful thoughts.
    Romeo and Juliet (1595) act 5, sc. 1, l. 3

3 Being holiday, the beggar's shop is shut.
    Romeo and Juliet (1595) act 5, sc. 1, l. 56

4 ROMEO: The world is not thy friend nor the world's
      law:
    The world affords no law to make thee rich;
    Then be not poor, but break it, and take this.
    APOTHECARY: My poverty, but not my will, consents.
    ROMEO: I pay thy poverty, and not thy will.
    Romeo and Juliet (1595) act 5, sc. 1, l. 72

5 Tempt not a desperate man.
    Romeo and Juliet (1595) act 5, sc. 3, l. 59

6 One writ with me in sour misfortune's book.
    Romeo and Juliet (1595) act 5, sc. 3, l. 82

7 How oft when men are at the point of death
Have they been merry! which their keepers call
A lightning before death.
    Romeo and Juliet (1595) act 5, sc. 3, l. 88

8   Beauty's ensign yet
Is crimson in thy lips and in thy cheeks,
And death's pale flag is not advancèd there.
    Romeo and Juliet (1595) act 5, sc. 3, l. 94

9   Shall I believe
That unsubstantial Death is amorous,
And that the lean abhorrèd monster keeps
Thee here in dark to be his paramour?
For fear of that I still will stay with thee,
And never from this palace of dim night
Depart again: here, here will I remain
With worms that are thy chambermaids; O! here
Will I set up my everlasting rest,
And shake the yoke of inauspicious stars
From this world-wearied flesh. Eyes, look your last!
Arms, take your last embrace! and, lips, O you
The doors of breath, seal with a righteous kiss
A dateless bargain to engrossing death!
    Romeo and Juliet (1595) act 5, sc. 3, l. 102

10 Seal up the mouth of outrage for a while,
Till we can clear these ambiguities.
    Romeo and Juliet (1595) act 5, sc. 3, l. 216

The Taming of the Shrew

11 Nothing comes amiss, so money comes withal.
    The Taming of the Shrew (1592) act 1, sc. 2, l. [82]

12 O! this learning, what a thing it is.
    The Taming of the Shrew (1592) act 1, sc. 2, l. [163]

13 She is your treasure, she must have a husband;
I must dance bare-foot on her wedding day,
And, for your love to her, lead apes in hell.
    The Taming of the Shrew (1592) act 2, sc. 1, l. 32

14 Say that she rail; why then I'll tell her plain
She sings as sweetly as a nightingale:
Say that she frown; I'll say she looks as clear
As morning roses newly washed with dew:
Say she be mute and will not speak a word;
Then I'll commend her volubility,
And say she uttereth piercing eloquence.
    The Taming of the Shrew (1592) act 2, sc. 1, l. 171

15   You are called plain Kate,
And bonny Kate, and sometimes Kate the curst;
But, Kate, the prettiest Kate in Christendom;
Kate of Kate-Hall, my super-dainty Kate,
For dainties are all cates; and therefore, Kate,
Take this of me, Kate of my consolation.
    The Taming of the Shrew (1592) act 2, sc. 1, l. 186

16 Kiss me Kate, we will be married o' Sunday.
    The Taming of the Shrew (1592) act 2, sc. 1, l. 318

17   She shall watch all night:
And if she chance to nod I'll rail and brawl,
And with the clamour keep her still awake.
This is the way to kill a wife with kindness.
    The Taming of the Shrew (1592) act 4, sc. 1, l. [208]

18 What say you to a piece of beef and mustard?
    The Taming of the Shrew (1592) act 4, sc. 3, l. [23]

19 PETRUCHIO: It shall be what o'clock I say it is.
    HORTENSIO: Why, so this gallant will command the
      sun.
    The Taming of the Shrew (1592) act 4, sc. 3, l. [197]

20   O vile,
Intolerable, not to be endured!
    The Taming of the Shrew (1592) act 5, sc. 2, l. 93

21 Fie, fie! unknit that threatening unkind brow,
And dart not scornful glances from those eyes,
To wound thy lord, thy king, thy governor.
    The Taming of the Shrew (1592) act 5, sc. 2, l. 137

22 A woman moved is like a fountain troubled,
Muddy, ill-seeming, thick, bereft of beauty.
    The Taming of the Shrew (1592) act 5, sc. 2, l. 143

23 Thy husband is thy lord, thy life, thy keeper,
Thy head, thy sovereign; one that cares for thee,
And for thy maintenance commits his body
To painful labour both by sea and land.
    The Taming of the Shrew (1592) act 5, sc. 2, l. 147

24 Such duty as the subject owes the prince,
Even such a woman oweth to her husband.
    The Taming of the Shrew (1592) act 5, sc. 2, l. 156

25 I am ashamed that women are so simple
To offer war where they should kneel for peace.
    The Taming of the Shrew (1592) act 5, sc. 2, l. 162

The Tempest

26 What cares these roarers for the name of king?
    The Tempest (1611) act 1, sc. 1, l. [18]

27 He hath no drowning mark upon him; his complexion
is perfect gallows.
    The Tempest (1611) act 1, sc. 1, l. [33]

28 Now would I give a thousand furlongs of sea for an
acre of barren ground; long heath, brown furze, any
thing. The wills above be done! but I would fain die a
dry death.
    The Tempest (1611) act 1, sc. 1, l. [70]

1   What seest thou else
In the dark backward and abysm of time?
The Tempest (1611) act 1, sc. 2, l. 49

2 Your tale, sir, would cure deafness.
The Tempest (1611) act 1, sc. 2, l. 106

3   My library
Was dukedom large enough.
The Tempest (1611) act 1, sc. 2, l. 109

4 The still-vexed Bermoothes.
The Tempest (1611) act 1, sc. 2, l. 229

5 As wicked dew as e'er my mother brushed
With raven's feather from unwholesome fen
Drop on you both! A southwest blow on ye,
And blister you all o'er!
The Tempest (1611) act 1, sc. 2, l. 321

6 For this, be sure, tonight thou shalt have cramps.
The Tempest (1611) act 1, sc. 2, l. 325

7 You taught me language; and my profit on't
Is, I know how to curse: the red plague rid you,
For learning me your language!
The Tempest (1611) act 1, sc. 2, l. 363

8 Come unto these yellow sands,
And then take hands:
Curtsied when you have, and kissed,—
The wild waves whist,—
Foot it featly here and there;
And, sweet sprites, the burden bear.
The Tempest (1611) act 1, sc. 2, l. 375

9 This music crept by me upon the waters,
Allaying both their fury, and my passion,
With its sweet air.
The Tempest (1611) act 1, sc. 2, l. 389

10 Full fathom five thy father lies;
Of his bones are coral made:
Those are pearls that were his eyes:
Nothing of him that doth fade,
But doth suffer a sea-change
Into something rich and strange.
Sea-nymphs hourly ring his knell:
Ding-dong.
Hark! now I hear them,—ding-dong, bell.
The Tempest (1611) act 1, sc. 2, l. 394

11 The fringèd curtains of thine eye advance,
And say what thou seest yond.
The Tempest (1611) act 1, sc. 2, l. 405

12   At the first sight
They have changed eyes.
The Tempest (1611) act 1, sc. 2, l. 437

13 He receives comfort like cold porridge.
The Tempest (1611) act 2, sc. 1, l. 10

14 Look, he's winding up the watch of his wit, by
and by it will strike.
The Tempest (1611) act 2, sc. 1, l. [12]

15 What's past is prologue.
The Tempest (1611) act 2, sc. 1, l. [261]

16 They'll take suggestion as a cat laps milk.
The Tempest (1611) act 2, sc. 1, l. [296]

17 When they will not give a doit to relieve a lame
beggar, they will lay out ten to see a dead Indian.
The Tempest (1611) act 2, sc. 2, l. [33]

18 Misery acquaints a man with strange bedfellows.
The Tempest (1611) act 2, sc. 2, l. [42]

19 Well, here's my comfort. [*Drinks.*]
The master, the swabber, the boatswain and I,
The gunner and his mate,
Loved Mall, Meg, and Marian and Margery,
But none of us cared for Kate;
For she had a tongue with a tang,
Would cry to a sailor, 'Go hang!'
The Tempest (1611) act 2, sc. 2, l. [48]

20 'Ban, 'Ban, Ca-Caliban,
Has a new master—Get a new man.
The Tempest (1611) act 2, sc. 2, l. [197]

21 FERDINAND: Wherefore weep you?
MIRANDA: At mine unworthiness, that dare not offer
What I desire to give; and much less take
What I shall die to want.
The Tempest (1611) act 3, sc. 1, l. 76

22 MIRANDA: My husband then?
FERDINAND: Ay, with a heart as willing
As bondage e'er of freedom.
The Tempest (1611) act 3, sc. 1, l. 89

23 Thou deboshed fish thou.
The Tempest (1611) act 3, sc. 2, l. [30]

24 Flout 'em, and scout 'em; and scout 'em, and flout
'em;
Thought is free.
The Tempest (1611) act 3, sc. 2, l. [133]

25 He that dies pays all debts.
The Tempest (1611) act 3, sc. 2, l. [143]

26 Be not afeard: the isle is full of noises,
Sounds and sweet airs, that give delight, and hurt not.
Sometimes a thousand twangling instruments
Will hum about mine ears, and sometime voices
That if I then had waked after long sleep
Will make me sleep again; and then in dreaming,
The clouds methought would open and show riches
Ready to drop upon me; that, when I waked
I cried to dream again.
The Tempest (1611) act 3, sc. 2, l. [135]

27 Thy banks with pionèd and twillèd brims,
Which spongy April at thy hest betrims,
To make cold nymphs chaste crowns.
The Tempest (1611) act 4, sc. 1, l. 64

28 Our revels now are ended. These our actors,
As I foretold you, were all spirits and
Are melted into air, into thin air:
And, like the baseless fabric of this vision,
The cloud-capped towers, the gorgeous palaces,
The solemn temples, the great globe itself,
Yea, all which it inherit, shall dissolve
And, like this insubstantial pageant faded,
Leave not a rack behind. We are such stuff
As dreams are made on, and our little life
Is rounded with a sleep.
The Tempest (1611) act 4, sc. 1, l. 148

29 I do begin to have bloody thoughts.
The Tempest (1611) act 4, sc. 1, l. [221]

30   We shall lose our time,
And all be turned to barnacles, or to apes
With foreheads villanous low.
The Tempest (1611) act 4, sc. 1, l. [250]

1 Ye elves of hills, brooks, standing lakes, and groves;
And ye, that on the sands with printless foot
Do chase the ebbing Neptune and do fly him
When he comes back; you demi-puppets, that
By moonshine do the green sour ringlets make
Whereof the ewe not bites; and you whose pastime
Is to make midnight mushrooms, that rejoice
To hear the solemn curfew; by whose aid,
Weak master though ye be, I have bedimmed
The noontide sun, called forth the mutinous winds,
And 'twixt the green sea and the azured vault
Set roaring war—to the dread rattling thunder
Have I given fire, and rifted Jove's stout oak
With his own bolt; the strong-based promontory
Have I made shake, and by the spurs plucked up
The pine and cedar; graves at my command
Have waked their sleepers, oped, and let 'em forth
By my so potent art. But this rough magic
I here abjure. And when I have required
Some heavenly music—which even now I do—
To work mine end upon their senses that
This airy charm is for, I'll break my staff,
Bury it certain fathoms in the earth,
And, deeper than did ever plummet sound,
I'll drown my book.
   The Tempest (1611) act 5, sc. 1, l. 33

2 Where the bee sucks, there suck I
In a cowslip's bell I lie;
There I couch when owls do cry.
On the bat's back I do fly
After summer merrily:
Merrily, merrily shall I live now
Under the blossom that hangs on the bough.
   The Tempest (1611) act 5, sc. 1, l. 88

3 How many goodly creatures are there here!
How beauteous mankind is! O brave new world,
That has such people in't.
   The Tempest (1611) act 5, sc. 1, l. 182

Timon of Athens

4 'Tis not enough to help the feeble up,
But to support him after.
   Timon of Athens (c.1607) act 1, sc. 1, l. 108

5 He that loves to be flattered is worthy o' the flatterer.
   Timon of Athens (c.1607) act 1, sc. 1, l. [233]

6   The strain of man's bred out
Into baboon and monkey.
   Timon of Athens (c.1607) act 1, sc. 1, l. [260]

7 I wonder men dare trust themselves with men.
   Timon of Athens (c.1607) act 1, sc. 2, l. [45]

8 Immortal gods, I crave no pelf;
I pray for no man but myself.
   Timon of Athens (c.1607) act 1, sc. 2, l. [64]

9 Like madness is the glory of this life.
   Timon of Athens (c.1607) act 1, sc. 2, l. [141]

10 Men shut their doors against a setting sun.
   Timon of Athens (c.1607) act 1, sc. 2, l. [152]

11 Nothing emboldens sin so much as mercy.
   Timon of Athens (c.1607) act 3, sc. 5, l. 3

12 You fools of fortune, trencher-friends, time's flies.
   Timon of Athens (c.1607) act 3, sc. 6, l. [107]

13 We have seen better days.
   Timon of Athens (c.1607) act 4, sc. 2, l. 27

14 O! the fierce wretchedness that glory brings us.
   Timon of Athens (c.1607) act 4, sc. 2, l. 30

15 The middle of humanity thou never knewest, but the
extremity of both ends.
   Timon of Athens (c.1607) act 4, sc. 2, l. [300]

16 Hadst thou like us from our first swath proceeded
The sweet degrees that this brief world affords
To such as may the passive drugs of it
Freely [command], thou would'st have plunged thyself
In general riot, melted down thy youth
In different beds of lust, and never learned
The icy precepts of respect, but followed
The sugared game before thee. But myself,
Who had the world as my confectionary,
The mouths, the tongues, the eyes, and hearts of men
At duty, more than I could frame employment;
That numberless upon me stuck as leaves
Do on the oak, have with one winter's brush
Fell from their boughs, and left me open, bare,
For every storm that blows.
   Timon of Athens (c.1607) act 4, sc. 3, l. 252

17   I'll example you with thievery:
The sun's a thief, and with his great attraction
Robs the vast sea; the moon's an arrant thief,
And her pale fire she snatches from the sun;
The sea's a thief, whose liquid surge resolves
The moon into salt tears; the earth's a thief,
That feeds and breeds by a composture stol'n
From gen'ral excrement.
   Timon of Athens (c.1607) act 4, sc. 3, l. 435

18 He has almost charmed me from my profession, by
persuading me to it.
   Timon of Athens (c.1607) act 4, sc. 3, l. [457]

19   My long sickness
Of health and living now begins to mend,
And nothing brings me all things.
   Timon of Athens (c.1607) act 5, sc. 1, l. [191]

20 ... Tell them, that, to ease them of their griefs,
Their fears of hostile strokes, their aches, losses,
Their pangs of love, with other incident throes
That nature's fragile vessel doth sustain
In life's uncertain voyage, I will some kindness do
them.
   Timon of Athens (c.1607) act 5, sc. 1, l. [203]

21 Timon hath made his everlasting mansion
Upon the beachèd verge of the salt flood;
Who once a day with his embossèd froth
The turbulent surge shall cover.
   Timon of Athens (c.1607) act 5, sc. 1, l. [220]

Titus Andronicus

22 She is a woman, therefore may be wooed;
She is a woman, therefore may be won;
She is Lavinia, therefore must be loved.
What, man! more water glideth by the mill
Than wots the miller of; and easy it is
Of a cut loaf to steal a shive, we know.
   Titus Andronicus (1590) act 2, sc. 1, l. 82. Cf. *Henry VI,
Part 1* 587:13

1 Come, and take choice of all my library,
And so beguile thy sorrow.
Titus Andronicus (1590) act 4, sc. 1, l. 34

2 TAMORA: Why hast thou slain thine only daughter
       thus?
TITUS: Not I, 'twas Chiron and Demetrius:
They ravished her and cut away her tongue,
And they, 'twas they, that did her all this wrong.
SATURNINUS: Go fetch them hither to us presently.
TITUS: Why, there they are, both bakèd in this pie
    Whereof their mother daintily hath fed,
    Eating the flesh that she herself hath bred.
Titus Andronicus (1590) act 5, sc. 3, l. 54

3 If one good deed in all my life I did,
I do repent it from my very soul.
Titus Andronicus (1590) act 5, sc. 3, l. [189]

Troilus and Cressida

4 I have had my labour for my travail.
Troilus and Cressida (1602) act 1, sc. 1, l. [73]

5   Women are angels, wooing:
Things won are done; joy's soul lies in the doing;
That she beloved knows nought that knows not this:
Men prize the thing ungained more than it is.
Troilus and Cressida (1602) act 1, sc. 2, l. [310]

6 The heavens themselves, the planets, and this centre
Observe degree, priority, and place,
Insisture, course, proportion, season, form,
Office, and custom, in all line of order.
Troilus and Cressida (1602) act 1, sc. 3, l. 85

7   O! when degree is shaked,
Which is the ladder to all high designs,
The enterprise is sick.
Troilus and Cressida (1602) act 1, sc. 3, l. 101

8 Take but degree away, untune that string,
And, hark! what discord follows; each thing meets
In mere oppugnancy. The bounded waters
Should lift their bosoms higher than the shores
And make a sop of all this sordid globe;
Strength should be lord of imbecility
And the rude son should strike his father dead.
Troilus and Cressida (1602) act 1, sc. 3, l. 109

9   The general's disdained
By him one step below, he by the next,
That next by him beneath; so every step,
Exampled by the first pace that is sick
Of his superior, grows to an envious fever
Of pale and bloodless emulation.
Troilus and Cressida (1602) act 1, sc. 3, l. 129

10   We are soldiers;
And may that soldier a mere recreant prove,
That means not, hath not, or is not in love!
Troilus and Cressida (1602) act 1, sc. 3, l. 286

11 And in such indexes, although small pricks
To their subsequent volumes, there is seen
The baby figure of the giant mass
Of things to come at large.
Troilus and Cressida (1602) act 1, sc. 3, l. 343

12 Achilles   who wears his wit in his belly, and his
guts in his head
Troilus and Cressida (1602) act 2, sc. 1, l. [78]

13   You have both said well;
And on the cause and question now in hand
Have glozed but superficially; not much
Unlike young men, whom Aristotle thought
Unfit to hear moral philosophy.
Troilus and Cressida (1602) act 2, sc. 2, l. 163

14   Thus to persist
In doing wrong extenuates not wrong,
But makes it much more heavy.
Troilus and Cressida (1602) act 2, sc. 2, l. 186

15 I am giddy, expectation whirls me round.
The imaginary relish is so sweet
That it enchants my sense.
Troilus and Cressida (1602) act 3, sc. 2, l. [17]

16 This is the monstruosity in love, lady, that the will is
infinite, and the execution confined; that the desire is
boundless, and the act a slave to limit.
Troilus and Cressida (1602) act 3, sc. 2, l. [85]

17   To be wise, and love,
Exceeds man's might.
Troilus and Cressida (1602) act 3, sc. 2, l. [163]

18 I am as true as truth's simplicity,
And simpler than the infancy of truth.
Troilus and Cressida (1602) act 3, sc. 2, l. [176]

19 Time hath, my lord, a wallet at his back,
Wherein he puts alms for oblivion,
A great-sized monster of ingratitudes:
Those scraps are good deeds past; which are devoured
As fast as they are made, forgot as soon
As done.
Troilus and Cressida (1602) act 3, sc. 3, l. 145

20   Perseverance, dear my lord,
Keeps honour bright: to have done, is to hang
Quite out of fashion, like a rusty mail
In monumental mockery.
Troilus and Cressida (1602) act 3, sc. 3, l. 150

21   Time is like a fashionable host
That slightly shakes his parting guest by the hand,
And with his arms outstretched, as he would fly,
Grasps in the comer: welcome ever smiles,
And farewell goes out sighing.
Troilus and Cressida (1602) act 3, sc. 3, l. 165

22   Beauty, wit,
High birth, vigour of bone, desert in service,
Love, friendship, charity, are subjects all
To envious and calumniating time.
One touch of nature makes the whole world kin,
That all with one consent praise new-born gawds,
Though they are made and moulded of things past,
And give to dust that is a little gilt
More laud than gilt o'er-dusted.
Troilus and Cressida (1602) act 3, sc. 3, l. 171

23 A plague of opinion! a man may wear it on both
sides, like a leather jerkin.
Troilus and Cressida (1602) act 3, sc. 3, l. [267]

24 How my achievements mock me!
Troilus and Cressida (1602) act 4, sc. 2, l. [72]

25 What a pair of spectacles is here!
Troilus and Cressida (1602) act 4, sc. 4, l. [13] (Pandarus, of
the lovers)

1 We two, that with so many thousand sighs
Did buy each other, must poorly sell ourselves
With the rude brevity and discharge of one.
Injurious time now with a robber's haste
Crams his rich thievery up, he knows not how:
As many farewells as be stars in heaven,
With distinct breath and consigned kisses to them,
He fumbles up into a loose adieu,
And scants us with a single famished kiss,
Distasted with the salt of broken tears.
    Troilus and Cressida (1602) act 4, sc. 4, l. [39]

2   Fie, fie upon her!
There's language in her eye, her cheek, her lip,
Nay, her foot speaks, her wanton spirits look out
At every joint and motive of her body.
    Troilus and Cressida (1602) act 4, sc. 5, l. 54

3 What's past, and what's to come is strewed with
    husks
And formless ruin of oblivion.
    Troilus and Cressida (1602) act 4, sc. 5, l. 165

4   The end crowns all,
And that old common arbitrator, Time,
Will one day end it.
    Troilus and Cressida (1602) act 4, sc. 5, l. 223

5 Lechery, lechery; still, wars and lechery: nothing else
holds fashion.
    Troilus and Cressida (1602) act 5, sc. 2, l. 192

6 Words, words, mere words, no matter from the heart.
    Troilus and Cressida (1602) act 5, sc. 3, l. [109]

7 Hector is dead; there is no more to say.
    Troilus and Cressida (1602) act 5, sc. 10, l. 22

8 O world! world! world! thus is the poor agent
despised. O traitors and bawds, how earnestly are you
set a-work, and how ill requited! why should our
endeavour be so loved, and the performance so
loathed?
    Troilus and Cressida (1602) act 5, sc. 10, l. [36]

Twelfth Night

9 If music be the food of love, play on;
Give me excess of it, that, surfeiting,
The appetite may sicken, and so die.
That strain again! it had a dying fall:
O! it came o'er my ear like the sweet sound
That breathes upon a bank of violets,
Stealing and giving odour! Enough! no more:
'Tis not so sweet now as it was before.
O spirit of love! how quick and fresh art thou,
That notwithstanding thy capacity
Receiveth as the sea, nought enters there,
Of what validity and pitch soe'er,
But falls into abatement and low price,
Even in a minute: so full of shapes is fancy,
That it alone is high fantastical.
    Twelfth Night (1601) act 1, sc. 1, l. 1

10 O! when mine eyes did see Olivia first,
Methought she purged the air of pestilence.
That instant was I turned into a hart,
And my desires, like fell and cruel hounds,
E'er since pursue me.
    Twelfth Night (1601) act 1, sc. 1, l. 19

11 And what should I do in Illyria?
My brother he is in Elysium.
    Twelfth Night (1601) act 1, sc. 2, l. 2

12 Methinks sometimes I have no more wit than a
Christian or an ordinary man has; but I am a great
eater of beef, and I believe that does harm to my wit.
    Twelfth Night (1601) act 1, sc. 3, l. [90]

13 I would I had bestowed that time in the tongues that I
have in fencing, dancing, and bear-baiting. O! had I
but followed the arts!
    Twelfth Night (1601) act 1, sc. 3, l. [99]

14 Wherefore are these things hid? wherefore have these
gifts a curtain before 'em? are they like to take dust,
like Mistress Mall's picture? why dost thou not go to
church in a galliard, and come home in a coranto?
My very walk should be a jig.
    Twelfth Night (1601) act 1, sc. 3, l. [135]

15 Is it a world to hide virtues in?
    Twelfth Night (1601) act 1, sc. 3, l. [142]

16   They shall yet belie thy happy years
That say thou art a man: Diana's lip
Is not more smooth and rubious; thy small pipe
Is as the maiden's organ, shrill and sound;
And all is semblative a woman's part.
    Twelfth Night (1601) act 1, sc. 4, l. 30

17 Many a good hanging prevents a bad marriage.
    Twelfth Night (1601) act 1, sc. 5, l. [20]

18 What says Quinapalus? 'Better a witty fool than a
foolish wit.'
    Twelfth Night (1601) act 1, sc. 5, l. [37]

19 Virtue that transgresses is but patched with sin; and
sin that amends is but patched with virtue.
    Twelfth Night (1601) act 1, sc. 5, l. [52]

20 Good my mouse of virtue, answer me.
    Twelfth Night (1601) act 1, sc. 5, l. [68]

21 A plague o' these pickle herring!
    Twelfth Night (1601) act 1, sc. 5, l. [127]

22 As a squash is before 'tis a peascod, or a codling when
'tis almost an apple: 'tis with him in standing water,
between boy and man. He is very well-favoured, and
he speaks very shrewishly: one would think his
mother's milk were scarce out of him.
    Twelfth Night (1601) act 1, sc. 5, l. [167]

23 I can say little more than I have studied, and that
question's out of my part.
    Twelfth Night (1601) act 1, sc. 5, l. [191]

24 Make me a willow cabin at your gate,
And call upon my soul within the house;
Write loyal cantons of contemnèd love,
And sing them loud even in the dead of night;
Halloo your name to the reverberate hills,
And make the babbling gossip of the air
Cry out, 'Olivia!' O! you should not rest
Between the elements of air and earth,
But you should pity me!
    Twelfth Night (1601) act 1, sc. 5, l. [289]

25 OLIVIA: What is your parentage?
VIOLA: Above my fortune, yet my state is well:
    I am a gentleman.
    Twelfth Night (1601) act 1, sc. 5, l. [310]

1 She is drowned already, sir, with salt water, though I
seem to drown her remembrance again with more.
Twelfth Night (1601) act 2, sc. 1, l. [31]

2 Disguise, I see thou art a wickedness
Wherein the pregnant enemy does much.
Twelfth Night (1601) act 2, sc. 2, l. 27

3 Not to be a-bed after midnight is to be up betimes.
Twelfth Night (1601) act 2, sc. 3, l. 1

4 O mistress mine! where are you roaming?
O! stay and hear; your true love's coming,
That can sing both high and low.
Trip no further, pretty sweeting;
Journeys end in lovers meeting,
Every wise man's son doth know . . .

What is love? 'tis not hereafter;
Present mirth hath present laughter;
What's to come is still unsure:
In delay there lies no plenty;
Then come kiss me, sweet and twenty,
Youth's a stuff will not endure.
Twelfth Night (1601) act 2, sc. 3, l. [42]

5 Am not I consanguineous? am I not of her blood?
Twelfth Night (1601) act 2, sc. 3, l. [85]

6 He does it with a better grace, but I do it more
natural.
Twelfth Night (1601) act 2, sc. 3, l. [91]

7 Is there no respect of place, persons, nor time, in you?
Twelfth Night (1601) act 2, sc. 3, l. [100]

8 Dost thou think, because thou art virtuous, there shall
be no more cakes and ale?
Twelfth Night (1601) act 2, sc. 3, l. [124]

9 I will drop in his way some obscure epistles of love;
wherein by the colour of his beard, the shape of his
leg, the manner of his gait, the expressure of his eye,
forehead, and complexion, he shall find himself most
feelingly personated.
Twelfth Night (1601) act 2, sc. 3, l. [171]

10 I was adored once too.
Twelfth Night (1601) act 2, sc. 3, l. [200]

11 My purpose is, indeed, a horse of that colour.
Twelfth Night (1601) act 2, sc. 3, l. [184]

12 Now, good Cesario, but that piece of song,
That old and antique song we heard last night;
Methought it did relieve my passion much,
More than light airs and recollected terms
Of these most brisk and giddy-pacèd times.
Twelfth Night (1601) act 2, sc. 4, l. 2

13 DUKE: If ever thou shalt love,
In the sweet pangs of it remember me;
For such as I am all true lovers are:
Unstaid and skittish in all motions else,
Save in the constant image of the creature
That is beloved. How dost thou like this tune?
VIOLA: It gives a very echo to the seat
Where love is enthroned.
Twelfth Night (1601) act 2, sc. 4, l. 15

14 Let still the woman take
An elder than herself, so wears she to him,
So sways she level in her husband's heart:
For, boy, however we do praise ourselves,
Our fancies are more giddy and unfirm,
More longing, wavering, sooner lost and worn,
Than women's are.
Twelfth Night (1601) act 2, sc. 4, l. 29

15 Then let thy love be younger than thyself,
Or thy affection cannot hold the bent.
Twelfth Night (1601) act 2, sc. 4, l. 36

16 Mark it, Cesario; it is old and plain.
The spinsters and the knitters in the sun
And the free maids that weave their thread with bones
Do use to chant it: it is silly sooth,
And dallies with the innocence of love,
Like the old age.
Twelfth Night (1601) act 2, sc. 4, l. 43

17 Come away, come away, death,
And in sad cypress let me be laid;
Fly away, fly away, breath:
I am slain by a fair cruel maid.
My shroud of white, stuck all with yew,
O! prepare it.
My part of death no one so true
Did share it.
Twelfth Night (1601) act 2, sc. 4, l. 51

18 Now, the melancholy god protect thee, and the tailor
make thy doublet of changeable taffeta, for thy mind is
a very opal.
Twelfth Night (1601) act 2, sc. 4, l. [74]

19 There is no woman's sides
Can bide the beating of so strong a passion
As love doth give my heart; no woman's heart
So big, to hold so much; they lack retention.
Alas! their love may be called appetite,
No motion of the liver, but the palate,
That suffer surfeit, cloyment, and revolt;
But mine is all as hungry as the sea,
And can digest so much.
Twelfth Night (1601) act 2, sc. 4, l. [95]

20 VIOLA: My father had a daughter loved a man,
As it might be, perhaps, were I a woman,
I should your lordship.
DUKE: And what's her history?
VIOLA: A blank, my lord. She never told her love,
But let concealment, like a worm i' the bud,
Feed on her damask cheek: she pined in thought;
And with a green and yellow melancholy,
She sat like patience on a monument,
Smiling at grief. Was not this love indeed?
We men may say more, swear more; but, indeed,
Our shows are more than will; for still we prove
Much in our vows, but little in our love.
Twelfth Night (1601) act 2, sc. 4, l. [108]

21 I am all the daughters of my father's house,
And all the brothers too.
Twelfth Night (1601) act 2, sc. 4, l. [122]

22 How now, my metal of India!
Twelfth Night (1601) act 2, sc. 5, l. [17]

23 Here comes the trout that must be caught with
tickling.
Twelfth Night (1601) act 2, sc. 5, l. [25]

1 Contemplation makes a rare turkey-cock of him: how
he jets under his advanced plumes!
Twelfth Night (1601) act 2, sc. 5, l. [35]

2 Now is the woodcock near the gin.
Twelfth Night (1601) act 2, sc. 5, l. [93]

3 I may command where I adore.
Twelfth Night (1601) act 2, sc. 5, l. [117]

4 But be not afraid of greatness: some men are born
great, some achieve greatness, and some have
greatness thrust upon them.
Twelfth Night (1601) act 2, sc. 5, l. [158]

5 Let thy tongue tang arguments of state; put thyself
into the trick of singularity. She thus advises thee that
sighs for thee. Remember who commended thy yellow
stockings, and wished to see thee ever cross-gartered.
Twelfth Night (1601) act 2, sc. 5, l. [165]

6 Jove and my stars be praised! Here is yet a postscript.
Twelfth Night (1601) act 2, sc. 5, l. [190]

7 Now Jove, in his next commodity of hair, send thee a
beard.
Twelfth Night (1601) act 3, sc. 1, l. [51]

8 This fellow's wise enough to play the fool,
And to do that well craves a kind of wit.
Twelfth Night (1601) act 3, sc. 1, l. [68]

9 Taste your legs, sir; put them to motion.
Twelfth Night (1601) act 3, sc. 1, l. [88]

10 'Twas never merry world
Since lowly feigning was called compliment.
Twelfth Night (1601) act 3, sc. 1, l. [110]

11 O world! how apt the poor are to be proud.
Twelfth Night (1601) act 3, sc. 1, l. [141]

12 O! what a deal of scorn looks beautiful
In the contempt and anger of his lip.
Twelfth Night (1601) act 3, sc. 1, l. [159]

13 Love sought is good, but giv'n unsought is better.
Twelfth Night (1601) act 3, sc. 1, l. [170]

14 You are now sailed into the north of my lady's
opinion; where you will hang like an icicle on a
Dutchman's beard.
Twelfth Night (1601) act 3, sc. 2, l. [29]

15 As many lies as will lie in thy sheet of paper, although
the sheet were big enough for the bed of Ware in
England, set 'em down.
Twelfth Night (1601) act 3, sc. 2, l. [51]

16 If he were opened, and you find so much blood in his
liver as will clog the foot of a flea, I'll eat the rest of
the anatomy.
Twelfth Night (1601) act 3, sc. 2, l. [68]

17 Look, where the youngest wren of nine comes.
Twelfth Night (1601) act 3, sc. 2, l. [73]

18 He does smile his face into more lines than are in the
new map with the augmentation of the Indies.
Twelfth Night (1601) act 3, sc. 2, l. [85]

19 In the south suburbs, at the Elephant,
Is best to lodge.
Twelfth Night (1601) act 3, sc. 3, l. 39

20 I think we do know the sweet Roman hand.
Twelfth Night (1601) act 3, sc. 4, l. [31]

21 Why, this is very midsummer madness.
Twelfth Night (1601) act 3, sc. 4, l. [62]

22 What, man! defy the devil: consider, he's an enemy to
mankind.
Twelfth Night (1601) act 3, sc. 4, l. [109]

23 Go, hang yourselves all! you are idle shallow things: I
am not of your element.
Twelfth Night (1601) act 3, sc. 4, l. [138]

24 If this were played upon a stage now, I could
condemn it as an improbable fiction.
Twelfth Night (1601) act 3, sc. 4, l. [142]

25 More matter for a May morning.
Twelfth Night (1601) act 3, sc. 4, l. [158]

26 Still you keep o' the windy side of the law.
Twelfth Night (1601) act 3, sc. 4, l. [183]

27 Fare thee well; and God have mercy upon one of our
souls! He may have mercy upon mine, but my hope is
better; and so look to thyself.
Twelfth Night (1601) act 3, sc. 4, l. [185]

28 Nay, let me alone for swearing.
Twelfth Night (1601) act 3, sc. 4, l. [204]

29 I hate ingratitude more in a man
Than lying, vainness, babbling drunkenness,
Or any taint of vice whose strong corruption
Inhabits our frail blood.
Twelfth Night (1601) act 3, sc. 4, l. [390]

30 In nature there's no blemish but the mind;
None can be called deformed but the unkind.
Twelfth Night (1601) act 3, sc. 4, l. [403]

31 Out, hyperbolical fiend!
Twelfth Night (1601) act 4, sc. 2, l. [29]

32 Leave thy vain bibble-babble.
Twelfth Night (1601) act 4, sc. 2, l. [106]

33 We took him for a coward, but he's the very devil
incarnate.
Twelfth Night (1601) act 5, sc. 1, l. [185]

34 Why have you suffered me to be imprisoned,
Kept in a dark house, visited by the priest,
And made the most notorious geck and gull
That e'er invention played on? Tell me why.
Twelfth Night (1601) act 5, sc. 1, l. [353]

35 Thus the whirligig of time brings in his revenges.
Twelfth Night (1601) act 5, sc. 1, l. [388]

36 I'll be revenged on the whole pack of you.
Twelfth Night (1601) act 5, sc. 1, l. [390]

37 When that I was and a little tiny boy,
With hey, ho, the wind and the rain;
A foolish thing was but a toy,
For the rain it raineth every day.

But when I came to man's estate,
With hey, ho, the wind and the rain;
'Gainst knaves and thieves men shut their gates,
For the rain it raineth every day.
Twelfth Night (1601) act 5, sc. 1, l. [401]

The Two Gentlemen of Verona

38 Home-keeping youth have ever homely wits.
The Two Gentlemen of Verona (1592–3) act 1, sc. 1, l. 2

1 He was more than over shoes in love.
The Two Gentlemen of Verona (1592–3) act 1, sc. 1, l. 24

2 I have no other but a woman's reason:
I think him so, because I think him so.
The Two Gentlemen of Verona (1592–3) act 1, sc. 2, l. 23

3 Fie, fie! how wayward is this foolish love
That, like a testy babe, will scratch the nurse
And presently all humbled kiss the rod!
The Two Gentlemen of Verona (1592–3) act 1, sc. 2, l. 55

4 O! how this spring of love resembleth
The uncertain glory of an April day,
Which now shows all the beauty of the sun,
And by and by a cloud takes all away!
The Two Gentlemen of Verona (1592–3) act 1, sc. 3, l. 84

5 Or as one nail by strength drives out another,
So the remembrance of my former love
Is by a newer object quite forgotten.
The Two Gentlemen of Verona (1592–3) act 2, sc. 4, l. 194

6 Except I be by Silvia in the night,
There is no music in the nightingale;
Unless I look on Silvia in the day,
There is no day for me to look upon.
The Two Gentlemen of Verona (1592–3) act 3, sc. 1, l. 178

7 Much is the force of heaven-bred poesy.
The Two Gentlemen of Verona (1592–3) act 3, sc. 2, l. 71

8 Who is Silvia? what is she,
That all our swains commend her?
Holy, fair, and wise is she;
The heaven such grace did lend her,
That she might admirèd be.

Is she kind as she is fair?
For beauty lives with kindness:
Love doth to her eyes repair,
To help him of his blindness;
And, being helped, inhabits there.
The Two Gentlemen of Verona (1592–3) act 4, sc. 2, l. 40

9 How use doth breed a habit in man!
The Two Gentlemen of Verona (1592–3) act 5, sc. 4, l. 1

10 O heaven! were man
But constant, he were perfect.
The Two Gentlemen of Verona (1592–3) act 5, sc. 4, l. 110

The Winter's Tale

11 We were, fair queen,
Two lads that thought there was no more behind
But such a day to-morrow as to-day,
And to be boy eternal.
The Winter's Tale (1610–11) act 1, sc. 2, l. 62

12 We were as twinned lambs that did frisk i' the sun,
And bleat the one at the other: what we changed
Was innocence for innocence; we knew not
The doctrine of ill-doing, no, nor dreamed
That any did.
The Winter's Tale (1610–11) act 1, sc. 2, l. 67

13 But to be paddling palms and pinching fingers,
As now they are, and making practised smiles,
As in a looking-glass.
The Winter's Tale (1610–11) act 1, sc. 2, l. 116

14 How like, methought, I then was to this kernel,
This squash this gentleman.
The Winter's Tale (1610–11) act 1, sc. 2, l. 160

15 Should all despair
That have revolted wives, the tenth of mankind
Would hang themselves.
The Winter's Tale (1610–11) act 1, sc. 2, l. 198

16 Make that thy question, and go rot!
The Winter's Tale (1610–11) act 1, sc. 2, l. 324

17 A sad tale's best for winter.
I have one of sprites and goblins.
The Winter's Tale (1610–11) act 2, sc. 1, l. 24

18 There may be in the cup
A spider steeped, and one may drink, depart,
And yet partake no venom, for his knowledge
Is not infected; but if one present
Th' abhorred ingredient to his eye, make known
How he hath drunk, he cracks his gorge, his sides,
With violent hefts. I have drunk, and seen the spider.
The Winter's Tale (1610–11) act 2, sc. 1, l. 39

19 It is a heretic that makes the fire,
Not she which burns in 't.
The Winter's Tale (1610–11) act 2, sc. 3, l. 114

20 I am a feather for each wind that blows.
The Winter's Tale (1610–11) act 2, sc. 3, l. 153

21 HERMIONE: My life stands in the level of your dreams,
Which I'll lay down.
LEONTES: Your actions are my dreams.
The Winter's Tale (1610–11) act 3, sc. 2, l. 81

22 What's gone and what's past help
Should be past grief.
The Winter's Tale (1610–11) act 3, sc. 2, l. [223]

23 *Exit, pursued by a bear.*
The Winter's Tale (1610–11) act 3, sc. 3 (stage direction)

24 When daffodils begin to peer,
With heigh! the doxy, over the dale,
Why, then comes in the sweet o' the year;
For the red blood reigns in the winter's pale.

The white sheet bleaching on the hedge,
With heigh! the sweet birds, O, how they sing!
Doth set my pugging tooth on edge;
For a quart of ale is a dish for a king.

The lark, that tirra-lirra chants,
With, heigh! with, heigh! the thrush and the jay,
Are summer songs for me and my aunts,
While we lie tumbling in the hay.
The Winter's Tale (1610–11) act 4, sc. 2, l. 1

25 My father named me Autolycus; who being, as I am,
littered under Mercury, was likewise a snapper-up of
unconsidered trifles.
The Winter's Tale (1610–11) act 4, sc. 2, l. [24]

26 For the life to come, I sleep out the thought of it.
The Winter's Tale (1610–11) act 4, sc. 2, l. [30]

27 Prig, for my life, prig; he haunts wakes, fairs, and
bear-baitings.
The Winter's Tale (1610–11) act 4, sc. 2, l. [109]

28 Jog on, jog on the foot-path way,
And merrily hent the stile-a:
A merry heart goes all the day,
Your sad tires in a mile-a.
The Winter's Tale (1610–11) act 4, sc. 2, l. [133]

29 For you there's rosemary and rue; these keep
Seeming and savour all the winter long.
The Winter's Tale (1610–11) act 4, sc. 3, l. 74

1   The fairest flowers o' the season
Are our carnations and streaked gillyvors,
Which some call nature's bastards.
  The Winter's Tale (1610–11) act 4, sc. 3, l. 81

2   I'll not put
The dibble in earth to set one slip of them.
  The Winter's Tale (1610–11) act 4, sc. 3, l. 99

3   Here's flowers for you;
Hot lavender, mints, savory, marjoram;
The marigold, that goes to bed wi' the sun,
And with him rises weeping.
  The Winter's Tale (1610–11) act 4, sc. 3, l. 103

4   O Proserpina!
For the flowers now that frighted thou let'st fall
From Dis's waggon! daffodils,
That come before the swallow dares, and take
The winds of March with beauty; violets dim,
But sweeter than the lids of Juno's eyes
Or Cytherea's breath; pale prime-roses,
That die unmarried, ere they can behold
Bright Phoebus in his strength,—a malady
Most incident to maids; bold oxlips and
The crown imperial; lilies of all kinds,
The flower-de-luce being one.
  The Winter's Tale (1610–11) act 4, sc. 3, l. 116

5 PERDITA: Sure this robe of mine
Doth change my disposition.
  FLORIZEL: What you do
Still betters what is done. When you speak, sweet,
I'd have you do it ever: when you sing,
I'd have you buy and sell so; so give alms;
Pray so; and, for the ordering your affairs,
To sing them too: when you do dance, I wish you
A wave o' the sea, that you might ever do
Nothing but that; move still, still so,
And own no other function: each your doing,
So singular in each particular,
Crowns what you are doing in the present deed,
That all your acts are queens.
  The Winter's Tale (1610–11) act 4, sc. 3, l. 134

6   Good sooth, she is
The queen of curds and cream.
  The Winter's Tale (1610–11) act 4, sc. 3, l. 160

7 Lawn as white as driven snow.
  The Winter's Tale (1610–11) act 4, sc. 3, l. [220]

8 I love a ballad in print, a-life, for then we are sure
they are true.
  The Winter's Tale (1610–11) act 4, sc. 3, l. [262]

9 The self-same sun that shines upon his court
Hides not his visage from our cottage, but
Looks on alike.
  The Winter's Tale (1610–11) act 4, sc. 3, l. [457]

10   This dream of mine,
Being now awake, I'll queen it no inch further,
But milk my ewes and weep.
  The Winter's Tale (1610–11) act 4, sc. 3, l. [462]

11 Prosperity's the very bond of love,
Whose fresh complexion and whose heart together
Affliction alters.
  The Winter's Tale (1610–11) act 4, sc. 3, l. [586]

12 Ha, ha! what a fool Honesty is! and Trust his sworn
brother, a very simple gentleman!
  The Winter's Tale (1610–11) act 4, sc. 3, l. [608]

13 Though I am not naturally honest, I am so sometimes
by chance.
  The Winter's Tale (1610–11) act 4, sc. 3, l. [734]

14 I will but look upon the hedge and follow you.
  The Winter's Tale (1610–11) act 4, sc. 3, l. [862]

15   Stars, stars!
And all eyes else dead coals.
  The Winter's Tale (1610–11) act 5, sc. 1, l. 67

16   Still, methinks,
There is an air comes from her: what fine chisel
Could ever yet cut breath?
  The Winter's Tale (1610–11) act 5, sc. 3, l. 77

17   O! she's warm.
If this be magic, let it be an art
Lawful as eating.
  The Winter's Tale (1610–11) act 5, sc. 3, l. 109

The Passionate Pilgrim (attribution doubtful)

18 Crabbed age and youth cannot live together:
Youth is full of pleasance, age is full of care.
  The Passionate Pilgrim (1599) no. 12

19 Age, I do abhor thee, youth, I do adore thee.
  The Passionate Pilgrim (1599) no. 12

The Rape of Lucrece

20 What I have done is yours; what I have to do is
yours; being part in all I have, devoted yours.
  The Rape of Lucrece (1594) dedication

21 Beauty itself doth of itself persuade
The eyes of men without an orator.
  The Rape of Lucrece (1594) l. 29

22 Who buys a minute's mirth to wail a week?
Or sells eternity to get a toy?
For one sweet grape who will the vine destroy?
  The Rape of Lucrece (1594) l. 213

23 Time's glory is to calm contending kings,
To unmask falsehood, and bring truth to light.
  The Rape of Lucrece (1594) l. 939

24 And now this pale swan in her watery nest
Begins the sad dirge of her certain ending.
  The Rape of Lucrece (1594) l. 1611

Sonnets

25 To the onlie begetter of these insuing sonnets,
Mr. W. H.
  Sonnets (1609) dedication (also attributed to Thomas
  Thorpe, the publisher)

26 From fairest creatures we desire increase,
That thereby beauty's rose might never die.
  Sonnet 1

1 When forty winters shall besiege thy brow,
   And dig deep trenches in thy beauty's field.
   Sonnet 2

2 Thou art thy mother's glass, and she in thee
   Calls back the lovely April of her prime.
   Sonnet 3

3 Music to hear, why hear'st thou music sadly?
   Sweets with sweets war not, joy delights in joy:
   Why lov'st thou that which thou receiv'st not gladly,
   Or else receiv'st with pleasure thine annoy?
   If the true concord of well-tunèd sounds,
   By unions married, do offend thine ear,
   They do but sweetly chide thee.
   Sonnet 8

4 When lofty trees I see barren of leaves,
   Which erst from heat did canopy the herd,
   And summer's green all girded up in sheaves,
   Borne on the bier with white and bristly beard.
   Sonnet 12

5 If I could write the beauty of your eyes
   And in fresh numbers number all your graces,
   The age to come would say, 'This poet lies;
   Such heavenly touches ne'er touched earthly faces.'
   So should my papers, yellowed with their age,
   Be scorned, like old men of less truth than tongue,
   And your true rights be termed a poet's rage
   And stretchèd metre of an antique song.
   Sonnet 17

6 Shall I compare thee to a summer's day?
   Thou art more lovely and more temperate:
   Rough winds do shake the darling buds of May,
   And summer's lease hath all too short a date:
   Sometimes too hot the eye of heaven shines,
   And often is his gold complexion dimmed;
   And every fair from fair sometime declines,
   By chance, or nature's changing course untrimmed;
   But thy eternal summer shall not fade,
   Nor lose possession of that fair thou ow'st,
   Nor shall death brag thou wander'st in his shade,
   When in eternal lines to time thou grow'st;
   So long as men can breathe, or eyes can see,
   So long lives this, and this gives life to thee.
   Sonnet 18

7 As an unperfect actor on the stage,
   Who with his fear is put beside his part,
   Or some fierce thing replete with too much rage,
   Whose strength's abundance weakens his own
     heart;
   So I, for fear of trust, forget to say
   The perfect ceremony of love's rite.
   Sonnet 23

8 O! let my books be then the eloquence
   And dumb presagers of my speaking breast.
   Sonnet 23

9 The painful warrior famousèd for fight,
   After a thousand victories once foiled,
   Is from the book of honour razèd quite
   And all the rest forgot for which he toil'd.
   Sonnet 25

10 When in disgrace with fortune and men's eyes
   I all alone beweep my outcast state,
   And trouble deaf heaven with my bootless cries,
   And look upon myself and curse my fate,
   Wishing me like to one more rich in hope,
   Featured like him, like him with friends possessed,
   Desiring this man's art, and that man's scope,
   With what I most enjoy contented least;
   Yet in these thoughts myself almost despising,
   Haply I think on thee,—and then my state,
   Like to the lark at break of day arising
   From sullen earth, sings hymns at heaven's gate;
   For thy sweet love remembered such wealth brings
   That then I scorn to change my state with kings.
   Sonnet 29

11 When to the sessions of sweet silent thought
   I summon up remembrance of things past,
   I sigh the lack of many a thing I sought,
   And with old woes new wail my dear times' waste.
   Sonnet 30

12 Full many a glorious morning have I seen
   Flatter the mountain-tops with sovereign eye,
   Kissing with golden face the meadows green,
   Gilding pale streams with heavenly alchemy.
   Sonnet 33

13 Roses have thorns, and silver fountains mud;
   Clouds and eclipses stain both moon and sun,
   And loathsome canker lives in sweetest bud.
   All men make faults.
   Sonnet 35

14 As a decrepit father takes delight
   To see his active child do deeds of youth,
   So I, made lame by fortune's dearest spite,
   Take all my comfort of thy worth and truth.
   Sonnet 37

15 Against that time when thou shalt strangely pass,
   And scarcely greet me with that sun, thine eye,
   When love, converted from the thing it was,
   Shall reasons find of settled gravity.
   Sonnet 49

16 What is your substance, whereof are you made,
   That millions of strange shadows on you tend?
   Sonnet 53

17 O! how much more doth beauty beauteous seem
   By that sweet ornament which truth doth give!
   Sonnet 54

18 Not marble, nor the gilded monuments
   Of princes, shall outlive this powerful rhyme;
   But you shall shine more bright in these contents
   Than unswept stone, besmeared with sluttish time.
   Sonnet 55

19 So true a fool is love that in your will,
   Though you do anything, he thinks no ill.
   Sonnet 57

20 Like as the waves make towards the pebbled shore,
   So do our minutes hasten to their end.
   Sonnet 60

21 Time doth transfix the flourish set on youth
   And delves the parallels in beauty's brow.
   Sonnet 60

22 Sin of self-love possesseth all mine eye.
   Sonnet 62

1 When I have seen by Time's fell hand defaced
The rich-proud cost of outworn buried age.
Sonnet 64

2 When I have seen the hungry ocean gain
Advantage on the kingdom of the shore.
Sonnet 64

3 Since brass, nor stone, nor earth, nor boundless sea,
But sad mortality o'ersways their power,
How with this rage shall beauty hold a plea,
Whose action is no stronger than a flower?
Sonnet 65

4 Tired with all these, for restful death I cry.
Sonnet 66

5 No longer mourn for me when I am dead
Than you shall hear the surly sullen bell
Give warning to the world that I am fled
From this vile world, with vilest worms to dwell.
Sonnet 71

6 That time of year thou mayst in me behold
When yellow leaves, or none, or few, do hang
Upon those boughs which shake against the cold,
Bare ruined choirs, where late the sweet birds sang.
In me thou see'st the twilight of such day
As after sunset fadeth in the west;
Which by and by black night doth take away,
Death's second self, that seals up all in rest.
Sonnet 73

7 O! know, sweet love, I always write of you,
And you and love are still my argument;
So all my best is dressing old words new,
Spending again what is already spent.
Sonnet 76

8 Time's thievish progress to eternity.
Sonnet 77

9 Was it the proud full sail of his great verse,
Bound for the prize of all too precious you,
That did my ripe thoughts in my brain inhearse,
Making their tomb the womb wherein they grew?
Sonnet 86

10   That affable familiar ghost
Which nightly gulls him with intelligence.
Sonnet 86

11 Farewell! thou art too dear for my possessing,
And like enough thou know'st thy estimate:
The charter of thy worth gives thee releasing;
My bonds in thee are all determinate.
Sonnet 87

12 Thus have I had thee, as a dream doth flatter,
In sleep a king, but, waking, no such matter.
Sonnet 87

13 Ah, do not, when my heart hath 'scaped this sorrow,
Come in the rearward of a conquered woe;
Give not a windy night a rainy morrow,
To linger out a purposed overthrow.
Sonnet 90

14 They that have power to hurt and will do none,
That do not do the thing they most do show,
Who, moving others, are themselves as stone,
Unmovèd, cold, and to temptation slow;
They rightly do inherit heaven's graces,
And husband nature's riches from expense.
Sonnet 94

15 They are the lords and owners of their faces,
Others but stewards of their excellence.
The summer's flower is to the summer sweet,
Though to itself it only live and die,
But if that flower with base infection meet,
The basest weed outbraves his dignity:
For sweetest things turn sourest by their deeds;
Lilies that fester smell far worse than weeds.
Sonnet 94

16 How like a winter hath my absence been
From thee, the pleasure of the fleeting year!
What freezings have I felt, what dark days seen!
What old December's bareness everywhere!
Sonnet 97

17 When in the chronicle of wasted time
I see descriptions of the fairest wights,
And beauty making beautiful old rime,
In praise of ladies dead and lovely knights.
Sonnet 106

18 For we, which now behold these present days,
Have eyes to wonder, but lack tongues to praise.
Sonnet 106

19 Not mine own fears, nor the prophetic soul
Of the wide world dreaming on things to come,
Sonnet 107

20 And thou in this shalt find thy monument,
When tyrants' crests and tombs of brass are spent.
Sonnet 107

21 Alas! 'tis true I have gone here and there,
And made myself a motley to the view,
Gored mine own thoughts, sold cheap what is most dear,
Made old offences of affections new;
Most true it is that I have looked on truth
Askance and strangely; but, by all above,
These blenches gave my heart another youth,
And worse essays proved thee my best of love.
Sonnet 110

22   My nature is subdued
To what it works in, like the dyer's hand.
Sonnet 111

23 Let me not to the marriage of true minds
Admit impediments. Love is not love
Which alters when it alteration finds,
Or bends with the remover to remove:
O, no! it is an ever-fixèd mark,
That looks on tempests and is never shaken.
Sonnet 116

24 Love alters not with his brief hours and weeks,
But bears it out even to the edge of doom.
If this be error, and upon me proved,
I never writ, nor no man ever loved.
Sonnet 116

25 What potions have I drunk of Siren tears,
Distilled from limbecks foul as hell within,
Applying fears to hopes, and hopes to fears,
Still losing when I saw myself to win!
Sonnet 119

1 The expense of spirit in a waste of shame
Is lust in action; and till action, lust
Is perjured, murderous, bloody, full of blame,
Savage, extreme, rude, cruel, not to trust;
Enjoyed no sooner but despisèd straight.
Sonnet 129

2 My mistress' eyes are nothing like the sun;
Coral is far more red than her lips' red:
If snow be white, why then her breasts are dun;
If hairs be wires, black wires grow on her head.
Sonnet 130

3 And yet, by heaven, I think my love as rare
As any she belied with false compare.
Sonnet 130

4 Whoever hath her wish, thou hast thy *Will*,
And *Will* to boot, and *Will* in over-plus.
Sonnet 135

5 When my love swears that she is made of truth,
I do believe her, though I know she lies.
Sonnet 138

6 Two loves I have of comfort and despair,
Which like two spirits do suggest me still:
The better angel is a man right fair,
The worser spirit a woman, coloured ill.
Sonnet 144

7 Poor soul, the centre of my sinful earth,
[Fooled by] these rebel powers that thee array,
Why dost thou pine within and suffer dearth,
Painting thy outward walls so costly gay?
Why so large cost, having so short a lease,
Dost thou upon thy fading mansion spend?
Sonnet 146

8 So shalt thou feed on Death, that feeds on men,
And Death once dead, there's no more dying then.
Sonnet 146

9 Past cure I am, now Reason is past care,
And frantic-mad with evermore unrest;
My thoughts and my discourse as madmen's are,
At random from the truth vainly expressed;
For I have sworn thee fair, and thought thee bright,
Who art as black as hell, as dark as night.
Sonnet 147

Venus and Adonis

10 If the first heir of my invention prove deformed, I shall
be sorry it had so noble a godfather.
Venus and Adonis (1593) dedication

11 Hunting he loved, but love he laughed to scorn.
Venus and Adonis (1593) l. 4

12 Bid me discourse, I will enchant thine ear,
Or like a fairy trip upon the green,
Or, like a nymph, with long dishevelled hair,
Dance on the sands, and yet no footing seen:
Love is a spirit all compact of fire,
Not gross to sink, but light, and will aspire.
Venus and Adonis (1593) l. 145

13 Love comforteth like sunshine after rain.
Venus and Adonis (1593) l. 799

14 For he being dead, with him is beauty slain,
And, beauty dead, black chaos comes again.
Venus and Adonis (1593) l. 1019

15 Good friend, for Jesu's sake forbear
To dig the dust enclosed here.
Blest be the man that spares these stones,
And curst be he that moves my bones.
Epitaph on his tomb, probably composed by himself

16 Item, I give unto my wife my second best bed, with
the furniture.
Will, 1616. See E. K. Chambers *William Shakespeare* (1930)
vol. 2, p. 169

Bill Shankly 1914–81
Scottish footballer

17 Some people think football is a matter of life and death
... I can assure them it is much more serious than
that.
In *Sunday Times* 4 October 1981

Tom Sharpe 1928–
English writer

18 The South African police would leave no stone
unturned to see that nothing disturbed the even terror
of their lives.
Indecent Exposure (1973) ch. 1

George Bernard Shaw 1856–1950
Irish playwright

19 All great truths begin as blasphemies.
Annajanska (1919) p. 262

20 One man that has a mind and knows it can always
beat ten men who haven't and don't.
The Apple Cart (1930) act 1

21 What Englishman will give his mind to politics as long
as he can afford to keep a motor car?
The Apple Cart (1930) act 1

22 You can always tell an old soldier by the inside of his
holsters and cartridge boxes. The young ones carry
pistols and cartridges; the old ones, grub.
Arms and the Man (1898) act 1

23 Oh, you are a very poor soldier—a chocolate cream
soldier!
Arms and the Man (1898) act 1

24 You're not a man, you're a machine.
Arms and the Man (1898) act 3

25 I enjoy convalescence. It is the part that makes illness
worth while.
Back to Methuselah (1921) pt. 2

26 He [the Briton] is a barbarian, and thinks that the
customs of his tribe and island are the laws of nature.
Caesar and Cleopatra (1901) act 2

27 When a stupid man is doing something he is ashamed
of, he always declares that it is his duty.
Caesar and Cleopatra (1901) act 3

28 A man of great common sense and good taste,
meaning thereby a man without originality or moral
courage.
Notes to Caesar and Cleopatra (1901) 'Julius Caesar'

1 We have no more right to consume happiness without
producing it than to consume wealth without
producing it.
   Candida (1898) act 1

2 Do you think that the things people make fools of
themselves about are any less real and true than the
things they behave sensibly about? They are more
true: they are the only things that are true.
   Candida (1898) act 1

3 It is easy—terribly easy—to shake a man's faith in
himself. To take advantage of that to break a man's
spirit is devil's work.
   Candida (1898) act 1

4 I'm only a beer teetotaller, not a champagne
teetotaller.
   Candida (1898) act 3

5 The worst sin towards our fellow creatures is not to
hate them, but to be indifferent to them: that's the
essence of inhumanity.
   The Devil's Disciple (1901) act 2

6 Martyrdom ... the only way in which a man can
become famous without ability.
   The Devil's Disciple (1901) act 3

7 I never expect a soldier to think.
   The Devil's Disciple (1901) act 3

8 SWINDON: What will history say?
   BURGOYNE: History, sir, will tell lies as usual.
   The Devil's Disciple (1901) act 3

9 Your friend the British soldier can stand up to
anything except the British War Office.
   The Devil's Disciple (1901) act 3

10 There is at bottom only one genuinely scientific
treatment for all diseases, and that is to stimulate the
phagocytes.
   The Doctor's Dilemma (1911) act 1

11 All professions are conspiracies against the laity.
   The Doctor's Dilemma (1911) act 1

12 A government which robs Peter to pay Paul can
always depend on the support of Paul.
   Everybody's Political What's What? (1944) ch. 30

13 It's all that the young can do for the old, to shock
them and keep them up to date.
   Fanny's First Play (1914) 'Induction'

14 Home life as we understand it is no more natural to us
than a cage is natural to a cockatoo.
   Getting Married (1911) preface 'Hearth and Home'

15 The one point on which all women are in furious
secret rebellion against the existing law is the saddling
of the right to a child with the obligation to become
the servant of a man.
   Getting Married (1911) preface 'The Right to Motherhood'

16 Physically there is nothing to distinguish human
society from the farm-yard except that children are
more troublesome and costly than chickens and
calves, and that men and women are not so
completely enslaved as farm stock.
   Getting Married (1911) preface 'The Personal Sentimental
   Basis of Monogamy'

17 What God hath joined together no man ever shall put
asunder: God will take care of that.
   Getting Married (1911) p. 216. Cf. Book of Common Prayer
   123:22

18 I am a woman of the world, Hector; and I can assure
you that if you will only take the trouble always to do
the perfectly correct thing, and to say the perfectly
correct thing, you can do just what you like.
   Heartbreak House (1919) act 1

19 Go anywhere in England where there are natural,
wholesome, contented, and really nice English people;
and what do you always find? That the stables are the
real centre of the household.
   Heartbreak House (1919) act 3

20 The captain is in his bunk, drinking bottled
ditch-water; and the crew is gambling in the
forecastle. She will strike and sink and split. Do you
think the laws of God will be suspended in favour of
England because you were born in it?
   Heartbreak House (1919) act 3

21 Money is indeed the most important thing in the
world; and all sound and successful personal and
national morality should have this fact for its basis.
   The Irrational Knot (1905) preface

22 Reminiscences make one feel so deliciously aged and
sad.
   The Irrational Knot (1905) ch. 14

23 A man who has no office to go to—I don't care who
he is—is a trial of which you can have no conception.
   The Irrational Knot (1905) ch. 18

24 An Irishman's heart is nothing but his imagination.
   John Bull's Other Island (1907) act 1

25 What really flatters a man is that you think him worth
flattering.
   John Bull's Other Island (1907) act 4

26 There are only two qualities in the world: efficiency
and inefficiency, and only two sorts of people: the
efficient and the inefficient.
   John Bull's Other Island (1907) act 4

27 The greatest of evils and the worst of crimes is
poverty...our first duty—a duty to which every other
consideration should be sacrificed—is not to be poor.
   Major Barbara (1907) preface

28 Nobody can say a word against Greek: it stamps a
man at once as an educated gentleman.
   Major Barbara (1907) act 1

29 I am a Millionaire. That is my religion.
   Major Barbara (1907) act 2

30 I can't talk religion to a man with bodily hunger in his
eyes.
   Major Barbara (1907) act 2

31 Wot prawce Selvytion nah?
   Major Barbara (1907) act 2

32 Alcohol is a very necessary article ... It makes life
bearable to millions of people who could not endure
their existence if they were quite sober. It enables
Parliament to do things at eleven at night that no
sane person would do at eleven in the morning.
   Major Barbara (1907) act 2

1 He knows nothing; and he thinks he knows everything. That points clearly to a political career.
Major Barbara (1907) act 3

2 Nothing is ever done in this world until men are prepared to kill one another if it is not done.
Major Barbara (1907) act 3

3 Like all young men, you greatly exaggerate the difference between one young woman and another.
Major Barbara (1907) act 3. Cf. Mencken 457:6

4 But a lifetime of happiness! No man alive could bear it: it would be hell on earth.
Man and Superman (1903) act 1

5 The more things a man is ashamed of, the more respectable he is.
Man and Superman (1903) act 1

6 Vitality in a woman is a blind fury of creation.
Man and Superman (1903) act 1

7 Of all human struggles there is none so treacherous and remorseless as the struggle between the artist man and the mother woman.
Man and Superman (1903) act 1

8 You think that you are Ann's suitor; that you are the pursuer and she the pursued . . . Fool: it is you who are the pursued, the marked down quarry, the destined prey.
Man and Superman (1903) act 2

9 MENDOZA: I am a brigand: I live by robbing the rich.
TANNER: I am a gentleman: I live by robbing the poor.
Man and Superman (1903) act 3

10 Hell is full of musical amateurs: music is the brandy of the damned.
Man and Superman (1903) act 3

11 Englishmen never will be slaves: they are free to do whatever the Government and public opinion allow them to do.
Man and Superman (1903) act 3

12 An Englishman thinks he is moral when he is only uncomfortable.
Man and Superman (1903) act 3

13 In the arts of life man invents nothing; but in the arts of death he outdoes Nature herself, and produces by chemistry and machinery all the slaughter of plague, pestilence and famine.
Man and Superman (1903) act 3

14 In the arts of peace Man is a bungler.
Man and Superman (1903) act 3

15 As an old soldier I admit the cowardice: it's as universal as sea sickness, and matters just as little.
Man and Superman (1903) act 3

16 When the military man approaches, the world locks up its spoons and packs off its womankind.
Man and Superman (1903) act 3

17 What is virtue but the Trade Unionism of the married?
Man and Superman (1903) act 3

18 Those who talk most about the blessings of marriage and the constancy of its vows are the very people who declare that if the chain were broken and the prisoners were left free to choose, the whole social fabric would fly asunder. You can't have the argument both ways. If the prisoner is happy, why lock him in? If he is not, why pretend that he is?
Man and Superman (1903) act 3

19 Beauty is all very well at first sight; but who ever looks at it when it has been in the house three days?
Man and Superman (1903) act 4

20 Revolutions have never lightened the burden of tyranny: they have only shifted it to another shoulder.
Man and Superman (1903) 'The Revolutionist's Handbook' foreword

21 The art of government is the organization of idolatry.
Man and Superman (1903) 'Maxims: Idolatry'

22 Democracy substitutes election by the incompetent many for appointment by the corrupt few.
Man and Superman (1903) 'Maxims: Democracy'

23 Liberty means responsibility. That is why most men dread it.
Man and Superman (1903)'Maxims: Liberty and Equality'

24 He who can, does. He who cannot, teaches.
Man and Superman (1903) 'Maxims: Education'

25 Marriage is popular because it combines the maximum of temptation with the maximum of opportunity.
Man and Superman (1903) 'Maxims: Marriage'

26 Titles distinguish the mediocre, embarrass the superior, and are disgraced by the inferior.
Man and Superman (1903) 'Maxims: Titles'

27 When domestic servants are treated as human beings it is not worth while to keep them.
Man and Superman (1903) 'Maxims: Servants'

28 If you strike a child take care that you strike it in anger, even at the risk of maiming it for life. A blow in cold blood neither can nor should be forgiven.
Man and Superman (1903) 'Maxims: How to Beat Children'

29 Beware of the man whose god is in the skies.
Man and Superman (1903) 'Maxims: Religion'

30 Self-denial is not a virtue: it is only the effect of prudence on rascality.
Man and Superman (1903) 'Maxims: Virtues and Vice'

31 A moderately honest man with a moderately faithful wife, moderate drinkers both, in a moderately healthy house: that is the true middle-class unit.
Man and Superman (1903) 'Maxims: Moderation'

32 The reasonable man adapts himself to the world: the unreasonable one persists in trying to adapt the world to himself. Therefore all progress depends on the unreasonable man.
Man and Superman (1903) 'Maxims: Reason'

33 The man who listens to Reason is lost: Reason enslaves all whose minds are not strong enough to master her.
Man and Superman (1903) 'Maxims: Reason'

34 Decency is Indecency's conspiracy of silence.
Man and Superman (1903) 'Maxims: Decency'

35 Life levels all men: death reveals the eminent.
Man and Superman (1903) 'Maxims: Fame'

1 Home is the girl's prison and the woman's workhouse.
  Man and Superman (1903) 'Maxims: Women in the Home'

2 Every man over forty is a scoundrel.
  Man and Superman (1903) 'Maxims: Stray Sayings'

3 Youth, which is forgiven everything, forgives itself nothing: age, which forgives itself everything, is forgiven nothing.
  Man and Superman (1903) 'Maxims: Stray Sayings'

4 Take care to get what you like or you will be forced to like what you get.
  Man and Superman (1903) 'Maxims: Stray Sayings'

5 Beware of the man who does not return your blow: he neither forgives you nor allows you to forgive yourself.
  Man and Superman (1903) 'Maxims: Stray Sayings'

6 Self-sacrifice enables us to sacrifice other people without blushing.
  Man and Superman (1903) 'Maxims: Self-Sacrifice'

7 There is nothing so bad or so good that you will not find Englishmen doing it; but you will never find an Englishman in the wrong. He does everything on principle. He fights you on patriotic principles; he robs you on business principles; he enslaves you on imperial principles; he bullies you on manly principles; he supports his king on loyal principles and cuts off his king's head on republican principles.
  The Man of Destiny (1898) p. 201

8 Anarchism is a game at which the police can beat you.
  Misalliance (1914) p. 85

9 The only way for a woman to provide for herself decently is for her to be good to some man that can afford to be good to her.
  Mrs Warren's Profession (1898) act 2

10 A great devotee of the Gospel of Getting On.
  Mrs Warren's Profession (1898) act 4

11 You'll never have a quiet world till you knock the patriotism out of the human race.
  O'Flaherty V.C. (1919) p. 178

12 The secret of being miserable is to have leisure to bother about whether you are happy or not. The cure for it is occupation.
  Parents and Children (1914) 'Children's Happiness'

13 A perpetual holiday is a good working definition of hell.
  Parents and Children (1914) 'Children's Happiness'

14 There is only one religion, though there are a hundred versions of it.
  Plays Pleasant and Unpleasant (1898) vol. 2, preface

15 The English have no respect for their language, and will not teach their children to speak it. They spell it so abominably that no man can teach himself what it sounds like. It is impossible for an Englishman to open his mouth without making some other Englishman hate or despise him.
  Pygmalion (1916) preface

16 I don't want to talk grammar, I want to talk like a lady.
  Pygmalion (1916) act 2

17 PICKERING: Have you no morals, man?
  DOOLITTLE: Can't afford them, Governor.
  Pygmalion (1916) act 2

18 I'm one of the undeserving poor . . . up agen middle-class morality all the time . . . What is middle-class morality? Just an excuse for never giving me anything.
  Pygmalion (1916) act 2

19 Gin was mother's milk to her.
  Pygmalion (1916) act 3

20 Walk! Not bloody likely. I am going in a taxi.
  Pygmalion (1916) act 3

21 If ever I utter an oath again may my soul be blasted to eternal damnation!
  Saint Joan (1924) sc. 2

22 No Englishman is ever fairly beaten.
  Saint Joan (1924) sc. 4

23 How can what an Englishman believes be heresy? It is a contradiction in terms.
  Saint Joan (1924) sc. 4

24 Must then a Christ perish in torment in every age to save those that have no imagination?
  Saint Joan (1924) epilogue

25 Assassination is the extreme form of censorship.
  The Showing-Up of Blanco Posnet (1911) 'Limits to Toleration'

26 'Do you know what a pessimist is?' 'A man who thinks everybody is as nasty as himself, and hates them for it.'
  An Unsocial Socialist (1887) ch. 5

27 The great advantage of a hotel is that it's a refuge from home life.
  You Never Can Tell (1898) act 2

28 The younger generation is knocking at the door, and as I open it there steps spritely in the incomparable Max.
  Saturday Review 21 May 1898 'Valedictory' (on handing over the theatre review column to Max Beerbohm)

29 The trouble, Mr Goldwyn, is that you are only interested in art and I am only interested in money.
  Telegraphed version of the outcome of a conversation between Shaw and Sam Goldwyn; in Alva Johnson *The Great Goldwyn* (1937) ch. 3

30 [Dancing is] a perpendicular expression of a horizontal desire.
  In *New Statesman* 23 March 1962

31 England and America are two countries divided by a common language.
  Attributed in this and other forms, but not found in Shaw's published writings

Sir Hartley Shawcross (Baron Shawcross) 1902–

British Labour politician

1 'But,' said Alice, 'the question is whether you can make a word mean different things.' 'Not so,' said Humpty-Dumpty, 'the question is which is to be the master. That's all.' We are the masters at the moment, and not only at the moment, but for a very long time to come.
> Speech, *Hansard* 2 April 1946, col. 1213 (often quoted 'We are the masters now'). Cf. Carroll 183:12

Charles Shaw-Lefevre (Viscount Eversley) 1794–1888

2 What is that fat gentleman in such a passion about?
> As a child, on hearing Charles James Fox speak in Parliament; in G. W. E. Russell *Collections and Recollections* (1898) ch. 11

Patrick Shaw-Stewart 1888–1917

3 I saw a man this morning
Who did not wish to die;
I ask and cannot answer
If otherwise wish I.
> Poem (1916) in M. Baring *Have You Anything to Declare?* (1936) p. 39

Mary Shelley (née Godwin) 1797–1851

English novelist

4 You seek for knowledge and wisdom as I once did; and I ardently hope that the gratification of your wishes may not be a serpent to sting you, as mine has been.
> *Frankenstein* (1818) Letter 4

5 It was the secrets of heaven and earth that I desired to learn.
> *Frankenstein* (1818) ch. 4

6 I beheld the wretch—the miserable monster whom I had created.
> *Frankenstein* (1818) ch. 5

7 All men hate the wretched; how, then, must I be hated, who am miserable beyond all living things! Yet you, my creator, detest and spurn me, thy creature, to whom thou art bound by ties only dissoluble by the annihilation of one of us.
> *Frankenstein* (1818) ch. 10

8 Everywhere I see bliss, from which I alone am irrevocably excluded.
> *Frankenstein* (1818) ch. 10

9 Teach him to think for himself? Oh, my God, teach him rather to think like other people!
> On her son's education, in Matthew Arnold *Essays in Criticism, Second Series* (1888) 'Shelley'

Percy Bysshe Shelley 1792–1822

English poet

10 The cemetery is an open space among the ruins, covered in winter with violets and daisies. It might make one in love with death, to think that one should be buried in so sweet a place.
> *Adonais* (1821) preface

11 I weep for Adonais—he is dead!
O, weep for Adonais! though our tears
Thaw not the frost which binds so dear a head!
> *Adonais* (1821) st. 1

12   He died,
Who was the Sire of an immortal strain,
Blind, old and lonely.
> *Adonais* (1821) st. 4

13 To that high Capital, where kingly Death
Keeps his pale court in beauty and decay,
He came.
> *Adonais* (1821) st. 7

14   The quick Dreams,
The passion-wingèd Ministers of thought.
> *Adonais* (1821) st. 9

15 Lost Angel of a ruined Paradise!
She knew not 'twas her own; as with no stain
She faded, like a cloud which had outwept its rain.
> *Adonais* (1821) st. 10

16 Ah, woe is me! Winter is come and gone,
But grief returns with the revolving year.
> *Adonais* (1821) st. 18

17 From the great morning of the world when first
God dawned on Chaos.
> *Adonais* (1821) st. 19

18 Alas! that all we loved of him should be,
But for our grief, as if it had not been,
And grief itself be mortal!
> *Adonais* (1821) st. 21

19 Whence are we, and why are we? Of what scene
The actors or spectators?
> *Adonais* (1821) st. 21

20 A pardlike Spirit, beautiful and swift—
A Love in desolation masked;—a Power
Girt round with weakness;—it can scarce uplift
The weight of the superincumbent hour;
It is a dying lamp, a falling shower,
A breaking billow;—even whilst we speak
Is it not broken?
> *Adonais* (1821) st. 32

21 He wakes or sleeps with the enduring dead;
Thou canst not soar where he is sitting now—
Dust to the dust! but the pure spirit shall flow
Back to the burning fountain whence it came,
A portion of the Eternal.
> *Adonais* (1821) st. 38

22 He hath awakened from the dream of life—
'Tis we, who lost in stormy visions, keep
With phantoms an unprofitable strife,
And in mad trance, strike with our spirit's knife
Invulnerable nothings.
> *Adonais* (1821) st. 39

1 He has out-soared the shadow of our night;
Envy and calumny and hate and pain,
And that unrest which men miscall delight,
Can touch him not and torture not again;
From the contagion of the world's slow stain
He is secure, and now can never mourn
A heart grown cold, a head grown grey in vain.
Adonais (1821) st. 40

2 He lives, he wakes,—'tis Death is dead, not he.
Adonais (1821) st. 41

3 He is a portion of the loveliness
Which once he made more lovely.
Adonais (1821) st. 43

4 The One remains, the many change and pass;
Heaven's light forever shines, Earth's shadows fly;
Life, like a dome of many-coloured glass,
Stains the white radiance of Eternity,
Until Death tramples it to fragments.
Adonais (1821) st. 52

5 A widow bird sat mourning for her love
Upon a wintry bough;
The frozen wind crept on above,
The freezing stream below.
Charles the First (1822) sc. 5, l. 9

6 That orbèd maiden, with white fire laden,
Whom mortals call the Moon.
'The Cloud' (1819)

7 I am the daughter of Earth and Water,
And the nursling of the Sky;
I pass through the pores of the ocean and shores;
I change, but I cannot die,
For after the rain when with never a stain
The pavilion of Heaven is bare,
And the winds and sunbeams with their convex
    gleams
Build up the blue dome of air,
I silently laugh at my own cenotaph,
And out of the caverns of rain,
Like a child from the womb, like a ghost from the
    tomb,
I arise and unbuild it again.
'The Cloud' (1819)

8 How wonderful is Death,
Death and his brother Sleep!
One pale as yonder wan and hornèd moon,
With lips of lurid blue,
The other glowing like the vital morn,
When throned on ocean's wave
It breathes over the world:
Yet both so passing strange and wonderful!
'The Daemon of the World' (1816) part 1, l. 1 (revision of
the opening lines of *Queen Mab*)

9 I never was attached to that great sect,
Whose doctrine is that each one should select
Out of the crowd a mistress or a friend,
And all the rest, though fair and wise, commend
To cold oblivion.
'Epipsychidion' (1821) l. 149

10   The beaten road
Which those poor slaves with weary footsteps tread,
Who travel to their home among the dead
By the broad highway of the world, and so
With one chained friend, perhaps a jealous foe,
The dreariest and the longest journey go.
'Epipsychidion' (1821) l. 154

11 I pant, I sink, I tremble, I expire!
'Epipsychidion' (1821) l. 591

12 Chameleons feed on light and air:
Poets' food is love and fame.
'An Exhortation' (1820)

13 Good-night? ah! no; the hour is ill
Which severs those it should unite;
Let us remain together still,
Then it will be *good* night.
'Good Night' (1822)

14 Let there be light! said Liberty,
And like sunrise from the sea,
Athens arose!
Hellas (1822) l. 682

15 The world's great age begins anew,
The golden years return,
The earth doth like a snake renew
Her winter weeds outworn;
Heaven smiles, and faiths and empires gleam,
Like wrecks of a dissolving dream.
Hellas (1822) l. 1060

16 O cease! must hate and death return?
Cease! must men kill and die?
Cease! drain not to its dregs the urn
Of bitter prophecy.
The world is weary of the past,
Oh, might it die or rest at last!
Hellas (1822) l. 1096

17 I pursued a maiden and clasped a reed.
Gods and men, we are all deluded thus!
It breaks in our bosom and then we bleed.
'Hymn of Pan' (1824)

18 The awful shadow of some unseen Power
Floats though unseen among us,—visiting
This various world with as inconstant wing
As summer winds that creep from flower to flower.
'Hymn to Intellectual Beauty' (1816)

19 The day becomes more solemn and serene
When noon is past—there is a harmony
In autumn, and a lustre in its sky,
Which through the summer is not heard or seen,
As if it could not be, as if it had not been!
'Hymn to Intellectual Beauty' (1816)

20   I love all waste
And solitary places; where we taste
The pleasure of believing what we see
Is boundless, as we wish our souls to be.
'Julian and Maddalo' (1818) l. 14

21 Thou Paradise of exiles, Italy!
'Julian and Maddalo' (1818) l. 57

22 *Me*—who am as a nerve o'er which do creep
The else unfelt oppressions of this earth.
'Julian and Maddalo' (1818) l. 449

1   Most wretched men
Are cradled into poetry by wrong:
They learn in suffering what they teach in song.
'Julian and Maddalo' (1818) l. 544

2 ... London, that great sea, whose ebb and flow
At once is deaf and loud, and on the shore
Vomits its wrecks, and still howls on for more.
'Letter to Maria Gisborne' (1820) l. 193

3 You will see Coleridge—he who sits obscure
In the exceeding lustre and the pure
Intense irradiation of a mind,
Which, with its own internal lightning blind,
Flags wearily through darkness and despair—
A cloud-encircled meteor of the air,
A hooded eagle among blinking owls—
You will see Hunt—one of those happy souls
Which are the salt of the earth, and without whom
This world would smell like what it is—a tomb.
'Letter to Maria Gisborne' (1820) l. 202

4   Have you not heard
When a man marries, dies, or turns Hindoo,
His best friends hear no more of him?
'Letter to Maria Gisborne' (1820) l. 235

5   His fine wit
Makes such a wound, the knife is lost in it.
'Letter to Maria Gisborne' (1820) l. 240 (of Thomas Love
Peacock)

6 When the lamp is shattered
The light in the dust lies dead—
When the cloud is scattered
The rainbow's glory is shed.
When the lute is broken,
Sweet tones are remembered not;
When the lips have spoken,
Loved accents are soon forgot.
'Lines: When the lamp' (1824)

7 Beneath is spread like a green sea
The waveless plain of Lombardy,
Bounded by the vaporous air,
Islanded by cities fair;
Underneath Day's azure eyes
Ocean's nursling, Venice lies,
A peopled labyrinth of walls,
Amphitrite's destined halls.
'Lines written amongst the Euganean Hills' (1818) l. 90

8 Sun-girt city, thou hast been
Ocean's child, and then his queen;
Now is come a darker day,
And thou soon must be his prey.
'Lines written amongst the Euganean Hills' (1818) l. 115
(of Venice)

9 The fountains mingle with the river,
And the rivers with the ocean;
The winds of heaven mix for ever
With a sweet emotion;
Nothing in the world is single;
All things, by a law divine,
In one spirit meet and mingle.
Why not I with thine?
'Love's Philosophy' (written 1819)

10 I met Murder on the way—
He had a mask like Castlereagh.
'The Mask of Anarchy' (1819) st. 2

11 His big tears, for he wept well,
Turned to mill-stones as they fell.
And the little children, who
Round his feet played to and fro,
Thinking every tear a gem,
Had their brains knocked out by them.
'The Mask of Anarchy' (1819) st. 4 (of 'Fraud' [Lord
Eldon])

12 Nought may endure but Mutability.
'Mutability' (1816)

13 I stood within the City disinterred;
And heard the autumnal leaves like light footfalls
Of spirits passing through the streets; and heard
The Mountain's slumberous voice at intervals
Thrill through those roofless halls.
'Ode to Naples' (1820) l. 1

14 O wild West Wind, thou breath of Autumn's being,
Thou, from whose unseen presence the leaves dead
Are driven, like ghosts from an enchanter fleeing,

Yellow, and black, and pale, and hectic red,
Pestilence-stricken multitudes: O thou,
Who chariotest to their dark wintry bed

The wingèd seeds, where they lie cold and low,
Each like a corpse within its grave, until
Thine azure sister of the spring shall blow

Her clarion o'er the dreaming earth, and fill
(Driving sweet buds like flocks to feed in air)
With living hues and odours plain and hill:

Wild Spirit, which art moving everywhere;
Destroyer and preserver; hear, oh, hear!
'Ode to the West Wind' (1819) l. 1

15   There are spread
On the blue surface of thine aëry surge,
Like the bright hair uplifted from the head

Of some fierce Maenad, even from the dim verge
Of the horizon to the zenith's height,
The locks of the approaching storm.
'Ode to the West Wind' (1819) l. 18

16 Thou who didst waken from his summer dreams
The blue Mediterranean, where he lay,
Lulled by the coil of his crystàlline streams

Beside a pumice isle in Baiae's bay,
And saw in sleep old palaces and towers
Quivering within the wave's intenser day,

All overgrown with azure moss and flowers
So sweet, the sense faints picturing them!
'Ode to the West Wind' (1819) l. 29

17 The sea-blooms and the oozy woods which wear
The sapless foliage of the ocean, know

Thy voice, and suddenly grow grey with fear,
And tremble and despoil themselves.
'Ode to the West Wind' (1819) l. 39

18 Oh, lift me as a wave, a leaf, a cloud!
I fall upon the thorns of life! I bleed!
'Ode to the West Wind' (1819) l. 53

19 Make me thy lyre, even as the forest is:
What if my leaves are falling like its own!
The tumult of thy mighty harmonies
Will take from both a deep, autumnal tone,
Sweet though in sadness.
'Ode to the West Wind' (1819) l. 57

1 And, by the incantation of this verse,

Scatter, as from an unextinguished hearth
Ashes and sparks, my words among mankind!
Be through my lips to unawakened earth

The trumpet of a prophecy! O, Wind,
If Winter comes, can Spring be far behind?
'Ode to the West Wind' (1819) l. 65

2 Its horror and its beauty are divine.
'On the Medusa of Leonardo da Vinci' (1824)

3 I met a traveller from an antique land
Who said: Two vast and trunkless legs of stone
Stand in the desert.
'Ozymandias' (1819)

4 'My name is Ozymandias, king of kings:
Look on my works, ye Mighty, and despair!'
Nothing beside remains. Round the decay
Of that colossal wreck, boundless and bare
The lone and level sands stretch far away.
'Ozymandias' (1819)

5 Hell is a city much like London—
A populous and smoky city.
'Peter Bell the Third' (1819) pt. 3, st. 1

6 But from the first 'twas Peter's drift
To be a kind of moral eunuch,
He touched the hem of Nature's shift,
Felt faint—and never dared uplift
The closest, all-concealing tunic.
'Peter Bell the Third' (1819) pt. 4, st. 11

7   Ere Babylon was dust,
The Magus Zoroaster, my dead child,
Met his own image walking in the garden,
That apparition, sole of men, he saw.
Prometheus Unbound (1819) act 1, l. 191

8 Cruel he looks, but calm and strong,
Like one who does, not suffers wrong.
Prometheus Unbound (1819) act 1, l. 238

9 It doth repent me: words are quick and vain;
Grief for awhile is blind, and so was mine.
Prometheus Unbound (1820) act 1, l. 303

10 Kingly conclaves stern and cold
Where blood with guilt is bought and sold.
Prometheus Unbound (1820) act 1, l. 530

11 The good want power, but to weep barren tears.
The powerful goodness want: worse need for them.
The wise want love; and those who love want
wisdom.
Prometheus Unbound (1820) act 1, l. 625

12   Peace is in the grave.
The grave hides all things beautiful and good:
I am a God and cannot find it there.
Prometheus Unbound (1820) act 1, l. 638

13 The dust of creeds outworn.
Prometheus Unbound (1820) act 1, l. 697

14 On a poet's lips I slept
Dreaming like a love-adept
In the sound his breathing kept.
Prometheus Unbound (1820) act 1, l. 737

15   To be
Omnipotent but friendless is to reign.
Prometheus Unbound (1820) act 2, sc. 4, l. 47

16 He gave man speech, and speech created thought,
Which is the measure of the universe.
Prometheus Unbound (1820) act 2, sc. 4, l. 72

17 My soul is an enchanted boat,
Which, like a sleeping swan, doth float
Upon the silver waves of thy sweet singing.
Prometheus Unbound (1820) act 2, sc. 5, l. 72

18 The loathsome mask has fallen, the man remains
Sceptreless, free, uncircumscribed, but man
Equal, unclassed, tribeless, and nationless,
Exempt from awe, worship, degree, the king
Over himself; just, gentle, wise: but man
Passionless?—no, yet free from guilt or pain,
Which were, for his will made or suffered them,
Nor yet exempt, though ruling them like slaves,
From chance, and death, and mutability,
The clogs of that which else might oversoar
The loftiest star of unascended heaven,
Pinnacled dim in the intense inane.
Prometheus Unbound (1820) act 3, sc. 4, l. 193

19 A traveller from the cradle to the grave
Through the dim night of this immortal day.
Prometheus Unbound (1820) act 4, l. 551

20 To suffer woes which Hope thinks infinite;
To forgive wrongs darker than death or night;
To defy Power, which seems omnipotent;
To love, and bear; to hope till Hope creates
From its own wreck the thing it contemplates;
Neither to change, nor falter, nor repent;
This, like thy glory, Titan, is to be
Good, great and joyous, beautiful and free;
This is alone Life, Joy, Empire and Victory.
Prometheus Unbound (1820) act 4, l. 570

21 That sweet bondage which is freedom's self.
Queen Mab (1813) canto 9, l. 76

22 I dreamed that, as I wandered by the way,
Bare Winter suddenly was changed to Spring,
And gentle odours led my steps astray,
Mixed with a sound of water's murmuring
Along a shelving bank of turf, which lay
Under a copse, and hardly dared to fling
Its green arms round the bosom of the stream,
But kissed it and then fled, as thou mightst in dream.
'The Question' (1822)

23 Daisies, those pearled Arcturi of the earth,
The constellated flower that never sets.
'The Question' (1822)

24 And in the warm hedge grew lush eglantine,
Green cowbind and the moonlight-coloured may.
'The Question' (1822)

25 With hue like that when some great painter dips
His pencil in the gloom of earthquake and eclipse.
The Revolt of Islam (1818) canto 5, st. 23

26 A Sensitive Plant in a garden grew.
'The Sensitive Plant' (1820) pt. 1, l. 1

27 And the rose like a nymph to the bath addressed,
Which unveiled the depth of her glowing breast,
Till, fold after fold, to the fainting air
The soul of her beauty and love lay bare.
'The Sensitive Plant' (1820) pt. 1, l. 29

1 And the jessamine faint, and the sweet tuberose,
  The sweetest flower for scent that blows.
   'The Sensitive Plant' (1820) pt. 1, l. 37

2 Rarely, rarely, comest thou,
  Spirit of Delight!
   'Song' (1824); epigraph to Elgar's Second Symphony

3 Men of England, wherefore plough
  For the lords who lay ye low?
   'Song to the Men of England' (written 1819)

4 The seed ye sow, another reaps;
  The wealth ye find, another keeps;
  The robes ye weave, another wears;
  The arms ye forge, another bears.
   'Song to the Men of England' (written 1819)

5 Lift not the painted veil which those who live
  Call Life.
   'Sonnet' (1824)

6 Through the unheeding many he did move,
  A splendour among shadows, a bright blot
  Upon this gloomy scene, a Spirit that strove
  For truth, and like the Preacher found it not.
   'Sonnet'

7 An old, mad, blind, despised, and dying king.
   'Sonnet: England in 1819' (written 1819)

8 Away! the moor is dark beneath the moon,
  Rapid clouds have drank the last pale beam of even:
  Away! the gathering winds will call the darkness
     soon,
  And profoundest midnight shroud the serene lights of
     heaven.
   'Stanzas—April 1814' (1816)

9 I see the waves upon the shore,
  Like light dissolved in star-showers, thrown.
   'Stanzas Written in Dejection, near Naples' (1818)

10 Alas! I have nor hope nor health,
   Nor peace within nor calm around,
   Nor that content surpassing wealth
   The sage in meditation found.
    'Stanzas Written in Dejection, near Naples' (1818)

11 Music, when soft voices die,
   Vibrates in the memory—
   Odours, when sweet violets sicken,
   Live within the sense they quicken.
    'To—: Music, when soft voices die' (1824)

12 The desire of the moth for the star,
   Of the night for the morrow,
   The devotion to something afar
   From the sphere of our sorrow.
    'To—: One word is too often profaned' (1824)

13 Hail to thee, blithe Spirit!
   Bird thou never wert,
   That from Heaven, or near it,
   Pourest thy full heart
   In profuse strains of unpremeditated art.
    'To a Skylark' (1819)

14 And singing still dost soar, and soaring ever singest.
    'To a Skylark' (1819)

15 Like an unbodied joy whose race is just begun.
    'To a Skylark' (1819)

16 Thou art unseen, but yet I hear thy shrill delight.
    'To a Skylark' (1819)

17 Like a Poet hidden
   In the light of thought,
   Singing hymns unbidden,
   Till the world is wrought
   To sympathy with hopes and fears it heeded not.
    'To a Skylark' (1819)

18 With thy clear keen joyance
   Languor cannot be:
   Shadow of annoyance
   Never came near thee:
   Thou lovest—but ne'er knew love's sad satiety.
    'To a Skylark' (1819)

19 We look before and after,
   And pine for what is not:
   Our sincerest laughter
   With some pain is fraught;
   Our sweetest songs are those that tell of saddest
      thought.
    'To a Skylark' (1819)

20 Teach me half the gladness
   That thy brain must know,
   Such harmonious madness
   From my lips would flow
   The world should listen then—as I am listening now.
    'To a Skylark' (1819)

21 Less oft is peace in Shelley's mind,
   Than calm in waters, seen.
    'To Jane: The Recollection' (written 1822)

22 Swiftly walk o'er the western wave,
   Spirit of Night!
   Out of the misty eastern cave,
   Where, all the long and lone daylight,
   Thou wovest dreams of joy and fear,
   Which make thee terrible and dear,—
   Swift be thy flight!
    'To Night' (1824)

23 Death will come when thou art dead,
   Soon, too soon—
   Sleep will come when thou art fled;
   Of neither would I ask the boon
   I ask of thee, belovèd Night
   Swift be thine approaching flight,
   Come soon, soon!
    'To Night' (1824)

24 Art thou pale for weariness
   Of climbing heaven, and gazing on the earth,
   Wandering companionless
   Among the stars that have a different birth,—
   And ever changing, like a joyless eye
   That finds no object worth its constancy?
    'To the Moon' (1824)

25 In honoured poverty thy voice did weave
   Songs consecrate to truth and liberty,—
   Deserting these, thou leavest me to grieve,
   Thus having been, that thou shouldst cease to be.
    'To Wordsworth' (1816)

26 And like a dying lady, lean and pale,
   Who totters forth, wrapped in a gauzy veil.
    'The Waning Moon' (1824)

27 A lovely lady, garmented in light
   From her own beauty.
    'The Witch of Atlas' (written 1820) st. 5

1 For she was beautiful—her beauty made
  The bright world dim, and everything beside
  Seemed like the fleeting image of a shade.
    'The Witch of Atlas' (written 1820) st. 12

2 The discussion of any subject is a right that you have
  brought into the world with your heart and tongue.
  Resign your heart's blood before you part with this
  inestimable privilege of man.
    An Address to the Irish People (1812)

3 Titles are tinsel, power a corrupter, glory a bubble,
  and excessive wealth a libel on its possessor.
    Declaration of Rights (1812) article 27

4 The vanity of translation; it were as wise to cast a
  violet into a crucible that you might discover the
  formal principle of its colour and odour, as seek to
  transfuse from one language to another the creations
  of a poet. The plant must spring again from its seed,
  or it will bear no flower.
    A Defence of Poetry (written 1821)

5 The great instrument of moral good is the
  imagination; and poetry administers to the effect by
  acting on the cause.
    A Defence of Poetry (written 1821)

6 A single word even may be a spark of inextinguishable
  thought.
    A Defence of Poetry (written 1821)

7 Poetry is the record of the best and happiest moments
  of the happiest and best minds.
    A Defence of Poetry (written 1821)

8 Poets are the hierophants of an unapprehended
  inspiration; the mirrors of the gigantic shadows which
  futurity casts upon the present; the words which
  express what they understand not; the trumpets
  which sing to battle, and feel not what they inspire;
  the influence which is moved not, but moves. Poets
  are the unacknowledged legislators of the world.
    A Defence of Poetry (written 1821). Cf. Johnson 369:20

9 What is Love? It is that powerful attraction towards
  all that we conceive, or fear, or hope beyond
  ourselves.
    'On Love' (notebook essay, c.1815), in D. L. Clark (ed.)
    Shelley's Prose (1966)

10 Tyranny entrenches itself within the existing interests
   of the most refined citizens of a nation and says 'If you
   dare trample upon these, be free.'
    A Philosophical View of Reform (written 1819–20) ch. 1

11 Thought can with difficulty visit the intricate and
   winding chambers which it inhabits. It is like a river
   whose rapid and perpetual stream flows
   outwards—like one in dread who speeds through the
   recesses of some haunted pile and dares not look
   behind.
    'Speculations on Metaphysics [On the Science of Mind]'
    (written 1815), in D. L. Clark (ed.) Shelley's Prose (1966)

William Shenstone 1714–63

English poet and essayist

12 The charm dissolves; th' aerial music's past;
   The banquet ceases, and the vision flies.
    'Elegy 11. He complains how soon the pleasing novelty of
    life is over' (1764)

13 Whoe'er has travelled life's dull round,
   Where'er his stages may have been,
   May sigh to think he still has found
   The warmest welcome, at an inn.
    'Written at an Inn at Henley' (1758). Cf. Johnson 374:10

14 Laws are generally found to be nets of such a texture,
   as the little creep through, the great break through,
   and the middle-sized are alone entangled in.
    Works in Verse and Prose (1764) vol. 2 'On Politics'. Cf.
    Anacharsis 11:5

15 A fool and his words are soon parted.
    Works ... (1764) vol. 2 'On Reserve'

16 The world may be divided into people that read, people
   that write, people that think, and fox-hunters.
    Works ... (1764) vol. 2 'On Writing and Books'

17 Every good poet includes a critic; the reverse will not
   hold.
    Works ... (1764) vol. 2 'On Writing and Books'

18 To endeavour, all one's days, to fortify our minds with
   learning and philosophy, is to spend so much in
   armour that one has nothing left to defend.
    Works ... (1764) vol. 2 'On Writing and Books'

Philip Henry Sheridan 1831–88

American Union cavalry commander in the Civil War

19 The only good Indian is a dead Indian.
    At Fort Cobb, January 1869 (attributed)

Richard Brinsley Sheridan 1751–1816

Anglo-Irish playwright

20 The newspapers! Sir, they are the most
   villainous—licentious—abominable—infernal—Not
   that I ever read them—No—I make it a rule never to
   look into a newspaper.
    The Critic (1779) act 1, sc. 1

21 If it is abuse,—why one is always sure to hear of it
   from one damned goodnatured friend or another!
    The Critic (1779) act 1, sc. 1

22 Egad I think the interpreter is the hardest to be
   understood of the two!
    The Critic (1779) act 1, sc. 2

23 I wish sir, you would practise this without me. I can't
   stay dying here all night.
    The Critic (1779) act 3, sc. 1

24 O Lord, Sir—when a heroine goes mad she always
   goes into white satin.
    The Critic (1779) act 3, sc. 1

25 An oyster may be crossed in love!
    The Critic (1779) act 3, sc. 1

26 I was struck all of a heap.
    The Duenna (1775) act 2, sc. 2

27 Conscience has no more to do with gallantry than it
   has with politics.
    The Duenna (1775) act 2, sc. 4

28 The throne we honour is the people's choice.
    Pizarro (1799) act 2, sc. 2

1 Illiterate him, I say, quite from your memory.
  The Rivals (1775) act 1, sc. 2

2 'Tis safest in matrimony to begin with a little aversion.
  The Rivals (1775) act 1, sc. 2

3 He is the very pineapple of politeness!
  The Rivals (1775) act 3, sc. 3

4 An aspersion upon my parts of speech!
  The Rivals (1775) act 3, sc. 3

5 If I reprehend any thing in this world, it is the use of my oracular tongue, and a nice derangement of epitaphs!
  The Rivals (1775) act 3, sc. 3

6 She's as headstrong as an allegory on the banks of the Nile.
  The Rivals (1775) act 3, sc. 3

7 Too civil by half.
  The Rivals (1775) act 3, sc. 4

8 Our ancestors are very good kind of folks; but they are the last people I should choose to have a visiting acquaintance with.
  The Rivals (1775) act 4, sc. 1

9 No caparisons, Miss, if you please!—Caparisons don't become a young woman.
  The Rivals (1775) act 4, sc. 2

10 You are not like Cerberus, three gentlemen at once, are you?
  The Rivals (1775) act 4, sc. 2

11 The quarrel is a very pretty quarrel as it stands—we should only spoil it by trying to explain it.
  The Rivals (1775) act 4, sc. 3

12 My valour is certainly going!—it is sneaking off!—I feel it oozing out as it were at the palms of my hands!
  The Rivals (1775) act 5, sc. 3

13 You shall see them on a beautiful quarto page where a neat rivulet of text shall meander through a meadow of margin.
  The School for Scandal (1777) act 1, sc. 1

14 You had no taste when you married me.
  The School for Scandal (1777) act 2, sc. 1

15 MRS CANDOUR: I'll swear her colour is natural—I have seen it come and go—
   LADY TEAZLE: I dare swear you have, ma'am; it goes of a night and comes again in the morning.
   The School for Scandal (1777) act 2, sc. 2

16 Here is the whole set! a character dead at every word.
   The School for Scandal (1777) act 2, sc. 2. Cf. Pope 523:25

17 I'm called away by particular business—but I leave my character behind me.
   The School for Scandal (1777) act 2, sc. 2

18 Here's to the maiden of bashful fifteen
   Here's to the widow of fifty
   Here's to the flaunting, extravagant queen;
   And here's to the housewife that's thrifty.
   Let the toast pass—
   Drink to the lass—
   I'll warrant she'll prove an excuse for the glass!
   The School for Scandal (1777) act 3, sc. 3

19 An unforgiving eye, and a damned disinheriting countenance!
   The School for Scandal (1777) act 4, sc. 1

20 ROWLEY: I believe there is no sentiment he has more faith in as that 'Charity begins at home'.
   SIR OLIVER SURFACE: And his I presume is of that domestic sort which never stirs abroad at all.
   The School for Scandal (1777) act 5, sc. 1

21 There is no trusting appearances.
   The School for Scandal (1777) act 5, sc. 2

22 You write with ease, to show your breeding,
   But easy writing's vile hard reading.
   'Clio's Protest' (written 1771, published 1819)

23 A man may surely be allowed to take a glass of wine by his own fireside.
   On being encountered drinking a glass of wine in the street, while watching his theatre, the Drury Lane, burn down; in T. Moore *Life of Sheridan* (1825) vol. 2, p. 20

24 The Right Honourable gentleman is indebted to his memory for his jests, and to his imagination for his facts.
   Speech in reply to Mr Dundas, in T. Moore *Life of Sheridan* (1825) vol. 2, p. 481

25 Won't you come into the garden? I would like my roses to see you.
   To a young lady (attributed)

Hugh Sherlock 1905–

26 Lord, thy church on earth is seeking
   Thy renewal from above;
   Teach us all the art of speaking
   With the accent of thy love.
   'Lord, thy church on earth is seeking' (hymn)

William Sherman 1820–91

American general in the Civil War

27 There is many a boy here to-day who looks on war as all glory, but, boys, it is all hell.
   Speech at Columbus, Ohio, 11 August 1880, in Lloyd Lewis *Sherman, Fighting Prophet* (1932)

28 I will not accept if nominated, and will not serve if elected.
   Telegram to General Henderson, on being urged to stand as Republican candidate in the 1884 US presidential election; in *Memoirs* (4th ed., 1891) ch. 27

Emanuel Shinwell (Baron Shinwell) 1884–1986

British Labour politician

29 We know that the organised workers of the country are our friends. As for the rest, they don't matter a tinker's cuss.
   Speech to the Electrical Trades Union conference at Margate, 7 May 1947; in *Manchester Guardian* 8 May 1947

Sir Arthur Shipley 1861–1927

English zoologist

1 When we were a soft amoeba, in ages past and gone,
Ere you were Queen of Sheba, or I King Solomon,
Alone and undivided, we lived a life of sloth,
Whatever you did, I did; one dinner served for both.
Anon came separation, by fission and divorce,
A lonely pseudopodium I wandered on my course.
  Life (1923) ch. 13 'Ere you were Queen of Sheba'

James Shirley 1596–1666

English playwright

2 The glories of our blood and state
Are shadows, not substantial things;
There is no armour against fate;
Death lays his icy hand on kings:
Sceptre and crown
Must tumble down,
And in the dust be equal made
With the poor crooked scythe and spade.
  The Contention of Ajax and Ulysses (1659) act 1, sc. 3

3 The garlands wither on your brow;
Then boast no more your mighty deeds!
  The Contention of Ajax and Ulysses (1659) act 1, sc. 3

4 Only the actions of the just
Smell sweet, and blossom in their dust.
  The Contention of Ajax and Ulysses (1659) act 1, sc. 3

5 I presume you're mortal, and may err.
  The Lady of Pleasure (1637) act 2, sc. 2

6   How little room
Do we take up in death, that, living know
No bounds?
  The Wedding (1629) act 4, sc. 4

The Shorter Catechism (1647)

7 'What is the chief end of man?'
'To glorify God and to enjoy him for ever'.

Walter Sickert 1860–1942

English painter

8 Nothing knits man to man, the Manchester School
wisely taught, like the frequent passage from hand to
hand of cash.
  'The Language of Art' in *New Age* 28 July 1910

Algernon Sidney 1622–83

*English conspirator, assassinated for his alleged part in the
Rye House Plot, 1683*

9 Liars ought to have good memories.
  Discourses concerning Government (1698) ch. 2, sect. 15

10 Men lived like fishes; the great ones devoured the
small.
  Discourses concerning Government (1698) ch. 2, sect. 18. Cf.
  Pericles 619:1

11 'Tis not necessary to light a candle to the sun.
  Discourses concerning Government (1698) ch. 2, sect. 23. Cf.
  Burton 165:8, Young 754:11

Sir Philip Sidney 1554–86

English soldier, poet, and courtier

12 Shallow brooks murmur most, deep silent slide away.
  Arcadia ('Old Arcadia', completed 1581) bk. 1 'First
  Eclogues: Lalus and Dorus'

13 Who shoots at the mid-day sun, though he be sure he
shall never hit the mark; yet as sure he is he shall
shoot higher than who aims but at a bush.
  Arcadia ('New Arcadia', 1590) bk. 2

14 My true love hath my heart and I have his,
By just exchange one for the other giv'n;
I hold his dear, and mine he cannot miss,
There never was a better bargain driv'n.
  Arcadia ('Old Arcadia', completed 1581) bk. 3

15 But words came halting forth, wanting Invention's
stay;
Invention, Nature's child, fled step-dame Study's
blows . . .
Biting my truant pen, beating myself for spite,
'Fool,' said my Muse to me; 'look in thy heart and
write.'
  Astrophil and Stella (1591) sonnet 1

16 With how sad steps, O Moon, thou climb'st the skies;
How silently, and with how wan a face.
What, may it be that even in heavenly place
That busy archer his sharp arrows tries?
  Astrophil and Stella (1591) sonnet 31

17   O moon, tell me,
Is constant love deemed there but want of wit?
Are beauties there as proud as here they be?
Do they above love to be loved, and yet
These lovers scorn whom that love doth possess?
Do they call virtue there ungratefulness?
  Astrophil and Stella (1591) sonnet 31

18 Come, sleep, O sleep, the certain knot of peace,
The baiting place of wit, the balm of woe,
The poor man's wealth, the prisoner's release,
Th' indifferent judge between the high and low.
  Astrophil and Stella (1591) sonnet 39

19 Take thou of me sweet pillows, sweetest bed,
A chamber deaf to noise and blind to light;
A rosy garland and a weary head.
  Astrophil and Stella (1591) sonnet 39

20 That sweet enemy, France.
  Astrophil and Stella (1591) sonnet 41

21 Dumb swans, not chattering pies, do lovers prove;
They love indeed who quake to say they love.
  Astrophil and Stella (1591) sonnet 54

22 Doubt you to whom my Muse these songs intendeth,
Which now my breast, o'ercharged, to music lendeth?
To you, to you, all song of praise is due;
Only in you my song begins and endeth.
  Astrophil and Stella (1591) first song

23 Oh heav'nly fool, thy most kiss-worthy face
Anger invests with such a lovely grace
That Anger's self I needs must kiss again.
  Astrophil and Stella (1591) sonnet 73

1 I never drank of Aganippe well,
  Nor ever did in shade of Tempe sit,
  And Muses scorn with vulgar brains to dwell;
  Poor layman I, for sacred rites unfit . . .
  I am no pick-purse of another's wit.
     Astrophil and Stella (1591) sonnet 74

2 Highway, since you my chief Parnassus be,
  And that my Muse, to some ears not unsweet,
  Tempers her words to trampling horses' feet
  More oft than to a chamber melody;
  Now blessed you, bear onward blessed me
  To her, where I my heart, safeliest, shall meet.
     Astrophil and Stella (1591) sonnet 84

3 Stella, think not that I by verse seek fame;
  Who seek, who hope, who love, who live, but thee:
  Thine eyes my pride, thy lips my history;
  If thou praise not, all other praise is shame.
     Astrophil and Stella (1591) sonnet 90

4 Leave me, O Love which reachest but to dust,
  And thou, my mind, aspire to higher things;
  Grow rich in that which never taketh rust;
  Whatever fades, but fading pleasure brings.
     Certain Sonnets (written 1577–81) no. 32

5 O fair! O sweet! When I do look on thee,
  In whom all joys so well agree,
  Heart and soul do sing in me,
  Just accord all music makes.
     'To the Tune of a Spanish Song' (written *c*.1581)

6 Nature never set forth the earth in so rich tapestry as
  diverse poets have done . . . her world is brazen, the
  poets only deliver a golden.
     The Defence of Poetry (1595)

7 Poetry therefore, is an art of *imitation* . . . that is to
  say, a representing, counterfeiting, or figuring forth to
  speak metaphorically. A speaking picture, with this
  end: to teach and delight.
     The Defence of Poetry (1595)

8 With a tale forsooth he [the poet] cometh unto you,
  with a tale which holdeth children from play, and old
  men from the chimney corner.
     The Defence of Poetry (1595)

9 Comedy is an imitation of the common errors of our
  life.
     The Defence of Poetry (1595)

10 Certainly I must confess mine own barbarousness, I
   never heard the old song of Percy and Douglas, that I
   found not my heart moved more than with a trumpet.
     The Defence of Poetry (1595)

11 Laughter almost ever cometh of things most
   disproportioned to our selves, and nature. Delight hath
   a joy in it either permanent or present. Laughter hath
   only a scornful tickling.
     The Defence of Poetry (1595)

12 Thy necessity is yet greater than mine.
     On giving his water-bottle to a dying soldier on the
     battle-field of Zutphen, 1586, in Sir Fulke Greville *Life of Sir
     Philip Sidney* (1652) ch. 12 (commonly quoted 'thy need is
     greater than mine')

Emmanuel Joseph Sieyès 1748–1836
French abbot and statesman

13 *La mort, sans phrases.*
   Death, without rhetoric.
     Attributed to Sieyès on voting in the French Convention for
     the death of Louis XVI, 16 January 1793, but afterwards
     repudiated by him. *Le Moniteur* 20 January 1793 records
     his vote as 'La mort'

14 *J'ai vécu.*
   I survived.
     When asked what he had done during the French
     Revolution. See F. A. M. Mignet *Notice historique sur la vie
     et les travaux de M. le Comte de Sieyès* (1836)

Maurice Sigler 1901–61 *and* Al Hoffman 1902–60
American songwriters

15 Little man, you've had a busy day.
     Title of song (1934)

Alan Sillitoe 1928–
English writer

16 The loneliness of the long-distance runner.
     Title of novel (1959)

Georges Simenon 1903–89
Belgian novelist

17 Writing is not a profession but a vocation of
   unhappiness.
     Interview in *Paris Review* Summer 1955

Paul Simon 1942–
American singer and songwriter

18 Like a bridge over troubled water
   I will lay me down.
     'Bridge over Troubled Water' (1970 song)

19 And here's to you, Mrs Robinson
   Jesus loves you more than you will know.
   God bless you please, Mrs Robinson
   Heaven holds a place for those who pray.
     'Mrs Robinson' (1967 song, from the film *The Graduate*)

20 People talking without speaking
   People hearing without listening . . .
   'Fools,' said I, 'You do not know
   Silence like a cancer grows.'
     'Sound of Silence' (1964 song)

Simonides *c*.556–468 BC
Greek poet

21 ὦ ξεῖν', ἀγγέλλειν Λακεδαιμονίοις ὅτι τῇδε
   κείμεθα τοῖς κείνων ῥήμασι πειθόμενοι.
   Go, tell the Spartans, thou who passest by,
   That here obedient to their laws we lie.
     In Herodotus *Histories* bk. 7, ch. 228 (attributed)

1 Τὴν μὲν ζωγραφίαν ποίησιν σιωπῶσαν, τὴν δὲ ποίησιν ζωγραφίαν λαλοῦσαν.

Painting is silent poetry, poetry is eloquent painting.
In Plutarch *Moralia* 'De Gloria Atheniensium' sect. 3

Harold Simpson

2 Down in the forest something stirred:
It was only the note of a bird.
'Down in the Forest' (1906 song)

Kirke Simpson

Associated Press reporter

3 [Warren] Harding of Ohio was chosen by a group of men in a smoke-filled room early today as Republican candidate for President.
News report, filed 12 June 1920 (usually attributed to Harry Daugherty, one of Harding's supporters, who appears merely to have concurred with this version of events, when pressed for comment by Simpson. See William Safire *New Language of Politics* (1968)

N. F. Simpson 1919–

English playwright

4 Knocked down a doctor? With an ambulance? How could she? It's a contradiction in terms.
One Way Pendulum (1960) act 1

5 In sentencing a man for one crime, we may well be putting him beyond the reach of the law in respect of those crimes which he has not yet had an opportunity to commit. The law, however, is not to be cheated in this way. I shall therefore discharge you.
One Way Pendulum (1960) act 2

6 And suppose we solve all the problems it presents? What happens? We end up with more problems than we started with. Because that's the way problems propagate their species. A problem left to itself dries up or goes rotten. But fertilize a problem with a solution—you'll hatch out dozens.
A Resounding Tinkle (1958) act 1, sc. 1

George R. Sims 1847–1922

English journalist and playwright

7 It is Christmas Day in the Workhouse.
'In the Workhouse—Christmas Day' (1879)

C. H. Sisson 1914–

English poet

8 Here lies a civil servant. He was civil
To everyone, and servant to the devil.
In *The London Zoo* (1961) p. 29

Dame Edith Sitwell 1887–1964

English poet and critic

9 Jane, Jane,
Tall as a crane,
The morning light creaks down again.
Façade (1923) 'Aubade'

10 The fire was furry as a bear.
Façade (1923) 'Dark Song'

11 Jumbo asleep!
Grey leaves thick-furred
As his ears, keep
Conversation blurred.
Façade (1923) 'Lullaby for Jumbo'

12 When
Sir
Beelzebub called for his syllabub in the hotel in Hell
Where Proserpine first fell,
Blue as the gendarmerie were the waves of the sea,
(Rocking and shocking the barmaid).
Façade (1923) 'Sir Beelzebub'

13 Still falls the Rain—
Dark as the world of man, black as our loss—
Blind as the nineteen hundred and forty nails
Upon the Cross.
'Still Falls the Rain' (1942)

14 Daisy and Lily,
Lazy and silly,
Walk by the shore of the wan grassy sea—
Talking once more 'neath a swan-bosomed tree.
'Waltz' (1948)

15 I have often wished I had time to cultivate modesty ... But I am too busy thinking about myself.
In *Observer* 30 April 1950

16 I enjoyed talking to her, but thought *nothing* of her writing. I considered her 'a beautiful little knitter'.
Of Virginia Woolf; letter to Geoffrey Singleton, 11 July 1955, in John Lehmann and Derek Palmer (eds.) *Selected Letters* (1970)

Sir Osbert Sitwell 1892–1969

English writer

17 The British Bourgeoise
Is not born,
And does not die,
But, if it is ill,
It has a frightened look in its eyes.
At the House of Mrs Kinfoot (1921) p. 8

18 In reality, killing time
Is only the name for another of the multifarious ways
By which Time kills us.
'Milordo Inglese' (1958). Cf. Boucicault 137:4

19 On the coast of Coromandel
Dance they to the tunes of Handel.
'On the Coast of Coromandel' (1943)

John Skelton c.1460–1529

English poet

20 The sovereign'st thing that any man may have
Is little to say, and much to hear and see.
The Bouge of Court (1499) l. 211

1 With solace and gladness,
  Much mirth and no madness,
  All good and no badness;
  So joyously,
  So maidenly,
  So womanly,
  Her demeaning.
    The Garland of Laurel (1523) 'To Mistress Margaret Hussey'

2 Far may be sought
  Erst that ye can find
  So courteous, so kind,
  As Merry Margaret,
  This midsummer flower,
  Gentle as falcon
  Or hawk of the tower.
    The Garland of Laurel (1523) 'To Mistress Margaret Hussey'

3 I blunder, I bluster, I blow, and I blother,
  I make on the one day, and I mar on the other.
  Busy, busy, and ever busy,
  I dance up and down till I am dizzy.
  I can find fantasies where none is:
  I will not have it so, I will have it this!
    Magnificence (1530) l. 1037

4 So many vagabonds, so many beggars bold;
  So much decay of monasteries and of religious places;
  So hot hatred against the Church, and charity so cold;
  So much of 'my Lord's Grace,' and in him no grace is;
  So much hollow hearts, and so double faces;
  So much sanctuary-breaking, and privilege-barred—
  Since Deucalion's flood was never seen nor lered.
    'Speak, Parrot' (written *c*.1520) l. 498

B. F. Skinner 1904–90

American psychologist

5 The real question is not whether machines think but
whether men do.
    Contingencies of Reinforcement (1969) ch. 9

6 Education is what survives when what has been
learned has been forgotten.
    New Scientist 21 May 1964

Christopher Smart 1722–71

English poet

7 Now the winds are all composure,
  But the breath upon the bloom,
  Blowing sweet o'er each enclosure,
  Grateful off'rings of perfume.

  Tansy, calaminth and daisies
  On the river's margin thrive;
  And accompany the mazes
  Of the stream that leaps alive.
    Hymns and Spiritual Songs (1765) 'St Mark'

8 Nature's decorations glisten
  Far above their usual trim;
  Birds on box and laurels listen,
  As so near the cherubs hymn.
    Hymns and Spiritual Songs (1765) 'The Nativity of Our Lord
    and Saviour Jesus Christ'

9 God all-bounteous, all-creative,
  Whom no ills from good dissuade,
  Is incarnate, and a native
  Of the very world he made.
    Hymns and Spiritual Songs (1765) 'The Nativity of Our Lord
    and Saviour Jesus Christ'

10 For in my nature I quested for beauty, but God, God
hath sent me to sea for pearls.
    Jubilate Agno (*c*.1758–63) Fragment B, l. 30

11 For sincerity is a jewel which is pure and transparent,
eternal and inestimable.
    Jubilate Agno (*c*.1758–63) Fragment B, l. 40

12 For Charity is cold in the multitude of possessions, and
the rich are covetous of their crumbs.
    Jubilate Agno (*c*.1758–63) Fragment B, l. 154

13 For I will consider my Cat Jeoffrey.
  For he is the servant of the Living God duly and daily
    serving him.
  For at the first glance of the glory of God in the East
    he worships in his way.
  For this is done by wreathing his body seven times
    round with elegant quickness.
    Jubilate Agno (*c*.1758–63) Fragment B, l. 695

14 For when his day's work is done his business more
    properly begins.
  For he keeps the Lord's watch in the night against the
    adversary.
  For he counteracts the powers of darkness by his
    electrical skin and glaring eyes.
  For he counteracts the Devil, who is death, by brisking
    about the life.
    Jubilate Agno (*c*.1758–63) Fragment B, l. 717

15 Ye beauties! O how great the sum
  Of sweetness that ye bring;
  On what a charity ye come
  To bless the latter spring!
  How kind the visit that ye pay,
  Like strangers on a rainy day.
    'On a Bed of Guernsey Lilies' (1764)

16 Lo, through her works gay nature grieves
  How brief she is and frail,
  As ever o'er the falling leaves
  Autumnal winds prevail.
  Yet still the philosophic mind
  Consolatory food can find,
  And hope her anchorage maintain:
  We never are deserted quite;
  'Tis by succession of delight
  That love supports his reign.
    'On a Bed of Guernsey Lilies' (1764)

17 He sung of God—the mighty source
  Of all things—the stupendous force
  On which all strength depends;
  From whose right arm, beneath whose eyes,
  All period, pow'r, and enterprise
  Commences, reigns, and ends.
    A Song to David (1763) st. 18

1 Strong is the lion—like a coal
His eye-ball—like a bastion's mole
His chest against his foes:
Strong, the gier-eagle on his sail,
Strong against tide, th' enormous whale
Emerges as he goes.
> *A Song to David* (1763) st. 76

2 But stronger still, in earth and air,
And in the sea, the man of pray'r;
And far beneath the tide;
And in the seat to faith assigned,
Where ask is have, where seek is find,
Where knock is open wide.
> *A Song to David* (1763) st. 77

3 Beauteous the fleet before the gale;
Beauteous the multitudes in mail,
Ranked arms and crested heads;
Beauteous the garden's umbrage mild,
Walk, water, meditated wild,
And all the bloomy beds.
> *A Song to David* (1763) st. 78

4 Glorious the northern lights astream;
Glorious the song, when God's the theme;
Glorious the thunder's roar:
Glorious hosanna from the den;
Glorious the catholic amen;
Glorious the martyr's gore.

Glorious—more glorious is the crown
Of Him that brought salvation down
By meekness, called thy Son;
Thou that stupendous truth believed,
And now the matchless deed's achieved,
Determined, dared, and done.
> *A Song to David* (1763) st. 85

5 Ah! Posthumus, the years, the years
Glide swiftly on, nor can our tears
Or piety the wrinkled age forefend,
Or for one hour retard th' inevitable end.
> Translation of Horace *Odes* bk. 2, no. 14. Cf. Horace 349:19

Elizabeth Smart 1913–86
American poet

6 By Grand Central Station I sat down and wept.
> Title of book (1945). Cf. Book of Common Prayer 134:17

Samuel Smiles 1812–1904
English writer

7 We each day dig our graves with our teeth.
> *Duty* (19) ch. 16

8 This   ary metal [iron], the soul of every
        d the mainspring perhaps of civilised

> *Industry* (1884) ch. 4

        the root of all genuine growth

10 As respects the great contrivances and inventions which have conferred so much power and wealth upon the nation, it is unquestionable that for the greater part of them we have been indebted to men of the humblest rank. Deduct what they have done in this particular line of action, and it will be found that very little indeed remains for other men to have accomplished.
> *Self-Help* (1859) ch. 2

11 The shortest way to do many things is to do only one thing at once.
> *Self-Help* (1859) ch. 9

12 Middle class people are apt to live up to their incomes, if not beyond them: affecting a degree of 'style' which is most unhealthy in its effects upon society at large.
> *Self-Help* (1859) ch. 9

13 Cheerfulness gives elasticity to the spirit. Spectres fly before it.
> *Self-Help* (1859) ch. 12

Adam Smith 1723–90
Scottish philosopher and economist

14 Wonder ... and not any expectation of advantage from its discoveries, is the first principle which prompts mankind to the study of Philosophy, of that science which pretends to lay open the concealed connections that unite the various appearances of nature.
> *Essays on Philosophical Subjects* (1795) 'The History of Astronomy' sect. 3, para. 3

15 And thus, *Place*, that great object which divides the wives of aldermen, is the end of half the labours of human life; and is the cause of all the tumult and bustle, all the rapine and injustice, which avarice and ambition have introduced into this world.
> *Theory of Moral Sentiments* (1759) pt. 1, sect. 3, ch. 2

16 Though our brother is on the rack, as long as we ourselves are at our ease, our senses will never inform us of what he suffers ... It is by imagination that we can form any conception of what are his sensations.
> *Theory of Moral Sentiments* (2nd ed., 1762) p. 2

17 It is not from the benevolence of the butcher, the brewer, or the baker, that we expect our dinner, but from their regard to their own interest. We address ourselves not to their humanity but to their self love.
> *Wealth of Nations* (1776) bk. 1, ch. 2

18 People of the same trade seldom meet together, even for merriment and diversion, but the conversation ends in a conspiracy against the public, or in some contrivance to raise prices.
> *Wealth of Nations* (1776) bk. 1, ch. 10, pt. 2

19 With the greater part of rich people, the chief enjoyment of riches consists in the parade of riches, which in their eyes is never so complete as when they appear to possess those decisive marks of opulence which nobody can possess but themselves.
> *Wealth of Nations* (1776) bk. 1, ch. 11

1 To found a great empire for the sole purpose of raising up a people of customers, may at first sight appear a project fit only for a nation of shopkeepers. It is, however, a project altogether unfit for a nation of shopkeepers; but extremely fit for a nation whose government is influenced by shopkeepers.

> *Wealth of Nations* (1776) bk. 4, ch. 7, pt. 3. Cf. Adams 3:9, Napoleon 490:5

2 Consumption is the sole end and purpose of production; and the interest of the producer ought to be attended to only so far as it may be necessary for promoting that of the consumer.

> *Wealth of Nations* (1776) bk. 4, ch. 8

3 The discipline of colleges and universities is in general contrived, not for the benefit of the students, but for the interest, or more properly speaking, for the ease of the masters.

> *Wealth of Nations* (1776) bk. 5, ch. 1, pt. 3

4 There is no art which one government sooner learns of another than that of draining money from the pockets of the people.

> *Wealth of Nations* (1776) bk. 5, ch. 2

5 If any of the provinces of the British empire cannot be made to contribute towards the support of the whole empire, it is surely time that Great Britain should free herself from the expense of defending those provinces in time of war, and of supporting any part of their civil or military establishments in time of peace, and endeavour to accommodate her future views and designs to the real mediocrity of her circumstances.

> *Wealth of Nations* (1776) bk. 5, ch. 3

Alfred Emanuel Smith 1873–1944

American politician

6 All the ills of democracy can be cured by more democracy.

> Speech in Albany, 27 June 1933, in *New York Times* 28 June 1933

7 Unpack.

> Telegraphed message to the Pope, 1932, who he had hoped would come to live in the United States, in the event of Smith's campaign for the presidency proving successful (attributed)

Sir Cyril Smith 1928–

British Liberal politician

8 The longest running farce in the West End.

> Of the House of Commons, in *Big Cyril* (1977) ch. 8

Dodie Smith 1896–1990

English novelist and playwright

9 The family—that dear octopus from whose tentacles we never quite escape.

> *Dear Octopus* (1938) p. 130

Edgar Smith 1857–1938

American songwriter

10 You may tempt the upper classes
With your villainous demi-tasses,
But; Heaven will protect a working-girl!

> 'Heaven Will Protect the Working-Girl' (1909 song)

F. E. Smith (1st Earl of Birkenhead) 1872–1930

British Conservative politician and lawyer

11 We have the highest authority for believing that the meek shall inherit the earth; though I have never found any particular corroboration of this aphorism in the records of Somerset House.

> *Contemporary Personalities* (1924) 'Marquess Curzon'

12 Nature has no cure for this sort of madness [Bolshevism], though I have known a legacy from a rich relative work wonders.

> *Law, Life and Letters* (1927) vol. 2, ch. 19

13 The world continues to offer glittering prizes to those who have stout hearts and sharp swords.

> Rectorial Address, Glasgow University, 7 November 1923, in *The Times* 8 November 1923

14 JUDGE: What do you suppose I am on the Bench for, Mr Smith?
SMITH: It is not for me, Your Honour, to attempt to fathom the inscrutable workings of Providence.

> In 2nd Earl of Birkenhead *F. E.* (1959 ed.) ch. 9

15 JUDGE: You are extremely offensive, young man.
SMITH: As a matter of fact, we both are, and the only difference between us is that I am trying to be, and you can't help it.

> In 2nd Earl of Birkenhead *Earl of Birkenhead* (1933) vol. 1, ch. 9

16 JUDGE DARLING: And who is George Robey?
SMITH: Mr George Robey is the Darling of the music halls, m'lud.

> In A. E. Wilson *The Prime Minister of Mirth* (1956) ch. 1

17 Good God, do you mean to say this place is a club?

> On being approached by the secretary of the Athenaeum, which he had been in the habit of using as a convenience on the way to his office (attributed)

Ian Smith 1919–

Rhodesian statesman; Prime Minister, 1964–79

18 I don't believe in black majority rule in Rhodesia—not in a thousand years.

> Broadcast speech, 20 March 1976, in *Sunday Times* 21 March 1976

Langdon Smith 1858–1908

19 When you were a tadpole, and I was a fish,
In the Palaeozoic time,
And side by side in the ebbing tide
We sprawled through the ooze and slime.

> 'A Toast to a Lady' in *The Scrap-Book* April 1906

Logan Pearsall Smith 1865–1946

American-born man of letters

1 There is more felicity on the far side of baldness than young men can possibly imagine.
   Afterthoughts (1931) 'Age and Death'

2 The denunciation of the young is a necessary part of the hygiene of older people, and greatly assists the circulation of their blood.
   Afterthoughts (1931) 'Age and Death'

3 The test of a vocation is the love of the drudgery it involves.
   Afterthoughts (1931) 'Art and Letters'

4 A best-seller is the gilded tomb of a mediocre talent.
   Afterthoughts (1931) 'Art and Letters'

5 To suppose, as we all suppose, that we could be rich and not behave as the rich behave, is like supposing that we could drink all day and keep absolutely sober.
   Afterthoughts (1931) 'In the World'

6 An improper mind is a perpetual feast.
   Afterthoughts (1931) 'Life and Human Nature'

7 People say that life is the thing, but I prefer reading.
   Afterthoughts (1931) 'Myself'

8 Those who set out to serve both God and Mammon soon discover that there is no God.
   Afterthoughts (1931) 'Other People'

9 Most people sell their souls, and live with a good conscience on the proceeds.
   Afterthoughts (1931) 'Other People'

10 All Reformers, however strict their social conscience, live in houses just as big as they can pay for.
   Afterthoughts (1931) 'Other People'

11 What I like in a good author is not what he says, but what he whispers.
   All Trivia (1933) 'Afterthoughts' pt. 5

12 There is one thing that matters—to set a chime of words tinkling in the minds of a few fastidious people.
   Said shortly before his death; in *New Statesman* 9 March 1946, obituary notice by Cyril Connolly

Samuel Francis Smith 1808–95

American poet and divine

13 My country, 'tis of thee,
   Sweet land of liberty,
   Of thee I sing:
   Land where my fathers died,
   Land of the pilgrims' pride,
   From every mountain-side
   Let freedom ring.
   'America' (1831)

Stevie Smith (Florence Margaret Smith) 1902–71

English poet and novelist

14 Oh I am a cat that likes to
   Gallop about doing good.
   'The Galloping Cat' (1972)

15 A good time was had by all.
   Title of book (1937)

16 Why does my Muse only speak when she is unhappy?
   She does not, I only listen when I am unhappy
   When I am happy I live and despise writing
   For my Muse this cannot but be dispiriting.
   'My Muse' (1964)

17 Oh, no no no, it was too cold always
   (Still the dead one lay moaning)
   I was much too far out all my life
   And not waving but drowning.
   'Not Waving but Drowning' (1957)

18 People who are always praising the past
   And especially the times of faith as best
   Ought to go and live in the Middle Ages
   And be burnt at the stake as witches and sages.
   'The Past' (1957)

19 Private Means is dead
   God rest his soul, officers and fellow-rankers said.
   'Private Means is Dead' (1962)

20 This Englishwoman is so refined
   She has no bosom and no behind.
   'This Englishwoman' (1937)

21 I long for the Person from Porlock
   To bring my thoughts to an end,
   I am growing impatient to see him
   I think of him as a friend.
   'Thoughts about the "Person from Porlock" ' (1962). Cf. Coleridge 210:8

22 If you cannot have your dear husband for a comfort and a delight, for a breadwinner and a crosspatch, for a sofa, chair or a hot-water bottle, one can use him as a Cross to be Borne.
   Novel on Yellow Paper (1936) p. 24

23 If there wasn't death, I think you couldn't go on.
   In *Observer* 9 November 1969 p. 21

Sydney Smith 1771–1845

English clergyman and essayist

24 The moment the very name of Ireland is mentioned, the English seem to bid adieu to common feeling, common prudence, and common sense, and to act with the barbarity of tyrants, and the fatuity of idiots.
   Letters of Peter Plymley (1807) letter 2

25 A Curate—there is something which excites compassion in the very name of a Curate!!!
   'Persecuting Bishops' in *Edinburgh Review* (1822)

26 Bishop Berkeley destroyed this world in one volume octavo; and nothing remained, after his time, but mind; which experienced a similar fate from the hand of Mr Hume in 1739.
   Sketches of Moral Philosophy (1849) introduction

27 We shall generally find that the triangular person has got into the square hole, the oblong into the triangular, and a square person has squeezed himself into the round hole. The officer and the office, the doer and the thing done, seldom fit so exactly that we can say they were almost made for each other.
   Sketches of Moral Philosophy (1849) Lecture 9

1 I never could find any man who could think for two
minutes together.
Sketches of Moral Philosophy (1849) Lecture 19

2 What bishops like best in their clergy is a
dropping-down-deadness of manner.
Works (1859) vol. 2 'First Letter to Archdeacon Singleton,
1837' p. 271 n.

3 I look upon Switzerland as an inferior sort of Scotland.
Letter to Lord Holland, 1815, in N. C. Smith (ed.) *Letters of
Sydney Smith* (1953)

4 Tory and Whig in turns shall be my host,
I taste no politics in boiled and roast.
Letter to John Murray, November 1834, in *Letters of Sidney
Smith* (1953)

5 I have no relish for the country; it is a kind of healthy
grave.
Letter to Miss G. Harcourt, 1838, in *Letters of Sidney Smith*
(1953)

6 I have seen nobody since I saw you, but persons in
orders. My only varieties are vicars, rectors, curates,
and every now and then (by way of turbot) an
archdeacon.
Letter to Miss Berry, 28 January 1843, in *Letters of Sidney
Smith* (1953)

7 It requires a surgical operation to get a joke well into
a Scotch understanding. Their only idea of wit . . . is
laughing immoderately at stated intervals.
In Lady Holland *Memoir* (1855) vol. 1, ch. 2

8 That knuckle-end of England—that land of Calvin,
oat-cakes, and sulphur.
In Lady Holland *Memoir* (1855) vol. 1, ch. 2 (of Scotland)

9 Take short views, hope for the best, and trust in God.
In Lady Holland *Memoir* (1855) vol. 1, ch. 6

10 No furniture so charming as books.
In Lady Holland *Memoir* (1855) vol. 1, ch. 9. Cf. Powell
528:4

11 How can a bishop marry? How can he flirt? The most
he can say is, 'I will see you in the vestry after
service.'
In Lady Holland *Memoir* (1855) vol. 1, ch. 9

12 Not body enough to cover his mind decently with; his
intellect is improperly exposed.
In Lady Holland *Memoir* (1855) vol. 1, ch. 9

13 As the French say, there are three sexes—men,
women, and clergymen.
In Lady Holland *Memoir* (1855) vol. 1, ch. 9

14 Daniel Webster struck me much like a steam-engine in
trousers.
In Lady Holland *Memoir* (1855) vol. 1, ch. 9

15 My definition of marriage . . . it resembles a pair of
shears, so joined that they cannot be separated; often
moving in opposite directions, yet always punishing
anyone who comes between them.
In Lady Holland *Memoir* (1855) vol. 1, ch. 11

16 He [Macaulay] is like a book in breeches.
In Lady Holland *Memoir* (1855) vol. 1, ch. 11

17 He [Macaulay] has occasional flashes of silence, that
make his conversation perfectly delightful.
In Lady Holland *Memoir* (1855) vol. 1, ch. 11

18 Let onion atoms lurk within the bowl,
And, scarce-suspected, animate the whole.
In Lady Holland *Memoir* (1855) vol. 1, ch. 11 'Receipt for a
Salad'

19 Serenely full, the epicure would say,
Fate cannot harm me, I have dined to-day.
In Lady Holland *Memoir* (1855) vol. 1, ch. 11 'Receipt for a
Salad'. Cf. Dryden 262:1

20 Deserves to be preached to death by wild curates.
In Lady Holland *Memoir* (1855) vol. 1, ch. 11

21 I never read a book before reviewing it; it prejudices a
man so.
In H. Pearson *The Smith of Smiths* (1934) ch. 3

22 Minorities . . . are almost always in the right.
In H. Pearson *The Smith of Smiths* (1934) ch. 9

23 My idea of heaven is, eating *pâté de foie gras* to the
sound of trumpets.
In H. Pearson *The Smith of Smiths* (1934) ch. 10

24 What a pity it is that we have no amusements in
England but vice and religion!
In H. Pearson *The Smith of Smiths* (1934) ch. 10

25 Let the Dean and Canons lay their heads together and
the thing will be done.
On a proposal to surround St Paul's with a wooden
pavement, in H. Pearson *The Smith of Smiths* (1934) ch. 10

26 Death must be distinguished from dying, with which it
is often confused.
In H. Pearson *The Smith of Smiths* (1934) ch. 11

27 What two ideas are more inseparable than Beer and
Britannia?
In H. Pearson *The Smith of Smiths* (1934) ch. 11

28 I am just going to pray for you at St Paul's, but with
no very lively hope of success.
In H. Pearson *The Smith of Smiths* (1934) ch. 13

29 Poverty is no disgrace to a man, but it is confoundedly
inconvenient.
In J. Potter Briscoe (ed.) *Sydney Smith: His Wit and Wisdom*
(1900) p. 89

30 Science is his forte, and omniscience his foible.
Of Whewell, in Isaac Todhunter *William Whewell* (1876)
vol. 1, p. 410

Walter Chalmers Smith 1824–1908
Scottish clergyman

31 Immortal, invisible, God only wise,
In light inaccessible hid from our eyes,
Most blessèd, most glorious, the Ancient of Days,
Almighty, victorious, thy great name we praise.

Unresting, unhasting, and silent as light,
Nor wanting, nor wasting, thou rulest in might.
'Immortal, invisible, God only wise' (1867 hymn)

32 We blossom and flourish as leaves on the tree,
And wither and perish; but naught changeth thee.
'Immortal, invisible, God only wise' (1867 hymn)

Tobias Smollett 1721–71
Scottish novelist

33 I think for my part one half of the nation is mad—and
the other not very sound.
The Adventures of Sir Launcelot Greaves (1762) ch. 6

1 The capital [London] is become an overgrown
monster; which, like a dropsical head, will in time
leave the body and extremities without nourishment
and support.
  Humphry Clinker (1771) vol. 1 (letter from Matthew
  Bramble, 29 May)

2 I am pent up in frowzy lodgings, where there is not
room enough to swing a cat.
  Humphry Clinker (1771) vol. 1 (letter from Matthew
  Bramble, 8 June)

3 'Begging your honour's pardon, (replied Clinker) may
not the new light of God's grace shine upon the poor
and the ignorant in their humility, as well as upon the
wealthy, and the philosopher in all his pride of human
learning?' 'What you imagine to be the new light of
grace, (said his master) I take to be a deceitful vapour,
glimmering through a crack in your upper storey.'
  Humphry Clinker (1771) vol. 2 (letter from Jery Melford,
  10 June)

4 Mourn, hapless Caledonia, mourn
Thy banished peace, thy laurels torn.
  'The Tears of Scotland' (1746)

5 That great Cham of literature, Samuel Johnson.
  Letter to John Wilkes, 16 March 1759, in James Boswell
  Life of Samuel Johnson (1934 ed.) vol. 1

C. P. Snow (*Baron Snow of Leicester*)
1905–80
English novelist and scientist

6 The official world, the corridors of power.
  Homecomings (1956) ch. 22

7 The intellectual life of the whole of western society is
increasingly being split into two polar groups . . .
Literary intellectuals at one pole—at the other
scientists, and as the most representative, the physical
scientists. Between the two a gulf of mutual
incomprehension.
  The Two Cultures and the Scientific Revolution (1959 Rede
  Lecture) p. 3

Philip Snowden (*Viscount Snowden*)
1864–1937
British Labour politician

8 This is not Socialism. It is Bolshevism run mad.
  Radio broadcast on the Labour Party's election programme,
  17 October 1931; in *The Times* 19 October 1931

Socrates 469–399 BC
Greek philosopher

9 πόσων ἐγὼ χρείαν οὐκ ἔχω.
How many things I can do without!
  On looking at a multitude of wares exposed for sale, in
  Diogenes Laertius *Lives of the Philosophers* bk. 2, ch. 25

10 καὶ εἰδέναι μὲν μηδὲν πλὴν αὐτὸ τοῦτο.
I know nothing except the fact of my ignorance.
  In Diogenes Laertius *Lives of the Philosophers* bk. 2, sect. 32

11 ὦ ἄριστε ἀνδρῶν, Ἀθηναῖος ὤν, πόλεως τῆς μεγίστης καὶ
εὐδοκιμωτάτης εἰς σοφίαν καὶ ἰσχύν, χρημάτων μὲν οὐκ
αἰσχύνει ἐπιμελούμενος, ὅπως σοι ἔσται ὡς πλεῖστα, καὶ
δόξης καὶ τιμῆς, φρονήσεως δὲ καὶ ἀληθείας καὶ τῆς
ψυχῆς, ὅπως ὡς βελτίστη ἔσται, οὐκ ἐπιμελεῖ οὐδὲ
φροντίζεις;
Most excellent man, are you who are a citizen of
Athens, the greatest of cities and the most famous for
wisdom and power, not ashamed to care for the
acquisition of wealth and for reputation and honour,
when you neither care nor take thought for wisdom
and truth and the perfection of your soul?
  In Plato *Apology* 29d

12 λέγων, ὅτι οὐκ ἐκ χρημάτων ἀρετὴ γίγνεται, ἀλλ' ἐξ
ἀρετῆς χρήματα καὶ τὰ ἄλλα ἀγαθὰ τοῖς ἀνθρώποις
ἅπαντα καὶ ἰδίᾳ καὶ δημοσίᾳ.
And I tell you that virtue does not come from money,
but from virtue comes money and all other good
things to man, both to the individual and to the state.
  In Plato *Apology* 30b

13 τότε μέντοι ἐγὼ οὐ λόγῳ ἀλλ' ἔργῳ αὖ ἐνεδειξάμην, ὅτι
ἐμοὶ θανάτου μὲν μέλει . . . οὐδ' ὁτιοῦν, τοῦ δὲ μηδὲν
ἄδικον μηδ' ἀνόσιον ἐργάζεσθαι, τούτου δὲ τὸ πᾶν μέλει.
Then I, however, showed again, by action, not in
word only, that I did not care a whit for death . . . but
that I did care with all my might not to do anything
unjust or unholy.
  On being ordered by the Thirty Commissioners to take part
  in the liquidation of Leon of Salamis; in Plato *Apology* 32d

14 ὁ δὲ ἀνεξέταστος βίος οὐ βιωτὸς ἀνθρώπῳ.
The unexamined life is not worth living.
  In Plato *Apology* 38a

15 ἀλλὰ γὰρ ἤδη ὥρα ἀπιέναι, ἐμοὶ μὲν ἀποθανουμένῳ, ὑμῖν
δὲ βιωσομένοις· ὁπότεροι δὲ ἡμῶν ἔρχονται ἐπὶ ἄμεινον
πρᾶγμα, ἄδηλον παντὶ πλὴν ἢ τῷ θεῷ.
But already it is time to depart, for me to die, for you
to go on living; which of us takes the better course, is
not known to anyone except God.
  In Plato *Apology* 42a

16 ὡς οὐδέποτε ὀρθῶς ἔχοντος οὔτε τοῦ ἀδικεῖν οὔτε τοῦ
ἀνταδικεῖν οὔτε κακῶς πάσχοντα ἀμύνεσθαι ἀντιδρῶντα
κακῶς.
It is never right to do wrong or to requite wrong with
wrong, or when we suffer evil to defend ourselves by
doing evil in return.
  In Plato *Crito* 49d

17 Παντὸς μᾶλλον ἄρα, ἔφη, ὦ Κέβης, ψυχὴ ἀθάνατον καὶ
ἀνώλεθρον, καὶ τῷ ὄντι ἔσονται ἡμῶν αἱ ψυχαὶ ἐν Ἅιδου.
It is perfectly certain that the soul is immortal and
imperishable, and our souls will actually exist in
another world.
  In Plato *Phaedo* 107a

1 ἀλλὰ τούτων δὴ ἕνεκα θαρρεῖν χρὴ περὶ τῇ ἑαυτοῦ ψυχῇ
ἄνδρα, ὅστις ἐν τῷ βίῳ τὰς μὲν ἄλλας ἡδονὰς τὰς περὶ τὸ
σῶμα καὶ τοὺς κόσμους εἴασε χαίρειν, ὡς ἀλλοτρίους τε
ὄντας, καὶ πλέον θάτερον ἡγησάμενος ἀπεργάζεσθαι, τὰς
δὲ περὶ τὸ μανθάνειν ἐσπούδασέ τε καὶ κοσμήσας τὴν
ψυχὴν οὐκ ἀλλοτρίῳ ἀλλὰ τῷ αὐτῆς κόσμῳ, σωφροσύνῃ
τε καὶ δικαιοσύνῃ καὶ ἀνδρείᾳ καὶ ἐλευθερίᾳ καὶ ἀληθείᾳ,
οὕτω περιμένει τὴν εἰς Ἅιδου πορείαν, ὡς πορευσόμενος
ὅταν ἡ εἱμαρμένη καλῇ.

A man should feel confident concerning his soul, who
has renounced those pleasures and fineries that go
with the body, as being alien to him, and considering
them to result more in harm than in good, but has
pursued the pleasures that go with learning and made
the soul fine with no alien but rather its own proper
refinements, moderation and justice and courage and
freedom and truth; thus he is ready for the journey to
the world below, ready to go when Fate calls him.

In Plato *Phaedo* 114d

2 Τί λέγεις, ἔφη, περὶ τοῦδε τοῦ πώματος πρὸς τὸ
ἀποσπεῖσαί τινι; ἔξεστιν ἢ οὔ; Τοσοῦτον, ἔφη, ὦ
Σώκρατες, τρίβομεν, ὅσον οἰόμεθα μέτριον εἶναι πιεῖν.
Μανθάνω, ἦ δ᾽ ὅς. ἀλλ᾽ εὔχεσθαί γέ που τοῖς θεοῖς ἔξεστί
τε καὶ χρή, τὴν μετοίκησιν τὴν ἐνθένδε ἐκεῖσε εὐτυχῆ
γενέσθαι· ἃ δὴ καὶ ἐγὼ εὔχομαί τε καὶ γένοιτο ταύτη.

'What do you say about pouring a libation to some
god from this cup? Is it allowed or not?' 'We only
prepare just the right amount to drink, Socrates,' he
[the jailer] said. 'I understand,' he went on; 'but it is
allowed and necessary to pray to the gods, that my
moving from hence to there may be blessed; thus I
pray, and so be it.'

In Plato *Phaedo* 117b

3 οὐ μὲν οὖν τῇ ἀληθείᾳ, φάναι, ὦ φιλούμενε Ἀγάθων,
δύνασαι ἀντιλέγειν, ἐπεὶ Σωκράτει γε οὐδὲν χαλεπόν.

But, my dearest Agathon, it is truth which you cannot
contradict; you can without any difficulty contradict
Socrates.

In Plato *Symposium* 201d

4 ὦ Κρίτων, τῷ Ἀσκληπιῷ ὀφείλομεν ἀλεκτρυόνα· ἀλλὰ
ἀπόδοτε καὶ μὴ ἀμελήσητε.

Crito, we owe a cock to Aesculapius; please pay it and
don't forget it.

In Plato *Phaedo* 118 *ad fin.*

Solon *c.*640–after 556 BC

Athenian statesman and poet

5 γηράσκω δ᾽ αἰεὶ πολλὰ διδασκόμενος.

I grow old ever learning many things.

Theodor Bergk (ed.) *Poetae Lyrici Graeci* (1843) no. 18

6 πρὶν δ᾽ ἂν τελευτήσῃ, ἐπισχεῖν μηδὲ καλέειν κω ὄλβιον,
ἀλλ᾽ εὐτυχέα.

Call no man happy before he dies, he is at best but
fortunate.

In Herodotus *Histories* bk. 1, ch. 32

Alexander Solzhenitsyn 1918–

Russian novelist

7 Вы сильны лишь постольку, поскольку отбираете
у людей не *всё*. Но человек, у которого вы
отбирали *всё* — уже не подвластен вам, он
снова свободен.

You only have power over people as long as you don't
take *everything* away from them. But when you've
robbed a man of *everything* he's no longer in your
power — he's free again.

The First Circle (1968) ch. 17

8 Архипелаг ГУЛаг.

The Gulag Archipelago.

Title of book (1973–5)

9 Работа — она как палка, конца в ней два: для
людей делаешь — качество дай, для дурака
делаешь — дай показуху.

Work was like a stick. It had two ends. When you
worked for the knowing you gave them quality; when
you worked for a fool you simply gave him eye-wash.

One Day in the Life of Ivan Denisovich (1962) p. 15
(translated by Ralph Parker)

10 Теплый зяблого разве когда поймет?

How can you expect a man who's warm to
understand one who's cold?

One Day in the Life of Ivan Denisovich (1962) p. 22
(translated by Ralph Parker)

11 Дума арестантская — и та несвободная, всё к
тому и возвращается.

The thoughts of a prisoner—they're not free either.
They keep returning to the same things.

One Day in the Life of Ivan Denisovich (1962) p. 34
(translated by Ralph Parker)

William Somerville 1675–1742

English country gentleman

12   My hoarse-sounding horn
Invites thee to the chase, the sport of kings;
Image of war, without its guilt.

The Chase (1735) bk. 1, l. 13. Cf. D'Avenant 231:19,
Surtees 672:8

13 Hail, happy Britain! highly favoured isle,
And Heaven's peculiar care!

The Chase (1735) bk. 1, l. 84

Anastasio Somoza 1925–80

Nicaraguan dictator

14 You won the elections, but I won the count.

Replying to an accusation of ballot-rigging, in *Guardian*
17 June 1977. Cf. Stoppard 669:14

Stephen Sondheim 1930–

American songwriter

15 Everything's coming up roses.

Gypsy (1959) title of song (music by Jule Styne)

1 Ev'ry day a little death
On the lips and in the eyes,
In the murmurs, in the pauses,
In the gestures, in the sighs.
Ev'ry day a little dies.
A Little Night Music (1973) 'Every Day a Little Death'

2 Isn't it rich?
Are we a pair?
Me here at last on the ground, you in mid-air . . .
Isn't it bliss?
Don't you approve?
One who keeps tearing around, one who can't move
. . .
Where are the clowns?
Send in the clowns.
A Little Night Music (1973) 'Send in the Clowns'

3 I like to be in America!
O.K. by me in America!
Ev'rything free in America
For a small fee in America!
West Side Story (1957) 'America' (music by Leonard Bernstein)

Susan Sontag 1933–

American writer

4 Interpretation is the revenge of the intellect upon art.
Evergreen Review December 1964

5 The camera makes everyone a tourist in other people's reality, and eventually in one's own.
New York Review of Books 18 April 1974

6 Illness is the night-side of life, a more onerous citizenship. Everyone who is born holds dual citizenship, in the kingdom of the well and in the kingdom of the sick.
New York Review of Books 26 January 1978

7 The white race *is* the cancer of human history, it is the white race, and it alone—its ideologies and inventions—which eradicates autonomous civilizations wherever it spreads, which has upset the ecological balance of the planet, which now threatens the very existence of life itself.
Partisan Review Winter 1967, p. 57

8 What pornography is really about, ultimately, isn't sex but death.
Partisan Review Spring 1967, p. 202

Donald Soper (Baron Soper) 1903–

British Methodist minister

9 It is, I think, good evidence of life after death.
On the quality of debate in the House of Lords, in *Listener* 17 August 1978

Sophocles c.496–406 BC

Greek dramatist

10 ὦ παῖ, γένοιο πατρὸς εὐτυχέστερος.
My son, may you be happier than your father.
Ajax l. 550

11 ἐχθρῶν ἄδωρα δῶρα κοὐκ ὀνήσιμα.
Enemies' gifts are no gifts and do no good.
Ajax l. 665

12 θεοῖς τέθνηκεν οὗτος, οὐ κείνοισιν, οὔ.
His death concerns the gods, not those men, no!
Ajax l. 970 (of Ajax's enemies, the Greek leaders)

13 πολλὰ τὰ δεινὰ κοὐδὲν ἀν-
θρώπου δεινότερον πέλει.
There are many wonderful things, and nothing is more wonderful than man.
Antigone l. 333

14 μὴ φῦναι τὸν ἅπαντα νι-
κᾷ λόγον.
Not to be born is, past all prizing, best.
Oedipus Coloneus l. 1225 (translation by R. C. Jebb)

15 '"πῶς," ἔφη, "ὦ Σοφόκλεις, ἔχεις πρὸς τἀφροδίσια; ἔτι οἷός τε εἶ γυναικὶ συγγίγνεσθαι;" καὶ ὅς, "εὐφήμει," ἔφη, "ὦ ἄνθρωπε· ἀσμενέστατα μέντοι αὐτὸ ἀπέφυγον, ὥσπερ λυττῶντά τινα καὶ ἄγριον δεσπότην ἀποδράς."
Someone asked Sophocles, 'How is your sex-life now? Are you still able to have a woman?' He replied, 'Hush, man; most gladly indeed am I rid of it all, as though I had escaped from a mad and savage master.'
In Plato *Republic* bk. 1, 329b

Charles Hamilton Sorley 1895–1915

English poet

16 We swing ungirded hips,
And lightened are our eyes,
The rain is on our lips,
We do not run for prize.
'Song of the Ungirt Runners' (1916)

17 When you see millions of the mouthless dead
Across your dreams in pale battalions go,
Say not soft things as other men have said,
That you'll remember. For you need not so.
Give them not praise. For, deaf, how should they know
It is not curses heaped on each gashed head?
'A Sonnet' (1916)

18 We have the evil spirits too
That shake our soul with battle-din.
But we have an eviller spirit than you,
We have a dumb spirit within:
The exceeding bitter agony
But not the exceeding bitter cry.
'To Poets' (1916)

John L. B. Soule 1815–91

American journalist

19 Go West, young man, go West!
Terre Haute [Indiana] *Express* (1851) editorial. Cf. Greeley 316:15

Robert South 1634–1716

English court preacher

1 An Aristotle was but the rubbish of an Adam, and Athens but the rudiments of Paradise.
   Twelve Sermons . . . (1692) vol. 1, no. 2

Thomas Southerne 1660–1746

Irish playwright

2   When we're worn,
Hacked hewn with constant service, thrown aside
To rust in peace, or rot in hospitals.
   The Loyal Brother (1682) act 1

3 Be wise, be wise, and do not try
How he can court, or you be won;
For love is but discovery:
When that is made, the pleasure's done.
   Sir Anthony Love (1690) act 2 'Song'

Robert Southey 1774–1843

English poet and writer

4 It was a summer evening,
Old Kaspar's work was done,
And he before his cottage door
Was sitting in the sun,
And by him sported on the green
His little grandchild Wilhelmine.
   'The Battle of Blenheim' (1800)

5 Now tell us all about the war,
And what they fought each other for.
   'The Battle of Blenheim' (1800)

6 'And everybody praised the Duke,
Who this great fight did win.'
'But what good came of it at last?'
Quoth little Peterkin.
'Why that I cannot tell,' said he,
'But 'twas a famous victory.'
   'The Battle of Blenheim' (1800)

7 Curses are like young chickens, they always come home to roost.
   The Curse of Kehama (1810) motto

8 Thou hast been called, O Sleep! the friend of Woe,
But 'tis the happy who have called thee so.
   The Curse of Kehama (1810) canto 15, st. 12

9 No stir in the air, no stir in the sea,
The ship was still as she could be.
   'The Inchcape Rock'

10 My name is Death: the last best friend am I.
   'The Lay of the Laureate' (1816) st. 87

11 Blue, darkly, deeply, beautifully blue.
   Madoc (1805) pt. 1, canto 5 'Lincoya' l. 102

12 We wage no war with women nor with priests.
   Madoc (1805) pt. 1, canto 15 'The Excommunication' l. 65

13 You are old, Father William, the young man cried,
The few locks which are left you are grey;
You are hale, Father William, a hearty old man,
Now tell me the reason, I pray.
   'The Old Man's Comforts' (1799). Cf. Carroll 182:3

14 In the days of my youth I remembered my God!
And He hath not forgotten my age.
   'The Old Man's Comforts' (1799)

15 The arts babblative and scribblative.
   Colloquies on the Progress and Prospects of Society (1829) no. 10, pt. 2

16 The march of intellect.
   Colloquies on the Progress and Prospects of Society (1829) no. 14

17 Your true lover of literature is never fastidious.
   The Doctor (1812) ch. 17

18 Show me a man who cares no more for one place than another, and I will show you in that same person one who loves nothing but himself. Beware of those who are homeless by choice.
   The Doctor (1812) ch. 34

19 Live as long as you may, the first twenty years are the longest half of your life.
   The Doctor (1812) ch. 130

20 The death of Nelson was felt in England as something more than a public calamity; men started at the intelligence, and turned pale, as if they had heard of the loss of a dear friend.
   The Life of Nelson (1813) ch. 9

21 She has made me in love with a cold climate, and frost and snow, with a northern moonlight.
   On Mary Wollstonecraft's letters from Sweden and Norway; letter to his brother Thomas, 28 April 1797, in Charles Southey *Life and Correspondence of Robert Southey* vol. 1 (1849)

Robert Southwell c.1561–95

English poet and Roman Catholic martyr

22 My faultless breast the furnace is,
The fuel wounding thorns;
Love is the fire, and sighs the smoke,
The ashes, shame and scorns;

The fuel Justice layeth on,
And Mercy blows the coals;
The metal in this furnace wrought
Are men's defiled souls:

For which, as now on fire I am
To work them to their good,
So will I melt into a bath
To wash them in my blood.
   'The Burning Babe' (*c.*1590)

23 To rise by other's fall
I deem a losing gain;
All states with others' ruins built
To ruin run amain.
   'Content and Rich' (1595)

24 Man's mind a mirror is of heavenly sights,
A brief wherein all marvels summèd lie;
Of fairest forms and sweetest shapes the store,
Most beautiful all, yet thought may grace them more.
   'Look Home' (1595)

1 Shun delays, they breed remorse;
  Take thy time while time doth serve thee;
  Creeping snails have weakest force,
  Fly their fault lest thou repent thee.
  Good is best when soonest wrought,
  Lingered labours come to naught.
  'Loss in Delays' (1595)

2 Times go by turns, and chances change by course,
  From foul to fair, from better hap to worse.
  'Times go by Turns' (1595). Cf. Anonymous 22:19

3 Before my face the picture hangs,
  That daily should put me in mind
  Of those cold qualms, and bitter pangs,
  That shortly I am like to find:
  But yet alas full little I
  Do think hereon that I must die.
  'Upon the Image of Death' (attributed)

Muriel Spark 1918–

British novelist

4 The one certain way for a woman to hold a man is to
  leave him for religion.
  The Comforters (1957) ch. 1

5 I am putting old heads on your young shoulders . . .
  all my pupils are the crème de la crème.
  The Prime of Miss Jean Brodie (1961) ch. 1

6 Give me a girl at an impressionable age, and she is
  mine for life.
  The Prime of Miss Jean Brodie (1961) ch. 1. Cf. Anonymous
  13:15

7 One's prime is elusive. You little girls, when you grow
  up, must be on the alert to recognise your prime at
  whatever time of your life it may occur.
  The Prime of Miss Jean Brodie (1961) ch. 1

8 To me education is a leading out of what is already
  there in the pupil's soul. To Miss Mackay it is a
  putting in of something that is not there, and that is
  not what I call education, I call it intrusion.
  The Prime of Miss Jean Brodie (1961) ch. 2

John Sparrow 1906–92

Warden of All Souls College, Oxford, 1952–77

9 Without you, Heaven would be too dull to bear,
  And Hell would not be Hell if you are there.
  Epitaph for Maurice Bowra, in *Times Literary Supplement*
  30 May 1975, p. 583

10 That indefatigable and unsavoury engine of pollution,
   the dog.
   Letter to *The Times* 30 September 1975

Herbert Spencer 1820–1903

English philosopher

11 Science is organized knowledge.
   Education (1861) ch. 2

12 People are beginning to see that the first requisite to
   success in life is to be a good animal.
   Education (1861) ch. 2

13 The Republican form of Government is the highest
   form of government; but because of this it requires the
   highest type of human nature—a type nowhere at
   present existing.
   Essays (1891) vol. 3 'The Americans'

14 Absolute morality is the regulation of conduct in such
   a way that pain shall not be inflicted.
   Essays (1891) vol. 3 'Prison Ethics'

15 The ultimate result of shielding men from the effects of
   folly, is to fill the world with fools.
   Essays (1891) vol. 3 'State Tamperings with Money and
   Banks'

16 Evolution . . . is—a change from an indefinite,
   incoherent homogeneity, to a definite coherent
   heterogeneity.
   First Principles (1862) ch. 16

17 It cannot but happen . . . that those will survive whose
   functions happen to be most nearly in equilibrium
   with the modified aggregate of external forces . . . This
   survival of the fittest implies multiplication of the
   fittest.
   Principles of Biology (1865) pt. 3, ch. 12, sect. 164. Cf.
   Darwin 231:9

18 How often misused words generate misleading
   thoughts.
   Principles of Ethics (1879) bk. 1, pt. 2, ch. 8, sect. 152

19 Progress, therefore, is not an accident, but a necessity
   . . . It is a part of nature.
   Social Statics (1850) pt. 1, ch. 2, sect. 4

20 A clever theft was praiseworthy amongst the
   Spartans; and it is equally so amongst Christians,
   provided it be on a sufficiently large scale.
   Social Statics (1850) pt. 2, ch. 16, sect. 3

21 Education has for its object the formation of character.
   Social Statics (1850) pt. 2, ch. 17, sect. 4

22 Opinion is ultimately determined by the feelings, and
   not by the intellect.
   Social Statics (1850) pt. 4, ch. 30, sect. 8

23 No one can be perfectly free till all are free; no one
   can be perfectly moral till all are moral; no one can be
   perfectly happy till all are happy.
   Social Statics (1850) pt. 4, ch. 30, sect. 16

24 French art, if not sanguinary, is usually obscene.
   In *Home Life with Herbert Spencer* (1906) ch. 4 (authorship
   unknown)

Raine, Countess Spencer 1929–

25 Alas, for our towns and cities. Monstrous carbuncles
   of concrete have erupted in gentle Georgian Squares.
   The Spencers on Spas (1983) p. 14. Cf. Charles 192:1

Stephen Spender 1909–

English poet

26 After the first powerful plain manifesto
   The black statement of pistons, without more fuss
   But gliding like a queen, she leaves the station.
   'The Express' (1933)

1 Born of the sun they travelled a short while towards the sun,
And left the vivid air signed with their honour.
'I think continually of those who were truly great' (1933)

2 My parents kept me from children who were rough
And who threw words like stones and who wore torn clothes.
'My parents kept me from children who were rough' (1933)

3 Never being, but always at the edge of Being.
Title of poem (1933)

4   Their collected
Hearts wound up with love, like little watch springs.
'The Past Values' (1939)

5 Pylons, those pillars
Bare like nude, giant girls that have no secret.
'The Pylons' (1933)

6 What I had not foreseen
Was the gradual day
Weakening the will
Leaking the brightness away.
'What I expected, was' (1933)

7 Who live under the shadow of a war,
What can I do that matters?
'Who live under the shadow of a war' (1933)

Edmund Spenser c.1552–99

English poet

8 The merry cuckoo, messenger of Spring,
His trumpet shrill hath thrice already sounded.
Amoretti (1595) sonnet 19

9 Most glorious Lord of life, that on this day
Didst make thy triumph over death and sin:
And, having harrowed hell, didst bring away
Captivity thence captive, us to win.
Amoretti (1595) sonnet 68

10 So let us love, dear Love, like as we ought,
—Love is the lesson which the Lord us taught.
Amoretti (1595) sonnet 68

11 One day I wrote her name upon the strand,
But came the waves and washèd it away:
Again I wrote it with a second hand,
But came the tide, and made my pains his prey.
Vain man, said she, that dost in vain assay,
A mortal thing so to immortalize,
For I myself shall like to this decay,
And eke my name be wipèd out likewise.
Not so, quoth I, let baser things devise
To die in dust, but you shall live by fame:
My verse your virtues rare shall eternize,
And in the heavens write your glorious name,
Where when as death shall all the world subdue,
Our love shall live, and later life renew.
Amoretti (1595) sonnet 75

12 So love is Lord of all the world by right.
Colin Clout's Come Home Again (1595) l. 883

13 So you great Lord, that with your counsel sway
The burden of this kingdom mightily,
With like delights sometimes may eke delays,
The rugged brow of careful Policy.
Dedicatory sonnet to Sir Christopher Hatton (1590)

14 Wake now, my love, awake; for it is time.
The rosy morn long since left Tithones bed,
All ready to her silver coach to climb,
And Phoebus gins to shew his glorious head.
Hark how the cheerful birds do chant their lays
And carol of love's praise.
The merry lark her matins sings aloft,
The thrush replies, the mavis descant plays,
The ouzel shrills, the ruddock warbles soft,
So goodly all agree with sweet consent,
To this day's merriment.
'Epithalamion' (1595) l. 74

15 Open the temple gates unto my love,
Open them wide that she may enter in.
'Epithalamion' (1595) l. 204

16 Ah! when will this long weary day have end,
And lend me leave to come unto my love?
How slowly do the hours their numbers spend!
How slowly does sad Time his feathers move!
'Epithalamion' (1595) l. 278

17 Song made in lieu of many ornaments,
With which my love should duly have been decked.
'Epithalamion' (1595) l. 427

18 The general end therefore of all the book is to fashion a gentleman or noble person in virtuous and gentle discipline.
The Faerie Queen (1596) preface

19 Fierce wars and faithful loves shall moralize my song.
The Faerie Queen (1596) bk. 1, introduction, st. 1

20 A gentle knight was pricking on the plain.
The Faerie Queen (1596) bk. 1, canto 1, st. 1

21 But on his breast a bloody cross he bore,
The dear remembrance of his dying Lord.
The Faerie Queen (1596) bk. 1, canto 1, st. 2

22 But of his cheer did seem too solemn sad;
Yet nothing did he dread, but ever was ydrad.
The Faerie Queen (1596) bk. 1, canto 1, st. 2

23 A bold bad man, that dared to call by name
Great Gorgon, Prince of darkness and dead night.
The Faerie Queen (1596) bk. 1, canto 1, st. 37. Cf. *Henry VIII* 588:13

24   Her angel's face
As the great eye of heaven shinèd bright,
And made a sunshine in the shady place;
Did never mortal eye behold such heavenly grace.
The Faerie Queen (1596) bk. 1, canto 3, st. 4

25 And all the hinder parts, that few could spy,
Were ruinous and old, but painted cunningly.
The Faerie Queen (1596) bk. 1, canto 4, st. 5

26 The noble heart, that harbours virtuous thought,
And is with child of glorious great intent,
Can never rest, until it have forth brought
Th' eternal brood of glory excellent.
The Faerie Queen (1596) bk. 1, canto 5, st. 1

27   A cruel crafty crocodile,
Which in false grief hiding his harmful guile,
Doth weep full sore, and sheddeth tender tears.
The Faerie Queen (1596) bk. 1, canto 5, st. 18

28 Still as he fled, his eye was backward cast,
As if his fear still followed him behind.
The Faerie Queen (1596) bk. 1, canto 9, st. 21

1 That darksome cave they enter, where they find
That cursèd man, low sitting on the ground,
Musing full sadly in his sullen mind.
  The Faerie Queen (1596) bk. 1, canto 9, st. 35

2 Sleep after toil, port after stormy seas,
Ease after war, death after life does greatly please.
  The Faerie Queen (1596) bk. 1, canto 9, st. 40

3 So double was his pains, so double be his praise.
  The Faerie Queen (1596) bk. 2, canto 2, st. 25

4 Upon her eyelids many Graces sate,
Under the shadow of her even brows.
  The Faerie Queen (1596) bk. 2, canto 3, st. 25

5 And all for love, and nothing for reward.
  The Faerie Queen (1596) bk. 2, canto 8, st. 2

6 So passeth, in the passing of a day,
Of mortal life the leaf, the bud, the flower,
No more doth flourish after first decay,
That erst was sought to deck both bed and bower,
Of many a lady, and many a paramour:
Gather therefore the rose, whilst yet is prime,
For soon comes age, that will her pride deflower:
Gather the rose of love, whilst yet is time,
Whilst loving thou mayst lovèd be with equal crime.
  The Faerie Queen (1596) bk. 2, canto 12, st. 75

7   The dunghill kind
Delights in filth and foul incontinence:
Let Grill be Grill, and have his hoggish mind.
  The Faerie Queen (1596) bk. 2, canto 12, st. 87

8   Whether it divine tobacco were,
Or panachaea, or polygony,
She found, and brought it to her patient dear.
  The Faerie Queen (1596) bk. 3, canto 5, st. 32

9 Hard is to teach an old horse amble true.
  The Faerie Queen (1596) bk. 3, canto 8, st. 26

10 And painful pleasure turns to pleasing pain.
  The Faerie Queen (1596) bk. 3, canto 10, st. 60

11 And as she looked about, she did behold,
How over that same door was likewise writ,
Be bold, be bold, and everywhere Be bold . . .
At last she spied at that room's upper end
Another iron door, on which was writ
Be not too bold.
  The Faerie Queen (1596) bk. 3, canto 11, st. 54

12 Dan Chaucer, well of English undefiled,
On Fame's eternal beadroll worthy to be filed.
  The Faerie Queen (1596) bk. 4, canto 2, st. 32

13 For all that nature by her mother wit
Could frame in earth.
  The Faerie Queen (1596) bk. 4, canto 10, st. 21

14 O sacred hunger of ambitious minds.
  The Faerie Queen (1596) bk. 5, canto 12, st. 1

15 A monster, which the Blatant beast men call,
A dreadful fiend of gods and men ydrad.
  The Faerie Queen (1596) bk. 5, canto 12, st. 37

16 The gentle mind by gentle deeds is known.
For a man by nothing is so well bewrayed,
As by his manners.
  The Faerie Queen (1596) bk. 6, canto 3, st. 1

17 What man that sees the ever-whirling wheel
Of Change, the which all mortal things doth sway,
But that thereby doth find, and plainly feel,
How Mutability in them doth play
Her cruel sports, to many men's decay?
  The Faerie Queen (1596) bk. 7, canto 6, st. 1

18 For all that moveth doth in Change delight:
But thenceforth all shall rest eternally
With Him that is the God of Sabbaoth hight:
O that great Sabbaoth God, grant me that Sabbaoth's
sight.
  The Faerie Queen (1596) bk. 7, canto 8, st. 2

19 That beauty is not, as fond men misdeem,
An outward show of things, that only seem.
  'An Hymn in Honour of Beauty' (1596) l. 90

20 For of the soul the body form doth take;
For soul is form, and doth the body make.
  'An Hymn in Honour of Beauty' (1596) l. 132

21 What more felicity can fall to creature,
Than to enjoy delight with liberty.
  'Muiopotmos' (1591) l. 209

22 Of such deep learning little had he need,
Ne yet of Latin, ne of Greek that breed
Doubts 'mongst Divines, and difference of texts,
From whence arise diversity of sects,
And hateful heresies.
  'Prosopopoia or Mother Hubbard's Tale' (1591) l. 385

23 Calm was the day, and through the trembling air,
Sweet breathing Zephyrus did softly play.
  Prothalamion (1596) l. 1

24 With that, I saw two swans of goodly hue,
Come softly swimming down along the Lee . . .
So purely white they were,
That even the gentle stream, the which them bare,
Seemed foul to them, and bade his billows spare
To wet their silken feathers, lest they might
Soil their fair plumes with water not so fair
And mar their beauties bright,
That shone as Heaven's light,
Against their bridal day, which was not long:
Sweet Thames, run softly, till I end my song.
  Prothalamion (1596) l. 37

25 To be wise and eke to love,
Is granted scarce to God above.
  The Shepherd's Calendar (1579) 'March. Willy's Emblem'

26 Bring hither the pink and purple columbine,
With gillyflowers:
Bring coronation, and sops in wine,
Worn of paramours.
Strew me the ground with daffadowndillies,
And cowslips, and kingcups, and loved lilies.
  The Shepherd's Calendar (1579) 'April' l. 136

27 And he that strives to touch the stars,
Oft stumbles at a straw.
  The Shepherd's Calendar (1579) 'July' l. 99

28 Uncouth unkist, said the old famous poet Chaucer.
  The Shepherd's Calendar (1579) 'Letter to Gabriel Harvey'

29 So now they have made our English tongue a
gallimaufry or hodgepodge of all other speeches.
  The Shepherd's Calendar (1579) 'Letter to Gabriel Harvey'

Steven Spielberg 1947–

American film director

1 Close encounters of the third kind.

Title of film (1977)

Baruch Spinoza 1632–77

Dutch philosopher

2 *Per Deum intelligo eus absolute infinitum, hoc est, substantiam constantem infinitis attributis, quorum unumquodque aeternam et infinitam essentiam exprimit.*

By *God* I mean a being absolutely infinite—that is, a substance consisting in infinite attributes, of which each expresses eternal and infinite essentiality.

Ethics (1677) pt. 1, para. 6 'Deus, sive Natura [God, or in other words, Nature]'

3 *Sedula curavi, humanas actiones non ridere, non lugere, neque detestare, sed intelligere.*

I have striven not to laugh at human actions, not to weep at them, nor to hate them, but to understand them.

Tractatus Politicus (1677) ch. 1, sect. 4

Benjamin Spock 1903–

American paediatrician

4 To win in Vietnam, we will have to exterminate a nation.

Dr Spock on Vietnam (1968) ch. 7

William Archibald Spooner 1844–1930

English clergyman; Warden of New College, Oxford, 1903–24

5 Mr Huxley assures me that it's no farther from the north coast of Spitzbergen to the North Pole than it is from Land's End to John of Gaunt.

Quoted by Julian Huxley in *SEAC* (Calcutta) 27 February 1944

6 You will find as you grow older that the weight of rages will press harder and harder upon the employer.

In William Hayter *Spooner* (1977) ch. 6

7 Her late husband, you know, a very sad death—eaten by missionaries—poor soul!

In William Hayter *Spooner* (1977) ch. 6

Sir Cecil Spring-Rice 1859–1918

British diplomat; Ambassador to Washington from 1912

8 I vow to thee, my country—all earthly things above—
Entire and whole and perfect, the service of my love,
The love that asks no question: the love that stands the test,
That lays upon the altar the dearest and the best:
The love that never falters, the love that pays the price,
The love that makes undaunted the final sacrifice.

'I Vow to Thee, My Country' (written on the eve of his departure from Washington, 13 January 1918)

9 And there's another country, I've heard of long ago—
Most dear to them that love her, most great to them that know.

'I Vow to Thee, My Country' (written 1918)

10 Her ways are ways of gentleness and all her paths are Peace.

'I Vow to Thee, My Country' (written 1918). Cf. Proverbs 5317

11 I am the Dean of Christ Church, Sir:
There's my wife; look well at her.
She's the Broad and I'm the High;
We are the University.

The Masque of Balliol (composed by and current among members of Balliol College, Oxford, in the 1870s) in W. G. Hiscock (ed.) *The Balliol Rhymes* (1939) p. 29. The first couplet was unofficially altered to: 'I am the Dean, and this is Mrs Liddell; / She the first, and I the second fiddle.' Cf. Anonymous 16:15, Beeching 59:7

12 Wilson is the nation's shepherd and McAdoo his crook.

Of President Woodrow Wilson and his secretary of the treasury, a remark considered unfortunate in the light of British attempts to draw the US into the First World War; in Robert Skidelsky *John Maynard Keynes* vol. 1 (1983) ch. 14, sect. 3

Bruce Springsteen 1949–

American rock singer and songwriter

13 Born down in a dead man's town
The first kick I took was when I hit the ground.

'Born in the USA' (1984 song)

14 We gotta get out while we're young,
'Cause tramps like us, baby, we were born to run.

'Born to Run' (1974 song)

15 Is a dream a lie if it don't come true,
Or is it something worse?

'The River' (1980 song)

C. H. Spurgeon 1834–92

English nonconformist preacher

16 If you want truth to go round the world you must hire an express train to pull it; but if you want a lie to go round the world, it will fly: it is as light as a feather, and a breath will carry it. It is well said in the old proverb, 'a lie will go round the world while truth is pulling its boots on'.

Gems from Spurgeon (1859) p. 74

Sir J. C. Squire 1884–1958

English man of letters

17 But I'm not so think as you drunk I am.

'Ballade of Soporific Absorption' (1931)

18 It did not last: the Devil howling 'Ho!
Let Einstein be!' restored the status quo.

'In continuation of Pope on Newton' (1926). Cf. Pope 521:2

Mme de Staël (Anne-Louise-Germaine Necker) 1766–1817

French writer

1 *Tout comprendre rend très indulgent.*

To be totally understanding makes one very indulgent.
   Corinne (1807) bk. 18, ch. 5

2 *Un homme peut braver l'opinion; une femme doit s'y soumettre.*

A man can brave opinion, a woman must submit to it.
   Delphine (1802) epigraph

3 Speech happens not to be his language.
   On being asked what she found to talk about with her new lover, a hussar (attributed)

Joseph Stalin (Iosif Vissarionovich Dzhugashvili) 1879–1953

Soviet dictator

4 The State is an instrument in the hands of the ruling class, used to break the resistance of the adversaries of that class.
   Foundations of Leninism (1924) section 4/6

5 The Pope! How many divisions has *he* got?
   On being asked to encourage Catholicism in Russia by way of conciliating the Pope, 13 May 1935; in W. S. Churchill *The Gathering Storm* (1948) ch. 8. Cf. Napoleon 490:6

Sir Henry Morton Stanley 1841–1904

British explorer

6 Dr Livingstone, I presume?
   How I found Livingstone (1872) ch. 11

Charles E. Stanton 1859–1933

American soldier

7 *Lafayette, nous voilà!*

Lafayette, we are here.
   At the tomb of Lafayette in Paris, 4 July 1917; in *New York Tribune* 6 September 1917

Edwin McMasters Stanton 1814–69

American lawyer

8 Now he belongs to the ages.
   Of Abraham Lincoln, following his assassination, 15 April 1865, in I. M. Tarbell *Life of Abraham Lincoln* (1900) vol. 2, p. 244

Elizabeth Cady Stanton 1815–1902

American suffragist

9 The Bible teaches that woman brought sin and death into the world, that she precipitated the fall of the race ... marriage for her was to be a condition of bondage, maternity a period of suffering and anguish, and in silence and subjection, she was to play the role of a dependant on man's bounty for all her material wants.
   The Woman's Bible (1895) pt. 1, introduction

10 Woman's degradation is in man's idea of his sexual rights. Our religion, laws, customs, are all founded on the belief that woman was made for man.
   Letter to Susan B. Anthony, 14 June 1860, in T. Stanton and H. Stanton Blatch (eds.) *Elizabeth Cady Stanton* (1922) vol. 2, p. 82

Frank L. Stanton 1857–1927

American journalist and poet

11 Sweetes' li'l' feller,
   Everybody knows;
   Dunno what to call him,
   But he's mighty lak' a rose!
   'Mighty Lak' a Rose' (1901 song)

John Stark 1728–1822

American Revolutionary officer

12 We beat them to-day or Molly Stark's a widow.
   Before the Battle of Bennington, 16 August 1777, in *Cyclopaedia of American Biography* vol. 5

Christina Stead 1902–83

Australian novelist

13 A self-made man is one who believes in luck and sends his son to Oxford.
   House of All Nations (1938) 'Credo'

Sir Richard Steele 1672–1729

Irish-born essayist and playwright

14 The insupportable labour of doing nothing.
   The Spectator no. 54 (2 May 1711)

15 A woman seldom writes her mind but in her postscript.
   The Spectator no. 79 (31 May 1711). Cf. Bacon 43:6

16 We were in some little time fixed in our seats, and sat with that dislike which people not too good-natured usually conceive of each other at first sight.
   The Spectator no. 132 (1 August 1711)

17 There are so few who can grow old with a good grace.
   The Spectator no. 263 (1 January 1712)

18 Will Honeycomb calls these over-offended ladies the outrageously virtuous.
   The Spectator no. 266 (4 January 1712)

19 It is to be noted that when any part of this paper appears dull there is a design in it.
   The Tatler no. 38 (7 July 1709)

20 To love her is a liberal education.
   The Tatler no. 49 (2 August 1709); of Lady Elizabeth Hastings

21 Reading is to the mind what exercise is to the body.
   The Tatler no. 147 (18 March 1710)

22 It was very prettily said, that we may learn the little value of fortune by the persons on whom heaven is pleased to bestow it.
   The Tatler no. 203 (27 July 1710). Cf. Luther 432:16, Swift 673:23

Lincoln Steffens 1866–1936
American journalist

1 I have seen the future; and it works.
   Following a visit to the Soviet Union in 1919, in *Letters* (1938) vol. 1, p. 463. See J. M. Thompson *Russia, Bolshevism and the Versailles Treaty* (1954) p. 176, where it is recalled that Steffens had composed the expression before he had even arrived in Russia

Gertrude Stein 1874–1946
American writer

2 Remarks are not literature.
   Autobiography of Alice B. Toklas (1933) ch. 7

3 Pigeons on the grass alas.
   Four Saints in Three Acts (1934) act 3, sc. 2

4 In the United States there is more space where nobody is than where anybody is. That is what makes America what it is.
   The Geographical History of America (1936)

5 Rose is a rose is a rose, is a rose.
   Sacred Emily (1913) p. 187

6 You are all a lost generation.
   Of the young who served in the First World War, the phrase having been borrowed (in translation) from a French garage mechanic, whom Stein heard address it disparagingly to an incompetent apprentice. Ernest Hemingway subsequently took it as his epigraph to *The Sun Also Rises* (1926)

7 A village explainer, excellent if you were a village, but if you were not, not.
   Of Ezra Pound, in Janet Hobhouse *Everyone who was Anybody* (1975) ch. 6

John Steinbeck 1902–68
American novelist

8 Man, unlike any other thing organic or inorganic in the universe, grows beyond his work, walks up the stairs of his concepts, emerges ahead of his accomplishments.
   The Grapes of Wrath (1939) ch. 14

9 Okie use' ta mean you was from Oklahoma. Now it means you're a dirty son-of-a-bitch. Okie means you're scum. Don't mean nothing itself, it's the way they say it.
   The Grapes of Wrath (1939) ch. 18

Gloria Steinem 1934–
American journalist

10 We are becoming the men we wanted to marry.
   Ms July/August 1982

11 Outrageous acts and everyday rebellions.
   Title of book (1983)

12 A woman without a man is like a fish without a bicycle.
   Attributed

Stendhal (Henri Beyle) 1783–1842
French novelist

13 *Un roman est un miroir qui se promène sur une grande route. Tantôt il reflète à vos yeux l'azur des cieux, tantôt la fange des bourbiers de la route.*

   A novel is a mirror which passes over a highway. Sometimes it reflects to your eyes the blue of the skies, at others the churned-up mud of the road.
   Le Rouge et le noir (1830) bk. 2, ch. 19

14 *J'aimais, et j'aime encore, les mathématiques pour elles-mêmes comme n'admettant pas l'hypocrisie et le vague, mes deux bêtes d'aversion.*

   I used to love mathematics for its own sake, and I still do, because it allows for no hypocrisy and no vagueness, my two *bêtes noires*.
   La Vie d'Henri Brulard (1890) ch. 10

Sir James Fitzjames Stephen 1829–94
English lawyer

15 The way in which the man of genius rules is by persuading an efficient minority to coerce an indifferent and self-indulgent majority.
   Liberty, Equality and Fraternity (1873) ch. 2

J. K. Stephen 1859–92
English journalist and writer of light verse

16 Ah! Matt.: old age has brought to me
   Thy wisdom, less thy certainty:
   The world's a jest, and joy's a trinket:
   I knew that once: but now—I think it.
   'Senex to Matt. Prior' (1891). Cf. Gay 300:11

17 Two voices are there: one is of the deep;
   It learns the storm-cloud's thunderous melody,
   Now roars, now murmurs with the changing sea,
   Now bird-like pipes, now closes soft in sleep:
   And one is of an old half-witted sheep
   Which bleats articulate monotony,
   And indicates that two and one are three,
   That grass is green, lakes damp, and mountains steep
   And, Wordsworth, both are thine.
   'A Sonnet' (1891). Cf. Wordsworth 748:9

18 Will there never come a season
   Which shall rid us from the curse
   Of a prose which knows no reason
   And an unmelodious verse . . .
   When there stands a muzzled stripling,
   Mute, beside a muzzled bore:
   When the Rudyards cease from kipling
   And the Haggards ride no more.
   'To R.K.' (1891)

James Stephens 1882–1950
Irish poet and writer

19 Finality is death. Perfection is finality. Nothing is perfect. There are lumps in it.
   The Crock of Gold (1912) bk. 1, ch. 4

1 I hear a sudden cry of pain!
There is a rabbit in a snare:
Now I hear the cry again,
But I cannot tell from where . . .
Little one! Oh, little one!
I am searching everywhere.
'The Snare' (1915)

Laurence Sterne 1713–68

English novelist

2 They order, said I, this matter better in France.
A Sentimental Journey (1768) opening words

3 As an Englishman does not travel to see Englishmen, I
retired to my room.
A Sentimental Journey (1768) 'Preface. In the Desobligeant'

4 I pity the man who can travel from Dan to Beersheba,
and cry, 'tis all barren.
A Sentimental Journey (1768) 'In the Street. Calais'

5 If ever I do a mean action, it must be in some interval
betwixt one passion and another.
A Sentimental Journey (1768) 'Montriul'

6 Vive l'amour! et vive la bagatelle!
A Sentimental Journey (1768) 'The letter'

7 Hail, ye small sweet courtesies of life.
A Sentimental Journey (1768) 'The Pulse. Paris'

8 There are worse occupations in this world than feeling
a woman's pulse.
A Sentimental Journey (1768) 'The Pulse. Paris'

9 God tempers the wind, said Maria, to the shorn lamb.
A Sentimental Journey (1768) 'Maria' (derived from a French
proverb, but familiar in this form of words)

10 Dear sensibility! source inexhausted of all that's
precious in our joys, or costly in our sorrows!
A Sentimental Journey (1768) 'The Bourbonnois'

11 I wish either my father or my mother, or indeed both
of them, as they were in duty both equally bound to
it, had minded what they were about when they begot
me.
Tristram Shandy (1759–67) bk. 1, ch. 1

12 'Pray, my dear,' quoth my mother, 'have you not
forgot to wind up the clock?'—'Good G—!' cried my
father, making an exclamation, but taking care to
moderate his voice at the same time,—'Did ever
woman, since the creation of the world, interrupt a
man with such a silly question?'
Tristram Shandy (1759–67) bk. 1, ch. 1

13 As we jog on, either laugh with me, or at me, or in
short do anything,—only keep your temper.
Tristram Shandy (1759–67) bk. 1, ch. 6

14 Have not the wisest of men in all ages, not excepting
Solomon himself,—have they not had their
Hobby-Horses . . . and so long as a man rides his
Hobby-Horse peaceably and quietly along the King's
highway, and neither compels you or me to get up
behind him,—pray, Sir, what have either you or I to
do with it?
Tristram Shandy (1759–67) bk. 1, ch. 7

15 He was in a few hours of giving his enemies the slip
for ever.
Tristram Shandy (1759–67) bk. 1, ch. 12

16 'Tis known by the name of perseverance in a good
cause,—and of obstinacy in a bad one.
Tristram Shandy (1759–67) bk. 1, ch. 17

17 What is the character of a family to an hypothesis?
my father would reply.
Tristram Shandy (1759–67) bk. 1, ch. 21

18 My uncle Toby would never offer to answer this by
any other kind of argument, than that of whistling
half a dozen bars of Lillabullero.
Tristram Shandy (1759–67) bk. 1, ch. 21

19 Digressions, incontestably, are the sunshine;—they
are the life, the soul of reading;—take them out of this
book for instance,—you might as well take the book
along with them.
Tristram Shandy (1759–67) bk. 1, ch. 22

20 I should have no objection to this method, but that I
think it must smell too strong of the lamp.
Tristram Shandy (1759–67) bk. 1, ch. 23

21 Writing, when properly managed (as you may be sure
I think mine is) is but a different name for
conversation.
Tristram Shandy (1759–67) bk. 2, ch. 11

22 'I'll not hurt thee,' says my uncle Toby, rising from
his chair, and going across the room, with the fly in
his hand,—'I'll not hurt a hair of thy head:—Go,'
says he, lifting up the sash, and opening his hand as
he spoke, to let it escape;—'go, poor devil, get thee
gone, why should I hurt thee?—This world surely is
wide enough to hold both thee and me.'
Tristram Shandy (1759–67) bk. 2, ch. 12

23 Whenever a man talks loudly against
religion,—always suspect that it is not his reason, but
his passions which have got the better of his creed.
Tristram Shandy (1759–67) bk. 2, ch. 17

24 It is the nature of an hypothesis, when once a man
has conceived it, that it assimilates every thing to
itself, as proper nourishment; and, from the first
moment of your begetting it, it generally grows the
stronger by every thing you see, hear, read, or
understand.
Tristram Shandy (1759–67) bk. 2, ch. 19

25 'Our armies swore terribly in Flanders,' cried my uncle
Toby,—'but nothing to this.'
Tristram Shandy (1759–67) bk. 3, ch. 11

26 The corregiescity of Corregio.
Tristram Shandy (1759–67) bk. 3, ch. 12.

27 Of all the cants which are canted in this canting
world,—though the cant of hypocrites may be the
worst,—the cant of criticism is the most tormenting!
Tristram Shandy (1759–67) bk. 3, ch. 12

28 Is this a fit time, said my father to himself, to talk of
Pensions and Grenadiers?
Tristram Shandy (1759–67) bk. 4, ch. 5

29 True *Shandeism*, think what you will against it, opens
the heart and lungs, and like all those affections which
partake of its nature, it forces the blood and other vital
fluids of the body to run freely through its channels,
and makes the wheel of life run long and cheerfully
round.
Tristram Shandy (1759–67) bk. 4, ch. 32

1 'There is no terror, brother Toby, in its [death's] looks, but what it borrows from groans and convulsions— and the blowing of noses, and the wiping away of tears with the bottoms of curtains, in a dying man's room—Strip it of these, what is it?'—''Tis better in battle than in bed', said my uncle Toby.
  Tristram Shandy (1759–67) bk. 5, ch. 3

2 There is a North-west passage to the intellectual World.
  Tristram Shandy (1759–67) bk. 5, ch. 42

3 'The poor soul will die:—' 'He shall not die, by G—', cried my uncle Toby.—The Accusing Spirit, which flew up to heaven's chancery with the oath, blushed as he gave it in;—and the Recording Angel, as he wrote it down, dropped a tear upon the word, and blotted it out for ever.
  Tristram Shandy (1759–67) bk. 6, ch. 8

4 To say a man is fallen in love,—or that he is deeply in love,—or up to the ears in love,—and sometimes even over head and ears in it,—carries an idiomatical kind of implication, that love is a thing below a man:—this is recurring again to Plato's opinion, which, with all his divinityship,—I hold to be damnable and heretical:—and so much for that.
  Let love therefore be what it will,—my uncle Toby fell into it.
  Tristram Shandy (1759–67) bk. 6, ch. 37

5 My brother Toby, quoth she, is going to be married to Mrs Wadman.
  Then he will never, quoth my father, lie *diagonally* in his bed again as long as he lives.
  Tristram Shandy (1759–67) bk. 6, ch. 39

6 Now hang it! quoth I, as I look'd towards the French coast—a man should know something of his own country too, before he goes abroad.
  Tristram Shandy (1759–67) bk. 7, ch. 2

7 And who are you? said he.—Don't puzzle me, said I.
  Tristram Shandy (1759–67) bk. 7, ch. 33

8 'A soldier,' cried my Uncle Toby, interrupting the corporal, 'is no more exempt from saying a foolish thing, Trim, than a man of letters.'—'But not so often, an' please your honour,' replied the corporal.
  Tristram Shandy (1759–67) bk. 8, ch. 19

9 Everything presses on—whilst thou art twisting that lock,—see! it grows grey; and every time I kiss thy hand to bid adieu, and every absence which follows it, are preludes to that eternal separation which we are shortly to make.
  Tristram Shandy (1759–67) bk. 9, ch. 10

10 —d! said my mother, 'what is all this story about?'— 'A Cock and a Bull,' said Yorick.
  Tristram Shandy (1759–67) bk. 9, ch. 33

11 This sad vicissitude of things.
  Sermons (1760) no. 16 'The Character of Shimei'

Brooks Stevens
American industrial designer

12 Our whole economy is based on planned obsolescence . . . we make good products, we induce people to buy them, and then the next year we deliberately introduce something that will make these products old-fashioned, out of date, obsolete.
  In Vance Packard *The Waste Makers* (1960) ch. 6

Wallace Stevens 1879–1955
American poet

13 The poet is the priest of the invisible.
  'Adagia' (1957)

14 I placed a jar in Tennessee,
  And round it was, upon a hill.
  It made the slovenly wilderness
  Surround that hill.
  'Anecdote of the Jar' (1923)

15 The prologues are over. It is a question, now,
  Of final belief. So, say that final belief
  Must be in a fiction. It is time to choose.
  'Asides on the Oboe' (1942)

16 Chieftain Iffucan of Azcan in caftan
  Of tan with henna hackles, halt!
  'Bantams in Pine Woods' (1923)

17 Only, here and there, an old sailor,
  Drunk and asleep in his boots,
  Catches tigers
  In red weather.
  'Disillusionment of Ten O'Clock' (1923)

18 Call the roller of big cigars,
  The muscular one, and bid him whip
  In kitchen cups concupiscent curds.
  Let the wenches dawdle in such dress
  As they are used to wear, and let the boys
  Bring flowers in last month's newspapers.
  Let be be finale of seem.
  The only emperor is the emperor of ice-cream.
  'The Emperor of Ice-Cream' (1923)

19 Frogs Eat Butterflies. Snakes Eat Frogs. Hogs Eat Snakes. Men Eat Hogs.
  Title of poem (1923)

20 Poetry is the supreme fiction, madame.
  'A High-Toned old Christian Woman' (1923)

21 Oh! Blessed rage for order, pale Ramón,
  The maker's rage to order words of the sea,
  Words of the fragrant portals, dimly-starred,
  And of ourselves and of our origins,
  In ghostlier demarcations, keener sounds.
  'The Idea of Order at Key West' (1936)

22 The man bent over his guitar,
  A shearsman of sorts. The day was green.

  They said, 'You have a blue guitar,
  You do not play things as they are.'
  The man replied, 'Things as they are
  Are changed upon the blue guitar.'
  'The Man with the Blue Guitar' (1937)

1 Twenty men crossing a bridge,
Into a village,
Are twenty men crossing twenty bridges,
Into twenty villages,
Or one man
Crossing a single bridge into a village.
    'Metaphors of a Magnifico' (1923)

2 The inconceivable idea of the sun.

You must become an ignorant man again
And see the sun again with an ignorant eye
And see it clearly in the idea of it.
    Notes Toward a Supreme Fiction (1947) 'It Must Be Abstract'
    no. 1

3 They will get it straight one day at the Sorbonne.
We shall return at twilight from the lecture
Pleased that the irrational is rational.
    Notes Toward a Supreme Fiction (1947) 'It Must Give
    Pleasure' no. 10

4 The palm at the end of the mind,
Beyond the last thought, rises . . .
A gold-feathered bird
Sings in the palm.
    'Of Mere Being' (1957)

5 We keep coming back and coming back
To the real: to the hotel instead of the hymns
That fall upon it out of the wind.
    'An Ordinary Evening in New Haven' (1950) no. 9

6   A more severe,
More harassing master would extemporize
Subtler, more urgent proof that the theory
Of poetry is the theory of life,

As it is, in the intricate evasions of as,
In things seen and unseen, created from nothingness,
The heavens, the hells, the worlds, the longed-for
    lands.
    'An Ordinary Evening in New Haven' (1950) no. 28

7 Just as my fingers on these keys
Make music, so the self-same sounds
On my spirit make a music, too.
Music is feeling, then, not sound;
And thus it is that what I feel,
Here in this room, desiring you,
Thinking of your blue-shadowed silk,
Is music.
    'Peter Quince at the Clavier' (1923) pt. 1

8 Beauty is momentary in the mind—
The fitful tracing of a portal;
But in the flesh it is immortal.
The body dies; the body's beauty lives.
    'Peter Quince at the Clavier' (1923) pt. 4

9 Susanna's music touched the bawdy strings
Of those white elders; but, escaping,
Left only Death's ironic scraping.
Now, in its immortality, it plays
On the clear viol of her memory,
And makes a constant sacrament of praise.
    'Peter Quince at the Clavier' (1923) pt. 4

10 Complacencies of the peignoir, and late
Coffee and oranges in a sunny chair,
And the green freedom of a cockatoo
Upon a rug mingle to dissipate
The holy hush of ancient sacrifice.
    'Sunday Morning' (1923) st. 1

11 We live in an old chaos of the sun,
Or old dependency of day and night,
Or island solitude, unsponsored, free,
Of that wide water, inescapable.
Deer walk upon our mountains, and the quail
Whistle about us their spontaneous cries;
Sweet berries ripen in the wilderness;
And, in the isolation of the sky,
At evening, casual flocks of pigeons make
Ambiguous undulations as they sink,
Downward to darkness, on extended wings.
    'Sunday Morning' (1923) st. 8

12 I do not know which to prefer,
The beauty of inflections
Or the beauty of innuendoes,
The blackbird whistling
Or just after.
    'Thirteen Ways of Looking at a Blackbird' (1923)

13 What makes the poet the potent figure that he is, or
was, or ought to be, is that he creates the world to
which we turn incessantly and without knowing it
and that he gives to life the supreme fictions without
which we are unable to conceive of it.
    The Noble Rider and the Sound of Words (1942)

Adlai Stevenson 1900–65

American Democratic politician

14 I suppose flattery hurts no one, that is, if he doesn't
inhale.
    Television broadcast, 30 March 1952, in N. F. Busch *Adlai
    E. Stevenson* (1952) ch. 5

15 If they [the Republicans] will stop telling lies about the
Democrats, we will stop telling the truth about them.
    Speech during 1952 Presidential campaign; in J. B. Martin
    Adlai Stevenson and Illinois (1976) ch. 8

16 Let's talk sense to the American people. Let's tell them
the truth, that there are no gains without pains.
    Speech of Acceptance at the Democratic National
    Convention, Chicago, Illinois, 26 July 1952; in *Speeches*
    (1952) p. 20

17 A hungry man is not a free man.
    Speech at Kasson, Minnesota, 6 September 1952; in
    Speeches (1952) 'Farm Policy'

18 There is no evil in the atom; only in men's souls.
    Speech at Hartford, Connecticut, 18 September 1952; in
    Speeches (1952) 'The Atomic Future'

19 In America any boy may become President.
    Speech in Indianapolis, 26 September 1952; in *Major
    Campaign Speeches . . . 1952* (1953) p. 174

20 A free society is a society where it is safe to be
unpopular.
    Speech in Detroit, 7 October 1952; in *Major Campaign
    Speeches . . . 1952* (1953) p. 218

21 The Republican party did not have to . . . encourage
the excesses of its Vice-Presidential nominee [Richard
Nixon]—the young man who asks you to set him one
heart-beat from the Presidency of the United States.
    Speech at Cleveland, Ohio, 23 October 1952, in *New York
    Times* 24 October 1952, p. 14 (commonly quoted 'just a
    heart-beat away . . . ')

1 A funny thing happened to me on the way to the White House.

> Speech in Washington, 13 December 1952, following his defeat in the Presidential election; in Alden Whitman *Portrait: Adlai E. Stevenson* (1965) ch. 1

2 We hear the Secretary of State [John Foster Dulles] boasting of his brinkmanship—the art of bringing us to the edge of the abyss.

> Speech in Hartford, Connecticut, 25 February 1956; in *New York Times* 26 February 1956, p. 64

3 She would rather light a candle than curse the darkness, and her glow has warmed the world.

> On learning of Eleanor Roosevelt's death, in *New York Times* 8 November 1962

Anne Stevenson 1933–

English poet

4 Blackbirds are the cellos of the deep farms.

> 'Green Mountain, Black Mountain' (1982)

Robert Louis Stevenson 1850–94

Scottish novelist

5 Every one lives by selling something.

> *Across the Plains* (1892) 'Beggars' pt. 3

6 A mortified appetite is never a wise companion.

> *Across the Plains* (1892) 'A Christmas Sermon' pt. 1

7 Here lies one who meant well, tried a little, failed much:—surely that may be his epitaph, of which he need not be ashamed.

> *Across the Plains* (1892) 'A Christmas Sermon' pt. 4

8 The harmless art of knucklebones has seen the fall of the Roman empire and the rise of the United States.

> *Across the Plains* (1892) 'The Lantern-Bearers' pt. 1

9 The bright face of danger.

> *Across the Plains* (1892) 'The Lantern-Bearers' pt. 4

10 The web, then, or the pattern; a web at once sensuous and logical, an elegant and pregnant texture: that is style, that is the foundation of the art of literature.

> *The Art of Writing* (1905) 'On some technical Elements of Style in Literature' (written 1885)

11 Politics is perhaps the only profession for which no preparation is thought necessary.

> *Familiar Studies of Men and Books* (1882) 'Yoshida-Torajiro'

12 Am I no a bonny fighter?

> *Kidnapped* (1886) ch. 10

13 I've a grand memory for forgetting, David.

> *Kidnapped* (1886) ch. 18

14 I have thus played the sedulous ape to Hazlitt, to Lamb, to Wordsworth, to Sir Thomas Browne, to Defoe, to Hawthorne, to Montaigne, to Baudelaire and to Obermann.

> *Memories and Portraits* (1887) ch. 4 'A College Magazine'

15 These are my politics: to change what we can; to better what we can; but still to bear in mind that man is but a devil weakly fettered by some generous beliefs and impositions; and for no word however sounding, and no cause however just and pious, to relax the stricture of these bonds.

> *More New Arabian Nights: The Dynamiter* (1885) 'Epilogue of the Cigar Divan'

16 He who was prepared to help the escaping murderer or to embrace the impenitent thief, found, to the overthrow of all his logic, that he objected to the use of dynamite.

> *More New Arabian Nights: The Dynamiter* (1885) 'The Superfluous Mansion'

17 I regard you with an indifference closely bordering on aversion.

> *New Arabian Nights* (1882) 'The Rajah's Diamond: Story of the Bandbox'

18 The devil, depend upon it, can sometimes do a very gentlemanly thing.

> *New Arabian Nights* (1882) 'The Suicide Club: Story of the Young Man with the Cream Tarts'

19 A faddling hedonist.

> *Travels with a Donkey* (1879) 'The Boarders'

20 For my part, I travel not to go anywhere, but to go. I travel for travel's sake. The great affair is to move.

> *Travels with a Donkey* (1879) 'Cheylard and Luc'

21 I own I like definite form in what my eyes are to rest upon; and if landscapes were sold, like the sheets of characters of my boyhood, one penny plain and twopence coloured, I should go the length of twopence every day of my life.

> *Travels with a Donkey* (1879) 'Father Apollinaris'

22 Fifteen men on the dead man's chest
Yo-ho-ho, and a bottle of rum!
Drink and the devil had done for the rest—
Yo-ho-ho, and a bottle of rum!

> *Treasure Island* (1883) ch. 1

23 Tip me the black spot.

> *Treasure Island* (1883) ch. 3

24 Many's the long night I've dreamed of cheese—toasted, mostly.

> *Treasure Island* (1883) ch. 15

25 Even if the doctor does not give you a year, even if he hesitates about a month, make one brave push and see what can be accomplished in a week.

> *Virginibus Puerisque* (1881) 'Aes Triplex'

26 There is no duty we so much underrate as the duty of being happy.

> *Virginibus Puerisque* (1881) 'An Apology for Idlers'

27 He sows hurry and reaps indigestion.

> *Virginibus Puerisque* (1881) 'An Apology for Idlers'

28 Old and young, we are all on our last cruise.

> *Virginibus Puerisque* (1881) 'Crabbed Age and Youth'

29 To travel hopefully is a better thing than to arrive, and the true success is to labour.

> *Virginibus Puerisque* (1881) 'El Dorado'

30 In marriage, a man becomes slack and selfish, and undergoes a fatty degeneration of his moral being.

> *Virginibus Puerisque* (1881) title essay, pt. 1

1 Even if we take matrimony at its lowest, even if we
regard it as no more than a sort of friendship
recognised by the police.
Virginibus Puerisque (1881) title essay, pt. 1

2 A little amateur painting in water-colour shows the
innocent and quiet mind.
Virginibus Puerisque (1881) title essay, pt. 1

3 Lastly (and this is, perhaps, the golden rule), no
woman should marry a teetotaller, or a man who does
not smoke.
Virginibus Puerisque (1881) title essay, pt. 1

4 Marriage is a step so grave and decisive that it attracts
light-headed, variable men by its very awfulness.
Virginibus Puerisque (1881) title essay, pt. 1

5 Marriage is like life in this—that it is a field of battle,
and not a bed of roses.
Virginibus Puerisque (1881) title essay, pt. 1

6 To marry is to domesticate the Recording Angel. Once
you are married, there is nothing left for you, not
even suicide, but to be good.
Virginibus Puerisque (1881) title essay, pt. 2

7 Man is a creature who lives not upon bread alone, but
principally by catchwords.
Virginibus Puerisque (1881) title essay, pt. 2

8 The cruellest lies are often told in silence.
Virginibus Puerisque (1881) title essay, pt. 4

9 What hangs people . . . is the unfortunate
circumstance of guilt.
The Wrong Box (with Lloyd Osbourne, 1889) ch. 7

10 Nothing like a little judicious levity.
The Wrong Box (with Lloyd Osbourne, 1889) ch. 7

11 Between the possibility of being hanged in all
innocence, and the certainty of a public and merited
disgrace, no gentleman of spirit could long hesitate.
The Wrong Box (with Lloyd Osbourne, 1889) ch. 10

12 I believe in an ultimate decency of things.
Letter to Sidney Colvin, 23 August 1893, in Sidney Colvin
(ed.) *Letters of Robert Louis Stevenson* (1911) vol. 4

13 In winter I get up at night
And dress by yellow candle-light.
In summer, quite the other way,—
I have to go to bed by day.
I have to go to bed and see
The birds still hopping on the tree,
Or hear the grown-up people's feet
Still going past me in the street.
A Child's Garden of Verses (1885) 'Bed in Summer'

14 The world is so full of a number of things,
I'm sure we should all be as happy as kings.
A Child's Garden of Verses (1885) 'Happy Thought'

15 When I was sick and lay a-bed,
I had two pillows at my head,
And all my toys beside me lay
To keep me happy all the day . . .
I was the giant great and still
That sits upon the pillow-hill,
And sees before him, dale and plain,
The pleasant land of counterpane.
A Child's Garden of Verses (1885) 'The Land of Counterpane'

16 When I am grown to man's estate
I shall be very proud and great,
And tell the other girls and boys
Not to meddle with my toys.
A Child's Garden of Verses (1885) 'Looking Forward'

17 Must we to bed indeed? Well then,
Let us arise and go like men,
And face with an undaunted tread
The long black passage up to bed.
A Child's Garden of Verses (1885) 'North-West Passage.
Good-Night'

18 The child that is not clean and neat,
With lots of toys and things to eat,
He is a naughty child, I'm sure—
Or else his dear papa is poor.
A Child's Garden of Verses (1885) 'System'

19 A birdie with a yellow bill
Hopped upon the window-sill,
Cocked his shining eye and said:
'Ain't you 'shamed, you sleepy-head?'
A Child's Garden of Verses (1885) 'Time to Rise'

20 A child should always say what's true,
And speak when he is spoken to,
And behave mannerly at table:
At least as far as he is able.
A Child's Garden of Verses (1885) 'Whole Duty of Children'

21 Whenever the moon and stars are set,
Whenever the wind is high,
All night long in the dark and wet,
A man goes riding by.
Late in the night when the fires are out,
Why does he gallop and gallop about?
A Child's Garden of Verses (1885) 'Bed in Summer'

22 But all that I could think of, in the darkness and the
cold,
Was that I was leaving home and my folks were
growing old.
Ballads (1890) 'Christmas at Sea'

23 In the highlands, in the country places,
Where the old plain men have rosy faces,
And the young fair maidens
Quiet eyes.
Songs of Travel (1896) 'In the highlands, in the country
places'

24 I will make you brooches and toys for your delight
Of bird-song at morning and star-shine at night.
I will make a palace fit for you and me
Of green days in forests and blue days at sea.
I will make my kitchen, and you shall keep your
room,
Where white flows the river and bright blows the
broom,
And you shall wash your linen and keep your body
white
In rainfall at morning and dewfall at night.
Songs of Travel (1896) 'I will make you brooches and toys
for your delight'

1 Trusty, dusky, vivid, true,
With eyes of gold and bramble-dew,
Steel-true and blade-straight,
The great artificer
Made my mate.
Songs of Travel (1896) 'My Wife'

2 Sing me a song of a lad that is gone,
Say, could that lad be I?
Merry of soul he sailed on a day
Over the sea to Skye.
Songs of Travel (1896) 'Sing me a song of a lad that is gone'

3 Be it granted to me to behold you again in dying,
Hills of home! and to hear again the call;
Hear about the graves of the martyrs the peewees crying,
And hear no more at all.
Songs of Travel (1896) 'To S. R. Crockett'

4 Give to me the life I love,
Let the lave go by me,
Give the jolly heaven above
And the byway nigh me.
Bed in the bush with stars to see,
Bread I dip in the river—
There's the life for a man like me,
There's the life for ever.
Songs of Travel (1896) 'The Vagabond'

5 Let the blow fall soon or late,
Let what will be o'er me;
Give the face of earth around
And the road before me.
Wealth I seek not, hope nor love,
Nor a friend to know me;
All I seek, the heaven above
And the road below me.
Songs of Travel (1896) 'The Vagabond'

6 Of all my verse, like not a single line;
But like my title, for it is not mine.
That title from a better man I stole;
Ah, how much better, had I stol'n the whole!
Underwoods (1887) foreword

7 If I have faltered more or less
In my great task of happiness;
If I have moved among my race
And shown no glorious morning face;
If beams from happy human eyes
Have moved me not; if morning skies,
Books, and my food, and summer rain
Knocked on my sullen heart in vain:—
Lord, thy most pointed pleasure take
And stab my spirit broad awake;
Or, Lord, if too obdurate I,
Choose thou, before that spirit die,
A piercing pain, a killing sin,
And to my dead heart run them in!
Underwoods (1887) 'The Celestial Surgeon'

8 Go, little book, and wish to all
Flowers in the garden, meat in the hall,
A bin of wine, a spice of wit,
A house with lawns enclosing it,
A living river by the door,
A nightingale in the sycamore!
Underwoods (1887) 'Envoy' (T. Chaucer 125:16)

9 Under the wide and starry sky
Dig the grave and let me lie.
Glad did I live and gladly die,
And I laid me down with a will.
This be the verse you grave for me:
'Here he lies where he longed to be;
Home is the sailor, home from sea,
And the hunter home from the hill.'
Underwoods (1887) 'Requiem'

10 The gauger walked with willing foot,
And aye the gauger played the flute;
And what should Master Gauger play
But 'Over the hills and far away'?
Underwoods (1887) 'A Song of the Road'

Caskie Stinnett 1911–

American writer

11 A diplomat ... is a person who can tell you to go to hell in such a way that you actually look forward to the trip.
Out of the Red (1960) ch. 4

Samuel John Stone 1839–1900

English clergyman

12 The Church's one foundation
Is Jesus Christ, her Lord;
She is his new creation
By water and the word:
From heaven he came and sought her
To be his holy bride,
With his own blood he bought her,
And for her life he died.
Lyra Fidelium (1866) 'The Church's one foundation'

Marie Stopes 1880–1958

English botanist and pioneer of birth-control clinics

13 An impersonal and scientific knowledge of the structure of our bodies is the surest safeguard against prurient curiosity and lascivious gloating.
Married Love (1918) ch. 5

Tom Stoppard 1937–

British playwright

14 It's not the voting that's democracy, it's the counting.
Jumpers (1972) act 1. Cf. Somoza 655:14

15 The House of Lords, an illusion to which I have never been able to subscribe—responsibility without power, the prerogative of the eunuch throughout the ages.
Lord Malquist and Mr Moon (1966) pt. 6. Cf. Kipling 402:13

16 The media. It sounds like a convention of spiritualists.
Night and Day (1978) act 1

17 I'm with you on the free press. It's the newspapers I can't stand.
Night and Day (1978) act 1

18 Comment is free but facts are on expenses.
Night and Day (1978) act 2. Cf. Scott 579:7

1 You're familiar with the tragedies of antiquity, are you? The great homicidal classics?
Rosencrantz and Guildenstern are Dead (1967) act 1

2 All your life you live so close to truth, it becomes a permanent blur in the corner of your eye, and when something nudges it into outline it is like being ambushed by a grotesque.
Rosencrantz and Guildenstern are Dead (1967) act 1

3 I can do you blood and love without the rhetoric, and I can do you blood and rhetoric without the love, and I can do you all three concurrent or consecutive, but I can't do you love and rhetoric without the blood. Blood is compulsory—they're all blood, you see.
Rosencrantz and Guildenstern are Dead (1967) act 1

4 Eternity's a terrible thought. I mean, where's it all going to end?
Rosencrantz and Guildenstern are Dead (1967) act 2

5 The bad end unhappily, the good unluckily. That is what tragedy means.
Rosencrantz and Guildenstern are Dead (1967) act 2. Cf. Wilde 734:1

6 Life is a gamble at terrible odds—if it was a bet, you wouldn't take it.
Rosencrantz and Guildenstern are Dead (1967) act 3

7 Death is not anything . . . death is not . . . It's the absence of presence, nothing more . . . the endless time of never coming back . . . a gap you can't see, and when the wind blows through it, it makes no sound.
Rosencrantz and Guildenstern are Dead (1967) act 3

8 War is capitalism with the gloves off and many who go to war know it but they go to war because they don't want to be a hero.
Travesties (1975) act 1

Harriet Beecher Stowe 1811–96
American novelist

9 'Never was born!' persisted Topsy . . . 'never had no father, nor mother, nor nothin'. I was raised by a speculator, with lots of others.'
Uncle Tom's Cabin (1852) ch. 20

10 I s'pect I growed. Don't think nobody never made me.
Uncle Tom's Cabin (1852) ch. 20

William Scott (Baron Stowell) 1745–1836
English jurist

11 The elegant simplicity of the three per cents.
In Lord Campbell *Lives of the Lord Chancellors* (1857) vol. 10, ch. 212. Cf. Disraeli 248:14

12 A precedent embalms a principle.
An opinion, while Advocate-General, 1788, quoted by Disraeli in *Hansard* 22 February 1848, col. 1066

Lytton Strachey 1880–1932
English biographer

13 Francis Bacon has been described more than once with the crude vigour of antithesis . . . He was no striped frieze; he was shot silk.
Elizabeth and Essex (1928) ch. 5

14 Ignorance is the first requisite of the historian—ignorance, which simplifies and clarifies, which selects and omits, with a placid perfection unattainable by the highest art.
Eminent Victorians (1918) preface

15 Was it he who had been supple and yielding? he who had won by art what he could never have won by force, and who had managed, so to speak, to be one of the leaders of the procession less through merit than through a superior faculty for gliding adroitly to the front rank?
Eminent Victorians (1918) 'Cardinal Manning' introduction

16 The time was out of joint, and he was only too delighted to have been born to set it right.
Eminent Victorians (1918) 'Cardinal Manning' pt. 2 (of Hurrell Froude). Cf. *Hamlet* 574:7

17 Her conception of God was certainly not orthodox. She felt towards Him as she might have felt towards a glorified sanitary engineer; and in some of her speculations she seems hardly to distinguish between the Deity and the Drains.
Eminent Victorians (1918) 'Florence Nightingale' pt. 4

18 The verses, when they were written, resembled nothing so much as spoonfuls of boiling oil, ladled out by a fiendish monkey at an upstairs window upon such passers-by whom the wretch had a grudge against.
Pope: The Leslie Stephen Lecture for 1925

19 [CHAIRMAN OF MILITARY TRIBUNAL:] What would you do if you saw a German soldier trying to violate your sister?
[STRACHEY:] I would try to get between them.
In Robert Graves *Good-bye to All That* (1929) ch. 23 (otherwise rendered: 'I should interpose my body')

20 Discretion is not the better part of biography.
In Michael Holroyd *Lytton Strachey* vol. 1 (1967) preface

21 If this is dying, then I don't think much of it.
On his deathbed, in Michael Holroyd *Lytton Strachey* vol. 2 (1968) pt. 2, ch. 6

Igor Stravinsky 1882–1971
Russian composer

22 Tradition is entirely different from habit, even from an excellent habit, since habit is by definition an unconscious acquisition and tends to become mechanical, whereas tradition results from a conscious and deliberate acceptance . . . Tradition presupposes the reality of what endures.
Poetics of Music (1947) ch. 3 (translated by A. Knodel and I. Dahl)

23 Conductors' careers are made for the most part with 'romantic' music. 'Classic' music eliminates the conductor; we do not remember him in it.
In Robert Craft *Conversations with Stravinsky* (1958) ch. 4

24 Academism results when the reasons for the rule change, but not the rule.
Attributed

Jan Struther (Joyce Placzek) 1901–53

English-born novelist and hymn-writer

1 Lord of all hopefulness, Lord of all joy,
  Whose trust, ever childlike, no cares could destroy,
  Be there at our waking, and give us, we pray,
  Your bliss in our hearts, Lord, at the break of the day.
    'All Day Hymn' (1931 hymn)

William Stubbs 1825–1901

English historian and prelate

2 Froude informs the Scottish youth
  That parsons do not care for truth.
  The Reverend Canon Kingsley cries
  History is a pack of lies.
  What cause for judgements so malign?
  A brief reflection solves the mystery—
  Froude believes Kingsley a divine,
  And Kingsley goes to Froude for history.
    Letter to J. R. Green, 17 December 1871, in *Letters* (1904)

G. A. Studdert Kennedy 1883–1929

British poet

3 Waste of Blood, and waste of Tears,
  Waste of youth's most precious years,
  Waste of ways the saints have trod,
  Waste of Glory, waste of God,
  War!
    More Rough Rhymes of a Padre by 'Woodbine Willie' (1919)
    'Waste'

4 When Jesus came to Birmingham they simply passed
    Him by,
  They never hurt a hair of Him, they only let Him die.
    Peace Rhymes of a Padre (1921) 'Indifference'

Sir John Suckling 1609–42

English poet and playwright

5 Women enjoyed (whatsoe'er before they've been)
  Are like romances read, or sights once seen:
  Fruition's dull, and spoils the play much more
  Than if one read or knew the plot before;
  'Tis expectation makes a blessing dear;
  It were not heaven, if we knew what it were.
    'Against Fruition' (1646)

6 Why so pale and wan, fond lover?
  Prithee, why so pale?
  Will, when looking well can't move her,
  Looking ill prevail?
  Prithee, why so pale? . . .

  Quit, quit, for shame, this will not move:
  This cannot take her.
  If of herself she will not love,
  Nothing can make her:
  The devil take her!
    Aglaura (1637) act 4, sc. 1 'Song'

7 Her feet beneath her petticoat,
  Like little mice, stole in and out,
  As if they feared the light.
    'A Ballad upon a Wedding' (1646) st. 8

8 Love is the fart
  Of every heart:
  It pains a man when 'tis kept close,
  And others doth offend, when 'tis let loose.
    'Love's Offence' (1646)

9 Out upon it, I have loved
  Three whole days together;
  And am like to love three more,
  If it prove fair weather.

  Time shall moult away his wings,
  Ere he shall discover
  In the whole wide world again
  Such a constant lover.
    'A Poem with the Answer' (1659)

10 Sure beauty's empires, like to greater states,
   Have certain periods set, and hidden fates.
    'Sonnet' (1646)

Louis Henri Sullivan 1856–1924

American architect

11 Form follows function.
    The Tall Office Building Artistically Considered (1896)

Terry Sullivan

12 She sells sea-shells on the sea-shore,
   The shells she sells are sea-shells, I'm sure,
   For if she sells sea-shells on the sea-shore,
   Then I'm sure she sells sea-shore shells.
    'She Sells Sea-Shells' (1908 song)

See also HARRY BEDFORD and TERRY SULLIVAN

Maximilien de Béthune, Duc de Sully 1559–1641

French statesman

13 *Labourage et pâturage sont les deux mamelles dont la France est alimenteé.*

   Tilling and grazing are the two breasts by which France is fed.
    Mémoires (1638) pt. 1, ch. 15

14 *Les Anglais s'amusent tristement selon l'usage de leur pays.*

   The English take their pleasures sadly after the fashion of their country.
    Attributed

Arthur Hays Sulzberger 1891–1968

American newspaper proprietor

15 We tell the public which way the cat is jumping. The public will take care of the cat.
    On journalism, in *Time* 8 May 1950

Edith Summerskill (Baroness Summerskill) 1901–80

British Labour politician

1 The housewife is the Cinderella of the affluent state ... She is wholly dependent on the whim of an individual to give her money for the essentials of life. If she complains she is a nagger—for nagging is the repetition of unpalatable truths.
  Speech to the Married Women's Association, House of Commons, 14 July 1960; in *The Times* 15 July 1960

Henry Howard, Earl of Surrey *c.*1517–47

English poet

2 Martial, the things for to attain
  The happy life be these, I find:
  The riches left, not got with pain;
  The fruitful ground, the quiet mind;

  The equal friend; no grudge nor strife;
  No charge of rule, nor governance;
  Without disease the healthful life;
  The household of continuance.
  'The Happy Life' (1547); translation of Martial *Epigrams* bk. 10, no. 47

3 The chaste wife, wise, without debate;
  Such sleeps as may beguile the night;
  Contented with thine own estate;
  Neither wish death nor fear his might.
  'The Happy Life' (1547)

4 Set me whereas the sun doth parch the green,
  Or where his beams may not dissolve the ice,
  In temperate heat, where he is felt and seen,
  With proud people, in presence sad and wise;
  Set me in base, or yet in high degree,
  In the long night, or in the shortest day,
  In clear weather, or where mists thickest be,
  In lusty youth, or when my hairs be grey ...
  Yours will I be, and with that only thought
  Comfort myself when that my hap is nought.
  'Set me whereas the sun doth parch the green' (1557)

R. S. Surtees 1805–64

English sporting journalist and novelist

5 More people are flattered into virtue than bullied out of vice.
  The Analysis of the Hunting Field (1846) ch. 1

6 The only infallible rule we know is, that the man who is always talking about being a gentleman never is one.
  Ask Mamma (1858) ch. 1

7 Major Yammerton was rather a peculiar man, inasmuch as he was an ass, without being a fool.
  Ask Mamma (1858) ch. 25

8 'Unting is all that's worth living for—all time is lost wot is not spent in 'unting—it is like the hair we breathe—if we have it not we die—it's the sport of kings, the image of war without its guilt, and only five-and-twenty per cent of its danger.
  Handley Cross (1843) ch. 7. Cf. D'Avenant 231:19, Somerville 655:12

9 Many a good run I have in my sleep. Many a dig in the ribs I gives Mrs J when I think they're running into the warmint ... No man is fit to be called a sportsman wot doesn't kick his wife out of bed on a haverage once in three weeks!
  Handley Cross (1843) ch. 11

10 I'll fill hup the chinks wi' cheese.
  Handley Cross (1843) ch. 15

11 It ar'n't that I loves the fox less, but that I loves the 'ound more.
  Handley Cross (1843) ch. 16

12 Three things I never lends—my 'oss, my wife, and my name.
  Hillingdon Hall (1845) ch. 33

13 Champagne certainly gives one werry gentlemanly ideas, but for a continuance, I don't know but I should prefer mild hale.
  Jorrocks's Jaunts and Jollities (1838) 'Mr Jorrocks in Paris'

14 Every man shouting in proportion to the amount of his subscription.
  Jorrocks's Jaunts and Jollities (1838) 'Swell and the Surrey'

15 Jorrocks, who is not afraid of 'the pace' so long as there is no leaping.
  Jorrocks's Jaunts and Jollities (1838) 'Swell and the Surrey'

16 Better be killed than frightened to death.
  Mr Facey Romford's Hounds (1865) ch. 32

17 Life would be very pleasant if it were not for its enjoyments.
  Mr Facey Romford's Hounds (1865) ch. 32. Cf. Lewis 420:19

18 These sort of boobies think that people come to balls to do nothing but dance; whereas everyone knows that the real business of a ball is either to look out for a wife, to look after a wife, or to look after somebody else's wife.
  Mr Facey Romford's Hounds (1865) ch. 56

19 The young ladies entered the drawing-room in the full fervour of sisterly animosity.
  Mr Sponge's Sporting Tour (1853) ch. 17

20 Women never look so well as when one comes in wet and dirty from hunting.
  Mr Sponge's Sporting Tour (1853) ch. 21

21 He was a gentleman who was generally spoken of as having nothing a-year, paid quarterly.
  Mr Sponge's Sporting Tour (1853) ch. 24

22 There is no secret so close as that between a rider and his horse.
  Mr Sponge's Sporting Tour (1853) ch. 31

David Sutton 1944–

English poet

23 Sorrow in all lands, and grievous omens.
  Great anger in the dragon of the hills,
  And silent now the earth's green oracles
  That will not speak again of innocence.
  'Geomancies' (1991)

Hannen Swaffer 1879–1962

British journalist

1 Freedom of the press in Britain means freedom to print such of the proprietor's prejudices as the advertisers don't object to.

In Tom Driberg *Swaff* (1974) ch. 2

Jonathan Swift (Dean Swift) 1667–1745

Anglo-Irish poet and satirist

2 I conceive some scattered notions about a superior power to be of singular use for the common people, as furnishing excellent materials to keep children quiet when they grow peevish, and providing topics of amusement in a tedious winter-night.

An Argument Against Abolishing Christianity (1708)

3 Satire is a sort of glass, wherein beholders do generally discover everybody's face but their own.

The Battle of the Books (1704) preface

4 Instead of dirt and poison we have rather chosen to fill our hives with honey and wax; thus furnishing mankind with the two noblest of things, which are sweetness and light.

The Battle of the Books (1704). Cf. Arnold 29:8

5 Laws are like cobwebs, which may catch small flies, but let wasps and hornets break through.

A Critical Essay upon the Faculties of the Mind (1709). Cf. Anarcharsis 11:5

6 There is nothing in this world constant, but inconstancy.

A Critical Essay upon the Faculties of the Mind (1709)

7 I have heard of a man who had a mind to sell his house, and therefore carried a piece of brick in his pocket, which he shewed as a pattern to encourage purchasers.

The Drapier's Letters (1724) no. 2

8 He [the emperor] is taller by almost the breadth of my nail than any of his court, which alone is enough to strike an awe into the beholders.

Gulliver's Travels (1726) 'A Voyage to Lilliput' ch. 2

9 He put this engine [a watch] to our ears, which made an incessant noise like that of a water-mill; and we conjecture it is either some unknown animal, or the god that he worships; but we are more inclined to the latter opinion.

Gulliver's Travels (1726) 'A Voyage to Lilliput' ch. 2

10 It is alleged indeed, that the high heels are most agreeable to our ancient constitution: but however this be, his Majesty hath determined to make use of only low heels in the administration of the government.

Gulliver's Travels (1726) 'A Voyage to Lilliput' ch. 4

11 I cannot but conclude the bulk of your natives to be the most pernicious race of little odious vermin that nature ever suffered to crawl upon the surface of the earth.

Gulliver's Travels (1726) 'A Voyage to Brobdingnag' ch. 6

12 And he gave it for his opinion, that whoever could make two ears of corn or two blades of grass to grow upon a spot of ground where only one grew before, would deserve better of mankind, and do more essential service to his country than the whole race of politicians put together.

Gulliver's Travels (1726) 'A Voyage to Brobdingnag' ch. 7

13 He had been eight years upon a project for extracting sun-beams out of cucumbers, which were to be put into vials hermetically sealed, and let out to warm the air in raw inclement summers.

Gulliver's Travels (1726) 'A Voyage to Laputa, etc.' ch. 5

14 These unhappy people were proposing schemes for persuading monarchs to choose favourites upon the score of their wisdom, capacity and virtue; of teaching ministers to consult the public good; of rewarding merit, great abilities and eminent services; of instructing princes to know their true interest by placing it on the same foundation with that of their people: of choosing for employment persons qualified to exercise them; with many other wild impossible chimeras, that never entered before into the heart of man to conceive, and confirmed in me the old observation, that there is nothing so extravagant and irrational which some philosophers have not maintained for truth.

Gulliver's Travels (1726) 'A Voyage to Laputa, etc.' ch. 6

15 He replied that I must needs be mistaken, or that I *said the thing which was not*. (For they have no word in their language to express lying or falsehood.)

Gulliver's Travels (1726) 'A Voyage to the Houyhnhnms' ch. 3

16 I told him ... that we ate when we were not hungry, and drank without the provocation of thirst.

Gulliver's Travels (1726) 'A Voyage to the Houyhnhnms' ch. 6

17 We are so fond of one another, because our ailments are the same.

Journal to Stella (in *Works*, 1768) 1 February 1711

18 Will she pass in a crowd? Will she make a figure in a country church?

Journal to Stella (in *Works*, 1768) 9 February 1711

19 I love good creditable acquaintance; I love to be the worst of the company.

Journal to Stella (in *Works*, 1768) 17 May 1711

20 He showed me his bill of fare to tempt me to dine with him; poh, said I, I value not your bill of fare, give me your bill of company.

Journal to Stella (in *Works*, 1768) 2 September 1711

21 We were to do more business after dinner; but after dinner is after dinner—an old saying and a true, 'much drinking, little thinking'.

Journal to Stella (in *Works*, 1768) 26 February 1712

22 Proper words in proper places, make the true definition of a style.

Letter to a Young Gentleman lately entered into Holy Orders (9 January 1720)

23 If Heaven had looked upon riches to be a valuable thing, it would not have given them to such a scoundrel.

Letter to Miss Vanhomrigh, 12–13 August 1720, in H Williams (ed.) *Correspondence of Jonathan Swift* vol. 2 (1963). Cf. Steele 662:22

1 I have ever hated all nations, professions and communities, and all my love is towards individuals ... But principally I hate and detest that animal called man; although I heartily love John, Peter, Thomas, and so forth.
   Letter to Pope, 29 September 1725, in H. Williams (ed.) *Correspondence of Jonathan Swift* vol. 3 (1963)

2 Not die here in a rage, like a poisoned rat in a hole.
   Letter to Bolingbroke, 21 March 1730, in H. Williams (ed.) *Correspondence of Jonathan Swift* vol. 3 (1963)

3 Surely mortal man is a broomstick!
   A Meditation upon a Broomstick (1710)

4 I have been assured by a very knowing American of my acquaintance in London, that a young healthy child well nursed is at a year old a most delicious, nourishing, and wholesome food, whether stewed, roasted, baked, or boiled, and I make no doubt that it will equally serve in a fricassee, or a ragout.
   A Modest Proposal for Preventing the Children of Ireland from being a Burden to their Parents or Country (1729)

5 I mean, you lie—under a mistake.
   Polite Conversation (1738) Dialogue 1

6 She wears her clothes, as if they were thrown on her with a pitchfork.
   Polite Conversation (1738) Dialogue 1

7 Faith, that's as well said, as if I had said it myself.
   Polite Conversation (1738) Dialogue 2

8 I always love to begin a journey on Sundays, because I shall have the prayers of the church, to preserve all that travel by land, or by water.
   Polite Conversation (1738) Dialogue 2

9 Books, like men their authors, have no more than one way of coming into the world, but there are ten thousand to go out of it, and return no more.
   A Tale of a Tub (1704) 'Epistle Dedicatory'

10 Satire, being levelled at all, is never resented for an offence by any.
   A Tale of a Tub (1704) 'Author's Preface'

11 What though his head be empty, provided his commonplace book be full.
   A Tale of a Tub (1704) ch. 7 'Digression in Praise of Digressions'

12 Last week I saw a woman flayed, and you will hardly believe, how much it altered her person for the worse.
   A Tale of a Tub (1704) ch. 9

13 I never saw, heard, nor read, that the clergy were beloved in any nation where Christianity was the religion of the country. Nothing can render them popular, but some degree of persecution.
   Thoughts on Religion (1765)

14 We have just enough religion to make us hate, but not enough to make us love one another.
   Thoughts on Various Subjects (1711)

15 When a true genius appears in the world, you may know him by this sign, that the dunces are all in confederacy against him.
   Thoughts on Various Subjects (1711)

16 What they do in heaven we are ignorant of; what they do *not* we are told expressly, that they neither marry, nor are given in marriage.
   Thoughts on Various Subjects (1711). Cf. St Matthew 92:3

17 The stoical scheme of supplying our wants, by lopping off our desires, is like cutting off our feet when we want shoes.
   Thoughts on Various Subjects (1711)

18 The reasons why so few marriages are happy, is, because young ladies spend their time in making nets, not in making cages.
   Thoughts on Various Subjects (1711)

19 Few are qualified to shine in company; but it is in most men's power to be agreeable.
   Thoughts on Various Subjects (1727 ed.)

20 Every man desires to live long; but no man would be old.
   Thoughts on Various Subjects (1727 ed.)

21 A nice man is a man of nasty ideas.
   Thoughts on Various Subjects (1727 ed.)

22 Old men and comets have been reverenced for the same reason; their long beards, and pretences to foretell events.
   Thoughts on Various Subjects (1727 ed.)

23 A coming shower your shooting corns presage.
   'A Description of a City Shower' (1710) l. 9

24 They never would hear,
   But turn the deaf ear,
   As a matter they had no concern in.
   'Dingley and Brent' (written 1724)

25 I often wished that I had clear,
   For life, six hundred pounds a-year,
   A handsome house to lodge a friend,
   A river at my garden's end,
   A terrace walk, and half a rood
   Of land, set out to plant a wood.
   'Imitation of Horace' (written 1714). Cf. Horace 351:9

26 How haughtily he lifts his nose,
   To tell what every schoolboy knows.
   'The Journal' (1727) l. 81

27 Nor do they trust their tongue alone,
   But speak a language of their own;
   Can read a nod, a shrug, a look,
   Far better than a printed book;
   Convey a libel in a frown,
   And wink a reputation down.
   'The Journal of a Modern Lady' (1729) l. 188

28 Hail, fellow, well met,
   All dirty and wet:
   Find out, if you can,
   Who's master, who's man.
   'My Lady's Lamentation' (written 1728) l. 165

29 Th' artillery of words.
   'Ode to Dr William Sancroft' (written 1692)

30 Philosophy! the lumber of the schools.
   'Ode to Sir W. Temple' (written 1692)

31 Say, Britain, could you ever boast,—
   Three poets in an age at most?
   Our chilling climate hardly bears
   A sprig of bays in fifty years.
   'On Poetry' (1733) l. 5

1 Then, rising with Aurora's light,
The Muse invoked, sit down to write;
Blot out, correct, insert, refine,
Enlarge, diminish, interline.
'On Poetry' (1733) l. 85

2 As learned commentators view
In Homer more than Homer knew.
'On Poetry' (1733) l. 103

3 So geographers, in Afric-maps,
With savage-pictures fill their gaps;
And o'er unhabitable downs
Place elephants for want of towns.
'On Poetry' (1733) l. 177

4 He gives directions to the town,
To cry it up, or run it down.
'On Poetry' (1733) l. 269

5 Hobbes clearly proves, that every creature
Lives in a state of war by nature.
'On Poetry' (1733) l. 319

6 So, naturalists observe, a flea
Hath smaller fleas that on him prey;
And these have smaller fleas to bite 'em,
And so proceed *ad infinitum*.
Thus every poet, in his kind,
Is bit by him that comes behind.
'On Poetry' (1733) l. 337

7 Walls have tongues, and hedges ears.
'A Pastoral Dialogue between Richmond Lodge
and Marble Hill' (written 1727) l. 8

8 Humour is odd, grotesque, and wild,
Only by affectation spoiled;
'Tis never by invention got,
Men have it when they know it not.
'To Mr Delany' (written 1718) l. 25

9 Hated by fools, and fools to hate,
Be that my motto and my fate.
'To Mr Delany' (written 1718) l. 171

10 In all distresses of our friends,
We first consult our private ends;
While nature, kindly bent to ease us,
Points out some circumstance to please us.
'Verses on the Death of Dr Swift' (1731) l. 7

11 Poor Pope will grieve a month, and Gay
A week, and Arbuthnot a day.
St John himself will scarce forbear
To bite his pen, and drop a tear.
The rest will give a shrug, and cry,
'I'm sorry—but we all must die!'
'Verses on the Death of Dr Swift' (1731) l. 207

12 Yet malice never was his aim;
He lashed the vice, but spared the name;
No individual could resent,
Where thousands equally were meant.
'Verses on the Death of Dr Swift' (1731) l. 512.
Cf. Pope 519:20

13 He gave the little wealth he had
To build a house for fools and mad;
And shewed, by one satiric touch
No nation wanted it so much.
'Verses on the Death of Dr Swift' (1731) l. 338

14 In Church your grandsire cut his throat;
To do the job too long he tarried,
He should have had my hearty vote,
To cut his throat before he married.
'Verses on the Upright Judge' (written 1724)

15 'Libertas et natale solum':
Fine words! I wonder where you stole 'em.
'Whitshed's Motto on his Coach' (written 1724) (*Libertas
... Freedom and my native skies*)

16 Good God! what a genius I had when I wrote that
book.
Of *A Tale of a Tub*, in Sir Walter Scott (ed.) *Works of Swift*
(1814) vol. 1, p. 90

17 I shall be like that tree, I shall die at the top.
In Sir Walter Scott (ed.) *Works of Swift* (1814) vol. 1,
p. 443

18 *Ubi saeva indignatio ulterius cor lacerare nequit.*
Where fierce indignation can no longer tear his heart.
Swift's epitaph. See S. Leslie *The Skull of Swift* (1928) ch. 15

Algernon Charles Swinburne 1837–1909
English poet

19 Superflux of pain.
'Anactoria' (1866) l. 27

20 Maiden, and mistress of the months and stars
Now folded in the flowerless fields of heaven.
Atalanta in Calydon (1865) l. 1

21 When the hounds of spring are on winter's traces,
The mother of months in meadow or plain
Fills the shadows and windy places
With lisp of leaves and ripple of rain;
And the brown bright nightingale amorous
Is half assuaged for Itylus,
For the Thracian ships and the foreign faces,
The tongueless vigil and all the pain.
Atalanta in Calydon (1865) chorus 'When the hounds
of spring'

22 For winter's rains and ruins are over,
And all the season of snows and sins;
The days dividing lover and lover,
The light that loses, the night that wins;
And time remembered is grief forgotten,
And frosts are slain and flowers begotten,
And in green underwood and cover
Blossom by blossom the spring begins.
Atalanta in Calydon (1865) chorus 'When the hounds
of spring'

23 And soft as lips that laugh and hide
The laughing leaves of the tree divide,
And screen from seeing and leave in sight
The god pursuing, the maiden hid.
Atalanta in Calydon (1865) chorus 'When the hounds
of spring'

24 Before the beginning of years
There came to the making of man
Time with a gift of tears,
Grief with a glass that ran,
Atalanta in Calydon (1865) chorus 'Before the beginning
of years'

1 Strength without hands to smite,
Love that endures for a breath;
Night, the shadow of light,
And Life, the shadow of death.
>   *Atalanta in Calydon* (1865) chorus 'Before the beginning
>   of years'

2 For words divide and rend;
But silence is most noble till the end.
>   *Atalanta in Calydon* (1865) chorus 'Who hath given man
>   speech'

3 For a day and a night Love sang to us, played with us,
Folded us round from the dark and the light;
And our hearts were fulfilled with the music he made
with us,
Made with our hands and our lips while he stayed
with us,
Stayed in mid passage his pinions from flight
For a day and a night.
>   'At Parting' (1878)

4 The deep division of prodigious breasts,
The solemn slope of mighty limbs asleep.
>   'Ave atque Vale' (1878) st. 6

5 Sleep; and if life was bitter to thee, pardon,
If sweet, give thanks; thou hast no more to live;
And to give thanks is good, and to forgive.
>   'Ave atque Vale' (1878) st. 17

6 Villon, our sad bad glad mad brother's name.
>   'Ballad of François Villon' (1878)

7 O slain and spent and sacrificed
People, the grey-grown speechless Christ.
>   'Before a Crucifix' (1871)

8 We shift and bedeck and bedrape us,
Thou art noble and nude and antique.
>   'Dolores' (1866) st. 7

9   Change in a trice
The lilies and languors of virtue
For the raptures and roses of vice.
>   'Dolores' (1866) st. 9

10 O splendid and sterile Dolores,
Our Lady of Pain.
>   'Dolores' (1866) st. 9

11 Ah beautiful passionate body
That never has ached with a heart!
>   'Dolores' (1866) st. 11

12 For the crown of our life as it closes
Is darkness, the fruit thereof dust;
No thorns go as deep as a rose's,
And love is more cruel than lust.
Time turns the old days to derision,
Our loves into corpses or wives;
And marriage and death and division
Make barren our lives.
>   'Dolores' (1866) st. 20

13 I shall remember while the light lives yet
And in the night time I shall not forget.
>   'Erotion' (1866)

14 In a coign of the cliff between lowland and highland,
At the sea-down's edge between windward and lee,
Walled round with rocks as an inland island,
The ghost of a garden fronts the sea.
>   'A Forsaken Garden' (1878)

15 As a god self-slain on his own strange altar,
Death lies dead.
>   'A Forsaken Garden' (1878)

16 Pale, beyond porch and portal,
Crowned with calm leaves, she stands
Who gathers all things mortal
With cold immortal hands.
>   'The Garden of Proserpine' (1866)

17 Fiddle, we know, is diddle: and diddle, we take it, is
dee.
>   *The Heptalogia* (1880) 'The Higher Pantheism in a
>   Nutshell'

18 But God, if a God there be, is the substance of men
which is man.
>   'Hymn of Man' (1871)

19 Glory to Man in the highest! for Man is the master of
things.
>   'Hymn of Man' (1871)

20 Yea, is not even Apollo, with hair and harpstring of
gold,
A bitter God to follow, a beautiful God to behold?
>   'Hymn to Proserpine' (1866)

21 Thou hast conquered, O pale Galilean; the world has
grown grey from Thy breath;
We have drunken of things Lethean, and fed on the
fullness of death.
>   'Hymn to Proserpine' (1866). Cf. Julian 382:9

22 Though these that were Gods are dead, and thou
being dead art a God,
Though before thee the throned Cytherean be fallen,
and hidden her head,
Yet thy kingdom shall pass, Galilean, thy dead shall
go down to thee dead.
>   'Hymn to Proserpine' (1866)

23 I remember the way we parted,
The day and the way we met;
You hoped we were both broken-hearted,
And knew we should both forget.
>   'An Interlude' (1866)

24 And the best and the worst of this is
That neither is most to blame,
If you have forgotten my kisses
And I have forgotten your name.
>   'An Interlude' (1866)

25 Swallow, my sister, O sister swallow,
How can thine heart be full of the spring?
A thousand summers are over and dead.
What hast thou found in the spring to follow?
What hast thou found in thine heart to sing?
What wilt thou do when the summer is shed?
>   'Itylus' (1864)

26 Till life forget and death remember,
Till thou remember and I forget.
>   'Itylus' (1864)

27 Ah, yet would God this flesh of mine might be
Where air might wash and long leaves cover me;
Where tides of grass break into foam of flowers,
Or where the wind's feet shine along the sea.
>   'Laus Veneris' (1866)

1 If love were what the rose is,
    And I were like the leaf,
    Our lives would grow together
    In sad or singing weather,
    Blown fields or flowerful closes,
    Green pleasure or grey grief.
      'A Match' (1866)

2 There was a poor poet named Clough,
    Whom his friends all united to puff,
    But the public, though dull,
    Had not such a skull
    As belonged to believers in Clough.
      Essays and Studies (1875) 'Matthew Arnold'

3 I will go back to the great sweet mother,
    Mother and lover of men, the sea.
    I will go down to her, I and no other,
    Close with her, kiss her and mix her with me.
      'The Triumph of Time' (1866)

4 I shall sleep, and move with the moving ships,
    Change as the winds change, veer in the tide.
      'The Triumph of Time' (1866)

5 There lived a singer in France of old
    By the tideless dolorous midland sea.
    In a land of sand and ruin and gold
    There shone one woman, and none but she.
      'The Triumph of Time' (1866)

John Addington Symonds 1840–93
English writer

6 These things shall be! A loftier race
    Than e'er the world hath known shall rise,
    With flame of freedom in their souls,
    And light of knowledge in their eyes.
      Hymn

John Millington Synge 1871–1909
Irish playwright

7 'A man who is not afraid of the sea will soon be
    drowned,' he said 'for he will be going out on a day
    he shouldn't. But we do be afraid of the sea, and we
    do only be drownded now and again.'
      The Aran Islands (1907) pt. 2

8 'A translation is no translation,' he said, 'unless it will
    give you the music of a poem along with the words of
    it.'
      The Aran Islands (1907) pt. 3

9 Oh my grief, I've lost him surely. I've lost the only
    Playboy of the Western World.
      The Playboy of the Western World (1907) act 3 *ad fin.*

Thomas Szasz 1920–
Hungarian-born psychiatrist

10 A child becomes an adult when he realizes that he has
    a right not only to be right but also to be wrong.
      The Second Sin (1973) 'Childhood'

11 A teacher should have maximal authority and
    minimal power.
      The Second Sin (1973) 'Education'

12 Happiness is an imaginary condition, formerly often
    attributed by the living to the dead, now usually
    attributed by adults to children, and by children to
    adults.
      The Second Sin (1973) 'Emotions'

13 The stupid neither forgive nor forget; the naïve forgive
    and forget; the wise forgive but do not forget.
      The Second Sin (1973) 'Personal Conduct'

14 If you talk to God, you are praying; if God talks to
    you, you have schizophrenia. If the dead talk to you,
    you are a spiritualist; if God talks to you, you are
    a schizophrenic.
      The Second Sin (1973) 'Schizophrenia'

15 Formerly, when religion was strong and science weak,
    men mistook magic for medicine; now, when science
    is strong and religion weak, men mistake medicine for
    magic.
      The Second Sin (1973) 'Science and Scientism'

16 Masturbation: the primary sexual activity of mankind.
    In the nineteenth century, it was a disease; in the
    twentieth, it's a cure.
      The Second Sin (1973) 'Sex'

17 Two wrongs don't make a right, but they make a good
    excuse.
      The Second Sin (1973) 'Social Relations'

Albert von Szent-Györgyi 1893–1986
Hungarian-born biochemist

18 Discovery consists of seeing what everybody has seen
    and thinking what nobody has thought.
      In Irving Good (ed.) *The Scientist Speculates* (1962) p. 15

Tacitus (Cornelius Tacitus)
AD *c.*56–after 117
Roman senator and historian

19 *Nunc terminus Britanniae patet, atque omne ignotum pro
    magnifico est.*
    Now the boundary of Britain is revealed, and
    everything unknown is held to be glorious.
      Agricola ch. 30 (reporting the speech of a British leader,
      Calgacus)

20 *Solitudinem faciunt pacem appellant.*
    They make a wilderness and call it peace.
      Agricola ch. 30

21 *Proprium humani ingenii est odisse quem laeseris.*
    It is part of human nature to hate the man you have
    hurt.
      Agricola ch. 42

22 *Tu vero felix, Agricola, non vitae tantum claritate, sed
    etiam opportunitate mortis.*
    You were indeed fortunate, Agricola, not only in the
    distinction of your life, but also in the lucky timing of
    your death.
      Agricola ch. 45

23 *Sine ira et studio.*
    With neither anger nor partiality.
      Annals bk. 1, ch. 1

1 *Elegantiae arbiter.*

The arbiter of taste.
   Annals bk. 16, ch. 18 (of Petronius)

2 *Rara temporum felicitate ubi sentire quae velis et quae sentias dicere licet.*

These times having the rare good fortune that you may think what you like and say what you think.
   Histories bk. 1, ch. 1

3 *Maior privato visus dum privatus fuit, et omnium consensu capax imperii nisi imperasset.*

He seemed much greater than a private citizen while he still was a private citizen, and by everyone's consent capable of reigning if only he had not reigned.
   Histories bk. 1, ch. 49 (of the Emperor Galba)

4 *Etiam sapientibus cupido gloriae novissima exuitur.*

Even for learned men, love of fame is the last thing to be given up.
   Histories bk. 4, ch. 6

5 *Deos fortioribus adesse.*

The gods are on the side of the stronger.
   Histories bk. 4, ch. 17. Cf. Bussy-Rabutin 165:19

Sir Rabindranath Tagore 1861–1941
Bengali poet and philosopher

6 Bigotry tries to keep truth safe in its hand
With a grip that kills it.
   Fireflies (1928) p. 29

Nellie Talbot

7 Jesus wants me for a sunbeam.
   Title of hymn (1921) in *CSSM Choruses* No. 1

Charles-Maurice de Talleyrand 1754–1838
French statesman

8 *Surtout, Messieurs, point de zèle.*

Above all, gentlemen, not the slightest zeal.
   In P. Chasles *Voyages d'un critique à travers la vie et les livres* (1868) vol. 2, p. 407

9 *Qui n'a pas vécu dans les années voisines de 1789 ne sait pas ce que c'est que le plaisir de vivre.*

He who has not lived during the years around 1789 can not know what is meant by the pleasure of life.
   In M. Guizot *Mémoires pour servir à l'histoire de mon temps* (1858) vol. 1, ch. 6

10 *Quelle triste vieillesse vous vous préparez.*

What a sad old age you are preparing for yourself.
   To a young diplomat who boasted of his ignorance of whist, in J. Amédée Pichot *Souvenirs Intimes sur M. de Talleyrand* (1870) 'Le Pour et le Contre'

11 *Ils n'ont rien appris, ni rien oublié.*

They have learnt nothing, and forgotten nothing.
   Oral tradition (attributed to Talleyrand by the Chevalier de Panat, January 1796). See A. Sayons (ed.) *Mémoires et correspondance de Mallet du Pan* (1851) vol. 2, p. 196. Cf. Dumouriez 264:1

12 *Voilà le commencement de la fin.*

This is the beginning of the end.
   On the announcement of Napoleon's defeat at Borodino, 1812, in Sainte-Beuve *M. de Talleyrand* (1870) ch. 3 (attributed)

Elizabeth, Lady Tanfield c.1565–1628

13 Love made me poet,
And this I writ;
My heart did do it,
And not my wit.
   Epitaph for her husband, in Burford Parish Church, Oxfordshire

Booth Tarkington 1869–1946
American novelist

14 There are two things that will be believed of any man whatsoever, and one of them is that he has taken to drink.
   Penrod (1914) ch. 10

Nahum Tate 1652–1715
English playwright

15 When I am laid in earth my wrongs create.
No trouble in thy breast,
Remember me, but ah! forget my fate.
   Dido and Aeneas (1689) act 3 ('Dido's Lament')

16 As pants the hart for cooling streams
When heated in the chase.
   New Version of the Psalms (1696) Psalm 42 (with Nicholas Brady). Cf. Book of Common Prayer 127:2

17 Through all the changing scenes of life,
In trouble and in joy,
The praises of my God shall still
My heart and tongue employ.
   New Version of the Psalms (1696) Psalm 34 (with Nicholas Brady)

18 While shepherds watched their flocks by night,
All seated on the ground,
The angel of the Lord came down,
And glory shone around.
   Supplement to the New Version of the Psalms (1700) 'While Shepherds Watched'

R. H. Tawney 1880–1962
British economic historian

19 The characteristic virtue of Englishmen is power of sustained practical activity and their characteristic vice a reluctance to test the quality of that activity by reference to principles.
   The Acquisitive Society (1921) ch. 1

20 Militarism . . . is fetish worship. It is the prostration of men's souls and the laceration of their bodies to appease an idol.
   The Acquisitive Society (1921) ch. 4

21 Those who dread a dead-level of income or wealth . . . do not dread, it seems, a dead-level of law and order, and of security for life and property.
   Equality (4th ed., 1931) ch. 3, sect. 3

1 Private property is a necessary institution, at least in a fallen world; men work more and dispute less when goods are private than when they are common. But it is to be tolerated as a concession to human frailty, not applauded as desirable in itself.

Religion and the Rise of Capitalism (1926) ch. 1, sect. 1

2 To take usury is contrary to Scripture; it is contrary to Aristotle; it is contrary to nature, for it is to live without labour; it is to sell time, which belongs to God, for the advantage of wicked men; it is to rob those who use the money lent, and to whom, since they make it profitable, the profits should belong.

Religion and the Rise of Capitalism (1926) ch. 1, sect. 2

3 Both the existing economic order, and too many of the projects advanced for reconstructing it, break down through their neglect of the truism that, since even quite common men have souls, no increase in material wealth will compensate them for arrangements which insult their self-respect and impair their freedom. A reasonable estimate of economic organisation must allow for the fact that, unless industry is to be paralysed by recurrent revolts on the part of outraged human nature, it must satisfy criteria which are not purely economic.

Religion and the Rise of Capitalism (1926) conclusion

4 What harm have I ever done to the Labour Party?

On declining the offer of a peerage, in *Evening Standard* 18 January 1962, p. 6

A. J. P. Taylor 1906–90

British historian

5 History gets thicker as it approaches recent times.

English History 1914–45 (1965) Bibliography

6 The First World War had begun—imposed on the statesmen of Europe by railway timetables. It was an unexpected climax to the railway age.

The First World War (1963) ch. 1

7 Like most of those who study history, he [Napoleon III] learned from the mistakes of the past how to make new ones.

Listener 6 June 1963 'Mistaken Lessons from the Past'

8 Human blunders usually do more to shape history than human wickedness.

The Origins of the Second World War (1961) ch. 10

9 If men are to respect each other for what they are, they must cease to respect each other for what they own.

Politicians, Socialism and Historians (1980) ch. 33

10 Crimea: The War That Would Not Boil.

Rumours of Wars (1952) ch. 6 (originally the title of an essay in *History Today* 2 February 1951)

Ann Taylor 1782–1866 *and Jane Taylor* 1783–1824

English writers of books for children

11 I thank the goodness and the grace
Which on my birth have smiled,
And made me, in these Christian days,
A happy English child.

Hymns for Infant Minds (1810) 'A Child's Hymn of Praise'

12 'Tis a *credit* to any good girl to be neat,
But quite a *disgrace* to be fine.

Hymns for Sunday Schools (1810) 'The Folly of Finery'

13 Who ran to help me when I fell,
And would some pretty story tell,
Or kiss the place to make it well?
My Mother.

Original Poems for Infant Minds (1804) 'My Mother'

14 Twinkle, twinkle, little star,
How I wonder what you are!
Up above the world so high,
Like a diamond in the sky!

Rhymes for the Nursery (1806) 'The Star'

15 How pleasant it is, at the end of the day,
No follies to have to repent;
But reflect on the past, and be able to say,
That my time has been properly spent.

Rhymes for the Nursery (1806) 'The Way to be Happy'

Bayard Taylor 1825–78

American traveller and writer

16 Till the sun grows cold,
And the stars are old,
And the leaves of the Judgement Book unfold.

'Bedouin Song'

Jeremy Taylor 1613–67

English divine

17 *Si fueris Romae, Romano vivito more; si fueris alibi, vivito sicut ibi.*

If you are at Rome, live in the Roman style; if you are elsewhere, live as they live elsewhere.

Ductor Dubitantium (1660) bk. 1, ch. 1, rule 5 (usually quoted: 'When in Rome, do as the Romans do'). Cf. St Ambrose 10:6

18 This thing . . . that can be understood and not expressed, may take a neuter gender;—and every schoolboy knows it.

The Real Presence . . . (1654) sect. 5, subsect. 1

19 As our life is very short, so it is very miserable, and therefore it is well it is short.

The Rule and Exercise of Holy Dying (1651) ch. 1, sect. 4

20 How many people there are that weep with want, or are mad with oppression, or are desperate by too quick a sense of a constant infelicity.

The Rule and Exercise of Holy Dying (1651) ch. 1, sect. 5

21 The union of hands and hearts.

XXV Sermons Preached at Golden Grove (1653) 'The Marriage Ring' pt. 1

Tom Taylor 1817–80

English playwright; editor of Punch from 1874

22 Hawkshaw, the detective.

The Ticket-of-leave Man (1863) act 4, sc. 1 (usually quoted 'I am Hawkshaw, the detective')

Norman Tebbit 1931–

British Conservative politician

1 I grew up in the Thirties with our unemployed father. He did not riot, he got on his bike and looked for work.

> Speech at Conservative Party Conference, 15 October 1981, in *Daily Telegraph* 16 October 1981

2 The cricket test—which side do they cheer for? . . . Are you still looking back to where you came from or where you are?

> On the loyalties of Britain's immigrant population; interview in *Los Angeles Times*, reported in *Daily Telegraph* 20 April 1990

Sir William Temple 1628–99

English diplomat and essayist

3 When all is done, human life is, at the greatest and the best, but like a froward child, that must be played with and humoured a little to keep it quiet till it falls asleep, and then the care is over.

> *Miscellanea. The Second Part* (1690) 'Of Poetry' *ad fin.*

William Temple 1881–1944

English theologian; Archbishop of Canterbury from 1942

4 Human status ought not to depend upon the changing demands of the economic process.

> In *The Life of the Church and the Order of Society* (Malvern, 1941) p. 221

5 It is a mistake to suppose that God is only, or even chiefly, concerned with religion.

> In R. V. C. Bodley *In Search of Serenity* (1955) ch. 12

6 Personally, I have always looked on cricket as organized loafing.

> Attributed

Sir John Tenniel 1820–1914

English draughtsman

7 Dropping the pilot.

> Cartoon caption, and title of poem, on Bismarck's departure from office, in *Punch* 29 March 1890

Alfred, Lord Tennyson 1809–92

English poet

8 For nothing worthy proving can be proven,
Nor yet disproven: wherefore thou be wise,
Cleave ever to the sunnier side of doubt.

> 'The Ancient Sage' (1885) l. 66

9 Break, break, break,
On thy cold grey stones, O Sea!
And I would that my tongue could utter
The thoughts that arise in me.

> 'Break, Break, Break' (1842)

10 And the stately ships go on
To their haven under the hill;
But O for the touch of a vanished hand,
And the sound of a voice that is still!

> 'Break, Break, Break' (1842)

11 I come from haunts of coot and hern,
I make a sudden sally
And sparkle out among the fern,
To bicker down a valley.

> 'The Brook' (1855) l. 23

12 For men may come and men may go,
But I go on for ever.

> 'The Brook' (1855) l. 33

13 Half a league, half a league,
Half a league onward,
All in the valley of Death
Rode the six hundred.

> 'The Charge of the Light Brigade' (1854)

14 'Forward, the Light Brigade!'
Was there a man dismayed?
Not though the soldier knew
Some one had blundered:
Their's not to make reply,
Their's not to reason why,
Their's but to do and die:
Into the valley of Death
Rode the six hundred.

Cannon to right of them,
Cannon to left of them,
Cannon in front of them
Volleyed and thundered.

> 'The Charge of the Light Brigade' (1854)

15 Into the jaws of Death,
Into the mouth of Hell.

> 'The Charge of the Light Brigade' (1854)

16 Come not, when I am dead,
To drop thy foolish tears upon my grave,
To trample round my fallen head,
And vex the unhappy dust thou wouldst not save.

> 'Come not, when I am dead' (1850)

17 Sunset and evening star,
And one clear call for me!
And may there be no moaning of the bar,
When I put out to sea.

> 'Crossing the Bar' (1889)

18 Twilight and evening bell,
And after that the dark!
And may there be no sadness of farewell,
When I embark;

For though from out our bourne of time and place
The flood may bear me far,
I hope to see my pilot face to face
When I have crossed the bar.

> 'Crossing the Bar' (1889)

19 O Love, what hours were thine and mine,
In lands of palm and southern pine;
In lands of palm, of orange-blossom,
Of olive, aloe, and maize and vine.

> 'The Daisy' (1855) st. 1

20 A daughter of the gods, divinely tall,
And most divinely fair.

> 'A Dream of Fair Women' (1832) l. 87

1 He clasps the crag with crookèd hands;
Close to the sun in lonely lands,
Ringed with the azure world, he stands.

The wrinkled sea beneath him crawls;
He watches from his mountain walls,
And like a thunderbolt he falls.
'The Eagle' (1851)

2 And when they buried him the little port
Had seldom seen a costlier funeral.
'Enoch Arden' (1864) *ad fin.*

3 The mellow lin-lan-lone of evening bells.
'Far-Far-Away' (1889)

4 O Love, O fire! once he drew
With one long kiss my whole soul through
My lips, as sunlight drinketh dew.
'Fatima' (1832) st. 3

5 More black than ashbuds in the front of March.
'The Gardener's Daughter' (1842) l. 28

6 A sight to make an old man young.
'The Gardener's Daughter' (1842) l. 140

7 Then she rode forth, clothed on with chastity.
'Godiva' (1842) l. 53

8 With twelve great shocks of sound, the shameless noon
Was clashed and hammered from a hundred towers.
'Godiva' (1842) l. 74

9   Ah! when shall all men's good
Be each man's rule, and universal peace
Lie like a shaft of light across the land?
'The Golden Year' (1846) l. 47

10 Through all the circle of the golden year.
'The Golden Year' (1846) l. 51

11 That a lie which is all a lie may be met and fought with outright,
But a lie which is part a truth is a harder matter to fight.
'The Grandmother' (1859) st. 8

12 That man's the true Conservative
Who lops the mouldered branch away.
'Hands all Round' (1882) l. 7

13 Pray God our greatness may not fail
Through craven fears of being great.
'Hands all Round' (1882) l. 31

14 Gigantic daughter of the West,
We drink to thee across the flood,
We know thee most, we love thee best,
For art thou not of British blood?
'Hands all Round' (1852) st. 4

15 Speak to Him thou for He hears, and Spirit with Spirit can meet—
Closer is He than breathing, and nearer than hands and feet.
'The Higher Pantheism' (1869)

16 Wearing the white flower of a blameless life,
Before a thousand peering littlenesses,
In that fierce light which beats upon a throne,
And blackens every blot.
Idylls of the King Dedication (1862) l. 24

17 Man's word is God in man.
Idylls of the King 'The Coming of Arthur' (1869) l. 132

18 Clothed in white samite, mystic, wonderful.
Idylls of the King 'The Coming of Arthur' (1869) l. 284;
'The Passing of Arthur' (1869) l. 199

19 Rain, rain, and sun! a rainbow in the sky!
A young man will be wiser by and by;
An old man's wit may wander ere he die.
Idylls of the King 'The Coming of Arthur' (1869) l. 402

20 From the great deep to the great deep he goes.
Idylls of the King 'The Coming of Arthur' (1869) l. 410

21 Blow trumpet, for the world is white with May.
Idylls of the King 'The Coming of Arthur' (1869) l. 481

22 Live pure, speak true, right wrong, follow the King—
Else, wherefore born?
Idylls of the King 'Gareth and Lynette' (1872) l. 117

23   The city is built
To music, therefore never built at all,
And therefore built for ever.
Idylls of the King 'Gareth and Lynette' (1872) l. 272

24 To reverence the King, as if he were
Their conscience, and their conscience as their King,
To break the heathen and uphold the Christ,
To ride abroad redressing human wrongs,
To speak no slander, no, nor listen to it,
To honour his own word as if his God's.
Idylls of the King 'Guinevere' (1859) l. 465

25 To love one maiden only, cleave to her,
And worship her by years of noble deeds,
Until they won her; for indeed I knew
Of no more subtle master under heaven
Than is the maiden passion for a maid,
Not only to keep down the base in man,
But teach high thought, and amiable words
And courtliness, and the desire of fame,
And love of truth, and all that makes a man.
Idylls of the King 'Guinevere' (1859) l. 472

26 I thought I could not breathe in that fine air
That pure severity of perfect light—
I yearned for warmth and colour which I found
In Lancelot.
Idylls of the King 'Guinevere' (1859) l. 640

27 It was my duty to have loved the highest:
It surely was my profit had I known:
It would have been my pleasure had I seen.
We needs must love the highest when we see it,
Not Lancelot, nor another.
Idylls of the King 'Guinevere' (1859) l. 652

28 For good ye are and bad, and like to coins,
Some true, some light, but every one of you
Stamped with the image of the King.
Idylls of the King 'The Holy Grail' (1869) l. 25

29 I will be deafer than the blue-eyed cat,
And thrice as blind as any noonday owl,
To holy virgins in their ecstasies,
Henceforward.
Idylls of the King 'The Holy Grail' (1869) l. 862

30 Elaine the fair, Elaine the loveable,
Elaine, the lily maid of Astolat.
Idylls of the King 'Lancelot and Elaine' (1859) l. 1

31 He is all fault who hath no fault at all.
For who loves me must have a touch of earth.
Idylls of the King 'Lancelot and Elaine' (1859) l. 131

1   In me there dwells
No greatness, save it be some far-off touch
Of greatness to know well I am not great.
Idylls of the King 'Lancelot and Elaine' (1859) l. 447

2 I know not if I know what true love is,
But if I know, then, if I love not him,
I know there is none other I can love.
Idylls of the King 'Lancelot and Elaine' (1859) l. 672

3 The shackles of an old love straitened him,
His honour rooted in dishonour stood,
And faith unfaithful kept him falsely true.
Idylls of the King 'Lancelot and Elaine' (1859) l. 870

4   Never yet
Was noble man but made ignoble talk.
He makes no friend who never made a foe.
Idylls of the King 'Lancelot and Elaine' (1859) l. 1080

5 The dirty nurse, Experience, in her kind
Hath fouled me.
Idylls of the King 'The Last Tournament' (1871) l. 317

6 The greater man, the greater courtesy.
Idylls of the King 'The Last Tournament' (1871) l. 628

7 Our hoard is little, but our hearts are great.
Idylls of the King 'The Marriage of Geraint' (1859) l. 352

8 For man is man and master of his fate.
Idylls of the King 'The Marriage of Geraint' (1859) l. 355

9 They take the rustic murmur of their bourg
For the great wave that echoes round the world.
Idylls of the King 'The Marriage of Geraint' (1859) l. 419

10 It is the little rift within the lute,
That by and by will make the music mute,
And ever widening slowly silence all.
Idylls of the King 'Merlin and Vivien' (1859) l. 388

11 And trust me not at all or all in all.
Idylls of the King 'Merlin and Vivien' (1859) l. 396

12 Man dreams of fame while woman wakes to love.
Idylls of the King 'Merlin and Vivien' (1859) l. 458

13 With this for motto, 'Rather use than fame.'
Idylls of the King 'Merlin and Vivien' (1859) l. 478

14   Where blind and naked Ignorance
Delivers brawling judgements, unashamed,
On all things all day long.
Idylls of the King 'Merlin and Vivien' (1859) l. 662

15 But every page having an ample marge,
And every marge enclosing in the midst
A square of text that looks a little blot.
Idylls of the King 'Merlin and Vivien' (1859) l. 667

16 And none can read the text, not even I;
And none can read the comment but myself.
Idylls of the King 'Merlin and Vivien' (1859) l. 679

17 I found Him in the shining of the stars,
I marked Him in the flowering of His fields,
But in His ways with men I find Him not.
Idylls of the King 'The Passing of Arthur' (1869) l. 9

18 So all day long the noise of battle rolled
Among the mountains by the winter sea.
Idylls of the King 'The Passing of Arthur' (1869) l. 170

19 On one side lay the Ocean, and on one
Lay a great water, and the moon was full.
Idylls of the King 'The Passing of Arthur' (1869) l. 179

20 Authority forgets a dying king.
Idylls of the King 'The Passing of Arthur' (1869) l. 289

21 Clothed with his breath, and looking, as he walked,
Larger than human on the frozen hills.
He heard the deep behind him, and a cry
Before.
Idylls of the King 'The Passing of Arthur' (1869) l. 350

22 And the days darken round me, and the years,
Among new men, strange faces, other minds.
Idylls of the King 'The Passing of Arthur' (1869) l. 405

23 The old order changeth, yielding place to new,
And God fulfils himself in many ways,
Lest one good custom should corrupt the world.
Idylls of the King 'The Passing of Arthur' (1869) l. 408

24 If thou shouldst never see my face again,
Pray for my soul. More things are wrought by prayer
Than this world dreams of. Wherefore, let thy voice
Rise like a fountain for me night and day.
For what are men better than sheep or goats
That nourish a blind life within the brain,
If, knowing God, they lift not hands of prayer
Both for themselves and those who call them friend?
For so the whole round earth is every way
Bound by gold chains about the feet of God.
Idylls of the King 'The Passing of Arthur' (1869) l. 414

25   I am going a long way
With these thou seëst—if indeed I go
(For all my mind is clouded with a doubt)—
To the island-valley of Avilion;
Where falls not hail, or rain, or any snow,
Nor ever wind blows loudly; but it lies
Deep-meadowed, happy, fair with orchard lawns
And bowery hollows crowned with summer sea,
Where I will heal me of my grievous wound.
Idylls of the King 'The Passing of Arthur' (1869) l. 424

26   Like some full-breasted swan
That, fluting a wild carol ere her death,
Ruffles her pure cold plume, and takes the flood
With swarthy webs.
Idylls of the King 'The Passing of Arthur' (1869) l. 434

27 Thou madest man, he knows not why,
He thinks he was not made to die;
And thou hast made him: thou art just.
In Memoriam A. H. H. (1850) Prologue

28 Our little systems have their day;
They have their day and cease to be:
They are but broken lights of thee,
And thou, O Lord, art more than they.
In Memoriam A. H. H. (1850) Prologue

29 Let knowledge grow from more to more,
But more of reverence in us dwell;
That mind and soul, according well,
May make one music as before.
In Memoriam A. H. H. (1850) Prologue

30 I held it truth, with him who sings
To one clear harp in divers tones,
That men may rise on stepping-stones
Of their dead selves to higher things.
In Memoriam A. H. H. (1850) canto 1

31 For words, like Nature, half reveal
And half conceal the Soul within.
In Memoriam A. H. H. (1850) canto 5

1 But, for the unquiet heart and brain,
A use in measured language lies;
The sad mechanic exercise,
Like dull narcotics, numbing pain.
In Memoriam A. H. H. (1850) canto 5

2 And common is the commonplace,
And vacant chaff well meant for grain.
In Memoriam A. H. H. (1850) canto 6

3   Never morning wore
To evening, but some heart did break.
In Memoriam A. H. H. (1850) canto 6

4 His heavy-shotted hammock-shroud
Drops in his vast and wandering grave.
In Memoriam A. H. H. (1850) canto 6

5 Dark house, by which once more I stand
Here in the long unlovely street,
Doors, where my heart was used to beat
So quickly, waiting for a hand.
In Memoriam A. H. H. (1850) canto 7

6 And ghastly through the drizzling rain
On the bald street breaks the blank day.
In Memoriam A. H. H. (1850) canto 7

7 The last red leaf is whirled away,
The rooks are blown about the skies.
In Memoriam A. H. H. (1850) canto 15

8 There twice a day the Severn fills;
The salt sea-water passes by,
And hushes half the babbling Wye,
And makes a silence in the hills.
In Memoriam A. H. H. (1850) canto 19

9 The Shadow cloaked from head to foot,
Who keeps the keys of all the creeds.
In Memoriam A. H. H. (1850) canto 23

10 And Thought leapt out to wed with Thought
Ere Thought could wed itself with Speech.
In Memoriam A. H. H. (1850) canto 23

11 I envy not in any moods
The captive void of noble rage,
The linnet born within the cage,
That never knew the summer woods.
In Memoriam A. H. H. (1850) canto 27

12 'Tis better to have loved and lost
Than never to have loved at all.
In Memoriam A. H. H. (1850) canto 27. Cf. Congreve
215:3

13 A solemn gladness even crowned
The purple brows of Olivet.
In Memoriam A. H. H. (1850) canto 31

14 Her eyes are homes of silent prayer.
In Memoriam A. H. H. (1850) canto 32

15 Short swallow-flights of song, that dip
Their wings in tears, and skim away.
In Memoriam A. H. H. (1850) canto 48

16 Be near me when my light is low,
When the blood creeps, and the nerves prick
And tingle; and the heart is sick,
And all the wheels of Being slow.

Be near me when the sensuous frame
Is racked with pains that conquer trust;
And Time, a maniac scattering dust,
And Life, a Fury slinging flame.
In Memoriam A. H. H. (1850) canto 50

17 Oh yet we trust that somehow good
Will be the final goal of ill.
In Memoriam A. H. H. (1850) canto 54

18 That nothing walks with aimless feet;
That not one life shall be destroyed,
Or cast as rubbish to the void,
When God hath made the pile complete.
In Memoriam A. H. H. (1850) canto 54

19 Behold, we know not anything;
I can but trust that good shall fall
At last—far off—at last, to all,
And every winter change to spring.

So runs my dream: but what am I?
An infant crying in the night:
An infant crying for the light:
And with no language but a cry.
In Memoriam A. H. H. (1850) canto 54

20 So careful of the type she seems,
So careless of the single life.
In Memoriam A. H. H. (1850) canto 55 (of Nature)

21   The great world's altar-stairs
That slope through darkness up to God.
In Memoriam A. H. H. (1850) canto 55

22 Man . . .
Who trusted God was love indeed
And love Creation's final law—
Though Nature, red in tooth and claw
With ravine, shrieked against his creed.
In Memoriam A. H. H. (1850) canto 56

23 Peace; come away: the song of woe
Is after all an earthly song:
Peace; come away: we do him wrong
To sing so wildly: let us go.
In Memoriam A. H. H. (1850) canto 57

24 O Sorrow, wilt thou live with me
No casual mistress, but a wife.
In Memoriam A. H. H. (1850) canto 59

25 As some divinely gifted man,
Whose life in low estate began
And on a simple village green;

Who breaks his birth's invidious bar,
And grasps the skirts of happy chance,
And breasts the blows of circumstance,
And grapples with his evil star.
In Memoriam A. H. H. (1850) canto 64

26 So many worlds, so much to do,
So little done, such things to be.
In Memoriam A. H. H. (1850) canto 73

27 Death has made
His darkness beautiful with thee.
In Memoriam A. H. H. (1850) canto 74

1 And round thee with the breeze of song
To stir a little dust of praise.
  In Memoriam A. H. H. (1850) canto 75

2 O last regret, regret can die!
  In Memoriam A. H. H. (1850) canto 78

3 Laburnums, dropping-wells of fire.
  In Memoriam A. H. H. (1850) canto 83

4 God's finger touched him, and he slept.
  In Memoriam A. H. H. (1850) canto 85

5 He brought an eye for all he saw;
He mixed in all our simple sports;
They pleased him, fresh from brawling courts
And dusty purlieus of the law.
  In Memoriam A. H. H. (1850) canto 89. Cf. Etherege
  278:16

6 You tell me, doubt is Devil-born.
  In Memoriam A. H. H. (1850) canto 96

7 There lives more faith in honest doubt,
Believe me, than in half the creeds.
  In Memoriam A. H. H. (1850) canto 96

8 Their meetings made December June,
Their every parting was to die.
  In Memoriam A. H. H. (1850) canto 97

9 He seems so near and yet so far.
  In Memoriam A. H. H. (1850) canto 97

10 Ring out, wild bells, to the wild sky,
The flying cloud, the frosty light:
The year is dying in the night;
Ring out, wild bells, and let him die.

Ring out the old, ring in the new,
Ring, happy bells, across the snow:
The year is going, let him go;
Ring out the false, ring in the true.
  In Memoriam A. H. H. (1850) canto 106

11 Ring out the want, the care, the sin,
The faithless coldness of the times;
Ring out, ring out my mournful rhymes,
But ring the fuller minstrel in.

Ring out false pride in place and blood,
The civic slander and the spite;
Ring in the love of truth and right,
Ring in the common love of good.

Ring out old shapes of foul disease;
Ring out the narrowing lust of gold;
Ring out the thousand wars of old,
Ring in the thousand years of peace.

Ring in the valiant man and free,
The larger heart, the kindlier hand;
Ring out the darkness of the land;
Ring in the Christ that is to be.
  In Memoriam A. H. H. (1850) canto 106

12   Not the schoolboy heat,
The blind hysterics of the Celt.
  In Memoriam A. H. H. (1850) canto 109

13 Now fades the last long streak of snow,
Now burgeons every maze of quick
About the flowering squares, and thick
By ashen roots the violets blow.
  In Memoriam A. H. H. (1850) canto 115

14 And drowned in yonder living blue
The lark becomes a sightless song.
  In Memoriam A. H. H. (1850) canto 115

15 There, where the long street roars, hath been
The stillness of the central sea.
  In Memoriam A. H. H. (1850) canto 123

16 And thou art worthy; full of power;
As gentle; liberal-minded, great,
Consistent; wearing all that weight
Of learning lightly like a flower.
  In Memoriam A. H. H. (1850) canto 131

17 One God, one law, one element,
And one far-off divine event,
To which the whole creation moves.
  In Memoriam A. H. H. (1850) canto 131

18 The voice of the dead was a living voice to me.
  'In the Valley of Cauteretz' (1864)

19 Below the thunders of the upper deep;
Far, far beneath in the abysmal sea,
His ancient, dreamless, uninvaded sleep
The Kraken sleepeth.
  'The Kraken' (1830)

20 There hath he lain for ages and will lie
Battening upon huge seaworms in his sleep,
Until the latter fire shall heat the deep.
  'The Kraken' (1830)

21 At me you smiled, but unbeguiled
I saw the snare, and I retired:
The daughter of a hundred Earls,
You are not one to be desired.
  'Lady Clara Vere de Vere' (1842) st. 1

22 From yon blue heavens above us bent
The gardener Adam and his wife
Smile at the claims of long descent.
Howe'er it be, it seems to me,
'Tis only noble to be good.
Kind hearts are more than coronets,
And simple faith than Norman blood.
  'Lady Clara Vere de Vere' (1842) st. 7

23 On either side the river lie
Long fields of barley and of rye,
That clothe the wold and meet the sky;
And through the field the road runs by
To many-towered Camelot.
  'The Lady of Shalott' (1832, revised 1842) pt. 1

24 Willows whiten, aspens quiver,
Little breezes dusk and shiver.
  'The Lady of Shalott' (1832, revised 1842) pt. 1

25 Only reapers, reaping early
In among the bearded barley,
Hear a song that echoes cheerly
From the river winding clearly,
Down to towered Camelot.
  'The Lady of Shalott' (1832, revised 1842) pt. 1

1 Or when the moon was overhead,
Came two young lovers lately wed;
'I am half sick of shadows,' said
The Lady of Shalott.
'The Lady of Shalott' (1832, revised 1842) pt. 2

2 A bow-shot from her bower-eaves,
He rode between the barley-sheaves,
The sun came dazzling through the leaves,
And flamed upon the brazen greaves
Of bold Sir Lancelot.
A red-cross knight for ever kneeled
To a lady in his shield,
That sparkled on the yellow field,
Beside remote Shalott.
'The Lady of Shalott' (1832, revised 1842) pt. 3

3 All in the blue unclouded weather
Thick-jewelled shone the saddle-leather,
The helmet and the helmet-feather
Burned like one burning flame together,
As he rode down to Camelot.
'The Lady of Shalott' (1832, revised 1842) pt. 3

4 She left the web, she left the loom,
She made three paces through the room,
She saw the water-lily bloom,
She saw the helmet and the plume,
She looked down to Camelot.
Out flew the web and floated wide;
The mirror cracked from side to side;
'The curse is come upon me,' cried
The Lady of Shalott.
'The Lady of Shalott' (1832, revised 1842) pt. 3

5 Slander, meanest spawn of Hell.
'The Letters' (1855)

6 Airy, fairy Lilian.
'Lilian' (1830)

7 In the spring a livelier iris changes on the burnished
dove;
In the spring a young man's fancy lightly turns to
thoughts of love.
'Locksley Hall' (1842) l. 19

8 And our spirits rushed together at the touching of the
lips.
'Locksley Hall' (1842) l. 38

9 He will hold thee, when his passion shall have spent
its novel force,
Something better than his dog, a little dearer than his
horse.
'Locksley Hall' (1842) l. 49

10   This is truth the poet sings,
That a sorrow's crown of sorrow is remembering
happier things.
'Locksley Hall' (1842) l. 75. Cf. Boethius 116:12, Dante
230:11

11 Like a dog, he hunts in dreams.
'Locksley Hall' (1842) l. 79

12 But the jangling of the guinea helps the hurt that
Honour feels.
'Locksley Hall' (1842) l. 105

13 Men, my brothers, men the workers, ever reaping
something new:
That which they have done but earnest of the things
that they shall do:

For I dipped into the future, far as human eye could
see,
Saw the vision of the world, and all the wonder that
would be;

Saw the heavens fill with commerce, argosies of magic
sails,
Pilots of the purple twilight, dropping down with
costly bales;

Heard the heavens fill with shouting, and there rained
a ghastly dew
From the nations' airy navies grappling in the central
blue;

Far along the world-wide whisper of the south-wind
rushing warm,
With the standards of the peoples plunging through
the thunder-storm;

Till the war-drum throbbed no longer, and the
battle-flags were furled
In the Parliament of man, the Federation of the world.
'Locksley Hall' (1842) l. 117

14 Science moves, but slowly slowly, creeping on from
point to point.
'Locksley Hall' (1842) l. 134

15 Yet I doubt not through the ages one increasing
purpose runs,
And the thoughts of men are widened with the
process of the suns.
'Locksley Hall' (1842) l. 137

16 Knowledge comes, but wisdom lingers.
'Locksley Hall' (1842) l. 141

17 I will take some savage woman, she shall rear my
dusky race.
'Locksley Hall' (1842) l. 168

18 I the heir of all the ages, in the foremost files of time.
'Locksley Hall' (1842) l. 178

19   Forward, forward let us range,
Let the great world spin for ever down the ringing
grooves of change.
'Locksley Hall' (1842) l. 181

20 Better fifty years of Europe than a cycle of Cathay.
'Locksley Hall' (1842) l. 184

21 Music that gentlier on the spirit lies,
Than tired eyelids upon tired eyes.
'The Lotos-Eaters' (1832) Choric Song, st. 1

22 There is no joy but calm!
'The Lotos-Eaters' (1832) Choric Song, st. 2

23 Death is the end of life; ah, why
Should life all labour be?
'The Lotos-Eaters' (1832) Choric Song, st. 4

1   Live and lie reclined
On the hills like Gods together, careless of mankind.
For they lie beside their nectar, and the bolts are
    hurled
Far below them in the valleys, and the clouds are
    lightly curled
Round their golden houses, girdled with the gleaming
    world.
  'The Lotos-Eaters' (1832) Choric Song, st. 8 (1842
  revision)

2 Surely, surely, slumber is more sweet than toil, the
    shore
Than labour in the deep mid-ocean, wind and wave
    and oar;
Oh rest ye, brother mariners, we will not wander
    more.
  'The Lotos-Eaters' (1832) Choric Song, st. 8

3   I saw the flaring atom-streams
And torrents of her myriad universe,
Ruining along the illimitable inane.
  'Lucretius' (1868) l. 38

4   Nor at all can tell
Whether I mean this day to end myself,
Or lend an ear to Plato where he says,
That men like soldiers may not quit the post
Allotted by the Gods.
  'Lucretius' (1868) l. 145

5 Passionless bride, divine Tranquillity,
Yearned after by the wisest of the wise,
Who fail to find thee, being as thou art
Without one pleasure and without one pain.
  'Lucretius' (1868) l. 265

6 Weeded and worn the ancient thatch
Upon the lonely moated grange.
She only said, 'My life is dreary,
He cometh not,' she said;
She said, 'I am aweary, aweary,
I would that I were dead!'

Her tears fell with the dews at even;
Her tears fell ere the dews were dried.
  'Mariana' (1830) st. 1. Cf. Measure for Measure 606:14

7 Faultily faultless, icily regular, splendidly null,
Dead perfection, no more.
  Maud (1855) pt. 1, sect. 2

8 The passionate heart of the poet is whirled into folly
    and vice.
  Maud (1855) pt. 1, sect. 4, st. 7

9 And most of all would I flee from the cruel madness of
    love,
The honey of poison-flowers and all the measureless
    ill.
  Maud (1855) pt. 1, sect. 4, st. 10

10 That jewelled mass of millinery,
That oiled and curled Assyrian Bull.
  Maud (1855) pt. 1, sect. 6, st. 6

11 She came to the village church,
And sat by a pillar alone;
An angel watching an urn
Wept over her, carved in stone.
  Maud (1855) pt. 1, sect. 8

12   I heard no longer
The snowy-banded, dilettante,
Delicate-handed priest intone.
  Maud (1855) pt. 1, sect. 8

13 Ah God, for a man with heart, head, hand,
Like some of the simple great ones gone
For ever and ever by,
One still strong man in a blatant land,
Whatever they call him, what care I,
Aristocrat, democrat, autocrat—one
Who can rule and dare not lie.
  Maud (1855) pt. 1, sect. 10, st. 5

14 I kissed her slender hand,
She took the kiss sedately;
Maud is not seventeen,
But she is tall and stately.
  Maud (1855) pt. 1, sect. 12, st. 4

15 Gorgonised me from head to foot
With a stony British stare.
  Maud (1855) pt. 1, sect. 13, st. 2

16 A livelier emerald twinkles in the grass,
A purer sapphire melts into the sea.
  Maud (1855) pt. 1, sect. 18, st. 6

17 Come into the garden, Maud,
For the black bat, night, has flown,
Come into the garden, Maud,
I am here at the gate alone;
And the woodbine spices are wafted abroad,
And the musk of the rose is blown.

For a breeze of morning moves,
And the planet of Love is on high,
Beginning to faint in the light that she loves
On a bed of daffodil sky.
  Maud (1855) pt. 1, sect. 22, st. 1

18 All night has the casement jessamine stirred
To the dancers dancing in tune;
Till a silence fell with the waking bird,
And a hush with the setting moon.
  Maud (1855) pt. 1, sect. 22, st. 3

19 Queen rose of the rosebud garden of girls.
  Maud (1855) pt. 1, sect. 22, st. 9

20 There has fallen a splendid tear
From the passion-flower at the gate.
She is coming, my dove, my dear;
She is coming, my life, my fate;
The red rose cries, 'She is near, she is near;'
And the white rose weeps, 'She is late;'
The larkspur listens, 'I hear, I hear;'
And the lily whispers, 'I wait.'

She is coming, my own, my sweet;
Were it ever so airy a tread,
My heart would hear her and beat,
Were it earth in an earthy bed;
My dust would hear her and beat,
Had I lain for a century dead;
Would start and tremble under her feet,
And blossom in purple and red.
  Maud (1855) pt. 1, sect. 22, st. 10

21 O that 'twere possible
After long grief and pain
To find the arms of my true love
Round me once again!
  Maud (1855) pt. 2, sect. 4, st. 1

1 But the churchmen fain would kill their church,
   As the churches have killed their Christ.
   Maud (1855) pt. 2, sect. 5, st. 2

2 O me, why have they not buried me deep enough?
   Is it kind to have made me a grave so rough,
   Me, that was never a quiet sleeper?
   Maud (1855) pt. 2, sect. 5, st. 11

3 My life has crept so long on a broken wing
   Through cells of madness, haunts of horror and fear,
   That I come to be grateful at last for a little thing.
   Maud (1855) pt. 3, sect. 6, st. 1

4 When the face of night is fair on the dewy downs,
   And the shining daffodil dies.
   Maud (1855) pt. 3, sect. 6, st. 1

5 The blood-red blossom of war with a heart of fire.
   Maud (1855) pt. 3, sect. 6, st. 4

6 It is better to fight for the good, than to rail at the ill;
   I have felt with my native land, I am one with my
      kind,
   I embrace the purpose of God, and the doom assigned.
   Maud (1855) pt. 3, sect. 6, st. 5

7 You must wake and call me early, call me early,
      mother dear;
   Tomorrow 'ill be the happiest time of all the glad
      New-year;
   Of all the glad New-year, mother, the maddest
      merriest day;
   For I'm to be Queen o' the May, mother, I'm to be
      Queen o' the May.
   'The May Queen' (1832)

8 Launch your vessel,
   And crowd your canvas,
   And, ere it vanishes
   Over the margin,
   After it, follow it,
   Follow The Gleam.
   'Merlin and The Gleam' (1889) st. 9

9 O mighty-mouthed inventor of harmonies,
   O skilled to sing of time or eternity,
   God-gifted organ-voice of England,
   Milton, a name to resound for ages.
   'Milton: Alcaics' (1863)

10 O you chorus of indolent reviewers.
   'Milton: Hendecasyllabics' (1863)

11   All that bowery loneliness,
   The brooks of Eden mazily murmuring.
   'Milton: Alcaics' (1863)

12 But I knaw'd a Quaäker feller as often 'as towd ma
      this:
   'Doänt thou marry for munny, but goä wheer munny
      is!'
   'Northern Farmer. New Style' (1869) st. 5

13 Taäke my word for it, Sammy, the poor in a loomp is
      bad.
   'Northern Farmer. New Style' (1869) st. 12

14 The last great Englishman is low
   'Ode on the Death of the Duke of Wellington' (1852) pt. 3

15 O good grey head which all men knew!
   'Ode on the Death of the Duke of Wellington' (1852) st. 4

16 O fall'n at length that tower of strength
   Which stood four-square to all the winds that blew!
   'Ode on the Death of the Duke of Wellington' (1852) st. 4

17 That world-earthquake, Waterloo!
   'Ode on the Death of the Duke of Wellington' (1852) st. 6

18 Who never sold the truth to serve the hour,
   Nor paltered with Eternal God for power.
   'Ode on the Death of the Duke of Wellington' (1852) st. 7

19 Naked they came to that smooth-swarded bower,
   And at their feet the crocus brake like fire,
   Violet, amaracus, and asphodel,
   Lotos and lilies.
   'Oenone' (1832, revised 1842) l. 93

20 I built my soul a lordly pleasure-house,
   Wherein at ease for aye to dwell.
   'The Palace of Art' (1832) st. 1

21 Still as, while Saturn whirls, his steadfast shade
   Sleeps on his luminous ring.
   'The Palace of Art' (1832) st. 4

22 An English home—grey twilight poured
   On dewy pasture, dewy trees,
   Softer than sleep—all things in order stored,
   A haunt of ancient Peace.
   'The Palace of Art' (1832) st. 22

23 Vex not thou the poet's mind
   With thy shallow wit:
   Vex not thou the poet's mind;
   For thou canst not fathom it.
   'The Poet's Mind' (1830)

24 With prudes for proctors, dowagers for deans,
   And sweet girl-graduates in their golden hair.
   The Princess (1847) 'Prologue' l. 141

25 And blessings on the falling out
   That all the more endears,
   When we fall out with those we love
   And kiss again with tears!
   The Princess (1847) pt. 2, song (added 1850)

26 A classic lecture, rich in sentiment,
   With scraps of thundrous epic lilted out
   By violet-hooded Doctors, elegies
   And quoted odes, and jewels five-words-long,
   That on the stretched forefinger of all Time
   Sparkle for ever.
   The Princess (1847) pt. 2, l. 352

27 Sweet and low, sweet and low,
   Wind of the western sea,
   Low, low, breathe and blow,
   Wind of the western sea!
   Over the rolling waters go,
   Come from the dying moon, and blow,
   Blow him again to me;
   While my little one, while my pretty one, sleeps.
   The Princess (1847) pt. 3, song (added 1850)

1 The splendour falls on castle walls
And snowy summits old in story:
The long light shakes across the lakes,
And the wild cataract leaps in glory.
Blow, bugle, blow, set the wild echoes flying,
Blow, bugle; answer, echoes, dying, dying, dying.

O hark, O hear! how thin and clear,
And thinner, clearer, farther going!
O sweet and far from cliff and scar
The horns of Elfland faintly blowing!
The Princess (1847) pt. 4, song (added 1850)

2 O love, they die in yon rich sky,
They faint on hill or field or river:
Our echoes roll from soul to soul,
And grow for ever and for ever.
The Princess (1847) pt. 4, song (added 1850)

3 Tears, idle tears, I know not what they mean,
Tears from the depth of some divine despair
Rise in the heart, and gather to the eyes,
In looking on the happy autumn-fields,
And thinking of the days that are no more.
The Princess (1847) pt. 4, l. 21, song (added 1850)

4 So sad, so fresh, the days that are no more.
The Princess (1847) pt. 4, l. 30, song (added 1850)

5 Ah, sad and strange as in dark summer dawns
The earliest pipe of half-awakened birds
To dying ears, when unto dying eyes
The casement slowly grows a glimmering square;
So sad, so strange, the days that are no more.

Dear as remembered kisses after death,
And sweet as those by hopeless fancy feigned
On lips that are for others; deep as love,
Deep as first love, and wild with all regret;
O Death in Life, the days that are no more.
The Princess (1847) pt. 4, l. 31, song (added 1850)

6 O Swallow, Swallow, flying, flying South,
Fly to her, and fall upon her gilded eaves,
And tell her, tell her, what I tell to thee.

O tell her, Swallow, thou that knowest each,
That bright and fierce and fickle is the South,
And dark and true and tender is the North.
The Princess (1847) pt. 4, l. 75, song (added 1850)

7 O tell her, Swallow, that thy brood is flown:
Say to her, I do but wanton in the South,
But in the North long since my nest is made.
The Princess (1847) pt. 4, l. 90, song (added 1850)

8 Man is the hunter; woman is his game:
The sleek and shining creatures of the chase,
We hunt them for the beauty of their skins;
They love us for it, and we ride them down.
The Princess (1847) pt. 5, l. 147

9 Home they brought her warrior dead.
She nor swooned, nor uttered cry:
All her maidens, watching said,
'She must weep or she will die.'
The Princess (1847) pt. 6, song (added 1850)

10 Rose a nurse of ninety years,
Set his child upon her knee—
Like summer tempest came her tears—
'Sweet my child, I live for thee.'
The Princess (1847) pt. 6, song (added 1850)

11   The woman is so hard
Upon the woman.
The Princess (1847) pt. 6, l. 205

12 Ask me no more: what answer should I give?
I love not hollow cheek or faded eye:
Yet, O my friend, I will not have thee die!
Ask me no more, lest I should bid thee live.
The Princess (1847) pt. 7, song (added 1850)

13 Now sleeps the crimson petal, now the white;
Nor waves the cypress in the palace walk;
Nor winks the gold fin in the porphyry font:
The fire-fly wakens: waken thou with me.

Now droops the milkwhite peacock like a ghost,
And like a ghost she glimmers on to me.

Now lies the Earth all Danaë to the stars,
And all thy heart lies open unto me.

Now slides the silent meteor on, and leaves
A shining furrow, as thy thoughts in me.

Now folds the lily all her sweetness up,
And slips into the bosom of the lake:
So fold thyself, my dearest, thou, and slip
Into my bosom and be lost in me.
The Princess (1847) pt. 7, l. 161, song (added 1850)

14 Come down, O maid, from yonder mountain
height:
What pleasure lives in height?
The Princess (1847) pt. 7, l. 177, song (added 1850)

15 For Love is of the valley, come thou down
And find him; by the happy threshold, he,
Or hand in hand with Plenty in the maize,
Or red with spirted purple of the vats,
Or foxlike in the vine; nor cares to walk
With Death and Morning on the silver horns.
The Princess (1847) pt. 7, l. 184, song (added 1850)

16   Sweet is every sound,
Sweeter thy voice, but every sound is sweet;
Myriads of rivulets hurrying through the lawn,
The moan of doves in immemorial elms,
And murmuring of innumerable bees.
The Princess (1847) pt. 7, l. 203, song (added 1850)

17 No little lily-handed baronet he,
A great broad-shouldered genial Englishman,
A lord of fat prize-oxen and of sheep,
A raiser of huge melons and of pine,
A patron of some thirty charities,
A pamphleteer on guano and on grain.
The Princess (1847) 'Conclusion' l. 84

1 At Flores in the Azores Sir Richard Grenville lay,
And a pinnace, like a fluttered bird, came flying from
far away:
'Spanish ships of war at sea! we have sighted
fifty-three!'
Then sware Lord Thomas Howard: ''Fore God I am no
coward;
But I cannot meet them here, for my ships are out of
gear,
And the half my men are sick. I must fly, but follow
quick.
We are six ships of the line; can we fight with
fifty-three?'

Then spake Sir Richard Grenville: 'I know you are no
coward;
You fly them for a moment to fight with them again.
But I've ninety men and more that are lying sick
ashore.
I should count myself the coward if I left them, my
Lord Howard,
To these Inquisition dogs and the devildoms of Spain.'

So Lord Howard passed away with five ships of war
that day,
Till he melted like a cloud in the silent summer
heaven.
'The Revenge' (1878) st. 1

2 And Sir Richard said again: 'We be all good English
men.
Let us bang these dogs of Seville, the children of the
devil,
For I never turned my back upon Don or devil yet.'
'The Revenge' (1878) st. 4

3 And the sun went down, and the stars came out far
over the summer sea,
But never a moment ceased the fight of the one and
the fifty-three.
'The Revenge' (1878) st. 9

4 'Sink me the ship, Master Gunner—sink her, split her
in twain!
Fall into the hands of God, not into the hands of
Spain!'

And the gunner said 'Ay, ay,' but the seamen made
reply:
'We have children we have wives,
And the Lord hath spared our lives.'
'The Revenge' (1878) st. 11

5 And they praised him to his face with their courtly
foreign grace;
But he rose upon their decks, and he cried:
'I have fought for Queen and Faith like a valiant man
and true;
I have only done my duty as a man is bound to do:
With a joyful spirit I Sir Richard Grenville die!'
And he fell upon their decks, and he died.
'The Revenge' (1878) st. 13

6 And the little Revenge herself went down by the island
crags
To be lost evermore in the main
'The Revenge' (1878) st. 14

7 My strength is as the strength of ten,
Because my heart is pure.
'Sir Galahad' (1842)

8 A man had given all other bliss,
And all his worldly worth for this,
To waste his whole heart in one kiss
Upon her perfect lips.
'Sir Launcelot and Queen Guinevere' (1842)

9 Alone and warming his five wits,
The white owl in the belfry sits.
'Song—The Owl' (1830)

10 The woods decay, the woods decay and fall,
The vapours weep their burthen to the ground,
Man comes and tills the field and lies beneath,
And after many a summer dies the swan.
Me only cruel immortality
Consumes: I wither slowly in thine arms,
Here at the quiet limit of the world.
'Tithonus' (1860, revised 1864) l. 1

11 Why wilt thou ever scare me with thy tears,
And make me tremble lest a saying learnt,
In days far-off, on that dark earth, be true?
'The gods themselves cannot recall their gifts.'
'Tithonus' (1860, revised 1864) l. 46

12 Of happy men that have the power to die,
And grassy barrows of the happier dead.
'Tithonus' (1860, revised 1864) l. 70

13 You'll have no scandal while you dine,
But honest talk and wholesome wine.
'To the Revd F. D. Maurice' (1855) st. 5

14 All the charm of all the Muses
often flowering in a lonely word.
'To Virgil' (1882) st. 3

15 I salute thee, Mantovano,
I that loved thee since my day began,
Wielder of the stateliest measure
ever moulded by the lips of man.
'To Virgil' (1882) st. 10

16 This truth within thy mind rehearse,
That in a boundless universe
Is boundless better, boundless worse.
'The Two Voices' (1842) st. 9

17 No life that breathes with human breath
Has ever truly longed for death.
'The Two Voices' (1842) st. 132

18 It little profits that an idle king,
By this still hearth, among these barren crags,
Matched with an aged wife, I mete and dole
Unequal laws unto a savage race.
'Ulysses' (1842) l. 1

1   I will drink
Life to the lees: all times I have enjoyed
Greatly, have suffered greatly, both with those
That loved me, and alone; on shore, and when
Through scudding drifts the rainy Hyades
Vext the dim sea: I am become a name;
For always roaming with a hungry heart
Much have I seen and known; cities of men
And manners, climates, councils, governments,
Myself not least, but honoured of them all;
And drunk delight of battle with my peers,
Far on the ringing plains of windy Troy.
I am a part of all that I have met;
Yet all experience is an arch wherethrough
Gleams that untravelled world, whose margin fades
For ever and for ever when I move.
How dull it is to pause, to make an end,
To rust unburnished, not to shine in use!
As though to breathe were life.
　　'Ulysses' (1842) l. 6

2   This grey spirit yearning in desire
To follow knowledge like a sinking star,
Beyond the utmost bound of human thought.
　　'Ulysses' (1842) l. 30

3 This is my son, mine own Telemachus.
　　'Ulysses' (1842) l. 33

4 There lies the port; the vessel puffs her sail:
There gloom the dark broad seas. My mariners,
Souls that have toiled, and wrought, and thought
　　with me—
That ever with a frolic welcome took
The thunder and the sunshine, and opposed
Free hearts, free foreheads—you and I are old;
Old age hath yet his honour and his toil;
Death closes all: but something ere the end,
Some work of noble note, may yet be done,
Not unbecoming men that strove with gods.
The lights begin to twinkle from the rocks:
The long day wanes: the slow moon climbs: the deep
Moans round with many voices. Come, my friends,
'Tis not too late to seek a newer world.
Push off, and sitting well in order smite
The sounding furrows; for my purpose holds
To sail beyond the sunset, and the baths
Of all the western stars, until I die.
It may be that the gulfs will wash us down:
It may be we shall touch the Happy Isles,
And see the great Achilles, whom we knew.
Though much is taken, much abides; and though
We are not now that strength which in old days
Moved earth and heaven; that which we are, we are;
One equal temper of heroic hearts,
Made weak by time and fate, but strong in will
To strive, to seek, to find, and not to yield.
　　'Ulysses' (1842) l. 44

5 Every moment dies a man,
Every moment one is born.
　　'The Vision of Sin' (1842) pt. 4, st. 9. Cf. Babbage
　　BABBOC

6 I grow in worth, and wit, and sense,
Unboding critic-pen,
Or that eternal want of pence,
Which vexes public men.
　　'Will Waterproof's Lyrical Monologue' (1842) st. 6

7 A land of settled government,
A land of just and old renown,
Where Freedom slowly broadens down
From precedent to precedent.
　　'You ask me, why, though ill at ease' (1842) st. 3

8 A louse in the locks of literature.
　　Of Churton Collins, in Evan Charteris Life and Letters of Sir
　　Edmund Gosse (1931) ch. 14

Terence (Publius Terentius Afer)

c.190–159 BC
Roman comic playwright

9 *Hinc illae lacrimae.*
Hence those tears.
　　Andria l. 126

10 *Amantium irae amoris integratio est.*
Lovers' rows make love whole.
　　Andria l. 555

11 *Nullumst iam dictum quod non dictum sit prius.*
Nothing has yet been said that's not been said before.
　　Eunuchus prologue l. 41

12 *Homo sum; humani nil a me alienum puto.*
I am a man, I count nothing human foreign to me.
　　Heauton Timorumenos l. 77

13 *Fortis fortuna adiuvat.*
Fortune assists the brave.
　　Phormio l. 203. Cf. Virgil 714:7

14 *Quot homines tot sententiae: suo quoique mos.*
There are as many opinions as there are people: each
has his own correct way.
　　Phormio l. 454

St Teresa of Ávila 1512–82

Spanish Carmelite nun and mystic

15 *Oh, válame Dios, Señor cómo apretáis a vuestros
amadores!*
Alas, O Lord, to what a state dost Thou bring those
who love Thee!
　　Interior Castle Mansion 6, ch. 11, para. 6 (translated by the
　　Benedictines of Stanbrook, 1921)

Tertullian (Quintus Septimius Florens Tertullianus) AD *c.160–c.225*

Latin Church father from Carthage

16 *O testimonium animae naturaliter Christianae.*
O evidence of a naturally Christian soul!
　　Apologeticus ch. 17, sect. 6

17 *Plures efficimur quoties metimur a vobis, semen est
sanguis Christianorum.*
As often as we are mown down by you, the more we
grow in numbers; the blood of Christians is the seed.
　　Apologeticus ch. 50, sect. 13 (traditionally 'The blood of the
　　martyrs is the seed of the Church')

18 *Certum est quia impossibile est.*
It is certain because it is impossible.
　　De Carne Christi ch. 5 (often quoted 'Credo quia impossibile')

A. S. J. Tessimond 1902–62

1 Cats, no less liquid than their shadows,
Offer no angles to the wind.
They slip, diminished, neat, through loopholes
Less than themselves.
Cats (1934) p. 20

William Makepeace Thackeray 1811–63

English novelist

2 He who meanly admires mean things is a Snob.
The Book of Snobs (1848) ch. 2

3 'Tis not the dying for a faith that's so hard, Master
Harry—every man of every nation has done that—'tis
the living up to it that is difficult.
The History of Henry Esmond (1852) bk. 1, ch. 6

4 'Tis strange what a man may do, and a woman yet
think him an angel.
The History of Henry Esmond (1852) bk. 1, ch. 7

5 What money is better bestowed than that of a
school-boy's tip?
The Newcomes (1853–5) vol. 1, ch. 16

6 He lifted up his head a little, and quickly said,
'Adsum!' and fell back . . . he, whose heart was as
that of a little child, had answered to his name, and
stood in the presence of The Master.
The Newcomes (1853–5) vol. 1, ch. 80

7 Yes, I am a fatal man, Madame Fribsbi. To inspire
hopeless passion is my destiny.
Pendennis (1848–50) ch. 23 (Mirobolant)

8 Remember, it is as easy to marry a rich woman as a
poor woman.
Pendennis (1848–50) ch. 28

9 For a slashing article, sir, there's nobody like the
Capting.
Pendennis (1848–50) ch. 32 (Mr Bungay)

10 The *Pall Mall Gazette* is written by gentlemen for
gentlemen.
Pendennis (1848–50) ch. 32

11 Business first; pleasure afterwards.
The Rose and the Ring (1855) ch. 1

12 A woman with fair opportunities and without a
positive hump, may marry whom she likes.
Vanity Fair (1847–8) ch. 4

13 Whenever he met a great man he grovelled before
him, and my-lorded him as only a free-born Briton
can do.
Vanity Fair (1847–8) ch. 13

14 If a man's character is to be abused, say what you
will, there's nobody like a relation to do the business.
Vanity Fair (1847–8) ch. 19

15 Them's my sentiments!
Vanity Fair (1847–8) ch. 21 (Fred Bullock)

16 Darkness came down on the field and city: and Amelia
was praying for George, who was lying on his face,
dead, with a bullet through his heart.
Vanity Fair (1847–8) ch. 32

17 Nothing like blood, sir, in hosses, dawgs, and men.
Vanity Fair (1847–8) ch. 35 (James Crawley)

18 How to live well on nothing a year.
Vanity Fair (1847–8) ch. 36 (title)

19 I think I could be a good woman if I had five thousand
a year.
Vanity Fair (1847–8) ch. 36

20 Ah! *Vanitas Vanitatum!* Which of us is happy in this
world? Which of us has his desire? or, having it, is
satisfied?—Come, children, let us shut up the box and
the puppets, for our play is played out.
Vanity Fair (1847–8) ch. 67

21 Werther had a love for Charlotte
Such as words could never utter;
Would you know how first he met her?
She was cutting bread and butter.
'Sorrows of Werther' (1855)

22 Oh, Vanity of vanities!
How wayward the decrees of Fate are;
How very weak the very wise,
How very small the very great are!
'Vanitas Vanitatum'

Margaret Thatcher 1925–

British Conservative politician; Prime Minister, 1979–90

23 We must try to find ways to starve the terrorist and
the hijacker of the oxygen of publicity on which they
depend.
Speech to American Bar Association in London, 15 July
1985, in *The Times* 16 July 1985

24 No one would remember the Good Samaritan if he'd
only had good intentions. He had money as well.
Television interview, 6 January 1986, in *The Times*
12 January 1986

25 It is exciting to have a real crisis on your hands, when
you have spent half your political life dealing with
humdrum issues like the environment.
On the Falklands campaign, 1982; Speech to Scottish
Conservative Party conference, 14 May 1982, in Hugo
Young *One of Us* (1990) ch. 13

26 There is no such thing as Society. There are individual
men and women, and there are families.
In *Woman's Own* 31 October 1987

27 We have become a grandmother.
In *The Times* 4 March 1989

William Roscoe Thayer 1859–1923

American biographer and historian

28 Log-cabin to White House.
Title of biography (1910) of James Garfield (1831–81)

Theocritus c.300–260 BC

Hellenistic poet

29 Ἁδύ τι τὸ ψιθύρισμα καὶ ἁ πίτυς αἰπόλε τήνα
ἁ ποτὶ ταῖς παγαῖσι μελίσδεται.
Something sweet is the whisper of the pine, O
goatherd, that makes her music by yonder springs.
Idylls no. 1

Louis Adolphe Thiers 1797–1877

French statesman and historian

1 [*Le roi*] *règne et le peuple se gouverne.*

The king reigns, and the people govern themselves.

Unsigned article in *Le National*, 20 January 1830 (a signed article, 4 February 1830, reads: '*Le roi n'administre pas, ne gouverne pas, il règne* [The king neither administers nor governs, he reigns]')

Thomas à Kempis c.1380–1471

German ascetical writer

2 *Opto magis sentire compunctionem: quam scire eius definitionem.*

I would far rather feel remorse than know how to define it.

De Imitatione Christi bk. 1, ch. 1, sect. 3

3 *O quam cito transit gloria mundi.*

Oh how quickly the glory of the world passes away!

De Imitatione Christi bk. 1, ch. 3, sect. 6. Cf. Anonymous 22:15

4 *Non quaeras quis hoc dixerit: sed, qvid diciatur attende.*

Seek not to know who said this or that, but take note of what has been said.

De Imitatione Christi bk. 1, ch. 5, sect. 1

5 *Multo tutius est stare in subiectione: quam in praelatura.*

It is much safer to be in a subordinate position than in authority.

De Imitatione Christi bk. 1, ch. 9, sect. 1

6 *Nam homo proponit, sed Deus disponit.*

For man proposes, but God disposes.

De Imitatione Christi bk. 1, ch. 19, sect. 2

7 *Numquam sis ex toto otiosus, sed aut legens, aut scribens, aut orans, aut meditans, aut aliquid utilitatis pro communi laborans.*

Never be completely idle, but either reading, or writing, or praying, or meditating, or at some useful work for the common good.

De Imitatione Christi bk. 1, ch. 19, sect. 4

8 *Hodie homo est: et cras non comparet. Cum autem sublatus fuerit ab oculis: etiam cito transit a mente.*

Today the man is here; tomorrow he is gone. And when he is 'out of sight', quickly also is he out of mind.

De Imitatione Christi bk. 1, ch. 23, sect. 1

9 *Utinam per unam diem bene essemus conversati in hoc mundo.*

Would that we had spent one whole day well in this world!

De Imitatione Christi bk. 1, ch. 23, sect. 2

10 *Passione interdum movemur: et zelum putamus.*

We are sometimes stirred by emotion and take it for zeal.

De Imitatione Christi bk. 2, ch. 5, sect. 1

11 *Si libenter crucem portas portabit te.*

If you bear the cross gladly, it will bear you.

De Imitatione Christi bk. 2, ch. 12, sect. 5

12 *De duobus malis minus est semper eligendum.*

Of the two evils the lesser is always to be chosen.

De Imitatione Christi bk. 3, ch. 12, sect. 2

St Thomas Aquinas c.1225–74

Italian Dominican friar and Doctor of the Church

13 *Pange, lingua, gloriosi*
Corporis mysterium,
Sanguinisque pretiosi,
Quem in mundi pretium
Fructus ventris generosi
Rex effudit gentium.

Now, my tongue, the mystery telling
Of the glorious Body sing,
And the Blood, all price excelling,
Which the Gentiles' Lord and King,
In a Virgin's womb once dwelling,
Shed for this world's ransoming.

'Pange Lingua Gloriosi' (Corpus Christi hymn, translated by J. M. Neale, E. Caswall, and others)

14 *Tantum ergo sacramentum*
Veneremur cernui;
Et antiquum documentum
Novo cedat ritui.

Therefore we, before him bending,
This great Sacrament revere;
Types and shadows have their ending,
For the newer rite is here.

'Pange Lingua Gloriosi' (Corpus Christi hymn, translated by J. M. Neale, E. Caswall, and others)

15 *Multo ergo magis ad moralem pertinet considerare de amicitia quam de justitia.*

Moral science is better occupied when treating of friendship than of justice.

Exposition of Aristotle's Ethics (c.1271) bk. 8, lecture 1

16 *Finis autem nostri desiderii Deus est; unde actus quo ei primo coniungimur, est originaliter et substantialiter nostra beatitudo. Primo autem Deo coniungimur per actum intellectus; et ideo ipsa Dei visio, quae est actus intellectus, est substantialiter et originaliter nostra beatitudo.*

Now, the end of our desires is God; hence, the act whereby we are primarily joined to Him is basically and substantially our happiness. But we are primarily united with God by an act of understanding; and therefore, the very seeing of God, which is an act of the intellect, is substantially and basically our happiness.

Quodlibetal Questions (c.1256) vol. 8, bk. 9, pt. 19 (translated by Bourke)

17 *Ergo necesse est devenire ad aliquod primum movens, quod a nullo movetur; et hoc omnes intellegunt Deum.*

Therefore it is necessary to arrive at a prime mover, put in motion by no other; and this everyone understands to be God.

Summa Theologicae (c.1265) pt. 3, qu. 2, art. 3 (translated by English Dominican Fathers)

1 *Si enim omnia mala impedirentur, multa bona deessent universo: non enim esset vita lionis, si non esset occisio animalium; nec esset patientia martyrum, si non esset persecutio tyrannorum.*

If all evil were prevented, much good would be absent from the universe. A lion would cease to live, if there were no slaying of animals; and there would be no patience of martyrs if there were no tyrannical persecution.

Summa Theologicae (c.1265) pt. 1, qu. 22, art. 2 (translated by English Dominican Fathers)

Brandon Thomas 1856–1914

English playwright

2 I'm Charley's aunt from Brazil—where the nuts come from.

Charley's Aunt (1892) act 1

Dylan Thomas 1914–53

Welsh poet

3 Though they go mad they shall be sane,
Though they sink through the sea they shall rise again;
Though lovers be lost love shall not;
And death shall have no dominion.

'And death shall have no dominion' (1936). Cf. Romans 99:29

4 Do not go gentle into that good night,
Old age should burn and rave at close of day;
Rage, rage against the dying of the light.

'Do Not Go Gentle into that Good Night' (1952)

5 Now as I was young and easy under the apple boughs
About the lilting house and happy as the grass was green.

'Fern Hill' (1946)

6 Oh as I was young and easy in the mercy of his means,
Time held me green and dying
Though I sang in my chains like the sea.

'Fern Hill' (1946)

7 The force that through the green fuse drives the flower
Drives my green age; that blasts the roots of trees
Is my destroyer.
And I am dumb to tell the crooked rose
My youth is bent by the same wintry fever.

'The force that through the green fuse drives the flower' (1934)

8 And I am dumb to tell the lover's tomb
How at my sheet goes the same crooked worm.

'The force that through the green fuse drives the flower' (1934)

9 The hand that signed the paper felled a city;
Five sovereign fingers taxed the breath,
Doubled the globe of dead and halved a country;
These five kings did a king to death.

'The hand that signed the paper felled a city' (1936)

10 The hand that signed the treaty bred a fever,
And famine grew, and locusts came;
Great is the hand that holds dominion over
Man by a scribbled name.

The hand that signed the paper felled a city' (1936)

11 Light breaks where no sun shines;
Where no sea runs, the waters of the heart
Push in their tides.

'Light breaks where no sun shines' (1934)

12 It was my thirtieth year to heaven
Woke to my hearing from harbour and neighbour wood
And the mussel pooled and the heron
Priested shore
The morning beckon.

'Poem in October' (1946)

13 Pale rain over the dwindling harbour
And over the sea wet church the size of a snail
With its horns through mist and the castle
Brown as owls
But all the gardens
Of spring and summer were blooming in the tall vales
Beyond the border and under the lark full cloud.
There could I marvel
My birthday
Away but the weather turned around.

'Poem in October' (1946)

14 Deep with the first dead lies London's daughter,
Robed in the long friends,
The grains beyond age, the dark veins of her mother,
Secret by the unmourning water
Of the riding Thames.
After the first death, there is no other.

'A Refusal to Mourn the Death, by Fire, of a Child in London' (1946)

15 There is only one position for an artist anywhere: and that is, upright.

Quite Early One Morning (1954) pt. 2 'Wales and the Artist'

16 To begin at the beginning: It is spring, moonless night in the small town, starless and bible-black.

Under Milk Wood (1954) p. 1

17 Chasing the naughty couples down the grassgreen gooseberried double bed of the wood.

Under Milk Wood (1954) p. 7

18 Before you let the sun in, mind it wipes its shoes.

Under Milk Wood (1954) p. 16

19 Gomer Owen who kissed her once by the pig-sty when she wasn't looking and never kissed her again although she was looking all the time.

Under Milk Wood (1954) p. 19

20 Oh, isn't life a terrible thing, thank God?

Under Milk Wood (1954) p. 30

21 The land of my fathers. My fathers can have it.

Of Wales, in *Adam* December 1953

22 [An alcoholic:] A man you don't like who drinks as much as you do.

In Constantine Fitzgibbon *Life of Dylan Thomas* (1965) ch. 6

Edward Thomas 1878–1917

English poet

23 Yes; I remember Adlestrop—
The name, because one afternoon
Of heat the express-train drew up there
Unwontedly. It was late June.

'Adlestrop' (1917)

1 The past is the only dead thing that smells sweet.
   'Early one morning in May I set out' (1917)

2 If I should ever by chance grow rich
I'll buy Codham, Cockridden, and Childerditch,
Roses, Pyrgo, and Lapwater,
And let them all to my elder daughter.
   'Household Poems: Bronwen' (1917)

3 I have come to the borders of sleep,
The unfathomable deep
Forest where all must lose
Their way, however straight
Or winding, soon or late;
They can not choose.
   'Lights Out' (1917)

4   As for myself,
Where first I met the bitter scent is lost.
I, too, often shrivel the grey shreds,
Sniff them and think and sniff again and try
Once more to think what it is I am remembering,
Always in vain. I cannot like the scent,
Yet I would gather up others more sweet,
With no meaning, than this bitter one.

I have mislaid the key. I sniff the spray
And think of nothing; I see and hear nothing;
Yet seem, too, to be listening, lying in wait
For what I should, yet never can, remember.
No garden appears, no path, no hoar-green bush
Of Lad's-love, or Old Man, no child beside,
Neither father nor mother, nor any playmate;
Only an avenue, dark, nameless, without end.
   'Old Man' (1917)

5 Out in the dark over the snow
The fallow fawns invisible go
With the fallow doe;
And the winds blow
Fast as the stars are slow.
   'Out in the dark' (1917)

6 As well as any bloom upon a flower
I like the dust on the nettles, never lost
Except to prove the sweetness of a shower.
   'Tall Nettles' (1917)

Elizabeth Thomas 1675–1731

English poet

7 From marrying in haste, and repenting at leisure;
Not liking the person, yet liking his treasure:
Libera nos.
   'A New Litany, occasioned by an invitation to a wedding'
   (1722). Cf. Congreve 215:25

Irene Thomas

British writer and broadcaster

8 Protestant women may take the pill. Roman Catholic
women must keep taking The Tablet.
   In *Guardian* 28 December 1990, p. 27

R. S. Thomas 1913–

Welsh poet and clergyman

9 To one kneeling down no word came,
Only the mind's song, saddening the lips
Of the grave saints, rigid in glass;
Or the dry whisper of unseen wings,
Bats not angels, in the high roof.
   'In a Country Church' (1955)

10   Doctors in verse
Being scarce now, most poets
Are their own patients, compelled to treat
Themselves first, their complaint being
Peculiar always.
   'The Cure' (1958)

11   Prompt me, God;
But not yet. When I speak
Though it be you who speak
Through me, something is lost.
The meaning is the waiting.
   'Kneeling' (1968)

12 In the darkness . . . the sound of a man
Breathing, testing his faith
On emptiness, nailing his questions
One by one to an untenanted cross.
   'Pietà' (1966)

13 There is no love
For such, only a willed
gentleness.
   'They' (1968)

14 . . . I never thought other than
That God is that great absence
In our lives, the empty silence
Within, the place where we go
Seeking, not in hope to
Arrive or find.
   'Via Negativa' (1972)

15 There is no present in Wales,
And no future;
There is only the past,
Brittle with relics . . .
And an impotent people,
Sick with inbreeding,
Worrying the carcase of an old song.
   'Welsh Landscape' (1955)

Francis Thompson 1859–1907

English poet

16 As the run-stealers flicker to and fro,
To and fro:—
O my Hornby and my Barlow long ago!
   'At Lord's' (1913)

17 The fairest things have fleetest end,
Their scent survives their close:
But the rose's scent is bitterness
To him that loved the rose!
   'Daisy' (1913)

18 Nothing begins, and nothing ends,
That is not paid with moan;
For we are born in other's pain,
And perish in our own.
   'Daisy' (1913)

1 I fled Him, down the nights and down the days;
 I fled Him, down the arches of the years;
 I fled Him, down the labyrinthine ways
 Of my own mind; and in the mist of tears
 I hid from Him, and under running laughter.
  'The Hound of Heaven' (1913) pt. 1

2 But with unhurrying chase,
 And unperturbèd pace,
 Deliberate speed, majestic instancy,
 They beat—and a Voice beat
 More instant than the Feet—
 All things betray thee, who betrayest Me.
  'The Hound of Heaven' (1913) pt. 1

3 I said to Dawn: Be sudden—to Eve:
 Be soon.
  'The Hound of Heaven' (1913) pt. 2

4 To all swift things for swiftness did I sue;
 Clung to the whistling mane of every wind.
  'The Hound of Heaven' (1913) pt. 2

5 Such is: what is to be?
 The pulp so bitter, how shall taste the rind?
  'The Hound of Heaven' (1913) pt. 4

6 Yet ever and anon a trumpet sounds
 From the hid battlements of Eternity;
 Those shaken mists a space unsettle, then
 Round the half-glimpsèd turrets slowly wash again.
  'The Hound of Heaven' (1913) pt. 4

7 Now of that long pursuit
 Comes on at hand the bruit;
 That Voice is round me like a bursting sea:
 'And is thy earth so marred,
 Shattered in shard on shard?
 Lo, all things fly thee, for thou fliest Me!'
  'The Hound of Heaven' (1913) pt. 5

8 There is no expeditious road
 To pack and label men for God,
 And save them by the barrel-load.
 Some may perchance, with strange surprise,
 Have blundered into Paradise.
  'A Judgement in Heaven' (1913) epilogue

9 O world invisible, we view thee,
 O world intangible, we touch thee,
 O world unknowable, we know thee,
 Inapprehensible, we clutch thee!
  'The Kingdom of God' (1913)

10 The angels keep their ancient places;—
 Turn but a stone, and start a wing!
 'Tis ye, 'tis your estrangèd faces,
 That miss the many-splendoured thing.
 But (when so sad thou canst not sadder)
 Cry;—and upon thy so sore loss
 Shall shine the traffic of Jacob's ladder
 Pitched betwixt Heaven and Charing Cross.
 Yea, in the night, my Soul, my daughter,
 Cry,—clinging Heaven by the hems;
 And lo, Christ walking on the water
 Not of Gennesareth, but Thames!
  'The Kingdom of God' (1913)

11 Look for me in the nurseries of heaven.
  'To My Godchild, Francis M.W.M.' (1913)

12 What heart could have thought you?—
 Past our devisal
 (O filigree petal!)
 Fashioned so purely,
 Fragilely, surely,
 From what Paradisal
 Imagineless metal,
 Too costly for cost?
  'To a Snowflake' (1913)

13 Insculped and embossed,
 With His hammer of wind,
 And His graver of frost.
  'To a Snowflake' (1913)

William Hepworth Thompson 1810–86

English classicist; Master of Trinity College, Cambridge, from 1866

14 What time he can spare from the adornment of his
 person he devotes to the neglect of his duties.
  Of Sir Richard Jebb, later Professor of Greek at Cambridge
  University, in M. R. Bobbit *With Dearest Love to All* (1960)
  ch. 7

James Thomson 1700–48

Scottish poet

15 When Britain first, at heaven's command,
 Arose from out the azure main,
 This was the charter of the land,
 And guardian angels sung this strain:
 'Rule, Britannia, rule the waves;
 Britons never will be slaves.'
  Alfred: a Masque (1740) act 2

16 A pleasing land of drowsyhead it was.
  The Castle of Indolence (1748) canto 1, st. 6

17 Soft quilts on quilts, on carpets carpets spread,
 And couches stretch around in seemly band;
 And endless pillows rise to prop the head.
  The Castle of Indolence (1748) canto 1, st. 33

18 A bard here dwelt, more fat than bard beseems.
  The Castle of Indolence (1748) canto 1, st. 68 (of himself)

19 A little round, fat, oily man of God,
 Was one I chiefly marked among the fry:
 He had a roguish twinkle in his eye.
  The Castle of Indolence (1748) canto 1, st. 69

20 Here lies a man who never lived,
 Yet still from death was flying;
 Who, if not sick, was never well;
 And died—for fear of dying!
  'Epitaph on Solomon Mendez' (published 1782)

21 A thousand shapes you wear with ease,
 And still in every shape you please.
  'Hymn on Solitude' (1729) l. 9

22 Still as I gazed new beauties met my sight.
  Letter to Elizabeth Young, 19 April 1743

23 But now those white unblemished minutes, whence
 The fabling poets took their golden age,
 Are found no more amid these iron times,
 These dregs of life!
  The Seasons (1746) 'Spring' l. 272

1 The daisy, primrose, violet, darkly blue,
And polyanthus of unnumbered dyes;
The yellow wall-flower, stained with iron brown;
And lavish stock that scents the garden round.
The Seasons (1746) 'Spring' l. 531

2 Delightful task! to rear the tender thought,
To teach the young idea how to shoot.
The Seasons (1746) 'Spring' l. 1152

3 An elegant sufficiency, content,
Retirement, rural quiet, friendship, books.
The Seasons (1746) 'Spring' l. 1161

4 O'er heaven and earth, far as the ranging eye
Can sweep, a dazzling deluge reigns; and all
From pole to pole is undistinguished blaze.
The Seasons (1746) 'Summer' l. 434

5 Ships, dim-discovered, dropping from the clouds.
The Seasons (1746) 'Summer' l. 946

6 Sighed and looked unutterable things.
The Seasons (1746) 'Summer' l. 1188

7 While listening senates hang upon thy tongue.
The Seasons (1746) 'Autumn' l. 15

8 For loveliness
Needs not the foreign aid of ornament,
But is when unadorned adorned the most.
The Seasons (1746) 'Autumn' l. 204

9 Poor is the triumph o'er the timid hare!
The Seasons (1746) 'Autumn' l. 401

10 Find other lands beneath another sun.
The Seasons (1746) 'Autumn' l. 1286

11 See, Winter comes to rule the varied year,
Sullen and sad.
The Seasons (1746) 'Winter' l. 1

12 Welcome, kindred glooms!
Congenial horrors, hail!
The Seasons (1746) 'Winter' l. 5

13 Studious let me sit,
And hold high converse with the mighty dead.
The Seasons (1746) 'Winter' l. 431

14 For ever, Fortune, wilt thou prove
An unrelenting foe to Love;
And, when we meet a mutual heart,
Come in between and bid us part?
'Song' (1732)

15 Even Light itself, which every thing displays,
Shone undiscovered, till his brighter mind
Untwisted all the shining robe of day.
'To the Memory of Sir Isaac Newton' (1727) l. 96 (on Newton's *Opticks*)

16 Did ever poet image aught so fair,
Dreaming in whispering groves, by the hoarse brook!
Or prophet, to whose rapture heaven descends!
'To the Memory of Sir Isaac Newton' (1727) l. 96 (on Newton's explanation of the rainbow in terms of refraction)

James Thomson 1834–82

Scottish poet

17 The City is of Night; perchance of Death,
But certainly of Night.
'The City of Dreadful Night' (written 1870–3)

18 As we rush, as we rush in the train,
The trees and the houses go wheeling back,
But the starry heavens above that plain
Come flying on our track.
'Sunday at Hampstead' (written 1863–5) st. 10

19 Give a man a horse he can ride,
Give a man a boat he can sail.
'Sunday up the River' (written 1865) st. 15

Roy Thomson (Baron Thomson of Fleet)
1894–1976

Canadian-born British newspaper proprietor

20 Like having your own licence to print money.
On the profitability of commercial television in Britain, in R. Braddon *Roy Thomson* (1965) ch. 32

Henry David Thoreau 1817–62

American writer

21 I heartily accept the motto, 'That government is best which governs least' . . . Carried out, it finally amounts to this, which I also believe,— 'That government is best which governs not at all.'
Civil Disobedience (1849) in *Writings* (1906 ed.) vol. 4, p. 356. Cf. O'Sullivan 502:4

22 Under a government which imprisons any unjustly, the true place for a just man is also a prison.
Civil Disobedience (1849) in *Writings* (1906 ed.) vol. 4, p. 370

23 Some circumstantial evidence is very strong, as when you find a trout in the milk.
Journal 11 November 1850, in *Writings* (1906 ed.) vol. 8, p. 94

24 We do not enjoy poetry unless we know it to be poetry.
Journal 1 October 1856, in *Writings* (1906 ed.) vol. 15, p. 96

25 Not that the story need be long, but it will take a long while to make it short.
Letter to Harrison Blake, 16 November 1857, in *Writings* (1906 ed.) vol. 6, p. 320. Cf. Pascal 507:8

26 I have travelled a good deal in Concord.
Walden (1854) 'Economy' in *Writings* (1906 ed.) vol. 2, p. 4

27 As if you could kill time without injuring eternity.
Walden (1854) 'Economy' in *Writings* (1906 ed.) vol. 2, p. 8

28 The mass of men lead lives of quiet desperation.
Walden (1854) 'Economy' in *Writings* (1906 ed.) vol. 2, p. 8. In *Histoire de ma vie* vol. 4 (1854) p. 439, George Sand described Chopin as being in a state of '*désespérance tranquille*'

29 In any weather, at any hour of the day or night, I have been anxious to improve the nick of time, and notch it on my stick too; to stand on the meeting of two eternities, the past and the future, which is precisely the present moment; to toe that line.
Walden (1854) 'Economy' in *Writings* (1906 ed.) vol. 2, p. 18

1 For more than five years I maintained myself thus solely by the labour of my hands, and I found, that by working about six weeks in a year, I could meet all the expenses of living.
Walden (1854) 'Economy' in *Writings* (1906 ed.) vol. 2, p. 76

2 As for Doing-good, that is one of the professions which are full.
Walden (1854) 'Economy' in *Writings* (1906 ed.) vol. 2, p. 80

3 The three-o'-clock in the morning courage, which Bonaparte thought was the rarest.
Walden (1854) 'Sounds' in *Writings* (1906 ed.) vol. 2, p. 131. Cf. Fitzgerald 285:5, Napoleon 490:2

4 Wherever a man goes, men will pursue him and paw him with their dirty institutions, and, if they can, constrain him to belong to their desperate oddfellow society.
Walden (1854) 'The Village' in *Writings* (1906 ed.) vol. 2, p. 190

5 I wanted to live deep and suck out all the marrow of life . . . to drive life into a corner, and reduce it to its lowest terms, and, if it proved to be mean, why then to get the whole and genuine meanness of it, and publish its meanness to the world; or if it were sublime, to know it by experience.
Walden (1854) 'Where I lived, and what I lived for' in *Writings* (1906 ed.) vol. 2, p. 101

6 Our life is frittered away by detail . . . Simplicity, simplicity.
Walden (1854) 'Where I lived, and what I lived for' in *Writings* (1906 ed.) vol. 2, p. 101

7 I once had a sparrow alight upon my shoulder for a moment while I was hoeing in a village garden, and I felt that I was more distinguished by that circumstance than I should have been by any epaulette I could have worn.
Walden (1854) 'Winter Animals' in *Writings* (1906 ed.) vol. 2, p. 304

8 If a man does not keep pace with his companions, perhaps it is because he hears a different drummer. Let him step to the music which he hears, however measured or far away.
Walden (1854) 'Conclusion' in *Writings* (1906 ed.) vol. 2, p. 358

9 The government of the world I live in was not framed, like that of Britain, in after-dinner conversations over the wine.
Walden (1854) 'Conclusion' in *Writings* (1906 ed.) vol. 2, p. 366

10 It takes two to speak the truth,—one to speak, and another to hear.
A Week on the Concord and Merrimack Rivers (1849) 'Wednesday'

11 It were treason to our love
And a sin to God above
One iota to abate
Of a pure impartial hate.
'Indeed, Indeed I Cannot Tell' (1852)

Jeremy Thorpe 1929–
British Liberal politician

12 Greater love hath no man than this, that he lay down his friends for his life.
On Harold Macmillan sacking seven of his Cabinet on 13 July 1962; in D. E. Butler and Anthony King *The General Election of 1964* (1965) ch. 1

James Thurber 1894–1961
American humorist

13 Her own mother lived the latter years of her life in the horrible suspicion that electricity was dripping invisibly all over the house.
My Life and Hard Times (1933) ch. 2

14 You might as well fall flat on your face as lean over too far backward.
'The Bear Who Let It Alone' in *New Yorker* 29 April 1939

15 Early to rise and early to bed makes a male healthy and wealthy and dead.
'The Shrike and the Chipmunks' in *New Yorker* 18 February 1939

16 The war between men and women.
Cartoon series title in *New Yorker* 20 January 28 April 1934

17 It's a naïve domestic Burgundy without any breeding, but I think you'll be amused by its presumption.
Cartoon caption in *New Yorker* 27 March 1937

18 Well, if I called the wrong number, why did you answer the phone?
Cartoon caption in *New Yorker* 5 June 1937

19 It's our *own* story *exactly*! He bold as a hawk, she soft as the dawn.
Cartoon caption in *New Yorker* 25 February 1939

20 Humour is emotional chaos remembered in tranquillity.
In *New York Post* 29 February 1960. Cf. Wordsworth 748:19

Edward, 1st Baron Thurlow 1731–1806
English jurist; Lord Chancellor, 1778–83, 1783–92

21 Corporations have neither bodies to be punished, nor souls to be condemned, they therefore do as they like.
In John Poynder *Literary Extracts* (1844) vol. 1, p. 268 (usually quoted 'Did you ever expect a corporation to have a conscience, when it has no soul to be damned, and no body to be kicked?')

Edward, 2nd Baron Thurlow 1781–1829
English poet

22 Nature is always wise in every part,
'To a Bird, that haunted the Waters of Lacken, in the Winter

Tibullus (Albius Tibullus) c.50–19 BC

Roman poet

1 *Te spectem, suprema mihi cum venerit hora,*
Et teneam moriens deficiente manu.

May I be looking at you when my last hour has come,
and dying may I hold you with my weakening hand.
Elegies bk. 1, no. 1, l. 59

2 *Te propter nullos tellus tua postulat imbres,*
Arida nec pluvio supplicat herba Iovi.

Because of you your land never pleads for showers,
nor does its parched grass pray to Jupiter the
Rain-giver.
Elegies bk. 1, no. 7, l. 25 (of the River Nile in Egypt)

Chidiock Tichborne c.1558–86

English Roman Catholic conspirator

3 My prime of youth is but a frost of cares;
My feast of joy is but a dish of pain;
My crop of corn is but a field of tares;
And all my good is but vain hope of gain.
The day is past, and yet I saw no sun;
And now I live, and now my life is done.
'Elegy' (composed in the Tower of London prior to his
execution)

Thomas Tickell 1686–1740

English poet

4 His shape o'ertakes me in the lonely grove:
'Twas there of just and good he reasoned strong,
Cleared some great truth, or raised some serious song
. . .
There taught us how to live; and (oh! too high
The price for knowledge) taught us how to die.
'To the Earl of Warwick. On the Death of Mr Addison'
(1721) l. 76

Paul Tillich 1886–1965

German-born Protestant theologian

5 Neurosis is the way of avoiding non-being by avoiding
being.
The Courage To Be (1952) pt. 2, ch. 3

6 Faith is the state of being ultimately concerned.
Dynamics of Faith (1957) ch. 1

Matthew Tindal 1657–1733

English deist

7 Matters of fact, which as Mr Budgell somewhere
observes, are very stubborn things.
The Will of Matthew Tindal (1733) p. 23

Titus (Titus Flavius Vespasianus) AD 39–81

Roman emperor from AD 79

8 *Amici, diem perdidi.*

Friends, I have lost a day.
On reflecting that he had done nothing to help anybody all
day, in Suetonius *Lives of the Caesars* 'Titus' ch. 8, sect. 1

Alexis de Tocqueville 1805–59

French historian and politician

9 *Seule [la liberté] substitue de temps à autre à l'amour du*
bien-être des passions énergiques et plus hautes, fournit à
l'ambition des objets plus grands que l'acquisition des
richesses, et crée la lumière qui permet de voir et de juger
les vices et les vertus des hommes.

Freedom alone substitutes from time to time for the
love of material comfort more powerful and more lofty
passions; it alone supplies ambition with greater
objectives than the acquisition of riches, and creates
the light that makes it possible to see and to judge the
vices and virtues of mankind.
L'Ancien régime (1856, ed. J. P. Mayer, 1951) p. 75
(translated by M. W. Patterson, 1933)

10 *Quel est l'homme qui, de nature, aurait l'âme assez base*
pour préférer dépendre des caprices d'un de ses semblables
à suivre les lois qu'il a contribué à établir lui-même?

Where is the man of soul so base that he would prefer
to depend on the caprices of one of his fellow men
rather than obey the laws which he has himself
contributed to establish?
L'Ancien régime (1856, ed. J. P. Mayer, 1951) p. 75
(translated by M. W. Patterson, 1933)

11 *Les despotes eux-mêmes ne nient pas que la liberté ne soit*
excellente; seulement ils ne la veulent que pour
eux-mêmes, et ils soutiennent que tous les autres en sont
tout à fait indignes.

Despots themselves do not deny that freedom is
excellent; only they desire it for themselves alone, and
they maintain that everyone else is altogether
unworthy of it.
L'Ancien régime (1856, ed. J. P. Mayer, 1951) p. 75
(translated by M. W. Patterson, 1933)

12 *La Révolution française a opéré par rapport à ce monde,*
précisément de la même manière que les révolutions
religieuses agissent en vue de l'autre; elle a considéré le
citoyen d'une façon abstraite, en dehors de toutes les
sociétés particulières de même que les religions considèrent
l'homme en général, indépendamment du pays et du temps.

The French Revolution operated in reference to this
world in exactly the same manner as religious
revolutions acted in view of the other world. It
considered the citizen as an abstract proposition apart
from any particular society, in the same way as
religions considered man as man, independent of
country and time.
L'Ancien régime (1856, ed. J. P. Mayer, 1951) p. 89
(translated by M. W. Patterson, 1933)

13 *On voit que l'histoire est une galerie de tableaux où il y a*
peu d'originaux et beaucoup de copies.

History is a gallery of pictures in which there are few
originals and many copies.
L'Ancien régime (1856, ed. J. P. Mayer, 1951) p. 133
(translated by M. W. Patterson, 1933)

14 *Qui cherche dans la liberté autre chose qu'elle-même est*
fait pour servir.

He who desires in liberty anything other than itself is
born to be a servant.
L'Ancien régime (1856, ed. J. P. Mayer, 1951) p. 217
(translated by M. W. Patterson, 1933)

1 *Ce n'est pas toujours en allant de mal en pis que l'on tombe en révolution ... Le régime qu'une révolution détruit vaut presque toujours mieux que celui qui l'avait immédiatement précédé, et l'expérience apprend que le moment le plus dangereux pour un mauvais gouvernement est d'ordinaire celui où il commence à se réformer.*

It is not always by going from bad to worse that a society falls into revolution ... The social order destroyed by a revolution is almost always better than that which immediately preceded it, and experience shows that the most dangerous moment for a bad government is generally that in which it sets about reform.

L'Ancien régime (1856, ed. J. P. Mayer, 1951) p. 223 (translated by M. W. Patterson, 1933)

2 *La Providence n'a créé le genre humain ni entièrement indépendant, ni tout à fait esclave. Elle trace, il est vrai, autour de chaque homme, un circle fatal dont il ne peut sortir; mais, dans ses vastes limites, l'homme est puissant et libre; ainsi des peuples.*

Providence has not created mankind entirely independent or entirely free. It is true that around every man a fatal circle is traced, beyond which he cannot pass; but within the wide verge of that circle he is powerful and free.

De la Démocratie en Amérique (1835–40, ed. J. P. Mayer, 1951) vol. 1, p. 339 (translated by H. Reeve, 1841)

3 *Les peuples chez lesqels la Civilisation parvient le plus difficilement à fonder son empire sont les peuples chasseurs.*

Of all nations, those submit to civilization with the most difficulty which habitually live by the chase.

De la Démocratie en Amérique (1835–40, ed. J. P. Mayer, 1951) vol. 1, p. 342 (translated by H. Reeve, 1841)

4 *Ce qu'on entend par république aux États-Unis, c'est l'action lente et tranquille de la société sur elle-même.*

What is understood by republican government in the United States is the slow and quiet action of society upon itself.

De la Démocratie en Amérique (1835–40, ed. J. P. Mayer, 1951) vol. 1, p. 412 (translated by H. Reeve, 1841)

5 *Il y a aujourd'hui sur la terre deux grands peuples qui, partis de points différents, semblent s'avancer vers le même but: ce sont les Russes et les Anglo-Américains ... leur point de départ est différent, leur voies sont diverses: néanmoins chacun d'eux semble appelé par un dessein secret de la Providence à tenir un jour dans ses mains les destinées de la moitié du monde.*

There are, at the present time, two great nations in the world, which seem to tend towards the same end, although they started from different points; I allude to the Russians and the Americans ... Their starting point is different, and their courses are not the same; yet each of them seems to be marked out by the will of Heaven to sway the destinies of half the globe.

De la Démocratie en Amérique (1835–40, ed. J. P. Mayer, 1951) vol. 1, p. 431 (translated by H. Reeve, 1841)

6 *Ne pouvant juger du premier coup d'œil quelle est la situation sociale de ceux qu'on rencontre, l'on évite prudemment d'entrer en contact avec eux. On redoute rendant de légers services de former malgré soi une amitié mal assortie; on craint les bons offices, et l'on se soustrait à la reconnaissance indiscrète d'un inconnu aussi soigneusement qu'à sa haine.*

Unable to judge at once of the social position of those he meets, an Englishman prudently avoids all contact with them. Men are afraid less some slight service rendered should draw them into an unsuitable acquaintance; they dread civilities, and they avoid the obtrusive gratitude of a stranger quite as much as his hatred.

De la Démocratie en Amérique (1835–40, ed. J. P. Mayer, 1951) vol. 2, p. 177 (translated by H. Reeve, 1841)

7 *L'esprit français est de ne pas vouloir de supérieur. L'esprit anglais est de vouloir des inférieurs. Le Français lève les yeux sans cesse au-dessus de lui avec inquiétude. L'Anglais les baisse au-dessous de lui avec complaisance. C'est de part et d'autre de l'orgueil, mais entendu de manière différente.*

The French want no-one to be their *superior*. The English want *inferiors*. The Frenchman constantly raises his eyes above him with anxiety. The Englishman lowers his beneath him with satisfaction. On either side it is pride, but understood in a different way.

Voyage en Angleterre et en Irlande de 1835 (ed. J. P. Mayer, 1958) 8 May 1835

8 *C'est au milieu de ce cloaque infect que le plus grand fleuve de l'industrie humaine prend sa source et va féconder l'univers. De cet égout immonde, l'or pur s'écoule. C'est là que l'esprit humain se perfectionne et s'abrutit; que la civilisation produit ses merveilles et que l'homme civilisé redevient presque sauvage.*

It is from the midst of this putrid sewer that the greatest river of human industry springs up and carries fertility to the whole world. From this foul drain pure gold flows forth. Here it is that humanity achieves for itself both perfection and brutalization, that civilization produces its wonders, and that civilized man becomes again almost a savage.

Voyage en Angleterre et en Irlande de 1835 (ed. J. P. Mayer, 1958) 2 July 1835 (of Manchester)

Alvin Toffler 1928–
American writer

9 'Future shock' ... the shattering stress and disorientation that we induce in individuals by subjecting them to too much change in too short a time.

Future Shock (1970). In Horizon Summer 1965, Toffler defined 'future shock' as 'the dizzying disorientation brought on by the premature arrival of the future'

1 Culture shock is what happens when a traveller suddenly finds himself in a place where yes may mean no, where a 'fixed price' is negotiable, where to be kept waiting in an outer office is no cause for insult, where laughter may signify anger.

Future Shock (1970) ch. 1 (the term 'culture shock' appears to have been already in use by the 1940s)

J. R. R. Tolkien 1892–1973
British philologist and writer

2 In a hole in the ground there lived a hobbit. Not a nasty, dirty, wet hole, filled with the ends of worms and an oozy smell, nor yet a dry, bare, sandy hole with nothing in it to sit down on or to eat: it was a hobbit-hole, and that means comfort.

The Hobbit (1937) ch. 1

3 Never laugh at live dragons.

The Hobbit (1937) ch. 12

4 One Ring to rule them all, One Ring to find them
One Ring to bring them all and in the darkness bind them.

The Lord of the Rings pt. 1 *The Fellowship of the Ring* (1954) epigraph

Leo Tolstoy 1828–1910
Russian novelist

5 Все счастливые семьи похожи друг на друга, каждая несчастливая семья несчастлива по-своему.

All happy families resemble one another, but each unhappy family is unhappy in its own way.

Anna Karenina (1875–7) pt. 1, ch. 1 (translated by A. and L. Maude)

6 Нет таких условий, к которым человек не мог бы привыкнуть, в особенности если он видит, что все окружающие его живут так.

There are no conditions of life to which a man cannot get accustomed, especially if he sees them accepted by everyone about him.

Anna Karenina (1875–7) pt. 7, ch. 13 (translated by Rosemary Edmonds)

7 Свеча, при которой она читала исполненную тревог, обманов, горя и зла книгу, вспыхнула более ярким, чем когда-нибудь, светом, осветила ей всё то, что прежде было во мраке, затрещала, стала меркнуть и навсегда потухла.

The candle by which she had been reading the book filled with trouble and deceit, sorrow and evil, flared up with a brighter light, illuminating for her everything that before had been enshrouded in darkness, flickered, grew dim, and went out for ever.

Anna Karenina (1875–7) pt. 7, ch. 31 (translated by Rosemary Edmonds)

8 Это новое чувство не изменила меня, не осчастливила, не просветила вдруг, как я мечтал ... чувство это так же незаметно вошло ... и твердо засело в душе.

This new feeling has not changed me, has not made me happy and enlightened me all of a sudden, as I dreamed it would ... This feeling has crept up just as imperceptibly into my heart and has lodged itself firmly there.

Anna Karenina (1875–7) pt. 8, ch. 9 (translated by Rosemary Edmonds)

9 жизнь моя теперь, вся моя жизнь, независимо от всего, что может случиться со мной, каждая минута ее — не только не бессмысленна, как была прежде, но имеет несомненный смысл добра, который я властен вложить в нее!

My life now, my whole life, independently of anything that can happen to me, every minute of it is no longer meaningless as it was before, but has a positive meaning of goodness with which I have the power to invest it.

Anna Karenina (1875–7) pt. 8, ch. 19 (translated by Rosemary Edmonds)

10 Герой же моей повести, которого я люблю всеми силами души, которого старался воспроизвести во всей красоте его и который всегда был, есть и будет прекрасен — правда.

The hero of my tale—whom I love with all the power of my soul, whom I have tried to portray in all his beauty, who has been, is, and will be beautiful—is Truth.

Sevastopol in May (1855) ch. 16 (translated by A. and L. Maude)

11 В исторических событиях так называемые великие люди суть ярлыки, дающие наименование событию, которые, так же как ярлыки, менее всего имеют связы с самым событием.

In historical events great men—so-called—are but labels serving to give a name to the event, and like labels they have the least possible connexion with the event itself.

War and Peace (1868–9) bk. 3, pt. 1, ch. 1 (translated by Rosemary Edmonds)

12 Дубина народной войны поднялась со всей грозной и величественной силой и, не спрашивая ничьих вкусов и правил, с глупой простотой, но с целесообразностью, не разбирая ничего, поднималась, опускалась.

The cudgel of the people's war was lifted with all its menacing and majestic might, and caring nothing for good taste and procedure, with dull-witted simplicity but sound judgement it rose and fell, making no distinctions.

War and Peace (1868–9) bk. 4, pt. 3, ch. 1 (translated by Rosemary Edmonds)

1 *Notre corps est une machine à vivre. Il est organisé pour cela, c'est sa nature; laissez-y la vie à son aise, qu'elle s'y défende elle-même: elle fera plus que si vous la paralysiez en l'encombrant de remèdes.*

Our body is a machine for living. It is organized for that, it is its nature. Let life go on in it unhindered and let it defend itself, it will do more than if you paralyse it by encumbering it with remedies.

   War and Peace (1865–9) bk. 10, ch. 29 (translated by A. and L. Maude). Cf. Le Corbusier 415:12

2 Я сижу на шее у человека, задавил его и требую, чтобы он вез меня, и, не слезая с него, уверяю себя и других, что я очень жалею и хочу облегчить его положение всеми возможными средствами, но только не тем, чтобы слезть с него.

I sit on a man's back, choking him and making him carry me, and yet assure myself and others that I am very sorry for him and wish to ease his lot by all possible means—except by getting off his back.

   What Then Must We Do? (1886) ch. 16 (translated by A. Maude)

3 All newspaper and journalistic activity is an intellectual brothel from which there is no retreat.

   Letter to Prince V. P. Meshchersky, 22 August 1871, in *Letters* (ed. R. F. Christian, 1978) vol. 1

Augustus Montague Toplady 1740–78
English clergyman

4 Rock of Ages, cleft for me,
Let me hide myself in Thee;
Let the water and the blood,
From Thy riven side which flowed,
Be of sin the double cure,
Cleanse me from its guilt and power.

   'Rock of Ages, cleft for me' (1776 hymn)

Robert Torrens 1780–1864
British economist

5 In the first stone which he [the savage] flings at the wild animals he pursues, in the first stick that he seizes to strike down the fruit which hangs above his reach, we see the appropriation of one article for the purpose of aiding in the acquisition of another, and thus discover the origin of capital.

   An Essay on the Production of Wealth (1821) ch. 2

Cyril Tourneur
See THOMAS MIDDLETON

A. Toussenel
French writer

6 *Plus on apprend à connaître l'homme, plus on apprend à estimer le chien.*

The more one gets to know of men, the more one values dogs.

   L'Esprit des bêtes (1847) ch. 3 (attributed to Mme Roland in the form 'The more I see of men, the more I like dogs'. See *Notes and Queries* 9 September 1871, p. 188)

Pete Townshend 1945–
British rock musician and songwriter

7 Hope I die before I get old.

   'My Generation' (1965 song)

Thomas Traherne c.1637–74
English mystic

8 An empty book is like an infant's soul, in which anything may be written. It is capable of all things, but containeth nothing.

   Centuries of Meditations 'First Century' opening line

9 You never enjoy the world aright, till the sea itself floweth in your veins, till you are clothed with the heavens, and crowned with the stars: and perceive yourself to be the sole heir of the whole world.

   Centuries of Meditations 'First Century' sect. 29

10 Will you see the infancy of this sublime and celestial greatness?

   Centuries of Meditations 'Third Century' sect. 1

11 All appeared new, and strange at first, inexpressibly rare and delightful and beautiful. I was a little stranger, which at my entrance into the world was saluted and surrounded with innumerable joys. My knowledge was divine.

   Centuries of Meditations 'Third Century' sect. 2

12 All things were spotless and pure and glorious . . . I knew not that there were any sins or complaints or laws. I dreamed not of poverties, contentions or vices. All tears and quarrels were hidden from my eyes. Everything was at rest, free and immortal.

   Centuries of Meditations 'Third Century' sect. 2

13 The corn was orient and immortal wheat, which never should be reaped, nor was ever sown. I thought it had stood from everlasting to everlasting.

   Centuries of Meditations 'Third Century' sect. 3

14 The green trees when I saw them first . . . transported and ravished me, their sweetness and unusual beauty made my heart to leap and almost mad with ecstasy, they were such strange and wonderful things.

   Centuries of Meditations 'Third Century' sect. 3

15 O what venerable creatures did the aged seem! Immortal cherubims! And young men glittering and sparkling angels, and maids strange seraphic pieces of life and beauty! Boys and girls tumbling in the street, and playing, were moving jewels. I knew not that they were born or should die; but all things abided eternally.

   Centuries of Meditations 'Third Century' sect. 3

16 The hands are a sort of feet, which serve us in our passage towards Heaven, curiously distinguished into joints and fingers, and fit to be applied to any thing which reason can imagine or desire.

   Meditations on the Six Days of Creation (1717) 'Sixth Day'

17 Contentment is a sleepy thing
If it in death alone must die;
A quiet mind is worse than poverty,
Unless it from enjoyment spring!
That's blessedness alone that makes a king!

   'Of Contentment'

1 I within did flow
With seas of life, like wine.
I nothing in this world did know,
But 'twas divine!
'Wonder'

Henry Duff Traill 1842–1900

British journalist

2 Look in my face. My name is Used-to-was;
I am also called Played-out and Done-to-death,
And It-will-wash-no-more.
'After Dilettante Concetti' (i.e. Dante Gabriel Rossetti) st. 8.
Cf. Rossetti 548:5

Joseph Trapp 1679–1747

English poet and pamphleteer

3 The King, observing with judicious eyes
The state of both his universities,
To Oxford sent a troop of horse, and why?
That learned body wanted loyalty;
To Cambridge books, as very well discerning
How much that loyal body wanted learning.
Lines written on George I's donation of the Bishop of Ely's
Library to Cambridge University, in John Nichols *Literary
Anecdotes* (1812–16) vol. 3, p. 330. Cf. Browne
146:25

Merle Travis 1917–83

American country singer

4 Sixteen tons, what do you get?
Another day older and deeper in debt.
Say brother, don't you call me 'cause I can't go
I owe my soul to the company store.
'Sixteen Tons' (1947 song)

Sir Herbert Beerbohm Tree 1852–1917

English actor–manager

5 He is an old bore. Even the grave yawns for him.
Of Israel Zangwill, in Max Beerbohm *Herbert Beerbohm Tree*
(1920) appendix 4

6 My poor fellow, why not carry a watch?
To a man in the street, carrying a grandfather clock, in
Hesketh Pearson *Beerbohm Tree* (1956) ch. 12

7 Sirs, I have tested your machine. It adds a new terror
to life and makes death a long-felt want.
When pressed by a gramophone company for a written
testimonial, in Hesketh Pearson *Beerbohm Tree* (1956)
ch. 19 (when asked to amend the statement, Tree insisted
'the immortalism must stand'). Cf. Wetherell 729:22

8 Ladies, just a little more virginity, if you don't mind.
To a motley collection of females, assembled to play
ladies-in-waiting to a queen; in Alexander Woollcott *Shouts
and Murmurs* (1923) 'Capsule Criticism'

Herbert Trench 1865–1923

Irish-born poet and playwright

9 Come, let us make love deathless.
Title of poem (1901)

G. M. Trevelyan 1876–1962

English historian

10 Disinterested intellectual curiosity is the life-blood of
real civilization.
English Social History (1942) introduction

11 If the French noblesse had been capable of playing
cricket with their peasants, their chateaux would
never have been burnt.
English Social History (1942) ch. 8

12 It [education] has produced a vast population able to
read but unable to distinguish what is worth reading,
an easy prey to sensations and cheap appeals.
English Social History (1942) ch. 18

13 In a world of voluble hates, he plotted to make men
like, or at least tolerate one another.
Of Stanley Baldwin, in *Dictionary of National Biography
1941–50* (1959) p. 51

William Trevor (William Trevor Cox) 1928–

Anglo-Irish novelist and short story writer

14 A disease in the family that is never mentioned.
Of the troubles in Northern Ireland, in *Observer*
18 November 1990, p. 20

Calvin Trillin

15 The shelf life of the modern hardback writer is
somewhere between the milk and the yoghurt.
In *Sunday Times* 9 June 1991 (attributed)

Lionel Trilling 1905–75

American literary critic

16 We are all [neurotically] ill: but even a universal
sickness implies an idea of health . . . And if we are all
ill, we are ill by a universal accident, not by a
universal necessity, by a fault in the economy of our
powers, not by the nature of the powers themselves.
The Liberal Imagination (1950) 'Art and Neurosis'

17 It can be said that all prose fiction is a variation on
the theme of *Don Quixote* . . . the poverty of the Don
suggests that the novel is born with the appearance of
money as a social element—money, the great solvent
of the solid fabric of the old society, the great
generator of illusion. Or, which is to say much the
same thing, the novel is born in response to snobbery.
The Liberal Imagination (1950) 'Manners, Morals and the
Novel'

18 The educated classes are learning to blame ideas for
our troubles, rather than . . . our own bad thinking.
This is the great vice of academicism, that it is
concerned with ideas rather than with thinking, and
nowadays the errors of academicism . . . make their
way into the world, and what begins as a failure of
perception among intellectual specialists finds its
fulfilment in policy and action.
The Liberal Imagination (1950) 'The Sense of the Past'

Tommy Trinder 1909–89

British comedian

1 Overpaid, overfed, oversexed, and over here.
   Of American troops in Britain during the Second World
   War (associated with Trinder, but probably not his
   invention)

Anthony Trollope 1815–82

English novelist

2 He must have known me had he seen me as he was
   wont to see me, for he was in the habit of flogging me
   constantly. Perhaps he did not recognize me by my
   face.
   Autobiography (1883) ch. 1

3 Take away from English authors their copyrights, and
   you would very soon take away from England her
   authors.
   Autobiography (1883) ch. 6

4 It is admitted that a novel can hardly be made
   interesting or successful without love . . . It is
   necessary because the passion is one which interests
   or has interested all. Everyone feels it, has felt it, or
   expects to feel it.
   Autobiography (1883) ch. 12

5 Three hours a day will produce as much as a man
   ought to write.
   Autobiography (1883) ch. 15

6 I think that Plantagenet Palliser, Duke of Omnium, is
   a perfect gentleman. If he be not, then I am unable to
   describe a gentleman.
   Autobiography (1883) ch. 20

7 A man's mind will very generally refuse to make itself
   up until it be driven and compelled by emergency.
   Ayala's Angel (1881) ch. 41

8 She was rich in apparel, but not bedizened with finery
   . . . she well knew the great architectural secret of
   decorating her constructions, and never descended to
   construct a decoration.
   Barchester Towers (1857) ch. 9

9 Those who have courage to love should have courage
   to suffer.
   The Bertrams (1859) ch. 27

10 Mr Palliser was one of those politicians in possessing
   whom England has perhaps more reason to be proud
   than of any other of her resources, and who, as a
   body, give to her that requisite combination of
   conservatism and progress which is her present
   strength and best security for the future.
   Can You Forgive Her? (1864) ch. 24

11 How I did respect you when you dared to speak the
   truth to me! Men don't know women, or they would
   be harder to them.
   The Claverings (1867) ch. 15

12 There is no road to wealth so easy and respectable as
   that of matrimony.
   Doctor Thorne (1858) ch. 16

13 Let no man boast himself that he has got through the
   perils of winter till at least the seventh of May.
   Doctor Thorne (1858) ch. 47

14 We cannot have heroes to dine with us. There are
   none. And were those heroes to be had, we should not
   like them . . . the persons whom you cannot care for
   in a novel, because they are so bad, are the very same
   that you so dearly love in your life, because they are
   so good.
   The Eustace Diamonds (1873) ch. 35

15 For the most of us, if we do not talk of ourselves, or at
   any rate of the individual circles of which we are the
   centres, we can talk of nothing. I cannot hold with
   those who wish to put down the insignificant chatter
   of the world.
   Framley Parsonage (1860) ch. 10

16 They who do not understand that a man may be
   brought to hope that which of all things is the most
   grievous to him, have not observed with sufficient
   closeness the perversity of the human mind.
   He Knew He Was Right (1869) ch. 38

17 She understood how much louder a cock can crow in
   its own farmyard than elsewhere.
   The Last Chronicle of Barset (1867) ch. 17

18 It's dogged as does it. It ain't thinking about it.
   The Last Chronicle of Barset (1867) ch. 61 (Giles Hoggett)

19 With many women I doubt whether there be any
   more effectual way of touching their hearts than
   ill-using them and then confessing it. If you wish to
   get the sweetest fragrance from the herb at your feet,
   tread on it and bruise it.
   Miss Mackenzie (1865) ch. 10

20 We cannot bring ourselves to believe it possible that a
   foreigner should in any respect be wiser than
   ourselves. If any such point out to us our follies, we at
   once claim those follies as the special evidences of our
   wisdom.
   Orley Farm (1862) ch. 18

21 It is because we put up with bad things that
   hotel-keepers continue to give them to us.
   Orley Farm (1862) ch. 18

22 As for conceit, what man will do any good who is not
   conceited? Nobody holds a good opinion of a man
   who has a low opinion of himself.
   Orley Farm (1862) ch. 22

23 A fainéant government is not the worst government
   that England can have. It has been the great fault of
   our politicians that they have all wanted to do
   something.
   Phineas Finn (1869) ch. 13

24 Mr Turnbull had predicted evil consequences . . . and
   was now doing the best in his power to bring about
   the verification of his own prophecies.
   Phineas Finn (1869) ch. 25

25 Perhaps there is no position more perilous to a man's
   honesty than that . . . of knowing himself to be quite
   loved by a girl whom he almost loves himself.
   Phineas Finn (1869) ch. 50

26 She knew how to allure by denying, and to make the
   gift rich by delaying it.
   Phineas Finn (1869) ch. 57

1 What man thinks of changing himself so as to suit his wife? And yet men expect that women shall put on altogether new characters when they are married, and girls think that they can do so.
  Phineas Redux (1874) ch. 3

2 It is the necessary nature of a political party in this country to avoid, as long as it can be avoided, the consideration of any question which involves a great change ... The best carriage horses are those which can most steadily hold back against the coach as it trundles down the hill.
  Phineas Redux (1874) ch. 4

3 Equality would be a heaven, if we could attain it.
  The Prime Minister (1876) ch. 68

4 To think of one's absent love is very sweet; but it becomes monotonous ... I doubt whether any girl would be satisfied with her lover's mind if she knew the whole of it.
  The Small House at Allington (1864) ch. 4

5 Why is it that girls so constantly do this,—so frequently ask men who have loved them to be present at their marriages with other men? There is no triumph in it. It is done in sheer kindness and affection. They intend to offer something which shall soften and not aggravate the sorrow that they have caused ... I fully appreciate the intention, but in honest truth, I doubt the eligibility of the proffered entertainment.
  The Small House at Allington (1864) ch. 9

6 It may almost be a question whether such wisdom as many of us have in our mature years has not come from the dying out of the power of temptation, rather than as the results of thought and resolution.
  The Small House at Allington (1864) ch. 14

7 Never think that you're not good enough yourself. A man should never think that. My belief is that in life people will take you very much at your own reckoning.
  The Small House at Allington (1864) ch. 32

8 The tenth Muse, who now governs the periodical press.
  The Warden (1855) ch. 14

9 Is it not singular how some men continue to obtain the reputation of popular authorship without adding a word to the literature of their country worthy of note? ... To puff and to get one's self puffed have become different branches of a new profession.
  The Way We Live Now (1875) ch. 1

10 Love is like any other luxury. You have no right to it unless you can afford it.
  The Way We Live Now (1875) ch. 84

Leon Trotsky (*Lev Davidovich Bronstein*) 1879–1940

Russian revolutionary

11 Old age is the most unexpected of all things that happen to a man.
  Diary in Exile (1959) 8 May 1935

12 Civilization has made the peasantry its pack animal. The bourgeoisie in the long run only changed the form of the pack.
  History of the Russian Revolution (1933) vol. 3, ch. 1

13 You [the Mensheviks] are pitiful isolated individuals; you are bankrupts; your role is played out. Go where you belong from now on — into the dustbin of history!
  History of the Russian Revolution (1933) vol. 3, ch. 10

14 Where force is necessary, there it must be applied boldly, decisively and completely. But one must know the limitations of force; one must know when to blend force with a manoeuvre, a blow with an agreement.
  What Next? (1932) ch. 14

Harry S. Truman 1884–1972

33rd President of the USA

15 All the President is, is a glorified public relations man who spends his time flattering, kissing and kicking people to get them to do what they are supposed to do anyway.
  Letter to his sister, 14 November 1947, in *Off the Record* (1980)

16 Wherever you have an efficient government you have a dictatorship.
  Lecture at Columbia University, 28 April 1959, in *Truman Speaks* (1960) p. 51

17 I never give them [the public] hell. I just tell the truth, and they think it is hell.
  In *Look* 3 April 1956

18 A politician is a man who understands government, and it takes a politician to run a government. A statesman is a politician who's been dead 10 or 15 years.
  In *New York World Telegram and Sun* 12 April 1958

19 It's a recession when your neighbour loses his job; it's a depression when you lose yours.
  In *Observer* 13 April 1958

20 I didn't fire him [General MacArthur] because he was a dumb son of a bitch, although he was, but that's not against the law for generals. If it was, half to three-quarters of them would be in jail.
  In Merle Miller *Plain Speaking* (1974) ch. 24

21 The buck stops here.
  Unattributed motto on Truman's desk

22 Always be sincere, even if you don't mean it.
  Attributed

Barbara W. Tuchman 1912–89

American writer

23 Dead battles, like dead generals, hold the military mind in their dead grip and Germans, no less than other peoples, prepare for the last war.
  August 1914 (1962) ch. 2

24 No more distressing moment can ever face a British government than that which requires it to come to a hard, fast and specific decision.
  August 1914 (1962) ch. 9

1 For one August in its history Paris was French—and silent.

August 1914 (1962) ch. 20

Sophie Tucker (*Sophia Abuza*)
1884–1966
Russian-born American vaudeville artiste

2 From birth to 18 a girl needs good parents. From 18 to 35, she needs good looks. From 35 to 55, good personality. From 55 on, she needs good cash.

In Michael Freedland *Sophie* (1978) p. 214

Martin Tupper 1810–89
English writer

3 A good book is the best of friends, the same to-day and for ever.

Proverbial Philosophy Series I (1838) 'Of Reading'

Ivan Turgenev 1818–23
Russian novelist

4 Лишний, лишний . . . Сверхштатный человек — вот и всё. На мое появление природа, очевидно, не рассчитывала и вследствие этого обошлась со мной, как с нежданным и незваным гостем.

Superfluous, superfluous . . . A supernumerary—that's all. Nature, obviously, hadn't counted on my showing up and consequently treated me as an unexpected and uninvited guest.

Diary of a Superfluous Man (1850) 23 March (translated by Franklin Reeve)

5 Природа не храм, а мастерская, и человек в ней работник.

Nature is not a temple, but a workshop, and man's the workman in it.

Fathers and Sons (1862) ch. 9 (translated by Rosemary Edmonds)

6 Я ничьих мнений не разделяю; я имею свои.

I share no one's ideas. I have my own.

Fathers and Sons (1862) ch. 13 (translated by Rosemary Edmonds)

7 Ваш брат, дворянин, дальше благородного смирения или благородного кипения дойти не может.

Your sort, the gentry, can never go farther than well-bred resignation or well-bred indignation.

Fathers and Sons (1862) ch. 26 (translated by Rosemary Edmonds)

8 Пойди, попробуй отрицать смерть. Она тебя отрицает, и баста!

Just try and set death aside. It sets you aside, and that's the end of it!

Fathers and Sons (1862) ch. 27 (translated by Rosemary Edmonds)

9 Сколько ты ни стучись природе в дверь, не отзовется она понятным словом, потому, что она немая. Будет звучать и ныть, как струна, а песни от нее не жди.

No matter how often you knock at nature's door, she won't answer in words you can understand—for Nature is dumb. She'll vibrate and moan like a violin, but you mustn't expect a song.

On the Eve (1860) ch. 1 (translated by Gilbert Gardiner)

10 Смерть, как рыбак, который поймал рыбу в свою сеть и оставляет ее на время в воде: рыба еще плавает, но сеть на ней, и рыбак выхватит ее — когда захочет.

Death is like a fisherman, who, having caught a fish in his net, leaves it in the water for a time; the fish continues to swim about, but all the while the net is round it, and the fisherman will snatch it out in his own good time.

On the Eve (1860) ch. 35 (translated by Gilbert Gardiner)

11 О чём бы не молился человек — он молится о чуде. — Всякая молитва сводится на следующую: «Великий боже, сделай, чтобы дважды два не было четыре.»

Whatever a man prays for, he prays for a miracle. Every prayer reduces itself to this: Great God, grant that twice two be not four.

Poems in Prose (1881) 'Prayer'

12 Непонятными остаются только те люди, которые либо еще сами не знают, чего хотят, либо не стоят того, чтобы их понимали.

The only people who remain misunderstood are those who either do not know what they want or are not worth understanding.

Rudin (1856) ch. 5 (translated by Richard Freeborn)

A. R. J. Turgot 1727–81
French economist and statesman

13 *Eripuit coelo fulmen, sceptrumque tyrannis.*

He snatched the lightning shaft from heaven, and the sceptre from tyrants.

Inscription for a bust of Benjamin Franklin, inventor of the lightning conductor. Cf. Manilius 444:8

Thomas Turner 1729–93
English diarist

14 Our diversion was dancing (or jumping about) without a violin or any music, singing of foolish and bawdy healths and more such-like stupidity, and drinking all the time as fast as could be poured down; and the parson of the parish was one amongst the mixed multitude, all the time.

Diary (ed. D. Vaisey, 1984) 22 February 1758

Walter James Redfern Turner 1889–1946
British writer and critic

15 When I was but thirteen or so
I went into a golden land,
Chimborazo, Cotopaxi
Took me by the hand.

'Romance' (1916)

Mark Twain (*Samuel Langhorne Clemens*)
1835–1910

American writer

1 There was things which he stretched, but mainly he told the truth.
The Adventures of Huckleberry Finn (1884) ch. 1

2 'Pilgrim's Progress', about a man that left his family it didn't say why ... The statements was interesting, but tough.
The Adventures of Huckleberry Finn (1884) ch. 17

3 All kings is mostly rapscallions.
The Adventures of Huckleberry Finn (1884) ch. 23

4 Hain't we got all the fools in town on our side? and ain't that a big enough majority in any town?
The Adventures of Huckleberry Finn (1884) ch. 26

5 Soap and education are not as sudden as a massacre, but they are more deadly in the long run.
A Curious Dream (1872) 'Facts concerning the Recent Resignation'

6 Barring that natural expression of villainy which we all have, the man looked honest enough.
A Curious Dream (1872) 'A Mysterious Visit'

7 Truth is the most valuable thing we have. Let us economize it.
Following the Equator (1897) ch. 7. Cf. Armstrong 26:13

8 It is by the goodness of God that in our country we have those three unspeakably precious things: freedom of speech, freedom of conscience, and the prudence never to practise either of them.
Following the Equator (1897) ch. 20

9 Man is the Only Animal that Blushes. Or needs to.
Following the Equator (1897) ch. 27

10 There are several good protections against temptations, but the surest is cowardice.
Following the Equator (1897) ch. 36

11 It takes your enemy and your friend, working together, to hurt you to the heart: the one to slander you and the other to get the news to you.
Following the Equator (1897) ch. 45

12 They spell it Vinci and pronounce it Vinchy; foreigners always spell better than they pronounce.
The Innocents Abroad (1869) ch. 19

13 Lump the whole thing! say that the Creator made Italy from designs by Michael Angelo!
The Innocents Abroad (1869) ch. 27. Cf. Ustinov 707:15

14 If you've got a nice *fresh* corpse, fetch him out!
The Innocents Abroad (1869) ch. 27

15 What a good thing Adam had. When he said a good thing he knew nobody had said it before.
Notebooks (1935) p. 67

16 Familiarity breeds contempt—and children.
Notebooks (1935) p. 237

17 Good breeding consists in concealing how much we think of ourselves and how little we think of the other person.
Notebooks (1935) p. 345

18 Adam was but human—this explains it all. He did not want the apple for the apple's sake; he wanted it only because it was forbidden.
Pudd'nhead Wilson (1894) ch. 2

19 Whoever has lived long enough to find out what life is, knows how deep a debt of gratitude we owe to Adam, the first great benefactor of our race. He brought death into the world.
Pudd'nhead Wilson (1894) ch. 3

20 Cauliflower is nothing but cabbage with a college education.
Pudd'nhead Wilson (1894) ch. 5

21 When angry, count four; when very angry, swear.
Pudd'nhead Wilson (1894) ch. 10

22 As to the Adjective: when in doubt, strike it out.
Pudd'nhead Wilson (1894) ch. 11

23 Few things are harder to put up with than the annoyance of a good example.
Pudd'nhead Wilson (1894) ch. 19

24 There is a sumptuous variety about the New England weather that compels the stranger's admiration—and regret. The weather is always doing something there; always attending strictly to business; always getting up new designs and trying them on the people to see how they will go.
Speech to New England Society, 22 December 1876, in *Speeches* (1910)

25 The report of my death was an exaggeration.
New York Journal 2 June 1897 (usually quoted 'Reports of my death have been greatly exaggerated')

26 At bottom he was probably fond of them [Americans], but he was always able to conceal it.
Of Thomas Carlyle, in *New York World* 10 December 1899 'Mark Twain's Christmas Book'

27 All you need in this life is ignorance and confidence; then success is sure.
Letter to Mrs Foote, 2 December 1887, in B. DeCasseres *When Huck Finn Went Highbrow* (1934)

Kenneth Tynan 1927–80

English theatre critic

28 Forty years ago he was Slightly in *Peter Pan*, and you might say that he has been wholly in *Peter Pan* ever since.
Curtains (1961) pt. 1, p. 59 (of Noel Coward)

29 He walks top-heavily, like a salmon standing on its tail.
Profiles (ed. Kathleen Tynan, 1989) 'Charles Laughton'

30 Drama criticism ... [is] a self-knowing account of the way in which one's consciousness has been modified during an evening in the theatre.
Tynan Right and Left (1967) foreword

31 A critic is a man who knows the way but can't drive the car.
In *New York Times Magazine* 9 January 1966, p. 27

32 A neurosis is a secret you don't know you're keeping.
In Kathleen Tynan *Life of Kenneth Tynan* (1987) ch. 19

33 There, standing at the piano, was the original good time who had been had by all.
At an Oxford Union Debate, while an undergraduate (attributed)

Ulpian (*Domitius Ulpianus*) d. 228

Roman jurist

1 *Nulla iniuria est, quae in volentem fiat.*
No injustice is done to someone who wants that thing done.
> In *Corpus Iuris Civilis* Digests bk. 47, ch. 10, sect. 1, subsect. 5 (usually quoted '*Volenti non fit iniuria*')

Miguel de Unamuno 1864–1937

Spanish philosopher and writer

2 *La vida es duda,*
y la fe sin la duda es sólo muerte.
Life is doubt,
And faith without doubt is nothing but death.
> *Poesías* (1907) 'Salmo II'

3 *Cúrate de la afección de preocuparte cómo apareces a los demás. Cuídate sólo de cómo apareces a Dios, cuídate de la idea que de ti Dios tenga.*
Cure yourself of the condition of bothering about how you look to other people. Concern yourself only with how you appear to God, with the idea that God has of you.
> *Vida de Don Quixote y Sancho* (1905) pt. 1

John Updike 1932–

American novelist and short-story writer

4 A healthy male adult bore consumes *each year* one and a half times his own weight in other people's patience.
> *Assorted Prose* (1965) 'Confessions of a Wild Bore'

5 The heart *prefers* to move against the grain of circumstance; perversity is the soul's very life.
> *Assorted Prose* (1965) 'More Love in the Western World'

6 A soggy little island huffing and puffing to keep up with Western Europe.
> Of England, in *Picked Up Pieces* (1976) 'London Life' (written 1969)

7 America is a land whose centre is nowhere; England one whose centre is everywhere.
> *Picked Up Pieces* (1976) 'London Life' (written 1969)

8 America is a vast conspiracy to make you happy.
> *Problems* (1980) 'How to love America and Leave it at the Same Time'

9 The artist brings something into the world that didn't exist before, and . . . he does it without destroying something else.
> In George Plimpton (ed.) *Writers at Work* (4th series, 1977) ch. 16

James Ussher 1581–1656

Irish prelate and scholar

10 Which beginning of time according to our Chronology, fell upon the entrance of the night preceding the twenty third day of Octob. in the year of the Julian Calendar, 710 [i.e. 4004 BC].
> *The Annals of the World* (1658) pt. 1 (on the Creation)

Sir Peter Ustinov 1921–

Russian-born actor, director, and writer

11 Laughter . . . the most civilized music in the world.
> *Dear Me* (1977) ch. 3

12 I do not believe that friends are necessarily the people you like best, they are merely the people who got there first.
> *Dear Me* (1977) ch. 5. Cf. Adams 2:7

13 I sometimes wished he would realize that he was poor instead of being that most nerve-racking of phenomena, a rich man without money.
> *Dear Me* (1977) ch. 6

14 Laughter would be bereaved if snobbery died.
> In *Observer* 13 March 1955

15 If Botticelli were alive today he'd be working for *Vogue*
> In *Observer* 21 October 1962 'Sayings of the Week'. Cf. Twain 706:13

16 At the age of four with paper hats and wooden swords we're all Generals. Only some of us never grow out of it.
> *Romanoff and Juliet* (1956) act 1

17 A diplomat these days is nothing but a head-waiter who's allowed to sit down occasionally.
> *Romanoff and Juliet* (1956) act 1

18 This is a free country, madam. We have a right to share your privacy in a public place.
> *Romanoff and Juliet* (1956) act 1

19 Talk as though you have a cathedral in your mouth.
> On imitating Harold Macmillan (attributed)

Paul Valéry 1871–1945

French poet, critic, and man of letters

20 *Un poème n'est jamais achevé — c'est toujours un accident qui le termine, c'est-à-dire qui le donne au public.*
A poem is never finished; it's always an accident that puts a stop to it—that is to say, gives it to the public.
> *Littérature* (1930) p. 46

21 *Il faut n'appeler Science que l'ensemble des recettes qui réussissent toujours. — Tout le reste est littérature.*
Science means simply the aggregate of all the recipes that are always successful. The rest is literature.
> *Moralités* (1932) p. 41. Cf. Verlaine 710:3

22 *Dieu créa l'homme, et ne le trouvant pas assez seul, il lui donne une compagne pour lui faire mieux sentir sa solitude.*
God created man and, finding him not sufficiently alone, gave him a companion to make him feel his solitude more keenly.
> *Tel Quel 1* (1941) 'Moralités'

23 *La politique est l'art d'empêcher les gens de se mêler de ce qui les regarde.*
Politics is the art of preventing people from taking part in affairs which properly concern them
> *Tel Quel 2* (1943) 'Rhumbs'

Sir John Vanbrugh 1664–1726

English architect and playwright

1 Much of a muchness.
   The Provoked Husband (1728) act 1, sc. 1

2 BELINDA: Ay, but you know we must return good for evil.
   LADY BRUTE: That may be a mistake in the translation.
   The Provoked Wife (1697) act 1, sc. 1

3 You men are unaccountable things; mad till you have your mistresses, and then stark mad till you are rid of 'em again.
   The Provoked Wife (1697) act 4, sc. 4

4 LADY BRUTE: 'Tis a hard fate I should not be believed.
   SIR JOHN: 'Tis a damned atheistical age, wife.
   The Provoked Wife (1697) act 5, sc. 2

5 Thinking is to me the greatest fatigue in the world.
   The Relapse (1696) act 2, sc. 1

6 When once a woman has given you her heart, you can never get rid of the rest of her body.
   The Relapse (1696) act 3, sc. 1

7 In matters of love men's eyes are always bigger than their bellies. They have violent appetites, 'tis true; but they have soon dined.
   The Relapse (1696) act 5, sc. 2

Vivian van Damm *c.*1889–1960

British theatre manager

8 We never closed.
   On the Windmill Theatre, London, during the Second World War; in *Tonight and Every Night* (1952) ch. 18

William Henry Vanderbilt 1821–85

American railway magnate

9 The public be damned!
   On whether the public should be consulted about luxury trains, in a letter from A. W. Cole to *New York Times* 25 August 1918

Bartolomeo Vanzetti 1888–1927

American anarchist, born in Italy

10 Sacco's name will live in the hearts of the people and in their gratitude when Katzmann's and yours bones will be dispersed by time, when your name, his name, your laws, institutions, and your false god are but a deem rememoring of a cursed past in which man was wolf to the man.
   Statement disallowed at his trial, with Nicola Sacco, for murder and robbery, in M. D. Frankfurter and G. Jackson *Letters of Sacco and Vanzetti* (1928) p. 380. Both were sentenced to death on 9 April 1927, and executed on 23 August 1927

11 If it had not been for these thing, I might have live out my life talking at street corners to scorning men. I might have die, unmarked, unknown, a failure. Now we are not a failure. This is our career and our triumph. Never in our full life could we hope to do such work for tolerance, for joostice, for man's onderstanding of man as now we do by accident.
   Statement after being sentenced to death, in M. D. Frankfurter and G. Jackson *Letters of Sacco and Vanzetti* (1928) preface

Charles John Vaughan 1816–97

English divine; headmaster of Harrow School, 1844–59

12 Must you go? Can't you stay?
   Formula for breaking up breakfast parties of schoolboys too shy to make a move; retold 'Can't you go? Must you stay?' in G. W. E. Russell *Collections and Recollections* (1898) ch. 24

Harry Vaughan

13 If you can't stand the heat, get out of the kitchen.
   In *Time* 28 April 1952 (associated with Harry S. Truman, but attributed by him to Vaughan, his 'military jester')

Henry Vaughan 1622–95

English poet

14 Man is the shuttle, to whose winding quest
   And passage through these looms
   God ordered motion, but ordained no rest.
   Silex Scintillans (1650–5) 'Man'

15 Wise Nicodemus saw such light
   As made him know his God by night.

   Most blest believer he!
   Who in that land of darkness and blind eyes
   Thy long expected healing wings could see
   When Thou didst rise!
   And, what can never more be done,
   Did at midnight speak with the Sun!
   Silex Scintillans (1650–5) 'The Night'

16 Dear Night! this world's defeat;
   The stop to busy fools; care's check and curb;
   The day of spirits; my soul's calm retreat
   Which none disturb!
   Silex Scintillans (1650–5) 'The Night'

17 My soul, there is a country
   Far beyond the stars,
   Where stands a wingèd sentry
   All skilful in the wars;
   There, above noise and danger,
   Sweet Peace is crowned with smiles,
   And One born in a manger
   Commands the beauteous files.
   Silex Scintillans (1650–5) 'Peace'

1 Happy those early days, when I
Shined in my angel-infancy.
Before I understood this place
Appointed for my second race,
Or taught my soul to fancy aught
But a white, celestial thought;
When yet I had not walked above
A mile or two from my first love,
And looking back—at that short space—
Could see a glimpse of His bright face.
Silex Scintillans (1650-5) 'The Retreat'

2 And in those weaker glories spy
Some shadows of eternity.
Silex Scintillans (1650-5) 'The Retreat'

3 But felt through all this fleshly dress
Bright shoots of everlastingness.
Silex Scintillans (1650 5) 'The Retreat'

4 Some men a forward motion love,
But I by backward steps would move,
And when this dust falls to the urn,
In that state I came, return.
Silex Scintillans (1650-5) 'The Retreat'

5 They are all gone into the world of light,
And I alone sit lingering here;
Their very memory is fair and bright,
And my sad thoughts doth clear.
Silex Scintillans (1650-5) 'They are all gone'

6 I see them walking in an air of glory,
Whose light doth trample on my days:
My days, which are at best but dull and hoary,
Mere glimmering and decays.
Silex Scintillans (1650-5) 'They are all gone'

7 Dear, beauteous death! the jewel of the just,
Shining nowhere but in the dark;
What mysteries do lie beyond thy dust,
Could man outlook that mark!
Silex Scintillans (1650-5) 'They are all gone'

8 And yet, as angels in some brighter dreams
Call to the soul when man doth sleep,
So some strange thoughts transcend our wonted themes,
And into glory peep.
Silex Scintillans (1650-5) 'They are all gone'

9 If a star were confined into a tomb
Her captive flames must needs burn there;
But when the hand that locked her up gives room,
She'll shine through all the sphere.
Silex Scintillans (1650-5) 'They are all gone'

10 Sure thou didst flourish once! and many springs,
Many bright mornings, much dew, many showers
Passed o'er thy head; many light hearts and wings
Which now are dead, lodged in thy living bowers.
Silex Scintillans (1650-5) 'The Timber'

11 I saw Eternity the other night,
Like a great ring of pure and endless light,
All calm, as it was bright;
And round beneath it, Time in hours, days, years,
Driv'n by the spheres
Like a vast shadow moved; in which the world
And all her train were hurled.
Silex Scintillans (1650-5) 'The World'

Thomas, Lord Vaux
(2nd Baron Vaux of Harrowden)
1510–56

English writer and courtier

12 My lusts they do me leave,
My fancies all be fled,
And tract of time begins to weave
Grey hairs upon my head.

For age with stealing steps
Hath clawed me with his clutch,
And lusty life away she leaps,
As there had been none such.
'The Aged Lover Renounceth Love' (1557); a garbled
version is sung by the gravedigger in *Hamlet* (1601) act 5,
sc. 1

13 When all is done and said, in the end thus shall you find,
He most of all doth bathe in bliss that hath a quiet mind;
And, clear from worldly cares, to deem can be content
The sweetest time in all his life in thinking to be spent.
'The Pleasures of Thinking' (1576)

Thorstein Veblen 1857–1929

American economist and social scientist

14 Conspicuous consumption of valuable goods is
a means of reputability to the gentleman of leisure.
Theory of the Leisure Class (1899) ch. 4

15 From the foregoing survey of conspicuous leisure and
consumption, it appears that the utility of both alike
for the purposes of reputability lies in the element of
waste that is common to both. In the one case it is a
waste of time and effort, in the other it is a waste of
goods.
Theory of the Leisure Class (1899) ch. 4

16 It is also a matter of common notoriety and byword
that in offences which result in a large accession of
property to the offender he does not ordinarily incur
the extreme penalty or the extreme obloquy with
which his offences would be visited on the ground of
the naïve moral code alone. The thief or swindler who
has gained great wealth by his delinquency has a
better chance than the small thief of escaping the
rigorous penalty of the law.
Theory of the Leisure Class (1899) ch. 6

17 The requirement of conspicuous wastefulness is not
commonly present, consciously, in our canons of taste,
but it is none the less present as a constraining norm,
selectively shaping and sustaining our sense of what is
beautiful, and guiding our discrimination with respect
to what may legitimately be approved as beautiful and
what may not.
Theory of the Leisure Class (1899) ch. 6

Vegetius (Flavius Vegetius Renatus)
AD 379–95

Roman military writer

1 *Qui desiderat pacem, praeparet bellum.*

Let him who desires peace, prepare for war.
> *Epitoma Rei Militaris* bk. 3, prologue (usually quoted '*Si vis pacem, para bellum* [If you want peace, prepare for war]').
> Cf. Anonymous 14:1, Aristotle 25:10

Pierre Verynlaud 1753–93
French revolutionary; executed with other Girondists

2 *Il a été permis de craindre que la Révolution, comme Saturne, dévorât successivement tous ses enfants.*

There was reason to fear that the Revolution, like Saturn, might devour in turn each one of her children.
> In Alphonse de Lamartine *Histoire des Girondins* (1847) bk. 38, ch. 20

Paul Verlaine 1844–96
French poet

3 *Et tout le reste est littérature.*

All the rest is mere fine writing.
> 'Art poétique' (1882). Cf. Valéry 707:21

4 *Les sanglots longs*
Des violons
De l'automne
Blessent mon cœur
D'une langueur
Monotone.

The drawn-out sobs of autumn's violins wound my heart with a monotonous languor.
> 'Chanson d'Automne' (1866)

5 *Et, Ô ces voix d'enfants chantants dans la coupole!*

And oh those children's voices, singing beneath the dome!
> 'Parsifal' A Jules Tellier (1886)

6 *Il pleure dans mon coeur*
Comme il pleut sur la ville.

Tears are shed in my heart like the rain on the town.
> *Romances sans paroles* (1874) 'Ariettes oubliées' no. 3

René Aubert, Abbé de Vertot 1655–1735
French historian

7 *Mon siège est fait.*

My siege is over.
> On receiving long-awaited documents for his history of the siege of Rhodes when it had already been completed; in J. Le Rond d'Alembert *Oeuvres* (1821 ed.) vol. 2, pt. 1, p. 5

Hendrik Frensch Verwoerd 1901–66
South African politician; Prime Minister from 1958

8 Up till now he [the Bantu] has been subjected to a school system which drew him away from his own community and practically misled him by showing him the green pastures of the European but still did not allow him to graze there . . . It is abundantly clear that unplanned education creates many problems, disrupts the communal life of the Bantu and endangers the communal life of the European.
> Speech in Senate, *Hansard* (South Africa) 7 June 1954, col. 2619

Vespasian (Titus Flavius Vespasianus)
AD 9–79

Roman emperor from AD 69

9 *Pecunia non olet.*

Money has no smell.
> Traditional summary of Suetonius *Lives of the Caesars* 'Vespasian' sect. 23, subsect. 3 (Vespasian replying to Titus's objection to his tax on public lavatories; holding a coin to Titus's nose and being told it didn't smell, he replied, '*Atque e lotio est* [Yes, that's made from urine]')

10 *Vae, puto deus fio.*

Woe is me, I think I am becoming a god.
> When fatally ill, in Suetonius *Lives of the Caesars* 'Vespasian' sect. 23, subsect. 4

Queen Victoria 1819–1901
Queen of the United Kingdom from 1837

11 The danger to the country, to Europe, to her vast Empire, which is involved in having all these great interests entrusted to the shaking hand of an old, wild, and incomprehensible man of 82, is very great!
> On Gladstone's last appointment as Prime Minister; letter to Lord Lansdowne, 12 August 1892, in T. Wodehouse Legh *Lord Lansdowne* (1929) p. 100

12 The future Vice Roy must . . . not be guided by the *snobbish* and vulgar, over-bearing and offensive behaviour of our Civil and Political Agents, if we are to go on peaceably and happily in India . . . not trying to trample on the people and continuously reminding them and making them feel they are a conquered people.
> Letter to Lord Salisbury, 27 May 1898, in Kenneth Rose *Superior Person* (1969) ch. 23

13 We are not interested in the possibilities of defeat; they do not exist.
> On the Boer War during 'Black Week', December 1899; in Lady Gwendolen Cecil *Life of Robert, Marquis of Salisbury* (1931) vol. 3, ch. 6

14 We are not amused.
> Attributed, in Caroline Holland *Notebooks of a Spinster Lady* (1919) ch. 21, 2 January 1900

15 I will be good.
> On being shown a chart of the line of succession, 11 March 1830; in Sir Theodore Martin *The Prince Consort* (1875) vol. 1, ch. 2

16 He speaks to Me as if I was a public meeting.
> Of Gladstone, in G. W. E. Russell *Collections and Recollections* (1898) ch. 14

1 Dirty, dark, and undevotional.

> Of St Paul's Cathedral, where a service of Thanksgiving had been held, following the recovery of the Prince of Wales from typhoid fever; attributed in this form, but recorded in her Journal, 27 February 1872, as 'so cold, dreary and dingy. It so badly lacks decoration and colour.' See G. E. Buckle (ed.) *Letters of Queen Victoria: 2nd Series* vol. 2 (1870–78) p. 195

Gore Vidal 1925–
American novelist and critic

2 [Commercialism is] doing well that which should not be done at all.

> In *Listener* 7 August 1975, p. 168

3 A triumph of the embalmer's art.

> Of Ronald Reagan, in *Observer* 26 April 1981

4 I'm all for bringing back the birch, but only between consenting adults.

> In *Sunday Times Magazine* 16 September 1973

5 Whenever a friend succeeds, a little something in me dies.

> In *Sunday Times Magazine* 16 September 1973

6 [On being asked what would have happened in 1963, had Khrushchev and not Kennedy been assassinated] With history one can never be certain, but I think I can safely say that Aristotle Onassis would not have married Mrs Khrushchev.

> In *Sunday Times* 4 June 1989, G2

7 He will lie even when it is inconvenient: the sign of the true artist.

> Attributed

King Vidor 1895–1982
American film director

8 Marriage isn't a word ... it's a *sentence*!

> *The Crowd* (1928 film)

José Antonio Viera Gallo 1943–
Chilean politician

9 El socialismo puede llegar solo en bicicleta.

> Socialism can only arrive by bicycle.
>
> In Ivan Illich *Energy and Equity* (1974) epigraph

Alfred de Vigny 1797–1863
French poet

10 J'aime le son du cor, le soir, au fond des bois.

> I love the sound of the horn, at night, in the depth of the woods.
>
> 'Le Cor' (1826)

11 J'aime la majesté des souffrances humaines.

> I love the majesty of human suffering
>
> La Maison du Berger (1844)

12 Seul le silence est grand; tout le reste est faiblesse ...
Fais énergiquement ta longue et lourde tâche ...
Puis, après, comme moi, souffre et meurs sans parler.

> Silence alone is great; all else is feebleness ... perform with all your heart your long and heavy task ... then as do I, say naught, but suffer and die.
>
> 'La mort du loup' (1843) pt. 3

Philippe-Auguste Villiers de L'Isle-Adam 1838–89
French writer

13 Vivre? les serviteurs feront cela pour nous.

> Living? The servants will do that for us.
>
> *Axël* (1890) pt. 4, sect. 2

François Villon b. 1431
French poet

14 Frères humains qui après nous vivez,
N'ayez les cœurs contre nous endurcis,
Car, si pitié de nous pauvres avez,
Dieu en aura plus tôt de vous mercis ...
Mais priez Dieu que tous nous veuille absoudre!

> Brothers in humanity who live after us, let not your hearts be hardened against us, for, if you take pity on us poor ones, God will be more likely to have mercy on you. But pray God that he may be willing to absolve us all.
>
> 'Ballade des pendus'

15 Mais où sont les neiges d'antan?

> But where are the snows of yesteryear?
>
> *Le Grand Testament* (1461) 'Ballade des dames du temps jadis' (translated by D. G. Rossetti)

16 En cette foi je veux vivre et mourir.

> In this faith I wish to live and to die.
>
> *Le Grand Testament* (1461) 'Ballade pour prier Nostre Dame'

St Vincent of Lerins d. AD c.450

17 Quod ubique, quod semper, quod ab omnibus creditum est.

> What is everywhere, what is always, what is by all people believed.
>
> *Commonitorium Primum* sect. 2

Virgil (Publius Vergilius Maro) 70–19 BC
Roman poet

18 Arma virumque cano, Troiae qui primus ab oris
Italiam fato profugus Laviniaque venit
Litora, multum ille et terris iactatus et alto
Vi superum, saevae memorem Iunonis ob iram.

> I sing of arms and the man who first from the shores of Troy came destined an exile to Italy and the Lavinian beaches, a man much buffeted on land and on the deep by force of the gods because of fierce Juno's never-forgetting anger.
>
> *Aeneid* bk. 1, l. 1

1 *Tantaene animis caelestibus irae?*

Why such great anger in those heavenly minds?
Aeneid bk. 1, l. 11

2 *Tantae molis erat Romanam condere gentem.*

So massive was the effort to found the Roman nation.
Aeneid bk. 1, l. 33

3 *Apparent rari nantes in gurgite vasto.*

Odd figures swimming were glimpsed in the waste of waters.
Aeneid bk. 1, l. 118

4 *Constitit hic arcumque manu celerisque sagittas*
Corripuit fidus quae tela gerebat Achates.

Hereupon he stopped and snatched up in his hand a bow and swift arrows, the weapons that trusty Achates carried.
Aeneid bk. 1, l. 187

5 *O passi graviora, dabit deus his quoque finem.*

O you who have borne even heavier things, God will grant an end to these too.
Aeneid bk. 1, l. 199

6 *Forsan et haec olim meminisse iuvabit.*

Maybe one day it will be cheering to remember even these things.
Aeneid bk. 1, l. 203

7 *Dux femina facti.*

The leader of the enterprise a woman.
Aeneid bk. 1, l. 364

8 *Dixit et avertens rosea cervice refulsit,*
Ambrosiaeque comae divinum vertice odorem
Spiravere; pedes vestis defluxit ad imos,
Et vera incessu patuit dea.

Thus she spoke and turned away with a flash of her rosy neck, and her ambrosial hair exhaled a divine fragrance; her dress flowed right down to her feet and her true godhead was evident from her walk.
Aeneid bk. 1, l. 402

9 *'En Priamus. Sunt hic etiam sua praemia laudi,*
Sunt lacrimae rerum et mentem mortalia tangunt.
Solve metus; feret haec aliquam tibi fama salutem.'
Sic ait atque animum pictura pascit inani.

'Look, there's Priam! Even here prowess has its due rewards, there are tears shed for things even here and mortality touches the heart. Abandon your fears; I tell you, this fame will stand us somehow in good stead.' So he spoke, and fed his thoughts on the unreal painting.
Aeneid bk. 1, l. 461

10 *Di tibi, si qua pios respectant numina, si quid*
Usquam iustitia est et mens sibi conscia recti,
Praemia digna ferant.

If the divine powers take note of the dutiful in any way, if there is any justice anywhere and a mind recognizing in itself what is right, may the gods bring you your earned rewards.
Aeneid bk. 1, l. 603

11 *Non ignara mali miseris succurrere disco.*

No stranger to trouble myself I am learning to care for the unhappy.
Aeneid bk. 1, l. 630

12 *Infandum, regina, iubes renovare dolorem.*

A grief too much to be told, O queen, you bid me renew.
Aeneid bk. 2, l. 3

13 *Quaeque ipse miserrima vidi*
Et quorum pars magna fui.

And the most miserable things which I myself saw and of which I was a major part.
Aeneid bk. 2, l. 5

14 *Equo ne credite, Teucri.*
Quidquid id est, timeo Danaos et dona ferentis.

Do not trust the horse, Trojans. Whatever it is, I fear the Greeks even when they bring gifts.
Aeneid bk. 2, l. 48

15 *. . . Crimine ab uno*
Disce omnis.

From the one crime recognize them all as culprits.
Aeneid bk. 2, l. 65

16 *Tacitae per amica silentia lunae.*

Through the friendly silence of the soundless moonlight.
Aeneid bk. 2, l. 255

17 *Tempus erat quo prima quies mortalibus aegris*
Incipit et dono divum gratissima serpit.

It was the time when first sleep begins for weary mortals and by the gift of the gods creeps over them most welcomely.
Aeneid bk. 2, l. 268

18 *Quantum mutatus ab illo*
Hectore qui redit exuvias indutus Achilli.

How greatly changed from that Hector who came back arrayed in the armour of Achilles!
Aeneid bk. 2, l. 274

19 *. . . Iam proximus ardet*
Ucalegon.

Ucalegon burns very near.
Aeneid bk. 2, l. 311

20 *Fuimus Troes, fuit Ilium et ingens*
Gloria Teucrorum.

We Trojans are at an end, Ilium has ended and the vast glory of the Trojans.
Aeneid bk. 2, l. 325

21 *Moriamur et in media arma ruamus.*
Una salus victis nullam sperare salutem.

Let us die even as we rush into the midst of the battle. The only safe course for the defeated is to expect no safety.
Aeneid bk. 2, l. 353

1   *Dis aliter visum.*

The gods thought otherwise.

   Aeneid bk. 2, l. 428

2 *Non tali auxilio nec defensoribus istis*
Tempus eget.

Neither the hour requires such help, nor those
defenders.

   Aeneid bk. 2, l. 521

3   *Quid non mortalia pectora cogis,*
Auri sacra fames!

To what do you not drive human hearts, cursed
craving for gold!

   Aeneid bk. 3, l. 56

4 *Monstrum horrendum, informe, ingens, cui lumen*
ademptum.

A monster horrendous, hideous and vast, deprived of
sight.

   Aeneid bk. 3, l. 658

5 *Quis fallere possit amantem?*

Who could deceive a lover?

   Aeneid bk. 4, l. 296

6   *Nec me meminisse pigebit Elissae*
Dum memor ipse mei, dum spiritus hos regit artus.

Nor will it ever upset me to remember Elissa so long as
I can remember who I am, so long as the breath of life
controls these limbs.

   Aeneid bk. 4, l. 335

7   *Varium et mutabile semper*
Femina.

Fickle and changeable always is woman.

   Aeneid bk. 4, l. 569 ('A windfane changabil huf puffe /
Always is a woomman' in Richard Stanyhurst's translation,
1582)

8 *Exoriare aliquis nostris ex ossibus ultor.*

Rise up from my dead bones, avenger!

   Aeneid bk. 4, l. 625 (translation by C. Day-Lewis)

9 *Hos successus alit: possunt, quia posse videntur.*

These success encourages: they can because they
think they can.

   Aeneid bk. 5, l. 231

10   *Bella, horrida bella,*
Et Thybrim multo spumantem sanguine cerno.

I see wars, horrible wars, and the Tiber foaming with
much blood.

   Aeneid bk. 6, l. 86

11   *Facilis descensus Averno:*
Noctes atque dies patet atri ianua Ditis;
Sed revocare gradum superasque evadere ad auras,
Hoc opus, hic labor est.

Easy is the way down to the Underworld: by night
and by day dark Hades' door stands open; but to
retrace one's steps and to make a way out to the
upper air, that is the task, that is the labour.

   Aeneid bk. 6, l. 126

12 *Procul, o procul este, profani.*

Far off, Oh keep far off, you uninitiated ones.

   Aeneid bk. 6, l. 258

13 *Ibant obscuri sola sub nocte per umbram*
Perque domos Ditis vacuas et inania regna.

Darkling they went under the lonely night through
the shadow and through the empty dwellings and
unsubstantial realms of Hades.

   Aeneid bk. 6, l. 268

14 *Vestibulum ante ipsum primisque in faucibus Orci*
Luctus et ultrices posuere cubilia Curae,
Pallentesque habitant Morbi tristisque Senectus,
Et Metus et malesuada Fames ac turpis Egestas,
Terribiles visu formae, Letumque Labosque.

Before the very forecourt and in the opening of the
jaws of hell Grief and avenging Cares have placed
their beds, and wan Diseases and sad Old Age live
there, and Fear and Hunger that urges to wrongdoing,
and shaming Destitution, figures terrible to see, and
Death and Toil.

   Aeneid bk. 6, l. 273

15 *Stabant orantes primi transmittere cursum*
Tendebantque manus ripae ulterioris amore.

They stood begging to be the first to make the voyage
over and they reached out their hands in longing for
the further shore.

   Aeneid bk. 6, l. 313

16 *Spiritus intus alit, totamque infusa per artus*
Mens agitat molem et magno se corpore miscet.

The spirit within nourishes, and mind instilled
throughout the living parts activates the whole mass
and mingles with the vast frame.

   Aeneid bk. 6, l. 726

17 *Excudent alii spirantia mollius aera*
(Credo equidem), vivos ducent de marmore vultus,
Orabunt causas melius, caelique meatus
Describent radio et surgentia sidera dicent:
Tu regere imperio populos, Romane, memento
(Hae tibi erunt artes), pacique imponere morem,
Parcere subiectis et debellare superbos.

Others shall shape bronzes more smoothly so that they
seem alive (yes, I believe it), shall mould from marble
living faces, shall better plead their cases in court, and
shall demonstrate with a pointer the motions of the
heavenly bodies and tell the stars as they rise: you,
Roman, make your task to rule nations by your
government (these shall be your skills), to impose
ordered ways upon a state of peace, to spare those
who have submitted and to subdue the arrogant.

   Aeneid bk. 6, l. 847

18 *Heu, miserande puer, si qua fata aspera rumpas,*
Tu Marcellus eris. Manibus date lilia plenis.

Alas, pitiable boy—if only you might break your cruel
fate!—you are to be Marcellus. [People,] give me lilies
in armfuls.

   Aeneid bk. 6, l. 882

1 *Sunt geminae Somni portae, quarum altera fertur*
Cornea, qua veris facilis datur exitus umbris,
Altera candenti perfecta nitens elephanto,
Sed falsa ad caelum mittunt insomnia Manes.

There are two gates of Sleep, one of which it is held is
made of horn and by it easy egress is given to real
ghosts; the other shining, fashioned of gleaming white
ivory, but the shades send deceptive visions that way
to the light.

Aeneid bk. 6, l. 893

2   *Geniumque loci primamque deorum*
Tellurem Nymphasque et adhuc ignota precatur
Flumina.

He prays to the spirit of the place and to Earth, the
first of the gods, and to the Nymphs and as yet
unknown rivers.

Aeneid bk. 7, l. 136

3 *Flectere si nequeo superos, Acheronta movebo.*

If I am unable to make the gods above relent, I shall
move Hell.

Aeneid bk. 7, l. 312

4 *O mihi praeteritos referat si Iuppiter annos.*

Oh if only Jupiter would give me back my past years.

Aeneid bk. 8, l. 560

5 *Quadripedante putrem sonitu quatit ungula campum.*

The hoof with a galloping sound is shaking the
powdery plain.

Aeneid bk. 8, l. 596

6 *Macte nova virtute, puer, sic itur ad astra.*

Blessings on your young courage, boy; that's the way
to the stars.

Aeneid bk. 9, l. 641

7 *Audentis Fortuna iuvat.*

Fortune assists the bold.

Aeneid bk. 10, l. 284 (often quoted 'Fortune favours the
brave'). Cf. Terence 690:13

8 *Et dulcis moriens reminiscitur Argos.*

And dying remembers his sweet Argos.

Aeneid bk. 10, l. 782

9 *Experto credite.*

Trust one who has gone through it.

Aeneid bk. 11, l. 283

10   *Pereat, qui crastina curat!*
Mors aurem vellens 'vivite' ait, 'venio.'

Away with him who heeds the morrow! Death,
plucking the ear, cries: 'Live; I come!'

Copa l. 37 (translated by H. Rushton Fairclough)

11 *Tityre, tu patulae recubans sub tegmine fagi*
Silvestrem tenui Musam meditaris avena.

Tityrus, you who lie under cover of the spreading
beech-tree, you are practising your pastoral music on
a thin stalk.

Eclogues no. 1, l. 1

12 *O Meliboee, deus nobis haec otia fecit.*

O Meliboeus, it is a god that has made this peaceful
life for us.

Eclogues no. 1, l. 6

13 *At nos hinc alii sitientis ibimus Afros,*
Pars Scythiam et rapidum cretae veniemus Oaxen
Et penitus toto divisos orbe Britannos.

But we from here are to go some to the parched
Africans, another group to Scythia and others of us
shall come to the Oaxes swirling with clay, and
amongst the Britons who are kept far away from the
whole world.

Eclogues no. 1, l. 64

14 *Formosum pastor Corydon ardebat Alexin,*
Delicias domini, nec quid speraret habebat.

The Shepherd, Corydon, burned with love for
handsome Alexis, his master's favourite, but he was
not getting what he hoped for.

Eclogues no. 2, l. 1

15 *O formose puer, nimium ne crede colori.*

Don't bank too much on your complexion, lovely boy.

Eclogues no. 2, l. 17

16 *Quem fugis, a! demens? Habitarunt di quoque silvas.*

Who are you running from, you crazy man? . . . Even
gods have lived in the woods like me.

Eclogues no. 2, l. 60

17 *Trahit sua quemque voluptas.*

Everyone is dragged on by their favourite pleasure.

Eclogues no. 2, l. 65

18 *Malo me Galatea petit, lasciva puella,*
Et fugit ad salices et se cupit ante videri.

Galatea aims at me with an apple, sexy girl, and runs
away into the willows and wants to have been
spotted.

Eclogues no. 3, l. 64

19 *Latet anguis in herba.*

There's a snake hidden in the grass.

Eclogues no. 3, l. 93

20 *Non nostrum inter vos tantas componere lites.*

It's not in my power to decide such a great dispute
between you.

Eclogues no. 3, l. 108

21 *Claudite iam rivos, pueri; sat prata biberunt.*

Close the sluices now, lads; the fields have drunk
enough.

Eclogues no. 3, l. 111

22 *Sicelides Musae, paulo maiora canamus!*
Non omnis arbusta iuvant humilesque myricae;
Si canimus silvas, silvae sint consule dignae.
Ultima Cumaei venit iam carminis aetas;
Magnus ab integro saeclorum nascitur ordo.
Iam redit et virgo, redeunt Saturnia regna,
Iam nova progenies caelo demittitur alto.

Sicilian Muses, let us sing of rather greater things.
Bushes and low tamarisks do not please everyone; if
we sing of the woods, let them be woods of consular
dignity. Now has come the last age according to the
oracle at Cumae; the great series of lifetimes starts
anew. Now too the virgin goddess returns, the golden
days of Saturn's reign return, now a new race is sent
down from high heaven.

Eclogues no. 4, l. 1

1 *Incipe, parve puer, risu cognoscere matrem.*

Begin, baby boy, to recognize your mother with a smile.

Eclogues no. 4, l. 60

2 *Incipe, parve puer: qui non risere parenti,*
Nec deus hunc mensa, dea nec dignata cubili est.

Begin, baby boy: if you haven't had a smile for your parent, then neither will a god think you worth inviting to dinner, nor a goddess to bed.

Eclogues no. 4, l. 62

3 *Ambo florentes aetatibus, Arcades ambo,*
Et cantare pares et respondere parati.

Both in the flower of their youth, Arcadians both, and matched and ready alike to start a song and to respond.

Eclogues no. 7, l. 4

4 *Saepibus in nostris parvam te roscida mala*
(Dux ego vester eram) vidi cum matre legentem.
Alter ab undecimo tum me iam acceperat annus,
Iam fragilis poteram a terra contingere ramos:
Ut vidi, ut perii, ut me malus abstulit error!

In our orchard I saw you as a child picking dewy apples with your mother (I was showing you the way). I had just turned twelve years old, I could reach the brittle branches even from the ground: how I saw you! how I perished [for love of you]! how an awful madness swept me away!

Eclogues no. 8, l. 37

5 *Nunc scio quid sit Amor.*

Now I know what Love is.

Eclogues no. 8, l. 43

6 *Non omnia possumus omnes.*

We can't all do everything.

Eclogues no. 8, l. 63. Cf. Lucilius 431:11

7   *Et me fecere poetam*
Pierides, sunt et mihi carmina, me quoque dicunt
Vatem pastores; sed non ego credulus illis.
Nam neque adhuc Vario videor nec dicere Cinna
Digna, sed argutos inter strepere anser olores.

Me too the Muses made write verse. I have songs of my own, the shepherds call me also a poet; but I'm not inclined to trust them. For I don't seem yet to write things as good either as Varius or as Cinna, but to be a goose honking amongst tuneful swans.

Eclogues no. 9, l. 32

8 *Omnia vincit Amor: et nos cedamus Amori.*

Love conquers all things: let us too give in to Love.

Eclogues no. 10, l. 69

9 *Ite domum saturae, venit Hesperus, ite capellae.*

Go on home, you have fed full, the evening star is coming, go on, my she-goats.

Eclogues no. 10, l. 77

10 *Ultima Thule.*

Farthest Thule.

Georgics no. 1, l. 30

11 *Nosque ubi primus equis Oriens adflavit anhelis*
Illic sera rubens accendit lumina Vesper.

And when the rising sun has first breathed on us with his panting horses, over there the red evening-star is lighting his late lamps.

Georgics no. 1, l. 250

12 *Ter sunt conati imponere Pelio Ossam*
Scilicet atque Ossae frondosum involvere Olympum;
Ter pater exstructos disiecit fulmine montis.

Three times they endeavoured to pile Ossa on Pelion, no less, and to roll leafy Olympus on top of Ossa; three times our Father broke up the towering mountains with a thunderbolt.

Georgics no. 1, l. 281

13 *O fortunatos nimium, sua si bona norint,*
Agricolas!

O farmers excessively fortunate if only they recognized their blessings!

Georgics no. 2, l. 458

14 *Felix qui potuit rerum cognoscere causas.*

Lucky is he who has been able to understand the causes of things.

Georgics no. 2, l. 490 (of Lucretius)

15 *Fortunatus et ille deos qui novit agrestis.*

Fortunate too is the man who has come to know the gods of the countryside.

Georgics no. 2, l. 493

16 *Optima quaeque dies miseris mortalibus aevi*
Prima fugit; subeunt morbi tristisque senectus
Et labor, et durae rapit inclementia mortis.

All the best days of life slip away from us poor mortals first; illnesses and dreary old age and pain sneak up, and the fierceness of harsh death snatches away.

Georgics no. 3, l. 66

17 *Sed fugit interea, fugit inreparabile tempus.*

But meanwhile it is flying, irretrievable time is flying.

Georgics no. 3, l. 284 (usually quoted '*tempus fugit* [time flies]')

18 *Hi motus animorum atque haec certamina tanta*
Pulveris exigui iactu compressa quiescent.

These movements of souls and these contests, however great, having been contained by the throwing of a little dust, will be quiet.

Georgics no. 4, l. 86 (of the battle of the bees)

19 *Non aliter, si parva licet componere magnis,*
Cecropias innatus apes amor urget habendi
Munere quamque suo.

Just so, if one may compare small things with great, an innate love of getting drives these Attic bees each with his own function.

Georgics no. 4, l. 176

20 *Sic vos non vobis mellificatis apes.*
Sic vos non vobis nidificatis aves.
Sic vos non vobis vellera fertis oves.

Thus you bees make honey not for yourselves. Thus you birds build nests not for yourselves. Thus you sheep bear fleeces not for yourselves.

On Bathyllus claiming authorship of certain lines by Virgil (continued)

Voltaire (François-Marie Arouet)
1694–1778
French writer and philosopher

1 *Dans ce meilleur des mondes possibles . . . tout est au mieux.*

In this best of possible worlds . . . all is for the best.
> *Candide* (1759) ch. 1 (usually quoted 'All is for the best in the best of all possible worlds')

2 *Si nous ne trouvons pas des choses agréables, nous trouverons du moins des choses nouvelles.*

If we do not find anything pleasant, at least we shall find something new.
> *Candide* (1759) ch. 17

3 *Dans ce pays-ci il est bon de tuer de temps en temps un amiral pour encourager les autres.*

In this country [England] it is thought well to kill an admiral from time to time to encourage the others.
> *Candide* (1759) ch. 23

4 *Il faut cultiver notre jardin.*

We must cultivate our garden.
> *Candide* (1759) ch. 30

5 *Ils ne se servent de la pensée que pour autoriser leurs injustices, et n'emploient les paroles que pour déguiser leurs pensées.*

[Men] use thought only to justify their injustices, and speech only to conceal their thoughts.
> *Dialogues* (1763) 'Le Chapon et la poularde'

6 *Le mieux est l'ennemi du bien.*

The best is the enemy of the good.
> *Contes* (1772) 'La Begueule' l. 2 (though often attributed to Voltaire, the notion in fact derives from an Italian proverb quoted in his *Dictionnaire philosophique* (1770 ed.) 'Art Dramatique': *'Le meglio è l'inimico del bene'*)

7 *La superstition met le monde entier en flammes; la philosophie les éteint.*

Superstition sets the whole world in flames; philosophy quenches them.
> *Dictionnaire philosophique* (1764) 'Superstition'

8 *Le secret d'ennuyer est . . . de tout dire.*

The secret of being a bore . . . is to tell everything.
> *Discours en vers sur l'homme* (1737) 'De la nature de l'homme' l. 172

9 *Tous les genres sont bons hors le genre ennuyeux.*

All styles are good except the tiresome kind.
> *L'Enfant prodigue* (1736) preface

10 *Si Dieu n'existait pas, il faudrait l'inventer.*

If God did not exist, it would be necessary to invent him.
> *Épîtres* no. 96 'A l'Auteur du livre des trois imposteurs'. Cf. Ovid 502:15

11 *Ce corps qui s'appelait et qui s'appelle encore le saint empire romain n'était en aucune manière ni saint, ni romain, ni empire.*

This agglomeration which was called and which still calls itself the Holy Roman Empire was neither holy, nor Roman, nor an empire.
> *Essai sur l'histoire générale et sur les moeurs et l'esprit des nations* (1756) ch. 70

12 *En effet, l'histoire n'est que le tableau des crimes et des malheurs.*

Indeed, history is nothing more than a tableau of crimes and misfortunes.
> *L'Ingénu* (1767) ch. 10. Cf. Gibbon 302:2

13 *C'est une des superstitions de l'esprit humain d'avoir imaginé que la virginité pouvait être une vertu.*

It is one of the superstitions of the human mind to have imagined that virginity could be a virtue.
> 'The Leningrad Notebooks' (c.1735–50) in T. Besterman (ed.) *Voltaire's Notebooks* (2nd ed., 1968) vol. 2, p. 455

14 *Quoi que vous fassiez, écrasez l'Infâme, et aimez qui vous aime.*

Whatever you do, stamp out abuses, and love those who love you.
> Letter to M. d'Alembert, 28 November 1762, in Voltaire Foundation (ed.) *Complete Works* vol. 25 (1973)

15 *Il est plaisant qu'on fait une vertu du vice de chasteté; et voilà encore une drôle de chasteté que celle qui mène tout droit les hommes au péché d'Onan, et les filles aux pâles couleurs!*

It is amusing that a virtue is made of the vice of chastity; and it's a pretty odd sort of chastity at that, which leads men straight into the sin of Onan, and girls to the waning of their colour.
> Letter to M. Mariott, 28 March 1766, in Voltaire Foundation (ed.) *Complete Works* vol. 30 (1973)

16 *Je ne suis pas comme une dame de la cour de Versailles, qui disait: c'est bien dommage que l'aventure de la tour de Babel ait produit la confusion des langues; sans cela tout le monde aurait toujours parlé français.*

I am not like a lady at the court of Versailles, who said: 'What a dreadful pity that the bother at the tower of Babel should have got language all mixed up; but for that, everyone would always have spoken French.'
> Letter to Catherine the Great, 26 May 1767, in Voltaire Foundation (ed.) *Complete Works* vol. 32 (1974)

17 *Le superflu, chose très nécessaire.*

The superfluous, a very necessary thing.
> *Le Mondain* (1736) l. 22

18 *Il faut qu'il y ait des moments tranquilles dans les grands ouvrages, comme dans la vie après les instants de passions, mais non pas des moments de dégoût.*

There ought to be moments of tranquillity in great works, as in life after the experience of passions, but not moments of disgust.
> 'The Piccini Notebooks' (c.1735–50) in T. Besterman (ed.) *Voltaire's Notebooks* (2nd ed., 1968) vol. 2, p. 500

19 *Il faut, dans le gouvernement, des bergers et des bouchers.*

Governments need both shepherds and butchers.
> 'The Piccini Notebooks' (c.1735–50) in T. Besterman (ed.) *Voltaire's Notebooks* (2nd ed., 1968) vol. 2, p. 517

20 *Dieu n'est pas pour les gros bataillons, mais pour ceux qui tirent le mieux.*

God is on the side not of the heavy battalions, but of the best shots.
> 'The Piccini Notebooks' (c.1735–50) in T. Besterman (ed.) *Voltaire's Notebooks* (2nd ed., 1968) vol. 2, p. 547. Cf. Anouilh 23:2, Bussy-Rabutin 165:19

1 *On doit des égards aux vivants; on ne doit aux morts que la vérité.*

We owe respect to the living; to the dead we owe only truth.

'Première Lettre sur Oedipe' in *Oeuvres* (1785) vol. 1, p. 15 n.

2 The composition of a tragedy requires *testicles*.

On being asked why no woman had ever written 'a tolerable tragedy'; letter from Byron to John Murray, 2 April 1817, in L. A. Marchand (ed.) *Byron's Letters and Journals* vol. 5 (1976)

3 The English plays are like their English puddings: nobody has any taste for them but themselves.

In Joseph Spence *Anecdotes* (ed. J. M. Osborn, 1966) no. 1033

4 *Habacuc était capable de tout.*

Habakkuk was capable of anything.

Attributed. See *Notes & Queries* vol. 181, p. 46

5 I disapprove of what you say, but I will defend to the death your right to say it.

Attributed to Voltaire, the words are in fact S. G. Tallentyre's summary of his attitude towards Helvétius following the burning of the latter's *De l'esprit* in 1759; in *The Friends of Voltaire* (1907) p. 199

6 What a fuss about an omelette!

What Voltaire *apparently* said on the burning of *De l'esprit*, in James Parton *Life of Voltaire* (1881) vol. 2, ch. 25

7 This is no time for making new enemies.

On being asked to renounce the Devil, on his deathbed (attributed)

Andrei Voznesensky 1933–

Russian poet

8 Я — Гойя!
Глазницы воронок мне выклевал ворог,
слетая на поле нагое.
Я — горе.
Я — голос.
Войны, городов головни
на снегу сорок первого года.
Я — голод.

I am Goya
of the bare field, by the enemy's beak gouged
till the craters of my eyes gape,
I am grief,
I am the tongue
of war, the embers of cities
on the snows of the year 1941
I am hunger.

'Goya' (published 1960) (translated by Stanley Kunitz)

Prince Peter Vyazemsky 1792–1878

Russian poet

9 Бог голодных, бог холодных,
нищих вплодь и поперег,
Бог имений недоходных,
Вот он, вот он русский бог.

God of frostbite, God of famine,
beggars, cripples by the yard,
farmers with no more to promise—
that's him, that's your Russian God.

'The Russian God' (1828) (translated by Alan Myers)

Richard Wagner 1813–83

German composer

10 *Frisch weht der Wind*
der Heimat zu:—
mein irisch Kind,
wo weilest du?

Freshly blows the wind homewards: my Irish child, where are you dwelling?

Tristan und Isolde (1865) act 1, sc. 1

Alice Walker 1944–

American poet

11 I love a man who is not worth
my love.
Did this happen to your mother? . . .

Did your sister throw up a lot?
Did your cousin complain
of a painful knot
in her back?
Did your aunt always
seem to have something else
troubling her mind?

I thought love would adapt itself
to my needs.
But needs grow too fast;
they come up like weeds.
Through cracks in the conversation.
Through silences in the dark.
Through everything you thought was concrete.

'Did This Happen to Your Mother? Did Your Sister Throw Up a Lot?' (1979)

12 Expect nothing. Live frugally
on surprise.

'Expect nothing' (1973)

13 The quietly pacifist peaceful
always die
to make room for men
who shout. Who tell lies to
children, and crush the corners
off of old men's dreams.

'The QPP' (1973)

14 We have a beautiful
mother
Her green lap
immense
Her brown embrace
eternal
Her blue body
everything
we know.

'We Have a Beautiful Mother' (1991)

Felix Walker

American politician

15 I'm talking to Buncombe ['bunkum'].

Excusing a long, dull, irrelevant speech in the House of Representatives, c 1820 (Buncombe being his constituency). See W. Safire *New Language of Politics* (2nd ed., 1972) p. 80. Cf. Carlyle 180:31

H. M. Walker

American screenwriter

1 You're here to stay until the rustle in your dying throat relieves you!

> Addressed to Laurel and Hardy in *Beau Hunks* (1931 film; re-named *Beau Chumps* for British audiences)

Edgar Wallace 1875–1932

English thriller writer

2 Dreamin' of thee! Dreamin' of thee!

> 'T. A. in Love' (1900); popularized by Cyril Fletcher in 1930s radio shows

3 What is a highbrow? He is a man who has found something more interesting than women.

> *New York Times* 24 January 1932, sect. 8, p. 6

George Wallace 1919–

American Democratic politician

4 Segregation now, segregation tomorrow and segregation forever!

> Inaugural speech as Governor of Alabama, January 1963, in *Birmingham World* 19 January 1963

Henry Wallace 1888–1965

American Democratic politician

5 The century on which we are entering—the century which will come out of this war—can be and must be the century of the common man.

> Speech, 8 May 1942, in *Vital Speeches* (1942) vol. 8, p. 483

William Ross Wallace d. 1881

American poet

6 A mighty power and stronger
Man from his throne has hurled,
For the hand that rocks the cradle
Is the hand that rules the world.

> 'What rules the world' (1865)

Graham Wallas 1858–1932

British politicial scientist

7 The little girl had the making of a poet in her who, being told to be sure of her meaning before she spoke, said, 'How can I know what I think till I see what I say?'

> *The Art of Thought* (1926) ch. 4

Edmund Waller 1606–87

English poet

8 So was the huntsman by the bear oppressed,
Whose hide he sold—before he caught the beast!

> 'The Battle of the Summer Islands' (1645) canto 2

9 Go, lovely rose!
Tell her, that wastes her time and me,
That now she knows,
When I resemble her to thee,
How sweet and fair she seems to be.

> 'Go, lovely rose!' (1645)

10 Small is the worth
Of beauty from the light retired;
Bid her come forth,
Suffer herself to be desired,
And not blush so to be admired.

> 'Go, lovely rose!' (1645)

11 Poets that lasting marble seek
Must carve in Latin or in Greek.

> 'Of English Verse' (1645)

12 Others may use the ocean as their road,
Only the English make it their abode.

> 'Of a War with Spain' (1658) l. 25

13 The soul's dark cottage, battered and decayed
Lets in new light through chinks that time has made;
Stronger by weakness, wiser men become,
As they draw near to their eternal home.
Leaving the old, both worlds at once they view,
That stand upon the threshold of the new.

> 'Of the Last Verses in the Book' (1685) l. 18

14 That which her slender waist confined
Shall now my joyful temples bind;
No monarch but would give his crown
His arms might do what this has done.

> 'On a Girdle' (1645)

15 Rome, though her eagle through the world had flown,
Could never make this island all her own.

> 'Panegyric to My Lord Protector' (1655) st. 17

16 Illustrious acts high raptures do infuse,
And every conqueror creates a Muse.

> 'Panegyric to My Lord Protector' (1655) st. 46

17 It is not that I love you less
Than when before your feet I lay:
But, to prevent the sad increase
Of hopeless love, I keep away.

In vain, alas! for every thing
Which I have known belong to you,
Your form does to my fancy bring
And makes my old wounds bleed anew.

> 'The Self-Banished' (1645)

18 Why came I so untimely forth
Into a world which, wanting thee,
Could entertain us with no worth,
Or shadow of felicity?

> 'To My Young Lady Lucy Sidney' (1645)

19 So all we know
Of what they do above,
Is that they happy are, and that they love.

> 'Upon the Death of My Lady Rich' (1645) l. 75

20 Under the tropic is our language spoke,
And part of Flanders hath received our yoke.

> 'Upon the Late Storm, and of the Death of His Highness Ensuing the Same' (1659) l. 21

Horace Walpole, 4th Earl of Orford
1717–97

English writer and connoisseur

1 Our supreme governors, the mob.
  Letter to Sir Horace Mann, 7 September 1743, in
  Correspondence (Yale ed. 1937–83) vol. 18

2 [Lovat] was beheaded yesterday, and died extremely
  well, without passion, affectation, buffoonery or
  timidity: his behaviour was natural and intrepid.
  Letter to Sir Horace Mann, 10 April 1747, in *Correspondence*
  (Yale ed.) vol. 19

3 [Strawberry Hill] is a little plaything-house that I got
  out of Mrs Chenevix's shop, and is the prettiest bauble
  you ever saw. It is set in enamelled meadows, with
  filigree hedges.
  Letter to Hon. Henry Conway, 8 June 1747, in
  Correspondence (Yale ed.) vol. 37

4 But, thank God! the Thames is between me and the
  Duchess of Queensberry.
  Letter to Hon. Henry Conway, 8 June 1747, in
  Correspondence (Yale ed.) vol. 37

5 Every drop of ink in my pen ran cold.
  Letter to George Montagu, 30 July 1752, in *Correspondence*
  (Yale ed.) vol. 9

6 At present, nothing is talked of, nothing admired, but
  what I cannot help calling a very insipid and tedious
  performance: it is a kind of novel, called *The Life and
  Opinions of Tristram Shandy*; the great humour of
  which consists in the whole narration always going
  backwards.
  Letter to Sir David Dalrymple, 4 April 1760, in
  Correspondence (Yale ed.) vol. 15

7 One of the greatest geniuses that ever existed,
  Shakespeare, undoubtedly wanted taste.
  Letter to Christopher Wren, 9 August 1764, in
  Correspondence (Yale ed.) vol. 40

8 At Madame du Deffand's, an old blind *débauchée* of wit
  [Charles-Jean-François Hénault].
  Letter to Hon. Henry Conway, 6 October 1765, in
  Correspondence (Yale ed.) vol. 39

9 What has one to do, when one grows tired of the
  world, as we both do, but to draw nearer and nearer,
  and gently waste the remains of life with friends with
  whom one began it?
  Letter to George Montagu, 21 November 1765, in
  Correspondence (Yale ed.) vol. 10

10 It is charming to totter into vogue.
  Letter to George Selwyn, 2 December 1765, in
  Correspondence (Yale ed.) vol. 30

11 The best sun we have is made of Newcastle coal.
  Letter to George Montagu, 15 June 1768, in *Correspondence*
  (Yale ed.) vol. 10

12 Everybody talks of the constitution, but all sides forget
  that the constitution is extremely well, and would do
  very well, if they would but let it alone
  Letter to Sir Horace Mann, 18 January 1770, in
  Correspondence (Yale ed.) vol. 23

13 One's mind suffers only when one is young and while
  one is ignorant of the world. When one has lived for
  some time, one learns that the young think too little
  and the old too much, and one grows careless about
  both.
  Letter to Sir Horace Mann, 14 January 1772, in
  Correspondence (Yale ed.) vol. 23

14 It was easier to conquer it [the East] than to know
  what to do with it.
  Letter to Sir Horace Mann, 27 March 1772, in
  Correspondence (Yale ed.) vol. 23

15 The way to ensure summer in England is to have it
  framed and glazed in a comfortable room.
  Letter to Revd William Cole, 28 May 1774, in
  Correspondence (Yale ed.) vol. 1

16 The next Augustan age will dawn on the other side of
  the Atlantic. There will, perhaps, be a Thucydides at
  Boston, a Xenophon at New York, and, in time, a
  Virgil at Mexico, and a Newton at Peru. At last, some
  curious traveller from Lima will visit England and give
  a description of the ruins of St Paul's, like the editions
  of Balbec and Palmyra.
  Letter to Sir Horace Mann, 24 November 1774, in
  Correspondence (Yale ed.) vol. 24. Cf. Macaulay 435:12

17 By the waters of Babylon we sit down and weep,
  when we think of thee, O America!
  Letter to Revd William Mason, 12 June 1775, in
  Correspondence (Yale ed.) vol. 28. Cf. Book of Common
  Prayer 134:17

18 This world is a comedy to those that think, a tragedy
  to those that feel.
  Letter to Anne, Countess of Upper Ossory, 16 August 1776,
  in *Correspondence* (Yale ed.) vol. 32

19 Tell me, ye divines, which is the most virtuous man,
  he who begets twenty bastards, or he who sacrifices
  an hundred thousand lives?
  Letter to Sir Horace Mann, 7 July 1778, in *Correspondence*
  (Yale ed.) vol. 24

20 When will the world know that peace and
  propagation are the two most delightful things in it?
  Letter to Sir Horace Mann, 7 July 1778, in *Correspondence*
  (Yale ed.) vol. 24

21 When men write for profit, they are not very delicate.
  Letter to Revd William Cole, 1 September 1778, in
  Correspondence (Yale ed.) vol. 2

22 When people will not weed their own minds, they are
  apt to be overrun with nettles.
  Letter to Caroline, Countess of Ailesbury, 10 July 1779, in
  Correspondence (Yale ed.) vol. 39

23 Prognostics do not always prove prophecies,—at least
  the wisest prophets make sure of the event first.
  Letter to Thomas Walpole, 19 February 1785, in
  Correspondence (Yale ed.) vol. 36

24 It is the story of a mountebank and his zany.
  Of Boswell's *Tour of the Hebrides*; letter to Hon. Henry
  Conway, 6 October 1785, in *Correspondence* (Yale ed.)
  vol. 39

25 All his own geese are swans, as the swans of others
  are geese.
  Of Sir Joshua Reynolds; letter to Anne, Countess of Upper
  Ossory, 1 December 1786, in *Correspondence* (Yale ed.)
  vol. 33

1 That hyena in petticoats, Mrs Wollstonecraft.
Letter to Hannah More, 26 January 1795, in *Correspondence* (Yale ed.) vol. 31

2 His speeches were fine, but as much laboured as his extempore sayings.
Memoirs of the Reign of King George II (ed. Lord Holland, 1846) vol. 1, p. 51 (of Lord Chesterfield, 1751)

3 Whoever knows the interior of affairs, must be sensible to how many more events the faults of statesmen give birth, than are produced by their good intentions.
Memoirs of the Reign of King George II (ed. Lord Holland, 1846) vol. 1, p. 372 (1754)

4 The keenness of his sabre was blunted by the difficulty with which he drew it from the scabbard; I mean, the hesitation and ungracefulness of his delivery took off from the force of his arguments.
Memoirs of the Reign of King George II (ed. Lord Holland, 1846) vol. 2, p. 148 (of Henry Fox, 1755)

5 While he felt like a victim, he acted like a hero.
Memoirs of the Reign of King George II (ed. Lord Holland, 1846) vol. 2, p. 369 (of Admiral Byng, on the day of his execution, 1757)

6 Perhaps those, who, trembling most, maintain a dignity in their fate, are the bravest: resolution on reflection is real courage.
Memoirs of the Reign of King George II (ed. Lord Holland, 1846) vol. 2, p. 370 (1757)

7 They seem to know no medium between a mitre and a crown of martyrdom. If the clergy are not called to the latter, they never deviate from the pursuit of the former. One would think their motto was, *Canterbury or Smithfield*.
Memoirs of the Reign of King George II (ed. Lord Holland, 1846) vol. 3, p. 114 (1758)

8 All his passions were expressed by one livid smile.
Memoirs of the Reign of King George III (ed. D. Le Marchant, 1845) vol. 1, p. 271 (of George Grenville, 1763)

9 His courage and his tenderness were never disunited. He was dauntless on every occasion, but when it was necessary to surmount his bashfulness.
Memoirs of the Reign of King George III (ed. D. Le Marchant, 1845) vol. 4, p. 176 (of the Marquis of Granby, 1770)

10 He lost his dominions in America, his authority over Ireland, and all influence in Europe, by aiming at despotism in England; and exposed himself to more mortifications and humiliations than can happen to a quiet Doge of Venice.
Memoirs of the Reign of King George III (ed. D. Le Marchant, 1845) vol. 4, p. 236 (of King George III, 1770)

11 Virtue knows to a farthing what it has lost by not having been vice.
In L. Kronenberger *The Extraordinary Mr Wilkes* (1974) pt. 3, ch. 2

Sir Hugh Walpole 1884–1941

British novelist

12 'Tisn't life that matters! 'Tis the courage you bring to it.
Fortitude (1913) bk. 1, ch. 1

Sir Robert Walpole, 1st Earl of Orford
1676–1745

English Whig statesman; first British Prime Minister, 1721–42

13 They now *ring* the bells, but they will soon *wring* their hands.
On the declaration of war with Spain, 1739, in W. Coxe *Memoirs of Sir Robert Walpole* (1798) vol. 1, p. 618

14 All those men have their price.
In W. Coxe *Memoirs of Sir Robert Walpole* (1798) vol. 1, p. 757 (of fellow parliamentarians)

15 Madam, there are fifty thousand men slain this year in Europe, and not one Englishman.
To Queen Caroline, 1734, in John Hervey *Memoirs* (written 1734–43, published 1848) vol. 1, p. 398 (on the war of Austrian succession, in which the English had refused to participate)

16 [Gratitude of place-expectants] is a lively sense of future favours.
In W. Hazlitt *Lectures on the English Comic Writers* (1819) 'On Wit and Humour'. Cf. La Rochefoucauld 410:20

William Walsh 1663–1708

English poet

17 A lover forsaken
A new love may get,
But a neck when once broken
Can never be set.
'The Despairing Lover' l. 17

18 By partners, in each other kind,
Afflictions easier grow;
In love alone we hate to find
Companions of our woe.
'Song: Of All the Torments'

19 I can endure my own despair,
But not another's hope.
'Song: Of All the Torments'

Izaak Walton 1593–1683

English writer

20 Angling may be said to be so like the mathematics, that it can never be fully learnt.
The Compleat Angler (1653) 'Epistle to the Reader'

21 And for winter fly-fishing it is as useful as an almanac out of date.
The Compleat Angler (1653) 'Epistle to the Reader'

22 As no man is born an artist, so no man is born an angler.
The Compleat Angler (1653) 'Epistle to the Reader'

23 I shall stay him no longer than to wish him a rainy evening to read this following discourse; and that if he be an honest angler, the east wind may never blow when he goes a-fishing.
The Compleat Angler (1653) 'Epistle to the Reader'

24 I am, Sir, a Brother of the Angle.
The Compleat Angler (1653) pt. 1, ch. 1

1 Sir Henry Wotton . . . was also a most dear lover, and
a frequent practiser of the art of angling; of which he
would say, 'it was an employment for his idle time,
which was then not idly spent . . . a rest to his mind, a
cheerer of his spirits, a diverter of sadness, a calmer of
unquiet thoughts, a moderator of passions, a procurer
of contentedness; and that it begat habits of peace and
patience in those that professed and practised it.'
The Compleat Angler (1653) pt. 1, ch. 1

2 Good company and good discourse are the very sinews
of virtue.
The Compleat Angler (1653) pt. 1, ch. 2

3 An excellent angler, and now with God.
The Compleat Angler (1653) pt. 1, ch. 4

4 I love such mirth as does not make friends ashamed to
look upon one another next morning.
The Compleat Angler (1653) pt. 1, ch. 5

5 A good, honest, wholesome, hungry breakfast.
The Compleat Angler (1653) pt. 1, ch. 5

6 No man can lose what he never had.
The Compleat Angler (1653) pt. 1, ch. 5

7 In so doing, use him as though you loved him.
The Compleat Angler (1653) pt. 1, ch. 8 (on baiting a hook
with a live frog)

8 This dish of meat is too good for any but anglers, or
very honest men.
The Compleat Angler (1653) pt. 1, ch. 8

9 I love any discourse of rivers, and fish and fishing.
The Compleat Angler (1653) pt. 1, ch. 18

10 Look to your health; and if you have it, praise God,
and value it next to a good conscience; for health is
the second blessing that we mortals are capable of; a
blessing that money cannot buy.
The Compleat Angler (1653) pt. 1, ch. 21

11 Let the blessing of St Peter's Master be . . . upon all
that are lovers of virtue; and dare trust in His
providence; and be quiet; and go a-Angling.
The Compleat Angler (1653) pt. 1, ch. 21

12 The great Secretary of Nature and all learning, Sir
Francis Bacon.
Life of Herbert (1670 ed.) p. 26

13 But God, who is able to prevail, wrestled with him, as
the Angel did with Jacob, and marked him; marked
him for his own.
Life of Donne (1670 ed.) p. 35

14 Of this blest man, let his just praise be given,
Heaven was in him, before he was in heaven.
Written in a copy of Dr Richard Sibbes's *The Returning
Backslider*, now preserved in Salisbury Cathedral Library.
See Geoffrey Keynes (ed.) *The Compleat Walton* (1929)
p. 584

William Warburton 1698–1779

English theologian; Bishop of Gloucester from 1759

15 Orthodoxy is my doxy; heterodoxy is another man's
doxy.
To Lord Sandwich, in Joseph Priestley *Memoirs* (1807)
vol. 1, p. 572

Artemus Ward (*Charles Farrar Browne*)
1834–67

American humorist

16 It is a pity that Chawcer, who had geneyus, was so
unedicated. He's the wuss speller I know of.
Artemus Ward in London (1867) ch. 4

17 Let us all be happy, and live within our means, even if
we have to borrer the money to do it with.
Artemus Ward in London (1867) ch. 7

18 I am happiest when I am idle. I could live for months
without performing any kind of labour, and at the
expiration of that time I should feel fresh and vigorous
enough to go right on in the same way for numerous
more months.
Artemus Ward in London (1867) ch. 9

19 He is dreadfully married. He's the most married man I
ever saw in my life.
Artemus Ward's Lecture (1869) 'Brigham Young's Palace'

20 Why is this thus? What is the reason of this thusness?
Artemus Ward's Lecture (1869) 'Heber C. Kimball's Harem'

Nathaniel Ward 1578–1652

English clergyman

21 The world is full of care, much like unto a bubble;
Woman and care, and care and women, and women
and care and trouble.
Epigram, attributed by Ward to a lady at the Court of the
Queen of Bohemia, in *The Simple Cobbler of Aggawam in
America* (1647) p. 25

Andy Warhol 1927–87

American artist

22 In the future everybody will be world famous for
fifteen minutes.
In *Andy Warhol* (1968) p. [12] (volume released to mark his
exhibition in Stockholm, February–March, 1968)

George Washington 1732–99

1st President of the USA

23 The time is now near at hand which must probably
determine whether Americans are to be freemen or
slaves; whether they are to have any property they
can call their own . . . The fate of unborn millions will
now depend, under God, on the courage and conduct
of this army. Our cruel and unrelenting enemy leaves
us only the choice of brave resistance, or the most
abject submission. We have, therefore, to resolve to
conquer or die.
General orders, 2 July 1776, in J. C. Fitzpatrick (ed.)
Writings of George Washington vol. 5 (1932) p. 211

24 'Tis our true policy to steer clear of permanent
alliances, with any portion of the foreign world.
President's Address . . . retiring from Public Life (17 September
1796)

25 Let me . . . warn you in the most solemn manner
against the baneful effects of the spirit of party
President's Address (17 September 1796)

1 The nation which indulges toward another an habitual hatred or an habitual fondness is in some degree a slave. It is a slave to its animosity or to its affection, either of which is sufficient to lead it astray from its duty and its interest.
President's Address ... (17 September 1796)

2 I can't tell a lie, Pa; you know I can't tell a lie. I did cut it with my hatchet.
In M. L. Weems *Life of George Washington* (10th ed., 1810) ch. 2

Ned Washington 1901–76
American songwriter

3 Hi diddle dee dee (an actor's life for me).
Title of song (1940) from the film *Pinocchio*

4 The night is like a lovely tune,
Beware my foolish heart!
How white the ever-constant moon,
Take care, my foolish heart!
There's a line between love and fascination
That's hard to see on an evening such as this,
For they both give the very same sensation
When you're lost in the magic of a kiss.
'My Foolish Heart' (1949 song); music by Victor Young

Edward Waterfield

5 Two men wrote a lexicon, Liddell and Scott;
Some parts were clever, but some parts were not.
Hear, all ye learned, and read me this riddle,
How the wrong part wrote Scott, and the right part wrote Liddell.
Of Henry Liddell (1811–98) and Robert Scott (1811–87) co-authors of the *Greek Lexicon* (1843), Liddell being in the habit of ascribing to his co-author usages which he criticised in his pupils, and which they said that they had culled from the *Lexicon*. See L. E. Tanner *Westminster School: A History* (1934) ch. 9

Rowland Watkyns c.1616–64

6 I love him not, but show no reason can
Wherefore, but this, *I do not love* the man.
'Antipathy'. Cf. Martial 449:12

7 For every marriage then is best in tune,
When that the wife is May, the husband June.
'To the most Courteous and Fair Gentlewoman, Mrs Elinor Williams'

William Watson c.1559–1603
English Roman Catholic conspirator

8 *Fiat justitia et ruant coeli.*
Let justice be done though the heavens fall.
A Decacordon of Ten Quodlibeticall Questions Concerning Religion and State (1602), being the first citation in an English work of a famous maxim. Cf. Ferdinand 281:9

William Watson 1858–1936
English poet

9 April, April,
Laugh thy girlish laughter.
'April'

10 His friends he loved. His direst earthly foes—
Cats—I believe he did but feign to hate.
My hand will miss the insinuated nose,
Mine eyes the tail that wagged contempt at Fate.
'An Epitaph'

Isaac Watts 1674–1748
English hymn-writer

11 One sickly sheep infects the flock,
And poisons all the rest.
Divine Songs for Children (1715) 'Against Evil Company'

12 How doth the little busy bee
Improve each shining hour,
And gather honey all the day
From every opening flower!
Divine Songs for Children (1715) 'Against Idleness and Mischief'

13 For Satan finds some mischief still
For idle hands to do.
Divine Songs for Children (1715) 'Against Idleness and Mischief'

14 Let me be dressed fine as I will,
Flies, worms, and flowers, exceed me still.
Divine Songs for Children (1715) 'Against Pride in Clothes'

15 Let dogs delight to bark and bite,
For God hath made them so.
Divine Songs for Children (1715) 'Against Quarrelling'

16 But, children, you should never let
Such angry passions rise;
Your little hands were never made
To tear each other's eyes.
Divine Songs for Children (1715) 'Against Quarrelling'

17 Birds in their little nests agree
And 'tis a shameful sight,
When children of one family
Fall out, and chide, and fight.
Divine Songs for Children (1715) 'Love between Brothers and Sisters'

18 'Tis the voice of the sluggard; I heard him complain,
'You have waked me too soon, I must slumber again'.
As the door on its hinges, so he on his bed,
Turns his sides and his shoulders and his heavy head.
Divine Songs for Children (1715) 'The Sluggard'

19 Come, let us join our cheerful songs
With angels round the throne;
Ten thousand thousand are their tongues,
But all their joys are one.

'Worthy the Lamb that died,' they cry,
'To be exalted thus;'
'Worthy the Lamb,' our lips reply,
'For he was slain for us.'
Hymns and Spiritual Songs (1707) 'Come, let us join our cheerful songs'

1 We are a garden walled around,
  Chosen and made peculiar ground;
  A little spot enclosed by grace,
  Out of the world's wide wilderness.
  > *Hymns and Spiritual Songs* (1707) 'The Church the Garden
  > of Christ'

2 When I survey the wondrous cross
  On which the prince of glory died,
  My richest gain I count but loss,
  And pour contempt on all my pride.
  > *Hymns and Spiritual Songs* (1707) 'Crucifixion to the World,
  > by the Cross of Christ'

3 Hark! from the tombs a doleful sound.
  > *Hymns and Spiritual Songs* (1707) 'Hark! from the Tombs'

4 There is a land of pure delight,
  Where saints immortal reign;
  Infinite day excludes the night,
  And pleasure banish pain.
  > *Hymns and Spiritual Songs* (1707) 'A Prospect of Heaven
  > makes Death easy'

5 Death like a narrow sea divides
  This heavenly land from ours.
  > *Hymns and Spiritual Songs* (1707) 'A Prospect of Heaven
  > makes Death easy'

6 Jesus shall reign where'er the sun
  Does his successive journeys run;
  His kingdom stretch from shore to shore,
  Till moons shall wax and wane no more.
  > *The Psalms of David Imitated* (1719) Psalm 72

7 Our God, our help in ages past
  Our hope for years to come,
  Our shelter from the stormy blast,
  And our eternal home.

  Beneath the shadow of Thy Throne
  Thy saints have dwelt secure;
  Sufficient is Thine Arm alone,
  And our defence is sure.

  Before the hills in order stood,
  Or earth received her frame,
  From everlasting Thou art God,
  To endless years the same.

  A thousand ages in Thy sight
  Are like an evening gone;
  Short as the watch that ends the night
  Before the rising sun.

  Time, like an ever-rolling stream,
  Bears all its sons away;
  They fly forgotten, as a dream
  Dies at the opening day.
  > *The Psalms of David Imitated* (1719) Psalm 90 ('Our God'
  > altered to 'O God' by John Wesley, 1738)

Evelyn Waugh 1903–66

English novelist

1 ████ ████ █ █████ ███ ████ ██ ██ █████ ████ ███ ███ █████
  > *Brideshead Revisited* (1945) 'Author's Note'

9 Something within me, long sickening, had quietly
  died, and [I] felt as a husband might feel, who, in the
  fourth year of his marriage, suddenly knew that he
  had no longer any desire, or tenderness, or esteem, for
  a once-beloved wife; no pleasure in her company, no
  wish to please, no curiosity about anything she might
  ever do or say or think; no hope of setting things
  right, no self-reproach for the disaster. I knew it all,
  the whole drab compass of marital disillusion; we had
  been through it together, the Army and I, from the
  first importunate courtship until now, when nothing
  remained to us except the chill bonds of law and duty
  and custom.
  > *Brideshead Revisited* (1945) Prologue

10 Charm is the great English blight. It does not exist
   outside these damp islands. It spots and kills anything
   it touches. It kills love, it kills art.
   > *Brideshead Revisited* (1945) bk. 3, ch. 2

11 Any who have heard that sound will shrink at the
   recollection of it; it is the sound of English county
   families baying for broken glass.
   > *Decline and Fall* (1928) 'Prelude'. Cf. Belloc 61:21

12 I expect you'll be becoming a schoolmaster, sir. That's
   what most of the gentlemen does, sir, that gets sent
   down for indecent behaviour.
   > *Decline and Fall* (1928) 'Prelude'

13 I haven't been to sleep for over a year. That's why I go
   to bed early. One needs more rest if one doesn't sleep.
   > *Decline and Fall* (1928) pt. 2, ch. 3

14 There is a species of person called a 'Modern
   Churchman' who draws the full salary of a beneficed
   clergyman and need not commit himself to any
   religious belief.
   > *Decline and Fall* (1928) pt. 2, ch. 4

15 Any one who has been to an English public school
   will always feel comparatively at home in prison. It is
   the people brought up in the gay intimacy of the
   slums, Paul learned, who find prison so
   soul-destroying.
   > *Decline and Fall* (1928) pt. 3, ch. 4

16 You never find an Englishman among the
   under-dogs—except in England, of course.
   > *The Loved One* (1948) ch. 1

17 He was an innocent, affable man who had somehow
   preserved his good humour ... throughout a life
   which to all outward observation had been overloaded
   with misfortune. He had like many another been born
   in full sunlight and lived to see night fall.
   > *Men at Arms* (1952) prologue, sect. 3

18 His strongest tastes were negative. He abhorred
   plastics, Picasso, sunbathing and jazz—everything in
   fact that had happened in his own lifetime.
   > *The Ordeal of Gilbert Pinfold* (1957) ch. 1

19 Ambrose lived in and for conversation; he rejoiced in
   the whole intricate art of it ... the changes of alliance,
   the betrayals, the diplomatic revolutions, the waxing
   and waning of dictatorships that could happen in an
   hour's session about a table.
   > *Put Out More Flags* (1942) ch. 1, sect. 7

20 *The Beast* stands for strong mutually antagonistic
   governments everywhere ... Self-sufficiency at home,
   self-assertion abroad.
   > *Scoop* (1938) bk. 1, ch. 1

1 Up to a point, Lord Copper.
>   *Scoop* (1938) bk. 1, ch. 1

2 'Feather-footed through the plashy fen passes the questing vole' . . . 'Yes,' said the Managing Editor. 'That must be good style.'
>   *Scoop* (1938) bk. 1, ch. 1

3 Remember that the Patriots are in the right and are going to win . . . But they must win quickly. The British public has no interest in a war that drags on indecisively. A few sharp victories, some conspicuous acts of personal bravery on the Patriot side and a colourful entry into the capital. That is *The Beast* Policy for the war.
>   *Scoop* (1938) bk. 1, ch. 3

4 News is what a chap who doesn't care much about anything wants to read. And it's only news until he's read it. After that it's dead.
>   *Scoop* (1938) bk. 1, ch. 5

5 I will not stand for being called a woman in my own house.
>   *Scoop* (1938) bk. 2, ch. 1

6 Other nations use 'force'; we Britons alone use 'Might'.
>   *Scoop* (1938) bk. 2, ch. 5

7 Is there any place that is free from evil? It is too simple to say that only the Nazis wanted war . . . Even good men thought that their private honour would be satisfied by war. They could assert their manhood by killing and being killed. They would accept hardship in recompense for having been selfish and lazy. Danger justified privilege.
>   *Unconditional Surrender* (1961) bk. 3, sect. 4

8 Punctuality is the virtue of the bored.
>   Michael Davie (ed.) *Diaries of Evelyn Waugh* (1976) 'Irregular Notes 1960–65', 26 March 1962

9 Randolph Churchill went into hospital . . . to have a lung removed. It was announced that the trouble was not 'malignant' . . . it was a typical triumph of modern science to find the only part of Randolph that was not malignant and remove it.
>   Michael Davie (ed.) *Diaries of Evelyn Waugh* (1976) 'Irregular Notes 1960–65', March 1964

10 Impotence and sodomy are socially O.K. but birth control is flagrantly middle-class.
>   'An Open Letter' pt. 3 in Nancy Mitford (ed.) *Noblesse Oblige* (1956)

11 Manners are especially the need of the plain. The pretty can get away with anything.
>   In *Observer* 15 April 1962

12 I drink for it.
>   When asked, while at Oxford, what he did for his college

Frederick Weatherly 1848–1929
English songwriter

13 Where are the boys of the old Brigade, Who fought with us side by side?
>   'The Old Brigade' (1886 song)

14 Roses are flowering in Picardy, But there's never a rose like you.
>   'Roses of Picardy' (1916 song)

Beatrice Webb (*née Potter*) 1858–1943
English socialist

15 I never visualised labour as separate men and women of different sorts and kinds . . . labour was an abstraction, which seemed to denote an arithmetically calculable mass of human beings, each individual a repetition of the other.
>   *My Apprenticeship* (1926) ch. 1

Sidney Webb (*Baron Passfield*) 1859–1947
English socialist

16 Once we face the necessity of putting our principles first into Bills, to be fought through committee clause by clause; and then into the appropriate machinery for carrying them into execution from one end of the kingdom to the other . . . the inevitability of gradualness cannot fail to be appreciated.
>   Presidential address to the annual conference of the Labour Party, 26 June 1923, in *The Labour Party on the Threshold* (Fabian Tract no. 207, 1923) p. 11

17 Marriage is the waste-paper basket of the emotions.
>   In Bertrand Russell *Autobiography* (1967) vol. 1, ch. 4

Max Weber 1864–1920
German sociologist

18 *Die protestantische Ethik und der Geist des Kapitalismus.*

The protestant ethic and the spirit of capitalism.
>   *Archiv für Sozialwissenschaft Sozialpolitik* vol. 20 (1904–5) (title of article)

19 *Nur wie 'ein dünner Mantel, den man jeder abwerfen könnte,' sollte nach Baxters Ansicht die Sorge um die äusseren Güter um die Schultern seiner Heiligen liegen. Aber aus dem Mantel liess das Verhängnis ein stahlhartes Gehäuse werden.*

In Baxter's view the care for external goods should only lie on the shoulders of the saint like 'a light cloak, which can be thrown aside at any moment.' But fate decreed that the cloak should become an iron cage.
>   *Gesammelte Aufsätze zur Religionssoziologie* (1920) vol. 1, p. 203 (translated by T. Parsons, 1930)

20 *Ein 'Stand' ist . . . eine durch die Art der Lebensführung, die konventionalen spezifischen Ehrbegriffe und die rechtlich monopolisierten ökonomischen Chancen . . . Menschengruppe.*

A 'status group' is a group societalized through its special styles of life, its conventional and specific notions of honour, and the economic opportunities it legally monopolizes.
>   *Gesammelte Aufsätze zur Religionssoziologie* (1920) vol. 1, p. 274 (translated by H. Gerth, 1948)

21 *Der Staat ist . . . ein auf das Mittel der legitimen (das heisst: als legitim angesehenen) Gewaltsamkeit gestütztes Herrschaftsverhältnis von Menschen über Menschen.*

The State is a relation of men dominating men, a relation supported by means of legitimate (i.e. considered to be legitimate) violence.
>   'Politik als Beruf' (1919) in *Gesammelte politische Schriften* (1921) p. 507 (translated by H. Gerth and C. Wright Mills, 1948)

1 *Die Autorität des 'ewig Gestrigen'.*

The authority of the 'eternal yesterday'.

'Politik als Beruf' (1919) in *Gesammelte politische Schriften* (1921) p. 507

2 *Die Erfahrung von der Irrationalität der Welt war ja die treibende Kraft aller Religionswicklung.*

The experience of the irrationality of the world has been the driving force of all religious revolution.

'Politik als Beruf' (1919) in *Gesammelte politische Schriften* (1921) p. 554

3 *Die massgebende Rolle der 'Lebensführung' für die ständische 'Ehre' bringt es mit sich, dass die 'Stände' die spezifischen Träger aller 'Konventionen' sind.*

The decisive role of a 'style of life' in status 'honour' means that status groups are the specific bearers of all 'conventions'.

'Politik als Beruf' (1919) in *Gesammelte politische Schriften* (1921) p. 637

4 *Der Begriff des 'Amtsgeheimnisses' ist ihre spezifische Erfindung.*

The concept of the 'official secret' is its [bureaucracy's] specific invention.

'Politik als Beruf' (1919) in *Gesammelte politische Schriften* (1921) p. 672

Daniel Webster 1782–1852

American politician

5 The people's government, made for the people, made by the people, and answerable to the people.

Second speech in the Senate on Foote's Resolution, 26 January 1830, in *Writings and Speeches* vol. 6 (1903). Cf. Lincoln 422:10

6 Liberty *and* Union, now and forever, one and inseparable!

Second speech in the Senate on Foote's Resolution, 26 January 1830, in *Writings and Speeches* vol. 6 (1903)

7 Fearful concatenation of circumstances.

Argument on the murder of Captain Joseph White, 6 April 1830, in *Writings and Speeches* vol. 11 (1903)

8 On this question of principle, while actual suffering was yet afar off, they [the Colonies] raised their flag against a power, to which, for purposes of foreign conquest and subjugation, Rome, in the height of her glory, is not to be compared; a power which has dotted over the surface of the whole globe with her possessions and military posts, whose morning drum-beat, following the sun, and keeping company with the hours, circles the earth with one continuous and unbroken strain of the martial airs of England.

Speech in the Senate on the President's Protest, 7 May 1834, in *Writings and Speeches* vol. 7 (1903)

9 Thank God, I—I also—am an American!

Speech on the completion of Bunker Hill Monument, 17 June 1843, in *Writings and Speeches* vol. 1 (1903)

10 The Law: It has honoured us, may we honour it.

Speech at the Charleston Bar Dinner, 10 May 1847, in *Writings and Speeches* vol. 4 (1903)

11 I was born an American; I will live an American; I shall die an American.

Speech in the Senate on 'The Compromise Bill', 17 July 1850, in *Writings and Speeches* vol. 10 (1903)

12 There is always room at the top.

On being advised against joining the overcrowded legal profession (attributed)

John Webster c.1580–c.1625

English playwright

13 Vain the ambition of kings
Who seek by trophies and dead things,
To leave a living name behind,
And weave but nets to catch the wind.

The Devil's Law-Case (1623) act 5, sc. 4

14 FERDINAND: And women like that part which, like the lamprey,
Hath never a bone in't.
DUCHESS: Fie, sir!
FERDINAND: Nay,
I mean the tongue; variety of courtship:
What cannot a neat knave with a smooth tale
Make a woman believe?

The Duchess of Malfi (1623) act 1, sc. 1

15 Unequal nature, to place women's hearts
So far upon the left side.

The Duchess of Malfi (1623) act 2, sc. 5

16   Why should only I . . .
Be cased up, like a holy relic? I have youth
And a little beauty.

The Duchess of Malfi (1623) act 3, sc. 2

17 Raised by that curious engine, your white hand.

The Duchess of Malfi (1623) act 3, sc. 2

18   O, that it were possible,
We might but hold some two days' conference
With the dead!

The Duchess of Malfi (1623) act 4, sc. 2

19 I have made a soap-boiler costive.

The Duchess of Malfi (1623) act 4, sc. 2

20 I am Duchess of Malfi still.

The Duchess of Malfi (1623) act 4, sc. 2

21 Glories, like glow-worms, afar off shine bright,
But looked to near, have neither heat nor light.

The Duchess of Malfi (1623) act 4, sc. 2

22 I know death hath ten thousand several doors
For men to take their exits.

The Duchess of Malfi (1623) act 4, sc. 2. Cf. Fletcher 285:15, Massinger 453:16, Seneca 563:2

23 FERDINAND: Cover her face; mine eyes dazzle: she died young.
BOSOLA: I think not so; her infelicity
Seemed to have years too many.

The Duchess of Malfi (1623) act 4, sc. 2

24 Physicians are like kings,—they brook no contradiction.

The Duchess of Malfi (1623) act 5, sc. 2

25 We are merely the stars' tennis-balls, struck and bandied
Which way please them.

The Duchess of Malfi (1623) act 5, sc. 4

26 Is not old wine wholesomest, old pippins toothsomest, old wood burn brightest, old linen wash whitest? Old soldiers, sweethearts, are surest, and old lovers are soundest.

Westward Hoe (1607) act 2, sc. 2

1   Fortune's a right whore:
If she give aught, she deals it in small parcels,
That she may take away all at one swoop.
  The White Devil (1612) act 1, sc. 1

2 'Tis just like a summer birdcage in a garden; the birds
that are without despair to get in, and the birds that
are within despair, and are in a consumption, for fear
they shall never get out.
  The White Devil (1612) act 1, sc. 2

3 A mere tale of a tub, my words are idle.
  The White Devil (1612) act 2, sc. 1

4 Only the deep sense of some deathless shame.
  The White Devil (1612) act 2, sc. 1

5 Cowardly dogs bark loudest.
  The White Devil (1612) act 3, sc. 2

6 A rape! a rape! . . .
Yes, you have ravished justice;
Forced her to do your pleasure.
  The White Devil (1612) act 3, sc. 2

7 Call for the robin-red-breast and the wren,
Since o'er shady groves they hover,
And with leaves and flowers do cover
The friendless bodies of unburied men.
  The White Devil (1612) act 5, sc. 4

8 But keep the wolf far thence that's foe to men,
For with his nails he'll dig them up again.
  The White Devil (1612) act 5, sc. 4

9 We think caged birds sing, when indeed they cry.
  The White Devil (1612) act 5, sc. 4. Cf. *King Lear* 597:16

10 And of all axioms this shall win the prize,—
'Tis better to be fortunate than wise.
  The White Devil (1612) act 5, sc. 6

11 There's nothing of so infinite vexation
As man's own thoughts.
  The White Devil (1612) act 5, sc. 6

12 My soul, like to a ship in a black storm,
Is driven, I know not whither.
  The White Devil (1612) act 5, sc. 6

13 Prosperity doth bewitch men, seeming clear;
But seas do laugh, show white, when rocks are near.
  The White Devil (1612) act 5, sc. 6

14   I have caught
An everlasting cold; I have lost my voice
Most irrecoverably.
  The White Devil (1612) act 5, sc. 6

Josiah Wedgwood 1730–95
English potter

15 Am I not a man and a brother.
  Legend on Wedgwood cameo, depicting a kneeling Negro
  slave in chains, reproduced in facsimile in E. Darwin *The
  Botanic Garden* pt. 1 (1791) facing p. 87

Simone Weil 1909–43
French essayist and philosopher

16 *Je voudrais proposer de considérer la barbarie comme un
caractère permanent et universel de la nature humaine, qui
se développe plus ou moins selon que les circonstances lui
donnent plus ou moins de jeu.*

I would suggest that barbarism be considered as a
permanent and universal human characteristic which
becomes more or less pronounced according to the
play of circumstances.
  Écrits Historiques et politiques (1960) 'Réflexions sur la
  barbarie' (written *c*,1939)

17 *Un droit n'est pas efficace par lui-même, mais seulement
par l'obligation à laquelle il correspond . . . Une obligation
ne serait-elle reconnue par personne, elle ne perd rien de la
plénitude de son être. Un droit qui n'est reconnu par
personne n'est pas grand-chose.*

A right is not effectual by itself, but only in relation to
the obligation to which it corresponds . . . An
obligation which goes unrecognized by anybody loses
none of the full force of its existence. A right which
goes unrecognized by anybody is not worth very
much.
  L'Enracinement (1949) 'Les Besoins de l'âme' (translated by
  A. F. Wills)

18 *Tous les Péchés sont des tentatives pour combler des vides.*
All sins are attempts to fill voids.
  La Pesanteur et la grâce (1948) p. 27

19 What a country calls its vital economic interests are
not the things which enable its citizens to live, but the
things which enable it to make war.
  In W. H. Auden *A Certain World* (1971) p. 384

Johnny Weissmuller 1904–84
American film actor

20 Me Tarzan, you Jane.
  Summing up his role in *Tarzan, the Ape Man* (1932 film).
  The words occur neither in the film nor the original, by
  Edgar Rice Burroughs. See *Photoplay Magazine* June 1932

Thomas Earle Welby 1881–1933
British writer

21 'Turbot, Sir,' said the waiter, placing before me two
fishbones, two eyeballs, and a bit of black mackintosh.
  The Dinner Knell (1932) 'Birmingham or Crewe?'

Orson Welles 1915–85
American actor and film director

22 In Italy for thirty years under the Borgias they had
warfare, terror, murder, bloodshed — they produced
Michelangelo, Leonardo da Vinci and the Renaissance.
In Switzerland they had brotherly love, five hundred
years of democracy and peace and what did that
produce . . . ? The cuckoo clock.
  The Third Man (1949 film); words added by Welles to
  Graham Greene's script

23 The biggest electric train set any boy ever had!
  Of the RKO studios, in Peter Noble *The Fabulous Orson
  Welles* (1956) ch. 7

Duke of Wellington 1769–1852

British soldier and statesman

1 All the business of war, and indeed all the business of life, is to endeavour to find out what you don't know by what you do; that's what I called 'guessing what was at the other side of the hill'.

> *The Croker Papers* (1885) vol. 3 ch. 28

2 As Lord Chesterfield said of the generals of his day, 'I only hope that when the enemy reads the list of their names, he trembles as I do.'

> Letter, 29 August 1810, in *Supplementary Despatches . . .* (1860) vol. 6, p. 582 (usually quoted 'I don't know what effect these men will have upon the enemy, but, by God, they frighten me')

3 Up Guards and at them!

> Letter from an officer in the Guards, 22 June 1815, in *The Battle of Waterloo* by a Near Observer [J. Booth] (1815) p. 57; later denied by Wellington. See *The Croker Papers* (1885) vol. 3, ch. 28

4 I never saw so many shocking bad hats in my life.

> On seeing the first Reformed Parliament, in Sir William Fraser *Words on Wellington* (1889) p. 12

5 You must build your House of Parliament upon the river . . . the populace cannot exact their demands by sitting down round you.

> In Sir William Fraser *Words on Wellington* (1889) p. 163

6 If you believe that, you'll believe anything.

> To a gentleman who had accosted him in the street saying, 'Mr Jones, I believe?'; in Elizabeth Longford *Pillar of State* (1972) ch. 10. George Jones RA (1786–1869), painter of military subjects, bore a striking resemblance to Wellington

7 The battle of Waterloo was won on the playing fields of Eton.

> Oral tradition, but not found in this form of words. See C. F. R. Montalembert *De l'avenir politique de l'Angleterre* (1856) ch. 10

8 I have no small talk and Peel has no manners.

> In G. W. E. Russell *Collections and Recollections* (1898) ch. 14

9 Hard pounding this, gentlemen; let's see who will pound longest.

> At the Battle of Waterloo, in Sir Walter Scott *Paul's Letters* (1816) Letter 8

10 Next to a battle lost, the greatest misery is a battle gained.

> In *Diary of Frances, Lady Shelley 1787–1817* (ed. R. Edgcumbe) vol. 1, ch. 9, p. 102. See S. Rogers *Recollections* (1859) p. 215 for variations on the theme

11 I used to say of him [Napoleon] that his presence on the field made the difference of forty thousand men.

> In Philip Henry Stanhope *Notes of Conversations with the Duke of Wellington* (1888) 2 November 1831

12 Ours [our army] is composed of the scum of the earth—the mere scum of the earth.

> In Philip Henry Stanhope *Notes of Conversations with the Duke of Wellington* (1888) 4 November 1831

13 Publish and be damned.

> Replying to a blackmail threat (attributed). See Elizabeth Longford *Wellington: The Years of the Sword* (1969) ch. 10

H. G. Wells 1866–1946

English novelist

14 It is leviathan retrieving pebbles. It is a magnificent but painful hippopotamus resolved at any cost, even at the cost of its dignity, upon picking up a pea which has got into a corner of its den.

> *Boon* (1915) ch. 4 (of Henry James)

15 He was a practical electrician but fond of whisky, a heavy, red-haired brute with irregular teeth. He doubted the existence of the Deity but accepted Carnot's cycle, and he had read Shakespeare and found him weak in chemistry.

> *Complete Short Stories* (1927) 'Lord of the Dynamos'

16 'Sesquippledan,' he would say. 'Sesquippledan verboojuice.'

> *The History of Mr Polly* (1909) ch. 1, pt. 5

17 'I'm a Norfan, both sides,' he would explain, with the air of one who had seen trouble.

> *Kipps* (1905) bk. 1, ch. 6, pt. 1

18 'I expect,' he said, 'I was thinking jest what a Rum Go everything is. I expect it was something like that.'

> *Kipps* (1905) bk. 3, ch. 3, pt. 8

19 The Social Contract is nothing more or less than a vast conspiracy of human beings to lie to and humbug themselves and one another for the general Good. Lies are the mortar that bind the savage individual man into the social masonry.

> *Love and Mr Lewisham* (1900) ch. 23

20 Human history becomes more and more a race between education and catastrophe.

> *The Outline of History* (1920) vol. 2, ch. 41, pt. 4

21 Bah! the thing is not a nose at all, but a bit of primordial chaos clapped on to my face.

> *Select Conversations with an Uncle* (1895) 'The Man with a Nose'

22 The shape of things to come.

> Title of book (1933)

23 The war that will end war.

> Title of book (1914). Cf. Lloyd George 424:7

24 Moral indignation is jealousy with a halo.

> *The Wife of Sir Isaac Harman* (1914) ch. 9, sect. 2

Arnold Wesker 1932–

English playwright

25 And then I saw the menu, stained with tea and beautifully written by a foreign hand, and on top it said — God I hated that old man — it said 'Chips with everything'. Chips with every damn thing. You breed babies and you eat chips with everything.

> *Chips with Everything* (1962) act 1, sc. 2

26 Education ent only books and music—it's asking questions, all the time. There are millions of us, all over the country, and no one, not one of us, is asking questions, we're all taking the easiest way out.

> *Roots* (1959) act 3

Charles Wesley 1707–88

English Methodist preacher and hymn-writer

1 Amazing love! How can it be
That thou, my God, shouldst die for me?
   'And can it be' (1738 hymn)

2 Long my imprisoned spirit lay
Fast bound in sin and nature's night;
Thine eye diffused a quickening ray—
I woke, the dungeon flamed with light,
My chains fell off, my heart was free,
I rose, went forth, and followed thee.
   'And can it be' (1738 hymn)

3 Hark! how all the welkin rings,
Glory to the King of kings.
Peace on earth and mercy mild,
God and sinners reconciled.
   Hymns and Sacred Poems (1739) 'Hymn for Christmas'; the
   first two lines altered to 'Hark! the herald-angels sing /
   Glory to the new born king' in George Whitefield's *Hymns
   for Social Worship* (1753)

4 Hail, the heaven-born Prince of Peace!
Hail, the Sun of Righteousness!
   Hymns and Sacred Poems (1739) 'Hymn for Christmas'

5 O for a thousand tongues to sing.
   Hymns and Sacred Poems (1740) 'For the Anniversary Day
   of one's Conversion'

6 Jesu, lover of my soul,
Let me to thy bosom fly,
While the nearer waters roll,
While the tempest still is high;
Hide me, O my Saviour, hide,
Till the storm of life is past;
Safe into the haven guide,
O receive my soul at last.
   Hymns and Sacred Poems (1740) 'In Temptation'

7 Gentle Jesus, meek and mild,
Look upon a little child;
Pity my simplicity,
Suffer me to come to thee.
   Hymns and Sacred Poems (1742) 'Gentle Jesus, Meek and
   Mild'

8 Come, O thou Traveller unknown,
Whom still I hold, but cannot see.
   Hymns and Sacred Poems (1742) 'Wrestling Jacob'

9 Wrestling, I will not let thee go,
Till I thy name, thy nature know.
   Hymns and Sacred Poems (1742) 'Wrestling Jacob'

10 Forth in thy name, O Lord, I go,
My daily labour to pursue;
Thee, only thee, resolved to know,
In all I think or speak or do.
   Hymns and Sacred Poems (1749) 'Forth in thy name, O
   Lord, I go'

11 Soldiers of Christ, arise,
And put your armour on.
   Hymns and Sacred Poems (1749) 'The Whole Armour of
   God'

12 God is gone up on high
With a triumphant noise.
   Hymns for our Lord's Resurrection (1746) 'God is gone up'

13 Rejoice, the Lord is King!
Your Lord and King adore;
Mortals, give thanks and sing,
And triumph evermore:
Lift up your heart, lift up your voice;
Rejoice, again, I say rejoice.
   Hymns for our Lord's Resurrection (1746) 'Rejoice, the Lord
   is King!'

14 Love divine, all loves excelling,
Joy of heav'n, to earth come down,
Fix in us thy humble dwelling,
All thy faithful mercies crown.
Jesu, thou art all compassion,
Pure unbounded love thou art;
Visit us with thy salvation,
Enter every trembling heart.
   Hymns for those that seek . . . Redemption (1747) 'Love
   divine' (based on Dryden's 'Fairest isle, all isles excelling',
   King Arthur, 1691). Cf. Dryden 260:34

15 Lo! He comes with clouds descending,
Once for favoured sinners slain;
Thousand thousand Saints attending
Swell the triumph of His train.
   Hymns of Intercession for all Mankind (1758) 'Lo! He comes'

John Wesley 1703–91

English preacher; founder of Methodism

16 Thou hidden love of God, whose height,
Whose depth unfathomed no man knows,
I see from far thy beauteous light,
Inly I sigh for thy repose.
   A Collection of Psalms and Hymns (1738) 'Divine Love' (a
   translation of G. Tersteegen's 'Verborgen Gottesliebe du',
   1729)

17 The Gospel of Christ knows of no religion but social;
no holiness but social holiness.
   Hymns and Sacred Poems (1739) Preface

18 I went to America to convert the Indians; but oh, who
shall convert me?
   Journal (ed. N. Curnock) 24 January 1738

19 I felt my heart strangely warmed. I felt I did trust in
Christ, Christ alone for salvation; and an assurance
was given me that He had taken away *my* sins, even
mine, and saved *me* from the law of sin and death.
   Journal (ed. N. Curnock) 24 May 1738 (on his conversion)

20 I look upon all the world as my parish.
   Journal (ed. N. Curnock) 11 June 1739

21 I have this day lived fourscore years . . . God grant
that I may never live to be useless!
   Journal (ed. N. Curnock) 28 June 1783

22 I design plain truth for plain people.
   Sermons on Several Occasions (1746) in *Works* (Centenary
   ed.) vol. 1, p. 104

23 Let it be observed, that slovenliness is no part of
religion; that neither this, nor any text of Scripture,
condemns neatness of apparel. Certainly this is a duty,
not a sin. 'Cleanliness is, indeed, next to godliness.'
   Sermons on Several Occasions (1788) Sermon 88

24 No circumstances can make it necessary for a man to
burst in sunder all the ties of humanity.
   Thoughts upon Slavery (1774) in *Works* (Centenary ed.)
   vol. 11, p. 72

1 I let you loose, George, on the great continent of America. Publish your message in the open face of the sun, and do all the good you can.
> Letter to a preacher, George Shadford, March 1773 in *Letters* (ed. J. Telford, 1931) vol. 6

2 Though I am always in haste, I am never in a hurry.
> Letter to Miss March, 10 December 1777, in *Letters* (ed. J. Telford, 1931) vol. 6

3 Those that desire to write or say anything to me have no time to lose; for time has shaken me by the hand and death is not far behind.
> Letter to Ezekiel Cooper, 1 February 1791, in *Letters* (ed. J. Telford, 1931) vol. 8

4 Men may call me a knave or a fool, a rascal, a scoundrel, and I am content; but they shall never by my consent call me a Bishop!
> In Betty M. Jarboe *Wesley Quotations* (1990)

Samuel Wesley 1662–1735

English clergyman and poet

5 Style is the dress of thought; a modest dress, Neat, but not gaudy, will true critics please.
> 'An Epistle to a Friend concerning Poetry' (1700). Cf. Pope 521:12

Mae West 1892–1980

American film actress

6 A man in the house is worth two in the street.
> *Belle of the Nineties* (1934 film)

7 I always say, keep a diary and some day it'll keep you.
> *Every Day's a Holiday* (1937 film)

8 Beulah, peel me a grape.
> *I'm No Angel* (1933 film)

9 It's not the men in my life that counts—it's the life in my men.
> *I'm No Angel* (1933 film)

10 Give a man a free hand and he'll try to put it all over you.
> *Klondike Annie* (1936 film)

11 'Goodness, what beautiful diamonds!'
'Goodness had nothing to do with it.'
> *Night After Night* (1932 film)

12 Is that a gun in your pocket, or are you just glad to see me?
> In Joseph Weintraub *Peel Me a Grape* (1975) p. 47 (usually quoted 'Is that a pistol in your pocket . . . ')

13 I used to be Snow White . . . but I drifted.
> In Joseph Weintraub *Peel Me a Grape* (1975) p. 47

14 Why don't you come up sometime, and see me?
> *She Done Him Wrong* (1933 film); usually quoted 'Why don't you come up and see me sometime?'

Rebecca West (Cicily Isabel Fairfield) 1892–1983

English novelist and journalist

15 She was not so much a person as an implication of dreary poverty, like an open door in a mean house that lets out the smell of cooking cabbage and the screams of children.
> *The Return of the Soldier* (1918) ch. 5

16 It is queer how it is always one's virtues and not one's vices that precipitate one into disaster.
> *There is No Conversation* (1935) ch. 1

17 The point is that nobody likes having salt rubbed into their wounds, even if it is the salt of the earth.
> *The Salt of the Earth* (1935) ch. 2

18 Every other inch a gentleman.
> Of Michael Arlen, in Victoria Glendinning *Rebecca West* (1987) pt. 3, ch. 5

Edward Noyes Westcott 1846–98

American novelist

19 They say a reasonable amount o' fleas is good fer a dog—keeps him from broodin' over bein' a dog, mebbe.
> *David Harum* (1898) ch. 32

John Fane, 10th Earl of Westmorland 1759–1841

20 *Merit*, indeed! . . . We are come to a pretty pass if they talk of *merit* for a bishopric.
> Noted in Lady Salisbury's diary, 9 December 1835; in C. Oman *The Gascoyne Heiress* (1968) pt. 5, p. 188

R. P. Weston 1878–1936 *and* Bert Lee 1880–1947

British songwriters

21 Good-bye-ee! — Good-bye-ee!
Wipe the tear, baby dear, from your eye-ee.
Tho' it's hard to part, I know,
I'll be tickled to death to go.
Don't cry-ee — don't sigh-ee!
There's a silver lining in the sky-ee!
Bonsoir, old thing! cheerio! chin-chin!
Nahpoo! Toodle-oo! Good-bye-ee!
> 'Good-bye-ee!' (c.1915 song)

Sir Charles Wetherell 1770–1846

English lawyer and politician

22 Then there is my noble and biographical friend who has added a new terror to death.
> Of Lord Campbell, in Lord St Leonards *Misrepresentations in Campbell's Lives of Lyndhurst and Brougham* (1869) p. 2. Cf. Arbuthnot 24:10, Lyndhurst 433:14

Robert Wever fl. 1550

1 In a harbour grene aslepe whereas I lay,
The byrdes sang swete in the middes of the day,
I dreamèd fast of mirth and play:
In youth is pleasure, in youth is pleasure.
'Lusty Juventus'

Edith Wharton 1862–1937

American novelist

2 An unalterable and unquestioned law of the musical
world required that the German text of French operas
sung by Swedish artists should be translated into
Italian for the clearer understanding of
English-speaking audiences.
The Age of Innocence (1920) bk. 1, ch. 1

3 If he paid for each day's comfort with the small
change of his illusions, he grew daily to value the
comfort more and set less store upon the coin.
The Descent of Man (1904) 'The Other Two' ch. 5

4 Almost everybody in the neighbourhood had
'troubles', frankly localized and specified; but only the
chosen had 'complications'. To have them was in itself
a distinction, though it was also, in most cases, a
death-warrant. People struggled on for years with
'troubles', but they almost always succumbed to
'complications'.
Ethan Frome (1911) ch. 7

5 Mrs Ballinger is one of the ladies who pursue Culture
in bands, as though it were dangerous to meet it
alone.
Xingu and Other Stories (1916) 'Xingu'

Thomas, 1st Marquess of Wharton 1648–1715

6 Ho, Brother Teague, dost hear de Decree?
Lilli Burlero Bullena-la.
Dat we shall have a new Debity,
Lilli Burlero Bullena-la.
'A New Song' (written 1687), in *Poems on Affairs of State*
(1704) vol. 3, p. 231 (*debity* deputy)

Richard Whately 1787–1863

*English philosopher and theologian; Archbishop of Dublin
from 1831*

7 Preach not because you have to say something, but
because you have something to say.
Apophthegms (1854)

8 Happiness is no laughing matter.
Apophthegms (1854)

9 It is a folly to expect men to do all that they may
reasonably be expected to do.
Apophthegms (1854)

10 Honesty is the best policy; but he who is governed by
that maxim is not an honest man.
Apophthegms (1854)

11 It is not that pearls fetch a high price *because* men
have dived for them; but on the contrary, men dive
for them because they fetch a high price.
Introductory Lectures on Political Economy (1832) p. 253

12 'Never forget, gentlemen,' he [Whateley] said, to his
astonished hearers, as he held up a copy of the
'Authorized Version' of the Bible, 'never forget that
this is *not* the Bible,' then, after a moment's pause, he
continued, 'This, gentlemen, is only a *translation* of the
Bible.'
To a meeting of his diocesan clergy, in H. Solly *These Eighty
Years* (1893) vol. 2, ch. 2

William Whewell 1794–1866

English philosopher and scientist

13 Nature, so far as it is the object of scientific research,
is a collection of facts governed by *laws*: our
knowledge of nature is our knowledge of laws.
*Astronomy and General Physics considered with reference to
Natural Theology* (1834) ch. 1

14 Hence no force however great can stretch a cord
however fine into an horizontal line which is
accurately straight: there will always be a bending
downwards.
Elementary Treatise on Mechanics (1819) ch. 4, problem 2
(often cited as an example of accidental metre and rhyme,
and changed in later editions)

15 Man is the interpreter of nature, science the right
interpretation.
Philosophy of the Inductive Sciences (1840) Aphorism 17

James McNeill Whistler 1834–1903

American-born painter

16 I am not arguing with you—I am telling you.
The Gentle Art of Making Enemies (1890) p. 51

17 Art is upon the Town!
Mr Whistler's 'Ten O'Clock' (1885) p. 7

18 Listen! There never was an artistic period. There never
was an Art-loving nation.
Mr Whistler's 'Ten O'Clock' (1885) p. 10

19 Nature is usually wrong.
Mr Whistler's 'Ten O'Clock' (1885) p. 14

20 I maintain that two and two would continue to make
four, in spite of the whine of the amateur for three, or
the cry of the critic for five.
Whistler v. Ruskin. Art and Art Critics (1878) p. 6

21 OSCAR WILDE: How I wish I had said that.
WHISTLER: You will, Oscar, you will.
In R. Ellman *Oscar Wilde* (1987) pt. 2, ch. 5

22 Yes madam, Nature is creeping up.
To a lady who had been reminded of his work by an
'exquisite haze in the atmosphere'; in D. C. Seitz *Whistler
Stories* (1913) p. 9

23 No, I ask it for the knowledge of a lifetime.
In his case against Ruskin, replying to the question 'For
two days' labour, you ask two hundred guineas?'; in D. C.
Seitz *Whistler Stories* (1913) p. 40

E. B. White 1899–1985

American humorist

1 Commuter—one who spends his life
In riding to and from his wife;
A man who shaves and takes a train,
And then rides back to shave again.
  'The Commuter' (1982)

2 MOTHER: It's broccoli, dear.
CHILD: I say it's spinach, and I say the hell with it.
  New Yorker 8 December 1928 (cartoon caption)

3 Democracy is the recurrent suspicion that more than
half of the people are right more than half of the time.
  New Yorker 3 July 1944

H. Kirke White 1785 1806

English poet

4 Oft in danger, oft in woe,
Onward, Christians, onward go;
Bear the toil, maintain the strife,
Strengthened with the Bread of Life.
  'Oft in danger, oft in woe' (1812 hymn)

Patrick White 1912–90

Australian novelist

5 Conversation is imperative if gaps are to be filled, and
old age, it is the last gap but one.
  The Tree of Man (1955) ch. 22

6 Few people of attainments take easily to a plan of
self-improvement. Some discover very early their
perfection cannot endure the insult. Others find their
intellectual pleasure lies in the theory, not the
practice. Only a few stubborn ones will blunder on,
painfully, out of the luxuriant world of their
pretensions into the desert of mortification and
reward.
  Voss (1957) ch. 4

T. H. White 1906–64

English novelist

7 The Victorians had not been anxious to go away for
the weekend. The Edwardians, on the contrary, were
nomadic.
  Farewell Victoria (1933) pt. 4

8 The once and future king.
  Title of novel (1958), taken from Sir Thomas Malory *Le
  Morte d'Arthur* bk. 21, ch. 7: '*Hic iacet Arthurus, rex
  quondam rexque futurus*'

Alfred North Whitehead 1861–1947

English philosopher and mathematician

9 Life is an offensive, directed against the repetitious
mechanism of the Universe.
  Adventures of Ideas (1933) pt. 1, ch. 4

10 It is more important that a proposition be interesting
than that it be true. This statement is almost
a tautology. For the energy of operation of
a proposition in an occasion of experience is its
interest, and is its importance. But of course a true
proposition is more apt to be interesting than a false
one.
  Adventures of Ideas (1933) pt. 4, ch. 16

11 There are no whole truths; all truths are half-truths.
It is trying to treat them as whole truths that plays
the devil.
  Dialogues (1954) prologue

12 Intelligence is quickness to apprehend as distinct from
ability, which is capacity to act wisely on the thing
apprehended.
  Dialogues (1954) 15 December 1939

13 What is morality in any given time or place? It is
what the majority then and there happen to like, and
immorality is what they dislike.
  Dialogues (1954) 30 August 1941

14 Art is the imposing of a pattern on experience, and our
aesthetic enjoyment is recognition of the pattern.
  Dialogues (1954) 10 June 1943

15 Civilization advances by extending the number of
important operations which we can perform without
thinking about them.
  Introduction to Mathematics (1911) ch. 5

16 The safest general characterization of the European
philosophical tradition is that it consists of a series of
footnotes to Plato.
  Process and Reality (1929) pt. 2, ch. 1

17 Since a babe was born in a manger, it may be doubted
whether so great a thing has happened with so little
stir.
  Science and the Modern World (1925) ch. 1 (on the scientific
  revolution in the sixteenth century)

Katharine Whitehorn 1926–

English journalist

18 An office party is not, as is sometimes supposed, the
Managing Director's chance to kiss the tea-girl. It is
the tea-girl's chance to kiss the Managing Director ...
Bringing down the mighty from their seats is an
agreeable and necessary pastime, but no one supposes
that the mighty, having struggled so hard to get
seated, will enjoy the dethronement.
  Roundabout (1962) 'The Office Party'

19 Hats divide generally into three classes: offensive hats,
defensive hats, and shrapnel.
  Shouts and Murmurs (1963) 'Hats'

20 I wouldn't say when you've seen one Western you've
seen the lot; but when you've seen the lot you get the
feeling you've seen one.
  Sunday Best (1976) 'Decoding the West'

George Whiting

American songwriter

21 My Blue Heaven.
  Title of song (1927)

1 When you're all dressed up and have no place to go.
  Title of song (1912)

William Whiting 1825–78

English teacher; master of the Quiristers of Winchester College from 1842

2 Eternal Father, strong to save,
  Whose arm doth bind the restless wave,
  Who bidd'st the mighty ocean deep
  Its own appointed limits keep:
  O hear us when we cry to thee,
  For those in peril on the sea.
  'Eternal Father, Strong to Save' (1869 hymn)

Walt Whitman 1819–92

American poet

3 I dreamed in a dream I saw a city invincible to the
  attacks of the whole of the rest of the earth,
  I dreamed that was the new city of Friends.
  'I dreamed in a dream' (1867)

4 I sing the body electric.
  Title of poem (1855)

5 Me imperturbe, standing at ease in Nature.
  'Me imperturbe' (1881)

6 O Captain! my Captain! our fearful trip is done,
  The ship has weathered every rack, the prize we
  sought is won,
  The port is near, the bells I hear, the people all
  exulting.
  'O Captain! My Captain!' (1871)

7 The ship is anchored safe and sound, its voyage closed
  and done.
  From fearful trip the victor ship comes in with object
  won;
  Exult O shores, and ring O bells! But I with mournful
  tread
  Walk the deck my Captain lies, Fallen cold and dead.
  'O Captain! My Captain!' (1871)

8 Out of the cradle endlessly rocking,
  Out of the mocking-bird's throat, the musical
  shuttle . . .
  A reminiscence sing.
  'Out of the cradle endlessly rocking' (1881)

9 Come my tan-faced children,
  Follow well in order, get your weapons ready,
  Have you your pistols? have you your sharp-edged
  axes?
  Pioneers! O pioneers!
  'Pioneers! O Pioneers!' (1881)

10 Camerado, this is no book,
  Who touches this touches a man,
  (Is it night? Are we here together alone?)
  It is I you hold and who holds you.
  I spring from the pages into your arms—decease calls
  me forth.
  'So Long!' (1881)

11 Where the populace rise at once against the
  never-ending audacity of elected persons.
  'Song of the Broad Axe' (1881) pt. 5, l. 12

12 Where the city of the healthiest fathers stands,
  Where the city of the best-bodied mothers stands,
  There the great city stands.
  'Song of the Broad Axe' (1881) pt. 5, l. 20

13 I celebrate myself, and sing myself.
  'Song of Myself' (written 1855) pt. 1

14 Urge and urge and urge,
  Always the procreant urge of the world.
  'Song of Myself' (written 1855) pt. 3

15 Has any one supposed it lucky to be born?
  I hasten to inform him or her, it is just as lucky to die
  and I know it.
  'Song of Myself' (written 1855) pt. 7

16 I also say it is good to fall, battles are lost in the same
  spirit in which they are won.
  'Song of Myself' (written 1855) pt. 18

17 I believe a leaf of grass is no less than the
  journey-work of the stars,
  And the pismire is equally perfect, and a grain of sand,
  and the egg of the wren,
  And the tree toad is a chef-d'oeuvre for the highest,
  And the running blackberry would adorn the parlours
  of heaven.
  'Song of Myself' (written 1855) pt. 31

18 I think I could turn and live with animals, they are so
  placid and self-contained,
  I stand and look at them long and long.
  They do not sweat and whine about their condition,
  They do not lie awake in the dark and weep for their
  sins,
  They do not make me sick discussing their duty to
  God,
  Not one is dissatisfied, not one is demented with the
  mania of owning things,
  Not one kneels to another, nor to his kind that lived
  thousands of years ago,
  Not one is respectable or unhappy over the whole
  earth.
  'Song of Myself' (written 1855) pt. 32

19 Behold, I do not give lectures or a little charity,
  When I give I give myself.
  'Song of Myself' (written 1855) pt. 40

20 My rendezvous is appointed, it is certain,
  The Lord will be there and wait till I come on perfect
  terms,
  The great Camerado, the lover true for whom I pine
  will be there.
  'Song of Myself' (written 1855) pt. 45

21 Do I contradict myself?
  Very well then I contradict myself,
  (I am large, I contain multitudes.)
  'Song of Myself' (written 1855) pt. 51

22 I sound my barbaric yawp over the roofs of the world.
  'Song of Myself' (written 1855) pt. 52

23 Afoot and light-hearted I take to the open road,
  Healthy, free, the world before me,
  The long brown path before me leading wherever I
  choose.
  'Song of the Open Road' (1871) pt. 1, l. 1

1 The earth does not argue,
Is not pathetic, has no arrangements,
Does not scream, haste, persuade, threaten, promise,
Makes no discriminations, has no conceivable failures,
Closes nothing, refuses nothing, shuts none out.
'A Song of the Rolling Earth' (1881) pt. 1

2 This dust was once the man,
Gentle, plain, just and resolute, under whose cautious hand,
Against the foulest crime in history known in any land or age,
Was saved the Union of these States.
'This dust was once the man' (1881)

3 When lilacs last in the dooryard bloomed,
And the great star early drooped in the western sky in the night,
I mourned, and yet shall mourn with ever-returning spring.
'When lilacs last in the dooryard bloomed' (1881) st. 1

4 Come lovely and soothing death,
Undulate round the world, serenely arriving, arriving,
In the day, in the night, to all, to each,
Sooner or later, delicate death.
'When lilacs last in the dooryard bloomed' st. 14

5 The United States themselves are essentially the greatest poem.
Leaves of Grass (1855) preface

John Greenleaf Whittier 1807–92
American poet

6 'Shoot, if you must, this old grey head,
But spare your country's flag,' she said.
A shade of sadness, a blush of shame,
Over the face of the leader came.
'Barbara Frietchie' (1863)

7 Dear Lord and Father of mankind,
Forgive our foolish ways!
Re-clothe us in our rightful mind,
In purer lives thy service find,
In deeper reverence praise.
'The Brewing of Soma' (1872)

8 For of all sad words of tongue or pen,
The saddest are these: 'It might have been!'
'Maud Muller' (1854). Cf. Harte 327:19

9 The Indian Summer of the heart!
'Memories' (1841)

10 O brother man! fold to thy heart thy brother.
'Worship' (1848)

Robert Whittington

11 As time requireth, a man of marvellous mirth and pastimes, and sometime of as sad gravity, as who say: a man for all seasons.
Of Sir Thomas More, in *Vulgaria* (1521) pt. 2 'De constructione nominum'. Erasmus famously applied the idea to More, writing in his preface letter to *In Praise of Folly* (1509) that he played 'omnium horarum hominem [a man of all hours]'

Charlotte Whitton 1896–1975
Canadian writer and politician

12 Whatever women do they must do twice as well as men to be thought half as good.
In *Canada Month* June 1963

Cornelius Whur

13 While lasting joys the man attend
Who has a faithful female friend.
'The Female Friend' (1837)

William H. Whyte 1917–
American writer

14 This book is about the organization man ... I can think of no other way to describe the people I am talking about. They are not the workers, nor are they the white-collar people in the usual, clerk sense of the word. These people only work for the Organization. The ones I am talking about *belong* to it as well.
The Organization Man (1956) ch. 1

George John Whyte-Melville 1821–78
Scottish-born novelist, killed in the hunting-field

15 But I freely admit that the best of my fun
I owe it to horse and hound.
'The Good Grey Mare' (1933)

Anna Wickham (Edith Alice Mary Harper) 1884–1947
English poet

16 It is well within the order of things
That man should listen when his mate sings;
But the true male never yet walked
Who liked to listen when his mate talked.
'The Affinity' (1915)

Samuel Wilberforce 1805–73
English prelate

17 If I were a cassowary
On the plains of Timbuctoo,
I would eat a missionary,
Cassock, band, and hymn-book too.
Impromptu verse (attributed)

18 Was it through his grandfather or his grandmother that he claimed his descent from a monkey?
Addressed to T. H. Huxley at a meeting of the British Association for the Advancement of Science, Oxford, June 1860; in *Macmillan's Magazine* vol. 50 (October 1898) p. 437

Richard Wilbur 1921–

American poet

1 When you come, as you soon must, to the streets of
    our city,
Mad-eyed from stating the obvious,
Not proclaiming our fall but begging us
In God's name to have self-pity.

Spare us all word of the weapons, their force and
    range,
The long numbers that rocket the mind;
Our slow, unreckoning hearts will be left behind,
Unable to fear what is too strange.
    'Advice to a Prophet' (1961)

2 There is a poignancy in all things clear,
    In the stare of the deer, in the ring of a hammer in the
        morning.
Seeing a bucket of perfectly lucid water,
We fall to imagining prodigious honesties.
    'Clearness' (1950)

3 We milk the cow of the world, and as we do
We whisper in her ear, 'You are not true.'
    'Epistemology' (1950)

4 It's hard to tell the purpose of a bird:
for relevance it does not seem to try.
No line can trace no flute exemplify
its travelling; it darts without the word.
Who wills devoutly to absorb, contain,
birds give him pain.
    'In a Bird Sanctuary' (1947)

5 Mind in its purest play is like some bat
That beats about in caverns all alone,
Contriving by a kind of senseless wit
Not to conclude against a wall of stone.

It has no need to falter or explore;
Darkly it knows what obstacles are there,
And so may weave and flitter, dip and soar
In perfect courses through the blackest air.

And has this simile a like perfection?
The mind is like a bat. Precisely. Save
That in the very happiest intellection
A graceful error may correct the cave.
    'Mind' (1956)

6 Love is the greatest mercy,
A volley of the sun
That lashes all with shade,
That the first day be mended;
And yet, so soon undone,
It is the lover's curse
Till time be comprehended
And the flawed heart unmade.
What can I do but move
From folly to defeat
And call that sorrow sweet
That teaches us to see
The final face of love
In what we cannot be?
    'Someone Talking to Himself' (1961)

Ella Wheeler Wilcox 1855–1919

American poet

7 Laugh and the world laughs with you;
Weep, and you weep alone;
For the sad old earth must borrow its mirth,
But has trouble enough of its own.
    'Solitude'

8 So many gods, so many creeds,
So many paths that wind and wind,
While just the art of being kind
Is all the sad world needs.
    'The World's Need'

Oscar Wilde 1854–1900

Anglo-Irish playwright and poet

9 Really, if the lower orders don't set us a good
example, what on earth is the use of them?
    The Importance of Being Earnest (1895) act 1

10 It is very vulgar to talk like a dentist when one isn't a
dentist. It produces a false impression.
    The Importance of Being Earnest (1895) act 1

11 The truth is rarely pure, and never simple.
    The Importance of Being Earnest (1895) act 1

12 In married life three is company and two none.
    The Importance of Being Earnest (1895) act 1

13 Ignorance is like a delicate exotic fruit; touch it and
the bloom is gone. The whole theory of modern
education is radically unsound. Fortunately, in
England, at any rate, education produces no effect
whatsoever.
    The Importance of Being Earnest (1895) act 1

14 To lose one parent, Mr Worthing, may be regarded as
a misfortune; to lose both looks like carelessness.
    The Importance of Being Earnest (1895) act 1

15 All women become like their mothers. That is their
tragedy. No man does. That's his.
    The Importance of Being Earnest (1895) act 1 (the same
    words occur in dialogue form in *A Woman of No Importance*
    (1893) act 2)

16 The good ended happily, and the bad unhappily. That
is what fiction means.
    The Importance of Being Earnest (1895) act 2. Cf. Stoppard
    670:5

17 I hope you have not been leading a double life,
pretending to be wicked and being really good all the
time. That would be hypocrisy.
    The Importance of Being Earnest (1895) act 2

18 Charity, dear Miss Prism, charity! None of us are
perfect. I myself am peculiarly susceptible to draughts.
    The Importance of Being Earnest (1895) act 2

19 CECILY: When I see a spade I call it a spade.
GWENDOLEN: I am glad to say that I have never seen
    a spade.
    The Importance of Being Earnest (1895) act 3

20 Thirty-five is a very attractive age. London society is
full of women of the very highest birth who have, of
their own free choice, remained thirty-five for years.
    The Importance of Being Earnest (1895) act 3

1 Every great man nowadays has his disciples, and it is always Judas who writes the biography.
Intentions (1891) 'The Critic as Artist' pt. 1

2 Meredith's a prose Browning, and so is Browning.
Intentions (1891) 'The Critic as Artist' pt. 1

3 The one duty we owe to history is to rewrite it.
Intentions (1891) 'The Critic as Artist' pt. 1

4 It is through Art, and through Art only, that we can realise our perfection; through Art, and through Art only, that we can shield ourselves from the sordid perils of actual existence.
Intentions (1891) 'The Critic as Artist' pt. 2

5 All art is immoral.
Intentions (1891) 'The Critic as Artist' pt. 2

6 A little sincerity is a dangerous thing, and a great deal of it is absolutely fatal.
Intentions (1891) 'The Critic as Artist' pt. 2

7 All that I desire to point out is the general principle that Life imitates Art far more than Art imitates Life.
Intentions (1891) 'The Decay of Lying'

8 I can resist everything except temptation.
Lady Windermere's Fan (1892) act 1

9 Many a woman has a past, but I am told that she has at least a dozen, and that they all fit.
Lady Windermere's Fan (1892) act 1

10 We are all in the gutter, but some of us are looking at the stars.
Lady Windermere's Fan (1892) act 3

11 There is nothing in the whole world so unbecoming to a woman as a Nonconformist conscience.
Lady Windermere's Fan (1892) act 3

12 CECIL GRAHAM: What is a cynic?
LORD DARLINGTON: A man who knows the price of everything and the value of nothing.
Lady Windermere's Fan (1892) act 3

13 Experience is the name every one gives to their mistakes.
Lady Windermere's Fan (1892) act 3

14 There is no such thing as a moral or an immoral book. Books are well written, or badly written.
The Picture of Dorian Gray (1891) preface

15 The nineteenth century dislike of Realism is the rage of Caliban seeing his own face in the glass.
The Picture of Dorian Gray (1891) preface

16 The moral life of man forms part of the subject matter of the artist, but the morality of art consists in the perfect use of an imperfect medium.
The Picture of Dorian Gray (1891) preface

17 There is only one thing in the world worse than being talked about, and that is not being talked about.
The Picture of Dorian Gray (1891) ch. 1

18 A man cannot be too careful in the choice of his enemies.
The Picture of Dorian Gray (1891) ch. 1

19 A cigarette is the perfect type of a perfect pleasure. It is exquisite, and it leaves one unsatisfied. What more can one want?
The Picture of Dorian Gray (1891) ch. 6

20 It is better to be beautiful than to be good. But . . . it is better to be good than to be ugly.
The Picture of Dorian Gray (1891) ch. 17

21 Anybody can be good in the country.
The Picture of Dorian Gray (1891) ch. 19

22 As for the virtuous poor, one can pity them, of course, but one cannot possibly admire them.
Sebastian Melmoth (1891) 'The Soul of Man under Socialism'

23 Democracy means simply the bludgeoning of the people by the people for the people.
Sebastian Melmoth (1891) 'The Soul of Man under Socialism'

24 A thing is not necessarily true because a man dies for it.
Sebastian Melmoth (1904 ed.) p. 12

25 MRS ALLONBY: They say, Lady Hunstanton, that when good Americans die they go to Paris.
LADY HUNSTANTON: Indeed? And when bad Americans die, where do they go to?
LORD ILLINGWORTH: Oh, they go to America.
A Woman of No Importance (1893) act 1. Cf. Appleton 23:19

26 The youth of America is their oldest tradition. It has been going on now for three hundred years.
A Woman of No Importance (1893) act 1

27 The English country gentleman galloping after a fox—the unspeakable in full pursuit of the uneatable.
A Woman of No Importance (1893) act 1

28 One should never trust a woman who tells one her real age. A woman who would tell one that, would tell one anything.
A Woman of No Importance (1893) act 1

29 LORD ILLINGWORTH: The Book of Life begins with a man and a woman in a garden.
MRS ALLONBY: It ends with Revelations.
A Woman of No Importance (1893) act 1

30 Children begin by loving their parents; after a time they judge them; rarely, if ever, do they forgive them.
A Woman of No Importance (1893) act 2

31 GERALD: I suppose society is wonderfully delightful!
LORD ILLINGWORTH: To be in it is merely a bore. But to be out of it simply a tragedy.
A Woman of No Importance (1893) act 3

32 You should study the Peerage, Gerald . . . It is the best thing in fiction the English have ever done.
A Woman of No Importance (1893) act 3

33 He did not wear his scarlet coat,
For blood and wine are red,
And blood and wine were on his hands
When they found him with the dead.
The Ballad of Reading Gaol (1898) pt. 1, st. 1

34 I never saw a man who looked
With such a wistful eye
Upon that little tent of blue
Which prisoners call the sky.
The Ballad of Reading Gaol (1898) pt. 1, st. 3

1 Yet each man kills the thing he loves,
By each let this be heard,
Some do it with a bitter look,
Some with a flattering word.
The coward does it with a kiss,
The brave man with a sword!
The Ballad of Reading Gaol (1898) pt. 1, st. 7

2 The Governor was strong upon
The Regulations Act:
The Doctor said that Death was but
A scientific fact:
And twice a day the Chaplain called,
And left a little tract.
The Ballad of Reading Gaol (1898) pt. 3, st. 3

3 Something was dead in each of us,
And what was dead was Hope.
The Ballad of Reading Gaol (1898) pt. 3, st. 31

4 And the wild regrets, and the bloody sweats,
None knew so well as I:
For he who lives more lives than one
More deaths than one must die.
The Ballad of Reading Gaol (1898) pt. 3, st. 37

5 How else but through a broken heart
May Lord Christ enter in?
The Ballad of Reading Gaol (1898) pt. 5, st. 14

6 All her bright golden hair
Tarnished with rust,
She that was young and fair
Fallen to dust.
'Requiescat' (1881)

7 Do you want to know the great drama of my life? It's
that I have put my genius into my life; all I've put
into my works is my talent.
In André Gide *Oscar Wilde* (1910) 'In Memoriam'

8 I have nothing to declare except my genius.
At the New York Custom House, in Frank Harris *Oscar
Wilde* (1918) p. 75

9 Chaos, illumined by flashes of lightning.
On Robert Browning's 'style', in Ada Leverson *Letters to the
Sphinx* (1930) pt. 1 'The Importance of Being Oscar'

10 Work is the curse of the drinking classes.
In H. Pearson *Life of Oscar Wilde* (1946) ch. 12

11 He has fought a good fight and has had to face every
difficulty except popularity.
Unpublished character sketch of W. E. Henley, written for
Rothenstein's *English Portraits*. See W. Rothenstein *Men and
Memories* vol. 1 (1931) ch. 25

12 He [Bernard Shaw] hasn't an enemy in the world, and
none of his friends like him.
In Bernard Shaw *Sixteen Self Sketches* (1949) ch. 17

13 Ah, well, then, I suppose that I shall have to die
beyond my means.
At the mention of a huge fee for a surgical operation, in
R. H. Sherard *Life of Oscar Wilde* (1906) ch. 18

Billy Wilder (Samuel Wilder) 1906–
American screenwriter and director

14 Hindsight is always twenty-twenty.
In J. R. Columbo *Wit and Wisdom of the Moviemakers* (1979)
ch. 7

Thornton Wilder 1897–1975
American novelist and playwright

15 Marriage is a bribe to make a housekeeper think she's
a householder.
The Merchant of Yonkers (1939) act 1

16 The fights are the best part of married life. The rest is
merely so-so.
The Merchant of Yonkers (1939) act 2

17 Literature is the orchestration of platitudes.
In *Time* 12 January 1953

Wilhelm II ('Kaiser Bill') 1859–1941
German emperor and King of Prussia, 1888–1918

18 We have...fought for our place in the sun and have
won it. It will be my business to see that we retain
this place in the sun unchallenged, so that the rays of
that sun may exert a fructifying influence upon our
foreign trade and traffic.
Speech in Hamburg, 18 June 1901; in *The Times* 20 June
1901. Cf. Bülow 155:2

John Wilkes 1727–97
English parliamentary reformer

19 [EARL OF SANDWICH:] 'Pon my soul, Wilkes, I don't
know whether you'll die upon the gallows or of the
pox.
[WILKES:] That depends, my Lord, whether I first
embrace your Lordship's principles, or your
Lordship's mistresses.
In Sir Charles Petrie *The Four Georges* (1935); probably
apocryphal

Emma Hart Willard 1787–1870
American pioneer of women's education

20 Rocked in the cradle of the deep.
Title of song (1840), inspired by a prospect of the Bristol
Channel

William III (William of Orange) 1650–1702
King of Great Britain and Ireland from 1688

21 'Do you not see your country is lost?' asked the Duke
of Buckingham. 'There is one way never to see it lost'
replied William, 'and that is to die in the last ditch.'
In Bishop Gilbert Burnet *History of My Own Time* (1838 ed.)
p. 218

22 Every bullet has its billet.
In John Wesley *Journal* (1827) 6 June 1765

Isaac Williams 1802–65
English clergyman

23 Be thou my Guardian and my Guide,
And hear me when I call;
Let not my slippery footsteps slide,
And hold me lest I fall.
'Be thou my Guardian and my Guide' (1842 hymn)

Tennessee Williams (Thomas Lanier Williams) 1911–83

American playwright

1 We have to distrust each other. It's our only defence against betrayal.
>*Camino Real* (1953) block 10

2 We're all of us guinea pigs in the laboratory of God. Humanity is just a work in progress.
>*Camino Real* (1953) block 12

3 What is the victory of a cat on a hot tin roof?—I wish I knew . . . Just staying on it, I guess, as long as she can.
>*Cat on a Hot Tin Roof* (1955) act 1

4 BRICK: Well, they say nature hates a vacuum, Big Daddy.
BIG DADDY: That's what they say, but sometimes I think that a vacuum is a hell of a lot better than some of the stuff that nature replaces it with.
>*Cat on a Hot Tin Roof* (1955) act 2. Cf. Rabelais 534:18

5 Mendacity is a system that we live in. Liquor is one way out an' death's the other.
>*Cat on a Hot Tin Roof* (1955) act 2

6 I didn't go to the moon, I went much further for time is the longest distance between two places.
>*The Glass Menagerie* (1945) p. 123

7 We're all of us sentenced to solitary confinement inside our own skins, for life!
>*Orpheus Descending* (1958) act 2, sc. 1

8 Turn that off! I won't be looked at in this merciless glare!
>*A Streetcar Named Desire* (1947) sc. 1

9 I have always depended on the kindness of strangers.
>*A Streetcar Named Desire* (1947) sc. 11

William Carlos Williams 1883–1963

American poet

10 Minds like beds always made up,
(more stony than a shore)
unwilling or unable.
>*Paterson* (1946) bk. 1, preface

11 so much depends
upon

a red wheel
barrow

glazed with rain
water

beside the white
chickens.
>'The Red Wheelbarrow' (1923)

12 Is it any better in Heaven, my friend Ford,
Than you found it in Provence?
>'To Ford Madox Ford in Heaven' (1944)

13 I will teach you my townspeople
how to perform a funeral
for you have it over a troop
of artists
unless one should scour the world
you have the ground sense necessary
>Tract (1917)

Love Maria Willis (née Whitcomb) 1824–1908

American doctor's wife

14 Father, hear the prayer we offer:
Not for ease that prayer shall be,
But for strength that we may ever
Live our lives courageously.

Not for ever in green pastures
Do we ask our way to be,
But the steep and rugged pathway
May we tread rejoicingly.
>'Father, hear the prayer we offer' (1864 hymn)

Wendell Willkie 1892–1944

American lawyer and politician

15 The constitution does not provide for first and second class citizens.
>*An American Programme* (1944) ch. 2

16 Freedom is an indivisible word. If we want to enjoy it, and fight for it, we must be prepared to extend it to everyone, whether they are rich or poor, whether they agree with us or not, no matter what their race or the colour of their skin.
>*One World* (1943) ch. 13

Angus Wilson 1913–91

English novelist and short-story writer

17 'God knows how you Protestants can be expected to have any sense of direction,' she said. 'It's different with us, I haven't been to mass for years, I've got every mortal sin on my conscience, but I know when I'm doing wrong. I'm still a Catholic, it's there, nothing can take it away from me.' 'Of course, duckie,' said Jeremy...'once a Catholic always a Catholic.'
>*The Wrong Set* (1949) p. 168

Charles E. Wilson 1890–1961

American industrialist; President of General Motors, 1941–53

18 For years I thought what was good for our country was good for General Motors and vice versa. The difference did not exist. Our company is too big. It goes with the welfare of the country.
>Testimony to the Senate Armed Services Committee on his proposed nomination for Secretary of Defence, 15 January 1953, in *New York Times* 24 February 1953, p. 8

Harold Wilson (Baron Wilson of Rievaulx) 1916–

British Labour politician; Prime Minister, 1964–70, 1974–6

19 All these financiers, all the little gnomes in Zurich and the other financial centres about whom we keep on hearing.
>Speech, *Hansard* 12 November 1956, col. 500

1 This party is a moral crusade or it is nothing.

Speech at the Labour Party Conference, 1 October 1962; in *The Times* 2 October 1962

2 The Smethwick Conservatives can have the satisfaction of having topped the poll, and of having sent here as their Member one who, until a further General Election restores him to oblivion, will serve his term here as a Parliamentary leper.

Speech, *Hansard* 3 November 1964, col. 71 (on the outcome of a by-election with racist overtones)

3 From now the pound abroad is worth 14 per cent or so less in terms of other currencies. It does not mean, of course, that the pound here in Britain, in your pocket or purse or in your bank, has been devalued.

Ministerial broadcast, 19 November 1967, in *The Times* 20 November 1967

4 If one buys land on which there is a slag heap 120 ft. high and it costs £100,000 to remove that slag, that is not land speculation in the sense that we condemn it. It is land reclamation.

Speech, *Hansard* 4 April 1974, col. 1441

5 The Monarchy is a labour-intensive industry.

In *Observer* 13 February 1977

6 A week is a long time in politics.

Probably first said at the time of the 1964 sterling crisis. See Nigel Rees *Sayings of the Century* (1984) p. 149

Harriette Wilson (née Dubochet)
1789–1846
English courtesan

7 I shall not say why and how I became, at the age of fifteen, the mistress of the Earl of Craven.

Memoirs (1825) opening words

John Wilson

See CHRISTOPHER NORTH

Sandy Wilson 1924–
English songwriter

8 We've got to have
We plot to have
For it's so dreary not to have
That certain thing called the Boy Friend.

The Boyfriend (1954) title song

Woodrow Wilson 1856–1924
28th President of the USA

9 Liberty has never come from the government. Liberty has always come from the subjects of government. The history of liberty is the history of resistance. The history of liberty is a history of the limitation of governmental power, not the increase of it.

Speech to the New York Press Club, 9 September 1912; in *Papers of Woodrow Wilson* (1978) vol. 25, p. 124

10 No nation is fit to sit in judgement upon any other nation.

Speech in New York, 20 April 1915; in *Selected Addresses* (1918) p. 79

11 There is such a thing as a man being too proud to fight; there is such a thing as a nation being so right that it does not need to convince others by force that it is right.

Speech in Philadelphia, 10 May 1915; in *Selected Addresses* (1918) p. 88

12 We have stood apart, studiously neutral.

Speech to Congress, 7 December 1915, in *New York Times* 8 December 1915, p. 4

13 America can not be an ostrich with its head in the sand.

Speech at Des Moines, 1 February 1916, in *New York Times* 2 February 1916, p. 1

14 It must be a peace without victory . . . Only a peace between equals can last.

Speech to US Senate, 22 January 1917, in *Messages and Papers* (1924) vol. 1, p. 352

15 A little group of wilful men representing no opinion but their own, have rendered the Great Government of the United States helpless and contemptible.

Statement, 4 March 1917, after a successful filibuster against his bill to arm American merchant ships; in *New York Times* 5 March 1917, p. 1

16 Armed neutrality is ineffectual enough at best.

Speech to Congress, 2 April 1917, in *Selected Addresses* (1918) p. 190

17 The world must be made safe for democracy.

Speech to Congress, 2 April 1917, in *Selected Addresses* (1918) p. 195

18 The right is more precious than peace.

Speech to Congress, 2 April 1917, in *Selected Addresses* (1918) p. 197

19 The programme of the world's peace . . . is this: 1. Open covenants of peace, openly arrived at.

Speech to Congress, 8 January 1918, in *Selected Addresses* (1918) p. 247

20 America is the only idealistic nation in the world.

Speech at Sioux Falls, South Dakota, 8 September 1919; in *Messages and Papers* (1924) vol. 2, p. 822

21 Once lead this people into war and they will forget there ever was such a thing as tolerance.

In John Dos Passos *Mr Wilson's War* (1917) pt. 3, ch. 12

Robb Wilton 1881–1957
British radio comedian

22 The day war broke out.

Customary preamble to radio monologues in the role of a Home Guard, from *c.*1940

Anne Finch, Lady Winchilsea 1661–1720
English poet

23 Thirst of wealth no quiet knows,
But near the death-bed fiercer grows.

'Enquiry after Peace' (1713) l. 30

24 Love (if such a thing there be)
Is all despair, or ecstasy.
Poetry's the feverish fit,
Th' o'erflowing of unbounded wit.

'Enquiry after Peace' (1713) l. 38

1 They tell us we mistake our sex and way;
Good breeding, fashion, dancing, dressing, play,
Are the accomplishments we should desire;
To write, or read, or think, or to enquire
Would cloud our beauty, and exhaust our time,
And interrupt the conquests of our prime;
While the dull manage of a servile house
Is held by some our utmost art and use.
'The Introduction' (1713) l. 13

2 Give me yet before I die
A sweet, yet absolute retreat,
'Mongst paths so lost and trees so high
That the world may ne'er invade
Through such windings and such shade.
'The Petition for an Absolute Retreat' (1713) l. 2

3 Now the jonquil o'ercomes the feeble brain;
We faint beneath the aromatic pain.
'The Spleen' (1701)

4 My hand delights to trace unusual things,
And deviates from the known and common way;
Nor will in fading silks compose
Faintly the inimitable rose.
'The Spleen' (1701)

William Windham 1750–1810
English politician

5 Those entrusted with arms . . . should be persons of
some substance and stake in the country.
Speech, *Hansard*, 22 July 1807, col. 897

Catherine Winkworth 1827–78
English translator of German hymns

6 Now thank we all our God,
With heart and hands and voices,
Who wondrous things hath done,
In whom his world rejoices;
Who from our mother's arms
Hath blessed us on our way
With countless gifts of love,
And still is ours to-day.

O may this bounteous God
Through all our life be near us,
With ever joyful hearts
And blessèd peace to cheer us;
And keep us in his grace,
And guide us when perplexed,
And free us from all ills
In this world and the next.
Lyra Germanica (1858) 'Now thank we all our God'
(translation of Martin Rinkart's 'Nun danket alle Gott',
c.1636)

7 Hast thou not seen?
All that is needful hath been
Granted in what he ordaineth.
'Praise to the Lord! the Almighty, the King of creation!'
(1863 hymn); translated from the German of Joachim
Neander (1650–80)

8 Ponder anew
What the Almighty can do
If with his love he befriend thee.
'Praise to the Lord! the Almighty . . . ' (1863 hymn)

9 *Peccavi*—I have Sindh.
Of Sir Charles Napier's conquest of Sindh, 1843 (*peccavi* I
have sinned); printed in *Punch* vol. 6, p. 209 (18 May
1844), supposedly sent by Napier to Lord Ellenborough

John Winthrop 1588–1649
American settler

10 We must consider that we shall be a city upon a hill,
the eyes of all people are on us; so that if we shall deal
falsely with our God in this work we have undertaken,
and so cause Him to withdraw His present help from
us, we shall be made a story and a byword through
the world.
Christian Charity, A Model Hereof (sermon, 1630) in
Massachusetts Historical Society *Winthrop Papers*
(1929–47) vol. 2

Robert Charles Winthrop 1809–94
American politician

11 A Star for every State, and a State for every Star.
Speech on Boston Common, 27 August 1862, in *Addresses
and Speeches* vol. 2 (1867) p. 534

Owen Wister 1860–1938
American novelist

12 When you call me that, *smile*!
The Virginian (1902) ch. 2 (*that* 'you son-of-a —')

George Wither 1588–1667
English poet and pamphleteer

13 When I behold the havoc and the spoil
Which, even within the compass of my days,
Is made through every quarter of this isle,
In woods and groves, which were this kingdom's
    praise;
And when I mind with how much greediness
We seek the present gain in everything,
Not caring (so our lust we may possess)
What damage to posterity we bring . . .
What our forefathers planted, we destroy:
Nay, all men's labours, living heretofore,
And all our own, we lavishly employ
To serve our present lusts, and for no more.
A Collection of Emblems (1635) bk. 1, no. 35

14 I loved a lass, a fair one,
As fair as e'er was seen;
She was indeed a rare one,
Another Sheba queen.
A Description of Love (1620) 'I loved a lass, a fair one'

Ludwig Wittgenstein 1889–1951
Austrian-born philosopher

15 *Die Philosophie ist ein Kampf gegen die Verhexung unsres
Verstandes durch die Mittel unserer Sprache.*

Philosophy is a battle against the bewitchment of our
intelligence by means of language.
Philosophische Untersuchungen (1953) pt. 1, sect. 109

1 *Der Philosoph behandelt eine Frage wie eine Krankheit.*

The philosopher's treatment of a question is like the treatment of an illness.
Philosophische Untersuchungen (1953) pt. 1, sect. 255

2 *Was ist dein Ziel in der Philosophie?—Der Fliege den Ausweg aus dem Fliegenglas zeigen.*

What is your aim in philosophy?—To show the fly the way out of the fly-bottle.
Philosophische Untersuchungen (1953) pt. 1, sect. 309

3 *Was sich überhaupt sagen lässt, lässt sich klar sagen; und wovon man nicht reden kann, darüber muss man schweigen.*

What can be said at all can be said clearly, and whereof one cannot speak thereof one must be silent.
Tractatus Logico-Philosophicus (1922) preface

4 *Die Welt ist alles, was der Fall ist.*

The world is everything that is the case.
Tractatus Logico-Philosophicus (1922) p. 30

5 *Die Grenzen meiner Sprache bedeuten die Grenzen meiner Welt.*

The limits of my language mean the limits of my world.
Tractatus Logico-Philosophicus (1922) p. 148

6 *Die Welt des Glücklichen ist eine andere als die des Unglücklichen.*

The world of the happy is quite different from that of the unhappy.
Tractatus Logico-Philosophicus (1922) p. 184

P. G. Wodehouse 1881–1975

English writer; an American citizen from 1955

7 Chumps always make the best husbands. When you marry, Sally, grab a chump. Tap his forehead first, and if it rings solid, don't hesitate. All the unhappy marriages come from the husbands having brains.
The Adventures of Sally (1920) ch. 10

8 At this point in the proceedings there was another ring at the front door. Jeeves shimmered out and came back with a telegram.
Carry On, Jeeves! (1925) 'Jeeves Takes Charge'

9 He spoke with a certain what-is-it in his voice, and I could see that, if not actually disgruntled, he was far from being gruntled.
The Code of the Woosters (1938) ch. 1

10 Slice him where you like, a hellhound is always a hellhound.
The Code of the Woosters (1938) ch. 1

11 It is no use telling me that there are bad aunts and good aunts. At the core, they are all alike. Sooner or later, out pops the cloven hoof.
The Code of the Woosters (1938) ch. 2

12 Roderick Spode? Big chap with a small moustache and the sort of eye that can open an oyster at sixty paces?
The Code of the Woosters (1938) ch. 2

13 To my daughter Leonora without whose never-failing sympathy and encouragement this book would have been finished in half the time.
The Heart of a Goof (1926) dedication

14 I turned to Aunt Agatha, whose demeanour was now rather like that of one who, picking daisies on the railway, has just caught the down express in the small of the back.
The Inimitable Jeeves (1923) ch. 4

15 Sir Roderick Glossop . . . is always called a nerve specialist, because it sounds better, but everybody knows that he's really a sort of janitor to the looney-bin.
The Inimitable Jeeves (1923) ch. 7

16 As a rule, you see, I'm not lugged into Family Rows. On the occasions when Aunt is calling to Aunt like mastodons bellowing across primeval swamps and Uncle James's letter about Cousin Mabel's peculiar behaviour is being shot round the family circle . . . the clan has a tendency to ignore me.
The Inimitable Jeeves (1923) ch. 16

17 It was my Uncle George who discovered that alcohol was a food well in advance of medical thought.
The Inimitable Jeeves (1923) ch. 16

18 It is a good rule in life never to apologize. The right sort of people do not want apologies, and the wrong sort take a mean advantage of them.
The Man Upstairs (1914) title story. Cf. Hubbard 353:9

19 She fitted into my biggest armchair as if it had been built round her by someone who knew they were wearing armchairs tight about the hips that season.
My Man Jeeves (1919) 'Jeeves and the Unbidden Guest'

20 What with excellent browsing and sluicing and cheery conversation and what-not, the afternoon passed quite happily.
My Man Jeeves (1919) 'Jeeves and the Unbidden Guest'

21 What a queer thing Life is! So unlike anything else, don't you know, if you see what I mean.
My Man Jeeves (1919) 'Rallying Round Old George'

22 Ice formed on the butler's upper slopes.
Pigs Have Wings (1952) ch. 5

23 The Right Hon. was a tubby little chap who looked as if he had been poured into his clothes and had forgotten to say 'When!'
Very Good, Jeeves (1930) 'Jeeves and the Impending Doom'

Charles Wolfe 1791–1823

Irish poet

24 Not a drum was heard, not a funeral note,
As his corse to the rampart we hurried.
'The Burial of Sir John Moore at Corunna' (1817)

25 We buried him darkly at dead of night,
The sods with our bayonets turning.
'The Burial of Sir John Moore at Corunna' (1817)

26 We carved not a line, and we raised not a stone—
But we left him alone with his glory.
'The Burial of Sir John Moore at Corunna' (1817)

Humbert Wolfe 1886–1940

British poet

1 You cannot hope
to bribe or twist,
thank God! the
British journalist.
But, seeing what
the man will do
unbribed, there's
no occasion to.
> 'Over the Fire' (1930)

James Wolfe 1727–59

British general; captor of Quebec

2 The General . . . repeated nearly the whole of Gray's
Elegy . . . adding, as he concluded, that he would
prefer being the author of that poem to the glory of
beating the French to-morrow.
> J. Playfair *Biographical Account of J. Robinson* in *Transactions
> of the Royal Society of Edinburgh* vol. 7 (1815) p. 499

3 Now God be praised, I will die in peace.
> Dying words, in J. Knox *Historical Journal of the Campaigns
> in North America* (ed. A. G. Doughty, 1914) vol. 2, p. 114

Thomas Wolfe 1900–38

American novelist

4 Most of the time we think we're sick, it's all in the
mind.
> *Look Homeward, Angel* (1929) pt. 1, ch. 1

5 'Where they got you stationed now, Luke?' said Harry
Tugman peering up snoutily from a mug of coffee. 'At
the p-p-p-present time in Norfolk at the Navy base,'
Luke answered, 'm-m-making the world safe for
hypocrisy.'
> *Look Homeward, Angel* (1929) pt. 3, ch. 36. Cf. Wilson
> 738:17

Tom Wolfe 1931–

American writer

6 The bonfire of the vanities.
> Title of novel (1987); deriving from Savonarola's 'burning
> of the vanities' in Florence, 1497

7 Electric Kool-Aid Acid test.
> Title of novel on hippy culture (1968)

8 We are now in the Me Decade—seeing the upward roll
of . . . the third great religious wave in American
history . . . and this one has the mightiest, holiest roll
of all, the beat that goes . . . *Me . . . Me . . . Me . . . Me.*
> *Mauve Gloves and Madmen* (1976) 'The Me Decade'

9 Radical Chic . . . is only radical in Style; in its heart it
is part of Society and its tradition—Politics, like Rock,
Pop, and Camp, has its uses.
> *New York* 8 June 1970, p. 26

Mary Wollstonecraft 1759–97

English feminist; mother of Mary Shelley

10 To give a sex to mind was not very consistent with the
principles of a man [Rousseau] who argued so
warmly, and so well, for the immortality of the soul.
> *A Vindication of the Rights of Woman* (1792) ch. 3 (often
> quoted 'Mind has no sex')

11 She [woman] was created to be the toy of man, his
rattle, and it must jingle in his ears whenever,
dismissing reason, he chooses to be amused.
> *A Vindication of the Rights of Woman* (1792) ch. 4

12 A king is always a king—and a woman always a
woman: his authority and her sex ever stand between
them and rational converse.
> *A Vindication of the Rights of Woman* (1792) ch. 4

13 I do not wish them [women] to have power over men;
but over themselves.
> *A Vindication of the Rights of Woman* (1792) ch. 4

14 When a man seduces a woman, it should, I think, be
termed a *left-handed* marriage.
> *A Vindication of the Rights of Woman* (1792) ch. 4

15 Taught from infancy that beauty is woman's sceptre,
the mind shapes itself to the body, and roaming round
its gilt cage, only seeks to adorn its prison.
> *A Vindication of the Rights of Woman* (1792) ch. 5

16 The pure animal spirits which make both mind and
body shoot out, and unfold the tender blossoms of
hope, are turned sour and vented in vain wishes, or
pert repinings, that contract the faculties and spoil the
temper; else they mount to the brain, and sharpening
the understanding before it gains proportional
strength, produce that pitiful cunning which
disgracefully characterizes the female mind and I fear
will characterize it whilst women remain the slaves of
power.
> *A Vindication of the Rights of Woman* (1792) ch. 9

17 A slavish bondage to parents cramps every faculty of
the mind.
> *A Vindication of the Rights of Woman* (1792) ch. 11

18 Was not the world a vast prison, and women born
slaves?
> *The Wrongs of Woman: or, Maria* (1798, ed. G. Kelly, 1976)
> p. 79

19 Minute attention to propriety stops the growth of
virtue.
> *Collected Letters* (ed. R. Wardle, 1979) p. 141

Thomas Wolsey c.1475–1530

English cardinal; Lord Chancellor, 1515–29

20 Father Abbot, I am come to lay my bones amongst
you.
> In George Cavendish *Negotiations of Thomas Wolsey* (1641)
> p. 108

21 Had I but served God as diligently as I have served the
King, he would not have given me over in my grey
hairs.
> In George Cavendish *Negotiations of Thomas Wolsey* (1641)
> p. 113

Mrs Henry Wood (née Ellen Price)
1814–87
English novelist

1 Dead! and . . . never called me mother.
   East Lynne (dramatized by T. A. Palmer, 1874, the words do not occur in the novel of 1861)

Woodbine Willie
See G. A. STUDDERT KENNEDY

Thomas Woodroofe 1899–1978
British naval officer

2 At the present moment, the whole Fleet's lit up. When I say 'lit up', I mean lit up by fairy lamps.
   First live outside broadcast, Spithead Review, 20 May 1937. See Asa Briggs *History of Broadcasting in the UK* vol. 2 (1965) pt. 2, ch. 2

Harry Woods

3 Oh we ain't got a barrel of money,
   Maybe we're ragged and funny,
   But we'll travel along
   Singin' a song,
   Side by side.
   'Side by Side' (1927 song)

Virginia Woolf 1882–1941
English novelist

4 Righteous indignation . . . is misplaced if we agree with the lady's maid that high birth is a form of congenital insanity, that the sufferer merely inherits diseases of his ancestors, and endures them, for the most part very stoically, in one of those comfortably padded lunatic asylums which are known, euphemistically, as the stately homes of England.
   The Common Reader (1925) 'Lady Dorothy Nevill'

5 We are nauseated by the sight of trivial personalities decomposing in the eternity of print.
   The Common Reader (1925) 'The Modern Essay'

6 Examine for a moment an ordinary mind on an ordinary day.
   The Common Reader (1925) 'Modern Fiction'

7 Life is not a series of gig lamps symmetrically arranged; life is a luminous halo, a semi-transparent envelope surrounding us from the beginning of consciousness to the end.
   The Common Reader (1925) 'Modern Fiction'

8 Let us record the atoms as they fall upon the mind in the order in which they fall, let us trace the pattern, however disconnected and incoherent in appearance, which each sight or incident scores upon the consciousness. Let us not take it for granted that life exists more fully in what is commonly thought big than in what is commonly thought small.
   The Common Reader (1925) 'Modern Fiction'

9 Each had his past shut in him like the leaves of a book known to him by heart; and his friends could only read the title.
   Jacob's Room (1922) ch. 5

10 A woman must have money and a room of her own if she is to write fiction.
   A Room of One's Own (1929) ch. 1

11 Women have served all these centuries as looking-glasses possessing the magic and delicious power of reflecting the figure of a man at twice its natural size.
   A Room of One's Own (1929) ch. 2

12 Literature is strewn with the wreckage of men who have minded beyond reason the opinions of others.
   A Room of One's Own (1929) ch. 3

13 This is an important book, the critic assumes, because it deals with war. This is an insignificant book because it deals with the feelings of women in a drawing-room.
   A Room of One's Own (1929) ch. 4

14 So that is marriage, Lily thought, a man and a woman looking at a girl throwing a ball.
   To the Lighthouse (1927) pt. 1, ch. 13

15 Things have dropped from me. I have outlived certain desires; I have lost friends, some by death—Percival—others through sheer inability to cross the street.
   The Waves (1931) p. 202

16 The scratching of pimples on the body of the bootboy at Claridges.
   Of James Joyce's *Ulysses*; letter to Lytton Strachey, 24 April 1922, in *Letters* (ed. N. Nicolson and J. Trautmann, 1976) vol. 2

Alexander Woollcott 1887–1943
American writer

17 I have no need of your God-damned sympathy. I only wish to be entertained by some of your grosser reminiscences.
   Letter to Rex O'Malley, 1942, in Samuel Hopkins Adams *Alexander Woollcott* (1945) ch. 34

18 A broker is a man who takes your fortune and runs it into a shoestring.
   In Samuel Hopkins Adams *Alexander Woollcott* (1945) ch. 15

19 All the things I really like to do are either illegal, immoral, or fattening.
   In R. E. Drennan *Wit's End* (1973)

Dorothy Wordsworth 1771–1855
English writer; sister of William Wordsworth

20 One only leaf upon the top of a tree—the sole remaining leaf—danced round and round like a rag blown by the wind.
   'Alfoxden Journal' 7 March 1798, in *Journals* (ed. E. de Selincourt, 1941)

21 Coleridge dined with us. He brought his ballad [*The Ancient Mariner*] finished. A beautiful evening, very starry, the horned moon.
   'Alfoxden Journal' 23 March 1798, in *Journals* (ed. E. de Selincourt, 1941)

1 We saw a raven very high above us. It called out, and the dome of the sky seemed to echo the sound. It called again and again as it flew onwards, and the mountains gave back the sound, seeming as if from their centre; a musical bell-like answering to the bird's hoarse voice.

'Grasmere Journal' 27 July 1800, in *Journals* (ed. E. de Selincourt, 1941)

2 When we were in the woods beyond Gowbarrow park we saw a few daffodils close to the waterside . . . But as we went along there were more and yet more and at last under the boughs of the trees, we saw that there was a long belt of them along the shore, about the breadth of a country turnpike road. I never saw daffodils so beautiful. They grew among the mossy stones about and about them; some rested their heads upon these stones as on a pillow for weariness; and the rest tossed and reeled and danced, and seemed as if they verily laughed with the wind that blew upon them over the lake.

'Grasmere Journal' 15 April 1802, in *Journals* (ed. E. de Selincourt, 1941). Cf. Wordsworth 744:15

3 We walked up to the house and stood some minutes watching the swallows that flew about restlessly, and flung their shadows upon the sunbright walls of the old building; the shadows glanced and twinkled, interchanged and crossed each other, expanded and shrunk up, appeared and disappeared every instant.

'Recollections of a Tour made in Scotland' 16 August 1803, in *Journals* (ed. E. de Selincourt, 1941)

Dame Elizabeth Wordsworth 1840–1932

English educationist; first Principal of Lady Margaret Hall, Oxford

4 If all the good people were clever,
And all clever people were good,
The world would be nicer than ever
We thought that it possibly could.
But somehow, 'tis seldom or never
The two hit it off as they should;
The good are so harsh to the clever,
The clever so rude to the good!

'Good and Clever'

William Wordsworth 1770–1850

English poet

5 My apprehensions come in crowds;
I dread the rustling of the grass;
The very shadows of the clouds
Have power to shake me as they pass.

'The Affliction of Margaret —' (1807)

6 And five times did I say to him
'Why, Edward, tell me why?'

'Anecdote for Fathers' (1798)

7 Action is transitory,—a step, a blow,
The motion of a muscle—this way or that—
'Tis done, and in the after vacancy
We wonder at ourselves like men betrayed:
Suffering is permanent, obscure and dark,
And shares the nature of infinity.

The Borderers (1842) act 3, l. 1539

8 Who is the happy Warrior? Who is he
Whom every man in arms should wish to be?
It is the generous spirit, who, when brought
Among the tasks of real life, hath wrought
Upon the plan that pleased his childish thought:
Whose high endeavours are an inward light
That makes the path before him always bright:
Who, with a natural instinct to discern
What knowledge can perform, is diligent to learn.

'Character of the Happy Warrior' (1807)

9 Earth has not anything to show more fair:
Dull would he be of soul who could pass by
A sight so touching in its majesty:
This City now doth like a garment wear
The beauty of the morning; silent, bare,
Ships, towers, domes, theatres, and temples lie
Open unto the fields, and to the sky;
All bright and glittering in the smokeless air.

'Composed upon Westminster Bridge' (1807)

10 Dear God! the very houses seem asleep;
And all that mighty heart is lying still!

'Composed upon Westminster Bridge' (1807)

11 Ah! THEN, if mine had been the Painter's hand,
To express what then I saw; and add the gleam,
The light that never was, on sea or land,
The consecration, and the Poet's dream.

'Elegiac Stanzas' (on a picture of Peele Castle in a storm, 1807)

12 Not in the lucid intervals of life
That come but as a curse to party-strife . . .
Is Nature felt, or can be.

'Evening Voluntaries' (1835) no. 4

13   By grace divine,
Not otherwise, O Nature! we are thine.

'Evening Voluntaries' (1835) no. 4

14 On Man, on Nature, and on Human Life,
Musing in solitude.

The Excursion (1814) Preface, l. 1

15   The Mind of Man—
My haunt, and the main region of my song.

The Excursion (1814) Preface, l. 40

16 Oh! many are the Poets that are sown
By Nature; men endowed with highest gifts,
The vision and the faculty divine;
Yet wanting the accomplishment of verse.

The Excursion (1814) bk. 1, l. 77

17 What soul was his, when from the naked top
Of some bold headland, he beheld the sun
Rise up, and bathe the world in light!

The Excursion (1827 ed.) bk. 1, l. 198

18   The good die first,
And they whose hearts are dry as summer dust
Burn to the socket.

The Excursion (1814) bk. 1, l. 500

19 This dull product of a scoffer's pen.

The Excursion (1814) bk. 2, l. 484 (of Voltaire's *Candide*)

20 The intellectual power, through words and things,
Went sounding on, a dim and perilous way!

The Excursion (1814) bk. 3, l. 700

21 Society became my glittering bride,
And airy hopes my children.

The Excursion (1814) bk. 3, l. 735

1   'Tis a thing impossible, to frame
Conceptions equal to the soul's desires;
And the most difficult of tasks to keep
Heights which the soul is competent to gain.
    The Excursion (1814) bk. 4, l. 136

2 'To every Form of being is assigned,'
Thus calmly spoke the venerable Sage,
'An *active* Principle.'
    The Excursion (1814) bk. 9, l. 1

3 How fast has brother followed brother,
From sunshine to the sunless land!
    'Extempore Effusion upon the Death of James Hogg' (1835)

4   The wiser mind
Mourns less for what age takes away
Than what it leaves behind.
    'The Fountain' (1800)

5 Bliss was it in that dawn to be alive,
But to be young was very heaven!
    'The French Revolution, as it Appeared to Enthusiasts'
    (1809); also *The Prelude* (1850) bk. 9, l. 108

6 A genial hearth, a hospitable board,
And a refined rusticity.
    'A genial hearth, a hospitable board' (1822)

7   Not choice
But habit rules the unreflecting herd.
    'Grant that by this unsparing hurricane' (1822)

8 The moving accident is not my trade;
To freeze the blood I have no ready arts:
'Tis my delight, alone in summer shade,
To pipe a simple song for thinking hearts.
    'Hart-Leap Well' (1800) pt. 2, l. 1

9   All shod with steel
We hissed along the polished ice, in games
Confederate.
    'Influence of Natural Objects' (1809); also *The Prelude*
    (1850) bk. 1, l. 414

10   Leaving the tumultuous throng,
To cut across the reflex of a star;
Image, that, flying still before me, gleamed
Upon the glassy plain.
    'Influence of Natural Objects' (1809)

11   Yet still the solitary cliffs
Wheeled by me—even as if the earth had rolled
With visible motion her diurnal round!
    'Influence of Natural Objects' (1809); also *The Prelude*
    (1850) bk. 1, l. 458

12 It is a beauteous evening, calm and free;
The holy time is quiet as a nun
Breathless with adoration.
    'It is a beauteous evening, calm and free' (1807)

13   In our halls is hung
Armoury of the invincible Knights of old:
We must be free or die, who speak the tongue
That Shakespeare spake; the faith and morals hold
Which Milton held. In every thing we are sprung
Of Earth's first blood, have titles manifold.
    'It is not to be thought of that the Flood' (1807)

14 I travelled among unknown men,
In lands beyond the sea;
Nor England! did I know till then
What love I bore to thee.
    'I travelled among unknown men' (1807)

15 I wandered lonely as a cloud
That floats on high o'er vales and hills,
When all at once I saw a crowd,
A host, of golden daffodils;
Beside the lake, beneath the trees,
Fluttering and dancing in the breeze.
    'I wandered lonely as a cloud' (1815 ed.). Cf.
    Wordsworth 743:2

16 A poet could not but be gay,
In such a jocund company:
I gazed—and gazed—but little thought
What wealth to me the show had brought:
For oft, when on my couch I lie
In vacant or in pensive mood,
They flash upon that inward eye
Which is the bliss of solitude;
And then my heart with pleasure fills,
And dances with the daffodils.
    'I wandered lonely as a cloud' (1815 ed.)

17   The gods approve
The depth, and not the tumult, of the soul.
    'Laodamia' (1815) l. 74

18 Of all that is most beauteous—imaged there
In happier beauty; more pellucid streams,
An ampler ether, a diviner air,
And fields invested with purpureal gleams.
    'Laodamia' (1815) l. 103

19   I have owed to them
In hours of weariness, sensations sweet,
Felt in the blood, and felt along the heart;
And passing even into my purer mind,
With tranquil restoration:—feelings too
Of unremembered pleasure: such, perhaps,
As may have had no trivial influence
On that best portion of a good man's life,
His little, nameless, unremembered, acts
Of kindness and of love.
    'Lines composed a few miles above Tintern Abbey'
    (1798) l. 26

20   That blessed mood
In which the burthen of the mystery,
In which the heavy and the weary weight
Of all this unintelligible world,
Is lightened.
    'Lines composed . . . above Tintern Abbey'
    (1798) l. 37

21   The sounding cataract
Haunted me like a passion: the tall rock,
The mountain, and the deep and gloomy wood,
Their colours and their forms, were then to me
An appetite; a feeling and a love,
That had no need of a remoter charm,
By thought supplied, nor any interest
Unborrowed from the eye.
    'Lines composed . . . above Tintern Abbey' (1798)
    l. 72

1   I have learned
To look on nature, not as in the hour
Of thoughtless youth; but hearing oftentimes
The still, sad music of humanity,
Nor harsh nor grating, though of ample power
To chasten and subdue. And I have felt
A presence that disturbs me with the joy
Of elevated thoughts; a sense sublime
Of something far more deeply interfused,
Whose dwelling is the light of setting suns,
And the round ocean and the living air,
And the blue sky, and in the mind of man.
> 'Lines composed . . . above Tintern Abbey' (1798)
> l. 88

2   All the mighty world
Of eye and ear, both what they half-create,
And what perceive.
> 'Lines composed   above Tintern Abbey' (1798)
> l. 106

3 And much it grieved my heart to think
What man has made of man.
> 'Lines Written in Early Spring' (1798)

4 Milton! thou shouldst be living at this hour:
England hath need of thee: she is a fen
Of stagnant waters: altar, sword, and pen,
Fireside, the heroic wealth of hall and bower,
Have forfeited their ancient English dower
Of inward happiness.
> 'Milton! thou shouldst be living at this hour' (1807)

5   Some happy tone
Of meditation, slipping in between
The beauty coming and the beauty gone.
> 'Most sweet it is' (1835)

6 My heart leaps up when I behold
A rainbow in the sky:
So was it when my life began;
So is it now I am a man;
So be it when I shall grow old,
Or let me die!
The Child is father of the Man;
And I could wish my days to be
Bound each to each by natural piety.
> 'My heart leaps up when I behold' (1807)

7 Nuns fret not at their convent's narrow room;
And hermits are contented with their cells.
> 'Nuns fret not at their convent's narrow room' (1807)

8 In sundry moods, 'twas pastime to be bound
Within the Sonnet's scanty plot of ground:
Pleased if some souls (for such there needs must be)
Who have felt the weight of too much liberty,
Should find short solace there, as I have found.
> 'Nuns fret not at their convent's narrow room' (1807)

9   Move along these shades
In gentleness of heart; with gentle hand
Touch—for there is a spirit in the woods.
> 'Nutting' (1800)

10 There was a time when meadow, grove, and stream,
The earth, and every common sight,
To me did seem
Apparelled in celestial light,
The glory and the freshness of a dream.
It is not now as it hath been of yore;—
Turn wheresoe'er I may,
By night or day,
The things which I have seen I now can see no more.

The rainbow comes and goes,
And lovely is the rose,
The moon doth with delight
Look round her when the heavens are bare;
Waters on a starry night
Are beautiful and fair;
The sunshine is a glorious birth;
But yet I know, where'er I go,
That there hath passed away a glory from the earth.
> 'Ode. Intimations of Immortality' (1807) st. 1

11 A timely utterance gave that thought relief,
And I again am strong.
> 'Ode. Intimations of Immortality' (1807) st. 3

12 The winds come to me from the fields of sleep.
> 'Ode. Intimations of Immortality' (1807) st. 3

13 Shout round me, let me hear thy shouts, thou happy
Shepherd Boy!
> 'Ode. Intimations of Immortality' (1807) st. 3

14 —But there's a tree, of many one,
A single field which I have looked upon,
Both of them speak of something that is gone:
The pansy at my feet
Doth the same tale repeat:
Whither is fled the visionary gleam?
Where is it now, the glory and the dream?

Our birth is but a sleep and a forgetting:
The Soul that rises with us, our life's Star,
Hath had elsewhere its setting,
And cometh from afar:
Not in entire forgetfulness,
And not in utter nakedness,
But trailing clouds of glory do we come
From God, who is our home:
Heaven lies about us in our infancy!
Shades of the prison-house begin to close
Upon the growing boy,
But he beholds the light, and whence it flows,
He sees it in his joy;
The youth, who daily farther from the east
Must travel, still is Nature's priest,
And by the vision splendid
Is on his way attended;
At length the man perceives it die away,
And fade into the light of common day.
> 'Ode. Intimations of Immortality' (1807) st. 4

15 As if his whole vocation
Were endless imitation.
> 'Ode. Intimations of Immortality' (1807) st. 7

16   Thou Eye among the blind,
That, deaf and silent, read'st the eternal deep,
Haunted for ever by the eternal mind.
> 'Ode. Intimations of Immortality' (1807) st. 8

1 Why with such earnest pains dost thou provoke
The years to bring the inevitable yoke,
Thus blindly with thy blessedness at strife?
Full soon thy Soul shall have her earthly freight,
And custom lie upon thee with a weight,
Heavy as frost, and deep almost as life!
    'Ode. Intimations of Immortality' (1807) st. 8

2 O joy! that in our embers
Is something that doth live,
That nature yet remembers
What was so fugitive!
The thought of our past years in me doth breed
Perpetual benediction.
    'Ode. Intimations of Immortality' (1832 ed.) st. 9

3 Not for these I raise
The song of thanks and praise;
But for those obstinate questionings
Of sense and outward things,
Fallings from us, vanishings;
Blank misgivings of a creature
Moving about in worlds not realised,
High instincts before which our mortal nature
Did tremble like a guilty thing surprised.
    'Ode. Intimations of Immortality' (1807) st. 9

4 Our noisy years seem moments in the being
Of the eternal Silence: truths that wake,
To perish never.
    'Ode. Intimations of Immortality' (1807) st. 9

5 Hence, in a season of calm weather,
Though inland far we be,
Our souls have sight of that immortal sea
Which brought us hither,
Can in a moment travel thither,
And see the children sport upon the shore,
And hear the mighty waters rolling evermore.
    'Ode. Intimations of Immortality' (1807) st. 9

6 Though nothing can bring back the hour
Of splendour in the grass, of glory in the flower;
We will grieve not, rather find
Strength in what remains behind . . .
In the faith that looks through death,
In years that bring the philosophic mind.
    'Ode. Intimations of Immortality' (1807) st. 10

7 Another race hath been, and other palms are won.
Thanks to the human heart by which we live,
Thanks to its tenderness, its joys, and fears,
To me the meanest flower that blows can give
Thoughts that do often lie too deep for tears.
    'Ode. Intimations of Immortality' (1807) st. 11

8 But Thy most dreaded instrument,
In working out a pure intent,
Is man—arrayed for mutual slaughter,—
Yea, Carnage is thy daughter!
    'Ode. The Morning of the Day Appointed for a General
    Thanksgiving' (1816)

9 Stern daughter of the voice of God!
O Duty! if that name thou love
Who art a light to guide, a rod
To check the erring, and reprove.
    'Ode to Duty' (1807)

10 Plain living and high thinking are no more:
The homely beauty of the good old cause
Is gone; our peace, our fearful innocence,
And pure religion breathing household laws.
    'O friend! I know not which way I must look' (1807)

11 Once did she hold the gorgeous East in fee,
And was the safeguard of the West.
    'On the Extinction of the Venetian Republic' (1807)

12 There's something in a flying horse,
There's something in a huge balloon;
But through the clouds I'll never float
Until I have a little Boat,
Shaped like the crescent-moon.
    Peter Bell (1819) prologue, l. 1

13 Is it some party in a parlour,
Crammed just as they on earth were crammed—
Some sipping punch, some sipping tea,
But as you by their faces see
All silent, and all damned?
    Peter Bell pt. 1, l. 541 in 1819 MS (subsequently deleted
    so as 'not to offend the pious')

14 Physician art thou?—one, all eyes,
Philosopher!—a fingering slave,
One that would peep and botanize
Upon his mother's grave?
    'A Poet's Epitaph' (1800)

15 A reasoning, self-sufficing thing,
An intellectual All-in-all!
    'A Poet's Epitaph' (1800)

16 In common things that round us lie
Some random truths he can impart,—
The harvest of a quiet eye
That broods and sleeps on his own heart.
    'A Poet's Epitaph' (1800)

17 Oh there is blessing in this gentle breeze,
A visitant that while it fans my cheek
Doth seem half-conscious of the joy it brings
From the green fields, and from yon azure sky.
Whate'er its mission, the soft breeze can come
To none more grateful than to me; escaped
From the vast city, where I long had pined
A discontented sojourner; now free,
Free as a bird to settle where I will.
    The Prelude (1850) bk. 1, l. 1

18   I recoil and droop, and seek repose
In listlessness from vain perplexity;
Unprofitably travelling toward the grave.
    The Prelude (1850) bk. 1, l. 265

19 Made one long bathing of a summer's day.
    The Prelude (1850) bk. 1, i. 290

20 Fair seed-time had my soul, and I grew up
Fostered alike by beauty and by fear.
    The Prelude (1850) bk. 1, l. 301

21 Dust as we are, the immortal spirit grows
Like harmony in music; there is a dark
Inscrutable workmanship that reconciles
Discordant elements, makes them cling together
In one society.
    The Prelude (1850) bk. 1, l. 340

22 And I was taught to feel, perhaps too much,
The self-sufficing power of Solitude.
    The Prelude (1850) bk. 2, l. 76

1   To thee
Science appears but what in truth she is,
Not as our glory and our absolute boast,
But as a succedaneum, and a prop
To our infirmity.
  The Prelude (1850) bk. 2, l. 211

2   The statue stood
Of Newton, with his prism, and silent face:
The marble index of a mind for ever
Voyaging through strange seas of Thought, alone.
  The Prelude (1850) bk. 3, l. 60

3   Spirits overwrought
Were making night do penance for a day
Spent in a round of strenuous idleness.
  The Prelude (1850) bk. 4, l. 376

4 Even forms and substances are circumfused
By that transparent veil with light divine;
And, through the turnings intricate of verse,
Present themselves as objects recognised,
In flashes, and with glory not their own.
  The Prelude (1850) bk. 5, l. 603

5   We were brothers all
In honour, as in one community,
Scholars and gentlemen.
  The Prelude (1850) bk. 9, l. 227

6   All things have second birth;
The earthquake is not satisfied at once.
  The Prelude (1850) bk. 10, l. 83

7 Not in Utopia,—subterranean fields,—
Or some secreted island, Heaven knows where!
But in the very world, which is the world
Of all of us,—the place where in the end
We find our happiness, or not at all!
  The Prelude (1850) bk. 11, l. 140

8   There is
One great society alone on earth,
The noble Living, and the noble Dead.
  The Prelude (1850) bk. 11, l. 393

9   I shook the habit off
Entirely and for ever, and again
In Nature's presence stood, as now I stand,
A sensitive being, a *creative* soul.
  The Prelude (1850) bk. 12, l. 204

10   Imagination, which in truth,
Is but another name for absolute power
And clearest insight, amplitude of mind,
And Reason, in her most exalted mood.
  The Prelude (1850) bk. 14, l. 190

11 I thought of Chatterton, the marvellous boy,
The sleepless soul that perished in its pride;
Of him who walked in glory and in joy
Behind his plough, upon the mountain side:
By our own spirits are we deified;
We poets in our youth begin in gladness;
But thereof comes in the end despondency and
  madness
  'Resolution and Independence' (1807) st. 7

12 His words came feebly, from a feeble chest,
Yet each in solemn order followed each,
With something of a lofty utterance drest;
Choice words, and measured phrase; above the reach
Of ordinary men; a stately speech!
Such as grave Livers do in Scotland use.
  'Resolution and Independence' (1807) st. 15

13   The fear that kills;
And hope that is unwilling to be fed;
Cold, pain, and labour, and all fleshly ills;
And mighty Poets in their misery dead.
—Perplexed, and longing to be comforted,
My question eagerly I did renew.
'How is it that you live, and what is it you do?'
  'Resolution and Independence' (1820 ed.) st. 17

14 Still glides the Stream, and shall for ever glide;
The Form remains, the Function never dies.
  'The River Duddon' (1820) no. 34 'After-Thought'

15 Enough, if something from our hands have power
To live, and act, and serve the future hour;
And if, as toward the silent tomb we go,
Through love, through hope, and faith's transcendent
  dower,
We feel that we are greater than we know.
  'The River Duddon' (1820) no. 34 'After-Thought'

16   The good old rule
Sufficeth them, the simple plan,
That they should take who have the power,
And they should keep who can.
  'Rob Roy's Grave' (1807) l. 37

17 Scorn not the Sonnet; Critic, you have frowned,
Mindless of its just honours; with this key
Shakespeare unlocked his heart.
  'Scorn not the Sonnet' (1827)

18 She dwelt among the untrodden ways
Beside the springs of Dove,
A maid whom there were none to praise
And very few to love:

A violet by a mossy stone
Half hidden from the eye!
—Fair as a star, when only one
Is shining in the sky.

She lived unknown, and few could know
When Lucy ceased to be;
But she is in her grave, and, oh,
The difference to me!
  'She dwelt among the untrodden ways' (1800)

19 And now I see with eye serene
The very pulse of the machine;
A being breathing thoughtful breath;
A traveller betwixt life and death;
The reason firm, the temperate will,
Endurance, foresight, strength, and skill;
A perfect woman; nobly planned,
To warn, to comfort, and command;
And yet a spirit still, and bright
With something of an angel light,
  'She was a phantom of delight' (1807)

1 A slumber did my spirit seal;
   I had no human fears:
   She seemed a thing that could not feel
   The touch of earthly years.

   No motion has she now, no force;
   She neither hears nor sees;
   Rolled round in earth's diurnal course,
   With rocks, and stones, and trees.
     'A slumber did my spirit seal' (1800)

2 O Man! that from thy fair and shining youth
   Age might but take the things Youth needed not!
     'The Small Celandine' (1807)

3 Behold her, single in the field,
   Yon solitary Highland lass!
     'The Solitary Reaper' (1807)

4 Will no one tell me what she sings?
   Perhaps the plaintive numbers flow
   For old, unhappy, far-off things,
   And battles long ago.
     'The Solitary Reaper' (1807)

5 What, you are stepping westward?
     'Stepping Westward' (1807)

6 Surprised by joy—impatient as the wind
   I wished to share the transport—Oh! with whom
   But thee, long buried in the silent tomb.
     'Surprised by joy—impatient as the wind' (1815)

7 One impulse from a vernal wood
   May teach you more of man,
   Of moral evil and of good,
   Than all the sages can.
     'The Tables Turned' (1798)

8 Our meddling intellect
   Mis-shapes the beauteous forms of things:—
   We murder to dissect.

   Enough of science and of art;
   Close up these barren leaves;
   Come forth, and bring with you a heart
   That watches and receives.
     'The Tables Turned' (1798)

9 Two Voices are there; one is of the sea,
   One of the mountains; each a mighty Voice:
   In both from age to age thou didst rejoice,
   They were thy chosen music, Liberty!
     'Thought of a Briton on the Subjugation of Switzerland'
     (1807)

10 O blithe new-comer! I have heard,
   I hear thee and rejoice:
   O Cuckoo! Shall I call thee bird,
   Or but a wandering voice?
     'To the Cuckoo' (1807)

11 Oft on the dappled turf at ease
   I sit, and play with similes,
   Loose types of things through all degrees.
     'To the Daisy' ('With little here to do or see', 1820 ed.)

12 Type of the wise who soar, but never roam;
   True to the kindred points of heaven and home!
     'To a Skylark' ('Ethereal minstrel! pilgrim of the sky',
     1827)

13 Though fallen thyself, never to rise again,
   Live, and take comfort. Thou hast left behind
   Powers that will work for thee; air, earth, and skies;
   There's not a breathing of the common wind
   That will forget thee; thou hast great allies;
   Thy friends are exultations, agonies,
   And love, and man's unconquerable mind.
     'To Toussaint L'Ouverture' (1807)

14 A simple child, dear brother Jim,
   That lightly draws its breath,
   And feels its life in every limb,
   What should it know of death?
     'We are Seven' (1798)

15 The world is too much with us; late and soon,
   Getting and spending, we lay waste our powers.
     'The world is too much with us' (1807)

16   Great God! I'd rather be
   A Pagan suckled in a creed outworn;
   So might I, standing on this pleasant lea,
   Have glimpses that would make me less forlorn;
   Have sight of Proteus rising from the sea;
   Or hear old Triton blow his wreathèd horn.
     'The world is too much with us' (1807)

17 The Poet writes under one restriction only, namely,
   the necessity of giving immediate pleasure to a human
   Being possessed of that information which may be
   expected from him, not as a lawyer, a physician, a
   mariner, an astronomer or a natural philosopher, but
   as a Man.
     Lyrical Ballads (2nd ed., 1802) Preface

18 Poetry is the breath and finer spirit of all knowledge;
   it is the impassioned expression which is in the
   countenance of all science.
     Lyrical Ballads (2nd ed., 1802) Preface

19 Poetry is the spontaneous overflow of powerful
   feelings: it takes its origin from emotion recollected in
   tranquillity.
     Lyrical Ballads (2nd ed., 1802) Preface

20 Never forget what I believe was observed to you by
   Coleridge, that every great and original writer, in
   proportion as he is great and original, must himself
   create the taste by which he is to be relished.
     Letter to Lady Beaumont, 21 May 1807, in E. de Selincourt
     (ed.) *Letters of William and Dorothy Wordsworth* vol. 2
     (revised by M. Moorman, 1969)

Sir Henry Wotton 1568–1639
English poet and diplomat

21 How happy is he born and taught
   That serveth not another's will;
   Whose armour is his honest thought,
   And simple truth his utmost skill!
     'The Character of a Happy Life' (1614)

1 Who God doth late and early pray
More of his grace than gifts to lend;
And entertains the harmless day
With a religious book, or friend.

This man is freed from servile bands,
Of hope to rise, or fear to fall:—
Lord of himself, though not of lands,
And having nothing, yet hath all.
'The Character of a Happy Life' (1614)

2 You meaner beauties of the night,
That poorly satisfy our eyes,
More by your number, than your light;
You common people of the skies,
What are you when the moon shall rise?
'On His Mistress, the Queen of Bohemia' (1624)

3 Untrue she was, yet I believed her eyes,
Instructed spies,
Till I was taught, that love was but a school
To breed a fool.
'Poem written in his youth' (1602)

4 He first deceased; she for a little tried
To live without him: liked it not, and died.
'Upon the Death of Sir Albertus Moreton's Wife' (1651)

5 Dazzled thus with height of place,
Whilst our hopes our wits beguile,
No man marks the narrow space
'Twixt a prison and a smile.
'Upon the sudden restraint of the Earl of Somerset' (1651)

6 In architecture as in all other operative arts, the end
must direct the operation. The end is to build well.
Well building hath three conditions. Commodity,
firmness, and delight.
Elements of Architecture (1624) pt. 1

7 Critics are like brushers of noblemen's clothes.
In Francis Bacon *Apophthegms New and Old* (1625) no. 64

8 Take heed of thinking, *The farther you go from the
church of Rome, the nearer you are to God.*
In Izaak Walton *Reliquiae Wottonianae* (1651) 'The Life of
Sir Henry Wotton'

9 An ambassador is an honest man sent to lie abroad for
the good of his country.
Written in the album of Christopher Fleckmore in 1604.
See Izaak Walton *Reliquiae Wottonianae* (1651) 'The Life of
Sir Henry Wotton'

Frank Lloyd Wright 1867–1959
American architect

10 The necessities were going by default to save the
luxuries until I hardly knew which were necessities
and which luxuries.
Autobiography (1945) bk. 2, p. 108

11 The physician can bury his mistakes, but the architect
can only advise his client to plant vines so they
should go as far as possible from home to build their
first buildings.
New York Times 4 Oct. 1953, sect. II, p. 17

Mehetabel ('Hetty') Wright (née Wesley)
1697–1750
English poet

12 Transient lustre, beauteous clay,
Smiling wonder of a day.
'To an Infant Expiring the Second Day of its Birth' (1733)

13 Thou tyrant whom I will not name,
Whom heaven and hell alike disclaim;
Abhorred and shunned, for different ends,
By angels, Jesuits, beasts and fiends!
What terms to curse thee shall I find,
Thou plague peculiar to mankind? . . .
That wretch, if such a wretch there be,
Who hopes for happiness from thee,
May search successfully as well
For truth in whores and ease in hell.
'Wedlock' (c.1730)

Lady Mary Wroth c.1586–c.1652
English poet

14 Love, a child, is ever crying:
Please him and he straight is flying,
Give him, he the more is craving,
Never satisfied with having.
'Love, a child, is ever crying' (1621)

Sir Thomas Wyatt c.1503–42
English poet

15 Farewell, Love, and all thy laws forever.
Thy baited hooks shall tangle me no more.
'Farewell, Love' (1557)

16   Go trouble younger hearts
And in me claim no more authority.
With idle youth go use thy property
And thereon spend thy many brittle darts:
For hitherto though I have lost all my time,
Me lusteth no longer rotten boughs to climb.
'Farewell, Love' (1557)

17 With serving still
This have I won:
For my good will
To be undone.

And for redress
Of all my pain
Disdainfulness
I have again.
'With serving still'

18 *Quondam* was I. She said, 'for ever'.
That 'ever' lasted but a short while,
A promise made not to dissever;
I thought she laughed, she did but smile.
Then *quondam* was I.
'Quondam was I'

19 They flee from me, that sometime did me seek
With naked foot, stalking in my chamber.
I have seen them gentle, tame, and meek,
That now are wild, and do not remember
That sometime they put themselves in danger
To take bread at my hand
'They flee from me' (1557)

1 Throughout the world, if it were sought,
Fair words enough a man shall find.
They be good cheap; they cost right naught;
Their substance is but only wind.
But well to say and so to mean—
That sweet accord is seldom seen.
'Throughout the world, if it were sought' (1557)

William Wycherley c.1640–1716

English playwright

2 A mistress should be like a little country retreat near the town, not to dwell in constantly, but only for a night and away.
The Country Wife (1675) act 1, sc. 1

3 A pox on 'em, and all that would force nature. Affectation is her greatest monster.
The Country Wife (1675) act 1, sc. 1

4 Go to your business, I say, pleasure, whilst I go to my pleasure, business.
The Country Wife (1675) act 2

5 Women and fortune are truest still to those that trust 'em.
The Country Wife (1675) act 5, sc. 4

6 Nay, you had both felt his desperate deadly daunting dagger:—there are your d's for you!
The Gentleman Dancing-Master (1672) act 5

7 Fy! madam, do you think me so ill bred as to love a husband?
Love in a Wood (1672) act 3, sc. 4

8 You who scribble, yet hate all who write . . .
And with faint praises one another damn.
The Plain Dealer (1677) Prologue (of drama critics)

William of Wykeham 1324–1404

English prelate and statesman

9 Manners maketh man.
Motto (proverbial since the mid-14th century)

Andrew of Wyntoun c.1350–c.1420

Scottish churchman

10 Quhen Alysander oure kyng wes dede,
That Scotland led in luve and le,
Away wes sons of ale and brede,
Of wyne and wax, of gamyn and gle;
Oure gold wes changyd into lede,
Cryst, borne into virgynyte,
Succour Scotland, and remede,
That stad is in perplexyte.
The Orygynale Cronykil (1795 ed.) vol. 1, bk. 7, ch. 10, l. 527

Xenophon c.428–c.354 BC

Greek historian

11 θάλαττα θάλαττα
The sea! the sea!
Anabasis bk. 4, ch. 7, sect. 24

Augustin, Marquis de Ximénèz 1726–1817

French poet

12 Attaquons dans ses eaux
La perfide Albion!
Let us attack in her own waters perfidious Albion!
'L'Ère des Français' (October 1793) in *Poésies Révolutionnaires et contre-révolutionnaires* (1821) vol. 1, p. 160. Cf. Bossuet 137:2

John Yates 1925–

English theologian; Bishop of Gloucester from 1975

13 There is a lot to be said in the Decade of Evangelism for believing more and more in less and less.
Gloucester Diocesan Gazette August 1991

Thomas Russell Ybarra b. 1880

14 A Christian is a man who feels
Repentance on a Sunday
For what he did on Saturday
And is going to do on Monday.
'The Christian' (1909)

W. F. Yeames 1835–1918

British painter

15 And when did you last see your father?
Title of painting (1878), now in the Walker Art Gallery, Liverpool

W. B. Yeats 1865–1939

Irish poet

16 I said 'a line will take us hours maybe,
Yet if it does not seem a moment's thought
Our stitching and unstitching has been naught.'
'Adam's Curse' (1904)

17 When I was young,
I had not given a penny for a song
Did not the poet sing it with such airs,
That one believed he had a sword upstairs.
'All Things can Tempt Me' (1910)

18 O chestnut-tree, great-rooted blossomer,
Are you the leaf, the blossom or the bole?
O body swayed to music, O brightening glance
How can we know the dancer from the dance?
'Among School Children' (1928)

19 Fifteen apparitions have I seen;
The worst a coat upon a coat-hanger.
'The Apparitions' (1939)

20 The unpurged images of day recede;
The Emperor's drunken soldiery are abed.
'Byzantium' (1933)

21 A starlit or a moonlit dome disdains
All that man is;
All mere complexities,
The fury and the mire of human veins.
'Byzantium' (1933)

1 Those images that yet
Fresh images beget,
That dolphin-torn, that gong-tormented sea.
 'Byzantium' (1933)

2 Now that my ladder's gone
I must lie down where all ladders start
In the foul rag and bone shop of the heart.
 'The Circus Animals' Desertion' (1939) pt. 3

3 I made my song a coat
Covered with embroideries
Out of old mythologies
From heel to throat;
But the fools caught it,
Wore it in the world's eye
As though they'd wrought it.
Song, let them take it
For there's more enterprise
In walking naked.
 'A Coat' (1914)

4 Though leaves are many, the root is one;
Through all the lying days of my youth
I swayed my leaves and flowers in the sun;
Now I may wither into the truth.
 'The Coming of Wisdom with Time' (1914)

5 We were the last romantics — chose for theme
Traditional sanctity and loveliness.
 'Coole and Ballylee, 1931' (1933)

6 The intellect of man is forced to choose
Perfection of the life, or of the work,
And if it take the second must refuse
A heavenly mansion, raging in the dark.
 'Coole Park and Ballylee, 1932' (1933)

7 The years like great black oxen tread the world,
And God the herdsman goads them on behind,
And I am broken by their passing feet.
 The Countess Cathleen (1895) act 4

8 A woman can be proud and stiff
When on love intent;
But Love has pitched his mansion in
The place of excrement;
For nothing can be sole or whole
That has not been rent.
 'Crazy Jane Talks with the Bishop' (1932)

9 Nor dread nor hope attend
A dying animal;
A man awaits his end
Dreading and hoping all.
 'Death' (1933)

10 He knows death to the bone—
Man has created death.
 'Death' (1933)

11 Down by the salley gardens my love and I did meet;
She passed the salley gardens with little snow-white feet.
She bid me take love easy, as the leaves grow on the tree;
But I, being young and foolish, with her would not agree.
 'Down by the Salley Gardens' (1889)

12 She bid me take life easy, as the grass grows on the weirs,
But I was young and foolish, and now am full of tears.
 'Down by the Salley Gardens' (1889)

13 I have met them at close of day
Coming with vivid faces
From counter or desk among grey
Eighteenth-century houses.
I have passed with a nod of the head
Or polite meaningless words.
 'Easter, 1916' (1921)

14 Too long a sacrifice
Can make a stone of the heart.
O when may it suffice?
 'Easter, 1916' (1921)

15 I write it out in a verse—
MacDonagh and MacBride
And Connolly and Pearse
Now and in time to be,
Wherever green is worn,
Are changed, changed utterly:
A terrible beauty is born.
 'Easter, 1916' (1921)

16 The rhetorician would deceive his neighbours,
The sentimentalist himself; while art
Is but a vision of reality.
 'Ego Dominus Tuus' (1917)

17 I see a schoolboy when I think of him
With face and nose pressed to a sweet-shop window,
For certainly he sank into his grave
His senses and his heart unsatisfied,
And made—being poor, ailing and ignorant,
Shut out from all the luxury of the world,
The ill-bred son of a livery stable-keeper—
Luxuriant song.
 'Ego Dominus Tuus' (1917); of Keats

18 The fascination of what's difficult
Has dried the sap out of my veins, and rent
Spontaneous joy and natural content
Out of my heart.
 'The Fascination of What's Difficult' (1910)

19 The friends that have it I do wrong
When ever I remake a song,
Should know what issue is at stake:
It is myself that I remake.
 'The friends that have it I do wrong' (1908)

20 Never to have lived is best, ancient writers say;
Never to have drawn the breath of life, never to have
  looked into the eye of day;
The second best's a gay goodnight and quickly turn
  away.
 'From *Oedipus at Colonus*' (1928). Cf. Sophocles 656:14

21 The ghost of Roger Casement
Is beating on the door.
 'The Ghost of Roger Casement' (1939)

22 Had I the heavens' embroidered cloths,
Enwrought with golden and silver light,
The blue and the dim and the dark cloths
Of night and light and the half light,
I would spread the cloths under your feet:
But I, being poor, have only my dreams;
I have spread my dreams under your feet;
Tread softly because you tread on my dreams
 'He Wishes for the Cloths of Heaven' (1899)

1 I mourn for that most lonely thing; and yet God's will
   be done,
   I knew a phoenix in my youth so let them have their
   day.
     'His Phoenix' (1919)

2 The light of evening, Lissadell,
   Great windows open to the south,
   Two girls in silk kimonos, both
   Beautiful, one a gazelle.
     'In Memory of Eva Gore Booth and Con Markiewicz' (1933)

3 The innocent and the beautiful
   Have no enemy but time.
     'In Memory of Eva Gore Booth and Con Markiewicz' (1933)

4 Some burn damp faggots, others may consume
   The entire combustible world in one small room
   As though dried straw, and if we turn about
   The bare chimney is gone black out
   Because the work had finished in that flare.
   Soldier, scholar, horseman, he,
   As 'twere all life's epitome.
   What made us dream that he could comb grey hair?
     'In Memory of Major Robert Gregory' (1919)

5 My country is Kiltartan Cross;
   My countrymen Kiltartan's poor!
     'An Irish Airman Foresees his Death' (1919)

6 Nor law, nor duty bade me fight,
   Nor public man, nor angry crowds,
   A lonely impulse of delight
   Drove to this tumult in the clouds;
   I balanced all, brought all to mind,
   The years to come seemed waste of breath,
   A waste of breath the years behind
   In balance with this life, this death.
     'An Irish Airman Foresees his Death' (1919)

7 I will arise and go now, and go to Innisfree,
   And a small cabin build there, of clay and wattles
   made;
   Nine bean rows will I have there, a hive for the honey
   bee,
   And live alone in the bee-loud glade.
     'The Lake Isle of Innisfree' (1893)

8 I hear lake water lapping with low sounds by the
   shore . . .
   I hear it in the deep heart's core.
     'The Lake Isle of Innisfree' (1893)

9 Land of Heart's Desire,
   Where beauty has no ebb, decay no flood,
   But joy is wisdom, Time an endless song.
     The Land of Heart's Desire (1894) p. 36

10 A sudden blow: the great wings beating still
   Above the staggering girl, her thighs caressed
   By the dark webs, her nape caught in his bill,
   He holds her helpless breast upon his breast.
   How can those terrified vague fingers push
   The feathered glory from her loosening thighs?
     'Leda and the Swan' (1928)

11 A shudder in the loins engenders there
   The broken wall, the burning roof and tower
   And Agamemnon dead.
     'Leda and the Swan' (1928)

12 Like a long-legged fly upon the stream
   His mind moves upon silence.
     'Long-Legged Fly' (1939)

13 We had fed the heart on fantasies,
   The heart's grown brutal from the fare,
   More substance in our enmities
   Than in our love; Oh, honey-bees
   Come build in the empty house of the stare.
     'Meditations in Time of Civil War' no. 6 'The Stare's Nest
     by my Window' (1928)

14 Think where man's glory most begins and ends
   And say my glory was I had such friends.
     'The Municipal Gallery Re-visited' (1939)

15 Why, what could she have done being what she is?
   Was there another Troy for her to burn?
     'No Second Troy' (1910)

16 I think it better that at times like these
   We poets keep our mouths shut, for in truth
   We have no gift to set a statesman right;
   He's had enough of meddling who can please
   A young girl in the indolence of her youth
   Or an old man upon a winter's night.
     'On being asked for a War Poem' (1919)

17 Where, where but here have Pride and Truth,
   That long to give themselves for wage,
   To shake their wicked sides at youth
   Restraining reckless middle age?
     'On hearing that the Students of our New University have
     joined the Agitation against Immoral Literature' (1910)

18 A pity beyond all telling,
   Is hid in the heart of love.
     'The Pity of Love' (1893)

19 Out of Ireland have we come.
   Great hatred, little room,
   Maimed us at the start.
   I carry from my mother's womb
   A fanatic heart.
     'Remorse for Intemperate Speech' (1933)

20 That is no country for old men. The young
   In one another's arms, birds in the trees—
   Those dying generations—at their song,
   The salmon-falls, the mackerel-crowded seas,
   Fish flesh or fowl, commend all summer long
   Whatever is begotten born and dies.
   Caught in that sensual music all neglect
   Monuments of unageing intellect.
     'Sailing to Byzantium' (1928)

21 An aged man is but a paltry thing,
   A tattered coat upon a stick, unless
   Soul clap its hands and sing, and louder sing
   For every tatter in its mortal dress.
     'Sailing to Byzantium' (1928)

22 And therefore I have sailed the seas and come
   To the holy city of Byzantium.
     'Sailing to Byzantium' (1928)

23 All shuffle there; all cough in ink;
   All wear the carpet with their shoes;
   All think what other people think;
   All know the man their neighbour knows.
   Lord, what would they say
   Did their Catullus walk that way?
     'The Scholars' (1919)

1 Turning and turning in the widening gyre
The falcon cannot hear the falconer;
Things fall apart; the centre cannot hold;
Mere anarchy is loosed upon the world,
The blood-dimmed tide is loosed, and everywhere
The ceremony of innocence is drowned;
The best lack all conviction, while the worst
Are full of passionate intensity.
    'The Second Coming' (1921)

2 The darkness drops again but now I know
That twenty centuries of stony sleep
Were vexed to nightmare by a rocking cradle,
And what rough beast, its hour come round at last,
Slouches towards Bethlehem to be born?
    'The Second Coming' (1921)

3 Far-off, most secret and inviolate Rose.
    'The Secret Rose' (1899)

4 A woman of so shining loveliness
That men threshed corn at midnight by a tress,
A little stolen tress.
    'The Secret Rose' (1899)

5 Romantic Ireland's dead and gone,
It's with O'Leary in the grave.
    'September, 1913' (1914)

6 Oh, who could have foretold
That the heart grows old?
    'A Song' (1919)

7 The woods of Arcady are dead,
And over is their antique joy;
Of old the world on dreaming fed;
Grey Truth is now her painted toy.
    'The Song of the Happy Shepherd' (1889)

8 And pluck till time and times are done,
The silver apples of the moon,
The golden apples of the sun.
    'Song of Wandering Aengus' (1899)

9 You think it horrible that lust and rage
Should dance attendance upon my old age;
They were not such a plague when I was young;
What else have I to spur me into song?
    'The Spur' (1939)

10 We Irish, born into that ancient sect
But thrown upon this filthy modern tide
And by its formless spawning, fury wrecked,
Climb to our proper dark, that we may trace
The lineaments of a plummet-measured face.
    'The Statues' (1939)

11 Swift has sailed into his rest;
Savage indignation there
Cannot lacerate his breast.
Imitate him if you dare,
World-besotted traveller; he
Served human liberty.
    'Swift's Epitaph' (1933). Cf. Swift 657:18

12 But where's the wild dog that has praised his fleas?
    'To a Poet, Who would have Me Praise certain bad Poets,
    Imitators of His and of Mine' (1910)

13 Red Rose, proud Rose, sad Rose of all my days!
Come near me, while I sing the ancient ways
    'To the Rose upon the Rood of Time' (1893)

14 What shall I do with this absurdity—
O heart, O troubled heart—this caricature,
Decrepit age that has been tied to me
As to a dog's tail?
    'The Tower' (1928) pt. 1

15 Michaelangelo left a proof
On the Sistine Chapel roof,
Where but half-awakened Adam
Can disturb globe-trotting Madam.
    'Under Ben Bulben' (1939) pt. 4

16 Irish poets, learn your trade,
Sing whatever is well made.
    'Under Ben Bulben' (1939) pt. 5

17 Cast your mind on other days
That we in coming days may be
Still the indomitable Irishry.
    'Under Ben Bulben' (1939) pt. 5

18 On limestone quarried near the spot
By his command these words are cut:
Cast a cold eye
On life, on death.
Horseman pass by!
    'Under Ben Bulben' (1939) pt. 6

19 When you are old and grey and full of sleep,
And nodding by the fire, take down this book
And slowly read and dream of the soft look
Your eyes had once, and of their shadows deep.
    'When You Are Old' (1893)

20 Unwearied still, lover by lover,
They paddle in the cold
Companionable streams or climb the air;
Their hearts have not grown old.
    'The Wild Swans at Coole' (1919)

21 We make out of the quarrel with others, rhetoric, but
of the quarrel with ourselves, poetry.
    Essays (1924) 'Anima Hominis' sect. 5

22 Even when the poet seems most himself . . . he is
never the bundle of accident and incoherence that sits
down to breakfast; he has been reborn as an idea,
something intended, complete.
    Essays and Introductions (1961) 'A General Introduction for
    my Work'

23 In dreams begins responsibility.
    Responsibilities (1914) epigraph

24 Think like a wise man but express yourself like the
common people.
    Letters on Poetry from W. B. Yeats to Dorothy Wellesley
    (1940) 21 December 1935

Sergei Yesenin 1895–1925
Russian poet

25 В этой жизни умирать не ново,
Но и жить, конечно, не новей.

In this life there's nothing new in dying,
But nor, of course, is living any newer.
    'Goodbye, my Friend, Goodbye' (Yesenin's final poem,
    written in his own blood the day before he hanged himself
    in his Leningrad hotel room, 28 December 1925)
    (tr. Gordon McVay)

1 И похабничал я и скандалил
Для того, чтобы ярче гореть.

Дар поэта — ласкать и карябать,
Роковая на нем печать.
Розу белую с черною жабой
Я хотел на земле повенчать.

I indulged in obscenities and scandals
In order to burn more bright.

The poet's gift is to soothe and harass,
He bears the stamp of fate.
On earth I wanted to marry
A white rose to a pitch-black toad.
      'I Have One Remaining Pastime' (1923) (translated by
      Gordon McVay)

2 Грубым дается радость.
Нежным дается печаль.

It's always the good feel rotten.
Pleasure's for those who are bad.
      'Pleasure's for the Bad' (1923) (translated by Gordon
      McVay)

Yevgeny Yevtushenko 1933–

Russian poet

3 Над Бабьим Яром памятников нет.
Крутой обрыв, как грубое надгробье.

Over Babiy Yar
There are no memorials.
The steep hillside like a rough inscription.
      'Babiy Yar' (1961) (translated by Robin Milner-Gulland)

4 Мы шли и шли,
забывая про отдых,
мимо воронок,
пожарищ мимо.
Шаталось небо сорок первого года, —
его подпирали
столбы дыма.

So on and on
we walked without thinking of rest
passing craters, passing fire,
under the rocking sky of '41
tottering crazy on its smoking columns.
      'The Companion' (1954) (translated by Robin
      Milner-Gulland)

5 Людей неинтересных в мире нет.
Их судьбы — как история планет.
У каждой всё особое, свое,
и нет планет, похожих на нее.

No people are uninteresting.
Their fate is like the chronicle of planets.
Nothing in them is not particular,
and planet is dissimilar from planet.
      'No People are Uninteresting' (1961) (translated by Robin
      Milner-Gulland)

Edward Young 1683–1765

English poet and playwright

6 Some for renown on scraps of learning dote,
And think they grow immortal as they quote.
      The Love of Fame (1725–8) Satire 1, l. 89

7 None think the great unhappy, but the great.
      The Love of Fame (1725–8) Satire 1, l. 238

8   Be wise with speed;
A fool at forty is a fool indeed.
      The Love of Fame (1725–8) Satire 2, l. 282

9 With skill she vibrates her eternal tongue,
For ever most divinely in the wrong.
      The Love of Fame (1725–8) Satire 6, l. 105

10 One to destroy, is murder by the law;
And gibbets keep the lifted hand in awe;
To murder thousands, takes a specious name,
'War's glorious art', and gives immortal fame.
      The Love of Fame (1725–8) Satire 7, l. 55. Cf. Rostand
      548:13

11 How science dwindles, and how volumes swell,
How commentators each dark passage shun,
And hold their farthing candle to the sun.
      The Love of Fame (1725–8) Satire 7, l. 96. Cf. Burton
      165:8, Johnson 372:17, Sidney 646:11

12 Tired Nature's sweet restorer, balmy sleep!
      Night Thoughts (1742–5) 'Night 1' l. 1

13   We take no note of Time
But from its loss.
      Night Thoughts (1742–5) 'Night 1' l. 55

14 Death! Great proprietor of all! 'Tis thine
To tread out empire, and to quench the stars.
      Night Thoughts (1742–5) 'Night 1' l. 204

15 Be wise to-day; 'tis madness to defer.
      Night Thoughts (1742–5) 'Night 1' l. 390

16 Procrastination is the thief of time.
      Night Thoughts (1742–5) 'Night 1' l. 393

17 At thirty a man suspects himself a fool;
Knows it at forty, and reforms his plan;
At fifty chides his infamous delay,
Pushes his prudent purpose to resolve;
In all the magnanimity of thought
Resolves; and re-resolves; then dies the same.
      Night Thoughts (1742–5) 'Night 1' l. 417

18 All men think all men mortal, but themselves.
      Night Thoughts (1742–5) 'Night 1' l. 424

19 By night an atheist half believes a God.
      Night Thoughts (1742–5) 'Night 5' l. 176

20 [The senses] Take in at once the landscape of the
      world,
At a small inlet, which a grain might close,
And half create the wondrous world they see.
      Night Thoughts (1742–5) 'Night 6' l. 425. Cf. Wordsworth
      745:2

21 To know the world, not love her, is thy point,
She gives but little, nor that little, long.
      Night Thoughts (1742–5) 'Night 8' l. 1276. Cf. Goldsmith
      310:20

22 Devotion! daughter of astronomy!
An undevout astronomer is mad.
      Night Thoughts (1742–5) 'Night 9' l. 769

23 How glorious, then, appears the mind of man,
When in it all the stars, and planets, roll.
And what it seems, it is: great objects make
Great minds.
      Night Thoughts (1742–5) 'Night 9' l. 1062

24 The course of Nature is the art of God.
      Night Thoughts (1742–5) 'Night 9' l. 1267

1 Life is the desert, life the solitude;
Death joins us to the great majority.
The Revenge (1721) act 4. Cf. Petronius 513:12

George W. Young 1846–1919

2 Your lips, on my own, when they printed 'Farewell',
Had never been soiled by the 'beverage of hell';
But they come to me now with the bacchanal sign,
And the lips that touch liquor must never touch mine.
'The Lips That Touch Liquor Must Never Touch Mine'
(*c..*1870) (also attributed, in a different form, to Harriet A.
Glazebrook, 1874)

Michael Young 1915–

British writer

3 Today we frankly recognize that democracy can be no
more than aspiration, and have rule not so much by
the people as by the cleverest people; not an
aristocracy of birth, not a plutocracy of wealth, but a
true meritocracy of talent.
The Rise of the Meritocracy (1958) pt. 1, ch. 1, sect. 1

Yevgeny Zamyatin 1884–1937

Russian writer

4 True literature can exist only where it is created not
by diligent and trustworthy officials, but by madmen,
heretics, dreamers, rebels and sceptics. But when a
writer must be sensible . . . there can be no bronze
literature, there can only be a newspaper literature,
which is read today, and used for wrapping soap
tomorrow.
Essays (1970, translated by M. Ginsberg) 'I am Afraid'
(1921)

5 Heretics are the only bitter remedy against the entropy
of human thought.
'Literature, Revolution and Entropy' quoted in *The Dragon
and other Stories* (1967, translated by M. Ginsberg)
Introduction

Israel Zangwill 1864–1926

Jewish spokesman and writer

6 Scratch the Christian and you find the pagan—spoiled.
Children of the Ghetto (1892) bk. 2, ch. 6

7 America is God's Crucible, the great Melting-Pot
where all the races of Europe are melting and
re-forming!
The Melting Pot (1908) act 1

Emiliano Zapata 1879–1919

Mexican revolutionary

0 Muchos de ellos, por complacer a tiranos, por un puñado
de monedas, o por cohecho o soborno, están derramando la
sangre de sus hermanos.

Many of them, so as to curry favour with tyrants, for
a fistful of coins, or through bribery or corruption, are
shedding the blood of their brothers.
Plan de Ayala 28 November 1911, para. 10 (on the
maderistas who, in Zapata's view, had betrayed the
revolutionary cause)

Frank Zappa 1940–

American rock musician and songwriter

9 Rock journalism is people who can't write
interviewing people who can't talk for people who
can't read.
In Linda Botts *Loose Talk* (1980) p. 177. Cf. Capp
178:15

Robert Zemeckis and Bob Gale

10 Back to the future.
Title of film (1985)

Ronald L. Ziegler 1939–

American government spokesman

11 Reminded of the President's previous statements that
the White House was not involved [in the Watergate
affair], Ziegler said that Mr Nixon's latest statement 'is
the Operative White House Position . . . and all
previous statements are inoperative.'
Boston Globe 18 April 1973

Grigori Zinoviev 1883–1936

Soviet politician

12 Armed warfare must be preceded by a struggle against
the inclinations to compromise which are embedded
among the majority of British workmen, against the
ideas of evolution and peaceful extermination of
capitalism. Only then will it be possible to count upon
complete success of an armed insurrection.
Letter to the British Communist Party, 15 September 1924,
in *The Times* 25 October 1924 (the 'Zinoviev Letter', said by
some to be a forgery. See *Listener* 17 September 1987)

Émile Zola 1840–1902

French novelist

13 Ne me regardez plus comme ça, parce que vous allez vous
user les yeux.
Don't go on looking at me like that, because you'll
wear your eyes out.
La Bête humaine (1889–90) ch. 5

14 J'accuse.
I accuse.
Title of an open letter to the President of the French
Republic, in connection with the Dreyfus affair; in *L'Aurore*
13 January 1898

INDEX

accidents: a. will happen NORTH 496:17
 A. will occur DICK 240:4
 chapter of a. CHES 198:22
 moving a. by flood and field SHAK 615:1
 problem of habitual a. BENC 62:10
 that he runs into a. MARQ 448:19
 Which shackles a., and bolts SHAK 566:19
accomplice: a. of liars and forgers PÉGUY 511:6
accomplished: a. man HOR 351:4
 desire a. is sweet BIBLE 78:28
 what can be a. in a week STEV 667:25
accomplishments: a. give lustre CHES 198:21
 a. we should desire WINC 739:1
 emerges ahead of his a. STEI 663:8
accord: Just a. all music SIDN 647:5
 Should of his own a. ANON 20:2
 sweet a. is seldom seen WYATT 750:17
account: a. thereof in the day BIBLE 90:33
 sent to my a. SHAK 573:20
 Such I a. thy love SHAK 601:5
accuracy: a. must be sacrificed JOHN 367:17
accursed: themselves a. they were not here
 SHAK 586:11
accuse: *I'a.* ZOLA 755:14
 thoughts a. the dead GREV 318:7
 yet I could a. me SHAK 575:18
accused: apology before you be a. CHAR 191:5
 security to persons who are a. DENM 237:1
 than a. of deficiency JOHN 374:19
accuser: not my A., but my judges
 NEWM 492:13
accusing: A. Spirit, which flew STER 665:3
accustomed: A. to her face LERN 419:4
ace: a. down his sleeve LAB 404:17
 a. of trumps and not CHUR 201:21
 was about to play the a. FIELD 281:15
aces: hands that hold the a. BETJ 67:9
Achaeans: A. have suffered HOMER 343:2
 myriad sufferings for the A. HOMER 342:22
Achates: *quae tela gerebat A.* VIRG 712:4
ached: never a. with a heart SWIN 676:11
acheronta: *A. movebo* VIRG 714:3
aches: sense a. at thee SHAK 617:16
achieve: a. of, the mastery HOPK 346:11
 I shall a. in time GILB 305:3
achieved: It is a. BIBLE 108:15
achievement: Great a. assured HEGEL 330:12
 she is the reward of a. GREER 317:13
achievements: a. mock me SHAK 622:24
achieving: Still a., still pursuing LONG 427:11
Achilles: A.' cursed anger sing HOMER 342:22
 A. . . . who wears his wit SHAK 627:12
 And see the great A. TENN 690:4
 arrayed in the armour of A. VIRG 712:18
 I've stood upon A.' tomb BYRON 171:10
 or what name A. assumed BROW 145:19
 work out A. his armour BROW 145:9
aching: A., shaking, crazy ROCH 543:17
 Desolate passions, a. hours JOHN 367:3
 O a. time KEATS 387:26
Achitophel: false A. was first DRYD 259:1
Achivi: *plectuntur A.* HOR 348:2
acid: Electric Kool-Aid A. test WOLFE 741:7
 though I wrote with a. MANS 445:7
'Ackney Marshes: could see to A. BAT 55:4
acknowledge: a. my faults BOOK 128:4
 next a. duly NEWM 493:12
 we a. thee to be the Lord BOOK 118:12
acknowledgement: a. passes for
 current payment BURN 160:12
acorns: Tall oaks from little a. EVER 279:9
acquaintance: A. I would have COWL 221:12
 A., *n.* A person whom BIER 109:2
 apology for dropping the a. SCOTT 560:24
 creditable a. SWIFT 673:9
 first an a., next a mistress CHEK 197:6
 have a visiting a. SHER 645:8
 I do not make a new a. JOHN 376:19
 man does not make new a. JOHN 371:21
 Should auld a. be forgot BURNS 161:4
acquainted: a. with grief BIBLE 84:11
 been one a. with the night FROST 294:8

acquainted: (*cont.*):
 Sentiment is what I am not a. FLEM 287:6
acquiesce: a. with silence JOHN 367:23
acquisition: aiding in the a. TORR 701:5
 personal a. but is inborn JUNG 382:12
acquitted: guilty party is a. PUBL 531:3
acre: a. in Middlesex is better MAC 435:2
 a. of barren ground SHAK 624:28
acres: few paternal a. bound POPE 523:11
 lass that has a. o' charms BURNS 162:3
 Three a. and a cow ANON 19:1
 Two wise a. and a cow COW 221:6
acrimonious: a. and surly republican
 JOHN 369:2
acrostic: peaceful province in A. Land
 DRYD 261:3
act: a. in the living Present LONG 427:9
 a. of darkness with her SHAK 596:9
 a. of dying is not JOHN 373:7
 And sleep an a. or two SHAK 589:18
 And the a. ELIOT 271:15
 Ay me! what a. SHAK 577:10
 character of the fifth a. LERM 418:16
 easier to a. than to think AREN 24:17
 Is in itself almost an a. ROSS 548:7
 it is the foolishest a. BROW 146:16
 last a. crowns QUAR 533:16
 princes to a. SHAK 584:16
 prologues to the swelling a. SHAK 600:11
 reference to fun in any A. HERB 333:22
 Regulations a. WILDE 736:2
 same in thine own a. SHAK 601:5
 sins they love to a. SHAK 618:23
 That does both a. and know MARV 450:16
 through the A. of Settlement RICE 540:4
 To see him a., is like COL 212:8
 which is capacity to a. WHIT 731:12
 within the meaning of the A. ANON 17:9
acted: a. so tragic the house HARG 326:9
 this our lofty scene be a. SHAK 591:17
acti: *Iucundi a. labores* CIC 203:26
acting: A. a masochistic form OLIV 498:15
 a. of a dreadful thing SHAK 590:15
 people in them, a. LARK 410:4
 when he was off he was a. GOLD 311:6
action: about the a. of the sky BYRON 170:9
 a. is a most dangerous CLOU 207:2
 A. is consolatory CONR 217:10
 A. is transitory WORD 743:7
 A man of a. forced GALS 297:6
 And lose the name of a. SHAK 575:16
 can only be grasped by a. BRON 141:17
 end of man is an a. CARL 181:8
 Every public a. CORN 219:7
 fulfilment in policy and a. TRIL 702:18
 imitate the a. of the tiger SHAK 585:7
 In a. faithful, and in honour POPE 520:32
 In a.'s dizzying eddy whirled ARN 27:23
 Is lust in a.; and till SHAK 635:1
 Let a single completed a. BOIL 117:4
 Makes that and th' a. fine HERB 334:18
 prefer the talents of a. BYRON 173:26
 suit the a. to the word SHAK 576:6
 Thought is the child of A. DISR 248:34
 true men of a. in our AUDEN 36:16
 with the liberty of a. MILL 460:14
 work, and cold for a SHAK 584:20
actions: a. are not always true BUTL 166:10
 a. are what they BUTL 165:22
 A. receive their tincture DEFOE 234:16
 a. that a man might play SHAK 572:10
 mutual a. of two bodies NEWT 494:4
 my a. are my ministers CHAR 191:12
 not to laugh at human a. SPIN 661:3
 Only the a. of the just SHIR 646:4
 person doing interesting a. BAG 47:5
 there are disinterested a. GIDE 303:6
 Your a. are my dreams SHAK 631:21
activated: A. Sludge JENN 365:7
active: An *a.* Principle WORD 744:2
active-valiant: More a. or SHAK 581:29
actor: a.'s life for me WASH 722:3
 As an a. does his part CAREY 179:17

actor: (*cont.*):
 Like a dull a. now SHAK 570:21
 unperfect a. on the stage SHAK 633:7
 well-graced a. leaves the stage SHAK 621:7
actors: a. or spectators SHEL 639:19
 best a. in the world SHAK 575:2
acts: first four a. already past BERK 65:13
 His a. being seven ages SHAK 568:16
 Our a. our angels FLET 287:16
 person a. his own creations BROW 151:18
 second a. in American FITZ 285:6
 That all your a. are queens SHAK 632:5
 unremembered, a. WORD 744:19
 which a. the most slowly DIMN 246:6
 who desires but a not BLAKE 112:18
actual: ideal distinguished from a. KEYN 395:13
actum: *Nil a. credens* LUCAN 431:6
adage: poor cat i' the a. SHAK 601:5
Adam: A. and Eve were dispossessed
 BOUL 137:16
 A. ate the apple HUGH 354:7
 A. from his fair spouse MILT 471:14
 A. Had 'em ANON 11:18
 A., the goodliest man MILT 471:7
 A. was but human TWAIN 706:18
 And A. was a gardener SHAK 587:25
 deep sleep to fall upon A. BIBLE 70:5
 For as in A. all die BIBLE 101:7
 gardener A. and his wife TENN 684:22
 grant that the old A. BOOK 122:20
 gratitude we owe to A. TWAIN 706:19
 Old A.'s likeness, set SHAK 620:15
 past Eve and A.'s JOYCE 380:21
 rubbish of an A. SOUTH 657:1
 That A. was not Adamant HOOD 344:5
 they hold up A.'s profession SHAK 578:16
 this is that doom that A. MILT 475:6
 we but the penalty of A. SHAK 567:24
 What a good thing A. had TWAIN 706:15
 When A. dalfe and Eve spane ROLLE 545:10
 Where but half-awakened A. YEATS 753:15
 Whilst A. slept, Eve from ANON 19:19
 whipped the offending A. SHAK 584:18
adamant: a. for drift, solid CHUR 202:4
 frame of a., a soul of fire JOHN 370:16
 That Adam was not A. HOOD 344:5
adazzle: sour; a., dim HOPK 345:20
adder: A.'s fork, and blind-worm's
 SHAK 603:18
 a. that stoppeth her ears BOOK 128:17
 golden beat, and an a. MAND 444:4
 go upon the lion and a. BOOK 131:5
 stingeth like an a. BIBLE 79:13
 that brings forth the a. SHAK 590:13
addicted: Salteena not very a. ASHF 31:7
addiction: Every form of a. bad JUNG 382:15
 prisoners of a. ILL 359:10
addictive: All sin tends to be a. AUDEN 36:14
Addison: Cato did, and A. approved
 BUDG 154:14
 volumes of A. JOHN 368:20
addled: a. delusion ELIOT 269:6
addresses: A. are given to us to conceal
 SAKI 553:12
adeste: *A., fideles* ANON 21:18
adieu: A., adieu, kind friends ANUN 18:11
 A., mes amis. Je vais DUNC 264:5
 A., she cries! GAY 300:17
 Bidding a.; and aching KEATS 389:7
 He fumbles up into a loose a. SHAK 628:1
ad infinitum: proceed *a.* SWIFT 675:6
adjective: As to the A. TWAIN 706:21
Adlestrop: I remember A. THOM 693:23
administered: best a. is best POPE 522:17
administration: a. of the government
 SWIFT 673:10
 made a criticism of a. BAG 46:16
admiral: a. from time to time VOLT 716:3
 Of some great a. MILT 468:14
admirals: A. extolled for standing still
 COWP 223:12
admiralty: blood the price of a. KIPL 401:2
admirari: *Nil a. prope res* HOR 348:7

admiration: As great in a. as herself
                     SHAK 589:17
  exciting a. by its resemblance PASC 507:11
  exercise our a. DONNE 253:11
  or disease of a. MAC 435:6
admirations: moulded by their a. BOWEN 138:9
admire: a. his sleight of hand BUTL 166:16
  a., we should not understand CONG 215:11
  cannot possibly a. them WILDE 735:22
  Let none a. MILT 469:5
  Not to a., is all the art POPE 522:28
  scarce begun to a. the one DRYD 262:14
  they at once a. and hate LEWIS 421:7
admired: not blush so to be a. WALL 718:10
  poet is to be a. COCT 208:11
  That she might a. be SHAK 631:8
admittance: No a. till the week after next
                     CARR 183:24
admitted: a. to that equal sky POPE 522:3
ado: heathen make much a. BOOK 127:16
adolescence: a. and obsolescence LINK 423:6
  vigour of a prolonged a. LEAV 415:5
Adonais: I weep for A. SHEL 639:11
Adonis: A. from his native rock MILT 468:20
adopted: by roads not a. BETJ 68:7
adoption: Spirit of a. BIBLE 99:35
adorable: a. tennis-girl's hand BETJ 68:9
adoration: a. which is paid MORE 484:4
  All a., duty, and observance SHAK 569:21
  Breathless with a. WORD 744:12
adore: command where I a. SHAK 630:3
  Pam, I a. you, Pam BETJ 68:3
  positively a. Miss Dombey DICK 240:12
adored: I was a. once too SHAK 629:10
adorings: a. from their loves KEATS 387:1
adorn: none that he did not a. JOHN 374:21
  To point a moral, or a. a tale JOHN 370:17
adorned: Christ a. and beautified BOOK 123:16
  when unadorned a. the most THOM 696:8
adornings: made their bends a. SHAK 565:6
adornment: a. of his person THOM 695:14
adorns: a. my legs HOUS 351:14
ads: He watched the a. NASH 490:13
adsuitur: A. pannus HOR 347:3
adsum: quickly said, 'A. THAC 691:6
adult: child becomes a. when SZASZ 677:10
  occupation of an a. OLIV 498:15
adulteration: Not quite adultery, but a.
                     BYRON 171:23
adulteries: all the a. of art JONS 378:18
adulterous: evil and a. generation BIBLE 90:34
  Mary was found in a. bed BLAKE 111:18
adultery: a. being a most conventional
                     NAB 488:20
  a. than in provincialism HUXL 357:8
  Die: die for a.! SHAK 597:4
  Do not a. commit CLOU 207:18
  gallantry, and gods a. BYRON 170:6
  Not quite a., but adulteration BYRON 171:23
  Thou shalt not commit a. BIBLE 72:16
  woman taken in a. BIBLE 96:29
adults: attributed by a. to children
                     SZASZ 677:12
  children produce a. DE VR 238:5
  only between consenting a. VIDAL 711:4
advance: retrograde if it does not a. GIBB 302:8
  say civilization don't a. ROG 545:4
  somewhat to a. POPE 522:26
advantage: a. of doing one's praising
                     BUTL 166:26
  A. rarely comes of it CLOU 207:18
  French are with equal a. CANN 178:3
  most naturally gain the a. POTT 525:17
  take a mean a. of them WOD 740:18
  thereout suck they no small a. BOOK 130:1
  undertaking of Great A. ANON 12:27
advantages: in hope of fair a. SHAK 608:13
  not had your a. BOTT 137:13
  stamp and counterfeit a. SHAK 615:21
advent: Hark to the a. voice OXRL 497:8
adventure: A. is only an inconvenience
                     CHES 198:13

adventure: (cont.):
  most beautiful a. in life FROH 294:5
  Our a. is ended ALAI 7:5
  out into a. and sunshine FORS 290:8
  will be an awfully big a. BARR 54:8
adventures: a. of his soul FRAN 292:8
  a. were by the fire-side GOLD 311:30
  hard a. t' undertake FITZ 283:9
adversitate: a. fortunae BOET 116:12
adversité: l'a. de nos meilleurs amis LA R 410:22
adversitee: For of fortunes sharpe a.
                     CHAU 195:20
adversities: a. which may happen BOOK 120:15
  all our troubles and a. BOOK 120:3
adversity: a. doth best discover BACON 42:21
  A., if a man is set down BUTL 166:24
  a. is not without comforts BACON 42:20
  a. is the blessing BACON 42:18
  A.'s sweet milk, philosophy SHAK 623:20
  bread of a. BIBLE 83:15
  brother is born for a. BIBLE 78:40
  day of a. consider BIBLE 80:14
  hundred that will stand a. CARL 180:29
  men contending with a. BURT 165:2
  sickness, or any other a. BOOK 122:3
  Sweet are the uses of a. SHAK 567:25
advertise: Finalize you or a. DYLAN 265:10
  shall call him and a. him BOOK 121:14
advertisement: soul of an a. JOHN 368:9
advertisers: proprietor's prejudices as the a.
                     SWAF 673:1
advertising: A. is the rattling ORW 501:4
advice: a. is good or bad only AUST 39:8
  a. is in nine cases out COLL 213:8
  A. is seldom welcome CHES 198:12
  A woman seldom asks a. ADD 4:21
  Can Love be controlled by a. GAY 299:13
  matrimony I never give any a. CHES 198:2
  tea and comfortable a. KEATS 391:22
advise: A. the prince ELIOT 272:5
  STREETS FLOODED. PLEASE A. BENC 62:13
  would a. no man to marry JOHN 377:6
advises: It's my old girl that a. DICK 239:12
advocate: intellect of an a. BAG 46:10
  our Mediator and A. BOOK 120:4
advocates: potent a. of peace GEOR 301:3
  you of a. the best CAT 186:6
Aeneas: A. shall want troops SHAK 566:9
aeon: a. after aeon HUGH 354:6
aeroplanes: it wasn't the a. CREE 226:17
aery: execute their a. purposes MILT 468:18
aes: Illi robur et a. triplex HOR 349:2
Aesculapius: owe a cock to A. SOCR 655:4
aesthetic: Between a. and religious BELL 60:19
  degree of my a. emotion BELL 60:19
  high a. band GILB 305:17
  our a. enjoyment WHIT 731:14
  shine in the high a. line GILB 305:15
aetas: A.: carpe diem HOR 349:9
  A. parentum peior avis tulit HOR 350:5
affable: sign of an a. man ROST 548:10
affair: love a. with America MAIL 442:8
affairs: amendment beginning in human a.
                     PRICE 528:17
  from taking part in a. VALÉ 707:23
  knows the interior of a. WALP 720:3
  There is a tide in the a. SHAK 593:12
  tide in the a. of women BYRON 171:15
affectation: A. is her greatest monster
                     WYCH 750:3
  hyperboles, spruce a. SHAK 599:7
  Only by a. spoiled SWIFT 675:8
  wits to sophistry and a. BACON 45:14
affection: A. beaming in one eye DICK 241:9
  Of any true a., but 'twas nipt MIDD 459:12
  Or thy a. cannot hold the bent SHAK 629:15
  rear of your a. SHAK 573:1
  Yet still he fills a.'s eye JOHN 375:29
  your a. on things above BIBLE 103:15
affections: a. dark as Erebus SHAK 610:3
  learnt's a. and the truth KEATS 391:5
  history of the a. IHV 360:14
  Made out of nothing of a. new SHAK 634:21

affections: (cont.):
  our selves into men's a. CAV 187:13
  our young a. run to waste BYRON 169:4
  T'a., and to faculties DONNE 251:26
  unruly wills and a. BOOK 120:18
affects: A. to nod DRYD 259:17
affinities: Elective a. GOET 309:13
afflicted: oppressed and a. BIBLE 84:12
affliction: A. alters SHAK 632:11
  A. is enamoured of thy parts SHAK 623:18
  bread of a. and with water BIBLE 76:13
  Of all a. taught a lover yet POPE 519:20
  Remembering mine a. BIBLE 85:17
  saveth in time of a. BIBLE 87:8
  thee in the furnace of a. BIBLE 84:4
  To try me with a., had SHAK 617:15
  waters of a. BIBLE 83:15
afflictions: A. easier grow WALSH 720:18
  A. sorted, anguish of all HERB 335:19
  describing the a. of Job BACON 42:19
  issue out of all their a. BOOK 120:7
affluence: A. a question of texture DRAB 257:7
afford: Can't a. them, Governor SHAW 638:17
  it unless you can a. it TROL 704:10
  parties could any way a. it EDG 266:10
  some man that can a. SHAW 638:9
  Whether we can a. it or no GAY 300:12
Afghanistan: left on A.'s plain KIPL 401:12
afire: bush a. with God BROW 147:9
afloat: A. We move CLOU 207:10
  full sea are we now a. SHAK 593:12
afraid: afraid of God, a. of me POPE 523:9
  a. to speak evil of dignities BIBLE 105:23
  a. to think what I have SHAK 602:4
  And in short, I was a. ELIOT 272:4
  And many are a. of God LOCK 425:13
  do what you are a. to do EMER 276:27
  got to be taught to be a. HAMM 323:2
  he was a. to look BIBLE 71:39
  I, a stranger and a. HOUS 351:20
  it is that he is a. FORS 290:1
  not so much a. of death BROW 146:11
  not that I'm a. to die ALLEN 9:15
  see all nor be a. BROW 152:6
  stop because you are a. NANS 489:8
  that he is a. of his enemy PLUT 517:15
  they were sore a. BIBLE 93:26
  things is to be a. FAUL 281:2
  we do be a. of the sea SYNGE 677:7
  whereof our conscience is a. BOOK 121:6
  whom then shall I be a. BOOK 125:24
  Who's A. of Virginia Woolf? ALBEE 7:8
Afric: geographers, in A.-maps SWIFT 675:3
  Where A.'s sunny fountains HEBER 330:3
Africa: A. and her prodigies BROW 146:6
  I speak of A. and golden joys SHAK 584:11
  something new out of A. PLINY 517:7
  Till China and A. meet AUDEN 34:3
  with A. than my own body ORTON 499:12
  yonder, silent over A. BROW 150:8
African: [A.] national consciousness
                     MACM 440:5
Africans: some to the parched A. VIRG 714:13
after: a. many a summer dies TENN 689:10
  A. the first death THOM 693:14
  Or just a. STEV 666:12
  tell them that come a. BOOK 127:23
afternoon: At five in the a. GARC 297:12
  could lose the war in an a. CHUR 203:6
  Lovely and willing every a. AUDEN 35:2
  rude multitude call the a. SHAK 599:5
  Summer a. JAMES 363:11
  With a. tea-cakes and scones BETJ 67:12
aftersight: mind to a. and foresight ELIOT 271:5
after-silence: But in the a. on the shore
                     BYRON 172:24
aftertimes: something so written to a.
                     MILT 476:5
Afton: Flow gently, sweet A. BURNS 161:3
again: help a. BOOK 128:6
  I'll see you a. COW 220:12
  n all bring the man over a. BARH 52:11
against: A. thee only have I sinned BOOK 128:4

against: (cont.):
anyone who wasn't a. war   LOW 429:9
because most people vote a.   ADAMS 2:5
hand will be a. every man   BIBLE 70:37
I always vote a.   FIEL 282:23
I have somewhat a. thee   BIBLE 106:3
not with me is a. me   BIBLE 90:29
that all life is 6 to 5 a.   RUNY 550:5
who can be a. us   BIBLE 99:39
Agamemnon: And A. dead   YEATS 752:11
When A. cried aloud   ELIOT 272:20
agate-stone: no bigger than an a.   SHAK 622:21
age: a. according to the oracle   VIRG 714:22
a. are threescore years   BOOK 131:1
A. cannot wither her   SHAK 565:8
a. demanded an image   POUND 526:13
a. fatal to Revolutionists   DESM 238:1
a. going to the workhouse   PAINE 504:21
a. has a kind of universal   DRYD 262:9
a. his sables and his weeds   SHAK 578:11
A., I do abhor thee   SHAK 632:19
a. in pilèd stones   MILT 466:17
a. is a dream that is dying   O'SH 501:23
a. is as a lusty winter   SHAK 567:28
A. is deformed, youth unkind   BAST 55:3
a. is rocking the wave   MAND 444:4
a. is the most unexpected   TROT 704:11
A. might but take the things   WORD 748:2
a. of chivalry is gone   BURKE 158:13
A. of Machinery   CARL 180:14
A. of man the waiters   BARN 53:18
a. of pamphleteers   HOGB 341:14
A. shall be able to destroy   OVID 503:2
A. shall not weary them   BINY 109:20
A. that brings along   FLAT 285:15
a. that has been tied   YEATS 753:14
a. to quit their clogs   MILT 474:22
a., which forgives itself   SHAW 638:3
A. will not be defied   BACON 44:14
An a. in her embraces passed   ROCH 543:8
And almost every one when a.   CLOU 207:15
And now in a. I bud again   HERB 335:3
away in the time of a.   BOOK 129:17
buried in a good old a.   BIBLE 70:36
companions for middle a.   BACON 44:5
Crabbed a. and youth cannot   SHAK 632:18
dawning of the a. of Aquarius   RADO 535:8
dead centre of middle a.   ADAMS 2:4
essentially a tragic a.   LAWR 411:12
fetch the a. of gold   MILT 467:8
flower of their a.   BIBLE 74:26
For a. with stealing steps   VAUX 709:12
For soon comes a.   SPEN 660:6
governed their rude a.   BAG 47:3
grief as a.   SHAK 595:17
harsh a. changed my course   AKHM 6:7
hath not forgotten my a.   SOUT 657:14
He died in a good old a.   BIBLE 76:33
He is of a.; ask him   BIBLE 96:35
He was not of an a.   JONS 380:4
His wealth a well-spent a.   CAMP 177:7
I can tell a woman's a.   GILB 306:14
If youth knew; if a. could   EST 278:15
infirmity of his a.   SHAK 594:25
invention of a barbarous a.   MILT 467:17
Is worth an a. without a name   MORD 483:18
labour with an a. of ease   GOLD 310:7
language of the a.   GRAY 316:11
less for what a. takes away   WORD 744:4
Let a. approve of youth   BROW 152:13
my a., still alive   LOW 430:14
Of cold a., narrow jealousy   ROCH 542:18
Of every a. and clime   JOHN 377:14
Old-a., a second child   CHUR 201:3
Old a. brings along   EMER 277:10
old a. crept over them   NAYL 491:3
Old a. hath yet his honour   TENN 690:4
Old a. should burn   THOM 693:4
poison for the a.'s tooth   SHAK 593:26
sad Old A. live there   VIRG 713:14
shall from a. to age endure   KETHE 394:13
should accompany old a.   SHAK 604:21
some smack of a. in you   SHAK 582:16

age: (cont.):
Soul of the A.   JONS 380:1
Spirit of the A.   HAZL 329:11
Stretch a.'s truth sometimes   JONS 378:7
stricken in a.   BIBLE 71:1
That men call a.; and those   BROO 143:3
Their a., not Charlemagne's   BROW 147:5
Then Old A., and Experience   ROCH 543:12
then the only end of a.   LARK 409:17
this a. best pleaseth   HERR 336:23
Thou hast nor youth nor a.   SHAK 606:8
'Tis well an old a. is out   DRYD 261:21
To complain of the a. we   BURKE 159:11
very attractive a.   WILDE 734:20
very staff of my a.   SHAK 608:6
virtuous in their old a.   POPE 524:6
when the a. is in   SHAK 614:6
who expect that a. will   JOHN 369:18
who tells one her real a.   WILDE 735:28
with a. and dust   RAL 536:3
With leaden a. o'ercargoed   FLEC 286:12
wrinkled a. forefend   SMART 650:5
youth and a. in common   ARN 29:6
aged: a. man is but a paltry   YEATS 752:21
allow this a. man his right   PEELE 511:5
An a. thrush, frail   HARDY 325:5
Certainly a.   BYRON 171:16
creatures did the a. seem   TRAH 701:15
deliciously a. and sad   SHAW 636:22
I saw an a., aged man   CARR 183:21
ageless-ancient: mother-naked and a.
  DAY-L 233:3
agenda: a. will be in inverse proportion
  PARK 507:4
agendum: *dum quid superesset a.*   LUCAN 431:6
agent: a. is a point that shifts   KLEE 402:20
living Power and prime A.   COL 212:1
agents: Civil and Political A.   VICT 710:12
Whiles nature's black a.   SHAK 603:5
ages: A. of hopeless end   MILT 469:15
a. of imagination this   BLAKE 113:1
a. past and gone   SHIP 646:1
For, as our different a. move   PRIOR 529:13
heir of all the a.   TENN 685:18
nations, and the next a.   BACON 46:3
Now he belongs to the a.   STAN 662:8
Our God, our help in a. past   WATTS 723:7
seven a.   SHAK 568:16
aggravating: was an a. child   BELL 61:8
aggression: menace of a.   ASQ 31:17
terrible weapon of a.   ADLER 5:7
Agincourt: affright the air at A.   SHAK 584:17
agitation: than to excite a.   PALM 505:12
agnostic: title of 'a.'   HUXL 358:2
agnosticism: all a. means   DARR 231:3
agnus: A. Dei, qui tollis   MISS 477:5
agog: a. at the plasterer   HEAN 329:17
agonies: friends are exultations, a.
  WORD 748:13
agony: a. is abated   MAC 435:25
Beyond is a.   GREV 318:3
But only a., and that has   BROO 143:17
check—intense the a.   BRON 142:14
it happen and am in a.   CAT 186:17
My soul in a.   COL 211:7
strong swimmer in his a.   BYRON 170:17
thine A. and bloody Sweat   BOOK 119:18
agree: a. in the truth of thy   BOOK 121:22
a. the kettle and the earthen   BIBLE 87:20
All colours will a. in the dark   BACON 45:3
they may a. like brothers   SHAK 587:23
things differ, all a.   POPE 523:33
thought that appear to a.   PAINE 505:2
When you did a., he was   LLOY 424:10
agreeable: most men's power to be a.
  SWIFT 674:19
agreed: except they be a.   BIBLE 86:10
agreement: blow with an a.   TROT 704:14
death and an a. with hell   GARR 298:13
with hell are we at a.   BIBLE 83:12
agrestis: *ille deos qui novit a.*   VIRG 715:15
agri: *modus a. non ita magnus*   HOR 351:9
ague-proof: I am not a.   SHAK 597:2

Ahab: ran before A.   BIBLE 76:5
a-hold: always keep a. of Nurse   BELL 61:2
a-hunting: And a. we will go   FIEL 282:1
We daren't go a.   ALL 10:1
aid: Apt Alliteration's artful a.   CHUR 201:8
whence doth come mine a.   SCOT 561:10
aik: leaned my back unto an a.   BALL 51:2
ail: can a. thee knight at arms   KEATS 388:7
ailes: *a. de géant l'empêchent*   BAUD 55:6
ailments: our a. are the same   SWIFT 673:17
aim: at which all things a.   ARIS 25:7
have forgotten your a.   SANT 555:15
you must a. a little above   LONG 426:15
aimai: *plus j'a. ma patrie*   BELL 62:9
aimez: *et a. qui vous aime*   VOLT 716:14
aiming: a. at a million   BROW 150;1
aims: other a. than my delight   HARDY 325:11
sick hurry, its divided a.   ARN 28:9
ain: hame to my a. countree   CUNN 229:3
ain't: a. a fit night out   FIEL 282:22
A. it all a bleedin shame   ANON 17:20
A. we got fun   KAHN 384:19
It a. necessarily so   HEYW 338:1
There a. gonna be no war   MACM 440:2
air: a., a chartered libertine   SHAK 584:19
a. a solemn stillness holds   GRAY 315:10
a. a voice without a face   AUDEN 36:2
a. broke into a mist   BROW 151:23
a. comes from her   SHAK 632:16
a. is delicate   SHAK 601:1
a. is full of our cries   BECK 58:2
a. might wash and long   SWIN 676:27
a. of delightful studies   MILT 476:7
a. which is now thoroughly   ELIOT 270:6
An ampler ether, a diviner a.   WORD 744:18
burning fills the startled A.   BELL 61:23
But merely vans to beat the a.   ELIOT 270:6
Clear the a.   ELIOT 272:11
conscience-stricken a.   HOUS 351:13
deep blue a.   LARK 409:18
excellent canopy, the a.   SHAK 574:28
fowls of the a.   BIBLE 89:9
Germans that of—the a.   RICH 540:17
He'd fly through the a.   LEYB 421:11
His happy good-night a.   HARDY 325:5
I am fire and a.; my other   SHAK 567:8
into air, into thin a.   SHAK 625:28
Into my heart an a. that kills   HOUS 352:15
nipping and an eager a.   SHAK 573:7
Now a. is hushed, save where   COLL 213:11
ocean and the living a.   WORD 745:1
one that beateth the a.   BIBLE 100:31
over the fowl of the a.   BIBLE 69:24
parching a.   MILT 470:2
path along the dusky a.   COL 211:21
pleasant seat; the a.   SHAK 601:1
streams or climb the a.   YEATS 753:20
There is music in the a.   ELGAR 268:14
This is the death of a.   ELIOT 271:4
through the trembling a.   SPEN 660:23
'twixt a. and angels' purity   DONNE 251:17
when take the a. I must   BECK 57:15
Wild air, world-mothering a.   HOPK 345:6
with pinions skim the a.   FRERE 293:16
air-balloons: Of a., and of the many bars
  BYRON 170:8
airconditioning: respectability and a.
  BAR 51:16
airing: toothbrush too is a.   BETJ 68:1
airline: a. ticket to romantic places
  MARV 451:14
airly: you've gut to git up a.   LOW 429:15
Airly Beacon: Shires and towns from A.
  KING 397:7
airman: a. finishing his time   HUGH 353:16
airports: a. almost deserted   AUDEN 34:13
airs: a. from heaven or blasts   SHAK 573:9
a. have brought me home   POE 518:9
don't give yourself a.   CARR 182:4
Lap me in soft Lydian a.   MILT 465:17
poet sing it with such a.   YEATS 750:17
shall silence all the a.   MILT 475:8

airs: (cont.):
Sounds and sweet a. — SHAK 625:26
airy: A., fairy Lilian — TENN 685:6
A. nothing, as they deemed — COL 209:8
divinity and a. subtleties — BROW 146:2
every bird that cuts the a. — BLAKE 112:30
aisles: on my heart monastic a. — EMER 276:10
Ajalon: valley of A. — BIBLE 73:32
Ajax: body is as good as A. — SHAK 571:15
When A. strives, some rock's — POPE 521:17
Akond: Is the A. of Swat — LEAR 413:17
alabaster: a. box of ointment — BIBLE 92:22
his grandsire cut in a. — SHAK 607:5
smooth as monumental a. — SHAK 618:5
alacrity: kind of a. in sinking — SHAK 610:18
alarm: little a. now and then — BURN 160:7
SPREAD A. AND DESPONDENCY — PEN 511:12
viewed the morning with a. — GERS 301:11
alarms: dwell in the midst of a. — COWP 224:15
swept with confused a. — ARN 27:1
alas: A., poor Yorick — SHAK 578:23
A., Time stays, *we* go — DOBS 249:23
a I we return — FORS 290:8
And some, a., with Kate — AUDEN 35:17
Hugo—a. — GIDE 303:9
May say A. but cannot help — AUDEN 36:8
Pigeons on the grass a. — STEIN 663:3
albatross: I shot the A. — COL 210:22
thought of the a. — LAWR 412:21
Albert: take a message to A. — DISR 249:14
takes to fill the A. Hall — LENN 417:17
Went there with young A. — EDGAR 266:8
Albion: *La perfide* A. — XIMÉ. 760:12
Alcestis: A. rises from shades — LAND 408:5
like A. from the grave — MILT 474:26
alchemy: By happy a. of mind — GREEN 316:19
alcohol: a. doesn't thrill me — PORT 524:19
a. has taken out of me — CHUR 203:15
A. is a very necessary article — SHAW 636:32
a. was a food well in advance — WOD 740:17
narcotic be a. or morphine — JUNG 382:15
aldermen: divides wives of a. — SMITH 650:15
Aldershot: burnish'd by A. sun — BETJ 68:6
ale: a. is a dish for a king — SHAK 631:24
a.'s the stuff to drink — HOUS 352:19
Away were sons of a. and brede — WYNT 750:10
be no more cakes and a. — SHAK 629:8
have fed purely upon a. — FARQ 280:8
my fame for a pot of a. — SHAK 585:11
Of jolly good a. and old — ANON 14:13
Sees bliss in a. — CRAB 224:24
Then to the spicy nut-brown a. — MILT 465:14
alehouse: In an a. in London — SHAK 585:11
Aleppo: Her husband's to A. gone — SHAK 600:1
in A. once — SHAK 618:20
Alexander: but A. women — LEE 416:6
If I were not A., I would — ALEX 8:8
She's gane, like A. — BURNS 160:7
Some talk of A., and some — ANON 18:3
Alexandrine: A needless A. ends the song — POPE 521:15
Alexin: *Corydon ardebat* A. — VIRG 714:14
alget: *Probitas laudatur et a.* — JUV 383:14
alibi: He always has an a. — ELIOT 272:12
Alice: Pass the sick bag, A. — JUNOR 383:10
you remember sweet A. — ENGL 277:24
alien: a. people clutching — ELIOT 271:14
amid the a. corn — KEATS 389:15
alieni: A. *appetens, sui profusus* — SALL 554:11
alienum: *humani nil a me a. puto* — TER 690:12
alike: a. and no one is alive — KING 398:8
light to thee are both a. — BOOK 134:19
Looks on a. — SHAK 632:9
aliter: *Dis a. visum* — VIRG 713:1
alive: alike and no one is a. — KING 398:8
a. and well and living — ANON 15:11
a. I shall be delighted — HOLL 342:3
a. so stout a gentleman — SHAK 582:7
Christ shall all be made a. — BIBLE 101:7
dead. I live again — BIBLE 95:5
half-a. — FORS 290:26
Half dead and half a. — BETJ 67:5
Hell below and I'm a. — ADD 6:11

alive: (cont.):
how it feels to be a. — BARZ 54:23
I am a. for evermore — BIBLE 106:2
if he gets out of it a. — LEON 236:14
it in that dawn to be a. — WORD 744:5
Life's not just being a. — MART 449:15
living which are yet a. — BIBLE 80:7
Looking as if she were a. — BROW 151:11
noise and tumult when a. — EDW 267:8
No one here gets out a. — MORR 485:20
Officiously to keep a. — CLOU 207:17
show that one's a. — BURN 160:17
there may be of being a. — DAWK 232:18
What still a. at twenty-two — KING 398:5
all: All, a. of a piece — DRYD 261:21
A. before my little room — BROO 143:9
A. by my own-alone self — HARR 327:2
A. for one, one for all — DUMAS 263:13
A. for your delight — SHAK 612:22
a. gone out of the way — BOOK 124:27
a. hell broke loose — MILT 471:18
a. in all for prose — CAREW 179:1
a. men are evil — MACH 438:6
A. men make faults — SHAK 633:13
A. my pretty ones — SHAK 604:9
a. our yesterdays have — SHAK 605:1
A. passes. Art alone — DOBS 249:20
a. shall be well and all — JUL 382:10
A.'s right with the world — BROW 151:28
A. that a man hath will — BIBLE 77:3
a. that's best of dark — BYRON 173:3
a. the rest forgot — SHAK 633:9
a. the silent manliness — GOLD 310:17
A. things are lawful — BIBLE 100.32
A. things bright and beautiful — ALEX 8:9
a. things to all men — ANON 15:20
A. things were made — BIBLE 95:36
a. to Heaven — JONES 378:2
A. we like sheep have gone — BIBLE 84:12
And a. for love, and nothing — SPEN 660:5
And a. shall be well — ELIOT 271:9
And nothing brings me a. — SHAK 626:19
Christ is a. — BIBLE 103:16
Fair shares for a. — JAY 363:23
Fool! A. that is, at all — BROW 152:10
From a. that terror teaches — CHES 199:3
have his a. neglected — JOHN 371:11
Her a. on earth, and more — BYRON 169:23
I am made a. things to all men — BIBLE 100:29
I'm a. right — BONE 117:18
It a. depends what you mean — JOAD 366:8
I would that you were a. to me — BROW 153:13
man for a. seasons — WHIT 733:11
not at all or all in a. — TENN 682:11
that we should at a. times — BOOK 122:10
think twice, it's a. right — DYLAN 265:13
upholdeth a. such as fall — BOOK 135:6
What! a. this for a song — CECIL 188:4
When a. the world is young — KING 397:17
Allah: A. is great, no doubt — CLOU 207:4
allaying: A. both their fury — SHAK 625:9
with not a drop of a. Tiber — SHAK 570:7
allegiance: Any victim demands a. — GREE 317:1
has not pledged a. to you — BALD 48:7
religious a. — BAG 46:11
allegory: headstrong as an a. — SHER 645:6
Which things are an a. — BIBLE 102:5
worth is a continual a. — KEATS 392:3
Alleluia: A.! sing to Jesus — DIX 249:18
alley: And she lives in our a. — CAREY 179:18
I think we are in rats' a. — ELIOT 273:4
alleys: vilest a. in London — DOYLE 256:5
alleyways: at the crossroads and in the a. — CAT 186:8
alliance: A., *n.* In international — BIER 109:3
changes of a. — WAUGH 723:19
rapture there is a family a. — BELL 60:18
rumours of a morganatic a. — HARD 323:15
alliances: entangling a. with none — JEFF 364:5
steer clear of permanent a. — WASH 721:24
allies: It is to be put — GEOR 301:9
thou hast great a. — WORD 748:13
We have no eternal a. — PALM 505:7

all-in-all: An intellectual A. — WORD 746:15
alliteration: A.'s artful aid — CHUR 201:8
allons: A., *enfants de la patrie* — ROUG 548:17
Allsopp: Guinness, A., Bass — CALV 175:12
allure: to a. by denying — TROL 703:26
alluring: a. than a levee from — CONG 215:36
almack: Carlisle's, and to A.'s — ANST 23:12
alma mater: And A. lie dissolved in port — POPE 518:22
almanac: Look in the a. — SHAK 611:23
May is a pious fraud of the a. — LOW 430:6
useful as an a. out of date — WALT 720:21
Almighty: a. dollar — IRV 360:18
A. placed it there — LAB 404:17
A.'s orders to perform — ADD 3:14
A, the King of Creation — WINK 739:7
A., victorious, thy great — SMITH 653:31
almond: a. tree shall flourish — BIBLE 81:1
almost: A. thou persuadest me — BIBLE 99:12
alms: accept our a. and oblations — BOOK 121:22
doth beg the a. — SHAK 606:8
he puts a. for oblivion — SHAK 627:19
thine a. may be in secret — BIBLE 89:3
alms-basket: a. of words — SHAK 599:4
aloe: a., and maize and vine — TENN 680:19
aloft: But now he's gone a. — DIBD 238:17
alone: a. against smiling enemies — BOWEN 138:12
A., alone, all, all alone — COL 211:7
a. and unsuspecting — DANTE 230:12
A. and palely loitering — KEATS 388:7
A. he rides, alone — JOHN 366:19
A. I did it — SHAK 570:27
A., poor maid. 'Tis but a stair — MFW 459:8
alone than when wholly a. — CIC 204:3
And all a. went she — KING 397:13
And be a. on earth — BYRON 168:11
And bear the palm a. — SHAK 590:2
are left a. with our day — AUDEN 36:8
Are we here together a. — WHIT 732:10
art, a. — ARN 27:10
dangerous to meet it a. — WHAR 730:5
experienced being a. together — LA BR 404:18
fastest who travels a. — KIPL 399:18
I must plough my furrow a. — ROS 546:17
I want to be a. — GARBO 297:11
left him a. with his glory — WOLFE 740:26
less a. than when alone — ROG 544:12
Let me a., that I may take — BIBLE 77:15
Lives not a., nor for itself — BLAKE 111:12
man who stands most a. — IBSEN 359:3
Nay, let me a. for swearing — SHAK 630:28
not sufficiently a. — VALÉ. 707:22
One is always a. — ELIOT 270:9
One is one and all a. — ANON 15:1
sitteth a. upon the house-top — BOOK 131:18
that the man should be a. — BIBLE 70:4
they would but let it a. — WALP 719:12
We live, as we dream — a. — CONR 217:3
were a. with the quiet day — JAMES 363:9
along: All a., down along — BALL 51:4
aloof: A. from the entire point — SHAK 594:23
aloud: Angels cry a. — BOOK 118:12
Before him I may think a. — EMER 276:24
Prayed a., as the hypocritical — AUBR 33:10
alp: a. of unforgiveness grew — PLOM 517:10
frozen, many a fiery a. — MILT 470:4
Alpes: *et saevas curre per* A. — JUV 384:9
Alpha: I am A. and Omega — BIBLE 105:32
alphabet: got to the end of the a. — DICK 243:15
alpine: As through an A. village passed — LONG 426:18
Alps: A. of green ice, in wild — PHIL 514:4
A. on Alps arise — POPE 521:9
beneath some snow-deep A. — ELIOT 270:10
fading a. and archipelagoes — ALDR 8:6
O'er the white A., alone — DONNE 250:14
passages through the A. — COLM 214:4
also: sun a. rises — HEM 331:17
thou art there a. — BOOK 134:19
altar: A high a. on the move — BOWEN 138:14
a. the dearest — SPR 661:8

altar: (*cont.*):	
a. with this inscription	BIBLE 98:31
self-slain on his own strange a.	SWIN 676:15
so will I go to thine a.	BOOK 125:22
that I may go unto the a.	BOOK 127:7
To what green a.	KEATS 388:29
altars: even thy a., O Lord	BOOK 130:16
threw our a. to the ground	JORD 380:13
altar-stairs: great world's a.	TENN 683:21
alte: *Es ist eine a. Geschichte*	HEINE 330:16
alter: tastes greatly a.	JOHN 372:26
alteram: *Audi partem a.*	AUG 37:5
alteration: A. though it be from worse	
	HOOK 344:15
Which alters when it a. finds	SHAK 634:23
alterations: Business as usual during a.	
	CHUR 202:1
alternatives: a. that are not their own	
	BONH 118:1
exhausted all other a.	EBAN 266:1
Althea: divine A. brings	LOV 429:1
altogether: righteous a.	BOOK 125:5
suit of clothes is a.	LOES 426:3
altrui: *Lo pane a.*	DANTE 230:20
alway: I am with you a.	BIBLE 93:6
They a. must be with us	KEATS 386:15
will not a. be chiding	BOOK 132:4
always: a. at the edge	SPEN 659:3
God is a. in the majority	KNOX 403:3
sometimes a.	RICH 540:16
There'll a. be an England	PARK 507:1
Alysander: Quhen A. oure kyng wes dede	
	WYNT 750:10
am: I a.—yet what I am	CLARE 204:25
I think, therefore I a.	DESC 237:18
Where I a., I don't know	BECK 57:18
ama: *a. et fac quod vis*	AUG 37:6
amaranth: a. on this side	LAND 408:9
amaranthus: Bid a. all his beauty shed	
	MILT 466:11
amare: *amans a.*	AUG 36:22
amari: *a. aliquid quod in ipsis*	LUCR 432:6
Amaryllis: To sport with A. in the shade	
	MILT 466:4
amateur: into a. sport	DOYLE 256:16
whine of the a. for three	WHIS 730:20
amateurs: Hell is full of musical a.	
	SHAW 637:10
that we are a nation of a.	ROS 546:16
amavi: *Sero te a., pulchritudo*	AUG 37:2
amaze: How vainly men themselves a.	
	MARV 450:5
these cogitations still a.	ELIOT 271:20
amazed: a. when others' tears begun	
	CONS 217:20
be wise, a., temperate	SHAK 602:18
glowr'd, a., and curious	BURNS 163:9
amazing: A. love!	WESL 728:1
a. the day is still here	LOW 430:8
Amazon: She was an A.	BLAN 115:1
ambassador: a. an honest man	WOTT 749:9
ambassadors: A. cropped up like hay	
	GILB 304:4
amber: prepared gold and a.	JONS 379:9
words, to lutes of a.	HERR 337:10
ambergris: Proclaim the a. on shore	
	MARV 449:20
ambiguities: Till we can clear these a.	
	SHAK 624:10
ambiguity: Seven types of a.	EMPS 277:21
ambition: a. can creep as well	BURKE 159:23
A. first sprung from	POPE 519:17
A., in a private man a vice	MASS 453:12
a. in rising in the state	BOSW 137:8
a. mock their useful toil	GRAY 315:13
A.'s debt is paid	SHAK 591:14
A. should be made of sterner	SHAK 592:7
a. to be a wag	JOHN 376:24
A. weed, but conscience till	MARV 451:9
Art not without a.	SHAK 600:15
charge thee, fling away a.	SHAK 589:1
Ill-weaved a., how much	SHAK 582:7
it alone supplies a.	TOCQ 698:9

ambition: (*cont.*):	
lofty pines were by a.	DRAY 258:3
lowliness is young a.'s ladder	SHAK 590:14
That make a. virtue	SHAK 616:20
To low a., and the pride	POPE 521:26
To reign is worth a.	MILT 468:13
Vain the a. of kings	WEBS 725:13
Vaulting a., which o'erleaps	SHAK 601:3
was this a.	SHAK 592:8
which avarice and a. have	SMITH 650:15
Who doth a. shun	SHAK 568:10
ambitions: a. are lawful except	CONR 217:13
deceives with whispering a.	ELIOT 271:11
ambitious: Brutus says he was a.	SHAK 592:6
Hath made Caesar was a.	SHAK 592:5
he was a., I slew him	SHAK 592:3
I would not be a. in my wish	DRAK 258:2
O sacred hunger of a. minds	SPEN 660:14
Sweet close of his a. line	CHAP 190:17
amble: teach an old horse a.	SPEN 660:9
ambo: *Arcades a.*	VIRG 715:3
Amboss: *A. oder Hammer*	GOET 309:9
Ambree: foremost in battle was Mary A.	
	BALL 50:2
ambrosial: a. hair	VIRG 712:8
Phallic and a.	POUND 526:14
ambulance: doctor? With an a.?	SIMP 648:4
ambushed: a. by a grotesque	STOP 670:2
âme: *grands n'ont point d'â.*	LA BR 405:1
Quelle â. est sans défauts	RIMB 541:9
amen: Glorious the catholic a.	SMART 650:4
Like the sound of a great A.	PROC 529:21
need of blessing, and 'A.'	SHAK 602:1
So goodbye dear, and A.	PORT 525:1
Will no man say, a.	SHAK 620:18
amend: wish for life, but to a.	GREV 318:7
amenities: say 'a.' used to say	CAT 186:16
amenity: all is a. and repose	CONS 217:24
amens: few mumbled a.	HUNT 356:16
America: America! A.!	BATES 55:5
A. can not be an ostrich	WILS 738:13
A. is a country of young men	EMER 277:15
A. is a land whose centre	UPD 707:7
A. is a vast conspiracy	UPD 707:8
A. is God's Crucible	ZANG 755:7
A. is just ourselves	ARN 29:7
A. is their oldest tradition	WILDE 735:26
A. is the only idealistic	WILS 738:20
A. is the way parents obey	EDW 267:6
A.'s present need is not	HARD 324:2
A., thou half-brother	BAIL 47:17
A. to convert the Indians	WESL 728:18
A. was thus clearly top	SELL 562:27
A. will think tomorrow	KIPL 401:13
content me, than *whole* A.	BURKE 157:22
England and A. are two	SHAW 638:31
glorious morning for A.	ADAMS 3:7
God bless A.	BERL 65:17
great continent of A.	WESL 729:1
I could come back to A.	JAMES 362:23
I like to be in A.	SOND 656:3
I, too, am A.	HUGH 354:1
I, too, sing A.	HUGH 354:1
It's morning again in A.	RINEY 541:11
loss of A. what can repay	FREE 293:15
next to of course god a. i	CUMM 228:6
O my A., my new found land	DONNE 250:16
politics ought to be in A.	HUMP 356:3
we think of thee, O A.	WALP 719:17
what A. will do for you	KENN 394:2
what makes A. what it	STEIN 663:4
which A. is the proof	MCC 436:19
You cannot conquer A.	PITT 515:11
American: A. beauty rose	ROCK 543:20
acts in A. lives	FITZ 285:6
A. as cherry pie	BROWN 144:11
A. people is business	COOL 218:7
A. women shoot the hippopotamus	
	FORS 289:19
elderly A. to leave	JENK 365:3
fallen in love with A. names	BENÉT 62:15
foreign oil controlling A.	DYLAN 265:21
I am a free man, an A.	JOHN 367:4

American: (*cont.*):	
I am A. bred	MILL 461:12
I am not a Virginian, but an A.	HENRY 333:6
intend to offer the A.	KENN 393:11
I shall die an A.	WEBS 725:11
justice and the A. way	ANON 13:8
process whereby A. girls	HAMP 323:3
send A. boys 9 or 10	JOHN 367:10
So, bye, bye, Miss A. Pie	MCL 439:8
texture of A. life	JAMES 362:19
Thank God, I also am an A.	WEBS 725:9
Americanism: McCarthyism is A. with	
its sleeves	MCC 436:18
Americans: A. are to be freemen	WASH 721:23
A. have taken umbrage	PUNCH 531:19
And when bad A. die	WILDE 705:26
Good A., when they die	APPL 23:19
new generation of A.	KENN 393:12
Russians and the A.	TOCQ 699:5
Than ignorant A.	MASS 453:13
To A., English manners	JARR 363:21
amertume: *fardeau et l'a.*	FLAU 286:5
amiable: good, a. or sweet	MILT 472:25
high thought, and a. words	TENN 681:25
how a. are thy dwellings	BOOK 130:16
amicably: a. if they can, violently	QUIN 534:12
amicus: A. Plato	ARIS 26:3
amid: a. the alien corn	KEATS 389:15
amis: *Nos a., les ennemis*	BÉR 65:2
amiss: mark what is done a.	BOOK 134:11
My rams speed not, all is a.	BARN 53:17
Nothing comes a., so money	SHAK 624:11
Nothing shall come a.	BUCK 154:13
thoughte it was a.	CHAU 194:1
amitié: *L'a. de la connaissance*	BUSS 165:17
l'a. ferme les yeux	ANON 20:16
amitti: *sciamus non a. sed praemitti*	CYPR 229:9
ammer: 'a. along the 'ard 'igh	PUNCH 531:14
ammunition: Praise the Lord and pass the a.	
	FORGY 289:18
amo: A., amas, I love a lass	O'KEE 498:8
Non a. te, Sabidi, nec possum	MART 449:12
Odi et a.: quare id faciam	CAT 186:17
amoeba: When we were a soft a.	SHIP 646:1
among: A. but not of them	BYRON 168:28
what are they a. so many	BIBLE 96:22
amongst: a. you and remain	BOOK 122:15
amor: A. vincit omnia	CHAU 192:16
come a. lo strinse	DANTE 230:12
L'a. che muove il sole	DANTE 230:21
Nunc scio quid sit A.	VIRG 715:5
Omnia vincit A.	VIRG 715:8
Suprema citius solvet a. die	HOR 349:10
amorous: a. ditties	MILT 468:20
And sweet reluctant a. delay	MILT 471:6
As a. of their strokes	SHAK 565:5
be a., but be chaste	BYRON 172:7
blame me for feeling a.	GERS 301:13
court an a. looking-glass	SHAK 621:15
excite my a. propensities	JOHN 371:8
long her a. descant sung	MILT 471:10
tangled in a. nets	MILT 473:15
That unsubstantial Death is a.	SHAK 624:9
What dire offence from a.	POPE 523:15
amour: beginning of an A.	BEHN 60:7
C'est tellement simple, l'a.	PRÉ.V 528:15
Il y a l'a. bien sûr	ANOU 23:5
L'a. de ma mie	ANON 21:5
L'a. est aveugle	ANON 20:16
L'a. vient de l'aveuglement	BUSS 165:17
sans soif et faire l'a.	BEAU 56:11
Vive l'a.! et vive la bagatelle	STER 664:6
Vous savez bien que l'a.	ANOU 23:6
amphibii: These rational a. go	MARV 451:13
amphibious: a. ill-born mob	DEFOE 234:21
ample: from an a. nation	DICK 244:18
Her cabined a. Spirit	ARN 27:20
ampulla: *in a. pendere*	PETR 513:13
ampullas: *a. et sesquipedalia*	HOR 347:8
amputate: Thank God they had to a.	
	SASS 557:12
Amurath: Not A. an Amurath succeeds	
	SHAK 584:7

amuse: talent to a.   COW 220:11
amused: a. by its presumption   THUR 697:17
  People mutht be a.   DICK 240:34
  We are not a.   VICT 710:14
amusement: a. in a tedious winter-night   SWIFT 673:2
amusements: tolerable but for its a.   LEWIS 420:19
Anabaptists: certain A. do falsely boast   BOOK 136:2
anaemia: emotional a.   POUND 526:10
anagram: In keen iambics, but mild a.   DRYD 261:3
analogies: A. decide nothing   FREUD 293:21
analytics: Sweet A.   MARL 446:13
analyze: A. you, categorize you   DYLAN 265:10
anapaestic: And the rolling a.   BROW 147:23
anarchism: A. is a game   SHAW 638:8
  A., stands for   GOLD 310:4
anarchist: small a. community   BENN 63:9
anarchy: a. and competition   RUSK 551:5
  a. is loosed upon the world   YEATS 753:1
  democracy, call it a.   HOBB 340:9
  servitude is the cure of a.   BURKE 157:27
anatomy: A mere a., a mountebank   SHAK 570:1
  A. is destiny   FREUD 293:19
  eat the rest of the a.   SHAK 630:16
ancestor: a. I should feel shame in recalling   HUXL 358:12
ancestors: a. are very good kind   SHER 645:8
  a. lost no time in abandoning   LANC 407:21
  look backward to their a.   BURKE 150:9
ancestral: A. voices prophesying war   COL 210:12
ancestry: a. back to a protoplasmal   GILB 304:20
  What, my Lord, is a.?   RICH 540:12
  without pride of a.   POWER 528:12
anchor: a. in nonsense   GALB 297:1
  My a. to let fall   ASKEW 31:16
anchorage: hope her a.   SMART 649:16
anchored: ship is a. safe and sound   WHIT 732:7
anchorite: saintship of an a.   BYRON 168:2
ancient: a. nobility   BACON 44:9
  A. of days did sit   BIBLE 86:1
  A. person of my heart   ROCH 543:17
  a. profession in the world   KIPL 401:14
  A. times were the youth   BACON 42:11
  And did those feet in a. time   BLAKE 113:4
  both so a. and so fresh   AUG 37:2
  Defender, the A. of Days   GRANT 314:6
  glorious, the A. of Days   SMITH 653:31
  In a. shadows and twilights   Æ 5:10
  It is an a. Mariner   COL 210:18
  totem poles—the a. terror   MACN 440:16
  while I sing the a. ways   YEATS 753:13
  With the a. is wisdom   BIBLE 77:19
ancients: a. dreaded death   HARE 326:4
  a. without idolatry   CHES 199:14
and: including 'a.' and 'the'   MCC 437:1
Andromache: kissed his sad A. goodbye   CORN 219:3
anecdotage: fell into his a.   DISR 248:23
anfractuosities: a. of the human mind   JOHN 375:12
angel: action how like an a.   SHAK 574:28
  A ministering a. shall   SHAK 578:26
  A ministering a. thou   SCOTT 560:9
  An a. satyr walks these hills   KILV 396:8
  An a. watching an urn   TENN 686:11
  A. did with Jacob   WALT 721:13
  a. is a man right fair   SHAK 635:6
  a. of the Lord came upon   BIBLE 93:26
  a. of the Lord came down   TATE 678:18
  a. took up a stone like   BIBLE 107:11
  a. travelling incognito   QUEN 534:7
  a. wakes me from my flowery   SHAK 611:26
  a. writing in a book   HUNT 356:4
  as an a. is the English child   DONNE 251:1
  beautiful and ineffectual a.   ARN 29:21
  If a. came from your door   BLAKE 110:20

angel: (*cont.*):
  enough for an a. to pass   FIRB 282:27
  Fresh as the A. o'er a new   BYRON 167:25
  Her a.'s face   SPEN 659:24
  Is man an ape or an a.   DISR 247:13
  Lost A. of a ruined Paradise   SHEL 639:15
  O! the more a. she   SHAK 618:10
  Recording A.   STER 665:3
  Recording A.   STEV 668:6
  She drew an a. down   DRYD 259:23
  Shined in my a.-infancy   VAUG 709:1
  That a. of the world   SHAK 571:14
  Though an a. should write   MOORE 482:19
  Who wrote like an a.   GARR 298:5
  With something of an a. light   WORD 747:19
  woman yet think him an a.   THAC 691:4
angelheaded: a. hipsters   GINS 306:28
angeli: *Non Angli sed A.*   GREG 317:17
angel of death: a. has been abroad   BRIG 141:6
  A. spread his wings   BYRON 169:29
angelorum: *A. chori*   ANON 22:9
angels: A. affect us oft   DONNE 251:16
  a. all were singing out   BYRON 173:13
  A alone, that soar above   LOV 429:4
  A. and ministers of grace   SHAK 573:9
  A. are bright still   SHAK 604:6
  A. came and ministered   BIBLE 88:21
  A. in jumpers   LEWIS 421:9
  a. in some brighter dreams   VAUG 709:8
  a. keep their ancient places   THOM 695:10
  a. of God ascending   BIBLE 71:13
  a. on the walls of heaven   MARL 448:6
  a. sing thee to thy rest   SHAK 579:14
  a. stood round about   BIBLE 106:10
  a. to be lookers on   BACON 42:6
  a. would be gods   POPE 522:4
  As make the a. weep   SHAK 605:18
  band of a. comin' after me   ANON 18:8
  Bats not a., in the high roof   THOM 694:9
  By that sin fell the a.   SHAK 589:1
  fools rush in where a.   POPE 521:25
  Four a. to my bed   ANON 16:9
  glittering and sparkling a.   TRAH 701:15
  glorious fault of a.   POPE 519:17
  Hear all ye a., progeny   MILT 471:28
  He maketh his a. spirits   BOOK 132:6
  his a. charge over thee   BOOK 131:4
  Let A. prostrate fall   PERR 513:1
  Liveried A. robed in green   LAND 408:3
  lower than the a.   BOOK 124:20
  Michael and his a. fought   BIBLE 106:30
  neglect God and his A.   DONNE 253:9
  nor a., nor principalities   BIBLE 100:1
  Not Angles but A.   GREG 317:17
  nothing to what the a. know   NEWM 493:8
  Our acts our a.   FLET 287:16
  So man did eat a.' food   BOOK 130:11
  some have entertained a.   BIBLE 104:20
  staring a. go through   HUGH 354:6
  then, if a. fight   SHAK 620:3
  To hear the a. sing   SEARS 561:12
  tongues of men and of a.   BIBLE 101:1
  To thee all A. cry aloud   BOOK 118:12
  treefull of a. at Peckham Rye   BENÉT 62:18
  'twixt air and a.   DONNE 251:17
  unto the world, and to a.   BIBLE 100:19
  Where a. tremble, while   GRAY 316:7
  with A. and Archangels   BOOK 122:10
  With a. round the throne   WATTS 722:19
  Ye holy a. bright   GURN 320:3
  yerks old a. out apace   GASC 298:17
angel-visits: Like a., few and far between   CAMP 176:19
anger: Achilles' cursed a. sing   HOMER 342:22
  A. and jealousy can no more   ELIOT 269:22
  a. as the flint bears fire   SHAK 593:9
  a. in the dragon   SUTT 672:23
  a. in those heavenly minds   VIRG 712:1
  A. invests with such   SIDN 646:23
  A. is a short madness   HOR 348:5
  A. is one of the sinews   FULL 296:6
  A. makes dull men witty   BACON 45:26
  A. maketh without an argument   HAL 321:12

anger: (*cont.*):
  a. of men who have no opinions   CHES 199:16
  A.'s self I needs must   SIDN 646:23
  He that is slow to a.   BIBLE 78:38
  his a. is not turned away   BIBLE 82:18
  In the contempt and a.   SHAK 630:12
  Juno's never-forgetting a.   VIRG 711:18
  keepeth he his a. for ever   BOOK 132:4
  laughter may signify a.   TOFF 700:1
  life of telegrams and a.   FORS 290:13
  Look Back In A.   OSB 501:12
  more in sorrow than in a.   SHAK 572:21
  principis mors est [The a....]   MORE 484:11
  rarely gave way to his a.   BECK 58:3
  that you strike it in a.   SHAW 637:28
  thy mistress some rich a.   KEATS 389:6
  Touch me with noble a.   SHAK 595:18
  With neither a. nor partiality   TAC 677:23
angiportis: *in quadriviis et a.*   CAT 186:8
angle: a. of forty-five degrees   JOYCE 382:4
  astonished-looking, a.-faced   HUNT 356:6
  Give me mine a.   SHAK 565:12
  I am, Sir, a Brother of the A.   WALT 720:24
  Themselves in every a. greet   MARV 450:3
angler: An excellent a.   WALT 721:3
  As the lone A., patient man   COLM 214:5
  so no man is born an a.   WALT 720:22
  that if he be an honest a.   WALT 720:23
anglers: too good for any but a.   WALT 721:8
angles: Not A. but Angels   GREG 317:17
  Offer no a. to the wind   TESS 691:1
Angli: *Non A. sed Angeli*   GREG 317:17
angling: A. may be said   WALT 720:20
  a. or float fishing I can   JOHN 377:1
  be quiet; and go a-A.   WALT 721:11
Anglo-Irishman: He was an A.   BEHAN 59:26
Anglo-Saxon: distorts the A. existence   LAWR 412:2
  natural idol of the A.   BAG 46:21
  those are A. attitudes   CARR 183:16
  vigour of our old A. breed   ARN 29:16
angry: a. at a slander makes it   JONS 378:13
  a. she is keen and shrewd   SHAK 612:5
  A. young man   PAUL 510:2
  Be ye a. and sin not   BIBLE 102:19
  dawn looking for an a. fix   GINS 306:28
  I was a. with my friend   BLAKE 114:11
  were a. and poor and happy   CHES 199:9
  When he was a., one   BECK 58:3
  when very a., swear   TWAIN 706:21
anguis: *Latet a. in herba*   VIRG 714:19
anguish: a. of a torturing hour   SHAK 612:18
  sorted, of all sizes   HERB 335:19
  With a. moist and fever dew   KEATS 388:8
angusta: *Res a. domi*   JUV 383:22
anheling: front the cive, a.   HOLM 342:9
anhelis: *Oriens adflavit a.*   VIRG 715:11
anima: Swift was a. Rabelaisii   COL 212:12
animae: *A. dimidium meae*   HOR 349:1
animal: A dying a.   YEATS 751:9
  After coition every a. is sad   ANON 22:12
  a. spirits which make both   WOLL 741:16
  Bang! Now the a.   DE L 236:4
  Be a good a., true   LAWR 412:9
  life is to be a good a.   SPEN 658:12
  Man is a noble a.   BROW 145:26
  Man is by nature a political a.   ARIS 25:15
  only a. in the world   LAWR 412:16
  Only A. that Blushes   TWAIN 706:9
  religious a.   BURKE 158:19
  that stirred like an a.   BABEL 41:12
  This a. is very bad   ANON 20:7
  vegetable, a., and mineral   GILB 306:9
animalculous: beings a.   GILB 306:9
animals: All a., except man   BUTL 166:25
  a. are equal but some animals   ORW 499:20
  A., whom we have made our   DARW 231:12
  a. will not look   AUDEN 36:8
  could turn and live with a.   WHIT 732:18
  distinguishes man from a.   OSLER 502:3
  distinguishes us from mere a.   LEIB 419:11
  it is written that no a.   BIBLE 100:8
  Man didn't find the a.   NIET 495:6

animals: (*cont.*):
production of the higher a.   DARW 231:10
animam: *Liberavi a. meam*   BERN 66:8
animate: a. the whole   SMITH 653:18
animated: what if all a. nature   COL 209:20
likeness of an a. thing   CANN 178:12
animosities: A. are mortal   NORTH 496:16
animosity: fervour of sisterly a.   SURT 672:19
animula: *A. vagula blandula*   HADR 320:8
animum: *Caelum non a.*   HOR 348:9
anise: mint and a. and cummin   BIBLE 92:5
Anjou: air the sweetness of A.   DU B 263:2
Ann: A., Ann! Come!   DE L 235:19
Anna: A. Livia! I want to hear   JOYCE 381:3
Annabel Lee: I and my A.   POE 518:1
annals: a. are blank in history-books   MONT 481:17
simple a. of the poor   GRAY 315:13
War's a. will cloud into night   HARDY 325:10
annibaptist: a. is a thing I am not   FLEM 287:5
annihilate: a. a man utterly   DOST 255:2
Ye gods! a. but space and time   POPE 523:10
annihilating: A. all that's made   MARV 450:11
annihilation: by the a. of one of us   SHEL 639:7
Oblivion is a kind of A.   BROW 145:5
anniversaries: secret a. of the heart   LONG 426:23
anno domini: a., the most fatal complaint   HILT 339:4
Sir, you shall taste my A.   FARQ 280:7
annoy: He only does it to a.   CARR 182:5
annoyance: a. and embarrassment   BAED 46:6
a. of a good example   TWAIN 706:23
Shadow of a.   SHEL 643:18
annuity: a. is a very serious business   AUST 39:20
annus: *monet a. et almum*   HOR 350:16
anointed: a. my head with oil   BOOK 125:15
wash the balm from an a.   SHAK 620:3
anointing: Thou the a. Spirit art   BOOK 135:21
anomaly: fancied herself such an a.   HARDY 324:19
another: A. nice mess you've gotten   LAUR 411:8
a. one walking beside you   ELIOT 273:12
a. shall gird thee   BIBLE 98:2
choose love by a.'s   SHAK 610:22
fair house built upon a.   SHAK 610:15
setteth up a.   BOOK 130:3
taste of a. man's bread   DANTE 230:20
that was in a. country   MARL 447:15
We are members one of a.   BIBLE 102:18
when comes such a.   SHAK 592:19
anser: *inter strepere a. olores*   VIRG 715:7
answer: A. a fool according   BIBLE 79:20
a. is blowin' in the wind   DYLAN 265:11
a. to a difficult situation   BEVAN 68:16
A. to the Great Question   ADAMS 2:7
But a. came there none   CARR 183:3
But a. came there none   SCOTT 559:7
But a. made it none   SHAK 572:20
He would a. to 'Hi!'   CARR 183:28
man's waitin' for an a.   DICK 239:25
please thee with my a.   SHAK 609:9
short a. is 'himself'   IBSEN 359:6
silver a. rang   BROW 147:18
soft a. turneth away wrath   BIBLE 78:33
than the wisest man can a.   COLT 214:8
They sent an a. back to me   CARR 183:15
way to a pertinent a.   BRON 141:18
what a dusty a. gets   MER 458:9
what a. should I give   TENN 688:12
why did you a. the phone   THUR 697:18
Winds of the World, give a.   KIPL 399:2
would not stay for an a.   BACON 44:36
answerable: a. for what we choose to believe   NEWM 493:16
answerably: a. to your Christian calling   BOOK 123:2
answered: grievously hath Caesar a.   SHAK 592:5
his prayer is a.   MER 457:28
I came, and no one a.   DE L 236:7

answered: (*cont.*):
They a., as they took   BELL 61:1
answering: a. that of God   FOX 292:3
a. to the bird's hoarse   WORD 743:1
answers: Kind are her a.   CAMP 177:9
ant: a.'s a centaur   POUND 527:7
a. thou sluggard   BIBLE 78:13
good husband, little a.   LOV 428:20
seem mountains, and the a.   COTT 220:3
antagonist: a. is our helper   BURKE 158:24
antagonistic: a. governments everywhere   WAUGH 723:20
antediluvian: one of your a. families   CONG 215:12
antennae: Artists are the a.   POUND 527:18
anthems: In service high, and a. clear   MILT 466:1
anthropology: most familiar facts of a.   FRAZ 293:9
anthropomorphic: a. view of the rat   KOES 403:20
anthropophagi: A., and men whose heads   SHAK 615:1
anti: a.-everythings   HOLM 342:14
antic: goat feet dance an a. hay   MARL 447:6
To put an a. disposition   SHAK 574:5
anti-christ: a. of Communism   BUCH 154:5
anti-destin: *L'art est un a.*   MALR 443:17
antidote: some sweet oblivious a.   SHAK 604:22
antipathy: strong a. of good to bad   POPE 523:8
antipodes: Diverse, sheer opposite, a.   KEATS 387:16
like A. in shoes   MARV 451:13
slightest errand now to the A.   SHAK 613:18
antiquarian: A mere a. is a rugged being   JOHN 374:29
antique: And over is their a. joy   YEATS 753:7
group that's quite a.   BYRON 170:21
noble and nude and a.   SWIN 676:8
traveller from an a.   SHEL 642:3
antiquitas: *A. saeculi juventus*   BACON 43:1
antiquities: A. are history defaced   BACON 41:18
antiquity: blasted with a.   SHAK 582:20
rejected all respect for a.   DISR 248:3
antithesis: And he himself one vile a.   POPE 520:5
Antony: A. brought drunken forth   SHAK 567:1
Is A. again, I will be Cleopatra   SHAK 565:23
O! my oblivion is a very A.   SHAK 564:26
people out upon her, and A.   SHAK 565:6
quick spirit that is in A.   SHAK 589:23
She shall be buried by her A.   SHAK 567:15
Should conquer A.   SHAK 566:12
there were an A.   SHAK 592:17
would catch a second A.   SHAK 567:13
anulus: *consumitur a. usu*   OVID 502:19
anvil: be the a. or the hammer   GOET 309:9
Church is an a.   MACL 439:7
England's on the a.   KIPL 398:12
My sledge and a. lie declined   ANON 16:16
anxiety: a. resolved itself   GONC 312:8
repose is taboo'd by a.   GILB 304:14
anxious: a. for to shine   GILB 305:15
any: A. old iron, any old iron   COLL 213:6
If a. of you know cause   BOOK 123:14
Ready to be a. thing   BROW 145:27
anybody: Is there a. there   DE L 236:6
Then no one's a.   GILB 304:6
anything: A. for a quiet life   MIDD 459:11
A. goes   PORT 524:18
nothing fall for a.   HAM 322:10
apart: man's life a thing a.   BYRON 170:13
We have stood a., studiously   WILS 738:12
apathy: dissolved into a.   GONC 312:8
ape: for his grandfather   HUXL 358:12
devil always God's a.   LUTH 432:12
gorgeous buttocks of the a.   HUXL 357:21
Is man an a. or an angel   DISR 247:13
naked a. self-named *Homo*   MORR 485:6
played the sedulous a.   STEV 667:4
apes: And a. are apes   JONS 378:24
a., and peacocks   BIBLE 75:25
A. of God   LEWIS 421:7

apes: (*cont.*):
barnacles, or to a.   SHAK 625:30
lead a. in hell   SHAK 624:13
Leave Now for dogs and a.   BROW 149:30
person and the peple his a.   CHAU 193:8
Well, I will scourge those a.   JONS 378:20
aphrodisiac: Power the great a.   KISS 402:14
Aphrodite: Blonde A. rose   AUDEN 34:1
a-plyin': you an' me a. up and down   KIPL 399:19
Apollo: A. from his shrine   MILT 467:11
A. hunted Daphne   MARV 450:8
As bright A.'s lute   SHAK 598:20
A young A., golden-haired   CORN 219:5
harsh after the songs of A.   SHAK 599:12
not even A., with hair   SWIN 676:20
Of Juve, A., of Mars   CHAU 196:2
Phoebus A. turned fasting   MER 457:21
Apollos: A. watered   BIBLE 100:17
apologies: people do not want a.   WOD 740:18
apologize: Never a.   FISH 283:5
rule in life never to a.   WOD 740:18
apology: An a. for the Devil   BUTL 167:2
a. before you be accused   CHAR 191:5
God's a. for relations   KING 398:7
apoplexy: Peace is a very a.   SHAK 570:18
This a. is, as I take it   SHAK 582:17
apostle: a. in the high aesthetic   GILB 305:17
great a. of the Philistines   ARN 29:19
apostles: am the least of the a.   BIBLE 101:4
A. would have done as they   BYRON 170:7
glorious company of the A.   BOOK 118:12
He gave some, a.; and some   BIBLE 102:17
true a. of equality   ARN 29:9
Twelve for the twelve a.   ANON 15:1
Apostolick: Catholic and A. Church   BOOK 121:20
apothecary: a. than a starved poet   LOCK 425:15
apparatus: *Persicos odi, puer, a.*   HOR 349:15
apparel: a. oft proclaims the man   SHAK 573:4
hath put on glorious a.   BOOK 131:6
She was rich in a.   TROL 703:8
woman in immodest thin a.   MIDD 459:19
apparelled: a. like the spring   SHAK 618:22
apparition: That a., sole of men, he saw   SHEL 642:7
apparitional: As a. as sails that cross   CRANE 225:25
apparitions: Fifteen a. have I seen   YEATS 750:19
appeal: a. against something   CAMUS 177:13
a. open from criticism   JOHN 369:9
I a. unto Caesar   BIBLE 99:8
Seedy a.   AUDEN 35:1
appear: a. considerable   JOHN 373:13
Blessed Cecilia, a. in visions   AUDEN 34:2
when thou leav'st to a.   NASHE 490:23
with how you a. to God   UNAM 707:3
appearance: a. of Your Majesty   BIBLE 69:19
less in reality than in a.   HUME 355:15
looketh on the outward a.   BIBLE 74:38
Thou hast a grim a.   SHAK 570:17
appearances: contrive to save a.   MILT 472:11
Keep up a.   CHUR 201:4
There is no trusting a.   SHER 645:21
appeared: a. and disappeared   WORD 743:3
appeareth: a. for a little time   BIBLE 105:4
appetite: a.; a feeling and a love   WORD 744:21
a. grows by eating   RAB 534:17
a. is never a wise companion   STEV 667:4
a. may sicken, and so die   SHAK 628:9
As if increase of a. had grown   SHAK 572:12
Doth not the a. alter   SHAK 613:26
Now good digestion wait on a.   SHAK 603:9
satisfying a voracious a.   FIEL 282:12
their love may be called a.   SHAK 629:19
With a more riotous a.   SHAK 597:5
appetites: And not their a.   SHAK 616:16
a. as apt to change   DRYD 260:1
men's carnal lusts and a.   BOOK 123:16
Subdue your a. my dears   DICK 242:4
They have violent a.   VANB 708:7
applaud: Till thou a. the deed   SHAK 603:5

applause: A., *n.* The echo of a platitude
    BIER 109:4
  cool ev'ning satiate of a. POPE 522:25
  everyone is forced to a. MILL 461:22
  sunshine and with a. BUNY 156:1
apple: aims at me with an a. VIRG 714:18
  An' there vor me the a. tree BARN 53:13
  a. falling towards England AUDEN 35:11
  a. for the apple's sake TWAIN 706:18
  a. of his eye BIBLE 73:21
  a. on its bough is her CRANE 225:21
  a. pressed with specious HOOD 344:5
  a. rotten at the heart SHAK 607:21
  a. which reddens upon ROSS 547:13
  sweet-a. SAPP 556:2
  What luckless a. did we taste MARV 451:8
  when 'tis almost an a. SHAK 628:22
  With a. pie and cheese FIELD 281:13
apple-pie: A was an a. ANON 12:9
  cabbage-leaf to make an a. FOOTE 288:15
apples: a. on the Dead Sea's BYRON 168:21
  child picking dewy a. VIRG 715:4
  golden a. of the sun YEATS 753:8
  knows Kent—a., cherries DICK 243:6
  On moon-washed a. of wonder DRIN 258:10
  Ripe a. drop about my head MARV 450:9
  spoken is like a. of gold BIBLE 79:15
  Stolen, stolen, be your a. HUNT 356:10
  tart a. to children RIMB 541:4
applications: a. for situations AUDEN 35:10
applied: no such things as a. sciences
    PAST 509:3
apply: a. our hearts unto wisdom BOOK 131:2
  know my methods. A. them DOYLE 256:19
appointed: even in the time a. BOOK 130:14
  house a. for all living BIBLE 77:30
  Its own a. limits keep WHIT 732:2
  Like pilgrims to th'a. place DRYD 261:13
appointment: a. at the end of the world
    DIN 246:7
  Every time I create an a. LOUI 428:15
  I had an a. with him LOW 429:13
  incompetent many for a. SHAW 637:22
  we have kept our a. BECK 57:27
apprehend: Intelligence is quickness to a.
    WHIT 731:12
  it would but a. some joy SHAK 612:17
apprehension: O, no! the a. of the good
    SHAK 619:14
  sense of death is most in a. SHAK 606:9
apprehensions: My a. come in crowds
    WORD 743:5
apprenticeship: cannot be any a. for freedom
    BAR 51:15
approach: If I a. he forward skips LODGE 426:1
approaching: To see the a. sacrifice MILM 462:7
approbation: A. from Sir Hubert Stanley
    MORT 486:17
appropriate: Nature gives to each what is a.
    AUCT 33:19
approve: a. it with a text SHAK 608:26
  But I do not a. MILL 461:6
  Isn't it bliss? Don't you a.? SOND 656:2
  My love doth so a. him SHAK 617:21
après: A. nous le déluge POMP 518:12
apricocks: yon dangling a. SHAK 620:14
apricot: blushing a. JONS 380:7
April: A., laugh thy girlish laughter
    WATS 722:9
  A. is the cruellest month ELIOT 272:11
  A. of your youth adorns HERB 334:2
  A. with his shoures soote CHAU 192:6
  bright cold day in A. ORW 500:8
  Calls back the lovely A. SHAK 633:2
  hill in an A. shroud KEATS 389:6
  Men are A. when they woo SHAK 569:18
  Now that A.'s there BROW 150:5
  sweet love seemed that A. BRID 141:5
  uncertain glory of an A. day SHAK 631:4
  Which spongy A. at thy best SHAK 665:97
  Appunni image thenceforth in BIBLE 77:10
apt: A. Alliteration's artful aid CHUR 201:8

apt: *(cont.)*:
  find myself so a. to die SHAK 591:20
aquarium: a. is gone. LOW 430:11
Aquarius: dawning of age of A. RADO 535:8
Arabia: all the perfumes of A. SHAK 604:14
  given of the gold of A. BOOK 129:21
  kings of A. and Saba BOOK 129:20
  with the spell of far A. DE L 235:21
Arabian: Drop tears as fast as the A.
    SHAK 618:20
  She is alone the A. bird SHAK 570:28
Arabians: Cretes and A. BIBLE 98:7
Arabs: their tents, like the A. LONG 426:14
Araby: burns in glorious A. DARL 231:2
Aral Sea: shine upon the A. ARN 28:18
aratro: *nullo contusus a.* CAT 186:9
Arbeit: A. macht frei ANON 21:9
arbiter: a. of others' fate BYRON 172:22
  Elegantiae a. TAC 678:1
  next him high a. MILT 470:11
arbitrary: *supreme power must be a.* HAL 321:14
arbitrate: Does a. the event MILT 463:28
arbitrator: that old common a., Time
    SHAK 628:4
arboreal: a. in its habits DARW 231:5
arbours: His private a. SHAK 592:18
arbusta: *a. iuvant humilesque* VIRG 714:22
Arcades: *florentes aetatibus*, A. ambo VIRG 715:3
Arcadia: *Et in A. ego* ANON 22:7
Arcadians: A. both, and matched VIRG 715:3
Arcady: woods of A. are dead YEATS 753:7
arceo: *Odi profanum vulgus et a.* HOR 349:22
arch: All experience is an a. ADAMS 2:9
  all experience is an a. TENN 690:1
  Tiber melt, and the wide a. SHAK 564:14
archangel: A. a little damaged LAMB 406:28
archangels: with Angels and A. BOOK 122:10
archbishop: a. had come to see me
    BURG 156:20
  Cardinal Lord A. of Rheims BARH 52:12
archdeacon: every now and then an a.
    SMITH 653:6
archèd: a. roof in words deceiving MILT 467:11
archer: a. his sharp arrows tries SIDN 646:16
  Finds mark the a. little meant SCOTT 559:18
arches: down the a. of the years THOM 695:1
  Underneath the A. FLAN 285:8
archetypes: are known as *a.* JUNG 382:12
archewyves: Ye a., stondeth at defense
    CHAU 193:11
arch-flatterer: a. with whom all the petty
    BACON 44:2
archipelagoes: fading alps and a. ALDR 8:6
architect: a. can only advise WRIG 749:11
  A. of the Universe now JFANS 363:27
  a. on those conditions DOST 254:6
  As an a., one of the greatest BARH 52:10
  or painter can be an a. RUSK 550:11
architectural: a. secret of decorating
    TROL 703:8
  respectable a. man-milliner RUSK 550:8
architecture: A. in general is frozen music
    SCH 557:19
  A. is the art of how JOHN 367:16
  A., of all the arts DIMN 246:6
  cuckoo clock style of a. HEM 332:2
  fall of English a. BETJ 68:11
  frolic a. of the snow EMER 276:12
  In a. as in all other operative arts WOTT 749:6
  New styles of a., a change AUDEN 36:6
arcs: broken a. BROW 147:26
arcturi: those pearled A. SHEL 642:23
Arden: Ay, now am I in A. SHAK 568:2
ardet: *paries cum proximus a.* HOR 348:13
ardeur: *a. dans mes veines* RAC 535:4
ardour: visit it with thine own a. LITT 423:9
ardua: *Per a. ad astra* ANON 22:11
arduis: *Aequam memento rebus in a.* HOR 349:17
are: Let them be as they a. CLEM 206:9
  that which we a. TENN 690:4
  we know what we a. SHAK 578:1
  will tell you what you a. BRIL 141:14
area: despondently at a. gates BROW 147:7

Argos: remembers his sweet A. VIRG 714:8
argosies: a. of magic sails TENN 685:13
  your a. with portly sail SHAK 607:2
argue: absurd to a. men NEWM 493:9
  a. freely according MILT 475:15
  a. the point with him MELV 456:16
  a. with someone who denies AUCT 33:15
  earth does not a. WHIT 733:1
  he could a. still GOLD 310:14
  hero is a man who would a. MAIL 442:9
argufies: What a. sniv'ling DIBD 238:15
arguing: a. with the inevitable LOW 430:7
  I am not a. with you WHIS 730:16
  necessity will be much a. MILT 475:13
argument: All a. is against it JOHN 374:25
  a. of the broken window PANK 506:1
  For Tories own no a. but force BROW 146:25
  height of this great a. MILT 467:21
  I have found you an a. JOHN 376:15
  impression, not an a. HARDY 324:14
  it is the a. of tyrants PITT 515:15
  love are still my a. SHAK 634:7
  never without an a. HAL 321:12
  stir without great a. SHAK 577:33
  than the staple of his a. SHAK 599:2
  their swords for lack of a. SHAK 585:8
  there's a nice knock-down a. CARR 183:11
  This is a rotten a. ANON 18:18
  Whigs admit no force but a. BROW 146:25
  would be a. for a week SHAK 580:8
argumentative: then a., then disputatious
    BYRON 174:2
arguments: force of his a. WALP 720:4
  tongue tang a. of state SHAK 630:5
Argus: A. were her eunuch SHAK 598:14
argutos: *a. inter strepere* VIRG 715:7
Ariadne: A. was a vintager KEATS 386:17
arias: a. of light thrilling over DAY-L 233:6
Ariel: Caliban casts out A. POUND 526:14
aright: that sought the Lord a. BURNS 161:16
arise: A., shine BIBLE 84:25
  I a. and unbuild it again SHEL 640:7
  I will a. and go now YEATS 752:7
  Let God a. BOOK 129:6
  Let us a. and go like men STEV 668:17
  My lady sweet, a. SHAK 571:3
aristocracy: displeased with *a.* HOBB 340:9
  a. and the true proletariat DIN 246:9
  a. in a republic is like MITF 478:6
  A. of the Moneybag CARL 180:24
  a. the most democratic MAC 435:16
  a. to what is decent HOPE 344.23
  is called *a.* PAINE 504:17
  natural a. among men JEFF 364:13
  not an a. of birth YOUNG 755:3
  while a. means government CHES 199:18
aristocrat: A., democrat, autocrat TENN 686:13
  A. who banks with Coutts GILB 304:1
aristocratic: a. class from the Philistines
    ARN 29:10
Aristotle: A. was but the rubbish of an Adam
    SOUTH 657:1
  follow this counsel of A. ASCH 31:3
  it is contrary to A. TAWN 679:2
  Of A. and his philosophie CHAU 192:20
  young man, whom A. thought SHAK 627:13
ark: a. of bulrushes BIBLE 71:34
  Noe entered into the a. BIBLE 92:13
  two unto Noah into the A. BIBLE 70:26
Arkangels: like he'd come from A. JOYCE 381:8
Arly: O My agèd Uncle A. LEAR 414:2
arm: And wound them on his a. MARL 447:11
  a. bent across your sullen SASS 557:8
  a. doth bind the restless WHIT 732:2
  A. it in rags, a pigmy's SHAK 597:8
  As lang's my a. BURNS 163:13
  As pearls upon an Ethiop's a. DYER 265:7
  by a stretched out a. BIBLE 73:14
  Give me your a., old toad LARK 410:9
  his reared a. crested SHAK 566:20
  lambs with his a. BIBLE 80:90
  lifting a. of conscience MILLER 460:16

arm: (cont.):
rebellious arm 'gainst a.   SHAK 599:17
seal upon thine a.   BIBLE 82:5
strength with his a.   BIBLE 93:23
Sufficient is Thine A. alone   WATTS 723:7
whom is the a.   BIBLE 84:10
Wi' the auld moon in her a.   BALL 50:11
with his holy a.   BOOK 131:13
arma: A. virumque cano   VIRG 711:18
Cedant a. togae, concedant   CIC 204:2
Moriamur et in media a.   VIRG 712:21
Silent enim leges inter a.   CIC 204:11
armadas: till the great A. come   NEWB 492:7
Armageddon: called in the Hebrew tongue A.   BIBLE 107:8
Lincoln County Road or A.   DYLAN 265:20
armaments: a. that cause wars   MAD 441:13
a. which only involve states   DISR 247:6
armchair: like a good a. which provides relaxation   MAT 454:1
Sure of the Fortieth spare A.   BROW 149:16
armchairs: wearing a. tight about the hips   WOD 740:19
armed: A. neutrality is ineffectual   WILS 738:16
a. so strong in honesty   SHAK 593:5
A. warfare must be preceded   ZIN 755:12
a. with more than complete   ANON 15:2
goeth on to meet the a.   BIBLE 77:38
want as an a. man   BIBLE 78:14
Armenteers: Mademoiselle from A.   ANON 16:6
armes: Aux a., citoyens   ROUG 548:17
armies: in all my pages   MAY 454:16
a. swore terribly in Flanders   STER 664:25
embattled a. clad in iron   MILT 474:4
ignorant a. clash by night   ARN 27:1
interested in a. and fleets   AUDEN 34:10
Kings with their a. did flee   BOOK 129:8
plenty of money and large a.   ANOU 23:2
stronger than all the a.   ANON 18:12
Arminian: A. clergy   PITT 515:10
armistice: it is an a. for twenty   FOCH 288:7
armonye: sterres, herkenyng a.   CHAU 196:1
Armoric: British and A. knights   MILT 469:1
armour: And put your a.   WESL 728:11
a. of a righteous cause   BRYAN 153:23
a. that one has nothing   SHEN 644:18
arrayed in the a. of Achilles   VIRG 712:18
his a. wherein he trusted   BIBLE 94:19
put on the a. of light   BIBLE 100:10
Put on the whole a. of God   BIBLE 102:26
upon us the a. of light   BOOK 120:10
Whose a. is his honest thought   WOTT 748:21
work out Achilles his a.   BROW 145:9
you the whole a. of God   BIBLE 103:1
armoured: a. cars of dreams   BISH 110:3
armourers: Now thrive the a.   SHAK 585:1
armoury: A. of the invincible Knights   WORD 744:13
arms: are the everlasting a.   BIBLE 73:24
a. against a sea of troubles   SHAK 575:16
A., and the man I sing   DRYD 262:7
a. and the man who first   VIRG 711:18
a. around him yes and drew   JOYCE 382:7
a. might do what this has   WALL 718:14
a. of a chambermaid   JOHN 375:6
A., take your last embrace   SHAK 624:9
a. went round her waist   MAS 453:5
a. with more right   LUCAN 431:4
a. ye forge, another bears   SHEL 643:4
But in my a. till break of day   AUDEN 35:5
corners of the world in a.   SHAK 594:16
defy the omnipotent to a.   MILT 467:23
Emparadised in one another's a.   MILT 471:9
For fear he a.   ROCH 543:13
haughty nation proud in a.   MILT 463:15
if my love were in my a.   ANON 19:14
I'll forswear a.   SHAK 579:28
in my a. burd Helen dropt   BALL 49:13
In one another's a.   YEATS 752:20
it hath very long a.   HAL 321:15
Its green a. round the bosom   SHEL 642:22
Leap to these a., untalked   SHAK 623:16
lord of folded a.   SHAK 598:13

arms: (cont.):
Made a. ridiculous   MILT 474:4
mightier than they in a.   MILT 472:4
muscles of his brawny a.   LONG 428:2
Of wit or a.   MILT 465:16
Ranked a. and crested heads   SMART 650:3
So he laid down his a.   HOOD 343:17
Those entrusted with a.   WIND 739:5
To find the a. of my true love   TENN 686:21
To war and a. I fly   LOV 429:6
Who from our mother's a.   WINK 739:6
youth of a state a.   BACON 45:5
army: against invasion by an a.   HUGO 354:15
An a. marches on its stomach   NAP 490:3
A. and I   WAUGH 723:9
A. is the non-commissioned   KIPL 399:1
a. of unalterable law   MER 458:6
a. which I oont among you   BIBLE 86:7
a. would be a base rabble   BURKE 157:32
contemptible little a.   ANON 13:7
either a. stilly sounds   SHAK 585:14
England brought the A. home   GUED 319:8
Grand A. never looked   MAHAN 442:3
noble a. of Martyrs   BOOK 118:12
[our a.] scum of the earth   WELL 727:12
terrible as an a. with banners   BIBLE 81:21
Your poor a., those poor   CROM 227:14
aroint: A. thee, witch!   SHAK 600:1
aroma: a. of performing seals   HART 327:11
aromatic: We faint beneath the a. pain   WINC 739:3
arose: he a. and followed him   BIBLE 90:4
a-roving: I'll go no more a.   ANON 12:8
arrangements: Is not pathetic, has no a.   WHIT 733:1
arranging: knack of so a. the world   FRIS 294:4
array: To summon his a.   MAC 436:9
arrears: pay glad life's a.   BROW 152:5
arrest: Is swift in his a.   SHAK 579:8
neither a. nor movement   ELIOT 270:16
arrested: a. one fine morning   KAFKA 384:15
arrival: a. there is what you   CAV 187:5
arrive: A. or find   THOM 694:14
barbarians are to a. today   CAV 187:7
been at to a. where I am   BUNY 156:16
better thing than to a.   STEV 667:29
I'll always a. like this   MOT 487:1
Will be to a. where we started   ELIOT 271:6
arrogant: subdue the a.   VIRG 713:17
arrow: a. from the Almighty's   BLAKE 112:5
a. that flies feels   LONG 426:15
I have shot mine a. o'er   SHAK 579:3
I shot an a. into the air   LONG 426:10
nor for the a. that flieth   BOOK 131:3
phrase 'time's a.'   EDD 266:2
arrows: a. in the hand of the giant   BOOK 134:7
a. of outrageous fortune   SHAK 575:16
Bring me my a. of desire   BLAKE 113:4
busy archer his sharp a.   SIDN 646:16
living a. are sent forth   GIBR 303:2
spend mine a. upon them   BIBLE 73:23
teeth are spears and a.   BOOK 128:15
ars: A. longa, vita brevis   HIPP 339:6
arse: a. for fifty years   MACN 440:14
politician is an a. upon   CUMM 228:9
with her big, fat a.   BLOK 115:8
arsenal: great a. of democracy   ROOS 546:2
art: All a. is immoral   WILDE 735:5
All passes. A. alone   DOBS 249:20
An a., in London only   DRYD 261:16
A. always serves beauty   PAST 508:6
a. and every investigation   ARIS 25:7
A. and Religion are means   BELL 60:18
A. and Science cannot exist   BLAKE 112:6
a. are of an infinite solitariness   RILKE 541:1
a. being all discrimination   JAMES 363:7
a. can wash her guilt away   GOLD 311:33
a. chatter turbulently   PIND 514:14
a. consists in the perfect   WILDE 735:16
a. constantly aspires towards   PATER 509:6
a. does not enlarge men's   ELIOT 270:2
A. does not reproduce   KLEE 402:19
A. for art's sake   CONS 218:1

art: (cont.):
a.-for-art's-sake   PRIT 529:19
a. has no importance whatever   NAB 489:4
A. has no other end   FLAU 286:5
A. has something to do   BELL 62:8
A. in its perfection   REYN 539:12
A. is a jealous mistress   EMER 276:17
A. is a revolt against fate   MALR 443:17
A. is born of humiliation   AUDEN 36:20
a. is but a vision of reality   YEATS 751:16
A. is in proportion   REYN 539:9
A. is long, and Time   LONG 427:8
A. is meant to disturb   BRAQ 139:17
A. is not a brassière   BARN 53:7
A. is only Nature operating   HOLB 341:19
A. is ... pattern informed   READ 537:7
A. is significant deformity   FRY 295:26
A. is the imposing   WHIT 731:14
A. is the objectification   LANG 408:18
a. is to limit and isolate   GOET 309:18
A. is to restore the decays   DENN 237:3
A. is upon the Town   WHIS 730:17
A. is vice   DEGAS 234:27
A. most cherishes   BROW 151:15
A. must be parochial   MOORE 482:10
a. of being wise   JAMES 363:17
a. of getting drunk   JOHN 375:8
a. of God   YOUNG 754:24
a. of our necessities   SHAK 596:2
a. of the possible   BISM 110:4
a.'s hid causes are not   JONS 378:18
a. the best is good enough   GOET 309:10
A. to fold her hands   ROSS 548:3
a. what he could never   STR 670:15
a. which one government   SMITH 651:4
bewitch me, than when A.   HERR 336:12
beyond the reach of a.   POPE 521:7
But hating, my boy, is an a.   NASH 490:17
By my so potent a.   SHAK 626:1
Desiring this man's a.   SHAK 633:10
Drawing is the true test of a.   INGR 360:9
Dying is an a.   PLATH 516:6
end and test of a.   POPE 521:6
Enough of science and of a.   WORD 748:8
est la probité de l'a.   INGR 360:9
every a. is its intensity   KEATS 391:9
failed in literature and a.   DISR 248:24
Fine a.   RUSK 550:28
For a. establishes   KENN 394:7
French a., if not sanguinary   SPEN 658:24
good a. than the pram   CONN 216:12
good grey guardians of a.   MERR 458:12
grandeur of the a. consists   REYN 539:8
great religious a.   CLARK 205:8
grotesque a. in English poetry   BAG 47:15
history of a.   BUTL 166:32
industry without a. is brutality   RUSK 550:12
In Spenser, and in Jonson, A.   DENH 236:19
intellect upon a.   SONT 656:4
Irish a.   JOYCE 381:19
It is the glory and good of A.   BROW 152:25
It is through A., and through   WILDE 735:4
It's clever, but is it A.   KIPL 398:17
I want that glib and oily a.   SHAK 594:21
kills love, it kills a.   WAUGH 723:10
know that A. is not truth   PIC 514:9
L'a. a pour objet de lui   ANOU 23:8
last and greatest a.   POPE 523:6
learn the hateful a.   KING 396:13
Life is short, the a. long   HIPP 339:6
Living is my job and my a.   MONT 481:4
Love is only Nature's a.   GREV 318:5
Minister that meddles with a.   MELB 456:6
models destroy genius and a.   HAZL 329:7
More matter with less a.   SHAK 574:13
murder and leave a.   EPST 278:5
nature is the a. of God   BROW 146:7
nature's handmaid a.   DRYD 260:3
Nature that is above all a.   DAN 229:13
new a. to them is natural   DAV 232:7
next to Nature, A.   LAND 408:2
noblest point of a.   GARR 298:3
not the a. of the possible   GALB 297:3

art: (cont.):

not works of a. at all	BLUNT 116:6
object of a. is actually	ANOU 23:8
offered you Conflict and A.	PRIE 528:18
only morality of a.	CONR 217:18
ornaments their want of a.	POPE 521:11
our utmost a. and use	WINC 739:1
people start on all this A.	HERB 333:17
Poetry is the universal a.	HEGEL 330:6
principle that Life imitates A.	WILDE 735:7
responsibility is to his a.	FAUL 281:4
rest is the madness of a.	JAMES 363:1
resuscitate the dead a.	POUND 526:11
Shakespeare wanted a.	JONS 380:8
so a. and morals	MURD 488:7
society a. is not a weapon	KENN 394:8
spoiled child of a.	JAMES 362:10
strains of unpremeditated a.	SHEL 643:13
supreme master of a.	CONR 217:14
Than all the adulteries of a.	JONS 378:18
triumph of the embalmer's a.	VIDAL 711:3
War's glorious a.	YOUNG 754:10
was almost lost in A.	COLL 213:16
where the a. resides	SCHN 558:7
Who talk about the Aims of A.	KIPL 399:12
with a. for art's sake	COUS 220:6
works of a., by being	ALB 7:9
writing comes from a.	POPE 521:16
you are only interested in a.	SHAW 638:29

artes: Hae tibi erunt a. VIRG 713:17

artful: Apt Alliteration's a. aid CHUR 201:8

Arthur: He's in A.'s bosom SHAK 585:5

talks of A.'s death	SHAK 594:11

article: being the correct a. ASHF 31:11

be snuffed out by an a.	BYRON 171:21
first a. of my faith	GAND 297:10
Fortieth A.	DENN 237:5

articles: These a. subscribed CONG 216:2

artifact: Death's a. ABSE 1:3

artifice: by every a. possible ANOU 23.8

artificer: Another lean unwashed a.

	SHAK 594:11
great a. made my mate	STEV 669:1
old a., stand me now	JOYCE 381:15

artificial: All things are a. BROW 146:7

breathe by a sort of a. inlet	FOST 291:9
said it was a. respiration	BURG 166:21

artillery: a. of words SWIFT 674:29

It is love's great a.	CRAS 226:10
terrible a.	FLAT 285:15

artisan: employment to the a. BELL 61:20

artist: a. brings something UPD 707:9

a. has no need to express	PROU 530:13
a. is a dreamer consenting	SANT 555:18
a. is his own fault	O'HARA 498:5
a., like the God	JOYCE 381:13
a. must be in his work	FLAU 286:3
a. never dies	LONG 427:5
no man is born an a.	WALT 720:22
Portrait of the A.	JOYCE 381:9
position for an a. anywhere	THOM 693:15
really only another a.	PIC 514:10
sign of the true a.	VIDAL 711:7
struggle between the a. man	SHAW 637:7
trust the a.	LAWR 412:8
West and from now on an a.	CONN 216:14
What an a. dies with me	NERO 491:20
Which dignifies the a.	DYER 265:4

artistic: give a. verisimilitude GILB 305:8

intellectual and a.	BERL 66:2
never was an a. period	WHIS 730:18

artists: A. are not engineers KENN 394:8

A. are the antennae	POUND 527:18
As a. they're rot	PARK 506:14
most a. and all humbugs	CONN 216:13

art-loving: There never was an A. nation

	WHIS 730:18

arts: a. in America a gigantic BEEC 59:4

a. of death	QUAW 537:12
a. of his man he seek	QUAW 537:13
a. of power and its minions	CLAY 206:1
a. reflect behaviour	FOOT 287:17
both a. and learning AAWH	QUAR 534:6

arts: (cont.):

But you 'a.' people	MCEW 437:15
Dear nurse of a., plenties	SHAK 586:16
famed in all great a.	ARN 29:2
Greece, mother of a.	MILT 473:20
had I but followed the a.	SHAK 628:13
His virtues were his a.	BURKE 160:1
interested in the a.	AYCK 40:8
mechanical and merchandise	BACON 45:5
mother of a., of warfare	DU B 262:23
No a.; no letters	HOBB 340:7

artus: dum spiritus hos regit a. VIRG 713:6

totamque infusa per a.	VIRG 713:16

Aryan: your A. eye PLATH 516:4

as: A. with gladness DIX 249:19

ascended: He a. into heaven BOOK 119:1

ascending: angels of God a. BIBLE 71:13

lark a.	MER 458:4

Ascension: glorious Resurrection and A.

	BOOK 119:18

ascribe: A. unto the Lord the honour

	BOOK 131:11

ash: A. on an old man's sleeve ELIOT 271:4

laughter of an empty a.	CRANE 225:20
Than Oak, and A., and Thorn	KIPL 400:10

ashamed: And be a. HUGH 354:1

a. and confounded	BOOK 129:15
a. of one another ever	CONG 216:1
a. to look upon one another	WALT 721:4
death, as a. thereof	BROW 146:11
doing something he is a.	SHAW 635:27
Hope maketh not a.	BIBLE 99:25
more things a man is a.	SHAW 637:5
Nor ever once a.	ARN 26:14
now-a-days men are a.	GAY 300:13
thing to feel a. of home	DICK 240:30

ashbuds: More black than a. TENN 681:5

ashes: All a. to the taste BYRON 168:21

all this glory unto a.	GREV 318:7
And into a. all my lust	MARV 451:3
Are a. under Uricon	HOUS 352:13
a. of an Oak	DONNE 253:7
a. to ashes, dust to dust	BOOK 124:5
But turn to a. on the lips	MOORE 483:15
fire and was burnt to a.	GRAH 313:12
For the a. of his fathers	MAC 436:10
Her a. new-create another heir	SHAK 589:17
I am a. where once I was fire	BYRON 173:10
past is a bucket of a.	SAND 555:7
Scatter my a.—strew them	GRAH 313:14
turn the universe to a.	MISS 477:11
unto them beauty for a.	BIBLE 84:27
will be sour grapes and a.	ASHF 31:12

Asia: churches which are in A. BIBLE 105:31

churches which are in A.	BIBLE 105:34
gaiety will end up in A.	BLY 116:7

Asian: what A. boys ought to be doing

for themselves	JOHN 367:10

aside: Just try and set death a. TURG 705:8

ask: all that we a. or think BIBLE 102:15

A., and it shall be given	BIBLE 89:17
a. faithfully we may obtain	BOOK 121:12
A. me no more	TENN 688:12
A. me no more where Jove	CAREW 179:11
a. not what your country	KENN 394:2
a. the hard question	AUDEN 36:9
a. why	AUDEN 34:9
blindness we cannot a.	BOOK 122:18
Don't a. me, ask	FREUD 293:22
I a. and cannot answer	SHAW- 639:3
I a. very little	CONN 216:10
I intend to a. of them	KENN 393:11
more we a., the more	COMP 214:16
Where is have, where	SMART 650:2

askance: looking a., other GOGOL 310:2

asked: And I have a. HOPK 345:14

asketh: Every one that a. BIBLE 89:18

asking: a. is not always easy COMP 214:16

offering too little and a.	CANN 178:3
or third time of a.	BOOK 123:14
refrain from a. it to dinner	HALS 322.8
release Dull on a learning dig	SHAK 588:16
But 'break a. and make	SHAK 594:26

asleep: (cont.):

Half a. as they stalk	HARDY 325:10
men were all a. the snow	BRID 141:3
quiet till it falls a.	TEMP 680:3
ships sail like swans a.	FLEC 286:12
That sucks the nurse a.	SHAK 567:11
those that are a. to speak	BIBLE 82:4
very houses seem a.	WORD 743:10
Where the winds are all a.	ARN 29:8

asp: on the hole of the a. BIBLE 83:3

asparagus: A. and it appeared DICK 241:4

Grew like a. in May	GILB 304:4

aspens: Willows whiten, a. quiver TENN 684:24

asperges: A. me, Domine MISS 476:11

A. me hyssopo	BIBLE 107:28

aspersion: a. upon my parts of speech

	SHER 645:4

aspes: a. leef she gan to quake CHAU 195:18

asphalt: Their only monument the a. road

	ELIOT 272:16

aspidistra: biggest a. in world HARP 326:15

Keep the a. flying	ORW 500:5
leaf of the a. that guards	GREE 317:6

aspiration: democracy can be no more

than a.	YOUNG 755:3
man of yearning thought and a.	ROSS 548:7

aspire: be that by due steps a. MILT 463:13

light, and will a.	SHAK 635:12
me gaze, and there a.	ARN 28:19
which when men a.	MARL 447:8

aspiring: all to have a. minds MARL 448:1

ass: a. will not mend his pace SHAK 578:18

inasmuch as he was an a.	SURT 672:7
jaw of an a. have I slain	BIBLE 74:17
kiss my a. in Macy's window	JOHN 367:11
law is a a.	DICK 242:29
law is such an a.	CHAP 190:20
Love a woman? You're an a.	ROCH 543:16
making him egregiously an a.	SHAK 615:22
nor his ox, nor his a.	BIBLE 72:16
thee call great Caesar a.	SHAK 567:11
was enamoured of an a.	SHAK 612:13

assailant: A. on the perched roosts MILT 474:14

assailed: A., fight, taken DONNE 250:14

assassin: copperheads and the a. SAND 555:3

you are an a.	ROST 548:13

assassination: absolutism moderated by a.

	ANON 13:3
A. has never changed	DISR 247:14
A. is the extreme form	SHAW 638:25
A. is the quickest way	MOL 479:10
if the a. could trammel	SHAK 601:2

assassins: que MM les a. commencent

	KARR 385:12

assault: as soon a. a Plush DICK 245:4

thoughts which may a.	BOOK 120:15

assaults: all a. of our enemies BOOK 119:3

crafts and a. of the devil	BOOK 119:17

assay: For by a. ther may no man it preve

	CHAU 194:29
Th'a. so hard, so sharp	CHAU 195:5

assemblies: calling of a. BIBLE 82:9

assent: a. with civil leer POPE 519:32

asses: a. quench their thirst BOOK 132:7

King Death hath a.' ears	BEDD 58:11
owls and cuckoos, apes	MILT 474:22
riches to those gross a.	LUTH 432:16
seeking a. found a kingdom	MILT 473:18

asshen: oure a. olde is fyr yreke CHAU 194:13

assis: Omnes unius aestimemus a. CAT 185:15

assume: A. a virtue SHAK 577:22

assurance: a. of a sleepwalker HITL 339:11

a. of incorruption	BIBLE 87:6
a. was given me that He	WESL 728:19
full a. given by looks	ROYD 549:14
I'll make a double sure	SHAK 604:1
One of the low on whom a.	ELIOT 273:9

Assyrian: A. came down like the wolf

	BYRON 169:28
That oiled and curled A. Bull	TENN 686:10
restoring my mind of a.	TENN 681:10

astonish: A, me DIAG 238:9

You must a. the bourgeois	BAUD 57:14

astonished: a. at my own moderation
CLIVE 206:16
a. to see him in Baghdad　　　LOW 429:13
astonishment: A. takes from us sense of pain
CONS 217:20
Dear Sir, Your a.'s odd　　　KNOX 403:10
astra: *Per ardua ad a.*　　　ANON 22:11
puer, sic itur ad a.　　　VIRG 714:6
astray: Like one that had been led a.
MILT 464:20
odours led my steps a.　　　SHEL 642:22
sheep have gone a.　　　BIBLE 84:12
were as sheep going a.　　　BIBLE 105:15
astrologers: separable into astronomers
and a.　　　QUINE 534:15
astronomer: undevout a. is mad　YOUNG 754:22
astronomers. Confounding her a.　HODG 340:17
astronomy: Devotion! daughter of a.
YOUNG 754:22
asunder: let not man put a.　　　BIBLE 91:22
let no man put a.　　　BOOK 123:22
My bones are smitten a.　　　BOOK 127:5
asure: a. were his legges　　　CHAU 194:5
asylum: a. run by lunatics　　　LLOY 424:12
in an a. and forgotten it　　　PALM 505:13
taken charge of the a.　　　ROWL 549:11
asylums: a. of this country　　　BENN 63:10
ate: a. a good supper at night　ANST 23:11
a. his bread in sorrow　　　GOET 309:15
a. when we were not hungry　SWIFT 673:16
With A. by his side　　　SHAK 591:24
Athalus: A., that made the game　CHAU 192:5
atheism: a., breast-feeding　　　ORTON 499:14
a. is against not only　　　BURKE 158:19
inclineth man's mind to a.　　　BACON 42:23
owlet A.　　　COL 210:2
atheist: a. half believes a God　YOUNG 754:19
a. is a man who has no　　　BUCH 154:2
a.-laugh's a poor exchange　BURNS 161:25
a. who does not so much　　　ORW 500:1
a. who finds creation　　　PROU 530:13
female a. talks you dead　　　JOHN 370:7
he was no a., but he could　CHAR 191:14
kept her from being an a.　SART 556:16
superstitious a., demirep　BROW 148:13
Thanks to God, I am still an a.　BUÑ 155:12
atheistical: damned a. age　　　VANB 708:4
atheists: no a. in the foxholes　CUMM 229:1
Athenians: A. and strangers　BIBLE 98:30
Athens: A. arose　　　SHEL 640:14
A. but the rudiments　　　SOUTH 657:1
A., the eye of Greece　　　MILT 473:20
Pericles felt of A.　　　KEYN 395:2
Truths as refined as ever A.　ARMS 26:8
who are a citizen of A.　　　SOCR 654:11
Ye men of A., I perceive　　　BIBLE 98:31
athirst: a. of the fountain　　　BIBLE 107:19
Atlantic: steep A. stream　　　MILT 463:16
Atlas: demi-A.　　　SHAK 565:1
disencumbered A. of the state　COWP 223:8
atmosphere: shove against an a.　EDD 266:4
atom: a. bomb is a paper tiger　MAO 446:2
a. has changed everything　EINS 268:4
carbon a. possesses　　　JEANS 363:26
defence against the a. bomb　ANON 12:13
grasped the mystery of the a.　BRAD 139:7
Melville who split the a.　LODGE 425:20
stars leads through the a.　EDD 266:5
There is no evil in the a.　STEV 666:18
atomic: primordial a. globule　GILB 304:20
atomies: as easy to count a.　SHAK 569:5
atoms: a. as they fall upon　WOOLF 742:8
a. of Democritus　　　BLAKE 113:6
A. or systems into ruin hurled　POPE 521:29
colourless movement of a.　BRAD 139:6
fortuitous concurrence of a.　PALM 505:9
where all these a.　　　GRAH 313:14
atom-streams: saw the flaring a.　TENN 686:3
atone: a. for our past　　　CHEK 196:9
atrabilious: bowl with a. liquor　HUXL 357:22
attach: Where people wish to a.　AUST 38:23
attachment: a. à la Plato　　　GILB 305:17

attack: a. the monkey when　BEVAN 68:17
both by his plan of a.　　　SASS 557:11
That dared a. my Chesterton　BELL 61:14
To lead such dire a.　　　MAC 436:13
attacked: a. it defends itself　ANON 20:7
attain: I cannot a. unto it　　　BOOK 134:19
attainable: We look at the a.　GLAD 307:13
attempt: a. and not the deed　SHAK 601:16
love can do that dares love a.　SHAK 622:31
attempts: sins a. to fill voids　WEIL 726:18
attend: Another to a. him　　　HERB 335:11
attendance: dance a. on their lordships'
pleasures　　　SHAK 589:13
attendant: Am an a. lord　　　ELIOT 272:5
attended: Is on his way a.　　　WORD 745:14
attention: a. in the midst of distraction
BELL 62:8
a. of the nation is concentrated　BAG 47:5
close the Valves of her a.　DICK 244:18
Enforce a., like deep harmony　SHAK 619:15
give their entire a. to it　BENN 63:20
serious a. than history　　　ARIS 25:13
So a. must be paid　　　MILL 461:16
attentions: a. proceed from the impulse
AUST 39:11
attentive: a. and favourable hearers
HOOK 344:13
attic: mellow glory of the A.　ARN 29:1
Not, at any rate, an A. grace　POUND 526:13
O A. shape! Fair attitude　KEATS 389:1
She sleeps up in the a. there　MEW 459:8
where the A. bird　　　MILT 473:20
attire: a. creeps rustling to her　KEATS 387:6
My Love in her a. doth show　ANON 16:14
or a bride her a.　　　BIBLE 85:3
attitude: O Attic shape! Fair a.　KEATS 389:1
attorney: gentleman was an *a.*　JOHN 373:11
love with a rich a.'s　　　GILB 306:22
office boy to an A.'s firm　GILB 305:26
attract: A. a Silver Churn　　　GILB 305:18
attracted: a. by God, or by Nature　INGE 359:15
attracting: rhythm of a. people　JOAD 366:9
attraction: A. and repulsion　BLAKE 112:13
a. towards all that we　　　SHEL 644:9
by sure a. led　　　POPE 518:23
that flies feels the a.　　　LONG 426:15
Why do we put a.　　　BEHN 60:9
attractions: costs register competing a.
KNIG 403:1
attribute: a. to God himself　SHAK 609:13
auburn: Sweet A.　　　GOLD 310:5
auctioneer: A., *n.* The man who proclaims
BIER 109:5
auctoritee: Experience, though noon a.
CHAU 194:19
audace: *et toujours de l'a.*　DANT 230:22
audacious: Of saucy and a. eloquence
SHAK 612:21
audacity: Arm me, a.　　　SHAK 570:28
a. is knowing how far　　　COCT 208:10
a. of elected persons　　　WHIT 732:11
aude: *coepit habet: sapere a.*　HOR 348:4
Auden: A., a sort of gutless　ORW 500:23
audendi: *a. semper fuit*　　　HOR 347:2
audi: A. *partem alteram.*　　　AUG 37:5
audible: a., and full of vent　SHAK 570:18
audience: a. look to their eyes　SHAK 611:4
event and whisks his a.　HOR 347:13
fit a. find　　　MILT 472:7
For which I crie in open a.　CHAU 193:10
audiences: English-speaking a.　WHAR 730:2
know two kinds of a. only　SCHN 558:6
audit: how his a. stands　　　SHAK 577:4
augmentation: a. of the Indies　SHAK 630:18
augur: He bored with his a.　BALL 49:11
augurs: A. and understood relations
SHAK 603:13
augury: Not a whit, we defy a.　SHAK 579:2
August: A. for the people　　　AUDEN 34:6
A. in its history Paris　　　TUCH 705:1
A. is a wicked month　　　O'BR 497:10
To recommence in A.　　　BYRON 171:26

Augustan: A. age will dawn　WALP 719:16
Augustus: A. was a chubby lad　HOFF 341:1
auld: 'tis a. it waxeth cauld　BALL 51:2
aunt: A. like mastodons　　　WOD 740:16
Charley's a. from Brazil　THOM 693:2
Did your a. always seem　WALK 717:11
aunts: bad a. and good a.　WOD 740:11
dull a., and croaking rooks　POPE 521:1
his cousins and his a.　GILB 305:25
auream: A. *quisquis mediocritatem*　HOR 349:18
auri: A. *sacra fames*　　　VIRG 713:3
Aurora: yonder shines A.'s harbinger
SHAK 612:6
austere: beauty cold and a.　RUSS 551:20
knewest that I was an a. man　BIBLE 95:16
autcrity: a. could never blight　BRON 142:5
Austerlitz: at A. and Waterloo　SAND 555:5
Austria: A. is going to the war　CHES 199:4
Ausweg: *Krieg findet immer einen A.*
BREC 140:10
authentic: a. mammon than a bogus
MACN 440:12
author: a. and we find a man　PASC 507:10
a. as you choose a friend　DILL 246:3
a. is not what he says　SMITH 652:11
a. of himself　　　SHAK 570:20
a. of his own disgrace　COWP 222:10
a. of peace and lover　BOOK 119:3
a.'s hands and feet　CHEK 197:8
a. that ever grazed　JOHN 372:5
a. to get at his meaning　RUSK 550:18
a. who speaks about　DISR 247:23
be but a shrimp of an a.　GRAY 316:13
characters in search of an a.　PIR 515:3
Jesus the a. and finisher　BIBLE 104:17
like a distinguished a.　NAB 489:3
majesty of the A. of things　LEIB 416:18
No a. ever spared a brother　GAY 299:32
Of the first a.　　　MARV 451:5
ruin half an a.'s graces　MORE 483:21
same steps as the a.　KEATS 391:18
than wit to become an a.　LA BR 405:5
This is indeed to be an a.　HAZL 329:10
who art the a. and giver　BOOK 121:5
authoritarian: triumph of an a. state
CLARK 205:9
authority: And the lie of A.　AUDEN 36:1
are put in a. under her　BOOK 122:1
A. doesn't work without　DE G 235:6
A. forgets a dying king　TENN 682:20
a. is oftenest likely　MILL 460:24
a. of the eternal yesterday　WEBER 725:1
a. uses not intellect　LEON 418:8
base a. from others' books　SHAK 598:7
Drest in a little brief a.　SHAK 605:18
faith that stands on a.　EMER 276:29
I am a man under a.　BIBLE 89:30
in me claim no more a.　WYATT 749:16
maximal a. and minimal power
SZASZ 677:11
Rulers have no a. from　MAYH 455:9
subordinate position than in a.　THOM 692:20
taught them as one having a.　BIBLE 89:28
authors: English a. their copyrights　TROL 703:3
great a. have their due　BACON 41:15
invades a. like a monarch　DRYD 202.12
praise of ancient a.　HOBB 340:13
They damn those a. whom　CHUR 200:14
'Till a. hear at length　COWP 223:11
authorship: reputation of popular a.
TROL 704:9
autobiography: a. is an obituary in serial
CRISP 227:2
autocrat: I shall be an a.　CATH 185:7
automatic: hair with a. hand　ELIOT 273:10
automaton: dragoon me into a lethal a.
MACN 441:1
automobile: And fix up his a.　CLAR 205:11
autres: *pour encourager les a.*　VOLT 716:3
autumn: a. and the falling fruit　LAWR 412:19
a. arrives in the early　BOWEN 138:8
a. was that grew the more　SHAK 566:20

autumn: (*cont.*):
cloudy days of a. — CLARE 204:28
happy a.–fields — TENN 688:3
In a., and a lustre in its sky — SHEL 640:19
I saw old A. in the misty morn — HOOD 344:3
long dark a.-evenings — BROW 148:21
sadly descends the a. evening. — ARN 28:1
sky breathed a., sombre — PUSH 532:16
This a. morning — BROW 150:17
thou breath of A.'s being — SHEL 641:14
autumnal: A. winds prevail — SMART 649:16
from both a deep, a. tone — SHEL 641:19
seen in one a. face — DONNE 250:10
avalanching: a. on the snow crust — FROST 294:9
avarice: A., spur of industry — HUME 355:8
beyond the dreams of a. — JOHN 375:23
beyond the dreams of a. — MOORE 482:7
discretion end, and a. begin — AUST 39:15
Is a. to itself — JONS 379:4
I think I must take up with a. — BYRON 170:15
which a. and ambition — SMITH 650:15
ave: a. atque vale — CAT 187:1
A. verum corpus — ANON 22:4
Ave Maria: A., gratia plena — ANON 22:3
A.! 'tis the hour of prayer — BYRON 171:0
Ave Marys: songs were A. — CORB 218:13
avenger: enemy, and the a. — BOOK 124:20
Rise up from my dead bones, a. — VIRG 713:8
avenue: Only an a., dark, nameless — THOM 694:4
avenues: seal up the a. of ill — EMER 276:13
average: A. made lethal — SHAF 563:19
averages: fugitive from th' law of a. — MAUL 454:14
Averno: Facilis descensus A. — VIRG 713:11
aversion: begin with a little a. — SHER 645:2
closely bordering on a — STEV 667:17
manner which is my a. — BYRON 171:4
avert: May the gods a. this omen — CIC 204:9
avertant: Quod di omen a. — CIC 204:9
aveugle: amour est a — ANON 20:16
avis: Rara a. in terris nigroque — JUV 383:24
avocados: Wives in the a. — GINS 306:29
avoid: a. what is to come — SHAK 577:19
who manages to a. them — HEIS 331:5
avoiding: non-being by a. being — TILL 698:5
Avon: Sweet Swan of A.! — JONS 380:5
awaits: A man a. his end — YEATS 751:9
awake: A., my soul, and with the sun — KEN 393:5
A., O north wind — BIBLE 81:16
Being now a., I'll queen — SHAK 632:10
clamour keep her still a. — SHAK 624:17
England! a.! awake! awake — BLAKE 112:8
myself will a. right early — BOOK 128:16
Onaway! A., beloved — LONG 427:17
They shall a. as Jacob did — DONNE 253:14
We are a. while sleeping — MONT 481:10
will he lie ten nights a. — SHAK 613:10
yet he durst attempt a. — JONS 379:15
awaked: a. as one out of sleep — BOOK 130:12
sleepeth, and must be a. — BIBLE 76:2
awakenings: bad dream between two a. — O'NEI 498:20
aware: infant child is not a. — HOUS 351:15
insignificant and is a. — BECK 57:10
single man sufficiently a. — LA R 410:18
awareness: a. of possibilities — LEAV 415:4
away: A kiss, a sigh, and so a. — CRAS 226:14
A., fear, with thy projects — ALAB 7:1
a.! for I will fly — KEATS 389:11
A. from me, all ye — BOOK 124:19
A.! the moor is dark beneath — SHEL 643:8
black night doth take a. — SHAK 634:6
Down and a. below — ARN 27:6
They can't take that a. — GERS 301:16
they get them a. together — BOOK 132:9
What! keep a week a. — SHAK 617:5
awe: a. into the beholders — SWIFT 673:8
a. of such a thing — SHAK 589:27
Exempt from a. worship — SHEL 642:18
eye whose bend doth a. — SHAK 590:1
increasing wonder and a — KANT 385:4

awe: (*cont.*):
keep the strong in a. — SHAK 622:14
Stand in a., and sin not — BOOK 124:12
aweary: Cassius is a. of the world — SHAK 593:8
I 'gin to be a. of the sun — SHAK 605:2
She said, 'I am a., aweary — TENN 686:6
awful: Anything a. makes me laugh — LAMB 406:26
Great God! this is an a. place — SCOTT 559:3
nobody goes, it's a. — BECK 57:22
together in a. silence — AKHM 6:8
Who wait the A. Day — CORN 219:2
awfully: To die will be an a. big adventure — BARR 54:8
awkward: a. squad fire over me — BURNS 164:4
awoke: a., and behold it was a dream — BUNY 156:7
a. one morning from uneasy — KAFKA 384:18
awry: at me for leaning all a. — FITZ 284:12
axe: a.'s edge did try — MARV 450:15
a. is laid unto the root — BIBLE 88:16
head off with a golden a. — SHAK 623:19
Lizzie Borden took an a. — ANON 15:22
offence is let the great a. — SHAK 578:10
then the a. to the root — PAINE 504:16
axes: your sharp-edged a. — WHIT 732:9
axioms: A. in philosophy — KEATS 391:18
axis: a. of the earth sticks — HOLM 342:7
sword is a. of the world — DE G 235:7
under-belly of the A. — CHUR 202:18
axle: His glowing a. doth allay — MILT 463:16
axletree: a. of the chariot-wheel — BACON 45:4
men feel the burning a. — CHAP 190:14
aye: Scylla and Charybdis of A. — NEWM 493:2
Azores: At Flores in the A. — TENN 689:1
azure: a. sister of the spring — SHEL 641:14
from out the a. main — THOM 695:15
overgrown with a. moss — SHEL 641:16
With a., white, and red — DRUM 258:13
azure-lidded: slept an a. sleep — KEATS 387:9

B

babblative: arts b. — SOUT 657:15
babble: Coffee house b. — DISR 249:12
babbled: a' b. of green fields — SHAK 585:5
babbler: What will this b. say — BIBLE 98:29
babe: B. looked up and showed — CRAS 226:6
b. was born in a manger — WHIT 731:17
Come little b., come silly — BRET 140:17
Finger of birth-strangled b. — SHAK 603:19
Hath laid her b. to rest — MILT 467:13
if my young b. were born — BALL 51:3
like a naked new-born b. — SHAK 601:3
tender 'tis to love the b. — SHAK 601:7
Babel: B. got language — VOLT 716:16
Of the great B., and not — COWP 223:32
babes: As newborn b., desire — BIBLE 105:10
very b. and sucklings — BOOK 124:20
babies: b. in the tomatoes — GINS 306:29
bit the b. in the cradles — BROW 151:26
hates dogs and b. — ROST 548:14
Other people's b. — HERB 333:18
than putting milk into b. — CHUR 202:20
Babiy Yar: Over B. — YEVT 754:3
Bab-lock-hithe: Thames at B. — ARN 28:5
baboon: Into b. and monkey — SHAK 626:6
baby: b. beats the nurse — SHAK 605:7
b. boy, to recognize — VIRG 715:1
b. doesn't understand English — KNOX 403:12
b. figure of the giant mass — SHAK 627:11
B. in an ox's stall — BETJ 67:4
b. laughed for the first — BARR 54:6
bats with b. faces — ELIOT 273:13
Burn, b., burn — ANON 12:19
I'm your little b. — LEWIS 421:1
Make it one for my b. — MERC 457:14
see my b. at my breast — SHAK 567:11
Thou cam'st, a little b. thing — MACD 437:11
with his b. on my knee — KING 397:8
you come from, b. dear — MACD 437:9

Babylon: B. in all its desolation — DAV 232:8
B. is fallen, is fallen — BIBLE 107:3
B. THE GREAT, THE MOTHER — BIBLE 107:10
B. we sit down and weep — WALP 719:17
city B. be thrown down — BIBLE 107:11
Ere B. was dust — SHEL 642:7
London is a modern B. — DISR 248:33
waters of B. we sat down — BOOK 124:12
bacchanal: come to me now with the b. sign — YOUNG 755:2
Bacchus: Not charioted by B. — KEATS 389:11
Of B. and his revellers — MILT 472:7
Baccus: dainty B. gross in taste — SHAK 598:20
'baccy: 'b. for the Clerk — KIPL 400:9
Bach: B. interwoven with Spohr — GILB 305:4
bachelor: b. never gets over — ROWL 549:9
b. of three-score again — SHAK 613:10
I said I would die a b. — SHAK 613:27
bachelors: All reformers are b. — MOORE 482:8
reasons for b. to go out — ELIOT 269:25
back: always give your b. a pat — LERN 419:3
And those before cried 'B.!' — MAC 436:13
B. and side go bare, go bare — ANON 14:13
b. but marched breast forward — BROW 148:6
b. from time to time — ELIOT 273:7
B. in the USSR — LENN 417:15
b. somewhere in our breast — ARN 26:17
b. three-quarter — DOYLE 256:15
B. to the future — GALE 755:10
B. to the garden — MITC 478:1
boys in the b. rooms — BEAV 57:7
boys in the b. room will — LOES 426:2
But at my b. I always hear — MARV 451:3
by one b. in the closet — FITZ 284:7
Empire strikes b. — LUCAS 431:9
gets stabbed in the b. — GARD 297:15
I counted them all b. — HANR 323:7
I have a beast on my b. — DOUG 255:10
I leaned my b. unto an aik — BALL 51:2
I sit on a man's b. — TOLS 701:2
looking b. — BIBLE 94:9
Not to go b., is somewhat — POPE 522:26
plowers plowed upon my b. — BOOK 134:10
safe to go b. in the water — ANON 15:13
stamp me b. to common — FITZ 284:14
backbone: b. of the Army — KIPL 399:1
backhand: wonderful b. drive — BETJ 68:3
backing: plague upon such b. — SHAK 580:16
backs: beast with two b. — SHAK 614:24
when maids lie on their b. — SHAK 622:22
backside: brain smoked like the b. — JONS 378:10
backward: b. and put to confusion — BOOK 129:15
b. parts of the proletariat — ANON 16:5
B. ran sentences until reeled — GIBBS 302:26
But I by b. steps would move — VAUG 709:4
drew me b. by the hair — BROW 147:18
For life goes not b. — GIBR 303:2
look b. to their ancestors — BURKE 158:9
look b. to with pride — FROST 294:14
revolutions never go b. — SEW 563:9
backwards: memory that only works b. — CARR 183:6
narration always going b. — WALP 719:6
backyards: clean American b. — MAIL 442:8
Bacon: B. has been described — STR 670:13
learning, Sir Francis B. — WALT 721:12
think how B. shined — POPE 522:21
When their lordships asked B. — BENT 64:9
bacon: b.'s not the only thing — KING 398:5
bacons: On b., on — SHAK 580:7
bad: animal is very b. — ANON 20:7
b. against the worse — DAY-L 233:7
b. as bad can — JOHN 376:11
b. aunts and good aunts — WOD 740:11
b. die late — DEFOE 234:14
b. end unhappily — STOP 670:5
b. it must be good to know — BRAD 139:5
B. laws are the worst sort — BURKE 158:34
b. movies when they can — GOLD 312:7
b. news infects the teller — SHAK 604:17
b. publicity except — BEHAN 60:6

bad: (cont.):
b.'s the best of us | FLET 287:14
b. taste is always | HOPK 346:17
b. things that hotel-keepers | TROL 703:21
b. to worse that a society | TOCQ 699:1
b. unhappily | WILDE 734:16
B. women never take | BROO 143:20
find the world ugly and b. | NIET 495:11
For good ye are and b. | TENN 681:28
hates dogs and babies can't be all bad | ROST 548:14
How sad and b. and mad | BROW 149:9
Mad, b., and dangerous | LAMB 406:2
make them feel b. | MONT 482:3
much b. in the best of us | ANON 18:13
neither good nor b. | BALZ 51:8
nothing either good or b. | SHAK 574:26
our sad b. glad mad brother's | EWIN 676:6
Pleasure's for those who are b. | YES 754:2
posterity as a brave b. | CLAR 205:5
resolved to do something b. | MCC 436:20
she was b. she was horrid | LONG 428:5
She was not really b. at heart | BELL 61:8
shocking b. hats in my life | WELL 727:4
they will come to a b. end | BEER 59:15
This bold b. man | SHAK 588:13
To make b. good, and good | SHAK 606:18
When b. men combine | BURKE 159:15
bade: b. betwixt their shores | ARN 29:4
There b. me gaze, and there | ARN 28:19
badge: b. of all our tribe | SHAK 607:22
red b. of courage | CRANE 225:27
badgers: When b. fight | CLARE 204:16
badly: it is worth doing b. | CHES 199:24
badness: All good and no b. | SKEL 649:1
bag: bottle and a b. | GASC 298:16
it into a b. with holes | BIBLE 86:18
though not with b. | SHAK 569:3
bagatelle: vive la b. | STER 664:6
baggage: b. loves me | CONG 215:19
one and all, bag and b. | GLAD 307:10
Baghdad: astonished to see him in B. | LOW 429:13
bagman: Cobden is an inspired b. | CARL 181:16
bagpipe: b. sings i' the nose | SHAK 609:8
bags: carry other people's b. | BRAC 138:19
bah: 'B.,' said Scrooge | DICK 239:17
Bailey: come home Bill B. | CANN 178:13
bailiff: loved the b.'s daughter | BALL 48:20
bainters: hate all Boets and B. | GEOR 300:22
baits: b. do fleetest fish entice | GASC 298:19
while good news b. | MILT 474:13
baked: both b. in this pie | SHAK 627:2
millionaires love a b. | FIRB 282:28
baker: b. rhymes for his pursuit | BROW 152:7
bakers: As b. and breweres | LANG 409:1
Baker Street: B. irregulars | DOYLE 256:20
Bakewell: every fool in B. | RUSK 550:16
balance: art of b. and weight | CERV 188:16
dream of is an art of b. | MAT 454:1
redress the b. of the Old | CANN 178:17
small dust of the b. | BIBLE 83:29
uncertain b. of proud time | GREE 317:7
weigh thy words in a b. | BIBLE 87:28
balances: Thou art weighed in the b. | BIBLE 85:31
bald: b. as the bare mountain | ARN 29:25
b. street breaks the blank | TENN 683:6
Go up, thou b. head | BIBLE 70:17
otherwise bald and unconvincing | GILB 305:8
two b. men over a comb | BORG 136:11
we found him b. too | BROW 149:28
baldheaded: Go into it b. | LOW 429:16
baldness: b. than young men | SMITH 652:1
with a b. full of grandeur | ARN 29:25
Baldwin: Mr B. denouncing sanctions | BEAV 57:5
bales: dropping down with costly b. | TENN 685:13
balkans: damned silly thing in the B. | BISM 110:7
ball: at a girl throwing a b. | WOOLF 742:14
b. is either to look out | SURT 672:18

ball: (cont.):
b. no question makes | FITZ 284:8
like a man yawning at a b. | LERM 418:17
Only wind it into a b. | BLAKE 112:7
that portion of the b. | POPE 518:19
ballad: And I met with a b. | CALV 175:10
I love a b. in print | SHAK 632:8
ballad-mongers: these same metre b. | SHAK 581:4
ballads: better than all the b. | LONG 426:12
permitted to make all the b. | FLET 287:10
ballet: b. in the evening | HACK 320:7
unearthly b. of bloodless | BRAD 139:6
ball-floor: Dance on this b. | BLUN 116:3
Balliol: B. made me | BELL 62:2
balloon: b. of experience | JAMES 361:6
something in a huge b. | WORD 746:12
ballot: b. is stronger than the bullet | LINC 421:17
ballots: peaceful b. only | LINC 421:17
balls: And elliptical billiard b. | GILB 305:5
b. stuck in her face | SHAK 598:14
B. will be lost always | BERR 66:16
our rackets to these b. | SHAK 584:23
balm: b. from an anointed | SHAK 620:3
B. of hurt minds, great | SHAK 602:2
b. th'hydroptic earth hath | DONNE 252:12
Is there no b. in Gilead | BIBLE 85:9
pours out a b. upon the world | KEATS 387:16
balmy: Ginger, you're b. | MURR 488:11
Baltimore: then you're in B. | GORD 312:13
banal: Eldorado b. | BAUD 55:10
banality: b. of evil | AREN 24:14
manufacture of b. | SARR 556:5
Banbury: To B. came I | BRAT 139:19
band: captain of this ruined b. | SHAK 585:15
heroes! heaven-born b. | HOPK 346:20
high aesthetic b. | GILB 305:17
rock 'n' roll b. | JAGG 361:12
twilight! importunate b. | BETJ 68:7
we b. of brothers | SHAK 586:11
When the b. commences playing | GROS 319:1
when the wearied B. swoons | HUXL 357:20
bandage: only b. might be chains | BYRON 172:14
bandaged: death b. my eyes | BROW 152:5
bandied: tennis-balls, struck and b. | WEBS 725:25
bands: I drew them . . . with b. of love | BIBLE 86:5
loose the b. of wickedness | BIBLE 84:22
or loose the b. of Orion | BIBLE 77:37
who pursue Culture in b. | WHAR 730:5
bandy: b. children nor fasting | BLAKE 114:10
b. civilities with my Sovereign | JOHN 372:27
bane: Deserve the precious b. | MILT 469:5
baneful: b. effects of the spirit | WASH 721:25
bang: B.! Now the animal | DE L 236:4
b. these dogs of Seville | TENN 689:2
b.—went saxpence | PUNCH 531:15
Bertha's got a b. on the boko | MARS 449:6
bigger b. for a buck | ANON 12:17
Not with a b. but a whimper | ELIOT 271:16
bangs: not him thy Harry's | SHAK 580:33
I b. you | SHAK 570:13
banish: b. not him thy Harry's | SHAK 580:33
I b. you | SHAK 570:13
banished: Alone, a b. man | BALL 50:4
my wilful crime art b. | MILT 473:13
Thy brother by decree is b. | SHAK 591:11
banishment: b. of its properly elected | CAIR 175:2
Eating the bitter bread of b. | SHAK 620:2
bank: b. is a place that will | HOPE 345:1
b. mightier than the sword | PLOM 517:11
b. whereon the wild thyme | SHAK 611:19
bitch not worth a B. token | BYRON 173:22
cry all the way to the b. | LIB 421:12
moonlight sleeps upon this b. | SHAK 610:1
pregnant b. swelled up | DONNE 251:24
robbing a b. compared with | BREC 140:5
this b. and shoal of time | SHAK 601:2
banknotes: fill bottles with b. | KEYN 395:9
bankrupt: B. of life, yet prodigal | DRYD 259:2

bankruptcy: blank cheques of intellectual b. | HOLM 342:18
bankrupts: you are b. | TROT 704:13
banks: b. with pionèd and twillèd | SHAK 625:27
bonnie b. o' Loch Lomon' | ANON 17:8
of thanks, letters from b. | AUDEN 35:10
Ye b. and braes o' bonny Doon | BURNS 161:9
banner: b. with the strange device | LONG 426:18
Freedom's b. streaming o'er us | DRAKE 257:13
'Tis the star-spangled b. | KEY 394:15
banners: b. of the king advance | FORT 291:2
b. on the outward walls | SHAK 604:23
Confusion on thy b. wait | GRAY 315:6
terrible as an army with b. | BIBLE 81:21
banquet: b. ceases, and the vision | SHEN 644:12
trifling foolish b. towards | SHAK 622:25
banqueter: like a b. fed full | LUCR 432:4
banqueting: beggar by b. upon borrowing | BIBLE 87:23
banquets: B. abroad by torchlight | MIDD 459:18
banter: how does fortune b. | BOL 117:11
Bantu: [B.] has been subject to | VERW 710:8
baptism: B., and the Supper | BOOK 123:10
B. be administered | BOOK 122:19
Godmothers in my B. | BOOK 123:3
may well be called a b. | ELIOT 268:18
baptize: b. I. with water | BIBLE 96:6
bar: be no moaning of the b. | TENN 680:17
But when was that ever a b. | FROST 295:6
door and b. for thy mouth | BIBLE 87:28
his birth's invidious b. | TENN 683:25
Mute at the b. | CHUR 201:10
treat if met where any b. | HARDY 325:12
When I have crossed the b. | TENN 680:18
Barabbas: At least we withstand B. now | BROW 150:4
crowd will always save B. | COCT 208:12
Now B. was a publisher | CAMP 177:2
Now B. was a robber | BIBLE 97:25
barajar: Digo, paciencia y b. | CERV 188:14
barbarian: He is a b. | SHAW 635:26
uncircumcision, B., Scythian | BIBLE 103:16
barbarians: b. arrive today | CAV 187:7
become of us without the b. | CAV 187:8
distributes itself into B. | ARN 29:7
Greeks, and to the B. | BIBLE 99:15
his young b. all at play | BYRON 169:8
name the former the B. | ARN 29:10
barbaric: b. yawp over roofs | WHIT 732:22
barbarism: b. a permanent characteristic | WEIL 726:14
barbarisms: clear it from colloquial b. | JOHN 369:17
barbarity: b. of tyrants | SMITH 652:24
barbarous: b. dissonance | MILT 464:3
invention of a b. age | MILT 467:17
me with the b. multitude | SHAK 608:16
barbarousness: must confess mine own b. | SIDN 647:10
barber: b.'s chair that fits all | SHAK 564:5
I must to the b.'s | SHAK 612:9
bard: B. triumphant | COWL 221:19
blame not the b. | MOORE 483:8
Hear the voice of the B. | BLAKE 114:4
more fat than b. beseems | THOM 695:18
this goat-footed b. | KEYN 395:7
bards: B. of Passion and of Mirth | KEATS 386:7
b. will not | CRAB 225:13
Lords too are b. | BYRON 172:10
worst of b. confessed | CAT 186:6
bare: Back and side go b. | ANON 14:13
bald as the b. mountain | ARN 29:25
B. like nude, giant girls | SPEN 659:5
B. ruined choirs, where | SHAK 634:6
beauty and love lay b. | SHEL 642:27
left me open, b. | SHAK 626:16
Though I go b., take ye | ANON 14:13
barefaced: bore him b. on the bier | SHAK 578:6
barefoot: b. friars singing | GIBB 302:18
I was born b. | LONG 426:4
that makes shoes go b. | BURT 164:18

bare-headed: grievances b.   MAND 444:5
bareness: old December's b.   SHAK 634:16
bargain: dateless b. to engrossing death
     SHAK 624:9
   fond of her most filthy b.   SHAK 618:12
   Necessity never made a good b.   FRAN 292:15
   never was a better b. driv'n   SIDN 646:14
bargains: Here's the rule for b.   DICK 241:12
   my b., and my well-won   SHAK 607:20
barge: The b. she sat in, like   SHAK 565:5
Baring: taken by Rothschild and B.   GILB 304:18
bark: bleat the b. bellow   BLAKE 111:7
   come out as I do, and b.   JOHN 376:2
   fatal and perfidious b.   MILT 466:6
   see, they b. at me   SHAK 596:19
   That dogs b. at me   SHAK 621:15
   they don't b.   NERV 492:3
   Though his b. cannot be lost   SHAK 600:2
   yond tall anchoring b.   SHAK 597:1
Barkis: B. is willin'   DICK 239:23
barks: Nicean b. of yore   POE 518:9
barley: among the bearded b.   TENN 684:26
   Long fields of b. and of rye   TENN 684:23
   Sitting on a heap of B.   LEAR 414:2
Barlow: Hornby and my B.   THOM 694:16
barmaid: Rocking and shocking the b.
     SITW 648:12
barmaids: Are B. Chaste   MAS 453:5
barn: from the b. and the forge   HOUS 352:11
barnacles: all be turned to b.   SHAK 626:30
barn-cocks: Ere the b. say   HARDY 325:13
barns: nor gather into b.   BIBLE 89:9
baronet: little lily-handed b.   TENN 688:17
Baronetage: took up any book but the B.
     AUST 39:2
barred: spot that's always b.   GILB 305:5
barrel: b. of Malmesey wine   FABY 279:17
   handful of meal in a b.   BIBLE 75:32
   language rhyme is a b.   MAY 455:2
   Oh we ain't got a b. of money   WOODS 742:3
   out of the b. of a gun   MAO 446:1
barrel-organ: kind of human b.   DICK 240:14
barrels: slurp into the b.   FISH 283:7
barreltone: Ben Dollard had a base b.
     JOYCE 382:1
barren: b. and dry land where no   BOOK 128:21
   b. sister all your life   SHAK 610:20
   b. superfluity of words   GARTH 298:15
   b. thing this Conservatism   DISR 248:6
   b. woman to keep house   BOOK 133:7
   Close up these barren leaves   WORD 748:8
   cry, 'tis all b.   STER 664:4
   fall was destined to a b.   JOHN 370:17
   I am but a b. stock   ELIZ 274:16
   Lo, the city is b.   DICK 239:11
   Make b. our lives   SWIN 676:12
   none is b. among them   BIBLE 81:13
barricade: some disputed b.   SEEG 561:18
Barrie: Sir James B.'s cans   GUED 319:9
barrier: escaped the b. of your teeth
     HOMER 343:3
barriers: impenetrable b. of our prison
     EDG 266:13
barrows: b. of the happier dead   TENN 689:12
bars: weary of these worldly b.   SHAK 590:12
Basan: fat bulls of B. close   BOOK 125:11
   Og the king of B.   BOOK 134:15
base: b. of heaven's deep organ   MILT 467:7
   b. that he would prefer   TOCQ 698:10
   had a b. barreltone voice   JOYCE 382:1
   he is a b. and ignoble   BACON 42:24
   keep down the b. in man   TENN 681:25
   Labour without joy is b.   RUSK 550:25
   Or art thou b., common   SHAK 585:21
   scorning the b. degrees   SHAK 590:14
   Things b. and vile   SHAK 611:1
   what b. uses we may return   SHAK 578:24
   Why bastard? wherefore b.   SHAK 594:26
baseless: b. fabric of this vision   SHAK 625:28
basely: spend that shortness b.   SHAK 582:2
baseness: child of ignorance and b.
     BACON 43:29

baseness: (cont.):
   Detraction is but b.' varlet   JONS 378:24
baser: lewd fellows of the b. sort   BIBLE 98:27
basest: b. of all things   FAUL 281:2
bashful: maiden of b. fifteen   SHER 645:18
   Plato for a b. young potato   GILB 305:17
bashfulness: in England a particular b.
     ADD 4:18
   necessary to surmount his b.   WALP 720:9
basia: Da mi b. mille   CAT 186:1
basil-pot: To steal my B. away   KEATS 388:4
basin: Stare, stare in the b.   AUDEN 34:4
Basingstoke: hidden meaning—like B.
     GILB 306:19
Bass: Guiness, Allsopp, B.!   CALV 175:12
bassoon: he heard the loud b.   COL 210:20
bastard: b. children than war's   SHAK 570:18
   b.! He doesn't exist   BECK 57:14
   putting all my eggs in one b.   PARK 506:21
   Well, we knocked the b. off   HILL 338:16
   Why b.? wherefore base   SHAK 594:26
bastardizing: firmament twinkled on my b.
     SHAK 595:2
bastards: b. at the monastery   PINT 514:17
   Don't let the b. grind   ANON 16:19
   he who begets twenty b.   WALP 719:19
   Now, gods, stand up for b.   SHAK 595:1
   Which some call nature's b.   SHAK 632:1
bastion: His eye-ball—like a b.'s mole
     SMART 650:1
bat: b. that flits at close   BLAKE 111:3
   beetle and the b.   JOHN 373:4
   Ere the b. hath flown   SHAK 603:4
   For the black b., night   TENN 606:17
   mind is like a b.   WILB 734:5
   On the b.'s back I do fly   SHAK 626:2
   Twinkle, twinkle, little b.   CARR 182:7
   where the weak-eyed b.   COLL 213:11
   Wool of b., and tongue of dog   SHAK 603:18
bated: With b. breath, and whispering
     SHAK 608:1
bath: I test my b. before I sit   NASH 490:19
   like a nymph to the b.   SHEL 642:27
   sore labour's b.   SHAK 602:2
   Then bring my b., and strew   ROCH 543:1
   who can ever be tired of B.   AUST 38:22
bathe: in reeking wounds   SHAK 599:16
   b. those beauteous feet   FLET 287:24
   there b. in his tears   DONNE 253:2
bathing: caught the Whigs b.   DISR 246:18
   large b. machine and a   GILB 304:15
   long b. of a summer's day   WORD 746:19
bathroom: church as he goes to the b.
     BLYT 116:9
   revolutionary in a b.   LINK 423:5
baths: sunset, and the b.   TENN 690:4
   Two walking b.; two weeping   CRAS 226:12
baton: cartridge-pouch the marshal's b.
     LOUI 428:17
bats: B. not angels, in the high   THOM 694:9
   b. will squeak and wheel   NIC 494:14
   b. with baby faces   ELIOT 273:13
   like bats amongst birds   BACON 44:31
batsman: b. and the bat   LANG 408:15
battalions: not of the heavy b.   VOLT 716:20
   your dreams in pale b. go   SORL 656:17
batten: And b. on this moor   SHAK 577:12
battening: B. upon huge seaworms
     TENN 684:20
batter: B. my heart   DONNE 250:24
Battery: but the B.'s down   COMD 214:11
battle: And drunk delight of b.   TENN 690:1
   b. fares like to the morning's   SHAK 587:29
   B., n. A method of untying   BIER 109:6
   b. sees the other's umbered   SHAK 585:14
   b. there was which I saw   MCL 439:11
   b. to the strong   DAV 231:22
   better in b. than in bed   STER 665:1
   brave that die in the b.   CLOU 207:6
   day long the noise of b.   TENN 682:18
   die well that die in a b.   SHAK 586:4
   even the Lord mighty in b.   BOOK 129:14
   first blow is half the b.   GOLD 311:26

battle: (cont.):
   foremost in b. was Mary   BALL 50:2
   France has lost a b.   DE G 234:28
   from b. and murder   BOOK 119:17
   into the midst of the b.   VIRG 712:21
   my tongue, the glorious b.   FORT 291:1
   Next to a b. lost   WELL 727:10
   nor the b. to the strong   BIBLE 80:21
   No war, or b.'s sound   MILT 467:3
   possibly happen to one in a b.   CARR 183:4
   prepare himself to the b.   BIBLE 101:2
   See the front o' b. lour   BURNS 163:1
   shake our soul with b.-din   SORL 656:18
   shall have borne the b.   LINC 422:9
   smelleth the b. afar off   BIBLE 77:39
   strife is o'er, the b. done   POTT 525:9
   that it is a field of b.   STEV 668:5
   that out of b. I escaped   OWEN 503:18
   There was a b. fought of late   HAR 326:10
   they make them ready to b.   BOOK 133:22
   We were defeated in a great b.   LIVY 423:13
   When the b.'s lost and won   SHAK 599:13
battledore: B. and shuttlecock   DICK 243:10
battlefield: b. is heart of man   DOST 254:3
battle-flags: b. were furled   TENN 685:11
battlements: came and perched on b.
     BEER 59:17
   Climb down from the white b.   HEAT 330:1
   fixed his head upon our b.   SHAK 599:15
   From the hid b. of Eternity   THOM 695:6
battles: And b. long ago   WORD 748:4
   b. and death   GAR 298:1
   B. and sex are the only   MCAR 434:1
   b. are lost in the same   WHIT 732:16
   b. of all subsequent wars   ORW 500:7
   b., sieges, fortunes   SHAK 615:1
   Dead b., like dead generals   TUCH 704:23
   mother of b.   HUSS 357:4
   O God of b.! steel my soldiers'   SHAK 586:9
   that I have fought his b.   BUNY 156:16
battu: de s'être bien b.   COUR 220:4
bauble: Pleased with this b.   POPE 522:16
   prettiest b. you ever saw   WALP 719:3
baubles: Take away these b.   CROM 227:11
Baum: des Lebens goldner B.   GOET 309:5
bavin: jesters and rash b.   SHAK 581:13
bawcock: The king's a b.   SHAK 585:22
bawdy: Bloody, b. villain   SHAK 575:12
   Susanna's music touched the b.   STEV 666:9
   While b. questions went about   MAS 453:4
bawdy-house: pretence of keeping a b.
     JOHN 375:16
bawling: b. what it likes   ARN 29:11
bay: dog, and b. the moon   SHAK 593:1
   steamer breaking from the b.   AUDEN 35:2
baying: b. for broken glass   WAUGH 723:11
bayonet: b. is a weapon with a worker
     ANON 12:10
bayonets: Chains worse than b.   JERR 366:4
   sods with our b. turning   WOLFE 740:25
   throne of b.   INGE 359:18
Bayonne: thy hams, B.!   POPE 519:9
bays: Have I no b. to crown it   HERB 334:11
   palm, the oak, or b.   MARV 450:5
   sprig of b. in fifty years   SWIFT 674:31
bay-tree: flourishing like a green b.
     BOOK 126:21
bazaar: Fate's great b.   MACN 441:3
be: As if it could not b.   SHEL 640:19
   b. as they are or not   CLEM 206:9
   b. the people never so   BOOK 131:5
   better to b. than not to be   AUCT 33:18
   Let b. be finale of seem   STEV 665:18
   poem should not mean but b.   MACL 439:10
   that which shall b.   BIBLE 80:1
   To b., or not to be   SHAK 575:18
   What from this day I shall b.   PRIOR 529:8
   what we cannot b.   WILB 734:6
beach: Along the hidden b.   KIPL 401:3
   walk upon the b.   ELIOT 272:6
beached: b. verge of the salt flood   SHAK 626:21
beaches: laying upon b.   QU FARQ
   We shall fight on the b.   CHUR 202:11

Beachy Head: Birmingham by way of B.
  CHES 199:5
beacon: b.-light is quenched in smoke
  SCOTT 560:1
beacons: b. of wise men HUXL 358:11
beaded: b. bubbles winking KEATS 389:9
beadroll: On Fame's eternal b. SPEN 660:12
beadsman: B., after thousand aves
  KEATS 387:13
  b. now that was your knight PEELE 511:5
beak: He takes in his b. MERR 458:14
  thy b. from out my heart POE 518:8
beaker: b. full of the warm South KEATS 389:9
Beale: Miss Buss and Miss B. ANON 16:11
be-all: b. and the end-all SHAK 601:2
beam: b. me up, Scotty RODD 543:22
  b. that is in thine own BIBLE 89:15
beaming: Leading onward, b. bright DIX 249:19
beamish: b. nephew, beware CARR 184:4
  Come to my arms, my b. boy CARR 182:19
beams: And tricks his b. MILT 466:13
  b. of his chambers BOOK 132:6
bean: Nine b. rows will I have YEATS 752:7
  home of the b. and the cod BOSS 137:1
  not too French French b. GILB 305:17
beanflowers: With the b.' boon BROW 149:13
bear: And b. the palm alone SHAK 590:2
  B. of Very Little Brain MILNE 462:11
  b. than you dare execute SHAK 587:21
  b. thee in their hands BOOK 131:4
  B. them we can, and if HOUS 351:18
  b. the yoke in his youth BIBLE 85:18
  B. up FORS 290:17
  b. up the pillars of it BOOK 130:4
  b. with a sore head MARR 449:3
  bush supposed a b. SHAK 612:17
  Cannot b. very much reality ELIOT 270:15
  Exit, pursued by a b. SHAK 631:23
  fire was furry as a b. SITW 648:10
  fitted by nature a b. AUR 37:17
  Grizzly B. is huge and wild HOUS 351:5
  huntsman by the b. WALL 718:8
  like the rugged Russian b. SHAK 603:11
  No dancing b. was so genteel COWP 222:16
  rather b. those ills we have SHAK 575:16
  so b. ourselves CHUR 202:12
  still less the b. FRERE 293:16
  We must b. all SHAK 586:6
  Who rode on the back of a b. LEAR 414:7
  wounded spirit who can b. BIBLE 79:2
  ye cannot b. them now BIBLE 97:19
bearable: makes life b. SHAW 636:32
bear-baiting: Puritan hated b. MAC 435:19
bear-baitings: fairs, and b. SHAK 631:27
beard: b. and blows it in my face SHAK 575:11
  b. of formal cut SHAK 568:16
  by the colour of his b. SHAK 629:9
  endure a husband with a b. SHAK 613:12
  grey b. and glittering eye COL 210:18
  hair, send thee a b. SHAK 630:7
  icicle on a Dutchman's b. SHAK 630:14
  I have a b. coming SHAK 611:7
  King of Spain's B. DRAKE 257:10
  Loose his b., and hoary hair GRAY 315:7
  There was an Old Man with a b. LEAR 413:18
  To pluck me by the b. SHAK 596:20
  with white and bristly b. SHAK 633:4
  womman hath no b. CHAU 194:1
bearded: b. like the pard SHAK 568:16
beards: their long b., and pretences
  SWIFT 674:22
  'Tis merry in hall when b. SHAK 584:10
bearer: b. of this letter ASHF 31:11
beareth: B. all things BIBLE 101:1
  that b. up things light BACON 44:13
bearing: b. down on me now JOYCE 381:8
bearings: b. of this observation DICK 240:20
bears: And dancing dogs and b. HODG 340:16
  b. might come with buns ISH 360:21
  jolly to call out, 'B. MILNE 462:16
  tap crude rhythms for b. FLAU 285:16
  Teddy B. have their Picnic BRAT 140:1

beast: A beast, but a just b. ANON 12:11
  And what rough b., its hour YEATS 753:2
  b. is deed he hath no peyne CHAU 193:18
  b. or a fool alone KILV 396:7
  b. so fierce but knows SHAK 621:17
  B. stands for strong mutually WAUGH 723:20
  b. to the truly genteel HARDY 324:10
  b. who is always spoiling MAC 435:26
  b. with many heads SHAK 570:16
  be either a b. or a god ARIS 25:16
  before he caught the b. WALL 718:8
  count the number of the b. BIBLE 107:1
  Feeds b. as man SHAK 564:14
  I have a b. on my back DOUG 255:10
  life of his b. BIBLE 78:25
  making the b. with two backs SHAK 614:24
  Man's life is cheap as b.'s SHAK 595:16
  more subtil than any b. BIBLE 70:8
  night out for man or b. FIEL 282:22
  or the name of the b. BIBLE 106:32
  people call this b. to mind BELL 60:22
  preeminence above a b. BIBLE 80:6
  serpent subtlest b. MILT 472:19
  solitude is either a wild b. BACON 43:20
  Some evil b. hath devoured BIBLE 71:23
  splendorous *blond b.* NIET 495:17
  was Beauty killed the B. CREE 226:17
  Who is like unto the b. BIBLE 106:31
  worship the b. and his image BIBLE 107:4
beastie: cow'rin', tim'rous b. BURNS 163:15
beasties: long-leggety b. ANON 13:12
beastly: How b. the bourgeois LAWR 412:14
  let's be b. to the Germans COW 220:9
beasts: b. and four and twenty BIBLE 106:14
  b. of the field drink thereof BOOK 132:7
  b. of the forest are mine BOOK 128:2
  b. of the forest do move BOOK 132:9
  be compared unto the b. BOOK 127:24
  elders and the four b. BIBLE 106:19
  fought with b. at Ephesus BIBLE 101:9
  four b. full of eyes before BIBLE 106:10
  like brute b. that have BOOK 123:16
  man is of kin to the b. BACON 42:24
  manner of four-footed b. BIBLE 98:19
beat: b. down Satan under our BOOK 119:20
  b. generation KER 394:12
  b. him when he sneezes CARR 182:5
  b. my people to pieces BIBLE 82:12
  b. the ground MILT 463:18
  b. their swords into plowshares BIBLE 82:11
  b. them to-day or Molly STARK 662:12
  B. wild on this world's shore NORT 497:1
  beauty b. on his conceits MARL 448:4
  could b. three Frenchmen ADD 4:15
  dread b. pulsing fire JOHN 366:16
  enemies have b. us to the pit SHAK 593:21
  So we b. on, boats against FITZ 285:4
  They beat—and a Voice in THOM 695:2
  Two hearts that b. as one HALM 322:7
  waves that b. on heaven BLAKE 111:7
beaten: b. road SHEL 640:10
  No Englishman is ever fairly b. SHAW 638:22
  Thrice was I b. with rods BIBLE 102:1
beateth: one that b. the air BIBLE 100:31
beating: b. in void his luminous ARN 29:21
  b. myself for spite SIDN 646:15
  Charity and b. begins at home FLET 287:23
  glory of b. the French WOLFE 741:2
  Greeks take the b. HOR 348:2
  hear the b. of his wings BRIG 141:6
  hearts b. each to each BROW 151:7
  Is b. on the door YEATS 751:21
  not mend his pace with b. SHAK 578:18
  than driven by b. ASCH 30:18
beatings: dread of b. BETJ 68:8
Beatles: And the B.' first LP LARK 409:12
beats: B. with light wing MORR 485:11
  Counting the slow heart b. GRAV 314:19
  light which b. upon a throne TENN 681:16
Beattock: Pulling up B. AUDEN 35:9
beatum: *Parte b.* HOR 349:20
  possit facere et servare b. HOR 348:7

beatum: (cont.):
  Recte b.: rectius occupat HOR 350:19
beatus: *B. ille, qui procul negotiis* HOR 348:22
  B. vir qui timet Dominum BIBLE 108:1
Beaumont: and rare B. lie BASSE 56:2
beaut: make a mistake, it's a b. LA G 405:16
beauteous: All b. things for which we live
  CORY 220:2
  B. the fleet before the gale SMART 650:3
  How b. mankind is! SHAK 626:3
  I see from far thy b. light WESL 728:16
  Of all that is most b. WORD 744:18
  Of b. and sublime AKEN 6:4
beauties: B. in vain their pretty POPE 523:31
  b. there as proud as here SIDN 646:17
  By their own b. SHAK 623:16
  concealed b. of a writer ADD 4:12
  gazed new b. met my sight THOM 695:22
  mar their b. bright SPEN 660:24
  Of common b. lived unknown CAREW 179:6
  saved by b. not his own POPE 518:16
  unripened b. of the north ADD 3:18
  When many b. grace a poem HOR 347:16
  Ye b.! O how great the sum SMART 649:15
  You meaner b. of the night WOTT 749:2
beautified: 'b.' is a vile phrase SHAK 574:14
  b. with his presence BOOK 123:16
beautiful: All things bright and b. ALEX 8:9
  b. and damned FITZ 284:21
  b. and death-struck year HOUS 352:16
  b. and ineffectual angel ARN 29:21
  b. and simple as all truly HENRY 333:3
  b. and the clever GREE 316:22
  b. and therefore SHAK 587:13
  b. and what may not VEBL 709:17
  b. are thy feet with shoes BIBLE 82:1
  b. cannot be the way COUS 220:6
  B. comical things HARV 327:23
  b. does not lead to extravagance PER 512:22
  B. dreamer, wake unto me FOST 291:11
  b. God to behold SWIN 676:20
  b. is all this visible BYRON 172:1
  B., one a gazelle YEATS 752:2
  b. things in the world RUSK 550:24
  b. upon the mountains BIBLE 84:8
  be b. than to be good WILDE 735:20
  Black is b. ANON 12:18
  deal of scorn looks b. SHAK 630:12
  Death is b. It alone gives ANOU 23:7
  entirely b. AUDEN 35:5
  Gently they go, the b. MILL 461:6
  His darkness b. with thee TENN 683:27
  innocent and b. YEATS 752:3
  it comes up more b. HOR 350:13
  joyous, b. and free SHEL 642:20
  not feel, how b. they are COL 209:12
  'Oh, how b.!' and sitting KIPL 399:7
  or believe to be b. MORR 485:16
  Ordinary made b. SHAF 563:19
  perpetual hunger to be b. RHYS 539:19
  see how b. I am HUGH 354:1
  slaying of a b. hypothesis HUXL 358:3
  When a woman isn't b. CHEK 197:7
  which indeed appear b. BIBLE 92:6
  will always make it b. CONS 217:23
  world was really b. CHEK 196:10
beauty: American b. rose can ROCK 543:20
  And a little b. WEBS 725:16
  And all that b. GRAY 315:13
  A terrible b. is born YEATS 751:15
  A thing of b. GILB 306:8
  be a b. without a fortune FARQ 280:12
  b. and a boy forever ROWL 549:19
  Beauty—B. that must die KEATS 389:7
  B. both so ancient AUG 37:2
  b. calls and glory leads LEE 416:3
  b. coming and the beauty WORD 745:5
  B. crieth in an attic BUTL 167:11
  b. draws us with a single POPE 523:21
  b. faded has no second PHIL 514:3
  B. for some provides escape HUXL 357:21
  b. in the works of a great ADD 5:1
  B. is all very well at first SHAW 637:19

beauty: (*cont.*):
B. is bought by judgement   SHAK 598:10
B. is but a flower   NASHE 491:1
B. is momentary in the mind   STEV 666:8
b. is mysterious as well   DOST 254:3
B. is Nature's brag   MILT 464:8
B. is Nature's coin   MILT 464:7
B. is no quality in things   HUME 355:16
b. is only sin deep   SAKI 553:10
B. [is that] at which a novelist   FORS 290:5
B. is the first test   HARDY 324:4
b. is the joy of possessing   PAST 508:6
B. is the lover's gift   CONG 215:34
b. is the mind diseased   BYRON 169:5
B. is truth, truth beauty   KEATS 389:3
B. itself doth of itself   SHAK 632:21
b. lives though lilies   FLEC 286:9
b. making beautiful old   SHAK 634:17
b. of inflections   STEV 666:12
b. of Israel is slain upon   BIBLE 75:8
b. of the good old cause   WORD 746:10
b. saith my sufferings   MARL 448:3
B.'s conquest of your face   AUDEN 35:3
B.'s ensign yet   SHAK 624:8
B. she was statue cold   FLEC 286:6
b. should never be half   KEATS 391:15
b.'s rose might never die   SHAK 632:26
b. that we should desire   BIBLE 84:11
B. took from those   DE L 236:2
B. too rich for use   SHAK 622:24
b. unadorned   BEHN 60:16
b. what could be more beaut-   CUMM 228:6
b. will be soon resolved   MARL 447:20
B. will not come   EMER 276:20
B., wit, high birth   SHAK 627:22
best part of b.   BACON 42:26
body's b. lives   STEV 666:8
But b.'s self she is   ANON 16:14
But b. vanishes; beauty passes   DE L 236:1
by b. and by fear   WORD 746:20
conscious stone to b. grew   EMER 276:11
deep trenches in thy b.'s   SHAK 633:1
delves the parallels in b.'s   SHAK 633:21
dreamed that life was b.   HOOP 344:16
England, home and b.   ARN 30:11
eternal image of true b.   ROUS 549:3
Exuberance is b.   BLAKE 112:27
fatal gift of b.   BYRON 169:2
fathers-forth whose b.   HOPK 345:20
For b. lives with kindness   SHAK 631:8
For in your b.'s orient deep   CAREW 179:11
ghosts of B. glide   POPE 520:11
He hath a daily b. in his life   SHAK 618:3
Helen's b. in a brow of Egypt   SHAK 612:17
Helen, thy b. is to me   POE 518:9
Her b. fed my common earth   MAS 453:4
horror and its b. are divine   SHEL 642:2
Individual b. from   AUDEN 35:5
issuing forth into b.   HUNT 356:19
June for b.'s heightening   ARN 28:25
Lord in the b. of holiness   BOOK 131:11
Lord in the b. of holiness   MONS 480:2
Losing both b. and utility   SHAK 586:17
loved the principle of b.   KEATS 392:13
March with b.   SHAK 632:4
more doth b. beauteous seem   SHAK 633:17
nature I quested for b.   SMART 649:10
near your b. with my nails   SHAK 587:17
No b. she doth miss   ANON 16:14
not befriended us with b.   CAV 187:13
Of b. from the light retired   WALL 718:10
principal b. in building   FULL 296:7
proportions we just b.   JONS 379:21
relationship with b. and truth   KEATS 391:9
seizes as b. must be truth   KEATS 391:5
She walks in b., like the night   BYRON 173:3
simple b. and naught else   BROW 149:24
simply order and b.   BAUD 55:9
smoothly with thy b.'s   CAMP 177:8
Sure b.'s empires, like   SUCK 671:10
That b. is not as fond   SPEN 660:19
that b. is woman's sceptre   WOLL 741:16
that b. shall consume   BOOK 139:1

beauty: (*cont.*):
there is no excellent b.   BACON 42:27
thick, bereft of b.   SHAK 624:22
thing of b. is a joy for   KEATS 386:13
thought that where B. was   GALS 297:5
Thy b. shall no more be found   MARV 451:3
'Tisn't b., so to speak   KIPL 402:12
truth, but supreme b.   RUSS 551:20
unmask her b. to the moon   SHAK 573:1
unto them b. for ashes   BIBLE 84:27
up into b. like a reed   LEWES 420:12
was beautiful—her b. made   SHEL 644:1
was B. killed the Beast   CREE 226:17
Where b. has no ebb   YEATS 752:9
Where perhaps some b. lies   MILT 465:11
with him is b. slain   SHAK 635:14
with this rage shall b.   SHAK 634:3
witty b. is a power   MER 457:17
Would cloud our b.   WINC 739:1
write the b. of your eyes   SHAK 633:5
Yet b., though injurious   MILT 474:10
Your infant b. could beget   SEDL 561:13
beaver: And cultivate a b.   HUXL 357:7
Cock up your b.   HOGG 341:15
young Harry, with his b.   SHAK 581:20
Beaverbrook: mind was that of Lord B.   ATTL 32:14
becalmed: As ships, b. at eve   CLOU 207:22
because: B. I do not hope to turn again   ELIOT 270:5
B. it's there   MALL 443:2
B. it was he; b. it was me   MONT 480:19
B. we're here   ANON 19:8
smashed it into b.   CUMM 228.13
think him so b. I think him   SHAK 631:2
We cannot do it, Sir, b.   CARR 183:15
beckon: The morning b.   THOM 693:12
becks: b., and wreathèd smiles   MILT 465:5
become: all that may b. a man   SHAK 601:6
What shall, alas! b. of me   LYLY 433:9
What shall b. of me   ANDR 11:11
becomes: nothing so. b. a man   SHAK 585:7
bed: And I in my b. again   ANON 19:14
and's newly gone to b.   MILT 467:16
And so to b.   PEPYS 512:3
Are the weans in their b.   MILL 462:3
bath, and strew my b.   ROCH 543:1
b. and procreant cradle   SHAK 601:1
b. at night, a chest   GOLD 310:15
b. at the same time   RAPH 536:17
b. be blest that I lie   ANON 16:9
b. for this huge birth   CRAS 226:7
B. in the bush with stars   STEV 669:4
b. I sought him whom   BIBLE 81:12
b. of Ware in England   SHAK 630:15
b. resting up from   RUNY 550:4
b. thou liest on despair   LYLY 433:12
b. with me and she said   ALLEN 9:14
b. with my catamite when   BURG 156:20
better in battle than in b.   STER 665:1
black passage up to b.   STEV 668:17
But me he mostly sent to b.   LAND 408:7
deck both b. and bower   SPEN 660:6
Down as upon a b.   MARV 450:15
dull, stale, tired b.   SHAK 594:26
Every b. is narrow   MILL 461:10
found in adulterous b.   BLAKE 111:18
from their lowly b.   GRAY 315:12
gooseberried double b.   THOM 693:17
grave as little as my b.   KEN 393:8
Has found out thy b.   BLAKE 114:12
His b. amidst my tender breast   LODGE 425:23
I drunk him to his b.   SHAK 565:13
I have to go to b. by day   STEV 668:13
In going to my naked b.   EDW 267:11
I should of stood in b.   JAC 361:7
I toward thy b.   FLEC 286:16
kick his wife out of b.   SURT 672:9
kneels at the foot of the b.   MILNE 462:18
migrations from the blue b.   GOLD 311:30
mind is not a b. to be made   AGATE 5:14
mother, make my b. soon   BALL 50:11
Must we to b. indeed   STEV 668:17

bed: (*cont.*):
My b. it is the cold   BALL 49:4
nor a goddess to b.   VIRG 715:2
not a b. of roses   STEV 668:5
Now can we go to b.   COPE 218:10
O mother, mother, make my b.   BALL 48:22
On a b. of daffodil sky   TENN 686:17
out for my b. and board   LOW 430:24
Out on the lawn I lie in b.   AUDEN 35:13
pluck me from my naked b.   KYD 404:10
Rise, take up thy b., and walk   BIBLE 96:19
stay in b. all day   BENC 62:10
sweat of an enseamèd b.   SHAK 577:15
That's why I go to b. early   WAUGH 723:13
This b. thy centre   DONNE 252:18
thy cold b.   KING 396:11
Tomnoddy went home to b.   BARH 52:11
Up to b.   DE L 236:5
used to go to b. early   PROU 530:6
wash I my b.   BOOK 124:18
we must all go to b.   HENS 333:9
When boys go first to b.   HERB 335:12
wife my second best b.   SHAK 635:16
bedding: Of the straw for a b.   BELL 62:1
bedevilment: man's b. and God's   HOUS 351:20
bedfellows: acquaints a man with strange b.   SHAK 625:18
bedlam: B. vision produced by   BYRON 174:8
with a sigh like Tom o' B.   SHAK 595:3
bedroom: b. as long as you don't frighten   CAMP 176:5
French widow in every b.   HOFF 341:13
Stranger, unless with b. eyes   AUDEN 35:16
beds: bearers weeping to their b.   CHAK 621:5
Minds like b. always made up   WILL 737:10
rejoice in their b.   BOOK 135:16
We have beat them to their b.   SHAK 566:2
bedside: very good b. manner   PUNCH 532:1
bed-staff: twinkling of a b.   SHAD 563:17
bed-time: I would it were b.   SHAK 581:30
bee: b. in conversation   JOHN 371:7
b. of sorrow had stung   BABEL 41:11
b.'s kiss, now   BROW 150:13
butterfly, sting like a b.   ALI 9:6
honeysuckle, I am the b.   FITZ 283:8
How doth the little busy b.   WATTS 722:12
Love in my bosom like a b.   LODGE 425:23
Where the b. sucks   SHAK 626:2
While the b. with honied thigh   MILT 464:25
beechen: plot of b. green   KEATS 389:8
beech-tree: cover of the spreading b.   VIRG 714:11
beef: am a great eater of b.   SHAK 628:12
Oh! The roast b. of England   FIEL 282:2
piece of b. and mustard   SHAK 624:18
beefsteak: as English an article as a b.   HAWT 328:8
beefy: As b. ATS   BETJ 67:10
bee-loud: live alone in the b. glade   YEATS 752:7
Beelzebub: B. called for his syllabub   SITW 648:12
bee-mouth: poison while the b.   KEATS 389:7
been: grief, as if it had not b.   SHEL 639:18
Thou hast b., shalt be, art   ARN 27:10
beer: B. and Britannia   SMITH 653:27
b. and skittles   CALV 175:13
chronicle small b.   SHAK 615:18
drink beer will think b.   IRV 360:16
felony to drink small b.   SHAK 587:23
I'm only a b. teetotaller   SHAW 636:4
I'm only here for the b.   LEV 419:16
like thine inspirer, B.   POPE 518:21
me to desire small b.   SHAK 583:5
muddy ecstasies of b.   CRAB 224:24
O B.! O Hodgson   CALV 175:12
torrent of gin and b.   GLAD 307:9
beerier: don't drink and get b.   LAWR 412:12
Beersheba: Dan even to B.   BIBLE 74:23
from Dan to B.   STER 664:4
bees: b. each with own function   VIRG 715:19
b. make honey not for yourselves   VIRG 715:20
half a number of b.   LONG 428:6

bellies: eyes bigger than their b.	VANB 708:7
such as for their b.' sake	MILT 466:8
bellman: B., perplexed	CARR 184:3
shrieked, the fatal b.	SHAK 601:15
Bellona: B.'s bridegroom	SHAK 599:17
bellows: My b. too have lost	ANON 16:16
bell-rope: b. that gathers God	CRANE 225:17
bells: b. and fire off pistols	MANN 445:1
b. brings back her old	JOHN 367:2
b. of Hell go ting-a-ling-a-ling	ANON 17:1
b. ringeth to evensong	HAWES 328:3
broke into a mist with b.	BROW 151:23
Camberley, heavy with b.	BETJ 68:7
Church-b. beyond the stars	HERB 335:13
From the b., bells	POE 518:3
Like sweet b. jangled	SHAK 576:4
lin-lan-lone of evening b.	TENN 681:3
near, the b. I hear	WHIT 732:6
Ring out, wild b.	TENN 684:10
so floating many b. down	CUMM 228:5
They now ring the b.	WALP 720:13
'Twould ring the b. of Heaven	HODG 340:16
with a tower and b.	CRAB 224:19
would ring the b. of Ecstasy	GINS 306:27
belly: b. God send thee good ale	ANON 14:13
b. will hardly mind anything	JOHN 372:19
filled his b. with the husks	BIBLE 95:3
his b. is as bright ivory	BIBLE 81:20
decreasing leg, increasing b.	SHAK 582:20
it was in Jonadge's b.	DICK 241:23
my b. was bitter	BIBLE 106:28
O wombe! O b.!	CHAU 194:10
Pee, po, b., bum, drawers	FLAN 285:11
something of a round b.	SHAK 582:21
thy b. is like an heap	BIBLE 82:2
wears his wit in his b.	SHAK 627:12
Whose God is their b.	BIBLE 103:10
bellyful: Rumble thy b.!	SHAK 595:21
bellyfuls: dainties, we want b.	GASK 299:5
belly-tension: b. between a man	GIBB 302:25
Belmont: In B. is a lady richly	SHAK 607:10
belong: about b. to it as well	WHYTE 733:14
B. TO ANY CLUB THAT WILL	MARX 451:16
that is where we really b.	GREE 316:25
To betray, you must first b.	PHIL 514:1
yet they b. not to you	GIBR 303:2
belongs: Where it b.	ALD 8:4
beloved: And 'tis b. of many	CHAL 189:1
b. come into his garden	BIBLE 81:16
b. knows nought that knows	SHAK 627:5
beloved more than another b.	BIBLE 81:18
bourn how far to be b.	SHAK 564:13
Cry, the b. country	PATON 509:15
Dearly b., we are gathered	BOOK 123:15
it is the voice of my b.	BIBLE 81:17
My b. is mine, and I am	BIBLE 81:11
My b. is white and ruddy	BIBLE 81:19
O Daniel, a man greatly b.	BIBLE 86:2
Shall never be b. by men	BLAKE 111:4
suspenders, Best B.	KIPL 402:1
This is my b., and this	BIBLE 81:20
This is my b. Son, in whom	BIBLE 88:17
below: above, between, b.	DONNE 250:16
b. the dignity of history	MAC 435:15
By him one step b.	SHAK 627:9
that love is a thing b.	STER 665:4
there is nobody b. decks	BARN 53:9
Thy element's b.	SHAK 595:14
belt: can't see a b. without	ASQ 32:4
belted: b. you and flayed you	KIPL 399:10
Belvoir: B.'s lordly terraces	MAC 436:2
Ben Bolt: sweet Alice, B.	ENGL 277:24
bench: drowsy b. protect	CRAB 225:16
bend: B. what is stiff	LANG 409:9
I b. and I break not	LA F 405:9
sidelong would she b. and sing	KEATS 388:11
Will b. to favour ev'ry client	GAY 300:5
bending: always be a b. downwards	WHEW 730:14
bends: That b. not as I tread	MILT 464:11
bene: Boner bene, for b.	SHAK 599:3
beneath: B. in the flood	SHAK 601:6

beneath: (cont.):	
some springing from b.	BACON 42:2
benedicite: B., omnia opera	BIBLE 108:8
benediction: clouds in b.	DAY-L 233:6
Perpetual b.	WORD 746:2
benedictus: B. qui venit in nomine patri	MISS 477:2
benefactor: first great b.	TWAIN 706:19
benefit: b. of the students	SMITH 651:3
benefits: As b. forgot	SHAK 568:17
forget not all his b.	BOOK 132:2
benevolence: b. of mankind	BAG 47:13
b. of the butcher	SMITH 650:17
b. of the passive order	MER 458:3
benevolent: Emporium of B. Knowledge	BORG 136:8
benight: b. our happiest day	DONNE 252:1
benighted: B. walks under the midday sun	MILT 463:27
pore b. 'eathen	KIPL 399:5
benign: under that b. sky	BRON 142:19
benison: For a b. to fall	HERR 336:5
Benjamin: tribe of B.	BIBLE 103:7
bent: b. to make some port	ARN 28:23
fool me to the top of my b.	SHAK 576:24
benumbed: feel b., and wish to be no more	BYRON 172:14
bereaved: black as if b. of light	BLAKE 114:1
would be b. if snobbery	UST 707:14
bereft: b. of wet and wildness	HOPK 345:15
Beresford: [Lord Charles B.]	CHUR 201:24
bergers: b. et des bouchers	VOLT 716:19
Berkeley: B. destroyed this world	SMITH 652:26
When Bishop B. said	BYRON 171:19
Berliner: Ich bin ein B.	KENN 304:6
Bermoothes: still-vexed B.	SHAK 625:4
Bermudas: remote B. ride	MARV 449:18
Bernard: B. always had a few prayers	ASHF 31:7
B. the monk ne saugh nat	CHAU 194:29
berries: b. moulded on one stem	SHAK 612:3
b. ripen in the wilderness	STEV 666:11
I come to pluck your b.	MILT 465:20
rowan b. red as blood	BLOK 115:3
berry: could have made a better b.	BUTL 167:12
O sweeter than the b.	GAY 299:9
berth: happened in his b.	HOOD 343:20
beryl: rings set with the b.	BIBLE 81:20
beseech: I pray and b. you	BOOK 118:6
We b. thee to hear us	BOOK 119:19
beset: b. by hardships	ATKI 32:13
beside: thou art b. thyself	BIBLE 99:10
thousand shall fall b.	BOOK 131:3
besiege: forty winters shall b.	SHAK 633:1
best: All is b., though we oft doubt	MILT 474:19
Always to be b.	HOMER 343:5
And so much bad in the b.	ANON 18:13
art the b. is good enough	GOET 309:10
bad's the b. of us	FLET 287:14
best administered is b.	POPE 522:17
b. and the worst of this	SWIN 676:24
b. chosen language	AUST 38:21
b. days of life slip away	VIRG 715:16
b. ends by the best means	HUTC 357:5
b. in this kind	SHAK 612:25
b. is the best	QUIL 534:9
b. is the enemy of the good	VOLT 716:6
b. is yet to be	BROW 152:6
b. lack all conviction	YEATS 753:1
b. of all possible worlds	CAB 174:12
b. of all possible worlds	VOLT 716:1
b. part of beauty	BACON 42:26
b. that is known and thought	ARN 29:17
B., of thought	BROW 150:18
b. way out is always through	FROST 295:12
company, that is the b.	AUST 39:5
doth seldom choose the b.	RAL 535:12
Fear not to touch the b.	RAL 535:15
It was the b. of times	DICK 244:1
lamentable change is from the b.	SHAK 596:23
nast all prizing, b.	KIPL 398:14
poetry — the b. words	COL 217:8

best: (cont.):	
record of the b.	SHEL 644:7
Sat we two, one another's b.	DONNE 251:24
Send forth the b. ye breed	KIPL 401:11
than any other person's b.	HAZL 329:10
Thou art tired; b. be still	ARN 27:11
virtuousest, discreetest, b.	MILT 472:15
where the b. is like	KIPL 400:3
which is the b. and soundest	DOYLE 256:16
wisest and justest and b.	PLATO 516:12
beste: der Kunst ist das B.	GOET 309:10
Inglissh in makyng was the b.	LYDG 433:3
Bestie: schweifende blonde B.	NIET 495:17
bestow: b. on every airth a limb	GRAH 313:14
bestride: b. the narrow world	SHAK 590:3
best seller: b. is gilded tomb	SMITH 652:4
best sellers: in all the great b.	PRIT 529:17
betake: b. myself to that course	PEPYS 512:20
bethel: O God of B., by whose	DODD 250:3
Bethlehem: At B. I had my birth	CART 184:13
B. Ephratah, though thou	BIBLE 86:13
But in B.'s home	ELL 275:8
O come ye, O come ye to B.	ANON 21:18
O Little town of B.	BROO 144:4
Slouches towards B.	YEATS 753:2
betray: All things b. thee	THOM 695:2
b. me to a lingering book	HERB 334:3
b. me to your mirth	FORD 289:14
else she'll b. more men	SHAK 618:5
encourage those who b.	GAY 299:25
guts to b. my country	FORS 290:29
honest trifles, to b.'s	SHAK 600:10
To b., you must first belong	PHIL 514:1
betrayal: b. of Ulster	CAIR 175:2
only defence against b.	WILL 737:1
succeed without any act of b.	REN 538:19
betrayals: b., the diplomatic	WAUGH 723:19
betrayed: b. by what is false within	MER 458:8
Betrothed, betrayer, and b.	SCOTT 560:14
by ourselves, b.	CONG 215:20
if she's fair, b.	LEAP 413:16
night that he was b.	BOOK 122:12
wonder at ourselves like men b.	WORD 743:7
betrayeth: which is he that b.	BIBLE 98:3
betrothed: B., betrayer, and betrayed	SCOTT 560:14
bright face of my b.	MIDD 459:16
better: always desires what is b.	AUCT 33:20
am getting b. and better	COUÉ 220:5
best way of going one b.	POTT 525:20
B. be courted and jilted	CAMP 176:14
B. by far you should forget	ROSS 547:8
b. day, the worse deed	HENRY 332:17
b. for worse, for richer	BOOK 123:20
b. hath in it inconveniences	HOOK 344:15
B. is the end of a thing	BIBLE 80:12
b. mouse-trap	EMER 277:17
b. nor the worse for wearing	CHES 198:5
b. part of biography	STR 670:20
b. parts must dance	DAV 232:7
B. red than dead	ANON 12:14
B. than a play	CHAR 191:13
b. than a thousand	BOOK 130:18
b. than light and safer	HASK 328:1
b. to be in chains	KAFKA 384:17
b. to have fought and lost	CLOU 207:21
b. to have loved and lost	BUTL 166:28
b. what we can	STEV 667:15
b. world than this	SHAK 567:20
confide in those who are b.	CAMUS 177:14
done b. but I don't mind	DYLAN 265:13
even from worse to b.	JOHN 367:19
far b. thing that I do	DICK 244:7
from b. hap to worse	SOUT 658:2
Gad! she'd b.	CARL 181:14
give place to b.	SHAK 593:11
have better spared a b.	SHAK 582:8
He is not b.—he is much	ANON 12:4
home I was in a b. place	SHAK 568:2
if they had been any b.	CHAN 190:6
If way to the B. there	HARDY 325:6
I see the b. things	OVID 502:24
It is a far better thing	MILT 464:18

better: (cont.):
I took thee for thy b. — SHAK 577:9
know b. as they grow older — SAKI 553:14
made b. by their presence — ELIOT 269:29
Many worse, b. few — LOCK 425:16
music is b. than it sounds — NYE 497:7
nae b. than he shou'd — BURNS 161:21
never b. than when I am mad — KYD 404:13
party breaks up the b. — AUST 38:9
see b. days — BEHN 60:12
Something b. than his dog — TENN 685:9
that which is truly b. — MILT 475:7
there was nothing b. — CARR 183:18
things I'd been b. without — PARK 506:7
'Tis b. to have loved and lost — TENN 683:12
We have seen b. days — SHAK 626:13
will b. the instruction — SHAK 608:23
You're a b. man than I am — KIPL 399:10
bettered: b. expectation — SHAK 613:5
betters: Still b. what is done — SHAK 632:5
between: b. his Darkness — BYRON 173:17
B. my finger and my thumb — HEAN 329:18
B. the idea — ELIOT 271:15
B. two worlds life hovers — BYRON 171:33
I would try to get b. them — STR 670:19
wasn't for the 'ouses in b. — BAT 55:4
betwixt: B. stirrup and ground — CAMD 176:3
Beulah: B., peel me a grape — WEST 729:8
Bevan: [B.] enjoys prophesying — MACM 440:8
bevelled: b. edge of a sunlit mirror — ABSE 1:3
beverage: sad, sour, sober b. — BYRON 170:24
soiled by the 'b. of hell' — YOUNG 755:2
Bevin: B. on a major occasion — FOOT 288:11
bewailed: b. at their birth — MONT 481:13
beware: all should cry, B.! — COL 210:14
B., lest in the worm you crush — BARB 52:3
B. my foolish heart — WASH 722:4
B. of desperate steps — COWP 222:15
B. of rudely crossing it — AUDEN 35:16
'B. of the dog — PETR 513:11
B. of the man who does not — SHAW 638:5
B. of the man whose god — SHAW 637:29
B. of the scribes — BIBLE 93:17
B. the ides of March — SHAK 589:21
Sisters, I bid you b. — KIPL 400:7
beweep: b. my outcast state — SHAK 633:10
bewildered: bothered, and b. — HART 327:14
unprincipled to the utterly b. — CAPP 178:15
bewitch: Do more b. me — HERR 336:12
bewitched: B., bothered, and — HART 327:14
b. for ever who has seen — SACK 552:16
b. with the rogue's company — SHAK 580:5
bewrapt: B. past knowing — HARDY 325:14
bewrayeth: Thy speech b. thee — BIBLE 93:2
beyond: is there anything b. — BROO 143:6
loved each other b. belief — HEINE 331:1
bias: Commodity, b. of world — SHAK 593:30
suggests forms of b. — SCH 558:10
biases: critic is a bundle of b. — BALL 51:5
bibble-babble: Leave thy vain b. — SHAK 630:32
bibendum: *Nunc est b.* — HOR 349:14
bibisti: *edisti satis atque b.* — HOR 348:21
Bible: B. as if it was a constable's — KING 398:1
B. only is the religion — CHIL 199:27
B. teaches that woman brought — STAN 662:9
big ha'-B. — BURNS 161:18
Both read the B. day and night — BLAKE 111:14
English B., a book — MAC 435:21
says Hebraism, 'his B. — ARN 29:13
that book is the B. — ARN 30:8
To read in de B. — HEYW 338:1
translation of the B. — WHAT 730:12
bible-black: starless and b. — THOM 693:16
bibles: B. laid open — HERB 335:19
Bible-Society: B. a machine — CARL 180:15
bicker: can safely afford to b. — BALF 48:17
To b. down a valley — TENN 680:11
bicycle: fish without a b. — STEI 663:12
Salisbury Plain on a b. — GILB 304:17
Socialism can only arrive by b. — VIER 711:9
so is a b. repair kit — CONN 216:9
To-morrow the b. races — AUDEN 36:7

bicycle-pump: poets b. the human heart — AMIS 10:18
bicyclists: illuminated trouser-clip for b. — MORT 486:15
bid: She b. me take love easy — YEATS 751:11
bier: barefaced on the b. — SHAK 578:6
float upon his watery b. — MILT 465:20
big: B. BROTHER IS WATCHING YOU — ORW 500:9
b. enough to take away — FORD 289:3
b. squadrons against — BUSS 165:19
b. than in what is commonly — WOOLF 742:8
b. words for little matters — JOHN 372:21
carry a b. stick — ROOS 546:9
he was too b. for them — BULM 155:1
I am b. It's the pictures — BRAC 138:20
If the b. bang does come — OSB 501:18
bigamy: And b., Sir, is a crime — MONK 479:18
B. is having one husband — ANON 12:16
bigger: b. bang for a buck — ANON 12:17
b. they are, the further — FITZ 285:7
seems no b. than his head — SHAK 597:1
biggest: b. aspidistra- — HARP 326:15
b. electric train set — WELL 726:23
biggin: brow with homely b. — SHAK 584:1
bigoted: superstitious, more b. — NEWM 492:15
bigotry: B. roughly defined — CHES 199:16
B. tries to keep truth — TAG 678:6
Big-Sea-Water: shining B. — LONG 427:15
bike: b. and looked for work — TEBB 680:1
Bilbo: B.'s the word — CONG 215:21
bill: b. of indemnity for raid — KRUG 404:5
b. of my divorce to all — DONNE 251:4
birdie with a yellow b. — STEV 668:19
called upon to pay the b. — HARD 323:15
give me your b. of company — SWIFT 673:20
her nape caught in his b. — YEATS 752:10
if God wrote the b. — EMER 276:13
billboard: b. lovely as a tree — NASH 490:20
billet: Every bullet has its b. — WILL 736:22
billet-doux: patches, bibles, b. — POPE 523:18
billiard: And elliptical b. balls — GILB 305:5
b. sharp any one catches — GILB 305:5
billiards: play b. well is sign — ROUP 549:1
billion: among that b. minus one — HUXL 357:19
Isn't this a b. dollar country — FOST 291:5
billow: A breaking b. — SHEL 639:20
Fierce was the wild b. — ANAT 11:6
billows: solid b. of enormous — PHIL 514:4
billowy: plunged into b. wave — GILB 305:13
bills: children and tradesmen's b. — MACN 440:18
inflammation of his weekly b. — BYRON 170:27
Just for paying a few b. — LARK 410:8
Receipted b. and invitations — AUDEN 35:10
Billy: B., in one of his nice — GRAH 313:12
That's the way for B. and me — HOGG 341:16
waited till his 'B.' boiled — PAT 509:9
bind: B. me at least, or set me — GOD 308:8
b. their kings in chains — BOOK 135:16
B.-their-kings-in-chains — MAC 436:3
b. the sweet influences — BIBLE 77:37
Go, b. your sons to exile — KIPL 401:11
I b. unto myself to-day — ALEX 8:15
My mother bids me b. my hair — HUNT 356:21
To b. another to its delight — BLAKE 114:7
binds: b. to himself a joy — BLAKE 113:11
binomial: about b. theorems — GILB 306:10
biographers: B., translators — MAC 435:6
Boswell is the first of b. — MAC 434:12
biographical: noble and b. friend — WETH 729:22
biographies: essence of innumerable b. — CARL 180:7
biography: B. is about Chaps — BENT 64:10
b. is ultimately fiction — MAL 442:15
Judas who writes the b. — WILDE 735:1
no history; only b. — EMER 276:28
nothing but b. — DISR 248:10
not the better part of b. — STR 670:20
birch: bringing back the b. — VIDAL 711:4
children nor fasting nor b. — BLAKE 114:10
bird: at the voice of the b. — BIBLE 81:1
b. can fly — MILNE 463:3
b. forlorn — HOOD 344:4
b. of dawning singeth all — SHAK 572:2

bird: (cont.):
b. of night did sit — SHAK 590:10
b. of Paradise — HERB 335:13
b. of wonder dies — SHAK 589:17
b. that cuts the airy way — BLAKE 112:30
b. that shunn'st the noise — MILT 464:19
b. that thinks two notes — DAV 232:9
B. thou never wert — SHEL 643:13
Both man and b. and beast — COL 211:17
catch a b. than a lady — RICH 540:9
catch the b. of paradise — KHR 395:17
death, immortal b. — KEATS 389:15
escaped even as a b. — BOOK 134:2
fell with the waking b. — TENN 686:18
forgets the dying b. — PAINE 504:15
further than a wanton's b. — SHAK 623:7
gold-feathered b. — STEV 666:4
household b. — DONNE 250:18
I know why the caged b. sings — DUNB 264:2
It's a b.! It's a plane — ANON 13:8
It was only the note of a b. — SIMP 648:2
I would I were thy b. — SHAK 623:7
least some b. would trust — HERB 334:4
like a b. on the wing — BOUL 137:17
Like that self-begotten b. — MILT 474:15
obscure b. clamoured — SHAK 602:13
O Cuckoo! Shall I call thee b. — WORD 748:10
rare b. on this earth — JUV 383:24
secular b. ages of lives — MILT 474:16
Stirred for a b. — HOPK 346:11
strong b. above its prey — HILL 338:10
that beats the bush the b. — OXF 504:2
Unto the sweet b.'s throat — SHAK 568:8
wakeful b. — MILT 470:16
were all like that wise b. — PUNCH 531:22
What b. so sings, yet — LYLY 433:10
birdcage: And a b., sir — DICK 243:23
summer b. in a garden — WEBS 726:2
bird-haunted: some wet b. English lawn — ARN 27:16
birdie: b. with a yellow bill — STEV 668:19
birds: And no b. sing — KEATS 388:7
are a nest of singing b. — JOHN 371:4
As the flight of b. — MACL 439:9
b. are faint with the hot — KEATS 390:5
B. build—but not I — HOPK 346:9
b. came home to roost — MILL 461:20
b. give him pain — WILB 734:4
B. in their little nests agree — WATTS 722:17
b. in the trees — YEATS 752:20
b. must find in freedom — SASS 557:9
b. of the air — BIBLE 90:1
b. of the air come — BIBLE 91:3
B. on box and laurels listen — SMART 649:8
b. sang swete in the middes — WEVER 730:1
b. sit brooding — SHAK 599:11
b. still hopping — STEV 668:13
b. that are without — WEBS 726:2
b. to the delicious time — HUNT 356:11
b., wild flowers, and Prime — BALD 48:14
But what these unobservant b. — ISH 360:21
cheerful b. do chant their lays — SPEN 659:14
Fish got to swim and b. — HAMM 322:17
If b. confabulate or no — COWP 222:28
I see all the b. are flown — CHAR 191:6
late the sweet b. sang — SHAK 634:6
like bats amongst b. — BACON 44:31
pipe of half-awakened b. — TENN 688:5
singing of b. is come — BIBLE 81:9
sing like b. i' the cage — SHAK 597:16
Thus you b. build nests — VIRG 715:20
Unhappy b.! what does it boot — MARV 451:11
very merciful to the b. — ANON 20:4
we'd be as happy as b. — BLAKE 114:10
We think caged b. sing — WEBS 726:9
birdsong: b. at morning — STEV 668:24
Birkenhead: B. is very clever — ASQ 32:2
Birmingham: B. by way of Beachy Head — CHES 199:5
no great hopes from B. — AUST 38:11
When Jesus came to B. — STUD 671:4
Birnam wood: Great B. to high Dunsinane — SHAK 604:2

blatant: still strong man in a b. TENN 686:13
 which the B. beast men SPEN 660:15
blaze: b. forth the death of princes SHAK 591:5
 pole is undistinguished b. THOM 696:4
 unclouded b. of living light BYRON 169:25
blazes: Exhales her odours, b. BYRON 172:12
blazon: But this eternal b. SHAK 573:14
 Their final b., and to prove LARK 409:13
bleaching: white sheet b. SHAK 631:24
bleak: In the b. mid-winter ROSS 547:4
bleat: b. the bark bellow BLAKE 111:7
 b. the one at the other SHAK 631:12
bleed: Caesar b. in sport SHAK 591:17
 Ile lay mee downe and b. BALL 50:9
 makes my old wounds b. WALL 718:17
 our bosom and then we b. SHEL 640:17
 painted devil. If he do b. SHAK 602:4
 prick us, do we not b. SHAK 609:22
 stabbed, b., fall DONNE 250:14
 then they b. JONS 379:13
 thorns of life! I b. SHEL 641:18
bleeding: Ain't it all a b. shame ANON 17:20
 Beneath the b. hands we feel ELIOT 270:22
 b. to death of time GRAV 314:19
 head and a dread beat b. JOHN 366:17
 instead of b., he sings GARD 297:15
 pageant of his b. heart ARN 28:21
 purple testament of b. war SHAK 620:10
 thou b. piece of earth SHAK 591:23
blemish: no b. but the mind SHAK 630:30
 Your lamb shall be without b. BIBLE 72:8
blenches: b. gave my heart SHAK 634:21
Blenheim: still fighting B. BEVAN 68:16
blent: in whose b. air all LARK 409:15
bless: B. 'em all HUGH 353:16
 B. her when she is riggish SHAK 565:8
 b. the hand that gave DRYD 261:28
 B. the Lord, all the works BIBLE 108:8
 except thou b. me BIBLE 71:18
 God b. the Prince of Wales LINL 423:7
 God b. us every one DICK 239:18
 how to load and b. KEATS 390:17
 Lord, b. ye the Lord BOOK 118:15
 Slow to chide, and swift to b. LYTE 433:17
 Will ask the Lord to b. me FIELD 281:13
blessed: always To be b. POPE 522:1
 And make us b. at last ROCH 543:9
 bear onward b. me SIDN 647:2
 bed be b. that I lie ANON 16:9
 B. are the dead which die BIBLE 107:5
 B. are the eyes which see BIBLE 94:12
 B. are the poor in spirit BIBLE 88:23
 B. are the pure in heart KEBLE 392:18
 b. art thou among women ANON 22:3
 b. art thou among women BIBLE 93:21
 B. be he that cometh BOOK 133:17
 b. be the name BIBLE 77:2
 B. is the man that endureth BIBLE 104:25
 B. is the man that hath BOOK 124:6
 b. is the man that trusteth BOOK 126:13
 B. is the man unto whom BOOK 126:8
 B. is the man whose strength BOOK 130:17
 b. mutter of the mass BROW 148:18
 B. pair of Sirens MILT 463:9
 b. they that master SHAK 610:20
 b. the latter end of Job BIBLE 78:6
 b. them these three times BIBLE 73:11
 b. to give than to receive BIBLE 99:4
 generations shall call me b. BIBLE 93:22
 hence to there may be b. SOCR 655:2
 His b. part to Heaven SHAK 589:5
 I b. them unaware COL 211:9
 Judge none b. before his death BIBLE 87:18
 Kings may be b., but Tam BURNS 163:5
 last promotion of the b. DRYD 261:32
 mortals always to be b. ARMS 26:7
 Of this b. man, let WALT 721:14
 Some b. Hope, whereof he knew HARDY 325:5
 supremely b. and happy ARIS 25:9
 That b. mood WORD 744:20
 that you should call b. HOR 350:19

blessed: (*cont.*):
 This b. plot, this earth SHAK 619:18
 Thou fall'st a b. martyr SHAK 589:1
 whom thou blessest is b. BIBLE 73:8
blessedness: b. alone that makes a King TRAH 701:17
 blindly with thy b. at strife WORD 746:1
 dies, in single b. SHAK 610:20
blessest: visitest the earth, and b. it BOOK 129:2
blesseth: b. him that gives SHAK 609:13
blessing: And truly it's a b. CLOU 207:14
 be to us a national b. HAM 322:11
 b. in this gentle breeze WORD 746:17
 b. of God Almighty BOOK 122:15
 b. of the Old Testament BACON 42:18
 b. that money cannot buy WALT 721:10
 boon and a b. to men ANON 18:16
 continual dew of thy b. BOOK 119:8
 contrariwise b. BIBLE 105:18
 expectation makes a b. SUCK 671:5
 hath taken away thy b. BIBLE 71:12
 Nothing is an unmixed b. HOR 349:20
 shall give us his b. BOOK 129:5
 simple b. of a rainbow ABSE 1:3
 Sweet was its b., kind COCK 208:3
 Thou have paid thy utmost b. DE L 236:2
 When thou dost ask me b. SHAK 597:16
 Yet possessing every b. EDM 266:17
blessings: b. on the falling out TENN 687:25
 For all the b. of the light KEN 393:7
 glass of b. HERB 335:14
 In b. on your head COWP 222:18
 they recognized their b. VIRG 715:13
blight: b. man was born for HOPK 346:4
 charm is the great English b. WAUGH 723:10
Blighty: Bound for Old B. HUGH 353:16
 Take me back to dear old B. MILL 462:6
Blimber: nonsense about Miss B. DICK 240:13
Blimp: Colonel B. LOW 429:8
blind: Altho' a poor b. boy CIBB 203:17
 b. and still by faith LIND 423:4
 b. as any noonday owl TENN 681:29
 b. life within the brain TENN 682:24
 b. man in a dark room BOWEN 138:3
 b. side of the heart CHES 198:29
 b. watchmaker DAWK 232:17
 country of the b. the one-eyed ERAS 278:12
 darkness and b. eyes VAUG 708:15
 eyes will gaze an eagle b. SHAK 598:20
 giveth sight to the b. BOOK 135:9
 halt, and the b. BIBLE 94:31
 if the b. lead the blind BIBLE 91:10
 I was eyes to the b. BIBLE 77:29
 Love is b.; friendship ANON 20:16
 mad, b., despised SHEL 643:7
 O b. entencioun! CHAU 195:7
 own internal lightning b. SHEL 641:3
 religion without science is b. EINS 268:6
 right to be b. sometimes NELS 491:12
 She won, and Cupid b. did rise LYLY 433:9
 splendid work for the b. SASS 557:6
 Thou Eye among the b. WORD 745:16
 though b., throbbing between ELIOT 273:8
 though she be b. BACON 43:19
 though she's painted b. BUTL 166:19
 unbelief is b. MILT 464:2
 Was b., but now I see NEWT 494:8
 whereas I was b. BIBLE 96:36
 which shall strike b. LYLY 433:12
 will accompany my being b. PEPYS 512:20
 winged Cupid painted b. SHAK 611:1
 Ye b. guides, which strain BIBLE 92:5
blinded: dulness of our b. sight BOOK 135:21
blindness: first love's impassioned b. PEAC 510:12
 From all b. of heart BOOK 119:17
 heathen in his b. HEBER 330:4
 'is b. bows down to wood KIPL 398:19
 Love comes from b. BUSS 165:17
 our b. we cannot ask BOOK 122:18
 To help him of his b. SHAK 631:8
 triple sight in b. KEATS 390:24
blinds: b. let through the day HOUS 351:21

blinds: (*cont.*):
 dusk a drawing-down of b. OWEN 503:13
blind-worm: and b.'s sting SHAK 603:18
blind-worms: Newts, and b. SHAK 611:20
blinked: other fellow just b. RUSK 550:7
blinking: portrait of a b. idiot SHAK 608:17
bliss: appreciate domestic b. SANT 555:17
 B. goes but to a certain bound GREV 318:3
 B. in our brows bent SHAK 564:25
 b. that hath a quiet mind VAUX 709:13
 B. was it in that dawn WORD 744:5
 body is in the b. AKHM 6:10
 certainty of waking b. MILT 463:24
 deprived of everlasting b. MARL 446:15
 each to his point of b. BROW 153:6
 Everywhere I see b. SHEL 600.8
 Gives promise of pneumatic b. ELIOT 273:16
 highest b. of human-kind KEATS 390:7
 Isn't it b.? Don't you approve? SOND 656:2
 man had given all other b. TENN 689:8
 Milk-soup men call domestic b. PATM 509:13
 mutual and partaken b. MILT 464:7
 Of bliss on b. MILT 471:9
 parted, b., or woe MILT 473:1
 Sees b. in ale CRAB 224:24
 Thou art a soul in b. SHAK 597:13
 Thou source of all my b. GOLD 310:19
 where ignorance is b. GRAY 316:3
 Which is the b. of solitude WORD 744:16
 winged hours of b. have been CAMP 176:19
 Your b. in our hearts STR 671:1
blissful: record of his old times BLAM 114:20
blister: And b. you all o'er SHAK 625:5
blithe: b. Irish lad so happy CAMP 176:13
 Hail to thee, b. Spirit SHEL 643:13
 No lark more b. BICK 108:20
 So buxom, b., and debonair MILT 465:4
blitz: b. of a boy is Timothy CAUS 187:3
blizzard: willingly to his death in a b. ATKI 32:13
block: And hew the b. off POPE 519:5
 chopper on a big black b. GILB 304:27
 I ain't lookin' to b. you up DYLAN 265:10
 old b. itself BURKE 160:2
blockhead: b.'s insult points JOHN 370:8
 bookful b., ignorantly read POPE 521:24
 diversion in a talking b. FARQ 280:11
 no man but a b. ever wrote JOHN 374:15
 very great b. CHAR 191:16
blocks: hew b. with a razor POPE 524:3
 You b., you stones SHAK 589:20
blond: B. comme un soleil BANV 51:13
 splendorous b. beast NIET 495:17
blonde: b. Bestie nicht zu NIET 495:17
 b. to make a bishop kick CHAN 190:2
blondes: Gentlemen Prefer B. LOOS 428:8
blood: against flesh and b. BIBLE 103:1
 am I not of her b. SHAK 629:5
 ancient troughs of b. HILL 338:11
 And flesh and b. so cheap HOOD 344:9
 And is this b., then BYRON 171:12
 And men are flesh and b. SHAK 591:12
 b. and iron BISM 110:6
 b. and love without STOP 670:3
 b. and wine were WILDE 735:33
 b. before your part SHEL 644:2
 b. be the price of admiralty KIPL 401:2
 b. drawn with the lash LINC 422:8
 b. further with the blood BROWN 144:13
 b. in his liver as will SHAK 630:20
 b. is fet from fathers SHAK 585:8
 b. is nipped and ways SHAK 599:11
 b. must have its course KING 397:17
 b. of an English-man NASHE 490:22
 B. of Jesus whispers peace BICK 108:22
 b. of martyrs is the seed TERT 690:17
 b. of patriots and tyrants JEFF 364:9
 b. of their brothers ZAP 755:8
 B. of the New Testament BOOK 122:12
 b. on my hands than water GREE 316:20
 b. reigns in the winter's SHAK 631:24
 b.'s a rover HOUS 352:7
 b. that's shed on earth BALL 50:17

blood: (*cont.*):
b. will have blood — SHAK 603:13
b. with guilt is bought — SHEL 642:10
by man shall his b. be shed — BIBLE 70:31
carrying a b.-red flag — BLOK 115:9
coughed-up b., laughter — RIMB 541:10
Dread Beat an B. — JOHN 366:16
drink the b. of goats — BOOK 128:3
drop my b. for drachmas — SHAK 593:6
effusion of Christian b. — LAUD 411:4
examine well your b. — SHAK 610:20
false pride in place and b. — TENN 684:11
For B., as all men know — HUXL 357:22
fountain filled with b. — COWP 222:21
getting b. out of a turnip — MARR 449:2
give me B. — DICK 240:2
glories of our b. and state — SHIR 646:2
guiltless of his country's b. — GRAY 315:15
haste to shed innocent b. — BIBLE 84:24
Hath redeemed us by his b. — DIX 249:18
have had so much b. in him — SHAK 604:12
Her b. is settled — SHAK 624:1
Here lies b.; and let it lie — CLEV 206:13
Here's the smell of the b. — SHAK 604:14
Her pure and eloquent b. — DONNE 251:10
hunter's b. was on their horn — BYRON 172:14
I am in b. stepp'd in so far — SHAK 603:14
I am innocent of the b. — BIBLE 93:3
Inhabits our frail b. — SHAK 630:29
king besmeared with b. — MILT 468:16
Let there be b.! — BYRON 171:17
make thick my b, — SHAK 600:16
man whose b. is snow-broth — SHAK 605:10
near in b., the nearer bloody — SHAK 602:19
Neptune's ocean wash this b. — SHAK 602:6
noble b. of all this world — SHAK 591:19
Nothing like b., sir — THAC 691:17
nothing to offer but b. — CHUR 202:8
now could I drink hot b. — SHAK 576:25
Of Earth's first b. — WORD 744:13
O! no more stirs — SHAK 579:34
pale by shedding of thy b. — CONS 217:21
poet's feverish b. — ARN 28:22
poison the whole b. — EMPS 277:20
Propinquity and property of b. — SHAK 594:19
purged away but with b. — BROWN 144:14
rivers of b. must yet flow — JEFF 364:16
shedding of b. is no remission — BIBLE 104:11
shente us and shedde oure b. — LANG 409:5
sleeping in the b. — SHAK 582:17
smeared in dust and b. — SHAK 588:6
smell the b. of a British — SHAK 596:17
summon up the b. — SHAK 585:7
That one drop of Negro b. — HUGH 354:2
that sheds his b. with me — SHAK 586:11
there's b. upon her gown — FLEC 286:6
they stream forth thy b. — SHAK 591:21
this tincture in the b. — DEFOE 234:17
Tiber foaming with much b. — POW 528:10
Tiber foaming with much b. — VIRG 713:10
To wash them in my b. — SOUT 657:22
voice of thy brother's b. — BIBLE 70:19
washed in the b. of the Lamb — LIND 423:3
We be one b., thou — KIPL 401:15
when b. is their argument — SHAK 586:4
When the b. creeps — TENN 683:16
Which all the while ran b. — SHAK 592:14
Which my God feels as b. — HERB 334:6
white in the b. of the Lamb — BIBLE 106:5
whose b. is warm within — SHAK 607:5
Who thicks man's b. with cold — COL 211:2
With his own b. he bought her — STONE 669:12
your b. was taken from you — MIDD 459:15
blood-dimmed: b. tide is loosed — YEATS 753:1
blood-guiltiness: Deliver me from b. — BOOK 128:7
bloodless: ballet of b. categories — BRAD 139:6
blood-red: sunset ran, one glorious b. — BROW 150:7
bloodshed: without b. — MACN 445:13
bloodthirsty: b. and deceitful man — BOOK 124:16
blood-tinctured: shows a heart within b. — SWIN 677:16

bloody: Abroad is b. — GEOR 301:8
Agony and b. Sweat — BOOK 119:18
And sang within the b. wood — ELIOT 272:20
Be b., bold, and resolute — SHAK 603:21
B. instructions — SHAK 601:2
b. noses and cracked crowns — SHAK 580:12
b. principles and practices — FOX 292:5
breast a b. cross he bore — SPEN 659:21
Brutes never meet in b. fray — GOLD 311:2
come out, thou b. man — BIBLE 75:15
Even so my b. thoughts — SHAK 616:23
I do begin to have b. thoughts — SHAK 625:29
last act is b. — PASC 507:15
Must often wipe a b. nose — GAY 300:2
My head is b., but unbowed — HENL 332:6
Not b. likely — SHAW 638:20
Sons of the dark and b. ground — O'HARA 498:6
subtle, sly, and b. — SHAK 622:5
What b. man is that — SHAK 599:14
with b. blameful blade — SHAK 612:23
Woe to the b. city — BIBLE 86:15
bloom: as any b. upon a flower — THOM 694:6
B. ate with relish — JOYCE 381:24
flowers that b. in the spring — GILB 305:9
Just now the lilac is in b. — BROO 143:9
look at things in b. — HOUS 352:6
opening sweet of earliest b. — COLL 213:10
risk of spoiling its b. — CONR 217:1
sort of b. on a woman — BARR 54:12
with b. along the bough — HOUS 352:5
with the b. go — ARN 28:26
ye b. sae fresh and fair — BURNS 161:9
blooming: b. well dead — SAR 556:4
stones and every b. thing — KAV 386:5
up for shame, the b. morn — HERR 336:9
were b. in the tall vales — THOM 693:10
blooms: blaster of freshest b. — MARS 449:8
bloomy: And all the b. beds — SMART 650:3
blossom: almond b. silent — REED 538:1
And bade it b. there — COL 210:1
And b. in purple and red — TENN 686:20
b. about me of something — BOSW 137:4
b. and flourish as leaves — SMITH 653:32
b. as the rose — BIBLE 83:19
B. by blossom the spring — SWIN 675:22
b. in their dust — SHIR 646:4
b. of war with a heart — TENN 687:5
b. on the tomb — CRAB 224:20
b. or the bole — YEATS /50:18
b. seethed and departed — BETJ 68:1
b. that hangs on the bough — SHAK 626:2
Letting a hundred flowers b. — MAO 446:3
may not b. into a Duchess — AIL 6:1
tongue b. into speech — BROW 149:1
blossoming: Florence b. in stone — LONG 426:21
blossoms: in the b. of my sin — SHAK 573:20
I sing of brooks, of b. — HERR 336:6
thousand b. with the day — FITZ 283:11
to-morrow b. — SHAK 588:19
blot: And blackens every b. — TENN 681:16
b. on the escutcheon — GRAY 315:4
B. out, correct, insert — SWIFT 675:1
b. out his name out — BIBLE 106:5
bright b. upon this gloomy — SHEL 643:6
greatest art, the art to b. — POPE 520:5
received from him a b. — HEMI 331:13
that looks a little b. — TENN 682:15
This world's no b. for us — BROW 149:25
vicious b. nor other foulness — SHAK 594:22
blotted: b. it out for ever — STER 665:3
one b. from life's page — BYRON 168:11
That ever b. paper — SHAK 609:3
Would he had b. a thousand — JONS 380:9
blow: And b. your own trumpet — GILB 306:16
A sudden b.: the great wings — YEATS 752:10
Blow, b., thou winter wind — SHAK 568:17
B., bugle, blow — TENN 688:1
b. from which he never — MCL 439:15
B. him up to the moon — TENN 687:22
B. in cold b. and neither — SHAW 637:20
b, me like thistledown — MACN 441:21
B. out, you bugles — BROO 143:3

blow: (*cont.*):
B., thou wind of God — KING 397:12
b. upon my garden — BIBLE 81:16
b. up the other half — LAING 405:18
B. up the trumpet — BOOK 130:14
B., winds, and crack — SHAK 595:20
b. with an agreement — TROT 704:14
does not return your b. — SHAW 638:5
first b. is half the battle — GOLD 311:26
great winds shorewards b. — ARN 27:7
hand that gave the b. — DRYD 261:28
Let the b. fall soon or late — STEV 669:5
otherwise you b. up — MARG 446:5
receive a knock-down b. — HUNT 356:14
themselves must strike the b. — BYRON 168:10
To b. on whom I please — SHAK 568:15
when will thou b. — ANON 19:14
bloweth: wind b. where it listeth — BIBLE 96:14
blowin': answer is b. in the wind — DYLAN 265:11
blowing: b. of a nose — FORS 290:22
B. sweet o'er each enclosure — SMART 649:7
blown: B. by surmises — SHAK 582:12
b. sky-high in a stanza — MAY 455:2
no sooner b. but blasted — MILT 466:18
once hath b. for ever dies — FITZ 284:1
rooks are b. about — TENN 683:7
blows: and buffets of the world — SHAK 603:1
B. out his brains upon — BROW 152:27
It b. so hard, 'twill soon — HOUS 352:13
never b. so red the rose — FITZ 283:16
Blücher: Napoleon forgot B. — CHUR 201:22
bludgeoning: b. of the people — WILDE 735:23
bludgeonings: b. of chance — HENL 332:6
blue: across the b. threshold — ROST 548:11
b. above the trees — KEATS 388:3
B. as the gendarmerie were — SITW 648:12
b. remembered hills — HOUS 352:15
B., silver-white, and budded — KEATS 389:18
deeply, beautifully b. — SOUT 657:11
Do I stand and stare? All's b. — BROW 148:8
drowned in yonder living b. — TENN 684:14
Eyes of most unholy b. — MOORE 483:3
Floating in the B. — MILNE 463:1
forests and b. days at sea — STEV 668:24
Her b. body — WALK 717:14
In his b. gardens — FITZ 285:1
migrations from the b. bed — GOLD 311:30
My b. heaven — WHIT 731:21
that b. is all in a rush — HOPK 346:1
Upon that little tent of b. — WILDE 735:34
Where the b. of the night — CROS 227:18
You have a b. guitar — STEV 666:22
Blue Beard: B.'s domestic chaplain — DICK 243:11
Bluebell: Mary, ma Scotch B. — LAUD 411:6
bluebirds: b. over the white cliffs — BURT 164:10
blueeyed: how do you like your b. boy — CUMM 228:14
blunder: At so grotesque a b. — BENT 64:18
I b., I bluster, I blow — SKEL 649:3
It wad frae mony a b. free us — BURNS 163:14
worse than a crime, it is a b. — BOUL 137:15
blundered: b. into Paradise — THOM 695:8
b. on some virtue unawares — CHUR 201:11
Some one had b. — TENN 680:14
blunders: Human b. usually — TAYL 679:8
Nature's agreeable b. — COWL 221:24
Natur never makes enny b. — BILL 109:18
blunt: b. his natural edge — SHAK 605:10
plain, b. man — SHAK 592:15
blur: b. in the corner — STOP 670:2
blush: And b. at what they hear — KING 398:6
And not b. so to be admired — WALL 718:10
b. into the cheek — DICK 242:34
b. with noble blood no — POPE 518:22
Else would a maiden b. bepaint — SHAK 622:32
flower is born to b. unseen — GRAY 315:15
For Greeks it b. — BYRON 171:2
blushed: Ne'er a b. unless — CHUR 201:11
water saw its God, and b. — CRAS 226:2
blushes: Only Animal that B. — TWAIN 706:9
Blushful B. Hippocrene — KEATS 389:9
Blushing: faint and woolly peach — JUNE 380:7

blushing: (*cont.*):
b. discontented sun   SHAK 620:9
b. either for a sign   CONG 215:30
b. honours thick upon him   SHAK 588:19
other people without b.   SHAW 638:6
Blut: *nur durch B. und Eisen*   BISM 110:6
board: carried on b. while asleep   HUME 355:12
genial hearth, a hospitable b.   WORD 744:6
heart out for my bed and b.   LOW 430:24
I struck the b., and cried   HERB 334:11
There wasn't any B., and now   HERB 333:19
boarded: Youth are b.   DICK 241:31
boarding-house: b. is a parallelogram   LEAC 413:10
boards: I sit upon her B.   DENN 237:5
Ships are but b.   SHAK 607:18
boar-pig: tidy Bartholomew b.   SHAK 583:9
boast: Anabaptists falsely h   BOOK 100:2
b. no more your mighty   SHIR 646:3
B. not thyself of to morrow   BIBLE 79:24
b. of heraldry   GRAY 315:13
girdeth on his harness b.   BIBLE 76:9
glory and our absolute b.   WORD 747:1
How many people can b.   BECK 57:27
Such is the patriot's b.   GOLD 311:9
boasteth: then he b.   BIBLE 79:8
boat: frail b. on rough sea   HOR 349:2
Give a man a b. he can sail   THOM 696:19
love b. has crashed   MAY 455:8
My soul is an enchanted b.   SHEL 642:17
Speed, bonnie b.   BOUL 137:17
They sank my b.   KENN 394:9
Until I have a little B.   WORD 746:12
boathook: diplomatic b.   SAL 553:19
boating: Jolly b. weather   CORY 219:13
boatman: B., do not tarry   CAMP 176:15
boats: b. against the current   FITZ 285:4
messing about in b.   GRAH 314:2
we seek happiness in b.   HOR 348:9
When b. or ships came near   LEAR 414:17
bobtail: bet my money on de b. nag   FOST 291:12
bodes: b. some strange eruption   SHAK 571:25
bodice: And lace my b.   HUNT 356:21
bodies: b. but not their souls   GIBR 303:2
b. high at Austerlitz   SAND 555:5
b. no sensible man directly   MACM 440:10
b. of those that made such   EDW 267:8
both outwardly in our b.   BOOK 120:15
changing of b. into light   NEWT 494:1
friendless b. of unburied   WEBS 726:7
knowledge of our b.   STOP 669:13
Our b. are our gardens   SHAK 615:10
our b. lay among   JARR 363:20
Our b. why do we forbear   DONNE 251:25
rough notes and our dead b.   SCOTT 559:6
small are men's poor b.   JUV 384:10
soul inhabiting two b.   ARIS 26:2
superficial contact of two b.   CHAM 189:13
We scorn their b.   BAST 55:3
with two seeming b.   SHAK 612:3
with well-developed b.   FORS 289:20
your b. a living sacrifice   BIBLE 100:3
your scattered b. go   DONNE 250:20
bodkin: With a bare b.?   SHAK 575:16
body: Absent in b., but present   BIBLE 100:20
alone is salutary to the b.   PROU 530:17
And in his b. there was   MAL 443:6
And though her b. die   MILT 474.16
b. and material substance   CARL 180:27
b. and the soul know how   ROET 544:8
b. continues in its state   NEWT 494:2
b. did contain a spirit   SHAK 582:7
b. dies; b.'s beauty lives   STEV 666:8
b. from the dominion   GOLD 310:4
b. gets its sop and holds   BROW 148:10
b. is a machine for living   TOLS 701:1
b. is even like melting   BOOK 125:12
b. is in the bliss   AKHM 6:10
b. is the temple   BIBLE 100:23
b. like a rough diamond   DEFOE 234:1
b. of a weak and feeble   ELIZ 274:3
b. of Benjamin Franklin   FRAN 293:6

body: (*cont.*):
b. of thought   CARL 181:7
b.'s delicate   SHAK 596:4
b. suffers the soul may   MER 457:20
b. than raiment   BIBLE 89:9
b. was as straight as Circe's   MARL 447:9
b. when it is with your   CUMM 228:16
brief loan of his own b.   CAB 174:11
But I keep under my b.   BIBLE 100:31
commit his b. to the deep   BOOK 135:20
commit his b. to the ground   BOOK 124:5
edifying of the b.   BIBLE 102:17
filling some other b.   KEATS 392:1
from the b. of this death   BIBLE 99:33
gigantic b., huge massy   MAC 434:14
Gin a body meet a b.   BURNS 161:13
give my b. to be burned   BIBLE 101:1
had tasted her sweet b.   SHAK 616:20
her b. thought   DONNE 251:10
holy of holies is the human b.   CHEK 197:11
If I had the use of my b.   BECK 57:17
In b. and in soul can bind   SCOTT 559:15
I should interpose my b.   STR 670:19
I sing the b. electric   WHIT 732:4
John Brown's b.   ANON 15:12
joint and motive of her b.   SHAK 628:2
left me but my b.'s length   SHAK 588:6
linen and keep your b.   STEV 668:24
Make less thy b. hence   SHAK 584:13
Marry my b. to that dust   KING 396:11
mind, b., or estate   BOOK 120:7
mind or b. to prefer   POPE 522:9
no b. to be kicked   THUR 697:21
O b. swayed to music   YEATS 750:18
Of the glorious B. sing   THOM 692:13
one's soul to keep one's b.   MACK 439:2
on thy b. slain I think on thee   CONS 217:21
Resurrection of the b.   BOOK 119:1
rid of the rest of her b.   VANB 708:6
shall change our vile b.   BOOK 124:5
shapes itself to the b.   WOLL 741:15
soul the b. form doth take   SPEN 660:20
sound mind in a sound b.   JUV 384:11
Take, eat; this is my b.   BIBLE 92:25
Thersites' b. is as good as Ajax   SHAK 571:15
This common b.   SHAK 564:27
Thy b. is all vice   JOHN 371:10
truly have none in the b.   LAWR 412:15
unacquainted with your b.   BACON 43:23
vast b. of the main Sea   ANDR 11:12
well proportioned b.   AUBR 33:6
what exercise is to the b.   STEE 662:21
Whose b., Nature   POPE 522:7
with Africa than my own b.   ORTON 499:12
with my b. I thee worship   BOOK 123:21
wreathing his b. seven times   SMART 649:13
young a b. with so old a head   SHAK 609:12
your b. between your knees   CORY 219:13
boets: hate all B. and Bainters   GEOR 300:22
boggy: dark, b., dirty   GOLD 311:24
Bognor: Bugger B.   GEOR 301:6
bogs: from b. and precipices   LOCKE 425:4
bogus: than a b. god   MACN 440:12
boil: b. breaking forth   BIBLE 72:6
War That Would Not B.   TAYL 679:10
We b. at different degrees   EMER 277:14
Boileau: B. was a little river   FLAU 286:2
boiled: safe pleasure for a parliamentarian is a bag of b. sweets   CRIT 227:3
taste no politics in b. and roast   SMITH 653:4
boilers: parcel of b. and vats   JOHN 375:23
boiling: b. bloody breast   SHAK 612:23
with b. oil in it   GILB 305:7
boire: *B. sans soif et faire*   BEAU 56:11
bois: *le soir, au fond des b.*   VIGNY 711:10
Nous n'irons plus aux b.   ANON 21:3
bok: Farewell my b. and my devocioun   CHAU 195:1
Go, litel b., go   CHAU 195:26
boko: Bertha's got bang on b.   MARS 449:6
bold: be b. and be sensible   HOR 348:4
be b., and everywhere   SPEN 660:11

bold: (*cont.*):
b. bad man, that dared   SPEN 659:23
b. spirit in a loyal breast   SHAK 619:7
drunk hath made me b.   SHAK 601:14
Fortune assists the b.   VIRG 714:7
Had you been as wise as b.   SHAK 608:14
He b. as a hawk, she soft   THUR 697:19
righteous are b. as a lion   BIBLE 79:28
This b. bad man   SHAK 588:13
boldest: b. held his breath   CAMP 176:9
boldly: b. go where no man   RODD 543:21
boldness: B., and again   DANT 230:22
b. at least will deserve   PROP 530:1
B. be my friend   SHAK 570:28
b. is a child of ignorance   BACON 42:29
B. is an ill keeper of promise   BACON 42:30
Bolingbroke: this canker, B.   SHAK 579:33
Bolshevism: It is B. run mad   SNOW 654:8
this sort of madness [B.]   SMITH 651:12
bolt: b. is shot back somewhere   ARN 26:17
like the b., and the breech   REED 538:1
bolts: b. are hurled   TENN 686:1
bomb: b. them back into the Stone Age   LEMAY 417:3
defence against the atom b.   ANON 12:13
ones we intended to b.   BLY 116:7
Bombay: troopship just leaving B.   HUGH 353:16
bombazine: B. would have shown a deeper   GASK 299:3
bombed: glad we've been b.   ELIZ 275:2
protect him from being b.   BALD 48:9
bomber: b. will always get through   BALD 48:9
bombers: In b. named for girls   JARR 363:20
bombs: b. redoubled on hills   MOT 487:2
Come, friendly b.   BETJ 68:5
Ears like b. and teeth   CAUS 187:3
poets exploding like b.   AUDEN 36:7
bon: *b. sens est la chose du*   DESC 237:17
bona: *sua si b. norint*   VIRG 715:13
Bonaparte: B. thought was rarest   THOR 697:3
bond: And take a b. of fate   SHAK 604:1
b. between two people   RILKE 541:3
b. nor free   BIBLE 103:16
I will have my b.   SHAK 609:4
Let him look to his b.   SHAK 608:21
pieces that great b.   SHAK 603:5
you break that sole b.   BURKE 157:31
bondage: B. is hoarse   SHAK 623:6
b. to parents cramps   WOLL 741:17
b. which is freedom's self   SHEL 642:21
Cassius from b. will deliver   SHAK 590:11
modern b. of rhyming   MILT 467:18
on his own obsequious b.   SHAK 614:19
out of the house of b.   BIBLE 72:16
spirit of b. again to fear   BIBLE 99:35
bondmaid: one by a b.   BIBLE 102:5
bondman: Checked like a b.   SHAK 593:8
so base that would be a b.   SHAK 592:4
wealth piled by the b.'s   LINC 422:8
bonds: b. in there are all determinate   SHAK 634:11
b. of civil society   LOCKE 425:8
b. of law and duty   WAUGH 723:9
He loves his b., who when   HERR 337:6
I am, except these b.   BIBLE 99:13
Let us break their b. asunder   BOOK 124:8
bondsmen: Hereditary b.!   BYRON 168:10
bone: *b.,* for *bene*   SHAK 599:3
B. of my bone thou art   MILT 473:1
b. to pick with graveyards   BECK 57:15
bright hair about the b.   DONNE 252:13
Hath never a b. in't   WEBS 725:14
He knows death to the b.   YEATS 751:10
rag and b. and a hank   KIPL 401:7
rag and b. shop   YEATS 751:2
This is now b. of my bones   BIBLE 70:6
vigour of b.   SHAK 627:22
boneless: b. wonder sitting   CHUR 202:3
bones: be he that moves my b.   SHAK 635:15
b. are smitten asunder   BOOK 127:5
b. that lay scattered   SHAK 621:23
b. that rattled   SACK 552:14

bones: (*cont.*):
b. which thou hast broken — BOOK 128:5
But to subsist in b. — BROW 145:20
Can these b. live — BIBLE 85:26
conjuring trick with b. — JENK 365:4
dead men lost their b. — ELIOT 273:4
England keep my b. — SHAK 594:13
full of dead men's b. — BIBLE 92:6
glas he hadde pigges b. — CHAU 193:8
have the tongs and the b. — SHAK 612:10
I may tell all my b. — BOOK 125:13
lay his weary b. among ye — SHAK 589:4
lay my b. amongst you — WOLS 741:20
my b. are out of joint — BOOK 125:12
my b. consumed away through — BOOK 126:8
my b. I feel it — ROET 544:3
nor hatchment o'er his b. — SHAK 578:9
Of his b. are coral made — SHAK 625:10
O ye dry b., hear — BIBLE 85:27
Rattle his b. over the stones — NOEL 496:10
valley which was full of b. — BIBLE 85:25
weave their thread with b. — SHAK 629:16
bonfire: b. of the vanities — WOLFE 741:6
way to the everlasting b. — SHAK 602:10
bong-tree: land where the B. grows
— LEAR 414:13
bonheur: b. seul est salutaire — PROU 530:17
bonhomie: Overcame his natural b. — BENT 64:16
bonjour: B. tristesse — ÉLUA 276:3
bon-mots: plucking b. from their places
— MORE 483:21
bonnet: h. of Bonny Dundee — SCOTT 559:8
bonnets: B. are bound for the Border
— SCOTT 560:25
bonnie: b. banks o' Loch Lomon' — ANON 17:8
bonny: Am I no a b. fighter — STEV 667:12
Belbroughton Road is b. — BETJ 68:1
bono: Cui b.? — CIC 204:12
bonum: Summum b. — CIC 204:1
bonus: b. homo et bonus civis — AUCT 33:21
Esse quam videri b. malebat — SALL 554:13
booby: give her b. for another — GAY 300:3
Boojum: If your Snark be a B.! — CARR 184:4
book: b. a devil's chaplain — DARW 231:11
b., and candle shall not — SHAK 594:3
b. because it deals — WOOLF 742:13
b. filled with trouble — TOLS 700:7
b. is like an infant's — TRAH 701:8
b. is the best of friends — TUPP 705:3
b. is the precious life-blood — MILT 475:5
b. is the purest essence — CARL 181:13
b. it is written — BOOK 126:25
b. known to him by heart — WOOLF 742:9
b. of honour razèd quite — SHAK 633:9
b. of knowledge — MILT 470:16
B. of Life begins — WILDE 735:29
b. of the living — BOOK 129:14
b. of verse — FITZ 283:13
b. polished dry with pumice — CAT 185:10
b. that ever took him out — JOHN 373:8
b. where men — SHAK 640:17
b. will be brought forth — MISS 477:12
Camerado, this is no b. — WHIT 732:10
dainties that are bred in a b. — SHAK 598:15
do not throw this b. about — BELL 60:21
doth best commend a b. — HEMI 331:12
encouragement this b. — WOD 740:13
Go, little b., and wish to all — STEV 669:8
Great b., great evil — CALL 175:8
had when I wrote that b. — SWIFT 675:14
hotch-potch of my little b. — JUV 383:16
I'll drown my b. — SHAK 626:1
I won't talk of his b. — JOHN 373:1
knows this out of the b. — DICK 242:5
leaves of the Judgement B. — TAYL 679:16
library to make one b. — JOHN 374:1
like a b. in breeches — SMITH 653:16
little volume, but large b. — CRAS 226:9
Making a b. is a craft — LA BR 405:5
mentioning a small b. — RFFD 538:10
mind afterwards—over a b. — LAMB 406:9
most valuable b., by chance — GRAY 316:14
My b. and thit this time — HALL 000:0

book: (*cont.*):
name out of the b. of life — BIBLE 106:5
Not on his picture, but his b. — JONS 379:18
novel is the one bright b. — LAWR 412:7
oldest rule in the b. — CARR 182:16
pain to pen the b. — OXF 504:2
read a b. before reviewing — SMITH 653:21
reader seldom peruses a b. — ADD 4:6
reading or non-reading a b. — BYRON 174:7
substance of a b. directly — KNOW 403:2
take down this b. — YEATS 753:19
take the b. along with them — STER 664:19
There is a b., who runs — KEBLE 392:21
thick, square b. — GLOU 308:3
things noted in thy b. — BOOK 128:13
this b. I directe — CHAU 196:3
thou seest, write in a b. — BIBLE 105:34
until he has written a b. — JOW 380:17
was the b. and writer too — DANTE 230:13
What is the use of a b. — CARR 181:23
when he can read the b. — BEVAN 68:15
where's the b. — CHUR 200:22
who destroys a good b. — MILT 475:4
With a religious b., or friend — WOTT 749:1
woman who wrote the b. — LINC 422:17
worthy to open the b. — BIBLE 106:13
Would shut the b., and sit — SHAK 583:14
book-case: last is a mere b. — DEFOE 233:15
book-club: B. bows the knee to Baal
— BYRON 172:5
bookful: b. blockhead — POPE 521:24
bookie: b. or of a clergyman — MUGG 487:8
book-keeping: inventor of double-entry b.
— MULL 487:15
books: authority from others' b. — SHAK 598:7
b. and talk that would — FORS 290:23
B. are a load of crap — LARK 410:5
b. are divisible into two — RUSK 550:17
b. are either dreams — LOW 429:14
B. are made not like children — FLAU 286:4
B. are not absolutely dead — MILT 475:3
b. are undeservedly forgotten — AUDEN 36:17
b. are weapons — ROOS 546:5
b. are well written — WILDE 735:14
b. be then the eloquence — SHAK 633:8
b. consumed the midnight — GAY 299:31
B. do furnish a room — POW 528:4
B. from Boots' and country — BETJ 67:15
b. in the running brooks — SHAK 567:25
b. lies the *soul* — CARL 180:27
B., like men their authors — SWIFT 674:9
B. make sense of life — BARN 53:8
B. must follow sciences — BACON 45:23
B. say: she did this because — BARN 53:8
b., the academes — SHAK 598:19
B. think for me — LAMB 406:17
B., we are told, propose — DE Q 237:14
b. were opened — BIBLE 86:1
b. which no one can read — CORN 219:6
B. will speak plain when — BACON 43:3
cannot learn men from b. — DISR 248:34
cream of others' b. — MORE 483:21
days is a collection of b. — CARL 180:28
Deep-versed in b. and shallow — MILT 473:22
do *you* read b. *through* — JOHN 373:22
Education ent only b. — WESK 727:26
equal skill to Cambridge b. — BROW 146:25
From reading far too many b. — BELL 61:13
gentleman is not in your b. — SHAK 613:8
has written all the b. — BUTL 167:2
He may live without b. — MER 458:11
her soul in new French b. — BROW 148:13
his b. were read — BELL 61:26
I never read b.—I *write* them — PUNCH 531:24
many b. there is no end — BIBLE 81:3
my b. had been any worse — CHAN 190:6
My only b. — MOORE 483:11
No furniture so charming as b. — SMITH 653:10
On b. for to rede I me delyte — CHAU 195:1
quiet, friendship, b. — THOM 696:3
read all the b. there — MALL 442:16
some b. are to be tasted — BACON 44:27
studied b. than men — BACON 45:11
study of mankind is b. — HUXL 357:11

books: (*cont.*):
their lean b. with the fat — BURT 164:14
Things in b.' clothing — LAMB 406:18
thumb each other's b. — RUSK 550:20
Twenty b., clad in blak — CHAU 192:20
we may live without b. — MER 458:11
Wherever b. will be burned — HEINE 330:13
write it in the b. of law — JOHN 367:6
written three b. on the soul — BROW 149:7
Your *borrowers of b.* — LAMB 406:13
booksellers: b. have put up with poets
— HOR 347:19
boom: groaning as the guns b. — CHES 199:4
boon: b. and a blessing to men — ANON 18:16
With the beanflowers' b. — BROW 149:13
boot: b. in the face — PLATH 516:5
B., saddle, to horse, and away — BROW 148:20
b. upon the summer's velvet — SHAK 584:22
imagine a b. stamping — ORW 500:17
squeak of a b. — FORS 290:22
bootboy: b. at Claridges — WOOLF 742:16
booted: b. and spurred to ride — RUMB 549:17
Booth: B. led boldly — LIND 423:3
boots: always have one's b. — MONT 480:14
Aristocrat who cleans the b. — GILB 304:1
Books from B.' — BETJ 67:15
b. it with uncessant pace — MILT 466:4
b.—movin' up and down again — KIPL 398:15
doormat in a world of b. — RHYS 539:22
He carries his heart in his b. — HERB 333:16
legs when I take my b. — DICK 240:23
pleasure me in his top-b. — MARL 446:9
Pulled off his b., and took — MILT 467:16
school without any b. — BULM 155:1
Their b. are heavy on the floor — AUDEN 35:15
truth is pulling its b. on — SPUR 661:16
booze: with b. until he's fifty — FAUL 281:5
boozes: b. by the company — BURT 164:8
border: As she gaed o'er the b. — BURNS 160:7
Bonnets are bound for the B. — SCOTT 560:25
B. and gi'e them a brush — HOGG 341:15
his b. see Israel set — BROW 150:3
Night Mail crossing the B. — AUDEN 35:9
nor West, B., nor Breed — KIPL 398:13
borders: come to the b. of sleep — THOM 694:3
bore: awhile they b. her up — SHAK 578:13
be in it is merely a b. — WILDE 735:31
b. consumes *each year* — UPD 707:4
Every hero becomes a b. at last — EMER 277:12
He is an old b. — TREE 702:5
He was not only a b. — MUGG 487:12
Mute, beside a muzzled b. — STEP 663:18
secret of being a b. — VOLT 716:8
bored: because I know that I am b. — JOAD 366:9
b. look on people's faces — MILL 461:23
Bores and B. — BYRON 171:27
Ever to confess you're b. — BERR 66:18
He b. with his augur — BALL 49:11
silent and indefinitely b. — KNOX 403:8
virtue of the b. — WAUGH 724:8
boredom: B. a vital problem — RUSS 551:9
b. on a large scale — INGE 359:13
Life is first b., then fear — LARK 409:17
bores: B. and *Bored* — BYRON 171:27
B. have succeeded to dragons — DISR 248:37
boring: b. about somebody else's happiness
— HUXL 357:16
Life, friends, is b. — BERR 66:18
born: already b. before my lips — MAND 444:7
And to the manner b. — SHAK 573:8
be b. is the best for man — AUDEN 34:7
been b. to set it right — STR 670:16
blight man was b. for — HOPK 346:4
b. about three of the clock — SHAK 582:21
b. an Englishman and remained — BEHAN 59:25
B. but to die, and reas'ning — POPE 522:9
b. falls into a dream like — CONR 217:7
B. for us on earth below — CASW 185:4
b. free and equal in dignity — ANON 11:19
B. in a cellar — FOOTE 288:14
b. in a... seventy years — JEANS 363:25
b. in days when wits were — ARN 28:9

born: (*cont.*):
b. in full sunlight — WAUGH 723:17
B. in the garret — BYRON 173:4
B. in the USA — SPR 661:13
b. King of the Jews — BIBLE 88:8
B. of the sun they travelled — SPEN 659:1
B. of the very sigh — KEATS 388:5
B. of the Virgin Mary — BOOK 119:1
B. on the fourth of July — COHAN 208:13
b. out of my due time — MORR 485:11
b. under a rhyming planet — SHAK 614:16
b. we cry that we are come — SHAK 597:11
b. with a different face — BLAKE 112:12
b. with a gift of laughter — SAB 552:11
b. with heavenly compassion — DICK 239:12
b. with your legs apart — ORTON 499:17
British Bourgeoise not b. — SITW 648:17
But I was free b. — BIBLE 00.0
Carry the lad that's b. — BOUL 137:17
Else, wherefore b. — TENN 681:22
ever b. in a conference — FITZ 284:22
every man who lives is b. — DRYD 261:13
Every moment one is b. — TENN 690:5
Except a man be b. again — BIBLE 96:13
For we are b. in other's pain — THOM 694:18
house where I was b. — HOOD 343:21
I am not yet b. — MACN 441:1
I've been b., and once — ELIOT 272:17
I was b. barefoot — LONG 426:6
I was b. free as Caesar — SHAK 589:28
I was b. in a cellar — CONG 215:8
I was b. sneering — GILB 304:20
man if he had not been b. — BIBLE 92:24
Man is b. to live — PAST 508:2
Man is b. unto trouble — BIBLE 77:12
Man that is b. of a woman — BIBLE 77:21
Man that is b. of a woman — BOOK 124:3
Man was b. free, and everywhere he is
  in chains — ROUS 549:2
men naturally were b. free — MILT 476:9
natural to die as to be b. — BACON 43:10
Never was b.! — STOWE 670:9
Not to be b. is — SOPH 656:14
Not to be b., or being born — BACON 46:2
one b. out of due time — BIBLE 101:4
One is not b. a woman — DE B 233:10
other powerless to be b. — ARN 28:20
perish wherein I was b. — BIBLE 77:6
person b. so unlucky — MARQ 448:19
seeing he had been b. — POUND 526:11
some men are b. great — SHAK 630:4
soon as we were b. — BIBLE 87:4
supposed it lucky to be b. — WHIT 732:15
That's b. into the world alive — GILB 304:10
that thou wast b. — SHAK 595:7
There's a sucker b. — BARN 53:19
They are b. three thousand — DEL 236:13
They can't be b. — DICK 240:6
they were b. or should die — TRAH 701:15
those who are to be b. — BURKE 158:2
Thou wast not b. for death — KEATS 389:15
thus was I b. again — LACK 405:7
time to be b., and a time — BIBLE 80:5
'Tis less than to be b. — BEAU 57:2
took the trouble to be b. — BEAU 56:12
To one of woman b. — SHAK 605:3
unto us a child is b. — BIBLE 82:27
virgin mother b. — MILT 466:20
was b. after the flesh — BIBLE 102:5
was b. to set it right — SHAK 574:7
was b. under other skies — LE C 415:13
We all are b. mad — BECK 57:28
were b. in a merry hour — SHAK 613:20
we were b. to run — SPR 661:14
We were not b. to sue — SHAK 619:8
Woman may b. you — HEYW 338:3
women are b. slaves — AST 32:9
work is not b. with him — LOW 429:19
borne: b. even heavier things — VIRG 712:5
b. it with a patient shrug — SHAK 607:22
b. me a man of strife — BIBLE 85:11
B. on our shoulders — BROW 149:27
I have b., and borne — SHAK 583:2

borne: (*cont.*):
It is b. in upon me I am — HARE 326:7
my mother had not b. me — SHAK 575:18
borogoves: mimsy were the b. — CARR 182:18
boroughs: bright b., the circle-citadels
— HOPK 346:5
borrer: b. the money to do it — WARD 721:17
borrow: *the men who b.* — LAMB 406:12
well enough to b. from — BIER 109:2
borrower: b. of the night — SHAK 602:22
Neither a b., nor a lender — SHAK 573:4
borrowers: Your b. *of books* — LAMB 406:13
borrowing: beggar by banqueting upon b.
— BIBLE 87:23
b. dulls the edge of husbandry — SHAK 573:4
b. only lingers and lingers — SHAK 582:25
boshaft: *aber b. ist er nicht* — EINS 268:1
bosom: And in your fragrant b. dies
— CAREW 179:13
angels into Abraham's b. — BIBLE 95:9
b.-friend of the maturing sun — KEATS 390:17
b.'s lord sits lightly — SHAK 624:2
b. that stirred like — BABEL 41:12
carry them in his b. — BIBLE 83:28
Cleanse the stuffed b. — SHAK 604:21
Close couched in your white b. — CRAS 226:10
Edward sleep in Abraham's b. — SHAK 622:4
guardage to the sooty b. — SHAK 614:28
her b. and half her side — COL 209:9
Into my b. and be lost in me — TENN 688:13
Let me to thy b. fly — WESL 728:6
little son into his b. — FLET 288:1
Love in my b. b. like a bee — LODGE 425:23
man take fire in his b. — BIBLE 78:15
seat is the b. of God — HOOK 344:14
She has no b. and no behind — SMITH 652:20
Through my burned b. — SHAK 594:15
unadornèd b. of the deep — MILT 463:14
bosomed: B. high in tufted trees — MILT 465:11
bosoms: b. higher than the shores — SHAK 627:8
b. of your actresses excite — JOHN 371:8
hang and brush their b. — BROW 153:11
Quiet to quick b. is a hell — BYRON 168:22
boss: b. there is always — MARQ 448:16
bossing: shorter hours and nobody b.
— ORW 500:22
Bossuet: excite the horror of B. — MAC 435:1
bossy: by the b. for the bully — SELD 562:14
Boston: And this is good old B. — BOSS 137:1
B. man is the east wind — APPL 23:18
O B. bells — ING 360:2
Boswell: B. is the first of biographers — MAC 434:12
Boswelliana: Lues B. — MAC 435:6
botanist: No, Sir, I am not a b. — JOHN 371:24
botanize: One that would peep and b.
— WORD 746:14
Botany Bay: New colonies seek for at B.
— FREE 293:15
botch: sundial, and I make a b. — BELL 61:25
botches: Leave no rubs nor b. — SHAK 603:2
both: life from b. sides now — MITC 477:19
long as ye b. shall live — BOOK 123:19
may wear it on b. sides — SHAK 627:23
bother: I never b. with people I hate
— HART 327:21
Though 'B. it' I may — GILB 305:24
bothered: b., and bewildered — HART 327:14
botté: *toujours b.* — MONT 480:14
Botticelli: B.'s a *cheese* — PUNCH 532:6
If B. were alive today — UST 707:15
bottle: b. and a bag — GASC 298:16
b. on the chimley-piece — DICK 241:13
great desire to a b. of hay — SHAK 612:11
little for the b. — DIBD 238:11
nor a b. to give him — DICK 240:16
put my tears into thy b. — BOOK 128:13
bottles: English have hot-water b. — MIKES 460:4
fill old b. with banknotes — KEYN 395:9
put new wine into old b. — ATTL 32:15
put new wine into old b. — BIBLE 90:8
with narrow-necked b. — POPE 524:5
bottom: b. of the monstrous world — MILT 466:12

bottom: (*cont.*):
fairies at b. of our garden — FYL 296:11
forgotten man at the b. — ROOS 545:14
I now sit down on my b. — FLEM 287:7
Which will reach the b. first — GRAH 313:9
bottomless: Burnt after them to the b. pit
— MILT 472:5
Law is a b. pit — ARB 24:8
smoke of the pit that is b. — JAM 361:17
bottoms: b. of my trousers rolled — ELIOT 272:6
bouchers: *des bergers et des b.* — VOLT 716:19
boue: *La nostalgie de la b.* — AUG 36:21
bough: blossom that hangs on the b.
— SHAK 626:2
bread beneath the b. — FITZ 283:13
Petals on a wet, black b. — POUND 527:5
with bloom along the b. — HOUS 352:5
boughs: b. and the brushwood sheaf
— BROW 150:5
b. which shake against — SHAK 634:6
Fell from their b. — SHAK 626:16
I got me b. off many a tree — HERB 334:15
longer rotten b. to climb — WYATT 749:16
on orchard b. they keep — DRIN 258:10
bought: blood with guilt is b. — SHEL 642:10
boum: all produce 'b.' — FORS 290:22
bounce: b. the reader — FORS 290:3
bound: b. for the same bourn — HOUS 352:16
b. him a thousand years — BIBLE 107:14
b. in the spirit unto Jerusalem — BIBLE 99:3
fast b. in misery — BOOK 132:15
my duty as a man is b. — TENN 689:5
one law, to another b. — GREV 318:8
tied and b. with the chain — BOOK 120:4
utmost b. of human thought — TENN 690:2
boundary: intimacy there is a secret b.
— AKHM 6:8
bounded: b. in a nut-shell — SHAK 574:27
bounden: b. duty and service — BOOK 122:13
meet, right, and our b. duty — BOOK 122:10
bounding: heart less b. at emotion — ARN 28:29
boundless: b., endless, and sublime
— BYRON 169:16
Is b., as we wish our souls — SHEL 640:20
Is b. better, boundless worse — TENN 689:16
My bounty is b. as the sea — SHAK 623:4
that the desire is b. — SHAK 627:16
bounds: b. which they shall not — BOOK 132:1
wider shall thy b. be set — BENS 63:23
bounteous: O may this b. God — WINK 739:6
bounties: morning b. ere I left — COWP 222:26
Bountiful: My Lady B. — FARQ 280:9
bounty: b. is as boundless — SHAK 623:4
By those his former b. fed — DRYD 259:19
For his b., there was no winter — SHAK 566:20
lust of the goat is the b. — BLAKE 112:24
bouquet: b. better than taste — POTT 525:15
bouquets: broken Anne of gathering b.
— FROST 295:11
bourg: rustic murmur of their b. — TENN 682:9
bourgeois: b. always bounces up — CONN 216:22
b. climb up on them — FLAU 286:4
B. . . . is an epithet — HOPE 344:23
b. montent dessus — FLAU 286:4
b. origin goes through — ORW 500:19
b. prefers comfort to pleasure — HESSE 337:16
How beastly the b. — LAWR 412:14
Il faut épater le b. — BAUD 55:14
Les b., ce sont les autres — REN 538:17
place of the old b. society — MARX 452:13
small-town b. at heart — NAB 488:20
bourgeoise: The British B. — SITW 648:17
bourgeoisie: b. in the long run — TROT 704:12
discreet charm of the b. — BUÑ 155:11
from the b. of all classes — DIN 246:9
bourn: bound for the same b. — HOUS 352:16
b. how far to be beloved — SHAK 564:13
country from whose b. — SHAK 575:16
see beyond our b. — KEATS 390:25
bourne: b. from which no hollingsworth
— MORT 486:13
our b. of time and place — TENN 680:18
bourreaux: *elles respectent leurs b.* — SART 557:2

boutique: b., and a swinging hot spot
    MITC 477:18
bow: B. down before him   MONS 480:2
  b. down thyself to them   BIBLE 72:16
  b. my knees unto the Father   BIBLE 102:13
  b. myself in the house   BIBLE 76:22
  b., ye tradesmen   GILB 304:6
  Bring me my b. of burning gold   BLAKE 113:4
  drew a b. at a venture   BIBLE 76:14
  from the Almighty's b.   BLAKE 112:5
  he breaketh the b.   BOOK 127:17
  Jesus every knee should b.   BIBLE 103:5
  Lord of the unerring b.   BYRON 169:11
  set my b. in the cloud   BIBLE 70:32
  strong men shall b.   BIBLE 81:1
  What of the b.   DOYLE 257:3
bowed: At her feet he b., he fell   BIBLE 74:5
  B. by the weight of centuries   MARK 446:7
bowels: b. of Christ   CROM 227:8
  b. of compassion from him   BIBLE 105:26
  b. of the earth were sought   DRAY 258:3
  Have molten b.   BOTT 137:11
bower: b. quiet for us   KEATS 386:13
  b. we shrined to Tennyson   HARDY 325:1
  deck both bed and b.   SPEN 660:6
  eyes doth build his b.   LODGE 426:1
  queen in a summer's b.   SHAK 581:9
  St Johnston's b.   BALL 49:14
  that smooth-swarded b.   TENN 687:19
  This lime-tree b. my prison   COL 211:20
bower-caves: bow-shot from her b.   TENN 685:2
bowers: England's green and pleasant b.
    BLAKE 112:9
  lodged in thy living b.   VAUG 709:10
bowl: atoms lurk within the b.   SMITH 653:18
  b. aloft and intoned   JOYCE 381:17
  b. with atrabilious   HUXL 357:22
  fill the flowing b.   ANON 12:24
  golden b. be broken   BIBLE 81:1
  inverted b. we call The Sky   FITZ 284:10
  Life is just a b. of cherries   BROWN 144:15
  Morning in the b. of night   FITZ 283:10
bowler: wild b. thinks he bowls   LANG 408:15
bowling: lies poor Tom B.   DIBD 238:16
bows: B. down to wood and stone   HEBER 330:4
  b. from which your children   GIBR 303:2
bow-shot: b. from her bower-eaves   TENN 685:2
bow-strings: Hold, or cut h.   SHAK 611:10
bow-windows: putting b. to the house
    DICK 239:27
bow-wow: B. strain I can do   SCOTT 561:1
  were it not for his b. way   PEMB 511:11
bow-wows: He has gone to the demnition b.
    DICK 242:16
box: b. where sweets compacted   HERB 336:1
  said 'B. about   AUBR 33:11
  twelve good men into a b.   BROU 144:7
boy: Alas, pitiable b.   VIRG 713:18
  And if I look the b. will lour   LODGE 426:1
  And to be b. eternal   SHAK 631:11
  Being read to by a b.   ELIOT 271:10
  b. brought the white sheet   GARC 297:12
  b. may become President   STEV 666:19
  b. playing on the sea-shore   NEWT 494:7
  b.'s love, or a whore's   SHAK 596:18
  b. stood on the burning   HEM 331:10
  b.'s will is the wind's will   LONG 427:4
  b. will ruin himself   GEOR 301:5
  compound a b., half-French   SHAK 587:2
  fifteen-year-old b.   ROTH 548:15
  Give to your b., your Caesar   DRYD 259:26
  I am the Yankee Doodle B.   COHAN 208:13
  Let the b. win his spurs   EDW 267:2
  Mad about the b.   COW 220:13
  misfortunes can befall a b.   MAUG 454:13
  O blackbird, what a b. you   BROWN 145:3
  [illegible]   GORD 312:13
  [illegible] roughly to your little b.   [illegible]
  schoolrooms for 'the b.'   COOK 218:5
  [illegible]   [illegible]
  Smiling the b. fell dead   [illegible]

boy: (cont.):
  squeaking Cleopatra b.   SHAK 567:1
  Take the thanks of a b.   BEEC 59:6
  thing of beauty and a b.   ROWL 549:9
  To be a soaring human b.   DICK 239:8
  Upon the growing b.   WORD 745:14
  was and a little tiny b.   SHAK 630:37
  When I was a little b.   ANON 19:17
  you like your blueeyed b.   CUMM 228:14
  You silly twisted b.   MILL 462:4
boyaux: étranglés avec les b.   MESL 458:15
boyfriend: certain thing called the B.   WILS 738:8
boyhood: lost b. of Judas   Æ 5:10
boys: And three merry b. are we   FLET 287:13
  As flies to wanton b.   SHAK 596:27
  B. and girls tumbling   TRAH 701:15
  b. and many girls long   CAT 186:9
  b. are not going to be sent   ROOS 546:1
  b. are still there   BAR 54:22
  b. get at one end they   JOHN 374:8
  b. in the back rooms   BEAV 57:7
  b. in the back room will   LOES 426:2
  b., it is all hell   SHER 645:27
  b. of the old Brigade   WEAT 724:13
  b. that swim on bladders   SHAK 588:19
  b. who will stop your little   PERRY 513:2
  By office boys for office b.   SAL 554:9
  Christian b. I can   ARN 30:12
  Deceive b. with toys   LYS 433:15
  lightfoot b. are laid   HOUS 352:18
  like loaded guns with b.   CRAB 225:10
  little b. with breeches   BARB 52:5
  Mealy b., and beef-faced   DICK 242:26
  send American b.   JOHN 367:10
  Till the b. come Home   FORD 289:16
  virgin girls and b.   HOR 349:22
  When b. go first to bed   HERB 335:12
bracelet: b. of bright hair   DONNE 252:13
braces: Damn. b.   BLAKE 112:26
  powerful liquid which rots b.   MORT 486:14
bracing: B. brain and sinew   KING 397:12
bracken: b. turning brown   BRAD 139:1
Bradford: hat on a B. millionaire   ELIOT 273:9
Bradshaw: vocabulary of 'B.'   DOYLE 257:1
braes: Ye banks and b.   BURNS 161:9
brag: Beauty is Nature's b.   MILT 464:8
  B., sweet tenor bull   BUNT 155:9
  Is left this vault to b.   SHAK 602:17
  list in bravery so to b.   GASC 298:16
  Nor shall death b. thou   SHAK 633:6
  vapour and fume and b.   KIPL 399:2
Brahmin: I the hymn the B. sings   EMER 276:6
braided: b. her yellow hair   BALL 50:13
braids: twisted b. of lilies   MILT 464:10
brain: alone immured in the b.   SHAK 598:20
  Bear of Very Little B.   MILNE 462:11
  b. about the action   BYRON 170:9
  b. attic stocked with all   DOYLE 256:6
  b. of feathers   POPE 518:18
  b. perplexes and retards   KEATS 389:11
  b. smoked like   JONS 378:10
  b. that won't believe   BLAKE 111:3
  b. to think again   BRON 142:14
  chimera in my b.   DONNE 253:10
  draughts intoxicate the b.   POPE 521:8
  drivel every drizzly b.   BYRON 169:27
  dry b. in a dry season   ELIOT 271:12
  fibre from the b. does tear   BLAKE 111:2
  fingerprints across his b.   HEND 332:4
  from the heat-oppressed b.   SHAK 601:12
  harmful to the b.   JAM 361:17
  has gleaned my teeming b.   KEATS 390:28
  instrumental to the b.   SHAK 572:5
  issue of my b.   MARS 449:8
  leave that b. outside   GILB 304:11
  My b.? my second favourite   ALLEN 9:13
  Owl hasn't exactly got B.   MILNE 463:6
  petrifactions of a plodding b.   BYRON 172:8
  schoolmasters puzzle their b.   GOLD 311:20
  should possess my b.   DRAY 258:4
  tares of mine own b.   BROW 140:10
  through which b. implores   JOUG 255:10

brain: (cont.):
  Which are the b. of heaven   MER 458:6
  young wife and a good b.   JONS 378:7
brained: large-b. woman   BROW 147:22
brains: And dash'd the b. out   SHAK 601:7
  b. knocked out by them   SHEL 641:16
  b. must beat on tickle   GASC 298:19
  b. of a Minerva   BARR 54:16
  cudgel thy b. no more   SHAK 578:18
  gentleman said a girl with b.   LOOS 428:8
  I mix them with my b., sir   OPIE 499:4
  Muses scorn with vulgar b.   SIDN 647:1
  out his b. upon the flute   BROW 152:27
  rifle and blow out your b.   KIPL 401:12
  sometimes his b. go to his head   ASQ 32:2
  steal away their b.   SHAK 616:6
brain-washing: called b.   GREER 317:16
brake: and his neck b.   BIBLE 74:31
  it bowed and syne it b.   BALL 51:2
brambles: b. in the fortresses   BIBLE 83:18
  That b. like tall cedars show   COTT 220:3
bran: this the Plebeian b.   DONNE 253:7
branch: b. shall grow out   BIBLE 83:1
  b. that might have grown   MARL 447:5
  reddens on the high b.   SAPP 556:2
  Who lops the mouldered b.   TENN 681:12
branches: b. of frankincense   BIBLE 88:4
  lodge in the b. thereof   BIBLE 91:3
  sing among the b.   BOOK 132:7
  Thy b. ne'er remember   KEATS 387:32
branchy: b. between towers   HOPK 345:9
brandy: B. for the Parson   KIPL 400:9
  b. of the damned   SHAW 637:10
  drink cold b., and water   LAMB 407:9
  must drink b.   JOHN 375:7
  pray get me a glass of b.   GEOR 301:1
  There's some are fou o' b.   BURNS 162:6
brass: All that was ever writ in b.   JONS 379:18
  am become as sounding b.   BIBLE 101:1
  feet like unto fine b.   BIBLE 106:1
  manners live in b.   SHAK 589:9
  Since b., nor stone   SHAK 634:3
brassière: Art is not a b.   BARN 53:7
brat: His spurious b., Tom Jones   RICH 540:15
brave: b. and one half cowards   JOHN 375:5
  b. causes left   OSB 501:18
  B. Macbeth   SHAK 599:15
  b. man with a sword   WILDE 736:1
  b. men lived before Agamemnon's time   HOR 350:18
  b. music of a distant drum   FITZ 283:14
  b. new world   SHAK 626:3
  b. push and see what can   STEV 667:25
  b.! that are no more   COWP 222:24
  b. world, Sir, full   BEHN 60:12
  depart the souls of the b.   CLOU 207:6
  Fears of the b., and follies   JOHN 370:20
  Fortune assists the b.   TER 690:13
  Fortune favours the b.   VIRG 714:7
  heard her cry, 'you are b.   GRAH 313:17
  home of the b.   KEY 394:15
  How sleep the b., who sink   COLL 213:12
  late to-morrow to be b.   ARMS 26:9
  None but the b. deserves   DRYD 259:16
  posterity as a b. bad   CLAR 205:5
  What's b., what's noble   SHAK 566:17
braved: b. by his brother   SHAK 593:8
braver: b. gentleman   SHAK 581:29
  I have done one b. thing   DONNE 252:20
bravery: b. on the Patriot side   WAUGH 724:3
  list in b. so to brag   GASC 298:16
  natural b. of your isle   SHAK 571:6
braw: b. bricht moonlicht nicht'   MORR 486:2
  He was a b. gallant   BALL 49:3
brawler: not a b., not covetous   BIBLE 103:26
brawling: b. woman   BIBLE 79:9
bray: I will be the Vicar of B.   ANON 15:5
brazen: her world is b.   SIDN 647:6
Brazil: Charley's aunt from B.   THOM 693:2
breach: More honoured in the b.   SHAK 573:8
  Once more unto the b.   SHAK 585:7
  [illegible]   WYNT 747:10

bread: (cont.):
bitter b. of banishment — SHAK 620:2
b. and butter that feels — MACK 439:4
b. beneath the bough — FITZ 283:13
b. eaten in secret — BIBLE 78:19
B. I dip in the river — STEV 669:4
b. of adversity — BIBLE 83:15
b. of affliction — BIBLE 76:13
b. of God is he which cometh — BIBLE 96:24
b. that goes into the oven — GUM 319:15
b. to strengthen man's — BOOK 132:8
b. to this intolerable — SHAK 580:35
breaking of b. — BIBLE 95:33
brought him b. and flesh — BIBLE 75:31
Cast thy b. upon the waters — BIBLE 80:25
crammed with distressful b. — SHAK 586:8
eat thy b. with joy — BIBLE 80:19
face shalt thou eat b — BIBLE 70:16
Give us this day our daily b. — BIBLE 89:5
He took the b. and brake it — ELIZ 274:11
I am the b. of life — BIBLE 96:25
Jesus took b., and blessed — BIBLE 92:25
learning is like b. — JOHN 374:3
lives not upon b. alone — STEV 668:7
living HOMER begged his b. — ANON 17:19
looked to government for b. — BURKE 159:10
Man shall not live by b. alone — BIBLE 88:18
my father's have b. — BIBLE 95:3
Royal slice of b. — MILNE 462:15
She was cutting b. and butter — THAC 691:21
Strengthened with the B. of Life — WHITE 731:4
taste of another man's b. — DANTE 230:20
that b. should be so dear — HOOD 344:9
that which is not b. — BIBLE 84:15
Thy b. is black, of ill — BARC 52:9
To eat dusty b. — BOGAN 116:13
To take b. at my hand — WYATT 749:19
unleavened b. — BIBLE 72:9
unleavened b. of sincerity — BIBLE 100:22
was betrayed, took B. — BOOK 122:12
when we did eat b. — BIBLE 72:15
who did also eat of my b. — BOOK 127:1
whom if his son ask b. — BIBLE 89:19
Who never ate his b. in sorrow — GOET 309:15
With the b. eaten up — CERV 188:10
breadth: Let me have length and b. — BALL 49:7
break: at the b. of the day — STR 671:1
b. a man's spirit is devil's — SHAW 636:3
b. an accepted social law — HARDY 324:16
B., break, break — TENN 680:9
b. the bloody glass you — MACN 440:15
b. their bonds asunder — BOOK 124:8
bruised reed shall he not b. — BIBLE 84:2
But b., my heart — SHAK 572:13
can b. them at pleasure — EDG 266:15
I bend and I b. not — LA F 405:9
I'll b. my staff — SHAK 626:1
it is good to b. the ice — BACON 43:5
lark at b. of day arising — SHAK 633:10
nature round him b. — ADD 4:5
Never give a sucker an even b. — FIEL 282:20
that ye b. every yoke — BIBLE 84:22
Thou thyself must b. at last — ARN 27:11
breakdown: approaching nervous b. — RUSS 551:10
Madness need not be all b. — LAING 405:19
breakers: like b. cliffward — CRANE 225:19
breaketh: he b. the bow, and knappeth — BOOK 127:17
Lord b. the cedar-trees — BOOK 126:2
breakfalls: rolls and throws and b. — REED 538:2
breakfast: embarrassment and b. — BARN 53:5
Hope is a good b. — BACON 45:25
impossible things before b. — CARR 183:8
incoherence that sits down to b. — YEATS 753:22
One doth but b. here — HENS 333:9
Where shall we our b. take — BALL 50:18
wholesome, hungry b. — WALT 721:5
breakfasted: I have b. with you — BRUCE 153:19
breakfast-time: critical period in matrimony is b. — HERB 333:23

breaking: b. what it likes — ARN 29:11
By b. of windows, or breaking — MORE 483:19
England take pleasure in b. — ANON 12:21
known of them in b. of bread — BIBLE 95:33
breaks: b. in our bosom — SHEL 640:17
something twangs and b. — MACN 440:17
break-through: may also be b. — LAING 405:19
breast: alas! in my b. — GOET 309:2
back somewhere in our b. — ARN 26:17
b. with freedom glowed — BARB 52:2
broached his boiling bloody b. — SHAK 612:23
charms to sooth a savage b. — CONG 215:16
depth of her glowing b. — SHEL 642:27
eternal in the human b. — POPE 522:1
helpless b. upon his breast — YEATS 752:10
His bed amidst my tender b. — LODGE 426:20
How smooth his b. was — MARL 447:9
leaned on his b. at supper — BIBLE 98:3
May toss him to My b. — HERB 335:16
my b., o'ercharged — SIDN 646:22
My faultless b. the furnace — SOUT 657:22
Oak was round his b. — HOR 349:2
Of thy chaste b., and quiet — LOV 429:6
soft hand, and softer b. — KEATS 386:11
stood b. high amid the corn — HOOD 344:6
that with dauntless b. — GRAY 315:15
void left aching in the b. — POPE 519:19
Wedding-Guest here beat his b. — COL 210:20
with her b. against a thorn — HOOD 344:4
World broods with warm b. — HOPK 345:11
breastie: what a panic's in thy b. — BURNS 163:15
breastless: b. creatures underground — ELIOT 273:15
breastplate: b. of faith and love — BIBLE 103:21
b. of judgement the Urim — BIBLE 72:18
b. of righteousness — BIBLE 103:1
b. than a heart untainted — SHAK 587:18
breasts: all night betwixt my b. — BIBLE 81:7
b. all perfume yes — JOYCE 382:7
b. are like two young roes — BIBLE 81:13
b. by which France is fed — SULLY 671:13
b. the blows of circumstance — TENN 683:25
division of prodigious b. — SWIN 676:4
Sestos and Abydos of her b. — DONNE 250:12
why then her b. are dun — SHAK 635:2
within their b. the grief — AYT 41:4
with wrinkled female b. — ELIOT 273:8
breath: A b. can make them — GOLD 310:6
a b. thou art — SHAK 606:6
Although thy b. be rude — SHAK 568:17
And having lost her b. — SHAK 565:7
And thou no b. at all — SHAK 598:3
are but the b. of kings — BURNS 161:19
ask how he left his b. — GREV 318:7
b. bigger than a circustent — CUMM 228:13
Breathe on me, B. of God — HATCH 328:2
breathes with human b. — TENN 689:17
b. goes now, and some — DONNE 252:21
b. he drew in he wished — LAMB 407:12
breathing thoughtful b. — WORD 747:19
b. of degradation — BYRON 172:17
b. of worldly men cannot — SHAK 620:3
B.'s a ware that will not keep — HOUS 352:7
But thus yields up his b. — GILB 303:11
Clothed with his b. — TENN 682:21
come seemed waste of b. — YEATS 752:6
Could ever yet cut b. — SHAK 632:16
deeds too cold b. gives — SHAK 601:13
Desire himself runs out of b. — RAL 535:12
dust expend an idle b. — CAT 187:1
each saving b. — LOW 430:17
every thing that hath b. — BOOK 135:17
Fly away, fly away, b. — SHAK 629:17
have drawn the b. of life — YEATS 751:20
healthy b. of morn — KEATS 387:22
hear her tender-taken b. — KEATS 386:10
I love thee with the b. — BROW 147:21
into his nostrils the b. — BIBLE 70:1
It fluttered and failed for b. — ARN 27:20
mansion call the fleeting b. — GRAY 315:14
mansionry that the heaven's b. — SHAK 601:1
sovereign fingers taxed the b. — THOM 693:9

breath: (cont.):
sweeter woman ne'er drew b. — ING 360:6
sweetness of man's b. — JAM 361:18
than b., he is set free — BERRY 66:15
That lightly draws its b. — WORD 748:14
this present b. may buy — SHAK 598:6
was down and out of b. — SHAK 582:9
world draw thy b. in pain — SHAK 579:11
year with toil of b. — COL 209:22
you have it use your b. — FLET 287:11
breathe: As though to b. were life — TENN 690:1
b. by a sort of artificial — FOST 291:9
b. not his name — MOORE 483:9
B. on me, Breath of God — HATCH 328:2
b. when I expire — BYRON 169:7
like the hair we b. — SURT 672:8
Low, low, b. and blow — TENN 687:27
not b. in that fine air — TENN 681:26
on a summer's morn to b. — MILT 472:21
So long as men can b. — SHAK 633:6
breathèd: This day I b. first — SHAK 593:17
breathes: B. like a bright-eyed face — HUNT 356:11
B. there the man — SCOTT 559:16
breathing: B. my name with a sigh — PAR 506:2
b. of the common wind — WORD 748:13
B., testing his faith — THOM 694:12
Closer is He than b. — TENN 681:15
health, and quiet b. — KEATS 386:13
In the sound his b. kept — SHEL 642:14
breathless: b. hush in the Close — NEWB 492:9
b. hush of evening — HAMM 322:14
B. with adoration — WORD 744:12
Is hanging b. on thy fate — LONG 426:11
thereby making the reader b. — KEATS 391:15
bred: B. en bawn in a brier-patch — HARR 327:4
Bredon: In summertime on B. — HOUS 352:10
'Tis Summer Time on B. — KING 398:6
bree: A little abune her b. — BALL 50:13
breeches: like a book in b. — SMITH 653:16
us little boys with b. — BARB 52:5
breed: Border, nor B., nor — KIPL 398:13
Feared by their b. — SHAK 619:18
it's a marvel they can b. — LAWR 412:24
not b. one work — HOPK 346:9
they most b. and haunt — SHAK 601:1
This happy b. of men — SHAK 619:18
wife for b. — GAY 300:18
breeder: b. of sinners — SHAK 575:18
breeding: b. consists in concealing — TWAIN 706:17
Burgundy without any b. — THUR 697:17
ease, to show your b. — SHER 645:22
Good b., fashion, dancing — WINC 739:1
guilt, or of ill b. — CONG 215:30
one quarrel with good b. — PUSH 532:14
true b. of a gentleman — BYRON 170:28
breeds: Chaos often b. life — ADAMS 2:14
Or lesser b. without the Law — KIPL 400:13
breeks: b. aff a wild Highlandman — SCOTT 560:18
breeze: As the b. rises — FROST 294:9
b. from foggy mount — BYRON 169:27
b. is on the sea — SCOTT 560:26
comes forth in every b. — DAV 232:14
Fluttering and dancing in the b. — WORD 744:15
For a b. of morning moves — TENN 686:17
one intellectual b. — COL 209:20
quivers in the sunny b. — GREN 318:2
volleying rain and tossing b. — ARN 28:26
with the b. of song — TENN 684:1
breezes: b. and the sunshine — CAMP 176:4
b. blown from the spice-islands — COL 212:17
Little b. dusk and shiver — TENN 684:24
breezy: b. call of incense-breathing — GRAY 315:12
B., Sneezy, Freezy — ELLIS 275:14
brekekekex: B. koax koax — ARIS 25:5
brethren: Behold my mother and my b. — BIBLE 90:38
b. and companions' sakes — BOOK 133:26
b., to dwell together — BOOK 134:14

brethren: (cont.):
Dearly beloved b.	BOOK 118:5
least of these my b.	BIBLE 92:21
thee and me . . . for we be b.	BIBLE 70:34
breuis: *Siquidem uita b.*	JOHN 366:15
brevis: *B. esse laboro*	HOR 347:4
Vitae summa b. spem nos	HOR 349:4
brevity: B. is sister of talent	CHEK 197:12
B. is the soul of lingerie	PARK 506:19
B. is the soul of wit	SHAK 574:11
b. of our life	JOHN 366:15
Its body b., and wit its soul	COL 209:21
brew: b. that is true	PANA 505:16
brewers: As bakeres and b.	LANG 409:1
brewery: O take me to a b.	ANON 14:15
bribe: b. or twist	WOLFE 741:1
b. to make a housekeeper	WILD 736:15
done without a b. I find	CENT 188:6
taking of a b. or gratuity	PENN 511:16
Too poor for a b.	GRAY 316:10
bribes: How many b. he had taken	BENT 64:9
man open to b.	GREE 316:23
our fingers with bare h	SHAK 592:27
bricht: braw b. moonlicht	MORR 486:2
brick: b. in his pocket	JOHN 369:7
b. without hitting	ORW 500:20
'Eave 'arf a b. at 'im	PUNCH 531:12
it b. and left it marble	AUG 37:13
piece of b. in his pocket	SWIFT 673:7
They threw it a b. at a time	HARG 326:9
bricks: carries the b. to Lewley	BETJ 68:4
brickwork: slimy posts, and b.	CONS 217:22
bridal: Against their b. day	SPEN 660.24
b. of the earth and sky	HERB 336:1
Or to dance at our b.	SCOTT 560:6
bride: all jealousy to the b.	BARR 54:10
became my glittering b.	WORD 743:21
b. adorned for her husband	BIBLE 107:17
Can ser' him for a b.	MACD 437:8
encounter darkness as a b.	SHAK 606:10
mistress, but a barren b.	POPE 520:9
mourning b.	DRYD 261:14
my life and my b.	POE 518:2
Never the blushing b.	LEIGH 417:1
or a b. her attire	BIBLE 85:3
Passionless b., divine	TENN 686:5
proud b. of a ducal coronet	DICK 241:29
read about his widowed b.	MCL 439:8
So though a virgin, yet a b.	CAREW 179:8
To be his holy b.	STONE 669:12
unravished b. of quietness	KEATS 388:23
bride-bed: thy b. to have decked	SHAK 578:28
bridegroom: Bellona's b.	SHAK 599:17
b. in my death	SHAK 566:10
b. out of his chamber	BOOK 125:4
funeral train which the b.	CLOU 207:3
Like a b. from his room	AYT 41:2
bridegrooms: Of b., brides	HERR 336:6
brides: The B. of Enderby	ING 360:3
bridesmaid: always the b.	LEIGH 417:1
bridge: Champagne, and B.	BELL 61:24
Come shooting through the b.	BETJ 67:10
How well Horatius kept the b.	MAC 436:16
keep the b. with me	MAC 436:11
Like a b. over troubled water	SIMON 647:18
might be going a b. too far	BROW 147:24
Railway B. of the Silv'ry Tay	MCG 437:17
Twenty men crossing a b.	STEV 666:1
bridle: be held with bit and b.	BOOK 126:10
b. not his tongue	BIBLE 104:28
brief: B. as the lightning	SHAK 610:23
b. wherein all marvels	SOUT 657:24
Drest in a little b. authority	SHAK 605:18
I strive to be b.	HOR 347:4
'Tis b., my lord	SHAK 576:15
To the end of a b. episode	MERC 457:14
tragical! tedious and b.	SHAK 612:19
brier: b. shall come up the myrtle	BIBLE 84:18
Thorough bush, thorough b.	SHAK 611:11
brier-pulling Down in a b	HARR 327:4
briers: h is this working-day	SHAK 667:29
brig: B, O Dread	DALL 50:1
brigade: boys of the old b.	WEAT 724:13

brigade: (cont.):
B. of Guards	MACM 440:10
brigand: I am a b.	SHAW 637:9
bright: All calm, as it was b.	VAUG 709:11
All things b. and beautiful	ALEX 8:9
Behold the b. original appear	GAY 300:9
bracelet of b. hair about	DONNE 252:13
b. and fierce and fickle	TENN 688:6
B. as the day, and like	GRAN 314:12
B. before it beat the water	LONG 427:15
b. day is done	SHAK 566:22
b. day that brings forth	SHAK 590:13
Bright effluence of b. essence	MILT 470:15
B. the vision that delighted	MANT 445:12
b. things come to confusion	SHAK 610:23
Dark with excessive b.	MILT 470:18
folds of a b. girdle furled	ARN 27:1
Goddess, excellently b.	JONS 378:16
Keep up your b. swords	SHAK 614:27
look, the land is b.	CLOU 207:25
Lucasta that b. northern star	LOV 428:19
northern climes, obscurely b.	BYRON 169:25
novel is the one b. book	LAWR 412:7
purpose and his eyes are b.	KEATS 392:6
b. face of danger	STEV 667.5
thought thee b.	SHAK 635:9
wishes to appear most b.	SHAK 606:5
you shall shine more b.	SHAK 633:18
brightest: B. and best of the sons	HEBER 330:2
bright-eyed: b. Mariner	COL 210:19
brightness: B. falls from the air	NASHE 491:1
b. of his glory	BIBLE 104:10
b. of his presence	BOOK 125:2
Clothed with transcendent b.	MILT 468:2
his Darkness and his B.	BYRON 173:17
Leaking the b. away	SPEN 659:6
Brignal: O, B. banks are wild	SCOTT 560:12
brilliance: world has achieved b.	BRAD 139:8
brilliant: dullard's envy of b.	BEER 59:15
hrillig: 'Twas b., and the slithy	CARR 182:18
brim: B., in a flash, full	HOPK 346:13
b. the bowl with atrabilious	HUXL 357:22
bubbles winking at the b.	KEATS 389:9
opaque vase fills to the b.	ROET 544:7
sparkles near the b.	BYRON 168:14
brimstone: b. and the burning lake	ALAB 7:1
rain snares, fire and b.	BOOK 124:23
bring: B. me my arrows of desire	BLAKE 113:4
B. out number weight	BLAKE 112:21
knowest not what a day may b.	BIBLE 79:24
They b. it to you, free	AMIS 11:3
would b. home knowledge	JOHN 375:1
bringer: b. of unwelcome news	SHAK 582:13
bringing: B. the cheque and the postal order	AUDEN 35:9
that her b. me up by hand	DICK 240:29
brink: b. and we looked it	DULL 263:11
that trembles on the b.	HAMM 322:14
brinkmanship: boasting of b.	STEV 667:2
brisk: b. as a bee in conversation	JOHN 371:7
b. little somebody	BROW 148:9
brisking: by b. about the life	SMART 649:14
Britain: boundary of B.	TAC 677:19
B. a fit country for heroes	LLOY 424:8
B. all the sun that shines	SHAK 571:11
Hail, happy B.!	SOM 655:13
Say, B., could you ever boast	SWIFT 674:31
When B. first, at heaven's	THOM 695:15
Britannia: Beer and B.	SMITH 653:27
Rule, B.	THOM 695:15
you've shouted 'Rule B.'	KIPL 398:11
brither: lo'ed him like a vera b.	BURNS 163:4
British: B. and Armoric knights	MILT 469:1
B. Grenadier	ANON 18:3
B. have the distinction	ATTL 32:15
B. Museum had lost	GERS 301:11
B. than these selfsame	BORR 136:13
destinies of the B. Empire	DISR 247:9
For art thou not of B. blood	TENN 681:14
greatness of the B.	ADD 4:15
I knell the blood of a B. man	SHAK 596:17
life for the B. female	CLOU 207:1
so also a B. subject	PALM 505:8

British: (cont.):
so ridiculous as the B.	MAC 434:19
useful to the B. nation	CART 184:11
We are B., thank God	MONT 481:19
With a stony B. stare	TENN 686:15
you B. soldier	KIPL 400:1
you broke a B. square	KIPL 399:5
Britishers: B. won't wear	COW 220:14
British Islands: selfsame B.	BORR 136:13
Briton: glory in the name of B.	GEOR 300:26
only a free-born B. can do	THAC 691:13
Britons: B. never will be slaves	THOM 695:15
B. were only natives	SELL 562:17
B. who are kept far away	VIRG 714:13
we B. alone use 'Might'	WAUGH 724:6
brittle: b. glory shineth in this	SHAK 621:2
spend thy many b. darts	WYATT 749:16
broad: b. is the way	BIBLE 89:21
B. of Church	BETJ 68:10
b. on the roots of things	BROW 147:25
By brooks too b. for leaping	HOUS 352:18
City of God, how b. and far	JOHN 377:14
make b. their phylacteries	BIBLE 92:4
She's the B. and I'm the High	SPR 661:11
broadened: b. into a brotherhood	JOHN 367:7
Broadway: sinners on this part of B.	RUNY 550:4
broccoli: It's b., dear	WHITE 731:2
brogues: not fit to tie his b.	SCOTT 561:3
broiled: piece of a b. fish	BIBLE 95:34
broke: If it ain't b., don't fix it	LANCE 407:22
Or b., but would not go	ROET 544:6
broken: baying for b. glass	WAUGH 723:11
bones thou hast b. may rejoice	BOOK 128:5
b. and contrite heart	BOOK 128:8
b. Anne of gathering bouquets	FROST 295:11
b. by their passing feet	YEATS 751:7
b. open on the most scientific	PFAC 510:6
b. the lock and splintered	AUDEN 35:15
b. with the storms of state	SHAK 589:4
But a week when once b.	WALSH 720:17
cord is not quickly b.	BIBLE 80:8
Don't tell me peace has b.	BREC 140:11
have taken up the b. blade	DE G 235:1
healeth those that are b.	BOOK 135:11
How else but through a b. heart	WILDE 736:5
Is it not b.	SHEL 639:20
Laws were made to be b.	NORTH 496:14
liked the Sound of B. Glass	BELL 61:21
mould. Can it be b.	JENK 365:5
Naught b. save this body	BROO 143:17
On the earth the b. arcs	BROW 147:26
When the lute is b.	SHEL 641:6
broken-hearted: bind up the b.	BIBLE 84:26
b. woman tends the grave	HAYES 328:10
You hoped we were both b.	SWIN 676:23
broker: b. is a man who takes	WOOL 742:18
more that of an honest b.	BISM 110:5
Bronx: B. is up but the Battery	COMD 214:11
bronze: monument more lasting than b.	HOR 350:9
bronzes: b. more smoothly	VIRG 713:17
brooch: b. of gold ful sheene	CHAU 192:16
brooches: and toys for your delight	STEV 668:24
brood: b. of folly without father	MILT 464:13
eternal b. of glory excellent	SPEN 659:26
fond of no second b.	SHAK 570:25
that thy b. is flown	TENN 688:7
broods: b. and sleeps on his own	WORD 746:16
b. with warm breast	HOPK 345:11
brook: b. doth an inland b.	SHAK 610:8
Fell in the weeping b.	SHAK 578:13
noise like of a hidden b.	COL 211:13
went and dwelt by the b.	BIBLE 75:31
Where the b. and river meet	LONG 427:2
wholesome salad from the b.	COWP 224:7
brooks: b. of Eden mazily	TENN 687:11
By b. too broad for leaping	HOUS 352:18
b. were frozen	AUDEN 34:13
broom: bright blows the b.	STEV 668:24
I am sent with b. before	SHAK 613:2
broomstick: mortal man is a b.	SWIFT 674:3

brothel: intellectual b. from which TOLS 701:3
metaphysical b. for emotions KOES 403:18
brothels: b. with bricks of Religion
BLAKE 112:23
Keep thy foot out of b. SHAK 596:10
brother: Am I my b.'s keeper BIBLE 70:18
Am I not a man and a b. WEDG 726:15
And hurt my b. SHAK 579:3
Be my b., or I kill you CHAM 189:16
be the white man's b. KING 396:14
BIG B. IS WATCHING YOU ORW 500:9
braved by his b. SHAK 593:8
b. and his lover have embraced SHAK 605:9
B. can you spare a dime HARB 323:10
b. is born for adversity BIBLE 78:40
b. of death exacteth BROW 146:22
b.'s soul you find BARB 52:3
b.'s tears have wet them CAT 187:1
B., thy tail hangs down KIPL 401:16
b. to the ox MARK 446:7
b. turns with ceaseless GOLD 311:8
Death and his b. Sleep SHEL 640:8
Esau my b. is a hairy BIBLE 71:10
far have him than his b. MARV 451:1
Had it been his b. ANON 14:6
hand of every man's b. BIBLE 70:30
has brother followed he WORD 744:3
hateth his b. BIBLE 105:29
his b. is dead BIBLE 71:29
I am a b. to dragons BIBLE 77:31
I am, Sir, a B. of the Angle WALT 720:24
I am the darker b. HUGH 354:1
marriage with his b.'s wife SHAK 588:12
marry with his b. SHAK 577:8
My b. he is in Elysium SHAK 628:11
O b. man WHIT 733:10
O my b., Chibiabos LONG 427:18
our dear b. here departed BOOK 124:5
our sad bad glad mad b.'s SWIN 676:6
seeth his b. have need BIBLE 105:26
shall my b. sin against me BIBLE 91:21
sticketh closer than a b. BIBLE 79:3
stick more close than a b. KIPL 400:16
Strong b. in God and last BELL 61:12
Though our b. is on the rack SMITH 650:16
Thy b. by decree is banishèd SHAK 591:11
Thy b. came with subtilty BIBLE 71:12
tyrant duke unto a tyrant b. SHAK 567:21
voice of thy b.'s blood BIBLE 70:19
brotherhood: b. of man is evoked LAING 405:18
crown thy good with b. BATES 55:5
doubly sweet a b. in song KEATS 390:23
has broadened into a b. JOHN 367:7
Love the b. BIBLE 105:13
together at the table of b. KING 397:1
brother-in-law: brother, not his b. KING 396:14
brotherly: Let b. love continue BIBLE 104:20
brothers: all men become b. SCH 558:1
And all the b. too SHAK 629:21
A noble pair of b. HOR 351:8
B. and sisters rocking JOHN 366:16
b. and their murdered man KEATS 388:2
B. in humanity who live VILL 711:14
forty thousand b. SHAK 578:29
happy few, we band of b. SHAK 586:11
men to feel they are b. GODW 308:12
they may agree like b. SHAK 587:23
together as b. or perish KING 397:2
We were b. all WORD 747:5
brought: b. forth her firstborn BIBLE 93:26
darkness safely b. KEBLE 392:19
government should be b. down MACM 440:9
brow: b. imperiously commands DAN 229:12
b. of labour this crown BRYAN 153:24
b. with homely biggin bound SHAK 584:1
hope to meet my Maker b. CORN 219:2
rugged b. of careful Policy SPEN 659:13
mighty Victor's b. KELLY 393:4
that threatening unkind b. SHAK 624:21
wanton with a velvet b. SHAK 598:14
Your bonny b. was brent BURNS 162:10
brown: b. be both at one price BARC 52:9

brown: (cont.):
b. coat, the black MAC 434:14
b. Greek manuscripts BROW 148:17
b. of her—her eyes MEW 459:8
B.'s body lies a mould'ring ANON 15:12
From those b. hills BRON 142:15
Her b. embrace WALK 717:14
Jeanie with the light b. FOST 291:13
She has b. hair, and speaks SHAK 610:10
smile o' the b. old earth BROW 150:17
browner: b. shade the evening GIBB 302:21
Browning: and so is B. WILDE 735:2
B.'s death is rather FITZ 284:18
B. some 'Pomegranate' BROW 147:15
God and Robert B. KLOP 402:21
Hang it all, Robert B. POUND 526:7
safety-catch of my B. JOHST 377.16
Wordsworth, Tennyson and B. BAG 47:15
brows: nodded with darkish b. HOMER 343:1
shadow of her even b. SPEN 660:4
browsing: b. and sluicing WOD 740:20
bruise: b. them with a rod of BOOK 124:10
It shall b. thy head BIBLE 70:14
tread on it and b. it TROL 703:19
bruised: be b. in a new place IRV 360:17
b. reed shall he not break BIBLE 84:2
staff of this b. reed BIBLE 76:31
was b. for our iniquities BIBLE 84:12
bruisers: sneer at the b. of England
BORR 136:15
bruit: Comes on at hand the b. THOM 695:7
Dont meurt le b. parmi le vent APOL 23:14
Brunetto: Are you here, Advocate B.
DANTE 230:14
brunt: Bear the b., in a minute BROW 152:5
brush: Border and gi'e them a b. HOGG 341:15
work with so fine a b. AUST 40:1
brushers: Critics are like b. WOTT 749:7
brushwood: lowest boughs and the b.
BROW 150:5
Brust: ach! in meiner B. GOET 309:2
bruta: B. fulmina PLINY 517:6
brutal: grown b. from the fare YEATS 752:13
brutality: industry without art is b.
RUSK 550:12
brutalization: perfection and b. TOCQ 699:8
brute: A b. I might have been BROW 152:7
Brute heart of a b. like you PLATH 516:5
Et tu, B.? CAES 174:21
Et tu, B.? SHAK 591:13
Feed the b. PUNCH 532:4
like b. beasts that have BOOK 124:21
such a cross-grained b. GOLD 311:27
brutes: B. never meet in bloody fray
GOLD 311:2
Exterminate all the b. CONR 217:4
not made to live as b. DANTE 230:16
brutish: nasty, b., and short HOBB 340:7
Unto some b. beast MARL 447:3
Brutus: B. makes mine greater SHAK 593:7
'B.' will start a spirit SHAK 590:4
For B. is an honourable man SHAK 592:5
Portia is B.' harlot SHAK 591:2
that Lord B. took to wife SHAK 591:3
What! is B. sick SHAK 590:2
You too, B. CAES 174:21
bubble: And now a b. burst POPE 521:29
Honour but an empty b DRYD 259:21
Life is mostly froth and b. GORD 312:12
light-blown b. vanished for ever BOLT 117:16
much like unto a b. WARD 721:21
Seeking the b. reputation SHAK 568:16
What is fame? an empty b. GRAI 314:4
world's a b. BACON 45:27
bubbles: beaded b. winking KEATS 389:9
bubus: Paterna rura b. HOR 348:22
Bücher: Dort, wo man B. HEINE 330:13
buck: bigger bang for a b. ANON 12:17
b. stops here TRUM 704:21
bucket: are as a drop of a b. BIBLE 83:29
b. down and full of tears SHAK 620:19
b. of perfectly lucid water WILB 734:2
past is a b. of ashes SAND 555:7

bucket: (cont.):
stick inside a swill b. ORW 501:4
buckets: b. into empty wells COWP 223:26
Buckingham: so much for B. CIBB 203:20
Buckingham Palace: changing guard at B.
MILNE 462:12
buckle: b. which fastens BAG 46:15
buckler: be thy shield and b. BOOK 131:3
bucklers: there hang a thousand b. BIBLE 81:13
buckram: eleven b. men SHAK 580:20
Four rogues in b. let SHAK 580:19
bud: be a b. again KEATS 387:8
b., and yet a rose full-blown HERR 337:11
b., the flower SPEN 660:6
I'll nip him in the b. ROCHE 542:17
now in age I b. again HERB 335:3
opening b. to Heaven COL 210:1
This b. of love SHAK 623:3
budding: b. morrow in midnight KEATS 390:24
budge: b. doctors of the Stoic MILT 464:6
'B.' says the fiend SHAK 608:5
buds: b. like flocks to feed SHEL 641:14
b. will go on swelling MAND 444:4
darling b. of May SHAK 633:6
green b. they were swellin BALL 48:21
That kneeled unto the b. SHAK 565:18
Buffalo Bill: B.'s defunct CUMM 228:14
buffeted: b. for your faults BIBLE 105:14
buffets: vile blows and b. SHAK 603:1
buffoon: statesman, and b. DRYD 259:8
bug: Skugg lies snug as a b. FRAN 292:19
this b. with gilded wings POPE 520:3
bugger: B. Bognor GEOR 301:6
buggers: b. can't be choosers BOWRA 138:18
bugle: Blow, b., blow TENN 688:1
bugles: Blow out, you b., over BROO 143:3
b. calling for them from OWEN 503:12
build: And easy to b., too IBSEN 358:16
Birds b.—but not I build HOPK 346:9
b. the house of death MONT 480:16
b. thou the walls of Jerusalem BOOK 128:8
end is to b. well WOTT 749:6
Except the Lord b. the house BOOK 134:6
how b., unbuild MILT 472:11
intending to b. a tower BIBLE 94:33
think that we b. for ever RUSK 550:23
To b. below the grass's root MARV 451:11
When we mean to b. SHAK 583:1
builder: he can only be a b. RUSK 550:11
maker of b. is God BIBLE 104:14
builders: stone the b. refused BOOK 133:16
building: it's a very old b. OSB 501:8
principal beauty in b. FULL 296:7
we have a b. of God BIBLE 101:18
builds: b. stronger than either SHAK 578:17
built: All we have b. do we discern ARN 27:15
And therefore b. for ever TENN 681:23
b. with stones of Law BLAKE 112:23
It is not what they b. FENT 281:7
bulk: b. in the dark LONG 427:20
bull: A Cock and a B. STER 665:10
are gone to milk the b. JOHN 372:11
Brag, sweet tenor b. BUNT 155:9
b. moose and you can use ROOS 546:14
curled Assyrian B. TENN 686:10
savage b. doth bear the yoke SHAK 613:11
bullet: ballot is stronger than the b.
LINC 421:17
b. may just as well have COLL 213:9
b. through his heart THAC 691:16
Every b. has its billet WILL 736:22
put a b. through his head ROB 542:11
speeding b. ANON 13:8
bullet-headed: b. many POUND 527:18
bullets: invulnerable where b. crossed
BLOK 115:9
not bloody b., but peaceful LINC 421:17
With b. made of platinum BELL 60:23
bull-fighters: b. of Spain BORR 136:15
bullied: are we to be b. KEATS 391:12
virtue than b. out of vice SURT 672:5
bullocks: whose talk is of b. BIBLE 87:36
young b. upon thine altar BOOK 128:9

C

Cambridge: (cont.):
C. to the ordinary visitor — BAED 46:5
For C. people rarely smile — BROO 143:13
gently back at Oxford or C. — BEER 59:12
skill to C. books he sent — BROW 146:25
To C. books, as very well — TRAPP 702:3
Ye fields of C., our dear — COWL 221:20
Cambyses: do it in King C.' vein — SHAK 580:28
came: He c. unto his own — BIBLE 96:3
I c., I saw, I conquered — CAES 174:20
I c. like water, and like — FITZ 284:2
I c., saw, and overcame — SHAK 583:25
I c. through and I shall return — MAC 434:3
Tell them I c., and no one — DE L 236:7
camel: c. has a single hump — NASH 490:9
c. is a horse designed — ISS 360:23
his raiment of c.'s hair — BIBLE 88:14
It is easier for a c. — BIBLE 91:25
swallow a c. — BIBLE 92:5
Take my c., dear — MAC 434:6
Camelot: As he rode down to C. — TENN 685:3
C. to minstrels seemed — BROW 147:6
To many-towered C. — TENN 684:23
ye cackling home to C. — SHAK 595:13
camera: c. makes everyone a tourist — SONT 656:5
I am a c. with its shutter — ISH 360:22
Camerado: C., this is no book — WHIT 732:10
great C., the lover true — WHIT 732:20
camp: From camp to c. — SHAK 585:14
camps: Courts and c. the only — CHES 198:8
can: c. because they think they — VIRG 713:9
c. must be so sweet — HOPK 345:13
C. something, hope — HOPK 345:7
He who c., does — SHAW 637:24
Pass me the c., lad — HOUS 351:16
talent which does what it c. — BAR 53:1
we wish to, but as we c. — MEN 457:3
What we c. we will — KING 397:10
you can't think you c. — INGE 359:11
youth replies, I c. — EMER 276:14
Cana: C. of Galilee — BOOK 123:16
canal: swimming along in the old c. — BETJ 68:4
Canalettos: Then the C. go — MACM 440:6
Canary: mine host's C. wine — KEATS 388:20
cancel: C. and tear to pieces — SHAK 603:5
c. half a line — FITZ 284:9
cancer: c. of human history — SONT 656:7
Silence like a c. grows — SIMON 647:20
candid: be c. where we can — POPE 521:27
from the c. friend — CANN 178:6
candidate: Republican c. for President — SIMP 648:3
candidates: when c. appeal — ADAMS 2:3
candied: Of c. apple, quince — KEATS 387:9
candle: box whose c. is the sun — FITZ 284:5
called him 'C.-ends' — CARR 184:1
c. by God's grace in England — LAT 411:3
c. by which she had been — TOLS 700:7
c. in that great turnip — CHUR 203:14
c. of understanding — BIBLE 86:24
c. shall not drive — SHAK 594:3
c. singed the moth — SHAK 608:19
c. than curse the darkness — STEV 667:3
farthing c. at Dover — JOHN 372:17
farthing c. to the sun — YOUNG 754:11
Fire and fleet and c.-lighte — BALL 49:18
hold a c. to my shames — SHAK 608:12
Is scarcely fit to hold a c. — BYROM 167:15
light a c. to the sun — SIDN 646:11
little c. throws his beams — SHAK 610:4
My c. burns at both ends — MILL 461:7
out, brief c. — SHAK 605:1
set a c. in the sun — BURT 165:8
Someone blew out the c. — ALAI 7:3
Two old chairs, and half a c. — LEAR 413:19
when he hath lighted a c. — BIBLE 94:20
candle-light: Colours seen by c. — BROW 147:16
dress by yellow c. — [illegible] 668:13
candles: c. and set chairs all — HERV 337:13
c. burn their sockets — HOUS 351:21
extinguishes c. and kindles fire — LA R 410:19

candles: (cont.):
Night's c. are burnt out — SHAK 623:23
Their c. are all out — SHAK 601:10
These blessed c. of the night — SHAK 610:8
candlestick: c. upon the plaister — BIBLE 85:30
candlestick-maker: C. much acquaints — BROW 152:27
candlesticks: I saw seven golden c. — BIBLE 105:35
candy: C. is dandy — NASH 490:18
cane: conduct of a clouded c. — POPE 523:30
canker: c. lives in sweetest bud — SHAK 633:13
c. of fair virtuous action — MARS 449:8
this c., Bolingbroke — SHAK 579:33
cankers: c. of a calm world — SHAK 581:23
cankerworm: c., and the caterpillar — BIBLE 86:7
cannibal: progress if a c. uses knife — LEC 415:10
cannibals: C. that each other — SHAK 615:1
with Caesars, and with C. — SHAK 583:8
cannon: C. to right of them — TENN 680:14
Even in the c.'s mouth — SHAK 568:16
vigour and a pulse like a c. — EMER 276:19
cannon-ball: But a c. took off his legs — HOOD 343:17
cannot: And I c., cannot go — BRON 142:11
cano: Arma virumque c. — VIRG 711:18
canoe: coffin clapt in a c. — BYRON 167:21
canoes: their heads in their c. — MARV 451:13
canonization: sort of natural c. — HAZL 329:8
canopied: enclosed lights, now c. — SHAK 571:1
canopies: Under the c. of costly state — SHAK 583:11
canopy: rich embroidered c. — SHAK 588:2
this most excellent c. — SHAK 574.20
cant: c. of criticism — STER 664:27
clear your mind of c. — JOHN 376:8
Let them c. about DECORUM — BURNS 162:14
pressed with specious c. — HOOD 344:5
stamp is the c. of Not men — BURKE 159:16
we have nothing but c. — PEAC 510:5
can't: C. help lovin' dat man — HAMM 322:17
cantate: C. Domino — BIBLE 107:29
Canterbury: C. or Smithfield — WALP 720:7
canting: canted in this c. — STER 664:27
cantons: c. of contemnèd love — SHAK 628:24
cantos: c. of unvanquished space — CRANE 225:18
canvas: And crowd your c. — TENN 687:8
With c. drooping, side by side — CLOU 207:22
canvasses: good in c. and factions — BACON 43:4
cap: riband and a cock of youth — SHAK 578:11
capability: Negative C. — KEATS 391:10
That a good-like reason — SHAK 577:31
capable: c. of reigning if only — TAC 678:3
Habacuc était c. de tout — VOLT 717:4
It is c. of all things — TRAH 701:8
capacity: c. and virtue — SWIFT 673:14
c. of taking trouble — CARL 180:18
which is c. to act wisely — WHIT 731:12
caparisons: No c., Miss — SHER 645:9
capax: c. imperii — TAC 678:3
cape: c. of a sudden came — BROW 151:21
capers: c. nimbly in a lady's — SHAK 621:15
He c., he dances — SHAK 610:16
lovers run into strange c. — SHAK 568:5
Cape Saint Vincent: nobly C. — BROW 150:7
capital: colourful entry into the c. — WAUGH 724:3
discover the origin of c. — TORR 701:5
Pandemonium, the high c. — MILT 469:9
say it is a c. offence — MARL 446:12
To that high C., where kingly — SHEL 639:13
capitalism: c. but a substitute — ROB 542:13
definition of c. — HAMP 323:3
ethic and the spirit of c. — WEBER 724:9
monopoly stage of c. — LENIN 417:5
peaceful extermination of c. — ZIN 755:12
unacceptable face of c. — HEATH 329:23
War is c. with the gloves — STOP 670:8
capitalist: forces of c. society — NEHRU 491:8
slave of c. society — CONN 216:24
capitulate: I will not c. — JOHN 376:20
Capolan you cannot had c. — SHAK 579:0

Capri: letter came from C. — JUV 384:6
caprices: c. of one of his fellow men — TOCQ 698:10
caps: C. tilted, fag drooping — BLOK 115:7
They threw their c. — SHAK 570:6
captain: c. of the Hampshire grenadiers — GIBB 302:17
c.'s but a choleric word — SHAK 606:1
c. is in his bunk — SHAW 636:20
C. of the Gate — MAC 436:10
Fighting in the c.'s tower — DYLAN 265:12
I am the c. of my soul — HENL 332:7
O C.! my Captain — WHIT 732:6
Our great captain's c. — SHAK 615:14
royal c. of this ruined band — SHAK 585:15
train-band c. eke was — COWP 222:12
Walk the deck my C. lies — WHIT 732:7
captains: All my sad c. — SHAK 565:22
c. and the kings depart — KIPL 400:11
c. and the kings depart — KNOX 403:7
c. courageous — BALL 50:2
C. of industry — CARL 181:3
Star c. glow — FLEC 286:7
thunder of the c. — BIBLE 77:39
capting: nobody like the C. — THAC 691:9
captive: c. required of us then — BOOK 134:17
thou hast led captivity c. — BOOK 129:10
when I am thy c. talk of chains — MILT 471:19
captives: liberty to the c. — BIBLE 84:26
upon all prisoners and c. — BOOK 120:1
captivity: C. thence captive — SPEN 659:9
no leading into c. — BOOK 135:5
prisoners out of c. — BOOK 129:7
turned again the c. of Sion — BOOK 134:4
Turn our c., O Lord — BOOK 134:5
car: afford to keep a motor c. — SHAW 635:21
And the gilded c. of day — MILT 463:16
c. has become an article — MCL 439:16
c. his perilous excursion — LEWIS 421:3
c., the furniture, the wife — MILL 461:18
commodious c. of the imagination — JAMES 362:14
expands to tinker with his c. — MACN 441:3
cara: *La c. e buona imagine paterna* — DANTE 230:15
caravan: Put up your c. — HODG 340:19
caravanserai: in this battered c. — FITZ 283:15
carbon: c. atom possesses — JEANS 363:26
carborundum: *Nil c. illegitimi* — ANON 16:19
carbuncle: monstrous c. on the face — CHAR 192:1
carbuncles: Monstrous c. of concrete — SPEN 658:25
carbuncular: young man c. — ELIOT 273:9
carcase: Wheresoever the c. — BIBLE 92:11
Worrying the c. of an old song — THOM 694:15
carcases: dead c. of unburied men — SHAK 570:13
carcass: c. fit for hounds — SHAK 590:18
card: c. to play for Honours — BENN 63:21
c. would be the one — CHUR 201:21
having a c. up his sleeve — LAB 404:17
we must speak by the c. — SHAK 578:21
cardboard: Sailing over a c. sea — HARB 323:12
cardinal: Jackdaw sat on the C.'s chair — BARH 52:12
card-indexes: Our memories are c. consulted — CONN 216:21
cards: And some were playing c. — BALL 49:11
At c. for kisses, Cupid paid — LYLY 433:8
c. and yet cannot play — BACON 43:4
c. than among people — LEWIS 420:16
Let's buy a pack of c. — COL 212:21
Never play c. with a man — ALGR 9:5
not learned to play at c. — JOHN 371:2
old age of c. — POPE 520:11
shuffle the c. — CERV 188:14
With a wicked pack of c. — ELIOT 272:24
care: age is full of c. — SHAK 632:18
And Heaven's peculiar c. — SOM 655:13
are now with the past c. — SHAK 620:3
beats c. with a [illegible] — MILT 466:4
c. and valour in this Welshman — SHAK 586:2

care: (*cont.*):
c. fifty times more — BAG 47:4
Careless she is with artful c. — CONG 216:4
c. of all the churches — BIBLE 102:1
C. of his Mother — MILNE 462:13
c.'s check and curb — VAUG 708:16
C. sits behind the horseman — HOR 349:24
c. to stay than will — SHAK 623:24
c. where the water goes — CHES 199:12
dark forgetting of my c. — DAN 229:16
disclaim all my paternal c. — SHAK 594:19
do buy it with much c. — SHAK 607:3
don't c. too much for money — LENN 417:16
enough in thee to kill c. — SHAK 614:15
forgather wi' Sorrow and C. — BURNS 161:14
Hast thou no c. of me — SHAK 566:15
Hippocleides doesn't c. — HIPP 339:5
I c. for nobody, not — RICK 100.21
I didn't c. who knew — CHAN 190:1
I don't c. — CROSS 227:19
Killing c. and grief of heart — SHAK 588:16
learning to c. for the unhappy — VIRG 712:11
least as feeling her c. — HOOK 344:14
Nor c. beyond to-day — GRAY 316:2
now Reason is past c. — SHAK 635:9
our anxious c. of thee — PEAC 510:11
ravelled sleave of c. — SHAK 602:2
she don't c. — LENN 418:2
Sport that wrinkled C. derides — MILT 465:6
Take c., my foolish heart — WASH 722:4
take c. of minutes — CHES 198:11
taken better c. of myself — BLAKE 110:16
Teach us to c. and not to care — ELIOT 270:6
then the c. is over — TEMP 680:3
things beyond our c. — DRYD 261:13
'twas nipt with c. — MIDD 459:12
We don't c. a fig — LEAR 414:4
with what c. Thou hast — HERB 335:19
women and c. and trouble — WARD 721:21
careas: c. quia cernere suave — LUCR 431:15
cared: C. not to be at all — MILT 469:11
career: boy's ideal of a manly c. — DISR 248:25
c. open to the talents — CARL 180:11
nothing in his long c. — ANON 19:11
our c. and our triumph — VANZ 708:11
careful: c. in the choice — WILDE 735:18
Horace's c. felicity — PETR 513:14
So c. of the type she seems — TENN 683:20
carefully: most c. upon your hour — SHAK 571:21
You've got to be c. taught — HAMM 323:2
careless: As 'twere a c. trifle — SHAK 600:14
C. she is with artful care — CONG 216:4
C. talk costs lives — ANON 12:20
Grow impudently c. — CENT 188:5
So c. of the single life — TENN 683:20
The first fine c. rapture — BROW 150:6
They were c. people — FITZ 285:3
carelessness: looks like c. — WILDE 734:14
With carefullest c. — BETJ 68:6
cares: anxious c., when past — ROCH 543:9
blessed than to put c. away — CAT 186:3
c. and pleasures of domestic — GIBB 302:3
c. can make the sweetest — GREE 317:11
c. that infest the day — LONG 426:14
c. were to increase — HOME 342:19
devil has ended his c. — BROW 151:6
ever against eating c. — MILT 465:17
hell Grief and avenging C. — VIRG 713:14
man is deprest with c. — GAY 200:20
Nobody c. — MORT 486:12
none c. or knows — CLARE 204:25
one c. for none of them — AUST 39:25
soft rest of c., come — CHAP 190:17
caressing: blessing, kind its c. — COCK 208:3
caret: golden cadence of poesy, c. — SHAK 598:17
careth: c. not for the sheep — BIBLE 97:1
Carew: grave of Mad C. — HAYES 328:10
carf: c. biforn his fader — CHAU 192:12
cargo: c. boats that sail — KIPL 399:19
With a c. of ivory — MAS 453:2
caricature: O troubled heart—this c. — YEATS 753:14
With a c. of a face — GILB 305:10

carl-hemp: Thou stalk o' c. in man — BURNS 163:18
Carlisle: roused the burghers of C. — MAC 436:2
You may go to C.'s — ANST 23:12
Carlyle: C. has led us all out — CLOU 207:26
very good of God to let C. — BUTL 166:29
carmina: *Pierides, sunt et mihi c.* — VIRG 715:7
placere diu nec vivere c. — HOR 348:15
carmine: *ubi plura nitent in c.* — HOR 347:16
carnage: stern strife, and c. drear — SCOTT 560:11
Yea, C. is thy daughter — WORD 746:8
carnal: A very heathen in the c. part — POPE 520:8
c. lusts and appetites — BOOK 123:16
carnally: For to be c. minded is death — BIBLE 99:34
carnations: c. and streaked gillyvors — SHAK 632:1
c. did o'erspread her face — DRUM 258:14
Soon will the musk c. break — ARN 28:27
Carnot: accepted C.'s cycle — WELLS 727:15
caro: *VERBUM C. FACTUM EST* — MISS 477:9
carol: And c. of love's praise — SPEN 659:14
chimes ring out with a c. — BOND 117:17
wild c. ere her death — TENN 682:26
Carolina: ham'n eggs in C. — GORD 312:13
carollings: So little cause for c. — HARDY 325:5
carouses: c. in this costly wine — DRAY 257:20
car park: c. the dance has begun — BETJ 68:7
carpe: *c. diem* — HOR 349:9
carpenter: c. who has made you a bad — JOHN 372:3
I said to the c. — CART 184:12
Walrus and the C. — CARR 183:1
Walrus and C. — LEVIN 420:4
carpet: c. with their shoes — YEATS 752:23
figure in the c. — JAMES 362:17
Mistake themselves for c. bags — RAL 536:11
carpets: c. rose along the gusty — KEATS 387:11
c. with a deadened force — BETJ 67:7
instead of fitted c. — FISH 283:7
carping: obnoxious to each c. tongue — BRAD 139:10
carrets: Sowe C. in your Gardens — GARD 297:14
carriage: C. held but just Ourselves — DICK 244:11
Making them women of good c. — SHAK 622:22
very small second class c. — GILB 304:15
carried: c. away with every blast — BOOK 121:12
carrier: set down from the c.'s cart — LEE 415:18
carrion: c. comfort, Despair — HOPK 345:7
With c. men, groaning — SHAK 591:24
carry: c. thee whither thou — BIBLE 98:2
c. them in his bosom — BIBLE 83:28
c. within us the wonders — BROW 146:6
certain we can c. nothing out — BIBLE 104:2
Do I c. the moon in my pocket — BROW 151:6
He'll c. a letter to my love — BALL 49:9
making him c. me — TOLS 701:2
must c. knowledge with him — JOHN 375:1
Speak softly and c. a big — ROOS 546:9
cars: c. today are almost — BART 54:18
they're crazy about c. — SAL 553:17
cart: Owl, and a useful C. — LEAR 414:5
Carthage: C. must be destroyed — CATO 185:8
carthaginian: With C. trustworthiness — SALL 554:15
carve: c. heads upon cherry-stones — JOHN 376:13
c. him as a dish fit — SHAK 590:18
Must c. in Latin or in Greek — WALL 718:11
Orlando: c. on every tree — SHAK 568:18
To c. out dials, quaintly — SHAK 588:1
ye c. my epitaph aright — BROW 148:17
case: c. is concluded — AUG 37:9
corpse in the c. with a sad — BARH 52:17
everything that is the c. — WITT 740:4
Have nothing to do with the c. — GILB 305:9
heard one side of the c. — BUTL 167:2
suitable for c. treatment — MERC 457:11
this c. is that case — ARAB 24:3
when a lady's in the c. — GAY 300:1
would have passed in any c. — BECK 57:25

cased: c. up, like a holy relic — WEBS 725:16
casement: c. high and triple-arched — KEATS 387:5
c. ledges where the moss — MACL 439:9
c. ope at night — KEATS 390:1
c. slowly grows a glimmering — TENN 688:5
ghost of Roger C. — YEATS 751:21
casements: Charmed magic c. — KEATS 389:15
cases: plead their c. in court — VIRG 713:17
cash: And takes your c. — CHUR 200:22
c. in hand and waive — FITZ 283:14
c. payment has become — CARL 180:2
from hand to hand of c. — SICK 646:8
pay you c. to go away — KIPL 401:8
she needs good c. — TUCK 705:2
casket: hushed c. of my soul — KEATS 390:15
casse: *tout c., tout lasse* — ANON 21:8
Cassidy: C.'s hanging hill — KAV 386:2
Cassiopeia: C. was over — KAV 386:2
Cassius: C. from bondage will deliver C. — SHAK 590:11
C. is aweary of the world — SHAK 593:8
cassock: C., band, and hymn-book too — WILB 733:17
cassocked: c. huntsman — COWP 223:1
cassowary: If I were a c. — WILB 733:17
cast: C. a cold eye — YEATS 753:18
c. away the works of darkness — BOOK 120:10
C. me not away from thy — BOOK 128:6
c. off the works of darkness — BIBLE 100:10
c. thy bread upon the waters — BIBLE 80:25
c. up again without effect — HOBB 340:11
c. ye your pearls before — BIBLE 89:16
C. your mind on other days — YEATS 753:17
Edom will I c. out my shoe — BIBLE 128:18
first c. a stone at her — BIBLE 96:30
have set my life upon a c. — SHAK 622:16
I shall never be c. down — BOOK 124:22
mighty is vilely c. — BIBLE 75:8
more he c. away — BUNY 156:12
suddenly c. down — BOOK 127:21
trouble me c. me in the teeth — BOOK 127:5
will in no wise c. out — BIBLE 96:26
castaway: c. wine-pots — CLOU 206:17
I myself should be a c. — BIBLE 100:31
castels: make c. thanne in Spayne — CHAU 195:6
casteth: c. out devils through — BIBLE 90:11
castigator: *c. censorque minorum* — HOR 347:14
Castilian: as might an old C. — BYRON 173:18
castitatem: *mihi c. et continentiam* — AUG 36:24
castle: c. hath a pleasant seat — SHAK 601:1
In the c. of my skin — LAMM 407:17
Look owre the C. Downe — BALL 49:3
man's house is his c. — COKE 209:1
my old lad of the c. — SHAK 579:19
rich man in his c. — ALEX 8:10
splendour falls on c. walls — TENN 688:1
Castlereagh: had a mask like C. — SHEL 641:10
intellectual eunuch C. — BYRON 170:2
castles: C. in the air — IBSEN 358:16
castrati: *dreamed* of reviving the c. — REED 538:8
casualties: Our c. were low — JARR 363:20
casualty: force and road of c. — SHAK 608:16
Truth is the first c. — JOHN 368:8
casuistry: c. heaped o'er her head — POPE 519:10
casuists: And soundest c. doubt — POPE 520:14
cat: C. of such deceitfulness — ELIOT 272:12
c. on a hot tin roof — WILL 737:3
C., the Rat, and Lovell — COLL 213:3
consider my C. Jeoffry — SMART 649:13
cosmic Cheshire c. — HUXL 358:1
endow a college, or a c. — POPE 520:15
Had Tiberius been a c. — ARN 27:19
Hanging of his c. on Monday — BRAT 139:19
I never do swing a c. — DICK 240:7
Lat take a c., and fostre — CHAU 193:26
Like the poor c. i' the adage — SHAK 601:5
mother's c. had but kittened — SHAK 581:1
Oh I am a c. that likes — SMITH 652:14
Old Foss is the name of his c. — LEAR 414:11
or a part to tear a c. — SHAK 611:5
room enough to swing a c. — SMOL 654:2

cat: (cont.):
Runcible C. with crimson	LEAR 414:18
see how the c. jumps	SCOTT 561:2
suggestion as a c. laps milk	SHAK 625:16
Touch not the c. but a glove	SCOTT 560:17
umpire, the pavilion c.	LANG 408:15
very fine c. indeed	JOHN 376:7
vigilant as a c. to steal cream	SHAK 581:24
When I play with my c.	MONT 481:7
will take care of the c.	SULZ 671:15

cataclysm: their c. but one poor Noah
HUXL 357:19

catalogue: Ay, in the c. ye go for men
SHAK 602:24
| dull c. of common things | KEATS 388:19 |
| lamentable c. of human crime | CHUR 202:9 |

catalyst: c. that sparks the revolution
DURY 264:13
catamite: in bed with my c.	BURG 156:20
cataract: sounding c.	WORD 744:21
wild c. leaps in glory	TENN 688:1
cataracts: You c. and hurricanoes	SHAK 595:20

catastrophe: between education and c.
WELLS 727:20
c. of the old comedy	SHAK 595:3
I'll tickle your c.	SHAK 583:3
toward unparalleled c.	EINS 268:4
catch: First c. your hare	GLAS 308:2
game of catch as c. can	FOOTE 288:15
hard to c. and conquer	MER 458:5
Catch-22: that was C.	HELL 331:6
catched: more wise, and not be c.	PEPYS 512:13
catcher: c. in the rye	SAL 553:18
catching: Passion, I see, is c.	SHAK 592:1
poverty's c.	BEHN 60:14
catchwords: principally by c.	STEV 668:7
catechism: so ends my c.	SHAK 582:1
categorical: This imperative is C.	KANT 385:7
categories: ballet of bloodless c.	BRAD 139:6
categorize: Analyze you, c.	DYLAN 265:10

category-habits: c. by category-disciplines
RYLE 552:9
caterpillar: cankerworm, and the c.	BIBLE 86:7
c. on the leaf	BLAKE 111:5
caterpillars: c. of commonwealth	SHAK 619:22
Fat c. drift around	BROO 143:8
cates: c. and have him talk	SHAK 581:7
Cathay: than a cycle of C.	TENN 685:20
cathedral: c. in your mouth	UST 707:19
Of C. Tunes	DICK 244:20
wander the c. lawn	CRANE 225:17
whole wide world is a c.	PAST 509:1
cathedrals: great Gothic c.	BART 54:18

Catherine the Great: child of Karl Marx
and C.   ATTL 32:17
| Catholic: always a C. | WILS 737:17 |
| C. and Apostolick Church | BOOK 121:20 |

[C. Church] holds that it were better
NEWM 493:6
currently did not attend was C.	AMIS 10:16
Gentlemen, I am a C.	BELL 62:5
holy C. Church	BOOK 119:1
I cannot be a good C.	NORF 496:11
now quite lawful for a C.	MENC 457:10
that he hold the C. Faith	BOOK 119:12
Catholicism: accessories of C.	HOPK 346:17
Catholics: C. and Communists	GREE 316:20
Hitler attacked the C.	NIEM 495:2
Catiline: abuse our patience, C.	CIC 204:5
Cato: C. is the voice of Rome	JONS 378:12
C.'s daughter	SHAK 591:3
losing one pleased C.	LUCAN 431:4
What C. did, and Addison	BUDG 154:14
cats: C. and monkeys	JAMES 362:24
C.—I believe he did but	WATS 722:10
C. is 'dogs' and rabbits	PUNCH 531:16
c. no less liquid	TESS 691:1
dogs and killed the c.	BROW 151:20
greater c. with golden eyes	SACK 550:15
little l'une c. under the moon	HUXL 357:10
where c. are safe	MARO 448:13
wild c. in your kitchens	SHAK 614:19
cattle: air, and over the c.	BIBLE 69:24

cattle: (cont.):
c. then are sick	KING 398:6
c. upon a thousand hills	BOOK 128:2
go and call the c. home	KING 397:13
grass for the c.	BOOK 132:8
unknown to the c.	CAT 186:9
cattle-shed: Stood a lowly c.	ALEX 8:11

Catullus: Did their C. walk that way
YEATS 752:23
Poor C., drop your silly	CAT 186:2
caught: 'Ah, ha!' you're c.	SHAK 565:12
But the fools c. it	YEATS 751:3
cauld: 'tis auld it waxeth c.	BALL 51:2
cauldron: Fire burn and c. bubble	SHAK 603:17
Round about the c. go	SHAK 603:17

cauliflower: C. is nothing but cabbage
TWAIN 706:20
causa: c. finita est	AUG 37:9
causality: law of c.	RUSS 551:18
causas: potuit rerum cognoscere c.	VIRG 715:14
vitam vivendi perdere c.	JUV 384:4
cause: beauty of good old c.	WORD 746:10
between c. and effect	LA BR 405:3
called amiss The good old C.	MILT 476:2
c. is in my will	SHAK 591:7
c. may be inconvenient	BENN 63:19
c. of dullness in others	FOOTE 288:17
c. that perishes	CLOU 207:6
c. that wit is in other men	SHAK 582:14
defendeth the c. of the widows	BOOK 129:7
defend my c. against	BOOK 127:6
effect was already in the c.	BERG 65:5
final c. of the human nose	COL 212:7
Freedom is the c. of God	BOWL 138:16
great c. of cheering	BENN 63:14
have full c. of weeping	SHAK 595:18
his c. being good	MORE 484:9
If any of you know c.	BOOK 123:14
it is the c., my soul	SHAK 618:5
judge thou my c.	BIBLE 85:20
man can shew any just c.	BOOK 123:18
myself and the just c.	NELS 491:15
Our c. is just, our union	DICK 245:7
perseverance in a good c.	STER 664:16
Rebel without a c.	LIND 423:1
Report me and my c. aright	SHAK 579:9
So little c. for carollings	HARDY 325:5
statistics that some c.	AUDEN 36:2
unites it with the secret c.	JOYCE 381:12
unpregnant of my c.	SHAK 575:10
Whose c. is God	COWP 224:6
winning c. pleased	LUCAN 431:4
causer: Heart's renying, c. of this	BARN 53:17
causes: And malice, to breed c.	JONS 379:12
brave c. left	OSB 501:18
c. was spinning from everlasting	AUR 38:2
c. which impel them	JEFF 364:1
Home of lost c., and forsaken	ARN 29:15
knowledge of c.	BACON 45:18
understand the c. of things	VIRG 715:14
Whatever is, is in its c. just	DRYD 261:8
caustic: voice which was more c.	ROLFE 545:8
caution: c. in love is perhaps	RUSS 551:13
cautiously: do c., and look	ANON 22:13
cavalier: c. who loves honour	SCOTT 559:8
cavalier: he was a perfect c.	BYRON 167:22
Cavaliers: C. (Wrong but Wromantic)	
	SELL 562:20
cave: burst stomach like a c.	DOUG 255:13
c. where Echo lies	SHAK 623:6
darksome c. they enter	SPEN 660:1
error may correct the c.	WILB 734:5
her vacant interlunar c.	MILT 474:2
littera scriptum 'C. canem	PETR 513:11
this our pinching c.	SHAK 571:8
caveant: C. consules	ANON 22:5
Cave of Adullam: his political C.	BRIG 141:10
cavern: c. sparkling with its native	
	BYRON 172:13
cavern: And out of the c. of rain	GIBL 640:7
beats about in c. all blank	MILR 734:5
c. measureless to man	COL 210:4
down within a vast c.	KEATS 390:6

caverns: (cont.):
Sand-strewn c., cool and deep	ARN 27:8
caves: Mendip's sunless c.	MAC 436:1
pleasure-dome with c. of ice	COL 210:11
unfathomed c. of ocean bear	GRAY 315:15
caviare: c. to the general	SHAK 575:5
Cawdor: Glamis thou art, and C.	SHAK 600:15
cawing: c. at the gun's report	SHAK 612:1
cease: C.! must men kill and die	SHEL 640:16
c. upon the midnight	KEATS 389:14
Fall and c.	SHAK 598:1
have fears that I may c.	KEATS 390:28
He maketh wars to c.	BOOK 127:17
not c. from exploration	ELIOT 271:6
not c. from mental fight	BLAKE 113:4
see me c. to live	ARN 29:5
storm to c.	BOOK 133:2
That things might change or c.	SHAK 595:19
thou shouldst c.	SHEL 643:25
War will c. when men refuse	ANON 19:5
ceased: it c. to be with Sarah	BIBLE 71:1
ceasing: Remembering without c.	BIBLE 103:19
Without c. I make mention	BIBLE 99:14
Cecilia: Blessed C., appear in visions	
	AUDEN 34:2
only C., or Camilla	AUST 38:21
cedar: numbdl c. what a burst	ARN 27:17
cedars: devour the c. of Lebanon	BIBLE 74:12
even the c. of Libanus	BOOK 132:8
excellent as the c.	BIBLE 81:20
cedar-trees: Lord breaketh the c.	BOOK 126:2
cedite: C. Romani scriptores	PROP 530:2
ceiling: lines of the c.	E.LUA 276:3
under a c. of commerce	OLIV 498:16
celebrate: just to c. the event	JERR 366:5
celerity: such a c. in dying	SHAK 564:19
celestial: And lighten with c. fire	BOOK 135:21
Apparelled in c. light	WORD 745:10
C. Emporium of Benevolent	BORG 136:8
For that c. light	MILT 468:11
sublime and c. greatness	TRAH 701:10
Celia: Come, my C., let us prove	JONS 379:10
Know, C.	CAREW 179:6
celibacy: c. has no pleasures	JOHN 369:22
c. is almost always a muddy	PEAC 510:8
cell: Content in the tight hot c.	BOGAN 116:13
narrow c. for ever laid	GRAY 315:12
cellar: Born in a c. and living	FOOTE 288:14
I was born in a c.	CONG 215:8
cellos: c. of the deep farms	STEV 667:4
cells: contented with their c.	WORD 745:7
Than c. and gibbets	COOK 218:5
These little grey c.	CHR 200:8
Celt: blind hysterics of the C.	TENN 684:12
cement: same c., ever sure	POPE 519:5
cemetery: c. is an open space	SHEL 639:10
Help me down C. Road	LARK 410:9
cenotaph: I silently laugh at my own c.	
	SHEL 640:7
censor: c. of the young generation	HOR 347:14
censorship: assassination the extreme	
form of c.	SHAW 638:25
censure: to read, and c.	HEMI 331:12
c. of a man's self is oblique	JOHN 375:3
c. this mysterious writ	DRYD 260:24
Take each man's c.	SHAK 573:4
cent: What he did with every c.	FROST 295:1
centaur: Into that moral c.	BYRON 171:14
Centaurs: from the waist they are C.	
	SHAK 597:5
central: navies grappling in the c. blue	
	TENN 685:13
centre: c. cannot hold	YEATS 753:1
dead c. of middle age	ADAMS 2:4
earth is the c.	DONNE 253:12
May sit i' the c., and enjoy	MILT 463:27
My c. is giving way	FOCH 288:6
now in the c. of politics	MOSL 486:20
real c. of the household	SHAW 636:19
This bed thy c.	DONNE 252:18
which the c. is everywhere	ANON 16:17
where c. is everywhere	UPD 707:7
centres: of which we are the c.	TROL 703:10

cents: I feel like thirty c. — ADE 5:5
centuries: All c. but this — GILB 304:22
 forty c. look down upon — NAP 490:1
 I shall lie through c. — BROW 148:18
 Through what wild c. — DE L 235:20
century: c. of common man — WALL 718:5
 last for more than a c. — CAT 185:12
 So the 20th C.—so whizzed — CRANE 225:23
 when a new c. begins — MANN 445:1
Cerberus: damn them with King C. — SHAK 583:8
 Of C., and blackest Midnight — MILT 465:3
 You are not like C. — SHER 645:10
cerebration: deep well of unconscious c. — JAMES 362:13
ceremonies: of dreams, and c. — SHAK 590:19
ceremony: C. is an invention — LAMB 406:5
 c. of innocence is drowned — YEATS 753:1
 c. that to great ones 'longs — SHAK 605:16
 It useth an enforcèd c. — SHAK 592:25
 perfect c. of love's rite — SHAK 633:7
 Save c., save general c. — SHAK 586:7
 thrice-gorgeous c. — SHAK 586:8
Ceres: laughing C. re-assume — POPE 520:22
certain: c. because impossible — TERT 690:18
 c. hope of the Resurrection — BOOK 124:5
 c. ill to leave assurèd — DRAY 258:3
 c. little lady comes by — GAY 300:19
 c. of nothing but the holiness — KEATS 391:5
 c. since Social Progress — KIPL 399:8
 c. thing called the Boy Friend — WILS 738:8
 dirge of her c. ending — SHAK 632:24
 lady of a 'c. age' — BYRON 171:16
 one thing is c. — FITZ 284:1
certainties: better than most people's c. — HARD 324:3
 man will begin with c. — BACON 41:16
 When hot for c. in this — MER 458:9
certainty: C. Feeling. Joy — PASC 508:1
 c. of power — DAY-L 233:5
 Such sober c. of waking bliss — MILT 463:24
 Thy wisdom, less thy c. — STEP 663:16
certamina: animorum atque haec c. — VIRG 715:18
certezza: Di doman non ci è c. — MED 456:3
certified: that I may be c. how long — BOOK 126:22
certifieth: one night c. another — BOOK 125:4
certitude: Nor c., nor peace — ARN 27:1
Cervantes: C. never petulant — MAC 435:1
 C. smiled Spain's chivalry — BYRON 171:25
cervicem: populus Romanus unam c. — CAL 175:5
cesspool: that great c. — DOYLE 256:21
Cetacean: Noble and generous C. — KIPL 402:2
Ceylon: Blow soft o'er C.'s isle — HEBER 330:4
chacals: c. pissent au bas — FLAU 286:4
chafe: Champ and c. and toss — ARN 27:7
chaff: c. well meant for grain — TENN 683:2
 see that the c. is printed — HUBB 353:11
 tastes like c. in my mouth — KEATS 392:14
chaffinch: c. sings on the orchard — BROW 150:5
chagrin: C. d'amour — FLOR 288:4
 c. qui développe les forces — PROU 530:17
chain: broke at once the vital c. — JOHN 375:30
 c. that is round us now — CORY 219:14
 flesh to feel the c. — BRON 142:14
 It gilds the lover's servile c. — ROCH 543:2
 remove a lengthening c. — GOLD 311:8
 that oak hangs a golden c. — PUSH 533:4
 with the c. of our sins — BOOK 120:4
chained: Over the c. bay waters — CRANE 225:25
chainless: Eternal spirit of the c. mind — BYRON 173:5
chains: adamantine c. and penal fire — MILT 467:23
 be in c. than to be free — KAFKA 384:17
 c. about the feet of God — TENN 682:24
 C. and slaverie — BURNS 163:1
 C. are worse than bayonets — JERR 366:4
 everywhere he is in c. — ROUS 549:2
 In c. and darkness — MONT 480:7
 kings in c. — BOOK 135:16
 Knock off the c. — GRAI 314:5
 My c. fell off, my heart — WESL 728:2

chains: (cont.):
 nothing to lose but their c. — MARX 452:14
 only bandage might be c. — BYRON 172:14
 only by the slightest c. — EDG 266:15
 sang in my c. like the sea — THOM 693:6
 since a woman must wear c. — FARQ 280:11
 thy captive talk of c. — MILT 471:19
chair: But has one vacant c. — LONG 427:12
 C. she sat in, like — ELIOT 273:2
 c. that fits all buttocks — SHAK 564:5
 Give Dayrolles a c. — CHES 198:26
 He fills a c. — JOHN 375:22
 La c. est triste, hélas — MALL 442:16
 Not to a true, but painted c. — HERB 335:6
 sat on the Cardinal's c. — BARH 52:13
 Seated in thy silver c. — JÖNS 378:16
chairs: carry candles and set c. — HERV 337:13
 empty c. in my drawing-room — BURN 160:10
chaise-longue: hurly-burly of the c. — CAMP 176:6
chalice: c. from the palace — PANA 505:16
chalices: treen priests and golden c. — JEWEL 366:7
chalked: c. up in Ballymurphy — HEAN 329:22
Cham: great C. of literature — SMOL 654:5
chamber: and in your c. — BOOK 124:12
 bridegroom out of his c. — BOOK 125:3
 cannot find a c. in the inn — ANON 20:3
 c. deaf to noise and blind — SIDN 646:19
 C. selected by the Whips — FOOT 288:12
 naked into the conference c. — BEVAN 69:1
 stalking in my c. — WYATT 749:19
Chamberlain: Listening to a speech by C. — BEVAN 69:3
 [Neville C.] able to gain — CHUR 202:6
chambermaid: c. as of a Duchess — JOHN 375:6
 more worth than his c. — GODW 308:10
chambermaids: worms that are thy c. — SHAK 624:9
chambers: his c. in the waters — BOOK 132:6
 perfumed c. of the great — SHAK 583:11
 Steel c., late the pyres — HARDY 325:3
 winding c. which it inhabits — SHEL 644:11
chameleon: add colours to the c. — SHAK 588:3
 c.'s dish — SHAK 576:9
chameleons: C. feed on light and air — SHEL 640:12
champ: C. and chafe and toss — ARN 27:7
champagne: c. and a chicken — MONT 480:5
 C., and Bridge — BELL 61:24
 c. and the stars — FITZ 285:1
 C. certainly gives one werry — SURT 672:13
 C. socialist — MORT 486:10
 I get no kick from c. — PORT 524:19
 It's like c. or high heels — BENN 63:19
 not a c. teetotaller — SHAW 636:4
Champmédy: bury my tongue at C. — BENÉ.T 62:16
chance: accident nor dart of c. — SHAK 617:13
 All c., direction — POPE 522:8
 And c. o'ertakes — MARV 451:11
 c. favours only the prepared — PAST 509:2
 C. governs all — MILT 470:11
 C. has appointed her — BUNT 155:8
 C. herself her nimble feet — DAV 232:7
 c. with one of the lords — LAWR 412:21
 Despair, law, c., hath slain — DONNE 250:21
 From c., and death — SHEL 642:18
 Give peace a c. — LENN 417:19
 main c. of things — SHAK 583:15
 Necessity and c. — MILT 472:8
 No gifts from c. — ARN 27:22
 or else, it was by c. — BRAD 139:10
 skirts of happy c. — TENN 683:25
 Under the bludgeonings of c. — HENL 332:6
 various turns of c. below — DRYD 259:20
 voice to come in as by c. — BACON 43:5
 Which erring men call c. — MILT 464:5
 will never eliminate c. — MALL 442:19
 would set my life on any c. — SHAK 603:1
Chancellor: C. of the Exchequer — LOWE 429:11
chances: c. change by course — SOUT 658:2
 changes and c. of this mortal — BOOK 122:16

chances: (cont.):
 have to take c. for peace — DULL 263:11
 spake of most disastrous c. — SHAK 615:1
 speak of c. and events — DRAY 257:18
change: and bolts up c. — SHAK 566:19
 architecture, a c. of heart — AUDEN 36:6
 But O the heavy c. — MILT 466:1
 certain relief in c. — IRV 360:17
 c. and chance he guideth — BRID 141:2
 C. and decay in all around — LYTE 433:16
 C. as the winds change — SWIN 677:4
 c. from Jane to Elizabeth — AUST 39:12
 c. in too short a time — TOFF 689:9
 C. is constant — DISR 247:16
 C. is not made without inconvenience — JOHN 367:19
 c. partners and dance — BERL 65:15
 c. something at once sordid — BAUD 55:12
 c. strike me and you — BROW 148:24
 c. that state by forces — NEWT 494:2
 C. the name and it's about — HOR 350:22
 c. we think we see in life — FROST 294:12
 c. what we can — STEV 667:15
 c. your mind and to follow — AUR 37:20
 Doth c. my disposition — SHAK 632:5
 Even God cannot c. the past — AGAT 5:15
 extremes by c. more fierce — MILT 470:3
 I c., but I cannot die — SHEL 640:7
 knavery, and c. — BEHN 60:12
 lamentable c. is from the best — SHAK 596:23
 leave it to a torrent of c. — CHES 199:21
 miserable c. now at my end — SHAK 566:14
 necessary not to c. — FALK 279:20
 Neither to c., nor falter — SHEL 642:20
 Of C., the which all mortal — SPEN 660:17
 point is to c. it — MARX 452:8
 ringing grooves of c. — TENN 685:19
 scorn to c. my state — SHAK 633:10
 shall c. our vile body — BOOK 124:5
 strange the c. from major — PORT 524:22
 that love could never c. — BRID 141:5
 that moveth doth in C. — SPEN 660:18
 That things might c. or cease — SHAK 595:19
 The more things c. — KARR 385:13
 things will have to c. — LAMP 407:18
 thou ever c. Kate into Nan — BLAKE 111:23
 To know the c. and feel it — KEATS 387:33
 vesture shalt thou c. — BOOK 132:1
 we c. with them — ANON 22:19
 which involves a great c. — TROL 704:2
 wind of c. is blowing — MACM 440:5
 wished to c. his place — GOLD 310:9
 wish to c. in the child — JUNG 383:2
 with fear of c. — MILT 469:2
 without the means of some c. — BURKE 158:7
changed: changed, c. utterly — YEATS 751:15
 c. upon the blue guitar — STEV 665:22
 But O how fallen! how c. — MILT 468:2
 c. from that Hector — VIRG 712:18
 new feeling has not c. — TOLS 700:8
 That all things are c. — BACON 42:10
 that it be not c. — BIBLE 85:32
 they shall be c. — BOOK 132:1
 Though c. in outward lustre — MILT 468:4
 we shall all be c. — BIBLE 101:14
changes: c. and chances of this — BOOK 122:16
 c. we fear be thus irresistible — JOHN 367:23
 Play all your c. — ING 360:7
 sundry and manifold c. — BOOK 120:18
 world's a scene of c. — COWL 221:14
changing: all the c. scenes of life — TATE 678:17
 And ever c. like a joyless eye — SHEL 643:24
 around them was c. — DID 245:11
 one fixed point in a c. — DOYLE 256:11
 stress on not c. one's mind — MAUG 454:10
 times they are a-c. — DYLAN 265:23
 What man thinks of c. himself — TROL 704:1
Chankly: Hills of the C. Bore — LEAR 413:20
channel: Flowing in a different c. — AKHM 6:7
 [the C.] is a mere ditch — NAP 489:9
 you are crossing the C. — GILB 304:15
channels: through the c. of the ear — AUDEN 35:4
chanted: c. snatches of old tunes — SHAK 578:13

chanticleer: My lungs began to crow like c.　SHAK 568:13

chanting: C. faint hymns to the cold　SHAK 610:20

chaos: bit of primordial c.　WELLS 727:21
black c. comes again　SHAK 635:14
C. and darkness heard　MARR 449:1
C., a rough and unordered mass　OVID 502:20
C., illumined by flashes　WILDE 736:9
C. is come again　SHAK 616:10
C. often breeds life　ADAMS 2:14
C. umpire sits　MILT 470:11
God dawned on C.　SHEL 639:17
Humour is emotional c.　THUR 697:20
In c. of vacancy shone　DE L 236:3
means of overcoming c.　RICH 540:8
Not c.-like　POPE 523:33
old c. of the sun　STEV 666:11
reign of C. and old Night　MILT 468:23
stillness in the midst of c.　BELL 62:8
thy dread empire, C.　POPE 519:12

chap: second eleven sort of c.　BARR 54:2

chapel: churchyard will have his c.　BANC 51:12
devil will build a c.　BECON 58:6
devil would also build a c.　LUTH 432:12

chapels: Stolen looks are nice in c.　HUNT 356:10

chaplain: And twice a day the C. called　WILDE 736:2

Chapman: C. & Hall　BENT 64:11

chapmen: base sale of c.'s tongues　SHAK 598:10

chaps: Biography is about C.　BENT 64:10
from the nave to the c.　SHAK 599:15

chapter: Attali, are a mere c.　MITT 478:9
c. of accidents is a very　CHES 198:22
now to write the next c.　JOHN 367:6
repeat a complete c.　JOHN 374:30

chapters: c. in your hand　PUSH 532:12

character: A man's c. is his fate　HFR 333:12
c. but the determination　JAMES 363:4
c. by his way of eating　REAG 537:11
c. dead at every word　SHER 645:16
c. in the full current　GOET 309:12
c. is destiny　ELIOT 269:26
c. of a family to an hypothesis　STER 664:17
content of their c.　KING 397:1
essential c. of the fifth act　LERM 418:16
fate and c. are the same　NOV 497:3
habit and you reap a c.　READE 537:9
I leave my c. behind me　SHER 645:17
man's c. is to be abused　THAC 691:14
object the formation of c.　SPEN 658:21
ourselves wise about his c.　ELIOT 268:15
personal c. and relations　NAP 489:12
whatever c. we choose　BOSW 137:3

characters: c. of hell to trace　GRAY 316:8
flat and round c.　FORS 290:4
from high life high c.　POPE 520:26
mean of the c. and conduct　ADAMS 2:25
my c. I despare for it　FLEM 287:4
Six c. in search of an author　PIR 515:3
Who have c. to lose　BURNS 162:14

charge: angels c. over thee　BOOK 131:4
C. his mind with meanings　COWP 223:24
Take thou in c. this day　MAC 436:14
When in c., ponder　BOREN 136:7

charged: c. the troops of error　BROW 145:29
thought c. with emotion　GIDE 303:8

charges: die to save c.　BURT 164:20
ought warily to begin c.　BACON 43:16

charging: marching, c. feet　JAGG 361:12

chariest: c. maid is prodigal　SHAK 573:1

Charing Cross: human existence is at C.　JOHN 373:28

Pitched betwixt Heaven and C.　THOM 695:10

chariot: Bring me my c. of fire　BLAKE 113:4
c. of Israel　BIBLE 76:15
c. of the mount Bear　CHAP 100:14
maketh the clouds his c.　[BOOK] 130:6
slap-up gal in a bang up c.　DICK 243:1
Turning wings go ... r.　ANON 18:8
Time's wingèd c. hurrying　[MARV] 449:8

charioted: Not c. by Bacchus　KEATS 389:11

chariotest: Who c. to their dark wintry bed　SHEL 641:14

chariots: burneth the c.　BOOK 127:17
put their trust in c.　BOOK 125:7
tarry the wheels of his c.　BIBLE 74:6

chariot-wheel: axletree of the c.　BACON 45:4

charitably: how can they c. dispose　SHAK 586:4

charities: cold c. of man to man　CRAB 225:15
Defer not c. till death　BACON 44:17
patron of some thirty c.　TENN 688:17

charity: and have not c.　BIBLE 101:1
C. and beating begins at home　FLEI 287:23
C. and Mercy　DICK 241:10
C. begins at home　SHER 645:20
C., dear Miss Prism　WILDE 734:18
c. edifieth　BIBLE 100:27
c. envieth not　BIBLE 101:1
C. is cold in the multitude　SMART 649:12
c. never faileth　BIBLE 101:1
C. shall cover the multitude　BIBLE 105:20
C. suffereth long　BIBLE 101:1
c. vaunteth not itself　BIBLE 101:1
c. will hardly water　BACON 44:4
c. with your neighbours　BOOK 122:5
Church, and c. so cold　SKEL 649:4
daughterly love and dear c.　MORE 484:16
faith, hope, c.　BIBLE 101:1
Give him a little earth for c.　SHAK 589:4
give with c. a stone　BLAKE 111:16
greatest of these is c.　BIBLE 101:1
lectures or a little c.　WHIT 732:19
Let holy c.　LITT 423:9
Love, friendship, c.　SHAK 627:22
Might there not be a c. in sin　SHAK 606:4
name to come called C.　MILT 473:12
need c. more than the dead　ARN 26:15
On what a c. ye come　SMART 649:15
with c. for all　LINC 422:9

Charlemain: C. with all his peerage　MILT 469:1

Charles: C. II was always very merry　SELL 562:22
In good King C.'s golden days　ANON 15:5

Charlie: o'er the water to C.　HOGG 341:18

Charlotte: Werther had a love for C.　THAC 691:21

charm: All the c. of all the Muses　TENN 689:14
c. can soothe her melancholy　GOLD 311:33
c. dissolves　SHEN 644:12
c. he never so wisely　BOOK 128:17
C. is the great English　WAUGH 723:10
C ..., it's a sort of bloom　BARR 54:12
C. thine eyes with sacred wand　LYLY 433:12
Completing the c.　ELIOT 270:12
discreet c. of the bourgeoisie　BUÑ 155:11
Each give each a double c.　DYER 265:7
For a c. of powerful trouble　SHAK 603:18
hard words like a c.　OSB 501:6
Museum had lost its c.　GERS 301:11
Oozing c. from every pore　LERN 419:7
powers of C. and Desire　CAT 185:13
such a c. in melancholy　ROG 544:14
What is c. then　LESS 419:11
You know what c. is　CAMUS 177:12

charmed: c. it with smiles and soap　CARR 184:5
c. me from my profession　SHAK 626:18

charmèd: Boil thou first i' the c. pot　SHAK 603:17
I bear a c. life　SHAK 605:3

charmer: voice of the c.　BOOK 128:17
Were t'other dear c. away　GAY 299:26

charming: C. spot　BECK 57:21
How c. is divine philosophy　MILT 464:1
So smoothes her c. tones　MILT 472:2

charms: C. strike the sight　POPE 523:31
c. unmarked by her alone　BYRON 167:27
Do not all c. fly　KEATS 388:19
fields and flocks have c.　CRAB 225:12
Freedom has a thousand c.　COWP 223:13
has c. to soothe a savage　CONG 215:16
land that has acres o' c.　BURNS 162:3
land our c. in the end　ROBIN 542:7

charms: (cont.):
Music alone with sudden c.　CONG 216:5
paid to mere external c.　MORE 484:4
those endearing young c.　MOORE 483:1
what drugs, what c.　SHAK 614:31

charter: c. of thy worth　SHAK 634:11
This was the c. of the land　THOM 695:15

charts: busied in c., exact in　BAG 46:20

chase: But with unhurrying c.　THOM 695:2
shining creatures of the c.　TENN 688:8
Thy c. had a beast in view　DRYD 261:21
When heated in the c.　TATE 678:16

chasing: always c. Rimbauds　PARK 506:13

chasm: great c. between　BERL 66:2

chassis: worl's in a state o' c.　O'CAS 497:16

chaste: Be thou as c. as ice　SHAK 576:1
c., and twenty-three　BYRON 170:5
C. as the icicle　SHAK 570:23
c. as unsunned snow　SHAK 571:5
c. polygamy　CAREW 179:8
c. to her husband　POPE 520:9
huntress, c., and fair　JONS 378:16
If I pronounce it c.　GILB 305:19
like a c. whore　MUGG 487:10
men ask, Are Barmaids C.　MAS 453:5
My English text is c.　GIBB 302:20
Nor ever c., except you　DONNE 250:3
To make cold nymphs c. crowns　SHAK 625:27
Was Jesus c.　BLAKE 111:18
wol nat kepe me c. in al　CHAU 194:20

chasten: To c. and subdue　WORD 745:1

chasteneth: Whom the Lord loveth he c.　BIBLE 104:18

chastised: c. you with whips　BIBLE 75:28
having been a little c.　BIBLE 86:28

chastisement: c. of our peace　BIBLE 84:12

chastity: C.—the most unnatural　HUXL 357:15
clothed on with c.　TENN 681:7
Eunuchs boasting of their c.　LEWIS 420:15
Even like thy c.　SHAK 618:18
Give any lessons of c.　BLAKE 111:18
Give me c. and continency　AUG 36:24
made of the vice of c.　VOLT 716:15
'Tis c., my brother, chastity　MILT 463:29

châteaux: Ô saisons, ô c.　RIMB 541:9

Chatham: Great C. with his sabre drawn　ANON 13:21

chats: spoiled the women's c.　BROW 151:26

Chattanooga: Pardon me boy is that the C.　GORD 312:13

chatter: c. about Harriet　FREE 293:14
idle c. of a transcendental　GILB 305:16
insignificant c. of the world　TROL 703:15

chattering: Dumb swans, not c. pies　SIDN 646:21

Chatterley: Between the end of the C. ban　LARK 409:12

Chatterton: C., the marvellous boy　WORD 747:11
Oh C.! how very sad thy fate　KEATS 390:22

Chaucer: [C.] is a perpetual fountain　DRYD 262:17
Dan C., well of English　SPEN 660:12
It is a pity that C.　WARD 721:16
lovely and fearless than C.　LAWR 412:2
mean Master Geoffrey C.　CAXT 188:1
old famous poet C.　SPEN 660:28
sufficient to say [of C.]　DRYD 262:16
To learnèd C., and rare　BASSE 55:2

chaunge: forme of speche is c.　CHAU 195:12

cheap: c. and chippy chopper　GILB 304:27
c. but wholesome salad　COWP 224:7
done as c. as other men　PEPYS 512:8
flesh and blood so c.　HOOD 344:9
hold their manhoods c.　SHAK 586:11
how potent c. music　COW 221:4
maketh himself c.　BACON 43:2
Man's life is c. as beast's　SHAK 595:16
sold c. what is most dear　SHAK 634:23
They be good c.　WYATT 750:1
them ... costs clap your hands　LENN 417:14
c. to do this than to drain　[LUTI] 167:6

795

cheaply: put him c. off — DRYD 259:26
Cheapside: in C. shall my palfrey — SHAK 587:23
cheat: And it is good to c. — BROW 149:1
  detecting what I think a c. — JOHN 373:24
  may c. at cards genteelly — BOSW 137:10
  so monosyllabic as to c. — FRY 295:25
  sweet c. gone — DE L 236:3
  To c. a man is nothing — GAY 299:23
  When it's so lucrative to c. — CLOU 207:19
cheated: C. of feature — SHAK 621:15
  enthusiasm I have been c. — KEATS 392:5
  Of being c., as to cheat — BUTL 166:16
  Old men who never c. — BETJ 67:8
  quality to be exceedingly c. — EVEL 279:6
cheating: Forbids the c. of our friends — CHUR 200:22
  period of c. between — BIER 109:13
cheats: He also c. with an oath — PLUT 517:15
check: dreadful is the c. — BRON 142:14
  To c. the erring, and reprove — WORD 746:9
checked: C. like a bondman — SHAK 593:8
cheek: call a blush into the c. — DICK 242:34
  c. that doth not fade — KEATS 387:19
  c. to him that smiteth — BIBLE 85:19
  Feed on her damask c. — SHAK 629:20
  give this c. a little red — POPE 520:30
  hangs upon the c. of night — SHAK 622:24
  He that loves a rosy c. — CAREW 179:2
  his c. to her cold grave — MALL 443:1
  hollow c. or faded eye — TENN 688:12
  iron tears down Pluto's c. — MILT 464:23
  leans her c. upon her hand — SHAK 622:28
  old ornament of his c. — SHAK 614:1
  smite thee on thy right c. — BIBLE 88:32
  that while it fans my c. — WORD 746:17
  together dancing c.-to-cheek — BERL 65:21
  yellow c., a white beard — SHAK 582:20
cheeks: c. of sorry grain — MILT 464:8
  c. strained by war — BLOK 115:5
  c. with artificial tears — SHAK 588:3
  crack your c. — SHAK 595:20
  Fat ruddy c. Augustus had — HOFF 341:4
  on thy c. a fading rose — KEATS 388:8
  Spoke in her c. — DONNE 251:10
cheer: be of good c. — BIBLE 97:21
  Be of good c. — BIBLE 91:7
  c. but not inebriate — BERK 65:8
  c. but not inebriate — COWP 223:31
  Could scarce forbear to c. — MAC 436:15
  Don't c., men — PHIL 514:2
  Greet the unseen with a c. — BROW 148:7
  let thy heart c. thee — BIBLE 80:30
  So c. up, my lads — HUGH 353:16
cheerer: c. of his spirits — WALT 721:1
cheerful: c. as any man could — PEPYS 512:4
  c. noise unto the God — BOOK 130:14
  Come, let us join our c. songs — WATTS 722:19
  God loveth a c. giver — BIBLE 101:21
  ground with c. thoughts — SHAK 624:2
  make him a c. countenance — BOOK 132:8
  maketh a c. countenance — BIBLE 78:34
cheerfulness: c. fixed and permanent — ADD 4:14
  C. gives elasticity — SMIL 650:13
  c. was always breaking — EDW 267:9
  this I testify for holy c. — DONNE 253:6
cheeriness: Chintzy c. — BETJ 67:5
cheering: great cause of c. us all up — BENN 63:14
cheerio: c. my deario — MARQ 440.12
cheerioh: 'c.' or 'cheeri-bye' — BETJ 67:10
cheerly: But c., cheerly — KEATS 386:18
cheers: Two c. for Democracy — FORS 290:30
cheese: Botticelli's a c. — PUNCH 532:6
  c. and garlic in a windmill — SHAK 581:7
  eggs and a pound of c. — CALV 175:10
  has 246 varieties of c. — DE G 235:10
  I'll fill hup the chinks wi' c. — SURT 672:10
  like some valley c. — AUDEN 36:4
  night I've dreamed of c. — STEV 667:24
  With apple pie and c. — FIELD 281:13
cheesed: humanity soon had me c. — BENN 63:11
cheeses: ate the c. out of the vats — BROW 151:26
chef-d'oeuvre: tree toad is a c. — WHIT 732:17

chemist: as objective as a c. — CHEK 197:9
  Was c., fiddler, statesman — DRYD 259:8
chemistry: by c. and machinery — SHAW 637:13
  found him weak in c. — WELLS 727:15
cheque: Bringing the c. and the postal — AUDEN 35:9
  give a political blank c. — GOSC 312:15
  statement is like a c. — POUND 527:14
chequer-board: c. of nights and days — FITZ 284:7
cheques: Blank c. of intellectual — HOLM 342:18
cherchez: c. la femme — DUMAS 263:12
cherish: c. those hearts that hate — SHAK 589:1
  love, c., and to obey — BOOK 123:20
  Then c. pity, lest you drive — BLAKE 113:20
cherished: My no longer c. — MILL 461:11
cherishing: kill thee with much c. — SHAK 623:7
  cheroot: whackin' white c. — KIPL 400:2
cherries: apples, c., hops — DICK 243:6
  Life is just a bowl of c. — BROWN 144:15
cherry: C.-ripe, ripe, ripe — HERR 336:8
  It is as American as c. — BROWN 144:11
  Like to a double c. — SHAK 612:3
  Loveliest of trees, the c. now — HOUS 352:5
  O ruddier than the c. — GAY 299:9
  To see the c. hung with snow — HOUS 352:6
cherry-stones: carve heads upon c. — JOHN 376:13
cherub: c.'s face, a reptile — POPE 520:6
  Proud limitary c. — MILT 471:19
cherubic: Soft—C. Creatures — DICK 245:4
cherubim: C. and Seraphim falling — HEBER 330:5
  c. does cease to sing — BLAKE 111:2
  heaven's c., horsed — SHAK 601:3
  helmèd c. and sworded — MILT 467:6
  That the C. may cry — ANON 22:9
cherubims: Immortal c. — TRAH 701:15
  rode upon the c. — BOOK 125:1
  sitteth between the c. — BOOK 131:16
Cherubin: To thee C., and Seraphin — BOOK 118:12
cherubins: quiring to the young-eyed c. — SHAK 610:1
cherubs: so near the c. hymn — SMART 649:8
cherubynnes: fyr-reed c. face — CHAU 193:5
ches: First of the c., so was — CHAU 192:5
Cheshire: smile of a cosmic C. cat — HUXL 358:1
chessboard: c. is the world — HUXL 358:7
  We called the c. white — BROW 148:12
chest: c. of drawers by day — GOLD 310:15
  His c. against his foes — SMART 650:1
  on the dead man's c. — STEV 667:22
Chesterton: dared attack my C. — BELL 61:14
chestnut: O c.-tree — YEATS 750:18
  Under a spreading c. tree — LONG 428:2
chestnuts: sailor's wife had c. — SHAK 600:1
chevalier: C. sans peur et sans — ANON 20:8
Chevy: Drove my C. to the levee — MCL 439:8
chew: fart and c. gum — JOHN 367:13
chewed: c., are cast up again — HOBB 340:11
cheweth: yet he c. not the cud — BIBLE 73:1
chewing gum: c. for the eyes — ANON 18:4
Chianti: C. to make into lamps — SHAF 563:18
chic: Radical C. — WOLFE 741:9
chicanery: c. of its vain pretence — LLOYD 424:2
chicken: c. in his pot every Sunday — HENR 332:10
  republic is like a c. — MITF 478:6
  Some c.! Some neck! — CHUR 202:16
  with champagne and a c. — MONT 480:5
chickens: beside the white c. — WILL 737:11
  Curses are like young c. — SOUT 657:7
  hen gathereth her c. — BIBLE 92:7
  pretty c. and their dam — SHAK 604:9
chid: He c. their wand'rings — GOLD 310:10
chide: Slow to c., and swift to bless — LYTE 433:17
  They do but sweetly c. thee — SHAK 633:3
chiding: c. of winter's wind — SHAK 567:24
  He will not alway be c. — BOOK 132:4
  I am a child to c. — SHAK 617:19
chief: c. of the ways of God — BIBLE 78:2

chief: (cont.):
  Cromwell, our c. of men — MILT 474:28
  Sinners; of whom I am c. — BIBLE 103:25
  What is the c. end of man — SHOR 646:7
chiefest: c. among ten thousand — BIBLE 81:19
Chief Justice: C. was rich, quiet — MAC 435:10
chieftain: C. Iffucan of Azcan — STEV 665:16
  c. to the Highlands bound — CAMP 176:15
  Great c. o' the puddin'-race — BURNS 163:13
chiere: c. as light as leef — CHAU 193:12
chiesa: Libera C. in libero — CAV 187:15
child: And mid-May's eldest c. — KEATS 389:13
  angel is the English c. — BLAKE 114:1
  As yet a c., nor yet a fool — POPE 519:28
  Become a C. on earth for me — BETJ 67:4
  But God bless the c. that's — HOL 342:1
  care for the c.'s rattle — JOHN 372:26
  c. becomes an adult when — SZASZ 677:10
  C.! do not throw this book — BELL 60:21
  c. even in the debased — ELIOT 268:20
  c. for the first seven — ANON 13:15
  c. imposes on the man — DRYD 260:26
  c. in the street I could — CLOU 207:1
  C. is father of the Man — WORD 745:6
  c. is known by his doings — BIBLE 79:6
  c. is owed the greatest — JUV 384:14
  c. is the sweetest thing — LAMB 406:3
  c. of glorious great intent — SPEN 659:26
  c. of God — BOOK 123:24
  c.'s a plaything for an hour — LAMB 407:8
  c. shall play on the hole — BIBLE 83:3
  c. should always say what's — STEV 668:20
  c.'s strength — LAMB 406:15
  c. take care that you strike — SHAW 637:28
  c. that is not clean — STEV 668:18
  c. well nursed — SWIFT 674:4
  Dear c. of sorrow — KEATS 390:22
  education bears upon the c.'s — HEGEL 330:11
  every formal visit a c. — AUST 39:21
  Every time a c. says — BARR 54:7
  father that knows his own c. — SHAK 608:7
  find I am to have his c. — BURG 156:21
  For unto us a c. is born — BIBLE 82:27
  Get with c. a mandrake root — DONNE 252:14
  had been any christom c. — SHAK 585:5
  happy English c. — TAYL 679:11
  hare's own c. — HOFF 341:10
  heard a wife sing to her c. — EDW 267:11
  heard one calling, 'C.' — HERB 334:12
  He has devoured the infant c. — HOUS 351:15
  Here a little c. I stand — HERR 336:5
  I am a c. to chiding — SHAK 617:19
  illegitimate c. of Karl Marx — ATTL 32:17
  Is it well with the c. — BIBLE 76:18
  I speak like a c. — NAB 489:3
  It's not fair to the c. — FROST 295:11
  I was a c. and she was a child — POE 518:1
  Jesus Christ her little c. — ALEX 8:11
  leave a c. alone — BROW 152:17
  like a c. who hasn't — HEND 332:4
  like a froward c. — TEMP 680:3
  like a three years' c. — COL 210:19
  little c., a limber elf — COL 209:11
  little c. shall lead them — BIBLE 83:2
  Love, a c., is ever crying — WROTH 749:14
  named the c. I-chabod — BIBLE 74:32
  O Lord, this thy C. — BOOK 123:13
  On a cloud I saw a c. — BLAKE 113:16
  or Old Man, no c. beside — THOM 694:4
  painted of dirt — POPE 520:3
  Perfection is the c. of Time — HALL 322:3
  Proves the c. ephemeral — AUDEN 35:5
  receive one such little c. — BIBLE 91:18
  Right . . . is the c. of law — BENT 64:2
  room up of my absent c. — SHAK 594:4
  see that every c. — RUSK 550:27
  Set his c. upon her knee — TENN 688:10
  She was an aggravating c. — BELL 61:8
  shocks the mind of a c. — PAINE 504:8
  spoiled c. of art — JAMES 362:10
  spoil the c. — BUTL 166:14
  that every c. may reach — JONS 380:7
  that of a little c. — THAC 691:6

child: (*cont.*):

that's governed by a c.	SHAK 621:25
There is a man c. conceived	BIBLE 77:6
thou show'st thee in a c.	SHAK 595:9
To have a thankless c.	SHAK 595:10
To see his active c. do	SHAK 633:14
Train up a c. in the way	BIBLE 79:11
use of a new-born c.	FRAN 293:5
was the mother for the c.	COL 211:19
When I was a c., I spake	BIBLE 101:1
when thy king is a c.	BIBLE 80:23
While the c. was yet alive	BIBLE 75:13
whimpering c. again	HART 327:14
wish to change in the c.	JUNG 383:2
woman forget her sucking c.	BIBLE 84:7

childbirth: Death, taxes and c.   MITC 478:2

Childe Roland: C. to the Dark Tower   BROW 149:3

childhood: And sleep as I in c.   CLARE 204:26

c., adolescence and obsolescence	LINK 423:6
C. is not from birth	MILL 461:5
c. shows the man	MILT 473:19
doing things in c.	GONC 312:10
For he is our c.'s pattern	ALEX 8:14
Her c., then her adolescence	COL 212:20
his c. onward this boy	HARD 323:15
moment in c. when the door	GREE 317:3
'tis the eye of c.	SHAK 602:4
We wove a web in c.	BRON 142:2
Where c. had strayed	Æ 5:10
Womanhood and c. fleet	LONG 427:2

childish: either knavish or c.   JOHN 375:9

c. treble, pipes and whistles	SHAK 568:16
c. valourous than manly	MARL 448:8
glamour of c. days	LAWR 412:17
I put away c. things	BIBLE 101:1
puts away c. things	MILL 461:5
these mild and c. pleasures	ALAI 7:3
Wordsworth chime his c.	BYRON 172:11

childishness: Is second c.   SHAK 568:16

childlike: Whose trust, ever c.   STR 671:1

children: airy hopes my c.   WORD 743:21

And oh those c.'s voices	VERL 710:5
And see his c. fed	PUDN 531:5
bandy c. nor fasting	BLAKE 114:10
be called the c. of God	BIBLE 88:23
become as little c.	BIBLE 91:17
becometh the c. of light	BOOK 123:2
better reasons for having c.	RUSS 551:27
breeds contempt—and c.	TWAIN 706:16
But, c., you should never let	WATTS 722:16
By c. and tradesmen's bills	MACN 440:18
by c. to adults	SZASZ 677:12
cabbage and the screams of c.	WEST 729:15
C. are dumb to say how	GRAV 314:17
c. are heard on the green	BLAKE 114:2
c. are more troublesome	SHAW 636:16
c. at play are not playing	MONT 480:18
C. begin by loving	WILDE 735:30
c. carried away	BOOK 121:12
c. cried in the streets	MOTL 487:3
c. hath given hostages	BACON 44:3
C. have never been very	BALD 48:1
c. in England take pleasure	ANON 12:21
c. in Holland take pleasure	ANON 12:21
c. in whom is no faith	BIBLE 73:22
c. like the olive-branches	BOOK 134:8
c. of a larger growth	DRYD 260:5
c. of a larger growth	CHES 198:16
C. of perdition are oft-times	JONS 378:5
c. of the devil	TENN 689:4
C. of the future age	BLAKE 114:9
c. of the kingdom shall	BIBLE 89:32
c. quiet when they grow	SWIFT 673:2
c. sport upon the shore	WORD 746:5
c.'s teeth set on edge	BIBLE 85:22
c. stood watching them	KING 397:15
C. sweeten labours	BACON 44:12
c. to be always and forever	DE S 553:2
of all I know	LARK 410:1
C. with Hyacinth's temperament	JAM 353:17
c. who then play	COWP 222:9
Christian of all must be	ALEX 8:10
Come, dear c., let us away	ARN 17:11

children: (*cont.*):

Come my tan-faced c.	WHIT 732:9
doeth for the c. of men	BOOK 132:15
dogs than of their c.	PENN 511:15
even so are the young c.	BOOK 134:7
father pitieth his own c.	BOOK 132:5
fathers thou shalt have c.	BOOK 127:14
fathers upon the c.	BIBLE 72:16
first class, and with c.	BENC 62:11
found in the thoughts of c.	LOCKE 424:16
from c. and from fools	DRYD 261:22
from c. who were rough	SPEN 659:2
hands of young c.	DYLAN 265:15
He has no c. All my pretty	SHAK 604:9
henceforth be no more c.	BIBLE 102:17
he reappears in your c.	CONN 216:22
I have gathered thy c.	BIBLE 92:7
I love my work and my c.	HILL 338:11
its c. to save its pride	MEYER 459:9
Joseph more than all his c.	BIBLE 71:20
kingdom, called you c.	SHAK 595:21
kitchen and their c.	FITZ 284:18
little c. died in the streets	AUDEN 34:10
maidens, old men and c.	BOOK 135:15
many women, and many c.	JOHN 372:1
Men fear death as c. fear	BACON 43:8
Myself and c. three	COWP 222:13
not much about having c.	LODGE 425:18
Nourish thy c., O thou good	BIBLE 86:22
peace to our c. when they fall	LOW 430:22
procreation of c.	BOOK 123:17
provoke not your c. to wrath	BIBLE 102:24
Rachel weeping for her c.	BIBLE 88:11
rich and the poor get c.	KAHN 384:19
sick persons, and young c.	BOOK 120:1
sleepless c.'s hearts are glad	BETJ 67:4
stars are my c.	KEATS 392:2
Suffer the little c.	BIBLE 93:16
tale which holdeth c.	SIDN 647:8
talks about their c.	DISR 247:23
teach their c. to speak it	SHAW 638:15
tell lies to c.	WALK 717:13
than c. love their parents	AUCT 33:24
that c. produce adults	DE VR 238:5
That is known as the C.'s Hour	LONG 426:13
that women and c. could	SELL 562:25
they bare c. to them	BIBLE 70:25
They were privileged c.	BROO 144:2
Thoughtful c., and the grave	AUDEN 35:5
thou shalt bring forth c.	BIBLE 70:16
thy c. kind and natural	SHAK 585:2
To beget c., nothing better	SART 556:14
turn each one of her c.	VERG 710:2
violations committed by c.	BOWEN 138:10
way parents obey their c.	EDW 267:6
We are c., playing	FORS 290:18
We are the c. of God	BIBLE 99:36
Weep, c., you no longer	NERV 492:1
We have c. we have wives	TENN 689:4
what you teach them [c.]	JOHN 372:15
When c. of one family	WATTS 722:17
wiser than the c. of light	BIBLE 95:6
ye hear the c. weeping	BROW 147:11
young c., were sooner	ASCH 30:18
Your c. are not your children	GIBR 303:2

child-wife: It's only my c.   DICK 240:8

Chile: small earthquake in C.   COCK 208:5

chill: bitter c. it was   KEATS 386:20

First—C.—then Stupor	DICK 244:10
So haunt thy days and c.	KEATS 390:16

chills: Of c. and fever she died   RANS 536:14

chilly: although the room grows c.

            GRAH 313:12

By c. fingered spring	KEATS 386:19
I feel c. and grown old	BROW 153:11
our c. women	BYRON 167:24

Chimborazo: C., Cotopaxi   TURN 705:15

chime: And let your silver c.   MILT 467:7

c. had stroked the air	JONS 379:16
c. of words tinkling	SMITH 652:12
in tune were the c.	JOHN 367:2
the c. buzzing in a vacuum	HUX 349:28

chimera: (*cont.*):

c. in my brain	DONNE 253:10

Chimeras: Hydras, and C. dire   MILT 470:4

Of dire c. and enchanted isles	MILT 464:2
other wild impossible c.	SWIFT 673:14

chimes: c. ring out with a carol gay

            BOND 117:17

heard the c. at midnight	SHAK 583:18

chimney: bare c. is gone black   YEATS 752:4

old men from the c.	SIDN 647:8

chimneys: good grove of c.   MORR 485:4

Our c. were blown down	SHAK 602:13
So your c. I sweep	BLAKE 113:17

chimney-sweepers: As c., come to dust

            SHAK 571:16

chin: c. upon an orient wave   MILT 467:12

China: from C. to Peru   JOHN 370:14

Till C. and Africa meet	AUDEN 34:3
up like thunder outer C.	KIPL 400:1
your land armies in C.	MONT 481:18

china: frail c. jar receive a flaw   POPE 523:23

though c. fall	POPE 520:12

Chinee: heathen C. is peculiar   HARTE 327:17

Chinese: C. wouldn't dare   COW 220:14

chinks: fill the c. wi' cheese   SURT 672:10

chintzy: C. cheeriness   BETJ 67:5

chip: c. of the old 'block'   BURKE 160:2

chippy: cheap and c. chopper   GILB 304:27

chips: C. with everything   WESK 727:25

given them nothing but c.	CHUR 201:18

chivalrie: He loved c.   CHAU 192:8

chivalry: age of c. is gone   BURKE 158:13

age of c. is past	DISR 248:37
Cervantes smiled Spain's c.	BYRON 171:25
Christian service and true c.	SHAK 610:18
I have a truant been to c.	SHAK 581:29
learn the noble acts of c.	CAXT 188:3
nine-tenths of the law of c.	SAY 557:15

Chloris: Ah, C.! that I now could sit

            SEDL 561:13

C., at worst, you'll in the end	ETH 278:19

chocolate: c. cream soldier   SHAW 635:23

choice: c. and master spirits   SHAK 591:20

c. dishes the Doctor has	GARR 298:7
c. of working or starving	JOHN 367:18
c. was any more than	DID 245:14
C. words, and measured	WORD 747:12
honour is the *people's* c.	SHER 644:28
If there were a sympathy in c.	SHAK 610:23
just the terrible c.	BROW 152:22
measure and the c.	JOHN 370:22
money and you takes your c.	PUNCH 531:8
parties having any c.	JOHN 374:11
simply *independent* c.	DOST 255:5
take c. of all my library	SHAK 627:1
with c. of all variety	BARN 53:18

choices: all the c. gone before   DID 245:14

choir: c. of heaven and furniture of earth

            BERK 65:12

c. of saints for evermore	DONNE 251:6
c. the small gnats mourn	KEATS 390:20
Oh may I join the c. invisible	ELIOT 269:29
Sweet singing in the c.	ANON 14:11
together as a c. of larks	DYER 265:3
To the full-voiced c. below	MILT 465:1
virgin-c.	KEATS 389:19

choirs: Bare ruined c.   SHAK 634:6

C. and Places where they sing	BOOK 119:5
demented c. of wailing shells	OWEN 503:12

choisir: *Gouverner, c'est c.*   LÉVIS 420:8

choke: c. the word   BIBLE 91:2

choked: thorns sprang up and c. them

            BIBLE 91:1

choking: c. him and making him carry me

            TOLS 701:2

choleric: captain's but a c.   SHAK 606:1

chommoda: C. dicebat   CAT 186:16

choose: *believe what we c*   NEWM 493:16

C. an author as you choose	DILL 246:3
c. love by another's eye	SHAK 610:22
c. the culprits	PAGN 504:6
c. the good	BIBLE 82:24
We cannot c, but hear	COL 210:13

choose: (cont.):
It is time to c. — STEV 665:15
leading wherever I c. — WHIT 732:23
Let's c. executors — SHAK 620:7
man is forced to c. — YEATS 751:6
multitude, that c. by show — SHAK 608:16
not c. not to be — HOPK 345:7
therefore c. life — BIBLE 73:20
They can not c. — THOM 694:3
To c. time is to save time — BACON 43:14
To govern is to c. — LÉVIS 420:8
woman can hardly ever c. — ELIOT 269:7
choosers: buggers can't be c. — BOWRA 138:18
choosing: c. between the disastrous — GALB 297:3
C. each stone, and poising — MARV 450:4
Freedom is not c. — MURD 488:6
just c. so — BROW 149:2
chopcherry: c. ripe within — PEELE 511:4
Chopin: I like C. and Bizet — FISH 283:7
chopper: c. on a big black block — GILB 304:27
chord: But I struck one c. of music — PROC 529:21
I feel for the common c. again — BROW 148:2
chords: c. in the human mind — DICK 239:9
c. of summer sustained — DAY-L 233:6
choristers: go the chanting c. — LAWR 412:13
chortled: He c. in his joy — CARR 182:19
chorus: c. of indolent reviewers — TENN 687:10
chose: c. him five smooth stones — BIBLE 75:3
chosen: best c. language — AUST 38:21
called, but few are c. — BIBLE 92:1
c. thee in the furnace — BIBLE 84:4
just after he has been c. — CHUR 203:4
Mary hath c. that good part — BIBLE 94:18
name is rather to be c. — BIBLE 79:10
ye are a c. generation — BIBLE 105:11
Ye have not c. me — BIBLE 97:17
choughs: crows and c. that wing — SHAK 597:1
Christ: all at once what C. is — HOPK 346:7
Are they ministers of C. — BIBLE 101:23
C. and his mother and all — HOPK 346:6
C. being raised from — BIBLE 99:29
C. borne into virgynyte — WYNT 750:10
[C.] came and preached peace — BIBLE 102:11
C. cannot find a chamber — ANON 20:3
C. erecteth his Church — BANC 51:12
C. follows Dionysus — POUND 526:14
C. is all, and in all — BIBLE 103:16
C. is born in Bethlehem — CASW 185:4
C. is the path and Christ — MONS 480:1
C. is thy strength — MONS 480:1
C. our passover is sacrificed — BIBLE 100:22
C. perish in torment — SHAW 638:24
C. risen from the dead — BIBLE 101:7
C. sailing to me in a boat — BLOK 115:3
C.'s blood streams — MARL 447:1
C.'s particular love's — BROW 152:17
C. walking on the water — THOM 695:10
C. was betrayed — Æ 5:10
C.! What are patterns — LOW 429:12
churches have killed their C. — TENN 687:1
depart, and to be with C. — BIBLE 103:3
estate C. adorned — BOOK 123:16
even so in C. shall all — BIBLE 101:7
faith and rejoice in C. — LUTH 432:9
For me to live is C. — BIBLE 103:2
glory in the church by C. Jesus — BIBLE 102:15
grey-grown speechless C. — SWIN 676:7
joint-heirs with C. — BIBLE 99:36
love of C. — BIBLE 102:14
May Lord C. enter — WILDE 736:5
now by Baptism put on C. — BOOK 123:2
Now call on C. to save — GILB 303:11
only we have hope in C. — BIBLE 101:6
Priest did offer C. — BOOK 135:25
Ring in the C. — TENN 684:11
stature of the fulness of C. — BIBLE 102:17
those I counted loss for C. — BIBLE 103:8
through C. which strengtheneth — BIBLE 103:14
unsearchable riches of C. — BIBLE 102:12
uphold the C. — TENN 681:24
Vision of C. that thou — BLAKE 111:13

Christ: (cont.):
We withstood C. then — BROW 150:4
Christ Church: line of festal light in C. — ARN 28:7
Christe: C. receive thy saule — BALL 49:18
Kyrie eleison. . .C. eleison — MISS 476:17
christened: pleasing you when she was c. — SHAK 569:8
Christian: As little as a C. can — DOYLE 257:5
C. blood amongst them — LAUD 411:4
C. boys I can scarcely — ARN 30:12
C. burial that wilfully — SHAK 578:15
C. can only fear dying — HARE 326:4
C. children all must — ALEX 8:13
C. hold for me the glass — ANON 22:9
C. ideal has not been tried — CHES 199:23
C. is a man who feels — YBAR 760:14
C. kisses on an 'eathen — KIPL 400:2
C. religion not only was — HUME 355:7
C. resolution to find — NIET 495:11
C.! seek not yet repose — ELL 275:11
C. service and true chivalry — SHAK 619:18
C., that's all — HUGH 354:10
forgive them as a c. — AUST 39:18
good C. at her heart — POPE 520:8
I die a C., according — CHAR 191:10
I hate him for he is a C. — SHAK 607:20
I mean the C. religion — FIEL 282:10
made me, in these C. days — TAYL 679:11
naturally C. soul — TERT 690:16
Onward, C. soldiers — BAR 53:2
persuadest me to be a C. — BIBLE 99:12
Scratch the C. and you — ZANG 755:6
See in what peace a C. can die — ADD 5:3
This Hebrew will turn C. — SHAK 608:3
three C. men — CAXT 188:2
tiger that hadn't got a C. — PUNCH 531:21
true warfaring C. — MILT 475:7
Christianity: C. is not so much — BUTL 165:20
C. is part of the laws — HALE 321:6
C. and journalism — BALF 48:16
C. was the religion — SWIFT 674:13
C. was to transfer — GIDE 303:7
His C. was muscular — DISR 248:12
local thing called C. — HARDY 324:5
loving C. better than Truth — COL 211:26
rock 'n' roll or C. — LENN 417:13
sinner in matters of C. — PÉ.GUY 511:8
sinner is at the heart of C. — PÉ.GUY 511:8
Christians: blood of C. is the seed — TERT 690:17
call themselves C. — BOOK 120:6
C., awake! Salute the happy — BYROM 167:14
C. have burnt each other — BYRON 170:7
English, that we are C. — AUST 39:1
forty generations of C. — MAC 435:18
what these C. are — SHAK 608:2
Christlike: C. in my behaviour — HUXL 357:7
Christmas: At C. I no more desire a rose — SHAK 598:8
C.-morning bells — BETJ 67:4
C. should fall out — ADD 4:11
C. stories tortured — BYRON 172:6
Do they know it's C. — GELD 300:21
I'm dreaming of a white C. — BERL 65:18
insulting C. card — GROS 319:6
'Twas the night before C. — MOORE 482:5
Christmas Day: C. in the Workhouse — SIMS 648:7
Christopher Robin: Nobody cares! C. has — MORT 486:12
C. went down with Alice — MILNE 462:12
Christ's College: called him the lady of C. — AUBR 33:7
chronicle: c. small beer — SHAK 615:18
like the c. of planets — YEVT 754:5
When in the c. of wasted time — SHAK 634:17
your c. as rich with praise — SHAK 584:21
chronicler: honest c. as Griffith — SHAK 589:12
chronicles: abstracts and brief c. — SHAK 575:6
chuckles: c. of the waves — AESC 5:12
chum: leagued with him, old c. — OWEN 503:16
chumps: C. make the best husbands — WOD 740:7
church: As some to c. repair — POPE 521:13

church: (cont.):
best harmony in a c. — MILT 475:10
Broad of C. — BETJ 68:10
Catholick and Apostolick C. — BOOK 121:20
Christ erecteth his C. — BANC 51:12
c. by Christ Jesus — BIBLE 102:15
C. can feed and sleep — ELIOT 271:13
c. he currently did not — AMIS 10:16
C. in continual godliness — BOOK 121:9
C. is an anvil which has — MACL 439:7
C. is said to want — NEWM 493:2
c. lewd hirelings climb — MILT 471:1
C. militant here in earth — BOOK 121:21
C.'s one foundation — STONE 669:12
C.'s Restoration in 1883 — BETJ 67:14
C. without pulling off his hat — JOHN 372:4
C. with psalms must shout — HERB 334:7
English C. shall be free — MAGN 441:19
estate of the Catholick C. — BOOK 120:6
figure in a country c. — SWIFT 673:18
free c. in a free state — CAV 187:15
hatred against the C. — SKEL 649:4
he goes to c. as he goes — BLYT 116:9
I like a c.; I like a cowl — EMER 276:10
literature and the Anglican C. — PYM 533:11
mere c. furniture at best — COWP 224:11
nearer the C. the further — ANDR 11:14
not the c. for his mother — CYPR 229:8
publick Prayer in the C. — BOOK 135:24
rock I will build my c. — BIBLE 91:14
salvation outside the c. — AUG 37:4
Say to the c., it shows — RAL 535:15
see a c. by daylight — SHAK 613:14
She came to the village c. — TENN 686:11
Stands the C. clock — BROO 143:15
there must be the C. — AMBR 10:5
thy c. on earth is seeking — SHER 645:26
wet c. the size of a snail — THOM 693:13
What is a c. — CRAB 224:19
where God built a c. — LUTH 432:12
wheresoever God buildeth a c. — BECON 58:6
who is always at c. — BLAKE 114:10
churches: care of all the c. — BIBLE 102:1
C. built to please the PRIEST — BURNS 162:13
c. have killed their Christ — TENN 687:1
he must build c. then — SHAK 576:12
seven c. which are in Asia — BIBLE 105:13
seven c. which are in Asia — BIBLE 105:34
Churchill: C. a perfect example — MUGG 487:8
Randolph C. to hospital — WAUGH 724:9
voice we heard that of C. — ATTL 32:14
[Winston C.] mobilized — MURR 488:12
churchman: British c. — BLYT 116:9
person called a 'Modern C.' — WAUGH 723:14
Would I that cowlèd c. — EMER 276:10
churchmen: c. fain would kill — TENN 687:1
life doth well with c. — BACON 44:4
Church of England: been the wisdom of the C. — BOOK 118:3
better satisfied in the C. — HOPK 346:17
If the C. were to fail — KEBLE 392:23
profession of the C. — CHAR 191:10
Protestant religion but the C. — FIEL 282:10
Church of Rome: thoroughly understands [the C.] — MAC 435:13
churchyard: beneath the elms in the c. — SCOTT 560:24
devil in the same c. — BANC 51:12
palsy-stricken, c. thing — KEATS 387:3
worse taste, than in a c. — JOW 380:18
churchyards: c. yawn and hell — SHAK 576:25
Troop home to c. — SHAK 612:6
churn: Attract a Silver C. — GILB 305:18
chute: une c. horizontale — COCT 208:8
Cicero: If I could have known C. — DICK 240:15
opinion can alienate C. — MAC 435:1
cigar: really good 5-cent c. — MARS 449:7
sweet post-prandial c. — BUCH 154:4
cigarette: c. is the perfect type — WILDE 735:19
c. that bears a lipstick's — MARV 451:14
cigars: Call the roller of big c. — STEV 665:18
Cinara: when good C. was my queen — HOR 350:11

Cinarae: *Sub regno C.* HOR 350:11
Cincinnatus: C. of the West BYRON 172:23
cinco: *c. en punto de la tarde* GARC 297:12
cinder: dry a c. this world DONNE 250:8
Cinderella: housewife is the C. SUMM 672:1
cinders: as the c. of the fire RAL 535:12
  c., ashes, dust KEATS 388:16
cinema: c. is truth 24 times GOD 308:4
cinerem: *nequiquam alloquerer c.* CAT 187:1
cinnamon: ginger, c. and cloves BEAU 56:13
  syrops, tinct with c. KEATS 387:9
circle: c. of our days is done BLOK 115:4
  c. of the golden year TENN 681:10
  c. of which the centre ANON 16:17
  c. that doth restless HERR 336:17
  man a fatal c. is traced TOCQ 699:2
  Round and round the c. ELIOT 270:12
  Thy firmness makes my c. just DONNE 252:22
  Weave a c. round him thrice COL 210:14
  wheel is come full c. SHAK 597:19
circles: c. of which we are TRÒL 703.15
  c. the earth with one WEBS 725:8
  Conversation is a game of c. EMER 276:21
circulate: To c. them round and round ALC 8:1
circulation: assists the c. of their blood
      SMITH 652:2
circumcised: C. the eighth day BIBLE 103:7
circumcision: breast-feeding, c. ORTON 499:14
  c. nor uncircumcision BIBLE 103:16
circumference: and the c. is nowhere
      ANON 16:17
circumfused: forms and substances are c.
      WORD 747:4
circumlocution: C. Office DICK 241:1
circumspectly: See then that ye walk c.
      BIBLE 102:22
circumspice: C., si Monumentum requiris
      BARH 52:10
  Si monumentum requiris, c. ANON 22:16
circumstance: And breasts the blows of c.
      TENN 683:25
  blindness or to the force of c. DID 245:10
  c. of glorious war SHAK 616:20
  escape from c. to ecstasy BELL 60:18
  In the fell clutch of c. HENL 332:6
  Of plastic c. BROW 152:12
circumstances: according to the play of c.
      WEIL 726:16
  C. beyond my individual control DICK 240:9
  Fearful concatenation of c. WEBS 725:7
circumstantial: c. evidence is very strong
      THOR 696:23
circumvent: one that would c. God
      SHAK 578:20
circunstancia: *Yo soy yo y mi c.* ORT 499:10
circus: breath bigger than a c. tent
      CUMM 228:13
  have no right in the c. MAXT 454:15
circuses: bread and c. JUV 384:7
cistern: Cold the seat and loud the c.
      BENN 63:12
citadel: mountain-built with peaceful c.
      KEATS 388:29
citadels: circle-c. there HOPK 346:5
  Where from c. on high AUDEN 35:3
cities: C. and their civilities PATM 509:14
  c. for our best morality AUST 38:17
  c. of men and manners TENN 690:1
  c. provides us with name BUNT 155:8
  c. we had learned about JARR 363:20
  hell to men, hell to c. AESC 5:11
  Of human c. torture BYRON 168:24
  Seven c. warred for Homer HEYW 338:6
  streets of a hundred c. HOOV 344:19
  thou art the flower of c. ANON 16:1
citizen: c. as an abstract proposition
      ROO 698:12
  c. in war, first in peace LEE 415.17
  c. in this world PHIL
  c. of no mean city AUH 30.3
  completely a c. of the world BOSW 137:5
  good man and a good c. AUCT 33:21

citizen: (cont.):
  greater than a private c. TAC 678:3
  he is a c. of the world BACON 43:26
  his wound, a c. of life SASS 557:12
  humblest c. of all BRYAN 153:23
  I am a Roman c. CIC 204:8
  John Gilpin was a c. COWP 222:12
  relation is a zealous c. BURKE 158:27
  To the c. or the police AUDEN 36:1
citizens: Before Man made us c. LOW 430:2
  c. kneading up the honey SHAK 584:22
  c. of death's grey land SASS 557:7
  first and second class c. WILL 737:15
  most refined c. SHEL 644:10
citizenship: c. in the kingdom of the well
      SONT 656:6
city: abstract and premeditated c. DOST 255:3
  all the c. on an uproar BIBLE 98:27
  Behold now this vast c. MILT 475:12
  citizen of no mean c. BIBLE 99:5
  c. and I see a man hurrying KEATS 392:6
  c.-builder DRAY 258:3
  c. is barren DICK 239:11
  c. is built to music TENN 681:21
  c. is not a concrete jungle MORR 485:5
  C. is of Night THOM 696:17
  C. now doth like a garment WORD 743:9
  C. of God, how broad and far JOHN 377:14
  C. of the Big Shoulders SAND 555:2
  c. on earth will be clean MAY 455:6
  c. that is set on an hill BIBLE 88:25
  c., thus I turn SHAK 570:15
  c. was pure gold BIBLE 107:20
  c. which hath foundations BIBLE 104:14
  c. will follow you CAV 187:9
  C. with her dreaming spires ARN 28:25
  c. with no more personality CHAN 190:3
  doth the c. sit solitary BIBLE 85:15
  each and every town or c. HOLM 342:7
  Except the Lord keep the c. BOOK 134:6
  fallen, that great c. BIBLE 107:3
  first c. Cain COWL 221:9
  For a c. consists in men NIC 494:13
  From the vast c., where WORD 746:17
  Happy is that c. ANON 14:1
  have we no continuing c. BIBLE 104:22
  Hell is a c. much like London SHEL 642:5
  I John saw the holy c. BIBLE 107:17
  Jerusalem is built as a c. BOOK 133:25
  London: a nation, not a c. DISR 248:21
  long in populous c. pent MILT 472:21
  Lord guards the c. BIBLE 108:4
  not be known, live in a c. COLT 214:9
  not say 'Dear c. of God' AUR 37:15
  Of this great hive, the c. COWL 221:16
  oppressing c. BIBLE 86:17
  people went up into the c. BIBLE 73:30
  perils of the c. BIBLE 102:1
  possession of truth as of a c. BROW 146:1
  rose-red c. half as old as BURG 156:24
  shall be a c. upon a hill WINT 739:10
  Shall there be evil in a c. BIBLE 86:11
  signed the paper felled a c. THOM 693:9
  streets and lanes of the c. BIBLE 94:31
  Sun-girt c., thou hast been SHEL 641:8
  than he that taketh a c. BIBLE 78:38
  that went about the c. BIBLE 81:18
  thou c. of God BOOK 130:21
  To feel, amid the c.'s jar ARN 27:12
  Unreal C. ELIOT 273:1
  Up and down the C. Road MAND 444:2
  was the new c. of Friends WHIT 732:3
  What is the c. but the people SHAK 570:12
  who has been long in c. KEATS 390:27
  within the C. disinterred SHEL 641:13
  Without a c. wall ALEX 8:16
  Woe to the bloody c. BIBLE 86:15
cive: His humid front the c. HOLM 342:9
  given c. me an ounce of c. SHAK 597:5
civil: Always be c. to the girls MITF 478.5
  c. to folk he ne'er saw ANST 18:19
  obey'd from discord ADD 3:24
  good people, be c. CINYN 320:6

civil: (cont.):
  In a c. war, a general REED 538:5
  In c. business BACON 42:29
  That the rude sea grew c. SHAK 611:16
  Too c. by half SHER 645:7
  wonderfully gifted c. servants CLARK 205:9
civilian: meet a mushroom rich c.
      BYRON 173:18
civilisation: present c. is composed HUGO 355:2
civilities: bandy c. with my Sovereign
      JOHN 372:27
  Cities and their c. PATM 509:14
  they dread c. TOCQ 699:6
civility: C. costs nothing MONT 480:10
  I see a wild c. HERR 336:12
  use the c. of my knee BROW 145:28
civilization: As c. advances, poetry MAC 434:16
  can't say c. don't advance ROG 545:4
  C. advances by extending WHIT 731:15
  C. and its discontents RIV 541:14
  C. and profits go hand in hand COOL 218:6
  c. has from time to time ELLIS 275:16
  C. has made the peasantry TROT 704:12
  C, is an active deposit CONN 216:16
  C. is nothing more ORT 499:11
  c. with the most difficulty TOCQ 699:3
  elements of modern c. CARL 180:17
  enumerate the items of high c. JAMES 362:19
  farmyard c. of the Fabians INGE 359:13
  For a botched c. POUND 527:3
  last product of c. RUSS 551:14
  life-blood of real c. TREV 702:10
  resources of c. against GLAD 307:12
  rottenness of our c. READ 537:6
  that c. produces its wonders TOCQ 699:8
civilizations: c. wherever it spreads SONT 656:7
civilized: c. man cannot live without
      MER 458:11
  last thing c. by Man MER 457.26
  mainspring of c. society SMIL 650:8
civilizers: two c. of man DISR 247:21
civil servant: c. doesn't make jokes ION 360:12
  Here lies a c. He was civil SISS 640:8
Civil Service: C. is profoundly deferential
      CROS 228:1
civis: C. Romanus sum CIC 204:8
  could say C. Romanus sum PALM 505:8
civium: *Non c. ardor* HOR 350:1
clad: naked every day he c. GOLD 310:22
claes: An' some upo' their c. BURNS 162:4
claiming: c. nothing for themselves MILL 461:2
clairvoyante: Madame Sosostris, famous c.
      ELIOT 272:24
clamavi: *De profundis c.* BIBLE 108:5
clamour: c. of the crowded street LONG 427:6
  which flees the worldly c. LUIS 432:7
clanging: C. from the Severn to the Tyne
      KIPL 398:12
clap: cheaper seats c. LENN 417:14
  C. her broad wings FRERE 293:17
  c. your hands BARR 54:9
  c. your hands together BOOK 127:18
  Don't c. too hard OSB 501:8
  Soul c. its hands YEATS 752:21
clapped-out: c., post-imperial DRAB 257:6
Clarence: fleeting, perjured C. SHAK 621:24
claret: C. is liquor for boys JOHN 375:7
Claridges: bootboy at C. WOOLF 742:16
clarion: c. o'er the dreaming earth SHEL 641:14
  cock's shrill c. GRAY 315:12
  Sound, sound the c. MORD 483:18
clashed: c. and hammered from TENN 681:8
clasped: C. by the golden light of morn
      HOOD 344:6
clasps: c. the crag with crookèd TENN 681:1
class: c. distinction is a proper BENN 63:4
  classes and c. antagonists MARX 452:13
  c. struggle necessarily MARX 452:9
  demarcate the upper c. ROSS 547:1
  flagrantly middle-c. WAUGH 724:10
  got a better c. of enemy MILL 462:5
  his flaws whatever his c. CHEK 197:2
  history of c. struggles MARX 452:12

class: *(cont.)*:

I could have had c.	SCH 558:9
passes, c. distinction	BETJ 67:15
use of *force* by one c.	LENIN 417:6
While there is a lower c.	DEBS 233:13
classes: all c. of society are trades	JEV 366:6
c. which need sanctuary	BALD 48:14
divisible into two great c.	BEER 59:8
masses against the c.	GLAD 307:17
two c. [educated and uneducated]	FOST 291:7
classic: 'C.' music eliminates	STR 670:23
C. music is th'kind	HUBB 353:12
tread on c. ground	ADD 4:2
classical: At c. Monday Pops	GILB 305:4
C. quotation is the *parole*	JOHN 375:24
great tragedy of the c.	MADAN 441:0
That's the c. mind at work	PIRS 515:4
classics: c. in paraphrase	POUND 526:13
man with a bellyful of the c.	MILL 462:1
clatter: c. of James Barrie's	GUED 319:9
claudite: C. iam rivos	VIRG 714:21
claw: red in tooth and c.	TENN 683:22
clawed: c. me with his clutch	VAUX 709:12
claws: c. that catch	CARR 182:18
How neatly spreads his c.	CARR 182:1
pair of ragged c.	ELIOT 272:3
clay: associate of this c.	HADR 320:8
c. and wattles made	YEATS 752:7
C. is the word and clay	KAV 386:3
C. lies still, but blood's	HOUS 352:7
c. say to him that fashioneth	BIBLE 84:3
covered thick with other c.	BYRON 168:20
grey stone and grassy c.	PEAC 510:11
grows my too refinèd c.	CLARE 204:20
make pure c. of time's mud	MAL 442:15
mire and c.	BOOK 126:24
potter and c. endure	BROW 152:11
potter power over the c.	BIBLE 100:2
They're only made of c.	GERS 301:15
thousand scattered into c.	FITZ 283:11
Transient lustre, beauteous c.	WRIG 749:12
clean: And keep their teeth c.	SHAK 570:8
c. and comfortable I sit	KEATS 392:11
C-l-e-a-n, c., verb active	DICK 242:5
c. the pasture spring	FROST 295:7
c. the sky	ELIOT 272:11
c. up the mess they had	FITZ 285:3
Every city on earth will be c.	MAY 455:6
fear of the Lord is c.	BOOK 125:5
hands ne'er be c.	SHAK 604:13
he did not love c. linen	JOHN 372:2
I shall be c.	BOOK 128:5
Make me a c. heart	BOOK 128:6
meadow for a c. place to die	KAV 386:4
Not a c. & in-between-	MCG 438:2
one more thing to keep c.	FRY 295:21
small and white and c.	MORR 485:12
that is not c. and neat	STEV 668:18
cleaned: c. the windows and I swept	GILB 305:26
cleanliness: C. is, indeed, next	WESL 728:23
c. of all the clean American	MAIL 442:8
Who of late for c.	CORB 218:12
cleanly: thus so c., I myself can free	DRAY 258:1
cleanness: swimmers into c. leaping	BROO 143:16
cleanse: C. me from its guilt and power	TOPL 701:4
c. me from my sin	BOOK 128:4
C. the stuffed bosom	SHAK 604:22
C. the thoughts of our	BOOK 121:16
c. thou me from my secret	BOOK 125:6
young man c. his way	BOOK 133:18
cleansed: doors of perception were c.	BLAKE 113:2
What God hath c., that call	BIBLE 98:20
clear: c. in his great office	SHAK 601:3
C. the air! clean the sky!	ELIOT 272:11
C. writers, like clear	LAND 408:12
c. your *mind* of cant	JOHN 376:8
literature c. and cold	LEWIS 421:2
night is as c. as the day	BOOK 134:19

clear: *(cont.)*:

poignancy in all things c.	WILB 734:2
What is not c. is not French	RIV 541:13
clearer: thinner, c., farther going	TENN 688:1
clearing: c. up the obscure corners	HUXL 358:8
clearing-house: c. of the world	CHAM 189:3
clears: A little water c. us	SHAK 602:7
cleave: c. the general ear	SHAK 575:9
c. the wood and there	ANON 17:16
shall c. unto his wife	BIBLE 70:7
tongue c. to the roof	BOOK 134:17
cleaveth: c. not stedfastly unto	BOOK 130:9
cleaving: c. the grass, gazelles	MOORE 482:17
cleft: Rock of Ages, c. for me	TOPL 701:4
Clemenceau: C. one of the greatest living orators	LLOY 424:9
Clementine: daughter, C.	MONT 482:4
Cleopatra: gone to gaze on C. too	SHAK 565:6
Is Antony again, I will be C.	SHAK 565:23
pleased with less than C.	DRYD 259:26
squeaking C. boy	SHAK 567:1
clercs: La trahison des c.	BENDA 62:14
clergy: c. is a dropping-down-deadness	SMITH 653:2
c. were beloved	SWIFT 674:13
If the c. are not called	WALP 720:7
without the benefit o' the C.	CONG 215:7
clergyman: bookie or of a c.	MUGG 487:8
c. and need not commit	WAUGH 723:14
good enough to be a c.	JOHN 373:18
clergymen: men, women, and c.	SMITH 653:13
with c. to do as little	DOYLE 257:5
cleric: C. before, Lay behind	BUTL 166:11
clerk: C. there was of Oxenford	CHAU 192:19
small house agent's c.	ELIOT 273:9
'twixt the Priest and C.	HERR 336:19
clerks: c. been noght wisest men	CHAU 194:14
statesmen or of c.	DISR 248:2
clever: c. and the successful	GREE 316:22
c. theft was praiseworthy	SPEN 658:20
c. to a fault	BROW 148:14
If all the good people were c.	WORD 743:4
It's c., but is it Art	KIPL 398:17
let who will be c.	KING 397:9
should rule over the c.	IBSEN 359:1
silliest woman can manage a c.	KIPL 402:8
Some parts were c.	WAT 722:5
Too c. by half	SAL 554:10
cleverness: c. is to be able to conceal it	LA R 410:17
cliché: c. and an indiscretion	MACM 440:7
click: c. upon themselves	FROST 294:9
cliff: In a coign of the c.	SWIN 676:14
cliffs: chalk c. of Dover	BALD 48:10
c. I never more must see	MAC 436:7
c. of fall frightful	HOPK 345:17
glittering c. on cliffs	BEAT 56:5
white c. of Dover	BURT 164:10
Yet still the solitary c.	WORD 744:11
climat: *donne à l'amour son vrai c.*	ANOU 23:7
climate: age too late, or cold C.	MILT 472:18
love with a cold c.	SOUT 657:21
now but a whole c. of opinion	AUDEN 34:12
Our chilling c. hardly bears	SWIFT 674:31
Our cloudy c., and our chilly	BYRON 167:24
climax: c. of all human ills	BYRON 170:27
climb: c. aloft by scales of courtly	GASC 298:17
c. out into the air	CONR 217:7
C. to our proper dark	YEATS 753:10
fails thee, c. not at all	ELIZ 274:12
Fain would I c., yet fear	RAL 536:2
I c. up into the heaven	BOOK 134:19
I must c. the tree	HERB 335:18
longer rotten boughs to c.	WYATT 749:16
She can teach ye how to c.	MILT 464:12
streams or c. the air	YEATS 753:20
climbed: While my love c. up to me	KING 397:7
climber-upward: Whereto the c. turns his face	SHAK 590:14
climbing: And, c., shakes his dewy wings	D'AV 231:20
c. after knowledge infinite	MARL 448:1
c. clear up to the sky	HAMM 322:16

climbing: *(cont.)*:

Of c. heaven, and gazing	SHEL 643:24
clime: after that sweet golden c.	BLAKE 114:5
All in this mottie, misty c.	BURNS 164:1
Of every age and c.	JOHN 377:14
They change their c.	HOR 348:9
this the soil, the c.	MILT 468:11
climes: cloudless c. and starry	BYRON 173:3
cling: c. to the old rugged cross	BENN 63:3
makes them c. together	WORD 746:21
clinging: blood-thirsty c. to life	ARN 29:14
Clive: What I like about C.	BENT 64:12
cloak: c. should become an iron	WEBER 724:19
not dissemble nor c.	BOOK 118:5
with the knyf under the c.	CHAU 193:21
clock: c. can't stop	LOW 430:17
c. is always slow	SERV 563:5
c. that clicked behind	GOLD 310:15
c. will strike	MARL 447:1
c. without the pendulum	RUSS 551:26
Court the slow c.	POPE 521:1
craft, as is making a c.	LA BR 405:5
forgot to wind up the c.	STER 664:12
Stands the Church c.	BROO 143:15
stop the church c.	KILV 396:6
turned into a sort of c.	HUXL 358:5
clocks: c. were striking	ORW 500:8
country houses hear c. ticking	BETJ 67:7
morning c. will ring	HOUS 352:8
clock-setter: Old Time the c.	SHAK 594:2
clockwork: c. orange	BURG 156:19
clod: c. of wayward marl	SHAK 613:13
clods: man harrowing c.	HARDY 325:10
clog: c. of his body	FULL 296:8
clogs: age to quit their c.	MILT 474:22
c. of that which else might	SHEL 642:18
cloister: be in shady c. mewed	SHAK 610:20
It is in c. or in scole	LANG 409:2
To walk the studious c.'s pale	MILT 464:26
cloistered: fugitive and c. virtue	MILT 475:7
cloisters: quiet collegiate c.	CLOU 207:5
close: c. ebbs out life's little	LYTE 433:16
C. encounters of the third kind	SPIE 661:1
c. the drama with the day	BERK 65:13
c. the wall up with our	SHAK 585:7
C. with her, kiss her	SWIN 677:3
c. your eyes before you	AYCK 40:7
Doth c. behind him tread	COL 211:14
ever beat found in the c.	MILT 474:19
Far away is c. at hand	GRAV 315:1
fatter man trying to c.	AMIS 10:15
peacefully towards its c.	DAWS 233:2
still hasten to a c.	COWP 222:1
closed: We never c.	VAN D 708:8
closer: c. is He than breathing	TENN 681:15
Come c., boys	CHIL 199:26
Oh! for a c. walk with God	COWP 222:22
sticketh c. than a brother	BIBLE 79:3
closes: Blown fields or flowerful c.	SWIN 677:1
C. nothing, refuses nothing	WHIT 733:1
it is about you that c.	CUMM 228:15
Satire is what c. Saturday	KAUF 385:14
closet: forth the c. brought a heap	KEATS 387:9
one by one back in the c.	FITZ 284:7
They put me in the c.	DICK 245:1
world, and not in a c.	CHES 198:6
closing: c. time in the gardens	CONN 216:14
cloth: c. coat is to look	BALM 51:7
having a fair white linen c.	BOOK 121:15
On a c. untrue	GILB 305:5
clothe: c. me round, the while my path	LITT 423:9
thus I c. my naked villany	SHAK 621:22
clothed: c., fed and educated	RUSK 550:27
C. in white samite	TENN 681:18
c. on with chastity	TENN 681:7
C. with his breath	TENN 682:21
C. with transcendent brightness	MILT 468:2
man c. in soft raiment	BIBLE 90:25
who c. you in scarlet	BIBLE 75:9
woman c. with the sun	BIBLE 106:29
ye c. me	BIBLE 92:20
clothes: been poured into his c.	WOD 740:23

clothes: (cont.):
brushers of noblemen's c.	WOTT 749:7
c. are good only as they	JOHN 374:12
C., or fortune gives the grace	JONS 379:14
c. that I have ever seen	LOES 426:3
Her c. spread wide	SHAK 578:13
his c. not be burned	BIBLE 78:15
Kindles in c. a wantonness	HERR 336:12
She wears her c., as if	SWIFT 674:6
That liquefaction of her c.	HERR 337:9
walked away with their c.	DISR 246:18
When he put on his c.	GOLD 310:22
Who touched my c.	BIBLE 93:12
who wore torn c.	SPEN 659:2
witnesses laid down their c.	BIBLE 98:12

clothing: c. for the soul divine BLAKE 111:6
come to you in sheep's c.	BIBLE 89:23
Gave thee c. of delight	BLAKE 113:21
her c. is of wrought gold	BOOK 127:13
lowliness become mine inner c.	LITT 423:9
sheep in sheep's c.	CHUR 203:11
sheep in sheep's c.	GOSSE 312:16
Things in books' c.	LAMB 406:18
which loose to go in long c.	BIBLE 93:17

cloths: heavens' embroidered c. YEATS 751:22
clotted: lump of c. nonsense DRYD 262:19
cloud: by a c. takes all away SHAK 631:4
c. instead, and ever-during dark	MILT 470:16
c. in trousers	MAY 454:17
c. of unknowing	ANON 12:22
c. that runs before	RAL 535:14
c. which had outwept	SHEL 639:15
core tore and flung c.	HUGH 364:5
day in a pillar of a c.	BIBLE 72:13
Don't you know each c. contains	BURKE 160:5
do set my bow in the c.	BIBLE 70:32
fair luminous c.	COL 209:15
Fall on the wat'ry c.	AKEN 6:5
Get off of my c.	JAGG 361:9
great a c. of witnesses	BIBLE 104:17
How sweet to be a C.	MILNE 463:1
I wandered lonely as a c.	WORD 744:15
Like a fiend hid in a c.	BLAKE 114:8
little c. out of the sea	BIBLE 76:4
On a c. I saw a child	BLAKE 113:16
or did a sable c.	MILT 463:21
see a c. that's dragonish	SHAK 566:6
shall be no C. nor Sun	DONNE 253:14
Stooping through a fleecy c.	MILT 464:20
Till he melted like a c.	TENN 689:1
Turn the dark c. inside out	FORD 289:16
under the lark full c.	THOM 693:13
When the c. is scattered	SHEL 641:6

cloud-continents: great c. of sunset-seas ALDR 8:6
cloudcuckooland: How about 'C.' ARIS 25:2
clouded: Shine forth upon our c. hills BLAKE 113:4
clouds: C. and eclipses stain SHAK 633:13
C. beyond clouds above me	BRON 142:11
c. blew off from a high	BRID 141:4
c. contend with growing	SHAK 587:29
c. have drank the last	SHEL 643:8
c. methought would open	SHAK 625:26
c. return after the rain	BIBLE 81:1
c. ye so much dread	COWP 222:18
comes with c. descending	WESL 728:15
cometh with c.	BIBLE 105:32
dropping from the c.	THOM 696:5
gift is like c. and wind	BIBLE 79:16
like the prince of the c.	BAUD 55:6
Looks in the c., scorning	SHAK 590:14
maketh the c. his chariot	BOOK 132:6
movement of c. in benediction	DAY L 233:6
Never d... hind c would break	BROW 148:6
O c., unfold	BLAKE 113:4
presence his... removed	BOOK 120:8
...shall not want	BIBLE 80:27
those c. will vanish	GRAY 316:0
through the c. I'll never float	WORD 744:1
thy c. drop fatness	BOOK 129:3
...c —how oft have	DE L 235:22

clouds: (cont.):
trailing c. of glory	WORD 745:14
White c. on the wing	ALL 10:2

cloudy: c. days of autumn CLARE 204:28
Clough: poor poet named C. SWIN 677:2
clouts: come thus into c. ANDR 11:12
stones and c. make martyrs	BROW 145:16

cloven: out pops the c. hoof WOD 740:11
cloven-footed: c., yet he cheweth not BIBLE 73:1
clover: sort of pig in c. LAWR 413:2
cloverleaf: national flower is the concrete c. MUMF 488:2
cloves: ginger, cinnamon and c. BEAU 56:13
clownage: conceits as c. keeps in pay MARL 447:19
clowns: Send in the c. SOND 656:2
cloy: all meats the soonest c. COWL 221:16
club: ANY C. THAT WILL ACCEPT MARX 451:16
savage wields his c.	HUXL 358:4
mean to say this place is a c.?	SMITH 651:17

clucked: c. thee to the wars SHAK 570:25
clue: almost invariably a c. DOYLE 256:4
Clun: Clungunford and C. HOUS 352:17
clung: c. into a kiss BYRON 170:20
clusters: luscious c. of the vine MARV 450:9
clutch: clawed me with his c. VAUX 709:12
Inapprehensive, we c. thee	THOM 695:9
In the fell c. of circumstance	HENL 332:6

clutching: alien people c. their gods ELIOT 271:18
Still c. the inviolable shade	ARN 28:10

Clyde: bonnie banks o' C. LAUD 411:7
C Major: C. of this life BROW 148:2
CMG: C. ('Call me God') SAMP 554:16
coach: c. and six horses through the Act RICE 540:4
her silver c. to climb	SPEN 659:14
hold back against the c.	TROL 704:2
rattling of a c.	DONNE 253:9

coach and six: give me indifference and a c. COLM 213:17
coachman: c.'s a privileged indiwidual DICK 243:28
coal: c. and surrounded by fish BEVAN 68:12
having a live c. in his hand	BIBLE 82:21
made of Newcastle c.	WALP 719:11
Strong is the lion—like a c.	SMART 650:1
whole world turn to c.	HERB 336:2

coalitions: England does not love c. DISR 247:4
coals: all eyes else dead c. SHAK 632:15
c. of fire	BOOK 125:2
c. of fire upon his head	BIBLE 79:18
I sleep on the c.	DICK 239:24
My c. are spent, my iron's	ANON 16:16
no more c. to Newcastle	GEOR 301:4

coarse: c. appropriates the finer HARDY 324:15
c., stupid, and unhappy	CHEK 196:7
c. complexions	MILT 464:8
one of them is rather c.	ROYD 549:13

coarseness: c. and vulgarity FORS 290:15
coast: c. of Coromandel LEAR 413:19
c. of Coromandel	SITW 648:19
gospel's pearl upon our c.	MARV 449:20

coaster: Dirty British c. MAS 453:3
coat: c. of many colours BIBLE 71:20
c. upon a coat-hanger	YEATS 750:19
eternal Footman hold my c.	ELIOT 272:4
Grab your c., and get your hat	FIEL 282:19
I made my song a c.	YEATS 751:3
riband to stick in his c.	BROW 150:25
tattered c. upon a stick	YEATS 752:21
that loves a scarlet c.	HOOD 343:19

coats: In c. of red DE L 236:5
coat-tails: see my c. flying GROS 319:1
cobble-stones: On c. I lay FLAN 285:8
cobweb: Learning, that c. of the brain BUTL 166:12
cobwebs: Laws ... like c. SWIFT 673:5
tickles with the c.	FROST 294:10
...old... whatever... blue jeans and C.	LEFČR 217:14

cock: before the c. crow BIBLE 92:26

cock: (cont.):
C. and a Bull, said Yorick	STER 665:10
c. can crow in its own	TROL 703:17
c. hadde in his governaunce	CHAU 194:5
c.'s shrill clarion	GRAY 315:12
c. who thought the sun	ELIOT 268:17
Diminished to her c.	SHAK 597:1
immediately the c. crew	BIBLE 93:2
levying of c.-tax	AMIS 10:10
Nationalism is a silly c.	ALD 8:3
on the crowing of the c.	SHAK 572:2
Our c. won't fight	BEAV 57:9
owe a c. to Aesculapius	SOCR 655:4
walks till the first c.	SHAK 596:13
While the c. with lively din	MILT 465:8

cockatoo: cage is natural to a c. SHAW 636:14
green freedom of a c.	STEV 666:10

cockatrice: on the c.' den BIBLE 83:3
cockerel: calls with c.'s tongue LEE 415:19
cockle: By his c. hat and staff SHAK 577:34
cockles: c. boiled in silver shells JONS 378:6
Cockney: C. impudence RUSK 550:10
cockpit: Can this c. hold SHAK 584:17
cocks: drowned the c. SHAK 595:20
cocktail: weasel under the c. cabinet PINT 515:2
cod: home of the bean and the c. BOSS 137:1
O bely! O stynkyng c.	CHAU 194:10

code: trail has its own stern c. SERV 563:4
Codlin: C.'s the friend DICK 242:19
codling: c. when 'tis almost an apple SHAK 628:22
codpiece: grace and a c. SHAK 595:24
codpieces: plackets, king of c. SHAK 598:13
coercion: effect of c. JEFF 364:17
coeur: Il pleure dans mon c. VERL 710:6
Coeur-de-Lion: reputed son of C. SHAK 593:24
co-exist: we must peacefully c. KHR 395:15
coffee: C. (which makes the politician wise) POPE 523:28
C. and oranges in a sunny	STEV 666:10
c. and other slop-kettle	COBB 207:27
C. house babble	DISR 249:12
if this is c., I want tea	PUNCH 532:6
measured out my life with c.	ELIOT 272:2

coffin: gorgeous c. laid low BYRON 173:14
grave in a Y-shaped c.	ORTON 499:17
like a c. clapt in a canoe	BYRON 167:21
Like the silver plate on a c.	CURR 229:5

cog: c. o' gude swats BURNS 161:14
make me a c. in a machine	MACN 441:1

cogitations: it still amaze ELIOT 271:20
cogito: C., ergo sum DESC 237:18
cognoscere: qui potuit rerum c. causas VIRG 715:14
coherent: C. miseries, a bite and sup HEAN 329:22
cohorts: c. gleaming in purple BYRON 169:28
coign: c. of the cliff between SWIN 676:14
coil: c. of crystalline streams SHEL 641:16
coin: Beauty is Nature's c. MILT 464:7
had rather c. my heart	SHAK 593:6
less store upon the c.	WHAR 730:3
The C., Tiberius	DOBS 249:20

coincidence: long arm of c. CHAM 189:10
coiner: c. of sweet words ARN 28:14
coins: fistful of c. ZAP 755:8
like to c., some true	TENN 681:28

coition: vulgar way of c. BROW 146:16
coitu: Foeda est in c. et brevis PETR 513:15
coitum: Post c. omne animal triste. ANON 22:12
cold: Aching, shaking, crazy, c. ROCH 543:17
And she alone were c.	SHAK 571:19
And straight is c. again	SHAK 593:9
art neither c. nor hot	BIBLE 106:7
As doth eternity: C. Pastoral	KEATS 389:2
Beauty she was statue c.	FLEC 286:6
blow in c. blood	SHAW 637:28
Cast a c. eye	YEATS 753:18
clear and c. and pure	LEWIS 421:2
...are not clothed	EIS 268:10
c. and heat, and summer	BIBLE 70:29
...and lonely as itself	ELIOT 508:6

cold: (*cont.*):
c. charities of man to man CRAB 225:15
Cold, c., my girl SHAK 618:18
c. coming they had of it ANDR 11:13
c. coming we had of it ELIOT 271:17
C. currents thrid HARDY 325:3
c. doesn't crouch over LAWR 413:1
c. had pierced the tender SACK 552:12
c. hearts and muddy understandings
BURKE 158:15
C. in the earth BRON 142:15
C. is the heart, fair Greece BYRON 168:6
C. lights hurting JOHN 366:17
c. metal of economic theory SCH 558:12
c. nymphs chaste crowns SHAK 625:27
C., pain, and labour WORD 747:13
c. performs the effect MILT 470:2
c. relation is a zealous BURKE 158:27
C. the seat and loud BFNN 63:12
comfort like c. porridge SHAK 625:13
darkness and the c. STEV 668:22
dwelleth i' the c. o' the moon BROW 149:1
Even till I shrink with c. SHAK 567:24
everlasting c. WEBS 726:14
Fallen c. and dead WHIT 732:7
I beg c. comfort SHAK 594:15
In c. grave she was lain BALL 51:1
ink in my pen ran c. WALP 719:5
it was too c. always SMITH 652:17
judgement, c. in blood SHAK 565:3
like rivers grow c. MONT 480:6
love with a c. climate SOUT 657:21
midst of a c. war BAR 54:19
Our sympathy is c. GIBB 302:6
Out, alas! she's c. SHAK 624:1
O ye Frost and C., bless BOOK 118:8
place is too c. for hell SHAK 602:10
Poor Tom's a-c. SHAK 596:16
spy who came in from the c. LE C 415:11
straight past the common c. AYRES 40:16
'tis bitter c. SHAK 571:22
To lie in c. obstruction SHAK 606:11
understand one who's c. SOLZ 655:10
colder: pleasanter, the c. BUTL 166:15
coldly: C., sadly descends ARN 28:1
coldness: faithless c. of the times TENN 684:11
Coleridge: C. dined with us WORD 742:21
C.—he who sits obscure SHEL 641:3
C. lull the babe at nurse BYRON 172:11
C., too, lately taken wing BYRON 170:1
Cultivate simplicity, C. LAMB 406:22
observed to you by C. WORD 748:20
Coliseum: While stands the C. BYRON 169:10
You're the top! You're the C. PORT 524:20
collapse: C. of Stout Party ANON 12:23
collar: braw brass c. BURNS 163:24
collateral: c. security CHES 198:19
collections: mutilators of c. LAMB 406:13
collective: c. unconscious JUNG 382:12
sense of c. responsibility ALD 8:3
collectors: great c. before me DOUG 255:11
collects: c. which had soothed MAC 435:18
college: cabbage with a c. education
TWAIN 706:20
Die, and endow a c., or a cat POPE 520:15
Than either school or c. BURNS 162:5
colleges: discipline of c. and universities
SMITH 651:1
collegiate: faces in quiet c. cloisters CLOU 207:5
colonel: C. Blimp LOW 429:8
C.'s Lady an' Judy O'Grady KIPL 399:15
colonies: C. do not cease to be colonies
DISR 247:8
c. will all be independent DISR 247:33
commerce with our c. BURKE 157:20
New c. seek at Botany Bay FREE 293:15
colonnade: whispering sound of the cool c.
COWP 222:29
Colonus: Singer of sweet C. ARN 29:1
colony: fuzzy wuzzy c. CAIR 175:2
colori: nimium ne crede c. VIRG 714:15
colossus: genius that could cut a C.
JOHN 376:13

colossus: (*cont.*):
narrow world like a C. SHAK 590:3
colour: Any c.—so long as it's black
FORD 289:5
cast thy nighted c. off SHAK 572:8
c. in his face hath had CHAU 193:25
c. of his hair HOUS 351:13
c. that of a tea-tray painter BLUNT 116:6
giveth his c. in the cup BIBLE 79:13
Her c. comes and goes DOBS 249:22
horse of that c. SHAK 629:11
I know the c. rose ABSE 1:2
Life is C. and Warmth GREN 318:2
not be judged by the c. KING 397:1
problem of the c. DU B 263:4
swear her c. is natural SHER 645:15
waning of their c. VOLT 716:15
yearned for warmth and c. TENN 681:26
coloured: And see the c. counties HOUS 352:10
black blood makes a man c. HUGH 354:2
'c.' signs on the foxholes KENN 394:5
colourless: C. green ideas CHOM 200:3
colours: All c. agree in the dark BACON 45:3
c. dont quite match ASHF 31:6
c. laid so thick DRYD 260:15
C. seen by candle-light BROW 147:16
I can add c. to the chameleon SHAK 588:3
made him a coat of many c. BIBLE 71:20
map-makers' c. BISH 110:2
tears have run the c. from my BROW 147:19
Their c. and their forms WORD 744:21
wrought about with divers c. BOOK 127:12
Columbia: C.! happy land HOPK 346:20
columbine: pink and purple c. SPEN 660:26
columbines: fennel for you, and c. SHAK 578:8
column: Now is the stately c. broke
SCOTT 560:1
stands like a black c. BABEL 41:10
columnae: non concessere c. HOR 347:19
columnists: political c. say ADAMS 2:3
columns: crazy on its smoking c. YEVT 754:4
enormous fluted Ionic c. MACN 440:16
comae: Arboribusque c. HOR 350:15
comb: that he could c. grey hair YEATS 752:4
two bald men over a c. BORG 136:11
combat: le triomphe mais le c. COUB 220:4
To c. may be glorious COWP 223:30
combatants: learned dust involves the c.
COWP 223:25
comber: c. wind-hounded KIPL 401:1
combination: You may call it c. PALM 505:9
combinations: c. have been tried FLAU 285:18
irregular c. JOHN 369:17
combine: When bad men c. BURKE 159:15
combining: cabinet is a c. committee BAG 46:15
combustible: c. world in one small room
YEATS 752:4
combustion: inside an internal c. engine
BEVAN 69:4
Of dire c. and confused events SHAK 602:13
With hideous ruin and c. down MILT 467:23
come: Amen. Even so, c., Lord Jesus
BIBLE 107:26
And, behold, I c. quickly BIBLE 107:24
And cannot c. again HOUS 352:15
an' I'll c. to you BURNS 162:26
be gone long.—You c. too FROST 295:7
believe in the life to c. BECK 57:13
be now, 'tis not to c. SHAK 579:2
c. all the way for this MORR 485:13
C., and he cometh BIBLE 89:30
C., come away, death SHAK 629:17
C., come, dear Night CHAP 190:17
C., dear children, let us away ARN 27:6
C. down, O Love divine LITT 423:9
C., Firm Resolve, take BURNS 163:18
C., friendly bombs BETJ 68:5
C., Holy Spirit, and send LANG 409:8
C. into the garden, Maud TENN 686:17
C., let us join our cheerful WATTS 722:19
C. little babe, come silly BRET 140:17
C., lovely Morning DAV 232:13

come: (*cont.*):
C. mothers and fathers DYLAN 265:23
C., my Celia, let us prove JONS 379:10
C. not between the dragon SHAK 594:20
C. out, thou bloody man BIBLE 75:15
C. over into Macedonia BIBLE 98:25
C. to me in my dreams ARN 27:5
c. to the end of a perfect BOND 117:17
C. unto me, all ye BIBLE 90:28
C. unto these yellow sands SHAK 625:8
c. up and see me sometime WEST 729:14
C. uppe, Whitefoot ING 360:5
C. what come may SHAK 600:13
C. when you do call SHAK 581:3
C. when you're called EDG 266:11
c. with old Khayyám FITZ 284:1
C. you back to Mandalay KIPL 400:1
dreaming on things to c. SHAK 634:19
For men may c. and men may go
TENN 680:12
Friend, wherefore art thou c. BIBLE 92:31
had better not c. at all KEATS 391:15
is in my will: I will not c. SHAK 591:7
it needn't c. to that CARR 183:14
King of glory shall c. BOOK 125:17
leave to c. unto my love SPEN 659:16
let him c. out as I do JOHN 376:2
Lo, I c. BOOK 126:25
mine hour is not yet c. BIBLE 96:10
my love is c. to me ROSS 547:2
O c., all ye faithful ANON 21:18
O c., let us sing unto BOOK 131:9
O c. to my heart, Lord Jesus ELL 275:8
Of things to c. at large SHAK 627:11
One to c., and one CARR 183:17
or c. without warning DAVIS 232:16
Out of Ireland have we c. YEATS 752:19
shape of things to c. WELLS 727:22
Suffer me to c. to thee WESL 728:7
That have c., that have gone RAL 536:1
That it should c. to this SHAK 572:12
therefore I cannot c. BIBLE 94:30
tho' they c. from the ends of KIPL 398:13
'twill c. in my father AUBR 33:11
war and nobody will c. SAND 555:9
We are c. for your good GEOR 300:24
We'd jump the life to c. SHAK 601:2
What's to c. is still unsure SHAK 629:4
what's to c. is strewed SHAK 628:3
wheel is c. full circle SHAK 597:19
When you c., as you soon WILB 734:1
When you c. back again RUB 549:16
Where all to c., is one GREV 318:7
where do they all c. from LENN 417:18
which is to c. BIBLE 105:31
Will come when it will c. SHAK 591:5
comedies: All c. are ended by a marriage
BYRON 170:26
comedy: catastrophe of the old c. SHAK 595:3
C. is an imitation SIDN 647:9
c. to those that think WALP 719:18
make a c. is a park CHAP 190:9
most lamentable c. SHAK 611:2
sende myght to make in som c. CHAU 195:26
tragedy, c., history SHAK 575:2
comeliness: hath no form nor c. BIBLE 84:11
comely: I am black, but c. BIBLE 81:6
comer: Grasps in the c. SHAK 627:21
comes: c. to the same thing BROW 148:4
goes of a night and c. SHER 645:15
He c. too near, that comes MONT 480:4
Look, where it c. again SHAK 571:24
nobody c., nobody goes BECK 57:22
then just as it c. BETJ 67:12
cometh: he c. with clouds BIBLE 105:32
he that c. in the Name BOOK 133:17
He that c. to me BIBLE 96:26
iceman c. O'NEI 498:18
master of the house c. BIBLE 93:4
no man c. unto the Father BIBLE 97:12
comets: Old men and c. SWIFT 674:22
there are no c. seen SHAK 591:5
Ye country c., that portend MARV 450:17

comfit-maker: You swear like a c.'s wife
                 SHAK 581:11
comfort: a' the c. we're to get   BURNS 163:23
   beside the waters of c.   BOOK 125:14
   carrion c., Despair   HOPK 345:7
   c. all that mourn   BIBLE 84:26
   c. and help   BOOK 119:20
   c. hath been in my people's   ELIZ 274:10
   c. more and set less store   WHAR 730:3
   c. more powerful and more   TOCQ 698:9
   C. myself when that my hap   SURR 672:4
   c. of thy help again   BOOK 128:6
   c. of thy worth and truth   SHAK 633:14
   C.'s a cripple and comes   DRAY 257:15
   c. serves in a whirlwind   HOPK 345:18
   c. that you will soon be out   EMER 277:10
   c. ye my people   BIBLE 83:25
   Continual c. in a face   ROYD 549:14
   From ignorance our c. flows   PRIOR 529:14
   good c. Master Ridley   LAT 411:3
   have of c. and despair   SHAK 635:6
   holy Sacrament to your c.   BOOK 122:5
   I beg cold c.   SHAK 594:15
   I tell you naught for your c.   CHES 198:27
   love her, c. her, honour   BOOK 123:19
   neither found I any to c. me   BOOK 129:12
   not ecstasy but it was c.   DICK 241:4
   Of c. no man speak   SHAK 620:7
   prefers c. to pleasure   HESSE 337:16
   receives c. like cold porridge   SHAK 626:13
   requireth further c. or counsel   BOOK 122:4
   That c. cruel men   CHES 199:3
   that I may take c. a little   BIBLE 77:15
   that means c.   TOLK 700:2
   they never knew c.   MAC 434:13
   To warn, to c., and command   WORD 747:19
   Well, here's my c.   SHAK 625:19
comfortable: baith grand and c.   BARR 54:4
   c. and the accepted   GALB 296:19
   c. estate of widowhood   GAY 299:16
   c. I sit down to write   KEATS 392:11
   c. words our Saviour Christ   BOOK 122:7
   What c. hour canst thou name   SHAK 622:5
comfortably: Are you sitting c.   LANG 408:17
   lived c. so long together   GAY 299:12
   Speak ye c. to Jerusalem   BIBLE 83:25
comforted: longing to be c.   WORD 747:13
   Lord hath c. his people   BIBLE 84:9
   they shall be c.   BIBLE 88:23
   would not be c.   BIBLE 88:11
comforter: A Guide, a C.   AUBER 32:20
   C. will not come unto you   BIBLE 97:18
   O C., draw near   LITT 423:9
comforters: Miserable c. are ye all   BIBLE 77:22
comforting: cloud of c. convictions
                 RUSS 551:21
   c. thought   MARQ 448:16
   where is your c.   HOPK 345:16
comfortless: All dark and c.   SHAK 596:22
   beseech thee, leave us not c.   BOOK 120:19
   Exceeding c., and worn   ROSS 547:5
comforts: But c. we despise   SHAK 566:11
   helpers fail, and c. flee   LYTE 433:16
   not without c. and hopes   BACON 42:20
   Our social c. drop away   JOHN 370:10
comic: c. poet to paint the vices   CONG 214:22
comical: Beautiful c. things   HARV 327:23
   I often think it's c.   GILB 304:10
coming: am c. to that holy room   DONNE 251:14
   c. after me is preferred   BIBLE 96:6
   cold c. we had of it   ELIOT 271:17
   c. down let me shift   MORE 484:14
   C. in on a wing and a pray'r   ADAM 3:11
   a of the King of Heaven   ANON 20:3
   c of the Son of Man   BIBLE 92:13
   C. thro' the rye   BURNS 161:13
   wing or their c. hither   MILK 597:15
   Anything's c. up roses   SOND 655:16
   He is c.! he is coming   HT 111:2
   Lord I am c. as fast   FAGE 111:4
   She is c., my dove, my dear   TENN 686:20
   There's a gude time c.   SCOTT 560:31

coming: (cont.):
   they will be c. for us   BALD 48:6
   We keep c. back and coming back   STEV 666:5
   what I thought his c.   BYRON 168:1
comma: c.-hunting   CORN 219:9
command: And hast c. of every part
                 HERR 337:3
   be able to c. the rain   PEPYS 512:7
   Bears a c. in't   SHAK 570:17
   born to sue, but to c.   SHAK 619:8
   c. of any kind as an exceptional   MILL 461:2
   commands move only in c.   SHAK 604:18
   gallant will c. the sun   SHAK 624:19
   give what you c.   AUG 37:3
   I may c. where I adore   SHAK 630:3
   left that c. sole daughter   MILT 472:23
   Less used to sue than to c.   SCOTT 559:9
   mortals to c. success   ADD 3:16
   up one's will to the c.   OSB 501:7
commandest: thing which thou c.   BOOK 120:18
commandment: c. of the Lord   BOOK 125:5
commandments: chiefly learn by these C.
                 BOOK 123:5
   Fear God, and keep his c.   BIBLE 81:4
   following the c. of God   BIBLE 122:5
   hearkened to my c.   BIBLE 84:5
   I'd set my ten c. in your face   SHAK 587:17
   love me, and keep my c.   BIBLE 72:16
   Ten for the ten c.   ANON 15:1
   thy c. we may please thee   BOOK 121:1
commands: C. the beauteous files   VAUG 708:17
   servant does not all c.   SHAK 571:10
commencement: le c. de la fin   TALL 678:12
commend: I c. my spirit   BIBLE 95:28
   Into thy hands I c. my spirit   BOOK 126:7
   some virtue, virtue to c.   CONG 216:7
commendable: Silence is only c.   SHAK 607:8
commendatio: Formosa facies muta c. est
                 PUBL 531:1
commendeth: obliquely c.   BROW 145:6
comment: C. is free but facts   STOP 669:18
   C. is free, but facts   SCOTT 559:2
   read the c. but myself   TENN 682:16
commentators: As learned c. view   SWIFT 675:2
   c. each dark passage shun   YOUNG 754:11
commerce: c., and honest friendship   JEFF 364:5
   c. the fault of the Dutch   CANN 178:3
   c. with our colonies   BURKE 157:20
   disinterested c. between equals   GOLD 311:17
   exist under a ceiling of c.   OLIV 498:16
   heavens fill with c.   TENN 685:13
commercialism: [C. is] doing well   VIDAL 711:2
commissary: Great Destiny the c. of God
                 DONNE 251:12
commit: c. his body to the deep   BOOK 135:20
   we therefore c. his body   BOOK 124:5
committed: [Earl Haig] c. suicide   BEAV 57:8
committee: cabinet is a combining c.   BAG 46:15
   C.—a group of men who individually
                 ALLEN 9:8
   c. is a group of the unwilling   ANON 12:26
   horse designed by a c.   ISS 360:23
commodious: c. car of the imagination
                 JAMES 362:14
   c. vicus of recirculation   JOYCE 380:21
commodity: C., firmness, and delight
                 WOTT 749:6
   c. of good names were   SHAK 579:23
   gentleman, tickling C.   SHAK 593:30
common: according to the c. weal   JAM 362:5
   are no members of the c. throng   GILB 306:12
   Ay, madam, it is c.   SHAK 572:9
   bound the c. of silence   EMER 276:21
   century of the c. man   WALL 718:5
   Christians are not c.   BOOK 136:2
   c. and popular   SHAK 585:21
   c. cormorant or shag   ISH 360:23
   c. man the great protection   BEVIN 69:14
   c. notions in an individual   HOR 347:10
   c. opinion and universal   BAG 46:9
   c. pursuit   ELIOT 115:3
   c. tax the multitude   BYRON 170:6
   concur with the c' finds   JOHN 366:27

common: (cont.):
   dull catalogue of c. things   KEATS 388:19
   express yourself like the c.   YEATS 753:24
   fade into the light of c.   WORD 745:14
   grazed the c. of literature   JOHN 372:5
   had all things c.   BIBLE 98:8
   have in c. being so poor   BLUN 116:1
   He nothing c. did or mean   MARV 450:15
   Horseguards and still be c.   RATT 537:3
   I am not in the roll of c. men   SHAK 581:2
   I feel for the c. chord again   BROW 148:2
   In c. things that round us lie   WORD 746:16
   Lazarus mystified, c. man   HILL 338:9
   loathe all things held in c.   CALL 175:7
   make it too c.   SHAK 582:23
   nay the c. law itself   COKE 208:17
   No c. thing to see   HAR 326:10
   nor lose the c. touch   KIPL 400:15
   not jump with c. spirits   SHAK 608:16
   Paradise of all things c. else   MILT 471:15
   prefers c.-looking people   LINC 422:15
   prevail, of a c. law   JEFF 364:11
   Should stamp me back to c.   FITZ 284:14
   speak as the c. people   ASCH 31:3
   Such Cloe is . . . and c. as the air
                 GRAN 314:12
   that call not thou c.   BIBLE 98:20
   they are not already c.   LOCKE 424:14
   trivial round, the c. task   KEBLE 392:20
   whom one has nothing in c.   PYM 533:10
   Who steals a c. from a goose   ANON 13:9
   You c. people of the skies   WOTT 749:2
commonalty: very dog to the c.   SHAK 570:2
Common Law: C. of England   HERB 334:1
   marry C. to Common Sense   LLOYD 424:2
commonplace: common is the c.   TENN 683:2
   c. things and characters   SCOTT 561:1
   featureless and c. a crime   DOYLE 256:4
   neither c., unmeaning   HARDY 324:12
   provided his c. book be full   SWIFT 674:11
Common Prayer: Because they hated C.
                 JORD 380:13
Commons: The C., faithful   MACK 439:6
common sense: admixture of insipid c.   SAL 554:2
   bring men back to c.   BERK 65:10
   c. tell lies to   WALK 717:13
   C. is the best distributed   DESC 237:17
   Defend me, therefore, c.   COWP 223:26
   from c., and observation   BROW 146:10
   great c. and good taste   SHAW 635:28
   marry Common Law to C.   LLOYD 424:2
   Nothing but c., and relatively   MORT 486:7
   trained and organized c.   HUXL 358:4
commonwealth: c. is fixed   BURKE 158:32
   c. of learning is not   LOCKE 424:15
   caterpillars of the c.   SHAK 619:22
   service and conduct of the c.   BURKE 159:17
   should arise in the C.   MILT 475:2
commonwealths: men's uniting into c.
                 LOCKE 425:7
   To raise up c. and ruin kings   DRYD 258:19
commune: c. with your own heart
                 BOOK 124:12
communia: Difficile est proprie c.   HOR 347:10
communicate: to c. was something positive
                 PRIT 529:18
   To do good and to c.   BIBLE 104:23
communicated: C. monthly, sit and stare
                 BETJ 67:8
communication: c. of the dead   ELIOT 271:3
communications: Evil c. corrupt good
   manners   BIBLE 101:10
communion: C. of Saints   BOOK 119:1
   one equal c. and identity   DONNE 253:14
   partakers of the holy C.   BOOK 121:14
   sense an act of holy c.   ROB 542:15
   should come to the holy C.   BOOK 122:4
   Table, at the C.-time   BOOK 121:15
   They plucked c. tables down   JORD 380:13
   weeks of perfect c.   AUDEN 36:7
Communism: against the anti-Christ of C.
                 BUCH 154:5
   C. is like prohibition   ROG 545:1

Communism: (*cont.*):
C. is Soviet power plus　　　　　LENIN 417:4
[Russian C. is] the illegitimate　ATTL 32:17
spectre of C.　　　　　　　　MARX 452:11
Communist: because I wasn't a C.　NIEM 495:2
What is a c.?　　　　　　　　ELL 275:12
communists: Catholics and C.　GREE 316:20
community: c. of thought, a rivalry of aim
　　　　　　　　　　　　　　ADAMS 2:16
c. will still be better　　　　　KALD 384:20
join and unite into a c.　　　　LOCKE 425:8
set up a small anarchist c.　　BENN 63:9
we are part of the c. of Europe　SAL 554:5
commuter: C.—one who spends his life
　　　　　　　　　　　　　　WHITE 731:1
compact: C. of ancient tales　BELL 61:15
c. which exists between　　　GARR 298:13
of imagination all c.　　　　　SHAK 612:17
They made a c. them between　BALL 49:8
compacted: box where sweets c. lie　HERB 336:1
compañía: El pan comido y la c. deshecha
　　　　　　　　　　　　　　CERV 188:10
companion: c. to owls　　　BIBLE 77:31
gave him a c. to make　　　　VALÉ. 707:22
It was even thou, my c.　　　BOOK 128:11
mortified appetite never a wise c.　STEV 667:6
old and agreeable c.　　　　GIBB 302:19
prince a better c.　　　　　SHAK 582:22
thy poor, earth-born c.　　　BURNS 163:16
companionless: Wandering c.　SHEL 643:24
companions: C. of our woe　WALSH 720:18
For my brethren and c.'　　　BOOK 133:26
His best c., innocence　　　　GOLD 310:6
company: before God and this c.　BOOK 123:23
be the worst of the c.　　　　SWIFT 673:19
"boozes" by the c. he chooses　BURT 164:8
colder rooms and worse c.　　AUST 38:8
c. and good discourse　　　　WALT 721:2
c. below your ambition　　　EMER 277:10
C. for carrying on an undertaking
　　　　　　　　　　　　　　ANON 12:27
c. of all faithful people　　　BOOK 122:14
c. of the heavenly host　　　BLAKE 114:18
c. of the preachers　　　　　BOOK 129:8
company, villanous c.　　　　SHAK 581:17
conversation in a mixed c.　　CHES 198:3
crowd is not c.　　　　　　BACON 43:21
fellows shall bear her c.　　BOOK 127:13
give me your bill of c.　　　SWIFT 673:20
I owe my soul to the c. store　TRAV 702:4
married life three is c.　　　WILDE 734:12
Punctual Delivery C.　　　　DICK 241:30
qualified to shine in c.　　　SWIFT 674:19
steal out of your c.　　　　SHAK 614:3
Take the tone of the c.　　　CHES 198:9
that is not good c.　　　　　AUST 39:5
To bear him c.　　　　　　LONG 428:3
up breaks the c.　　　　　CERV 188:10
very good c., and of a ready　AUBR 33:12
When c. comes　　　　　　HUGH 354:1
whose c. I delight myself　　BUNY 156:17
with all the c. of heaven　　BOOK 122:10
compare: c. small things with great
　　　　　　　　　　　　　　VIRG 715:19
c. thee to a summer's day　SHAK 633:6
c. this prison where I live　SHAK 621:10
reason and c.　　　　　　BLAKE 112:1
she belied with false c.　　SHAK 635:3
compared: c. unto the beasts　BOOK 127:24
comparisons: C. are odorous　SHAK 614:5
C. doon offte gret greuaunce　LYDG 433:4
Confronted him with self-c.　SHAK 599:17
compass: c. of the world　　BOOK 125:16
My life is run his c.　　　　SHAK 593:17
note to the top of my c.　　SHAK 576:22
op'ning wide, and c. lost　　COWP 222:27
when the fire did c. him　　GILB 303:11
compassed: c. about with so great　BIBLE 104:17
snares of death c. me　　　BOOK 133:11
compassion: c. in the very name　SMITH 652:25
c. on the son of her womb　BIBLE 84:7
full of c. and mercy　　　　BIBLE 87:8
full of c. and mercy　　　　BOOK 132:4

compassion: (*cont.*):
Jesu, thou art all c.　　　　WESL 728:14
sharp c. of the healer's art　ELIOT 270:22
shutteth up his bowels of c.　BIBLE 105:26
compel: c. thee to go a mile　BIBLE 88:33
compendious: Portable, and c. oceans
　　　　　　　　　　　　　　CRAS 226:12
competence: C. with pain　　HEAN 329:22
competency: c. lives longer　SHAK 607:11
competing: c. attractions　　KNIG 403:1
competition: Approves all forms of c.
　　　　　　　　　　　　　　CLOU 207:20
c., and mutual envy　　　　HOBB 340:13
c. the laws of death　　　　RUSK 551:5
complacencies: C. of the peignoir　STEV 666:10
complacency: Built on c.　　GAUNT 299:7
complain: c. of the age we live　BURKE 159:11
farmers, flourish and c.　　CRAB 225:5
Never c. and never explain　DISR 249:10
then c. we cannot see　　　BERK 65:11
complainers: c. for the public　BURKE 157:14
complaining: no c. in our streets　BOOK 135:5
through my daily c.　　　　BOOK 126:8
triple-towered sky, the dove c.　DAY-L 233:4
complaint: from the words of my c.　BOOK 125:9
most fatal c. of all　　　　HILT 339:4
their c. being peculiar always　THOM 694:10
voice of my c.　　　　　　BOOK 134:11
complaints: c. of ill-usage　MELB 456:9
sins or c. or laws　　　　　TRAH 701:12
when c. are freely heard　　MILT 475:2
complementarity: understood c. and relative
time　　　　　　　　　　MCEW 437:15
completed: c. labours are pleasant　CIC 203:26
complex: ugly, heavy and c.　FLAU 286:5
complexes: *feeling-toned* c.　JUNG 382:12
complexion: bank too much on your c.
　　　　　　　　　　　　　　VIRG 714:15
different c. or slightly flatter　CONR 217:2
Mislike me not for my c.　　SHAK 608:4
often is his gold c. dimmed　SHAK 633:6
own clime, c., and degree　SHAK 616:15
complexities: All mere c.　YEATS 750:21
compliance: All I wanted was c.　CHUR 203:5
by a timely c.　　　　　　FIEL 282:3
join c. with reason　　　　BURKE 158:29
complicated: phrases of your c. state
　　　　　　　　　　　　　　GILB 305:16
complications: only the chosen had 'c.'
　　　　　　　　　　　　　　WHAR 730:4
complies: He that c. against his will
　　　　　　　　　　　　　　BUTL 166:18
compliment: farewell c.　　SHAK 622:33
feigning was called c.　　　SHAK 630:10
componere: *inter vos tantas c. lites*　VIRG 714:20
parva licet c. magnis　　　VIRG 715:19
composed: Cruel, but c. and bland　ARN 27:19
composer: c. is to be dead　HON 343:14
composition: mad kings! mad c.　SHAK 593:29
one mind but in one c.　　JOHN 369:9
compound: c. a boy　　　　SHAK 587:2
comprehend: Time we may c.　BROW 146:4
When she begins to c.　　　PRIOR 529:13
comprehended: darkness c. it　BIBLE 95:37
comprehends: c. them wholly　NEWT 493:21
It c. some bringer of that joy　SHAK 612:17
comprendre: *Tout c. rend très indulgent*
　　　　　　　　　　　　　　STAËL 662:1
compris: *Je vous ai c.*　　DE G 235:2
compromise: c. when I'm on his side
　　　　　　　　　　　　　　HUGH 354:11
inclinations to c.　　　　　ZIN 755:12
compulsion: fools by heavenly c.　SHAK 595:2
Give you a reason on c.　　SHAK 580:22
Made happy by c.　　　　COL 211:22
sweet c. doth in music lie　MILT 463:8
compulsions: all our c. meet　LARK 409:15
compulsive: Whose icy current and c. course
　　　　　　　　　　　　　　SHAK 616:23
compunctious: no c. visitings of nature
　　　　　　　　　　　　　　SHAK 600:16
computer: foul things up requires a c.
　　　　　　　　　　　　　　ANON 19:2

concatenation: Fearful c. of circumstances
　　　　　　　　　　　　　　WEBS 725:7
conceal: And half c. the Soul within
　　　　　　　　　　　　　　TENN 682:31
cleverness is to be able to c.　LA R 410:17
c. a fact with words　　　　MACH 438:5
c. our whereabouts　　　　SAKI 553:12
express our wants as to c.　GOLD 311:13
Fate tried to c. him　　　　HOLM 342:12
should c. it as well　　　　AUST 38:23
was always able to c. it　　TWAIN 706:26
yet cannot all c.　　　　　BYRON 169:13
concealing: hazard of c.　　BURNS 161:24
Rive your c. continents　　SHAK 596:1
concealment: let c., like a worm i' the bud
　　　　　　　　　　　　　　SHAK 629:20
conceit: curst c. o' bein' richt　MACD 437:7
he be wise in his own c.　　BIBLE 79:20
man wise in his own c.　　BIBLE 79:22
never forgive any c.　　　DRYD 262:18
wiser in his own c.　　　　BIBLE 79:23
With forms to his c.　　　SHAK 575:8
with self and vain c.　　　SHAK 620:8
conceited: do any good who is not c.
　　　　　　　　　　　　　　TROL 703:22
conceits: c. do prove the greatest　DRAY 257:17
current and accepted for c.　BACON 42:4
not wise in your own c.　　BIBLE 100:5
conceive: towards all that we c.　SHEL 644:9
virgin shall c.　　　　　　BIBLE 82:24
conceived: c. by the Holy Ghost　BOOK 119:1
in sin hath my mother c. me　BOOK 128:5
There is a man child c.　　BIBLE 77:6
conceives: C. by idleness　　SHAK 586:17
concentrated: c. in you　　KEATS 392:14
concentrates: it c. his mind wonderfully
　　　　　　　　　　　　　　JOHN 374:23
conception: dad present at the c.　ORTON 499:13
conceptions: C. equal to the soul's desires
　　　　　　　　　　　　　　WORD 744:1
conceptual: our c. scheme　POPP 524:17
concern: life and its largest c.　ARN 30:3
matter they had no c. in　SWIFT 674:24
Since our c. was speech　ELIOT 271:5
concerned: being ultimately c.　TILL 698:6
concerns: Think only what c. thee　MILT 472:12
concert: self-imposed torture, the c.
　　　　　　　　　　　　　　MILL 461:23
concessions: c. of the weak　BURKE 157:19
knowing what c. to make　METT 459:5
conciseness: accuracy must be sacrificed to c.
　　　　　　　　　　　　　　JOHN 367:17
conclaves: Kingly c. stern and cold　SHEL 642:10
concluded: Rome has spoken; the case is c.
　　　　　　　　　　　　　　AUG 37:9
conclusion: other is a c.　JOHN 371:17
conclusions: narrow c.　　MILL 460:6
She hath pursued c. infinite　SHAK 567:14
concord: c. of well-tunèd sounds　SHAK 633:3
Love-quarrels oft in pleasing c.　MILT 474:11
peace and lover of c.　　　BOOK 119:3
travelled a good deal in C.　THOR 696:26
truth, unity, and c.　　　　BOOK 121:22
with c of sweet sounds　SHAK 610:3
concordia: C. discors　　　HOR 348:10
concrete: city not a c. jungle　MORR 485:5
everything you thought was c.　WALK 717:11
flower is the c. cloverleaf　MUMF 488:2
concupiscent: In kitchen cups c. curds
　　　　　　　　　　　　　　STEV 665:18
concupiscite: *sine dolo lac c.*　BIBLE 108:17
concurrence: sweet c. of the heart　HERR 336:14
condamner: *de songer à c. les gens*　MOL 479:6
condemn: C. the fault and not　SHAK 605:15
c. you to death　　　　　CARR 182:2
does some delights c.　　MOL 479:12
Neither do I c. thee　　　BIBLE 96:31
condemned: c. to have an itching palm
　　　　　　　　　　　　　　SHAK 592:26
I am c. to be free　　　　SART 556:9
condemns: c. whatever he disapproves
　　　　　　　　　　　　　　BURN 160:18

condescend: c. to men of low estate   BIBLE 100:5
condition: c. upon which God hath given liberty
                                      CURR 229:4
devils in life and c.   ASCH 31:2
man could do in that c.   PEPYS 512:4
O hard c.   SHAK 586:6
O wearisome c. of humanity   GREV 318:8
primordial c. of liberty   BAK 47:23
conditions: all sorts and c. of men   BOOK 120:5
c. of life to which a man   TOLS 700:6
govern our c.   SHAK 596:30
material c. for its solution   MARX 452:3
conduct: C. is three-fourths of our life
                                        ARN 30:3
c. of a losing party   BURKE 157:2
C. . . . to the prejudice of   ANON 12:28
c. unbecoming   ANON 12:5
nice c. of a clouded cane   POPE 523:30
on the c. of the women   MORE 484:2
rottenness begins in his c.   JEFF 364:10
conductors: third-rate foreign c.   BEEC 59:1
cone: despot is an inverted c.   JOHN 374:31
cones: c. under his pines   FROST 295:4
confabulate: If birds c. or no   COWP 222:28
confectionary: world as my c.   SHAK 626:16
confederacy: dunces all in c.   SWIFT 674.15
confederate: in games C.   WORD 744:9
conference: c. a ready man   BACON 44:28
hold some two days' c.   WEBS 725:18
naked into the c. chamber   BEVAN 69:1
was ever born in a c.   FITZ 284:22
confess: c. them with an humble   BOOK 118:5
C. yourself to heaven   SHAK 577:19
I c. to almighty God   MISS 476:16
confessed: c. that they were strangers
                                      BIBLE 104:15
confessing: ill-using them and then c. it
                                      TROL 703:19
confession: after the sweetness of c.
                                      FIRB 282:29
humble c. to Almighty God   BOOK 122:5
let's be there at the C.   DONNE 253:6
confessions: trench c.   POUND 527:2
confide: c. in those who are better
                                      CAMUS 177:14
confidence: c. in their understandings
                                      JOHN 369:26
C. is a plant of slow growth   PITT 515:7
ignorance and c.   TWAIN 706:27
In quietness and in c. shall   BIBLE 83:14
confident: Never glad c. morning again
                                      BROW 151:2
confine: verge of her c.   SHAK 595:15
confined: execution c.   SHAK 627:16
wander, but c. him home   CLEV 206:14
confinement: c. which hedges us in only
                                      LOCKE 425:4
sentenced to solitary c.   WILL 737:7
confiscation: We have legalized c.   DISR 247:18
confiteor: C. Deo omnipotenti   MISS 476:16
conflagration: What message, years of c.
                                      BLOK 115:5
conflict: c. of its elements   BYRON 172:17
c. of physical strength   MILL 460:23
Never in the field of human c.
                                      CHUR 202:13
offered you C. and Art   PRIE 528:18
risks of spreading c.   JOHN 367:9
this c. of opinions   JOHN 377:2
We are in an armed c.   EDEN 266:7
conflicts: solution of all disputes or c.
                                      BRIA 141:1
conform: c., or be more wise   PEPYS 512:13
confound: C. their politics   ANON 13:19
world in a the wise   BIBLE 100:16
confounded: Confusion wurse   MILT 470:15
h[...] n[...]ar in g.   BOOK [...]
confounding: [...] the integration[...] DONG 340:17
Neither c. the Persons   [...]NK 114:10
confundar: non c. in aeternum   ANON [...]
confused: isn't c. doesn't really understand
                                      MURR 488:13

confusion: bright things come to c.
                                      SHAK 610:23
C. now hath made his masterpiece
                                      SHAK 602:14
C. on thy banners wait   GRAY 315:6
C. worse confounded   MILT 470:13
from a couch in some c.   CONG 215:36
confute: can tell how to c. him   SELD 562:5
congeals: When love c.   HART 327:11
Congo: C., creeping through the black
                                      LIND 423:2
congregation: C. be thereby offended
                                      BOOK 121:14
c. of the poor for ever   BOOK 130:3
face of this c.   BOOK 123:15
landlord to the whole c.   ADD 4:8
latter has the largest c.   DEFOE 234:19
pestilent c. of vapours   SHAK 574:28
praise the Lord in the c.   BOOK 125:23
congregations: C. committed to their charge
                                      BOOK 119:8
Congress: C. makes no progress   LIGNE 421:14
conies: stony rocks for the c.   BOOK 132:9
conjecture: not beyond all c.   BROW 145:19
Now entertain c. of a time   SHAK 585:14
conjectures: dogmatically to our c.
                                      POPP 524:16
conjunction: c. of the mind   MARV 450:3
conjuration: What c., and what mighty
magic   SHAK 614:31
conjuring: c. trick with bones   JENK 365:4
Parson left c.   SELD 562:9
connect: Only c.   FORS 290:14
connected: c. to the busy world   AUDEN 35:1
connections: c. that unite the various
                                      SMITH 650:14
conned: learned, and c. by rote   SHAK 593:8
conning: pro-ing and c.   POTT 525:20
connive: Who would c.   HEAN 329:20
connubial: c. love refused   MILT 471:14
connubiality: victim o' c.   DICK 243:11
conquer: c. it [the East]   WALP 719:14
die here, and we will c.   BEE 58:15
hard to catch and c.   MER 458:5
In this sign shalt thou c.   CONS 218:2
Like Douglas c.   HOME 342:20
resolve to c. or die   WASH 721:23
Should c. Antony   SHAK 566:12
that did his master c.   SHAK 565:19
that was wont to c.   SHAK 619:18
conquered: c. and peopled half   SEEL 562:1
c.; I will not capitulate   JOHN 376:20
feel they are a c. people   VICT 710:12
I came, I saw, I c.   CAES 174:20
perpetually to be c.   BURKE 157:21
Thou hast c., O pale Galilean   SWIN 676:21
conquering: C. kings their titles take
                                      CHAN 189:17
See, the c. hero comes   MOR 484:17
conqueror: And every c. creates a Muse
                                      WALL 718:16
c. of every other description   BURKE 159:1
Lie at the proud foot of a c.   SHAK 594:16
you are a c.   ROST 548:13
conquest: Beauty's c. of your face   AUDEN 35:3
c. of the earth   CONR 217:2
fanned by C.'s crimson wing   GRAY 315:6
foreign c. and subjugation   WEBS 725:8
Hath made a shameful c.   SHAK 619:18
powerful the urge for c.   ADLER 5:8
conquests: all thy c., glories   SHAK 591:18
interrupt the c. of our prime   WINC 739:1
To spread her c. farther   BURNS 161:12
consanguineous: Am not I c.?   SHAK 629:5
conscia: iustitia est et mens sibi c.   VIRG 712:10
conscience: catch the c. of the king
                                      SHAK 575:14
C. avaunt, Richard's himself   GIBB 203:22
c. doth make cowards   SHAK 575:16
c. first   NEWM [...]
c. had thee to do   CHER 644:27
c. hath a thousand several   SHAK 577:11

conscience: (cont.):
C. is but a word that cowards   SHAK 622:14
C. is thoroughly well-bred   BUTL 167:8
c. round from body to body   BEVIN 69:13
C., that heaven-nursèd plant   MARV 451:9
C.: the inner voice   MENC 457:9
c. void of offence toward   BIBLE 99:7
c. with injustice is corrupted   SHAK 587:18
corporation to have a c.   THUR 697:21
cruelty with a good c.   RUSS 551:22
dominion of reason and c.   PRICE 528:17
evidences of a good c.   DONNE 253:6
freely according to c.   MILT 475:15
good c. on the proceeds   SMITH 652:9
happiness or a quiet c.   BERL 66:4
Has crept too near his c.   SHAK 588:12
if it were c. money   LEV 420:1
My c. says   SHAK 608:5
O coward c.   SHAK 622:10
power without c.   BRAD 139:8
speech, freedom of c.   TWAIN 706:8
still and quiet c.   SHAK 588:20
strict their social c.   SMITH 652:10
Sufficient c. to bother him   LLOY 424:13
their c. as their King   TENN 681:24
thus be c.-calmed   KEATS 390:16
try to ease your c.   ALAI 7:4
uncreated c. of my race   JOYCE 381:15
value it next to a good c.   WALT 721:10
wearing such a c.-stricken   HOUS 351:13
We may live without c.   MER 458:11
whereof our c. is afraid   BOOK 121:6
will not cut my c.   HELL 331:8
with a quiet c.   BOOK 122:4
woman as a Nonconformist c.   WILDE 735:11
consciences: c. of the citizens   JOHN 366:10
conscious: c. of the hopelessness   DOST 255:4
c. stone to beauty grew   EMER 276:11
To be c. is an illness   DOST 255:6
consciousness: c. has been modified during
                                      TYNAN 706:30
C. the phenomenon whereby   PENR 512:1
flow of our sympathetic c.   LAWR 411:13
from the beginning of c. to the end
                                      WOOLF 742:7
multiplicity of agreeable c.   JOHN 372:24
that determines their c.   MARX 452:4
consecrated: habits which have been c.
                                      GIBB 302:9
kind of 'c. obstruction'   BAG 47:6
consecration: c., and the Poet's dream
                                      WORD 743:11
consent: agree with sweet c.   SPEN 659:14
c. began to make excuse   BIBLE 94:29
c. either expressed by   CAMD 176:2
c. of the governed   PAGE 504:4
inferior without your c.   ROOS 545:13
like enough to c.   SHAK 569:16
Rome is the c. of heaven   JONS 378:12
Thou shalt not c.   BIBLE 73:18
whispering 'I will ne'er c.'   BYRON 170:10
consented: c. together in holy wedlock
                                      BOOK 123:23
'I will ne'er consent'—c.   BYRON 170:10
consenting: only between c. adults   VIDAL 711:4
Saul was c. unto his death   BIBLE 98:13
consequence: c. of cabinet government
                                      BAG 46:16
If it's business of c.   BARH 52:19
It's of no c.   DICK 240:19
consequences: c. will be what they will be
                                      BUTL 165:22
mystic terror of the c.   LAWR 412:2
not regard political c.   MANS 445:10
prevent it and to damn the c.   MILN 463:7
punishments—there are c.   ING 360:8
renounce war for its c.   FOSD 291:4
conservation: without the means of its c.
                                      BURKE 158:7
conservatism: barren thing this C.   DISR 248:6
c. and progress   TROL 703:10
C. discard. Prescription   DISR 248:3
c. is based upon the idea   GHES 199.21

conservatism: (*cont.*):
What is c.? Is it not adherence　LINC 422:1
conservative: C. Government is　DISR 246:20
C. ideal of freedom　MADAN 441:11
c. man in this world　BEVIN 69:12
C., *n.* A statesman　BIER 109:8
[C. Party] found it hard　JOS 380:16
C. Party at prayer　ROYD 549:12
Or else a little C.　GILB 304:10
revolutionary will become a c.　AREN 24:16
sound C. government　DISR 248:4
That man's the true C.　TENN 681:12
which makes a man more c.　KEYN 395:5
would make me c. when old　FROST 295:8
conservatives: C. being by the law　MILL 460:9
C. do not believe　HAIL 320:13
more formalistic than c.　CALV 175:18
They are c. after dinner　EMER 277:6
consider: C. anything, only don't cry
　　　　　　　　　　　　　　CARR 183:7
c. her ways, and be wise　BIBLE 78:13
c. how my light is spent　MILT 474:24
C. the lilies of the field　BIBLE 89:11
day of adversity c.　BIBLE 80:14
For I will c. thy heavens　BOOK 124:20
O let thine ears c. well　BOOK 134:11
Stop and c.! life is but a day　KEATS 390:10
weigh and c.　BACON 44:26
considerable: appear c. in his native place
　　　　　　　　　　　　　　JOHN 373:13
considerate: C. *la vostra semenza*　DANTE 230:16
consideration: C. like an angel　SHAK 584:18
considered: c. the days of old　BOOK 130:7
consiliis: *Misce stultitiam c. brevem*　HOR 350:20
consistency: C. is contrary to nature
　　　　　　　　　　　　　　HUXL 357:12
c. is the hobgoblin　EMER 277:2
consistent: c. people are the dead　HUXL 357:12
consolation: c. in a distressed　AUST 39:2
Kate of my c.　SHAK 624:15
that's one c.　DICK 243:13
console: C.-*toi*　PASC 507:21
To be consoled as to c.　FRAN 292:12
consoles: Anything that c. is fake　MURD 488:8
conspicuous: c. by its presence　RUSS 552:3
C. consumption　VEBL 709:14
c. wastefulness　VEBL 709:17
Vega c. overhead　AUDEN 35:13
conspiracies: c. against the laity　SHAW 636:11
conspiracy: c. against the public　SMITH 650:18
c. of human beings to lie　WELLS 727:19
imagines a perpetual c.　SAL 554:4
Indecency's c. of silence　SHAW 637:34
maintaining the 'c. of silence'　COMTE 214:20
O c.! Sham'st thou　SHAK 590:16
conspirators: All the c.　SHAK 593:23
conspiring: C. with him how to load
　　　　　　　　　　　　　　KEATS 390:17
constable: if it was a c.'s handbook　KING 398:1
constabulary: When c. duty's to be done
　　　　　　　　　　　　　　GILB 306:11
constancy: c. lives in realms above　COL 209:10
is but c. in a good　BROW 146:8
no object worth its c.　SHEL 643:24
O c.! be strong upon my side　SHAK 591:9
Of c. to a bad, ugly woman　BYRON 173:15
Tell me no more of c.　ROCH 542:18
witness to their c.　DID 245:11
constant: But c., he were perfect　SHAK 631:10
But if thou wilt be c. then　GRAH 313:16
c. as the northern star　SHAK 591:12
c. image of the creature　SHAK 629:13
C. in human sufferings　JOYCE 381:12
C. in Nature were inconstancy　COWL 221:14
c. love deemed there　SIDN 646:17
c. service of the antique　SHAK 568:1
C. you are　SHAK 580:13
Friendship is c. in all　SHAK 613:16
Like to a c. woman　FORD 289:9
nothing in this world c.　SWIFT 673:6
One here will c. be　BUNY 156:14
sense of a c. infelicity　TAYL 679:20
She is so c. to me　KEATS 386:18

constant: (*cont.*):
Such a c. lover　SUCK 671:9
To one thing c. never　SHAK 613:24
constellated: c. flower that never sets
　　　　　　　　　　　　　　SHEL 642:23
constellation: c. which has gone before
　　　　　　　　　　　　　　JEFF 364:6
constellations: c. of feeling　DOUG 255:10
constitit: C. *hic arcumque manu celerisque*
　　　　　　　　　　　　　　VIRG 712:4
constitution: c. does not provide　WILL 737:15
C., in all its provisions　CHASE 192:3
c. is extremely well　WALP 719:12
C. or laws by any hypercritical　LINC 422:3
country has its own c　ANON 13:3
I invoke the genius of the C.　PITT 515:12
Our C. works　FORD 289:2
part of an Englishman's c.　AUST 38:19
principle of the English c.　BLAC 110:13
principles of a free c.　GIBB 302:1
proportioned to the human c.　BERK 65:8
support its C.　PAGE 504:4
very essence of the c.　JUN 383:4
constitutional: c. right of amending it
　　　　　　　　　　　　　　LINC 422:4
have no eyes but c. eyes　LINC 422:18
constitutions: c. of later Greece　BAG 47:3
constrained: c. to dwell with Mesech
　　　　　　　　　　　　　　BOOK 133:21
violence c. to do anything　ELIZ 274:1
construction: mind's c. in the face　SHAK 600:14
constructions: secret of decorating her c.
　　　　　　　　　　　　　　TROL 703:8
consuetudo: C. *est altera natura*　AUCT 33:14
consul: born when I was c.　CIC 204:15
consuls: c. see to it that no harm　ANON 22:5
consulted: right to be c.　BAG 47:8
consume: born to c. resources　HOR 348:3
more history than they can c.　SAKI 553:7
shall c. in the sepulchre　BOOK 128:1
consumed: bush was not c.　BIBLE 71:37
c. away through my daily　BOOK 126:8
consumer: c. isn't a moron　OGIL 498:3
c. is the king　SAM 555:1
in a c. society　ILL 359:10
consumere: *numerus sumus et fruges c.*
　　　　　　　　　　　　　　HOR 348:3
consumes: c. without producing　ORW 499:18
consuming: ashes in its heat c.　LITT 423:9
consummation: c. devoutly to be wished
　　　　　　　　　　　　　　SHAK 575:16
Quiet c. have　SHAK 571:16
consummatum: C. *est*　BIBLE 108:15
consumption: Conspicuous c.　VEBL 709:14
c. by an equal *absolute*　KEYN 395:8
c. has to be artificially　SAY 557:14
C. is the sole end and purpose　SMITH 651:2
c. of the purse　SHAK 582:25
contact: Fly hence, our c. fear　ARN 28:9
superficial c. of two bodies　CHAM 189:13
contagion: c. of the world's slow　BOGAN 116:1
C. to this world　SHAK 576:25
foul c. spread　MILT 466:9
vile c. of the night　SHAK 590:22
contaminate: C. our fingers　SHAK 592:27
contemned: c. and flattered　SHAK 596:23
would utterly be c.　BIBLE 82:6
contemneth: he that c. small things
　　　　　　　　　　　　　　BIBLE 87:24
contemplation: Beneath thy c.　NEALE 491:5
by action, not by c.　BRON 141:17
C. makes a rare turkey-cock　SHAK 630:1
For c. he and valour formed　MILT 471:5
Has left for c. not what　BETJ 67:14
mind serene for c.　GAY 300:8
Of all the solemn talk of c.　KAV 386:5
Where with her best nurse C.　MILT 463:27
contemplative: fools should be so deep-c.
　　　　　　　　　　　　　　SHAK 568:13
contempt: C., farewell!　SHAK 613:30
c. of fear　JONS 378:20
c. too high　COWL 221:11
Familiarity breeds c. and　TWAIN 706:16

contempt: (*cont.*):
In the c. and anger of his lip　SHAK 630:12
moderns without c.　CHES 198:14
pour c. on all my pride　WATTS 723:2
religion when in rags and c.　BUNY 156:1
wagged c. at Fate　WATS 722:10
was only an Object of C.　AUST 38:15
contemptible: complaints of ill-usage c.
　　　　　　　　　　　　　　MELB 456:9
French's c. little army　ANON 13:7
sacrifice in a c. struggle　BURKE 163:16
those poor c. men　CROM 227:14
contendi: c. no more, Love　BROW 153:16
contender: could have been a c.　SCH 558:9
contending: C. with the fretful elements
　　　　　　　　　　　　　　SHAK 595:19
let fierce c. nations know　ADD 3:24
content: And cry 'C.!'　SHAK 588:3
C. in the tight hot cell　BOGAN 116:13
C. to breathe his native air　POPE 523:11
c. with half knowledge　KEATS 391:10
c. with his fortunes fit　SHAK 596:3
c. with my harm　SHAK 569:1
ease, c.! whate'er thy　POPE 522:19
land of lost c.　HOUS 352:15
money, means, and c.　SHAK 568:19
Nor that c. surpassing wealth　SHEL 643:10
Nothing less will c. me　BURKE 157:22
O sweet c.　DEKK 235:15
Spontaneous joy and natural c.
　　　　　　　　　　　　　　YEATS 751:18
contented: But he was c. there　ARIS 25:4
C. wi' little and cantie　BURNS 161:4
C. with thine own estate　SURR 672:3
Half-pleased, c. will　GREV 318:4
Ireland was c. when　LAND 408:3
king shall be c.　SHAK 620:12
one lives c. with his lot　HOR 350:21
To be c.—that's for the cows　CHAN 190:8
With what I most enjoy c.　SHAK 633:10
contentedness: procurer of c.　WALT 721:1
contention: Let the long c. cease　ARN 27:11
strife and a man of c.　BIBLE 85:11
contentions: c. or vices　TRAH 701:12
contentious: rainy day and a c. woman
　　　　　　　　　　　　　　BIBLE 79:27
contentment: C. is a sleepy thing　TRAH 701:17
Or all enjoying, what c. find　MILT 472:14
Preaches c. to that toad　KIPL 400:6
withdraw with c. and rest　LUCR 432:4
contentus: C. *vivat*　HOR 350:21
contest: Great c. follows　COWP 223:25
victory but the c.　COUB 220:4
contests: c. rise from trivial things　POPE 523:15
continency: chastity and c.　AUG 36:24
continent: C. people have good food
　　　　　　　　　　　　　　MIKES 460:3
C. will not suffer England　DISR 246:15
destiny to overspread the c.　O'SUL 502:5
man is a piece of the C.　DONNE 253:5
mountains level, and the c.　SHAK 583:13
Thou knowest of no strange c.　DAV 232:14
upon this c. a new nation　LINC 422:10
continental: C. people have sex life　MIKES 460:4
on the hand may be quite c.　ROBIN 542:7
contingent: c. and the unforeseen　FISH 283:1
continual: c. dew of thy blessing　BOOK 119:8
continuance: gentlemanly ideas, but for a c.
　　　　　　　　　　　　　　SURT 672:13
household of c.　SURR 672:2
Patient c. in well doing　BIBLE 99:18
which in c. of time hath　BOOK 118:4
continue: c. thine for ever　BOOK 123:13
runagates c. in scarceness　BOOK 129:7
which once begun will c.　BACON 43:6
continued: c., and ended in thee　BOOK 122:17
long soever it hath c.　COKE 208:16
continuing: c. unto the end　DRAKE 257:9
here have we no c. city　BIBLE 104:22
contraception: fast word about oral c.
　　　　　　　　　　　　　　ALLEN 9:14
contract: C. into a span　HERB 335:14
c. into which men enter　CHUR 201:23

contract: (*cont.*):
movement *from Status to C.* — MAINE 442:11
nothing but a civil c. — SELD 562:7
Social C. is nothing — WELLS 727:19
Society is indeed a c. — BURKE 158:21
tugging at every c. — EMER 276:16
verbal c. isn't worth — GOLD 312:3
contracting: c. powers solemnly declare — BRIA 141:1
contradict: Do I c. myself — WHIT 732:21
I never c.; I sometimes forget — DISR 249:4
Never c., never explain — FISH 283:5
Read not to c. and confute — BACON 44:26
truth which you cannot c. — SOCR 655:3
contradicted: I dogmatise and am c. — JOHN 377:2
contradiction: c. in terms — SHAW 638:23
It's a c. in terms — SIMP 648:4
they brook no c. — WEBS 725:24
Woman's at best a c. still — POPE 520:13
contradictions: c. cover such a range — EMPS 277:19
hath been one chain of c. — CLARE 204:18
Omnipotence cannot work c. — JENY 365:8
paradox, a bundle of c. — COLT 214:10
reconcile the most glaring c. — HUME 355:14
contraries: Without c. is no progression — BLAKE 112:13
contrariwise: 'C.,' continued Tweedledee — CARR 182:24
contrary: c. to the decrees of Caesar — BIBLE 98:28
directed to c. parts — NEWT 494:4
everythink goes c. with me — DICK 239:20
trial is by what is c. — MILT 475:7
usury is c. to Scripture — TAWN 679:2
what is most c. to custom — HUME 355:7
contrast: intense enjoyment from a c. — FREUD 293:18
contrite: broken and c. heart — BOOK 128:8
sighing of a c. heart — BOOK 120:3
contrive: Nature always does c. — GILB 304:10
control: beyond my individual c. — DICK 240:9
Ground c. to Major Tom — BOWIE 138:15
ought to c. our thoughts — DARW 231:4
unless it is kept under c. — MARQ 448:17
Who can c. his fate — SHAK 618:16
controls: c. the past controls — ORW 500:11
controversy: c. is either superfluous — NEWM 493:10
man of c. is looked upon — GALB 296:19
contumely: proud man's c. — SHAK 575:16
convalescence: I enjoy c. — SHAW 635:25
convenience: C. next suggested elbow-chairs — COWP 221:4
c. to liberty, and a pleasant — HESSE 337:16
'Twixt treason and c. — CLEV 206:13
convenient: c. that there be gods — OVID 502:15
feed me with food c. — BIBLE 79:32
nor jesting, which are not c. — BIBLE 102:20
convent: fret not at their c.'s — WORD 745:7
The C. of the Sacred Heart — ELIOT 272:20
convention: To the Lords of C. — SCOTT 559:8
conventional: adultery a most c. — NAB 488:20
They are merely c. signs — CARR 184:2
conventionality: C. is not morality — BRON 142:3
conventions: specific bearers of all 'c.' — WEBER 725:3
conversation: Ambrose lived in and for c. — WAUGH 723:19
brisk as a bee in c. — JOHN 371:7
C. blurred — SITW 648:11
C. is a game of circles — EMER 276:21
C. is imperative if gaps — WHITE 731:5
different name for c. — STER 064:21
have a great deal of c. — AUST 39:5
subject of c. in a mixed — CHES 198:3
that thing I've perfectly — SMITH 653:1?
those soft parts of c. — SHAK 616:16
who is always spoiling c. — WAU ...
you stick on c.'s burrs — HOLM 342.10
conversations: after-dinner c. — THOR 697:9
without pictures or c. — CARR 181:23

conversation-scraps: Intrigues half-gathered, c. — CRAB 224:21
converse: between them and rational c. — WOLL 741:12
c. and love so dearly joined — MILT 472:26
c. of an innocent mind — KEATS 390:7
c. with everlasting groans — MILT 469:15
c. with the mighty dead — THOM 696:13
conversion: Till the c. of the Jews — MARV 451:2
convert: oh, who shall c. me — WESL 728:18
converted: c. from the thing it was — SHAK 633:15
Except ye be c. — BIBLE 91:17
You have not c. a man — MORL 485:2
converting: c. the soul — BOOK 125:5
converts: Charming women can true c. — FARQ 280:19
convey: 'C.,' the wise it call — SHAK 610:11
conviction: best lack all c. — YEATS 753:1
c. begins as a whim — BROUN 144:10
open to what is called c. — HUNT 356:14
pretence of a personal c. — METT 459:1
convictions: cloud of comforting c. — RUSS 551:21
Such Dimity C. — DICK 245:4
convince: To c. the whole race — KNOX 403:9
we c. ourselves — JUN 383:6
convinced: know too much and c. of too little — ELIOT 273:21
convinces: man who c. the world — DARW 231:15
convincing: And thought of c. — GOLD 311:4
Oh! too c.—dangerously dear — BYRON 169:22
two excuses always less c. — HUXL 357:17
convivia: *plenus vitae c. recedis* — LUCR 432:4
convoy: And crowns for c. put — SHAK 586:11
convulsions: gall'ry in c. hurled — POPE 519:26
conviviality: kindled at the taper of c. — DICK 242:17
cook: C. is a little unnerved — DETJ 67:11
cookery: Kissing don't last: c. do — MER 458:1
cooks: c. chop neither herbs — HEYW 338:5
Devil sends c. — GARR 298:7
entrusted to 'plain' c. — MORP 485:3
good c. go, she went — SAKI 553:9
had there been a Synod of C. — JOHN 372:20
He liked those literary c. — MORE 483:21
man cannot live without c. — MER 458:11
should praise it, not the c. — HAR 326:11
cool: Be still and c. in thy — FOX 292:4
c. gales shall fan — POPE 523:13
c. web of language winds — GRAV 314:18
garden in the c. of the day — BIBLE 70:10
So c. a purple — KEATS 386:17
sound of the c. colonnade — COWP 222:29
Sweet day, so c., so calm — HERB 336:1
cooled: C. a long age — KEATS 389:9
Coolidge: C. only snored — MENC 457:4
C.'s genius for inactivity — LIPP 423:8
my admiration for Mr C. — ANON 18:19
cooling: for c. the blood — FLAN 285:10
coomb: c. was redder — CHAU 194:5
Cooper: Gary C. killing off the Indians — BALD 48:7
co-operation: Government and c. — RUSK 551:5
coot: haunts of c. and hern — TENN 680:11
copier: c. of nature can never — REYN 539:6
copies: few originals and many c. — TOCQ 698:13
copperheads: c. and the assassin — SAND 555:3
coppers: like the old time 'c.' — COLL 213:7
copula: *Quos irrupta tenet c. nec malis* — HOR 349:10
copulating: skeletons c. on a corrugated — BEEC 58:17
copulation: Birth, and c., and death — ELIOT 272:17
Let c. thrive — SHAK 597:4
copyrights: English authors their c. — TROL 703:3
coque: *L'eau vive pénétra ma c.* — RIMB 541:4
coquetry: as tiresome as c. — LA FRM 418:14
... I rub and I will c. — MARQ 448:1?
Gay c., and all ... — SANC 555:14
cor: *J'aime le son du c.* — VIG ...

coral: c. aboute hire arm she — CHAU 192:16
c. in all of the neighbour — REED 537:18
C. is far more red — SHAK 635:2
From India's c. strand — HEBER 330:3
Of his bones are c. made — SHAK 625:10
redder than the fyn c. — CHAU 194:5
coranto: come home in a c. — SHAK 628:14
corbies: twa c. making a mane — BALL 50:20
cord: c. however fine — WHEW 730:14
c. is not quickly broken — BIBLE 80:8
silver c. be loosed — BIBLE 81:1
triple c., which no — BURKE 157:7
corda: *Sursum c.* — MISS 476:24
cordial: c. drop heaven in our cup — ROCH 543:6
What I have lost with c. fruit — HERB 334:11
cords: cast away their c. from us — BOOK 124:8
scourge of small c. — BIBLE 96:12
core: c. tore and flung cloud — HUGH 354:5
deep heart's c. — YEATS 752:8
unerringly upon the human c. — JAMES 363:15
Corinna: Come, my C., come — HERR 336:11
Corinth: lucky enough to get to C. — HOR 348:11
Corinthian: C. capital of polished — BURKE 158:22
Corinthum: *homini contingit adire C.* — HOR 348:11
cork: c. out of my lunch — FIEL 282:21
corkscrew: clean tumbler, and a c. — DICK 242:13
corkscrews: heart are as crooked as c. — AUDEN 34:7
cormorant: common c. or shag — ISH 360:21
Sat like a c. — MILT 471:1
spite of c. devouring Time — SHAK 598:6
corn: amid the alien c. — KEATS 389:15
breast high amid the c. — HOOD 344:6
c. and begin raising hell — LEASE 415:2
c. at midnight by a tress — YEATS 753:4
c. is as high as an elephant's — HAMM 322:16
c. that makes the holy — MAS 453:6
c. was orient and immortal — TRAH 701:13
could make two ears of c. — SWIFT 673:12
did dry it; there was c. — HERB 334:11
In our sustaining c. — SHAK 596:31
lower the price of c. — MELB 466:5
My crop of c. is but a field — TICH 698:3
raise the price of c. — BYRON 167:19
stand so thick with c. — BOOK 129:3
that there was c. in Egypt — BIBLE 71:27
Was yellow like ripe c. — ROSS 547:15
cornea: C., *qua veris facilis* — VIRG 714:1
Corneille: C. is to Shakespeare — JOHN 377:3
corner: At every c. I meet my father — LOW 430:14
c. in the thing I love — SHAK 616.16
c. to look for a friend — MILNE 462:16
drive life into a c. — THOR 697:5
head-stone in the c. — BOOK 133:16
in a c., some untidy spot — AUDEN 35:7
lew c. of airth to lie — PHIL 514:8
round the c. of nonsense — COL 212:15
Sits the wind in that c. — SHAK 613:25
some c. of a foreign field — BROO 143:18
thing was not done in a c. — BIBLE 99:11
corners: all the c. of the earth — BOOK 131:10
and crush the c. off of old men's — WALK 717:13
clearing up the obscure c. — HUXL 358:8
fantastical Duke of dark c. — SHAK 606:22
into the c. of the evening — ELIOT 272:1
polished c. of the temple — BOOK 135:4
round earth's imagined c. — DONNE 250:3
sheet knit at the four c. — BIBLE 98:19
three c. of the world — SHAK 594:16
Unregarded age in c. thrown — SHAK 567:27
cornet: hear the sound of the c. — BIBLE 85:28
cornfield: o'er the green c. did pass — SHAK 569:23
cornfields: c., and ballet in the evening — HACK 320:7
Cornish: twenty thousand C. men — HAWK 328:4
corns: shower your shooting c. — SWIFT 674:23
corny: c. as Kansas in August — HAMM 323:1
Coromandel: coast of C. — LEAR 413:19
coronation: Bring c., and sops in wine — SPEN 660:26

coronet: proud bride of a ducal c.   DICK 241:29
coronets: Kind hearts are more than c.
                                    TENN 684:22
corporation: c. to have a conscience
                                    THUR 697:21
corporations: [c.] cannot commit treason
                                    COKE 209:3
corpore: mens sana in c. sano   JUV 384:11
  molem et magno se c. miscet   VIRG 713:16
corps: c. of impudent snobs   AGNEW 5:16
corpse: frozen c. was he   LONG 428:4
  good wishes to the c.   BARR 54:10
  got a nice fresh c.   TWAIN 706:14
  He'd make a lovely c.   DICK 241:17
  here's a c. in the case   BARH 52:17
  like a c. within its grave   SHEL 641:14
  slovenly, unhandsome c.   SHAK 579:40
corpses: c. are set to banquet   POUND 526:4
  loves into c. or wives   SWIN 676:12
  riddled c. round Bapaume   SASS 557:5
corpus: Ave verum c.   ANON 22:4
corpuscula: Quantula sint hominum c.
                                     JUV 384:10
correct: All present and c.   ANON 12:1
  being the c. article   ASHF 31:11
  Blot out, c., insert, refine   SWIFT 675:1
  perfectly c. thing   SHAW 636:18
  than be c. with those men   CIC 204:14
corrected: C. and amended   FRAN 293:6
correcteth: whom the Lord loveth he c.
                                    BIBLE 78:7
corrects: first often c.   FOOTE 288:16
Correggios: Raphaels, C.   GOLD 311:7
Corregio: corregiescity of C.   STER 664:26
correlative: objective c.   ELIOT 273:17
correspondent: describes London like a
  special c.   BAG 47:14
corridors: admit princes to the c. DOUG 255:10
  c. of power   SNOW 654:6
  c. under nothing but sleep   DRIN 258:10
corroborative: Merely c. detail   GILB 305:8
corrugated: copulating on a c.   BEEC 58:17
corrupcioun: Fulfilled of dong and of c.
                                    CHAU 194:10
corrupt: Among a people generally c.
                                    BURKE 157:12
  be equally wicked and c.   BURKE 159:14
  c. government on the earth   JEFF 364:11
  moth and rust doth c.   BIBLE 89:6
  one good custom should c.   TENN 682:23
  Peace to c. no less than war   MILT 473:10
  That do c. my air   SHAK 570:13
  They are c., and become   BOOK 124:26
  Unlimited power is apt to c.   PITT 515:8
corrupted: conscience with injustice is c.
                                    SHAK 587:18
  c. by this stinking smoke   JAM 361:18
  C. honest men   SHAK 566:1
  c. the youth of the realm   SHAK 587:26
  had been c. by sentiment   GREE 316:23
  time hath not been c.   BOOK 118:4
corruptible: c. must put on incorruption
                                    BIBLE 101:14
  to obtain a c. crown   BIBLE 100:31
corruption: be turned into c.   BOOK 135:20
  C., the most infallible   GIBB 302:4
  C. wins not more than honesty   SHAK 589:1
  generation to c. turns   GREV 318:7
  in danger of great c.   KNOX 403:15
  It is sown in c.   BIBLE 101:12
  Stewed in c., honeying   SHAK 577:15
  thy Holy One to see c.   BOOK 124:31
  vice whose strong c.   SHAK 630:29
corrupts: absolute power c.   ACTON 1:10
cors: Les souvenirs sont c. de chasse APOL 23:14
corse: c. again in complete steel   SHAK 573:9
  c. to the rampart we hurried   WOLFE 740:24
  Like to a c., whose monument   CONS 217:21
Cortez: like stout C. when   KEATS 390:3
coruscations: c. of summer lightning
                                    GOUL 313:1
Corydon: For Time, not C.   ARN 28:28

Corydon: (cont.):
  pastor C. ardebat Alexin   VIRG 714:14
cosiness: c. and irritation   PYM 533:10
cosmopolitan: become c. in the end
                                   MOORE 482:10
  C. critics   DISR 247:26
cost: But at what c.   BECK 57:12
  c. of setting him up in poverty NAIDU 489:8
  c. of the erection   SHAK 583:1
  counteth the c.   BIBLE 94:33
  not to count the c.   IGN 359:8
  Some c. a passing bell   BEDD 58:12
  they c. right naught   WYATT 750:1
  Why should he c. thee   CRAO 226:1
  Why so large c,   SHAK 635:7
costing: C. not less than everything ELIOT 271:9
costive: made a soap-boiler c.   WEBS 725:19
costly: C. thy habit as thy purse   SHAK 573:4
  or c. in our sorrows   STER 664:10
  Too c. for cost   THOM 695:12
costs: C. merely register   KNIG 403:1
  c. more than it [the territory]   MAC 435:8
  duke c. as much   LLOY 424:5
costume: same c. will be   LAVER 411:10
cot: c. with a pot of pink geraniums
                                   MACN 440:14
  I paint the c.   CRAB 225:13
Cotopaxi: Chimborazo, C.   TURN 705:15
Cotswold: As of C.   GURN 320:2
cottage: his visage from our c.   SHAK 632:9
  left as a c. in a vineyard   BIBLE 82:8
  Love and a c.   COLM 213:17
  poorest man may in his c.   PITT 515:6
  soul's dark c.   WALL 718:13
  straw c. to a palace turns   DYER 265:4
  though from court to c.   PEELE 511:5
  Wherever there's a c. small   PARK 507:1
Cottleston Pie: Cottleston, C.   MILNE 463:3
cotton: an' the c. is high   HEYW 338:2
cotton-grass: Past c. and moorland border
                                   AUDEN 35:9
couch: flinty and steel c. of war   SHAK 615:7
  For oft, when on my c. I lie   WORD 744:16
  There I c. when owls do cry   SHAK 626:2
  water my c. with my tears   BOOK 124:14
couche: make his c. of silk   CHAU 193:26
couché: je me suis c. de bonne   PROU 530:6
couched: Close c. in your white bosom
                                   CRAS 226:10
couches: c. stretch around in seemly band
                                   THOM 695:17
  stilly c. she   HARDY 325:3
cough: all c. in ink   YEATS 752:23
  falls into a c.   SHAK 611:12
  Keep a c. by them ready made   CHUR 200:20
coughing: c. drowns the parson's saw
                                   SHAK 599:11
  one c., and one not coughing   SCHN 558:6
coughs: C. and sneezes spread   ANON 12:29
could: c. ye not watch with me   BIBLE 92:29
coulter: while that the c. rusts   SHAK 586:17
council: In c. rooms apart   RICE 540:2
counsel: c. in his face yet shone   MILT 469:18
  c. of the ungodly   BOOK 124:6
  darkeneth c. by words   BIBLE 77:33
  Dost sometimes c. take   POPE 523:24
  execution than for c.   BACON 45:9
  follow this c. of Aristotle   ASCH 31:3
  keep my c.   GLAD 307:15
  lightly regarded the c.   BOOK 132:15
  requireth further comfort or c.   BOOK 122:4
  spirit of c. and might   BIBLE 83:1
  To hear good c.   SHAK 623:21
  We took sweet c. together   BOOK 128:11
  Who cannot give good c.   BURT 165:4
  women to keep c.   SHAK 591:9
  you c. well   SHAK 608:5
counsellor: C., The mighty God   BIBLE 82:27
  this c. is now most still   SHAK 577:26
counsellors: speak plain when c. blanch
                                   BACON 43:3
  With kings and c.   BIBLE 77:7
counsels: designs and crooked c. fit DRYD 259:1

counsels: (cont.):
  from whom all good c.   BOOK 119:10
  United thoughts and c.   MILT 469:3
count: c. myself in nothing else   SHAK 619:20
  c. the number of the beast   BIBLE 107:1
  C. to ten, and man is bored   PARK 506:6
  I c. it not an inn   BROW 146:19
  I won the c.   SOM 655:14
  Let me c. the ways   BROW 147:20
  let us c. our spoons   JOHN 372:9
  tho' some did c. him mad   BUNY 156:12
  To give and not to c. the cost   IGN 359:8
  when angry, c. four   TWAIN 706:21
counted: c. as the small dust of the balance
                                   BIBLE 83:29
  c. them all out and I counted   HANR 323:7
  faster we c. our spoons   EMER 276:18
  those I c. loss for Christ   BIBLE 103:8
countenance: And did the C. Divine
                                   BLAKE 113:4
  bright c. of truth   MILT 476:7
  damned disinheriting c.   SHER 645:9
  heart maketh a cheerful c.   BIBLE 78:34
  his c. is as Lebanon   BIBLE 81:20
  his c. was as the sun   BIBLE 106:1
  I trow that c. cannot lie   ROYD 549:14
  Knight of the Doleful C.   CERV 188:8
  light of his c.   BOOK 129:4
  light of thy c. upon   BOOK 124:13
  Lord lift up his c.   BIBLE 73:4
  make him a cheerful c.   BOOK 132:8
  shew the light of thy c.   BOOK 130:13
  Till grim, grim grew his c.   BALL 49:5
  which is the help of my c.   BOOK 127:8
  withal of a beautiful c.   BIBLE 74:39
counter: All things c., original   HOPK 345:20
countercheck: c. quarrelsome   SHAK 569:26
counterfeit: c. sad looks   SHAK 612:4
  laughed with c. glee   GOLD 310:12
  stamp and c. advantages   SHAK 615:21
  Teach light to c. a gleam   MILT 464:22
counterpane: pleasant land of c.   STEV 668:15
counterpoint: Too much c.   BEEC 59:3
counters: Words are wise men's c. HOBB 340:1
counties: see the coloured c.   HOUS 352:10
  six c. overhung with smoke   MORR 485:12
counting: C. the beats   GRAV 314:19
  democracy, it's the c.   STOP 669:14
countless: With c. gifts of love   WINK 739:6
countree: hame to my c.   CUNN 229:3
countries: no c. in the world less known
                                   BORR 136:13
  preferreth all c. before his own OVER 502:10
country: all airs make unto me one c.
                                   BROW 146:14
  America is a c. of young men   EMER 277:15
  And there's another c.   SPR 661:9
  Anybody can be good in the c.   WILDE 735:21
  Anyone who loves his c.   GAR 298:1
  best c. ever is, at home   GOLD 311:9
  be understood by my c.   MAY 455:4
  body of my c. to its death   OSB 501:20
  Britain a fit c. for heroes   LLOY 424:8
  But sucked on c. pleasures   DONNE 252:4
  but that was in another c.   MARL 447:15
  By all their c.'s wishes blest   COLL 213:12
  c. and betraying my friend   FORS 290:29
  c. and the age we live in   AUST 39:1
  c. and they only saved the world
                                   CHES 199:1
  c. as good as he had found   COBB 208:1
  country for his c.'s sake   FITZ 283:9
  country for our c.'s good   CART 184:11
  c. governed by a despot   JOHN 374:31
  c. habit has me   SACK 552:16
  c. has its own constitution   ANON 13:3
  c. has the government it   MAIS 442:14
  C. in the town   MART 494:17
  c. in which the office   HUXL 357:9
  c. loves such sweet desires   GREE 317:11
  c. of the blind the one-eyed   ERAS 278:17
  c. retreat near the town   WYCH 750:2
  c. through which the river   GLAD 307:8

country: (cont.):
c. 'tis of centuries come — CUMM 228:6
c. town is my detestation — BURN 160:20
c. which is continually — KEATS 391:17
c. will be called upon — HARD 323:15
Cry, the beloved c. — PATON 509:15
defence of one's c. — HOMER 343:8
departed into their own c. — BIBLE 88:10
die for one's c. — HOR 349:25
ever exist in a free c. — BURKE 157:29
every c. but his own — CANN 178:4
every c. but his own — GILB 304:22
families in a c. village — AUST 39:26
fight for its King and C. — GRAH 313:7
For your King and your C. — RUB 549:16
friends of every c. — DISR 247:26
From yon far c. blows — HOUS 352:15
God made the c. and man — BRAD 139:1
God made the c., and man — COWP 223:18
good news from a far c. — BIBLE 79:19
good of his c. — WOTT 749:9
good of one's c. — FARQ 280:14
good to be had in the c. — HAZL 329:1
great deal of unmapped c. — ELIOT 268:23
grow up with the c. — GREE 316:15
halved a c. — THOM 693:9
has to understand the c. — LESS 419:8
have no relish for the c. — SMITH 653:5
He likes the c. — COWP 223:9
highlands, in the c. places — STEV 666:23
his journey into a far c. — BIBLE 95:2
How can you govern a c. — DE G 235:10
how I leave my c. — PITT 515:19
I love thee still—My c. — COWP 223:20
I love to serve my c. — GIBR 303:1
In a half-savage c. — POUND 526:11
Indeed I tremble for my c. — JEFF 364:18
In this frozen whited c. — HUGH 354:8
Isn't this a billion dollar c. — FOST 291.5
know it's a different c. — LARK 410:1
life to lose for my c. — HALE 321:7
Love of our c. is another — GODW 308:11
Love thy c., wish it well — DOD 250:4
man should know of own c. — STER 665:6
may our c. be always successful — ADAMS 3:6
My c. is Kiltartan Cross — YEATS 752:5
My c. is the world — PAINE 505:1
My c., right or wrong — SCH 558:13
My c., 'tis of thee — SMITH 652:13
My soul, there is a c. — VAUG 708:17
not see your c. is lost — WILL 736:21
Old C. must wake up — GEOR 301:2
once to serve our c. — ADD 3:21
Our c. is the world — GARR 298:12
our c., right or wrong — DEC 233:14
past is a foreign c. — HART 327:22
prepare the mind of the c. — DISR 247:15
pride that pulls the c. — SHAK 615:25
quarrel in a far away c. — CHAM 189:7
senators and I pray for the c. — HALE 321:5
service of their c. — PAINE 504:12
she is my c. still — CHUR 200:17
That is no c. for old men — YEATS 752:20
that will not love his c. — SHAK 592:4
these c. patriots born — BYRON 167:19
They touch our c. — COWP 223:19
they've undone his c. — ADD 3:20
This c. needs good farmers — NIXON 496:6
this c. of ours where — AUDEN 36:18
This was my c. — BLUN 116:5
thou aim'st at be thy c.'s — SHAK 589:1
valour, the c. of worth — BURNS 162:23
was to all the c. dear — GOLD 310:9
what was good for our c. — WILS 737:18
While there's a lane — PARK 507:1
you call do for your c. — FENN 394:2
countryman; c. must have prime — PLYT 116:10
[...] lend me your ears — SHAK 581:8
hearts of [...] — LEE 415:17
our c. are all mankind — [...]
perils by mine own c. — BIBLE 100:1
countryside: know the gods of the c. — VIRG 715:15
smiling and beautiful c. — DOYLE 256:5

county: Ah! C. Guy — SCOTT 560:26
English c. families baying — WAUGH 723:11
coup: c. de dés jamais n'abolira — MALL 442:19
coupés: les lauriers sont c. — ANON 21:3
cœur: voit bien qu'avec le c. — DE S 553:3
courage: Blessings on your young c. — VIRG 714:6
But screw your c. — SHAK 601:7
C. in your own — GORD 312:12
C. is not simply one — LEWIS 420:17
C., mon ami, le diable — READE 537:8
C. mounteth with occasion — SHAK 593:27
c. never to submit or yield — MILT 468:5
c. of my companions — SCOTT 559:6
c. you bring to it — WALP 720:12
fearful saints fresh c. — COWP 222:18
keener, c. the greater — ANON 21:20
make can aught my c. quail — ALAB 7:1
must have the c. to dare — DOST 254:11
on reflection is real c. — WALP 720:6
originality or moral c. — SHAW 635:28
piety, c.—they exist — FORS 290:24
red badge of c. — CRANE 225:27
should have c. to suffer — TROL 703:9
strong and of a good c. — BIBLE 73:27
Than C. of Heart or Holiness — BELL 61:9
therefore should our c. — SHAK 585:19
three-o'-clock in the morning c. — THOR 697:3
two o'clock in the morning c. — NAP 490:2
unto him with a good c. — BOOK 126:11
vain faith, and c. vain — MAC 436:6
which inspired c. whilst — BURKE 158:14
With constant c., and contempt — JONS 378:20
courageous: captains c. — BALL 50:2
couriers: sightless c. of the air — SHAK 601:3
Vaunt-c. to oak-cleaving — SHAK 595:20
cours: Suspendez votre c. — LAM 406:1
course: betake myself to that c. — PEPYS 512:20
c. of human events — JEFF 364:1
c. of true love never did — SHAK 610:21
giant to run his c. — BOOK 125:4
have them served to him c. — CHUR 202:6
I have finished my c. — BIBLE 104:8
I must stand the c. — SHAK 596:21
Of c., of course — JAMES 363:10
takes the better c. — SOCR 654:15
Take thou what c. thou wilt — SHAK 592:20
courses: c. through the blackest — WILB 734:5
court: c. awards it — SHAK 609:18
c. for owls — BIBLE 83:18
C., him, elude him — BLUN 116:3
c. in beauty and decay — SHEL 639:13
c. is obliged to submit — CHEK 197:13
c. to cottage he depart — PEELE 511:5
How he can c., or you be won — SOUT 657:3
I c. others in verse — PRIOR 529:4
Let her alone, she will c. you — JONS 379:19
peril than the envious c. — SHAK 567:24
Say to the c., it glows — RAL 535:15
Talk of the c. — SHAK 597:16
that shines upon his c. — SHAK 632:9
courted: Better be c. and jilted — CAMP 176:14
courteous: c. to strangers — BACON 43:26
courtesies: and for these c. — SHAK 608:1
Hail, ye small sweet c. of life — STER 664:7
courtesy: c. help a lame dog over — CHIL 199:28
greater man, the greater c. — TENN 682:6
I am the very pink of c. — SHAK 623:9
Showed thy dear mother any c. — SHAK 570:25
That the Grace of God is in C. — BELL 61:9
trust thy honest-offered c. — MILT 463:25
Why, what a candy deal of c. — SHAK 580:2
courtier: Here lies a noble c. — ANON 14:5
near the heel of the c. — SHAK 578:22
courtiers: c. who surround him — DUM 264:1
courtly: by scales of c. grace — GASC 298:17
courtmartialled: c. in my absence — BEHAN 60:2
courts: And c. of princes — MILT 463:25
Applaud [...] with joy his c. unto — KETHE 394:13
C. and camps are the only — CHES 196.0
[...] towards were erected — BURNS 168:10
day la [...] — BOOK 130:18
fresh from brawling c. — [...] 694:h

courts: (cont.):
into the c. of the Lord — BOOK 130:16
still before the c. — HOR 347:7

courtship: C. to marriage — CONG 215:27
importunate c. until now — WAUGH 723:9
variety of c. — WEBS 725:14
cousin: Did your c. complain — WALK 717:11
cousins: his c. and his aunts — GILB 305:25
Coutts: Aristocrat who banks with C. — GILB 304:1
covenant: c. between me and the earth — BIBLE 70:32
c. with death and an agreement — GARR 298:13
have made a c. with death — BIBLE 83:12
covenanted: c. with him for thirty — BIBLE 92:23
covenants: c. to those that buy — DRAY 257:18
Open c. of peace — WILS 738:19
cover: C. her face — WEBS 725:23
c. the universe with mud — FORS 290:6
I am the grass; I c. all — SAND 555:5
jewels c. ev'ry part — POPE 521:11
neither turn again to c. — BOOK 132:7
covered: c. it all over with these two — RAL 536:6
with twain he c. his face — BIBLE 82:19
covert: c. from the tempest — BIBLE 83:17
covet: c.; but tradition approves — CLOU 207:20
c. thy neighbour's house — BIBLE 72:16
coveted: ever c. his neighbour's goods — KING 398:2
covetous: not a brawler, not c. — BIBLE 103:26
covetousness: all uncleanness, or c. — BIBLE 102:20
c. is the root of all evil — DEFOE 234:4
cow: c. is of the bovine ilk — NASH 490:10
I never saw a Purple C. — BURG 166:22
isn't grass to graze a c. — BETJ 68:5
it was an open c. — HERB 333:24
than to keep a c. — BUTL 167:5
Three acres and a c. — ANON 19:1
Truth, Sir, is a c. — JOHN 372:11
Two wise acres and a c. — COW 221:6
We milk the c. of the world — WILB 734:3
coward: Am I a c. — SHAK 575:11
c. does it with a kiss — WILDE 736:1
c. in thine own esteem — SHAK 601:5
c.'s castle, and the sluggard's — CHAP 190:16
c.'s weapon, poison — FLET 288:3
'Fore God I am no c. — TENN 689:1
His c. lips did from their — SHAK 590:1
I was a c. on instinct — SHAK 580:25
May c. shame distain his name — BURNS 162:17
No c. soul is mine — BRON 142:12
sea hates a c. — O'NEI 499:1
Shaked like a c. — SHAK 581:1
We took him for a c. — SHAK 630:33
cowardice: mutual c. keeps us in peace — JOHN 375:5
soldier I admit the c. — SHAW 637:15
surest is c. — TWAIN 706:10
cowardly: C. dogs bark loudest — WEBS 726:5
Not c. put off my helmet — SHAK 566:14
cowards: As many other mannish c. — SHAK 567:23
being all c. — JOHN 375:5
conscience doth make c. — SHAK 575:16
Conscience is but a word that c. — SHAK 622:14
Courts for c. were erected — BURNS 162:13
C. die many times before — SHAK 591:5
C. in scarlet pass — GRAN 314:14
plague of all c. — SHAK 580:17
such c. in reasoning — SHAF 563:21
would be c. if they durst — ROCH 543:11
cowbird: c. and the moonlight-coloured — SHEL 642:24
cowl: I like a church; I like a c. — EMER 276:10
cowled: that c. churchman — EMER 276:10
Cowley: Who now reads C.? — POPE 523:1
cows: contented—that's for the c. — CHAN 190:8
C. are my passion — DICK 240:18
cowslip: [...] and shad-blow — CRANE 225:19
In a c.'s bell I lie — SHAK 626:2

cowslip: (*cont.*):	
I' the bottom of a c.	SHAK 571:2
O'er the c.'s velvet head	MILT 464:11
cowslips: c. tall her pensioners	SHAK 611:11
c. wan that hang the pensive	MILT 466:11
coxcombs: c. Nature meant but fools	
	POPE 521:4
coy: coming, sometimes c.	SEDL 561:16
make me c. and tender	HERB 335:23
Then be not c.	HERR 337:8
coyness: This c., lady, were no crime	
	MARV 451:2
cozenage: c. that men can put	CROM 227:13
crabbed: C. age and youth	SHAK 632:18
crabs: c. had scrawled their crooked	
	CRAB 224:23
roasted c. hiss in the bowl	SHAK 590:11
crab-tree: grievous c. cudgel	BUNY 156:3
crack: canst hear the mighty c.	POPE 519:26
C. and sometimes break	ELIOT 270:17
c. in the tea-cup opens	AUDEN 34:4
c. in your upper storey	SMOL 654:3
C. nature's moulds	SHAK 595:20
heaven's vaults should c.	SHAK 597:21
sans c. or flaw	SHAK 599:8
sometimes, and c. it too	JONS 378:7
would hear the mighty c.	ADD 4:5
cracked: bloody noses and c. crowns	
	SHAK 580:12
crackling: c. of thorns under a pot	BIBLE 80:11
cracks: c. and crazes their enamel	FROST 294:9
Now c. a noble heart	SHAK 579:14
Through c. in the conversation	WALK 717:11
cradle: Between the c. and the grave	
	DYER 265:6
c. endlessly rocking	WHIT 732:8
c. rocks above an abyss	NAB 489:2
For the hand that rocks the c.	WALL 718:6
from the c. to the grave	CHUR 202:19
from the c. to the grave	SHEL 642:19
high mountain c. in Pamere	ARN 28:18
nightmare by a rocking c.	YEATS 753:2
pendent bed and procreant c.	SHAK 601:1
Rocked in the c. of the deep	WILL 736:20
rocking a grown man in the c.	BURKE 157:11
craft: Between c. and credulity	BURKE 157:9
c. so long to lerne	CHAU 195:5
craftier: Ful c. to pley she was	CHAU 192:5
crafts: c. and assaults	BOOK 119:17
crag: c. with crookèd hands	TENN 681:1
craggy: c. government there was	DAN 229:12
past the c. paths of study	JONS 379:5
crags: among these barren c.	TENN 689:18
crammed: C. just as they on earth	
	WORD 746:13
cramps: tonight thou shalt have c.	SHAK 625:6
Cranberry Tart: pound of Rice, and a C.	
	LEAR 414:5
crane: Jane, Jane, Tall as a c.	SITW 648:9
cranes: Warred on by c.	MILT 468:25
crank: apprenticeship as a c.	BROUN 144:10
cranks: philosophers into sages and c.	
	QUINE 534:15
Quips and c., and wanton wiles	MILT 465:5
cras: C. *amet qui nunquam amavit*	ANON 22:6
C. *ingens iterabimus aequor*	HOR 349:6
crastina: *Pereat, qui c. curat*	VIRG 714:10
Sera nimis vita est c.	MART 449:11
craters: passing c., passing fire	YEVT 754:4
crave: still my mind forbids to c.	DYER 264:15
too much, yet still do c.	DYER 265:1
craved: who c. no crumb	GILB 306:24
craven: c. fears of being great	TENN 681:13
craving: And full as c. too	DRYD 260:1
c. in the world	PEAR 510:15
Give him, he the more is c.	WROTH 749:14
crawling: c. between heaven and earth	
	SHAK 575:18
crawls: sea-worm c.	HARDY 325:3
crazed: c. with the spell of far	DE L 235:21
crazier: World is c. and more	MACN 441:2
crazy: Aching, shaking, c., cold	ROCH 543:17
C. like a fox	PER 512:21

crazy: (*cont.*):	
Just two c. people together	HART 327:13
creaking: Came c. to the barn	LOW 430:15
creaks: morning light c. down	SITW 648:9
cream: c. and mantle like a	SHAK 607:6
queen of curds and c.	SHAK 632:6
Skim milk masquerades as c.	GILB 306:3
vigilant as a cat to steal c.	SHAK 581:24
cream-faced: thou c. loon	SHAK 604:20
crease: not a c., not a mark	ROST 548:11
create: half c. the wondrous world	
	YOUNG 754:20
Her ashes new-c. another heir	SHAK 589:17
himself c. the taste	WORD 748:20
I must c. a system	BLAKE 112:1
what they half-c.	WORD 745:2
created: all men are c. equal	ANON 19:7
all men are c. equal	JEFF 364:2
c. him in his own image	DOST 254:4
C. sick, commanded to be sound	GREV 318:8
Nothing can be c. out	LUCR 431:14
Thou hast c. all things	BIBLE 106:12
creating: c. a whole tribe of fops	SHAK 594:26
creation: And love C.'s final law	TENN 683:22
atheist who finds c.	PROU 530:13
been present at the C.	ALF 9:2
c. groaneth and travaileth	BIBLE 99:37
c. in the infinite I AM	COL 212:1
c. rises again to make	MISS 477:12
C. to a stunned repose	HILL 338:10
Is pilf'ring from the first c.	LLOYD 424:3
mars c.'s plan	CANN 178:8
not got your niche in c.	HALL 322:4
Now I hold C. in my foot	HUGH 354:4
She is his new c.	STONE 669:12
speak before you think c.'s	FORS 290:28
To which the whole c. moves	TENN 684:17
We bless thee for our c.	BOOK 120:8
woman is a blind fury of c.	SHAW 637:6
creations: person acts his own c.	BROW 151:18
creative: destruction is also a c.	BAK 47:22
sensitive being, a c. soul	WORD 747:9
creator: can dispense with a c.	PROU 530:13
C. and Preserver of all	BOOK 120:5
C. and the relief of man's	BACON 41:17
c. from his work returned	MILT 472:10
C. made Italy from designs	TWAIN 706:13
creature more than the C.	BIBLE 99:17
myself and my C.	NEWM 492:14
now he hasn't been a c.	CHEK 197:5
Remember now thy C.	BIBLE 81:1
creature: base and ignoble c.	BACON 42:24
c. hath a purpose	KEATS 392:6
c. more than the Creator	BIBLE 99:17
c.'s at his dirty work	POPE 519:27
c. whose life is not worth	DEFOE 234:8
God's first C., which was Light	BACON 45:17
I am a lone lorn c.	DICK 239:20
in this world no lyves c.	CHAU 195:15
Let the living c. lie	AUDEN 35:5
Y'are the deed's c.	MIDD 459:14
creatures: All c. great and small	ALEX 8:9
c. set upon tables	JOHN 374:6
goodly c. are there here	SHAK 626:3
meanest of his c.	BROW 151:17
take unto other living c.	BACON 43:25
widows the most perverse c.	ADD 4:13
credat: C. *Iudaeus Apella*	HOR 351:5
credence: gave no c. to his word	BOOK 132:13
yive I feyth and ful c.	CHAU 195:1
credit: And it's greatly to his c.	GILB 306:4
c. in this world much wrong	FITZ 284:15
c. to any good girl	TAYL 679:12
I never seek to take the c.	PARK 506:10
In science the c. goes	DARW 231:15
let the c. go	FITZ 283:14
Of c. and renown	COWP 222:12
people who get the c.	MORR 486:3
There an't much c.	DICK 241:8
creditable: love good c. acquaintance	
	SWIFT 673:19
credite: *Experto c.*	VIRG 714:9
creditor: or trembling at a c.	JOHN 368:22

credo: *C. in unum Deum*	MISS 476:21
C. quia impossibile	TERT 690:18
credulities: upwards on the miseries or c.	
	CONR 217:13
credulity: Between craft and c.	BURKE 157:9
c. below the milkiness	BURKE 159:14
c. increases his impudence	HUME 355:5
C. is the man's weakness	LAMB 406:15
present age is craving c.	DISR 247:10
youth is the season of c.	PITT 515:7
credulous: positive men are the most c.	
	POPE 524:7
credulus: *sed non ego c. illis*	VIRG 715:7
creed: got the better of his c.	STER 664:23
His c. no parson ever knew	DOYLE 257:5
it is the c. of slaves	PITT 515:15
last article of my c.	GAND 297:10
mustn't monkey with the C.	BELL 61:13
Pagan suckled in a c.	WORD 748:16
political c. is that despotism	ADAMS 3:4
shrieked against his c.	TENN 683:22
solemn c. with solemn sneer	BYRON 168:26
creeds: dust of c. outworn	SHEL 642:13
half-believers in our casual c.	ARN 28:8
keys of all the c.	TENN 683:9
So many gods, so many c.	WILC 734:8
than in half the c.	TENN 684:7
creep: ambition can c. as well as soar	
	BURKE 159:23
And bade me c. past	BROW 152:5
c. again, leap again	DE L 236:4
c. and intrude, and climb	MILT 466:8
C. in our ears	SHAK 610:1
C. into thy narrow bed	ARN 27:11
oft c. in one dull line	POPE 521:14
creeper-nails: c. are rust	HARDY 325:1
creeping: c. things, and fowls	BIBLE 98:19
c. things innumerable	BOOK 132:9
c. thing that creepeth	BIBLE 69:24
creeps: C. in this petty pace	SHAK 605:1
c. rustling to her knees	KEATS 387:6
it c. like a rat	BOWEN 138:11
crème: are the c. de la crème	SPARK 658:5
crept: c. too near his conscience	SHAK 588:12
crested: Ranked arms and c. heads	
	SMART 650:3
Crete: people of C. make more history	
	SAKI 553:7
Cretes: C. and Arabians	BIBLE 98:7
crevasse: like a scream from a c.	GREE 317:2
crew: darling of our c.	DIBD 238:16
industrious c. to build in hell	MILT 469:8
Mirth, admit me of thy c.	MILT 465:7
We were a ghastly c.	COL 211:12
cribbed: Now I am cabined, c.	SHAK 603:18
cribs: liest thou in smoky c.	SHAK 583:11
cricket: C.—a game which the English	
	MANC 444:1
c. as organized loafing	TEMP 680:6
C. civilizes people	MUG 487:7
c. with their peasants	TREV 702:11
Save the c. on the hearth	MILT 464:22
The c. test	TEBB 680:2
cried: And still she c., and still	ELIOT 273:3
c. the little children died	AUDEN 34:10
from the depths I have c.	BIBLE 108:5
I c. to dream again	SHAK 625:26
little children c.	MOTL 487:3
that the poor have c.	SHAK 592:7
cries: air is full of our c.	BECK 58:2
c., and falls into a cough	SHAK 611:12
heaven with my bootless c.	SHAK 633:10
Night and day on me she c.	BALL 49:13
crieth: c. in the wilderness	BIBLE 83:26
Crillon: brave C.	HENR 332:11
crime: c. of being a young man	PITT 515:5
c. recognize them all	VIRG 712:15
c. so shameful as poverty	FARQ 280:10
c.'s so great as daring	CHUR 200:16
c. they like and transgress	DOST 254:9
c. to love too well	POPE 519:15
c. you haven't committed	POW 528:8

crucify: (*cont.*):
you shall not c. mankind — BRYAN 153:24
cruel: C., but composed and bland — ARN 27:19
C. he looks, but calm — SHEL 642:8
C. necessity — CROM 227:7
horridly c. works of nature — DARW 231:11
I must be c. only to be kind — SHAK 577:23
jealousy is c. as the grave — BIBLE 82:5
Let me be c., not unnatural — SHAK 577:1
mercies of the wicked are c. — BIBLE 78:25
Not that he's c. — LEAC 413:12
Such c. glasses — HOW 353:5
That comfort c. men — CHES 199:3
truth is c. — SANT 555:20
you c. men of Rome — SHAK 589:20
cruellest: April is the c. month — ELIOT 272:21
cruelty: C. has a human heart — BLAKE 114:10
c. with a good conscience — RUSS 551:22
gratification of c. — FOST 291:10
main sources of c. — RUSS 551:25
top full of direst c. — SHAK 600:16
'Tis a c. to load — SHAK 589:14
cruise: are all on our last c. — STEV 667:28
crumble: c. to the dust beneath — BROW 147:14
crumbling: C. between the fingers — MACN 440:17
rock that was c. to dust — DID 245:11
crumbs: bags to hold the c. — ISH 360:21
covetous of their c. — SMART 649:12
c. which fell from — BIBLE 95:9
dogs eat of the c. — BIBLE 91:11
picker-up of learning's c. — BROW 149:19
crumpet: Hot Muffin and C. Baking — DICK 241:30
thinking man's c. — MUIR 487:14
crusade: Labour Party a moral c. — WILS 738:1
cruse: c. best fits my little — HERR 336:25
little oil in a c. — BIBLE 75:32
crush: To c., to annihilate — DOST 255:2
crushing: C. out life — HOPE 345:3
crust: c. over a volcano of revolution — ELLIS 275:16
c. so fresh — HOPK 345:13
other, upper c. — GILB 306:6
These men are all upper c. — HAL 321:9
cry: anything, only don't c. — CARR 183:7
continually do c. — BOOK 118:12
c. all the way to the bank — LIB 421:12
C.;—and upon thy so sore loss — THOM 695:10
C.,—clinging Heaven — THOM 695:10
c. is still 'They come' — SHAK 604:23
C. not when his father dies — JOHN 377:4
c. of his hounds has me — GRAV 314:16
c. of the Little Peoples — LE G 416:9
C., the beloved country — PATON 509:15
cuckoo's parting c. — ARN 28:26
deep behind him, and a c. — TENN 682:21
Forgot the c. of gulls — ELIOT 273:11
he said, What shall I c. — BIBLE 83:27
his little son should c. — CORN 219:3
I c. in the day-time — BOOK 125:9
I hear a sudden c. of pain — STEP 664:1
let our c. come unto thee — BOOK 123:12
little baby, don' yo' c. — HEYW 338:2
righteousness, but behold a c. — BIBLE 82:15
shriek, the bubbling c. — BYRON 170:17
Some must c. so that others — RHYS 539:18
Speechless still, and never c. — CLEV 206:13
stones would immediately c. — BIBLE 95:17
that c. over me, There — BOOK 129:15
That the Cherubim may c. — ANON 22:9
that we still should c. — BACON 46:2
To c. it up, or run it down — SWIFT 675:4
Truth is the c. of all — BERK 65:9
was a great c. in Egypt — BIBLE 72:11
We waul and c. — SHAK 597:10
when indeed they c. — WEBS 726:9
When we are born we c. — SHAK 597:11
with no language but a c. — TENN 683:19
your bald c. — PLATH 516:7
crying: And then not hear it c. — HERB 334:13
Love, a child, is ever c. — WROTH 749:14
one c. in the wilderness — BIBLE 88:13

crying: (*cont.*):
we came c. hither — SHAK 597:10
crystal: c. branches on his forehead — PHIL 514:5
c. frolicked in the ray — BYRON 172:14
C. sincerity hath found — HOPK 346:15
makes them shed c. shells — FROST 294:9
Of golden sands, and c. brooks — DONNE 251:19
sea of glass like unto c. — BIBLE 106:10
water of life, clear as c. — BIBLE 107:22
Why name the c. when — BEVAN 68:15
crystals: instants become c. — BLY 116:7
cubes: c. in two different ways — RAM 536:13
cubili: *dea nec dignata c. est* — VIRG 715:2
cubit: one c. unto his stature — BIBLE 89:10
cuckold: c. to make him a monarch — SHAK 618:1
cuckoo: c. clock — WELL 726:22
c. clock style of architecture — HEM 332:2
C.-echoing — HOPK 345:9
c. is in June — SHAK 581:14
c. then, on every tree — SHAK 599:10
heard the c.'s parting cry — ARN 28:26
hear the pleasant c. — DAV 232:9
Lhude sing c. — ANON 18:6
merry c., messenger — SPEN 659:8
O C.! Shall I call thee bird — WORD 748:10
rainbow and a c.'s song — DAV 232:10
Responsive to the c.'s note — GRAY 316:5
weather the c. likes — HARDY 326:1
cuckoo-buds: c. of yellow hue — SHAK 599:10
cucumber: c. should be well sliced — JOHN 371:1
when c. is added to it — MACK 439:4
cucumbers: lodge in a garden of c. — BIBLE 82:8
sun-beams out of c. — SWIFT 673:13
they are but c. after all — JOHN 375:14
cud: cheweth not the c. — BIBLE 73:1
Cuddesdon: Hey for C.! — KETT 394:14
cudgel: c. of the people's war — TOLS 700:12
grievous crab-tree c. — BUNY 156:3
cue: With a twisted c. — GILB 305:5
cui: C. bono? — CIC 204:12
cully: by Nature Woman's c. — CONG 215:20
culpa: *mea c., mea culpa* — MISS 476:16
O felix c., quae talem — MISS 477:16
culprits: better to choose the c. — PAGN 504:6
recognize them all as c. — VIRG 712:15
cult: What's a c.? — ALTM 10:4
cultivate: And c. a beaver — HUXL 357:7
c. a few inhibitions — LOOS 428:11
C. simplicity, Coleridge — LAMB 406:22
c. your friendship — JOHN 375:27
We must c. our garden — VOLT 716:4
culture: c. lives by sympathies — JAMES 363:15
C. shock is what happens — TOFF 700:1
don't swallow the c. bait — LAWR 412:12
elaborate defence of c. — ARN 29:13
man of c. rare — GILB 305:15
men of c. are true apostles — ARN 29:9
possible stage in moral c. — DARW 231:4
Whenever I hear the word c. — JOHST 377:16
whole vast intuitive c. — SHAF 563:18
who pursue C. in bands — WHAR 730:5
Cumaei: *Ultima C.* — VIRG 714:22
cumber: c. you good Margaret — MORE 484:16
cumbered: was c. about much serving — BIBLE 94:17
cumbrous: easiest of this c. charge — MILT 473:7
cummin: mint and anise and c. — BIBLE 92:5
cunctando: *nobis c. restituit* — ENN 278:2
cunning: C. is the dark sanctuary — CHES 198:4
c. men pass for wise — BACON 43:7
c. which disgracefully — WOLL 741:16
right hand forget her c. — BOOK 134:17
silence, exile, and c. — JOYCE 381:14
that c. whore of Venice — SHAK 617:18
cunningly: little world made c. — DONNE 251:1
cup: after supper he took the C. — BOOK 122:12
Ah, fill the c. — FITZ 284:3
Come fill up my c. — SCOTT 560:30
c. but sparkles near — BYRON 168:14
fill the c. that clears today — FITZ 283:17
Freely welcome to my c. — OLDYS 498:11

cup: (*cont.*):
giveth his colour in the c. — BIBLE 79:13
let this c. pass from me — BIBLE 92:28
my c. overflows — SCOT 561:8
my c. shall be full — BOOK 125:15
my glory in a shallow c. — FITZ 284:15
Perfect the c. as planned — BROW 152:13
There may be in the c. — SHAK 631:18
There's death in the c. — BURNS 162:8
We'll tak a c. o' kindness yet — BURNS 161:5
cupboard: our c. of food — HERB 335:10
Cupid: C. and my Campaspe — LYLY 433:8
C. is a knavish lad — SHAK 612:7
C.'s darts do not feel — ANON 16:11
giant-dwarf, Dan C. — SHAK 598:13
winged C. painted blind — SHAK 611:1
cupidinibus: *Responsare c.* — HOR 351:11
cupido: *c. gloriae novissima exuitur* — TAC 678:4
cupidons: away all the little c. — BURN 160:13
cups: flowing c. run swiftly — LOV 429:2
steamy column, and the c. — COWP 223:31
cur: half lurcher and half c. — COWP 224:2
I spurn thee like a c. out — SHAK 591:11
cura: *Post equitem sedet atra C.* — HOR 349:24
curantur: *Similia similibus c.* — HAHN 320:10
curate: c. faced the laurels — GRAH 313:17
c. something between a eunuch — FIRB 282:26
c. who has strayed by mistake — AUDEN 36:16
I was a pale young c. then — GILB 306:21
very name of a C. — SMITH 652:25
curates: abundant shower of c. — BRON 142:7
all Bishops and C. — BOOK 122:2
C., and all Congregations — BOOK 119:8
C., long dust, will come and go — BROO 143:11
preached to death by wild c. — SMITH 653:20
curb: c. a runaway young star — BYRON 173:13
snaffle and the c. — CAMP 176:8
curbing: C. his lavish spirit — SHAK 599:17
curds: queen of c. and cream — SHAK 632:6
cure: Be of sin the double c. — TOPL 701:4
But wilt thou c. thine heart — BEDD 58:9
c. for admiring the House — BAG 46:22
c. for it is occupation — SHAW 638:12
c. for this ill is not to sit still — KIPL 401:23
c. of all diseases — BROW 146:18
c. of a romantic first — BURN 160:11
c. the disease and kill — BACON 43:23
labour against our own c. — BROW 146:18
love's a malady without a c. — DRYD 261:9
no C. for this Disease — BELL 61:1
palliate what we cannot c. — JOHN 367:23
To c. this deadly grief — SHAK 604:9
twentieth, it's a c. — SZASZ 677:16
cured: c. by hanging from a string — KING 398:17
c. by more democracy — SMITH 651:6
C. yesterday of my disease — PRIOR 529:11
cures: if a lot of c. — CHEK 196:6
Like c. like — HAHN 320:10
curfew: begins at c., and walks — SHAK 596:13
c. tolls the knell of parting — GRAY 315:10
I hear the far-off c. sound — MILT 464:21
curia: *semper celebrat superna c.* — ABEL 1:1
curiosa: *Horatii c. felicitas* — PETR 513:14
curiosities: c. would be quite forgot — AUBR 33:2
curiosity: Disinterested intellectual c. — TREV 702:10
eminent degree of c. — JOHN 370:4
Love, c., freckles, and doubt — PARK 506:2
curious: amaz'd, and c. — BURNS 163:9
c. in unnecessary matters — BIBLE 87:10
Raised by that c. engine — WEBS 725:17
curiouser: C. and curiouser! — CARR 181:24
curis: *quid solutis est beatius c.* — CAT 186:3
curl: Who had a little c. — LONG 428:5
curled: C. like vapour over shrines — BROW 147:23
C. minion, dancer — ARN 28:14
curlèd: wealthy c. darlings — SHAK 614:28
curlew: c.'s tear turned its edge — HUGH 354:5
curls: And Frocks and C. — DICK 245:3
currency: c. that buys all things — CERV 188:16
Debasing the moral c. — ELIOT 269:10
than to debauch the c. — KEYN 395:4

current: boats against the c.   FITZ 285:4
  c. and compulsive course   SHAK 616:23
  giving a c. to the whole   HOPK 346:14
  take the c. when it serves   SHAK 593:12
currents: Cold c. thrid   HARDY 325:3
  regard their c. turn awry   SHAK 575:16
curs: You common cry of c.   SHAK 570:13
curse: And the c. be ended   ELIOT 270:12
  An open foe may prove a c.   GAY 300:4
  began he to c. and to swear   BIBLE 93:2
  blessing, is to me a c.   MASS 453:14
  C. God, and die   BIBLE 77:5
  c. is come upon me   TENN 685:4
  c. of the drinking   WILDE 736:10
  C. on his virtues   ADD 3:20
  C. the blasted, jelly-boned   LAWR 412:24
  c. thee shall I find   WRIG 749:13
  c. thine own inconstancy   CAREW 179:14
  c. to party-strife   WORD 743:12
  c. with their heart   BOOK 128:19
  heard such a terrible c.   BARH 52:15
  I know how to c.   SHAK 625:7
  look upon myself and c.   SHAK 633:10
  loved which is the real c.   RHYS 539:19
  My c., which shall strike   LYLY 433:12
  thee to c. mine enemies   BIBLE 73:11
  'Tis the c. of service   SHAK 614:18
cursed: c. man, low sitting   SPEN 660:1
  c. past in which man   VANZ 708:10
  He c. him in sleeping   BARH 52:14
  whom thou cursest is c.   BIBLE 73:8
curses: C. are like young chickens   SOUT 657:7
  c. heaped on each gashed   SORL 656:17
  C., not loud but deep   SHAK 604:21
  Writ with c. from pole to pole   BLAKE 111:19
cursing: c. his staff for incompetent   SASS 557:11
  death, blessing and c.   BIBLE 73:20
curst: all succeeding ages c.   DRYD 259:1
  c. be he that moves   SHAK 635:15
curt: c. societies whose deaths   MOT 487:2
curtain: Adriatic an iron c.   CHUR 202:22
  c. of the night sinks down   PUSH 533:5
  draw the c. close   SHAK 587:19
  lets the c. fall   POPE 519:12
  sensuous c. is a deception   BRAD 139:6
  these gifts a c. before 'em   SHAK 628:14
  Up with the c.   BROW 149:28
curtained: C. with cloudy red   MILT 467:12
curtains: c. of Solomon   BIBLE 81:6
  Damp c. glued against   HILL 338:10
  fringèd c. of thine eye   SHAK 625:11
  gap between the lace c.   GREE 317:6
  Nottingham lace of the c.   BETJ 67:3
curteis: C. he was, lowely   CHAU 192:12
curteisie: honour, fredom and c.   CHAU 192:8
curteisye: mirour of alle c.   CHAU 192:4
curtiosity: full of 'satiable c.   KIPL 401:20
curtsey: C. while you're thinking   CARR 182:20
curtsies: Low-crooked c.   SHAK 591:11
curve: with inviolate c.   CRANE 225:25
Curzon: George Nathaniel C.   ANON 16:15
Cusha: C.!' calling   ING 360:4
cushion: c. and soft Dean invite   POPE 520:21
cuss: don't matter a tinker's c.   SHIN 645:29
custodes: custodiet ipsos C.?   JUV 384:2
custodierit: Dominus c. civitatem   BIBLE 108:4
custom: contrary to c. and experience   HUME 355:7
  C. calls me to 't   SHAK 570:10
  c. lie upon thee   WORD 746:1
  c. loathsome to the eye   JAM 361:17
  c. made this life more   SHAK 567:24
  c. reconciles us to everything   BURKE 158:4
  c. should call upon the world   TENN 682:23
  c. rule prevails   JOU 632:14
  c., the tie helping all law   DAN 220:4
  c. of the world   U HH 701:16
  C., that unwritten law   HIIU 056:4
  C., then, is the great guide   HUME 355:3
  custom to whom c.   BIBLE 100:5
  c., who all sense doth   SHAK 577:22
  law and duty and c.   WAUGH 723:9

custom: (cont.):
  sitting at the receipt of c.   BIBLE 90:4
  wither her, nor c. stale   SHAK 565:8
  you also follow the c.   AMBR 10:6
customer: c. is never wrong   RITZ 541:12
customers: raising up a people of c.   SMITH 651:1
customs: ancient c. and its manhood   ENN 278:1
  c. of his tribe and island   SHAW 635:26
cut: c. his throat before   SWIFT 675:14
  c. my conscience to fit   HELL 331:8
  C. off, and for the book   MILT 470:16
  c. off Israel out   BIBLE 75:22
  c. off out of the land   BIBLE 84:13
  evening it is c. down   BOOK 130:23
  guardsman's c. and thrust   HUXL 358:4
  Look at the c., the style   LOES 426:3
  that shall not be c. off   BIBLE 84:19
  they will c. off my head   CHAR 191:7
  was the most unkindest c.   SHAK 592:14
  You can c., or you can drug   LOW 429:14
cutlets: suggested we play 'C.'   GROS 319:4
cut-purse: c. of the empire   SHAK 577:16
cuts: C. off so many years   SHAK 591:16
cutting: c. edge of the mind   BRON 141:17
cuttlefish: c. squirting out ink   ORW 501:1
Cutty-sark: Weel done, C.!   BURNS 163:10
cycle: C. and epicycle, orb in   MILT 472:1
  c. of deprivation   JOS 380:15
  Europe than a c. of Cathay   TENN 685:20
cycle-clips: My c. in awkward reverence   LARK 409:14
cyclone: South Bend c.   RICE 540:3
cygnets: swan her downy c.   SHAK 587:12
cymbal: or a tinkling c.   BIBLE 101:1
  talk but a tinkling c.   BACON 43:21
cymbals: upon the well-tuned c.   BOOK 135:17
cynic: precepts from the C. tub   MILT 464:6
  What is a c.   WILDE 735:12
cynicism: C. is intellectual dandyism   MFR 457:23
cynosure: c. of neighbouring eyes   MILT 465:11
Cynthia: He that lets his C. lie   GREV 318:5
cypress: c. in the palace walk   TENN 688:13
  in sad c. let me be laid   SHAK 629:17
  little noise outside the c.   LAWR 412:11
cypresses: Along the avenue of c.   LAWR 412:13
Cyprus: rings black C. with a lake   FLEC 286:12
Cyrene: parts of Libya about C.   BIBLE 98:7
Cythera: It's C., so they say   BAUD 55:10
Cytherea: C., how bravely thou   SHAK 571:1
Czechoslovakia: able to gain for C.   CHUR 202:6

D

d: I never use a big, big D   GILB 305:24
  there are your d's for you   WYCH 750:6
da: D. mi basia mille   CAT 186:1
  d. quod iubes et iube quod   AUG 37:3
dad: d. present at the conception   ORTON 499:13
  girls in slacks remember D.   BETJ 67:4
  To meet their D., wi' flichterin'   BURNS 161:15
dada: mama of d.   FAD 279:19
daddy: My heart belongs to D.   PORT 525:4
  yo' d.'s rich, and yo'   HEYW 338:2
daffadowndillies: Strew me the ground with d.   SPEN 660:26
daffed: that d. the world aside   SHAK 581:19
daffodil: On a bed of d. sky   TENN 686:17
  shining d. dies   TENN 687:4
daffodillies: d. fill their cups   MILT 466:11
daffodils: d. that come before the swallow   SHAK 632:4
  d. were for Wordsworth   LARK 410:12
  D. in d. we weep to see   HERR 337:4
  host, of golden d.   WORD 744:15
  dawn, pour d, so beautiful   WORD 743:2
  with d. I begin to see   SHAK 631:4
daft: warld daft wi' their d.   BURN 590:28
dagger: d. of the mind, a false   SHAK 601:12

dagger: (cont.):
  d. which I see before me   SHAK 601:12
  desperate deadly daunting d.   WYCH 750:6
daggers: fighting with d. in a hogshead   SCOTT 561:5
  Give me the d.   SHAK 602:4
  I will speak d. to her   SHAK 577:1
  There's d. in men's smiles   SHAK 602:19
dahin: D.! Dahin   GOET 309:16
daily: d. beauty in his life   SHAK 618:3
  d. increase in thy   BOOK 123:13
  Give us this day our d. bread   BIBLE 89:5
  My d. labour to pursue   WESL 728:10
  through my d. complaining   BOOK 126:8
  which cometh upon me d.   BIBLE 102:1
dainties: For d. are all cates   SHAK 624:15
  hath not fed of the d.   SHAK 598:15
  spiced d., every one   KEATS 387:9
  We donnot want d.   GASK 299:5
daintily: D. alights Elaine   BETJ 68:2
  must have things d. served   BETJ 67:11
dainty: Nothing's so d. sweet   FLET 287:17
dairy: doth nightly rob the d.   JONS 378:17
dairymaid: Queen asked the D.   MILNE 462:15
  That strapping d.   PAST 508:9
daisies: Buttercups and d.   HOW 353:6
  d. and discourse in novel   GILB 305:16
  d. growing over me   KEATS 392:16
  D. smell-less, yet most quaint   FLET 287:19
  D., those pearlèd Arcturi   SHEL 642:23
  men callen in our toun   CHAU 195:2
  Meadows trim with d. pied   MILT 465:11
  Tansy, calaminth and d.   SMART 649:7
  When d. pied and violets blue   SHAK 599:10
daisy: D. and Lily   SITW 648:14
  'd.,' or 'ye of day'   CHAU 195:3
  d., primrose, violet   THOM 696:1
dalliance: d. in the wardrobe lies   SHAK 585:1
  primrose path of d.   SHAK 573:2
dam: pretty chickens and their d.   SHAK 604:9
  She did not give a singel d.   FLEM 286:19
damage: can pay for the d. if   CLOU 207:12
  moral or intellectual d.   KRUG 404:5
damaged: Archangel a little d.   LAMB 406:28
  D. people are dangerous   HART 327:10
damages: He first d. his mind   ANON 21:15
Damascus: rivers of D.   BIBLE 76:21
damasked: tiger-moth's deep-d.   KEATS 387:5
dame: And modest d. Lurch   BLAKE 114:10
  belle d. sans merci   KEATS 388:12
  belle d. sans mercy   KEATS 387:10
dames: d. in whom he did delight   BYRON 168:2
  Stoutly struts his d. before   MILT 465:8
  Ye high, exalted, virtuous d.   BURNS 161:1
dammed: saved by being d.   HOOD 344:12
damn: d. her at a venture   LAMB 407:11
  d. the consequences   MILN 463:7
  D. the torpedoes   FARR 281:1
  d. those authors whom they   CHUR 200:14
  D. with faint praise   POPE 519:32
  d. you England   OSB 501:20
  I care not a d.   CLOU 207:12
  I don't give a d.!   MITC 478:3
  old man who said, 'D.   HARE 326:7
  praises one another d.   WYCH 750:8
  with a spot I d. him   SHAK 592:23
damnation: blasted to eternal d.   SHAW 638:21
  deep d. of his taking-off   SHAK 601:3
  from everlasting d.   BOOK 119:17
  From sleep and from d.   CHES 199:3
  Heap on himself d.   MILT 468:10
damnations: Twenty-nine distinct d.   BROW 152:28
damned: All silent, and all d.   WORD 746:13
  beautiful and d.   FITZ 284:21
  brandy of the d.   SHAW 637:10
  d. and luxurious mountain   SHAK 586:12
  D. below Judas   COWP 222:7
  d. for never a king's son   SHAK 579:26
  D. from here to Eternity   KIPL 399:6
  d. lies and statistics   DISR 249:13
  d. to everlasting fame   POPE 522:21
  d. would make no noise   HERR 337:10

damned: (cont.):
Faustus must be d. — MARL 447:1
foremost shall be d. to Fame — POPE 518:20
have written a d. play — REYN 539:3
health or goblin d. — SHAK 573:9
Life is just one d. thing — HUBB 353:10
public be d. — VAND 708:9
Publish and be d. — WELL 727:13
those who shall be d. — JOHN 376:12
will be d. if you don't — DOW 256:1
damning: careless of the d. sin — COWP 222:5
d. those they have no mind — BUTL 166:7
damnosa: D. hereditas. — GAIUS 296:18
D. quid non imminuit dies — HOR 350:5
damns: d. the vast majority — MACD 437:7
damozel: blessed d. leaned out — ROSS 547:14
damp: d. souls of housemaids — ELIOT 272:7
lakes d., and mountains — STEP 663:17
or years d. my intended — MILT 472:18
poisonous d. of night — SHAK 566:3
damsel: A d. with a dulcimer — COL 210:13
Dan: D. even to Beer-sheba — BIBLE 74:23
Danaë: lies the Earth all D. — TENN 688:13
Danaos: timeo D. et dona ferentis — VIRG 712:14
dance: at least before they d. — POPE 522:26
change partners and d. — BERL 65:15
d. attendance — SHAK 589:13
d. attendance upon my old — YEATS 753:9
D., dance, dance, little lady — COW 220:8
d. e'er cam to the land — BURNS 161:22
d., for the figure — AUDEN 34:7
d. in the old dame yet — MARQ 448:15
d. is a measured pace — BACON 42:5
D. on the sands, and yet — SHAK 635:12
D. on this ball-floor thin — BLUN 116:3
dancer from the d. — YEATS 750:18
d. round in a ring — FROST 295:10
D. then wherever you may — CART 184:13
d. to the music of time — POW 528:6
d. up and down till I am — SKEL 649:3
departs too far from the d. — POUND 527:13
from the car-park the d. — BETJ 68:7
He fixed thee 'mid this d. — BROW 152:12
Learn then to d., you — DAV 232:7
Let's face the music and d. — BERL 65:16
Love makes them d. — DAV 232:6
Mystical d., which yonder — MILT 472:2
On with the d.! let joy — BYRON 168:16
Or to d. at our bridal — SCOTT 560:6
see me d. the Polka — GROS 319:1
there the d. is — ELIOT 270:16
When you d. it bust to bust — GREN 318:1
when you do d., I wish — SHAK 632:5
who have learned to d. — POPE 521:16
will you join the d. — CARR 182:14
danced: d. before the Lord — BIBLE 75:10
d. by the light — LEAR 414:15
d. round and round like — WORD 742:20
his didn't he d. his did — CUMM 228:5
I d. in the morning — CART 184:13
ye have not d. — BIBLE 90:26
dancer: Curled minion, d. — ARN 28:14
Degas d. pirouettes — MERR 458:12
know the d. from the dance — YEATS 750:18
dancers: d. are all gone under — ELIOT 270:20
nation of d., singers — EQUI 278:10
To the d. dancing in tune — TENN 686:18
dances: d. with the daffodils — WORD 744:16
He capers, he d. — SHAK 610:16
makes no progress; it d. — LIGNE 421:14
Their d. were procession — CORB 218:13
We shall have no time for d. — MACN 441:5
danceth: hope d. without music — HERB 336:4
dancing: And d. dogs and bears — HODG 340:16
are d. not on a volcano — FLAU 285:17
D. in the chequered shade — MILT 465:13
[D.] a perpendicular expression — SHAW 638:30
d. is love's proper exercise — DAV 232:5
Fluttering and d. in the breeze — WORD 744:15
manners of a d. master — JOHN 371:16
Our diversion was d. — TURN 705:14
Say I am a d.; if in mirth — SHAK 564:22
Singing, d. to itself — COL 209:11

dancing: (cont.):
together d. cheek-to-cheek — BERL 65:21
You and I are past our d. days — SHAK 622:23
dandy: Candy is d. — NASH 490:18
I'm a Yankee Doodle D. — COHAN 208:13
dandyism: Cynicism is intellectual d. — MER 457:23
Dane: antique Roman than a D. — SHAK 579:10
You never get rid of the D. — KIPL 401:8
Dane-geld: paying the D. — KIPL 401:8
danger: bright face of d. — STEV 667:9
But only when in d. — OWEN 503:8
d. chiefly lies in acting — CHUR 200:16
D. justified privilege — WAUGH 724:7
D. knows full well — SHAK 591:6
d. of her former tooth — SHAK 603:3
d. of Popery so long — ADD 4:15
d. of the past was — FROMM 294:7
D., the spur of all great — CHAP 191:3
d. to the country — VICT 710:11
Happy am I who out of d. sit — AST 32:6
having any share in the d. — LUCR 431:15
much as to be out of d. — HUXL 358:6
Oft in d., oft in woe — WHITE 731:4
Oh, woeful state, oh d. deep — GILB 303:11
One would be in less d. — NASH 490:11
Out of this nettle, d. — SHAK 580:10
per cent of its d. — SURT 672:8
Pleased with the d. — DRYD 259:1
run into any kind of d. — BOOK 119:4
scared by an imaginary d. — HUME 355:8
shall be in d. of hell — BIBLE 88:29
that we are in great d. — SHAK 585:19
There is d. from all men — ADAMS 2:26
There is no d. to a man — CHAP 190:15
they put themselves in d. — WYATT 749:19
which everything is in d. — NIET 495:8
dangerous: All delays d. in war — DRYD 261:34
Damaged people are d. — HART 327:10
d. deceits — BOOK 135:25
d. moment for bad government — TOCQ 699:1
interest's on the d. edge — BROW 148:13
Into the d. world I leapt — BLAKE 114:8
literature is that it is d. — MORT 486:8
little knowledge is d. — HUXL 358:6
Mad, bad, and d. to know — LAMB 406:2
more d. than an idea — ALAIN 7:2
so many a d. thing — BISH 110:3
such men are d. — SHAK 590:6
To a most d. sea — SHAK 609:1
were d. to meet it alone — WHAR 730:5
dangers: D. by being despised — BURKE 159:8
d. I had passed — SHAK 615:3
d. thou canst make us scorn — BURNS 163:8
fear of tomorrow's d. — DONNE 253:10
No d. fright him, and no — JOHN 370:16
On the d. of the seas — PARK 506:25
perils and d. of this night — BOOK 119:11
so many and great d. — BOOK 120:14
dangling: yon d. apricocks — SHAK 620:14
Daniel: D. come to judgement — SHAK 609:16
spoken of by D. the prophet — BIBLE 92:10
Dan McGrew: Dangerous D. — SERV 563:8
Danny: hangin' D. Deever — KIPL 398:18
Dante: D. never stays too long — MAC 435:1
D., who loved well — BROW 151:16
That highte D. — CHAU 194:4
dapper: d. from your napper — COLL 213:6
dappled: Glory be to God for d. things — HOPK 345:19
dapple-dawn-drawn: d. Falcon — HOPK 346:10
dapples: D. the drowsy east — SHAK 614:17
dare: Do I d. to eat a peach — ELIOT 272:6
do menace heaven and d. — MARL 447:22
have the courage to d. — DOST 254:11
I can d. to be poor — GAY 300:13
Letting 'I d. not' wait — SHAK 601:5
licence to d. anything — HOR 347:2
Nobody'll d. — HUGH 354:1
none d. call it treason — HAR 326:12
Take me if you d. — PANK 505:17
unworthiness we d. not — BOOK 122:18
What man dare, I d. — SHAK 603:11

dare: (cont.):
what men d. do — SHAK 614:8
dared: Determined, d., and done — SMART 650:4
dares: do that d. love attempt — SHAK 622:31
Who d. do more is none — SHAK 601:6
Who d. wins — ANON 19:20
Darien: Silent, upon a peak in D. — KEATS 390:3
daring: d. young man on the flying — LEYB 421:11
dark: All d. and comfortless — SHAK 596:22
Among these d. Satanic mills — BLAKE 113:4
And we are for the d. — SHAK 566:22
At one stride comes the d. — COL 211:3
blind man in a d. room — BOWEN 138:3
children fear to go in the d. — BACON 43:8
Climb to our proper d. — YEATS 753:10
colours will agree in the d. — BACON 45:3
damned long, d., boggy — GOLD 311:24
d., amid the blaze — MILT 474:1
d. and go into the dark — MANN 445:3
d. and true and tender — TENN 688:6
D. as the world of man — SITW 648:13
d. backward and abysm — SHAK 625:1
d. inscrutable workmanship — WORD 746:21
d. is light enough — FRY 295:20
d. night of the soul it — FITZ 285:5
D. the sky and dark the night — PUSH 532:11
D. was the nyght as pich — CHAU 194:1
D. with excessive bright — MILT 470:18
d. world where gods have — ROET 544:8
day of his death was a d. — AUDEN 34:13
ever-during d. — MILT 470:16
fantastical Duke of d. corners — SHAK 606:22
great leap in the d. — HOBB 340:14
hell, as d. as night — SHAK 635:9
he that hides a d. soul — MILT 463:27
I knew you in this d. — OWEN 503:20
In the nightmare of the d. — AUDEN 34:15
i' the d. to rise — BROW 152:19
Kept in a d. house — SHAK 630:34
Lady is as good i' th' d. — HERR 336:19
made a leap into the d. — BROWN 144:16
murmur and the poring d. — SHAK 585:14
Out in the d. over the snow — THOM 694:5
raging in the d. — YEATS 751:6
Roland to the D. Tower — BROW 149:3
Sons of the dark and bloody — O'HARA 498:6
strange as in d. summer dawns — TENN 688:5
than vision, he goes d. — BERRY 66:15
That for ways that are d. — HARTE 327:17
They all go into the d. — ELIOT 270:21
this d. world of sin — BICK 108:22
through the blanket of the d. — SHAK 600:16
through the spaces of the d. — ELIOT 272:14
want to go home in the d. — HENRY 333:4
We work in the d. — JAMES 363:1
What in me is d. — MILT 467:21
Yet in thy d. streets shineth — BROO 144:4
darken: Never d. my Dior — LILL 421:15
darkeneth: d. counsel by words without — BIBLE 77:33
darkening: night is d. round me — BRON 142:11
darker: express our d. purpose — SHAK 594:17
darkest: d. day (Live till tomorrow) — COWP 222:15
darkies: d., how my heart grows weary — FOST 291:15
darkling: as on a d. plain — ARN 27:1
D. I listen — KEATS 389:14
darkly: through a glass, d. — BIBLE 101:1
darkness: act of d. with her — SHAK 596:9
against the rulers of this d. — BIBLE 103:1
And universal d. buries all — POPE 519:12
away the works of d. — BIBLE 70:35
Aye on the shores of d. — KEATS 390:24
between two eternities of d. — NAB 489:2
candle than curse the d. — STEV 667:3
cast off the works of d. — BIBLE 100:10
cast out into outer d. — BIBLE 89:32
Chaos and d. heard — MARR 449:7
d. and in the shadow — BIBLE 93:24
d. and put your hand — HASK 328:1

darkness: (*cont.*):
d. and the cold　　　　　　STEV 668:22
d. bind them　　　　　　　TOLK 700:4
d. brings not sleep　　　　PUSH 533:5
d. by his electrical skin　SMART 649:14
D. came down on the field　THAC 691:16
d. comprehended it not　BIBLE 95:37
d. drops again but now　YEATS 753:2
d. falls at Thy behest　　ELL 275:6
d. is no darkness with thee　BOOK 134:19
d. of mere being　　　　JUNG 382:14
d. over the land of Egypt　BIBLE 72:7
d. that it may be night　BOOK 132:9
d. was upon the face　　BIBLE 69:20
Dawn on our d. and lend　HEBER 330:2
detail leafed from the d.　HUGH 354:5
Downward to d., on extended　STEV 666:11
far as light excelleth d.　BIBLE 80:4
his D. and his Brightness　BYRON 173:17
His d. beautiful with thee　TENN 683:27
In chains and d., wherefore　MONT 480:7
In spite of d., it was day　CRAS 226:6
instruments of d. tell us truths　SHAK 600:10
into the d. of the grave　MILL 461:6
Is d., the fruit thereof dust　SWIN 676:12
I will encounter d. as a bride　SHAK 606:10
jaws of d. do devour it up　SHAK 610:23
land of d. and the shadow　BIBLE 77:15
Lighten our d., we beseech　BOOK 119:11
little d. upon nature　LAUD 411:4
loved d. rather than light　BIBLE 96:16
Love's glory doth in d. shine　CHAP 190:17
lump bred up in d.　KYD 404:14
make d. more visible　EDG 266:13
No light, but rather d. visible　MILT 468:1
passed the dense d.　FITZ 284:6
people that walked in d.　BIBLE 82:26
Peradventure the d. shall　BOOK 134:19
pestilence that walketh in d.　BOOK 131:3
Prince of d. and dead　SPEN 659:23
prince of d. is a gentleman　SHAK 596:15
race that long in d. pined　SCOT 561:11
Ring out the d. of the land　TENN 684:11
Scatters the rear of d. thin　MILT 465:8
Shares the d.—presently　MILL 461:10
silent d. born　DAN 229:16
slope through d. up to God　TENN 683:21
Such as sit in d.　BOOK 132:15
then d. again and a silence　LONG 428:1
there is d. everywhere　NEHRU 491:6
there was an ocean of d.　FOX 292:1
To sit in d. here　MILT 469:19
When awful d. and silence reign　LEAR 413:20
where the light is as d.　BIBLE 77:16
winds will call the d.　SHEL 643:8
with the d. all the night　COL 210:7
world to d. and to me　GRAY 315:10
darksome: along the d. road　CAT 185:14
Who never spent the d. hours　GOET 309:15
darlin': oh, he's a d. man　O'CAS 497:15
darling: call you d. after sex　BARN 53:11
d. buds of May　SHAK 633:6
d. of our crew　DIBD 238:16
green lap was Nature's d.　GRAY 316:6
Mayst find thy d. in an urn　CAREW 179:10
my d. from the lions　BOOK 126:17
my d., my life　POE 518:2
Robey is the D. of the music　SMITH 651:16
She is the d. of my heart　CAREY 179:18
darlings: wealthy curlèd d.　SHAK 614:28
dart: And shook a dreadful d.　MILT 470:5
Time shall throw a d. at thee　BROW 146:24
darter: d.'s youngest darter　PHIL 514:8
darts: fiery d. of the wicked　BIBLE 103:1
mend thy many brittle d.　WYATT 749:16
dastard: tower a lend. in war　SCOTT 560:5
dater d. will live in infamy　ROOS 546:4
keep them up to d.　SHAW 636:13
Standard d. air, ye rue out of d.　BENN 63:8
dateless: d. bargain to engrossing dust　SHAK 624:0
dates: Manna and d.　KEATS 387:9
daubed. d. it with slime　BIBLE 71:34

daughter: all to my elder d.　THOM 694:2
As is the mother, so is her d.　BIBLE 85:21
D. am I in my mother's house　KIPL 400:5
d. hath soft brown hair　CALV 175:10
d. of a hundred Earls　TENN 684:21
d. of debate　ELIZ 274:17
d. of the gods, divinely　TENN 680:20
D. of the Moon, Nokomis　LONG 427:15
d. of Zion is left　BIBLE 82:8
Don't put your d. on the stage　COW 220:15
Elderly ugly d.　GILB 306:22
ever rear a d.　GAY 299:11
father would wish his d.　ANON 13:10
first dead lies London's d.　THOM 693:14
Gigantic d. of the West　TENN 681:14
had taken his little d.　LONG 428:3
He loved the bailiff's d. dear　BALL 48:20
His d. went through　BUNY 156:15
I am the d. of Earth and Water　SHEL 640:7
King's d. is all glorious　BOOK 127:13
landlord's black-eyed d.　NOYES 497:5
My father had a d. loved　SHAK 629:20
O my ducats! O my d.　SHAK 608:15
One fair d. and no more　SHAK 575:3
slain thine only d. thus　SHAK 627:2
Sole of his voice　MILT 472:23
Stern d. of the voice of God　WORD 746:9
Still harping on my d.　SHAK 574:20
virgin-d. of the skies　DRYD 261:32
well-reputed, Cato's d.　SHAK 591:3
Yea, Carnage is thy d.　WORD 746:8
daughterly: d. love and dear charity　MORE 484:16
daughters: all the d. of music　BIBLE 81:1
came in unto the d. of men　BIBLE 70:25
d. may be as the polished　BOOK 135:4
d. of my father's house　SHAK 629:21
d. of the Philistines rejoice　BIBLE 75:8
d. were among thy honourable　BOOK 127:12
forget that words are the d.　JOHN 367:20
O ye d. of Jerusalem　BIBLE 81:6
thunder, fire, are my d.　SHAK 595:21
Words are men's d.　MADD 441:14
dauntless: D. the slug-horn　BROW 149:3
so d. in war　SCOTT 560:4
that with d. breast　GRAY 315:15
was d. on every occasion　WALP 720:9
dauphin: kingdom of daylight's d.　HOPK 346:10
David: D. his ten thousands　BIBLE 75:6
King D. wrote the Psalms　NAYL 491:3
Once in royal D.'s city　ALEX 8:11
Davy: Sir Humphrey D.　BENT 64:13
daw: I am no wiser than a d.　SHAK 587:8
dawn: brown fog of winter d.　ELIOT 273:1
catch and to reflect the d.　MAC 435:4
d. comes up like thunder　KIPL 400:1
d. of life unto the grave　EGER 267:12
d. of the morning after　ADE 5:5
D. on our darkness　HEBER 330:2
dusk and d. many a head　MÜLL 487:16
grey d. breaking　MAS 453:7
Hail, redemption's happy d.　CASW 185:4
music of its trees at d.　ARN 27:16
Rosy-fingered d.　HOMER 343:12
see by the d.'s early　CUMM 228:6
that d. to be alive　WORD 744:5
through night hooting at d.　BEER 59:17
We'd see truth d. together　BROW 148:10
Will sing at d.,—and yet　BROW 147:2
dawning: bird of d. singeth all　SHAK 572:2
d. of the age of Aquarius　RADO 535:8
dawns: How many d., chill　CRANE 225:25
strange as in dark summer d.　TENN 688:5
day: alternate night and d.　FITZ 283:15
And d.'s at the morn　BROW 151:28
And named a trysting d.　MAC 436:9
arrow that flieth by d.　BOOK 131:3
benight our happiest d.　DONNE 252:1
blight cold d. in April　PYM 529:8
bright d. is done　SHAK 566:22
burden and heat of the d.　BIBLE 81:28
close the drama with the d.　THOM 65:13

day: (*cont.*):
compare thee to a summer's d.　SHAK 633:6
d. and a night Love sang　SWIN 676:3
d. and night shall　BIBLE 70:29
d. becomes more solemn　SHEL 640:19
d. be time enough to mourn　DAN 229:16
d. brought back my night　MILT 474:27
Day by d. like us he grew　ALEX 8:14
D. by day: we magnify thee　BOOK 118:14
d. dawned clear and untroubled　RAC 535:5
d. for me to look upon　SHAK 631:6
d. in a pillar of a cloud　BIBLE 72:13
d. is at hand　BIBLE 100:10
d. is gone, and all　KEATS 386:11
d. is past, and yet　TICH 698:3
d. is still here　LOW 430:8
d. joins the past eternity　BYRON 169:1
d. long from 10 till 4　BELL 61:22
d. of his death was a dark　AUDEN 34:13
d. of his wrath is come　BIBLE 106:17
d. of salvation　BIBLE 101:19
d. of small nations has　CHAM 189:4
d. of the Lord　BIBLE 86:9
d. of vengeance　BIBLE 84:26
d. of wrath, will　MISS 477:11
d. older and deeper in debt　TRAV 702:4
d. or a brief period　ARIS 25:9
D., or the sweet approach　MILT 470:16
d. o' the Oppressor　KIPL 401:13
d. perish wherein I was　BIBLE 77:6
d. star arise in your hearts　BIBLE 105:22
d. that has dawned　HOR 348.6
d. the music died　MCL 439:8
d. there cometh the dark　HAWES 328:3
d. Thou gavest　ELLI 275:6
d. war broke out　WILT 738:22
d. warn us not to hope　HOR 350:16
d. when heaven was falling　HOUS 351:22
d. which the Lord hath　BOOK 133:16
death of each d.'s life　SHAK 602:2
each d. dies with sleep　HOPK 345:18
ebbs out life's little d.　LYTE 433:16
end of a perfect d.　BOND 117:17
end of this d.'s business　SHAK 593:16
Ev'ry d. a little dies　SOND 656:1
first d. of our Jubilee　BROW 146:12
Friends, I have lost a d.　TITUS 698:8
Gets her through her busy d.　JAGG 361:10
Go ahead, make my d.　FINK 282:24
Good things of d. begin　SHAK 603:5
greater light to rule the d.　BIBLE 69:23
Hide me from d.'s garish eye　MILT 464:25
I have met them at close of d.　YEATS 751:13
it is not yet near d.　SHAK 623:22
it perfect d. nor night　SHAK 587:29
It was Thy d., sweet　CRAS 226:6
it were a d. very meet　MORE 484:16
Joy ruled the d.　DRYD 261:20
knell of parting d.　GRAY 315:10
lark at break of d.　SHAK 633:10
last, everlasting d.　DONNE 251:18
left alone with our d.　AUDEN 36:8
long d.'s journey into night　O'NEI 498:19
long d. wanes　TENN 690:4
long weary d. have end　SPEN 659:14
mind on an ordinary d.　WOOLF 742:6
more unto the perfect d.　BIBLE 78:11
morning were the first d.　BIBLE 69:21
murmur of a summer's d.　ARN 28:3
my night be turned to d.　BOOK 134:19
night do penance for a d.　WORD 747:3
night of this immortal d.　SHEL 642:19
not a second on the d.　COOK 218:3
not what a d. may bring　BIBLE 79:24
Now's the d., and now's　BURNS 163:1
one d. in thy courts　BOOK 130:18
One d. telleth another　BOOK 125:4
one place, all in one d.　BOIL 117:4
or in the shortest d.　SURR 672:4
posteriors of this d.　SHAK 599:5
precincts of the cheerful d.　GRAY 315:18
profit every d. doth live　HUN 040:7
seize the d., put no　HOR 040:9

day: (*cont.*):

shall not burn thee by d.	BOOK 133:23
singer of an empty d.	MORR 485:11
So foul and fair a d.	SHAK 600:4
Spirit on the Lord's d.	BIBLE 105:33
stand at the latter d.	BIBLE 77:25
street breaks the blank d.	TENN 683:6
succeeds thy little d.	PEAC 510:11
take the whole long d.	ROSS 547:11
that tarrieth but a d.	BIBLE 87:5
their d. and cease	TENN 682:28
There's night and d.	BORR 136:14
this d. as if thy last	KEN 393:6
This is the d. of prayer	ELL 275:7
This'll be the d. that I die	MCL 439:8
thou d. in night	SHAK 623:17
thousand blossoms with the d.	FITZ 283:11
tomorrow is another d.	MITC 478:4
Underneath D.'s azure eyes	SHEL 641:7
Until the d. break	BIBLE 81:11
unto the d. is the evil	BIBLE 89:13
upon every d. to be lost	JOHN 376:19
vital, fine d.: today	MALL 442:18
wave's intenser d.	SHEL 641:16
week, a natural d.	MARL 447:1
welcome d.	BUNY 156:15
w'en de great d. comes	HARR 327:9
when our d. was fair	HARDY 325:15
Which heaven to gaudy d.	BYRON 173:3
who dwell in realms of d.	BLAKE 111:10
whole d. well in this world	THOM 692:9
Without all hope of d.	MILT 474:1
with some streaks of d.	SHAK 603:6
with which thoughts the d.	KING 396:13

day-blind: feel above me the d. stars

	BERRY 66:13

daydreams: d. do not prevent

	NAB 488:20
d. of melancholy men	DRYD 261:18

day-labour: Doth God exact d.

	MILT 474:24

daylight: all the long and lone d.

	SHEL 643:22
can see a church by d.	SHAK 613:14
kind of d. in the mind	ADD 4:14
kingdom of d.'s dauphin	HOPK 346:10
methinks is but the d. sick	SHAK 610:6
not let in d. upon magic	BAG 47:7
We burn d.	SHAK 610:13

Dayrolles: Give D. a chair

	CHES 198:26

days: And drawing d. out

	SHAK 591:15
And the d. grow short	AND 11:8
because the d. are evil	BIBLE 102:22
behold these present d.	SHAK 634:18
best d. of life slip away	VIRG 715:16
burnt-out ends of smoky d.	ELIOT 272:13
Cast your mind on other d.	YEATS 753:17
cause that the former d.	BIBLE 80:13
chequer-board of nights and d.	FITZ 284:7
d. after he has been chosen	CHUR 203:4
d. are swifter than a weaver's	BIBLE 77:13
D. are where we live	LARK 409:16
d. darken round me	TENN 682:22
d. go by, I remain	APOL 23:15
d. of gathering flowers	PEAC 510:12
d. of golden dreams had	BRON 142:17
d. of Methuselah were nine	BIBLE 70:24
d. of our youth	BYRON 173:8
d. of wine and roses	DOWS 256:3
d. that are no more	TENN 688:3
d. will finish up the year	SHAK 588:1
end my d. in a tavern	ANON 22:9
finished in the first 1000 d.	KENN 393:15
good d. speed and depart	MART 449:14
In the brave d. of old	MAC 436:12
itself only three d. old	JEANS 363:25
Length of d. is in her right	BIBLE 78:8
length of d. understanding	BIBLE 77:19
life with multitude of d.	JOHN 370:18
me all the d. of my life	BOOK 125:15
midst of his d.	BIBLE 85:13
My d. are in the yellow leaf	BYRON 173:1
number of my d.	BOOK 126:22
number our d.	BOOK 131:2
our d. on the earth	BIBLE 76:32
O ye Nights, and D.	BOOK 118:18

days: (*cont.*):

seemed unto him but a few d.	BIBLE 71:16
shall shortly see better d.	BEHN 60:12
Six d. shalt thou labour	BIBLE 72:16
teach much which the d.	EMER 277:5
that thy d. may be long	BIBLE 72:16
these fair well-spoken d.	SHAK 621:16
We have seen better d.	SHAK 626:13
woman is of few d.	BIBLE 77:21
would fain see good d.	BOOK 126:15

day-star: d. in the ocean bed

	MILT 466:13

daytime: my God, I cry in the d.

	BOOK 125:9

day-to-day: d. business life

	LAF 405:15

dazzle: d. for an hour

	MORR 484:3
mine eyes d.	WEBS 725:23

dazzled: D. thus with height of place

	WOTT 749:5
Eyes still d. by the ways	LIND 423:4
flowed in it d. their eyes	BALL 49:14

dea: *Et vera incessu patuit d.*

	VIRG 712:8

deacons: Priests, and D.

	BOOK 119:19

dead: act as if d. already

	POUND 527:6
After that it's d.	WAUGH 724:4
all our best men are d.	PUNCH 532:5
already three parts d.	RUSS 551:16
And he is d., who will not	GREN 318:2
And I mysel' were d. and gane	BALL 51:3
And simplify me when I'm d.	DOUG 255:12
And what was d. was Hope	WILDE 736:3
Ay, d.! and were yourself	BROW 153:18
barrows of the happier d.	TENN 689:12
Beautiful Evelyn Hope is d.	BROW 149:20
be blooming well d.	SAR 556:4
been d. these two years	CHES 198:24
being d. unto sin	BOOK 123:1
besides, the wench is d.	MARL 447:15
Better be with the d.	SHAK 603:3
Better red than d.	ANON 12:14
better than a d. lion	BIBLE 80:18
Blessed are the d.	BIBLE 107:5
Books are not absolutely d.	MILT 475:3
Born down in a d. man's town	SPR 661:13
But two months d.: nay	SHAK 572:12
character d. at every word	SHER 645:16
charity more than the d.	ARN 26:15
Chile. Not many d.	COCK 208:5
cold and pure and very d.	LEWIS 421:2
Come not, when I am d.	TENN 680:16
composer is to be d.	HON 343:14
conference with the d.	WEBS 725:18
consistent people are the d.	HUXL 357:12
converse with the mighty d.	THOM 696:13
D.! and never called me mother	WOOD 742:1
D. battles, like dead generals	TUCH 704:23
d., but in the Elysian	DISR 249:8
D., for a ducat, dead	SHAK 577:7
d. had no speech	ELIOT 271:3
D. he is not, but departed	LONG 427:5
d. he would like to see	HOLL 342:3
d. level of provincial	ELIOT 269:23
d. lies London's daughter	THOM 693:14
d. men lost their bones	ELIOT 273:4
d. more than the living	BIBLE 80:7
d., quick	DYER 264:14
d. rest well who lived	CLARE 204:21
D., Right Reverends	DICK 239:14
d. selves to higher things	TENN 682:30
d. shall be raised incorruptible	BIBLE 101:14
d. shall go down to thee	SWIN 676:22
d. shall live, the living	DRYD 261:26
d. shall not have died	LINC 422:10
d. sinner revised	BIER 109:15
d. sound on the final stroke	ELIOT 273:1
d. there is no rivalry	MAC 435:1
d. to rapture and despair	MARK 446:7
d. we owe only truth	VOLT 717:1
d. which he slew	BIBLE 74:21
d. woman bites not	GRAY 315:5
d. writers are remote from	ELIOT 273:19
democracy of the d.	CHES 199:19
dew on the face of the d.	BEERS 59:22
Down among the d. men let	DYER 265:9

dead: (*cont.*):

Either he's d., or my watch	MARX 451:17
ere I am laid out d.	HERR 336:7
Faith without works is d.	BIBLE 104:29
Fame is a food that d. men	DOBS 249:21
famous calm and d.	BROW 149:27
fell at his feet as d.	BIBLE 106:1
female atheist talks you d.	JOHN 370:7
fire live—and we d.	BYRON 171:12
For Lycidas is d., dead	MILT 465:20
For y'cr a lang time d.	ANON 12:12
found, when she was d.	GOLD 310:21
From the throat of a d. man	GRAV 314:20
full of d. men's bones	BIBLE 92:6
Had I lain for a century d.	TENN 686:20
has been d. many times	PATER 509:5
healthy and wealthy and d.	THUR 697:15
Hector is d.	SHAK 628:7
He is d. and gone, lady	SHAK 577:35
He is d., the sweet musician	LONG 427:18
heroic happy d.	CUMM 228:6
if the d. rise not	BIBLE 101:9
If the d. talk to you	SZASZ 677:14
imagined for the mighty d.	KEATS 386:14
I'm d. behind these eyes	OSB 501:11
immortal d. who live again	ELIOT 269:22
In the long run we are all d.	KEYN 395:11
Is d. and dumb and done	DE L 236:4
I would that I were d.	TENN 686:6
judge the quick and the d.	BOOK 119:1
King of all these the d.	HOMER 343:13
kissed by the English d.	OWEN 503:15
ladies and lovely knights	SHAK 634:17
Lady Dalhousie are d.	MCG 437:16
lasting mansions of the d.	CRAB 224:25
Let the d. bury their dead	BIBLE 90:2
Let the dead Past bury its d.	LONG 427:9
Lilacs out of the d. land	ELIOT 272:21
living among the d.	BIBLE 95:30
madman shakes a d. geranium	ELIOT 272:4
maid is not d.	BIBLE 90:10
millions of the mouthless d.	SORL 656:17
Mindful of th' unhonoured d.	GRAY 315:19
Mistah Kurtz—he d.	CONR 217:6
more to say when I am d.	ROB 542:9
noble Living, and the noble D.	WORD 747:8
not d.—but gone before	ROG 544:12
number of the d.	D'AV 231:19
once d. by fate	BEAU 56:15
or himself must be d.	AUST 39:24
over the rich D.	BROO 143:3
past is the only d.	THOM 694:1
Phoenician, a fortnight d.	ELIOT 273:11
pleasure we'd rather be d.	COW 220:10
Protection is not only d.	DISR 249:5
quick, and the d.	DEWAR 238:7
quite for ever d.	CONG 215:18
recoil from things gone d.	LAWR 411:13
resurrection of the d.	BIBLE 101:13
sculptured d., on each	KEATS 386:21
sea gave up the d.	BIBLE 107:16
Sea shall give up her d.	BOOK 135:20
servant's cut in half; he's d.	GRAH 313:11
she is dead; she's d.	DONNE 250:8
sleeping and the d.	SHAK 602:4
sleeps with the enduring d.	SHEL 639:21
Smiling the boy fell d.	BROW 150:14
somewhere that falls down d.	BARR 54:7
Strike them all d.	DICK 242:30
tenantless and the sheeted d.	SHAK 571:26
ten to see a d. Indian	SHAK 625:17
that are d. to sin	BIBLE 99:27
that's a d. donkey	DICK 243:25
that thou wert d. before	CONS 217:20
their home among the d.	SHEL 640:10
their wages and are d.	HOUS 351:22
There are no d.	MAET 441:17
they found him with the d.	WILDE 735:33
they told me you were d.	CORY 219:15
This my son was d.	BIBLE 95:5
those who are d.	BURKE 158:21
to be said for being d.	BENT 64:12
towns contend for HOMER d.	ANON 17:19

dead: (*cont.*):
up with our English d.   SHAK 585:7
vastly more ways of being d.   DAWK 232:18
very d. of Winter   ANDR 11:13
very d. of winter   ELIOT 271:17
voice of the d. was   TENN 684:18
Weep me not d., in thine   DONNE 252:23
When I am d., I hope it   BELL 61:26
When I am d., my dearest   ROSS 547:12
when only the d. smiled   AKHM 6:11
Where d. men meet, on lips   BUTL 167:10
where the d. leaf fell   KEATS 387:23
where there was not one d.   BIBLE 72:11
Who was alive and is d.   ANON 14:6
you remind me of the d.   SASS 557:8
dead-born: d. from the press   HUME 355:18
deadened: carpets with d. force   BETJ 67:7
deadener: habit is a great d.   BECK 58:2
dead-level: d. of income or wealth
  TAWN 678:21
deadlock: Holy d.   HERB 333:21
deadly: more d. in the long run   TWAIN 706:5
more d. than the male   KIPL 399:3
deadness: dropping-down-d.   SMITH 653:2
Dead Sea: Like D. fruits   MOORE 483:15
Deadwood: Tucson and D.   BENÉT 62.15
deaf: But turn the d. ear   SWIFT 674:24
d., how should they know   SORL 656:17
d. pillows will discharge   SHAK 604:17
would prove me d. and blind   BROW 153:8
deafer: d. than the blue-eyed cat   TENN 681:29
deafness: tale, sir, would cure d.   SHAK 625:2
deal: be given a square d.   ROOS 546:10
new d. for the American   ROOS 545:15
There was a faith-healer of D.   ANON 18:15
dealbabor: et super nivem d.   BIRLE 107:28
dealing: whose own hard d.   SHAK 608:2
dean: cushion and soft D.   POPE 520:21
D. of Christ Church   SPR 661:11
no dogma, no D.   DISR 249:6
sly shade of a Rural D.   BROO 143:11
deans: dowagers for d.   TENN 687:24
dear: dangerously d.   BYRON 169:22
d., deluding woman   BURNS 163:21
d. in the sight   BOOK 133:14
D. Lord and Father of mankind   WHIT 733:7
D. One is mine as mirrors   AUDEN 35:18
d. to me as are the ruddy   SHAK 591:2
d. to them that love her   SPR 661:9
fault, d. Brutus   SHAK 590:3
make thee terrible and d.   SHEL 643:22
Plato is d. to me   ARIS 26:3
Serve it right for being so d.   DICK 242:2
sold cheap what is most d.   SHAK 634:21
that bread should be so d.   HOOD 344:9
this dear, d. land   SHAK 619:18
too d. for my possessing   SHAK 634:11
dearer: d. still is truth   ARIS 26:3
D. than self, possesses   BYRON 168:7
d. to a man who is deprived   DOST 255:1
d. was the mother   COL 211:19
little d. than his horse   TENN 685:9
thy mouth is d. unto me   BOOK 133:19
dearest: d., you're a dunce   JOHN 375:25
I assure you she's the d. girl   DICK 240:3
My near'st and d. enemy   SHAK 581:15
To throw away the d. thing   SHAK 600:14
dearie: For thinking on my d.   BURNS 161:8
dearly: D. beloved brethren   BOOK 118:5
D. beloved, we are gathered   BOOK 123:15
dearth: measure in a year of d.   BLAKE 112:21
pine within and suffer d.   SHAK 635:7
death: added a new terror to d.   WETH 729:22
added another terror to d.   LYND 433:14
After the first d.   THOM 693:14
ancients dreaded d.   HARE 326:4
And d. unloads thee   BLAK 606:7
And d., not had the soldier   DOUG 255:19
And Life, the shadow of d.   SWIN 676:1
And make d. proud to take us   SHAK 601:17
are at the point of d.   SHAK 624:7
back resounded D.   MILT 470:9
bargain to engrossing d.   SHAK 624:9

death: (*cont.*):
Be absolute for d.   SHAK 606:6
be carnally minded is d.   BIBLE 99:34
been studied in his d.   SHAK 600:14
Be thou faithful unto d.   BIBLE 106:4
better to be eaten to d.   SHAK 582:24
Birth, and copulation, and d.   ELIOT 272:17
birth and d., we do   MANN 445:3
birth, and not at their d.   MONT 481:13
Black Widow, d.   LOW 430:16
bleeding to d. of time   GRAV 314:19
bridegroom in my d.   SHAK 566:10
brother of d.   BROW 146:22
Brother to D.   FLET 287:20
Brother to D., in silent   DAN 229:16
Brought d. into the world   MILT 467:19
brought d. into the world   TWAIN 706:19
build the house of d.   MONT 480:16
but no one his d.   SEN 563:2
Capital, where kingly D.   SHEL 639:13
captains courageous whom d.   BALL 50:2
Come away, come away, d.   SHAK 629:17
Come lovely and soothing d.   WHIT 733:4
Comes D., and takes   BARN 53:18
competition the laws of d.   RUSK 551:5
consenting unto his d.   BIBLE 98:13
darkness and the shadow of d.   BIBLE 77:15
day of our Jubilee is d.   BROW 146:12
days shall men seek d.   BIBLE 106:26
dead in silence like to d.   BROW 147:14
Dear, beauteous d.   VAUG 709:7
d. after life does greatly   SPEN 660:2
D. alone reveals how small   JUV 384:10
d. and he forgets to live   LA BR 405:2
d., and Hell that was   BUNY 156:11
D. and his brother Sleep   SHEL 640:8
d., and I will coquette   MARQ 448:15
D. and Morning on the silver   TENN 688:15
d., and mutability   SHEL 642:18
D. and taxes and childbirth   MITC 478:2
death and the sole d.   BROW 149:11
D. and Toil   VIRG 713:14
d., a necessary end   SHAK 591:5
d. approached unlocked   GIBB 302:22
d. as children fear   BACON 43:8
D. be not proud   DONNE 250:22
d. brag thou wander'st   SHAK 633:6
D. breaks into the cottages   HOR 349:3
D. broke at once the vital   JOHN 375:30
D. came with friendly care   COL 210:1
D. cancels everything   HAZL 329:8
D. closes all   TENN 690:4
[D.] comes equally to us   DONNE 253:7
D. cometh soon or late   MAC 436:10
d. complete the same   BROW 152:13
D. destroys a man   FORS 290:15
D. devours all lovely things   MILL 461:10
d. does end and each day   HOPK 345:18
D., ere thou hast slain   BROW 146:24
d. ever life devouring   ALAB 7:1
d. gnaweth upon them   BOOK 128:1
D.! Great proprietor   YOUNG 754:14
d. had been his neighbour   SCOTT 560:1
D. has a thousand doors   MASS 453:16
D. has got something   AMIS 11:3
D. has made his darkness   TENN 683:27
d. hath no more dominion   BIBLE 99:29
D. hath so many doors   FLET 287:15
d. hath ten thousand several   WEBS 725:22
D. hath this also   BACON 43:11
d. in a blizzard to try   ATKI 32:13
D., in itself, is nothing   DRYD 260:5
d., in thy possession   SHAK 567:12
D. is a fearful thing   SHAK 606:11
d. is as a lover's pinch   SHAK 567:7
D. is beautiful   ANOU 23:7
D. is like a fisherman   TURG 705:10
d. is most in apprehension   SHAK 606:9
[D. is] nature's way   ANON 12:31
d. is no such terrible   BACON 43:9
d. is not anything   STOP 670:7
D. is nothing at all   HOLL 342:4
D. is nothing if one can   CORN 999:7

death: (*cont.*):
D. is still working like   HERB 335:5
d. is the cure   BROW 146:18
D. is the end of life   TENN 688:8
D. is the only great emotion   FULL 296:3
D. is the privilege   ROWE 549:7
d. is to lose belief   DU B 263:3
D. joins us to the great   YOUNG 755:1
D. lays his icy hand on kings   SHIR 646:2
D. lies dead   SWIN 676:15
D. lies on her like   SHAK 624:1
D. like a narrow sea divides   WATTS 723:5
d. lives, and nature breeds   MILT 470:4
d. makes us think about   DE G 235:9
D. must be distinguished   SMITH 653:26
D. my life and fortune   CAMP 177:4
D. never takes the wise   LA F 405:13
d. no more dreadfully   SHAK 606:20
d. obscured that eye   KEATS 390:22
d. of a political economist   BAG 47:9
d. of each day's life   SHAK 602:2
d. of his saints   BOOK 133:14
d. on the hunting-field   MORT 486:5
D. opens unknown doors   MAS 453:10
d. part thee and me   BIBLE 74:25
d. reveals the eminent   SHAW 637:35
d.'s counterfeit   SHAK 602:15
d. shall have no dominion   THOM 693:3
d.'s pale flag is not advanced   SHAK 624:8
D.'s second self   SHAK 634:6
D.'s shadow at the door   BLUN 116:1
D. stands above me   LAND 408:1
d.'s wing flashed ahead   AKHM 6:6
d. that is immortal has   LUCR 432:3
d. the journey's end   DRYD 261:13
D. therefore is nothing   LUCR 432:2
d. they were not divided   BIBLE 75:9
D. thou shalt die   DONNE 250:23
D. tramples it to fragments   SHEL 640:4
D. was never enemy of ours   OWEN 503:16
d. what dreams may come   SHAK 575:16
D. will be aghast   MISS 477:12
D. will come when thou   SHEL 643:23
d. will have his day   SHAK 620:6
D. will make thee lay it   FLAT 285:15
d. will provide the meaning   ALAI 7:5
D., without rhetoric   SIEY 647:13
d. your vital twist shall   DAV 232:7
direful d. indeed they had   FLEM 286:19
disappointed by stroke of d.   JOHN 369:3
disgrace of d.   SHAK 598:6
disqualified by accident of d.   CHES 199:20
Doctor said that D. was   WILDE 736:2
does d. lie heavily   SEN 563:3
doth but gain his d.   RAL 535:12
doubt is nothing but d.   UNAM 707:2
Do we take up in d.   SHIR 646:6
dread of something after d.   SHAK 575:16
dull cold ear of d.   GRAY 315:14
dust, across which d.   BERRY 66:12
E'en D., to die for thee   HERR 337:3
enormously improved by d.   SAKI 553:6
envy of the cruel d.   BIBLE 86:27
even hard at d.'s door   BOOK 132:16
Ev'ry day a little d.   SOND 656:1
except d. and taxes   FRAN 293:3
faith that looks through d.   WORD 746:6
Fear d.?—to feel the fog   BROW 152:4
fed on the fullness of d.   SWIN 676:21
feet go down to d.   BIBLE 78:12
Finality is d. Perfection   STEP 663:19
flower-bell, some one's d.   BROW 148:11
For d. and life, in ceaseless   NORT 497:1
for restful d. I cry   SHAK 634:4
For since by man came d.   BIBLE 101:7
forth the d. of princes   SHAK 591:5
Found d. in life, may here   COL 209:22
friend and enemy is but D.   BROO 143:17
from sudden d.   BOOK 119:17
from the body of this d.   BIBLE 99:33
Glad to d.'s mystery   HOOD 343:16
half dead, a living d.   MILT 474:3
Larch d. snatches away   VIRG 715:16

deceive: (cont.):
d. even from their earliest   IRWIN 360:20
d. you with vain words   BIBLE 102:21
don't d. me   ANON 12:34
no sin, we d. ourselves   BIBLE 105:25
they lie in wait to d.   BIBLE 102:17
When first we practise to d.   SCOTT 560:8
Who could d. a lover   VIRG 713:5
deceived: by bad women been d.   MILT 474:5
should we desire to be d.   BUTL 165:22
still d. with ornament   SHAK 608:26
deceiver: I'm a gay d.   COLM 214:2
Welcome, thou kind d.   DRYD 260:2
deceivers: Men were d. ever   SHAK 613:24
deceiveth: d. his own heart   BIBLE 104:28
deceiving: D. world, that with   GREE 317:8
d. your own selves   BIBLE 104:27
She d., I believing   SEDL 561:17
December: D. when they wed   SHAK 569:18
From May to D.   AND 11:8
In drear nighted D.   KEATS 387:32
old D.'s bareness everywhere   SHAK 634:16
rain and wind beat dark D.   SHAK 571:8
Their meetings made D. June   TENN 684:8
Decembers: fifteen wild D.   BRON 142:15
decencies: dwell in d. for ever   POPE 520:10
decency: believe in an ultimate d.   STEV 668:12
D. is Indecency's conspiracy   SHAW 637:34
Terrible that old life of d.   LOW 430:10
want of d. is want of sense   DILL 246:4
decent: aristocracy to what is d.   HOPE 344:23
d. obscurity   GIBB 302:20
d. people live beyond their incomes   SAKI 553:8
decently: done d. and in order   BIBLE 101:3
deceptive: d. visions that way   VIRG 714:1
decide: comes the moment to d.   LOW 430:3
d. such a great dispute   VIRG 714:20
decision: fast and specific d.   TUCH 704:24
make a 'realistic d.'   MCC 436:20
monologue is not a d.   ATTL 32:19
questions of will or d.   CHOM 200:5
valley of d.   BIBLE 86:9
decisions: d. he is allowed to take   PARK 507:5
deck: boy stood on the burning d.   HEM 331:10
d. her mistress' head   BYRON 173:4
d. my Captain lies   WHIT 732:7
d. on each occasion   LODGE 425:19
d. put on its leaves again   FLEC 286:13
why do we d.   BEHN 60:9
decked: should duly have been d.   SPEN 659:17
thy bride-bed to have d.   SHAK 578:28
decks: fell upon their d.   TENN 689:5
declamatio: Ut pueris placeas et d. fias   JUV 384:9
declaration: make up the D. of Independence   CHOA 200:2
There has been no d. of war   EDEN 266:7
declarations: And timid lovers' d.   AUDEN 35:10
declare: And then, I d.   HOFF 341:3
d. except my genius   WILDE 736:8
d., if thou hast understanding   BIBLE 77:34
d. the wonders   BOOK 132:15
heavens d. the glory   BOOK 125:4
Matrimony, ye are to d. it   BOOK 123:14
declension: by this d. into madness   SHAK 574:17
decline: d. and fall of the city   GIBB 302:18
height, are ready to d.   SHAK 593:12
Morn in weary Night's d.   BLAKE 111:23
declined: Carrie rightly d.   GROS 319:4
decomposing: d. in the eternity of print   WOOLF 742:5
decoration: descended to construct a d.   TROL 703:8
decorative: d. and to do right   FIRB 282:25
decorum: Dulce et d. est   HOR 349:25
Goes all d.   SHAK 605:7
hunt D. down   BYRON 172:9
Let none … about D.   BURNS 162:11
decoyed: these poor fools d.   FLE⊓⊓   ⊓⊓
des… d. from Caesar Augustus   BIBLE 93:25
coℓatiⁿ⊓⊓ ⊓⊓, d.   DIBL⊓ 85:⊓⊓
Teague, dost hear dé D.   WⁿⁿⁿⁿR 7⊓⊓,⊓

decrees: contrary to the d. of Caesar   BIBLE 98:28
dedicate: d. your volumes to Prince   CLAR 205:12
dedis: gentil that dooth gentil d.   CHAU 194:27
dee: Across the sands of D.   KING 397:13
Hi diddle dee d.   WASH 722:3
Lived on the river D.   BICK 108:20
deed: attempt and not the d.   SHAK 601:16
better day, the worse d.   HENRY 332:17
bloody d.! almost as bad   SHAK 577:8
both in will and d.   BOOK 121:1
d. is all, the glory nothing   GOET 309:7
d. of dreadful note   SHAK 603:4
d. without a name   SHAK 603:20
good d. in a naughty world   SHAK 610:4
horrid d. in every eye   SHAK 601:3
If one good d. in all   SHAK 627:3
leff woord and tak the d.   LYDG 433:5
right d. for the wrong   ELIOT 272:10
so I may do the d.   KEATS 390:11
Y'are the d.'s creature   MIDD 459:14
deeds: because their d. were evil   BIBLE 96:16
be nameless in worthy d.   BROW 145:22
d. that some knights used   CAXT 188:3
d. that ye do upon   MORR 485:15
D. to thy knowledge answerable   MILT 473:12
Foul d. will rise   SHAK 572:24
My d. upon my head   SHAK 609:14
no more your mighty d.   SHIR 646:3
Our d. determine us   ELIOT 268:15
though the sager sort our d.   CAMP 177:3
deem: better d. t'have lived to be   DAN 229:18
doubt to d. himself a god   POPE 522:9
deemed: d. necessary that I should   BROWN 144:13
Some d. him wondrous wise   BEAT 56:4
deep: commit his body to the d.   BOOK 135:20
day have I been in the d.   BIBLE 102:1
d. almost as life   WORD 746:1
d. are dumb   RAL 535.19
D. as first love, and wild   TENN 688:5
d. have I called   BOOK 134:11
D. in the shady sadness   KEATS 387:22
d. is the silence   DRIN 258:10
d. like as with a garment   BOOK 132:6
d. moans round   TENN 690:4
d. peace of the double-bed   CAMP 176:6
d. sense of some deathless   WEBS 726:4
d. silent slide away   SIDN 646:12
d. upon her peerless eyes   KEATS 389:6
D.-versed in books   MILT 473:22
face of the d.   BIBLE 69:20
From the great d.   TENN 681:20
gentle motion with the d.   DAV 232:14
glory forth tell in d. tone   BAKER 47:21
heard the d. behind him   TENN 682:21
his wonders in the d.   BOOK 133:1
lowest d. a lower deep   MILT 470:25
Not d. the Poet sees, but wide   ARN 27:21
often lie too d. for tears   WORD 746:7
One d. calleth another   BOOK 127:4
one is of the d.   STEP 663:17
Plunge it in d. water   HOR 350:13
Rocked in the cradle of the d.   WILL 736:20
unadornèd bosom of the d.   MILT 463:14
very d. did rot   COL 211:1
They cannot look in d.   FROST 295:6
Though d., yet clear   DENH 236:17
thunders of the upper d.   TENN 684:19
'tis not so d. as a well   SHAK 623:13
too d. for his hearers   GOLD 311:4
when the remorseless d.   MILT 466:3
deepens: d. like a coastal shelf   LARK 410:7
deeper: day older and d. in debt   TRAV 702:4
d. sense of her loss   GASK 299:3
d. than did ever plummet   SHAK 626:1
In d. reverence praise   WHIT 733:7
what is d. than the ave   BALL 50:7
deep-hearted. ⁿⁿ ⁿⁿ, ⁿⁿⁿⁿⁿⁿⁿ   BROW 147.14
deep meadowed: D., happy   TENN 682:16
⊓⊓⊓⊓, ⊓⊓⊓⊓ ⊓⊓ running of the d.   ANON 14:11

deer: (cont.):
Around the dying d.   AYT 41:3
D. walk upon our mountains   STEV 666:11
In the stare of the d.   WILB 734:2
I was a stricken d.   COWP 223:23
let the stricken d. go   SHAK 576:20
deeth: d. moot wepe and pleyne   CHAU 193:18
Toward his d., wher as hym   CHAU 193:25
défauts: Quelle âme est sans d.   RIMB 541:9
defeat: are triumph and d.   LONG 427:6
Dear Night! this world's d.   VAUG 708:16
d. is an orphan   CIANO 203:16
In d.: defiance   CHUR 203:3
In d. unbeatable   CHUR 203:13
possibilities of d.   VICT 710:13
we know we should d. you   KIPL 401:8
defeated: Down with the d.   LIVY 423:12
History to the d.   AUDEN 36:8
safe course for the d.   VIRG 712:21
We were d. in a great battle   LIVY 423:13
defect: did make d. perfection   SHAK 565:7
this fair d. of Nature   MILT 473:5
defence: And our d. is sure   WATTS 723:7
at one gate to make d.   MILT 474:8
cheap d. of nations   BURKE 158:14
d. against the atom bomb   ANON 12:13
D., not defiance   ANON 12:32
d. of England you no longer   BALD 48:10
d. of the country   ARIS 26:6
d. of the indefensible   ORW 500:26
d. or apology before you   CHAR 191:5
extremism in the d. of liberty   GOLD 312:1
fight in d. of one's country   HOMER 343:8
house of d. very high   BOOK 131:4
Lord is thy d. upon   BOOK 133:23
only d. against betrayal   WILL 737:1
only d. is in offence   BALD 48:9
defend: D. me, therefore, common sense   COWP 223:26
d. my cause against   BOOK 127:6
D., O Lord, this thy Child   BOOK 123:13
d. ourselves with guns   GOEB 308:14
D. the bad against the worse   DAY-L 231:7
d. to the death your right   VOLT 717:5
d. us from all perils   BOOK 119:11
D. us thy humble servants   BOOK 119:3
has nothing left to d.   SHEN 644:18
defended: What God abandoned, these d.   HOUS 351:22
defends: attacked it d. itself   ANON 20:7
defensoribus: Non tali auxilio nec d. istis   VIRG 713:2
defer: 'tis madness to d.   YOUNG 754.15
defiance: Defence, not d.   ANON 12:32
d. in their eye   GOLD 311:10
In defeat: d.   CHUR 203:3
défier: d. de ses amis   LA R 410:14
defiled: pitch shall be d.   BIBLE 87:19
defileth: into the mouth d. a man   BIBLE 91:9
define: remorse than know how to d. it   THOM 692:2
To d. true madness   SHAK 574:12
defined: ill-d., ill-cultivated   MAC 435:23
definition: capable of exact legal d.   RUSS 551:23
d. is the enclosing a wilderness   BUTL 167:3
good working d. of hell   SHAW 638:13
definitions: which they call D.   HOBB 339:18
deflower: her pride d.   SPEN 660:6
deformed: called d. but the unkind   SHAK 630:30
my invention prove d.   SHAK 635:10
deformity: Art is significant d.   FRY 295:26
shall see the time's d.   JONS 378:20
defrauding: d. of the State   PENN 511:16
defy: d. the devil   SHAK 630:22
d. the foul fiend   SHAK 596:10
d. the omnipotent to arms   MILT 467:23
dégagé: Or half so d.   COWP 222:16
degeneration: fatty d. of his moral being   STEV 667:30
dégoût: des moments de d.   VOLT 716:18
⊓ⁿⁿⁿⁿⁿⁿⁿ; breath of d. and of pride   BYRON 172:17

degree: exalted them of low d.   BIBLE 93:23
Observe d., priority   SHAK 627:6
or yet in high d.   SURR 672:4
O! when d. is shaked   SHAK 627:7
degrees: d. that this brief world   SHAK 626:16
things through all d.   WORD 748:11
Dei: Ad majorem D. gloriam   ANON 22:1
Introibo ad altare D.   JOYCE 381:17
Vox populi, vox D.   ALC 8:2
deified: By our own spirits are we d.
  WORD 747:11
deil: d.'s awa wi' th'Exciseman   BURNS 161:22
deities: some other new d.   PLATO 516:9
deity: D. and the Drains   STR 670:17
D. but accepted Carnot's   WELLS 727:15
D. disowns me   COWP 222:8
For D. offended   BURNS 161:25
deject: ladies most d.   SHAK 576.4
dejected: d. 'haviour of the visage   SHAK 572:10
lowest and most d. thing   SHAK 596:23
delay: chides his infamous d.   YOUNG 754:17
In d. there lies no plenty   SHAK 629:4
In me is no d.   MILT 473:13
Nothing was ever lost by d.   GREE 316:21
or d., right or justice   MAGN 442:2
sweet reluctant amorous d.   MILT 471:6
think not much of my d.   KING 396:11
delayed: d. till I am indifferent   JOHN 371:13
delaying: d. put the state to rights   ENN 278:2
make the gift rich by d.   TROL 703:26
delays: d. are dangerous in war   DRYD 261:34
D. have dangerous ends   SHAK 587:10
Shun d., they breed remorse   SOUT 658:1
delectable: came to the D. Mountains
  BUNY 156:4
delectando: Lectorem d.   HOR 347:15
delegate: When in trouble, d.   BOREN 136:7
delenda: D. est Carthago   CATO 185:8
deleted: Expletive d.   ANON 13:6
Delia: While D. is away   JAGO 361:15
deliberate: D. speed, majestic instancy
  THOM 695:2
O, these d. fools   SHAK 608:19
Where both d., the love   MARL 447:10
deliberates: woman that d. is lost   ADD 3:19
deliberation: D. sat and public care   MILT 469:18
delicate: mind's free, body's d.   SHAK 596:4
So d. his motions   BRID 141:5
Sooner or later, d. death   WHIT 733:4
these d. creatures ours   SHAK 616:16
they are not very d.   WALP 719:21
deliciae: d. meae puellae   CAT 185:13
delicias: D. domini   VIRG 714:14
delicious: Thou art to me a d. torment
  EMER 276:23
To this d. solitude   MARV 450:7
We move: D.!   CLOU 207:10
delight: And go to 't with d.   SHAK 565:24
And turn d. into a sacrifice   HERB 334:8
Ay, in the very temple of D.   KEATS 389:7
best gift, my ever new d.   MILT 471:21
But ever to do ill our sole d.   MILT 468:7
d. and ends in wisdom   FROST 295:14
d. at once and lash   POPE 521:3
D. hath a joy in it either   SIDN 647:11
d. in conceiving an Iago   KEATS 391:23
d. is in proper young men   BURNS 162:11
d. of battle with my peers   TENN 690:1
d. of her husband, her aunts   RANS 536:14
d. of her thought   ROET 544:5
D. of lust is gross and brief   PETR 513:15
Energy is Eternal D.   BLAKE 112:14
firmness, and d.   WOTT 749:6
Had other aims than my d.   HARDY 325:11
He did me the d.   JONS 379:15
Him in whose company I d.   BUNY 156:17
immense world of d.   BLAKE 112:30
intent is. All for your d.   SHAK 612:22
labour as in physics   SHAK 602:12
Let dogs d. to bark and bite   WATTS 722:15
lonely impulse of d.   YEATS 752:6
Moved to d. by the melody   AUDEN 34:1

delight: (cont.):
Rose with d. to us   KING 396:13
She was a phantom of d.   WORD 747:19
source of little visible d.   BRON 142:18
Spirit of D.   SHEL 643:2
Studies serve for d.   BACON 44:23
sweet airs, that give d.   SHAK 625:26
sweetest d. of gardens   BROW 145:12
Than to enjoy d. with liberty   SPEN 660:21
Their d. is in lies   BOOK 128:19
There is a land of pure d.   WATTS 723:4
There is d. in singing   LAND 408:6
thing met conceives d.   MILT 472:21
'Tis by succession of d.   SMART 649:16
'Tis never too late for d.   MOORE 483:13
To bind another to its d.   BLAKE 114:7
top-gallant d. is to him   MELV 456:15
truest which men miscall d.   SHEL 640:1
yet I hear thy shrill d.   SHEL 643:16
delighted: d. in solitude is either   BACON 43:20
delightest: d. not in burnt-offerings   BOOK 128:8
delighteth: king d. to honour   BIBLE 76:36
neither d. he in any man   BOOK 135:12
delightful: And almost as d.   LOCK 425:12
inexpressibly rare and d.   TRAH 701:11
marriages, but no d. ones   LA R 410:15
delighting: But, O! d. me   HODG 340:17
by d. the reader   HOR 347:15
delights: D. in filth and foul   SPEN 660:7
does some d. condemn   MOL 479:12
more by reaping; his d.   SHAK 566:20
thee king of intimate d.   COWP 223:33
To scorn d., and live laborious   MILT 466:4
delineation: happiest d. of its varieties
  AUST 38:21
delinquencies: naturally indulge in a few d.
  ELIOT 269:28
delinquent: condemns a less d.   BUTL 166:22
delirant: d. reges plectuntur Achivi   HOR 348:2
delitabill: Storys to rede ar d.   BARB 52:7
deliver: D. Israel, O God   BOOK 125:20
d. me from the body   BIBLE 99:33
d. me from the deceitful   BOOK 127:6
d. my soul from the calamities   BOOK 126:17
d. us from evil   BIBLE 89:5
d. us from evil   MISS 477:3
D. us, good Lord   CHES 199:3
Good Lord, d. us   BOOK 119:17
let him d. him, if   BOOK 125:10
neither shall he d.   BOOK 126:12
delivered: d. them into the hands   BIBLE 73:34
hast d. my soul from death   BOOK 133:12
hath d. him into mine hand   BIBLE 75:6
delivereth: d. them out of their distress
  BOOK 133:2
delivery: ungracefulness of his d.   WALP 720:4
delphiniums: d. blue and geraniums red
  MILNE 462:14
Delphos: shriek the steep of D.   MILT 467:11
deluded: kind of heaven to be d.   LEE 416:2
we are all d. thus   SHEL 640:17
deluding: dear, d. woman   BURNS 163:21
deluge: dazzling d. reigns   THOM 696:4
d. subsides and the waters   CHUR 202:2
déluge: Après nous le d.   POMP 518:12
delusion: added d.   ELIOT 269:6
d., a mockery, and a snare   DENM 237:1
delusive: d. seduction of martial   BURN 160:19
demand: He'll make d. of her   SHAK 567:11
demands: cannot exact their d.   WELL 727:5
demarcations: In ghostlier d.   STEV 665:21
demeaning: So womanly, her d.   SKEL 649:1
demens: Quem fugis, a! d.?   VIRG 714:16
demented: not one is d.   WHIT 732:18
demerit: preacher's merit or d.   BROW 149:6
demesne: private pagus or d.   AUDEN 35:16
demeure: Les jours s'en vont, je d.   APOL 23:15
demi-paradise: This other Eden, d.
  SHAK 619:18
demi-puppets: you d.   SHAK 626:1
demi-tasses: your villainous d.   SMITH 651:10
democracies: in d. the only sacred thing
  FRAN 292:6

democracy: [Blackstone's] D.   BENT 64:5
can be cured by more d.   SMITH 651:6
capacity for justice makes d.   NIEB 495:1
D. and proper drains   BETJ 67:15
D. and socialism are means   NEHRU 491:7
d. can afford among   BEV 69:8
d. can be no more   YOUNG 755:3
d. in a republic   PAGE 504:4
D. is a State which recognizes   LENIN 417:6
D. is the name we give   FLERS 287:9
D. is the recurrent suspicion   WHITE 731:3
D. is the theory   MENC 457:8
d. is the worst form   CHUR 202:23
D. means government   CHES 199:18
D. means government by discussion
  ATTL 32:18
D. means bludgeoning   WILDE 735:23
d. or absolute oligarchy   ARIS 25:18
D. resumed her reign   BELL 61:24
D. substitutes election   SHAW 637:22
D. will not be salvaged   HOGB 341:14
great arsenal of d.   ROOS 546:2
holy name of liberty or d.   GAND 297:8
It is the d. of the dead   CHES 199:19
little less d. to save   ATK 32:12
must be made safe for d.   WILS 738:17
perfect d. is therefore   BURKE 158:20
political aspirant under d.   MENC 457:5
puts in the place of d.   FOSD 291:4
thanks to wine-lees and d.   BROW 148:5
themselves grieved under a d.   HOBB 340:9
Thus our d. was, from   MAC 435:16
Two cheers for D.   FORS 290:30
voting that's d.   STOP 669:14
Democrat: D., in that order   JOHN 367:4
democrats: D. object to men being disqualified
  CHES 199:20
telling lies about the D.   STEV 666:15
Democritus: D. would laugh   HOR 348:18
demon: wailing for her d.-lover   COL 210:10
demonstrandum: Quod erat d.   EUCL 278:20
Demosthenes: D. is not more decidedly
  MAC 434:12
D. never comes unseasonably   MAC 435:1
demur: Don't be surprised if I d.   HEAN 329:19
den: hand on the cockatrice' d.   BIBLE 83:3
made it a d. of thieves   BIBLE 91:30
denial: d. dash my wished desire   ALAB 7:1
d. of Him by the atheist   PROU 530:13
Hence with d. vain   MILT 465:21
denied: Cannot be d.   HARB 323:9
faintly and would be d.   SHAK 621:9
that comes to be d.   MONT 480:4
denies: I am the spirit that always d.
  GOET 309:3
deniges: Who d. of it   DICK 241:25
denizen: spider is sole d.   HARDY 325:1
Denmark: rotten in the state of D.   SHAK 573:12
sure it may be so in D.   SHAK 573:23
Than is the throne of D.   SHAK 572:5
dens: d. and in the rocks   BIBLE 106:17
lay them down in their d.   BOOK 132:9
On the dowie d. o' Yarrow   BALL 49:8
dentist: out of the d.'s hands   EMER 277:10
vulgar to talk like a d.   WILDE 734:10
denunciation: d. of the young   SMITH 652:2
deny: And so ingrateful you d.   SHAK 594:15
d. that faintly prays   QUAR 534:2
I never d.; I never contradict   DISR 249:4
Room to d. ourselves; a road   KEBLE 392:20
sell, or d., or delay   MAGN 442:2
thou shalt d. me thrice   BIBLE 92:26
yet will I not d. thee   BIBLE 92:27
You must d. yourself   GOET 309:4
denying: how to allure by d.   TROL 703:26
deo: D. gratias   MISS 476:20
Ille mi par esse d. videtur   CAT 186:7
Jubilate D., omnis terra   BIBLE 107:30
deoch-an-doris: Just a wee d.   MORR 486:2
deorum: Parcus d. cultor et infrequens
  HOR 349:13
depart: already it is time to d.   SOCR 654:15

DEPARTED DESPOIL

depart: (*cont.*):
D.,—be off HOLM 342:10
Having a desire to d. BIBLE 103:3
he will not d. from it BIBLE 79:11
thy servant d. in peace BIBLE 93:29
departed: Dead he is not, but d. LONG 427:5
dear brother here d. BOOK 124:5
d. into their own country BIBLE 83:10
D., never to return BURNS 161:10
d. this life in thy faith BOOK 122:3
glory is d. from Israel BIBLE 74:32
He d., he withdrew CIC 204:7
not that the Lord was d. BIBLE 74:19
Remembered knolling a d. SHAK 582:13
departing: someone who's d. RILKE 541:2
departure: point of d. is defined by METT 459:2
their d. is taken BIBLE 86:28
depend: did on false thee d. ROCH 543:4
dependant: d. on man's bounty STAN 662:9
dependency: Or old d. of day and night STEV 666:11
depends: It all d. what you mean JOAD 366:8
so much d. upon a red wheel WILL 737:11
That d. on the tip BRAC 138:19
deponere: *longum subito d. amorem* CAT 186:13
depopulating: d. his dominions BECK 58:3
deportment: celebrated for his D. DICK 239:6
To adapt her methods and d. CRANE 225:22
depose: glories and my state d. SHAK 620:20
deposit: Civilization is an active d. CONN 216:16
d. in my name at a Swiss ALLEN 9:17
depositary: d. of power is always unpopular DISR 248:7
depraved: No one ever suddenly became d. JUV 383:18
depravity: innate d. and original MELV 456:12
proof of stupidity than d. JOHN 373:9
depression: d. when you lose yours TRUM 704:19
deprivation: cycle of d. JOS 380:15
D. is for me what daffodils LARK 410:12
depth: And in the d. be praise NEWM 493:13
But far beyond my d. SHAK 588:19
d., and not the tumult WORD 744:17
d. in philosophy bringeth BACON 42:23
hundred feet d. of every acre GURN 320:2
depths: d. I have cried to thee BIBLE 108:5
his d. and his shallows BURNS 163:3
deputy: d. elected by the Lord SHAK 620:3
may be read by d. BACON 44:27
deracinate: That should d. such savagery SHAK 586:17
derangement: nice d. of epitaphs SHER 645:5
derelict: my splendid d., my age MAND 444:4
deride: d. tears I cannot hide HARB 323:9
derision: Lord shall have them in d. BOOK 124:9
Time turns the old days to d. SWIN 676:12
descansada: *Que d. vida* LUIS 432:7
descant: mavis d. plays SPEN 659:14
descend: we too into the dust d. FITZ 283:18
descending: Lo! He comes with clouds d. WESL 728:15
descensus: *Facilis d. Averno* VIRG 713:11
descent: claimed his d. from a monkey WILB 733:18
d. of their last end JOYCE 380:20
Smile at the claims of long d. TENN 684:22
descriptions: I see d. of the fairest wights SHAK 634:17
desert: all out into the d. CLOU 207:26
And the Blast of the D. LONG 427:14
d. of mortification WHITE 731:6
d. shall rejoice BIBLE 83:19
d. sighs in the bed AUDEN 34:4
d. were my dwelling-place BYRON 169:12
every man after his d. SHAK 575:7
Found him in a d. land BIBLE 73:21
its sweetness on the d. GRAY 315:15
Life is the d., life YOUNG 755:1
myself with my own d. places FROST 294:16
[illegible] but the d. [illegible]
owl that is in the d. [illegible]
desert: (*cont.*):
Stand in the d. SHEL 642:3
straight in the d. a highway BIBLE 83:26
streams in the d. BIBLE 83:21
went unrewarded, but d. DRYD 259:9
deserted: D. at his utmost need DRYD 259:19
We never are d. quite SMART 649:16
deserts: D. are there, and different SACK 552:15
D. of vast eternity MARV 451:3
In the d. of the heart AUDEN 34:16
It's my d.; I'm a second BARR 54:2
Or his d. are small GRAH 313:15
When she d. the night MILT 474:2
deserve: d. any thanks from anyone CAT 186:11
d. to get it good and hard MENC 457:8
Sempronius; we'll d. it ADD 3:16
those who really d. them FIEL 282:8
war, but only d. it CHUR 202:14
you somehow haven't to d. FROST 294:15
design: dull there is a d. in it STEE 662:19
designing: Gay coquette, and all d. SANS 555:14
designs: d. were strictly honourable FIEL 282:14
instruments of their crooked d. GODW 308:11
ladder to all high d. SHAK 627:7
large to his own dark d. MILT 468:10
Lofty d. must close in like BROW 150:2
desinat: *D. in piscem mulier formosa* HOR 347:1
desine: *D. de quoquam quicquam* CAT 186:11
desipere: *Dulce est d. in loco* HOR 350:20
desire: all a wonder and a wild d. BROW 152:15
And weariness treads on d. PETR 513:15
As thou art in d.? SHAK 601:5
beauty that we should d. BIBLE 84:11
But D. gratified BLAKE 113:14
d. accomplished is sweet BIBLE 78:28
d. and longing to enter BOOK 130:16
d. at last and vain regret ROSS 548:4
D. attained is not desire RAL 535:12
d. for preventing the things PROU 530:12
d. of power after power HOBB 340:3
d. of the moth SHEL 643:12
d. shall fail BIBLE 81:1
d. should so many years SHAK 583:10
exceed all that we can d. BOOK 121:4
From what I've tasted of d. FROST 294:17
it provokes the d. SHAK 602:11
Land of Heart's D. YEATS 752:9
lineaments of gratified d. BLAKE 113:12
many men d.! that 'many' SHAK 608:16
Memory and d., stirring ELIOT 272:21
nor d. other men's goods BOOK 123:9
on its bough is her d. CRANE 225:21
pleasing hope, this fond d. ADD 3:23
powers of Charm and D. CAT 185:13
shall d. to die BIBLE 106:26
shot and danger of d. SHAK 573:1
than for the d. of the man COL 212:10
that the d. is boundless SHAK 627:16
This grey spirit yearning in d. TENN 690:2
when the d. cometh BIBLE 78:26
Which of us has his d. THAC 691:20
desired: d. are they than gold BOOK 125:5
d. by all healthy and good CIC 204:13
I have d. to go where springs HOPK 345:14
Suffer herself to be d. WALL 718:10
You are not one to be d. TENN 684:21
You who d. so much CRANE 225:26
desires: Ah! two d. toss about ARN 28:22
And my d., like fell SHAK 628:10
by lopping off our d. SWIFT 674:17
consists in doing what one d. MILL 460:19
cradle than nurse unacted d. BLAKE 112:28
d. and other hopes beset BRON 142:16
d. and petitions of thy BOOK 119:9
d. of the heart AUDEN 34:7
d. that only fear GREV 318:7
d. which thereof did ensue DONNE 250:13
devices and d. BOOK 118:7
end of our d. is God THOM 692:16
enough to answer back to d. [illegible]
from whom all holy d. BOOK 110:19
hearts be open, all d. known BOOK 121:16
desires: (*cont.*):
He who d. but acts not BLAKE 112:18
into our minds good d. BOOK 120:16
proportion to our d. MANN 444:13
Question your d. SHAK 610:20
shows of things to the d. BACON 42:1
we fondly flatter our d. DRAY 257:17
desirest: thou d. no sacrifice BOOK 128:8
desireth: hart d. the water-brooks BOOK 127:2
desiring: D. this man's art SHAK 633:10
desirous: d. of being the correct article ASHF 31:11
ought else on earth d. GAY 299:19
desk: From counter or d. YEATS 751:13
Is but a d. to write upon BUTL 166:13
subservience to the d. FRAN 293:7
Turn upward from the d. ELIOT 273:8
votary of the d. LAMB 406:10
desks: stick close to your d. GILB 306:2
desolate: all that are d. BOOK 120:1
d. places for themselves BIBLE 77:7
whisperings around d. shores KEATS 390:6
desolated: have d. and profaned GLAD 307:10
desolation: abomination of d. BIBLE 92:10
D. in immaculate public places ROET 544:4
Love in d. masked SHEL 639:20
My d. does begin to make SHAK 566:19
witnesses to the d. of war GEOR 301:3
years of d. pass over JEFF 364:16
despair: bed thou liest on be d. LYLY 433:12
begins on the far side of d. SART 556:17
Bid me d., and I'll despair HERR 337:3
builds a Heaven in Hell's d. BLAKE 114:6
carrion comfort, D. HOPK 345:7
depth of some divine d. TENN 688:3
D. a smilingness assume BYRON 168:10
d. there are the most intense DOST 255:4
D. was powerless to destroy BRON 142:17
D. yawns HUGO 355:1
Do not d. PUDN 531:5
Drowned with d., with fleshly GREV 318:6
eminence; and from d. MILT 469:10
foundation of unyielding d. RUSS 551:19
have of comfort and d. SHAK 635:6
I can endure my own d. WALSH 720:19
Is all d., or ecstasy WINC 738:24
I shall d. There is no SHAK 622:12
It was begotten by D. MARV 450:2
Lead me from d. to hope KUMAR 404:8
Magnanimous D. alone MARV 450:2
minor form of d. BIER 109:12
now fiercer by d. MILT 469:11
Now Giant D. had a wife BUNY 156:2
or the quality of his d. CONN 216:14
racked with deep d. MILT 468:6
reganing my charecter I d. FLEM 287:4
Should all d. SHAK 631:15
thou needst not then d. ARN 27:4
what resolution from d. MILT 468:9
ye Mighty, and d. SHEL 642:4
despairer: Too quick d. ARN 28:27
despairs: And leaden-eyed d. KEATS 389:10
desperandum: *Nil d.* HOR 349:5
desperate: Beware of d. steps COWP 222:15
Diseases d. grown SHAK 577:27
Tempt not a d. man SHAK 624:5
desperately: d. mortal SHAK 606:20
desperation: lives of quiet d. THOR 696:28
despise: ere you d. the other DRYD 262:14
shalt thou not d. BOOK 128:8
despised: Dangers by being d. BURKE 159:8
d., and dying king SHEL 643:7
d. and rejected of men BIBLE 84:11
d. Mr Tattle of all things CONG 215:15
d. old man SHAK 595:21
Enjoyed no sooner but d. SHAK 635:1
not having hated and d. HAZL 328:15
despising: d. all manner of *éclat* BAG 46:20
d. the shame BIBLE 104:17
thoughts myself almost d. SHAK 633:10
despite: builds a Hell in Heaven's d. BLAKE 114:7
despoil: tremble and d. themselves SHEL 641:17

despond: slough was D.   BUNY 155:14
despondency: end d. and madness
        WORD 747:11
    last words of Mr D. were   BUNY 156:15
    SPREAD ALARM AND D.   PEN 511:12
despot: country governed by a d.   JOHN 374:31
despotism: aiming at d. in England
        WALP 720:10
    D. accomplishes great things   BALZ 51:10
    France was long a d. tempered   CARL 180:23
    or d. will come from either   ARIS 25:18
    political creed is that d.   ADAMS 3:4
    root of d. as virtue   ROB 542:5
despots: D. themselves do not   TOCQ 698:11
destined: Amphitrite's d. halls   SHEL 641:7
    d. by the mysterious powers   GOGOL 310:1
destinies: d. of half the globe   TOCQ 699:5
    d. of the British Empire   DISR 247:3
    d. the play of the contingent   FISH 283:1
    recognised, and robed as d.   LARK 409:15
destiny: Anatomy is d.   FREUD 293:19
    character is d.   ELIOT 269:26
    come I am, the dreary d.   SACK 552:13
    creating a fabric of human d.   DOST 254:6
    D., n. A tyrant's authority   BIER 109:9
    d. to overspread the continent   O'SUL 502:5
    D. with Men for pieces   FITZ 284:7
    Great D. the commissary of God
        DONNE 251:12
    homely joys, and d. obscure   GRAY 315:13
    sea the tide of d.   PAST 508:10
    We hug our little d. again   HEAN 329:22
destitution: shaming D.   VIRG 713:14
destroy: after my skin worms d.   BIBLE 77:25
    age shall be able to d.   OVID 503:2
    Despair was powerless to d.   BRON 142:17
    d. in all my holy mountain   BIBLE 83:3
    d. in mankind the belief   DOST 254:2
    Doth the winged life d.   BLAKE 113:17
    forefathers planted, we d.   WITH 739:13
    hovers o'er, impatient to d.   JOHN 370:18
    I am come not to d.   BIBLE 88:27
    necessary to d. the town   ANON 15:7
    One to d., is murder   YOUNG 754:10
    when man determined to d.   CUMM 228:13
    Whom God would d. He first   DUP 264:8
    Whom the gods wish to d.   CONN 216:11
    Whom the mad would d.   LEVIN 420:6
destroyed: Carthage must be d.   CATO 185:8
    d. by Time's devouring   BRAM 139:16
    made great is a name d.   HILL 339:1
    That not one life shall be d.   TENN 683:18
    that shall be d. is death   BIBLE 101:8
    treated generously or d.   MACH 438:7
destroyer: D. and preserver   SHEL 641:14
    hasn't been a creator, only a.d.   CHEK 197:5
    Is my d.   THOM 693:7
destroyeth: d. in the noon-day   BOOK 131:3
destroying: without d. something else
        UPD 707:9
destroys: Death d. a man   FORS 290:15
    he who d. a good book   MILT 475:4
destruction: d. is also a creative   BAK 47:22
    d. is wrought under   GAND 297:8
    d. of the poor   BIBLE 78:21
    d. of the whole world   HUME 356:1
    economic law on the side of d.   KEYN 395:4
    from us to be utter d.   BIBLE 86:28
    Pride goeth before d.   BIBLE 78:37
    rush and rumble of d.   NIC 494:14
    startles at d.   ADD 3:23
    that leadeth to d.   BIBLE 89:21
    their d. draw   DONNE 251:18
    To say that for d. ice   FROST 294:17
destructive: are essentially d.   CHUR 201:17
    d. element submit yourself   CONR 217:7
    d. of the manhood of living   JERR 366:4
    smiling, d. man   LEE 416:7
desuper: coeli, d., et nubes pluant   BIBLE 108:7
detail: d. leafed from the darkness   HUGH 354:5
    frittered away by d.   THOR 697:6
    Merely corroborative d.   GILB 305:8

detail: (cont.):
    occupied in trivial d.   BAG 46:20
details: d. of every kind   REYN 539:8
    mind which reveres d.   LEWIS 421:5
detect: lose it in the moment you d.
        POPE 520:25
detection: D. is, or ought   DOYLE 256:17
detective: d. novel is   PRIT 529:19
    Hawkshaw, the d.   TAYL 679:22
deteriora: D. sequor   OVID 502:24
determination: d. of incident   JAMES 363:4
determine: much as we d. our deeds
        ELIOT 268:15
determined: D., dared, and done   SMART 650:4
    I am d. to prove a villain   SHAK 621:16
detest: but they d. at leisure   BYRON 171:24
    d. that animal called man   SWIFT 674:1
detestari: neque d., sed intelligere   SPIN 661:3
detestation: country town is my d.
        BURN 160:20
dethrimental: temper till it would be d.
        O'CAS 497:19
detraction: D. is but baseness' varlet
        JONS 378:24
    D. will not suffer it   SHAK 582:1
    Envy's abhorrèd child, D.   MARS 449:8
detrimenti: res publica d. caperet   ANON 22:5
deuce: d. they ever could have   BYRON 170:8
deuil: est le fond même du d.   HUGO 355:1
deum: D. de Deo, lumen de lumine   MISS 476:22
deus: d. nobis haec otia fecit   VIRG 714:12
    Nec d. hunc mensa, dea nec   VIRG 715:2
    Sit D. propitius   ANON 22:9
    Vae, puto d. fio   VESP 710:10
Deutschland: D. über alles   HOFF 340:21
de Valera: Negotiating with d.   LLOY 424:11
devastating: d. or redeeming fires   GONC 312:9
development: d. is allowed to multiply
        NAIRN 489:7
De Vere: name and dignity of D.   CREWE 226:19
deviates: Shadwell never d. into sense
        DRYD 261:2
device: banner with the strange d.
        LONG 426:18
    imagined such a d.   BOOK 125:8
    invention breeds a raw d.   GASC 298:19
devices: d. and desires   BOOK 118:7
    man of many d.   HOMER 343:11
devil: apology for the D.   BUTL 167:2
    assaults of the d.   BOOK 119:17
    because your adversary the d.   BIBLE 105:21
    But the D. whoops   KIPL 398:17
    D. always builds a chapel   DEFOE 234:19
    d. a monk would   MOTT 487:5
    d. and all his works   BOOK 123:4
    d. can cite Scripture   SHAK 607:21
    d. damn thee black   SHAK 604:20
    d., depend upon it   STEV 667:18
    d. haunts thee in the likeness   SHAK 580:30
    d. have all the good tunes   HILL 338:15
    d. in the same churchyard   BANC 51:12
    d. is dead   READE 537:8
    d.-porter it no further   SHAK 602:10
    D. sends cooks   GARR 298:7
    D. should have right   MORE 484:9
    d.'s most devilish when   BROW 147:8
    D. so must we overthrow   GASC 298:18
    D.'s party   BLAKE 112:15
    d. take her   SUCK 671:6
    d. taketh him up   BIBLE 88:20
    d., taking him up into   BIBLE 94:1
    D. that prompts 'em   BROW 151:5
    d. understands Welsh   SHAK 581:10
    d. where he is known   JOHN 370:24
    d. will come, and Faustus   MARL 447:1
    D. with devil damned   MILT 469:22
    Drink and the d. had done   STEV 667:22
    English and the D. knows Latin   KNOX 403:12
    envy of the d. came death   BIBLE 86:27
    fears a painted d.   SHAK 602:4
    first Whig was the D.   JOHN 375:4
    For he counteracts the D.   SMART 649:14
    given the d. a foul fall   MORE 484:10

devil: (cont.):
    hoard of gold kept by a d.   SHAK 583:27
    how the d. they got there   POPE 519:30
    I dreamed of the d.   ANST 23:11
    If the d. doesn't exist   DOST 254:4
    if the d. dress her not   SHAK 567:6
    last: the D. howling   SQUI 661:18
    laughing d. in his sneer   BYRON 169:19
    Let the d. be sometime honoured
        SHAK 606:24
    let us call thee d.   SHAK 616:5
    make a moral of the d.   SHAK 585:20
    man! defy the d.   SHAK 630:22
    man is to go to the d.   NORF 496:11
    man's spirit is d.'s work   SHAW 636:2
    mind that man is but a d.   STEV 667:15
    my back upon Don or d.   TENN 689:2
    name a synonym for the D.   MAC 434:15
    not serve God if the d.   SHAK 614:23
    Old D. Moon in your eyes   HARB 323:11
    Or who cleft the D.'s foot   DONNE 252:14
    poor d. has ended his cares   BROW 151:6
    problem must puzzle the d.   BURNS 163:3
    sacrifice to God of the d.'s leavings
        POPE 524:6
    serpent, which is the D.   BIBLE 107:14
    should dream of the d.   BARH 52:14
    that d.'s madness—War   SERV 563:7
    there the d. would also   LUTH 432:3
    very d. incarnate   SHAK 630:33
    we do sugar o'er the d. himself   SHAK 575:15
    we'll face the d.   BURNS 163:8
    What! can the d. speak true   SHAK 600:9
    when most I play the d.   SHAK 621:22
    world, the flesh, and the d.   BOOK 119:17
    young and sweating d.   SHAK 617:1
    your father the d.   BIBLE 96:33
    You tell me, doubt is D.-born   TENN 684:6
    you the blacker d.   SHAK 618:10
devildoms: Inquisition dogs and the d.
        TENN 689:1
devilish: d. thing is 8 times 8   FLEM 287:1
    Tough, and d. sly   DICK 240:11
devils: become d. in life   ASCH 31:2
    d. being offended   SHAK 615:15
    d. to contest his vision   MAIL 442:9
    d. would set on me in Worms   LUTH 432:11
    He casteth out d. through   BIBLE 90:11
    still 'tis d. must print   MOORE 482:19
    wolves and fight like d.   SHAK 585:13
devious: howling winds drive d.   COWP 222:27
devisal: Past our d.   THOM 695:12
devised: wit of man so well d.   BOOK 118:4
devoid: D. of sense and motion   MILT 469:14
Devon: If the Dons sight D.   NEWB 492:6
    started that morning from D.   GILB 304:16
    'Twas Devon, glorious D.   BOUL 137:16
devotion: D.! daughter of astronomy
        YOUNG 754:22
    d. should not be encouraged   JOHN 372:25
    d. to something afar   SHEL 643:12
    Farewell my bok and my d.   CHAU 195:1
    Matrimonial d.   GILB 305:2
    object of universal d.   IRV 360:18
    Tell zeal it wants d.   RAL 535:16
devour: seeking whom he may d.   BIBLE 105:21
    tears when they would d.   BACON 45:8
    Which d. widows' houses   BIBLE 93:17
devourer: Time the d. of everything   OVID 503:1
devourers: become so great d.   MORE 484:5
devout: less human for being d.   MOL 479:11
    One cannot be d. in dishabilly   FARQ 280:26
dew: begotten the drops of d.   BIBLE 77:36
    continual d. of thy blessing   BOOK 119:8
    d. as e'er my mother brushed   SHAK 625:5
    d. bespangling herb   HERR 336:10
    d. of heaven drops now   FORD 289:8
    d. of yon high eastern   SHAK 572:3
    d. shall weep thy fall   HERB 336:1
    d. will rust them   SHAK 614:27
    drenched with d.   DE L 236:10
    Drop down d., heavens   BIBLE 108:7
    fades awa' like morning d.   BALL 51:2

dew: (*cont.*):
let there be no d.   BIBLE 75:8
meet the morning d.   ARN 28:29
more smell the d. and rain   HERB 335:3
O ye Showers, and D.   BOOK 118:17
resolve itself into a d.   SHAK 572:12
sunlight drinketh d.   TENN 681:4
there rained a ghastly d.   TENN 685:13
Thins to a d. and steams off   HUGH 354:8
dewdrop: fragile on its perilous way   KEATS 390:10
Starlight and d. are waiting   FOST 291:11
dewdrops: I must go seek some d. here   SHAK 611:11
dewfall: rainfall at morning and d.   STEV 668:24
dews: E'er the early d. were falling   ING 360:4
fell ere the d. were dried   TENN 686:6
Nor ask amid the d. of morning   HOUS 352:1
dewy: from noon to d. eve   MILT 469:7
night is fair on the d.   TENN 687:4
On d. pasture, dewy trees   TENN 687:22
shakes his d. wings   D'AV 231:20
deyntee: d. that is in that hous   CHAU 193:26
di: *Quod d. omen avertant*   CIC 204:9
diable: *mon ami, le d. est mort*   READE 537:8
diadem: A royal d. adorns   KELLY 393:4
Bring forth the royal d.   PERR 513:1
flowery d. of frost   BLOK 115:9
diagnostician: rectum makes a good d.   OSLER 502:1
diagonally: d. in his bed again   STER 665:5
dialect: Babylonish d.   BUTL 166:2
d. I understand very little   PEPYS 512:12
picturesque use of d. words   HARDY 324:10
To purify the d. of the tribe   ELIOT 271:5
dial-plate: by looking on the d.   JOHN 372:28
dials: To carve out d.   SHAK 588:1
diamond: body like a rough d.   DEFOE 234:1
D.! thou little knowest   NEWT 494:6
Like a d. in the sky   TAYL 679:14
matchwood, immortal d.   HOPK 346:7
Ours the d. mines of stars   MAY 455:7
rough than polished d.   CHES 198:17
diamonded: d. with panes of quaint   KEATS 387:5
diamonds: D. are a girl's best   ROBIN 542:7
Goodness, what beautiful d.   WEST 729:11
Dian: And hangs on D.'s temple   SHAK 570:23
her as D. had hot dreams   SHAK 571:19
Diana: Great is D. of the Ephesians   BIBLE 99:2
Let us be D.'s foresters   SHAK 579:18
diapason: d. closing full in Man   DRYD 261:23
diary: d. and some day it'll keep me   WEST 729:7
life of every man is a d.   BARR 54:3
diatonic: common d. little numbers   REED 538:3
diavolo: *è un d. incarnato*   ASCH 31:2
dibble: d. in earth to set one   SHAK 632:2
dic: *sed tantum d. verbo*   MISS 477:6
dice: d. dearly   SHAK 596:9
d. will never eliminate   MALL 442:19
God does not play d.   EINS 268:2
some were playing d.   BALL 49:11
dicere: *et quae sentias d. licet*   TAC 678:2
Dick: And D. the shepherd   SHAK 599:11
Dickens: put to D. as children   BENN 63:11
dicky-bird: D., why do you sit   GILB 305:11
dictate: suggest, never to d.   BRON 142:10
who may one day d. to him   JOHN 370:1
dictates: d. to me slumbering   MILT 472:17
woman d. before marriage   ELIOT 269:12
dictation: at d. speed what he knew   AMIS 10:14
dictator: German d.   CHUR 202:6
proclamations of a d.   AMIS 10:10
dictators: D. ride to and fro   CHUR 202:5
which d. may cultivate   BEV 69:8
dictatorship: d. in order to safeguard   ORW 500:16
d. of the proletariat   MARX 452:9
government you have a d.   TRUM 704:16
dictatorship ... in place of democracy   TRO 291:9
d. that could impose for an hour   MILL 463:10

dictionaries: d., a harmless drudge   JOHN 368:1
d. are like watches   JOHN 371:19
To make d. is dull work   JOHN 367:24
dictionary: He will be but a walking d.   CHAP 191:4
seen before outside of a d.   LODGE 425:20
dictum: *dictum quod non d. sit prius*   TER 690:11
D. sapienti sat est   PLAU 517:4
did: d. for them both   SASS 557:11
didn't he danced his d.   CUMM 228:5
ripped her and d. her   MORR 486:1
well, d. you evah   PORT 525:5
didacticism: tempted by d.   BARN 53:9
diddle: d., we take it, is dee   SWIN 676:17
High d. diddle   GILB 305:19
Dido: D. and her Aeneas shall   SHAK 566:9
D. with a willow in her   SHAK 609:24
die: about to d.   JOHN 377:13
about to d. salute you   ANON 22:2
am prepared to d.   SHAK 606:6
and, dear, I d. as often   DONNE 252:8
And d. in music   SHAK 618:15
And how can man d. better   MAC 436:10
And love me, till I was sure to d.   MOORE 483:14
And shall Trelawny d.   HAWK 328:4
And thou must d.   HERB 336:1
And yet I love her till I d.   ANON 18:10
back to America...to d.   JAMES 362:23
because they d.   CORY 220:2
believe they d. to vex me   MELB 456:8
But ye shall d. like men   BOOK 130:15
clean place to d.   KAV 386:4
Cowards d. many times before   SHAK 591:5
Curse God, and d.   BIBLE 77:6
Dar'st thou d.   SHAK 606:9
determine to d. here   BEE 58:15
d. all, die merrily   SHAK 581:21
D., and endow a college   POPE 520:15
d., and go we know   SHAK 606:11
d. before we go quite off   POPE 524:2
d. before we have explained   ADAMS 3:3
d. but do not surrender   CAMB 176:1
d. but once to serve our   ADD 3.21
d. by famine die by inches   HENRY 333:1
Die: d. for adultery! No   SHAK 597:4
d. eating ortolans   DISR 248:36
d. even as we rush   VIRG 712:21
d. for one's country   HOR 349:25
D. he or justice must   MILT 470:17
d. in that man's company   SHAK 586:11
d. in the flower   BIBLE 74:26
d. in the last ditch   WILL 736:21
D. in the lost, lost fight   CLOU 207:6
d. is cast   CAES 174:19
d. is gain   BIBLE 103:2
d. like a true-blue rebel   HILL 338:13
D., my dear Doctor   PALM 505:15
D. not, poor death   DONNE 250:22
d. of that roar which lies   ELIOT 269:17
d. on your feet   IBAR 358:14
d. sweetly was only belonging   DRYD 262:21
d. twenty times upon far   SHAK 564:19
d. well that die in a battle   SHAK 586:4
d. when the trees were   CLARE 204:17
d. who complains of misery   BROW 146:13
d. will be an awfully big   BARR 54:8
d. with harness on our   SHAK 605:2
d. with kissing of my Lord   MARL 448:7
do now not basely d.   SHAK 566:14
Do think hereon that I must d.   SOUT 658:3
Easy live and quiet d.   SCOTT 560:15
ever seems it rich to d.   KEATS 389:14
fall, and d.   DONNE 250:14
Fall asleep, or hearing d.   SHAK 588:16
Few d. and none resign   JEFF 364:12
fifteen-year-old boy until *they* d.   ROTH 548:15
find myself so apt to d.   SHAK 591:20
For as in Adam all d.   BIBLE 101:7
D. we needs must d.   BIBLE 75:11
Glad did I live and gladly d.   STEV 669:8
greatly think, or bravely d.   POPE 519:16

die: (*cont.*):
harder lesson! how to d.   PORT 525:8
have to d. beyond my means   WILDE 736:13
he had to d. in my week   JOPL 380:12
He shall not d.   STER 665:3
He will, he must d.   NICH 494:11
honour I will d. with them   NELS 491:13
Hope I d. before I get old   TOWN 701:7
I change, but I cannot d.   SHEL 640:7
I d. a Christian, according   CHAR 191:10
I die because I do not d.   JOHN 366:13
I d. happy   FOX 291:19
I d., if he die not   ANDR 11:11
I d. pronouncing it   SHAK 619:18
if he d., I die too   ANDR 11:11
If I should d. before I wake   ANON 16:24
If I should d., think only   BROO 143:18
If it were now to d.   SHAK 615:20
If we are marked to d.   SHAK 586:10
If we must d., let it not   MCKAY 439:1
I'll d. for him to-morrow   BALL 48:22
I'm sorry—but we all must d.   SWIFT 675:11
I shall d. at the top   SWIFT 675:17
I shall not altogether d.   HOR 350:10
I sink I'd d. down over   JOYCE 381:8
It is most grand to d.   MAS 453:10
I will d. in peace   WOLFE 741:3
I will not have thee d.   TENN 688:12
Jerusalem shall Harry d.   SHAK 584:5
Let me d. a youngman's death   MCG 438:2
Let us do—or d.   BURNS 163:2
live, begins to d.   QUAR 634:4
live, but to d.   BROW 146:19
live, or dare to d.   POPE 522:19
look about us and to d.   POPE 521:26
lucky to d. and I know it   WHIT 732:16
man can d. but once   SHAK 583:19
might it d. or rest at last   SHEL 640:16
morrow we d.   BIBLE 101:9
Muse forbids to d.   HOR 350:17
must be with us, or we d.   KEATS 386:15
Must d. of love   SHAK 564:2
myself to d. upon a kiss   SHAK 618:21
natural to d. as to be born   BACON 43:10
night to d. upon the sand   ARN 28:15
Not d. here in a rage   SWIFT 674:2
not so difficult to d.   BYRON 172:19
not that I'm afraid to d.   ALLEN 9:15
not willingly let it d.   MILT 476:5
Now that I come to d.   BROW 149:8
Of easy ways to d.   SHAK 567:14
Old soldiers never d.   FOLEY 288:8
or being born, to d.   BACON 46:2
Or bid me d., and I will dare   HERR 337:3
or like Douglas d.   HOME 342:20
passing-bells for these who d.   OWEN 503:12
peace a Christian can d.   ADD 5:3
People can't d., along   DICK 240:6
People d., but books never   ROOS 546:5
Perhaps when we come to d.   ALAI 7:5
poison us, do we not d.   SHAK 608:22
resolve to conquer or d.   WASH 721:23
shall desire to d.   BIBLE 106:26
She answered, "I would d."   PETR 513:13
She must weep or she will d.   TENN 688:9
should d. for the people   BIBLE 97:6
shouldst d. for me   WESL 728:1
Sir Richard Grenville d.   TENN 689:5
sit him down and d.   SHAK 583:14
sky when you d.   HILL 338:12
something he will d.   KING 396:17
sometimes d. to save charges   BURT 164:20
stand the hazard of the d.   SHAK 622:16
suffer and d.   VIGNY 711:12
taught us how to d.   TICK 698:4
that d. ere they be born   GREE 317:8
that have the power to d.   TENN 689:12
that I shall d. to-day   MORE 484:11
that I've longed to d.   PROU 530:9
That we shall d., we know   SHAK 591:15
Their every parting was to d.   TENN 684:8
Their's but to do and d.   TENN 689:14
Then d., dear, d.   REDD 538:9

die: (*cont.*):

thereof thou shalt surely d.	BIBLE 70:3
they d. in yon rich sky	TENN 688:2
They d. not,—for their life	ROSS 548:1
they only let Him d.	STUD 671:4
thinks he was not made to d.	TENN 682:27
Though I should d. with thee	BIBLE 92:27
Thus by feigned deaths to d.	DONNE 252:15
Thus unlamented let me d.	POPE 523:12
time to d.	BIBLE 80:5
To d. and know it	LOW 430:16
To d. the death, for nought	SACK 552:12
To go away is to d. a little	HAR 323:8
To-morrow let us do or d.	CAMP 176:12
to morrow we shall d.	BIBLE 83:7
unwise they seemed to d.	BIBLE 86:28
We d. in earnest, that's	RAL 535:17
We must love one another or d.	AUDEN 36:1
We shall d. alone	PASC 507:14
What I shall d. to want	SHAK 625:21
What 'tis to d.	BEAU 57:2
When beggars d.	SHAK 591:5
when they d., go to Paris	APPL 23:19
when you have to d.	MOL 479:7
Who did not wish to d.	SHAW- 639:3
Who went abroad to d.	LETTS 419:15
who would wish to d.	BORR 136:14
why then, we'll d.	PUSH 533:2
wisdom shall d.	BIBLE 77:18
Wise men also d., and perish	BOOK 127:24
wish to live and to d.	VILL 711:16
wretch that dares not d.	BURNS 162:17
yet d. we must	SHAK 588:6
Yet she must d., else she'll	SHAK 618:5
you asked this man to d.	AUDEN 34:9
youth who must fight and d.	HOOV 344:20

Dieb: *war sie, er war ein D.* | HEINE 331:1

died: d. an hour before this | SHAK 602:17

d. by the hand of the Lord	BIBLE 72:15
d. extremely well	WALP 719:2
d.—for fear of dying	THOM 695:20
d. last night of my physician	PRIOR 529:11
d. some, pro patria	POUND 527:1
d. to save their country	CHES 199:1
d. to succour me	BALL 49:13
dog it was that d.	GOLD 311:1
eyes dazzle: she d. young	WEBS 725:23
grandam ere she d.	SHAK 599:6
He d. in a good old age	BIBLE 76:33
he d. unto sin once	BIBLE 99:29
He that d. o' Wednesday	SHAK 582:1
I could have d. contented	DICK 240:15
If any question why we d.	KIPL 398:16
liked it not, and d.	WOTT 749:4
Mithridates, he d. old	HOUS 352:20
Mother d. today. Or perhaps	CAMUS 177:16
She should have d. hereafter	SHAK 605:1
than to have d. to have	DAN 229:18
These all d. in faith	BIBLE 104:15
thought it of grieving	KEATS 380:17
Who d. to save us all	ALEX 8:16
would God I had d. for thee	BIBLE 75:17

diem: *Amici, d. perdidi* | TITUS 698:8

carpe d., quam minimum	HOR 349:9
d. tibi diluxisse supremum	HOR 348:6

dienen: *Oder d. und verlieren* | GOET 309:9

dies: begotten born and d. | YEATS 752:20

D. irae, dies illa	MISS 477:11
d., or turns Hindoo	SHEL 644:4
d. this year is quit	SHAK 583:20
d. to himself unknown	SEN 563:3
Every moment a. a man	BABB 41:6
Every moment a. a man	TENN 690:5
hath blown for ever d.	FITZ 284:1
He that d. pays all debts	SHAK 625:25
kingdom where nobody d.	MILL 461:5
little something in me d.	VIDAL 711:5
man happy before he d.	SOLON 655:6
man who d. rich dies	CARN 181:18
matters not how a man d.	JOHN 373:7
One d. only once	MOL 478:20
Optima quaeque d. miseris	VIRG 715:16
then d. the same	YOUNG 754:17

dies: (*cont.*):

true because a man d. for it	WILDE 735:24
Who d. if England live	KIPL 399:4
Whom the gods love d. young	MEN 457:2

diesel: D.-engined | FLAN 285:14

diest: Where thou d., will I die | BIBLE 74:25

diet: d. unparalleled | DICK 241:31

that oft with gods doth d.	MILT 464:17

Dieu: *D. est d'ordinaire pour* | BUSS 165:19

D. est mort! le ciel est vide	NERV 492:1
le bon D. me pardonnera	CATH 185:7
le bon D. who drives it	CHR 200:9
Si D. n'existait pas	VOLT 716:10

differ: though all things d. | POPE 523:33

difference: and, oh, the d. to me | WORD 747:18

But internal d.	DICK 244:20
d. between your grace	MORE 484:11
d. does it make	GAND 297:8
d. of forty thousand men	WELL 727:11
d. of taste in jokes	ELIOT 268:22
Divines, and d. of texts	SPEN 660:22
greatly exaggerate the d.	SHAW 637:3
has made all the d.	FROST 295:9
only d., after all	CHUR 200:15
Strange the d. of men's talk	PEPYS 512:2
wear your rue with a d.	SHAK 578:8

different: d. from the home life | ANON 14:12

How d. from us	ANON 16:11
only on d. subjects	ROG 545:3
other naturs thinks d.	DICK 241:14
praises those who follow d.	HOR 350:21
They are d. from you	FITZ 284:20
We boil at d. degrees	EMER 277:14

differential: integral and d. calculus | GILB 306:9

differently: one who thinks d. | LUX 433:1

they do things d. there	HART 327:22

difficile: *D. est longum subito deponere*

CAT 186:13

D. est saturam non scribere	JUV 383:13

difficult: D. do you call it | JOHN 377:12

d. is what takes a little time	NANS 489:8
d. we do immediately	CAL 175:9
fascination of what's d.	YEATS 751:18
first step that is d.	DU D 263:8
It has been found d.	CHES 199:23
must be d. poets	ELIOT 273:23
Old man! 'tis not so d. to die	BYRON 172:19
too d. for artists	SCHN 558:8
which it is d. to speak	BURKE 159:5

difficulties: d. do not make one doubt

NEWM 493:3

d. for several generations	NAP 489:14
little local d.	MACM 440:4

difficulty: every d. except popularity

WILDE 736:11

with d. and labour	MILT 470:14
with great d. I am got hither	BUNY 156:16

diffidence: her name was D. | BUNY 156:2

diffugere: *D. nives* | HOR 350:15

dig: d. till you gently perspire | KIPL 401:23

I'll d. with it	HEAN 329:18
Let 'D. for Victory'	DORM 254:1
Many a d. in the ribs	SURT 672:9
with his nails he'll d.	WEBS 726:8

digest: And can d. so much | SHAK 629:19

inwardly d. them	BOOK 120:11

digestion: from pure d. bred | MILT 471:20

Now good d. wait on appetite	SHAK 603:9
sweet to taste prove in d.	SHAK 619:11

diggeth: d. a pit shall fall | BIBLE 80:22

dignified: d. parts | BAG 46:12

dignify: Dared the labor | CRANE 225:26

dignitate: *cum d. otium* | CIC 204:13

dignities: afraid to speak evil of d. | BIBLE 105:23

indignities men come to d.	BACON 43:29

dignity: below the d. of history | MAC 435:15

d. composed and high exploit	MILT 469:13
d. of a person is acknowledged	JOHN 366:12
d. of thinking beings	JOHN 368:14
d. of this high calling	BURKE 158:2
d. tends to increase	HUXL 357:9
equal in d. and rights	ANON 11:19
hath no new to purchase d.	GASC 298:17

dignity: (*cont.*):

maintain a d.	WALP 720:6
maintained the d. of history	BOL 117:8
May reach the d. of crimes	MORE 483:20
my bosom for the d.	SHAK 604:15
our d. as human beings	CHEK 196:10
room with silent d.	GROS 319:5
write trifles with d.	JOHN 375:19

dignum: *D. et justum est* | MISS 477:1

D. laude virum Musa	HOR 350:17

dignus: *d. ut intres sub tectum* | MISS 477:6

digression: there began a lang d. | BURNS 163:25

digressions: d. and skilled appeals | HUXL 358:12

D. are the sunshine	STER 664:19

digs: d. my grave at each remove | HERB 335:5

Dijon: was a young man of D. | ANON 20:11

dilectione: *d. hominum et odio vitiorum* | AUG 37:8

dilettante: snowy-banded, d. | TENN 686:12

dilige: *D. et quod vis fac* | AUG 37:6

diligence: D. is the mother of good | CERV 188:15

dillied: But I d. and dallied | COLL 213:7

dilly-dally: d. on the way | COLL 213:7

dim: bright world d. | SHEL 644:1

d. and perilous way	WORD 743:20
d. in the intense inane	SHEL 642:18
doth the greater glory d.	SHAK 610:4
grew d., and went out	TOLS 700:7
Nor d. nor red, like God's	COL 210:23

dime: can you spare a d. | HARB 323:10

dimension: this world's true d. | GREV 318:9

dimensions: Time has three d. | HOPK 346:14

When my d. are as well	SHAK 594:26

dimidium: *Animae d. meae* | HOR 349:1

D. facti qui coepit habet	HOR 348:4

diminish: Enlarge, d., interline | SWIFT 675:1

diminished: D. to her cock | SHAK 597:1

ought to be d.	DUNN 264:7

dimity: Such D. Convictions | DICK 245:4

dimming: gradual d. of the lights | NIC 494:16

dimpled: pretty-d. boys | SHAK 565:5

dine: cannot have heroes to d. | TROL 703:14

d. exact at noon	POPE 521:1
d. somewhere among	JERR 366:5
going to d. with some men	BENT 64:17
hang that jury-men may d.	POPE 523:26
no scandal while you d.	TENN 689:13
Where sall we gang and d.	BALL 50:20

dined: I have d. to-day | SMITH 653:19

more d. against than dining	BOWRA 138:17

diner-out: And philosophic d. | BROW 151:10

dining: dined against than d. | BOWRA 138:17

that can live without d.	MER 458:11
while they thought of d.	GOLD 311:4

dinner: after d. is after dinner | SWIFT 673:21

best number for a d.	GULB 319:14
conservatives after a d.	EMER 277:6
d. and feasting reconciles	PEPYS 512:15
d. had there been a *Synod*	JOHN 372:20
D. in the diner nothing	GORD 312:13
d. of herbs where love	BIBLE 78:35
doubtful of his d.	JOHN 368:22
expect if we haven't any d.	LEAR 414:20
if you'd watch a d. out	BROW 148:10
I get too hungry for d.	HART 327:12
one d. served for both	SHIP 646:1
refrain from asking it to d.	HALS 322:8
soul—the d. bell	BYRON 171:13
So we may make our d. sweet	BALL 50:20
sufficient for a kite's d.	QUAR 533:15
that we expect our d.	SMITH 650:17
They would ask him to d.	CARL 181:17
three hours' march to d.	HAZL 329:14
you worth inviting to d.	VIRG 715:2

dinner-knives: gravel paths with broken d.

KIPL 399:7

dint: with many a curious d. | MARL 447:9

diocese: All the air is thy D. | DONNE 250:17

Diogenes: Alexander, I would be D. | ALEX 8:8

Dior: Never darken my D. | LILL 421:15

diplomacy: D. is to do and say | GOLD 310:9

diplomat: d. can tell you to go to hell

STIN 669:11

d. nothing but a head-waiter	UST 707:17

diplomatic: d. boathook   SAL 553:19
d. revolutions   WAUGH 723:19
dipping: age o'ercargoed, d. deep   FLEC 286:12
his oar was d.   COKE 208:15
direct: d. and honest is not safe   SHAK 616:21
d. and rule our hearts   BOOK 121:7
we were all going d.   DICK 244:1
directed: all d. your way   HOR 348:1
direction: All chance, d.   POPE 522:8
one positive pitch or d.   HOPK 346:14
directions: By indirections find d. out   SHAK 574:8
He gives d. to the town   SWIFT 675:4
rode madly off in all d.   LEAC 413:13
direful: d. death indeed   FLEM 286:19
something d. in the sound   AUST 38:11
to Greece the d. spring   HOMER 342:22
dirge: By forms unseen their d.   COLL 213:13
d. of her certain ending   SHAK 632:24
with d. in marriage   SHAK 572:4
dirt: child of d. that stinks   POPE 520:3
D. is only matter out   GRAY 315:4
d. succeed where sweetness   FORS 290:6
d. the reasoning engine   ROCH 543:12
first four years the d.   CRISP 227:1
If d. were trumps   LAMB 407:10
In poverty, hunger, and d.   HOOD 344:7
insult sex, to do d. on it   LAWR 412:5
she borne the d. and rain   MORR 485:13
thicker will be the d.   GALB 297:2
dirty: creature's at his d. work   POPE 519:27
d., dangerous way   GOLD 311:24
D., dark, and undevotional   VICT 711:1
d. for the light of day   CLARE 204:20
d. work for the rest   RUSK 550:19
'Jug Jug' to d. ears   ELIOT 273:3
Dirty Dick: At D.'s and Sloppy Joe's   AUDEN 35:17
dirty-mindedness: deliberate, journalistic d.   LAWR 413:3
dis: D. aliter visum   VIRG 713:1
disagree: men only d.   MILT 469:22
disagreeable: tell him d. truths   BULW 155:6
disagreeables: all d. evaporate   KEATS 391:9
disappeared: He d. in the dead of winter   AUDEN 34:13
disappointed: d. by that stroke of death   JOHN 369:3
Sir! you have d. us   BELL 61:4
disappointeth: d. him not   BOOK 124:29
disappointing: he'll be the least d.   BAR 54:21
disappointment: D. all I endeavour end   HOPK 346:8
d. to their children   POW 528:5
disapproval: special sort of moral d.   AYER 40:13
disapprove: d. of what you say   VOLT 717:5
disapproves: condemns whatever he d.   BURN 160:18
disaster: meet with triumph and d.   KIPL 400:14
precipitate one into d.   WEST 729:16
disasters: d. in his morning face   GOLD 310:12
make guilty of our own d.   SHAK 595:2
So weary with d., tugged   SHAK 603:1
disastrous: d. and the unpalatable   GALB 297:3
win a war is as d. as to lose   CHR 200:7
disbelief: willing suspension of d.   COL 212:2
discandy: do d., melt their sweets   SHAK 566:4
disce: D. omnis   VIRG 712:15
discern: All we have built do we d.   ARN 27:15
discerning: Gives genius a better d.   GOLD 311:20
discharge: no d. in that war   BIBLE 80:16
discharged: Indebted and d.   MILT 470:24
disciple: d. is not above his master   BIBLE 90:17
d. whom Jesus loved following   BIBLE 98:3
only in the name of a d.   BIBLE 90:23
other d. did outrun Peter   BIBLE 97:31
disciples: nowadays has his d.   WILDE 735:1
discipline: D. must be maintained   DICK 239:12
d. of colleges and universities   SMITH 661:2
good order and military d.   ANON 12:28

discipline: (cont.):
virtuous and gentle d.   SPEN 659:18
disciplines: category-d.   RYLE 552:9
disclaim: d. her for a mother   GIBB 302:10
disco: mali miseris succurrere d.   VIRG 712:11
Discobbolos: Darling Mr D.   LEAR 414:9
discomfort: great d. of my soul   BOOK 126:16
discommendeth: d. others obliquely commendeth   BROW 145:6
discontent: discontented with the divine d.   KING 397:18
In pale contented sort of d.   KEATS 388:18
Now is the winter of our d.   SHAK 621:14
To youth and age in common—d.   ARN 29:6
discontented: blushing d. sun   SHAK 620:9
discontents: Civilization and its d.   RIV 541:14
source of all our d.   LEACH 413:8
discord: dire effects from civil d.   ADD 3:24
that eke d. doth sow   ELIZ 274:17
what d. follows   SHAK 627:8
discordant: reconciles D. elements   WORD 746:21
still-d. wavering multitude   SHAK 582:12
discors: Concordia d.   HOR 340:10
discount: sells us life at a d.   FRY 295:22
discouragement: There's no d.   BUNY 156:14
discourse: d. and nearest prose   DRYD 261:17
d. in novel phrases   GILB 305:16
Good company and good d.   WALT 721:2
I love any d. of rivers   WALT 721:9
Miss not the d. of the elders   BIBLE 87:14
pinching cave, shall we d.   SHAK 571:8
discover: end to d. life   GUIB 319:12
further to d. truth   BACON 41:15
discoverers: ill d. that think   BACON 42:3
discovereth: d. the thick bushes   BOOK 126:3
discoveries: virtue and consequence of d.   BACON 45:21
discovery: are the portals of d.   JOYCE 382:2
D. consists of seeing what   SZEN 677:18
d. of reality   MURD 488:7
For love is but d.   SOUT 657:3
Medicinal d.   AYRES 40:16
discreet: d. and learned Minister   BOOK 122:4
d. charm of the bourgeoisie   BUN 155:11
discretion: D. is not the better part   STR 670:20
guide his words with d.   BOOK 133:6
inform their d. by education   JEFF 364:15
surety to subsequent d.   BURN 160:11
their happiness in thy d.   ELIZ 274:10
Where does d. end   AUST 39:15
woman which is without d.   BIBLE 78:23
your own d. be your tutor   SHAK 576:6
discriminate: do learn to d.   LAWR 412:12
discrimination: art being all d.   JAMES 363:7
discriminations: Makes no d.   WHIT 733:1
discunt: Homines dum docent d.   SEN 562:29
discussion: d. of any subject   SHEL 644:2
means government by d.   ATTL 32:18
wishes after reasonable d.   CHUR 203:5
disdain: burning pride and high d.   SCOTT 559:12
dear Lady D.   SHAK 613:9
D. and scorn ride sparkling   SHAK 613:3
fixed mind and high d.   MILT 468:4
Give me more love or more d.   CAREW 179:9
little d. is not amiss   CONG 215:35
disdained: general's d. by him   SHAK 627:9
If now I be d.   ANON 17:21
disdainfulness: D. I have again   WYATT 749:12
disdains: d. all things above   OVER 502:10
disease: be prepared when d.   OVID 503:3
Confront at its onset   PERS 513:5
Cured yesterday of my d.   PRIOR 529:11
cure the d. and kill   BACON 43:23
d. in the family   TREV 702:14
d. is incurable   CHEK 196:6
d is incurable   SHAK 582:25
d of not listening   SHAK 582:18
D., or sorrow strike him   CLOU 207:15
d. requires a dangerous   MAR 281:6
d. that gave death him   GUIB 319:12
incurable d. of writing   JUV 390:9

disease: (cont.):
Life is an incurable d.   COWL 221:21
me through this long d.   POPE 519:29
nineteenth century, it was a d.   SZASZ 677:16
or d. of admiration   MAC 435:6
others are D.   BEV 69:10
our national d.   JAMES 363:14
Progress is a comfortable d.   CUMM 228:11
remedy is worse than the d.   BACON 44:21
Ring out old shapes of foul d.   TENN 684:11
sexually transmitted d.   ANON 15:18
strange d. of modern life   ARN 28:9
There is no Cure for this D.   BELL 61:1
Without d. the healthful life   SURR 672:2
diseased: minister to a mind d.   SHAK 604:22
own beauty is the mind d.   BYRON 169:5
diseases: death the cure of all d.   BROW 146:18
D. and sad Old Age live   VIRG 713:14
D. desperate grown   SHAK 577:27
inherits d. of his ancestors   WOOLF 742:4
scientific treatment for all d.   SHAW 636:10
sneezes spread d.   ANON 12:29
subject to the same d.   SHAK 608:22
disenchantment: I mistook d. for truth   SART 556:12
disentangle: and cannot d.   ANON 17:21
disfigure: in a moment can so d. us   BROW 146:11
disgrace: But quite a d. to be fine   TAYL 679:12
d. and ignominy of our natures   BROW 146:11
d. with fortune and men's   SHAK 633:10
Even to a full d.   SHAK 570:21
grace us in the d. of death   SHAK 598:6
Intellectual d.   AUDEN 34:15
It's no d. t'be poor   HUBB 353:13
Its private life is a d.   ANON 17:15
public and merited d.   STEV 668:11
sole author of his own d.   COWP 222:10
with a passing d.   DID 245:10
disgraced: dies rich dies d.   CARN 181:18
disgraceful: something d. in mind   JUV 384:14
disgruntled: if not actually d.   WOD 740:9
disguise: As to go naked is the best d.   CONG 215:5
D. fair nature with hard-favoured   SHAK 585:7
D., I see thou art a wickedness   SHAK 629:2
My love with no d.   ROET 544:9
You'd better go in d.   BRAT 140:1
disguised: England is a d. republic   BAG 47:1
disguiser: O! death's a great d.   SHAK 606:21
disguises: troublesome d. which we wear   MILT 4/1:14
disgust: d. this refined age   EVEL 279:8
not moments of d.   VOLT 716:18
Our capacity for d.   MANN 444:13
dish: dinner—some stirring d.   MIDD 459:17
forth butter in a lordly d.   BIBLE 74:4
Let's carve him as a d.   SHAK 590:18
woman is a d. for the gods   SHAK 567:6
dishabilly: cannot be devout in d.   FARQ 280:26
dishclout: Romeo's a d. to him   SHAK 623:27
dishcover: or d. the riddle   CARR 183:26
dishes: Are these the choice d.   GARR 298:7
d. were ill-sorted   DRYD 262:18
there's no washing of d.   ANON 14:4
were the d. wherein to me   AUG 36:23
dishonour: another unto d.   BIBLE 100:2
down in honour or d.   LINC 422:5
dishonourable: find ourselves d. graves   SHAK 590:3
dishonoured: No unchaste action, or d. step   SHAK 594:22
disiecti: Etiam d. membra poetae   HOR 351:3
disillusion: marital d.   WAUGH 723:9
one d.—mankind   KEYN 395:2
disinclination: d. to inflict pain   MER 458:3
disinherited: d. by the out of pocket   BENN 63:10
disinheriting: damned d. countenance   SHER 645:19
disintegration: d. and dismemberment   GLAD 307:14
disinterested: d. endeavour to learn   ARN 29:17

disinterested: (cont.):
D. intellectual curiosity — TREV 702:10
that there are d. actions — GIDE 303:6
dislike: d. everything writ by — CENT 188:7
hint a fault, and hesitate d. — POPE 519:32
I d. what I fancy I feel — ANON 18:15
I, too, d. it — MOORE 482:13
not much d. the matter — SHAK 565:4
sat with that d. — STEE 662:16
dislikes: not by d. and disdains — JAMES 363:15
dismal: d. Mapperly Hills — ARN 29:16
D. Science — CARL 180:32
with a d. headache — GILB 304:14
With d. stories — BUNY 156:14
dismayed: neither be thou d. — BIBLE 73:27
Was there a man d. — TENN 680:14
dismemberment: d. of the Empire — GLAD 307:14
dismiss: Lord, d. us with Thy — BUCK 154:12
dismounts which they dare not d. — CHUR 202:5
disobedience: Civil D. — THOR 696:21
man's first d. — MILT 467:19
upon the children of d. — BIBLE 102:21
disorder: A sweet d. in the dress — HERR 336:12
bounds with brave d. part — POPE 521:7
d. by authorities whom — CONN 216:21
D., horror, fear and mutiny — SHAK 620:17
in wild d. rise — PHIL 514:4
disparity: Just such d. — DONNE 251:17
dispatch: more requisite in business than d. — ADD 4:1
dispatchful: d. looks in haste — MILT 471:24
dispiriting: For my Muse this cannot but be d. — SMITH 652:16
display: does a human form d. — BLAKE 111:10
displeased: so wrathfully d. at us — BOOK 134:1
displeasing: something which is not d. to us — LA R 410:22
dispoged: when I am so d. — DICK 241:13
disponit: Nam homo proponit, sed Deus d. — THOM 692:6
disposable: everything has to be d. — MILL 461:18
dispose: d. the way of thy servants — BOOK 122:16
disposed: way she d. of an empire — HARL 326:13
disposes: man proposes, but God d. — THOM 692:6
disposition: Doth change my d. — SHAK 632:5
lay his goatish d. — SHAK 595:2
mild or choleric d. — ADD 4:6
To put an antic d. — SHAK 574:5
truant d., good my lord — SHAK 572:14
dispossessed: imprisoned or d. — MAGN 442:1
dispraised: d. were no small praise — MILT 473:16
To be d., is the most perfect — JONS 378:15
disputants: d. put me in mind — ADD 4:22
disputation: that's a feeling d. — SHAK 581:8
disputations: Doubtful d. — BIBLE 100:12
dispute: decide such a great d. — VIRG 714:20
D. it like a man — SHAK 604:10
work more and d. less — TAWN 679:1
disputes: all d. or conflicts — BRIA 141:1
disquieted: Never to be d. — KING 396:11
so d. within me — BOOK 127:3
disquieteth: d. himself in vain — BOOK 126:23
dissatisfaction: D. with the world — DICK 245:6
dissatisfied: Not one is d. — WHIT 732:18
dissect: thro' creatures you d. — POPE 520:25
We murder to d. — WORD 748:8
dissemble: d. in their double — BOOK 124:24
d. nor cloke them before — BOOK 118:5
d. sometimes your knowledge — BACON 43:12
right to d. your love — BICK 108:19
dissembling: Cheated of feature by d. — SHAK 621:15
dissent: dissidence of d. — BURKE 157:24
dissentious: you d. rogues — SHAK 570:4
dissimulation: defined by one word—d. — DISR 248:11
dissipation: d. without pleasure — GIBB 302:16
dissociation: d. of sensibility — ELIOT 273:22
dissolution: And wait my d. — KING 396:12
from d. and the grave — DAN 229:18
lingering d. — BECK 57:11
patiently attend my d. — MILT 473:7

dissolve: D. me into ecstasies — MILT 465:1
Fade far away, d., and quite — KEATS 389:10
dissolved: tabernacle were d. — BIBLE 101:18
dissonance: air with barbarous d. — MILT 464:3
far off the barbarous d. — MILT 472:7
distaff: mind the d., or the spit — LEWIS 420:18
distains: or a moonlit dome d. — YEATS 750:21
distance: d. between Russia and British India — SAL 554:1
d. is nothing — DU D 263:8
d. lends enchantment — CAMP 176:16
longest d. between two places — WILL 737:6
or prestige without d. — DE G 235:6
seconds' worth of d. run — KIPL 400:15
distant: d. from Heaven alike — BURT 165:6
d. scene — NEWM 493:14
music of a d. drum — FITZ 283:14
prospect of a d. good — DRYD 260:25
distasted: D. with the salt of — SHAK 628:1
distastes: fears and d. — BACON 42:20
distemperature: And thorough this d. we see — SHAK 611:15
distempered: questions the d. part — ELIOT 270:22
distillation: History a d. of rumour — CARL 180:20
distinction: British have the d. — ATTL 32:15
d. between virtue and vice — JOHN 372:9
distinctive: man's d. mark — BROW 149:12
distinguished: be d. above — HOMER 343:5
d. by that circumstance — THOR 697:7
d. thing — JAMES 363:12
man is d. from all other — ADD 4:23
distinguishes: it d. nothing — DONNE 253:7
distortions: d. of ingrown virginity — AUDEN 36:5
distraction: attention in the midst of d. — BELL 62:8
d. in 's aspect — SHAK 575:8
Into a fine d. — HERR 336:12
distress: All pray in their d. — BLAKE 113:18
Aside, but in d. — GOOGE 312:11
delivereth them out of their d. — BOOK 133:2
Far as d. the soul can wound — GREV 318:3
one incapable of her own d. — SHAK 578:13
partake of the d. of another — RICH 540:13
distressed: afflicted, or d., in mind — BOOK 120:7
distresses: In all d. of our friends — SWIFT 675:10
insurmountable d. of humanity — JOHN 367:23
distribute: d. as fairly as he can — LOWE 429:11
distrust: have to d. each other — WILL 737:1
disturb: Art is meant to d. — BRAQ 139:17
me to d. your season due — MILT 465:20
ourselves doesn't d. — HESSE 337:15
Which none d. — VAUG 708:16
dit: pas la peine d'être d. — BEAU 56:9
ditch: [Channel] is a mere d. — NAP 489:9
die in the last d. — WILL 736:21
environed with a great d. — CROM 227:15
he wasn't as dull as d. water — DICK 243:2
shall fall into the d. — BIBLE 91:10
ditch-delivered: D. by a drab — SHAK 603:19
ditchers: d. and grave-makers — SHAK 578:16
ditches: water-land of Dutchmen and of d. — BYRON 171:18
ditties: In amorous d. — MILT 468:20
spirit d. of no tone — KEATS 388:25
ditty: He played an ancient d. — KEATS 387:10
diurnal: her d. round — WORD 744:11
diurnity: D. is a dream and folly — BROW 145:25
dive: Heav'n's great lamps do d. — CAMP 177:3
search for pearls must d. — DRYD 259:24
divers: sundry times and in d. manners — BIBLE 104:10
diversa: laudet d. sequentis — HOR 350:21
diversity: arise d. of sects — SPEN 660:22
them and servants some d. — BARC 52:9
divide: rejoice when they d. the spoil — BIBLE 82:26
though he d. the hoof — BIBLE 73:1
divided: death they were not d. — BIBLE 75:9
d. by a common language — SHAW 638:31
D. by the morning tea — MACN 440:18
d. self — LAING 405:17
He d. the sea, and let them — BOOK 130:10

divided: (cont.):
household d. the spoil — BOOK 129:8
I do perceive here a d. duty — SHAK 615:4
If a house be d. against — BIBLE 93:8
sick hurry, its d. aims — ARN 28:9
what common use has harshly d. — SCH 558:1
whole is d. into three — CAES 174:14
dividend: d. from time's tomorrows — SASS 557:7
divideth: d. his spoils — BIBLE 94:19
dividing: by d. we fall — DICK 245:8
days d. lover and lover — SWIN 675:22
divination: d. too will perish them — MAND 444:6
divine: Ah, what the form d. — LAND 408:4
All things, by a law d. — SHEL 641:9
And Love, the human form d. — BLAKE 113:19
And one far-off d. event — TENN 684:17
But 'twas d. — TRAH 702:1
by a d. thrusting — SHAK 595:2
Come down, O Love d. — LITT 423:9
could d. his real thought — BYRON 170:28
depth of some d. despair — TENN 688:3
d. enchanting ravishment — MILT 463:23
D. of Kings to govern wrong — POPE 519:3
d. than the physician — SHAK 604:17
d. that follows his own — SHAK 607:12
Fanny Kelly's d. plain face — LAMB 407:2
Froude believes Kingsley a d. — STUB 671:2
handful of the D. Inert — MELV 456:18
hand that made us is d. — ADD 4:20
horror and its beauty are d. — SHEL 642:2
human; to forgive, d. — POPE 521:21
inspired by d. revelation — BACON 42:2
little heavy, but no less d. — BYRON 171:3
My knowledge was d. — TRAH 701:11
some are fou o' love d. — BURNS 162:6
spirit of man, is d. — BYRON 167:26
To her d. Majority — DICK 244:17
vision and the faculty d. — WORD 743:16
worshipped by the names d. — BLAKE 111:23
You look d. as you advance — NASH 490:21
divinely: And most d. fair — TENN 680:20
For ever most d. in the wrong — YOUNG 754:9
divineness: some participation of d. — BACON 42:1
divines: Doubts 'mongst D. — SPEN 660:22
eternal reproach of our d. — MILT 476:3
divinest: d. things this world has — HUNT 356:12
diving-bell: in a religious d. — FOST 291:9
divinity: d. that shapes our ends — SHAK 578:30
d. that stirs within us — ADD 3:23
mysteries in d. and airy — BROW 146:2
such d. doth hedge a king — SHAK 578:5
surely a piece of d. — BROW 146:20
There is d. in odd numbers — SHAK 610:19
division: D. is as bad — ANON 16:13
marriage and death and d. — SWIN 676:12
divisos: Et penitus toto d. orbe — VIRG 714:13
divorce: d. of steel falls on me — SHAK 588:11
this bill of my d. — DONNE 251:4
divorced: this golden rigol hath d. — SHAK 584:2
dizzy: d. 'tis to cast one's eyes — SHAK 597:5
do: am to d. what I please — FRED 293:11
And d. what thou wouldst do — HATCH 328:2
And what I d. in any thing — HERB 334:16
are supposed to d. anyway — TRUM 704:15
consequence, D. IT YOURSELF — BARH 52:19
Diplomacy is to d. and say — GOLD 310:3
D. as I say, not — SELD 562:13
d. as much for my true-love — BALL 51:1
D. as you would be done — CHES 198:10
do cautiously — ANON 22:13
D. not expect again a phoenix — DAY-L 233:4
d. not fold, spindle — ANON 12:33
d. nothing and get something — DISR 248:25
d. only one thing at once — SMIL 650:11
D. other men, for they — DICK 241:12
d. the perfectly correct — SHAW 636:18
D. this, and he doeth — BIBLE 89:30
d. were as easy as to know — SHAK 607:12
D. what thou wilt shall — CROW 228:3
d. ye even so to them — BIBLE 89:20
fine pleasure is not to d. — HOPK 346:19
Government is not to d. — KEYN 395:6

do: *(cont.):*

HOW NOT TO D. IT	DICK 241:1
I can d. no other	LUTH 432:10
I'll do, I'll do, and I'll d.	SHAK 600:1
I'll d.'t before I speak	SHAK 594:21
I would they should d.	BOOK 123:6
Let's d. it, let's fall	PORT 525:2
Let us d.—or die	BURNS 163:2
Love and d. what you will	AUG 37:6
not d. things themselves	RAV 537:4
not knowing what they d.	SHAK 614:8
one that will d. the deed	SHAK 598:14
So little done, so much to d.	RHOD 539:17
they know not what they d.	BIBLE 95:25
To-morrow let us d. or die	CAMP 176:12
true and d. what is right	HUXL 358:5
We cannot d. it, Sir	CARR 183:15
We can't all d. everything	VIRG 715:6
what is it you d.	WORD 747:13
What must I d. to be saved	BIBLE 98:26
what you are afraid to d.	EMER 276:27

Doc: with a man called D.   ALGR 9:5
docent: *Homines dum d. discunt*   SEN 562:29
docile: d. instruments in its hands   MILL 460:20
docks: hateful d., rough thistles   SHAK 586:17
doctor: d. does not give you   STFV 667:25

d. for a nauseous draught	DRYD 260:16
d. found, when she was dead	GOLD 310:21
d. full of phrase and fame	ARN 29:5
God and the d. we alike adore	OWEN 503:8
Knocked down a d.	SIMP 648:4
my d., what do you say	ROTH 548:16
or any other d.	HOBB 340:1
therein d. but himself	MILT 474:7
When the artless d. sees	HERR 336:15

doctors: D. in verse   THOM 694:10

d. of the Stoic fur	MILT 464:6
If you believe the d.	SAL 554:2
There might be medical d.	DICK 244:6
violet-hooded D., elegies	TENN 687:26
We d. know	CUMM 228:12
when d. disagree	POPE 520:14

doctrine: d. lies under this little   FANS 280:1

d. never was there school	MILT 474:7
d. of ignoble ease	ROOS 546:8
d. set forth thy true	BOOK 122:2
d. were let loose to play	MILT 475:16
every blast of vain d.	BOOK 121:12
loved the d. for the teacher	DEFOE 234:15
Not for the d.	POPE 521:13
with every wind of d.	BIBLE 102:17

doctrines: d. plain and clear   BUTL 166:17
   artful D.   DICK 242:24
dodger: artful D.   DICK 242:24
doers: be ye d. of the word   BIBLE 104:27
   talkers, and not of d.   HAZL 329:9
does: who d., not suffers wrong   SHEL 642:8
doest: That thou d., do quickly   BIBLE 97:9
doeth: Whoso d. these things   BOOK 124:29
dog: Am I a d., that thou   BIBLE 75:4

And every d. his day	KING 397:17
As to a d.'s tail	YEATS 753:14
beaten d. beneath the hail	POUND 527:8
been working like a d.	LENN 417:20
black d. I hope always	JOHN 368:17
But if a man bites a d.	BOG 116:14
courtesy help a lame d.	CHIL 199:28
d. is better than a dead lion	BIBLE 80:18
d. is turned to his own vomit	BIBLE 105:24
d. it was that died	GOLD 311:1
d. returneth to his vomit	BIBLE 79:21
D. returns to his Vomit	KIPL 399:8
d. shall bear him company	POPE 522:3
d.'s obeyed in office	SHAK 597:7
d. starved at his master's	BLAKE 111:2
d. that has praised his fleas	YEATS 753:12
d., to d.'s come private cude	SPAR 658.10
engine of pollution, the d.	ROHR (illeg.)
you y a lim, his day	WEST 729:19
flame is good for a d,	KIPL 400.7
giving your heart to a d.	KIPL 400.7
If you call a d. Hervey	JOHN 371:5
I had rather be a d.	SHAK 593:1
incident of the d. in the night	DOYLE 256:14

dog: *(cont.):*

I never heard thy d. once bark	HEYW 338:5
infidel as a d. is an infidel	JOHN 373:5
I ope my lips let no d. bark	SHAK 607:6
Is thy servant a d.	BIBLE 76:24
jumps over the lazy d.	ANON 17:14
Like a d., he hunts in dreams	TENN 685:11
limps the hungry d.	BLOK 115:9
lost d. somewhere	ANOU 23:10
Lovell our d.	COLL 213:3
Mine enemy's d.	SHAK 597:12
misbeliever, cut-throat d.	SHAK 607:22
more ridiculous than a d.	NERV 492:3
My d.! what remedy remains	COWP 222:23
preaching is like a d.'s	JOHN 372:18
Something better than his d.	TENN 685:9
This mad d. of the Middle East	REAG 537:14
very d. to the commonalty	SHAK 570:2
very flea of his d.	JONS 378:19
went was my poor d. Tray	CAMP 176:13
whose d. are you	POPE 519:23
Wool of bat, and tongue of d.	SHAK 603:18
You called me d.	SHAK 608:1

Doge: quiet D. of Venice   WALP 720:10
dogfight: regaled by a d.   MAC 435:26
dogged: It's d. as does it   TROL 703:18
dogma: d. has been the fundamental   principle   NEWM 493:1

no d., no Dean	DISR 249:6
will serve to beat a d.	GUED 319:7

dogmatise: d. and am contradicted   JOHN 377:2
dogs: All the d. of Europe bark   AUDEN 34:15

bang these d. of Seville	TENN 689.2
Cowardly d. bark loudest	WEBS 726:5
d. and killed the cats	BROW 151:26
d. delight to bark	WATTS 722:16
d. eat of the crumbs	BIBLE 91:11
d. go on with their doggy	AUDEN 35:7
d. shall drink him 'till	POPE 520:17
d. who don't understand	CALV 175:17
extravagant for seeing d.	JENY 365:10
For without are d.	BIBLE 107:25
hates d. and babies	ROST 548:14
Lame d. over stiles	KING 397:10
laughter, like dancing d.	JOHN 374:6
let's go to the d. tonight	HERB 333:14
let slip the d. of war	SHAK 591:24
little d. and all	SHAK 596:19
Mad d. and Englishmen	COW 220:14
more one values d.	TOUS 701.6
moreover the d. licked	BIBLE 95:9
Now for d. and apes	BROW 149:30
That d. bark at me	SHAK 621:15
they were na men, but d.	BURNS 163:26
Things are but as straw d.	LAO-T 409:10
Throw physic to the d.	SHAK 604:22

dog-star: The d. rages   POPE 519:25
doileys: I'm soiling the d.   BETJ 67:12
doing: d. things rightly   RUSK 550:20

joy's soul lies in the d.	SHAK 627:5
Patient continuance in well d.	BIBLE 99:18
put me to d.	METH 458:6
see what she's d.	PUNCH 531:20
still be d., never done	BUTL 166:6
This is the Lord's d.	BOOK 133:16
weary in well d.	BIBLE 102:9
What was he d., the great	BROW 147:17

doing-good: As for D.   THOR 697:2
doings: child is known by his d.   BIBLE 79:6
dole: Born as I doubt to all our d.   BRET 140:17
   muffleered men in the 1930s d.   JOS 380:16
doleful: Knight of the D. Countenance   CERV 188:8
dolendum: *Si vis me flere, d. est*   HOR 347:9
doll: A living d.   PLATH 516:2
   doll in the d.'s house   DICK 243:3
dollar: almighty d.   IRV 360:18
   d. is the only object   ANON 12:3
dollars: billion d. country   FOST 291:5
dolore: *Nessun maggior d.*   DANTE 230:11
   Per me si va nell' città ETERNO D.   DANTE 230.0
dolorem: *infies renovare d.*   VIRG 712:12
Dolores: splendid and sterile D.   SWIN 676:10

dolorous: strike a stroke most d.   MAL 443:4
dolour: d. of pad and paper-weight   ROET 544:4
   have wept to see the d.   MAL 443:12
dolphin: delights were d.-like   SHAK 566:20
   heard a mermaid on a d.'s   SHAK 611:16
Dolphin-chamber: sitting in my D.   SHAK 583:4
dolphins: gentler d. of kindlier waves   MOORE 482:17
   rare butter made of d.' milk   JONS 378:6
dolphin-torn: That d., that gong-tormented sea   YEATS 751:1
dome: Build up the blue d. of air   SHEL 640:7

d. of heaven had fallen	FROST 294:9
d. of the sky seemed	WORD 743:1
like a d. of many-coloured	SHEL 640:4
moonlit d. distains	YEATS 750:21
singing beneath the d.	VERL 710:5

domestic: cares and pleasures of d. life   GIBB 302:3

d. business is no less	MONT 480:20
d. sort which never stirs	SHER 645:20
Milk-soup men call d. bliss	PATM 509:13
respectable d. establishment	BENN 63:6

domesticate: d. the Recording Angel   STEV 668:6
domi: *Res angusta d.*   JUV 383:22
dominant: d.'s persistence   BROW 153:9
dominating: men d. men   WEBER 724:21
domination: d. of Prussia   ASQ 31:17
   d. over them in the morning   BOOK 128:1
domine: D., defende nos   GODL 308:7
dominion: And death shall have no d.   THOM 693:3

changed for the d. of laws	PRICE 528:17
death hath no more d.	BIBLE 99:29
d. of kings changed	PRICE 528:17
d. of the master	HUME 355:12
d. of the sea	COV 220:7
d. of the world	MAHAN 442:3
d. over the fish	BIBLE 69:24
d. shall be also from	BOOK 129:20
from the d. of religion	GOLD 310:4
hand that holds d.	THOM 693:10
I'm truly sorry Man's d.	BURNS 163:16
inglorious period of our d.	BURKE 159:1
they get the d. over me	BOOK 125:6

dominions: depopulating his d.   BECK 58:3
   His Majesty's d.   NORTH 496:13
   sun does not set in my d.   SCH 558:2
domino: 'falling d.' principle   EIS 268:11
dominus: D. custodierit civitatem   BIBLE 108:4
   D. illuminatio mea   BIBLE 107:27
   D. vobiscum   MISS 476:12
domum: *Ite d. saturae, venit*   VIRG 715:9
don: D.'s room, like the nest   MADAN 441:10

English critic is a d.	LAMB 407:15
good is the typical D.	GODL 308:6
my back upon D. or devil	TENN 689:2
Remote and ineffectual D.	BELL 61:14

dona: *d. nobis pacem*   MISS 477:5
   Requiem aeternam d. eis   MISS 477:10
   timeo Danaos et d. ferentis   VIRG 712:14
donations: limiting his d.   BAED 46:6
done: Apostles would have d.   BYRON 170:7

at present are not d. at all	KEYN 395:6
betters what is d.	SHAK 632:5
Determined, dared, and d.	SMART 650:4
Do as you would be d.	CHES 198:10
D. because we are too menny	HARDY 324:9
d. the state some service	SHAK 618:20
d. those things which we	BOOK 118:8
d. very well out of the war	BALD 48:13
have d. being what she is	YEATS 752:15
he d. her wrong	ANON 13:11
he might have d. with us	CLOU 207:14
Inasmuch as ye have d. it	BIBLE 92:21
much is to be d. and little	JOHN 369:14
Nay, I have d.: you get	DRAY 258:1
Nothing to be d.	BECK 57:19
petty d., the undone vast	BROW 150:23
Playng—till and D. to death	TRAI 702;2
should not be d. at all	(illeg.) 711;2

done: (*cont.*):
surprised to find it d. at all   JOHN 372:18
that nothing can be d.   ALLEN 9:8
that which is d.   BIBLE 80:1
thou hast not d.   DONNE 251:7
was not d. in a corner   BIBLE 99:11
were d. when 'tis done   SHAK 601:2
We thought we were d.   BENET 62:17
What is this that thou hast d.   BIBLE 70:12
What is to be d.   LENIN 417:8
What's d. cannot be undone   SHAK 604:16
what's d. is done   SHAK 603:3
which gets things d.   LLOY 424:9
while anything remained to be d.
   LUCAN 431:6
won are d.   SHAK 627:5
dong: d. and of corrupcioun   CHAU 104.10
D. with a Luminous Nose   LEAR 414:1
donkey. d. wot wouldn't go   DICK 242:20
that's a dead d.   DICK 243:27
donkeys: lions led by d.   HOFF 341:12
Donne: another Newton, a new D.
   HUXL 357:19
D., for not keeping   JONS 380:8
D.'s verses are like   JAM 362:6
D., whose muse on dromedary   COL 210:16
Don Quixote: excepting *D.*   JOHN 377:9
dons: D. admirable!   BELL 61:15
If the D. sight Devon   NEWB 492:6
don't: But d. think twice   DYLAN 265:13
D. ask me, ask the horse   FREUD 293:22
D. tell my mother I'm living   HERB 333:15
d. think you can't think   INGE 359:11
persons about to marry.—'D.   PUNCH 531:7
doodle: Yankee D. came to town   ANON 20:1
doom: d. assigned   TENN 687:8
d. that Adam fell   MILT 475:6
even to the edge of d.   SHAK 634:24
great d.'s image   SHAK 602:15
His d.'s extremely hard   GILB 305:5
Our d. is, to be sifted   BUNT 155:10
regardless of their d.   GRAY 316:2
To the scaffold and the d.   AYT 41:2
would have changed his d.   CLEV 206:14
doomed: And d. to death   DRYD 260:19
D. for a certain term   SHAK 573:13
dooms: grandeur of the d.   KEATS 386:14
doomsday: D. is near   SHAK 581:21
Then is d. near   SHAK 574:25
Doon: and braes o' bonny D.   BURNS 161:9
door: And at the d. too   SHAK 589:13
back at mine hostess' d.   SHAK 593:28
butt'ry d. I hear not creak   HEYW 338:5
coming in at one d.   BEDE 58:13
Converses at the d. apart   ELIOT 272:20
d. flew open, in he ran   HOFF 341:6
d. opens and lets the future   GREE 317:3
d. we never opened   ELIOT 270:14
drive an angel from your d.   BLAKE 113:20
even hard at death's d.   BOOK 132:16
generation is knocking at the d.
   SHAW 638:28
handle of the big front d.   GILB 305:26
I am the d.   BIBLE 96:37
interest a knock at the d.   LAMB 406:14
Is beating on the d.   YEATS 751:21
I stand at the d.   BIBLE 106:8
knocking at Preferment's d.   ARN 28:4
like an open d. in a mean   WEST 729:15
lock and splintered the d.   AUDEN 35:15
made my sin their d.   DONNE 251:7
make a d. and bar   BIBLE 87:28
my d. stayed shut   RAC 535:6
No d. can keep them out   HERB 334:7
On the wrong side of the d.   CHES 198:29
opening and closing of a d.   SAND 555:10
opening of a D.   DICK 244:14
passed the d. of darkness   FITZ 284:6
prejudices through the d.   FRED 293:10
rapping at my chamber d.   POE 518:6
Shut the d. after you   EDG 266:11
so wide as a church d.   SHAK 623:13
Then—shuts the D.   DICK 244:17

door: (*cont.*):
whining of a d.   DONNE 253:9
door-keeper: d. in the house of my God
   BOOK 130:18
doormat: d. in a world of boots   RHYS 539:22
doors: Death opens unknown d.   MAS 453:10
d. of perception were cleansed   BLAKE 113:2
d. shall be shut   BIBLE 81:1
D., where my heart was   TENN 683:5
heavens, your living d.   MILT 472:10
infernal d.   MILT 470:10
In Little Girls is slamming D.   BELL 61:7
many d. to let out life   FLET 287:15
My d. are widely flung   ROET 544:9
taxi-cab with both d.   HUGH 353:15
ten thousand several d.   WEBS 725:22
their d. against a setting sun   SHAK 626:10
thousand d. open   SEN 563:2
thousand d. to let out life   MASS 453:16
ye everlasting d.   BOOK 125:17
yielding like swinging d.   DOUG 255:10
doorstep: go and do this on the d.
   JUNOR 383:11
Leave your worry on the d.   FIEL 282:19
doorways: d. are alternate night   FITZ 283:15
dooryard: lilacs last in the d.   WHIT 733:3
Dorcas: D.: this woman was   BIBLE 98:18
Dorchester: Safe in the D. Hotel   BETJ 67:4
Dorian: perfect phalanx to the D. mood
   MILT 468:24
Doric: warbling his D. lay   MILT 466:15
dormienda: *Nox est perpetua una d.*   CAT 185:15
Dorset: funeral Monday D.   BEER 59:18
dotage: eyes the streams of d.   JOHN 370:20
Pedantry the d. of knowledge   JACK 361:4
dote: D. on his imperfections   EPH 278:4
d. on his very absence   SHAK 607:17
nor so old to d. on her   SHAK 595:5
dotting: D. the shoreless watery wild   ARN 29:3
double: been leading a d. life   WILDE 734:17
dissemble in their d.   BOOK 124:24
Double, d. toil and trouble   SHAK 603:17
D.-lived in regions new   KEATS 386:7
so d. be his praise   SPEN 660:3
double-bed: d. after the hurly-burly
   CAMP 176:6
doubles: d. your chances for a date   ALLEN 9:8
doublet: bought his d. in Italy   SHAK 607:15
tailor make thy d.   SHAK 629:18
with his d. all unbraced   SHAK 574:9
doublethink: *D.* means   ORW 500:15
doubly: D. redoubled strokes   SHAK 599:16
doubt: But never d. I love   SHAK 574:15
Did Jesus teach d.   BLAKE 111:21
difficulties do not make one d.   NEWM 493:3
d. diversified by faith   BROW 148:12
d. is our passion   JAMES 363:1
d. to act or rest   POPE 522:9
freckles, and d.   PARK 506:7
Humility is only d.   BLAKE 111:17
Life is d.   UNAM 707:2
mind is clouded with a d.   TENN 682:25
more faith in honest d.   TENN 684:7
night of d. and sorrow   BAR 53:3
No possible d. whatever   GILB 303:15
Oh! let us never, never d.   BELL 61:19
philosophy calls all in d.   DONNE 250:7
shameful to d. one's friends   LA R 410:14
sunnier side of d.   TENN 680:8
time will d. of Rome   BYRON 171:10
We are not enabled to d. Thee   KNOX 403:9
When in d., mumble   BOREN 136:7
when in d., strike it out   TWAIN 706:22
wherefore didst thou d.   BIBLE 91:8
wisdom, dying in d.   LOW 430:21
You tell me, d. is Devil-born   TENN 684:6
doubter: I am the d. and the doubt   EMER 276:6
doubtful: D. disputations   BIBLE 100:12
doubtless: d. God never did   BUTL 167:12
shall d. come again   BOOK 134:5
doubts: d. aboot the meenister   PUNCH 531:27
d. better than most people's certainties
   HARD 324:3

doubts: (*cont.*):
D. 'mongst Divines   SPEN 660:22
he shall end in d.   BACON 41:16
Kind jealous d., tormenting   ROCH 543:9
To saucy d. and fears   SHAK 603:8
douceur: *la d. angevine*   DU B 263:2
Douglas: doughty D.   BALL 49:1
Like D. conquer   HOME 342:20
dove: and the sweet d. died   KEATS 387:31
be as the wings of a d.   BOOK 129:8
Beside the springs of D.   WORD 747:18
changes on the burnished d.   TENN 685:7
d. complaining   DAY-L 233:4
d. found no rest   BIBLE 70:27
eagle in thee, all the d.   CRAS 226:4
hawk at eagles with a d.   HERB 335:17
that I had wings like a d.   BOOK 128:10
dove-cote: like an eagle in a d.   SHAK 570:27
Dover: chalk cliffs of D.   BALD 48:10
farthing candle at D.   JOHN 372:17
white cliffs of D.   BURT 164:10
Dover Road: milestones on the D.   DICK 241:3
doves: d.' eyes within thy locks   BIBLE 81:13
harmless as d.   BIBLE 90:16
dovetailedness: kind of universal d.
   DICK 242:11
dowagers: d. for deans   TENN 687:24
dower: earth its d. of river   KEATS 386:16
faith's transcendent d.   WORD 747:15
their ancient English d.   WORD 745:4
thy truth then be thy d.   SHAK 594:19
dowie: d. dens o' Yarrow   BALL 49:8
down: D. a-down the deeps of thought
   COL 209:8
D. among the dead men let   DYER 265:9
D. and away below   ARN 27:6
D. and Out in Paris   ORW 500:1
D. by the salley gardens   YEATS 751:11
d. express in the small of the back
   WOD 740:14
d.' from Jimmy's university   OSB 501:15
D. in the forest something   SIMP 648:2
d. into the darkness   MILL 461:6
d. needs fear no fall   BUNY 156:10
d. the nights and down   THOM 695:1
D., thou climbing sorrow   SHAK 595:14
D. to Gehenna or up   KIPL 399:18
D. to the sea in ships   BOOK 133:1
Finds the d. pillow hard   SHAK 571:12
go d. to the sea again   MAS 453:7
Had me low and had me d.   GERS 301:11
he putteth d. one   BOOK 130:5
If you go d. in the woods today   BRAT 140:1
many kicked d. stairs   HAL 322:1
meet 'em on your way d.   MIZN 478:10
quite, quite, d.   SHAK 576:4
soft young d. of her   MEW 459:8
was d. and out of breath   SHAK 582:9
way d. to the Underworld   VIRG 713:11
downcast: people to feel a little d.   MCG 437:16
downfall: regress is either a d.   BACON 43:29
down-gyvèd: d. to his ancle   SHAK 574:9
downhearted: Are we d.   KNIG 402:22
Are we d.? No   ANON 12:7
We are not d.   CHAM 189:5
Downing Street: Germany to D. peace
   CHAM 189:8
downs: All in the D. the fleet   GAY 300:15
down-sitting: knowest my d.   BOOK 134:18
downstairs: But—why did you kick me d.
   BICK 108:19
downwards: could look no way but d.
   BUNY 156:8
my gross flesh sinks d.   SHAK 621:13
dozens: Mother to d.   HERB 333:18
Whom he reckons up by d.   GILB 305:25
dozes: d. one against the wall   MERR 458:12
drab: Ditch-delivered by a d.   SHAK 603:19
drachmas: drop my blood for d.   SHAK 593:24
dragging: d. themselves through negro streets
   GINS 306:28
drag-net: swept like a d.   DRYD 262:18

dragon: And as an evening d.   MILT 474:14
angels fought against the d.   BIBLE 106:30
between the d. and his wrath   SHAK 594:20
d. shalt thou tread under   BOOK 131:4
Great anger in the d.   SUTT 672:23
he laid hold on the d.   BIBLE 107:14
mother under the d.'s tail   SHAK 595:2
O to be a d.   MOORE 482:12
that swingèd the d.   SHAK 593:28
dragon-fly: d. hangs like a blue thread
  ROSS 547:21
dragon-green: d., the luminous   FLEC 286:8
dragons: be an habitation of d.   BIBLE 83:18
Bores have succeeded to d.   DISR 248:37
d. in their pleasant palaces   BIBLE 83:4
I am a brother to d.   BIBLE 77:31
Never laugh at live d.   TOLK 700:3
ye d., and all deeps   BOOK 135:14
drags: d. at each remove   GOLD 311:8
drain: d. pure god flows forth   TOCU 689:8
drains: Deity and the D.   STR 670:17
Democracy and proper d.   BETJ 67:15
some dull opiate to the d.   KEATS 389:8
Drake: D. he's in his hammock   NEWB 492:7
drama: close the d. with the day   BFRK 65:13
D. criticism   TYNAN 706:30
d. onto the moral plane   GIDE 303:7
d.'s laws the drama's patrons   JOHN 370:12
general d. of pain   HARDY 324:11
dramas: climax of other people's d.
  LERM 418:16
d. of a grandeur and unity   HARDY 324:20
dramatist: d. only wants more liberties
  JAMES 362:15
dramatists: the first of d.   MAC 434:12
dramatize: ever-importunate murmur,
'D. it'   JAMES 362:9
Drang: *Sturm und D.*   KAUF 386:1
drank: And still my body d.   COL 211:11
d. without the provocation   SWIFT 673:16
have eat my ale, d. my ale   FARQ 280:8
he d. of the brook   BIBLE 75:31
I never of Aganippe well   SIDN 647:1
drastic: D. measures is Latin   ANST 23:13
draughts: peculiarly susceptible to d.
  WILDE 734:18
draw: began to d. to our end   BIBLE 87:4
cable can so forcibly d.   BURT 165:9
d. but twenty miles a day   MARL 448:9
d. hearts after them   MILT 473:15
D. near with faith   BOOK 122:5
D. not up seas to drown   DONNE 252:23
d. you to her *with a single hair*   DRYD 262:6
drawbacks: everything has its d.   JER 365:16
drawers: and d. of water unto   BIBLE 73:31
Pee, po, belly, bum, d.   FLAN 285:11
drawing: d. days out, that men   SHAK 591:15
d. is on the level   BLUNT 116:6
D. is the true test of art   INGR 360:9
Mrs Gaskell! no d. back   BRON 143:1
drawing-room: feelings of women in a d.
  WOOLF 742:13
drawn: d. amidst the frozen pools   MARL 447:20
that was briefly d. out   MAL 443:9
dread: and fear of kings   SHAK 609:13
d. beat pulsing fire   JOHN 366:16
d. of beatings   BETJ 68:8
d. who speeds through   SHEL 644:11
From Brig o' D. when thou   BALL 50:1
let him be your d.   BIBLE 82:25
Nor d. nor hope attend   YEATS 751:9
Or whence this secret d.   ADD 3:23
That is why most men d. it   SHAW 637:23
What d. hand   BLAKE 114:14
Yet nothing did I d.   SPEN 659:22
dreaded. Thy most d. instrument   WORD 746:8
dreadful: I deed of a note   SHAK 603:4
Between the action of a d. thing
  SHAK 610:15
d. fiend of gods and men   SPEN 660:18
d. is the check   BRON 142:14
dreading: D. and hoping all   YEATS 751:9

Dreadnoughts: cost as much to keep
up as two D.   LLOY 424:5
dream: And slowly read and d.   YEATS 753:19
As love's young d.   MOORE 483:6
awakened from the d. of life   SHEL 639:22
Because thou must not d.   ARN 27:4
behold it was a d.   BUNY 156:7
born falls into a d.   CONR 217:7
Diurnity is a d. and folly   BROW 145:25
d. a lie if it don't come true   SPR 661:15
d. all night without a stir   KEATS 387:27
d. between two awakenings   O'NEI 498:20
d. but of a shadow   CHAP 190:12
d. doth flatter   SHAK 634:12
d. not in the first half   BROW 146:23
D. of Fair Women   TENN 680:20
d. of money-bags to-night   SHAK 608:9
d. of reason produces monsters   GOYA 313:5
d. of the days when work   CHES 199:9
d. of the south and west   HARDY 326:1
d. that he could comb grey   YEATS 752:4
D. the impossible dream   DAR 231:1
d. you are crossing   GILB 304:15
Everlasting peace is a d.   MOLT 479:17
For each age is a d.   O'SH 501:23
freshness of a d.   WORD 745:10
from a deep d. of peace   HUNT 356:4
glory and the d.   WORD 745:14
hope I dreamed of was a d.   ROSS 547:5
I cried to d. again   SHAK 625:26
I d. my dreams away   FLAN 285:8
if I d. I have you   DONNE 261:23
I have a d.   KING 397:1
In a d. you are never eighty   SEXT 563:11
is but a brief d.   PETR 513:10
Is but a d. within a dream   POE 518:4
Life is but an empty d.   LONG 427:7
life, without a d.   ROST 548:12
likened our life to a d.   MONT 481:10
like unto them that d.   BOOK 134:4
Like wrecks of a dissolving d.   SHEL 640:15
lost traveller's d.   BLAKE 111:23
Love in a subtle d. disguised   JONS 379:15
My d. thou brok'st not   DONNE 251:22
noble things, not d. them   KING 397:9
perceived they had dreamed a d.   BROW 153:5
perchance to d.   SHAK 575:16
perfectibility as a d.   MILL 460:21
phantasma, or a hideous d.   SHAK 590:15
quiet sleep and a sweet d.   MAS 453:9
report, what my d. was   SHAK 612:16
salesman is got to d.   MILL 461:17
shadow, short as any d.   SHAK 610:23
should d. of the devil   BARH 52:14
sight to d. of, not to tell   COL 209:9
Soft! I did but d.   SHAK 622:10
So runs my d.   TENN 683:19
speaking silence of a d.   ROSS 547:3
that insane d. we take   BROW 149:18
They fly forgotten, as a d.   WATTS 723:1
This d. of mine   SHAK 632:10
thou mightst in d.   SHEL 642:22
True to the d. I am dreaming   COW 221:1
vanished like a d.   CARL 180:27
vision and the old men's d.   DRYD 259:4
vision, or a waking d.   KEATS 389:17
We live, as we d. — alone   CONR 217:3
Where we used to sit and d.   ARMS 26:5
wit of man to say what d.   SHAK 612:15
dreamed: d., and behold   BIBLE 71:13
d. in a dream I saw a city   WHIT 732:3
d. that Greece might still   BYRON 171:1
d. that I dwelt in marble halls   BUNN 155:7
d. that life was beauty   HOOP 344:16
I d. fast of mirth and play   WEVER 730:1
I d. of the devil, and waked   ANST 23:11
right I've d. of choose   STEV 667:24
or can be d.   HALD 321:2
perceived they had d. a dream   BROW 153:5
Abrahm, artist is a d. consenting   SANT 555:10
Beautiful d., wake unto me   FOST 291:11
Behold, this d. cometh   BIBLE 70:22

dreamer: (cont.):
D. of dreams, born out   MORR 485:11
He is a d.; let us leave   SHAK 589:22
or a d. of dreams   BIBLE 73:17
poet and the d.   KEATS 387:16
dreamers: d. of another existence
  BYRON 173:26
heretics, d., rebels   ZAMY 755:4
We are the d. of dreams   O'SH 501:22
dreaming: City with her d. spires   ARN 28:25
D. of thee! Dreamin' of thee   WALL 718:2
d. on the verge of strife   CORN 219:5
I'm of a white Christmas   BERL 65:18
little d., a little dyin'   PHIL 514:8
Of old the world on d. fed   YEATS 753:7
whether I was then a man d.   CHUA 200:10
dreams: affliction of these terrible d.
  SHAK 603:3
angels in some brighter d.   VAUG 709:8
are either d. or swords   LOW 429:14
are to me sick men's d.   BROW 146:23
armoured cars of d.   BISH 110:3
awoke from uneasy d.   KAFKA 384:18
because you tread on my d.   YEATS 751:22
before us like a land of d.   ARN 27:1
beyond the d. of avarice   JOHN 375:23
beyond the d. of avarice   MOORE 482:7
City of perspiring d.   RAPH 536:18
Come to me in my d., and then   ARN 27:5
dreamed his white Platonic d.   JOHN 367:1
d., and ceremonies   SHAK 590:19
d. are dreams   CALD 175:4
d. good works are not wasted   CALD 175:5
d. happy as her day   BROO 143:18
d. is the royal road   FREUD 293:20
d. of a poet doomed   JOHN 367:22
d. their children dreamed   COL 209:8
Fanatics have their d.   KEATS 387:14
forgotten scream for help in d.   CAN 178:2
her as Dian had hot d.   SHAK 571:19
If there were d. to sell   BEDD 58:12
Inaudible as d.   COL 210:4
In d. begins responsibility   YEATS 753:23
Into the land of my d.   KING 397:6
level of your d.   SHAK 631:21
Like a dog, he hunts in d.   TENN 685:11
Like transitory d. given o'er   ROCH 543:7
Made holy by their d.   GIBS 303:5
not make d. your master   KIPL 400:14
not that I have bad d.   SHAK 574:27
off of old men's d.   WALK 717:13
old men shall dream d.   BIBLE 86:8
or dreamt of in d.   BARH 52:12
quick D., the passion-winged   SHEL 639:14
Real are the d. of Gods   KEATS 388:15
such stuff as d. are made on   SHAK 625:28
Sure I had drunken in my d.   COL 211:1
That we who lived by honest d.   DAY-L 233:7
Thou wovest d. of joy and fear   SHEL 643:22
thy d., long care   LYLY 433:12
we see it in our d.   CHEK 196:12
when the days of golden d.   BRON 142:17
wicked d. abuse   SHAK 601:13
dreamt: d. of in your philosophy   SHAK 574:4
I d. I went to Manderley   DU M 263:14
drear: down the vast edges d.   ARN 27:1
nothing d. can move me   BRON 142:11
dreary: come I am, the d. destiny   SACK 552:13
d. length before the Court   DICK 239:1
d. subject of world's tragedy   DRAY 258:3
She only said, 'My life is d.   TENN 686:6
dregs: among the d. of Romulus   CIC 203:24
from the d. of life   DRYD 260:6
These d. of life   THOM 695:23
drench: d. to bring 'em off   LAMB 407:1
dress: And Peace, the human d.   BLAKE 113:19
do we deck, why do we d.   BEHN 60:9
d. after the sweetness   FIRB 282:29
d. by yellow candle-light   STEV 668:13
d. without which we feel   MCL 439:16
Expression is the d. of thought   POPE 521:12
Full evening d. is a must   GREN 318:1
noble youth did n.   SHAK 583:7

dress: (cont.):
Style is the d. of thought WESL 729:5
sweet disorder in the d. HERR 336:12
through all this fleshly d. VAUG 709:3
You will put on as I will MCG 438:1
dressed: D. in a little brief authority
SHAK 605:18
D. in style, brand new tile COLL 213:6
d. up and have no place WHIT 732:1
d. up and no place to go BURT 164:9
Let me be d. fine as I will WATTS 722:14
temper when he's well d. DICK 241:8
dresser: Slept under the d. BENT 64:15
dresses: neat-handed Phyllis d. MILT 465:12
dressing: best is d. old words new SHAK 634:7
dressings: every season she hath d. fit
ANON 16:14
drew: d. a bow at a venture BIBLE 76:14
She d. an angel down DRYD 259:23
Dr Fell: I do not love thee, D. BROWN 145:1
dried: d. up, and withered BOOK 130:23
little life with d. tubers ELIOT 272:21
would at once be d. up DOST 254:2
drift: adamant for d. CHUR 202:4
d. toward catastrophe EINS 268:4
drifted: Snow White...but I d. WEST 729:13
drifts: Strewn with its dank yellow d. ARN 28:1
drink: ale's the stuff to d. HOUS 352:19
And men and dogs shall d. POPE 520:17
Barring d. and the girls LOCK 425:16
beasts of the field d. BOOK 132:7
be their portion to d. BOOK 124:23
But sure I think, that I can d. ANON 14:13
debt, and in a BROME 141:15
d. all day and keep absolutely SMITH 652:5
d., and be merry BIBLE 94:23
d. and get beerier LAWR 412:12
D. and the devil had done STEV 667:22
d., and to be merry BIBLE 80:17
D. deep, or taste not POPE 521:8
D. fair, wotever you do DICK 241:27
D.! for you know not whence FITZ 284:11
d. shall be prepared gold JONS 379:9
D., sir, is a great provoker SHAK 602:11
d. the blood of goats BOOK 128:3
d. thy wine BIBLE 80:19
D. to me only with thine eyes JONS 379:20
d. unto one of these little BIBLE 90:23
D. ye all of this BOOK 122:12
eat and d. BIBLE 83:7
eat with you, d. with you SHAK 607:19
five reasons we should d. ALDR 8:5
Gently d., and drink OLDYS 498:11
Give strong d. unto him BIBLE 79:34
his hous of mete and d. CHAU 192:24
I d. for it WAUGH 724:12
I d. well, and I sleep MORT 486:18
If ever thou gavest meat or d. BALL 50:1
intelligence to buy a d. CUMM 228:7
I will d. life to the lees TENN 690:1
Leeze me on d.! BURNS 162:5
let us eat and d. BIBLE 101:9
man may d. and no be drunk BURNS 163:12
Man wants but little d. below HOLM 342:17
meaning is my meat and d. BROW 149:25
Nor any drop to d. COL 211:1
or sleep or d. again DE L 236:4
sat down to eat and to d. RIBLE 72:20
Should every creature d. COWL 221:8
strong d. is raging BIBLE 79:4
that he has taken to d. TARK 678:14
That I might d., and leave KEATS 389:9
they do who d. their last BYRON 172:14
They never taste who always d.
PRIOR 529:16
thirsty and ye gave me d. BIBLE 92:20
We'll teach you to d. deep SHAK 572:15
drinkers: d. drink, and swearers BURNS 162:7
drinketh: he d. up a river BIBLE 78:3
drinking: And d. largely sobers us again
POPE 521:8
A very merry, dancing, d. DRYD 261:19
constant d. fresh and fair COWL 221:7

drinking: (cont.):
curse of the d. classes WILDE 736:10
d. all the time as fast TURN 705:14
d. at somebody else's expense LEIGH 417:2
D. is the soldier's pleasure DRYD 259:18
D. my griefs, whilst you SHAK 620:19
d. that is to be blamed SELD 562:4
D. the blude-red wine BALL 50:10
D. when we are not thirsty BEAU 56:11
much d., little thinking SWIFT 673:21
my days in a tavern d. ANON 22:9
Now for d., now the Earth HOR 349:14
There is no d. after death FLET 287:11
they were eating and d. BIBLE 92:13
thought surpass eating and d. CLOU 207:13
unhappy brains for d. SHAK 615:23
drinks: man you don't like who d.
THOM 693:22
Now the king d. to Hamlet SHAK 579:4
dripping: electricity was d. THUR 697:13
drive: but difficult to d. BROU 144:9
lest you d. an angel from BLAKE 113:20
way but can't d. the car TYNAN 706:31
drivel: d. every drizzly brain BYRON 169:27
driver: he was in the d.'s seat BEAV 57:6
drives: And d. away his fear NEWT 494:10
d. fat oxen should himself JOHN 376:14
one nail by strength d. SHAK 631:5
driveth: he d. furiously BIBLE 76:26
driving: d. briskly in a post-chaise JOHN 374:22
like the d. of Jehu BIBLE 76:26
drizzly: drivel every d. brain BYRON 169:27
droghte: d. of March hath perced CHAU 192:6
drollery: d. called representative government
DISR 248:30
dromedary: The d., two NASH 490:2
whose muse on d. trots COL 210:16
drone: lazy yawning d. SHAK 584:22
droning: beetle wheels his d. GRAY 315:16
droon: I d. twa ANON 17:17
droop: D. in a hundred A.B.C.'s ELIOT 270:10
d. men and beasts NASHE 490:23
droopingly: Lady Jane, a little d. LAWR 412:1
droops: D. on the little hands MILNE 462:18
drop: are as a d. of a bucket BIBLE 83:29
clouds d. fatness BOOK 129:3
dance till you d. AUDEN 34:7
Drop, d., slow tears FLET 287:24
Nor any d. to drink COL 211:1
One d. would save my soul MARL 447:1
should like very well to d. JOHN 375:20
That one d. of Negro blood HUGH 354:2
Then d. into thyself POPE 522:11
tune in and d. out LEARY 415:1
world am like a d. of water SHAK 569:30
dropped: D. from the ruined BEAU 56:15
heavens d. at the presence BOOK 129:7
Things have d. from me WOOLF 742:15
When in my arms burd Helen d. BALL 49:13
would not wish to be d. by JOHN 375:20
dropping: d. a rose petal MARQ 448:20
d.-down-deadness SMITH 653:2
d. in a very rainy day BIBLE 79:27
D. the pilot TENN 680:7
drops: changed into little water d. MARL 447:4
D. earliest to the ground SHAK 609:11
d. on gate-bars hang HARDY 326:2
me as are the ruddy d. SHAK 591:2
soft with the d. of rain BOOK 129:3
these are gracious d. SHAK 592:14
dropsical: like a d. head SMOL 654:1
dross: d. that is not Helena MARL 446:17
stoops not to shows of d. SHAK 608:13
drought: d. is destroying his roots HERB 333:16
drove: he d. them all out BIBLE 96:12
drown: D. all my faults and fears FLET 287:25
I'll d. my book SHAK 626:1
I will incontinently d. SHAK 615:9
tears that d. the wind SHAK 601:3
what pain it was to d. SHAK 621:23
drownded: do only be d. now SYNGE 677:7
drowned: And d. in yonder living blue
TENN 684:14

drowned: (cont.):
d. my glory in a shallow FITZ 284:15
D. THAN DUFFERS IF NOT RANS 536:16
d. with us in endless night HERR 336:11
She is d. already SHAK 629:1
That he was d. GILB 303:11
that he were d. BIBLE 91:18
drowning: By d. their speaking BROW 151:26
hath no d. mark upon him SHAK 624:27
maid is like death by d. FERB 281:9
not waving but d. SMITH 652:17
drowns: d. things weighty and solid
BACON 44:13
drowsy: Dapples the d. east SHAK 614:17
dozing sages drop the d. COWP 222:2
d. approaches of sleep BROW 145:13
d. numbness pains KEATS 389:8
d. syrups of the world SHAK 616:19
Vexing the dull ear of a d. man SHAK 594:5
drowsyhead: pleasing land of d. THOM 695:16
drudge: a harmless d. JOHN 368:1
drudgery: Makes a d. divine HERB 334:18
vocation is the love of the d. SMITH 652:3
drug: literature is a d. BORR 136:16
'O d.!' said I aloud DEFOE 234:8
or you can d., with words LOW 429:14
Poetry's a mere d., Sir FARQ 280:22
drugs: may the passive d. of it SHAK 626:16
Sex and d. and rock and roll DURY 264:12
drum: A d.! a drum SHAK 600:3
brave music of a distant d. FITZ 283:14
d. them up the Channel NEWB 492:6
Dumb as a d. vith a hole DICK 243:14
Not a d. was heard WOLFE 740:24
pulse, like a soft d. KING 396:12
spirit-stirring d. SHAK 616:20
still the most effective d. GIR 307:2
Take my d. to England NEWB 492:6
drum-beat: whose morning d. WEBS 725:8
drummer: hears a different d. THOR 697:8
drumming: Down in the valley d. AUDEN 35:14
drums: en de bangin' er de d. HARR 327:9
like muffled d., are beating LONG 427:8
trumpets, beat the d. MOR 484:17
when the d. begin to roll KIPL 401:5
drunk: And partly she was d. BURNS 162:12
being reasonable, must get d. BYRON 170:19
Be not d. with wine BIBLE 102:23
D. and asleep in his boots STEV 665:17
d. deep of the Pierian DRAY 258:5
d. hath made me bold SHAK 601:14
d. old wine straightway BIBLE 94:4
d. with sight of power KIPL 400:13
eaten and d. enough HOR 348:21
fields have d. enough VIRG 714:21
genteel when he gets d. BOSW 137:10
I d. him to his bed SHAK 565:13
if it be d. moderately BIBLE 87:31
I have d., and seen the spider SHAK 631:18
inarticulate, and then d. BYRON 174:2
man may drink and no be d. BURNS 163:12
not so think as you d. SQUI 661:17
not the art of getting d. JOHN 375:8
Philip d. to Philip sober ANON 12:6
that this meeting is d. DICK 243:18
Then hasten to be d. DRYD 260:14
Was the hope d. SHAK 601:5
when d., gentlemen often ROSS 547:1
when men have well d. BIBLE 96:11
Wordsworth d. and Porson sober
HOUS 353:1
drunkard: Reel in a d. CHUR 201:5
rolling English d. made CHES 199:5
drunken: but as a d. sleep SHAK 606:20
Shall be brought d. forth SHAK 567:1
stagger like a d. BOOK 133:2
Sure I had d. in my dreams COL 211:11
drunkenness: branch of the sin of d.
JAM 361:16
d. of things being various MACN 441:2
dry: But oh! I am so d. FARM 280:5
But oh, I am so d. ANON 14:15
d. as the remainder biscuit SHAK 568:14

dry: (*cont.*):
d. brain in a dry season — ELIOT 271:12
d. land where no water — BOOK 128:21
how d. a cinder this world is — DONNE 250:8
Israelites passed over on d. — BIBLE 73:29
O d. your eyes — KEATS 390:9
old man in a d. month — ELIOT 271:10
O ye d. bones, hear — BIBLE 85:27
Rabelais dwelling in a d. place — COL 212:12
refresh it when it was d. — BOOK 120:9
rivers of water in a d. place — BIBLE 83:17
shall be done in the d. — BIBLE 95:24
they whose hearts are d. — WORD 743:18
wine—a friend—or being d. — ALDR 8:5
would fain die a d. death — SHAK 624:28

dryad: light-winged D. of the trees — KEATS 389:8

Dryden: D. fails to render him — ARN 30:6
Ev'n copious D., wanted — POPE 523:5
poetry and the poetry of D. — ARN 29:23

dubious: petty fortress, and a d. hand — JOHN 370:17

ducats: O my d.! O my daughter — SHAK 608:15

duce: *quot libras in d. summo* — JUV 384:8

duchess: chambermaid as of a D. — JOHN 375:6
D. painted on the wall — BROW 151:11
every D. in London — MACD 437:13
I am D. of Malfi still — WEBS 725:20
may not blossom into a D — AIL 6:1

duchesses: what Grand D. are doing — NAP 489:13

duck: d. on a lake in the midst — AUG 36:21
Honey, I just forgot to d. — DEMP 236:15

ducks: country stealing d. — ARAB 24:5
Four d. on a pond — ALL 10:2
I turn to d. — HARV 327:23

duda: *La vida es d.* — UNAM 707:2

dude: d. who lets the girl down — LARK 410:5

due: d. season we shall — BIBLE 102:9
d. time we may enjoy them — BOOK 120:2
render to every one his d. — JUST 383:12

dues: simple d. of fellowship — BROW 147:4
therefore to all their d. — BIBLE 100:9

duffers: BETTER D. THAN DUFFERS — RANS 536:16

dug: never palates more the d. — SHAK 566:19

dugs: old man with wrinkled d. — ELIOT 273:9

duke: And everybody praised the D. — SOUT 657:6
D. of Fife left off using — BENT 64:14
D. of Plaza Toro — GILB 303:14
d.'s revenues on her back — SHAK 587:16
d. unto a tyrant brother — SHAK 567:21
knows enough who knows a d. — COWP 224:10

dukedom: d. large enough — SHAK 625:3

dukes: drawing room full of d. — AUDEN 36:16
d. are just as great — LLOY 424:5
d. were thrice a penny — GILB 304:4

dulce: D. *est desipere in loco* — HOR 350:20
D. *et decorum est pro patria* — HOR 349:25
D. *ridentem Lalagen amabo* — HOR 349:12
D. *ridentem, misero* — CAT 186:7

dulcet: d. and harmonious breath — SHAK 611:16

dulcimer: A damsel with a d. — COL 210:13
d., and all kinds of music — BIBLE 85:28

dulcius: *Sed nil d. est* — LUCR 431:15

dull: Anger makes d. men witty — BACON 45:26
appears d. there is a design — STEE 662:19
at best but d. and hoary — VAUG 709:6
can be d. in Fleet Street — LAMB 406:23
d. and deep potations — GIBB 302:11
d. and muddy-mettled rascal — SHAK 575:10
D. is the eye that will — BYRON 168:6
D. 'mongst the dullest — CHUR 201:10
d. opiate to the drains — KEATS 389:8
d. product of a scoffer's — WORD 743:19
d. scum o' produce — CRAB 224:23
D. would he be of soul — WORD 742:9
He was d. in a new way — GILB 302:26
How d. it is to pause — TENN 690:1
make dictionaries is d. work — JOHN 367:24
not only d. in himself — FOOTE 288:11
Of his d. life — BEAU 56:14
Sherry is d., naturally — JOHN 372:16
so d. but she can learn — SHAK 609:2

dull: (*cont.*):
so smoothly d. — POPE 518:21
statesman is that he be d. — ACH 1:7
venerably d. — CHUR 201:13
wasn't as d. as ditch water — DICK 243:2
What's this d. town to me — KEPP 394:11

dullard: d.'s envy of brilliant — BEER 59:15

duller: d. shouldst thou — SHAK 573:17
d. spectacle this earth — DE Q 237:8

dullness: cause of d. — FOOTE 288:17
d. of our blinded sight — BOOK 135:21
d. of our senses — JOHN 366:15
ones of d. and stupidity — AST 32:7

dumb: before her shearers is d. — BIBLE 84:12
Children are d. to say how — GRAV 314:17
deep are d. — RAL 535:19
D. as a drum with a hole — DICK 243:14
d. as old medallions — MACL 439:9
d. he can't fart and chew — JOHN 367:13
D., inscrutable and grand — ARN 27:19
d. presagers of my speaking — SHAK 633:8
d. to tell the crooked — THOM 693:7
d. to tell the lover's tomb — THOM 693:8
otherwise I shall be d. — KEATS 392:4
swell in the havens d. — HOPK 345:14
tongue of the d. — BIBLE 83:21
understand—for Nature is d. — TURG 705:9
We have a d. spirit within — SORL 656:18

dumb-show: fatal d. of our misery — DRAY 258:3

dumb-shows: inexplicable d. and noise — SHAK 576:5

Dummheit: *D. kämpfen Götter selbst* — SCH 558:3

dummy: risk and a d. for sex — MACH 438:13

dun: then her breasts are d. — SHAK 635:2

Duncan: fatal entrance of D. — SHAK 600:16

dunce: dearest, you're a d. — JOHN 375:25
d. that has been kept — COWP 223:5
d. with wits — POPE 519:1
thou art but a d. — DLAKE 111:23

duncery: inquisitorial and tyrannical d. — MILT 476:6

dunces: d. all in confederacy — SWIFT 674:15

Dundee: bonnets of Bonny D. — SCOTT 559:8
stay langer in bonny D. — SCOTT 560:30

Dunfermline: king sits in D. town — BALL 50:10

dung: d.-heaps play a part in — CHEK 197:9

dungeon: d. flamed with light — WESL 728:2
d. horrible, on all sides — MILT 468:1
Himself is his own d. — MILT 463:27
In a d. cell — GILB 305:5
life-sentence in the d. of self — CONN 216:19
This D., that I'm rotting in — CANN 178:9

dungeons: Brightest in d. — BYRON 173:5

dungfork: man with a d. in his hand — HOPK 346:16

dunghill: cock crowing on its own d. — ALD 8:3
d. kind delights in filth — SPEN 660:7

Dunkirk: in the epic of D. — PRIE 529:1

dunnest: d. smoke of hell — SHAK 600:16

Dunsinane: Birnam wood to high D. — SHAK 604:2
Till Birnam wood remove to D. — SHAK 604:1

duodecimos: humbler band of d. — CRAB 224:26

dupe: The d. of friendship — HAZL 328:15

duped: than to be d. by them — LA R 410:14

dupes: If hopes were d. — CLOU 207:24

duration: fallacy in d. — BROW 145:20

dusk: Betwen d. and dawn many a head — MÜLL 487:16
d. with a light behind — GILB 306:23
with the falling of the d. — HEGEL 330:10

dusky: D. like night, but night — BYRON 172:13
she shall rear my d. race — TENN 685:17
straight path along the d. air — COL 211:21
Trusty, d., vivid, true — STEV 669:1

dust: are they like to take a d. — SHAK 628:14
ashes to ashes, d. to dust — BOOK 124:5
blow in their d. — SHIR 646:4
but writes in d. — BACON 15:28
chimney-sweepers, come to d. — SHAK 571:16
d. all ... in its heat — LIT 423.0
D. as we are, the immortal — WORD 740.21
d. expend an idle breath — RAL 535.17

dust: (*cont.*):
D. hath closed Helen's eye — NASHE 491:1
D. inbreathed was a house — ELIOT 271:4
D. in the air suspended — ELIOT 271:4
d., in the cool tombs — SAND 555:3
d. of exploded beliefs — MADAN 441:12
d. of great persons' graves — DONNE 253:7
d. on antique time would — SHAK 570:10
d. return to the earth — BIBLE 81:1
d. that is a little gilt — SHAK 627:22
D. thou art, to dust returnest — LONG 427:7
d. to the dust — SHEL 639:21
d. upon the paper eye — DOUG 255:13
D. was Gentlemen and Ladies — DICK 245:3
enemies shall lick the d. — BOOK 129:20
English d. — MAC 436:7
even by our mother's d. — FORD 289:14
Excuse My D. — PARK 506:24
Fallen to d. — WILDE 736:6
fear in a handful of d. — ELIOT 272:23
first raised a d. — BERK 65:11
For d. thou art, and unto — BIBLE 70:17
fruit thereof to d. — SWIN 676:12
God formed man of the d. — BIBLE 70:1
Half d., half deity — BYRON 172:17
handful of d. — CONR 217:17
Here lies wise and valiant d. — CLEV 206:13
Hope raises no d. — E.LUA 276:2
in the d. be equal made — SHIR 646:2
in the d. my vice is laid — ANON 16:16
into the d. descend — FITZ 283:18
itself crumble to the d. — BROW 147:14
Less than the d., beneath — HOPE 345:4
like the d. on the nettles — THOM 694:6
maniac scattering d. — TENN 683:16
Marry my body to that d. — KING 396:11
much learned d. — COWP 223:25
My d. would hear her and beat — TENN 686:20
not without d. and heat — MILT 475:7
o'er the d. they loved — BYRON 168:6
off the d. of your feet — BIBLE 90:15
our proud and angry d. — HOUS 351:18
palm without the d. — HOR 347:21
quaint honour turn to d. — MARV 451:3
remembereth we are but d. — BOOK 132:5
rich earth a richer d. — BROO 143:18
shouldst give d. a tongue — HERB 334:13
small d. of the balance — BIBLE 83:29
smeared in d. and blood — SHAK 588:6
So nigh is grandeur to our d. — EMER 276:14
Tell flesh it is but d. — RAL 535:16
this d. falls to the urn — VAUG 709:4
This d. was once the man — WHIT 733:2
this quintessence of d. — SHAK 574:28
thou'lt recover once my d. — GRAH 313:14
throwing of a little d. — VIRG 715:18
T'impark the wanton mote of d. — MARV 451:6
To dig the d. enclosed here — SHAK 635:15
To stir a little d. of praise — TENN 684:1
To sweep the d. behind — SHAK 613:2
Upon the fulcrum d. — BERRY 66:12
vex the unhappy d. thou — TENN 680:16
voiced those rhymes is d. — HARDY 325:1
voice provoke the silent d. — GRAY 315:14
what a d. do I raise — BACON 45:4
which reachest but to d. — SIDN 647:4
with age and d. — RAL 536:3
with a piece of valiant d. — SHAK 613:13
You are not worth the d. — SHAK 596:28

dustbin: into the d. of history — TROT 704:13

dust-heap: great d. called 'history' — BIRR 109:23

dusty: d. answer gets the soul — MER 458:9

Dutch: commerce the fault of the D. — CANN 178:3

Dutchman: icicle on a D.'s beard — SHAK 630:14

Dutchmen: of D. and ditches — BYRON 171:18

duteous: d. and knee-crooking knave — SHAK 614:19

duties: If I had no d. — JOHN 374:22
neglect of his d. — THOM 695:14
our ... sions teach new d. — LOW 430:5
Properly has its d. — DRUM 258:11

dutiful: powers take note of the d. — WORD 712:19

earth: (*cont.*):

all the ends of the e.	BOOK 129:1
And e. is but a star	FLEC 286:10
And I danced on the e.	CART 184:13
And is thy e. so marred	THOM 695:7
And we will stay on e.	PRE.V 528:16
are the salt of the e.	BIBLE 88:24
are the scum of the e.	CHES 199:15
As low as where this e.	ROSS 547:16
between the e. and skies	CAMP 176:7
blow the e. into the sea	SHAK 595:19
bowels of the harmless e.	SHAK 579:32
bring food out of the e.	BOOK 132:8
But did thee feel the e. move	HEM 331:15
canst work i' the e.	SHAK 574:3
Cold in the e.	BRON 142:15
conquest of the e.	CONR 217:2
Could frame in m.	SPEN 660:13
created the heaven and the e.	BIBLE 69:20
dust return to the e.	BIBLE 81:1
E. to Danaë to the stars	TENN 688:13
e. a richer dust concealed	BROO 143:18
e., a sterile promontory	SHAK 574:28
e. breaks up and heaven	BROW 148:24
E. changes, but thy soul	BROW 152:10
e. compels, upon it	MACN 441:5
e. does not argue	WHIT 733:1
e. doth like a snake renew	SHEL 640:15
E. felt the wound	MILT 472:24
E. has not anything to show	WORD 743.9
e. his sober inn	CAMP 177:7
e. in fast thick pants	COL 210:10
e. is all the home I have	AYT 41:5
e. is covered thick	BYRON 168:20
e. is full of his glory	BIBLE 82:19
e. is hell when thou leav'st	NASHE 490:23
e. is not too low	HERB 334:7
e. is the centre	DONNE 253:12
e. is the Lord's	BIBLE 100:33
e. is the Lord's	BOOK 125:16
e. is warm with Spring	GREN 318:2
e. is weak	BOOK 130:4
e. must borrow its mirth	WILC 734:17
E., receive an honoured guest	AUDEN 34:15
e.'s a thief	SHAK 626:17
E.'s crammed with heaven	BROW 147:9
e.'s diurnal course	WORD 748:1
e. shall be filled	AING 6:3
e. shall be full	BIBLE 83:3
e. shall melt away	BOOK 127:16
E.'s shadows fly	SHEL 640:4
e. shook, and the heavens	BOOK 129:7
e.'s human shores	KEATS 386:9
E.'s the right place	FROST 294:11
E. stood hard as iron	ROSS 547:4
e. the broken arcs	BROW 147:26
e. to earth, ashes	BOOK 124:5
e. to heaven as quickly	PLATO 517:2
Everything on e. is flying past	GOGOL 310:2
feel the cold e. upon me	KEATS 392:16
first man is of the e.	BIBLE 101:13
foundation of the e.	BOOK 132:1
foundations of the e.	BIBLE 77:34
general balm th'hydroptic e.	DONNE 252:12
girdle round about the e.	SHAK 611:18
Give the face of e. around	STEV 669:5
going the way of all the e.	BIBLE 73:33
going to and fro in the e.	BIBLE 76:37
hath made heaven and e.	BOOK 134:2
head upon the lap of E.	GRAY 315:20
heaven and e. is named	BIBLE 102:13
Her all on e., and more	BYRON 169:23
huge foundation of the e.	SHAK 581:1
If all the e. were paper white	LYLY 433:13
I find e. not grey but rosy	BROW 148:8
if the e. had rolled	WORD 744:11
In the deep-delvèd e.	KEATS 389:9
it f'll to e., I knew not where	LONG 420.18
I will warm life, or	ANCH 24:13
kindreds of the e. shall wail	BIBLE 105:32
Lay her i' the e.	SHAK 570:16
Let me enjoy the e. no less	HARDY 325:11
let the E. bless the Lord	BOOK 118:19

earth: (*cont.*):

Lie heavy on him, E.	EVANS 279:4
like to get away from e.	FROST 294:11
little e. for charity	SHAK 589:4
make terms with the e.	ALAI 7:6
make the e. my hell	SHAK 622:5
meek shall inherit the e.	SMITH 651:11
meek-spirited shall possess the e.	
	BOOK 126:19
must have a touch of e.	TENN 681:31
my lips to unawakened e.	SHEL 642:1
names of e. and Heaven	COWL 221:18
new heaven and a new e.	BIBLE 107:17
new heaven, new e.	SHAK 564:13
new heavens and a new e.	BIBLE 85:2
nor e. have been at peace	SHAK 591:4
O E., lie heavily upon her	ROSS 547:9
Of E.'s first blood	WORD 744:13
on e. I wait forlorn	ARN 28:20
On e. nothing great but man	HAM 322:13
on e. peace, good	BIBLE 93:28
On the cool flowery lap of e.	ARN 27:13
Or e. received her frame	WATTS 723:7
our dungy e. alike	SHAK 564:14
paces of the vilest e.	SHAK 582:7
pilgrims on the e.	BIBLE 104:15
poetry of e. is never dead	KEATS 390:5
rejoicing with heaven and e.	MILT 476:1
replenish the e.	BIBLE 69:26
round e.'s imagined corners	DONNE 250:20
round e.'s shore	ARN 27:1
serious house on serious e.	LARK 409:15
sleepers in that quiet e.	BRON 142:19
smile o' the brown old e.	BROW 150:17
some say the e. was feverous	SHAK 602:13
spirit of the place and to E.	VIRG 714:2
Standing on e., not rapt	MILT 472:6
substance from the common e.	FITZ 284:14
Than anywhere else on e.	GURN 319:17
that creepeth upon the e.	BIBLE 69:24
There were giants in the e.	BIBLE 70:25
they shall inherit the e.	BIBLE 88:23
th' inhabitants o' the e.	SHAK 600:5
thirsty e. soaks up the rain	COWL 221:7
This e. of majesty	SHAK 619:18
this e., this realm	SHAK 619:18
This litel spot of e.	CHAU 196:1
thou bleeding piece of e.	SHAK 591:23
Though e. and moon were gone	
	BRON 142:13
though the e. be moved	BOOK 127:15
Thou visitest the e.	BOOK 129:2
tread on E. unguessed	ARN 28:13
water under the e.	BIBLE 72:16
Were it e. in an earthy bed	TENN 686:20
What have they done to the e.	MORR 486:1
What if e. be but the shadow	MILT 471:27
When I am laid in e.	TATE 678:15
When thou camest to e. for me	ELL 275:8
Which men call e.	MILT 463:12
While e.'s foundations stand	HOUS 352:4
While the e. remaineth	BIBLE 70:29
Who hath made heaven and e.	BOOK 123:11
whole e. as their memorial	PER 512:23
whole round e. is every way	TENN 682:24
Yours is the E.	KIPL 400:15
earth-born: poor e. companion	BURNS 163:16
earthen: with an e. voider	BARN 53:18
earthly: e. godfathers of Heaven's	SHAK 598:7
well all e. things born	SACK 552:12
earthquake: e. is not satisfied	WORD 747:6
e. were to engulf England	JERR 366:5
eruption prevents an e.	BYRON 173:25
gloom of e. and eclipse	SHEL 642:25
Lord was not in the e.	BIBLE 76:7
Small e. in Chile	COCK 208:5
smiling back—that's an e.	MILL 461:17
were very good against an e.	ADD 5:2
earthy: thou in of the earth, e.	BIBLE 101:13
ease: he never at heart's e.	SHAK 590:7
If 'twere equal e. unto my pain	CAREW 180:9
But for unquiet at in its e.	BLAKE 114:6
Counselled ignoble e.	MILT 469:16

ease: (*cont.*):

doctrine of ignoble e.	ROOS 546:8
E. after war, death after	SPEN 660:2
e. in hell	WRIG 749:13
e. in writing comes from	POPE 521:16
e. of the masters	SMITH 651:3
e. that prayer shall be	WILL 737:14
e. the anguish of a torturing	SHAK 612:18
e. them of their griefs	SHAK 626:20
If thou wilt e. thine heart	BEDD 58:8
inability to be at e. in a room	PASC 507:12
Joys in another's loss of e.	BLAKE 114:7
kindly bent to e. us	SWIFT 675:10
labour with an age of e.	GOLD 310:7
ourselves are at our e.	SMITH 650:16
Some come to take their e.	SHAK 589:18
Studious of elegance and e.	GAY 300:6
Studious of laborious e.	COWP 223:29
take thine e., eat	BIBLE 94:23
To e. my breast of melodies	KEATS 390:9
To e. thine heaviness	GOOGE 312:11
Virtue shuns e. as a companion	MONT 481:5
was done with so much e.	DRYD 258:18
Wherein at e. for aye to dwell	TENN 687:20
with the greatest of e.	LEYB 421:11
world is at e. with them	RENN 63:4
You write with e.	SHER 645:22
easeful: in love with e. Death	KEATS 389:14
easer: thou e. of all woes	FLET 287:20
easier: e. for a camel	BIBLE 91:25
e. to make war	CLEM 206:7
It will be e. for you	CHIL 199:26
tyranny it is far e. to act	AREN 24:17
easiest: all taking the e. way out	WESK 727:26
easing: call it e. the Spring	REED 534:1
east: Boston man is the e. wind	APPL 23:18
cometh neither from the e.	BOOK 130:5
Dapples the drowsy e.	SHAK 614:17
e. all the way into Mississippi	KIPL 399:20
E. is a career	DISR 248:32
E. is East, and West	KIPL 398:13
e. wind may never	WALT 720:23
fiery portal of the e.	SHAK 620:9
hold the gorgeous E. in fee	WORD 746:11
I' the e. my pleasure lies	SHAK 565:10
It is the e., and Juliet	SHAK 622:27
Look how wide also the e.	BOOK 132:5
me somewheres e. of Suez	KIPL 400:3
Not from the E., but from	CRAS 226:6
on the e. of Eden	BIBLE 70:22
practice of politics in the E.	DISR 248:11
through the e.-wind	BOOK 127:22
tried to hustle the E.	KIPL 400:4
wind's in the e.	DICK 239:3
East End: look the E. in the face	ELIZ 275:2
eastern: Out of the misty e. cave	SHEL 643:22
Right against the e. gate	MILT 465:9
Eastertide: Wearing white for E.	HOUS 352:5
eastward: garden e. in Eden	BIBLE 70:1
easy: e. as one's discourse	OSB 501:6
E. is the way down	VIRG 713:11
e. it is to call rogue	DRYD 262:20
E. live and quiet die	SCOTT 560:15
e. to shake a man's faith	SHAW 636:3
e. writing's vile hard	SHER 645:22
If to do were as e.	SHAK 607:12
Of e. ways to die	SHAK 567:14
on the rack of a too e. chair	POPE 519:8
She bid me take love e.	YEATS 751:11
so e. to take refuge	IBSEN 358:16
summer time an' the livin' is e.	HEYW 338:2
Too e. for children	SCHN 558:8
type of the normal and e.	JAMES 363:6
eat: And e. into it self, for lack	BUTL 166:8
Butter and honey shall he e.	BIBLE 82:24
did also e. of my bread	BOOK 127:1
down to e. and to drink	BIBLE 72:20
e. and drunk and lived	JOHN 373:15
e. but ye have not enough	BIBLE 86:18
e. his heart in the market-place	SHAK 614:10
E. in the kitchen	HUGH 354:1
e. like wolves and fight	SHAK 585:13
E. not of it raw, nor sodden	BIBLE 72.5

eat: (cont.):
E. or sleep or drink again   DE L 236:4
E. slowly: only men in rags   RAL 536:11
e. the fat of the land   BIBLE 71:30
e. up and swallow down   MORE 484:5
face shalt thou e. bread   BIBLE 70:16
great ones e. up the little ones   SHAK 619:1
I can not e. but little meat   ANON 14:13
I e. well, and I drink   MORT 486:18
I have e. my ale   FARQ 280:8
I'll e. the rest   SHAK 630:16
I see what I e.   CARR 182:6
I will e. bulls' flesh   BOOK 128:3
I will not e. with you   SHAK 607:19
Let them e. cake   MAR 446:6
Let us e. and drink   BIBLE 83:7
let us e. and drink   BIBLE 101.5
neither should he e,   BIBLE 103:24
One should e. to live   MOL 478:14
Some have meat and cannot e.
    BURNS 162:15
Take, e., this is my Body   BOOK 122:12
Take, e.; this is my body   BIBLE 92:25
Tell me what you e.   BRIL 141:14
than to e., and to drink   BIBLE 80:17
thine ease, e., drink   BIBLE 94:23
thou shalt not e. of it   BIBLE 70:3
tree, and I did e.   BIBLE 70:11
will e. our meal in fear   SHAK 603:3
ye shall e. it in haste   BIBLE 72:10
You will e., bye and bye   HILL 338:12
eaten: e. and drunk enough   HOR 348:21
e. by missionaries   SPOO 661:7
e. to death with rust   SHAK 582:24
He has been e. by the bear   HOUS 351:15
He was e. of worms   BIBLE 98:22
see God made and e.   BROW 148:18
They'd e. every one   CARR 183:3
eater: e. came forth meat   BIBLE 74:14
I am a great e. of beef   SHAK 628:12
eateth: e. your Master with publicans
    BIBLE 90:5
he e. grass as an ox   BIBLE 78:1
eating: appetite grows by e.   RAB 534:17
e. or opening a window   AUDEN 35:6
E. people is wrong   FLAN 285:12
surpass e. and drinking   CLOU 207:13
they were e. and drinking   BIBLE 92:13
eats: Man is what he e.   FEUE 281:12
eave: 'E. 'arf a brick at 'im   PUNCH 531:12
Whether the e.-drops fall   COL 210:6
eaves: fall upon her gilded e.   TENN 688:6
ebb: ne'er e. to humble love   SHAK 616:23
ebbed: e. man, ne'er loved   SHAK 564:27
ebbing: steady than an e. sea   FORD 289:15
Ebenezer: E. thought it wrong   BELL 61:27
ebony: e. as if done in ivory   FULL 296:4
ecce: E. homo   BIBLE 108:14
eccentric: centric and e. scribbled o'er
    MILT 472:11
E. intervolved, yet regular   MILT 472:2
ecclesia: Ubi Petrus, ibi ergo e.   AMBR 10:5
ecclesiam: Salus extra e. non est   AUG 37:4
ecclesiastic: E. tyranny's the worst
    DEFOE 234:25
ecclesiologist: A keen e.   BETJ 68:10
echo: As any challenged e. clear   CAMP 177:5
e. arose from the suicide's   GILB 305:13
E. beyond the Mexique Bay   MAHV 450:1
e. of a platitude   BIER 109:4
Footfalls e. in the memory   ELIOT 270:14
It gives a very e. to the seat   SHAK 629:13
seem an e. to the sense   POPE 521:16
Still left an e. in the sense   JONS 379:16
Sublimity is the e. of a noble   LONG 428:7
Sweet E., sweetest nymph   MILT 463:22
tear the cave where E.   SHAK 623:6
waiting for the e.   MARQ 448:20
echoes: By heaven, he e. me   SHAK 616:11
e. back the public voice   JOHN 370:12
e. which he made relent   DRUM 258:12
great wave that e.   TENN 682:9
Our e. roll from soul to soul   TENN 688:2

echoes: (cont.):
set the wild e. flying   TENN 688:1
echoing: e. straits between us thrown   ARN 29:3
éclat: é. and eloquence   BAG 46:20
eclipse: Built in th' e.   MILT 466:6
e. disastrous twilight   MILT 469:2
E. first, the rest nowhere   O'KEL 498:10
gloom of earthquake and e.   SHEL 642:25
In a merciful e.   GILB 304:3
Irrecoverably dark, total e.   MILT 474:1
or at least an e.   BACON 43:29
Slivered in the moon's e.   SHAK 603:19
eclipsed: which has e. the gaiety   JOHN 369:3
eclipses: Clouds and e. stain   SHAK 600.13
ecological: e. balance of the planet   SONT 656:7
economic: cold metal of e. theory   SCH 558:12
demands of the e. process   TEMP 680:4
e. interests are not   WEIL 726:19
e. law of motion   MARX 452:6
e. law on the side of destruction   KEYN 395:4
e. opportunities   WEBER 724:20
social and e. experiment   HOOV 344:17
which are not purely e.   TAWN 679:3
economical: e. with the truth   ARMS 26:13
economics: about e. than my examiners
    KEYN 395:12
E. is the science   ROBB 541:15
economist: death of a political e.   BAG 47:9
need for the e. to prove   KALD 384:20
slaves of some defunct e.   KEYN 395:10
economists: e., and calculators   BURKE 158:13
e. and political philosophers   KEYN 395:10
economize: Let us e. it   TWAIN 706:7
economy: E. is going without something
    HOPE 344:21
E. was always elegant   GASK 299:2
e. where there is no efficiency   DISR 247:17
fear of Political E.   SELL 562:23
Principles of Political E.   BENT 64:16
ecstasies: Dissolve me into e.   MILT 465:1
To holy virgins in their e.   TENN 681:29
ecstasy: almost mad with e.   TRAH 701:14
Blasted with e.: O! woe is me   SHAK 576:4
E. and Forever be Itself   GINS 306:27
e. of being ever   BROW 145:27
escape from circumstance to e.   BELL 60:18
In restless e. Duncan   SHAK 603:3
Is all despair, or e.   WINC 738:24
maintain this e.   PATER 509:7
My thoughts with e. unknown   DODD 250:2
not e. but it was comfort   DICK 241:4
think thereof without an e.   BROW 146:4
This is the very e. of love   SHAK 574:10
Upon the seraph-wings of e.   GRAY 316:7
What wild e.   KEATS 388:24
ecstatic: Of such e. sound   HARDY 325:5
eddy: In action's dizzying e.   ARN 27:23
Eden: E.'s dread probationary   COWP 223:6
E. took their solitary way   MILT 473:14
garden eastward in E.   BIBLE 70:1
happier E.   MILT 471:9
on the east of E.   BIBLE 70:22
This other E., demi-paradise   SHAK 619:18
voice that breathed o'er E.   KEBLE 392:22
With loss of E.   MILT 467:19
edge: always at the e. of being   SPEN 659:3
blunt his natural e.   SHAK 605:10
children's teeth are set on e.   BIBLE 85:22
e. of the abyss   STEV 667:2
e. yet does not flow over   ROET 544:7
interest's on the dangerous e.   BROW 148:13
my teeth nothing on e.   SHAK 581:5
turned its e. on the silence   HUGH 354:5
edged: Science is an e. tool   EDD 266:6
edges: down the vast e. drear   ARN 27:1
edifieth: charity e.   BIBLE 100:27
edifying: e. of the body   BIBLE 102:17
edisti: e. satis atque bibisti   HOR 348:21
edition: And more beautiful e.   FRAN 293:6
new e. of human nature   HAZL 329:10
editions: like the e. of Balbec   WALP 719:16
editor: E.: a person employed   HUBB 353:11
Edom: over E. will I cast out   BOOK 128:18

educate: e. our masters   LOWE 429:10
e. our party   DISR 247:15
educated: Cabinet ministers are e.   BENN 63:21
clothed, fed and e.   RUSK 550:27
e. classes are learning   TRIL 702:18
e. man's!   BROW 152:23
'e.' people tend to come   ORW 500:19
government by the badly e.   CHES 199:18
once as an e. gentleman   SHAW 636:28
two classes [the e....]   FOST 291:7
women are not e. as they   CAV 187:14
education: between e. and catastrophe
    WELLS 727:20
By e. most have been misled   DRYD 260:26
cabbage with a college e.   TWAIN 706:20
chief hand in their own e.   SCOTT 561:6
ease was produced by e.   BENN 63:4
e. bears upon the child's   HEGEL 330:11
e. between the male   ADAMS 1:12
e. creates many problems   VERW 710:8
E. ent only books and music   WESK 727:26
e. forms the common mind   POPE 520:27
E. has been theirs   AUST 39:6
E. has for its object   SPEN 658:21
[e.] has produced a vast   TREV 702:12
e. is a little too pedantic   CONG 215:14
e. is not that girls should   NAP 489:11
e. is so astonishing   ADAMS 2:20
e. is the knowledge not of facts   INGE 360:1
E. is what survives when   SKIN 649:6
E. made us what we are   HELV 331:9
E. makes a people easy to lead   BROU 144:9
e. must ultimately be limited   POUND 527:16
e. of the people of this   DISR 247:24
e. produces no effect   WILDE 734:13
e. serves as a rattle   ARIS 26:1
e. that which fits a man   MILT 475:19
just as in the case of e.   JAY 363:24
lack of proper e.   BEVAN 69:4
movies, and that is e.   ROG 544:17
Soap and e.   TWAIN 706:5
thank your e.   JONS 379:12
that is not what I call e.   SPARK 658:8
To love her is a liberal e.   STEE 662:20
travel ... is a part of e.   BACON 44:35
unfit of any to be used in e.   LOCKE 425:10
What poor e. I have received   BOTT 137:13
with the e. of the heart   SCOTT 561:7
educe: e. the man   BROW 150:12
Edward: E. may be still fair England's king
    MARL 447:7
E. the Confessor   BENT 64:15
Edwardians: E. were nomadic   WHITE 731:7
Edward VIII: [the future E.]   HARD 323:15
eel: I have seen but an e.   DICK 239:11
eels: I gat e. boil'd in broo   BALL 49:17
effacerai: j'en e. trois   BOIL 117:5
effect: between cause and e.   LA BR 405:3
bring the same to good e.   BOOK 120:16
e. was already in the cause   BERG 65:5
little e. after much labour   AUST 40:1
Nature is but a name for an e.   COWP 224:6
effects: e. from civil discord flow   ADD 3:24
slow preparation of e.   ELIOT 269:16
effectually: faithfully we may obtain e.
    BOOK 121:10
effeminate: He that in e. invention
    MARS 449:10
efficacy: e. and extraction   MILT 475:3
efficiency: economy where there is no e.
    DISR 247:17
e. and inefficiency   SHAW 636:26
efficient: dignified parts and e. parts   BAG 46:12
e. government you have dictatorship
    TRUM 704:16
effluence: e. of bright essence   MILT 470:15
effort: e. nor the failure tires   EMPS 277:20
e. when you have forgotten   SANT 555:15
if that e. be too great   ANON 16:12
What is written without e.   JOHN 377:11
effugere: Soles e. atque   MART 449:14
effugies: At non e. meos iambos   CAT 187:2

effusions: e. of wit and humour   AUST 38:21
egg: afraid you've got a bad e.   PUNCH 532:7
    eating a demnition e.   DICK 242:9
    e. boiled very soft   AUST 38:5
    e. is full of meat   SHAK 623:12
    e. of a North African Empire   GLAD 307:11
    e. of the wren   WHIT 732:17
    e. right through   HOR 351:2
    fatal e. by pleasure laid   COWP 223:3
    like eating an e. without salt   KIPL 402:11
    radish and an e.   COWP 223:34
    See this e. It is with this   DID 245:13
    sitting on one addled e.   ELIOT 269:6
    Wall St. lays an e.   ANON 19:4
    white and hairless as an e.   HERR 336:22
eggs: all my e. in one bastard   PARK 506:21
    eighty-five ways to dress e.   MOORE 482:18
    I'm glad it sits to lay its e.   NASH 490:15
    Lays e. inside a paper bag   ISH 360:21
    partridge sitteth on e.   BIBLE 85:13
    song as a weasel sucks e.   SHAK 568:9
    To boil e. in your shoes   LEAR 414:8
    were but to roast their e.   BACON 45:7
eglantine: musk-roses, and with e.
                                   SHAK 611:19
    warm hedge grew lush e.   SHEL 642:24
ego: Et in Arcadia e.   ANON 22:7
egotist: engendered in the whims of an e.
                                   KEATS 391:12
egotistical: Wordsworthian or e. sublime
                                   KEATS 391:23
egregiously: For making him e. an ass
                                   SHAK 615:22
Egypt: all the first-born of E.   SHAK 568:11
    darkness over the land of E.   BIBLE 72:7
    E.'s might is tumbled down   COL 209:8
    firstborn in the land of E.   BIBLE 72:10
    Our first site in E.   GLAD 307:11
    that there was corn in E.   BIBLE 71:27
    thee out of the land of E.   BIBLE 72:16
    there was a great cry in E.   BIBLE 72:11
    We do not want E.   PALM 505:10
    When Israel came out of E.   BOOK 133:8
    wonders in the land of E.   BIBLE 72:3
Egyptian: Did an E. to my mother give
                                   SHAK 617:2
Egyptians: spoiled the E.   BIBLE 72:12
eheu: E. fugaces, Postume   HOR 349:19
Eichmann: [E.] was summing up   AREN 24:14
eight: want e., and we won't wait   ANON 19:13
eighty: In a dream you are never e.
                                   SEXT 563:11
    rottenness of e. years in gold   BYRON 173:14
ein: E. Reich, ein Volk, ein Führer.   ANON 21:10
Einstein: Let E. be   SQUI 661:18
Eisen: Blut und E.   BISM 110:6
either: How happy could I be with e.
                                   GAY 299:26
    their troth e. to other   BOOK 123:23
Elaine: E., the lily maid of Astolat   TENN 681:30
élan: L'é. vital   BERG 65:6
elbow: e. has a fascination   GILB 305:6
elbow-chairs: Convenience next
    suggested e.   COWP 223:16
eld: Of palsied e.   SHAK 606:8
elder: An e. than herself   SHAK 629:14
    e. man not at all   BACON 44:6
    five days e. than ourselves   BROW 146:4
    I said an e. soldier   SHAK 593:3
    I the e. and more terrible   SHAK 591:6
elderly: e. lady who mutters   CAREY 179:15
    imported, e. American   JENK 365:3
    Mr Salteena an e. man of 42   ASHF 31:4
    elders; at listening to their e.   BALD 48:1
    discourse of three   RIBLE 87:14
    and the four beasts   BIBLE 106:13
    four and twenty e.   BIBLE 106:7
    Of those things e.   STEV 666:9
eldest: Sable-vested Night, e. of things
                                   MILT 470:11
eldorado: E. banal de tous les vieux   BAUD 55:10
eldritch: e. light of sundown   DAY-L 233:4

Eleanor Rigby: E. picks up the rice   LENN 417:18
elect: I was e., I was born fit   GURN 320:2
    knit together thine e.   BOOK 121:13
elected: audacity of e. persons   WHIT 732:11
    will not serve if e.   SHER 645:28
election: An e. is coming   ELIOT 269:4
    e. by the incompetent   SHAW 637:22
    e. is the very essence   JUN 383:4
elections: E. are won by men and women
                                   ADAMS 2:5
    it's no go the e.   MACN 440:14
    You won the e., but I won   SOM 655:14
elective: E. affinities   GOET 309:13
electric: biggest e. train set   WELL 726:23
    E. Kool-Aid Acid Test   WOLFE 741:7
    I sing the body e.   WHIT 732:4
    tried to mend the E. Light   BELL 61:20
electrical: e. skin and glaring eyes
                                   SMART 649:14
electrician: E. is no longer there   BELL 61:23
    practical e. but fond of whisky   WELLS 727:15
electricity: e. dripping invisibly   THUR 697:13
electrification: Soviet power plus the e.
                                   LENIN 417:4
electronic: e. interdependence   MCL 439:13
elegance: casque has outdone your e.
                                   POUND 527:7
    Observed the e. of Circe's hair   POUND 526:12
    Studious of e. and ease   GAY 300:6
elegant: Economy always 'e.'   GASK 299:2
    e. and pregnant texture   STEV 667:10
    e. but not ostentatious   JOHN 368:20
    e. simplicity of the three   STOW 670:11
    e. sufficiency   THOM 696:3
    It's so e., so intelligent   ELIOT 273:5
    Most intelligent, very e.   RUBY 154:7
    round with e. quickness   SMART 649:13
    You e. fowl   LEAR 414:13
elegy: character of his E.   JOHN 368:27
    whole of Gray's E.   WOLFE 741:2
eleison: Kyrie e.   MISS 476:17
element: e. of fire is quite put   DONNE 250:7
    I am not of your e.   SHAK 630:23
    still you watches of the e.   MARL 447:7
    Thy e.'s below   SHAK 595:14
elementary: E., my dear Watson   DOYLE 256:12
elements: Become our e.   MILT 469:17
    But, with the motion of all e.   SHAK 598:20
    Can every element our e. mar   BYRON 171:12
    conflict of its e.   BYRON 172:17
    Contending with the fretful e.   SHAK 595:19
    e. of modern civilization   CARL 180:17
    e. so mixed in him   SHAK 593:23
    Of e., and an angelic sprite   DONNE 251:1
elephant: Appears a monstrous e.   COTT 220:3
    corn is as high as an e.'s eye   HAMM 322:16
    E.'s Child   KIPL 401:20
    great masterpiece, an e.   DONNE 251:14
    herd of e. pacing along   DIN 246:7
    He thought he saw an E.   CARR 184:7
    south suburbs, at the E.   SHAK 630:19
    unwieldy e.   MILT 471:8
elephanto: candenti perfecta nitens e.   VIRG 714:1
elephants: e. for want of towns   SWIFT 675:3
elevated: generous and e. mind   JOHN 370:4
    joy of e. thoughts   WORD 745:1
elevates: e. above the vulgar herd   GAIS 296:15
elevators: Till e. drop us from our day
                                   CRANE 225:25
eleven: e. buckram men   SHAK 580:20
    e. o'clock in the morning   CHAN 190:1
    tells you he's only e.   GILB 304:16
eleven-plus: at e., sixteen-plus   LODGE 425:19
elf: A little child, a limber e.   COL 209:11
    famed to do, deceiving e.   KEATS 389:16
    too often a negligent e.   BARH 52:19
Elginbrodde: Here lie I, Martin E.   MACD 437:10
Eli: E., lama sabachthani   BIBLE 93:5
Elijah: E. doth rest on Elisha   BIBLE 76:16
    E. passed by him, and cast   BIBLE 76:6
    E. went up by a whirlwind   BIBLE 76:15
eliminated: e. the impossible   DOYLE 256:11

Elisha: Elijah doth rest on E.   BIBLE 76:16
Elizabeth: Queen E. of most happy   BIBLE 69:18
    Than my sonne's wife, E.   ING 360:6
elle: e. est comme les autres   DE G 235:12
Ellen: Was to wed the fair E.   SCOTT 560:5
elliptical: And e. billiard balls   GILB 305:5
elm: makes the vine about the e.   DAV 232:6
    tell me, tell me, e.!   JOYCE 381:4
elms: Behind the e. last night   PRIOR 529:15
    Beneath those rugged e.   GRAY 315:12
    doves in immemorial e.   TENN 688:16
    Of withered leaves, and the e.   ARN 28:1
elm-tree: e. bole are in tiny leaf   BROW 150:5
elope: must e. methodically   GOLD 311:19
elopement: love-story or an e.   DOYLE 256:17
eloquence: bag of parliamentary e.   CARL 181:1
    Continual e. is tedious   PASC 507:19
    e. that which gets things done   LLOY 424:9
    e., native to famous wits   MILT 473:20
    For e. the soul, song charms   MILT 469:23
    manner of éclat and e.   BAG 46:20
    Of saucy and audacious e.   SHAK 612:21
    O! let my books be then the e.   SHAK 633:8
    ornate e. in our English   CAXT 188:1
    should say that e. is heard   MILL 460:17
    Talking and e. are not   JONS 380:11
eloquent: e. in a more sublime language
                                   MAC 434:18
    else: e. would I give it thee   BOOK 128:8
    happening to Somebody E.   ROG 544:20
    elsewhere: Altogether,   AUDEN 34:11
    Elsinore: By thy wild and stormy sleep, E.
                                   CAMP 176:10
elude: Court him, e. him   BLUN 116:3
elves: all the criticizing e.   CHUR 201:14
    And the e. also   HERR 336:18
    Ye e. of hills, brooks   SHAK 626:1
Elysian: dead, but in the E. fields   DISR 249:8
Elysium: Keep alive our lost E.   BETJ 68:2
    My brother he is in E.   SHAK 628:11
    Sleeps in E.   SHAK 586:8
    What E. have ye known   KEATS 388:20
emancipator: every e. save his apprenticeship
                                   BROUN 144:10
embalmer: e. of the still midnight   KEATS 390:14
    triumph of the e.'s art   VIDAL 711:3
embalming: For my E.   HERR 337:1
embarras: L'e. des richesses   ALL 9:7
    l'e. où l'on est de se   LA BR 404:18
embarrassment: e. of riches   ALL 9:7
    land of e. and breakfast   BAHN 53:5
    source of annoyance and e.   BAED 46:6
    what keeps us in our place is e.   BENN 63:4
embers: glowing e. through the room
                                   MILT 464:22
    O joy! that in our e.   WORD 746:2
emblem: Take away that e. of mortality
                                   DISR 249:2
embrace: But none, I think, do there e.
                                   MARV 451:3
    But oh as to e. me she inclined   MILT 474:27
    e. your Lordship's principles   WILK 736:19
    Her brown e.   WALK 717:14
    then pity, then e.   POPE 522:13
embraceable: my sweet e. you   GERS 301:14
embracements: e. round   DAV 232:6
embraces: age in her e. passed   ROCH 543:8
    old sire, to his e. runs   DENH 236:16
embraceth: mercy e. him on every side
                                   BOOK 126:10
embroidered: heavens' e. cloths   YEATS 751:22
embroideries: Covered with e.   YEATS 751:3
embroidery: e. had been a constant   ELIOT 269:5
Emelye: up roos E.   CHAU 193:22
emendation: e. wrong   JOHN 369:12
emerald: As green as e.   COL 210:21
    e. twinkles in the grass   TENN 686:16
    sight like unto an e.   BIBLE 106:9
Emerald Isle: men of The E.   DREN 258:9
emeralds: E. big as half a county   LAND 408:3
    E. is paved with yellow   BAUM 55:15
emerge: E., and shine up   AHN 10:19

ending: *(cont.)*:
e. a war is to lose it — ORW 500:18
Never e., still beginning — DRYD 259:21
endite: songes make and wel e. — CHAU 192:11
endless: Closed his eyes in e. night — GRAY 316:7
Lies drowned with us in e. — HERR 336:11
nowhere, and is e. — LARK 409:18
endow: worldly goods I thee e. — BOOK 123:21
ends: all the e. of the earth — BOOK 129:1
best e. by the best means — HUTC 357:5
burnt-out e. of smoky days — ELIOT 272:13
divinity that shapes our e. — SHAK 578:30
e. and scarce means — ROBB 541:15
e. as beyond the province — POPP 524:14
e. by our beginnings know — DENH 236:18
e. for which we live — KING 397:3
e. I think criminal — KEYN 395:1
e. of the world are come — PATER 509:4
e. thou aim'st at be thy — SHAK 589:1
extremity of both e. — SHAK 626:15
into the e. of the world — BOOK 124:4
More are men's e. marked — SHAK 619:16
nature of the e. produced — HUXL 357:13
no e. nor beginnings — DONNE 253:14
Out to the undiscovered e. — BELL 62:3
To do that thing that e. — SHAK 566:19
worthy e. and expectations — BACON 43:11
endue: E. her plenteously — BOOK 119:6
endurance: e., and courage — SCOTT 559:6
patient e. is godlike — LONG 426:17
endure: all that human hearts e. — JOHN 370:13
e. the toothache patiently — SHAK 614:13
E. the winter's cold — SHAK 589:28
e. thyself, those clouds — GREV 318:6
heaviness may e. for a night — BOOK 126:5
I can e. my own despair — WALSH 720:19
love is worth, or may e. — CHAU 195.15
man will not merely e. — FAUL 281:3
Men must e. — SHAK 597:15
nature itselfe cant e. — FLEM 287:1
potter and clay e. — BROW 152:11
therefore, or e. them — AUR 38:1
thou shalt e. — BOOK 132:1
We first e., then pity — POPE 522:13
Youth's a stuff will not e. — SHAK 629:4
endured: not to be e. with patient
resignation — RUSS 551:12
which much is to be e. — JOHN 369:21
endureth: e. all things — BIBLE 101:1
mercy e. for ever — BOOK 134:16
praise of it e. for ever — BOOK 133:5
Endymion: In E., I leaped headlong — KEATS 391:22
enemies: against the common e. of man — KENN 394:1
all assaults of our e. — BOOK 119:3
alone against smiling e. — BOWEN 138:12
by the number of his e. — FLAU 285:19
called thee to curse mine e. — BIBLE 73:11
choice of his e. — WILDE 735:8
E.' gifts are no gifts — SOPH 656:11
e. of Caesar shall say — SHAK 591:22
e. of Freedom do not argue — INGE 359:12
e. shall lick the dust — BOOK 129:20
e. will not believe you — HUBB 353:9
friendship with thine e. — SHAK 591:21
have been e. of liberty — HUME 355:13
Have left me naked to mine e. — SHAK 589:2
his e. the slip for ever — STER 664:15
let his e. be scattered — BOOK 129:6
Love your e., do good — BIBLE 94:6
More than your e. — SHAK 567:19
Our e. have beat us to the pit — SHAK 593:21
People wish their e. dead — MONT 480:11
superiority are utter e. — GAIN 296:13
Such men fitly do e. than e. — DHAK 593:20
they will be e. to laws — BURKE 159:24
Philip and their footstool — BOOK 133:1
time for making fitte e. — VOLT 717:7
To forgive e. H— does pretend — HOWE 113:8
trophies unto the e. of truth — BROW 148.00
we have no perpetual e. — PALM 506:7
with their e. in the gate — BOOK 134:7

enemy: belong the spoils of the e. — MARCY 446:4
be taught by the e. — OVID 502:23
classics is an e. to the human — MILL 462:1
Death was never e. of ours — OWEN 503:16
effect. . .upon the e. — WELL 727:2
E. ears are listening — ANON 21:6
e. faints not, nor faileth — CLOU 207:23
e. if you want to save — BALD 48:9
e. increaseth every day — SHAK 593:12
e. in their mouths to steal — SHAK 616:6
e. of good art — CONN 216:12
E. of the People — IBSEN 359:1
e. of thought — CONR 217:10
e. that will run me through — BURN 160:8
e. who speaks ill of your king — NELS 491:10
friend and e. is but Death — BROO 143:17
got a better class of e. — MILL 462:5
hasn't an e. in the world — WILDE 736:12
Hast thou found me, O mine e. — BIBLE 76:11
Have no e. but time — YEATS 752:3
he is afraid of his e. — PLUT 517:15
he's an e. to mankind — SHAK 630:22
high speed toward the e. — HALS 322:9
Hush! Here comes the e. — CONDÉ. 214:21
I am the e. you killed — OWEN 503:20
If thine e. be hungry — BIBLE 79:18
Is mortals' chiefest e. — SHAK 603:16
Is my vision's greatest e. — BLAKE 111:13
last e. that shall be destroyed — BIBLE 101:8
mightest still the e. — BOOK 124:20
Mine e.'s dog — SHAK 597:12
My near'st and dearest e. — SHAK 581:15
No e. but winter — SHAK 568:8
Our friends, the e. — BÊR 65:2
pregnant e. does much — SHAK 629:2
Sir, no man's e., forgiving all — AUDEN 36:5
that great e. of reason — BROW 146:15
That sweet e., France — SIDN 646:20
then there's life, its e. — ANOU 23:5
while the e. oppresseth — BOOK 127:5
your e. and your friend — TWAIN 706:11
energy: E. is Eternal Delight — BLAKE 112:14
majestic march, and e. divine — POPE 523:4
reason and e., love — BLAKE 112:13
Symbol or e., the Virgin — ADAMS 2:1
enfants: Allons, e. de la patrie — ROUG 548:17
Faire des e., rien de — SART 556:14
Les e. terribles — GAV 299:8
se font pas comme les e. — FLAU 286:4
enforced: useth an e. ceremony — SHAK 592:25
engagement: from every honourable e. — BURKE 159:16
Engels: teaching of Marx, E. and Lenin — KHR 395:14
engine: An e. that moves — HARE 326:7
e. [a watch] to our ears — SWIFT 673:9
Raised by that curious e. — WEBS 72b:17
tremendous from her great e. — AUDEN 34:1
two-handed e. at the door — MILT 469:8
unsavoury e. of pollution — SPAR 658:10
you'll be a Really Useful E. — AWDRY 40:6
engineering: Piecemeal social e. — POPP 524:1
engineers: Artists are not e. — KENN 394:8
It is the age of the e. — HOGB 341:14
engineer: e. hoist with his own — SHAK 577:24
engines: e. to play a little — BURKE 158:6
nor did he scape by all his e. — MILT 469:8
On swiftly-circling e. — DYER 265:3
powers the e. of science — QUINE 534:14
England: Be E. what she will — CHUR 200:17
But in E.'s song for ever — NEWB 492:8
compared to E.'s bruisers — BORR 136:15
damn you E. — OSB 501:20
deep sleep of E. — ORW 500:2
E.—a happy land we know — CHUR 200:19
E, and America two countries separated — SHAW 638:31
E. will do it George — SHAK 585:10
E. a particular battalion — AUD 41:8
I awake! awake! awake — BLAKE 112:8
E. beneath you are born — SHAW 638.20
E. but vice and religion — SMITH 653:24

England: *(cont.)*:
E. expects that every man — NELS 491:16
E. forget her precedence — MILT 475:17
E. has saved herself — PITT 515:17
E. hath need of thee — WORD 745:4
E., home and beauty — ARN 30:11
E. invented the phrase — BAG 46:16
E. is a disguised republic — BAG 47:1
E. is a nation of shopkeepers — NAP 490:5
E. is a paradise for women — BURT 165:12
E. is finished and dead — MILL 461:12
E. is the paradise of women — FLOR 288:5
E. keep my bones — SHAK 594:13
E., my England — HENL 332:9
E. people have good table — MIKES 460:3
E. . . .resembles a family — ORW 500:6
E.'s green and pleasant bowers — BLAKE 112:9
E.'s green and pleasant land — BLAKE 113:4
E. should be free — MAGEE 441:18
E.'s not a bad country — DRAB 257:6
E.'s on the anvil — KIPL 398:12
E. take pleasure in breaking — ANON 12:21
E., their England — MACD 437:14
E. to be the workshop — DISR 246:15
E. was too pure an Air — ANON 17:5
England who only E. know — KIPL 399:2
E. will have her neck wrung — CHUR 202:16
E. will protect him against — PALM 505:8
E., with all thy faults — COWP 223:20
Establishment which we call E. — DENN 237:5
faithless E. — BOSS 137:2
falling towards E. — AUDEN 35:11
fashion of the court of E. — SHAK 587:15
Florence, Elizabethan E. — INGE 359:17
For E.'s the one land, I know — BROO 143:12
France and E. is—the sea — JERR 365:19
Gott strafe E.! — FUNKE 296:10
Heart of E. well may call — DRAY 258:2
heart of E. — QUIL 534:11
he bored for E. — MUGG 487:12
here did E. help me — BROW 150:8
History is now and E. — ELIOT 271:8
history of E. is emphatically — MAC 435:5
I am sure no man in E. — CHAR 191:19
Ireland gives E. her soldiers — MFR 457:18
jurisdiction in this Realm of E. — BOOK 135:26
landscape of E. — AUST 38:13
lot that make up E. today — LAWR 412:24
Noon strikes on E. — FLEC 286:6
Nor E.! did I know till then — WORD 744:14
O E.! full of sin — HERB 334:9
O E.! model to thy inward — SHAK 586:2
Oh, to be in E. — BROW 150:5
old E.'s winding sheet — BLAKE 111:9
ordained that E. shall perish — ELIZ 274:7
Our E. is a garden — KIPL 399:7
regard to this aged E. — EMER 276:19
road that leads him to E. — JOHN 372:7
Rule all E. under a hog — COLL 213:3
Slaves cannot breathe in E. — COWP 223:19
Speak for E. — AMERY 10:8
stately homes of E. — HEM 331:11
Such is E. herself — CANN 178:12
summer in E. — WALP 719:15
That is for ever E. — BROO 143:18
There'll always be an E. — PARK 507:1
think of E. — HILL 339:3
think of the defence of E. — BALD 48:10
This E. never did, nor never — SHAK 594:16
this realm, this E. — SHAK 619:18
thoughts by E. given — BROO 143:18
Wake up, E. — GEOR 301:2
Walk upon E.'s mountains — BLAKE 113:4
we are the people of E. — CHES 199:7
What do you think about E. — AUDEN 36:18
Who dies if E. live — KIPL 399:4
You gentlemen of E. — PARK 506:25
You that love E., who have — DAY-L 233:6
youth of E. are on fire — SHAK 585:1
Englanders: Little E. — ANON 15:21
English: angel is the E. child — BLAKE 114:1
the thing to your E — SHAK 615:24
be the scourif of the saint — HALL 322:2

English: (cont.):

breathing E. air	BROO 143:18
Breeds hard E. men	KING 397:11
But marks our E. dead	KIPL 401:2
Charm is the great E. blight	WAUGH 723:10
E. and the Devil knows Latin	KNOX 403:12
E. are best	FLAN 285:13
E. are busy	MONT 481:16
E. . . . are paralysed	LAWR 412:2
E. are very little . . . inferior	NORTH 496:12
E. as she is spoke	FONS 288:9
E. have hot-water bottles	MIKES 460:4
E. have no respect	SHAW 638:15
E. home—grey twilight poured	TENN 687:22
E. in taste, in opinions	MAC 435:20
E. make it their abode	WALL 718:12
E. manners are far more	JARR 363:21
E. never smash in a face	HALS 322:8
E. plays are like . . puddings	VOLT 717:3
E. subject's sole prerogative	DRYD 261:30
E. sweete upon his tonge	CHAU 192:18
E. take their pleasures	SULLY 671:14
E. talk is a quadrille	JAMES 362:16
E. that of the sea	RICH 540:17
E. tongue a gallimaufry	SPEN 660:29
E. unofficial rose	BROO 143:8
E. up with which I will	CHUR 203:9
E. want inferiors	TOCQ 699:7
E. will long maintain our	CARL 180:26
E. would manage to meet	JERR 366:5
forfeited their ancient E. dower	WORD 745:4
game which the E.	MANC 444:1
half-French, half-E.	SHAK 587:2
happy E. child	TAYL 679:11
Johnson's morality was as E.	HAWT 328:8
king's E.	SHAK 610:12
Like a fine old E. gentleman	ANON 15:19
My native E., now I must	SHAK 619:9
not the expression in E.	ARN 29:18
O noble E.! that could entertain	SHAK 584:20
On, on you noblest E.	SHAK 585:8
principle of the E. constitution	BLAC 110:13
really nice E. people	SHAW 636:19
Remember that we are E.	AUST 39:1
rolling E. drunkard made	CHES 199:5
Saxon-Danish-Norman E.	DEFOE 234:22
seven feet of E. ground	HAR 326:14
shed one E. tear	MAC 436:7
so gret diversite in E.	CHAU 195:26
sort of licence that E.	MANS 445:7
stones kissed by the E. dead	OWEN 503:15
Student of our sweet E. tongue	FLEC 286:15
talent of our E. nation	DRYD 261:15
think of the E. for a thing	CARR 182:22
This is the E., not the Turkish	SHAK 584:7
trick of our E. nation	SHAK 582:23
We be all good E. men	TENN 689:2
wet bird-haunted E. lawn	ARN 27:16
wishes to attain an E. style	JOHN 368:20

Englishman: broad-shouldered genial E.

	TENN 688:17
Either for E. or Jew	BLAKE 111:20
E. a combination of qualities	DICK 242:34
E. among the under-dogs	WAUGH 723:16
E. as ever coveted	KING 398:2
E., being flattered	CHAP 190:11
E. believes be heresy	SHAW 638:23
E. could beat three Frenchmen	ADD 4:15
E. does not travel to see	STER 664:3
E., even if he is alone	MIKES 460:5
E. hate or despise him	SHAW 638:15
E. is content to say nothing	JOHN 375:15
E. prudently avoids all	TOCQ 699:6
E.'s heaven-born privilege	ARN 29:11
E. thinks he is moral when	SHAW 637:12
E. unmoved that statement	GILB 306:13
E. will give his mind	SHAW 638:5
Europe, and not one E.	WALP 720:15
find an E. in the wrong	SHAW 638:7
He is an E.	GILB 306:4
He remains an E.	GILB 306:5
He was born an E. and remained	
	BEHAN 59:25

Englishman: (cont.):

ill-natured thing, an E.	DEFOE 234:21
last great E. is low	TENN 687:14
No E. is ever fairly beaten	SHAW 638:22
religious rights of an E.	JUN 383:3
smell the blood of an E.	NASHE 490:22
that the E. can't feel	FORS 290:1
truth-telling E.	HUGH 354:10

Englishmen: absurd nature of E. | PEPYS 512:9

characteristic virtue of E.	TAWN 678:19
E. act better than Frenchmen	BENN 63:15
E. never will be slaves	SHAW 637:11
first to his E.	MILT 475:11
Honest E.	KING 397:10
Mad dogs and E.	COW 220:14
our very name as E.	PITT 515:16
they would prefer to be E.	RHOD 539:16
When two E. meet	JOHN 368:7

Englishwoman: This E. is so refined

	SMITH 652:20

Englishwomen: Frenchwomen better

than E.	BENN 63:15

engrafted: with meekness the e. word

	BIBLE 104:27

enigma: e. of the fever chart | ELIOT 270:22

mystery inside an e.	CHUR 202:7

enjoy: business of life is to e. | BUTL 166:25

due time we may e.	BOOK 120:2
e. poetry unless we know	THOR 696:24
I can e. her while she's kind	DRYD 262:3
I e. convalescence	SHAW 635:25
inherent will to e.	HARDY 324:17
Let me e. the earth no less	HARDY 325:11
most e. contented least	SHAK 633:10
taught and yet not to e.	ELIOT 269:20
that private men e.	SHAK 586:7
To glorify God and to e.	SHOR 646:7
who can e. alone	MILT 472:14
world to e. Paradise	BECK 58:4

enjoyed: all times I have e. | TENN 690:1

E. no sooner but despisèd	SHAK 635:1
little to be e.	JOHN 369:21
warm and still to be e.	KEATS 388:28

enjoying: others from e. themselves

	RUSS 551:24
Think, oh think, it worth e.	DRYD 259:21

enjoyment: aesthetic e. is | WHIT 731:14

e. as the greatest orator	HUME 355:11
e. of riches consists	SMITH 650:19
Unless it from e. spring	TRAH 701:17
Was it done with e.	RUSK 550:21

enjoyments: Fire-side e. | COWP 223:33

in despair the most intense e.	DOST 255:4
insufficiency of human e.	JOHN 369:24
it were not for its e.	SURT 672:17

enlarge: E., diminish, interline | SWIFT 675:1

enlargement: stability or e. of the language

	JOHN 367:21

enmities: More substance in our e.

	YEATS 752:13
reconciliation where the e.	MAC 435:11

enmity: e. among seekers after | AUCT 33:23

ennemies: Les oreilles e. vous écoutent

	ANON 21:6
Nos amis, les e.	BER 65:2

ennuie: L'éloquence continue e. | PASC 507:19

ennuyer: Le secret d'e. est | VOLT 716:8

Enoch: E. walked with God | BIBLE 70:23

enormity: womb and bed of e. | JONS 378:9

enormous: At the far end of the e. room

	AUDEN 34:5

enough: but ye have not e. | BIBLE 86:18

dark is light e.	FRY 295:20
eaten and drunk e.	HOR 348:21
e. for fifty hopes	BROW 148:11
e. in the world for everyone's	BUCH 154:6
e. people to make a minority	ALTM 10:4
E. that he heard it once	BROW 148:1
'tis e., 'twill serve	SHAK 623:13
When thou hast e., remember	BIBLE 87:22

enquiries: or remote e. | JOHN 368:22

enraged: E. I write | DYER 264:14

ense: sit calamus saevior e. | BURT 164:22

ensign: imperial e., which full high

	MILT 468:22

enskyed: thing e. and sainted | SHAK 605:8

enslave: impossible to e. | BROU 144:9

enslaved: completely e. as farm stock

	SHAW 636:16
e. than any other of Nature's	CAV 187:13

ensnare: web as this will I e. | SHAK 615:19

ensue: seek peace, and e. it | BOOK 126:15

entangled: middle-sized are alone e.

	OHEN 644:14

entbehren: E. sollst Du! | GOET 309:4

entente: Th' e. is al | CHAU 195:25

enter: Abandon all hope, you who e.

	DANTE 230:6
e. into the kingdom	BIBLE 88:28
e. into the kingdom	BIBLE 91:17
e. into the kingdom of God	BIBLE 91:25
E. not into judgement	BOOK 135:3
e. who does not know geometry	ANON 21:16
King of England cannot e.	PITT 515:6
threshold about to e. a room	EDD 266:4
wide that she may e. in	SPEN 659:15

entered: iron e. into his soul | BOOK 132:11

enterprise: All period, pow'r, and e.

	SMART 649:17
And hazard in the glorious e.	MILT 468:3
e. is sick	SHAK 627:7
For there's more e.	YEATS 751:3
starship E.	RODD 543:21

enterprised: therefore not by any to be e.

	BOOK 123:16

enterprises: And e. of great pith and moment

	SHAK 575:16
impediments to great e.	BACON 44:3

entertain: And for an inn to e. | MARV 451:7

Could e. us with no worth	WALL 718:18
e. an idea than to take	JARR 363:22
e. four royalties	SAL 554:3
e. him all the saints above	MILT 466:14
e., when they might instruct	MORE 484:3
Tickle and e. us, or we die	COWP 223:11
To e. divine Zenocrate	MARL 448:6
To e. the lag-end of my life	SHAK 581:27
To e. this starry stranger	CRAS 226:7

entertained: e. by some of your grosser

	WOOL 742:17
have e. angels unawares	BIBLE 104:20

entertainment: A mere gossiping e.

	HUNT 356:16
eligibility of the proffered e.	TROL 704:5
exotic and irrational e.	JOHN 368:28
e. this week cost me above	PEPYS 512:19
Pictures are for e.	GOLD 312:5
some other custom of e.	SHAK 615:23

entertains: e. the harmless day | WOTT 749:1

enthral: Except you e. me | DONNE 250:25

enthralled: unjust force, but not e. | MILT 464:5

enthronèd: e. in the hearts of kings

	SHAK 609:13

enthusiasm: Above all no e. | LAMB 407:15

e. I have been cheated	KEATS 392:5
inspires us with a holy e.	ROUS 549:3
little ordinary human e.	OSB 501:12
that e. moves the world	BALF 48:19

enthusiasts: e. can be trusted to speak

	BALF 48:19
how to deal with e.	MAC 435:13

entia: E. non sunt multiplicanda | OCCAM 498:1

entice: e. thee secretly | BIBLE 73:18

enticing: Mirth can do with her e. | ANON 15:6

entire: E. and whole and perfect | SPR 661:8

entirely: The e. beautiful | AUDEN 35:5

entirety: who would dissipate my e.

	MACN 441:1

entitled: than that no man is e. | ROOS 546:10

entrails: In our own proper e. | SHAK 593:19

In the poisoned e. throw	SHAK 603:17
men her golden e. did espy	DRAY 258:9

entrance: give back my e. ticket | DOST 254:5

To e. the prophet's ear	MANT 445:12
which at my e. into the world	TRAH 701:11

entrances: their exits and their e.   SHAK 568:16
entrancing: most e. sight of all   RODG 544:1
entrap: To e. the wisest   SHAK 609:1
entreat: e. heaven daily   ELIZ 274:10
entropy: e. of human thought   ZAMY 755:5
entrusted: Those e. with arms   WIND 739:5
entwine: e. itself verdantly still   MOORE 483:1
envelope: e. of its technical forms   MAINE 442:12
semi-transparent e.   WOOLF 742:7
envelopes: On backs of tattered e.   HOPE 345:2
envie: e. de recevoir de plus   LA R 410:20
envies: are only the various e.   AUDEN 34:17
envious: beats back the e. siege   SHAK 619:18
grows to an e. fever   SHAK 627:9
To silence e. tongues   SHAK 589:1
environed: e. with a great ditch   CROM 227:15
environment: humdrum issues like the e.   THAT 691:25
no law known to the e.   HARDY 324:16
envy: did in e. of great Caesar   SHAK 593:23
E. and wrath shorten the life   BIBLE 87:29
e. of less happier lands   SHAK 619:18
e. of the devil came death   BIBLE 86:27
E.'s abhorrèd child   MARS 449:8
E.'s a sharper spur than pay   GAY 299:32
E.'s greener than the grass   BALL 50:7
extinguisheth e.   BACON 43:11
from e., hatred, and malice   BOOK 119:17
I e. not in any moods   TENN 683:11
moved with e., took unto them   BIBLE 98:27
mutual of the living   HOBB 359:10
prisoners of e.   ILL 359:10
thoughts and E.'s raging hate   MARS 449:9
through e. of thy happy lot   KEATS 389:8
Toil, e., want   JOHN 370:15
Too low for e., for contempt   COWL 221:11
up with e. and revenge   MILT 467:22
enwrought: E. with golden and silver   YEATS 751:22
épater: Il faut é. le bourgeois   BAUD 55:14
epaulette: any e. I could have worn   THOR 697:7
Ephesians: Great is Diana of the E.   BIBLE 99:2
Ephesus: fought with beasts at E.   BIBLE 101:9
Ephraim: E. also is the strength   BOOK 128:18
grapes of E. better than   BIBLE 74:10
epic: An e. of the eyes   ROET 544:9
name of E.'s no misnomer   BYRON 170:14
thundrous e. lilted out   TENN 687:26
epicure: e. would say   SMITH 653:19
sighs this e. doth burn   DRAY 257:20
Epicuri: voles E. de grege porcum   HOR 348:6
Epicurus: For he was E. owene sone   CHAU 192:23
one of E.'s herd of pigs   HOR 348:6
epigram: Impelled to try an e.   PARK 506:10
until it purrs like an e.   MARQ 448:21
What is an E.? a dwarfish   COL 209:21
Epigramm: Witz ist das E.   NIET 495:16
epigrams: despotism tempered by e.   CARL 180:23
epilogue: good play needs no e.   SHAK 569:29
epiphany: e., a sudden spiritual   JOYCE 381:16
episcopal: lays down his e. hat   AUBR 33:1
episode: e. in a general drama   HARDY 324:11
To the end of a brief e.   MERC 457:14
epistles: obscure e. of love   SHAK 629:9
epistula: Verbosa et grandis e. venit   JUV 384:6
epitaph: are no e. of that Oak   DONNE 253:7
But not remembered in thy e.   SHAK 582:8
e. than their ill report   SHAK 575:6
surely that may be his e.   STEV 667:7
That's if ye carve my e.   BROW 148:17
were an e. to be my story   FROST 295:2
Wit is the e. of an emotion   NIET 495:16
epitaphs: thick derangement of e.   SHER 645:5
worms, and   SHAK 620:7
epithet: Fair is too foul an e.   MARL 448:5
epi mor As 'twere all life's e.   YEATS 751:4
Not one, but all his kind's e.   DRYD 259:8
eppur: E. si muove   497:4
equal: all e. when it comes   DONNE 255:7
all men are created e.   JEFF 364:2

equal: (cont.):
all men are created e.   LINC 422:10
All shall e. be   GILB 304:1
And faith shines e.   BRON 142:12
And in the dust be e. made   SHIR 646:2
country about e. rights   JOHN 367:6
e. division of unequal earnings   ELL 275:12
E. in strength, and rather   MILT 469:11
e. to any living now   PAST 508:12
e. to any other person   PRIE 529:3
E., unclassed, tribeless   SHEL 642:18
free and in dignity   ANON 11:19
freedom we are all e.   JUN 383:7
hast made them e. unto us   BIBLE 91:28
like to consider our e.   DARW 231:12
one e. eternity   DONNE 253:14
robbery to be e. with God   BIBLE 103:4
separate and e. station   JEFF 364:1
Though e. to all things   GOLD 311:4
which is e. to anything   LEAC 413:10
equality: e. in fact as corollary   BAK 47:23
e. in the servants' hall   BARR 54:1
E. would be a heaven   TROL 704:3
general state of e.   JOHN 374:16
idea of e. or inequality   HUGH 354:9
majestic e. of the law   FRAN 292:7
not e. or fairness   BERL 66:4
true apostles of e.   ARN 29:9
equalize: attempt to level never e.   BURKE 168:10
equals: commerce between e.   GOLD 311:17
least of all between e.   BACON 43:17
live together as e.   MILL 461:2
Only a peace between e.   WILS 738:14
equanimity: No man can face with e.   GILB 304:12
equation: Each e. in the book   HAWK 328.5
e. is something for eternity   EINS 268:7
equators: North Poles and E.   CARR 184:2
equi: lente currite noctis e.   MARL 447:1
équilibre: c'est un art d'é.   MA1 454:1
equilibrium: held in perfect e.   JENN 365:7
while than is he keep   BROW 148:13
equinox: who knows when was the e.   BROW 145:24
equipment: e. always deteriorating   ELIOT 271:1
equitem: Post e. sedet atra Cura   HOR 349:24
equity: people with e.   BOOK 131:15
equivocate: I will not e.   GARR 298:17
equivocation: e. will undo us   SHAK 578:21
equivocator: here's an e., that could   SHAK 602:9
equo: E. ne credite, Teucri   VIRG 712:14
ere: Oon e. it herde, at tother   CHAU 195:21
erect: e. and manly foe   CANN 178:6
erecting: there e. new   MARV 450:4
erection: rate the cost of the e.   SHAK 583:1
Eremite: nature's patient, sleepless E.   KEATS 386:9
eripuit: E. coelo fulmen   TURG 705:13
eris: don thyn e. glowe   CHAU 195:14
err: e. as grossly as the few   DRYD 259:11
e. while yet he strives   GOET 309:1
people that do e.   BOOK 131:10
reas'ning but to e.   POPE 522:9
To e. with her   ANON 19:24
To e. is human   POPE 521:21
To e. is human but to really   ANON 19:2
you're mortal, and may e.   SHIR 646:5
errand: e. now to the Antipodes   SHAK 613:18
joyous e. reach the spot   FITZ 284:17
errands: e. for the Ministers   GILB 304:2
Meet to be sent on e.   SHAK 592:24
erred: have e. exceedingly   BIBLE 75:7
We have e., and strayed   BOOK 118:7
erreur: L'e. n'a jamais approché   METT 459:6
erring: e. on ventiferous ripes   HOLM 342:9
error: All men are liable to e.   LOCKE 425:2
charged the troops of e,   BROW 145:29
endless e. must   POPE 522:10
e. be too highly heaped   MILK 570:10
e. never approached   METT 459:6
e. is immense   BOL 117:10

error: (cont.):
It is the very e. of the moon   SHAK 618:8
made the e. double   CLARE 204:19
man that he is in e.   LOCKE 424:19
O hateful e., melancholy's   SHAK 593:18
positive in e. as in truth   LOCKE 425:1
stalking-horse to e.   BOL 117:7
than all the hosts of e.   BRYAN 153:23
ut me malus abstulit e.   VIRG 715:4
errors: common e. of our life   SIDN 647:9
E., like straws, upon   DRYD 259:24
E. look so very ugly   ELIOT 269:28
e. of a wise man make   BLAKE 113:9
e. of those who think   BID 109:1
harmful than reasoned e.   HUXL 358:10
His e. are volitional   JOYCE 382:2
share some female e. fall   POPE 523:20
talk of e. and absurdities   BURN 160:9
erstwhile: After all, my e. dear   MILL 461:11
erudite: e. Verger translated   BARH 52:10
erump: evade,—e.   HOLM 342:10
erupit: excessit, evasit, e.   CIC 204:7
eruption: bodes some strange e.   SHAK 571:25
Esau: E. my brother is a hairy   BIBLE 71:10
E. selleth his birthright   BIBLE 71:7
E. was a cunning hunter   BIBLE 71:8
hands are the hands of E.   BIBLE 71:11
escadrons: gros e. contre les petits   BUSS 165:19
escalier: L'esprit de l'e.   DID 245:12
escamoter: e. le fardeau et   FLAU 286:5
escape: And nothing to e.   ELIOT 270:9
Beauty for some provides e.   HUXL 357:21
But you shall not e. my iambics   CAT 187:2
earnest wish to e.   FOST 291:8
e. complex   MCAR 434:1
e. from emotion   ELIOT 273:20
e. from those whom they   FORS 290:11
let me ever e. them   BOOK 135:2
Let no guilty man e.   GRANT 314:11
make our e. into the calm   HUME 355:17
What struggle to e.   KEATS 388:24
escaped: e. even as a bird out   BOOK 134:2
e. with the skin   BIBLE 77:24
that out of battle I e.   OWEN 503:18
through language and e.   BROW 152:9
eschew: E. evil, and do good   BOOK 126:1b
escutcheon: blot on the e.   GRAY 315:4
Eskdale: E. and Liddesdale   SCOTT 560:25
especial: The sweet e. scene   HOPK 345:5
esperance: Now, E.! Percy!   SHAK 582:3
Stands still in e.   SHAK 596:23
espoused: Methought I saw my late
e. saint   MILT 474:26
my e., my latest found   MILT 471:21
esprit: il faut plus que de l'e.   LA R 405:5
jamais approché de mon e.   METT 459:6
L'e. de l'escalier   DID 245:12
Le peuple n'a guère d'e.   LA BR 405:1
esquires: We are all e. now   GOW 313:4
essays: e. proved thee my best   SHAK 634:21
essence: e. of the true sublime   BYRON 172:6
Existence precedes and rules e.   SART 556:8
History the e. of innumerable   CARL 180:7
purest e. of a human soul   CARL 181:13
uncompounded is their e. pure   MILT 468:17
essenced: with his long e. hair   MAC 436:5
essential: what is e. is invisible   DE S 553:3
essentiality: eternal and infinite e.   SPIN 661:2
established: like an e. society   GREE 316:20
or so sure e.   BOOK 118:4
establishment: E. which we call England   DENN 237:5
estate: And ordered their e.   ALEX 8:10
condescend to men of low e.   BIBLE 100:5
e. Christ adorned and beautified   BOOK 123:16
e. of the Catholick Church   BOOK 120:6
e. o' the world were now   SHAK 605:2
has become a fourth e.   MAC 434:10
low e. of his handmaiden   BIBLE 93:22
mind, body, or e.   BOOK 120:7
relief of man's e.   BACON 41:17
When I am grown to man's e.   STEV 668:16
esteemed: We e. him not   BIBLE 84:11

ESTIMATE EVERYTHING

estimate: enough thou know'st thy e. SHAK 634:11
estranging: salt, e. sea ARN 29:4
esuriens: *Graeculus e.* JUV 383:20
esurientes: *E. implevit bonis* BIBLE 108:10
état: *L'É. c'est moi* LOUI 428:13
éteint: *petite flamme qui ne s'é.* REN 539:2
eternal: And our e. home WATTS 723:7
And to be boy e. SHAK 631:11
authority of the 'e. yesterday' WEBER 725:1
draw near to their e. home WALL 718:13
E. Father, strong to save WHIT 732:2
e. Footman hold my coat ELIOT 272:4
e. in the heavens BIBLE 101:18
E. Passion ARN 27:18
e. summer shall not fade SHAK 633:6
Grant them e. rest MISS 477:10
himself and her of an e. tie AUDEN 35:11
Hope springs e. in the human POPE 522:1
It keeps e. whisperings around KEATS 390:6
lay hold on e. life BIBLE 104:4
lose not the things e. BOOK 121:2
Or of the e. co-eternal beam MILT 470:15
portion of the E. SHEL 639:21
Promised from e. years CASW 185:4
resembles the e. rocks beneath BRON 142:18
stereotype is the E. Feminine GREER 317:13
think ye have e. life BIBLE 96:21
Thou, whose e. Word MARR 449:1
To see itself in that e. glass GREV 318:7
way to e. suffering DANTE 230:6
eternally: all things abided e. TRAH 701:15
eternities: I play for Seasons; not E. MER 458:7
on the meeting of two e. THOR 696:29
eternity: And e. in an hour BLAKE 110:18
And lovers' hours be full e. DONNE 252:8
And make us heirs of all e. SHAK 598:6
Are from e., and shall not fail HOUS 351:18
A teacher affects e. ADAMS 2:15
Damned from here to E. KIPL 399:6
day joins the past e. BYRON 169:1
decomposing in the e. of print WOOLF 742:5
Deserts of vast e. MARV 451:3
equation is something for e. EINS 268:7
e. hath triumphed over RAL 536:4
E. is in love with BLAKE 112:20
e. or infinitude ADD 4:16
E.'s a terrible thought STOP 670:4
E. shut in a span CRAS 226:8
E.! thou pleasing ADD 3:23
E. was in our lips and eyes SHAK 564:25
E. was in that moment CONG 215:23
e. without a solecism BROW 146:4
For oh! E.'s too short ADD 4:17
From the hid battlements of E. THOM 695:6
Horses Heads Were toward E. DICK 244:12
image of e. BYRON 169:16
In the same sweet e. of love HERR 336:17
I saw E. the other night VAUG 709:11
Like mortal life to meet e. DENH 236:16
Lives in E.'s sunrise BLAKE 113:11
one equal e. DONNE 253:14
Or sells e. to get a toy SHAK 632:22
Passing through nature to e. SHAK 572:9
Silence is deep as E. CARL 180:10
some conception of e. MANC 444:1
Some shadows of e. VAUG 709:2
That opes the palace of e. MILT 463:13
that wander through e. MILT 469:14
they are candidates for e. MORE 484:3
time is a pinprick of e. AUR 37:18
Time's thievish progress to e. SHAK 634:8
time without injuring e. THOR 696:27
white radiance of E. SHEL 640:4
eternize: your virtues rare shall e. SPEN 659:11
eterno: PER ME SI VA NELL' E. DOLORE DANTE 230:6
ether: ampler e., a diviner air WORD 744:18
etherized: Like a patient e. upon a table ELIOT 271:21
ethical: giants and e. infants BRAD 139:8
ethics: drew a system of e. MAC 434:20
etiquette: isn't e. to cut any one CARR 183:25
Eton: playing fields of E. WELL 727:7
Etonians: Hail him like E. KNOX 403:8
étonne: *É.-moi* DIAG 238:9
Etrurian: where the E. shades MILT 468:15
Etruscans: secret of the long-nosed E. LAWR 412:11
Euclid: fifth proposition of E. DOYLE 256:17
Eugene Aram: How E., though a thief CALV 175:16
eunuch: between a e. and a snigger FIRB 282:26
can now see the Female E. GREER 317:14
intellectual e. Castlereagh BYRON 170:2
prerogative of the e. STOP 669:15
Though Argus were her e. SHAK 598:14
time's e. and never to beget HOPK 346:19
Time's e., and not breed HOPK 346:9
To be a kind of moral e. SHEL 642:6
eunuchs: A seraglio of e. FOOT 288:12
E. boasting of their chastity LEWIS 420:15
eureka: E.! [I've got it!] ARCH 24:12
Europe: All the dogs of E. bark AUDEN 34:15
alterations on the map of E. CHUR 202:1
And E. made his woe her own ARN 28:21
community of E. SAL 554:5
E. is a continent of energetic FISH 283:2
E. is the unfinished negative MCC 436:19
E. of the ancient parapets RIMB 541:7
E. than a cycle of Cathay TENN 685:20
glory of E. BURKE 158:13
it is the whole of E. DE G 235:3
keep up with Western E. UPD 707:6
lamps are going out all over E. GREY 318:10
last gentleman in E. LEV 419:17
noblest river in E. ADD 4:15
poor are E.'s blacks CHAM 189:15
save E. by her example PITT 515:17
Since E. took their gold CHUR 201:1
smaller nationalities of E. ASQ 31:17
whole map of E. has been changed CHUR 202:2
European: characteristic of a E. CHAN 190:8
communal life of the E. VERW 710:8
Europeans: You are learned E. and we worse MASS 453:13
Eurydice: His half-regained E. MILT 465:18
Euston: flushpots of E. JOYCE 381:2
now three in E. waiting-room CORN 219:3
evangelists: and some, e. BIBLE 102:17
evasion: admirable e. of whoremaster man SHAK 595:2
evasions: intricate e. STEV 666:6
evasit: *excessit, e., erupit* CIC 204:7
eve: E. ate Adam HUGH 354:7
E. from his side arose ANON 19:19
fairest of her daughters E. MILT 471:7
fallen sons of E. CHES 199:10
From far, from e. and morning HOUS 352:14
past E. and Adam's JOYCE 380:21
spouse, nor E. the rites MILT 471:14
When Adam dalfe and E. ROLLE 545:10
When E. upon the first of Men HOOD 344:5
Evelyn: E. Hope is dead BROW 149:20
even: E. as you and I! KIPL 401:7
E. less am I HOPE 345:4
e. terror of their lives SHAR 635:18
last pale beam of e. SHEL 643:8
When the grey-hooded E. MILT 463:19
evening: And yet the E. listens KEATS 390:8
Are like an e. gone WATTS 723:7
beautiful e., very starry WORD 742:21
bright exhalation in the e. SHAK 588:18
browner shade the e. GIBB 302:21
e. and the morning were BIBLE 69:21
e. is spread out against ELIOT 271:21
e. it is cut down BOOK 130:23
e. satiate of applause POPE 522:25
e. star is coming VIRG 715:9
e. star, love's harbinger MILT 473:9
e. withhold not thine hand BIBLE 80:28
For note, when e. shuts BROW 152:8
evening: (*cont.*):
hands be an e. sacrifice BOOK 135:1
hush of e. that trembles HAMM 322:14
into the corners of the e. ELIOT 272:1
It is a beauteous e. WORD 744:12
light of e., Lissadell YEATS 752:2
Now came still e. MILT 471:10
Of grateful e. mild MILT 471:12
over there the red e. star VIRG 715:11
sadly descends the autumn e. ARN 28:1
see on an e. such as this WASH 722:4
Softly along the road of e. DE L 236:10
welcome peaceful e. COWP 223:31
When e.'s come, you homeward COLL 212:23
When it is e., ye say BIBLE 91:12
winter e. settles down ELIOT 272:13
evensong: bells ringeth to e. HAWES 328:3
In a full-hearted e. HARDY 325:5
event: How much the greatest e. FOX 291:18
hurries to the main e. HOR 347:13
only as the e. decides AUST 39:8
eventide: fast falls the e. LYTE 433:16
events: category of objective e. MANN 445:3
e. in the womb of time SHAK 615:11
e., mostly unimportant BIER 109:11
that e. have controlled me LINC 422:13
We cannot make e. ADAMS 3:8
ever: 'e.' lasted but a short WYATT 749:18
For e. panting, and for ever KEATS 388:28
Lasts e., past recall BROW 152:10
things to last for e. HOR 350:16
What, *never*? Hardly e. GILB 305:23
ever-fixèd: an e. mark SHAK 634:23
everlasting: And the life e. BOOK 119:1
caught an e. cold WEBS 726:14
come unto thy e. kingdom BOOK 123:13
From e. Thou art God WATTS 723:7
from e. to everlasting TRAH 701:13
hath e. life BIBLE 96:27
have e. life BIBLE 96:15
hath made his e. mansion SHAK 626:21
In e. watch and moveless woe BROW 147:14
mighty God, The e. Father BIBLE 82:27
Seems here her e. rest FANS 280:2
Thy e. mercy, Christ MAS 453:6
underneath are the e. arms BIBLE 73:24
unto e. time AUR 37:19
will give them an e. name BIBLE 84:19
everlastingness: Bright shoots of e. VAUG 709:3
evermore: and e. shalt be HEBER 330:5
E. be led to thee DIX 249:19
mighty waters rolling e. WORD 746:5
their name liveth for e. BIBLE 88:3
this time forth for e. BOOK 133:24
every: e. common bush afire BROW 147:9
E. Day a Little Death SOND 656:1
E. day, in every way COUÉ 220:5
e. thing there is a season BIBLE 80:5
'E. thinking man' ADAMS 2:3
E. time a child says BARR 54:7
E. time we say goodbye PORT 524:22
E. which way but loose KRON 404:4
everybody: e. will be world famous WARH 721:22
You know e. is ignorant ROG 545:3
everyday: crashed against the e. MAY 455:8
everyman: E., I will go with thee ANON 13:4
everyone: e. is alike and no one KING 398:8
E. suddenly burst out singing SASS 557:9
When e. is wrong, everyone LA CH 405:6
everything: E. has been said LA BR 405:4
e. has been tried at least BENN 63:1
e. in its place and nothing BEVAN 69:3
E. is fitting for me AUR 37:15
E. is funny as long as it ROG 544:20
Greek can do e. JUV 383:20
it is for e. dear PITT 515:16
it said 'Chips with e.' WESK 727:25
make myself laugh at e. BEAU 56:10
place for e. and everything BEET 59:24
robbed a man of *e.* SOLZ 655:7

everything: (*cont.*):
sans taste, sans e. — SHAK 568:16
Universe and E. — ADAMS 2:1
we cannot all do e. — LUC 431:11
We can't all do e. — VIRG 715:6
world is e. that is the case — WITT 740:4
everywhere: e. and the circumference
— ANON 16:17
E. I hear the sound — JAGG 361:12
his behaviour is — SHAK 607:15
Out of the e. into here — MACD 437:9
evidence: before you have all the e.
— DOYLE 256:22
clearer e. than this — ARAB 24:3
e. of life after death — SOPER 656:9
e. of things not seen — BIBLE 104:13
'it's not e. — DICK 243:20
Some circumstantial e. — THOR 696:23
speech than to give e. — HAL 321:13
evil: all e. shed away — BROO 143:18
all government is e. — O'SUL 502:4
All partial e., universal good — POPE 522:8
all that we are e. in — SHAK 595:2
aware to know all the e. — LA R 410:18
banality of e. — AREN 24:14
because the days are e. — BIBLE 102:22
because their deeds were e. — BIBLE 96:16
confusion that wish me e. — BOOK 129:15
Created e., for evil only good — MILT 470:4
deliver us from e. — BIBLE 89:5
deliver us from e. — MISS 477:3
doeth e. hath not seen God — BIBLE 105:30
Do e. in return — AUDEN 35:19
done e. to his neighbour — BOOK 124:28
done this e. in thy sight — BOOK 128:4
don't think that he's e. — ALLEN 9:12
Eschew e., and do good — BOOK 126:15
e. and adulterous generation — BIBLE 90:34
E., be thou my good — MILT 470:26
E. be to him who evil thinks — ANON 20:9
E. communications corrupt — BIBLE 101:10
e. empire — REAG 537:12
e. is simply ignorance — FORD 289:6
e. is wrought by want — HOOD 343:23
e. manners live in brass — SHAK 589:9
e. that men do lives after — SHAK 592:5
e. which I would not — BIBLE 99:32
face of 'e.' is always — BURR 164:5
far deeper than the e. — FORS 290:16
Few and e. have the days — BIBLE 71:32
For e. news rides post — MILT 474:13
good of e. shall produce — MILT 473:11
heart is e. from his youth — BIBLE 70:28
Her rash hand in e. hour — MILT 472:24
If all e. were prevented — THOM 693:1
Ignorance is an e. weed — BEV 69:8
it is a necessary e. — BRAD 139:4
it is an unruly e. — BIBLE 105:2
knowing good and e. — BIBLE 70:9
knowing good by e. — MILT 475:6
know to refuse the e. — BIBLE 82:24
Let us do e., that good — BIBLE 99:21
money is the root of all e. — BIBLE 104:3
must return good for e. — VANB 708:2
necessary e. — PAINE 504:10
no e. happen unto thee — BOOK 131:4
nothing for e. to triumph — BURKE 160:4
notorious e. liver — BOOK 121:14
Not rendering evil for e. — BIBLE 105:18
Obscures the show of e. — SHAK 608:26
only e. that walks — MILT 470:21
on the e. and on the good — BIBLE 88:34
ourselves by doing e. in return — SOCR 654:16
overcome e. with good — BIBLE 100:7
perplexity of radical e. — AREN 24:15
place that is free from e. — WAUGH 724:7
presuppose that all men are e. — MACH 438:6
prevention from e. — MANN 444:11
provoked, thinketh no e. — BIBLE 101:1
punishment in itself is e. — BENT 61:6
represent poverty as no e. — BURN 160:10
[illegible line] — BIBLE 88:32
rewarded me e. for good — BOOK 124:18

evil: (*cont.*):
Shall there be e. in a city — BIBLE 86:11
sometimes meet e.-willers — ELIZ 274:2
speak e. of dignities — BIBLE 105:23
still to find means of e. — MILT 468:8
supernatural source of e. — CONR 217:16
that call e. good — BIBLE 82:17
that e. passions — CHEK 197:9
There is no e. in the atom — STEV 666:18
though fall'n on e. days — MILT 472:6
unto the day is the e. — BIBLE 89:13
what people call e. — GIDE 303:6
Whenever God prepares e. — ANON 21:15
withstand in the e. day — BIBLE 103:1
Wi' tippenny, we fear nae e. — BURNS 163:8
evils: enamoured of existing e. — BIER 109:8
e. and the worst of crimes — SHAW 636:27
E., Theodorus, can never — PLATO 517:2
greater e. than the first — CHUR 201:3
live only by fighting e. — BERL 66:1
of two e. the lesser is always — THOM 692:12
remedies must expect new e. — BACON 43:33
they are necessary e. — JOHN 369:13
Two e., monstrous either — RANS 536:15
When e. are most free — SHAK 590:16
evil-speaking: my tongue from e. — BOOK 123:8
evoke: To e. posterity — GRAV 315:2
evolution: e. and peaceful extermination
— ZIN 755:12
E. is change from indefinite — SPEN 658:16
Some call it e. — CARR 184:9
ewe: Is tupping your white e. — SHAK 614:22
Whereof the e. not bites — SHAK 626:1
ewer: safe in a golden e. — BROW 149:6
ewes: my e. breed not — BARN 53:17
ewig: 'e. Gestrigen' — WEBER 725:1
ewige: e. Friede ist ein Traum — MOLT 479:1
exact: Detection an e. science — DOYLE 256:17
greatness not to be e. — BURKE 157:15
understand the e. and tribal — HEAN 329:20
writing an e. man — BACON 44:28
exactitude: L'e. est la politesse des rois
— LOUI 428:18
exaggerate: interesting are obliged to e.
— FORS 290:23
exaggerated: have been greatly e.
— TWAIN 706:25
exaggeration: e. a truth that has lost its temper
— GIBR 303:4
exalt: e. us unto the same place — BOOK 120:19
exalted: Every valley shall be e. — BIBLE 83:26
e. among the heathen — BOOK 127:17
e. them of low degree — BIBLE 93:23
God hath also highly e. — BIBLE 103:5
her most e. mood — WORD 747:10
Sorrow proud to be e. — ANON 15:6
To be e. thus — WATTS 722:19
exalteth: himself shall be abased — BIBLE 94:28
exalts: what man does which e. him
— BROW 152:26
examinations: E. are formidable even
— COLT 214:8
in e. those who do not wish to know
— RAL 536:10
examine: E. for a moment an ordinary mind
— WOOLF 742:6
E. me, O Lord, and prove — BOOK 125:21
e. my thoughts — BOOK 134:22
e. well your blood — SHAK 610:20
examiners: knew more about economics than
my e. — KEYN 395:12
example: annoyance of a good e. — TWAIN 706:23
don't set us a good e. — WILDE 734:9
E. is always more efficacious — JOHN 369:23
E. is the school of mankind — BURKE 159:21
My great e., as it is my theme — DENH 236:17
save Europe by her e. — PITT 515:17
examples: History is philosophy from e.
— DION 246:12
exaudi: e. vocem meam — BIBLE 108:5
exceed: e. all that we can desire — BOOK 121:4
reach should e. his grasp — BROW 149:2
[illegible] bitter agony — SORL 656:18

excel: so great as daring to e. — CHUR 200:16
thou shalt not e. — BIBLE 71:33
excellence: conformity with e. — ARIS 25:9
ne'er will reach an e. — DRYD 261:33
so nearly allied to e. — GOLD 311:15
excellencies: upon e. than imperfections
— ADD 4:12
excellent: e. thing in woman — SHAK 598:2
e. things are spoken — BOOK 130:21
e. things for mean or no — LOCKE 424:17
his Name only is e. — BOOK 135:15
mediocrity when the e. — D'ISR 249:15
too wonderful and e. — BOOK 134:19
excellently: Goddess, e. bright — JONS 378:16
I see them all so e. fair — COL 209:12
excelling: Love divine, all loves e. — WESL 728:14
Excelsior: strange device, E.! — LONG 426:18
excelsis: Gloria in e. Deo — MISS 476:18
except: E. the Lord build the house — BOOK 134:6
exception: glad to make an e. in your case
— MARX 452:1
excess: blasted with e. of light — GRAY 316:7
e. leads to the palace — BLAKE 112:16
Give me e. of it — SHAK 628:9
intimidated by an e. of joy — ALAI 7:7
Is wasteful and ridiculous e. — SHAK 594:9
not drinking to be blamed, but the e.
— SELD 562:4
Nothing in e. — ANON 21:14
should surprise by a fine e. — KEATS 391:14
so much poverty and e. — PENN 511:14
Such an e. of stupidity — JOHN 372:16
excessit: Abiit, e., evasit — CIC 204:7
excessive: Dark with e. bright — MILT 470:18
right of an e. wrong — BROW 152:18
exchange: By just e. — SIDN 646:14
excise: E. A hateful tax levied — JOHN 367:25
exciseman: deil's awa wi' th'E. — BURNS 161:22
excite: e. my amorous propensities — JOHN 371:8
exciting: films. They are too e. — BERR 66:19
too e. to be pleasant — DICK 243:10
excluded: am irrevocably e. — SHEL 639:8
exclusion: e. and prohibition — MILL 461:14
excommunicate: nor be outlawed, nor e.
— COKE 209:3
When thou, poor e. — CAREW 179:14
excrement: From gen'ral e. — SHAK 626:17
in the place of e. — YEATS 751:8
excrucior: Nescio, sed fieri sentio et e. — CAT 186:17
excursion: car his perilous e. — LEWIS 421:3
e. to hell and came back — PRIE 529:1
poem, called the 'E.' — BYRON 171:4
excuse: denial vain, and coy e. — MILT 465:21
e. every man will plead — SELD 562:5
E. My Dust — PARK 506:24
I will not e.—I will not — GARR 298:11
prove an e. for the glass — SHER 645:18
they make a good e. — SZASZ 677:17
with one consent began to make e.
— BIBLE 94:29
excuses: several e. less convincing than one
— HUXL 357:17
execrable: e. shape — MILT 470:6
execute: people who e. them — MILL 461:1
executing: thought-e. — SHAK 595:20
execution: and the e. confined — SHAK 627:16
effective as their stringent e. — GRANT 314:10
e. than for counsel — BACON 45:9
fascination of a public e. — FOOT 288:11
Which smoked with bloody e. — SHAK 599:15
executioner: I am mine own E. — DONNE 253:4
executioners: victims who respect their e.
— SART 557:2
executive: nominated by the e. — GIBB 302:1
executives: where e. would never want
to tamper — AUDEN 34:14
executors: Delivering o'er to e. pale
— SHAK 584:22
Let's choose e., and talk — SHAK 620:7
exercise: cure, on e. depend — DRYD 260:16
dancing is love's proper e. — DAV 232:5
e. for a reasonable soul — LOD 428:13

exercise: (*cont.*):
e. myself in great matters   BOOK 134:13
e. of his soul's faculties   ARIS 25:9
mind what e. is to the body   STEE 662:21
sad mechanic e.   TENN 683:1
exertion: extraordinary, unceasing e.
                                    CHEK 196:9
exhalation: bright e. in the evening
                                    SHAK 588:18
Rose like an e.   MILT 469:6
exhausted: enemies are not yet e.   GLAD 307:12
exhaustion: e. of weaning   AUDEN 36:5
exhibitionism: Acting is a masochistic
form of e.   OLIV 498:15
exile: e. to Italy and the Lavinian   VIRG 711:18
silence, e., and cunning   JOYCE 381:14
therefore I die in e.   GREG 317:18
exiled: or outlawed or e.   MAGN 442:1
exiles q. from our fathers' land   GALT 297:7
Thou Paradise of e., Italy   SHEL 640:21
Which none save e. feel   AYT 41:4
exist: Art and Science cannot e.   BLAKE 112:6
bastard! He doesn't e.   BECK 57:14
e. in order to save us   DE VR 238:4
I e. by what I think   SART 557:1
impression that we e.   BECK 57:26
Laski that He doesn't e.   PRIE 529:2
questioned its right to e.   SCH 558:11
they e., but are identical   FORS 290:24
existence: Every e. would exist in thee
                                    BRON 142:13
e. and this which befalls you   AUR 38:2
e. is but a brief crack   NAB 489:2
e. is itself an illusion   BELL 62:7
e. or when hope is gone   AUST 39:7
E. precedes and rules essence   SART 556:8
how e. could be cherished   BRON 142:17
justifying their own e.   FORS 290:23
Let us contemplate e.   DICK 241:11
must contribute is her e.   GREER 317:13
our e. as a nation   PITT 515:16
paint on the face of E.   BYRON 174:1
prefer mere e. to honour   JUV 384:4
sole purpose of human e.   JUNG 382:14
Struggle for E.   DARW 231:8
Their e. only adds   MOUN 487:6
'Tis woman's whole e.   BYRON 170:13
universe's very e.   PENR 512:1
very e. of life itself   SONT 656:7
exists: And no one e. alone   AUDEN 36:1
understood no longer e.   ÉLUA 276:4
exit: E., pursued by a bear   SHAK 631:23
Such a graceful e.   JUNOR 383:11
exits: e. and their entrances   SHAK 568:16
For men to take their e.   WEBS 725:22
exitus: e. multos   SEN 563:1
exorciser: No e. harm thee   SHAK 571:16
exordium: th'e. of our woes   DRAY 258:3
exoriare: E. aliquis nostris   VIRG 713:8
exotic: e. follies o'er the town   BYRON 172:9
expatiate: E. free o'er all this scene   POPE 521:26
expect: E. nothing. Live frugally on surprise
                                    WALK 717:12
know more of mankind I e. less   JOHN 376:9
people e. most from others   AUST 38:16
expectancy: e. and rose of the fair   SHAK 576:4
expectation: dream and folly of e.   BROW 145:25
e. whirls me round   SHAK 627:15
For now sits E. in the air   SHAK 585:1
indeed better bettered e.   SHAK 613:5
Singing songs of e.   BAR 53:3
'Tis e. makes a blessing dear   SUCK 671:5
expectations: ends and e.   BACON 43:11
revolution of rising e.   CLEV 206:12
expediency: always be sacrificed to e.
                                    MAUG 454:5
expedient: all things are not e.   BIBLE 100:32
consider that it is e. for us   BIBLE 97:6
e. for you that I go away   BIBLE 97:18
may be most e. for them   BOOK 119:9
not a principle, but an e.   DISR 246:19
expedit: E. esse deos   OVID 502:15
expeditious: He's an e. man   MOL 479:7

expeditious: (*cont.*):
There is no e. road   THOM 695:8
expelles: Naturam e. furca   HOR 348:41
expende: E. Hannibalem   JUV 384:8
expenditure: annual e.   DICK 239:28
E. rises to meet income   PARK 507:2
expense: drinking at somebody else's e.
                                    LEIGH 417:2
e. damnable   CHES 198:25
e. of spirit in a waste   SHAK 635:1
repay the trouble and e.   BELL 60:24
use alone that sanctifies e.   POPE 520:23
Would be at the e. of two   CLOU 207:16
expenses: but facts are on e.   STOP 669:18
meet all the e. of living   THOR 697:1
expensive: how e. it is to be poor   BALD 48:2
experience: All e. is an arch to build upon
                                    ADAMS 2:9
are perfected by e.   BACON 44:26
balloon of e.   JAMES 362:14
contrary to custom and e.   HUME 355:7
death we do not e.   MANN 445:3
dirty nurse, E.   TENN 682:5
elder, a part of e.   BACON 44:35
e. and trial of this world   ELIZ 274:2
e. has no value   METT 459:1
e. is an arch wherethrough   TENN 690:1
E. is never limited   JAMES 363:3
E. is the child of Thought   DISR 248:34
E. is the name every one   WILDE 735:13
E., though noon auctoritee   CHAU 194:19
flower of any kind of e.   HUNT 356:19
full of e. and good sense   DU B 263:1
go beyond his e.   LOCKE 424:18
great e. one thing is essential   BAG 47:11
I have e.: I have a wife   CONG 215:29
I know it from e.   ARAB 24:4
imposing of a pattern on e.   WHIT 731:14
know it by e.   THOR 697:5
knowledge but recorded e.   CARL 180:6
never had much e.   MARQ 448:11
system to be refuted by e.   POPP 524:10
Then Old Age, and E.   ROCH 543:12
Till old e. do attain   MILT 465:2
triumph of hope over e.   JOHN 373:12
which e. gives is a lantern   COL 212:14
world that we need not e. it   FRIS 294:4
experiences: lie the e. of our life   MANN 445:3
experientia: E. does it—   DICK 239:26
experiment: best scale for an e.   FISH 283:3
never tried an e. in his life   DARW 231:13
social and economic e.   HOOV 344:17
tide of successful e.   JEFF 364:4
experimental: contain any e. reasoning
                                    HUME 355:4
experimentalists: e. bungle things   EDD 266:3
expers: Vis consili e.   HOR 350:4
expert: e. is someone who knows   HEIS 331:5
e. one who knows more and more
                                    BUTL 165:23
experto: E. credite   VIRG 714:9
experts: never trust e.   SAL 554:2
expiate: And I have something to e.
                                    LAWR 412:21
expire: I tremble, I e.   SHEL 640:11
expiring: on the point of e.   FORS 290:7
explain: e. a thing till all men   POPE 519:4
e. why it didn't happen   CHUR 203:7
Never complain and never e.   DISR 249:10
Never e. Never apologize   FISH 283:5
Never e.—your friends do not   HUBB 353:9
spoil it by trying to e.   SHER 645:11
would e. his explanation   BYRON 170:1
explained: die before we have e. ourselves
                                    ADAMS 3:3
Shut up he e.   LARD 409:11
explainer: A village e.   STEIN 663:7
explaining: forever e. things to them   DE S 553:2
explanation: fuss and no e.   BLYT 116:9
sometimes saves tons of e.   SAKI 553:13
expletive: E. deleted   ANON 13:6
exploit: dignity composed and high e.
                                    MILT 469:13

exploit: (*cont.*):
I'm sure you'd never e. one   COPE 218:10
explore: no need to falter or e.   WILB 734:5
explorers: endeavours are unlucky e.
                                    DOUG 255:11
exploring: end of all our e.   ELIOT 271:6
explosive: 'philosopher': a terrible e.   NIET 495:8
exposed: intellect improperly e.   SMITH 653:12
exposes: e. himself when he is intoxicated
                                    JOHN 375:8
exposition: e. of sleep   SHAK 612:12
exposure: unseemly e. of the mind   HAZL 329:6
express: e. image of his person   BIBLE 104:10
e. in the small of the back   WOD 740:14
e. myself in some mode   JOYCE 381:14
e. our wants as to conceal   GOLD 311:13
e.-train drew up there   THOM 693:23
e. yourself like the common   YEATS 753:24
To e. what then I saw   WORD 743:11
What I can ne'er e.   BYRON 169:13
which a picture cannot e.   BACON 42:26
expressed: ne'er so well e.   POPE 521:11
expresser: most gentle e. of it   HEMI 331:13
expression: E. is the dress of thought
                                    POPE 521:12
e. which is in the countenance   WORD 748:18
have not the e. in English   ARN 29:18
expressive: e. of his eye   SHAK 629:9
exquisite: e. touch   SCOTT 561:1
pleasure so e.   HUNT 356:17
exquisitely: Autumn sunsets e. dying
                                    HUXL 357:21
extant: be but pyramidally e.   BROW 145:20
extempore: laboured as his e. sayings
                                    WALP 720:2
extemporize: More harassing master
would e.   STEV 666:6
extension: e. which lends utility   SANT 555:19
extenuate: nothing e.   SHAK 618:20
extenuates: e. not wrong   SHAK 627:14
exterminate: E. all the brutes   CONR 217:4
will have to e. a nation   SPOCK 661:4
extinguished: sometimes overcome,
seldom e.   BACON 44:7
extol: all ye creatures to e.   MILT 471:23
e. thee who are born   BENS 63:23
extra: some e., just for you   LARK 410:6
extraction: e. of that living intellect   MILT 475:3
extraordinary: e. people have the right
                                    DOST 254:9
this is an e. man   JOHN 376:10
extravagance: beautiful does not lead to e.
                                    PER 512:22
extravagant: e. and irrational   SWIFT 673:14
e. with his own   SALL 554:11
extreme: e. to mark what is done amiss
                                    BOOK 134:11
extremes: e. appear like man   CHUR 201:15
'E. meet', as the whiting   HOOD 344:11
E. meet—it's the only way   MACD 437:7
I could lean to wild e.   DURY 264:13
mean between the two e.   BOOK 118:3
Of fierce e.   MILT 470:3
toil in other men's e.   KYD 404:12
extremism: e. in the defence of liberty
                                    GOLD 312:1
extremity: e. of both ends   SHAK 626:15
extricate: unable to e. himself   ADD 4:22
exuberance: E. is beauty   BLAKE 112:27
exuitur: cupido gloriae novissima e.   TAC 678:4
exult: E. O shores   WHIT 732:7
exultations: Thy friends are e.   WORD 748:13
exulting: hear people all e.   WHIT 732:6
exuvias: redit e. indutus Achilli   VIRG 712:18
eye: apple of his e.   BIBLE 73:21
auspicious and one dropping e.   SHAK 572:4
beam that is in thine own e.   BIBLE 89:15
bought by judgement of the e.   SHAK 598:10
brought an e. for all he saw   TENN 684:5
Cast a cold e.   YEATS 753:7
Cocked his shining e.   STEV 668:19
corner of your e.   STOP 670:2

eye: (cont.):
custom loathsome to the e.   JAM 361:17
death obscured that e.   KEATS 390:22
Dull is the e. that will   BYRON 168:6
dust upon the paper e.   DOUG 255:13
every e. shall see   BIBLE 105:32
e. and the strong arm   PALM 505:8
e. begins to see   BRON 142:14
e. correct the heart   GARR 298:3
e. diffused a quickening   WESL 728:2
E. for eye, tooth for tooth   BIBLE 72:17
e. is not satisfied   BIBLE 80:1
e. of a needle   BIBLE 91:25
e. of heaven shinèd bright   SPEN 659:24
e. of heaven to garnish   SHAK 594:9
e. of man hath not heard   SHAK 612:16
e. of peninsulas and islands   CAT 186:3
e. sinks inward   ARN 26:17
e. that can open an oyster   WOD 740:12
e. that scorcheth   BYRON 168:4
e. was in itself a Soul   BYRON 167:27
e. whose bend doth awe   SHAK 590:1
Fair nature's e.   MARL 447:1
Far away from heart and e.   CLARE 204.20
fettered to her e.   LOV 429:1
friend one must close one e.   DOUG 255:14
fringèd curtains of thine e.   SHAK 625:11
God caught his e.   MCC 437:3
Green E. of the Yellow God   HAYES 328:10
harvest of a quiet e.   WORD 746:16
have neither e. to see   LENT 418:6
heavenly rhetoric of thine e.   SHAK 598:18
He had but one e.   DICK 242:1
Hide me from day's garish e.   MILT 464:25
His e. a dark grey   AUBR 33:7
his e. was backward cast   SPEN 659:28
hot the e. of heaven shines   SHAK 633:6
If thine e. offend thee   BIBLE 91:19
incarnation to the e. of God   OLIV 498:14
learning more than the fond c.   SHAK 608:16
like a joyless e.   SHEL 643:24
Locked and frozen in each e.   AUDEN 34:15
looked into the e. of day   YEATS 751:20
man has cast a longing e.   JEFF 364:10
mighty world of e. and ear   WORD 745:2
mild and magnificent e.   BROW 151:1
My tiny watching e.   DE L 236:12
neither a wit in his own e.   CONG 215:13
now mine e. seeth   BIBLE 78:5
one e. is weeping   FROST 294:10
On it may stay his e.   HERB 334:17
Only the chosen seer's e.   PATM 509:11
or he that made the e.   BOOK 131:8
saving those that e. thee   SHAK 570:24
seeing e.   BIBLE 79:7
sniv'ling and piping your e.   DIBD 238:15
still-soliciting e.   SHAK 594:22
There's language in her e.   SHAK 628:2
they shall see e. to eye   BIBLE 84:9
Thou E. among the blind   WORD 745:16
thoughts are legible in the e.   ROYD 549:14
twinkling of an e.   BIBLE 101:14
twinkling of an e.   BOOK 126:5
Unborrowed from the e.   WORD 744:21
unforgiving e.   SHER 645:19
Was never e., did see   ROYD 549:15
Who sees with equal e.   POPE 521:29
with his e. on the object   ARN 30:6
with its soft black e.   MOORE 483:14
with not through the e.   BLAKE 111:17
Wore it in the world's e.   YEATS 751:3
eyeball: e. like a bastion's mole   SMART 650:1
e. owns the mystic rod   BROW 153:3
We're e. to eyeball   RUSK 550:7
eyeballs: two fishbones, two e.   WELBY 726:21
eyebrow: Made to his mistress' e.   SHAK 568:16
eyebrows: e. made of platinum   FORS 289:19
eyelashes: lose our teeth and e.   LEAR 414:20
eyeless: E. in Gaza at the mill   MILT 473:25
eyelids: c. into a lull manner   PATER 509:4
marble e. are not   BROW 147:11
lifted e. upon tired eyes   TENN 685:21
Upon her e. MANY tracts sate   SPEN 661:11

eyelids: (cont.):
wilt weigh mine e. down   SHAK 583:11
With e. heavy and red   HOOD 344:7
eyes: And all e. else dead coals   SHAK 632:15
And each man fixed his e.   ELIOT 273:1
And her e. were wild   KEATS 388:9
And lightened are our e.   SORL 656:16
And mock our e. with air   SHAK 566:6
And their e. are burning   AUDEN 35:15
And those e., the break of day   SHAK 606:17
another's e. read clear   ARN 26:17
As fills a father's e.   COL 209:11
At last he set her both his e.   LYLY 433:9
audience look to their e.   SHAK 611:4
bald too, e. like lead   BROW 149:28
bein' only e., my wision   DICK 243:21
Blessed are the e. which see   BIBLE 94:12
bodily hunger in his e.   SHAW 636:30
brown of her—her e.   MEW 459:8
Closed his e. in endless night   GRAY 316:7
close my e., open my legs   HILL 339:3
close your e. before you   AYCK 40:7
cocking their medical e.   DICK 244:6
Crumbling behind the e.   MACN 440:17
cynosure of neighbouring e.   MILT 465:11
death bandaged my e.   BROW 152:5
deep upon her peerless e.   KEATS 389:6
Drink to me only with thine e.   JONS 379:20
electrical skin and glaring e.   SMART 649:14
e. are always bigger   VANB 708:7
e. are fixed upon the earth   MARL 447:22
e. are homes of silent   TENN 683:14
e. are nothing like   SHAK 635:2
e. are quickened   GRAV 314:20
e. as thou hast wounds   SHAK 591:21
e. as wide as a football-pool   CAUS 187:3
e. at the full midday beam   MILT 475:14
eyes but constitutional e.   LINC 422:18
e. did see Olivia first   SHAK 628:10
e. doth build his bower   LODGE 426:1
e. have seen the glory   HOWE 353:2
e. have seen what my hand   LOW 430:9
e. have they, and see   BOOK 133:10
E., look your last   SHAK 624:9
e. might be shining   LAWR 413:6
e. of gold and bramble-dew   STEV 669:1
E. of most unholy blue   MOORE 483:3
E. still dazzled   LIND 423:4
e. suffice to wail   DAN 229:16
e. that were a language   BYRON 172:13
e. to ask again yes   JOYCE 382:7
e. to behold the sun   BIBLE 80:29
e. were deeper   ROSS 547:14
Foolish e., thy streams   SANS 555:14
four beasts full of e.   BIBLE 106:10
friend to close his e.   DRYD 259:19
frightened look in its e.   SITW 648:17
from star-like e.   CAREW 179:2
from thine e.   CRAS 226:6
From women's e. this doctrine   SHAK 598:19
From women's e. this doctrine   SHAK 599:1
gather to the e.   TENN 688:3
Get thee glass e.   SHAK 597:9
God be in my e.   ANON 13:16
good Lord made your e.   LEHR 416:11
Have e. to wonder   SHAK 634:18
her e. the gazers strike   POPE 523:19
Her e. the glow-worm lend thee   HERR 336:18
hills will lift mine e.   SCOT 561:10
his e. are bright with it   KEATS 392:6
his e. became so terrible   BECK 58:3
his e. were as a flame   BIBLE 106:1
I'd say I had e. again   SHAK 596:25
If at times my e. are lenses   DOUG 255:10
If beams from happy human e.   STEV 669:7
I'm dead behind these e.   OSB 501:11
inaccessible hid from our e.   SMITH 653:31
it dazzled their e.   BALL 49:11
It is engendered in the e.   SHAK 608:25
I was e. to the blind   BIBLE 77:29
kinah not . J · · · · · ?   SHAK 608:22
king's e., that so long   SHAK 588:13
Tove darting fire in his house   MILT 464:8

eyes: (cont.):
Love in her sunny e.   COWL 221:13
Love looks not with the e.   SHAK 611:1
lover's e. will gaze an eagle   SHAK 598:20
Love's tongue is in the e.   FLET 287:26
marvellous in our e.   BOOK 133:16
Mine e. are full of tears   SHAK 621:1
Mine e. do itch   SHAK 617:23
mine e. he makes his nest   LODGE 425:23
mine e. into my very soul   SHAK 577:14
My e. are bleared, my coppers   ADE 5:5
night has a thousand e.   BOUR 138:2
Night hath a thousand e.   LYLY 433:11
no e., but fountains fraught   KYD 404:11
Not with e. service   BIBLE 102:25
one, all e., Philosopher!   WORD 746:14
one whose subdued e.   SHAK 618:20
Or was it his bees-winged e.   BETJ 67:3
other's dark e. darting light   BYRON 170:20
our e. upon his graces   JOHN 369:11
Our gloom-pleased e.   KEATS 390:14
pearls that were his e.   SHAK 625:10
people whose e. are oddly   HAMM 323:2
Pure e. and Christian hearts   KEBLE 392:21
Quiet e.   STEV 668:23
scribble on our e. the frosty   CRANE 225:18
Seal her sweet e. weary   ROSS 547:9
see nothing with my e.   SAPP 556:1
Smoke gets in your e.   HARB 323:9
So much chewing gum for the e.   ANON 18:4
stuck in her face for e.   SHAK 598:14
Take a pair of sparkling e.   GILB 304.3
tempts your wand'ring e.   GRAY 316:4
their e. purging thick   SHAK 574:22
Their e. were feverish   BYRON 172:14
therefore want in e.   SHAK 596:24
these e. to behold felicity   BROW 146:12
they are hid from thine e.   BIBLE 95:18
They have changed e.   SHAK 625:12
They strike mine e.   JONS 378:18
thine e. and seek his face   MONS 480:1
thine e. like the fishpools   BIBLE 82:3
thought of Donna Julia's e.   BYRON 170:8
thou hast doves' e. within   BIBLE 81:13
through another man's e.   SHAK 569:20
turn my ravished e.   ADD 4:2
very e. of me   HERR 337:3
voice of your e.   CUMM 228:15
were full of e. within   BIBLE 106:11
when unto dying e.   TENN 688:5
Will you put out mine e.   SHAK 594:8
with cold commemorative e.   ROSS 548:6
With e. up-raised   COLL 213:14
with fortune and men's e.   SHAK 633:10
with his half-shut e.   POPE 523:28
with sad and wand'ring e.   MILM 462:7
world to turn thine e.   JOHN 370:15
write the beauty of your e.   SHAK 633:5
yet I believed her e.   WOTT 749:3
you'll wear your e. out   ZOLA 755:13
Your e. are lodestars   SHAK 610:24
Your e. had once   YEATS 753:19
your e. that looked so mild   BALL 49:15
your e. with holy dread   COL 210:14
You see her e. are open   SHAK 604:11
youth's e. burned at thine   ROSS 547:22

F

faber: F. est suae quisque fortunae   CAEC 205:15
Fabians: civilization of the F.   INGE 359:13
good man fallen among F.   LENIN 417:10
fable: f., song, or fleeting   HERR 336:11
that thai be nocht bot f.   BARB 52:7
when life's sweet f. ends   CRAS 226:14
wonderful what f. will not do   BYRON 171:32
fables: all the f. in the legend   BACON 42:22
Hesperian f. true   MILT 471:2
profane and old wives' f.   BIBLE 104:1
Them f. yet have feigned   MILT 476:4
were blasphemous f.   DONN 166:11

fabric: baseless f. of this vision | SHAK 625:28
f. of human destiny | DOST 254:6
out of the earth a f. huge | MILT 469:6
solid f. of the old society | TRIL 702:17
fabula: F. narratur | HOR 350:22
face: Accustomed to her f. | LERN 419:4
Am I in f. to-day | GOLD 311:21
And it is not always f. | JONS 379:14
and seek his f. | MONS 480:1
Anoint and cheer our soilèd f. | BOOK 135:21
Beauty's conquest of your f. | AUDEN 35:3
born with a different f. | BLAKE 112:12
Breathes like a bright-eyed f. | HUNT 356:11
can hear my Thisby's f. | SHAK 612:24
case with a sad swelled f. | BARH 52:17
construction in the f. | SHAK 600:14
Cover her f. | WEBS 725:23
dew on the f. of the dead | BEERS 50:22
disasters in his morning f. | GOLD 310:12
dont quite match your f. | ASHF 31:6
draw a full f. | DRYD 262:20
English never smash in a f. | HALS 322:8
f. and state of things | BACON 45:21
f. burns and tickles | FROST 294:10
f. is a mute recommendation | PUBL 531:1
f. looks like a wedding-cake | AUDEN 36:19
f. of 'evil' | BURR 164:5
f. of my betrothèd lady | MIDD 459:16
f. of the world would have | PASC 507:13
f. of this congregation | BOOK 123:15
f. peered. All the grey night | DE L 236:3
f. that launched a thousand | MARL 446:17
f. the index of a feeling | CRAB 225:9
Fair f. show friends | GOOGE 312:11
False f. must hide | SHAK 601:9
Fanny Kelly's divine plain f. | LAMB 407:2
final f. of love | WILB 734:6
flat on your f. as lean | THUR 697:14
frame my f. to all occasions | SHAK 588:3
garden of your f. | HERB 334:2
Give me a look, give me a f. | JONS 378:18
glimpse of His bright f. | VAUG 709:1
glory shineth in this f. | SHAK 621:2
God hath given you one f. | SHAK 576:2
good f. is a letter | ADD 4:10
Has he not a rogue's f.? | CONG 215:7
has the f. he deserves | ORW 499:22
have seen God f. to face | BIBLE 71:19
have the f. of a Venus | BARR 54:16
He hides a smiling f. | COWP 222:19
Her f., at first . . . just ghostly | REID 535:5
hide us from the f. | BIBLE 106:17
his listless form and f. | HARDY 325:14
his natural f. in a glass | BIBLE 104:27
his prism, and silent f. | WORD 747:2
I am the family f. | HARDY 325:8
I never forget a f. | MARX 452:1
I see ye have a singing f. | FLET 287:21
It had a lonely f. | HARDY 324:12
I wish I loved its silly f. | RAL 536:12
long wilt thou hide thy f. | BOOK 124:25
Look in my f. | TRAI 702:2
Look on her f., and you'll | POPE 523:20
Lord make his f. shine | BIBLE 73:4
mist in my f. | BROW 152:4
Moses hid his f. | BIBLE 71:39
never f. so pleased my mind | ANON 18:10
night's starred f. | KEATS 391:1
not recognize me by my f. | TROL 703:2
one to f. the world | BROW 151:17
open f. of the sun | WESL 729:1
or human f. divine | MILT 470:16
paint in the public's f. | RUSK 550:10
Pity a human f. | BLAKE 113:9
plummet-measured f. | YEATS 753:10
rabbit has a charming f. | ANON 17:15
saved you only must save f. | HEAN 329:21
seyn somtyme a pale f. | CHAU 193:25
shouldst never see my f. again | TENN 682:24
showed the paint, but hid the f. | DRYD 260:15
Since first I saw your f. | ANON 17:21
sing in the robber's f. | JUV 384:5

face: (cont.):
smile on the f. of the tiger | ANON 17:13
spirit passed before my f. | BIBLE 77:10
stamping on a human f. | ORW 500:17
Stares from every human f. | AUDEN 34:15
sullen, cold, exhausted f. | SASS 557:8
taking your f. in your hands | ANON 15:9
then f. to face | BIBLE 101:1
there glorifies your f. | BROW 153:18
thing with one f. | MACN 441:1
thy f. bears a command | SHAK 570:17
To get very red in the f. | BENT 64:9
turn away thy f. | SHAK 593:22
turning your f. to the light | SASS 557:6
twain he covered his f. | BIBLE 82:19
two strong men stand f. | KIPL 398:13
unacceptable f. of capitalism | HEATH 320.20
upon the f. of the deep | BIBLE 69:20
upon the f. of the waters | BIBLE 69:20
Visit her f. too roughly | SHAK 572:12
way plain before my f. | BOOK 124:16
wearing the f. that she | LENN 417:18
Where's the f. one would meet | KEATS 387:20
will pass nor turn my f. | BROW 153:17
with how wan a f. | SIDN 646:16
would not lose its human f. | DUBC 262:22
Your f., my thane | SHAK 600:17
your honest, sonsie f. | BURNS 163:13
faces: baby f. in the violet | ELIOT 273:13
Bid them wash their f. | SHAK 570:8
cantan', grace-proud f. | BURNS 163:22
Coming with vivid f. | YEATS 751:13
f. are but a gallery | BACON 43:21
gild the f. of the grooms | SHAK 602:4
grind the f. of the poor | BIBLE 82:12
hollow hearts, and loose double f. | SKEL 649:4
In nice clean f., and nice | BARH 52:13
know the f. I shall see | ROSS 548:2
monastic f. in quiet collegiate | CLOU 207:5
not having any f. | PRIE 528:19
old familiar f. | LAMB 407:7
owners of their f. | SHAK 634:15
public f. in private places | AUDEN 35:12
red f., and loose hair | EQUI 278:11
slope of f. | COWP 224:1
that their f. are wrinkled | SHAK 574:22
these f. in the crowd | POUND 527:5
'tis your estrangèd f. | THOM 695:10
wears everywhere two f. | DRYD 262:14
we hid as it were our f. | BIBLE 84:11
facets: This iceberg cuts its f. | BISH 110:1
facilis: F. descensus Averno | VIRG 713:11
fact: And were judges of f. | PULT 531:6
Death but a scientific f. | WILDE 736:2
f. for the most airy fabric | BYRON 174:5
fatal futility of F. | JAMES 363:8
hypothesis by an ugly f. | HUXL 358:3
irritable reaching after f. | KEATS 391:10
knowe his f. that was bistad | CHAU 193:25
Matters of f. | TIND 698:7
physical f. into a legal right | MILL 460:23
faction: it made them a f. | MAC 435:17
Liberty is to f. what air | MAD 441:15
whisper of a f. | RUSS 552:1
factions: good in canvasses and f. | BACON 43:4
religious f. are volcanoes | BURKE 159:7
factitious: tremble for something f. | CLOU 207:2
facts: consists in ignoring f. | ADAMS 2.19
Corruption of the f. | HUGH 354:7
F. alone are wanted | DICK 240:32
f. are sacred | SCOTT 559:2
f. but to re-allocate them | RYLE 552:8
f. governed by laws | WHEW 730:13
F. were never pleasing | BARR 54:5
form of inert f. | ADAMS 2:20
free but f. are on expenses | STOP 669:18
imagination for his f. | SHER 645:24
not of f. but of values | INGE 360:1
Science is built up of f. | POIN 518:10
will give you all the f. | AUDEN 36:3
faculties: diversity in the f. of men | MAD 441:16
each according to his f. | BAK 47:23
exercise of his soul's f. | ARIS 25:9

faculties: (cont.):
Hath borne his f. so meek | SHAK 601:3
T'affections, and to f. | DONNE 251:26
faculty: bondage to parents cramps every f. | WOLL 741:17
faddling: A f. hedonist | STEV 667:19
fade: f. away into the forest | KEATS 389:9
F. far away, dissolve | KEATS 389:10
F. into dimness apace | ARN 28:1
f. into the light of common | WORD 745:14
They simply f. away | FOLEY 288:8
we all do f. as a leaf | BIBLE 84:28
faded: f. on the crowing | SHAK 572:2
not hollow cheek or f. eye | TENN 688:12
fades: f. awa' like morning dew | BALL 51:2
F. o'er the waters blue | BYRON 168:3
Now f. the glimmering | GRAY 315:10
Whatever f., but fading | SIDN 647:4
fading: Nor will in f. silks compose | WINC 739:4
now to lend thy f. joys | GREE 317:8
Soft silken primrose f. | MILT 466:18
faenore: Solutus omni f. | HOR 348:22
faery: and sing a f.'s song | KEATS 388:11
f. lands forlorn | KEATS 389:15
Full beautiful, a f.'s child | KEATS 388:9
fag: Caps tilted, f. drooping | BLOK 115:7
faggots: Some burn damp f. | YEATS 752:4
faiblesse: tout le reste est f. | VIGNY 711:12
fail: And we'll not f. | SHAK 601:7
F. not our feast | SHAK 602:22
I will not f. thee | BIBLE 73:26
Let no man's heart f. | BIBLE 75:1
Some night you'll f. us | BROW 152:2
We shall not flag or f. | CHUR 202:11
when ye f., they may receive | BIBLE 95:7
yet not ashamed to f. | JOHN 370:5
failed: f. in literature and art | DISR 248:24
It fluttered and f. for breath | ARN 27:20
tried a little, f. much | STEV 667:7
faileth: f. thing that fooles | CHAU 195:7
when my strength f. me | BOOK 129:17
failing: from f. hands we throw | MCCR 437:6
failings: blind to my small f. | DENN 237:5
fails: life seemed meant for, f. | BROW 150:19
One sure, if another f. | BROW 152:28
failure: f. of hope | GIBB 302:21
f.'s no success at all | DYLAN 265:17
His f. is ignominious | MENC 457:5
not the effort nor the f. | EMPS 277:20
Now we are not a f. | VANZ 708:11
perhaps a tragic f. | ELIOT 269:11
Women can't forgive f. | CHEK 196:13
failures: f. in life arise from | HARE 326:5
has no conceivable f. | WHIT 733:1
fain: would f. see good | BOOK 126:15
faint: eating hay when you're f. | CARR 183:18
f. cold fear thrills through | SHAK 623:28
f. heart ne'er wan | BURNS 163:18
f. in the light that she | TENN 686:17
f. on hill or field | TENN 688:2
f. praises one another | WYCH 750:8
F., yet pursuing | BIBLE 74:11
pray, and not to f. | BIBLE 95:13
shall reap, if we f. not | BIBLE 102:9
shall walk, and not f. | BIBLE 84:1
fainted: f. Alternately on a Sofa | AUST 38:14
should utterly have f. | BOOK 126:1
faints: sense f. picturing them | SHEL 641:16
fair: all so excellently f. | COL 209:12
anything to show more f. | WORD 743:9
be a black man or a f. | ADD 4:6
brave deserves the f. | DRYD 259:16
Do it in hope of f. advantages | SHAK 608:13
F. and fair, and twice so fair | PEELE 511:2
f. and fatal king | JOHN 366:19
f. and smell'st so sweet | SHAK 617:16
f. as an Italian sun | BANV 51:13
f. as is the rose in May | CHAU 195:4
f. as the moon | BIBLE 81:21
F. be their wives | ANON 16:2
f. from fame sometime declines | SHAK 633:6
F. is foul, and foul is fair | SHAK 599:13
F. is too foul an epithet | MARL 448:5

fair: (cont.):	
F. laughs the morn	GRAY 315:9
F. shares for all	JAY 363:23
F. stood the wind for France	DRAY 258:8
f. terms and a villain's	SHAK 608:3
Fat, f. and forty	O'KEE 498:9
For I have sworn thee f.	SHAK 635:9
foul and f. a day	SHAK 600:4
hand that hath made you f.	SHAK 606:12
having a f. white linen	BOOK 121:15
How sweet and f. she seems	WALL 718:9
huntress, chaste and f.	JONS 378:16
If it prove f. weather	SUCK 671:9
Is she kind as she is f.	SHAK 631:8
it's not f. to the child	FROST 295:11
noble, historically f.	LERN 419:3
Outward be f., however	CHUR 201:4
pitiful as she is f.	GREE 317:9
possession of that f. thou ow'st	SHAK 633:6
remained at 'set f.'	BENN 63:13
Sabrina f.	MILT 464:10
She f., divinely fair	MILT 472:22
She is not f. to outward view	COL 209:6
this f. defect of nature	MILT 473.5
Thou art all f., my love	BIBLE 81:14
thou art f., my love	BIBLE 81:13
thou love, and she be f.	KEATS 388:26
thousand times more f.	SHAK 609:2
what's right and f.	HUGH 354:1
With you f. maid	ANON 12:8
fairer: f. person lost not heaven	MILT 469:13
f. than the word	SHAK 607:10
Is f. far, in May	JONS 379:21
surely the f. way	BACON 42:9
fairest: f. creatures we desire	SHAK 632:26
f. forms and sweetest shapes	SOUT 657:24
F. Isle, all isles excelling	DRYD 260:34
f. things have fleetest	THOM 694:17
O f of creation, last and best	MILT 472:25
O thou f. among women	BIBLE 81:18
fairies: Do you believe in f.	BARR 54:9
f. at the bottom of our	FYL 296:11
F. of the old profession	CORB 218:13
Farewell, rewards and F.	CORB 218:11
I don't believe in f.	BARR 54:7
merry world since the f.	SELD 562:9
She is the f.' midwife	SHAK 622:21
was the beginning of f.	BARR 54:6
fairly: No Englishman is ever f. beaten	
	SHAW 638:22
fairness: equality or f. or justice	BERL 66:4
fairs: f., and bear-baitings	SHAK 631:27
fairy: And I serve the f. queen	SHAK 611:11
Come not near our f. queen	SHAK 611:20
f. hands their knell	COLL 213:13
f. kind of writing	DRYD 260:32
F. me thoghte	LANG 408:20
f. thing with red round	COL 209:11
Like f. gifts fading away	MOORE 483:1
Lilly believes it was a f.	AUBR 33:13
loves a f. when she's forty	HENL 332:5
myth is not a f. story	RYLE 552:8
there is a little f. somewhere	BARR 54:7
'tis almost f. time	SHAK 612:26
fairytale: f. of olden times	HEINE 330:15
fait: un seul f. accompli	BOIL 117:4
faith: And f. shines equal	BRON 142:12
And in the seat to f. assigned	SMART 650:2
And now abideth f.	BIBLE 101:1
And purged its f., and trimmed	ARN 28:19
As puts me from my f.	SHAK 581:6
both are left to f.	BYRON 170:26
breastplate of f. and love	BIBLE 103:21
Breathing, testing his f.	THOM 694:12
children in whom is no f.	BIBLE 73:22
died blind and still by f.	LIND 423:4
doubt diversified by f.	BROW 148:12
Draw near with f.	BOOK 122:5
ꞌ. and me n.l. ꞌꞌ	HARDY 325:13
ꞌꞌꞌꞌ ꞌꞌꞌꞌꞌꞌꞌꞌ ꞌꞌꞌ	WORD 744.13
f and rejoice in Christ	ꞏꞏꞏ
f as a grain of mustard	BIBLE 91:16
f. chiefly in the Spirit	ANON 10:16

faith: (cont.):	
f. in a nation of sectaries	DISR 248:8
f. in the people governing	DICK 244:8
F. is kneeling by his bed	DRAY 258:1
F. is the state of being	TILL 698:6
F. is the substance	BIBLE 104:13
f. means nothing to him	METT 459:1
f. of the heart alone make	LUTH 432:14
f. of the Saviour spread	BOSS 137:2
f.'s transcendent dower	WORD 747:15
f. that looks through death	WORD 746:6
f. that right makes might	LINC 422:2
f. that stands on authority	EMER 276:29
f. unfaithful kept him	TENN 682:3
f. without doubt is nothing	UNAM 707:2
F. without works is dead	BIBLE 104:29
fanatic F., once wedded	MOORE 483:16
Fight the good fight of f.	BIBLE 104:4
finisher of our f.	BIBLE 104:17
first article of my f.	GAND 297:10
fright my f.	DRYD 260:21
have not found so great f.	BIBLE 89:31
he hold the Catholic F.	BOOK 119:12
If ye break f. with us who die	MCCR 437:6
I have kept the f.	BIBLE 104:8
In this f. I wish to live	VILL 711:16
judgement, mercy, and f.	BIBLE 92:5
just shall live by f.	BIBLE 99:16
life in thy f. and fear	BOOK 122:3
Love in dying, F. is defying	BARN 53:17
made of f. and service	SHAK 569.21
more f. in honest doubt	TENN 684:7
moved by f. to assent to it	HUME 355:7
My f. shall wax, when thou	DAN 229:15
My staff of f. to walk upon	RAL 535:18
not the dying for a f.	THAC 691:3
O thou of little f.	BIBLE 91:8
plain and simple f.	SHAK 592:25
Queen and F. like a valiant	TENN 689:5
scientific f.'s absurd	BROW 149:17
Sea of F.	ARN 27:1
shake a man's f.	SHAW 636:3
simple f. than Norman blood	TENN 684:22
Stole many a man's soul and f.	JAGG 361:13
strong f. shall purchase me	CAREW 179:14
sudden explosions of f.	BREN 140:13
taking the shield of f.	BIBLE 103:1
These all died in f.	BIBLE 104:15
though I have all f.	BIBLE 101:1
Thy f. hath made thee whole	BIBLE 90:9
unity of the f.	BIBLE 102:17
vain f., and courage vain	MAC 436:6
yive I f. and ful credence	CHAU 195:1
you have kept f.	HARDY 325:7
your work of f. and labour	BIBLE 103:19
faithful: All thy f. mercies crown	WESL 728:14
Be thou f. unto death	BIBLE 106:4
blessed company of all f.	BOOK 122:14
Ever f., ever sure	MILT 465:19
f. and just to me	SHAK 592:6
f. are minished from among	BOOK 124:24
F. are the wounds of a friend	BIBLE 79:26
F., below, he did his duty	DIBD 238:17
f. friend is the medicine	BIBLE 87:12
f. in that which is least	BIBLE 95:8
f. soul would walk	CARB 178:17
good and f. servant	BIBLE 92:16
I have been f. to thee	DOWS 256:2
mentally to himself	PAINE 504:7
O come, all ye f.	ANON 21:18
So f. in love, and so dauntless	SCOTT 560:4
these words are true and f.	BIBLE 107:18
was called F. and True	BIBLE 107:12
Who has a f. female friend	WHUR 733:13
faithfully: ask f. we may obtain effectually	
	BOOK 121:10
faithfulness: Great is thy f.!	CHIS 200:1
faith-healer: was a f. of Deal	ANON 18:15
faithless: Be not f., but	BIBLE 97:36
f. ꞏꞏ stubborn generation	BOOK 130:9
f. ꞏꞏꞏ son of the times	ꞏꞏꞏ
Human on my f. arm	ꞏꞏꞏ
faiths: men's f. are wafer-cakes	SHAK 585:6

fake: Anything that consoles is f.	MURD 488:8
falcon: dapple-dawn-drawn F.	HOPK 346:10
f. cannot hear the falconer	YEATS 753:1
f., towering in her pride	SHAK 602:20
Gentle as f.	SKEL 649:2
falconer: O! for a f.'s voice	SHAK 623:6
Falklands: F. thing was a fight between two	
bald men	BORG 136:11
fall: And hold me lest I f.	WILL 736:23
Another thing to f.	SHAK 605:12
by dividing we f.	DICK 245:8
chance that you will f. out	BENC 62:10
dew shall weep thy f.	HERB 336:1
diggeth a pit shall f.	BIBLE 80:22
down needs fear no f.	BUNY 156:10
Et tu, Brute? Then f., Caesar	SHAK 591:13
F. and cease	SHAK 598:1
f. by little and little	BIBLE 87:24
f. flat on your face	THUR 697:14
f. for anything	HAM 322:10
F. into the hands of God	TENN 689:4
f. into the hands of the living	BIBLE 104:12
f. into the hands of the Lord	BIBLE 87:9
f. of mountain-stream	BEAT 56:6
F. on the wat'ry cloud	AKEN 6:5
F. on us, and hide us	BIBLE 106:17
f. out with those we love	TENN 687:25
f. the people unto them	BOOK 130:1
f. upon it out of the wind	STEV 666:5
f. was destined to a barren	JOHN 370:17
further they have to f.	FITZ 285:7
going to f. like rain	AUDEN 36.13
great was the f.	BIBLE 89:27
grieve at my declining f.	MARL 447:8
hard rain's a gonna f.	DYLAN 265:15
haughty spirit before a f.	BIBLE 78:37
human nature by the f.	DENN 237:3
I meditated on the F.	BETJ 67:13
I shall f. like a bright	SHAK 588:18
Is less likely to f.	GAY 299:28
it had a dying f.	SHAK 628:9
it is good to f.	WHIT 732:16
Life is a horizontal f.	COCT 208:8
precipitated the f. of the race	STAN 662:9
proclaiming our f. but begging us	WILB 734:1
raise up them that f.	BOOK 119:20
shall never f.	BOOK 124:29
that can f. without shaking	MONT 480:3
Things f. apart	YEATS 753:1
thousand shall f. beside	BOOK 131:3
To rise by other's f.	SOUT 657:23
upholdeth all such as f.	BOOK 136:6
Weak men must f.	SHAK 620:3
We f. not in such sin	GILB 303:11
we f. to rise	BROW 148:6
we should happen to f.	LEAR 414:9
what a f. was there	SHAK 592:14
worship and f. down	BOOK 131:10
ye f. not out by the way	BIBLE 71:31
yet fear I not f.	RAL 536:2
fallacy: Pathetic F.	RUSK 550:14
fallen: are f. into the midst	BOOK 128:15
art thou f. from heaven	BIBLE 83:5
Babylon is f., is fallen	BIBLE 107:3
f. by the edge of the sword	BIBLE 87:27
F. cold and dead	WHIT 732:7
F. from his high estate	DRYD 259:19
follow with allegiance a f. lord	SHAK 565:19
good man f. among Fabians	LENIN 417:10
have never f. or stumbled	PAST 508:4
How are the mighty f.	BIBLE 75:9
lay great and greatly f.	HOMER 343:9
lot is f. unto me	BOOK 124:30
say a man is f. in love	STER 665:4
scribbled lines like f. hopes	HOPE 345:2
though f. on evil days	MILT 472:6
Though f. thyself, never	WORD 748:13
throned Cytherean be f.	SWIN 676:22
Yc are f. from grace	BIBLE 102:6
fallentis: F. semita vitae	HOR 348:14
fallere: ꞏꞏꞏ possit amare	VIRG 713:5
falling: ꞏ domini principio	FIS 268:11

falling: (*cont.*):
f. out of faithful friends — EDW 267:11
f. towards England — AUDEN 35:11
Go, and catch a f. star — DONNE 252:14
he hath the f. sickness — SHAK 590:8
my feet from f. — BOOK 133:12
secure amidst a f. world — ADD 4:5
To load a f. man — SHAK 589:14
fallings: F. from us, vanishings — WORD 746:3
fall lall: fuss of these f. people — BURN 160:20
fallow: female mind like a rude f. lies — IRWIN 360:19
falls: By shallow rivers, to whose f. — MARL 447:18
f. do hinder hasty joys — GASC 298:19
F. the Shadow — ELIOT 271:15
F. with the leaf still — FLET 287:12
false: all is f. that I advance — COWP 221:29
betrayed by what is f. — MER 458:8
Beware of f. prophets — BIBLE 89:23
But all was f. and hollow — MILT 469:13
F. face must hide what — SHAK 601:9
f. gift is like clouds — BIBLE 79:16
f. grief hiding his harmful — SPEN 659:27
F. guilt is guilt felt — LAING 405:20
f. sincere — POPE 520:28
f. step involves her — AUST 39:16
F. to my nature — SHAK 570:14
f. witness against thy — BIBLE 72:16
Followed f. lights — DRYD 260:21
Framed to make women f. — SHAK 615:12
If she be f., O! then heaven — SHAK 616:17
interesting than a f. one — WHIT 731:10
Man, f. man, smiling — LEE 416:7
mind, a f. creation — SHAK 601:12
not then be f. to any man — SHAK 573:4
perils among f. brethren — BIBLE 102:1
perish with our f. theories — POPP 524:16
philosopher, as equally f. — GIBB 301:18
produces a f. impression — WILDE 734:10
Ring out the f. — TENN 684:10
thou be not f. to others — BACON 45:6
unweaving of f. impressions — ELIOT 270:1
Were women never so f. — LYLY 433:7
wouldst not play f. — SHAK 600:15
falsehood: express lying or f. — SWIFT 673:15
F. has a perennial spring — BURKE 157:16
goodly outside f. hath — SHAK 607:21
Let her and F. grapple — MILT 475:16
neither Truth nor F. — HOBB 339:17
right of honour cuts f. — GURN 320:1
strife of Truth with f. — LOW 430:3
To some dear f., hugs it — MOORE 483:16
falsehoods: f. which interest — JOHN 368:8
falsely: Anabaptists do f. boast — BOOK 136:2
prophets prophesy f. — BIBLE 85:6
unfaithful kept him f. true — TENN 682:3
falseness: f. in all our impressions — RUSK 550:19
falser: f. than vows made in wine — SHAK 569:14
falsifiability: f. of a system — POPP 524:10
Falstaff: F. shall die of a sweat — SHAK 584:15
F. sweats to death — SHAK 580:9
sweet Jack F. — SHAK 580:33
falter: nor f., nor repent — SHEL 642:20
Who hesitate and f. life away — ARN 28:8
faltered: If I have f. more or less — STEV 669:7
falters: love that never f. — SPR 661:8
fama: aliquam tibi f. salutem — VIRG 712:9
Famagusta: For F. and the hidden sun — FLEC 286:12
fame: also call the Temple of F. — LICH 421:13
blush to find it f. — POPE 523:7
body die, her f. survives — MILT 474:16
carelessly smiling at F. — MOORE 483:8
damned to everlasting f. — POPE 523:7
desire of f. — TENN 681:25
doctor full of phrase and f. — ARN 29:5
dreams of f. while woman — TENN 682:12
establishment of my f. — GIBB 302:19
F. and tranquillity can — MONT 481:3
F. is a food that dead — DOBS 249:21
F. is like a river — BACON 44:13
F. is no plant that grows — MILT 466:5

fame: (*cont.*):
F. is the spur — MILT 466:4
F.'s eternal beadroll worthy — SPEN 660:12
foremost shall be damned to F. — POPE 518:20
gives immortal f. — YOUNG 754:10
his f. the ocean sea — BARN 53:16
Let f., that all hunt after — SHAK 598:6
love and f. to nothingness — KEATS 391:2
love of f. is the last — TAC 678:4
my f. for a pot of ale — SHAK 585:11
no one shall work for f. — KIPL 401:9
nor yet a fool to f. — POPE 519:28
not to purchase f. — DRYD 261:3
Oh my f. — CHAP 190:14
openeth the gate to good f. — BACON 43:11
Physicians of the Utmost F. — BELL 61:1
Poets' food is love and f, — SHEL 640:12
Rather use than f. — TENN 682:13
servants of f. — BACON 43:27
That f. can never heal — AYT 41:4
Thou art virtue, f. — JONS 379:1
We came here for f. — DISR 248:38
What is f.? an empty bubble — GRAI 314:4
you shall live by f. — SPEN 659:11
youth to fortune and to f. — GRAY 315:20
famed: f. in all great arts — ARN 29:2
fames: Auri sacra f. — VIRG 713:3
F. ac turpis Egestas — VIRG 713:14
familiar: Be thou f. — SHAK 573:3
even mine own f. friend — BOOK 127:1
F. in his mouth as household — SHAK 586:11
f. with her face — POPE 522:13
mine own f. friend — BOOK 128:11
old f. faces — LAMB 407:7
That once f. word — BAYLY 56:3
familiarity: F. breeds contempt—and children — TWAIN 706:16
familiarly: Talks as f. of John a Gaunt — SHAK 583:23
families: All happy f. resemble — TOLS 700:5
And mothers of large f. — BELL 60:24
and there are f. — THAT 691:26
best-regulated f. — DICK 240:4
best-regulated f. — NORTH 496:10
f. in a country village — AUST 39:26
Great f. of yesterday — DEFOE 234:24
occasionally to run in f. — LEWES 420:10
old f. last not three — BROW 145:21
Whole f. shopping at night — GINS 306:29
your antediluvian f. — CONG 215:12
family: brought up a large f. — GOLD 311:28
dominion [of the f.] — HOBB 340:10
➤f. in heaven and earth — BIBLE 102:13
f. of rare, long-stemmed — DIN 246:8
f. than in that of an entire — MONT 480:20
f.—that dear octopus — SMITH 651:9
f. that prays together — SCAL 557:16
f. to an hypothesis — STER 664:17
f. was not unworthy — DISR 248:19
f., with its narrow privacy — LEACH 413:8
f. with wrong members in control — ORW 500:6
I am the f. face — HARDY 325:8
man that left his f. — TWAIN 706:2
my f. pride is something — GILB 304:20
not lugged into F. Rows — WOD 740:16
famine: die by f. die by inches — HENRY 333:1
f. in his face — CHUR 201:10
from plague, pestilence, and f. — BOOK 119:17
God of frostbite, God of f. — VYAZ 717:9
famous: And f. by my sword — GRAH 313:16
become f. without ability — SHAW 636:6
Be f. then by wisdom — MILT 473:19
f. calm and dead — BROW 149:27
f. for fifteen minutes — WARH 721:22
f. men have the whole earth — PER 512:10
Feared by their breed and f. — SHAK 619:18
Let us now praise f. men — BIBLE 87:37
morning and found myself f. — BYRON 174:9
Not a f.-last-words — MCG 438:2
that time I was too f. — BENC 62:12
fan: f. spread and streamers — CONG 215:32
F. the sinking flame — DICK 242:18
fanatic: f. heart — YEATS 752:19

fanatic: (*cont.*):
f. is a great leader — BROUN 144:10
fanaticism: f. and intolerance — LEVIN 420:3
F. consists in redoubling — SANT 555:15
fanatics: F. have their dreams — KEATS 387:14
fancies: can many f. feign — GREE 317:15
drop your silly f. — CAT 186:2
f. are more giddy and unfirm — SHAK 629:14
f. outwork nature — SHAK 565:5
F. that broke through language — BROW 152:9
proud, and full of f. — KEATS 391:3
With a heart of furious f. — ANON 19:23
fancy: But keep your f. free — HOUS 352:9
credulity to the whispers of f. — JOHN 369:18
dorgs is some men's f. — DICK 239:31
Ever let the f. roam — KEATS 387:17
F. a thousand wondrous — BEAT 56:5
f. cannot cheat so well — KEATS 389:16
f. is the sails — KEATS 391:4
f.'s maze and clue — COL 210:16
I dislike what I f. I feel — ANON 18:15
invention and makes f. — COWP 223:11
most excellent f. — SHAK 578:23
odoriferous flowers of f. — SHAK 598:17
so full of shapes is f. — SHAK 628:9
spring a young man's f. — TENN 685:7
Tell me where is f. bred — SHAK 608:25
those by hopeless f. — TENN 688:5
Your form does to my f. bring — WALL 718:17
fancy-free: In maiden meditation, f. — SHAK 611:17
fans: With divers-coloured f. — SHAK 565:5
Wi' their f. into their hand — BALL 50:12
fantasies: f. and the superficial — CHAM 189:13
I can find f. where none — SKEL 649:3
We had fed the heart on f. — YEATS 752:13
fantastic: In a light f. round — MILT 463:18
On the light f. toe — MILT 465:6
thinking on f. summer's heat — SHAK 619:14
fantastical: all our joys are but f. — DONNE 251:23
That it alone is high f. — SHAK 628:9
fantasy: all made of f. — SHAK 569:21
f., of dreams, and ceremonies — SHAK 590:19
much too strong for f. — DONNE 251:22
We live in a f. world — MURD 488:9
fan-vaulting: F. from an aesthetic standpoint — LANC 407:20
far: audacity is knowing how f. — COCT 208:10
be going a bridge too f. — BROW 147:24
big stick; you will go f. — ROOS 546:9
f. above the great — GRAY 316:9
F. and few, far and few — LEAR 414:3
F. away is close at hand — GRAV 315:1
F. be that fate from us — OVID 502:11
f. end of the enormous — AUDEN 34:5
F. from the madding crowd's — GRAY 315:17
F. from sun and summer-gale — GRAY 316:6
for ever f. away — CLARE 204:28
He seems so near and yet so f. — TENN 684:9
It is a f., far better — DICK 244:7
It is a f., far better — GALB 297:1
I was much too f. out all — SMITH 652:17
keep f. from me, you grim — OVID 502:12
news from a f. country — BIBLE 79:19
Oh keep f. off, you uninitiated — VIRG 713:12
Over the hills and f. away — GAY 299:17
so f. from God — DIAZ 238:10
Faraday: plain Michael F. — FAR 280:3
farce: la f. est jouée — RAB 534:21
longest running f. in the West End — SMITH 651:1
second as f. — MARX 452:7
second time as f. — BARN 53:10
wine was a f. and the food — POW 528:3
fardeau: le f. et l'amertume — FLAU 286:5
fardels: Who would f. bear — SHAK 575:16
fare: f. and just a trifle — GORD 312:13
value not your bill of f. — SWIFT 673:20
farewell: Ae f., and then for ever — BURNS 161:2
And f. goes out sighing — SHAK 627:21
and f. king! — SHAK 620:8
F.! a long farewell — SHAK 588:19
f. compliment — SHAK 622:33

farewell: (*cont.*):
f. content	SHAK 616:20
F., great painter of mankind	GARR 298:3
F., happy fields	MILT 468:12
f., he is gon	CHAU 193:13
F., Leicester Square	JUDGE 382:8
F., Love, and all thy laws	WYATT 749:15
F. my bok and my devocioun	CHAU 195:1
F. night, welcome day	BUNY 156:15
F., rewards and Fairies	CORB 218:11
F. to the Highlands	BURNS 162:23
f. to the shade	COWP 222:29
hail, and f. evermore	CAT 187:1
must bid the company f.	RAL 536:9
nor bade f. to him	SHAK 599:15
So f. hope, and with hope	MILT 470:26
than waving me f.	HOPE 345:3
there be no sadness of f.	TENN 680:18
Too-late, F.	ROSS 548:5

farewells: Everlasting f.!
f. as be stars in heaven	DE Q 237:10
	SHAK 628:1

farm: keep 'em down on the f.   LEWIS 420:21
farmer: f. that hanged himself   SHAK 602:8
F. will never be happy	HERB 333:16

farmers: And now the f. swear
	KING 398:6
embattled f. stood	EMER 276:7
f. excessively fortunate	VIRG 715:13
Our f. round, well pleased	CRAB 225:5
This country needs good f.	NIXON 496:6

farms: cellos of the deep f.
	STEV 667:4
gazes or for him that f.	CRAB 225:12
What spires, what f. are those	HOUS 352:15
wi' the weel-stockit f.	BURNS 162:3

farmyard: crow in its own f.   TROL 703:17
distinguish human society from the f.
	SHAW 636:16

far-off: old, unhappy, f. things   WORD 748:4
farrago: *Gaudia discursus nostri f.*   JUV 383:16
farrow: sow that eats her f.   JOYCE 381:11
fart: can't f. and chew gum   JOHN 367:13
Love is the f.	SUCK 671:8
My Lord, I had forgot the f.	ELIZ 274:5

farther: *f. you go from the church*   WOTT 749:8
farthest: F. Thule   VIRG 715:10
farthing: done what I do for a f. less   ADD 3:25
hast paid the uttermost f.	BIBLE 88:30
old men as worth one f.	CAT 185:15
Virtue knows to a f.	WALP 720:11

farthings: sold for two f.   BIBLE 94:22
fascination: f. of a public execution
	FOOT 288:11
f. of what's difficult	YEATS 751:18
line between love and f.	WASH 722:4
There's a f. frantic	GILB 305:14

Fascism: American F.   ROS 546:20
Fascist: Every woman adores a F.   PLATH 516:5
fashion: appear a little out of f.   SHAK 586:2
carving the f. of a new	SHAK 613:22
Cynara! in my f.	DOWS 256:2
f. a gentleman or noble	SPEN 659:18
f. must excite your languid	GILB 305:17
f. of these times	SHAK 568:1
f. of this world passeth	BIBLE 100:26
F., though Folly's child	CRAB 225:1
first style of f.	AUST 39:22
garment out of f.	SHAK 571:10
Gives the lover weight and f.	JONS 379:14
glass of f.	SHAK 576:4
laws of markets and f.	ALB 7:9
men in shape and f.	ASCH 31:2
nothing else holds f.	SHAK 628:5
out of the f.	CIBB 203:19
tell you the leading f.	RUSK 550:8
will deeply put the f.	SHAK 584:8

fashionable: join the f. madmen   DID 246:1
fashioned: F. so purely   THOM 695:12
F. so slenderly	HOOD 343:15
Which day by day were f.	BOOK 134:21

fashions: conscience to fit this year's f.
fast: being f. bound in misery   BOOK 122:16
can nevir in dame too f.	GOLD 311:19
Faith in a little remedy	COL unknown

fast: (*cont.*):
F. as the stars are slow	THOM 694:5
F. by their native shore	COWP 222:24
f. that I have chosen	BIBLE 84:22
f. word about oral contraception	ALLEN 9:14
fun grew f. and furious	BURNS 163:9
he talks it so very f.	FARQ 280:15
Lord I am coming as f.	LAUD 411:4
my heart is f., and cannot	ANON 17:21
none so f. as stroke	COKE 208:15
or come he f.	SCOTT 560:2
sadness, then into a f.	SHAK 574:17
Silently and very f.	AUDEN 34:11
Snip! They go so f.	HOFF 341:7
Spare F., that oft	MILT 464:17
study and f.	SHAK 605:10
wherefore should I f.	BIBLE 75:13
who will not f. in peace	CRAB 225:3

fasten: F. your seat-belts   MANK 444:9
if they think, they f.	HOUS 351:19

faster: F. than a speeding bullet   ANON 13:8
fastest: f. who travels alone   KIPL 399:18
fastidious: f. as though I wrote with acid
	MANS 445:7
literature is never f.	SOUT 657:17
minds of a few f.	SMITH 652:12

fasting: And thank heaven, f.   SHAK 569:13
Apollo turned f. friar	MER 457:21
between a fou man and a f.	SCOTT 560:27
children nor f. nor birch	BLAKE 114:10
lives upon hope will die f.	FRAN 292:17

fasts: that come in f. divine   HOPK 345:13
fat: ain't over 'til the f. lady   COOK 218:4
all f., without nerve	LEWIS 421:8
all people a feast of f.	BIBLE 83:8
Butter merely makes us f.	GOER 308:15
eat the f. of the land	BIBLE 71:30
f. and grows old	SHAK 580:15
f. and long-haired fellows	PLUT 517:16
f. and look young till	DRYD 261:4
f. bulls of Basan close	BOOK 125:11
F., fair and forty were	O'KEE 498:9
f. gentleman in such	SHAW- 639:2
f. greedy owl of the Remove	RICH 540:7
F. is a feminist issue	ORB 499:6
f. white woman whom nobody	CORN 219:4
if you're f., is a minefield	MARG 446:5
Imprisoned in every f. man	CONN 216:17
lean books with the f.	BURT 164:14
men about me that are f.	SHAK 590:6
Outside every f. man there	AMIS 10:15
oxen should himself be f.	JOHN 376:14
round, f., oily man of God	THOM 695:19
seven f. kine	BIBLE 71:25
thin man inside every f.	ORW 499:23
Who's your f. friend	BRUM 153:20

fatal: fair and f. king   JOHN 366:19
f. bellman	SHAK 601:15
f. futility of Fact	JAMES 363:8
f. gift of beauty	BYRON 169:2
f. shadows that walk	FLET 287:16
great deal of it is absolutely f.	WILDE 735:6
I am a f. man, Madame	THAC 691:7
most f. complaint of all	HILT 339:4
most f. to true happiness	RUSS 551:13
So sweet was ne'er so f.	SHAK 618:5
that f. and perfidious bark	MILT 466:6
Their f. hands	MILT 470:8

fatalistic: Beats like a f. drum   ELIOT 272:14
fate: ah! forget my f.   TATE 678:15
And take a bond of f.	SHAK 604:1
arbiter of others' f.	BYRON 172:22
Art is a revolt against f.	MALR 443:17
at length my f. I know	BROW 150:19
But F. so enviously debars	MARV 450:3
cannot suspend their f.	DEFOE 234:14
decide the f. of the world	DE G 235:3
down the torrent of his f.	JOHN 370:21
Ever hung my f.	MIDD 459:15
For he that f. from us	OVID 502:11
F. and character	NOV 497:3
F. cannot harm me	SMITH 653:19
f. change me for worms	ROCH 543:1

fate: (*cont.*):
f. has torn your living	CAT 187:1
f. is like the chronicle	YEVT 754:5
F. is not an eagle	BOWEN 138:11
f. never wounds more deep	JOHN 370:8
f. not to be too cruel	ALAI 7:7
f. of a nation was riding	LONG 427:20
f. of this country depends	DISR 247:24
f. of unborn millions	WASH 721:23
F.'s great bazaar	MACN 441:3
f. that cannot be surmounted	CAMUS 177:20
F. tried to conceal him	HOLM 342:12
f. wilfully misunderstand	FROST 294:11
F. wrote her a most tremendous	BEER 59:21
Fixed f., free will	MILT 469:23
go when F. calls him	SOCR 655:1
hands and sealed his f.	JAGG 361:13
hanging breathless on thy f.	LONG 426:11
have conquered f.	ARN 27:22
He either fears his f. too	GRAH 313:15
how very sad thy f.	KEATS 390:22
I am the master of my f.	HENL 332:7
I have a bone to pick with F.	NASH 490:14
limits of a vulgar f.	GRAY 316:9
makers of our f.	POPP 524:11
man and master of his f.	TENN 682:8
man's character is his f.	HER 333:12
might read the book of f.	SHAK 583:13
My grief to thy too rigid f.	GRAH 313:13
once dead by f.	BEAU 56:15
our folly, or our f.	DENH 236:20
over-ruled by f.	MARL 447:10
profit every day that F.	HOR 349:7
should they know their f.	GRAY 316:3
that waggèd contempt at F.	WATS 720:1
There is no armour against f.	SHIR 646:2
Till I thy f. shall overtake	KING 396:11
transient is the smile of f.	DYER 265:6
war our f. has consummation	MAND 444:6
wayward the decrees of F.	THAC 691:22
what I will is f.	MILT 472:8
when f. summons	DRYD 261:1
Who can control his f.	SHAK 618:16
Why, I hold f.	FORD 289:15
With a heart for any f.	LONG 427:11
With the severity of f.	FORD 289:7
would F. but mend it	PRIOR 529:13

fated: though f. not to die   DRYD 260:19
fates: are masters of their f.   SHAK 590:3
periods set, and hidden f.	SUCK 671:10

fat-head: F. poet nobody reads   CHES 199:2
father: about my F.'s business   BIBLE 93:30
ance his f.'s pride	BURNS 161:18
As a decrepit f. takes delight	SHAK 633:14
As my poor f. used to say	HERB 333:12
because I go to the F.	BIBLE 97:20
be happier than your f.	SOPH 656:10
bow my knees unto the F.	BIBLE 102:13
brood of folly without f.	MILT 464:13
cannot have God for his f.	CYPR 229:8
Child is f. of the Man	WORD 745:6
Dear Lord and F. of mankind	WHIT 733:7
down from the F. of lights	BIBLE 104:26
either my f. or my mother	STER 664:11
even as your F.	BIBLE 89:2
f. and first founder	CAXT 188:1
f. answered never a word	LONG 428:4
f. had a daughter loved	SHAK 629:20
f. had an accident there	POTT 525:13
F., hear the prayer we offer	WILL 737:14
F., I have sinned against	BIBLE 95:3
f. is gone wild	SHAK 584:9
F. is rather vulgar	DICK 241:6
F.-like, he tends and spares	LYTE 433:17
f. married the ae warst	BALL 49:16
f. of English criticism	JOHN 368:25
f. of many nations	BIBLE 99:24
f. pitieth his own children	BOOK 132:5
f.'s eyes with light	COL 209:11
F.'s house are many mansions	BIBLE 97:11
f. that knows his own child	SHAK 608:7
f. when the son swore	BURT 165:11
f. would wish his daughter	ANON 13:10

father: (*cont.*):

Glory be to the F.	BOOK 118:11
Had it been his f.	ANON 14:6
Hath the rain a f.?	BIBLE 77:36
Have a turnip than his f.	JOHN 377:4
He took my f. grossly	SHAK 577:4
Honour thy f. and thy mother	BIBLE 72:16
I am thy f.'s spirit	SHAK 573:13
I had it from my f.	SHAK 588:10
I meet my F.	LOW 430:14
leave his f. and his mother	BIBLE 70:7
limp f. of thousands	JOYCE 381:25
lively picture of his f.'s	FLET 288:1
Lloyd George knew my f.	ANON 15:23
man cometh unto the F.	BIBLE 97:12
My f. as he slept I had done't	SHAK 601:17
My f. feeds his flocks	HOME 342:19
My mother groaned! my f. wept	BLAKE 114:8
Neither f. nor mother	THUM 694:4
no more like my f.	SHAK 572:12
of your f. the devil	BIBLE 96:33
one God the F. Almighty	BOOK 121:19
only begotten of the F.	BIBLE 96:4
Our F. which art in heaven	BIBLE 89:5
Our F. which art in heaven	PREV 528:16
polite f. of his people	JAM 362:2
servants of my f.'s have bread	BIBLE 95:3
She gave her f. forty-one	ANON 15:22
son should strike his f.	SHAK 627:8
There is no good f.	SART 556:14
thicker than my f.'s loins	BIBLE 75:27
Thy f.'s fortunes	CORB 218:14
Thy f.'s shame, thy mother's	BRET 140:17
thy F. which seeth in secret	BIBLE 89:3
Thy wish was f., Harry	SHAK 584:3
'Tis the F.'s pleasure	NOEL 496:9
'twill come to my f. anon	AUBR 33:11
when did you last see your f.	YEAM 750:15
will cut off thy f.'s head	CHAR 191:7
wise son maketh a glad f.	BIBLE 78:20
withered all when my f. died	SHAK 578:8
you no longer have a f.	NERV 492:1

fathered: so f. and so husbanded — SHAK 591:3

fatherhood: Mirrors and f. — BORG 136:10

fatherless: defendeth the f. and widow — BOOK 135:10

f. children, and widows	BOOK 120:1
He is a Father of the f.	BOOK 129:7
visit the f. and widows	BIBLE 104:28

fatherly: commend to thy f. goodness — BOOK 120:7

fathers: f. and makes friends — MUMF 488:1

f. brought forth upon	LINC 422:10
f. by the prophets	BIBLE 104:10
f.-forth whose beauty is past	HOPK 345:20
f. have eaten sour grapes	BIBLE 85:22
f. thou shalt have children	BOOK 127:14
f. upon the children	BIBLE 72:16
fet from f. of war-proof	SHAK 585:8
healthiest f. stands	WHIT 732:12
He slept with his f.	BIBLE 75:30
I am going to my F.	BUNY 156:16
Lord God of your f.	BIBLE 71:42
My f. can have it	THOM 693:21
our f. have told us	BOOK 127:9
such as our f. have	BOOK 130:8
Tell them, because our f. lied	KIPL 398:16
To our f. in distress	LYTE 433:17
Victory has a hundred f.	CIANO 203:16
were all our f.	BIBLE 76:32
When your f. tempted me	BOOK 131:10
Ye f., provoke not	BIBLE 102:24

Father William: You are old, F. — CARR 182:3

You are old, F.	SOUT 657:13

fathom: f. inscrutable workings — SMITH 651:14

For thou canst not f. it	TENN 687:23
Full f. five thy father lies	SHAK 625:10
Full many a f. deep	CAMP 176:10

fathom-line: f. could never touch — SHAK 580:1

fathoms: 'Tis fifty f. deep — BALL 50:12

fatigue: Thinking the greatest f. — VANB 708:5

fatling: young lion and the f. — BIBLE 83:2

fatness: thy clouds drop f. — BOOK 129:3

---

fatted: Bring hither the f. calf — BIBLE 95:4

fattening: immoral, or f. — WOOL 742:19

fatter: Would he were f. — SHAK 590:7

fatti: F. *non foste a viver come* — DANTE 230:16

fatuity: f. of idiots — SMITH 652:24

faucibus: *f. Orci* — VIRG 713:14

Faulconbridge: Hadst thou rather be a F. — SHAK 593:24

fault: An artist is his own f. — O'HARA 498:5

But see thy f.	SHAK 585:2
clever to a f.	BROW 148:14
Condemn the f. and not	SHAK 605:15
f., dear Brutus	SHAK 590:3
f. is great in man or woman	ANON 13:9
f. of angels and of gods	POPE 519:17
f. when someone else	BROO 143:20
f. who hath no fault	TENN 681:21
fellow f. came to match it	SHAK 569:10
It has no kind of f. or flaw	GILB 304:7
it was a grievous f.	SHAK 592:5
Just hint a f., and hesitate	POPE 519:32
O happy f.	MISS 477:16
scarce weed out the f.	GOLD 311:15
through my most grievous f.	MISS 476:16
'tis Nature's f. alone	CHUR 201:16
To hide the f. I see	POPE 523:32
What soul is without f.	RIMB 541:9

faultless: Faultily f. — TENN 686:7

F. to a fault	BROW 152:20
thinks a f. piece to see	POPE 521:10

faults: acknowledge my f. — BOOK 128:4

all acknowledge our f.	BURN 160:12
all his f. observed	SHAK 593:8
All men make f.	SHAK 633:13
be buffeted for your f.	BIBLE 105:14
Be to her f. a little blind	PRIOR 529:5
Drown all my f. and fears	FLET 287:25
England, with all thy f.	COWP 223:20
f. are such that one loves	GOLD 311:16
f. of statesmen give birth	WALP 720:3
f. true critics dare not	POPE 521:7
his f. lie gently on him	SHAK 589:6
men are moulded out of f.	SHAK 607:1
secret f.	BOOK 125:6
Some f. to make us men	SHAK 566:18
their f. confessing	BUCK 154:12
They fill you with the f.	LARK 410:6
vile ill-favoured f.	SHAK 610:17
what f. they commit	QUAR 534:5
With all her f.	CHUR 200:17
with all thy f. I love	BUTL 167:7

faune: *l'après-midi d'un f.* — MALL 442:17

faute: *qu'un crime, c'est une f.* — BOUL 137:15

fauteuil: *f. qui le délasse* — MAT 454:1

favete: *F. linguis* — HOR 349:22

favilla: *Solvet saeclum in f.* — MISS 477:11

favour: f. with God — BIBLE 93:31

Have grace and f. in them	SHAK 617:21
me of your grace and f.	SHAK 594:22
out of f. grudge at knaves	DEFOE 234:18
par in f. of the people	BURKE 159:2
Praise him for his grace and f.	LYTE 433:17
truths being in and out of f.	FROST 294:12
Will bend to f. ev'ry client	GAY 300:5

favourable: f. and gracious unto Sion — BOOK 128:8

favoured: that art highly f. — BIBLE 93:21

favourite: second f. organ — ALLEN 9:13

favourites: persuading monarchs to choose f. — SWIFT 673:14

Topography displays no f.	BISH 110:2

favours: f. swims with fins of lead — SHAK 570:5

felt all its f.	COCK 208:3
lively sense of future f.	WALP 720:16
middle of her f.	SHAK 574:25
necessity a bad recommendation to f.	FIEL 282:8
secret hope for greater f.	LA R 410:20
that hangs on princes' f.	SHAK 588:19

fawning: base spaniel f. — SHAK 591:11

How like a f. publican	SHAK 607:20

fawns: fallow f. invisible go — THOM 694:5

---

fay: *F. ce que vouldras* — RAB 534:19

fear: acting and reasoning as f. — BURKE 158:3

alike by beauty and by f.	WORD 746:20
And drives away his f.	NEWT 494:10
And their one f., Death's	BLUN 116:1
are paralysed by f.	LAWR 412:2
are the concessions of f.	BURKE 157:19
be just, and f. not	SHAK 589:1
By f., to fear, successively	ROCH 543:13
by means of pity and f.	ARIS 25:12
contempt of f.	JONS 378:20
Cuckoo, cuckoo; O, word of f.	SHAK 599:10
direction of our f.	BERR 66:17
down needs f. no fall	BUNY 156:10
dread and f. of kings	SHAK 609:13
equal poise of hope and f.	MILT 463:28
F. and Hunger	VIRG 713:14
f. first in the world made	JONS 378:25
F. God. Honour the King	BIBLE 105:13
F. God. Honour the King	KITC 402:17
F. God, and keep his	BIBLE 81:4
F. God, and take your own part	BORR 136:18
f. in a handful of dust	ELIOT 272:23
F. is the foundation	ADAMS 3:2
F. is the main source	RUSS 551:25
f. my name shall the Sun	BIBLE 86:19
F. no more the heat o' the sun	SHAK 571:16
f. of finding something	BELL 61:2
f. of having to weep	BEAU 56:10
f. of the Lord is clean	BOOK 125:5
f. of the Lord is the beginning	BOOK 133:5
f. of tomorrow's dangers	DONNE 253:10
f., or hope beyond ourselves	SHEL 644:9
f. still followed him behind	SPEN 659:28
f. that kills	WORD 747:13
f. to be we know not what	DRYD 260:5
f. to whom fear	BIBLE 100:9
f. usually ends in folly	COL 212:13
f. what is too strange	WILB 734:1
f., with thy projects	ALAB 7:1
Fly hence, our contact f.	ARN 28:9
For f. of little men	ALL 10:1
For I am keepet by thy f.	BURNS 162:7
fourth is freedom from f.	ROOS 546:3
given us the spirit of f.	BIBLE 104:5
had I cannot f. to lose	AST 32:6
hate, so long as they f.	ACC 1:4
hate that which we often f.	SHAK 564:24
Him serve with f., his praise	KETHE 394:13
hope that never had a f.	COWP 224:13
I cannot taint with f.	SHAK 604:19
I f. thee, ancient Mariner	COL 211:6
I f. those big words	JOYCE 381:21
I have a faint cold f.	SHAK 623:28
include me in their f.	MOT 487:2
I will f. no evil	BOOK 125:5
knowledge and of the f.	BIBLE 83:1
let him be your f.	BIBLE 82:25
life in thy faith and f.	BOOK 122:3
Life is first boredom, then f.	LARK 409:17
lives not in f.	SHAK 596:23
masters the f. of death	BACON 43:9
much joy or too much f.	GRAV 314:18
name were liable to f.	SHAK 590:7
natural f. in children	BACON 43:8
never f. to negotiate	KENN 393:14
nobility is exempt from f.	SHAK 587:21
ocean in the eventide of f.	MORR 485:9
only thing we have to f.	ROOS 545:16
Perfect f. casteth out love	CONN 216:23
Possess them not with f.	SHAK 586:9
salvation with f. and trembling	BIBLE 103:6
Severity breedeth f.	BACON 43:30
so whom shall I f.	BIBLE 107:27
state as required by its f.	MAD 441:13
suddenly grow grey with f.	SHEL 641:17
Thawing cold f.	SHAK 585:16
There is no f. in love	BIBLE 105:28
there is not a word of f.	LAND 408:1
those who f. life	RUSS 551:16
till the f. of the Law	JOYCE 381:5
trembled with f. at your frown	ENGL 277:24

fear: (cont.):
watch not one another out of f.	DONNE 252:5
whom then shall I f.	BOOK 125:24
Why f. death	FROH 294:5
will eat our meal in f.	SHAK 603:3
with hope farewell f.	MILT 470:26
without f. the lawless roads	MUIR 487:13
yet will I f. none ill	SCOT 561:8

feared: f. nor flattered any flesh — DOUG 255:9
safer for a prince to be f. — MACH 438:8

fearful: f. symmetry — BLAKE 114:13
f. thing to fall — BIBLE 104:12
our f. trip is done — WHIT 732:6
To be a lovely and a f. thing — BYRON 170:22

fearfully: f. and wonderfully made — BOOK 134:20

fearing: many years of f. death — SHAK 591:16

fearless: F., blameless knight — ANON 20:8

fears: Applying f. to hopes — SHAK 634:25
are their griefs and f. — BACON 44:11
doubts, tormenting f. — ROCH 543:9
Drown all my faults and f. — FLET 287:25
f. his fellowship to die — SHAK 586:11
f. may be liars — CLOU 207:24
F. of the brave, and follies — JOHN 370:20
f. that I may cease — KEATS 390:28
forgot the taste of f. — SHAK 604:24
Happy is the man who f. — BIBLE 108:1
have grown from sudden f. — BYRON 173:2
He either f. his fate too much — GRAH 313:15
hopes and f. of all the years — BROO 144:4
I had no human f. — WORD 748:1
More pangs and f. than wars — SHAK 588:19
Not mine own f. — SHAK 634:19
Our f. do make us traitors — SHAK 604:3
past regrets and future f. — FITZ 283:17
Present f. — SHAK 600:12
sympathy with hopes and f. — SHEL 643:17
tie up thy f. — HERB 334:12
To saucy doubts and f. — SHAK 603:8
who f. dishonour more — HUR 350:19
without many f. and distastes — BACON 42:20

feast: As you were going to a f. — JONS 378:18
Chief nourisher in life's f. — SHAK 602:2
f. at ease on dainty fare — DUCK 263:6
f. of fat things — BIBLE 83:8
f. of joy is but a dish — TICH 698:3
great f. of languages — SHAK 599:4
improper mind a perpetual f. — SMITH 652:6
LIBERTY's a glorious f. — BURNS 162:13
my senses to a solemn f. — DRAY 257:20
Paris is a movable f. — HEM 331:16
perpetual f. of nectared sweets — MILT 464:1
scramble at the shearers' f. — MILT 466:8
vigil f. his neighbours — SHAK 586:11
well compared to a f. — BARN 53:18
When I make a f. — HAR 326:11

feast-day: upon our solemn f. — BOOK 130:14

feasts: uppermost rooms at f. — BIBLE 92:4
uppermost rooms at f. — BIBLE 93:17

feather: Blade on the f. — CORY 219:13
f. for each wind that blows — SHAK 631:20
f. to tickle the intellect — LAMB 406:20
friendship never moults a f. — DICK 242:17
my foot, my each f. — HUGH 354:4
Stuck a f. in his cap — ANON 20:1
wit's a f. — POPE 522:20

feather-beds: go to heaven in f. — MORE 484:8

feathered: f. glory from her — YEATS 752:10
f. race with pinions skim — FRERE 293:16

feather-footed: F. through the plashy fen — WAUGH 724:2

feathers: her f. like gold — BOOK 129:8
shalt be safe under his f. — BOOK 131:3
To wet their silken f. — SPEN 660:24

featly: Foot it f. here and there — SHAK 625:8

feats: What f. he did that day — SHAK 586:11

feature: every f. works — AUST 38:7

featured: F. like him, like him — SHAK 633:10

February: not Puritanism but F. — KRUT 404:6

fed: But it is f. and man. — CAMP 176:4
f. a. I ruminated till it — RUSK 550:27
f. of the dainties — ....
f. on the fullness — SWIN 676:21

fed: (cont.):
f. our sea for a thousand — KIPL 401:2
f. with the same food — SHAK 608:22
We both have f. as well — SHAK 589:28
you have f. full — VIRG 715:9

federal: Our F. Union — JACK 361:2

federation: F. of the world — TENN 685:13

fee: For a small f. in America — SOND 656:3
gorgeous East in f. — WORD 746:11
though it were a doctor's f. — LEV 420:1

feeble: confirm the f. knees — BIBLE 83:20
f. can seldom persuade — GIBB 302:7
jonquil o'ercomes the f. brain — WINC 739:3
Most forcible F. — SHAK 583:17
not enough to help the f. — SHAK 626:4
such a f. temper should — SHAK 590:2
Well our f. frame he knows — LYTE 433:17

feebly: His words came f. — WORD 747:12

feed: And f. deep, deep — KEATS 389:6
Church can f. and sleep — ELIOT 271:13
doth this our Caesar f. — SHAK 590:4
f. his flock like a shepherd — BIBLE 83:28
f. me in a green pasture — BOOK 125:14
F. my lambs — BIBLE 97:40
f. on thoughts that voluntary — MILT 470:16
F. the brute — PUNCH 532:4
f. with the rich — JOHN 373:2
Gave thee life and bid thee f. — BLAKE 113:21
shalt thou f. on Death — SHAK 635:8
will you still f. me — LENN 418:3

feedeth: he f. among the lilies — BIBLE 81:11

feel: because I don't f. a thing — OSB 501:11
But I must also f. it as a man — SHAK 604:10
can f. that he is dying — CAL 175:6
do a thing but to f. — HOPK 346:19
Englishman can't f. — FORS 290:1
feel a feeling which I f. — RIDD 540:18
f. for the common chord — BROW 148:2
f. it happen and am — CAT 186:17
f. the earth move — HEM 331:15
f. the heart-break — GIBS 303:5
f. what wretches feel — SHAK 596:7
I believe to One does f. — KNOX 403:5
I dislike what I fancy I f. — ANON 18:15
make one f. more at home — FREUD 293:21
see and hear and f. — JOYCE 381:27
something more to do than f. — LAMB 406:21
Speak what we f. — SHAK 598:5
thing that could not f. — WORD 748:1
Those who would make us f. — CHUR 201:14
tragedy to those that f. — WALP 719:18
women feel just as men f. — BRON 142:4

feeling: And petrifies the f. — BURNS 161:24
appeals to diffused f. — BAG 47:5
Certainty. F. Joy — PASC 508:1
constellations of f. — DOUG 255:10
depth of f. to embrace — BYRON 172:1
f. and a love — WORD 744:21
f. is more soft and sensible — SHAK 598:20
f. of Sunday is the same — RHYS 539:21
f.-toned complexes — JUNG 382:12
f. which I feel you all — RIDD 540:18
formal f. comes — DICK 244:9
generous and honest f. — BURKE 159:17
mess of imprecision of f. — ELIOT 271:1
Music is f., then, not sound — STEV 666:7
new f. has not changed me — TOLS 700:8
more true f. and worse taste — JOW 380:18
pulse of f. stirs again — ARN 26:17
school that f. is bad form — FORS 290:1
To f. as to sight — SHAK 601:12
without f. gay — CHUR 201:6

feelings: define f. in language — HARDY 324:7
f. these dull scenes produce — CRAB 224:23
f. which ought to taste — AUST 39:4
overflow of powerful f. — WORD 748:19
their f. than by reason — ADAMS 3:8
ultimately determined by the f. — SPEN 658:22

feels: Everyone f. it, has felt it — TROL 703:4

feet: accompanied by a few f. — HUNT 356:16
... ... f. ... but of his f. — HERR 336:15
they took their F. and said — ....
feet: ... ... f. — ARN 27:15

feet: (cont.):
And bathe those beauteous f. — FLET 287:24
And did those f. — BLAKE 113:4
And palms before my f. — CHES 198:30
At her f. he bowed — BIBLE 74:5
beautiful are thy f. with shoes — BIBLE 82:1
broken by their passing f. — YEATS 751:7
But let my due f. never fail — MILT 464:26
clothes at a young man's f. — BIBLE 98:12
die down over his f. — JOYCE 381:8
down Satan under our f. — BOOK 119:20
f., and the palms — BIBLE 76:30
f. are always in the water — AMES 10:9
f. chill on steps — CRANE 225:17
f. have they, and walk — BOOK 133:10
f. into the way of peace — BIBLE 93:24
f. like unto fine brass — BIBLE 106:1
f. of him that bringeth — BIBLE 84:8
f. shall stand in thy gates — BOOK 133:25
f. shod with the preparation — BIBLE 103:1
f. they hurt in the stocks — BOOK 132:11
f. was I to the lame — BIBLE 77:29
fell at his f. as dead — BIBLE 106:1
gold chains about the f. — TENN 682:24
grown-up people's f. — STEV 668:13
hands are a sort of f. — TRAH 701:16
Her f. beneath her petticoat — SUCK 671:7
Her f. go down to death — BIBLE 78:12
his eyes before his f. — ELIOT 273:1
iron f. can print no ruin — MONT 482:1
Its f. were tied — KEATS 387:31
Just direct your f. — FIEL 282:19
lantern unto my f. — BOOK 133:20
Lord, dost thou wash my f. — BIBLE 97:8
marching, charging f. — JAGG 361:12
moon under her f. — BIBLE 106:29
My f. begin to go — GROS 319:1
my f. from falling — BOOK 133:12
nations under our f. — BOOK 127:19
nothing walks with aimless f. — TENN 683:18
on little cat f. — SAND 555:4
on three f. — SACK 552:14
on your f. than to live — IBAR 358:14
our f. when we want shoes — SWIFT 674:17
pierced my hands and my f. — BOOK 125:13
set my f. upon the rock — BOOK 126:24
seven f. of English ground — HAR 326:14
shake off the dust of your f. — BIBLE 90:15
slipping underneath our f. — FITZ 284:3
spring up between the f. — EMER 276:20
stablish their f. — BIBLE 86:22
Standing, with reluctant f. — LONG 427:2
stranger's f. may find — HOUS 352:1
tempt with wandering f. — MILT 469:20
Than when before your f. I lay — WALL 718:17
their f. than their head — CAV 187.14
Thus I set my printless f. — MILT 464:11
thy shoes from off thy f. — BIBLE 71:38
Til crowes f. be growe under — CHAU 195:13
To his f. thy tribute bring — LYTE 433:17
tremble under her f. — TENN 686:20
twain he covered his f. — BIBLE 82:19
wash their f. in soda water — ELIOT 273:7
what dread f. — BLAKE 114:14
Wi' the Scots lords at his f. — BALL 50:12

feigned: nedeth f. loves for to seke — CHAU 196:2

feigning: f. called compliment — SHAK 630:10

felice: Che ricordarsi del tempo f. — DANTE 230:11

felicem: genus infortunii, fuisse f. — BOET 116:12

felices: F. ter et amplius — HOR 349:10

felicities: Job than the f. of Solomon — BACON 42:19

felicitous: F. phenomenon — MOORE 482:12

felicity: Absent thee from f. — SHAK 579:11
And none can boast sincere f. — DRYD 261:13
approaches f. — MER 457:24
eyes to behold f. — BROW 146:12
f. can fall to creature — SPEN 660:21
Horace's careful f. — PETR 513:14
Or shadow of f. — WALL 718:18
Our own f. we make or find — JOHN 370:13
Their green f. — KEATS 387:32
To respect of the pleyn f. — 196:1

felix: *F. qui potuit rerum* VIRG 715:14
fell: f. among thieves BIBLE 94:13
  f. at his feet as dead BIBLE 106:1
  f. before the throne BIBLE 106:19
  f. in love with a rich GILB 306:22
  f. into his anecdotage DISR 248:23
  God forgot me, and I f. BROW 148:19
  my uncle Toby f. into it STER 665:4
  though the brightest f. SHAK 604:6
  To noon he f. MILT 469:7
  Who ran to help me when I f. TAYL 679:13
feller: Sweetes' li'l' f. STAN 662:11
fellow: as one that loves his f.-men HUNT 356:5
  His f. traveller ANON 18:7
  testy, pleasant f. ADD 4:7
fellow-feeling: f. makes one wond'rous kind GARR 298:6
fellow-mortal: companion to an' f. BURNS 163:16
fellows: For f. whom it hurts to think HOUS 352:19
  shoes that were not f. DEFOE 234:7
  these f. of infinite tongue SHAK 587:1
fellowship: F. is heaven MORR 485:15
  learnt the simple dues of f. BROW 147:4
  one communion and f. BOOK 121:13
  right hands of f. BIBLE 102:4
felonious: some f. end MILT 463:20
felony: f. to drink small beer SHAK 587:23
felt: darkness which may be f. BIBLE 72:7
  f. along the heart WORD 744:19
female: f. atheist talks you dead JOHN 370:7
  F. Eunuch GREER 317:14
  f. mind WOLL 741:16
  f. mind like a rude fallow IRWIN 360:19
  f. mind not capable KNOX 403:14
  f. of the species is more KIPL 399:3
  f. physique and alarming LANC 407:19
  f. upon the male LAWR 412:6
  f. worker is the slave CONN 216:24
  flaming racket of the f. OSB 501:14
  involved with the f. principle CLARK 205:8
  life for the British f. CLOU 207:1
  Male and f. created he them BIBLE 69:25
  male and the f. created he BIBLE 70:26
  now shall know a f. reign EGER 267:13
  These stores supply the f. pen ALC 8:1
  they cast on f. wits BRAD 139:10
  Who has a faithful f. friend WHUR 733:13
females: with eighty mile o' f. DICK 243:28
femina: *Dux f. facti* VIRG 712:7
feminine: Eternal F. GREER 317:13
  F. Mystique FRIE 294:3
  Taste is the f. of genius FITZ 284:19
  this beautiful f. tissue HARDY 324:15
feminist: Fat is a f. issue ORB 499:6
femme: *Cherchez la f.* DUMAS 263:12
fen: she is a f. of stagnant waters WORD 745:4
  through the plashy f. WAUGH 724:2
fence: f. just too high MAUG 454:4
  jonquils by sunny garden f. BETJ 68:1
  o'er the f. leaps Sunny Jim HANFF 323:5
fences: And tied her with f. MORR 486:1
  f. and their whole array HERB 335:20
  f. make good neighbours FROST 295:4
fennel: There's f. for you SHAK 578:8
fens: As reek o' the rotten f. SHAK 570:13
fercula: *Et illa erant f.* AUG 36:23
feri: *Ita f. ut se mori sentiat* CAL 175:6
feriam: *Sublimi f. sidera vertice* HOR 348:24
Fermanagh: steeples of F. and Tyrone CHUR 202:2
ferments: F. and frets, until BUTL 166:21
fern: sparkle out among the f. TENN 680:11
fern-seed: have the receipt of f. SHAK 580:4
ferny: Of the forest's f. floor DE L 236:6
ferocity: whilst it mitigated f. BURKE 158:14
feros: *mores nec sinit esse f.* OVID 502:17
fers: *partout il est dans les f.* ROUS 549:2
fertile: In such a fix to be so f. NASH 490:8
fervent: f. prayer of a righteous BIBLE 105:7
fessi: *f. venimus larem ad nostrum* CAT 186:3

festal: f. light in Christ-Church ARN 28:7
fester: Lilies that f. smell far SHAK 634:15
  limbs that f. are not springlike ABSE 1:2
festina: *F. lente* AUG 37:12
fetch: f. the age of gold MILT 467:8
  fresh corpse, f. him out TWAIN 706:14
fetish: Militarism is f. worship TAWN 678:20
fetters: be in love with his f. BACON 42:16
  F. of gold are still fetters AST 32:8
  his f. fall GAND 297:9
  reason Milton wrote in f. BLAKE 112:15
feuds: Forget all f., and shed MAC 436:7
feux: *f. qui s'enflamment* FRAN 292:10
fever: After life's fitful f. SHAK 603:3
  bent by the same wintry f. THOM 693:7
  f., and the fret KEATS 389:10
  f. called 'Living' POE 518:5
  f. is to the physicians MILT 476:3
  f. of life is over NEWM 493:11
  f. when he was in Spain SHAK 590:1
  Of chills and f. she died RANS 536:14
  Resolving the enigma of the f. ELIOT 270:22
  signed the treaty bred a f. THOM 693:10
  That this her f. might be it DONNE 252:2
feverish: Poetry's the f. fit WINC 738:24
feverous: Was f. and did shake SHAK 602:13
fevers: Time and f. burn away AUDEN 35:5
février: Generals Janvier and F. NICH 494:12
few: Far and f., far and few LEAR 414:3
  F. and evil have the days BIBLE 71:32
  f. and far between CAMP 176:19
  f. are chosen BIBLE 92:1
  f. child's squalls HUNT 356:16
  F. thought he was even ATTL 32:16
  f. words are the best men SHAK 585:12
  fit audience find, though f. MILT 472:7
  Gey f., and they're a' deid ANON 14:7
  owed by so many to so f. CHUR 202:13
  therefore let thy words be f. BIBLE 80:9
  we happy f., we band SHAK 586:11
fewer: there was merely one man f. METT 459:3
fiancée: wish his f. to see ANON 13:10
fiat: bound to say *'f. justitia* MANS 445:10
  F. justitia et pereat mundus FERD 281:9
  F. justitia et ruant coeli WATS 722:8
  f. voluntas tua sicut MISS 477:3
  I have a bit of F. in my soul BEDD 58:10
fickle: fierce and f. is the South TENN 688:6
  Whatever is f., freckled HOPK 345:20
fico: *Diga ao povo que f.* PEDR 510:16
  f. for the phrase SHAK 610:11
fiction: biography ultimately f. MAL 442:15
  But in a f., in a dream SHAK 575:8
  f. is a necessity CHES 199:14
  f. lags after truth BURKE 157:20
  f. the English have ever done WILDE 735:32
  house of f. JAMES 363:5
  I hate things all *f.* BYRON 174:5
  it as an improbable f. SHAK 630:24
  It is sometimes f. MAC 435:23
  Must be in a f. STEV 665:15
  one form of continuous f. BEVAN 69:7
  Poetry is the supreme f. STEV 665:20
  Stranger than f. BYRON 171:29
  That is what f. means WILDE 734:16
fictions: air of truth to their f. HUME 355:19
  f. without which we STEV 666:13
  that f. only and false heir HERB 335:6
fiddle: f., sir, and spade SCOTT 560:16
  F., we know, is diddle SWIN 676:17
  important beyond all this f. MOORE 482:13
  I the second f. SPR 661:11
fiddler: chemist, f., statesman DRYD 259:8
fiddling: and a f. priest COWP 223:1
fide: *Punica f.* SALL 554:15
  sed fortius f. et gaude LUTH 432:9
Fidele: fair F.'s grassy tomb COLL 213:10
fideles: *Adeste, f.* ANON 21:18
fidelity: f. is not having more RAPH 536:17
  stone f. they hardly meant LARK 409:13
fidgety: But f. Phil HOFF 341:3
fidus: *f. quae tela gerebat Achates* VIRG 712:4

field: Beside a f. of grain PARK 507:1
  comes and tills the f. TENN 689:10
  Consider the lilies of the f. BIBLE 89:11
  corner of a foreign f. BROO 143:18
  f. ful of folk fond I ther LANG 408:21
  f. is won MORE 484:12
  f. of Golgotha SHAK 620:17
  f. ring again and again BOWEN 138:6
  For Vaguery in the F. OSB 501:13
  From the wet f. ARN 28:26
  F. strewn with its dank yellow ARN 28:1
  man of the f. BIBLE 71:8
  Never in the f. of human CHUR 202:13
  Not that fair f. MILT 471:4
  sickle in the fruitful f. BLAKE 113:13
  simple as to cross a f. PAST 508:8
  that lay f. to field BIBLE 82:16
  What though the f. be lost MILT 468:5
fields: Blown f. or flowerful SWIN 677:1
  f. and catch a glimpse KEATS 392:6
  f. and flocks have charms CRAB 225:12
  f. invested with purpureal WORD 744:18
  f. so fade that flourished SACK 552:12
  flowerless f. of heaven SWIN 675:20
  In f. where roses fade HOUS 352:18
  me from the f. of sleep WORD 745:12
  Open unto the f. WORD 743:9
  Poetic f. encompass me ADD 4:2
  Strawberry f. forever LENN 418:1
  through the f. in gloves CORN 219:4
  till his ancestral f. HOR 348:22
  walks the f. and the waters MER 457:29
  We plough the f., and scatter CAMP 176:4
  whispering of f. half-sown OWEN 503:14
fiend: A foul F. coming over BUNY 155:17
  As soon as she the f. did name BALL 50:7
  dark dominion swung the f. MER 458:6
  defy the foul f. SHAK 596:10
  f. walked up and down MILT 470:19
  frightful f. doth close behind COL 211:14
  Like a f. hid in a cloud BLAKE 114:8
  Out, hyperbolical f. SHAK 630:31
fiends: Beneath is all the f.' SHAK 597:5
  foreigners are f. MITF 478:8
fierce: bright and f. and fickle TENN 688:6
  extremes by change more f. MILT 470:3
  F. as ten Furies MILT 470:5
  f. blaze of riot cannot SHAK 619:17
  f. light which beats upon TENN 681:16
  F. was the wild billow ANAT 11:6
  grew more f. and wild HERB 334:12
  look not so f. on me MARL 447:4
fiere: a hand, my trusty f. BURNS 161:6
fiery: burning f. furnace BIBLE 85:28
  f. portal of the east SHAK 620:9
  f. ramparts rise BEAT 56:5
  quench all the f. darts BIBLE 103:1
  that very f. particle BYRON 171:21
  throne was like the f. flame BIBLE 86:1
fife: Thane of F. had a wife SHAK 604:13
  That practised on a f. CARR 184:7
fifteen: always f. years older BAR 54:20
  famous for f. minutes WARH 721:22
  F. men on dead man's chest STEV 667:22
  f. wild Decembers BRON 142:15
fifth: came f. and lost the job JOYCE 301:26
  remember the F. of November ANON 17:11
fifties: tranquillized F. LOW 430:13
fifty: After f. the clock can't stop LOW 430:17
  enough for f. hopes and fears BROW 148:11
  f. chides his infamous delay YOUNG 754:17
  F. million Frenchmen GUIN 319:13
  fool with booze until he's f. FAUL 281:5
fig: f. for those by law protected BURNS 162:13
  sewed f. leaves together BIBLE 70:10
  We don't care a f. LEAR 414:4
fight: And then Ile rise and f. BALL 50:9
  bade me f. had told me so EWER 279:10
  better to f. for the good TENN 687:6
  cannot f. against the future GLAD 307:6
  can we f. with fifty-three TENN 689:1
  cease when men refuse to f. ANON 19:5

fight: (*cont.*):
dead, who will not f.	GREN 318:2
Fall out, and chide, and f.	WATTS 722:17
f. and everyone's a foe	CLARE 204:16
f. and fight and fight	GAIT 296:16
f. and not to heed	IGN 359:8
f. begins within himself	BROW 148:15
f. for freedom and truth	IBSEN 359:2
f. for its King and Country	GRAH 313:7
f. in defence of one's	HOMER 343:8
f. is a tombstone white	KIPL 400:4
f. it out on this line	GRANT 314:8
f. longer than he sees	SHAK 579:28
f. of the one and the fifty-three	TENN 689:3
F. on, my men, sayes Sir	BALL 50:9
F. the good fight	MONS 480:1
F. the good fight of faith	BIBLE 104:4
fought a good f.	WILDE 736:11
fought the better f.	MILT 472:4
Good at a f., but better	ANON 13:20
hath no stomach to this f.	SHAK 586.11
have fought a good f.	BIBLE 104:8
I dare not f.; but I will	SHAK 585:3
I give the f. up	BROW 151:20
I have not yet begun to f.	JONES 377:19
man being too proud to f.	WILS 738:11
man may f. and no be slain	BURNS 163:12
moment to f.	TENN 689:1
must f. on to the end	HAIG 320:12
Never give up the f.	MARL 446:11
no peril in the f.	CORN 218:15
Nor law, nor duty bade me f.	YEATS 752:6
shall f. on the beaches	CHUR 202:11
so f. I, not as one	BIBLE 100:31
that crowns us, not the f.	HERR 336:13
then say it was in f.	SHAK 580:24
They would go f. tomorrow	BALL 49:8
thought it wrong to f.	BELL 61:27
Ulster will f.; Ulster	CHUR 201:19
wolves and f. like devils	SHAK 585:13
yourselves like men, and f.	BIBLE 74:30
youth who must f. and die	HOOV 344:20

fighter: Am I no a bonny f.
	STEV 667:12
I was ever a f.	BROW 152:5

fighting: are not fifty ways of f.
	MALR 443:15
between two periods of f.	BIER 109:13
consisteth not in actual f.	HOBB 340:6
f. Blenheim all over again	BEVAN 68:16
f. for this woman's honour	KALM 385:1
F. in the captain's tower	DYLAN 265:12
f. man shall from the sun	GREN 318:2
F. still, and still destroying	DRYD 259:21
f. with daggers in a hogshead	SCOTT 561:5
time is right for f.	JAGG 361:12
What are WE f.	SERV 563:7
who dies f. has increase	GREN 318:2
wilt thou leave f. o' days	SHAK 583:9

fights: the best part of married
	WILD 736:16
that knows what he f.	CROM 227:6

figs: long life better than f.
	SHAK 564:15
or f. of thistles	BIBLE 89:24

figurative: f., a metaphorical God DONNE 253:3

figure: extraordinary f. of our time KEYN 395:7
f. a poem makes	FROST 295:14
f. in a country church	SWIFT 673:18
f. in the carpet	JAMES 362:17
f. is easy	AUDEN 34:7
f. of Juno	BARR 54:16
f. that thou here seest	JONS 379:18

figures: f. they at once admire LEWIS 421:7
f. to be filed away	CRANE 225:25
might prove anything by f.	CARL 179:20

filches: f. from me my good name SHAK 616:12

filed: beadroll worthy to be f. SPEN 660:12

files: Commands the beauteous f. VAUG 708:17
foremost f. of time	TENN 685:18

filigree: meadows, with f. hedges WALF 710:3

fill: Come f. up my cup SCOTT 559:8
f. all f' in for wine	GAY 299:19
f. hup the chalice of liquor	SURT 672:10
F. me with life anew	HATCH 327:1
f. the cup	FITZ 284:3
f. you with the faults	LARK 410:6

fill: (*cont.*):
I am not yet born; O f. me	MACN 441:1
take our f. of love until	BIBLE 78:16
To f. the hour	EMER 277:4

filled: be f. with the Spirit BIBLE 102:23
f. his belly with the husks	BIBLE 95:3
mouth f. with laughter	BOOK 134:4
they shall be f.	BIBLE 88:23

filles: les f. aux pâles couleurs VOLT 716:15

fillest: f. all things living BOOK 135:7

filling: f. the world, and emptying
	SCOTT 560:16

fills: He f. a chair JOHN 375:22

film: f. of death obscured KEATS 390:22
like f. stars and royalty	LESS 419:9
Only that f., which fluttered	COL 210:5

films: f. are too exciting BERR 66:19

filth: f. and foul incontinence SPEN 660:7
identical, and so is f.	FORS 290:24

filthiness: f. and superfluity of naughtiness
	BIBLE 104:27
Neither f., nor foolish	BIBLE 102:20

filths: F. savour but themselves SHAK 596:29

filthy: fond of her most f. bargain SHAK 618.12
greedy of f. lucre	BIBLE 103:26
righteousnesses are as f. rags	BIBLE 84:28
that is f. and polluted	BIBLE 86:17

fin: f. in the porphyry font TENN 688:13
Voilà le commencement de la f.	TALL 678:12

final: f. belief must be in a fiction STEV 665:5
f. face of love	WILB 734:6
f. message of India	FORS 290:27

finale: Let be be f. of seem STEV 665:18

finality: F. is not the language DISR 247:5
Perfection is f.	STEP 663:19

finalize: F. you or advertise you DYLAN 265:10

Finals: This is called F. LODGE 425:19

finance: F. is, as it were GLAD 307:5

financiers: f., all the little gnomes WILS 737:19

Finchley: F. tried to mend the Electric
	BELL 61:20

find: Erst that ye can f. SKEL 649:2
f. a friend one must close	DOUG 255:14
f., and not to yield	TENN 690:4
f. someone to worship	DOST 254:7
His ways with men I f.	TENN 682:17
if ye f. my beloved	BIBLE 81:18
not f. anything pleasant	VOLT 716:2
places you will not f.	CAV 187:9
returns home to f. it	MOORE 482:9
searching f. out God	BIBLE 77:17
Someday I'll f. you	COW 221:1
there thou shalt f. me	ANON 17:16
thou shalt f. it after	BIBLE 80:25
We always f. something	BECK 57:26
Who fail to f. thee	TENN 686:5

findeth: f. his life shall lose BIBLE 90:22
he that seeketh f.	BIBLE 89:18

finds: always f., and never seeks COL 209:11
Who f. himself, loses	ARN 28:11

fine: bring in f. things BUCK 154:9
But quite a disgrace to be f.	TAYL 679:12
F. art	RUSK 550:28
f. madness still he did	DRAY 258:4
f. point of his soul taken	KEATS 391:8
f. romance with no kisses	FIEL 282:18
f. writing is next to fine	KEATS 392:10
purple and f. linen	BIBLE 95:9
stretch a cord however f.	WHEW 730:14
than much f. gold	BOOK 125:5
think is particularly f.	JOHN 373:23
too f. a point upon it	DICK 239:4
very f. cat indeed	JOHN 376:7

fine arts: murder as one of the f. DE Q 237:11

finem: F. di dederint HOR 349:8
prudenter agas, et respice f.	ANON 22:13

finer: appropriates the f. thus HARDY 324:15
diligent nothing could be f.	GORD 312:13
thoce're no love song f.	PORT 524:22

finery: not bedizened with f. TROL 707:8

fines: interest and f. on sorrow MILT 465:3
spent their f. hour	CHUR 202:12
Yes, this is our f. rhyme	OSB 501:9

finger: Between my f. and my thumb
	HEAN 329:18
burnt Fool's bandaged f.	KIPL 399:8
chills the f. not a bit	NASH 490:19
cold f. closer to her lips	KEATS 387:24
f. do you want on the trigger	ANON 19:21
f. in the throat and one	OSLER 502:1
F. of birth-strangled babe	SHAK 603:19
God's f. touched him	TENN 684:4
his slow and moving f.	SHAK 617:15
like a rugged f. to Heaven	LLOY 424:6
little f. shall be thicker	BIBLE 75:27
measured by the f. and thumb	SAL 554:1
moving f. writes	FITZ 284:9
ring without the f.	MIDD 459:13
scratching of my f.	HUME 356:1

fingernails: paring his f. JOYCE 381:13

fingerprints: f. across his brain HEND 332:4

fingers: cool stream thy f. wet ARN 28:5
Crumbling between the f.	MACN 440:17
cut their own f.	EDD 266:6
dead men's f. call them	SHAK 578:13
f. of cold	LAWR 413:1
forth f. of a man's hand	BIBLE 85:30
immortal f. did imprint	MARL 447:9
Just as my f. on these keys	STEV 666:7
our f. with base bribes	SHAK 592:2/
smile upon his f.' ends	SHAK 585:5
sovereign f. taxed the breath	THOM 693:9
Stop twisting in your yellow f.	HEAT 330:1
those terrified vague f.	YEATS 752:10
thrust his icy f. in my maw	SHAK 694:15
with careful f. and benign	KEATS 390:14
with forced f. rude	MILT 465:20
With f. weary and worn	HOOD 344:7
works of thy f.	BOOK 124:20

finger-stalls: In fitless f. GILB 305:5

finger-tips: accomplished to his f. HOR 351:4

finish: Nice guys. F. last DUR 264:11
start together and f.	BEEC 58:16
tools and we will f. the job	CHUR 202:15

finished: All that is f., finished BLOK 115:4
f. in half the time	WOD 740.13
f. in the first 100 days	KENN 393:15
I have f. my course	BIBLE 104:8
It is f.	BIBLE 97:29
married. Then he's f.	GABOR 296:12
world where England is f.	MILL 461:12

finisher: f. of our faith BIBLE 104:17

finite: are neither f. quantities BERK 65:7
Of f. hearts that yearn	BROW 153:5
quite bury under the F.	CARL 181:10
should like it to be f.	LEIB 416:18

finned: f. cars nose forward LOW 430:11

fins: swims with f. of lead SHAK 570:5

fir: thorn shall come up the f. BIBLE 84.18

fire: adamant, a soul of f. JOHN 370:16
adamantine chains and	
penal f.	MILT 467:23
And nodding by the f.	YEATS 753:19
And when the f. did compass him	
	GILB 303:11
anger as the flint bears f.	SHAK 593:9
be in danger of hell f.	BIBLE 88:29
Bennet was stirring the f.	AUST 39:12
broad gate and the great f.	SHAK 564:10
bush burned with f.	BIBLE 71:37
But gold shines like f.	PIND 514:13
candles and kindles f.	LA R 410:19
cloven tongues like as of f.	BIBLE 98:6
C'mon, baby, light my f.	MORR 485:19
dare seize the f.	BLAKE 114:14
deathly inner consuming f.	HESSE 337:16
dropping-wells of f.	TENN 684:3
every time She shouted 'F.	BELL 61:6
f. and brimstone	BOOK 124:23
F. and fleet and candle-lighte	BALL 49:18
F. and hail, snow and vapours	BOOK 135:14
f. and the rose are one	ELIOT 271:9
f. and was burnt to ashes	GRAH 313:12
f. answers fire, and through	SHAK 585:14
F. burn and cauldron bubble	SHAK 600.17

fire: (cont.):
f. can burn when all — DAN 229:15
f. come out of the bramble — BIBLE 74:12
f. has caught throughout — SAPP 556:1
f. in the head and a dread — JOHN 366:17
f. is quickly trodden out — SHAK 588:5
f. next time — ANON 13:17
f. of my loins — NAB 488:21
f. of my nature continually — BRON 142:5
f. of soul is kindled — DICK 242:17
f. sall never make thee — BALL 50:1
f. seven times tried this — SHAK 608:18
f. shall heat the deep — TENN 684:20
f. until you see the white — PUTN 533:6
f. was furry as a bear — SITW 648:10
f. which so often inflamed — ROUS 549:3
F. your little gun — DE L 236:4
fretted with golden f. — 3HAK 574:28
Gie me ae spark o' Nature's f. — BURNS 161:26
glass mingled with f. — BIBLE 107:6
great a matter a little f. — BIBLE 105:1
hailstones, and coals of f. — BOOK 125:2
heretic that makes the f. — SHAK 631:19
his wheels as burning f. — BIBLE 86:1
I am ashes where once I was f. — BYRON 173:10
I am f. and air — SHAK 567:8
I didn't f. him because — TRUM 704:20
It is a f., it is a coal — PEELE 511:3
little torches at his f. — COK 208:14
Lord was not in the f. — BIBLE 76:7
Love is ane fervent f. — SCOTT 559:1
Love is the f., and sighs — SOUT 657:22
man take f. in his bosom — BIBLE 78:15
may f. when you are ready — DEWEY 238:8
ministers a flaming f. — BOOK 132:6
Muse of f. — SHAK 584:16
My f.'s extinct, my forge — ANON 16:16
neighbour's house is on f. — BURKE 158:6
night in a pillar of f. — BIBLE 72:13
no false f. — ALAB 7:1
No light, no f. — SHAK 619:3
Now stir the f., and close — COWP 223:31
oure asshen olde is f. — CHAU 194:13
pale f. — SHAK 626:17
performs the effect of f. — MILT 470:2
right Promethean f. — SHAK 599:1
roast with f. — BIBLE 72:9
shall be found by the f. — BROW 148:22
shalt heap coals of f. — BIBLE 79:18
sheaves of sacred f. — CHAP 190:17
spirit all compact of f. — SHAK 635:12
steep-down gulfs of liquid f. — SHAK 618:18
take a walk into the f. — ENG 277:23
that are set on f. — BOOK 128:15
Thorough flood, thorough f. — SHAK 611:11
Till Skiddaw saw the f. — MAC 436:2
tongued with f. — ELIOT 271:3
trimmed its f. — ARN 28:19
Upon a wheel of f. — SHAK 597:13
wabbling back to the F. — KIPL 399:8
war with a heart of f. — TENN 687:5
What! frighted with false f. — SHAK 576:19
What of the faith and f. — HARDY 325:3
will set a house on f. — BACON 45:7
world will end in f. — FROST 294:17
youth of England are on f. — SHAK 585:1
firebrand: f. plucked out of — BIBLE 86:12
fired: hand that f. the shot — BALL 49:13
fire-fly: The f. wakens — TFNN 088:13
fire-folk: f. sitting in the air — HOPK 346:5
fires Big f. flare up in a wind — FRAN 292:10
devastating or redeeming f. — GONC 312:9
f. soon burn out themselves — SHAK 619:17
f. the length of Ophiuchus — MILT 470:7
Fuel to maintain his f. — CAREW 179:2
misled by wandering f. — DRYD 260:21
Of her salamandrine f. — HARDY 325:3
thought-executing f. — SHAK 595:20
fireside: adventures by the f. — GOLD 311:30
F. enjoyments, home-born — COWP 223:33
glass of wine by his own f. — SHER 645:23
There is no f., howsoe'er — LONG 427:12
firm: F. Resolve, take thou — BURNS 163:18

firm: (cont.):
old f. is selling out — OSB 501:16
firmament: blood streams in the f. — MARL 447:1
f. sheweth his handy-work — BOOK 125:4
now glowed the f. — MILT 471:10
spacious f. on high — ADD 4:19
There is no fellow in the f. — SHAK 591:12
this brave o'erhanging f. — SHAK 574:28
Waters that be above the F. — BOOK 118:16
firmly: F. I believe and truly — NEWM 493:12
firmness: Commodity, f., and delight — WOTT 749:6
Thy f. makes my circle just — DONNE 252:22
first: be done for the f. time — CORN 219:7
cure of a romantic f. flame — DUHN 160:11
Eclipse f,, the rest nowhere — O'KEL 498:10
f. and second class citizens — WILL 737:15
f. blow is half the battle — GOLD 311:26
f. day of our Jubilee — BROW 146:12
f. destroys their mind — DRYD 260:28
f. four years the dirt — CRISP 227:1
f. fruits of them — BIBLE 101:7
f. impulses — MONT 482:2
f. in a village than second — CAES 174:17
f. in the hearts — LEE 415:17
f. man is of the earth — BIBLE 101:13
f. step that is difficult — DU D 263:8
f. time that we smell — SHAK 597:10
f. to catch and to reflect — MAC 435:4
f. true gentleman — DEKK 235:14
he'd have been here f. — CARR 183:19
if they speak f. — CONG 215:6
know the place for the f. — ELIOT 271:6
last shall be f. — BIBLE 91:27
Non-violence is the f. article — GAND 297:10
not degrade a F. Cause — HARDY 324:13
people who got there f. — UST 707:12
That the f. day be mended — WILB 734:6
there is no last nor f. — BROW 152:1
We were the f. that ever burst — COL 210:24
work is what to put f. — PASC 507:9
first-born: against all the f. of Egypt — SHAK 568:11
brought forth her f. son — BIBLE 93:26
will smite all the f. — BIBLE 72:10
first class: f., and with children — BENC 62:11
fish: black and ugly f. — HOR 347:1
cars nose forward like f. — LOW 430:11
coal and surrounded by f. — BEVAN 68:12
f. and fishing — WALT 721:9
F. are jumpin' an' — HEYW 338:2
F. fiddle de-dee! — LEAR 414:16
F. got to swim and birds — HAMM 322:17
F. say, they have — BROO 143:6
f. the last food — BASSE 55:1
f. with the worm that hath — SHAK 577:29
f. would have bright mail — KEATS 386:16
have dominion over the f. — BIBLE 69:24
Impaling worms to torture f. — COLM 214:5
It's no f. ye're buying — SCOTT 560:13
Ives says the smell of f. — KILV 396:6
like a f. without a bicycle — STEI 663:12
piece of a broiled f. — BIBLE 95:34
tadpole, and I was a f. — SMITH 651:19
There's a f. that *talks* — DE L 235:19
Thou deboshed f. thou — SHAK 625:23
Un-dish-cover the f. — CARR 183:26
fishbone: monument sticks like a f. — LOW 430:12
fishbones: two f., two eyeballs — WELBY 726:21
fished: f. by obstinate isles — POUND 526:12
fisher: Oh, the gallant f.'s life — CHAL 189:1
fisherman: Death is like a f. — TURG 705:10
fishermen: f. hold flowers — DYLAN 265:12
f. that walk upon the beach — SHAK 597:1
fishers: Blest f. were — BASSE 55:1
f. went sailing away — KING 397:15
will make you f. of men — BIBLE 88:22
fishes: And welcomes little f. — CARR 182:1
f. first to shipping — DRYD 260:3
f. live in the sea — SHAK 619:1
F., that tipple in the deep — LOV 429:3
little f. of the sea — CARR 183:15
Men lived like f. — SIDN 646:10

fishes: (cont.):
men that f. gnawed upon — SHAK 621:23
notes like little f. — MACN 441:3
Tawny-finned f. — SHAK 565:12
two small f. — BIBLE 96:22
uncommunicating muteness of f. — LAMB 406:11
Where the flyin'-f. play — KIPL 400:1
fishified: flesh, how art thou f. — SHAK 623:8
fishing: angling or float f. — JOHN 377:1
blow when he goes a-f. — WALT 720:23
saith unto them, I go a f. — BIBLE 97:39
fish-knives: Phone for the f. — BETJ 67:11
fishmonger: Excellent well; you are a f. — SHAK 574:18
fishpond: great f. (the sea) — DEKK 235:13
fishpools: thine eyes like the f. — BIBLE 82:3
fist: f. most valiant — SHAK 585:22
f. still knocking at Death's — SACK 552:14
fistful: f. of coins — ZAP 755:8
fists: groan and shake their f. — HOUS 351:13
fit: become f. for this world — KEATS 391:8
f. audience find — MILT 472:7
f. for nothing but to carry — HERV 337:13
f. for the kingdom of God — BIBLE 94:9
Huddled up, 'twixt f. and just — CLEV 206:13
It isn't f. for humans now — BETJ 68:5
only the F. survive — SERV 563:6
when the f. was on him — SHAK 590:1
fitchew: f. nor the soiled horse — SHAK 597:5
fitful: life's f. fever — SHAK 603:3
fitless: in f. finger-stalls — GILB 305:5
fitly: word f. spoken is like — BIBLE 79:15
fittest: multiplication of the f. — SPEN 658:17
Survival of the F. — DARW 231:9
survival of the f. — ROCK 543:20
fitting: It is right and f. — MISS 477:1
Fitzgerald: F. strung them on — LOW 430:1
five: At f. in the afternoon — GARC 297:12
chirche dore he hadde f. — CHAU 192:25
f. dull hours in another — AUST 38:8
f. minutes too late all — COWL 221:22
f. o'clock in an evening — BOWEN 138:8
f. per cent is the natural — MAC 434:21
F. to one, baby, one in five — MORR 485:20
Full fathom f. thy father lies — SHAK 625:10
god that I have wedded f. — CHAU 194:20
'tis but f. days elder — BROW 146:4
fivepence: We have saved f. — BECK 57:12
five-pound: Wrapped up in a f. note — LEAR 414:12
fix: And f. up his automobile — CLAR 205:11
F. in us thy humble dwelling — WESL 728:14
If it ain't broke, don't f. it — LANCE 407:22
looking for an angry f. — GINS 306:28
fixed: f. point in a changing — DOYLE 256:11
He f. thee 'mid this dance — BROW 152:12
may surely there be f. — BOOK 120:18
there is a great gulf f. — BIBLE 95:10
flag: an f. debt, an' a f. — LOW 429:17
And death's pale f. is not — SHAK 624:8
carrying a blood-red f. — BLOK 115:9
f. as the race wore — COKE 208:16
f. to which you have pledged — BALD 48:7
out a f. and sign of love — SHAK 614:25
plyin' an' the old f. flyin' — NEWB 492:7
respect its f. — PAGE 504:4
spare your country's f. — WHIT 733:6
their f. against a power — WEBS 725:8
vagabond f. upon the stream — SHAK 564:27
We'll keep the red f. flying — CONN 216:8
We shall not f. or fail — CHUR 202:11
flagellation: Not f., not pederasty — RATT 537:2
flag-flapper: Jelly-bellied F. — KIPL 402:10
flagitium: *Peiusque leto f. timet* — HOR 350:19
flame: And feed his sacred f. — COL 210:15
And Life, a Fury slinging f. — TENN 683:16
And the roof-lamp's oily f. — HARDY 325:14
Both moth and f.? — ROET 544:10
But Chloe is my real f. — PRIOR 529:9
f. of the taper — SHAK 571:1
f. out like shining from — HOPK 345:10
f. which burnt his bulwarks — DRAY 258:3

flame: (cont.):

f. which is not to be snuffed	REN 539:2
gemlike f.	PATER 509:7
He flew awa' in a bleezing f.	BALL 50:7
his eyes were as a f.	BIBLE 106:1
into f. from smoke to run	ALAB 7:1
Kindled a f. I still deplore	GARR 298:10
one burning f. together	TENN 685:3
romantic first f.	BURN 160:11
so full of subtil f.	BEAU 56:14
so in a shapeless f.	DONNE 251:16
Still plays about the f.	GAY 299:10
Though spent thy f.	DAN 229:15
thy holy f. bestowing	LITT 423:9
tongues of f. are in-folded	ELIOT 271:9
tongues of living f.	AUBER 32:20
was like the fiery f.	BIBLE 86:1
When a lovely f. dies	HARB 323:9

flamed: And f. upon the brazen greaves

                                    TENN 685:2

flames: Commit it to the f.   HUME 355:4

explains itself as f.	MOT 487:2
f. and hired tears they	BROW 145:15
f. must needs burn there	VAUG 709:9
So his f. must waste away	CAREW 179:2
Went by her like thin f.	ROSS 547:17

flaming: f. bounds of place   GRAY 316:7

ministers a f. fire	BOOK 132:6
thou f. minister	SHAK 618:5
Waved over by that f. brand	MILT 473:14

flamme: f. qui ne s'éteint pas   REN 539:2

Flanders: F. hath received our yoke

                                    WALL 718:20

had brought him a F. mare	HENR 332:15
In F. fields the poppies blow	MCCR 437:5

flanks: f. with garlands dressed   KEATS 388:29

flap-dragon: easier swallowed than a f.

                                    SHAK 599:4

flare: f. was up in the gymn   BETJ 68:4

   had finished in that f.   YEATS 752:4

flash: f. through the flowery   CHES 199:2

flashes: In f., and with glory   WORD 747:4

   occasional f. of silence   SMITH 653:17

flashing: f. eyes, his floating   COL 210:14

flask: A f. of wine, a book   FITZ 283:13

flat: characters into f. and round   FORS 290:4

F. and flexible truths	BROW 145:9
half so f. as Walter Scott	ANON 17:7
very dangerous f.	SHAK 608:20
Very f., Norfolk	COW 221:3

flat-earth: f. view of the mind   KOES 403:20

flats: different sharps and f.   BROW 151:26

flatten: hide is sure to f. 'em   BELL 60:23

flatter: f. a man so grossly   JOHN 376:23

F. the mountain-tops	SHAK 633:12
f. with their lips	BOOK 124:24
we fondly f. our desires	DRAY 257:17

flattered: Being f., is a lamb   CHAP 190:11

being then most f.	SHAK 590:20
feared nor f. any flesh	DOUG 255:9
f. into virtue than bullied	SURT 672:5
He that loves to be f.	SHAK 626:5
not f. its rank breath	BYRON 168:27
still contemned and f.	SHAK 596:23

flatterer: hypocrite and f.   BLAKE 112:6

   worthy o' the f.   SHAK 626:5

flatterers: And all the fawning f. hate

                                    CHUD 200:13

I tell him he hates f.   SHAK 590:20

surrounded by sycophants and f.

                                    HARD 323:15

flatteries: securing yourself against f.

                                    MACH 438:12

flattering: f. unction to your soul   SHAK 577:18

Some with a f. word	WILDE 736:1
who spends his time f.	TRUM 704:15
you think flattery worth f.	SHAW 609:25
flattery! everyone likes f.	DICR 249:11
everybody f. of one's own	LODGE 425:22
f. is worth his flattery	JOHN 376:20
f. soothe the dull cold	GRAY 316:11
paid with f.	JOHN 368:4
suppose f. hurts no one	STEV 666:14

---

flattery: (cont.):

This is no f.	SHAK 567:24
to tout for f.	COLL 213:8
Was f. lost on poet's ear	SCOTT 559:14

Flaubert: true Penelope was F.   POUND 526:12

flavour: from its high celestial f.   BYRON 170:24

   general f. of mild decay   HOLM 342:13

flaw: has no kind of fault or f.   GILB 304:7

   sans crack or f.   SHAK 599:8

flawed: f. heart unmade   WILB 734:6

flaws: wished the f. fewer   BROW 149:6

flax: smoking f. shall he not   BIBLE 84:2

flayed: saw a woman f.   SWIFT 674:12

flea: between a louse and a f.   JOHN 376:6

honour the very f. of his dog	JONS 378:19
literature's performing f.	O'CAS 497:20
So, naturalists observe, a f.	SWIFT 675:6
will clog the foot of a f.	SHAK 630:16

fleas: Even educated f. do it   PORT 525:2

F. know not whether they	LAND 408:13
f. that tease in the High	BELL 62:1
o' f. is good fer a dog	WEST 729:19
that has praised his f.	YEATS 753:12

flectere: F. si nequeo superos   VIRG 714:3

fled: But kissed it and then f.   SHEL 642:22

f. far, far away	COCK 208:3
F. is that music	KEATS 389:17
I f. Him, down the nights	THOM 695:1
sea saw that, and f.	BOOK 133:8
Still as he f., his eyes	SPEN 659:28
world that I am f.	SHAK 634:5

flee: death shall f. from   BIBLE 106:26

f. from the wrath to come	BIBLE 88:15
F. fro the prees, and dwelle	CHAU 196:4
f. when no man pursueth	BIBLE 79:28
sorrow and sighing shall f.	BIBLE 83:22
then would I f. away	BOOK 128:10

They f. from me, that sometime

                                    WYATT 749:19

with their armies did f.   BOOK 129:8

fleece: F. and then came home   DU B 263:1

forest f. the Wrekin heaves	HOUS 352:12
Its f. was white as snow	HALE 321:8

fleeces: Thus you sheep bear f.   VIRG 715:20

fleet: All in the Downs the f.   GAY 300:15

Beauteous the f. before	SMART 650:3
Fire and f. and candle-lighte	BALL 49:18
F. in which we serve	BOOK 135:18
f. of stars is anchored	FLEC 286:7
F.'s lit up	WOOD 742:2
F. the time carelessly	SHAK 567:16
we took care of our f.	ADD 4:15

fleetest: fairest things have f.   THOM 694:17

fleeth: soul f. unto the Lord   BOOK 134:12

fleeting: fable, song, or f. shade   HERR 336:11

   F., unsubstantial, vain   COL 209:8

fleets: f. sweep over thee in vain   BYRON 169:14

Fleet Street: F. has a very animated

   appearance   JOHN 373:28

F. to our poets	BROW 147:6
who can be dull in F.	LAMB 406:23

flere: Si vis me f., dolendum est   HOR 347:9

flesh: All f. is as grass   BIBLE 105:9

All f. is grass, and all	BIBLE 83:27
all f. shall see it	BIBLE 83:26
And f. and blood so cheap	HOOD 344:9
And men are f. and blood	SHAK 591:12

bondwoman was born after the f.

                                    BIBLE 102:5

brought him bread and f.	BIBLE 75:31
bulls' f.	BOOK 128:3
But in the f. it is immortal	STEV 666:8
carrion f. than to receive	SHAK 609:7
closed up the f. instead	BIBLE 70:5
could not all this f.	SHAK 582:8
delicate white human f.	FIEL 282:12
east wind made f.	APPL 23:18
eat the f. in that night	BIBLE 72:9
fair and unpolluted f.	SHAK 578:20
feared not flattered any f.	DOUG 255:9
f., alas, is wearied	MALL 442:16
f. and the devil	BOOK 119:17
f., how art thou fashioned	SHAK 570:9

---

flesh: (cont.):

F. of flesh	MILT 473:1
f. of my flesh	BIBLE 70:6
F. perishes, I live	HARDY 325:8
f. sinks downwards here	SHAK 621:13
f. that she herself hath	SHAK 627:2
f. to feel the chain	BRON 142:14
f. which walls about our	SHAK 620:8
For him f. was sacramental	ROB 542:15
Frail f. and the	CROS 228:22
From this world-wearied f.	SHAK 624:9
he might trust in the f.	BIBLE 103:7
human f. subsisting	BOOK 119:15
in my f. shall I see God	BIBLE 77:25
In that land of f. and bone	AUDEN 35:3
I wants to make your f. creep	DICK 243:7
makes man and wife one f.	CONG 215:2
me a thorn in the f.	BIBLE 102:2
mind the things of the f.	BIBLE 99:34
more f. than another man	SHAK 581:18
my heart and my f. rejoice	BOOK 130:16
Neither f. nor fleshless	ELIOT 270:16
not against f. and blood	BIBLE 103:1
One f.	MILT 473:2
provision for the f.	BIBLE 100:11
sinful lusts of the f.	BOOK 123:4
ta'en out thy heart o' f.	BALL 50:14
Tell f. it is but dust	RAL 535:16
these our f. upright	DONNE 250:15
they shall be one f.	BIBLE 70:7
too solid f. would melt	SHAK 572:12
unto thee shall all f.	BOOK 128:23
which can outlive all f.	BYRON 172:2
willing but the f. is weak	BIBLE 92:30
Wisdom must bear what our f.	GREV 318:6
word and clay is the f.	KAV 386:3
Word was made f.	BIBLE 96:4
WORD WAS MADE F.	MISS 477:9
yet would God this f.	SWIN 676:27

fleshly: through all this f. dress   VAUG 709:3

   with f. lustings shaken   GREV 318:6

flesh pots: sat by the f.   BIBLE 72:15

fletu: fraterno multum manantia f.   CAT 187:1

flew: f. between me and the sun   BLUN 116:5

flexible: Flat and f. truths   BROW 145:9

Flibbertigibbet: foul fiend F.   SHAK 596:13

flicker: moment of my greatness f.   ELIOT 272:4

flies: As f. to wanton boys   SHAK 596:27

F., worms, and flowers	WATTS 722:14
Full fast he f., and dares	BLAIR 110:15
like f. on a summer day	RUSS 551:21
murmurous haunt of f.	KEATS 389:13
on his skin the swart f.	DOUG 255:13
pedantical; these summer f.	SHAK 599:7
Unfading moths, immortal f.	BROO 143:8
which may catch small f.	SWIFT 673:5

fliest: fly thee, for thou f. Me   THOM 695:7

flight: alarms of struggle and f.   ARN 27:1

And took their f.	MARR 449:1
And will not take their f.	MILT 467:4
His cloistered f., ere	SHAK 603:4
His f. was madness	SHAK 604:3
now wing thy distant f.	HADR 320:8
Swift be thine approaching f.	SHEL 643:23
Swift be thy f.	SHEL 643:22
that puts the stars to f.	FITZ 283:10
Were not attained by sudden f.	LONG 427:1

flights: f. upon the banks of Thames

                                    JONS 380:5

fling: F. but a stone, the giant dies

                                    GREEN 316:18

f. the ringleaders from	HARDY 325:5
Had chosen thus to f. his soul	HARDY 325:5

flint: as the f. bears fire   SHAK 593:9

   Clearly through a f. wall see   GRAV 314:20

flints: soul would walk the f.   CARB 178:17

flippant: when I behold thee f.   KEATS 391:3

flirtation: Merely innocent f.   BYRON 171:23

flittings: Thou tellest my f.   BOOK 128:13

float: English policy is to f.   SAL 553:19

f. like a butterfly	ALI 8:3
f. upon his watery bier	MILT 465:20
Forever f. that standard sheet	DRAKE 257:13

float: (cont.):
through the clouds I'll never f.   WORD 746:12
floating: f. bulwark of the island   BLAC 110:12
F. in the Blue   MILNE 463:1
His flashing eyes, his f. hair   COL 210:14
floats: f. on high o'er vales   WORD 744:15
She f., she hesitates   RAC 535:3
flock: feed his f. like a shepherd   BIBLE 83:28
hair is as a f. of goats   BIBLE 81:13
keeping watch over their f.   BIBLE 93:26
tainted wether of the f.   SHAK 609:11
There is no f., however   LONG 427:12
was the f. in woolly fold   KEATS 386:20
flocks: My father feeds his f.   HOME 342:19
My f. feed not, my ewes   BARN 53:17
shepherds watched their f.   TATE 678:18
Flodden: Of F.'s fatal field   SCOTT 560:11
flog: f. the rank and file   AHN 30:14
flogging: f. in our great schools   JOHN 374:8
habit of f. me constantly   TROL 703:2
flood: and takes the f.   TENN 682:26
beachèd verge of the salt f.   SHAK 626:21
days that were before the f.   BIBLE 92:13
fellows the f. could not wash   CONG 215:12
f. unto the world's end   BOOK 129:20
plunged beneath that f.   COWP 222:21
second f. we are spreading   MAY 455:6
Since Deucalion's f.   SKEL 649:4
swam the brackish f.   DRAY 258:3
taken at the f.   SHAK 593:12
ten years before the f.   MARV 451:2
Thorough f., thorough fire   SHAK 611:11
vapour and return it as a f.   GLAD 308:1
flooded: STREETS F. PLEASE ADVISE   BENC 62:13
floodgate: f. and o'bearing nature   SHAK 614:20
F. of the deeper heart   FLEC 286:17
floods: Beside the haystack in the f.
  MORR 485:13
f. are risen, O Lord   BOOK 131:7
governess of f.   SHAK 611:15
neither can the f. drown it   BIBLE 82:6
passions are most like to f.   RAL 535:19
She quells the f. below   CAMP 177:1
floor: how the f. of heaven   SHAK 610:1
nicely sanded f.   GOLD 310:15
Of the forest's ferny f.   DE L 236:6
oiled his way around the f.   LERN 419:7
rose along the gusty f.   KEATS 387:11
spit upon my curious f.   HERB 335:24
floors: across the f. of silent seas   ELIOT 272:3
flop: f. and roll about   MANS 445:7
flopping: go f. yourself down   DICK 244:4
Flopshus: F. Cad   KIPL 402:10
Flora: F. and the country green   KEATS 389:9
floraisons: O mois des f.   ARAG 24:6
Florence: F. ran fastest of a'   MCL 439:11
Rode past fair F.   KEATS 388:2
Flores: at F. in the Azores   TENN 689:3
florid: Let the f. music praise   AUDEN 35:3
flotilla: Where the old f. lay   KIPL 400:1
flourish: f. after first decay   SPEN 660:6
f. and complain   CRAB 225:5
f. where you turn   POPE 523:13
Princes and lords may f.   GOLD 310:6
shall f. out of the earth   BOOK 130:20
Sure thou didst f. once   VAUG 709:10
transfix f. set on youth   SHAK 633:21
flourisheth: he f. as a flower   BOOK 132:5
flourishing: f. like a green bay-tree
  BOOK 126:21
flout: scout 'em, and f. 'em   SHAK 625:24
flow: blood must yet f.   JEFF 364:16
F. down the woods and stipple   SACK 552:16
F. gently, sweet Afton   BURNS 161:3
I within did f.   TRAH 702:1
Now the salt tides seawards f.   ARN 27:7
O could I f. like thee   DENH 236:17
What need you f. so fast   ANON 19:6
flower: beauteous f. when next we meet
  SHAK 623:3
bud, the f.   SPEN 660:6
cometh forth like a f.   BIBLE 77:21
constellated f.   SHEL 642:23

flower: (cont.):
creep from flower to f.   SHEL 640:18
die in the f. of their age   BIBLE 74:26
fairer f. by gloomy Dis   MILT 471:4
f.-de-luce being one   SHAK 632:4
f. fadeth   BIBLE 83:27
f. for scent that blows   SHEL 643:1
f. grows concealed   CAT 186:9
f. is born to blush unseen   GRAY 315:15
f. no sooner blown   MILT 466:18
f. of a blameless life   TENN 681:16
f. of any kind of experience   HUNT 356:19
f. of roses in the spring   BIBLE 88:4
f. that once hath blown   FITZ 284:1
f. that sad embroidery   MILT 466:11
f. thereof falleth   BIBLE 105:9
f. with base infection   SHAK 634:15
From every opening f.   WATTS 722:12
goodliness thereof is as the f.   BIBLE 83:27
green fuse drives the f.   THOM 693:7
he flourisheth as a f.   BOOK 132:5
look like the innocent f.   SHAK 600:17
meanest f. that blows can give   WORD 746:7
no stronger than a f.   SHAK 634:3
Of learning lightly like a f.   TENN 684:16
or it will bear no f.   SHEL 644:4
plant and f. of light   JONS 379:21
pleasing but a short-lived f.   LEAP 413:16
same f. that smiles to-day   HERR 337:7
stem of the contained f.   ROET 544:7
summer's f.   SHAK 634:15
this is the noble f.   DONNE 253:7
thou art the f. of cities   ANON 16:1
upon a little western f.   SHAK 611:17
we pluck this f.   SHAK 580:10
When once they find her f.   DAN 229:14
flowering: About the f. squares   TENN 684:13
I marked Him in the f.   TENN 682:17
flowers: all amongst the f.   LUCR 432:6
And fishermen hold f.   DYLAN 265:12
And it won't be f.   AUDEN 36:5
are f. but fading seen   PEELE 511:5
bunch of other men's f.   MONT 481:11
cool-rooted f., fragrant-eyed   KEATS 389:18
droop-headed f. all   KEATS 389:6
emperice and flour of f.   CHAU 195:3
Ensnared with f., I fall   MARV 450:9
fairest f. o' the season   SHAK 632:1
f. and fruits of love   BYRON 173:1
f. appear on the earth   BIBLE 81:9
f. gynnen for to sprynge   CHAU 195:1
f. in last month's newspapers   STEV 665:18
F. in the garden, meat   STEV 669:8
f. now that frighted thou   SHAK 632:4
F. of all hue, and without   MILT 471:3
f. of the forest are a'   COCK 208:4
f. of the forest are a'   ELL 275:9
f. that bloom in the spring   GILB 305:9
f. the tenderness of patient   OWEN 503:13
frosts are slain and f.   SWIN 675:22
gigantic f. slowly advancing   DIN 246:8
grass break into foam of f.   SWIN 676:27
her f. to love, her ways   BROO 143:18
I got me f. to strew Thy way   HERB 334:15
No f., by request   AING 6:2
odoriferous f. of fancy   SHAK 598:17
Of al the f. in the mede   CHAU 195:2
Say it with f.   O'KEE 498:7
That f. would bloom   KEATS 386:16
Time did beckon to the f.   HERB 335:7
Too many f. . . . too little fruit   SCOTT 561:4
were but as a bed of f.   DONNE 253:8
what f. are at my feet   KEATS 389:12
Where have all the f. gone   SEEG 561:19
Where souls do couch on f.   SHAK 566:9
wild f., and Prime Ministers   BALD 48:14
worms, and f., exceed   WATTS 722:14
flowery: come to the f. plains   JONS 379:5
f. way that leads   SHAK 564:10
On the cool f. lap of earth   ARN 27:13
That at her f. work doth sing   MILT 464:25
you flash through the f.   CHES 199:2
flowing: f. with milk and honey   BIBLE 71:40

flowing: (cont.):
Robes loosely f., hair as free   JONS 378:18
wet sheet and a f. sea   CUNN 229:2
flown: I see all the birds are f.   CHAR 191:6
whither f. again   FITZ 284:16
flows: Everything f. and nothing stays
  HER 333:10
fluidity: f. of self-revelation   JAMES 362:11
solid for f.   CHUR 202:4
flung: f. himself from the room   LEAC 413:13
flush: Gush!– f. the man   HOPK 346:12
Oh roses for the f. of youth   ROSS 547:6
flushing: constant sound of f.   BETJ 68:1
flushpots: f. of Euston   JOYCE 381:2
flute: cornet, f., harp   BIBLE 85:28
f. and the trumpet   AUDEN 35:3
gauger played the f.   STEV 669:10
Gibbon moved to f.   COLM 214:4
his brains upon the f.   BROW 152:27
No line can trace no f.   WILB 734:4
soft complaining f.   DRYD 261:25
flutes: Of f. and soft recorders   MILT 468:24
tune of f. kept stroke   SHAK 565:5
flutter: F. and bear him up   BETJ 67:6
fluttered: f. and failed for breath   ARN 27:20
fluttering: F. and dancing in the breeze
  WORD 744:15
flutters: Still f. there, the sole   COL 210:5
fly: all things f. thee   THOM 695:7
birds their wings to f.   CLARE 204:20
Busy, curious, thirsty f.   OLDYS 498:11
but to f. is safe   COWP 223:30
F. at your Lord's command   GURN 320:3
f. can't bird, but a bird   MILNE 463:3
F. envious Time, till thou   MILT 467:15
F. fishing may be a very   JOHN 377:1
F. hence, our contact fear   ARN 28:9
f. sat upon the axletree   BACON 45:4
f., Sir, may sting   JOHN 371:14
f., them for a moment   TENN 689:1
f. the way out of the fly-bottle   WITT 740:2
f. through the air   LEYB 421:11
F. to her, and fall upon   TENN 688:6
f. to India for gold   MARL 446:14
f. where men feel   CHAP 190:14
He wouldn't hurt a f.   LEAC 413:12
I must f., but follow   TENN 689:1
I will f. to thee   KEATS 389:11
long-legged f. upon the stream   YEATS 752:12
man is not a f.   POPE 522:5
noise of a f.   DONNE 253:4
often have seen spiders f.   EDW 267:7
said a spider to a f.   HOW 353:7
small gilded f.   SHAK 597:4
they ever f. by twilight   BACON 44:31
They f. forgotten, as a dream   WATTS 723:7
To f. from, need not   BYRON 168:23
try to f. by those nets   JOYCE 381:10
which way shall I f.   MILT 470:25
with the f. in his hand   STER 664:22
with twain he did f.   BIBLE 82:19
fly-blown: f. phylacteries   ROS 546:18
fly-fishing: for winter f.   WALT 720:21
flying: f. upon the wings   BOOK 125:1
he straight is f.   WROTH 749:14
irretrievable time is f.   VIRG 715:17
Keep the aspidistra f.   ORW 500:5
There is nor f. hence   SHAK 605:2
young man on the f. trapeze   LEYB 421:11
Flying Scotsman: F. is no less splendid
  BEAV 57:5
foam: F. glimmered white   ANAT 11:6
opening on the f.   KEATS 389:15
was wild and dank with f.   KING 397:13
foaming: Tiber f. with much blood   POW 528:10
foamless: grey, f., enormous   KIPL 401:1
foe: another to let in the f.   MILT 474:8
Call no man f., but never   BENS 64:1
erect and manly f.   CANN 178:6
everyone's a f.   CLARE 204:16
first f. in the field   LOV 429:6
f. but falls before us   DRAKE 257:13
f. was folly and his weapon   HOPE 344:24

foe: (*cont.*):

friend than as a f.	GLAD 307:19
friend who never made a f.	TENN 682:4
I was angry with my f.	BLAKE 114:11
my dearest f. in heaven	SHAK 572:16
not a furnace for your f.	SHAK 588:9
open f. may prove a curse	GAY 300:4
perhaps a jealous f.	SHEL 640:10
redoubled strokes upon the f.	SHAK 599:16
Scratch a lover, and find a f.	PARK 506:4
unrelenting f. to Love	THOM 696:14
willing f. and sea room	ANON 19:22
wolf far thence that's f.	WEBS 726:8
ye sail to meet the f.	NEWB 492:7

foeda: *F. est in coitu et brevis*   PETR 513:15

foes: judge of a man by his f.   CONR 217:8

Keep far our f., give peace	BOOK 135:21
man's f. shall be they	BIBLE 90:21
Thou art in the midst of f.	ELL 275:11

fog: brown f. of a winter dawn   ELIOT 273:1

feel the f. in my throat	BROW 152:4
f. comes on little cat feet	SAND 555:4
f. of philistinism	MAY 455:3
f. of the good man's mind	BROW 149:4
London particular … A f., miss	DICK 239:2
morning f. may chill the air	CROSS 227:19
through the f. and filthy air	SHAK 599:13
yellow f. that rubs	ELIOT 272:1

foggy: Faustus like a f. mist   MARL 447:2

f. day in London Town   GERS 301.11

fogs: f. prevail upon the day   DRYD 261:2

foible: omniscience his f.   SMITH 653:30

foil: like shining from shook f.   HOPK 345:10

foining: f. o' nights   SHAK 583:9

fold: f., spindle or mutilate   ANON 12:33

f. after fold	SHEL 642:27
f. stands empty	SHAK 611:14
f. to thy heart thy brother	WHIT 733:10
In glittering fold on f.	DAV 232:13
like the wolf on the f.	BYRON 169:28
So f. thyself, my dearest	TENN 688:13
which are not of this f.	BIBLE 97:2

folded: F. us round from the dark   SWIN 676:3

sweetest leaves yet f.	BYRON 171:31
To undo the f. lie	AUDEN 36:1

folders: misery of manilla f.   ROET 544:4

folding: little f. of the hands   BIBLE 78:14

folds: f. shall be full of sheep   BOOK 129:3

spring has kept in its f.	ARAG 24:6
tinklings lull the distant f.	GRAY 315:10

folio: whole volumes in f.   SHAK 598:9

folios: And mighty f. first   CRAB 224:26

folk: music is f. music   ARMS 26:10

And how civil to f. he ne'er	ANST 23:12
f. to goon on pilgrimages	CHAU 192:7
Is emptied of this f.	KEATS 388:29
trouble with a f. song	LAMB 407:14

folk-dancing: incest and f.   ANON 20:5

folkes: O yonge, fresshe f.   CHAU 196:2

folks: f. git ole en strucken   HARR 326:16

F. *prefer* in fact a hovel	CALV 175:15
my f. were growing old	STEV 668:22
There's where the old f. stay	FOST 291:14

follies: f., and misfortunes   GIBB 302:2

f. of the wise	JOHN 370:20
f. that themselves commit	SHAK 608:11
f. which a man regrets	ROWL 549:10
No f. to have to repent	TAYL 679:15
Of all human f.	MOL 479:5
paint the vices and f.	CONG 214:22
point out to us our f.	TROL 703:20
Pour her exotic f. o'er	BYRON 172:9
Where f. naturally grow	CHUR 200:19

follow: f. at convenience   BURT 164:11

F. me, and I will make	BIBLE 88:22
f. thine own teaching	SHAK 607:12
f. the custom of which you	AMBR 10:0
f. thee with all the good	KING 101:11
F. The f thum	[illegible] 687:8
F. up	BOWEN 130:0
F. well in order, get	WHIT 79:10
f. with allegiance a fall'n	SHAK 565:19
F. your Saint, follow	CAMP 177:6

follow: (*cont.*):

F. your spirit	SHAK 585:10
I f. but myself	SHAK 614:20
I f. the worse	OVID 502:24
I really had to f. them	LEDR 415:14
My old man said, 'F. the van	COLL 213:7
So, f. me, follow	FLAN 285:10
their works do f.	BIBLE 107:5
Whom he to f. him hath chose	BASSE 55:1

followed: first he f. it hymselve   CHAU 193:3

he arose and f. him   BIBLE 90:4

follows: Cannot come, lie f.   PROU 530:15

f. or what went before   BEDE 58:13

folly: all a too presumptuous f.   HARTE 327:16

And f.'s all they've taught me	MOORE 483:11
brood of f. without father	MILT 464:13
But F. sat full length	BRER 140:14
fear usually ends in f.	COL 212:13
foe was f. and his weapon	HOPE 344:24
F. comes from something	LOW 430:23
f. he hath committed	BROW 146:16
f. like a stalking-horse	SHAK 569:28
f. like the back	AUDEN 34:10
f. of expectation	BROW 145:25
f. of people's not staying	AUST 38:8
fool according to his f.	BIBLE 79:20
fool and the f.	JOHN 376:25
fool returneth to his f.	BIBLE 79:21
From f. to defeat	WILB 734:6
from the effects of f.	SPEN 658:15
God calleth preaching f.	HERB 334:10
lovely woman stoops to f.	ELIOT 273:10
lovely woman stoops to f.	GOLD 311:33
moved to f. by a noise	LAWR 413:5
our f., or our fate	DENH 236:20
profit by the f.	PLINY 517:8
remember'st not the slightest f.	SHAK 568:4
schools 'tis public f.	COWP 224:9
shoot F. as it flies	POPE 521:27
shunn'st the noise of f.	MILT 464:19
though F.'s child	CRAB 225:1
'Tis f. to be wise	GRAY 316:3
whirled into f. and vice	TENN 686:8
Wisdom excelleth f.	BIBLE 80:4
would persist in his f.	BLAKE 112:22

fond: *au f. des bois*   VIGNY 711:10

false, men would be f.	LYLY 432:3
f. maid run mad	ALC 8:1
f. of her most filthy bargain	SHAK 618:12
I should be f. to live	ELIZ 274:2
learning more than the f. eye	SHAK 608:16
over-f. of resisting	BECK 58:5
reason to be f. of grief	SHAK 594:4
should grow too f. of it	LEE 416:8
so f. of one another	SWIFT 673:17
When men were f., I smiled	SHAK 606:3

fonder: makes heart grow f.   ANON 11:17

fondness: hatred or habitual f.   WASH 722:1

fons: *Salva me, f. pietatis*   MISS 477:13

font: fin in the porphyry f.   TENN 688:13

second-hand f., would   KNOX 403:11

food: bring f. out of the earth   BOOK 132:8

But finds its f. in music	LILLO 421:16
chief of Scotia's f.	BURNS 161:17
Continent people have good f.	MIKES 460:3
discovered that alcohol was a f.	WOD 740:17
either our cupboard of f.	HERB 335:10
Fame is a f. that dead	DOBS 249:21
farce and the f. a tragedy	POW 528:3
fed with the same f.	SHAK 608:22
feed me with f. convenient	BIBLE 79:32
fish the last F. was	BASSE 55:1
f. and not fine words	MOL 478:22
F. comes first, then morals	BREC 140:4
F. enough for a week	MERR 458:14
f. for powder	SHAK 581:25
f. that raises	HANFF 323:5
gave them f. from heaven	BOOK 130:11
f. for f.	BIBLE 70:2
f. ly bread, the f. unprinted	MAS 453.0
homely wall f. f.	GALL 189:14
lays out f. in f.	JOT 273:8
music be the f. of love	SHAK 606:0

food: (*cont.*):

problem is f.	DONL 250:6
struggle for room and f.	MALT 443:19
wholesome f.	SWIFT 674:4

fool: Busy old f., unruly sun   DONNE 252:16

But the heart of the f.	MILT 474:7
By the f. multitude	SHAK 608:16
clever woman to manage a f.	KIPL 402:8
Dost thou call me f., boy	SHAK 595:7
drop into thyself, and be a f.	POPE 522:11
Every f. will be meddling	BIBLE 79:5
f. according to his folly	BIBLE 79:20
f. all the people some	LINC 422:14
f. and his words are soon	SHEN 644:15
f. at forty is a f. indeed	YOUNG 754:8
f. at least in every married	FIEL 281:17
f. can play upon the word	SHAK 609:5
f. consistent and the false	POPE 520:28
F. had stuck himself up	BENT 64:5
f. hath said in his heart	BOOK 124:26
f. his whole life long	LUTH 432:17
f. in Buxton can	RUSK 550:10
f. is a greater fool	MOL 479:1
f. is a man who never tried	DARW 231:13
f. is happy that he knows	POPE 522:14
f. is love	SHAK 633:19
f. lies here who tried	KIPL 400:4
f. may ask more	COLT 214:8
f. may write a most valuable	GRAY 316:14
f. me to the top	SHAK 576:24
f. must now and then	COWP 221:29
f. of love	HAZL 328:15
F.'s bandaged finger goes	KIPL 399:8
f. sees not the same tree	BLAKE 112:19
f.'s excuse for failure	BIER 109:9
f. there was and he made	KIPL 401:7
f. uttereth all his mind	BIBLE 79:30
f. would persist	BLAKE 112:22
f. you simply gave him	SOLZ 665:9
greater f. to admire him	BOIL 117:3
had resolved to live a f.	BEAU 56:14
hardly be a beast or a f.	KILV 396:7
haste of a f. is the slowest	SHAD 563:15
he hated a f.	JOHN 377:5
he is a wise man or a f.	BLAKE 112:10
He's a muddle-headed f.	CERV 188:12
I have played the f.	BIBLE 75:7
laughter of a f.	BIBLE 80:11
life time's f.	SHAK 582:6
longer I live the more f.	ANON 19:13
make a man appear a f.	DRYD 262:20
man suspects himself a f.	YOUNG 754:17
nor a f. in the eye	CONG 215:13
perfections of a f.	BLAKE 113:9
Prove to me that you're no f.	RICE 540:5
shelter but in a f.'s cap	HOPK 346:15
shouldn't f. with booze	FAUL 281:5
smarts so little as a f.	POPE 519:26
so a f. returneth	BIBLE 79:21
stupendous genius! damned f.	BYRON 174:3
Take away that f.'s bauble	CROM 227:11
That every f. is not a poet	POPE 519:24
that's a wise man and a f.	SHAK 595:24
There is more hope of a f.	BIBLE 79:22
thou art death's f.	SHAK 606:6
Thou f., shall be in danger	BIBLE 88:29
Thou f., this night thy	BIBLE 94:24
Till he's become the golden f.	BLAKE 113:7
To breed a f.	WOTT 749:3
wise enough to play the f.	SHAK 630:8
wisest f. in Christendom	HENR 332:13
without being a f.	SURT 672:7
witty f. than a foolish wit	SHAK 628:18
worm at one end and a f.	JOHN 377:1

foolery: f. governs the whole world   OXEN 503:21

hateful form of f.   BROW 151:10

foolish: being young and f.   YEATS 751:11

be likened unto a f. man	BIBLE 89:27
Beware my f. heart	WASH 722:4
f. son is the heaviness	BIBLE 78:20
f. things of the world	BIBLE 100:16
f. thing to make a wine	BIBLE 88:0

foolish: (*cont.*):
f. thing was but a toy — SHAK 630:37
f. thing well done — JOHN 373:20
f. when he had not a pen — JOHN 375:17
Forgive our f. ways — WHIT 733:7
from saying a f. thing — STER 665:8
He never said a f. thing — ROCH 543:5
I am a very f., fond old man — SHAK 597:14
I could be mighty f. — FARQ 280:24
ignorant and f. — BOOK 127:24
lot of f. ideas — FITZ 284:22
These f. things — MARV 451:14
foolishest: f. act a wise man — BROW 146:16
foolishly: don't *think* f. — JOHN 376:8
foolishness: Mix a little f. — HOR 350:20
fools: all tongues are called f. — SHAK 569:24
And f., who came to scoff — GOLD 310:11
Beggared by f., whom still — DRYD 259:9
But the f. caught it — YEATS 751:3
coxcombs Nature meant but f. — POPE 521:4
fill the world with f. — SPEN 658:15
F. are my theme, let satire — BYRON 172:3
f. at the wicket — KIPL 399:13
f. by heavenly compulsion — SHAK 595:2
f. decoyed into our condition — PEPYS 512:16
F.! For I also had my hour — CHES 198:30
f. in a majority — IBSEN 359:1
f. in town on our side — TWAIN 706:4
F. out of favour grudge — DEFOE 234:18
f. rush in where angels — POPE 521:25
f. said would happen has — MELB 456:10
f. should be so deep-contemplative
— SHAK 568:13
For f. admire, but men — POPE 521:18
For f. to sing — BURNS 164:1
For ye suffer f. gladly — BIBLE 101:22
from children and from f. — DRYD 261:22
Hated by f., and fools to hate — SWIFT 675:9
house for f. and mad — SWIFT 675:13
I am two f., I know — DONNE 252:19
Invented to awe f. — JONS 379:11
leaves 'em still two f. — CONG 215:2
Lord, what f. these mortals — SHAK 612:2
melted f. — SHAK 591:11
most part of f. and knaves — BUCK 154:8
one half the world f. — JEFF 364:17
or perish together as f. — KING 392:2
O, these deliberate f — SHAK 608:19
Paradise of F. — MILT 470:20
Poems are made by f. like me — KILM 396:3
proved plain f. at last — POPE 521:5
scarecrows of f. and the beacons
— HUXL 358:11
shoal of f. — CONG 215:32
Silence is the virtue of f. — BACON 42:14
they are the money of f. — HOBB 340:1
things people make f. — SHAW 636:2
To this great stage of f. — SHAK 597:11
utmost industry bred f. — CHUD 200:11
yesterdays have lighted f. — SHAK 605:1
foot: accent of a coming F. — DICK 244:14
And the Forty-second F. — HOOD 343:18
caught my f. in the mat — GROS 319:5
f. already in the stirrup — CERV 188:18
f. from thy neighbour's — BIBLE 79:17
F. it featly here and there — SHAK 625:8
f. less prompt to meet — ARN 28:29
hand for hand, f. for foot — BIBLE 72:17
her f. speaks — SHAK 628:2
his f. upon the stirrup — DE L 236:4
hurt not thy f. — BOOK 131:4
Love is swift of f. — HERB 334:14
My f. standeth right — BOOK 125:23
needlessly sets f. upon a worm — COWP 224:8
nor can f. feel, being — HOPK 345:10
Now I hold Creation in my f. — HUGH 354:4
on an 'eathen idol's f. — KIPL 400:2
One f. in sea, and one — SHAK 613:24
O! so light a f. — SHAK 623:11
print of a man's naked f. — DEFOE 234:9
shining f. shall pass — FITZ 284:17
sole of her f. — BIBLE 70:27
squeeze a right-hand f. — CARR 183:23

foot: (*cont.*):
suffer thy f. to be moved — BOOK 133:23
walked with willing f. — STEV 669:10
was long, her f. was light — KEATS 388:9
football: f. crazy, he's f. mad — MCGR 438:4
f. is a matter of life and death — SHAN 635:17
f. team was swept over — RICE 540:3
footed: and f. like a hart — MAL 443:6
footfalls: autumnal leaves like light f.
— SHEL 641:13
F. echo in the memory — ELIOT 270:14
footing: yet no f. seen — SHAK 635:12
foot-in-the-grave: F. young man — GILB 305:21
footman: eternal F. hold my coat — ELIOT 272.4
footmen: *literary f.* — HAZL 329:3
footnotes: series of f. to Plato — WHIT 731:16
footpath: jog on the f. way — SHAK 631:28
footprints: Because those f. scare me — HOR 348:1
F. on the sands of time — LONG 427:10
footsteps: And our f. guideth — BAKER 47:19
He plants his f. in the sea — COWP 222:17
Let not my slippery f. slide — WILL 736:23
footstool: it is his f. — BIBLE 88:31
make thine enemies thy f. — BOOK 133:3
foppery: f. of the world — SHAK 595:2
sound of shallow f. — SHAK 608:10
fops: whole tribe of f. — SHAK 594:26
for: f. whom the bell tolls — DONNE 252:5
F. you but not for me — ANON 17:1
F. your tomorrows these — EDM 267:1
not for myself who is f. — HILL 339:2
forasmuch: f. as without thee — BOOK 121:7
forbearance: f. ceases to be a virtue
— BURKE 157:13
forbid: f. them not — BIBLE 93:16
God f. How shall we — BIBLE 99:27
He shall live a man f. — SHAK 600:2
My lips are now f. to speak — BAYLY 56:3
they said, God f. — BIBLE 95:19
forbidden: Of that f. tree — MILT 467:19
only because it was f. — TWAIN 706:18
force: achieve more than our f. — BURKE 158:25
blend f. with a manoeuvre — TROT 704:14
By f., hath overcome — MILT 469:3
By verray f., he rafte hire — CHAU 194:25
carpets with a deadened f. — BETJ 67:7
could never have won by f. — STR 670:15
f. alone is but *temporary* — BURKE 157:21
f. and beauty must — POPE 521:6
F., and fraud, are in war — HOBB 340:8
f. by one class against — LENIN 417:6
f. however great can stretch — WHEW 730:14
F. is not a remedy — BRIG 141:12
'F.' is the food that raises — HANFF 323:5
f. maintaining the life — DOST 254:2
f. of all religious revolution — WEBER 725:2
f. that through the green — THOM 693:7
f. the Western world had — ADAMS 2:21
f. to the last resort — ORT 499:11
F., unaided by judgement — HOR 350:4
have spent its novel f. — TENN 685:9
may the f. be with you — LUCAS 431:10
motive f. impressed — NEWT 494:3
nations use 'f.' — WAUGH 724:6
No motion has she now, no f. — WORD 748:1
own no argument but f. — BROW 146:25
snails have weakest f. — SOUT 658:1
Surprised by unjust f. — MILT 464:5
thy strong oppressive f. — BARB 52:2
unofficial f. — DOYLE 256:20
very f. entangles — SHAK 566:9
forced: F. her to do your pleasure — WEBS 726:6
forces: change that state by f. — NEWT 494:2
f. are held in perfect — JENN 365:7
f. were at work here — HARDY 324:17
forcibly: f. if we must — CLAY 205:18
Ford: Heaven, my friend F. — WILL 737:12
I am a F., not a Lincoln — FORD 289:1
forefathers: f. of the hamlet sleep — GRAY 315:12
Not to be as their f. — BOOK 130:9
Think of your f.! Think — ADAMS 3:5
forefinger: stretched f. of all Time — TENN 687:26
foregone: f. conclusion — SHAK 616:22

forehead: burning f., and a parching
— KEATS 388:28
f. of the morning sky — MILT 466:13
His f. was prodigious — HUNT 356:13
Right in the middle of her f. — LONG 428:5
Upon the f. of the age to come — KEATS 386:6
foreheads: Free hearts, free f. — TENN 690:4
With f. villanous low — SHAK 625:30
foreign: be sent into any f. wars — ROOS 546:1
enriched with f. matter — REYN 539:11
From wandering on a f. strand — SCOTT 605:16
jowled or hawk-like f. faces — MACN 440:16
Life is a f. language — MORL 484:19
my f. policy: I wage war — CLEM 206:6
past is a f. country — HART 327:22
some corner of a f. field — BROO 143:18
their courtly f. grace — TENN 689:5
third-rate f. conductors — BEEC 59:1
Thracian ships and the f. — SWIN 675:21
wish to avoid f. collision — CLAY 205:17
foreigner: f. wiser than ourselves — TROL 703:20
foreigners: and f. are fiends — MITF 478:8
f. always spell Better — TWAIN 706:12
more f. I saw, the more I loved — BELL 62:9
Foreign Secretary: F. naked into the
conference — BEVAN 69:1
whatsoever in attacking the F. — BEVAN 68:17
foremost: f. fighting — BYRON 168:19
f. in battle was Mary Ambree — BALL 50:2
Was none who would be f. — MAC 436:13
foreplay: No f. No afterplay — BENN 63:5
foreseen: What I had not f. — SPEN 659:6
foresight: to aftersight and f. — ELIOT 271:5
forest: All the beasts of the f. — BOOK 128:2
all the beasts of the f. — BOOK 132:9
carry timber to the f. — HOR 351:6
clipped hedge is to a f. — JOHN 377:3
Dark behind it rose the f. — LONG 427:15
fade away into the f. — KEATS 389:9
flowers of the f. — ELL 275:9
flowers of the f. — COCK 208:4
f. laments in order — CHUR 201:17
f.'s ferny floor — DE L 236:6
f. something stirred — SIMP 648:2
F. where all must lose — THOM 694:3
f. with a golden track — LIND 423:2
He is lost to the f. — SCOTT 559:10
This is the f. primeval — LONG 426:16
forests: f., with their myriad — LONG 427:14
God has given us vast f. — CHEK 196:8
green days in f. — STEV 668:24
In the f. of the night — BLAKE 114:13
foretold: f. that the heart grows old
— YEATS 753:6
for ever: f. hold his peace — BOOK 123:18
F. panting, and for ever young — KEATS 388:28
his mercy endureth f. — BOOK 134:16
houses shall continue f. — BOOK 127:24
Round the world f. and aye — ARN 27:9
shall not be destroyed f. — ANON 22:18
thine f. — BOOK 123:13
thing of beauty is a joy f. — KEATS 386:13
forever: Man has F. — BROW 149:30
picket's off duty f. — BEERS 59:22
Strawberry fields f. — LENN 418:1
that vast f. — KING 397:9
forfeit: deadly f. should release — MILT 466:20
f. fair renown — SCOTT 559:17
forfended: music of f. spheres — PATM 509:14
forgave: f. the offence — DRYD 260:13
forge: f. and the mill — HOUS 352:11
f. and working-house — SHAK 586:13
f. in the smithy — JOYCE 381:15
man can't f. his own will — GILB 306:18
my f. decayed — ANON 16:16
forgers: accomplice of liars and f. — PÉGUY 511:6
forget: And if thou wilt, f. — ROSS 547:12
And knew we should both f. — SWIN 676:23
And we f. because we must — ARN 26:16
best sometimes f. — SHAK 616:2
conversing I f. all time — MILT 471:11
do not quite f. — CHES 199:7

forget: (*cont.*):
do not thou f. me	ASTL 32:10
F. all feuds	MAC 436:7
F. her pray'rs, or miss	POPE 523:23
f. not all his benefits	BOOK 132:2
F. six counties overhung	MORR 485:12
f. the lilac and the roses	ARAG 24:6
f. what I have been	SHAK 620:11
f. who we are	MCC 436:21
forgive, if I f. thee	BRON 142:16
hateful art, how to f.	KING 396:13
honour doth f. men's names	SHAK 593:25
How long wilt thou f. me	BOOK 124:25
If I f. thee, O Jerusalem	BOOK 134:17
I never f. a face	MARX 452:1
into war and they will f.	WILS 738:21
learn so little and f.	DAV 232:2
Lest we f. —lest we forget	KIPL 400:11
might all f. the human race	BYRON 169:12
must *not* f. the suspenders	KIPL 402:1
night time I shall not f.	SWIN 676:13
nor worms f.	DICK 241:28
not to f. we are gentlemen	BURKE 159:17
Old men f.	SHAK 586:11
shall ye f. your tears	MORR 485:10
sometimes f.	DISR 249:4
Sun himself cannot f.	ANON 18:7
teach the unforgetful to f.	ROSS 548:4
Till thou remember and I f.	SWIN 676:26
to communicate f. not	BIBLE 104:23
wise forgive but do not f.	SZASZ 677:13
yet will I not f. thee	BIBLE 84:7
you'll f. 'em all	POPE 523:20
you should f. and smile	ROSS 547:8

forgetfulness: Not in entire f.   WORD 745:14
steep my senses in f.   SHAK 583:11
to dumb F. a prey   GRAY 315:18
forgets: F. the shows of love   SHAK 589:25
forgetteth: f. what manner of man
                                        BIBLE 104:27
forgetting: F. those things   BIBLE 103:9
I've a grand memory for f.   STEV 667:13
sleep and a f.   WORD 745:14
With dark f. of my care return   DAN 229:16
world f., by the world forgot   POPE 519:21
forgive: allows you to f. yourself   SHAW 638:5
but mercy to f.   DRYD 260:22
can f. a man for the harm   MAUG 454:9
do they f. them   WILDE 735:30
Father, f. them   BIBLE 95:25
f. him? till seven times?   BIBLE 91:21
f., if I forget them   BRON 142:16
F., O Lord, my little jokes   FROST 294:13
F. our foolish ways   WHIT 733:7
f. that sin where I begun   DONNE 251:7
f. them as a Christian   AUST 39:18
f. us our debts   BIBLE 89:5
f. us our trespasses   BOOK 118:10
f. wrongs darker than death   SHEL 642:20
good Lord will f. me   CATH 185:7
lambs could not f.   DICK 241:28
ought to f. our friends   MED 456:2
somewhere would f. you   ALAI 7:4
To err is human; to f., divine   POPE 521:21
To f. enemies H—   BLAKE 113:8
wise f. but do not forget   SZASZ 677:13
Women can't f. failure   CHEK 196:13
forgiven: age is f. nothing   SHAW 638:3
Ransomed, healed, restored, f.   LYTE 433:17
sins, which are many, are f.   BIBLE 94:8
forgiveness: And ask of thee f.   SHAK 597:16
F. of sins   BOOK 119:1
F. to the injured does belong   DRYD 260:9
Mutual F. of each vice   BLAKE 111:22
much knowledge, what f.   ELIOT 271:11
forgiving: f. all   AUDEN 36:5
forgot: all the rest f.   SHAK 633:9
things f. the taste of fears   SHAK 604:11
born to be f.   COWP 222:25
curiosities would be quite f.   WORR 33:2
forgetting, by the world f.   POPE 519:21
f. as soon as done   SHAK 627:19
F. it not, nay, but got   ROSS 547:13

forgot: (*cont.*):
Honey, I just f. to duck	DEMP 236:15
I have f. my part	SHAK 570:21
My Lord, I had f. the fart	ELIZ 274:5
proposed as things f.	POPE 521:23
she f. the stars	KEATS 388:3
They never f.	AUDEN 35:7

forgotten: been learned has been f.   SKIN 649:6
books undeservedly f.   AUDEN 36:17
f. as a nameless number   PAST 508:7
f. before God   BIBLE 94:22
f. man at the bottom   ROOS 545:14
f. nothing and learnt nothing   DUM 264:1
f. scream for help in dreams   CAN 178:2
f. this day we must part   CRAW 226:16
He hath not f. my age   SOUT 657:14
I am all f.   SHAK 564:26
Is by a newer object quite f.   SHAK 631:5
I want to be f. even by God   BROW 151:20
learned nothing, f. nothing   TALL 678:11
ruins of f. times   BROW 145:14
sooner f. than an insult   CHES 198:7
There is always a f. thing   CHES 198:29
fork: pick up mercury with f.   LLOY 424:11
When he left off using a f.   BENT 64:14
forked: f. animal as thou art   SHAK 596:11
forks: pursued it with f.   CARR 184:5
forlorn: F.! the very word   KEATS 389:16
Like these, on earth I wait f.   ARN 28:20
that would make me less f.   WORD 748:16
form: earth was without f.   BIBLE 69:20
Fain would I dwell on f.   SHAK 622:33
fast the f. of sound words   BIBLE 104:6
f. does or fancy bring   WALL 718:17
F. follows function   SULL 671:11
f. in what my eyes   STEV 667:21
F. *is* substance   JAMES 362:22
f. is the key to organic   PAST 508:8
f. like Aphrodite's   BYRON 172:13
f. of an object   CONS 217:23
f. of a servant   BIBLE 103:4
F. of being is assigned   WORD 744:2
F. remains   WORD 747:14
hath no f. nor comeliness   BIBLE 84:11
mould of f.   SHAK 576:4
silent f, dost tease us   KEATS 389:2
take thy f. from off   POE 518:8
Terror the human f. divine   BLAKE 114:16
time to lick it into f.   BURT 164:16
formal: f. feeling comes   DICK 244:9
formalistic: more f. than conservatives
                                        CALV 175:18
forme: *mais cela n'a pas de f.*   ANOU 23:8
formed: Shall the thing f.   BIBLE 100:2
small, but perfectly f.   COOP 218:9
former: f. and the latter rain   BOOK 120:9
f. days were better   BIBLE 80:13
f. things are passed away   BIBLE 107:18
thy f. light restore   SHAK 618:5
formerly: what we were f. told   BLUN 116:4
formosa: F. facies   PUBL 531:1
forms: amber to observe the f.   POPE 519:30
By f. unseen their dirge   COLL 213:13
f. are circumfused   WORD 747:4
f. of government let fools   POPE 522:17
f. of things unknown   SHAK 612:17
f. which can outlive all   BYRON 172:2
forneys: greet was as a greet f.   CHAU 193:4
fornication: f., and all other   BOOK 119:17
F., and all uncleanness   BIBLE 102:20
forsake: fail thee, nor f. thee   BIBLE 73:26
f. me not when my strength   BOOK 129:17
F. not an old friend   BIBLE 87:16
forsaken: never righteous f.   BOOK 126:20
rathe primrose that f.   MILT 466:11
why hast thou f. me   BIBLE 93:5
why hast thou f. me   BOOK 125:9
forsaking: f. all other   BOOK 123:19
forsworn: so sweetly were f.   SHAK 560:17
f. *cynthia:* Of promise and f.   BETJ 68:1
fort: Hold the f.   BLISS 115:2
forth: F. in thy name, O God   WESL 728:10

forth: (*cont.*):
Pilgrim, forth	CHAU 196:5
Man goeth f. to his work	BOOK 132:9
fortieth: become her F. Article	DENN 237:5
fortissimo: F. at last	MAHL 442:4
fortitude: f. the Soul contains	DICK 244:14
fortnight: beyond the next f.	CHAM 189:2
Phoenician, a f. dead	ELIOT 273:11
fortress: f. built by Nature	SHAK 619:18
petty f. and a dubious hand	JOHN 370:17
fortresses: brambles in the f.	BIBLE 83:18
fortuna: *Audentis F. iuvat*	VIRG 714:7
fortunate: he is at best but f.	SOLON 655:6
'Tis better to be f. than wise	WEBS 726:10
With the same f. man	BERL 65:15
fortunatus: *F. et ille deos qui novit*	VIRG 715:15
fortune: arrows of outrageous f.	SHAK 575:16
Base F., now I see	MARL 447:8
be a beauty without a f.	FARQ 280:12
Blind F. still bestows	JONS 378:22
Disdaining f.	SHAK 599:15
disgrace with f.	SHAK 633:10
do F. what she can	DRAY 257:16
ere f. made him so	DRYD 260:18
fools of f., trencher-friends	SHAK 626:12
For ever, F., wilt thou prove	THOM 696:16
F. assists the brave	TER 690:13
f. gives the grace	JONS 379:14
F. is merry	SHAK 592:21
F. made his sword	SHAK 587:4
f. may naturally indulge	ELIOT 269:28
F.'s a right whore	WEBS 726:1
F.'s cap we are not	SHAK 574:25
F., that favours fools	JONS 378:4
good f. to others	BIER 109:7
good f. where I find it	MOI 479:15
happily upon a plentiful f.	JOHN 372:10
hast Caesar and his f.	CAES 174:18
her f. by way of marriage	FIEL 282:14
he's but F.'s knave	SHAK 566:19
he shall see F.	BACON 43:19
hostages to f.	BACON 44:3
how does f. banter us	BOL 117:11
leads on to f.	SHAK 593:12
little value of f.	STEE 662:22
made lame by f.'s dearest	SHAK 633:14
man who takes your f.	WOOL 742:18
method of making a f.	GRAY 316:10
mock the good housewife F.	SHAK 567:17
mother of good f.	CERV 188:15
mould of a man's f.	BACON 43:18
O! I am F.'s fool	SHAK 623:15
possession of a good f.	AUST 39:9
secret parts of F.	SHAK 574:25
seen the smiling of F.	COCK 208:3
smith of his own f.	CAEC 205:15
whan that F. list to flee	CHAU 194:2
when we are sick in f.	SHAK 595:2
Whom F., in this maze	SACK 552:13
Women and f. are truest	WYCH 750:5
world's great f. and affairs	DAV 232:7
youth f. and to fame	GRAY 315:20

fortunes: f. sharpe adversitee   CHAU 195:20
make content with his f.   SHAK 596:3
my f. have corrupted   SHAK 566:1
with those my former f.   SHAK 566:14
forty: at f., the judgement   FRAN 292:16
Fat, fair and f.   O'KEE 498:9
fool at f. is a fool indeed   YOUNG 754:8
f. winters shall besiege   SHAK 633:1
F. years long was I grieved   BOOK 131:10
F. years on   BOWEN 138:5
In f. minutes   SHAK 611:18
Knows it at f., and reforms   YOUNG 754:17
look young till f.   DRYD 261:4
loves a fairy when she's f.   HENL 332:5
man over f. is a scoundrel   SHAW 638:2
forty-five: At f. what next?   LOW 430:14
forty-three: may pass for f.   GILB 306:23
forward: F. and backward rapt   DAV 232:7
For ward, f, let us range   TENN 685:19
from this day f.   BOOK 123:20
look f. to with hope   FROST 294:14

forward: (*cont.*):
looking f. to the past — OSB 501:17
marched breast f. — BROW 148:6
not look f. to posterity — BURKE 158:9
Some men a f. motion love — VAUG 709:4
those behind cried 'F.!' — MAC 436:13
Foss: Old F. the name of his cat — LEAR 414:11
fossil: Language is f. poetry — EMER 277:8
foster-child: f. of silence — KEATS 388:23
fostered: F. by beauty and fear — WORD 746:20
fou: I wasna f., but just had — BURNS 161:20
There's some are f. o' brandy — BURNS 162:6
fought: angels f. the dragon — BIBLE 106:30
but to have f. well — COUB 220:4
courses f. against Sisera — BIBLE 74:3
f. against me from my youth — BOOK 134:9
f. a long hour by Shrewsbury — SHAK 592:9
f. the dogs and killed — BROW 151:26
I have f. a good fight — BIBLE 104:8
Than never to have f. at all — CLOU 207:21
they f. each other — SOUT 657:5
we f. at Arques — HENR 332:11
Who f. with us side by side — WEAT 724:13
foul: Fair is foul, and f. is fair — SHAK 599:13
Fair is too f. an epithet — MARL 448:5
f. and fair a day I have — SHAK 600:4
F. as their soil, and frigid — BYRON 169:27
f. deed shall smell above — SHAK 591:24
F. deeds will rise — SHAK 572:24
f. Fiend coming over — BUNY 155:17
f. rag and bone shop — YEATS 751:2
however f. within — CHUR 201:4
I doubt some f. play — SHAK 572:23
less f. profanation — SHAK 605:19
Murder most f. — SHAK 573:16
Seemed f. to them — SPEN 660:24
thank the gods I am f. — SHAK 569:12
to really f. things up — ANON 19:2
fouled: Experience hath f. me — TENN 682:5
foulest: shortest way the f. — BACON 42:9
foully: play'dst most f. for't — SHAK 602:21
found: asses f. a kingdom — MILT 473:18
awoke and f. me here — KEATS 388:13
awoke and f. myself famous — BYRON 174:9
country as good as he had f. it — COBB 208:1
f. Him in the shining — TENN 682:17
f. my sheep which was lost — BIBLE 94:35
f. no more of her — BIBLE 76:30
f. the Roman nation — VIRG 712:2
Hast thou f. me, mine enemy — BIBLE 76:11
he was lost, and is f. — BIBLE 95:5
not yet f. a role — ACH 1:6
place could no where be f. — BOOK 126:21
shall be f. by the fire — BROW 148:22
tragedy of a man who has f. — BARR 54:14
When f., make a note — DICK 240:16
when thou mayest be f. — BOOK 126:9
foundation: f. of morals — BENT 64:4
f. of most governments — ADAMS 3:2
f. of unyielding despair — RUSS 551:19
Good order is the f. — BURKE 158:28
laid the f. of the earth — BOOK 132:1
foundations: city which hath f. — BIBLE 104:14
hour when earth's f. fled — HOUS 351:22
laid the f. of the earth — BIBLE 77:34
laid the f. of the earth — BOOK 132:6
founder: father and first f. — CAXT 188:1
founding: compared with f. a bank — BREC 140:5
F. a firm state by proportions — MARV 450:4
fount: Virtue is the f. — MARL 448:2
Slow, slow, fresh f. — JONS 378:14
fountain: burning f. — SHEL 639:21
f. filled with blood — COWP 222:21
f. from the which my current — SHAK 617:15
f. momently was forced — COL 210:10
f. of all goodness — BOOK 119:7
f. of delights — LUCR 432:6
f. of honour — BAG 46:14
f. of the water of life — BIBLE 107:19
f. send forth at the same — BIBLE 105:3
He is the f. of honour — BACON 42:17
Here at the f.'s sliding foot — MARV 450:12
It is that f. and that well — RAL 535:13

fountain: (*cont.*):
Let the healing f. start — AUDEN 34:16
Like a summer-dried f. — SCOTT 559:10
next a f. — POPE 520:17
perpetual f. of good sense — DRYD 262:17
spring shut up, a f. sealed — BIBLE 81:15
Thou f., at which drink — COWP 223:6
Whose f. who shall tell — MILT 470:15
woman moved is like a f. — SHAK 624:22
fountains: f. mingle with the river — SHEL 641:9
living f. contains — AKEN 6:4
silver f. mud — SHAK 633:13
Weep you no more, sad f. — ANON 19:6
Where Afric's sunny f. — HEBER 330:3
whose f. are within — COL 209:13
writers, like clear f. — LAND 408:12
four: f. beasts full of eyes — BIBLE 106:10
f. essential human freedoms — ROOS 546:3
f.-footed beasts of the earth — BIBLE 98:19
F. lagging winters — SHAK 619:10
F. legs good, two legs bad — ORW 499:19
that twice two be not f. — TURG 705:11
that two plus two make f. — ORW 500:13
four-in-hand: f. round corner — COL 212:15
fourscore: come to f. years — BOOK 131:1
fourteenth: f. Mr Wilson — HOME 342:21
fourth: f. estate of the realm — MAC 434:10
High as a flag on the F. of — HAMM 323:1
foutra: f. for the world — SHAK 584:11
fowl: Of tame villatic f. — MILT 474:14
over the f. of the air — BIBLE 69:24
You elegant f. — LEAR 414:13
fowler: snare of the f. — BOOK 134:2
fowls: Behold the f. of the air — BIBLE 89:9
f. came and devoured — BIBLE 91:1
f. of the air — BIBLE 98:19
f. of the air — BOOK 132:7
f. singis on the spray — DOUG 255:8
smale f. maken melodye — CHAU 192:7
that I here the f. synge — CHAU 195:1
fox: ar'n't that I loves the f. — SURT 672:11
Crazy like a f. — PER 512:21
f. from his lair — GRAV 314:16
f. jumps over the lazy dog — ANON 17:14
f. knows many things — ARCH 24:11
f. said once upon a time — HOR 348:1
gentleman galloping after a f. — WILDE 735:27
historical f. — HUXL 358:2
mentality of a f. at large — LEVIN 420:5
prince must be a f. — MACH 438:10
They've shot our f. — BIRCH 109:22
foxed: If ever I was f. — PEPYS 512:6
foxes: f. have a sincere interest — ELIOT 269:4
f. have holes — BIBLE 90:1
little f. — BIBLE 81:10
portion for f. — BOOK 128:22
second to the f. — BERL 66:2
foxholes: no atheists in the f. — CUMM 229:1
on f. or graveyards — KENN 394:5
fox-hunters: people that think, and f. — SHEN 644:16
fox-hunting: simplest prefer f. — HAIL 320:13
foxlike: Or f. in the vine — TENN 688:15
frabjous: O f. day! — CARR 182:19
fraction: Thou wretched f. — CARL 180:5
fragile: nature's f. vessel — SHAK 626:20
fragments: I have f. shored — ELIOT 273:14
Gather up the f. that remain — BIBLE 96:23
Until Death tramples it to f. — SHEL 640:4
fragrance: Isles of f. — POPE 519:6
fragrant: Words of f. portals — STEV 665:21
frailties: f. with a lover's care — CENT 188:5
frailty: concession to human f. — TAWN 679:1
f. of our nature — BOOK 120:14
F., thy name is woman — SHAK 572:12
gie poor F. names — BURNS 161:1
love's the noblest f. — DRYD 260:29
noblest f. of the mind — SHAD 563:14
therefore more f. — SHAK 581:18
frame: Could f. in earth — SPEN 660:13
f. of adamant — JOHN 370:16
f. of nature round him — ADD 4:5
f. perish even in conquering — BYRON 169:7

frame: (*cont.*):
mighty f. of the world — BERK 65:12
sensuous f. is racked — TENN 683:16
shakes this fragile f. at eve — HARDY 325:9
universal f. is without a mind — BACON 42:22
framed: to have it f. and glazed — WALP 719:15
France: between F. and England — JERR 365:19
Fair stood the wind for F. — DRAY 258:8
forces the full pride of F. — SHAK 584:20
F., famed in all great arts — ARN 29:2
F. has lost a battle — DE G 234:28
F. is adequately secured — ASQ 31:17
F., mother of arts — DU B 262:23
F. was long a despotism — CARL 180:23
F. will say that I am — EINS 268:3
He had one illusion—F. — KEYN 395:2
his round hose in F. — SHAK 607:15
Our fertile F. — SHAK 586:16
political thought in F. — ARON 30:15
That sweet enemy, F. — SIDN 646:20
There lived a singer in F. — SWIN 677:5
this matter better in F. — STER 664:2
two breasts by which F. — SULLY 671:13
vasty fields of F. — SHAK 584:17
wield the sword of F. — DE G 235:1
Francesca di Rimini: F., miminy — GILB 305:20
Frankie: F. and Albert — ANON 13:11
frankincense: branches of f. — BIBLE 88:4
f., and myrrh — BIBLE 88:9
frankly: F., my dear, I don't give a damn! — MITC 478:3
frantic: fascination f. — GILB 305:14
f.-mad with evermore unrest — SHAK 635:9
frater: *f., ave atque vale* — CAT 187:1
fraternize: I beckon you to f. — AUDEN 35:16
fratrum: *Par nobile f.* — HOR 351:8
fraud: Force, and f. — HOBB 340:8
Grown old in f. — CHUR 201:10
pious f. of the almanac — LOW 430:6
fraudatrix: *f. scientiae* — JOHN 366:15
fray: eager for the f. — CIBB 203:22
freaks: Darting with f. — HUNT 356:11
freckled: f. Human Nature — DICK 245:4
Whatever is fickle, f. — HOPK 345:20
zebra, f. like a pard — KEATS 388:14
freckles: In those f. live their savours — SHAK 611:11
Love, curiosity, f., and doubt — PARK 506:7
Fred: Here lies F. — ANON 14:6
free: better chains than to be f. — KAFKA 384:17
better that England should be f. — MAGEE 441:18
Bind me at least, or set me f. — GOD 308:8
bond nor f. — BIBLE 103:16
born f. and equal in dignity — ANON 11:19
But I was f. born — BIBLE 99:6
English Church shall be f. — MAGN 441:19
everywhere f. born — LINC 422:12
Ev'rything f. in America — SOND 656:3
exist in a f. country — BURKE 157:29
f. agent that you were — AUR 37:20
f. and immortal — TRAH 701:12
F. as a bird to settle — WORD 746:17
f. as Caesar — SHAK 589:28
f. as nature first made — DRYD 260:8
f. as they want to be — BALD 48:3
f. development of each — MARX 452:13
freedom to the f. — LINC 422:6
F. hearts, free foreheads — TENN 690:4
f. he strives for nothing — DOST 254:7
F. me, I pray, to go — MERR 458:13
f. society is a society — STEV 666:20
F. speech, free passes — BETJ 67:15
f. themselves must strike — BYRON 168:10
f. to do as they please — HOFF 340:20
f. verse as play tennis — FROST 295:17
give a man a f. hand — WEST 729:10
Greece might still be f. — BYRON 171:1
half slave and half f. — LINC 421:18
he's f. again — SOLZ 655:7
hungry man not a f. man — STEV 666:17
I am a f. man, an American — JOHN 367:4
I am condemned to be f. — SART 556:9

free: (*cont.*):
I am not f.	DEBS 233:13
ignorant and f.	JEFF 364:14
leaves f. to all	MILT 471:14
Long Live F. Quebec	DE G 235:5
Love is a thyng as any spirit f.	CHAU 193:13
Love Virtue, she alone is f.	MILT 464:12
makes f. those who loved it	SANT 555:20
man is either f. or he is not	BAR 51:15
Man was born f.	ROUS 549:2
maxim of a f. government	ADAMS 2:26
Mother of the F.	BENS 63:23
My lines and life are f.	HERB 334:11
naturally were born f.	MILT 476:9
no f. man shall be taken	MAGN 442:1
nominally f., but really	BOOTH 136:5
no such thing as a f. lunch	ANON 18:14
not only to be f.	PANK 505:18
O'er the land of the f.	KEY 394:15
people let him go f.	BOOK 132:12
perfectly f. till all are free	SPEN 658:23
powerful and f.	TOCQ 699:2
Thou art f.	ARN 28:12
Ring in the valiant man and f.	TENN 684:11
set f. his half-gained Eurydice	MILT 465:18
set f. in our remembering	BERRY 66:15
should themselves be f.	BROO 143:2
so far kept us f. and firm	JEFF 364:4
Teach the f. man how to praise	AUDEN 34:16
that moment they are f.	COWP 223:19
they are f. to do whatever	SHAW 637:11
They bring it to you, f.	AMIS 11:3
This is a f. country	UST 707:18
trample upon these, be f.	SHEL 644:10
truth shall make you f.	BIBLE 96:32
truth which makes men f.	AGAR 5:13
Was he f.? Was he happy?	AUDEN 36:12
We *know* our will is f.	JOHN 373:3
We must be f. or die	WORD 744:13
When the mind's f.	SHAK 596:4
wholly slaves or wholly f.	DRYD 260:23
worth nothin', but it's f.	KRIS 404:3
yearning to breathe f.	LAZ 413:7

free-born: f. mouse detain — BARB 52:2

freed: f. his soul the nearest way — JOHN 375:30
hour which f. us from sleep — BROW 145:13
I have f. my soul — BERN 66:8

freedom: apprenticeship for f. — BAR 51:15
are fit to use their f.	MAC 434:17
better organised than f.	PÉGUY 511:7
bondage which is f.'s self	SHEL 642:21
But what is F.?	COL 209:5
can do for the f. of man	KENN 394:2
desire their liberty and f.	CHAR 191:9
enemies of F. do not argue	INGE 359:12
fight for f. and truth	IBSEN 359:2
flame of f. in their souls	SYM 677:6
F. alone substitutes	TOCQ 698:9
f. and chief place of seclusion	MONT 481:1
f. and curteisie	CHAU 192:8
F. and not servitude	BURKE 157:27
F. and power	DOST 254:10
F. and slavery	GAND 297:9
F. and Whisky	BURNS 161:7
F. cannot exist without	METT 459:2
f. for the one who thinks	LUX 433:1
F., f.! Down with cross	BLOK 115:8
F. has a thousand charms	COWP 223:13
F. is an indivisible word	WILL 737:16
f. is a noble thing	BARB 52:8
f. is but a light	GUM 319:16
f. is excellent	TOCQ 698:11
F. is not choosing	MURD 488:6
f. is reserved	COLL 213:5
F. is slavery	ORW 500:10
f. is something people take	BALD 48:3
F. is the cause of God	BOWL 138:16
F. is the freedom to say	ORW 500:13
f. of pres.	JEFF 361:6
f. of speech	THOM 710:0
f. of speech	TWAIN 706:8
F. of the press in Britn.	SWAF 673:1
F. shrieked	CAMP 176:17

freedom: (*cont.*):
F.'s just another word	KRIS 404:3
F. slowly broadens down	TENN 690:7
F.'s soil beneath our feet	DRAKE 257:13
f. there will be no State	LENIN 417:7
f. to the slave	LINC 422:6
f. we are all equal	JUN 383:7
F. which in no other land	DRYD 261:30
F., which stamps him image	GRAI 314:5
green f. of a cockatoo	STEV 666:10
ideal of f. and progress	MADAN 441:11
If I have f. in my love	LOV 429:4
I gave my life for f.	EWER 279:10
impair their f.	TAWN 679:3
Let f. ring	SMITH 652:13
most absolute f.	CHEK 197:11
not f. from, but freedom to	BERL 66:5
obtained I this f.	BIBLE 99:6
O F., what liberties	GEOR 301:10
Our f. as free lances	MACN 441:5
preserve and enlarge f.	LOCKE 425:4
rest love not f.	MILT 476:8
service is perfect f.	BOOK 119:3
this participation of f.	BURKE 157:31
those principles of f.	PAGE 504:4
To earn you f.	LAWR 413:6
We must plan for f.	POPP 524:12
What stands if f. fall	KIPL 399:4

freedoms: four essential f. — ROOS 546:3
F. you'll not to me allow — BEHN 60:11

freehold: life given to none f. — LUCR 432:5

freeing: f. some and leaving others — LINC 422:12

freely: f. we serve — MILT 471:26
F. ye have received — BIBLE 90:14
O let it f. burn — LITT 423:9

Freeman: F. butters Stubbs — ROG 544:16

freemasonry: kind of bitter f. — BEER 59:16

freemen: f. are the only slaves — MASS 453:14
f. or slaves — WASH 721:23
To rule o'er f. — BROO 143:2
true thy chartered f. are — JOHN 377:14

freer: f., and more loving — BALD 48:5

freewoman: other by a f. — BIBLE 102:5

freeze: f. my humanity — MACN 441:1
f., thou bitter sky — SHAK 568:17
f. thy young blood — SHAK 573:14
froze as if to f. us all — HILL 338:10
To f. the blood — WORD 744:8

freezes: Yours till Hell f. — FISH 283:6

freezing: As F. persons — DICK 244:10

freezings: What f. have I felt — SHAK 634:16

frei: *Arbeit macht f.* — ANON 21:9

freight: have her earthly f. — WORD 746:1

French: boy, half-F. — SHAK 587:2
F. are wiser than they seem	BACON 44:22
F. are with equal advantage	CANN 178:3
F. art, if not sanguinary	SPEN 658:24
F. noblesse had been capable	TREV 702:11
F. of Parys was to hire	CHAU 192:4
F., or Turk, or Proosian	GILB 306:5
F. Revolution operated	TOCQ 698:8
F. the empire of the land	RICH 540:17
F. want no-one to be	TOCQ 699:7
F. widow in every bedroom	HOFF 341:13
glory of beating the F.	WOLFE 741:2
how it's improved her F.	GRAH 313:8
No more Latin, no more F.	ANON 16:21
not too French F. bean	GILB 305:17
Paris was F.—and silent	TUCH 705:1
professor of F. letters	JOYCE 382:5
soul in new F. books	BROW 148:13
Speak in F. when you can't	CARR 182:22
to women Italian, to men F.	CHAR 191:21
We are not F.	MONT 481:19
What is not clear is not F.	RIV 541:13
would always have spoken F.	VOLT 716:16

Frenchman: F. always talking — JOHN 375:15
hate a F. as you hate devil — NELS 491:3

Frenchmen: could beat three F. — ADD 4:15
Englishmen act better than F. — BENN 63:15
Fifty million F. can't be wrong — GUIN 319:13

Frenchwomen: F. better than — BENN 63:13
Am I a Demoniac f. — MILT 473:6

frenzy: (*cont.*):
fine f. rolling	SHAK 612:17
What is life? a f.	CALD 175:4
frequency: very fact of f.	ELIOT 269:18
frequent: For f. tears have run	BROW 147:19
frère: *mon semblable,—mon f.*	BAUD 55:7
frères: F. humains après nous	VILL 711:14
fresh: both so ancient and so f.	AUG 37:2
f. air should be kept	MAC 434:4
f. as is the month of May	CHAU 192:10
F. as the Angel o'er	BYRON 167:25
f. lap of the crimson rose	SHAK 611:15
F. shalt thou see in me	DAN 229:15
nice f. corpse	TWAIN 706:14
noted for f. air and fun	EDGAR 266:8
O yonge, f. folkes	CHAU 196:2
So sad, so f., the days	TENN 688:4
Tomorrow to f. woods	MILT 466:16
women of that ever-f.	AMIS 11:4

freshening: F. in the wind — BROW 150:21

fret: fever, and the f. — KEATS 389:10
f. a passage through — FULL 296:8
f. not after knowledge — KEATS 390:8
F. not thyself — BOOK 126:18
oh i should worry and f. — MARQ 448:15
though you can f. me — SHAK 576:23

frets: f. the saints in heaven — BROW 147:4
struts and f. his hour — SHAK 605:1

fretted: F. pigmy body — DRYD 259:1

Freud: F. said all I needed — LOOS 428:11
trouble with F. — DODD 249:24

Freude: F., schöner Götterfunken — SCH 558:1

Freudian: her F. papa — LOW 430:10

friar: Apollo turned fasting f. — MER 457:21

friars: f. were singing vespers — GIBB 302:18
We cannot all be f. — CERV 188:11

fricassee: in a f., or a ragout — SWIFT 674:4

Friday: My man F. — DEFOE 234:10
on a F. fil al this meschaunce — CHAU 194:8
One F. morn when we set sail — ANON 17:6

friend: As f. remembered not — SHAK 568:17
At luncheon with a city f.	BELL 61:22
author as you choose a f.	DILL 246:3
betraying my f.	FORS 290:29
blunt man that love my f.	SHAK 592:15
Boldness be my f.	SHAK 570:28
change your Lover for a f.	ETH 278:19
equal f.	SURR 672:2
faithful f. is the medicine	BIBLE 87:12
Forsake not an old f.	BIBLE 87:16
F. and associate of this clay	HADR 320:8
f. and enemy is but Death	BROO 143:3
f.-and-relation	MILNE 462:9
F., go up higher	BIBLE 94:27
f. he drops into poetry	DICK 242:32
f. in power is a friend lost	ADAMS 2:10
f. is a person with whom	EMER 276:24
friendless name the f.	JOHN 375:29
f. loveth at all times	BIBLE 78:40
f. may spit upon my floor	HERB 335:24
f. of every country	CANN 178:4
f. of flattering illusions	CONR 217:10
f. of my better days	HALL 322:6
f. should bear f.'s infirmities	SHAK 593:7
f. sincere enough to tell	BULW 155:6
f. that sticketh closer	BIBLE 79:3
f. that will go to jail	BURN 160:8
f. to close his eyes	DRYD 259:19
f. we lose a part of ourselves	POPE 524:2
F., wherefore art thou come	BIBLE 92:31
f. who never made a foe	TENN 682:4
handsome house to lodge a f.	SWIFT 674:25
have a f. is to be one	EMER 276:25
He was my f., faithful	SHAK 592:6
homes without a f.	CLARE 204:23
In every mess I finds a f.	DIBD 238:13
Is such a f., that one had need	COWP 222:6
I think of him as a f.	SMITH 652:21
I was angry with my f.	BLAKE 114:11
I would not use a f.	HERB 335:23
lost best f. amn I	SOUT 657:10
l r down his wife for his f.	JOYCE 382:5
Little F. of all the World	KIPL 402:4

fruits: (cont.):
flowers and f. of love	BYRON 173:1
f. of life and beauty	BLAKE 113:14
kindly f. of the earth	BOOK 120:2
Like Dead Sea f.	MOORE 483:15
frustra: f. vigilat qui custodit	BIBLE 108:4
frustrate: each f. ghost	BROW 153:7
F. their knavish tricks	ANON 13:19
fry: Such as 'F. me!'	CARR 183:28
frying-pan: fish that talks in the f.	DE L 235:19
frizzled in my f.	ENG 277:23
fubbed: have been f. off	SHAK 583:2
fuck: And f. all in between	BENN 63:5
f. you up, your mum and dad	LARK 410:6
zipless f.	JONG 378:3
fudge: two-fifths sheer f.	LOW 429:18
fuel: F. to maintain his fires	CAREW 179:2
f. wounding thorns	SOUT 657:22
fugaces: Eheu f.	HOR 349:19
fugit: f. inreparabile tempus	VIRG 715:17
fugitive: f. and cloistered virtue	MILT 475:7
f. from th' law of averages	MAUL 454:14
What was so f.	WORD 746:2
fugues: masses and f. and 'ops'	GILB 305:4
Führer: Ein Reich, ein Volk, ein F.	ANON 21:10
fuimus: F. Troes	VIRG 712:20
fuisse: f. felicem	BOET 116:12
fulcrum: Upon the f. dust	BERRY 66:12
fulfil: f. lusts thereof	BIBLE 100:11
F. now, O Lord, the desires	BOOK 119:9
not to destroy, but to f.	BIBLE 88:27
power faithfully to f.	BOOK 120:13
fulfilled: f. a long time	BIBLE 87:2
hearts were f. with the music	SWIN 676:3
fulfilling: f. his word	BOOK 135:14
fulfilment: image of f.	MUGG 487:11
full: All then is f.	POPE 519:19
Brim, in a flash, f.	HOPK 346:13
commonplace book be f.	SWIFT 674:11
F. fathom five thy father lies	SHAK 625:10
F. many a fathom deep	CAMP 176:11
F. speed ahead	FARR 281:1
f. stop just at right place	BABEL 41:8
f. tide of human existence	JOHN 373:28
let me be f.	METH 458:16
Lord God, we ha' paid in f.	KIPL 401:2
Reading maketh a f. man	BACON 44:28
Serenely f., the epicure	SMITH 653:19
that hath his quiver f.	BOOK 134:7
full-blown: yet a rose f.	HERR 337:11
fuller: f.'s earth for reputations	GAY 299:15
full-throated: in f. ease	KEATS 389:8
fulmina: Bruta f.	PLINY 517:6
fulness: and the f. thereof	BIBLE 100:33
stature of the f. of Christ	BIBLE 102:17
fum: Fy, fa, f.	NASHE 490:22
fumbles: f. up into a loose adieu	SHAK 628:1
fume: stinking f. thereof	JAM 361:17
fumitor: Crowned with rank f.	SHAK 596:31
fumum: F. et opes Romae	HOR 350:8
fun: Ain't we got f.	KAHN 384:19
f. enough for far into night	BETJ 68:9
f. in any Act of Parliament	HERB 333:22
F. is fun but no girl wants	LOOS 428:10
f. nine-tenths of the law	SAY 557:15
f. to be in the same decade	ROOS 546:6
f. where I've found it	KIPL 399:14
Gladstone read Homer for f.	CHUR 203:2
It's less f. and it lasts	ANOU 23:9
It was great f.	PORT 525:1
much less f. if we were	RHYS 539:18
Oh, what f.	DE L 236:4
people have f.	MONT 481:15
Polka the jolliest f. I know	GROS 319:1
[sex] was the most f.	ALLEN 9:9
What on earth was all the f. for?	BETJ 68:9
function: each with his own f.	VIRG 715:19
Form follows f.	SULL 671:11
F. never dies	WORD 747:14
must f. to perfection	MUSS 489:19
imple state of man that f.	SHAK 600:12
This frightful world in	LE C 415:13
functions: their f. and offices	SHAK 599:10

fundament: frigid upon the f.	NASH 490:19
fundamental: f. things apply	HUPF 357:2
funeral: Disposed upon a f. chair	MERR 458:12
f. baked meats	SHAK 572:16
f. expenses	JER 365:16
F. marches to the grave	LONG 427:8
f. train which the bridegroom	CLOU 207:3
how to perform a f.	WILL 737:13
mirth in f. and with dirge	SHAK 572:4
not a f. note	WOLFE 740:24
Prepare vault for f. Monday	BEER 59:18
present is the f. of the past	CLARE 204:27
seldom seen a costlier f.	TENN 681:2
to speak in Caesar's f.	SHAK 592:5
funk: poor world in a blue f.	CRANE 225:22
funny: Everything is f.	ROG 544:20
Funny-peculiar or f. ha-ha	HAY 328:9
f. thing happened to me	STEV 667:1
Isn't it f.	MILNE 462:19
It's a f. old world	LEON 236:14
Whatever is f. is subversive	ORW 500:3
fur: fresh beneath her sable f.	PUSH 532:10
On some other f.	ANON 19:24
furies: with inward f. blasted	GREV 318:6
furious: fun grew fast and f.	BURNS 163:9
temperate, and f.	SHAK 602:18
furiously: green ideas sleep f.	CHOM 200:3
heathen so f. rage together	BOOK 124:7
he driveth f.	BIBLE 76:26
furled: folds of bright girdle f.	ARN 27:1
furnace: As one great f. flamed	MILT 468:1
burning fiery f.	BIBLE 85:28
f. of affliction	BIBLE 84:4
Heat not a f. for your foe	SHAK 588:9
if they burned in a f.	BIBLE 106:1
lover, sighing like f.	SHAK 568:16
My faultless breast the f.	SOUT 657:22
furnaces: worship is your f.	BOTT 137:11
furnish: Books do f. a room	POW 528:4
Would f. all we ought to ask	KEBLE 392:20
furnished: F. and burnish'd	BETJ 68:6
know how poorly f. you are	PERS 513:6
large upper room f.	BIBLE 95:20
who live in f. souls	CUMM 228:17
furniture: f. of earth	BERK 65:12
f. on the deck of the Titanic	MORT 486:16
f. that used to be in saloon	MACM 440:6
new f. of friends	MARV 451:7
No f. so charming as books	SMITH 653:10
piece of mere church f.	COWP 224:11
stocked with f.	DOYLE 256:6
furor: Ira f. brevis est	HOR 348:5
furrow: half-reaped f. sound asleep	KEATS 390:18
I must plough my f. alone	ROS 546:17
leaves a shining f.	TENN 688:13
furrows: made long f.	BOOK 134:10
smite the sounding f.	TENN 690:4
Thou waterest her f.	BOOK 129:3
furry: fire was f. as a bear	SITW 648:10
further: f. away than	RAPH 537:1
f. from God	ANDR 11:14
f. they have to fall	FITZ 285:7
f. us with thy continual help	BOOK 122:17
gates of Hell—but no f.	PIUS 515:20
fury: blind f. of creation	SHAW 637:6
full of sound and f.	SHAK 605:1
f. and mire of human veins	YEATS 750:21
f. like a non-combatant	MONT 480:12
f., lustings out of man	GREV 318:6
f. of a patient man	DRYD 259:13
F. with th' abhorrèd shears	MILT 466:4
In her prophetic f. sewed	SHAK 617:3
Life, a f. slinging flame	TENN 683:16
Nor Hell a f.	CONG 215:17
fuse: green f. drives the flower	THOM 693:7
line is a f.	MAY 455:2
fuss: f. about an omelette	VOLT 717:6
minimum of f.	BLYT 116:9
fustian: f.'s so sublimely bad	POPE 519:31
futility: fatal f. of Fact	JAMES 363:8
f. of our emotion	JOHN 366:15

future: Back to the f.	GALE 755:10
cast spells over the f.	AKHM 6:9
Children of the f. age	BLAKE 114:9
danger of the f.	FROMM 294:7
door opens and lets the f. in	GREE 317:3
empires of the f.	CHUR 202:21
everything for the f.	KHR 395:16
extravagant hopes of the f.	BURKE 159:11
fight against the f.	GLAD 307:6
For I dipped into the f.	TENN 685:13
F. as a promised land	LEWIS 420:13
f. everybody will be famous	WARH 721:22
F., n. That period of time	BIER 109:10
f. of the human race	JEANS 363:25
F. shock	TOFF 699:9
f. states of both left to faith	BYRON 170:26
I never think of the f.	EINS 268:9
lively sense of f. favours	WALP 720:16
once and f. king	WHITE 731:8
orgastic f. that year by year	FITZ 285:4
past controls the f.	ORW 500:11
plan the f. by the past	BURKE 157:5
present in time f.	ELIOT 270:13
preparation for the f.	DISR 248:3
put no trust in the f.	HOR 349:9
seen the f. and it works	STEF 663:1
serve the f. hour	WORD 747:15
that scaffold sways the f.	LOW 430:4
Trust no F.	LONG 427:9
want a picture of the f.	ORW 500:17
we call on past and f.	O'NEI 499:2
Fuzzy-Wuzzy: 'ere's to you, F.	KIPL 399:5
Fyfe: David Patrick Maxwell F.	ANON 16:18

G

gabardine: my Jewish g.	SHAK 607:22
gable: skimming our g.	HEAN 329:17
gad: liberty to g.	BIBLE 87:25
gadding: thyme and the g. vine	MILT 466:2
Gaels: great G. of Ireland	CHES 198:28
gag: tight g. of place	HEAN 329:21
gai: toujours g. toujours g.	MARQ 448:15
Gaierty: back to the G. hotel	ASHF 31:13
gaiety: eclipsed the g. of nations	JOHN 369:3
Our own g. will end up	BLY 116:7
gaily: G. into Ruislip Gardens	BETJ 68:2
gain: comes to him from his g.	BROW 149:11
For g., not glory,	POPE 522:30
hath not the g., but pain	OXF 504:1
I deem a losing g.	SOUT 657:23
My richest g. I count but loss	WATTS 723:2
present g. in everything	WITH 739:13
shall g. the whole world	BIBLE 93:14
So might I g.	BROW 150:22
soul is competent to g.	WORD 744:1
to die is g.	BIBLE 103:2
vain hope of g.	TICH 698:3
what things were g. to me	BIBLE 103:8
gained: misery is a battle g.	WELL 727:10
gainful: g. employment	ACH 1:8
gains: Light g. make heavy purses	BACON 43:1
no g. without pains	STEV 666:16
owners always reap the g.	COLL 213:1
gait: manner of his g.	SHAK 629:9
gaiters: All is gas and g.	DICK 242:14
Galatea: G. aims at me	VIRG 714:18
Galatians: great text in G.	BROW 152:28
gale: g., it plies the saplings	HOUS 352:13
Galeotto: G. was the book	DANTE 230:13
Galilean: pilot of the G. lake	MILT 466:7
You have won, G.	JUL 382:9
Galilee: nightly on deep G.	BYRON 169:28
gall: take my milk for g.	SHAK 600:16
They gave me g. to eat	BOOK 129:12
wormwood and the g.	BIBLE 85:17
gallant: died a g. gentleman	ATKI 32:13
He was a braw g.	BALL 49:3
top a delight	MELV 169:15
gallantry: What men call g.	BYRON 170:6

gallantry: (cont.):
with g. than politics SHER 644:27
galleon: Stately as a g. GREN 318:1
gallery: faces are but a g. BACON 43:21
History is a g. of pictures TOCQ 698:13
Gallia: G. est omnis divisa CAES 174:14
galliard: go to church in a g. SHAK 628:14
gallimaufry: our tongue a g. SPEN 660:29
gallop: G. about doing good SMITH 652:14
G. apace, you fiery-footed SHAK 623:16
Why does he g. and g. about? STEV 668:21
galloped: we g. all three BROW 150:10
galloping: g. sound is shaking VIRG 714:5
gallows: at length it grew a g. KYD 404:15
complexion is perfect g. SHAK 624:27
g. standing in England SHAK 579:21
see nothing but the g. BURKE 158:16
Under the G.-Tree FLET 307.13
upon the g. or of the pox WILK 736:19
gallows-maker: g.; for that frame SHAK 578:17
gallows-tree: Jack on the g. SCOTT 560:19
galumphing: He went g. back CARR 182:19
gambit: by ploy or g. POTT 525:17
gamble: g. at terrible odds STOP 670:6
gambler: whore and g. BLAKE 111:9
game: But war's a g. COWP 224:3
Conversation is a g. of circles EMER 276:21
g. at which the police SHAW 638:8
g. at which two can play BEER 59:19
g. is never lost till won CRAB 225:8
g. of the few BERK 65:9
g. on these lone heaths HAZL 329:14
g.'s afoot SHAK 585:10
g. within the view LEAC 413:14
how you played the G. RICE 540:1
Is the nature of my g. JAGG 361:13
It is but giving over of a g. BEAU 57:2
man is hunter; woman his g. TENN 688:8
play up! and play the g. NEWB 492:9
sugared g. before thee SHAK 626:16
time to win this g. DRAKE 257:12
will stop your little g. PERRY 513:2
gamecocks: Wits are g. GAY 299:32
games: dread of g. BETJ 68:8
G. people play BERNE 66:10
g. should be seen MONT 480:18
it is better than g. SCOTT 559:5
gamesmanship: g. or The art of POTT 525:21
gamesome: I am not g. SHAK 589:23
gammon: g. and spinnage DICK 240:1
gamut: g. of the emotions PARK 506:23
gamyn: of g. and gle WYNT 750:10
Gandhi: [G.] knew the cost NAIDU 489:6
gang: may g. a kennin wrang BURNS 161:1
Ganges: Indian G.' side MARV 451:2
gangsters: always acted like g. KUBR 404:7
gaol: or the world's thy g. DONNE 252:25
gap: And made a g. in nature SHAK 565:6
g. between the lace curtains GREE 317:6
g. you can't see STOP 670:7
it is the last g. WHITE 731:5
through a g. in a raped tomb HEAT 329:24
gaping: g. wretches of the sea HUNT 356:6
Garcia Lorca: and you, G. GINS 306:29
garden: Almighty planted a g. BACON 43:24
Back to the g. MITC 478:1
Beauteous g.'s umbrage SMART 650:3
beloved come into his g. BIBLE 81:16
best g. of the world SHAK 586:10
Come into the g., Maud TENN 686:11
concealed in an enclosed g. CAT 186:9
energized the G.-Suburb LEAV 415:5
fairies at the bottom of our g. FYL 296:11
g. inclosed is my sister BIBLE 81:15
g. is a lovesome thing BROWN 145:2
g. of the world MARV 451:8
g. of your face HERB 334:2
ghost of a g. SWIN 676:14
Glory of the G. KIP 399:7
God the first g. made COWL 221:9
I have a g. of my own MARV 450:19
imperfections of my g. MONT 480:15
In a g. shady this holy lady AUDEN 34:1

garden: (cont.):
land where a g. should be HOR 351:9
lodge in a g. of cucumbers BIBLE 82:8
man and a woman in a g. WILDE 735:29
Muses' g. with pedantic weeds CAREW 179:3
nearer God's Heart in a g. GURN 319:17
No g. appears, no path THOM 694:4
Our England is a g. KIPL 399:7
planted a g. eastward in Eden BIBLE 70:1
rosebud g. of girls TENN 686:19
set to dress this g. SHAK 620:15
sunlight on the g. MACN 441:4
through his g. walketh God BROW 153:3
'tis an unweeded g. SHAK 572:12
walking in the g. in the cool BIBLE 70:10
We are a g. walled around WATTS 723:1
Garden City: G. Café BETJ 67:13
gardener: Adam was a g. SHAK 587:25
supposing him to be the g. BIBLE 97:33
gardeners: g., ditchers and SHAK 578:16
gardening: g. is landscape-painting POPE 524:8
gardens: all the g. of spring THOM 693:13
g. with real toads in them MOORE 482:14
In his blue g. FITZ 285:1
Leaving the g. tidy LARK 410:3
Our bodies are our g. SHAK 615:10
Sowe Carrets in your G. GARD 297:14
sweetest delight of g. BROW 145:12
time in the g. of the West CONN 216:14
trim g. takes his pleasure MILT 464:18
garden-state: that happy g. MARV 450:13
garden-trees: through vext g. ARN 28:26
garish: day's g. eye MILT 464:25
I loved the g. day NEWM 493:15
no worship to the g. sun SHAK 623:17
garland: green willow my g. HEYW 338:4
green willow must be my g. SHAK 617:22
rosy g. and a weary head SIDN 646:19
where that immortal g. MILT 475:7
withered is the g. of the war SHAK 566:15
garlanded: All g. with carven imag'ries KEATS 387:5
garlands: g. wither on your brow SHIR 646:3
her silken flanks with g. KEATS 388:29
may gather g. there SCOTT 560:12
There with fantastic g. SHAK 578:13
they are g. BENN 63:5
To weave the g. of repose MARV 450:5
garlic: g. in a windmill SHAK 581:7
Wel loved he g., oynons CHAU 193:6
garment: g. of praise BIBLE 84:27
know the g. from the man BLAKE 111:23
Language the g. of thought CARL 181:7
left his g. in her hand BIBLE 71:24
like as with a g. BOOK 132:6
shall wax old as doth a g. BOOK 132:1
whose g. was white as snow BIBLE 86:1
garments: borders of their g. BIBLE 92:4
Reasons are not like g. ESSEX 278:14
Stuffs out his vacant g. SHAK 594:4
They part my g. among them BOOK 125:13
garnished: swept, and g. BIBLE 90:36
garret: Born in the g. BYRON 173:4
Genius in a g. starving ROB 542:16
living in a g. FOOTE 288:14
Garrick: Here lies David G. GOLD 311:5
Our G.'s a salad GOLD 311:3
garrison: hath friends in the g. HAL 321:10
gars: What g. ye rin sae still ANON 17:17
Garsington: Hey for G. KETT 394:14
garters: own heir-apparent g. SHAK 580:6
gas: All is g. and gaiters DICK 242:14
g. off before leaving home LEVIN 420:2
G. smells awful PARK 506:11
g. was on in the Institute BETJ 68:4
gash: Give me a g. SHAK 619:5
gashed: heaped on each g. head SORL 656:17
gas masks: trying on g. CHAM 189:7
gasp: g. of Love's latest breath DRAY 258:1
When he was at the last g. BIBLE 88:7
gat: g. me to my Lord right BIBLE 88:7
gate: A-sitting on a g. CARR 183:21
broad g. and the great fire SHAK 564:10

gate: (cont.):
dreams out of the ivory g. BROW 146:23
g. where they're turning AUDEN 35:15
keep the g. of hell SHAK 617:18
latch ter de golden g. HARR 327:9
matters not how strait the g. HENL 332:7
November at the g. PUSH 532:16
one g. to make defence MILT 474:8
openeth the g. to good fame BACON 43:11
poor man at his g. ALEX 8:10
stood at the g. of the year HASK 328:1
that flaming brand, the g. MILT 473:14
that g. they shall enter DONNE 253:14
their enemies in the g. BOOK 134:7
this is the g. of heaven BIBLE 71:15
watchful at his g. DODD 250:1
which was laid at his g. BIBLE 95:9
Wide is the g., and broad BIBLE 89:21
gates: despondently at area g. ELIOT 272:7
enter his g. with praise KETHE 394:13
feet shall stand in thy g. BOOK 133:25
g. are mine to open KIPL 400:5
g. of hell shall not prevail BIBLE 91:14
g. of it shall not be shut BIBLE 107:21
g. of mercy on mankind GRAY 315:16
g. to the glorious FORS 290:8
go to the g. of Hell PIUS 515:20
hearses shall besiege your g. POPE 519:18
Lift up your heads, O ye g. BOOK 125:17
stranger that is within thy g. BIBLE 72:16
temple g. unto my love SPEN 659:15
There are two g. of Sleep VIRG 714:1
Gath: Tell it not in G. BIBLE 75:8
gather: G. ye rosebuds HERR 337:7
he shall g. the lambs BIBLE 83:28
who shall g. them BOOK 126:23
gathered: flowers, g. at six DONNE 253:8
g. thy children together BIBLE 92:7
when two or three are g. BOOK 119:9
where two or three are g. BIBLE 91:20
which cannot be g. up BIBLE 75:14
gathering: g. where thou hast BIBLE 92:17
gat-toothed: G. I was CHAU 194:24
gaude: g. in Christo LUTH 432:9
gaudeamus: G. igitur ANON 22:8
gaudy: doffed her g. trim MILT 467:2
g., blabbing, and remorseful SHAK 587:20
have one other g. night SHAK 565:22
Neat, but not g. WESL 729:5
rich, not g. SHAK 573:4
gauger: g. walked with willing STEV 669:10
gaul: G. as a whole is divided CAES 174:14
To G., to Greece COWP 223:10
Gaunt: familiarly of John a G. SHAK 583:23
Old John of G. SHAK 619:6
on G.'s embattled pile MAC 436:2
gauntlet: g. with a gift in't BROW 147:3
gave: she g. me of the tree BIBLE 70:11
What wee g., wee have ANON 19:15
gawds: praise new-born g. SHAK 627:22
gay: g. Lothario ROWE 549:5
Gay rich, and Rich g. JOHN 368:26
g. villains rise CHUR 201:10
He has a g. appeal COW 220:13
Her heart was warm and g. HAMM 322:15
I'm a g. deceiver COLM 214:2
I would not, if I could, be g. ROG 544:14
outward walls so costly g. SHAK 635:7
profane and impiously g. CRAB 225:2
second best's a g. goodnight YEATS 751:20
So g. the band GREN 318:1
without feeling g. CHUR 201:6
Gaza: Eyeless in G. at the mill MILT 473:25
gaze: Of the inward g. POUND 526:13
Stand fixed in steadfast g. MILT 467:4
There bade me g. ARN 28:19
gazelle: I never loved a dear G. CARR 184:6
I never nursed a dear G. DICK 242:21
I never nursed a dear G. MOORE 483:14
gazelles: g. appear MOORE 482:1
gazer: Bids the rash g. HERB 336:1
gazes: g. or for him that farms CRAB 225:12
Yellow God forever g. HAYES 328:10

gazing: does not consist in g. — DE S 553:4
  stand ye g. up into heaven — BIBLE 98:5
géant: ailes de g. l'empêchent — BAUD 55:6
gear: my ships are out of g. — TENN 689:1
geck: notorious g. and gull — SHAK 630:34
Gedanke: Zwei Seelen, ein G. — HALM 322:7
geese: G. are swans — ARN 27:11
  Like g. about the sky — AUDEN 34:3
  swans of others are g. — WALP 719:25
  wild g. — PUSH 532:16
Gehenna: Down to G. — KIPL 399:18
Geist: der G. der stets verneint — GOET 309:3
gem: considered a perfect g. — CALV 175:11
  g. of purest ray serene — GRAY 315:15
  Thinking every tear a g. — SHEL 641:11
geminae: Sunt g. Somni portae — VIRG 714:1
gems: prow-promoted g. — BETJ 67:10
  Rich and rare were the g. — MOORE 483:10
  rich and various g. inlay — MILT 463:14
  these the g. of heaven — MILT 471:12
gender: she's of feminine g. — O'KEE 498:8
general: abstract and g. terms — KAMES 385:3
  caviare to the g. — SHAK 575:5
  feet of the great g. — OVID 503:5
  G. good is the plea — BLAKE 112:6
  G. notions are generally wrong — MONT 480:9
  g.'s disdained by him — SHAK 627:9
  Sole imperator and great g. — SHAK 598:13
  will you find in that great g. — JUV 384:8
generalities: g. of natural right — CHOA 200:2
  Glittering g.! — EMER 277:16
General Motors: good for G. — WILS 737:18
generals: against the law for g. — TRUM 704:20
  bite some of my other g. — GEOR 300:25
  dead battles, like dead g. — TUCH 704:23
  in g. than in particulars — HUME 355:15
  Our G. now — POPE 522:25
  Russia has two g. — NICH 494:12
  wooden swords we're all G. — UST 707:16
generation: beat g. — KER 394:12
  But ye are a chosen g. — BIBLE 105:11
  faithless and stubborn g. — BOOK 130:9
  g. destroyed by madness — GINS 306:28
  g. of them that hate me — BIBLE 72:16
  g. of vipers — BIBLE 88:15
  g. revolts against fathers — MUMF 488:1
  g. seeketh after a sign — BIBLE 90:34
  g. to corruption turns — GREV 318:7
  g. wiser than the children — BIBLE 95:6
  Had it been the whole g. — ANON 14:6
  I grieved with this g. — BOOK 131:10
  leaves is a g. of men — HOMER 343:4
  lost g. — STEIN 663:6
  One g. passeth away — BIBLE 79:36
  very froward g. — BIBLE 73:22
generations: G. have trod — HOPK 345:10
  G. pass while some trees — BROW 145:21
  g. shall call me blessed — BIBLE 93:22
  manners of future g. — JOHN 369:20
  No hungry g. tread thee down — KEATS 389:15
  shirtsleeves in three g. — ANON 13:13
  Those dying g.—at their song — YEATS 752:20
generator: Tortured with the telephone g. — BLY 116:7
generosity: to exercise our g. — SART 556:15
generous: g. and elevated mind — JOHN 370:4
  g. and honest feeling — BURKE 159:17
  g. sentiments — JOHN 372:12
  It is the g. spirit — WORD 743:8
  My mind as g., and my shape — SHAK 594:26
  they are always g. — MONT 482:2
generously: treated g. or destroyed — MACH 438:7
genes: go by the name of g. — DAWK 233:1
Geneva: grim G. ministers — AYT 41:3
genius: doth yourself to be a great g. — BEAU 56:12
  Eccentricities of g. — DICK 243.10
  g. nothing but g. and virtue — HAZL 328.10
  G., all over [it, out.] — MELV 456:13
  g. a mind of general power — JOHN 368:23
  g. and regularity are enemies — GAIN 296.10
  g. and the mortal instruments — SHAK 590:15

genius: (cont.):
  g. appears in the world — SWIFT 674:15
  g. . . . does what it must — BAR 53:1
  G. does what it must — MER 458:10
  g. has been slow of growth — LEWES 420:12
  g. I had when I wrote — SWIFT 675:16
  G. in a garret starving — ROB 542:16
  G. is one per cent inspiration — EDIS 266:16
  G. is only a greater aptitude — BUFF 154:16
  G. . . . is the child of imitation — REYN 539:10
  g. makes no mistakes — JOYCE 382:2
  G. (which means — CARL 180:18
  g. of Einstein — PIC 514:11
  g. of its scientists — EIS 268:10
  g. of the Constitution — PITT 515:12
  g. of the place — POPE 520:19
  g. rules is by persuading — STEP 663:15
  g. that could cut a Colossus — JOHN 376:13
  g. who is ignorant of all — ADD 5:1
  Gives g. a better discerning — GOLD 311:20
  instantly recognizes g. — DOYLE 257:2
  I think like a g. — NAB 489:3
  kind of universal g. — DRYD 262:9
  lawful G. from the throne — BYRON 172:5
  models destroy g. and art — HAZL 329:7
  Mr Wordsworth's g. — HAZL 329:11
  no longer taste and g. — REYN 539:9
  nothing to declare except g. — WILDE 736:8
  Philistine of g. in religion — ARN 30:5
  put my g. into my life — WILDE 736:7
  Ramp up my g. — JONS 378:23
  stupendous g. — BYRON 174:3
  Taste is the feminine of g. — FITZ 284:19
  Three-fifths of him g. — LOW 429:18
  times in which a g. would — ADAMS 1:13
  To raise the g. — POPE 523:14
  True G., like Armida's wand — LLOYD 424:3
  was g. found respectable — BROW 147:7
  Whence g. wildly flashed — KEATS 390:22
  when rash g. fires — CHUR 201:7
genres: g. sont bons — VOLT 716:9
gent: gentleman is to a g. — BALD 48:15
  was indeed a valiant G. — EVEL 279:5
gente: LA PERDUTA G. — DANTE 230:6
genteel: beast to the truly g. — HARDY 324:10
  He is a man of g. appearance — JOHN 375:22
  No dancing bear was so g. — COWP 222:16
  not g. when he gets drunk — BOSW 137:10
gentes: omnes g. — BIBLE 108:3
Gentiles: preach among the G. — BIBLE 102:12
  Such boasting as the G. use — KIPL 400:13
gentility: Give any marks of g. — BLAKE 111:15
gentle: G. as falcon — SKEL 649:2
  G. Child of gentle Mother — DEAR 233:8
  g. into that good night — THOM 693:4
  G. Jesus, meek and mild — WESL 728:7
  g. mind by g. deeds — SPEN 660:16
  g. motion with the deep — DAV 232:14
  g. rain from heaven — SHAK 609:13
  g. that dooth gentil dedis — CHAU 194:27
  His life was g. — SHAK 593:23
  I have seen them g. — WYATT 749:19
  parfit g. knyght — CHAU 192:9
  shall g. his condition — SHAK 586:11
  yet clear, though g. — DENH 236:17
gentleman: Be a little g. — HOFF 341:2
  Bears not alive so stout a g. — SHAK 582:7
  book is to fashion a g. — SPEN 659:18
  died a very gallant g. — ATKI 32:3
  Every other inch a g. — WEST 729:18
  first true g. that ever — DEKK 235:14
  g. and nothing else — CROM 227:6
  g. and scholar — BURNS 163:24
  g. in Whitehall really — JAY 363:24
  g. is not in your books — SHAK 613:8
  g. should never go beyond — ETH 278:18
  g. to say that he is one — NEWM 493:5
  g. who had a great estate — ANON 17:3
  g. who was genteelly spoken — SURT 672:21
  God send us merry g. — BALL 50:19
  he cannot make a g. — BURKE 159:26
  I am g. — SHAK 628:20
  I am a g. — SHAW 637:9

gentleman: (cont.):
  I am not quite a g. — ASHF 31:5
  kissing, kind-hearted g. — COWP 224:18
  last g. in Europe — LEV 419:17
  lay in linen like a g. — JOHN 368:11
  Like a fine old English g. — ANON 15:19
  little too pedantic for a g. — CONG 215:14
  mariner with the g. — DRAKE 257:11
  No real English g. — BAG 47:9
  officer and a g. — ANON 12:5
  Once a g., and always a g. — DICK 241:7
  prince of darkness is a g. — SHAK 596:15
  Since every Jack became a g. — SHAK 621:21
  soul of this g.'s way — ANON 22:9
  stamps a man as an educated g. — SHAW 636:28
  such true breeding of a g. — BYRON 170:28
  talking about being a g. — SURT 672:6
  This squash, this g. — SHAK 631:14
  unable to describe a g. — TROL 703:6
  what a g. is to a gent — BALD 48:15
  what a g. should be — DEFOE 233:15
  who was then the g.? — ROLLE 545:10
gentlemanly: g. conduct — ARN 30:13
  gives one werry g. ideas — SURT 672:13
  sometimes do a very g. thing — STEV 667:18
gentlemen: behave like g. — MACK 439:3
  Cricket creates good g. — MUG 487:7
  Dust was G. and Ladies — DICK 245:3
  G. do not take soup — CURZ 229:7
  g. in England, now a-bed — SHAK 586:11
  g. often become amorous — ROSS 547:1
  G. Prefer Blondes — LOOS 428.8
  Good morning, g. both — CARL 181:12
  Great-hearted g. — BROW 151:5
  none of us g. any more — COW 313:4
  not a religion for g. — CHAR 191:15
  not to forget we are g. — BURKE 159:17
  Scholars and g. — WORD 747:5
  Three jolly g. — DE L 236:5
  what most of the g. does — WAUGH 723:12
  while the G. go by — KIPL 400:9
  written by gentlemen for g. — THAC 691:10
  You g. of England — PARK 506:2b
gentlemen-rankers: G. out on the spree — KIPL 399:6
gentleness: longsuffering, g. — BIBLE 102:7
  only a willed g. — THOM 694:13
  that g. and show of love — SHAK 589:24
  ways are ways of g. — SPR 661:10
gentlewomen: These G. — DICK 245:4
gently: dig till you g. perspire — KIPL 401:23
  g. as any sucking dove — SHAK 611:8
  g. they go, the beautiful — MILL 461:6
  his faults lie g. on him — SHAK 589:6
genuflexion: at same time a g. — ALAI 7:7
  will never grudge a g. — OLIV 498:12
genuine: g. poetry is conceived — ARN 29:23
  place for the g. — MOORE 482:13
genus: Hoc g. omne — HOR 351:1
geographers: g., in Afric-maps — SWIFT 675:3
geographical: Italy is a g. expression — METT 459:7
geography: G. is about Maps — BENT 64:10
  Is different from G. — BENT 64:10
geometrical: in a g. ratio — MALT 443:18
geometricians: we are g. only — JOHN 369:1
geometry: does not know g. — ANON 21:16
  G. (the only science — HOBB 339:18
  subject as precise as g. — FLAU 286:1
  There is no 'royal road' to g. — EUCL 279:2
George: Amelia praying for G. — THAC 691:16
  And if his name be G. — SHAK 593:25
  Any good of G. the Third — LAND 408:8
  England and Saint G. — SHAK 585:10
  G. the First knew nothing — JOHN 373:29
  G. the First was always — LAND 408:8
  G. the Third ought never — BENT 64:18
  G. III a 'consecrated obstruction' — BAG 47:6
  King G., passing slowly — MADAN 441:7
  saint G., that swinged — SHAK 593:28
Georges: God be praised, the G. ended — LAND 408:8

Georgia: G. on my mind   GORR 312:14
on the red hills of G.   KING 397:1
Georgian: all the G. silver goes   MACM 440:6
geranium: g. windows   LEE 415:19
madman shakes a dead g.   ELIOT 272:14
geraniums: cot with a pot of pink g.   MACN 440:14
delphiniums (blue) and g. (red)   MILNE 462:14
German: G. dictator   CHUR 202:6
G. soldier trying to violate   STR 670:19
to my horse—G.   CHAR 191:21
Germans: beastly to the G.   COW 220:9
G. to pay every penny   GEDD 300:20
to the G.—the air   RICH 540:17
Germany: G. above all   HOFF 340:21
G. to Downing Street peace   CHAM 189:8
G. will declare   EINS 268:3
his bonnet in G.   SHAK 607:15
offering G. too little   NEV 492:5
rebellious G.   OVID 503:5
germens: all g. spill at once   SHAK 595:20
germs: g. in your handkerchief   ANON 12:29
Gershwin: G. songs   FISH 283:7
Gert: G.'s writings are punk   ANON 14:14
Gesang: *Wein, Weib und G.*   LUTH 432:17
Gesetz: *solle allgemeines G.*   KANT 385:6
Gestern: *G. liebt' ich*   LESS 419:12
gestrigen: *Autorität des 'ewig G.'*   WEBER 725:1
gesture: Morality's a g.   BOLT 117:14
gestures: In the g., in the sighs   SOND 656:1
get: better g. out of the way   EIS 268:12
do nothing and g. something   DISR 248:25
g. anywhere in a marriage   MURD 488:5
g. out and get under   CLAR 205:11
G. out as early as you can   LARK 410:7
g. out of these wet clothes   ANON 15:16
g. out while we're young   SPR 661:14
G. thee behind me, Satan   BIBLE 91:15
g. up for shame   HERR 336:9
G. up, stand up   MARL 446:11
g. what you like   SHAW 638:4
getting: Gospel of G. On   SHAW 638:10
G. and spending   WORD 748:15
g. drives these Attic bees   VIRG 715:19
Getty: Paul G. went about   LEVIN 420:2
gewgaw: This g. world   DRYD 259:26
ghastly: G. good taste   BETJ 68:11
g. through drizzling rain   TENN 683:6
neither g., hateful nor ugly   HARDY 324:12
We were a g. crew   COL 211:12
ghost: and woke a g.   ROET 544:8
For love is like a g.   PATM 509:11
gave up the g.   BIBLE 98:22
g. ful blisfully is went   CHAU 196:1
G. in the Machine   RYLE 552:10
g. of a garden   SWIN 676:14
g. of a great name   LUCAN 431:5
g. of Roger Casement   YEATS 751:21
g. of the deceased Roman   HOBB 340:12
g. she glimmers on to me   TENN 688:13
G. unlaid forbear thee   SHAK 571:16
impute to each frustrate g.   BROW 153:7
kind of g.   DONNE 251:20
make a g. of him that lets me   SHAK 573:11
Moves like a g.   SHAK 601:13
raise up the g. of a rose   BROW 145:12
That affable familiar g.   SHAK 634:10
There needs no g.   SHAK 574:1
to police the earth, a g.   LOW 430:22
Turn thou g. that way   DONNE 252:1
Vex not his g.   SHAK 598:4
What beck'ning g.   POPE 519:14
with some old lover's g.   DONNE 252:10
ghosties: From ghoulies and g.   ANON 13:12
ghostly: Her face, at first . . . just g.   REID 538:15
ghosts: egress given to real g.   VIRG 714:1
g. from an enchanter   SHEL 641:14
g. of departed quantities   BERK 65:7
g., wandering here   SHAK 612:6
sprightly port make the g.   SHAK 566:9
ghoul: dug them up like a G.   DICK 240:13

ghoulies: g. and ghosties   ANON 13:12
giant: As when a g. dies   SHAK 606:9
baby figure of the g. mass   SHAK 627:11
Fling but a stone, the g. dies   GREEN 316:18
G. on the mountain stands   BYRON 168:4
g. refreshed with wine   BOOK 130:12
g.'s robe upon dwarfish thief   SHAK 604:18
g. to run his course   BOOK 125:4
in the hand of the g.   BOOK 134:7
I was the g. great and still   STEV 668:15
Now G. Despair had a wife   BUNY 156:2
one g. leap for mankind   ARMS 26:12
sees farther than the g.   COL 212:4
To have a g.'s strength   SHAK 605:17
upon the body of a g.   LAND 408:13
giants: g. in the earth   BIBLE 70:25
grasshoppers are g. there   MARV 451:10
on the shoulders of g.   BERN 66:9
on the shoulders of g.   NEWT 493:19
surely we ought to be g.   CHEK 196:8
there we saw the g.   BIBLE 73:6
Want is one only of five g.   BEV 69:10
world of nuclear g.   BRAD 139:8
gibber: Did squeak and g.   SHAK 571:26
gibbets: cells and g.   COOK 218:5
g. keep the lifted hand   YOUNG 754:10
Gibbon: G. moved to flute   COLM 214:4
scribble! Eh! Mr G.   GLOU 308:3
Gibeon: stand thou still upon G.   BIBLE 73:32
giberne: *dans sa g. le bâton*   LOUI 428:17
gibes: g. and flouts and jeers   DISR 247:25
giblet: He liked thick g. soup   JOYCE 381:24
Gibraltar: g. may tumble   GERS 301:15
giddy: g. line midway   BROW 148:13
Our fancies are more g.   SHAK 629:14
So g. the sight   GREN 318:1
giddy-pacèd: brisk and g. times   SHAK 629:12
Gideon: Lord came upon G.   BIBLE 74:8
gier-eagle: g. on his sail   SMART 650:1
gift: Beauty is the lover's g.   CONG 215:34
gauntlet with a g. in't   BROW 147:3
g. of God may be purchased   BIBLE 98:14
g. of oneself   ANOU 23:6
g. rich by delaying it   TROL 703:26
Heaven's last best g.   MILT 471:21
perfect g. is from above   BIBLE 104:26
You have a g., sir   JONS 379:12
your g. survived it all   AUDEN 34:14
gifted: some divinely g. man   TENN 683:25
Young, g. and black   IRV 360:13
giftie: wad some Pow'r the g. gie us   BURNS 163:14
gifts: adore my g. instead of Me   HERB 335:15
cannot recall their g.   TENN 689:11
contempt of God's good g.   JAM 361:18
Enemies' gifts are no g.   SOPH 656:11
even when they bring g.   VIRG 712:14
g. of God are strown   HEBER 330:4
g. of goodly golden Muse   OXF 504:2
g. on such as cannot use   JONS 378:22
g. that mortal men commend   GRIM 318:12
love your goodly g.   SHAK 619:2
No g. from chance   ARN 27:22
received g. for men   BOOK 129:10
Saba shall bring g.   BOOK 129:20
there are diversities of g.   BIBLE 100:35
They presented unto him g.   BIBLE 88:9
With countless g. of love   WINK 739:6
Yet take these g.   CAT 187:1
gig: Life not a series of g. lamps   WOOLF 742:7
gigantic: g. body, huge massy face   MAC 434:14
Oh, good g. smile   BROW 150:17
when I saw g. shadows   BYRON 168:1
gild: G., but to flout, the ruins   SCOTT 559:13
g. it with the happiest   SHAK 582:10
g. the faces of the grooms   SHAK 602:4
To g. refinèd gold   BYRON 170:29
To g. refinèd gold   SHAK 594:9
gilded: g. loam or painted clay   SHAK 619:7
gilding: G. pale streams   SHAK 633:12
Gilead: G. is mine   BOOK 128:18
Is there no balm in G.   BIBLE 85:9

Gilpin: John G. was a citizen   COWP 222:12
gilt: dust that is a little g.   SHAK 627:22
gin: G. by pailfuls   SCOTT 560:19
g. joints in all the towns   EPST 278:6
G. less than a' the world   MACD 437:8
G. was mother's milk to her   SHAW 638:19
Now is woodcock near the g.   SHAK 630:2
proper union of g.   DE V 238:3
sooner we can get out the g.   REED 538:7
torrent of g. and beer   GLAD 307:9
Ginger: G., you're balmy   MURR 488:11
Nutmegs and g., cinnamon   BEAU 56:13
Gioconda: one isn't the real G.   CRANE 225.22
Giotto: G.'s tower   LONG 426:21
Gipfeln: *Über allen G.*   GOET 309:14
Gipper: one for G.   GIPP 307:1
gipsy: bring out the g. in me   GERS 301:14
Time, you old g. man   HODG 340:19
Two-wheeled g. queen   DYLAN 265:14
vagrant g. life   MAS 453:9
giraffe: g., in their queer, inimitable   DIN 246:8
giraffes: G.!—a People who   CAMP 176:7
girded: and g. with praise   GRANT 314:6
g. about with power   BOOK 129:1
g. himself with strength   BOOK 131:6
He g. up his loins   BIBLE 76:5
girdedst: thou g. thyself   BIBLE 98:2
girdeth: g. on his harness   BIBLE 76:9
girdle: bright g. furled   ARN 27:1
g. do the Gods inherit   SHAK 597:5
g. round about the earth   SHAK 611:18
g. when your hips stick   NASH 490:16
leathern g. about   BIBLE 88:14
girdled: g. with the gleaming world   TENN 686:1
girl: Above the staggering g.   YEATS 752:10
any good g. to be neat   TAYL 679:12
be quite loved by a g.   TROL 703:25
g. at an impressionable age   SPARK 658:6
g. graduates in their golden hair   TENN 687:24
g. in the indolence of youth   YEATS 752:16
g. needs good parents   TUCK 705:2
g. next door   AUDEN 35:9
g. throwing a ball   WOOLF 742:14
g. with brains   LOOS 428:8
I can't get no g. reaction   JAGG 361:11
Is an unlessoned g.   SHAK 609:2
no g. wants to laugh all time   LOOS 428:10
Once in a lifetime, do a g. in   ELIOT 272:18
policeman and a pretty g.   CHAP 190:9
Poor little rich g.   COW 220:16
pretty g. is like a melody   BERL 65:19
There was a little g.   LONG 428:5
To the sweetest g. I know   JUDGE 382:8
You speak like a green g.   SHAK 573:5
girlish: brim with g. glee   GILB 304:23
Laugh thy g. laughter   WATS 722:9
girls: Barring drink and g.   LOCK 425:16
g. and the lads   HOUS 352:11
G. aren't like that   AMIS 10:18
g. in slacks remember Dad   BETJ 67:4
g. that have no secret   SPEN 659:5
g. turn into American women   HAMP 323:3
g. who wear glasses   PARK 506:8
In Little G. is slamming Doors   BELL 61:7
like g. and roses   DE G 235:4
Men grow cold as g. grow old   ROBIN 542:7
not that g. should think   NAP 489:11
Of all the g. that are so smart   CAREY 179:18
rosebud garden of g.   TENN 686:19
rose-lipt g. are sleeping   HOUS 352:18
Secrets with g.   CRAB 225:10
gist: g. and sum of it   PARK 506:6
git: you've gut to g. up airly   LOW 429:15
give: freely g.   BIBLE 90:14
G., and it shall be given   BIBLE 94:7
g. and not to count cost   IGN 359:8
g. a war and nobody come   SAND 555:9
G. crowns and pounds   HOUS 352:9
G. him, he the more is craving   WROTH 749:14
G. me a look, give me a face   JONS 378:18
g. me back my legions   AUG 37:11

give: (cont.):
  G. me more love — CAREW 179:9
  'G. me,' quoth I — SHAK 600:1
  G. me yet before I die — WINC 739:2
  G. this man place — BIBLE 94:26
  G. to me the life I love — STEV 669:4
  g. to the poor — BIBLE 91:23
  g. up their liberties — BURKE 159:3
  G. us the tools — CHUR 202:15
  G. us this day our daily bread — BIBLE 89:5
  g. what you command — AUG 37:3
  I couldn't g. it up — BENC 62:12
  more blessed to g. than to receive — BIBLE 99:4
  receive but what we g. — COL 209:14
  She did not g. a singel dam — FLEM 286:19
  such as I have g. I thee — BIBLE 98:9
  What I desire to g. — SHAK 625:21
  which the world cannot g. — BOOK 119:10
  world giveth, g. I unto you — BIBLE 97:15
given: g. away by a novel — KEATS 392:8
  g. gladly not to be standing — JOHN 367:5
  g. me ever in my grey hairs — WOLS 741:21
  one that hath shall be g. — BIBLE 92:18
  sister is g. to government — DICK 240:26
  To whom nothing is g. — FIEL 282:4
giver: g. of all good things — BOOK 121:5
  God loveth a cheerful g. — BIBLE 101:21
  Lord and g. of life — BOOK 121:20
gives: He g. twice who g. soon — PUDL 531:2
  who ever g., takes liberty — DONNE 251:3
giving: g. and receiving of a Ring — BOOK 123:23
  Godlike like g. — ANON 13:20
  I am not in the g. vein to-day — SHAK 622:3
glacier: g. knocks in the cupboard — AUDEN 34:4
glad: G. did I live and gladly die — STEV 669:9
  g. green leaves like wings — HARDY 324:22
  g. me with its soft black eye — MOORE 483:14
  g. of other men's good — SHAK 569:1
  g. when they said unto me — BOOK 133:25
  I'm g. we've been bombed — ELIZ 275:2
  just g. to see me — WEST 729:12
  Never g. confident morning — BROW 151:2
  shew ourselves g. — BOOK 131:9
  solitary place shall be g. — BIBLE 83:19
  son maketh a g. father — BIBLE 78:20
  that maketh g. the heart — BOOK 132:8
  was made to make men g. — BIBLE 87:31
  will rejoice and be g. — BOOK 133:16
glade: alone in the bee-loud g. — YFATS 752:7
  That crown the wat'ry g. — GRAY 315:21
gladiators: g. of Rome — BORR 136:15
gladly: given g. not to be standing here — JOHN 367:5
  g. wolde he lerne — CHAU 192:21
gladness: anointed thee with g. — BOOK 127:11
  As with g. men of old — DIX 249:19
  he shareth in our g. — ALEX 8:14
  serve the Lord with g. — BIBLE 107:30
  serve the Lord with g. — BOOK 131:17
  shall obtain joy and g. — BIBLE 83:22
  solemn g. even crowned — TENN 683:13
  Teach me thy g. — SHEL 643:20
gladsome: g. light of Jurisprudence — COKE 208:18
  Let us with a g. mind — MILT 465:19
Gladstone: G. read Homer for fun — CHUR 203:2
  G. spent his declining years — SELL 562:26
  that Mr G. may perspire — CHUR 201:17
Glamis: G. hath murdered sleep — SHAK 602:3
  G. thou art, and Cawdor — SHAK 600:15
glamorous: made my life so g. — GERS 301:13
glamour: g. of childish days — LAWR 412:17
glance: g. from heaven to earth — SHAK 612:17
  g. of great politeness — BYRON 173:17
  g. of supernatural hate — BYRON 173:16
  O brightening g. — YEATS 759:18
  whose g. was glum — GILB 306:24
glassee: Phil g. a' Frindlaw looked — MAC 436:2
  strange unheavenly g — KRIU 141:1
  this merciless g. — WILL 737:8
  To protect you from the g. — COW 220:14
Glasgow: G. Empire on a Saturday — DODD 249:24

glass: double g. o' the inwariable — DICK 243:17
  broken g. to sweep away — FROST 294:9
  dome of many-coloured g. — SHEL 640:4
  families baying for broken g. — WAUGH 723:11
  Get thee g. eyes — SHAK 597:9
  g. I drink from — MUSS 488:14
  g. is falling hour by hour — MACN 440:15
  g. like unto crystal — BIBLE 106:10
  g. mingled with fire — BIBLE 107:6
  g. of blessings — HERB 335:14
  g. when I am shrinking — ANON 22:9
  grave saints, rigid in g. — THOM 694:9
  Grief with a g. that ran — SWIN 675:24
  hate you through the g. — BLUN 116:3
  He was indeed the g. — SHAK 583:7
  his natural face in a g. — BIBLE 104:27
  his own face in the g. — WILDE 735:15
  I look into my g. — HARDY 325:9
  itself in that eternal g. — GREV 318:7
  man that looks on g. — HERB 334:17
  No g. of ours was ever raised — HEAN 329:19
  prove an excuse for the g. — SHER 645:18
  Satire is a sort of g. — SWIFT 663:18
  she made mouths in a g. — SHAK 595:22
  Sound of Broken G. — BELL 61:21
  sun-comprehending g. — LARK 409:18
  through a g. darkly — BIBLE 101:1
  till I set you up a g. — SHAK 577:6
  To g. the opulent — HARDY 325:3
  turn down an empty g. — FITZ 284:17
  when he looked into the g. — DISR 248:19
glass-bottomed: sewer in a g. boat — MIZN 470:12
glasses: broke our painted g. — JORD 380:13
  Fill all the g. there — COWL 221:8
  girls who wear g. — PARK 506:8
  peeps over the g.' edge — BROW 148:10
  Such cruel g. — HOW 353:5
  with plenty of looking g. — ASHF 31:9
  Wiv a ladder and some g. — BAT 65:4
glasshouse: blood-coloured g. — HUGH 354:8
glassy: crowns around g. sea — HEBER 330:5
  g., cool, translucent wave — MILT 464:10
  Upon the g. plain — WORD 744:10
gle: wax, of gamyn and g. — WYNT 750:10
gleam: Follow The G. — TENN 687:8
  spent lights quiver and g. — ARN 27:8
  then I saw; and add the g. — WORD 743:11
gleamed: g. upon the glassy plain — WORD 744:10
gleaming: girdled with the g. world — TENN 686:1
gleams: with their convex g. — SHEL 640:7
gleaning: g. of the grapes — BIBLE 74:10
glee: At their tempestuous g. — LONG 427:14
  brim with girlish g. — GILB 304:23
  I watched with g. while — JAGG 361:14
  Piping songs of pleasant g. — BLAKE 113:16
glen: Down the rushy g. — ALL 10:1
glib: I want that g. and oily art — SHAK 594:21
gliding: But g. like a queen — SPEN 658:26
  g. adroitly to the front — STR 670:15
glimmering: Mere g. and decays — VAUG 709:6
  Now fades the g. landscape — GRAY 315:10
glimmers: like a ghost she g. — TENN 688:13
glimpse: g. of His bright face — VAUG 709:1
glimpses: g. of the moon — SHAK 573:9
  g. that would make me less — WORD 748:16
glittering: g. and sounding generalities — CHOA 200:2
  g. in the smokeless air — WORD 743:9
  g. prizes — SMITH 651:13
  He holds him with his g. eye — COL 210:19
  O how that g. taketh me — HERR 337:9
gloaming: In the g. — ORRED 499:9
  Roamin' in the g. — LAUD 411:7
global: image of a g. village — MCL 439:13
  We're g. from the start — REED 538:2
globe: g. of dead and halved — THOM 693:9
  great g. itself — SHAK 625:28
  rattle of a g. to play — DRYD 269:26
  sup of all this sordid g. — BLAK 627:8
  unhappy wealth of g. people — KEATS 389:8
globe-trotting: drawn'g, globe — YEATS 750:15
globule: atomic g. — THK 701:80

gloire: g. et repos sont choses — MONT 481:3
gloom: g. of earthquake — SHEL 642:25
  g. the dark broad seas — TENN 690:4
  inspissated g. — JOHN 373:4
  light to counterfeit a g. — MILT 464:22
  Our g.-pleased eyes — KEATS 390:14
  this mournful g. — MILT 468:11
glooms: Welcome, kindred g. — THOM 696:12
gloomy: fairer flower by g. Dis — MILT 471:4
  G. night embraced the place — CRAS 226:6
  Upon this g. scene — SHEL 643:6
gloria: G. in excelsis Deo — MISS 476:18
  G. Patri, et Filio — MISS 476:15
gloriam: Ad majorem Dei g. — ANON 22:1
  sed nomini tuo da g. — BIBLE 108:2
glories: g. and my state depose — SHAK 620:20
  G., like glow-worms — WEBS 725:21
  g. of our blood and state — SHIR 646:2
  in those weaker g. spy — VAUG 709:2
  its g. pass away — LYTE 433:16
glorious: but Tam was g. — BURNS 163:5
  daughter is all g. within — BOOK 127:13
  g. and the unknown — FORS 290:8
  G. things of thee are spoken — NEWT 494:9
  I'll make thee g. by my pen — GRAH 313:16
  King, all-g. above — GRANT 314:6
  most blessed, most g. — SMITH 653:31
  Mud! Mud! G. mud — FLAN 285:10
  reach at the g. gold — SHAK 587:14
  Sheds not its g. ray — MARR 449:1
  To combat may be g. — COWP 223:30
  'Twas Devon, g. Devon — BOUL 137:16
  What a g. morning is this — ADAMS 3:7
glory: All g., laud, and honour — NEALE 491:4
  all his g. was not arrayed — BIBLE 89:11
  all things give him g. — HOPK 346:16
  And g. shone around — TATE 678:18
  And into g. peep — VAUG 709:8
  And the g. of them — BIBLE 88:20
  away a g. from the earth — WORD 745:10
  brightness of his g. — BIBLE 104:10
  calls the g. from the grey — BROW 157:8
  count the g. of my crown — ELIZ 274:4
  crown him with g. — BOOK 124:20
  day of g. has arrived — ROUG 548:17
  declare the g. of God — BOOK 125:4
  deed is all, the g. nothing — GOET 309:7
  drowned my g. in shallow cup — FITZ 284:15
  earth is full of his g. — BIBLE 82:19
  eternal brood of g. — SPEN 659:26
  fierce wretchedness that g. — SHAK 626:14
  fill thy breast with g. — HERB 334:9
  find her flower, her g. — DAN 229:14
  For what g. is it — BIBLE 105:14
  from another star in g. — BIBLE 101:11
  full course of their g. — SHAK 587:4
  g. a bubble — SHEL 644:3
  gout and g. seat me there — BROW 154:9
  G. and loveliness — KEATS 390:26
  g. and nothing of name — BYRON 169:17
  g. and our absolute boast — WORD 747:1
  g. and shame — MILT 470:1
  g. and the dream — WORD 745:14
  g. and the freshness — WORD 745:10
  g. as of the only begotten — BIBLE 96:4
  G. be to God for dappled — HOPK 345:19
  G. be to the Father — BOOK 118:11
  g. dropped from their youth — BROW 153:5
  g. in the church by Christ — BIBLE 102:15
  g. in the name of Briton — GEOR 300:26
  g. is departed from Israel — BIBLE 74:32
  g. is not to be inferior — PER 512:24
  g. lead but to the grave — GRAY 315:13
  g. leads the way — LEE 416:3
  g., like the phoenix — BYRON 172:12
  g. nothing but success — LERM 418:13
  g. of Europe is extinguished — BURKE 158:13
  g. of Lord shall be revealed — BIBLE 83:26
  g. of man as the flower — BIBLE 105:9
  g. of rulers or of races — BEV 69:9
  g. of the Creator — BACON 41:17
  g. of the Lord is risen — BIBLE 84:25

glory: (cont.):
g. of the Lord shone round — BIBLE 93:26
g. of the winning — MER 458:5
g. of the world passes — THOM 692:3
g. of this world is appearance — BRAD 139:6
g. shineth in this face — SHAK 621:2
g. smeared in dust — SHAK 588:6
G., the grape — BYRON 170:19
G. to God in the highest — BIBLE 93:28
G. to Man in the highest — SWIN 676:19
G. to thee, my God — KEN 393:7
g. was I had such friends — YEATS 752:14
Heaven and earth full of thy g. — BOOK 122:10
his g. forth tell in deep tone — BAKER 47:21
hope of g. — BOOK 120:8
I felt it was g. — BYRON 173:9
I go to g. — DLINC 204:5
Is crowned with g. now — KELLY 393:4
it is a g. to her — BIBLE 100.34
King of g. shall come — BOOK 125:17
Land of Hope and G. — BENS 63:23
left him alone with his g. — WOLFE 740:26
looks on war as all g. — SHER 645:27
madness is the g. of this life — SHAK 626:9
Majesty: of thy G. — BOOK 118:12
mellow g. of the Attic stage — ARN 29:1
Mine eyes have seen the g. — HOWE 353:2
My gown of g. — RAL 535:18
no g. in the triumph — CORN 218:15
our best g. shall be sent — DAN 230:2
O what their joy and g. — ABEL 1:1
passes the g. of the world — ANON 22:15
peacock is the g. — BLAKE 112:24
power and g., or happiness — ARIS 25:11
sea of g. streams along — BYRON 169:1
short of the g. of God — BIBLE 99:22
There's g. for you — CARR 183:11
this g. unto ashes must — GREV 318:7
To the greater g. of God — ANON 22:1
to thy name give g. — BIBLE 108:2
trailing clouds of g. — WORD 745:14
unspeakable and full of g. — BIBLE 105:8
Vain pomp and g. of this — SHAK 588:19
vast g. of Trojans — VIRG 712:20
walked in g. and in joy — WORD 747:11
walking in an air of g. — VAUG 709:6
What price g. — ANDE 11:9
whose g. in their shame — BIBLE 103:10
Why in the name of G. were — KEATS 388:1
with g. not their own — WORD 747:4
yields the true g. — DRAKE 257:9
youth the days of our g. — BYRON 173:8
Gloucester: tailor in G. — POTT 525:10
thy name is G. — SHAK 597:10
Gloucestershire: stranger here in G.
— SHAK 619:19
glove: g. upon that hand — SHAK 622:28
gloves: capitalism with the g. — STOP 670:8
down the Strand with my g. — HARG 326:8
people in g. — CHES 199:2
through the fields in g. — CORN 219:4
glow: don thyn eris g. — CHAU 195:14
g. in the heart — CONR 217:17
her g. has warmed — STEV 667:3
glowing: g. like the vital morn — SHEL 640:8
Who many a g. kiss had won — HOOD 344:6
glow-worm: g. shows matin — SHAK 573:21
Her eyes the g. lend thee — HERR 336:18
glow-worms: Glories, like g. — WEBS 725:21
glozed: g. but superficially — SHAK 627:13
glubit: G. Remi nepotes — CAT 186:8
glut: g. thy sorrow on morning — KEATS 389:6
gluts: G. twice ten thousand — KEATS 390:6
glutton: g. of wordes — LANG 408:22
gluttons: g. dainties carving — ROB 542:16
gluve: played at the g. — BALL 49:3
Glyn: sin with Elinor G. — ANON 19:24
gnashing: g. of teeth — BIBLE 89:32
gnat: which strain at a g. — BIBLE 92:5
gnats: small g. mourn — KEATS 390:20
gnaw: g. you so your nether lip — SHAK 618:6
gnaweth: death g. upon them — BOOK 128:1
gnomes: little g. in Zurich — WILS 737:19

go: because I g. to the Father — BIBLE 97:20
better 'ole, g. to it — BAIR 47:18
boldly g. where no man — RODD 543:21
But I g. on for ever — TENN 680:12
come, and one to g. — CARR 183:17
could never g. back again — MORE 484:10
expedient for you that I g. — BIBLE 97:18
G. ahead, make my day — FINK 282:24
G., and catch a falling star — DONNE 252:14
G., and do thou likewise — BIBLE 94:16
G., and he goeth — BIBLE 89:30
g., and sin no more — BIBLE 96:31
G., and the Lord be with thee — BIBLE 75:2
g. anywhere I please — BEVIN 69:15
g. away is to die a little — HAR 323:8
G. down where lumps of lead — HODG 340:18
G. down, Moses — ANON 19:16
G., for they call you — ARN 28:2
g. into the house — BOOK 133:25
G., litel bok — CHAU 195:26
G., little book — STEV 669:8
G., lovely rose — WALL 718:9
Goodnight and g. to it — MORR 485:18
G. out into the highways — BIBLE 94:32
g. to him but he shall — BIBLE 75:13
g. to Innisfree — YEATS 752:7
G. to the ant thou sluggard — BIBLE 78:13
g. to the devil where — JOHN 370:24
g. unto the altar of God — BOOK 127:7
g. we know not where — SHAK 606:11
G. West, young man — GREE 316:15
G. ye into all the world — BIBLE 93:20
have no place to g. — WHIT 732:1
hell I g. — MILL 460:13
How you do g. it — BROWN 145:3
I can't g. on, I'll go on — BECK 57:18
I g. to glory — DUNC 264:5
I have a g., lady, don't I? — OSB 501:10
In the name of God, g. — CROM 227:10
I will not, cannot g. — BRON 142:11
I will not let me g. — BIBLE 71:18
I will not let thee g. — WESL 728:9
Let my people g. — BIBLE 72:5
Let us g. then, you and I — ELIOT 271:21
Must you g.? Can't you stay? — VAUG 708:12
neither g. nor hang — BIGOD 109:16
Nowhere to g. but out — KING 396:10
shalt thou g. and no further — PARN 507:7
so cheap a death, as saying, G. — DONNE 252:1
There g. the ships — BOOK 132:9
To g. away at any rate — ANON 16:12
unto Caesar shalt thou g. — BIBLE 99:9
we'll g. no more a-roving — BYRON 173:6
we think you ought to g. — RUB 549:16
what a Rum G. everything is — WELLS 727:18
Whither shall I g. then — BOOK 134:19
Will g. with thee along — HERR 337:4
with thee to g. is to stay — MILT 473:13
goads: words of wise are as g. — BIBLE 81:2
goal: g. of grief — RAL 535:14
moving freely without a g. — KLEE 402:20
Will be the final g. of ill — TENN 683:17
goals: muddied oafs at the g. — KIPL 399:13
'theories' and 'g.' — KIPL 399:12
They live by positive g. — BERL 66:1
goat: Gall of g. — SHAK 603:19
g. feet dance an antic hay — MARL 447:6
g. is the bounty — BLAKE 112:24
luxurious mountain g. — SHAK 586:12
sort of fleecy hairy g. — BELL 61:17
goatish: g. disposition — SHAK 595:2
goats: Cadwallader and his g. — SHAK 586:14
drink the blood of g. — BOOK 128:3
g. on the left — BIBLE 92:19
hair is as a flock of g. — BIBLE 81:13
refuge for the wild g. — BOOK 132:9
separate me from the g. — MISS 477:14
gobbledygoo: your g. — PLATH 516:4
goblet: navel like a round g. — BIBLE 82:2
upon a parcel-gilt g. — SHAK 583:4
goblin: health or g. damned — SHAK 573:9
goblins: one of sprites and g. — SHAK 631:17

God: acceptable unto G. — BIBLE 100:3
afraid to look upon G. — BIBLE 71:39
All praise to thee, my G. — KEN 393:7
among the children of G. — BIBLE 87:3
And others call it G. — CARR 184:9
angler, and now with G. — WALT 721:3
answering that of G. — FOX 292:3
apprehension how like a g. — SHAK 574:28
Assumes the g. — DRYD 259:17
atheist half believes a G. — YOUNG 754:19
attracted by G. — INGE 359:15
bell-rope that gathers G. — CRANE 225:17
best thing G. invents — BROW 149:24
bitter G. to follow — SWIN 676:20
But for the grace of G. — BRAD 139:2
By G. I mean a being — SPIN 661:2
By G.'s almighty hand — CAMP 176:4
by searching find out G. — BIBLE 77:17
Cabots talk only to G. — BOSS 137:1
cannot have G. for father — CYPR 229:8
cannot serve G. and mammon — BIBLE 89:8
children of G. — BIBLE 88:23
choose a Jewish G. — BROW 145:4
Church the further from G. — ANDR 11:14
common bush afire with G. — BROW 147:9
conscious water saw its G. — CRAS 226:2
course of Nature the art of G. — YOUNG 754:24
daughter of the voice of G. — WORD 746:9
Did not G. withhold in mercy — MORE 483:22
discover that there is no G. — SMITH 652:8
discussing their duty to G. — WHIT 732:18
doeth evil hath not seen G. — BIBLE 105:30
door-keeper in house of my G. — BOOK 130:18
doth G. respect any person — BIBLE 75:14
Doth Job fear G. for naught — BIBLE 77:1
dumb g. that giv'st — JONS 379:1
Ef you want to take in G. — LOW 429:15
either a beast or a g. — ARIS 25:16
end of our desires is G. — THOM 692:16
Enoch walked with G. — BIBLE 70:23
establishes the being of a g. — HUME 356:2
even G. was born too late — LOW 430:21
everyone understands to be G. — THOM 692:17
existence of transcendent g. — AYER 40:14
Fear G., and keep — BIBLE 81:4
Fear G. Honour the King — BIBLE 105:13
Fear G., take your own part — BORR 136:18
For G. hath made them — WATTS 722:15
For G.'s sake let's go — DONNE 253:6
for G. took him — BIBLE 70:23
forgotten before G. — BIBLE 94:22
forgotten even by G. — BROW 151:20
Freedom is the cause of G. — BOWL 138:16
From G., who is our home — WORD 745:14
from the love of G. — BIBLE 100:1
gift of G. may be purchased — BIBLE 98:14
glorify G. and to enjoy him — SHOR 646:7
G. all-bounteous, all-creative — SMART 649:9
G. and devil are fighting — DOST 254:3
G. and I both knew — KLOP 402:21
G. and nature do nothing — AUCT 33:16
G. and the doctor we alike — OWEN 503:8
G. be in my head — ANON 13:16
G. be merciful to a soul — ANON 22:9
G. be merciful to me a sinner — BIBLE 95:15
G. be thanked, the meanest — BROW 151:17
G. be thanked who matched — BROO 143:16
G. be with you, Balliol men — BELL 62:2
G. bless America — BERL 65:17
G. bless the child — HOL 342:1
G. bless the Prince of Wales — LINL 423:7
G. bless us every one — DICK 239:18
G. calleth preaching folly — HERB 334:10
G. Calls Me God — SAMP 554:16
G. came in unto the daughters — BIBLE 70:25
G. cannot alter the past — BUTL 166:23
G. cannot change the past — AGAT 5:15
G. can stand being told — PRIE 529:2
G. caught his eye — MCC 437:3
G. commonly gives riches — LUTH 432:16
G. created man — VALE 707:22
G. dawned on Chaos — SHEL 639:17

God: (*cont.*):

G. destroy man's nobility — BACON 42:24
G. disposes — THOM 692:6
G. does not play dice — EINS 268:2
G. doth not need either — MILT 474:24
G. erected into a system — GLAD 307:4
G. erects a house of prayer — DEFOE 234:19
G. forbid — BIBLE 95:19
G. forbid — BIBLE 99:27
G. forgot me, and I fell — BROW 148:19
G. fulfils himself in many — TENN 682:23
G. gave Noah rainbow sign — ANON 13:17
G. has any validity or use — BALD 48:5
G. has been replaced — BAR 51:16
G. has given good abilities — ARAB 24:5
G. has more right — JOHN 366:10
G. has written all — BUTL 167:2
G. hath also highly exalted — BIBLE 103:5
G. hath joined together — BIBLE 91:22
G. hath joined together — BOOK 123:22
G. hath joined together — SHAW 636:17
G. help the Minister — MELB 456:6
G., *Immortality, Duty* — ELIOT 270:4
G. in human form — BONH 118:2
G. in Three Persons — HEBER 330:5
G.-intoxicated man — NOV 497:4
G. is always in the majority — KNOX 403:3
G. is a Spirit — BIBLE 96:17
G. is beginning to resemble — HUXL 358:1
G. is blameless — PLATO 516:16
G. *is dead* — FROMM 294:7
G. is dead — NERV 492:1
G. is dead — NIET 495:9
G. is distant, difficult — HILL 338:11
G. is gone up on high — WESL 728:12
G. is his own interpreter — COWP 222:17
G. is in the midst of — BOOK 127:16
G. is just — JEFF 364:18
G. is love — BIBLE 105:27
G. is love, but get it in — LEE 415:15
G. is no respecter of persons — BIBLE 98:21
G. is not a man — BIBLE 73:9
G. is not mocked — BIBLE 102:8
G. is on everyone's side — ANOU 23:4
G. is only another artist — PIC 514:10
G. is on side of big squadrons — BUSS 165:19
G. is on side of the best shots — VOLT 716:20
G. is our hope and strength — BOOK 127:15
G. is subtle not malicious — EINS 268:1
G. is that great absence — THOM 694:14
G. is the Judge — BOOK 130:5
G. is the perfect poet — BROW 151:18
G. is Three, and God is One — NEWM 493:12
G. is thy law, thou mine — MILT 471:11
G. is working his purpose out — AING 6:3
G. knows where — BYRON 171:15
G. lost, hell found — ALAB 7:1
G. loveth, and to love — CHAU 195:15
G. made me to know Him — CAT 185:6
G. made the country — COWP 223:18
G. moves in a mysterious way — COWP 222:17
G. must think it exceedingly — KNOX 403:10
G. now accepteth thy works — BIBLE 80:19
G. numbered thy kingdom — BIBLE 85:31
G. of Abraham — PASC 508:1
G. of Bethel, by whose hand — DODD 250:3
G. of frostbite, God of famine — VYAZ 717:9
G. of gods appeareth — BOOK 130:17
G. of Jacob — BOOK 127:16
G. of life, and poesy — BYRON 169:11
G. of love my Shepherd — HERB 335:22
g. of love was born — DONNE 252:10
G. of Things as They are — KIPL 401:9
G., or in other words, Nature — SPIN 661:2
G. prepares evil — ANON 21:15
G. proved them — BIBLE 86:28
G. punish England — FUNKE 296:10
g. [assuming] the maiden hid — SWIN 675:23
[it] reigned from the wood — FORT 291:3
G. reigns, and if government — GARL 197:19
G. save king Solomon — BIBLE 75:01
G. save our gracious king — ANON 13:18
G. save the king — BIBLE 74:34

God: (*cont.*):

G. save the king — HOGG 341:17
G. save the king — SHAK 620:18
G. saw that it was good — BIBLE 69:22
g. self-slain on his own — SWIN 676:15
G. send every gentleman — BALL 50:19
G.'s first blunder — NIET 495:6
G.'s first Creature — BACON 45:17
G. shall give us his blessing — BOOK 129:5
G. shall wipe away all tears — BIBLE 106:23
G. shall wipe away all tears — BIBLE 107:18
G. si Love — FORS 290:27
G.'s in his heaven — BROW 151:28
G. so loved the world — BIBLE 96:15
G.'s own name upon a lie — COWP 223:14
G. spake all these words — BIBLE 72:16
G.'s revenge against vanity — FOOTE 288:18
G.'s sake look after our people — SCOTT 559:4
g. that he worships — SWIFT 673:9
G. the first garden made — COWL 221:9
G., to me, is a verb — FULL 296:1
G. unknown, He alone — BRID 141:2
G. was certainly not orthodox — STR 670:17
G. was very merciful — ANON 20:4
G. who is the ultimate — LEIB 416:13
G. who made thee mighty — BENS 63:23
G. whom he hath not seen — BIBLE 105:29
G. will grant an end — VIRG 712:5
G. will pardon me — HEINE 331:4
G. will provide himself — BIBLE 71:5
G. wills the things — LEIB 416:17
G. won't, and we can't mend it — CLOU 207:11
G. would destroy He first — DUP 264:8
G. would make man miserable — CHAR 191:14
good of G. to let Carlyle — BUTL 166:29
good to them that love G. — BIBLE 99:38
granted scarce to G. above — SPEN 660:25
Had G. on his side — DYLAN 265:24
Had I but served my G. — SHAK 589:2
hand into the Hand of G. — HASK 328:1
hands of the living G. — BIBLE 104:12
Have G. to be his guide — BUNY 156:10
Heart within, and G. o'erhead — LONG 427:9
he liveth unto G. — BIBLE 99:29
He sung of G. — SMART 649:17
he thinks little of G. — PLUT 517:15
He trusted in G. — BOOK 125:10
honest G. is the noblest — ING 360:7
Honest to G. — ROB 542:14
How do you know you're . . . G. — BARN 53:12
How odd of G. to choose — EWER 279:11
how should G. perceive it — BOOK 130:1
how you appear to G. — UNAM 707:3
I am a G. and cannot find it — SHEL 642:12
idea of G. — ELIOT 270:3
if a G. there be — SWIN 676:18
If G. be for us — BIBLE 99:39
If G. did not exist — VOLT 716:10
if G. talks to you — SZASZ 677:14
if G. wrote the bill — EMER 276:13
If it turns out there is a G. — ALLEN 9:12
if only G. would give sign — ALLEN 9:17
if there be a G. — ANON 17:2
in the sight of G. — BOOK 123:15
It's G. they ought to crucify — CART 184:12
justify the ways of G. — MILT 467:21
know his G. by night — VAUG 708:15
Knowledge makes a g. — KEATS 387:30
known to anyone except G. — SOCR 654:15
laboratory of G. — WILL 737:2
last and best of all G.'s works — MILT 472:25
lay wrestling with my G. — HOPK 345:8
leaping, and praising G. — BIBLE 98:10
leave the word of G. — BIBLE 98:11
Let G. arise — BOOK 129:4
Let G. be true — BIBLE 99:20
light but the shadow of G. — BROW 145:8
Like a g. he seems to me — CAT 186:7
little tribal G. — BURR 164:6
Lord G. made them all — ALEX 9:0
Lord G. of your fathers — BIBLE 71:42
[and I] will wipe — BIBLE 83:9
love of G. is shed abroad — BIBLE 99:10

God: (*cont.*):

make both G. and an idol — LUTH 432:14
maker and builder is G. — BIBLE 104:14
man be more just than G. — BIBLE 77:11
Man's word is G. in man — TENN 681:17
many are afraid of G. — LOCK 425:13
May G. us keep — BLAKE 112:11
May the Great G. — NELS 491:15
Men not afraid of G. — POPE 523:9
mills of G. grind slowly — LOGAU 426:4
my duty towards G. — BOOK 123:5
my flesh shall I see G. — BIBLE 77:25
My G. and King — HERB 334:7
My G., I love Thee — CASW 185:3
my G., look not so fierce — MARL 447:4
my G., look upon me — BOOK 125:9
My God, my G., why hast — BIBLE 93:5
my King and my G. — BOOK 130:16
My Lord and my G. — BIBLE 97:37
nature is the art of G. — BROW 146:7
nature of G. is a circle — ANON 16:17
Nearer, my G., to thee — ADAMS 3:10
nearer you are to G. — WOTT 749:8
neglect G. and his Angels — DONNE 253:9
next of course G. america — CUMM 228:6
noblest work of G. — BURNS 161:19
No man hath seen G. — BIBLE 96:5
none other but the house of G. — BIBLE 71:15
not the G. of Nature — HERB 335:15
Now G. be praised — WOLFE 741:3
O G., for as much as without — KNOX 403:9
Oh! for a closer walk with G. — COWP 222:22
One G., one law, one element — TENN 684:17
only G. can make a tree — KILM 396:3
Our G., our help in ages past — WATTS 723:7
Our G.'s forgotten — QUAH 530:3
Our sufficiency is of G. — BIBLE 101:16
peace of G. — JAM 362:6
Perfect G., and perfect Man — BOOK 119:15
power belongeth unto G. — BOOK 128:20
powers that be ordained of G. — BIBLE 100:8
presents the g. unshorn — HERR 336:9
presume not G. to scan — POPE 522:9
principle of G. to turn mind — FOX 292:4
Put on the whole armour of G. — BIBLE 102:26
put thy trust in G. — BOOK 127:8
Put your trust in G. — BLAC 110:9
ranks the same with G. — BROW 152:1
reader of the works of G. — COWP 223:27
Read G. aright — QUAR 534:3
reason and the will of G. — ARN 29:8
reserved for G. and angels — BACON 42:6
respect for the idea of G. — DUH 263:10
righteousness of G. — BIBLE 104:27
robbery to be equal with G. — BIBLE 103:4
sacraments to a dying g. — HEINE 331:2
safe stronghold our G. — LUTH 432:13
seek their meat from G. — BOOK 132:9
seen G. face to face — BIBLE 71:19
Sees G. in clouds — POPE 522:2
served G. as diligently — WOLS 741:5
shalt have one G. only — CLOU 207:16
she for G. in him — MILT 471:5
short of the glory of G. — BIBLE 99:22
soul and G. stand sure — BROW 152:10
spell G. with wrong blocks — ROB 542:12
spend and G. will send — GASC 298:16
Spirit of the Lord G. — BIBLE 84:26
spirit shall return unto G. — BIBLE 81:1
stamps him image of his G. — GRAI 314:5
Standeth G. within the shadow — LOW 430:4
Strong brother in G. — BELL 61:12
strong brown g. — ELIOT 271:2
suppose that G. is only — TEMP 680:5
Teach me, my G. and King — HERB 334:16
thank G. He has spared me — BELL 62:5
Thanks to G., I am still — BUÑ 155:12
that is really your G. — LUTH 432:15
that Thou, my G., art in't — HERR 337:5
that would circumvent G. — SHAK 578:20
There is no G — BOOK 124:26
There is no G. — CLOU 207:14
they shall see G. — BIBLE 88:25

God: (*cont.*):
think I am becoming a g.   VESP 710:10
think there is a G.   CLOU 207:15
this g. did shake   SHAK 590:1
this is G.'s hill   BOOK 129:9
thou art a direct G.   DONNE 253:3
thou being dead art a G.   SWIN 676:22
thou city of G.   BOOK 130:21
three-personed G.   DONNE 250:24
through darkness up to G.   TENN 683:21
through his garden walketh G.   BROW 153:3
throws himself on G.   BROW 150:1
thy God is a jealous G.   BIBLE 73:16
thy God my G.   BIBLE 74:25
Thy G. reigneth   BIBLE 84:8
To bring us, daily, nearer G.   KEBLE 392:20
To G. I speak Spanish   CHAR 191:21
To justify G.'s ways to man   HOUS 362:19
tomorrow long I to go to G.   MORE 484:16
To see G. only, I go out   DONNE 251:5
To the greater glory of G.   ANON 22:1
triangles were to make a G.   MONT 481:14
UNKNOWN G.   BIBLE 98:31
unto G. things that are G.'s   BIBLE 92:2
Verb is G.   HUGO 354:13
Very God of very G.   BOOK 121:19
voice of G.   POPE 523:2
voice of people the voice of G.   ALC 8:2
was a man sent from G.   BIBLE 96:1
We are the children of G.   BIBLE 99:36
We give thanks to G. always   BIBLE 103:19
Well, G.'s a good man   SHAK 614:7
we owe G. a death   SHAK 583:19
whan G. first maked man   CHAU 194:7
What G. abandoned   HOUS 351:22
What G. hath cleansed   BIBLE 98:20
What hath G. wrought   BIBLE 73:10
When G. at first made man   HERB 335:14
when G.'s the theme   SMART 650:4
when you've sung 'G. save   KIPL 398:11
Where G. paints the scenery   HART 327:13
Where is now thy G.   BOOK 127:5
Whose cause is G.   COWP 224:6
whose g. is in the skies   SHAW 637:29
Whose G. is their belly   BIBLE 103:10
who think not G. at all   MILT 474:6
Who trusted G. was love   TENN 683:22
Why, then, G.'s soldier   SHAK 605:5
wild beast, or a g.   BACON 43:20
with Eternal G. for power   TENN 687:18
with G. all things   BIBLE 91:26
with the grandeur of G.   HOPK 345:10
woman is the work of G.   BLAKE 112:24
Word was with G.   BIBLE 95:35
worship one G. in Trinity   BOOK 119:13
would G. this flesh of mine   SWIN 676:27
would know the mind of G.   HAWK 328:7
yearning like a G.   KEATS 387:2
ye believe in G.   BIBLE 97:10
you are a g.   ROST 548:13
your false g. are but a   VANZ 708:10
youth I remembered my G.   SOUT 657:14
God Almighty: G. first planted   BACON 43:24
G. would never have given   DEFOE 234:2
nobody cries, Hey for G.   KETT 394:14
Goddamm: Lhude sing G.   POUND 526:2
goddess: G., excellently bright   JONS 378:16
goddesses: immortal g.   HOMER 343:2
godfather: so noble a g.   SHAK 635:10
godfathers: G. and Godmothers   BOOK 123:3
These earthly g. of Heaven's   SHAK 598:7
godhead: g. was evident   VIRG 712:8
touching his G.   BOOK 119:15
godless: decent g. people   ELIOT 272:16
godliness: Church in continual g.   BOOK 121:9
Cleanliness next to g.   WESL 728:23
exercise thyself unto g.   BIBLE 104:1
godly: he ran his g. race   GOLD 310:9
live in unity and g. love   BOOK 121:22
may hereafter live a g.   BOOK 118:9
not one g. man left   BOOK 124:24
godmothers: Godfathers and G.   BOOK 123:3
Godot: We're waiting for G.   BECK 57:21

gods: By the Nine G. he swore   MAC 436:9
convenient that there be g.   OVID 502:15
daughter of the g.   TENN 680:20
decades for the g. they made   JAGG 361:14
dish fit for the g.   SHAK 590:18
first in the world made g.   JONS 378:25
fit love for g.   MILT 472:22
girdle do the G. inherit   SHAK 597:5
g. are come down to us   BIBLE 98:23
g. are on the side   TAC 678:5
g.' gifts wisely   HOR 350:19
g. have lost their way   ROET 544:8
g. of the countryside   VIRG 715:15
g., that mortal beauty chase   MARV 450:8
g. that the city recognizes   PLATO 516:9
G., that wanton in the air   LOV 429:1
g. themselves cannot recall   TENN 689:11
g. themselves struggle   SCH 558:3
g. thought otherwise   VIRG 713:1
g. who sits in your company   SAPP 556:1
g. wish to destroy   CONN 216:11
he creates g.   MONT 481:9
himself they are called g.   JAM 362:1
His death concerns the g.   SOPH 656:12
holy loved by the g.   PLATO 516:10
irregular worshipper of the g.   HOR 349:13
It lies in the lap of the g.   HOMER 343:10
Kings it makes g.   SHAK 622:8
leave the outcome to the G.   CORN 218:16
make the g. above relent   VIRG 714:3
May the g. avert this omen   CIC 204:9
nature gave birth to the G.   HOLB 341:20
not know much about g.   ELIOT 271:2
people clutching their g.   ELIOT 271:18
shalt have no other g.   BIBLE 72:16
So many g., so many creeds   WILC 734:8
These be thy g., O Israel   BIBLE 72:19
they first make g.   LEVIN 420:6
utterance of the early g.   KEATS 387:25
What men or g. are these?   KEATS 388:24
Whom the g. love dies young   MEN 457:2
woman a dish for the gods   SHAK 567:6
Ye are g.   BOOK 130:15
Ye shall be as g.   BIBLE 70:9
God's-Acre: burial-ground G.   LONG 426:22
goes: g. of a bund and comes   SHER 645:15
goest: g. whithersoever thou g.   BIBLE 73:27
whither thou g.   BIBLE 74:25
goeth: g. after her straightway   BIBLE 78:17
now g. on his way weeping   BOOK 134:5
Goethe: G. had an aversion   NERV 492:3
going: g. down of the sun   BINY 109:20
g. the way of all the earth   BIBLE 73:33
g. to and fro in the earth   BIBLE 76:37
He is gone, and we are g.   JOHN 368:16
Their g. hence   SHAK 597:15
tough get g.   KENN 394:10
upon the order of your g.   SHAK 603:12
were long and loath at g.   RANS 536:15
goings: ordered my g.   BOOK 126:24
goings-on: numberless g. of life   COL 210:4
gold: apples of g. in pictures   BIBLE 79:15
bringing g., and silver   BIBLE 75:25
builded over with pillars of g.   BLAKE 112:3
burned g. was his colour   CHAU 194:5
but litel in cofre   CHAU 192:20
city was pure g.   BIBLE 107:20
clothing is of wrought g.   BOOK 127:13
cursed craving for g.   VIRG 713:3
fetch the age of g.   MILT 467:8
fetters, though of g.   BACON 42:16
fly to India for g.   MARL 446:14
From the g. bar of Heaven   ROSS 547:14
get much g. by her   BIBLE 88:5
given of the g. of Arabia   BOOK 129:21
gleaming in purple and g.   BYRON 169:28
glistering g. but more to shine   BRAD 139:12
g., and frankincense   BIBLE 88:9
g. and silver becks me   SHAK 594:3
g. gathers light against it   POUND 526:8
g. kept by a devil   SHAK 583:27
G. never starts aside   GOOGE 312:11

gold: (*cont.*):
g. of obedience and incense   MONS 480:2
g. or gret richesse   LYDG 433:6
g. shines like fire blazing   PIND 514:13
G.? transient, shining trouble   GRAI 314:4
g. with plenty of looking   ASHF 31:9
hands are as g. rings   BIBLE 81:20
harpstring of g.   SWIN 676:20
heaven's pavement, trodden g.   MILT 469:4
her feathers like g.   BOOK 129:8
If g. ruste, what shall iren   CHAU 193:2
jewel of g. in a swine   BIBLE 78:23
little hands little g. head   MILNE 462:18
mankind upon a cross of g.   BRYAN 153:24
Meets the g. of the day   CROS 227:18
Monarchy is the g. filling   OSB 501:21
more desired are they than g.   BOOK 125:5
Nor all, that glisters, g.   GRAY 316:4
Oure g. wes changyd into lede   WYNT 750:10
Plate sin with g.   SHAK 597:8
prepared g. and amber   JONS 379:9
queen in a vesture of g.   BOOK 127:12
rarer gifts than g.   BROO 143:3
reach at the glorious g.   SHAK 587:14
realms of g.   KEATS 390:2
religion of g.   BAG 46:21
rottenness of eighty years in g.   BYRON 173:14
sand and ruin and g.   SWIN 677:5
streets are paved with g.   COLM 214:1
stuffed their mouths with g.   BEVAN 69:2
That seldom handles g.   DAV 232:13
this foul drain pure g.   TOCQ 699:8
This g., my dearest   LEAP 413:15
thousands of g. and silver   BOOK 133:19
To gild refinèd g.   BYRON 170:29
To gild refinèd g.   SHAK 594:9
what's become of all the g.   BROW 153:11
with patines of bright g.   SHAK 610:1
Would he have g.?   HERB 335:24
golden: after that sweet g. clime   BLAKE 114:5
Among her g. pillars high   BLAKE 112:4
chalices and g. priests   JEWEL 366:7
circle of the g. year   TENN 681:10
Clasped by the g. light   HOOD 344:6
days of g. dreams   BRON 142:17
fruit burnished with g. rind   MILT 471:2
girl-graduates in their g. hair   TENN 687:24
g. bowl   BLAKE 111:11
g. bowl be broken   BIBLE 81:1
g.-calf of self-love   CARL 180:3
g. crowns around the glassy   HEBER 330:5
g. days of Saturn's   VIRG 714:22
G. lads and girls all must   SHAK 571:16
g. locks time hath to silver   PEELE 511:5
g. mind stoops not to shows   SHAK 608:13
g. moments of our history   GLAD 307:16
G. opinions from all sorts   SHAK 601:4
G. Road to Samarkand   FLEC 286:11
g. years return   SHEL 640:15
good King Charles's g. days   ANON 15:5
hand that lays the g. egg   GOLD 312:4
Happy the g. mean   MASS 453:14
He has observed the g. rule   BLAKE 113:7
her g. entrails did espy   DRAY 258:3
I went into a g. land   TURN 705:15
Jerusalem the g.   NEALE 491:5
latch ter de g. gate   HARR 327:9
lift my lamp beside g. door   LAZ 413:7
Like g. lamps in a green night   MARV 449:19
Miles and miles of g. moss   AUDEN 34:11
round oak hangs g. chain   PUSH 533:4
Of g. sands, and crystal   DONNE 251:19
poets only deliver a g.   SIDN 647:6
poets took their g. age   THOM 695:23
Red hair she had and g. skin   BETJ 67:16
Roll down their g. sand   HEBER 330:3
safe in a g. ewer   BROW 149:6
seven g. candlesticks   BIBLE 105:35
shout to him g. shouts   MER 457:2
Someone who loves g. mean   HOR 349:18
they did in the g. world   SHAK 567:16
through forest with g. track   LIND 423:2

golden: (*cont.*):
wander in that g. maze — DRYD 261:18
We are g. — MITC 478:1
Golden Gate: west to the G. — KIPL 399:20
Goldengrove: Over G. unleaving — HOPK 346:2
Golden Vanity: by name of G. — BALL 49:10
Goldsmith: Here lies Nolly G. — GARR 298:5
This G.'s fine feast — GARR 298:7
To Oliver G., A Poet — JOHN 374:21
golf: American people than G. — ROG 544:19
g. may be played on Sunday — LEAC 413:14
thousand lost g. balls — ELIOT 272:16
too young to take up g. — ADAMS 2:4
Golgotha: field of G. — SHAK 620:17
memorize another G. — SHAK 599:16
gondola: Did'st ever see a g. — BYRON 167:21
g. of London — DISR 248:22
What else is like the g. — CLOU 207:10
gone: all are g. — LAMB 407:7
g.: aye, ages long ago — KEATS 387:12
G. before to that unknown — LAMB 407:6
G. far away into the silent — ROSS 547:5
g. from original righteousness — BOOK 135:23
g. here and there — SHAK 634:21
g. into the world of light — VAUG 709:5
g. to the demnition bow-wows — DICK 242:16
g. up with a merry noise — BOOK 127:20
g. with the wind — DOWS 256:2
He is g., and we are going — JOHN 368:16
I shan't be g. long — FROST 295:7
I would have thee g. — SHAK 623:7
lo, he was g. — BOOK 126:21
not dead—but g. before — ROG 544:12
Not lost but g. before — NORT 497:1
Now thou art g., and never — MILT 466:1
She's g. for ever — SHAK 597:21
something that is g. — WORD 745:14
There's a great spirit g. — SHAK 564:18
they are g. forever — MANN 444:12
welcomest when they are g. — SHAK 587:7
what haste I can to be g. — CROM 227:17
What's g. and past help — SHAK 631:22
Wilt thou be g.? — SHAK 623:22
gongs: g. groaning as the guns — CHES 199:4
struck regularly, like g. — COW 221:5
gong-tormented: that g. sea — YEATS 751:1
good: All g. things vanish — NASHE 490:23
annoyance of a g. example — TWAIN 706:23
another for the general G. — WELLS 727:19
Any g. of George the Third — LAND 408:8
apprehension of the g. — SHAK 619:14
Be g., sweet maid — KING 397:9
be g. than to be ugly — WILDE 735:20
being really g. all the time — WILDE 734:17
Beneath the g. how far — GRAY 316:9
best is the enemy of the g. — VOLT 716:6
better to fight for the g. — TENN 687:6
call a man a g. man — JOHN 376:9
choose the g. — BIBLE 82:24
common g. to all — SHAK 593:23
corrupt g. manners — BIBLE 101:10
country as g. as he had found — COBB 208:1
crown thy g. with brotherhood — BATES 55:5
discretion for the public g. — LOCKE 425:9
do g. and to communicate — BIBLE 104:23
Do g. by stealth — POPE 523:7
do g. to them which hate — BIBLE 94:6
Even in dreams g. works — CALD 175:3
evil and on the g. — BIBLE 88:34
Evil, be thou my g. — MILT 470:26
evil for g. — BOOK 126:16
evil good, and g. evil — BIBLE 82:17
evil turn to g. — MILT 473:11
For g. ye are and bad — TENN 681:28
f... m g will — WYATT 749:17
f... our country g — CART 184:11
Gallop about doing g. — JOHN 662:14
giver of all g things — BOOK 121:5
A... g.. t it was g. — BIBLE 69:22
g. action by stealth — LAMB 407:1
g. and bad at the same — WARLL ? ?
g. and bad of every land — BAIL 47:17
g and evil much they argued — MILT 470:1

good: (*cont.*):
g. and faithful servant — BIBLE 92:16
G., and great, I'm a Don — GODL 308:6
g. animal — SPEN 658:12
G., but not religious-good — HARDY 324:19
g. come of water and mud — BROO 143:7
g. compensate bad in man — BROW 152:22
g. deed in all my life — SHAK 627:3
g. deed in a naughty world — SHAK 610:4
g. die early — DEFOE 234:14
g. die first — WORD 743:18
g. ended happily — WILDE 734:16
g. enough to be a clergyman — JOHN 373:18
g. face is a letter — ADD 4:10
G. fences make g. neighbours — FROST 295:4
g. for a Pobble's toes — LEAR 414:16
g. for our country — WILS 737:18
g. for people — JAY 363:24
g. for that man if he had — BIBLE 92:24
g. for the people of England — GLAD 307:13
G., great and joyous — SHEL 642:20
g. he must be pole-axed — CHUR 203:4
g. in canvasses and factions — BACON 43:4
g. Indian is a dead Indian — SHER 644:19
g. in the country — WILDE 735:21
G. is best when soonest — SOUT 658:1
g. is but vain hope — TICH 698:3
G. is oft interrèd — SHAK 592:5
G. is That at which all — ARIS 25:7
g. man and a good citizen — AUCI 33:21
g. man is merciful — BOOK 133:6
g. man to do nothing — BURKE 160:4
g. minute goes — BROW 153:14
G. morning, gentlemen both — CARL 181:12
g. name rather to be chosen — BIBLE 79:10
g. never will be our task — MILT 468:7
G. of man is the active — ARIS 25:9
g. of man must be the end — ARIS 25:8
g. of one's country — FARQ 280:14
g. of subjects is the end — DEFOE 234:26
g. of the people — CIC 203:27
g. old Cause — MILT 476:2
g. or so bad as their opinions — MACK 439:5
g. people were clever — WORD 743:4
g. poet includes a critic — SHEN 644:17
g. provoke to harm — SHAK 606:18
g. still to find means — MILT 468:8
g. that I would I do not — BIBLE 99:32
g. they inculcate live after — SAKI 553:5
g. thing come out of Nazareth — BIBLE 96:8
g. thing left to me — MUSS 488:16
G. things of day begin — SHAK 603:5
g. time coming — SCOTT 560:31
g. time was had by all — SMITH 652:15
g. time who had been had — TYNAN 706:33
g. to be had in the country — HAZL 329:1
g. to cheat the pair — BROW 149:1
G., to forgive — BROW 150:18
g. to some man that can — SHAW 638:9
g. to them that love God — BIBLE 99:38
g. unluckily — STOP 670:5
g. will be the final goal of ill — TENN 683:17
g. will toward men — BIBLE 93:28
g. without qualification — KANT 385:5
g. woman if I had five — THAC 691:19
G. women always think — BROO 143:20
g. words, I think — SHAK 594:14
great who are truly g. — CHAP 191:1
g. want power — SHEL 642:11
half as g. — WHIT 733:12
hand hath made you g. — SHAK 606:12
Hanging is too g. for him — BUNY 165:9
hath this world's g. — BIBLE 105:26
heaviness foreruns the g. — SHAK 583:24
He was a g. man, and a just — BIBLE 95:29
He who would do g. — BLAKE 112:6
He wos wery g. to me — DICK 239:5
Her own g., oujol, or moral — MILL 460:15
hold fast that which is g. — BIBLE 103:23
it they have a g. thing — SHAK 582:23
Hillight. to a — MANN 444:11
in art the best in g thought — GOET 300:10

good: (*cont.*):
it cannot come to g. — SHAK 572:13
It's always the g. feel rotten — YES 754:2
I will be g. — VICT 710:15
I will call no being g. — MILL 460:13
kept the g. wine until now — BIBLE 96:11
knowing g. and evil — BIBLE 70:9
knowing g. by evil — MILT 475:6
Know their own g. — DRYD 262:4
luxury of doing g. — CRAB 225:7
Man is neither g. nor bad — BALZ 51:8
mankind does most g. or harm — BAG 47:13
man loves what he is g. — SHAD 563:16
much g. in the worst of us — ANON 18:13
much g. would be absent — THOM 693:1
never had it so g. — MACM 440:3
none that doeth g. — BOOK 124:26
not g. enough yourself — TROL 704:7
nothing either g. or bad — SHAK 574:26
Nothing we see means our g. — HERB 335:10
obscurely g. — ADD 3:22
Only g. and only true — BRID 141:2
overcome evil with g. — BIBLE 100:7
policy of the g. neighbour — ROOS 545:17
prospect of a distant g. — DRYD 260:25
rather than to seem g. — SALL 554:13
return g. for evil — VANB 708:2
Ring in the common love of g. — TENN 684:11
Roman Conquest a G. Thing — SELL 562:17
satisfieth thy mouth with g. — BOOK 132:3
scraps are g. deeds past — SHAK 627:19
see g. days — BOOK 126:15
Seek to be g. — LYTT 433:18
see your g. works — BIBLE 88:26
some future apparent g. — HOBB 340:2
sovereign g. of human nature — BACON 45:2
stars and isles where g. — FLEC 286:9
strong antipathy of g. — POPE 523:8
that doeth g. is of God — BIBLE 105:30
that g. may come — BIBLE 99:21
that is not g. company — AUST 39:5
that to the public g. — MILT 474:9
their luxury was doing g. — GARTH 298:14
things are of g. report — BIBLE 103:13
this woman was full of g. — BIBLE 98:18
those who go about doing g. — CREI 226:18
Time makes ancient g. — LOW 430:5
'Tis only noble to be g. — TENN 684:22
We are come for your g. — GEOR 300:24
We love, Fool, for the g. we do — PATM 509:10
What earthly g. can come of it — PARK 506:6
what g. came of it at last — SOUT 657:6
What's g., and doth no good — RAL 535:15
When he said a g. thing — TWAIN 706:16
when shall all men's g. be — TENN 681:9
When she was g. — LONG 428:5
while g. news baits — MILT 474.13
Whom no ills from g. dissuade — SMART 649:9
worst speaks something g. — HERB 334:10
good-bye: G., moralitee — HERB 333:17
G., Piccadilly — JUDGE 382:8
G., proud world! — EMER 276:8
G. to all — GRAV 315:3
kissed his sad Andromache g. — CORN 219:3
good-bye-ee: G.! — G.! — WEST 729:21
goodliness: g. is as the flower — BIBLE 83:27
goodly: g. fellowship of the Prophets — BOOK 118:12
g. to look to — BIBLE 74:39
I have a g. heritage — BOOK 124:30
goodman: g. is not at home — BIBLE 78:16
good morrow: I bade g. — KEATS 386:18
now g. to our waking souls — DONNE 252:5
goodness: And g. only knowses — CHES 199:11
fountain of all g. — BOOK 119:7
g. entirely human — ELIOT 270:3
G. had nothing to do with it — WEST 729:11
G. is not the same thing — PLATO 516:15
g. never fearful — SHAK 606:13
g. of the Lord in the land of — BOOK 126:1
If g. lead him not — HERB 335:16
inclination to g. — BACON 43:25
long-suffering, and of great g. — BOOK 132:4

graves: (*cont.*):
they watch from their g. BROW 151:1
graveyards: no bone to pick with g. BECK 57:15
signs on the foxholes or g. KENN 394:5
gravity: g., profound conceit SHAK 607:6
old man's g. JONS 378:7
reasons find of settled g. SHAK 633:15
strong impulsive g. of head POPE 518:23
What doth g. out of his bed SHAK 580:26
gravy: g. with the spoon RAL 536:11
It's the rich wot gets the g. ANON 17:20
Gray: G.'s Elegy WOLFE 741:2
Graymalkin: I come, G. SHAK 599:13
graze: not allow him to g. there VERW 710:8
grease: slides by on g. LOW 430:11
greasy: top of the g. pole DISR 249:7
great: aim not to be g. LYTT 433:18
All creatures g. and small ALEX 8:9
All g. men make mistakes CHUR 201:22
All things both g. and small COL 211:17
between the small and g. COWP 224:12
But he is always g. DRYD 262:11
compare small things with g. VIRG 715:19
craven fears of being g. TENN 681:13
darkly wise, and rudely g. POPE 522:9
desireth g. matters QUAR 533:15
far above the g. GRAY 316:9
few really g. novelists LEAV 415:4
forgive Thy g. big one on me FROST 294:13
For he was g., ere fortune DRYD 260:18
g. a matter a little fire BIBLE 105:1
G. and good is the typical GODL 308:6
g. a thing has happened WHIT 731:17
g. break through SHEN 644:14
g. deep to the great deep TENN 681:20
G., Good and Just GRAH 313:13
G. hatred, little room YEATS 752:19
g. have kindness in reserve POPE 520:1
g. illusion ANG 11:15
G. is Diana of the Ephesians BIBLE 99:2
G. is the hand that holds THOM 693:10
g. is to be misunderstood EMER 277:3
g. is truth BROO 144:5
g. life if you don't weaken BUCH 154:1
g. man he grovelled before THAC 691:11
g. man helped the poor MAC 436:12
g. man nowadays WILDE 735:1
g. men are but labels TOLS 700:11
G. men are not always wise BIBLE 77:32
g. men contending BURT 165:2
g. no heart LA BR 405:1
g. objects make g. minds YOUNG 754:23
g. ones devoured the small SIDN 646:10
g. party not to be brought down HAIL 321:1
g. seemed to him little MAC 435:7
g. than ever pencil drew BEAT 56:5
G. Villiers lies POPE 520:18
g. was the fall of it BIBLE 89:27
How very small the very g. THAC 691:22
it kindles the g. BUSS 165:18
know well I am not g. TENN 682:1
lay g. and greatly fallen HOMER 343:9
Lives of g. men all remind us LONG 427:10
made g. is a name destroyed HILL 339:1
Man is only truly g. when DISR 248:9
many people think him g. JOHN 373:26
most g. to them that know SPR 661:9
None think the g. unhappy YOUNG 754:7
our hearts are g. TENN 682:7
Rightly to be g. SHAK 577:33
some men are born g. SHAK 630:4
That he is grown so g. SHAK 590:4
there is a g. gulf fixed BIBLE 95:10
there is nothing g. but man HAM 322:13
those who were truly g. SPEN 659:1
though fallen, g. BYRON 168:9
thou wouldst be g. SHAK 600:15
truly g. who are truly good CHAP 191:1
upward to the G. Society JOHN 367:8
with small men no g. thing MILL 460:20
Great Britain: G. going to make war BETH 67:2
G. has lost an empire ACH 1:6
G. should free herself SMITH 651:5

Great Britain: (*cont.*):
seem to be natives of G. CHES 198:17
greater: behold a g. than themselves SHAK 590:7
g. glory dim the less SHAK 610:4
G. love hath no man BIBLE 97:16
G. love than this JOYCE 382:5
g. man, greater courtesy TENN 682:6
g. prey upon the less GREEN 316:17
g. than a private citizen TAC 678:3
g. than Solomon is here BIBLE 90:35
half is g. than the whole HES 337:14
sing of rather g. things VIRG 714:22
that he is g. than they RUSK 551:1
Thy necessity is yet g. SIDN 647:12
we are g., than we know WORD 747:15
greatest: g. event it is that ever FOX 291:18
g. happiness for g. numbers HUTC 357:6
g. happiness principle CARL 180:13
g. thing in the world MONT 481:2
happiness of the g. number BENT 64:4
great-hearted: G. gentlemen BROW 151:5
greatly: g. to his credit GILB 306:4
who would g. win BYRON 172:20
greatness: all g. not to be exact BURKE 157:15
farewell, to all my g. SHAK 588:19
G. knows itself SHAK 581:26
g. of the British Nation ADD 4:15
g. thrust upon them SHAK 630:4
g. within them do not go CAMUS 177:11
G., with private men MASS 453:14
having intended g. for men ELIOT 269:21
moment of my g. flicker ELIOT 272:4
No g., save it be some far-off TENN 682:1
Pray God our g. may not fail TENN 681:13
sublime and celestial g. TRAH 701:10
Than g. going off SHAK 566:5
under the shade of g. MARS 449:10
greaves: flamed upon brazen g. TENN 685:2
Greece: constitutions of later G. BAG 47:3
Fair G.! sad relic of departed BYRON 168:9
For G. a tear BYRON 171:2
G. is fallen and Troy town COL 209:8
isles of G., the isles of G.! BYRON 170:30
that G. might still be free BYRON 171:1
To Gaul, to G. COWP 223:10
greed: enough for everyone's g. BUCH 154:6
greediness: with how much g. WITH 739:13
greedy: G. for the property of SALL 554:11
not g. of filthy lucre BIBLE 103:26
thank goodness, I am g. PUNCH 531:25
Greek: brown G. manuscripts BROW 148:17
can say a word against G. SHAW 636:28
carve in Latin or in G. WALL 718:11
it was G. to me SHAK 590:9
little G. can do everything JUV 383:20
loving, natural, and G. BYRON 170:21
neither G. nor Jew BIBLE 103:16
not G. in its origin MAINE 442:13
pay at the G. Kalends AUG 37:14
small Latin, and less G. JONS 380:3
straw for G. particles HUGH 354:10
study of G. literature GAIS 296:15
That questioned him in G. CARR 184:8
Greeks: debtor both to the G. BIBLE 99:15
fear G. when they bring gifts VIRG 712:14
For G. a blush BYRON 171:2
G. had a word for it AKINS 6:13
G. take the beating HOR 348:2
Let G. be Greeks BRAD 139:11
make way, G.! PROP 530:2
When G. joined Greeks LEE 416:5
green: As g. as emerald COL 210:21
believed in the g. light FITZ 285:4
bordered by its gardens g. MORR 485:12
By slow Meander's margent g. MILT 463:22
children are heard on the g. BLAKE 114:2
Colourless g. ideas sleep CHOM 200:3
day was g. STEV 665:22
Drives my g. age THOM 693:7
feed me in a g. pasture BOOK 125:14
Flora and the country g. KEATS 389:9
g. and pleasant bowers BLAKE 112:9

green: (*cont.*):
g. and pleasant land BLAKE 113:4
g. arms round the bosom SHEL 642:22
g. banks of Shannon CAMP 176:13
g. buds they were swellin' BALL 48:21
g. casque has outdone POUND 527:7
g. days in forests STEV 668:24
g. days telling QUIL 534:11
G. grow the rashes, O BURNS 162:1
G. grow the rushes O ANON 15:5
g. herb for the service BOOK 132:8
G. how I love you green GARC 297:13
golden lamps in a g. night MARV 449:19
g. lap of the new SHAK 621:8
g. lap was Nature's darling GRAY 316:6
g. mantle of standing pool SHAK 596:14
G. pleasure or grey grief SWIN 677:1
g. swell is in the havens HOPK 345:14
G. Things upon the Earth BOOK 118:20
g. thought in a green shade MARV 450:11
Her g. lap immense WALK 717:14
How g. was my valley LLEW 423:14
In a harbour g. WEVER 730:1
In the morning it is g. BOOK 130:23
laid him on the g. BALL 49:2
laughs to see the g. man HOFF 341:8
look so g. and pale SHAK 601:5
Making the g. one red SHAK 602:6
Not for ever in g. pastures WILL 737:14
on a simple village g. TENN 683:25
On the dry smooth-shaven g. MILT 464:20
pierced the tender g. SACK 552:12
Praise the g. earth BUNT 155:8
springs ever g. GOET 309:5
summer's g. all girded SHAK 633:4
sun doth parch the g. SURR 672:4
There is a g. hill far away ALEX 8:16
these things in a g. tree BIBLE 95:24
Time held me g. and dying THOM 693:6
wearin' o' the G. ANON 15:4
When I was g. in judgement SHAK 565:3
when the trees were g. CLARE 204:17
When wheat is g. SHAK 610:24
Wherever g. is worn YEATS 751:15
green-coat: sleepy, g. man HOFF 341:9
greener: What is g. than grass BALL 50:7
greenery: In a mountain g. HART 327:13
greenery-yallery: g., Grosvenor Gallery GILB 305:21
green-eyed: g. monster SHAK 616:13
greening: g. of America REICH 538:14
Greenland: G.'s icy mountains HEBER 330:3
greenly: We have done but g. SHAK 578:4
greenness: recovered g. HERB 335:2
rust amid g. MELV 456:19
greens: healing g. ABSE 1:2
Greensleeves: G. was all my joy ANON 13:22
greenwood: I must to the g. go BALL 50:4
Under the g. tree SHAK 568:8
greet: G. the unseen with a cheer BROW 148:7
How should I g. thee BYRON 173:21
scarely g. me with that sun SHAK 633:15
Greise: *mancher Kopf zum* G. MÜLL 487:16
grenadier: British G. ANON 18:3
grenadiers: Pensions and G. STER 664:28
Grenville: Sir Richard G. lay TENN 689:1
Grenzen: G. meiner Sprache WITT 740:5
Greta: G. woods are green SCOTT 560:12
greuaunce: Comparisouns doon ofte
gret g. LYDG 433:4
grew: a gallows g. KYD 404:15
So we g. together SHAK 612:3
grey: calls glory from g. BROW 152:8
given me over in my g. WOLS 741:21
Green pleasure or g. grief SWIN 677:1
g. and full of sleep YEATS 753:19
g. hairs with sorrow BIBLE 71:29
G. leaves thick-furred SITW 648:11
G. silent fragments HUGH 354:5
head grown g. in vain SHEL 640:1
lend me your g. mare BALL 51:4
little g. cells CHR 200:8
philosophy paints its g. HEGEL 330:10

grey: (*cont.*):
  suddenly grow g. with fear　SHEL 641:17
  this old g. head　WHIT 733:6
  world has grown g.　SWIN 676:21
greyhound: g. did proffer me　SHAK 580:2
greyhounds: like g. in the slips　SHAK 585:10
grief: acquainted with g.　BIBLE 84:11
  After long g. and pain　TENN 686:21
  As full of g. as age　SHAK 595:17
  As is my g.　SHAK 620:11
  Can I see another's g.　BLAKE 114:3
  every one can master a g.　SHAK 613:32
  father's shame, mother's g.　BRET 140:17
  feel the g. I did sustain　CONS 217:20
  Green pleasure or grey g.　SWIN 677:1
  G. and avenging Cares　VIRG 713:14
  G. fills the room up　SHAK 594:4
  g. flieth to it　BACON 43:9
  G. for awhile is blind　SHEL 642:9
  G. for thy dead in silence　BROW 147:14
  g. for which the wisest　RAL 535:14
  g. hiding his harmful guile　SPEN 659:27
  G. is a species of idleness　JOHN 368:15
  G. is itself a med'cine　COWP 221:26
  g. itself be mortal　SHEL 639:18
  g. returns with the revolving　SHEL 639:16
  g. that does not speak　SHAK 604:8
  g. too much to be told　VIRG 712:12
  G. with a glass that ran　SWIN 675:24
  hopeless g. is passionless　BROW 147:13
  I am g. I am the tongue　VOZN 717:8
  into the bottom of my g.　SHAK 623:26
  it was pain and g.　BOOK 126:22
  journeyman to g.　SHAK 619:12
  Killing care and g. of heart　SHAK 588:16
  My g. to thy too rigid fate　GRAH 313:13
  My particular g.　SHAK 614:29
  Of g. I died　ROET 544:10
  open his g.　BOOK 122:4
  Patch g. with proverbs　SHAK 614:12
  Pitched past pitch of g.　HOPK 345:16
  plague of sighing and g.　SHAK 580:27
  quickened so with g.　GRAV 314:20
  Should be past g.　SHAK 631:22
  shows of g.　SHAK 572:10
  Silence augmenteth g.　DYER 264:14
  silent manliness of g.　GOLD 310:17
  Smiling at g.　SHAK 629:20
  Thine be the g.　AYT 41:1
  thirsty g. in wine we steep　LOV 429:3
  thy mother's g.　BLAKE 111:5
  time remembered is g.　SWIN 675:22
  To cure this deadly g.　SHAK 604:9
  unmanly g.　SHAK 572:11
  with forethought of g.　BERRY 66:13
  within their breasts the g.　AYT 41:4
  you must first feel g.　HOR 347:9
griefs: all g. which bow　ARN 28:13
  cutteth g. in halves　BACON 43:22
  Drinking my g.　SHAK 620:19
  ease then of their g.　SHAK 626:20
  ere England's g. began　GOLD 310:6
  Great g., I see　SHAK 571:13
  g. of forty generations　MAC 435:18
  g. that harrass the distressed　JOHN 370:8
  I am sick of many g.　SHAK 593:10
  isolation and the busy g.　AUDEN 34:14
  my state depose, but not my g.　SHAK 620:20
  so are their g. and fears　BACON 44:11
  solitary g.　JOHN 367:3
  Surely he hath borne our g.　BIBLE 84:11
grievances: g. bare-headed　MAND 444:5
grieve: g. at my declining fall　MARL 447:8
  lose, g. or triumph　GOET 309:9
  make the judicious g.　SHAK 576:6
  Nor joy nor g. too much　DRYD 261:13
  Poor Pope will g. a month　SWIFT 670:11
  than a nation g.　DIJ 096:6
  thou leavest me to g.　CHEF 643:25
  what could it g.　KEATS 382:31
grieved: g. with this generation　BOOK 121:10
grieves: g. not and never hopes　MARK 446:7
grieving: Márgarét, áre you g.　HOPK 346:2

grievous: g. crab-tree cudgel　BUTV 166:3
  of all things the most g.　TROL 703:16
  remembrance of them is g.　BOOK 122:6
  through my most g. fault　MISS 476:16
Griffith: honest chronicler as G.　SHAK 589:12
grill: Let Grill be G.　SPEN 660:7
grim: Ay, there, look g. as hell　SHAK 617:15
  g. grew his countenance　BALL 49:5
  Thou hast a g. appearance　SHAK 570:17
grimace: Of its accelerated g.　POUND 526:13
grimness: what element of g.　ARN 29:16
grin: backward with a lipless g.　ELIOT 273:15
  How cheerfully he seems to g.　CARR 182:1
  Relaxed into a universal g.　COWP 224:1
  wears one universal g.　FIEL 282:16
grind: bastards g. you down　ANON 16:19
  g. in the prison house　BIBLE 74:20
  g. the faces of the poor　BIBLE 82:12
  Laws g. the poor　GOLD 311:11
  mills of God g. slowly　LOGAU 426:4
  My life is one demd horrid g.　DICK 242:15
grinders: incisors and g.　BAG 47:10
  g. cease　BIBLE 81:1
grinding: some g. monopoly　MARS 449:10
grinning: such g. honour　SHAK 582:4
grip: With a g. that kills it　TAG 678:6
Grishkin: G. is nice　ELIOT 273:16
Grisilde: G. is deed　CHAU 193:10
groan: bitter g. of martyr's woe　BLAKE 112:5
  Condemned alike to g.　GRAY 316:3
  depths with bubbling g.　BYRON 169:15
  g. and shake their fists　HOUS 351:13
  hear each other g.　KEATS 389:10
groaneth: creation g.　BIBLE 99:37
groaning: g. for burial　SHAK 591:24
  kill sick people g.　MARL 447:14
  weary of my g.　BOOK 124:18
groans: converse with everlasting g.　MILT 469:15
  g. of love to those of dying　LOWRY 431:3
  sovereign of sighs and g.　SHAK 598:13
groined: titanic wars had g.　OWEN 503:18
Gromboolian: great G. plain　LEAR 413:20
groom: death is but a g.　DONNE 251:9
grooms: gild faces of g.　SHAK 602:4
grooves: In determinate g.　HARE 326:7
  ringing of change　TENN 685:19
grope: buildings g. the sky　AUDEN 36:1
gross: g. as a mountain　SHAK 580:21
  Not g. to sink　SHAK 635:12
  things rank and g.　SHAK 572:12
grosser: your g. reminiscences　WOOL 742:17
grossness: g. with fair ornament　SHAK 608:26
Grosvenor Gallery: greenery-yallery, G.　GILB 305:21
grotesque: ambushed by a g.　STOP 670:2
Groucho: G. tendency　ANON 20:13
ground: acre of barren g.　SHAK 624:28
  Betwixt the stirrup and the g.　CAMD 176:15
  Chosen and made peculiar g.　WATTS 723:1
  commit his body to the g.　BOOK 124:5
  crieth unto me from the g.　BIBLE 70:19
  fallen unto me in a fair g.　BOOK 124:30
  gain a little patch of g.　SHAK 577:30
  Grammer, the g. of al　LANG 409:4
  G. control to Major Tom　BOWIE 138:15
  g. I se thee stare　CHAU 194:16
  g. maintained its man　GOLD 310:6
  g. to fight their battle　SCOTT 561:5
  g. won to-day　ARN 28:8
  here at last on the g.　SOND 656:2
  He swalloweth the g.　BIBLE 77:39
  holy g.　BIBLE 71:38
  In his own g.　POPE 523:11
  let us sit upon the g.　SHAK 620:8
  other fell into good g.　BIBLE 91:1
  seek the g. of my heart　BOOK 134:22
  keep feet of English g.　HAR 326:14
  should see no traces on the g.　GNOS 319:1
  They till the g. the books　DIJAK 598:19
  wood the classic g.　ADD 4:?
  water spilt on the g.　BIBLE 75:44

ground: (*cont.*):
  when I hit the g.　SPR 661:13
  will hardly water the g.　BACON 44:4
grouse: g. against life　ELIOT 273:24
grove: deep windings of the g.　BEAT 50:0
  good g. of chimneys　MORR 485:4
  olive g. of Academe　MILT 473:20
grovelled: he g. before him　THAC 691:13
groves: forsake her Cyprian g.　DRYD 260:34
  g. of Academe　HOR 348:19
  g. of their academy　BURKE 158:16
  G. whose rich trees wept　MILT 471:2
  whispering g.　THOM 696:16
grow: g. for ever　TENN 688:2
  g. up with the country　GREE 316:15
  hand wrought to make it g.　FITZ 284:2
  I g. in worth, and wit　TENN 690:6
  that ye may g. thereby　BIBLE 105:10
  then I should g. to fruit　HERB 334:4
  They shall g. not old　BINY 109:20
growed: I s'pect I g.　STOWE 670:10
growing: It is not g. like a tree　JONS 379:21
growl: but sit and g.　JOHN 376:2
grown: g. accustomed to her face　LERN 419:4
  When I am g. to man's estate　STEV 668:16
grows: g. beyond his work　STEI 663:8
growth: children of a larger g.　CHES 198:16
  children of a larger g.　DRYD 260:1
  genuine g. in the individual　SMIL 650:9
  quick g. to meet decay　HERR 337:4
  their g., their manhood　LAND 408:11
grub: old ones, g.　SHAW 635:22
grubs: Paradisal g. are found　BROO 143:8
grudge: ancient g. I bear him　SHAK 607:20
gruel: Make the g. thick　SHAK 603:19
grumbling: rhythmical g.　ELIOT 273:24
Grundy: And more of Mrs G.　LOCK 425:13
  What will Mrs G. think　MORT 486:19
gruntled: far from being g.　WOD 740:9
guard: Be on your g.　ANON 21:6
  g. a title that was rich　SHAK 594:9
  G. us, guide us, keep us　EDM 266:17
  Must g. themselves　LARK 409:19
guarda: *di lor, ma g., e passa*　DANTE 230:7
guardian: Be thou my G.　WILL 736:23
  Thou G. of my soul　BODE 116:11
guardians: good grey g. of art　MERR 458:12
guards: G. die but do not　CAMB 176:1
  Up G. and at them!　WELL 727:3
guardsman: g.'s cut and thrust　HUXL 358:4
gudeman: When our g.'s awa　MICK 459:10
gudgeon: For this fool g.　SHAK 607:7
guenille: *ma g. m'est chère*　MOL 478:23
guerdon: But the fair g.　MILT 468:4
guerre: *Je fais toujours la g.*　CLEM 206:6
  mais ce n'est pas la g.　BOSQ 136:19
guess: G. now who holds thee　BROW 147:18
guessing: G. so much　CHES 199:2
  g. what was at other side　WELL 727:1
  It's better only g.　CLOU 207:14
guest: Earth, receive an honoured g.　AUDEN 34:15
  Go, Soul, the body's g.　RAL 535:15
  Invites heart to be chiefest g.　DRAY 257:20
  I too awaited the expected g.　ELIOT 273:9
  Like some poor nigh-related g.　COL 211:25
  remembrance of g. that tarrieth　BIBLE 87:5
  second inn, built by the g.　DONNE 251:13
  slightly shakes his parting g.　SHAK 627:21
  Some second g. to entertain　DONNE 252:13
  speed the going g.　POPE 522:24
  unexpected and uninvited g.　TURG 705:4
  worthy bidden g.　MILT 466:8
  your g. tomorrow night　ANON 20:2
guests: g. star-scattered　FITZ 284:17
  my g. should praise it　HAR 326:11
  two classes: hosts and g.　BEER 59:8
  Unbidden g.　SHAK 587:7
guide: being our ruler and g.　BOOK 121:2
  g. our feet　BIBLE 93:24
  g. what goes off the road　LANG 409:9
  G. where our Infant Redeemer　HEBER 330:2
  Have God to be his g.　BUNY 156:10

guide: (*cont.*):
None need a g. — PUPE 518:23
probability in the very g. — BUTL 165:21
Who art a light to g. — WORD 746:9
guided: g. by wiser — CARL 180:1
g. missiles and misguided — KING 397:3
guides: G. us by vanities — ELIOT 271:11
Ye blind g. — BIBLE 92:5
guiding: Did the g. star behold — DIX 249:19
g. star of a whole brave nation — MOTL 487:3
guile: hiding his harmful g. — SPEN 659:27
in whom is no g. — BIBLE 96:9
in whose spirit there is no g. — BOOK 126:8
packed with g. — BROO 143:13
that they speak no g. — BOOK 126:15
guilt: blood with g. is bought — SHEL 642:10
Cleanse me from its g. — TOPL 701:4
For it must seem their g. — SHAK 602:4
free from g. or pain — SHEL 642:18
g. at the obligation she owes — LAING 405:20
G. in his heart, and famine — CHUR 201:10
Image of war, without its g. — SOM 655:12
Life without industry is g. — RUSK 550:12
pens dwell on g. and misery — AUST 38:20
punishment of his g. — CURR 229:4
put on a dress of g. — MCG 438:1
sign of g. or ill breeding — CONG 215:30
unfortunate circumstance of g. — STEV 668:9
What art can wash her g. away — GOLD 311:33
guiltier: G. than him they try — SHAK 605:12
guiltless: will not hold him g. — BIBLE 72:16
guilts: Close pent-up g. — SHAK 596:1
guilty: crimes of this g. land — BROWN 144:14
g. creatures sitting — SHAK 575:13
g. man is acquitted if — JUV 384:12
G. of dust and sin — HERB 335:8
g. of our own disasters — SHAK 595:2
g. party is acquitted — PUBL 531:3
g. persons escape — BLAC 110:14
Let no g. man escape — GRANT 314:11
like a g. thing surprised — WORD 746:3
Make mad the g. — SHAK 575:9
Mortal, g., but to me — AUDEN 35:5
started like a g. thing — SHAK 572:1
Suspicion always haunts the g. — SHAK 588:7
guinea: g. helps the hurt — TENN 685:12
g. pigs in the laboratory — WILL 737:2
g. you have in your pocket — RUSK 551:3
rank is but the g.'s stamp — BURNS 160:2
round disc of fire like a g. — BLAKE 114:18
to one g. — JOHN 377:7
Guinness: O Hodgson, G. — CALV 175:12
guitar: changed upon the blue g. — STEV 665:22
sang to a small g. — LEAR 414:12
Gulag: G. Archipelago — SOLZH 655:8
gulf: great g. fixed — BIBLE 95:10
g. of mutual incomprehension — SNOW 654:7
redwood forest to the G. — GUTH 320:5
Shook the g. open — HUGH 354:5
gulfs: g. will wash us down — TENN 690:4
steep-down g. of liquid fire — SHAK 618:18
whelmed in deeper g. — COWP 221:25
gull: notorious geck and g. — SHAK 630:30
gullet: g. of New York — MILL 461:19
gulls: Forgot the cry of g. — ELIOT 273:11
g. him with intelligence — SHAK 634:10
gum: fart and chew g. — JOHN 367:13
gums: wept odorous g. — MILT 471:2
gun: barrel of a g. — MAO 446:1
Every g. that is made — EIS 268:10
Fire your little g. — DE L 236:4
Grip your g. like a man — BLOK 115:8
I have no g., but I can spit — AUDEN 35:16
we have got the Maxim G. — BELL 61:16
gun-boat: send a g. — BEVAN 68:16
Gunga: than I am, G. Din — KIPL 399:10
gunner: g. said 'Ay, ay,' — TENN 689:4
gunpowder: g., and the magnet — BACON 45:21
G., Printing and Protestant — CARL 180:17
G. Treason and Plot — ANON 17:11
till the g. ran out — FOOTE 288:15
guns: butter, not without g. — GOEB 308:14
butter or g. — GOER 308:15

guns: (*cont.*):
defend ourselves with g. — GOEB 308:14
groaning as the g. boom — CHES 199:4
G. aren't lawful — PARK 506:11
g. but we got the numbers — MORR 485:20
heard amid the g. below — MCCR 437:5
hundred men with g. — PUZO 533:8
like loaded g. with boys — CRAB 225:10
monstrous anger of the g. — OWEN 503:12
saw g. and sharp swords — DYLAN 265:15
these vile g. — SHAK 579:32
when the g. begin to shoot — KIPL 401:6
with g. we kill the crow — GASC 298:18
gunshot: With g. of belief — GASC 298:18
gurgite: in g. vasto — VIRG 712:3
gurgle: g. he gave — GILB 305:13
gurly: g. grew the sea — BALL 49:5
gush: they g. — PARK 506:16
gusts: our g. and storms — ELIOT 268:23
Gute: ist das G. zu geniessen — GOET 309:10
gutless: sort of g. Kipling — ORW 500:23
guts: g. at Goose Green — KINN 398:10
g. should hale souls — SHAK 613:23
his g. in his head — SHAK 627:12
lug the g. into the — SHAK 577:25
strangled with the g. of priests — MESL 458:15
gutta: G. cavat lapidem — OVID 502:19
gutter: so I lay down in the g. — BURT 164:8
We are all in the g. — WILDE 735:10
guttural: g. sorrow of refugees — MACN 440:16
guys: G. and dolls — RUNY 550:1
Nice g. Finish last — DUR 264:11
gymn: flare was up in the g. — BETJ 68:4
gyre: Did g. and gimble — CARR 182:18
turning in the widening g. — YEATS 753:1

H

ha: among the trumpets, H., ha — BIBLE 77:39
Habakkuk: H. was capable — VOLT 717:4
habeas corpus: protection of h. — JEFF 364:6
habileté: savoir cacher son h. — LA R 410:17
habit: different from h. — STR 670:22
h. is a great deadener — BECK 58:2
H. is second nature — AUCT 33:14
h. of living indisposeth — BROW 145:18
h. rules the unreflecting — WORD 744:7
H. with him was all — CRAB 224:22
I shook the h. off — WORD 747:9
Sow a h., reap a character — READE 537:9
use doth breed a h. in man — SHAK 631:9
when order breeds h. — ADAMS 2:14
habitarunt: H. di quoque silvas — VIRG 714:16
habitat: gives love its true h. — ANOU 23:7
habitation: fowls have their h. — BOOK 132:7
God in his holy h. — BOOK 129:7
h. among the tents of Kedar — BOOK 133:21
Let their h. be void — BOOK 129:13
local h. and a name — SHAK 612:17
shall be an h. of dragons — BIBLE 83:18
soul's h. safely built — RUSS 551:9
habitations: into everlasting h. — BIBLE 95:7
habits: Of h. devil — SHAK 577:22
prejudices and h. — GIBB 302:9
Small h., well pursued — MORE 483:20
habitual: h. hatred — WASH 722:1
nothing is h. but indecision — JAMES 363:16
hack: Do not h. me as you did — MONM 479:19
hacked: H. hewn — SOUT 657:2
had: good time who h. been h. by all — TYNAN 706:33
ne'er h. I cannot fear to lose — AST 32:6
Hades: dark H.' door — VIRG 713:11
H. is that man who hides — HOMER 343:7
unsubstantial realms of H. — VIRG 713:13
haedis: ab h. me sequestra — MISS 477:14
hag: h. obscene — BEAT 56:6
haggard: h. hawks mislike — GASC 298:17
If I do prove her h. — SHAK 616:16
Whene'er with h. eyes I view — CANN 178:9
Haggards: H. ride no more — STEP 663:18

hags: midnight h. — SHAK 603:20
haie: H.! H.! — POUND 527:9
Haig: [H.] committed suicide — BEAV 57:8
hail: beaten dog beneath the h. — POUND 527:8
Fire and h. — BOOK 135:14
flies no sharp and sided h. — HOPK 345:14
h., and farewell — CAT 187:1
H., fellow, well met — SWIFT 674:28
H. him like Etonians — KNOX 403:8
H., holy Light — MILT 470:16
H. holy queen — ANON 22:14
H. Mary, full of grace — ANON 22:3
h. the power of Jesus' — PERR 513:1
H., thou ever-blessèd morn — CASW 185:4
H., thou that art highly — BIBLE 93:21
H. to thee, blithe Spirit — SHEL 643:13
Where falls not h. — TENN 682:25
hailstones: h., and coals of fire — BOOK 125:2
hair: All her bright golden h. — WILDE 736:6
bids me bind my h. — HUNT 356:21
braided her yellow h. — BALL 50:13
bright h. about the bone — DONNE 252:13
colour of his h. — HOUS 351:13
dead woman, with such h. — BROW 153:11
draws us with a single h. — POPE 523:21
draw you with a single h. — DRYD 262:6
drew her long black h. — ELIOT 273:13
drew me backward by the h. — BROW 147:18
from his horrid h. — MILT 470:7
gowd kames in their h. — BALL 50:12
h. as free — JONS 378:18
h. has become very white — CARR 182:3
h. in long yellow string — BROW 152:3
h. is as a flock of goats — BIBLE 81:13
h. of a woman can draw — HOW 353:4
h. of his head — BIBLE 86:1
h. of my flesh stood up — BIBLE 77:10
h. soft-lifted by the — KEATS 390:18
h. to stand an end — SHAK 573:14
h. uplifted from the head — SHEL 641:15
h. with automatic hand — ELIOT 273:10
her h., her hair! — MEW 459:8
Her h. that lay along her back — ROSS 547:15
Her h. was long — KEATS 388:9
his next commodity of h. — SHAK 630:7
image doth unfix my h. — SHAK 600:12
like the h. we breathe — SURT 672:8
My h. is grey — BYRON 173:2
never hurt a h. of Him — STUD 671:4
one strangling golden h. — ROSS 547:22
Our h. turns white — BERRY 66:14
part my h. behind — ELIOT 272:6
pin up my h. with prose — CONG 215:33
raiment of camel's h. — BIBLE 88:14
red faces, and loose h. — EQUI 278:11
ruddy limbs and flaming h. — BLAKE 113:14
stars in her h. — ROSS 547:14
subtle wreath of h. — DONNE 252:3
sunlight in your h. — ELIOT 271:19
thy amber-dropping h. — MILT 464:10
When I lie tangled in her h. — LOV 429:1
with his long essenced h. — MAC 436:5
with long dishevelled h. — SHAK 635:12
woman have long h. — BIBLE 100:34
you have lovely h. — CHEK 197:7
hairless: h. as an egg — HERR 336:22
hairs: grey h. with sorrow — BIBLE 71:29
h. of your head are numbered — BIBLE 90:18
his h. were white — BIBLE 106:1
If h. be wires, black wires — SHAK 635:2
or when my h. be grey — SURR 672:4
They set our h. — DONNE 250:15
hairy: Esau is a h. man — BIBLE 71:10
marvellous h. about the face — SHAK 612:9
halcyon: h. days — SHAK 587:6
hale: guts should h. souls out — SHAK 613:23
You are h., Father William — SOUT 657:13
half: h. angel and half bird — BROW 152:15
h. as old as Time — BURG 166:24
h. as old as Time — ROG 544:13
H. dead and half alive — BETJ 67:5
Half dust, h. deity — BYRON 172:17

half: (cont.):

h. his height	LEON 418:11
h. in love with easeful Death	KEATS 389:14
h. is greater than the whole	HES 337:14
H. my own soul	HOR 349:1
h. of the warld thinks	SCOTT 560:28
H. our days we pass	BROW 146:22
h. slave and half free	LINC 421:18
h. that's got my keys	GRAH 313:11
h. the power to do me harm	SHAK 618:13
h. to rise, and h. to fall	POPE 522:10
h. was not told me	BIBLE 75:24
hath overcome but h.	MILT 469:3
have been finished in h.	WOD 740:13
I knew h. of her	O'BR 497:13
image of myself and dearer h.	MILT 471:22
longest h. of your life	SOUT 657:19
One h. of the world	AUST 38:6
Too clever by h.	SAL 554:10

half-a-crown: Or help to h. — HARDY 325:12

half-alive: h. things that try — FORS 290:26

half-brother: h. of the world — BAIL 47:17

half-knowledge: content with h. — KEATS 391:10

half-pence: like as h. — SHAK 569:10

half-truths: all truths are h. — WHIT 731:11

halfway: H. House to Rome — PUNCH 531:9

I'll ha'e nae h. hoose	MACD 437:7
run h. to meet it	JERR 366:3
should never be h.	KEATS 391:15

hall: fly swiftly into the h. — BEDE 58:13

He slept in the h.	BENT 64:15
vasty h. of death	ARN 27:20

hallelujah: H. I'm alive! — OSB 501:12

hallow: cannot h. this ground — LINC 422:10

hallowed: h. and so gracious — SHAK 572:2

H. be thy name	BIBLE 89:5

halls: Amphitrite's destined b — SHEL 641:7

I dwelt in marble h.	BUNN 156:7
In our h. is hung	WORD 744:13
in tap'stry h.	MILT 463:25

halo: jealousy with a h. — WELLS 727:24

What is a h.?	FRY 295:21
life is a luminous h.	WOOLF 742:7

halt: h., and the blind — BIBLE 94:31

h. ye between two opinions	BIBLE 76:1
with henna hackles, h.	STEV 665:16

halting: words came h. forth — SIDN 646:15

ham: case when there's h. — DICK 242:33

your h.'n eggs in Carolina	GORD 312:13

hame: Hame's h., be it never — ARB 24:9

O, h., hame, hame	CUNN 229:3

Hamlet: H. is so much paper — PRIE 528:18

H. without the Prince	SCOTT 560:32
I am not Prince H.	ELIOT 272:5
I'll call thee H.	SHAK 573:9
I saw H. played	EVEL 279:8
Lord H. is a prince	SHAK 574:16
Now the king drinks to H.	SHAK 579:4

hammer: be the anvil or the h. — GOET 309:9

h. that he has picked	BIER 109:5
ring of a h.	WILB 734:2
took an h. in her hand	BIBLE 74:1

hammered: clashed and h. — TENN 681:8

h. into line	KIPL 398:12

hammers: h. closing rivets up — SHAK 585:14

worn out many h.	MACL 439:7

hammock: Drake he's in his h. — NEWB 492:7

heavy-shotted h.-shroud	TENN 683:4

Hampshire: Hertford, Hereford, and H.

— LERN 419:5

hams: thy h., Bayonne — POPE 519:9

hand: adorable tennis-girl's h. — BETJ 68:7

beloved h. is laid in ours	ARN 26:17
bite the h. that fed them	BURKE 159:10
bloody and invisible h.	SHAK 603:5
by Time's devouring h.	BRAM 139:16
I WILL do ... un h	SHAK 602:6
curious engine, your Wille l	WEBS 726:17
Death lays his icy h. on kings	SHIL 640:2
delivered from mine h.	DIBLE 75:6
died by the h. of the Lord	BIBLE 72:15
Emprison her soft h.	KEATS 389:4
every man's h. against	BIBLE 70:37

hand: (cont.):

eyes have seen what my h.	LOW 430:9
from h. to hand of cash	SICK 646:8
gie's a h. o'thine	BURNS 161:6
Give a man a free h.	WEST 729:10
hair with automatic h.	ELIOT 273:10
h. a needle better fits	BRAD 139:10
h. dare seize the fire	BLAKE 114:14
h. delights to trace	WINC 739:4
h. findeth to do	BIBLE 80:20
h. for hand	BIBLE 72:17
h., head and heart of man	RUSK 550:28
h. in hand	MILT 473:14
h. is not able to taste	SHAK 612:16
h. is stretched out still	BIBLE 82:18
h. is the cutting edge	BRON 141:17
h. more instrumental	SHAK 572:5
h. of every man's brother	BIBLE 70:30
h. of Rousseau	HEINE 331:3
h. of the physician	BIBLE 87:34
h. on the cockatrice' den	BIBLE 83:3
h. that fired the shot	BALL 49:13
h. that hath made you fair	SHAK 606:12
h. that holds dominion	THOM 693:10
h. that lays the golden egg	GOLD 312:4
h. that made us is divine	ADD 4:20
h. that rocks the cradle	WALL 718:6
h. that signed the paper	THOM 693:9
h. then of the potter shake	FITZ 284:12
h. to execute	GIBB 302:5
h. to execute any mischief	CLAR 205:2
hawks mislike an empty h.	GASC 298:17
Heaving up my either h.	HERR 336:5
Her h. on her bosom	SHAK 617:22
His hand and h. went together	HEMI 331:13
his right h. seven stars	BIBLE 106:1
if my h. were at its throat	LOW 430:20
I kissed her slender h.	TENN 686:14
In his h. are all the corners	BOOK 131:10
it hurts my h.	SHAK 617:9
it will go into his h.	BIBLE 78:31
kingdom of heaven is at h.	BIBLE 88:12
kiss on the h. may be quite	ROBIN 542:7
know the sweet Roman h.	SHAK 630:20
larger heart, kindlier h.	TENN 684:11
left his garment in her h.	BIBLE 71:24
lily in your medieval h.	GILB 305:17
My h. in yours	CRANE 225:19
my hat, and h.	BROW 145:28
My strict h.	JONS 378:21
my sword sleep in my h.	BLAKE 113:4
My times be in Thy h.	BROW 152:13
my weakening h.	TIB 698:1
O! let me kiss that h.	SHAK 597:5
On this side my h.	SHAK 620:19
Our times are in His h.	BROW 152:6
put your h. into the H. of God	HASK 328:1
right h. forget her cunning	BOOK 134:17
right h. of the Majesty	BIBLE 104:10
sheep of his h.	BOOK 131:10
soft h., and softer breast	KEATS 389:11
So quickly, waiting for a h.	TENN 683:5
spirit-small h.	BROW 148:23
'Tes the h. of Nature	GIBB 302:23
thence through a mighty h.	BIBLE 73:14
thine h. toward heaven	BIBLE 72:7
This living h., now warm	KEATS 390:16
thousand at thy right h.	BOOK 131:3
thrust my h. into his side	BIBLE 97:35
Time's fell h.	SHAK 634:1
'Tis a good h.	SHAK 617:1
Took me by the h.	TURN 705:15
touch of a vanished h.	TENN 680:10
unto you with mine own h.	BIBLE 102:10
was the h. that wrote it	CRAN 225:28
waved her lily h.	GAY 300:17
were a glove upon that h.	SHAK 622:28
what thy right h. doeth	BIBLE 89:3
With his flail is his h.	JOHN 376:26
With his one right h.	BOOK 131:13
withhold not thine h.	BIBLE 80:28
Woe unto... constable's h	KING 404:1

handclasp: h.'s a little stronger — CHAP 190:10

handcuffs: sinner with the h.	HOUS 351:13

handed: H. they went — MILT 471:14

Handel: compared to H. — BYROM 167:15

Dance they to the tunes of H.	SITW 648:19

handful: fear in a h. of dust — ELIOT 272:23

h. of meal in a barrel	BIBLE 75:32
life in the h. of dust	CONR 217:17

handicraft: out of the sphere of h. — SARR 556:5

handiwork: God's h. — BROW 149:19

handkerchief: damp h. — MACK 439:4

h. binding her hair	CONN 216:20
That h. did an Egyptian	SHAK 617:2
tie and display h.	CHAN 190:1
Trap the germs in your h.	ANON 12:29

handle: I polished up the h. — GILB 305:26

handles: hath two h. — BURT 165:3

There are no h. to a horse	LEAC 413:11

handmaid: nature's h. art — DRYD 260:3

Riches are a good h.	BACON 42:12

handmaiden: low estate of h. — BIBLE 93:22

handmaidens: With her five h. — ROSS 547:18

hands: aching h. and bleeding feet — ARN 27:15

All h. to work	ANON 20:2
Beneath the bleeding h.	ELIOT 270:20
by joining of h.	BOOK 123:23
caught the world's great h.	HUNT 356:8
chained up the h. of the loyal	ANON 20:14
clasps the crag with crooked h.	TENN 681:1
Come, knit h.	MILT 463:18
fold her h. and pray	ROSS 548:3
fortune is in his own h.	BACON 43:18
h. are as gold rings	BIBLE 81:20
h. are a sort of feet	TRAH 701:16
h. are the hands of Esau	BIBLE 71:11
h. could lay hold on	BENET 62:18
h. from picking and stealing	BOOK 123:8
h. I commend my spirit	BIBLE 95:28
h. I commend my spirit	BOOK 126:7
h. I loved beside the Shalimar	HOPE 345:3
h. of peasants	SHAK 593:6
h. that hold the aces	BETJ 67:9
h. wrought in the work	BIBLE 76:34
has such small h.	CUMM 228:15
hath not a Jew h.	SHAK 608:22
He hath shook h. with time	FORD 289:11
Holding h. at midnight	GERS 301:12
horny h. of toil	LOW 429:19
house not made with h.	BIBLE 101:18
house not made with h.	BROW 148:24
into the h. of spoilers	BIBLE 73:34
into the h. of the living	BIBLE 104:12
Let the lifting up of my h.	BOOK 135:1
Licence my roving h.	DONNE 250:16
Lift not thy h. to It	FITZ 284:10
little folding of the h.	BIBLE 78:14
Made with our h.	SWIN 676:3
nearer than h. and feet	TENN 681:15
not into the h. of men	BIBLE 87:9
not into the h. of Spain	TENN 689:4
own h. I give away my crown	SHAK 620:22
pierced my h. and my feet	BOOK 125:13
Pilate washed his h.	JAGG 361:13
reached out h. in longing	VIRG 713:16
reveals the author's h.	CHEK 197:8
right h. of fellowship	BIBLE 102:4
Shake h. for ever	DRAY 258:1
Soul clap its h. and sing	YEATS 752:21
spits on h. and goes to work	SAND 555:12
Strengthen ye the weak h.	BIBLE 83:20
temples made with h.	BIBLE 98:12
Their fatal h.	MILT 470:8
Their h. upon their hearts	HOUS 351:19
These h. are not more like	SHAK 572:19
these h. ne'er be clean	SHAK 604:13
They have h., and handle	BOOK 133:10
thieves who have their h.	BIER 109:3
union of h. and hearts	TAYL 679:21
violent h. upon themselves	BOOK 124:2
washed his h. before	BIBLE 93:3
wash my h. in innocency	BOOK 125:2
what h. you would hold	LAMB 407:10
Work yours h. ... day to day	MASN 440:15

hands: (*cont.*):
Your little h. were never made   WATTS 722:16
handsaw: hawk from a h.   SHAK 575:1
handsome: h. in three hundred pounds
  SHAK 610:17
he was a h. man   CUMM 228:14
Hi! h. hunting man   DE L 236:4
handy-work: firmament sheweth his h.
  BOOK 125:4
hang: all h. together   FRAN 293:1
h. a pearl in every cowslip's   SHAK 611:11
h. in a row   HARDY 326:2
H. it all, Robert Browning   POUND 526:7
h. my hat is home sweet   JER 365:17
h. that jury-men may dine   POPE 523:26
h. the man over again   BARH 52:11
h. upon him that hangs   DONNE 253:2
H. yourself, brave Crillon   HENR 332:11
neither go nor h.   BIGOD 109:16
that you would h. yourself   JOHN 373:19
There his head   CRAB 224:23
they h. a man first   MOL 479:8
When they come to h. you   KING 398:5
Would h. themselves   SHAK 631:15
hanged: farmer that h. himself   SHAK 602:8
h., drawn, and quartered   PEPYS 512:4
h. for stealing horses   HAL 321:18
h. himself   BIBLE 75:16
h. in a fortnight   JOHN 374:23
h. in all innocence   STEV 668:11
h. that swear and lie   SHAK 604:5
my poor fool is h.   SHAK 598:3
our harps, we h. them up   BOOK 134:17
hanging: bare h.   DRYD 262:21
H. and marriage   FARQ 280:23
h. Danny Deever   KIPL 398:18
h. garments of Marylebone   JOYCE 381:2
H. is too good for him   BUNY 155:19
h. look to me   CONG 215:7
H. of his cat on Monday   BRAT 139:19
h.' men an' women   ANON 15:4
h. prevents a bad marriage   SHAK 628:17
hangman: h.'s thrusting the final nail
  BLOK 115:3
naked to the h.'s noose   HOUS 352:8
only the arm of the h.   ANON 20:14
hangs: And thereby h. a tale   SHAK 568:12
H. in the uncertain balance   GREE 317:7
h. on princes' favours   SHAK 588:19
What h. people   STEV 668:9
hank: and a h. of hair   KIPL 401:7
Hannibalem: *Expende H.*   JUV 384:8
hansom: helped to a h. outside   BETJ 67:3
hap: when that my h. is nought   SURR 672:4
happen: Did this h. to your mother?
  WALK 717:11
fools said would h.   MELB 456:10
It can't h. here   LEWIS 421:6
more things h. to you   EMPS 277:19
There shall no evil h.   BOOK 131:4
Things h.   HILL 338:11
happened: after they have h.   ION 360:11
happening: way of h., a mouth   AUDEN 34:14
happens: be there when it h.   ALLEN 9:15
dependent on what h. to her   ELIOT 269:7
like something, h. anywhere   LARK 410:2
Nothing h., nobody comes   BECK 57:22
happier: be h. than your father   SOPH 656:10
I am h. than I know   MILT 472:13
No h. state   MILT 471:16
remembering h. things   TENN 685:10
happiest: gild it with h. terms   SHAK 582:10
h. and best minds   SHEL 644:7
h. marriages on earth   DE V 238:3
h. people in the world   OSB 501:5
h. time of all the glad   TENN 687:7
h. women, like h. nations   ELIOT 269:24
parsons like the h. men alive   LLOYD 424:1
yet h. if ye seek   MILT 471:16
happily: live very h. upon   JOHN 372:10
happiness: all the h. mankind can gain
  DRYD 260:31
best recipe for h.   AUST 38:18

happiness: (*cont.*):
brief period of h.   ARIS 25:9
By no greatest h. principle   CARL 180:13
consume h. without producing   SHAW 636:1
flaw in h.   KEATS 390:25
For such a short-lived h.   BEHN 60:9
great enemy to human h.   JOHN 376:1
h. alone is salutary   PROU 530:17
H. consists in   JOHN 372:24
h. does that sometimes   MAUG 454:8
h. for the greatest numbers   HUTC 357:6
H., for you we walk   MONT 481:12
h. in eyeing the gorgeous buttocks
  HUXL 357:21
H. is an imaginary condition   SZASZ 677:12
H. is no laughing matter   WHAT 730:8
H. is not an ideal of reason   KANT 386:9
H. makes up in height   FROST 294:19
h. of an individual   JOHN 373:16
h. of society   ADAMS 3:1
h. of the common man   BEV 69:9
h. of the greatest number   BENT 64:4
h. of the human race   BURKE 158:2
h. of the next world   BROW 145:17
h. or a quiet conscience   BERL 66:4
H.! our being's end and aim   POPE 522:19
h. produced by a good tavern   JOHN 374:10
h. the occasional episode   HARDY 324:11
h. through another man's eyes   SHAK 569:20
h. too swiftly flies   GRAY 316:3
home-born h.   COWP 223:33
In my great task of h.   STEV 669:7
lifetime of h.   SHAW 637:4
most fatal to true h.   RUSS 551:13
most suited to human h.   DEFOE 234:6
my people's h.   ELIZ 274:10
Of h. and final misery   MILT 470:1
only thing for h.   EDG 266:10
our h. is assured   BIER 109:10
politics of h.   HUMP 356:3
power and glory, or h.   ARIS 25:11
pursuit of h.   ANON 19:7
pursuit of h.   JEFF 364:2
result h.   DICK 239:28
salutation to h.   ALAI 7:7
seem to find the h. I seek   BERL 65:21
somebody else's h.   HUXL 357:16
To fill the hour—that is h.   EMER 277:4
too happy in thine h.   KEATS 389:8
Travelling is the ruin of all h.   BURN 160:14
uncertain of giving h.   AUST 39:14
unrivalled h.   ARN 29:16
very seeing of God our h.   THOM 692:16
virtue and the secret of h.   MORE 484:1
We find our h., or not at all   WORD 747:7
we seek h. in boats   HOR 348:9
What h.? who can enjoy alone   MILT 472:14
Who hopes for h. from thee   WRIG 749:13
Withdraws into its h.   MARV 450:10
you take away his h.   IBSEN 359:7
happy: angry and poor and h.   CHES 199:9
as h. as kings   STEV 668:14
attain the h. seat   SURR 672:2
Be h. while y'er leevin   ANON 12:12
conspiracy to make you h.   UPD 707:8
duty of being h.   STEV 667:26
Farmer will never be h.   HERB 333:16
Hail, redemption's h. dawn   CASW 185:4
h. as birds in the spring   BLAKE 114:10
h. as the grass was green   THOM 693:5
H. birthday to you   HILL 338:14
h. families resemble   TOLS 700:5
H. field or mossy cavern   KEATS 388:20
Happy, happy, h., pair   DRYD 259:16
h. he who crowns in shades   GOLD 310:7
H. he who like Ulysses   DU B 263:1
h. highways where I went   HOUS 352:15
h. I live and despise writing   SMITH 652:16
h. in arms of a chambermaid   JOHN 375:6
h. in their peace   AKHM 6:11
h. in this world   THAC 691:20
h. is he who comes top   LODGE 425:19
h. issue out   BOOK 120:7

happy: (*cont.*):
H. is that city   ANON 14:1
H. is the man who fears   BIBLE 108:1
h. is the rose distilled   SHAK 610:20
h. men that have the power   TENN 689:12
h. noise to hear   HOUS 352:10
h. now the savage race   CHUR 201:1
h. on being environed   CROM 227:15
H. people are ignoramuses   LERM 418:13
H. the hare at morning   AUDEN 34:8
H. the man, happy he alone   DRYD 262:1
H. the man, his quiver full   ROOK 134:7
H. the man who, far away   HOR 346:22
H. the man, whose wish   POPE 523:11
H. the people whose annals   MONT 481:17
H. those early days   VAUG 709:1
His h. good-night air   HARDY 325:5
How h. could I be with either   GAY 299:26
How h. is he born and taught   WOTT 748:21
How h. some o'er other   SHAK 611:1
I die h.   FOX 291:19
Made h. by compulsion   COL 211:22
making men h. in the end   DOST 254:6
methinks it were a h. life   SHAK 588:1
myself in nothing else so h.   SHAK 619:20
no man h. before he dies   SOLON 655:6
nor as h. as one hopes   LA R 410:23
O h. Rome   CIC 204:15
one thing to make me h.   HAZL 328:14
one who has been h.   BOET 116:12
pain to remember a h. time   DANTE 230:11
perfectly happy till all are h.   SPEN 658:23
policeman's lot is not a h. one   GILB 306:11
prevent me from being h.   ANOU 23:10
remote from the h.   AUDEN 33:28
So I'm h. tonight   KING 397:5
so late their h. seat   MILT 473:14
someone, somewhere, may be h.   MENC 457:7
splendid and a h. land   GOLD 310:16
stayed me in a h. hour   SHAK 614:9
That all who are h.   JOHN 372:24
that can make a man h.   HOR 348:7
that none should be h.   JOHN 374:16
They are to be h.   LARK 409:16
they h. are, and they love   WALL 718:19
This h. breed of men   SHAK 619:18
To make men h., and to keep   POPE 522:28
too h. in thine happiness   KEATS 389:8
'Twere now to be most h.   SHAK 615:20
Was he h.?   AUDEN 36:12
was the carver h.   RUSK 550:21
We can't all be h.   RHYS 539:18
Well, I've had a h. life   HAZL 329:15
What makes a nation h.   MILT 473:23
whether you are h.   MILL 460:7
whether you are h. or not   SHAW 638:12
Whoever wants to be h.   MED 456:3
world of the h.   WITT 740:6
would in general be as h.   JOHN 374:1
You ask if they were h.   CHAN 190:8
Happy Isles: shall touch the H.   TENN 690:4
harbinger: Love's h.   MILT 473:9
harbour: h. grene aslepe   WEVER 730:1
Though the h. bar be moaning   KING 397:16
hard: ask the h. question   AUDEN 36:9
Between a rock and a h. place   ANON 12:15
Breeds h. English men   KING 397:11
h. dealing teaches them   SHAK 608:2
h. it is to hide the sparks   SHAK 571:9
h. rain's a gonna fall   DYLAN 265:15
h. to catch and conquer   MER 458:5
h. to make a man appear   DRYD 262:20
H. was their lodging   GARTH 298:14
h. words like a charm   OSB 501:6
It's been a h. day's night   LENN 417:20
it was too h.   BOOK 130:2
Long is the way and h.   MILT 469:21
never is so h. hearted man   MAL 443:12
never think I have hit h.   JOHN 373:21
that thou art an h. man   BIBLE 92:17
theirs thine own h. case   CAREW 179:10
very h. guy, indeed   RUNY 550:3
when you're h. up you pawn   CUMM 228:7

hard: (cont.):
will declare h. sentences   BOOK 130:8
woman is so h.   TENN 688:11
hard-boiled: h. city   CHAN 190:3
harden: h. not your hearts   BOOK 131:10
will h. Pharaoh's heart   BIBLE 72:3
harder: or they would be h.   TROL 703:11
hard-faced: lot of h. men   BALD 48:13
hardly: Johnny, I h. knew ye   BALL 49:15
hardships: beset by h.   ATKI 32:13
hare: Caught the Pubic H.   BEHAN 60:1
Happy the h. at morning   AUDEN 34:8
h. limped trembling   KEATS 386:20
h.'s own child   HOFF 341:10
h. sits snug in leaves   HOFF 341:8
h. sitting up   LAWR 412:10
outcry of the hunted h.   BLAKE 111:2
Take your h. when it is cased   GLAS 308:2
than to start a h.   SHAK 579:34
That is why the h. wins   BROO 143:19
thou woldest fynde an h.   CHAU 194:16
triumph o'er the timid h.   THOM 696:9
hare-brained: h. chatter   DISR 247:30
harelip: and makes the h.   SHAK 596:13
hares: little hunted h.   HODG 340:16
hark: H., my soul! it is the Lord   COWP 222:20
H., the dominant's persistence   BROW 153:9
H.! the herald-angels sing   WESL 728:3
harlot: Every h. was a virgin   BLAKE 111:23
h.'s cry from street   BLAKE 111:9
h. we have got hold of   BYRON 174:1
Portia is Brutus' h.   SHAK 591:2
prerogative of the h.   KIPL 402:13
harlotries: of synne and h.   CHAU 193:4
harlots: MOTHER OF H.   BIBLE 107:10
harm: content with my h.   SHAK 569:1
forgive a man for the h.   MAUG 454:9
h. as those who go about   CREI 226:18
h. that is spoken of it   FLAU 285:19
h. to the mene peple   LANG 409:1
I fear we'll come to h.   BALL 50:11
mankind does most good or h.   BAG 47:13
may do you extreme h.   MORT 486:8
no h. come to the state   ANON 22:5
no h. happen unto me   BOOK 124:22
prevent h. to others   MILL 460:15
Shall h. Macbeth   SHAK 603:21
supposed to do no h.   RUSS 551:18
that does h. to my wit   SHAK 628:12
win us to our h.   SHAK 600:10
world meaning no h.   GREE 317:4
harmless: entertains the h. day   WOTT 749:1
h. as doves   BIBLE 90:16
only h. great thing   DONNE 251:14
harmonical: h. and ingenious soul   AUBR 33:6
harmonies: inventor of h.   TENN 687:9
tumult of thy mighty h.   SHEL 641:19
harmonious: best and most h.   LEIB 416:17
such dulcet and h. breath   SHAK 611:16
Such h. madness   SHEL 643:20
harmony: best h. in a church   MILT 475:10
Discordant h.   HOR 348:10
discord, h., not understood   POPE 522:8
Enforce attention, like deep h.   SHAK 619:15
From harmony, heavenly h.   DRYD 261:23
h., and even justice   BELL 62:7
h. in autumn   SHEL 640:19
heaven drowsy with the h.   SHAK 598:20
her voice the h.   HOOK 344:14
in their motions h. divine   MILT 474:2
other h. of prose   DRYD 262:15
price is asked for h.   DOST 254:5
Sentimentally disposed to h.   LAMB 406:7
Such h. is in immortal souls   SHAK 610:1
touched with the h. of music   REYN 539:13
touches of sweet h.   SHAK 610:1
untaught h. of spring   GRAY 316:5
wherever there is a h.   BROW 146:17
with your true field h.   MILT 467:9
harmow between th. limits of the h.
   BIBLE 78:19
die with h. on our back   SHAK 603:8
h. and not the horses   CANN 178:10

harness: (cont.):
him that girdeth on his h.   BIBLE 76:9
harp: awake, lute and h.   BOOK 128:16
clear h. in divers tones   TENN 682:30
flute, h., sackbut   BIBLE 85:28
H. not on that string   SHAK 622:7
h. on a weeping willow-tree   ANON 18:11
h. that once through Tara's   MOORE 483:5
merry h. with the lute   BOOK 130:14
No h. like my own   CAMP 176:13
sing to the h. with a psalm   BOOK 131:14
sweet h., the story of what   BAKER 47:21
upon the h. will I give thanks   BOOK 127:7
wild h. slung behind him   MOORE 483:7
Harpic: As I read the H. tin   BENN 63:12
harping: h. on my daughter   SHAK 574:20
harps: As for our h.   BOOK 134:17
harpers harping with their h.   BIBLE 107:2
having every one of them h.   BIBLE 106:14
organic h. diversely framed   COL 209:20
To touch their h. of gold   SEARS 561:12
harpy: conference with this h.   SHAK 613:18
harrass: all the griefs that h.   JOHN 370:8
Harriet: chatter about H.   FREE 293:14
harrow: H. the house of dead   AUDEN 36:6
Would h. up thy soul   SHAK 573:14
harrowing: man h. clods   HARDY 325:10
Harry: banish not him thy H.'s company
   SHAK 580:33
But H., Harry   SHAK 584:7
Cry 'God for H.! England   SHAK 585:10
H. and his followers   SHAK 585:1
In that Jerusalem shall H. die   SHAK 584:5
touch of H. in the night   SHAK 585:17
harsh: h. and embittered manhood
   GOGOL 309:21
Nor h. nor grating   WORD 745:1
harshness: no h. gives offence   POPE 521:16
hart: footed like a h.   MAL 443:6
h. for cooling streams   TATE 678:16
h. ungallèd play   SHAK 576:20
lame man leap as an h.   BIBLE 83:21
Like as the h. desireth   BOOK 127:2
like to a roe or young h.   BIBLE 82:7
was I turned into a h.   SHAK 628:10
harts: milk-white h. upon   MARL 447:20
Harvard: glass flowers at H.   MOORE 482:15
Yale College and my H.   MELV 456:17
harvest: according to joy in h.   BIBLE 82:26
all the h. that I reaped   FITZ 284:2
h. is past   BIBLE 85:8
h. of a quiet eye   WORD 746:16
h. truly is plenteous   BIBLE 90:12
no h. but a thorn   HERB 334:11
reapèd h. of the light   CHAP 190:17
seedtime and h.   BIBLE 70:29
she laughs with a h.   JERR 366:1
shine on, h. moon   NORW 497:2
harvests: Deep h. bury all   POPE 520:22
Harwich: steamer from H.   GILB 304:15
Hasdrubale: lost with H.   HOR 350:14
haste: H. still pays haste   SHAD 563:15
H. still pays haste   SHAK 606:25
I said in my h.   BOOK 133:13
Make h. slowly   AUG 37:12
maketh h. to be rich   BIBLE 79:29
Men love in h.   BYRON 171:24
No h. but good   GASC 298:19
repent in h.   CONG 215:25
Though I am always in h.   WESL 729:2
what h. I can to be gone   CROM 227:17
Without h., but without rest   GOET 309:17
ye shall eat it in h.   BIBLE 72:10
hasten: So do our minutes h.   SHAK 633:20
To h. or control   BODE 116:11
hasting: Until the h. day   HERR 337:4
hat: hang my h. is home sweet   JER 365:17
hang your h. on a pension   MACN 440:14
He can't think without his h.   BECK 57:23
knee, my h., and hand   BROW 146:29
looking for a black h.   BOWEN 128:3
My hat and his head   SHAK 574:9
way you wear your h.   FITZG 290:18

hat: (cont.):
with my h. upon my head   JOHN 376:26
without pulling off his h.   JOHN 372:4
your h. upon your brows   SHAK 604:8
hatches: continually under h.   KEATS 391:17
hatchet: I did cut it with my h.   WASH 722:2
hatching: H. vain empires   MILT 469:19
hate: betray me to your mirth or h.
   FORD 289:14
cherish hearts that h.   SHAK 589:1
do good to them which h.   BIBLE 94:6
Each sequestered in its h.   AUDEN 34:15
energy, love and h.   BLAKE 112:13
Envy's raging h.   MARS 449:9
For nought did I in h.   SHAK 618:19
frighten those who might h. her   AUST 38:4
generation of them that h.   BIBLE 72:16
glance of supernatural h.   BYRON 173:16
h. a fellow whom pride   JOHN 376:2
h. all that don't love   FARQ 280:17
h. all the people your   HAMM 323:2
h. and detest that animal   SWIFT 674:1
h. any one that we know   HAZL 329:13
h. him as I do hell-pains   SHAK 614:25
h. him flee before him   BOOK 129:6
h. something in him   HESSE 337:15
h. that which we often   SHAK 564:24
h. the common herd   HOR 349:22
h. the fine lawn   BLAM 114:20
h. the idle pleasures   SHAK 621:16
h. the man you have hurt   TAC 677:21
h. what every poet hates   KAV 386:5
h. your neighbour   MAC 433:9
h. you through the glass   BLUN 116:3
have seen much to h. here   MILL 461:12
Hence, ye profane; I h. ye all   COWL 221:10
how I h. them   LAWR 412:24
I h. all Boets and Bainters   GEOR 300:22
I h. and I love   CAT 186:17
I h. him for he is a Christian   SHAK 607:20
implacable in h.   DRYD 259:3
I think I know enough of h.   FROST 294:17
Lead me from h. to love   KUMAR 404:8
Let them h.   ACC 1:4
man you love to h.   ANON 16:8
must h. and death return   SHEL 640:16
need not be to h. mankind   BYRON 168:23
never bother with people I h.   HART 327:12
no h. lost between us   MIDD 460:2
not h. them, but be indifferent   SHAW 636:5
Of a pure impartial h.   THOR 697:11
religion to make us h.   SWIFT 674:14
revenge, immortal h.   MILT 468:5
roughness breedeth h.   BACON 43:30
sprung from my only h.   SHAK 622:26
they at once admire and h.   LEWIS 421:7
This is a letter of h.   OSB 501:20
time to h.   BIBLE 80:5
Wonder hinders love and h.   GREV 318:5
you must h. a Frenchman   NELS 491:10
hated: H. by fools   SWIFT 675:9
H. by one he loves   SHAK 593:8
h. the ruling few   BENT 64:8
how, then, must I be h.   SHEL 639:7
loved well because he h.   BROW 151:16
not having h. the world enough   HAZL 328:15
She might have h.   BROW 150:22
hateful: And shamed life a h.   SHAK 606:11
Must learn the h. art   KING 396:13
hater: he was a very good h.   JOHN 377:5
hates: h. dogs and babies   ROST 548:14
h. them for it   SHAW 638:26
He h. our sacred nation   SHAK 607:20
In a world of voluble h.   TREV 702:13
just heaven now h.   ANON 14:5
man who h. his mother   BENN 63:22
hateth: h. his brother   BIBLE 105:29
hath: that h. shall be given   BIBLE 92:18
hating: By h. vices too much   BURKE 158:26
don't give way to h.   KIPL 400:14
h. all other nations   GASK 299:6
h., my boy is an art   NASH 490:17
hatless: H., I take off   LARK 409:14

hatless: (cont.):
young man lands h. from the air   BETJ 67:8
hatred: envy, h., and malice   BOOK 119:17
force, h., history   JOYCE 382:3
Great h., little room   YEATS 752:19
h. for the Tory Party   BEVAN 68:13
H. is a tonic   BALZ 51:9
h. is the longest pleasure   BYRON 171:24
h. or an habitual fondness   WASH 722:1
h. or bitterness towards   CAV 187:10
hot h. against the Church   SKEL 649:4
into the most deadly h.   HUME 355:10
It is bound up with h.   ORW 500:25
like love to h. turned   CONG 215:17
mind with perpetual h.   GODW 308:12
odium and the public h.   CLAY 206:1
quite as much as his h.   TOCQ 699:6
Regulated h.   HARD 324:1
stalled ox and h.   BIBLE 78:35
undying h. it arouses   FOSD 291:4
hatreds: organization of h.   ADAMS 2:6
hats: H. divide generally   WHIT 731:19
inside men's Sunday h.   BROW 151:26
so many shocking bad h.   WELL 727:4
they have h. like plates   COW 220:14
haughtiness: h. of soul   ADD 3:17
haughty: h. spirit before   BIBLE 78:37
haunches: on silent h.   SAND 555:4
haunt: And all the h. be ours   SHAK 566:9
h. of flies on summer eves   KEATS 389:13
h. thy days and chill thy   KEATS 390:16
haunted: H. for ever by   WORD 745:16
h. town it is to me   LANG 408:14
On summer eves by h. stream   MILT 465:17
recesses of some h. pile   SHEL 644:11
haunts: h. of coot and hern   TENN 680:11
h. of horror and fear   TENN 687:3
he h. wakes, fairs   SHAK 631:27
That h. you night and day   BERL 65:19
hause-bane: sit on his white h.   BALL 50:20
have: died to h.   DAN 229:18
h. and to hold from this day   BOOK 123:20
h. it when they know it   SWIFT 675:8
H. more than thou showes?   SHAK 595:6
H. Some Madeira, M'dear   FLAN 285:9
if he will h. him   BOOK 125:10
I h. thee not   SHAK 601:12
I'll h. her   SHAK 621:19
I will not h. it   SKEL 649:3
so long as you h. your life   JAMES 362:12
They h. to take you in   FROST 294:15
will not let you h. it   HAZL 329:1
have-his-carcase: h., next to perpetual
motion   DICK 243:25
haven: Safe into the h. guide   WESL 728:6
To their h. under the hill   TENN 680:10
haves: h. and the have-nots   CERV 188:13
having: Never satisfied with h.   WROTH 749:14
havoc: Cry, 'H.!' and let slip   SHAK 591:24
h. and the spoil   WITH 739:13
Strokes of h. únselve   HOPK 345:5
hawk: But his h., his hound   BALL 50:20
h. at eagles with a dove   HERB 335:17
h. to fetch the wild-fowl   BALL 50:20
know a h. from a handsaw   SHAK 575:1
Or h. of the tower   SKEL 649:2
hawks: such h., and such leman   BALL 50:19
Hawkshaw: H., the detective   TAYL 679:22
hawthorn: h. bush a sweeter shade   SHAK 588:2
Under the h. in the dale   MILT 465:10
hay: desire to a bottle of h.   SHAK 612:11
eating h. when you're faint   CARR 183:18
In latter August when the h.   LOW 430:15
laid himself sheets with h.   JOHN 368:11
lie tumbling in the h.   SHAK 631:24
Work and pray, live on h.   HILL 338:12
haystack: h. in the floods   MORR 485:13
hazard: h. in glorious enterprise   MILT 468:3
Men that h. all   SHAK 608:13
stand the h. of the die   SHAK 622:16
hazards: h. whence no tears   HARDY 325:13
he: H. that hath wife   BACON 44:3
H. that is without sin   BIBLE 96:30

he: (cont.):
h. that should come   BIBLE 90:24
H. would, wouldn't he?   RIC 540:6
life to live as the greatest h.   RAIN 535:10
While H. is mine   HERB 335:22
head: And under my h. a sod   BALL 49:7
An' she takes my laily h.   BALL 49:16
Are still inside my h.   RODG 544:1
As with my hat upon my h.   JOHN 376:26
bear with a sore h.   MARR 449:3
blew his h. off   BLY 116:7
body with so old a h.   SHAK 609:12
bullet through his h.   ROB 542:11
But bowed his comely h.   MARV 450:15
get one's h. cut off   CARR 183:4
God be in my h.   ANON 13:16
Go up, thou bald h.   BIBLE 76:17
grey h. which all men knew   TENN 687:15
hand, the h., and the heart   RUSK 550:28
hath not where to lay his h.   BIBLE 90:1
h. and his hairs were white   BIBLE 106:1
h. could carry all he knew   GOLD 310:14
h. is as full of quarrels   SHAK 623:12
h. is not more native   SHAK 572:5
h. of a family off   DICK 243:4
h. off with a golden axe   SHAK 623:19
h. of your loved Lycidas   MILT 466:3
h. stuffed with the jargon   DEFOE 233:15
h. that once was crowned   KELLY 393:4
h. thou dost with oil anoint   SCOT 561:8
h. to contrive   CLAR 205:2
h. to contrive   GIBB 302:5
h. upon our battlements   SHAK 599:15
Here is the h. upon which   PATER 509:4
her h. on her knee   SHAK 617:22
hidden her h.   SWIN 676:22
his brains go to his h.   ASQ 32:2
his guts in his h.   SHAK 627:12
his h. with his legs   BIBLE 72:9
If you can keep your h.   KIPL 400:14
ignorance bumping its h.   FORD 289:6
I'll hold my h. so high   HOR 348:24
incessantly stand on your h.   CARR 182:3
Is there any room at your h.   BALL 49:4
It shall bruise thy h.   BIBLE 70:14
laid your wretched h.   OVID 503:5
Lay your sleeping h., my love   AUDEN 35:5
learned lumber in his h.   POPE 521:24
like God's own h.   COL 210:23
make you shorter by the h.   ELIZ 274:8
many a h. has turned white   MÜLL 487:16
matter which way the h. lies   RAL 536:8
My deeds upon my h.   SHAK 609:14
my h. is a map   FIEL 282:9
My h. is bloody, but unbowed   HENL 332:6
nowhere yet to rest my h.   ARN 28:20
Off with his h.   CIBB 203:20
On my h.   DISR 246:13
Or in the heart or in the h.   SHAK 608:25
parboiled h. upon a stake   GRAH 313:14
psychiatrist should have his h.   GOLD 310:6
repairs his drooping h.   MILT 466:13
rise and cut off his h.   JOHN 373:17
seems no bigger than his h.   SHAK 597:1
sex ever rears its ugly h.   AYCK 40:7
shake of his poor little h.   GILB 305:12
shew his glorious h.   SPEN 659:14
show my h. to the people   DANT 230:23
snorted or jerked its h.   HUGH 354:5
that sacred h. of thine   MILT 466:6
their feet than their h.   CAV 187:14
their h. the prow   DRYD 260:3
though his h. be empty   SWIFT 674:11
To keep your h.   PUDN 531:5
To shake his sapient h.   ARN 29:5
Uneasy lies the h.   SHAK 583:12
very hairs of your h.   BIBLE 90:18
what seemed his h.   MILT 470:5
which binds so dear a h.   SHEL 639:11
which the h. and which   BRIG 141:11
wrong man's h. off   DICK 243:13
your good h.   ELIZ 274:9
headache: awake with dismal h.   GILB 304:21

headin': know where we're h.   DYLAN 265:20
headland: top of some bold h.   WORD 743:17
headlong: h. sent to build in hell   MILT 469:8
H. themselves they threw   MILT 472:5
Hurled h. flaming   MILT 467:23
headpiece: H. filled with straw   ELIOT 271:14
heads: Canons lay h. together   SMITH 653:25
had ever very empty h.   BACON 45:24
h. replete with thoughts   COWP 224:4
Hide their diminished h.   MILT 470:22
I first surmised the Horses H.   DICK 244:12
Its h. o'ertaxed   ARN 20.9
Lift up your h.   BOOK 125:17
stood them on their h.   BARR 54:5
headstone: h. in the corner   BOOK 133:16
headstrong: h. as an allegory   SHER 645:6
head waiter: h. allowed to sit   UST 707:17
heady: H., not strong   POPE 518:21
heal: h. me of my grievous wound   TENN 682:25
h. what is wounded   LANG 409:9
Physician, h. thyself   BIBLE 94:2
time to h.   BIBLE 80:5
What wound did ever h.   SHAK 616:8
When there is none to h. it   KEATS 387:33
healed: h. also the hurt   BIBLE 85:7
Ransomed, h., restored   LYTE 433:17
with his stripes we are h.   BIBLE 84:12
healer: compassion of the h.'s   ELIOT 270:22
It is not a great h.   COMP 214:13
healeth: h. those that are broken   BOOK 135:11
healing: expected h. wings   VAUG 708:15
h. greens   ABSE 1:2
H. is a matter of time   HIPP 339:8
h. of the nations   BIBLE 107:23
Let the h. fountain start   AUDEN 34:16
no h. has been necessary   COMP 214:13
not heroics, but h.   HARD 324:2
with h. in his wings   BIBLE 86:19
health: art so far from my h.   BOOK 125:9
case of nutrition and h.   JAY 363:24
for h. unbought   DRYD 260:16
h. and living now begins   SHAK 626:19
h. and plenty cheered   GOLD 310:5
h., and quiet breathing   KEATS 386:13
h. and wealth have missed   HUNT 356:9
h. and wealth long to live   BOOK 119:6
h. of his wife   CONN 216:18
h. shall spring forth speedily   BIBLE 84:23
His h., his honour   BLUN 116:4
horse's h., a boy's love   SHAK 596:18
Importing h. and graveness   SHAK 578:11
innocence and h.   GOLD 310:6
in sickness and in h.   BOOK 123:20
Look to your h.   WALT 721:10
overthroweth your h.   BACON 43:23
spirit of h. or goblin   SHAK 573:9
there is no h. in us   BOOK 118:8
thy saving h.   BOOK 129:4
When you have both it's h.   DONL 250:6
healthful: h. Spirit of thy grace   BOOK 119:8
Without disease the h. life   SURR 672:2
healths: h. and draughts go free   LOV 429:3
healthy: all h. instinct for it   BUTL 167:4
h. and wealthy and dead   THUR 697:15
h. state of political life   MILL 460:17
Remorse cuts away h. tissue   FORS 290:15
heap: rude h. together hurled   MARV 451:12
struck all of a h.   SHER 644:26
waters to stand on an h.   BOOK 130:10
heapeth: he h. up riches   BOOK 126:23
hear: And h. no more at all   STEV 669:3
And h. the larks so high   HOUS 352:10
another to h.   THOR 697:10
can h. my Thisby's face   SHAK 612:24
come when you will h. me   DISR 246:14
h. more good things   HAZL 329:12
H. my law, O my people   BOOK 130:8
H. not my steps   SHAK 601:13
H., O Israel   BIBLE 73:15
H. the other side   AUG 37:5
h. the pleasant cuckoo   DAV 232:9
h. the sins they love   SHAK 618:23

hear: (*cont.*):

h. the word of the Lord	BIBLE 85:27
H. us, we humbly pray	MARR 449:1
He cannot choose but h.	COL 210:19
He that hath ears to h.	BIBLE 93:9
I h. a smile	CROSS 227:20
I h. a sudden cry of pain	STEP 664:1
I h. thy shrill delight	SHEL 643:16
Lord, h. our prayers	BOOK 123:12
may in such wise h. them	BOOK 120:11
O h. us when we cry to thee	WHIT 732:2
O let me h. thee speaking	BODE 116:11
see and h. and feel	JOYCE 381:27
shall he not h.	BOOK 131:8
swift to h., slow to speak	BIBLE 104:27
They never would h.	SWIFT 674:24
To h. the angels sing	SEARS 561:12
to make you h.	CONR 217:9
We beseech thee to h. us	BOOK 119:19
we shall h. it by-and-by	BROW 148:1
which men prefer not to h.	AGAR 5:13
who do not wish to h. it	BUTL 167:8
would h. the mighty crack	ADD 4:5

heard: And then is h. no more   SHAK 605:1

have not h. them	BIBLE 94:12
Have you h. it's in the stars	PORT 525:5
have ye not h.?	BIBLE 83:30
h. for their much speaking	BIBLE 89:4
H., not regarded	SHAK 581:14
h. of thee by the hearing	BIBLE 78:5
h. one side of the case	BUTL 167:2
I never h. thy fire once spark	HEYW 338:5
I will be h.!	GARR 298:11
more he h., the less he spoke	PUNCH 531:22
Oon ere it h., at tother	CHAU 195:21
Scarce h. amid the guns below	MCCR 437:5
should certainly have h.	AUDEN 36:12
twice I have also h.	BOOK 128:20
voice of the turtle is h.	BIBLE 81:9
Which we have h. and known	BOOK 130:8
you ain't h. nuttin' yet	JOLS 377:17

hearers: favourable h.   HOOK 344:13

not h. only	BIBLE 104:27
too deep for his h.	GOLD 311:4

heareth: thy servant h.   BIBLE 74:28

hearing: delicate h. saves   MOORE 482:17

Fall asleep, or h. die	SHAK 588:16
passionate my sense of h.	SHAK 598:12
People h. without listening	SIMON 647:20
Woke to my h. from harbour	THOM 693:12

hearken: h. than fat of rams   BIBLE 74:37

hearkened: he h. not   BIBLE 72:4

h. not unto the voice	BOOK 132:13
h. to my commandments	BIBLE 84:5

hears: She neither h. nor sees   WORD 748:1

hearsay: lived by h. and faith   BUNY 156:17

walls have h.	FONS 288:9

hearse: h. be vexed   CAMP 177:4

laureate h. where Lycid lies	MILT 466:11
Underneath this sable h.	BROW 146:24
walk before the h.	GARR 298:8

hearses: h. besiege your gates   POPE 519:18

heart: aboute myn h. roote   CHAU 194:22

abundance of the h.	BIBLE 90:32
abundance weakens his own h.	SHAK 633:7
accompany me with a pure h.	BOOK 118:6
Ah! ás the h. grows older	HOPK 346:3
Ah God, for a man with h.	TENN 686:13
And I am sick at h.	SHAK 571:22
And my h. beats so that I can	BERL 65:21
And put in a h. o' stane	BALL 50:14
And the flawed h. unmade	WILB 734:6
and the h. is sick	TENN 683:16
And to my dead h. run them	STEV 669:7
And when thy h. began to beat	BLAKE 114:14
And with a well-tuned h.	GURN 320:4
and . . . ories of the h.	LONG 426:23
As my poor h. doth think	IVY Y 433:13
As well as want of h.	HOOD 343:21
at the h. of all identity	PEGUY 511:8
autumn's violins wound my h.	VERL 710:4
awful warmth about my h.	KEATS 391:31
Batter my h.	DONNE 250:24

heart: (*cont.*):

battlefield is the h.	DOST 254:3
Because my h. is pure	TENN 689:7
bicycle-pump the human h.	AMIS 10:18
bitter insights of the h.	PUSH 532:12
blind side of the h.	CHES 198:29
book known to him by h.	WOOLF 742:9
bring with you a h.	WORD 748:8
broken h. lies here	MAC 436:7
Brute h. of a brute like you	PLATH 516:5
Bury my h. at Wounded Knee	BENÉT 62:16
But above all, the h.	HERB 334:7
But break, my h.	SHAK 572:13
But my h.'s right there	JUDGE 382:8
But not your h. away	HOUS 352:9
But now from the h. of joy	BEEC 59:6
Call home the h. you gave me	DRAY 258:6
Calls my h. to be his own	BRID 141:2
Can make a stone of the h.	YEATS 751:14
can no longer tear his h.	SWIFT 675:18
carries his h. in his boots	HERB 333:16
Cold is the h., fair Greece	BYRON 168:6
confidence and faith of the h.	LUTH 432:14
corrupt the h.	BYRON 172:9
curse with their h.	BOOK 128:19
deceiveth his own h.	BIBLE 104:28
deferred maketh the h. sick	BIBLE 78:26
Did not our h. burn within us	BIBLE 95:32
Divided, with but half a h.	KING 396:12
education of the h.	SCOTT 561:7
engraved on her h.	SELL 562:19
eye correct the h.	GARR 298:3
faint h. ne'er wan	BURNS 163:18
fanatic h.	YEATS 752:19
fed the h. on fantasies	YEATS 752:13
felt along the h.	WORD 744:19
Floodgate of the deeper h.	FLEC 286:17
fold to thy h. thy brother	WHIT 733:10
For h. and voice would fail me	CLAR 205:6
For Mercy has a human h.	BLAKE 113:19
Fourteen h. attacks	JOPL 380:12
glad the h. of man	BOOK 132:8
God be in my h.	ANON 13:16
great have no h.	LA BR 405:1
harden Pharaoh's h.	BIBLE 72:3
hast cleft my h. in twain	SHAK 577:21
have garnered up my h.	SHAK 617:15
having war in his h.	BOOK 128:12
h. al holly on hym leye	CHAU 196:2
h. and eye and for ever	CLARE 204:28
h. and hand once belonged	MARL 446:10
h. and my flesh rejoice	BOOK 130:16
H. and soul do sing in me	SIDN 647:5
h. and stomach of a king	ELIZ 274:3
h. as crooked as corkscrews	AUDEN 34:7
h. as sound as a bell	SHAK 613:31
h. be full of the spring	SWIN 676:25
h. *bleeds for his country*	JOHN 371:26
h. break asunder	AKHM 6:8
heart-break in the h.	GIBS 303:5
h. cheer thee in the days	BIBLE 80:30
h. clings to and confides	LUTH 432:15
h. demands its quittance	PUSH 533:2
h. doeth good like a medicine	BIBLE 79:1
h. doth need a language	COL 210:17
h. expands to tinker	MACN 441:3
h. fail because of him	BIBLE 75:1
h. for harping	POUND 527:11
h. grown cold, a head	SHEL 640:1
h. grows old	YEATS 753:6
h. has its reasons	PASC 507:17
h. hath 'scaped this sorrow	SHAK 634:13
h. high-sorrowful and cloyed	KEATS 388:28
h. in my bosom	SHAK 604:15
h. is a blessing that	RICH 540:13
h. is a lonely hunter	MCL 439:12
h. is a small thing	QUAR 533:15
h. is deceitful above all	BIBLE 85:12
h. is Highland	GALT 297:7
h. is inditing	BOOK 127:10
h. is on the left	MUS 170:2
h. for courage greater	ANON 18:20
h. less bounding at e맣oud	ARN 28:25

heart: (*cont.*):

h. lies plain	ARN 26:17
h. moved more	SIDN 647:10
h. of a man is deprest	GAY 299:20
h. of a true Englishman	ADD 4:15
H. of England	DRAY 258:2
h. of kings is unsearchable	BIBLE 79:14
h. of lead	POPE 518:18
h. of man is made to reconcile	HUME 355:14
H. of oak are our ships	GARR 298:4
h. of the poet is whirled	TENN 686:8
h. of the ridiculous	MAHON 442:5
h. *prefers* to move against	UPD 707:5
H. questions was it He	DICK 244:9
h.'s first ease	DAY-L 233:4
h. speaks to h.	FRAN 292:11
H.'s renying, causer of this	BARN 53:17
h.'s stalled motor	MAY 455:5
h. that has truly loved	MOORE 483:2
h. that none is left	SHAK 614:9
h. that one can see rightly	DE S 553:3
h. that wanted somehow	HEAT 329:25
h. to be the chiefest guest	DRAY 257:20
heart to h., and mind to mind	SCOTT 559:15
h. to poke poor Billy	GRAH 313:12
h. turns to travel	POUND 527:11
h. unfortified	SHAK 572:11
h. untravelled fondly turns	GOLD 311:8
h. was piercèd through	SHAK 615:6
h. was to thy rudder tied	SHAK 565:16
H. within, and God o'erhead	LONG 427:9
h. within blood-tinctured	BROW 147:15
hell's h. I stab at thee	MELV 456:20
Her h. was warm and gay	HAMM 322:15
hides one thing in his h.	HOMER 343:7
His flawed h.	SHAK 597:20
his h. in the market-place	SHAK 614:10
his little h.	JAMES 363:9
holiness of the h.'s affections	KEATS 391:5
human h. is strong	BAG 47:5
I feel my h. new opened	SHAK 588:19
If thou wilt ease thinc h.	BEDD 58:8
If thy h. fails thee	ELIZ 274:12
I had rather coin my h.	SHAK 593:6
I left my h. in San Francisco	CROSS 227:19
I live to own h.	RICH 540:12
imagination of man's h. is evil	BIBLE 70:28
in laughter the h. is sorrowful	BIBLE 78:30
In my h.'s core	SHAK 576:7
In the deserts of the h.	AUDEN 34:16
Into my h. an air that kills	HOUS 352:15
Irishman's h. is nothing	SHAW 636:24
I said to H. 'How goes it?'	BELL 61:10
Is your h. at rest	FLET 287:18
hear it in the deep h.'s core	YEATS 752:8
I wish my h. had never	ANON 17:21
Land of H.'s Desire	YEATS 752:9
larger h., kindlier hand	TENN 684:11
laughter of her h.	HAMM 322:15
lay his h. out for my bed	LOW 430.24
lent out my h. with usury	LAMB 406:24
Let no love-desiring h.	GREV 318:5
Let not your h. be troubled	BIBLE 97:10
let your h. be strong	LAUD 411:5
Lift up your h.	WESL 728:13
light h. lives long	SHAK 599:6
little body with a mighty h.	SHAK 585:2
live without h.	MER 458:11
look in thy h. and write	SIDN 646:15
loosed our h. in tears	ARN 27:13
Lord looketh on the h.	BIBLE 74:38
Love, give me back my h.	GRAN 314:15
loving h. to thee	HERR 337:2
lying in my h.	MARY 453:1
Make me a clean h.	BOOK 128:6
makes the h. grow fonder	ANON 11:17
making melody in your h.	BIBLE 102:23
man after his own h.	BIBLE 74:35
mend the h.	POPE 523:14
merry h. maketh a cheerful	BIBLE 78:34
mighty h. is lying still	WORD 743:10
mine eye, but not my h.	JONS 378:18
mischief he had a h.	CIBB 302:5

hell: *(cont.):*

cold for h.	SHAK 602:10
come hot from h.	SHAK 591:24
Down, down to h.	SHAK 588:8
dunnest smoke of h.	SHAK 600:16
ease in h.	WRIG 749:13
even h., with thee to boot	JONS 379:1
eye-deep in h.	POUND 527:1
from h.'s heart I stab	MELV 456:20
gates of H.	PIUS 515:20
God lost, h. found	ALAB 7:1
having harrowed h.	SPEN 659:9
He descended into h.	BOOK 119:1
h. fire	BIBLE 88:29
h. for horses	BURT 165:12
H. in Heaven's despite	BLAKE 114:7
H. is a city much like London	SHEL 642:5
h. is deeper than the sea	BALL 50:7
H. is full of musical amateurs	SHAW 637:10
H. is murky	SHAK 604:12
H. is oneself	ELIOT 270:9
H. is other people	SART 556:11
h. itself will pass away	MILT 467:9
H., madam, is to love no more	BERN 66:7
h. of heaven	MILT 468:12
h. of horses	FLOR 288:5
h. of this world to enjoy	BECK 58:4
H. that was to him	BUNY 156:11
H. to ships, hell to men	AESC 5:11
H. trembled at the hideous	MILT 470:9
H. would not be Hell if	SPAR 658:9
her steps take hold on h.	BIBLE 78:12
if I go down to h.	BOOK 134:19
I myself am h.	LOW 430:20
industrious crew to build in h.	MILT 469:8
In h. they'll roast thee like	BURNS 163:11
injured lover's h.	MILT 471:25
Into the mouth of H.	TENN 680:15
I say the h. with it	WHITE 731:2
I shall move H.	VIRG 714:3
I that in h. wes	DUNB 264:3
it would be h. on earth	SHAW 637:4
jaws of h.	VIRG 713:14
joy in hevene and peyne in h.	CHAU 194:29
keep the gate of h.	SHAK 617:18
keys of h. and of death	BIBLE 106:2
lack of fellowship is h.	MORR 485:15
lead apes in h.	SHAK 624:13
lie in the h. like sheep	BOOK 128:1
made an excursion to h.	PRIE 529:1
make the earth my h.	SHAK 622:5
mentions H. to ears polite	POPE 520:21
never married, and that's his h.	BURT 165:1
Nor H. a fury, like a woman	CONG 215:17
not leave my soul in h.	BOOK 124:31
pains of h. gat hold upon	BOOK 133:11
panoramic view of h.	BYRON 170:14
printing house in H.	BLAKE 113:3
Quiet to quick bosoms is a h.	BYRON 168:22
riches grow in h.	MILT 469:5
Sent to H., Sir	JOHN 376:12
shout that tore h.'s concave	MILT 468:23
Slander, meanest spawn of H.	TENN 685:5
society would be a h.	MILL 461:1
summons thee to heaven or h.	SHAK 601:13
tell you to go to h. in such a way	STIN 669:11
that out of h. leads up	MILT 469:21
that there was a way to H.	BUNY 156:6
There's h., there's darkness	SHAK 597:5
they think it is h	TRUM 704:17
this is h., nor am I out of it	MARL 446:15
though h. should bar the way	NOYES 497:6
thou profoundest h.	MILT 468:12
threats of H.	FITZ 284:1
to fly in hell; myself am h.	MILT 470:25
to h. I will go	MILL 460:13
torment, there's the h.	KYD 404:13
where we are is H.	MARL 446:16
why they invented H.	RUSS 551:22
with h. are we at agreement	BIBLE 83:12
working definition of h.	SHAW 638:13
Yours till H. freezes	FISH 283:6

hell-broth: h. boil and bubble — SHAK 603:18
Hellenism: Hebraism and H. — ARN 29:12
Hellespont: straight H. — DONNE 250:12
hell-gate: porter of h. — SHAK 602:8
hellhound: h. is always a h. — WOD 740:10
hell-kite: O h.! — SHAK 604:9
hell-pains: hate him as I do h. — SHAK 614:25
helluva: New York,—a h. town — COMD 214:11
helmet: h. and the h.-feather — TENN 685:3

h. now shall make a hive	PEELE 511:5
h., the hope of salvation	BIBLE 103:21
Not cowardly put off my h.	SHAK 566:14
She saw the h. and the plume	TENN 685:4

help: and h. there's none — HODG 340:18

cannot h. or pardon	AUDEN 36:8
Can't h. lovin' dat man	HAMM 322:17
comfort of thy h.	BOOK 128:6
For we have no h. but Thee	EDM 266:17
from whence cometh my h.	BOOK 133:23
God h. me	LUTH 432:10
God shall h. her	BOOK 127:16
heaven will h. you	LA F 405:8
h. and support of the woman	EDW 267:5
h. is in the name	BOOK 123:11
h. me, heaven	FIRB 282:25
h. of my countenance	BOOK 127:8
H. of the helpless	LYTE 433:16
h. standeth in the Name	BOOK 134:2
h. the feeble up	SHAK 626:4
hour that requires such h.	VIRG 713:2
little h. from my friends	LENN 418:4
nor h. for pain	ARN 27:1
place where h. wasn't hired	ANON 14:4
power of ourselves to h.	BOOK 120:15
present h. in time of trouble	ANON 11:16
scream for h. in dreams	CAN 178:2
Since there's no h.	DRAY 258:1
there is no h. in them	BOOK 135:8
very present h. in trouble	BOOK 127:15
Who ran to h. me when I fell	TAYL 679:13
will make him an h. meet	BIBLE 70:4
you can't h. it	SMITH 651:15
your countrymen cannot h.	JOHN 371:25

helped: over, and can't be h. — DICK 243:13
 We shall have h. it — DICK 244:5
helper: mother's little h. — JAGG 361:10
 my h. and redeemer — BOOK 126:26
 Our antagonist is our h. — BURKE 158:24
helpers: When other h. fail — LYTE 433:16
helpless: H., naked — BLAKE 114:8
 Help of the h. — LYTE 433:16
 they h. are undone — GREE 317:8
helps: What h. it now — ARN 28:21
hem: h. of Nature's shift — SHEL 642:6
hemlock: of h. I had drunk — KEATS 389:8
hempen: sing in a h. string — FLET 287:13
 What h. home-spuns have we — SHAK 611:24
hen: better take a wet h. — KHR 395:17
 h. gathereth her chickens — BIBLE 92:7
 of that text a pulled h. — CHAU 192:17
hence: H., loathèd Melancholy — MILT 465:3
 H., vain deluding joys — MILT 464:13
henceforth: h. all generations — BIBLE 93:22
 h. in his holy ways — BOOK 122:5
henna: Of tan with h. hackles — STEV 665:16
hen-pecked: h. you all — BYRON 170:4
Henri: *Je dirais au roi H.* — ANON 21:5
Heraclitus: They told me, H. — CORY 219:15
herald: Hark! the h.-angels sing — WESL 728:3
 I wish no other h. — SHAK 589:12
heraldry: boast of h. — GRAY 315:13
herb: dew bespangling h. — HERR 336:10

from the h. at your feet	TROL 703:19
h. for the service of men	BOOK 132:8
h. of grace o' Sundays	SHAK 578:8
some single h. or tree	MARV 450:5
sour h. of grace	SHAK 620:16

herbs: dinner of h. — BIBLE 78:35

greatest among h.	BIBLE 91:3
have it for a garden of h.	BIBLE 76:10
h., and other country messes	MILT 465:12
with bitter h. they shall eat	BIBLE 72:9

Hercules: and some of H. — ANON 18:3
 is not love a H. — SHAK 598:20
 Than I to H. — SHAK 572:12
herd: above the vulgar h. — GAIS 296:15
 h. of swine ran violently — BIBLE 90:3
 lowing h. wind slowly o'er — GRAY 315:10
 rules the unreflecting h. — WORD 744:7
herd-instinct: Morality is h. — NIET 495:10
herdman: faithful h.'s art — MILT 466:8
herdsman: h. goads them on — YEATS 751:7
here: Are *you* h., Advocate — DANTE 230:14

H. am I; send me	BIBLE 82:22
H., a sheer hulk, lies	DIBD 238:16
H. I am, and here I stay	MACM 440:1
H.'s a how-de-doo	GILB 304:28
H.'s looking at you, kid	FPST 270:0
H.'s tae us	ANON 14:7
H.'s to thee, Corbet	AUBR 33:1
H.'s to the widow of fifty	SHER 645:18
H. today—in next week	GRAH 314:3
h.'s to you, Mrs Robinson	SIMON 647:19
H. were decent godless	ELIOT 272:16
I have been h. before	ROSS 548:8
I'm only h. for the beer	LEV 419:16
It can't happen h.	LEWIS 421:6
We're h. because we're here	ANON 19:8
We're h. because we're queer	BEHAN 60:5
What you seek is h.	HOR 348:9

hereafter: h. hold his peace — BOOK 123:18
 She should have died h. — SHAK 605:1
 that points out an h. — ADD 3:23
hereditary: H. bondsmen! — BYRON 168:10
 h. government — PAINE 504:20
 h. monarch was insane — BAG 46:19
hereditas: *Damnosa h.* — GAIUS 296:18
Hereford: In Hertford, H. — LERN 419:6
heresies: hateful h. — SPEN 660:22
 new truths to begin as h. — HUXL 358:9
 Religions are kept alive by h. — BREN 140:13
heresy: Englishman believes in h.? — SHAW 638:23

h. signifies no more	HOBB 340:4
No h. can excite the horror	MAC 435:1

heretic: h. makes the fire — SHAK 631:19
 oppressor or a h. — CAMUS 177:19
heretics: H. the only remedy — ZAMY 755:5
heritage: h. unto Israel — BOOK 134:15
 I have a goodly h. — BOOK 124:30
 we have come into our h. — BROO 143:4
hermit: A rake turned h. — ALC 8:1
 More torment than a h.'s fast — KEATS 388:16
hermitage: palace for a h. — SHAK 620:12
 take that for an h. — LOV 429:4
hermits: h. are contented — WORD 745:7
Hermon: little hill of H. — BOOK 127:4
hern: haunts of coot and h. — TENN 680:11
hero: Came the h. from his prison — AYT 41:2

Every h. becomes a bore	EMER 277:12
he acted like a h.	WALP 720:5
h. is a man who would argue	MAIL 442:9
h. of my tale	TOLS 700:10
h. perish, or sparrow fall	POPE 521:29
Millions a h.	PORT 525:6
No man is a h. to his valet	CORN 219:10
See, the conquering h. comes	MOR 484:17
Show me a h. and I will	FITZ 284:23
they don't want to be a h.	STOP 670:8
very valet seemed a h.	BYRON 167:22
who aspires to be a h.	JOHN 375:7

Herod: it out-herods H. — SHAK 576:5
 Oh, for an hour of H. — HOPE 344:25
heroes: all the world's brave h. — ANON 18:3
 And its h. were made — Æ 5:10
 Britain a fit country for h. — LLOY 424:8
 hand in hand with my strange h. — GOGOL 310:1

have h. to dine with us	TROL 703:14
h. as good as warming-pans	MER 457:16
h. of old	BROW 152:5
h. that the world can know	COLL 213:2
h. up the line to death	SASS 557:4
land that needs h.	BREC 140:6

heroic: finished a life h. — MILT 474:17
first of h. poets — MAC 434:12
h. for earth too hard — BROW 148:1
h. poem of its sort — CARL 180:9
H. womanhood — LONG 427:13
One equal temper of h. hearts — TENN 690:4
heroically: h. mad — DRYD 259:14
heroics: present need is not h. — HARD 324:2
heroine: h. goes mad — SHER 644:24
Herren-Moral: H. und Sklaven-Moral. — NIET 495:15
Herrgott: Raffiniert ist der H. — EINS 268:1
herring: plague o' these pickle h. — SHAK 628:21
they'll roast there like a h. — BURNS 163:11
herrschen: Du musst h. — GOET 309:9
Hertford: In H., Hereford — LERN 419:6
Hervey: If you call a dog H. — JOHN 371:5
Herveys: women, and H. — MONT 480:8
Herzen: Zwei H. und ein Schlag — HALM 322:7
hesitate: spirit could long h. — STEV 668:11
Who h. and falter life away — ARN 28:8
hesitates: She floats, she h. — RAC 535:3
Hesperides: climbing trees in H. — SHAK 598:20
Hesperus: H. entreats thy light — JONS 378:16
It was the schooner H. — LONG 428:3
venit H. — VIRG 715:9
heterodoxy: h. is another man's doxy — WARB 721:15
My doxy and H. or Thy-doxy — CARL 180:21
heterogeneity: coherent h. — SPEN 658:16
heures: et vous, h. propices — LAM 406:1
hew: h. him as a carcass fit — SHAK 590:18
some body to h. and hack — BUTL 166:8
hewers: h. of wood — BIBLE 73:31
hewn: h. out her seven pillars — BIBLE 78:18
hey: H. for God Almighty — KETT 394:14
Then h. for boot and horse — KING 397:17
hey-day: h. in the blood is tame — SHAK 577:13
hi: He would answer to 'H.!' — CARR 183:28
H. diddle dee dee — WASH 722:3
hic: H. jacet — RAL 536:6
Quod petis h. est — HOR 348:9
hick: Sticks nix h. pix — ANON 18:5
hid: h. as it were our faces — BIBLE 84:11
h. from thine eyes — BIBLE 95:18
h. themselves in the dens — BIBLE 106:17
I h. from Him — THOM 695:1
set on an hill cannot be h. — BIBLE 88:25
to keep that h. — DONNE 252:20
Wherefore are these things h. — SHAK 628:14
hidden: fallen, and h. her head — SWIN 676:22
follows the h. path — LUIS 432:7
For Famagusta and the h. sun — FLEC 286:12
Half h. from the eye — WORD 747:18
h. in each other's hearts — DICK 241:20
h. persuaders — PACK 504:3
teems with h. meaning — GILB 306:19
Thou h. love of God — WESL 728:16
hide: h. in cooling trees — KEATS 390:5
H. me from day's garish eye — MILT 464:25
H. me, O my Saviour, hide — WESL 728:6
h. of a rhinoceros — BARR 54:16
h. us from the face — BIBLE 106:17
h. with ornaments — POPE 521:11
His h. is sure to flatten 'em — BELL 60:23
Is it a world to h. virtues — SHAK 628:15
Let me h. myself in Thee — TOPL 701:4
Prime Minister has nothing to h. — CHUR 203:8
thou h. thy face from me — BOOK 124:25
Whose h. he sold — WALL 718:8
wrapped in a woman's h. — SHAK 587:28
hideous: h. notes of woe — BYRON 171:28
Making night h. — SHAK 573:9
hides: that h. a dark soul — MILT 463:27
H. h. himself his state — JOHN 370:18
H. not his visage — SHAK 632:9
h. one thing in his heart and — HOMER 340:11
hungry h. plane from the wind — BIBLE 83:17
h. in the cleanness with him — DYLAN 608:26
My heart in h. — HOPK 346:11
hiding-place: dark lonely h. — COL 210:7
hier: H. stehe ich — LUTH 432:10

Hierusalem: H., my happy home — ANON 14:10
high: Cannot be heard so h. — SHAK 597:1
Every man who is h. up — BARR 54:15
for contempt too h. — COWL 221:11
h. altar on the move — BOWEN 138:14
h. and frosty heaven — BRID 141:4
H. as a flag on the Fourth — HAMM 323:1
h. as an elephant's eye — HAMM 322:16
h. birth a form of congenital — WOOLF 742:4
H. diddle diddle — GILB 305:19
h. heels are most agreeable — SWIFT 673:10
h. life high characters — POPE 520:26
h. road that leads — JOHN 372:7
h. that proved too high — BROW 148:1
h. the heaven in comparison — BOOK 132:5
h. time to awake out — BIBLE 100:10
h. with a little help from — LENN 418:4
house of defence very h. — BOOK 131:4
knowledge in the most H. — BOOK 130:1
like champagne or h. heels — BENN 63:19
no h. flyer — PEPYS 512:11
O Lord most H. — BOOK 122:10
She's the Broad and I'm the H. — SPR 661:11
slain in thine h. places — BIBLE 75:9
stand in your account — SHAK 609:2
This h. man, with a great — BROW 150:1
upon the h. horse — BROWN 144:12
which arc too h. for me — BOOK 134:13
wickedness in h. places — RIBLE 103:1
ye'll tak' the h. road — ANON 17:8
highbrow: What is a h.? — WALL 718:3
higher: find my own the h. — CORN 219:2
Friend, go up h. — BIBLE 94:27
production of the h. animals — DARW 231:10
Stuart or Nassau go h. — PRIOR 529:6
subject unto the h. powers — BIBLE 100:8
their dead selves to h. things — TENN 682:30
highest: children of most H. — BOOK 130:15
h. good — CIC 204:1
needs must love the h. — TENN 681:27
not down in the h. room — BIBLE 94:26
Highland: heart is H. — GALT 297:7
Yon solitary H. lass — WORD 748:3
Highlandman: breeks aff a wild H. — SCOTT 560:18
highlands: Farewell to the H. — BURNS 162:23
In the h., in the country — STEV 668:23
My heart's in the H. — BURNS 162:22
to the H. bound — CAMP 176:15
Ye H. and ye Lawlands — BALL 49:2
highly: what thou wouldst h. — SHAK 600:15
high-minded: I am not h. — BOOK 134:13
high-mindedness: honourable h. — BRAM 139:15
highway: broad h. of world — SHEL 640:10
h. for our God — BIBLE 83:26
H., since you my chief — SIDN 647:2
which passes over a h. — STEN 663:13
highways: happy h. where I went — HOUS 352:15
out into the h. and hedges — BIBLE 94:32
hijacker: h. of the oxygen — THAT 691:23
hilarity: h. was like a scream — GREE 317:2
h. with the wing of friendship — DICK 242:18
hill: all gone under the h. — ELIOT 270:20
bring me unto thy holy h. — BOOK 127:7
Cassidy's hanging h. — KAV 386:2
city set on an h. cannot be hid — BIBLE 88:25
city upon a h. — WINT 739:10
every mountain and h. — BIBLE 83:26
green h. in an April shroud — KEATS 389:6
High on a h. it calls to me — CROSS 227:19
hunter home from the h. — STEV 669:9
into the life of the h. — BERRY 66:15
laughing is heard on the h. — BLAKE 114:2
little h. of Hermon — BOOK 127:4
Mahomet will go to the h. — BACON 42:31
nursed upon the self-same h. — MILT 465:22
On a huge h. — DONNE 251:15
On the cold h.'s side — KEATS 388:13
on the last h. — BUKE 541:7
other side of the h. — WELL 727:1
round it was upon a h. — STEV 665:14
shall rest upon thy holy h. — BOOK 174:22

hill: (cont.):
this is God's h. — BOOK 129:9
To their haven under the h. — TENN 680:10
hills: Along Morea's h. — BYRON 169:25
angel satyr walks these h. — KILV 396:8
Before the h. in order stood — WATTS 723:7
blue remembered h. — HOUS 352:15
cattle upon a thousand h. — BOOK 128:2
he do but touch the h. — BOOK 132:10
h. are a refuge — BOOK 132:9
h. like Gods together — TENN 686:1
h. of Georgia — KING 397:1
H. of home — STEV 669:3
H. of the Chankly Bore — LEAR 413:20
H. of the North, rejoice — OAKL 497:8
h. of the South Country — BELL 61:28
H. peep o'er hills — POPE 521:9
h. shall rejoice — BOOK 129:3
h. stand about Jerusalem — BOOK 134:3
I to the h. will lift mine eyes — SCOT 561:10
lift up mine eyes unto the h. — BOOK 133:23
little h. like young sheep — BOOK 133:8
little h. righteousness — BOOK 129:19
out on the h. alone — KILV 396:7
Over the h. and far away — GAY 299:17
Over the h. and far away — STEV 669:10
strength of the h. is his also — BOOK 131:10
though the h. be carried — BOOK 127:15
to the reverberate h. — SHAK 628:24
waters stand in the h. — BOOK 132:6
Why hop ye so, ye high h. — BOOK 129:9
yon are the h. o' Heaven — BALL 49:6
hill-side: h.'s dew-pearled — BROW 151:28
him: H. first, him last — MILT 471:23
That's h.! — BARH 52:16
himself: Ech man for h. — CHAU 193:17
He h. said it — CIC 203:28
he shall speak for h. — BIBLE 96:35
my short answer is 'h.' — IBSEN 359:6
Poor Brutus, with h. at war — SHAK 589:25
subdue all things to h. — BOOK 124:5
hind: h. that would be mated — SHAK 564:2
hinder: And all the h. parts — SPEN 659:25
hindered: h. in running the race — BOOK 120:12
hinders: wickedness h. loving — BROW 151:16
Hindoo: dies, or turns H. — SHEL 641:4
hindrance: to his own h. — BOOK 124:29
hinds: h. to bring forth young — BOOK 126:3
hindsight: H. is twenty-twenty — WILD 736:14
hinges: As the door on its h. — WATTS 722:18
on their h. grate — MILT 470:10
hinky: H., dinky, parley-voo — ANON 16:6
hip: catch him once upon h. — SHAK 607:20
He smote them h. and thigh — BIBLE 74:16
H. is the sophistication — MAIL 442:10
Hippocrene: blushful H. — KEATS 389:9
hippopotamus: h. resolved at any cost — WELLS 727:14
h.'s day — ELIOT 271:13
shoot the H. — BELL 60:23
shoot the h. — FORS 289:19
hips: armchairs tight about the h. — WOD 740:19
We swing ungirded h. — SORL 656:16
when your h. stick — NASH 490:16
whole quire hold their h. — SHAK 611:12
hipsters: angelheaded h. — GINS 306:28
hire: labourer worthy of his h. — BIBLE 94:10
hired: flames and h. tears — BROW 145:15
h. servants of my father's — BIBLE 95:3
They h. the money — COOL 218:8
hireling: h. fleeth — BIBLE 97:1
h. for treason to his country — JOHN 368:5
hirelings: lewd h. — MILT 471:1
Hiroshima: Einstein leads to H. — PIC 514:11
hiss: dismal universal h. — MILT 473:4
hissed: h. along polished ice — WORD 744:9
historian: first requisite of h. — STR 670:14
h. of the Roman empire — GIBB 302:17
h. short and precarious — GIBB 302:19
h. wants more documents — JAMES 362:15
h. must inquire for an h. — JOHN 372:6
one safe rule for the h. — FISH 283:1
historians: h. can utter the past — BUTL 168:8

home: (*cont.*):

h. his footsteps turned	SCOTT 559:16
Home, home, sweet, sweet h.	PAYNE 510:4
H. is home, though it	CLAR 205:14
H. is the girl's prison	SHAW 638:1
H. is the place where	FROST 294:15
H. is the sailor	STEV 669:9
H. James, and don't spare	HILL 339:17
H. life as we understand	SHAW 636:14
h. life of our own dear Queen	ANON 14:12
H. of lost causes	ARN 29:15
h. of the bean and the cod	BOSS 137:1
h. of the brave	KEY 394:15
h., rejoicing, brought me	BAKER 47:20
H. they brought her warrior	TENN 688:9
H. was no home to him	COL 211:23
h. will be quaint	FISH 283:7
h., you idle creatures	SHAK 589:19
house is not a h.	ADLER 5:9
hunter h. from the hill	STEV 669:9
it never is at h.	COWP 222:4
land is not the sweet h.	AUDEN 35:1
leaving h. and my folks	STEV 668:22
Look as much like h. as	FRY 295:24
make one feel more at h.	FREUD 293:21
man goeth to his long h.	BIRLE 81:1
My h. it is the Sule Skerry	BALL 49:12
My h. policy	CLEM 206:6
never felt myself from h.	BOSW 137:5
never h. came she	KING 397:14
points of heaven and h.	WORD 748:12
that drive one from h.	HOOD 343:24
that has been kept at h.	COWP 223:5
that it's a refuge from h.	SHAW 638:27
their h. among the dead	SHEL 640:10
there's nobody at h.	POPE 519:22
there's no place like h.	PAYNE 510:4
Till the boys come H.	FORD 289:16
to feel ashamed of h.	DICK 240:30
want to go h. in the dark	HENRY 333:4
what is it to be at h.	BECK 57:11
What's the good of a h.	GROS 319:2
won't go h. till morning	BUCK 154:13
won't you come h. Bill Bailey	CANN 178:13
home-acre: hearth-fire and h.	KIPL 400:8
home-fires: Keep H. burning	FORD 289:16
home-keeping: H. youth	SHAK 630:38
homeland: more I loved my h.	BELL 62:9
homeless: Send these, the h.	LAZ 413:7
those who are h. by choice	SOUT 657:18
homely: h. was their food	GARTH 298:14
It is for h. features	MILT 464:8
though it be never so h.	CLAR 205:14
youth have ever h. wits	SHAK 630:38
home-made: H. dishes that drive one	
	HOOD 343:24
Homer: excellent H. nods	HOR 347:17
Gladstone read H. for fun	CHUR 203:2
H. invariably composes	ARN 30:6
H. is not more decidedly	MAC 434:12
H. smote 'is bloomin' lyre	KIPL 401:10
H. sometimes sleeps	BYRON 171:5
In Homer more than H. knew	SWIFT 675:2
living H. begged his bread	ANON 17:19
Seven cities warred for H.	HEYW 338:6
towns contend for H. dead	ANON 17:19
you must not call it H.	BENT 64:20
homes: From quiet h. and first	BELL 62:3
h. without a friend	CLARE 204:23
Stately H. of England	COW 221:2
stately h. of England	HEM 331:11
whose h. are nothing more	MOT 487:2
home-spuns: hempen h.	SHAK 611:24
homeward: h. take your way	COLL 212:23
Look h. angel	MILT 466:12
ploughman h. plods	GRAY 315:10
rooks in families h. go	HARDY 326:9
L mindful gleam h. classics	STOI 0:11
hommage l'hypocrisie est l'h	I A R 410:16
homme: le style est l'h.	BUFF 154:16
homo: Ecce h.	BIBLE 110:14
ET H. FACTUS EST	MISS 476:23
naked ape self-named H. sapiens	MORR 485:6

homogeneity: incoherent h.	SPEN 658:16
honest: As h. madam's issue	SHAK 594:26
beat the h. men	SHAK 604:5
buy it like an h. man	NORT 496:20
Corrupted h. men	SHAK 566:1
Fair fa' your h., sonsie face	BURNS 163:13
general h. thought	SHAK 593:23
h. broker who really wants	BISM 110:5
h. chronicler as Griffith	SHAK 589:12
H. God is the noblest work	ING 360:7
H. labour bears a lovely face	DEKK 235:15
h. man's the noblest work	BURNS 161:19
h. man's the noblest work	POPE 522:20
h. men are better	CROM 227:5
h. tale speeds best	SHAK 622:6
h. talk and wholesome wine	TENN 689:13
H. to God	ROB 542:14
least h. themselves	AUST 38:16
man looked h. enough	TWAIN 706:6
maxim is not an h. man	WHAT 730:10
myself indifferent h.	SHAK 575:18
Report be an h. woman	SHAK 608:20
She was poor but she was h.	ANON 17:20
thinks men h. that but seem	SHAK 615:12
Though I am not naturally h.	SHAK 632:13
To be direct and h. is not	SHAK 616:21
to be h., as this world goes	SHAK 574:19
very h. woman	SHAK 567:4
we who lived by h. dreams	DAY-L 233:7
whatsoever things are h.	BIBLE 103:13
Win us with h. trifles	SHAK 600:10
world's grown h.	SHAK 574:25
honester: no h. than I	SHAK 614:4
honesties: imagining prodigious h.	WILB 734:2
honestly: If possible h.	HOR 347:22
honesty: armed so strong in h.	SHAK 593:5
h. and love doth mince	SHAK 616:3
h. dwells like a miser	SHAK 569:25
h. is a good thing	MARQ 448:17
h. is *not* to be based either	RUSK 550.26
H. is praised and left	JUV 383:14
H. is the best policy	WHAT 730:10
make thine h. a vice	SHAK 616:21
parted so much h. among 'em	SHAK 589:13
perilous to a man's h.	TROL 703:25
saving of thine h.	MORE 484:15
what a fool H.	SHAK 632:12
yet I hold it not h.	SHAK 574:22
honey: As the h. of Hybla	SHAK 579:19
Butter and h. shall he eat	BIBLE 82:24
citizens kneading up the h.	SHAK 584:22
did but taste a little h.	BIBLE 74:36
flowing with milk and h.	BIBLE 71:40
gather h. all the day	WATTS 722:12
gather h. from the weed	SHAK 585:20
hive for the h. bee	YEATS 752:7
h. of his music vows	SHAK 576:6
h. of poison-flowers	TENN 686:9
H. of roses	HERB 335:4
H., your silk stocking's	SELL 562:18
How a bear likes h.	MILNE 462:19
is there h. still for tea	BROO 143:15
It's no go my h. love	MACN 440:15
locusts and wild h.	BIBLE 88:14
make h. not for yourselves	VIRG 715:20
my mouth sweet as h.	BIBLE 106:28
our hives with h. and wax	SWIFT 673:4
sun drips h.	LEE 415:19
surfeited with h.	SHAK 581:14
sweeter also than h.	BOOK 125:5
took some h., and plenty of	LEAR 414:12
very h. of all earthly joy	COWL 221:16
With milk and h. blessed	NEALE 491:5
honey-bees: h. come build	YEATS 752:13
so work the h.	SHAK 584:22
honeycomb: gave him of an h.	BIBLE 95:34
strange woman drop as an h.	BIBLE 78:12
than h. row and the h.	BOOK 125:5
honey-dew: he on h. hath fed	COL 210:14
honeyed: h. middle of the night	KEATS 407:1
honey heavy dew of slumber	SHAK 590:21
honeyless: And leave them h.	SHAK 593:14

honeysuckle: h., I am the bee	FITZ 283:8
honi: H. soie qui mal y pense	SELL 562:18
H. soit qui mal y pense	ANON 20:9
honorificabilitudinitatibus: long by	
the head as h.	SHAK 599:4
honour: air signed with their h.	SPEN 659:1
All is lost save h.	FRAN 292:9
Ascribe unto the Lord the h.	BOOK 131:11
as he was valiant, I h. him	SHAK 592:3
cannot be maintained with h.	RUSS 552:2
drowned h. by the locks	SHAK 580:1
either property or h.	MACH 438:11
Fear God. H. the King	KITC 402:17
fighting for this woman's h.	KALM 385:1
fountain of h.	BACON 42:17
fountain of h.	BAG 46:14
fount whence h.	MARL 448:2
Give h. unto Luke Evangelist	ROSS 548:3
Giving h. unto the wife	BIBLE 105:13
greater share of h.	SHAK 586:10
helps the hurt that H. feels	TENN 685:12
his end to be without h.	BIBLE 87:3
H. all men	BIBLE 105:13
H., and all things else	JONS 379:1
h., and keep her in sickness	BOOK 123:19
h. and life have been spared	FRAN 292:9
h., and welfare of this	CHAR 191:11
h. a physician	BIBLE 87:33
h. aspireth to it	BACON 43:9
H. but an empty bubble	DRYD 259:21
h. doth forget men's names	SHAK 593:25
H. from the pale-faced moon	SHAK 580:1
H. has come back	BROO 143:4
h. in one eye	SHAK 589:26
H. is like a match	PAGN 504:5
H. is the subject	SHAK 589:27
h. or dishonour	LINC 422:5
H. pricks me	SHAK 582:1
h. rooted in dishonour	TENN 682:3
h.'s voice provoke	GRAY 315:14
H. the greatest poet	DANTE 230:9
h. the very flea	JONS 378:19
h. those whom they have slain	DOST 254:8
H. thy father and thy mother	BIBLE 72:16
honour to whom h.	BIBLE 100:9
H.! tut, a breath	JONS 379:11
h. we had forgotten	LLOY 424:6
h. which shall bate	SHAK 598:6
H., without money	RAC 535:7
h. would be satisfied	WAUGH 724:7
in h. clear	POPE 520:32
In h. I gained them	NFLS 491:13
I resolved to h. and renown	ANON 17:21
Is from the book of h. razèd	SHAK 633:9
journey be his, and h. therof	EDW 267:2
Keeps h. bright	SHAK 627:20
king delighteth to h.	BIBLE 76:36
Leave not a stain in thine h.	BIBLE 87:32
left hand riches and h.	BIBLE 78:8
leisure with h.	CIC 204:3
Let us h. if we can	AUDEN 36:10
like not such grinning h.	SHAK 582:4
loss of h. was a wrench	GRAH 313:8
louder he talked of his h.	EMER 276:18
Loved I not h. more	LOV 429:6
make one vessel unto h.	BIBLE 100:2
man will not abide in h.	BOOK 127:24
may we h. it	WEBS 725:10
mine h. from corruption	SHAK 589:12
Mine h. is my life	SHAK 619:7
nought in hate, all in h.	BIBLE 618:19
Of h. and the sword	CHES 199:3
peace I hope with h.	DISR 247:27
peace with h.	CHAM 189:8
perfect ways of h.	SHAK 589:16
places where their h. died	POPE 520:11
plains of h. and reputation	JONS 379:5
post of h. a private station	ADD 3:22
prefer mere existence to h.	JUV 384:4
prophet is not without h.	BIBLE 91:5
quinol h. turn to dust	MARV 451:3
republic a roll of h.	CLEV 208:10

honour: (cont.):
reputation and h.   SOCR 654:11
right of h. cuts falsehood   GURN 320:1
some smatch of h.   SHAK 593:22
specific notions of h.   WEBER 724:20
that chastity of h.   BURKE 158:14
this state of temporary h.   JOHN 370:1
throne *we* h. is the *people*   SHER 644:28
tide is ready her to h.   BEST 67:1
Trouthe and h., fredom   CHAU 192:8
When h.'s at the stake   SHAK 577:33
Ye take mine h. from me if   KIPL 399:16
honourable: among thy h. women
    BOOK 127:12
Brutus is an h. man   SHAK 592:5
Brutus is an h. man   SHAK 592:6
designs were strictly h.   FIEL 287:14
h. alike in what we give   LINC 422:6
h. among men   BOOK 123:16
lest a more h. man than   BIBLE 94:26
Let us make an h. retreat   SHAK 569:3
honoured: hath h. me of late   SHAK 601:4
h. in the breach   SHAK 573:8
h. of them all   TENN 690:1
honours: bears his blushing h.   SHAK 588:19
despise h.   HOR 351:11
good card to play for H.   BENN 63:21
his h. to the world again   SHAK 589:5
Mindless of its just h.   WORD 747:17
neither h. nor wages   GAR 298:1
Hood: *Here lies bold Robin H.!*   BALL 49:7
hoof: though he divide the h.   BIBLE 73:1
hoofs: h. in a village street   LONG 427:20
h. of a swinish multitude   BURKE 158:18
When plunging h. were gone   DE L 236:8
hook: great h. nose like thine   BLAKE 111:13
h. where he suspends   BYRON 167:18
leviathan with an h.   BIBLE 78:4
my bended h. shall pierce   SHAK 565:12
thy h. spares the next swath   KEATS 390:18
hookah-mouth: sliding puffs from the h.
    KIPL 398:14
hook-nosed: h. fellow of Rome   SHAK 583:25
hooks: his h. and his crooks   BURNS 163:3
h. shall tangle me no more   WYATT 749:15
hoot: literary mornings with its h.   AUDEN 35:2
hooting: H. and shrieking   SHAK 590:10
h. at dawn flew away   BEER 59:17
h. at the glorious sun   COL 210:2
shunting and h.   BURR 164:7
Hoover: onto the board of H.   GREER 317:15
hooves: No mad h. galloping   KAV 386:4
hop: H. forty paces through   SHAK 565:7
Why h. ye so, ye high hills   BOOK 129:9
hope: Abandon all h.   DANTE 230:6
against hope believed in h.   BIBLE 99:24
Alas! I have nor h. nor health   SHEL 643:10
All my h. on God is founded   BRID 141:2
All our h. is fallen   HOR 350:14
Beautiful Evelyn H. is dead   BROW 149:20
best h. of earth   LINC 422:6
But not another's h.   WALSH 720:19
Can something, h., wish   HOPK 345:7
certain h. of the Resurrection   BOOK 124:5
death of h. and despair   ELIOT 271:4
either h. and agitation   BAR 52:1
equal h.   MILT 468:3
equal poise of h. and fear   MILT 463:28
failure of h.   GIBB 302:21
fair day warn us not to h.   HOR 350:16
faith, h., charity   BIBLE 101:1
God is our h. and strength   BOOK 127:15
heirs through h.   BOOK 122:14
H. (like thy fool)   LYLY 433:12
H. again for aught   MORR 485:10
H. could ne'er have flown   MARV 450:2
h. danceth without music   HERB 336:4
H. deferred maketh   BIBLE 78:26
h., fear, rage, pleasure   JUV 383:16
H., for a season, bade   CAMP 176:17
h. for greater favours   LA R 410:20
h. for the best   SMITH 653:9

hope: (cont.):
h. full of immortality   BIBLE 86:28
h. grew round me   COL 209:16
h. I dreamed of was a dream   ROSS 547:5
h. in Christ   BIBLE 101:6
h. in our Lord Jesus   BIBLE 103:19
H. is a good breakfast   BACON 45:25
h. I will be religious   FLEM 287:4
Hopeless h. hopes   CLARE 204:23
h. maketh not ashamed   BIBLE 99:25
h. never comes that comes to   MILT 468:1
h. of all the ends   BOOK 129:1
h. of glory   BOOK 120:8
h. of the ungodly   BIBLE 87:6
h. of unbending Tories   MAC 435:3
h., once crushed   ARN 28:29
H., politeness, the blowing   FORS 290:22
H. raises no dust   E.LUA 276:2
h.'s delusive mine   JOHN 370:10
H. springs eternal   POPE 522:1
h. that is unwilling   WORD 747:13
h. that keeps up a wife's spirits   GAY 299:16
h. that never had a fear   COWP 224:13
hope till H. creates   SHEL 642:20
H. withering fled   BYRON 169:19
h. without an object   COL 211:24
I have h. to live   SHAK 606:6
Land of H. and Glory   BENS 63:23
Lead me from despair to h.   KUMAR 404:8
leaves of h.   SHAK 588:19
look forward to with h.   FROST 294:14
more h. of a fool than of him   BIBLE 79:22
my h. is better   SHAK 630:27
my h. is perished   BIBLE 85:17
Never to h. again   SHAK 588:19
Nor dread nor h. attend   YEATS 751:9
nursing the unconquerable h.   ARN 28:10
one more rich in h.   SHAK 633:10
or h. beyond ourselves   SHEL 644:9
Our h. for years to come   WATTS 723:7
phantoms of h.   JOHN 369:18
Poetry is a religion with no h.   COCT 208:6
reinforcement gain from h.   MILT 468:9
Some blessed H., whereof   HARDY 325:5
Take back the h. you gave   BROW 150:19
Through love, through h.   WORD 747:15
Thus high uplifted beyond h.   MILT 469:10
triumph of h. over experience   JOHN 373:12
True h. is swift   SHAK 622:8
unsettled is there any h.   EMER 276:22
upon h. will die fasting   FRAN 292:17
Was the h. drunk   SHAK 601:5
Whatever is yours   OWEN 503:19
what is h. but deceiving   MER 458:11
What is h.?   BYRON 174:1
what was dead was H.   WILDE 736:3
whence this pleasing h.   ADD 3:23
when existence or when h. is gone   AUST 39:7
Where there is despair, h.   FRAN 292:12
wish for what I faintly h.   DRYD 261:18
with h. farewell fear   MILT 470:20
Youth and H.   COL 212:17
hoped: substance of things h.   BIBLE 104:13
hoped-for: heaven   MILL 461:4
hopeful: with the h. past   BROW 150:23
hopefully: To travel h.   STEV 667:29
hopefulness: Lord of all h.   STR 671:1
hopeless: Ages of h. end   MILT 469:15
h. grief is passionless   BROW 147:13
h. he'd lie down and trace   CRAB 224:23
H. hope hopes on   CLARE 204:23
h. longing of the day   ARN 27:5
h. passion is my destiny   THAC 691:7
h. than a scheme of merriment   JOHN 368:10
Only the h. are starkly sincere   RHYS 539:20
perennially h.   DICK 239:1
We doctors know a h. case   CUMM 228:12
hopelessness: agitation, or h.   BAR 52:1
h. of one's position   DOST 255:4
undone years, the h.   OWEN 503:19
hopes: airy h. my children   WORD 743:21
Applying fears to h.   SHAK 634:25
enter on far-reaching h.   HOR 349:4

hopes: (cont.):
have set my h. in thee   ANON 22:18
h. and fears of all the years   BROO 144:4
h. of all men   BYRON 170:19
h. of its children   EIS 268:10
H. which obscure   BRON 142:16
If h. were dupes   CLOU 207:24
I've seen my fondest h. decay   MOORE 483:14
no great h. from Birmingham   AUST 38:11
no h. but from power   BURKE 159:24
nor as happy as one h.   LA R 410:20
partly is and wholly h.   BROW 149:12
scribbled lines like fallen h.   HOPE 346:2
sympathy with h. and fears   SHEL 643:17
vanity of human h.   JOHN 369:16
Whilst our h. our wits beguile   WOTT 749:5
without comforts and h.   BACON 42:20
hopeth: h. all things   BIBLE 101:1
hoping: Dreading and h. all   YEATS 751:9
hops: cherries, h., and women   DICK 243:6
hop-yards: for what were h. meant
    HOUS 352:19
hora: *quae non sperabitur h.*   HOR 348:6
Quae rapit h. diem   HOR 350:16
Horatius: H. kept the bridge   MAC 436:16
Then out spake brave H.   MAC 436:10
horizon: h. adorning   HEBER 330:2
h. recedes as we advance   PATT 510:1
rode across the h.   KAV 386:2
somebody else's h.   GRAH 314:3
horizontal: But the h. one   AUDEN 36:10
expression of a h. desire   SHAW 638:30
Life is a h. fall   COCT 208:8
Looks through the h. misty air   MILT 469:2
horn: His small but sullen h.   COLL 213:11
h. called me from my bed   GRAV 314:16
h. of the hunter is heard   CRAW 226:16
love the sound of the h.   VIGNY 711:10
lusty h. is not a thing   SHAK 569:19
mellow h. her pensive soul   COLL 213:14
one of which is made of h.   VIRG 714:1
south to the blind H.'s hate   KIPL 399:20
Triton blow his wreathèd h.   WORD 748:16
won't come out of your h.   PARK 506:3
Hornby: my H. and my Barlow   THOM 694:16
hornets: let wasps and h. break   SWIFT 673:5
Hornie: Auld H., Satan   BURNS 160:23
hornpipes: h. and strathspeys   BURNS 161:22
horns: h. in fog of philistinism   MAY 455:3
h. of Elfland faintly blowing   TENN 688:1
h. through mist   THOM 693:13
Memories are hunting h.   APOL 23:14
Morning on the silver h.   TENN 688:15
with crescent h.   MILT 468:19
horny: are the h. hands of toil   LOW 429:19
H.-handed sons of toil   SAL 554:7
horrible: also out of the h. pit   BOOK 126:24
h. pleasure of pleasing   CLOU 206:18
less than h. imaginings   SHAK 600:12
O, h.! most horrible   SHAK 573:20
Your h. pleasure   SHAK 595:21
horrid: 'Mongst h. shapes   MILT 465:3
she was bad she was h.   LONG 428:5
With h. warning gapèd wide   KEATS 388:13
horror: h. and its beauty   SHEL 642:2
h. of a deep night   RAC 535:2
h. of great darkness fell   BIBLE 70:35
h. of the Twentieth Century   MAIL 442:7
h.! The horror   CONR 217:5
I have a h. of sunsets   PROU 530:14
imagination there is no h.   DOYLE 256:23
needed to hide that h.   COL 212:21
Or image of that h.   SHAK 598:1
present h. from the time   SHAK 601:13
scaly h. of his folded tail   MILT 467:10
secret dread, and inward h.   ADD 3:23
horrors: Congenial h.   THOM 696:12
have supped full with h.   SHAK 604:24
stained with mystic h.   RIMB 541:6
horse: And a h. of air   ANON 19:23
behold a pale h.   BIBLE 106:16
behold a white h.   BIBLE 107:12
between a rider and his h.   SURT 672:22

hysteria: thin whine of h.   DID 246:1
hysterical: starving h. naked   GINS 306:28
hysterics: blind h. of the Celt   TENN 684:12

I

I: altogether such as I am   BIBLE 99:13
I am a camera   ISH 360:22
I am a free man, an American   JOHN 367:4
I am fearfully wonderfully   BOOK 134:20
I am not I   WAUGH 723:8
I AM THAT I AM   BIBLE 71:41
I am the family face   HARDY 325:8
I am the State   LOUI 428:13
I grow old . . . I grow old   ELIOT 272:6
in the infinite I AM   COL 212:1
I plus my surroundings   ORT 499:10
I shall not escape my I.   BOOK 124:22
I, too, am America   HUGH 354:1
I want to be alone   GARBO 297:11
that can tell me who I am   SHAK 595:8
this solitude is I   DE L 236:9
Thou a person becomes I   BUBER 153:25
Why not I with thine   SHEL 641:9
Iago: I. as an Imogen   KEATS 391:23
I.'s soliloquy   COL 212:5
iam: I. redit et virgo   VIRG 714:22
iambics: fame in keen i.   DRYD 261:3
you shall not escape my i.   CAT 187:2
ianua: dies patet atri i. Ditis   VIRG 713:11
ibant: I. obscuri sola sub nocte   VIRG 713:13
ibit: in caelum iusseris i.   JUV 383:20
ice: Alps of green i.   PHIL 514:4
break the i. by some   BACON 43:5
hissed along the polished i.   WORD 744:9
his urine is congealed i.   SHAK 606:15
hot i. and wondrous strange   SHAK 612:19
I. formed on the butler's   WOD 740:22
i. like morsels   BOOK 135:13
i., mast-high   COL 210:21
i. on a hot stove   FROST 295:16
loaded with i.   FROST 294:9
may not dissolve the i.   SURR 672:4
O ye I. and Snow   BOOK 118:18
pleasure-dome with caves of i.   COL 210:11
skating over thin i.   EMER 276:30
Some say in i.   FROST 294:17
thin i. that cracks   MONT 481:12
to i. a wedding cake   ASQ 32:3
To smooth the i.   SHAK 594:9
iceberg: i. cuts its facets from   BISH 110:1
ice-cream: emperor of i.   STEV 665:18
iced: three parts i. over   ARN 29:26
Iceland: Natural History of I.   JOHN 374:30
iceman: i. cometh   O'NEI 498:18
I-chabod: named the child I.   BIBLE 74:32
ichor: perspiration was but i.   BYRON 173:16
icicle: Chaste as the i.   SHAK 570:23
i. on a Dutchman's beard   SHAK 630:14
icicles: hang up in silent i.   COL 210:6
When i. hang by the wall   SHAK 599:11
icumen: Sumer is i. in   ANON 18:6
icy: i. silence of the tomb   KEATS 390:16
id: PUT THE I. BACK IN YID   ROTH 548:16
idea: against invasion by an i.   HUGO 354:15
better to entertain an i.   JARR 363:22
Between the i. and the reality   ELIOT 271:15
good i. but it won't work   ROG 545:1
he had only one i.   DISR 248:27
i. cannot well be accompanied   FOST 291:8
i. is accepted it is time   JACK 361:5
i. of death saves   FORS 290:15
i. whose time has come   ANON 18:12
i. within a wall of words   BUTL 167:3
no grand i. was ever born in   FITZ 284:22
pain of a new i.   BAG 47:12
politician does get an i.   MARQ 448:18
possess but one i.   JOHN 373:10
see it clearly in the i.   STEV 666:2
teach the young i. to shoot   THOM 696:2

idea: (cont.):
to whom the i. first occurs   DARW 231:15
when you have only one i.   ALAIN 7:2
ideal: Christian i. has not been tried   CHES 199:23
Happiness not an i. of reason   KANT 385:9
i. as distinguished from   KEYN 395:13
i. reader suffering from   JOYCE 381:1
softly sleeps the calm I.   DICK 241:22
idéal: paletot aussi devenait i.   RIMB 541:8
idealism: morphine or i.   JUNG 382:15
idealist: I am an i.   SAND 555:8
idealistic: America the only i. nation   WILO 738:20
ideals: with broken high l.   MCG 438:1
ideas: are but the signs of i.   JOHN 367:20
blame i. for our troubles   TRIL 702:18
i. like bad sixpences   BUTL 167:1
i. rather than with thinking   TRIL 702:18
inner time of i.   HEGEL 330:6
instead of genuine i.   BENT 64:19
I share no one's i.   TURG 705:6
identical: i. if one can be substituted   LEIB 416:16
Pathos, piety, courage—are i.   FORS 290:24
identity: because he has no i.   KEATS 392:1
equal communion and i.   DONNE 253:14
ides: Beware the i. of March   SHAK 589:21
i. of March are come   SHAK 591:10
idiom: i. of words very little   PRIOR 529:7
idioms: barbarisms, licentious i.   JOHN 369:17
i. appropriate to another   RYLE 552:8
idiot: i. who praises   GILB 304:22
portrait of a blinking i.   SHAK 608:17
tale told by an i.   SHAK 605:1
idiots: fatuity of i.   SMITH 652:24
idle: be not i.   JOHN 375:11
Be not solitary, be not i.   BURT 165:14
convey five i. creatures   AUST 38:8
employment for his i. time   WALT 721:1
For i. hands to do   WATTS 722:13
happiest when I am i.   WARD 721:18
i. and unprofitable   GIBB 302:10
i. as a painted ship   COL 210:25
i. chatter of a transcendental   GILB 305:16
i. if hunger didn't pinch   ELIOT 269:8
i. smoke of praise   DAN 229:17
i. spear and shield   MILT 467:3
idle than when wholly i.   CIC 204:3
i. word that men shall   BIBLE 90:33
little profits that an i. king   TENN 689:18
mock the air with i. state   GRAY 315:6
Never be completely i.   THOM 692:7
seemed to them as i. tales   BIBLE 95:31
We would all be i. if we could   JOHN 374:14
you are i. shallow things   SHAK 630:23
you i. creatures   SHAK 589:19
idleness: Conceives by i.   SHAK 586:17
good fortune, and i.   CERV 188:15
Grief is a species of i.   JOHN 368:15
I. is only the refuge   CHES 198:18
pains and penalties of i.   POPE 519:8
round of strenuous i.   WORD 747:3
idlers: i. of the Empire   DOYLE 256:21
progress is a doctrine of i.   BAUD 56:13
idling: impossible to enjoy i.   JER 365:13
idol: bodies to appease an i.   TAWN 678:20
Erects a shrine and i.   BYRON 172:5
make both God and an i.   LUTH 432:14
natural i. of the Anglo-Saxon   BAG 46:21
one-eyed yellow i.   HAYES 328:10
idolaters: murderers, and i.   BIBLE 107:25
idolatries: To its i. a patient knee   BYRON 168:27
idolatry: ancients without i.   CHES 198:14
organization of i.   SHAW 637:21
idols: i. I have loved so long   FITZ 284:15
like old i., lost obscenes   BOTT 137:11
idyll: Will rank as an i.   GILB 305:19
if: I. it moves, salute it   ANON 14:17
much virtue in 'i.'   SHAK 569:27
ifs: Talk'st thou to me of 'i.'   SHAK 622:2
ignara: Non i. mali   VIRG 712:11
ignis: i. fatuus of the mind   ROCH 543:11

ignoble: base and i. creature   BACON 42:24
doctrine of i. ease   ROOS 546:8
noble man but made i. talk   TENN 682:4
To names i., born to be forgot   COWP 222:25
ignominy: i. of our natures   BROW 146:1
i. sleep with thee   SHAK 582:8
ignoramuses: people are i.   LERM 418:13
ignorance: Alike in i.   POPE 522:9
And putting us to i. again   BROW 149:7
child of i. and baseness   BACON 42:30
distinguished for i.   DISR 248:27
except the fact of my i.   SOCR 654:10
From i. our comfort flows   PRIOR 529:14
from i. the Western World   JOHN 370:6
from knowledge i.   BROW 149:11
helpless man, in i. sedate   JOHN 370:21
i. and simple-heartedness   LERM 418:14
I. excuses from sin   AUCT 33:17
I. is an evil weed   BEV 69:8
I. is like a delicate exotic   WILDE 734:13
I. is not innocence but sin   BROW 150:15
I. is strength   ORW 500:10
I. is the first requisite   STR 670:14
i. it accumulates   ADAMS 2:20
I., madam   JOHN 371:18
i. of nature gave birth   HOLB 341:20
I. of the law   SELD 562:5
life is i. and confidence   TWAIN 706:27
O! more than Gothic i.   FIEL 282:13
smallest allowance for i.   HUXL 358:7
there is no sin but i.   MARL 447:12
understand a writer's i.   COL 211:27
What we call evil is simply i.   FORD 289:6
Where blind and naked I.   TENN 682:14
where i. is bliss, 'tis folly   GRAY 316:3
With a knowing i.   JOHN 366:14
women in a state of i.   KNOX 403:16
ignorant: Confound the i.   SHAK 575:9
expects to be i. and free   JEFF 364:14
i. have prescribed   DUPPA 264:9
i. man to be guided   CARL 180:1
i. of any thing in a great   BIBLE 87:11
i., unweighing fellow   SHAK 606:16
know everybody is i.   ROG 545:3
must become an i. man again   STEV 666:2
they should always be i.   AUST 38:23
well as the i. and foolish   BOOK 127:24
Where i. armies clash by night   ARN 27:1
where many i. men are sure   DARR 231:3
ignorantly: ye i. worship   BIBLE 98:31
ignore: i. most poetry   MITC 477:17
ignotus: I. moritur sibi   SEN 563:3
I. pecori, nullo contusus   CAT 186:9
ile: cette î. triste et noire   BAUD 55:10
Iliad: greater than the I.   PROP 530:2
Ilium: Fuimus Troes, fuit I.   VIRG 712:20
ill: all the measureless i.   TENN 686:9
Boldness is an i. keeper   BACON 42:30
But, if it is i., it has a   SITW 648:17
For certain i. to leave   DRAY 258:3
he thinks no i.   SHAK 633:19
i. a-brewing towards   SHAK 608:9
i. discoverers that think   BACON 42:3
I. fares the land   GOLD 310:6
i. he cannot cure a name   ARN 29:5
I. met by moonlight   SHAK 611:13
I. news hath wings   DRAY 257:15
i. report while you live   SHAK 575:6
it is i.-fed, ill-killed   JOHN 376:11
Looking i. prevail   SUCK 671:6
no i. can come   BOOK 135:21
Nothing i. come near thee   SHAK 571:16
sight of means to do i.   SHAK 594:12
than to rail at the i.   TENN 687:6
to do i. our sole delight   MILT 468:7
warn you not to fall i.   KINN 398:9
we are all i.   TRIL 702:16
Will be the final goal of i.   TENN 683:17
illacrimabiles: sed omnes i.   HOR 350:18
ill-bred: i. son   YEATS 751:17
so i. as to love a husband   WYCH 750:7
so illiberal and so i.   CHES 198:10

ill-doing: doctrine of i.   SHAK 631:12
ille: *I. mi par esse deo videtur*   CAT 186:7
illegal: i., immoral, or fattening   WOOL 742:19
   means that it is not i.   NIXON 496:7
illegally: accomplishes things i.   BALZ 51:10
illegitimate: i. child of Karl Marx   ATTL 32:17
   malpractice of heart and i.   CLOU 207:2
   strangled i. child   ARN 29:16
illegitimi: *Nil carborundum i.*   ANON 16:19
ill-favoured: i. thing, sir   SHAK 569:25
ill-housed: one-third of nation i.   ROOS 545:19
illiberal: nothing so i. and so ill-bred   CHES 198:15
illiterate: I. him, I say   SHER 645:1
ill-luck: i. of my dear country   CHES 198:23
   i. that they run half-way   JERR 366:3
illness: i. in stages   GUIB 319:12
   I is the night-side of life   SONT 656:6
   i. should attend it   SHAK 600:15
   i. to which sleep provides   CHAM 189:11
   like the treatment of an i.   WITT 740:1
   that makes i. worth while   SHAW 635:25
   To be conscious is an i.   DOST 255:6
illnesses: i. and dreary old age   VIRG 715:16
ill-nourished: ill-clad, i.   ROOS 545:19
   well-nourished and an i. love   COL 212:22
ills: climax of all human i.   BYRON 170:27
   free us from all i.   WINK 739:6
   i. of democracy can   SMITH 651:6
   i. o' life victorious   BURNS 163:5
   i. the scholar's life assail   JOHN 370:15
   marvelling sweetly on her i.   RANS 536:14
   no sense have they of i. to come   GRAY 316:2
ill-tempered: i. and queer   LEAR 414:10
illuminate: i. all Bishops   BOOK 119:19
illuminating: i. for her everything   TOLS 700:7
illuminatio: *Dominus i. mea*   BIBLE 107:27
illuming: the while my path i.   LITT 423:9
ill-usage: complaints of i.   MELB 456:9
illusion: He had one i.—France   KEYN 395:2
   great generator of i.   TRIL 702:17
   great i.   ANG 11:15
   nothing but sophistry and i.   HUME 355:4
   visible universe was an i.   BORG 136:10
   what i., and what power   BLOK 115:4
illusions: friend of flattering i.   CONR 217:10
   It's life's i. I recall   MITC 477:19
   small change of his i.   WHAR 730:3
illustration: i. of character   JAMES 363:4
illustrious: I. acts high raptures   WALL 718:16
Illyria: what should I do in I.   SHAK 628:11
Ilsley: that looks on I. downs   ARN 28:24
image: age demanded an i.   POUND 526:13
   created him in his own i.   DOST 254:4
   dear and kindly paternal i.   DANTE 230:15
   express i. of his person   BIBLE 104:10
   fleeting i. of a shade   SHEL 644:1
   great i. of authority   SHAK 597:7
   i. if not in usage   BART 54:18
   i. of eternity   BYRON 169:16
   i. of his Maker   SHAK 589:1
   i. of myself and dearer   MILT 471:22
   i. of passion   BART 54:17
   I., that, flying still before me   WORD 744:10
   i. that Nebuchadnezzar   BIBLE 85:28
   i. walking in the garden   SHEL 642:7
   kills the i. of God   MILT 475:4
   kiss the i. of my death   DRUM 258:15
   knowledge after the i.   BIBLE 103:16
   make man in our i.   BIBLE 69:24
   nevertheless his i.   FULL 296:4
   Save in the constant i.   SHAK 629:13
   Scattered his Maker's i.   DRYD 258:17
   stamps him i. of his God   GRAI 314:5
   licat i. of death   ELIOT 269:27
   unto thee any graven i.   BIBLE 72:19
   will thou i. of the King   LENN 001:00
   worship the graven i.   BIBLE 107:4
imagery: plundered science ...   MOEW 14:19
   produced no religious i.   CLARK 205:8
images: Fresh i. beget   YEATS 751:1

images: (*cont.*):
   i. and scenes of early life   COL 212:17
   I., which are the life   KAMES 385:3
   i. without absorbing them   ADAMS 2:13
   unpurged i. of day recede   YEATS 750:20
imaginary: Happiness is an i. condition   SZASZ 677:12
imagination: relish is so sweet   SHAK 627:15
   ages of i.   BLAKE 113:1
   always f–gg–g his i.   BYRON 174:8
   by i. that we can form   SMITH 650:16
   commodious car of the i.   JAMES 362:14
   force of i.   DRYD 260:32
   heart is nothing but his i.   SHAW 636:24
   his i. for his facts   SHER 645:24
   hunting-grounds for the poetic i.   ELIOT 269:13
   ideal of reason but of i.   KANT 385:9
   if i. amend them   SHAK 612:25
   i. bodies forth   SHAK 612:17
   i, cold and barren   BURKE 157:20
   i. droops her pinion   BYRON 171:7
   i. I hold to be the living   COL 212:1
   i. is not required   JOHN 372:0
   I., not invention   CONR 217:14
   i. of a boy is healthy   KEATS 386:12
   i. of man's heart is evil   BIBLE 70:28
   i. resembled the wings   MAC 435:22
   i. than the study of law   GIR 307:3
   i. the rudder   KEATS 391:4
   i. to the proper pitch   LACK 405:7
   I., which in truth   WORD 747:10
   i. which preys incessantly   JOHN 369:24
   Instrument of moral good is the i.   SHEL 644:5
   it is the lava of the i.   BYRON 173:25
   literalists of the i.   MOORE 482:14
   My shaping spirit of i.   COL 209:17
   no i. there is no horror   DOYLE 256:23
   of i. all compact   SHAK 612:17
   Reason and the I.   MAC 435:23
   save those that have no i.   SHAW 638:24
   scattered the proud in the i.   BIBLE 93:23
   sweeten my i.   SHAK 597:5
   truth of i.   KEATS 391:5
   Vision or I. is   BLAKE 114:17
   whispering chambers of I.   DICK 241:22
imaginations: my i. are as foul   SHAK 576:8
   perish through their own i.   BOOK 124:17
imagine: I. there's no heaven   LENN 417:12
   La cara e buona i. paterna   DANTE 230:15
   people i. a vain thing   BOOK 124:7
imagined: i. such a device   BOOK 125:8
imaginibus: *Ex umbris et i.*   NEWM 493:17
imaginings: less than horrible i.   SHAK 600:12
imitate: I i. the Saviour   HUXL 357:7
   I. him if you dare   YEATS 753:11
   i. the action of the tiger   SHAK 585:7
   I. them, and thereof take   DAV 232:7
   Immature poets i.   ELIOT 273:18
   never failed to i. them   BALD 48:1
   they usually i. each other   HOFF 340:20
imitated: he can be i. by none   CHAT 192:4
   i. humanity so abominably   SHAK 576:6
imitation: art of i.   SIDN 647:7
   Genius is the child of i.   REYN 539:10
   Of servile i. thrown away   CAREW 179:3
   Were endless i.   WORD 745:15
   While all the art of I.   LLOYD 424:3
imitator: happy i. of Nature   HEMI 331:13
imitatores: *O i., servum pecus*   HOR 348:16
immanent: I. Will that stirs   HARDY 325:4
Immanuel: call his name I.   BIBLE 82:24
immemorial: doves in i. elms   TENN 688:16
immense: error is i.   BOL 117:10
   Last night at twelve I felt i.   ADE 5:5
immensity: I. cloistered in thy dear womb   DONNE 251:8
   vortex of i.   DICK 241:22
immolation: ... so belied   SASS 557:13
immoral: All art is i.   WILDE 735:5
   i. ... or ugly   SCH 000:00
   i. as fattening   WOOL 742:19
   moral or an i. book   WILDE 736:00

immoral: (*cont.*):
   people looked on it as i.   GALS 297:5
immoralité: *L'i. est la base du despotisme*   ROB 542:5
immorality: i. is what they dislike   WHIT 731:13
immortal: Being a thing i.   SHAK 573:10
   believe that the soul is i.   PLATO 517:1
   do not seek i. life   PIND 514:15
   free and i.   TRAH 701:12
   grew i. in his own despite   POPE 522:30
   have sight of that i. sea   WORD 746:5
   I have lost the i. part   SHAK 616:4
   I., invisible, God only wise   SMITH 653:31
   I. longings in me   SHAK 567:7
   i. spirit grows   WORD 746:21
   I., though no more   BYRON 168:9
   I. youth to mortal maids   LAND 408:5
   make me i. with a kiss   MARL 446:17
   pleasures in a long i. dream   KEATS 388:15
   they grow i. as they quote   YOUNG 754:6
   What i. hand or eye   BLAKE 114:13
   when death that is i.   LUCR 432:3
   Who was the Sire of an i.   SHEL 639:12
   With cold i. hands   SWIN 676:16
immortalia: *I. ne speres*   HOR 350:16
immortality: achieve i.   ALLEN 9:19
   destroy the belief in i.   DOST 254:2
   God, I., Duty   ELIOT 270:4
   If I. unveil   DICK 244:16
   just ourselves—and I.   DICK 244:11
   like a load of i.   KEATS 391:21
   Me only cruel i. consumes   TENN 689:10
   Milk's leap toward i.   FAD 279:18
   millions long for i.   ERTZ 278:13
   Now, in its i., it plays   STEV 666:9
   Sinews of concord, earthly i.   FORD 289:9
   their hope full of i.   BIBLE 86:28
   Their sons they gave, their i.   BROO 143:3
   This longing after i.   ADD 3:23
   this mortal must put on i.   BIBLE 101:14
immortalize: mortal thing so to i.   SPEN 659:11
immured: alone i. in the brain   SHAK 598:20
Imogen: Iago as an I.   KEATS 391:23
imp: lad of life, an i. of fame   SHAK 585:22
impaling: I. worms to torture fish   COLM 214:5
impartial: its i. administration   PEEL 511:1
   neutrality of an i. judge   BURKE 160:3
   Of a pure i. hate   THOR 697:11
impatience: i. so much fretted   JOHN 373:19
impatient: i. to see him   SMITH 652:21
   people never so i.   BOOK 131:16
impavidum: *I. ferient ruinae*   HOR 350:2
impediment: just i.   BOOK 123:14
impediments: i. to great enterprises   BACON 44:3
impenetrable: dark i. wood   SCOTT 560:10
imperasset: *nisi i.*   TAC 678:3
imperative: i. is Categorical   KANT 385:7
imperator: Sole i. and great general   SHAK 598:13
imperatur: *Natura enim non i.*   BACON 45:22
imperfect: I. Enjoyment   ROCH 543:3
   my substance, yet being i.   BOOK 134:21
   perfect use of an i. medium   WILDE 735:16
imperfections: But pass my i.   EVER 279:9
   Dote on his i.   EPH 278:4
   upon excellencies than i.   ADD 4:12
   With all my i. on my head   SHAK 573:20
imperial: Her i. standards fly   AUDEN 35:3
   Of the i. theme   SHAK 600:11
   service of our great I. family   ELIZ 274:20
imperialism: I. is the monopoly stage   LENIN 417:5
   wild-cat I.   ROS 546:15
imperium: *I. et Libertas*   DISR 247:31
impertinent: ask an i. question   BRON 141:18
   don't ask i. questions   DARW 231:14
   privileged to be very i.   FARQ 280:25
imperturbe: *Me i.*   WHIT 732:5
impious: i. hand to the Crown   BRON 142:3
   i. men bear sway   ADD 3:22
implacable: ... in hate   DRYD 259:3
implore: Queen, we ...   ANON 16:12

Indian: (cont.):
Veiling an I. beauty SHAK 609:1
Indians: I. are you BALD 48:7
to America to convert I. WESL 728:18
indictment: i. against an whole people
BURKE 157:25
Indies: augmentation of the I. SHAK 630:18
indifference: i. and a coach and six
COLM 213:17
i. closely bordering on STEV 667:17
on the i. or the frozen stare ELIOT 269:16
torpor of our i. JOHN 366:15
indifferent: but to be i. to them SHAW 636:5
delayed till I am i. JOHN 371:13
universe is simply i. HOLM 342:6
indifferently: i. minister justice BOOK 122:1
I will look on both i. SHAK 589:26
indigestion: sows hurry and reaps i.
STEV 667:27
indignatio: I. principis mors est MORE 484:11
indignation: i. can no longer tear SWIFT 675:18
i. makes me write verse JUV 383:15
mists of righteous i. MUGG 487:9
Moral i. is jealousy WELLS 727:24
resignation or well-bred i. TURG 705:7
Savage i. YEATS 753:11
they had i. BIBLE 92:22
indignities: by i. men come to dignities
BACON 43:29
indignity: spared me the i. BELL 62:5
indirection: By any i. SHAK 593:6
their art proceeds by i. BARN 53:9
indirections: By i. find directions SHAK 574:8
indiscretion: between a cliché and an i.
MACM 440:7
lover without i. is no lover HARDY 324:8
indisposeth: living i. us for dying BROW 145:18
indistinct: dislimns, makes it i. SHAK 566:7
host with someone i. ELIOT 272:20
inditing: i. of a good matter BOOK 127:10
individual: common notions in an i.
HOR 347:10
definition of the i. KOES 403:19
each i. a repetition WEBB 724:15
i. reader Is important NAB 489:4
injustice done to an i. JUN 383:8
liberty of the i. MILL 460:18
No I. could resent SWIFT 675:12
not an i., but a species FIEL 282:5
not the i., but the species JOHN 369:19
individualism: rugged i. HOOV 344:18
individuals: all my love is towards i.
SWIFT 674:1
I. pass like shadows BURKE 158:32
indivisible: Freedom an i. word WILL 737:16
Peace is i. LITV 423:11
indocilis: I. pauperiem pati HOR 348:23
indolence: i. of her youth YEATS 752:16
indolent: i. expression BELL 61:17
indomitable: Still the i. Irishry YEATS 753:17
indoors: i. and out-of-doors MAC 434:4
indubitably: so very i. are BEER 59:9
indulgent: makes one very i. STAEL 662:1
industrial: I. Revelation SELL 562:25
industries: solemnest of i. DICK 244:13
industry: Avarice, spur of i. HUME 355:8
birth commonly abateth i. BACON 44:10
Captains of i. CARL 181:3
greatest river of human i. TOCQ 699:8
I. dignifies the artist DYER 265:4
i. will supply their deficiency REYN 539:5
i. without art RUSK 550:12
national i. of Prussia MIR 476:10
not his i. only BURKE 158:31
unless i. is to ? paralysed TAWN 679:3
indutus: éxúvías i. Achilli VIRG 712:18
inebriate: cheer but not i. BERK 69:0
Cups but not i. COWP 228:31
ineffectual: beautiful ii angel ARN 29:21
Remote and i. Don DUU 61:14
inefficiency: efficiency and i. SHAW 636:06
inert: handful of the Divine I. MELV 456:18
inertia: Strennia nos exercet i. HOR 348:9

inescapable: end of the way i. PAST 508:8
inestimable: thine i. love BOOK 120:8
inevitability: i. of gradualness WEBB 724:16
inevitable: arguing with the i. LOW 430:7
inexactitude: terminological i. CHUR 201:23
inexcusable: done something i. ALAI 7:4
inexperienced: i. house JER 365:15
inextinguishable: i. thought SHEL 644:6
infallible: only i. rule SURT 672:6
infâme: écrasez l'i. VOLT 716:14
infamous: quiet, and i. MAC 435:10
infamy: which will live in i. ROOS 546:4
infancy: Heaven lies about us in our i.
WORD 745:14
i., childhood, adolescence LINK 423:6
Nations . . . have their i. BOL 117:9
simpler than the i. of truth SHAK 627:18
wayward was thy i. SHAK 622:5
We dug a spring in i. BRON 142:2
Will you see the i. of this sublime
TRAH 701:10
infant: i. crying in the night TENN 683:19
i., mewling and puking SHAK 568:16
i. phenomenon DICK 242:10
Sooner murder an i. BLAKE 112:28
Your i. beauty could beget SEDL 561:1
infantry: That small i. MILT 468:25
infants: nuclear giants and ethical i.
BRAD 139:8
infected: his knowledge is not i. SHAK 631:18
i. minds to their deaf pillows SHAK 604:17
i. that th'infected spy POPE 521:22
infection: i. and the hand of war SHAK 619:18
i. of things gone LOW 430:23
that flower with base i. SHAK 634:15
infects: bad news i. the teller SHAK 564:17
something that i. the world ARN 27:23
infelicity: her i. seemed to have WEBS 725:23
sense of a constant i. TAYL 679:20
inferias: fraier, ad i. CAT 18/:1
inferior: disgraced by the i. SHAW 637:26
feel i. without your consent ROOS 545:13
knowing myself i. to myself MILT 476:4
pleasure of pleasing i. people CLOU 206:18
inferiority: conscious of an i. JOHN 374:17
i. that has been experienced ADLER 5:8
i. to the choice hidden MELV 456:18
minds so impatient of i. JOHN 369:15
inferiors: English want i. TOCQ 699:7
infernal: I. world MILT 468:12
inferno: i. of his passions JUNG 382:13
infidel: infidel as a dog is an i. JOHN 373:5
infidelity: I. does not consist PAINE 504:7
infinite: both are i. SHAK 623:4
eternal silence of these i. spaces PASC 507:14
God . . . a being absolutely i. SPIN 661:2
idea of the i. torments me MUSS 488:15
I. day excludes the night WATTS 723:4
i. I AM COL 212:1
i.-resource-and-sagacity KIPL 402:3
I. riches in a little room MARL 447:13
I. wrath, and infinite despair MILT 470:25
that the will is i. SHAK 627:16
there is an I. in him CARL 181:10
Though i., can never meet MARV 450:3
infinities: you numberless i. DONNE 260:20
infinitive: when I split an i. CHAN 190:7
infinity: Hold i. in the palm BLAKE 110:18
shares the nature of i. WORD 743:7
infirmi: i. est animi exiguique JUV 384:13
infirmitie: And feblit with i. DUNB 264:3
infirmities: i. were not noxious JOHN 372:2
should bear his friend's i. SHAK 593:7
infirmity: i. of others HOBB 339:16
prop to our i. WORD 747:1
That last i. of noble mind MILT 466:4
Its the i. f his age SHAK 594:25
inflamed I. will i. you SHAK 592:12
inflammation: i. of his weekly bills
BYRON 178:07
infectious honours are i. CTFV 666:12
inflicted: pain shall not be i. BENT 658:14

influence: i. of the Crown DUNN 264:7
i. on human life MULL 487:15
no slight or trivial i. WORD 744:19
obedience of planetary i. SHAK 595:2
one way their precious i. MILT 467:4
Rain i., and judge the prize MILT 465:16
tell where his i. stops ADAMS 2:15
under the name of I. BURKE 159:13
win friends and i. people CARN 181:19
influences: bind the sweet i. BIBLE 77:37
in-folded: tongues of flame i. ELIOT 271:9
inform: all occasions do i. SHAK 577:31
i. his princes BOOK 132:12
i. the reader but to protect ACH 1:9
I will i. thee BOOK 126:10
information: I only ask for i. DICK 239:32
knowledge we have lost in i. ELIOT 272:15
mean understanding, little i. AUST 39:10
we can find i. upon it JOHN 374:4
informed: one i. by the light BACON 42:2
ingeminate: i. the word Peace CLAR 205:3
Inglese: I. Italianato ASCH 31:2
Inglissh: I. in makyng was the beste
LYDG 433:3
inglorious: i. period of our dominion
BURKE 159:1
ingots: We don't take i. CHAM 189:1
ingrateful: so i. you deny me SHAK 594:15
That make i. man SHAK 595:20
ingratitude: As man's i. SHAK 568:17
I hate i. more in a man SHAK 630:29
I., more strong than traitors' SHAK 592:14
I , thou marble-hearted fiend SHAK 595:9
ingratitudes: monster of i. SHAK 627:19
inhabitants: i. o' the earth SHAK 600:5
inhale: if he doesn't i. STEV 666:14
inhearse: thoughts in my brain i. SHAK 634:9
inherit: do i. heaven's graces SHAK 634:14
they shall i. the earth BIBLE 88:23
To-night it doth i. ARN 27:20
inheritance: Ruinous i. GAIUS 296:18
inherited: i. it brick and left it AUG 37:13
inheritor: i. of the kingdom of heaven
BOOK 123:3
inhibitions: cultivate a few i. LOOS 428:11
inhumanity: i. meant cruelty FROMM 294:7
Man's i. to man BURNS 162:19
that's the essence of i. SHAW 636:5
inimitable: Faintly the i. rose WINC 739:4
iniquities: bruised for our i. BIBLE 84:12
iniquity: and hated i. BOOK 127:11
I lack i. SHAK 614:26
i. of oblivion BROW 145:23
loved justice and hated i. GREG 317:18
reverend vice, that grey i. SHAK 580:31
right hand of i. BOOK 135.4
visiting the i. of the fathers BIBLE 72:16
initiation: i. into a new state ELIOT 268:18
injured: Forgiveness to the i. DRYD 260:9
from sense of i. merit MILT 468:4
i. lover's hell MILT 471:25
Yes, i. Woman! BARB 52:4
injuries: i. of other men LOCKE 425:5
take revenge for slight i. MACH 438:7
This is adding insult to i. MOORE 482:6
injury: i. sooner forgotten CHES 198:7
possible to love without i. GREE 317:5
injustice: against i. and wrong PALM 505:8
all the rapine and i. SMITH 650:15
conscience with i. is corrupted SHAK 587:18
I. anywhere is a threat KING 396:15
i. done to an individual JUN 383:8
i. is done to someone ULP 707:1
i. makes democracy necessary NIEB 495:1
I., poverty, slavery BERL 66:1
justice or i. JOHN 370:23
so finely felt, as i. DICK 240:28
That's social i. BRAC 138:19
injustices: to justify their i. VOLT 716:5
ink: all a gh in j, YEATS 752:23
all thu are were i. LYLY 433:13
he hath not drunk i. SHAK 611:15

intelligencies: we are the i. DONNE 251:25
intelligent: Every i. voter ADAMS 2:3
  i. are to the intelligentsia BALD 48:15
  Most i., very elegant RUBY 154:7
  so elegant, So i. ELIOT 273:5
intelligentsia: intelligent are to the i. BALD 48:15
intelligere: neque detestare, sed i. SPIN 661:3
intelligible: i. government BAG 47:2
intemperance: potations excused the brisk i. GIBB 302:11
intend: i. to lead a new life BOOK 122:5
  since what I well i. SHAK 594:21
intended: damp my i. wing MILT 472:18
intense: i. the agony BRON 142:14
intensity: every art is its i. KEATS 391:9
  full of passionate i. YEATS 753:1
intent: child of glorious great i. SPEN 659:26
  His first avowed i. BUNY 156:14
  Our true i. CHAK 612:22
  prick the sides of my i. SHAK 601:3
  truth that's told with bad i. BLAKE 111:6
intentions: only had good i. THAT 691:24
  produced by their good i. WALP 720:3
  vacuum can devour second i. RAB 534:20
intents: Be thy i. wicked or SHAK 573:9
inter: hugger-mugger to i. him SHAK 578:4
intercession: i. for the transgressors BIBLE 84:14
interchanging: pleasing game of i. praise HOLM 342:11
interest: by passion or i. LOCKE 425:2
  from its duty and its i. WASH 722.1
  i. always will prevail DRYD 259:10
  i.'s on the dangerous edge BROW 148:13
  it's i. that keeps peace CROM 227:12
  natural i. of money MAC 434:21
  regard to their own i. SMITH 650:17
  Since i. neither have designed BEHN 60:11
  unbound by any i. to pay HOR 348:22
interested: only i. in money SHAW 638:29
  subsequent proceedings i. him HARTE 327:21
  whatever he is most i. in BARR 54:11
  you're i. in the arts AYCK 40:8
interesting: person doing i. actions BAG 47:5
  proposition be i. than that it be WHIT 731:10
  something more i. than women WALL 718:3
  statements was i. TWAIN 706:2
interests: Our i. are eternal PALM 505:7
  pursue their respective i. JEV 366:6
interfering: i. with the liberty MILL 460:14
interfused: far more deeply i. WORD 745:1
interior: pries not to the i. SHAK 608:16
interjection: present life is but an I. BYRON 171:30
interline: Enlarge, diminish, i. SWIFT 675:1
interlude: present is an i. O'NEI 499:2
intermission: i. of pain SELD 562:11
international: dependable i. emotion ALSOP 10:3
internationals: Blackheath, and five I. DOYLE 256:15
interpose: i. my body STR 670:19
  who in quarrels i. GAY 300:2
interpretation: I. is the revenge of intellect SONT 656:4
  what is lost in i. FROST 295:19
interpreted: i. the world MARX 452:8
interpreter: God is his own i. COWP 222:17
  i. is hardest to be understood SHER 644:22
  Man is the i. of nature WHEW 730:15
interpreters: crowd they need i. PIND 514:14
  i. between us and the millions MAC 435:20
interred: good is oft i. SHAK 592:5
intersum: ignorant i. spacca ELIOT 270:21
interstices: i. between the i. erections JOHN 379:2
interval: and make a lucid i. DRYD 261:2
  save to enjoy the i. SAN 556:11
intervals: lucid i. and happy pauses BACON 45:10
  Not in the lucid i. of life WORD 743:12

interview: strange and fatal i. DONNE 250:13
intestine: This is the dark i. HUGH 354:7
intestines: product of smaller i. CARL 180:16
intimacy: every old authentic i. LAMB 406:4
  i. there is a secret boundary AKHM 6:8
  that is to determine i. AUST 39:23
  without unseemly i. LOW 430:10
  you should avoid any i. KITC 402:17
intimate: i. when he is rich or famous BIER 109:2
  i. with him by instinct AUST 38:19
  tribal, i. revenge HEAN 329:20
into: i. the dust descend FITZ 283:18
intolerable: burden of them is i. BOOK 122:6
  i. neutral itch AUDEN 36:5
  I., not to be endured SHAK 624:20
intolerance: fanaticism and i. LEVIN 420:3
intoxicated: A God-i. man NOV 497:4
  exposes himself when he is i. JOHN 375:8
  i. with power BURKE 157:3
intoxication: best of life is but i. BYRON 170:19
intreasurèd: weak beginnings lie i. CHAK 583:15
intreat: I. me not to leave thee BIBLE 74:25
intricated: Poor i. soul DONNE 253:13
intrigues: I. half-gathered CRAB 224:21
intrinsicate: this knot i. SHAK 567:11
introduce: allow me to i. myself JAGG 361:13
introduced: And when I'm i. RAL 536:12
  cut any one you've been i. to CARR 183:25
introduction: i. to any literary work JOHN 371:17
introibo: I. ad altare Dei JOYCE 381:17
  I. ad altare Dei MISS 476:14
introitum: i. nobis ad vitam dedit SEN 563:1
intruding: i. fool, farewell SHAK 577:9
intrusion: education, I call it i. SPARK 658:8
inutterable: Abominable, i. MILT 470:4
invades: horrid stillness first i. DRYD 260:4
  i. authors like a monarch DRYD 262:12
invasion: i. by an idea HUGO 354:15
invective: insolence is not i. DISR 247:3
invent: be necessary to i. him VOLT 716:10
  Everything you i. is true FLAU 286:1
  fitter to i. than to judge BACON 45:9
  inalienable right to i. GREER 317:16
  i. some other custom SHAK 615:23
  To remember or i. FROST 295:1
  when god decided to i. CUMM 228:13
invented: England i. the phrase BAG 46:16
  Truth exists; only lies are i. BRAQ 139:18
invention: And fresh i. planted CAREW 179:3
  As rash i. breeds a raw device GASC 298:19
  Beggars i. and makes COWP 223:11
  brightest heaven of i. SHAK 584:16
  [bureaucracy's] specific i. WEBER 725:4
  Imagination, not i. CONR 217:14
  In scaled i. or true artistry POUND 527:7
  i. is but the talent BYRON 174:5
  i. is unfruitful BURKE 157:20
  i. of a barbarous age MILT 467:17
  it is a happy i. ANON 21:17
  jerks of i. SHAK 598:17
  Marriage is a wonderful i. CONN 216:9
  my i. prove deformed SHAK 635:10
  'Tis never by i. got SWIFT 675:8
  wanting I.'s stay SIDN 646:15
inventions: have sought out many i. BIBLE 80:15
  i. which have conferred SMIL 650:10
  whoring with their own i. BOOK 132:14
inventor: To plague the i. SHAK 601:2
invents: arts of life man i. SHAW 637:13
inversion: will his negative i. AUDEN 36:5
inverted: i. bowl we call The Sky FITZ 284:10
investigation: Every art and i. ARIS 25:7
invincible: i. to the attacks WHIT 732:3
invincibly: snatching the i. abode ARN 28:10
inviolate: secret and i. row YEATS 750.2
invisible: all things visible and i. BOOK 121:10
  better thy musician in that of i. I FON 418:12
  Immortal, i., God only wise SMITH 650:11

invisible: (cont.):
  i. and all-powerful FLAU 286:3
  I., except to God alone MILT 470:21
  man who has no i. means BUCH 154:2
  Oh may I join the choir i. ELIOT 269:29
  priest of the i. STEV 665:13
  thy bloody and i. hand SHAK 603:5
  we walk i. SHAK 580:4
  What does remains i., is lost MOT 487:2
  what is essential is i. DE S 553:3
  yet she is not i. BACON 43:19
invitations: don't accept our i. KHR 395:15
  Receipted bills and i. AUDEN 35:10
invite: Friendly himself i. ANON 20:2
invites: I. my step, and points POPE 519:14
invocation: By i. of the same ALEX 8:15
involuntary: It was i. They sank my boat KENN 394:9
invulnerable: I. nothings SHEL 639:22
inward: i. and spiritual grace BOOK 123:10
  They flash upon that i. eye WORD 744:16
  truth in the i. parts BOOK 128:5
inwardly: i. in our souls BOOK 120:15
inwards: looked i., and found DRYD 262:11
inwariable: double glass o' the i. DICK 243:17
iocos: Nec ut soles dabis i. HADR 320:8
iota: One i. to abate THOR 697:17
ipse: I. dixit CIC 203:28
  I. docet quid agam OVID 502:23
Ipswich: I. and Oxford SHAK 589:11
ira: Ça i. ANON 20:6
  I. furor brevis est HOR 348:5
  Sine i. et studio TAC 677:23
irae: Dies i., dies illa MISS 477:11
  i. amoris integratio est TER 690:10
  Tantaene animis caelestibus i. VIRG 712:1
Ireland: great Gaels of I. CHES 198:28
  How's poor ould I. ANON 15:4
  I. gives England her soldiers MER 457:18
  I. hurt you into poetry AUDEN 34:14
  I. is the old sow that eats JOYCE 381:11
  I. never was contented LAND 408:3
  My mission is to pacify I. GLAD 307:7
  name of I. is mentioned SMITH 652:24
  Out of I. have we come YEATS 752:19
  Romantic I.'s dead and gone YEATS 753:5
  we are bound to lose I. GLAD 307:19
  what I have got for I. COLL 213:9
iris: livelier i. changes TENN 685:7
  Melted to one vast I. BYRON 169:1
irisch: mein i. Kind WAGN 717:10
Irish: answer to the I. Question SELL 562:26
  howling of I. wolves against SHAK 569:22
  I. poets, learn your trade YEATS 753:16
  Let the I. vessel lie AUDEN 34:15
  my I. child WAGN 717:10
  now the I. are ashamed MARV 450:16
  symbol of I. art JOYCE 381:19
  That is the I. Question DISR 246:16
  We I., born into that ancient YEATS 753:10
Irishman: I.'s heart is nothing SHAW 636:24
Irishry: Still the indomitable I. YEATS 753:13
iron: Any old i. COLL 213:6
  Are strong as i. bands LONG 428:2
  blood and i. BISM 110:6
  bound in misery and i. BOOK 132:15
  bruise them with a rod of i. BOOK 124:10
  extraordinary metal [i.] SMIL 650:8
  i. can stab the heart BABEL 41:8
  i. curtain has descended CHUR 202:22
  i. entered into his soul BOOK 132:11
  i. feet can print no ruin-trace MONT 482:1
  i. shuts amain MILT 466:7
  i. tears down Pluto's cheek MILT 464:23
  i. while it is hot DRYD 262:8
  more amid these i. times THOM 695:23
  my i.'s gone ANON 16:16
  nobles with links of i. BOOK 135:16
  Nor i. bars a cage LOV 429:4
  On i., wood and glass DAV 232:13
  painted to look like i. BISM 110:8
  should become an i. cage WEBER 724:19
  sound of i. on stone DE L 236.8

journey: (cont.):
j. all the human emotions GOGOL 309:21
j. I prepare as though for death MANS 445:9
j. to the world below SOCR 655:1
j.-work of the stars WHIT 732:17
long day's j. into night O'NEI 498:19
long j. towards oblivion LAWR 412:19
take a j., and specially ANDR 11:13
Up, lad: when the j.'s over HOUS 352:7
Where the traveller's j. BLAKE 114:5
worst time of year for a j. ELIOT 271:17
journeying: j. boy HARDY 325:14
journeyman: j. to grief SHAK 619:12
journeymen: j. had made men SHAK 576:6
journeys: J. end in lovers meeting SHAK 629:4
jours: Les j. s'en vont APOL 23:15
jousted: J. in Aspramont MILT 469:1
Jove: J.'s planet rises yonder BROW 150:8
Of J., Appollo, of Mars CHAU 180.2
Jowett: my name is J. BEEC 59:7
joy: all the passages of j. JOHN 370:18
And dreme of j. CHAU 195:6
And J., whose hand is ever KEATS 389:7
And snatch a fearful j. GRAY 316:1
at the expense of j. FORS 290:10
Break forth into j. BIBLE 84:9
But j. is wisdom, Time YEATS 752:9
excess of j. ALAI 7:7
fed without the aid of j. BRON 142:17
Feeling. J. Peace PASC 508:1
good tidings of great j. BIBLE 93:27
half-conscious of the j. it WORD 746:17
Hath really neither j. ARN 27:1
He sees it in his j. WORD 745:14
He who binds to himself a j. BLAKE 113:11
hopefulness, Lord of all j. STR 671:1
I wish you all j. of the worm SHAK 567:5
J. always came after pain APOL 23:15
J. and all prosperity HAWES 328:3
J. and woe are woven fine BLAKE 111:6
J., arises in the mind employed DYER 265:3
J., beautiful radiance SCH 558:1
j. cometh in the morning BOOK 126:5
j. delights in joy SHAK 633:3
J., Empire and Victory SHEL 642:20
j. from girl and boy AUDEN 35:10
j. in hevene and peyne CHAU 194:29
j. is but a dish of pain TICH 698:3
j. is ever on the wing MILT 473:24
j. nor grieve too much DRYD 261:13
J. of heav'n, to earth WESL 728:14
J. of love is too short MAL 443:7
j. of the working KIPL 401:9
J. ruled the day, and Love DRYD 261:20
j.'s a trinket STEP 663:16
J.'s grape against KEATS 389:7
J. shall be in heaven over BIBLE 95:1
j.'s soul lies in the doing SHAK 627:5
j. that the day has brought BOND 117:17
j. the world can give like BYRON 173:7
j. unspeakable and full BIBLE 105:8
j. whose race is just begun SHEL 643:15
kisses the j. as it flies BLAKE 113:11
Labour without j. is base RUSK 550:25
let j. be unconfined BYRON 168:16
much j. or too much fear GRAV 314:18
My scrip of j., immortal diet RAL 535:18
no earthly j. may dure SACK 552:13
not increased the j. BIBLE 82:26
obtain j. and gladness BIBLE 83:22
Of crimson j. BLAKE 114:12
Of j. illimited HARDY 325:5
oil of j. for mourning BIBLE 84:27
O j.! that in our embers WORD 746:2
politics of j. HUMP 356:3
shall reap in j. BOOK 134:5
sons of God shouted for j. BIBLE 77:35
stern j. which warriors feel SCOTT 559:11
Strength through j. LEY 421:10
Such perfect j. therein I find DYER 264:15
Surprised by j. WORD 748:6
their j. and glory must ABEL 1:1
There is no j. but calm TENN 685:22

joy: (cont.):
thing of beauty is a j. for ever KEATS 386:13
Thy j. and crown eternally MONS 480:1
'twere with a defeated j. SHAK 572:4
walked in glory and in j. WORD 747:11
weep at joy than to j. SHAK 613:6
Where j. for ever dwells MILT 468:12
Where's all the j. and mirth KEPP 394:11
Where there is sadness, j. FRAN 292:12
who for the j. that was BIBLE 104:17
would but apprehend some j. SHAK 612:17
Writhed not of passèd j. KEATS 387:33
joyance: j. everywhere COL 209:19
With thy clear keen j. SHEL 643:18
Joyce: olla putrida James J. LAWR 413:3
joyful: be a j. mother BOOK 133:7
day of prosperity be j. BIBLE 80:14
how good and j. a thing it is BOOK 134:14
J. and triumphant ANON 21:18
j. rain upon thine inheritance BOOK 120:9
Let the saints be j. BOOK 135:16
O be j. in the Lord BOOK 131:17
joyfully: Sing j. to God BIBLE 107:30
joyicity: on akkant of his j. JOYCE 381:7
joys: Africa and golden j. SHAK 584:11
All my j. to this are folly BURT 164:12
But all their j. are one WATTS 722:19
Earth's j. grow dim LYTE 433:16
falls do hinder hasty j. GASC 298:19
For present j. are more DRYD 260:25
go in search of j. MERR 458:13
Hence, vain deluding j. MILT 464:13
In whom all j. so well agree SIDN 647:5
It redoubleth j., and cutteth BACON 43:22
j. are but fantastical DONNE 251:23
j. did on false thee depend ROCH 543:4
J. in another's loss of ease BLAKE 114:7
j. of marriage FORD 289:9
j. of parents are secret BACON 44:11
surrounded with innumerable j.
TRAH 701:11
that's precious in our j. STER 664:10
Their homely j., and destiny GRAY 315:13
Thou minds me o' departed j. BURNS 161:10
Thy j. when shall I see ANON 14:10
What j. await us there NEALE 491:5
where true j. are to be BOOK 120:18
While lasting j. the man attend WHUR 733:13
who lived for j. in vain CLARE 204:21
Youth's the season made for j. GAY 299:22
jubilant: Each j. chord re-echo BAKER 47:21
jubilate: J. Deo, omnis terra BIBLE 107:30
jubilee: day of our J. is death BROW 146:12
Judah: J. is my law-giver BOOK 128:18
J. was his sanctuary BOOK 133:8
Once the sight of J.'s seer MANT 445:12
Judas: Damned below J. COWP 222:7
In the lost boyhood of J. Æ 5:10
J. saith unto him BIBLE 97:14
J. who writes the biography WILDE 735:1
Whether J. Iscariot DYLAN 265:24
judge: after a time they j. them WILDE 735:30
can be decided by the j. JOHN 370:23
fitter to invent than to j. BACON 45:9
Forbear to j., for we SHAK 587:19
God is the J. BOOK 130:5
I'll be j., I'll be jury CARR 182:2
j. between the high and low SIDN 646:18
j. is condemned when PUBL 531:3
J. none blessed before BIBLE 87:18
J. not, that ye be not judged BIBLE 89:14
J. not the preacher HERB 334:10
J. of all the earth BIBLE 71:2
j. of a man by his foes CONR 217:8
j. the quick and the dead BOOK 119:1
j. this movement kindly READ 537:6
J. thou my cause BIBLE 85:20
Justly to j. BROO 143:2
neutrality of an impartial j. BURKE 160:3
nor the j.'s robe SHAK 605:16
prince and a j. over us BIBLE 71:35
righteousness shall he j. BOOK 131:15
Sole j. of truth, in endless POPE 522:10

judge: (cont.):
thine own mouth will I j. thee BIBLE 95:16
judged: j. by the colour KING 397:1
j. every man according BIBLE 107:16
no man is acquitted if j. JUV 384:12
judgement: at forty, the j. FRAN 292:16
breastplate of j. the Urim BIBLE 72:18
bring every work into j. BIBLE 81:4
day of j. BIBLE 90:33
day of j. BOOK 119:18
Daniel come to j. SHAK 609:16
Don't wait for the last j. CAMUS 177:15
Force, unaided by j. HOR 350:4
For the Last J. draweth nigh BLAKE 111:5
He j. brings, and victory OAKL 497:8
he looked for j. BIBLE 82:15
history is the world's j. SCH 558:4
industry only, but his j. BURKE 158:31
into j. with thy servant BOOK 135:3
It biases the j. DOYLE 256:22
j. fouk woud hae a doubt FERG 281:10
j. I had increases rather DRYD 262:15
j. of his peers MAGN 442:1
j. of our scientific age HOLM 342:6
j. of the great whore BIBLE 107:9
j. tempers when rash genius CHUR 201:7
j. was set BIBLE 86:1
j. will probably be right MANS 445:11
law, j., mercy BIBLE 92:5
leaves of the J. Book unfold TAYL 679:16
names of j. and solidity AST 32:7
no nation is fit to sit in j. WILS 738:10
not give his j. rashly ADD 4:9
O j.! thou art fled to brutish SHAK 592:10
people's j. always true DRYD 259:11
reserve thy j. SHAK 573:4
right j. in all things BOOK 120:20
their j. is a mere lottery DRYD 262:13
waits upon the j. SHAK 577:13
What j. shall I dread SHAK 609:10
will replace reasoned j. JUV 384:1
judgements: Delivers brawling j. TENN 682:14
Give the King thy j. BOOK 129:18
j. about great and lofty MONT 480:13
j. of the Lord are true BOOK 125:5
j. serve but to declare COWP 222:11
What cause for j. so malign STUB 671:2
judges: And were j. of fact PULT 531:6
j. have declared it QUIL 534:9
j. soon the sentence sign POPE 523:26
my Accuser, but my j. NEWM 492:13
judging: considers j. others MOL 479:6
judicious: make the j. grieve SHAK 576:6
Nothing like a little j. levity STEV 668:10
tale should be j. COWP 222:1
Judy O'Grady: Colonel's Lady an' J. KIPL 399:15
jug: it git loose fum de j. HARR 327:7
J., jug, jug LYLY 433:10
'J. Jug' to dirty ears ELIOT 273:3
One old j. without a handle LEAR 413:19
juggler: perceive a j.'s sleight BUTL 166:16
threadbare j., and a fortune SHAK 570:1
juggling: There's j. of all sides MIDD 459:19
juices: living j. out of them DOST 254:12
juin: J. poignardé ARAG 24:6
Julia: kiss my J.'s dainty leg HERR 336:22
missed the point J. ELIOT 270:8
Whenas in silks my J. goes HERR 337:9
Where my J.'s lips do smile HERR 336:8
Julius Caesar: To J.'s ill-erected tower
SHAK 621:3
July: Born on the fourth of J. COHAN 208:13
Next J. we collide with Mars PORT 525:5
Jumblies: where the J. live LEAR 414:3
jumbo: J. asleep? SITW 648:11
jump: j. with common spirits SHAK 608:16
We'd j. the life to come SHAK 601:2
what Trojan 'orses will j. BEVIN 69:16
jumpers: Angels in j. LEWIS 421:9
jumping: dancing or j. about TURN 705:14
June: In the leafy month of J. COL 211:13
J. that was stabbed ARAG 24:6
meetings made December J. TENN 684:8

June: (*cont.*):
Unwontedly. It was late J.   THOM 693:23
When J. is past, the fading   CAREW 179:11
jungle: not a concrete j.   MORR 485:5
primitive in a giant j.   MAIL 442:10
this is the Law of the J.   KIPL 402:9
juniper: sat down under a j.   BIBLE 76:6
sat under a j.-tree   ELIOT 270:7
junk: Ep's statues are j.   ANON 14:14
Juno: J.'s never-forgetting anger   VIRG 711:18
Jupiter: *J. est quodcumque vides*   LUCAN 431:8
J. from on high laughs   OVID 502:14
J. the Rain-giver   TIB 698:2
jurisdiction: Bishop of Rome hath no j.   BOOK 135:26
jurisprudence: gladsome light of J.   COKE 208:18
jury: I'll be judge, I'll be j.   CARR 182:2
j. do the deciding   CHEK 197:13
j., passing on the prisoner's   SHAK 605:12
just: all j. works do proceed   BOOK 119:10
be j., and fear not   SHAK 589:1
Be j., my lovely swain   BEHN 60:11
faithful and j. to me   SHAK 592:6
gods are j.   SHAK 597:18
He was a good man, and a j.   BIBLE 95:29
in its causes j.   DRYD 261:8
jewel of the j.   VAUG 709:7
j. and good he reasoned   TICK 698:4
J. are the ways of God   MILT 474:6
J. as I am, without one plea   ELL 276:10
j. enough of learning   BYRON 172:4
j. man having a firm grasp   HOR 350:1
j. man is also a prison   THOR 696:22
j. one of those things   PORT 525:1
j. shall live by faith   BIBLE 99:16
J. when we are safest   BROW 148:11
J. when you thought it was   ANON 15:13
land of j. and old renown   TENN 690:7
man be more j. than God   BIBLE 77:11
ninety and nine j. persons   BIBLE 95:1
Only the actions of the j.   SHIR 646:4
path of the j.   BIBLE 78:11
rain, it raineth on the j.   BOWEN 138:4
rain on the j. and on the unjust   BIBLE 88:34
reflect that God is j.   JEFF 364:18
scrupulous and the j.   CONR 217:15
spirits of j. men made   BIBLE 104:19
that hath his quarrel j.   SHAK 587:18
that 'j.' or 'right'   PLATO 516:13
Thou art indeed j.   HOPK 346:8
thou art j.   TENN 682:27
thou'lt raise me with the j.   GRAH 313:14
whatsoever things are j.   BIBLE 103:13
justest: wisest and j. and best   PLATO 516:12
justice: at my hands call for j.   MORE 484:9
deny, or delay, right or j.   MAGN 442:2
devoted to order than to j.   KING 396:16
Die he or j. must   MILT 470:1
For J., though she's painted   BUTL 166:19
friendship than of j.   THOM 692:15
fuel J. layeth   SOUT 657:22
handy-dandy, which is j.   SHAK 597:6
harmony, and even j.   BELL 62:7
have never obstructed j.   NIXON 496:5
humanity, reason, and j.   BURKE 157:26
indifferently minister j.   BOOK 122:1
j. and the American way   ANON 13:8
j. anywhere and a mind   VIRG 712:10
j. be done though the heavens   WATS 722:8
j., in fair round belly   SHAK 568:16
j. is eternal publicity   BENN 63:18
J. is in one scale   JEFF 364:20
j. is open to all   MATH 453:17
J. is truth in action   DISR 247:1
j. makes democracy possible   NIEB 495:1
j. of my quarrel   ANON 15:2
j. or injustice of the cause   JOHN 370:23
j. should not only be done   HEW 337:17
J. the constant and perpetual   JUST 383:12
'J' was done   HARDY 321:19
J. with mercy   MILT 473:3
Let j. be done   FERD 281:9
till you plucked j. by the nose   SHAK 608:1

justice: (*cont.*):
like the old line about j.   OSB 501:19
loved j. and hated iniquity   GREG 317:18
moral good and of j.   JOHN 366:12
or j. or human happiness   BERL 66:4
pursuit of j. is no virtue   GOLD 312:1
Revenge is a kind of wild j.   BACON 44:15
sad-eyed j.   SHAK 584:22
strong lance of j.   SHAK 597:8
sword of j. first lay down   DEFOE 234:26
This ain't the shop for j.   DICK 242:28
this even-handed j.   SHAK 601:2
Thou shalt have j.   SHAK 609:19
threat to j. everywhere   KING 396:15
Thwackum was for doing j.   FIEL 282:11
What use of J., if God   ANDR 11:11
what you think j. requires   MANS 445:11
When mercy seasons j.   SHAK 609:13
you have ravished j.   WEBS 726:6
justifiable: And j. to men   MILT 474:6
justification: j., in short   ARN 30:1
justified: no man living be j.   BOOK 135:3
Wisdom is j. of her children   BIBLE 90:27
justifies: end j. the means   BUS 165:11
justify: j. the ways of God to men   MILT 467:21
j. God's ways to man   HOUS 352:19
yet men j. him   BIBLE 87:21
justifying: j. his position   AMERY 10:7
j. their own existence   FORS 290:23
justitia: *Fiat j. et pereat mundus*   FERD 281:9
justly: do j., and to love mercy   BIBLE 86:14
justum: *Dignum et j. est*   MISS 477:1
et nubes pluant J.   BIBLE 108:7
jutting: beside j. rock the few   BYRON 172:14
juventus: *Antiquitas saeculi j. mundi*   BACON 42:11
juxtaposition: J. his prophet   CLOU 207:4

K

kaim: kaims it wi' a siller k.   BALL 49:16
Kaiser: kibosh on the K.   ELL 275:5
Kalends: pay at the Greek K.   AUG 37:14
kames: gowd k. in their hair   BALL 50:12
kann: *Ich k. nicht anders*   LUTH 432:10
Kansas: corny as K. in August   HAMM 323:1
K. had better stop raising   LEASE 415:2
What the horses o' K. think   KIPL 401:13
Karshish: K., the picker-up of learning's   BROW 149:19
Kaspar: Old K.'s work was done   SOUT 657:4
Kate: And some, alas, with K.   AUDEN 35:17
But none of us cared for K.   SHAK 624:15
K. of my consolation   SHAK 624:15
Kathleen: K. Mavourneen!   CRAW 226:16
K. Ní Houlihan, your road's   CARB 178:17
kaught: For k. is proud   CHAU 196:7
Keats: K. five feet high likes   KEATS 391:20
K.'s vulgarity with a   LEAV 415:5
out-glittering K.   BULW 155:4
Kedar: among the tents of K.   BOOK 133:21
tents of K., curtains of Solomon   BIBLE 81:6
keel: Joan doth k. the pot   SHAK 599:11
keen: quite as k. a sense of duty   GILB 306:8
keener: But with his k. eye   MARV 450:15
demarcations, k. sounds   STEV 665:21
edged tool that grows k.   IRV 360:15
keep: And k. the gate of hell   SHAK 617:18
And k. us in his grace   WINK 739:6
And they should k. who can   WORD 747:16
diary and some day it'll k. you   WEST 729:7
Except the Lord k. the city   BOOK 134:6
intention to k. my counsel   GLAD 307:15
I will not k. her   SHAK 621:19
k. 'em down on the farm   LEWIS 420:21
k. her in sickness   BOOK 123:19
K. right on to the end   LAUD 411:5
K' the aspidistra flying   ORW 500:5
k, the bridge with me   MAC 436:11
k. thee in all thy   BOOK 131:4
K. the Home-fires burning   FORD 289:16

keep: (*cont.*):
K. violence in the mind   ALD 8:4
k. your head when all about   KIPL 400:14
little to earn, and many to k.   KING 397:16
mercy k. us in the same   BOOK 121:5
Of hopeless love, I k. away   WALL 718:17
shall k. your hearts   BIBLE 103:12
ware that will not k.   HOUS 352:7
keeper: Am I my brother's k.   BIBLE 70:18
ill k. of promise   BACON 42:30
Lord himself is thy k.   BOOK 133:23
keepers: k. of the house   BIBLE 81:1
k. of the walls took away   BIBLE 81:18
keepeth: he that k. thee will   BOOK 133:23
keeping: art of k.   MARQ 448:10
keeps: And gave it us for k.   AYRES 40:16
He jus' k. rollin'   HAMM 322:18
Kelly: K. from the Isle of Man   MURP 488:10
ken: k. John Peel with his coat   GRAV 314:16
kenne: *k. mich auch nicht*   GOET 309:19
Kennedys: Who killed the K.   JAGG 361:14
kennst: *K. du das Land, wo die*   GOET 309:16
K. du es wohl   GOET 309:16
kennt: *Der k. euch nicht*   GOET 309:19
Kensal Green: by way of K.   CHES 199:6
Kent: everybody knows K.   DICK 243:6
Kentish: K. Sir Byng   BROW 151:5
Kentish-town: Pancras and K.   BLAKE 112:4
kept: I have k. the faith   BIBLE 104:8
I k. them in thy name   BIBLE 97:22
That I k. my word,' he said   DE L 236:7
What wee k., wee lost   ANON 19:15
kernel: I then was to this k.   SHAK 631:14
kettle: back to the tea-k.   DISR 246:21
filled with the k.'s breath   HILL 338:10
k. and the earthen pot   BIBL F 87:20
speech is like a cracked k.   FLAU 285:16
kettle-drums: Johnson marched to k.   COLM 214:4
key: hands on that golden k.   MILT 463:13
I have mislaid the k.   THOM 694:4
k. deftly in the oiled   KEATS 390:15
k. of India is London   DISR 247:32
k. of knowledge   BIBLE 94:21
minor k., to existence   DIN 246:9
out of k. with his time   POUND 526:11
while I keep the k.   MONT 480:7
who, with an easy k.   DRYD 260:2
with this k. Shakespeare   WORD 747:17
keys: half that's got my k.   GRAH 313:11
his k. at a great rate   BYRON 173:16
k. he bore of metals twain   MILT 466:7
k. of all the creeds   TENN 683:9
k. of hell and of death   BIBLE 106:2
kharki: gentleman in K. ordered South   KIPL 398:11
Khatmandu: idol to the north of K.   HAYES 328:10
Khayyám: come with old K.   FITZ 284:1
Khrushchev: not have married Mrs K.   VIDAL 711:6
kibe: courtier, he galls his k.   SHAK 578:22
kibosh: put the k. on the Kaiser   ELL 275:5
kick: be a great k. at misery   LAWR 412:25
did you k. me downstairs   BICK 108:19
I get a k. out of you   PORT 524:19
I'll k. you downstairs   CARR 182:4
k. against the pricks   BIBLE 98:16
k. I took was when I hit   SPR 661:13
lion who dies of an ass's k.   BROW 151:14
water I would scarcely k.   KEATS 391:19
wot doesn't k. his wife   SURT 672:9
kicked: was k. up stairs before   HAL 322:1
kicking: K. you seems the common lot   BROW 153:18
kissing and k. people   TRUM 704:15
kickshaws: pretty little tiny k.   SHAK 584:6
kid: Here's looking at you, k.   EPST 278:8
shall lie down with the k.   BIBLE 83:2
kiddies: k. have crumpled the serviettes   BETJ 67:11
kidding: k. Mister Hitler   PERRY 513:2
kids: don't know any k. yourself   LARK 410:7

kids: (*cont.*):
k. when they got married   HOL 342:2
kill: As k. a king, and marry   SHAK 577:8
Be my brother, or I k. you   CHAM 189:16
churchmen fain would k.   TENN 687:1
disease and k. the patient   BACON 43:23
enough in thee to k. care   SHAK 614:15
get out and k. something   LEAC 413:12
I'll k. you if you quote it   BURG 156:23
I will k. thee   SHAK 618:5
k. a good book   MILT 475:4
K. a man, and you   ROST 548:13
k. animals and stick   NIC 494:17
k. a wife with kindness   SHAK 624:17
K. me to-morrow   SHAK 618:7
k. more women and children   BALD 48:9
K. not the moth nor butterfly   BLAKE 111:5
k. one another if it   SHAW 637:2
k. shall be thy kill if   KIPL 401:15
k. sick people groaning   MARL 447:14
k. thee with much cherishing   SHAK 623:7
k. with looks   SHAK 620:8
let's k. all the lawyers   SHAK 587:23
Meet for nothing, but to k.   HERR 336:15
nor yet canst thou k. me   DONNE 250:22
Otherwise k. me   MACN 441:1
These poor half-kisses k.   DRAY 258:7
They k. us for their sport   SHAK 596:27
they k. you in a new way   ROG 545:4
Thou shalt not k.   BIBLE 72:16
Thou shalt not k.; but need'st   CLOU 207:17
time to k., and a time to heal   BIBLE 80:5
to k. a mockingbird   LEE 415:16
killed: as you jabbed and k.   OWEN 503:20
don't mind your being k.   KITC 402:18
have so many people k.   AUST 39:25
I am the enemy you k.   OWEN 503:20
I kissed thee ere I k.   SHAK 618:21
k. than frightened to death   SURT 672:16
k. with my own treachery   SHAK 579:6
we had k. and never seen   JARR 363:20
who k. him   BELL 61:27
killer: lover and k. are mingled   DOUG 255:13
killest: that k. the prophets   BIBLE 92:7
killeth: letter k.   BIBLE 101:16
killing: assert their manhood by k.
  WAUGH 724:7
For k. of a mouse on Sunday   BRAT 139:19
K. myself to die upon a kiss   SHAK 618:21
K. no murder briefly discourst   SEXBY 563:10
k. time is only the name   SITW 648:18
Men talk of k. time   BOUC 137:14
kills: but to that which k.   DE B 233:9
It both sustains and k.   SHAF 563:19
It spots and k. anything   WAUGH 724:7
man k. the thing he loves   WILDE 736:1
pity k., it makes   BALZ 51:9
With a grip that k. it   TAG 678:6
yet it is waking that k.   BROW 146:21
kilometres: Peeling off the k.   CONN 216:20
Kiltartan: country is K. Cross   YEATS 752:5
kilted: has k. her green kirtle   BALL 50:13
kimonos: Two girls in silk k.   YEATS 752:2
kin: A little more than k.   SHAK 572:6
If one's own k. and kith   NASH 490:11
k. with kin and kind   SHAK 620:17
makes the whole world k.   SHAK 627:22
kind: been early, had been k.   JOHN 371:13
Christian, he grows k.   SHAK 608:3
constant in me, and so k.   KEATS 386:18
I am one with my k.   TENN 687:6
I can enjoy her while she's k.   DRYD 262:3
I must be cruel only to be k.   SHAK 577:23
Is she k. as she is fair   SHAK 631:8
K. are her answers   CAMP 177:9
K. hearts are more   TENN 684:22
k. to have made me a grave   TENN 687:2
less than k.   SHAK 572:6
makes one wond'rous k.   GARR 298:6
not k. sir usual   ASHF 31:8
people will always be k.   SASS 557:6
Shall kin with kin and k.   SHAK 620:17
Too kind, too k.   NIGH 496:2

kind: (*cont.*):
While just the art of being k.   WILC 734:8
wise, and coarsely k.   JOHN 375:29
kindergarten: kind of k.   ROB 542:12
kindest: k. and the best   BURNS 162:20
thou wert the k. man   MAL 443:13
kind-hearted: k. gentleman   COWP 224:18
kindle: existence is to k. a light   JUNG 382:14
k. it, thy holy flame bestowing   LITT 423:9
kindled: if his wrath be k.   BOOK 124:11
K. he was, and blasted   BYRON 168:25
thus musing the fire k.   BOOK 126:22
kindliness: cool k. of sheets   BROO 143:5
kindly: K. Call Me God   SAMP 554:16
to our use the k. fruits   BOOK 120:2
kindness: kill a wife with k.   SHAK 624:17
k. and consolidates society   JOHN 371:2
K. in another's trouble   GORD 312:12
k. of strangers   WILL 737:9
K. only can persuade   ROCH 543:2
milk of human k.   SHAK 600:15
Of k. and of love   WORD 744:19
still the great have k.   POPE 520:1
think it k. to his Majesty   HALL 322:5
value on spontaneous k.   JOHN 375:27
We'll tak a cup o' k. yet   BURNS 161:5
will some k. do them   SHAK 626:20
with the milk of human k.   GUED 319:9
kindnesses: thought of k. done   CAT 186:12
kindred: Good to the poor, to k. dear
  CAREW 179:7
haunts two k. spirits flee   KEATS 390:7
kindreds: all k. of the earth   BIBLE 105:32
kine: first seven fat k.   BIBLE 71:25
king: ale is a dish for a k.   SHAK 631:24
And the k. was much moved   BIBLE 75:17
And when I am k.   SHAK 587:23
As kill a k., and marry   SHAK 577:8
As to the K., the laws   CHAR 191:9
Authority forgets a dying k.   TENN 682:20
Ay, every inch a k.   SHAK 597:3
banners of the k. advance   FORT 291:2
blessedness alone that makes a K.
  TRAH 701:17
born K. of the Jews   BIBLE 88:8
coming of the K. of Heaven   ANON 20:3
conscience are the K.   TENN 681:24
despised, and dying k.   SHEL 643:7
divinity doth hedge a k.   SHAK 578:5
fair and fatal k.   JOHN 366:19
Fear God. Honour the k.   BIBLE 105:13
fight for its K. and Country   GRAH 313:7
five kings did a k. to death   THOM 693:9
Give the K. thy judgements   BOOK 129:18
God bless the K., I mean   BYROM 167:17
God save k. Solomon   BIBLE 75:21
God save our gracious k.   ANON 13:18
God save the k.   BIBLE 74:34
God save the k.   HOGG 341:17
God save the k.   SHAK 620:18
government without a k.   BANC 51:11
hath not offended the k.   MORE 484:6
heart and stomach of a k.   ELIZ 274:3
heaven's k. matchless k.   MILT 470:23
He played the K.   FIELD 281:15
Here lies a great and mighty k.   ROCH 543:5
Here lies a k., that ruled   CAREW 179:4
He that plays the k. shall   SHAK 574:29
how like a k. I looked   DEFOE 234:11
I have made unto the K.   BOOK 127:10
I have served the K.   WOLS 741:21
I served my k., he would   SHAK 589:2
It was a' for our rightfu' K.   BURNS 162:9
k. and officers of sorts   SHAK 584:22
K. and your Country both   RUB 549:16
K. asked the Queen   MILNE 462:15
k. besmeared with blood   MILT 468:24
K. born of all England   MAL 443:3
k. can do no wrong   BLAC 110:13
K. David and King Solomon   NAYL 491:3
k. delighteth to honour   BIBLE 76:36
K. enjoys his own again   PARK 506:26
k. I offered free from   MAC 436:6

king: (*cont.*):
k. is always a king   WOLL 741:12
k. is a thing men have   SELD 562:8
k. is strongest   BIBLE 86:20
k. is truly *parens patriae*   JAM 362:2
k. may make a nobleman   BURKE 159:26
k. never dies   BLAC 110:11
K., observing with judicious   TRAPP 702:3
K. of all these the dead   HOMER 343:13
k. of codpieces   SHAK 598:13
K. of England cannot enter   PITT 515:6
K. of glory now   NOEL 496:9
K. of glory shall   BOOK 125:17
K. of Great Britain   REED 538:12
K. of heaven   LYTE 433:17
k. of infinite space   SHAK 574:27
k. of intimate delights   COWP 223:33
K. OF KINGS, AND LORD   BIBLE 107:13
k. of love my shepherd   BAKER 47:20
k. of shreds and patches   SHAK 577:17
K. of tremendous majesty   MISS 477:13
K. over the Water   ANON 15:14
k. reigns, and the people   THIE 692:1
k.'s a bawcock   SHAK 585:22
King's a K., do Fortune   DRAY 257:16
K.'s daughter is all glorious   BOOK 127:13
k.'s English   SHAK 610:12
k.'s eyes, that so long   SHAK 588:13
k. sits in Dunfermline town   BALL 50:10
K.'s life is moving peacefully   DAWS 233:2
K.'s Moll Reno'd in Wolsey's   ANON 15:15
k.'s name is a tower   SHAK 622:9
k.'s name twenty thousand   SHAK 620:5
K. thought mair o' Marie   BALL 50:5
K. to have things done   PEPYS 512:8
K. to Oxford sent a troop   BROW 146:25
K. will never leave   ELIZ 275:4
lessened my esteem of a k.   PEPYS 512:7
Like a k. in exile   LAWR 412:21
Lord is K., and hath   BOOK 131:5
loses the k. in the tyrant   MAYH 455:10
man who would be k.   KIPL 402:6
mile of kingdom, I am k.   KAV 386:5
much a k. as a Monarch   SELL 562:22
my K. and my God   BOOK 130:16
my life to make you K.   CHAR 191:19
No bishop, no K.   JAM 362:4
Northcliffe has sent for the K.   ANON 14:2
Now the k. drinks to Hamlet   SHAK 579:4
Offends the k. no law, k. indeed   CHAP 190:13
Og the k. of Basan   BOOK 134:15
once and future k.   WHITE 731:8
one-eyed man is k.   ERAS 278:12
our sins lay on the k.   SHAK 586:6
passing fair to be a k.   MARL 447:24
right wrong, follow the K.   TENN 681:22
Ruin seize thee, ruthless K.   GRAY 315:6
shines brightly as a k.   SHAK 610:4
Sir Byng stood for his K.   BROW 151:5
skipping k., he ambled   SHAK 581:13
smote the k. of Israel   BIBLE 76:14
still am I k. of those   SHAK 620:20
still fair England's k.   MARL 447:7
subject's duty is the k.'s   SHAK 586:5
that there is another k.   BIBLE 98:28
That whatsoever K. shall reign   ANON 15:5
their K., refused   MARY 452:16
There was a k. of Yvetot   BÉR 65:3
there was no k. in Israel   BIBLE 74:22
They all were looking for a k.   MACD 437:11
think the k. is but a man   SHAK 586:3
thy k., thy governor   SHAK 624:21
'Tis done—but yesterday a K.   BYRON 172:21
To be a Pirate K.   GILB 306:7
What is a K.?—a man   PRIOR 529:12
What must the k. do now   SHAK 620:12
when thy k. is a child   BIBLE 80:23
Whilst thou I sing, I am a K.   CIBB 203:17
who speaks ill of your k.   NELS 491:10
with the image of the K.   TENN 681:28
worm that hath eat of a k.   SHAK 577:29
worship, degree, the k.   SHEL 642:18
Would shake hands with a k.   HALL 322:5

king: (cont.):

you must not be a k.	CHAR 191:7

kingdom: I never gave you k.

	SHAK 595:21
In this k. by the sea	POE 518:1
k. against kingdom	BIBLE 92:9
k. for a stage, princes	SHAK 584:16
k. for it was too small	SHAK 582:7
k. of the well	SONT 656:6
k. stretch from shore	WATTS 723:6
k. where nobody dies	MILL 461:5
large k. for a little grave	SHAK 620:12
Like to a little k.	SHAK 590:15
mind his k. and his will	COWP 224:14
my k. for a horse	SHAK 622:15
My k., safeliest when	DONNE 250:16
My mind to me a k.	DYER 264:15
on the k. of the shore	SHAK 634:2
seeking asses found a k.	MILT 473:18
thou comest into thy k.	BIBLE 95:26
Thy k. come	BIBLE 89:5
Thy k. is divided	BIBLE 85:31
Yet thy k. shall pass	SWIN 676:22

kingdom of god: fit for the k.

	BIBLE 94:9
he cannot see the k.	BIBLE 96:13
k. is within you	BIBLE 95:11
man to enter into the k.	BIBLE 91:25
Seek ye first the k.	BIBLE 89:12
such is the k.	BIBLE 93:16

kingdom of heaven: enter into the k.

	BIBLE 88:28
inheritor of the k.	BOOK 123:3
k. is at hand	BIBLE 88:12
k. is like to a grain	BIBLE 91:3
K. to all believers	BOOK 118:13
shall not enter into the k.	BIBLE 91:17
theirs is the k.	BIBLE 88:23

kingdoms: all the k. of the world

	BIBLE 88:20
K. are clay	SHAK 504:14
k. of the world in a moment	BIBLE 94:1
many goodly states and k.	KEATS 390:2

kingly: And thy k. crown

	ELL 275:8
K. conclaves stern and cold	SHEL 642:10
runnable stag, a k. crop	DAV 231:21
this k. seal	SHAK 565:21

kings: are but the breath of k.

	BURNS 161:19
bind their k. in chains	BOOK 135:16
captains and the k. depart	KIPL 400:11
chase, the sport of k.	SOM 655:12
commonwealths and ruin k.	DRYD 258:19
Conquering k. their titles take	CHAN 189:17
dread and fear of k.	SHAK 609:13
good of subjects is the end of k.	DEFOE 234:26
heart of k. is unsearchable	BIBLE 79:14
into the castles of k.	HOR 349:3
it's the sport of k.	SURT 672:8
K. and all beautiful Queens	DONNE 253:8
k. and counsellors	BIBLE 77:7
k. barbaric pearl and gold	MILT 469:10
k. crept out again to feel	BROW 147:10
K.' daughters were among	BOOK 127:12
k. governed their rude age	BAG 47:3
k. have cares that wait	GREE 317:11
k. have sat down upon	BIBLE 87:17
k. is mostly rapscallions	TWAIN 706:3
K. may be blest, but Tam	BURNS 163:5
k. not only God's lieutenants	JAM 362:1
k. of the earth	BIBLE 100:17
k. of the earth	BOOK 127:21
k. shall fall down before	BOOK 129:20
k. that fear their subjects'	SHAK 588:2
K. will be tyrants from	BURKE 158:17
K. with their armies did	BOOK 129:8
K. would not play	COWP 224:3
mad k. mad composition	SHAK 593:29
madness their k. commit	HOR 348:2
meanest from ... mor k.	SHAK 622:8
Must K. ... that private	SHAK 586:7
Of cabbages—and k.	CARR 183:2
only five K. left	FAR 280:0
people keep even in awe	D'AV 231:16
Physicians are like k.	WEBS 725:24
politeness of k.	LOUI 420:19
puller down of k.	SHAK 588:4

kings: (cont.):

ruined sides of k.	BEAU 56:15
saddest of all K.	JOHN 366:18
shall be accounted poet k.	KEATS 390:13
should all be as happy as k.	STEV 668:14
So many English k.	SHAK 584:2
stories of the death of k.	SHAK 620:8
that many prophets and k.	BIBLE 94:12
That part which laws or k.	GOLD 311:12
That part which laws or k.	JOHN 370:13
Vain the ambition of k.	WEBS 725:13
walk with K.	KIPL 400:15

Kingsley: Froude believes K. — STUB 671:2

kipling: Rudyards cease from k. — STEP 663:18

kirk: Marie Hamilton's to the k. gane

	BALL 50:5

Kirkconnell: On fair K. lea — BALL 49:13

kirtle: has kilted her green k. — BALL 50:13

kiss: Ae fond k.

	BURNS 161:2
all humbled k. the rod	SHAK 631:3
And if I k. he stingeth me	LODGE 426:1
And k. again with tears	TENN 687:25
Anger's self I needs must k.	SIDN 646:23
another with an holy k.	BIBLE 100:14
clung into a k.	BYRON 170:20
Colder thy k.	BYRON 173:20
come let us k. and part	DRAY 258:1
coward does it with a k.	WILDE 736:1
his whole heart in one k.	TENN 689:8
human souls did never k.	KEATS 386:16
I k. his dirty shoe	SHAK 585:22
I saw you take his k.	PATM 509:12
I want him to k. my ass	JOHN 367:1
k., a sigh, and so away	CRAS 226:14
k. 'em one day	KIPL 402:13
k. her and mix her	SWIN 677:3
k. is still a kiss	HUPF 357:2
k. me and never no more	MAL 443:12
K. me as if you made believe	BROW 150:14
K. me, Hardy	NELS 491:19
K. me Kate	SHAK 624:16
k. my Julia's dainty leg	HERR 336:22
k. my whole soul through	TENN 681:4
k. of the sun for pardon	GURN 319:17
k. on the hand may be quite	ROBIN 542:7
K. the book's outside	COWP 222:5
k. the image of my death	DRUM 258:16
K. the place to make it	TAYL 679:13
K. the Son, lest	BOOK 124:11
k.-worthy face	SIDN 646:23
Leans to the sun's k. glorying	GREN 318:2
lost in the magic of a k.	WASH 722:4
make me immortal with a k.	MARL 446:17
man may k. a bonnie lass	BURNS 163:12
might take occasion to k.	SHAK 569:17
myself to die upon a k.	SHAK 618:21
O! a k.	SHAK 570:22
O! let me k. that hand	SHAK 570:3
Or leave a k. but in the cup	JONS 379:20
rough male k.	BROO 143:5
She took the k. sedately	TENN 584:4
spend that k.	SHAK 567:11
stop his mouth with a k.	SHAK 613:19
thank you, k. you	RUB 549:16
Then come k. me, sweet	SHAK 629:4
this last lamenting k.	DONNE 252:1
To part at last without a k.	MORR 485:13
will be wanting to k. me	MACD 437:13
with a single famished k.	SHAK 628:1
You are the promised k.	HAMM 322:14

kissed: But k. it and then fled

	SHEL 642:22
Hasn't been k. for forty years	ANON 16:3
k. by a man who *didn't* wax	KIPL 402:11
k. her again although she	THOM 693:19
k. sad Andromache goodbye	CORN 219:3
k. thee ere I killed thee	SHAK 618:21
righteousness and peace have k.	BOOK 130:20
we k. beside the thorn	BRID 141:5

kisses: At Lord's ... k.

	LYLY 433:8
But my k. bring again	CHAP 600:11
consigned k. to them	SHAK 628:1
fine romance with no k.	FIEL 282:18

kisses: (cont.):

Give me a thousand k.	CAT 186:1
half-k. kill me	DRAY 258:7
If you have forgotten my k.	SWIN 676:24
I gave her k. back	ROET 544:8
I understand thy k.	SHAK 581:8
Love's mart of k.	CHAP 190:17
more than k., letters mingle	DONNE 252:24
My k. are his daily feast	LODGE 425:23
reaps a thousand k.	COWL 221:13
remembered k. after death	TENN 688:5
Stolen k. much completer	HUNT 356:10
thousand k. the poor last I lay	SHAK 566:13
wastin' Christian k.	KIPL 400:2
with the k. of his mouth	BIBLE 81:5

kissing: die with k. of my Lord

	MARL 448:7
For k., lady, not for such	SHAK 621:18
I wonder who's k. her now	ADAMS 2:2
K. don't last: cookery do	MER 458:1
k., kind-hearted gentleman	COWP 224:18
K. with golden face	SHAK 633:12
when the k. had to stop	BROW 153:10

kit-bag: troubles in your old k. — ASAF 30:17

kitchen: in the k. bred

	BYRON 173:4
get out of the k.	VAUG 708:13
In k. cups concupiscent curds	STEV 665:18
I will make my k.	STEV 668:24
mind the k. and their children	FITZ 284:18
They send me to eat in the k.	HUGH 354:1
Thy k. cumbreth not by heat	HEYW 338:5

kitchen-cabals: K., and nursery — CRAB 224:21

Kitchener: K. is a great poster — ASQ 31:20

kitchens: wild cats in your k. — SHAK 615:15

kites: fatted all the region k. — SHAK 575:12

kith: If one's own kin and k. — NASH 490:11

kitten: be a k. and cry mew — SHAK 581:4

Kitty: K., fair, but frozen maid — GARR 298:10

knack: k. of so arranging — FRIS 294:4

knapeth: k. the spear in sunder — BOOK 127:17

knave: But he's an arrant k.

	SHAK 574:1
coined an epithet for a k.	MAC 434:15
duteous and knee-crooking k.	SHAK 614:19
he's but Fortune's k.	SHAK 566:19
How absolute the k.	SHAK 570:21
life a foolish prating k.	SHAK 577:26
makes an honest man a k.	DEFOE 234:13
neat k. with a smooth tale	WEBS 725:14
rascally yea-forsooth k.	SHAK 582:15
slipper and subtle k.	SHAK 615:21
To feed the titled k.	BURNS 163:23

knaves: called them untaught k.

	SHAK 579:30
favour grudge at k.	DEFOE 234:18
He calls the k., Jacks	DICK 240:27
k. and thieves men shut	SHAK 630:37
most part of fools and k.	BUCK 154:8
We are arrant k.	SHAK 575:18

knavish: either k. or childish — JOHN 375:9

knee: A little abune her k.

	BALL 50:13
And set upon the nurse's k.	BALL 51:3
civility of my k.	BROW 145:28
Every k. shall bow	NOEL 496:9
Jesus every k. should bow	BIBLE 103:5
Lord Primate on bended k.	BARH 52:12
Picture you upon my k.	CAES 174:13
straw under my k.	DONNE 253:10

kneel: K. and adore him

	MONS 480:2
k. before the Lord	BOOK 131:10
they should k. for peace	SHAK 624:25
wilderness shall k. before him	BOOK 129:20

kneeling: meekly k. upon your knees

	BOOK 122:5

kneels: Not one k. to another — WHIT 732:18

knees: bow my k. unto the Father

	BIBLE 102:13
confirm the feeble k.	BIBLE 83:20
creeps rustling to her k.	KEATS 387:6
heart, not in the k.	JERR 365:18
than to live on your k.	IBAR 358:14
your body between your k.	CORY 219:13

knell: By fairy hands their k.

	COLL 213:13
curfew tolls the k.	GRAY 315:10
it is a k. that summons thee	SHAK 601:13
... surly ring his k.	SHAK 625:10
strikes like a ... k.	BYRON 168:15

knell: (cont.):
though I dropped down the k. CRANE 225:17
knelt: K. down with angry prayers
          HODG 340:16
knew: He said it that k. it best BACON 42:28
I k. that once STEP 663:16
I k. you once: but in Paradise BROW 153:17
k. almost as much at eighteen JOHN 372:13
Och, Johnny, I hardly k. ye BALL 49:15
They asked me how I k. HARB 323:9
world k. him not BIBLE 96:3
knife: fawning looks the deadly k. FANS 280:1
k. is lost in it SHEL 641:15
k. see not the wound it makes SHAK 600:16
k. that probes far deeper FORS 290:16
Left off using a k. BENT 64:14
progress if a cannibal uses k. LEC 415:10
strike with our spirit's k. SHEL 641:22
War to the k. PAL 505:4
we walk on a k. edge MONT 481:12
Wind's like a whetted k. MAS 453:9
with the k. under the cloke CHAU 193:21
knight: beadsman now that was your k.
          PEELE 511:5
earl and a k. of the garter ATTL 32:16
Fearless, blameless k. ANON 20:8
k. like the young Lochinvar SCOTT 560:4
K. of the Doleful Countenance CERV 188:8
k. shall not be whole MAL 443:4
k. that ever bare shield MAL 443:13
k. was indeed a valiant EVEL 279:5
k. was pricking SPEN 659:20
Like as the armèd k. ASKEW 31:15
parfit gentil k. CHAU 192:9
red-cross k. for ever kneeled TENN 685:2
there lies a new-slain k. BALL 50:20
what can ail thee k. KEATS 388:7
knight-errantry: K. is religion CERV 188:11
knights: accomplishing the k. SHAK 585:14
Armoury of the invincible K. WORD 744:13
ladies dead and lovely k. SHAK 634:17
virtuous deeds that some k. CAXT 188:3
knit: k. together thine elect BOOK 121:13
sheet k. at the four corners BIBLE 98:19
stuff of life to k. me HOUS 352:14
knits: k. me to thy rugged strand SCOTT 559:17
k. up the ravelled sleave SHAK 602:2
Nothing k. man to man SICK 646:8
knitter: beautiful little k. SITW 648:16
knitters: spinsters and the k. SHAK 629:16
knitting: In twisted braids of lilies k.
          MILT 464:10
knives: night of the long k. HITL 339:10
knock: As yet but k., breathe DONNE 250:24
Don't k. masturbation ALLEN 9:10
k., and it shall be opened BIBLE 89:17
K. as you please POPE 519:22
K. at a star with my exalted HERR 336:7
k. at the door LAMB 406:14
k. it never is at home COWP 222:4
right to k. him down for it JOHN 375:13
Shock or k. or lock you up DYLAN 265:10
should k. him down first JOHN 374:13
stand at the door, and k. BIBLE 106:8
Where k. is open wide SMART 650:2
knock-down: nice k. argument CARR 183:11
knocked: K. down a doctor SIMP 648:4
ruin that Cromwell k. about BEDF 58:14
we k. the bastard off HILL 338:16
what they k. down TENN 281:7
knocker: Tie up the k. POPE 519:25
knocking: Here's a k., indeed SHAK 602:8
k. at Preferment's door ARN 28:4
K. on the moonlit door DE L 236:6
Whence is that k. SHAK 602:5
withered fist still k. SACK 552:14
knocks: he k. you down GOLD 311:34
knolling: k. a departed friend SHAK 582:13
knot: crowned k. of fire ELIOT 271:9
So let the be unknotted ELIOT 270:12
this k. intrinsicate SHAK 567:11
untying with teeth political k. BIER 109:6
knot-grass: bunches of k. KEATS 387:5

knots: pokers into true-love k. COL 210:16
knotted: Sat and k. all the while SEDL 561:15
knotty: k. as a root of heath BRON 142:9
know: all ye need to k. KEATS 389:3
Behold, we k. not anything TENN 683:19
don't k. by what you do WELL 727:1
God made me to k. Him CAT 185:6
go we k. not where SHAK 606:11
hate any one that we k. HAZL 329:13
have much ado to k. myself SHAK 607:2
He must k. sumpin' HAMM 322:18
he that kan hymselven k. CHAU 194:3
How do they k. PARK 506:15
How do you k. you're God BARN 53:12
how may I k. him MILT 472:13
How shall I k. your true love RAL 536:1
How well I k. what I mean to BROW 148:21
I do not k. myself GOET 309:19
I don't k. where I'm going SAND 555:8
if you would k., and not COLT 214:9
I k. not the Lord, neither BIBLE 72:2
I k. not the man BIBLE 93:2
I k. thee not, old man SHAK 584:12
I think I k. enough of hate FROST 294:17
k. a thing or two MOL 478:17
k. enough who know how ADAMS 2:17
k. is what I read ROG 545:2
k. more of mankind I expect JOHN 376:9
K. most of the rooms FULL 296:5
k. nothing except the fact SOCR 654:10
k. such a frightful lot CHES 199:2
k. that I am God BOOK 127:17
k. that my redeemer liveth BIBLE 77:25
k. that which we are BYRON 171:33
k. that you know not BACON 43:12
K. their own good DRYD 262:4
k. the man their neighbour YEATS 752:23
K. then thyself, presume POPE 522:9
k. the place for the first ELIOT 271:6
knows the universe and does not k.
          LA F 405:12
K. thy contree, look up CHAU 196:5
K. thyself ANON 21:13
k. to know no more MILT 471:16
k. too much and are convinced ELIOT 273:21
k. what I think till WALL 718:7
k. what we are talking RUSS 551:17
k. where many ignorant DARR 231:3
K. you the land where GOET 309:16
let me k. mine end BOOK 126:22
master of those who k. DANTE 230:10
men naturally desire to k. AUCT 33:22
more than to k. little BACON 44:32
neither shall his place k. BIBLE 77:14
no one to k. what ANON 12:27
only k. two sorts of boys DICK 242:26
others that we k. not SHAK 575:16
People of quality k. everything MOL 479:9
place saying you want to k. DICK 241:2
So all we k. WALL 718:19
that he nought did k. DAV 232:3
they are that which we k. ELIOT 273:19
they do not k. what they CHUR 201:24
they k. not what they do BIBLE 95:25
they merely k. more SAKI 553:14
things they didn't k. POUND 526:9
those who do not wish to k. RAL 536:10
thought so once; but now k. it GAY 300:11
To be we k. not what DRYD 260:5
To k. the change and feel it KEATS 387:33
To k. the world, not love YOUNG 754:21
To k. this only MILT 473:21
unless we k. it to be poetry THOR 696:24
We k. our will is free JOHN 373:3
We may not k., we cannot tell ALEX 8:16
What do I k. MONT 481:8
what we would, we k. ARN 26:17
when it came to k. me well MOORE 483:14
Where I am, I don't k. BECK 57:18
which you yourselves do k. SHAK 592:16
knowest: Speak less than thou k. SHAK 595:6
thou k. all things BIBLE 98:1

knowest: (cont.):
thou k. my down-sitting BOOK 134:18
thou k. not what BIBLE 79:24
knoweth: k. not God BIBLE 105:17
knowing: Bewrapt past k. HARDY 325:14
For lust of k. what should not FLEC 286:11
k. and understanding MURD 488:6
k. what would make us prized CHUD 200:11
misfortune of k. any thing AUST 38:23
one who INSISTS on k. POUND 527:16
proud of k. nothing MCEW 437:15
With a k. ignorance JOHN 366:14
knowingly: Never k. undersold LEWIS 420:20
knowledge: After such k., what
forgiveness ELIOT 271:11
all k. to be my province BACON 45:12
all mysteries, and all k. BIBLE 101:1
All our k. is, ourselves POPE 522:23
And light of k. in their eyes SYM 677:6
Benevolent K. BORG 136:8
But of the tree of the k. BIBLE 70:3
close the five ports of k. BROW 145:10
communicate k. DE Q 237:14
counsel by words without k. BIBLE 77:33
Debarred from k., banished CHUD 200:11
Deeds to thy k. answerable MILT 473:12
desire more love and k. SHAK 567:20
dissemble sometimes your k. BACON 43:12
dreaded and envied kind of k. ADAMS 2:25
Exceeds his k. CHAP 190:15
finer spirit of all k. WORD 748:18
follow virtue and k. DANTE 230:16
For all k. and wonder BACON 41:14
For also k. itself is power BACON 45:15
foundation is the k. of causes BACON 45:18
Friendship from k. BUSS 165:17
from k. ignorance BROW 149:11
full of the k. of the Lord BIBLE 83:3
he would bring home k. JOHN 375:1
If k. and understanding DEFOE 234:2
increaseth k. increaseth sorrow BIBLE 80:3
is there k. in the most High BOOK 130:1
Is woman's happiest k. MILT 471:11
K. advances by steps MAC 435:10
k. and wisdom as I once SHEL 639:4
K. comes, but wisdom lingers TENN 685:16
K. dwells in heads COWP 224:4
K. enormous makes a god of KEATS 387:30
k. for the sceptic side POPE 522:9
k. here can go beyond LOCKE 424:18
k. is bought in the market CLOU 207:9
K. is of two kinds JOHN 374:11
k. is proud that he has COWP 224:5
k. is the ability to teach AUCT 33:25
k. is the measure GREV 318:9
k. is transmitted from BLAKE 113:3
k. like a sinking star TENN 690:2
K. may give weight CHES 198:6
k. of a lifetime WHIS 730:23
k. of God is no less the LEIB 416:13
K. of good and evil COWP 223:6
k. of man is as the waters BACON 42:2
k. of nature is destined HOLB 341:20
k. of nothing DICK 243:29
k. of the ancient languages BRIG 141:13
k. of the boundless skies BYRON 170:8
k. of the Son BIBLE 102:17
k. of the world is only CHES 198:6
k. of truth BACON 45:2
K. puffeth up, but charity BIBLE 100:27
k. shall be increased BIBLE 86:3
k. that they are so OSB 501:5
k. too but recorded experience CARL 180:6
k. we have lost in information ELIOT 272:15
k. when the day was done KEATS 388:3
k. which they cannot lose OPP 499:5
k. without integrity JOHN 369:25
Let k. grow from more to more TENN 682:29
literature of k. DE Q 237:13
little k. is dangerous HUXL 358:6
My k. was divine TRAH 701:11
O fret not after k. KEATS 390:8
opinion in good men is but k. MILT 475:13

knowledge: (*cont.*):

our k. of nature is our	WHEW 730:13
Out-topping k.	ARN 28:12
partake no venom, for his k.	SHAK 631:18
Pedantry is the dotage of k.	JACK 361:4
province of k. to speak	HOLM 342:8
raising us to k. of ourselves	LEIB 416:14
renewed in k. after the image	BIBLE 103:16
Science is organized k.	SPEN 658:11
Sorrow is k.	BYRON 172:16
Soul of the world, k.	DAN 230:1
spirit of k. and of the fear	BIBLE 83:1
Such k. is too wonderful	BOOK 134:19
taken away the key of k.	BIBLE 94:21
that lies in the way of k.	LOCKE 424:15
There's no k. but I know it	BEEC 59:7
thorough k. of human nature	AUST 38:21
too high the price for k.	TICK 698:4
Unto this k. to aspire	DONNE 252:2
what is k. but grieving	MER 458:11
What k. can perform	WORD 743:8
whether there be k.	BIBLE 101:1
which passeth k.	BIBLE 102:14
with the objects of k.	PLATO 516:15

known: And then the end is k.

	SHAK 593:16
be unknown than to be k.	HOPK 346:18
child is k. by his doings	BIBLE 79:6
devil where he is k.	JOHN 370:24
done and little to be k.	JOHN 369:14
don't choose to have it k.	CHES 198:24
from the k. and common way	WINC 739:4
Have ye not k.?	BIBLE 83:30
If you would be k.	COLT 214:9
Jewry is God k.	BOOK 130:6
know even as also I am k.	BIBLE 101:1
k. and the unknown	PINT 515:1
k. no more than other men	AUBR 33:3
k. of them in breaking	BIDLE 95:33
safer than a k. way	HASK 328:1
So I had nothing k.	SHAK 616:20
That thy way may be k. upon	BOOK 129:4
this is all that is k.	NEWM 493:8
till I am k., and do not want	JOHN 371:13
unknown, and k. too late	SHAK 622:26
Which we have heard and k.	BOOK 130:8
yet hast thou not k. me	BIBLE 97:13
you 'ave k. o' the others	KIPL 399:14

knows: HE k.—HE knows

	FITZ 284:8
He k. nothing	SHAW 637:1
he K. Things	MILNE 463:6
He k. ye not, ye heavenly	GOET 309:15
if you k. of a better 'ole	BAIR 47:18
k. nothing whatever about	KNOX 403:9
sits in the middle and k.	FROST 295:10
that has a mind and k. it	SHAW 635:20
knucklebones: k. has seen the fall	STEV 667:8
knuckle-end: k. of England	SMITH 653:8
Kopf: *Ward mancher K. zum Greise*	MÜLL 484:6
Kraken: The K. sleepeth	TENN 684:19
Krieg: *K. findet immer einen Ausweg*	
	BREC 140:10
K. ist nichts als eine	CLAU 205:16
Krorluppia: Nasticreechia K.	LEAR 414:6
Kruger: killing K. with your mouth	KIPL 398:11
krummem: *Aus so k. Holze*	KANT 385:11
Kubla: In Xanadu did K. Khan	COL 210:9
kummervollen: *Wer nie die k. Nächte*	
	GOET 309:15
Kunst: *K. ist das Beste gut genug*	GOET 309:10
zuletzt die grösste K.	GOET 309:18
Kurtz: Mistah K.—he dead	CONR 217:6
kynde: fordon the lawe of k.	CHAU 195:8
kyrie: *K. eleison*	MISS 476:17

L

label: l. to cover himself	HUXL 378:2
l. ... I to join a name to	TOLS 700:11
labor: *Hoc opus, hic l. est*	VIRG 713:11
laboratory: guinea pigs in the l. of God	
	WILL 737:2

---

laboraverunt: *vanum l. qui aedificant*	
	BIBLE 108:4
laborem: *magnum alterius spectare l.*	
	LUCR 431:15
laboribus: *unum est pro l. tantis*	CAT 186:3
laborious: Studious of l. ease	COWP 223:29
labour: All things are full of l.	BIBLE 80:1
brow of l. this crown	BRYAN 153:24
Cold, pain, and l.	WORD 747:13
'Fair Shares for All' is L.'s call	JAY 363:23
faith and l. of love	BIBLE 103:19
his work, and to his l.	BOOK 132:9
Honest l. bears a lovely face	DEKK 235:15
I have had my l. for my travail	SHAK 627:4
I l. for peace, but when	BOOK 133:22
In all l. there is profit	BIBLE 78:31
it is to live without l.	TAWN 679:2
l. against our own cure	BROW 146:18
l. and are heavy laden	BIBLE 90:28
l. and not to ask	IGN 359:8
l. as separate men	WEBB 724:15
l. both by sea and land	SHAK 624:23
l. for that which satisfieth not	BIBLE 84:15
l. in the deep mid-ocean	TENN 686:2
l. of doing nothing	STEE 662:14
l. of your life is to build	MONT 480:16
l. spread her wholesome	GOLD 310:6
l. we delight in physics	SHAK 602:12
l. which he taketh under	BIBLE 79:36
L. without joy is base	RUSK 550:25
Learn to l. and to wait	LONG 427:11
man to l. in his vocation	SHAK 579:27
many still must l. for the one	BYRON 169:18
mental l. employed in it	REYN 539:9
My daily l. to pursue	WESL 728:10
Now all l. mars	SHAK 566:9
reward of l. is life	MORR 485:17
Should life all l.	TENN 685:23
Six days shalt thou l.	BIBLE 72:16
solely by the l. of my hands	THOR 697:1
sore l.'s bath	SHAK 602:2
strength then but l. and sorrow	BOOK 131:1
their l. is but lost	BOOK 134:6
true success is to l.	STEV 667:29
We l. soon, we labour late	BURNS 163:23
with difficulty and l.	MILT 470:14
youth of l. with an age of ease	GOLD 310:7
labourage: *L. et pâturage sont*	SULLY 671:13
laboured: builders have l. in vain	BIBLE 108:4
l. as his extempore sayings	WALP 720:2
l. more abundantly	BIBLE 101:5
labourer: l. to take his pension	RUSK 551:2
l. worthy of his hire	BIBLE 94:10
labourers: l. are few	BIBLE 90:12
labouring: entrails of yon l. cloud	MARL 447:2
l. man, that tills	OXF 504:1
Sleep is sweet to the l. man	BUNY 156:5
sleep of a l. man is sweet	BIBLE 80:10
women l. of child	BOOK 120:1
labour-intensive: Monarchy is a l. industry	
	WILS 738:5
Labour Party: L. owes more to Methodism	
	PHIL 514:6
right kind of leader for the L.	BEVAN 69:4
what have I ever done to the L.	TAWN 679:4
labours: Children sweeten l.	BACON 44:12
fright him, and no l. tire	JOHN 370:16
line too l.	POPE 521:17
Lingered l. come to naught	SOUT 658:1
may rest from their l.	BIBLE 107:5
their uncessant l. see	MARV 450:5
laburnums: L., dropping-weels of fire	
	TENN 684:3
labyrinth: peopled l. of walls	SHEL 641:7
labyrinthical: l. soul	DONNE 253:13
labyrinthine: fled Him, down the l. ways	
	THOM 695:1
Still more l. buds the rose	BROW 153:2
lace: And l. my bodice blue	HUNT 356:21
lacerate: Cannot l. his breast	YEATS 744:11
lacerations: l. of their bodies	TAWN 678:20

---

lacessit: *Nemo me impune l.*	ANON 22:10
lack: I nothing l. if I am his	BAKER 47:20
I sigh the l. of many	SHAK 633:11
l. of love from love made	BROW 149:11
lions do l., and suffer	BOOK 126:14
therefore can I l. nothing	BOOK 125:14
They l., I leave; they pine	DYER 265:1
lacked: If I l. any thing	HERB 335:8
lacking: in her inventions nothing is l.	
	LEON 418:10
lacrimae: *l. rerum et mentem mortalia*	
	VIRG 712:9
lad: l. does not care	JOHN 372:26
l. that's born to be king	BOUL 137:17
Sing me a song of a l.	STEV 669:2
When I was a l. I served a term	GILB 305:26
ladder: behold a l. set up	BIBLE 71:13
l. out of our vices if	AUG 37:10
l. to all high designs	SHAK 627:7
Now that my l.'s gone	YEATS 751:2
plasterer on his l.	HEAN 329:17
Wiv a l. and some glasses	BAT 55:4
young ambition's l.	SHAK 590:14
laden: labour and are heavy l.	BIBLE 90:28
l. with time expired men	HUGH 353:16
Then I should ever l.	HERB 335:1
ladies: Come from a l.' seminary	GILB 304:25
Dust was Gentlemen and L.	DICK 245:3
l. apparently rolled along	HUXL 357:18
l. dead and lovely knights	SHAK 634:17
L., just a little more	TREE 702:8
l. most deject and wretched	SHAK 576:4
l. of St James's	DOBS 249:2
l should ever sit down	MORE 484:3
Ladies were l. in those days	RAV 537:4
lion among l.	SHAK 611:22
lords of l. intellectual	BYRON 170:4
O lang, lang may the l. sit	BALL 50:12
rhyme themselves into l.'	SHAK 587:1
seminaries of young l.	KNOX 403:15
when he has l. to please	AUST 38:7
With store of l.	MILT 465:16
you would remember the l.	ADAMS 1:11
lads: Come lasses and l.	ANON 12:25
Golden l. and girls all must	SHAK 571:16
l. in their hundreds	HOUS 352:11
l. that will never be old	HOUS 352:11
lady: And when a l.'s in the case	GAY 300:1
called her his l. fair	KIPL 401:7
capers nimbly in a l.'s chamber	SHAK 621:15
catch a bird but a l.	RICH 540:9
first learnèd in a l.'s	SHAK 598:20
full-blown l.	CLOU 207:1
hound, and his l. fair	BALL 50:20
I met a l. in the meads	KEATS 388:9
in case a certain little l.	GAY 300:19
I saw my l. weep	ANON 15:6
Joan as my L. is as good	HERR 336:19
Laces for a l., letters	KIPL 400:9
l. doth protest too much	SHAK 576:16
l. of a 'certain age'	BYRON 171:3
l. of beauty and high degree	RANS 536:14
l. of Christ's College	AUBR 33:7
L. of Spain, I adore you	REAV 537:15
l. that's known as Lou	SERV 563:8
L. with a Lamp shall stand	LONG 427:13
l. would not love a shepherd	GREE 317:11
Liner she's a l.	KIPL 399:19
love for any l.	PEELE 511:2
lovely l., garmented in light	SHEL 643:7
many holiday and l. terms	SHAK 579:30
My L. Bountiful	FARQ 280:9
ne'er wan a l. fair	BURNS 163:18
Of many a l., and many	SPEN 660:6
O lang will his L.	BALL 49:3
Our L. of Pain	SWIN 676:10
Said our L. of the Snows	KIPL 400:5
see it as an elderly l.	CAREY 179:15
That's why the l. is a tramp	HART 327:12
There is a l. sweet and kind	ANON 16:9
This l. of the West Country	DE L 236:1
waulk in a l. like a l.	SHAW 638:16

lady: (*cont.*):
young l. named Bright · BULL 154:17
lady-smocks: l. all silver-white · SHAK 599:10
Lafayette: *L., nous voilà!* · STAN 662:7
laff'd: mus speck ter be l. · HARR 326:16
lag-end: l. of my life · SHAK 581:27
laggard: For a l. in love · SCOTT 560:5
laid: He l. us as we lay at birth · ARN 27:13
l. in earth my wrongs create · TATE 678:15
l. the foundations · BIBLE 77:34
when I'm l. by thee · HERR 337:1
where they have l. him · BIBLE 97:32
where thou hast l. him · BIBLE 97:33
laily: has made me the l. worm · BALL 49:16
lain: In cold grave she was l. · BALL 51:1
l. for ages and will lie · TENN 684:20
l. still and been quiet · BIBLE 77:7
laisser-faire: L. · ANON 20:16
L. · ARG 24:18
laisser passer et de l. · QUES 534:8
laity: conspiracies against the l. · SHAW 636:11
To tell the l. our love · DONNE 252:21
lake: black Cyprus with a l. · FLEC 286:12
into the bosom of the l. · TENN 688:13
l. water lapping with low · YEATS 752:8
waters of the Lydian l. · CAT 186:3
lakes: light shakes across the l. · TENN 688:1
lama: l. sabachthani · BIBLE 93:5
lamb: Behold the L. of God · BIBLE 96:7
blood of thé L. · BIBLE 106:21
blood of the L. · LIND 423:3
But one dead l. is there · LONG 427:12
Did he who made the L. make · BLAKE 114:15
fell down before the L. · BIBLE 106:14
from the wrath of the L. · BIBLE 106:17
holy L. of God · BLAKE 113:4
l. shall be without blemish · BIBLE 72:8
l. should be made parchment · SHAK 587:24
l. to the slaughter · BIBLE 84:12
Little L. who made thee · BLAKE 113:21
Maria, to the shorn l. · STER 664:9
Mary had a little l. · HALE 321:8
Pipe a song about a L. · BLAKE 113:16
save one little ewe l. · BIBLE 75:11
shall dwell with the l. · BIBLE 83:2
That leads me to the L. · COWP 222:22
will provide another l. · BIBLE 71:5
Worthy the L. that died · WATTS 722:19
you are yokèd with a l. · SHAK 593:9
lambent: l. but innocuous · GOUL 313:1
lambs: Feed my l. · BIBLE 97:40
gather the l. with his arm · BIBLE 83:28
l. that did frisk i' the sun · SHAK 631:12
l. who've lost our way · KIPL 399:6
lame: feet was I to the l. · BIBLE 77:29
l. by fortune's dearest · SHAK 633:14
L. dogs over stiles · KING 397:10
l. man leap as an hart · BIBLE 83:21
without religion is l. · EINS 268:6
lamentable: l. catalogue of human crime · CHUR 202:9
Tell thou the l. tale of me · SHAK 621:5
lamentation: l., weeping · BIBLE 88:11
lamented: ye have not l. · BIBLE 90:26
lamentings: L. heard i' the air · SHAK 602:13
laments: forest l. in order that · CHUR 201:17
Lammastide: It fell about the L. · BALL 49:1
lamp: Every street l. that I pass · ELIOT 272:14
It is a dying l., a falling · SHEL 630:24
Lady with a L. shall stand · LONG 427:13
l. and the ungirt loin · BROW 153:7
l. beside the golden door · LAZ 413:7
lord of lycht and l. · DOUG 255:8
Slaves of the L. · ARN 26:14
smell too strong of the l. · STER 664:20
When the l. is shattered · SHEL 641:6
lampada: *quasi cursores vitai l.* · LUCR 432:1
lamp-post: I'm leaning on a l. · GAY 300:19
lamprey: part which, like the l. · WEBS 725:14
surfeit by eating of a l. · FABY 279:16
lamps: filled their l. · MILT 463:20
Heav'n's great l. do dive · CAMP 177:3
l. are going out all over · GREY 318:10

lamps: (*cont.*):
old l. for new · ARAB 24:1
Ye living l., by whose dear · MARV 450:17
Lancaster: time-honoured L. · SHAK 619:6
lance: l. of justice hurtless · SHAK 597:8
Lancelot: reading for pleasure about L. · DANTE 230:12
land: And seems a moving l. · MILT 472:9
came down and hid the l. · KING 397:14
Ceres re-assume the l. · POPE 520:22
citizens of death's grey l. · SASS 557:7
even to the l. of darkness · BIBLE 77:15
French the empire of the l. · RICH 540:17
from l. to land · COL 211:16
good and bad of every l. · BAII 47:17
great rock in a weary l. · BIBLE 83:17
green and pleasant l. · BLAKE 113:4
hands prepared the dry l. · BOOK 131:10
heaven by sea as by l. · GILB 303:12
hum of that low l. · ARN 28:17
Ill fares the l., to hast'ning · GOLD 310:6
In that l. of flesh and bone · AUDEN 35:3
It is l. reclamation · WILS 738:4
l. flowing with milk and honey · BIBLE 71:40
l. is not the sweet home · AUDEN 35:1
L. of brown heath and shaggy · SCOTT 559:17
l. of embarrassment · BARN 53:5
L. of Heart's Desire · YEATS 752:9
L. of Hope and Glory · BENS 63:23
l. of lost content · HOUS 352:15
l. of meanness, sophistry · BYRON 169:26
l. of my fathers · THOM 693:21
l. of sand and ruin · SWIN 677:5
l. of the living · BIBLE 84:13
l. of the shadow · BIBLE 82:26
l. of Vainglory · BUNY 155:15
L. that I love · BERL 65:17
l. was made for you · GUTH 320:5
l. was ours before we were · FROST 294:18
L. where my fathers died · SMITH 652:13
l. . . . where the light is as darkness · BIBLE 77:16
lane to the l. of the dead · AUDEN 34:4
nakedness of the l. · BIBLE 71:28
O'er the l. of the free · KEY 394:15
on this windy sea of l. · MILT 470:19
piece of l. not so very · HOR 351:9
pleasant l. of counterpane · STEV 668:15
possessed his l. · BIBLE 73:7
presence and no l. beside · SHAK 593:24
ready by water as by l. · ELST 276:1
scorn of that pleasant l. · BOOK 132:13
sent to spy out the l. · BIBLE 73:5
splendid and a happy l. · GOLD 310:16
that think there is no l. · BACON 42:3
There is a l. of pure delight · WATTS 723:4
There shall be no more l. · BROO 143:8
There's the l., or cherry-isle · HERR 336:8
They love their l. · HALL 322:5
This heavenly l. from ours · WATTS 723:5
This l. of such dear souls · SHAK 619:18
to enjoy thy l. · SHAK 593:24
travel by l. or by water · BOOK 120:1
Truth is a pathless l. · KRIS 404:1
Woe to the l. that's governed · SHAK 621:25
Ye shall eat the fat of the l. · BIBLE 71:30
landing: fight on the l. grounds · CHUR 202:11
landlady: l. of a boarding-house · LEAC 413:10
landlord: Bess, the l.'s daughter · NOYES 497:5
Come, l., fill the flowing bowl · ANON 12:24
I'll marry a l.'s daughter · LAMB 407:9
l. for the use of the original · RIC 539:23
l. to the whole congregation · ADD 4:8
land-lubbers: l. lying down below · ANON 17:6
landmark: Remove not the ancient l. · BIBLE 79:12
lands: By many l. and over many a wave · CAT 187:1
envy of less happier l. · SHAK 619:18
gone out into all l. · BOOK 125:4
l. after their own names · BOOK 127:24
l. beneath another sun · THOM 696:10

lands: (*cont.*):
l. of palm · TENN 680:19
longed-for l. · STEV 666:6
Lord of himself, not of l. · WOTT 749:1
Then l. were fairly portioned · MAC 436:12
landscape: Claude's l. all is lovely · CONS 217:24
gardening is l.-painting · POPE 524:8
l. of England in general · AUST 38:13
once the l. of the world · YOUNG 754:20
reasonable part in a l. · CHEK 197:9
landscapes: if l. were sold · STEV 667:21
Land's End: L. to John of Gaunt · SPOO 661:5
landslide: going to pay for a l. · KENN 393:10
land-thieves: l. and water-thieves · SHAK 607:18
lane: l. to the land of the dead · AUDEN 34:4
lanes: streets and l. of the city · BIBLE 94:31
language: best chosen l. · AUST 38:21
beyond the l. of the living · ELIOT 271:3
But speak a l. of their own · SWIFT 674:27
But the l., and the truth · JONS 379:14
clear l. is insincerity · ORW 501:1
clear view of our l. · POPP 524:7
conceive you may use any l. · GILB 304:14
define her feelings in l. · HARDY 324:7
divided by a common l. · SHAW 638:31
fancies broke through l. · BROW 152:9
heart doth need a l. · COL 210:17
In l., the ignorant have · DUPPA 264:9
instead of l., we have jargon · BENT 64:19
In such lovely l. · LAWR 412:23
intelligence by means of l. · WITT 739:15
l. and sent it into battle · MURR 488:12
l. and ways of behaving · JUV 383:19
l. an opera is sung in · APPL 23:17
l. convey more than they · CONN 216:13
l. he was the lodesterre · LYDG 433:2
l. I have learned these forty · SHAK 619:9
L. is a form of human reason · LÉV 420:9
L. is called the garment of · CARL 181:7
L. is fossil poetry · EMER 277:8
L. is only the instrument · JOHN 367:20
L. is the dress of thought · JOHN 368:24
l. of another world · BYRON 172:18
l. of priorities · BEVAN 68:14
l. of the age is never · GRAY 316:11
l. of the heart · POPE 520:7
l. of the unheard · KING 397:4
l. only speaks to the ears · FRAN 292:11
l. plain, and incidents · COWP 222:1
l. to another the creations · SHEL 644:4
L. was not powerful enough · DICK 242:10
l. which I spake like thee · MAC 436:7
Learned his great l. · BROW 151:1
Life is a foreign l. · MORL 484:19
limits of my l. mean · WITT 740:5
literature is simply l. · POUND 527:17
Lovely enchanting l. · HERB 335:4
Money speaks sense in a l. · BEHN 60:15
natural l. of the heart · SHAD 563:13
neither speech nor l. · BOOK 125:4
no respect for their l. · SHAW 638:15
obscurity of a learned l. · GIBB 302:20
Of his strange l. all I know · LAND 408:1
or enlargement of the l. · JOHN 367:21
our l. should perish · MAC 435:21
Political l.—with variations · ORW 501:2
refine our l. to grammatical · JOHN 369:17
some entrance into the l. · BACON 44:35
Speech happens not to be his l. · STAËL 662:3
spoken in their own l. · BIBLE 87:7
That l., by your skill made · GAY 300:5
There's a cool web of l. · GRAV 314:18
There's l. in her eye · SHAK 628:2
Under the tropic is our l. · WALL 718:20
with no l. but a cry · TENN 683:19
You taught me l. · SHAK 625:7
languages: at a great feast of l. · SHAK 599:4
gave l. just as she needed · PRIOR 529:7
knowledge of the ancient l. · BRIG 141:13
l. are the pedigree · JOHN 370:27
live l. for Miss Blimber · DICK 240:13
silent in seven l. · BAG 46:20
wit in all l. · DRYD 262:10

languid: excite your l. spleen — GILB 305:17
languish: Relieve my l. — DAN 229:16
languor: L. cannot be — SHEL 643:18
with a monotonous l. — VERL 710:4
languors: lilies and l. of virtue — SWIN 676:9
Lansbury: telling L. what he — BEVIN 69:13
lantern: l. on the stern — COL 212:14
l. whereof tales are told — JONS 380:6
socket of his earthly l. — GREV 318:7
word is a l. unto my feet — BOOK 133:20
lap: Carrie to sit on his l. — GROS 319:4
flowery l. of earth — ARN 27:13
fresh l. of the crimson rose — SHAK 611:15
head upon the l. of Earth — GRAY 315:20
It lies in the l. of the gods — HOMER 343:10
l. of the new come spring — SHAK 621:8
Stark calm on the l. — KIPL 401:1
lap-dogs: l. give themselves — POPE 523:16
When husbands or when l. — POPE 523:29
lapidary: l. inscriptions — JOHN 374:7
lapping: lake water l. with low — YEATS 752:8
lapwing: Beatrice, like a l. — SHAK 613:28
lard: l. their lean books — BURT 164:14
lards: l. the lean earth — SHAK 580:9
larem: Labore fessi venimus l. — CAT 186:3
large: are at l. and unrelated — JAMES 362:14
It's as l. as life — CARR 183:20
l. a letter I have written — BIBLE 102:10
l.-brained woman — BROW 147:22
little volume, l. book — CRAS 226:9
too small to live in and too l. — ANON 19:3
larger: l., freer, and more loving — BALD 48:5
L. than human on the frozen — TENN 682.21
largess: l. universal, like the sun — SHAK 585:16
lark: bisy l., messager of day — CHAU 193:19
l. ascending — MER 458:4
l. at break of day arising — SHAK 633:10
l. at heaven's gate sings — SHAK 571:3
l. becomes a sightless — TENN 684:14
l.-charmèd — HOPK 345:9
l. her matins sings aloft — SPEN 659:14
l. now leaves his wat'ry — D'AV 231:20
l. somewhere begin to sing — PORT 524:22
l.'s on the wing — BROW 151:28
l., that tirra-lirra — SHAK 631:24
More tuneable than l. — SHAK 610:24
No l. more blithe — BICK 108:20
sing as sweetly as the l. — SHAK 610:5
Some late l. singing — HENL 332:8
swallow for the holy l. — BROW 147:2
We rise with the l. — BRET 140:15
larks: And hear the l. so high — HOUS 352:10
Four L. and a Wren — LEAR 413:18
l., still bravely singing — MCCR 437:5
together as a choir of l. — DYER 265:3
larkspur: The l. listens — TENN 686:20
Lars Porsena: L. of Clusium — MAC 436:9
lascivious: l. gloating — STOP 669:13
To the l. pleasing of a lute — SHAK 621:15
lash: blood drawn with the l. — LINC 422:8
delight at once and l. — POPE 521:3
dost thou l. that whore — SHAK 597:7
rum, sodomy, and the l. — CHUR 203:10
lashes: That l. all with shade — WILB 734:6
Laski: Ayer and Marghanita L. — PRIE 529:2
lass: A l. unparalleled — SHAK 567:12
And every l. a queen — KING 397:17
And the l. that loves a sailor — DIBD 238:14
Drink to me l. — SHER 645:18
It came with a l. — JAM 362:8
It was a lover and his l. — SHAK 569:23
l. that has acres o' charms — BURNS 162:3
Sweet l. of Richmond Hill — MACN 440:11
lasse: tout casse, tout l. — ANON 21:8
lasses: Come l. and lads — ANON 12:25
then she made the l., O — BURNS 162:2
lassie: I love a l., a bonnie — LAUD 411:6
Wae my l. by my side — LAUD 411:7
young l., ... on auld man — BURNS 164.2
lost: bears the marks of the l. — AARO 569:19
bring a man foul in thy l. — BOOK 126:21
creation, I will bear — MILT 472:16

last: (cont.):
families l. not three oaks — BROW 145:21
Heaven's l. best gift — MILT 471:21
Him first, him l., him midst — MILT 471:23
It did not l.: the Devil — SQUI 661:18
It will l. my time — CARL 180:4
l. article of my creed — GAND 297:10
L. came, and last did go — MILT 466:7
l. for more than a century — CAT 185:12
l. gentleman in Europe — LEV 419:17
l. great Englishman is low — TENN 687:14
l. have wrought but one — BIBLE 91:28
L. night I dreamt I went — DU M 263:14
l. red leaf is whirled — TENN 683:7
l. romantics — YEATS 751:5
L. scene of all — SHAK 568:16
l. shall be first — BIBLE 91:27
l. state of that man — BIBLE 90:37
L.-supper-carved-on-a-peach — LANC 407:20
l. syllable of recorded — SHAK 605:1
l. taste of sweets — SHAK 619:16
l. thing I shall do — PALM 505:15
l. time I saw Paris — HAMM 322:15
live this day as if thy l. — KEN 393:6
Look thy l. on all things lovely — DE L 236:2
Nice guys. Finish l. — DUR 264:11
nought long time may l. — SACK 552:12
present were the world's l. — DONNE 251:2
that has dawned is your l. — HOR 348:6
that I could l. for ever — CONR 217:17
there is no l. nor first — BROW 152:1
they l. while they last — DE G 235:4
Tristram Shandy did not l. — JOHN 374:9
unto this l. — BIBLE 91:29
wait for the l. judgement — CAMUS 177:15
When he was at the l. gasp — BIBLE 88:7
latch: Lingering he raised his l. — COL 211:23
no l. ter de golden gate — HARR 327:9
latchet: shoe's l. I am not worthy — BIBLE 96:6
late: Dread of being l. — BETJ 68:8
five minutes too l. all my life — COWL 221:22
l. came I to love thee — AUG 37:2
l. into a world too old — MUSS 488:17
never come l. — HART 327:12
No, you were l. — LERN 419:2
offering even that too l. — NEV 492:5
So l. into the night — BYRON 173:6
too l. to-morrow to be brave — ARMS 26:9
years of human thought too l. — LA BR 405:4
later: It is l. than you think — SERV 563:5
lateral: l. thinking — DE B 233:11
latet: *L. anguis in herba* — VIRG 714:19
lath: l. of wood painted to look — BISM 110:8
Latin: Devil knows L. — KNOX 403:12
he speaks L. — SHAK 587:27
measures is L. for a whopping — ANST 23:13
no L. word for Tea — BELL 62:4
No more L., no more French — ANON 16:21
Then you understand L. — FARQ 280:15
Thou hadst small L. — JONS 380:3
latrine: mouth had been used as a l. — AMIS 10:13
rotten seat of a l. — FLAU 285:17
latrone: *vacuus coram l. viator* — JUV 384:5
latter: and the l. rain — BOOK 120:9
stand at the l. day — BIBLE 77:25
laud: we l. and magnify thy glorious — BOOK 122:10
laudamus: L. te — MISS 476:18
Te Deum l.: Te Dominum — ANON 22:17
laudant: L. illa sed ista legunt — MART 449:13
laudate: L. Dominum — BIBLE 108:3
l. et superexaltate eum — BIBLE 108:8
laudator: l. temporis acti — HOR 347:14
laudi: concedant laurea l. — CIC 204:2
laugh: An atheist-l.'s — BURNS 161:25
And I did l. sans intermission — SHAK 568:13
Anything awful makes me l. — LAMB 406:26
But I l. and eat well — HUGH 354:1
dismissed with a l. — HOR 351:7
either l. with me — STER 664:13
In not a thing to l. to scorn — GILM 569:19
L. and be well — GREEN 316:18
l. ... old laughs — WILC 734:7

laugh: (cont.):
L. at all you trembled — COWP 223:7
l. at any mortal thing — BYRON 171:8
l. at human actions — SPIN 661:3
l. at them in our turn — AUST 39:19
l. broke into a thousand — BARR 54:6
L. no man to scorn — BIBLE 87:13
l. out aloud all — CAT 186:3
l. that spoke the vacant — GOLD 310:8
l. the more heartily — RHYS 539:18
L. where we must, be candid — POPE 521:27
make the unskilful l. — SHAK 576:6
making decent people l. — MOL 478:18
man cannot make him l. — SHAK 583:26
man of quality than to l. — CONG 215:1
myself l. at everything — BEAU 56:10
Never l. at live dragons — TOLK 700:3
no girl wants to l. all of the — LOOS 428:10
silently l. at my own cenotaph — SHEL 640:7
sillier than a silly l. — CAT 186:4
that see me l. me to scorn — BOOK 125:10
their squeaking l. — MARV 451:10
They l. uproariously in youth — BROO 143:14
they shall l. and sing — BOOK 129:3
tickle us, do we not l. — SHAK 608:22
time to l. — BIBLE 80:5
unextinguishable l. in heaven — BROW 145:7
Wanna l. like a loon — HARB 323:11
laughable: schemes of political
improvement l. — JOHN 373:6
laughed: I l. him into patience — SHAK 565:13
l. at in the second — NAP 489:10
l. with counterfeited glee — GOLD 310:12
they l. consumedly — FARQ 280:13
When he l., respectable — AUDEN 34:10
laughing: Happiness is no l. matter — WHAT 730:8
hear you sweetly l. — CAT 186:7
l. and jeering at everything — PEPYS 512:9
l. devil in his sneer — BYRON 169:19
l. immoderately at stated — SMITH 653:7
l. is heard on the hill — BLAKE 114:2
l. queen that caught — HUNT 356:8
Minnehaha, L. Water — LONG 427:16
most fun I ever had without l. — ALLEN 9:9
speaking sweetly and l. sexily — SAPP 556:1
waked herself with l. — SHAK 613:21
laughs: at lovers' perjury — DRYD 261:10
l. to see the green man — HOFF 341:8
she l. with a harvest — JERR 366:1
laughter: anything that tends to l. — SHAK 582:14
born with a gift of l. — SAB 552:11
But l. and the love of friends — BELL 62:3
creatures by the faculty of l. — ADD 4:23
grail of l. of an empty ash — CRANE 225:20
ill-bred, as audible l. — CHES 198:15
l. and sorrow — JOHN 369:9
l. at their quaint opinions — MILT 472:11
l. for a month — SHAK 580:8
L. hath only a scornful — SIDN 647:11
L. holding both his sides — MILT 465:6
L. is nothing else but sudden — HOBB 339:16
L. is pleasant — PEAC 510:9
l., learnt of friends — BROO 143:18
l. of her heart in ev'ry street — HAMM 322:15
l. out of dead bellies — POUND 527:2
l. seen by the world — GOGOL 310:1
l. the heart is sorrowful — BIBLE 78:30
L. . . . the most civilized music — UST 707:11
L. would be bereaved if — UST 707:14
Laugh thy girlish l. — WATS 722:9
more frightful than l. — SAGAN 552:17
mouth filled with l. — BOOK 134:4
Our sincerest l. — SHEL 643:19
Present mirth hath present l. — SHAK 629:4
so is the l. of a fool — BIBLE 80:11
under running l. — THOM 695:1
Was l. and ability and Sighing — DICK 245:3
weeping and the l. — DOWS 256:3
where l. may signify anger — TOFF 700:1
With weeping and with l. — MAC 436:16
worst returns to l. — SHAK 596:23
launch: l. your vessel — TENN 687:8
launched: l. ... ... chins — MARL 446:17

leaf: (cont.):
Falls with the l. still	FLET 287:12
He can watch a grass or l.	GRAV 314:20
last red l. is whirled	TENN 683:7
l. upon the top of a tree	WORD 742:20
My days are in the yellow l.	BYRON 173:1
Of mortal life the l.	SPEN 660:6
prickling l. it bears	MARV 451:9
sear, the yellow l.	SHAK 604:21
we all do fade as a l.	BIBLE 84:28

league: Half a l. onward — TENN 680:13
She hadna sailed a l. — BALL 49:5
Will keep a l. till death — SHAK 621:4
leak: One l. will sink a ship — BUNY 156:9
lean: flat on your face as l. — THUR 697:14
has a l. and hungry look — SHAK 590:6
l. and tight-lipped mufflered — JOS 380:16
l. on a garden urn — ELIOT 271:19
l. on one another — BURKE 159:18
l. to wild extremes — DURY 264:13
on which if a man l. — BIBLE 76:31
leaning: l. on a lamp-post — GAY 300:19
sneer at me for l. all awry — FITZ 284:12
leap: creep again, l. again — DE L 236:4
great l. in the dark — HOBB 340:14
lame man l. as an hart — BIBLE 83:21
L. to these arms, untalked — SHAK 623:16
made a l. into the dark — BROWN 144:16
methinks it were an easy l. — SHAK 580:1
Milk's l. toward immortality — FAD 279:18
must l. into the ocean — HUME 356:12
one giant l. for mankind — ARMS 26:12
shall l. over the wall — BOOK 125:3
worthy to l. in ourselves — SHAK 693:21
leaped: God have I l. over a wall — BIBLE 75:18
leaping: By brooks too broad for l. — HOUS 352:18
l., and praising God — BIBLE 98:10
l. from place to place — HARDY 325:8
l. light for your delight — AUDEN 36:5
long as there is no l. — SURT 672:15
one's horse as he is l. — HARE 326:5
swimmers into cleanness l. — BROO 143:16
leaps: It moves in mighty l. — AYRES 40:16
learn: craft so long to l. — CHAU 195:5
diligent to l. — WORD 743:8
Even while they teach, men l. — SEN 562:29
I l. two things — BOOK 123:5
Irish poets, l. your trade — YEATS 753:16
l., and inwardly digest — BOOK 120:11
l. in suffering what they — SHEL 641:1
l. so little and forget — DAV 232:2
L. to write well, or not — BUCK 154:11
places to l. the world — CHES 198:8
so dull but she can l. — SHAK 609:2
so much to l. so little — DICK 243:15
there is much desire to l. — MILT 475:13
thirty who don't want to l. — SELL 562:15
We cannot l. men from — DISR 248:34
We live and l. — POMF 518:11
wolde he l. and gladly teche — CHAU 192:21
learned: discreet and l. Minister — BOOK 122:4
Even for l. men, love — TAC 678:4
forgotten nothing and l. — DUM 264:1
grew within this l. man — MARL 447:5
l. anything from history — HEGEL 330:7
l. has been forgotten — SKIN 649:6
l. lumber in his head — POPE 521:24
L. without sense — CHUR 201:13
much l. dust — COWP 223:25
obscurity of a l. language — GIBB 302:20
opinion with the l. — CONG 215:6
prescribed laws to the l. — DUPPA 264:9
taught, and easiest l. — MILT 473:23
They have l. nothing — TALL 678:11
Things l. on earth — BROW 151:15
learning. and in l, rules — CRAB 225:1
and l. of a sort — BELL 61:15
attain good l. — ASCH 30:10
be written for our l. — BOOK 120:11
calling. 'rolth of l. — LOCKE 424:15
deep l. little had he — SPEN 660:?
encourage a will to l. — AOUI 41:?
enough of l. to misquote — BYRON 172:4

learning: (cont.):
I grow old ever l. many things — SOLON 655:5
l., a mere hoard — SHAK 583:27
l. belongs not to the female — KNOX 403:14
l. is a dangerous thing — POPE 521:8
l. is like bread in a besieged — JOHN 374:3
l. more than the fond eye — SHAK 608:16
l.'s triumph o'er her barb'rous — JOHN 370:11
L., that cobweb of the brain — BUTL 166:12
l. the instrument — BUTL 167:9
L. will be cast — BURKE 158:18
l. with a great sum — BIBLE 88:5
liberty, and of l. — DISR 247:22
middle age of a state, l. — BACON 45:5
mind by that traitor to l. — JOHN 366:15
much l. doth make thee — BIBLE 99:10
nonsense, and l. — GOLD 311:20
Of l. lightly like a flower — TENN 684:16
O! this l., what a thing it is — SHAK 624:12
our rights in l.'s world — EGER 267:13
O, what l. — SHAK 623:21
picker-up of l.'s crumbs — BROW 149:19
pleasures that go with l. — SOCR 655:1
polite l. and a mere scholar — DEFOE 233:15
renown on scraps of l. — YOUNG 754:6
that loyal body wanted l. — TRAPP 702:3
That's a' the l. I desire — BURNS 161:26
They can't be alwayth a l. — DICK 240:34
Those twins of l. — SHAK 589:11
'till l. fly the shore — POPE 518:22
Wear your l., like — CHES 198:13
We'll cry both arts and l. — QUAR 534:6
Whence is thy l.? Hath thy toil — GAY 299:31
lease: And summer's l. hath — SHAK 633:6
having so short a l. — SHAK 635:7
leasehold: it is l. for all — LUCR 432:5
least: faithful in that which is l. — BIBLE 96:8
l. of all seeds — BIBLE 91:3
l. of these my brethren — BIBLE 92:21
promises l. — BAR 54:21
leathern: l. girdle about — BIBLE 88:14
Their l. boats begin to hoist — MARV 451:13
leave: And l. me there to die — ANON 14:16
be ready to l. — MONT 480:14
couldn't l. without the King — ELIZ 275:4
ever taking l. — RILKE 541:2
Intreat me not to l. thee — BIBLE 74:25
I pray thee l., love me — DRAY 258:6
l. a child alone — BROW 152:17
l. her far away behind — KEATS 386:18
l. his father and his mother — BIBLE 70:7
l. in a taxi you can leave — KALM 385:2
l. it to a moment of change — CHES 199:21
L. me, O Love which reachest — SIDN 647:4
L. not a rack behind — SHAK 625:28
L. not a stain in thine honour — BIBLE 87:32
L. off first for manners' sake — BIBLE 87:30
l. something so written — MILT 476:5
l. their riches — BOOK 127:24
l. them in the midst — BIBLE 85:13
L. them while you're looking — LOOS 428:9
l. the outcome — CORN 218:16
L. writing plays — DRYD 261:3
not l. my soul in hell — BOOK 124:3
Oh, never l. me — ANON 12:34
repeat his past nor l. it — AUDEN 36:15
should l. the word of God — BIBLE 98:11
Thou didst l. thy throne — ELL 275:8
To l. a living name behind — WEBS 725:13
We asked none l. to love — DONNE 252:1
leaven: l. leaveneth the whole — BIBLE 100:21
l. of malice and wickedness — BIBLE 100:22
l. of malice and wickedness — BOOK 120:17
leaves: burning of the l. — BINY 109:21
Close up these barren l. — WORD 748:8
Crowned with calm l. — SWIN 676:16
fields and l. to the trees — HOR 350:15
flaps its glad green l. — HARDY 324:22
In shady l. of destiny — CRAS 226:15
laughing l. of the tree divide — SWIN 675:23
and flowers in the sun — YEATS 753:?
l. are falling like — SHEL 641:18
l. column a part of oneself — HOR 323:8

leaves: (cont.):
l. dead are driven — SHEL 641:14
l. fall early — POUND 527:10
l. hast never known — KEATS 389:10
l. is a generation of men — HOMER 343:4
l. like light footfalls — SHEL 641:13
l. of the tree were — BIBLE 107:23
l. that strew the brooks — MILT 468:15
l. to a tree — KEATS 391:15
long l. cover me — SWIN 676:27
noiseless noise among the l. — KEATS 388:5
Of withered l., and the elms — ARN 28:1
Shatter your l. before — MILT 465:20
tender l. of hope — SHAK 588:19
Than what it l. behind — WORD 744:4
Though l. are many — YEATS 751:4
trees I see barren of l. — SHAK 633:4
When yellow l., or none — SHAK 634:6
whole deck put on its l. — FLEC 286:13
woods and stipple l. — SACK 552:16
leave-taking: It is not worth l. — SHAK 567:10
leaving: Became him like the l. it — SHAK 600:14
L. his country for his — FITZ 283:9
Lebanon: cedars of L. — BIBLE 74:12
Samarcand to cedared L. — KEATS 387:9
leben: Ehrfurcht vor dem L. — SCHW 558:14
Ihr Racker, wollt ihr ewig l.? — FRED 293:12
Lebens: des L. goldner Baum — GOET 309:5
lecher: Does l. in my sight — SHAK 597:4
lecherous: I am rough and l. — SHAK 595:2
l. as a sparwe — CHAU 193:5
lechery: L., sir, it provokes — SHAK 602:11
wars and l. — SHAK 628:5
lecto: Desideratoque acquiescimus l. — CAT 186:3
lectorem: L. delectando pariterque — HOR 347:15
lecture: at twilight from the l. — STEV 666:3
classic l., rich in sentiment — TENN 687:26
l., love, in love's philosophy — DONNE 252:6
lectures: l. or a little charity — WHIT 732:19
lecturing: l. had convinced me — HUXL 358:8
led: L. go. You are hurtig be — KIPL 401:21
think we l., we are most l. — BYRON 173:12
were we l. all that way — ELIOT 271:18
Leda: And L.'s goose a swan — ANON 14:9
leek: By this l., I will most — SHAK 586:15
lees: drink life to the l. — TENN 690:1
feast of wine on the l. — BIBLE 83:8
leeward: l. run or strike my sail — ALAB 7:1
left: better to be l. than — CONG 215:31
everything is l. out — JAMES 362:19
hast l. thy first love — BIBLE 106:3
he l. the thorn wi' me — BURNS 161:11
I l. my heart in San Francisco — CROSS 227:19
l. a lot o' little things behind — KIPL 398:11
l. and is now in the centre — MOSL 486:20
l. hand know what thy right — BIBLE 89:3
l. her husband because — MURD 488:3
l. our country for our — CART 184:11
l. thee all her lovely hues — DAV 232:11
l. to treat my friends — MALL 442:20
my l. hand — MILT 476:4
O let them be l., wildness — HOPK 345:15
one shall be taken and the other l.
— BIBLE 92:14
So far upon the l. side — WEBS 725:15
that never l. the ground — LOW 430:21
Thou hast l. behind — WORD 748:13
We l. fair Scotland's strand — BURNS 162:9
we that are l. grow old — BINY 109:20
left-handed: a l. marriage — WOLL 741:14
leg: decreasing l. — SHAK 582:20
For here I leave my second l. — HOOD 343:18
kiss my Julia's dainty l. — HERR 336:22
l. has often as much — HUNT 356:18
l. you shall put into breeches — JOHN 372:15
ne'er lift a lawless l. — BURNS 162:7
shape of his l. — SHAK 629:9
legacy: l. from a rich relative — SMITH 651:12
legal: exact l. definition — RUSS 551:23
physical fact into a l. right — MILL 460:23
legally: accomplishing small things l.
— BALZ 51:10
lege: Tolle l., tolle lege — AUG 37:1

legend: all the fables in the l.   BACON 42:22
past exudes l.   MAL 442:15
leges: *Silent enim l. inter arma*   CIC 204:11
leggemmo: *giorno più non vi l. avante*
  DANTE 230:13
leggiavamo: *Noi l. un giorno per diletto*
  DANTE 230:12
legion: L. and Social Club   BETJ 67:9
My name is L.   BIBLE 93:11
legions: give me back my l.   AUG 37:11
legislation: foundation of morals and l.
  BENT 64:4
imports and exports, l.   ARIS 25:6
legislative: l. power is   GIBB 302:1
legislator: l. of mankind   JOHN 369:20
people is the true l.   BURKE 159:19
legislators: unacknowledged l. of
the world   SHEL 644:8
legs: adorns my l,   HOUS 351:14
born with your l. apart   ORTON 499:17
cannon-ball took off his l.   HOOD 343:17
dclighteth he in any man's l.   BOOK 135:12
fold his l. and have out   JOHN 374:26
Four legs good, two l. bad   ORW 499:19
His l. bestrid the ocean   SHAK 566:20
It has such long and lofty l.   NASH 490:15
l. an instrument capable   BEEC 59:5
l. are as pillars of marble   BIBLE 81:20
l. when I take my boots off   DICK 240:23
lie between maids' l.   SHAK 576:11
not for your bad l.   ELIZ 274:9
open my l., and think of   HILL 339:3
recuvver the use of his l.   DICK 242:8
strongest l. in Pontefract   BETJ 67:16
Taste your l., sir   SHAK 630:9
Two vast and trunkless l.   SHEL 642:3
walking on his hinder l.   JOHN 372:18
Walk under his huge l.   SHAK 590:3
legunt: *Laudant illa sed ista l.*   MART 449:13
Leicester: Farewell, L. Square   JUDGE 382:8
Here lies the Earl of L.   ANON 14:5
leiden: *L. oder triumphieren*   GOET 309:9
Leidenschaften: *seiner L. gegangen ist*
  JUNG 382:13
leisure: add to these retirèd L.   MILT 464:18
At l. married, they repent   CONG 215:25
cometh by opportunity of l.   BIBLE 87:35
conspicuous l.   VEBL 709:15
detest at l.   BYRON 171:24
fill l. intelligently   RUSS 551:14
he is never at l.   JOHN 374:26
improvement arises from l.   JOHN 373:21
l. answers leisure   SHAK 606:25
l. are the two civilizers   DISR 247:21
l. with honour   CIC 204:13
miserable is to have l. to   SHAW 638:12
Politicians also have no l.   ARIS 25:11
trusted with a life of l.   MORE 484:1
we may polish it at l.   DRYD 262:8
leman: such hawks, and such l.   BALL 50:19
lemon: be squeezed as a l.   GEDD 300:20
squeezing of a l.   GOLD 311:23
lemon-trees: where the l. bloom   GOET 309:16
lend: L. less than thou owest   SHAK 595:6
l. me your ears   SHAK 592:5
l. you thus much moneys   SHAK 608:1
men who l.   LAMB 406:12
not well enough to l.   BIER 109:2
lender: borrower, nor a l. be   SHAK 573:4
lenders: thy pen from l.' books   SHAK 596:10
leudeth: merciful, and l.   BOOK 133:6
lendings: off, you l.!   SHAK 596:11
lends: Three things I never l.   SURT 672:12
length: drags its slow l. along   POPE 521:15
have l. and breadth enough   BALL 49:7
L. of days is in her right   BIBLE 78:8
l. of days understanding   BIBLE 77:19
still drags its dreary l.   DICK 239:1
what it lacks in l.   FROST 294:19
lengthen: To l. our days   MOORE 483:13
lengthening: at each remove a l. chain
  GOLD 311:8

Lenin: Engels and L.   KHR 395:14
L. was right   KEYN 395:4
lenses: my eyes are l.   DOUG 255:10
lent: one thing only has been l. to youth
  ARN 29:6
lente: *Festina l.*   AUG 37:12
O lente l. currite noctis equi   MARL 447:1
leoni: *vulpes aegroto cauta l.*   HOR 348:1
Léonie: Weep not for little L.   GRAH 313:8
leopard: l. shall lie down   BIBLE 83:2
or the l. his spots   BIBLE 85:10
leopards: l. sat under a juniper-tree   ELIOT 270:7
leper: as a Parliamentary l.   WILS 738:2
innocence is like a dumb l.   GREE 317:4
leprosy: skin was white as l.   COL 211:2
Lesbia: L. let us live and love   CAMP 177:3
I, whom Catullus once loved   CAT 186:8
L. with her sparrow   MILL 461:10
Vivamus, mea L.   CAT 185:15
Lesley: O saw ye bonnie L.   BURNS 161:12
less: And the little l.   BROW 148:25
believing more and more in l.   YATES 750:13
had he pleased us l.   ADD 3:12
How l. what we may be!   BYRON 171:33
Is l. likely to fall   GAY 299:28
l. is learned there   JOHN 374:8
L. than the dust, beneath   HOPE 345:4
L. than themselves   TESS 691:1
l. we love her   PUSH 532:15
Make l. thy body hence   SHAK 584:13
mean you can't take l.   CARR 182:8
more about less and l.   BUTL 165:23
nothing l. than thee   DONNE 251:22
rather than be l.   MILT 469:11
small Latin, and l. Greek   JONS 380:3
lessen: they l. from day to day   CARR 182:12
lesser: Of the two evils the l.   THOM 692:12
Or l. breeds without the Law   KIPL 400:13
refused a l. sacrifice   MARY 452:16
lesson: l. of the fearsome   AREN 24:14
l. which the Lord us taught   SPEN 659:10
lessons: they're called l.   CARR 182:12
lest: L. we forget   KIPL 400:11
let: L. justice be done   FERD 281:9
L. my people go   ANON 19:16
L. my people go   BIBLE 72:5
l. them all to my elder   THOM 694:2
L. there be light   BIBLE 69:20
l. the sounds of music   SHAK 610:1
L. the word go forth from   KENN 393:12
L. the words of my mouth   BOOK 125:6
L. us with a gladsome mind   MILT 465:19
L. what will be o'er me   STEV 669:5
sore l. and hindered   BOOK 120:12
lethal: Average made l.   SHAF 563:19
lethargy: a kind of l.   SHAK 582:17
Lethe: go not to L., neither   KEATS 389:4
itself in ease on L. wharf   SHAK 573:17
Lethean: drunken of things L.   SWIN 676:21
letter: deal by speech than by l.   BACON 44:8
He'll carry a l. to my love   BALL 49:9
huge wordy l. came from Capri   JUV 384:6
large a l. I have written   BIBLE 102:10
letter by strange l.   HEAN 329:17
l. from his wife   CARR 184:7
l. killeth   BIBLE 101:16
[l.] longer than usual   PASC 507:8
l. of recommendation   ADD 4:10
l. to the world   DICK 245:2
that when he wrote a l.   BACON 43:6
thou unnecessary l.   SHAK 595:12
until you have had a l.   LEV 419:18
letters: All l., methinks, should   OSB 501:6
And pause awhile from l.   JOHN 370:15
French l. to the university   JOYCE 382:5
L. for the rich, letters   AUDEN 35:9
l. get in the wrong places   MILNE 463:5
l. mingle souls   DONNE 252:24
L. of thanks, letters from   AUDEN 35:10
like women's l.; all pith   HAZL 328:17
nat the l. space   CHAU 195:25
No arts; no l.; no society   HOBB 340:7

letters: *(cont.):*
receive no l. in the grave   JOHN 376:22
than a man of l.   STER 665:8
letter-writing: uncertain process of l.
  ELIOT 270:1
letting: Stupor—then the l. go   DICK 244:10
lettuce: l. is 'soporific'   POTT 525:12
Letumque: *L. Labosque*   VIRG 713:14
levee: Drove my Chevy to the l.   MCL 439:8
more alluring than a l.   CONG 215:36
level: attempt to l. never equalize   BURKE 158:10
dead l. of provincial   ELIOT 269:22
l. of your dreams   SHAK 631:21
one dead l. ev'ry mind   POPE 519:5
Our low life was the l.'s   BROW 149:26
levellers: l. wish to level *down*   JOHN 372:14
levelling: bear l. *up*   JOHN 372:15
lever: l. should rest   BABEL 41:7
leviathan: draw out l. with an hook   BIBLE 78:4
l. retrieving pebbles   WELLS 727:14
there is that L.   BOOK 132:9
There L. hugest of   MILT 472:9
levity: like a little judicious l.   STEV 668:10
lewd: l. fellows of the baser   BIBLE 98:27
L., tiny, careless lives   ROET 544:6
Lewley: carries the bricks to L.   BETJ 68:4
lex: *Salus populi suprema est l.*   CIC 203:27
Salus populi suprema l.   SELD 562:10
lexicographer: doomed at last to
wake a l.   JOHN 367:22
L. A writer of dictionaries   JOHN 368:1
lexicon: Two men wrote a l.   WAT 722:5
liar: easy virtue and a proved l.   HAIL 321:1
every man a l.   BIBLE 99:20
he is a l.   BIBLE 96:33
l. gone to burning hell   SHAK 618:10
l. is he who makes   BUTL 166:2
only answered 'Little L.!'   BELL 61:6
liars: All men are l.   BOOK 133:13
do prove the greatest l.   DRAY 257:17
fears may be l.   CLOU 207:24
Income Tax has made more L.   ROG 544:19
l. and swearers are fools   SHAK 604:5
L. need good memories   SIDN 646:9
though l. by profession   HUME 355:19
Libanus: cedars of L.   BOOK 126:2
even the cedars of L.   BOOK 132:8
libation: l. to some god   SOCR 655:2
libel: Convey a l. in a frown   SWIFT 674:27
excessive wealth a l.   SHEL 644:3
libellum: *Cui dono lepidum novum l.*   CAT 185:10
liber: *L. scriptus proferetur*   MISS 477:12
libera: *L. Chiesa in libero Stato*   CAV 187:15
liberal: Is either a little L.   GILB 304:10
Just like an old l.   PLOM 517:11
l. of another man's   BACON 44:17
L. who wishes to replace   BIER 109:8
panted for a l. profession   COLM 214:3
you are l. in offers   SHAK 609:22
liberality: l. frequently becomes   BAED 46:6
win the world with l.   GASC 298:17
liberal-minded: l., great   TENN 684:16
liberate: we shall l. this country   MAND 444:3
liberates: Work l.   ANON 21:9
liberation: l. of the human mind   GOLD 310:4
liberavi: *L. animam meam*   BERN 66:8
libertas: *L. et natale solum*   SWIFT 675:15
Imperium et L.   DISR 247:31
liberté: *L.! Égalité! Fraternité!*   ANON 21:1
liberties: dramatist only wants more l.
  JAMES 362:15
never give up these l.   BURKE 159:3
what l. are taken in thy name   GEOR 301:10
libertine: air, a chartered l.   SHAK 584:19
puffed and reckless l.   SHAK 573:2
liberty: Abstract l., like other   BURKE 157:23
And play not with my l.   GOD 308:8
at l. when of Devils and Hell   BLAKE 112:15
between l. and slavery   CAMD 176:2
Brightest in dungeons, L.   BYRON 173:5
can be no effective l.   BELL 60:20
consecrate to truth and l.   SHEL 643:25
convenience to l.   HESSE 337:16

liberty: (cont.):
defence of l. is no vice — GOLD 312:1
desires in l. anything other — TOCQ 698:14
desire their l. and freedom — CHAR 191:9
endanger the public l. — ADAMS 2:26
end to a woman's l. — BURN 160:21
enjoy delight with l. — SPEN 660:21
Enjoy such l. — LOV 429:4
give me l., or give me — HENRY 333:7
Give me the l. to know — MILT 475:15
have been enemies of l. — HUME 355:13
I must have l. — SHAK 568:15
individual l. as an idol — SAL 554:6
insolent and L. to be saucy — HAL 321:17
interfering with l. of action — MILL 460:14
it certainly destroys l. — JOHN 376:1
known rules of ancient l. — MILT 474:22
Let there be light! said L. — SHEL 640:14
l. amuses the people — JOHN 371:26
l., and of learning — DISR 247:22
l. and prosperity of their — JENY 365:9
l. and the pursuit of — ANON 19:7
l., and the pursuit of — JEFF 364:2
L. and Union, now and — WEBS 725:6
L. cannot be preserved — ADAMS 2:25
l. cannot long exist — BURKE 157:12
l. catching and spreading — PRICE 528:17
L. consists in doing what — MILL 460:19
l. doesn't go to the trouble — BALZ 51:10
L. has never come from — WILS 738:9
L. is always unfinished — ANON 15:17
L. is liberty, not equality — BERL 66:4
l. is not licence — SCAN 557:17
L. is precious — LENIN 417:11
L. is to faction lowest air — MAD 441:15
L. is, to the lowest rank — JOHN 367:18
L. means responsibility — SHAW 637:23
l. of the individual must — MILL 460:18
l. of the press — JUN 383:3
l. plucks justice — SHAK 605:7
L.'s a glorious feast — BURNS 162:13
L.'s in every blow — BURNS 163:2
l. till they become wise — MAC 434:17
l. to man is eternal vigilance — CURR 229:4
L. too must be limited — BURKE 157:10
l. which we can hope — MILT 475:2
loudest yelps for l. — JOHN 370:3
love of l. is the love — HAZL 328:16
make them so easy as l. — AST 32:8
manly, moral, regulated l. — BURKE 158:5
mansion-house of l. — MILT 475:12
Money is coined l. — DOST 255:1
mountain nymph, sweet L. — MILT 465:6
name of l. or democracy — GAND 297:8
nation, conceived in l. — LINC 422:10
natural l. and puts on — LOCKE 425:8
O l.! what crimes — ROL 545:7
Over the chained bay waters L. — CRANE 225:25
people contend for their l. — HAL 321:16
primordial condition of l. — BAK 47:23
proclaim l. to the captives — BIBLE 84:26
seek power and to lose l. — BACON 43:28
Served human l. — YEATS 753:11
Shouted of l. — LONG 427:14
So loving-jealous of his l. — SHAK 623:7
survival and the success of l. — KENN 393:12
Sweet land of l. — SMITH 652:13
symptom of constitutional l. — GIBB 302:4
they mean when they cry l. — MILT 474:23
thy chosen music, L. — WORD 748:9
tree of l. must — JEFF 364:9
voices of l. be mute — CUMM 228:6
weight of too much l. — WORD 745:8
When love is l., and nature — POPE 519:19
who ever gives, takes l. — DONNE 251:3
womenl. is god abroad — BIBLE 87:25
Wommen, of kynde, Alkynn l. — CHAU 193:13
Lib'ty-Hall; This is L. — GOLD 311:18
libraries: books our circulating l. — COWP 550:20
library: half a l. to make one book — JOHN 377:4
l. and make use of her — AYCK 40:9

library: (cont.):
l. is thought in cold storage — SAM 554:17
Like one of his l. books — AYCK 40:11
lumber room of his l. — DOYLE 256:6
My l. was dukedom — SHAK 625:3
take choice of all my l. — SHAK 627:1
than a public l. — JOHN 369:16
libre: Je suis condamné à être l. — SART 556:9
L'homme est né l. — ROUS 549:2
libro: il l. e chi lo scrisse — DANTE 230:13
licence: L. my roving hands — DONNE 250:16
l. that English people — MANS 445:7
L. they mean when they — MILT 474:23
l. to print money — THOM 696:20
love not freedom, but l. — MILT 476:8
of course liberty is not l. — SCAN 557:17
universal l. to be good — COL 209:5
licences: L. POÉTIQUES — BANV 51:14
licensed: based upon l. premises — O'BR 497:11
licentious: all l. passages — GIBB 302:20
rapacious and l. soldiery — BURKE 159:2
Licht: ein L. anzuzünden in der Mehr L.! — JUNG 382:14 / GOET 309:20
lick: enemies shall l. the dust — BOOK 129:20
time to l. it into form — BURT 164:16
licorice: l. fields at Pontefract — BETJ 67:16
Liddell: right part wrote L. — WAT 722:5
this is Mrs L. — SPR 661:11
Liddesdale: Eskdale and L. — SCOTT 560:25
lids: Drops his blue-fringèd l. — COL 210:2
with eternal l. apart — KEATS 386:9
lie: after all, what is a l. — BYRON 171:20
And give the world the l. — RAL 535:15
And I l. down alone — HOUS 352:2
And leads you to believe a l. — BLAKE 111:17
And the l. of Authority — AUDEN 36:1
Art is a l. that makes — PIC 514:9
came home, home to a l. — POUND 527:1
Cannot come, l. follows — PROU 530:15
circumstantial . . . the l. direct — SHAK 569:26
compulsion doth in music l. — MILT 463:8
dost thou l. so low — SHAK 591:18
every word she writes is a l. — MCC 437:1
fain wald l. down — BALL 49:17
fall victim to a big l. — HITL 339:14
gives me the l. i' — SHAK 575:11
God's own name upon a l. — COWP 223:14
He makes me down to l. — SCOT 561:8
Here l. I, Martin Elginbrodde — MACD 437:10
History becomes a l. — COCT 208:7
Is a dream a l. if it don't — SPR 661:15
know I can't tell a l. — WASH 722:2
l. abroad for the good — WOTT 749:9
l. as quietly among — EDW 267:8
l. between maids' legs — SHAK 576:11
l. circumstantial — SHAK 569:26
l. diagonally in his bed — STER 665:5
l. doth ever add pleasure — BACON 44:37
l. down in peace — DONNE 253:2
l. down where all ladders — YEATS 751:2
l. even among the children — BOOK 128:15
l. even when it is inconvenient — VIDAL 711:7
L. follows by post — BER 65:4
L. heavy on him, Earth — EVANS 279:4
l. in cold obstruction — SHAK 606:11
l. in the soul is a true — JOW 380:19
l. low Brer Rabbit — JENK 365:2
l. may do thee grace — SHAK 582:10
l. than a truth misunderstood — JAMES 363:18
l. that sinketh — BACON 45:1
l. usefully should lie — HERV 337:12
l. which is part a truth — TENN 681:11
l. will go round the world — SPUR 661:16
L. with me — BIBLE 71:24
l. with your legs ungainly — SASS 557:8
Live and l. reclined — TENN 686:1
loveth and maketh a l. — BIBLE 107:25
May l. left seven — CLAR 205:13
misleading impression, not a l. — ARMS 26:13
not I easy at Winchelsea — BENET 62:16
obedient to their lawès we l. — SIM 64:21
l. virsilje to l. for the truth — ALL EN 6:7
shall l. through names — BROW 148:18

lie: (cont.):
something given to l. — SHAK 567:4
that he should l. — BIBLE 73:9
There's a real love of a l. — BROW 151:9
To undo the folded l. — AUDEN 36:1
wenen every thing a l. — CHAU 194:29
When he speaketh a l. — BIBLE 96:33
When I l. tangled in her hair — LOV 429:1
Who can rule and dare not l. — TENN 686:13
Who loves to l. with me — SHAK 568:8
Who readily can l. with art — GAY 300:7
you.—under a mistake — SWIFT 674:7
lieb: sich beide so herzlich l. — HEINE 331:1
Liebe: Was ist denn L.? — HALM 322:7
Wo die L. herrscht — JUNG 383:1
lied: because our fathers l. — KIPL 398:16
But it l. — BELL 61:10
lien: have l. among the pots — BOOK 129:8
lies: bare earth exposed he l. — DRYD 259:19
Beats all the l. you can invent — BLAKE 111:6
believing their own l. — ARB 24:7
From l. of tongue and pen — CHES 199:3
full of l. and robbery — BIBLE 86:15
he l. to the heart — SHAK 618:12
Here l. a most beautiful lady — DE L 236:1
Here l. the Earl of Leicester — ANON 14:5
History is a pack of l. — STUB 671:2
It produces l. like sand — ANON 21:11
I wish I were where Helen l. — BALL 49:13
l. about the Democrats — STEV 666:15
l. are like the father — SHAK 580:21
l. are often told in silence — STEV 668:8
L. are the mortar — WELLS 727:19
l. as will lie in thy sheet — SHAK 630:15
l., damned lies and statistics — DISR 249:13
l. it lives on — FOSD 291:4
l. sound truthful and murder — ORW 501:2
l. to ice a wedding cake — ASQ 32:3
l. where he longed — STEV 669:9
Matilda told such Dreadful L. — BELL 61:5
only l. are invented — BRAQ 139:18
open truth to cover l. — CONG 215:5
rest is l. — FITZ 284:1
spring of endless l. — COWP 223:6
That lust had l. — GREE 317:10
Their delight is in l. — BOOK 128:19
There l. the Doctor — AUBR 33:1
though I know she l. — SHAK 635:5
Who l. beneath your spell — HOPE 345:3
who shout. Who tell l. — WALK 717:13
will tell l. as usual — SHAW 636:8
lieto: Chi vuol esser l. sia — MED 456:3
lieutenants: God's l. — JAM 362:1
life: about l. beyond the grave — KHR 395:16
accounted his l. madness — BIBLE 87:3
actor's l. for me — WASH 722:3
all human l. is there — JAMES 362:24
all l. is 6 to 5 against — RUNY 550:5
All my past l. is mine no more — ROCH 543:7
All the best days of l. — VIRG 715:16
amended his former naughty l. — BOOK 121:14
And feels its l. in every limb — WORD 748:14
And for her l. he died — STONE 669:12
And L., a Fury slinging flame — TENN 683:16
And L., the shadow of death — SWIN 676:1
And slits the thin-spun l. — MILT 466:4
And then there's l. — ANOU 23:5
And the Pride of L. — HARDY 325:3
Anyone can stop a man's l. — SEN 563:2
are born to eternal l. — FRAN 292:12
are no conditions of l. — TOLS 700:6
As our l. is very short — TAYL 679:19
As though to breathe were l. — TENN 690:1
awakened from the dream of l. — SHEL 639:22
banqueter fed full of l. — LUCR 432:4
before you l. and death — BIBLE 73:20
believe in l. — DU B 263:3
believe in the l. to come — BECK 57:13
believe that since my l. began — COW 220:11
bitterness of l. — CARR 184:7
blood-thirsty clinging to l. — ARN 29:14
Book of L. begins — WILDE 735:29
beginning a criticism of l. — ARN 29:24

life: *(cont.)*:

bound to way of l. as	LEVIN 420:3
brevity of our l.	JOHN 366:15
brother will I require the l.	BIBLE 70:30
business of l. is to enjoy	BUTL 166:25
But l., being weary of these	SHAK 590:12
certain, that l. flies	FITZ 284:1
changing scenes of l.	TATE 678:17
Chief nourisher in l.'s feast	SHAK 602:2
colours from my l.	BROW 147:19
Could she not live who l.	BYRON 168:8
crowded hour of glorious l.	MORD 483:18
Crushing out l.	HOPE 345:3
cuts off twenty years of l.	SHAK 591:16
daily for your longer l.	ELIZ 274:10
dawn of l. unto the grave	EGER 267:12
days of my l.	BOOK 125:15
days of the years of my l.	BIBLE 71:32
day-to-day business l.	LAF 405:15
devils in l. and condition	ASCH 31:2
distinction of your l.	TAC 677:22
doctrine of the strenuous l.	ROOS 546:8
Does thy l. destroy	BLAKE 114:12
Do vainly wish for l.	GREV 318:7
drive l. into a corner	THOR 697:5
entertain the lag-end of my l.	SHAK 581:27
eternal l.	BIBLE 96:21
every day is a l.	O'NEI 498:20
evidence of l. after death	SOPER 656:9
except a little l.	BYRON 172:24
except my l., except	SHAK 574:24
fear love is to fear l.	RUSS 551:16
Fill me with l. anew	HATCH 328:2
findeth his l. shall lose it	BIBLE 90:22
following l. thro' creatures you	POPE 520:25
football is a matter of l.	SHAN 635:17
fool, the rest of his dull l.	BEAU 56:14
force maintaining the l.	DOST 254:2
For each one l. to give	KIPL 399:4
forfeit my l.	BROWN 144:13
For the l. to come	SHAK 631:26
For what is your l.	BIBLE 105:4
found that l. was duty	HOOP 344:16
fountain of the water of l.	BIBLE 107:19
freezes up the heat of l.	SHAK 623:28
Friday I tasted l.	DICK 245:5
From l., that insane dream	BROW 149:18
gave my l. for freedom	EWER 279:10
Gave thee l. and bid thee feed	BLAKE 113:21
given us one way in to l.	SEN 563:1
give thee a crown of l.	BIBLE 106:4
giveth his l. for the sheep	BIBLE 96:38
giveth l. to the world	BIBLE 96:24
giving l. but in risking l.	DE B 233:9
glory of this l.	SHAK 626:9
going to turn over a new l.	FLEM 287:3
golden tree of actual l.	GOET 309:5
Good l. be now my task	DRYD 260:21
great l. if you don't weaken	BUCH 154:1
have everlasting l.	BIBLE 96:15
have set my l. upon a cast	SHAK 622:16
he is tired of l.	JOHN 374:24
he ne'er saw in his l.	ANST 23:12
he studied from the l.	ARMS 26:6
he took a man's l. along	CARL 180:12
his friends for his l.	THOR 697:12
His l. was gentle	SHAK 593:23
Human l. a process of	BERNE 66:11
human l. is, at the greatest	TEMP 680:3
I bear a charmèd l.	SHAK 605:3
I count l. just a stuff	BROW 150:12
if l. was bitter	SWIN 676:9
In balance with this l.	YEATS 752:6
In l.'s uncertain voyage	SHAK 626:20
I paid the prices of l.	GURN 320:1
I pass my whole l.	DICK 244:2
I really don't know l. at all	MITC 477:19
Is it not l., is it not *the thing*	BYRON 174:6
isn't l. a terrible thing	THOM 693:20
is there a l. before death	HEAN 329:22
it is a tree of l.	BIBLE 78:26
It is not a L. at all	GLAD 307:20
it's the l. in my men	WEST 729:9

life: *(cont.)*:

jump the l. to come	SHAK 601:2
Just gave what l. required	GOLD 310:6
lad of l., an imp of fame	SHAK 585:22
last of l., for which the first	BROW 152:6
later l. renew	SPEN 659:11
lay down his l. for his friends	BIBLE 97:16
Lead me from death to l.	KUMAR 404:8
l. alone does Nature live	COL 209:14
l. and power that took	FOX 292:2
L. and these lips have	SHAK 624:1
l. as it is in ways	BACON 42:9
l. as on a summer's day	KEATS 387:23
l., a very rebel	SHAK 566:3
l. began by flickering	GONC 312:9
l. being all inclusion	JAMES 363:7
l. can little more supply	POPE 521:26
l. closed twice before its close	DICK 244:16
L. death does end and each	HOPK 345:18
l. doth well with churchmen	BACON 44:4
L. exists in the universe	JEANS 363:26
L. feeding death, death	ALAB 7:1
L., force and beauty must	POPE 521:6
l. forget and death remember	SWIN 676:26
L. for life	BIBLE 72:17
l. for the British female	CLOU 207:1
L., friends, is boring	BERR 66:18
l. from the glowing earth	GREN 318:2
l. goes not backward	GIBR 303:2
l. had been ruined by literature	BROO 144:3
l. has crept so long	TENN 687:3
l. hath been one chain	CLARE 204:18
l. he has been in the wrong	ROCH 543:12
l. her husband makes	ELIOT 269:19
l. heroic	MILT 474:17
L. imitates Art far more	WILDE 735:7
l. in another life	ELIOT 268:20
l. in the village began	LEE 415:18
L. is a foreign language	MORL 484:19
L. is a gamble at terrible odds	STOP 670:6
l. is a glorious cycle	PARK 506:5
L. is a great surprise	NAB 489:1
L. is a horizontal fall	COCT 208:8
L. is a jest	GAY 300:11
L. is a joke that's just begun	GILB 304:24
L. is all a VARIORUM	BURNS 162:14
L. is a maze in which we	CONN 216:15
L. is an incurable disease	COWL 221:21
L. is an offensive	WHIT 731:9
L. is a sexually transmitted	ANON 15:18
L. is as tedious as a twice-told	SHAK 594:5
L. is a top which whipping	GREV 318:6
l. is but a day	KEATS 390:10
L. is but an empty dream	LONG 427:7
l. is but an Interjection	BYRON 171:30
L. is Colour and Warmth	GREN 318:2
L. is doubt	UNAM 707:2
l. is everywhere a state	JOHN 369:21
L. is first boredom, then fear	LARK 409:17
l. is from the body fled	GREV 318:7
l. is given to none freehold	LUCR 432:5
l. is in the past and future	O'NEI 499:2
L. is just a bowl of cherries	BROWN 144:15
L. is just one damned thing	HUBB 353:10
L. is like a sewer	LEHR 416:12
L. is like a very short visit	MORR 485:7
L. is like playing a violin	BUTL 167:9
L. is made up of sobs	HENRY 333:2
L. is mostly froth and bubble	GORD 312:12
L. is not a series of gig	WOOLF 742:7
L. isn't finished for us	CHEK 197:4
l. is of a mingled yarn	SHAK 564:8
L. is one long process	BUTL 166:30
L. is real! Life is earnest	LONG 427:7
L. is really a One Way Street	CHR 200:6
L. is short, the art long	HIPP 339:6
l. is so dull that there is	FORS 290:23
L. is something to do when	LEB 415:9
l. is that which flees	LUIS 432:7
L. is the desert, life	YOUNG 755:1
L. is the other way round	LODGE 425:18
l. is the thing, but I prefer	SMITH 652:7
L. is too much like a pathless	FROST 294:10

life: *(cont.)*:

L. is too precious	ELIOT 270:1
L. is too short to stuff	CONR 217:19
L. is very nice, but it	ANOU 23:8
l. is washed	BARZ 54:23
l. is well comparèd	BARN 53:18
L. itself is but the shadow	BROW 145:8
L. levels all men	SHAW 637:35
l., liberty, and the pursuit	ANON 19:7
L., like a dome of many-coloured	SHEL 640:4
l. neither as it is nor as	CHEK 196:12
l. of any worth is a continual	KEATS 392:3
l. of doubt diversified	BROW 148:12
l. of every man is a diary	BARR 54:3
l. of man less than	BACON 45:27
l. of man, solitary, poor	HOBB 340:7
l. of only one of them	GODW 308:10
l. of sensations rather	KEATS 391:7
l. only we have hope	BIBLE 101:6
l. on the whole is far	LEAR 414:19
l. protracted is protracted	JOHN 370:18
l. ran gaily as the sparkling	ARN 28:9
l.'s a pain and but a span	DAV 232:4
L. says: she did this	BARN 53:8
L.'s but a walking shadow	SHAK 605:1
l.'s dim windows	BLAKE 111:17
l.'s fitful fever he sleeps	SHAK 603:3
l.'s last scene what prodigies	JOHN 370:20
L.'s not just being alive	MART 449:15
l. so fast doth fly	DAV 232:2
l. so short, the craft	CHAU 195:5
l. stands in the level	SHAK 631:21
l. that breathes with human	TENN 689:17
l. the subject of thy scorn	GREE 317:8
L., the Universe and Everything	ADAMS 2:1
l. time's fool	SHAK 582:6
l. to a dream were more	MONT 481:10
L., to be sure, is nothing	HOUS 352:3
l. to lose for my country	HALE 321:7
l. too near the bones	DRAB 257:7
l. to the lees	TENN 690:1
l. unto the bitter	BIBLE 77:9
l. was coming to consist of	AMIS 10:14
L. we have lost in living	ELIOT 272:15
l. well spent is long	LEON 418:7
l. went through with death	FORT 291:2
l. will be sour grapes	ASHF 31:12
l. will suit itself	BYRON 168:21
l. within us and abroad	COL 209:19
L. with its way before us lies	MONS 480:1
L. without industry is guilt	RUSK 550:12
l. without it were not	ROWE 549:7
L. without theory	DISR 248:10
L. would be tolerable	LEWIS 420:19
L. would be very pleasant	SURT 672:17
L. would ring the bells	GINS 306:27
lines and l. are free	HERB 334:11
little l. with dried tubers	ELIOT 272:21
long l. better than figs	SHAK 564:15
long l. will I satisfy	BOOK 131:5
looked at l. from both sides	MITC 477:19
Lord and giver of l.	BOOK 121:20
low l. was the level's	BROW 149:26
Mad from l.'s history	HOOD 343:16
makes the wheel of l.	STER 664:29
makes us think about l.	DE G 235:9
man's l. a thing apart	BYRON 170:13
man's l. it is reserved	BACON 42:6
many-coloured l. he drew	JOHN 370:11
many doors to let out l.	FLET 287:15
married my husband for l.	ANON 15:3
may here find l. in death	COL 209:22
measured out my l. with coffee	ELIOT 272:2
measures l. may perfect	JONS 379:21
me hath everlasting l.	BIBLE 96:27
midst of l. we are in death	BOOK 124:4
midst of l. we are in debt	MUMF 487:17
Midway along the path of our l.	DANTE 230:5
more a way of l.	ANON 16:23
most loathèd worldly l.	SHAK 606:11
mourning for my l.	CHEK 196:11
My l. is dreary	TENN 686:6
my l. is preserved	BIBLE 71:19

life: (cont.):
My l. is run his compass — SHAK 593:17
My l. now, my whole life — TOLS 700:9
my l. seemed meant — BROW 150:19
my l. to Him who made me — NELS 491:15
my l. to make you King — CHAR 191:19
My l. within this band — HERB 335:7
my whole l. whether it be long — ELIZ 274:20
name out of the book of l. — BIBLE 106:5
nauseous draught of l. — ROCH 543:6
nearest thing to death in l. — ANON 16:18
Nobody can write the l. — JOHN 373:15
no l., but lively form — KYD 404:11
no, no l. — SHAK 598:3
nor l., nor angels — BIBLE 100:1
Nor love thy l., nor hate — MILT 473:8
Nothing in his l. became him — SHAK 600:14
Nothing in l. shall sever — CORY 219:14
not lead a pleasant l. — RAL 536:11
not the l. more than meat — BIBLE 89:9
now my l. is done — TICH 698:3
O Death in L., the days — TENN 688:5
Of l., of crown, of queen — SHAK 573:20
Of poetry is the theory of l. — STEV 666:6
one l. and one death — BROW 150:11
one l. shall be destroyed — TENN 683:18
On l., on death — YEATS 753:18
only honour and l. have — FRAN 292:9
on the tree of l. — MILT 471:1
or stand aside from l. — COMP 214:18
Our end is L. Put out to sea — MACN 441:6
our little l. — SHAK 625:28
outer l. of telegrams — FORS 290:13
part of l.'s rich pageant — MARS 449:6
passion and the l. — COL 209:13
Perfection of the l. — YEATS 751:6
perhaps only a l. of mistakes — ELIOT 269:11
Pip; such is L. — DICK 240:31
pleasure is l. — BOOK 126:5
present l. of men on earth — BEDE 58:13
preservation of l. — JEFF 364:2
priceless gift of l. — ROS 546:19
purpose to a life beyond l. — MILT 475:5
put my genius into my l. — WILDE 736:7
queer thing L. — WOD 740:21
rather the l. we share — MOT 487:1
readers better to enjoy l. — JOHN 368:6
Reason is the l. of the law — COKE 208:17
receive the crown of l. — BIBLE 104:25
regardeth the l. of his beast — BIBLE 78:25
Replaced one l. with another — AKHM 6:7
resurrection, and the l. — BIBLE 97:4
Reverence for L. — SCHW 558:14
reward of labour is l. — MORR 485:17
right to a dignified l. — JOHN 366.12
river of water of l. — BIBLE 107:22
runners relay the torch of l. — LUCR 432:1
sech is l. — DICK 241:19
security is the denial of l. — GREER 317:12
sells us l. — FRY 295:22
set my l. at a pin's fee — SHAK 573:10
set my l. on any chance — SHAK 603:1
Shall l. succeed — BROW 152:7
shilling l. will give you all the — AUDEN 36:6
Should l. all labour — TENN 685:23
should walk in newness of l. — BIBLE 99:28
sketchy understanding of l. — CRICK 226:20
So careless of the single l. — TENN 683:20
So have I loitered my l. — HAZL 328:14
So in my veins red l. might — KEATS 390:16
so long as you have your l. — JAMES 362:12
sons and daughters of L.'s — GIBR 303:2
sounds the l. and element — COL 209:15
spare all I have, and take my l. — FARQ 280:16
spirit giveth l. — BIBLE 101:16
strange disease of modern l. — ARN 28:9
Style lo l. r — FLAN 286:2
style of l — WEBER 725:3
take r l. and all — SHAK 609:20
take my l. from thee night — KIPL 401:15
taken over one's mortal l. — Quar 122:3
taking l. by the throat — FROST 290:16
tears, of all my l. — BROW 147:21

life: (cont.):
terror to l. and makes death — TREE 702:7
That was how his l. happened — KAV 386:4
That which we call l. — DONNE 253:1
their l. was death — ROSS 548:1
there is a space of l. — KEATS 386:12
There is no l. of a man — CARL 180:9
There is no wealth but l. — RUSK 551:7
There's the l. for ever — STEV 669:4
this gives l. to thee — SHAK 633:6
This is alone L., Joy — SHEL 642:20
This l. is most jolly — SHAK 568:17
this long disease, my l. — POPE 519:29
thorns of l. — SHEL 641:18
Thorough the iron gates of l. — MARV 451:4
Thou art my l.; if thou — QUAR 534:1
Thou art my l., my love — HERR 337:3
thousand doors to let out l. — MASS 453:16
time of l. is short — SHAK 582:2
Time to taste l. — BROW 149:28
'Tisn't l. that matters — WALP 720:12
To live a l. half dead — MILT 474:3
travelled l.'s dull round — SHEN 644:13
traveller betwixt l. and death — WORD 747:19
tree of l. — BIBLE 70:2
try to crowd out real l. — FORS 290:26
University of l. — BOTT 137:13
value of l. lies not — MONT 480:17
Variety's the very spice of l. — COWP 223:22
viewing l. in all — GOGOL 310:1
voyage of their l. — SHAK 593:12
warm full blooded l. — JOYCE 381:27
waste the remains of l. — WALP 719:9
Well, I've had a happy l. — HAZL 329:15
well-written L. is almost — CARL 180:8
What is l.? a frenzy — CALD 175:4
What is l., without — ROST 548.12
What is this l. if — DAV 232:12
What l. and death — CHAP 190:15
what l. is then to a man — BIBLE 87:31
Where all l. dies, death — MILT 470:4
which he slew in his l. — BIBLE 74:21
which leadeth unto l. — BIBLE 89:22
wholesome of l. and free of — HOR 349:11
Who saw l. steadily — ARN 29:1
will he give for his l. — BIBLE 77:3
wine of l. is drawn — SHAK 602:17
With Nature, to out-do the l. — JONS 379:18
With seas of l., like wine — TRAH 702:1
Women and wine should l. — GAY 299:19
worlds l. hovers like a star — BYRON 171:33
Yes! in the sea of l. enisled — ARN 29:3
life-blood: book is the precious l. — MILT 475:5
life-jacket: brassière is the French for l. — BARN 53:7
lifeless: virtue is l. — PAST 508:4
life-lie: l. away from the average — IBSEN 359:7
life-sentence: l. in the dungeon of self — CONN 216:19
l. which fate carries — LAWR 413:4
lifetime: But a l. of happiness — SHAW 637:4
knowledge of a l. — WHIS 730:23
must occupy a complete l. — ARIS 25:9
Once in a l., do a girl in — ELIOT 272:18
lifetimes: series of l. starts anew — VIRG 714:22
lift: floods l. up their waves — BOOK 131:7
L. her with care — HOOD 343:15
l. me as a wave, a leaf — SHEL 641:18
L. not thy hands to It — FITZ 284:10
l. thou up — BOOK 124:13
l. up his countenance — BIBLE 73:4
l. up mine eyes unto — BOOK 133:23
L. up your heads — BOOK 125:17
L. up your heart — WESL 728:13
L. up your hearts — BOOK 122:8
lifting: l. up of my hands — BOOK 135:1
light: against the dying of the l. — THOM 693:4
And let thy glorious l. — LITT 423:9
and l. but the shadow — BROW 145:8
And Newton particles of l. — BLAKE 113:6
angels, progeny of l. — MILT 471:28
As if they feared the l. — SUCK 671:7
bathe the world in l. — WORD 743:17

light: (cont.):
bear witness of that L. — BIBLE 96:2
becometh the children of l. — BOOK 123:2
Be near me when my l. is low — TENN 683:16
be the new l. of grace — SMOL 654:3
black as if bereaved of l. — BLAKE 114:1
blasted with excess of l. — GRAY 316:7
burning and a shining l. — BIBLE 96:20
But he beholds the l. — WORD 745:14
But if once we lose this l. — JONS 379:8
can again thy former l. — SHAK 618:5
Casting a dim religious l. — MILT 465:1
close up thou my little l. — CAMP 177:4
C'mon, baby, l. my fire — MORR 485:19
Colour and Warmth and L. — GREN 318:2
come in may see the l. — BIBLE 94:20
contend with growing l. — SHAK 587:29
Creature, which was L. — BACON 45:17
dark is l. enough — FRY 295:20
darkness have seen a great l. — BIBLE 82:26
darkness rather than l. — BIBLE 96:16
dusk with a l. behind — GILB 306:23
Enable with perpetual l. — BOOK 135:21
endeavours are an inward l. — WORD 743:8
Even L. itself — THOM 696:15
everlasting oil, to give due l. — MILT 463:20
festal l. in Christ-Church — ARN 28:7
fire, to give them l. — BIBLE 72:13
For that celestial l. — MILT 468:11
giveth l. unto the eyes — BOOK 125:5
gladsome l. of Jurisprudence — COKE 208:18
God appears and God is L. — BLAKE 111:10
God said, Let there be l. — BIBLE 69:20
gone into the world of l. — VAUG 709:5
gust of l. explains itself — MOT 487:2
Had she been l., like you — SHAK 599:6
happy realms of l. — MILT 468:2
hath reft the sonne his l. — CHAU 193:14
have neither heat nor l. — WEBS 725:21
have seen a glorious l. — SCOT 561:11
holy L., offspring — MILT 470:15
hours of l. return — ARN 27:15
In a l. fantastic round — MILT 463:18
infant crying for the l. — TENN 683:19
infinite ocean of l. and love — FOX 292:1
informed by the l. of nature — BACON 42:2
It is the l. of Terewth — DICK 239:10
Jeanie with the l. brown hair — FOST 291:13
just is as the shining l. — BIBLE 78:11
kindle a l. in the darkness — JUNG 382:14
Lamp; Servants of L. — ARN 26:14
Lead, kindly L., amid the — NEWM 493:14
leaping l. — AUDEN 35:4
let me not be l. — SHAK 610:7
let perpetual l. shine — MISS 477:10
Let there be l. — MARR 449:1
'Let there be l.!' said God — BYRON 171:17
Let there be l.! said Liberty — SHEL 640:14
levelled rule of streaming l. — MILT 463:26
L. God's eldest daughter — FULL 296:7
l. after smoke — HOR 347:12
l., a glory, a fair luminous — COL 209:15
L. and joy receiveth — BAKER 47:19
l. and the half light — YEATS 751:22
l., and will aspire — SHAK 635:12
l. at the end of the tunnel — DICK 245:9
l. at the end of the tunnel — LOW 430:19
l. between two eternities — NAB 489:2
l. break forth as the morning — BIBLE 84:23
L. breaks where no sun shines — THOM 691:11
l. did him harm — AMIS 10:13
l. dissolved in star-showers — SHEL 643:9
l. excelleth darkness — BIBLE 80:4
l. given to him — BIBLE 77:9
l. gleams an instant — BECK 58:1
l. has gone out of our lives — NEHRU 491:6
l. heart lives long — SHAK 599:6
l. in mine eye — DONNE 253:10
l. in sound, a sound-like — COL 209:19
l. in the dust lies dead — SHEL 641:6
l. into bodies — NEWT 494:1
l. of a whole life dies — BOUR 138:2
l. of evening, Lissadell — YEATS 752:2

911

light: (*cont.*):

l. of his countenance	BOOK 129:4
L. of step and heart was she	DE L 236:1
l. of the world	BIBLE 88:25
l. of thy countenance	BOOK 124:13
l. of thy countenance	BOOK 130:13
l. of thy Holy Spirit	BOOK 120:20
l. or leading received	MILT 475:18
l., shade, and perspective	CONS 217:23
l. shineth in darkness	BIBLE 95:37
l. so shine before men	BIBLE 88:26
l. that I may tread safely	HASK 328:1
l. that loses, the night	SWIN 675:22
l. that makes it possible	TOCQ 698:9
l. that never was	WORD 743:11
l. them for themselves	SHAK 605:6
l. through chinks	WALL 718:13
l. through yonder window	SHAK 622:27
l. to counterfeit a gloom	MILT 464:22
l. to shine upon the road	COWP 222:22
l. to thee are both alike	BOOK 134:19
l. to them that sit in darkness	BIBLE 93:24
l. unto my paths	BOOK 133:20
l. which experience gives	COL 212:14
l. within his own clear	MILT 463:27
Lord is my l.	BOOK 125:24
lost to l. for evermore	BYRON 169:20
lovely lady, garmented in l.	SHEL 643:2
mend the Electric L.	BELL 61:20
More l.!	GOET 309:20
Night, the shadow of l.	SWIN 676:1
noise and blind to l.	SIDN 646:19
No l., no fire. Th' unfriendly	SHAK 619:3
No l. propitious shone	COWP 224:1
Of beauty from the l. retired	WALL 718:10
once our brief l. has set	CAT 185:15
once set is our little l.	CAMP 177:3
one equal l.	DONNE 253:14
On the l. fantastic toe	MILT 465:6
Or through the realms of l.	GURN 320:3
O! so l. a foot	SHAK 623:11
Our freedom is but a l.	GUM 319:16
out thy l. and thy truth	BOOK 127:7
plant and flower of l.	JONS 379:21
pure and endless l.	VAUG 709:11
pursuit of sweetness and l.	ARN 29:8
put on the armour of l.	BIBLE 100:10
Put out the l., and then	SHAK 618:5
remember while the l. lives	SWIN 676:13
severity of perfect l.	TENN 681:26
shew l. at Calais	JOHN 372:17
should be a place of l.	DISR 247:22
shows sufficient of His l.	BROW 152:19
source of my l. and my safety	BIBLE 107:27
sweetness and l.	SWIFT 673:4
than the children of l.	BIBLE 95:6
that l. falls and fills	ROET 544:7
There's a certain Slant of l.	DICK 244:20
Thou art my l.	QUAR 534:1
thy l. is come	BIBLE 84:25
took away the l.	MILT 467:16
transparent veil with l.	WORD 747:4
trees by the eldritch l.	DAY-L 233:4
Truly the l. is sweet	BIBLE 80:29
turning your face to the l.	SASS 557:6
turret in a noose of l.	FITZ 283:10
unapproachèd l.	MILT 470:15
unclouded blaze of living l.	BYRON 169:25
universal l.	POPE 521:6
upon them hath the l.	BIBLE 82:26
upon us the armour of l.	BOOK 120:10
waited for the l.	ROB 542:11
was far faster than l.	BULL 154:17
We all *know* what l. is	JOHN 374:18
What l. beyond compare	NEALE 491:5
When I consider how my l.	MILT 474:24
where the l. is as darkness	BIBLE 77:16
while the l. fails	ELIOT 271:8

Light Brigade: Forward, the L.   TENN 680:14

lighten: l. with celestial fire   BOOK 135:21

let thy mercy l. upon us	BOOK 118:14
L. our darkness	BOOK 119:11

lighter: l. than vanity   BOOK 128:20

l. than vanity   BUNY 155:18

Lightfoot: come uppe L.   ING 360:5

light-headed: l., variable men   STEV 668:4

lighthouse: l. with his eyes   CAMP 176:7

sitivation at the l.   DICK 243:26

lightly: And l. as it comth   CHAU 194:12

And l. skims the midge	BETJ 67:10
l. regarded the counsel	BOOK 132:15
unadvisedly, l., or wantonly	BOOK 123:16

lightness: depth of its uncompacted l.

    BRID 141:4

Thence to a l.	SHAK 574:17
unbearable l. of being	KUND 404:9

lightning: Brief as the l.   SHAK 610:23

Bring in the bottled l.	DICK 242:13
coruscations of summer l.	GOUL 313:1
Fear no more the l. flash	SHAK 571:16
From l. and tempest	BOOK 119:17
Have known the l.'s hour	DAY-L 233:5
He snatched the l. shaft	TURG 705:13
I beheld Satan as l. fall	BIBLE 94:11
illumined by flashes of l.	WILDE 736:9
It's to keep the l. out	ISH 360:21
l. of his terrible swift	HOWE 353:2
like l. on an open field	LOW 430:8
O at l. and lashed rod	HOPK 346:12
Shakespeare by flashes of l.	COL 212:8
snatched from Jove the l.	MAN 444:8
Too like the l., which doth	SHAK 623:3

lights: all-the-l.-on man   REED 538:9

And God made two great l.	BIBLE 69:23
Followed false l.	DRYD 260:21
from the Father of l.	BIBLE 104:26
Glorious the northern l.	SMART 650:4
gradual dimming of the l.	NIC 494:16
l. around the shore	ROSS 548:8
l. begin to twinkle from	TENN 690:4
L. left, right, left	BLOK 115:6
may bear all l.	SHAF 563:22
serene l. of heaven	SHEL 643:8
spent l. quiver and gleam	ARN 27:8
tail l. widen and converge	CRANE 225:23
They are but broken l. of thee	TENN 682:28
Turn up the l.	HENRY 333:4
When the l. are dim and low	ORRED 499:8
your l. burning	BIBLE 94:25

ligno: *Regnavit a l. Deus.*   FORT 291:3

like: can do just what you l.   SHAW 636:18

Do what you l.	RAB 534:19
forced to l. what you get	SHAW 638:4
husband could have made me l.	
	CONG 215:15
L. as the hart desireth	BOOK 127:2
L. cures like	HAHN 320:10
L. doth quit like	SHAK 606:25
l. is not necessarily good	BELL 60:20
l. one another as half-pence	SHAK 569:10
l. this sort of thing will	LINC 422:16
l. to do are either illegal	WOOL 742:19
l. to get away from earth	FROST 294:11
No wonder we l. them	AMIS 11:2
people you l. best	UST 707:12
plotted to make men l.	TREV 702:13
shall not look upon his l. again	SHAK 572:17
That l. I best, that flies	MARL 447:16
then were we l. unto them	BOOK 134:4
there was nothing l. it	CARR 183:18
These hands are not more l.	SHAK 572:19
want it the most always l.	CHES 198:2

liked: l. it not, and died   WOTT 749:4

l. whate'er she looked on	BROW 151:12
People wish to be l.	RUSS 551:12
that loved and you that l.	ANON 17:21

likely: A mighty l. speech   GAY 299:14

Walk! Not bloody l.!   SHAW 638:20

likeness: devil haunts thee in the l.

    SHAK 580:30

l. of men	BIBLE 98:23
or any l. of any thing	BIBLE 72:16
our image, after our l.	BIBLE 69:24

likeness: (*cont.*):

was made in the l.	BIBLE 103:4

likerous: l. mouth moste han   CHAU 194:21

likes: weather the cuckoo l.   HARDY 326:1

likewise: Canst thou do l.   DICK 240:24

Go, and do thou l.   BIBLE 94:16

liking: Hath lost me in your l.   SHAK 594:22

l. for war	BENN 63:6
l. or gratitude	ELIOT 269:1
Not l. the person, yet liking	THOM 694:7

lilac: forget the l. and the roses   ARAG 24:6

Just now the l. is in bloom   BROO 143:9

lilacs: l. last in the dooryard   WHIT 733:3

L. out of the dead land   ELIOT 272:21

Lilian: Airy, fairy L.   TENN 685:6

lilies: And a few l. blow   HOPK 345:14

beauty lives though l. die	FLEC 286:9
Consider the l. of the field	BIBLE 89:11
give me l. in armfuls	VIRG 713:18
he feedeth among the l.	BIBLE 81:11
l. of all kinds	SHAK 632:4
kingcups, and loved l.	SPEN 660:26
l. and languors of virtue	SWIN 676:9
l. by the rivers of waters	BIBLE 88:4
l. of ambition	DOUG 255:11
L. that fester smell far	SHAK 634:15
L. without, roses within	MARV 450:20
lost l. out of mind	DOWS 256:2
Lotos and l.	TENN 687:19
peacocks and l. for instance	RUSK 550:24
She had three l. in her hand	ROSS 547:14
wheat set about with l.	BIBLE 82:2
which feed among the l.	BIBLE 81:13
Ye L. male! think	CRAB 224:21

Lilli Burlero: L. Bullena-la   WHAR 730:6

lilting: l. house and happy   THOM 693:5

lily: A l. of a day   JONS 379:21

And the l. whispers, 'I wait.'	TENN 686:20
Elaine, the l. maid of Astolat	TENN 681:30
folds the l. all her sweetness	TENN 688:13
gold, or paint the l.	BYRON 170:29
gold, to paint the l.	SHAK 594:9
I see a l. on thy brow	KEATS 388:8
It trembles to a l.	DOBS 249:22
l. of Florence blossoming	LONG 426:21
l. of the valleys	BIBLE 81:8
l. rears its gouged face	HILL 338:8
or a l. in my medieval hand	GILB 305:17
She's as pure as the l.	LAUD 411:6
That lies across the l. leven	BALL 50:16
waved her l. hand	GAY 300:17

lily-white: l. boys   ANON 15:1

limb: feels its life in every l.   WORD 748:14

l. by limb still as they   MILT 475:9

limbecks: l. foul as hell within   SHAK 634:25

limber: A little child, a l. elf   COL 209:11

limbo: l. large and broad   MILT 470:20

limbs: great smooth marbly l.   BROW 148:17

keep these l., her provinces	DONNE 252:3
life controls these l.	VIRG 713:6
l. of a poet	HOR 351:3
l. that fester are not	ABSE 1:2
l. were made in England	SHAK 585:9
my l. may issue from you	MARL 447:2
ruddy l. and flaming hair	BLAKE 113:14
slope of mighty l. asleep	SWIN 676:4
Yours are the l., my sweeting	NASH 490:21

limestone: On l. quarried near   YEATS 753:18

lime-tree: l. bower my prison   COL 211:20

limit: act a slave to l.   SHAK 627:16

greatest art is to l. and isolate	GOET 309:18
quiet l. of the world	TENN 689:10

limitary: Proud l. cherub   MILT 471:19

limitation: l. of governmental power

    WILS 738:9

limited: Liberty too must be l.   BURKE 157:10

so whizzed the L.   CRANE 225:23

limits: l. of my language   WITT 740:5

stony l. cannot hold love   SHAK 622:31

limns: But l. the water   BACON 45:28

limousine: l. and a ticket   MACN 440:13

One perfect l., do you suppose   PARK 506:9

limp: l. father of thousands   JOYCE 381:25
limpid: stag in l. currents   PHIL 514:5
Lincoln: I am a Ford, not a L.   FORD 289:1
   L. County Road or Armageddon
         DYLAN 265:20
   L. was shovelled   SAND 555:3
   sign to L. sent   MAC 436:2
Linden Lea: down low in L.   BARN 53:13
line: active l. on a walk   KLEE 402:20
   back to cancel half a l.   FITZ 284:9
   cut, the style, the l.   LOES 426:3
   fine into an horizontal l.   WHEW 730:14
   full-resounding l.   POPE 523:4
   giddy l. midway   BROW 148:13
   high aesthetic l.   GILB 305:15
   l. can trace no flute exemplify   WILB 734:4
   l. in which that force   NEWT 494:3
   l. is length without breadth   EUCL 279:1
   l. too labours   POPE 521:17
   l. upon line, line upon   BIBLE 83:11
   l. will take us hours maybe   YEATS 760:16
   lives along the l.   POPE 522:6
   oft creep in one dull l.   POPE 521:14
   or quarrelling on the l.   FORS 290:18
   season-ticket on the l.   AMERY 10:7
   six ships of the l.   TENN 689:1
   This l. of scarlet thread   BIBLE 73:28
   towards that thin red l.   RUSS 552:5
   We carved not a l.   WOLFE 740:26
lineaments: l. of a plummet-measured
         YEATS 753:10
   l. of Gospel books   ROYD 549:14
   l. of gratified desire   BLAKE 113:12
linen: clean l.   JOHN 372:2
   clothed in purple and fine l.   BIBLE 95:9
   fair white l. cloth upon   BOOK 121:15
   In blanchèd l., smooth   KEATS 387:9
   l. like a gentleman   JOHN 368:11
   Love is like l. often changed   FLET 288:2
   not l. you're wearing out   HOOD 344:8
   old l. wash whitest   WEBS 725:26
   very fine l.   BRUM 153:22
   wash your l. and keep your   STEV 668:24
liner: The L. she's a lady   KIPL 399:19
lines: As l. (so loves)   MARV 460:3
   consisted of l. like these   CALV 175:10
   l. are fallen unto me   BOOK 124:30
   liquid l. mellifluously bland   BYRON 171:11
   May no l. pass, except they   HERB 335:6
   My l. and life are free   HERB 334:11
   Prose is when all the l.   BENT 64:7
   scribbled l. like fallen   HOPE 345:2
   town-crier spoke my l.   SHAK 576:5
   walk on the l. or squares   MILNE 462:16
linger: l. out a purposed overthrow
         SHAK 634:13
lingered: I l. round them   BRON 142:19
lingerie: Brevity the soul of l.   PARK 506:19
lingering: alone sit l. here   VAUG 709:5
   l. and consumptive passion   ETH 278:17
   l. dissolution   BECK 57:11
   L. he raised his latch at eve   COL 211:23
   Something l., with boiling   GILB 305:7
lingua: *Pange, l., gloriosi*   FORT 291:1
   Pange, l., gloriosi   THOM 692:13
linguam: Et l. et mores   JUV 383:19
linguistic: l. philosophy   RUSS 551:26
lining: softest l. can never   AST 32:8
   Turn forth her silver l.   MILT 463:21
lin-lan-lone: mellow l. of evening bells
         TENN 681:3
linnet: l. born within the cage   TENN 683:11
linsy-woolsy: lawless l. brother   BUTL 166:11
lion: better than a dead l.   BIBLE 80:18
   buttocked like a l. and footed   MAL 443:6
   devil, as a roaring l.   BIBLE 105:21
   go upon the l. and adder   BOOK 131:4
   l. among ladies   SHAK 611:27
   l. and the fatling together   BIBLE 83:2
   l. is the wisdom   BLAKE 112:24
   l. shall eat straw like   BIBLE 80:7
   l. to frighten the wolves   MACH 438:10

lion: (*cont.*):
   l. who dies of an ass's kick   BROW 151:14
   Now the hungry l. roars   SHAK 613:1
   Of some pained desert l.   ARN 28:15
   righteous are bold as a l.   BIBLE 79:28
   rouse a l. than to start a hare   SHAK 579:34
   Rouse the l. from his lair   SCOTT 560:33
   Strong is the l.—like a coal   SMART 650:1
   threatened, a l.   CHAP 190:11
   upon a time to the sick l.   HOR 348:1
   would be mated with the l.   SHAK 564:2
lions: And, on the other, l.   PATM 509:14
   laughing l. must come   NIET 495:5
   l. do lack, and suffer   BOOK 126:14
   l. led by donkeys   HOFF 341:12
   l. littered in one day   SHAK 591:6
   l., or Vanity-Fair   BUNY 156:11
   l. roaring after   BOOK 132:9
   l. to the roaring slaughter   CUMM 228:6
   my darling from the l.   BOOK 126:17
   my soul is among l.   BOOK 128:15
   stronger than l.   BIBLE 75:9
lip: gnaw you so your nether l.   SHAK 618:6
   Teach not thy l. such scorn   SHAK 621:18
   vermeil-tinctured l.   MILT 464:8
   Whose l. mature is ever new   KEATS 387:19
lipless: Leaned backward with a l. grin
         ELIOT 273:15
lips: already born before my l.   MAND 444:7
   But turn to ashes on the l.   MOORE 483:15
   flatter with their l.   BOOK 124:24
   hand is ever at his l.   KEATS 389:7
   Her l. suck forth my soul   MARL 446:17
   Her l. were red, *her* looks   COL 211:2
   His coward l. did from   SHAK 590:1
   keep the door of my l.   BOOK 135:1
   Life and these l. have long   SHAK 624:1
   l. are like a thread   BIBLE 81:13
   l. are not yet unsealed   BALD 48:11
   l. be joined together   AKHM 6:8
   l. cannot fail of taking   BURG 167:1
   l. in anger or penitent   RIMB 541:10
   l. it was that I called   FLEM 287:2
   l. ne'er act the winning   HERR 336:14
   l. of a strange woman drop   BIBLE 78:12
   l. of those that are asleep   BIBLE 82:4
   l. that are for others   TENN 688:5
   l. that laugh and hide   SWIN 675:23
   l., that they speak no guile   BOOK 126:15
   l. that touch liquor must   YOUNG 755:2
   l. the mould falls close   ROSS 548:1
   l. to it when I am so dispoged   DICK 241:13
   l. were shaped for sin   BETJ 67:16
   mammets and to tilt with l.   SHAK 580:12
   My l. are now forbid to speak   BAYLY 56:3
   on l. of living men   BUTL 167:10
   ope my l. let no dog bark   SHAK 607:6
   people of unclean l.   BIBLE 82:20
   poor Jim's l. once more   FARM 280:5
   Read my l.: no new taxes   BUSH 165:16
   Red l. are not so red   OWEN 503:15
   saddening the l.   THOM 694:9
   sits upon the l. of dying   ARN 28:16
   Spitting from l. once sanctified   BROW 153:18
   starved l. in the gloam   KEATS 388:13
   sweet l., soft hand   KEATS 386:11
   Take, O take those l. away   SHAK 606:17
   Their l. drew near   BYRON 170:20
   they shoot out their l.   BOOK 125:10
   this hath touched thy l.   BIBLE 82:21
   Thou shalt open my l.   BOOK 128:8
   touching of the l.   TENN 685:8
   Upon her perfect l.   TENN 689:8
   very good words for the l.   DICK 241:6
   When the l. have spoken   SHEL 641:6
   Where my Julia's l. do smile   HERR 336:8
   winds kiss my parchèd l.   SHAK 594:15
   With l. of lurid blue   SHEL 640:8
lipsed: Somewhat he l.   CHAU 192:18
lipstick: team o l.'s traces   MARV 451:14
   you've got on too much l.   NASH 490:16
liquefaction: l. of her clothes   HERR 337:0
liquid: less l. than their shadows   TESS 691:1

liquid: (*cont.*):
   let their l. siblings fall   ELIOT 272:20
   l. lines mellifluously   BYRON 171:11
   l. which rots braces   MORI 400:11
   severed signs I white and l.   CONS 217:21
   Thames is l. history   BURNS 160:22
liquidity: A purpose in l.   BROO 143:7
liquor: bowl with atrabilious l.   HUXL 357:22
   But l. is quicker   NASH 490:18
   Good l., I stoutly maintain   GOLD 311:20
   lads for the l.   HOUS 352:11
   lips that touch l.   YOUNG 755:2
   L. is one way out an'   WILL 737:5
   L. talks mighty loud   HARR 327:7
   Livelier l. than the Muse   HOUS 352:19
   Love is that l. sweet   HERB 334:6
   such other spiritual l.   BYRON 173:16
   We drank our l. straight   AUDEN 35:17
   which wanteth not l.   BIBLE 82:2
lisp: l. of leaves and ripple   SWIN 675:21
lisped: l. in numbers   POPE 519:28
list: I've got a little l.   GILB 304:21
   list, O, l.!   SHAK 573:14
listen: Darkling I l.   KEATS 389:14
   l. all day to such stuff   CARR 182:4
   L., my children, and you   LONG 427:19
   l. when his mate talked   WICK 733:16
   only l. when I am unhappy   SMITH 652:10
   O speak, and make me l.   BODE 116:11
   privilege of wisdom to l.   HOLM 342:8
   world should l. then   SHEL 643:20
listened: l. and looked sideways   COL 211:4
listening: disease of not l.   SHAK 582:18
   Enemy ears are l. to you   ANON 21:6
   l., lying in wait   THOM 694:4
   People hearing without l.   SIMON 647:20
listens: l. like a three years'   COL 210:19
listeth: bloweth where it l.   BIBLE 96:14
listless: on his l. form and face   HARDY 325:14
listlessness: In l. from vain perplexity
         WORD 746:18
lit: whole Fleet's l. up   WOOD 742:2
literal: may I not say a l. God   DONNE 253:3
literalists: l. of imagination   MOORE 482:14
literary: beloved by l. pundits   CONN 216:13
   He liked those l. cooks   MORE 483:21
   Like an unsuccessful l. man   BELL 61:17
   l. and scientific opinion   ARN 29:20
   l. attempt more unfortunate   HUME 355:18
   L. intellectuals at one pole   SNOW 654:7
   l. man—*with a wooden leg*   DICK 242:31
   l. mornings with its hoot   AUDEN 35:7
   lowest class is l. *footmen*   HAZL 329:3
   Of all the l. scenes   PRES 528:14
   quotation is the *parole* of l.   JOHN 375:24
   St Paul are l. terms   ARN 30:1
   uncorrupted with l. prejudices   JOHN 368:27
literate: If, with the l., I am   POPE 506:10
literature: English l.'s performing flea
         O'CAS 497:20
   failed in l. and art   DISR 248:24
   grazed the common of l.   JOHN 372:5
   life had been ruined by l.   BROO 144:3
   l. and the Anglican Church   PYM 533:11
   l. clear and cold and pure   LEWIS 421:2
   l. is a drug   BORR 136:16
   L. is a luxury   CHES 199:14
   l. is mostly about having   LODGE 425:18
   l. is my mistress   CHEK 197:10
   l. is never fastidious   SOUT 657:17
   l. is news that STAYS news   POUND 527:15
   l. is simply language charged   POUND 527:17
   L. is strewn with the wreckage
         WOOLF 742:12
   l. is that it is dangerous   MORT 486:8
   L. is the orchestration   WILD 736:17
   l. of *power*   DE Q 237:13
   L.'s always a good card   BENN 63:21
   l. seeks to communicate   DE Q 237:14
   louse in the locks of l.   TENN 690:8
   must wash l. off ourselves   ART 30:16
   only be a newspaper l.   ZAMY 755:4
   Our l. is a substitute   ELIOT 273:21

literature: (*cont.*):
Philistine of genius in l ... ARN 30:5
produce ... little l. ... JAMES 362:18
profession of l. ... JOHN 369:26
Remarks are not l. ... STEIN 663:2
rest is l. ... COL 212:22
rest is l. ... VALE 707:21
That great Cham of l. ... SMOL 654:5
tip's a good one, as for l. ... POUND 527:4
When once the itch of l. ... LOVER 429:7
lites: *vos tantas componere l.* ... VIRG 714:20
litigious: l. lady that a man has ... NEWT 493:20
litter: overwhelmed all her l. ... SHAK 582:14
littered: l. under Mercury ... SHAK 631:25
little: And though she be but l. ... SHAK 612:5
big words for l. matters ... JOHN 372:21
breed of men, this l. world ... SHAK 619:18
But wants that l. strong ... HOLM 342:17
cry of the L. Peoples ... LE G 416:9
done and I to be known ... JOHN 369:14
drink unto one of these l. ... BIBLE 90:23
Ev'ry day a l. death ... SOND 656:1
Go, l. bok ... CHAU 195:26
grateful at last for a l. thing ... TENN 687:3
great a matter a l. fire ... BIBLE 105:1
great ones eat up the l. ... SHAK 619:1
happened with so l. stir ... WHIT 731:17
he only knew a l. of law ... ANON 14:16
here a l., and there ... BIBLE 83:11
He was l., weak, and helpless ... ALEX 8:14
hobgoblin of l. minds ... EMER 277:2
I ask very l. Some fragments ... CONN 216:10
I l. have, and seek no more ... DYER 265:1
Is l. to say, and much ... SKEL 648:20
it was a very l. one ... MARR 449:4
L. boxes on the hillside ... REYN 539:15
L. Boy kneels at the foot ... MILNE 462:18
l. child, a limber elf ... COL 209:11
L. creep through ... SHEN 644:14
L. drops of water ... CARN 181:20
L. Englanders ... ANON 15:21
l. finger shall be thicker ... BIBLE 75:27
L. Friend of all the World ... KIPL 402:4
l. grey cells ... CHR 200:8
l. hill of Hermon ... BOOK 127:4
l. in our love ... SHAK 629:20
little l. grave, an obscure ... SHAK 620:12
l. man! thy father had he ... ELIZ 274:13
L. man, you've had a busy day ... SIGL 647:15
l. may be diffused ... BOSW 137:7
l. more, and how much ... BROW 148:25
L. one! Oh, little one ... STEP 664:1
l. philosophy inclineth ... BACON 42:23
l. saint best fits a little ... HERR 336:25
l. seemed to him great ... MAC 435:7
l. ships of England brought ... GUED 319:8
L. subject, little wit ... CAREY 179:16
l. the mind is actually ... JOHN 373:30
L. to do, and plenty ... DICK 243:20
l. we think of the other ... TWAIN 706:17
l. while, and ye shall ... BIBLE 97:20
l. woman who wrote ... LINC 422:17
Lo here a l. volume ... CRAS 226:9
Man wants but l. here below ... GOLD 310:20
mother's l. helper ... JAGG 361:10
nearly as much as too l. ... COMP 214:15
no wonder we have so l. ... COMP 214:16
offering Germany too l. ... NEV 492:5
our l. life is rounded ... SHAK 625:28
own child, the l. hare ... HOFF 341:10
shall we turn to l. things ... GIBS 303:5
She gives but l. ... YOUNG 754:21
So l. done, so much to do ... RHOD 539:17
So l. done, such things ... TENN 683:26
sweetness, whereof a l. ... SHAK 581:14
these l. local difficulties ... MACM 440:4
things shall fall by l. ... BIBLE 87:24
littleness: long l. of life ... CORN 219:5
ruined by the l. of those who ... BREC 140:9
littlenesses: thousand peering l. ... TENN 681:16
liturgy: her Publick L. ... BOOK 118:3
live: And l. or die wi' Charlie ... HOGG 341:18
And there my love will l. ... CLARE 204:22

live: (*cont.*):
As you l., believe ... DU B 263:3
Bid me to l., and I will live ... HERR 337:2
cannot l. without cooks ... MER 458:11
Can these bones l. ... BIBLE 85:26
certified how long I have to l. ... BOOK 126:22
Come l. with me ... DONNE 251:19
Come l. with me ... MARL 447:17
Days are where we l. ... LARK 409:16
death and he forgets to l. ... LA BR 405:2
don't know how to l. right ... HOR 348:21
Easy l. and quiet die ... SCOTT 560:15
enable its citizens to l. ... WEIL 726:19
Expect nothing. L. frugally ... WALK 717:12
For in him we l., and move ... BIBLE 99:00
For me to l. is Christ ... BIBLE 103:2
For we that l. to please ... JOHN 370:12
For which we bear to l. ... POPE 522:19
Glad did I l. and gladly die ... STEV 669:9
health and wealth long to l. ... BOOK 119:6
he isn't fit to l. ... KING 396:17
He shall l., and unto him ... BOOK 129:21
He shall not l. ... SHAK 592:23
He that begins to l. ... QUAR 534:4
How can I l. without thee ... MILT 472:26
How is it that you l. ... WORD 747:13
I am content to l. ... KING 396:12
I cannot l. with you ... MART 449:16
I have hope to l. ... SHAK 606:6
I l. for thee ... TENN 688:10
I l. not in myself ... BYRON 168:24
I must l. ... ARG 24:19
I shall l. to do that ... MART 449:11
It is silliness to l. when ... SHAK 615:9
I wish to l. and to die ... VILL 711:16
I would l. to study ... BACON 45:16
just shall l. by faith ... BIBLE 99:16
leave sack, and l. cleanly ... SHAK 582:11
lest I should bid thee l. ... TENN 688:12
let me l. to-night ... SHAK 618:7
Let us l., my Lesbia ... CAT 185:15
l. after them if it is to l. at all ... SAKI 553:5
L. all you can ... JAMES 362:12
l. alone and smash ... ANON 20:17
l. and last for more ... CAT 185:12
L. and he reclined ... TENN 686:1
L., and take comfort ... WORD 748:13
l. any longer in sin ... BIBLE 99:27
L. a thousand years ... SHAK 591:20
l. beyond its income ... BUTL 166:31
l. dangerously ... NIET 495:12
l. deep and suck out all ... THOR 697:5
L. in despite of murder ... CHAP 190:14
l. on this Crumpetty Tree ... LEAR 414:19
L. our lives courageously ... WILL 737:14
L. till tomorrow ... COWP 222:15
l. together as brothers ... KING 397:2
l. together as equals ... MILL 461:2
l. under the shadow ... SPEN 659:7
L. well, how long or short ... MILT 473:8
l. well on nothing a year ... THAC 691:18
l. who life eternal gave ... BYRON 168:8
l. with a good conscience ... SMITH 652:9
l. without labour ... TAWN 679:2
L. with yourself ... PERS 513:6
living he'd learn how to l. ... BROW 149:20
long as ye both shall l. ... BOOK 123:19
longer I l. the more fool ... ANON 19:17
lusteth to l. ... BOOK 126:15
man desires to l. long ... SWIFT 674:20
Man is born to l. ... PAST 508:2
means whereby I l. ... SHAK 609:20
must l. or bear no life ... SHAK 617:15
My self now l. ... HERR 336:23
never l. to be useless ... WESL 728:21
None would l. past years again ... DRYD 260:6
not l. to eat ... MOL 478:14
not to l., but to die ... BROW 146:19
Rascals, would you l. for ever ... FRED 293:12
resolved to l. a fool ... BEAU 56:14
see me cease to l. ... ARN 29:5
shall find out why we l. ... CHEK 197:4
Shall make me l. ... SHAK 564:9

live: (*cont.*):
shall no man see me and l. ... BIBLE 72:22
short time to l. ... BOOK 124:3
small to l. in and too large ... ANON 19:3
So longe mote ye l. ... CHAU 195:13
so much, nor l. so long ... SHAK 598:5
teaching nations how to l. ... MILT 475:17
Teach me to l., that I may ... KEN 393:8
than to l. on your knees ... IBAR 358:14
that can l. without dining ... MER 458:11
that we may l. in peace ... ARIS 25:10
There taught us how to l. ... TICK 698:4
they sometimes l. apart ... SAKI 553:15
thou hast no more to l. ... SWIN 676:5
Thus let me l., unseen ... POPE 523:12
To l. and die for thee ... HERR 337:3
To l. is like to love ... BUTL 167:4
To l. without him ... WOTT 749:4
To l. with thee ... RAL 535:11
turn and l. with animals ... WHIT 732:18
unable to l. in society ... ARIS 25:16
was gonna l. this long ... BLAKE 110:16
We l. and learn ... POMF 518:11
We l., as we dream — alone ... CONR 217:3
We l. in a fantasy world ... MURD 488:9
We l., not as we wish ... MEN 457:3
we l. our lives, for ever ... RILKE 541:2
We mortal millions l. *alone* ... ARN 29:3
were a martyrdom to l. ... BROW 145:17
where I shall l. by sight ... BUNY 156:17
which will l. in infamy ... ROOS 546:4
who love, who l., but thee ... SIDN 647:3
Work and pray, l. on hay ... HILL 338:12
wouldn't l. under Niagara ... CARL 181:15
write too much, and l. too long ... DAN 230:3
years a mortal man may l. ... SHAK 588:1
You might as well l. ... PARK 506:11
you shall l. by fame ... SPEN 659:11
lived: Had we l., I should have ... SCOTT 559:6
have eat and drunk and l. ... JOHN 373:15
Holmes where *have* you l. ... DOYLE 256:15
I have l. long enough ... SHAK 604:21
L. in his mild and magnificent ... BROW 151:1
never loved, has never l. ... GAY 299:27
Never to have l. is best ... YEATS 751:20
To have l. light in the spring ... ARN 27:3
lively: l. Oracles ... COR 219:11
thy true and l. Word ... BOOK 122:2
liver: l. on the right ... MOL 479:3
L. of blaspheming Jew ... SHAK 603:19
l. spotted, the brain ... JONS 378:10
open and notorious evil l. ... BOOK 121:14
so much blood in his l. ... SHAK 630:16
livered: But I am pigeon-l. ... SHAK 575:12
livers: grave L. do in Scotland ... WORD 747:12
livery: all in one l. ... SHAK 587:23
careless l. that it wears ... SHAK 578:11
ill-bred son of a l. ... YEATS 751:17
l. of the burnished sun ... SHAK 608:4
sober l. all things clad ... MILT 471:10
lives: but how he l. ... JOHN 373:7
Careless talk costs l. ... ANON 12:20
ends marked than their l. ... SHAK 619:16
Everything that l. ... BLAKE 111:12
evil that men do l. after ... SHAK 592:5
He l., he wakes,—'tis Death ... SHEL 640:2
Lewd, tiny, careless l. ... ROET 544:6
l. along the line ... POPE 522:6
l. have been taken away ... MCG 437:17
L. in Eternity's sunrise ... BLAKE 113:11
l. of quiet desperation ... THOR 696:28
l. upon hope will die fasting ... FRAN 292:17
no second acts in American l. ... FITZ 285:6
one really l. no where ... BURN 160:15
Our l. would grow together ... SWIN 677:1
passing their l. together ... HUME 355:10
pleasant in their l. ... BIBLE 75:9
right way to conduct our l. ... PLATO 516:14
sinking as the light wind l. ... KEATS 390:20
Till our l. we end ... JARR 363:20
We can make our l. sublime ... LONG 427:10
Went in jeopardy of their l. ... BIBLE 75:20
who lives more l. than one ... WILDE 736:4

lives: (cont.):
woman who l. for others — LEWIS 420:14
liveth: he l. unto God — BIBLE 99:29
I am he that l., and was — BIBLE 106:2
I know that my redeemer l. — BIBLE 77:25
l. longest doth but sup — HENS 333:9
name l. for evermore — BIBLE 88:3
living: alive and well and l. — ANON 15:11
all the l. and the dead — JOYCE 380:20
between those who are l. — BURKE 158:21
bodies a l. sacrifice — BIBLE 100:3
body is a machine for l. — TOLS 701:1
Disdain, are you yet l. — SHAK 613:9
even for the l. God — BOOK 127:2
fever called 'L.' — POE 518:5
For ye are l. poems — LONG 426:12
habit of l. indisposeth — BROW 145:18
hands of the l. God — BIBLE 104:12
house appointed for all l. — BIBLE 77:30
language of the l. — ELIOT 271:3
Life we have lost in l. — ELIOT 272:15
L. and partly living — ELIOT 272:9
l. by taking in one another's — ANON 13:1
l. dog is better — BIBLE 80:18
l. doll — PLATH 516:2
L. for today — LENN 417:12
l., had no roof to shroud — HEYW 338:6
l. is abnormal — ION 360:10
L. is an illness — CHAM 189:11
L. is my job and my art — MONT 481:4
l. need charity more — ARN 26:15
l. peaceably — BIBLE 88:1
l. unto righteousness — BOOK 123:1
l. up to it that is difficult — THAC 691:3
L., we fret — BROW 150:18
l. which are yet alive — BIBLE 80:7
lose the reasons for l. — JUV 384:4
man became a l. soul — BIBLE 70:1
mutual envy of the l. — HOBB 340:13
noble L., and the noble Dead — WORD 747:8
no l. people in it — CHEK 196:12
Of health and l. now begins — SHAK 626:19
out of the book of the l. — BOOK 129:14
out of the land of the l. — BIBLE 84:13
Plain l. and high thinking — WORD 746:10
respect to the l. — VOLT 717:1
riotous l. — BIBLE 95:2
shadows of the l. — BROW 145:8
shall no man l. be justified — BOOK 135:3
shouldst be l. at this hour — WORD 745:4
So start by l. — ANOU 23:9
Summer time an' the l. is easy — HEYW 338:2
that, l. know no bounds — SHIR 646:6
their preaching and l. — BOOK 119:19
There is no l. with thee — ADD 4:7
things l. with plenteousness — BOOK 135:7
This l. buried man — DONNE 251:13
truly to get mine own l. — BOOK 123:9
two revolutions is l. — PAINE 505:3
unexamined life is not worth l. — SOCR 654:14
withdrawn from l.'s store — PUSH 533:2
ye the l. among the dead — BIBLE 95:30
you to go on l. — SOCR 654:15
living-dead: A l. man — SHAK 570:1
Livingstone: Dr L., I presume — STAN 662:6
livres: l. cadrent mal avec — MOL 479:2
l. ne se font pas comme — FLAU 286:4
lizard: L.'s leg, and howlet's — SHAK 603:18
Lizzie Borden: L. took an axe — ANON 15:22
llama: L. is a woolly sort — BELL 61:17
Lloyd George: [L.] did not seem to care — BEAV 57:6
L. knew my father — ANON 15:23
[L.] thinks he is Napoleon — CLEM 206:8
lo: L.! He comes with clouds — WESL 728:15
then said I, L., I come — BOOK 126:25
load: Deserves his l. — HERB 334:12
him to l. and bless — KEATS 390:17
like a l. of immortality — KEATS 391:21
every rift with ore — KEATS 382:18
l. many out of many — SHAK 588:21
To l. a falling man — SHAK 584:14
loaf: cut l. to steal a shive — SHAK 580:17

loaf: (cont.):
l. of bread beneath — FITZ 283:13
loafing: cricket as organized l. — TEMP 680:6
loam: From the provided l. — HILL 338:9
loan: brief l. of his own body — CAB 174:11
l. oft loses both itself — SHAK 573:4
Norman that I have him on l. — AYCK 40:11
loathe: I l. all things held — CALL 175:7
Must be to l. her — SHAK 616:16
loathed: performance so l. — SHAK 628:8
loathing: My l. was prophet to — MIDD 459:15
shortcomings weeps with l. — LITT 423:9
loaves: five barley l. — BIBLE 96:22
halfpenny l. sold for a penny — SHAK 587:23
lobby: into the l. against us — BALD 48:11
lobster: has seen the mailed l. — FRERE 293:17
l. more ridiculous than a dog — NERV 492:3
local: little l. difficulties — MACM 440:4
l., but prized elsewhere — AUDEN 36:4
l. habitation and a name — SHAK 612:17
l. thing called Christianity — HARDY 324:5
Loch: banks o' L. Lomon' — ANON 17:8
Lochinvar: L. is come out of the west — SCOTT 560:3
loci: Geniumque l. primamque — VIRG 714:2
lock: broken the l. and splintered — AUDEN 35:15
happy, why l. — SHAW 637:18
Wi' ae l. o' his gowden hair — BALL 50:20
locked: L. and frozen in each eye — AUDEN 34:15
L. up from mortal eye — CRAS 226:15
that l. her up gives room — VAUG 709:9
locks: combined l. to part — SHAK 573:14
l. of the approaching storm — SHEL 641:15
l. which are left you — SOUT 657:13
louse in the l. of literature — TENN 690:8
shaking her invincible l. — MILT 475:14
Thy gory l. at me — SHAK 603:10
until his l. grew grey — CARB 178:17
Your l. were like the raven — BURNS 162:10
loco: Es un entreverado l. — CERV 188:12
locust: hath the l. eaten — BIBLE 86:6
years that the l. hath eaten — BIBLE 86:7
locusts: famine grew, and l. came — THOM 693:10
meat was l. and wild honey — BIBLE 88:14
locuta: Roma l. est — AUG 37:9
lodesterre: language he was the l. — LYDG 433:2
lodestone: l. to the north advance — DAV 232:6
lodge: Is best to l. — SHAK 630:19
l. in a garden — BIBLE 82:8
still l. Him in the manger — ANON 20:3
thou lodgest, I will l. — BIBLE 74:25
uncomfortable inn to l. — MELV 456:16
lodged: L. with me useless — MILT 474:24
lodging: Hard was their l. — GARTH 298:14
lodgings: pent up in frowzy l. — SMOL 654:2
Such as take l. in a head — BUTL 166:5
loftier: A l. race — SYM 677:6
loftily: L. lying — BROW 150:2
lofty: about great and l. things — MONT 480:13
L. and sour to them — SHAK 589:10
L. designs must close — BROW 150:2
l. utterance drest — WORD 747:12
log: To fall a l. at last — JONS 379:21
log-cabin: L. to White House — THAY 691:28
logic: grape that can with l. — FITZ 284:4
It is the l. of our times — DAY-L 233:7
l. and rhetoric, able — BACON 44:29
Of science and l. he chatters — PRAED 528:13
overthrow of all his l. — STEV 667:16
That's l. — CARR 182:24
This Second L. then — ARIS 25:3
too, L., of course — CLOU 207:8
logicians: If we believe our l. — ADD 4:23
logs: Tom bears l. into the hall — SHAK 599:11
loin: lamp and the ungirt l. — BROW 153:7
loins: He girded up his l. — BIBLE 76:5
l. girt about with truth — BIBLE 103:1
shudder in the l. engenders — YEATS 752:11
thicker than my father's l. — BIBLE 75:27
With your l. girded — BIBLE 72:10
your l. be girded about — BIBLE 94:25
l'dieu my Gallic L. more — BY R 263:2
loiterly: have l. l. my life, away — HAZL 328:14

loiterers: l. and malecontents — SHAK 598:13
loitering: Alone and palely l. — KEATS 388:7
Lolita: L., light of my life — NAB 488:21
lollipop: Monkey with l. paws — LEAR 414:5
Lombardy: waveless plain of L. — SHEL 641:7
London: And dream of L. — MORR 485:12
art, in L. only is a trade — DRYD 261:16
As he gazed at the L. skies — BETJ 67:3
'Cause in sleepy L. town — JAGG 361:12
Certainly L. fascinates — FORS 290:12
dead lies L.'s daughter — THOM 693:14
foggy day in L. Town — GERS 301:11
Hell is a city much like L. — SHEL 642:5
L.: a nation, not a city — DISR 248:21
L. doth pour out her citizens — SHAK 586:13
L. is a modern Babylon — DISR 248:33
[L.] is become an overgrown — SMOL 654:1
L. like a special correspondent — BAG 47:14
L. spread out in the sun — LARK 410:10
L., that great cesspool — DOYLE 256:21
L., that great sea — SHEL 641:2
L., thou art of townes — ANON 15:24
L., thou art the flower — ANON 16:1
man is tired of L. — JOHN 374:24
Oh, L. is a fine town — COLM 214:1
parks are the lungs of L. — PITT 515:13
than a rainy London in L. — DE Q 237:8
that should go on in L. — PYM 533:9
This is a L. particular — DICK 239:2
vilest alleys in L. — DOYLE 256:5
Yankee Doodle came to L. — COHAN 208:13
London Bridge: A crowd flowed over L. — ELIOT 273:1
L. a greater piece of work — ADD 4:15
L. to sketch the ruins — MAC 435:12
London Transport: L. Diesel-engined — FLAN 285:14
lone: I am a l. lorn creetur — DICK 239:20
l. shieling of the misty — GALT 297:7
l. unhaunted place possessed — DONNE 251:13
walking by his wild l. — KIPL 401:19
loneliness: All that bowery l. — TENN 687:11
l. of the long-distance runner — SILL 647:16
Well of L. — HALL 322:4
lonely: All the l. people — LENN 417:18
as mirrors are l. — AUDEN 35:18
for fear I may be l. — JOAD 366:9
heart is a l. hunter — MCL 439:12
l. impulse of delight — YEATS 752:6
l. sea and the sky — MAS 453:7
Only the l. — ORBI 499:7
rapture on the l. shore — BYRON 169:13
that most l. thing — YEATS 752:1
troubled with her l. life — PEPYS 512:10
lonesome: Like one, that on a l. road — COL 211:14
lonesomeness: starlight lit my l. — HARDY 326:3
long: And thou art l., and lank — COL 211:6
ask that your way be l. — CAV 187:4
But it's a l., long while — AND 11:8
certified how l. I have to live — BOOK 126:22
For y'er a l. time deid — ANON 12:12
fulfilled a l. time — BIBLE 87:2
has been l. in city pent — KEATS 390:27
How l. a time lies in one little — SHAK 619:10
how l. or short permit — MILT 473:8
I am going a l. way — TENN 682:25
In the l. night — SURR 672:4
In the l. run we are all dead — KEYN 395:11
it hath very l. arms — HAL 321:15
It's a l. way to Tipperary — JUDGE 382:8
Life is one l. process — BUTL 166:30
l. and the short — HUGH 353:16
l. dark autumn-evenings — BROW 148:21
l. day's task is done — SHAK 566:8
l. for scenes where man — CLARE 204:26
l. hot summer — RAVE 537:8
L. is the way and hard — MILT 469:21
l. life will I satisfy — BOOK 131:5
l. littleness of life — CORN 219:5
L. my imprisoned spirit lay — WESL 728:2
long, l. thoughts — LONG 427:4

long: (*cont.*):
l. time I used to go to bed   PROU 530:6
l. trail awinding   KING 397:6
l. will you abuse our patience   CIC 204:5
l. wilt thou forget me   BOOK 124:25
l., withdrawing roar   ARN 27:1
Love me little, love me l.   ANON 16:4
man goeth to his l. home   BIBLE 81:1
night of the l. knives   HITL 339:10
Nor wants that little l.   GOLD 310:20
So l. as men can breathe   SHAK 633:6
so l. as ye both shall live   BOOK 123:19
So l. mote ye lyve   CHAU 195:13
that if a man have l. hair   BIBLE 100:34
that the story need be l.   THOR 696:25
Then said I, Lord, how l.   BIBLE 82:23
to make a l. prologue   BIBLE 88:6
tomorrow l. I to go to God   MORE 484:16
Too l. a sacrifice   YEATS 751:14
was gonna live this l.   BLAKE 110:16
week is a l. time in politics   WILS 738:6
witty and it sha'n't be l.   CHES 197:14
words a foot and a half l.   HOR 347:8
long-cramped: l. scroll   BROW 150:21
longen: l. folk to goon on pilgrimages
  CHAU 192:7
longer: daily for your l. life   ELIZ 274:10
I am no l. my own   METH 458:16
l. I live the more fool   ANON 19:17
O what is l. than the wave   BALL 50:7
takes a little l.   NANS 489:8
wished l. by its readers   JOHN 377:9
longest: l. journey go   SHEL 640:10
l. running farce in the West End   SMITH 651:8
l. suicide note in history   KAUF 385:15
Must bear the l. part   HERB 334:7
longeth: flesh also l. after thee   BOOK 128:21
so l. my soul after thee   BOOK 127:2
long-haired: consort with l. things   KIPL 399:12
longing: Cross as focus of l.   MUGG 487:11
has cast a l. eye on them   JEFF 364:10
hopeless l. of the day   ARN 27:5
l. ling'ring look behind   GRAY 315:18
Sir Richard, l. to be at 'em   ANON 13:21
soul hath a desire and l.   BOOK 130:16
This l. after immortality   ADD 3:23
longings: Immortal l. in me   SHAK 567:7
longitude: l. with no platitude   FRY 295:23
long-nosed: l., sensitive-footed   LAWR 412:11
long-suffering: l., and of great goodness
  BOOK 132:4
l., and very pitiful   BIBLE 87:8
peace, l., gentleness   BIBLE 102:7
longtemps: *et c'est pour si l.*   MOL 478:20
L., je me suis couché   PROU 530:6
look: afraid to l. upon God   BIBLE 71:39
And they all l. just the same   REYN 539:15
Can read a nod, a shrug, a l.   SWIFT 674:27
dares not l. behind   BLAIR 110:15
dares not l. behind   SHEL 644:11
full l. at the worst   HARDY 325:6
God's sake l. after our people   SCOTT 559:4
Hit l. lak sparrer-grass   HARR 327:1
Let him l. to his bond   SHAK 608:21
l. about us and to die   POPE 521:26
l., and pass on   DANTE 230:7
l. as much like home as   FRY 295:24
L. at it, it's all in bits   AYCK 40:10
l. at the senators   HALE 321:5
l. at things in bloom   HOUS 352:6
L. for me by moonlight   NOYES 497:6
L. for me in the nurseries of   THOM 695:11
l. forward to the trip   STIN 669:11
l. grim as hell   SHAK 617:15
L. in my face   TRAI 702:2
l. in thy heart and write   SIDN 646:15
l. no way but downwards   BUNY 156:8
l. on both indifferently   SHAK 589:26
l. shining at new styles   AUDEN 36:6
L., stranger, at this island   AUDEN 35:4
l. the East End in the face   ELIZ 275:2
L. thy last on all things lovely   DE L 236:2
L. to it   LINC 422:11

look: (*cont.*):
l. to the end   ANON 22:13
L. to your Moat   HAL 321:19
L.! Up in the sky!   ANON 13:8
l. upon his like again   SHAK 572:17
l. upon myself and curse   SHAK 633:10
l. upon the hedge and follow   SHAK 632:14
L. with thine ears   SHAK 597:6
one longing ling'ring l.   GRAY 315:18
Only a l. and a voice   LONG 428:1
or do we l. for another   BIBLE 90:24
shall tremble at the l. of him   BOOK 132:10
sweet to l. into the fair   KEATS 390:27
that row one way and l.   BURT 164:17
that we may l. upon thee   BIBLE 81:22
They cannot l. out far   FROST 296:6
They l. on and help   LAWR 412:27
We l. before and after   SHEL 643:19
When I do l. on thee   SIDN 647:5
where to l. for it   DONNE 250:7
you l. to other people   UNAM 707:3
looked: l. at in this merciless   WILL 737:8
l. at life from both sides now   MITC 477:19
l. for a city which hath   BIBLE 104:14
l. inside the more Piglet   MILNE 462:8
l. upon Peter   BIBLE 95:23
She l. at me as she did love   KEATS 388:10
lookers on: God and angels to be l.   BACON 42:6
looking: go on l. at me like that   ZOLA 755:13
Here's l. at you, kid   EPST 278:8
Leave them while you're l. good   LOOS 428:9
l. at you when my last hour   TIB 698:1
l. beyond the next fortnight   CHAM 189:2
l. one way, and rowing   BUNY 155:20
l. together in same direction   DE S 553:4
plough, and l. back   BIBLE 94:9
she was l. all the time   THOM 693:19
that someone may be l.   MENC 457:20
with plenty of l. glasses   ASHF 31:9
looking-glass: As in a l.   SHAK 631:13
court an amorous l.   SHAK 621:15
cracked l. of a servant   JOYCE 381:19
looking-glasses: l. possessing the magic
  WOOLF 742:11
looks: even in heaven his l.   MILT 469:4
her l. went everywhere   BROW 151:12
I discerned her l.   PATM 509:11
I have no proud l.   BOOK 134:13
l. do menace heaven   MARL 447:22
she needs good l.   TUCK 705:2
Stolen l. are nice in chapels   HUNT 356:10
loom: labours of the l.   DYER 265:2
left the web, she left the l.   TENN 685:4
looms: passage through these l.   VAUG 708:14
loon: some false l. betrayed   ALC 8:1
thou cream-faced l.   SHAK 604:20
Wanna laugh like a l.   HARB 323:11
looney: L. Tunes, and squalid   REAG 537:13
looney-bin: janitor to the l.   WOD 740:15
loophole: l. through which pervert   BRON 142:1
loopholes: l. less than themselves   TESS 691:1
through the l. of retreat   COWP 223:32
loose: all hell broke l.   MILT 471:18
Every which way but l.   KRON 404:4
For the man who should l.   LOW 429:12
I let you l., George   WESL 729:1
L. his beard, and hoary hair   GRAY 315:7
l. the hands of wickedness   BIBLE 84:22
l. the seals thereof   BIBLE 106:13
L. types of things through   WORD 748:11
or l. the bands of Orion   BIBLE 77:37
loosed: l. our heart in tears   ARN 27:13
looted: All has been l.   AKHM 6:6
lops: l. the mouldered branch   TENN 681:12
loquendi: *est et ius et norma l.*   HOR 347:6
lord: absent long, your L. is nigh   OAKL 497:8
acceptable year of the L.   BIBLE 84:26
And I replied, 'My L.'   HERB 334:12
And the L. turned, and looked   BIBLE 95:23
Because you are a great l.   BEAU 56:12
cometh in the Name of the L.   BOOK 133:17
coming of the L.   HOWE 353:2

lord: (*cont.*):
day which the L. hath made   BOOK 133:16
dear L. was crucified   ALEX 8:16
Deliver us, good L.   CHES 199:3
died by the hand of the L.   BIBLE 72:15
die with kissing of my L.   MARL 448:7
earth is the L.'s   BOOK 125:16
entertain its l. a while   MARV 451:7
Even so, come, L. Jesus   BIBLE 107:26
Even the L. of hosts   BOOK 125:18
Fresh from the L.   FARJ 280:4
Go, and the L. be with thee   BIBLE 75:2
Good L., deliver us   BOOK 119:17
Great l. of all things   POPE 522:10
house of the L.   BOOK 125:15
I am the L. thy God   BIBLE 72:16
into the house of the L.   BOOK 133:25
It would talk: L. how it talk't   BEAU 57:4
KING OF KINGS, AND L. OF LORDS   BIBLE 107:13
know not what hour your L.   BIBLE 92:15
lesson which the L.   SPEN 659:10
L., dismiss us with Thy   BUCK 154:12
L., dost thou wash my feet?   BIBLE 97:8
L. gave, and the Lord   BIBLE 77:2
L. guards the city   BIBLE 108:4
L. has built the house   BIBLE 108:4
L. hath not spoken   BIBLE 76:13
L. hath spared our lives   TENN 689:4
L. I am coming as fast   LAUD 411:4
L. is a man of war   BIBLE 72:14
L. is his name   MONS 480:2
L. is King, and hath   BOOK 131:6
L. is my light   BOOK 125:24
L. is my shepherd   BOOK 125:14
L. is the source of my light   BIBLE 107:27
L. looketh on the heart   BIBLE 74:38
L. loveth he chasteneth   BIBLE 104:18
L. make his face shine   BIBLE 73:4
L., make me coy and tender   HERB 335:23
L. mighty in battle   BOOK 125:17
L., now lettest thou thy servant depart
  BIBLE 93:29
L. of all hopefulness   STR 671:1
l. of fat prize-oxen   TENN 688:17
L. of folded arms   SHAK 598:13
L. of himself, though not   WOTT 749:1
l. of lycht and lamp   DOUG 255:8
L. of the Dance   CART 184:13
l. of the foul and the brute   COWP 224:15
L. of thy presence   SHAK 593:24
L. once own the happy lines   POPE 521:19
L. our God is good   KETHE 394:13
L. our God is one   BIBLE 73:15
L. Randal, my Son   BALL 49:17
L., remember me when thou   BIBLE 95:26
L. require of thee   BIBLE 86:14
L.'s and the fulness thereof   BIBLE 100:33
L. said unto my Lord   BOOK 133:3
L.'s anointed temple   SHAK 602:14
L. set a mark upon Cain   BIBLE 70:21
L. shall be revealed   BIBLE 83:26
L. shall raise me up   RAL 536:3
L.'s my shepherd   SCOT 561:8
L. survives the rainbow   LOW 430:18
L. thy God is with thee   BIBLE 73:27
L., thy word abideth   BAKER 47:19
l. to leggen in his bedde   CHAU 193:29
L. Tomnoddy went home   BARH 52:11
L. was departed from him   BIBLE 74:19
L. watch between me   BIBLE 71:17
L., what fools these mortals   SHAK 612:2
L. will be there and wait   WHIT 732:20
L., with what care Thou   HERB 335:19
L., ye know, is God indeed   KETHE 394:13
Love is our L.'s meaning   JUL 382:11
Love, thou art absolute sole L.   CRAS 226:5
mouth of the L. hath spoken   BIBLE 83:26
My L. and my God   BIBLE 97:37
My L. should take   CROS 228:2
My soul doth magnify the L.   BIBLE 93:22
nurture of the L.   BOOK 123:17
O L., art more than they   TENN 682:28
O L., have mercy upon us   BOOK 118:14

lord: (*cont.*):

O L., to what a state	TER 690:15
Prepare ye the way of the L.	BIBLE 83:26
Prepare ye the way of the L.	BIBLE 88:13
Rejoice in the L. alway	BIBLE 103:11
Rejoice, the L. is King	WESL 728:13
remembrance of his dying L.	SPEN 659:21
Sae let the L. be thankit	BURNS 162:15
Seek ye the L.	BIBLE 84:16
servant above his l.	BIBLE 90:17
shall we sing the L.'s song	BOOK 134:17
So love is L. of all	SPEN 659:12
Spirit on the L.'s day	BIBLE 105:33
that sought the L. aright	BURNS 161:16
that the L. is gracious	BIBLE 105:10
their L. himself bespake	MILT 467:4
Then said I, L., how long	BIBLE 82:23
They have taken away my L.	BIBLE 97:32
those who love the L.	HUNT 356:4
To wound thy l., thy king	SHAK 624:21
wait upon the L. shall renew	BIBLE 84:1
we own thee L.	ANON 22:17
We should call him L.	NOEL 496:9
when they crucified my L.	ANON 19:9
Lord Copper: Up to a point, L.	WAUGH 724:1
Lord Howard: L. passed away	TENN 689:1
lordliest: Lords are l. in their wine	MILT 474:12
lords: About the l. o' the creation	
	BURNS 163:25
chance with one of the L.	LAWR 412:21
For the l. who lay ye low	SHEL 643:3
l. and owners	SHAK 634:15
l. drinking at the wine	BALL 49:8
l. have their pleasures	MUNT 481.15
L. in ermine, beggars freezing	ROB 542:16
L. of Convention	SCOTT 559:8
l. of human kind	GOLD 311:10
L. too are bards	BYRON 172:10
l. whose parents were	DEFOE 234:24
l. will alway that people note	BARC 52:9
only a wit among L.	JOHN 371:16
Wi' the Scots l. at his feet	BALL 50:12
with those L. I had gone so far	MORE 484:10
lordships: l. on a hot summer afternoon	
	ANON 18:18
lore: l. its scholars need	KEBLE 392:21
lose: And l. me the name of action	SHAK 575:16
as disastrous as to l. one	CHR 200:7
findeth his life shall l. it	BIBLE 90:22
had I cannot fear to l.	AST 32:6
hope and nothing to l.	BURKE 159:24
l. but their chains	MARX 452:14
l. her as a friend	GLAD 307:19
l. his own soul	BIBLE 93:14
l. itself in the sky	BROW 148:1
l. it that do buy it	SHAK 607:3
l. myself in a mystery	BROW 146:3
l. thee were to l. myself	MILT 473:6
l. the war in an afternoon	CHUR 203:6
l., though full of pain	MILT 469:14
l. to-morrow the ground	ARN 28:8
l. what he never had	WALT 721:6
l. you but we think you	RUB 549:16
nobly save, or meanly l.	LINC 422:6
nothing to l. but our aitches	ORW 500:24
Or l. our ventures	SHAK 593:12
seek power and to l. liberty	BACON 43:28
Them that's not shall l.	HOL 342:1
To l. one parent, Mr Worthing	WILDE 734:14
To win or l. it all	GRAH 313:15
way to l. him	SHAK 564:23
wish that one should l.	MARL 447:10
losers: all are l.	CHAM 189:6
So both should l. be	HERB 335:15
loses: l. his misery	ARN 28:11
Who l., and who wins	SHAK 597:16
losing: conduct of a l. party	BURKE 157:2
Does it matter?—l. your sight	SASS 557:6
Hath but a l. office	SHAK 582:13
I deem a l. gain	SOUT 657:23
l. one pleased Cato	LUCAN 431:4
l. trade, I assure you	BORR 136:18
l. l. of I now myself	SHAK 604:25

loss: And the profit and l.	ELIOT 273:11
But from its l.	YOUNG 754:13
counted l. for Christ	BIBLE 103:8
deeper sense of her l.	GASK 299:3
l. comes to him from	BROW 149:11
My richest gain I count but l.	WATTS 723:2
To do our country l.	SHAK 586:10
lost: All is not l.	MILT 468:5
Balls will be l. always	BERR 66:16
battles are l.	WHIT 732:16
better to have fought and l.	CLOU 207:21
better to have loved and l.	BUTL 166:28
better to have loved and l.	TENN 683:12
Britain has l. an empire	ACH 1:6
Die in the lost, l. fight	CLOU 207:6
found my sheep which was l.	BIBLE 94:35
France has not l. the war	DE G 234:28
Friends, I have l. a day	TITUS 698:8
Hath l. me in your liking	SHAK 594:22
he was l., and is found	BIBLE 95:5
Home of l. causes	ARN 29:15
horse the rider was l.	FRAN 292:18
I have l. all the names	JOHN 375:26
In search of l. time	PROU 530:5
in the l. boyhood of Judas	Æ 5:10
Into my bosom and be l. in me	TENN 688:13
I once was l., but now am	NEWT 494:8
Is the year only l. to me	HERB 334:11
land of l. content	HOUS 352:15
l. but the son of perdition	BIBLE 97:22
l. daddy I arsked tenderly	LARD 409:11
l. generation	STEIN 663:6
l. in stormy visions	SHEL 639:22
l. in the magic of a kiss	WASH 722:4
l. my edifice by mistaking	SHAK 610.15
l. sheep of the house	BIBLE 90:13
l., that is unsought	CHAU 195:10
l. the only Playboy	SYNGE 677:9
l. the world for love	DRYD 261:11
l. to us and counted against	MART 449:14
l. traveller's dream under	BLAKE 111:23
L., yesterday, somewhere	MANN 444:12
make wherever we're l.	FRY 295:24
never l. till won	CRAB 225:8
Next to a battle l.	WELL 727:10
Not l. but gone before	NORT 497:1
not that you won or l.	RICE 540:1
paradises that we have l.	PROU 530:16
Praising what is l.	SHAK 564:11
see is lost let it be l.	CAT 186:2
see your country is l.	WILL 736:21
such victory and we are l.	PYRR 533:12
than never to have l. at all	BUTL 166:28
That all was l.	MILT 472:24
that nothing be l.	BIBLE 96:23
this body, l. but breath	BROO 143:17
Through me, something is l.	THOM 694:11
To be l. evermore in the main	TENN 689:6
upon every day to be l.	JOHN 376:19
what is l. in translation	FROST 295:19
When all is l.	BYRON 172:24
woman that deliberates is l.	ADD 3:19
lot: cast my l. in an island	DICK 244:3
l. for to bemoan of those	SACK 552:13
l. is fallen unto me	BOOK 124:30
Not milder is the general l.	ARN 27:23
policeman's l. is not a happy	GILB 306:11
Remember L.'s wife	BIBLE 95:12
Their l. forbad	GRAY 315:16
Lothario: gallant, gay L.	ROWE 549:5
lotos: L. and lilies	TENN 687:19
lots: cast l. upon my vesture	BOOK 125:13
lottery: judgement is a mere l.	DRYD 262:13
Lou: lady that's known as L.	SERV 563:8
loud: upon the l. cymbals	BOOK 135:17
louder: and play it rather l.	LAMB 407:14
l. he talked of his honour	EMER 276:18
loungers: l. and idlers of the Empire	
	DOYLE 256:21
lounjun: L. 'roun' an' suffer'n'	HARR 327:5
louse: between a l. and a flea	JOHN 376:8
l. in the locks of literature	TENN 690:6

lousy: L. but loyal	ANON 16:3
l. skin scabbed here	BUNT 155:8
Louvre: You're the L. Museum	PORT 524:20
love: absent l. is very sweet	TROL 704:4
against the reasons of my l.	FORD 289:13
Ah, l., let us be true	ARN 27:1
Alas! the l. of women	BYRON 170:22
All are but ministers of L.	COL 210:15
all for l. and a little	DIBD 238:11
All l., all liking, all delight	HERR 336:11
All l. at first, like generous	BUTL 166:21
all she loves is l.	BYRON 170:23
All that matters is l. and work	FREUD 294:2
Amazing l.!	WESL 728:1
Amo, amas, I l. a lass	O'KEE 498:8
And all for l.	SPEN 660:5
And carol of l.'s praise	SPEN 659:14
And his dark secret l.	BLAKE 114:12
And l. Creation's final law	TENN 683:22
And l. is more cruel than lust	SWIN 676:12
And l. thee after	SHAK 618:5
And L., the human form divine	BLAKE 113:19
And putting L. away	DICK 244:13
And the planet of L.	TENN 686:17
And there my l. will live	CLARE 204:22
And very few to l.	WORD 747:18
And when L. speaks	SHAK 598:20
And yet I l. her till I die	ANON 18:10
And yet I l. this false	EPH 278:4
As great in l. as in religion	COWL 221:15
asked none leave to l.	DONNE 252:1
As woman's l.	SHAK 576:15
Ave Maria! 'tis the hour of l.	BYRON 171:6
Because we freely l.	MILT 471:26
better than secret l.	BIBLE 79:25
between l. and fascination	WASH 722:4
boy's l., or a whore's	SHAK 596:18
bred as to l. a husband	WYCH 750:7
bring those who know l. Thee	TER 690:15
But l., first learnèd	SHAK 598:20
'But l.,' quoth he, 'says truth'	GREE 317:10
But never doubt I l.	SHAK 574:15
But never taint my l.	SHAK 617:20
But quick-eyed L., observing	HERB 335:8
But yet in l. he sought me	BAKER 47:20
Can L. be controlled by advice	GAY 299:13
cantons of contemnèd l.	SHAK 628:24
caution in l. is perhaps	RUSS 551:13
Christ's particular l.'s sake	BROW 152:17
Come, let us make l. deathless	TREN 702:9
comely in nothing but in l.	BACON 44:1
come to l. men too little	BURKE 158:26
corner in the thing I l.	SHAK 616.16
cruel madness of l.	TENN 686:9
daughterly l. and dear charity	MORE 484:16
dearest l. in all the world	RODG 544:1
Dear l., for nothing less	DONNE 251:22
Deep as first l.	TENN 688:5
do not fall in l. with me	SHAK 569:14
Dreaming like a l.-adept	SHEL 642:14
earth could never living l.	ANON 14:5
essence of real human l.	ELIOT 268:20
Farewell, L., and all thy	WYATT 749:15
fear l. is to fear life	RUSS 551:16
figure is the same as for l.	FROST 295:14
fit l. for gods	MILT 472:22
fitter l. for me	DONNE 252:15
flowers and fruits of l.	BYRON 173:1
fool of l.	HAZL 328:15
For a day and a night L.	SWIN 676:3
For ever wilt thou l.	KEATS 388:26
Forgets the shows of l.	SHAK 589:25
fruit of the Spirit is l.	BIBLE 102:7
Gather the rose of l.	SPEN 660:6
give up my darling's l.	ANON 21:5
God is l., but get it in writing	LEE 415:15
God of l. my Shepherd is	HERB 336:22
God si [is] L.	FORS 290:27
good man's l.	SHAK 569:13
good to them that l. God	BIBLE 99:38
Greater l. hath no man	BIBLE 97:16
greater l. hath no man	THOR 697:12

love: (*cont.*):

l. swears that she is made	SHAK 635:5
Love! sweet l.! was thought	BLAKE 114:9
l.'s young dream	MOORE 483:6
l. than matrimony in them	GOLD 311:32
l. that asks no question	SPR 661:8
l. that can be reckoned	SHAK 564:13
L. that cordial drop	ROCH 543:6
L. that dare not speak its	DOUG 255:7
L. that endures for a breath	SWIN 676:1
l. that loves a scarlet	HOOD 343:19
l. that moves the sun	DANTE 230:21
L. that never told can	BLAKE 113:15
l. that we have loved together	MAL 443:11
l. the babe that milks	SHAK 601:7
L. the Beloved Republic	FORS 290:30
L. the brotherhood	BIBLE 105:13
l. thee better after death	BROW 147:21
l. the highest when we	TENN 681:19
l. their land because it	HALL 322:5
love them which l. you	BIBLE 89:1
L. the night	DRYD 261:20
l. the precepts	FARQ 280:19
L. the sinner but hate the sin	AUG 37:8
l. the uppermost rooms	DIDLE 92:4
L.-thirty, love-forty	BETJ 68:6
l. those who love you	VOLT 716:14
L., thou art absolute sole Lord	CRAS 226:5
l. thy neighbour as thyself	BIBLE 73:3
L. thyself last	SHAK 589:1
l. to hatred turned	CONG 215:17
L. to the loveless shown	CROS 228:2
l. to those of the dying	LOWRY 431:3
l. up groweth with youre	CHAU 196:2
l. upon the honest square	BEHN 60:11
l. was but a school	WOTT 749:3
l. was passion's essence	BYRON 168:25
l. what thou dost love	HATCH 328:2
l. will be seen at its height	FORS 290:14
l. will change in growing	BRID 141:5
l. will yield to business	OVID 503:4
l. with a cold climate	SOUT 657:21
l. with himself at first	POW 528:2
l. with his fetters	BACON 42:16
L. without his wings	BYRON 172:15
l. without the rhetoric	STOP 670:3
l. with the productions	BLAKE 112:20
L. with unconfinèd wings	LOV 429:1
L. wol nat been constreyned	CHAU 193:13
l. your enemies, do good	BIBLE 94:6
l. your goodly gifts	SHAK 619:2
l. your neighbour's wife	MAC 434:20
L. you ten years before	MARV 451:2
make us l. one another	SWIFT 674:14
making l. all year round	BEAU 56:11
Man torn with l., with inward	GREV 318:6
man who is not worth my l.	WALK 717:11
man you l. to hate	ANON 16:8
means l. without marriage	CLARK 205:7
Men l. in haste, but they	BYRON 171:24
might love, loving to l.	AUG 36:22
more l. or more disdain	CAREW 179:9
more than over shoes in l.	SHAK 631:1
most important thing is l.	BREN 140:12
Most people experience l.	PAST 508:3
music be the food of l.	SHAK 628:9
My l. and I did meet	BETJ 67:16
My l. and I would lie	HOUS 352:10
My l. has died for me to-day	BALL 48:22
My l. is of a birth as rare	MARV 450:2
My l.'s a noble madness	DRYD 259:25
my L.'s like a red, red rose	BURNS 162:27
My l. to thee is sound	SHAK 599:8
My l. with no disguise	ROET 544:9
My song is l. unknown	CROS 228:2
Mysterious of connubial l.	MILT 471:14
My vegetable l. should grow	MARV 451:2
Need we say it was not l.	MILL 461:11
ne'er knew l.'s sad satiety	SHEL 643:18
never l. a stranger	BENS 64:1
new l. may b'	WALSH 720:17
No man is in l. when	BURN 100:10
None knew thee but to l. thee	HALL 322:6

love: (*cont.*):

none other I can l.	TENN 682:2
Now I know what L.	VIRG 715:5
Now what is l.?	RAL 535:13
Now with his l.	CHAU 193:23
obscure epistles of l.	SHAK 629:9
O cruel L., on thee I lay	LYLY 433:12
office and affairs of l.	SHAK 613:16
Of kindness and of l.	WORD 744:19
Of l. and all its smart	BEDD 58:8
Oh mighty l.!	HERB 335:11
O, if thou car'st not whom I l.	DONNE 251:3
O L.! has she done this	LYLY 433:9
O lyric L., half-angel	BROW 152:15
O my l. is slain	DONNE 250:14
Only l. can apprehend	RILKE 541:1
Only our l. hath no decay	DONNE 251:18
Only to l. is naturally mine	DRAY 257:19
Or l. in a golden bowl	BLAKE 111:11
Or l. me less, or love me more	GOD 308:8
or successful without l.	TROL 703:4
O spirit of l.! how quick	SHAK 628:9
our l. is here to stay	GERS 301:15
our l. repeating itself	MOT 487:1
Our l. shall live, and later	SPEN 659:11
O waly, waly, gin I be bonnie	BALL 51:2
oyster may be crossed in l.	SHER 644:25
Pains of l. be sweeter far	DRYD 261:35
pangs of disprized l.	SHAK 575:16
passing the l. of women	BIBLE 75:9
perfect ceremony of l.'s	SHAK 633:7
Perfect fear casteth out l.	CONN 216:2
perfect l. casteth out fear	BIBLE 105:28
Poets' food is l. and fame	SHEL 640:12
possible to l. without injury	GREE 317:5
presume too much upon my l.	SHAK 593:4
Prosperity's the very bond of l.	SHAK 632:11
proved thee my best of l.	SHAK 634:21
Regent of l. rhymes	SHAK 598:13
remembrance of my former l.	SHAK 631:5
renewing is of l.	EDW 267:11
right place for l.	FROST 294:11
right to dissemble your l.	BICK 108:19
right true end of l.	DONNE 250:11
salley gardens my l. and I	YEATS 751:11
same sweet eternity of l.	HERR 336:17
save the Party we l.	GAIT 296:16
See how l. and murder will out	CONG 215:4
separate us from the l. of God	BIBLE 100:1
sets l. a task	HUNT 356:7
sex with someone I l.	ALLEN 9:10
shackles of an old l.	TENN 682:3
She bid me take l. easy	YEATS 751:11
She looked at me as she did l.	KEATS 388:10
She never told her l.	SHAK 629:20
show out a flag and sign of l.	SHAK 614:25
sit down says L.	HERB 335:9
soft philosopher of l.	DRYD 260:35
So let us l., dear Love	SPEN 659:10
some are fou o' l. divine	BURNS 162:6
some l. but little policy	SHAK 621:6
sooner allured by l.	ASCH 30:18
So true a fool is l.	SHAK 633:19
sports of l.	JONS 379:10
stars and fate, to manage l.	BUTL 166:20
stony limits cannot hold l.	SHAK 622:31
substance of his house for l.	BIBLE 82:6
Such a morning it is when l.	LEE 415:19
Sweetest l., I do not go	DONNE 252:5
Sweet L. of youth, forgive	BRON 142:16
sweet l. seemed that April	BRID 141:5
take our fill of l.	BIBLE 78:16
Tell l. it is but lust	RAL 535:16
temple gates unto my l.	SPEN 659:15
that doesn't l. a wall	FROST 295:3
that l. could never change	BRID 141:5
that l. endures no tie	DRYD 261:10
That l. my friend	SHAK 592:15
That l. supports his reign	SMART 649:16
that they l.	WALL 718:19
There is l. of course	ANOU 23:5
There is no l.; there are only	AUDEN 04:17
There is no l. for such	HILL 00:17

love: (*cont.*):

There's a real l. of a lie	BROW 151:9
They l. the Good	BROO 143:14
They l. us for it, and we	TENN 688:8
This is the very ecstasy of l.	SHAK 574:10
this youth what 'tis to l.	SHAK 569:21
those who l. the Lord	HUNT 356:4
those who l. want wisdom	SHEL 642:11
though l. and beauty fail	ETH 278:19
Though lovers be lost l.	THOM 693:3
Thou hidden l. of God	WESL 728:16
Through l., through hope	WORD 747:15
thy l. is better than wine	BIBLE 81:5
Thy sweet converse and l.	MILT 472:26
To be wise and eke to l.	SPEN 660:25
To be wise, and l.	SHAK 627:17
To find the arms of my true l.	TENN 686:21
To let the warm l.	KEATS 390:1
To l. one maiden only	TENN 681:25
Too late came I to l. thee	AUG 37:2
To see her is to l. her	BURNS 161:12
To tell the laity our l.	DONNE 252:21
true l. hath my heart	SIDN 646:14
truth, unity, and godly l.	BOOK 121:22
turns to thoughts of l.	TENN 685:7
'Twixt women's l., and men's	DONNE 251:17
Use him as though you l. him	BLUN 116:3
want l.'s majesty	SHAK 621:15
wayward is this foolish l.	SHAK 631:3
We l., Fool, for the good	PATM 509:10
we l. our House of Peers	GILB 306:1
We men have got l. well	AMIS 1
We must l. one another or die	AUDEN
we one jot of former l. retain	DRAY
What is commonly called l.	FIF ..12
What is L.?	SH 644:9
what is l.! a pretty thing	GREE 317:11
What is l.? 'tis not hereafter	SHAK 629:4
What l. I bore to thee	WORD 744:14
What's death? You'll l. me yet	BROW 151:29
What thing is l.	PEELE 511:3
What will survive of us is l.	LARK 409:13
When l. congeals	HART 327:11
When l., converted from	SHAK 633:15
When l. grows diseased	ETH 278:17
When l. is liberty	POPE 519:19
Where l. is enthroned	SHAK 629:13
Where l. rules	JUNG 383:1
where there is no l.	BACON 43:21
while woman wakes to l.	TENN 682:12
who does not l. Scotland	JOHN 368:12
who lost the world for l.	DRYD 261:11
Whom the gods l. die young	BYRON 171:9
whom they no longer l.	FORS 290:11
wilder shores of l.	BLAN 115:1
will not l. his country	SHAK 592:4
Wilt thou l. her	BOOK 123:19
Withouten l. is worth	CHAU 195:15
with the innocence of l.	SHAK 629:16
with this lost l. of mine	SCOTT 560:7
woman's l. for us increases	PUSH 532:15
Wonder hinders l. and hate	GREV 318:5
Work is l. made visible	GIBR 303:3
You all did l. him once	SHAK 592:9
You cannot call it l.	SHAK 577:13
your true l.'s coming	SHAK 629:4
loved: better to have l. and lost	BUTL 166:28
better to have l. and lost	TENN 683:12
disciple whom Jesus l.	BIBLE 98:3
for she l. much	BIBLE 94:8
God so l. the world	BIBLE 96:15
heart that has truly l.	MOORE 483:2
holy l. by the gods	PLATO 516:10
idols I have l. so long	FITZ 284:15
I have l. him too much	RAC 535:1
I l. a lass, a fair one	WITH 739:14
I l. Ophelia	SHAK 578:29
I l. thee once	AYT 41:1
I l. you, so I drew these	LAWR 413:6
I saw and l.	GIBB 302:14
it can be l.	SANT 555:20
I wish I l. the Human Race	RAL 536:12
left than never to have been l.	CONG 215:31

loved: (*cont.*):

l. by a girl whom he almost TROL 703:25
l. each other beyond belief HEINE 331:1
l. passing well SHAK 575:3
l. the bailiff's daughter BALL 48:20
l. the doctrine DEFOE 234:15
l. which is the real curse RHYS 539:19
men who have l. them TROL 704:5
Might she have l. me BROW 150:22
most l., despised SHAK 594:24
Not that I l. Caesar less SHAK 592:2
our endeavour be so l. SHAK 628:8
Out upon it, I have l. SUCK 671:9
prince to be feared than l. MACH 438:8
Shall never be by woman l. BLAKE 111:4
She who has never l. GAY 299:27
Solomon l. many strange BIBLE 75:26
sour to them that l. SHAK 589:10
that l. not at first sight MARL 447:10
that l. not at first sight SHAK 569:15
therefore must be l. SHAK 626:22
they above love to be l. SIDN 646:17
time and the place and the l. one
BROW 151:13
time to l., and a time to hate BIBLE 80:5
To have l., to have thought ARN 27:3
Twice or thrice had I l. thee DONNE 251:16
use him as though you l. him WALT 721:7
we l. of him should SHEL 639:18
We l., sir—used to meet BROW 149:9
We that had l. him BROW 151:1
what thou and I did till we l. DONNE 252:4
Whilst loving thou mayst l. be SPEN 660:6
who l. well BROW 151:16
who never l. before ANON 22:6
love-in-idleness: maidens call it, L.
SHAK 611:17
love-knot: l. into her long black NOYES 497:5
loveless: Love to the l. shown CROS 228:2
loveliness: feature of l. and perfection
MILT 475:9
For l. needs not foreign THOM 696:8
Glory and l. have passed away KEATS 390:26
He is a portion of the l. SHEL 640:3
Her l. I never knew COL 209:6
I am weak from your l. BETJ 68:6
Its l. increases; it will never KEATS 386:13
l. and the hour of my death KEATS 392:9
Of dim and solitary l. BYRON 172:18
That fashioned forth its l. HARDY 325:11
that is a miracle of l. GILB 305:6
Traditional sanctity and l. YEATS 751:5
woman of so shining l. YEATS 753:4
lovely: And l. is the rose WORD 745:10
As you are known, so be l. GRAV 314:22
Claude's landscape all is l. CONS 217:24
he is altogether l. BIBLE 81:20
How l. is thy dwelling-place SCOT 561:9
It gives a l. light MILL 461:7
left thee all her l. hues DAV 232:11
Look thy last on all things l. DE L 236:2
L. and willing every afternoon AUDEN 35:2
l. April of her prime SHAK 633:2
L. enchanting language HERB 335:4
more l. and more temperate SHAK 633:6
Oh what a l. war LITT 423:10
Saul and Jonathan were l. BIBLE 75:9
That they might l. be CROS 228:2
To be a l. and a fearful thing BYRON 170:22
whatsoever things are l. BIBLE 103:13
When l. woman stoops to folly GOLD 311:33
Which once he made more l. SHEL 640:3
woods are l. FROST 295:13
You have l. eyes CHEK 197:7
your complexion, l. boy VIRG 714:15
love-making: l., or wooing BACON 45:2
love powders: rogue gives you L. LAMB 407:1
love-quarrels: L. oft in pleasing concord end
MILT 474:11
lover: abhor, too, the roaming l. CALL 175:7
affliction taught a l. POPE 519:20
Beauty is the l.'s gift CONG 215:34
change your L. for a friend ETH 278:19

lover: (*cont.*):

days dividing lover and l. SWIN 675:22
has done the l. mortal hurt DOUG 255:13
injured l.'s hell . MILT 471:25
I sighed as a l. GIBB 302:15
It was a l. and his lass SHAK 569:23
Jesu, l. of my soul WESL 728:6
l. and killer are mingled DOUG 255:13
l. of a sinful man MAL 443:13
l.'s eyes will gaze SHAK 598:20
l., sighing like a furnace SHAK 568:16
l.'s quarrel with the world FROST 295:2
l. true for whom WHIT 732:20
l. weight and fashion JONS 379:14
l. without indiscretion HARDY 324:8
lunatic, the l., and the poet SHAK 612:17
magnetic, peripatetic L. GILB 305:18
my fause l. stole my rose BURNS 161:11
propositions of a l. SHAK 569:5
Scratch a l., and find a foe PARK 506:4
she was a true l. MAL 443:10
since I cannot prove a l. SHAK 621:16
Such a constant l. SUCK 671:9
thou wast as true a l. SHAK 568:3
Unwearied still, l. by lover YEATS 753:20
what is left of a l. ROWL 549:8
Who could deceive a l. VIRG 713:5
Wine, not water, binds the l. SANS 555:14
with some old l.'s ghost DONNE 252:10
woman says to her lusting l. CAT 186:10
woman loves her l. BYRON 170:23
Your brother and his l. SHAK 605:9
lovers: All lovers young SHAK 571:16
And make two l. happy POPE 523:10
At l.' perjuries SHAK 623:1
Came two young l. lately wed TENN 685:1
Frankie and Albert were l. ANON 13:11
Journeys end in l. meeting SHAK 629:4
laughs at l.' perjury DRYD 261:10
let all l., rich in triumph CAMP 177:4
l.' absent hours SHAK 617:5
l. cannot see SHAK 608:11
L. can see to do their SHAK 623:16
l. find their peace FLEC 286:10
l. fled away into the storm KEATS 387:12
l. run into strange capers SHAK 568:5
l. scorn whom that love SIDN 646:17
L., to bed; 'tis almost SHAK 612:26
old l. are soundest WEBS 725:26
pair of star-crossed l. SHAK 622:17
sleepless l., just at twelve POPE 523:16
such as I am all true l. SHAK 629:13
though l. be lost love shall not THOM 693:3
Thy l. were all untrue DRYD 261:21
What need l. wish for more SEDL 561:17
loves: all she l. is love BYRON 170:23
And our l., must I remember APOL 23:15
A-waiting for their ain dear l. BALL 50:12
believe the baggage l. me CONG 215:19
die to that which one l. HAR 323:8
faithful l. shall moralize SPEN 659:19
faults are such that one l. GOLD 311:16
For who l. that, must first MILT 474:23
grete god of L. name CHAU 194:28
Hated by one he l. SHAK 593:8
have reigned with your l. ELIZ 274:4
He l. us not SHAK 604:4
He that l. a rosy cheek CAREW 179:2
I l. the fox less SURT 672:11
l. around her on the deep BYRON 172:13
l. me must have a touch of TENN 681:31
l. nothing but himself SOUT 657:18
l. to hear himself talk SHAK 623:10
l. what he is good at SHAD 563:16
l. what he knows CROM 227:6
man kills the thing he l. WILDE 736:1
Our l. into corpses or wives SWIN 676:12
solace ourselves with l. BIBLE 78:16
so l. oblique may well MARV 450:3
There is no creature l. me SHAK 622:12
truly l. on to the close MOORE 483:2
What nedeth feynede l. CHAU 196:2
white woman whom nobody l. CORN 219:4

lovesick: winds were l. SHAK 565:5
lovesome: garden is a l. thing BROWN 145:2
lovest: l. thou me more than these BIBLE 97:40
love story: l. or an elopement DOYLE 256:17
loveth: Lord l. he chasteneth BIBLE 104:18
Lord l. he correcteth BIBLE 78:7
l. another hath fulfilled BIBLE 100:9
l. not knoweth not God BIBLE 105:27
prayeth well, who l. well COL 211:17
sought him whom my soul l. BIBLE 81:12
loving: For l., and for saying so DONNE 252:19
heart be still as l. BYRON 173:6
I ain't had no l. NORW 497:2
l. himself better COL 211:26
l. longest, when existence AUST 39:7
l. the land that has taught MOORE 482:18
l. thou mayst lovèd be SPEN 660:6
l. to love AUG 36:22
most l. mere folly SHAK 568:17
perfectly sore with l. DICK 240:22
wickedness that hinders l. BROW 151:16
loving-kindness: l. and mercy shall follow
BOOK 125:15
low: As l. as where this earth ROSS 547:16
brought l. for you METH 458:16
cast one's eyes so l. SHAK 597:1
condescend to men of l. estate BIBLE 100:5
dost thou lie so l. SHAK 591:18
exalted them of l. degree BIBLE 93:23
Had me l. and had me down GERS 301:11
hum of that l. land ARN 28:17
l. estate of his handmaiden BIBLE 93:22
l. life was the level's BROW 149:26
l. man seeks a little thing BROW 150:1
l. on whom assurance sits ELIOT 273:9
l. raise and support MILT 467:21
Malice is of a l. stature HAL 321:15
man who has a l. opinion of TROL 703:22
Seem to murmur sweet and l. ARMS 26:5
Sweet and l., sweet and low TENN 687:27
Too l. for envy, for contempt COWL 221:11
upper station of l. life DEFOE 234:6
Whose life in l. estate began TENN 683:25
with l. sounds by the shore YEATS 752:8
lowbrow: first militant l. BERL 66:3
Lowells: L. talk to the Cabots BOSS 137:1
lower: l. orders don't set a good example
WILDE 734:9
l. organs of the Party ANON 16:5
l. than the angels BOOK 124:20
l. than vermin BEVAN 68:13
lowering: once a l. day GOOGE 312:11
lowest: l. and most dejected thing SHAK 596:23
shame to take the l. room BIBLE 94:26
lowlands: As she sails by the L. low BALL 49:10
Ye Highlands and ye L. BALL 49:2
lowliness: l. become mine inner clothing
LITT 423:9
l. is young ambition's SHAK 590:14
obedience and incense of l. MONS 480:2
True l. of heart LITT 423:9
lowly: As in the l. air GILB 304:9
be l. wise MILT 472:12
I am meek and l. BIBLE 90:28
lowness: l. is unsafe as height MARV 451:11
loyal: Lousy but l. ANON 16:3
L. and neutral, in a moment SHAK 602:18
loyalties: Impossible l. ARN 29:15
l. which centre upon number CHUR 203:4
loyalty: I want l. JOHN 367:11
L. is the Tory's secret weapon KILM 396:4
l. we all feel to unhappiness GREE 316:25
sovereign which constitute l. BOSW 137:6
That learned body wanted l. TRAPP 702:3
Lucasta: L. that bright northern star
LOV 428:19
my L. might I crave LOV 429:5
lucem: *sed ex fumo dare l.* HOR 347:12
lucent: l. as a rounded moon LOW 430:1
lucid: l. intervals and happy BACON 45:10
make a l. interval DRYD 261:1
Not in the l. intervals of life WORD 743:12

lucid: (cont.):
  with frequent l. intervals   CERV 188:12
Lucifer: he falls like L.   SHAK 588:19
  L. that often warned them   MILT 467:4
  O L., son of the morning   BIBLE 83:5
  starred night Prince L.   MER 458:6
luck: but it is l.   FORS 290:18
  have wished you good l.   BOOK 133:17
  just my l. to get one perfect   PARK 506:9
  l. and sends his son   STEAD 662:13
  l. of our name lost   HOR 350:14
  l. was his light-o'-love   SERV 563:8
  nae l. about the house   MICK 459:10
lucky: man's l. if he gets out   LEON 236:14
  supposed it l. to be born   WHIT 732:15
lucrative: so l. to cheat   CLOU 207:19
lucro: dierum cumque dabit l.   HOR 349:7
Lucy: When L. ceased   WORD 747:18
Ludlow: their hundreds to L.   HOUS 352:11
Luftwaffe: With your L.   PLATH 516:4
lug: l. the guts into the neighbour room
     SHAK 577:25
lugere: non l., neque detestare   SPIN 661:3
lugete: L., O Veneres Cupidinesque   CAT 185:13
lugger: forcing her on board the l.   JOHN 377:15
lukewarm: because thou art l.   BIBLE 106:7
lukewarmness: L. I account a sin   COWL 221:15
lullaby: And I will sing a l.   DEKK 235:11
  Once in a l.   HARB 323:13
lulled: l. with sound of sweetest   SHAK 583:11
lumber: learned l. in his head   POPE 521:24
  l. of the schools   SWIFT 674:30
  l. room of his library   DOYLE 256:6
lumen: l. de lumine   MISS 476:22
luminous: Dong with a L. Nose   LEAR 414:1
  l. home of waters opens   ARN 28:18
  void his l. wings   ARN 29:21
lump: A l. bred up in darkness   KYD 404:14
  leaveneth the whole l.   BIBLE 100:21
  L. the whole thing   TWAIN 706:13
  poor in a l. is bad   TENN 687:13
lumps: Go down like l. of lead   HODG 340:18
  There are l. in it   STEP 663:19
luna: inferebantur sol et l.   AUG 36:23
lunae: Tacitae per amica silentia l.   VIRG 712:16
lunatic: l. asylums known as the stately
  homes of England   WOOLF 742:4
  l. fringe in all reform   ROOS 546:13
  l., the lover, and the poet   SHAK 612:17
lunatics: asylum run by l.   LLOY 424:12
  l. have taken charge   ROWL 549:11
lunch: for life, not for l.   ANON 15:3
  no such thing as a free l.   ANON 18:14
  she's unable to l. today   PORT 525:3
  took the cork out of my l.   FIFL 282:21
luncheon: At l. with a city friend   BELL 61:22
  Breakfast, supper, dinner, l.   BROW 151:27
  do not take soup at l.   CURZ 229:7
lungs: dangerous to the l.   JAM 361:17
  l. began to crow like   SHAK 568:13
  l. of the tobacconist   JONS 378:10
  parks are the l. of London   PITT 515:13
Lupercal: On the L. I thrice   SHAK 592:8
lupus: L. est homo homini   PLAU 517:3
lurcher: half l. and half cur   COWP 224:2
lurching: L. to rag-time tunes   SASS 557:5
lure: l. it back to cancel half   FITZ 284:9
  l. this tassel-gentle back   SHAK 623:6
luscious: canopied with l. woodbine
     SHAK 611:19
  l. clusters of the vine   MARV 450:9
Lushington: Here's to thee, L.   AUBR 33:1
lusisti: L. satis, edisti satis   HOR 348:21
lust: Delight of l. is gross   PETR 513:15
  Die L. der Zerstörung   BAK 47:22
  horrible that l. and rage   YEATS 753:9
  I'm feeb'd wi' fleshly l.   BURNS 162:7
  In different bouts of l.   SHAK 609:16
  into ashes all my l.   MARV 451:3
  Is l. in action   SHAK 635:1
  light of human l.   HARV 14:17
  love is more cruel than l.   SWIN 670:12
  l., and fleshly seeming   MARS 449:10

lust: (cont.):
  l. of knowing what should   FLEC 286:11
  l. of my mistress's heart   SHAK 596:9
  l. of the goat is the bounty   BLAKE 112:24
  Men, when they l.   GREE 317:10
  narrowing l. of gold   TENN 684:11
  Palate, the hutch of tasty l.   HOPK 345:13
  something generous in mere l.   ROCH 543:10
  Tell love it is but l.   RAL 535:16
lusteth: that l. to live   BOOK 126:15
lustily: sing praises l. unto
  him   BOOK 126:11
lustings: l. out of man are taken   GREV 318:6
lustre: obscure in the exceed-
  ing l.   SHEL 641:3
  Though changed in out-
  ward l.   MILT 468:4
  Where is thy l. now   SHAK 596:22
lusts: Abstain from fleshly l.   BIBLE 105:12
  fulfil the l. thereof   BIBLE 100:11
  l. of your father   BIBLE.96:33
  My l. they do me leave   VAUX 709:12
  sinful l. of the flesh   BOOK 123:4
  To serve our present l.   WITH 739:13
lust'st: l. to use her in that
  kind   SHAK 597:7
lusty: l. leas, forlorn   SACK 552:12
  l. life away she leaps   VAUX 709:12
  l. stealth of nature take   SHAK 594:26
  Of l. folk   CHAU 194:23
  young and l. as an eagle   BOOK 132:3
lute: As bright Apollo's l.   SHAK 598:20
  lascivious pleasing of a l.   SHAK 621:15
  little rift within the l.   TENN 682:10
  l. and harp   BOOK 128:16
  merry harp with the l.   BOOK 130:14
  Orpheus with his l. made
  trees   SHAK 588:15
  or the l. its tones   KEATS 386:16
  When the l. is broken   SHEL 641:6
  When to her l. Corinna sings   CAMP 177:5
lutes: l. of amber   HERR 337:10
Luther: genius in religion—L.   ARN 30:5
  Grand rough old Martin L.   BROW 153:12
Lutheran: A spleeny L.   SHAK 588:17
lux: et l. perpetua luceat   MISS 477:10
luxe: L., calme et volupté   BAUD 55:9
luxuriant: L. song   YEATS 751:17
luxuries: Give us the l. of life   MOTL 487:4
  were necessities and which l.   WRIG 749:10
luxurious: l. mountain goat   SHAK 586:12
luxury: all the l. of the world   YEATS 751:17
  doth snort in fat-fed l.   MARS 449:10
  He tried the l. of doing good   CRAB 225:7
  languages is mainly a l.   BRIG 141:13
  Literature is a l.   CHES 199:14
  Love is like any other l.   TROL 704:10
  l., peace and sensual   BAUD 55:9
  l. the accomplished sofa last   COWP 223:16
  l. was lavished on you   ORTON 499:14
  private and costly l.   ADAMS 2:18
  their l. was doing good   GARTH 298:14
  They knew l.   MAC 434:13
  To trust people is a l.   FORS 290:9
Lycidas: For L. is dead   MILT 465:20
  So L. sunk low, but mounted   MILT 466:13
lying: been l. till noon   JOHN 370:25
  be listening, in wait   THOM 694:4
  express l. or falsehood   SWIFT 673:15
  l., and slandering   BOOK 123:4
  l. awake with a dismal   GILB 304:14
  l. days of my youth   YEATS 751:4
  One of you is l.   PARK 506:12
  smallest amount of l.   BUTL 166:27
  this vice of l.   SHAK 583:21
  this world is given to l.   SHAK 582:9
Lyme: was an old man of L.   MONK 479:18
Lyonnesse: When I set out for L.   HARDY 326:3
lyre: Make me thy l.   SHEL 641:19
  Una more 'is bloomin' l.   KIPL 401:10
lyres: turn to rhythmic l.   HARDY 326:2
  With laughter, me among the l. poets
     HOR 348:24

M

ma: M.'s out, Pa's out   FLAN 285:11
Mab: This is M.   JONS 378:17
Macaroni: And called it M.   ANON 20:1
MacArthur: didn't fire him [General M.]
     TRUM 704:20
Macaulay: apostle of the Philistines, M.
     ARN 29:19
  [M.] has occasional flashes   SMITH 653:17
  [M.] is like a book in breeches   SMITH 653:16
  M. is well for a while   CARL 181:15
Macavity: M. WASN'T THERE   ELIOT 272:12
Macbeth: Brave M.   SHAK 599:15
  M. does murder sleep   SHAK 602:2
  M. shall never vanquished   SHAK 604:3
  M. shall sleep no more   SHAK 602:3
  Shall harm M.   SHAK 603:21
  There to meet with M.   SHAK 599:13
Macduff: Lay on, M.   SHAK 605:4
  M. was from his mother's   SHAK 605:3
mace: fool's bauble, the m.   CROM 227:11
Macedonia: Come over into M.   BIBLE 98:25
macerations: Made way for m.   POUND 526:14
Macheath: jack-knife has M.   BREC 140:3
Machiavel: murderous M.   SHAK 588:3
machine: body is a m. for living   TOLS 701:1
  Ghost in the M.   RYLE 552:10
  house is a m. for living   LE C 415:12
  I have tested your m.   TREE 702:7
  ingenious m. for turning   DIN 246:10
  m. for converting the Heathen   CARL 180:15
  m. slipping from our hands   LOW 430:19
  very pulse of the m.   WORD 747:19
  You're not a man, you're a m.   SHAW 635:24
machinery: dynamo in the m. of the night
     GINS 306:28
  It is the Age of M.   CARL 180:14
  [Our] whole political m.   BALF 48:17
  whole m. of the State   BROU 144:7
machines: M. for making more machines
     BOTT 137:11
  m. think but whether men do   SKIN 649:5
  we are their survival m.   DAWK 233:1
macht: Arbeit m. frei   ANON 21:9
  die M. den Vorrang hat   JUNG 383:1
Mächte: ihr himmlischen M.   GOET 309:15
mackerel: m. of the sea   BALL 49:16
  Not so the m.   FRERE 293:16
mackintosh: bit of black m.   WELBY 726:21
mad: All poets are m.   BURT 164:19
  almost m. with ecstasy   TRAH 701:14
  And in one word, heroically m.   DRYD 259:14
  And makes men m.   SHAK 618:8
  bad glad m. brother's   SWIN 676:6
  better than when I am m.   KYD 404:13
  Channel in the m. March days   MAS 453:3
  destroy He first sends m.   DUP 264:8
  go m. they shall be sane   THOM 693:3
  half of the nation is m.   SMOL 653:33
  house for fools and m.   SWIFT 675:13
  How m. I am, sad I am   BETJ 68:6
  How sad and bad and m. it was   BROW 149:9
  In being m., which none but   DRYD 261:27
  it will make you m.   SHAK 592:12
  learning doth make thee m.   BIBLE 99:10
  let me not be m.   SHAK 595:11
  M. about the boy   COW 220:13
  m. all are in God's keeping   KIPL 402:5
  m. and savage master   SOPH 656:15
  m. as the vexed sea   SHAK 596:31
  M., bad, and dangerous to know   LAMB 406:2
  m. dog of the Middle East   REAG 537:14
  M. dogs and Englishmen   COW 220:14
  made me m. all my life   JOHN 370:26
  Made us nobly wild, not m.   HERR 336:20
  M.-eyed from staring   WILB 734:1
  m. north-north-west   SHAK 575:1
  m. that loves in the tameness   SHAK 596:18
  m. till you have your mistresses   VANB 708:3
  M. world! Mad kings   SHAK 593:29

MADAM MAJORITY

mad: (*cont.*):
Make m. the guilty SHAK 575:9
man is m., Sir BYRON 173:22
men that God made m. CHES 198:28
O fool! I shall go m. SHAK 595:18
old, m., blind, despised SHEL 643:7
or less m. on one point KIPL 402:7
sense that the world was m. SAB 552:11
some believed him m. BEAT 56:4
tho' some did count him m. BUNY 156:12
to make poor females m. SHAK 612:7
We all are born m. BECK 57:28
Went m. and bit the man GOLD 310:23
when a heroine goes m. SHER 644:24
Whom the m. would destroy LEVIN 420:6
madam: M. I may not call you ELIZ 274:14
madame: m.! truly it's not right CRANE 225:22
maddest: m. merriest day TENN 687:7
madding: Far from the m. crowd GRAY 315:17
made: All things were m. by him BIBLE 95:36
almost m. for each other SMITH 652:27
Begotten, not m. BOOK 121:19
Dost thou know who m. thee BLAKE 113:21
earth and the world were m. BOOK 130:22
fearfully and wonderfully m. BOOK 134:20
it is he that hath m. us BOOK 131:17
knoweth whereof we are m. BOOK 132:5
M. with our hands and our lips SWIN 676:3
mind is not a bed to be m. AGATE 5:14
see God m. and eaten all BROW 148:18
That man was m. to mourn BURNS 162:18
Who hath m. heaven and earth BOOK 123:11
who m. the Lamb make thee BLAKE 114:15
Who m. you? God made me CAT 185:6
Why hast thou m. me thus BIBLE 100:2
Madeira: Have Some M., M'dear FLAN 285:9
madeleine: little crumb of m. PROU 530:7
mademoiselle: M. from Armenteers ANON 16:6
madhouse: in a m. there exists no law CLARE 204:20
You don't want m. EMPS 277:19
madhouses: M., prisons CLARE 204:18
madman: m. shakes a dead geranium ELIOT 272:14
m. were to come into this room JOHN 374:13
Victor Hugo was a m. COCT 208:9
madmen: by m., heretics ZAMY 755:4
join the fashionable m. DID 246:1
M. in authority, who hear KEYN 395:10
m. is a saint run mad POPE 522:29
They were m. REN 539:2
which none but m. know DRYD 261:27
madness: accounted his life m. BIBLE 87:3
And moon-struck m. MILT 473:6
Doth work like m. in the brain COL 209:10
end despondency and m. WORD 747:11
Even to m. SHAK 615:22
For that fine m. still DRAY 258:4
from the cruel m. of love TENN 686:9
generation destroyed by m. GINS 306:28
Great wits are sure to m. DRYD 259:1
His flight was m. SHAK 604:3
If this be not love, it is m. CONG 215:22
Ireland has her m. AUDEN 34:14
m. is the glory of this SHAK 626:9
M.! madness! FOR 289:17
M. need not be all breakdown LAING 405:19
m. of many for the gain POPE 524:1
m. of the people BOOK 129:1
m. or hope? BLOK 115:5
m. their kings commit HOR 348:2
m. wherein now he raves SHAK 574:17
midsummer m. SHAK 630:21
My love's a noble m. DRYD 259:25
rest is the m. of art JAMES 363:1
sort of m. [Bolshevism] SMITH 651:12
Such harmonious m. SHEL 643:20
that way m. lies SHAK 596:5
Though this be m. SHAK 574:23
Through cells of m. TENN 687:3
till m. strike thee dead LYLY 433:12
To define true m. SHAK 574:12
madonna: motorcycle black m. DYLAN 265:14
madrigal: descant on Rawthey's m. BUNT 155:9
woeful stuff this m. is POPE 521:19
madrigals: Melodious birds sing m. MARL 447:18
Maenad: Of some fierce M. SHEL 641:15
maestro: *Il m. di color che sanno* DANTE 230:10
magazines: graves of little m. PRES 528:14
Magdalen: fourteen months at M. College GIBB 302:10
maggot: full of m. ostentation SHAK 599:7
know how to create a m. MONT 481:9
m. must be born i' the ELIOT 268:16
maggot-pies: m. and choughs SHAK 603:13
magic: house rose like m. HARG 326:9
If this be m., let it be an art SHAK 632:17
let in daylight upon m. BAG 47:7
lost in the m. of a kiss WASH 722:4
m. in a pint bottle DICK 241:4
m. shadow-show FITZ 284:5
mistake medicine for m. SZASZ 677:15
rough m. SHAK 626:1
secret m. of numbers BROW 146:5
That old black m. MERC 457:15
there's m. in the web of it SHAK 617:3
what mighty m. SHAK 614:31
magical: purely m. object BART 54:18
Maginn: bright, broken M. LOCK 425:16
magistrate: anything that shocks the m. RUSS 551:23
Between the muse and the m. FOOTE 288:16
m. corruptible ROB 542:4
magistrates: like m., correct at home SHAK 584:22
magistri: *iurare in verba m.* HOR 347:20
magna: *M. est veritas* BIBLE 108:18
Magna Charta: M. is such a fellow COKE 209:4
magnanimity: In all the m. of thought YOUNG 754:17
In victory: m. CHUR 203:3
M. in politics is not seldom BURKE 158:1
magnet: Can m. ever attract GILB 305:18
gunpowder, and the m. BACON 45:21
magnetic: m., peripatetic lover GILB 305:18
magnificat: *M. anima mea Dominum* BIBLE 108:9
magnificent: Lived in his mild and m. eye BROW 151:1
Mute and m., without a tear DRYD 261:29
magnifico: *atque omne ignotum pro m. est* TAC 677:19
magnifique: *m., mais ce n'est pas* BOSQ 136:19
magnify: m. him for ever BOOK 118:17
My soul doth m. the Lord BIBLE 93:22
My soul doth m. the Lord BIBLE 108:9
we laud and m. thy glorious BOOK 122:10
we m. thee BOOK 118:14
worthily m. thy holy Name BOOK 121:16
magnis: *parva licet componere m.* VIRG 715:19
magnus: *M. ab integro saeclorum* VIRG 714:22
magpie: swollen m. in a fitful sun POUND 527:8
Maguire: M. and his men KAV 386:3
Mahomet: M. will go to the hill BACON 42:31
maid: fair pretty m. ANON 17:6
I once was a m. BURNS 162:11
Kitty, a fair, but frozen m. GARR 298:10
likewise the m. in the kitchen COWP 224:18
m. forget her ornaments BIBLE 85:3
m. is mine JOHN 377:15
m. is not dead BIBLE 90:10
m. not vendible SHAK 607:8
m. ov all maïdens BARN 53:15
m. sing in the valley below ANON 12:34
m. whom there were none WORD 747:18
many a youth, and many a m. MILT 465:13
no differ, being a m. MAC 434:5
old m. is like death FERB 281:8
or neglected m. LEAP 413:16
She could not live a m. PEELE 511:4
this virtuous m. SHAK 606:3
way of a man with a m. BIBLE 79:33
way of a man with a m. KIPL 399:17
maid: (*cont.*):
Where's the m. whose lip KEATS 387:19
Whether a m. so tender SHAK 614:28
Yonder a m. and her wight HARDY 325:10
maiden: god pursuing, the m. hid SWIN 675:23
In m. meditation SHAK 611:17
Is as the m.'s organ SHAK 628:16
m. blush bepaint my cheek SHAK 622:32
m. never bold SHAK 614:31
m. of bashful fifteen SHER 645:18
m. she lived with no other POE 517:17
m. whom the angels name POE 518:7
pursued m. and clasped SHEL 640:17
To love one m. only TENN 681:25
undergo such m. pilgrimage SHAK 610:20
maidenly: So m., womanly SKEL 649:1
maidens: And all the m. pretty COLM 214:1
And lang, lang may the m. sit BALL 50:12
Conserved of m.' hearts SHAK 617:3
What m. loth KEATS 388:24
Young men and m. BOOK 135:15
maids: If seven m. with seven mops CARR 183:1
Immortal youth to mortal m. LAND 408:5
m. are May when they SHAK 569:18
m. strange seraphic pieces TRAH 701:15
Most incident to m. SHAK 632:4
Nastys or fine ladies' m. HUGH 354:9
Three little m. from school GILB 304:23
when m. lie on their backs SHAK 622:22
maidservant: nor thy m. BIBLE 72:16
maidservants: M. getting instructed in the 'ologies' CARL 180:30
mail: fashion, like a rusty m. SHAK 627:20
mailed: seen the m. lobster rise FRERE 293:17
maimed: m., and the halt BIBLE 94:31
M. us at the start YEATS 752:19
main: Into the m. of waters SHAK 610:4
To be lost evermore in the m. TENN 689:6
mainspring: m. of civilised society SMIL 650:8
maintain: m. mine own ways BIBLE 77:20
maior: *M. erat natu* LUC 431:11
M. privato visus dum privatus TAC 678:3
Maisie: Proud M. is in the wood SCOTT 560:22
maison: *m. est une machine-à-habiter* LE C 415:12
maize: olive, aloe, and m. TENN 680:19
with Plenty in the m. TENN 688:15
majesté: *m. des souffrances humaines* VIGNY 711:11
majestic: But m. river floated ARN 28:17
Deliberate speed, m. instancy THOM 695:2
m. equality of the law FRAN 292:7
M. though in ruin MILT 469:18
majestical: laid in bed m. SHAK 586:8
majesty: appearance of Your M. BIBLE 69:19
as his m. is, so is his money BIBLE 87:9
full of the M. of thy Glory BOOK 118:12
his m. our sovereign lord ANON 20:2
Ride on! ride on in m. MILM 462:7
right hand of the M. BIBLE 104:10
sight so touching in its m. WORD 743:9
This earth of m. SHAK 619:18
Thy M. how bright FABER 279:12
want love's m. SHAK 621:15
major: from m. to minor PORT 524:22
Ground control to M. Tom BOWIE 138:15
M. Major HELL 331:7
major-general: very model of a modern M. GILB 306:9
majorities: Wisdom goes by m. MER 457:27
majority: big enough m. in any town TWAIN 706:4
Death joins us to the great m. YOUNG 755:1
God is always in the m. KNOX 403:3
great silent m. NIXON 496:3
join the m. [the dead] PETR 513:12
m. are wrong DEBS 233:12
m. happen to like WHIT 731:13
m. is always the best repartee DISR 248:31
m. never has right IBSEN 359:1
minority to the m. LENIN 417:6
self-indulgent m. STEP 663:15
though the will of the m. JEFF 364:3

majority: (*cont.*):
To her divine M. — DICK 244:17
majors: scarlet M. at the Base — SASS 557:4
make: Go ahead, m. my day — FINK 282:24
king may m. a nobleman — BURKE 159:26
lest he should m. an end — JONS 380:10
m. his sword to approach — BIBLE 78:2
M. IT NEW — POUND 526:5
M. me a clean heart — BOOK 128:6
M. mouths upon me — SHAK 612:4
m. myself laugh at everything — BEAU 56:10
m. the most of what we — FITZ 283:18
m. thine own — ARN 27:10
M. yourself necessary — EMER 276:15
Scotsman on the m. — BARR 54:13
We cannot m. events — ADAMS 3:8
You cannot m. him out at all — BELL 61:18
maker: before the Lord our M. — BOOK 131:10
be more pure than his m. — BIBLE 77:11
m. is hymself ybeten — CHAU 195:9
M. of heaven and earth — BOOK 119:1
M. of heaven and earth — BOOK 121:19
M.'s image through — DRYD 258:17
meet my M. brow to brow — CORN 219:2
striveth with his m. — BIBLE 84:3
that sinneth before his M. — BIBLE 87:34
whose m. and builder is God — BIBLE 104:14
makes: m. me or fordoes me — SHAK 618:4
man who m. no mistakes — PHEL 513:17
makest: What m. thou — BIBLE 84:3
making: Holland take pleasure in m. — ANON 12:21
m. the world safe for hypocrisy — WOLFE 741:5
There came to the m. of man — SWIN 675:24
makings: royal m. of a queen — SHAK 589:3
makyng: Inglissh in m. was the beste — LYDG 433:3
mal: *connaître tout le m. qu'il fait* — LA R 410:18
mala: *Usque ad m.* — HOR 351:2
malady: love's a m. without a cure — DRYD 261:9
m. of not marking — SHAK 582:18
male: impulse of the m. — LAWR 412:6
M. and female created he them — BIBLE 69:25
M. and the female — BIBLE 70:26
m. of the species — LAWR 412:14
more deadly than the m. — KIPL 399:3
true m. never yet walked — WICK 733:16
Ye Lilies m.! — CRAB 224:21
malecontents: loiterers and m. — SHAK 598:13
malefactions: proclaimed their m. — SHAK 575:13
males: Nothing but m. — SHAK 601:8
malesuada: *Metus et m. Fames* — VIRG 713:14
Malherbe: At last came M. — BOIL 117:2
malheurs: *tableau des m.* — VOLT 716:12
mali: *Non ignara m. miseris succurrere* — VIRG 712:11
malice: leaven of m. — BOOK 120:17
m., and all uncharitableness — BOOK 119:17
M. is of a low stature — HAL 321:15
m. mingled with a little wit — DRYD 260:24
m., to breed causes — JONS 379:12
Nor set down aught in m. — SHAK 618:20
When fortune's m. — BROW 149:14
With m. toward none — LINC 422:9
Yet m. never was his aim — SWIFT 675:12
malicious: God is subtle but he is not m. — EINS 268:1
malignant: only part of Randolph that was not m. — WAUGH 724:9
malignity: motiveless m. — COL 212:5
with a m. truly diabolical — BURKE 159:14
Mall: Mistress M.'s picture — SHAK 628:14
mallard: swapping m. — ANON 18:9
mallecho: this is miching m. — SHAK 576:14
malmesey: drowned in a barrel of M. — FABY 279:17
malo: M. me Galai petit — VIRG 714:18
malo practice: m. of heart — *illegible* 207:2
illegible does juved than Milton — HOUS 352:19
Malvernham old M illegible — *illegible* 99:2
mama: M. may have, papa — *illegible*
m. of dada — FAD 279:19

mammas: What is it our m. bewitches — BARB 52:5
mammets: play with m. — SHAK 580:12
mammon: authentic m. — MACN 440:12
cannot serve God and m. — BIBLE 89:8
M. led them — MILT 469:4
m. of unrighteousness — BIBLE 95:7
M. pine amidst his store — POPE 520:17
serve both God and M. — SMITH 652:8
mammy: Mammy, M., look at me — LEWIS 421:1
man: all that makes a m. — TENN 681:25
all that may become a m. — SHAK 601:6
Am I not a m. and a brother — WEDG 726:15
And only m. is vile — HEBER 330:4
Any m. has to, needs to — ELIOT 272:18
apparel oft proclaims the m. — SHAK 573:4
Arms and the m. — DRYD 262:7
arms and the m. — VIRG 711:18
artist m. and the mother — SHAW 637:7
be a m. — ARN 27:2
be M. and Wife together — BOOK 123:23
better angel is a m. — SHAK 635:6
Blessed is the m. that hath — BOOK 124:6
Blessed is the m. unto whom — BOOK 126:8
bold bad m. — SHAK 508:13
bold bad m., that dared — SPEN 659:23
Both m. and bird and beast — COL 211:17
But if a m. bites a dog — BOG 116:14
But when I came to m.'s estate — SHAK 630:37
call a m. *a good man* — JOHN 376:9
Cannot a plain m. live — SHAK 621:20
Can't help lovin' dat m. — HAMM 322:17
century of the common m. — WALL 718:5
childhood shows the m. — MILT 473:19
Child is father of the M. — WORD 745:6
coming of the Son of M. — BIBLE 92:13
debased, degraded m. — ELIOT 268:20
delighteth he in any m.'s legs — BOOK 135:12
detest that animal called m. — SWIFT 674:1
distinguishes m. from animals — OSLER 502:3
Ech m. for hymself — CHAU 193:17
encompassed but one m. — SHAK 590:5
Eustace is a m. no longer — KING 398:3
every m. against every man — HOBB 340:5
every m. is surrounded by — AUST 39:1
everyone has sat except a m. — CUMM 228:9
Except a m. be born again — BIBLE 96:13
extraordinary m. — JOHN 376:10
family to the m. only — HOBB 340:10
first m. is of the earth — BIBLE 101:13
fit night out for m. or beast — FIEL 282:22
forgetteth what manner of m. — BIBLE 104:27
For m. proposes, but God — THOM 692:6
fou m. and a fasting — SCOTT 560:27
fresh as when m. first broke — LOW 430:8
friendly, honest m. — BURNS 161:27
garment from the m. — BLAKE 111:23
get out the m. — POPE 519:5
get to a m. in the case — KIPL 399:15
gibbets for 'the m.' — COOK 218:5
God created m. — VALE 707:22
God is not a m. — BIBLE 73:9
Good Lord, what is m. — BURNS 163:3
good m. and a good citizen — AUCT 33:21
Greater love hath no m. — BIBLE 97:16
hand will be against every m. — BIBLE 70:37
hang the m. over again — BARH 52:11
Happy is the m. that hath — BOOK 134:7
have you ever tasted M. — KIPL 402:2
Here lies a m. who never lived — THOM 695:20
He's no a m. ava' — MACD 437:8
He was a good m., and a just — BIBLE 95:29
He was a m., take him for all — SHAK 572:17
He was a spare m. — AUBR 33:6
He was her m., but he done — ANON 13:11
hour is come, but not the m. — SCOTT 560:20
I am a m. upon the land — BALL 49:12
I have a m.'s mind — SHAK 591:9
I know myself a m. — DAV 232:4
It... to m. who is not worth — WALK 717:11
I'm a m. of wealth illegible taste — JAGG 361:12
I'm a simple m. — illegible 191:2
illegible when wasn't there — MEAR 456:1

man: (*cont.*):
I'm truly sorry M.'s dominion — BURNS 163:16
in m. there is nothing great but mind — HAM 322:13
I saw a m. this morning — SHAW- 639:3
it is the number of a m. — BIBLE 107:1
It's that m. again — ANON 15:10
I was an austere m. — BIBLE 95:16
large-hearted m. — BROW 147:22
lassie do wi' an auld m. — BURNS 164:2
last thing civilized by M. — MER 457:26
let him pass for a m. — SHAK 607:13
let no m. put asunder — BOOK 123:22
let no m. put asunder — BOOK 125:10
Let no m. stop to plunder — MAC 436:8
Let the end try the m. — SHAK 583:6
like a m.'s hand — BIBLE 76:4
like m., slighted and enduring — HARDY 324:12
Lord is a m. of war — BIBLE 72:14
Love's a m. of war — HERB 334:14
make a m. a woman — PEMB 511:10
make m. in our image — BIBLE 69:24
makes a m. coloured — HUGH 354:2
makes m. and wife one flesh — CONG 215:2
m. a free hand and he'll — WEST 729:10
m. after his own heart — BIBLE 74:35
m., a man! — MARS 449:10
m. and a woman looking — WOOLF 742.14
m. and I ain't together — KOEH 403:17
m. and me hath all this — MAL 443:11
M. and this Woman in holy — BOOK 123:15
m. and wife — BYRON 171:14
M. being by nature all free — LOCKE 425:6
m. be more just than God — BIBLE 77:11
M., biologically considered — JAMES 363:13
M. comes and tills — TENN 689:10
m. delights not me — SHAK 574:28
M. did not make, and cannot — ARN 27:12
M. didn't find the animals — NIET 495:6
M. disavows, and Deity disowns — COWP 222:8
m. dreaming I was a butterfly — CHUA 200:10
M. dreams of fame while — TENN 682:12
M., false man, smiling — LEE 416:7
m. fixed his eyes before — ELIOT 273:1
m. for all seasons — WHIT 733:11
m. for others — BONH 118:2
M. goeth forth to his work — BOOK 132:9
m. goeth to his long home — BIBLE 81:1
M. hands on misery to man — LARK 410:7
m. has a right to utter — JOHN 375:13
M. has created death — YEATS 751:10
M. has Forever — BROW 149:30
m. hates to be moved — LAWR 413:5
m. hath no preeminence — BIBLE 80:6
m. hath seen God — BIBLE 96:5
m. have the upper hand — BOOK 124:21
m. hurrying along—to what? — KEATS 392:6
m. I am — SHAK 570:14
m. in his own proud esteem — COWP 224:14
m. in love is incomplete — GABOR 296:12
m. in the house is worth — WEST 729:6
M. is a history-making creature — AUDEN 36:15
M. is a nasty creature — MOL 479:14
M. is an embodied paradox — COLT 214:10
M. is a noble animal — BROW 145:26
M. is a tool-using animal — CARL 181:5
M. is a useless passion — SART 556:10
M. is born unto trouble — BIBLE 77:12
m. is but a devil weakly — STEV 667:15
M. is but earth — DONNE 253:12
m. is dead — FROMM 294:7
m. is either free or he is not — BAR 51:15
M. is Heaven's masterpiece — QUAR 533:19
m. is in love when he marries — BURN 160:13
m. is man and master — TENN 682:8
M. is man's A.B.C — QUAR 534:3
M. is Nature's sole mistake — GILB 306:15
m. is of kin to the beasts — BACON 42:24
M. is one world, and hath — HERB 335:11
M. is quite insane — MONT 481:9
m. is seldom ashamed — ELIOT 269:21
m. in is in the way — GASK 299:1

mankind: (cont.):
M. is a dream of a shadow	PIND 514:16
M. is divisible into two	BEER 59:8
M. must put an end to war	KENN 394:3
need not be to hate, m.	BYRON 168:23
our countrymen are all m.	GARR 298:12
shut the gates of mercy on m.	GRAY 315:16
superfluities of m.	GAY 299:18
proper study of m. is books	HUXL 357:11
proper study of m. is man	POPE 522:9
There is no history of m.	POPP 524:13

manliness: silent m. of grief — GOLD 310:17
manly: be a m. man — MAL 443:5
| more valourous than m. wise | MARL 448:8 |
man-milliner: respectable architectural m.
| | RUSK 550:8 |

manna: his tongue dropped m. — MILT 469:13
Exalted m., gladness	HERB 335:13
He rained down m. also upon	BOOK 130:11
'Tis m. to the hungry soul	NEWT 494:10
We loathe our m., and we	DRYD 261:6

manned: safeliest when with one man m.
| | DONNE 250:16 |

manner: All m. of thing shall be well
	ELIOT 271:9
m. of his speech	SHAK 565:4
m. of men I have fought	BIBLE 101:9
m. which is my aversion	BYRON 171:4
shall be well and all m.	JUL 382:10
to the m. born	SHAK 573:8

Männer: stolzen M. der Tat — HFINE 331:3
manners: As by his m. — SPEN 660:16
catch the M. living as	POPE 521:27
communications corrupt good m.	
	BIBLE 101:10
Edward III had very good m.	SELL 562:18
English m. are far more	JARR 363:21
evil m. live in brass	SHAK 589:9
Leave off first for m,' sake	BIBLE 87:30
M. maketh man!	WYK 750:9
m. of a dancing master	JOHN 371:16
m. of a Marquis	GILB 306:17
m. of future generations	JOHN 369:20
M. the need of the plain	WAUGH 724:11
not men, but m.	FIEL 282:5
Of m. gentle, of affections	POPE 521:3
Oh, the times! Oh, the m.	CIC 204:6
Peel has no m.	WELL 727:8
people have good table m.	MIKES 460:3
polished m. and fine sense	COWP 224:8
thereby to rectify m.	MILT 475:8
To soften m., not corrupt	BYRON 172:9

Manningtree: M. ox — SHAK 580:31
manoeuvre: blend force with a m. — TROT 704:14
man-o'-war: M.'s 'er 'usband — KIPL 399:19
manque: Un être seul vous m. — LAM 405:21
manservant: m., nor thy maidservant
| | BIBLE 72:16 |

mansion: heavenly m., raging — YEATS 751:6
Love has pitched his m.	YEATS 751:8
made his everlasting m.	SHAK 626:21
m. call the fleeting breath	GRAY 315:14
to rectify my m.	MILT 463:11
upon thy fading m. spend	SHAK 635:7

mansion-house: m. of liberty — MILT 475:12
mansions: are many m. — BIBLE 97:11
| dolorous m. to the peering day | MILT 467:9 |
| lasting m. of the dead | CRAB 224:25 |

mantle: cast his m. upon him — BIBLE 76:8
dark her silver m. threw	MILT 471:10
Her purple m. to the light	RONS 545:11
m. like a standing pond	SHAK 607:6
m. muffling up his face	SHAK 592:14
m. that covers all	CERV 188:16
russet m. clad	SHAK 572:3
twitched his m. blue	MILT 466:16
You all do know this m.	SHAK 592:13

mantled: M. in mist, remote — AUDEN 33:28
Mmmann: old M.! — QUAK 598:16
ffffff; facture; soul of every m. — SMIL 650:8
manunkind: all fully Little monsters, iii.
| | Cummi 228:11 |

manure: It is its natural m. — JEFF 364:5

---

manuscript: youth's sweet-scented m.
| | FITZ 284:16 |

manuscripts: brown Greek m. — BROW 148:17
many: death had undone so m. — ELIOT 273:1
For m. are called, but few are	BIBLE 92:1
for we are m.	BIBLE 93:11
he makes so m. of them	LINC 422:15
How m. things I can do without	SOCR 654:9
m. for the remission	BOOK 122:12
m.-splendoured thing	THOM 695:10
m. still must labour	BYRON 169:18
m. ways out	SEN 563:1
owed by so m. to so few	CHUR 202:13
So m. worlds, so much to do	TENN 683:26
what are they among so m.	BIBLE 96:22
What m. men desire	SHAK 608:16

map: Lord would use a larger m. — SAL 554:1
m.-makers' colours	BISH 110:2
M. me no maps	FIEL 282:9
m. of Europe has been changed	CHUR 202:2
m. with the augmentation	SHAK 630:18
Roll up that m.	PITT 515:18

maps: Geography is about M. — BENT 64:10
| m. on a small scale | SAL 554:1 |
| So geographers, in Afric-m. | SWIFT 675:3 |

mar: I m. on the other — SKEL 649:3
| m. all with this starting | SHAK 604:13 |
| not make, and cannot m. | ARN 27:12 |

Marathon: M. looks on the sea — BYRON 171:1
| skirmish fought near M. | GRAV 314:21 |

marble: dwelt in m. halls — BUNN 155:7
from their m. caves repent	DRUM 258:12
Glowed on the m.	ELIOT 273:2
great piece of placid m.	HUNT 356:13
hovel to your dreary m.	CALV 175:15
I am m.-constant	SHAK 567:2
inherited it brick and left it m.	AUG 37:13
in thy m. vault, shall sound	MARV 451:3
legs are as pillars of m.	BIBLE 81:20
m. eyelids are not wet	BROW 147:14
m. index of a mind	WORD 747:2
m. to retain	BYRON 167:23
mould from m. living faces	VIRG 713:17
Not m., nor the gilded	SHAK 633:18
Poets that lasting m. seek	WALL 718:11
slate more than hard m.	DU B 263:2
What need of all this m. crust	MARV 451:6

marbly: great smooth m. limbs — BROW 148:17
Marcellus: Tu M. eris — VIRG 713:18
March: ashbuds in the front of M. — TENN 681:5
Beware the ides of M.	SHAK 589:21
droghte of M. hath perced	CHAU 192:6
ides of M. are come	SHAK 591:10
That highte M., whan God	CHAU 194:7
winds of M. with beauty	SHAK 632:4

march: Do not m. on Moscow — MONT 481:18
long majestic m.	POPE 523:4
M., march, Ettrick	SCOTT 560:25
m. of a nation	PARN 507:7
m. of intellect	SOUT 657:16
m. of mind has marched	PEAC 510:6
m. on their stomachs shouting	SELL 562:24
m. through rapine to disintegration	
	GLAD 307:14
m. to the siege	BALL 50:2
m. with sovereign tread	BLOK 115:9
Men who m. away	HARDY 325:13
three hours' m. to dinner	HAZL 329:14

March-bloom: Look! M. — HOPK 346:6
marche: Le congrès ne m. pas — LIGNE 421:14
marched: m. breast forward — BROW 148:6
| M. them along, fifty-score | BROW 151:5 |

Märchen: Ein M. aus alten Zeiten — HEINE 330:15
marches: forced m., battles — GAR 298:1
| Funeral m. to the grave | LONG 427:8 |
| slow howe'er my m. | KING 396:12 |

marching: hear the sound of m. — JAGG 361:12
His soul is m. on	ANON 15:12
His truth is m. on	HOWE 353:2
M. as to war	BAR 53:2
M. in the Promised Land	BAR 53:3
m. where it likes	ARN 29:11

---

marching: (cont.):
'Tis the people m.	MORR 485:9

mare: animum mutant qui trans m. — HOR 348:9
brought him a Flanders m.	HENR 332:15
lend me your grey m.	BALL 51:4
man shall have his m.	SHAK 612:8

mares: M. eat oats — DRAKE 257:14
Margaret: As Merry M. — SKEL 649:2
| he called on M.'s name | MALL 443:1 |
| It is M. you mourn | HOPK 346:4 |

marge: having an ample m. — TENN 682:15
Margery: Some went upstairs with M.
| | AUDEN 35:17 |

margin: meadow of m. — SHER 645:13
| untravelled world, whose m. | TENN 690:1 |

Maria: ex M. Virgine — MISS 476:23
| M. flung herself on him | GRAH 313:17 |

Mariana: dejected M. — SHAK 606:14
Marias: wheels of black M. — AKHM 6:12
Marie: I am M. of Roumania — PARK 506:5
Maries: Queen had four M. — BALL 50:6
marigold: m., that goes to bed wi' the sun
| | SHAK 632:3 |

Marilyn: M. who was every man's — MAIL 442:8
mariner: haul and draw with the m.
| | DRAKE 257:11 |
| It is an ancient M. | COL 210:18 |

mariners: rest ye, brother m. — TENN 686:2
| My m. souls that have | TENN 690:4 |

Marion: M.'s nose looks red — SHAK 599:11
marital: m. disillusion — WAUGH 723:9
marjoram: savory, m. — SHAK 632:3
mark: He hath no drowning m. — SHAK 624:27
If you would hit the m.	LONG 426:15
I press toward the m.	BIBLE 103:9
Lord set a m. upon Cain	BIBLE 70:21
man's distinctive m. alone	BROW 149:12
m. is a long one	SHAK 583:2
m. me how I will undo myself	SHAK 620:21
M. well her bulwarks	BOOK 127:23
m. what is done amiss	BOOK 134:11
not a crease, not a m.	ROST 548:11
read, m., learn	BOOK 120:11
save the beast that had the m.	BIBLE 106:32

market: knowledge is bought in the m.
| | CLOU 207:9 |
| salutations in the m. places | BIBLE 93:17 |

market-place: eat his heart in the m.
	SHAK 614:10
Enthroned i' the m.	SHAK 565:6
gathered in the m.	CAV 187:7

markets: m. by the sea shut fast — FLEC 286:10
| of m. and fashion | ALB 7:9 |

marking: malady of not m. — SHAK 582:18
marks: sorrow m. the last — HAIG 320:11
| m. and scars I carry | BUNY 156:16 |
| terrible m. of the beast | HARDY 324:10 |

marl: clod of wayward m. — SHAK 613:13
| Over the burning m. | MILT 468:14 |

Marlbro: M.'s mighty soul — ADD 3:13
Marlb'rough: M.'s eyes — JOHN 370:20
Marlowe: or M.'s mighty line — JONS 380:2
marmasyte: Call Tullia's ape a m. — ANON 14:9
Marquis: Abducted by a French M. — GRAH 313:8
| manners of a M. with | GILB 306:17 |

marred: All that's spoke is m. — SHAK 618:21
| married is a man that's m. | SHAK 564:6 |

marriage: All comedies are ended by a m.
	BYRON 170:20
And m. and death and division	SWIN 676:12
companionship as in m.	ADAMS 2:7
Courtship to m.	CONG 215:27
curse of m.!	SHAK 616:16
furnish forth the m. tables	SHAK 572:16
get anywhere in a m.	MURD 488:5
Hanging and m.	FARQ 280:23
hanging prevents a bad m.	SHAK 628:17
her fortune by way of m.	FIEL 282:14
I'll frighten her into m.	JOHN 377:15
In m., a man becomes slack	STEV 667:30
Is not m. an open question	EMER 277:11
Joys of m., are the heaven	FORD 289:9
left-handed m.	WOLL 741:14

marriage: (cont.):
live in a state of m.   JOHN 373:14
long monotony of m.   GIBB 302:25
love and m. rarely can   BYRON 170:24
M. always demands the finest   BAUM 56:1
m. and the constancy   SHAW 637:18
m. for her was   STAN 662:9
m. had always been her   AUST 39:14
M. has many pains   JOHN 369:22
M. is a bribe to make   WILD 736:15
M. is a step so grave   STEV 668:4
M. is a wonderful invention   CONN 216:9
M. is like life   STEV 668:5
M. is nothing but a civil   SELD 562:7
m. is not that adults produce   DE VR 238:5
M. isn't a word, it's a *sentence*   VIDOR 711:8
M. is popular because   SHAW 637:25
M. is the grave or tomb of wit   CAV 187:12
M. is the waste-paper basket of the emotions
    WEBB 724:17
m. makes man and wife one   CONG 215:2
M. may often be a stormy   PEAC 510:8
m. of true minds   SHAK 634:23
m. than a ministry   BAG 47:4
m. then is best in tune   WATK 722:7
m. with his brother's wife   SHAK 588:12
m. without love means love   CLARK 205:7
marrying and giving in m.   BIBLE 92:13
My definition of m.   SMITH 653:15
nor are given in m.   BIBLE 92:3
nor are given in m.   SWIFT 674:16
primal m. blessing   KEBLE 392:22
Reading and m. don't go   MOL 479:2
retrieve his fortunes by m.   DICK 241:5
So that is m., Lily thought   WOOLF 742:14
think there is any in m.   GAY 299:24
To speke of wo that is in m.   CHAU 194:19
who drags the m. chain   CENT 188:5
with dirge in m.   SHAK 572:4
woman dictates before m.   ELIOT 269:12
marriage-procession: fall in with the m.
    CLOU 207:3
marriages: God, the best maker of all m.
    SHAK 587:3
I say, we will have no more m.   SHAK 576:3
m. is selling one's soul to   MACK 439:2
M. would in general   JOHN 374:11
one of the happiest m.   DE V 238:3
their m. with other men   TROL 704:5
There are good m.   LA R 410:15
thousands of m.   LARK 410:3
unhappy m. come from   WOD 740:7
why so few m. are happy   SWIFT 674:18
married: cut his throat before he m.
    SWIFT 675:14
fights the best part of m. life   WILD 736:16
fool at least in every m.   FIEL 281:17
if ever we had been m.   GAY 299:12
if m. life were all that it   MILL 461:1
I m. beneath me, all women do ASTOR 32:11
imprudently m. the barber   FOOTE 288:15
incomplete until he has m.   GABOR 296:12
in m. life three is company   WILDE 734:12
I would be m. to a single life   CRAS 226:11
like other m. couples   SAKI 553:15
m. and brought up a large   GOLD 311:28
M., charming, chaste   BYRON 170:5
M. in haste, we may repent   CONG 215:25
m. is a man that's marred   SHAK 564:6
m. past redemption   DRYD 261:5
m. people have to see these   PEPYS 512:16
m. to a poem   KEATS 392:8
m. to a sponge   SHAK 607:16
M. to immortal verse   MILT 465:17
m. with mine uncle   SHAK 572:12
Miss will soon be m.   HAYW 328:11
Mocks m. men   SHAK 599:10
most m. man I ever saw   WARD 721:9
no taste when you m. me   SHER 645:14
O let us be m.!   LEAR 414:13
Once you are m.   STEV 668:6
One was never m.   BURT 165:1
Reader, I m. him   BRON 142:6

married: (cont.):
should live till I were m.   SHAK 613:27
So they were m.   MACN 440:18
Trade Unionism of the m.   SHAW 637:17
Unpleasing to a m. ear   SHAK 599:10
Ven you're a m. man   DICK 243:15
well-bred as if we were not m.   CONG 216:1
wench who is just m.   GAY 299:14
You, that are going to be m.   GOLD 311:19
marries: signify whom one m.   ROG 544:15
When a man m., dies   SHEL 641:4
marrow: fat things full of m.   BIBLE 83:8
out all the m. of life   THOR 697:5
marry: advise no man to m.   JOHN 377:6
And while ye may, go m.   HERR 337:0
better to m. than to burn   BIBLE 100:24
Carlyle and Mrs Carlyle m.   BUTL 166:29
Doänt thou m. for munny   TENN 687:12
find it in my heart to m. thee   CONG 215:26
get away to m. you today   LEIGH 416:19
How can a bishop m.   SMITH 653:11
if you do *not* m. Mr Collins   AUST 39:13
Man may not m. his Mother   BOOK 136:3
man should m.   BACON 44:6
m. a man who hates his   BENN 63:22
m. a market-gardener   DICK 242:21
m. any vun among them   DICK 243:28
m. a rich woman as a poor   THAC 691:8
m. is to domesticate   STEV 668:6
M. my body to that dust   KING 396:11
m. with his brother   SHAK 577:8
may m. whom she likes   THAC 691:12
men that women m.   LONG 427:3
men we wanted to m.   STEI 663:10
neither m., nor are given in   SWIFT 674:16
never know who they may m.   MITF 478:5
not taken in when they m.   AUST 38:16
persons about to m.   PUNCH 531:7
resurrection they neither m.   BIBLE 92:3
should m. a teetotaller   STEV 668:3
should m. twenty husbands   SHAK 607:14
Will you m. it, marry it   PLATH 516:2
You don't m. it legitimately   DEGAS 234:27
marrying: m. and giving in marriage
    BIBLE 92:13
m. in haste, and repenting   THOM 694:7
Mars: Appollo, of M.   CHAU 196:2
Next July we collide with M.   PORT 525:5
marshal: m.'s baton   LOUI 428:17
Martha: M. was cumbered about much
    BIBLE 94:17
martial: become valiant and m.   BACON 44:34
have a swashing and a m.   SHAK 567:23
m. airs of England   WEBS 725:8
M., the things for to attain   SURR 672:2
Sonorous metal blowing m.   MILT 468:23
Martin: Saint M.'s summer   SHAK 587:6
Martini: medium Vodka dry M.   FLEM 286:13
wet clothes and into a dry M.   ANON 15:16
Martinis: M. did the work for me   ADE 5:5
martlet: like the m.   SHAK 568:16
temple-haunting m.   SHAK 601:1
martyr: And if thow deye a m.   CHAU 195:22
Glorious the m.'s gore   SMART 650:4
m. of the people   CHAR 191:9
m. with the intellect   BAG 46:10
Thou fall'st a blessed m.   SHAK 589:1
martyrdom: dreadful m. must run its course
    AUDEN 35:7
it were a m. to live   BROW 145:17
M. is the test   JOHN 375:13
M....the only way to become   SHAW 636:6
mitre and a crown of m.   WALP 720:7
martyrs: graves of the m.   STEV 669:3
love their m. and honour   DOST 254:8
noble army of M.   BOOK 118:12
no patience of m.   THOM 693:1
stones and clouts make m.   BROW 145:16
marvel: m. at nothing   HOR 348:7
Match me such m.   BURG 156:24
There could I m.   THOM 693:13
They m. more and more   BELL 60:22
marvelled: m. to see such things   BOOK 127:21

marvellous: Chatterton, the m. boy
    WORD 747:11
he has done m. things   BIBLE 107:29
he hath done m. things   BOOK 131:13
it is m. in our eyes   BOOK 133:16
mankind towards the m.   HUME 355:6
marvels: wherein all m. summèd   SOUT 657:24
who alone workest great m.   BOOK 119:8
Marx: child of Karl M. and   ATTL 32:17
teaching of M.   KHR 395:14
wholly wrong to blame M.   BENN 63:2
Marxism: Methodism than to M.   PHIL 514.0
Marxist: M.—of the Groucho tendency
    ANON 20:13
know is that I am not a M.   MARX 452:10
Mary: Hail M., full of grace   ANON 22:3
M. Ambree   BALL 50:2
M. found in adulterous bed   BLAKE 111:18
M. had a little lamb   HALE 321:8
M. hath chosen   BIBLE 94:18
M. Queen the praise   COL 211:10
M. was that mother mild   ALEX 8:11
Where the lady M.   ROSS 547:18
Mary-buds: And winking M. begin   SHAK 571:3
Mary Jane: *What* is the matter with M.
    MILNE 462:17
Marylebone: hanging garments of M.
    JOYCE 381:2
Mary Magdalene: cometh M. early   BIBLE 97:30
masculine: With spirits m.   MILT 473:5
Masefield: To M. something more   BEER 59:10
mask: loathsome m. has fallen   SHEL 642:18
m. like Castlereagh   SHEL 641:10
m. like open truth to cover   CONG 215:5
m. of night is on my face   SHAK 622:32
masochism: spirit of national m.   AGNEW 5:16
masochistic: m. form of exhibitionism
    OLIV 498:15
masonry: man into the social m.   WELLS 727:19
masons: m. building roofs of gold   SHAK 584:22
masquerade: m., a murdered peer   ALC 8:1
or miss a m.   POPE 523:23
truth in m.   BYRON 171:20
masquerades: Skim milk m. as cream
    GILB 306:3
mass: After two thousand years of m.
    HARDY 325:2
blessed mutter of the m.   BROW 148:18
broad m. of a nation   HITL 339:14
calculable m. of human beings   WEBB 724:15
Chaos, a rough and unordered m.
    OVID 502:20
dead level of the m.   MELV 456:18
m. and multitude   VIRG 713:16
m. of broken and castaway   CLOU 206:17
Paris is well worth a m.   HENR 332:12
massacre: not as sudden as a m.   TWAIN 706:5
masses: call them the m.   PRIE 528:19
m. against the classes   GLAD 307:17
m. yearning to breathe   LAZ 413:7
Of m. and fugues and 'ops'   GILB 305:4
sacrifices of M.   BOOK 135:25
these stupendous m.   CANN 178:12
mass-production: methods of m.   LANC 407:21
massy: huge m. face   MAC 434:14
mast: bends the gallant m.   CUNN 229:2
m. burst open with a rose   FLEC 286:13
m. of some great admiral   MILT 468:14
master: choice and m. spirits   SHAK 591:20
disciple is not above his m.   BIBLE 90:17
dominion of the m.   HUME 355:12
eateth your M. with publicans   BIBLE 90:5
from a mad and savage m.   SOPH 656:15
great m. so to sympathize   MILT 467:2
great mocking m.   DAV 232:3
great soul of an ancient M.   BROW 151:14
harassing m.   STEV 666:6
Has a new m.—Get a new man   SHAK 625:20
I am M. of this college   BEEC 59:7
I am the m. of my fate   HENL 332:7
love is m. wher he wile   GOWER 313:2
man and m. of his fate   TENN 682:8

master: (*cont.*):
Man is the m. of things	SWIN 676:19
m. a grief	SHAK 613:32
m. of the house cometh	BIBLE 93:19
m. of money	BEV 69:11
m. of those who know	DANTE 230:10
M. shall praise us	KIPL 401:9
M., we have toiled all	BIBLE 94:3
more subtle m. under heaven	TENN 681:25
peace, who slew his m.	BIBLE 76:28
presence of The M.	THAC 691:6
swear allegiance to any m.	HOR 347:20
This is our m., famous calm	BROW 149:27
Thrice blessèd they that m.	SHAK 610:20
To the M. of all singing	LONG 427:18
which is to be m.	CARR 183:12
which I would fain call m.	SHAK 595:4
Who's m., who's man	SWIFT 674:28
You must be m. and win	GOET 309:9

master-builders: without m. LOCKE 424:15
master morality: M. and slave-morality
	NIET 495:15

masterpiece: Man is Heaven's m. QUAR 533.13
Nature's great m., an elephant
	DONNE 251:14
one knows, at sight, a m.	POUND 527:4

masters: ease of the m. SMITH 651:3
m. of their fates	SHAK 590:3
never wrong, the Old M.	AUDEN 35:6
people are the m.	BURKE 158:33
serve two m.	BIBLE 89:8
spiritual pastors and m.	BOOK 123:7
their victory but new m.	HAL 321:16
We are the m. now	SHAW 639:1
We must educate our m.	LOWF 429:10

master-spring: m. controlled them all
	COWP 224:1

mastery: been constreyned by m. CHAU 193:13
m. of the thing	HOPK 346:11
voice said in m.	BROW 147:18

mastiff: leal and trusty m. LLOY 424:4
mastodons: Aunt calling to Aunt like m.
	WOD 740:16

masturbation: don't knock it ALLEN 9:10
M.: the primary sexual	SZASZ 677:16
sort of mental m.	BYRON 174:8

mat: As an old rough m. HUGH 354:3
match: blue spurt of a lighted m. BROW 151:7
bread and the big m.	JUV 384:7
dont quite m. your face	ASHF 31:6
Honour is like a m.	PAGN 504:5
M. me such marvel	BURG 156:24
m. was the only thing	EDG 266:10
Ten to make and the m. to win	NEWB 492:9

matched: m. of earthly knight's MAL 443:13
Who are m. us with His hour	BROO 143:16

matches: plays extravagant m. GILB 305:5
With that stick of m.	MAND 444:3

matchless: now the m. deed's achieved
	SMART 650:4

matchwood: m., immortal diamond
	HOPK 346:7

mate: lady's ta'en anither m. BALL 50:20
listen when his m. sings	WICK 733:16
Made my m.	STEV 669:1
there walked without a m.	MARV 450:13

mater: *Magna ista scientiarum m.* BACON 45:20
Stabat M. dolorosa JAC 361:8
materialism: deteriorate into m. MOLT 479:17
materials: I use simple m. LOWRY 431:2
maternity: m. a period of suffering STAN 662:9
mathematician: pure m. JEANS 363:27
mathematics: Angling…so like the m.
	WALT 720:20
love m. for its own sake	STEN 663:14
M. may be defined	RUSS 551:17
M., rightly viewed	RUSS 551:20
m. subtile	BACON 44:29
order and mysucal m	BROW 148:11
place in the world for ugly m.	HARDY 324:4
nicely by a resort to m.	MFNC 457:10

Matilda: M. told acful dreadful Lies BELL 60:16
matin: glow-worm shows the m. SHAK 611:21

---

matins: merry lark her m. sings SPEN 659:14
matrimonial: M. devotion GILB 305:2
m. preparations that drive	BURN 160:13

matrimony: argument in favour of m.
	AUST 40:2
critical period in m.	HERB 333:23
had more of love than m.	GOLD 311:32
joined together in holy M.	BOOK 123:14
matters of religion and m.	CHES 198:2
respectable as that of m.	TROL 703:12
safest in m. to begin	SHER 645:2
we take m. at its lowest	STEV 668:1

matron: Thou sober-suited m. SHAK 623:16
matter: altering the position of m. RUSS 551:15
beginning of any great m.	DRAKE 257:9
Dirt is only m. out of place	GRAY 315:4
Does it m.?—losing your sight	SASS 557:6
if it is it doesn't m.	GILB 306:20
inditing of a good m.	BOOK 127:10
m. enough to save one's	BROW 150:24
m. she drove at succeeded	PRIOR 529:7
M., the wickedest offspring	ROCH 543:19
More m, with less art	SHAK 574:13
order this m. better in France	STER 664:2
our speculations upon m.	JOHN 380:1
seeing the root of the m.	BIBLE 77:26
sum of m. remains	BACON 42:10
take away the m. of them	BACON 44:19
What is M.?—Never mind	PUNCH 531:13
What is the m. with Mary Jane	MILNE 462:17
when all the m.'s spent	DAN 229:15
wretched m. and lame metre	MILT 467:17

matters: exercise myself in great m.
	BOOK 134:13
big words for little m.	JOHN 372:21
m. just as little	SHAW 637:15
What can I do that m.	SPEN 659:7

Matthew: M., Mark ANON 16:9
named M., sitting	BIBLE 90:4

mattress: don't crack it open on a m.
	MILL 461:15

maturing: think my mind is m. NASH 490:14
Maud: Come into the garden, M. TENN 686:17
maugree: m. hir heed CHAU 194:25
mausoleum: then as its m. AMIS 10:13
mavult: *enim m. homo verum esse* BACON 45:19
maw: his icy fingers in my m. SHAK 594:15
mawkish: So sweetly m. POPE 518:21
mawkishness: thence proceeds m.
	KEATS 386:12

Max: incomparable M. SHAW 638:28
maxim: M. Gun, and they have not BELL 61:16
my m. should become	KANT 385:6
only m. of a free government	ADAMS 2:26
That grounded m.	MILT 474:9

maxima: *mea m. culpa* MISS 476:16
maximum: m. of temptation SHAW 637:25
May: darling buds of M. SHAK 633:6
fayr as the rose in M.	CHAU 195:4
fressh as is the month of M.	CHAU 192:10
From M. to December	AND 11:8
in the merry month of M.	BALL 48:21
Is fairer far, in M.	JONS 379:21
Is the merry month of M.	BALL 50:8
least the seventh of M.	TROL 703:13
maids are M. when they	SHAK 569:18
M. is a pious fraud	LOW 430:6
M.-mess, like on orchard	HOPK 346:6
M. month flaps its glad	HARDY 324:22
M. will be fine next year	HOUS 351:17
M. without cloud and June	ARAG 24:6
moonlight-coloured m.	SHEL 642:24
More matter for a M. morning	SHAK 630:25
on a M. mornyng	LANG 408:20
Than wish a snow in M.'s	SHAK 598:8
there's an end of M.	HOUS 351:16
whan that the month of M.	CHAU 195:1
world is white with M.	TENN 681:21

may: know whal we m. SHAK 578:1
lawyer tells me I m.	BURKF 157:26

maydenhed: he rafte hire m. CHAU 194:25
Maying: come, let's go a-M. HERR 336:11

---

maypole: away to the M. hie ANON 12:25
organ and the m.	JORD 380:13
where's the M. in the Strand	BRAM 139:16

maypoles: I sing of M., Hock-carts HERR 336:6
maze: law seems like a sort of m. MORT 486:4
Life is a m.	CONN 216:15
m. wherein affection finds	RAL 535:14
mighty m.! but not without a plan	
	POPE 521:26
Now burgeons every m.	TENN 684:13
wander in that golden m.	DRYD 261:18

mazes: And accompany the m. SMART 649:7
in wandering m. lost	MILT 469:23
m. intricate	MILT 472:2
pleasant m. of her hair	COWL 221:13

mazy: A merry road, a m. road CHES 199:5
McCarthyism: M. is Americanism MCC 436:18
McGregor: Mr M.'s garden POTT 525:13
me: are now in the M. Decade WOLFE 741:8
For you but not for me.	ANON 17:1
Keep m., O keep me	KEN 393:7
let m. ever escape them	BOOK 135:2
M. imperturbe, standing	WHIT 732:5
M. Tarzan, you Jane	WEIS 726:20
M. too the Muses made write	VIRG 715:7
no harm happen unto m.	BOOK 124:22
queer save thee and m.	OWEN 503:9

mead: By the stream and o'er the m.
	BLAKE 113:21

meadow: m. traversed by men BABEL 41:13
painted m., or a purling stream	ADD 4:3
stranger's feet may find the m.	HOUS 352:1
through a m. of margin	SHER 645:13

meadows: Do paint the m. with delight
	SHAK 599:10
m. runnels, runnels	KEATS 386:16
M. trim with daisies pied	MILT 465:11
with golden face the m. green	SHAK 633:12

meal: handful of m. in a barrel BIBLE 75:32
no man gets a full m.	JOHN 374:3

mean: admires m. things is a Snob THAC 691:2
be seated in the m.	SHAK 607:11
citizen of no m. city	BIBLE 99:5
Down these m. streets	CHAN 190:5
Happy the golden m.	MASS 453:14
He nothing common did or m.	MARV 450:15
If ever I do a m. action	STER 664:5
It all depends what you m.	JOAD 366:8
no m. of death	SHAK 591:20
poem should not m. but be	MACL 439:10
should say what you m.	CARR 182:6
sincere, even if you don't m. it	TRUM 704:22
Someone who loves the golden m.	
	HOR 349:18
They m. well	DISR 248:17
things for m. or no uses	LOCKE 424:17
Though m. and mighty rotting	SHAK 571:14
what we m., we say	ARN 26:17
woman of m. understanding	AUST 39:10

Meander: By slow M.'s margent green
	MILT 463:22

meaner: leave all m. things POPE 521:26
m. things are within her	ELIOT 269:7

meanest: m. of mankind POPE 522:21
meaning: although I take your m. BROW 153:8
And as to the m.	CALV 175:11
author to get at his m.	RUSK 550:18
death will provide the m.	ALAI 7:5
faint m. make pretence	DRYD 261:2
Free from all m., whether	DRYD 259:14
hidden m.—like Basingstoke	GILB 306:19
it promises us m.	BELL 62:7
language charged with m.	POUND 527:17
Love is our Lord's m.	JUL 382:1
m. doesn't matter if	GILB 305:16
m. is my meat and drink	BROW 149:25
m. is the waiting	THOM 694:11
m. of a proposition	SCHL 558:5
m. of religion is thus	ARN 30:2
m.'s press and screw	COL 210:16
plain man in his plain m.	SHAK 609:6
richest without m.	RUSK 550:22

melody: (*cont.*):
God with the voice of m.   BOOK 127:18
making m. in your heart   BIBLE 102:23
m., in our heaviness   BOOK 134:17
m. lingers on   BERL 65:20
Moved to delight by the m.   AUDEN 34:1
pretty girl is like m.   BERL 65:19
smale foweles maken m.   CHAU 192:7
This m., which I've never   ALAI 7:7
with sound of sweetest m.   SHAK 583:11
melons: huge m. and of pine   TENN 688:17
Stumbling on m., as I pass   MARV 450:9
Melrose: view fair M. aright   SCOTT 559:13
melt: crown o' the earth doth m.   SHAK 566:15
earth shall m.   BOOK 127:16
m. itself into the sun   SHAK 583:13
m. with ruth   MILT 466:12
So let us m., and make no   DONNE 252:21
So will I m. into a bath   SOUT 657:22
too too solid flesh would m.   SHAK 572:12
vanish, fade, and m. away   BOLT 117:16
melted: Are m. into air   SHAK 625:28
m. like a cloud   TENN 689:1
M. to one vast Iris   BYRON 169:1
With that which m. fools   SHAK 591:11
melting: body is even like m. wax   BOOK 125:12
must ride on its own m.   FROST 295:16
melting-pot: great M. where   ZANG 755:7
melts: then m. for ever   BURNS 163:6
Melville: Herman M. who split   LODGE 425:20
member: Distinguishable in m.   MILT 470:5
thing I am not a m. of   FLEM 287:5
together every joint and m.   MILT 475:9
was made a m. of Christ   BOOK 123:3
WILL ACCEPT ME AS A M.   MARX 451:16
members: m. incorporate in the mystical
  BOOK 122:14
m. of the common throng   GILB 306:12
We are m. one of another   BIBLE 102:18
were all my m. written   BOOK 134:21
membra: disiecti m. poetae   HOR 351:3
même: plus c'est la m. chose   KARR 385:13
meminisse: Forsan et haec olim m. iuvabit
  VIRG 712:6
Nec me m. pigebit Elissae   VIRG 713:6
memoirs: m. is to speak ill of everybody
  PÉT 513:7
memor: *Dum m. ipse mei*   VIRG 713:6
memorable: Upon that m. scene   MARV 450:15
memorandum: m. is written not to inform
  ACH 1:9
memorial: which have no m.   BIBLE 88:3
whole earth as their m.   PER 512:23
memorials: There are no m.   YEVT 754:3
memories: Liars ought to have good m.
  SIDN 646:9
m. are card-indexes consulted   CONN 216:21
M. are hunting horns   APOL 23:14
M. are not shackles   BENN 63:7
M. have three epochs   AKHM 6:10
memorize: m. another Golgotha   SHAK 599:16
memory: Fond M. brings the light
  MOORE 483:17
Footfalls echo in the m.   ELIOT 270:14
For my name and m.   BACON 46:3
forsake me like a m. lost   CLARE 204:25
grand m. for forgetting   STEV 667:13
his m. for his jests   SHER 645:24
His m. is going   JOHN 376:4
It brings back a m. ever green   PORT 524:21
M. and desire, stirring   ELIOT 272:21
m. a rooted sorrow   SHAK 604:22
m. may outlive his life   SHAK 576:12
m. of all that   GERS 301:16
m. of a Macaulay   BARR 54:16
m. of men without distinction   BROW 145:23
m. of yesterday's pleasures   DONNE 253:10
m. remains sceptreless   SHEL 642:18
m. revealed itself   PROU 530:7
m. that only works backwards   CARR 183:6
Midnight shakes the m.   ELIOT 272:14
no force can abolish m.   BOOK 546:5
nui intellect but rather m.   LEON 418:8

memory: (*cont.*):
O! it comes o'er my m.   SHAK 617:6
Only a m. of the same   BROW 150:19
plucking the fruit of m.   CONR 217:1
Quick, thy tablets, M.   ARN 27:14
Thanks for the m.   ROBIN 542:8
Thru' the mist of a m. you   PAR 506:2
very m. is fair and bright   VAUG 709:5
Vibrates in the m.   SHEL 643:11
while m. holds a seat   SHAK 573:22
women'll stay in a man's m.   KIPL 402:12
Yea, from the table of my m.   SHAK 573:22
men: all m. are created equal   ANON 19:7
All m. naturally desire to know   AUCT 33:22
all our best m. are dead   PUNCH 532:5
all things to all m.   ANON 15:20
all things to all m.   BIBLE 100:29
among the children of m.   BOOK 128:15
As though he had 200,000 m.   NAP 490:6
boon and a blessing to m.   ANON 18:16
But m. at whiles are sober   HOUS 351:19
But ye shall die like m.   BOOK 130:15
danger from all m.   ADAMS 2:26
days shall m. seek death   BIBLE 106:26
deals with the memory of m.   BROW 145:23
delight is in proper young m.   BURNS 162:11
Either war is obsolete or m.   FULL 295:27
For fear of little m.   ALL 10:1
form Christian m.   ARN 30:12
great Nature made us m.   LOW 430:2
half my m. are sick   TENN 689:1
hearts of m.   SHAK 626:16
hell to m., hell to cities   AESC 5:11
herb for the service of m.   BOOK 132:8
Hogs Eat Snakes, M. Eat Hogs   STEV 665:19
I describe not m.   FIEL 202:6
If all m. are born free   AST 32:9
in the catalogue ye go for m.   SHAK 602:24
I see m. as trees, walking   BIBLE 93:13
issue not towards m.   BACON 43:25
it's m.'s lives   SCOTT 560:13
it's the life in my m.   WEST 729:9
learn m. from books   DISR 248:34
leaves is a generation of m.   HOMER 343:4
likeness of m.   BIBLE 98:23
looking upon m. as virtuous   BOL 117:12
make you fishers of m.   BIBLE 88:22
mak'st m. do all things   JONS 379:1
many m., many women   JOHN 372:1
m. alone are quite capable   CONR 217:16
m. and malice to breed   JONS 379:12
m. and nations behave wisely   EBAN 266:1
m. and women, and there are   THAT 691:26
m. and women are not so   SHAW 636:16
M. are April when they woo   SHAK 569:18
M. are but children   DRYD 260:1
m. are created equal   JEFF 364:2
m. are deceitful upon   BOOK 128:20
M. are everything   CANN 178:10
m. are generally more careful   PENN 511:15
M. are so honest, so thoroughly   LERN 419:3
m. are unaccountable things   VANB 708:3
m. better than sheep   TENN 682:24
M. deal with life   COWP 222:9
M. decay   GOLD 310:6
m. despise   CHUD 200:3
M. don't know women   TROL 703:11
m. from the barn   HOUS 352:11
m. from the chimney corner   BOOK 647:8
M. grow cold as girls grow old   ROBIN 542:7
m. have got love well weighed   AMIS 11:1
M. have had every advantage   AUST 39:6
M. have precedency   BRAD 139:11
M. in great place are thrice   BACON 43:27
m. in shape and fashion   ASCH 31:2
M. into monsters   FORD 289:12
m. in women do require   BLAKE 113:12
men know so little of m.   DU B 263:5
M. lived like fishes   SIDN 646:10
M. loved darkness rather   BIBLE 96:16
m. made perfect   BIBLE 104:19
m. may be as positive   LOCKE 425:1
m. may come and m.   TENN 680:12

men: (*cont.*):
M. must be taught as if   POPE 521:23
m. must work, and women   KING 397:16
M., my brothers, men   TENN 685:13
m. naturally were born   MILT 476:9
m. of action in our time   AUDEN 36:16
m. of like passions   BIBLE 98:24
m. only disagree   MILT 469:22
M. seldom make passes   PARK 506:8
m. that women marry   LONG 427:3
M.! The only animal   LAWR 412:16
m. think all men mortal   YOUNG 754:18
m. to some one quality   DRAY 257:19
m. were all asleep   BRID 141:3
M. were deceivers ever   SHAK 613:24
m. we wanted to marry   STEI 663:10
M., when they lust   GREE 317:10
m. who have loved them   TROL 704:5
M. who march away   HARDY 325:13
m. who will support me   MELB 456:7
m., women, and clergymen   SMITH 653:13
m., women, and Herveys   MONT 480:8
M. would be angels   POPE 522:4
m. would be false   LYLY 433:7
m. would be tyrants if they
could   DEFOE 234:17
Millions of innocent m.   JEFF 364:17
Mocks married m.   SHAK 500:10
more I see of m.   TOUS 701:6
much nicer than m.   AMIS 11:2
mufflered m. in the 1930s   JOS 380:16
My m., like satyrs grazing   MARL 447:6
need of a world of m.   BROW 151:21
Not m., but measures   BURKE 159:16
not stones, but m.   SHAK 592:12
no way for m. to be   SHAK 571:4
Old m. who never cheated   BET.I 67:8
Philip fought m.   LEE 416:6
power over m.   WOLL 741:13
precisely as m. would suffer   BRON 142:4
purgatory of m.   FLOR 288:5
rather studied books than m.   BACON 45:11
rejected of m.   BIBLE 84:11
Rejoiced they were no m.   BURNS 163:26
schemes o' mice an' m.   BURNS 163:17
should be by the m. despised   CHUD 200:11
Some faults to make us m.   SHAK 566:18
Some m. are born mediocre   HELL 331:7
some m. have good hap   GASC 298:17
sorts and conditions of m.   BOOK 120:5
So they be ill m.   JONS 378:15
State which dwarfs its m.   MILL 460:20
strong m. stand face to face   KIPL 398:13
to m. French   CHAR 191:21
too late that m. betray   GOLD 311:33
trust themselves with m.   SHAK 626:7
unscrupulous m. for unhealthy   BEEC 59:1
unto the daughters of m.   BIBLE 70:25
want to be m. above all   ART 30:16
war between m. and women   THUR 697:12
We are the hollow m.   ELIOT 271:14
What m. or gods are these   KEATS 388:24
when m. and mountains meet   BLAKE 113:10
Where Destiny with M.   FITZ 284:7
with m. he can be rational   AUST 38:7
with m. I find Him not   TENN 682:17
menace: looks do m. heaven   MARL 447:22
m. of aggression   ASQ 31:17
men-children: Bring forth m. only   SHAK 601:8
mend: God won't, and we can't m. it
  CLOU 207:11
shine, and seek to m.   DONNE 250:24
To m. it or be rid on't   SHAK 603:1
mendacities: Better m.   POUND 526:13
mendacity: M. is a system   WILL 737:5
mendax: *Splendide m. et in omne virgo*
  HOR 350:6
mended: For nothing else but to be m.
  BUTL 166:6
Think but this, and all is m.   SHAK 613:3
mendicus: *M. es?*   PLAU 517:5
Mendip: M.'s sunless caves   MAC 436:1
Mene: M., Tekel, Upharsin   BIBLE 85:31

menpleasers: as m.   BIBLE 102:25
mens: *M. agitat molem et magno*   VIRG 713:16
   M. cuiusque is est quisque   CIC 204:4
   m. sana in corpore sano   JUV 384:11
   m. sibi conscia recti   VIRG 712:10
mensa: *Nec deus hunc m.*   VIRG 715:2
Mensch: *Es irrt der M.*   GOET 309:1
   Unaufrichtigkeit zwischen M.   BAUM 56:1
mental: m. pleasure produced   REYN 539:9
   slavery are m. states   GAND 297:9
   will not cease from m. fight   BLAKE 113:4
mention: m. of you in our prayers   BIBLE 103:19
   Oh! no! we never m. her   BAYLY 56:3
   Without ceasing I make m.   BIBLE 99:14
Mercator: *M.'s*   CARR 184:2
mercenary: Followed their m. calling   HOUS 351:22
   m. and the prudent move   AUST 39:15
merchandise: mechanical arts and m.   BACON 48:5
merchant: m. shall hardly keep himself   BIBLE 87:26
   m., to secure his treasure   PRIOR 529:9
merchantman: heaven is like unto a m.   BIBLE 91:4
   monarchy is a m.   AMES 10:9
merchants: like m., venture trade abroad   SHAK 584:22
mercies: All thy faithful m. crown   WESL 728:14
   by morning new m. I see   CHIS 200:1
   For his m. ay endure   MILT 465:19
   tender m. of the wicked   BIBLE 78:25
   Thanks for m. past receive   BUCK 154:12
merciful: Blessed are the m.   BIBLE 88:23
   God be m. to a soul   ANON 22:9
   God be m. to me a sinner   BIBLE 95:15
   God be m. unto us, and bless   BOOK 129:4
   In a m. eclipse   GILB 304:3
   M. as constant, constant as   GRAV 314:22
   was very m. to the birds   ANON 20:4
merciless: black and m. things   JAMES 362:21
   looked at in this m. glare   WILL 737:8
Mercuries: as English M.   SHAK 585:1
mercury: like feathered M.   SHAK 581:20
   littered under M.   SHAK 631:25
   m. sank in the mouth   AUDEN 34:13
   pick up m. with a fork   LLOY 424:11
   words of M. are harsh   SHAK 599:12
mercy: big with m.   COWP 222:18
   Charity and M.   DICK 241:10
   compassion and m.   BIBLE 87:8
   crowning m.   CROM 227:9
   emboldens sin so much as m.   SHAK 626:11
   For M. has a human heart   BLAKE 113:19
   gates of m. on mankind   GRAY 315:16
   Hae m. o' my soul, Lord God   MACD 437:10
   hand folks over to God's m.   ELIOT 268:19
   his m. endureth for   BOOK 134:16
   His m. is for ever sure   KETHE 394:13
   judgement, m., and faith   BIBLE 92:5
   Justice with m.   MILT 473:3
   La belle dame sans m.   KEATS 387:10
   leaving m. to heaven   FIEL 282:11
   likely to have m. on you   VILL 711:14
   Lord, have m. upon us   BOOK 118:14
   Love is the greatest m.   WILB 734:6
   love m., and to walk humbly   BIBLE 86:14
   m. also toward them   BOOK 132:5
   m. and protection we commit   BOOK 124:1
   M. and truth are met together   BOOK 130:20
   M. blows the coals   SOUT 657:22
   m. embraceth him   BOOK 126:10
   M. I asked, mercy I found   CAMD 176:3
   m. I to others show   POPE 523:32
   M....laboured much   BUNY 156:13
   m. of his means   THOM 693:6
   M. sighed farewell   BYRON 169:19
   m. to forgive   DRYD 260:22
   m. unto thousands of them   BIBLE 72:16
   m. upon one of our souls   SHAK 630:27
   m. upon us miserable sinners   BOOK 119:16
   most tender m. is neglect   CRAB 225:16

mercy: (*cont.*):
   property is ever to have m.   BOOK 120:4
   quality of m. is not strained   SHAK 609:13
   so good a grace as m. does   SHAK 605:16
   so is his m.   BIBLE 87:9
   There's a wideness in God's m.   FABER 279:14
   they shall obtain m.   BIBLE 88:23
   Thy everlasting m.   MAS 453:6
   to the m. of a rude stream   SHAK 588:19
   When m. seasons justice   SHAK 609:13
   Widely as his m. flows   LYTE 433:17
   will have m. on Jacob yet   BROW 150:3
Meredith: M.'s a prose Browning   WILDE 735:2
   M., we're in   KITC 402:16
mereri: *quicquam bene velle m.*   CAT 186:11
meridian: under any m.   BROW 146:14
merit: from sense of injured m.   MILT 468:4
   How he esteems your m.   COWP 222:6
   m. but mere knack of rhyme   CHUR 201:7
   m. for a bishopric   WEST 729:20
   m.'s all his own   CHUR 201:16
   m. wins the soul   POPE 523:31
   preacher's m. or demerit   BROW 149:6
   What is m.? The opinion   PALM 505:11
meritocracy: true m. of talent   YOUNG 755:3
merits: not weighing our m.   BOOK 122:13
mermaid: Choicer than the M. Tavern   KEATS 388:20
   Done at the M.!   BEAU 56:14
   M. in the Zodiac   KEATS 388:21
   m. on a dolphin's back   SHAK 611:16
mermaids: heard the m. singing   ELIOT 272:6
   So many m.   SHAK 565:6
merrily: die all, die m.   SHAK 581:21
   m. hent the stile-a   SHAK 631:28
   m. shall I live now   SHAK 626:2
   Sing we m. unto God our   BOOK 130:14
   we may m. meet in heaven   MORE 484:16
merriment: m. of parsons   JOHN 375:21
   scheme of m.   JOHN 368:10
   To this day's m.   SPEN 659:14
merry: All in the m. month of May   BALL 48:21
   chances men are ever m.   SHAK 583:24
   drink, and be m.   BIBLE 94:23
   drink, and to be m.   BIBLE 80:17
   For all their wars are m.   CHES 198:28
   For to-night we'll m. be   ANON 12:24
   gone up with a m. noise   BOOK 127:20
   Have they been m.   SHAK 624:7
   I am not m., but I do beguile   SHAK 615:17
   Is the m. month of May   BALL 50:8
   M. and tragical   SHAK 612:19
   m. day once or twice   PEPYS 512:19
   m. heart doeth good like   BIBLE 79:1
   m. heart goes all the day   SHAK 631:28
   m. heart maketh a cheerful   BIBLE 78:34
   m. in hall when beards   SHAK 584:10
   m. road, a mazy road   CHES 199:5
   m. when I hear sweet music   SHAK 610:2
   m. world in England since   SHAK 587:22
   m. world since the fairies   SELD 562:9
   you were born in a m. hour   SHAK 613:20
merrygoround: no go the m.   MACN 440:13
merryman: It's a song of a m.   GILB 306:24
merses: *M. profundo*   HOR 350:13
meschaunce: on a Friday fil al this m.   CHAU 194:8
Mesech: constrained to dwell with M.   BOOK 133:21
Meshach: M., and Abed-nego   BIBLE 85:29
mess: Another nice m. you've   LAUR 411:8
   birthright for a m. of potage   BIBLE 71:7
   In every m. I finds a friend   DIBD 238:13
   m. of pottage with love   BIBLE 78:35
   m. we have made of things   ELIOT 270:11
   m. with Mister In-between   MERC 457:12
   other people clean up the m.   FITZ 285:3
   who has made an awful m.   BURR 164:6
message: final m. of India   FORS 290:27
   medium is the m.   MCL 439:14
   take a m. to Albert   DISR 249:14
   your m. in the open face   WESL 729:1
messager: bisy larke, m. of day   CHAU 193:19

messages: m. should be delivered   GOLD 312:5
   receive fair speechless m.   SHAK 607:10
   sending of general m.   DOYLE 257:1
   you get m. of sympathy   AYCK 40:8
messenger: musician, if he's a m.   HEND 332:4
   m. of Satan   BIBLE 102:2
   shape and m. of Death   SACK 552:14
messes: Of herbs, and other country m.   MILT 465:12
messing: m. about in boats   GRAH 314:2
met: Are m. in thee to-night   BROO 144:4
   day and the way we m.   SWIN 676:23
   Hail, fellow, well m.   SWIFT 674:28
   Ill m. by moonlight   SHAK 611:13
   know how first he m. her   THAC 691:21
   m. us in your Son   BOOK 122:14
   M. you not with my true love   BAL 530.1
   never be m. with again   CARR 184:4
   truth are m. together   BOOK 130:20
   We m. at nine   LERN 419:2
metal: cold m. of economic theory   SCH 558:12
   Here's m. more attractive   SHAK 576:10
   How now, my m. of India   SHAK 629:22
   Imagineless m.   THOM 695:12
métamorphoses: *mois des m.*   ARAG 24:6
metaphor: whaling a universal m.   LODGE 425:20
metaphorical: m. God   DONNE 253:3
metaphysic: As m. wit can fly   BUTL 166:4
   M. calls for aid   POPE 519:10
metaphysical: m. brothel   KOES 403:18
metaphysicians: tempted to say of m.   CHAM 189:14
metaphysics: Explaining m. to the nation   BYRON 170:1
   M. is the finding of bad   BRAD 139:3
mete: With what measure ye m.   BIBLE 93:10
metempsychosis: Pythagoras' m.   MARL 447:3
meteor: cloud-encircled m.   SHEL 641:3
   like a m., to the troubled   GRAY 315:7
   m. streaming to the wind   MILT 468:22
   slides the silent m.   TENN 688:13
meters: Watch the parkin' m.   DYLAN 265:22
method: yet there is m. in't   SHAK 574:23
methodically: must elope m.   GOLD 311:19
Methodism: more to M. than to Marxism   PHIL 514:6
Methodist: morals of a M.   GILB 306:17
methought: M. I saw my late espousèd saint   MILT 474:26
   m. what pain it was   SHAK 621:23
Methuselah: all the days of M.   BIBLE 70:24
métier: *c'est son m.*   CATH 185:7
   c'est son m.   HEINE 331:4
   m. que de faire un livre   LA BR 405:5
   Mon m. et mon art c'est vivre   MONT 481:4
metope: o to be a m.   CUMM 228:8
metre: laws of God and man and m.   LOCK 425:17
   same m. ballad-mongers   SHAK 581:4
   stretchèd m. of an antique   SHAK 633:5
   though its m. was to tackle   QUIL 534:10
   wretched matter and lame m.   MILT 467:17
metropolis: m. of the empire   COBB 208:2
mettle: m. in death   SHAK 564:19
   m. of your pasture   SHAK 585:9
   undaunted m. should compose   SHAK 601:8
metuant: *dum m.*   ACC 1:4
metus: *M. et malesuada Fames*   VIRG 713:14
meum: *M. est propositum*   ANON 22:9
mew: be a kitten and cry m.   SHAK 581:4
mewling: M. and puking in the nurse's   SHAK 568:16
Mexico: Poor M., so far from God   DIAZ 238:10
Mexique Bay: Echo beyond the M.   MARV 450:1
mezzo: *m. del cammin di nostra*   DANTE 230:5
mice: Appear like m.   SHAK 597:1
   Like little m.   SUCK 671:7
   schemes o' m. an' men   BURNS 163:17
Michael: M. and his angels   BIBLE 106:30
Michelangelo: from designs by M.   TWAIN 706:13

Michelangelo: (*cont.*):
M. left a proof — YEATS 753:15
might be the name of—M. — REYN 539:14
Talking of M. — ELIOT 272:1
Michelin: she with the M. — CONN 216:20
Michelle: M. *ma belle* — LENN 417:21
micher: m. and eat blackberries — SHAK 580:29
miching: this is m. mallecho — SHAK 576:14
Mickey Mouse: You're M. — PORT 524:20
microbe: M. is so very small — BELL 61:18
microscopes: gas m. of hextra power — DICK 243:21
microscopic: Why has not man a m. eye — POPE 522:5
mid-air: you in m. — SOND 656:2
middenpit: workshop, larder, m. — BUNT 155:8
middle: beginning, a m. and an end — GOD 308:5
companions for m. age — BACON 44:5
dead centre of m. age — ADAMS 2:4
grant me, Heaven, a m. state — MALL 442:20
M. of Next Week — CARR 184:8
most safely by the m. way — OVID 502:21
sits in the m. and knows — FROST 295:10
stay in the m. of the road — BEVAN 69:6
Tenants of life's m. state — COWP 224:12
that in politics the m. — ADAMS 2:28
that mine was the m. state — DEFOE 234:6
Middle Age: last enchantments of the M. — ARN 29:15
last enchantments of the M. — BEER 59:14
Restraining reckless m. — YEATS 752:17
middle-ageing: m. care — POUND 527:12
Middle Ages: Ought to go and live in the M. — SMITH 652:18
middle class: great English m. — ARN 29:14
M. people are apt to live — SMIL 650:12
M. was quite prepared — BELL 61:4
Philistines proper, or m. — ARN 29:10
that is the true m. unit — SHAW 637:31
We of the sinking m. — ORW 500:24
What is m. morality — SHAW 630:18
middle classes: bow, ye lower m. — GILB 304:6
Middle East: mad dog of the M. — REAG 537:14
Middlesex: acre in M. — MAC 435:2
Elysium—rural M. again — BETJ 68:2
middle-sized: m. are alone entangled — SHEN 644:14
midge: lightly skims the m. — BETJ 67:10
Spins like a fretful m. — ROSS 547:16
Midian: host of M. — BIBLE 74:9
Midlands: When I am living in the M. — BELL 61:28
midnight: a bed after m. is to — SHAK 629:3
And still her woes at m. rise — LYLY 433:10
blackest M. born — MILT 465:3
budding morrow in m. — KEATS 390:24
chimes at m. — SHAK 583:18
Did at m. speak with the Sun — VAUG 708:15
embalmer of the still m. — KEATS 390:14
Holding hands at m. — GERS 301:12
It came upon the m. clear — SEARS 561:12
iron tongue of m. — SHAK 612:26
Let's mock the m. bell — SHAK 565:22
midday sweat, our m. oil — QUAR 533:17
m. and the noon's repose — ELIOT 271:20
m. never come — MARL 447:1
m. oil — GAY 299:31
M. shakes the memory — ELIOT 272:14
m. shroud the serene lights — SHEL 643:8
Of the m. ride of Paul Revere — LONG 427:19
Once upon a m. dreary — POE 518:6
sighed upon a m. pillow — SHAK 568:3
'Tis the year's m. — DONNE 252:11
Upon the m. hours — KEATS 389:19
upon the m. with no pain — KEATS 389:14
visions before m. — BROW 146:23
who watch at that m. hour — LEAR 414:1
midst: God is in the m. of her — BOOK 127:16
go up in the m. of thee — BIBLE 72:21
of life we are in death — BOOK 124:4
there am I in the m. — BIBLE 91:20
midsummer high M. pomps — ARN 28:27
while dull cold m. junkhead — SHAK 609:21

midway: M. along the path of our life — DANTE 230:5
midwife: m. slapped your footsoles — PLATH 516:7
She is the fairies' m. — SHAK 622:21
mid-winter: In the bleak m. — ROSS 547:4
mie: *J'aime mieux ma m.* — ANON 21:5
mieux: m. est l'ennemi du bien — VOLT 716:6
pour ceux qui tirent le m. — VOLT 716:20
tout est au m. — VOLT 716:1
might: all-enacting M. — HARDY 325:11
Britons alone use 'M.' — WAUGH 724:6
do it with thy m. — BIBLE 80:20
Egypt's m. is tumbled down — COL 209:8
Exceeds man's m. — SHAK 627:17
faith that right makes m. — LINC 422:2
It m. have been — HARTE 327:19
It m. have been — WHIT 733:8
Lord of all power and m. — BOOK 121:5
m. of Him that walked — MILT 466:13
mirth used all his m. — MILT 471:8
my name is M.-have-been — ROSS 548:5
our m. lessens — ANON 18:20
spirit of counsel and m. — BIBLE 83:1
woman's m. — SHAK 591:9
mightier: make thee m. yet — BENS 63:23
pen is m. than the sword — BULW 155:5
spark-gap is m. than the pen — HOGB 341:14
mightiest: 'Tis m. in the mightiest — SHAK 609:13
mighty: according to the m. working — BOOK 124:5
bringeth m. things to pass — BOOK 133:15
But he's m. lak' a rose — STAN 662:11
Lord m. in battle — BOOK 125:17
M. and dreadful — DONNE 250:22
m. fallen in the midst — BIBLE 76:9
m. from their seats — BIBLE 93:23
m. from their seats — WHIT 731:18
m. God, The everlasting — BIBLE 82:27
m. hand and by a stretched — BIBLE 73:14
m. is vilely cast — BIBLE 75:8
m. men which were of old — BIBLE 70:25
m. roar of London's traffic — ANON 17:4
m. things from small — DRYD 260:3
m. Victor's brow — KELLY 393:4
Nimrod the m. hunter — BIBLE 70:33
or Marlowe's m. line — JONS 380:2
rushing m. wind — BIBLE 98:6
things which are m. — BIBLE 100:16
thou art m. yet — SHAK 593:19
Though mean and m. rotting — SHAK 571:14
thou m. man of valour — BIBLE 74:7
mignonne: M., allons voir si la rose — RONS 545:11
migrations: m. from the blue bed — GOLD 311:30
mild: brought reg'lar and draw'd m. — DICK 241:16
his m. and magnificent eye — BROW 151:1
I should prefer m. hale — SURT 672:13
m. as she is seeming — GREE 317:9
M., obedient, good — ALEX 8:13
mildest: m. mannered man — BYRON 170:28
mildews: m. the white wheat — SHAK 596:13
mild-mannered: m. reporter — ANON 13:8
mile: compel thee to go a m. — BIBLE 88:33
m. or two from my first love — VAUG 709:1
miles: can ye draw but twenty m. — MARL 448:9
m. to go before I sleep — FROST 295:13
milestones: m. on the Dover Road — DICK 241:3
militant: Poets M. below — COWL 221:19
state of Christ's Church m. — BOOK 121:21
was the first m. lowbrow — BERL 66:3
militarism: M. is fetish worship — TAWN 678:20
military: arms race has no m. purpose — MOUN 487:6
Doing the M. Two-step — GREN 318:1
hold the m. mind — TUCH 704:23
matter to entrust to m. men — CLEM 206:5
order and m. discipline — ANON 12:28
When the m. man approaches — SHAW 637:16
milk: And take my m. for gall — SHAK 600:16
are gone to m. the bull — JOHN 372:11
as it fine by m. — SHAK 623:10
But m. my ewes and weep — SPEN 661:19

milk: (*cont.*):
buy wine and m. without — BIBLE 84:15
drunk the m. of Paradise — COL 210:14
find a trout in the m. — THOR 696:23
flowing with m. and honey — BIBLE 71:40
Gin was mother's m. to her — SHAW 638:19
M. and then just as it comes — BETJ 67:12
m. and the yoghurt — TRIL 702:15
m. comes frozen home — SHAK 599:11
m. is more likely — BUTL 167:5
m. of human kindness — GUED 319:9
m. of human kindness — SHAK 600:15
M.'s leap toward immortality — FAD 279:18
m. the cow of the world — WILB 734:3
m. were scarce out of him — SHAK 628:22
m.-white steed — BALL 50:15
One end is moo, the other, m. — NASH 490:10
putting m. into babies — CHUR 202:20
she gave him m. — BIBLE 74:4
sincere m. of the word — BIBLE 105:10
sincere m. of the word — BIBLE 108:17
weyveth m. and flessh and al — CHAU 193:26
white curd of ass's m. — POPE 520:2
With m. and honey blessed — NEALE 491:5
milking: Jetty, to the m. shed — ING 360:5
milkmaid: And the m. singeth — MILT 465:10
milk-soup: M. men call domestic bliss — PATM 509:13
milky: M. Way, the bird of Paradise — HERB 335:13
or m. way — POPE 522:2
steeped in stars, and m. — RIMB 541:5
mill: at the m. with slaves — MILT 473:25
forge and the m. — HOUS 352:11
John Stuart M. — BENT 64:16
neither a m., a fermenting vat — HUNT 357:1
old m. by the stream — ARMS 26:5
water glideth by the m. — SHAK 626:22
mille: clappeth as a m. — CHAU 193:11
Da mi basia m. — CAT 186:1
millenium: believes in a calico m. — CARL 181:16
miller: hackneyed jokes from M. — BYRON 172:4
Than wots the m. — SHAK 626:22
There was a jolly m. once — DICK 108:70
millinery: jewelled mass of m. — TENN 686:10
million: Fifty m. Frenchmen — GUIN 319:13
m. million spermatozoa — HUXL 357:19
multitude of one m. — KOES 403:19
really want to make a m. — HUBB 353:14
millionaire: I am a M. That is my religion — SHAW 636:29
old-fashioned m. — FISH 283:7
silk hat on a Bradford m. — ELIOT 273:9
millionaires: All m. love a baked apple — FIRB 282:28
millions: m. long for immortality — ERTZ 278:13
m. of strange shadows — SHAK 633:16
m. of the mouthless dead — SORL 656:17
our yearly multiplying m. — O'SUL 502:5
tear-wrung m. — BYRON 167:20
We mortal m. live *alone* — ARN 29:3
What m. died — CAMP 176:18
mills: dark Satanic m. — BLAKE 113:4
m. of God grind slowly — LOGAU 426:1
millstone: m. round our necks — DISR 247:33
m. were hanged about his — BIBLE 91:18
mill-stones: Turned to m. as they fell — SHEL 641:11
Milton: inglorious M. — GRAY 315:15
malt does more than M. can — HOUS 352:19
M., a name to resound for ages — TENN 687:9
M., Madam, was a genius — JOHN 376:13
M.'s the prince of poets — BYRON 171:3
M.! thou shouldst be living — WORD 745:4
M. was for us — BROW 151:7
M. wrote in fetters when — BLAKE 112:15
morals hold which M. held — WORD 744:13
mimic: m. of the sun — CRANE 225:21
miminy: m., piminy — GILB 305:20
mimsy: All m. were the borogoves — CARR 182:18
mince: dined on m. — LEAR 414:15
love doth m. this matter — SHAK 616:3
mind: amplitude of m. — WORD 747:10

mint: mark of the m.	CHES 199:9
m. which coined our misery	DRAY 258:3
tithe of m. and anise	BIBLE 92:5
mints: m., savory	SHAK 632:3
minute: And his first m.	DONNE 252:7
do it in m. particulars	BLAKE 112:6
leave in a m. and a huff	KALM 385:2
M. after minute, aeon after	HUGH 354:6
Then the good m. goes	BROW 153:14
We cannot cage the m.	MACN 441:4
minutes: care of m.	CHES 198:11
could think for two m.	SMITH 653:1
five m. too late all my life	COWL 221:22
m. hasten to their end	SHAK 633:20
see the m. how they run	SHAK 588:1
set with sixty diamond m.	MANN 444:12
those white unblemished m.	THOM 695:23
world famous for fifteen m.	WARH 721:22
Mirabeau: *Sous le pont M.*	APOL 23:15
mirabilia: *quia m. fecit*	BIBLE 107:29
miracle: continued m. in his own	
person	HUME 355:7
first m. that he wrought	BOOK 123:16
It was a m. of rare device	COL 210:11
shall find this m. in me	DAN 229:15
Take the m. of our age	CAREW 179:1
That m. of a youth	EVEL 279:7
wondrous m. did Love devise	DAV 232:5
would seem a M.	DONNE 253:11
miracles: age of m. hadn't passed	GERS 301:11
miraculous: most m. organ	SHAK 575:13
Miranda: remember an inn, M.	BELL 62:1
mire: out of the m. and clay	BOOK 126:24
Sow returns to her M.	KIPL 399:8
will be cast into the m.	BURKE 158:18
mirk: It was m., mirk night	BALL 50:17
mirror: alone and smash his m.	ANON 20:17
bevelled edge of a sunlit m.	ABSE 1:3
courteous eyes oppose a m.	JONS 378:20
in a m. we perceive	MARL 448:3
Man's mind a m. is of	SOUT 657:24
m. cracked from side	TENN 685:4
m. of all Christian kings	SHAK 585:1
m. up to nature	SHAK 576:6
novel is a m. which passes	STEN 663:13
She is m. of alle curteisye	CHAU 193:24
mirrored: Lie m. on her sea	HODG 340:17
mirrors: as m. are lonely	AUDEN 35:18
M. and fatherhood	BORG 136:10
m. of the gigantic shadows	SHEL 644:8
m. of the sea are strewn	FLEC 286:14
most woeful m.	SACK 552:13
Over the m. meant	HARDY 325:3
mirth: Bards of Passion and of M.	KEATS 386:7
betray me to your m. or hate	FORD 289:14
buys a minute's m. to wail	SHAK 632:22
earth must borrow its m.	WILC 734:7
Far from all resort of m.	MILT 464:22
In m., that after no repenting	MILT 464:25
M., admit me of thy crew	MILT 465:7
m. as does not make friends	WALT 721:4
M. can do with her enticing	ANON 15:6
m. hath present laughter	SHAK 629:4
m. in funeral	SHAK 572:4
M. is short and transient	ADD 4:14
m. used all his might	MILT 471:8
song of the birds for m.	GURN 319:17
misbeliever: You call me m.	SHAK 607:22
miscarriage: success and m.	JOHN 371:20
misce: *M. stultitiam consiliis*	HOR 350:20
mischief: All punishment is m.	BENT 64:6
either of virtue or m.	BACON 44:3
For Satan finds some m. still	WATTS 722:13
From all evil and m.	BOOK 119:17
hand to execute any m.	CLAR 205:2
Intended m. against thee	BOOK 125:8
m. means m.	SHAK 576:14
little knowest thou m. time	NEWT 491:6
little neglect may breed m.	FRAN 297:10
m. befall him by the way	BIBLE 71:29
m. he had a heart to resolve	GIBB 302:5
m. then into the world	DRAY 258:5

mischief: *(cont.):*	
m., thou art afoot	SHAK 592:20
Spectatress of the m.	ROWE 549:6
think what m. is in hand	BYRON 171:11
To m. trained, e'en from	CHUR 201:10
tree on which our m.	DRAY 258:3
mischiefs: M. feed like beasts	JONS 379:13
will heap m. upon them	BIBLE 73:23
misconceive: I can hardly m. you	BROW 153:8
miscuit: *m. utile dulci*	HOR 347:15
misdoings: these our m.	BOOK 122:6
miserable: arise and make them m.	
	HUXL 357:14
God would make a man m.	CHAR 191:14
make only two people m.	BUTL 166:29
Me m.! which way shall I fly	MILT 470:25
mercy upon us m. sinners	BOOK 119:16
M. comforters are ye all	BIBLE 77:22
m. have no other medicine	SHAK 606:6
m. human being than one	JAMES 363:16
m. is to have leisure	SHAW 638:12
m. things which I myself	VIRG 712:13
of all men most m.	BIBLE 101:6
so it is very m.	TAYL 679:19
miserande: *m. puer*	VIRG 713:18
miserere: *m. nobis*	MISS 477:5
miseria: *Nella m.*	DANTE 230:11
miseries: Coherent m.	HEAN 329:22
Is bound in shallows and in m.	SHAK 593:12
m. or credulities of mankind	CONR 217:13
whom the m. of the world	KEATS 387:15
misery: affliction and my m.	BIBLE 85:17
bound in m. and iron	BOOK 132:15
child of sorrow! son of m.	KEATS 390:22
departure is taken for m.	BIBLE 86:28
fatal dumb-show of our m.	DRAY 258:3
finds himself, loses his m.	ARN 28:11
full of m.	BOOK 124:3
given to him that is in m.	BIBLE 77:9
greatest m. is a battle gained	WELL 727:10
great kick at m.	LAWR 412:25
guilt and m.	AUST 38:20
Man heaps on m. to man	LARK 410:7
mint which coined our m.	DRAY 258:3
miseries of the world are m.	KEATS 387:15
M. acquaints a man	SHAK 625:18
m. of being it	DRAB 257:8
m. of manilla folders	ROET 544:4
m. use it for a well	BOOK 130:17
m. which it is his duty	LOWE 429:11
nothing but pure m.	JOHN 375:18
Of happiness and final m.	MILT 470:1
relation of distant m.	GIBB 302:6
result m.	DICK 239:28
time when one is in m.	DANTE 230:11
with m., grief, and fear	CRAB 224:23
misfits: collection of m.	REAG 537:13
misfortune: m. it is to be born a woman	
	EDG 266:13
m. of our best friends	LA R 410:22
m. to ourselves, and good	BIER 109:7
writ with me in sour m.'s	SHAK 624:6
misfortunes: if a man talks of his m.	
	JOHN 375:18
make m. more	BACON 44:12
m. can befall a boy	MAUG 454:13
m. of mankind	GIBB 302:2
m. of men derive from one	PASC 507:12
strong enough to bear the m.	LA R 410:13
tableau of crimes and m.	VOLT 716:12
misgivings: Blank m. of a creature	WORD 746:3
misguided: guided missiles and m.	KING 397:3
mislead: one to m. the public	ASQ 31:19
misleading: words generate m. thoughts	
	SPEN 658:18
misled: By education most have been m.	
	DRYD 260:26
mislike: M. me not for my complexion	
	SHAK 608:4
misnomer: name of Epic's no m.	BYRON 170:14
misquoted: M. is	PEAR 510:14
misquote: enough of learning to m.	
	BYRON 172:4

misrepresentation: live under some degree of m.	
	ELIOT 270:1
miss: little m., dressed in a new	HUME 355:11
m. but a tree where we	BLAM 114:20
m. for pleasure	GAY 300:18
M. not the discourse	BIBLE 87:14
or rather did not m. it out	SAPP 556:2
So might I gain, so might I m.	BROW 150:22
missa: *Ite m. est.*	MISS 477:7
missed: he m. the bus	CHAM 189:9
m. the point completely	ELIOT 270:8
No one would have m. her	ANON 14:6
who never would be m.	GILB 304:21
wonder what you've m.	AUDEN 34:4
missing: And m. thee, I walk	MILT 464:20
M. so much and so much	CORN 219:4
mission: Its five-year m.	RODD 543:21
m. workers came out too	RUNY 550:4
My m. is to pacify Ireland	GLAD 307:7
Whate'er its m., the soft	WORD 746:17
missionaries: eaten by m.	SPOO 661:7
missionary: I would eat a m.	WILB 733:17
Mississippi: all the way into M.	KIPL 399:20
mis-spent: Redeem thy m. time	KEN 393:6
missus: The M., my Lord	PUNCH 531:26
mist: broke into a m. with bells	BROW 151:23
For every drizzling m.	ASKEW 31:15
He spent his time here in a m.	CLEV 206:13
m. and hum of that low	ARN 28:17
m. came down and hid	KING 397:14
m. in my face	BROW 152:4
m. is dispelled when	GAY 299:20
m. of a memory you wander	PAR 506:2
sophistry, and m.	BYRON 169:26
mistake: Among all forms of m.	ELIOT 269:14
he never overlooks a m.	HUXL 358:7
I mean, you lie—under a m.	SWIFT 674:5
Man is Nature's sole m.	GILB 306:15
m. in the translation	VANB 708:2
When I make a m., it's a beaut	LA G 405:16
when she made any such m.	DICK 242:6
mistaken: possible you may be m.	CROM 227:8
mistakes: genius makes no m.	JOYCE 382:2
great men make m.	CHUR 201:22
man who makes no m.	PHEL 513:17
m. of the past how to make	TAYL 679:7
m. that can be made	HEIS 331:5
m. they must be covered	CHUR 203:4
name every one gives to their m.	
	WILDE 735:13
nothing that make no m.	CONR 217:11
search for our m.	POPP 524:16
mistress: Art is a jealous m.	POPE 520:12
But m. in my own	EMER 276.17
crowd a m. or a friend	KIPL 400:5
I'll change a m. till I'm dead	SHEL 640:9
In ev'ry port a m. find	ROCH 543:1
literature is a m.	GAY 300:16
m. I am ashamed to call	CHEK 197:10
m. of the Earl of Craven	ELIZ 274:14
m. of the months and stars	WILS 738:7
m. should be like a little	SWIN 675:20
m. some rich anger shows	WYCH 750:2
new m. now I chase	KEATS 389:6
next a m.	LOV 429:6
No casual m., but a wife	CHEK 197:6
O m. mine	TENN 683:24
served the lust of my m.'s	SHAK 629:4
So court a m., she denies you	SHAK 596:9
teeming m., but a barren bride	JONS 379:19
thence to deck her m.' head	POPE 520:9
worst m.	BYRON 173:4
	BACON 42:12
mistresses: I shall have m.	GEOR 300:23
mad till you have your m.	VANB 708:3
m. with great smooth marbly	BROW 148:17
or your Lordship's m.	WILK 736:19
Wives are young men's m.	BACON 44:5
mists: low the m. of evening lie	BETJ 67:10
m. of righteous indignation	MUGG 487:9
season of m. and mellow	KEATS 390:17
thicken m. a space unsettle	THOM 695:6

mists: (cont.):
when the m. in autumn KING 398:6
where m. thickest be SURR 672:4
misty: seyn of a ful m. morwe CHAU 195:17
misunderstood: admired through
being m. COCT 208:11
m. are those who either TURG 705:12
To be great is to be m. EMER 277:3
worse lie than a truth m. JAMES 363:18
misuse: Who first m., then cast COWP 222:9
misused: m. the king's press SHAK 581:22
m. words generate misleading SPEN 658:18
mites: she threw in two m. BIBLE 93:18
mither: When my m. she did die BALL 49:16
Mithridates: M., he died old HOUS 352:20
mitre: m. and a crown WALP 720:7
Mittel: niemals bloss als M. brauchest
KANT 385:10
unentbehrlich nothwendige M. KANT 386:9
mix: I m. them with my brains OPIE 499:4
kiss her and m. her SWIN 677:3
M. a little foolishness HOR 350:20
mixed: conversation in a m. company
CHES 198:3
mixture: m. of a lie doth ever BACON 44:37
Moab: M. is my wash-pot BOOK 128:18
moan: And made sweet m. KEATS 388:10
m. of doves in immemorial TENN 688:16
That is not paid with m. THOM 694:18
to make delicious m. KEATS 389:19
moanday: m., tearsday, wailsday JOYCE 381:5
moaning: no m. of the bar TENN 680:17
moat: Look to your M. HAL 321:19
moated: at the m. grange SHAK 606:14
Upon the lonely m. grange TENN 686:6
mob: amphibious ill-born m. DEFOE 234:21
do what the m. do DICK 243:8
M., Parliament, Rabble COBB 207:28
remonstrative whisper to a m. HUNT 356:15
supreme governors, the m. WALP 719:1
mock: How my achievements m. me
SHAK 627:24
m. at our accursed lot MCKAY 439:1
Mock on m. on Voltaire BLAKE 113:5
m. our eyes with air SHAK 566:6
M. thee, till madness strike LYLY 433:12
mocked: As if he m. himself SHAK 590:7
God is not m. BIBLE 102:8
mocker: Wine is a m. BIBLE 79:4
mockeries: by what their m. be SHAK 585:18
No m. now for them OWEN 503:12
mockery: In monumental m. SHAK 627:20
seemed the m. of hell to fold BYRON 173:14
mocking: m. master mocked DAV 232:3
mockingbird: Out of the m.'s throat WHIT 732:8
to kill a m. LEE 415:16
mocks: M. married men SHAK 599:10
model: m. of a man DICK 241:21
m. of a modern Major-General GILB 306:9
when they come to m. heaven MILT 472:11
models: Rules and m. destroy genius
HAZL 329:7
they have no other m. BALD 48:1
moderate: £40,000 a year a m. income
LAMB 407:16
white m. more devoted to KING 396:16
moderately: drunk m. BIBLE 87:31
m. honest man with SHAW 637:31
moderation: astonished at my own m.
CLIVE 206:16
easier than perfect m. AUG 37:7
m. in politics is just HUNT 356:15
m. in the pursuit of justice GOLD 312:1
m. in war is imbecility MAC 434:11
m. is a sort of treason BURKE 157:8
No term of m. takes place BACON 42:13
There is m. in everything HOR 350:23
modern: called a 'M. Churchman'
WAUGH 723:14
model of a m. Major-General GILB 306:9
m. hardback writer TRIL 702:15
strange disease of m. life ARN 28:9
moderns: m. without contempt CHES 198:14

modest: M.? My word REED 538:9
modesty: in the m. of fearful duty SHAK 612:21
it is cold m. SHAK 591:22
Enough for m.—no more BUCH 154:3
o'erstep not the m. of nature SHAK 576:6
time to cultivate m. SITW 648:15
modified: M. rapture GILB 304:26
modus: Est m. in rebus HOR 350:23
moenia: flammantia m. mundi LUCR 431:12
Möglichen: Politik ist die Lehre vom M.
BISM 110:4
moins: m. des choses nouvelles VOLT 716:2
mois: m. des floraisons ARAG 24:6
moist: Have you not a m. eye SHAK 582:20
mole: like a bastion's m. SMART 650:1
m. cinque-spotted SHAK 571:7
still working like a m. HERB 335:5
Well said, old m.! SHAK 574:3
molecules: without understanding m.
CRICK 226:20
molehills: M. seem mountains COTT 220:3
moles: rudis indigestaque m. OVID 502:20
moll: King's M. Reno'd ANON 15:15
Moloch: right of that great M. MEYER 459:9
Mom: at a place called M.'s ALGR 9:5
mome: m. raths outgrabe CARR 182:18
moment: Eternity was in that m. CONG 215:23
Every m. dies a man BABB 41:6
Every m. dies a man TENN 690:5
from the impulse of the m. AUST 39:11
kingdoms of the world in a m. BIBLE 94:1
m. can so disfigure BROW 146:11
m. in childhood when GREE 317:3
m. of my greatness flicker ELIOT 272:4
momentary: Beauty is m. in the mind
STEV 666:8
pleasure is m. CHES 198:25
moments: O m. big as years KEATS 387:26
timeless m. ELIOT 271:8
Wagner has lovely m. ROSS 548:9
Mona: M. did researches in original sin
PLOM 517:13
monade: n'avelant pas de m. NERV 492:3
monarch: cuckold to make him a m.
SHAK 618:1
hereditary m. was insane BAG 46:19
I am m. of all I survey COWP 224:15
invades authors like a m. DRYD 262:12
merry m., scandalous and poor ROCH 543:15
m. better than his crown SHAK 609:13
m. clothed with majesty COWP 224:14
m. hears, assumes the god DRYD 259:17
m. of the road FLAN 285:14
No m. but would give his WALL 718:14
not so much a king as a M. SELL 562:22
monarchize: To m., be feared SHAK 620:8
monarchs: fate summons, m. must
obey DRYD 261:1
For righteous m. justly to BROO 143:2
m. to behold the swelling SHAK 584:16
m. to choose favourites SWIFT 673:14
Perplexes m. MILT 469:2
monarchy: constitutional m. BAG 47:8
discontented under m. HOBB 340:9
English M. BAG 47:3
essential to a true m. BAG 46:11
M. is a labour-intensive WILS 738:5
m. is a merchantman AMES 10:9
M. is a strong government BAG 47:2
M. is the gold filling OSB 501:21
m. is the supremest thing JAM 362:1
universal m. of wit CAREW 179:4
monasteries: decay of m. SKEL 649:4
monastery: bastards at the m. PINT 514:17
monastic: m. faces in quiet collegiate
CLOU 207:5
Monday: At classical M. Pops GILB 305:4
going to do on M. YBAR 750:14
monendo: delectando pariterque m. HOR 347:15
money: blessing that m. cannot buy
WALT 721:10
corrupted by m. GREE 316:23

money: (cont.):
employed than in getting m. JOHN 373:25
ever wrote, except for m. JOHN 374:15
For lack of m. LARK 409:19
For m. has a power above BUTL 166:20
given his m. upon usury BOOK 124:29
goä wheer m. is TENN 687:12
he gat hym moore m. CHAU 193:8
He had m. as well THAT 691:24
Her voice is full of m. FITZ 285:2
he that hath no m. BIBLE 84:15
He that wants m. SHAK 568:19
Hollywood m. isn't money PARK 506:17
Honour, without m. RAC 535:7
I have spent all the m. JOHN 375:26
leave them now is m. LARK 410:1
lend you m. if you can prove HOPE 345:1
licence to print m. THOM 696:20
love of m. is the root BIBLE 104:3
m. and large armies ANOU 23:2
m. answereth all things BIBLE 80:24
m. can't buy me love LENN 417:16
M. couldn't buy friends MILL 462:5
M. doesn't talk, it swears DYLAN 265:16
m. for that which is not BIBLE 84:15
m. from the pockets SMITH 651:4
M. gives me pleasure all BELL 61:11
M. has no smell VESP 710:9
m. is better bestowed THAC 691:5
M. is better than poverty ALLEN 9:16
M. is coined liberty DOST 255:1
M. is like a sixth sense MAUG 454:12
M. is like muck BACON 44:20
M. is none of the wheels of HUME 355:9
M. is the most important SHAW 636:21
M. is the sinews of love FARQ 280:21
m. of fools HOBB 340:1
m. or their vast carelessness FITZ 285:3
M. speaks sense in a language BEHN 60:15
m., the great solvent TRIL 702:17
m. the sinews of war BACON 44:33
m. wall to wall FISH 283:7
M. was exactly like sex BALD 48:4
M., wife, is the true fuller's GAY 299:15
Never ask of m. spent FROST 295:1
No m., no service RAC 535:6
no one shall work for m. KIPL 401:9
not spending m. alone EIS 268:10
Oh we ain't got a barrel of m. WOODS 742:3
only interested in m. SHAW 638:29
Papa! What's m. DICK 240:12
pleasant it is to have m. CLOU 207:13
poor know that it is m. BREN 140:12
pretty to see what m. PEPYS 512:18
private parts, his m. BUTL 167:6
rich man without m. UST 707:13
sinews of war, unlimited m. CIC 204:10
somehow, make m. HOR 347:22
some m. nothing of Swiss FONS 288:10
so m. comes withal SHAK 624:11
state is or can be master of m. BEV 69:11
Stealing m. is wrong AYER 40:13
That's the way the m. goes MAND 444:2
there shall be no m. SHAK 587:23
They hired the m., didn't they COOL 218:8
Thy m. perish with thee BIBLE 98:14
time is m. FRAN 292:13
try to rub up against m. RUNY 550:6
virtue does not come from m. SOCR 654:12
We haven't got the m. RUTH 552:7
we have to borrer the m. WARD 721:17
When you have m. DONL 250:6
who uses his m. as votes SAM 555:1
You pays your m. and you PUNCH 531:8
moneybag: Aristocracy of the M. CARL 180:24
moneybags: I did dream of m. SHAK 608:8
moneys: m. are for values BACON 42:4
mongrels: continent of energetic m. FISH 283:2
monk: devil a m. he'd be MOTT 487:5
I said to this m. PINT 514:18
m. who shook the world MONT 481:20
monkey: attack the m. when the organ grinder
BEVAN 68:17

morality: (*cont.*):
m. in any given time — WHIT 731:13
M. in the novel is — LAWR 412:4
M. is a private and costly — ADAMS 2:18
M. is the herd-instinct — NIET 495:10
m. is the regulation — SPEN 658:14
m. loses the foundation — SAM 554:18
m. of *art* apart from *subject* — CONR 217:18
m. of art consists — WILDE 735:16
m. should have this fact — SHAW 636:21
M.'s *not* practical — BOLT 117:14
m. touched by emotion — ARN 30:2
periodical fits of m. — MAC 434:19
some people talk of m. — EDG 266:9
unawares M. expires — POPE 519:11
moralize: shall m. my song — SPEN 659:19
morally: does nothing m. — ELIOT 270:2
morals: art and m. — MURD 488:7
basing m. on myth — SAM 554:10
faith and m. hold — WORD 744:13
Food comes first, then m. — BREC 140:4
foundation of m. — BENT 64:4
Have you no m., man — SHAW 638:17
pictured m. charm the mind — GARR 298:3
teach the m. of a whore — JOHN 371:16
Why, man of m., tell me why — COWL 221:8
with the m. of a Methodist — GILB 306:17
morbo: *Venienti occurrite m.* — PERS 513:5
mordre: M. wol out — CHAU 194:6
more: and m. than all — NEWM 493:8
art m. than they — TENN 682:28
believing m. and more in less — YATES 750:13
For, I have m. — DONNE 251:7
I am m. — BIBLE 101:23
little M. than a little — SHAK 581:14
m. about less and less — BUTL 165:23
m. Piglet wasn't there — MILNE 462:8
m. things a man is ashamed — SHAW 637:5
m. things are shewed — BIBLE 87:10
m. things in heaven — SHAK 574:4
M. to be desired are they — BOOK 125:5
M. will mean worse — AMIS 10:11
No m. o' that, my lord — SHAK 604:13
O m. than moon — DONNE 252:23
Please, sir, I want some m. — DICK 242:23
probably m. than she ever did — KALM 385:1
some animals are m. equal — ORW 499:20
take *m.* than nothing — CARR 182:8
there is no m. to say — SHAK 628:7
mores: *Et linguam et m.* — JUV 383:13
m. nec sinit esse feros — OVID 502:17
O tempora, O m.! — CIC 204:6
morganatic: m. alliance will follow — HARD 323:15
Morgen: *M. sterb' ich* — LESS 419:12
mori: *In taberna m.* — ANON 22:9
laude virum Musa vetat m. — HOR 350:17
pro patria m. — HOR 349:25
moriamur: *M. et in media* — VIRG 712:21
moriar: *Non omnis m.* — HOR 350:10
Moriarty: M. of mathematical — DOYLE 256:13
moribus: *M. antiquis res stat Romana* — ENN 278:1
morientis: *M. ori* — ANON 22:9
morituri: *m. te salutant* — ANON 22:2
morn: grey eyed M. perfumes — CHAP 190:14
incense-breathing M. — GRAY 315:12
m. a thousand roses brings — FITZ 283:12
m., in russet mantle — SHAK 572:3
m. of bright carnations — DRUM 258:14
m. went out with sandals — MILT 466:15
new m. she saw not — KEATS 388:3
Son of M. in weary Night — BLAKE 111:23
this the happy m. — MILT 466:20
morning: All in one M. — DONNE 253:8
Almost at odds with m. — SHAK 603:13
arrested one fine m. — KAFKA 384:15
beauty of the m. — WORD 743:9
before the m. watch — BOOK 134:12
Come, lovely M., rich in frost — DAV 232:13
disasters in his m. face — GOLD 310:12
domination over them in the m. — BOOK 128:1
Early in the m. our song — HEBER 330:5
Early one m. — ANON 12:34

morning: (*cont.*):
evening and the m. — BIBLE 69:21
fares like to the m.'s war — SHAK 587:29
glorious m. have I seen — SHAK 633:12
grey dawn of the m. after — ADE 5:5
He's for the m. — BROW 149:26
if m. skies, books — STEV 669:7
In the m. it is green — BOOK 130:23
In the m. sow thy seed — BIBLE 80:28
It's m. again in America — RINEY 541:11
I viewed the m. with alarm — GERS 301:11
joy cometh in the m. — BOOK 126:5
Lucifer, son of the m. — BIBLE 83:5
methinks I scent the m. — SHAK 573:19
m. blushed fiery red — BLAKE 111:18
m. cometh, and also — BIBLE 83:6
M. has broken — FARJ 280:4
M. in the bowl of night — FITZ 283:10
m. light creaks down again — SITW 648:9
m. of the world when first — SHEL 639:17
M. on the silver horns — TENN 688:15
M.'s at seven — BROW 151:28
m. stars sang together — BIBLE 77:35
m.-walks — POPE 521:1
m. well-aired before — BRUM 153:21
Never glad confident m. again — BROW 151:2
Never m. wore — TENN 683:3
New every m. is the love — KEBLE 392:19
started that m. from Devon — GILB 304:16
Such a m. it is when love — LEE 415:19
take the wings of the m. — BOOK 134:19
they take you in the m. — BALD 48:6
this morning m.'s minion — HOPK 346:10
thy princes eat in the m. — BIBLE 80:23
thy sorrow on a m. rose — KEATS 389:6
To pay thy m. sacrifice — KEN 393:5
To Thee our m. hymns — ELL 275:6
What a glorious m. is this — ADAMS 3:7
When m. gilds the skies — CASW 185:5
Your shadow at m. striding — ELIOT 272:23
mornings: literary m. with its hoot — AUDEN 35:2
Many bright m., much dew — VAUG 709:10
Mornington: present of M. Crescent — HARG 326:9
Morocco: we're M. bound — BURKE 160:6
moron: consumer isn't a m. — OGIL 498:3
See the happy m. — ANON 17:18
morphine: alcohol or m. or — JUNG 382:15
morris: nine men's m. — SHAK 611:14
morrow: Eagerly I wished the m. — POE 518:7
no thought for the m. — BIBLE 89:13
Weeping and watching for the m. — GOET 309:15
mors: *Illi m. gravis incubat* — SEN 563:3
Indignatio principis m. est — MORE 484:11
M. aurem vellens — VIRG 714:10
m. cum immortalis ademit — LUCR 432:3
m. est ad nos neque pertinet — LUCR 432:2
M. stupebit et natura — MISS 477:12
Pallida M. aequo pulsat — HOR 349:3
morsel: I found you as a m. — SHAK 565:20
It was a vast m. — DICK 245:5
morsels: his ice like m. — BOOK 135:13
mort: *La m. est belle* — ANOU 23:7
La m. est le remède — CHAM 189:11
La m., sans phrases — SIEY 647:13
m. ne surprend point le — LA F 405:13
veut abolir la peine de m. — KARR 385:12
mortal: All men think m. m. — YOUNG 754:18
And if I laugh at any m. thing — BYRON 171:8
But 'twas beyond a m.'s share — MARV 450:14
chances of this m. life — BOOK 122:16
desperately m. — SHAK 606:20
every tatter in its m. dress — YEATS 752:21
For m. tongue — GURN 320:3
genius and the m. instruments — SHAK 590:15
He raised a m. to the skies — DRYD 259:23
Her last disorder m. — GOLD 310:21
Immortal youth to m. maids — LAND 408:5
I presume you're m. — SHIR 646:5
M., guilty, but to me — AUDEN 35:5
m. men, mortal men — SHAK 581:25
m. mixture of earth's mould — MILT 463:23

mortal: (*cont.*):
m. thing so to immortalize — SPEN 659:11
possess is something m. — LUCR 432:2
shuffled off this m. coil — SHAK 575:16
this m. must put — BIBLE 101:14
time of this m. life — BOOK 120:10
To make us m., and thee waste — MARV 451:8
Who gathers all things m. — SWIN 676:16
mortality: frail m. shall trust — BACON 45:28
insensible of m. — SHAK 606:20
it smells of m. — SHAK 597:5
M. weighs heavily — KEATS 390:4
O'erbear the shores of my m. — SHAK 619:5
Old m., the ruins of forgotten — DROW 145:14
sad m. o'ersways — SHAK 634:3
Take away that emblem of m. — DISR 249:2
There's nothing serious in m. — SHAK 602:17
things even here and m. — VIRG 712:9
urns and sepulchres of m. — CREWE 226:19
mortals: Composing m. with immortal fire — AUDEN 34:2
greatest good that m. know — ADD 4:4
Is m.' chiefest enemy — SHAK 603:16
Lord, what fools these m. be — SHAK 612:2
m. always to be blest — ARMS 26:7
M., give thanks and sing — WESL 728:13
m. to command success — ADD 3:16
mortar: Lies are the m. — WELLS 727:19
mortification: desert of m. — WHITE 731:6
mortifications: m. and humiliations — WALP 720:10
mortis: *etiam opportunitate m.* — TAC 677:22
postremo donarem munere m. — CAT 187:1
Timor m. conturbat me — DUNB 264:3
morts: *Il n'y a pas de m.* — MAET 441:17
mortuus: *Passer m. est meae puellae* — CAT 185:13
Moscow: Do not march on M. — MONT 481:18
M.: those syllables can start — PUSH 533:1
Moses: And M. hid his face — BIBLE 71:39
As I was with M., so I will — BIBLE 73:26
Go down, M. — ANON 19:16
Jesus was sitting in M. chair — BLAKE 111:19
M. sent to spy out — BIBLE 73:5
moss: miles of golden m. — AUDEN 34:11
mossy: Happy field or m. cavern — KEATS 388:20
mote: m. that is in thy brother's — BIBLE 89:15
motes: m. that people the sunbeams — MILT 464:14
moth: m. of peace — SHAK 615:8
Both m. and flame — ROET 544:10
candle singed the m. — SHAK 608:19
desire of the m. — SHEL 643:12
Kill not the m. nor butterfly — BLAKE 111:5
like a m., the simple maid — GAY 299:10
m. and rust doth corrupt — BIBLE 89:6
m.'s kiss — BROW 150:13
mother: And gave her m. forty whacks — ANON 15:22
And, m., do not cry — FARM 280:5
As is the m., so is her daughter — BIBLE 85:21
back to the great sweet m. — SWIN 677:3
be a joyful m. — BOOK 133:7
Behold my m. — BIBLE 90:38
Behold thy m. — BIBLE 97:27
Care of his M. — MILNE 462:13
Christ and his m. — HOPK 346:6
Dead! and never called me m. — WOOD 742:1
Did this happen to your m. — WALK 717:11
Don't tell my m. I'm living in sin — HERB 333:15
either my father or my m. — STER 664:11
even by our m.'s dust — FORD 289:14
father and thy m. — BIBLE 72:16
father's shame, thy m.'s grief — BRET 140:17
For m. will be there — HERB 333:14
From whence his m. rose — SEDL 561:14
Gentle Child of gentle M. — DEAR 233:8
great m. of sciences — BACON 45:20
half knew my m. — O'BR 497:13
has not the church for his m. — CYPR 229:8
heaviness of his m. — BIBLE 78:20
his father and his m. — BIBLE 70:7
I arose a m. in Israel — BIBLE 74:2

mother: (*cont.*):
If that was a m., nobody	AMIS 10:17
it is the m.'s safeguard	NAP 489:11
man and the m. woman	SHAW 637:7
Man may not marry his M.	BOOK 136:3
man who hates his m.	BENN 63:22
m. bore me in the southern	BLAKE 114:1
M. died today	CAMUS 177:16
M., give me the sun	IBSEN 359:4
M. needs something today	JAGG 361:10
m. of arts, of warfare	DU B 262:23
m. of battles	HUSS 357:4
M. OF HARLOTS	BIBLE 107:10
m. of mankind	MILT 467:22
m. of months in meadow	SWIN 675:21
m. of Parliaments	BRIG 141:9
m. of Sisera looked out	BIBLE 74:6
M. of the Free	BENS 63:23
M. Russia	BLOK 115:8
m.'s head off	DICK 243:4
m.'s little helper	JAGG 361:10
m.'s sake the child was	COL 211:19
m.'s yearning	ELIOT 268:20
M. to dozens	HERB 333:18
m. was a decent family	ASHF 31:11
m. who talks about her	DISR 247:23
My M.	TAYL 679:13
My m. bids me bind my hair	HUNT 356:21
my m. cried	SHAK 613:20
My m., groaned! my father wept	BLAKE 114:8
My m.'s life made me a man	MAS 453:4
my m. taught me as a boy	BERR 66:18
No m., God forgot me	BROW 148:19
O m., mother	SHAK 570:26
O mother, m., make my bed	BALL 48:22
really affectionate m.	MAUG 454:13
recognize your m. with a smile	VIRG 715:1
There was their Dacian m.	BYRON 168:8
Thou art thy m.'s glass	SHAK 633:2
thou hast murdered thy m.	MAL 443:5
thy dear m. any courtesy	SHAK 570:25
universal m.	CHES 199:24
Upon his m.'s grave	WORD 746:14
We have a beautiful m.	WALK 717:14
Where a m. laid her baby	ALEX 8:11
Where yet was ever found a m.	GAY 300:3
wish thee all thy m.'s graces	CORB 218:14
Your m. will never see you	AUST 39:13

mother-in-law: man said when his m. died
	JER 365:16
savage contemplates his m.	FRAZ 293:9

mother-naked: m. and ageless-ancient
	DAY-L 233:3

mothers: best-bodied m. stands | WHIT 732:12
Come m. and fathers	DYLAN 265:23
m. of large families	BELL 60:24
women become like their m.	WILDE 734:15
Younger than she are happy m.	SHAK 622:20

mother-wits: rhyming m. | MARL 447:19

moths: Unfading m., immortal | BROO 143:8

motion: Between the m. and the act
	ELIOT 271:15
Devoid of sense and m.	MILT 469:14
Ev'ry m. has some end	BYROM 167:16
gentle m. with the deep	DAV 232:14
her m. blushed	SHAK 614:31
God ordered m., but ordained	VAUG 708:14
meets all m. and becomes	COL 209:19
m. is ever proportional	NEWT 494:3
m. of modern society	MARX 452:6
next to the perpetual m.	DICK 243:25
No m. has she now, no force	WORD 748:1
Of time's eternal m.	FORD 289:15
oil which renders the m.	HUME 355:9
Poetry in m.	KAUF 385:16
poetry of m.	GRAH 314:3
put them to m.	SHAK 630:9
Tell me it metes but m.	RAL 535:16
this m. like an angel sings	SHAK 610:1
uniform m. in a right line	NEWT 494:2
visible in her diurnal round	WORD 744:11

motions: m. of his spirit are dull | ... 810:9
secret m. of things	BACON 45:18

motions: (*cont.*):
So delicate his m.	BRID 141:5
two weeping m.	CRAS 226:12

motive: joint and m. of her body | SHAK 628:2
m.-hunting	COL 212:5
noble in m. and far-reaching	HOOV 344:17

motley: M.'s the only wear | SHAK 568:13
myself a m. to the view	SHAK 634:21

motor: heart's stalled m. | MAY 455:5

motorcycle: Art of M. Maintenance | PIRS 515:4
m. black madonna	DYLAN 265:14

motoribus: Cincti Bis M. | GODL 308:7

mots: m. qui vont bien ensemble | LENN 417:21

motto: my m. and my fate | SWIFT 675:9
scouts' m. is founded	BAD 46:4
that is my m.	MARQ 448:14
With this for m.	TENN 682:13

mottoes: m. on sundials | POUND 526:12

motus: m. animorum atque haec | VIRG 715:18

mould: can the m. be broken? | JENK 365:5
mortal mixture of earth's m.	MILT 463:23
m. of a man's fortune	BACON 43:18
m. them into an immortal	MILT 475:9
quite fresh from Natur's m.	DICK 241:21
their narrow lips the m.	ROSS 548:1
then broke the m.	ARIO 25:1

moulded: men are m. out of faults | SHAK 607:1
m. by their admirations	BOWEN 138:9
m. by the lips of man	TENN 689:15

mouldering: in many a m. heap | GRAY 315:12

moulds: Crack nature's m. | SHAK 595:20

mount: Mount, m., my soul | SHAK 621:13
rejected the Sermon on the M.	BRAD 139:7
they shall m. up with wings	BIBLE 84:1

Mount Abora: Singing of M. | COL 210:13

mountain: bald as the bare m. | AHN 29:25
destroy in all my holy m.	BIBLE 83:3
every m. and hill	BIBLE 83:26
fool alone on a great m.	KILV 396:7
from yonder m. height	TENN 688:14
go up to the m.	KING 397:5
gross as a m.	SHAK 580:21
He is gone on the m.	SCOTT 559:10
He watches from his m. walls	TENN 681:1
If the m. will not come	BACON 42:31
In a m. greenery	HART 327:13
into an exceeding high m.	BIBLE 88:20
M.'s slumberous voice	SHEL 641:13
m. 'tween my heart	SHAK 591:9
river jumps over the m.	AUDEN 34:3
sun looked over the m.'s rim	BROW 151:21
taking him up into a high m.	BIBLE 94:1
Tching prayed on the m.	POUND 526:5
this fair m. leave to feed	SHAK 577:12
tiptoe on the misty m.	SHAK 623:23
Up the airy m.	ALL 10:1

mountainous: m. sports girl | BETJ 68:3

mountains: Among the m. by the
winter sea	TENN 682:18
came to the Delectable M.	BUNY 156.4
High m. are a feeling	BYRON 168:24
lakes damp, and m. steep	STEP 663:17
Make m. level	SHAK 583:13
m. also shall bring peace	BOOK 129:19
M. are the beginning	RUSK 550:15
m. gave back the sound	WORD 743:1
m. look on Marathon	BYRON 171:1
m. skipped like rams	BOOK 133:8
m. were brought forth	BOOK 130:22
M. will go into labour	HOR 347:11
One of the m.	WORD 748:9
rocks of the m.	BIBLE 106:19
scale the icy m.' lofty tops	MARL 447:20
strength setteth fast the m.	BOOK 129:1
that I could remove m.	BIBLE 101:1
towering m. with a thunderbolt	VIRG 715:12
when men and m. meet	BLAKE 113:10
Where rose the m.	BYRON 168:17
Ye m. of Gilboa	BIBLE 75:8

mountain-tops: Flatter the m. | SHAK 633:12
m. that freeze	SHAK 588:15

mountebank: m. who sold pills | ADD 5:2
story of a m. and his monkey	HUXL 719:24

mountebanks: prosperous m. | LEWIS 421:7

mourir: M. ce n'est rien | ANOU 23:9
Partir c'est m. un peu	HAR 323:8

mourn: And m. in prison | MONT 480:7
Blessed are they that m.	BIBLE 88:23
But each will m. her own	ING 360:6
comfort all that m.	BIBLE 84:26
don't m. for me never	ANON 14:4
here is no cause to m.	OWEN 503:19
It is Margaret you m.	HOPK 346:4
love you, an' m. you	HEYW 338:3
Makes countless thousands m.	BURNS 162:19
m. all at her grave	BALL 51:1
m. for me when I am dead	SHAK 634:5
M., hapless Caledonia, mourn	SMOL 654:4
m. with ever-returning	WHIT 733:3
M., you powers of Charm	CAT 185:13
now can never m.	SHEL 640:1
summer skies to m.	KEATS 390:25
That man was made to m.	BURNS 162:18
time enough to m.	DAN 229:16
time to m., and a time to dance	BIBLE 80:5

mourned: we have m. unto you | BIBLE 90:26
Would have m. longer	SHAK 572:12

mournful: m. ever weeping Paddington
	BLAKE 112:2
Tell me not, in m. numbers	LONG 427:7

mourning: great m. | BIBLE 88:11
I'm in m. for my life	CHEK 196:11
m. that either his mother	AUST 39:24
oil of joy for m.	BIBLE 84:27
voice of m. save the choirs	OWEN 503:12
waste any time in m.	HILL 338:13
when she doth of m. speak	CAMP 177:5
widow bird sat m.	SHEL 640:5

mouse: appetit hath he to ete a m. | CHAU 193:26
For killing of a m. on Sunday	BRAT 139:19
free-born m. deation	BARB 52:2
Good m. of virtue	SHAK 628:20
if that she saugh a m.	CHAU 192:15
little m. will be born	HOR 347:11
Not a m. shall disturb	SHAK 613:2
Not a m. stirring	SHAK 571:23
seen a m. go by the wal	CHAU 193:26
usual to catch a m. or two	GRAY 316:12
wainscot and the m.	ELIOT 271:4

mouse-trap: or make a better m. | EMER 277:17
The M.	SHAK 576:17

moustache: And your neat m. | PLATH 516:4
Big chap with a small m.	WOD 740:12
man who didn't wax his m.	KIPL 402:11

mouth: cathedral in your m. | UST 707:19
door and bar for thy m.	BIBLE 87:28
God be in my m.	ANON 13:16
her m. is smoother	BIBLE 78:12
His m. is most sweet	BIBLE 81:20
just whispering in her m.	MARX 451:15
keeping your m. shut	EINS 268:5
Keep your m. shut	ANON 21:6
kisses of his m.	BIBLE 81:5
Let the words of my m.	BOOK 125:6
m. as greet was as a greet	CHAU 193:4
m. filled with laughter	BOOK 134:4
m. had been used as a latrine	AMIS 10:13
m. of the Lord hath spoken	BIBLE 83:26
m. of very babes and sucklings	BOOK 124:20
m. shall shew thy praise	BOOK 128:8
m. speaketh	BIBLE 90:32
m. went a sharp two-edged	BIBLE 106:1
Englishman to open his m.	SHAW 638:15
my m. sweet as honey	BIBLE 106:28
no m. to put it in	DICK 243:4
out of the m. of God	BIBLE 88:18
own m. will I judge thee	BIBLE 95:16
praises of God be in their m.	BOOK 135:16
purple-stainèd m.	KEATS 389:9
roof of my m.	BOOK 134:17
sank in the m. of the dying	AUDEN 34:13
slap-dash down in the m.	CONG 215:24
so he openeth not his m.	BIBLE 84:12
spew thee out of my m.	BIBLE 106:7

mouth: (cont.):
tastes like chaff in my m.   KEATS 392:14
musky, tusky m.   KIPL 401:21
way of happening, a m.   AUDEN 34:14
which cometh out of the m.   BIBLE 91:9
yet he opened not his m.   BIBLE 84:12
mouthed: m. to flesh-burst   HOPK 346:13
mouths: Blind m.! that scarce   MILT 466:8
enemy in their m. to steal   SHAK 616:6
issue from your smoky m.   MARL 447:2
Make m. upon me when I turn   SHAK 612:4
m., the tongues   SHAK 626:16
she made m. in a glass   SHAK 595:22
stuffed their m. with gold   BEVAN 69:2
They have m., and speak   BOOK 133:10
to m. like mine   BROW 152:25
We poets keep our m. shut   YEATS 752:16
movable: M. Types   CARL 181:4
Paris is a m. feast   HEM 331:16
move: But it does m,   GAL 297:4
great affair is to m.   STEV 667:20
high altar on the m.   BOWEN 138:14
If I could pray to m.   SHAK 591:12
in just order m.   DAV 232:6
I will m. the earth   ARCH 24:13
m., and have our being   BIBLE 98:33
M. him into the sun   OWEN 503:14
m. with the moving ships   SWIN 677:4
one who can't m.   SOND 656:2
that it never should m.   BOOK 132:6
this will not m.   SUCK 671:6
What can I do but m.   WILB 734:6
whichever way you m.   LUCAN 431:8
moved: earth be m.   BOOK 127:15
foot to be m.   BOOK 133:23
hates to be m. to folly   LAWR 413:5
I do not like being m.   CLOU 207:2
king was much m.   BIBLE 75:17
m. by what is not unusual   ELIOT 269:18
We shall not be m.   ANON 19:10
moveless: m. woe   BROW 147:14
movement: neither arrest nor m.   ELIOT 270:16
Time is the measure of m.   AUCT 33:27
mover: arrive at a prime m.   THOM 692:17
movere: Quieta m. magna merces   SALL 554:12
movers: m. and shakers   O'SH 501:22
moves: If it m., salute it   ANON 14:17
m. in this world   MAINE 442:13
m. with its own organs   SHAK 565:15
which is moved not, but m.   SHEL 644:8
moveth: all that m. doth in Change   SPEN 660:18
movies: M. should have a beginning   GOD 308:5
pay to see bad m.   GOLD 312:7
thing that can kill the m.   ROG 544:17
moving: King's life is m. peacefully   DAWS 233:2
m. accident is not my trade   WORD 744:8
m. as the restless spheres   MARL 448:1
m. finger writes   FITZ 284:9
m. from hence to there   SOCR 655:2
m. toyshop of their heart   POPE 523:17
stopped the m. stairs   MACN 440:19
which art m. everywhere   SHEL 641:14
mower: m. whets his scythe   MILT 465:10
Mozart: M. and Salieri we see   BAR 53:1
MPs: dull M. in close proximity   GILB 304:12
When in that House M. divide   GILB 304:11
much: Guessing so much and so m.   CHES 199:2
He that is too m. in anything   BACON 43:2
I'll do as m. for my true-love   BALL 51:1
just so m., no more   BROW 153:13
Missing so m. and so much   CORN 219:4
M. as you said you were   HARDY 325:7
M. have I seen and known   TENN 690:1
M. in our vows, but little   SHAK 629:20
m. is to be done and little   JOHN 369:14
m. to hear and see   SKEL 648:20
m. too far out all my life   SMITH 652:17
seem m. for them to be   COMP 214:14
So little done, so m. to do   RHOD 539:17
So many worlds, so m. to do   TENN 683:26
so m. owed by so many   CHUR 202:13
muchness: Much of a m.   VANB 708:1

muck: Money is like m.   BACON 44:20
Sing 'em m.!   MELBA 456:4
when to stop raking the m.   ROOS 546:11
muckrake: with a m. in his hand   BUNY 156:8
mud: cover the universe with m.   FORS 290:6
crawled about in the m.   BECK 57:24
Longing to be back in the m.   AUG 36:21
morris is filled up with m.   SHAK 611:14
m. against a wall   BLUNT 116:6
M.! Mud! Glorious mud   FLAN 285:10
M.'s sister, not himself   HOUS 351:14
on the people builds on m.   MACH 438:9
pure clay of time's m.   MAL 442:15
Shall come of water and of m.   BROO 143:7
muddle: beginning, a m., and an end   LARK 410:11
Fro' first to last, a m.   DICK 240:33
manage somehow to m. through   BRIG 141:8
Meddle and m.   DERBY 237:16
muddy: celibacy a m. horsepond   PEAC 510:8
M., ill-seeming, thick   SHAK 624:22
m. understandings   BURKE 158:5
this m. vesture of decay   SHAK 610:1
muero: Muero porque no m.   JOHN 366:13
muffin: Hot M. and Crumpet Baking   DICK 241:30
mufflered: tight-lipped m. men   JOS 380:16
muffling: his mantle m. up   SHAK 592:14
mug: graceful air and heavenly m.   FLEM 287:8
muir-men: m. win their hay   BALL 49:1
mulatto: Grape is my m. mother   HUGH 354:8
mule: like to horse and m.   BOOK 126:10
m. of politics   DISR 248:6
that Sicilian m. was to me   GLAD 307:18
mules: The m. of politics   POWER 528:12
mulier: Desinat in piscem m.   HOR 347:1
m. cupido quod dicit amanti   CAT 186:10
mullets: We will eat our m.   JONS 378:6
Mulligan: plump Buck M.   JOYCE 381:7
multas: M. per gentes et multa   CAT 187:1
multiplication: M. is vexation   ANON 16:13
m. of the fittest   SPEN 658:17
multiplicity: m. of agreeable consciousness   JOHN 372:24
multiplied: Thou hast m. the nation   BIBLE 82:26
multiply: Increase and m.   BOOK 121:2
m., and replenish   BIBLE 69:26
m. my signs   BIBLE 72:3
multitude: barbarous m.   SHAK 608:16
By the fool m.   SHAK 608:16
great m.   BIBLE 106:18
hoofs of a swinish m.   BURKE 158:18
m. is always in the wrong   DILL 246:5
m. of one million   KOES 403:19
m. of the isles   BOOK 131:12
m., that numerous piece of   BROW 146:15
m. the blind instruments   GODW 308:11
my life with m. of days   JOHN 370:18
or m., such as Mob   COBB 207:28
vast despairing m.   BOOTH 136:5
multitudes: Beauteous the m.   SMART 652:13
I am large, I contain m.   WHIT 732:21
m. in the valley of decision   BIBLE 86:9
Pestilence-stricken m.   SHEL 641:14
Weeping, weeping m.   ELIOT 270:10
mum: fuck you up, your m. and dad   LARK 410:6
oafish louts remember M.   BETJ 67:4
mumble: When in doubt, m.   BOREN 136:7
mumbled: few m. cakes   HUNT 356:16
mummy: dyed in m.   SHAK 617:3
munch: So m. on, crunch on   BROW 151:27
munched: m., and munched   SHAK 600:1
mundi: Antiquitas saeculi juventus m.   BACON 42:11
cito transit gloria m.   THOM 692:3
qui tollis peccata m.   MISS 477:5
Sic transit gloria m.   ANON 22:15
mundus: justitia et pereat m.   FERD 281:9
munere: sunt tristi m.   CAT 187:1
muneribus: M. sapienter uti   HOR 350:19

muove: Eppur si m.   GAL 297:4
L'amor che m. il sole   DANTE 230:21
murals: Garden City Café with its m.   BETJ 67:13
murder: brought back m. into the home   HITC 339:9
For m., though it have no   SHAK 575:13
foul and most unnatural m.   SHAK 573:15
from battle and m.   BOOK 119:17
I met M. on the way   SHEL 641:10
indeed should m. sanctuarize   SHAK 578:12
indulges himself in m.   DE Q 237:12
I wanted to m.   DOST 254:12
Killing no m.   SEXBY 563:10
Live in despite of m.   CHAP 190:14
Macbeth does m. sleep   SHAK 602:2
Most sacrilegious m.   SHAK 602:14
m. an infant in its cradle   BLAKE 112:28
m. by the law   YOUNG 754:10
m. cannot be hid long   SHAK 608:8
M. considered as one   DE Q 237:11
m. for the truth   ADLER 5:7
M. is a serious business   ILES 359:9
M., like talent   LEWES 420:10
M. most foul   SHAK 573:16
m. respectable   ORW 501:2
M.'s out of tune   SHAK 618:9
m. whiles I smile   SHAK 588:3
M. will out   CHAU 194:6
m. yet is but fantastical   SHAK 600:12
One m. made a villain   PORT 525:6
See how love and m. will out   CONG 215:4
stick to m. and leave art to us   EPST 278:5
Thou shalt do no m.   BOOK 121:18
To do no contrived m.   SHAK 614:26
To m. thousands   YOUNG 754:10
Vanity, like m., will out   COWL 221:23
We hear war called m.   MACD 437:12
We m. to dissect   WORD 748:8
withered m.   SHAK 601:13
murdered: Each one a m. self   ROSS 548:2
masquerade, a m. peer   ALC 8:1
m. reputations of the week   CONG 215:28
Our royal master's m.   SHAK 602:16
two brothers and their m. man   KEATS 388:2
murderer: help the escaping m.   STEV 667:16
honest thief, the tender m.   BROW 148:13
honourable m.   SHAK 618:19
m. from the beginning   BIBLE 96:33
m. would shudder at it   DOST 255:2
that art a m. so young   MAL 443:5
murderers: let the m. take the first   KARR 385:12
m., and idolaters   BIBLE 107:25
murders: upon the stroke that m.   SHAK 623:19
murd'rous: m. hand   CRAB 225:16
murmur: creeping m.   SHAK 585:14
ever-importunate m.   JAMES 362:9
live m. of a summer's day   ARN 28:3
rustic m. of their bourg   TENN 682:9
Seem to m. sweet and low   ARMS 26:5
shallow m., but the deep are   RAL 535:19
with reason m. at his case   COWP 222:10
murmured: m. in their tents   BOOK 132:13
murmuring: mazily m.   TENN 687:11
m. of innumerable bees   TENN 688:16
suffice me that my m. rhyme   MORR 485:11
murmurs: In hollow m. died   COLL 213:15
In the m., in the pauses   SOND 656:1
m. of more censorious old   CAT 185:15
m. of self-will   BODE 116:11
Murray: slain the Earl of M.   BALL 49:2
mus: nascetur ridiculus m.   HOR 347:11
musarum: Audita M. sacerdos   HOR 349:22
muscle: motion of a m.   WORD 743:7
take the m. from bone   ELIOT 272:11
muscles: M. better and nerves   CUMM 228:16
m. of his brawny arms   LONG 428:2
muscular: Christianity was m.   DISR 248:12
muse: conqueror creates a M.   WALL 718:16
gifts of goodly golden M.   OXF 504:2
He talked shop like a tenth m.   ANON 14:8

muse: (cont.):
Livelier liquor than the M.   HOUS 352:19
meditate the thankless m.   MILT 466:4
m. and the magistrate   FOOTE 288:16
M. first trod the stage   POPE 523:14
m. in silence sings aloud   CLARE 204:22
M. invoked, sit down   SWIFT 675:1
M. Oblivion's curtain draw   CLARE 204:20
m. of fire exist under   OLIV 498:16
M. of fire, that would ascend   SHAK 584:16
M. of heav'nly birth inspires   CHUR 201:7
m. only speak when she   SMITH 652:16
praise the M. forbids to die   HOR 350:17
tenth M.   TROL 704:8
whose m. on dromedary   COL 210:16
muses: charm of all the M.   TENN 689:14
M. made write verse   VIRG 715:7
M. never knew their pains   CRAB 225:11
M. scorn with vulgar brains   SIDN 647:1
mushroom: I am ... a m.   FORD 289:8
Life is too short to stuff a m.   CONR 217:19
meet a m. rich civilian   BYRON 173:18
m. of a night's growth   DONNE 253:8
shape of a supramundane m.   LAUR 411:9
mushrooms: make midnight m.   SHAK 626:1
music: aerial m.'s past   SHEN 644:12
all kinds of m.   BIBLE 85:28
All m. is folk music   ARMS 26:10
all the daughters of m.   BIBLE 81:1
And die in m.   SHAK 618:15
brave m. of a *distant* drum   FITZ 283:14
Caught in that sensual m.   YEATS 752:20
city is built to m.   TENN 681:23
Classic m. is th'kind   HUBB 353:12
dance to the m. of time   POW 528:6
Darling of the m. halls   SMITH 651:16
day the m. died   MCL 439:8
doctrine, but the m. there   POPE 521:13
Fading in m.   SHAK 608:24
finds its food in m.   LILLO 421:16
Fled is that m.   KEATS 389:17
frozen m.   SCH 557:10
fulfilled with the m. he made   SWIN 676:3
Give me some m.   SHAK 565:11
heavy part the m. bears   JONS 378:14
he hears no m.   SHAK 590:7
hope danceth without m.   HERB 336:4
how potent cheap m. is   COW 221:4
How sour sweet m. is   SHAK 621:11
If m. be the food of love   SHAK 628:9
In sweet m. is such art   SHAK 588:16
I shall be made thy m.   DONNE 251:6
Just accord all m. makes   SIDN 647:5
Let him step to the m.   THOR 697:8
Let's face the m. and dance   BERL 65:16
let the sounds of m. creep   SHAK 610:1
Like m. on my heart   COL 211:15
maintain the m. of the spheres   BROW 146:17
make the m. mute   TENN 682:10
man that hath no m.   SHAK 610:3
May make one m. as before   TENN 682:29
merry when I hear sweet m.   SHAK 610:2
most civilized m.   UST 707:11
M. alone with sudden charms   CONG 215:16
M. and women I cannot   PEPYS 512:17
m. at the close   SHAK 619:16
m. begins there   MILL 461:23
m. begins to atrophy when   POUND 527:13
M. breathing from her face   BYRON 167:27
m. crept by me upon   SHAK 625:9
m. crept into our ears   ROET 544:8
m. divides, measures   MANN 445:5
m. Dr Johnson used to say   JOHN 376:27
M. has charms to sooth   CONG 215:16
m. in its roar   BYRON 169:13
M. is essentially useless   SANT 555:19
M. is feeling, then, not sound   STEV 666:7
m. is the brandy of the damned   SHAW 637:10
M. is your own experience   PARK 506:3
m. of a poem   SYNGE 677:8
m. of forfended spheres   PATM 509:14
m. of its trees at dawn   IDN 77:16
m. of men's lives   SHAK 621:11

music: (cont.):
m. oft hath such a charm   SHAK 606:18
m. of the Gospel leads   FABER 279:13
m. sent up to God   BROW 148:1
M. shall untune the sky   DRYD 261:26
m. that excels is the sound of   FISH 283:7
M. that gentlier on the spirit   TENN 685:21
m. that I care to hear   HOPK 345:12
M., the greatest good   ADD 4:4
m. touched the bawdy strings   STEV 666:9
M., when soft voices die   SHEL 643:11
m., yearning like a God   KEATS 387:2
My m. playing far off   SHAK 565:12
no m. in the nightingale   SHAK 631:6
O body swayed to m.   YEATS 750:18
one equal m.   DONNE 253:14
own m. when they stray   CAMP 177:9
pine that makes her m.   THEO 691:29
practising your pastoral m.   VIRG 714:11
reasonable good ear in m.   SHAK 612:10
seduction of martial m.   BURN 160:19
shriller than all the m.   SHAK 589:21
Silent m., either other   CAMP 177:8
since the m. began   BERL 65:15
softest m. to attending ears   SHAK 623:6
sound of soft m.   DISR 248:36
still, sad m. of humanity   WORD 745:1
There is m. in the air   ELGAR 268:14
They were thy chosen m.   WORD 748:9
thou hast thy m. too   KEATS 390:19
to m. lendeth   SIDN 646:22
To the Master of all m.   LONG 427:18
towards the condition of m.   PATER 509:6
uproar's your only m.   KEATS 391:11
We are the m. makers   O'SH 501:22
What passion cannot M. raise   DRYD 261:24
why hear'st thou m. sadly   SHAK 633:3
musical: his m. finesse was such   COWP 223:15
Most m., most melancholy   MILT 464:19
m. as is Apollo's lute   MILT 464:1
m. Malcolm Sargent   BEEC 58:18
Silence more m. than any song   ROSS 547:10
So m. a discord, such sweet   SHAK 612:14
Such as found out m. tunes   BIBLE 88:1
music-hall: m. singer attends a series   GILB 305:4
musician: dead, the sweet m.   LONG 427:18
far below the m.   LEON 418:12
m., if he's a messenger   HEND 332:4
No better a m. than the wren   SHAK 610:5
musing: Love of peace, and lonely m.   COLL 213:15
M. full sadly in his sullen   SPEN 660:1
M. in solitude   WORD 743:14
thus m. the fire kindled   BOOK 126:22
musk: m. carnations break   ARN 28:27
musket: Sam, pick up tha' m.   HOLL 342:5
musk-rose: coming m.   KEATS 389:13
m., and the well-attired woodbine   MILT 466:11
musk-roses: With sweet m.   SHAK 611:19
musky: m., tusky mouth   KIPL 401:21
muss: M. es sein?   BEET 59:23
mussel: And the m. pooled   THOM 693:12
mussels: Where gaping m.   CRAB 224:23
Mussolini: Even Hitler and M.   LOW 429:9
must: Duty whispers low, *Thou m.*   EMER 276:14
forget because we m.   ARN 26:16
genius which does what it m.   BAR 53:1
It m. be so   ADD 3:23
m. a word to be addressed   ELIZ 274:13
Must it be?   BEET 59:23
mustard: faith as a grain of m.   BIBLE 91:16
like to a grain of m.   BIBLE 91:3
say 'Pass the m.'   GILB 306:25
We sowed in youth a m. seed   BRON 142:2
musty: proverb is something m.   SHAK 576:21
mutabile: *Varium et m. semper*   VIRG 713:7
mutability: From chance, and death, and m.   SHEL 642:18
How M. in them doth play   SPEN 660:17
Nought may endure but M.   SHEL 641:12
mutamur: *et illos m. in illis*   ANON 22:19

mutant: *animum m. qui*   HOR 348:9
mutantur: *spatio m. saecla*   LUCR 432:1
mutato: *M. nomine de te*   HOR 350:22
mutatus: *Quantum m. ab illo*   VIRG 712:18
mute: beautiful face is a m.   PUBL 531:1
except that of m.   MACM 440:8
M. and magnificent   DRYD 261:29
muteness: uncommunicating m. of fishes   LAMB 406:11
mutilate: fold, spindle or m.   ANON 12:33
mutiny: horror, fear and m.   SHAK 620:17
Rome to rise and m.   SHAK 592:17
mutter: blessed m. of the mass   BROW 148:18
mutton-pies: make them into m.   CARR 183:22
mutual: m. cowardice keeps us   JOHN 375:5
when we meet a m. heart   THOM 696:14
muzzle: m. on the window-panes   ELIOT 272:1
muzzled: beside a m. bore   STEP 663:18
my-doxy: M. and Heterodoxy   CARL 180:21
my-lorded: m. him as only a free-born   THAC 691:13
myriad: There died a m.   POUND 527:3
myriad-minded: m. Shakespeare   COL 212:3
myriads: M. of rivulets   TENN 688:16
M. though bright   MILT 468:2
myrrh: frankincense, and m.   BIBLE 88:9
m. is my wellbeloved   BIBLE 81:7
myrtle: brier shall come up the m.   BIBLE 84:18
m. and turkey part of it   AUST 38:18
myself: find I'm talking to m.   BARN 53:12
I celebrate m., and sing   WHIT 732:13
I do not know m., and God   GOET 309:19
In awe of such a thing as I m.   SHAK 589:27
I pray for no man but m.   SHAK 626:8
It is m. that I remake   YEATS 751:19
love him as m.   BOOK 123:6
M. alone I seek to please   GAY 300:6
m. a traitor with the rest   SHAK 621:1
not for m. who is for me   HILL 339:2
thought of thinking for m.   GILB 306:1
When I give I give m.   WHIT 732:19
mysteries: m. of Hecate   SHAK 594:19
m. of our religion   HOBB 340:11
Stewards of the m. of God   BIBLE 100:18
What m. do lie beyond thy dust   VAUG 709:7
wingy m. in divinity   BROW 146:2
mysterious: God moves in a m. way   COWP 222:17
m. as well as terrible   DOST 254:3
m. or supernatural   HUME 355:6
mystery: Behold, I shew you a m.   BIBLE 101:14
from the penetralium of m.   KEATS 391:10
In which the burthen of the m.   WORD 744:20
Its m. is its life   BAG 47:7
lose myself in a m.   BROW 146:3
marvel and a m.   LONG 427:3
M., BABYLON THE GREAT   BIBLE 107:10
m. inside an enigma   CHUR 202:7
m. of the atom   BRAD 139:7
m. of the cross   FORT 291:2
m. of the king's power   JAM 362:3
my tongue, the m. telling   THOM 692:13
out the heart of my m.   SHAK 576:22
reflection solves the m.   STUB 671:2
upon 's the m. of things   SHAK 597:16
Your mystery, your m.   SHAK 617:14
mystic: scaled eyeball owns the m.   BROW 153:3
white samite, m., wonderful   TENN 681:18
mystical: m. body of the Son   BOOK 122:14
m. body of thy Son   BOOK 121:13
m. way of Pythagoras   BROW 146:5
order and m. mathematics   BROW 145:1
mystique: Feminine M.   FRIE 294:3
myth: lend a m. to God   CRANE 225:24
most potent m. of all   BROO 143:19
m. is not a fairy story   RYLE 552:8
m. is recognized for what   SAM 554:18
myths: Science must begin with m.   POPP 524:15

N

Naboth: N. the Jezreelite — BIBLE 76:10
Nächte: *nie die kummervollen N.* — GOET 309:15
nag: gait of a shuffling n. — SHAK 581:5
nagging: n. is the repetition — SUMM 672:1
Naiad: N. 'mid her reeds — KEATS 387:24
nail: blows his n. — SHAK 599:11
  final n. with bony thud — BLOK 115:3
  for want of a n. — FRAN 292:18
  n. by strength drives out — SHAK 631:5
  n. into his temples — BIBLE 74:1
  n. my pictures together — SCHW 558:16
  walks away with the n. — LAWR 412:3
nails: And three cloves like n. — HEAT 330:1
  blowing of his n. — SHAK 587:29
  Can pay attention to his n. — PUSH 532:14
  into the print of the n. — BIBLE 97:35
  My n. are drove — ANUN 16:16
  n. bitten and pared — MAC 434:14
  n. he'll dig them up again — WEBS 726:8
  n. whitter than the lylye — CHAU 194:5
  near your beauty with my n. — SHAK 587:17
  nineteen hundred and forty n. — SITW 648:13
  relatively clean finger n. — MORT 486:7
naître: *êtes donné la peine de n.* — BEAU 56:12
naïve: n. domestic Burgundy — THUR 697:17
  n. forgive and forget — SZASZ 677:13
naked: drear and n. shingles — ARN 27:1
  Half n., loving, natural — BYRON 170:21
  In walking n. — YEATS 751:3
  kiste hir n. ers — CHAU 194:1
  left me n. to mine enemies — SHAK 589:2
  N., and ye clothed me — BIBLE 92:20
  n. ape self-named *Homo* — MORR 485:6
  n. every day he clad — GOLD 310:22
  n. into the conference chamber — BEVAN 69:1
  n. is the best disguise — CONG 215:5
  N. on a bed of play — GREV 318:5
  N. they came to that smooth — TENN 687:19
  n. to the hangman's noose — HOUS 352:8
  orchid she rode quite n. — AUDEN 34:1
  pluck me from my n. bed — KYD 404:10
  stark n. truth — CLEL 206:4
  starving hysterical n. — GINS 306:28
  thus I clothe my n. villany — SHAK 621:22
  When a' was n. — SHAK 583:22
  With n. foot, stalking — WYATT 749:19
nakedness: And not in utter n. — WORD 745:14
  n. of woman is the work — BLAKE 112:24
  see the n. of the land — BIBLE 71:28
Namby-Pamby: N.'s little rhymes — CAREY 179:17
name: And I have forgotten your n. — SWIN 676:24
  at the n. of Jesus — BIBLE 103:5
  At the n. of Jesus — NOEL 496:9
  bless your n. in pride and — BROW 150:19
  breathe not his n. — MOORE 483:9
  Breathing my n. with a sigh — PAR 506:2
  But only differ in the n. — CHUD 200:12
  Change the n. — HOR 350:22
  cometh in the N. of the Lord — BOOK 133:17
  Conveys it in a borrowed n. — PRIOR 529:9
  Corsair's n. to other times — BYRON 169:24
  coward shame distain his n. — BURNS 162:17
  deed without a n. — SHAK 603:20
  Democracy is the n. we give — FLERS 287:9
  everlasting n. — BIBLE 84:19
  ev'n for his own n.'s sake — SCOT 561:8
  fear my n. shall the Sun — BIBLE 86:19
  filches from me my good n. — SHAK 616:12
  For my n. and memory — BACON 46:3
  gable and writing our n. — HEAN 329:17
  gathered together in my n. — BIBLE 91:20
  ghost of a great n. — LUCAN 431:5
  glory in the n. of Briton — GEOR 300:26
  God's own n. upon a lie — COWP 223:14
  have left a n. behind them — BIBLE 88:2
  He left the n. — JOHN 370:17
  help standeth in the N. — BOOK 134:2

name: (*cont.*):
  Her n. is never heard — BAYLY 56:3
  her n. upon the strand — SPEN 659:11
  his N. is great in Israel — BOOK 130:6
  his N. only is excellent — BOOK 135:15
  his n. shall be called Wonderful — BIBLE 82:27
  I am become a n. — TENN 690:1
  I do not like her n. — SHAK 569:8
  I kept them in thy n. — BIBLE 97:22
  In the n. of God — CROM 227:10
  Is not the king's n. twenty — SHAK 620:5
  king's n. is a tower — SHAK 622:9
  Let me not n. it to you — SHAK 618:5
  liberties are taken in thy n. — GEOR 301:10
  local habitation and a n. — SHAK 612:17
  may prefer a self-made n. — HAND 323:4
  my n. is Jowett — BEEC 59:7
  My n. is Legion — BIBLE 93:11
  my wife, and my n. — SURT 672:12
  n. is rather to be chosen — BIBLE 79:10
  n. liveth for evermore — BIBLE 88:3
  n. made great is a name — HILL 339:1
  n. of a man is a numbing blow — MCL 439:15
  N. of the Lord our God — BOOK 125:7
  n. of the Lord thy God — BIBLE 72:16
  n. to all succeeding ages curst — DRYD 259:1
  n. too will be linked — OVID 502:16
  n. to the reverberate hills — SHAK 628:24
  n. were not so terrible — SHAK 582:24
  nothing but to n. his tools — BUTL 166:1
  nothing of a n. — BYRON 169:17
  or the number of his n. — BIBLE 106:32
  out his n. out of the book — BIBLE 106:5
  praise of his holy N. — BOOK 123:17
  problem that has no n. — FRIE 294:3
  provides us with n. and nation — BUNT 155:8
  redeem my n. from dissolution — DAN 229:18
  roarers for the n. of king — SHAK 624:26
  shakes up everyone's n. — HOR 349:23
  spared the n. — SWIFT 675:12
  talk not to me of a n. — BYRON 173:8
  that dare not speak its n. — DOUG 255:7
  that slow sweet n.'s sake — BROW 149:23
  Their n. liveth for ever — SASS 557:13
  thy great n. we praise — SMITH 653:31
  thy n. give glory — BIBLE 108:2
  thy N. give the praise — BOOK 133:9
  Till I thy n., thy nature know — WESL 728:9
  To leave a living n. behind — WEBS 725:13
  trembled at the hideous n. — MILT 470:9
  What's in a n. — SHAK 622:30
  which is above every n. — BIBLE 103:5
  whose n. was writ in water — KEATS 392:17
  With a n. like yours — CARR 183:9
  with the whistling of a n. — POPE 522:21
  write upon him my new n. — BIBLE 106:6
  yet can't quite n. — LARK 410:4
named: heaven and earth is n. — BIBLE 102:13
  she n. the child I-chabod — BIBLE 74:32
nameless: intolerably n. names — SASS 557:13
  N. here for evermore — POE 518:7
  n. in worthy deeds — BROW 145:22
  n., unremembered, acts — WORD 744:19
names: calleth them all by their n. — BOOK 135:11
  commodity of good n. — SHAK 579:23
  honour doth forget men's n. — SHAK 593:25
  I have lost all the n. — JOHN 375:26
  in love with American n. — BENÉ.T 62:15
  instinct bring back the old n. — COL 210:17
  lands after their own n. — BOOK 127:24
  n. ignoble, born to be forgot — COWP 222:25
  n. in many a musèd rhyme — KEATS 389:14
  n. of those who love — HUNT 356:4
  N. that should be on every — CALV 175:12
  n. to be mentioned — AUST 39:18
  things with their n. — SART 556:13
  worshipped by the n. divine — BLAKE 111:23
naming: n. of parts — REED 537:18
Nan: change Kate into N. — BLAKE 111:23
nap: short n. at sermon — ADD 4:8
nape: her n. caught in his bill — YEATS 752:10
Napoleon: N. forgot Blücher — CHUR 201:22

Napoleon: (*cont.*):
  N. of crime — DOYLE 256:13
  N.'s armies — SELL 562:24
  [N.] that his presence — WELL 727:11
  thinks he is N. — CLEM 206:8
Napoleons: Caesars and N. — HUXL 357:14
narcotic: n. be alcohol or — JUNG 382:15
narcotics: Like dull n., numbing pain — TENN 683:1
Narr: *ein N. sein Leben lang* — LUTH 432:17
narration: n. always going backwards — WALP 719:6
  time is the medium of n. — MANN 445:5
narrative: bald and unconvincing n. — GILB 305:8
narratur: *Fabula n.* — HOR 350:22
narrow: its neck is n. — NASH 490:15
  n. is the way — BIBLE 89:22
  niggard n. way — DAN 229:12
  O make it saft and n. — BALL 48:22
narrower: n. kind of life — PYM 533:11
narrow-souled: n. people — POPE 524:5
Nassau: Can Stuart or N. go — PRIOR 529:6
Nasticreechia: N. Krorluppia — LEAR 414:6
nastiest: n. thing in the nicest way — GOLD 310:3
nasty: everybody is as n. as himself — SHAW 638:26
  Man is a n. creature — MOL 479:14
  n., brutish, and short — HOBB 340:7
  nice man is a man of n. ideas — SWIFT 674:21
  Something n. in the woodshed — GIBB 302:24
natale: *Libertas et n. solum* — SWIFT 675:15
nation: against the voice of a n. — RUSS 552:1
  bind up the n.'s wounds — LINC 422:9
  boundary of the march of a n. — PARN 507:7
  broad mass of a n. — HITL 339:14
  exterminate a n. — SPOCK 661:4
  faith in a n. of sectaries — DISR 248:8
  fate of a n. was riding — LONG 427:20
  from an ample n. — DICK 244:18
  general happiness of the n. — PEDR 510:16
  hast multiplied the n. — BIBLE 82:26
  haughty n. proud in arms — MILT 463:15
  holy n., a peculiar people — BIBLE 105:11
  king and government and n. — KAV 386:5
  Licensed build that n.'s fate — BLAKE 111:9
  London: a n., not a city — DISR 248:21
  make war on a kindred n. — BETH 67:2
  n. expects to be ignorant — JEFF 364:14
  n. is fit to sit in judgement — WILS 738:10
  n. is not governed — BURKE 157:21
  n. of dancers, singers — EQUI 278:10
  n. of shopkeepers — NAP 490:5
  n. of shopkeepers — SMITH 651:1
  n. of shopkeepers — ADAMS 3:9
  n. shall not lift up sword — BIBLE 82:11
  n. shall rise against nation — BIBLE 92:9
  N. shall speak peace unto — REND 538:18
  N. spoke to a Nation — KIPL 400:5
  n. talking to itself — MILL 461:21
  n. which indulges toward — WASH 722:1
  noble and puissant n. — MILT 475:14
  No n. wanted it so much — SWIFT 675:13
  Once to every man and n. — LOW 430:3
  one-third of a n. ill-housed — ROOS 545:19
  our existence as a n. — PITT 515:16
  places the n. at his service — POMP 518:13
  public burden of the n.'s — PRIOR 529:12
  Righteousness exalteth a n. — BIBLE 78:32
  Still better for the n. — ANON 14:6
  temptation to a rich and lazy n. — KIPL 401:8
  this continent a new n. — LINC 422:10
  top n. — SELL 562:27
  we are a n. of amateurs — ROS 546:16
  what our N. stands for — BETJ 67:15
  whole n. perish not — BIBLE 97:6
national: above n. prejudices — NORTH 496:12
  n. debt . . . a national blessing — HAM 322:11
  N. Debt is a very Good — SELL 562:23
  our n. disease — JAMES 363:14
nationalism: N. is an infantile sickness — EINS 268:8
  N. is a silly cock crowing — ALD 8:3

nationalities: smaller n. of Europe ASQ 31:17
tangle of squabbling n. ROOS 546:12
nationality: n. he would prefer RHOD 539:16
You talk to me of n. JOYCE 381:10
nationless: tribeless, and n. SHEL 642:18
nations: And the living n. wait AUDEN 34:15
become the father of many n. BIBLE 99:24
belong to two different n. FOST 291:7
day of small n. CHAM 189:4
friendship with all n. JEFF 364:5
gossip from all the n. AUDEN 35:10
hating all other n. GASK 299:6
healing of the n. BIBLE 107:23
let fierce contending n. ADD 3:24
n. are as a drop of a bucket BIBLE 83:29
n. by your government VIRG 713:17
N., like men BOL 117:9
n. shall do him service BOOK 129:20
N. touch at their summits BAG 46:23
n. under our feet BOOK 127:19
n. which have put mankind INGE 359:17
other n. and states draw GOGOL 310:2
Other n. use 'force' WAUGH 724:6
pedigree of n. JOHN 370:27
small n. like prostitutes KUBR 404:7
smote divers n. BOOK 134:15
teaching n. how to live MILT 475:17
To belong to other n. GILB 306:5
two great n. in the world TOCQ 699:5
Two N. DISR 248:28
Two n. DISR 248:26
unknowing n. with our stores DAN 230:2
native: adieu! my n. shore BYRON 168:3
comes n. with the warmth KEATS 390:8
considerable in his n. place JOHN 373:13
Fast by their n. shore COWP 222:24
found him a n. of the rocks JOHN 371:12
have felt with my n. land TENN 687:6
n. of the very world he made SMART 649:9
not more n. to the heart SHAK 572:5
our ideas about the n. LESS 419:8
This is my own, my n. land SCOTT 559:16
With thunders from her n. oak CAMP 177:1
natives: Britons were only n. SELL 562:17
nativity: At my n. SHAK 581:1
For thy holy n. ELL 275:8
n. was under *ursa major* SHAK 595:2
natura: N. *enim non imperatur* BACON 45:2
N. *il fece, e poi roppe* ARIO 25:1
natural: and twice as n. CARR 183:20
behaviour was n. and intrepid WALP 719:2
boy interested in n. history SCOTT 559:5
He wants the n. touch SHAK 604:4
I do it more n. SHAK 629:6
n. for a man and woman JOHN 373:14
n. man has only two primal OSLER 502:2
N. rights is simple nonsense BENT 64:3
N. Selection DARW 231:7
[N. selection] has no vision DAWK 232:17
n. to die as to be born BACON 43:10
n. to us than a cage SHAW 636:14
On the stage he was n. GOLD 311:6
something in this more than n. SHAK 574:30
swear her colour is n. SHER 645:15
naturam: N. *expelles furca* HOR 348:8
nature: accordant with man's n.
HARDY 324:12
against n. not to go out MILT 476:1
All n. is but art POPE 522:8
All N. was degraded BLAKE 110:17
all that would force n. WYCH 750:3
Art is only N. operating HOLB 341:19
Auld n. swears BURNS 162:2
Beauty is N.'s brag MILT 464:8
course of N. is the art of God YOUNG 754:24
[Death is] n.'s way of ANON 12:31
death lives, and n. breeds MILT 470:4
double vigour, art and n. SHAK 606:3
drive out n. with a pitchfork HOR 348:8
experiencing it. BAG 47:11
n... N.'s walks POPE 521:27
fancy outwork n. SHAK 566:5

nature: *(cont.)*:
Finally he paid the debt of n. FABY 279:15
For n., heartless, witless HOUS 352:1
For N. made her what she BURNS 161:12
frame of n. round him break ADD 4:5
From the war of n. DARW 231:10
fulfils great N.'s plan BURNS 161:27
Gie me ae spark o' N.'s fire BURNS 161:26
God and n. do nothing in vain AUCT 33:16
Good painters imitate n. CERV 188:17
great N. made us men LOW 430:2
great n.'s second course SHAK 602:2
great Secretary of N. WALT 721:12
hand of N. and we women GIBB 302:23
happy imitator of N. HEMI 331:13
happy n. to explore POPE 522:14
horridly cruel works of n. DARW 231:11
How N. always does contrive GILB 304:10
human n. is finer KEATS 391:16
If ignorance of n. gave HOLB 341:20
I linger yet with n. BYRON 172:18
informed by the light of n. BACON 42:2
intellectual n. is necessary JOHN 369:1
interpreter of n. JOHN 369:20
interpreter of n. WHEW 730:15
Is N. felt, or can WORD 743:12
It can't be N., for it CHUR 200:18
It is a part of n. SPEN 658:19
keep the fire of my n. BRON 142:5
law of n. and of nations BURKE 159:9
learned to look on n. WORD 745:1
like N. to go no further LEIB 416:18
looks thro' N. POPE 522:22
Love is only N.'s art GREV 318:5
lusty stealth of n. SHAK 594:26
made a gap in n. SHAK 565:6
Man is N.'s sole mistake GILB 306:15
man the less, but n. more BYRON 169:13
mere copier of n. REYN 539:6
mirror up to n. SHAK 576:6
more direct than does N. LEON 418:10
My n. is subdued SHAK 634:22
N. abhors a vacuum RAB 534:18
N. always desires AUCT 33:20
N., and Nature's laws POPE 521:2
n. as freely as a lawyer GIR 307:3
n. by her mother wit SPEN 660:13
N. cannot be ordered about BACON 45:22
N. did never put her precious BACON 45:24
N. does nothing in vain NEWT 493:21
N. does nothing without ARIS 25:17
n. est un temple BAUD 55:8
N. first doth cause all DAV 232:6
N. gave me at my birth COL 209:17
N. gives to each what AUCT 33:19
N. had not befriended us CAV 187:13
N. hadn't counted on my showing up
TURG 705:4
N. has no cure for this SMITH 651:12
N. hath provided and left LOCKE 425:3
n. her custom holds SHAK 578:14
N. in awe to him MILT 467:2
N. in him was almost lost COLL 213:16
N. in you stands SHAK 595:15
N. is always wise THUR 697:22
N. is but a name for an effect COWP 224:6
N. is creeping up WHIS 730:22
N. is dumb TURG 705:9
N. is not a temple TURG 705:5
N. is often hidden BACON 44:7
n. is the art of God BROW 146:7
N. is tugging at every EMER 276:16
N. is usually wrong WHIS 730:19
n. itselfe cant endure FLEM 287:1
N. made him, and then broke ARIO 25:1
n. makes the whole world SHAK 627:22
n. more than nature needs SHAK 595:16
N. must obey necessity SHAK 593:13
N. never makes enny blunders BILL 109:18
N. never makes excellent LOCKE 424:17
N. never set forth the earth SIDN 647:6
n. of all greatness not to be BURKE 157:15
n. of God is a circle XENO 16:17

nature: *(cont.)*:
n. of war consisteth not HOBB 340:6
N., red in tooth and claw TENN 683:22
n. replaces it WILL 737:4
N.'s agreeable blunders COWL 221:24
N. say one thing and Wisdom BURKE 159:22
n.'s changing course SHAK 633:6
N.'s decorations glisten SMART 649:8
N. seems dead SHAK 601:13
n.'s fragile vessel SHAK 626:20
N.'s great masterpiece DONNE 251:14
n.'s handmaid art DRYD 260:3
N.'s law BURNS 162:18
N.'s social union BURNS 163:16
N.'s works to me expunged MILT 470:16
N. that framed us of four MARL 448:1
N. that is above all art DAN 229:13
n. there are neither rewards ING 360:8
N. wears one universal grin FIEL 282:16
N. were inconstancy COWL 221:14
N., with all her cruelty FORS 290:12
n. yet remembers WORD 746:2
next to N., Art LAND 408:2
Not otherwise, O N. WORD 743:13
observe n. OSLER 501:24
Of slower N. got the start DENH 236:19
open from criticism to n. JOHN 369:9
our knowledge of n. WHEW 730:13
our life alone does N. COL 209:14
Passing through n. to eternity SHAK 572:9
pattern of excelling n. SHAK 618:5
perfect n. and are perfected BACON 44:25
priketh hem n. in hir corages CHAU 192:7
rest in N., not the God of HERB 335:15
rest on N. fix COKE 209:2
spectacles of books to read N. DRYD 262:11
standing at ease in N. WHIT 732:5
still is N.'s priest WORD 745:14
subjectification of n. LANG 408:18
through her works gay n. SMART 649:16
Till I have name, thy n. know WESL 728:9
Tired N.'s sweet restorer YOUNG 754:12
'Tis n., full of spirits HUNT 356:11
True wit is N. to advantage POPE 521:11
Uncrring N., still divinely POPE 521:6
various appearances of n. SMITH 650:14
Vows can't change n. BROW 152:14
weakness of our mortal n. BOOK 121:7
what if all animated n. COL 209:20
While n., kindly bent SWIFT 675:10
With N., to out-do the life JONS 379:18
World, N., Universe's Essence PAST 509:1
natures: ignominy of our n. BROW 146:11
naught: it is n., saith the buyer BIBLE 79:8
n. for your comfort CHES 198:27
struggle n. availeth CLOU 207:23
naughtiness: n. of thine heart BIBLE 74:40
superfluity of n. BIBLE 104:29
naughty: former n. life BOOK 121:14
good deed in a n. world SHAK 610:4
He is a n. child, I'm sure STEV 668:18
'Tis a n. night to swim SHAK 596:12
nauseous: n. draught of life ROCH 543:6
naval: n. tradition CHUR 203:10
nave: from the n. to the chaps SHAK 599:15
navel: n. is like a round goblet BIBLE 82:2
navibus: *n. atque quadrigis* HOR 348:9
navies: Far-called our n. melt KIPL 400:12
n. grappling in the central TENN 685:13
navita: N. *de ventis* PROP 529:22
navy: came the n. of Tharshish BIBLE 75:25
load would sink a n. SHAK 588:21
n. of England hath ever BLAC 110:12
n. under the good Providence CHAR 191:11
put at the head of the N. CARS 184:1
Ruler of the Queen's N. GILB 305:26
thoroughly efficient n. ROOS 546:9
your n. nothing BURKE 157:32
nay: And Mr Hall's n. was nay BENT 64:11
your n., nay BIBLE 105:6
Nazareth: good thing come out of N. BIBLE 96:8
Nazi: finally N. Germany NEV 492:5
Nazis: only the N. wanted war WAUGH 724:7

Neaera: tangles of N.'s hair — MILT 466:4
near: Be n. me when my light is low — TENN 683:16
come not n. to me — BIBLE 85:1
n. in blood — SHAK 602:19
She is n., she is near — TENN 686:20
so n. and yet so far — TENN 684:9
when you're n. there's such — PORT 524:22
nearer: n. God's Heart in a garden — GURN 319:17
N., my God, to thee — ADAMS 3:10
n. than hands and feet — TENN 681:15
n. the Church the further — ANDR 11:14
n. *you are to God* — WOTT 749:8
nearest: n. and dearest enemy — SHAK 581:15
nearly: I was n. kept waiting — LOUI 428:14
neat: any good girl to be n. — TAYL 679:12
I was n., clean, shaved — CHAN 190:1
N., but not gaudy — WESL 729:5
Still to be n., still to be dressed — JONS 378:18
that is not clean and n. — STEV 668:18
You look n., Talk about a treat — COLL 213:6
Nebuchadnezzar: golden image that N. — BIBLE 85:28
necessarily: It ain't n. so — HEYW 338:1
necessary: it is n. not to change — FALK 279:20
Make yourself n. to someone — EMER 276:15
n. evil — BRAD 139:4
n. evil — PAINE 504:10
n. evils — JOHN 369:13
n. to destroy the town — ANON 15:7
superfluous, a very n. thing — VOLT 716:17
things n. to salvation — BOOK 135:22
visible delight, but n. — BRON 142:18
necessities: art of our n. is strange — SHAK 596:2
n. call out great virtues — ADAMS 1:13
were n. and which luxuries — WRIG 749:10
will dispense with its n. — MOTL 487:4
necessity: always at the door of n. — DEFOE 234:3
Cruel n. — CROM 227:7
fiction is a n. — CHES 199:14
first n. invented stools — COWP 223:16
grim N. — SHAK 621:4
I do not see the n. — ARG 24:19
N. and chance — MILT 472:8
N. has no law — PUBL 531:4
N. hath no law — CROM 227:13
N. is a bad recommendation — FIEL 282:8
N. is the plea — PITT 515:15
N. makes an honest man a knave — DEFOE 234:3
nature must obey n. — SHAK 593:13
N. never made a good bargain — FRAN 292:15
There is no virtue like n. — SHAK 619:13
Thy n. is yet greater than mine — SIDN 647:12
urgent n. of intense speed — LEV 419:19
villains by n. — SHAK 595:2
neck: hanged about his n. — BIBLE 91:18
his n. brake — BIBLE 74:31
his n. unto a second yoke — HERR 337:6
its n. is narra — NASH 490:15
left his straight n. bent — ROSS 547:22
my n. is very short — MORE 484:15
n. God made for other use — HOUS 352:8
n. is as a tower of ivory — BIBLE 82:3
n. is like the tower — BIBLE 81:13
n. when once broken — WALSH 720:17
Roman people had but one n. — CAL 175:5
Some chicken! Some n. — CHUR 202:16
strecche forth the n — CHAU 194:9
neckcurls: n., limp and damp — ROET 544:5
necklace: with our n., we shall — MAND 444:3
necklaces: n. of gleaming fruit — BABEL 41:10
nectar: lie beside their n. — TENN 686:1
sipped out n. from his hand — MARL 447:9
To comprehend a n. — DICK 244:19
Work without hope draws n. — COL 211:24
nectarine: n., and curious peach — MARV 450:9
need: all ye n. to know — KEATS 389:3
all you n. in this life — TWAIN 706:27
everyone's n., but not enough — BUCH 154:6
face of total n. — BURR 164:5

need: *(cont.)*:
living n. charity more — ARN 26:15
n. of a world of men — BROW 151:21
people whenever we n. them — FLERS 287:9
reason not the n. — SHAK 595:16
Requires sorest n. — DICK 244:19
sorrow, n., sickness — BOOK 122:3
thy n. is greater than mine — SIDN 647:12
To suit and serve his n. — HERB 334:12
What can I want or n. — HERB 335:22
Will you still n. me — LENN 418:3
needful: All that is n. hath been — WINK 739:7
But one thing is n. — BIBLE 94:18
needle: Plying her n. and thread — HOOD 344:7
through the eye of a n. — BIBLE 91:25
Who says my hand a n. — BRAD 139:10
Why are the n. and the pen — LEWIS 420:18
needlework: raiment of n. — BOOK 127:13
needs: But n. grow too fast — WALK 717:11
each according to his n. — BAK 47:23
each according to his n. — MARX 452:5
needy: the poor and n. — BOOK 126:27
world was wilfulliche n. — LANG 409:7
negation: n. of God — GLAD 307:4
negative: N. Capability — KEATS 391:10
n. of which America — MCC 436:19
prefers a n. peace — KING 396:16
will his n. inversion — AUDEN 36:5
neglect: most tender mercy is n. — CRAB 225:16
n. arises in some measure — ADAMS 1:12
n. may breed mischief — FRAN 292:18
n. of his duties — THOM 695:14
Such sweet n. more taketh me — JONS 378:18
neglected: to have his all n. — JOHN 371:11
negligent: servant's too often a n. elf — BARH 52:19
negotiate: never n. out of fear — KENN 393:14
negotiating: N. with de Valera — LLOY 424:11
negotiation: finish a difficult n. — SAL 553:3
negotiis: *qui procul n.* — HOR 348:22
nègres: *Les pauvres sont les n.* — CHAM 189:15
Negro: drop of N. blood — HUGH 354:2
N. could never *hope* — DAVIS 232:15
N.'s great stumbling block — KING 396:6
negroes: drivers of n. — JOHN 370:3
neiges: *où sont les n. d'antan?* — VILL 711:15
neighbour: coveted his n.'s goods — KING 398:2
hate your n. — MAC 434:20
I am a n. and near bred — SHAK 608:4
lug the guts into the n. room — SHAK 577:25
my duty to my N. — BOOK 123:5
My duty towards my N. — BOOK 123:6
n.'s house is on fire — BURKE 158:6
neighed after his n.'s wife — BIBLE 85:4
next-door n. for so many years — SCOTT 560:24
nor done evil to his n. — BOOK 124:28
our unintroduced n. — ELIOT 269:16
policy of the good n. — ROOS 545:17
Thou shalt love thy n. — BIBLE 73:3
Thou shalt not covet thy n.'s — BIBLE 72:16
thy foot from thy n.'s house — BIBLE 79:17
neighbourhood: n. before it has broadened — JOHN 367:7
n. of voluntary spies — AUST 39:1
neighbouring: aspiring rock, n. the skies — DAN 229:12
cynosure of n. eyes — MILT 465:11
peaceable n. state — AMIS 10:10
neighbours: charity with your n. — BOOK 122:5
Good fences make good n. — FROST 295:4
make sport for our n. — AUST 39:19
n. say, 'He was a man who used — HARDY 324:22
peace to all his n. — SHAK 589:15
upon his n. to do his work — BAUD 55:13
vigil feast his n. — SHAK 586:11
what is happening to our n. — CHAM 189:5
what to have good n. — ELIZ 274:2
neighed: n. after his neighbour's wife — BIBLE 85:4
neighs: high and boastful n. — SHAK 585:14
neither: I will n. go nor hang — BIGOD 109:16
'Tis n. here nor there — SHAK 617:23

Nell: Pretty witty N. — PEPYS 512:14
Nellie: by the stream, N. Dean — ARMS 26:5
Nelly: Let not poor N. starve — CHAR 191:17
Nelson: N. touch — NELS 491:14
N. was felt in England — SOUT 657:20
nemo: N. me impune lacessit — ANON 22:10
Neptune: As N.'s park, ribbed — SHAK 571:6
nequiores: Nos n., mox daturos — HOR 350:5
Nero: N. fiddled, but Coolidge — MENC 457:4
nerve: after the n. has been — ROWL 549:8
all fat, without n. — LEWIS 421:8
always called a n. specialist — WOD 740:15
Anatomised in every n. — JONS 378:20
n. o'er which do creep — SHEL 640:22
nerves: and the n. prick — TENN 683:16
his vitals and his n. — HUNT 366:10
N. sit ceremonious — DICK 244:9
strengthens our n. — BURKE 168:24
that, and my firm n. — SHAK 603:11
Nervii: he overcame the N. — SHAK 592:13
nervous: n. breakdown — RUSS 551:10
nervousness: only n. or death — LEB 415:8
nest: her soft and chilly n. — KEATS 387:7
like the n. of a foolish bird — MADAN 441:10
long since my n. is made — TENN 688:7
mine eyes he makes his n. — LODGE 425:23
n. of singing birds — JOHN 371:4
now leaves his wat'ry n. — D'AV 231:20
swallow a n. — BOOK 130:16
warm n. of renaissance — DAY-L 233:3
We'll theek our n. when — BALL 50:20
nestling: N. me everywhere — HOPK 345:6
nests: Birds in their little n. agree — WATTS 722:17
birds of the air have n. — BIBLE 90:1
built their n. in my beard — LEAR 413:18
Thus you birds build n. — VIRG 715:20
net: have laid a n. for my feet — BOOK 128:15
I will let down the n. — BIBLE 94:3
play tennis with the n. down — FROST 295:17
too old to rush up to the n. — ADAMS 2:4
nets: holdeth fast the n. — OXF 504:2
into their own n. together — BOOK 135:2
n. and stratagems to catch — HERB 335:19
n. of such a texture — SHEN 644:14
n. to catch the wind — WEBS 725:13
tangled in amorous n. — MILT 473:15
their time in making n. — SWIFT 674:18
try to fly by those n. — JOYCE 381:10
nettle: Out of this n., danger — SHAK 580:10
Tender-handed stroke a n. — HILL 338:8
nettles: like the dust on the n. — THOM 694:6
n. and brambles — BIBLE 83:18
overrun with n. — WALP 719:22
network: N. Anything reticulated — JOHN 368:2
neurosis: n. is a secret you don't know — TYNAN 706:32
N. is the way of avoiding — TILL 698:5
neurotics: come to us from n. — PROU 530:11
neutral: intolerable n. itch — AUDEN 36:5
Loyal and n. — SHAK 602:18
stood apart, studiously n. — WILS 738:12
neutrality: Armed n. — WILS 738:16
Just for a word 'n.' — BETH 67:2
n. of an impartial judge — BURKE 160:3
neutralize: White shall not n. the black — BROW 152:22
never: and n. go to sea — GILB 306:2
And n. home came she — KING 397:14
N. do to-day what you can — PUNCH 531:11
N. explain — FISH 283:5
N. explain — HUBB 353:9
N. give a sucker an even break — FIEL 282:20
N. glad confident morning — BROW 151:2
n. had it so good — MACM 440:3
N. in the field of human — CHUR 202:13
N. knowingly undersold — LEWIS 420:20
N., never, never, never — SHAK 598:3
N. play cards with a man called — ALGR 9:5
n. should move at any time — BOOK 132:6
N. the time and the place — BROW 151:13
n. thought of thinking — GILB 306:1

never: (*cont.*):
N. to have lived is best — YEATS 751:20
n. use a big, big D — GILB 305:24
n. was and never will be — JEFF 364:14
N. was born — STOWE 670:9
people n. so impatient — BOOK 131:16
She who has n. loved — GAY 299:27
sometimes always, by God, n. — RICH 540:16
than n. to have been loved — CONG 215:31
Than n. to have fought at all — CLOU 207:21
This will n. do — JEFF 365:1
We n. closed — VAN D 708:8
What, n.? No, never! — GILB 305:23
nevermore: N. to peep again — DE L 236:4
Quoth the Raven, 'N.' — POE 518:8
new: against the n. and untried — LINC 422:1
All appeared n., and strange — TRAH 701:11
America, my n. found land — DONNE 250:16
Among n. men, strange faces — TENN 682:22
blessing of the N. — BACON 42:18
Blow up the trumpet in the n. moon
   — BOOK 130:14
brave n. world — SHAK 626:3
change old lamps for n. — ARAB 24:1
have put on the n. man — BIBLE 103:16
I make all things n. — BIBLE 107:18
intend to lead a n. life — BOOK 122:5
make a n. acquaintance — JOHN 376:19
MAKE IT N. — POUND 526:5
needs find out n. heaven — SHAK 564:13
n. deal for the American — ROOS 545.15
N. every morning is the love — KEBLE 392:19
n. friend is as new wine — BIBLE 87:16
n. heaven and a new earth — BIBLE 107:17
n. heavens and a new earth — BIBLE 85:2
n. man may be raised up — BOOK 122:20
N. nobility is — BACON 44:9
N. opinions — LOCKE 424:14
n. race is sent down from — VIRG 714:22
n. thing under the sun — BIBLE 80:1
n. what ev'ry body knows — COWP 222:1
n. wine into old bottles — ATTL 32:15
n. wine into old bottles — BIBLE 90:8
offences of affections n. — SHAK 634:21
or to hear some n. thing — BIBLE 98:30
piping songs for ever n. — KEATS 388:27
ring in the n. — TENN 684:10
shall find something n. — VOLT 716:2
shock of the n. — DUNL 264:6
so quite n. a thing — CUMM 228:16
there's nothing n. in dying — YES 753:25
threshold of the n. — WALL 718:13
time for making n. enemies — VOLT 717:7
unto the Lord a n. song — BOOK 126:11
unto the Lord a n. song — BOOK 131:13
we'll find the n. — BAUD 55:11
Whether it be n. or old — ANON 14:13
write upon him my n. name — BIBLE 106:6
Yet somehow always n. — HEINE 330:16
new-bathed: n. stars — ARN 28:18
newborn: What is the use of a n. child
   — FRAN 293:5
Newcastle: made of N. coal — WALP 719:11
no more coals to N. — GEOR 301:4
newcomer: O blithe n.! — WORD 748:10
New England: brought against N. — KRUT 404:6
N. weather that compels — TWAIN 706:24
newer: n. object quite forgotten — SHAK 631:5
newest: oldest sins the n. kind — SHAK 584:4
newness: in n. of life — BIBLE 99:28
news: All the n. that's fit to print — OCHS 498:2
bad n. infects the teller — SHAK 564:17
man bites a dog, that is n. — BOG 116:14
bringer of unwelcome n. — SHAK 582:13
For evil n. rides post — MILT 474:13
get the n. to you — TWAIN 706:11
good n. from a far country — BIBLE 79:19
Ill n. hath wings — DRAY 257:10
All nature is news that stays n.
   — POUND 527:15
n. and Prince of Peace — FITZ 287:24
n. to hear and bitter tears — CURT 241:14
n. yet to hear and fine — CHES 199:6

news: (*cont.*):
only n. until he's read it — WAUGH 724:4
passion is the love of n. — CRAB 225:4
What n. on the Rialto — SHAK 607:19
New South Wales: govern N. — BELL 61:4
newspaper: good n. is a nation talking
   to itself — MILL 461:21
never to look into a n. — SHER 644:20
n. is of necessity something — SCOTT 559:2
only be a n. literature — ZAMY 755:4
newspapers: I read the n. avidly — BEVAN 69:7
It's the n. I can't stand — STOP 669:17
where roads and n. — AUST 39:1
Newspeak: N. is — ORW 500:12
Newstatesmanship: In N. — POTT 525:20
newt: Eye of n., and toe of frog — SHAK 603:18
Newton: another N., a new Donne
   — HUXL 357:19
Let N. be — POPE 521:2
make us as N. was — AUDEN 35:11
N. at Peru — WALP 719:16
N., childlike sage — COWP 223:27
Single vision and N.'s sleep — BLAKE 112:11
statue stood of N. — WORD 747:2
newts: N., and blind-worms — SHAK 611:20
New World: N. into existence — CANN 178:11
New York: California to the N. Island
   — GUTH 320:5
N.,—a helluva town — COMD 214:11
N. swallowing the tonnage — MII L 461:19
next: n. to Nature, Art — LAND 408:2
n. to course god america i — CUMM 228:6
What n., what next — LOW 430:14
nexus: sole n. of man to man — CARL 180:2
Niagara: wouldn't *live* under N. — CARL 181:15
nice: N. but nubbly — KIPL 402:2
n. clean faces — BARH 52:13
N. guys finish last — DUR 264:11
n. man is a man of nasty — SWIFT 674:21
n. people with whom one — PYM 533:10
n. to people on your way up — MIZN 478:10
N. work if you can get it — GERS 301:12
Too n. for a statesman — GOLD 311:4
nicens: n. little boy named baby — JOYCE 381:9
nicest: nastiest thing in the n. — GOLD 310:3
niche: got your n. in creation — HALL 322:4
Nicholas: St N. soon would be there
   — MOORE 482:5
Nick: Satan, N., or Clootie — BURNS 160:23
nick: improve the n. of time — THOR 696:29
nickname: every n. is a title — PAINE 504:18
n. is the heaviest stone — HAZL 329:4
Nicodemus: Wise N. — VAUG 708:15
nidificatis: *Sic vos non vobis n.* — VIRG 715:20
niece: hitting the n. of a bishop — ORW 500:20
niggard: n. narrow way — DAN 229:12
nigger: woman is the n. of the world — ONO 499:3
nigh: shall any plague come n. — BOOK 131:4
they shall not come n. — BOOK 126:9
night: acquainted with the n. — FROST 294:8
after noon, in n. — DONNE 242:7
ain't a fit n. out for man — FIEL 282:22
all n. by troops of stars — COL 210:7
All n. it fell, and when — BRID 141:4
alternate n. and day — FITZ 283:15
And n. with different stars — SACK 552:15
And when n. darkens — MILT 468:21
as a watch in the n. — BOOK 130:23
ate a good supper at n. — ANST 23:11
become a borrower of the n. — SHAK 602:22
black bat, n. — TENN 686:17
black n. doth take away — SHAK 634:6
blessed candles of the n. — SHAK 610:8
by Silvia in the n. — SHAK 631:6
call it perfect day nor n. — SHAK 587:29
City is of N. — THOM 696:17
Closed his eyes in endless n. — GRAY 316:7
cloudy n. immediately — SHAK 623:16
Come, civil n. — SHAK 623:16
cottle, door N. — CHAP 190:17
covered by the long n. — HÖR 350.19
dangers of this n. — BOOK 119:11
darkness hides n. may be n. — BOOK 132:9

night: (*cont.*):
dark n. of the soul — FITZ 285:5
day brought back my n. — MILT 474:27
Dear N.! this world's defeat — VAUG 708:16
desolate n. in search of him — BYRON 168:1
dog in the n.-time — DOYLE 256:14
dusky n. rides down the sky — FIEL 282:1
everlasting n. is to be slept — CAT 185:15
everlasting n. — DONNE 251:5
Every n. and alle — BALL 49:18
Farewell n., welcome — BUNY 156:15
filmy curtain of the n. — PUSH 533:5
fourth watch of the n. — BIBLE 91:6
from this palace of dim n. — SHAK 624:9
gentle into that good n. — THOM 693:4
genuine n. admits no ray — DRYD 261:2
goes of a n. and comes — SHER 645:15
hangs upon the cheek of n. — SHAK 622:24
haunts you n. and day — BERL 65:19
have toiled all the n. — BIBLE 94:3
heaviness may endure for a n. — BOOK 126:5
honeyed middle of the n. — KEATS 387:1
horror of a deep n. — RAC 535:2
I ask of thee, belovèd N. — SHEL 643:23
ignorant armies clash by n. — ARN 27:1
Illness is the n.-side of life — SONT 656:6
infant crying in the n. — TENN 683:19
Infinite day excludes the n. — WATTS 723:4
in the n., my Soul — THOM 695:10
I pass like n., from land — COL 211:16
Is it n.? Are we here together — WHIT 732:10
It's been a hard day's n. — LENN 417:20
It was mirk, mirk n. — BALL 50:17
know his God by n. — VAUG 708:15
know'st the mask of n. — SHAK 622:32
last out a n. in Russia — SHAK 605:13
lesser light to rule the n. — BIBLE 69:23
Let n. come, ring out the hour — APOL 23:15
Let no n. seal thy sense — DE L 236:2
lived to see n. fall — WAUGH 723:17
long day's journey into n. — O'NEI 498:19
long n. of waiting — KING 397:6
Long n. succeeds thy little day — PEAC 510:11
love my ever-during n. — CAMP 177:4
love-performing n. — SHAK 623:16
Love the n. — DRYD 261:20
loving, black-browed n. — SHAK 623:17
machinery of the n. — GINS 306:28
Making n. hideous — SHAK 573:9
moonless n. in the small — THOM 693:16
Morning in the bowl of n. — FITZ 283:10
Morn in weary N.'s decline — BLAKE 111:23
muche to seye as it was n. — CHAU 193.14
my n. be turned to day — BOOK 134:19
mysteries of Hecate and the n. — SHAK 594:19
nation was riding that n. — LONG 427:20
neither the moon by n. — BOOK 133:23
Never sees horrid n. — SHAK 586.8
n. after tonight — AMIS 11:4
N. and day on me she cries — BALL 49:13
N. and day, you are the one — PORT 524:23
n. before Christmas — MOORE 482:5
n. cometh, when no man — BIBLE 96:34
n. do penance for a day — WORD 747:3
n. has a thousand eyes — BOUR 138:2
N. hath a thousand eyes — LYLY 433:11
n. in a palace of fire — BIBLE 72:13
n. in her silver shoon — DE L 236:11
n. is crept upon our talk — SHAK 593:13
n. is darkening round me — BRON 142:11
n. is fair on the dewy — TENN 687:4
n. is far spent — BIBLE 100:10
n. long in the dark — STEV 668:21
N. Mail crossing the Border — AUDEN 35:9
N. makes no difference — HERR 336:19
n. methinks is but the daylight — SHAK 610:6
n. of the long knives — HITL 339:10
n. of this immortal day — SHEL 642:19
n. of time far surpasseth — BROW 145:24
n. of tropical splendour — PORT 524:21
n. of tyranny had descended — MURR 488:12
n.'s black agents — SHAK 603:5
N.'s candles are burnt — SHAK 623:23

night: (*cont.*):
n. she'll hae but little   BALL 50:6
two swift dragons cut   SHAK 612:6
n. stands like a black   BABEL 41:10
n. that he was betrayed   BOOK 122:12
n. that wins   SWIN 675:22
N., the shadow of light   SWIN 676:1
n. time I shall not forget   SWIN 676:13
n. to die upon the sand   ARN 28:15
n. were falling fast   LONG 426:18
n. we went to Birmingham   CHES 199:5
n. will more than pay   ARN 27:5
n. you sit feasting   BEDE 58:13
one n. certifieth   BOOK 125:4
only for a n. and away   WYCH 750:2
O thievish N.   MILT 463:20
Out of the n. that covers me   HENL 332:6
Queen of the silent n.   BEST 67:1
reign of Chaos and old N   MILT 468:23
returned on the previous n.   BULL 154:17
rung n.'s yawning peal   SHAK 603:4
Sable-vested N.   MILT 470:12
Ships that pass in the n.   LONG 428:1
sin and nature's n.   WESL 728:2
sleep one ever-during n.   CAMP 177:3
So late into the n.   BYRON 173:6
sound lovers' tongues by n.   SHAK 623:6
sound of revelry by n.   BYRON 168:15
spend the n. with the other   CHEK 197:10
Spirit of N.   SHEL 643:22
stayed here all the n.   SHAK 623:21
Stay out all n., but take   CHUR 201:5
such a n. as this   SHAK 609:23
tender is the n.   KEATS 389:11
terror by n.   BOOK 131:3
then it's n. once more   BECK 58:1
there cometh the dark n.   HAWES 328:3
there shall be no n. there   BIBLE 107:21
There's n. and day   BORR 136:14
things that go bump in the n.   ANON 13:12
This is the n.   SHAK 618:4
through the foul womb of n.   SHAK 585:14
Through the n. of doubt and   BAR 53:3
thy dangerous brow by n.   SHAK 590:16
tire the n. in thought   QUAR 533:17
'Tis a naughty n. to swim   SHAK 596:12
'Tis with us perpetual n.   JONS 379:8
touch of Harry in the n.   SHAK 585:17
under the lonely n.   VIRG 713:13
upon the n.'s starred face   KEATS 391:1
vast and middle of the n.   SHAK 572:18
very witching time of n.   SHAK 576:25
vile contagion of the n.   SHAK 590:22
Watchman, what of the n.   BIBLE 83:6
Were toiling upward in the n.   LONG 427:1
What hath n. to do with sleep   MILT 463:17
What is the n.   SHAK 603:13
Where the blue of the n.   CROS 227:18
wide womb of uncreated n.   MILT 469:14
Yesterday the bird of n.   SHAK 590:10
yet it is not n.   BYRON 169:1
You meaner beauties of the n.   WOTT 749:2
nighted: cast thy n. colour off SHAK 572:8
night-flies: buzzing n.   SHAK 583:11
nightingale: all but the wakeful n. MILT 471:10
brown bright n.   SWIN 675:21
brown n. bills his best   HARDY 326:1
Hark! ah, the N.   ARN 27:17
It was the n., and not   SHAK 623:22
My n.   SHAK 566:2
newe abaysed n.   CHAU 195:19
n. does sit so late   MARV 450:17
n., if she should sing   SHAK 610:5
n. in the sycamore   STEV 669:8
n. that in the branches   FITZ 284:16
n. when May is past   CAREW 179:12
O 'tis the ravished n.   LYLY 433:10
roar you as 'twere any n.   SHAK 611:8
She sings as sweetly as a n.   SHAK 624:14
spoils the singing of the n.   KEATS 390:25
There is no music in the n.   SHAK 631:6
Where the n. doth sing   KEATS 386:8
nightingales: n. are singing near ELIOT 272:20

nightlight: I was just a tiny n. FORS 290:7
nightmare: History is a n. JOYCE 381:22
In the n. of the dark   AUDEN 34:15
long national n. is over   FORD 289:2
n. by a rocking cradle   YEATS 753:2
nights: chequer-board of n. and days
                                FITZ 284:7
Love not such n. as these   SHAK 595:25
n. are wholesome   SHAK 572:2
n. which appear too long   HEAT 329:25
O n. and feasts divine   HOR 351:10
O ye N., and Days   BOOK 118:18
night-season: n. also I take no rest BOOK 125:9
night-wind: breath of the n. ARN 27:1
nihil: *Aut Caesar, aut n.* BORG 136:12
N. est sine ratione   LEIB 416:15
Vox et praeterea n.   ANON 23:1
nil: *N. actum credens*   LUCAN 431:6
N. admirari prope res est   HOR 348:7
N. carborundum illegitimi   ANON 16:19
N. desperandum   HOR 349:5
N. posse creari   LUCR 431:14
Nile: on the banks of the N. SHER 645:6
pour the waters of the N.   CARR 181:25
Where's my serpent of old N.   SHAK 565:1
nimble: n. and airy servitors MILT 475:1
nimbler: n. much than hinds MARV 450:18
nimini-pimini: pronouncing to yourself n.
                                BURG 157:1
Nimrod: N. the mighty hunter BIBLE 70:33
nine: N. bean rows will I have YEATS 752:7
n. men's morris is filled   SHAK 611:14
n. worthy and the best   CAXT 188:2
nineteen: it doesn't mean n. BENN 63:16
ninety: n. and nine in the wilderness
                                BIBLE 94:34
n. men and more   TENN 689:1
Nineveh: one with N., and Tyre KIPL 400:12
ninny: Compared to Handel's a mere n.
                                BYROM 167:15
Niobe: Like N., all tears   SHAK 572:12
nip: I'll n. him in the bud ROCHE 542:17
nipping: n. and an eager air SHAK 573:7
nipple: Have plucked my n.   SHAK 601:7
nisi: *N. Dominus aedificaverit* BIBLE 108:4
nives: *Diffugere n., redeunt* HOR 350:15
nix: Sticks n. hick pix   ANON 18:5
no: everlasting N.   CARL 181:9
land of the omnipotent No   BOLD 117:6
man who says n.   CAMUS 177:17
n. go the merrygoround   MACN 440:13
N.! I am not Prince Hamlet   ELIOT 272:5
N. money, no service   RAC 535:6
N. more o' that, my lord   SHAK 604:13
N. pain, no palm; no thorns   PENN 511:13
N. sun—no moon   HOOD 344:1
There is n. God   BOOK 124:26
there is n. more to say   SHAK 628:7
'twas n. matter what he said   BYRON 171:19
Noah: but one poor N.   HUXL 357:19
God gave N. the rainbow sign   ANON 13:17
into N.'s ark   COWP 223:10
N. he often said   CHES 199:12
nobile: *Par n. fratrum*   HOR 351:8
nobility: ancient n. is the act of time
                                BACON 44:9
Betwixt the wind and his n.   SHAK 579:30
But leave us still our old n.   MANN 445:6
God destroy man's n.   BACON 42:24
Here all were noble, save N.   BYRON 168:5
in others n.   PAINE 504:17
N. has its obligations   LÉVIS 420:7
N. is a graceful ornament   BURKE 158:22
N. of birth commonly abateth   BACON 44:10
order of n. is of great use   BAG 46:21
True n. is exempt from fear   SHAK 587:21
nobis: *Non n., Domine*   BIBLE 108:2
noble: death so n.   MILT 474:18
Do n. things, not dream   KING 397:9
Eternally n., historically fair LERN 419:3
fredome is a n. thing   BARB 52:8
Here all were n., save Nobility BYRON 168:5

noble: (*cont.*):
Is this the n. nature   SHAK 617:13
Man is a n. animal   BROW 145:26
My love's a n. madness   DRYD 259:25
n. acts of chivalry   CAXT 188:3
n. and nude and antique   SWIN 676:8
n. grounds for the noble   RUSK 550:13
n. heart, that harbours   SPEN 659:26
n. Living, and the noble Dead   WORD 747:8
n. man but made ignoble   TENN 682:4
n. mind is here o'erthrown   SHAK 576:4
n. savage   DRYD 260:8
n., the grand style   ARN 30:9
n. to myself   SHAK 566:2
ruins that of a n. mind   DOYLE 256:10
silence is most n. till   SWIN 676:2
Some work of n. note   TENN 690:4
Sublimity is the echo of a n.   LONG 428:7
'Tis only n. to be good   TENN 684:22
What's brave, what's n.   SHAK 566:1
nobleman: king may make a n. BURKE 159:26
underrated N.   GILB 303:14
noblemen: n. who have gone wrong
                                GILB 306:12
nobleness: allied with perfect n. ARN 30:8
And N. walks in our ways   BROO 143:4
n. of life   SHAK 564:14
Thy thoughts with n.   SHAK 570:24
nobler: n. in the mind to suffer SHAK 575:16
nobles: n. by the right of an earlier MAC 434:18
their n. with links of iron   BOOK 135:16
noblesse: *N. oblige*   LÉVIS 420:7
noblest: amongst the n. of mankind
                                CALV 175:16
honest God is the n. work of   ING 360:7
honest man's the n. work of   BURNS 161:19
honest man's the n. work of   POPE 522:20
n. prospect which a Scotchman   JOHN 372:7
n. Roman of them all   SHAK 593:23
ruins of the n. man   SHAK 591:23
nobly: I am n. born   DEKK 235:18
n. Cape Saint Vincent   BROW 150:7
Spurn not the n. born   GILB 304:8
We shall n. save   LINC 422:6
nobody: gave a war & N. came GINS 306:27
give a war and n. will come   SAND 555:9
n. comes, nobody goes   BECK 57:22
n. left to be concerned   NIEM 495:2
n.'s here   LOW 430:20
n. should be sad   SHAK 594:7
n. walks much faster   CARR 183:19
noctes: *O n. cenaeque deum* HOR 351:10
noctis: *O lente lente currite n.* MARL 447:1
nocturnal: Tunes her n. note MILT 470:16
nod: dwelt in the land of N. BIBLE 70:22
Old N., the shepherd   DE L 236:10
others n., pretending   MAHON 442:5
passed with a n. of the head   YEATS 751:13
read a n., a shrug, a look   SWIFT 674:27
nodded: n. with his darkish brows
                                HOMER 343:1
noddle: barmie n.'s working BURNS 163:19
nods: even excellent Homer n. HOR 347:11
it n. a little   FARQ 280:24
N., and becks   MILT 465:5
noes: yeas and honest kersey n. SHAK 599:8
noire: *cette île triste et n.* BAUD 55:10
noise: barbarous n. environs me MILT 474:22
chamber deaf to n.   SIDN 646:19
dumb-shows and n.   SHAK 576:5
gone up with a merry n.   BOOK 127:20
happy n. to hear   HOUS 352:10
make a cheerful n. unto   BOOK 130:14
moved to folly by a n.   LAWR 413:5
n. at one end and no sense   KNOX 403:13
n. in mine ear   DONNE 253:10
noiseless n. among the leaves   KEATS 388:5
n. like of a hidden brook   COL 211:13
n. like that of a water-mill   SWIFT 673:9
n., my dear! And the people   ANON 16:20
n. of battle rolled   TENN 682:18
n. of water in mine ears   SHAK 621:23
n. outside the cypress   LAWR 412:11

944

noise: (cont.):

n. they make in pouring	POPE 524:5
no n. mine ease to break	HEYW 338:5
Nursed amid her n.	LAMB 406:24
So let us melt, and make no n.	DONNE 252:21
such n. that beast	MAL 443:6
valued till they make a n.	CRAB 225:10
when every n. appals me	SHAK 602:5
wi' flichterin' n. an'	BURNS 161:15

noiseless: n. noise among the leaves

	KEATS 388:5
n. tenor of their way	GRAY 315:17

noises: isle is full of n.   SHAK 625:26

noisome: from the n. pestilence	BOOK 131:3
noisy: n. years seem moments	WORD 746:4
noli: N. me tangere	BIBLE 108:16
nomadic: Edwardians were n.	WHITE 731:7
no-meaning: channel of n.	NEWM 493:2
nominate: boldly n. a spade	JONS 378:23
nominated: not accept if n.	SHER 645:28
nomine: In N. Patris, et Filii	MISS 476:13
nomini: sed n. tuo da gloriam	BIBLE 108:2
nominis: Stat magni n. umbra	LUCAN 431:5
nom'native: Is her n. case	O'KEE 498:8
No-more: I am also called N.	ROSS 548:5
non: saturam n. scribere	JUV 383:13

non-being: avoiding n. by avoiding being

	TILL 698:5

non-combatant: War hath no fury like a n.

	MONT 480:12

non-commissioned: backbone of the
   Army is the n. man   KIPL 399:1

nonconformist: woman as a N. conscience

	WILDE 735:11
would be a man must be a n.	EMER 276.31

nonconformity: history of N. behind him

	ORW 500:21

none: answer came there n.   SCOTT 559:7

But answer made it n.	SHAK 572.20
malice toward n.	LINC 422:9
N. but the brave	DRYD 259:16
n. that doeth good	BOOK 124:26

non-fiction: make use of her n. tickets

	AYCK 40:9

nonsense: All time and n.   BUCK 154:13

damned n. will I put twice	RICH 540:16
good lump of clotted n.	DRYD 262:19
have a firm anchor in n.	GALB 297:1
His n. suits their nonsense	CHAR 191:16
n., and learning	GOLD 311:20
n. upon stilts	BENT 64:3
n. which was knocked out	BEER 59:16
round the corner of n.	COL 212:15
Through sense and n.	DRYD 259:14

nonsensical: are equally n.   CHOM 200:3

Non-U: U and N.   ROSS 547:1

non-violence: N. the first article   GAND 297:10

organization of n.	BAEZ 46:8

nook: obscure n. for me   BROW 151:20

noon: after n., is night   DONNE 252:7

amid the blaze of n.	MILT 474:1
been lying till n.	JOHN 370:25
Far from the fiery n.	KEATS 387:22
N. strikes on England	FLEC 286:6
obscene wings athwart the n.	COL 210:2
returned before n.	SAIN 553:1
shameless n.	TENN 681:8
troubled midnight and the n.'s	ELIOT 271:20
When n. is past	SHEL 640:19

noonday: My heart at some n.   BROW 150:13

that destroyeth in the n.	BOOK 131:3

noontide: With throbbings of n.   HARDY 325:9

noose: naked to the hangman's n.   HOUS 352:8

turret in a n. of light	FITZ 283:10

Norfan: I'm a N., both sides   WELLS 727:17

Norfolk: bear him up the N. sky   BETJ 67:6

(faded/illegible lines)

    COW 221:3

normal: N. ...   CHAF 563:19

Thank God we're n.

    JAMES 363.0

normally ...   HARD 324:2

Norman: And simple faith ...   TENN 664.20

Norman: (cont.):

I always feel with N.	AYCK 40:11

normative: n. or regular science   KEYN 395:13

North: heart of the N. is dead   LAWR 413:1

n. of my lady's opinion	SHAK 630:14
N.'s as near as West	BISH 110:2
n. you may run to the rime-ringed	
	KIPL 399:20
O n. wind	BIBLE 81:16
ship I have got in the N.	BALL 49:10
triumph from the n.	MAC 436:4
true and tender is the N.	TENN 688:6
unripened beauties of the n.	ADD 3:18

North African: egg of a N. Empire   GLAD 307:11

Northcliffe: N. has sent for the king   ANON 14:2

northern: constant as the n. star   SHAK 591:12

Glorious the n. lights astream	SMART 650:4
Lucasta that bright n. star	LOV 428:19
N. reticence	HEAN 329:21

north-north-west: mad n.   SHAK 575:1

north-west: N. passage to the intellectual

	STER 665:2

Norval: My name is N.   HOME 342:19

nose: Any n. may ravage   BROW 153:4

caught him by his little n.	KIPL 401:21
Cleopatra's n. been shorter	PASC 507:13
Dong with a Luminous N.	LEAR 414:1
down his innocent n.	SHAK 567:26
Entuned in hir n. ful semely	CHAU 192:14
final cause of the human n.	COL 212:7
Had a very shiny n.	MARKS 446:8
hateful to the n.	JAM 361:17
Heaven stops the n. at it	SHAK 617:17
He hadde a semely n.	CHAU 194:17
How haughtily he lifts his n.	SWIFT 674:26
make the n. and cheeks stand	DRYD 262:20
Marion's n. looks red	SHAK 599:11
may they stop their n.	SHAK 565:18
miss the insinuated n.	WATS 722:10
Must often wipe a bloody n.	GAY 300:2
n. dead against the Pope	BALD 48:12
n. is as the tower of Lebanon	BIBLE 82:3
n. is in fact the sign	ROST 548:10
Nose, nose, jolly red n.	BEAU 56:13
N. of Turk, and Tartar's lips	SHAK 603:19
n., the hook where he	BYRON 167:18
n. was as sharp as a pen	SHAK 585:5
plucks justice by the n.	SHAK 605:7
ring at the end of his n.	LEAR 414:13
Some thirty inches from my n.	AUDEN 35:16
Thine has a great hook n.	BLAKE 111:13
thing is not n. at all	WELLS 727:21
Tweaks me by the n.	SHAK 575:11

noselessness: The N. of Man   CHES 199:11

nose-painting: n., sleep, and urine

	SHAK 602:11

noses: eyes is deeper than all n.   CUMM 228:15

His n. cast is of the roman	FLEM 287:8
men's n. as they lie asleep	SHAK 622:21
n. have they, and smell	BOOK 133:10
or slightly flatter n.	CONR 217:2
They haven't got no n.	CHES 199:10
Where do the n. go	HEM 331:14

nostalgia: N. isn't what it used   ANON 16:22

nostalgie: La n. de la boue   AUG 36:21

noster: Pater n., qui es in coelis   MISS 477:3

nostra: qui ante nos n. dixerunt   DON 250:5

nostrils: his n. the breath of life   BIBLE 70:1

n. blake were and wyde	CHAU 193:4

nostrums: not n. but normalcy   HARD 324:2

not: but if you were not, n.   STEIN 663:7

n. I, but the wind	LAWR 412:22
N. so much a programme	ANON 16:23
N. unto us, O Lord	BOOK 133:9
n. wisely but too well	SHAK 618:20

notch: n. it on my stick too   THOR 696:29

note: living had no n.   GIBB 302:22

only the n. of a bird	SIMP 648:2

note-book: Set in a n., learned   SHAK 593:8

(faded line)   BOOK 128:13

notes: englich ...   DYER 265:3

(faded lines)

    JOHN 369:13

---

notes: (cont.):

n. by distance made more	COLL 213:14
n. I handle no better	SCHN 558:7
n. like little fishes vanish	MACN 441:3
n. tremendous from her	AUDEN 34:1
sad n., fall at her flying	CAMP 177:6
thick-warbled n.	MILT 473:20

nothing: Analogies decide n.   FREUD 293:21

And can say n.	SHAK 575:10
brought n. into this world	BIBLE 104:2
can n. be required	FIEL 282:4
desired to know n.	JOHN 373:29
didn't say there was n. better	CARR 183:18
do n. for ever and ever	ANON 14:4
do n. for evil	BURKE 160:4
don't resent having n.	COMP 214:15
Dying is n.	ANOU 23:9
easy to take more than n.	CARR 182:8
For n. can be sole or whole	YEATS 751:8
For saying n.	SHAK 607:6
gives to airy n.	SHAK 612:17
glory and the n. of a name	BYRON 169:17
growing old in drawing n.	COWP 223:26
have not charity, I am n.	BIBLE 101:1
Have n. to do with the case	GILB 305:9
having n., and yet possessing	BIBLE 101:20
having n. a-year	SURT 672:21
having n., yet hath all	WOTT 749:1
he n. knew	MILT 473:21
How to live well on n. a year	THAC 691:18
I have n. to say	CAGE 174:22
insupportable labour of doing n.	STEE 662:14
Is it n. to you	BIBLE 85:16
I will say n.	SHAK 595:23
let me have n.	METH 458:16
N. ain't worth nothin'	KRIS 404:3
N., and is nowhere	LARK 409:18
N. begins, and nothing ends	THOM 694:18
n. brings me all things	SHAK 626:19
N. can be created out of	LUCR 431:14
n. could be finer	GORD 312:13
n. done for the first time	CORN 219:7
n. done while anything	LUCAN 431:6
n. done while aught remains	ROG 544:11
N. doth more hurt in a state	BACON 43:7
n. ever ran quite straight	GALS 297:5
n. extenuate	SHAK 618:20
N. for nothink 'ere	PUNCH 531:17
N. goes on at all	BENN 63:5
N. happens, nobody comes	BECK 57:22
N. happens to anybody	AUR 37:17
N. in excess	ANON 21:14
n. in his long career	ANON 19:11
N. is ever done in this	SHAW 637:2
N. is here for tears	MILT 474:18
n. is law that is not reason	POW 528:11
N. is more dangerous	ALAIN 7:2
N. is wasted	HERB 333:20
n. left remarkable	SHAK 566:15
N., like something	LARK 410:2
N. some money	FONS 288:10
n. that make no mistakes	CONR 217:11
N., thou elder brother	ROCH 543:18
N. to be done	BECK 57:19
N. to do but work	KING 396:9
n. to look backward to	FROST 294:14
n. to what I could say	CARR 182:11
N. will come of nothing	SHAK 594:18
n. with a deal of skill	COWP 223:12
she was n. Nothing at all	AYCK 40:9
shook us all—but n. came	BYRON 168:1
Signifying n.	SHAK 605:1
smothered in surmise, and n.	SHAK 600:12
stand for n. fall for anything	HAM 322:10
strain at achieving n.	HOR 348:9
Tar-baby ain't sayin' n.	HARR 327:6
To marvel at n. is just	HOR 348:7
whatever you say, you say n.	HEAN 329:21
when he has n. to say	JOHN 375:15
when there's n. to be said	JOHN 371:22
when they can see n.	BACON 42:3
When you have n. to say	COLT 214:7
(faded line) n. ... is strong	BOOK 121:2

nothing: (cont.):
Ye know n. at all — BIBLE 97:6
You Ain't Heard N. Yet — JOLS 377:17
nothingness: Pass into n. — KEATS 386:13
Till love and fame to n. — KEATS 391:2
nothings: Invulnerable n. — SHEL 639:22
notice: man who used to n. such things — HARDY 324:22
not-incurious: n. in God's handiwork — BROW 149:19
notion: Doesn't seem to suit her n. — GILB 305:2
notions: General n. are generally wrong — MONT 480:9
notorious: n. evil liver — BOOK 121:14
Nottingham: N. lace of the curtains — BETJ 67:3
nought: aspiration, to do n. — ROSS 548:7
For n. did I in hate — SHAK 618:19
N. but vast Sorrow — DE L 236:3
n. enters there — SHAK 620.5
n. shall make us rue — SHAK 594:16
So much a thing of n. — CRAS 226.1
noun: verb not a n. — FULL 296:1
nouns: N. of number — COBB 207:28
nourish: n. all the world — SHAK 599:1
N. thy children — BIBLE 86:22
n. us with all goodness — BOOK 121:5
nourisher: n. in life's feast — SHAK 602:2
nourishes: n. them, incites — MONT 481:6
novel: atom of the traditional n. — LODGE 425:20
cannot care for in a n. — TROL 703:14
given away by a n. — KEATS 392:8
it is only a n. — AUST 38:21
Morality in the n. — LAWR 412:4
n. can hardly be interesting — TROL 703:4
n. gets up and walks away — LAWR 412:3
n. is a mirror which passes — STEN 663:13
n. is an impression — HARDY 324:14
n. is a balanced between — BELL 62:7
n. is born in response — TRIL 702:17
n. is the one bright book — LAWR 412:7
n. tells a story — FORS 290:2
vast importance of the n. — LAWR 411:13
novelist: Beauty [is that] at which a n. — FORS 290:5
novelists: n. know their art — BARN 53:9
really great—the major n. — LEAV 415:4
novelty: This n. on earth — MILT 473:5
November: no birds,—N. — HOOD 344:2
remember the Fifth of N. — ANON 17:11
Who hear N. at the gate — PUSH 532:16
novissima: cupido gloriae n. — TAC 678:4
novo: N. cedat ritui — THOM 692:14
novum: Reddiderit iunctura n. — HOR 347:5
now: He who sees what is n. — AUR 37:19
If it be n., 'tis not to come — SHAK 579:2
If not n. when — HILL 339:2
Leave N. for dogs and apes — BROW 149:30
N. fades the glimmering — GRAY 315:10
N. I lay me down to sleep — ANON 16:24
n. is the accepted time — BIBLE 101:19
N. is the time for the burning — BINY 109:21
N. more than ever seems it — KEATS 389:14
n. she is like everyone else — DE G 235:12
N. thank we all our God — WINK 739:6
nowhere: circumference is n. — ANON 16:17
Eclipse first, the rest n. — O'KEL 498:10
N. to fall but off — KING 396:9
nox: N. est perpetua — CAT 185:15
noxious: Of all n. animals — KILV 396:5
nubbly: Nice but n. — KIPL 402·2
nuclear: n. arms race — MOUN 487:6
n. freeze proposals — REAG 537:12
world of n. giants — BRAD 139:8
nude: noble and n. and antique — SWIN 676:8
To keep one from going n. — KING 396:9
nudula: Pallidula rigida n. — HADR 320:8
nugas: esse aliquid putare n. — CAT 185:11
nuisance: n. for another nuisance — ELLIS 275:15
n. to other people — MILL 460:18
null: N. an' Void — O'CAS 497:17
regular, splendidly n. — TENN 686:7
nullius: N. in verba — HOR 347:20
NUM: the Pope or the N. — BALD 48:12

number: Bring out n. weight — BLAKE 112:21
count the n. of the beast — BIBLE 107:1
forgotten as a nameless n. — PAST 508:7
greatest n. is the foundation — BENT 64:4
loyalties which centre upon n. — CHUR 203:4
Not on the n., but the choice — COWL 221:12
Nouns of n., or multitude — COBB 207:28
n. for a dinner party — GULB 319:14
n. of my days — BOOK 126:22
n. of your years — MONT 480:17
numbers n. all your graces — SHAK 633:5
or the n. of his name — BIBLE 106:32
root of half a n. of bees — LONG 428:6
teach us to n. our days — BOOK 131:2
very interesting n. — RAM 536:13
world is so full of a n. — STEV 608.14
numbered: God hath n. thy kingdom — BIBLE 85:31
hairs of your head are all n. — BIBLE 90:18
n. with the transgressors — BIBLE 84:14
numberless: As thick and n. — MILT 464:14
From death, you n. infinities — DONNE 250:20
n. goings-on of life — COL 210:4
numbers: diatonic little n. — REED 538:3
guns but we got the n. — MORR 485:20
happiness for the greatest n. — HUTC 357:6
Here are only n. ratified — SHAK 598:17
men are better than n. — CROM 227:5
numbers, for the n. came — POPE 519:28
n. that rocket the mind — WILB 734:1
secret magic of n. — BROW 146:5
There is divinity in odd n. — SHAK 610:19
To add to golden n. — DEKK 235:15
numbness: drowsy n. pains — KEATS 389:8
numerous: n. piece of monstrosity — BROW 146:15
numerus: n. sumus et fruges — HOR 348:3
nun: holy time is quiet as a n. — WORD 744:12
pensive n., devout — MILT 464:16
nunc: et n., et semper — MISS 476:15
N. est bibendum, nunc pede — HOR 349:14
nunc dimittis: N. servum tuum — BIBLE 108:11
sweetest canticle is N. — BACON 43:11
nunnery: Get thee to a n. — SHAK 575:18
That from the n. of thy chaste — LOV 429:6
nuns: N. fret not at their convent's — WORD 745:7
nuptials: any iteration of n. — CONG 216:3
day set apart for her n. — KELLY 393:2
nurse: always keep a-hold of N. — BELL 61:2
And set upon the n.'s knee — BALL 51:3
baby beats the n. — SHAK 605:7
beggar's n. and Caesar's — SHAK 566:19
Dear n. of arts — SHAK 586:16
dirty n., Experience — TENN 682:5
Nature's soft n. — SHAK 583:11
n. of manly sentiment — BURKE 158:14
n. sleeps sweetly — COWP 223:17
n. unacted desires — BLAKE 112:28
priest continues what the n. — DRYD 260:26
Rose a n. of ninety years — TENN 688:10
sucks the n. asleep — SHAK 567:11
what a n. should be — NIGH 496:1
will scratch the n. — SHAK 631:3
nursed: never n. a dear gazelle — MOORE 483:14
n. upon the self-same hill — MILT 465:22
nurseries: in the n. of heaven — THOM 695:11
public schools are the n. of all vice — FIEL 282:6
nursery: Kitchen-cabals, and n. mishaps — CRAB 224:21
n. of future revolutions — BURKE 158:8
nurses: old men's n. — BACON 44:5
So the n. get by heart — CAREY 179:17
nursing: n. the unconquerable hope — ARN 28:10
nursling: And the n. of the Sky — SHEL 640:7
nurture: fear and n. of the Lord — BOOK 123:17
nutmegs: N. and ginger — BEAU 56:13
nutrition: case of n. and health — JAY 363:24
nuts: N.! — MCAU 436:17
where the n. come from — THOM 693:2
nut-shell: bounded in a n. — SHAK 574:27
nymph: Not as a n., but for a reed — MARV 450:8

nymph: (cont.):
N., in thy orisons — SHAK 575:17
n. shall break Diana's — POPE 523:23
nymphs: N. and as yet unknown rivers — VIRG 714:2
N. and tribal deities — LANC 407:19
Where were ye n. — MILT 466:3

O

O: O Death, where is thy sting — ANON 17.1
O Little town of Bethlehem — BROO 144:4
o o o o that Shakespeherian — ELIOT 273.5
pursue my reason to an O altitudo — BROW 146:3
Within this wooden O — SHAK 584:17
oafish: o. louts remember Mum — BETJ 67:4
oafs: muddied o. at the goals — KIPL 399:13
oak: as leaves do on the o. — SHAK 626:16
Heart of o. are our ships — GARR 298:4
o. hangs a golden chain — PUSH 533:4
O. was round his breast — HOR 349:2
Or standing long an o. — JONS 379:21
Than O., and Ash, and Thorn — KIPL 400:10
thunders from her native o. — CAMP 177:1
To thee the reed is as the o. — SHAK 571:16
where English o. and holly — HARTE 327:16
oak-cleaving: Vaunt-couriers to o. thunderbolts — SHAK 595:20
oaks: families last not three o. — BROW 145:21
hews down o. with rushes — SHAK 570:5
o. from little acorns grow — EVER 279:9
O. that flourish — LEWES 420:12
Tall o., branch-charmèd — KEATS 387:27
oar: o. was dipping — COKE 208:15
oars: o. laboured heavily — ANAT 11:6
oat-cakes: Calvin, o., and sulphur — SMITH 653:8
Oates: O. of the Inniskilling — ATKI 32:13
oath: good mouth-filling o. — SHAK 581:12
He who cheats with an o. — PLUT 517:15
If ever I utter an o. again — SHAW 638:21
I have an o. in heaven — SHAK 609:17
man is not upon o. — JOHN 374:7
o. was but by Seinte Loy — CHAU 192:13
whore's o. — SHAK 596:18
oaths: but men with o. — LYS 433:15
Full of strange o. — SHAK 568:26
O. are but words, and words — BUTL 166:15
o. are straws — SHAK 585:6
oats: Mares eat o. — DRAKE 257:14
O. A grain, which in England — JOHN 368:3
Oaxen: rapidum cretae veniemus O. — VIRG 714:13
Obadiah: O. Bind-their-kings — MAC 436:3
obdurate: Or, Lord, if too o. — STEV 669:7
obedience: gold of o. and incense — MONS 480:2
lead a life of strict o. — DOST 254:9
o. of distant provinces — MAC 435:8
o. of planetary influence — SHAK 595:2
Rebellion to tyrants is o. — BRAD 139:9
obedient: Mild, o., good — ALEX 8:13
o. to their laws we lie — SIM 647:21
penitent, and o. heart — BOOK 118:5
obeisance: made o. to my sheaf — BIBLE 71:21
obey: o. is better than sacrifice — BIBLE 74:37
ó., till death us do part — BOOK 123:20
with the laws but to o. — HORS 351:12
obeyed: I o. as a son — GIBB 302:15
right to be o. than man — JOHN 366:10
She who must be o. — HAGG 320:9
obeying: except by o. her — BACON 45:22
obituary: o. in serial form — CRISP 227:2
publicity except your own o. — BEHAN 60:6
object: My o. all sublime — GILB 305:3
o. as in itself it really is — ARN 30:7
o. worth its constancy — SHEL 643:24
only an O. of Contempt — AUST 38:15
with his eye on the o. — ARN 30:6
objectification: Art is the o. of feeling — LANG 408:18
objectionable: it is doubtless o. — ANON 18:2
objective: o. correlative — ELIOT 273:17

objectivity: o. and again o. POUND 528:1
objects: o. cannot occupy MILL 461:14
oblation: o. of himself once offered
BOOK 122:11
oblations: Bring no more vain o. BIBLE 82:9
our alms and o. BOOK 121:22
obligation: o. is a pain JOHN 369:15
o. which goes unrecognized WEIL 726:17
Possession without o. MER 457:24
sequel of o. JOHN 369:5
obligations: Nobility has its o. LEVIS 420:7
oblige: Noblesse o. LEVIS 420:7
oblivion: alms for o. SHAK 627:19
cold o. SHEL 640:9
formless ruin of o. SHAK 628:3
childishness, and mere o. SHAK 568:16
Here let the Muse O.'s curtain CLARE 204:20
iniquity of o. BROW 145:23
long journey towards o. LAWR 412:19
O. is a kind of Annihilation BROW 145:5
O! my o. is a very Antony SHAK 564:26
place to place over o. HARDY 325:8
sank unwept into o. ELIOT 269:11
stepmother to memory, o. JOHN 366:15
oblivious: sweet o. antidote SHAK 604:22
obnoxious: o. to each carping tongue
BRAD 139:10
obscene: hag o., and grisly phantom BEAT 56:6
is usually o. SPEN 658:24
o. wings athwart the noon COL 210:2
obscenes: old idols, lust o. BOTT 137:11
obscenities: o. and scandals YES 754:1
obscenity: 'o.' is not a term RUSS 551:23
obscure: Coleridge—he who sits o. SHEL 641:3
I become o. HOR 347:4
o. nook BROW 151:20
o. reveries POUND 526:13
palpable o. MILT 469:20
obscurely: Content thyself to be o. good
ADD 3:22
northern climes, o. bright BYRON 169:25
obscuri: Ibant o. sola sub nocte VIRG 713:13
obscurity: o. of a learned language GIBB 302:20
rise out of o. JUV 383:22
snatches a man from o. REYN 539:3
obscurus: O. flo HOR 347:4
obsequies: solemnized their o. BROW 145:15
observance: All adoration, duty, and o.
SHAK 569:21
observation: bearings of this o. DICK 240:20
commonsense and o. BROW 146:10
Let o. with extensive view JOHN 370:14
Where o. is concerned PAST 509:2
With o., the which he vents SHAK 568:14
observe: You see, but you do not o.
DOYLE 256:8
observed: o. of all observers SHAK 576:4
observer: He is a great o. SHAK 590:7
Is a keen o. of life AUDEN 35:8
more partial for th' o.'s POPE 520:24
o. of human nature DICK 243:5
observeth: o. the wind BIBLE 80:27
obsolescence: adolescence and o. LINK 423:6
based on planned o. STEV 665:12
obsolete: war is o. or men FULL 295:27
obstacles: knows what o. are there WILB 734:5
o. in order to get repose ADAMS 2:23
obstinacy: O. in a bad cause BROW 146:8
o. in a bad one STER 664:16
obstruction: consecrated o. BAG 47:6
not as a boon, but an o. MANN 445:2
obtain: faithfully we may o. BOOK 121:10
obtruding: O. false rules MILT 464:9
obvious: Mad-eyed from stating the o.
WILB 734:1
statement of the o. KNOX 403:6
Abrasion (turns) mounteth with o.
[illegible] POY 707:2
o.'s forelock MILT 473:17
occasions: o. do inform against me
SHAK 577:31

occasions: (cont.):
upon their lawful o. BOOK 135:19
occident: yet unformed O. DAN 230:2
occidental: that bright O. Star BIBLE 69:18
occidit: o. spes omnis HOR 350:14
occupation: cure for it is o. SHAW 638:12
found o. for an idle hour AUST 39:2
o. of an adult OLIV 498:15
Othello's o.'s gone SHAK 616:20
shall find that diligent o. MORE 484:1
occupations: let us love our o. DICK 239:16
occupy: o. their business BOOK 133:1
ocean: day-star in the o. bed MILT 466:13
had better abandon the o. CLAY 205:17
have seen the hungry o. SHAK 634:2
I'll love you till the o. is folded AUDEN 34:3
In the o.'s bosom unespied MARV 449:18
like o. on a western beach LANG 408:16
loved of all the O.'s sons DENH 236:16
mind is tossing on the o. SHAK 607:2
must leap into the o. HUME 355:12
Neptune's o. wash this blood SHAK 602:6
o. for orient pearl MARL 446:14
o. in the eventide of fear MORR 485:9
o. of darkness and death FOX 292:1
o. of life we pass LONG 428:1
O.'s child, and then his queen SHEL 641:8
o.'s margin this innocent AUDEN 34:1
O.'s nursling, Venice SHEL 641:7
O. to attend upon her BEST 67:1
On one side lay the O. TENN 682:19
rivers with the o. SHEL 641:9
round o. and the living air WORD 745:1
sail again on the vast o. HOR 349:6
sapless foliage of the o. SHEL 641:17
Spread like a rosy o. BYRON 170:20
thou deep and dark blue O. BYRON 169:14
thou, vast o.! on whose MONT 482:1
Upon a painted o. COL 210:25
use the o. as their road WALL 718:12
Where rolled the o. BYRON 168:17
Who bidd'st the mighty o. deep WHIT 732:2
Yet for his fame the o. BARN 53:16
oceanic: depths of his own o. mind COL 212:16
oceans: Portable, and compendious o.
CRAS 226:12
To the o. white with foam BERL 65:17
o'clock: what o. I say it is SHAK 624:19
octavos: o. fill a spacious plain CRAB 224:26
October: heard O.'s strife GURN 320:1
What of O., that ambiguous LESS 419:10
octopus: dear o. SMITH 651:9
odd: But not so o. BROW 145:4
divinity in o. numbers SHAK 610:19
How o. of God EWER 279:11
It's an o. job, making MOL 478:18
Must think it exceedingly o. KNOX 403:10
Nothing o. will do long JOHN 374:9
oddfellow: desperate o. society THOR 697:4
oddly: people whose eyes are o. made
HAMM 323:2
odds: at o. with morning SHAK 603:13
facing fearful o. MAC 436:10
gamble at terrible o. STOP 670:6
how am I to face the o. HOUS 351:20
o. are five to six DICK 245:9
what o. so long as Caesar's CRAS 226:13
Ode: O. on a Grecian Urn FAUL 281:4
oderint: O., dum metuant ACC 1:4
odes: And quoted o. TENN 687:26
odi: O. et amo CAT 186:17
O. profanum vulgus et arceo HOR 349:22
odio: dilectione hominum et o. vitiorum AUG 37:8
odious: O.! in woollen POPE 520:29
odisse: ingenii est o. TAC 677:21
odium: He lived in the o. of BENT 64:13
odoriferous: o. flowers SHAK 598:17
odorous: Comparisons are o. SHAK 614:5
o. [illegible] of [illegible]-sticks BRAM 139:15
Stealing and [illegible] SHAK 628:9
odours: and the o. tangle [illegible]
Exhales from o. BYRON 172:12

odours: (cont.):
golden vials full of o. BIBLE 106:14
o. led my steps astray SHEL 642:22
O., when sweet violets sicken SHEL 643:11
star-led wizards haste with o. MILT 467:1
With living hues and o. SHEL 641:14
Odysseus: Like O., the President KEYN 395:3
Odyssey: surge and thunder of the O.
LANG 408:16
o'erflowing: o. of unbounded wit WINC 738:24
oeuf: Voyez-vous cet o. DID 245:13
off: O. with his head CIBB 203:20
O. with his head SHAK 622:2
walk down again with them o. HARG 326:8
offal: With this slave's o. SHAK 575:12
offence: conscience void of o. BIBLE 99:7
forgave the o. DRYD 260:13
innocent from the great o. BOOK 125:6
I shall not take o. HOR 347:16
men yow doon o. CHAU 193:11
my o. is rank, it smells SHAK 577:2
o. against virtue HAZL 329:5
o. from am'rous causes POPE 523:15
only defence is in o. BALD 48:9
resented for an o. SWIFT 674:10
rock of o. BIBLE 82:25
th'o. ne'er reach the offender's CENT 188:5
where the o. is let the great axe SHAK 578:10
whom I was like to give o. FROST 295:5
yet detest th'o. POPE 519:20
offences: Made old o. of affections new
SHAK 634:21
more o. at my beck SHAK 575:18
o. which result in a large VEBL 709:16
sins and o. of my youth BOOK 125:19
offend: And others doth o. SUCK 671:8
coy and tender to o. HERR 335:23
o. one of these little ones BIBLE 91:18
we come not to o. SHAK 612:22
offendar: O. maculis HOR 347:16
offended: him have I o. SHAK 592:4
If we shadows have o. SHAK 613:3
This hath not o. the king MORE 484:6
offender: hugged the o., and forgave
DRYD 260:13
love th'o. POPE 519:20
offenders: society o. who might GILB 304:21
offendeth: oft he o. BOOK 125:6
offensive: Life is an o. WHIT 731:9
You are extremely o. SMITH 651:15
offer: dare not o. what I desire to give
SHAK 625:21
instantly close with the o. HUXL 358:5
o. he can't refuse PUZO 533:7
o. the American people KENN 393:11
offering: last o. in death CAT 187:1
o. too little and asking CANN 178:3
offerings: nor fields of o. BIBLE 79:8
offers: you are liberal in o. SHAK 609:22
office: By office boys for o. boys SAL 554:9
Each in his o. wait DODD 250:1
insolence of o. SHAK 575:16
in which the o. is held HUXL 357:9
man who has no o. SHAW 636:23
o. boy to an Attorney's GILB 305:26
o. party is not WHIT 731:18
o. was his pirate ship LEWIS 421:3
Tall O. Building SULL 671:11
officer: art thou o.? SHAK 585:21
doth fear each bush an o. SHAK 588:7
o. and a gentleman shall ANON 12:5
officers: They have a king and o. SHAK 584:22
offices: functions and their o. SHAK 598:20
official: concept of the 'o. secret' WEBER 725:4
This high o., all allow HERB 333:19
What is o. is incontestable FRY 295:22
officialism: where there is o. FORS 290:25
officials: diligent and trustworthy o.
ZAMY 755:4
o. are the servants of the public GOW 313:3
officious: O., innocent, sincere JOHN 375:29
officiously: O. to keep alive CLOU 207:17
[illegible] of [illegible] MILT 470:15

offspring: (cont.):

Of human o., sole propriety	MILT 471:15
Time's noblest o.	BERK 65:13
wickedest o. of thy race	ROCH 543:19
oft: by o. falling	LAT 411:2
o. as ye shall drink	BOOK 122:12
O. in danger, oft in woe	WHITE 731:4
tell how o. he offendeth	BOOK 125:6
What o. was thought	POPE 521:11
often: Vote early and vote o.	BILL 109:19
Og: O. the king of Basan	BOOK 134:15
oil: anointed my head with o.	BOOK 125:15
consumed the midnight o.	GAY 299:31
head thou dost with o.	SCOT 561:8
it is the o. which renders	HUME 355:9
little o. in a cruse	BIBLE 75:32
mix like o. and vinegar	GAIN 296:13
mouth is smoother than o.	BIBLE 78:12
o. controlling American soil	DYLAN 208.21
o. of gladness	BOOK 127:11
u. ol joy for mourning	BIBLE 84:27
o. out of the tabernacle	BIBLE 75:21
u. to make him a cheerful	BOOK 132:8
O., vinegar, sugar	GOLD 311:3
Pour o. into their ears	JONS 379:3
providers they're o. wells	PARK 506:16
sound of o. wells	FISH 283:7
spoonfuls of boiling o.	STR 670:18
with boiling o. in it	GILB 305:7
words were smoother than o.	BOOK 128:12
oiled: key deftly in the o. wards	KEATS 390:15
o. and curled Assyrian	TENN 686:10
o. his way around the floor	LERN 419:7
oily: I want that glib and o. art	SHAK 594:21
ointment: o. might have been sold	BIBLE 92:22
Okie: O. means you're scum	STEI 663:9
old: adherence to the o. and tried	LINC 422:1
any number of o. ladies	FAUL 281:4
Any o. iron, any old iron	COLL 213:6
are planned by o. men	RICE 540:2
body with so o. a head	SHAK 609:12
boys of the o. Brigade	WEAT 724:13
buried in a good o. age	BIBLE 70:36
change in growing o.	BRID 141:5
change o. lamps for new ones	ARAB 24:1
conservative when o.	FROST 295:8
considered the days of o.	BOOK 130:7
country for o. men	YEATS 752:20
dance attendance upon my o.	YEATS 753:9
declare hard sentences of o.	BOOK 130:8
died in a good o. age	BIBLE 76:33
Diseases and sad O. Age	VIRG 713:14
Don't let the o. folks know	HERB 333:15
dreary o. age and pain	VIRG 715:16
dressing o. words new	SHAK 634:7
feel chilly and grown o.	BROW 153:11
foolish, fond o. man	SHAK 597:14
growing o. in drawing nothing	COWP 223:26
Grown o. before my time	ROSS 547:6
Grow o. along with me	BROW 152:6
grow o. with a good grace	STEE 662:17
heart grows o.	YEATS 753:6
Hope I die before I get o.	TOWN 701:7
I cannot sing the o. songs	CLAR 205:6
I grow o. . . . . I grow old	ELIOT 272:6
in judgement o.	SHAK 608:14
it is o. and plain	SHAK 629:16
It is so o. a story	HEINE 330:16
lads that will never be o.	HOUS 352:11
late into a world too o.	MUSS 488:17
Leaving the o., both worlds	WALL 718:13
make an o. man young	TENN 681:6
may crucify the o. man	BOOK 123:1
Men grow cold as girls grow o.	ROBIN 542:7
Mithridates, he died o.	HOUS 352:20
my folks were growing o.	STEV 668:22
no man would be o.	SWIFT 674:20
now am not too o.	BLUN 116:4
o. Adam in this Child	BOOK 122:20
O. Age, and Experience	ROCH 543:12
O. Age a regret	DISR 248:5
O.-age, a second child	CHUR 201:3
O. age brings along	EMER 277:10

old: (cont.):

O. age hath yet his honour	TENN 690:4
o. age is always fifteen years	BAR 54:20
O. age is the most unexpected	TROT 704:11
o. age, it is the last gasp but one	WHITE 731:5
o. age of cards	POPE 520:11
O. age should burn	THOM 693:4
o. and faded as I am	MARL 446:10
o. and grey and full	YEATS 753:19
O. and young, we are all	STEV 667:28
o. as we to keep the peace	SHAK 622:19
o. black magic	MERC 457:15
O. Country must wake up	GEOR 301:2
o. December's bareness	SHAK 634:16
o. ever learning many things	SOLON 655:5
o. familiar faces	LAMB 407:1
o. friends are best	SELD 562:3
o. have rubbed it into the young	MAUG 454:3
o. heads on your young	SPARK 658:5
o. is better	BIBLE 94:4
o. is having lighted rooms	LARK 410:4
o. is like being increasingly	POW 528:8
o., mad, blind, despised	SHEL 643:7
o. maid is like death	FERB 281:8
o. man and no honester	SHAK 614:4
o. man decayed in his intellects	JOHN 376:4
o. man does not care for the	JOHN 372:26
o. man in a dry month	ELIOT 271:10
o. man in a hurry	CHUR 201:20
o. man of Thermopylae	LEAR 414:8
o. man upon a winter's night	YEATS 752:16
o. man who said, 'Damn!	HARE 326:7
O. Masters	AUDEN 35:6
O. men and children	BOOK 135:15
O. men and comets	SWIFT 674:22
o. men have grey beards	SHAK 574:22
o. men of less truth	SHAK 633:5
o. order changeth	TENN 682:23
O. soldiers never die	FOLEY 288:8
O, sir! you are o.	SHAK 595:15
redress the balance of the O.	CANN 178:11
Ring out the o.	TENN 684:10
Say I'm growing o.	HUNT 356:9
shaking hand of an o.	VICT 710:11
she is not yet so o.	SHAK 609:2
should accompany o. age	SHAK 604:21
so o., and so profane	SHAK 584:12
teach an o. horse	SPEN 660:9
Tell me the o., old story	HANK 323:6
They shall grow not o.	BINY 109:20
think too little and the o.	WALP 719:13
times begin to wax o.	BIBLE 86:23
too o. to rush up to the net	ADAMS 2:4
warn you not to grow o.	KINN 398:9
wax o. as doth a garment	BOOK 132:1
Were ruinous and o.	SPEN 659:25
What a sad o. age you	TALL 678:10
when they get to feeling o.	BROO 143:14
when thou shalt be o.	BIBLE 98:2
Whether it be new or o.	ANON 14:13
wine into o. bottles	ATTL 32:15
worn, and o.	ROSS 547:5
Ye have put off the o. man	BIBLE 103:16
You are o., Father William	CARR 182:3
You are o., Father William	SOUT 657:13
young, and now am o.	BOOK 126:20
young can do for the o.	SHAW 636:13
your o. men shall dream	BIBLE 86:8
You think of o. people	ALAI 7:4
older: always fifteen years o.	BAR 54:20
I was so much o. then	DYLAN 265:19
O. men declare war	HOOV 344:20
o. than the rocks among	PATER 509:5
o. we do not get any younger	REED 537:16
richer still, the o.	BUTL 166:21
oldest: o. hath borne most	SHAK 598:5
o. rule in the book	CARR 182:16
o. sins the newest kind	SHAK 584:4
old-fashioned: I want an o. house	FISH 283:7
Old Testament: blessing of the O.	BACON 42:18
oligarchy: aristocracy, call it o.	HOBB 340:9
democracy or absolute o.	ARIS 25:18
olive: Of o., aloe, and maize	TENN 680:19

olive-branches: o. round about thy table	
	BOOK 134:8
Olivet: purple brows of O.	TENN 683:13
Olivia: Cry out, 'O.!'	SHAK 628:24
when mine eyes did see O.	SHAK 628:10
olla putrida: clumsy o. James Joyce	LAWR 413:3
ologies: instructed in the 'o.'	CARL 180:30
olores: inter strepere anser o.	VIRG 715:7
Olympian: O. bolts	DISR 247:2
Olympus: leafy O. on top of Ossa	VIRG 715:12
made great O. tremble	HOMER 343:1
Pelion on top of shady O.	HOR 350:3
Omar: O. plucked them	LOW 430:1
Omega: I am Alpha and O.	BIBLE 105:32
omelette: What a fuss about an o.	VOLT 717:6
omen: May the gods avert this o.	CIC 204:9
Procul o. abesto	OVID 502:11
This is the one best o.	HOMER 343:8
omens: lands, and grievous o.	SUTT 672:23
omitted: O., all the voyage	SHAK 593:12
omne: o. immensum peragravit	LUCR 431:12
omnes: o. gentes	BIBLE 108:3
O. homines naturaliter	AUCT 33:22
omnia: non o. possumus omnes	LUC 431:11
Non o. possumus omnes	VIRG 715:5
O. vincit Amor	VIRG 715:8
omnibus: Ninety-seven horse power O.	
	FLAN 285:14
omnipotence: O. cannot work	
contradictions	JENY 365:8
o. that he need not exist	DE VR 238:4
omnipotent: O. but friendless	SHEL 642:15
Scotland, land of the o. No	BOLD 117:6
Who durst defy the o. to arms	MILT 467:23
omnis: Non o. moriar	HOR 350:10
omniscience: o. his foible	SMITH 653:30
Omnium: Duke of O.	TROL 703:6
Onan: into the sin of O.	VOLT 716:15
Onassis: O. would not have married	
	VIDAL 711:6
onaway: O.! Awake, beloved	LONG 427:17
once: if it were done but o.	DONNE 253:11
I was adored o. too	SHAK 629:10
oblation of himself o. offered	BOOK 122:11
o. and future king	WHITE 731:8
o. familiar word	BAYLY 56:3
o. in a great while	PEPYS 512:19
O. in royal David's city	ALEX 8:11
o. is enough	ELIOT 272:17
O. lead this people	WILS 738:21
O. more unto the breach	SHAK 585:7
O. to every man and nation	LOW 430:3
O. upon a time and a very	JOYCE 381:9
pass through this world but o.	GREL 317:19
oncoming: headlight of an o. train	DICK 245:9
It's the light of the o. train	LOW 430:19
one: All for one, o. for all	DUMAS 263:13
apparel them all in o. livery	SHAK 587:23
But the O. was Me	HUXL 357:19
Dear O. is mine as mirrors	AUDEN 35:18
doeth good, no not o.	BOOK 124:26
do only o. thing at once	SMIL 650:11
encompassed but o. man	SHAK 590:5
For o. day in thy courts	BOOK 130:18
given us o. way in to life	SEN 563:1
he putteth down o.	BOOK 130:5
How to be o. up	POTT 525:16
incorporate and make us o.	SHAK 591:1
it ought to be Number O.	CARR 182:16
Make it o. for my baby	MERC 457:14
merely o. man fewer	METT 459:3
more than o. a bed	DONNE 252:13
o. by one back in the closet	FITZ 284:7
o. man picked out of ten	SHAK 574:19
O. man shall have one vote	CART 184:14
o. near one is too far	BROW 148:26
O. realm, one people	ANON 21:10
O. remains, the many	SHEL 640:4
O. Way Street	CHR 200:6
O. who never turned	BROW 148:6
Only o. being is wanting	LAM 405:21
she who but trifles with o.	GAY 299:28

one: (*cont.*):
stranger to o. of your parents   AUST 39:13
Win just o. for the Gipper   GIPP 307:1
one-and-twenty: Long-expected o.
   JOHN 376:21
When I was o.   HOUS 352:9
one-eyed: o. man is king   ERAS 278:12
o. yellow idol to the north   HAYES 328:10
onion: o. atoms lurk within   SMITH 653:18
tears live in an o.   SHAK 564:21
onions: Wel loved he garleek, o.   CHAU 193:6
only: glory as of the o. begotten   BIBLE 96:4
It's the o. thing   SAND 555:13
keep thee o. unto her   BOOK 123:19
o. begetter of these insuing sonnets
   SHAK 632:25
o.-begotten Son of God   BOOK 121:19
O. connect   FORS 290:14
O. the lonely   ORBI 499:7
o. thing we have to fear   ROOS 545:16
o. to stand high   SHAK 609:2
pint of plain is your o. man   O'BR 497:12
say o. the word   MISS 477:6
onori: *offrirgli né o. né stipendi*   GAR 298:1
onset: Vain thy o.!   ARN 27:11
onward: O., Christian soldiers   BAR 53:2
O. goes the pilgrim band   BAR 53:3
'O.,' the sailors cry   BOUL 137:17
upward still, and o.   LOW 430:5
Yet this will go o. the same   HARDY 325:10
ooze: scarcely coffined, in o.   SHAK 619:3
through the o. and slime   SMITH 651:19
oozing: O. charm from every pore   LERN 419:7
o. out as it were   SHER 645:12
oozy: sea-blooms and the o. woods
   SHEL 641:17
opal: thy mind is a very o.   SHAK 629:18
opals: Whose cream does look like o.
   JONS 378:6
open: great o. spaces   MARQ 448:13
only function when they are o.   DEWAR 238:6
o. and notorious evil liver   BOOK 121:14
o. covenants of peace   WILS 738:19
o. cow   HERB 333:24
o. his grief   BOOK 122:4
O. not thine heart   BIBLE 87:15
O. rebuke is better   BIBLE 79:25
O. Sesame   ARAB 24:2
o. that Pandora's Box   BEVIN 69:16
o. the Kingdom of Heaven   BOOK 118:13
O. the temple gates   SPEN 659:15
O. to me, my sister   BIBLE 81:17
o. to the poor   ANON 13:14
o. unto the fields   WORD 743:9
O., ye everlasting gates   MILT 472:10
Secret thoughts and o.   ALB 7:10
take to the o. road   WHIT 732:23
Thou shalt o. my lips   BOOK 128:8
You see her eyes are o.   SHAK 604:11
opened: had o. the seventh seal   BIBLE 106:24
If he were o., and you   SHAK 630:16
opening: o. of the prison   BIBLE 84:26
opera: don't mind what language an o.
   APPL 23:17
omnia o. Domini   BIBLE 108:8
o. ain't over 'til the fat lady   COOK 218:4
O. is when a guy gets stabbed   GARD 297:15
operas: o. sung by Swedish   WHAR 730:2
operatic: so romantic, so o.   PROU 530:14
operation: end must direct the o.   WOTT 749:6
operations: o. which we can perform
   WHIT 731:15
operative: O. White House Position ZIEG 755:11
opes: *Fumum et o.*   HOR 350:8
golden o., the iron shuts   MILT 466:7
Magnas t' tar o. inops   HOR 350:7
Ophelia. I loved O.   SHAK 578:29
water hast thou, poor O.   SHAK 579:14
inter. dull o. to the drains   KEAT 399:8
opinion: had acd l 'r o. with quotations
   PRIOR 529:10
conforming to majority o.   SCAL 567:11
expected of him by prevalent o.   OLIV 498:12

opinion: (*cont.*):
For this fool gudgeon, this o.   SHAK 607:7
gross and scope of my o.   SHAK 571:25
His o. of himself   BENN 63:13
independent of public o.   HEGEL 330:12
Is of his own o. still   BUTL 166:18
justifies that ill o.   BURNS 163:16
literary and scientific o.   ARN 29:20
main o. he held once   SHAK 590:19
man can brave o.   STAËL 662:2
matters of o. and science   HUME 355:15
men representing no o.   WILS 738:15
north of my lady's o.   SHAK 630:14
of one o.   MILL 460:16
o. and uncommon abilities   BAG 46:9
o. in good men is but knowledge MILT 475:13
O. is ultimately determined   SPEN 658:22
o. of a man who has a low   TROL 703:22
o. one man entertains   PALM 505:11
o. with the learned   CONG 215:6
plague of o.!   SHAK 627:23
poor itch of your o.   SHAK 570:4
researchers into Public O.   AUDEN 36:11
respect public o.   RUSS 551:11
sacrifices it to your o.   BURKE 158:31
scorching world's o.   FLET 287:18
that approve a private o.   HOBB 340:4
think the last o. right   POPE 521:20
vagrant o. without visible   BIER 109:14
whole climate of o.   AUDEN 34:12
world's o.   EMER 277:1
opinions: anger of men who have no o.
   CHES 199:16
anyone's o. but your own   PERS 513:3
conflict of o. and sentiments JOHN 377:2
Golden o. from all sorts   SHAK 601:4
good or so bad as their o.   MACK 439:5
halt ye between two o.   BIBLE 76:1
held the proper o.   AUDEN 36:11
his religious o.   BUTL 167:6
killed with your hard o.   SHAK 584:15
minded beyond reason the o.   WOOLF 742:12
o. are always suspected   LOCKE 424:14
o. as there are people   TER 690:14
o. as though he were living   CIC 203:24
public buys its o.   BUTL 167:5
Stiff in o.   DRYD 259:8
opium: o.-dose for keeping   KING 398:1
o. of the people   MARX 452:2
subtle, and mighty o.   DE Q 237:9
opponents: its o. eventually die   PLAN 516:1
opportunitate: *sed etiam o. mortis* TAC 677:22
opportunity: commit when he
had the o.   ROWL 549:10
maximum of o.   SHAW 637:25
meanness of o.   ELIOT 269:11
o. is that wherein   HIPP 339:7
O. makes a thief   BACON 45:13
o. of leisure   BIBLE 87:35
sometimes also a matter of o. HIPP 339:8
Thou strong seducer, o.   DRYD 260:10
oppose: o. everything, and propose
   DERBY 237:15
opposing: And by o. end them   SHAK 575:16
opposite: O. is also a profound truth
   BOHR 117:1
opposites: o. are obviously absurd BOHR 117:1
opposition: And o. of the stars   MARV 450:3
duty of an O.   DERBY 237:15
Her Majesty's O.   BAG 46:16
His Majesty's O.   HOBH 340:15
without a formidable O.   DISR 248:1
oppressed: He was o.   BIBLE 84:12
let the o. go free   BIBLE 84:22
oppresseth: the enemy o. me   BOOK 127:5
oppressing: o. city   BIBLE 86:17
oppression: behold o.   BIBLE 82:15
mad with o.   TAYL 679:20
O. and in the wise man mad   BROW 151:4
To make o. bitter   SHAK 575:12
to violate would be in   JEFF 364:3
oppressions: not in doing many o.   CUMB 218:14
useful in, of o. in earth   SHEL 640:22

oppressor: day o' the O. is ended   KIPL 401:13
ends as an o. or a heretic   CAMUS 177:19
o.'s wrong   SHAK 575:16
oppugnancy: In mere o.   SHAK 627:8
optavere: *multae o. puellae*   CAT 186:9
optics: o. of these eyes   BROW 146:12
optima: *O. quaeque dies*   VIRG 715:16
optimism: pessimism as agreeable as o.
   BENN 63:17
optimist: o. is a guy   MARQ 448:11
o. proclaims that we live   CAB 174:12
opulence: o. nobody can possess SMITH 650:19
opulent: To glass the o.   HARDY 325:3
opus: *Hoc o., hic labor est*   VIRG 713:11
Iamque o. exegi   OVID 503:2
orabunt: *O. causas melius*   VIRG 713:9
Oracle: I am Sir O.   SHAK 607:6
oracles: earth's green o.   SUTT 672:23
o. are dumb   MILT 467:11
these are the lively O.   COR 219:11
oracular: use of my o. tongue   SHER 645:5
oral: fast word about o. contraception
   ALLEN 9:14
orange: clockwork o.   BURG 156:19
o. flower perfumes   SCOTT 560:26
shades the o. bright   MARV 449:19
orange-blossom: lands of palm, of o.
   TENN 680:19
orange-tree: Oh that I were an o. HERB 335:1
orang-outang: o. or the tiger   BURKE 159:1
orantes: *Stabant o. primi transmittere*
   VIRG 713:15
oration: not studied as an o.   OSB 501:6
orator: enjoyment as the greatest o.
   HUME 355:11
eyes of men without an o.   SHAK 632:21
I am no o.   SHAK 592:16
No o. ever made an impression BAG 46:13
o. as well as Nestor   SHAK 588:3
orators: decidedly the first of o. MAC 434:12
one of those o. of whom   CHUR 201:24
swords shall play the o.   MARL 447:21
oratory: o. alone is not truth   MAC 434:8
orb: epicycle, o. in orb   MILT 472:11
orbis: *Si fractus illabatur o.*   HOR 350:2
orbs: glimmering o. did glow   MILT 467:4
o. shoots shafts divine   LODGE 426:1
orchard: chaffinch sings on the
o. bough   BROW 150:5
orchards: new-planted o.   SHAK 592:18
orchestra: o. is playing to the rich AUDEN 34:5
two golden rules for an o.   BEEC 58:16
orchestration: o. of platitudes   WILD 736:17
orchid: White as an o. she rode AUDEN 34:1
orci: *primisque in faucibus O.*   VIRG 713:14
ordained: powers that be are o.   BIBLE 100:8
'Tis so o.   PRIOR 529:13
ordainer: o. of order   BROW 145:11
order: all in o. stand   CRAB 224:26
all is in o.   MANS 445:9
all line of o.   SHAK 627:6
All things began in o.   BROW 145:11
all things in o. stored   TENN 687:22
defined by the word 'o.'   METT 459:2
Democrat, in that o.   JOHN 367:4
devoted to o. than to justice   KING 396:16
done decently and in o.   BIBLE 101:3
each in solemn o.   WORD 747:12
good o. and military   ANON 12:28
Half of one o., half another   BUTL 166:11
not necessarily in that o.   GOD 308:5
old o. changeth   TENN 682:22
only war creates o.   BREC 140:7
ordainer of o. and mystical BROW 145:11
o. and beauty   BAUD 55:9
o. and beauty   NEWT 493:21
o. breeds habit   ADAMS 2:14
o. destroyed by a revolution TOCQ 699:1
o. in variety we see   POPE 523:33
o. is the foundation   BURKE 158:28
o. of Melchisedech   BOOK 133:4
o. of the acts is plann'd   PAST 508:8

order: (*cont.*):
o. or proportion　　　　　　　　　　BROW 146:17
O. reigns in Warsaw　　　　　　　　ANON 21:2
o., security and peace　　　　　　　JOHN 366:11
o. to a peopled kingdom　　　　　　SHAK 584:22
o. words of the sea　　　　　　　　STEV 665:21
party of o. or stability　　　　　　MILL 460:17
put his household in o.　　　　　　BIBLE 75:16
Set thine house in o.　　　　　　　BIBLE 83:23
so I o. it done　　　　　　　　　　JUV 384:1
straining o. into tyranny　　　　　GODW 308:13
They o., said I, this matter　　　　STER 664:2
upon the o. of your going　　　　　SHAK 603:12
within the o. of things　　　　　　WICK 733:16
ordered: And o. their estate　　　ALEX 8:10
o. my goings　　　　　　　　　　　BOOK 126:24
ordering: better o. of the universe　ALF 9:2
orderly: keep themselves o.　　　LARK 409:19
orders: Almighty's o. to perform　ADD 3:14
o. unless they is 'is own　　　　　KIPL 398:19
ordinance: God's holy o.　　　　　BOOK 123:20
ordinary: o. mind on an ordinary day
　　　　　　　　　　　　　　　　WOOLF 742:6
o. one seem original　　　　　　　HOR 347:5
o. people must lead a life　　　　　DOST 254:9
warn you not to be o.　　　　　　KINN 398:9
ordo: *integro saeclorum nascitur o.*　VIRG 714:22
ore: load every rift with o.　　　　KEATS 392:15
with new spangled o.　　　　　　　MILT 466:13
oremus: O.　　　　　　　　　　　MISS 476:19
organ: great o. of public opinion　DISR 247:2
heaven's deep o.　　　　　　　　　MILT 467:7
Is as the maiden's o.　　　　　　　SHAK 628:16
mellering to the o.　　　　　　　　DICK 242:33
my second favourite o.　　　　　　ALLEN 9:13
o. and the maypole　　　　　　　　JORD 380:13
o. grinder is present　　　　　　　BEVAN 68:17
o. to enlarge her prayer　　　　　AUDEN 34:1
playing of the merry o.　　　　　　ANON 14:11
Seated one day at the o.　　　　　PROC 529:20
There let the pealing o. blow　　　MILT 465:1
organic: form is the key to o. life　PAST 508:6
o. harps diversely framed　　　　　COL 209:20
o. or inorganic　　　　　　　　　　STEI 663:8
organization: o. is and must be　MILL 461:14
o. of idolatry　　　　　　　　　　SHAW 637:21
o. of non-violence　　　　　　　　BAEZ 46:8
o. man　　　　　　　　　　　　　WHYTE 733:14
systematic o. of hatreds　　　　　ADAMS 2:6
organize: any time in mourning—o.
　　　　　　　　　　　　　　　　HILL 338:13
organized: Party is o. opinion　　DISR 247:12
organs: His 'owls was o.　　　　　DICK 241:26
Loud o., his glory forth tell　　　　BAKER 47:21
moves with its own o.　　　　　　SHAK 565:15
o. of beasts and fowls　　　　　　JOYCE 381:24
other o. take their tone　　　　　　GLAD 307:5
organ-voice: God-gifted o. of England
　　　　　　　　　　　　　　　　TENN 687:9
orgasm: o. has replaced the Cross
　　　　　　　　　　　　　　　　MUGG 487:11
orgastic: o. future that year　　　FITZ 285:4
orgy: o. looks particularly alluring　MUGG 487:9
Oriens: *equis O. adflavit anhelis*　VIRG 715:11
orient: o. and immortal wheat　　TRAH 701:13
origin: not Greek in its o.　　　　MAINE 442:13
stamp of his lowly o.　　　　　　　DARW 231:6
original: Behold the bright o.　　GAY 300:9
depravity and o. sin　　　　　　　MELV 456:12
either o. or instrumental　　　　　HOBB 340:2
every great and o. writer　　　　　WORD 748:20
I have nothing o. in me　　　　　　CAMP 176:20
ordinary one seem o.　　　　　　　HOR 347:5
o. is unfaithful　　　　　　　　　BORG 136:9
o. perused mankind　　　　　　　ARMS 26:6
o. righteousness　　　　　　　　　BOOK 135:23
o. writer is not　　　　　　　　　CHAT 192:4
originality: O. is deliberate and forced
　　　　　　　　　　　　　　　　HOFF 340:20
o. is taken to be a mark　　　　　GALB 296:19
without o. or moral courage　　　SHAW 635:28
originals: few o. and many copies　TOCQ 698:13
we do not admire the o.　　　　　PASC 507:11

origins: Consider your o.　　　　DANTE 230:16
Orion: O. plunges prone　　　　　HOUS 352:2
orison: mid his o. hears　　　　　DYER 265:8
orisons: patter out their hasty o.　OWEN 503:12
orisonte: th'o. hath reft the sonne　CHAU 193:14
Orlando: Run, run, O.　　　　　　SHAK 568:18
ornament: esteem'st the o. of life　SHAK 601:5
grossness with fair o.　　　　　　SHAK 608:26
My study's o.　　　　　　　　　　MIDD 459:16
Nobility is a graceful o.　　　　　BURKE 158:22
not the foreign aid of o.　　　　　THOM 696:8
O. is but the guilèd shore　　　　SHAK 609:1
o. of a meek and quiet　　　　　　BIBLE 105:16
o. of his cheek　　　　　　　　　SHAK 614:1
o. to her profession　　　　　　　BUNY 156:13
o. which truth doth give　　　　　SHAK 633:17
respecting all o.　　　　　　　　　RUSK 550:21
Silence is a woman's finest o.　　AUCT 33:26
still deceived with o.　　　　　　SHAK 608:26
ornaments: maid forget her o.　　BIBLE 85:3
Song made in lieu of many o.　　SPEN 659:17
with o. their want of art　　　　　POPE 521:11
Orontes: Syrian O.　　　　　　　JUV 383:19
orphan: defeat is an o.　　　　　CIANO 203:16
Orpheus: bid the soul of O. sing　MILT 464:23
O. with his lute made trees　　　SHAK 588:15
orthodoxy: O. is my doxy　　　　WARB 721:15
O. or My-doxy　　　　　　　　　CARL 180:21
ortolans: Let me die eating o.　　DISR 248:36
Oscar: assume that O. said it　　PARK 506:10
You will, O., you will　　　　　　WHIS 730:21
osprey: As is the o. to the fish　　SHAK 570:19
Ossa: pile O. on Pelion　　　　　VIRG 715:12
ostentation: full of maggot o.　　SHAK 599:7
ostrich: America can not be an o.　WILS 738:13
O. roams the great Sahara　　　　NASH 490:15
Othello: O.'s occupation's gone　　SHAK 616:20
other: desire o. men's goods　　　BOOK 123:9
Every o. inch a gentleman　　　　WEST 729:18
forsaking all o.　　　　　　　　　BOOK 123:19
I am not as o. men　　　　　　　　BIBLE 95:14
on the o. side　　　　　　　　　　BUNY 156:16
o. side of the hill　　　　　　　　WELL 727:1
O. voices, other rooms　　　　　　CAP 178:14
quite o. than ourselves　　　　　　MURD 488:6
strange faces, o. minds　　　　　　TENN 682:22
their troth either to o.　　　　　　BOOK 123:23
This o. Eden, demi-paradise　　　SHAK 619:18
turn to him the o. also　　　　　　BIBLE 88:32
Were t'o. dear charmer away　　　GAY 299:26
others: by their hunted expression
　　　　　　　　　　　　　　　　LEWIS 420:14
otherwise: gods thought o.　　　　VIRG 713:1
otia: *deus nobis haec o. fecit*　　VIRG 714:12
otiosus: *otiosum esse quam cum o.*　CIC 204:3
Otis: Miss O. regrets　　　　　　PORT 525:3
otium: *cum dignitate o.*　　　　CIC 204:13
ought: criteria of what o. to be　KEYN 395:13
It is, but hadn't o. to be　　　　　HARTE 327:19
meritus, 'so he o. to be'　　　　LEAC 413:9
o. never to have done it　　　　　BEVIN 69:17
o. or an *ought not*　　　　　　HUME 356:2
tells me I o. to do　　　　　　　　BURKE 157:26
what things they o. to do　　　　BOOK 120:13
which we o. to have done　　　　BOOK 118:8
our: O. Father which art　　　　　BIBLE 89:5
ours: And still is o. to-day　　　　WINK 739:6
ourselves: better be changed in o.　JUNG 383:2
five days elder than o.　　　　　　BROW 146:4
made us, and not we o.　　　　　　BOOK 131:17
Our remedies oft in o. do lie　　　SHAK 564:4
o. to help ourselves　　　　　　　BOOK 120:15
power is the love of o.　　　　　　HAZL 328:16
out: are o. wish to get in　　　　　EMER 277:11
at tother o. it wente　　　　　　　CHAU 195:21
down and o. of breath　　　　　　SHAK 582:9
Gentlemen, include me o.　　　　GOLD 312:2
I counted them all o.　　　　　　HANR 323:7
I o. of myself　　　　　　　　　　AUG 37:2
many ways o.　　　　　　　　　　SEN 563:1
Mordre wol o.　　　　　　　　　CHAU 194:6
never o. of the way　　　　　　　CHAR 191:18

out: (*cont.*):
one is in, the other o.　　　　　　CHUR 200:15
o., brief candle　　　　　　　　　SHAK 605:1
O. of the deep have I called　　　BOOK 134:11
o. of the fashion　　　　　　　　CIBB 203:19
O. of this wood do not　　　　　　SHAK 611:27
O. where the handclasp's　　　　CHAP 190:10
o. . . . with the Stuarts　　　　　DISR 248:15
shall preserve thy going o.　　　BOOK 133:24
To be o. of the war　　　　　　　EMER 277:10
out-argue: out-vote them we will o.
　　　　　　　　　　　　　　　　JOHN 374:27
out-babying: O. Wordsworth　　BULW 155:4
outcast: bewerp my o. state　　　SHAK 633:10
o. by nature　　　　　　　　　　　BARN 53:6
o. of the people　　　　　　　　　BOOK 125:10
outcasts: o. of Israel　　　　　　BOOK 135:11
outcries: o. pluck me　　　　　　KYD 404:10
outcry: Each o. of the hunted hare　BLAKE 111:2
outer: o. life of telegrams and anger
　　　　　　　　　　　　　　　　FORS 290:13
out-glittering: o. Keats　　　　BULW 155:4
outgrabe: mome raths o.　　　　CARR 182:18
outlast: last for ever, o. the sea　CONR 217:17
outlaw: o. of his own dark mind　BYRON 168:13
o. states run by the strangest　REAG 537:13
outlawed: nor be o., nor excommunicate
　　　　　　　　　　　　　　　　COKE 209:3
or o. or exiled　　　　　　　　　MAGN 442:1
outlive: o. this powerful rhyme　SHAK 633:18
outlives: He that o. this day　　SHAK 586:11
outlook: Could man o. that mark　VAUG 709:7
out-paramoured: woman o. the Turk
　　　　　　　　　　　　　　　　SHAK 596:9
outrage: civilised o.　　　　　　HEAN 329:20
Seal up the mouth of o.　　　　　SHAK 624:10
outrageous: O. acts and everyday rebellions
　　　　　　　　　　　　　　　　STEI 663:11
outrageously: o. virtuous　　　STEE 662:18
outside: o. and may be some time
　　　　　　　　　　　　　　　　MAHON 442:5
o. and may be some time　　　　OATES 497:9
O. every fat man　　　　　　　　AMIS 10:15
than o. pissing in　　　　　　　　JOHN 367:12
outspread: O. thy walls sublime　JOHN 377:14
out-topping: O. knowledge　　ARN 28:12
out-vote: o. them we will out-argue
　　　　　　　　　　　　　　　　JOHN 374:27
outward: every o. and inward sense
　　　　　　　　　　　　　　　　CARL 180:14
hope from o. forms to win　　　　COL 209:13
looketh on the o. appearance　　BIBLE 74:38
mark of virtue on his o. parts　　SHAK 608:26
Of sense and o. things　　　　　　WORD 746:3
o. and visible sign　　　　　　　　BOOK 123:10
O. be fair, however foul　　　　　CHUR 201:4
o. parts Love's always seen　　　COWL 221:13
o. show of things　　　　　　　　SPEN 660:19
o. shows be least themselves　　SHAK 608:26
weather on the o. wall　　　　　　SHAK 608:16
outwardly: o. in our bodies　　BOOK 120:15
outweighs: o. ability　　　　　　SHAK 583:1
outworn: cost of o. buried age　SHAK 634:1
oval: O. face. His eye a dark　　AUBR 33:7
over: opera ain't o. 'til the fat lady　COOK 218:4
O. hill, over dale　　　　　　　　SHAK 611:11
o. on this side the tomb　　　　　BYRON 168:18
oversexed, and o. here　　　　　　TRIN 703:1
O. the hills and far away　　　　　GAY 299:17
O. the hills and far away　　　　　STEV 669:10
O. the sea to Skye　　　　　　　BOUL 137:17
try to put it all o. you　　　　　　WEST 729:10
overbearing: o. and offensive behaviour
　　　　　　　　　　　　　　　　VICT 710:12
overbought: that thou hast o.　CRAS 226:1
overcame: came, saw, and o.　SHAK 583:25
That day he o. the Nervii　　　　SHAK 592:13
overcoat: my o. also was entering　RIMB 541:8
put on your o.　　　　　　　　　LOW 430:7
overcome: Be not o. of evil, but overcome
　　　　　　　　　　　　　　　　BIBLE 100:7
I have o. the world　　　　　　　BIBLE 97:21
o. the sharpness of death　　　　BOOK 118:13

overcome: (*cont.*):
sometimes o., seldom extinguished
    BACON 44:7
We shall o.   ANON 19:12
what is else not to be o.   MILT 468:5
overcomes: Who o. by force   MILT 469:3
overdone: anything so o.   SHAK 576:6
overgrown: o. with azure moss   SHEL 641:16
so with roses o.   MARV 450:19
overheard: poetry is *o.*   MILL 460:11
overlook: art of knowing what to o.
    JAMES 363:17
overmastered: o. with a piece of valiant
    SHAK 613:13
overpaid: Is grossly o.   HERB 333:19
O., overfed, oversexed   TRIN 703:1
over-past: until this tyranny be o. BOOK 128:14
over-prepared: o. the event   POUND 527:12
oversexed: o., and over here   TRIN 703:1
overtake: Till I thy fate shall o. KING 396:11
overthroweth: o. your health   BACON 43:23
overthrown: I have o. some of you BIBLE 86:12
overwhelm: o. myself in poesy KEATS 390:11
overwrought: Spirits o.   WORD 747:3
oves: *Inter o. locum praesta* MISS 477:14
Ovid: As O. has sweetly   MONT 480:6
O., the soft philosopher   DRYD 260:35
Venus clerk O.   CHAU 194:28
Ovidius: O. Naso was the man SHAK 598:17
ovo: *Ab o.*   HOR 351:2
owe: O. no man anything   BIBLE 100:9
we o. everything to him   JOHN 369:11
we o. God a death   SHAK 583:19
You o. me no subscription   SHAK 595:21
owed: I have o. to them   WORD 744:19
owest: Lend less than thou o. SHAK 595:6
Why, thou o. God a death   SHAK 581:30
oweth: woman o. to her husband SHAK 624:24
owing: By o. owes not   MILT 470:24
owl: fat greedy o. of the Remove RICH 540:7
He respects O.   MILNE 462:10
nightly sings the staring o.   SHAK 599:11
old o. lived in an oak   PUNCH 531:22
O. and the Pussy-Cat   LEAR 414:12
O., and the Waverley pen   ANON 18:16
o. does to the moon complain GRAY 315:11
o., for all his feathers   KEATS 386:20
o. hawked at and killed   SHAK 602:20
o. of Minerva   HEGEL 330:10
o. that is in the desert   BOOK 131:18
o. that shrieked   SHAK 601:15
white o. in the belfry sits   TENN 688:14
will fight . . . against the o.   SHAK 604:4
owlet: o. Atheism   COL 210:2
owls: companion to o.   BIBLE 77:31
court for o.   BIBLE 83:18
eagle among blinking o.   SHEL 641:3
o. came and perched   BEER 59:17
There I couch when o. do cry SHAK 626:2
Two O. and a Hen   LEAR 413:18
own: at least it is my o.   MUSS 488:14
child that's got his o.   HOL 342:1
every country but his o.   CANN 178:4
his o. received him not   BIBLE 96:3
marked him for his o.   WALT 721:13
my words are my o.   CHAR 191:12
respect each other for what they o.
    TAYL 679:9
room of her o.   WOOLF 742:10
own-alone: All by my o. self   HARR 327:2
owners: o. always reap the gains COLL 213:1
owning: mania of o.   WHIT 732:18
owse: o. and bottom of the sea SHAK 584:21
ox: brother to the o.   MARK 446:7
fat o. with evil will   BIBLE 78:35
he eateth grass as an o.   BIBLE 78:1
Manningtree o.   SHAK 580:31
nor his o., . . his ass   BIBLE 72:16
o. goeth to the slaughter   BIBLE 78:17
. to wrath has moved   BLAKE 111:1
shall eat straw like the o.   BIBLE 83:3
stalled o. and hatred   BIBLE 78:35
oxen: fields with his own o.   HOR 350:17

oxen: (*cont.*):
Many o. are come about me BOOK 125:11
o. may be strong to labour   BOOK 135:5
than a hundred pair of o.   HOW 353:4
Who drives fat o.   JOHN 376:14
years like great black o.   YEATS 751:7
Oxenford: Clerk there was of O. CHAU 192:19
Oxford: airing in this new North O. air
    BETJ 68:1
Half-Way House to Rome, O. PUNCH 531:9
Ipswich and O.   SHAK 589:11
My heart was with the O. men LETTS 419:15
noon on O. town   FLEC 286:6
O. has made me insufferable BEER 59:11
O. is on the whole more   BAED 46:5
O. sent a troop   BROW 146:25
O. sent a troop   TRAPP 702:3
poetry, which is in O. made DRYD 261:19
put back at O. or Cambridge BEER 59:12
secret in the O. sense   FRAN 293:8
sends his son to O.   STEAD 662:13
stagecoach from London to O. HAZL 329:12
To O. I acknowledge no   GIBB 302:10
what a *whole* O. is!   COL 209:7
Oxford Street: O., stony-hearted
stepmother   DE Q 237:7
oxlips: bold o.   SHAK 632:4
o. and the nodding violet   SHAK 611:19
Oxonian: being an O.   FARQ 280:25
Oxus: O., forgetting the bright ARN 28:18
oxygen: o. of publicity   THAT 691:23
oyster: open an o. at sixty paces WOD 740:12
o. may be crossed in love   SHER 644:25
o. shell on top   AUDEN 34:1
world is an o.   MILL 461:15
world's mine o.   SHAK 610:14
your pearl in your foul o.   SHAK 569:25
oysters: poverty and o.   DICK 243:12
Ozymandias: My name is O. SHEL 642:4

P

pace: And unperturbèd p.   THOM 695:2
Creeps in this petty p.   SHAK 605:1
dance is a measured p.   BACON 42:5
not afraid of 'the p.'   SURT 672:15
Requiescant in p.   MISS 477:15
sua volontade è nostra p. DANTE 230:19
pacem: *dona nobis p.*   MISS 477:5
paces: open an oyster at sixty p. WOD 740:12
three p. through the room   TENN 685:4
Pacific: He stared at the P. KEATS 390:3
pacific: except by p. means   BRIA 141:1
repose of a p. station   ADAMS 1:13
pacifist: quietly p. peaceful   WALK 717:13
pacify: My mission is to p. Ireland GLAD 307:7
pack: human p. is shuffled LODGE 426:19
I will p., and take a train   BROO 143:12
p., and follow at convenience BURT 164:11
p. the cards and yet cannot BACON 43:4
p. up your troubles   ASAF 30:17
peasantry its p. animal   TROT 704:12
revenged on the whole p. SHAK 630:36
To p. and label men for God THOM 695:8
packets: like a post with p.   SHAK 589:13
packhorse: p. on the down MORR 485:12
posterity is p.   DISR 247:7
packhorses: Shall p.   SHAK 583:8
packs: p. and sets of great ones SHAK 597:16
Paddington: As London is to P. CANN 178:7
Ever weeping P.   BLAKE 112:2
paddles: p. chunkin' from Rangoon KIPL 400:1
paddling: p. palms and pinching fingers
    SHAK 631:13
paddocks: Cold as p. though they be
    HERR 336:5
padlock: clap your p.—on her mind
    PRIOR 529:5
jingling p.—the mind   POPE 519:2
padre: *vittoria trova cento p.* CIANO 203:10
p. ... laurels to p.   CIC 204:8

paene: *P. insularum, Sirmio* CAT 186:3
pagan: find the p.—spoiled ZANG 755:6
P. suckled in a creed outworn WORD 748:16
page: And I turn the p.   BROW 146:22
p. having an ample marge TENN 682:15
Reading this indignant p. BLAKE 114:9
pageant: like this insubstantial p. SHAK 625:28
p. of his bleeding heart   ARN 28:21
part of life's rich p.   MARS 449:6
pageantry: masque, and antique p.
    MILT 465:17
pageants: black vesper's p. SHAK 566:6
pages: armies of my p.   MAY 454:16
I spring from the p.   WHIT 732:10
pagoda: old Moulmein P.   KIPL 400:1
pagus: private p. or demesne AUDEN 35:16
paid: attention must be p.   MILL 461:16
Lord God, we ha' p. in full KIPL 401:2
p. his subjects with a royal BROO 143:4
p. the uttermost farthing   BIBLE 88:30
well p. that is well satisfied SHAK 609:21
pain: After great p., a formal DICK 244:9
After long grief and p.   TENN 686:21
almost to amount to p.   HUNT 356:17
Although p. isn't real   ANON 18:15
and she hasn't a p.   MILNE 462:17
assuage the unforgotten p. ROSS 548:4
beneath the aromatic p.   WINC 739:3
birds give him p.   WILB 734:4
Bring equal ease unto my p. CAREW 179:9
Competence with p.   HEAN 329:22
cost Ceres all that p.   MILT 471:4
cures all p.   CLARE 204:21
disinclination to inflict p. MER 458:3
dreary old age and p.   VIRG 715:16
Eternal P.   ARN 27:18
For we are born in other's p. THOM 694:18
general drama of p.   HARDY 324:11
groaneth and travaileth in p. BIBLE 99:37
grown with pleasant p.   KEATS 389:20
I am quite sure she felt no p. BROW 152:3
I feel no p. dear mother now ANON 14:15
I have no p., dear mother, now FARM 280:5
Infinite passion, and the p. BROW 153:15
intermission of p.   SELD 562:11
Joy always came after p.   APOL 23:15
joy in hevene and p. in helle CHAU 194:29
joy is but a dish of p.   TICH 698:3
labour we delight in physics p. SHAK 602:12
life's a p. and but a span   DAV 232:4
midnight with no p.   KEATS 389:14
momentary intoxication with p. BRON 142:1
narcotics, numbing p.   TENN 683:1
Never p. to tell thy love BLAKE 113:15
nor help for p.   ARN 27:1
not because it gave p.   MAC 435:19
not in deed the gain, but p. OXF 504:1
obligation is a p.   JOHN 369:15
Of all my p.   WYATT 749:17
Of all pains, the greatest p. GRAN 314:13
Of p., darkness and cold BROW 152:5
one who never inflicts p. NEWM 493:5
Our Lady of P.   SWIN 676:9
p. and anguish wring   SCOTT 560:9
p. and grief to me   BOOK 126:22
p. of a new idea   BAG 47:12
p. shall not be inflicted   SPEN 658:14
p. than to remember a happy time
    DANTE 230:11
piercing p., a killing sin   STEV 669:7
pleasure and without one p. TENN 686:5
pleasure banish p.   WATTS 723:4
pleasures to another's p. COWP 223:28
pleasure turns to pleasing p. SPEN 660:10
put me to present p.   SHAK 619:5
relieved their p.   GOLD 310:10
rest from p.   DRYD 260:31
shall there be any more p. BIBLE 107:18
Superflux of p.   SWIN 675:19
Sweet is pleasure after p. DRYD 259:18
takes from us sense of p. CONS 217:20
tender for another's p.   GRAY 316:3

pain: (*cont.*):

Though full of p.	MILT 469:14
tongueless vigil and all the p.	SWIN 675:21
what p. it was to drown	SHAK 621:23
What triumph! hark—what p.	ARN 27:17
with no throbs of fiery p.	JOHN 375:30
With some p. is fraught	SHEL 643:19

painful: one is as p. as the other | BACON 43:10
| p. pleasure turns to pleasing | SPEN 660:10 |

pains: by p. men come | BACON 43:29
His present and your p.	SHAK 584:23
let our p. be less	BROME 141:16
made my p. his prey	SPEN 659:11
Marriage has many p.	JOHN 369:22
Muses never knew their p.	CRAB 225:11
no gains without p.	STEV 666:16
p. a man when 'tis kept	SUCK 671:8
p. of hell gat hold upon	BOOK 133:11
P. of love be sweeter far	DRYD 261:35
p. the immortal spirit	ARN 28:13
pleasure in poetic p.	COWP 223:21
So double was his p.	SPEN 660:3
sympathize with people's p.	HUXL 357:16
What p. he had to bear	ALEX 8:16
with p. that conquer trust	TENN 683:16

paint: As only showed the p. | DRYD 260:15
can't pick it up, p. it	ANON 14:17
I p. with my prick	REN 539:1
or p. the lily	BYRON 170:29
p. 'em truest praise 'em	ADD 3:15
p. in the public's face	RUSK 550:10
p. objects as I think them	PIC 514:12
p. on the face of Existence	BYRON 174:1
p. the meadows with delight	SHAK 599:10
refinèd gold, to p. the lily	SHAK 594:9

painted: As idle as a p. ship | COL 210:25
Duchess p. on the wall	BROW 151:11
gilded loam or p. clay	SHAK 619:7
p. child of dirt that stinks	POPE 520:3
p. cunningly	SPEN 659:25
p. meadow, or a purling stream	ADD 4:3
p. veil which those	SHEL 643:5
She p. her face, and tired	BIBLE 76:27
so young as they are p.	BEER 59:20
That fears a p. devil	SHAK 602:4
wood p. to look like iron	BISM 110:8

painter: colour that of a tea-tray in | BLUNT 116:6
Farewell, great p. of mankind	GARR 298:3
had been the P.'s hand	WORD 743:11
I, too, am a p.	CORR 219:12
or p. can be an architect	RUSK 550:11
p. and I nail my pictures	SCHW 558:16
ranks far below the p.	LEON 418:12
some great p. dips his pencil	SHEL 642:25
those scenes made me a p.	CONS 217:22

painters: Good p. imitate | CERV 188:17
| P. and poets alike | HOR 347:2 |
| Poets like p. | POPE 521:11 |

painting: How vain p. is | PASC 507:11
p. and punctuality mix	GAIN 296:13
p. in water-colour shows	STEV 668:2
P. is silent poetry	SIM 648:1
P. thy outward walls	SHAK 635:7
poem is like a p.	HOR 347:18
thoughts on the unreal p.	VIRG 712:9
Whose mother was her p.	SHAK 571:10

paintings: heard of your p. too | SHAK 576:2
paint-pots: p. and his words | HOR 347:8
paints: want to know a butcher p. | BROW 152:27
| Where God p. the scenery | HART 327:13 |

pair: p. of ragged claws | ELIOT 272:3
p. so famous	SHAK 567:15
Sleep on, blest p.	MILT 471:16
Take a p. of sparkling eyes	GILB 304:3

palace: at the p. door one day | DICK 243:5
Be thine own p.	DONNE 252:25
chalice from the p.	PANA 505:16
from this p. of dim night	SHAK 624:9
gorgeous p. for a hermitage	SHAK 620:12
leads to the p. of wisdom	BLAKE 112:16
Love in a p. is perhaps	KEATS 388:16

palace: (*cont.*):

making his p. desolate	BECK 58:3
man armed keepeth his p.	BIBLE 94:19
p. built upon the sand	MILL 461:8
p. fit for you and me	STEV 668:24
p. is more than a house	COL 212:11
purple-linèd p. of sweet sin	KEATS 388:17
straw cottage to a p.	DYER 265:4

palaces: dragons in their pleasant p. | BIBLE 83:4
fair, frail p.	ALDR 8:6
gorgeous p.	SHAK 625:28
Mid pleasures and p.	PAYNE 510:4
plenteousness with thy p.	BOOK 133:26
sleep old p. and towers	SHEL 641:16

paladin: Sidney's self, the starry p. | BROW 153:1
Palaeozoic: In the P. time | SMITH 651:19
palate: no motion of the liver, but | the p. | SHAK 629:19
| P., the hutch of tasty lust | HOPK 345:13 |
| steps down the p. to tap | NAB 488:21 |

palates: never p. more the dug | SHAK 566:19
| p. both for sweet and sour | SHAK 618:2 |

Palatine: more than the P. Hill | DU B 263:2
pale: behold a p. horse | BIBLE 106:16
bond which keeps me p.	SHAK 603:5
intelligence, and turned p.	SOUT 657:20
I was a p. young curate then	GILB 306:21
look so green and p.	SHAK 601:5
P. as thy smock	SHAK 618:18
p. as yonder wan and hornèd	SHEL 640:8
P., beyond porch and portal	SWIN 676:16
p. by shedding of thy blood	CONS 217:21
p. contented sort of discontent	KEATS 388:18
p. fire she snatches	SHAK 626:17
P. grew thy cheek and cold	BYRON 173:20
P. hands I loved beside	HOPE 345:3
p. prime-roses	SHAK 632:4
p., unripened beauties	ADD 3:18
Prithee, why so p.	SUCK 671:8
seyn somtyme a p. face	CHAU 193:25
whiter shade of p.	REID 538:15
world grew p.	JOHN 370:17

palely: Alone and p. loitering | KEATS 388:7
paler: I become p. than grass | SAPP 556:1
paletot: p. aussi devenait idéal | RIMB 541:8
paling: piece-bright p. | HOPK 346:6
Palladium: press is the P. | JUN 383:3
pallets: Upon uneasy p. | SHAK 583:11
palliate: p. what we cannot cure | JOHN 367:23
pallid: p., cheerless, and forlorn | HADR 320:8
pallida: P. Mors aequo | HOR 349:3
pallidula: P. rigida nudula | HADR 320:8
Palliser: Plantagenet P. | TROL 703:6
Pall Mall Gazette: P. is written by | gentlemen | THAC 691:10
pallor: p. of girls' brows | OWEN 503:13
palls: perishes, everything p. | ANON 21:8
palm: And bear the p. alone | SHAK 590:2
has won it bear the p.	JORT 380:14
Hold infinity in the p.	BLAKE 110:18
itching p.	SHAK 592:26
p. and southern pine	TENN 680:19
p. at the end of the mind	STEV 666:4
p. the hangman's thrusting	BLOK 115:3
p. without the dust	HOR 347:21
Quietly sweating p. to palm	HUXL 357:20
To win the p., the oak	MARV 450:5

palmae: dulcis sine pulvere p. | HOR 347:21
palmer: sad votarist in p.'s weed | MILT 463:19
palmerworm: which the p. hath left BIBLE 86:6
palms: And p. before my feet | CHES 198:30
other p. are won	WORD 746:7
p. of her hands	BIBLE 76:30
p. on the staircase	BETJ 67:3

palmy: p. state of Rome | SHAK 571:26
palpable: A Poem should be p. | MACL 439:9
palsied: alms of p. eld | SHAK 606:8
| its p. hearts | ARN 28:9 |

palsy: ole en strucken wid de p. | HARR 326:16
| p.-stricken, churchyard thing | KEATS 387:3 |
| Where p. shakes a few | KEATS 389:10 |

paltered: p. with Eternal God | TENN 687:18
paltry: aged man is but a p. thing YEATS 752:21

paltry: (*cont.*):

'Tis p. to be Caesar	SHAK 566:19

Pam: P., I adore you | BETJ 68:3
pampered: Holla, ye p. jades of Asia | MARL 448:9
pamphleteer: p. on guano and on grain | TENN 688:17
pamphleteers: not the age of p. | HOGB 341:14
Pan: P. did after Syrinx speed | MARV 450:8
| great god P. | BROW 147:17 |

panachaea: Or p., or polygony | SPEN 660:8
panache: c'est... Mon p. | ROST 548:11
Pancras: P. and Kentish-town | BLAKE 112:4
pandemonium: P., the high capital MILT 469:9
Pandora: open that P.'s Box | BEVIN 69:16
pane: A tap at the p., the quick | BROW 151:7
| Lo p. altrui, e com'è duro | DANTE 230:20 |

panes: And diamonded with p. | KEATS 387:5
pang: sufferance finds a p. | SHAK 606:9
pange: P., lingua, gloriosi | FORT 291:1
| P., lingua, gloriosi | THOM 692:13 |

pangs: p. and fears | SHAK 588:19
qualms, and bitter p.	SOUT 658:3
sweet p. of it remember me	SHAK 629:13
Their p. of love	SHAK 626:20

panic: what a p.'s in thy breastie | BURNS 163:15
panjandrum: grand P. himself | FOOTE 288:15
panoramic: p. view of hell | BYRON 170:14
pansies: p., that's for thoughts | SHAK 578:7
pansy: p. at my feet | WORD 745:14
| p. freaked with jet | MILT 466:11 |

pant: I p., I sink, I tremble | SHEL 640:11
pantaloon: lean and slippered p. | SHAK 568:16
Panther: Black P. | NEWT 493:18
panting: For ever p., and for ever young | KEATS 388:28
pants: earth in fast thick p. | COL 210:10
| p. the hart for cooling | TATE 678:16 |
| your lower limbs in p. | NASH 490:21 |

papa: else his dear p. is poor | STEV 668:18
| The word P. | DICK 241:6 |

papacy: p. is not other than | HOBB 340:12
paper: age of four with p. hats | UST 707:16
All reactionaries are p. tigers	MAO 446:3
contract isn't worth the p.	GOLD 312:3
he hath not eat p.	SHAK 598:15
If all the earth were p. white	LYLY 433:13
just for a scrap of p.	BETH 67:2
more personality than a p. cup	CHAN 190:3
only a p. moon	HARB 323:12
p. appears dull there is	STEE 662:19
p. work down to a minimum	ORTON 499:16
That ever blotted p.	SHAK 609:3
virtue of p. government	BURKE 157:18

paper-mill: thou hast built a p. | SHAK 587:26
papers: He's got my p. | PINT 514:19
| what I read in the p. | ROG 545:2 |

Papist: P., yet a Calvinist | CLEV 206:13
par: P. nobile fratrum | HOR 351:3
parable: open my mouth in a p. | BOOK 130:8
parachutes: Minds are like p. | DEWAR 238:6
parade: Deploying in a p. | MAY 454:16
| p. of riches | SMITH 650:19 |

paradisal: P. Imagineless metal | THOM 695:12
paradise: All P. opens | DISR 248:36
And drunk the milk of P.	COL 210:14
And wilderness is p. enow	FITZ 283:13
catch the bird of p.	KHR 395:17
England is a p. for women	BURT 165:12
England is the p. of women	FLOR 288:5
enjoy P. in the next	BECK 58:4
For I was taught in P.	KEATS 390:9
Have blundered into P.	THOM 695:8
I knew you once: but in P.	BROW 153:17
Life's p.	FORD 289:9
Lost Angel of a ruined P.	SHEL 639:15
P. by way of Kensal Green	CHES 199:6
p. for a sect	KEATS 387:14
P. of Fools	MILT 470:20
p. reserved for me	DODD 250:2
P., so late their happy seat	MILT 473:14
p. within thee, happier far	MILT 473:12
rudiments of P.	SOUTH 657:1

paradise: (cont.):
shalt thou be with me in p.   BIBLE 95:27
Such are the Gates of P.   BLAKE 111:22
They paved p.   MITC 477:18
Thou hast the keys of P.   DE Q 237:9
Thou P. of exiles, Italy   SHEL 640:21
Thou p. of four seas   MARV 451:8
paradises: God's compassion with P.   NIET 495:6
p. we have lost   PROU 530:16
Two p. 'twere in one   MARV 450:14
paradox: Man is an embodied p.   COLT 214:10
p. but a statement of the obvious   KNOX 403:6
parallel: But ours so truly p.   MARV 450:3
parallelism: certain p. of life   ADAMS 2:16
parallelogram: boarding-house is a p.   LEAC 413:10
parallelograms: Princess of P.   BYRON 173:23
parallels: p. in beauty's brow   SHAK 633:21
paramour: lady, and many a p.   SPEN 660:6
paramours: sustres and his p.   CHAU 194:5
Worn of p.   SPEN 660:26
parapets: Europe of the ancient p.   RIMB 541:7
parasites: p. or sub-parasites   JONS 379:7
parasol: quaint as an old p.   FISH 283:7
parboiled: my p. head   GRAH 313:14
parcels: she deals it in small p.   WEBS 726:1
parcere: P. subiectis et debellare   VIRG 713:17
parch: sun doth p. the green   SURR 672:4
parchment: features bound in stale p.   MER 457:19
lamb should be made p.   SHAK 587:24
rotten p. bonds   SHAK 619:18
parcus: P. deorum cultor   HOR 349:13
pardlike: p. Spirit, beautiful   SHEL 639:20
pardon: Bretful of p.   CHAU 193:7
cannot help or p.   AUDEN 36:8
faithful people and peace   BOOK 121:8
God may p. you, but I   ELIZ 274:15
God will p. me, it is His trade   HEINE 331:4
kiss of the sun for p.   GURN 319:17
P. all, their faults confessing   BUCK 154:12
P. me boy is that the   GORD 312:13
they ne'er p., who have   DRYD 260:9
To p. or to bear it   COWP 222:6
We cannot beg for p.   MACN 441:4
With a thousand Ta's and P.'s   BETJ 68:2
pardoned: praised than to be p.   JONS 380:9
pardoning: p. our offences   BOOK 122:13
parens: king is truly p. patriae   JAM 362:2
parent: had a smile for your p.   VIRG 715:2
Revolution a p. of settlement   BURKE 158:8
That would put any p. mad   FLEM 286:19
To lose one p., Mr Worthing   WILDE 734:14
parentage: What is your p.   SHAK 628:25
parents: And left his p. in dismay   BLAKE 111:15
And lords whose p. were   DEFOE 234:24
begin by loving their p.   WILDE 735:30
contingent preferences of p.   HEGEL 330:11
girl needs good p.   TUCK 705:2
Jewish man with p. alive   ROTH 548:15
joys of p. are secret   BACON 44:11
Of p. good, of fist most   SHAK 585:22
Our p.' age has produced us   HOR 350:5
P.—especially step-parents   POW 528:5
P. first season us   HERB 335:19
p. kept me from children who   SPEN 659:2
P. love their children more   AUCT 33:24
p. obey their children   EDW 267:6
p. take more care   CAV 187:14
slavish bondage to p.   WOLL 741:17
stranger to one of your p.   AUST 39:13
parentum: Aetas p. peior avis tulit   HOR 350:5
parfit: p. gentil knyght   CHAU 192:9
paries: p. cum proximus ardet   HOR 348:13
l'udor after they've seen P.   LEWIS 420:21
die, go to P.   APPL 23:19
die they go to P   WILDE 735:25
is P. burning?   HITL 339:10
'Joa 'twe I saw P.   HAMM 321:19
king had given me P   ANON 21:5
no more Hoares to P.   CROR 301:4
P. is a movable feast   HEM 891:18
P. vaut bien une messe   HENR 332:12

Paris: (cont.):
P. was French—and silent   TUCH 705:1
parish: all the world as my p.   WESL 728:20
his pension from his p.   RUSK 551:2
p. of rich women   AUDEN 34:14
'paritors: Of trotting p.   SHAK 598:13
park: p., a policeman and a pretty girl   CHAP 190:9
parking: And put up a p. lot   MITC 477:18
parks: p. are the lungs of London   PITT 515:13
parley-voo: Hinky, dinky, p.   ANON 16:6
parliament: crop-headed P.   BROW 151:5
In the P. of man   TENN 685:13
Mob, p., Rabble   COBB 207:28
[p.] are a lot of hard-faced   BALD 48:13
p. can do any thing   PEMB 511:10
P. itself would not exist   SCAR 557:18
P. speaking through reporters   CARL 180:31
P. to do things at eleven   SHAW 636:32
parliamentarian: only safe pleasure for a p.   CRIT 227:3
parliamentary: P. leper   WILS 738:2
unhappy bag of p. eloquence   CARL 181:1
parliaments: the mother of P.   BRIG 141:9
parlour: Is it some party in a p.   WORD 746:13
Will you walk into my p.   HOW 353:7
Parnassus: my chief P.   SIDN 647:2
parochial: Art must be p.   MOORE 482:10
hopelessly p. when not   LAMB 407:15
worse than provincial—he was p.   JAMES 362:20
parole: p. of literary men   JOHN 375:24
paroles: p. que pour déguiser leurs
sortir de confuses p.   VOLT 716:5 / BAUD 55:8
pars: Et quorum p. magna fui   VIRG 712:13
parson: after him the p. ran   CHES 199:5
coughing drowns the p.'s saw   SHAK 599:11
If P. lost his senses   HODG 340:16
p. knows enough who knows   COWP 224:10
P. left conjuring   SELD 562:9
p. of the parish was one   TURN 705:14
see a Whig in a p.'s gown   JOHN 370:28
Then the P. might preach   BLAKE 114:10
parsons: merriment of p.   JOHN 375:21
p. are the happiest men   LLOYD 424:1
p. are very like men   CHES 198:5
p. do not care for truth   STUB 671:2
part: come let us kiss and p.   DRAY 258:1
every man must play a p.   SHAK 607:4
Fear God, and take your own p.   BORR 136:18
For we know in p.   BIBLE 101:1
hath chosen that good p.   BIBLE 94:18
if ought but death p.   BIBLE 74:25
more willingly p. withal   SHAK 574:24
My soul, bear thou thy p.   GURN 320:4
of which I was a major p.   VIRG 712:13
one leaves behind a p.   HAR 323:8
p. my garments among them   BOOK 125:13
p. of all that I have met   TENN 684:9
p. of life's rich pageant   MARS 449:6
p. of ourselves doesn't   HESSE 337:15
p. of the solution or you're   CLEA 206:3
P. steals, lets part abide   HARDY 325:9
p. to tear a cat in   SHAK 611:5
prepared to play a p.   MACM 440:8
Shall I p. my hair behind   ELIOT 272:6
shall meet and never p.   KING 396:12
till death us do p.   BOOK 123:20
To p. at last without a kiss   MORR 485:13
Yet meet we shall, and p.   BUTL 167:10
partagée: chose la mieux p.   DESC 237:17
partakers: p. of the holy Communion   BOOK 121:14
parted: fool and his words are soon p.   SHEN 644:15
I remember the way we p.   SWIN 676:23
P. are those who are singing   BOWEN 138:5
When we two p.   BYRON 173:20
parterre: God on the p.   POPE 520:22
Parthian: P. and Medes   BIBLE 98:7
partial: p. for th' observer's sake   POPE 520:24
partiality: neither anger nor p.   TAC 677:23
particoloured: p. of divineness   BACON 42:1

particles: instants became P.   BLY 116:7
Newton's p. of light   BLAKE 113:6
particular: introducing p. objects   KAMES 385:3
love a bright p. star   SHAK 604:1
particularities: p., and details   REYN 539:8
particulars: generals than in p.   HUME 355:15
must do it in minute p.   BLAKE 112:6
parties: Like other p.   BYRON 174:2
p. having any choice   JOHN 374:11
P. must ever exist in a free   BURKE 157:29
warns the heads of p.   ARB 24:7
parting: Ere the p. hour go   ARN 27:14
P. is all we know of heaven   DICK 244:16
p. is such sweet sorrow   SHAK 623:7
p. there is an image of death   ELIOT 269:27
rive not more in p.   SHAK 566:5
stood at the p. of the ways   BIBLE 85:24
Their every p. was to die   TENN 684:8
this p. was well made   SHAK 593:15
Upon the p. of his hair   MERR 458:12
partir: P. c'est mourir un peu   HAR 323:8
partly: And p. she was drunk   BURNS 162:12
Living and p. living   ELIOT 272:9
partners: change p. and dance   BERL 65:15
partridge: Always p.   ANON 21:7
p. sitteth on eggs   BIBLE 85:13
parts: dignified and efficient p.   BAG 46:12
his time plays many p.   SHAK 568:16
P. answering parts   POPE 520:20
P. of it are excellent   PUNCH 532:7
p. of one stupendous whole   POPE 522:7
Today we have naming of p.   REED 537:18
truth in the inward p.   BOOK 128:5
parturient: P. montes   HOR 347:11
party: Collapse of Stout P.   ANON 12:23
conduct of a losing p.   BURKE 157:2
educate our p.   DISR 247:15
effects of the spirit of p.   WASH 721:25
I always voted at my p.'s call   GILB 306:1
Is it some p. in a parlour   WORD 746:13
lower organs of p.   ANON 16:5
maintain the p. of the truth   SHAK 587:9
nature of a political p.   TROL 704:2
Not a select p.   KEATS 392:12
not p. men, but sensible   NEWM 493:2
p. is not to be brought down   HAIL 321:1
P. is organized opinion   DISR 247:12
p. is worse than the other   ROG 544:18
p. of order or stability   MILL 460:17
p. of two is like the Scotch   BRIG 141:11
p.'s over   COMD 214:12
without p. Parliamentary   DISR 247:19
passion and p. blind   COL 212:14
save the P. we love   GAII 296:16
sooner a p. breaks up   AUST 38:9
Stick to your p.   DISR 249:3
stupidest p.   MILL 460:9
Then none was for a p.   MAC 436:12
party-spirit: P., which at best   POPE 524:1
parva: p. licet componere magnis   VIRG 715:19
pasarán: No p.   IBAR 358:15
pass: cunning men p. for wise   BACON 43:7
Generations p. while   BROW 145:21
I keep, and p., and turn again   EMER 276:5
I p., like night, from land   COL 211:16
let him p. for a man   SHAK 607:13
let this cup p. from me   BIBLE 92:28
look, and p.   DANTE 230:7
my words shall not p.   BIBLE 92:12
narrow way for men to p.   DAN 229:12
O! let him p.   SHAK 598:4
p. by me as the idle wind   SHAK 593:5
p. for forty-three   GILB 306:23
p. her time 'twixt reading   POPE 521:1
P. into nothingness   KEATS 386:13
p. man's understanding   BOOK 121:4
P. me the can, lad   HOUS 351:16
p. the ammunition   FORGY 289:18
p. the mustard   GILB 306:25
P. the sick bag, Alice   JUNOR 383:10
p. through this world   GREL 317:19
pay us, p. us   CHES 199:7

pass: (*cont.*):

Ships that p. in the night	LONG 428:1
these things must come to p.	BIBLE 92:8
They shall not p.	ANON 20:10
They shall not p.	IBAR 358:15
thou shalt strangely p.	SHAK 633:15
through it p.	HERB 334:17
Try not the P.!	LONG 426:19
we may so p. through things	BOOK 121:2
which they shall not p.	BOOK 132:7
will p. nor turn my face	BROW 153:17
Will she p. in a crowd	SWIFT 673:18
with shining foot shall p.	FITZ 284:17

passa: *ma guarda, e p.*   DANTE 230:7

passage: carved out his p.   SHAK 599:15

fret a p. through	FULL 296:8
long black p. up to bed	STEV 668:17
North-west p. to the intellectual	STER 665:2
p. from hand to hand	DICK 646:8
p. which we did not take	ELIOT 270:14

passages: cheated into some fine p.

	KEATS 392:5
History has many cunning p.	ELIOT 271:11
imaginative or domestic p.	KEATS 391:12
shuts up all the p. of joy	JOHN 370:18

passageways: smell of steaks in p. ELIOT 272:13

passe: *Tout p., tout casse*   ANON 21:8

passed: Has p. away   PEAC 510:12

He p. by on the other side	BIBLE 94:14
p. the door of darkness	FITZ 284:6
remembren, whan it p.	CHAU 195:20
That p. the time	BECK 57:25
Writhed not of p. joy	KEATS 387:33

passer: *p. et de laisser faire*   QUES 534:8

P. mortuus est meae puellae   CAT 185:13

passeront: *Ils ne p. pas*   ANON 20:10

passes: beauty vanishes; beauty p. DE L 236:1

Everything p.	ANON 21:8
free p., class distinction	BETJ 67:15
Men seldom make p.	PARK 506:8
Thus p. the glory of the world	ANON 22:15

passeth: p. all understanding   BIBLE 103:12

which p. knowledge   BIBLE 102:14

passi: *O p. graviora*   VIRG 712:5

passing: I did but see her p.   ANON 18:10

Is it not p. fair to be a king	MARL 447:24
p. of the third floor back	JER 365:14
p. the love of women	BIBLE 75:9
So be my p.!	HENL 332:8
So passeth, in the p. of a day	SPEN 660:6

passing-bells: p. for these who die

	OWEN 503:12

passion: All breathing human p. KEATS 388:28

All made of p.	SHAK 569:21
all p. spent	MILT 474:20
Bards of P. and of Mirth	KEATS 386:7
betwixt one p. and another	STER 664:5
by p. or interest	LOCKE 425:2
Cows are my p.	DICK 240:18
Cross and P.	BOOK 119:18
desolate and sick of an old p.	DOWS 256:2
did relieve my p. much	SHAK 629:12
dream of p.	SHAK 575:8
Eternal P.	ARN 27:18
fellow tear a p. to tatters	SHAK 576:5
gentleman in such a p.	SHAW- 639:2
His love was p.'s essence	BYRON 168:25
I have no p. for it	JOHN 372:2
Infinite p., and the pain	BROW 153:15
lingering and consumptive p.	ETH 270.17
maiden p. for a maid	TENN 681:25
Man is a useless p.	SART 556:10
no p. in the human soul	LILLO 421:16
our p. is our task	JAMES 363:1
O well-painted p.	SHAK 617:12
P. and apathy, and glory	MILT 470:1
p. and party blind our	COL 212:14
p. and the life	COL 209:13
p. and the power to roam	BYRON 168:17
p. as the maid that milks	SHAK 566:16
p. cannot Music raise	DRYD 261:24
p. doth expel another still	CHAP 190:19
p. for a man	KELLY 393:2

passion: (*cont.*):

p. for hunting something	DICK 242:25
p. in the mind of man	BACON 43:9
P., I see, is catching	SHAK 592:1
passion, not p. itself	BART 54:17
p. shakes your very frame	SHAK 618:6
p. shall have spent	TENN 685:9
p. so effectually robs	BURKE 158:3
P. speechless lies	DRAY 258:1
p. that left the ground	BROW 148:1
p. to which he has always	POW 528:2
p. turn into respect	ETH 278:19
p. woman loves her lover	BYRON 170:23
prose and the p.	FORS 290:14
ruling p. conquers reason	POPE 520:10
science of the tender p.	PUSH 532:13
Search then the Ruling P.	POPE 520:28
sentimental p. of a vegetable	GILB 305:17
so obstinate a p.	HUME 355:8
That is not p.'s slave	SHAK 576:7
Till earthly p. turn	LITT 423:9
'Tis a most insipid p.	ROCH 543:16
To inspire hopeless p.	THAC 691:7
vows his p. is infinite	PARK 506:12
what is p. but pining	MER 458:11
What is p.? That sickness	LERM 418:18
Whom p. could not shake	SHAK 617:13
with all the p. that a woman	EPH 278:4
With the ardour and the p.	JONS 379:14

passionate: beautiful p. body SWIN 676:11

full of p. intensity   YEATS 753:1

passione: *P. interdum movemur* THOM 692:10

passion-flower: p. at the gate TENN 686:20

passionless: hopeless grief is p. BROW 147:13

man p.?—no   SHEL 642:18

passions: Absence diminishes commonplace p.

	LA R 410:19
after experience of p.	VOLT 716:18
All thoughts, all p.	COL 210:15
concentrated p.	HARDY 324:20
Desolate p., aching hours	JOHN 367:3
governs the p. and resolutions	HUME 355:11
his p. which have	STER 664:23
inferno of his p.	JUNG 382:13
Love is only one of many p.	JOHN 369:8
men of like p.	BIBLE 98:24
moderator of p.	WALT 721:1
p. are most like to floods	RAL 535:19
p. of his fellow men	HOR 350:1
P. spin the plot	MER 458:8
p. expressed by one lurid smile	WALP 720:8
powerful and more lofty p.	TOCQ 698:9
slave of the p.	HUME 355:20
two primal p., to get and beget	OSLER 502:2
when he acts from the p.	DISR 248:9

passive: apparently p. and motionless

	CANN 178:12
Much benevolence of the p. order	MER 458:3

passives: Love's p. are his activ'st part

	CRAS 226:3

passover: Christ our p. is sacrificed

	BIBLE 100:22
it is the Lord's p.	BIBLE 72:10

passport: his p. shall be made   SHAK 586:11

My p.'s green	HEAN 329:19
p. is sometimes asked	BAED 46:7

past: always praising the p.   SMITH 652:18

As changed itself to p.	LARK 410:3
borne back into the p.	FITZ 285:4
dote on p. achievement	HAZL 329:9
first atone for our p.	CHEK 196:9
funeral of the p.	CLARE 204:27
give me back my p. years	VIRG 714:4
God cannot alter the p.	BUTL 166:23
God cannot change the p.	AGAT 5:15
lament the p.	BURKE 159:11
Let the dead P. bury its dead	LONG 429:7
looking forward to the p.	OSB 501:17
Many a woman has a p.	WILDE 735:9
more than things long p.	SHAK 619:16
moulded of things p.	SHAK 627:22
nothing more than the p.	BERG 65:5
or nothing but the p.	KEYN 395:5

past: (*cont.*):

p. and future to bear witness	O'NEI 499:2
p. are condemned to repeat it	SANT 555:16
p. as a watch in the night	BOOK 130:23
p. exudes legend	MAL 442:15
p. is a bucket of ashes	SAND 555:7
p. is a foreign country	HART 327:22
p. is the only dead thing	THOM 694:1
p. our dancing days	SHAK 622:23
p. redress are now with	SHAK 620:1
p. shut in him like	WOOLF 742:9
P., when you have gone	BLOK 115:4
p. years in me doth breed	WORD 746:2
plan the future by the p.	BURKE 157:5
present controls the p.	ORW 500:11
Present with the P.	CONN 216:16
remember what is p.	HAL 321:11
remembrance of things p.	SHAK 633:11
repeat his p. nor leave	AUDEN 36:15
scraps are good deeds p.	SHAK 627:19
soul of the whole P.	CARL 180:27
There is only the p.	THOM 694:18
Time present and time p.	ELIOT 270:13
upon the p. has power	DRYD 262:2
What's p., and what's to come	SHAK 628:3
What's p. is prologue	SHAK 625:15
world is weary of the p.	SHEL 640:16
years that are p.	BOOK 130:7

pastime: take his p. therein   BOOK 132:9

'twas p. to be bound   WORD 745:8

pastoral: Cold P.   KEATS 389:2

p. music on a thin stalk   VIRG 714:11

pastors: p. and teachers   BIBLE 102:17

P. she sends to help them	CHUR 201:1
some ungracious p. do	SHAK 573:2
spiritual p. and masters	BOOK 123:7

pasture: clean the p. spring   FROST 295:7

mettle of your p.	SHAK 585:9
people of his p.	BOOK 131:10
shall feed me in a green p.	BOOK 125:14
sheep of his p.	BOOK 131:17

pastures: fresh woods, and p. new MILT 466:16

green p. of the European	VERW 710:8
Pipe me to p. still	HOPK 345:12

pat: Now might I do it p.   SHAK 577:3

P. he comes   SHAK 595:3

patch: P. grief with proverbs SHAK 614:12

p. up thine old body	SHAK 583:9
potsherd, p., matchwood	HOPK 346:7

patched: is but p. with sin SHAK 628:19

patches: king of shreds and p. SHAK 577:17

thing of shreds and p.   GILB 304:19

pate: made by an aged old p.   ANON 17:3

p. of a politician   SHAK 578:20

pâté de foie gras: p. to the sound of trumpets

	SMITH 653:23

pater: *P. noster*   MISS 477:3

paterna: *buona imagine p.*   DANTE 230:15

P. rura bubus   HOR 348:22

paternal: dear and kindly p. image

	DANTE 230:15
disclaim all my p. care	SHAK 594:19

paternalism: p. ought to be unlearned

	CLEV 206:11

paternity: bond of p., which is rotten

	SART 556:14

path: beaten p. to his door   EMER 277:17

cannot approach it by any p.	KRIS 404:1
heavenly p., with many a	MARL 447:9
p. before him always bright	WORD 743:8
p. before me leading wherever	WHIT 732:23
p. emerges for a while	DOWS 256:3
p. of the just	BIBLE 78:11
P. of Wickedness	BALL 50:16
rough and thorny p.	MONT 481:5
was a p. of gold for him	BROW 151:21

pathetic: P. Fallacy   RUSK 550:14

Is not p., has no arrangements	WHIT 733:1
too p. for the feelings of	AUST 38:14

pathless: heaven's wide p. way MILT 464:20

Life is too much like a p.	FROST 294:10
pleasure in the p. woods	BYRON 169:13

pathos: P., piety, courage   FORS 290:24

paths: all her p. are peace — BIBLE 78:9
all her p. are Peace — SPR 661:10
craggy p. of study — JONS 379:5
light unto my p. — BOOK 133:20
make his p. straight — BIBLE 88:13
p. of glory lead — GRAY 315:13
So many p. that wind and wind — WILC 734:8
pathway: p. of a life unnoticed — HOR 348:14
steep and rugged p. — WILL 737:14
patience: All humbleness, all p. — SHAK 569:21
and eek hire p. — CHAU 193:10
drop of p. — SHAK 617:15
greater aptitude for p. — BUFF 154:16
habits of peace and p. — WALT 721:1
His wyves p. in trust to fynde — CHAU 193:10
I laughed him into p. — SHAK 565:13
Let p. have her perfect work — BIBLE 104:24
long will you abuse our p. — CIC 204:5
my p. is now at an end — HITL 339:13
old abusing of God's p. — SHAK 610:12
other people's p. — UPD 707:4
p., and shuffle the cards — CERV 189:14
P., n. A minor form — BIER 109:12
p. of hope in our Lord — BIBLE 103:19
p. of Job — BIBLE 105:5
P., thou young and rose-lipped — SHAK 617:15
p. to appreciate domestic — SANT 555:17
p. under their sufferings — BOOK 120:7
p. will achieve more — BURKE 158:25
pattern of all p. — SHAK 595:23
preached up p. — PRIOR 579:10
preacheth p. — HERB 334:10
sat like p. on a monument — SHAK 629:20
they that have not p. — SHAK 616:8
patient: Beware the fury of a p. man — DRYD 259:13
brought it to her p. dear — SPEN 660:8
but not so p. — SHAK 582:19
kill the p. — BACON 43:23
P. continuance in well doing — BIBLE 99:18
p. etherized upon a table — ELIOT 271:21
p. must minister to himself — SHAK 604:22
p., not a brawler — BIBLE 103:26
Thou must be p. — SHAK 597:10
patientia: Catilina, p. nostra — CIC 204:5
patiently: waited p. for the Lord — BOOK 126:24
ye take it p. — BIBLE 105:14
patients: Are their own p. — THOM 694:10
likes to hurry his p. along — MOL 479:7
patines: with p. of bright gold — SHAK 610:1
patria: pro p. mori — HOR 349:25
patriarchal: wi' p. grace — BURNS 161:18
patrician: A regular p. — GILB 306:6
This is the P. — DONNE 253:7
patrie: Allons, enfants de la p. — ROUG 548:17
plus j'aimai ma p. — BELL 62:9
patrimony: was all his p. — SAB 552:11
patriot: Never was p. yet — DRYD 259:12
only a p. to heaven — MELV 456:15
steady p. of the world — CANN 178:4
Such is the p.'s boast — GOLD 311:9
Would the honest p. — JEFF 364:4
patriotism: call of p. — CANN 178:12
knock the p. out of the human race — SHAW 638:11
larger p. — ROS 546:15
P. is a lively sense — ALD 8:3
P. is not enough — CAV 187:10
P. is the last refuge — JOHN 374:2
p. which consists in hating — GASK 299:6
patriots: blood of p. and tyrants — JEFF 364:9
P. are in the right — WAUGH 724:3
so to be p. — BURKE 159:17
True p. we — CART 184:11
were all these country p. born — BYRON 167:19
patrol: P. the halls on spongy shoes — MERR 458:12
[illegible] of some thirty [illegible] — TENN 688:17
[illegible] — JOHN [illegible]
p., and the [illegible] — [illegible]
P. Commonly a wretch — [illegible]
patronage: p. is swayed — ALD 7:0

patroness: My celestial p. — MILT 472:17
patronum: omnium's p. — CAT 186:6
patter: unintelligible p. — GILB 306:20
pattern: dance's p. — AUDEN 34:7
For he is our childhood's p. — ALEX 8:14
history is a p. — ELIOT 271:8
imposing of a p. on experience — WHIT 731:14
let us trace the p. — WOOLF 742:8
our p. to live and to die — BROW 151:1
p. as it was doomed — HARDY 324:15
p. informed by sensibility — READ 537:7
p. of all patience — SHAK 595:23
p. of excelling nature — SHAK 618:5
p. to encourage purchasers — SWIFT 673:7
predetermined p. — FISH 283:1
web, then, or the p. — STEV 667:10
patterns: Christ! What are p. — LOW 429:12
pâturage: Labourage et p. — SULLY 671:13
paucity: p. of human pleasures — JOHN 377:8
p. of its reverberation — MAIL 442:7
pauper: He's only a p. — NOEL 496:10
pause: How dull it is to p. — TENN 690:1
I p. for a reply — SHAK 592:4
p. in the day's occupations — LONG 426:3
speak, and p. again — CUWP 222:2
pauses: But the p. between — SCHN 558:7
intervals and happy p. — BACON 45:10
paved: streets are p. with gold — COLM 214:1
pavement: P. slippery — ROB 542:16
riches of heaven's p. — MILT 469:4
Stand on the highest p. — ELIOT 271:19
pavilioned: P. in splendour — GRANT 314:6
paweth: He p. in the valley — BIBLE 77:38
pawn: p. your intelligence — CUMM 228:7
pax: et in terra p. hominibus — MISS 476:18
P. Domini sit semper vobiscum — MISS 477:4
P. Vobis — BIBLE 108:12
'P. vobiscum' will answer all — SCOTT 560:23
pay: And wonders what's to p. — HOUS 351:21
cut each other's throats for p. — GOLD 311:2
devil to p. — ANON 13:20
Envy's a sharper spur than p. — GAY 299:32
for what p.? — RUSK 550:19
I p. thy poverty — SHAK 624:4
Not a penny off the p. — COOK 218:3
p. a million priests — HARDY 325:2
p. any price, bear any burden — KENN 393:12
p. at the Greek Kalends — AUG 37:14
P. every debt, as if God — EMER 276:13
p. for one by one — KIPL 401:4
p. for the damage if ever — CLOU 207:12
P. given to a state hireling — JOHN 368:5
p. glad life's arrears — BROW 152:5
P., pack, and follow — BURT 164:11
Smile at us, p. us, pass us — CHES 199:7
sum of things to p. — HOUS 351:22
paycock: mornin' till night like a p. — O'CAS 497:14
paying: p. the Dane-geld — KIPL 401:8
payment: passes for current p. — BURN 160:12
paynims: That is to wit three p. — CAXT 188:2
pays: owes not, but still p. — MILT 470:24
scent wich p. the best — LOW 429:16
pea: p. which has got into — WELLS 727:14
peace: all her paths are p. — BIBLE 78:9
all her paths are P. — SPR 661:10
and slept in p. — SHAK 589:5
arch of p. is morticed — NIC 494:14
are like the p. of God — JAM 362:6
blessèd p. to cheer us — WINK 739:6
blessing of p. — BOOK 126:4
bring a man p. at the last — BOOK 126:21
But not the easy p. — GAUNT 299:7
calm world and a long p. — SHAK 581:23
certain knot of p. — SIDN 646:18
Certainty. Feeling. Joy. P. — PASC 508:1
chastisement of our p. — BIBLE 84:12
cowardice keeps us in p. — JOHN 375:5
deep p. of the double-bed — CAMP 176:6
even though I find their p. — ELEG 286:10
[illegible] ring p. is a dream — MOLT 479:17
[illegible] — BOOK [illegible]

peace: (cont.):
gain our p., have sent to — SHAK 603:3
Give p. a chance — LENN 417:19
give p. at home — BOOK 135:21
Give p. in our time, O Lord — BOOK 119:2
good war makes a good p. — HERB 336:3
good war, or a bad p. — FRAN 293:2
Grace be unto you, and p. — BIBLE 105:31
habits of p. and patience — WALT 721:1
Had Zimri p. — BIBLE 76:28
hard and bitter p. — KENN 393:12
hast thou to do with p. — BIBLE 76:25
haunt of ancient P. — TENN 687:22
heaven-born Prince of P. — WESL 728:4
his goods are in p. — BIBLE 94:19
I came not to send p. — BIBLE 90:20
if thou return at all in p. — BIBLE 76:13
If you want p., prepare for war — VEGE 710:1
I labour for p. — BOOK 133:22
Imperishable p. — HOUS 352:4
ingeminate the word P. — CLAR 205:3
In His will is our p. — DANTE 230:19
In p.: goodwill — CHUR 203:3
instrument of Your p. — FRAN 292:12
interest that keeps p. — CROM 222:12
into the way of p. — BIBLE 93:24
in what p. a Christian can die — ADD 5:3
join with thee calm P. — MILT 464:17
lasting p. among ourselves — LINC 422:9
lazy P. will hide her drowsy head — D'AV 231:19
Let p. fill our heart — KUMAR 408:8
Let us have p. — GRANT 314:9
Let war yield to p. — CIC 204:2
Love of p., and lonely musing — COLL 213:15
make war than to make p. — CLEM 206:7
more precious than p. — WILS 738:18
moth of p. — SHAK 615:8
mountains also shall bring p. — BOOK 129:19
mountain tops is p. — GOET 309:14
multitude of p. — BOOK 126:19
My p. is gone — GOET 309:6
Nation shall speak p. unto — REND 538:18
news and Prince of P. — FLET 287:24
nor earth have been at p. — SHAK 591:4
Nor p. within nor calm around — SHEL 643:10
no such thing as inner p. — LEB 415:8
Not p. — MILT 469:16
not p. at any price — JERR 366:4
old as we to keep the p. — SHAK 622:19
on earth p. — BIBLE 93:28
Only a p. between equals — WILS 738:14
Open covenants of p. — WILS 738:19
pardon and p. — BOOK 121:8
p. above all earthly dignities — SHAK 588:20
p. and lover of concord — BOOK 119:3
p. and propagation — WALP 719:20
p. and rest at last — DOST 254:6
p. and rest can never dwell — MILT 468:1
p. and sensual indulgence — BAUD 55:9
P. be to this house — BOOK 123:24
P. be unto you — BIBLE 108:12
p. cannot be maintained — RUSS 552:2
P.; come away — TENN 683:23
P., commerce, and honest — JEFF 364:5
p. for our time — CHAM 189:8
p. has broken out — BREC 140:11
P. hath her victories — MILT 474:29
P. I leave with you — BIBLE 97:15
P.! impudent and shameless — SHAK 588:4
p. in Shelley's mind — SHEL 643:21
P. is a very apoplexy — SHAK 570:18
P. is crowned with smiles — VAUG 708:17
P. is indivisible — LITV 423:11
P. is in the grave — SHEL 642:12
P. is nothing but slovenliness — BREC 140:7
P. is poor reading — HARDY 324:6
P. is the way — MUSTE 488:19
P.! it is I — ANAT 11:6
P. its ten thousands — PORT 525:7
p. Man is a bungler — SHAW 637:14
P., n. . . .period of cheating — BIER 109:13
p of God, which passeth — BIBLE 103:12
p. of Jerusalem — BOOK 133:26

peace: (cont.):
p. of wild things BERRY 66:13
P. on earth and mercy mild WESL 728:3
P., perfect peace BICK 108:22
P., plenty, pleasure NASHE 490:23
P., retrenchment, and reform BRIG 141:7
P. shall go sleep SHAK 620:17
p. the historical calm AUDEN 35:1
P., the human dress BLAKE 113:19
p. there's nothing so becomes SHAK 585:7
p. to all his neighbours SHAK 589:15
P. to corrupt no less MILT 473:10
P. to him that is far off BIBLE 84:21
p. to our children LOW 430:22
p. to you which were afar BIBLE 102:11
P. upon earth HARDY 325:2
p. which the world cannot BOOK 119:10
p. with honour CHAM 189:8
p. with honour DISR 247:2/
poor, and mangled P. SHAK 586:16
potent advocates of p. GEOR 301:3
practising upon his p. and quiet SHAK 615:22
righteousness and p. have kissed
BOOK 130:20
right hand carry gentle p. SHAK 589:1
security and p. of each JOHN 366:11
seek p., and ensue it BOOK 126:15
So enamoured on p. CLAR 205:4
take chances for p. DULL 263:11
that publisheth p. BIBLE 84:8
that we may live in p. ARIS 25:10
there abides a p. of thine ARN 27:12
There is no p., saith the Lord BIBLE 84:6
they are in p. BIBLE 86:28
they should kneel for p. SHAK 624:25
This is not a p. treaty FOCH 288:7
this p. sleep with her SHAK 589:17
thousand years of p. TENN 684:11
Thy banished p., thy laurels SMOL 654:4
thy p. been as a river BIBLE 84:5
thy servant depart in p. BIBLE 93:29
time of p. thinks of war ANON 14:1
time of war, and a time of p. BIBLE 80:5
To rust in p., or rot SOUT 657:2
universal p. TENN 681:9
want p. so much that EIS 268:12
War is p. ORW 500:10
ways upon a state of p. VIRG 713:17
weak piping time of p. SHAK 621:15
What is p.? Is it war DICK 239:7
when there is no p. BIBLE 85:7
When there was p., he was AUDEN 36:11
which belong unto thy p. BIBLE 95:16
White P. FANS 280:2
who prefers a negative p. KING 396:16
wilderness and call it p. TAC 677:20
will lay me down in p. BOOK 124:14
with the soft phrase of p. SHAK 614:30
work, my friend, is p. ROOS 546:7
work us a perpetual p. MILT 466:20
peaceably: p. if we can CLAY 205:18
p. ordered by thy governance BOOK 121:3
peaceful: made this p. life VIRG 714:12
peacefully: moving p. towards its close
DAWS 233:2
peacemakers: Blessed are the p. BIBLE 88:23
peach: blushing apricot and woolly p.
JONS 380:7
carved-on-a-p.-stone LANC 407:20
Do I dare to eat a p. ELIOT 272:6
nectarine, and curious p. MARV 450:9
peaches: What p. and what penumbras
GINS 306:29
peacock: Eyed like a p. KEATS 388:14
milkwhite p. like a ghost TENN 688:13
pride of the p. is the glory BLAKE 112:24
peacocks: apes, and p. BIBLE 75:25
p. and lilies for instance RUSK 550:24
pea-green: beautiful p. boat LEAR 414:12
peal: rung night's yawning p. SHAK 603:4
pear: go round the prickly p. ELIOT 271:15
pearl: gospel's p. upon our coast MARV 449:20
hang a p. in every cowslip's ear SHAK 611:11

pearl: (cont.):
her tears to p. he turned MARL 447:11
ocean for orient p. MARL 446:14
on her kings barbaric p. MILT 469:10
p. in your foul oyster SHAK 569:25
p. of great price BIBLE 91:4
threw a p. away SHAK 618:20
pearls: As p. upon an Ethiop's arm DYER 265:7
Give p. away and rubies HOUS 352:9
p. before swine BIBLE 89:16
p. fetch a high price because WHAT 730:11
p. of thought in Persian LOW 430:1
p. that were his eyes SHAK 625:10
search for p. must dive below DRYD 259:24
sent me to sea for p. SMART 649:10
string the p. were strung on JAMES 362.17
pearly: shows them p. white BREC 140:3
pears: our French withered p. SHAK 564:3
peartree: glassy p. leaves HOPK 346:1
peas: If p. were eaten with RAL 536:11
peasant: p. and a philosopher JOHN 372:24
that the toe of the p. SHAK 578:22
what a rogue and p. slave SHAK 575:8
peasantry: But a bold p. GOLD 310:6
has made the p. its pack TROT 704:12
peasants: hands of p. their vile trash
SHAK 593:6
p. now resign their pipes CRAB 225:11
playing cricket with their p. TREV 702:11
peascod: squash is before 'tis a p. SHAK 628:22
pebble: each p. its part BUNT 155:9
p. or a prettier shell NEWT 494:7
pebbles: leviathan retrieving p. WELLS 727:14
unnumbered idle p. chafes SHAK 597:1
peccata: qui tollis p. mundi MISS 477:5
peccator: Esto p. et pecca LUTH 432:9
peccavi: P.—I have Sindh WINK 739:9
quia p. nimis cogitatione MISS 476:16
pecker: his p. in my pocket JOHN 367:11
Peckham: angels at P. BENÉT 62:18
peculiar: holy nation, a p. people BIBLE 105:11
was the p. grace BROW 149:29
pecunia: P. non olet VESP 710:9
pecuniam: p. infinitam CIC 204:10
pecuniary: immense p. Mangle DICK 244:2
pedant: apothegmatical P. NASHE 490:22
pedantic: Muses' garden with p. weeds
CAREW 179:3
too p. for a gentleman CONG 215:14
pedantical: Figures p. SHAK 599:7
pedantry: P. is the dotage of knowledge
JACK 361:4
pedants: Which learned p. much affect
BUTL 166:2
peddle: shoddier than what they p. BECK 57:16
pede: nunc p. libero HOR 349:14
pederasty: Not flagellation, not p. RATT 537:2
pedestalled: p. in triumph BROW 152:21
pedestrians: two classes of p. DEWAR 238:7
pedigree: languages are the p. of nations
JOHN 370:27
pee: P., po, belly, bum FLAN 285:11
Peel: and P. has no manners WELL 727:8
peel: p. me a grape WEST 729:8
peeling: P. off the kilometres CONN 216:20
peep: And into glory p. VAUG 709:8
Nevermore to p. again DE L 236:4
that would p. and botanize WORD 746:14
To p. at such a world COWP 223:32
peepers: where you get them p. MERC 457:13
peeping: Came p. in at morn HOOD 343:21
peepshow: ticket for the p. MACN 440:13
peer: hath not left his p. MILT 465:20
many a p. of England brews HOUS 352:19
masquerade, a murdered p. ALC 8:1
p. is exalted into MAN PAINE 504:17
peerage: Charlemain with all his p. MILT 469:1
shall have gained a p. NELS 491:11
want a p., I shall buy one NORT 496:20
You should study the P. WILDE 735:32
peering: dolorous mansions to the p. day
MILT 467:9
peerless: unveiled her p. light MILT 471:10

peerless: (cont.):
p. paper peer LOCK 425:17
peers: flattery of one's p. LODGE 425:22
House of P. GILB 304:13
House of P. GILB 306:13
in the P. will take his place BROU 144:6
P.: a kind of eye-shade MADAN 441:9
praise in p. to write at all BYRON 172:10
peewees: graves of the martyrs the p. crying
STEV 669:3
Pegasus: And thought it P. KEATS 390:12
To turn and wind a fiery P. SHAK 581:20
Complacencies of the p. STEV 666.10
pelf: I crave no p. SHAK 626:8
pelican: p. in the wilderness BOOK 131:18
wondrous bird is the p. MERR 458:14
Pelion: P. imposuisse Olympo HOR 350:3
pile Ossa on P. VIRG 715:12
pellet: p. with the poison's PANA 505:16
pellucid: more p. streams WORD 744:18
Pemberley: shades of P. to be thus polluted
AUST 39:17
pen: bite his p., and drop a tear SWIFT 675:11
Biting my truant p. SIDN 646:15
foolish when he had not a p. JOHN 375:17
From lies of tongue and p. CHES 199:3
glorious by my p. GRAH 313:16
mightier than the p. HOGB 341:14
nose was as sharp as a p. SHAK 585:5
p. has been in their hands AUST 39:6
p. has gleaned my teeming KEATS 390:28
p. is mightier than the sword BULW 155:5
p. is worse than the sword BURT 164:22
p. weighs heavier in the LEWES 420:11
prevents his holding a p. DICK 242:8
product of a scoffer's p. WORD 743:19
rough and all-unable p. SHAK 587:4
scratching of a p. LOVER 429:7
squat p. rests HEAN 329:18
stores supply the female p. ALC 8:1
take a p. in his hand JOHN 371:7
tongue is the p. BOOK 127:10
Waverley p. ANON 18:16
Why are the needle and the p. LEWIS 420:18
woman's p. presents you BOOT 136:6
penalty: p. of Adam SHAK 567:24
rigorous and p. of the law VEBL 709:16
penance: night do p. for a day WORD 747:3
pence: He took out two p. BIBLE 94:15
Or that eternal want of p. TENN 690:6
Take care of the p. LOWN 431:1
pencil: p. of the Holy Ghost BACON 42:19
pencils: inexorable sadness of p. ROET 544:4
pendulum: vibration of a p. JUN 383:5
pendulums: discontented p. EMER 277:10
Penelope: His true P. POUND 526:12
penetralium: p. of mystery KEATS 391:10
peninsulas: eye of p. CAT 186:3
penitent: p., and obedient heart BOOK 118:5
p. drunkenness RIMB 541:10
Restore thou them that are p. BOOK 118:9
penitus: p. toto divisos orbe VIRG 714:13
pennies: P. from heaven BURKE 160:5
Pennsylvania: P. station GORD 312:13
penny: Not a p. off the pay COOK 218:3
one p. the worse BARH 52:15
p. for a song YEATS 750:17
p. in the way of trade COWP 223:14
p. plain and twopence coloured STEV 667:21
worn p. in the window MADAN 441:7
pens: p. dwell on guilt and misery AUST 38:20
p. that ever poets held MARL 448:3
pensée: Ma p., c'est moi SART 557:1
Penshurst: P., to envious show JONS 380:6
pensieri: p. stretti ed il viso ALB 7:10
pension: hang your hat on a p. MACN 440:14
his p. from his parish RUSK 551:2
p. jingle in his pockets COWP 224:16
p. list of the republic CLEV 206:10
P. Pay given to a state JOHN 368:5
pensions: talk of P. and Grenadiers STER 664:28
pensive: cowslips wan that hang the p. head
MILT 466:11

pensive: (*cont.*):
In vacant or in p. mood   WORD 744:16
mellow horn her p. soul   COLL 213:14
Pentagon: P., that immense monument
   FRAN 293:7
penthouse: Hang upon his p. lid   SHAK 600:2
Pentridge: P. by the river   BARN 53:14
peonies: wealth of globèd p.   KEATS 389:6
people: All p. that on earth do dwell
   KETHE 394:13
August for the p.   AUDEN 34:6
beat my p. to pieces   BIBLE 82:12
Before we were her p.   FROST 294:18
bludgeoning of the p.   WILDE 735:23
builds on the p. builds on mud   MACH 438:9
by the cleverest p.   YOUNG 755:3
by the p., for the people   LINC 422:10
by the p., for the people   PAGE 504:4
debauch her p.   JENY 365:9
divided into p. that read   SHEN 644:16
Eating p. is wrong   FLAN 285:12
For God's sake look after our p.   SCOTT 559:4
give strength unto his p.   BOOK 126:4
good of the p. is the chief law   CIC 203:27
government, made for the p.   WEBS 725:5
Hell is other p.   SART 556:11
I am myself the p.   ROB 542:1
Imagine all the p.   LENN 417:12
include the support of the p.   CLEV 206:11
indictment against an whole p.
   BURKE 157:25
in favour of the p.   BURKE 159:12
It is the love of the p.   BURKE 157:32
I would be of the p.   LA BR 405:1
Let my p. go   ANON 19:16
Let my p. go   BIBLE 72:5
Let the p. praise thee   BOOK 129:4
madness of the p.   BOOK 129:1
man should die for the p.   BIBLE 97:0
Most p. ignore most poetry   MITC 477:17
My faith in the p. governing   DICK 244:8
my p. love to have it   BIBLE 85:6
new p. takes the land   CHES 199:8
no doubt but ye are the p.   BIBLE 77:18
noise, my dear! And the p.   ANON 16:20
One realm, one p., one leader   ANON 21:10
opinions as there are p.   TER 690:14
p. are only human   COMP 214:14
p. are right more than half of   WHITE 731:3
p. are the masters   BURKE 158:33
p. arose as one man   BIBLE 74:24
p. don't do such things   IBSEN 359:5
p. govern themselves   THIE 692:1
p. imagine a vain thing   BOOK 124:7
p. is the true legislator   BURKE 159:19
p. know what they want   MENC 457.8
p. looked he then would speak   GILB 303:11
p. of his pasture   BOOK 131:10
p. overlaid with taxes   BACON 44:34
p.'s choice   SHER 644:28
p. that do err   BOOK 131:10
p. that walked in darkness   BIBLE 82:26
p. went up into the city   BIBLE 73:30
p. were a kind of solution   CAV 187:8
p. which call upon thee   BOOK 120:13
p. who do things and people   MORR 486:3
p. who got there first   UST 707:12
p. who inhabit it   LINC 422:4
p. whom one should like   JOHN 375:20
p. whose eyes are oddly made   HAMM 323:2
p. will always be kind   SASS 557:6
p. without history   ELIOT 271:8
P. you know, yet can't quite name
   LARK 410:4
Power to the p.   ANON 17:12
same as if they was p.   DUREM 264:10
suppose the p. good   ROB 542:4
surely the p. is grass   BIBLE 83:27
that was full of p.   BIBLE 85:15
thy p. who shall be my p.   BIBLE 74:28
'Tis the p. law-abiding   MARR 195:9
understanded of the p.   BOOK 106:24
voice of the p. is the voice of God   ALC 6.1

people: (*cont.*):
we are the p. of England   CHES 199:7
What is the city but the p.   SHAK 570:12
When wilt thou save the p.   ELL 275:13
whole world is bereft of p.   LAM 405:21
You may fool all the p.   LINC 422:14
peopled: p. half the world   SEEL 562:1
world must be p.   SHAK 613:27
peoples: cry of the Little P.   LE G 416:9
Peoria: It'll play in P.   ANON 15:8
peppered: have p. two of them   SHAK 580:19
per: P. ME SI VA NELLA CITTÀ   DANTE 230:6
peradventure: P. the darkness shall cover
   BOOK 134:19
perceive: p. and know what things
   BOOK 120:13
percentage: It's a reasonable p.   BECK 57:20
perception: doors of p. were cleansed
   BLAKE 113:2
begins as failure of p.   TRIL 702:18
prime Agent of all human P.   COL 212:1
perch: p. and not their terror   SHAK 605:11
perchance: p. to dream   SHAK 575:16
perdition: children of p.   JONS 378:5
lost out the son of p.   BIBLE 97:22
P. catch my soul   SHAK 616:10
To bottomless p.   MILT 467:23
perditum: perisse p. ducas   CAT 186:2
père: P., et le Fils, et le Pigeon   ANON 20:11
pereant: P., inquit   DON 250:5
pereat: justitia et p. mundus   FERD 281:9
P., qui crastina curat   VIRG 714:10
peremptory: p. and absolute the third
   ELIOT 270:4
perennial: Falsehood has a p. spring
   BURKE 157:16
Peres: P.; Thy kingdom is divided   BIBLE 85:31
pereunt: Qui nobis p.   MART 449:14
perfect: Be ye therefore p.   BIBLE 89:2
But constant, he were p.   SHAK 631:10
end of a p. day   BOND 117:17
Entire and whole and p.   SPR 681:8
If thou wilt be p.   BIBLE 91:23
Let patience have her p. work   BIBLE 104:24
made p. in a short time   BIBLE 87:2
more unto the p. day   BIBLE 78:11
None of us are p.   WILDE 734:18
Nothing is p.   STEP 663:19
nothing p. in this world   DONNE 253:10
p. democracy   BURKE 158:20
P. fear casteth out love   CONN 216:23
P. God, and perfect Man   BOOK 119:15
p. nature and are perfected   BACON 44:25
p. round   BROW 147:26
P. the cup as planned   BROW 152:13
p. use of an imperfect medium   WILDE 735:16
pismire is equally p.   WHIT 732:17
read the p. ways of honour   SHAK 589:16
service is p. freedom   BOOK 119:3
short measures life may p. be   JONS 379:21
spirits of just men made p.   BIBLE 104:19
strength is made p. in weakness   BIBLE 102:3
that which is p. is come   BIBLE 101:1
unto a p. man   BIBLE 102:17
perfectibility: P. is   GODW 308:9
speak of p. as a dream   MILL 460:21
perfecting: p. of the saints   BIBLE 102:17
perfection: both p. and brutalization
   TOCQ 699:8
Dead p., no more   TENN 686:7
delightful thing to think of p.   BURN 160:9
everything must function to p.   MUSS 488:18
feature of loveliness and p.   MILT 475:9
p. cannot endure the insult   WHITE 731:6
p. is not the true basis   GLAD 307:13
P. is the child of Time   HALL 322:3
P., of a kind, was what   AUDEN 34:10
P. of the life, or of the work   YEATS 751:6
p. unattainable   STR 670:14
pictures of p. as you know   AUST 40:3
pursuit of p.   ARN 29:8
right praise and true p.   SHAK 610:5
soul of all p.   MARS 449:10

perfection: (*cont.*):
That she did make defect p.   SHAK 565:7
that we can realise our p.   WILDE 735:4
very pink of p.   GOLD 311:22
What's come to p. perishes   BROW 151:15
which is the p. of reason   COKE 208:17
perfections: eyes where all p. keep   ANON 15:6
Rather than the p. of a fool   BLAKE 113:9
Were with his sweet p. caught   ROYD 549:15
perfectly: small, but p. formed   COOP 218:9
that we may p. love thee   BOOK 121:16
perfide: la p. Angleterre   BOSS 137:2
perfidious: fatal and p. bark   MILT 466:6
p. Albion   XIMÉ 750:12
p. friends   MED 456:2
perform: Almighty's orders to p.   ADD 3:14
fits a man to p. justly   MILT 475:19
Lord of hosts will p. this   BIBLE 82:28
operations which we can p.   WHIT 731:15
they are not able to p.   BOOK 125:8
performance: And no p.   MASS 453:15
her p. keeps no day   CAMP 177:9
his p., as he is now   SHAK 589:8
insipid and tedious p.   WALP 719:6
it takes away the p.   SHAK 602:11
p. every thing   HUNT 356:20
p. so loathed   SHAK 628:8
so many years outlive p.   SHAK 583:10
performed: vow be p. in Jerusalem
   BOOK 128:23
performing: aroma of p. seals   HART 327:11
perfume: Grateful off'rings of p.   SMART 649:7
invisible p. hits the sense   SHAK 565:6
p. and most melodious twang   AUBR 33:13
To throw a p. on the violet   SHAK 594:9
perfumed: delicately p.   QUIL 534:10
perfumes: all the p. of Arabia   SHAK 604:14
No p., but very fine linen   BRUM 153:22
perhaps: grand P.   BROW 148:11
P. it may turn out a sang   BURNS 161:23
to seek a great p.   RAB 534:21
Pericles: what P. felt of Athens   KEYN 395:2
Perigord: Thy truffles, P.!   POPE 519:9
perii: P., nisi homo moriatur   ANDR 11:11
ut p., ut me malus abstulit   VIRG 715:4
peril: For those in p. on the sea   WHIT 732:2
P. was nigh   ANAT 11:6
there is no p. in the fight   CORN 218:15
perilous: dim and p. way   WORD 743:20
perils: in p. of waters   BIBLE 102:1
p. and dangers of this night   BOOK 119:11
What p. past, what crosses   SHAK 583:14
period: All p., pow'r, and enterprise
   SMART 649:17
inglorious p. of our dominion   BURKE 159:1
p. of cheating between two   BIER 109:13
periods: Have certain p. set   SUCK 671:10
peripatetic: P. Lover   GILB 305:18
periphrastic: p. study in a worn-out
   ELIOT 270:19
perish: And if I p., I perish   BIBLE 76:35
And p. in our own   THOM 694:18
believeth in him should not p.   BIBLE 96:15
day p. wherein I was born   BIBLE 77:6
if it had to p. twice   FROST 294:17
I p. with hunger   BIBLE 95:3
Must then a Christ p.   SHAW 638:24
or p. together as fools   KING 397:2
people p.   BIBLE 79:31
P. the thought   CIBB 203:21
p. through their own imaginations
   BOOK 124:17
shall p. with the sword   BIBLE 93:1
speak again, and it will p.   JOHN 370:2
that is ready to p.   BIBLE 79:34
They shall p.   BOOK 132:1
They too shall p. unconsoled   LANG 408:15
though the world p.   FERD 281:9
Thy money p. with thee   BIBLE 98:14
To p. rather   MILT 469:14
venal city ripe to p.   SALL 554:14
ye p. from the right way   BOOK 124:11

pine: (*cont.*):
p. that makes her music	THEO 691:29
p. within and suffer dearth	SHAK 635:7
they p., I live	DYER 265:1
This spray of Western p.	HARTE 327:16

pineapple: p. of politeness — SHER 645:3
pines: p. shall murmur — KEATS 389:20
  p. were by ambition hewn — DRAY 258:3
pinguem: *p. et nitidum bene* — HOR 348:6
pinion: imagination droops her p. — BYRON 171:7
pinions: race with p. skim the air — FRERE 293:16
  Stayed in mid passage his p. — SWIN 676:3
pink: Lavender water tinged with p.
          LEAR 414:16
  very p. of courtesy — SHAK 623:9
  very p. of perfection — GOLD 311:22
  With a p. hotel — MITC 477:18
pinkly: p. bursts the spray — BETJ 68:1
pinko-grey: white races are really p.
          FORS 290:20
pinnacled: P. dim in the intense inane
          SHEL 642:18
pinprick: time is a p. of eternity — AUR 37:18
pins: p. extend their shining — POPE 523:18
pint: p. of plain is your only man — O'BR 497:12
pioneers: P.! O pioneers — WHIT 732:9
pious: as he was rarther p. — ASHF 31:7
  this p. morn — KEATS 388:29
pipe: p. and exhaled in a pun — LAMB 407:12
  p. a simple song for thinking — WORD 744:8
  P. a song about a Lamb — BLAKE 113:16
  P. me to pastures still — HOPK 345:12
  p. might fall out if he did — FORS 290:1
  p. of half-awakened birds — TENN 688:5
  p. with solemn interposing — COWP 222:2
  Rumour is a p. — SHAK 582:12
  So put that in your p. — BARH 52:18
  thy small p. — SHAK 628:16
piped: We have p. unto you — BIBLE 90:26
pipes: Grate on their scrannel p. — MILT 466:9
  therefore, ye soft p., play on — KEATS 388:25
  What p. and timbrels — KEATS 388:24
piping: For ever p. songs — KEATS 388:27
  Helpless, naked, p. loud — BLAKE 114:8
  P. songs of pleasant glee — BLAKE 113:16
  sniv'ling and p. your eye — DIBD 238:15
  weak p. time of peace — SHAK 621:15
Pippa: P. passes — BEER 59:13
Pippin: Ribstone P. — BELL 61:10
pippins: old p. toothsomest — WEBS 725:26
pips: until the p. squeak — GEDD 300:20
pirate: To be a P. King — GILB 306:7
piscem: *Desinat in p. mulier formosa* — HOR 347:1
pismire: p. is equally perfect — WHIT 732:17
piss: May'st thou ne'er p. — ROCH 543:4
  P. off, he said to me — PINT 514:18
  worth a pitcher of warm p. — GARN 298:2
pissing: inside the tent p. out — JOHN 367:12
pistol: p. in your pocket, or — WEST 729:12
  pun is a p. let off — LAMB 406:20
  reach for my p. — JOHST 377:16
  when his p. misses — GOLD 311:34
pistols: carry p. and cartridges — SHAW 635:22
  Have you your p.? — WHIT 732:9
  ring bells and fire off p. — MANN 445:1
piston: snorting steam and p. stroke
          MORR 485:12
pistons: black statement of p. — SPEN 658:26
pit: diggeth a p. shall fall — BIBLE 80:22
  From p. to crucifix — CRANE 225:17
  have beat us to the p. — SHAK 593:21
  have digged a p. before me — BOOK 128:15
  know what is in the p. — BLAKE 111:11
  Law is a bottomless p. — ARB 24:8
  many-headed monster of the p. — POPE 523:6
  out of the horrible p. — BOOK 126:24
  there is the sulphurous p. — SHAK 597:5
  they'll fill a p. as well — SHAK 581:25
pitch: bumping p. and a
  imagination to the proper p. — LACK 405:7
  Of what validity and p. soe'er — SHAK 628:9
  Pitched past p. of grief — HOPK 345:16
  positive p. or direction — HOPK 346:14

pitch: (*cont.*):
toucheth p. shall be defiled	BIBLE 87:19

pitched: Love has p. his mansion — YEATS 751:8
pitcher: or the p. be broken — BIBLE 81:1
  worth a p. of warm piss — GARN 298:2
pitchfork: drive out nature with a p. — HOR 348:8
  thrown on her with a p. — SWIFT 674:6
  use my wit as a p. — LARK 410:8
pith: p. is in the postscript — HAZL 328:12
pitieth: father p. his own children — BOOK 132:5
pitiful: lips say, 'God be p.' — BROW 147:12
  long-suffering, and very p. — BIBLE 87:8
  'twas wondrous p. — SHAK 615:2
  were she p. as she is fair — GREE 317:9
pitifulness: p. of thy great mercy — BOOK 120:4
Pitt: P. is to Addington — CANN 178:7
pity: But yet the p. of it — SHAK 617:11
  But you should p. me — SHAK 628:24
  cherish p., lest you drive an angel
          BLAKE 113:20
  dint of p. — SHAK 592:14
  Find in myself no p. to myself — SHAK 622:12
  knows some touch of p. — SHAK 621:17
  more than all they p. most — MOT 487:2
  never a saint took p. — COL 211:7
  P. a human face — BLAKE 113:19
  p. and fear bringing about — ARIS 25:12
  p. beyond all telling — YEATS 752:18
  P. from blust'ring wind — LOV 429:5
  p. him afterwards — JOHN 374:13
  P. is the feeling — JOYCE 381:12
  p. kills — BALZ 51:9
  p., like a naked new-born — SHAK 601:3
  p. never ceases to be — DRYD 259:10
  p. of War — OWEN 503:10
  p. renneth soone in gentil — CHAU 193:20
  p. sitting in the clouds — SHAK 623:26
  P. the planet, all joy gone — LOW 430:22
  P. the reapers — DUCK 263:6
  Poetry is in the p. — OWEN 503:10
  save me, O source of p. — MISS 477:13
  seas of p. lie locked and frozen — AUDEN 34:15
  some to have p. on me — BOOK 129:12
  that she did p. them — SHAK 615:3
  then p., then embrace — POPE 522:13
pix: Sticks nix hick p. — ANON 18:5
place: all in one p. — BOIL 117:4
  all other things give p. — GAY 300:1
  could have no p. — BIBLE 87:21
  degree, priority, and p. — SHAK 627:6
  earns a p. i' the story — SHAK 565:19
  exalt us unto the same p. — BOOK 120:19
  genius of the p. — POPE 520:19
  Get p. and wealth — POPE 522:27
  great p. is by a winding stair — BACON 43:31
  He loved no other p., and yet — COL 211:23
  I go to prepare a p. — BIBLE 97:11
  In p. of strife — CAST 184:15
  keep in the same p. — CARR 182:21
  know the p. for the first time — ELIOT 271:6
  lone unhaunted p. — DONNE 251:13
  Lord is in this p. — BIBLE 71:14
  Men in great p. are thrice — BACON 43:27
  neither shall his p. know — BIBLE 77:14
  Never the time and the p. — BROW 151:13
  one p. than another — SOUT 657:18
  our bourne of time and p. — TENN 680:18
  p. could no where be found — BOOK 126:21
  p. for everything — BEET 59:24
  p. in the sun — BÜLOW 155:2
  p. in the sun — WILH 736:18
  p., not to live, but to die in — BROW 146:19
  p. of understanding — BIBLE 77:27
  P., that great object — SMITH 650:15
  p. thereof shall know it — BOOK 132:5
  p. where a story ended — ELIOT 271:4
  p. where we go seeking — THOM 694:14
  right man in the right p. — JEFF 364:19
  rising unto p. is laborious — BACON 43:29
  spirit of the p. — VIRG 714:2
  stand in the holy p. — BIBLE 92:10
  suffer a man of his p. — SHAK 589:13
  superior to time and p. — JOHN 369:20

place: (*cont.*):
till there be no p.	BIBLE 82:16

  To know their p., and not — BELL 61:3
  water in a dry p. — BIBLE 83:17
places: All p., all airs — BROW 146:14
  all p. were alike — KIPL 401:18
  Are the quietest p. — HOUS 352:17
  distance between two p. — WILL 737:6
  New p. you will not find — CAV 187:9
  p. that the eye of heaven — SHAK 619:13
  P. they guarded, or kept — LARK 409:19
  Proper words in proper p. — SWIFT 673:22
  Quires and P. where they sing — BOOK 119:5
  slain in thine high p. — BIBLE 75:9
  under heaven, all p. thou — MILT 473:13
  We returned to our p. — ELIOT 271:18
  which built desolate p. — BIBLE 77:7
plackets: Dread prince of p. — SHAK 598:13
  thy hand out of p. — SHAK 596:10
placuisse: *Principibus p. viris non* — HOR 348:11
plafond: *dans les lignes du p.* — E.LUA 276:3
plagiarism: from one author, it's p.
          MIZN 478:11
plagiarist: situation of the p. — MUSS 488:14
plagiarize: P.! Let no one else's work
          LEHR 416:11
plague: Make instruments to p. us — SHAK 597:18
  O may 't ne'er be a living p. — BURNS 162:7
  p. and pestilence — NASHE 491:2
  p. come nigh thy dwelling — BOOK 131:4
  p. o' both your houses — SHAK 623:14
  p., pestilence, and famine — BOOK 119:17
  p. us little boys with breeches — BARB 52:5
  such a p. when I was young — YEATS 753:9
  that's his p. — BURT 165:1
  Thou p. peculiar to mankind — WRIG 749:13
  To p. the inventor — SHAK 601:2
plagues: omit those two main p. — BURT 164:21
  p. remain for the ungodly — BOOK 126:10
  p. with which mankind — DEFOE 234:25
plain: And he will make it p. — COWP 222:1
  as on a darkling p. — ARN 27:1
  best p. set — BACON 42:25
  design plain truth for p. — WESL 728:22
  especially the need of the p. — WAUGH 724:11
  Fanny Kelly's divine p. face — LAMB 407:2
  it is old and p. — SHAK 629:16
  make it p. upon tables — BIBLE 86:16
  Make thy way p. before — BOOK 124:16
  Over the great Gromboolian p. — LEAR 413:20
  'p.' cooking cannot — MORP 485:3
  pint of p. is your only man — O'BR 497:12
  p., blunt man — SHAK 592:15
  p. Kate — SHAK 624:15
  P. living and high thinking — WORD 746:10
  plain man in his p. meaning — SHAK 609:6
  p. man live and think no — SHAK 621:20
  p. Michael Faraday — FAR 280:3
  p. to uninstructed people — HUXL 358:8
  P. women he regarded — ELIOT 269:15
  pricking on the p. — SPEN 659:20
  rough places p. — BIBLE 83:26
  speak p. when counsellors — BACON 43:3
  stays mainly in the p. — LERN 419:5
plainness: p. of speech is allied — ARN 30:8
plains: flowery p. of honour — JONS 379:5
  ringing p. of windy Troy — TENN 690:1
plain-speaking: p. with Mr Snagsby — DICK 239:4
plaintive: p. numbers flow — WORD 748:4
  p. treble of the Treasury — DISR 247:2
plaire: *règles n'est pas de p.* — MOL 478:19
plaisir: P. d'amour — FLOR 288:4
plaister: upon p. of the wall — BIBLE 85:30
plaisters: which there are no p. — GARR 298:5
plan: both by his p. of attack — SASS 557:11
  Commends a most practical p. — INGE 359:11
  fulfils great Nature's p. — BURNS 161:27
  mars creation's p. — CANN 178:8
  not without a p. — POPE 521:26
  p. the future by the past — BURKE 157:5
  rebuild it on the old p. — MILL 460:10
  rest on its original p. — BURKE 157:11
  wagon of his 'P.' — PAST 508:12

plane: It's a bird! It's a p.!	ANON 13:8	
p. trees going sha-sha-sha	CONN 216:20	
planet: born under a rhyming p.	SHAK 614:16	
hanging from a round p.	EDD 266:4	
Jove's p. rises yonder	BROW 150:8	
new p. swims into his ken	KEATS 390:3	
Pity the p., all joy gone	LOW 430:22	
p. of Love is on high	TENN 686:17	
planetary: obedience of p. influence		
	SHAK 595:2	
planets: big p. hanging	HUGH 354:5	
heavens themselves, the p.	SHAK 627:6	
like the chronicle of p.	YEVT 754:5	
other p. circle other suns	POPE 521:28	
people p. of its own	BYRON 172:2	
p. in their stations listening	MILT 472:10	
then no p. strike	SHAK 572:2	
planks: willows, old rotten p.	CONS 217:22	
planned: based on p. obsolescence	STEV 665:12	
Perfect the cup as p.	BROW 152:13	
Who saith, 'A whole I p.	BROW 152:6	
plans: are always ruined	BREC 140:9	
plant: Confidence is a p. of slow	PITT 515:7	
Fame is no p. that grows	MILT 466:5	
O wicked, wicked p.	KYD 404:15	
p. and flower of light	JONS 379:21	
p. must spring again from	SHEL 644:4	
p. on his peculiar spot	POPE 522:12	
P. thou no roses at my head	ROSS 547:12	
p. whose virtues have	EMER 277:9	
Sensitive P. in a garden	SHEL 642:26	
That busy p.	HERB 335:1	
time to p., and a time	BIBLE 80:5	
Plantagenet: where is P.	CREWE 226:19	
planted: I have p., Apollos	BIBLE 100:17	
planting: p. my cabbages	MONT 480:15	
plants: as the young p.	BOOK 135:4	
p. suck in the earth	COWL 221:7	
They are forced p.	JOHN 375:14	
plashy: through the p. fen	WAUGH 724:2	
plasterer: p. on his ladder	HEAN 329:17	
plasters: back to 'p., pills	LOCK 425:15	
plastic: Of p. circumstance	BROW 152:12	
plastics: abhorred p., Picasso	WAUGH 723:18	
plat: on a p. of rising ground	MILT 464:21	
plate: P. sin with gold	SHAK 597:8	
plates: hats like p.	COW 220:14	
p. dropped from his pocket	SHAK 566:20	
platinum: bullets made of p.	BELL 60:23	
eyebrows made of p.	FORS 289:19	
platitude: APPLAUSE, n. The echo of a p.		
	BIER 109:4	
longitude with no p.	FRY 295:23	
p. is simply a truth repeated	BALD 48:8	
stroke a p. until it purrs	MARQ 448:21	
platitudes: orchestration of p.	WILD 736:17	
Plato: attachment à la P.	GILB 305:17	
lend an ear to P.	TENN 686:4	
P. is dear to me, but dearer	ARIS 26:3	
P. is never sullen	MAC 435:1	
P.'s Republic rather than	CIC 203:24	
P.'s retirement	MILT 473:20	
P., thou reason'st well	ADD 3:23	
p. told him	CUMM 228:10	
rather be wrong with P.	CIC 204:14	
series of footnotes to P.	WHIT 731:16	
taught out of the rule of P.	MILT 475:20	
plaudits: shouts and p. of the throng		
	LONG 427:6	
play: actions that a man might p.	SHAK 572:10	
better at a p.	ANON 13:20	
Better than a p.	CHAR 191:13	
children at p. are not playing	MONT 480:18	
children with their p.	COWP 222:9	
could p. Ercles rarely	SHAK 611:5	
creatures sitting at a p.	SHAK 575:13	
edifice I p. than no play at all	REYN 539:3	
discourse than see a p.	BUH 106:7	
do not p. things as they are	STEV 666:02	
fool cried p. upon the word	SHAK 609:5	
game at which two can p.	BECH 60:14	
Games people p.	BERNE 68:10	

play: (cont.):		
good p. needs no epilogue	SHAK 569:29	
House Beautiful is p. lousy	PARK 506:18	
I doubt some foul p.	SHAK 572:23	
It'll p. in Peoria	ANON 15:8	
Kings would not p.	COWP 224:3	
let me not p. a woman	SHAK 611:7	
life's poor p.	POPE 522:16	
little victims p.	GRAY 316:2	
old come forth to p.	MILT 465:13	
our p. is played out	THAC 691:20	
pack the cards and yet cannot p.	BACON 43:4	
P. all your changes	ING 360:2	
p. before the play is done	QUAR 533:16	
p. began to disgust this	EVEL 279:8	
P. it again, Sam	EPST 278:7	
p. it over again and play it	LAMB 407:14	
P. out the play	SHAK 580:34	
p.'s the thing	SHAK 575:14	
p. the game	NEWB 492:9	
p. the wantons with our	SHAK 620:13	
p. without a woman in it	KYD 404:16	
presents you with a p.	BOOT 136:6	
prologue to a very dull p.	CONG 215:27	
rest of the p. may	PASC 507:15	
rose up to p.	BIBLE 72:20	
structure of a p.	MILL 461:20	
thing to p. with souls	BROW 150:24	
When I p. with my cat	MONT 481:7	
Work is x; y is p.	EINS 268:5	
wouldst not p. false	SHAK 600:15	
you cannot p. upon me	SHAK 576:23	
Your p.'s hard to act	CHEK 196:12	
You would p. upon me	SHAK 576:22	
playbills: no time to read p.	BUHN 160:17	
playboy: P. of the Western	SYNGE 677:9	
played: And he p. at the gluve	BALL 49:3	
I have p. the fool	BIBLE 75:7	
P.-out and Done-to-death	TRAI 702:2	
p. the King as though under	FIELD 281:15	
your role is p. out	TROT 704:13	
player: as strikes the p.	FITZ 284:8	
p. on the other side	HUXL 358:7	
poor p., that struts	SHAK 605:1	
players: men and women merely p.		
	SHAK 568:16	
P., Sir! I look upon them	JOHN 374:6	
p. that I have seen play	SHAK 576:6	
see the p. well bestowed	SHAK 576:6	
playfellow: My p., your hand	SHAK 565:21	
playing: from the purpose of p.	SHAK 576:6	
on the p. fields of Eton	WELL 727:7	
p. or quarrelling	FORS 290:18	
work terribly hard at p.	MORT 486:6	
playmate: nor mother, nor any p.	THOM 694:4	
plays: English p. are like	VOLT 717:3	
he loves no p.	SHAK 590:7	
p. the king shall be welcome	SHAK 574:29	
plaything: child's a p. for an hour	LAMB 407:8	
Strawberry Hill is a little p.-house		
	WALP 719:3	
Plaza Toro: Duke of P.	GILB 303:14	
plea: Just as I am, without one p.	ELL 275:10	
p. so tainted and corrupt	SHAK 608:26	
Though justice be thy p.	SHAK 609:13	
plead: For which I would not p.	SHAK 605:14	
pleasance: Youth is full of p.	SHAK 632:18	
pleasant: abridgement of all that was p.		
	GOLD 311:5	
But a few think him p. enough	LEAR 414:10	
completed labours are p.	CIC 203:26	
fallen unto me in p. places	BOOK 124:30	
gets too excitin' to be p.	DICK 243:10	
green and p. bowers	BLAKE 112:9	
hear the p. cuckoo	DAV 232:9	
how p., Lord, they be!	SCOT 561:9	
if we do not find anything p.	VOLT 716:2	
Life would be very p. if	SURT 672:17	
Oh the p. sight to see	KING 397:7	
p. it is to have money	CLOU 207:12	
p. thing it is to be thankful	BOOK 135:11	
scorn of that p. land	BOOK 132:19	
something happens to you	MUIR 489:9	

pleasant: (cont.):		
that is p. to the sight	BIBLE 70:2	
Who is to do the p. work?	RUSK 550:19	
pleasanter: And proves the p.	BUTL 166:21	
pleasantness: Her ways are ways of p.		
	BIBLE 78:9	
please: Contented, half to p.	GREV 318:4	
death after life does greatly p.	SPEN 660:2	
For we that live to p.	JOHN 370:12	
I am to do what I p.	FRED 293:11	
Love seeketh only Self to p.	BLAKE 114:7	
Myself alone I seek to p.	GAY 300:6	
Nothing can p. many	JOHN 369:6	
P. him and he straight	WROTH 749:14	
p. thee with my answer	SHAK 609:9	
p. the touchy breed	HOR 348:20	
some circumstance to p. us	SWIFT 675:10	
To tax and to p., no more	BURKE 157:17	
Towered cities p. us then	MILT 465:15	
'twas natural to p.	DRYD 258:18	
Uncertain, coy, and hard to p.	SCOTT 560:9	
when he has ladies to p.	AUST 38:7	
Yet she never fails to p.	SEDL 561:16	
pleased: All seemed well p.	MILT 472:1	
And p. with what he gets	SHAK 568:10	
have p. leading men	HOR 348:11	
He more had p. us	ADD 3:12	
in whom I am well p.	BIBLE 88:17	
p. not the million	SHAK 575:5	
pleasing consists in being p.	HAZL 329:2	
pleases: Though every prospect p.	HEBER 330:4	
pleaseth: this age best p. me	HERR 336:23	
which it p. him to dwell	BOOK 129:9	
pleasing: p. consists in being pleased		
	HAZL 329:2	
pleasure of p. inferior	CLOU 206:18	
pleasure turns to p. pain	SPEN 660:10	
surest method that I know of p.	CHES 198:10	
pleasure: aching P. nigh	KEATS 389:7	
And p. banish pain	WATTS 723:4	
Business first; p. afterwards	THAC 691:11	
But the privilege and p.	GILB 304:2	
cabinet of p.	HERB 335:10	
dragged on by their favourite p.	VIRG 714:17	
fading p. brings	SIDN 647:4	
fatal egg by p. laid	COWP 223:3	
Forced her to do your p.	WEBS 726:6	
gave p. to the spectators	MAC 435:19	
general read without p.	JOHN 377:11	
greatest p. I know	LAMB 407:4	
greatest rule of all to give p.	MOL 478:19	
Green p. or grey grief	SWIN 677:1	
his p. is life	BOOK 126:5	
Holland take p. in making	ANON 12:21	
horrible p.	SHAK 596:23	
If they have p., the servant	BARC 52:9	
I have no p. in them	BIBLE 81:1	
I make poetry and give p.	HOR 350:12	
impression of p. itself	BACON 41:14	
In youth is p.	WEVER 730:1	
Is not in p., but in rest	DRYD 260:31	
I' the east my p. lies	SHAK 565:10	
lie doth ever add p.	BACON 44:37	
little p. out of the way	CHAR 191:14	
Lord, thy most pointed p. take	STEV 669:7	
Love ceases to be a p.	BEHN 60:8	
make a bait of p.	HERB 334:8	
meant by the p. of life	TALL 678:9	
mind, from p. less	MARV 450:10	
miss for p., and a wife	GAY 300:18	
mixed profit with p.	HOR 347:15	
my heart with p. fills	WORD 744:16	
necessity of giving immediate p.		
	WORD 748:17	
No p., nor no pain	SEDL 561:13	
Of unremembered p.	WORD 744:19	
painful p. turns to pleasing	SPEN 660:10	
perfect type of a perfect p.	WILDE 735:19	
p. and without one pain	TENN 686:5	
P. at the helm	GRAY 315:9	
p. if it were realized	MILL 460:21	
p. in poetic pains	COWP 223:21	
p. in recalling the thought	CAT 186:12	

pleasure: (cont.):
p. in the pathless woods — BYRON 169:13
p. in the strength — BOOK 135:12
P. is a *thief* to business — DEFOE 233:16
p. is momentary — CHES 198:25
p. is not enhanced — AUST 38:10
P. is nothing else — SELD 562:11
p. is not to do a thing — HOPK 346:19
p. me in his top-boots — MARL 446:9
P. never is at home — KEATS 387:17
p. of drinking at somebody else's — LEIGH 417:2
p. of feeling and exhibiting — FOST 291:10
p. of the fleeting year — SHAK 634:16
p. of thought is the pleasure — CLOU 207:13
P.'s a sin — BYRON 170:12
P.'s for those who are bad — YES 754:2
p. so exquisite as almost — HUNT 356:17
p. they are and were created — BIBLE 106:12
p. was his business — EDG 266:17
p. we'd rather be dead — COW 220:10
prefers comfort to p. — HESSE 337:16
public stock of harmless p. — JOHN 369:3
receiv'st with p. thine annoy — SHAK 633:3
Short p., long displeasure — SCOTT 559:1
source of p. is variety — JOHN 368:21
suburbs of your good p. — SHAK 591:2
Sweet is p. after pain — DRYD 259:18
There is a p. sure — DRYD 261:27
There's little p. in the house — MICK 459:10
They turn to p. all they find — GREEN 316:19
though on p. she was bent — COWP 222:14
'Tis full of p. — CHAL 189:1
trim gardens takes his p. — MILT 464:18
upon the p. of the palace — MIDD 459:18
Variety is the soul of p. — BEHN 60:13
we not pay a debt to p. — ROCH 543:3
What p. lives in height — TENN 688:14
When that is made, the p.'s done — SOUT 657:3
when Youth and P. meet — BYRON 168:16
Where p. and repentance dwell — RAL 535:13
Where P. lies, carelessly — MOORE 483:8
whilst I go to my p. — WYCH 750:4
would have been my p. — TENN 681:27
pleasure-dome: A stately p. — COL 210:9
pleasure-house: I built my soul a lordly p. — TENN 687:20
pleasures: all the p. of life — HAYW 328:11
but not with their p. — HUXL 357:16
celibacy has no p. — JOHN 369:22
childish p. — ALAI 7:3
common p. — SHAK 592:18
English take their p. sadly — SULLY 671:14
Great lords have their p. — MONT 481:15
hate the idle p. of these days — SHAK 621:16
In unreprovèd p. free — MILT 465:7
No man is a hypocrite in his p. — JOHN 376:16
owes its p. to another's pain — COWP 223:28
paucity of human p. — JOHN 377:8
p. and fineries that go — SOCR 655:1
p. and palaces though we — PAYNE 510:4
p. are like poppies spread — BURNS 163:6
p. in a long immortal dream — KEATS 388:15
p. that to verse belong — KEATS 390:23
purest of human p. — BACON 43:24
Summers p. they are gone — CLARE 204:28
understand the p. of the other — AUST 38:6
we will all the p. prove — MARL 447:17
we will some new p. prove — DONNE 251:19
plebeian: this the P. bran — DONNE 253:7
plectuntur: *reges p. Achivi* — HOR 348:2
pledge: And I will p. with mine — JONS 379:20
p. our Empire vast across — HUXL 357:22
pledged: p. their troth either — BOOK 123:23
pledging: P. with contented smack — KEATS 388:21
Pleiads: rainy P. wester — HOUS 352:2
pleni: *P. sunt coeli et terra* — MISS 477:2
plenteous: thou makest it very p. — BOOK 129:2
plenteously: Endue her p. — BOOK 119:6
p. bringing forth the fruit — BOOK 121:11
plenteousness: all things living with p. — BOOK 135:7
p. with thy palaces — BOOK 133:26

plenty: hand with P. in the maize — TENN 688:15
here is God's p. — DRYD 262:16
In delay there lies no p. — SHAK 629:4
I wasna fou, but just had p. — BURNS 161:20
Little to do, and p. to get — DICK 243:20
on the expectation of p. — SHAK 602:8
Peace, p., pleasure — NASHE 490:23
P. has made me poor — OVID 502:22
Where health and p. cheered — GOLD 310:5
Where P. smiles — CRAB 225:14
pleut: *Comme il p. sur la ville* — VERL 710:6
plie: fail of taking their p. — BURG 157:1
plight: I p. thee my troth — BOOK 123:20
plighter: And p. of high hearts — SHAK 565:21
plod: p. behind the plough — CRAB 225:11
plodders: continual p. ever won — SHAK 598:7
plods: ploughman homeward p — GRAY 315:10
plonking: 'p.' tone of voice — POTT 525:19
plot: devil is the p. good for — BUCK 154:9
discerned in history a p. — FISH 283:1
excellent p. — SHAK 580:11
Gunpowder Treason and P. — ANON 17:11
Passions spin the p. — MER 458:8
p. for a short story — CHEK 197:1
p. thickens very much upon — BUCK 154:10
Sonnet's scanty p. — WORD 745:8
This blessèd p. — SHAK 619:18
We first survey the p. — SHAK 583:1
plots: All my plays' p. — CAV 187:11
P., true or false — DRYD 258:19
plough: Behind his p. — WORD 747:11
bruised by no p. — CAT 186:9
I must p. my furrow alone — ROS 546:17
Men of England, wherefore p. — SHEL 643:3
plod behind the p. — CRAB 225:11
put his hand to the p. — BIBLE 94:9
this morning held the p. — BETJ 67:9
We p. the fields, and scatter — CAMP 176:4
ploughman: p. homeward plods his weary — GRAY 315:10
While the p. near at hand — MILT 465:10
Whilst the heavy p. snores — SHAK 613:1
wrong even the poorest p. — CHAR 191:8
ploughshare: Soldiers of the P. — RUSK 551:4
ploughed: p. with my heifer — BIBLE 74:15
ploughers: p. plowed upon my back — BOOK 134:10
ploughshares: swords into p. — BIBLE 82:11
ploy: by p. or gambit — POTT 525:17
pluck: I'll p. it down — SHAK 588:3
offend thee, p. it out — BIBLE 91:19
p. till time and times — YEATS 753:8
p. your berries harsh — MILT 465:20
To p. me by the beard — SHAK 596:20
plucked: p. my nipple — SHAK 601:7
plucking: p. the fruit of memory — CONR 217:1
plum: or confectionary p. — COWP 222:26
plumage: He pities the p. — PAINE 504:15
plumbers: good p., good carpenters — NIXON 496:6
plume: In blast-beruffled p. — HARDY 325:5
Ruffles her pure cold p. — TENN 682:26
plumes: jets under his advanced p. — SHAK 630:1
p. with water not so fair — SPEN 660:24
plummet: like a leaden p. — FORD 289:10
plunder: cannot separately p. a third — BIER 109:3
Let no man stop to p. — MAC 436:8
What a place to p.! — BLÜC 115:10
plunge: p. your hands in water — AUDEN 34:4
plunged: p. himself into the billowy — GILB 305:13
plunging: When the p. hoofs were gone — DE L 236:8
plural: Incorribly p. — MACN 441:2
pluralitas: *P. non est ponenda* — OCCAM 498:1
plures: *Abiit ad p.* — PETR 513:12
plus: *P. ça change* — KARR 385:13
plush: as soon assault a P. — DICK 245:4
Pluto: won the ear of P. — MILT 465:18
plutocracy: not a p. of wealth — YOUNG 755:3
Plymouth Hoe: dreamin' arl the time o' P. — NEWB 492:7

pneumatic: promise of p. bliss — ELIOT 273:16
pobble: P. who has no toes — LEAR 414:16
pocket: disinherited by the out of p. — BENN 63:10
Do I carry the moon in my p. — BROW 151:6
hand in its breeches p. — KEATS 391:13
Is that a gun in your p. — WEST 729:12
money is jingling in his p. — DOST 255:1
not scruple to pick a p. — DENN 237:2
picked a p. with his tongue — BIER 109:5
plates dropped from his p. — SHAK 566:20
p. or purse — WILS 738:3
p. that they cannot separately put it in his p. — BIER 109:3
want his pecker in my p. — SHAK 577:10
your neighbour's p. — JOHN 367:11
pockets: hands in holey p. — RUSK 551:3
pension jingle in his p. — RIMB 541:8
young man feels his p. — COWP 224:16
Poe: P. with his raven — HOUS 351:21
poem: bathed in the P. of the Sea — LOW 429:18
drowsy frowzy p. — RIMB 541:5
figure a p. makes — BYRON 171:4
give you the music of a p. — FROST 295:14
heroic p. of its sort — SYNGE 677:8
ice on a hot stove the p. — CARL 180:9
It is a pretty p. — FROST 295:16
made one p.'s period — BENT 64:20
many beauties grace a p. — MARL 448:3
married to a p. — HOR 347:16
ornament of p. or good verse — KEATS 392:8
ought himself to be a true p. — MILT 467:17
p. is a test of invention — MILT 474:30
p. is like a painting — KEATS 391:4
p. is never finished — HOR 347:18
p. lovely as a tree — VALÉ 707:20
P. should be palpable — KILM 396:2
p. should not mean, but be — MACL 439:9
p., whose subject is not — MACL 439:10
prefer being the author of that p. — CHAP 191:2
poems: For ye are living p. — WOLFE 741:2
P. are made by fools like me — LONG 426:12
we all scribble p. — KILM 396:3
poesy: call p. *vinum daemonum* — HOR 348:17
force of heaven-bred p. — BACON 42:7
golden cadence of p. — SHAK 631:7
overwhelm myself in p. — SHAK 598:17
P. was ever thought to have — KEATS 390:11
subgit be to alle p. — BACON 42:1
viewless wings of P. — CHAU 195:26
poet: All a p. can do today is warn — KEATS 389:11
because he was a true P. — OWEN 503:11
better p. than Porson — BLAKE 112:15
business of a p. — HOUS 353:1
comic p. to paint the vices — JOHN 369:19
consecration, and the p.'s dream — CONG 214:22
dreams of a p. — WORD 743:11
every fool is not a p. — JOHN 367:22
Fat-head p. that nobody reads — POPE 519:24
flattery lost on p.'s ear — CHES 199:2
For what is left the p. here — SCOTT 559:14
found no sacred p. — BYRON 171:2
God is the perfect p. — ELIOT 269:11
himself the p. and the theme — BROW 151:18
Honour the greatest p. — COWP 224:14
I was a p., I was young — DANTE 230:9
Lawn Tennyson, gentleman p. — FLEC 286:15
Like a P. hidden in the light — JOYCE 381:23
limbs of a p. — SHEL 643:17
Love made me p. — HOR 351:3
lunatic, the lover, and the p. — TANF 678:13
No p. ever interpreted — SHAK 612:17
Not deep the P. sees, but wide — GIR 307:3
On a p.'s lips I slept — ARN 27:21
passionate heart of the p. — SHEL 642:14
P. and Saint — TENN 686:8
p. and the dreamer — COWL 221:18
p. could not but be gay — KEATS 387:16
Spare the p. for his subject — WORD 744:16
                      COWP 221:28

poet: (cont.):

p. image aught so fair	THOM 696:16
p. is always indebted	MAY 455:3
p. is like the prince	BAUD 55:6
p. is the most unpoetical	KEATS 392:1
p. is the priest	STEV 665:13
p. is to be admired	COCT 208:11
p. ranks far below	LEON 418:12
p. seems most himself	YEATS 753:22
p.'s eye, in a fine frenzy	SHAK 612:17
p.'s feverish blood	ARN 28:22
p.'s gift is to soothe	YES 754:1
p.'s hope; to be like	AUDEN 36:4
p. sing it with such airs	YEATS 750:17
p.'s inward pride	DAY-L 233:5
p.'s pen, all scorn	BRAD 139:10
p.'s soul starts like	PUSH 533:3
p. the potent figure that he	STEV 666:13
p. touch a pen to write	SHAK 598:20
p. whose right of honour	GURN 320:1
P. writes under one restriction	WORD 748:17
poor p. named Clough	SWIN 677:2
Redeth the grete p. of Ytaille	CHAU 194:4
rights be termed a p.'s rage	SHAK 633:5
shall be accounted p. kings	KEATS 390:13
shepherds call me also a p.	VIRG 715:7
should possess a p.'s brain	DRAY 258:4
skilled p. is one	PIND 514:14
starved p.	LOCK 425:15
Sure the p. spewed up	DRYD 262:19
they lack their sacred p.	HOR 350:18
This is truth the p. sings	TENN 685:10
This p. lies	SHAK 633:5
Thus every p., in his kind	SWIFT 675:6
true p. that you are	BROW 152:2
Vex not the the p.'s mind	TENN 687.23
What is a modern p.'s fate	HOOD 343:22
poetic: Meet nurse for a p. child	SCOTT 559:17
P. fields encompass me around	ADD 4:2
P. Justice, with her lifted	POPE 518:14
P. LICENCE	BANV 51:14
P. souls delight in prose	BYRON 172:6
which constitutes p. faith	COL 212:2
poetical: all claim to b. honours	JOHN 368:27
As to the p. character itself	KEATS 391:23
gods had made thee p.	SHAK 569:11
worn-out p. fashion	ELIOT 270:9
poetry: and that is p.	CAGE 174:22
car was p. and tragedy	LEWIS 421:3
cradled into p. by wrong	SHEL 641:1
Emptied of its p.	AUDEN 34:15
friend the phoso into p.	DICK 242:32
give p. a proper flow	BOIL 117:2
grand style arises in p.	ARN 30:9
grotesque art in English p.	BAG 47:15
Images, which are the life of p.	KAMES 385:3
In p., no less	ARN 29:21
In winning p.	DONNE 252:19
Ireland hurt you into p.	AUDEN 34:14
It is not p., but prose	POPE 519:31
Jonson his best piece of p.	JONS 379:17
Language is fossil p.	EMER 277:8
Made p. a mere mechanic art	COWP 223:15
make p. and give pleasure	HOR 350:12
misfortune of p. to be	AUST 39:4
most p. ignores most people	MITC 477:17
neither p. nor any thing else	BYRON 174:8
never the language of p.	GRAY 316:11
Nothing so much as mincing p.	SHAK 581:5
p. administers to the effect	SHEL 644:5
p. almost necessarily declines	MAC 434:16
P. and Religion are a product	CARL 180:16
p. begins to atrophy	POUND 527:13
p. cannot celebrate them	AUDEN 36:16
p. comes not as naturally	KEATS 391:15
p. does not matter	ELIOT 270:19
p. he invented was easy	AUDEN 34:10
p. high in the scale	BYRON 173:25
P. in motion	KAUF 385:14
P. is a religion with no hope	COET 208:6
P. is a subject no precise	FLAU 286:1
P. is as hortma as artficial	ARN 29:24
P. is a way of taking life	FROST 295:18

poetry: (cont.):

p. is conceived and composed	ARN 29:23
p. is eloquent painting	SIM 648:1
P. is in the pity	OWEN 503:10
P. is the medium of past literatures	FLAU 285:18
P. is more than good sense	COL 212:11
P. is not a turning loose	ELIOT 273:20
p. is overheard	MILL 460:11
p. is something more	ARIS 25:13
P. is the achievement	SAND 555:11
P. is the breath and finer	WORD 748:18
P. is the opening and closing	SAND 555:10
P. is the record	SHEL 644:7
P. is the spontaneous overflow	WORD 748:19
P. is the supreme fiction	STEV 665:20
P. is the universal art	HEGEL 330:6
P. is what is lost in translation	FROST 295:19
P. is when some of them	BENT 64:7
P. makes nothing happen	AUDEN 34:14
P. must be as well written as	POUND 527:19
p. of earth is never dead	KEATS 390:5
p. of motion	GRAH 314:3
P.'s a mere drug, Sir	FARQ 280:22
P. shall tune her sacred voice	JOHN 370:6
P. should be great	KEATS 391:12
P. should surprise	KEATS 391:14
p. sinks and swoons	LAND 408:10
P.'s the feverish fit	WINC 738:24
p. that has a palpable	KEATS 391:13
p. = the best words	COL 212:9
P. the flower of experience	HUNT 356:19
P. therefore, is an art	SIDN 647:7
p. to interpret life for us	ARN 29:22
P. unearths	HILL 338:9
p. would be made subsequent	MILT 475:20
polar star of p.	KEATS 391:4
power corrupts, p. cleanses	KENN 394:7
publicity rather than of p.	LEAV 415:6
quarrel with ourselves, p.	YEATS 753:21
repeat p. as well as other folk	CARR 183:14
resuscitate the dead art of p.	POUND 526:11
She that with p. is won	BUTL 166:13
Sir, what is p.	JOHN 374:18
So p., which is in Oxford made	DRYD 261:16
Superstition is the p. of life	GOET 309:11
theory of p. is the theory of life	STEV 666:6
unless we know it to be p.	THOR 696:24
was trying to say was p.	OVID 503:6
We may live without p.	MER 458:11
What is p.?	RUSK 550:13
poets: All p. are mad	BURT 164:19
amatory p. sing	BYRON 171:11
booksellers have put up with p.	HOR 347:19
first for wits, then p. passed	POPE 521:5
he the worst of p. ranks	CAT 186:6
impossible to hold the p. back	GIR 307:2
Irish p., learn your trade	YEATS 753:16
Latin p., I could never	CAV 187:11
mature p. steal	ELIOT 273:18
Milton's the prince of p.	BYRON 171:3
most p. are their own patients	THOM 694:10
Painters and p. alike	HOR 347:2
P. are the hierophants	SHEL 644:8
p. bicycle-pump the human	AMIS 10:18
p. exploding like bombs	AUDEN 36:7
P.' food is love and fame	SHEL 640:12
P. in our civilization	ELIOT 273:23
p. in our youth begin	WORD 747:11
p. in their misery dead	WORD 747:13
p. is sunk in his reputation	DRYD 262:18
p. keep our mouths shut	YEATS 752:16
P. like painters	POPE 521:11
P. Militant below	COWL 221:19
p. only deliver a golden	SIDN 647:6
p. painful vigils keep	POPE 518:15
P. that are sown by Nature	WORD 743:16
P. that lasting marble seek	WALL 718:11
p. though liars by profession	HUME 355:19
p. took their golden age	THOM 695:23
p. witty	BACON 44:29
powerful p. of the century	ELIOT 273:22
room for p. in this world	BROW 147:6

poets: (cont.):

Souls of p. dead and gone	KEATS 388:20
spite of all romantic p.	LEAP 413:15
Such sights as youthful p.	MILT 465:17
theft in other p.	DRYD 262:12
Three p. in an age at most	SWIFT 674:31
touchy breed of p.	HOR 348:20
We p. of the proud old lineage	FLEC 286:9
Which only p. know	COWP 223:21
point: agent is a p. that shifts	KLEE 402:20
Aloof from the entire p.	SHAK 594:23
creeping on from p. to point	TENN 685:14
each to his p. of bliss	BROW 153:6
Not to put too fine a p.	DICK 239:4
Point against p.	SHAK 599:17
p. envenomed too	SHAK 379:9
p. his slow and moving	SHAK 617:15
still p. of the turning world	ELIOT 270:16
That was the p.	ELIOT 270:8
They do not p. on me	SHAK 618:6
To p. a moral, or adorn a tale	JOHN 370:17
Up to a p., Lord Copper	WAUGH 724:1
You've hit the p.	PLAU 517:5
poised: p. between a cliché	MACM 440:7
poising: p. every weight	MARV 450:4
poison; coward's weapon, p.	FLET 288:3
if you p. us, do we not die	SHAK 608:22
I go about and p. wells	MARL 447:14
p. imposed by the authorities	PLATO 516:11
p. in jest	SHAK 576:17
p. quite o'ercrows my spirit	SHAK 579:12
p. the wells	NEWM 492:12
p. the whole blood stream	EMPS 277:20
p. while the bee-mouth	KEATS 389:7
strongest p. ever known	BLAKE 111:8
sweet p. for the age's tooth	SHAK 593:26
With its sickening p.	LARK 410:8
poisoned: In the p. entrails throw	SHAK 603:17
like a p. rat in a hole	SWIFT 674:2
of our p. chalice	SHAK 601:2
poison-flowers: honey of p.	TENN 686:9
poison-gas: got as far as p.	HARDY 325:2
poisonous: its p. wine	KEATS 389:4
p. damp of night disponge	SHAK 566:3
poisons: And p. all the rest	WATTS 722:11
poke: to p. poor Billy	GRAH 313:12
pokers: p. into true-love knots	COL 210:16
polar: p. star of poetry	KEATS 391:4
pole: Beloved from pole to p.	COL 211:10
curses from pole to p.	BLAKE 111:19
not rapt above the p.	MILT 472:6
p. is undistinguished blaze	THOM 696:4
returning from the P.	ATKI 32:13
top of the greasy p.	DISR 249:7
polecat: semi-house-trained p.	FOOT 288:13
police: among p. officers	ORTON 499:16
friendship recognised by the p.	STEV 668:1
game at which the p.	SHAW 638:8
p. the earth	LOW 430:22
To the citizen or the p.	AUDEN 36:1
policeman: p.'s lot is not a happy one	GILB 306:11
It would not do for a p.	NIGH 496:1
park, p. and a pretty girl	CHAP 190:9
scheme of things than a p.	SAL 554:8
terrorist and the p.	CONR 217:12
policemen: P., like red squirrels	ORTON 499:15
policy: either on religion or p.	RUSK 550:26
fulfilment in p. and action	TRIL 702:18
home p.: I wage war	CLEM 206:6
my p. is to be able to take	BEVIN 69:15
p. is to float lazily downstream	SAL 553:19
p. of the good neighbour	ROOS 545:17
rugged brow of careful P.	SPEN 659:13
some love but little p.	SHAK 621:6
will be tyrants from p.	BURKE 158:17
polis: The P. as Polis	O'CAS 497:17
polish: contented to p.	MORE 484:3
we may p. it at leisure	DRYD 262:8
polished: as the p. corners	BOOK 135:4
O p. perturbation! golden care	SHAK 584:1
p. up the handle	GILB 305:26

polite: don't have time to be p.   MONT 481:16
   have no allies to be p. to   GEOR 301:9
   Or p. meaningless words   YEATS 751:13
   p. father of his people   JAM 362:2
politeness: mutual glance of great p.
                                BYRON 173:17
   pineapple of p.   SHER 645:3
   p., the blowing of a nose   FORS 290:22
   Punctuality is the p. of kings   LOUI 428:18
   When suave p., tempering   KNOX 403:5
political: death of a p. economist   BAG 47:9
   fear of P. Economy   SELL 562:23
   healthy state of p. life   MILL 460:17
   his p. Cave of Adullam   BRIG 141:10
   history of p. power   POPP 524:13
   Man is by nature a p. animal   ARIS 25:15
   points clearly to a p. career   SHAW 637:1
   p. aspirant under democracy   MENC 457:5
   p. columnists say   ADAMO 2:3
   p. creed is that deopollsin   ADAMS 3:4
   P. language   ORW 501:2
   p. leader must keep looking   BAR 54:22
   p. life dealing with humdrum   THAT 691:25
   p. machinery pre-supposes   BALF 48:17
   p. party in this country   TROL 704:2
   P. power grows out of   MAO 446:1
   p. power of another   LOCKE 425:6
   p. speech and writing   ORW 500:26
   P. thought, in France   ARON 30:15
   regard p. consequences   MANS 445:10
   schemes of p. improvement   JOHN 373:6
   species of p. villainy   PEAC 510:7
politician: like a scurvy p.   SHAK 597:9
   pate of a p.   SHAK 578:20
   p. is a man who understands   TRUM 704:18
   p. is an arse upon which   CUMM 228:9
   p. is a statesman   POMP 518:13
   p. is to render vice serviceable   BOL 117:13
   p. never believes   DE G 235:11
   p. ought to sacrifice   BURKE 158:29
   p. was a person with whose   LLOY 424:10
   p. will never grudge   OLIV 498:12
   That p. tops his part   GAY 300:7
   when a p. does get an idea   MARQ 448:18
   which makes the p. wise   POPE 523:28
politicians: fault of our p.   TROL 703:23
   not the p. and statesmen   AUDEN 36:16
   Old p. chew on wisdom past   POPE 520:31
   Palliser was one of those p.   TROL 703:10
   P. also have no leisure   ARIS 25:11
   race of p. put together   SWIFT 673:12
   to be left to the p.   DE G 235:8
politics: Confound their p.   ANON 13:19
   do not go in for p.   CAMUS 177:11
   From p., it was an easy step   AUST 38:24
   gallantry than it has with p.   SHER 644:27
   give his mind to p.   SHAW 635:21
   In international p.   BIER 109:3
   In p., there is no use   CHAM 189:2
   In p., what begins in fear   COL 212:13
   Magnanimity in p. is not   BURKE 158:1
   men enter local p. solely   PARK 507:6
   Modern p. is, at bottom   ADAMS 2:22
   mule of p. that engenders   DISR 248:6
   not the language of p.   DISR 247:5
   now in the centre of p.   MOSL 486:20
   observe about this P. thing   ROG 544:18
   Philistine of genius in p.   ARN 30:5
   playful moderation in p.   HUNT 356:15
   P. are now nothing more   JOHN 374:5
   P. are too serious a matter   DE G 235:8
   P., as a practice   ADAMS 2:6
   p. as well as in religion   JUN 383:6
   p. by other means   CLAU 205:16
   p. consists in ignoring   ADAMS 2:19
   p. in boiled and roast   SMITH 653:4
   p. in the East may be defined   DISR 248:11
   P. is not the art of the   GALB 297:3
   P. is perhaps the only   STEV 667:11
   p. is present history   FREE 293:13
   P. is the art of preventing   VALÉ 707:23
   P. is war without bloodshed   MAO 445:13

politics: (cont.):
   p. of happiness   HUMP 356:3
   p. of the left and centre   JENK 365:5
   P. the second oldest profession   REAG 537:10
   p. the middle way is none   ADAMS 2:28
   science of p.   ARIS 25:8
   theory of p. was Bismarck's   KEYN 395:2
   They p. like ours profess   GREEN 316:17
   week is a long time in p.   WILS 738:6
Polka: see me dance the P.   GROS 319:1
polluted: Pemberley to be thus p.   AUST 39:17
   that is filthy and p.   BIBLE 86:17
pollution: beastly source of all p.   MARS 449:10
   unsavoury engine of p.   SPAR 658:10
Polly: Our P. is a sad slut   GAY 299:11
polyanthus: p. of unnumbered dyes
                                THOM 696:1
polygamous: Man is p.   JAMES 363:19
polygamy: Before p. was made a sin
                                DRYD 258:16
   chaste p.   CAREW 179:8
polygony: Or panachaea, or p.   SPEN 660:8
polyphiloprogenitive: P.   ELIOT 272:8
pomegranate: from Browning some 'P.'
                                BROW 147:15
   p. within thy locks   BIBLE 81:13
pomp: bright p. ascended   MILT 472:10
   grinning at his p.   SHAK 620:8
   Here's a world of p. and state   BEAU 56:15
   Lo, all our p. of yesterday   KIPL 400:12
   nor the tide of p.   SHAK 586:8
   pleasure, p. and plenty   JOHN 376:21
   p., and circumstance   SHAK 616:20
   p. and glory of this world   SHAK 588:19
   p. and majesty   BARN 53:18
   p. of pow'r   GRAY 315:13
   possessed with double p.   SHAK 594:9
   sultan after sultan with his p.   FITZ 283:15
   Take physic, p.   SHAK 596:7
   Their p., their power   SACK 552:13
   what is p., rule, reign   SHAK 588:6
   with p. of waters   DAN 229:11
Pompey: base of P.'s statua   SHAK 592:14
   Knew you not P.   SHAK 589:20
   wars of P. the Great   SHAK 586:1
pompous: p. in the grave   BROW 145:26
pomps: high Midsummer p.   ARN 28:27
   p. and vanity of this wicked   BOOK 123:4
pond: Four ducks on a p.   ALL 10:2
   have their stream and p.   BROO 143:6
   mantle like a standing p.   SHAK 607:6
ponder: P. anew   WINK 739:8
   When in charge, p.   BOREN 136:7
ponies: Five and twenty p.   KIPL 400:9
   wretched, blind, pit p.   HODG 340:16
Pontefract: licorice fields at P.   BETJ 67:16
poodle: right hon. Gentleman's p.   LLOY 424:4
Pooh: yawn, or 'P.!'   BYRON 171:30
pool: it must first fill a p.   BACON 44:4
   Walk across my swimming p.   RICE 540:5
pools: drawn amidst the frozen p.   MARL 447:20
   p. are bright and deep   HOGG 341:16
   p. are filled with water   BOOK 130:17
poop: p. was beaten gold   SHAK 565:5
poor: all the senses from p. me   CAT 186:7
   As for the virtuous p.   WILDE 735:22
   backward steward for the p.   POPE 520:17
   being p., have only my dreams   YEATS 751:22
   Blessed are the p. in spirit   BIBLE 88:23
   bring in hither the p.   BIBLE 94:31
   congregation of the p.   BOOK 130:3
   considereth the p. and needy   BOOK 126:27
   cottages of the p.   HOR 349:3
   destruction of the p. is   BIBLE 78:21
   expensive it is to be p.   BALD 48:2
   feel for the p.   LAND 407:23
   forbids the rich as well as the p.   FRAN 292:7
   found'st me p. at first   GOLD 310:19
   Give me your tired, your p.   LAZ 413:7
   give to the p.   BIBLE 91:23
   Good to the p., to kindred   CAREW 179:7
   grind the faces of the p.   BIBLE 82:12
   have in common being so p.   BLUN 116:1

poor: (cont.):
   help the many who are p.   KENN 393:13
   I can dare to be p.   GAY 300:13
   inconvenient to be p.   COWP 221:27
   It's no disgrace t'be p.   HUBB 353:13
   It's the p. wot gets the blame   ANON 17:20
   Laws grind the p.   GOLD 311:11
   let the p., and Thou within them
                                HERB 335:24
   live by robbing the p.   SHAW 637:9
   makes me p. indeed   SHAK 616:12
   makes them doubly p.   CRAB 225:14
   marry a rich woman as a p.   THAC 691:8
   murmuring p.   CRAB 225:3
   My countrymen Kiltartan's p.   YEATS 752:5
   no peasant so p. that   HENR 332:10
   not that men are p.   DU B 263:5
   not to be p.   SHAW 636:27
   object is p. or obscure   BIER 109:2
   one of the undeserving p.   SHAW 638:18
   open to the p. and the rich   ANON 13:14
   Or else his dear papa is p.   STEV 668:18
   Plenty has made me p.   OVID 502:22
   p. always ye have with you   BIBLE 97:7
   p. and unhappy brains   SHAK 615:23
   p. are Europe's blacks   CHAM 189:15
   p. are to be proud   SHAK 630:11
   p. cannot afford it   FORS 290:9
   p. cannot always reach   FORS 290:11
   p. don't know   SART 556:15
   p. get children   KAHN 384:19
   p. have cried, Caesar hath wept   SHAK 592:7
   p. have no right   RUSK 551:6
   p. in a loomp is bad   TENN 687:13
   p. know that it is money   BREN 140:12
   P. little rich girl   COW 220:16
   p. man at his gate   ALEX 8:10
   p. man had nothing   BIBLE 75:11
   p. man loved the great   MAC 436:12
   p. man's dearest friend   BURNS 162:20
   p. man slipped   BIBLE 87:21
   p. relation   LAMB 406:19
   p. relations who are horribly   ORW 500:6
   p. soul sat sighing   SHAK 617:22
   p. to do him reverence   SHAK 592:11
   p. who die   SART 556:6
   prey of the rich on the p.   JEFF 364:7
   propensity for being p.   AUST 40:2
   realize that he was p.   UST 707:13
   Resolve not to be p.   JOHN 376:1
   RICH AND THE P.   DISR 248:26
   rich richer and the p. poorer   NEHRU 491:8
   She was p. but she was honest   ANON 17:20
   simple annals of the p.   GRAY 315:13
   stately frontispiece of p.   MARV 451:7
   They p., I rich   DYER 265:1
   Too p. for a bribe   GRAY 316:10
   what can a p. boy do   JAGG 361:12
   With the p. and mean and lowly   ALEX 8:12
poorer: richer for p.   BOOK 123:20
poorest: p. he that is in England   RAIN 535:10
   p. man may in his cottage   PITT 515:6
poorly: P. he lived; poorly   FLET 287:27
pop: P. goes the weasel   MAND 444:2
Pope: against the P. or the NUM   BALD 48:12
   poetry of Dryden, P.   ARN 29:23
   P. afterwards   NEWM 493:7
   P. composes with his eye   ARN 30:6
   P. will grieve a month   SWIFT 675:11
   The P.! How many divisions   STAL 662:5
Popery: in danger of P.   ADD 4:15
popinjay: So pestered with a p.   SHAK 579:31
Popish: P. liturgy   PITT 515:10
poplars: p. are felled, farewell   COWP 222:29
poppies: fume of p.   KEATS 390:18
   In Flanders fields the p. blow   MCCR 437:5
   pleasures are like p.   BURNS 163:6
   p. was nothing to it   DICK 243:24
poppy: Not p., nor mandragora   SHAK 616:19
   Piccadilly with a p. or a lily   GILB 305:17
pops: At classical Monday P.   GILB 305:4
populace: Philistines, and P.   ARN 29:7
   propriety give the name of P.   ARN 29:11

popular: base, common and p.   SHAK 585:21
   p. humanity is treason   ADD 3:20
popularity: every difficulty except p.
     WILDE 736:11
population: p. against another   LENIN 417:6
   P., when unchecked   MALT 443:18
   single and only talked of p.   GOLD 311:28
populi: *Salus p. suprema est lex*   CIC 203:27
   Salus p. suprema lex esto   SELD 562:10
   Vox p., vox Dei   ALC 8:2
porcelain: dainty rogue in p.   MER 457:22
porcupines: couple of p. under you   KHR 396:1
pores: p. of the ocean   SHEL 640:7
pork: vision produced by raw p.   BYRON 174:8
Porlock: Person from P.   SMITH 652:21
   person on business from P.   COL 210:8
pornographic: p. show   BLUNT 116:6
pornography: P. is the attempt to insult
   sex   LAWR 412:5
   p. of war   RAE 535:9
   What p. is really about   SONT 656:8
porpentine: quills upon the fretful p.
     SHAK 573:14
porpoise: p. close behind us   CARR 182:13
porridge: comfort like cold p.   SHAK 625:13
   healsome p.   BURNS 161:17
Porson: better poet than P.   HOUS 353:1
port: ancient tales, and p.   BELL 61:15
   buried him the little p.   TENN 681:2
   I'll quit the p. o' Heaven   NEWB 492:6
   In every p. a wife   DIBD 238:13
   In ev'ry p. a mistress   GAY 300:16
   It would be p. if it could   BENT 64:21
   mater lie dissolved in p.   POPE 518:22
   p. after stormy seas   SPEN 660:2
   p., for men   JOHN 376:7
   p. is near, the bells I hear   WHIT 732:6
   sprightly p. make the ghosts   SHAK 566:9
   Still bent to make some p.   ARN 28:23
   There lies the p.   TENN 690:4
   which p. one is sailing   SEN 562:28
portable: P., and compendious   CRAS 226:12
portal: fiery p. of the east   SHAK 620:9
   fitful tracing of a p.   STEV 666:8
portents: These are p.   SHAK 618:6
porter: devil-p. it no further   SHAK 602:10
   p. of hell-gate   SHAK 602:8
   Sweeney to Mrs P.   ELIOT 273:7
porters: mechanic p. crowding   SHAK 584:22
Portia: P. is Brutus' harlot   SHAK 591:2
portion: p. of a good man's life   WORD 744:19
   P. of that around me   BYRON 168:24
   shall be their p. to drink   BOOK 124:23
   they may be a p. for foxes   BOOK 128:22
portmanteau: it's like a p.   CARR 183:13
portrait: paint a p. I lose a friend   SARG 556:3
   p., in frame, of the Bishop   KNOX 403:11
   p. not too stale to record   PLOM 517:11
   p. of a blinking idiot   SHAK 608:17
   P. of the Artist   JOYCE 381:9
   two styles of p. painting   DICK 242:7
portraits: take down p. all day long   LICH 421:13
ports: five p. of knowledge   BROW 145:10
   p. of slumber open wide   SHAK 584:1
pose: you didn't love a p.   GREE 316:24
position: hopelessness of one's p.   DOST 255:4
   Its human p.   AUDEN 35:6
   p. must be held   HAIG 320:12
   p. of matter at or near   RUSS 551:15
   p. ridiculous   CHES 198:25
positions: p. of considerable emolument
     GAIS 296:15
positive: ac-cent-tchu-ate the p.   MERC 457:12
   p. men are the most credulous   POPE 524:7
   p. peace which is the presence   KING 396:16
   p. science may be defined   KEYN 395:13
   p. value has its price   PIC 514:11
   power of p. thinking   PEALE 510:13
possess: shall p. the earth   BOOK 126:19
   possess'd of world in order to be p.
     BUNY 157:10
   Love once p.   MILT 470:16

possessed: *(cont.)*:
   p. his land   BIBLE 73:7
   Webster was much p. by death   ELIOT 273:15
possessing: too dear for my p.   SHAK 634:11
   yet p. all things   BIBLE 101:20
   Yet p. every blessing   EDM 266:17
possession: hurt is in the act of p.   GREE 317:5
   one equal p.   DONNE 253:14
   O that I could have p.   KEATS 392:9
   p. of a good fortune   AUST 39:9
   p. of the same   BOOK 136:2
   p. of truth as of a city   BROW 146:1
   P. without obligation   MER 457:24
   Than in the glad p.   JONS 379:2
possessions: all my p. for a moment   ELIZ 274:19
   behind the great p.   JAMES 362:21
   he had great p.   BIBLE 91:24
   multitude of p.   SMART 649:12
   p. that you should call blessed   HOR 350:19
possessor: Receive thy new p.   MILT 468:12
possibilities: awareness of the p. of life
     LEAV 415:4
   infinite number of all p.   LEIB 416:17
   preferred to improbable p.   ARIS 25:4
possibility: sceptic to deny the p.   HUXL 358:13
possible: can only effect all p. things   JENY 365:8
   effecting of all things p.   BACON 45:18
   exhaust the realm of the p.   PIND 514:15
   if a thing is p.   CAL 175:9
   Politics is not the art of the p.   GALB 297:3
   Politics is the art of the p.   BISM 110:4
   p. you may be mistaken   CROM 227:8
   says that something is p.   CLAR 205:10
   with God all things are p.   BIBLE 91:26
   world is the best of all p.   BRAD 139:4
Possum: Honourable P.   BERR 66:19
possumus: *Non omnia p. omnes*   VIRG 715:6
post: For evil news rides p.   MILT 474:1
   Lie follows by p.   BER 65:4
   like a p. with packets   SHAK 589:13
   P. coitum omne animal triste   ANON 22:12
   p. o'er land and ocean   MILT 474:24
   p. of honour is a private   ADD 3:22
   soldiers may not quit the p.   TENN 686:4
postal: Bringing the cheque and the p. order
     AUDEN 35:9
   p. districts packed like   LARK 410:10
postboy: see a dead p.   DICK 243:27
post-chaise: driving briskly in a p.   JOHN 374:22
posted: p. presence of the watcher   JAMES 363:5
poster: Kitchener is a great p.   ASQ 31:20
posteri: *Credite p.*   HOR 349:21
posteriors: p. of this day   SHAK 599:5
posterity: decided to write for p.   ADE 5:4
   hope of p.   POWER 528:12
   looked upon by p. as brave bad   CLAR 205:5
   mankind and p. in their debt   INGE 359:17
   not look forward to p.   BURKE 158:9
   P. do something for us   ADD 4:24
   p. is a pack-horse   DISR 247:7
   p. talking bad grammar   DISR 249:1
   Think of your p.   ADAMS 3:5
   To evoke p.   GRAV 315:2
   trustees of P.   DISR 248:29
   What damage to p. we bring   WITH 739:13
postern: Present has latched its p.
     HARDY 324:22
posters: P. of the sea and land   SHAK 600:3
posthumous: Ah! P., the years   SMART 650:5
post-impressionist: P. pictures   BLUNT 116:6
postman: p. always rings twice   CAIN 175:1
post-prandial: sweet p. cigar   BUCH 154:4
postscript: Here is yet a p.   SHAK 630:6
   her mind but in her p.   STEE 662:15
   most material in the p.   BACON 43:6
   pith is in the p.   HAZL 328:12
posy: Do I stoop? I pluck a p.   BROW 148:8
   made p. while the day ran   HERB 335:7
pot: greasy Joan doth keel the p.   SHAK 599:11
   have a chicken in his p.   HENR 332:10
   kettle and the cauldron p.   BIBLE 87:20
   make them in the one p.   JOYCE 381:20
   p. shall have ten hoops   SHAK 587:23

pot: *(cont.)*:
   potter pray, and who the p.   FITZ 284:13
   There is death in the p.   BIBLE 76:19
   thorns under a p.   BIBLE 80:11
potage: for a mess of p.   BIBLE 71:7
potations: forswear thin p.   SHAK 583:28
   Their dull and deep p.   GIBB 302:11
potato: bashful young p.   GILB 305:17
   p.-gatherers   KAV 386:3
potatori: *Huic p.*   ANON 22:9
potent: are most p. in potting   SHAK 615:24
   how p. cheap music is   COW 221:4
   p. advocates of peace   GEOR 301:3
potentially: what he is p.   FROMM 294:6
potion: his p. and his pill   HERR 336:15
potions: p. have I drunk of Siren   SHAK 634:25
Potomac: All quiet along the P.   MCCL 437:2
   All quiet along the P.   BEERS 59:22
potoribus: *scribuntur aquae p.*   HOR 348:15
pots: have lien among the p.   BOOK 129:8
potsherd: joke, poor p., patch   HOPK 346:7
   Let the p. strive   BIBLE 84:3
   p. to scrape himself withal   BIBLE 77:4
potter: hand then of the p.   FITZ 284:12
   pieces like a p.'s vessel   BOOK 124:10
   p. and clay endure   BROW 152:11
   p. power over the clay   BIBLE 100:2
   Who *is* the p., pray   FITZ 284:9
potting: most potent in p.   SHAK 615:24
pouch: and p. on side   SHAK 568:16
poultry: prolonging the lives of the p.
     ELIOT 269:4
pounces: p. upon the human core
     JAMES 363:15
pound: p. here in Britain   WILS 738:3
pounding: Hard p. this   WELL 727:9
pounds: crowns and p.   HOUS 352:9
   handsome in three hundred p.   SHAK 610:17
   p. will take care   LOWN 431:1
   p. will you find   JUV 384:8
   six hundred p. a-year   SWIFT 674:25
   two hundred p. a year   BUTL 166:1
pour: P. into our hearts such   BOOK 121:4
   p. out my spirit upon all   BIBLE 86:8
poured: I am p. out like water   BOOK 125:12
   P. forth her song in perfect   AUDEN 34:1
   p. into his clothes   WOD 740:23
pouring: noise they make in p.   POPE 524:5
poverties: I dreamed not of p.   TRAH 701:12
poverty: And in his squadrons P.   FLAT 285:15
   Come away; p.'s catching   BEHN 60:14
   crime so shameful as p.   FARQ 280:10
   endure harsh p.   HOR 350:19
   Give me not p. lest I steal   DEFOE 234:5
   implication of dreary p.   WEST 729:15
   in honoured p. thy voice   SHEL 643:25
   In p., hunger, and dirt   HOOD 344:7
   misfortunes of p. carry   JUV 383:21
   Money is better than p.   ALLEN 9:16
   My p., but not my will   SHAK 624:4
   neither p. nor riches   BIBLE 79:32
   poor is their p.   BIBLE 78:21
   p. and oysters always seem   DICK 243:12
   p. come as one that travelleth   BIBLE 78:14
   P. is a great enemy   JOHN 376:1
   P. is no disgrace to a man   SMITH 653:29
   p. is the worst of all   DEFOE 234:4
   p. knows how expensive it is   BALD 48:2
   quiet mind is worse than p.   TRAH 701:17
   represent p. as no evil   JOHN 372:10
   setting him up in p.   NAIDU 489:6
   she scorns our p.   SHAK 587:16
   suffer so much p. and excess   PENN 511:14
   Untaught to bear p.   HOR 348:23
   worst of crimes is p.   SHAW 636:27
   worth, by p. depressed   JOHN 370:9
powder: food for p.   SHAK 581:25
   keep your p. dry   BLAC 110:9
   when your p.'s runnin' low   NEWB 492:6
powdered: Still to be p.   JONS 378:18
power: absolute p.   ADAMS 3:4
   acquisition of p.   RUSS 551:24
   All hail the p. of Jesus' Name   PERR 513:1

power: (*cont.*):
all p. is a trust	DISR 248:35
another name for absolute p.	WORD 747:10
arts of p.	CLAY 206:1
authority and minimal p.	SZASZ 677:11
balance of p.	NIC 494:14
because we had p.	BENÉT 62:17
Between his p. and thine	JONS 378:25
certainty of p.	DAY-L 233:5
corridors of p.	SNOW 654:6
depository of p.	DISR 248:7
effect of p. and publicity	ADAMS 2:11
Everyone who desires p.	MILL 460:24
every power a double p.	SHAK 598:20
force of temporal p.	SHAK 609:13
friend in p. is a friend lost	ADAMS 2:10
girded about with p.	BOOK 129:1
good want p.	SHEL 642:11
gratefully sing his p.	GRANT 314:6
greater the p.	BURKE 160.30
have given a p. over us	OSB 501:7
Him the almighty p. hurled	MILT 467:23
Horses and P. and War	KIPL 398:14
knowledge itself is p.	BACON 45:15
lies not in our p. to love	MARL 447:10
limitation of governmental p.	WILS 738:9
literature of *p.*	DE Q 237:13
Lord of all p. and might	BOOK 121:5
man who has the p. and skill	ANON 19:18
mighty p. and stronger	WALL 718:6
more contracted that p. is	JOHN 374:31
mystery of the king's p.	JAM 362:3
neither hath he p.	BIBLE 80:16
nobility is but the act of p.	BACON 44:9
no hopes but from p.	BURKE 159:24
no more than p. in trust	DRYD 259:5
not exempted from her p.	HOOK 344:14
notions about a superior p.	SWIFT 673:2
once intoxicated with p.	BURKE 157:3
outrun our spiritual p.	KING 397:3
pains be less, or p. more	BROME 141:16
p. a corrupter	SHEL 644:3
p. and glory, or happiness	ARIS 25:11
P. and prime Agent of	COL 212:1
p., and the glory	BIBLE 89:5
p. at the top	LUCR 431:15
p. belongeth unto God	BOOK 128:20
p. breathe forth	SHAK 565:7
p. can be rightfully exercised	MILL 460:15
p. faithfully to fulfil	BOOK 120:13
P. girt round with weakness	SHEL 639:20
p. grows out of the barrel of	MAO 446:1
p. into the hands of husbands	ADAMS 1:11
p. is apt to corrupt	PITT 515:8
P. is given only to him	DOST 254:11
p. is nominated	GIBB 302:1
P. is not a means, it is an end	ORW 500:16
P. is so apt to be insolent	HAL 321:17
P. is the great aphrodisiac	KISS 402:14
p. is the love of ourselves	HAZL 328:16
p. of a lower moral quality	HARDY 324:13
p. of a man, to take	HOBB 340:2
p. of no calamity	BROW 146:13
p. of our senses	JOHN 368:14
p. of positive thinking	PEALE 510:13
p. of the crown	BURKE 159:13
p. of the press is very great	NORT 496:19
p. of the written word	CONR 217:9
P. over all the tumbling	DOST 254:10
p. over men, but over themselves	
	WOLI 741:13
p. over other beings	FOST 291:10
p. over people as long	SOLZ 655:7
p. should always be distrusted	JONES 378:1
P. tends to corrupt	ACTON 1:10
p. that worketh in us	BIBLE 102:15
p. thrown away	LESS 419:11
p. to act according	LOCKE 425:9
p. to be put forth	CANN 178:12
p. to die	TENN 689:12
p. to execute his purposes	JOHN 370:2
p. to hurt and will do	SHAK 634:14
p. to hurt us that we love	BEAU 57:1

power: (*cont.*):
p. to keep them all	HOBB 340:5
p. to live and act and serve	WORD 747:15
P. to the people	ANON 17:12
p. which erring men call chance	MILT 464:5
p. which has dotted over	WEBS 725:8
p. which stands on Privilege	BELL 61:24
P. without responsibility	KIPL 402:13
responsibility without p.	STOP 669:15
restless desire of p.	HOBB 340:3
Restored to life, and p.	KEBLE 392:19
seek p. and to lose liberty	BACON 43:28
seeks to communicate p.	DE Q 237:14
Send to us p. and light	AUDEN 36:5
shadow of some unseen P.	SHEL 640:18
should take who have the p.	WORD 747:16
sound-like p. in light	COL 209:19
subjected to the political p.	LOCKE 425:6
supreme p. must be arbitrary	HAL 321:14
Their pomp, their p.	SACK 552:13
though injurious, hath strange p.	
	MILT 474:10
though stripped of p.	SCOTT 559:19
Thou hast not half the p.	SHAK 618:13
To defy P., which seems	SHEL 642:20
too weak for p.	LEAP 413:16
trust no man living with p.	ADAMS 2:26
upon the past has p.	DRYD 262:2
utility of monarchical p.	BOSW 137:6
virtue of that life and p.	FOX 292:2
When p. corrupts	KENN 394:7
where p. predominates	JUNG 383:1
with Eternal God for p.	TENN 687:18
witty beauty is a p.	MER 457:17
women remain the slaves of p.	WOLL 741:16
world desires to have—P.	BOUL 138:1
powerful: All-p. as the wind	AUBER 32:20
p. goodness want	SHEL 642:11
powerless: p. to be born	ARN 28:20
powers: All period, p., and enterprise	
	SMART 649:17
high contracting p.	BRIA 141:1
jurisdiction of two hostile p.	MAC 435:23
nor p., nor things present	BIBLE 100:1
p. of the society	JEFF 364:15
p. that be are ordained	BIBLE 100:8
P. that will work for thee	WORD 748:13
princedoms, virtues, p.	MILT 471:28
principalities, against p.	BIBLE 103:1
wad some P. the giftie gie us	BURNS 163:14
we lay waste our p.	WORD 748:15
ye heavenly p.	GOET 309:15
pox: A p. on 'em	WYCH 750:3
gallows or of the p.	WILK 736:19
practical: Commends a most p. plan	
	INGE 359:11
Morality's *not* p.	BOLT 117:14
P. men, who believe	KEYN 395:10
sustained p. activity	TAWN 678:19
we look at the p.	GLAD 307:13
practice: And P. drives me mad	ANON 16:13
not wear them out in p.	BEAU 56:8
practices: bloody principles and p.	FOX 292:5
practise: Go p. if you please	BROW 152:17
never to p. either of them	TWAIN 706:8
we shall p. in heaven	BROW 151:15
would p. this without me	SHER 644:23
practised: making p. smiles	SHAK 631:13
p. what he preached	ARMS 26:8
practising: p. the hundredth psalm	
	BYRON 173:19
praemia: *P. digna ferant*	VIRG 712:10
Sunt hic etiam sua p.	VIRG 712:9
praemitti: *sciamus non amitti sed p.*	CYPR 229:9
praevalet: *Magna est veritas, et p.*	BIBLE 108:18
praise: All p. to thee, my God	KEN 393:7
all song of p. is due	SIDN 646:22
countryman must have p.	BLYT 116:10
Damn with faint p.	POPE 519:32
dispraised were no small p.	MILT 473:16
game of interchanging p.	HOLM 342:11
garment of p. for the spirit	BIBLE 84:27
girded with p.	GRANT 314:6

praise: (*cont.*):
going for p. to Mount Sion	BUNY 155:15
Hubert Stanley is p. indeed	MORT 486:17
husband's first p.	BARB 52:6
idle smoke of p.	DAN 229:17
if there be any p.	BIBLE 103:13
lack tongues to p.	SHAK 634:18
let his just p. be given	WALT 721:14
Let the florid music p.	AUDEN 35:3
Let the people p. thee	BOOK 129:4
Let us now p. famous men	BIBLE 87:37
most perfect p.	JONS 378:15
mouth shall shew thy p.	BOOK 128:8
Nor named thee but to p.	HALL 322:6
no such whetstone as p.	ASCH 31:1
oblique p.	JOHN 375:3
Oh let our voice his p. exalt	MARV 450:1
O p. ye the Lord	BAKER 47:21
p. any man that will praise	SHAK 565:14
p. at morning what they	POPE 521:20
P. be to Nero's Neptune	DYLAN 265:12
P. for the singing	FARJ 280:4
p. him, and magnify him	BOOK 118:17
p. is paid by perception	JOHN 369:11
P., laud, and bless	KETHE 394:13
P. my soul, the King of heaven	LYTE 433:17
p. new-born gawds	SHAK 627:22
p. of ancient authors	HOBB 340:13
p. of God consists	PROU 530:13
p. of his holy Name	BOOK 123:17
p. thee	BOOK 118:12
P. the everlasting King	LYTE 433:17
P. the green earth	BUNT 155:8
P. the Lord, all nations	BIBLE 108:3
P. the Lord and pass the	FORGY 289:18
P. the Lord, for he is kind	MILT 465:19
p. the Lord for his goodness	BOOK 132:15
P. the Lord, O my soul	BOOK 132:2
p. the Muse forbids	HOR 350:17
P. they that will times past	HERR 336:23
P. to the Holiest	NEWM 493:13
p. to the Lord	WINK 739:7
pudding against empty p.	POPE 518:14
right p. and true perfection	SHAK 610:5
so double be his p.	SPEN 660:3
song of thanks and p.	WORD 746:3
Teach the free man how to p.	AUDEN 34:16
they only want p.	MAUG 454:11
They p. those works	MART 449:13
Thy p. shall sanctify our rest	ELL 275:6
To stir a little dust of p.	TENN 684:1
To utter all thy P.	ADD 4:17
unto thy Name give the p.	BOOK 133:9
We p. thee, God	ANON 22:17
We p. thee, O God	BOOK 118:12
Who like me his p. should sing	LYTE 433:17
whom there were none to p.	WORD 747:18
who paint 'em truest p.	ADD 3:15
praised: everybody p. the Duke	SOUT 657:6
p. him to his face	TENN 689:5
p. than to be pardoned	JONS 380:9
p. the dead which are already	BIBLE 80:7
Who ne'er said, 'God be p.'	BROW 147:12
praiser: p. of past times	HOR 347:14
praises: faint p. one another damn	WYCH 750:8
His p. there may grow	HERB 334:7
p. from the men, whom all men	COWL 221:17
p. those who follow different	HOR 350:21
Sing p. unto the Lord	BOOK 126:5
These p. are not small nor few	HEYW 338:5
praising: doing one's p. for oneself	BUTL 166:26
P. all alike, is praising none	GAY 300:10
P. the lean and sallow	MILT 464:6
P. what is lost	SHAK 564:11
who are always p. the past	SMITH 652:18
pram: p. in the hall	CONN 216:12
pranks: it heaven see the p.	SHAK 616:14
prata: *pueri; sat p. biberunt*	VIRG 714:21
prater: p. of the northern race	CHUR 201:10
pray: All p. in their distress	BLAKE 110:1
fervently do we p.	LINC 422:8
fold her hands and p.	ROSS 548:3
God doth late and early p.	WOTT 749:1

President: (cont.):
more than any other P.   MENC 457:4
P. is a glorified public relations TRUM 704:15
P. of the Immortals   HARDY 324:18
rather be right than be P.   CLAY 206:2
their P. is a crook   NIXON 496:5
We are the P.'s men   KISS 402:15
When the P. does it   NIXON 496:7
press: dead-born from the p.   HUME 355:18
freedom of the p.   JEFF 364:6
Freedom of the p. in Britain   SWAF 673:1
god of our idolatry, the p.   COWP 223:6
governs the periodical p.   TROL 704:8
have misused the king's p.   SHAK 581:22
I p. toward the mark   BIBLE 103:9
lose your temper with the P.   PANK 505:17
power of the p.   NORT 496:19
p. is the Palladium   JUN 383:3
racket is back in its p.   BETJ 68:6
turned him about in the p.   BIBLE 97:12
with you on the free p.   STOP 669:17
pressed: p. down my soul   BOOK 128:15
service means p. out of shape   FROST 295:11
presses: University printing up. CORN 219:6
press-men: P.; Slaves of the Lamp ARN 26:14
pressure: Grace under p.   HEM 332:1
p. and resistance   NIC 494:14
prestige: p. without distance   DE G 235:6
presume: P. not that I am the thing
                                   SHAK 584:14
p. too much upon my love   SHAK 593:4
presumption: amused by its p.   THUR 697:17
Of surquidrie and foul p.   CHAU 195:7
presumptuous: from p. sins   BOOK 125:6
rash, refined, p. man   CANN 178:8
prêt: Il est toujours p. à partir LA F 405:13
pretence: p. make long prayers BIBLE 93:17
some faint meaning make p.   DRYD 261:2
pretend: We shall not p.   ANON 19:11
why p. that he is?   SHAW 637:18
pretended: p. friend is worse   GAY 300:4
pretender: and the Old P.   GUED 319:10
who P. is, or who is King   BYROM 167:17
pretending: to be wicked   WILDE 734:17
pretension: p. is nothing   HUNT 356:20
pretexts: Tyrants seldom want p. BURKE 157:4
pretio: Cum p.   JUV 383:23
pretty: And all the maidens p. COLM 214:1
He is a very p. woeman   FLEM 287:8
It is a p., pretty thing   PEELE 511:3
It is a p. thing   GREE 317:11
park, a policeman and a p. girl   CHAP 190:9
p. can get away with   WAUGH 724:11
p. chickens and their dam   SHAK 604:9
p. girl is like a melody   BERL 65:19
P.! in amber to observe   POPE 519:30
p. to see what money will   PEPYS 512:18
Puts on his p. looks   SHAK 594:4
should be p. of its kind   LAMB 406:3
Which is sometimes so p.   PRÉ.V 528:16
prevail: great is truth, and shall p. BROO 144:5
not merely endure, he will p.   FAUL 281:3
prevailed: have not p. against me BOOK 134:10
prevails: Great is truth, and it p. BIBLE 108:18
prevarication: last dyke of p. BURKE 159:6
prevent: duty to try to p. it   MILN 463:7
P. us, O Lord, in all our   BOOK 122:17
preventing: by thy special grace p.
                                   BOOK 120:16
prevents: p. the rule of wealth BAG 46:21
prey: bent on his p.   MILT 470:19
expects his evening p   GRAY 315:9
greater p. upon the less   GREEN 316:17
hast'ning ills a p.   GOLD 310:6
made my pains his p.   SPEN 659:11
p. departeth not   BIBLE 86:15
p. of the rich on the poor   JEFF 364:7
quarry, the destined p.   SHAW 637:8
roaring after their p.   BOOK 132:9
thou soon must be his p.   SHEL 641:8
to drive a p.   BALL 49:1
yet a p. to all   POPE 522:10
preys: p. systematically   JAMES 363:13

Priamus: En P.   VIRG 712:9
price: abatement and low p.   SHAK 628:9
All those men have their p.   WALP 720:14
because they fetch a high p.   WHAT 730:11
blood be the p. of admiralty   KIPL 401:2
bought it at any p.   CLAR 205:4
'fixed p.' is negotiable   TOFF 700:1
her p. is far above rubies   BIBLE 79:35
love that pays the p.   SPR 661:8
pearl of great p.   BIBLE 91:4
positive value has its p.   PIC 514:11
p. is asked for harmony   DOST 254:5
p. of everything   WILDE 735:12
p. of insubordination   MACG 438:3
p. of justice is eternal   BENN 63:18
p. of wisdom is above rubies   BIBLE 77:28
What p. glory   ANDE 11:9
Wot p. Selvytion nah   SHAW 636:31
without money and without p.   BIBLE 84:15
prices: contrivance to raise p. SMITH 650:18
I paid the p. of life   GURN 320:1
prick: If you p. us, do we not   SHAK 608:22
I paint with my p.   REN 539:1
It is a p., it is a sting   PEELE 511:3
p. the sides of my intent   SHAK 601:3
pricking: By the p. of my thumbs SHAK 603:20
knight was p. on the plain   SPEN 659:20
prickly: Here we go round the p. pear
                                   ELIOT 271:15
pricks: although small p.   SHAK 627:11
kick against the p.   BIBLE 98:16
pride: all the p., cruelty   RAL 536:6
burning and high disdain   SCOTT 559:12
burn its children to save its p.   MEYER 459:9
false p. in place and blood   TENN 684:11
from p., vain-glory   BOOK 119:17
He that is low no p.   BUNY 156:10
his father's p.   BURNS 161:18
I know thy p., and the naughtiness
                                   BIBLE 74:40
look backward to with p.   FROST 294:14
maiden's, adieu   SHAK 613:30
my high-blown p.   SHAK 588:19
name in p. and thankfulness   BROW 152:17
On either side it is p.   TOCQ 699:7
poet's inward p.   DAY-L 233:5
pour contempt on all my p.   WATTS 723:2
P. and pleasure, pomp   JOHN 376:21
P. AND PREJUDICE   BURN 160:16
P. and Truth   YEATS 752:17
P. goeth before destruction   BIBLE 87:37
P. in their port, defiance   GOLD 311:10
p. is something in-conceivable   GILB 304:20
P. make such a stir   DAN 230:1
P. of Life that planned   HARDY 325:3
p. of the peacock   BLAKE 112:24
P. ruled my will   NEWM 493:15
P. still is aiming   POPE 522:4
p. struck out new sparkles   DRYD 260:21
p. that apes humility   COL 209:18
p. that pulls the country   SHAK 615:25
rank p., and haughtiness   ADD 3:17
Such is our p., our folly   DENH 236:20
that perished in its p.   WORD 747:11
that will her p. deflower   SPEN 660:6
Thine eyes my p., thy lips   SIDN 647:3
pridie: A day that hath no p.   DONNE 253:8
priest: As a p., a piece of mere COWP 224:11
built to please the p.   BURNS 162:13
Delicate-handed p. intone   TENN 686:12
huntsman and a fiddling p.   COWP 223:1
I will be thy p.   KEATS 389:20
Presbyter is but old P. writ   MILT 467:14
p. continues what the nurse   DRYD 260:26
P. did offer Christ   BOOK 135:25
P. for ever after the order   BOOK 133:4
P. of the invisible   STEV 665:13
p. of the Muses   HOR 349:22
rid me of this turbulent p.   HENR 332:14
still is Nature's p.   WORD 745:14
take my religion from the p.   GOLD 311:35
Than he listen'd to the p.   BALL 50:5

priest: (cont.):
'twixt the P. and Clerk   HERR 336:19
visited by the p.   SHAK 630:34
priestcraft: ere p. did begin   DRYD 258:16
priesthood: royal p., an holy   BIBLE 105:11
priestlike: at their p. task   KEATS 386:9
priests: And pay a million p.   HARDY 325:2
Bishops, P., and Deacons   BOOK 119:19
p. are only men   BROW 152:14
p. bear rule   BIBLE 86:6
p. by the imposition of   MAC 434:18
p. giving way to the dominion   PRICE 528:17
p. have been enemies   HUME 355:13
p. in gold and black   LAWR 412:13
strangled with the guts of p.   MESL 458:16
treen p. and golden chalices   JEWEL 366:7
with women nor with p.   SOUT 657:12
Prig: P., I term the sort   SHAK 631:27
primal: taught us from the p. state SHAK 564:27
Primate: Lord P. on bended knee BARH 52:12
prime: arrive at a p. mover   THOM 692:17
barmie noddle's p.   BURNS 163:19
having lost but once your p.   HERR 337:8
laurel for the perfect p.   ROSS 547:6
One's p. is elusive   SPARK 658:7
p. of youth is but a frost   TICH 698:3
spent my youthfu' p.   BURNS 164:1
Prime Minister: next P. but three BELL 61:4
P. has nothing to hide from   CHUR 203:8
P. has resigned and Northcliffe   ANON 14:2
turned-out P.   MELB 456:9
Unknown P.   ASQ 31:18
Prime Ministers: P. and such   GILB 304:4
P. are wedded to the truth   SAKI 553:15
wild flowers, and P.   BALD 48:14
prime-roses: pale p.   SHAK 632:4
primeval: This is the forest p. LONG 426:16
primitive: wise p. in a giant jungle MAIL 442:10
primordial: p. chaos   WELLS 727:21
p. condition of liberty   BAK 47:23
protoplasmal p. atomic   GILB 304:20
primrose: p. by the mourning river
                                   BOLT 117:16
P. first born child of Ver   FLET 287:19
p. path of dalliance   SHAK 573:2
rathe p. that forsaken dies   MILT 466:11
silken p. fading timelessly   MILT 466:18
that go the p. way   SHAK 602:10
Primrose Hill: To P. and Saint John's Wood
                                   BLAKE 112:3
primroses: Wan as p.   KEATS 386:19
prince: Advise the p.   ELIOT 272:5
companion a better p.   SHAK 582:22
Dread p. of plackets   SHAK 598:13
Else a great p. in prison lies   DONNE 251:26
Good-night, sweet p.   SHAK 579:14
greatest p. o' the world   SHAK 566:14
Hamlet without the P.   SCOTT 560:32
Is in a p. the virtue   MASS 453:12
Lord Hamlet is a p.   SHAK 574:16
madcap P. of Wales   SHAK 581:19
news and P. of Peace   FLET 287:24
On which the p. of glory died   WATTS 723:2
p. and a judge over us   BIBLE 71:35
P. calls in the good old   LAMB 406:4
P. I am not, yet I am nobly   DEKK 235:18
p. of Aquitaine   NERV 492:2
P. of darkness and dead   SPEN 659:23
p. of darkness is a gentleman   SHAK 596:15
P. of Peace   BIBLE 82:27
p. sets himself up above   MAYH 455:10
p. who gets a reputation   NAP 489:10
P. whom thou couldest not   DONNE 253:7
under the dominion of a p.   HUME 355:12
princedoms: dominations, p.   MILT 471:28
Prince of Wales: God bless the P. LINL 423:7
princes: admit p. to the corridors DOUG 255:10
blaze forth the death of p.   SHAK 591:5
fall like one of the p.   BOOK 130:15
he might inform his p.   BOOK 132:4
into the weakness of P.   JAM 362:3
make p. in all lands   BOOK 127:14
P. and Lords are but   BURNS 161:19

princes: (*cont.*):
P. and lords may flourish   GOLD 310:6
p. are come home again   SHAK 594:16
p. of the Empire   MELV 456:18
p. to act   SHAK 584:16
put not your trust in p.   BOOK 135:8
That sweet aspect of p.   SHAK 588:19
princess: My P. of Parallelograms
                                   BYRON 173:23
principal: There were none p. SHAK 569:10
principalities: against p.   BIBLE 103:1
nor p., nor powers   BIBLE 100:1
principibus: P. placuisse viris HOR 348:11
principiis: P. obsta   OVID 503:3
principio: In p. erat Verbum   MISS 477:8
principis: Indignatio p. mors est MORE 484:11
principle: active P.   WORD 744:2
'falling domino' p.   EIS 268:11
first human p.   SHAK 583:28
good men to rise above p.   LONG 426:9
He does everything on p.   SHAW 638:7
involved with the female p.   CLARK 205:8
precedent embalms a p.   STOW 670:12
p. of beauty in all things   KEATS 392:10
p. of God to turn thy mind   FOX 292:4
p. of the English constitution   BLAC 110:13
p. of the English law   DICK 239:13
p. sacrificed to expediency   MAUG 454:5
Protection is not a p.   DISR 246:19
rights is the basic p.   FOUR 291:16
shrinks from P., disavows   DISR 248:3
subjects are rebels from p.   BURKE 158:17
that sensibility of p.   BURKE 158:14
principles: ain't by p. nor men LOW 429:16
bloody p. and practices   FOX 292:5
Damn your p.!   DISR 249:3
instead of p., slogans   BENT 64:19
Lordship's p. or your mistress   WILK 736:19
p. of a free constitution   GIBB 302:1
P. of Political Economy   BENT 64:16
reference to p.   TAWN 678:19
shows that he has good p.   JOHN 372:4
Their p. are the same   JOHN 375:28
who denies the first p.   AUCT 33:15
print: All the news that's fit to p. OCHS 498:2
delight me for to p. my book   HERR 337:5
decomposing in the eternity of p.
                                   WOOLF 742:5
I love a ballad in p.   SHAK 632:8
licence to p. money   THOM 696:20
p. of a man's naked foot   DEFOE 234:9
p. such of the proprietor's   SWAF 673:1
seeing our names in p.   CHES 199:9
'tis devils must p.   MOORE 482:19
wickedness of the world is p.   DICK 241:18
printing: caused p. to be used SHAK 587:26
invented the art of p.   CARL 181:4
P., and the Protestant   CARL 180:17
p., gunpowder, and the magnet
                                   BACON 45:21
p. house in Hell   BLAKE 113:3
University p. presses   CORN 219:6
we think to regulate p.   MILT 475:8
printless: lissom, clerical, p. toe BROO 143:11
on the sands with p. foot   SHAK 626:1
priorities: language of p.   BEVAN 68:14
priority: degree, p., and place SHAK 627:6
prisca: Ut p. gens mortalium   HOR 348:22
Priscian: P. a little scratched SHAK 599:3
prism: Of Newton, with his p. WORD 747:2
prison: And mourn in p.   MONT 480:7
Came the hero from his p.   AYT 41:2
Come, let's away to p.   SHAK 597:16
comparatively at home in p.   WAUGH 723:15
Else a great prince in p. lies   DONNE 251:26
He did grind in the p. house   BIBLE 74:20
In the p. of his days   AUDEN 34:16
I was in p , and ye came   BIBLE 92:20
Just man is also a p.   THOR 696:22
Lord looseth men out of p   BOOK 133.0
only to ha to adorn its p.   WULL 711.15
prettiest of the p,   BIBLE 84:26
p. and the woman'n workhouse   SHAW 800:1

prison: (*cont.*):
prison in a p.   DICK 243:23
p. where I live unto   SHAK 621:10
Stone walls do not a p. make   LOV 429:4
This lime-tree bower my p.   COL 211:20
'Twixt a p. and a smile   WOTT 749:5
was not the world a vast p.   WOLL 741:18
What is a ship but a p.   BURT 165:5
while there is a soul in p.   DEBS 233:13
world is not a 'p. house'   ROB 542:12
prisoner: If the p. is happy   SHAW 637:18
object to your being taken p.   KITC 402:18
passing on the p.'s life   SHAK 605:12
p. in his twisted gyves   SHAK 623:7
p. of the Lord   BIBLE 102:16
p.'s release   SIDN 646:18
That takes the reason p.   SHAK 600:8
thoughts of a p. are not free   SOLZ 655:11
prisoners: p. of addiction   ILL 359:10
p. out of captivity   BOOK 129:7
p. underneath her wings   SHAK 587:12
upon all p. and captives   BOOK 120:1
weapons and virtues of all p.   COL 212:20
Which p. call the sky   WILDE 735:34
prison-house: Shades of the p. WORD 745:14
To tell the secrets of my p.   SHAK 573:14
prisons: Madhouses, p.   CLARE 204:18
P. are built with stones   BLAKE 112:23
privacy: gnaw upon one's monadic p.
                                   NERV 492:3
p., an obscure nook for me   BROW 151:20
narrow p. and tawdry secrets   LEACH 413:8
your p. in a public place   UST 707:18
private: grave's a fine and p. place MARV 451:3
his p. parts, his money   BUTL 167:6
honour is a p. station   ADD 3.22
invade the sphere of p. life   MELB 456:11
Its p. life is a disgrace   ANON 17:15
kind heaven, a p. station   GAY 300:8
lovely in p. life   BURKE 159:17
no p. life which has not been   ELIOT 269:3
P. faces in public places   AUDEN 35:12
P. Means is dead   SMITH 652:19
P. property is a necessary   TAWN 679:1
P. respects must yield   MILT 474:9
P. will governs each separate   ROB 542:2
silk hat at a p. view   EDW 267:3
that p. men enjoy   SHAK 586:7
to serve our p. ends   CHUR 200:22
We first consult our p. ends   SWIFT 675:10
privately: I indulge them p.   DENN 237:5
privates: Faith, her p., we   SHAK 574:25
privato: Maior p. visus   TAC 678:3
privilege: Danger justified p. WAUGH 724:7
Death is the p. of human   ROWE 549:7
Englishman's heaven-born p.   ARN 29:11
power which stands on P.   BELL 61:24
p. and pleasure that we   GILB 304:2
p. I claim for my own sex   AUST 39:7
p. only of seeing one another   JENY 365:10
this inestimable p. of man   SHEL 644:2
privileged: coachman's a p. individual
                                   DICK 243:28
P. and the People formed   DISR 248:28
p. to be very impertinent   FARQ 280:25
They were p. children   BROO 144:2
privileges: stand for your p. HEMI 331:12
prize: all a purchase, all is a p. HOPK 346:6
Christ the p.   MONS 480:1
is lawful p.   GRAY 316:4
judge the p.   MILT 465:16
Let old Timotheus yield the p.   DRYD 259:23
one receiveth the p.   BIBLE 100:30
p. of all too precious you   SHAK 634:9
p. the thing ungained more   SHAK 627:5
We do not run for p.   SORL 656:16
prized: knowing what would make us p.
                                   CHUD 200:11
local, but p. elsewhere   AUDEN 36:4
prizes: glittering p.   SMITH 651:13
probability: p. is the very guide BUTL 165:21
probable: P. impossibilities   ARIS 25:14
probationary: Eden's dress p. had COWP 223:6

probitas: P. laudatur et alget JUV 303:14
problem: not a single p. is solved CHEK 197:13
or you're part of the p.   CLEA 206:3
p. is food   DONL 250:6
p. left to itself dries up   SIMP 648:6
p. must puzzle the devil   BURNS 163:3
p. of the colour line   DU B 263:4
p. that has no name   FRIE 294:3
three-pipe p.   DOYLE 256:7
problematical: The p. world   FRY 295:22
problems: such p. as it can solve MARX 452:3
proboscis: His lithe p.   MILT 471:8
procedure: interstices of p.   MAINE 442:12
proceed: all just works do p. BOOK 119:10
p. no further in this business   SHAK 601:4
proceedeth: Who p. from the Father
                                   BOOK 121:20
proceedings: p. interested him no more
                                   HARTE 327:21
proceeds: good conscience on the p.
                                   SMITH 652:9
procession: torchlight p.   O'SUL 502:6
Their dances were p.   CORB 218:13
proclaims: apparel oft p. the man SHAK 573:4
p. with a hammer   BIER 109:5
proclamation: To avoid p.   MIDD 459:19
procrastination: p. is the art MARQ 448:10
P. is the thief of time   YOUNG 754:16
to incivility and p.   DE Q 237:12
procreant: bed and p. cradle   SHAK 601:1
p. urge of the world   WHIT 732:14
procreation: p. of children   BOOK 123:17
proctors: With prudes for p.   TENN 687:24
procul: P. hinc, procul este, severae OVID 502:12
P. omen abesto   OVID 502:11
Procul, o p. este, profani   VIRG 713:12
prodigal: chariest maid is p. enough
                                   SHAK 573:1
oppression of their p. weight   SHAK 620:14
played the p.   DRAY 257:20
yet p. of ease   DRYD 269:2
prodigies: all Africa and her p. BROW 146:6
prodigious: all p. things   MILT 470:4
produce: p. it in God's name   CARL 181:11
producing: P. what? A pair of slippers
                                   BROW 147:1
product: infinitesimal fraction of a p.
                                   CARL 181:11
production: sole end and purpose of p.
                                   SMITH 651:2
productions: in love with the p. of time
                                   BLAKE 112:20
profanation: From sale and p. CHES 199:3
in the less foul p.   SHAK 605:19
'Twere p. of our joys   DONNE 252:21
profane: Coldly p.   CRAB 225:2
Hence, ye p.; I hate ye all   COWL 221:10
P., erroneous, and vain   BUTL 166:12
so old, and so p.   SHAK 584:12
To Banbury came I, O p. one   BRAT 139:19
profaned: desolated and p.   GLAD 307:10
profani: o procul este, p.   VIRG 713:12
profanum: Odi p. vulgus   HOR 349:22
profess: p. and call themselves BOOK 120:6
profession: charmed me from my p.
                                   SHAK 626:18
different branches of a new p.   TROL 704:9
discharge of any p.   JOHN 373:30
man a debtor to his p.   BACON 42:15
most ancient p.   KIPL 401:14
not a p. but a vocation   SIM 647:17
ornament to her p.   BUNY 156:13
panted for a liberal p.   COLM 214:3
second oldest p.   REAG 537:10
professional: P. men, they have no cares
                                   NASH 490:12
professionally: P. he declines and falls
                                   DICK 242:32
professions: let in some of all p. SHAK 602:10
one of the p. which are full   THOR 697:2
p. are conspiracies against   SHAW 636:11
professor: called a p. emeritus LEAC 413:9

prose: (*cont.*):
pin up my hair with p.   CONG 215:33
Poetic souls delight in p.   BYRON 172:6
p. and the passion   FORS 290:14
p. is verse, and verse   BYRON 172:6
P. is when all the lines   BENT 64:7
p. run mad   POPE 519:31
P. was born yesterday   FLAU 285:18
P. = words in their best   COL 212:9
speaking p. without knowing it   MOL 478:16
They shut me up in p.   DICK 245:1
unattempted yet in p. or rhyme   MILT 467:20
Proserpine: P. gathering flowers   MILT 471:4
prospect: dull p. of a distant good   DRYD 260:25
noblest p. which a Scotchman   JOHN 372:7
Though every p. pleases   HEBER 330:4
prospects: affording delightful p.   HOFF 341:13
Charming spot. Inspiring p.   BECK 57:2
gilded scenes and shining p.   ADD 4:2
p. are as pleasing   ADD 4:16
prosper: I grow, I p.   SHAK 595:1
in which our affairs p.   BIER 109:10
Treason doth never p.   HAR 326:12
Why do sinners' ways p.   HOPK 346:8
prosperity: day of p. be joyful   BIBLE 80:14
end of joy and all p.   HAWES 328:3
I will wish thee p.   BOOK 133:26
jest's p. lies in the ear   SHAK 599:9
liberty and p.   JENY 365:9
man to han ben in p.   CHAU 195:20
one man who can stand p.   CARL 180:29
p. arrived at in a single   BUTL 166:24
P. doth best discover vice   BACON 42:21
P. doth bewitch men   WEBS 726:13
P. is not without many fears   BACON 42:20
P. is the blessing   BACON 42:18
P.'s the very bond of love   SHAK 632:11
prostitute: I puff the p. away   DRYD 262:3
prostitutes: small nations like p.   KUBR 404:7
prostitution: P. Selling one's body   MACK 439:2
protect: And I'll p. it now   MORR 485:8
Heaven will p. a working   SMITH 651:10
p. its own existence   ASIM 31:14
p. us from the full glare   MADAN 441:9
to p. the writer   ACH 1:9
protection: calls mutely for p.   GREE 317:4
God's gracious mercy and p.   BOOK 124:1
great p. against war   BEVIN 69:14
P. is not a principle   DISR 246:19
P. is not only dead, but damned   DISR 249:5
such strength and p.   BOOK 120:14
protective: Impartially p.   MERR 458:12
protector: praise is a Friend and P.   BARB 52:6
p. of all that trust in thee   BOOK 121:2
protest: lady doth p. too much   SHAK 576:16
partakes of the nature of a p.   HOFF 340:20
that none is left to p.   SHAK 614:9
Protestant: attacked me and the P. church   NIEM 495:2
I am the P. whore   GWYN 320:6
Printing, and the P. Religion   CARL 179:7
P. counterpoint   BEEC 59:3
p. ethic and the spirit of   WEBER 724:18
P., if he wants aid   DISR 248:20
P. with a horse   BEHAN 59:26
Thy P. to be   HERR 337:2
Protestantism: All P.   BURKE 157:24
P. of the Protestant religion   BURKE 157:24
Protestants: religion of P.   CHIL 199:27
Proteus: P. rising from the sea   WORD 748:16
protoplasmal: p. primordial atomic   GILB 304:20
protracted: life protracted is p. woe   JOHN 370:18
proud: always p. of the fact   RUSS 551:8
Are beauties there as p.   SIDN 646:17
be p. if you'll be wise   CHUD 200:13
Death be not p.   DONNE 250:22
how apt the poor are to be p.   SHAK 630:11
I have no p, looks   BOOK 134:13
I will the p. and mighty have   DYER 265:6
It makes him very p.   MILNE 463:1
milk-hath p. to take us   SHAK 580:17
mine being too p. to fight   WILS 738:11

proud: (*cont.*):
mote ye lyve, and alle p.   CHAU 195:13
nation p. in arms   MILT 463:15
p. and yet a wretched thing   DAV 232:4
proudest of the p.   CHUR 201:10
p. full sail of his great   SHAK 634:9
p. in heart and mind   SHAK 596:9
p. in the imagination   BIBLE 93:23
p. me no prouds   SHAK 623:25
p. of one another the first week   CONG 216:1
p. of seeing our names in   CHES 199:9
P. Wellington   BYRON 167:18
rather p. of knowing nothing   MCEW 437:15
since thou art so p.   CAREW 179:6
too p. for a wit   GOLD 311:4
too p. to importune   GRAY 316:10
where's the sense in being p.   CHEK 196:7
Who was so p., so witty   ROCH 543:12
Why were they p.?   KEATS 388:1
woman can be p. and stiff   YEATS 751:8
proudly: p. raised there stands   DAN 229:12
prove: I could p. everything   PINT 514:19
lend you money if you can p.   HOPE 345:1
P. all things   BIBLE 103:23
p. anything by figures   CARL 179:20
p. me, and examine my   BOOK 134:22
p. me: try out my reins   BOOK 125:21
since I cannot p. a lover   SHAK 621:16
proved: God p. them   BIBLE 86:28
Marlbro's mighty soul was p.   ADD 3:13
p. me, and saw my works   BOOK 131:10
p. to be much as you said   HARDY 325:7
To have p. most royally   SHAK 579:16
proven: worthy proving can be p.   TENN 680:8
Provençal: P. song   KEATS 389:9
Provence: found it in P.   WILL 737:12
provender: For nought but p.   SHAK 614:19
proverb: p. is one man's wit   RUSS 552:4
p. is something musty   SHAK 576:21
shall be a p. and a byword   BIBLE 75:22
Proverbs: King Solomon wrote the P.   NAYL 491:3
Patch grief with p.   SHAK 614:12
provide: God will p. himself a lamb   BIBLE 71:5
provided: 'P. for'   DICK 240:5
providence: Behind a frowning p.   COWP 222:19
I may assert eternal p.   MILT 467:21
inscrutable workings of P.   SMITH 651:14
Of p., foreknowledge   MILT 469:23
P. dictates with the assurance   HITL 339:11
P. had sent a few men   RUMB 549:17
P. has given human wisdom   BAR 52:1
P. has not created mankind   TOCQ 699:2
provident: They are p. instead   BOGAN 116:13
providers: as p. they're oil wells   PARK 506:16
province: all knowledge to be my p.   BACON 45:12
backward and dilapidated p.   AUDEN 35:1
p. they have desolated   GLAD 307:10
provinces: these limbs, her p.   DONNE 252:3
those p. in time of war   SMITH 651:5
provincial: dead level of p. existence   ELIOT 269:23
worse than p., he was parochial   JAMES 362:20
provincialism: taken in adultery than in p.   HUXL 357:8
provision: Make not p. for the flesh   BIBLE 100:11
provocation: as in the p.   BOOK 131:10
Ask you what p. I have had   POPE 523:8
provoke: p. not your children   BIBLE 102:24
provoker: p. of three things   SHAK 602:11
provokes: No one p. me with impunity   ANON 22:10
proximus: *paries cum p. ardet*   HOR 348:13
proxy: p. for risk and a dummy   MACH 438:13
prudence: effect of p. on rascality   SHAW 637:30
forced into p. in her youth   AUST 39:3
P. bring thee back to early   CHUR 201:5
P. is a rich, ugly, old maid   BLAKE 112:17
prudent: mercenary and the p   AUST 39:15
My p. course is *made?*   LOW 429:18

prudenter: *p. agas*   ANON 22:13
prudes: With p. for proctors   TENN 687:24
prunes: p. and prism   DICK 241:6
pruninghooks: spears into p.   BIBLE 82:11
prunus: p. and forsythia across   BETJ 68:1
Prussia: military domination of P.   ASQ 31:17
national industry of P.   MIR 476:10
prymerole: She was a p.   CHAU 193:29
psalm: like a p. of green days   QUIL 534:11
My ear the echo of a p.   PAST 509:1
practising the hundredth p.   BYRON 173:19
reverent cadence and subtle p.   AUDEN 34:1
sing to the harp with a p.   BOOK 131:14
Take the p., bring hither   BOOK 130:14
psalmist: sweet p. of Israel   BIBLE 75:19
Psalms: Church with p. must   HERB 334:7
glad in him with p.   BOOK 131:9
King David wrote the P.   NAYL 491:3
p. and hymns and spiritual   BIBLE 102:23
sonnets turned to holy p.   PEELE 511:5
psaltery: sackbut, p., dulcimer   BIBLE 85:28
pseudopodium: lonely p.   SHIP 646:1
Psyche: Your mournful P.   KEATS 389:5
psychiatrist: Any man who goes to a p.   GOLD 312:6
psychology: p. of human relationships   BERNE 66:10
pub: wasn't a p. open in the city   BEHAN 60:4
puberty: thinking p. assisted   BYRON 170:9
pubic: that Caught the P. Hare   BEHAN 60:1
public: as if I was a p. meeting   VICT 710:16
complainers for the p.   BURKE 157:14
consult the p. good   SWIFT 673:14
describe holding p. office   ACH 1:8
Desolation in immaculate p.   ROET 544:4
determined by a wider p. life   ELIOT 269:3
discretion for the p. good   LOCKE 425:9
fascination of a p. execution   FOOT 208:11
I and the p. know   AUDEN 35:19
It's not a p. conveyance   MURD 488:5
man assumes a p. trust   JEFF 364:21
one to mislead the p.   ASQ 31:19
Private faces in p. places   AUDEN 35:12
p. and merited disgrace   STEV 668:11
p. be damned   VAND 708:9
p. doesn't give   BEEC 58:16
p. odium and the public   CLAY 206:1
p. Prayer in the Church   BOOK 135:24
p. school will always feel   WAUGH 723:15
p. will take care of the cat   SULZ 671:15
researchers into P. Opinion   AUDEN 36:11
servants of the p.   GOW 313:3
share your privacy in a p.   UST 707:18
solo in p. and learning   BUTL 167:9
to the p. good private respects   MILT 4/4:9
things on which the p. thinks long   JOHN 368:19
whatever the Government and p.   SHAW 637:11
Which vexes p. men   TENN 690:6
publican: How like a fawning p.   SHAK 607:20
publicans: Master with p. and sinners   BIBLE 90:5
not even the p. the same   BIBLE 89:1
publicity: oxygen of p.   THAT 691:23
power and p.   ADAMS 2:11
price of justice is eternal p.   BENN 63:18
p. except your own obituary   BEHAN 60:6
p. rather than of poetry   LEAV 415:6
public relations: glorified p. man   TRUM 704:15
public school: p. men   FORS 289:20
with a P. accent   LEAV 415:5
public schools: P. are the nurseries   FIEL 282:6
P. 'tis public folly feeds   COWP 224:9
publish: I'll p., right or wrong   BYRON 172:3
P. and be damned   WELL 727:13
p. it not in the streets   BIBLE 75:8
P. your message   WESL 729:1
publisher: Barabbas was a p.   CAMP 177:2
pudding: Manningtree ox with the p.   SHAK 580:31
p. against empty praise   POPE 518:14

quail: q. whistle about us — STEV 666:11
quailing: No q., Mrs Gaskell — BRON 143:1
quails: we long for q. — DRYD 261:6
quaint: q. and curious war — HARDY 325:12
q. as an old parasol — FISH 283:7
quake: aspes leef she gan to q. — CHAU 195:18
They love indeed who q. — SIDN 646:21
qualities: great q. — BAG 46:18
In whom his q. are reigning — BYRON 173:15
Q. too elevated often unfit — CHAM 189:12
such q. as would wear well — GOLD 311:29
quality: give us a taste of your q. — SHAK 575:4
his honour and his q. — BLUN 116:4
knowing you gave them q. — SOLZ 655:9
More composition and fierce q. — SHAK 594:26
People of q. know everything — MOL 479:9
Persons of q. to be cheated — EVEL 279:6
q. of mercy is not strained — SHAK 609:13
to some one q. incline — DRAY 257:19
qualms: cold q., and bitter pangs — SOUT 658:3
quantities: ghosts of departed q. — BERK 65:7
quantum: I waive the q. o' the sin — BURNS 161:24
quarks: Three q. for Muster Mark — JOYCE 381:6
quarrel: false q. there is no true valour — SHAK 614:14
find q. in a straw — SHAK 577:33
justice of my q. — ANON 15:2
lover's q. with the world — FROST 295:2
only one to make a q. — INGE 359:16
pretty q. as it stands — SHER 645:11
q. in a far away country — CHAM 189:7
q. with others, rhetoric — YEATS 753:21
that hath his q. just — SHAK 587:18
therefore a perpetual q. — DURKE 157:28
quarrelled: man who has q. — PEAC 510:10
quarrelling: find that they had been q. — HUME 355:15
q. wi' the equawtor — NORTH 496:15
set them a q. — HUME 355:17
quarrels: All tears and q. were — TRAH 701:12
full of q. as an egg — SHAK 623:12
never strained by nasty q. — HOR 349:10
q. and disgusts are there — HUME 355:10
unseemly intimacy or q. — LOW 430:10
quarry: marked down q. — SHAW 637:8
quarterly: nothing a-year, paid q. — SURT 672:21
quarto: beautiful q. page — SHER 645:13
quartos: q. their well-ordered ranks — CRAB 224:26
Quebec: Long Live Free Q. — DE G 235:5
queen: Ere you were Q. of Sheba — SHIP 646:1
flaunting, extravagant q. — SHER 645:18
Hail holy q. — ANON 22:14
I am your anointed Q. — ELIZ 274:1
I have been to the Q. — GLAD 307:18
I'll q. it no inch further — SHAK 632:10
I'm to be Q. o' the May — TENN 687:7
I would not be a q. — SHAK 588:14
laughing q. that caught — HUNT 356:8
life of our own dear Q. — ANON 14:12
Most Gracious Q., we thee — ANON 16:12
Ocean's child, and then his q. — SHEL 641:8
O he was the Q.'s luve — BALL 49:3
pale Q. of the silent night — BEST 67:1
Q. and Faith like a valiant — TENN 689:5
Q. and huntress — JONS 378:16
Q. had four Maries — BALL 50:6
q. in a summer's bower — SHAK 581:9
q. in a vesture of gold — BOOK 127:12
q. of curds and cream — SHAK 632:6
q. of heaven, with crescent — MILT 468:19
q. of Scots is this day — ELIZ 274:16
q. of Sheba had seen all — BIBLE 75:23
q. unveiled her peerless — MILT 471:10
remembrance of a weeping q. — SHAK 620:16
royal makings of a q. — SHAK 589:3
Ruler of the Q.'s Navee — GILB 305:26
sometime sister, now our q. — SHAK 572:4
To toast The Q. — HILL 890:10
Two-wheeled gypsy q. — DYLAN 265:14

queen: (cont.):
when good Cinara was my q. — HOR 350:11
Would grace a summer q. — SCOTT 560:12
Queen Mab: Q. hath been with you — SHAK 622:21
queens: all your acts are q. — SHAK 632:5
beautiful Q. of this world — DONNE 253:8
Q. have died young and fair — NASHE 491:1
Queensberry: Duchess of Q. — WALP 719:4
queer: q. save thee and me — OWEN 503:9
q. sort of thing — BARH 52:17
We're here because we're q. — BEHAN 60:5
What a q. thing Life is — WOD 740:21
queerer: q. than we can suppose — HALD 321:2
quells: She q. the floods below — CAMP 177:1
quench: If I q. thee — SHAK 618:5
Many waters cannot q. love — BIBLE 82:6
q. all the fiery darts — BIBLE 103:1
smoking flax shall he not q. — BIBLE 84:2
quenched: What hath q. them — SHAK 601:14
querulous: God's q. calling — HUGH 354:7
quest: to whose winding q. — VAUG 708:14
questing: passes the q. vole — WAUGH 724:2
twenty couple of hounds q. — MAL 443:6
question: ask an impertinent q. — BRON 141:18
having asked any clear q. — CAMUS 177:12
If any q. why we died — KIPL 398:16
Make that thy q., and go rot — SHAK 631:16
Others abide our q. — ARN 28:12
q. causes it to disappear — FORS 290:21
q. is absurd — AUDEN 36:12
q. not to be asked — SHAK 580:29
secretly changed the Q. — SELL 562:26
that q.'s out of my part — SHAK 628:23
To ask the hard q. is simple — AUDEN 36:9
with such a silly q. — STER 664:12
questionable: com'st in such a q. shape — SHAK 573:9
questionings: But for those obstinate q. — WORD 746:3
questions: all q. are open — BELL 60:20
answered three q. — CARR 182:4
it's asking q., all the time — WESK 727:26
nailing his q. one by one — THOM 694:12
q. of those who cannot tell — RAL 536:10
That q. the distempered part — ELIOT 270:22
queue: beautiful q. of one — MIKES 460:5
quibble: q. is to Shakespeare — JOHN 369:10
quick: burgeons every maze of q. — TENN 684:13
Come! q. as you can — DE L 235:19
dead, q., I know not — DYER 264:14
judge the q. and the dead — BOOK 119:1
less q. to spring again — ARN 28:29
q., and the dead — DEWAR 238:7
q. spirit that is in Antony — SHAK 589:23
Touched to the q., he said — BROW 150:14
quicken: turn again, and q. us — BOOK 130:19
quickened: eyes are q. so with grief — GRAV 314:20
Yet q. now with fire — DYER 264:14
quickeneth: spirit that q. — BIBLE 96:28
quickening: Thine eye diffused a q. ray — WESL 728:2
quicker: But liquor is q. — NASH 490:18
quickly: That thou doest, do q. — BIBLE 97:9
'twere well it were done q. — SHAK 601:2
quickness: our q. of thought — AST 32:7
quicksands: q., and the rocks — KEATS 391:22
quiddities: in thy quips and thy q. — SHAK 579:20
quidquid: Q. agis, prudenter — ANON 22:13
Q. agunt homines — JUV 383:16
quiet: All q. along the Potomac — MCCL 437:2
All q. along the Potomac — BEERS 59:22
All q. on the western front — REM 538:16
alone with the q. day — JAMES 363:9
Anythin' for a q. life — DICK 243:26
Anything for a q. life — MIDD 459:11
be q.; and go a-Angling — WALT 721:11
bliss that hath a q. mind — VAUX 709:13
calm Peace, and Q. — MILT 464:17
days telling with a q. beat — QUIL 534:11
Easy live and q. die — SCOTT 560:15
Fair Q., have I found thee — MARV 450:9

quiet: (cont.):
Fie upon this q. life — SHAK 580:14
fruitful ground, the q. mind — SURR 672:2
Give me my scallop-shell of q. — RAL 535:18
lain still and been q. — BIBLE 77:7
lives of q. desperation — THOR 696:28
monopoly profits is a q. life — HICKS 338:7
never have a q. world till — SHAW 638:11
O for this q. — KEATS 392:16
q., grave man — BAG 46:20
q. his own conscience herein — BOOK 122:4
q. mind is worse than poverty — TRAH 701:17
q., pilfering, unprotected race — CLARE 204:24
Q. to quick bosoms is a hell — BYRON 168:22
q. us in a death so noble — MILT 474:18
serve thee with a q. mind — BOOK 121:8
Study to be q. — BIBLE 103:20
Thirst of wealth no q. knows — WINC 738:23
With q. hours — SHAK 581:27
quieta: Q. movere magna — SALL 554:12
quietest: q. places under the sun — HOUS 352:17
quietly: Q. shining to the quiet moon — COL 210:6
Q. they go, the intelligent — MILL 461:6
quietness: q. and in confidence — BIBLE 83:14
serve thee in all godly q. — BOOK 121:3
unravished bride of q. — KEATS 388:23
quietus: himself might q. make — SHAK 575:16
quillets: sharp q. of the law — SHAK 587:8
quills: q. upon the fretful porpentine — SHAK 573:14
tender stops of various q. — MILT 466:15
quilts: Soft q. on quilts — THOM 695:17
Quinapalus: What says Q. — SHAK 628:18
quince: slices of q. — LEAR 414:15
quincunx: q. of heaven runs low — BROW 145:10
Quinquireme: Q. of Nineveh — MAS 453:2
quinsy: weaning, the liar's q. — AUDEN 36:5
quip: q. modest — SHAK 569:26
quips: thy q. and thy quiddities — SHAK 579:20
quiring: q. to the young-eyed cherubins — SHAK 610:1
quis: Sed q. custodiet ipsos — JUV 384:2
quit: I q. such odious subjects — AUST 38:20
Q. yourselves like men — BIBLE 74:30
that dies this year is q. — SHAK 583:20
quiver: man that hath his q. full — BOOK 134:7
quivers: q. in the sunny breeze — GREN 318:2
quo: Q. vadis? — BIBLE 108:13
quondam: Q. was I — WYATT 749:18
quotation: q. constitutes — JOHN 367:21
quotations: Backed his opinion with q. — PRIOR 529:10
q. from the Bible — LAWR 413:3
quote: and q. aptly — HOGB 341:14
grow immortal as they q. — YOUNG 754:6
I'll kill you if you q. it — BURG 156:23

R

R: pronounced the letter R — AUBR 33:8
rabbit: r. has a charming face — ANON 17:15
There is a r. in a snare — STEP 664:1
rabble: army would be a base r. — BURKE 157:32
Parliament, R., House — COBB 207:28
Rabelais: R. dwelling in a dry — COL 212:12
race: Another r. hath been — WORD 746:7
avails the sceptred r. — LAND 408:4
happiness of the human r. — BURKE 158:2
hindered in running the r. — BOOK 120:12
like the rest of my r. — BLAKE 112:12
loftier r. — SYM 677:6
lovely ere his r. be run — BYRON 169:25
Nor did he flag as the r. — COKE 208:15
now a new r. is sent down — VIRG 714:22
pilfering, unprotected r. — CLARE 204:24
Purity of r. does not exist — FISH 283:2
r. between education — WELLS 727:20
r. is not to the swift — BIBLE 80:21
r. is to the swift — DAV 232:21
r. of little odious vermin — SWIFT 673:11
r. or the colour of their skin — WILL 737:16

race: (cont.):
r. that long in darkness SCOT 561:11
r. through God's good grace MONS 480:1
run the r. with Death JOHN 376:18
run with patience the r. BIBLE 104:17
slinks out of the r. MILT 475:7
they which run in a r. BIBLE 100:30
till thou run out thy r. MILT 467:1
tree did end their r. MARV 450:8
unbodied joy whose r. SHEL 643:15
white r. *is* the cancer SONT 656:7
races: r. of men in Asia and Africa DU B 263:4
Some r. increase, others LUCR 432:1
white r. are really pinko-grey FORS 290:20
Rachel: R. weeping for her children
  BIBLE 88:11
served seven years for R. BIBLE 71:16
rack: Leave not a r. behind SHAK 625:28
r. dislimns SHAK 566:7
r. of a too easy chair POPE 519:8
r. of this tough world SHAK 558:4
racked: r. with deep despair MILT 468:6
racket: flaming r. of the female OSB 501:14
r. is back in its press BETJ 68:6
r. run by unscrupulous men BEEC 59:4
rackets: matched our r. to these balls
  SHAK 584:23
radiance: shadowy r. lies on the earth
  BABEL 41:10
white r. of Eternity SHEL 640:4
radiances: R. know him BERRY 66:15
radiancy: What r. of glory NEALE 491:5
radical: dared be r. when young FROST 295:8
R. Chic WOLFE 741:9
r. revolutionary will become a
  conservative AREN 24:16
radio: car r. bleats LOW 430:20
R. and television SARR 556:5
r. *et surgentia sidera* VIRG 713:17
radish: like a forked r. SHAK 583:22
r. and an egg COWP 223:34
raft: republic is a r. AMES 10:9
rafters: stars come down with the r.
  AUDEN 34:7
rag: foul r. and bone shop YEATS 751:2
r. and a bone and a hank KIPL 401:7
r. blown by the wind WORD 742:20
That Shakespearian r. RUBY 154:7
that Shakespeherian R. ELIOT 273:5
rage: Blessed r. for order STEV 665:21
captive void of noble r. TENN 683:11
heathen so furiously r. BOOK 124:7
Heaven has no r. CONG 215:17
horrible that lust and r. YEATS 753:9
humour temp'ring virtuous r. POPE 521:3
nature with hard-favoured r. SHAK 585:7
Not die here in a r. SWIFT 674:2
Puts all Heaven in a r. BLAKE 111:1
r. against the dying of the light THOM 693:4
r. shall beauty hold SHAK 634:3
Realism is the r. of Caliban WILDE 735:15
replete with too much r. SHAK 633:7
rights be termed a poet's r. SHAK 633:5
Strong without r. DENH 236:17
writing increaseth r. DYER 264:14
rages: weight of r. SPOO 661:6
ragged: pair of r. claws ELIOT 272:3
raggedness: windowed r. SHAK 596:6
raging: r. in the dark YEATS 751:6
strong drink is r. BIBLE 79:4
Who stilleth the r. BOOK 129:1
ragout: fricassee, or a r. SWIFT 674:4
rags: Arm it in r. SHAK 597:8
filthy r. BIBLE 84:28
fond of my r. and tatters MOL 478:23
when in r. and contempt BUNY 156:1
which are the r. of time DONNE 252:17
ragtime: R. . . . but when the wearied
  Band HUXL 357:20
raid: r. by Dr Jameson KRUG 404:5
r. on the inarticulate ELIOT 271:1
rail: any body else to r. at me CONG 215:19
her six young on the r. BROW 150:16

rail: (cont.):
Say that she r. SHAK 624:14
than to r. at the ill TENN 687:6
railing: or railing for r. BIBLE 105:18
R. at life, and yet afraid CHUR 201:3
railroad: You enterprised a r. RUSK 550:16
railway: imposed by r. timetables TAYL 679:6
R. termini FORS 290:8
threatened its life with a r. share CARR 184:5
raiment: body than r. BIBLE 89:9
his r. of camel's hair BIBLE 88:14
King in r. of needlework BOOK 127:13
man clothed in soft r. BIBLE 90:25
rain: able to command the r. PEPYS 512:7
all in the spring r. PAST 508:11
And soft refreshing r. CAMP 176:4
boy, waiting for r. ELIOT 271:10
clouds and wind without r. BIBLE 79:16
clouds return after the r. BIBLE 81:1
droppeth as the gentle r. SHAK 609:13
former and the latter r. BOOK 120:9
going to fall like r. AUDEN 36:13
hard r.'s a gonna fall DYLAN 265:15
Hath the r. a father BIBLE 77:36
Jupiter the R.-giver TIB 698:2
like sunshine after r. SHAK 635:13
more smell the dew and r. HERB 335:3
neither let there be r. BIBLE 75:8
not even the r., has such CUMM 228:15
r. in Spain stays mainly LERN 419:5
r. is destroying his grain HERB 333:16
r. is on our lips SORL 656:16
r. is over and gone BIBLE 81:9
r. it raineth every day SHAK 596:3
r. it raineth every day SHAK 630:37
r., it raineth on the just BOWEN 138:4
r. maketh a hole LAT 411:2
r. of gold and heart's DAY-L 233:4
r. over the dwindling harbour THOM 693:13
Rain! R.! KEATS 391:17
r. when with never a stain SHEL 640:7
sendeth r. on the just BIBLE 88:34
send my roots r. HOPK 346:9
slanted r. passes MAY 455:4
small rain down can r. ANON 19:14
sound of abundance of r. BIBLE 76:3
Still falls the R. SITW 648:13
thirsty earth soaks up the r. COWL 221:7
thou sendest r. BOOK 129:3
through the drizzling r. TENN 683:6
wedding-cake left out in the r. AUDEN 36:19
Which cries against the r. GASC 298:18
which had outwept its r. SHEL 639:15
rainbow: awful r. once in heaven KEATS 388:19
God gave Noah the r. sign ANON 13:17
It was the R. gave thee birth DAV 232:11
Lord survives the r. LOW 430:18
r. and a cuckoo's song DAV 232:10
r. comes and goes WORD 745:10
r. in the sky WORD 745:6
r. in the sky TENN 681:15
r. of the salt sand-wave KEATS 389:6
r. round about the throne BIBLE 106:9
r.'s glory is shed SHEL 641:6
r.'s vernal-tinctured hues AKEN 6:5
simple blessing of a r. ABSE 1:3
Somewhere over the r. HARB 323:13
Unto the r., or with taper SHAK 594:9
rained: r. down manna BOOK 130:11
raineth: R. drop and staineth slop POUND 526:2
rainfall: r. at morning STEV 668:24
rain-green: over the r. grass LEE 415:19
rains: r. pennies from heaven BURKE 160:5
rainy: r. day and a contentious woman
  BIBLE 79:27
r. evening to read this WALT 720:23
r. morrow SHAK 634:13
r. Pleiads wester HOUS 352:2
scudding drifts the r. Hyades TENN 690:1
strangers on a r. day SMART 649:15
raise: Lord shall r. me up RAL 536:3
r. the price of corn BYRON 167:19
R. the stone ANON 17:16

raise: (cont.):
thou'lt r. me with the just GRAH 313:14
raised: r. by a speculator STOWE 670:9
raising: had better stop r. corn LEASE 415:2
raison: *La r. tonne en cratère* POTT 526:1
rake: r. among scholars MAC 435:14
r. turned hermit ALC 8:1
ram: r. caught in a thicket BIBLE 71:6
Rama: In R. was there a voice BIBLE 88:11
ramas: *Verde viento. Verdes r.* GARC 297:13
rampage: On the R. DICK 240:31
rampart: As his corse to the r. WOLFE 740:24
ramparts: fiery r. rise BEAT 56:5
rams: fat of r. BIBLE 74:37
mountains skipped like r. BOOK 133:8
My r. speed not BARN 53:17
Ramsbottom: Mr and Mrs R. EDGAR 266:8
ran: r. before Ahab BIBLE 76:5
So they r., both together BIBLE 97:31
they r. awa', Man! MCL 439:11
ranches: r. of isolation AUDEN 34:14
Randal: your dinner, Lord R. BALL 49:17
random: many a word, at r. spoken
  SCOTT 559:18
rangers: eight bold r. ANON 15:1
Rangoon: R. to Mandalay KIPL 400:1
rank: distinguished by r. or property JUN 383:7
my offence is r. SHAK 577:2
r. is but the guinea's BURNS 161:28
r. me with whom you will METH 458:16
r. pride, and haughtiness ADD 3:17
things r. and gross SHAK 572:12
track marched, r. on rank MER 458:6
unassailable holds on his r. SHAK 591:12
Will r. as an idyll GILB 305:19
ranks: even the r. of Tuscany MAC 436:15
r. of death you'll find MOORE 483:7
r. with wings displayed MILT 467:6
ransack: R. the ocean MARL 446:14
ransom: Of the world's r. SHAK 619:18
ransomed: r., healed, restored LYTE 433:17
rap: r. and knock and enter BROW 148:11
rapacious: r. and licentious soldiery
  BURKE 159:2
rape: A r.! a rape! WEBS 726:6
don't marry it, you r. it DEGAS 234:27
principle of procrastinated r. PRIT 529:17
Raphaels: talked of their R. GOLD 311:7
rapid: This particularly r. GILB 306:20
rapidly: Yes, but not so r. BECK 57:25
rapine: all the r. and injustice SMITH 650:15
through r. to disintegration GLAD 307:14
rapping: r. at my chamber door POE 518:6
rapscallions: kings is mostly r. TWAIN 706:3
rapture: aesthetic and religious r. BELL 60:18
each gay turn thy r. move POPE 521:18
first fine careless r. BROW 150:6
Modified r. GILB 304:26
r. on the lonely shore BYRON 169:13
raptures: r. and roses of vice SWIN 676:9
Illustrious acts high r. WALL 718:16
rara: *R. avis in terris nigroque* JUV 383:24
rare: man of culture r. GILB 305:15
miracle of r. device COL 210:11
r. and delightful and beautiful TRAH 701:11
r. in our pockets the mark CHES 199:9
Rich and r. were the gems MOORE 483:10
She was indeed a r. one WITH 739:14
raree-show: r. of Peter's successor BROW 149:5
rarely: Rarely, r., comest thou SHEL 643:2
rarer: r. spirit never did steer SHAK 566:18
r. than the unicorn JONG 378:3
rari: *r. nantes in gurgite vasto* VIRG 712:3
rascal: rather be called a r. JOHN 374:19
rascality: prudence on r. SHAW 637:30
rascally: r. yea-forsooth knave SHAK 582:15
rascals: R., would you live for ever FRED 293:12
rash: Her r. hand in evil hour MILT 472:24
He was not r. GRAH 313:17
It is too r., too unadvised SHAK 623:3
You look rather r. my dear ASHF 31:6
rat: Cat, the R., and Lovell COLL 213:3
giant r. of Sumatra DOYLE 256:9

reason: *(cont.)*:
r. of the strongest — LA F 405:11
r. produces monsters — GOYA 313:5
R. still keeps its throne — FARQ 280:24
r. themselves out again — SHAK 587:1
R. to rule, but mercy — DRYD 260:22
r. why gunpowder treason — ANON 17:11
right deed for the wrong r. — ELIOT 272:10
ruling passion conquers r. — POPE 520:16
show no r. can — WATK 722:6
suspect that it is not his r. — STER 664:23
That takes the r. prisoner — SHAK 600:8
that wants discourse of r. — SHAK 572:12
their feelings than by r. — ADAMS 3:8
Their's not to r. why — TENN 683:15
There is nothing without a r. — LEIB 416:15
To rules of r., holy messengers — HERB 335:19
ultimate r. of things — LEIB 416:13
ultimate triumph of human r. — HAWK 328:7
voice of r. is stifled — BURKE 157:9
What I. I should be the same — AYT 41:1
which r. knows nothing of — PASC 507:17
who listens to R. is lost — SHAW 637:33
will not r. and compare — BLAKE 112:1
words clothed in r.'s garb — MILT 469:16
worse appear the better r. — MILT 469:13
reasonable: figure of 'The R. Man' — HERB 334:1
r. man adapts himself — SHAW 637:32
r. soul and human flesh — BOOK 119:15
rightful must be r. — JEFF 364:3
They were r. people — BROO 144:1
reasonableness: sweet r. — ARN 30:4
reasoning: cowards in r. — SHAF 563:21
contain any abstract r. — HUME 355:4
Huddled in dirt the r. engine — ROCH 543:12
r., self-sufficing thing — WORD 746:15
truth by consecutive r. — KEATS 391:6
reasons: against the r. of my love — FORD 289:13
five r. we should drink — ALDR 8:5
Good r. must, of force — SHAK 593:11
lose the r. for living — JUV 384:4
R. are not like garments — ESSEX 278:14
r. find of settled gravity — SHAK 633:15
r. for having children — RUSS 551:27
r. for the rule change — STR 670:24
r. for what we believe — BRAD 139:3
r. will certainly be wrong — MANS 445:11
reason'st: Plato, thou r. well — ADD 3:23
reassure: O speak to r. me — BODE 116:11
rebecks: jocund r. sound — MILT 465:13
rebel: die like a true-blue r. — HILL 338:13
R. without a cause — LIND 423:1
There's an experienced r. — FLAT 285:15
very r. to my will — SHAK 566:3
What is a r.? — CAMUS 177:17
rebelled: r. against the words — BOOK 132:15
rebellion: furious secret r. — SHAW 636:15
little r. now and then — JEFF 364:8
r. is as the sin of witchcraft — BIBLE 74:37
R. lay in his way — SHAK 581:28
R. to tyrants is obedience — BRAD 139:9
r. was the certain consequence — MANS 445:10
ruin, Romanism, and r. — BURC 156:18
rebellions: everyday r. — STEI 663:11
rebellious: r. arm 'gainst arm — SHAK 599:17
revolting and a r. heart — BIBLE 85:5
waves, that in r. bands — DAN 229:12
rebels: r. from principle — BURKE 158:17
reborn: r. as an idea — YEATS 753:22
rebounds: hit hard, unless it r. — JOHN 373:27
rebuild: r. it on the old plan — MILL 460:10
rebuke: Open r. is better than — DIDLE 79.25
r. hath broken my heart — BOOK 129:12
r. the people — BOOK 135:16
recall: cannot r. their gifts — TENN 689:11
word takes wing beyond r. — HOR 348:12
recalled: once spoke can never be r. — DILL 246:2
receipt: at the r. of custom — BIBLE 90:4
receive: more blessed to give than to r. — BIBLE 99:4
r. one such little child — BIBLE 91:18
we r. but what we give — COL 209:14

received: by him best r. — MILT 471:6
Freely ye have r. — BIBLE 90:14
his own r. him not — BIBLE 96:3
receiver: left the r. off the hook — KOES 403:21
r. is always thought as bad — CHES 198:1
receives: That watches and r. — WORD 748:8
receiveth: that asketh r. — BIBLE 89:18
receiving: giving and r. of a Ring — BOOK 123:23
recesses: r. in my mind — BRON 142:5
recession: r. when your neighbour — TRUM 704:19
recherche: *A la r. du temps perdu* — PROU 530:5
recipes: r. that are always successful — VALÉ 707:21
recirculation: vicus of r. — JOYCE 380:21
recited: r. verses in writing — BIBLE 88:1
reckless: I am r. what I do — SHAK 603:1
reckoned: love that can be r. — SHAK 564:13
reckoning: No r. made — SHAK 573:20
O, weary r. — SHAK 617:5
sense of r. — SHAK 600.9
very much at your own r. — TROL 704:7
recks: And r. not his own rede — SHAK 573:2
reclamation: It is land r. — WILS 738:4
reclothe: R. us in our rightful mind — WHIT 733:7
recognition: one shock of r. — MELV 456:13
recognize: did not r. me by my face — SHAK 573:2
only a trial if I r. it as such — KAFKA 384:16
recognized: Present themselves as objects r. — WORD 747:4
recoil: I r. and droop — WORD 746:18
recommendation: face is a letter of r. — ADD 4:10
recompense: r. is a pleasure — JOHN 369:15
reconciles: dinner and feasting r. — PEPYS 512:15
reconciliation: silence and r. — MAC 435:11
reconnaissance: *La r. de la plupart* — LA R 410:20
record: r. of blissful old times — BLAM 114:20
r. on the gramophone — ELIOT 273:10
recordanti: *r. benefacta priora* — CAT 186:12
recorded: r. experience — CARL 180:6
recorders: Of flutes and soft r. — MILT 468:24
recording: domesticate the R. Angel — STEV 668:6
records: all trivial fond r. — SHAK 573:22
recover: r. the use of his legs — DICK 242:8
seldom or never r. — SHAK 567:3
thou might'st him yet r. — DRAY 258:1
recovered: tyme ylost may nought r. — CHAU 195:23
recreant: that soldier a mere r. prove — SHAK 627:10
recreate: r. yourselves — SHAK 592:18
recrudescence: R. of Puritanism — RUSS 551:23
rectangular: Her proceedings are quite r. — BYRON 173:23
recte: *Si possis r.* — HOR 347:22
Vivere r. nescis — HOR 348:21
rectum: finger in the throat and one in the r. — OSLER 502:1
recurret: *tamen usque r.* — HOR 348:8
red: Better r. than dead — ANON 12:14
In r. weather — STEV 665:17
it's not even r. brick — OSB 501:15
Making the green one r. — SHAK 602:6
more red than her lips' r. — SHAK 635:2
my Luve's like a r. red rose — BURNS 162:27
Nor dim nor r. — COL 210:23
Nose, nose, jolly r. nose — BEAU 56:13
r. flag flying here — CONN 216:8
R. hair she had and golden — BETJ 67:16
r. in my mind — DICK 245:5
r. in tooth and claw — TENN 683:22
R. lips are not so red — OWEN 503:15
r. men scalped each other — MAC 434:7
r. rose from off this thorn — SHAK 587:9
r. wheel barrow — WILL 737:11
that never blows so r. — FITZ 283:16
thin r. line tipped with steel — RUSS 552:5
this cheek a little r. — POPE 520:30
To get very r. in the face — BENT 64:9
your raiment all r. — MAC 436:4
redbreast: r. whistles from a garden-croft — KEATS 390:21

red deer: last remnant of the r.'s herd — BYRON 172:14
rede: And recks not his own r. — SHAK 573:2
redeem: R. thy mis-spent time — KEN 393:6
redeemed: hath r. Jerusalem — BIBLE 84:9
were r. from the earth — BIBLE 107:2
redeemer: earned such a mighty R. — MISS 477:16
Guide where our infant R. — HEBER 330:2
I know that my r. liveth — BIBLE 77:25
my strength, and my r. — BOOK 125:6
Our blest R., ere he breathed — AUBER 32:20
To thee, R., King — NEALE 491:4
redeeming: r. fires — GONC 312:9
R. the time — BIBLE 102:22
redemption: married past r. — DRYD 261:5
r. from above did bring — MILT 466:20
r.'s happy dawn — CASW 185:4
redemptorem: *tantum meruit habere R.* — MISS 477:16
red-haired: r. girls scamper — LEE 415:19
redress: And for r. of all my pain — WYATT 749:17
Things past r. are now — SHAK 620:1
redtape: r. talking-machine — CARL 181:1
redwood: r. forest to the Gulf Stream — GUTH 320:5
re-echo: Each jubilant chord r. around — BAKER 47:21
reed: and clasped a r. — SHEL 640:17
bruised r. shall he not break — BIBLE 84:2
Man is only a r. — PASC 507:18
Not as a nymph, but for a r. — MARV 450:8
r. shaken with the wind — BIBLE 90:25
spring up into beauty like a r. — LEWES 420:12
staff of this bruised r. — BIBLE 76:31
To thee the r. is as the oak — SHAK 571:16
reeds: Down in the r. by the river — BROW 147:17
surf floods over the r. — PAST 508:10
reeking: r. into Cadiz Bay — BROW 150:7
reel: R. in a drunkard — CHUR 201:5
They r. to and fro — BOOK 133:2
reeled: until r. the mind — GIBBS 302:26
reels: There's threesome r. — BURNS 161:22
references: verify your r. — ROUTH 549:4
refine: correct, insert, r. — SWIFT 675:1
r. our language to grammatical — JOHN 369:17
refined: disgust this r. age — EVEL 279:8
r. citizens of a nation — SHEL 644:10
R. himself to soul — DRYD 260:7
r. out of existence — JOYCE 381:13
r. sentiments are the most — KELLY 393:3
r. with th'accents — DAN 230:2
This Englishwoman is so r. — SMITH 652:20
reflections: bloody r. still remain — BLOK 115:5
reflex: cut across the r. of a star — WORD 744:10
reform: cured by r. or revolution — BERL 66:1
lunatic fringe in all r. — ROOS 546:13
party of progress or r. — MILL 460:17
retrenchment, and r. — BRIG 141:7
that in which it sets about r. — TOCQ 699:1
To innovate is not to r. — BURKE 157:6
when they are able to r. — MORE 484:3
reformation: plotting some new r. — DRYD 261:15
reforming of R. itself — MILT 475:11
reformer: r. is a guy who — MIZN 478:12
reformers: All r. are bachelors — MOORE 482:8
All R., however strict — SMITH 652:10
consolations of middle-aged r. — SAKI 553:5
refresh: r. it when it was dry — BOOK 120:9
refreshed: giant r. with wine — BOOK 130:12
refuge: eternal God is thy r. — BIBLE 73:24
God of Jacob is our r. — BOOK 127:16
home is his safest r. — COKE 209:1
Idleness is only the r. of weak — CHES 198:18
last r. of a scoundrel — JOHN 374:2
r. for the wild goats — BOOK 132:9
r. from home life — SHAW 638:27
so easy to take r. in — IBSEN 358:16
thou hast been our r. — BOOK 130:22
refugees: guttural sorrow of the r. — MACN 440:16
refusal: The great r. — DANTE 230:8

refuse: if you please, r.　MARV 451:2
make him an offer he can't r.　PUZO 533:7
may know to r. the evil　BIBLE 82:24
R. his age the needful hours　DRYD 259:2
r. of your teeming shore　LAZ 413:7
when men r. to fight　ANON 19:5
Which he did thrice r.　SHAK 592:8
refused: stone which the builders r.
　BOOK 133:16
refuses: Closes nothing, r. nothing　WHIT 733:1
refute: I r. it *thus*　JOHN 372:22
Who can r. a sneer　PALEY 505:6
regarder: *On doit se r. soi-même*　MOL 479:6
regardeth: he that r. the clouds　BIBLE 80:27
regardless: r. of their doom　GRAY 316:2
regards: mingled with r.　SHAK 594:23
regeneration: baptism, a r.　ELIOT 268:18
regent: R. of love rhymes　SHAK 598:13
reges: *delirant r. plectuntur*　HOR 348:2
regiment: Monstrous R. of Women　KNOX 403:4
then comes up the R.　KIPL 398:19
within our breasts for r.　MARL 448:1
regina: *Salve,*　ANON 22:14
region: Is this the r.　MILT 468:11
main r. of my song　WORD 746:7
untrodden r. of my mind　KEATS 389:20
regions: Double-lived in r. new　KEATS 386:7
register: r. is either　GIBB 302:2
registered: r. upon our brazen tombs
　SHAK 598:6
regnavit: *R. a ligno Deus*　FORT 291:3
regnum: *adveniat r. tuum*　MISS 477:3
regress: r. is either　BACON 43:29
regret: O last r.　TENN 684:2
Old Age a r.　DISR 248:5
vain r.　ROSS 548:4
wild with all r.　TENN 688:6
regrets: And the wild r.　WILDE 736:4
Miss Otis r.　PORT 525:3
past and future fears　FITZ 283:17
series of congratulatory r.　DISR 247:28
regular: brought r. and draw'd mild
　DICK 241:15
icily r., splendidly null　TENN 686:7
normative or r., science　KEYN 395:13
regularity: genius and r. are enemies
　GAIN 296:13
regulate: r. all recreations　MILT 475:8
regulated: R. hatred　HARD 324:1
Regulations Act: was strung upon the R.
　WILDE 736:2
Reich: *Ein R., ein Volk*　ANON 21.10
reign: Better to r. in hell　MILT 468:13
but friendless is to r.　SHEL 642:15
Long to r. over us　HOGG 341:17
r. is worth ambition　MILT 468:18
r. of Chaos and old Night　MILT 468:23
Than r. in this horrible place　COWP 224:15
reigned: r. with your loves　ELIZ 274:4
reigning: capable of r. if only　TAC 678:3
he answered 'r.'　BENT 64:5
reigns: For the red blood r.　SHAK 631:24
king r.　THIE 692:1
reindeer: Herds of r. move　AUDEN 34:11
Rudolph, the Red-Nosed R.　MARKS 446:8
reinforcement: r. we may gain from hope
　MILT 468:9
reins: try out my r.　BOOK 125:21
reject: If you r. me　BELL 62:5
time to r. it　JACK 361:5
rejected: despised and r. of men　BIBLE 84:11
rejoice: daughters of the Philistines r.
　BIBLE 75:8
desert shall r.　BIBLE 83:19
have faith and r. in Christ　LUTH 432:9
let us heartily r.　BOOK 131:9
little hills shall r.　BOOK 129:3
R. evermore　BIBLE 103:22
R. in the Lord alway　BIBLE 103:11
r. the heart　BOOK 125:5
R., the Lord is King　WESL 728:13
r. when they divide　BIBLE 82:26

rejoice: (cont.):
R. with them that do rejoice　BIBLE 100:4
we will r. and be glad　BOOK 133:16
which thou hast broken may r.　BOOK 128:5
rejoiced: R. they were na men, but dogs
　BURNS 163:26
rejoiceth: r. as a giant to run　BOOK 125:4
r. in his strength　BIBLE 77:38
rejoicing: And home, r., brought me
　BAKER 47:20
r. with heaven and earth　MILT 476:1
relation: cold r. is a zealous citizen
　BURKE 158:27
nobody like a r. to do　THAC 691:14
poor r.　LAMB 406:19
State is a r. of men dominating　WEBER 724:21
relations: God's apology for r.　KING 398:7
offensive in personal r.　RUSS 551:12
or to visit r.　AUDEN 35:10
personal character and r.　NAP 489:12
Personal r. are the important　FORS 290:13
r. they find already existing　MILL 460:23
relationship: officialism every human r.
suffers　FORS 290:25
relationships: psychology of human r.
　BERNE 66:10
relative: In a r. way　BULL 154:17
Success is r.　ELIOT 270:11
relatives: hate all the people your r. hate
　HAMM 323:2
relativity: If my theory of r. is proven
　EINS 268:3
relax: r. the stricture of these bonds
　STEV 667:15
relaxes: Bless r.　BLAKE 112:26
release: Ensured r.　HOUS 352:4
relent: make the gods above r.　VIRG 714:3
Shall make him once r.　BUNY 156:14
relevance: r. it does not seem to try　WILB 734:4
relic: cased up, like a holy r.　WEBS 725:16
sad r. of departed worth　BYRON 168:9
relics: hallowed r. should be hid　MILT 466:17
unhonoured his r. are laid　MOORE 483:9
with thise r.　CHAU 193:8
relief: And not seek for kind r.　BLAKE 114.3
Browning's death is rather a r.　FITZ 284:18
For spoiling our r.　GASC 298:18
my r. must be to loathe her　SHAK 616:16
r. of man's estate　BACON 41:17
utterance gave that thought r.　WORD 745:11
relieve: comfort and r. them　BOOK 120:7
relieved: By desperate appliances are r.
　SHAK 677:27
religion: affront her r. and debauch　JENY 365:9
airy subtleties in r.　BROW 146:2
are all of the same r.　DISR 248:13
are really but of one r.　SHAF 563:20
Art and R. are means　BELL 60:18
As great in love as in r.　COWL 221:15
As if R. were intended　BUTL 166:6
As rum and true r.　BYRON 170:16
As to r., I hold it to be　PAINE 504:11
becomes an act of duty and r.　OSB 501:7
brothels with bricks of R.　BLAKE 112:23
can't talk r. to a man with　SHAW 636:30
England but vice and r.　SMITH 653:24
enough r. to make us hate　SWIFT 674:14
fox-hunting—the wisest r.　HAIL 320:13
Freedom of r.　JEFF 364:6
from the dominion of r.　GOLD 310:4
full of r., knavery　BEHN 60:12
genius in r.　ARN 30:5
handmaid to r.　BACON 42:8
honesty not to be based either on r.
　RUSK 550:26
I count r. but a childish toy　MARL 447:12
impossibilities enough in r.　BROW 146:2
increase in us true r.　BOOK 121:5
indirect way to plant r.　BROW 146:9
in every thing that regards r.　ADD 4:18
In their r. they are so uneven　DEFOE 234:20
inward tranquillity which r.　FORB 288:19
Knight-errantry *is* r.　CERV 188:11

religion: (cont.):
knows of no r. but social　WESL 728:17
leave him for r.　SPARK 658:4
men's minds about to r.　BACON 42:23
Millionaire. That is my r.　SHAW 636:29
more fierce in its r. than　NEWM 492:15
my r. is to do good　PAINE 505:1
mysteries of our r.　HOBB 340:11
no reason to bring r. into it　O'CAS 497:18
not a r. for gentlemen　CHAR 191:15
One r. is as true as another　BURT 165:13
original feature of *any* r.　PAINE 504:19
Poetry and R. a product of　CARL 180:16
Poetry is a r. with no hope　COCT 208:6
politics as well as in r.　JUN 383:6
reject me on account of my r.　BELL 62:5
r. and matrimony I never　CHES 198:2
r., and not atheism　BURKE 157:27
r. and philosophy will be　ARN 29:22
r., as a mere sentiment　NEWM 493:1
r. at the lowest　CHES 198:19
r. becomes really frantic　MELV 456:16
R. blushing veils her sacred　POPE 519:11
r. breathing household　WORD 746:10
r. for religion's sake　COUS 220:6
r. into after-dinner toasts　NEWM 493:7
r. is allowed to invade　MELB 456:11
R. is an all-important matter　NAP 489:11
R. is by no means a proper　CHES 198:3
r. is made so as to wipe　MONT 481:6
r. is not circumambient　FOST 291:9
R. is the frozen thought　KRIS 404:2
R. is the opium of the people　MARX 452:2
r. is whatever he is most　BARR 54:11
r., justice, counsel　BACON 44.18
r. most prevalent in our　BURKE 157:24
r. of gold　BAG 46:21
r. of humanity　PAINE 504:14
r. of Socialism　BEVAN 68:14
R.'s in the heart　JERR 365:18
r. that has any thing in it　PAINE 504:8
r. when in rags and contempt　BUNY 156:1
r. without a prelate　BANC 51:11
r. without science is blind　EINS 268:6
R.? Yes; but which of all　BYRON 171:32
reproach to r. and government　PENN 511:14
science is strong and r. weak　SZASZ 677:15
slovenliness is no part of r.　WESL 728:23
So much wrong could r. induce　LUCR 431:13
start your own r.　HUBB 353:14
substitute for r.　ELIOT 273:21
Superstition is the r.　BURKE 158:23
take my r. from the priest　GOLD 311:35
talks loudly against r.　STER 664:23
There is only one r.　SHAW 638:14
this man's r. is vain　BIBLE 104:28
To become a popular r.　INGE 359:14
too late to trust the old r.　LOW 430:21
true meaning of r.　ARN 30:2
When I mention r.　FIEL 282:10
Who had only a little r.　ANON 20:11
religions: are sixty different r.　CAR 178:16
neurotics have founded r.　PROU 530:11
R. are kept alive by heresies　BREN 140:13
r. considered man as man　TOCQ 698:12
r. have produced no religious　CLARK 205:8
religious: appeals to r. prejudice　HUXL 358:12
between aesthetic and r. rapture　BELL 60:18
commit himself to any r. belief
　WAUGH 723:14
decay of monasteries and of r.　SKEL 649:4
driving force of all r.　WEBER 725:2
his money and his r. opinions　BUTL 167:6
I hope I will be r. again　FLEM 287:4
intellect in r. enquiries　NEWM 493:4
Man is a r. animal　BURKE 158:19
r. alacrity　DONNE 253:6
r. and moral principles　ARN 30:13
r. art of the world　CLARK 205:8
r. factions are volcanoes　BURKE 159:7
R. persecution may shield　BURKE 159:13
r. wave in American history　WOLFE 741:8
seem to be r.　BIBLE 104:28

religious: (*cont.*):
suspended my r. enquiries — GIBB 302:13
With a r. book, or friend — WOTT 749:1
religious-good: Good, but not r. — HARDY 324:19
relish: some r. of the saltness — SHAK 582:16
relished: taste by which he is to be r.
— WORD 748:20
reluctance: r. to sit for a picture — JOHN 375:12
rem: *quocumque modo r.* — HOR 347:22
remain: amongst you and r. with you
— BOOK 122:15
days go by, I r. — APOL 23:15
fragments that r. — BIBLE 96:23
things have been, things r. — CLOU 207:23
remained: else perished, and he r. — BRON 142:18
remains: look on love's r. — BROW 151:29
nothing done while aught r. — ROG 544:11
r., *however improbable* — DOYLE 256:18
Strength in what r. behind — WORD 746:6
waste the r. of life — WALP 719:9
remake: It is myself that I r. — YEATS 751:19
remark: Which I wish to r. — HARTE 327:17
remarkable: nothing left r. — SHAK 566:15
This very r. man — INGE 359:11
remarks: R. are not literature — STEIN 663:2
said our r. before — DON 250:5
remedies: encumbering it with r. — TOLS 701:1
Our r. oft in ourselves do lie — SHAK 564:4
that will not apply new r. — BACON 43:33
remedy: Force is not a r. — BRIG 141:12
Heretics are the only bitter r. — ZAMY 755:5
know not how to r. our own — KYD 404:12
My dog! what r. remains — COWP 222:23
r. is death — CHAM 189:11
r. is worse than the disease — BACON 44:21
requires a dangerous r. — FAWK 281:6
Things without all r. — SHAK 603:3
'Tis a sharp r. — RAL 536:7
remember: Ah yes! I r. it well — LERN 419:2
And if thou wilt, r. — ROSS 547:12
But he'll r. with advantages — SHAK 586:11
don't you r. sweet Alice — ENGL 277:24
Do you r. an Inn, Miranda — BELL 62:1
If I do not r. thee — BOOK 134:17
I r., I remember — HOOD 343:21
I r. the way we parted — SWIN 676:23
I would r. Him — BEEC 59:6
long as I can r. who I am — VIRG 713:6
Must I r.? — SHAK 572:12
no greater pain than to r. — DANTE 230:11
nor long r., what we say — LINC 422:10
Or not r. what I must be now — SHAK 620:11
r. even these things — VIRG 712:6
R. me, but ah! forget my fate — TATE 678:15
R. me when I am dead — DOUG 255:12
R. me when I am gone away — ROSS 547:7
r. me when thou comest — BIBLE 95:26
r. not past years — NEWM 493:15
R. now thy Creator — BIBLE 81:1
r. of this unstable world — MAL 443:8
R. that we are English — AUST 39:1
r. the black wharves — LONG 427:4
R. thee! Ay, thou poor ghost — SHAK 573:22
r. the Fifth of November — ANON 17:11
R. the sabbath day — BIBLE 72:16
r. what is past — HAL 321:11
r. while the light lives — SWIN 676:13
should, yet never can, r. — THOM 694:4
Till thou r. and I forget — SWIN 676:26
To r. or invent — FROST 295:1
To r. with tears — ALL 10:2
We will r. them — BINY 109:20
Yes; I r. Adlestrop — THOM 693:23
You must r. this, a kiss — HUPF 357:2
you should r. and be sad — ROSS 547:8
remembered: blue r. hills — HOUS 352:15
flowing cups freshly r. — SHAK 586:11
my youth I r. my God — SOUT 657:14
none are undeservedly r. — AUDEN 36:17
r. for a very long time — MCG 437:17
would have made myself r. — KEATS 392:13
remembering: R. without ceasing — BIBLE 103:19
soul r. my good friends — SHAK 619:20

remembers: R. me of all his gracious
— SHAK 594:4
remember'st: r. not the slightest folly
— SHAK 568:4
remembrance: almost a r. — KEATS 391:14
dear r. of his dying Lord — SPEN 659:21
Do this in r. of me — BOOK 122:12
Down in the flood of r. — LAWR 412:17
In the r. of a weeping queen — SHAK 620:16
Makes the r. dear — SHAK 564:11
r. more than things long — SHAK 619:16
r. of a guest that tarrieth — BIBLE 87:5
r. of his holiness — BOOK 126:5
r. of my former love — SHAK 631:5
r. of them is grievous — BOOK 122:6
R. of things past — PROU 530:5
r. of things past — SHAK 633:11
rosemary, that's for r. — SHAK 578:7
shall be had in everlasting r. — BOOK 133:6
remembren: it r., whan it passed is
— CHAU 106:20
remind: R. me of you — MARV 451:14
reminiscence: A r. sing — WHIT 732:8
reminiscences: R. make one feel — SHAW 636:22
some of your grosser r. — WOOL 742:17
remission: for the r. of sins — BOOK 122:12
r. of pain or guilt — BOOK 135:25
shedding of blood is no r. — BIBLE 104:11
remnant: Here will I smell my r. out
— HERB 335:7
r. of the red-deer's herd — BYRON 172:14
remorse: access and passage to r. — SHAK 600:16
rather feel r. than know — THOM 692:2
R. is surely the most wasteful — FORS 290:16
R., the fatal egg by pleasure — COWP 223:3
R.! Those dry Martinis — ADE 5:5
Shun delays, they breed r. — SOUT 658:1
remorseful: r. day — SHAK 587:20
remote: r. my enquiries — JOHN 368:22
R. and ineffectual Don — BELL 61:14
remoter: no need of a r. charm — WORD 744:21
removals: infidelity and household r.
— BAUD 55:12
remove: fat greedy owl of the R. — RICH 540:7
not malignant and r. it — WAUGH 724:9
R. hence to yonder place — BIBLE 91:16
R. not the ancient landmark — BIBLE 79:12
remover: bends with the r. — SHAK 634:23
renaissance: English R. — LAWR 412:2
Wake in her warm nest of r. — DAY-L 233:3
renard: *Certain r. voulut* — LA F 405:14
render: r. the deeds of mercy — SHAK 609:13
R. therefore to all their — BIBLE 100:9
R. therefore unto Caesar — BIBLE 92:2
rendezvous: I have a r. with Death — SEEG 561:18
My r. is appointed — WHIT 732:20
renew: r. a right spirit — BOOK 128:6
shall r. their strength — BIBLE 84:1
renewed: r. in knowledge — BIBLE 103:16
renewing: r. is of love — EDW 267:11
Reno'd: King's Moll R. — ANON 15:15
renounce: the devil and all — BOOK 123:4
r. war for its consequences — FOSD 291:4
renown: land of just and old r. — TENN 690:7
r. on scraps of learning dote — YOUNG 754:6
'Twas I that gave thee thy r. — CAREW 179:6
were of old, men of r. — BIBLE 70:25
rent: R. is that portion — RIC 539:23
That has not been r. — YEATS 751:8
why? for r. — BYRON 167:20
repair: friendship in constant r. — JOHN 371:21
repartee: majority is best r. — DISR 248:31
repay: I will r., saith the Lord — BIBLE 100:6
I will r. thee — BIBLE 94:15
Will find a Tiger well r. — BELL 60:24
repeal: r. of bad or obnoxious — GRANT 314:10
repeat: Historians r. each other — GUED 319:11
neither r. his past nor leave it — AUDEN 36:15
past are condemned to r. it — SANT 555:16
repeateth: a matter separateth — BIBLE 78:39
repeats: r. his words — SHAK 594:4
repel: retard what we cannot r. — JOHN 367:23

repelled: only r. by man — INGE 359:15
repent: from their marble caves r.
— DRUM 258:12
have no strength to r. — SHAK 581:16
I do r. it from my very soul — SHAK 627:3
It doth r. me — SHEL 642:9
No follies to have to r. — TAYL 679:15
nor falter, nor r. — SHEL 642:20
R. what's past — SHAK 577:19
R. ye — BIBLE 88:12
truly and earnestly r. — BOOK 122:5
weak alone r. — BYRON 169:21
we may r. at leisure — CONG 215:25
repentance: morning cool r. came
— SCOTT 560:29
R. is but want of power to sin — DRYD 261:12
R. is the hire — SCOTT 559:1
R. is the virtue of weak minds — DRYD 260:30
R. on a Sunday — YBAR 750:14
sinners to r. — BIBLE 90:7
Where pleasure and r. dwell — RAL 535:13
repente: *Nemo r. fuit turpissimus* — JUV 383:18
repented: strove, and much r. — BYRON 170:10
repenteth: Me r., said Merlin — MAL 443:4
over one sinner that r. — BIBLE 95:1
repenting: r. at leisure — THOM 694:7
that after no r. draws — MILT 474:25
repetition: nagging is the r. — SUMM 672:1
repetitions: Use not vain r. — BIBLE 89:4
repetitious: r. mechanism of the Universe
— WHIT 731:9
replenish: r. the earth — BIBLE 69:26
replete: r. with too much rage — SHAK 633:7
reply: I pause for a r. — SHAK 592:4
r. churlish — SHAK 569:26
Their's not to make r. — TENN 680:14
report: are of good r. — BIBLE 103:13
R. me and my cause aright — SHAK 579:9
Who hath believed our r. — BIBLE 84:10
reporters: through r. to Buncombe
— CARL 180:31
reports: Bring me no more r. — SHAK 604:19
R. of my death have been — TWAIN 706:25
repose: Creation to a stunned r. — HILL 338:10
Inly I sigh for thy r. — WESL 728:16
r. is insupportable — ADAMS 2:23
r. is taboo'd by anxiety — GILB 304:14
r. of a pacific station — ADAMS 1:13
sleep should be his last r. — ANON 19:19
To weave the garlands of r. — MARV 450:5
representation: Taxation and r. — CAMD 176:2
Taxation without r. — OTIS 502:7
representations: just r. of general nature
— JOHN 369:6
representative: called a r. government
— DISR 248:30
indignity of being your r. — BELL 62:5
Your r. owes you — BURKE 158:31
repress: r. the speech they know — ELIOT 269:2
repression: forced r. — MILL 460:25
reproach: eternal r. of our divines — MILT 476:3
reproche: *Chevalier sans peur et sans r.*
— ANON 20:8
reproof: r. valiant — SHAK 569:26
reproofs: r. from authority — BACON 43:30
reprove: To check the erring, and r.
— WORD 746:9
reptile: r. all the rest — POPE 520:6
turn myself into a r. — JOHN 371:24
republic: England is a disguised r. — BAG 47:1
essence of the R. — ROB 542:5
Love the Beloved R. — FORS 290:30
R. is a Government of laws — FORD 289:2
r. is a raft which would — AMES 10:9
r. is like a chicken — MITF 478:6
republican: acrimonious and surly r.
— JOHN 369:2
R. form of Government is — SPEN 658:13
r. government in the United — TOCQ 699:4
Republicans: stop telling the truth about the R.
— STEV 666:15
We are R. — BURC 156:18

rich: *(cont.)*:
r. in a more precious treasure   MAC 434:18
R. in the simple worship   KEATS 388:22
r. man in his castle   ALEX 8:10
r. man to enter into   BIBLE 91:25
r. man without money   UST 707:13
R. men furnished with ability   BIBLE 88:1
r. men rule the law   GOLD 311:11
r., not gaudy   SHAK 753:4
r. richer and the poor   NEHRU 491:8
r. shall not be innocent   BIBLE 79:29
r. society and the powerful   JOHN 367:8
r. wage war it's the poor   SART 556:6
save the few who are r.   KENN 393:13
seems it r. to die   KEATS 389:14
ten thousand times more r.   SHAK 609:2
that art most r.   SHAK 594:24
There was a certain r. man   BIBLE 96:9
very r. in subjects   DEFOE 234:11
When a r. man is fallen   BIBLE 87:21
Richard: Did scowl on R.   SHAK 621:7
R.'s himself again   CIBB 203:22
To put down R.   SHAK 579:33
Richardson: read R. for the story   JOHN 373:19
richer: Becomes the r. still   BUTL 166:21
for r. for poorer   BOOK 123:20
R. than all his tribe   SHAK 618:20
riches: beggar amidst great r.   HOR 350:7
best r., ignorance of wealth   GOLD 305:6
deceitfulness of r.   BIBLE 91:2
earth is full of thy r.   BOOK 132:9
embarrassment of r.   ALL 9:7
he heapeth up r.   BOOK 126:23
he that getteth r.   BIBLE 85:13
if r. increase   BOOK 128:20
Infinite r. in a little room   MARL 447:13
leave their r. for other   BOOK 127:24
left hand r. and honour   BIBLE 78:8
Let the world's r.   HERB 335:14
material and spiritual r.   KHR 395:16
parade of r.   SMITH 650:19
poverty nor r.   BIBLE 79:32
R. are a good handmaid   BACON 42:12
R. are for spending   BACON 43:15
r. grow in hell   MILT 469:5
r. left, not got with pain   SURR 672:2
r. of heaven's pavement   MILT 469:4
R., the dumb god that giv'st   JONS 379:1
r. to be a valuable thing   SWIFT 670:2
r. to those gross asses   LUTH 432:16
that of the titled for r.   PEAR 510:15
unsearchable r. of Christ   BIBLE 102:12
When r. do abound   GOOGE 312:11
richest: r. without meaning   RUSK 550:22
richly: lady r. left   SHAK 607:10
Richmond: lass of R. Hill   MACN 440:11
richness: all in a rush with r.   HOPK 346:1
Here's r.   DICK 242:3
ricordarsi: *Che r. del tempo*   DANTE 230:11
rid: mad till you are r. of 'em   VANB 708:8
purely to be r. of thee   CONG 215:26
time we got r. of Him   BALD 48:5
To mend it or be r. on't   SHAK 603:1
riddance: die and be a r.   DICK 239:21
riddle: had not found out my r.   BIBLE 74:15
or dishcover the r.   CARR 183:26
read me this r.   WAT 722:5
r. of the sands   CHIL 199:25
r. of the world   POPE 522:10
r. wrapped in a mystery   CHUR 202:7
riddles: R. lie here   CLEV 206:13
ride: Haggards r. no more   STEP 663:18
if you cannot r. two horses   MAXT 454:15
Just to r. the ponies   COHAN 208:13
midnight r. of Paul Revere   LONG 427:19
r. in a hole in the ground   COMD 214:11
r. in triumph through Persepolis
    MARL 447:24
R. on! ride on in majesty   MILM 462:7
She's got a ticket to r.   LENN 418:2
we r. them down   TENN 688:8
Who went for a r. on a tiger   ANON 17:13
ridentem: *Dulce r.*   HOR 349:12

ridentem: *(cont.)*:
Dulce r.   CAT 186:7
rider: between a r. and his horse   SURT 672:22
want of a horse the r. was lost   FRAN 292:18
rides: And r. upon the storm   COWP 222:17
ridete: *R. quidquid est domi*   CAT 186:3
rideth: r. upon the heavens   BOOK 129:7
ridicule: liable to r. in any subject   SHAF 563:22
r. is the best test of truth   CHES 198:20
stand the test of r.   SHAF 563:21
ridiculos: *r. homines facit*   JUV 383:21
ridiculous: fine sense of the r.   ALBEE 7:8
from the sublime to the r.   NAP 489:16
heart of the r., the sublime   MAHON 442:5
one step above the r.   PAINE 504:9
position r.   CHES 198:25
R. and lovely   BUNT 155:9
spectacle so r. as the British   MAC 434:19
Sublime to the R.   GRAH 313:10
wasteful and r. excess   SHAK 594:9
riding: man goes r. by   STEV 668:21
nation was r. that night   LONG 427:20
r. at breakneck speed towards   BLAN 115:1
r. on a smile and a shoeshine   MILL 461:17
Ridley: good comfort Master R.   LAT 411:3
riff-raff: r. apply to what is respectable
    HOPE 344:23
rifle: r. all the breathing spring   COLL 213:10
r. and blow out your brains   KIPL 401:12
r.-butts   BLOK 115:6
rift: little r. within the lute   TENN 682:10
load every r. with ore   KEATS 392:15
rigged: r. with curses dark   MILT 466:6
riggish: Bless her when she is r.   SHAK 565:8
right: All's r. with the world   BROW 151:28
all the earth do r.   BIBLE 71:2
almost always in the r.   SMITH 653:22
because not all was r.   CRAD 226:6
decorative and to do r.   FIRB 282:25
defend to the death your r.   VOLT 717:5
discussion of any subject is a r.   SHEL 644:2
doeth the thing which is r.   BOOK 124:28
do what is r.   HUXL 358:5
everyone is r.   LA CH 405:6
every single one of them is r.   KIPL 399:11
generalities of natural r.   CHOA 200:2
grounded on just and r.   MILT 472:16
half of the people are r.   WHITE 731:3
has no more r. to be obeyed   JOHN 366:10
heaven still guards the r.   SHAK 620:3
if r., to be kept right   SCH 558:13
It must be r.: I've done it   CRAB 224:22
it's all r. with me   BELL 62:6
Damn you, Jack — I'm all r.   BONE 117:18
love of truth and r.   TENN 684:11
majority never has r. on its side   IBSEN 359:1
meet, r., and our bounden duty   BOOK 122:10
must now and then be r.   COWP 221:29
My foot standeth r.   BOOK 125:23
my r. is retreating   FOCH 288:6
My r. there is none to dispute   COWP 224:15
nation being so r. that   WILS 738:11
no r. in the circus   MAXT 454:15
Of r. and wrong he taught   ARMS 26:8
Only if it's done r.   ALLEN 9:11
or 'r.' means nothing   PLATO 516:13
our country, r. or wrong   DEC 233:14
our r. as well as our duty   PANK 505:18
rather be r. than be President   CLAY 206:2
recognizing in itself what is r.   VIRG 712:10
renew a r. spirit within   BOOK 128:6
R. as a Ribstone Pippin   BELL 61:10
r. but also to be wrong   SZASZ 677:17
R. but Repulsive   SELL 562:20
r. can be determined without   HOBB 340:10
r. deed for the wrong reason   ELIOT 272:10
r. hand of iniquity   BOOK 135:4
r. hands of fellowship   BIBLE 102:4
r. have they to butcher me   DICK 242:30
r. in his own eyes   BIBLE 74:22
r. is more precious   WILS 738:18
R. . . . is the child of law   BENT 64:2
r. little, tight little island   DIBD 238:18

right: *(cont.)*:
r. makes might   LINC 422:2
r. man in the right place   JEFF 364:19
r. of an excessive wrong   BROW 152:18
r. of the ignorant man   CARL 180:1
r. side of the blanket   ASHF 31:11
r. to a child   SHAW 636:15
r. to a fair portion   BURKE 158:11
r. to be consulted   BAG 47:8
r. to consume happiness   SHAW 636:1
r. to dissemble your love   BICK 108:19
r. to do wrong or to requite   SOCR 654:16
r. to invent themselves   GREER 317:16
r. to that most dreaded   ADAMS 2:25
r. which goes unrecognized   WEIL 726:17
r. wrong, follow the King   TENN 681:22
sat down on the r. hand   BIBLE 104:10
secure of private r.   DRYD 259:11
Sit thou on my r. hand   BOOK 133:3
that r. early   BOOK 127:16
that which they will, is r.   ADAMS 2:8
their constitutional r.   LINC 422:4
To do a great r., do a little   SHAK 609:15
two wrongs don't make a r.   SZASZ 677:17
Whatever is, is R.   POPE 522:8
whatever you do is r.   ALAI 7:4
what's r. and fair   HUGH 354:11
which is lawful and r.   BIBLE 85:23
with firmness in the r.   LINC 422:9
Woman! rise, assert thy r.!   BARB 52:4
worldlings prate of r. and wrong
    DRAY 257:18
righteous: armour of a r. cause   BRYAN 153:23
fervent prayer of a r. man   BIBLE 105:7
not come to call the r.   BIBLE 90:7
r., and sober life   BOOK 118:9
r. are bold   BIBLE 79:28
r. man regardeth the life   BIBLE 78:25
r. perisheth   BIBLE 84:20
r. shall be had in everlasting   BOOK 133:6
saw I never the r. forsaken   BOOK 126:20
seen the r. forsaken   BLUN 116:4
souls of the r.   BIBLE 86:28
righteousness: breastplate of r.   BIBLE 103:1
clouds rain down r.   BIBLE 108:7
for r., but behold a cry   BIBLE 82:15
Hail, the Sun of R.   WESL 728:4
hunger and thirst after r.   BIBLE 88:23
living unto r.   BOOK 123:1
r. and peace have kissed   BOOK 130:20
r. arise with healing   BIBLE 86:19
R. exalteth a nation   BIBLE 78:32
r. of the scribes and Pharisees   BIBLE 88:28
r. shall he judge the world   BOOK 131:15
r. with wisdom always   PLATO 517:1
Thou hast loved r.   BOOK 127:11
thy r. as the waves   BIBLE 84:5
what r. really is   ARN 30:4
Within the paths of r.   SCOT 561:8
worketh not the r. of God   BIBLE 104:27
righteousnesses: our r. are as filthy rags
    BIBLE 84:28
rightful: Re-clothe us in our r. mind
    WHIT 733:7
r. must be reasonable   JEFF 364:3
righting: good for r. wrongs   LOCK 425:14
rights: certain unalienable r.   ANON 19:7
duties as well as its r.   DRUM 258:11
equal in dignity and r.   ANON 11:19
extension of women's r.   FOUR 291:16
Natural r. is simple nonsense   BENT 64:3
real laws come real r.   BENT 64:2
religious r. of an Englishman   JUN 383:3
r. are disregarded by wicked   BROWN 144:13
r. inherent and inalienable   JEFF 364:2
r. in learning's world   EGER 267:13
r. of man   ROB 542:3
r. of the smaller nationalities   ASQ 31:17
sensible of his natural r.   PRIE 529:3
talked long enough about equal r.
    JOHN 367:6
rigol: golden r. hath divorced   SHAK 584:12
riled: In gittin' r.   HARTE 327:18

Rimbauds: always chasing R. PARK 506:13
rime: r. was on the spray HARDY 326:3
Rimmon: in the house of R. BIBLE 76:22
rin: What gars ye r. sae still ANON 17:17
rind: how shall taste the r. THOM 695:5
   r. of one apple tasted MILT 475:6
ring: dance round in a r. FROST 295:10
   giving and receiving of a R. BOOK 123:23
   One R. to rule them all TOLK 700:4
   only pretty r. time SHAK 569:23
   r. at the end of his nose LEAR 414:13
   r. of pure and endless light VAUG 709:11
   r. on her wand she bore MOORE 483:10
   R. out the false TENN 684:10
   r. out the hour APOL 23:9
   R. out, wild bells TENN 684:10
   R. out, ye crystal spheres MILT 467:7
   r. without the finger MIDD 459:13
   Sleeps on his luminous r. TENN 687:21
   They now r. the bells WALP 720:13
   'Twould r. the bells of Heaven HODG 340:16
   what shall we do for a r. LEAR 414:13
   With this R. I thee wed BOOK 123:21
Ring-Bo-Ree: forty bottles of R. LEAR 414:5
ringed: R. with the azure world TENN 681:1
ringleaders: fling the r. from ARN 30:14
ringlets: green sour r. SHAK 626:1
rings: gold r. set with the beryl BIBLE 81:20
   r. black Cyprus FLEC 286:12
rinky-dink: r. of a voice MAIL 442:8
Rio: Go rolling down to R. KIPL 401:17
riot: In general r., melted down thy
   youth SHAK 626:16
   rash fierce blaze of r. SHAK 619:17
   r. is at bottom the language KING 397:4
riotous: with r. living BIBLE 95:2
ripe: rotten before it is r. CORN 219:8
   we r. and ripe SHAK 568:12
ripeness: R. is all SHAK 597:15
ripening: hair turns white with our r.
    BERRY 66:14
   His greatness is a-r. SHAK 588:19
ripens: not when it r. in a tumour ABSE 1:2
riper: amuse his r. stage POPE 522:16
ripes: erring on ventiferous r. HOLM 342:9
ripple: r. of rain SWIN 675:21
rise: dead r. not BIBLE 101:9
   For us i' the dark to r. by BROW 152:19
   half to r. and half to fall POPE 522:10
   Held we fall to r. BROW 148:6
   Ile r. and fight againe BALL 50:9
   men may r. on stepping-stones TENN 682:30
   Must r. at five CLAR 205:13
   nation shall r. against nation BIBLE 92:9
   nobody who does not r. early JOHN 370:25
   resistible r. of Arturo Ui BREC 140:2
   r., assert thy right BARB 52:4
   r. at once against WHIT 732:11
   r. at ten thirty and saunter HARG 326:8
   r. by other's fall SOUT 657:23
   r. out of obscurity JUV 383:22
   R. up, my love, my fair BIBLE 81:9
   r. with the lark and go BRET 140:15
risen: floods are r., O Lord BOOK 131:7
rises: Jove's planet r. yonder BROW 150:8
   sun also r. HEM 331:17
rising: evening r. to meet you ELIOT 272:23
   means of r. in the world JOHN 374:5
   revolution of r. expectations CLEV 206:12
   R. and cawing at the gun's SHAK 612:1
   r. to great place BACON 43:31
risk: proxy for r. and a dummy MACH 430:13
risking: not in giving life but in r. DE B 233:9
rite: For the newer r. is here THOM 692:14
   r. nor formal ostentation SHAK 578:9
rites: payens corsed olde r. CHAU 196:2
   r. for which I love him SHAK 615:8
Ritz: open to all—like the R. MATH 453:17
rivalry: dead there is no r. MAC 435:1
   r. of aim ADAMS 2:16
rivals: Three for the r. ANON 15:1
   ungenerous jealousy of r. ADAMS 1:12

rive: body r. not more in parting SHAK 566:5
riven: From Thy r. side TOPL 701:4
river: Among the r. sallows KEATS 390:20
   As if I were a r. AKHM 6:7
   But the majestic r. floated ARN 28:17
   daughter went through the r. BUNY 156:15
   Down in the reeds by the r. BROW 147:17
   Fame is like a r. BACON 44:13
   fountains mingle with the r. SHEL 641:9
   fruitful r. in the eye SHAK 572:10
   he drinketh up a r. BIBLE 78:3
   I see upon the r.'s reaches BLOK 115:3
   living r. by the door STEV 669:8
   noblest r. in Europe ADD 4:15
   Ol' man r. HAMM 322:18
   on a r. of crystal light FIELD 281:14
   On a tree by a r. a little tom-tit GILB 305:11
   On either side the r. lie TENN 684:23
   On the r.'s margin thrive SMART 649:7
   Parliament upon the r. WELL 727:5
   Pentridge by the r. BARN 53:14
   pure r. of water of life BIBLE 107:22
   r. at my garden's end SWIFT 674:25
   r. is a strong brown god ELIOT 273:2
   r. jumps over the mountain AUDEN 34:3
   r. of human industry TOCQ 699:8
   r. of things passing AUR 37:16
   rook-racked, r.-rounded HOPK 345:9
   Sleepless as the r. under thee CRANE 225:24
   thy peace been as a r. BIBLE 84:5
   time for r. in the tree DICK 245:5
   twice into the same r. HER 333:11
   we'll to the r. SHAK 565:12
   Where the brook and r. meet LONG 427:2
   white flows the r. STEV 668:24
riverrun: r., past Eve JOYCE 380:21
rivers: By shallow r. MARL 447:18
   kingdom's r. take their course SHAK 594:15
   like r. grow cold MONT 480:6
   lilies by the r. of waters BIBLE 88:4
   love any discourse of r. WALT 721:9
   Nymphs and as yet unknown r. VIRG 714:2
   R. and mountain-spring OAKL 497:8
   r. cannot quench SHAK 588:5
   r. in the south BOOK 134:5
   r. of blood must yet flow JEFF 364:16
   r. of Damascus BIBLE 76:21
   r. of water in a dry BIBLE 83:17
   r. run into the sea BIBLE 79:37
   springs into the r. BOOK 132:7
rivets: hammers closing r. SHAK 585:14
rivulet: r. of text SHER 645:13
rivulets: meadow r. overflow HARDY 326:2
road: light to shine upon the r. COWP 222:22
   along the 'ard 'igh r. PUNCH 531:14
   Don't leave them on the r. GOGOL 309:21
   goes along the darksome r. CAT 185:14
   Golden R. to Samarkand FLEC 286:11
   hard the r. may be CHUR 202:10
   I take to the open r. WHIT 732:23
   Like one, that on a lonesome r. COL 211:14
   look ahead up the white r. ELIOT 273:12
   middle of the r. BEVAN 69:6
   one more for the r. MERC 457:14
   on to the end of the r. LAUD 411:5
   r. below me STEV 669:5
   r. of excess leads BLAKE 112:16
   r. that leads him to England JOHN 372:7
   r. through the woods KIPL 400:17
   r. to bring us daily nearer KEBLE 392:20
   R. to Heaven BALL 50:16
   r. to the City of Emeralds BAUM 55:15
   r. to wealth so easy TROL 703:12
   r. up and the road down HER 333:13
   rolling English r. CHES 199:5
   Softly along the r. of evening DE L 236:10
   watched the ads, and not the r. NASH 490:13
   who takes no private r. POPE 522:22
   winding r. before me HAZL 329:14
   ye'll tak' the high r. ANON 17:8
   yon braid, braid r. BALL 50:16
   Your old r. is rapidly agin' DYLAN 265:23

road: (cont.):
   your r.'s a thorny way CARB 178:17
roads: lawless r. ran wrong MUIR 487:13
   By r. 'not adopted' BETJ 68:7
   How many r. must a man DYLAN 265:11
   Two r. diverged in a wood FROST 295:9
roam: don't know where to r. COLL 213:7
   dunce that has been sent to r. COWP 223:5
   Everywhere I r. FOST 291:15
   passion and the power to r. BYRON 168:17
   Where'er I r. GOLD 311:8
   who soar, but never r. WORD 748:12
roamin': R. in the gloamin' LAUD 411:7
roaming: r. with a hungry heart TENN 690:1
   where are you r. SHAK 629:4
roar: die of that r. which lies ELIOT 269:7
   long, withdrawing r. ARN 27:1
   mighty r. of London's traffic ANON 17:4
   most like the r. of some ARN 28:15
   r. you as gently as any SHAK 611:8
   Swinging slow with sullen r. MILT 464:21
   they r. their ribs out GILB 306:25
roarers: r. for the name of king SHAK 624:26
roareth: What is this that r. thus GODL 308:7
roaring: But R. Bill BELL 61:27
   lions r. after their prey BOOK 132:9
   r. of the wind is my wife KEATS 392:2
roast: politics in boiled and r. SMITH 653:4
   r. me in sulphur SHAK 618:18
   r. with fire BIBLE 72:9
   they'll r. thee like a herrin BURNS 163:11
   were but to r. their eggs BACON 45:7
rob: If a writer has to r. his mother FAUL 281:4
   r. a lady of her fortune FIEL 282:14
   r. those who use the money TAWN 679:2
robbed: We was r. JAC 361:6
robber: Barabbas was a r. BIBLE 97:25
   now with a r.'s haste SHAK 628:1
robbers: in perils of r. BIBLE 102:1
robbery: all full of lies and r. BIBLE 86:15
   In scandal, as CHES 198:1
   r. to be equal with God BIBLE 103:4
   trust not in wrong and r. BOOK 128:20
robbing: Forbids the r. of a foe CHUR 200:22
   r. a bank compared with BREC 140:5
   r. he comes next to drinking DE Q 237:12
robe: Give me my r. SHAK 567:7
   like a giant's r. SHAK 604:18
   nor the judge's r. SHAK 605:16
   Untwisted all the shining r. THOM 696:15
robed: R. in the long friends THOM 693:14
robes: arrayed in white r. BIBLE 106:20
   have washed their r. BIBLE 106:21
   R. loosely flowing JONS 378:14
   r. ye weave, another wears SHEL 643:4
   When all her r. are gone ANON 16:14
Robespierre: R. was nothing HEINE 331:3
Robey: R. is the Darling SMITH 651:16
robin: bonny sweet R. SHAK 578:8
   Call for the r.-red-breast WEBS 726:7
   r. red breast in a cage BLAKE 111:1
   R.'s not near KEPP 394:11
   Sweet R. sits in the bush SCOTT 560:22
Robin Adair: fled with thee, R. KEPP 394:11
Robinson: here's to you, Mrs R. SIMON 647:19
Robinson Crusoe: Don Quixote, R. JOHN 377:9
robot: r. may not injure ASIM 31:14
robotics: Rules of R. ASIM 31:14
robots: men may become r. FROMM 294:7
robs: R. not one light seed KEATS 387:23
   r. Peter to pay Paul SHAW 636:12
rock: Beside the jutting r. BYRON 172:14
   Between a r. and a hard place ANON 12:15
   founded upon a r. BIBLE 89:26
   great r. in a weary BIBLE 83:17
   huge aspiring r. DAN 229:12
   I've gotten a r. BLAM 114:19
   Rhyme the r. DRYD 259:15
   R. journalism is people ZAPPA 755:9
   R. of Ages, cleft for me TOPL 701:4
   r. of offence BIBLE 82:25
   Rock them, r. them, lullaby DEKK 235:17
   serpent upon a r. BIBLE 79:33

rock: (cont.):

set my feet upon the r.	BOOK 126:24
Sex and drugs and r. and roll	DURY 264:12
upon this r. I will build my	BIBLE 91:14

rocked: R. in the cradle of the deep WILL 736:20
She r. it, and rated it — EDW 267:11

rocket: As he rose like a r. — PAINE 504:13
every r. fired signifies — EIS 268:10
long numbers that r. the mind — WILB 734:1

Rockies: R. may crumble — GERS 301:15

rocking: Brothers and sisters r. — JOHN 366:16
Out of the cradle endlessly r. — WHIT 732:8
r. a grown man in the cradle — BURKE 157:11

rocking horse: swayed about upon a r.
— KEATS 390:12

rocks: eternal r. beneath — BRON 142:18
hand that r. the cradle — WALL 718:6
native of the r. — JOHN 371:12
older than the r. — PATER 509:5
R., caves, lakes — MILT 470:4
r. of the mountains — BIBLE 106:17
R., torrents, gulfs — BEAT 56:5
r. whose entrance leads — MILT 464:2
r. won't lose their shape — ROBIN 542:7
seas roll over but the r. — HERB 333:20
stony r. for the conies — BOOK 132:9
when r. are near — WEBS 726:13
With r., and stones, and trees — WORD 748:1
With r. unscalable — SHAK 571:6

rod: Aaron's r. swallowed up — BIBLE 72:4
at lightning and lashed r. — HOPK 346:12
all humbled kiss the r. — SHAK 631:3
bruise them with a r. of iron — BOOK 124:10
r. out of the stem of Jesse — BIBLE 83:1
spare the r., and spoil the child — BUTL 166:14
spareth his r. hateth his son — BIBLE 180:8
r. becomes more mocked than — SHAK 605:7
r., which is the only — LOCKE 425:10
thy r. and staff comfort me — SCOT 561:8
thy r. and thy staff comfort me — BOOK 125:15

rode: r. madly off in all directions — LEAC 413:13
r. upon the cherubims — BOOK 125:1

rods: was I beaten with r. — BIBLE 102:1

roe: be thou like to a r. — BIBLE 82:7

roes: breasts are like two young r. BIBLE 81:13

Roger: R. is landlord to — ADD 4:8

rogue: dainty r. in porcelain — MER 457:22
Has he not a r.'s face — CONG 215:7
How easy it is to call r. — DRYD 262:20
r. and peasant slave am — SHAK 575:8

rogues: r. in buckram let drive — SHAK 580:19
see the r. flourish — BROW 151:5

roi R. m'avait donné Paris — ANON 21:5

Roland: R. to the dark tower — SHAK 596:17

role: has not yet found a r. — ACH 1:6

roll: All away began to r. — BLAKE 111:19
r. all our strength — MARV 451:4
R. on, thou deep and dark — BYRON 169:14
R. up that map — PITT 515:18
Sex and drugs and rock and r. — DURY 264:12
spread over and flop and r. — MANS 445:7

rolled: bottoms of my trousers r. — ELIOT 272:6
r. along on wheels — HUXL 357:18

roller: r., pitch, and stumps — LANG 408:15

rollicking: r. romping Polka — GROS 319:1

rolling: And the r. anapaestic — BROW 147:23
Go r. down to Rio — KIPL 401:17
He jus' keeps r. along — HAMM 322:18
r. English drunkard — CHES 199:5

rolls: r. back the restless stone — DUCK 263:7
R. impotently on as Thou or I — FITZ 284:10
r. it about with the swaddling — ANDR 11:12
r. it under his tongue — HENRY 332:18

Roman: after the high R. fashion — SHAK 566:17
antique R. than a Dane — SHAK 579:10
Before the R. came to Rye — CHES 199:5
Butchered to make a R. holiday — BYRON 169:8
found the R. nation — VIRG 712:2
His noses cast is of the r. — FLEM 287:8
I am a R. citizen — CIC 204:8
I'm a R. for that — FARQ 280:14
know the sweet R. hand — SHAK 630:20
Make way, you R. writers — PROP 530:2

Roman: (cont.):

neither holy, nor R. — VOLT 716:11
Roman by a R. valiantly — SHAK 566:14
R. Conquest was a *Good Thing* — SELL 562:17
R. meal . . . a radish and an egg — COWP 223:34
R. people had but one neck — CAL 175:5
R.'s life, a Roman's arms — MAC 436:14
R. thought hath struck him — SHAK 564:16
so rude that would not be a R. — SHAK 592:4
Than such a R. — SHAK 593:1
This was the noblest R. — SHAK 593:23
Thundered out on the R. air — AUDEN 34:1
To-day the R. and his trouble — HOUS 352:13
virtue with the R. clergy — KING 398:4

Romana: *Moribus antiquis res stat R.* ENN 278:1

Roman Catholic: [R. Church] may still
exist — MAC 435:12
R. Church, the Brigade of Guards
— MACM 440:10
R. women must keep — THOM 694:8

romance: any historical r. — CLAR 205:12
cloudy symbols of a high r. — KEATS 391:1
fine r. with no kisses — FIEL 282:18
learned r. as she grew older — AUST 39:3
music and love and r. — BERL 65:16
not a little given to r. — EVEL 279:5

romances: like r. read — SUCK 671:5

Roman Empire: ghost of the deceased R.
— HOBB 340:12
R. and the rise — STEV 667:8

Romanism: rum, R., and rebellion
— BURC 156:18

Romans: Friends, R., countrymen — SHAK 592:5
R. call it stoicism — ADD 3:17
R. were like brothers — MAC 436:12

romantic: In a ruin that's r. — GILB 305:14
In spite of all r. poets sing — LEAP 413:15
R. Ireland's dead and gone — YEATS 753:5
r. lie in the brain — AUDEN 36:1
'r.' music — STR 670:23
ticket to r. places — MARV 451:14
was once r. to burlesque — BYRON 171:7
Wrong but R. — SELL 562:20

romantics: We were the last r. — YEATS 751:5

Romanus: *Civis R. sum* — CIC 204:8
Civis R. sum — PALM 505:8

Rome: Cato is the voice of R. — JONS 378:12
comen from R. al hoot — CHAU 193:7
conquest and subjugation, R. — WEBS 725:8
For R. so near us — DAY-L 233:3
go from the church of R. — WOTT 749:8
grandeur that was R. — POE 518:9
high and palmy state of R. — SHAK 571:26
hook-nosed fellow of R. — SHAK 583:25
I'm getting out of R. — GAR 298:1
Let R. in Tiber melt — SHAK 564:14
O happy R. — CIC 204:15
Oh R.! my country — BYRON 169:3
R. has spoken — AUG 37:9
R. hath lost her crown — COL 209:8
R. hath no jurisdiction — BOOK 135:26
R. immortal heard October's — GURN 320:1
R. indeed and room enough — SHAK 590:5
R. . . . is like its own Monte — CLOU 206:17
R., though her eagle through — WALL 718:15
strangers of R. — BIBLE 98:7
that I loved R. more — SHAK 592:2
time with full doubt of R. — BYRON 171:10
village than second at R. — CAES 174:17
wealth and din of R. — HOR 350:8
When I go to R., I fast — AMBR 10:6
When in R. — TAYL 679:17
when R. falls—the World — BYRON 169:10
you cruel men of R. — SHAK 589:20

Romeo: wherefore art thou R. — SHAK 622:29

Ronsard: *R. me célébrait* — RONS 545:12

rood: terrace walk, and half a r. — SWIFT 674:25

roof: cat on a hot tin r. — WILL 737:3
cleave to the r. of my mouth — BOOK 134:17
love the high embowèd r. — MILT 465:1
no r. to shroud his head — HEYW 338:6
on a corrugated tin r. — BEEC 58:17
shouldest come under my r. — BIBLE 89:29

roof: (cont.):

shouldst enter under my r. — MISS 477:6
this majestical r. fretted — SHAK 574:28
until my r. whirl around — JONS 379:9

roofless: those r. halls — SHEL 641:13

roofs: as there are tiles on the r. — LUTH 432:11

roof-tree: heavens my wide r. — AYT 41:5

roof-wrecked: Is r. — HARDY 325:1

rook: r.-racked — HOPK 345:9
When the last r. — COL 211:21

rooks: choughs and r. — SHAK 603:13
r. are blown about — TENN 683:7
r. in families homeward go — HARDY 326:2

room: about to enter a r. — EDD 266:4
All before my little r. — BROO 143:9
although the r. grows chilly — GRAH 313:12
boys in the back r. — LOES 426:2
down in the highest r. — BIBLE 94:26
end of the enormous r. — AUDEN 34:5
engine-r. was never installed — BARN 53:9
Fifty springs are little r. — HOUS 352:6
fill the r. my heart keeps empty — KING 396:11
Great hatred, little r. — YEATS 752:19
Here in this r., desiring you — STEV 666:7
How little r. — SHIR 646:6
inability to be at ease in a r. — PASC 507:12
In every grave make r. — D'AV 231:17
Infinite riches in a little r. — MARL 447:13
is there any r. at your head — BALL 49:4
just entering the r. — BROUN 144:10
make r. for men — WALK 717:13
nowhere beyond your r. — MOT 487:1
Rome indeed and r. enough — SHAK 590:5
r. at the top — WEBS 725:12
r. confining mighty men — SHAK 587:4
r. for them in the inn — BIBLE 93:26
r. in my heart for thee — ELL 275:8
r. of her own — WOOLF 742:10
R. to deny ourselves — KEBLE 392:20
r. to swing a cat — DICK 240:7
r. where he must lodge — MILT 467:16
shame to take the lowest r. — BIBLE 94:26
sitting in the smallest r. — REGER 538:13
slipped away into the next r. — HOLL 342:4
smoke-filled r. — SIMP 648:3
struggle for r. and food — MALT 443:19
taper to the outward r. — DONNE 251:9
upper r. furnished — BIBLE 95:20
was not sufficient r. — BARN 53:16
Was there room no r. — ELL 275:8
you shall keep your r. — STEV 668:24

rooms: boys in the back r. — BEAV 57:7
colder r. and worse company — AUST 38:8
Know most of the r. — FULL 296:5
lighted r. inside your head — LARK 410:4
Other voices, other r. — CAP 178:14
uppermost r. at feasts — BIBLE 92:4
uppermost r. at feasts — BIBLE 93:17

Rooshans: may be R. — DICK 241:14

Roosian: might have been a R. — GILB 306:5

roost: always come home to r. — SOUT 657:7
birds came home to r. — MILL 461:20

rooster: Hongry r. don't cackle — HARR 327:8

roosts: perchèd r. — MILT 474:14

root: because they had no r. — BIBLE 91:1
eaten on the insane r. — SHAK 600:8
knotty as a r. — BRON 142:9
March hath perced to the r. — CHAU 192:6
money is the r. of all evil — BIBLE 104:3
nips his r. — SHAK 588:19
r. is one — YEATS 751:4
r. of the matter is found — BIBLE 77:26
some fruit-tree's mossy r. — MARV 450:12
square r. of half a number — LONG 428:6
then the axe to the r. — PAINE 504:16
Thy r. is ever in its grave — HERB 336:1
unto the r. of the trees — BIBLE 88:16

rooting: r. for Gary Cooper — BALD 48:9

roots: blasts the r. of trees — THOM 693:7
broad on the r. of things — BROW 147:25
drought is destroying his r. — HERB 333:16
Dull r. with spring rain — ELIOT 272:21
r., and ever green — PEELE 511:5

roots: (cont.):
r. that can be pulled up | ELIOT 269:1
send my r. rain | HOPK 346:9
shall grow out of his r. | BIBLE 83:1
rope: by the r. we know where we are | JAMES 362:14
fourfold r. of nerves | HEAT 330:1
set his hand to a r. | DRAKE 257:11
rorate: R., coeli, desuper | BIBLE 108:7
Rosalind: No jewel is like R. | SHAK 569:2
rose: Against the blown r. may they | SHAK 565:18
American beauty r. | ROCK 543:20
beauty's r. might never die | SHAK 632:26
blossom as the r. | BIBLE 83:19
Christmas I no more desire a r. | SHAK 598:8
dropping a r. petal down | MARQ 448:20
earthlier happy is the r. | SHAK 610:20
English unofficial r. | BROO 143:10
fading r. | CAREW 179:11
Faintly the inimitable r. | WINC 739:4
fayr as is the r. in May | CHAU 195:4
fire and the r. are one | ELIOT 271:9
fresh lap of the crimson r. | SHAK 611:15
Gather therefore the r. | SPEN 660:6
Go, lovely r. | WALL 718:9
He wears the r. | SHAK 565:19
I am the r. of Sharon | BIBLE 81:8
If love were what the r. | SWIN 677:1
If you gave Ruth a r. | AYCK 40:10
I know the colour r. | ABSE 1:2
I pluck the r. | BROW 153:14
I r., went forth, and followed | WESL 728:2
It wavers to a r. | DOBS 249:22
labyrinthine buds the r. | BROW 153:2
last r. of summer | MOORE 483:12
late r. may yet linger | HOR 349:16
leaves the r. of yesterday | FITZ 283:12
lovely is the r. | WORD 745:10
mast burst open with a r. | FLEC 286:13
May ravage with impunity a r. | BROW 153:4
mighty lak' a r. | STAN 662:11
Mignonne, allons voir si la r. | RONS 545:11
musk of the r. is blown | TENN 686:17
my fause luver stole my r. | BURNS 161:11
my Luve's like a red, red r. | BURNS 162:27
never promised you a r. garden | GREEN 316:16
No thorns go as deep as a r.'s | SWIN 676:12
One perfect r. | PARK 506:9
O R., thou art sick | BLAKE 114:12
Pluck a red r. from off | SHAK 587:9
pluck a white r. with me | SHAK 587:9
raise up the ghost of a r. | BROW 145:12
r. as where some buried | FITZ 283:16
r. by any other name | SHAK 622:30
r. full-blown | HERR 337:11
R. is a rose is a rose | STEIN 663:5
r. like a nymph | SHEL 642:27
r. of the fair state | SHAK 576:4
r. of the rosebud garden | TENN 686:19
r.'s scent is bitterness | THOM 694:17
R. the black and gloomy | LONG 427:15
r. to a pitch-black toad | YES 754:1
R., were you not extremely | PRIOR 529:15
r. with all its sweetest | BYRON 171:31
r. without the thorn | HERR 336:24
Roves back the r. | DE L 235:20
sad R. of all my days | YEATS 753:13
scent is of the summer's r. | GRAV 314:17
secret and inviolate R. | YEATS 753:3
sorrow on a morning r. | KEATS 389:6
Sweet r., whose hue angry | HERB 336:1
tell the crooked r. | THOM 693:7
third day he r. again | BOOK 119:1
though a r. should shut | KEATS 387:8
vanish with the r. | FITZ 284:16
When I have plucked the r. | SHAK 618:5
white r. weeps | TENN 686:20
without thorn the r. | MILT 471:3
rosea: avertens r. cervice | VIRG 712:8
rosebuds: crown ourselves with r. | BIBLE 86:26
Gather ye r. while ye may | HERR 337:7

rosemary: r. and rue | SHAK 631:29
r., that's for remembrance | SHAK 578:7
Rosencrantz: R. and Guildenstern | SHAK 579:15
rose-red: r. city half as old as | BURG 156:24
r. sissy half as old as time | PLOM 517:14
roses: ash the burnt r. leave | ELIOT 271:4
days of wine and r. | DOWS 256:3
Do r. stick like burrs | BROW 153:12
Each morn a thousand r. | FITZ 283:12
Everything's coming up r. | SOND 655:15
flower of r. in the spring | BIBLE 88:4
forget the lilac and the r. | ARAG 24:6
girls and r. | DE G 235:4
Honey of r. | HERB 335:4
In fields where r. fade | HOUS 352:18
Lilies without, r. within | MARV 450:20
Love guards the r. of thy lips | LODGE 426:1
not a bed of r. | STEV 668:5
Plant thou no r. at my head | ROSS 547:12
raptures and r. of vice | SWIN 676:9
R. are flowering in Picardy | WEAT 724:14
r. for the flush of youth | ROSS 547:6
R. have thorns | SHAK 633:13
roses, r., all the way | BROW 151:22
scent of the r. will hang | MOORE 483:4
smells like r. | JOHN 367:11
Two red r. across the moon | MORR 485:14
virgins are soft as the r. | BYRON 167:26
would like my r. to see you | SHER 645:25
rosy: plain men have r. faces | STEV 668:23
r. morn long since left | SPEN 659:14
rosy-fingered: R. dawn | HOMER 343:12
rot: As artists they're r. | PARK 506:16
cold obstruction and to r. | SHAK 606:11
go r. | SHAK 631:16
or r. in hospitals | SOUT 657:2
R. half a grain a day | SHAK 618:12
R. inwardly | MILT 466:9
r. itself with motion | SHAK 564:27
we r. and rot | SHAK 568:12
rote: conned by r. | SHAK 593:8
Rothschild: R. and Baring | GILB 304:18
rots: liquid which r. braces | MORT 486:14
rotted: Or simply r. early | NASH 490:14
rotten: hypocrite is really r. | AREN 24:15
It's always the good feel r. | YES 754:2
r. before it is ripe | CORN 219:8
r. in the state of Denmark | SHAK 573:12
shines like r. wood | RAL 535:15
rottenness: r. begins in his conduct | JEFF 364:10
r. of eighty years in gold | BYRON 173:14
r. of our civilization | READ 537:6
rotundity: thick r. o' the world | SHAK 595:20
rough: al r. and long yherd | CHAU 194:1
I am r. and lecherous | SHAK 595:2
children who were r. | SPEN 659:2
r. and ready man who write | BROW 148:14
r. diamond | DEFOE 234:1
R. he may be | DICK 241:21
r. magic | SHAK 626:1
r. places plain | BIBLE 83:26
r. than polished diamond | CHES 198:17
R. winds do shake the darling | SHAK 633:6
with r. and all-unable pen | SHAK 587:4
rough-hew: R. them how | SHAK 578:30
roughness: r. breedeth hate | BACON 43:30
roughs: among his fellow r. | DOYLE 257:4
round: heaven, a perfect r. | BROW 147:26
himself into the r. hole | SMITH 652:27
made the r. world so sure | BOOK 131:6
R. and round the circle | ELIOT 270:12
R. both the shires they | HOUS 352:10
r. earth's imagined corners | DONNE 250:20
r., fat, oily man | THOM 695:19
r. it was, upon a hill | STEV 665:14
R. the world for ever and aye | ARN 27:9
r. unvarnished tale deliver | SHAK 614:31
R. up the usual suspects | EPST 278:9
test of a r. character | FORS 290:4
rounded: Our little life is r. with a sleep | SHAK 625:28
polished and well-r. | HOR 351:11

Roundheads: R. (Right but Repulsive) | SELL 562:20
roundly: r., but hollowly | POTT 525:19
rouse: r. a lion than to start | SHAK 579:34
R. the lion from his lair | SCOTT 560:33
r. them from their lowly | GRAY 315:12
Rousseau: mock on Voltaire R. | BLAKE 113:5
R. was the first militant | BERL 66:3
shall not ask Jean Jacques R. | COWP 222:28
whose soul R. had created | HEINE 331:3
rout: r. send forth a joyous | MAC 436:4
rove: she may r. as well as you | BEHN 60:11
rover: blood's a r. | HOUS 352:7
roves: R. back the rose | DE L 235:20
roving: we'll go no more a-r. | BYRON 173:6
row: gate-bars hang in a r. | HARDY 326:2
Gently, sweetly, r. by row | CAREY 179:16
nor canst boast a r. | JONS 380:6
that r. one way and look | BURT 164:17
rowan: r. leaves are dank | BLUC 115:3
Rowe: R.'s Rule | DICK 245:9
rowed: All r. fast | COKE 208:15
rowing: and r. another | BUNY 155:20
rows: Lovers' r. | TER 690:10
not lugged into Family R. | WOD 740:16
royal: interpretation of dreams is the r. road | FREUD 293:20
r. banners forward go | FORT 291:2
r. captain of this ruined | SHAK 585:15
r. priesthood | BIBLE 105:11
There is no 'r. road' | EUCL 279:2
this is the r. Law | COR 219:11
This r. throne of kings | SHAK 619:18
with a r. wage | BROO 143:4
royaliste: plus r. que le roi | ANON 20:14
royally: proved most r. | SHAK 579:16
Sorrow so r. in you appears | SHAK 584:8
Royal Society: honour which the R. | FAR 280:3
royalties: entertain four r. | SAL 554:3
royalty: full glare of R. | MADAN 441:9
like film stars and r. | LESS 419:9
R. is a government | BAG 47:5
r. is to be reverenced | BAG 47:7
R. . . . lay it on with a trowel | DISR 249:11
R. will be strong | BAG 47:5
rub: ay, there's the r. | SHAK 575:16
if you r. up against money | RUNY 550:6
What r. or what impediment | SHAK 586:16
rubbish: cast as r. to the void | TENN 683:18
r. that lies in the way | LOCKE 424:15
was but the r. of an Adam | SOUTH 657:1
What r.! | BLÜC 115:10
rubies: Give pearls away and r. | HOUS 352:9
her price is far above r. | BIBLE 79:35
price of wisdom is above r. | BIBLE 77:28
R. unparagoned | SHAK 571:1
Shouldst r. find | MARV 451:2
rubs: r. nor botches in the work | SHAK 603:2
rudder: My heart was to thy r. tied | SHAK 565:16
rhyme the r. is of verses | BUTL 166:9
Their tail the r. | DRYD 260:3
ruddier: O r. than the cherry | GAY 299:9
ruddy: beloved is white and r. | BIBLE 81:19
Now he was r. | BIBLE 74:39
rude: let's talk r. | FLAN 285:11
only rather r. and wild | BELL 61:8
R. am I in my speech | SHAK 614:30
r. heap together hurled | MARV 451:12
rudest: r. work that tells a story | RUSK 550:22
Rudolph: R., the Red-Nosed | MARKS 446:8
Rudyards: R. cease from kipling | STEP 663:18
rue: nought shall make us r. | SHAK 594:16
R., even for ruth | SHAK 620:16
there's rosemary and r. | SHAK 631:29
there's r. for you | SHAK 578:8
ruffian: by the menaces of a r. | JOHN 373:24
that father r. | SHAK 580:31
ruffle: Would r. up your spirits | SHAK 592:17
rug: cockatoo upon a r. | STEV 666:10
rugged: cling to the old r. cross | BENN 63:3
harsh cadence of a r. line | DRYD 261:31

rugged: *(cont.)*:
mere antiquarian is a r. — JOHN 374:29
r. individualism — HOOV 344:18
steep and r. pathway — WILL 737:14
unpolished r. verse I chose — DRYD 261:17
ruin: feet can print no r.-trace — MONT 482:1
hideous r. and combustion — MILT 467:23
In a r. that's romantic — GILB 305:14
Majestic though in r. — MILT 469:18
r. each wish of my heart — MOORE 483:1
r. of all happiness — BURN 160:14
r. or to rule the state — DRYD 259:3
R. seize thee, ruthless King! — GRAY 315:6
r. that Cromwell knocked — BEDF 58:14
r. that it feeds upon — COWP 223:4
ruin upon r. — MILT 470:13
sand and r. and gold — SWIN 677:5
Spreading r. and scattering — BROW 147:17
Thou its r. didst not share — DOD 250:4
What had his r. lost thee — CRAS 226:1
whom God to r. has designed — DRYD 260:28
will r. himself in twelve — GEOR 301:5
yet what r.! — BYRON 169:9
ru-i-n: roving's been my r. — ANON 12:8
ruined: r. at our own request — MORE 483:22
r. by the littleness of those — BREC 140:9
from the r. sides of kings — BEAU 56:15
home of r. reputations — ELIOT 269:9
O r. piece of nature — SHAK 597:5
r. on the side of their — BURKE 159:20
ruining: R. along the illimitable inane — TENN 686:3
ruinous: R. inheritance — GAIUS 296:18
Were r. and old — SPEN 659:25
ruins: but to flout, the r. grey — SCOTT 559:13
have shored against my r, — ELIOT 273:14
human mind in r. — DAV 232:8
r. of the noblest man — SHAK 591:23
r. that of a noble mind — DOYLE 256:10
r. would strike him unafraid — HOH 350:2
states with others' r. built — SOUT 657:23
Ruislip: Gaily into R. Gardens — BETJ 68:2
rult: *consili expers mole r.* — HOR 350:4
rule: bear r. in their kingdoms — BIBLE 87:38
Be each man's r. — TENN 681:9
good old r. sufficeth them — WORD 747:16
greater light to r. the day — BIBLE 69:23
greatest r. of all — MOL 478:19
He has observed the golden r. — BLAKE 113:9
levelled r. of streaming light — MILT 463:26
little r., a little sway — DYER 265:6
No charge of r. — SURR 672:2
oldest r. in the book — CARR 182:16
only infallible r. we know — SURT 672:6
prevents the r. of wealth — BAG 46:21
priests bear r. — BIBLE 85:6
reasons for the r. — STR 670:24
Reason to r., but mercy to — DRYD 260:22
Resolved to ruin or to r. — DRYD 259:3
rich men r. the law — GOLD 311:11
Rowe's R. — DICK 245:9
R., Britannia, rule the waves — THOM 695:15
r. in life never to apologize — WOD 740:18
r. of speech — HOR 347:6
R. of Three doth puzzle me — ANON 16:13
Shall all be done by the r. — SHAK 565:9
To r. o'er freemen — BROO 143:2
Who can r. and dare not lie — TENN 686:13
wise man make your r. — BLAKE 113:9
ruled: God their severance r. — ARN 29:4
ruler: being our r. and guide — BOOK 121:2
r. of all his substance — BOOK 132:12
R. of the Queen's Navee — GILB 305:26
that is to be r. in Israel — BIBLE 86:13
thee a r. over many things — BIBLE 92:16
rulers: brought about by r. — BIER 109:11
conduct of their r. — ADAMS 2:25
R. have no authority from — MAYH 455:9
r. of the darkness — BIBLE 103:1
rules: by any hypercritical r. — LINC 422:3
different set of r. of the game — ROB 542:13
disregard of all the r. — ORW 500:25
false r. pranked in reason — MILT 464:9

rules: *(cont.)*:
golden r. for an orchestra — BEEC 58:16
hand that r. the world — WALL 718:6
keep making up these sex r. — SAL 553:16
known r. of ancient liberty — MILT 474:22
people wouldn't obey the r. — BENN 63:9
pretences to break known r. — CROM 227:13
R. and models destroy genius — HAZL 329:7
R. of Robotics — ASIM 31:14
r. of the game — HUXL 358:7
teach taste or genius by r. — REYN 539:7
rulest: thou r. in might — SMITH 653:31
ruleth: r. his spirit — BIBLE 78:38
ruling: hands of the r. class — STAL 662:4
He rather hated the r. — BENT 64:8
r. passion conquers reason — POPE 520:16
Search then the R. Passion — POPE 520:28
rum: r. and true religion — BYRON 170:16
r., Romanism, and rebellion — BURC 156:18
r., sodomy, and the lash — CHUR 203:10
what a R. Go everything is — WELLS 727:18
Yo-ho-ho, and a bottle of r. — STEV 667:22
rumble: r. of a distant drum — FITZ 283:14
R. thy bellyful — SHAK 595:21
rumour: History a distillation of r. — CARL 180:20
R. is a pipe — SHAK 582:12
sound and r. — MORR 485:9
rumours: hear of wars and r. — BIBLE 92:8
rump: The R. Parliament — SELL 662:21
run: And to my dead heart r. — STEV 669:7
as they r. they look behind — GRAY 316:1
chance to r. over a cad — CLOU 207:12
For frequent tears have r. — BROW 147:19
I therefore so r. — BIBLE 100:31
Many shall r. to and fro — BIBLE 86:3
r. from me and the child — BALL 49:15
R., run, Orlando — SHAK 568:18
r., though not to soar — MAC 436:22
r. to and fro like sparks — BIBLE 87:1
r. with patience the race — BIBLE 104:17
that he may r. that readeth — BIBLE 86:16
They get r. down — BEVAN 69:6
they which r. in a race run all — BIBLE 100:30
till thou r, out thy race — MILT 467:15
To cry it up, or r. it down — SWIFT 675:4
true love never did r. smooth — SHAK 610:21
we were born to r. — SPR 661:14
Who can r. the race with Death — JOHN 376:18
yet we will make him r. — MARV 451:4
runagates: r. continue in scarceness — BOOK 129:7
runaway: curb a r. young star — BYRON 173:13
runcible: ate with a r. spoon — LEAR 414:15
He weareth a r. hat — LEAR 414:11
R. Cat with crimson whiskers — LEAR 414:8
runic: In a sort of R. rhyme — POE 518:3
runnable: r. stag — DAV 231:21
runnels: r. pebble-stones — KEATS 386:6
runner: long-distance r. — SILL 647:16
running: first sprightly r. — DRYD 260:6
from r. over with any little — KEATS 392:4
R. it never runs from us away — DONNE 251:18
shaken together, and r. over, shall — BIBLE 94:7
she'll be constantly r. back — HOR 348:8
takes all the r. *you* can do — CARR 182:17
Who are you r. from — VIRG 714:16
runs: who r. may read — KEBLE 392:21
Rupert: R. of Debate — BULW 155:8
R. of Parliamentary discussion — DISR 246:17
R. of the Rhine — MAC 436:5
rural: lovely woman in a r. spot — HUNT 356:12
r. quiet, friendship — THOM 696:3
r. virtues leave the land — GOLD 310:18
sweet especial r. scene — HOPK 345:5
rus: R. *in urbe* — MART 449:17
rush: r. jaded with the r. — ARN 26:17
r. through the fields — CHES 199:2
rushed: He r. into the field — BYRON 168:19
rushes: *Green grow the r. O* — ANON 15:1
Green grow the r., O — BURNS 162:1
rushing: r. mighty wind — BIBLE 98:6
russet: r. yeas — SHAK 599:8

russet-coated: r. captain — CROM 227:6
Russia: distance between R. — SAL 554:1
innocent R. squirmed — AKHM 6:12
last out a night in R. — SHAK 605:13
R. has two generals in whom — NICH 494:12
R. with her big, fat arse — BLOK 115:8
Russian: furnished with a R. soul — LERM 419:1
Grishkin is nice: her R. eye — ELIOT 273:16
that's your R. God — VYAZ 717:9
tumult in the R. heart — PUSH 533:1
Russians: R. and the Americans — TOCQ 699:5
rust: moth and r. doth corrupt — BIBLE 89:6
r. amid greenness — MELV 456:19
Tarnished with r. — WILDE 736:6
that which never taketh r. — SIDN 647:4
To r. in peace, or rot — SOUT 657:2
To r. unburnished — TENN 690:1
wear out than to r. — CUMB 228:4
rustic: r. murmur of their bourg — TENN 682:9
rusticity: And a refined r. — WORD 744:6
rustics: gazing r. ranged — GOLD 310:14
rustle: r. in your throng throat — WALK 718:1
rustling: I dread the r. of the grass — WORD 743:5
rusty: fighting was grown r. — BUTL 166:8
Ruth: sad heart of R. — KEATS 389:15
ruthful: Heaven and Earth are not r. — LAO-T 409:10
ruthless: Ruin seize thee, r. King! — GRAY 315:6
rutting: lean as a r. Stag — BYRON 173:22
rye: catcher in the r. — SAL 553:18
Comin thro' the r. — BURNS 161:13
fields of barley and of r. — TENN 684:23
Roman came to R. — CHES 199:5
r. reach to the chin — PEELE 511:4

S

Saba: S. shall bring gifts — BOOK 129:20
sabachthani: lama s. — BIBLE 93:5
Sabaoth: grant me that S.'s sight — SPEN 660:18
Lord God of S. — BOOK 118:12
sabbath: Remember the s. day — BIBLE 72:16
S. eves I am oppressed — BABEL 41:9
s. was made for man — BIBLE 93:7
seventh day is the s. — BIBLE 72:16
sabbaths: endless s. — ABEL 1:1
new moons and s. — BIBLE 82:9
Sabidi: *Non amo te, S.* — MART 449:12
sable: And paint the s. skies — DRUM 258:13
son of the s. Night — DAN 229:16
sable-vested: S. Night — MILT 470:12
sabre: Great Chatham with his s. — ANON 13:21
s. was blunted by the difficulty — WALP 720:4
Sabrina: S. fair — MILT 464:10
Sacco: S.'s name will live — VANZ 708:10
sack: intolerable deal of s. — SHAK 580:35
leave s., and live cleanly — SHAK 582:11
s. and sugar be a fault — SHAK 580:32
S. the lot — FISH 283:4
sackbut: harp, s., psaltery — BIBLE 85:28
sacrament: constant s. of praise — STEV 666:9
holy S. to your comfort — BOOK 122:5
This great S. revere — THOM 692:14
sacramental: flesh was s. of the spirit — ROB 542:15
sacraments: S. hath Christ ordained — BOOK 123:10
S. in a tongue not — BOOK 135:24
s. to a dying god — HEINE 331:2
sacred: facts are s. — SCOTT 559:2
s. rites unfit — SIDN 647:1
wealth is a s. thing — FRAN 292:6
sacrifice: blood of human s. — MILT 468:16
full, perfect, and sufficient s. — BOOK 122:11
great pinnacle of S. — LLOY 424:6
hands be an evening s. — BOOK 135:1
obey is better than s. — BIBLE 74:37
ought to s. to the graces — BURKE 158:29
refused a lesser s. — MARY 452:1
s. for sin — BOOK 126:25

SALTEENA SAVE

salt: (*cont.*):
s. tides seawards flow ARN 27:7
seasoned with s. BIBLE 103:18
Salteena: Mr S. was an elderly man of 42 ASHF 31:4
saltness: s. of time SHAK 582:16
sugar, and s. agree GOLD 311:3
saltpetre: villainous s. SHAK 579:32
salus: *S. populi suprema est lex* CIC 203:27
S. populi suprema lex est SELD 562:10
salutant: *morituri te s.* ANON 22:2
salutations: s. in the marketplaces BIBLE 93:17
salute: If it moves, s. it ANON 14:17
I s. thee, Mantovano TENN 689:15
S. one another BIBLE 100:14
S. the happy morn BYROM 167:14
who are about to die s. ANON 22:2
saluted: s. and surrounded with innumerable joys TRAH 701:11
salva: *S. me, fons pietatis* MISS 477:13
salvaged: ships have been s. HALS 322:9
salvation: for an helmet, the hope of s. BIBLE 103:21
Him that brought s. down SMART 650:4
My bottle of s. RAL 535:18
my light, and my s. BOOK 125:24
necessary to s. BOOK 123:10
necessary to s. BOOK 135:22
none of us should see s. SHAK 609:13
no s. outside the church AUG 37:4
now is our s. nearer BIBLE 100:10
now is the day of s. BIBLE 101:19
s. of our own souls JOHN 372:25
s. with fear and trembling BIBLE 103:6
show him my s. BOOK 131:5
strength of our s. BOOK 131:9
that publisheth s. BIBLE 84:8
There cannot be s. CYPR 229:10
Visit us with thy s. WESL 728:14
Wot prawce S. nah SHAW 636:31
salve: *S., regina* ANON 22:14
Sam: nephew of my Uncle S. COHAN 208:13
S., pick up tha' musket HOLL 342:5
Samarcand: silken S. KEATS 387:9
Samaritan: remember the good S. THAT 691:24
Samarkand: Golden Road to S. FLEC 286:11
Samarra: tonight in S. LOW 429:13
same: Christ the s. yesterday BIBLE 104:21
he is much the s. ANON 12:4
s. a hundred years hence DICK 242:6
s. in thine own act SHAK 601:5
s. the whole world over ANON 17:20
s. thing at the end BROW 148:4
s. thing in different words REED 538:6
tell them I'm having the s. LOES 426:2
things don't seem the s. HEND 332:3
thou art the s. BOOK 132:1
we must all say *the s.* MELB 456:5
What reason I should be the s. AYT 41:1
you are the s. you MART 449:16
samite: Clothed in white s. TENN 681:18
samphire: one that gathers s. SHAK 597:1
sampler: serve to ply the s. MILT 464:8
Samson: S. hath quit himself MILT 474:17
Samuel: Lord called S. BIBLE 74:27
sancta: *sed s. simplicitas* JER 365:11
sanctified: husband is s. by the wife BIBLE 100:25
sanctify: S. the Lord of hosts BIBLE 82:25
sanctuarize: should murder s. SHAK 578:12
sanctuary: dark s. of incapacity CHES 198:4
he shall be for a s. BIBLE 82:25
so much s.-breaking SKEL 649:4
three classes which need s. BALD 48:14
sanctus: *S., sanctus, sanctus* MISS 477:2
sand: at night to die upon the s. ARN 28:15
built his house upon the s. BIBLE 89:27
grain of s. WHIT 732:17
land of s. and ruin SWIN 677:5
on the edge of the s. LEAR 414:15
palace built upon the s. MILL 461:8
plain to be seen in the s. DEFOE 234:9
s. against the wind BLAKE 113:5
sand: (*cont.*):
s. in the porridge COW 220:10
S.-strewn caverns ARN 27:8
see a world in a grain of s. BLAKE 110:18
Such quantities of s. CARR 183:1
tide crept up along the s. KING 397:14
sandal: And his s. shoon SHAK 577:34
sandals: still morn went out with s. grey MILT 466:15
sandalwood: S., cedarwood MAS 453:2
sands: Across the s. of Dee KING 397:13
Footprints on the s. of time LONG 427:10
Here are s., ignoble things BEAU 56:15
level s. stretch far away SHEL 642:4
riddle of the s. CHIL 199:25
s. upon the Red sea shore BLAKE 113:6
s. with printless foot SHAK 626:1
smoothed down like silly s. BUNT 155:10
sandwich: s. in her hand DICK 243:4
s. it swallowed centuries ago BARN 53:10
sane: go mad they shall be s. THOM 693:3
no s. person would do at eleven SHAW 636:32
sang: s. his didn't he danced CUMM 228:5
s. in my chains THOM 693:6
s. within the bloody wood ELIOT 272:20
Sangreal: story of the S. MAL 443:9
sanguis: *semen est s. Christianorum* TERT 690:17
sanitary: glorified s. engineer STR 670:17
sanitas: *S. sanitatum* MEN 457:1
sank: he s. into his grave YEATS 751:17
s. by the Low-lands low BALL 49:11
Sighted sub, s. same MASON 453:11
They s. my boat KENN 394:9
sano: *mens sana in corpore s.* JUV 384:11
sans: s. End FITZ 283:18
S. teeth, sans eyes SHAK 568:16
Sansculotte: *bon S. Jésus* DESM 238:1
sap: also are full of s. BOOK 132:8
s. out of my veins YEATS 751:18
world's whole s. is sunk DONNE 252:12
sapient: s. sutlers of the Lord ELIOT 272:8
shake his s. head ARN 29:5
sapienti: *Dictum s. sat est* PLAU 517:4
sapless: s. foliage of the ocean SHEL 641:17
saplings: wind it plies the s. HOUS 352:12
sapphire: purer s. melts TENN 686:16
sapphires: ivory overlaid with s. BIBLE 81:20
Sappho: burning S. loved BYRON 170:30
Dark S.! could not verse BYRON 168:8
Sarah: it ceased to be with S. BIBLE 71:1
sardine: jasper and a s. stone BIBLE 106:9
Sargent: musical Malcolm S. BEEC 58:18
Sarum: had you upon S. plain SHAK 595:13
sashes: one of his nice new s. GRAH 313:12
sassy: sickly but s. HARR 327:3
sat: I s. down and wept SMART 650:6
I s. upon a promontory SHAK 611:16
S. and knotted all the while SEDL 561:15
s. down under a juniper tree BIBLE 76:6
s. too long here CROM 227:10
upon which everyone has s. CUMM 228:9
we s. down and wept BOOK 134:17
Satan: As S. seems to show GILB 303:10
Auld Hornie, S., Nick BURNS 160:23
beat down S. under our feet BOOK 119:20
Get thee behind me, S. BIBLE 91:15
Incensed with indignation S. MILT 470:7
Lord said unto S. BIBLE 76:37
messenger of S. BIBLE 102:2
my S., thou art but a dunce BLAKE 111:23
Of S. and his peers MILT 469:9
S. as lightning fall BIBLE 94:11
S. exalted sat, by merit raised MILT 469:10
S. finds some mischief WATTS 722:13
S. met his ancient friend BYRON 173:18
S., so call him now MILT 472:3
Satanic: dark S. mills BLAKE 113:4
'satiable: full of s. curtiosity KIPL 401:20
satiety: another occasion of s. BACON 43:2
ne'er knew love's sad s. SHEL 643:18
satire: It's hard not to write s. JUV 383:13
let s. be my song BYRON 172:3
S., being levelled at all SWIFT 674:10
satire: (*cont.*):
s. indeed is entirely our QUIN 534:16
S. is a sort of glass SWIFT 673:3
S. is what closes Saturday KAUF 385:14
S. or sense, alas POPE 520:2
s. out of time CHUR 201:7
satiric: by one s. touch SWIFT 675:13
satirical: s. rogue says here SHAK 574:22
sign of a s. wit AUBR 33:8
satirist: s. may laugh GIBB 302:9
second English s. HALL 322:2
satisfaction: I can't get no s. JAGG 361:11
murder, for my own s. DOST 254:12
to give you s. GAY 299:24
satisfied: Never s. with having WROTH 749:14
philosopher may be equally *s.* JOHN 372:24
well paid that is well s. SHAK 609:21
satisfies: Where most she s. SHAK 565:8
satisfieth: he s. the empty soul BOOK 132:15
labour for that which s. BIBLE 84:15
s. thy mouth with good things BOOK 132:3
satisfy: poorly s. our eyes WOTT 749:2
with long life will I s. him BOOK 131:5
satisfying: s. a voracious appetite FIEL 282:12
Saturday: date on S. night ALLEN 9:18
For what he did on S. YBAR 750:14
Glasgow Empire on a S. DODD 249:24
Satire is what closes S. night KAUF 385:14
Saturn: grey-haired S. KEATS 387:22
while S. whirls TENN 687:21
Saturnia: *redeunt S. regna* VIRG 714:22
Saturnus: S., with his frosty face SACK 552:12
satyr: angel s. walks these hills KILV 396:8
Hyperion to a s.: so loving SHAK 572:12
satyrs: like s. grazing MARL 447:6
sauce: Hunger is the best s. CERV 188:9
religions, and only one s. CAR 178:16
saucy: deep-searched with s. SHAK 598:7
s. and audacious eloquence SHAK 612:21
Saul: S. also among the prophets BIBLE 74:33
S. and Jonathan were lovely BIBLE 75:9
S. hath slain his thousands BIBLE 75:5
S. was consenting unto BIBLE 98:13
S., why persecutest thou BIBLE 98:15
weep over S. BIBLE 75:9
whose name was S. BIBLE 98:12
savage: becomes again almost a s. TOCQ 699:8
does not allow it to be s. OVID 502:17
in which a s. wields his club HUXL 358:4
mad and s. master SOPH 656:15
s. contemplates his mother-in-law FRAZ 293:9
sooth a s. breast CONG 215:16
Standing among s. scenery HOFF 341:13
thrice happy now the s. CHUR 201:1
Unequal laws unto a s. race TENN 689:18
wild in woods the noble s. DRYD 260:8
will take some s. woman TENN 685:17
savaged: s. by a dead sheep HEAL 329:16
savageness: sing the s. out SHAK 617:10
savages: love of s. LERM 418:14
save: destroy the town to s. it ANON 15:7
God s. king Solomon BIBLE 75:21
God s. the king HOGG 341:17
he shall s. his soul alive BIBLE 85:23
himself he cannot s. BIBLE 93:4
little less democracy to s. ATK 32:12
matter enough to s. one's own BROW 150:24
need not exist in order to s. us DE VR 238:4
s. me from the candid friend CANN 178:6
s. me, O source of pity MISS 477:13
s. my soul ANON 17:2
s. them by the barrel-load THOM 695:8
s. the Party we love GAIT 296:16
s. those that have no imagination SHAW 638:24
struggle is to s. the Union LINC 422:12
That can, but will not, s. me DRAY 258:6
To choose time is to s. time BACON 43:14
To s. your world you asked AUDEN 34:9
vain thing to s. a man BOOK 126:12
We shall nobly s. LINC 422:6
When wilt thou s. the people ELL 275:13

save: (*cont.*):
you only must s. face HEAN 329:21
saved: could have s. sixpence BECK 57:12
He s. others BIBLE 93:4
s. in this World HAL 321:19
s. you only must save face HEAN 329:21
they only s. the world CHES 199:1
we are not s. BIBLE 85:8
What must I do to be s. BIBLE 98:26
Whosoever will be s. BOOK 119:12
saves: idea of death s. him FORS 290:15
saveth: s. in time of affliction BIBLE 87:8
saving: poetry is capable of s. us RICH 540:8
thy s. health BOOK 129:4
saviour: first men that our S. BASSE 55:1
I imitate the S. HUXL 357:7
it's 'S. of 'is country' KIPL 401:6
Lived on earth our s. holy ALEX 8:12
S. of the world was born BYROM 167:14
S.'s birth is celebrated SHAK 572:2
s. spring to life BIBLE 108:7
'Tis thy S., hear his word COWP 222:20
savory: mints, s., marjoram SHAK 632:3
savour: salt have lost his s. BIBLE 88:24
Seeming and s. all the winter SHAK 631:29
saw: drowns the parson's s. SHAK 599:11
grave hum, and formal s. LLOYD 424:2
He s., he sighed, he loved GAY 299:29
I came, s., and overcame SHAK 583:25
I s. and loved GIBB 302:14
I s. the Sibyl at Cumae PETR 513:13
I stumbled when I s. SHAK 596:24
Nor do not s. the air SHAK 576:5
saws: s. and modern instances SHAK 568:16
Saxon: that ancient S. phrase LONG 426:22
saxpence: *bang*—ten s. PUNCH 531:15
say: before the morning watch, I s.
BOOK 134:12
don't s. nothin' HAMM 322:18
Englishman is content to s. JOHN 375:15
Have something to s. ARN 30:10
I have nothing to s. CAGE 174:22
I s. the hell with it WHITE 731:2
many things to s. unto you BIBLE 97:19
more to s. when I am dead ROB 542:9
nothing to say, s. nothing COLT 214:7
nothing to what I could s. CARR 182:11
Preachers say, Do as I s. SELD 562:13
S. I'm weary, say I'm sad HUNT 356:9
S. it with flowers O'KEE 498:7
s. the perfectly correct thing SHAW 636:18
s. what you mean CARR 182:6
s. what you think TAC 678:2
s. why and how I became WILS 738:7
someone else has got to s. GASK 299:4
Some s. the world will end FROST 294:17
there is no more to s. SHAK 628:7
There's some s. that we wan MCL 439:11
They are to s. what they please FRED 293:11
till I see what I s. WALL 718:7
we must all s. *the same* MELB 456:5
We must not s. so BERR 66:18
whatever you s., say nothing HEAN 329:21
what they are going to s. CHUR 201:24
you have something to s. WHAT 730:7
saying: and I am s. it CAGE 174:22
For loving, and for s. so DONNE 252:19
not worth s., people sing it BEAU 56:9
rage for s. something JOHN 371:22
We were s. yesterday LUIS 432:8
says: author is not what he s. SMITH 652:11
scabbard: threw away the s. CLAR 205:1
scabs: Make yourselves s. SHAK 570:4
scaffold: s. from a throne FANS 280:1
To the s. and the doom AYT 41:2
Truth forever on the s. LOW 430:4
scald: Do s. like molten lead SHAK 597:13
scale: best s. for an experiment FISH 283:3
not made on a human s. MALR 443:16
s. the icy mountains' lofty MARL 447:20
sink i' the s. BROW 152:7
sufficiently large s. SPEN 658:20
thumb in the s. LAWR 412:4

scales: climb aloft by s. of courtly GASC 298:17
could swear in both the s. SHAK 602:9
someone is practising s. MACN 441:3
scalp: s. all pilled SACK 552:14
scaly: s. horror of his folded MILT 467:10
scan: s. your brother man BURNS 161:1
scandal: have no s. while you dine TENN 689:13
In s., as in robbery CHES 198:1
Love and s. are the best FIEL 282:7
Retired to their tea and s. CONG 214:23
s. by a woman of easy virtue HAIL 321:1
s. that constitutes offence MOL 479:13
There is no s. like rags FARQ 280:10
scandalous: s. and poor ROCH 543:15
scapegoat: Let him go for a s. BIBLE 73:2
scar: s. that whiter skin SHAK 618:5
We can find no s. DICK 244:20
scarcely: s. greet me with that sun SHAK 633:15
scarceness: runagates continue in s.
BOOK 129:7
scaret ever o. me with thy tears TENN 689:11
s. me with their empty FROST 294:16
those footprints s. me HOR 348:1
scarecrow: s. of the law SHAK 605:11
scarecrows: like mechanized s. KAV 386:3
s. of fools and the beacons HUXL 358:11
scared: always been s. of *you* PLATH 516:4
scarf: S. up the tender eye SHAK 603:5
scarlet: are like a thread of s. BIBLE 81:13
Cowards in s. pass for men GRAN 314:14
He did not wear his s. coat WILDE 735:33
His sins were s. BELL 61:26
love that loves a s. coat HOOD 343:19
Only the s. soldiers, dear AUDEN 35:14
raise the s. standard high CONN 216:8
This line of s. thread BIBLE 73:28
though clothed in s. JONS 378:24
Though your sins be as s. BIBLE 82:10
who clothed you in s. BIBLE 75:9
scars: He jests at s., that never SHAK 622:27
My marks and s. I carry BUNY 156:16
show his s. SHAK 586:11
scatter: S., as from an SHEL 642:1
scattered: he hath s. the proud BIBLE 93:23
let his enemies be s. BOOK 129:6
thousand s. into clay FITZ 283:11
scatterest: soon as thou s. them BOOK 130:23
scatters: the rear of darkness MILT 465:8
scelerisque: *vitae s. purus* HOR 349:11
scene: behold the swelling s. SHAK 584:16
every day speaks a new s. QUAR 533:16
In life's last s. what prodigies JOHN 370:20
Last s. of all SHAK 568:16
Live o'er each s. POPE 523:14
lofty s. be acted o'er SHAK 591:17
start a s. or two ELIOT 272:5
scenery: And the s.'s divine CALV 175:14
end of all natural s. RUSK 550:15
S. is fine KEATS 391:16
Standing among savage s. HOFF 341:13
Where God paints the s. HART 327:13
you talk to me about s. BECK 57:24
scenes: long for s. where man CLARE 204:20
no more behind your s. JOHN 371:8
s. and shining prospects ADD 4:2
scent: first I met the bitter s. THOM 694:4
How hot the s. GRAV 314:17
methinks I s. the morning air SHAK 573:19
s. comes forth DAV 232:14
s. of the roses will hang MOORE 483:4
sweetest flower for s. SHEL 643:1
Their s. survives their close THOM 694:17
whose s. the fair annoys COWP 222:3
sceptic: too much of a s. to deny HUXL 358:13
What ever s. could inquire BUTL 166:3
scepticism: s. kept her from being SART 556:16
s. of the intellect NEWM 493:4
which at first lead to s. BERK 65:10
sceptre: His the s., his the throne DIX 249:18
S. and crown SHIR 646:2
s. and the ball SHAK 586:8
s. shows the force of temporal SHAK 609:13

sceptred: this s. isle SHAK 619:18
what avails the s. race LAND 408:4
sceptreless: S., free SHEL 642:18
schemes: s. of political improvement
JOHN 373:6
s. o' mice an' men BURNS 163:17
scherzando: *S.! ma non troppo ppp* GILB 303:13
schizoid: s. self-alienation FROMM 294:7
schizophrenic: you are a s. SZASZ 677:14
scholar: better s. than Wordsworth
HOUS 353:1
gentleman and s. BURNS 163:24
He was a s. SHAK 589:10
infinitely before a great s. LOCKE 425:11
mere s. DEFOE 233:15
s. all Earth's volumes carry CHAP 191:4
s. among rakes MAC 435:14
Soldier, s., horseman YEATS 752:4
what ills the s.'s life assail JOHN 370:15
scholars philosophers and s. PASC 508:1
S. and gentlemen WORD 747:5
S. dispute HOR 347:7
school: erecting a grammar s. SHAK 587:26
Example is the s. of mankind BURKE 159:21
in cloistre or in s. LANG 409:2
language, goeth in s. BACON 44:35
never was there s. MILT 474:7
nonsense knocked out of them at s.
BEER 59:12
s. of Manchester DISR 248:39
Than either s. or college BURNS 162:5
that love was but a s. WOTT 749:3
till he's been to a good s. SAKI 553:1
Unwillingly to s. SHAK 568:16
vixen when she went to s. SHAK 612:5
went to s. without any boots BULM 155:1
What is he sent to s. for? HUGH 354:10
schoolboy: Every s. knows MAC 435:9
every s. knows it TAYL 679:18
I see a s. when I think of him YEATS 751:17
Not the s. heat TENN 684:12
s. who wipes his fingers BLUNT 116:6
s. with a satchel BLAIR 110:15
tell what every s. knows SWIFT 674:26
than that of a s.'s tip THAC 691:5
then the whining s. SHAK 568:16
schoolboys: duty to delight s. JUV 384:9
s. from their books SHAK 623:5
s. playing in the stream PEELE 511:4
schoolchildren: What all s. learn AUDEN 35:19
schooldays: Thy s. frightful SHAK 622:5
schoolgirl: Pert as a s. GILB 304:23
schoolman: no s.'s subtle art POPE 520:7
schoolmaster: s. is abroad BROU 144:8
you'll be becoming a s. WAUGH 723:12
schoolmasters: Let s. puzzle their brain
GOLD 311:20
s. deliver us to laws HERB 335:19
schoolrooms: build s. for 'the boy' COOK 218:5
schools: banished from the s. CHUD 200:11
bewildered in the maze of s. POPE 521:4
blossom and a hundred s. MAO 446:3
flogging in our great s. JOHN 374:8
lumber of the s. SWIFT 674:30
Oh wrangling s. DONNE 252:2
schooner: s. Hesperus LONG 428:3
sciatica: S.: he cured it AUBR 33:9
science: Art and S. cannot exist BLAKE 112:6
beams of s. fall POPE 518:19
countenance of all s. WORD 748:18
Dismal S. CARL 180:32
Enough of s. and of art WORD 748:8
essence of s. BRON 141:18
How s. dwindles YOUNG 754:11
human s. is at a loss CHOM 200:5
investigated by s. ELIOT 269:15
Language is only the instrument of s.
JOHN 367:20
matters of opinion and s. HUME 355:15
new s. for their imagery MCEW 437:15
no less the beginning of s. LEIB 416:13
Of s. and logic he chatters PRAED 528:13

SCIENCES SEA

science: (*cont.*):
only applications of s. PAST 509:3
only s. that it hath pleased God HOBB 339:18
positive s. may be defined KEYN 395:13
redefined the task of s. HAWK 328:6
s. and study of man CHAR 192:2
S. appears WORD 747:1
S. appears intuitive METT 459:1
S. frowned not on his humble GRAY 315:20
S. is an edged tool EDD 266:6
S. is built up of facts POIN 518:10
s. is either physics or stamp RUTH 552:6
S. is his forte SMITH 653:30
S. is nothing but HUXL 358:4
S. is organized knowledge SPEN 658:11
s. is strong and religion weak SZASZ 677:15
S. means simply the aggregate VALÉ 707:21
S. moves, but slowly slowly TENN 685:14
S. must begin with myths POPP 524:15
S. never taught to stray POPE 522:2
s. of politics ARIS 25:8
s. of the tender passion PUSH 532:13
s. pointed out the path AKEN 6:5
s. reassures BRAQ 139:17
s. the credit goes to the man DARW 231:15
s. the right interpretation WHEW 730:15
s. which pretends to lay open SMITH 650:14
s. will appear incomplete ARN 29:22
S. without religion is lame EINS 268:6
tragedy of S. HUXL 358:3
typical triumph of modern s. WAUGH 724:9
sciences: advancing the s. LOCKE 424:15
Books must follow s. BACON 45:23
gives us *Reason* and the s. LEIB 416:14
That great mother of s. BACON 45:20
scientia: *S. potestas est.* BACON 45:15
scientiae: *fraudatrix s.* JOHN 366:15
scientiarum: *Magna ista s. mater* BACON 45:20
scientific: as if they were s. terms ARN 30:1
broken open on the most s. PEAC 510:6
Death was but a s. fact WILDE 736:2
judgement of our s. age HOLM 342:6
literary and s. opinion ARN 29:20
possible for an empirical s. POPP 524:10
s. faith's absurd BROW 149:17
s. names of beings GILB 306:9
s. power has outrun our KING 397:3
s. questions HUXL 358:12
s. truth does not triumph PLAN 516:1
scientis: *Signum s. est posse* AUCT 33:25
scientist: research s. to discard LOR 428:12
s. says that something CLAR 205:10
s.'s laws and his own attempted QUINE 534:14
scientists: in the company of s. AUDEN 36:16
physical s. SNOW 654:7
scintillations: s. of your wit GOUL 313:1
scire: *s. nefas* HOR 349:8
scissor-man: long, red-legged s. HOFF 341:6
scoff: who came to s. GOLD 310:11
scoffer: product of a s.'s pen WORD 743:19
scoffing: S. his state SHAK 620:8
scones: afternoon tea-cakes and s. BETJ 67:12
Over buttered s. and crumpets ELIOT 270:10
scope: that man's s. SHAK 633:10
scorched: they were s. BIBLE 91:1
scorer: One Great S. comes RICE 540:1
scorn: cannot be surmounted by s. CAMUS 177:20
deal of s. looks beautiful SHAK 630:12
Disdain and s. ride sparkling SHAK 613:29
figure for the time of s. SHAK 617:15
Laugh no man to s. BIBLE 87:13
life the subject of thy s. GREE 317:8
little s. is alluring CONG 215:35
love he laughed to s. SHAK 635:11
Nor treat with virtuous s. GILB 304:8
S. not the Sonnet WORD 747:17
s. of that pleasant land BOOK 132:13
s. that Parma or Spain ELIZ 274:3
s. to change my state SHAK 633:10
s. which mocked the smart ARN 28:21
sound of public s. MILT 472:4
scorn: (*cont.*):
Teach not thy lip such s. SHAK 621:18
thereof take no s. DAV 232:7
very s. of men BOOK 125:10
We s. their bodies BAST 55:3
scorned: like a woman s. CONG 215:17
s. his spirit SHAK 590:7
was s. and died GAY 299:29
scornful: only a s. tickling SIDN 647:11
sat in the seat of the s. BOOK 124:6
s. glances from those eyes SHAK 624:21
scorning: s. the base degrees SHAK 590:14
scorpions: chastise you with s. BIBLE 75:28
Scot: Had Cain been S. CLEV 206:14
Scotch: inferior to the S. NORTH 496:12
joke well into a S. understanding SMITH 653:7
Mary, ma S. Bluebell LAUD 411:6
scotched: s. the snake SHAK 603:3
Scotchman: noblest prospect which a S. JOHN 372:7
Scotia: chief of S.'s food BURNS 161:17
old S.'s grandeur springs BURNS 161:19
Scotland: fair S.'s spear SCOTT 560:11
from S. but I cannot help it JOHN 371:25
grave Livers do in S. use WORD 747:12
I'll be in S. afore ye ANON 17:8
inferior sort of S. SMITH 653:3
in S. supports the people JOHN 368:3
left fair S.'s strand BURNS 162:9
love S. better than truth JOHN 368:12
S., land of the omnipotent No BOLD 117:6
S. led in luve and le WYNT 750:10
Stands S. where it did SHAK 604:7
Scots: dozen of S. at breakfast SHAK 580:14
S., wha hae wi' Wallace bled BURNS 163:1
Wi' the S. lords at his feet BALL 50:12
Scotsman: S. on the make BARR 54:13
Scott: half so flat as Walter S. ANON 17:7
wrong part wrote S. WAT 722:5
Scottish: auld S. sang BURNS 161:14
Froude informs the S. youth STUB 671:2
scoundrel: Every man over forty is a s. SHAW 638:2
given them to such a s. SWIFT 673:23
good is the plea of the s. BLAKE 112:6
last refuge of a s. JOHN 374:2
scoured: s. to nothing SHAK 582:24
scourge: s. of small cords BIBLE 96:12
scout: s. 'em, and flout 'em SHAK 625:24
scouts: s.' motto is founded BAD 46:4
scowl: Did s. on Richard SHAK 621:7
With anxious s. drew near AYT 41:3
scramble: s. at the shearers' feast MILT 466:8
scrap: just for a s. of paper BETH 67:2
scrape: potsherd to s. himself BIBLE 77:4
scraping: Death's ironic s. STEV 666:9
scraps: stolen the s. SHAK 599:4
scratch: all you can do is s. it BEEC 59:5
quick sharp s. BROW 151:7
S. a lover, and find a foe PARK 506:4
S. the Christian and you ZANG 755:6
s. the nurse SHAK 631:3
scratched: Priscian a little s. SHAK 599:3
scratches: S. its innocent behind AUDEN 35:7
scratching: but the s. of a pen LOVER 429:7
s. of pimples on the body WOOLF 742:16
world to the s. of my finger HUME 356:1
scream: Does not s. WHIT 733:1
like a s. from a crevasse GREE 317:2
more thrilling than a s. ROLFE 545:8
screams: strange s. of death SHAK 602:13
screen: s. from seeing SWIN 675:23
screw: s. your courage SHAK 601:7
scribblative: arts babblative and s. SOUT 657:15
scribble: Always s., scribble GLOU 308:3
s., to a man POPE 523:3
scribbled: Man by a s. name THOM 693:10
s. lines like fallen hopes HOPE 345:2
scribendi: *S. cacoethes et aegro* JUV 384:3
scribere: *Difficile est saturam non s.* JUV 383:13
In vento et rapida s. oportet CAT 186:10
scribes: Beware of the s. BIBLE 93:17
scribes: (*cont.*):
s. and Pharisees BIBLE 88:28
s. and Pharisees BIBLE 92:5
scribimus: *S. indocti doctique* HOR 348:17
scrip: with s. and scrippage SHAK 569:3
scriptores: *Cedite Romani s.* PROP 530:2
scripture: devil can cite S. SHAK 607:21
Hooly writ is the s. of puples JER 365:12
I will better it in S. JAM 362:7
S. containeth all things BOOK 135:22
S. moveth us in sundry BOOK 118:5
usury is contrary to S. TAWN 679:2
scriptures: caused all Holy S. BOOK 120:11
Search the s. BIBLE 96:21
scrivener: cropt s. LAMB 406:10
scroll: long-cramped s. BROW 150:21
with punishments the s. HENL 332:7
scrotumtightening: s. sea JOYCE 381:18
scruple: Some craven s. SHAK 577:32
scrupulosity: oriental s. JOHN 369:4
scrupulous: s. and the just CONR 217:15
scrutamini: *S. scripturas* SELD 562:2
scullion: Away, you s.! SHAK 583:3
sculptor: great s. or painter RUSK 550:11
sculpture: like that of s. RUSS 551:20
s. is the true school PEAC 510:5
sculptured: s. dead KEATS 386:21
scum: dungy muddy s. MARS 449:9
Okie means you're s. STEI 663:9
s. of the earth CHES 199:15
s. of the earth WELL 727:12
scutcheon: honour is a mere s. SHAK 582:1
scuttling: S. across the floors ELIOT 272:3
Scylla: S. and Charybdis of Aye and No NEWM 493:2
scythe: mower whets his s. MILT 465:10
poor crooked s. and spade SHIR 646:2
Wanting the s., all uncorrected SHAK 586:17
which shall bate his s.'s SHAK 598:6
scythes: last year's s. flung MELV 456:19
Scythia: another group to S. VIRG 714:13
sea: all as hungry as the s. SHAK 629:19
all gone under the s. ELIOT 270:20
all the s. were ink LYLY 433:13
Alone on a wide wide s. COL 211:7
beneath in the abysmal s. TENN 684:19
blow the earth into the s. SHAK 595:19
bottom of the s. SHAK 621:23
boundless as the s. SHAK 623:4
But I beneath a rougher s. COWP 221:25
Call him on the deep s. NEWB 492:7
crowned with summer s. TENN 682:25
crowns around the glassy s. HEBER 330:5
Death like a narrow s. divides WATTS 723:5
deep s. keep you up CONR 217:7
do be afraid of the s. SYNGE 677:7
Down to a sunless s. COL 210:9
down to the s. in ships BOOK 133:1
English that of the s. RICH 540:17
far over the summer s. TENN 689:3
forests and blue days at s. STEV 668:24
For those in peril on the s. WHIT 732:2
frail boat on the rough s. HOR 349:2
France and England is—the s. JERR 365:19
From s. to shining sea BATES 55:5
full s. are we now afloat SHAK 593:12
gaping wretches of the s. HUNT 356:6
gong-tormented s. YEATS 751:1
great and wide s. also BOOK 132:9
gurly grew the s. BALL 49:5
has something of the s. SEDL 561:14
heaven by s. as by land GILB 303:12
He divided the s., and let BOOK 130:10
his trunk spouts out a s. MILT 472:9
if we gang to s. master BALL 50:11
if Ye take away the s. KIPL 399:16
In a solitude of the s. HARDY 325:3
in the s. of life enisled ARN 29:3
in the s., the man SMART 650:2
Into a s. of dew FIELD 281:14
Into that silent s. COL 210:24
into the midst of the s. BOOK 127:15
leaped headlong into the s. KEATS 391:22

shadow: (cont.):
mere s. of death — LAUD 411:4
neither s. of turning — BIBLE 104:26
one is the s. of the other — JUNG 383:1
Or s. of felicity — WALL 718:18
out-soared the s. of our night — SHEL 640:1
s. at morning striding — ELIOT 272:23
S. cloaked from head — TENN 683:9
s. of a great rock — BIBLE 83:17
s. of death — BIBLE 77:15
s. of death — BIBLE 93:24
s. of death — BOOK 132:15
s. of some unseen Power — SHEL 640:18
s. of the earth — BROW 146:22
Swift as a s. — SHAK 610:23
Under the s. of her even brows — SPEN 660:4
valley of the s. of death — BOOK 125:15
walketh in a vain s. — BOOK 126:23
Who live under the s. of a war — SPEN 659:7
shadowing: depth of s. — DRYD 262:20
shadowless: s. like Silence — HOOD 344:3
shadows: all I have loved were s. — HEAT 029.24
best in this kind are but s. — SHAK 612:25
chase hurdling s. — BUNT 155:9
half sick of s. — TENN 685:1
If we s. have offended — SHAK 613:3
In ancient s. and twilights — Æ 5:10
Individuals pass like s. — BURKE 158:32
less liquid than their s. — TESS 691:1
millions of strange s. — SHAK 633:16
Our fatal s. that walk — FLET 287:16
s. and types to the reality — NEWM 493:17
s. flee away — BIBLE 81:11
s., not substantial things — SHIR 646:2
s. now so long do grow — COTT 220:3
s. numberless — KEATS 389:8
s., that showed at noon — LEE 416:1
s. to-night — SHAK 622:13
s. upon the sunbright walls — WORD 743:3
Some there be that s. kiss — SHAK 608:18
splendour among s. — SHEL 643:6
Styled but the s. of us men — JONS 379:19
Types and s. have their ending — THOM 692:14
very s. of the clouds — WORD 743:5
shadow-show: magic s. — FITZ 284:5
shadowy: with a s. third — BROW 148:26
Shadrach: S., Meshach — BIBLE 85:29
shady: s. trees cover him — BIBLE 78:3
shaft: many a s., at random — SCOTT 559:18
s. of light across — TENN 681:9
Shaftesbury: Lord S. — CHES 198:20
shafts: Its s. remain — ROET 544:2
shoots s. divine — LODGE 426:1
shag: cormorant (or s.) — ISH 360:21
shaggy: S., and lean — COWP 224:2
shake: now the Earth must s. — HOR 349:14
power to s. me as they pass — WORD 743:5
s. hands with a king — HALL 322:5
S. off dull sloth — KEN 393:5
s. off the dust — BIBLE 90:15
s. of his poor little head — GILB 305:12
s. their heads — BOOK 125:10
s. their wicked sides — YEATS 752:17
s. the laughing heart's — BROO 143:17
s. the saintship — BYRON 168:2
'tis true, this god did s. — SHAK 590:1
To s. his sapient head — ARN 29:5
Upon those boughs which s. — SHAK 634:6
shaken: S. and not stirred — FLEM 286:18
So s. as we are — SHAK 579:17
tempests and is never s. — SHAK 634:23
time has s. me — WESL 729:3
To be well s. — COLM 214:6
shakers: movers and s. — O'SH 501:22
shakes: Midnight s. the memory — ELIOT 272:14
s. his parting guest — SHAK 627:21
S. so my single state — SHAK 600:12
Shakespeare: already S. is morbid — LAWR 412:2
Corneille is to S. — JOHN 377:3
immortal S. rose — JOHN 370:11
It was for gentle S. cut — JONS 379:18
less S. he — BROW 150:9
make more room for S. — BASSE 55:2

Shakespeare: (cont.):
Or sweetest S. fancy's child — MILT 465:17
Our myriad-minded S. — COL 212:3
quibble is to S. — JOHN 369:10
S. also says, 'tis very silly — BYRON 170:29
S. and Fletcher all they have — DENH 236:19
S., another Newton — HUXL 357:19
S. by flashes of lightning — COL 212:8
S. for his honoured bones — MILT 466:17
S. has united the powers — JOHN 369:9
S. is not more decidedly — MAC 434:12
S. . . . is of no age — COL 212:16
S. one gets acquainted with — AUST 38:19
S. that in his writing — JONS 380:9
S.—the nearest thing — OLIV 498:14
S. undoubtedly wanted taste — WALP 719:7
S. unlocked his heart — WORD 747:17
S. wanted art — JONS 380:8
S. was of us, Milton was — BROW 151:1
S. weak in chemistry — WELLS 727:15
S. (whom you and ev'ry — POPE 622.00
S. would have grasped wave — MCEW 437:15
stuff as great part of S. — GEOR 300:27
talk of my being like S. — SCOTT 561:3
tongue that S. spake — WORD 744:13
When I read S. — LAWR 412:23
Shakespearian: That S. rag — RUBY 154:7
Shakespeherian: o that S. Rag — ELIOT 273:5
shaking: Aching, s., crazy — ROCH 543:17
s. hand of an old man — VICT 710:11
that can fall without s. — MONT 480:3
Shalimar: loved beside the S. — HOPE 345:3
shall: His absolute 's.' — SHAK 570:11
s. and finding only why — CUMM 228:13
shallow: S. brooks murmur most — SIDN 646:12
s. in himself — MILT 473:22
s. murmur, but the deep — RAL 535:19
you are idle s. things — SHAK 630:23
shallows: s. and in miseries — SHAK 593:12
With his depths and his s. — BURNS 163:3
shame: Ain't it all a bleedin s. — ANON 17:20
ashamed with the noble s. — KING 397:18
blush of s. — WHIT 733:6
coward s. distain his name — BURNS 162:17
despising the s. — BIBLE 104:17
fruit of my vanity is s. — PETR 513:10
it is a s. unto him — BIBLE 100:34
now bound in with s. — SHAK 619:18
O s. to men — MILT 469:22
sense of some deathless s. — WEBS 726:4
s. to take the lowest room — BIBLE 94:26
spirit in a waste of s. — SHAK 635:1
still have to ask . . . s. on you — ARMS 26:11
Thy father's s. — BRET 140:17
To s. unvulnerable — SHAK 570:24
whose glory is in their s. — BIBLE 103:10
shamed: Ain't you 's., you sleepy-head — STEV 668:19
shameful: s. conquest of itself — SHAK 619:18
s. to doubt one's friends — LA R 410:14
shameless: most s. thing — BURKE 158:20
shames: hold a candle to my s. — SHAK 608:12
s., on my bare head — SHAK 617:15
Shandeism: True S. — STER 664:29
shank: For his shrunk s. — SHAK 568:16
Shannon: green banks of S. — CAMP 176:13
shape: But in what s. they choose — MILT 468:18
every s. you please — THOM 695:21
execrable s. — MILT 470:6
If s. it might be called — MILT 470:5
it has no s. — ANOU 23:8
men in s. and fashion — ASCH 31:2
pressed out of s. — FROST 295:11
rocks won't lose their s. — ROBIN 542:7
s. in the moonlight — LONG 427:20
s. o'ertakes me — TICK 698:4
s. of things to come — WELLS 727:22
subtly wrought me into s. — FITZ 284:14
such a questionable s. — SHAK 573:9
Take any s. but that — SHAK 603:11
you might be any s. — CARR 183:9
shaped: It is s., sir, like itself — SHAK 565:15
shapen: s. in wickedness — BOOK 128:5

shapes: heaven was full of fiery s. — SHAK 581:1
s. of giant size — BEAT 56:5
s. with Proteus for advantages — SHAK 588:3
shaping: s. spirit of imagination — COL 209:17
shard: s. on shard — THOM 695:7
share: greater s. of honour — SHAK 586:10
I s. no one's ideas — TURG 705:6
Thou its ruin didst not s. — DOD 250:4
wished to s. the transport — WORD 748:6
shares: Fair s. for all — JAY 363:23
s. are a penny — GILB 304:18
shark: s. has pretty teeth — BREC 140:3
Sharon: I am the rose of S. — BIBLE 81:8
sharp: s. as a two-edged sword — BIBLE 78:12
so s. the conquerynge — CHAU 195:5
'Tis a s. remedy — RAL 536:7
sharper: s. than a serpent's tooth — DICK 243:2
s. than a serpent's tooth — SHAK 595:10
sharpness: s. of death — BOOK 118:13
sharps: different s. and flats — BROW 151:26
shatter: S. your leaves before — MILT 465:20
you may s. the vase — MOORE 483:4
shaved: s. and sober — CHAN 190:1
shaves: s. and takes a train — WHITE 731:1
Shaw: Bernard S. hasn't an enemy — WILDE 736:12
shawms: trumpets also, and s. — BOOK 131:14
she: S. sells sea-shells — SULL 671:12
S., she is dead — DONNE 250:8
S. went, to plain-work — POPE 521:1
S. who must be obeyed — HAGG 320:9
S. who trifles with all — GAY 299:28
s. who voiced those rhymes — HARDY 325:1
That not impossible s. — CRAS 226:15
unexpressive s. — SHAK 568:18
sheaf: made obeisance to my s. — BIBLE 71:21
shearers: at the s.' feast — MILT 466:8
sheep before her s. is dumb — BIBLE 84:12
shears: abhorrèd s. — MILT 466:4
resembles a pair of s. — SMITH 653:15
shearsman: s. of sorts — STEV 665:22
sheath: never s. the sword — ASQ 31:17
sheathed: s. their swords — SHAK 585:8
sheaves: bring his s. with him — BOOK 134:5
He rode binding the barley-s. — TENN 685:2
in s. of sacred fire — CHAP 190:17
your s. stood round about — BIBLE 71:21
Sheba: Another S. queen — WITH 739:14
S. had seen all Solomon's — BIBLE 75:23
shed: prepare to s. them now — SHAK 592:13
shall his blood be s. — BIBLE 70:31
s. for you and for many — BOOK 122:12
s. innocent blood — BIBLE 84:24
with Burke under a s. — JOHN 376:10
Yet I'll not s. her blood — SHAK 618:5
shedding: s. of blood — BIBLE 104:11
sheds: found in lowly s. — MILT 463:25
sheep: Among the s. set me — MISS 477:14
black s. who've gone astray — KIPL 399:6
care of s., the labours — DYER 265:2
careth not for the s. — BIBLE 97:1
come you in s.'s clothing — BIBLE 89:23
craved the life of a s. — LA F 405:14
Feed my s. — BIBLE 97:41
folds shall be full of s. — BOOK 129:3
found my s. which was lost — BIBLE 94:35
from thy ways like lost s. — BOOK 118:7
get back to these s. — ANON 21:4
giveth his life for the s. — BIBLE 96:38
Go rather to the lost s. — BIBLE 90:13
His silly s. — COWP 223:2
hungry s. look up — MILT 466:9
lie in the hell like s. — BOOK 128:1
like s. have gone astray — BIBLE 84:12
little hills like young s. — BOOK 133:8
looking on their silly s. — SHAK 588:2
men better than s. — TENN 682:24
noble ensample to his s. — CHAU 193:1
old half-witted s. — STEP 663:17
One sickly s. infects — WATTS 722:11
Other s. I have — BIBLE 97:2
savaged by a dead s. — HEAL 329:16

sickness: (*cont.*):
Till age, or grief, or s. must — KING 396:11
universal as sea s. — SHAW 637:15
Sidcup: I could get down to S. — PINT 514:19
side: Are on our s. to-day — MAC 436:8
embraceth him on every s. — BOOK 126:10
Eve from his s. arose — ANON 19:19
good or evil s. — LOW 430:3
had not been on our s. — BOOK 134:1
Hear the other s. — AUG 37:5
He passed by on the other s. — BIBLE 94:14
her bosom and half her s. — COL 209:9
move over to the other s. — REED 538:5
on the other s. — BUNY 156:16
on the s. of the angels — DISR 247:13
S. by side — WOODS 742:3
s. by side in the ebbing tide — SMITH 651:19
s. of those with plenty — ANOU 23:2
Strait s. by side were laid — MILT 471:14
This s. the tomb — DAV 232:10
thrust my hand into his s. — BIBLE 97:35
Which S. Are You On — DYLAN 265:12
Who is on my s. — BIBLE 76:29
side-arms: keeps 'is s. awful — KIPL 398:19
side-fall: s. of the hill — KAV 386:3
sidelong: s. would she bend — KEATS 388:14
sidera: s. vertice — HOR 348:24
sides: I'm a Norfan, both s. — WELLS 727:17
looked at life from both s. — MITC 417:19
might be said on both s. — ADD 4:9
sideways: up and down than s. — HEM 332:2
We listened and looked s. up — COL 211:4
Sidney: our age, Sir Philip S. — CAREW 179:1
S.'s self, the starry paladin — BROW 153:1
S., whom we yet admire — COK 207:4
siege: beats back the envious s. — SHAK 619:18
Did march to the s. — BALL 50:2
My s. is over — VERT 710:7
She kept the s. — HILL 338:10
Will laugh a s. to scorn — SHAK 604:23
Siegfried: washing on the S. line — KENN 393:9
siesta: Englishmen detest a s. — COW 220:14
sieve: in a s. I'll thither sail — SHAK 600:1
Our S. ain't big — LEAR 414:4
they went to sea in a S. — LEAR 414:3
siftings: let their liquid s. fall — ELIOT 272:20
sigh: Inly I s. for thy repose — WESL 728:16
I to s. for her — SHAK 598:14
prompts th' eternal s. — POPE 522:19
resolved itself into a s. — GONC 312:8
s. is just a sigh — HUPF 357:2
s. is the sword of an Angel — BLAKE 112:5
s. like Tom o' Bedlam — SHAK 595:3
S. no more, ladies — SHAK 613:24
s. the lack of many a thing — SHAK 633:11
telling this with a s. — FROST 295:9
very s. that silence heaves — KEATS 388:5
sighed: He sobbed and he s. — GILB 305:13
I s. as a lover — GIBB 302:15
S. and looked, and sighed — DRYD 259:22
S. and looked unutterable — THOM 696:6
s. for the love of a ladye — GILB 306:24
s. his soul toward — SHAK 609:23
sighing: plague of s. and grief — SHAK 580:27
poor soul sat s. — SHAK 617:22
s. of a contrite heart — BOOK 120:3
sorrow and s. shall flee — BIBLE 83:22
Was laughter and ability and S. — DICK 245:3
sighs: all made of s. and tears — SHAK 569:21
In the gestures, in the s. — SOND 656:1
my pains a world of s. — SHAK 615:2
S. are the natural language — SHAD 563:13
s. the strings do break — CAMP 177:5
sovereign of s. and groans — SHAK 598:13
sight: admit them in your s. — AUST 39:18
dares not come within my s. — JONS 379:15
deprived of s. — VIRG 713:4
done this evil in thy s. — BOOK 128:4
each other at first s. — STEE 662:16
gimleted and neatly out of s. — CRANE 225:23
giveth s. to the blind — BOOK 135:9
In the s. of the unwise — BIBLE 86:28
in thy s. shall no man — BOOK 135:3

sight: (*cont.*):
keeps it out of s. — BREC 140:3
leave in s. — SWIN 675:23
losing your s. — SASS 557:6
My dying s. to space remote — BLOK 115:3
possession of this heavenly s. — SHAK 618:18
right dear in the s. — BOOK 133:14
s. of means to do ill deeds — SHAK 594:12
s. of vernal bloom — MILT 470:16
s. so touching in its majesty — WORD 743:9
s. to dream of, not to tell — COL 209:9
sensible to feeling as to s. — SHAK 601:12
s. to make an old man young — TENN 681:6
that is pleasant to the s. — BIBLE 70:2
thousand years in thy s. — BOOK 130:23
together here in the s. of God — BOOK 123:15
triple s. in blindness — KEATS 390:24
where I shall live by s. — BUNY 156:17
sightless: lark becomes a s. song — TENN 684:14
sights: Her s. and sounds — BROO 143:18
impressive s. in the world — BARR 54:13
Such s. as youthful poets dream — MILT 465:17
sign: generation seeketh after a s. — BIBLE 90:34
In this s. shalt thou conquer — CONS 218:2
s. of the true artist — VIDAL 711:7
s. you must not touch — DONNE 252:3
visible s. of an inward — BOOK 123:10
would give me some clear s. — ALLEN 9:17
signal: s. shown and a distant — LONG 428:1
signal-elm: s., that looks on Ilsley — ARN 28:24
signalling: thin one is wildly s. — CONN 216:17
signed: hand that s. the paper — THOM 693:9
s. my death warrant — COLL 213:9
significance: No personal s. — LINC 422:5
What is the s. of Man — BECK 57:10
significant: Art is s. deformity — FRY 295:26
signiors: s. and rich burghers — SHAK 607:2
signo: *In hoc s. vinces* — CONS 218:2
signs: are but the s. of ideas — JOHN 367:20
discern the s. of the times — BIBLE 91:13
Except ye see s. and wonders — BIBLE 96:18
merely conventional s. — CARR 184:2
my s. and my wonders — BIBLE 72:3
silence: all in s., all in order — CRAB 224:26
answered best with s. — JONS 379:6
bound the common of s. — EMER 276:21
bright towers of s. — DE L 235:22
conspiracy of s. — COMTE 214:20
darkness again and a s. — LONG 428:1
dead in s. like to death — BROW 147:14
easy step to s. — AUST 38:24
Elected S., sing to me — HOPK 345:12
empty s. within — THOM 694:14
foster-child of s. — KEATS 388:23
golden Gospel of S. — MORL 485:1
His mind moves upon s. — YEATS 752:12
icy s. of the tomb — KEATS 390:16
I kept s., yea, even from — BOOK 126:22
Indecency's conspiracy of s. — SHAW 637:34
in the s. you don't know — BECK 57:18
lies are often told in s. — STEV 668:8
makes a s. in the hills — TENN 683:8
My gracious, hail — SHAK 570:9
occasional flashes of s. — SMITH 653:17
Of the eternal S. — WORD 746:4
on the other side of s. — ELIOT 269:17
private s. in which we live — PRIT 529:18
rest is s. — SHAK 579:13
Seul le s. est grand — VIGNY 711:12
Shall s. shroud such sin — GILB 303:10
s. all the airs and madrigals — MILT 475:8
s. also does not necessarily — ELIOT 269:6
S. augmenteth grief — DYER 264:14
S. a woman's finest ornament — AUCT 33:26
S. become his mother tongue — GOLD 311:18
s. deep as death — CAMP 176:9
s., exile, and cunning — JOYCE 381:14
s. fell with the waking — TENN 686:18
s. in heaven — BIBLE 106:24
S. is deep as Eternity — CARL 180:10
s. is most noble till — SWIN 676:2
S. is only commendable — SHAK 607:8
S. is the virtue of fools — BACON 42:14

silence: (*cont.*):
S. like a cancer grows — SIMON 647:20
S. more musical than any — ROSS 547:10
s. of these infinite spaces — PASC 507:14
s. of the soundless moonlight — VIRG 712:16
s. sank like music — COL 211:15
s. surged softly backward — DE L 236:8
S. that dreadful bell — SHAK 616:1
S.! Voilà l'ennemi! — CONDÉ 214:21
S. was pleased — MILT 471:10
s. was the song of love — ROSS 547:21
s. we the tempest fear — DRYD 260:4
s. yet I picked a welcome — SHAK 612:21
small change of s. — MER 458:2
Sorrow and s. are strong — LONG 426:17
Sound of S. — SIMON 647:20
speaking s. of a dream — ROSS 547:3
Stand shadowless like S. — HOOD 344:3
Still-born S.! — FLEC 286:1
together in awful s. — AKHM 6:8
trembles into s. as before — BYRON 169:20
turned its edge on the s. — HUGH 354:5
very sigh that s. heaves — KEATS 388:5
visible s. — ROSS 547:20
When awful darkness and s. — LEAR 413:20
widening slowly s. all — TENN 682:10
With s. and tears — BYRON 173:21
silenced: you have s. him — MORL 485:2
silences: Through s. in the dark — WALK 717:11
silencing: s. mankind — MILL 460:16
silent: All s., and all damned — WORD 746:13
all the s. manliness — GOLD 310:17
and s. as light — SMITH 653:31
And s. be — AUDEN 35:4
evening mild, then s. night — MILT 471:12
Gone far away into the s. land — ROSS 547:7
Grey s. fragments — HUGH 354:5
impossible to be s. — BURKE 159:5
Laws are s. in time of war — CIC 204:11
Paris was French—and s. — TUCH 705:1
s. and indefinitely bored — KNOX 403:8
S. as the sleeve-worn stone — MACL 439:9
s. in seven languages — BAG 46:20
s. majority — NIXON 496:3
s. now the earth's green — SUTT 672:23
s. over Africa — BROW 150:8
s. too as space — BYRON 172:1
s. touches of time — BURKE 159:25
S., upon a peak in Darien — KEATS 390:3
s. witnesses to the desolation — GEOR 301:3
strong, s. man — MORL 485:1
thereof one must be s. — WITT 740:3
t is s., as in *Harlow* — ASQ 32:1
unlocked her s. throat — GIBB 302:22
why art thou s. — CRAW 226:16
silentia: *Tacitae per amica s.* — VIRG 712:16
silently: How s., and with how wan — SIDN 646:16
S. and very fast — AUDEN 34:11
Slowly, s., now the moon — DE L 236:11
silk: hallowed that did breed the s. — SHAK 617:3
he was shot s. — STR 670:13
s. hat at a private view — EDW 267:3
s. hat on a Bradford millionaire — ELIOT 273:9
s. makes the difference — FULL 296:9
s. purse out of your wife's — MORT 486:11
s. stockings — JOHN 371:8
s. thread plucks it back — SHAK 623:7
soft as s. remains — HILL 338:8
that thing of s. — POPE 520:2
your blue-shadowed s. — STEV 666:7
silken: s. terms precise — SHAK 599:7
silver link, the s. tie — SCOTT 559:15
With s. lines, and silver — DONNE 251:19
silks: in fading s. compose — WINC 739:4
Whenas in s. my Julia goes — HERR 337:9
silkworm: of s. size — MOORE 482:12
s. expend her yellow labours — MIDD 460:1
siller: pinned it wi' a s. pin — BALL 51:3
sillier: s. than a silly laugh — CAT 186:4
sillies: s. believe their talk — MILNE 462:16
silliest: s. part of God's creation — ROCH 543:16
s. woman can manage — KIPL 402:8

silliness: s. to live | SHAK 615:9
silly: also says, 'tis very s. | BYRON 170:29
s. at the right moment | HOR 350:20
s. thoughts so busy keep | MILT 467:5
thou s. gentleman | SHAK 615:9
with such a s. question | STER 664:12
You were s. like us | AUDEN 34:14
silvae: *Et paulum s. super his* | HOR 351:9
s. sint consule dignae | VIRG 714:22
silvam: *In s. . . . ligna feras* | HOR 351:6
silvas: *Habitarunt di quoque s.* | VIRG 714:16
s. Academi quaerere verum | HOR 348:19
silver: Attract a S. Churn | GILB 305:18
Between their s. bars | FLEC 286:14
bringing gold, and s., ivory | BIBLE 75:25
Can wisdom be put in a s. rod | BLAKE 111:11
covered with s. wings | BOOK 129:8
ever the s. cord be loosed | BIBLE 81:1
Georgian s. goes | MACM 440:6
golden locks time hath to s. | PEELE 511:5
gold in pictures of s. | BIBLE 79:15
handful of s. he left us | BROW 150:25
silken lines, and s. hooks | DONNE 251:19
S. and gold have I none | BIBLE 98:9
s. apples of the moon | YEATS 753:8
s. answer rang | BROW 147:18
s. lining in the sky-ee | WEST 729:21
s. lining on the night | MILT 463:21
s. link, the silken tie | SCOTT 559:15
s. plate on a coffin | CURR 229:5
s., snarling trumpets | KEATS 386:22
spread your s. sunsets out | DAV 232:13
take s. or small change | CHAM 189:12
There's a s. lining | FORD 289:16
thirty pieces of s. | BEVAN 69:5
thirty pieces of s. | BIBLE 92:23
thousands of gold and s. | BOOK 133:19
Walks the night in her s. | DE L 236:11
When gold and s. becks me | SHAK 594:3
silver-sweet: s. sound | SHAK 623:6
silvery: so s. is thy voice | HERR 337:10
silvestrem: *S. tenui Musam* | VIRG 714:11
Silvia: Except I be by S. | SHAK 631:6
Who is S.? what is she | SHAK 631:8
simile: this s. a like perfection | WILB 734:5
similes: I sit, and play with s. | WORD 748:11
most unsavoury s. | SHAK 579:22
similia: *S. similibus curantur.* | HAHN 320:10
simpering: s., whimpering child again | HART 327:14
simple: *C'est s., l'amour* | PRÉ.V 528:15
giveth wisdom unto the s. | BOOK 125:5
I use s. materials | LOWRY 431:2
rarely pure, and never s. | WILDE 734:11
s. as all truly great swindles | HENRY 333:3
s. as to cross a field | PAST 508:8
s. dues of fellowship | BROW 147:4
S. tastes, you will agree | CONN 216:10
S. this tale | QUIL 534:10
s. truth must be abused | SHAK 621:20
To ask the hard question is s. | AUDEN 36:9
very s. gentleman | SHAK 632:12
women are so s. | SHAK 624:25
simpleness: When s. and duty | SHAK 612:20
simpler: than the infancy | SHAK 627:18
simplicitas: *O sancta s.!* | HUSS 357:3
simplicity: complete s. | ELIOT 271:9
Cultivate s. | LAMB 406:22
holy s. | HUSS 357:3
holy s. | JER 365:11
I am as true as truth's s. | SHAK 627:18
Pity my s. | WESL 728:7
s., a child | POPE 521:3
s. of the three per cents | DISR 248:14
s. of the three per cents | STOW 670:11
s. or with severity a serious | ARN 30:9
S., simplicity | THOR 697:6
That makes s. a grace | JONS 378:18
simplify: s. me when I'm dead | DOUG 255:12
simulacrum: dark s. | BROW 145:8
sin: abolish the whole body of s. | BOOK 123:1
almost a s. of abstinence | DRYD 260:7

sin: (*cont.*):
beauty is only s. deep | SAKI 553:10
being dead unto s. | BOOK 123:1
Be of s. the double cure | TOPL 701:4
Be ye angry and s. not | BIBLE 102:19
brother s. against me | BIBLE 91:21
By that s. fell the angels | SHAK 589:1
careless of the damning s. | COWP 222:5
charity in s. | SHAK 606:4
commit one single venial s. | NEWM 493:6
day we fall into no s. | BOOK 119:4
depravity and original s. | MELV 456:12
dreadful record of s. | DOYLE 256:5
emboldens s. so much as mercy | SHAK 626:11
Excepting Original S. | CAMP 176:20
full of s., but most of sloth | HERB 334:9
go, and s. no more | BIBLE 96:31
go away and s. no more | ANON 16:12
hate the s. | AUG 37:8
he bare the s. | BIBLE 84:14
he died unto s. once | BIBLE 99:29
He that is without s | DIDLE 80.30
How shall I lose the s. | POPE 519:20
Ignorance excuses from s. | AUCT 33:17
I had not known s. | BIBLE 99:31
I'm living in s. | HERB 333:15
in secret s. | CHUR 201:4
I waive the quantum o'the s. | BURNS 161:24
keep us this day without s. | BOOK 118:14
lips were shaped for s. | BETJ 67:16
Lord imputeth no s. | BOOK 126:8
Lukewarmness I account a s. | COWL 221:15
made my s. their door | DONNE 251:7
my s. is ever before me | BOOK 128:4
My s., my soul | NAB 488:21
no s. but ignorance | MARL 447:12
not innocence but s. | BROW 150:15
one s. will destroy | BUNY 156:9
physicists have known s. | OPP 499:5
piercing pain, a killing s. | STEV 669:7
Plate s. with gold | SHAK 597:8
purple-linèd palace of sweet s. | KEATS 388:17
repent me now of s. | MILT 473:11
researches in original s. | PLOM 517:13
sacrifice for s. | BOOK 126:25
say that we have no s. | BIBLE 105:25
say there is no s. | SHAK 594:1
Shall we continue in s. | BIBLE 99:27
silence shroud such s. | GILB 303:10
s. blows quite away | HERB 335:20
s. could blight or sorrow | COL 210:1
s., death, and hell | BUNY 156:11
s. I impute to each frustrate | BROW 153:7
s. in secret is not to sin | MOL 479:13
S. is behoved | JUL 382:10
S. of self-love possesseth | SHAK 633:22
s. of witchcraft | BIBLE 74:37
S.'s rotten trunk | COWP 221:12
s. tends to be addictive | AUDEN 36:14
s. that amends | SHAK 628:19
s. to God above | THOR 697:11
s. towards our fellow creatures | SHAW 636:5
s. ye do by two and two | KIPL 401:4
sometimes s.'s a pleasure | BYRON 170:12
sorrow dogging s. | HERB 335:19
Stand in awe, and s. not | BOOK 124:12
they who s. with caution | CENT 188:5
this dark world of s. | BICK 108:22
To s. in loving virtue | SHAK 606:3
triumph over death and s. | SPEN 659:9
wages of s. is death | BIBLE 99:30
want of power to s. | DRYD 261:12
We fall not in such s. | GILB 303:11
We wallow in our s. | ANON 20:3
Where s. abounded, grace | BIBLE 99:26
Which is my s., though it were | DONNE 251:7
which taketh away the s. | BIBLE 96:7
woman brought s. and death | STAN 662:9
world's as ugly, ay, as s. | LOCK 425:12
Would you like to s. | ANON 19:24
your s. will find you out | BIBLE 73:12
since: dearest, s. 'tis so | BROW 150:19
sincere: hopeless are starkly s. | RHYS 539:20

sincere: (*cont.*):
person with whom I may be s. | EMER 276:24
s., even if you don't mean it | TRUM 704:22
s. enough to tell him | BULW 155:6
sincerely: s. want to be rich | CORN 219:1
sincerity: bread of s. and truth | BIBLE 100:22
Crystal s. hath found no | HOPK 346:15
s. is a dangerous thing | WILDE 735:6
s. is a jewel | SMART 649:11
Sindh: *Peccavi*—I have S. | WINK 739:9
sindon: thy s. wrapped | CONS 217:21
sinecure: It gives no man a s. | POUND 527:4
part of the world is no s. | BYRON 174:4
sinews: Money is the s. of love | FARQ 280:21
Neither is money the s. of war | BACON 44:33
one of the s. of the soul | FULL 296:6
S. of concord | FORD 289:9
s. of virtue | WALT 721:2
s. of war | CIC 204:10
Stiffen the s. | SHAK 585:7
twist the s. of thy heart | BLAKE 114:14
sinewy: large and s. hands | LONG 428:2
sinful: deceit, or any s. games | HARTE 327:20
sing: crow doth s. as sweetly | SHAK 610:5
Elected Silence, s. to me | HOPK 345:12
found in thine heart to s. | SWIN 676:25
her flowery work doth s. | MILT 464:25
I cannot s. the old songs | CLAR 205:6
I know ye s. well | FLET 287:21
I'll s. you twelve O | ANON 15:1
in ev'ry corner s. | HERB 334:7
I s. of brooks, of blossoms | HERR 336:6
I s. the body electric | WHIT 732:4
I, too, s. America | HUGH 354:1
I will s. of the sun | POUND 526:6
let us s. unto the Lord | BOOK 131:9
More safe I s. | MILT 472:6
never heard no horse s. | ARMS 26:10
O for a thousand tongues to s. | WESL 728:5
Of the glorious Body s. | THOM 692:13
Places where they s. | BOOK 119:5
sidelong would she bend and s. | KEATS 388:11
s. among the branches | BOOK 132:7
s. both high and low | SHAK 629:4
S. 'em muck | MELBA 456:4
s. for a rock 'n' roll | JAGG 361:12
s. in a hempen string | FLET 287:13
s. in the robber's face | JUV 384:5
s. like birds i' the cage | SHAK 597:16
S. me a song of a lad | STEV 669:2
s. myself | WHIT 732:13
S., my tongue | FORT 291:1
S. no sad songs for me | ROSS 547:12
s. of time or eternity | TENN 687:9
s. praises unto his name | BOOK 129:7
s. so wildly | TENN 683:23
s. the progress of a deathless | DONNE 251:11
s. the savageness out | SHAK 617:10
S. thou smoothly | CAMP 177:8
S. thou the songs of love | GURN 320:4
S. through all Jerusalem | CASW 185:4
s. to find your hearts | FLEC 286:9
S. to the harp with a psalm | BOOK 131:14
S. to the Lord a new song | BIBLE 107:29
s. unto God with the voice | BOOK 127:18
S. unto the Lord a new song | BOOK 126:1
s. unto the Lord a new song | BOOK 131:13
S. us one of the songs | BOOK 134:17
S. we merrily unto God | BOOK 130:14
S. whatever is well made | YEATS 753:16
Soul clap its hands and s. | YEATS 752:21
they shall laugh and s. | BOOK 129:3
think that they will s. to me | ELIOT 272:6
whan she bygynneth to s. | CHAU 195:19
when you s. | SHAK 632:5
while I s. the ancient ways | YEATS 753:13
Whilst thus I s., I am a King | CIBB 203:17
Will s. at dawn | BROW 147:2
worth saying, people s. it | BEAU 56:9
would not s. for Lycidas | MILT 465:20
singe: S. my white head | SHAK 595:20
That it do s. yourself | SHAK 588:9

singeing: s. of the King of Spain's Beard   DRAKE 257:10
singer: Beside the s.   LAND 408:6
  idle s. of an empty day   MORR 485:10
  lived a s. in France of old   SWIN 677:5
  sans song, sans s.   FITZ 283:18
  s. not the song   ANON 18:1
  s. of an empty day   MORR 485:11
  S. of sweet Colonus   ARN 29:1
singers: well-known s.   REED 538:8
singeth: s. with her breast   HOOD 344:4
singing: angels all were s. out   BYRON 173:13
  Beside me s. in the wilderness   FITZ 283:13
  delight in s.   LAND 408:6
  Everyone suddenly burst out s.   SASS 557:9
  I see ye have a s. face   FLET 287:21
  love a woman for s.   SHAK 595:5
  nest of s. birds   JOHN 371:4
  silver waves of thy sweet s.   SHEL 642:17
  s. and making melody   BIBLE 102:23
  S., dancing to itself   COL 209:11
  s. in their glory move   MILT 466:14
  s. of foolish and bawdy   TURN 705:14
  S. so rarely   SCOTT 560:22
  s. still dost soar   SHEL 643:14
  s. will never be done   SASS 557:9
  six little S.-boys   BARH 52:13
  time of the s. of birds   BIBLE 81:9
  To the Master of all s.   LONG 427:18
  Why is there always a secret s.   SAND 555:6
single: In a s. night   BYRON 173:2
  married to a s. life   CRAS 226:11
  Nothing in the world is s.   SHEL 641:9
  s. and only talked of population   GOLD 311:28
  s. blessedness   SHAK 610:20
  s. completed action   BOIL 117:4
  s. in the field   WORD 748:3
  s. life doth well   BACON 44:4
  s. man in possession   AUST 39:9
  S. vision and Newton's   BLAKE 112:11
  S. women have a dreadful   AUST 40:8
  they come not s. spies   SHAK 578:3
  Two souls with but a s.   HALM 322:7
  with a s. hair   DRYD 262:6
singles: s. we played after tea   BETJ 68:6
sings: he s. each song twice   BROW 150:6
  in me s. no more   MILL 461:9
  instead of bleeding, he s.   GARD 297:15
  motion like an angel s.   SHAK 610:1
  S. in the palm   STEV 666:4
  tell me what she s.   WORD 748:4
singular: it was s.   NELS 491:14
  So s. in each particular   SHAK 632:5
singularity: not by s.   KEATS 391:14
  S. is almost invariably   DOYLE 256:4
  thyself into the trick of s.   SHAK 630:5
sinister: strange and s.   JAMES 363:6
sink: I pant, I s., I tremble   SHEL 640:11
  load would s. a navy   SHAK 588:21
  Not gross to s., but light   SHAK 635:12
  raft which would never s.   AMES 10:9
  S. me the ship   TENN 689:4
  s. through the sea   THOM 693:3
  To s. or soar   BYRON 172:17
  would not s. i' the scale   BROW 152:7
sinking: kind of alacrity in s.   SHAK 610:18
  suddenly with a s. feeling   MILNE 463:2
  when they see me s.   ANON 22:9
sinks: s. into thy depths   BYRON 169:15
Sinn: *nicht aus dem S.*   HEINE 330:15
sinned: all have s.   BIBLE 99:22
  He would have s. incessantly   ROB 542:10
  I have s. against heaven   BIBLE 95:3
  More s. against than sinning   SHAK 596:1
  people s. against   COMP 214:17
  s. exceedingly in thought   MISS 476:16
sinner: Be a s. and sin strongly   LUTH 432:9
  dead s. revised   BIER 109:15
  God be merciful to me a s.   BIBLE 95:15
  Love the s.   AUG 37:8
  one sin will destroy a s.   BUNY 156:9
  Or I of her a s.   CONG 216:6
  over one s. that repenteth   BIBLE 95:1

sinner: (*cont.*):
  Say, poor s., lov'st thou me   COWP 222:20
  s. is at the heart of Christianity   PÉGUY 511:8
  s. with the handcuffs   HOUS 351:13
sinners: God and s. reconciled   WESL 728:3
  Master with publicans and s.   BIBLE 90:5
  mercy upon us miserable s.   BOOK 119:16
  Once for favoured s. slain   WESL 728:15
  s.'ll be kotched out late   HARR 327:9
  S.; of whom I am chief   BIBLE 103:25
  s. on this part of Broadway   RUNY 550:4
  s., plunged beneath   COWP 222:21
  s. to repentance   BIBLE 90:7
  stood in the way of s.   BOOK 124:6
  thou be a breeder of s.   SHAK 575:18
  we are s. all   SHAK 587:19
  Why do s.' ways prosper   HOPK 346:8
sinning: more s. a little later   RUNY 550:4
  sinned against than s.   SHAK 596:1
sins: Be all my s. remembered   SHAK 575:17
  by himself purged our s.   BIBLE 104:10
  chain of our s.   BOOK 120:4
  Compound for s.   BUTL 166:7
  cover the multitude of s.   BIBLE 105:20
  dark and weep for their s.   WHIT 732:18
  far hath he set our s.   BOOK 132:5
  forgiveth us   BIBLE 87:8
  half the s. of mankind   RUSS 551:9
  Her s., which are many   BIBLE 94:8
  His s. were scarlet   BELL 61:26
  oldest s. the newest kind   SHAK 584:4
  root of all s.   JAM 361:16
  s. and offences of my youth   BOOK 125:19
  s. are attempts to fill   WEIL 726:18
  s. or complaints or laws   TRAH 701:12
  s. they love to act   SHAK 618:23
  thinkin' on their s.   BURNS 162:4
  Though your s. be as scarlet   BIBLE 82:10
sint: *S. ut sunt aut non sint*   CLEM 206:9
Sion: art praised in S.   BOOK 128:23
  captivity of S.   BOOK 134:4
  gracious unto S.   BOOK 128:8
  his dwelling in S.   BOOK 130:6
  one of the songs of S.   BOOK 134:17
  praise to Mount S.   BUNY 155:15
  Walk about S.   BOOK 127:23
  we remembered thee, O S.   BOOK 134:17
sip: way you s. your tea   GERS 301:16
sipped: Who s. no sup   GILB 306:24
Sir-come-spy-see: S.   BARH 52:10
sire: S. of an immortal strain   SHEL 639:12
  s. the son shall hear   SCOTT 560:11
Siren: drunk of S. tears   SHAK 634:25
Sirens: Blest pair of S.   MILT 463:9
  What song the S. sang   BROW 145:19
Sirion: S., like a young unicorn   BOOK 126:2
Sisera: fought against S.   BIBLE 74:3
sister: azure s. of the spring   SHEL 641:14
  Did your s. throw up a lot   WALK 717:11
  done to our fair s.   MORR 486:1
  garden inclosed is my s.   BIBLE 81:15
  Had it been his s.   ANON 14:6
  My s. and my sister's child   COWP 222:13
  my s. Masery   BALL 49:16
  s. hath left me to serve   BIBLE 94:17
  sometime s., now our queen   SHAK 572:4
  To live a barren s. all   SHAK 610:20
  trying to violate your s.   STR 670:19
sisterhood: s. is powerful   MORG 484:18
sisterly: s. animosity   SURT 672:19
sisters: s. under their skins   KIPL 399:15
  so do his s.   GILB 305:25
  Sphere-born harmonious s.   MILT 463:9
  weird s., hand in hand   SHAK 600:3
Sistine: On the S. Chapel roof   YEATS 753:15
Sisyphus: S. is happy   CAMUS 178:1
  S., proletarian   CAMUS 177:20
sit: at last s. down by thee   KING 396:12
  head-waiter allowed to s.   UST 707:17
  Here I s., alone and sixty   BENN 63:12
  I'll s. and mourn   BALL 51:1
  let us s. upon the ground   SHAK 620:8
  May s. i' the centre   MILT 463:27

sit: (*cont.*):
  s. and hear each other   KEATS 389:10
  s. down on my botom   FLEM 287:7
  s. not down in the highest   BIBLE 94:26
  S. thou on my right hand   BOOK 133:3
  So I did s. and eat   HERB 335:9
  superstitious reluctance to s.   JOHN 375:12
  Teach us to s. still   ELIOT 270:6
  them that s. in darkness   BIBLE 93:24
  Though I s. down now   DISR 246:14
  To s. still for once at table   HOFF 341:2
  we used to s. and dream   ARMS 26:5
sits: It s. looking   SAND 555:4
  Sometimes I s. and thinks   PUNCH 532:9
sitteth: s. on the right hand   BOOK 119:1
sitting: Are you s. comfortably   LANG 408:17
  exact their demands by s.   WELL 727:5
  got as far as actually s. up   REED 538:4
  Lord s. upon a throne   BIBLE 82:19
  not soar where he is s.   SHEL 639:21
  s. careless on a granary   KEATS 390:18
situation: *s. excellente*   FOCH 288:6
situations: applications for s.   AUDEN 35:10
Sitwells: S. belong   LEAV 415:6
six: All's set at s. and seven   ANON 20:3
  his number is s. hundred   BIBLE 107:1
  Rode the s. hundred   TENN 680:13
  S. days shalt thou labour   BIBLE 72:16
  s. little Singing-boys   BARH 52:13
  s. ships of the line   TENN 689:1
  world on s. and sevene   CHAU 195:22
sixpence: Finds s. in her shoe   CORB 218:12
  nothing above s.   BEVAN 69:3
  precious little for s.   PUNCH 531:17
  We could have saved s.   BECK 57:12
  Whoso has s. is sovereign   CARL 181:6
sixpences: Our ideas like bad s.   BUTL 167:1
  there go two-and-forty s.   JOHN 377:7
sixteen: S. tons   TRAV 702:4
sixth: s. age shifts   SHAK 568:16
sixties: they divided up the S.   LEVIN 420:4
sixty: Here I sit, alone and s.   BENN 63:12
  rate of s. minutes an hour   LEWIS 420:13
  When I'm s.-four   LENN 418:3
skating: In s. over thin ice   EMER 276:30
  S. across still water   BLY 116:8
skeletons: s. copulating   BEEC 58:17
skelp: I gie them a s.   BURNS 161:14
Skiddaw: S. saw the fire   MAC 436:2
skies: born under other s.   LE C 415:13
  paint the sable s.   DRUM 258:13
  s. are painted with unnumbered   SHAK 591:12
  soaring claim the s.   FRERE 293:17
  some watcher of the s.   KEATS 390:3
  virgin-daughter of the s.   DRYD 261:32
  whose god is in the s.   SHAW 637:29
  You common people of the s.   WOTT 749:2
skill: Has, or none, or little s.   HERR 336:15
  his s. runs on the lees   HERR 336:15
  nothing with a deal of s.   COWP 223:12
  Short Time and Little S.   HAR 326:10
  S. comes so slow, and life   DAV 232:2
  S. in the weapon is nothing   SHAK 583:27
  who has the power and s.   ANON 19:18
skilled: S. or unskilled   HOR 348:17
skim: s. away   TENN 683:15
  S. milk masquerades   GILB 306:3
skimble-skamble: s. stuff   SHAK 581:6
skimming: S. our gable   HEAN 329:17
skin: Ethiopian change his s.   BIBLE 85:10
  In the castle of my s.   LAMM 407:17
  Nor scar that whiter s.   SHAK 618:5
  punctures my s.   ANON 18:15
  s. is a different shade   HAMM 323:2
  s. of an innocent lamb   SHAK 587:24
  s. the swart flies move   DOUG 255:13
  skull beneath the s.   ELIOT 273:15
  take the s. from the arm   ELIOT 272:11
  through his apostolic s.   BYRON 173:16
  throws her enamelled s.   SHAK 611:19
  viewing wasting s.   HARDY 325:19
  with the s. of my teeth   BIBLE 77:24

skinny: I fear thy s. hand COL 211:6
skins: beauty of their s. TENN 688:8
sisters under their s. KIPL 399:15
skip: to s. like a calf BOOK 126:2
skipped: mountains s. BOOK 133:8
skipper: s. had taken his little LONG 428:3
skipping: s. king, he ambled SHAK 581:13
they all went s. about BARR 54:6
With what a pretty s. grace MARV 450:18
skirmish: s. fought near GRAV 314:21
skirts: s. of happy chance TENN 683:25
skittish: Unstaid and s. SHAK 629:13
skittles: all beer and s. CALV 175:13
Sklaven-Moral: S. NIET 495:15
Skugg: Here S. lies snug FRAN 292:19
skull: more of her than the s. BIBLE 76:30
s. beneath the skin ELIOT 273:15
skuttle fish: in mind of the s. ADD 4:22
sky: about the action of the s. BYRON 170:9
above, the vaulted s. CLARE 204:26
admitted to that equal s. POPE 522:3
And the blue s. WORD 745:1
blue-grey October s. RICE 540:3
blue s. of spring ALL 10:2
clean the s. ELIOT 272:11
clear blue s. over my head HAZL 329:14
climbin' clear up to the s. HAMM 322:16
discern the face of the s. BIBLE 91:13
Freeze, freeze, thou bitter s. SHAK 568:17
inverted bowl we call The S. FITZ 284:10
lose itself in the s. BROW 148:1
Music shall untune the s. DRYD 261:26
On a bed of daffodil s. TENN 686:17
sent him down the s. CORY 219:15
Shine upon the starry s. BLAKE 112:4
shoulders held the s. HOUS 351:22
Shoulder the s., my lad HOUS 351:18
s. and sea and land HOUS 352:4
s. breathed autumn PUSH 532:16
s. changes when they SHAK 569:18
s., earth, and sea HUNT 356:11
s. grows darker yet CHES 198:27
s. is darkening like AUDEN 36:13
s. is red BIBLE 91:12
spread out against the s. ELIOT 271:20
This northern s. DE L 236:9
triple-towered s. DAY-L 233:4
twelve-winded s. HOUS 352:14
under the rocking s. of '41 YEVT 754:4
Under the wide and starry s. STEV 669:9
Which prisoners call the s. WILDE 735:34
With all the blue ethereal s. ADD 4:19
Skye: Over the sea to S. BOUL 137:17
Over the sea to S. STEV 669:2
skylark: s. wounded BLAKE 111:2
slab: Beneath this s. NASH 490:13
slacks: girls in s. remember Dad BETJ 67:4
slag-heap: post-industrial s. DRAB 257:6
s. 120 ft high WILS 738:4
slain: Despair, law, chance, hath s.
                                        DONNE 250:21
ere thou hast s. another BROW 146:24
Full many a gallant man was s. ANON 17:7
I am hurt but I am not s. BALL 50:9
I am s. by a fair cruel maid SHAK 620:9
jaw of an ass have I s. BIBLE 74:17
man may fight and no be s. BURNS 163:12
new-s. knight BALL 50:20
Or if the s. think he is slain EMER 276:5
own eyes might see him s. MORR 485:13
Saul hath s. his thousands BIBLE 75:5
s. in thine high places BIBLE 75:9
s. this year in Europe WALP 720:15
slamming: In Little Girls is s. Doors BELL 61:7
S. their doors OSB 501:14
slander: civic s. and the spite TENN 684:11
Fear not s. SHAK 571:16
one to s. you TWAIN 706:11
S., meanest spawn of Hell TENN 685:5
To speak no s. TENN 681:24
Who's angry at a s. makes JONS 378:13
slandered: s. his neighbour BOOK 124:28

slandering: lying, and s. BOOK 123:8
slang: S. is a language that SAND 555:12
slant: certain S. of light DICK 244:20
slap-dash: s. down in the mouth CONG 215:24
slap-up: s. gal DICK 243:1
slashing: For a s. article, sir THAC 691:9
slate: his thoughts upon a s. HOOD 343:22
wiping something off a s. KIPL 398:11
slaughter: arrayed for mutual s. WORD 746:8
as a lamb to the s. BIBLE 84:12
machinery all the s. of plague SHAW 637:13
ox goeth to the s. BIBLE 78:17
s. will ensue CONG 215:21
some for love of s. POUND 527:1
through s. to a throne GRAY 315:16
Yet was the s. small HAR 326:10
slaughterous: my s. thoughts SHAK 604:24
slave: Better be a s. at once BRON 142:8
fingering s. WORD 746:14
giving freedom to the s. LINC 422:6
half s. and half free LINC 421:18
here I stand, your s. SHAK 588:21
moment the s. resolves GAND 297:9
one is always the s. LERM 418:15
s. grow pleased and vain ROCH 543:2
s. is a slave to the same MILL 460:26
slave of that s. CONN 216:24
s. of the passions HUME 355:20
s. to its animosity WASH 722:1
S. to no sect POPE 522:2
s. to thousands SHAK 616:12
soundly as the wretched s. SHAK 586:8
Till he faced the s. SHAK 599:15
What a s. art thou SHAK 580:24
without freeing any s. LINC 422:12
womankind's in every state a s. EGER 267:12
slave-morality: Master-morality and s.
                                        NIET 495:15
slavery: between liberty and s. CAMD 176:2
Chains and s. BURNS 163:1
Freedom and s. are mental GAND 297:9
Of heart-debasing s. GRAI 314:5
s. in the extreme acceptance CHUR 201:23
s. in which a man does GILL 306:26
s. of the tea and coffee COBB 207:27
S. they can have anywhere BURKE 157:30
wise and good in s. MAC 434:17
slaves: are to be freemen or s. WASH 721:23
at the mill with s. MILT 473:25
Britons never will be s. THOM 695:15
creed of s. PITT 515:15
Englishmen never will be s. SHAW 637:11
freemen, are the only s. MASS 453:14
inevitably two kinds of s. ILL 359:10
S. cannot breathe in England COWP 223:19
s., howe'er contented COWP 223:13
S. of the Lamp ARN 26:14
s. that dig the golden CRAB 225:14
s. with weary footsteps SHEL 640:10
sons of former s. KING 397:1
too pure an Air for S. ANON 17:5
wholly s. or wholly free DRYD 260:23
whom we have made our s. DARW 231:12
women are born s. AST 32:9
women born s. WOLL 741:18
slavish: you s. herd HOR 348:16
slay: But s., and slay, and slay MAC 436:8
s. more gazers SHAK 588:3
Though he s. me BIBLE 77:20
slayer: If the red s. think EMER 276:5
slaying: s. of a beautiful hypothesis HUXL 358:3
slays: red slayer think he s. EMER 276:5
sledge: great s. drops in vain ROET 544:2
My s. and anvil lie declined ANON 16:16
sleek: s. and shining creatures TENN 688:8
sleek-headed: S. men SHAK 590:6
sleekit: Wee, s., cow'rin' BURNS 163:15
sleep: after-dinner's s. SHAK 606:8
azure-lidded s. KEATS 387:9
been to s. for over a year WAUGH 723:13
Care-charmer S., son DAN 229:16
Care-charming S., thou easer FLET 287:20

sleep: (cont.):
Church can feed and s. ELIOT 271:13
Come, s., O sleep, the certain SIDN 646:18
come to the borders of s. THOM 694:3
darkness brings not s. PUSH 533:5
Death and his brother S. SHEL 640:8
deep and dreamless s. BROO 144:4
deep s. of England ORW 500:2
deep s. to fall upon Adam BIBLE 70:5
desire of s. again JONS 379:15
do I wake or s. KEATS 389:17
dreadfully but as a drunken s. SHAK 606:20
dreamless, uninvaded s. TENN 684:19
drink well, and I s. well MORT 486:18
drowsy approaches of s. BROW 145:13
each day dies with s. HOPK 345:18
Eat or s. or drink again DE L 236:4
Entice the dewy-feathered S. MILT 464:25
exposition of s. SHAK 612:23
first approach of s. BYRON 172:13
from everlasting s. BROW 145:13
From s. and from damnation CHES 199:3
good run I have in my s. SURT 672:9
green ideas s. furiously CHOM 200:3
grey and full of s. YEATS 753:19
His s. was aery light MILT 471:20
How long wilt thou s. BIBLE 78:14
How s. the brave COLL 213:12
I always s. upon ale FARQ 280:8
I'll go to s. if I can SHAK 568:11
In s. a king SHAK 634:12
in soot I s. BLAKE 113:17
I s., but my heart waketh BIBLE 81:17
I s. out the thought SHAK 631:26
keepeth thee will not s. BOOK 133:23
lasting s. BEAU 57:2
Let us s. now OWEN 503:20
life is rounded with a s. SHAK 625:28
Macbeth does murder s. SHAK 602:2
Macbeth shall s. no more SHAK 602:3
Me biful for to s. LANG 408:20
medicine thee to that sweet s. SHAK 616:19
me from the fields of s. WORD 745:12
men who s. badly RUSS 551:8
miles to go before I s. FROST 295:13
Never may s. with velvet hand LYLY 433:12
Never s. with a woman whose ALGR 9:5
nose-painting, s., and urine SHAK 602:11
Now I lay me down to s. ANON 16:24
Oh S.! it is a gentle thing COL 211:10
One short s. past DONNE 250:23
on him who invented s. CERV 188:16
Only s.! BROW 153:16
O sleep! O gentle s. SHAK 583:11
O S., the friend of Woe SOUT 657:8
season of all natures, s. SHAK 603:15
Shake off this downy s. SHAK 602:15
She looks like s. SHAK 567:13
single vision and Newton's s. BLAKE 112:11
Six hours in s. COKE 209:2
S. after toil SPEN 660:2
s. al the nyght with open ye CHAU 192:7
s. an act or two SHAK 589:18
s. and a forgetting WORD 745:14
s. and a sweet dream MAS 453:9
s. and darkness safely brought KEBLE 392:19
S.; and if life was bitter SWIN 676:5
s. as I in childhood sweetly CLARE 204:26
s. at last on the field MELV 456:19
s. before evening PATER 509:8
s. begins for weary mortals VIRG 712:19
s. between term and term SHAK 569:9
S. I can get nane BURNS 161:8
s. in Abraham's bosom SHAK 622:4
sleeping, and waking s. MONT 481:10
s. in it [the church] ADD 4:8
S. is sweet to the labouring BUNY 156:5
S. no more SHAK 602:2
s. of a labouring man BIBLE 80:10
S. on Blest pair MILT 471:16
s. one ever-during night CAMP 177:3
s. on (my Love!) KING 396:11
s. out this great gap SHAK 564:28

sleep: (cont.):
s. provides relief — CHAM 189:11
S. shall neither night nor day — SHAK 600:2
s. should be his last repose — ANON 19:19
s. so soundly as the wretched — SHAK 586:8
S. to wake — BROW 148:6
S. will come when thou — SHEL 643:23
Softer than s. — TENN 687:22
such as s. o'nights — SHAK 590:6
sweet restorer, balmy s. — YOUNG 754:12
Then sleep, dear, s. — BEDD 58:8
There are two gates of S. — VIRG 714:1
there is nothing but s. — DRIN 258:10
There'll be time enough to s. — HOUS 352:7
they are even as a s. — BOOK 130:23
This s. is sound indeed — SHAK 584:2
thou s. the sleep of death — BLAKE 112:8
Thy s., fond dreams — LYLY 433:12
time to awake out of s. — BIBLE 100:10
To s.: perchance to dream — SHAK 575:16
twenty centuries of stony s. — YEATS 753:2
unwilling s. — KEATS 390:4
We shall not all s. — BIBLE 101:14
We shall not s. — MCCR 437:6
What hath night to do with s. — MILT 463:17
when you can't get to s. — LEB 415:9
when you s. you remind me — SASS 557:8
Where fain, fain I would s. — BALL 49:4
while some must s. — SHAK 576:20
would make anyone go to s. — DICK 243:24
yet I would not s. — SHAK 601:11
sleeper: never a quiet s. — TENN 687:2
sleepers: slumbers for the s. — BRON 142:19
sleepeth: maid is not dead, but s. — BIBLE 90:10
or peradventure he s. — BIBLE 76:2
sleepin': art tha s. there below — NEWB 492:7
sleeping: He cursed him in s. — BARH 52:14
kind of s. in the blood — SHAK 582:17
Lay your s. head, my love — AUDEN 36:6
s. and the dead — SHAK 602:4
s., by a brother's hand — SHAK 573:20
s. hound to wake — CHAU 195:16
suddenly he find you s. — BIBLE 93:19
sleepless: O S. as the river — CRANE 225:24
s. soul that perished — WORD 747:11
S. themselves, to give their — POPE 518:15
S. with cold commemorative — ROSS 548:6
sleeps: He wakes or s. — SHEL 639:21
Homer sometimes s. — BYRON 171:5
Now s. the crimson petal — TENN 688:13
s. as may beguile the night — SURR 672:3
s. feels not the toothache — SHAK 571:19
S. in Elysium — SHAK 586:8
s. on his luminous ring — TENN 687:21
S. sound, secure — MARS 449:10
s. within their pretty — LODGE 426:1
That broods and s. — WORD 746:16
Till tired he s. — POPE 522:16
while my pretty one, s. — TENN 687:27
sleepwalker: assurance of a s. — HITL 339:11
sleepy: Contentment is a s. thing — TRAH 701:17
in s. London town — JAGG 361:12
s. and there is no place — DYLAN 266:18
who in the s. region stay — MORR 485:11
sleepy-head: 'shamed, you s. — STEV 668:19
sleeve: Ash on an old man's s. — ELIOT 271:4
wear my heart upon my s. — SHAK 614:21
sleeves: Americanism with its s. — MCC 436:18
language that rolls up its s. — SAND 555:12
Tie up my s. with ribbons rare — HUNT 356:21
sleigh: s. glides in the moonlight — PUSH 532:10
sleight: by the s. of men — BIBLE 102:17
more th' admire his s. — BUTL 166:16
sleights: And never see thy s. — GREE 317:8
slenderly: s. known himself — SHAK 594:25
slept: everlasting night is to be s. — CAT 185:15
fruits of them that s. — BIBLE 101:7
He s. in the hall — BENT 64:15
He s. with his fathers — BIBLE 75:30
I should have s. — BIBLE 77:7
s. more than any other — MENC 457:4
thought he thought I s. — PATM 509:12
Whilst Adam s. — ANON 19:19

slew: I s. him — SHAK 592:3
s. mighty kings — BOOK 134:15
which he s. at his death — BIBLE 74:21
who s. his master — BIBLE 76:28
slice: S. him where you like — WOD 740:10
slid: That s. into my soul — COL 211:10
slight: Away, s. man — SHAK 593:2
friendship called s. — BIER 109:2
s. all that do — FARQ 280:17
slightly: S. in *Peter Pan* — TYNAN 706:28
slime: daubed it with s. — BIBLE 71:34
through the ooze and s. — SMITH 651:19
slimy: s. channel slowly glide — CRAB 224:23
s. things did crawl — COL 211:1
thousand thousand s. things — COL 211:8
slings: s. and arrows — SHAK 575:16
slip: catch no s. — BUNY 155:16
giving his enemies the s. — STER 664:15
in earth to set one s. — SHAK 632:2
s. into my bosom — TENN 688:13
s., slide, perish — ELIOT 270:17
Then s. I from her bum — SHAK 611:12
then s. out of the world — DRYD 261:4
They s., diminished — TESS 691:1
slipper: s. and subtle knave — SHAK 615:21
slippers: pair of s., sir — BROW 147:1
walks in his golden s. — BUNY 156:1
slippery: s. footsteps slide — WILL 736:23
standing is s. — BACON 43:29
slipping: s. gimleted — CRANE 225:23
slit: S. your girl's, and swing — KING 398:5
slits: s. the thin-spun life — MILT 466:4
sliver: envious s. broke — SHAK 578:13
sloe: lush-kept plush-capped s. — HOPK 346:13
slogans: instead of principles, s. — BENT 64:19
slogged: s. up to Arras — SASS 557:11
slope: s. of faces — COWP 224:1
S. their slow passage — CRAB 224:23
slopes: on the butler's upper s. — WOD 740:2
slop-kettle: coffee and other s. — COBB 207:27
slop-pail: with a s. — HOPK 346:16
Sloppy Joe: Dirty Dick's and S.'s — AUDEN 35:17
sloth: but most of s. — HERB 334:9
ease, and peaceful s. — MILT 469:16
much time in studies is s. — BACON 44:24
Shake off dull s. — KEN 393:5
s. finds the down pillow — SHAK 571:12
we lived a life of s. — SHIP 646:1
slouches: S. towards Bethlehem — YEATS 753:2
Slough: bombs, and fall on S. — BETJ 68:5
slough: name of the s. was Despond — BUNY 155:14
slovenliness: nothing but s. — BREC 140:7
s. is no part of religion — WESL 728:23
slow: But I am s. of speech — BIBLE 72:1
come he s., or come — SCOTT 560:2
cripple and comes ever s. — DRAY 257:15
Slow, s., fresh fount — JONS 378:14
s. to anger is better — BIBLE 78:38
S. to chide, and swift to — LYTE 433:17
s. to speak, slow to wrath — BIBLE 104:27
telling you to s. down — ANON 12:31
slowest: haste of a fool is the s. — SHAD 563:15
slowly: angel to pass, flying s. — FIRB 282:27
Make haste s. — AUG 37:12
mills of God grind s. — LOGAU 426:4
Science moves, but s. slowly — TENN 685:14
s. do the hours their numbers — SPEN 659:16
s. in the wind — EHRL 267:14
S., silently, now the moon — DE L 236:11
sludge: Activated S. — JENN 365:7
slug: Get up, sweet S.-a-bed — HERR 336:10
sluggard: foul s.'s comfort — CARL 180:4
Go to the ant thou s. — BIBLE 78:13
s. is wiser in his own — BIBLE 79:23
s.'s cradle — CHAP 190:16
'Tis the voice of the s. — WATTS 722:18
slug-horn: s. to my lips — BROW 149:3
sluices: Close the s. now, lads — VIRG 714:21
sluicing: browsing and s. — WOD 740:20
slum: diversions in s. life — MCAR 434:1
swear-word in a rustic s. — BEER 59:10

slumber: Ere S.'s chain has bound me — MOORE 483:17
honey-heavy dew of s. — SHAK 590:21
keep'st the ports of s. — SHAK 584:1
little sleep, a little s. — BIBLE 78:14
neither s. nor sleep — BOOK 133:23
Seal thy sense in deathly s. — DE L 236:2
s. did my spirit seal — WORD 748:1
s. is more sweet than toil — TENN 686:2
soothing s. seven — JONES 378:2
slumbered: you have but s. — SHAK 613:3
slumbering: s. still — CRAW 226:16
slumbers: soul is dead that s. — LONG 427:7
Golden s. kiss — DEKK 235:17
unquiet s. for the sleepers — BRON 142:19
yet hast thou golden s. — DEKK 235:15
slums: gay intimacy of the s. — WAUGH 723:15
slurp: As they s., slurp, slurp — FISH 283:7
slut: I am not a s. — SHAK 569:12
sluts: foul s. in dairies — CORB 218:11
sluttish: besmeared with s. time — SHAK 633:18
sly: s. shade of a Rural Dean — BROO 143:11
smack: with contented s. — KEATS 388:21
yet some s. of age in you — SHAK 582:16
small: All creatures great and s. — ALEX 8:9
All things both great and s. — COL 211:17
Almost too s. for sight — SHAK 597:1
between the s. and great — COWP 224:12
commonly thought s. — WOOLF 742:8
compare s. things with great — VIRG 715:19
day of s. nations — CHAM 189:4
deals it in s. parcels — WEBS 726:1
express in the s. of the back — WOD 740:14
extinguishes the s. — BUSS 165:18
grind exceeding s. — LOGAU 426:4
How very s. the very great — THAC 691:22
In s. proportions we just — JONS 379:21
Is it so s. a thing — ARN 27:3
Microbe is so very s. — BELL 61:18
no s. talk and Peel has no — WELL 727:8
now thoroughly s. and dry — ELIOT 270:6
one s. step for man — ARMS 26:12
pictures that got s. — BRAC 138:20
shows how s. the world is — GROS 319:3
s. and selfish is sorrow — ELIZ 275:3
s., but perfectly formed — COOP 218:9
s. change of silence — MER 458:2
s. Latin and less Greek — JONS 380:3
s. men no great thing can — MILL 460:20
s. nations like prostitutes — KUBR 404:7
speaks s. like a woman — SHAK 610:10
squadrons against the s. — BUSS 165:19
still s. voice — BIBLE 76:7
That s. infantry — MILT 468:25
Too s. to live — ANON 19:3
we are too s. in mind — GREE 317:5
smaller: s. fleas that on him — SWIFT 675:6
smallest: s. amount of lying — BUTL 166:27
s. room of my house — REGER 538:13
small talk: s. flows from lip — CRAB 224:21
small-talking: this s. world — FRY 295:23
smart: Of love and all its s. — BEDD 58:8
scorn which mocked the s. — ARN 28:21
stranger shall s. — BIBLE 78:22
smarter: thought themselves s. — ATTL 32:16
smash: never s. in a face — HALS 322:8
smashed: s. up things and creatures — FITZ 285:3
smatch: some s. of honour — SHAK 593:22
smattering: s. of everything — DICK 243:29
smell: I s. a rat — ROCHE 542:17
Money has no s. — VESP 710:9
shares man's s. — HOPK 345:10
s. and hideous hum — GODL 308:7
s. of burning fills — BELL 61:23
s. of fish — KILV 396:6
s. of steaks in passageways — ELIOT 272:13
s. of the blood still — SHAK 604:14
s. the blood of a British — SHAK 596:17
s. too strong of the lamp — STER 664:20
sweet keen s. — ROSS 548:8
this foul deed shall s. — SHAK 591:24
smelleth: he s. the battle afar — BIBLE 77:39

soap: S. and education — TWAIN 706:5
used your s. two years ago — PUNCH 532:2
What? no s.? — FOOTE 288:15
with smiles and s. — CARR 184:5
soap-boiler: made a s. costive — WEBS 725:19
soar: can creep as well as s. — BURKE 159:23
run, though not to s. — MAC 435:22
s. where he is sitting — SHEL 639:21
Type of the wise who s. — WORD 748:12
soaring: s. ever singest — SHEL 643:14
sob: S., heavy world — AUDEN 33:28
sobbed: He s. and he sighed — GILB 305:13
sober: and Porson s. — HOUS 353:1
at least not s. — JOHN 370:26
Be s., be vigilant — BIBLE 105:21
compulsorily s. — MAGEE 441:18
he that will go to bed s. — FLET 287:12
keep absolutely s. — SMITH 652:5
men at whiles are s. — HOUS 351:19
Philip drunk to Philip s. — ANON 12:6
righteous, and s. life — BOOK 118:9
shaved and s. — CHAN 190:1
s., of good behaviour — BIBLE 103:26
S., steadfast, and demure — MILT 464:16
To-morrow we'll be s. — ANON 12:24
when I was one-third s. — BURT 164:8
sobrely: looked holwe, and therto s. — CHAU 192:19
sobs: s. of autumn's violins — VERL 710:4
s., sniffles, and smiles — HENRY 333:2
sociable: I am a s. worker — BEHAN 60:3
social: bade self-love and s. — POPE 522:18
connected with the s. progress — JOHN 366:11
knows of no religion but s. — WESL 728:17
Legion and S. Club — BETJ 67:9
s. and economic experiment — HOOV 344:17
S. Contract is nothing — WELLS 727:19
s. engineering resembles — POPP 624:14
s. fabric would fly asunder — SHAW 637:18
s. position of those he meets — TOCQ 699:6
socialism: Democracy and s. — NEHRU 491:7
priorities the religion of S. — BEVAN 68:14
S. can only arrive by bicycle — VIER 711:9
S. does not mean much more — ORW 500:22
s. is not a stage beyond — ROB 542:13
s. would not lose its human — DUBC 262:22
This is not S. It is Bolshevism — SNOW 654:8
socialist: Champagne s. — MORT 486:10
s. culture in our land — MAO 446:3
S. is a prim little man — ORW 500:23
S. literature is W. H. Auden — ORW 500:23
socialists: We are all s. now — HARC 323:14
societies: curt s. whose deaths — MOT 487:2
In solemn troops, and sweet s. — MILT 466:14
society: action of s. upon itself — TOCQ 699:4
altering the *shape* of s. — ORW 500:4
And woman made S. — BRAD 139:1
bonds of civil s. — LOCKE 425:8
capital of polished s. — BURKE 158:22
cling together in one s. — WORD 746:21
consolidates s. — JOHN 371:2
desperate oddfellow s. — THOR 697:4
effects upon s. at large — SMIL 650:12
fair portion of all which s. — BURKE 158:11
first duty to serve s. — JOHN 372:25
free s. it is master of — BEV 69:11
law of motion of modern s. — MARX 452:6
Man was formed for s. — BLAC 110:10
no importance whatever to s. — NAB 489:4
no letters; no s. — HOBB 340:7
no such thing as S. — THAT 691:26
One great s. alone on earth — WORD 747:8
Ourself will mingle with s. — SHAK 603:7
planned order of s. — MEAD 455:11
S. became my glittering bride — WORD 743:21
s. cannot help the many — KENN 393:13
s. distributes itself — ARN 29:7
s. founded on trash — SAY 557:14
S. is all but rude — MARV 450:7
S. is based on the assumption — KING 398:8
S. is indeed a contract — BURKE 158:21
S. is now one polished horde — BYRON 171:27

society: (*cont.*):
s. is the end of government — ADAMS 3:1
s. is wonderfully delightful — WILDE 735:31
s. requires to be rebuilt — MILL 460:10
s. where it is safe — STEV 666:20
s., where none intrudes — BYRON 169:13
s. would be a hell upon earth — MILL 461:1
solid fabric of the old s. — TRIL 702:17
solitude sometimes is best s. — MILT 472:20
Soul selects her own S. — DICK 244:17
unable to live in s. — ARIS 25:16
unfit a man for s. — CHAM 189:12
upward to the Great S. — JOHN 367:8
sock: If Jonson's learnèd s. — MILT 465:17
socket: Burn to the s. — WORD 743:18
s. of his earthly lantern — GREV 318:7
sockets: candles burn their s. — HOUS 351:21
set upon s. of fine gold — BIBLE 81:20
socks: inability to put on your s. — GONC 312:10
In your shirt and your s. — GILB 304:17
Socrates: contradict S. — SOCR 655:3
S. breaks the law by — PLATO 516:9
S., I shall not accuse — PLATO 516:11
Socratic: S. manner — BEER 59:19
sod: under my head a s. — BALL 49:7
withered in the s. — BRON 142:2
soda water: Sermons and s. — BYRON 170:18
wash their feet in s. — ELIOT 273:7
sodden: nor s. at all with water — BIBLE 72:9
That are s. and unkind — BELL 61:28
sodium: having discovered S. — BENT 64:13
Sodom: S. and Gomorrah — BIBLE 86:12
sodomy: Impotence and s. — WAUGH 724:10
rum, s., and the lash — CHUR 203:10
sods: s. with our bayonets — WOLFE 740:25
sofa: accomplished s. last — COWP 223:16
fainted Alternately on a S. — AUST 38:14
s. upholstered in panther — PLOM 517:13
wheel the s. round — COWP 223:31
soft: does not make us s. — PER 512:22
her s. and chilly nest — KEATS 387:7
O make It s. and narrow — BALL 48:22
she s. as the dawn — THUR 697:19
s. answer turneth away wrath — BIBLE 78:33
s. falls the dew — BEERS 59:22
s. philosopher — DRYD 260:35
s. phrase of peace — SHAK 614:30
s., unhappy sex — BEHN 60:17
whan s. was the sonne — LANG 408:19
When we were a s. amoeba — SHIP 646:1
softer: s. than butter — BOOK 128:12
softest: s. lining can never — AST 32:8
s. thing about him — RUNY 550:3
softly: run s., till I end — SPEN 660:24
s. all my years — BIBLE 83:24
S. along the road of evening — DE L 236:10
s. and suddenly vanish — CARR 184:4
S. come and softly go — ORRED 499:9
Tread s. because you tread — YEATS 751:22
softness: of my body — LOW 429:12
s. she and sweet attractive — MILT 471:5
that whisper s. in chambers — MILT 475:8
soggy: little island huffling — UPD 707:6
soil: Foul as their s. — BYRON 169:27
indestructible powers of the s. — RIC 539:23
rather be tied to the s. — HOMER 343:13
s. is bare now — HOPK 345:10
s. may best deserve — MILT 469:5
s. which is soon exhausted — REYN 539:11
that grows in every s. — BURKE 157:30
this the s., the clime — MILT 468:11
soilèd: cheer our s. face — BOOK 135:21
soiling: I'm s. the doileys — BETJ 67:12
soils: Six days of the week it s. — LARK 410:8
sojourner: discontented s. — WORD 746:17
sojourners: s., as were all our — BIBLE 76:32
sol: *inferebantur s. et luna* — AUG 36:23
solace: find short s. there — WORD 745:8
s. ourselves with loves — BIBLE 78:16
With s. and gladness — SKEL 649:1
sold: I'd not have s. her for it — SHAK 618:11
s. his birthright — BIBLE 71:9
s. my reputation — FITZ 284:15

sold: (*cont.*):
s. the truth to serve — TENN 687:18
went and s. all — BIBLE 91:4
soldats: *vingt-quatre s.* — ANON 20:12
soldier: arm our s. — SHAK 570:3
Ben Battle was a s. — HOOD 343:17
can always tell an old s. — SHAW 635:22
chocolate cream s. — SHAW 635:23
death, who had the s. singled — DOUG 255:13
Drinking is the s.'s pleasure — DRYD 259:18
For a s. I listed — DIBD 238:12
God's s. be he — SHAK 605:5
go to your Gawd like a s. — KIPL 401:12
great s. of today — BAG 46:20
himself have been a s. — SHAK 579:32
I never expect a s. to think — SHAW 636:7
in the s. is flat blasphemy — SHAK 606:1
I said an elder s. — SHAK 593:3
not having been a s. — JOHN 374:28
side of the Unknown S. — ASQ 31:18
s. a mere recreant prove — SHAK 627:10
s., and afeard — SHAK 604:12
s. can stand up to anything — SHAW 636:9
s. details his wounds — PROP 529:22
s. full of strange oaths — SHAK 568:16
s. is better accommodated — SHAK 583:16
s. is no more exempt — STER 665:8
S., scholar, horseman — YEATS 752:4
s.'s life is terrible hard — MILNE 462:12
s.'s paid to kick against — OWEN 503:16
s.'s pole is fall'n — SHAK 566:15
s.'s ribbon on a tunic — ABSE 1:3
summer s. and the sunshine — PAINE 504:12
what the s. said — DICK 243:20
soldiers: bring the s. home — LARK 409:19
god of s. — SHAK 570:24
having s. under me — BIBLE 89:30
if you believe the s. — SAL 554:2
Ireland gives England her s. — MER 457:18
Old s. never die — FOLEY 288:8
Old s., sweethearts — WEBS 725:26
our s. slighted — QUAR 533:13
S. are citizens of death's — SASS 557:7
s., armèd in their stings — SHAK 584:22
s. bore dead bodies — SHAK 579:30
s. by two and by three — BALL 50:2
s. coming — AUDEN 35:14
s. he smiled at are most — SASS 557:11
s. home for lack of money — LARK 410:1
s. may not quit the post — TENN 686:4
s., mostly fools — BIER 109:11
S. of Christ, arise — WESL 728:11
S. of the ploughshare — RUSK 551:4
S., this solitude — DE L 236:9
steel my s.' hearts — SHAK 586:9
substance of ten thousand s. — SHAK 622:13
twenty-six lead s. — ANON 20:12
s. what is the world, O s. — DE L 236:9
soldier-saints: s., who row on row — BROW 153:6
soldiery: Emperor's drunken s. — YEATS 750:20
rapacious and licentious s. — BURKE 159:2
sole: *muove il s. e l'altre stelle* — DANTE 230:21
nothing can be s. or whole — YEATS 751:8
rest for the s. of her foot — BIBLE 70:27
solecism: eternity without a s. — BROW 146:4
soleil: *comme un s. d'Italie* — BANV 51:13
J'ai vu le s. bas — RIMB 541:6
solemn: s. creed with solemn sneer — BYRON 168:26
upon our s. feast-day — BOOK 130:14
world in s. stillness lay — SEARS 561:12
solemnized: s. their obsequies — BROW 145:15
soles: Nor the s. of her shoe — SHAK 574:25
S. *effugere atque abire sentit* — MART 449:14
S. *occidere et redire possunt* — CAT 185:15
soli: S. *eravamo, e sanza alcun* — DANTE 230:12
soliciting: still-s. eye — SHAK 594:22
This supernatural s. — SHAK 600:12
viciously s. — BYRON 174:8
solicitor: can only go to his s. — DISR 248:20
solid: Safe upon s. rock — MILL 461:8
s. for fluidity — CHUR 202:4
solidity: appearance of s. — ORW 501:2

solitary: Be not s., be not idle — BURT 165:14
How doth the city sit s. — BIBLE 85:15
if you are s., be not idle — JOHN 375:11
sentenced to s. confinement — WILL 737:7
s. places; where we taste — SHEL 640:20
spill her s. tea — POPE 521:1
Through Eden took their s. way — MILT 473:14
till I am s. — JOHN 371:13
To wander s. there — MARV 450:14
wilderness and the s. — BIBLE 83:19
Yon s. Highland lass — WORD 748:3
solitude: easy in s. to live after our own — EMER 277:1
endure our own s. — PRIT 529:18
feel his s. more keenly — VALÉ. 707:22
How sweet is harmless s. — MOLL 479:16
In a s. of the sea — HARDY 325:3
In s. what happiness — MILT 472:14
island s., unsponsored — STEV 666:11
life the s. — YOUNG 755:1
Musing in s. — WORD 743:14
Oft seeks to sweet retirèd s. — MILT 463:27
one to s. — ARN 28:22
O s. where are the charms — COWP 224:15
place of seclusion and s. — MONT 481:1
protects the s. of the other — RILKE 541:3
resonance of his s. — CONN 216:14
self-sufficing power of S. — WORD 746:22
Soldiers, this s. — DE L 236:9
s. is either a wild beast — BACON 43:20
s. sometimes is best society — MILT 472:20
To this delicious s. — MARV 450:7
Which is the bliss of s. — WORD 744:16
solitudinem: S. faciunt pacem — TAC 677:20
Solomon: greater than S. — BIBLE 90:35
had seen all S.'s wisdom — BIBLE 75:23
in the proverbs of S. — DICK 240:16
King S. wrote the Proverbs — NAYL 491:3
S. in all his glory — BIBLE 89:11
S. loved many strange women — BIBLE 75:26
S. of saloons — BROW 151:10
tabernacle, and anointed S. — BIBLE 75:21
than the felicities of S. — BACON 42:19
solus: solum quam cum s. esset — CIC 204:3
solution: fertilize a problem with a s. — SIMP 648:6
material conditions for its s. — MARX 452:3
s. for the problem of habitual — BENC 62:10
Those people were a kind of s. — CAV 187:8
total s. of the Jewish — GOER 308:16
you're either part of the s. — CLEA 206:3
solutis: O quid s. — CAT 186:3
solutus: S. omni faenore — HOR 348:22
solve: S. metus — VIRG 712:9
solvent: money, the great s. — TRIL 702:17
solventur: S. risu tabulae — HOR 351:7
some: s., alas, with Kate — AUDEN 35:17
S. chicken! Some neck! — CHUR 202:16
s. of the people all the time — LINC 422:14
S. say the world will end — FROST 294:1
somebodee: When every one is s. — GILB 304:5
somebody: brisk little s. — BROW 148:9
someday: S. I'll find you — COW 221:1
someone: haunting fear that s. — MENC 457:7
Make yourself necessary to s. — EMER 276:15
that it was s. else — ROG 544:15
something: s. for Posterity — ADD 4:24
S. here inside — HARB 323:9
S. must be done — EDW 267:4
s. that infects the world — ARN 27:23
s. to say — WHAT 730:7
S. you somehow haven't — FROST 294:15
Time for a little s. — MILNE 463:4
sometime: that s. did me seek — WYATT 749:19
woman is a s. thing — HEYW 338:3
sometimes: s. always, by God — RICH 540:16
S. coming, sometimes coy — SEDL 561:16
somewhat: have s. against thee — BIBLE 106:3
tough joints more than s. — RUNY 550:2
somewhere: S. over the rainbow — HARB 323:13
to get s. else — CARR 182:21
sommeil: s. nous soulage — CHAM 189:11

son: coming of the S. of Man — BIBLE 92:13
conceive, and bear a s. — BIBLE 82:24
dumb s. of a bitch — TRUM 704:20
Fitzdotterel's eldest s. — BROU 144:6
forth her firstborn s. — BIBLE 93:26
gallows and did bear our s. — KYD 404:15
gave his only begotten S. — BIBLE 96:15
his little s. should cry — CORN 219:3
keep his only s., myself — HOME 342:19
Kiss the S. — BOOK 124:11
leichter of a fair s. — ELIZ 274:16
my s., mine own Telemachus — TENN 690:3
My s. shall not go down — BIBLE 71:29
O Absalom, my s. — BIBLE 75:17
righteousness unto the King's s. — BOOK 129:18
s. into his bosom creeps — FLET 288:1
s. of Adam and of Eve — PRIOR 529:6
s. of his old age — BIBLE 71:20
S. of man hath not where — BIBLE 90:1
S. of Morn in weary Night's — BLAKE 111:23
S. of Saint Louis — FIRM 202:30
s. should strike his father — SHAK 627:8
spareth his rod hateth his s. — BIBLE 78:29
spoken unto us by his S. — BIBLE 104:10
Take now thy s. — BIBLE 71:4
This is my beloved S. — BIBLE 88:17
This my s. was dead — BIBLE 95:5
two-legged thing, a s. — DRYD 259:2
unto us a s. is given — BIBLE 82:27
what's a s.? A thing — KYD 404:14
whom if his s. ask bread — BIBLE 89:19
wise s. maketh a glad father — BIBLE 78:20
Woman, behold thy s. — BIBLE 97:27
worthy to be called thy s. — BIBLE 95:3
you'll be a Man, my s. — KIPL 400:15
younger s. gathered all — BIBLE 95:2
your s.'s tender years — JUV 384:14
song: after all an earthly s. — TENN 683:23
all this for a s. — CECIL 188:4
Assist our s. — GURN 320:3
auld Scotish s. — BURNS 161:14
beyond a s. or a billet — ETH 278:18
breeze of s. — TENN 684:1
burden of my s. — ANON 16:4
burthen of his s. — BICK 108:21
carcase of an old s. — THOM 694:15
end of ane old s. — OGIL 498:4
glorious s. of old — SEARS 561:12
Glorious the s. — SMART 650:4
goodly manor for a s. — SHAK 564:7
Hear a s. that echoes cheerly — TENN 684:25
his presence with a s. — BOOK 131:17
if such holy s. — MILT 467:8
I hear but their low lone s. — CARP 181:21
I made my s. a coat — YEATS 751:3
joyful S. I'll raise — ADD 4:17
lark becomes a sightless s. — TENN 684:14
let satire be my s. — BYRON 172:3
loves shall moralize my s. — SPEN 659:19
Luxuriant s. — YEATS 751:17
main region of my s. — WORD 743:15
my reputation for a s. — FITZ 284:15
my s. begins and endeth — SIDN 646:22
My s. is love unknown — CROS 228:2
old s. made by an aged — ANON 17:3
O let the s. of praise be sung — POTT 525:9
One grand, sweet s. — KING 397:9
On wings of s. — HEINE 330:14
penny for a s. — YEATS 750:17
Perhaps it may turn out a s. — BURNS 161:23
Pipe a s. about a Lamb — BLAKE 113:16
play a s. for me — DYLAN 265:18
Poured forth her s. in perfect — AUDEN 34:1
raised some serious s. — TICK 698:4
required of us then a s. — BOOK 134:17
sans s., sans singer — FITZ 283:18
self-same s. that found a path — KEATS 389:15
Short swallow-flights of s. — TENN 683:15
sing unto the Lord a new s. — BOOK 134:1
sing unto the Lord a new s. — BOOK 131:13
s. charms the sense — MILT 469:23

song: (cont.):
s. comes native — KEATS 390:8
s. is considered a perfect gem — CALV 175:11
s. is ended — BERL 65:20
S. made in lieu of many — SPEN 659:17
s. of songs — BIBLE 81:5
s. of the birds for mirth — GURN 319:17
S. of the Shirt — HOOD 344:7
s. that never ends — GOET 309:4
s. was wordless — SASS 557:10
s. we heard last night — SHAK 629:12
s. would come in the right — OVID 503:6
spur me into s. — YEATS 753:9
start a s. and to respond — VIRG 715:3
Still all my s. would — ADAMS 3:10
subject for heroic s. — MILT 472:17
subject will I frame my s. — CHES 197:14
suck melancholy out of a s. — SHAK 568:9
suffering what they teach in s. — SHEL 641:1
sung as it were a new s. — BIBLE 107:2
sword he sung a s. of death — BLAKE 113:13
think two notes a s. — DAV 232:9
till I end my s. — SPEN 660:24
Time an endless s. — YEATS 752:9
Time is our tedious s. — MILT 467:13
twofold silence was the s. — ROSS 547:21
What is the Syrens sang — BROW 145:19
When ever I remake a s. — YEATS 751:19
woman, wine, and s. — LUTH 432:17
songs: after the s. of Apollo — SHAK 599:12
all their s. are sad — CHES 198:28
Her matchless s. — MARV 450:17
hymns and spiritual s. — BIBLE 102:23
I cannot sing the old s. — CLAR 205:6
I have s. of my own — VIRG 715:7
I sing s. never heard — HOR 349:22
lean and flashy s. — MILT 466:9
Muse these s. intendeth — SIDN 646:22
one of the s. of Sion — BOOK 134:17
Our sweetest s. — SHEL 643:19
piping s. for ever new — KEATS 388:27
Piping s. of pleasant glee — BLAKE 113:16
Sing no sad s. for me — ROSS 547:12
Sing thou the s. of love — GURN 320:4
s. beguile your pilgrimage — FLEC 286:9
S. consecrate to truth — SHEL 643:25
s. for me and my aunts — SHAK 631:24
s. make and wel endite — CHAU 192:11
Their s. were Ave Marys — CORB 218:13
Where are the s. of Spring — KEATS 390:19
sonitu: putrem s. quatit ungula — VIRG 714:5
sonne: Platz an der S. — BÜLOW 155:2
Vienne la nuit, s. l'heure — APOL 23:15
sonnet: Scorn not the S. — WORD 747:17
s. is a moment's monument — ROSS 547:19
S.'s scanty plot of ground — WORD 745:8
sonneteer: starved hackney s. — POPE 521:19
sonnetter: I shall turn s. — SHAK 598:9
sonnets: S. and birds descend — MACN 441:5
s. turned to holy psalms — PEELE 511:5
written s. all his life — BYRON 170:25
sonorous: S. metal blowing — MILT 468:23
sons: Abraham had two s. — BIBLE 102:5
Bears all its s. away — WATTS 723:7
Brightest and best of the s. — HEBER 330:2
cruel s. of Cain — LE G 416:9
fallen s. of Eve — CHES 199:10
God's s. are things — MADD 441:14
If I had a thousand s. — SHAK 583:28
many s. as I have hairs — SHAK 605:5
s. and daughters of Life's — GIBR 303:2
s. and your daughters shall — BIBLE 86:8
s. may grow up as the young — BOOK 135:4
s. of God came in unto — BIBLE 70:25
s. of God shouted for joy — BIBLE 77:35
S. of the dark and bloody — O'HARA 498:6
then wander forth the s. — MILT 468:21
Your s. and your daughters — DYLAN 265:23
soon: Be s. — THOM 695:3
Come s., soon — SHEL 643:23
s. as one is unhappy — PROU 500:17
sooner: make an end the s. — BACON 43:13
s. every party breaks up — AUST 38:9

soonest: best when s. wrought SOUT 658:1
soot: in s. I sleep BLAKE 113:17
sooth: it is silly s. SHAK 629:16
  thing is never the lasse s. CHAU 194:29
soothing: these are s. hints EMER 277:10
sooty: to the s. bosom SHAK 614:28
sop: body gets its s. BROW 148:10
  s. of all this sordid globe SHAK 627:8
sophist: saint nor s.-led ARN 27:2
sophistication: s. of the wise primitive
                                                             MAIL 442:10
sophistry: Destroy his fib, or s. POPE 519:27
  nothing but s. and illusion HUME 355:4
  So s., cleaves close COWP 223:4
  Their s. I can control AST 32:5
  wits to s. and affectation BACON 45:14
soporific: lettuce is 's.' POTT 525:12
sops: s. in wine SPEN 660:26
sorcerers: s. and whoremongers BIBLE 107:25
Sordello: but the one 'S.' POUND 526:7
sore: bear with a s. head MARR 449:3
  perfectly s. with loving her DICK 240:22
  s. let and hindered BOOK 120:12
sores: at his gate, full of s. BIBLE 95:9
sorest: our need was the s. SCOTT 559:10
sorriness: s. underlying HARDY 324:21
sorrow: and the s. thereof MAL 443:7
  bee of s. had stung BABEL 41:11
  call that s. sweet WILB 734:6
  Down, thou climbing s. SHAK 595:14
  Ere the s. comes with years BROW 147:11
  forgather wi' S. and Care BURNS 161:14
  From the sphere of our s. SHEL 643:12
  Give s. words SHAK 604:8
  glut thy s. on a morning KEATS 389:6
  hairs with s. to the grave BIBLE 71:29
  heart hath 'scaped this s. SHAK 634:13
  in s. thou shalt bring forth BIBLE 70:15
  interest and fines on s. MAY 455:3
  in trouble, s., need BOOK 122:3
  knowledge increaseth s. BIBLE 80:3
  Labour without s. is base RUSK 550:25
  Lycidas your s. is not dead MILT 466:13
  memory a rooted s. SHAK 604:22
  more in s. than in anger SHAK 572:21
  night of doubt and s. BAR 53:3
  not be in s. too BLAKE 114:3
  Nought but vast S. DE L 236:3
  O S., wilt thou live with me TENN 683:24
  parting is such sweet s. SHAK 623:7
  Regions of s., doleful shades MILT 468:1
  selfish is s. ELIZ 275:3
  sin could blight or s. fade COL 210:1
  so beguile thy s. SHAK 627:1
  s. and sighing shall flee BIBLE 83:22
  S. and silence are strong LONG 426:17
  s. dogging sin HERB 335:19
  s. enough in the natural KIPL 400:17
  s. for the lost Lenore POE 518:7
  S. in all lands SUTT 672:23
  S. is knowledge BYRON 172:16
  S. is tranquillity remembered PARK 506:14
  s. lasts all through life FLOR 288:4
  sorrow like unto my s. BIBLE 85:16
  s. never comes too late GRAY 316:3
  S. proud to be exalted ANON 15:6
  s.'s crown of sorrow TENN 685:10
  S.'s most detested fruit BYRON 168:21
  S. so royally in you appears SHAK 584:8
  s.'s tribute to the passing CAT 187:1
  then but labour and s. BOOK 131:1
  think is to be full of s. KEATS 389:10
  this s.'s heavenly SHAK 618:5
  top which whipping S. GREV 318:6
  To S., I bade good-morrow KEATS 386:18
  Who never ate his bread in s. GOET 309:15
  Write s. on the bosom SHAK 620:7
sorrowful: He went away s. BIBLE 91:24
  laughter the heart is s. BIBLE 78:30
  such as be s. BOOK 120:3
  way to the s. city DANTE 230:6
sorrowing: s. I to see the summer flowers
                                                             SACK 552:12

sorrows: carried our s. BIBLE 84:11
  costly in our s. STER 664:10
  Desire can make, or s. breed KING 396:11
  Disease, or s. strike him CLOU 207:15
  engluts and swallows other s. SHAK 614:29
  It soothes his s., heals NEWT 494:10
  man of s., and acquainted BIBLE 84:11
  s. of women would be averted ELIOT 269:2
  Then all my s. are at an end GAY 299:14
  When shall my s. have an end ANON 14:10
  When s. come, they come SHAK 578:3
  world's great s. were born Æ 5:10
sorry: I'm s., now, I wrote it BURG 156:23
  S. for itself LAWR 412:18
  s. for these our misdoings BOOK 122:6
  that I shall be s. for SHAK 593:4
  Very s. can't come BER 65:4
sort: see a s. of traitors here SHAK 621:1
  s. of person you and I CARL 179:19
  s. of treason BURKE 157:8
sortem: nemo, quam sibi s. HOR 350:21
sortir: à vous à l'en faire s. LOUIS 428:17
sorts: s. and conditions of men BOOK 120:5
so-so: rest is merely s. WILD 736:16
Sosostris: Madame S. ELIOT 272:24
sospetto: sanza alcun s. DANTE 230:12
sot: s. savant est sot plus MOL 479:1
  s. trouve toujours un plus BOIL 117:3
souffre: s. et meurs VIGNY 711:12
sought: Love s. is good SHAK 630:13
  many a thing I s. SHAK 633:11
  s. him whom my soul loveth BIBLE 81:12
  s. in vain that sought BURNS 161:16
  They s. with thimbles CARR 184:5
  those men that s. him SHAK 589:10
soul: adventures of his s. FRAN 292:8
  assault and hurt the s. BOOK 120:15
  At once the s. of each COL 209:20
  bitterness of his s. BIBLE 87:13
  bitterness of my s. BIBLE 83:24
  bright s. of the sad year NASHE 490:23
  brother's s. you find BARB 52:3
  buried s. and all its gems BLAKE 111:17
  but because he has a s. FAUL 281:3
  Calm s. of all things ARN 27:12
  chosen thus to fling his s. HARDY 325:5
  city of the s. BYRON 169:3
  clothing for the s. divine BLAKE 111:6
  complete s. of all perfection MARS 449:10
  composed in the s. ARN 29:23
  Conceptions equal to the s.'s WORD 744:1
  confident concerning his s. SOCR 655:1
  dark night of the s. FITZ 285:5
  eye was in itself a S. BYRON 167:27
  fine point of his s. KEATS 391:8
  freed his s. the nearest way JOHN 375:30
  furnished with a Russian s. LERM 419:1
  God rest his s., officers SMITH 652:19
  God the s. POPE 522:7
  Go, S., the body's guest RAL 535:15
  half conceal the S. within TENN 682:31
  Half my own s. HOR 349:1
  Hang there like fruit, my s. SHAK 571:20
  harmonical and ingenious s. AUBR 33:6
  haughtiness of s. ADD 3:17
  Heart and s. do sing in me SIDN 647:5
  Heaven take my s. SHAK 594:13
  he has the s. of a martyr BAG 46:10
  he shall save his s. alive BIBLE 85:23
  he that hides a dark s. MILT 463:27
  his eager s. FULL 296:8
  His s. is marching on ANON 15:12
  hurl my s. from heaven SHAK 618:18
  hushèd casket of my s. KEATS 390:15
  I am the captain of my s. HENL 332:7
  I have a bit of FIAT in my s. BEDD 58:10
  I have freed my s. BERN 66:8
  In books lies the s. CARL 180:27
  I pray the Lord my s. to keep ANON 16:24
  I pray the Lord my s. to take ANON 16:24
  iron entered into his s. BOOK 132:11

soul: (cont.):
  Jesu, lover of my s. WESL 728.0
  knock and enter in our s. BROW 148:11
  leave my s. in hell BOOK 124:31
  leaves s. free a little BROW 148:10
  lie in the s. is a true lie JOW 380:19
  life's dim windows of the s. BLAKE 111:17
  life unto the bitter in s. BIBLE 77:9
  lift my s. to heaven SHAK 588:11
  like an infant's s. TRAH 701:8
  little babe, come silly s. BRET 140:17
  lose his own s. BIBLE 93:14
  man became a living s. BIBLE 70:1
  man, with s. so dead SCOTT 559:16
  Marlbro's mighty s. ADD 3:13
  meeting s. may pierce MILT 465:17
  Memorial from the S.'s ROSS 547:19
  Merry of s. he sailed on a day STEV 669:2
  mind and s. TENN 682:29
  most comprehensive s. DRYD 262:11
  most surely, on the s. DIMN 246:6
  my outward s. DONNE 252:3
  My s., bear thou thy part GURN 320:4
  My s. doth magnify the Lord BIBLE 93:22
  My s. he doth restore again SCOT 561:8
  my soul, if I have a s. ANON 17:2
  My s. in agony COL 211:7
  My s. is an enchanted boat SHEL 642:17
  my s. is white BLAKE 114:1
  My s., like to a ship WEBS 726:12
  My s.'s in arms, and eager CIBB 203:22
  My s., sit thou a patient QUAR 533:16
  My s. smoothed itself out BROW 150:21
  my s. within the house SHAK 628:24
  my unconquerable s. HENL 332:6
  No coward s. is mine BRON 142:12
  nor the prophetic s. SHAK 634:19
  no s. to be damned THUR 697:21
  oath again may my s. SHAW 638:21
  one's s. to keep one's body MACK 439:2
  Only a sweet and virtuous s. HERB 336:2
  Oppressed the s.! CRAB 224:23
  O s., be changed into little MARL 447:4
  Our echoes roll from s. to s. TENN 688:2
  Perdition catch my s. SHAK 616:10
  perfection of your s. SOCR 654:11
  Poor intricated s. DONNE 253:13
  progress of a deathless s. DONNE 251:11
  purest essence of a human s. CARL 181:13
  purest s. that e'er was sent CAREW 179:5
  receive my s. at last WESL 728:6
  Refined himself to s. DRYD 260:7
  repose of His s. ROLFE 545:9
  return to the depth of your s. ROUS 549:3
  Revolving in his altered s. DRYD 259:20
  seek the hurt of my s. BOOK 128:22
  Seek thou this s. of mine LITT 423:9
  Shall I lay perjury upon my s. SHAK 609:17
  shivering human s. PAST 508:5
  sighed his s. toward SHAK 609:23
  sinews of the s. FULL 296:6
  slid into my s. COL 211:10
  so longeth my s. after BOOK 127:2
  s. above buttons COLM 214:3
  s. a lordly pleasure-house TENN 687:20
  S. and body part like friends CRAS 226:14
  s. clap its hands and sing YEATS 762:7
  s. doth magnify the Lord BIBLE 108:9
  s. fleeth unto the Lord BOOK 134:12
  s. has to itself decreed KEATS 390:11
  s. inhabiting two bodies ARIS 26:2
  s. in new French books BROW 148:13
  s. into the boughs MARV 450:12
  s. is Christ's abode KEBLE 392:18
  s. is dead that slumbers LONG 427:7
  s. is form SPEN 660:20
  s. is immortal and capable PLATO 517:1
  s. is immortal and imperishable SOCR 654:17
  s. is placed in the body DEFOE 234:1
  s. is under their blessed AKHM 6:10
  s. itself must issue forth COL 209:15
  s. may but ascend to heaven MARL 447:2
  s. of a man is born JOYCE 381:10

Spanish: I must learn S.   BROW 149:23
S. ships of war at sea   TENN 689:1
taken by a S. Ga-la-lee   BALL 49:10
To God I speak S.   CHAR 191:21
spare: bread enough and to s.   BIBLE 95:3
Brother can you s. a dime   HARB 323:10
don't s. the horses   HILL 338:17
He was a s. man   AUBR 33:6
S. all I have, and take my life   FARQ 280:16
s. the beechen tree   CAMP 176:11
s. those who have submitted   VIRG 713:17
S. us all word of the weapons   WILB 734:1
s. your country's flag   WHIT 733:6
Woodman, s. that tree   MORR 485:8
spared: better s. a better man   SHAK 582:8
s. me the indignity   BELL 62:5
spares: that s. these stones   SHAK 635:15
spareth: s. his rod hateth his   BIBLE 78:29
spark: shows a hasty s.   SHAK 593:9
s. from heaven   ARN 28:8
s. from heaven to fall   ARN 28:6
s. of inextinguishable   SHEL 644:6
s. o' Nature's fire   BURNS 161:26
spark-gap: s. is mightier   HOGB 341:14
sparkle: S. for ever   TENN 687:26
s. out among the fern   TENN 680:11
s. still the right Promethean   SHAK 599:1
sparkles: s. near the brim   BYRON 168:14
sparks: hard it is to hide the s.   SHAK 571:9
like s. among the stubble   BIBLE 87:1
painted with unnumbered s.   SHAK 591:12
s. fly upward   BIBLE 77:12
sparrer-grass: bless ef 'taint a   HARR 327:1
sparrow: even as it were a s.   BOOK 131:18
hero perish, or a s. fall   POPE 521:29
My lady's s. is dead   CAT 185:13
providence in the fall of a s.   SHAK 579:2
s. alight upon my shoulder   THOR 697:7
s. hath found her an house   BOOK 130:16
s. should fly swiftly   BEDE 58:13
sparrows: more value than many s.   BIBLE 90:19
s. sold for two farthings   BIBLE 94:22
Spartans: Go, tell the S.   SIM 647:21
spat: s. on me Wednesday last   SHAK 608:1
spawn: meanest s. of Hell   TENN 685:5
spawning: by its formless s.   YEATS 753:10
speak: Books will s. plain   BACON 43:3
dare not s. its name   DOUG 255:7
did you s. to him again   BROW 151:8
grief that does not s.   SHAK 604:8
he shall s. for himself   BIBLE 96:35
I also could s. as ye do   BIBLE 77:23
I'll do't before I s.   SHAK 594:21
In all I think or s. or do   WESL 728:10
I only s. right   SHAK 592:16
it is difficult to s.   BURKE 159:5
I will s. now   BROW 148:23
let him now s., or else   BOOK 123:18
Let us not s. of them   DANTE 230:7
men shall s. well of you   BIBLE 94:5
mute and will not s. a word   SHAK 624:14
My lips are now forbid to s.   BAYLY 56:3
one to s., and another   THOR 697:10
O s. to reassure me   BODE 116:11
province of knowledge to s.   HOLM 342:8
slow to s.   BIBLE 104:27
s., and pause again   COWP 222:2
s. as the common people   ASCH 31:3
s. before you think   FORS 290:28
S. for England   AMERY 10:8
s. ill of everybody   PÉT 513:7
s. in Caesar's funeral   SHAK 592:5
s. in our tongues the wonderful   BIBLE 98:7
S. less than thou knowest   SHAK 595:6
S., Lord; for thy servant   BIBLE 74:28
s. low, if you speak love   SHAK 613:15
s. of eternity without   BROW 146:4
s. of the somwhat   CHAU 195:14
S. roughly to your little boy   CARR 182:5
S. softly and carry   ROOS 546:9
S. the speech, I pray you   SHAK 576:5

speak: (cont.):
s. they through their throat   BOOK 133:10
S. to Him thou for He hears   TENN 681:15
s. to the wise   PIND 514:14
S. unto us smooth things   BIBLE 83:13
S. what we feel   SHAK 598:5
s. when he is spoken to   STEV 668:20
s. with their enemies   BOOK 134:7
S. ye comfortably to Jerusalem   BIBLE 83:25
those that are asleep to s.   BIBLE 82:4
To s. and purpose not   SHAK 594:21
to speak, and to s. well   JONS 380:11
What should we s.   SHAK 571:8
when I s. unto them   BOOK 133:22
when I think, I must s.   SHAK 569:6
When you s., sweet   SHAK 632:5
whereof one cannot s.   WITT 740:3
You were better s. first   SHAK 569:17
you who s. through me   THOM 694:11
speaker: s. of my living actions   SHAK 589:12
speaketh: he s. of his own   BIBLE 96:33
s. things not to be spoken   BIBLE 87:21
speaking: adepts in the s. trade   CHUR 200:20
By drowning their s.   BROW 151:26
heard for their much s.   BIBLE 89:4
People talking without s.   SIMON 647:20
s. picture   SIDN 647:7
S. to yourselves in psalms   BIBLE 102:23
Teach us all the art of s.   SHER 645:26
speaks: and s. another   HOMER 343:7
Gladstone s. to Me as if   VICT 710:16
her foot s.   SHAK 628:2
She s. poniards   SHAK 613:17
s. small like a woman   SHAK 610:10
When he s.   SHAK 584:19
when Love s., the voice   SHAK 598:20
spear: Bring me my s.   BLAKE 113:4
His s., to equal which   MILT 468:14
knappeth the s. in sunder   BOOK 127:17
put s. in the rest   MAL 443:13
With a burning s.   ANON 19:23
with sharpened s. points   MAY 455:7
spear-men: stubborn s.   SCOTT 560:10
spears: s. was like stars   BYRON 169:28
stars threw down their s.   BLAKE 114:15
teeth are s. and arrows   BOOK 128:15
their s. into pruninghooks   BIBLE 82:11
special: s. grace preventing us   BOOK 120:16
We are all s. cases   CAMUS 177:13
specials: 's.' like the old time   COLL 213:7
species: female of the s.   KIPL 399:3
individual, but a s.   FIEL 282:5
individual, but the s.   JOHN 369:19
systematically on its own s.   JAMES 363:13
specimen: brick as a s.   JOHN 369:7
spectacle: present at this great s. of life   ELIOT 269:20
s. so ridiculous   MAC 434:19
s. unto the world   BIBLE 100:19
spectacles: s. have a function   POPP 524:17
s. of books to read Nature   DRYD 262:11
s., to shoot the hare   HOFF 341:8
What a pair of s. is here   SHAK 627:25
With s. on nose and pouch   SHAK 568:16
spectantia: adversum s.   HOR 348:1
spectat: S. et audit   CAT 186:7
spectators: actors or s.   SHEL 639:19
spectatress: S. of the mischief   ROWE 549:6
spectatum: S. veniunt   OVID 502:1
spectre: s. of Communism   MARX 452:11
spectres: S. fly before it   SMIL 650:13
spectre-thin: pale, and s.   KEATS 389:10
speculation: land s.   WILS 738:4
speculations: s. upon matter   JOHN 369:1
wrung from s. and subtleties   BROW 146:10
speculator: I was raised by a s.   STOWE 670:9
speech: as it does in one's s.   LA R 410:21
aspersion upon my parts of s.   SHER 645:4
But I am slow of s.   BIBLE 72:1
could wed itself with S.   TENN 683:10
dead had no s.   ELIOT 271:3
deal by s. than by letter   BACON 44:8
forme of s. is chaunge   CHAU 195:12

speech: (cont.):
freedom of s. and expression   ROOS 546:3
freedom of s.   TWAIN 706:8
I have strange power of s.   COL 211:16
manner of his s.   SHAK 565:4
neither s. nor language   BOOK 125:4
our concern was s.   ELIOT 271:5
perfect plainness of s.   ARN 30:8
rule of s.   HOR 347:6
sensibly refrain from s.   GRAH 314:1
Speak the s., I pray you   SHAK 576:5
s. by Chamberlain is like   BEVAN 69:3
s. created thought   SHEL 642:16
s. has escaped the barrier   HOMER 343:3
s. in that victorious brow   ARN 28:13
s. is like a cracked kettle   FLAU 285:16
S. is often barren   ELIOT 269:6
s. is shallow as Time   CARL 180:10
S. is the small change   MER 458:2
S. . . . not his language   STAËL 662:3
s. only to conceal   VOLT 716:5
s. than to give evidence   HAL 321:13
s. they have resolved not   ELIOT 269:2
stately s.   WORD 747:12
Thy s. bewrayeth thee   BIBLE 93:2
thy s. is comely   BIBLE 81:13
tongue blossom into s.   BROW 149:1
true use of s. is not   GOLD 311:13
utterance, nor power of s.   SHAK 592:16
verse is a measured s.   BACON 42:5
where s. is not   HOBB 339:17
your s. be alway with grace   BIBLE 103:18
speeches: From all the easy s.   CHES 199:3
His s. were fine   WALP 720:2
speechless: among the s. dead   HILL 338:9
great persons' graves is s.   DONNE 253:7
grey-grown s. Christ   SWIN 676:7
S. still, and never cry   CLEV 206:13
washed in the s. real   BARZ 54:23
speech-making: practising s.   JUV 384:9
speed: forgetting the bright s.   ARN 28:18
necessity of intense s.   LEV 419:19
our safety is in our s.   EMER 276:30
S., bonnie boat   BOUL 137:17
s. glum heroes up the line   SASS 557:4
s. the going guest   POPE 522:24
s. towards the wilder shores   BLAN 115:1
S. with the light-foot   GREN 318:2
time shall teach me s.   SHAK 594:10
Unsafe at any s.   NADER 489:5
Speed: our English S.   CAV 187:11
speeding: Faster than a s. bullet   ANON 13:8
spell: foreigners always s. better   TWAIN 706:12
s. it with a "V"   DICK 243:19
Thy s. through him   ROSS 547:22
who can s. TUESDAY   MILNE 462:10
Who lies beneath your s.   HOPE 345:3
with the s. of far Arabia   DE L 235:21
speller: fancy of the s.   DICK 243:19
wuss s. I know   WARD 721:1
spelling: My s. is Wobbly   MILNE 463:5
spells: cast s. over the future   AKHM 6:9
spem: Vitae summa brevis s.   HOR 349:4
spend: so wol we s.   CHAU 194:12
s. and God will send   GASC 298:16
whatever you have, s. less   JOHN 376:1
whatsoever thou s. more   BIBLE 94:15
what we yet may s.   FITZ 283:18
spender: s. thinks it went   FROST 295:1
spending: Getting and s.   WORD 748:15
money-s. always 'vulgar'   GASK 299:2
Riches are for s.   BACON 43:15
S. again what is already spent   SHAK 634:7
Spenser: In S., and in Jonson   DENH 236:19
little nearer s.   BASSE 55:2
Renownèd S.   BASSE 55:2
Thee gentle S. fondly led   LAND 408:7
spent: I have s. all the money   JOHN 375:26
Of a s. day   CRANE 225:17
s. lights quiver and gleam   ARN 27:8
What wee s., wee had   ANON 19:15
sperabitur: quae non s. hora   HOR 348:6

speranza: LASCIATE OGNI S. — DANTE 230:6
sperare: *salus victis nullam s.* — VIRG 712:21
speraret: *nec quid s. habebat* — VIRG 714:14
speravi: *In te Domine, s.* — ANON 22:18
spermatozoa: million s. — HUXL 357:19
spes: *S. omnis et fortuna nostri* — HOR 350:14
spew: bad ones s. it up — CERV 188:17
s. thee out of my mouth — BIBLE 106:7
spewed: s. up a good lump — DRYD 262:19
sphere: how gird the s. — MILT 472:11
shine through all the s. — VAUG 709:9
their motion in one s. — SHAK 582:5
these walls thy s. — DONNE 252:18
they the s. — DONNE 251:25
yonder starry s. — MILT 472:2
spheres: all the tuned s. — SHAK 566:20
Driv'n by the s. — VAUG 709:11
maintain the music of the s. — BROW 146:17
music of forfended s. — PATM 509:14
seems to shake the s. — DRYD 259:17
spherical: body is perfectly s. — LEAR 414:11
Sphinx: Subtle as S. — SHAK 598:20
spice: very s. of life — COWP 223:22
spices: land of s. — HERB 335:13
No S. wanting — HERR 337:1
s. thereof may flow out — BIBLE 81:16
upon the mountains of s. — BIBLE 82:7
spicy: s. nut-brown ale — MILT 465:14
What though the s. breezes — HEBER 330:4
spider: laws are like s.'s webs — ANAC 11:5
said a s. to a fly — HOW 353:7
s. catching them all — DOST 254:12
s. is sole denizen — HARDY 325:1
s.'s touch, how exquisitely — POPE 522:6
spiders: No more s. in my bath — ANON 16:21
often have seen s. fly — EDW 267:7
s. marching through — LOW 430:15
Weaving s. come not here — SHAK 611:21
spider-web: kind of huge s. — JAMES 363:3
spies: As if we were God's s. — SHAK 597:16
Instructed s. — WOTT 749:3
neighbourhood of voluntary s. — AUST 39:1
they come not single s. — SHAK 578:3
Ye are s. — BIBLE 71:28
spill: let them not s. me — MACN 441:1
spilt: water s. on the ground — BIBLE 75:14
spin: Go s., you jades — PEMB 511:9
Let the great world s. — TENN 685:19
neither do they s. — BIBLE 89:11
Sob as you s. — AUDEN 33:28
spinach: I say it's s. — WHITE 731:2
world of gammon and s. — DICK 240:1
spindle: fold, s. or mutilate — ANON 12:33
spine: s. has been shattered — MAND 444:4
spinis: *iuvat s. de pluribus una* — HOR 348:21
spinners: long-legged s., hence — SHAK 611:21
spinning: evening s. by the fire — RONS 545:12
spinning-wheel: wee bit s. — BLAM 114:19
spinster: saved many an English s. — MITF 478:5
spinsters: s. and the knitters — SHAK 629:16
spirantia: *Excudent alii s.* — VIRG 713:17
spires: dreaming s. — ARN 28:25
I saw the s. of Oxford — LETTS 419:15
What s., what farms are those — HOUS 352:15
Ye distant s., ye antique — GRAY 315:21
spirit: be filled with the S. — BIBLE 102:23
Blessed are the poor in s. — BIBLE 88:23
bold s. in a loyal breast — SHAK 619:7
break a man's s. is devil's — SHAW 636:3
'Brutus' will start a s. — SHAK 590:4
characteristics of the modern s. — DICK 245:6
Come, Holy S. — LANG 409:8
Curbing his lavish s. — SHAK 599:17
elasticity to the s. — SMIL 650:13
eviller s. than you — SORL 656:18
fair s. for my minister — BYRON 169:12
female s. begot the wheel — LAWR 412:6
fruit of the S. is love — BIBLE 102:7
gifts, but the same S. — BIBLE 100:35
given us the s. of fear — BIBLE 104:5
God is a S. — BIBLE 96:17
grey s. yearning in desire — TENN 690:2
Hail to thee, blithe S. — SHEL 643:13

spirit: (*cont.*):
haughty s. before a fall — BIBLE 78:37
heard the angry s.'s yell — BEAT 56:6
Her cabined ample S. — ARN 27:20
he that ruleth his s. — BIBLE 78:38
his S. in the inner man — BIBLE 102:13
holy-day rejoicing s. down — LAMB 407:3
humble, tranquil s. — DEKK 235:14
I am the s. that always denies — GOET 309:3
I commend my s. — BIBLE 95:28
I commend my s. — BOOK 126:7
ill-s. sob in each blood cell — LOW 430:20
immortal s. must endure — ARN 28:13
I will pour out my s. — BIBLE 86:8
kin to God by his s. — BACON 42:24
least erected s. that fell — MILT 469:4
light of thy Holy S. — BOOK 120:20
meek and quiet s. — BIBLE 105:16
motions of his s. — SHAK 610:3
My shaping s. of imagination — COL 209:17
nature of the s. we possess — LUCR 432:2
never approached my s. — METT 459:6
nimble, stirring s. — SHAK 599:6
no more s. in her — BIBLE 75:23
no s. can walk abroad — SHAK 572:2
Of s. so still and quiet — SHAK 614:31
On my s. make a music — STEV 666:7
pardlike S., beautiful — SHEL 639:20
present in s. — BIBLE 100:20
quick s. that is in Antony — SHAK 589:23
received the S. of adoption — BIBLE 99:35
renew a right s. within me — BOOK 128:6
retentive to the strength of s. — SHAK 590:12
sacramental of the s. — ROB 542:15
save the s. of man — BYRON 167:26
shall I go then from thy S. — BOOK 134:19
slumber did my s. seal — WORD 748:1
s. all compact of fire — SHAK 635:12
s. burning but unbent — BYRON 169:21
s. capable of compassion — FAUL 281:3
s. giveth life — BIBLE 101:16
s. hath rejoiced in God — BIBLE 93:22
s. indeed is willing — BIBLE 92:30
s. is the true self — CIC 204:4
S. of Delight — SHEL 643:2
s. of Elijah doth rest — BIBLE 76:16
S. of God moved upon — BIBLE 69:20
s. of health or goblin — SHAK 573:9
s. of heaviness — BIBLE 84:27
s. of national masochism — AGNEW 5:16
s. of party — WASH 721:25
S. of the Age — HAZL 329:11
S. of the chainless mind — BYRON 173:5
S. of the Lord God is upon — BIBLE 84:26
s. of the Lord shall rest — BIBLE 83:1
S. of the time shall teach — SHAK 594:10
S. on the Lord's day — BIBLE 105:33
s. passed before my face — BIBLE 77:10
s. scorns Detraction's — MARS 449:8
s. shall return unto God — BIBLE 81:1
S. that quickeneth — BIBLE 96:28
S. that strove for truth — SHEL 643:6
spirit to retain the s. — BIBLE 80:16
s. unto Jerusalem — BIBLE 99:3
s. within nourishes — VIRG 713:16
S. with Spirit can meet — TENN 681:15
stablish me with thy free S. — BOOK 128:6
stab my s. broad awake — STEV 669:7
strongest and the fiercest s. — MILT 469:11
take not thy holy S. — BOOK 128:6
there is a s. in the woods — WORD 745:9
There's a great s. gone — SHAK 564:18
things of the S. — BIBLE 99:34
this body did contain a s. — SHAK 582:7
Thy s. walks abroad — SHAK 593:19
troubled s. — BOOK 128:8
unaccustomed s. lifts me — SHAK 624:2
vanity and vexation of s. — BIBLE 80:2
vital strength of his s. — LUCR 431:12
watch the startled s. flee — GRAV 314:20
When the unclean s. is gone — BIBLE 90:36
whether a good s. or a bad — AUBR 33:13
Wild S., which art moving — SHEL 641:14

spirit: (*cont.*):
worship him in s. and in truth — BIBLE 96:17
wounded s. who can bear — BIBLE 79:2
yet a s. still, and bright — WORD 747:19
spirits: By our own s. are we deified — WORD 747:11
choice and master s. — SHAK 591:20
day of s. — VAUG 708:16
drooping s. can raise — COWL 221:17
footfalls of s. passing — SHEL 641:13
For s. when they please — MILT 468:17
He maketh his angels s. — BOOK 132:6
her wanton s. look out — SHAK 628:2
not jump with common s. — SHAK 608:16
other s. there are standing — KEATS 386:6
seven other s. more wicked — BIBLE 90:37
s. from the vasty deep — SHAK 581:3
s. of just men made perfect — BIBLE 104:19
S. of well-shot woodcock — BETJ 67:6
S. overwrought — WORD 747:3
s. rushed together — TENN 685:8
s. which are the house of life — BROW 146:21
thy haunts two kindred s. — KEATS 390:7
Would ruffle up your s. — SHAK 592:17
spiritu: *Et cum s. tuo* — MISS 476:12
spiritual: inward and s. grace — BOOK 123:10
not being a s. people — MANC 444:1
nothing in s. things — DONNE 253:10
some such other s. liquor — BYRON 173:16
s. creatures walk the earth — MILT 471:13
s. grandeur ill-matched — ELIOT 269:11
spiritualist: you are a s. — SZASZ 677:14
spiritualists: convention of s. — STOP 669:16
spiritus: *dum s. hos regit artus* — VIRG 713:6
S. intus alit, totamque — VIRG 713:16
Veni, Sancte S. — LANG 409:8
spiro: *Quod s. et placeo* — HOR 350:12
spit: I have no gun, but I can s. — AUDEN 35:16
s. in my face — SHAK 580:19
s. upon my curious floor — HERB 335:24
s. upon my Jewish gabardine — SHAK 607:22
spite: civic slander and s. — TENN 684:11
delight, or s. — JONS 379:15
what 'scapeth s. — MARV 451:11
spiteful: write when I feel s. — LAWR 412:26
spitting: S. from lips — BROW 153:18
splay-foot: smock by the s. — JONS 378:8
spleen: excite your languid s. — GILB 305:17
splendeat: *late qui s.* — HOR 347:3
splendid: s. and a happy land — GOLD 310:16
S. Isolation — FOST 291:6
S. to eat and sleep — SASS 557:12
splendide: *S. mendax* — HOR 350:6
splendour: Pavilioned in s. — GRANT 314:6
s. among shadows — SHEL 643:6
s. borrows all her rays — POPE 520:23
s. falls on castle walls — TENN 688:1
s. hung aloft the night — KEATS 386:8
s. in the grass — WORD 746:6
Stung by the s. of a sudden — BROW 149:10
splendoured: many-s. thing — THOM 695:10
splintered: s. the door — AUDEN 35:15
split: I s. it so it will stay s. — CHAN 190:7
s. her in twain — TENN 689:4
s. the ears of the groundlings — SHAK 576:5
to make all s. — SHAK 611:5
Spohr: With S. and Beethoven — GILB 305:4
spoil: hath been the s. of me — SHAK 581:17
household divided the s. — BOOK 129:8
s. it by trying to explain — SHER 645:11
when they divide the s. — BIBLE 02:28
spoiled: s. the Egyptians — BIBLE 72:12
s. the women's chats — BROW 151:26
spoilers: into the hands of s. — BIBLE 73:34
spoiling: For s. our relief — GASC 298:18
spoils: divideth his s. — BIBLE 94:19
s. of the enemy — MARCY 446:4
s. the singing of the nightingale — KEATS 390:25
Then s. were fairly sold — MAC 436:12
spoke: he who s., and the world — JOHN 370:2
less he s., the more — PUNCH 531:22
S. in her cheeks — DONNE 251:10

spoken: excellent things are s.   BOOK 130:21
  Lord hath not s.   BIBLE 76:13
  mouth of the Lord hath s.   BIBLE 83:26
  possible to the s. one   CONN 216:13
  Rome has s.   AUG 37:9
  s. unto us by his Son   BIBLE 104:10
  that never have s. yet   CHES 199:7
  When the lips have s.   SHEL 641:6
  word fitly s. is like apples   BIBLE 79:15
sponge: will be married to a s.   SHAK 607:16
spongy: humour of such s. souls   JONS 378:21
  Patrol the halls on s. shoes   MERR 458:12
  s. April at thy hest betrims   SHAK 625:27
spontaneous: S. joy   YEATS 751:18
spoon: ate with a runcible s.   LEAR 414:15
  Why doesn't he use a s.?   LLOY 424:11
spoons: counted our s.   EMER 276:18
  let us count our s.   JOHN 372:9
  world locks up its s.   SHAW 637:16
sport: Detested s.   COWP 223:28
  ended his s. with Tess   HARDY 324:18
  into amateur s.   DOYLE 256:16
  make s. for our neighbours   AUST 39:19
  shall Caesar bleed in s.   SHAK 591:17
  s. nothing to do with fair play   ORW 500:25
  s. of kings   D'AV 231:19
  s. of kings   SOM 655:12
  s. of kings   SURT 672:8
  S. that wrinkled Care derides   MILT 465:6
  They kill us for their s.   SHAK 596:27
  To s. with Amaryllis   MILT 466:4
  To s. would be as tedious   SHAK 579:29
sported: s. on the green   SOUT 657:4
sporting: why this cruel s.   COCK 208:4
sportive: shaped for s. tricks   SHAK 621:15
sports: He mixed in all our simple s.   TENN 684:5
  mountainous s. girl   BET.I 68:3
  play her cruel s.   SPEN 660:17
  While we can, the s. of love   JONS 379:10
sportsman: s. is a man who   LEAC 413:12
  s. wot doesn't kick   SURT 672:9
Sporus: Let S. tremble   POPE 520:2
spot: Charming s.   BECK 57:21
  little s. enclosed by grace   WATTS 723:1
  On a s. that's always barred   GILB 305:5
  Out, damned s.! out   SHAK 604:12
  penned in an inglorious s.   MCKAY 439:1
  some untidy s.   AUDEN 35:7
  sumpshous s. all done up   ASHF 31:9
  there is no s. in thee   BIBLE 81:14
  Tip me the black s.   STEV 667:23
  with a s. I damn him   SHAK 592:23
spotless: s. and pure   TRAH 701:12
spots: or the leopard his s.   BIBLE 85.10
  s. and kills anything it touches   WAUGH 723:10
spotted: s. snakes with double   SHAK 611:20
  wants to have been s.   VIRG 714:18
spouse: my sister, my s.   BIBLE 81:15
  shuts the s. Christ home   HOPK 346:6
  s. occasion to complain   CENT 188:5
spout: hurricanoes, s.   SHAK 595:20
sprang: I s. to the stirrup   BROW 150:10
sprats: kegs of salted s.   BROW 151:26
spray: chafe and toss in the s.   ARN 27:7
  fowlys singis on the s.   DOUG 255:8
  I sniff the s.   THOM 694:4
  pinkly bursts the s.   BETJ 68:1
  rime was on the s.   HARDY 326:3
  thy hand a withered s.   ARN 28:6
spread: Masters, s. yourselves   SHAK 611:3
  not good except it be s.   BACON 44:20
  S. ALARM AND DESPONDENCY   PEN 511:12
  s. my dreams under   YEATS 751:22
spreading: S. ruin   BROW 147:1
sprightly: s. running   DRYD 260:6
sprig-muslin: s. drest   HARDY 326:1
spring: apparelled like the s.   SHAK 618:22
  azure sister of the s.   SHEL 641:14
  Blossom by blossom the s.   SWIN 675:22
  By chilly fingered s.   KEATS 386:19
  can S. be far behind   SHEL 642:1

spring: (cont.):
  clean the pasture s.   FROST 295:7
  commonly called the s.   COWP 224:17
  deep of the Pierian s.   DRAY 258:5
  easing the S.   REED 538:1
  every winter change to s.   TENN 683:19
  Falsehood has a perennial s.   BURKE 157:16
  fells' late s.   BUNT 155:9
  first hour of s. strikes   BOWEN 138:8
  flower of roses in the s.   BIBLE 88:4
  flowers that bloom in the s.   GILB 305:9
  found in the s. to follow   SWIN 676:25
  hounds of s. are on winter's   SWIN 675:21
  In the s. a young man's fancy   TENN 685:7
  It is s., moonless night   THOM 693:16
  lap of the new come s.   SHAK 621:8
  less quick to s. again   ARN 28:29
  naked earth is warm with S.   GREN 318:2
  No s., nor summer beauty   DONNE 250:10
  Now S. restores balmy warmth   CAT 186:5
  over us all in the s. rain   PAST 508:11
  rifle all the breathing s.   COLL 213:10
  seethes in the hands of s.   PAST 508:9
  s. breaks through again   COW 220:12
  s. comes her hour is upon her   GIBB 302:23
  s. from the pages   WHIT 732:10
  s. has kept in its folds   ARAG 24:6
  s. is wound up tight   ANOU 23:3
  s. of endless lies   COWP 223:6
  s. of hope, the winter of   DICK 244:1
  s. of light   COL 209:6
  s. should vanish   FITZ 284:16
  s. shut up, a fountain   BIBLE 81:15
  s. summer autumn winter   CUMM 228:5
  s. up between the feet   EMER 276:20
  such an air of s. about it   PORT 524:22
  suddenly was changed to S.   SHEL 642:22
  Sweet lovers love the s.   SHAK 569:23
  Sweet s., full of sweet   HERB 336:1
  this s. of love resembleth   SHAK 631:4
  To bless the latter s.   SMART 649:15
  To have lived light in the s.   ARN 27:3
  Treasury is the s. of business   BAG 46:14
  untaught harmony of s.   GRAY 316:5
  We have as short a S.   HERR 337:4
  Where are the songs of S.   KEATS 390:19
  with ever-returning s.   WHIT 733:3
  with his vision, S.   SACK 552:16
springe: woodcock to mine own s.   SHAK 579:6
springes: Ay, s. to catch woodcocks   SHAK 573:6
springlike: fester are not s.   ABSE 1:2
springs: Fifty s. are little room   HOUS 352:6
  many s., many bright   VAUG 709:10
  O faintly, gentle s.   JONS 378:14
  old Scotia's grandeur s.   BURNS 161:19
  sendeth the s. into the rivers   BOOK 132:7
  s. o' that countrie   BALL 50:17
  Wastes without s.   CLARE 204:23
  Where s. not fail   HOPK 345:14
springtide: brings back her old s.   JOHN 367:2
springtime: S.'s Harbinger   FLET 287:19
sprinkle: s. me with hyssop   BIBI F 107:28
sprite: fleeting, wav'ring s.   HADR 320:8
sprites: one of s. and goblins   SHAK 631:17
sprouting: S. despondently   ELIOT 270:2
spumantem: Thybrim multo s.   VIRG 713:10
spun: ships are twirled and s.   HODG 340:18
spunk: their s. is that watery   LAWR 412:24
spur: Fame is the s.   MILT 466:4
  I have no s.   SHAK 601:3
  s. me into song   YEATS 753:9
  s. of all great minds   CHAP 191:3
spurious: His s. brat, Tom Jones   RICH 540:15
spurn: But s. the Jews   BROW 145:4
  S. not the nobly born   GILB 304:8
  s. thee like a cur   SHAK 591:11
spurs: to wynne his s.   EDW 267:2
spy: letters for a s.   KIPL 400:9
  sent to s. out the land   BIBLE 73:5
  s. who came in from the cold   LE C 415:11
squabbling: s. nationalities   ROOS 546:12
squad: awkward s. fire over me   BURNS 164:4
squadrons: side of the big s.   BUSS 165:19

squadrons: (cont.):
  wingèd s. of the sky   MILM 462:7
squandering: s. wealth   DRYD 259:9
square: I have not kept the s.   SHAK 565:9
  love upon the honest s.   BEHN 60:11
  slowly grows a glimmering s.   TENN 688:5
  so thoroughly s.   LERN 419:3
  s. cut or pear shape   ROBIN 542:7
  s. deal   ROOS 546:10
  s. on the hypotenuse   GILB 306:10
  s. person has squeezed   SMITH 652:27
  s. root of half a number   LONG 428:6
squares: Tree-muffled s.   LARK 410:1
  walking in all the s.   MILNE 462:16
squash: s. is before 'tis a peascod   SHAK 628:22
  This s., this gentleman   SHAK 631:14
squat: S. like a toad   MILT 471:17
  s. pen rests   HEAN 329:18
  urban, s. and packed with   BROO 143:13
squawking: seven stars go s.   AUDEN 34:3
squeak: s. and gibber   SHAK 571:26
  s. of a boot   FORS 290:22
squeaking: s. Cleopatra boy   SHAK 567:1
  With shrieking and s.   BROW 151:26
squeeze: s. a right-hand foot   CARR 183:23
squeezed: as a lemon is s.   GEDD 300:20
squeezes: she s. your hand   PUSH 532:10
squeezing: s. of a lemon   GOLD 311:23
squinch-owl: say ter der s.   HARR 327:3
squint: banish s. suspicion   MILT 463:28
squints: s. the eye   SHAK 596:13
squire: Bless the s.   DICK 239:16
squires: s. ride slowly towards   CHES 199:8
squirrels: Policeman, like red s.   ORTON 499:15
stab: from hell's heart I s.   MELV 456:20
  No iron can s. the heart   BABEL 41:8
  s. my spirit broad awake   STEV 669:7
stabant: S. orantes   VIRG 713:15
stabat: S. Mater dolorosa   JAC 361.8
stabbed: guy gets s. in the back   GARD 297:15
stability: party of order or s.   MILL 460:17
  s. or enlargement   JOHN 367:21
stable: good horse in the s.   GOLD 311:14
  In a s. born our Brother   DEAR 233:8
  nothing s. in the world   KEATS 391:11
stables: s. are the real centre   SHAW 636:10
stablish: s. me with thy free   BOOK 128:6
stabs: every word s.   SHAK 613:17
stacher: s. through   BURNS 161:15
stad: That s. is in perplexyte   WYNT 750:10
staff: By his cockle hat and s.   SHAK 577:34
  I'll break my s.   SHAK 626:1
  s. of this bruised reed   BIBLE 76:31
  thy rod and thy s. comfort me   BOOK 125:15
  very s. of my age   SHAK 608:6
  your s. in your hand   BIBLE 72:10
stag: lean as a rutting S.   BYRON 173:22
  runnable s.   DAV 231:21
  S. at Bay with the mentality   LEVIN 420:5
  s. in limpid currents   PHIL 514:5
stage: All the world's a s.   SHAK 568:16
  daughter on the s.   COW 220:15
  drown the s. with tears   SHAK 575:9
  kingdom for a s.   SHAK 584:16
  lags the vet'ran on the s.   JOHN 370:19
  On the s. he was natural   GOLD 311:6
  s. where every man must   SHAK 607:4
  to the well-trod s. anon   MILT 465:17
  To this great s. of fools   SHAK 597:11
  well-graced actor leaves the s.   SHAK 621:7
  were played upon a s. now   SHAK 630:24
  wonder of our s.   JONS 380:1
stagecoach: s. from London to Oxford   HAZL 329:12
stages: four s. of man are   LINK 423:6
stagger: s. like a drunken man   BOOK 133:2
staggered: He s.—and, terrible-eyed   BETJ 67:3
stagnant: fen of s. waters   WORD 745:4
  s. grows my too refinèd   CLARE 204:20
stagnation: keeps life from s.   BURN 160:7
St Agnes: S.' Eve   KEATS 386:20
stain: felt a s. like a wound   BURKE 158:14
  Leave not a s. in thine honour   BIBLE 87:32

stain: (*cont.*):
Or s. her honour — POPE 523:23
sky is darkening like a s. — AUDEN 36:13
s. the stiff dishonoured shroud — ELIOT 272:20
with no s. she faded — SHEL 639:15
world's slow s. — SHEL 640:1
stained: hole in a s. glass — CHAN 190:2
s. with their own works — BOOK 132:14
stains: Lose all their guilty s. — COWP 222:21
s. and splendid dyes — KEATS 387:5
S. the white radiance — SHEL 640:4
washed the gory s. — BYRON 172:14
stair: by a winding s. — BACON 43:31
'Tis but a s. betwixt us — MEW 459:8
staircase: S. wit — DID 245:12
stairs: another man's s. — DANTE 230:20
kicked up s. — HAL 322:1
rotten-runged rat-riddled s. — BROW 151:6
s. of his concepts — STEI 663:8
stopped the moving s. — MACN 440:19
stake: I am tied to the s. — SHAK 596:21
some substance and s. — WIND 739:5
s. they have in such — BURKE 157:32
what it is we have at s. — PITT 515:16
stale: How weary, s., flat — SHAK 572:12
Poor I am s. — SHAK 571:10
Tho' s., not ripe — POPE 518:21
staled: S. are my thoughts — DYER 264:14
stalk: Half asleep as they s. — HARDY 325:10
men do not weigh the s. — DAN 229:14
stalking: s. in my chamber — WYATT 749:19
stalking-horse: s. to error — BOL 117:7
uses his folly like a s. — SHAK 569:28
stalks: starvation that s. — FOSD 291:4
stall: Baby in an ox's s. — BETJ 67:4
stalled: than a s. ox — BIBLE 78:35
stallion: water-smooth silver s. — CUMM 228:14
stalls: Tank come down the s. — SASS 557:5
stamp: physics or s. collecting — RUTH 552:6
rank is but the guinea's s. — BURNS 161:28
s. me back to common earth — FITZ 284:14
stamped: S. with the image of the King — TENN 681:28
stamps: and stick in s. — NIC 494:17
stand: British soldier can s. up to — SHAW 636:9
By uniting we s. — DICK 245:8
feet shall s. in thy gates — BOOK 134:5
firm spot on which to s. — ARCH 24:13
Get up, s. up — MARL 446:11
He alone can s. apart — BECK 57:10
Here s. I. I can do no other — LUTH 432:10
If you can't s. the heat — VAUG 708:13
I s. at the door — BIBLE 106:8
Now who will s. on either hand — MAC 436:11
on what he intended *to* s. — DISR 246:13
serve who only s. and wait — MILT 474:24
s. and look at them long — WHIT 732:18
s. aside from life — COMP 214:18
s. at the latter day — BIBLE 77:25
S. by thyself — BIBLE 85:1
s. for nothing fall for — HAM 322:10
s. in the holy place — BIBLE 92:10
s. me now and ever — JOYCE 381:15
S. on the highest pavement — ELIOT 271:19
s. or fall — MILT 471:26
S. out of my sun a little — DIOG 246:11
s. secure amidst a falling — ADD 4:5
S. stable here — AUDEN 35:4
S. still, you ever-moving — MARL 447:1
S. still you watches — MARL 447:7
S. therefore, having — BIBLE 103:1
s. up for bastards — SHAK 595:1
Stand up!—s. up for Jesus — DUFF 263:9
strengthen such as do s. — BOOK 119:20
that men s. upon — SHAK 591:15
time to s. and stare — DAV 232:12
who shall be able to s. — BIBLE 106:17
standard: Forever float that s. — DRAKE 257:13
Then raise the scarlet s. high — CONN 216:8
standards: Her imperial s. fly — AUDEN 35:3
S. are always out of date — BENN 63:8
s. of the peoples — TENN 685:13
standeth: foot s. right — BOOK 125:23

standeth: (*cont.*):
help s. in the Name — BOOK 134:2
standing: mantle of the s. pool — SHAK 596:14
not to be s. here today — JOHN 367:5
s. for some false impossible — ARN 28:23
St Andrews: S. by the Northern sea — LANG 408:14
stands: man who s. most alone — IBSEN 359:3
s. about the woodland ride — HOUS 352:5
S. Scotland where it did — SHAK 604:7
S. the Church clock at — BROO 143:15
Stanley: how S. scorns — BULW 155:3
stanza: blown sky-high in a s. — MAY 455:2
staple: s. of his argument — SHAK 599:2
star: across the reflex of a s. — WORD 744:10
Being a s. made it possible — DAVIS 232:15
bright northern s. — LOV 428:19
bright Occidental S. — BIBLE 69:18
bright particular s. — SHAK 564:1
Bright s., would I were — KEATS 386:9
By a high s. our course is set — MACN 441:6
constant as the northern s. — SHAK 591:12
curb a runaway young s. — BYRON 173:13
disposition to the charge of a s. — SHAK 595:2
each, in his separate s. — KIPL 401:9
earth is but a s. — FLEC 286:10
eve's one s. — KEATS 387:22
Fair as a s., when only one — WORD 747:18
Go, and catch a falling s. — DONNE 252:14
grapples with his evil s. — TENN 683:25
Hitch your wagon to a s. — EMER 277:13
Knew you, and named a s. — BROW 152:2
Knock at a s. — HERR 336:7
My only s. is dead — NERV 492:2
name to every fixèd s. — SHAK 598:7
O eastern s. — SHAK 567:11
one bright s. — COL 211:5
our life's S. — WORD 745:14
prince, out of thy s. — SHAK 574:16
seen his s. in the east — BIBLE 88:8
s. arise in your hearts — BIBLE 105:22
S. captains glow — FLEC 286:7
s. differeth from another — BIBLE 101:11
s. early drooped — WHIT 733:3
S. for every State — WINT 739:11
s. in the firmament twinkled — SHAK 595:2
s. is called Wormwood — BIBLE 106:25
S. of the east, the horizon — HEBER 330:2
s. of unascended heaven — SHEL 642:18
s. were confined into a tomb — VAUG 709:9
Sunset and evening s. — TENN 680:17
tall ship and a s. to steer her — MAS 453:7
there was a s. danced — SHAK 613:20
This s. of England — SHAK 587:4
Twinkle, twinkle, little s. — TAYL 679:14
Westward the s. of empire — BERK 65:13
white s. of Truth — ARN 28:19
worlds life hovers like a s. — BYRON 171:33
you've *got* to come back a s. — SEYM 563:12
zenith like a falling s. — MILT 469:7
Star-Chamber: S. matter of it — SHAK 610:9
star-crossed: pair of s. lovers — SHAK 622:17
stardust: We are s. — MITC 478:1
stare: s. in a million adults — SHAF 563:19
empty house of the s. — YEATS 752:13
indifference or the frozen s. — ELIOT 269:16
no time to stand and s. — DAV 232:12
s. of the deer — WILB 734:2
S., stare in the basin — AUDEN 34:4
stony British s. — TENN 686:15
upon the ground I s. thee s. — CHAU 194:16
We s. dumb — BERRY 66:12
with one bold s. — ELIOT 273:9
stares: S. from every human face — AUDEN 34:15
starfighters: Black S. — BLY 116:7
staring: s. and looking upon me — BOOK 125:13
Truth is s. at the sun — BELL 60:25
Stark: or Molly S.'s a widow — STARK 662:12
stark: s. insensibility — JOHN 371:3
s. mad till you are rid of 'em — VANB 708:3
we are s. naught all — FLET 287:14
starless: s. and bible-black — THOM 693:16
starlight: Into the frosty s. — ARN 28:17

starlight: (*cont.*):
S. and dewdrop are waiting — FOST 291:11
s. lit my lonesomeness — HARDY 326:3
there was nae s. — BALL 50:17
starlit: s. or a moonlit dome — YEATS 750:21
starred: s. night Prince Lucifer — MER 458:6
starry: her s. shade — BYRON 172:18
her s. train — MILT 471:12
Shine upon the s. sky — BLAKE 112:4
Sidney's self, the s. paladin — BROW 153:1
s. dynamo — GINS 306:28
To entertain this s. stranger — CRAS 226:7
very s., the hornèd moon — WORD 742:21
stars: At whose sight all the s. — MILT 470:22
charmèd by the earnest s. — KEATS 387:27
by troops of s. — COL 210:7
calculate the s. — MILT 472:11
champagne and the s. — FITZ 285:1
chaste s. — SHAK 618:5
climb half-way to the s. — CROSS 227:19
crowned with the s. — TRAH 701:0
crown of twelve s. — BIBLE 106:29
cut him out in little s. — SHAK 623:17
day-blind s. — BERRY 66:13
erratik s., herkenyng — CHAU 196:1
Fast as the s. are slow — THOM 694:5
forth to see the s. again — DANTE 230:17
Have you heard it's in the s. — PORT 525:5
he made the s. also — BIBLE 69:23
high it'll strike the s. — HOR 348:24
his right hand seven s. — BIBLE 106:1
imitate the s. celestial — DAV 232:7
its paw with mites of s. — MAY 455:1
journey-work of the s. — WHIT 732:17
lantern thus close up the s. — MILT 463:20
Look at the s. — HOPK 346:5
looking at the s. — WILDE 735:10
mistress of the months and s. — SWIN 675:20
moon and the s. — BOOK 124:20
music that will melt the s. — FLAU 285:16
new-bathed s. emerge — ARN 28:18
not in our s. — SHAK 590:3
opposition of the s. — MARV 450:3
Ours the diamond mines of s. — MAY 455:7
quench the s. — YOUNG 754:14
ready to mount to the s. — DANTE 230:18
same bright, patient s. — KEATS 387:29
seven s. go squawking — AUDEN 34:3
seven s. in the sky — ANON 15:1
shining of the s. — TENN 682:17
silent s. go by — BROO 144:5
s. above us, govern our — SHAK 596:30
s. and sunbeams know — ARN 28:13
s. are dead — AUDEN 36:8
s. . . . are my children — KEATS 392:2
s. are old — TAYL 679:16
s. begin to flicker — PAR 506:2
s. came otherwise — BROW 149:1
s. came out far over — TENN 689:3
s. come down with the rafters — AUDEN 34:7
s. hung with humid nightblue — JOYCE 382:6
s. in her hair were seven — ROSS 547:14
s. in their courses fought — BIBLE 74:3
s. keep not their motion — SHAK 582:5
s. leads through the atom — EDD 266:5
s. move still — MARL 447:1
S. of death stood over us — AKHM 6:12
s. rush out — COL 211:3
S. scribble on our eyes — CRANE 225:18
s. shot madly — SHAK 611:16
Stars, s.! and all eyes else — SHAK 632:15
s. that reigned at my nativity — MARL 447:2
s. threw down their spears — BLAKE 114:15
s. where no human race is — FROST 294:16
s., which are the brain — MER 458:6
s. with deep amaze — MILT 467:4
steeped in s., and milky — RIMB 541:5
strives to touch the s. — SPEN 660:27
sun and the other s. — DANTE 230:21
telleth the number of the s. — BOOK 135:11
tell the s. as they rise — VIRG 713:17
Tempt not the s. — FORD 289:7
that puts the s. to flight — FITZ 283:10

stars: (cont.):
that's the way to the s. — VIRG 714:6
Through struggle to the s. — ANON 22:11
When the morning s. sang — BIBLE 77:35
where all the s. bow down — HUGH 354:6
with how splendid s. — FLEC 286:14
Your chilly s. I can forgo — CORY 220:1
star-scattered: s. on the grass — FITZ 284:17
star-shine: s. at night — STEV 668:24
starship: s. Enterprise — RODD 543:21
star-showers: dissolved in s. — SHEL 643:9
star-spangled: 'Tis the s. banner — KEY 394:15
start: 'Brutus' will s. a spirit — SHAK 590:4
end is where we s. from — ELIOT 271:7
stand afraid and s. at us — BROW 146:11
s. a scene or two — ELIOT 272:5
s. from their spheres — SHAK 573:14
s. of the majestic world — SHAK 590:2
s. together and finish — BEEC 58:16
s. your own religion — HUBB 353:14
Stop it at the s. — OVID 503:3
started: it s. like a guilty thing — SHAK 572:1
s. that morning from Devon — GILB 304:16
to arrive where we s. — ELIOT 271:8
starter: thought he was even a s. — ATTL 32:16
starting: mar all with this s. — SHAK 604:13
startle: come down and s. — AUDEN 34:2
s. it or amaze it — KEATS 391:13
startled: once s. into talk — ROET 544:5
starts: Was everything by s. — DRYD 259:8
starvation: s. that stalks — FOSD 291:4
starve: Let not poor Nelly s. — CHAR 191:17
s. at door — HERB 335:24
s. for want of impudence — DRYD 260:11
whom he helped to s. — POPE 520:1
starved: s. poet — LOCK 425:15
starving: choice of working or s. — JOHN 367:18
s. hysterical naked — GINS 306:28
you have a s. population — DISR 246:16
star-ypointing: s. pyramid — MILT 466:17
state: ambition in rising in the s. — BOSW 137:8
broken with the storms of s. — SHAK 589:4
complicated s. of mind — GILB 305:16
done the s. some service — SHAK 618:20
duty in that s. of life — BOOK 123:9
first duty of a S. — RUSK 550:27
free church in a free s. — CAV 187:15
from thy s. mine never shall — MILT 473:1
glories and my s. depose — SHAK 620:20
glories of our blood and s. — SHIR 646:2
great sun begins his s. — MILT 465:9
Here's a s. of things — GILB 305:1
Here's a world of pomp and s. — BEAU 56:15
I am the S. — LOUI 428:13
initiation into a new s. — ELIOT 268:18
In that s. I came, return — VAUG 709:4
I scorn to change my s. — SHAK 633:10
little from a s. of things — FREUD 293:18
middle age of a s. — BACON 45:5
mine was the middle s. — DEFOE 234:6
more hurt in a s. — BACON 43:9
no harm come to the s. — ANON 22:5
no such thing as the S. — AUDEN 36:1
obscure sequestered s. — BROW 152:24
Oh happy s.! when souls — POPE 519:19
Our s. cannot be severed — MILT 473:2
Predicts the ruin of the S. — BLAKE 111:2
put the s. to rights for us — ENN 278:2
reinforcement of the S. — CAMUS 177:18
sail on, O Ship of S. — LONG 426:11
Scoffing his s. and grinning — SHAK 620:8
shun that wretched s. — CHUD 200:13
sovereign or s. — BACON 43:27
s. does man have a rational — HEGEL 330:8
S. for every Star — WINT 739:11
S. in wonted manner keep — JONS 378:16
S. is an instrument — STAL 662:4
S. is a relation of men — WEBER 724:21
S. is not 'abolished' — ENG 277:22
s. is or can be master — BEV 69:11
s. of that man is worse — BIBLE 90:37
s. where your small talents — CRAB 224:21
S. which dwarfs its men — MILL 460:20

state: (cont.):
s. without the means — BURKE 158:7
s. with the prettiest name — BISH 109:24
Then all were for the s. — MAC 436:12
They mock the air with idle s. — GRAY 315:6
to what a s. dost Thou bring — TER 690:15
While the S. exists — LENIN 417:7
whole machinery of the S. — BROU 144:7
worl's in a s. o' chassis — O'CAS 497:16
stateliest: s. measure — TENN 689:15
stately: But she is tall and s. — TENN 686:14
S. as a galleon, I sail — GREN 318:1
S. Homes of England — COW 221:2
s. homes of England — HEM 331:11
s. homes of England — WOOLF 742:4
s. park and the fence — MAUG 454:6
S., plump Buck Mulligan — JOYCE 381:17
s. tents of war — MARL 447:19
statement: black s. of pistons — SPEN 658:26
s. is like a cheque drawn — POUND 527:14
unmoved that s. hears — GILB 306:13
states: goodly s. and kingdoms — KEATS 390:2
indestructible S. — CHASE 192:3
In s. unborn, and accents — SHAK 591:17
like to greater s. — SUCK 671:10
Nation of many sovereign S. — PAGE 504:4
saved the Union of these S. — WHIT 733:2
slavery are mental s. — GAND 297:9
S., like men — LAND 408:11
s. with her imperious sway — DAV 232:7
statesman: constitutional s. — BAG 46:9
fiddler, s., and buffoon — DRYD 259:8
gift to set a s. right — YEATS 752:16
s. is a politician — POMP 518:13
s. is a politician — TRUM 704:18
s. is that he be dull — ACH 1:7
s. rests not in knowing — METT 459:5
s. who is enamoured — BIER 109:8
S., yet friend to Truth — POPE 520:32
Too nice for a s. — GOLD 311:4
when you did agree, he was a s. — LLOY 424:10
statesmen: faults of s. — WALP 720:3
government of s. or of clerks — DISR 248:2
like great S., we encourage — GAY 299:25
station: At the cross her s. — JAC 361:8
By Grand Central S. I sat down — SMART 650:6
Hurries down the concrete s. — BETJ 68:2
post of honour is a private s. — ADD 3:22
she leaves the s. — SPEN 658:26
walls of that antique s. — BEER 59:14
stations: know our proper s. — DICK 239:16
statistical: s. improbability — DAWK 232:19
statistics: damned lies and s. — DISR 249:13
Proved by s. that some cause — AUDEN 36:2
We are just s. — HOR 348:3
statua: base of Pompey's s. — SHAK 592:14
statuary: s. which no careful father — ANON 13:10
statue: Beauty she was s. cold — FLEC 286:6
Most like a monumental s. — BROW 147:14
statues: disfigured the public s. — AUDEN 34:13
Ep's s. are junk — ANON 14:14
s. will be standing — LARK 410:1
stature: add one cubit unto his s. — BIBLE 89:10
increased in wisdom and s. — BIBLE 93:31
Malice is of a low s. — HAL 321:15
s. of the fulness of Christ — BIBLE 102:17
status: from S. to Contract — MAINE 442:11
's. group' is a group — WEBER 724:20
s. groups are the specific — WEBER 725:3
s. ought not to depend — TEMP 680:4
status quo: restored the s. — SQUI 661:18
statutes: s. of the Lord — BOOK 125:5
staves: comest to me with s. — BIBLE 75:4
stay: behind my tremulous s. — HARDY 324:22
care to s. than will to go — SHAK 623:24
Must you go? Can't you s.? — VAUG 708:12
our love is here to s. — GERS 301:15
S. a little — BACON 43:13
S. for me — SHAK 566:9
S. for me there — KING 396:1
S. out all night — CHUR 201:5
s. until the hasting day — HERR 337:4

stay: (cont.):
want things to s. as they are — LAMP 407:18
will not s. in place — ELIOT 270:17
without thee here to s. — MILT 473:13
stay-at-home: Sweet S. — DAV 232:14
stayed: S. in mid passage — SWIN 676:3
staying: Tell the people I'm s. — PEDR 510:16
stays: nothing s. — HER 333:10
prays together s. together — SCAL 557:16
stead: soul were in my soul's s. — BIBLE 77:23
steadfast: I were s. as thou — KEATS 386:9
steady: S., boys, steady — GARR 298:4
more s. than an ebbing sea — FORD 289:15
steaks: smell of s. in passageways — ELIOT 272:13
steal: And as silently s. away — LONG 426:14
Even s. us from ourselves — DRYD 260:2
Give me not poverty lest I s. — DEFOE 234:5
if you s. from many — MIZN 478:11
most cunningly did s. away — HERB 335:7
s. a few hours from — MOORE 483:13
s. away their brains — SHAK 616:6
s. away your hearts — SHAK 592:15
s. bread — FRAN 292:7
S. from the world — POPE 523:12
s. more than a hundred men — PUZO 533:8
s. my Basil-pot — KEATS 388:4
s. one poor farthing — NEWM 493:6
s. out of your company — SHAK 614:3
s. the very teeth — ARAB 24:4
thieves break through and s. — BIBLE 89:6
Thou shalt not s. — BIBLE 72:16
Thou shalt not s. — CLOU 207:19
stealing: not hanged for s. — HAL 321:18
picking and s. — BOOK 123:8
s. dey gits you in jail — O'NEI 498:17
s. ducks — ARAB 24:5
S. money is wrong — AYER 40:13
steals: s. my purse steals trash — SHAK 616:12
s. something from the thief — SHAK 615:5
stealth: do a good action by s. — LAMB 407:4
Do good by s. — POPE 523:7
lusty s. of nature — SHAK 594:26
steam: Shovelling white s. — AUDEN 36:9
steam-engine: s. always back to the tea-kettle — DISR 246:21
s. in trousers — SMITH 653:14
steamer: s. breaking from the bay — AUDEN 35:2
in a s. from Harwich — GILB 304:15
This little s. — PRIE 529:1
steamers: Daily the s. sidle up — AUDEN 34:6
Great s., white and gold — KIPL 401:17
steaming: s. phrases — SCH 558:12
steamy: Throws up a s. column — COWP 223:31
steed: beneath me as a s. — BYRON 168:12
his s. was the best — SCOTT 560:3
I set her on my pacing s. — KEATS 388:11
mounted on her milk-white s. — BALL 50:15
Our s. the leg — SHAK 70:3
s. flying fearless — LONG 427:20
Steed threatens s. — SHAK 585:14
steeds: mounting barbèd s. — SHAK 621:15
steel: All shod with s. — WORD 744:9
clad in complete s. — MILT 463:29
corse again in complete s. — SHAK 573:9
Give them the cold s., boys — ARM 26:4
In foemen worthy of their s. — SCOTT 559:11
long divorce of s. — SHAK 588:11
S. chambers, late the pyres — HARDY 325:3
S.-true and blade-straight — STEV 669:1
tipped with a line of s. — RUSS 552:5
with his brandished s. — SHAK 599:15
with more than complete s. — ANON 15:2
wounded surgeon plies the s. — ELIOT 270:22
steep: But the s. and rugged pathway — WILL 737:14
hastens to the monstrous s. — KEATS 390:10
s. my senses in forgetfulness — SHAK 583:11
steeple: lone religious s. — CAMP 176:7
steeples: In s. far and near — HOUS 352:10
s. of Fermanagh and Tyrone — CHUR 202:2
you have drenched our s. — SHAK 595:20
steer: they s. their courses — BUTL 166:9
ugly 'ead it's time to s. — ALL 9:20

Stein: Gertrude S.'s prose-song · LEWIS 421:8
I don't like the family S. · ANON 14:14
Stella: S., think not · SIDN 647:3
stem: rod out of the s. of Jesse · BIBLE 83:1
s. of the contained flower · ROET 544:7
s. the torrent of a woman's · ANON 19:18
step: one s. enough for me · NEWM 493:14
s. is short from the Sublime · GRAH 313:10
That's one small s. for man · ARMS 26:12
To s. aside is human · BURNS 161:1
stepmother: s. to memory · JOHN 366:15
step-parents: especially s. · POW 528:5
stepped: S. in so far · SHAK 603:14
stepping: s. westward · WORD 748:5
s. where his comrade stood · SCOTT 560:10
stepping-stones: rise on s. · TENN 682:30
steps: Hear not my s. · SHAK 601:13
her s. take hold on hell · BIBLE 78:12
Knowledge advances by s. · MAC 435:24
s. that led assuredly to death · GUIB 319:12
Who countest the s. of the Sun · BLAKE 114:5
with wandering s. and slow · MILT 473:14
sterile: o. promontory · SHAK 574:28
sterner: made of s. stuff · SHAK 592:7
steward: backward s. · POPE 520:17
commended the unjust s. · BIBLE 95:6
stewards: s. of their excellence · SHAK 634:15
S. of the mysteries of God · BIBLE 100:18
stewed: Get s. · LARK 410:5
S. in corruption · SHAK 577:15
St George: England and S. · SHAK 585:10
S. that swinged the dragon · SHAK 593:28
stick: carry a big s. · ROOS 546:9
going to make it s. · MACG 438:3
he fell like the s. · PAINE 504:13
I am a kind of burr; I shall s. · SHAK 606:23
notch it on my s. · THOR 696:29
S. close to your desks · GILB 306:2
s. inside a swill bucket · ORW 501:4
s. more close than a brother · KIPL 400:16
s. that he seizes to strike · TORR 701:5
tattered coat upon a s. · YEATS 752:21
Work like a s. · SOLZ 655:9
sticketh: friend that s. closer · BIBLE 79:3
sticks: S. nix hick pix · ANON 18:5
stiff: woman can be proud and s. · YEATS 751:8
stiffnecked: s. people · BIBLE 72:21
stiffness: much s. in refusing · BOOK 118:3
stigma: Any s. will serve to beat · GUED 319:7
still: And do them s. · DONNE 251:7
And s. they gazed · GOLD 310:14
Because they liked me 's.' · DICK 245:1
be s. · BOOK 124:12
Be s. then · BOOK 127:17
How s. we see thee lie · BROO 144:4
If you s. have to ask · ARMS 26:11
mighty heart is lying s. · WORD 743:10
ship was s. as she could be · SOUT 657:9
sound of a voice that is s. · TENN 680:10
s. and cool in thy own mind · FOX 292:4
S. falls the Rain · SITW 648:13
S. glides the Stream · WORD 747:14
s. it is not we · CHES 199:8
S. point of the turning world · ELIOT 270:16
s., sad music of humanity · WORD 745:1
s. small voice · BIBLE 76:7
Thou art tired; best be s. · ARN 27:11
thou mightest s. the enemy · BOOK 124:20
waves thereof are s. · BOOK 133:2
What gars ye rin sae s. · ANON 17:17
still-born: S. Silence! · FLEC 286:17
stilleth: s. the raging of the sea · BOOK 129:1
stillness: all the air a solemn s. · GRAY 315:10
And do a wilful s. entertain · SHAK 607:6
As modest s. and humility · SHAK 585:7
s. first invades the ear · DRYD 260:4
s. in the midst of chaos · BELL 62:8
s. of the central sea · TENN 684:15
that s. ultimately best · CRANE 225:26
still-vexed: s. Bermoothes · SHAK 625:4
stilly: Oft, in the s. night · MOORE 483:17
s. couches she · HARDY 325:3

Stilton Cheese: no end of S. · LEAR 414:5
stilts: nonsense upon s. · BENT 64:3
stimulate: s. the phagocytes · SHAW 636:10
stimulation: unnatural s. · MILL 460:25
sting: It is a prick, it is a s. · PEELE 511:3
s. like a bee · ALI 9:6
Thy s. is not so sharp · SHAK 568:17
where is thy s. · BIBLE 101:15
sting-a-ling-a-ling: where is thy s. · ANON 17:1
stingeth: s. like an adder · BIBLE 79:13
stings: armèd in their s. · SHAK 584:22
s. and motions of the sense · SHAK 605:10
s. in their tails · BIBLE 106:27
s. you for your pains · HILL 338:8
Who for it can endure the s. · COWL 221:16
stinker: Outrageous s. · KIPL 402:10
stinks: child of dirt that s. · POPE 520:3
stipendi: né onori né s. · GAR 298:1
stir: Above the smoke and s. · MILT 463:12
How should we s. ourselves · ANON 20:2
No s. in the air · SOUT 657:0
No s. of air was there · KEATS 387:23
s. it and stump it · GILB 306:16
s. men's blood · SHAK 592:16
s. up undisputed matters · SALL 554:12
S. up, we beseech thee · BOOK 121:11
s. without great argument · SHAK 577:33
stirbt: er s. ab · ENG 277:22
stirred: forest something s. · SIMP 648:2
Shaken and not s. · FLEM 286:18
stirring: Mrs Bennet was s. the fire · AUST 39:12
stirrup: I sprang to the s. · BROW 150:10
one foot already in the s. · CERV 188:18
s. and the ground · CAMD 176:3
stirrup-pump: simple s. · REED 537:17
stirs: lost pulse of feeling s. · ARN 26:17
Will that s. and urges · HARDY 325:4
stitch: S.! stitch! stitch · HOOD 344:7
stitching: s. and unstitching · YEATS 750:16
stithy: As Vulcan's s. · SHAK 576:8
St James: ladies of S.'s · DOBS 249:22
St Martin: Expect S.'s summer · SHAK 587:6
St Mary Woolnoth: S. kept · ELIOT 273:1
stock: s. that scents the garden · THOM 696:1
stocking: glimpse of s. · PORT 524:18
your silk s.'s hanging down · SELL 562:18
stockings: thy yellow s. · SHAK 630:5
his s. fouled · SHAK 574:9
s. were hung by the chimney · MOORE 482:5
stocks: feet they hurt in the s. · BOOK 132:11
stoic: doctors of the S. fur · MILT 464:6
stoical: s. scheme of supplying · SWIFT 674:17
stoicism: Romans call it s. · ADD 3:17
stole: S. many a man's soul · JAGG 361:13
wonder where you s. 'em · SWIFT 675:15
stolen: had I s. the whole · STEV 669:6
receiver of s. goods · JOHN 375:16
Stolen, s., be your apples · HUNT 356:10
S. sweets are best · CIBB 203:23
S. the scraps · SHAK 594:4
S. waters are sweet · BIBLE 78:19
They have s. his wits away · DE L 235:21
stoles: nice white s. · BARH 52:13
stolid: S. and stunned · MARK 446:7
stomach: army marches on its s. · NAP 490:3
burst s. like a cave · DOUG 255:13
hath no s. to this fight · SHAK 586:11
heart and s. of a king · ELIZ 274:3
I have no s. for such meat · DOBS 249:21
My s. is not good · ANON 14:13
Of an unbounded s. · SHAK 589:7
s., gentlemen · HUNT 357:1
s. of the country · GLAD 307:5
s. sets us to work · ELIOT 269:8
stomacher: bird, with the red s. · DONNE 250:18
stomachs: march on their s. · SELL 562:24
stone: are themselves as s. · SHAK 634:14
At his heels a s. · SHAK 577:35
brass, nor s., nor earth · SHAK 634:3
Can make a s. of the heart · YEATS 751:14

stone: (cont.):
conscious s. to beauty · EMER 276:11
first s. which he flings · TORR 701:5
Fling but a s. · GREEN 316:18
Florence blossoming in s. · LONG 426:21
give them the s. · MONT 480:11
hurt not thy foot against a s. · BOOK 131:4
jasper and a sardine s. · BIBLE 106:9
lay s. on stone · ARN 27:15
let him first cast a s. · BIBLE 96:30
lies under this little s. · FANS 280:1
make me a s. · MACN 441:1
mighty angel took up a s. · BIBLE 107:11
nickname is the heaviest s. · HAZL 329:4
not a s. tell where · POPE 523:12
Raise the s. · ANON 17:16
rolls back the restless s. · DUCK 263:7
Saturn, quiet as a s. · KEATS 387:22
seeth the s. taken away · BIBLE 97:30
standing like a s. wall · BEE 58:15
s. of stumbling · BIBLE 82:25
s. set in the silver sea · SHAK 619:18
s. that puts the stars · FITZ 283:10
s. the twenty-first · BROW 149:2
S. walls do not a prison make · LOV 429:4
s. which the builders refused · BOOK 133:16
s. world thins to a dew · HUGH 354:8
take the s. from stone · ELIOT 272:1
Turn but a s. · THOM 695:10
Virtue is like a rich s. · BACON 42:25
water hollows out a s. · OVID 502:19
Wept over her, carved in s. · TENN 686:11
we raised not a s. · WOLFE 740:26
will he give him a s. · BIBLE 89:21
with a shower of s. fruit · LANC 407:19
written of me on my s. · FROST 295:2
Stone Age: bomb them back into the S. · LEMAY 417:3
stoned: once was I s. · BIBLE 102:1
stones: croys of latoun ful of s. · CHAU 193:8
five smooth s. · BIBLE 75:3
man that spares these s. · SHAK 635:15
no s. in heaven · SHAK 618:14
Sermons in s. · SHAK 567:25
s. and clouts make martyrs · BROW 145:16
s. kissed by the English dead · OWEN 503:15
s. of Rome to rise · SHAK 592:17
s. prate of my whereabout · SHAK 601:18
S. towards the earth descend · BYROM 167:16
s. would immediately cry · BIBLE 95:17
That scuttled under s. · ROET 544:6
you are not s., but men · SHAK 592:12
stonest: s. them · BIBLE 92:7
stony: more s. than a shore · WILL 737:10
Some fell upon s. places · BIBLE 91:1
s. limits cannot hold love · SHAK 622:31
s. path the senses pave · MERR 458:13
stood: should of s. in bed · JAC 361:7
s. against the world · SHAK 592:14
s. four-square · TENN 687:16
s. them on their heads · BARR 54:5
s. upon Achilles' tomb · BYRON 171:10
stool: three-foot s. mistaketh · SHAK 611:12
stools: necessity invented s. · COWP 223:16
stoop: Do I s.? · BROW 148:8
stooping: S. through a fleecy · MILT 464:20
stop: come to the end: then s. · CARR 182:15
could not s. for Death · DICK 244:11
did he s. and speak to you · BROW 151:8
easy and so plain a s. · SHAK 582:12
s. a hole to keep the wind · SHAK 578:26
S. and consider · KEATS 390:10
s. because you are afraid · NANS 489:8
s. his mouth with a kiss · SHAK 613:19
S. it at the start · OVID 503:3
S. the world, I want to get off · NEWL 492:10
s. to buoy fools · VAUG 708:16
s. to think they died instead · CUMM 228:6
when the kissing had to s. · BROW 153:10
stops: s. of various quills · MILT 466:15
would seem to know my s. · SHAK 576:22
storage: thought in cold s. · SAM 554:17
store: seen thee oft amid thy s. · KEATS 390:18

store: (cont.):
spread her wholesome s. — GOLD 310:6
storehouse: s. for the glory — BACON 41:17
storey: crack in your upper s. — SMOL 654:3
storied: S. of old — MILT 464:2
stories: sad s. of the death — SHAK 620:8
seaman tells s. — PROP 529:22
S. to rede ar delitabill — BARB 52:7
With dismal s. — BUNY 156:14
storm: And rides upon the s. — COWP 222:17
directs the s. — ADD 3:14
For every s. that blows — SHAK 626:16
locks of the approaching s. — SHEL 641:15
lovers fled away into the s. — KEATS 387:12
maketh the s. to cease — BOOK 133:2
No voice divine the s. allayed — COWP 221:25
pelting of this pitiless s. — SHAK 596:6
sleek-barrelled swell before s. — KIPL 401:1
S. and stress — KAUF 386:1
s. nor in ie strife — BYRON 172:24
Till the s. of life is past — WESL 728:6
to me is but a ceaseless s. — SHAK 619:4
wind and s., fulfilling — BOOK 135:14
storm-clouds: S. whirl — PUSH 532:11
When s. brood — LEAR 413:20
storms: all thy waves and s. — BOOK 127:4
He sought the s. — DRYD 259:1
s. of passion — BODE 116:11
sudden s. are short — SHAK 619:17
Where no s. come — HOPK 345:14
storm-troubled: s. sphere — BRON 142:12
stormy: in bloody s. stours — DRAY 258:3
O s. peple — CHAU 193:9
S. weather — KOEH 403:17
to 'scape s. days, I choose — DONNE 251:5
story: earns a place i' the s. — SHAK 565:19
Every picture tells a s. — ANON 13:5
he means to write one s. — BARR 54:3
it's about you, that s. — HOR 350:22
It's our *own* s. *exactly* — THUR 697:19
Not that the s. need be long — THOR 696:25
novel tells a s. — FORS 290:2
plot for a short s. — CHEK 197:1
read Richardson for the s. — JOHN 373:19
short in the s. itself — BIBLE 88:6
Shuts up the s. of our days — RAL 536:3
s. always old and always new — BROW 152:16
s. and a byword — WINT 739:10
s. chronicled for one of the — MAL 443:9
S. is the spoiled child of art — JAMES 362:10
s. of what he hath done — BAKER 47:21
To tell my s. — SHAK 579:11
truths lacking which any s. — FAUL 281:2
were an epitaph to be my s. — FROSI 295:2
would some pretty s. tell — TAYL 679:13
stout: Collapse of S. Party — ANON 12:23
stove: ice on a hot s. — FROST 295:16
St Pancras: Towers of S. Station — BEEC 59:2
St Paul's: ruins of S. — WALP 719:16
Say I am designing S. — BENT 64:17
sketch the ruins of S. — MAC 435:12
Strabismus: Dr S. — MORT 486:15
Strachan: Sir Richard S. — ANON 13:21
Strafford S., who was hurried — CLEV 206:13
straight: crooked shall be made s. — BIBLE 83:26
make his paths s. — BIBLE 88:13
make s. in the desert — BIBLE 83:26
no s. thing can ever be made — KANT 385:11
nothing ever ran quite s. — GALS 297:5
stiff and unflexible as s. — LOCKE 425:1
s. one day at the Sorbonne — STEV 666:3
street which is called S. — BIBLE 98:17
which is accurately s. — WHEW 730:14
straightway: goeth after her s. — BIBLE 78:17
strain: no, but s. — HOPK 346:9
s. of man's bred out — SHAK 626:6
That s. again — SHAK 628:9
To something like prophetic s. — MILT 465:2
which s. at a gnat — BIBLE 92:5
Words s. — ELIOT 270:17
strains: s. of unpremeditated art — SHEL 643:13
s. that might create — MILT 464:4
Such s. as would have won — MILT 465:18

strait: S. is the gate — BIBLE 89:22
straits: echoing s. between — ARN 29:3
strand: Come sailing to the s. — BALL 50:12
I walk down the S. — HARG 326:8
I walked along the S. — JOHN 376:26
That knits me to thy rugged s. — SCOTT 559:17
We left fair Scotland's s. — BURNS 162:9
where's the Maypole in the S. — BRAM 139:16
wrote her name upon the s. — SPEN 659:11
strands: these last s. of man — HOPK 345:7
strange: everything that looks s. — PEPYS 512:9
foul, s., and unnatural — SHAK 573:16
from among the s. people — BOOK 133:8
hand of s. children — BOOK 135:4
Into something rich and s. — SHAK 625:10
Lord's song: in a s. land — BOOK 134:17
millions of s. shadows — SHAK 633:16
new, and s. at first — TRAH 701:11
now wonder nyce and s. — CHAU 195:12
owe this s. intelligence — SHAK 600:7
pair of very s. beasts — SHAK 569:24
passing s. and wonderful — SHEL 640:8
real thing s. — EMPS 277:19
s. and sinister — JAMES 363:6
s. and terrible events — SHAK 566:11
s. as in dark summer dawns — TENN 688:5
s., astonished-looking — HUNT 356:6
s. faces, other minds — TENN 682:22
'S. friend,' I said — OWEN 503:19
s. interlude — O'NEI 499:2
strangely sweet, it was not s. — BRID 141:5
stranger in a s. land — BIBLE 71:36
s. that one so young — BYRON 170:9
s. the change from major — PORT 524:22
such s. and wonderful things — TRAH 701:14
too stubborn and too s. — SHAK 589:24
Unable to fear what is too s. — WILB 734:1
very s. and well-bred — CONG 216:1
strangeness: some s. in the proportion — BACON 42:27
stranger: entertain Him always like a s. — ANON 20:3
From the wiles of the s. — NASH 490:11
I, a s. and afraid — HOUS 351:20
I was a little s. — TRAH 701:11
I was a s., and ye took me in — BIBLE 92:20
Look, s., at this island now — AUDEN 35:4
never love a s. — BENS 64:1
obtrusive gratitude of a s. — TOCQ 699:6
On earth I am a s. grown — BURNS 162:16
s.! 'Eave 'arf a brick at 'im — PUNCH 531:4
s. here in Gloucestershire — SHAK 619:19
s. in a strange land — BIBLE 71:36
S. than fiction — BYRON 171:29
s. that is within thy gates — BIBLE 72:16
s. to my heart and me — SHAK 594:19
s. to one of your parents — AUST 39:13
S., unless with bedroom eyes — AUDEN 35:16
surety for a s. shall smart — BIBLE 78:22
would turn to a mighty s. — BRON 142:18
strangers: Athenians and s. — BIBLE 98:30
forgetful to entertain s. — BIBLE 104:20
gracious and courteous to s. — BACON 43:26
I do desire we may be better s. — SHAK 569:7
kindness of s. — WILL 737:9
Lord careth for the s. — BOOK 135:10
s. of Rome, Jews — BIBLE 98:7
s. on a rainy day — SMART 649:15
they were s. and pilgrims — BIBLE 104:15
we are s. before thee — BIBLE 76:32
strangled: And s. her — BROW 152:3
s. with the guts of priests — MESL 458:15
strangling: one s. golden hair — ROSS 547:22
Than s. in a string — HOUS 352:8
stratagems: Fine nets and s. — HERB 335:19
Stratford atte Bowe: scole of S. — CHAU 192:14
strathspeys: hornpipes and s. — BURNS 161:22
Strauss: symphony by S. — PORT 524:20
straw: He gets the s. — OXF 504:1
Of the s. for a bedding — BELL 62:1
Oft stumbles at a s. — SPEN 660:27
pigmy's s. doth pierce — SHAK 597:8

straw: (cont.):
shall eat s. like the ox — BIBLE 83:3
s. under my knee — DONNE 253:10
Take a s. and throw it up — SELD 562:6
Things are but as s. dogs — LAO-T 409:10
strawberries: S. swimming in the cream — PEELE 511:4
strawberry: Like s. wives — ELIZ 274:6
S. fields forever — LENN 418:1
Strawberry Hill: [S.] is — WALP 719:3
strawed: where thou hast not s. — BIBLE 92:17
straws: For oaths are s. — SHAK 585:6
stray: what wonder if they s. — COWP 223:2
with me you'd fondly s. — GAY 299:17
strayed: s. from thy ways — BOOK 118:7
streaks: some s. of day — SHAK 603:6
stream: By the s. and o'er the mead — BLAKE 113:21
cool s. thy fingers wet — ARN 28:5
long-legged fly upon the s. — YEATS 752:12
make thy s. my great example — DENH 236:17
meadow, or a purling s. — ADD 4:3
old mill by the s. — ARMS 26:5
pure ethereal s. — MILT 470:15
salt weed sways in the s. — ARN 27:8
Still glides the S. — WORD 747:14
s. came tumbling from — BYRON 172:14
s. issued and came forth — BIBLE 86:1
s. that leaps alive — SMART 649:7
s. that must for ever hide — SHAK 588:19
they have their s. and pond — BROO 143:6
Time, like an ever-rolling s. — WATTS 723:7
streamers: s. waving — GAY 300:15
streams: Companionable s. — YEATS 753:20
crystàlline s. — SHEL 641:16
Gilding pale s. with heavenly — SHAK 633:12
horses when crossing s. — LINC 422:7
more pellucid s. — WORD 744:18
pants the hart for cooling s. — TATE 678:16
s. in the desert — BIBLE 83:21
s. of dotage flow — JOHN 370:20
s. run dimpling all the way — POPE 520:4
s. to quench a country's thirst — POPE 520:17
That shrunk thy s. — MILT 466:10
street: breaks at the end of the s. — MACN 440:17
done by jostling in the s. — BLAKE 113:10
Here in the long unlovely s. — TENN 683:5
Life is really a One Way S. — CHR 200:6
On the bald s. — TENN 683:6
place for a s. fighting man — JAGG 361:12
Still going past me in the s. — STEV 668:13
s. and frighten the horses — CAMP 176:5
s. of the city was pure gold — BIBLE 107:20
s. which is called Straight — BIBLE 98:17
talking at s. corners — VANZ 708:11
where the long s. roars — TENN 684:15
worth two in the s. — WEST 729:6
street-bred: s. people — KIPL 399:2
streets: children died in the s. — AUDEN 34:10
Down these mean s. — CHAN 190:5
negro s. at dawn — GINS 306:28
s. and lanes of the city — BIBLE 94:31
s. are paved with gold — COLM 214:1
S. FLOODED. PLEASE ADVISE — BENC 62:13
s. of a hundred cities — HOOV 344:19
s. of our city — WILB 734:1
s. that no longer exist — FENT 281:7
ten thousands in our s. — BOOK 135:5
took you off the s. — BEHAN 60:4
when night darkens the s. — MILT 468:21
strength: any man by his great s. — BOOK 126:12
But for s. that we may ever — WILL 737:14
confidence shall be your s. — BIBLE 83:14
Even if s. fail — PROP 530:1
full of the s. of five — BETJ 68:3
girded himself with s. — BOOK 131:6
give s. unto his people — BOOK 126:4
God is our hope and s. — BOOK 127:15
go from s. to strength — BOOK 130:17
His s. the more is — BUNY 156:14
king's name is a tower of s. — SHAK 622:9
length that tower of s. — TENN 687:16
Let us roll all our s. — MARV 451:4

strength: (cont.):
Lord shall renew their s. — BIBLE 84:1
My s. and my hope is perished — BIBLE 85:17
On which all s. depends — SMART 649:17
pleasure in the s. of an horse — BOOK 135:12
rejoiceth in his s. — BIBLE 77:38
retentive to the s. of spirit — SHAK 590:12
shewed s. with his arm — BIBLE 93:23
S. in what remains behind — WORD 746:6
strength is as the s. of ten — TENN 689:7
s. is made perfect in weakness — BIBLE 102:3
s. of his spirit won through — LUCR 431:12
s. of my head — BOOK 128:18
s.'s abundance weakens — SHAK 633:7
S. should be lord of imbecility — SHAK 627:8
S. through joy — LEY 421:10
S. without hands to smite — SWIN 676:1
sucklings hast thou ordained s. — BOOK 124:20
Sun in his s. — BIBLE 69:19
that s. which in old days — TENN 690:4
their s. then but labour — BOOK 131:1
Though the s. is lacking — OVID 502:10
To have a giant's s. — SHAK 605:17
triumphant conviction of s. — CONR 217:17
which is her present s. — TROL 703:10
strengthen: bread to s. man's — BOOK 132:8
s. such as do stand — BOOK 119:20
S. ye the weak hands — BIBLE 83:20
strengthened: S., and fed — BRON 142:17
s. with might by his Spirit — BIBLE 102:13
strengtheneth: Christ which s. — BIBLE 103:14
strengthens: s. our nerves — BURKE 158:24
strenua: S. nos exercet inertia — HOR 348:9
strenuous: doctrine of the s. life — ROOS 546:8
round of s. idleness — WORD 747:3
strepitumque: opes s. Romae — HOR 350:8
stress: Storm and s. — KAUF 386:1
stretch: S. him out longer — SHAK 598:4
stretched: by a s. out arm — BIBLE 73:14
his hand is s. out — BIBLE 82:18
s. metre of an antique — SHAK 633:5
There was things which he s. — TWAIN 706:1
strewed: s. thy grave — SHAK 578:28
strewn: S. with its dank yellow — ARN 28:1
stricken: I was a s. deer — COWP 223:23
let the s. deer go weep — SHAK 576:20
old and well s. in age — BIBLE 71:1
stride: At one s. comes the dark — COL 211:3
strides: Tarquin's ravishing s. — SHAK 601:13
strife: curse to party-s. — WORD 743:12
hast borne me a man of s. — BIBLE 85:11
In place of s. — CAST 184:15
Is it s.? No — DICK 239:7
Let there be no s. — BIBLE 70:34
maintain the s. — WHITE 731:4
none was worth my s. — LAND 408:2
Of the stern s. — SCOTT 560:11
pleasure, void of s. — CHAL 189:1
promise heavens free from s. — CORY 220:1
s. is o'er, the battle done — POTT 525:9
thraldom, or a double s. — BACON 46:1
together for the sake of s. — CHUR 201:15
Wherein the graver had a s. — JONS 379:18
with thy blessedness at s. — WORD 746:1
strike: S. flat the thick — SHAK 595:20
S. him so that he can feel — CAL 175:6
s. his father's crown — SHAK 584:23
s. it in anger — SHAW 637:28
s. it out — JOHN 373:23
therefore thou s. not awry — MORE 484:15
They s. mine eyes — JONS 378:18
when in doubt, s. it out — TWAIN 706:22
yet afraid to s. — POPE 519:32
striker: no s., not greedy — BIBLE 103:26
strikes: as s. the player goes — FITZ 284:8
Empire s. back — LUCAS 431:9
puny subject s. — SHAK 620:5
string: end of a golden s. — BLAKE 112:7
s. that ties them together — MONT 481:11
Than strangling in a s. — HOUS 352:8
untune that s. — SHAK 627:8
stringent: s. execution — GRANT 314:10

stringing: s. blethers — BURNS 164:1
strings: s. in the human heart — DICK 238:20
whisper music on those s. — ELIOT 273:13
with her sighs the s. do break — CAMP 177:5
strip: s. his sleeve and show — SHAK 586:11
S. thine own back — SHAK 597:7
stripe: s. for stripe — BIBLE 72:17
striped: He was no s. frieze — STR 670:13
S. like a zebra — KEATS 388:14
stripes: forty s. save one — BIBLE 102:1
with his s. we are healed — BIBLE 84:12
strive: need'st not s. — CLOU 207:17
seem to s. again — POPE 523:33
To s., to seek, to find — TENN 690:4
strives: Man will err while yet he s. — GOET 309:1
striveth: that s. with his maker — BIBLE 84:3
striving: s. evermore — GREN 318:2
strode: he s. off — CIC 204:7
stroke: greater s. astonisheth — CONS 217:20
none so fast as s. — COKE 208:15
on the final s. of nine — ELIOT 273:1
s. a platitude — MARQ 448:21
s. most dolorous — MAL 443:4
s. of midnight ceases — HOUS 352:2
upon the s. that murders me — SHAK 623:19
strokes: amorous of their s. — SHAK 565:5
redoubled s. upon the foe — SHAK 599:16
strong: advantage of s. people — BONH 118:1
And grow s. — HUGH 354:1
And I again am s. — WORD 745:11
battle to the s. — DAV 231:22
but s. in will — TENN 690:4
But wants that little s. — HOLM 342:17
Eternal Father, s. to save — WHIT 732:2
first to keep the s. in awe — SHAK 622:14
nor the battle to the s. — BIBLE 80:21
only the s. shall thrive — SERV 563:6
Sorrow and silence are s. — LONG 426:17
s. and of a good courage — BIBLE 73:27
S. brother in God — BELL 61:12
s. came forth sweetness — BIBLE 74:14
S. drink is raging — BIBLE 79:4
s. drink unto him — BIBLE 79:34
S. gongs groaning — CHES 199:4
S. is the lion — SMART 650:1
s. man armed keepeth — BIBLE 94:19
s. man in a blatant land — TENN 686:13
s. men shall bow themselves — BIBLE 81:1
s. name of the Trinity — ALEX 8:15
s., silent man — MORL 485:1
s. that they come to fourscore — BOOK 131:1
S. without rage — DENH 236:7
those who think they are s. — BID 109:1
without whom nothing is s. — BOOK 121:2
stronger: But s. still, in earth — SMART 650:2
I am no s. than my sex — SHAK 591:3
interest of the s. party — PLATO 516:13
no s. than a flower — SHAK 634:3
on the side of the s. — TAC 678:5
s. by every thing you see — STER 664:24
S. by weakness — WALL 718:13
s. than all the armies — ANON 18:12
s. than all the hosts — BRYAN 153:23
s. than he shall come — BIBLE 94:19
they were s. than lions — BIBLE 75:9
strongest: reason of the s. — LA F 405:11
s. man in the world — IBSEN 359:3
Wine is the s. — BIBLE 86:20
stronghold: safe s. our God is still — LUTH 432:13
strongly: sinner and sin s. — LUTH 432:9
strove: I s. with none — LAND 408:2
little still she s. — BYRON 170:10
unbecoming men that s. — TENN 690:4
struck: I s. the board — HERB 334:11
I was s. all of a heap — SHER 644:26
s. the father when the son — BURT 165:11
women should be s. — COW 221:5
structure: s. in a winding stair — HERB 335:6
s. of a play — MILL 461:20
struggle: alarms of s. — ARN 27:1
burden of a long twilight s. — KENN 394:1

struggle: (cont.):
class s. necessarily leads — MARX 452:9
gods themselves s. in vain — SCH 558:3
perpetual s. for room and food — MALT 443:19
sacrifice in a contemptible s. — BURKE 159:15
Say not the s. naught availeth — CLOU 207:23
s. between the artist man — SHAW 637:7
S. for Existence — DARW 231:8
s. itself towards the heights — CAMUS 178:1
s. not of men but of forces — ADAMS 2:22
to-day the s. — AUDEN 36:7
What s. to escape — KEATS 388:24
struggles: history of class s. — MARX 452:12
struggling: her s. ceases — PUSH 532:15
strumpet: Into a s.'s fool — SHAK 564:12
she is a s. — SHAK 574:25
She was a s., he was a thief — HEINE 331:1
'Tis the s.'s plague — SHAK 617:8
struts: Stoutly s. his dames — MILT 466:10
s. and frets his hour — SHAK 605:1
Stuart: S. or Nassau go higher — PRIOR 529:6
stubble: sparks among the s. — BIBLE 87:1
stubborn: are very s. things — TIND 698:7
faithless and s. generation — BOOK 130:9
s. and too strange a hand — SHAK 589:24
s. bootless striveth — GREV 318:6
stubbornness: impious s. — SHAK 572:11
That even his s., his checks — SHAK 617:21
Stubbs: S. butters Freeman — ROG 544:16
stuck: S. her with knives — MORR 486:1
S. in my throat — SHAK 602:1
students: benefit of the s. — SMITH 651:3
studied: he s. from the life — ARMS 26:6
little more than I have s. — SHAK 628:23
rather s. books than men — BACON 45:11
studies: much time in s. is sloth — BACON 44:24
some particular s. — DRYD 262:9
still air of delightful s. — MILT 476:7
S. serve for delight — BACON 44:23
studieth: man that s. revenge — BACON 44:16
studio: Sine ira et s. — TAC 677:23
studious: S. let me sit — THOM 696:13
S. of elegance and ease — GAY 300:6
S. of laborious ease — COWP 223:29
S. to please, yet not ashamed — JOHN 370:5
walk the s. cloister's pale — MILT 464:26
studiously: s. neutral — WILS 738:12
study: craggy paths of s. — JONS 379:5
did nothing s. but the way — KING 396:13
much s. is a weariness — BIBLE 81:3
My s.'s ornament — MIDD 459:16
not s. to live — BACON 45:16
proper s. of mankind is books — HUXL 357:11
proper s. of mankind is man — POPE 522:9
result of previous s. — AUST 39:11
science and s. of man is man — CHAR 192:2
s. and fast — SHAK 605:10
s. in a worn-out poetical — ELIOT 270:19
S. is like the heaven's — SHAK 598:7
s. of Greek literature — GAIS 296:15
S. to be quiet — BIBLE 103:20
studying: s. all the summer night — MARV 450:17
s. how I may compare — SHAK 621:10
stuff: bosom of that perilous s. — SHAK 604:22
I count life just a s. — BROW 150:12
I s. my skin — ANON 14:13
man might write such s. — JOHN 376:5
mean and unrefinèd s. — BRAD 139:12
our s. can get by without it — AMIS 11:1
should be made of sterner s. — SHAK 592:7
s. as great part of Shakespeare — GEOR 300:27
s. of life to knit me — HOUS 352:14
too short to s. a mushroom — CONR 217:19
What s. 'tis made of — SHAK 607:2
stuffed: s. their mouths with gold — BEVAN 69:2
We are the s. men — ELIOT 271:14
stuffs: S. out his vacant garments — SHAK 594:4
stultitiam: Misce s. consiliis — HOR 350:20
stumbled: I s. when I saw — SHAK 596:24
stumbles: Oft s. at a straw — SPEN 660:27
stumbling: stone of s. — BIBLE 82:25
S. on melons — MARV 450:9

stump: stir it and s. it	GILB 306:16	**sublime:** (cont.):		**success:** (cont.):	
stumps: pitch, and s., and all	LANG 408:15	or if it were s.	THOR 697:5	s. in war	CHUR 202:14
stung: S. by the splendour	BROW 149:10	our monotonous s.	LOW 430:22	S. is counted sweetest	DICK 244:19
stunned: one that hath been s.	COL 211:18	s. and celestial greatness	TRAH 701:10	S. is relative	ELIOT 270:11
stunt: just another amusing s.	READ 537:6	s. dashed to pieces	COL 212:15	s. is sure	TWAIN 706:27
stupefying: s. incense-smoke	BROW 148:18	S. to the ridiculous	GRAH 313:10	s. perhaps may crown us	COWP 223:30
stupendous: these s. masses	CANN 178:12	s. to the ridiculous	NAP 489:16	Sweet smell of s.	LEHM 416:10
stupid: s. neither forgive	SZASZ 67:13	to maintain 'the s.'	POUND 526:11	to our good s. refer the rest	DRAY 257:18
s. should rule over	IBSEN 359:1	You're s.	HARG 326:9	to vulgar judgements—s.	BURKE 157:2
When a s. man	SHAW 635:27	**sublimity:** S. is the echo of a noble		true s. is to labour	STEV 667:29
stupidest: s. party	MILL 460:9	mind	LONG 428:7	very lively hope of s.	SMITH 653:28
stupidity: proof of s. than	JOHN 373:9	**submerged:** S. Tenth	BOOTH 136:5	**successful:** clever and the s.	GREE 316:22
Such an excess of s.	JOHN 372:16	**submission:** appetite for s.	ELIOT 269:12	full tide of s. experiment	JEFF 364:4
With s. the gods themselves	SCH 558:3	Yielded with coy s.	MILT 471:6	S. crimes alone are justified	DRYD 261:7
stupor: First—Chill—then S.	DICK 244:10	**submit:** Must be s.	SHAK 620:12	s. writer or picture-painter	LEWIS 421:4
Sturm: S. und Drang	KAUF 386:1	s. myself to all my governors	BOOK 123:7	whether s. or otherwise	ADAMS 3:6
stuttering: s. rifles' rapid rattle	OWEN 503:12	to the destructive element s.	CONR 217:7	**successive:** his s. journeys run	WATTS 723:6
sty: No better than a s.	SHAK 566:15	**subordinate:** safer to be in a s.	THOM 692:5	**successor:** of Peter's s.	BROW 149:5
Over the nasty s.	SHAK 577:15	**subordination:** s. of one sex	MILL 460:22	**successus:** Hos s. alit	VIRG 713:9
Stygian: In S. cave forlorn	MILT 465:3	**subscribers:** list of s.	JOHN 375:26	**succour:** And died to s. me	BALL 49:13
S. smoke of the pit	JAM 361:17	**subscription:** amount of his s.	SURT 672:14	comfort and s. all them	BOOK 122:3
style: attain an English s.	JOHN 368:20	You owe me no s.	SHAK 595:21	**such:** As there had been none s.	VAUX 709:12
cut, the s., the line	LOES 426:3	**subsistence:** S. only increases	MALT 443:18	s. as I am	BIBLE 99:13
grand s. arises in poetry	ARN 30:9	s. without a mind	BERK 65:12	S. as I am	SHAK 609:2
He has no real s.	PIC 514:10	too near the bones of s.	DRAB 287:9	s. is the kingdom of God	BIBLE 93:16
how the s. refines	POPE 521:19	**subsisting:** human flesh s.	BOOK 119:15	S. knowledge is too wonderful	BOOK 134:19
only secret of s.	ARN 30:10	**substance:** body and material s.	CARL 180:27	**suck:** I have given s., and know	SHAK 601:7
S. is life	FLAU 286:2	Form is s.	JAMES 362:22	s. they no small advantage	BOOK 130:1
S. is the dress of thought	WESL 729:5	mind can make S.	BYRON 172:2	**sucked:** s. on country pleasures	DONNE 252:4
s. is the man	BUFF 154:15	More s. in our enmities	YEATS 752:13	**sucker:** s. an even break	FIEL 282:20
s. of life	WEBER 725:3	nor dividing the S.	BOOK 119:13	s. born every minute	BARN 53:19
's.' which is most unhealthy	SMIL 650:12	ruler of all his s.	BOOK 132:12	**sucking:** s. child shall play	BIBLE 83:3
that is s.	STEV 667:10	s. and stake in the country	WIND 739:5	you as gently as any s. dove	SHAK 611:8
true definition of a s.	SWIFT 673:22	s. from the common earth	FITZ 284:14	**suckle:** s. fools and chronicle	SHAK 615:18
When we see a natural s.	PASC 507:10	s. of his house for love	BIBLE 82:6	**sucklings:** babes and s.	BOOK 124:20
with his eye on his s	ARN 30:6	s. of men which is man	SWIN 676:18	**sucks:** one that s. his substance	LAMB 406:10
styles: All s. are good except	VOLT 716:9	s. of ten thousand soldiers	SHAK 622:13	weasel s. eggs	SHAK 568:9
its special s. of life	WEBER 724:20	summed with all his s.	CHAP 190:12	**Sudan:** at your 'ome in the S.	KIPL 399:5
suave: S., mari magno	LUCR 431:15	Thine eyes did see my s.	BOOK 134:21	**sudden:** I said to Dawn: Be s.	THOM 695:3
suavity: deceitfulness and s.	ELIOT 272:12	wasted his s. with riotous	BIBLE 95:2	nothing else but s. glory	HOBB 339:16
sub: Sighted s., sank same	MASON 453:11	What is your s.	SHAK 633:16	splendour of a s. thought	BROW 149:10
subdue: may s. for a moment	BURKE 157:21	**substances:** forms and s.	WORD 747:4	s. storms are short	SHAK 619:17
replenish the earth, and s. it	BIBLE 69:26	**substantial:** My ship s.	ASKEW 31:15	too unadvised, too s.	SHAK 623:3
s. all things to himself	BOOK 124:5	**substantive:** s. law	MAINE 442:12	**suddenly:** s. became depraved	JUV 383:18
s. the arrogant	VIRG 713:17	**substitute:** no s. for victory	MAC 434:2	s. cast down	BOOK 127:21
s. the people under us	BOOK 127:19	**substitutes:** age of s.	BENT 64:19	s., I saw you there	GERS 301:11
To chasten and s.	WORD 745:1	**subterranean:** s. fields	WORD 747:7	**Sudeten:** S. Germans	HITL 339:13
To teach, convince, s.	AUBER 32:20	**subtle:** God is s. but he is not	EINS 268:1	**sue:** Less used to s. than	SCOTT 559:9
subdued: My nature is s.	SHAK 634:22	His s. point	DAV 232:6	**suet-pudding:** cold, black s.	LEWIS 421:8
subdues: S. me quite	SHAK 606:3	more s. than any beast	BIBLE 70:8	**Suez:** somewhere east of S.	KIPL 400:3
subeunt: s. morbi tristisque	VIRG 715:16	proud, s., sly, and bloody	SHAK 622:5	**suffer:** Better one s.	DRYD 259:6
subiectis: Parcere s.	VIRG 713:17	slipper and s. knave	SHAK 615:21	courage to s.	TROL 703:9
subject: Grasp the s.	CATO 185:9	**subtleties:** airy s. in religion	BROW 146:7	doth s. a sea-change	SHAK 625:10
honour is the s. of my story	SHAK 589:27	from speculations and s.	BROW 146:10	do well, and s. for it	BIBLE 105:14
know what it is to be a s.	ELIZ 274:2	**subtlety:** Human s.	LEON 418:10	let's s. on the heights	HUGO 354:14
Lies the s. of all verse	BROW 146:24	Thy brother came with s.	BIBLE 71:12	prepared to s. for it	BENN 63:19
Little s., little wit	CAREY 179:16	**Subtopia:** bestows a name—s	NAIRN 489:7	s. a man of his place	SHAK 589:13
My s. is War, and the pity	OWEN 503:10	**suburb:** s. stretched beyond	BETJ 67:8	s. and die	VIGNY 711:12
Spare the poet for his s. sake	COWP 221:28	**suburbia:** I come from s. . . . and I don't		s. fools gladly	BIBLE 101:22
s. and a sovereign	CHAR 191:9		RAPH 537:1	S. the little children	BIBLE 93:16
s. of conversation	CHES 198:3	**suburbs:** Dwell I but in the s.	SHAK 591:2	s. thy foot to be moved	BOOK 133:23
s.'s duty is the king's	SHAK 586:5	In the south s.	SHAK 630:19	s. thy Holy One to see	BOOK 124:31
s. unto the higher powers	BIBLE 100:8	**subversion:** complaining about s.	JUV 383:17	**sufferance:** S. is a soverayn vertue	LANG 409:3
We know a s. ourselves	JOHN 374:4	**subversive:** is funny is s.	ORW 500:3	s. is the badge of all	SHAK 607:22
whose s. is not truth	CHAP 191:2	**succedaneum:** as a s., and a prop	WORD 747:1	**suffered:** Achaeans have s.	HOMER 343:2
with severity a serious s.	ARN 30:9	**succeed:** How to s. in business	MEAD 455:12	S. under Pontius Pilate	BOOK 119:1
subjectification: s. of nature	LANG 408:18	Shall life s.	BROW 152:7	**sufferer:** s., a soft, meek	DEKK 235:14
subjectivity: S. is a terrible thing	CHEK 197:8	s. without any act of betrayal	REN 538:19	unites it with the human s.	JOYCE 381:12
subjects: most important s.	ARIS 25:6	**succeeded:** matter she drove at s.	PRIOR 529:7	**suffering:** About s. they were never	
my self very rich in s.	DEFOE 234:11	**succeeds:** Whenever a friend s.	VIDAL 711:5	wrong	AUDEN 35:6
s. are rebels from principle	BURKE 158:17	Where he s., the merit's	CHUR 201:16	atone for it by s.	CHEK 196:9
s. of government	WILS 738:9	**success:** and yours is S.	BARR 54:11	Doing or s.	MILT 468:7
subjugation: conquest and s.	WEBS 725:8	bitch-goddess s.	JAMES 363:14	learn in s. what they teach	SHEL 641:1
sublimation: s. of the work instinct		For an actress to be a s.	BARR 54:16	Lounjun 'roun' en s.	HARR 327:5
	LODGE 425:21	given me earnest of s.	SHAK 600:12	loved the s. many	BENT 64:8
sublime: egotistical s.	KEATS 391:23	glory is nothing else but s.	LERM 418:13	majesty of human s.	VIGNY 711:11
essence of the true s.	BYRON 172:6	his s. is disgraceful	MENC 457:5	put me to s.	METH 458:16
heart of the ridiculous, the s.	MAHON 442:5	If A is a s. in life	EINS 268:5	s. ennobles the character	MAUG 454:8
Howls the s.	DICK 241:22	mortals to command s.	ADD 3:16	S. is permanent, obscure	WORD 743:7
My object all s.	GILB 305:3	no s. like failure	DYLAN 265:17	s. may well be called	ELIOT 268:18
Of beauteous and s.	AKEN 6:4	s. and miscarriage	JOHN 371:20	s., privation, or injustice	BEVAN 69:4
One step above the s.	PAINE 504:9	s. in life	PATER 509:7	take the s. upon ourselves	DOST 254:10
		s. in life is to be a good	SPEN 658:12	To each his s.	GRAY 316:3

sufferings: constant in human s.   JOYCE 381:12
  myriad s. for the Achaeans   HOMER 342:22
  patience under their s.   BOOK 120:7
suffers: does, not s. wrong   SHEL 642:8
  inform us of what he s.   SMITH 650:16
suffice: And would s.   FROST 294:17
  O when may it s.   YEATS 751:14
sufficiency: elegant s.   THOM 696:3
  Our s. is of God   BIBLE 101:16
sufficient: S. is Thine Arm   WATTS 723:7
  s. sacrifice   BOOK 122:11
  s. to finish it   BIBLE 94:33
  s. to keep him straight   LLOY 424:13
  S. unto the day   BIBLE 89:13
sufficiently: s. decayed   GILB 305:14
suffocated: s. in its own wax   FORS 290:7
sugar: If sack and s. be a fault   SHAK 580:32
  pious action, we do s. o'er   SHAK 575:15
  s., and saltness agree   GOLD 311:3
suggest: suffer reality to s.   BRON 142:10
suggestion: s. as a cat laps milk   SHAK 625:16
suicide: from the s.'s grave   GILD 308:13
  It is not: it is s.   MACD 437:12
  It is s. to be abroad   BECK 57:11
  longest s. note in history   KAUF 385:15
  nothing left for you, not even s.   STEV 668:6
  s. 25 years after his death   BEAV 57:8
  s. is a great source of comfort   NIET 495:14
  s. kills two people   MILL 461:13
sui generis: s. and let it go   LONG 426:7
suis: J'y s., j'y reste   MACM 440:1
Suisse: point de S.   RAC 535:6
suit: could see ye wi' a s.   FERG 281:10
  Doesn't seem to s. her notion   GILB 305:2
  Shall I be still in s.   HERB 334:11
suitable: s. case for treatment   MERC 457:11
suits: s. of woe   SHAK 572:10
suivre: il fallait bien les s.   LEDR 415:14
sukebind: s. hangs heavy from   GIBB 302:23
Sule Skerry: it is the S.   BALL 49:12
sullen: in his s. mind   SPEN 660:1
  S. and sad   THOM 696:11
  s., untamed and intractable   ELIOT 271:2
sulphur: oat-cakes, and s.   SMITH 653:8
sulphurous: s. and thought-executing   SHAK 595:20
sultan: sultan after s.   FITZ 283:15
sultry: where the climate's s.   BYRON 170:6
sum: Cogito, ergo s.   DESC 237:18
  s. obtained I this freedom   BIBLE 99:6
  s. of matter remains exactly   BACON 42:10
  sum of me is s. of nothing   SHAK 609:2
  s. of things for pay   HOUS 351:22
Sumatra: giant rat of S.   DOYLE 256:9
summas: s. emergere opes   LUCR 431:15
summer: after many a s. dies the swan   TENN 689:10
  After s. merrily   SHAK 626:2
  chords of s.   DAY-L 233:6
  compare thee to a s.'s day   SHAK 633:6
  Eternal s. gilds them yet   BYRON 170:30
  Fair s. droops   NASHE 490:23
  Far from the sun and s. gale   GRAY 316:6
  far over the s. sea   TENN 689:3
  fruitful s. of his blisses   CHAP 190:17
  guest of s.   SHAK 601:1
  if it takes all s.   GRANT 314:8
  In a s. seson   LANG 408:19
  Indian S. of the heart   WHIT 733:9
  In s., quite the other way   STEV 668:13
  last rose of s.   MOORE 483:12
  long bathing of a s.'s day   WORD 746:10
  long hot s.   RAVE 537:5
  lordships on a hot s. afternoon   ANON 18:18
  murmur of a s.'s day   ARN 28:3
  never knew the s. woods   TENN 683:11
  nor s. beauty hath such   DONNE 250:10
  On s. eves by haunted stream   MILT 465:17
  Saint Martin's s.   SHAK 587:6
  see in a s.'s day   SHAK 611:9
  Singest of s. in full-throated   KEATS 389:8
  s. afternoon   JAMES 363:11

summer: (cont.):
  s. and winter   BIBLE 70:29
  s. birdcage in a garden   WEBS 726:2
  s. has set in with its usual   COL 212:18
  s. in England   WALP 719:15
  s. is ended   BIBLE 85:8
  S. is icumen in   ANON 18:6
  s. is not heard or seen   SHEL 640:19
  s. or winter are lucky   CHEK 197:3
  s. sang in me   MILL 461:9
  s.'s beauty yields to winter's   SACK 552:12
  s.'s flower is to the summer   SHAK 634:15
  s.'s green all girded up   SHAK 633:4
  s.'s here and the time is   JAGG 361:12
  S.'s joys are spoilt by use   KEATS 387:18
  s. skies to mourn   KEATS 390:25
  s.'s lease   SHAK 633:6
  S. time an' the livin' is easy   HEYW 338:2
  S. Time on Bredon   KING 398:6
  s. winds that creep   SHEL 640:18
  sweet as s.   SHAK 600:10
  thinking on fantastic s.'s   SHAK 619:14
  thy eternal s.   SHAK 633:6
  tree in the time of s.   BIBLE 88:4
  upon a trancèd s.-night   KEATS 387:27
  waken from his s. dreams   SHEL 641:16
  when the s. is shed   SWIN 676:25
summers: ful ofte a myrie s. day   CHAU 195:17
  s. in a sea of glory   SHAK 588:19
  S. pleasures they are gone   CLARE 204:28
summertime: s. on Bredon   HOUS 352:10
summits: Nations touch at their s.   BAG 46:23
summoner: S. was ther with us   CHAU 193:5
summoners: These dreadful s.   SHAK 596:1
summons: s. lies like lead   SHAK 601:11
  s. thee to heaven   SHAK 601:13
  Upon a fearful s.   SHAK 572:1
summum: S. bonum   CIC 204:1
sumpshous: s. spot all done up   ASHF 31:9
sums: exact in s.   BAG 46:20
sun: all, except their s., is set   BYRON 170:30
  all the beauty of the s.   SHAK 631:4
  bedimmed the noontide s.   SHAK 626:1
  Before the rising s.   WATTS 723:7
  Before you let the s. in   THOM 693:18
  best s. we have is made of   WALP 719:14
  black s. of melancholy   NERV 492:2
  blushing discontented s.   SHAK 620:9
  brighte s. loste his hewe   CHAU 193:14
  Busy old fool, unruly s.   DONNE 252:16
  clear as the s., and terrible   BIBLE 81:21
  countenance was as the s.   BIBLE 106:1
  doors against a setting s.   SHAK 626:10
  ere the set of s.   SHAK 599:13
  eyes to behold the s.   BIBLE 80:29
  farthing candle to the s.   YOUNG 754:11
  Fear no more the heat o' the s.   SHAK 571:16
  flew between me and the s.   BLUN 116:5
  gallant will command the s.   SHAK 624:19
  glorious S. uprist   COL 210:23
  going down of the s.   BINY 109:20
  Go out in the midday s.   COW 220:14
  great s. begins his state   MILT 465:9
  Hail, the S. of Righteousness   WESL 728:4
  Hath Britain all the s.   SHAK 571:11
  heaven's glorious s.   SHAK 598:7
  he beheld the s.   WORD 743:17
  he taketh under the s.   BIBLE 79:36
  hooting at the glorious s.   COL 210:2
  I am too much i' the s.   SHAK 572:7
  I 'gin to be aweary of the s.   SHAK 605:2
  I have seen the s. set   NIMB 541:6
  inconceivable idea of the s.   STEV 666:2
  I will sing of the s.   POUND 526:6
  Juliet is the s.   SHAK 622:27
  lands beneath another s.   THOM 696:10
  let not the s. go down   BIBLE 102:19
  Let the hot s.   AUDEN 35:3
  light a candle to the s.   SIDN 646:11
  Light breaks where no s.   THOM 693:11
  like the s., they shine   POPE 523:19
  livery of the burnished s.   SHAK 608:4
  loves to live i' the s.   SHAK 568:10

sun: (cont.):
  maturing s.   KEATS 390:17
  midnight speak with the S.   VAUG 708:15
  Mother, give me the s.   IBSEN 359:4
  Move him into the s.   OWEN 503:14
  new thing under the s.   BIBLE 80:1
  nothing like the s.   SHAK 635:2
  Now the s. is laid to sleep   JONS 378:16
  on which the s. never sets   NORTH 496:13
  open face of the s.   WESL 729:1
  out again to feel the s.   BROW 147:10
  Pees 'most shene is the s.   LANG 409:6
  place in the s.   BÜLOW 155:2
  place in the s.   WILH 736:18
  quietest places under the s.   HOUS 352:17
  rising of the s.   ANON 14:11
  run to the rime-ringed s.   KIPL 399:20
  sacred radiance of the s.   SHAK 594:19
  setting s., and music   SHAK 619:16
  shall the s. light on them   BIBLE 106:22
  shoots at the mid-day s.   SIDN 646:13
  short while towards the s.   SPEN 659:1
  So when the s. in bed   MILT 467:12
  s. also rises   HEM 331:17
  s. and moon were served   AUG 36:23
  s. and the other stars   DANTE 230:21
  s. ariseth   BOOK 132:9
  s. came dazzling through   TENN 685:2
  s. does not set in my dominions   SCH 558:2
  s. enough for lazing upon   BETJ 68:9
  s. from weeping fountains   BOLT 117:16
  s. goes down with a flaming   BOND 117:17
  s. has first breathed   VIRG 715:11
  S. himself cannot forget   ANON 18:7
  S. in his strength   BIBLE 69:19
  s. in lonely lands   TENN 681:1
  s. is coming down to earth   MER 457:29
  s. is lost, and th'earth   DONNE 250:7
  s. knoweth his going down   BOOK 132:9
  s. looked over the mountain's   BROW 151:21
  s. makes strong   CAT 186:9
  s. not shining and a look   CHAN 190:1
  s. of heaven prove a micher   SHAK 580:29
  S. of righteousness   BIBLE 86:19
  s. of York   SHAK 621:14
  s. orange, red, red   HUGH 354:5
  s. rises do you not see   BLAKE 114:18
  s.'s a thief   SHAK 626:17
  s. shall not burn thee   BOOK 133:23
  s. showing up the dust   PERR 512:25
  S.'s rim dips   COL 211:3
  S., stand thou still upon   BIBLE 73:32
  s. that shines upon   SHAK 632:9
  s. to me is dark   MILT 474:2
  s. to rise on the evil   BIBLE 88:34
  s. was shining everywhere   GERS 301:11
  s. will not haver   HEAT 329:25
  swollen magpie in a fitful s.   POUND 527:8
  tabernacle for the s.   BOOK 125:4
  though we cannot make our s.   MARV 451:4
  Till the s. grows cold   TAYL 679:16
  tired the s. with talking   CORY 219:15
  To have enjoyed the s.   ARN 27:3
  Truth is staring at the s.   BELL 60:25
  Up roos the s., and up roos   CHAU 193:22
  volley of the s.   WILB 734:6
  walks under the midday s.   MILT 463:27
  whan softe was the s.   LANG 408:19
  whereas the s. doth parch   SURR 672:4
  where the s. reigns supreme   LE C 415:13
  whose candle is the s.   FITZ 284:5
  with the s. to match   BROW 149:1
  woman clothed with the s.   BIBLE 106:29
  worship to the garish s.   SHAK 623:17
  yet I saw no s.   TICH 698:3
  you stand out of my s.   DIOG 246:11
sunbathing: s. and jazz   WAUGH 723:18
sunbeam: Jesus wants me for a s.   TALB 678:7
  s. in a winter's day   DYER 265:6
sunbeams: didst the stars and s. know   ARN 28:13
  motes that people the s.   MILT 464:14
  s. out of cucumbers   SWIFT 673:13

tales: seemed to them as idle t.   BIBLE 95:31
T., marvellous tales   FLEC 286:9
tell old t., and laugh   SHAK 597:16
tali: t. auxilio nec defensoribus   VIRG 713:2
talk: And the t. slid north   KIPL 398:14
by men who t. fluently   HOGB 341:14
Careless t. costs lives   ANON 12:20
chance to t. a little wild   SHAK 588:10
difference of men's t.   PEPYS 512:2
English t. is a quadrille   JAMES 362:16
gotta use words when I t.   ELIOT 272:19
have out his t., as I do   JOHN 374:26
he knows when not to t.   ROG 545:6
If you t. to God, you   SZASZ 677:14
It can talk, talk, t.   PLATH 516:2
It's very easy to t.   DICK 242:9
It would t.: Lord how it talk't   BEAU 57:4
I want to t. like a lady   SHAW 638:16
I won't t. of his book   JOHN 373:1
loves to hear himself t.   SHAK 623:10
Money doesn't t., it swears   DYLAN 265:16
night is crept upon our t.   SHAK 593:13
nor to find t. and discourse   BACON 44:26
No use to t. to me   HOUS 352:9
once startled into t.   ROET 544:5
people who can't t.   ZAPPA 755:9
t. and go so far about   EMPS 277:19
t. as they please about   CLOU 207:13
t. but a tinkling cymbal   BACON 43:21
t. not to me of a name   BYRON 173:8
t. of Swann at the Verdurins'   PROU 530:8
t. of wills   SHAK 620:7
t. on 'Sex and Civics'   BETJ 67:13
t. six times with the same   BYRON 174:2
t. with crowds and keep   KIPL 400:15
t. with some old lover's   DONNE 252:10
t. with you, walk   SHAK 607:19
Then he will t., Good Gods   LEE 416:4
They always t., who never   PRIOR 529:16
think too little and who t. too   DRYD 259:7
To t. about the rest of us   ANON 18:13
To t. of many things   CARR 183:2
we do not t. of ourselves   TROL 703:15
wished him to t. on for ever   HAZL 328:13
world may t. of hereafter   COLL 213:4
You may t. in this manner   JOHN 376:8
talked: he t. with us by the way   BIBLE 95:32
I believe they t. of me   FARQ 280:13
least t. by men   PER 512:24
listen when his mate t.   WICK 733:16
only t. of population   GOLD 311:28
So much they t., so very   CHUR 201:12
t. like poor Poll   GARR 298:5
t. shop like a tenth muse   ANON 14:8
that is not being t. about   WILDE 735:17
they t. of their Raphaels   GOLD 311:7
We have t. for a hundred   JOHN 367:6
talkers: present is an age of t.   HAZL 329:9
t. whose tongues were all   DYLAN 265:15
talking: find I'm t. to myself   BARN 53:12
Frenchman must be always t.   JOHN 375:15
nation t. to itself   MILL 461:21
never know what we are t.   RUSS 551:17
nor foolish t., nor jesting   BIBLE 102:20
People t. without speaking   SIMON 647:20
soon leaves off t.   BUTL 167:8
T. and eloquence are not   JONS 380:11
t. at street corners   VANZ 708:11
tired the sun with t.   CORY 219:15
wonder that you will still be t.   SHAK 613:9
you can stop people t.   ATTL 32:18
talking-machine: redtape t.   CARL 181:1
talks: Licker t. mighty loud   HARR 327:7
t. it so very fast   FARQ 280:15
t. of Arthur's death   SHAK 594:11
t. of his misfortunes there   JOHN 375:18
tall: But she is t. and stately   TENN 686:14
gods, divinely t.   TENN 680:20
long and the short and the t.   HUGH 353:16
T. as a crane   SITW 648:9
t. men had ever very empty   BACON 45:24
t. rock, the mountain   WORD 744:21

tall: (cont.):
t. ship and a star to steer   MAS 453:7
'Tis a t. building   CRAB 224:19
taller: t. by almost the breadth   SWIFT 673:8
t. than other men   HAR 326:14
Talmuds: rotted T. of my childhood   BABEL 41:9
Tam: T. was glorious   BURNS 163:5
tambourine: Hey! Mr T. Man   DYLAN 265:18
t. on her other knee   DICK 242:12
tame: Be not too t. neither   SHAK 576:6
hey-day in the blood is t.   SHAK 577:13
Of t. villatic fowl   MILT 474:14
tongue can no man t.   BIBLE 105:2
tamed: see themselves in one year t.   MARV 450:16
tameness: trusts in t. of a wolf   SHAK 596:18
taming: T. my wild heart to thy   SHAK 613:30
Tam Lin: I ken this night, T.   BALL 50:14
tamper: Would never want to t.   AUDEN 34:14
Tandy: I met wid Napper T.   ANON 15:4
tangere: Noli me t.   BIBLE 108:16
tangerine: peel and portion a t.   MACN 441:2
tangle: and the odors t.   DICK 245:5
Thy baited hooks shall t.   WYATT 749:15
tangles: t. of Neaera's hair   MILT 466:3
tank: T. come down the stalls   SASS 557:5
tantae: T. molis erat Romanam   VIRG 712:2
tantum: T. ergo sacramentum   THOM 692:14
T. religio potuit suadere   LUCR 431:13
taper: or with t. light   SHAK 594:9
t. as she hurried   KEATS 387:4
t. to the outward room   DONNE 251:9
tapestry: so rich t. as poets   SIDN 647:6
wrong side of a Turkey t.   HOW 353:3
tapping: suddenly there came a t.   POE 518:6
tar: [T. water] is of a nature   BERK 65:8
wine that tasted of the t.   BELL 62:1
Tara: that once through T.'s   MOORE 483:5
when T. rose so high   LAND 408:3
taratantara: tuba terribili sonitu t.   ENN 278:3
tar-baby: T. ain't sayin' nuthin'   HARR 327:6
tarde: cinco en punto de la t.   GARC 297:12
tares: corn is but a field of t.   TICH 698:3
t. of mine own brain   BROW 146:10
tarnished: neither t. nor afraid   CHAN 190:5
Tarquin: T.'s ravishing strides   SHAK 601:13
tarried: do the job too long he t.   SWIFT 675:14
too long we have t.   LEAR 414:13
tarrieth: guest that t. but a day   BIBLE 87:5
tarry: Boatman, do not t.   CAMP 176:15
t. the wheels of his chariots   BIBLE 74:6
that he t. till I come   BIBLE 98:4
You may for ever t.   HERR 337:8
tarrying: make no long t.   BOOK 126:26
nor t. here   SHAK 605:2
Tarsus: which am a Jew of T.   BIBLE 99:5
tart: t. who has finally married   BAXT 56:2
this t. cathartic virtue   EMER 276:26
Tartar: T.'s lips   SHAK 603:19
tarts: by the action of two t.   MACM 440:9
Tarzan: Me T., you Jane   WEIS 726:20
task: All with weary t. fordone   SHAK 613:1
long day's t. is done   SHAK 566:8
sets love a t. like   HUNT 356:7
t. accomplished   HENL 332:8
t. in life is to give birth   FROMM 294:6
There is but one t. for all   KIPL 399:4
Thou thy worldly t. hast done   SHAK 571:16
what he reads as a t.   JOHN 372:8
your long and heavy t.   VIGNY 711:12
tasks: Among the t. of real life   WORD 743:8
tassel-gentle: lure this t. back   SHAK 623:6
tassie: An' fill it in a silver t.   BURNS 162:21
taste: arbiter of t.   TAC 678:1
bad t. is always meeting   HOPK 346:17
bad t. of the smoker   ELIOT 268:21
bouquet is better than the t.   POTT 525:15
common sense and good t.   SHAW 635:28
dainty Baccus gross in t.   SHAK 598:20
difference of t. in jokes   ELIOT 268:22
forgot the t. of fears   SHAK 604:24
Ghastly good t.   BETJ 68:11
good sense and good t.   LA BR 405:3

taste: (cont.):
Good t. and humour   MUGG 487:10
good t. and procedure   TOLS 700:12
held together by a sense of t.   BALL 51:5
his own inch-rule of t.   ADAMS 2:12
last t. of sweets   SHAK 619:16
let me t. the whole of it   BROW 152:5
must himself create the t.   WORD 748:20
never t. who always drink   PRIOR 529:16
nobody has any t. for them   VOLT 717:3
no longer t. and genius   REYN 539:7
nowhere worse t. than in   JOW 380:18
O t. and see, how gracious   BOOK 126:13
ought to t. it sparingly   AUST 39:4
our canons of t.   VEBL 709:17
Shakespeare wanted t.   WALP 719:7
shall t. my Anno Domini   FARQ 280:7
t. a little honey   BIBLE 74:36
T. is the feminine of genius   FITZ 284:9
t. my meat   HERB 335:9
t. of your quality   SHAK 575:4
t. prove in digestion   SHAK 619:11
t. when you married me   SHER 645:14
T. your legs, sir   SHAK 630:9
tasted: had t. her sweet body   SHAK 616:20
Some books are to be t.   BACON 44:27
t. that the Lord is gracious   BIBLE 105:10
tastes: Our t. greatly alter   JOHN 372:26
Simple t., you will agree   CONN 216:10
strongest t. were negative   WAUGH 723:18
tasting: T. of Flora and the country green   KEATS 389:9
Tat: Die T. ist alles   GOET 309:7
Ihr stolzen Männer der T.   HEINE 331:3
tatter: t. in its mortal dress   YEATS 752:21
tattered: t. coat upon a stick   YEATS 752:21
tatters: fond of my rags and t.   MOL 478:23
taught: and afterward he t.   CHAU 193:1
In them is plainest t.   MILT 473:23
nor heeds what we have t. her   GAY 299:11
right to be t. by the enemy   OVID 502:23
t. and yet not to enjoy   ELIOT 269:20
taught as if you t. them not   POPE 521:23
t.; but first he folwed it   CHAU 193:3
t. them as one having authority   BIBLE 89:28
t. to any purpose who have   REYN 539:4
t. to think that moderation   BURKE 157:8
without ever having been t. anything   MOL 479:9
You t. me first to beg   SHAK 609:22
You t. me language   SHAK 625:7
You've got to be carefully t.   HAMM 323:2
taunting: be grave, and not t.   BACON 43:30
tavern: by a good t. or inn   JOHN 374:10
end my days in a t.   ANON 22:9
opened a t. for his friends   DOUG 255:15
So is the London T.   ANON 13:14
There is a t. in the town   ANON 18:11
tax: Excise. A hateful t.   JOHN 367:25
I t. not you, you elements   SHAK 595:21
To t. and to please   BURKE 157:17
When it doth t. itself   SHAK 606:5
taxation: T. and representation   CAMD 176:2
T. without representation   OTIS 502:7
taxed: world should be t.   BIBLE 93:25
taxes: as true as t. is   DICK 239:33
Death and t. and childbirth   MITC 478:2
except death and t.   FRAN 293:3
people overlaid with t.   BACON 44:34
Read my lips: no new t.   BUSH 165:16
taxi: Like a t. throbbing   ELIOT 273:8
you can't leave in a t.   KALM 385:2
taxi-cab: t. with both doors open   HUGH 353:15
taxing: or less of a t. machine   LOWE 429:11
Tay: Bridge of the Silv'ry T.   MCG 437:17
te: T. Deum laudamus   ANON 22:17
tea: ain't going to be no t.   MANS 445:8
And is there honey still for t.   BROO 143:15
best sweeteners of t.   FIEL 282:7
counsel take and sometimes t.   POPE 523:24
if this is t., then I want coffee   PUNCH 532:8
no Latin word for T.   BELL 62:4
slavery of the t. and coffee   COBB 207:27

TEACH TEMPERANCE

tea: (*cont.*):
some sipping t. WORD 746:13
Take some more t. CARR 182:8
t. and comfortable advice KEATS 391:22
t. and sympathy AND 11:10
t. for two and two for tea CAES 174:13
t. solaces the midnight JOHN 368:18
t.'s out of the way REED 538:7
their t. and scandal CONG 214:23
when I makes t. I makes tea JOYCE 381:20
teach: apt to t. BIBLE 103:26
Even while they t. SEN 562:29
for every person who wants to t. SELL 562:15
he lerne and gladly t. CHAU 192:21
knowledge is the ability to t. AUCT 33:25
May t. you more of man WORD 748:7
She can t. ye how to climb MILT 464:12
suffering what they t. in song SHEL 641:1
t. and delight SIDN 647:7
t. an old horse amble true SPEN 660:9
T. him how to live PORT 525:8
t. his senators wisdom BOOK 132:12
T. me, my God and King HERB 334:16
T. me thy way, O Lord BOOK 125:25
T. me to feel another's woe POPE 523:32
T. me to live, that I may dread KEN 393:8
t. thee in the way BOOK 126:10
T. the free man how to praise AUDEN 34:16
t. them [children] first JOHN 372:15
t. the torches to burn SHAK 622:24
t. the young idea how to THOM 696:2
T. us to care and not to care ELIOT 270:6
t. you to drink deep SHAK 572:15
Those that do t. young babes SHAK 617:19
To t., convince, subdue AUBER 32:20
we but t. bloody instructions SHAK 601:2
years t. much which the days EMER 277:5
teacher: A t. affects eternity ADAMS 2:15
doctrine for the t.'s sake DEFOE 234:15
love the precepts for the t.'s FARQ 280:19
t. should have maximal SZASZ 677:11
teachers: not been their own t. REYN 539:4
rigorous t. seized my youth ARN 28:19
some, pastors and t. BIBLE 102:17
t., spiritual pastors BOOK 123:7
teaches: From all that terror t. CHES 199:3
He who cannot, t. SHAW 637:24
teachest: Thou t. like a fool SHAK 564:23
teaching: t. nations how to live MILT 475:17
twenty to follow mine own t. SHAK 607:12
tea-cup: crack in the t. opens AUDEN 34:4
tea-drinker: hardened and shameless t. JOHN 368:18
tea-girl: t.'s chance to kiss WHIT 731:18
teapot: further than warming the t. MANS 445:8
tear: claims the homage of a t. BYRON 168:7
dropped a t. upon the word STER 665:3
eye the unanswerable t. BYRON 169:22
Forbade the rising t. to flow SCOTT 559:12
for Greece a t. BYRON 171:2
magnificent, without a t. DRYD 261:29
meed of some melodious t. MILT 465:20
No t.-floods, nor sigh DONNE 252:21
of that divine t. HUGO 355:2
shed one English t. MAC 436:7
T. him for his bad verses SHAK 592:22
t. is an intellectual thing BLAKE 112:5
t. our pleasures with rough MARV 451:4
There has fallen a splendid t. TENN 686:20
Thinking every t. a gem SHEL 641:11
To t. each other's eyes WATTS 722:16
Wipe the t., baby dear WEST 729:21
tears: all made of sighs and t. SHAK 569:21
All t. and quarrels were TRAH 701:12
amazed when others' t. CONS 217:20
And foolish t. would flow CLAR 205:6
And keep your t. PUDN 531:5
And kiss again with t. TENN 687:25
And wipe the t. for ever MILT 466:14
big round t. coursed SHAK 567:26
blood, toil, t. and sweat CHUR 202:8
brother's t. have wet CAT 187:1
tears: (*cont.*):
cheeks with artificial t. SHAK 588:3
Come back in t. ROSS 547:3
Drop, drop, slow t. FLET 287:24
drop t. as fast as the Arabian SHAK 618:20
edifice on its unavenged t. DOST 254:6
ever scare me with thy t. TENN 689:11
foolish t. upon my grave TENN 680:16
For frequent t. have run BROW 147:19
fountains fraught with t. KYD 404:11
have I drunk of Siren t. SHAK 634:25
Hence those t. TER 690:9
her t. to pearl he turned MARL 447:11
hired t. they solemnized BROW 145:15
His big t., for he wept SHEL 641:11
If you have t., prepare SHAK 592:13
iron t. down Pluto's cheek MILT 464:23
keep time with my salt t. JONS 378:14
Like Niobe, all t. SHAK 572:12
loosed our heart in t. ARN 27:13
Lord God will wipe away t. BIBLE 83:9
match with shedding t. SHAK 620:13
Mine eyes are full of t. SHAK 621:1
mine eyes from t. BOOK 133:12
mine own t. do scald like SHAK 597:13
mist of t. THOM 695:1
natural t. they dropped MILT 473:14
news to hear and bitter t. CORY 219:15
No t. in the writer FROST 295:15
Nothing is here for t. MILT 474:18
now am full of t. YEATS 751:12
often lie too deep for t. WORD 746:7
put my t. into thy bottle BOOK 128:13
resolves the moon into salt t. SHAK 626:17
sacrifice, and parents' t. MILT 468:16
See sin, but through my t. FLET 287:25
shall wipe away all t. BIBLE 106:23
shall wipe away all t. BIBLE 107:18
shall ye forget your t. MORR 485:10
sheddeth tender t. SPEN 659:27
shed t. when they would devour BACON 45:8
sink'st in thine own t. DEKK 235:16
Smiling through her t. HOMER 343:6
sow in t. BOOK 134:5
summer tempest came her t. TENN 688:10
T. and smiles like us he knew ALEX 8:14
t. distilling from mine DRAY 257:20
t. fell with the dews TENN 686:6
t. I cannot hide HARB 323:9
T., idle tears, I know TENN 688:3
T. in his eyes, distraction SHAK 575:8
t. I wash away my balm SHAK 620:22
t. live in an onion SHAK 564:21
t. out the heart of it KNOW 403:2
t. shall drown the wind SHAK 601:3
t. shed for things even VIRG 712:9
t. unseen and unknown GOGOL 310:1
t. wash out a word of it FITZ 284:9
that dip their wings in t. TENN 683:15
therefore I forbid my t. SHAK 578:14
Time with a gift of t. SWIN 675:24
To hazards whence no t. HARDY 325:13
To remember with t. ALL 10:2
view the world as a vale of t. BROW 149:8
watered heaven with their t. BLAKE 114:15
water my couch with my t. BOOK 124:18
weeping in this vale of t. ANON 22:14
With silence and t. BYRON 173:21
with t. unto the core KEATS 388:3
with the salt of broken t. SHAK 628:1
tease: dost t. us out of thought KEATS 389:2
t. in the High Pyrenees BELL 62:1
teases: Because he knows it t. CARR 182:5
tea-shops: Emperor in the low-class t. BRAM 139:13
tea-tray: colour that of a t. painter BLUNT 116:6
Like a t. in the sky CARR 182:7
Technik: *Vorsprung durch T.* ANON 21:12
technology: beyond the province of t. POPP 524:14
Progress through t. ANON 21:12
T. . . . the knack of so arranging FRIS 294:4
tecum: *T. habita* PERS 513:6
t. possum vivere nec sine MART 449:16
tedding: t. and the spreading BELL 62:1
teddy: T. Bears have their Picnic BRAT 140:1
tedious: as t. as a tired horse SHAK 581:7
Continual eloquence is t. PASC 507:19
more t. than the dial eight SHAK 617:5
t. and brief SHAK 612:19
t. as a twice-told tale SHAK 594:5
tedium: t. is the very basis HUGO 355:1
teeming: gleaned my t. brain KEATS 390:28
teems: t. with hidden meaning GILB 306:19
teeth: about him is his front t. RUNY 550:3
And keep their t. clean SHAK 570:8
barrier of your t. HOMER 343:3
children's t. are set on edge BIBLE 85:22
Ears like bombs and t. like CAUS 187:3
happily strike out his t. RAL 536:5
lose our t. and eyelashes LEAR 414:20
old bitch gone in the t. POUND 527:3
our graves with our t. SMIL 650:7
set my t. nothing on edge SHAK 581:5
shark has pretty t. BREC 140:3
t. are like a flock of sheep BIBLE 81:13
thy t. able it to break BARC 52:9
To cast into my t. SHAK 593:8
trouble me cast me in the t. BOOK 127:5
untying with the t. BIER 109:6
weeping and gnashing of t. BIBLE 89:32
which makes my t. watter FLEM 287:3
whose t. are spears BOOK 128:15
will steal the very t. ARAB 24:4
with the skin of my t. BIBLE 77:24
teetotaller: I'm only a beer t. SHAW 636:4
t. and often with vegetarian ORW 500:21
woman should marry a t. STEV 668:3
tekel: T.; Thou art weighed BIBLE 85:31
telegrams: life of t. and anger FORS 290:13
Telemachus: mine own T. TENN 690:3
television: Radio and t. SARR 556:5
see bad t. for nothing GOLD 312:7
T. has brought back murder HITC 339:9
tell: Go, t. the Spartans SIM 647:21
I'll t. thee everything I can CARR 183:21
poem itself to t. how it can FROST 295:14
sight to dream of, not to t. COL 209:9
t. her she mustn't PUNCH 531:20
T. it not in Gath BIBLE 75:8
T. me all JOYCE 381:3
T. me not, Sweet, I am unkind LOV 429:6
Tell me, t. me, tell me JOYCE 381:4
T. me the old, old story HANK 323:6
T. me what you eat BRIL 141:14
T. out my soul BIBLE 93:22
t. sad stories of the death SHAK 620:8
T. them, because our fathers KIPL 398:16
T. them I came, and no one DE L 236:7
t. them of us and say EDM 267:1
t. the most heart-easing KEATS 390:13
t. the towers thereof BOOK 127:23
those who cannot t. RAL 536:10
telleth: One day t. another BOOK 125:4
t. the number of the stars BOOK 135:11
telling: A pity beyond all t. YEATS 752:18
arguing with you—I am t. you WHIS 730:16
I shall be t. this with a sigh FROST 295:9
Téméraire: Fighting T. NEWB 492:8
temper: Keep me in t. SHAK 595:11
lose your t. with the Press PANK 505:17
One equal t. of heroic hearts TENN 690:4
only keep your t. STER 664:13
t. justice with mercy MILT 473:3
t. never mellows with age IRV 360:15
t. that if I were under water KEATS 391:19
t. till it would be dethrimental O'CAS 497:19
truth that has lost its t. GIBR 303:4
temperament: disqualified them was t. BENN 63:4
temperance: beget a t. SHAK 576:5
But what availed this t. MILT 474:8
Meekness, t. BIBLE 102:7
t. would be difficult JOHN 377:10

temperate: amazèd, t., and furious
                          SHAK 602:18
  In t. heat, where   SURR 672:4
  more lovely and more t.   SHAK 633:6
  reason firm, the t. will   WORD 747:19
  t. affords me none   CAREW 179:9
temperature: pleasant t.   HESSE 337:16
  t. not naturally its own   SCH 558:12
tempered: t. by war, disciplined by
                          KENN 393:12
tempest: covert from the t.   BIBLE 83:17
  Dark lowers the t. overhead LONG 426:19
  lightning and t.   BOOK 119:17
  Like summer t. came her tears TENN 688:10
  that silence we the t. fear DRYD 260:4
  While the t. still is high WESL 728:6
tempestas: me cumque rapit t. HOR 347:20
tempests: nor sigh-t. move DONNE 252:21
  On whom Thy t. fell all night HERB 335:3
  t. and is never shaken   SHAK 634:23
tempest-tost: Yet it shall be t. SHAK 600:2
tempestuous: O'er the world's t. sea
                          EDM 266:17
temple: all out of the t.   BIBLE 96:12
  Ay, in the very t. of Delight KEATS 389:7
  his train filled the t.   BIBLE 82:19
  Lord's anointed t.   SHAK 602:14
  nature is a t.   BAUD 55:8
  Open the t. gates unto my love SPEN 659:15
  polished corners of the t. BOOK 135:4
  t. of silence and reconciliation MAC 435:11
  t. of the Holy Ghost   BIBLE 100:23
temples: And the t. of his Gods MAC 436:10
  not in t. made with hands BIBLE 98:32
  out of which they build t. KRIS 404:2
  Shall now my joyful t. bind WALL 718:14
  smote the nail into his t. BIBLE 74:1
  solemn t., the great globe SHAK 625:28
  theatres, and t. lie   WORD 743:9
  thy t. are like a piece   BIBLE 81:13
  tous les t. de la terre   DID 245:13
tempora: O t., O mores!   CIC 204:6
  T. mutantur, et nos mutamur ANON 22:19
temporal: pass through things t. BOOK 121:2
temporary: force alone is but t. BURKE 157:21
temps: la recherche du t. perdu PROU 530:5
  Ô t.! suspend ton vol   LAM 406:1
tempt: not t. the Lord thy God BIBLE 88:19
  shall t. with wandering feet MILT 469:20
  T. me no more   DAY-L 233:5
  T. not a desperate man   SHAK 624:5
  T. not the stars   FORD 289:7
temptation: combines maximum of t.
                          SHAW 637:25
  comes t. but for man to meet BROW 152:21
  insist on their resisting t. KNOX 403:16
  lead us not into t.   BIBLE 89:5
  man that endureth t.   BIBLE 104:25
  oughtn't to yield to t.   HOPE 344:22
  out of the power of t.   TROL 704:6
  over-fond of resisting t. BECK 58:5
  resist everything except t. WILDE 735:8
  t. in the wilderness   BOOK 131:10
  t. is the greatest treason ELIOT 272:10
  t. that you have not yet LEWIS 420:15
  t. to a rich and lazy nation KIPL 401:8
  that ye enter not into t. BIBLE 92:30
  to get the better of t.   GRAH 313:6
  under t. to it   LOCKE 425:2
  Unmovèd, cold, and to t. slow SHAK 634:14
  Ye're aiblins nae t.   BURNS 161:1
temptations: But in spite of all t. GILB 306:5
  carry us through all t.   BOOK 120:14
  protections against t.   TWAIN 706:10
  t. both in wine and women KITC 402:17
tempted: fathers t. me   BOOK 131:10
  tempter or the t.   SHAK 606:2
  'Tis one thing to be t.   SHAK 605:12
tempter: t. or the tempted SHAK 606:2
tempus: fugit inreparabile t. VIRG 715:17
  T. abire tibi est   HOR 348:21
  T. edax rerum   OVID 503:1

tempus: (cont.):
  T. erat quo prima quies VIRG 712:17
ten: Church clock at t. to three BROO 143:15
  only t. or twelve strokes HOPK 345:5
  T. Commandments an' a man KIPL 400:3
  T. days that shook the world REED 538:11
  t. men who haven't and don't SHAW 635:20
  t. thousands in our streets BOOK 135:5
  t. thousand times   BIBLE 86:1
tenacem: Iustum et t. propositi HOR 350:1
tenantless: graves stood t. SHAK 571:26
tenants: T. of life's middle state COWP 224:12
  T. of the house   ELIOT 271:12
tendebantque: T. manus ripae VIRG 713:15
tendency: Groucho t.   ANON 20:13
tender: coy and t. to offend HERB 336:23
  His t. last farewell   AUBER 32:20
  I'll be irreproachably t. MAY 454:17
  t. for another's pain   GRAY 316:3
  t. is the night   KEATS 389:11
  t. mercies   BIBLE 78:25
  t. years of youth   GOGOL 309:21
  that are t. and unpleasing BACON 43:5
  true and t. is the North TENN 688:6
tenderly: Take her up t.   HOOD 343:15
tenderness: spiritual species of t. BYRON 173:24
  Thanks to its t., its joys WORD 746:7
  Want of t., he always alleged JOHN 373:9
tendrils: limp and damp, as t. ROET 544:5
tends: he t. and spares us LYTE 433:17
ténébreux: Je suis le t.   NERV 492:2
tenement: Into a clayey t. CAREW 179:5
  Like to a t. or pelting farm SHAK 619:18
  o'er informed the t. of clay DRYD 259:1
  t. dweller's subconscious MCAR 434:1
tener: son el t. y el no tener CERV 188:13
Tennessee: I placed a jar in T. STEV 665:14
tennis: t. with the net down FROST 295:17
tennis-balls: merely the stars' t. WEBS 725:25
Tennyson: bower we shrined to T.
                          HARDY 325:1
  Lawn T.   JOYCE 381:23
  T. and Browning   BAG 47:15
  T. was not Tennysonian JAMES 363:2
Tennysonianness: no T. of speech
                          POUND 528:1
tenor: noiseless t. of their way GRAY 315:17
tent: inside the t. pissing out JOHN 367:12
  Upon that little t. of blue WILDE 735:34
tenth: Submerged T.   BOOTH 136:5
  talked shop like a t. muse ANON 14:8
tents: among the t. of Kedar BOOK 133:21
  Israel's t. do shine so bright BLAKE 113:6
  lead you to the stately t. MARL 447:19
  man to dwell in their t. BOOK 129:13
  murmured in their t.   BOOK 132:13
  plain man, dwelling in t. BIBLE 71:8
  Shall fold their t.   LONG 426:14
  t. of Kedar   BIBLE 81:6
  t. of ungodliness   BOOK 130:18
  To your t., O Israel   BIBLE 75:29
tepores: ver egelidos refert t. CAT 186:5
ter: T. sunt conati imponere VIRG 715:12
teres: t., atque rotundus HOR 351:11
term: sleep between term and t. SHAK 569:9
  mere t. invented to awe fools JONS 379:11
  t. of moderation takes BACON 42:13
  When I was a lad I served a t. GILB 305:26
termagant: whipped for o'erdoing T.
                          SHAK 576:5
terminations: terrible as her t. SHAK 613:17
termini: t. which bound the common
  of silence   EMER 276:21
terminological: t. inexactitude CHUR 201:23
terms: gild it with the happiest t. SHAK 582:10
  hard to come to t. with Him MOL 479:12
  make t. with the earth   ALAI 7:6
  T. like grace, new birth ARN 30:1
  wait till I come on perfect t. WHIT 732:20
terra: et in t. pax hominibus MISS 476:18
terrace: t. walk, and half a rood SWIFT 674:25
terraces: Belvoir's lordly t. MAC 436:2
terrible: appear most long and t. LEE 416:1

terrible: (cont.):
  being just the t. choice BROW 152:22
  his eyes became so t.   BECK 58:3
  isn't life a t. thing   THOM 693:20
  I the elder and more t. SHAK 591:6
  It would not be t.   JOHN 372:21
  my name were not so t. SHAK 582:24
  mysterious as well as t. DOST 254:3
  our t. notions of duty   CLOU 207:2
  ten Furies, t. as hell   MILT 470:5
  t. as an army   BIBLE 81:21
  t. as her terminations SHAK 613:17
  t. beauty is born   YEATS 751:15
  t. events are welcome SHAK 566:11
  T. that old life of decency LOW 430:10
  T. Vaudeville   ACE 1:5
  that t. football club   MCGR 438:4
  Then lend the eye a t. aspect SHAK 585:7
  Which make thee t. and dear SHEL 643:22
terrified: t. vague fingers YEATS 752:10
territorial: last t. claim   HITL 339:12
territory: It comes with the t. MILL 461:17
  more than the t. is worth MAC 435:8
terror: added a new t. to death WETH 729:22
  added another t. to death LYND 433:14
  adds a new t. to life   TREE 702:7
  afraid for any t. by night BOOK 131:3
  children's sight for t.   SHAK 605:7
  dukes are just as great a t. LLOY 424:5
  From all that t. teaches CHES 199:3
  make thee a t. to thyself BIBLE 85:14
  nothing disturbed the even t. SHAR 635:18
  t. in death that I should fear ELIZ 274:2
  T. is the feeling   JOYCE 381:12
  T. the human form divine BLAKE 114:16
  t. to the soul of Richard SHAK 622:13
  Their perch and not their t. SHAK 605:11
  There is no t., brother STER 665:1
  There is no t., Cassius SHAK 593:5
  Thy t., O Christ, O God HOPK 346:12
terrorist: t. and the hijacker THAT 691:23
  t. and the policeman both CONR 217:12
terrors: new t. of Death   ARB 24:10
  t. of the earth   SHAK 595:18
Tess: ended his sport with T. HARDY 324:18
test: Beauty is the first t. HARDY 324:4
testament: Have you your t. BEHAN 60:3
  ministers of the new t. BIBLE 101:16
  purple t. of bleeding war SHAK 620:10
testicles: tragedy requires t. VOLT 717:2
testify: they are which t. of me BIBLE 96:21
testimonies: Thy t., O Lord BOOK 131:7
testimony: our t. to the whole world FOX 292:5
  t. of the Lord   BOOK 125:5
testing: virtue at the t. point LEWIS 420:17
tetigisti: T. acu   PLAU 517:5
teutonophile: when not exaggeratedly t.
                          LAMB 407:15
Tewkesbury: Between T. and Stroudway
                          GURN 320:2
text: approve it with a t. SHAK 608:26
  God takes a t., and preacheth HERB 334:10
  great t. in Galatians   BROW 152:28
  t. that looks a little   TENN 682:15
  that t. a pulled hen   CHAU 192:17
  where a neat rivulet of t. SHER 645:13
texture: question of t.   DRAB 257:7
Thackeray: T. settled like a meat-fly
                          RUSK 550:9
Thames: flights upon the banks of T.
                          JONS 380:5
  Not of Gennesareth, but T. THOM 695:10
  Of the riding T.   THOM 693:14
  Oh shall I see the T. again BETJ 67:10
  stripling T. at Bab-lock-hithe ARN 28:5
  Sweet T., run softly   SPEN 660:24
  T. bordered by its gardens MORR 485:12
  T. is between me   WALP 719:4
  T. is liquid history   BURNS 160:22
  T. see Eton's sons   POPE 518:22
  T., the most loved of all DENH 236:16
  T. was the noblest river ADD 4:15
  With no allaying T.   LOV 429:2

Thames: (cont.):
youthful T.   ARN 28:24
thank: And t. heaven, fasting   SHAK 569:13
I t. thee, that I am not   BIBLE 95:14
I t. the goodness and the grace   TAYL 679:11
Now t. we all our God   WINK 739:6
T. me no thankings   SHAK 623:25
thanked: When I'm not t. at all   FIEL 282:17
thankful: pleasant thing to be t.   BOOK 135:11
thankfulness: name in pride and t.   BROW 150:19
thankless: To have a t. child   SHAK 595:10
Upon a t. arrant   RAL 535:15
thanks: And to give t. is good   SWIN 676:5
Catullus gives you warmest t.   CAT 186:6
give t. unto thee   BOOK 122:10
How to return your t. would   BROW 153:18
In everything give t.   BIBLE 103:22
O give t. unto the Lord   BOOK 134:16
song of t. and praise   WORD 746:3
Take the t. of a boy   BEEC 59:6
T. for mercies past receive   BUCK 154:12
T. for the memory   ROBIN 542:8
t. to God always for you   BIBLE 103:19
T. to the human heart   WORD 746:7
upon the harp will I give t.   BOOK 127:7
wanting to deserve any t.   CAT 186:11
when he had given t.   BOOK 122:12
will give t. unto thee   BOOK 134:20
thanksgiving: presence with t.   BOOK 131:9
shew the voice of t.   BOOK 125:22
Tharsis: Kings of T. and of   BOOK 129:20
thatch: Weeded and worn the ancient t.   TENN 686:6
thatch-eaves: vines that round the t.   KEATS 390:17
thawed: t. from the true quality   SHAK 591:11
thawing: T. cold fear   SHAK 585:16
thcream: t. and thcream and thcream   CROM 227:4
theatre: As in a t., the eyes   SHAK 621:7
during an evening in the t.   TYNAN 706:30
keep the t. packed   BOIL 117:4
like the t., but never come late   HART 327:12
t. of man's life   BACON 42:6
t. where no-one is allowed   MILL 461:22
theatres: t., and temples lie   WORD 743:9
thee: Dreamin' of t.!   WALL 718:2
queer save t. and me   OWEN 503:9
theek: t. our nest when it grows   BALL 50:20
theft: clever t. was praiseworthy   SPEN 658:20
Property is t.   PROU 530:4
suspicious head of t. is stopped   SHAK 598:20
t. from those who hunger   EIS 268:10
would be t. in other poets   DRYD 262:12
theist: t. the same comfort   AYER 40:14
them: Let t. say   KEITH 393:1
T. that's got shall get   HOL 342:1
theme: Fools are my t.   BYRON 172:3
glad diviner's t.   DRYD 259:4
himself the poet and the t.   COWP 224:14
It was a t. for reason   DONNE 251:22
Or else the t. too high doth   GURN 320:3
pudding — it has no t.   CHUR 203:12
themes: transcend our wonted t.   VAUG 709:8
themselves: A law unto t.   BIBLE 99:19
laid violent hands upon t.   BOOK 124:2
they did not do things t.   RAV 537:4
theologians: if you believe the t.   SAL 554:2
t. have employed as if   ARN 30:1
theology: t. and all the temples   DID 245:13
t. as well as in arithmetic   MILT 475:10
theorem: About binomial t.   GILB 306:10
theories: And 't.' and 'goals'   KIPL 399:12
false t. die in our stead   POPP 524:16
theorize: mistake to t. before   DOYLE 256:22
theory: All t., dear friend   GOET 309:5
It is sometimes t.   MAC 435:23
pleasure lies in the t.   WHITE 731:6
that is life without t.   DISR 248:10
t. is found to be against   EDD 266:3
t. of poetry is the t. of life   STEV 666:6
t. of relativity is proven   EINS 268:3

there: Because it's t.   MALL 443:2
be t. when it happens   ALLEN 9:15
heaven, thou art t.   BOOK 134:19
I met a man who wasn't t.   MEAR 456:1
that cry over me, T., there   BOOK 129:15
T. but for the grace of God   BRAD 139:2
T. go the ships   BOOK 132:9
t. vor me the apple tree   BARN 53:13
t. when they crucified   ANON 19:9
thereby: O! t. hangs a tail   SHAK 616:9
therein: and all that t. is   BOOK 125:16
thereout: t. suck they no small   BOOK 130:1
thereto: t. I give thee my troth   BOOK 123:20
thermodynamics: against the second law of t.   EDD 266:3
Thersites: T.'s body is as good as Ajax   SHAK 571:15
they: t. are not they   WAUGH 723:8
thick: As t. and numberless   MILT 464:14
dashed through t. and thin   DRYD 259:14
shall stand so t. with corn   BOOK 129:3
thcream till I'm t.   CROM 227:4
t. and exactly in the right   BUTL 166:26
t. on Severn snow the leaves   HOUS 352:12
thickens: now the plot t.   BUCK 154:10
thicker: History gets t. as it approaches   TAYL 679:5
little finger shall be t.   BIBLE 75:27
thicket: ram caught in a t.   BIBLE 71:6
thief: Behold, I come as a t.   BIBLE 107:7
embrace the impenitent t.   STEV 667:16
first cries out stop t.   CONG 215:10
grand t. into God's fold   MILT 471:1
honest t., the tender murderer   BROW 148:13
if you do take a t.   SHAK 614:3
justice, which is the t.?   SHAK 597:6
man's apparel fits your t.   SHAK 606:19
Opportunity makes a t.   BACON 45:13
Pleasure is a t. to business   DEFOE 233:16
Procrastination is the t. of time   YOUNG 754:16
She was a strumpet, he was a t.   HEINE 331:1
steals something from the t.   SHAK 615:5
sun's a t.   SHAK 626:17
t. doth fear each bush   SHAK 588:7
t. or swindler who has gained   VERI 709:16
thought as bad as the t.   CHES 198:1
time the subtle t. of youth   MILT 474:21
thievery: Crams his rich t. up   SHAK 628:1
thieves: fell among t.   BIBLE 94:13
'Gainst knaves and t.   SHAK 630:37
have made it a den of t.   BIBLE 91:30
Her t. are never hung   FERG 281:11
One of the t. was saved   BECK 57:20
T. respect property   CHES 199:17
t. who have their hands   BIER 109:3
Thou best of t.   DRYD 260:2
where t. break through   BIBLE 89:6
thievish: Time's t. progress   SHAK 634:8
thigh: on his t. a name written   BIBLE 107:13
smote them hip and t.   BIBLE 74:16
While the bee with honied t.   MILT 464:25
thighs: glory from her loosening t.   YEATS 752:10
thimbles: sought it with t.   CARR 184:5
thin: My heart had shrunk as t.   HARDY 325:9
t. ears devoured the seven   BIBLE 71:26
t. man inside every fat   ORW 499:23
t. one is wildly signalling   CONN 216:17
T. red line of 'eroes   KIPL 401:5
t. red line tipped   RUSS 552:5
those pale and t. ones   PLUT 517:16
tho' t., yet never clear   POPE 518:21
thine: continue t. for ever   BOOK 123:13
For t. is the kingdom   BIBLE 89:5
not my will, but t.   BIBLE 95:22
Why not I with t.   SHEL 641:9
thing: do only one t. at a time   SMIL 650:11
do t. that ends all other   SHAK 566:19
firm persuasion that a t. is so   BLAKE 113:1
is it not the t.   BYRON 174:6
love only means one t.   BENN 63:16

thing: (cont.):
machine, a t. with one face   MACN 441:1
most unattractive old t.   GILB 305:10
National Debt a Good T.   SELL 562:17
only t. we have to fear   ROOS 545:16
play's the t.   SHAK 575:14
Simply the t. I am   SHAK 564:9
sort of t. they like   LINC 422:16
that if a t. is worth doing   CHES 199:24
T. as he sees It   KIPL 401:9
t. enskyed and sainted   SHAK 605:8
t. of beauty is a joy for ever   KEATS 386:13
t. they most do show   SHAK 634:14
t. we have prayed   BROW 147:3
thingish: thing which seemed T.   MILNE 462:11
things: And t. are not what they seem   LONG 427:7
as t. have been, things remain   CLOU 207:23
bright t. come to confusion   SHAK 610:23
confused t. with their names   SART 556:13
deeds are concerned with t.   AUDEN 36:16
done but earnest of the t.   TENN 685:13
excellent t. are spoken   BOOK 130:21
God's sons are t.   MADD 441:14
I am made all t. to all men   BIBLE 100:29
I mean for t. they didn't know   POUND 526:9
infection of t. gone   LOW 430:23
It means twenty t.   BENN 63:16
more t. in heaven and earth   SHAK 574:4
O all ye Green T. upon   BOOK 118:20
Of t. to come at large   SHAK 627:11
people don't do such t.   IBSEN 359:5
present, nor t. to come   BIBLE 100:1
shape of t. to come   WELLS 727:22
So little done, such t. to be   TENN 683:26
there are tears shed for t.   VIRG 712:9
These t. shall be!   SYM 677:6
T. ain't what they used   PERS 513:8
T. are in the saddle   EMER 276:9
T. are seldom what they seem   GILB 306:3
t. are the sons of heaven   JOHN 367:20
t. are wrought by prayer   TENN 682:24
T. fall apart   YEATS 753:1
t. people make fools   SHAW 636:2
t. that are not   SHAK 593:18
t. through Christ   BIBLE 103:14
t. unknown proposed   POPE 521:23
t. which belong unto thy   BIBLE 95:18
what T. think about men   JENN 365:6
think: above all that we ask or t.   BIBLE 102:15
All t. what other people think   YEATS 752:23
always talk, never t.   PRIOR 529:16
And t. by fits and starts   HOUS 351:19
And t., this heart   BROO 143:18
because I have time to t.   DARW 231:14
Before him I may t. aloud   EMER 276:24
But don't t. twice   DYLAN 265:13
But I can't t. for you   DYLAN 265:24
comedy to those that t.   WALP 719:18
commonly attains to t. right   JOHN 368:19
don't t. foolishly   JOHN 376:8
easier to act than to t.   AREN 24:17
fellows whom it hurts to t.   HOUS 352:19
For those who greatly t.   POPE 519:16
Haply I t. on thee   SHAK 633:10
He can't t. without his hat   BECK 57:23
In all I t. or speak or do   WESL 728:10
I never expect a soldier to t.   SHAW 636:7
I paint objects as I t.   PIC 514:3
I t., therefore I am   DESC 237:18
know what I t. till I see   WALL 718:7
money, so we've got to t.   RUTH 552:7
not whether machines t.   SKIN 649:5
open my legs and t. of England   HILL 339:3
or read, or t., or to enquire   WINC 739:1
people that t., and fox-hunters   SHEN 644:16
something with them besides t.   LOOS 428:8
so t. as you drunk I am   SQUI 661:17
then I don't t. much   STR 670:21
think alike who t. at all   PAINE 505:2
t. as wise men do   ASCH 31:3
T. before you speak   FORS 290:28
t. for two minutes together   SMITH 653:1

think: (cont.):
t. him so, because I t. him	SHAK 631:2
t. is to be full of sorrow	KEATS 389:10
T. like a wise man but express	YEATS 753:24
t. like other people	SHEL 639:9
t. now before	DONNE 251:6
T. of your forefathers	ADAMS 3:5
t. only this of me	BROO 143:18
T. only what concerns thee	MILT 472:12
t. on these things	BIBLE 103:13
t. perhaps even less	BROW 148:14
t. too little and the old	WALP 719:13
t. too little and who talk	DRYD 259:7
t. up to the height	CHES 199:22
t. what is true and do	HUXL 358:5
t. what you like and say	TAC 678:2
t. ye have eternal life	BIBLE 96:21
time we t. we're sick	WOLFE 741:4
when I t., I must speak	SHAK 569:6
will make you t. again	PERRY 513:2
you can't make her t.	PARK 506:20

thinking: All t. for themselves
as well as an art of t.	GILB 304:12
columnists say 'Every t. man'	D'ISR 249:17
	ADAMS 2:3
dignity of t.	JOHN 368:14
he is a t. reed	PASC 507:18
ideas rather than with t.	TRIL 702:18
It ain't t. about it	TROL 703:18
life in t. to be spent	VAUX 709:14
lateral t.	DE B 233:11
modes of t. are different	JOHN 375:28
much drinking, little t.	SWIFT 673:21
pipe a simple song for t.	WORD 744:8
Plain living and high t.	WORD 746:10
power of positive t.	PEALE 510:13
prevent myself from t.	SART 557:1
She's been t. of the old 'un	DICK 239:22
t. and we thus drift toward	EINS 268:4
T. is to me the greatest	VANB 708:5
t. makes it so	SHAK 574:26
t. man's crumpet	MUIR 487:14
t. what a Rum Go everything	WELLS 727:18
t. what nobody has thought	SZEN 677:18
this gentleman's way of t.	ANON 22:9
thought is the pleasure of t.	CLOU 207:13
thought of t. for myself	GILB 306:1

thinks: he t. no ill
He t. too much	SHAK 633:19
Sometimes I sits and t.	SHAK 590:6
unhappy as one t.	PUNCH 532:9
Whether he t. too little	LA R 410:23
	POPE 522:9

thinner: And t., clearer, farther
keep on growing t.	TENN 688:1
	LEAR 414:20

third: Close encounters of the t. kind
passing of the t. floor back	SPIE 661:1
separately plunder a t.	JER 365:14
t. day he rose again	BIER 109:3
t. who walks always beside	BOOK 119:1
with a shadowy t.	ELIOT 273:12
	BROW 148:26

third-rate: t. foreign conductors
	BEEC 59:1

thirst: an' a man can raise a t.
believeth on me shall never t.	KIPL 400:3
I t.	BIBLE 96:25
My soul is a t. for God	BIBLE 97:28
neither t. any more	BOOK 127:2
t. after righteousness	BIBLE 106:22
t., forced marches	BIBLE 88:23
T. of wealth no quiet knows	GAR 298:1
without the provocation of t.	WINC 738:23
	SWIFT 673:16

thirsteth: every one that t.
My soul t. for thee	BIBLE 84:15
	BOOK 128:21

thirsty: As cold waters to a t. soul
if he be t., give	BIBLE 79:19
I was t. and ye gave me	BIBLE 79:18
t. they gave me vinegar	BIBLE 92:20
	BOOK 129:12

thirteen: clocks were striking t.
	ORW 500:8

thirtieth: my t. year to heaven
	THOM 693:12

thirty: at t., the wit
I am past t., and three parts	FRAN 292:16
t. a man suspects himself	ARN 29:26
T. days hath September	YOUNG 754:17
t. pieces of silver	ANON 18:17
t. pieces of silver	BEVAN 69:5
	BIBLE 92:23

thirty-five: remained t. for years WILDE 734:20
thirty-one: Days and nights hast t.
	SHAK 603:17

this: T. happy breed of men
T. was a man	SHAK 619:18
	SHAK 593:23

thistles: thorns, or figs of t.
	BIBLE 89:24

thither: For t. the tribes go up
	BOOK 133:25

Thomas: ta'en true T. up
T., because thou hast seen	BALL 50:15
T. says good-night to Lady	BIBLE 97:38
	LAWR 412:1

thorn: ah! he left the t. wi' me
Have I no harvest but a t.	BURNS 161:11
her breast against a t.	HERB 334:11
rid of one t. out of many	HOOD 344:4
rose without the t.	HOR 348:21
Than Oak, and Ash, and T.	HERR 336:24
t. in the flesh	KIPL 400:10
t. shall come up the fir	BIBLE 102:2
without t. the rose	BIBLE 84:18
	MILT 471:3

thorns: And some fell among t.
crackling of t. under a pot	BIBLE 91:1
crown of t. and the thirty	BIBLE 80:11
fall upon the t. of life	BEVAN 69:5
labour this crown of t.	SHEL 641:18
men gather grapes of t.	BRYAN 153:24
t. shall come up in her	BIBLE 89:24
	BIBLE 83:18

thorny: life is t.; and youth is vain COL 209:10
your road's a t. way	CARB 178:17

thoroughfare: t. for all thoughts KEATS 392:12
thou: T. a person becomes I
t. art not he or she	BUBER 153:25
T. art the man	WAUGH 723:8
T. shalt have no other	BIBLE 75:12
T. swell! Thou witty	BIBLE 72:16
	HART 327:15

thought: beautiful clean t.
Beyond the last t.	LAWR 412:10
But a white, celestial t.	STEV 666:4
but he t. another	VAUG 709:1
But teach high t., and amiable	CHAU 193:16
By t. supplied	TENN 681:25
called the garment of t.	WORD 744:21
carry all that t.	CARL 181:7
constitution of their modes of t.	HUNT 356:13
could divine his real t.	MILL 460:8
delight of her t.	BYRON 170:28
dost tease us out of t.	ROET 544:5
ears, and ev'ry t.	KEATS 389:2
enemy of t. and the friend	ROYD 549:15
Expression is the dress of t.	CONR 217:10
father, Harry, to that t.	POPE 521:12
Grave without t., and without	SHAK 584:3
green t. in a green shade	CHUR 201:6
have loved, to have t.	MARV 450:11
heart that thought the t.	ARN 27:3
he went, for want of t.	BALL 49:13
In all the magnanimity of t.	DRYD 260:12
inextinguishable t.	YOUNG 754:7
In the light of t.	SHEL 644:6
I thought he t. I slept	SHEL 643:17
I t. so once	PATM 509:12
Language is the dress of t.	GAY 300:11
library is t. in cold storage	JOHN 368:24
lived with no other t.	SAM 554:17
My t. is me	POE 517:17
never t. of thinking	SART 557:1
never t. upon the subject	GILB 306:1
not seem a moment's t.	JOHN 373:5
One single grateful t.	YEATS 750:16
One t., one grace, one wonder	LESS 419:13
passion-wingèd Ministers of t.	MARL 448:3
Perish the t.	SHEL 639:14
rear the tender t.	CIBB 203:21
Religion is the frozen t.	THOM 696:2
results of t. and resolution	KRIS 404:2
Rhythm in all t.	TROL 704:6
Roman t. hath struck him	COL 209:19
sessions of sweet silent t.	SHAK 564:16
sinned exceedingly in t.	SHAK 633:11
speech created t.	MISS 476:16
splendour of a sudden t.	SHEL 642:16
Style is the dress of t.	BROW 149:10
that harbours virtuous t.	WESL 729:5
	SPEN 659:26

thought: (cont.):
That tremble into t.	COL 209:20
therefore no t. for the morrow	BIBLE 89:13
t. can add one cubit unto	BIBLE 89:10
T. can with difficulty visit	SHEL 644:11
t. charged with emotion	GIDE 303:8
T. does not crush to stone	ROET 544:2
t.-executing	SHAK 595:20
T. is free	SHAK 625:24
T. is the child of Action	DISR 248:34
t. is unhappy until	GALS 297:6
T. leapt out to wed	TENN 683:10
t. may grace them more	SOUT 657:24
t. more steady	FORD 289:15
t. of hath worn the crown	BIBLE 87:17
t. of you with kindness	PEAC 510:12
t. only to justify	VOLT 716:5
T. shall be the harder	ANON 18:20
t.'s the slave of life	SHAK 582:6
t. surpass eating and drinking	CLOU 207:13
t. we were done with these	BENÉT 62:17
t. which saddens while	BROW 151:25
through strange seas of T.	WORD 747:2
troubled seas of t.	BRYAN 153:24
unmeaning thing they call a t.	POPE 521:15
utmost bound of human t.	TENN 690:2
utterance gave that t. relief	WORD 745:11
very life-blood of t.	FLAU 286:2
what he t., he uttered	HEMI 331:13
What oft was t., but ne'er	POPE 521:11
with the pale cast of t.	SHAK 575:16
words are slippery and t.	ADAMS 2:24
working-house of t.	SHAK 586:13
wrought by want of t.	HOOD 343:23
years of human t. too late	LA BR 405:4
you sit alone with your t.	BOND 117:17

thoughtcrime: t. impossible ORW 500:12
thoughts: All t., all passions COL 210:15
amongst t. are like bats	BACON 44:31
And my sad t. doth clear	VAUG 709:5
As man's own t.	WEBS 726:11
Cleanse the t. of our	BOOK 121:16
Even so my bloody t.	SHAK 616:23
examine my t.	BOOK 134:22
familiar to my slaughterous t.	SHAK 604:24
found in the t. of children	LOCKE 424:16
furrow, as thy t. in me	TENN 688:13
generate misleading t.	SPEN 658:18
Give thy t. no tongue	SHAK 573:3
Good t. his only friends	CAMP 177:7
Gored mine own t.	SHAK 634:21
ground with cheerful t.	SHAK 624:2
Hunter's waking t.	AUDEN 34:8
I do begin to have bloody t.	SHAK 625:29
In heads replete with t.	COWP 224:4
My t. with ecstasy unknown	DODD 250:2
not make t. your aim	KIPL 400:14
only to conceal their t.	VOLT 716:5
ought to control our t.	DARW 231:4
pansies, that's for t.	SHAK 578:7
sensations rather than of t.	KEATS 391:7
Staled are my t.	DYER 264:14
that did their silly t.	MILT 467:5
Then feed on t. that voluntary	MILT 470:16
thoroughfare for all t.	KEATS 392:12
t. accuse the dead	GREV 318:7
t. and actions when we	CHEK 196:10
t. and manners of future	JOHN 369:20
t. are legible in the eye	ROYD 549:14
t. are not your thoughts	BIBLE 84:17
t. beyond the reaches	SHAK 573:9
T., boundless, deep	BYRON 172:1
t. by England given	BROO 143:18
t. in my brain inhearse	SHAK 634:9
t. of a prisoner	SOLZ 655:11
T. of heroes were as good	MER 457:16
t. of men are widened	TENN 685:15
t. that arise in me	TENN 680:9
T., that breathe, and words	GRAY 316:8
T. that do often lie too	WORD 746:7
t. that wander through	MILT 469:14
t. transcend our wonted	VAUG 709:8
t. which may assault	BOOK 120:15

thoughts: (*cont.*):
t. which were not — BYRON 168:28
To bring my t. to an end — SMITH 652:21
Where branchèd t., new grown — KEATS 389:20
words are images of t. — KEATS 390:7
Words without t. never — SHAK 577:5
your love but not your t. — GIBR 303:2
youth are long, long t. — LONG 427:4

thousand: After two t. years of mass — HARDY 325:2
better than a t. — BOOK 130:18
cattle upon a t. hills — BOOK 128:2
Death has a t. doors — MASS 453:16
difference of forty t. — WELL 727:11
end of a t. years of history — GAIT 296:17
Give me a t. kisses — CAT 186:1
man picked out of ten t. — SHAK 574:19
night has a t. eyes — BOUR 138:2
Night hath a t. eyes — LYLY 433:11
not in a t. years — SMITH 651:18
O for a t. tongues to sing — WESL 728:5
picture is worth ten t. words — BARN 53:4
ten t. times ten thousand — BIBLE 86:1
t. ages in Thy sight — WATTS 723:7
t. blossoms with the day — FITZ 283:11
t. doors open — SEN 563:2
t. shall fall beside thee — BOOK 131:3
t. shapes you wear with ease — THOM 695:21
t. thousand are their tongues — WATTS 722:19
T. thousand Saints attending — WESL 728:15
t. thousand slimy things — COL 211:8
t. times more fair — SHAK 609:2
t. years in thy sight — BOOK 130:23
woman if I had five t. — THAC 691:19
Would he had blotted a t. — JONS 380:9

thousands: From the t. He hath freed — CHAN 189:17
limp father of t. — JOYCE 381:25
Saul hath slain his t. — BIBLE 75:5
showing mercy unto t. — BIBLE 72:16
ten t. in our streets — BOOK 135:5
than t. of gold and silver — BOOK 133:19
T. at his bidding speed — MILT 474:24
T., careless of the damning sin — COWP 222:5
Where t. equally were meant — SWIFT 675:12

thraldom: single t., or a double — BACON 46:1
thrall: Thee hath in t. — KEATS 388:12
thread: And with a silk t. — SHAK 623:7
love can do with a twined t. — BURT 165:9
strung them on an English t. — LOW 430:1
This line of scarlet t. — BIBLE 73:28
t. of his verbosity finer — SHAK 599:2
t. of my own hand's weaving — KEATS 387:31
t.-paper — POTT 525:11
weave their t. with bones — SHAK 629:16
threat: Whiles I t. he lives — SHAK 601:13
threaten: persuade, t., promise — WHIT 733:1
threatened: t. its life with a railway-share — CARR 184:5
threats: Cassius, in your t. — SHAK 593:5
nor his t. unexecuted — JOHN 370:2
three: always t. o'clock in the morning — FITZ 285:5
And t. merry boys are we — FLET 287:13
fright my faith than T. in One — DRYD 260:1
handsome in t. hundred pounds — SHAK 610:17
married life is company — WILDE 734:12
roared by and left t. men — CRANE 225:23
tell you t. times is true — CARR 183:27
There are t. kinds of lies — DISR 249:13
Though he was only t. — MILNE 462:13
t. corners of the world — SHAK 594:16
t. events in his life — LA BR 405:2
t. gentlemen at once — SHER 645:10
T. hours a day will produce — TROL 703:5
T. in One and One in Three — ALEX 8:15
T. little maids from school — GILB 304:23
T. quarks for Muster Mark — JOYCE 381:6
t. ravens sat on a tree — BALL 50:18
t. words' conference — SHAK 613:18
t. years old is half his height — LEON 418:11
two or t. are gathered — BOOK 119:9

three: (*cont.*):
When shall we t. meet again — SHAK 599:13
whole is divided into t. — CAES 174:14
write, I strike out t. — BOIL 117:5
threefold: t. cord is not quickly broken — BIBLE 80:8
three-fourths: Conduct is t. of our life — ARN 30:3
three o'-clock: t. in the morning courage — THOR 697:3
three-pipe: quite a t. problem — DOYLE 256:7
threescore: t. years and ten — BOOK 131:1
threshold: over the t. thereof — FULL 296:5
starry t. of Jove's Court — MILT 463:11
upon the t. of the new — WALL 718:13
threw: stars t. down their spears — BLAKE 114:15
thrice: thou shalt deny me t. — BIBLE 92:26
T. is he armed that hath — SHAK 587:18
T. was I beaten with rods — BIBLE 102:1
thrift: my well-won t. — SHAK 607:20
Thrift, t., Horatio — SHAK 572:16
thrill: T. through those roofless — SHEL 641:13
thrilling: more t. than a scream — ROLFE 545:8
thrills: sound which so t. the ear — AUDEN 35:14
thrive: He that would t. — CLAR 205:13
t. without one grain — DRYD 260:11
throat: cut his t. before he married — SWIFT 675:14
down the t. of Old Time — DICK 240:25
feel the fog in my t. — BROW 152:4
fishbone in the city's t. — LOW 430:12
For in your sweet dividing t. — CAREW 179:12
From the t. of a dead man — GRAV 314:20
if my hand were at its t. — LOW 430:20
rather felt you round my t. — HOPE 345:3
rustle in your dying t. — WALK 718:1
scuttled ship or cut a t. — BYRON 170:28
Stuck in my t. — SHAK 602:1
taking life by the t. — FROST 295:18
t. just cut from ear — ALC 8:1
times her little t. around — BROW 152:3
unlocked her silent t. — GIBB 302:22
your t. 'tis hard to slit — KING 398:5
throats: Nor cut each other's t. — GOLD 311:2
throbbing: t. between two lives — ELIOT 273:8
throbs: with no t. of fiery pain — JOHN 375:30
throne: Beneath the shadow of Thy T. — WATTS 723:7
Bust outlasts the t. — DOBS 249:20
everyone before the t. — MISS 477:12
fell before the t. — BIBLE 106:19
Gehenna or up to the T. — KIPL 399:18
His the sceptre, his the t. — DIX 249:18
his t. was like the fiery — BIBLE 86:1
honoured for his burning t. — SHAK 606:24
it is God's t. — BIBLE 88:31
light which beats upon a t. — TENN 681:16
like a burnished t. — ELIOT 273:2
like a burnished t. — SHAK 565:5
living t., the sapphire-blaze — GRAY 316:7
Lord sitting upon a t. — BIBLE 82:19
Man from his t. has hurled — WALL 718:6
midst of the t. — BIBLE 106:10
on a t. of royal state — MILT 469:10
rainbow round about the t. — BIBLE 106:9
saw a great white t. — BIBLE 107:15
scaffold from a t. — FANS 280:1
something behind the t. — PITT 515:9
stood before the t. — BIBLE 106:18
that sitteth upon the t. — BIBLE 106:17
This royal t. of kings — SHAK 619:18
Thou didst leave thy t. — ELL 275:8
t. he sits on, nor the tide of pomp — SHAK 586:8
t. of bayonets — INGE 359:18
t. of Denmark to thy father — SHAK 572:5
T. sent word to a Throne — KIPL 400:5
t. we honour is the *people's* — SHER 644:28
through slaughter to a t. — GRAY 315:16
unto the t. of the heavenly — BOOK 118:6
thrones: Not t. and crowns, but men — ELL 275:13
T., dominations, princedoms — MILT 471:28
throng: Leaving the tumultuous t. — WORD 744:10

through: best way out is always t. — FROST 296:12
No, Sir, do *you* read books t. — JOHN 373:22
T. all the changing scenes — TATE 678:17
T. them we pass out — FORS 290:8
T. the night of doubt — BAR 53:3
t. you but not from you — GIBR 303:2
Trust one who has gone t. it — VIRG 714:9
throughly: Wash me t. from my wickedness — BOOK 128:4
throw: Did your sister t. up — WALK 717:11
t. away the dearest thing — SHAK 600:14
t. away the worser part — SHAK 577:21
t. myself down in my Chamber — DONNE 253:9
thrown: all *this* t. away for *that* — MARY 452:15
then t. out, as good for nothing — JOHN 371:1
throws: t. himself on God — BROW 150:1
thrush: aged t., frail, gaunt — HARDY 325:5
That's the wise t. — BROW 150:6
t. replies, the mavis descant — SPEN 659:14
with, heigh! t. and the jay — SHAK 631:24
thrust: guardsman's cut and t. — HUXL 358:4
t. my hand — BIBLE 97:35
Thule: *Ultima T.* — VIRG 715:10
thumb: puts his t. in the scale — LAWR 412:4
t. each other's books out — RUSK 550:20
thumbs: By the pricking of my t. — SHAK 603:20
his t. are off at last — HOFF 341:7
Thummim: Urim and the T. — BIBLE 72:18
thumps: by t. upon your back — COWP 222:6
thunder: But what serve for t. — SHAK 618:14
comes up like t. outer China — KIPL 400:1
discord, such sweet t. — SHAK 612:14
dread rattling t. — SHAK 626:1
Glorious the t.'s roar — SMART 650:4
Harsh t. — MILT 470:10
Here falling houses t. — JOHN 370:7
He was as rattling t. — SHAK 566:20
surge and t. of the Odyssey — LANG 408:16
they steal my t. — DENN 237:4
T. like a mighty flood — DIX 249:18
t. of the captains — BIBLE 77:39
voice of a great t. — BIBLE 107:2
thunderbolt: like a t. he falls — TENN 681:1
towering mountains with a t. — VIRG 715:12
thunderbolts: Harmless t. — PLINY 517:6
Vaunt-couriers oak-cleaving t. — SHAK 595:20
thundered: T. on Roman air — AUDEN 34:1
thunders: t. in the index — SHAK 577:10
With t. from her native oak — CAMP 177:1
thunder-stone: Nor the all-dreaded t. — SHAK 571:16
thunder-storm: plunging through the t. — TENN 685:13
thus: T. have I had thee — SHAK 634:12
To be t. is nothing — SHAK 602:23
thusness: reason of this t. — WARD 721:20
Thybrim: *T. multo spumantem sanguine* — VIRG 713:10
thy-doxy: Heterodoxy or T. — CARL 180:21
thyme: And sweet t. true — FLET 287:19
bank whereon the wild t. — SHAK 611:19
t. and the gadding vine — MILT 466:2
thyself: beside t. — BIBLE 99:10
thou t. to all eternity — ROSS 548:2
Tiber: been pouring into the T. — JUV 383:19
not a drop of allaying T. — SHAK 570:7
Oh, T.! father Tiber — MAC 436:14
T. foaming with much blood — POW 528:10
T. foaming with much blood — VIRG 713:10
Tiberius: Had T. been a cat — ARN 27:19
The Coin, T. — DOBS 249:20
ticket: give back my entrance t. — DOST 254:5
In his hat a Railway-T. — LEAR 414:2
She's got a t. to ride — LENN 418:2
t. at Victoria Station — BEVIN 69:15
t. for the peepshow — MACN 440:13
tickle: if you t. us, do we not — SHAK 608:22
I'll t. your catastrophe — SHAK 583:3
T. and entertain us, or we die — COWP 223:11
t. her with a hoe and she — JERR 366:1
tickled: I'll be t. to death to go — WEST 729:21

tickled: (*cont.*):
  rattle, t. with a straw   POPE 522:15
tickles: He t. this age that can   ANON 14:9
tickling: hath only a scornful t.   SIDN 647:11
  must be caught with t.   SHAK 629:23
  t. Commodity   SHAK 593:30
ticky-tacky: all made out of t.   REYN 539:15
tiddle-taddle: no t. nor pibble-pabble
       SHAK 586:1
tide: But came the t., and made   SPEN 659:11
  call of the running t.   MAS 453:8
  change, veer in the t.   SWIN 677:4
  full t. of human existence   JOHN 373:28
  going out with the t.   DICK 240:6
  lackeying the varying t.   SHAK 564:27
  Nae man can tether time or t.   BURNS 163:7
  perhaps under the whelming t.   MILT 466:12
  t. crept up along the sand   KING 397:14
  t. in the affairs of men   SHAK 593:12
  t. in the affairs of women   BYRON 171:15
  t. is ready her to honour   BEST 67:1
  t.'s pretty nigh out   DICK 240:6
  upon this filthy modern t.   YEATS 753:10
tides: Now the salt t. seawards   ARN 27:7
  Push in their t.   THOM 693:11
  so I drew these t.   LAWR 413:6
tidings: good t. of great joy   BIBLE 93:27
  that bringeth good t.   BIBLE 84:8
tie: father's old green t.   COLL 213:6
  not fit to t. his brogues   SCOTT 561:3
  that love endures no t.   DRYD 261:10
tied: t. and bound with the chain   BOOK 120:4
  t. to the soil as another   HOMER 343:13
ties: all the t. of humanity   WESL 728:24
  only the string that t.   MONT 481:11
tiger: atom bomb is a paper t.   MAO 446:2
  Beth egre as is a t.   CHAU 193:11
  imitate the action of the t.   SHAK 585:7
  On a t. skin   ANON 19:24
  orang-outang or the t.   BURKE 159:1
  rhinoceros or the Hyrcan t.   SHAK 603:11
  smile on the face of the t.   ANON 17:13
  t.'s heart wrapped   SHAK 587:28
  t.'s terrible heart   BENÉT 62:18
  T. Tyger, burning bright   BLAKE 114:13
  T. well repay the trouble   BELL 60:24
  Who went for a ride on a t.   ANON 17:13
tiger-moth: t.'s deep-damasked wings
       KEATS 387:5
tigers: Catches t. in red weather   STEV 665:17
  For tamed and shabby t.   HODG 340:16
  There *were* no t.   ELIOT 270:8
  t. are getting hungry   CHUR 202:5
  t. of wrath are wiser   BLAKE 112:25
tight: his shoes were far too t.   LEAR 414:2
  t. gag of place   HEAN 329:21
  t. little Island   DIBD 238:18
tight-lipped: t. mufflered men   JOS 380:16
tights: she played in t.   BEER 59:21
tile: red brick, but white t.   OSB 501:15
tiles: there are t. on the roofs   LUTH 432:11
Till: Says Tweed to T.   ANON 17:17
tilt: and to t. with lips   SHAK 580:12
tilth: his full t. and husbandry   SHAK 605:9
timber: crooked t. of humanity   KANT 385:11
  Like seasoned t., never gives   HERB 336:2
  navy nothing but rotten t.   BURKE 157:32
Timbuctoo: On the plains of T.   WILB 733:17
time: abbreviation of t.   GIBB 302:21
  accepted t.   BIBLE 101:19
  aching t.   KEATS 387:26
  against her, but she's on t.   AUDEN 35:9
  age, but for all t.   JONS 380:4
  Aghast the voice of T.   DYER 265:8
  Ah, Sun-flower! weary of t.   BLAKE 114:5
  Alas, T. stays, *we* go   DOBS 249:23
  all my possessions for a moment of t.
       ELIZ 274:19
  All of the olden t.   ANON 15:19
  All t. and nonsense scorning   BUCK 154:13
  all t. of our tribulation   BOOK 119:18
  And pluck till t. and times   YEATS 753:8
  And T., a maniac scattering   TENN 683:16

time: (*cont.*):
  And t. is setting with me, Oh   BURNS 162:25
  And t., that takes survey   SHAK 582:6
  And tract of t. begins to weave   VAUX 709:12
  annihilate but space and t.   POPE 523:10
  antique t. would lie unswept   SHAK 570:10
  appeareth for a little t.   BIBLE 105:4
  articulates t., and can   MANN 445:5
  As old T. makes these decay   CAREW 179:2
  As t. goes by   HUPF 357:2
  backward and abysm of t.   SHAK 625:1
  because t. is long   DU B 263:3
  been a t. for such a word   SHAK 605:1
  been so long t. with you   BIBLE 97:13
  besmeared with sluttish t.   SHAK 633:18
  bid t. return   SHAK 620:4
  bleeding to death of t.   GRAV 314:19
  bourne of t. and place   TENN 680:18
  Breaks t., as dancers   CAMP 177:9
  But T., to make me grieve   HARDY 325:9
  By the t. you say you're   PARK 506:12
  by T.'s fell hand defaced   SHAK 634:1
  By which T. kills us   SHAK 648:18
  chronicle of wasted t.   SHAK 634:17
  common arbitrator, T.   SHAK 628:4
  conversing I forget all t.   MILT 471:11
  cormorant devouring T.   SHAK 598:6
  count t. by heart-throbs   BAIL 47:16
  destroyed by T.'s devouring   BRAM 139:16
  down the throat of Old T.   DICK 240:25
  drew from the womb of t.   HEINE 331:3
  entertain conjecture of a t.   SHAK 585:14
  envious t. is fleeing   HOR 349:9
  escaped the shipwreck of t.   BACON 41:18
  Even such is T., which takes   RAL 536:3
  events in the womb of t.   SHAK 615:11
  Every t. we say goodbye   PORT 524:22
  exhaust our t.   WINC 739:1
  experienced rebel, T.   FLAT 285:15
  Fleet the t. carelessly   SHAK 567:16
  Fly envious T., till thou   MILT 467:15
  Footprints on the sands of t.   LONG 427:10
  foremost files of t.   TENN 685:18
  For he loved the t. too well   CLARE 204:17
  For T., not Corydon   ARN 28:28
  Give peace in our t., O Lord   BOOK 119:2
  good t. was had by all   SMITH 652:15
  good t. who had been had   TYNAN 706:33
  Grown old before my t.   ROSS 547:6
  had my world as in my t.   CHAU 194:22
  half as old as T.   BURG 156:24
  hath triumphed over t.   RAL 536:4
  Have no enemy but t.   YEATS 753:2
  Healing is a matter of t.   HIPP 339:8
  Heavily laden with t. expired   HUGH 353:16
  He hath shook hands with t.   FORD 289:11
  Hurry up please it's t.   ELIOT 273:6
  I backward mus'd on wasted t.   BURNS 164:1
  Indecent . . . 10 years before its t.
       LAVER 411:10
  In search of lost t.   PROU 530:5
  irretrievable t. is flying   VIRG 715:17
  it is peace for our t.   CHAM 189:8
  it is t. for you to go   HOR 348:21
  it is t. to be in earnest   JOHN 368:13
  it is to sell t.   TAWN 679:2
  it no longer told the t.   RUSS 551:26
  It saves t.   CARR 182:20
  It's t., my dear, it's time   PUSH 533:2
  It will last my t.   CARL 180:4
  I was on t.   LERN 419:2
  Just the worst t. of the year   ELIOT 271:17
  Keeping t., time, time   POE 518:3
  lines to t. thou grow'st   SHAK 633:6
  look into the seeds of t.   SHAK 600:6
  Look like the t.   SHAK 600:17
  me more than t. and space   LAMB 406:25
  Nae man can tether t. or tide   BURNS 163:7
  Never the t. and the place   BROW 151:13
  new direction of T.   LAWR 412:22
  night of t. far surpasseth   BROW 145:24
  nobility is the act of t.   BACON 44:9

time: (*cont.*):
  not coy, but use your t.   HERR 337:8
  No t. like the present   MANL 444:10
  no t. to read play-bills   BURN 160:17
  no t. to stand and stare   DAV 232:12
  now doth t. waste me   SHAK 621:12
  Of t.'s eternal motion   FORD 289:15
  Old T. the clock-setter   SHAK 594:2
  one born out of due t.   BIBLE 101:4
  O T.! arrest your flight   LAM 406:1
  O t. too swift, O swiftness   PEELE 511:5
  outside and may be some t.   MAHON 442:5
  outside and may be some t.   OATES 497:9
  Perfection is the child of T.   HALL 322:3
  Principle of Unripe T.   CORN 219:8
  Procrastination is the thief of t.
       YOUNG 754:16
  ravages of t. not injure   HOR 350:5
  Redeeming the t.   BIBLE 102:22
  relish of the saltness of t.   SHAK 582:16
  Remember that t. is money   FRAN 292:13
  sad T. his feathers move   SPEN 659:16
  shall see the t.'s deformity   JONG 379:20
  Short T. and Little Skill   HAR 326:10
  silent touches of t.   BURKE 159:25
  speech is shallow as T.   CARL 180:10
  spirit of the t. shall   SHAK 594:10
  stretched forefinger of all T.   TENN 687:26
  superior to t. and place   JOHN 369:20
  syllable of recorded t.   SHAK 605:1
  Teacheth t. to run away   GREV 318:5
  Tell t. it metes but motion   RAL 535:16
  temple half as old as T.   ROG 544:13
  that is an idea whose t.   ANON 18:12
  That passed the t.   BECK 57:25
  Then while t. serves   HERR 336:11
  There'll be t. enough to sleep   HOUS 352:7
  this bank and shoal of t.   SHAK 601:2
  Till t. be comprehended   WILB 734:6
  T. and fevers burn away   AUDEN 35:5
  T. and the hour runs through   SHAK 600:13
  T. an endless song   YEATS 752:9
  t. brings in his revenges   SHAK 630:35
  T. did beckon to the flowers   HERB 335:7
  t. didst teach the hearts   BOOK 120:20
  T. doth transfix the flourish   SHAK 633:21
  T. flies   VIRG 715:17
  T. for a little something   MILNE 463:4
  t. has been properly spent   TAYL 679:15
  t. has come for all good   LONG 426:9
  't. has come,' the Walrus said   CARR 183:2
  T. has no divisions to mark   MANN 445:1
  t. has shaken me   WESL 729:3
  T. has three dimensions   HOPK 346:14
  T. has too much credit   COMP 214:13
  T. has transfigured them   LARK 409:13
  t. hath his revolution   CREWE 226:19
  T. hath, my lord, a wallet   SHAK 627:19
  T. held me green and dying   THOM 693:6
  T. hovers o'er, impatient   JOHN 370:18
  T. in hours, days   VAUG 709:11
  t. is a pinprick of eternity   AUR 37:17
  T. is a violent torrent   AUR 37:16
  t. is come round   SHAK 593:17
  T. is fleeting   LONG 427:8
  T. is like a fashionable host   SHAK 627:21
  T. is on our side   GLAD 307:6
  t. is our tedious song   MILT 467:13
  t. is out of joint   SHAK 574:7
  t. is right for fighting   JAGG 361:12
  t. is running out   KOES 403:21
  t. is slipping underneath   FITZ 284:3
  T. is that wherein there   HIPP 339:7
  t. is the greatest innovator   BACON 43:33
  T. is the great physician   DISR 248:16
  t. is the longest distance   WILL 737:6
  T. is the measure of movement   AUCT 33:27
  T., like an ever-rolling   WATTS 723:7
  T. makes ancient good   LOW 430:5
  t. now with a robber's   SHAK 628:1
  t. of asking   BOOK 123:14
  t. of swords and periwigs   POTT 525:10
  t. of the singing of birds   BIBLE 81:9

time: (*cont.*):
t. of trouble	BOOK 126:27
t. of year thou mayst in me	SHAK 634:6
T. present and time past	ELIOT 270:13
t. remembered is grief	SWIN 675:22
t. runs, the clock will	MARL 447:1
t.'s arrow	EDD 266:2
T.'s eunuch, and not breed	HOPK 346:9
T.'s glory to calm contending	SHAK 632:23
T. shall moult away his wings	SUCK 671:9
T. shall throw a dart at thee	BROW 146:24
T.'s noblest offspring	BERK 65:13
T. spent on any item	PARK 507:4
T.'s thievish progress	SHAK 634:8
T.'s wheel runs back	BROW 152:11
T.'s wingèd chariot hurrying	MARV 451:3
t. that shall surely be	AING 6:3
T. that's lost may all	BUCK 154:12
T., the avenger! unto thee	BYRON 169:6
T. the devourer of everything	OVID 503:1
t. the subtle thief	MILT 474:21
time, it is all I lacked	DOUG 255:11
t. to awake out of sleep	BIBLE 100:10
t. to cultivate modesty	SITW 648:15
t. to discover time	GUIB 319:12
t. to take that individual	MELV 456:16
t. to think before I speak	DARW 231:14
t. to win this game	DRAKE 257:12
T. travels in divers paces	SHAK 569:9
t. until the arrival	BERNE 66:11
T. was away and somewhere	MACN 440:19
T. was out of joint	STR 670:16
t. we have rushed through	ROG 545:5
T. we may comprehend	BROW 146:4
t. we shall not know	PEAC 510:12
t. when only the dead smiled	AKHM 6:11
t. when thou mayest	BOOK 126:9
t. which is the author of authors	
	BACON 41:15
t. will come when	DISR 246:14
t. will doubt of Rome	BYRON 171:10
T. will run back, and fetch	MILT 467:8
T. with a gift of tears	SWIN 675:24
t. without injuring eternity	THOR 696:27
T. ylost may nought recovered	CHAU 195:23
T., you old gipsy man	HODG 340:19
T., you thief, who love to get	HUNT 356:9
'tis but the t. and drawing days	SHAK 591:15
To choose time is to save t.	BACON 43:14
To envious and calumniating t.	SHAK 627:22
To it comes T.	BARN 53:18
trencher-friends, t.'s flies	SHAK 626:12
uncertain balance of proud t.	GREE 317:7
unconscionable t. dying	CHAR 191:20
unthinking t.	DRYD 261:19
waste of t. and effort	VEBL 709:15
Wears out his t., much like	SHAK 614:19
week is a long t. in politics	WILS 738:6
we have not the t.	KIPL 401:8
We have short t. to stay	HERR 337:4
We take no note of T.	YOUNG 754:13
what takes a little t.	NANS 489:8
When t. is broke, and no	SHAK 621:11
Where t. doth end, and thoughts	GREV 318:7
which are the births of t.	BACON 43:32
which are the rags of t.	DONNE 252:17
Which beginning of t. according	
	USSH 707:10
while t. doth serve thee	SOUT 658:1
while t. quietly kills	BOUC 137:14
whips and scorns of t.	SHAK 575:16
With leaden foot t. creeps	JAGO 361:15
with the productions of t.	BLAKE 112:20
world enough, and t.	MARV 451:2
timebo: *et salus mea, quem t.* BIBLE 107:27
timeless: Of t. moments ELIOT 271:8
timely: by a t. compliance FIEL 282:3
| t. utterance gave | WORD 745:11 |
timeo: *t. Danaos et dona ferentis* VIRG 712:14
times: brisk and giddy-pacèd t. SHAK 629:12
discern the signs of the t.	BIBLE 91:13
five t. did I say to him	WORD 743:6
For the t. they are a-changin'	DYLAN 265:23

times: (*cont.*):
It is the logic of our t.	DAY-L 233:7
It was the best of t.	DICK 244:1
My t. be in Thy hand	BROW 152:13
nature of the t. deceased	SHAK 583:15
Oh, the t.! Oh, the manners	CIC 204:6
one year's experience 30 t.	CARR 181:22
Our t. are in His hand	BROW 152:6
praiser of past t.	HOR 347:14
Praise they that will t.	HERR 336:23
record of blissful old t.	BLAM 114:20
revolution of the t.	SHAK 583:13
t. begin to wax	BIBLE 86:23
T. change, and we change	ANON 22:19
T. go by turns, and chances	SOUT 658:2
T. has made many ministries	BAG 46:17
t. have I herd men telle	CHAU 194:29
t. in which a genius would	ADAMS 1:13
t. that try men's souls	PAINE 504:12
t. will not mend	PARK 506:26
wail my dear t.' waste	SHAK 633:11
timet: *Beatus vir qui t.* BIBLE 108:1
| *Peiusque leto flagitium t.* | HOR 350:19 |
timetables: imposed by railway t. TAYL 679:6
timing: lucky t. of your death TAC 677:22
timor: *T. mortis conturbat me* DUNB 264:3
Timothy: T. Winters CAUS 187:3
tin: cheap t. trays MAS 453:3
tincture: Actions receive their t. DEFOE 234:16
| left this t. in the blood | DEFOE 234:17 |
ting-a-ling-a-ling: bells of Hell go t. ANON 17:1
tingle: that heareth it shall t. BIBLE 74:29
tingling: a whoreson t. SHAK 582:17
tinker: don't matter a t.'s cuss SHIN 645:29
| expands to t. with his car | MACN 441:3 |
tinkling: talk but a t. cymbal BACON 43:21
| words t. in the minds | SMITH 652:12 |
tinklings: t. lull the distant folds GRAY 315:10
tins: lays out food in t. ELIOT 273:8
tinsel: flapped its t. wing MARV 450:2
tintinnabulation: t. that so musically wells
| | POE 518:3 |
tiny: Lewd, t., careless lives ROET 544:6
| My t. watching eye | DE L 236:12 |
| Your t. hand is frozen | GIAC 301:17 |
tip: That depends on the t. BRAC 138:19
| that of a school-boy's t. | THAC 691:5 |
| Within the nether t. | COL 211:5 |
Tipperary: long way to T. JUDGE 382:8
tipple: that t. in the deep LOV 429:3
tippled: t. drink more fine KEATS 388:20
tipsy: my heart grew t. in me GERS 301:14
tiptoe: Dance t., bull BUNT 155:9
on t. for a flight	KEATS 388:6
t. on the misty mountain	SHAK 623:23
t. when this day is named	SHAK 586:11
tired: and t. her head BIBLE 76:27
Give me your t., your poor	LAZ 413:7
He was so t.	ROLFE 545:9
I'm t. of Love	BELL 61:11
long process of getting t.	BUTL 166:30
Oh! who can ever be t. of Bath	AUST 38:22
one grows t. of the world	WALP 719:9
Thou art t.; best be still	ARN 27:11
Tho' you're t. and weary	LAUD 411:5
T. of his dark dominion	MER 458:6
t. the sun with talking	CORY 219:15
T. with all these, from these	SHAK 634:4
t. with labour of far travel	CAT 186:3
When a man is t. of London	JOHN 374:24
woman who always was t.	ANON 14:4
tires: t. betimes that spurs too SHAK 619:17
Tiresias: T., though blind ELIOT 273:8
tiresome: styles are good except the t. |
| | VOLT 716:9 |
tiring: T. thy wits and toiling DAN 229:17
| Wooing, so t. | MITF 478:7 |
tissue: beautiful feminine t. HARDY 324:15
Titan: thy glory, T. SHEL 642:20
titanic: furniture on the deck of the T. |
	MORT 486:16
T. sails at dawn	DYLAN 265:12
which t. wars had groined	OWEN 503:18

tite: *T. tute Tati tibi tanta* ENN 277:25
tithe: ye pay t. of mint BIBLE 92:5
Titian: much at heart about T. RUSK 551:1
title: could only read the t. WOOLF 742:9
now does he feel his t.	SHAK 604:18
O thou! whatever t. suit thee	BURNS 160:23
t., and possession	BOOK 136:2
t. from a better man	STEV 669:6
t. running 'fore the king	SHAK 586:8
To guard a t. that was rich	SHAK 594:9
Who gained no t.	POPE 520:32
titles: And lawyers talk of t. DRAY 257:18
Conquering kings their t. take	CHAN 189:17
Despite those t., power	SCOTT 559:17
have t. manifold	WORD 744:13
that of the rich for t.	PEAR 510:15
T. are but nick-names	PAINE 504:18
T. are shadows, crowns	DEFOE 234:26
T. are tinsel, power	SHEL 644:3
T. distinguish the mediocre	SHAW 637:26
T. thou hast given away	SHAK 595:7
tittle: Such a set of t. tattle BURN 160:20
titwillow: Sang 'Willow, t.' GILB 305:11
Tityre: *T., tu patulae recubans* VIRG 714:11
toad: Give me your arm, old t. LARK 410:9
I had rather be a t.	SHAK 616:16
rose to a pitch-black t.	YES 754:1
Squat like a t.	MILT 471:17
t. beneath the harrow knows	KIPL 400:6
t. is a chef-d'oeuvre	WHIT 732:17
T., that under cold stone	SHAK 603:17
Which like the t., ugly	SHAK 567:25
Why should I let the t. *work*	LARK 410:8
toads: imaginary gardens with real t.
	MOORE 482:14
toast: Let the t. pass SHER 645:18
My t. would be	ADAMS 3:9
never had a piece of t.	PAYN 510:3
t. that pleased the most	DIBD 238:14
toasted-cheese: his enemies, 'T.' CARR 184:1
tobacco: For thy sake, T. LAMB 407:5
going to leave off t.	LAMB 406:27
snuff, and sleep	DICK 239:31
that tawney weed t.	JONS 378:11
t. is not worthy to live	MOL 478:21
t. to explain it to me	LONG 426:8
Whether it divine t. were	SPEN 660:8
tobacconist: lungs of the t. JONS 378:10
tocsin: t. of the soul BYRON 171:13
Tod: *auf den T. eines Gefühls* NIET 495:16
today: about them if T. be sweet FITZ 284:3
But such a day to-morrow as t.	SHAK 631:11
I have lived t.	DRYD 262:1
life's too late; live t.	MART 449:11
t. I am fifty-five	REED 537:16
T. I feel like thirty cents	ADE 5:5
T. if ye will hear	BOOK 131:10
t. I suffer, tomorrow	LESS 419:12
T. shalt thou be with me	BIBLE 95:27
t. the struggle	AUDEN 36:7
T. we have naming of parts	REED 537:18
t. which the world may	COLL 213:4
tomorrows these gave their t.	EDM 267:1
yesterday—but never jam t.	CARR 183:5
toe: clerical, printless t. BROO 143:11
| t. of the peasant comes | SHAK 578:22 |
| t. that line | THOR 696:29 |
toes: Pobble who has no t. LEAR 414:16
toff: saunter along like a t. HARG 326:8
togae: *Cedant arma t.* CIC 204:2
together: all that believed were t. BIBLE 98:8
Are we here t. alone	WHIT 732:10
comfortably so long t.	GAY 299:12
Let us remain t. still	SHEL 640:13
never again so much t.	MACN 440:18
Our lives would grow t.	SWIN 677:1
persons acting t.	ARAB 24:3
sufficient to keep them t.	JOHN 373:14
t. is worshipped and glorified	BOOK 121:20
toil: ambition mock their useful t. GRAY 315:13
| As on we t. from day to day | JOHN 370:10 |

toil: (cont.):

Bear the t., maintain	WHITE 731:4
bleared, smeared with t.	HOPK 345:10
Death and T.	VIRG 713:14
Double, double t. and trouble	SHAK 603:17
Horny-handed sons of t.	SAL 554:7
horny hands of t.	LOW 429:19
if for all his t. he gets the straw	OXF 504:1
In her strong t. of grace	SHAK 567:13
slumber is more sweet than t.	TENN 686:2
some men t. after virtue	LAMB 407:13
they t. not, neither do	BIBLE 89:11
they waste their t.	SCOTT 559:14
thought, the day in t.	QUAR 533:17
T., envy, want	JOHN 370:15
t. in other men's extremes	KYD 404:12
t., tears and sweat	CHUR 202:8
To t. and not to seek for rest	IGN 359:8
unrequited t. shall be sunk	LINC 422:8
year with t. of breath	COL 209:22

toiled: we have t. all the night — BIBLE 94:3

toiling: Tiring thy wits and t. — DAN 229:17
Were t. upward in the night — LONG 427:1

toils: alone is worth all these t. — CAT 186:3
recompense their t. and pains — COLL 213:1

token: t. of a covenant between — BIBLE 70:32

tokens: Words are the t. current — BACON 42:4

tolbooth-gate: passive resistance of the T. — SCOTT 560:21

told: I t. my wrath, my wrath — BLAKE 114:11
I t. you so — BYRON 171:28
our fathers have t. us — BOOK 127:9
They t. me, Heraclitus — CORY 219:15
t. you from the beginning — BIBLE 83:30
what we were formerly t. — BLUN 116:4
When all is t. — MACN 441:4

Toledo: T. trusty — BUTL 166:8

tolerable: Life would be t. — LEWIS 420:19

tolerance: t. and mutual acceptance — LEVIN 420:3
was such a thing as t. — WILS 738:21

tolerate: at least t. one another — TREV 702:13

toleration: thus t. produced not — GIBB 301:18

toll: T. for the brave — COWP 222:24
t. me back from thee — KEATS 389:16

tolle: T. lege, tolle lege — AUG 37:1

tollis: qui t. peccata mundi — MISS 477:5

tolls: it t. for thee — DONNE 253:5

Tom: Ground control to Major T. — BOWIE 138:15
Old Uncle T. Cobbleigh and all — BALL 51:4
Poor T.'s a-cold — SHAK 596:16
T. Pearse, lend me — BALL 51:4

tomatoes: babies in the t. — GINS 306:29

tomb: blossom on the t. — CRAB 224:20
buried in the silent t. — WORD 748:6
grave or t. of wit — CAV 187:12
icy silence of the t. — KEATS 390:16
My heart keeps empty in thy t. — KING 396:11
over on this side the t. — BYRON 168:18
pastimes grace my happy t. — CAMP 177:4
sea was made his t. — BARN 53:16
smell like what it is—a t. — SHEL 641:3
tell the lover's t. — THOM 693:8
This side the t. — DAV 232:10
threefold, fourfold t. — BASSE 55:2
through a gap in a raped t. — HEAT 329:24
To fair Fidele's grassy t. — COLL 213:10
t. by the side of the sea — POE 518:2
t. of a mediocre talent — SMITH 652:4
t. the womb wherein they — SHAK 634:9
were confined into a t. — VAUG 709:9

tombs: dust, in the cool t. — SAND 555:3
registered upon our brazen t. — SHAK 598:6
sit ceremonious, like T. — DICK 244:9
through the t. of all regions — MISS 477:12
t. a doleful sound — WATTS 723:3

tombstone: end of the fight is a t. — KIPL 400:4
on the t. where he lies — LONG 427:5

tomcat: this t. lies stretched flat — HUGH 354:3

Tom Jones: His spurious brat, T. — RICH 540:15

Tomnoddy: My Lord T. is — BROU 144:6
my Lord T. went home to bed — BARH 52:11

tomorrow: Boast not thyself of t. — BIBLE 79:24

tomorrow: (cont.):

dwell in the house of t.	GIBR 303:2
Here today—in next week t.	GRAH 314:3
jam t. and jam yesterday	CARR 183:5
Leave it behind	COW 220:8
no t. hath, nor yesterday	DONNE 251:18
question what t. may bring	HOR 349:7
such a day t. as to-day	SHAK 631:11
today I suffer, t. I die	LESS 419:12
T., and to-morrow	SHAK 605:1
T. do thy worst	DRYD 262:1
T. every Duchess in London	MACD 437:13
T. for the young the poets	AUDEN 36:7
T. I'll sit at the table	HUGH 354:1
t. is another day	MITC 478:4
t. shall not drive it out	DONNE 253:8
t.'s life's too late	MART 449:11
t. there's no knowing	MED 456:3
t. we shall die	BIBLE 83:7
T. we shall sail again	HOR 349:6
To-morrow! —Why, t. I may	FITZ 283:17
too late t. to be brave	ARMS 26:9
Unborn T., dead YESTERDAY	FITZ 284:3
you can put off till t.	PUNCH 531:11

tomorrows: dividend from time's t. — SASS 557:7
For your t. these gave — EDM 267:1

tom-tit: by a river a little t. — GILB 305:11

tone: deep, autumnal t. — SHEL 641:19
that t. of voice — PUNCH 532:3
t. of the company — CHES 198:9

tones: Sweet t. remembered not — SHEL 641:6
t. as dry and level — AUDEN 36:2
t. of a loved voice caressed — ARN 26:17

tongs: the t. and the bones — SHAK 612:10

tongue: bridleth not his t. — BIBLE 104:28
fellows of infinite t. — SHAK 587:1
For she had a t. with a tang — SHAK 625:19
For while I held my t. — BOOK 126:8
From lies of t. and pen — CHES 199:3
God's sake hold your t. — DONNE 251:21
have fallen by the t. — BIBLE 87:27
her and cut away her t. — SHAK 627:2
his t. dropped manna — MILT 469:13
his t. is the clapper — SHAK 613:31
his t. to conceive — SHAK 612:16
I have no need for t. — ROET 544:9
I held my t., and spake — BOOK 126:22
I mean the t.; variety — WEBS 725:14
I must hold my t. — SHAK 572:13
Keep thy t. from evil — BOOK 126:15
Kepe wel they t., and thenk — CHAU 193:27
let my t. cleave — BOOK 134:17
Love's t. is in the eyes — FLET 287:26
men of less truth than t. — SHAK 633:5
My heart and t. employ — TATE 678:17
my t. from evil-speaking — BOOK 123:8
My t. is the pen — BOOK 127:10
My t. swore, but my mind's — EUR 279:3
nor t. to speak here — LENT 418:6
obnoxious to each carping t. — BRAD 139:10
our t. with joy — BOOK 134:4
parching t. — KEATS 388:28
picked a pocket with his t. — BIER 109:5
put a t. in every wound — SHAK 592:17
senates hang upon thy t. — THOM 696:7
shouldst give dust a t. — HERB 334:13
Silence become his mother t. — GOLD 311:18
Sing, my t., the glorious — FORT 291:1
slow of speech, and a slow t. — BIBLE 72:1
speak the t. Shakespeare — WORD 744:13
such a t. that I am glad — SHAK 594:22
their t. a sharp sword — BOOK 128:15
t. blossom into speech — BROW 149:1
t. can no man tame — BIBLE 105:2
t. freezes into silence — SAPP 556:1
t. into the corners — ELIOT 272:1
t. is the only edged tool — IRV 360:15
t. not understanded — BOOK 135:24
t. of midnight hath told — SHAK 612:26
t. of the dumb — BIBLE 83:21
t. our trumpeter — SHAK 570:3
t. proves dainty Baccus — SHAK 598:20
t. taking a trip of three steps — NAB 488:21

tongue: (cont.):

t. to persuade	CLAR 205:2
treasure of our t.	DAN 230:2
'tween my heart and t.	SHAK 591:9
under his t. as a sweet	HENRY 332:18
understanding, but no t.	SHAK 572:22
use of my oracular t.	SHER 645:5
vibrates her eternal t.	YOUNG 754:9
vulgar t.	BOOK 122:19
whose strenuous t.	KEATS 389:7
would not yield to the t.	BIER 109:6
would that my t. could utter	TENN 680:9
writyng of oure t.	CHAU 195:26
your t.'s sweet air	SHAK 610:24

tongued: t. with fire beyond — ELIOT 271:3

tongueless: t. vigil — SWIN 675:21

tongues: cloven t. like as of fire — BIBLE 98:6
Finds t. in trees, books — SHAK 567:25
hath a thousand several t. — SHAK 622:11
He came in t. of living flame — AUBER 32:20
Hush your t. — HOR 349:22
lack t. to praise — SHAK 634:18
O for a thousand t. to sing — WESL 728:5
our t. the wonderful works — BIBLE 98:7
sale of chapmen's t. — SHAK 598:10
Sweet the countless t. united — MANT 445:12
They say the t. of dying men — SHAK 619:15
thousand talkers whose t. — DYLAN 265:15
thousand thousand are their t. — WATTS 722:19
t. of men and of angels — BIBLE 101:1
t. that have not Thee — KIPL 400:13
t. that I have in fencing — SHAK 628:13
Walls have t., and hedges ears — SWIFT 675:7
whether there be t. — BIBLE 101:1
whispering t. can poison truth — COL 209:10

tonic: Hatred is a t. — BALZ 51:9

tonight: be but a short time t. — BALD 48:11
Not t., Josephine — NAP 490:7
t. thou shalt have cramps — SHAK 625:6

tonnage: swallowing the t. of the world — MILL 461:19

too: because we are t. menny — HARDY 324:9
T. kind, too kind — NIGH 496:2
T. small to live — ANON 19:3

took: 'E went an' t. — KIPL 401:19
person you and I t. me for — CARL 179:19
stranger, and ye t. me in — BIBLE 92:20
t. a man's life along — CARL 180:12

tool: Science is an edged t. — EDD 266:6
t. that grows keener — IRV 360:15

tooled: t. in a post-chaise — BYRON 174:6

tool-making: Man a t. animal — FRAN 293:4

tools: For secrets are edged t. — DRYD 261:27
nothing but to name his t. — BUTL 166:1
t. and we will finish — CHUR 202:15
t. to him that can handle — CARL 180:1
Without t. he is nothing — CARL 181:5

tooth: danger of her former t. — SHAK 603:3
Doth set my pugging t. on edge — SHAK 631:14
hadde alwey a coltes t. — CHAU 194:24
poison for the age's t. — SHAK 593:26
red in t. and claw — TENN 683:22
sharper than a serpent's t. — SHAK 595:10
t. for tooth, hand — BIBLE 72:17
where each t.-point goes — KIPL 400:6

toothache: could endure the t. — SHAK 614:13
He that sleeps feels not the t. — SHAK 571:18
Venerable Mother T. — HEAT 330:1

toothbrush: t. too is airing — BETJ 68:1

toothpaste: t. is out of the tube — HALD 321:4

top: always room at the t. — WEBS 725:12
Life is a t. which whipping — GREV 318:6
t. of it reached to heaven — BIBLE 71:13
t. thing in the world — KEATS 392:10

toper: t. whose untutored sense — CRAB 224:14

topics: you have but two t. — JOHN 374:20

topless: t. towers of Ilium — MARL 446:17

topmost: A-top on the t. twig — ROSS 547:13

topography: T. displays no favourites — BISH 110:2

tops: t. and help there's none — HODG 340:18

torch: bright t., and a casement — KEATS 390:1
runners relay the t. of life — LUCR 432:1

torch: (cont.):
t.; be yours to hold it high | MCCR 437:6
t. borne in the wind | CHAP 190:12
t. has been passed | KENN 393:12
Truth, like a t. | HAM 322:12
torches: our little t. at his fire | COK 208:14
she doth teach the t. | SHAK 622:24
with us as we with t. do | SHAK 605:6
torchlight: t. procession | O'SUL 502:6
Tories: are T. born wicked | ANON 16:7
Boswell and Johnson both T. | BOSW 137:6
revolutionaries are potential T. | ORW 500:4
stern and unbending T. | MAC 435:3
T. are atrophied Englishmen | JOHN 367:14
T. own no argument | BROW 146:25
torment: shall no t. touch them | BIBLE 86:28
smoke of their t. ascendeth | BIBLE 107:4
Thou art to me a delicious t. | EMER 276:23
t. of the night's untruth | DAN 229:16
t. than a hermit's fast | KEATS 388:16
tormented: has t. us to the full | GUM 319:15
tormenting: t. the people with trivia | NAP 489:14
torments: t. also may in length | MILT 469:17
t. lie in the small circle | CIBB 203:18
T. not moved, unheard | ALAB 7:1
torpedo: it becomes a t. to him | JOHN 371:7
torpedoes: Damn the t.! | FARR 281:1
torrent: down the t. of his fate | JOHN 370:21
leave it to a t. of change | CHES 199:21
stem the t. of a woman | ANON 19:18
torrents: t. of her myriad universe | TENN 686:3
torrid: t. or the frozen zone | CAREW 179:9
tort: *Quand tout le monde a t.* | LA CH 405:6
tortoise: this 'ere 'T.' is a insect | PUNCH 531:16
t. as a worthy adversary | BROO 143:19
t.-like but not so slow | MARV 451:13
torture: polite form of self-imposed t. | MILL 461:23
shall tire T. and Time | BYRON 169:7
t. of the mind to lie | SHAK 603:3
t. one poor word ten thousand | DRYD 261:3
t. them into believing | NEWM 493:9
t. to death only one tiny | DOST 254:6
torturer: life and the t.'s horse | AUDEN 35:7
Tory: burning hatred for the T. | BEVAN 68:13
I may be a T. | PEEL 511:1
T. and Whig in turns shall | SMITH 653:4
T. men and Whig measures | DISR 248:4
T.'s secret weapon | KILM 396:4
wise T. and a wise Whig | JOHN 375:28
toss: chafe and t. in the spray | ARN 27:7
good enough to t. | SHAK 581:25
tossed: children, t. to and fro | BIBLE 102:17
t. and gored several persons | BOSW 137:9
tossing: t. about in a steamer | GILB 304:15
Your mind is t. on the ocean | SHAK 607:2
total: t. absolution of the Jewish | GOER 308:16
totalitarianism: under the name of t. | GAND 297:8
totem: And under the t. poles | MACN 440:16
totter: charming to t. into vogue | WALP 719:10
totters: Who t. forth, wrapped | SHEL 643:26
totus: *et in se ipso t.* | HOR 351:11
touch: Can t. him further | SHAK 603:3
Do not t. me | BIBLE 108:16
exquisite t. | SCOTT 561:1
he do but t. the hills | BOOK 132:10
live to see thee in my t. | SHAK 596:25
natural t. | SHAK 604:4
That puts it not unto the t. | GRAH 313:15
T. me not | BIBLE 97:34
T. not the cat but a glove | SCOTT 560:17
t. of earthly years | WORD 748:1
t. of Harry in the night | SHAK 585:17
t. of nature makes | SHAK 627:22
with gentle hand t. | WORD 745:9
touched: this hath t. thy lips | BIBLE 82:21
t. none that he did not adorn | JOHN 374:21
T. to the quick, he said | BROW 150:14
Who t. my clothes | BIBLE 93:12
touches: silent t. of time | BURKE 159:25
Such heavenly t. ne'er touched | SHAK 633:5

touches: (cont.):
t. of sweet harmony | SHAK 610:1
Who t. this touches a man | WHIT 732:10
toucheth: t. pitch shall be defiled | BIBLE 87:19
tough: T., and devilish sly | DICK 240:11
t. get going | KENN 394:10
toujours: t. gai toujours gai | MARQ 448:15
Toulouse: suspicious of T. | MERR 458:12
tourist: camera makes everyone a t. | SONT 656:5
loathsome is the British t. | KILV 396:5
t. the last enchantments | BEER 59:14
tournament: We in the t.—you against me | BETJ 68:6
tous: *T. pour un, un pour tous* | DUMAS 263:13
tout le monde: *Quand t. a tort* | LA CH 405:6
toves: slithy t. | CARR 182:18
towards: Neither from nor t. | ELIOT 270:16
tower: Caesar's ill-erected t. | SHAK 621:3
Childe Roland to the Dark T. | BROW 149:3
Child Roland to the dark t. | SHAK 596:17
Fighting in the captain's t. | DYLAN 265:12
Giotto's t. | LONG 426:21
intending to build a t. | BIBLE 94:33
length that t. of strength | TENN 687:16
name is a t. of strength | SHAK 622:9
thy nose is as the t. | BIBLE 82:3
with a t. and bells | CRAB 224:19
with the blasted t. | NERV 492:2
towered: T. cities please us | MILT 465:15
towering: his own t. style | CHES 199:22
towers: branchy between t. | HOPK 345:9
bright t. of silence steal | DE L 235:22
built in heaven high t. | MILT 469:8
cloud-capped t. | SHAK 625:28
exult, and London's t. | BLAKE 112:9
hammered from a hundred t. | TENN 681:8
sleep old palaces and t. | SHEL 641:16
spires, ye antique t. | GRAY 315:21
tell the t. thereof | BOOK 127:23
then entrenched his t. | DRAY 258:3
T., and battlements it sees | MILT 465:11
t. the last enchantments | ARN 29:15
Two t. of sail at dawn of day | CLOU 207:22
With walls and t. were girdled | COL 210:9
towery: T. city and branchy | HOPK 345:9
town: Come sounding through the t. | BALL 49:3
Country in the t. | MART 449:17
country retreat near the t. | WYCH 750:2
country is my detestation | BURN 160:20
destroy the t. to save it | ANON 15:7
down to the end of the t. | MILNE 462:13
each and every t. or city | HOLM 342:7
go seaward from the t. | HUNT 356:11
haunted it is to me | LANG 408:14
He gives directions to the t. | SWIFT 675:4
man made the t. | BRAD 139:1
man made the t. | COWP 223:18
pretty how t. | CUMM 228:5
spreading of the hideous t. | MORR 485:12
There is a tavern in the t. | ANON 18:11
took the way that takes the t. | HERB 334:3
t. and village, dome and farm | DYER 265:7
t. by river or sea shore | KEATS 388:29
What's this dull t. to me | KEPP 394:11
when he studies it in t. | COWP 223:9
town-crier: t. spoke my lines | SHAK 576:5
towns: Seven wealthy t. contend | ANON 17:19
thou art of t. *A per se* | ANON 15:24
t. he ran his godly race | GOLD 310:9
t. that we believe | AUDEN 34:14
townspeople: I will teach you my t. | WILL 737:13
toy: created to be the t. of man | WOLL 741:11
foolish thing was but a t. | SHAK 630:37
Or sells eternity to get a t. | SHAK 632:22
Truth is now her painted t. | YEATS 753:7
toys: All is but t. | SHAK 602:17
And all my t. beside me lay | STEV 668:15
Deceive boys with t. | LYS 433:15
make you brooches and t. | STEV 668:24
must beat on tickle t. | GASC 298:19
Not to meddle with my t. | STEV 668:16

toys: (cont.):
prayer-books are the t. of age | POPE 522:16
that with alluring t. | GREE 317:8
then cast their t. away | COWP 222:9
t. and things to eat | STEV 668:18
toyshop: moving t. of the heart | POPE 523:17
t. between birth and death | MORR 485:7
trace: delights to t. unusual things | WINC 739:4
Projecting trait and t. | HARDY 325:8
t. my ancestry back | GILB 304:20
traces: on winter's t. | SWIN 675:21
tracing: fitful t. of a portal | STEV 666:8
track: ancient t. marched | MER 458:6
Come flying on our t. | THOM 696:18
T. twenty nine | GORD 312:13
tracks: staring at its own t. | MAND 444:4
still hungry on the t. | CRANE 225:23
tract: And left a little t. | WILDE 736:2
trade: And all is seared with t. | HOPK 345:10
And arts of t., I sing | DYER 265:2
art in London only is a t. | DRYD 261:16
autocrat: that's my t. | CATH 185:7
great t. will always | BURKE 157:15
heel of the North-East T. | KIPL 399:17
Irish poets, learn your t. | YEATS 753:16
It is not your t. to make | JOHN 372:3
Of us that t. in love | SHAK 565:11
pardon me, it is His t. | HEINE 331:4
penny in the way of t. | COWP 223:14
pre-eminence in her Colonial t. | GEOR 301:2
samphire, dreadful t. | SHAK 597:1
There isn't any T. | HERB 333:19
t. of war I have slain men | SHAK 614:26
t. seldom meet together | SMITH 650:18
traffic from the vulgar t. | MARL 447:13
War is the t. of kings | DRYD 260:33
wheels of t. | HUME 355:9
tradesmen: bow, ye t., bow | GILB 304:6
Trade Unionism: T. of the married | SHAW 637:17
trade unionist: T. when you want to change him | BEVIN 69:12
trade unions: first snarl of the t. | LLOY 424.4
tradition: t. approves all forms | CLOU 207:20
T. is entirely different | STR 670:22
T. means giving votes | CHES 199:19
We don't want t. | FORD 289.4
youth of America is their oldest t. | WILDE 735:26
traditional: T. sanctity and loveliness | YEATS 751:5
traditions: shares in the old t. | OSB 501:16
traduced: t. Joseph K. | KAFKA 384:15
traffic: Hushing the latest t. | BRID 141:3
Is now the two hours' t. | SHAK 622:18
mighty roar of London's t. | ANON 17:4
t. and all the noise | PUSH 533:5
t. from the vulgar trade | MARL 447:13
tragedies: All t. are finished by a death | BYRON 170:26
with the t. of antiquity | STOP 670:1
tragedy: be out of it simply a t. | WILDE 735:31
blustering about Imperial T. | BROWN 144:12
dreary subject of world's t. | DRAY 258:3
either for t., comedy | SHAK 575:2
first time as t. | BARN 53:10
first time as t. | MARX 452:7
go, litel myn t. | CHAU 195:26
great t. of Science | HUXL 358:3
I will write you a t. | FITZ 284:23
lies the t. of the age | DU B 263:5
so convenient in t. | ANOU 23:3
That element of t. | ELIOT 269:18
That is their t. | WILDE 734:15
That is what t. means | STOP 670:5
t., and she played it in tights | BEER 59:21
t. and therefore not worth | AUST 38:12
t. for a poet | COCT 208:11
T. is clean, it is restful | ANOU 23:4
T. is thus a representation | ARIS 25:12
t. means unpleasantness | DIN 246:9
t. of a man who could not | OLIV 498:13
t. of a man who has found | BARR 54:14

tragedy: (*cont.*):
t. of the classical languages MADAN 441:8
T. ought really LAWR 412:25
t. requires *testicles* VOLT 717:2
t. to those that feel WALP 719:18
washy way of true t. KAV 386:4
wine a farce and the food a t. POW 528:3
You *may* abuse a t. JOHN 372:3
tragic: acted so t. HARG 326:9
essentially a t. age LAWR 411:12
In t. life, God wot MER 458:8
perhaps a t. failure ELIOT 269:11
tragical: Merry and t. SHAK 612:19
suggesting t. possibilities HARDY 324:12
trahit: *T. sua quemque voluptas* VIRG 714:17
trail: long, long t. awinding KING 390:6
t. has its own stern code SERV 563:4
trailing: t. clouds of glory WORD 745:14
T. in the cool stream ARN 28:5
train: biggest electric t. set WELL 726:23
headlight of an oncoming t. DICK 245:9
his t. filled the temple BIBLE 82:19
light of the oncoming t, LOW 430:19
next t. has gone PUNCH 540:7
Runs the red electric t. BETJ 68:2
t. is arriving on time MUSS 488:18
t. of events has carried AMERY 16:5
T. up a child in the way BIBLE 79:11
Trust the t., Mademoiselle CHR 200:9
we rush in the t. THOM 696:18
who shaves and takes a t. WHITE 731:1
will pack, and take a t. BROO 143:12
world and all her t. VAUG 709:11
trains: through the fields in t. CHES 199:2
trait: Projecting t. and trace HARDY 325:8
traitor: by that t. to learning JOHN 366:15
Do hate the t., though they DAN 230:4
I find myself a t. SHAK 621:1
traitors: fears do make us t. SHAK 604:3
they can see a sort of t. SHAK 621:1
t. and the treason love DRYD 260:27
tram: not even a bus, I'm a t. HARE 326:7
tramp: the lady is a t. HART 327:12
t. of the twenty-two men BOWEN 138:6
trample: If you bare t. upon these SHEL 644:10
t. round my fallen head TENN 680:16
t. the vices AUG 37:10
Whose light doth t. on my days VAUG 709:6
trance: And in mad t., strike SHEL 639:22
He fell into a t. BIBLE 98:19
trancèd: t. summer-night KEATS 387:27
trances: t. of the blast COL 210:6
Tränen: *Wer nie sein Brot mit T.* GOET 309:15
tranquil: Farewell the t. mind SHAK 616:20
tranquillity: chaos remembered in t. THUR 697:20
emotion recollected in t. WORD 748:19
Fame and t. can never MONT 481:3
moments of t. in great works VOLT 716:18
Passionless bride, divine T. TENN 686:5
Sorrow is t. remembered PARK 506:14
T. Base here ALDR 8:7
t. which religion is powerless FORB 288:19
tranquillized: t. *Fifties* LOW 430:13
transaction: both ignored the t. LEV 420:1
transcendental: idle chatter of a t. kind GILB 305:16
T. moonshine CARL 181:2
transform: those who t. the world AUDEN 36:16
t. ourselves into beasts SHAK 616:6
transformed: t. into a gigantic insect KAFKA 384:18
transgress: t. the law DOST 254:9
transgression: there is no t. BIBLE 90:23
transgressions: was wounded for our t. BIBLE 84:12
transgressors: numbered with the t. BIBLE 84:14
way of t. is hard BIBLE 78:27
transient: terra firma and t. LOW 430:8
t. is the smile of fate DYER 265:6
T. lustre, beauteous clay WRIG 749:12
transit: *Sic t. gloria mundi* ANON 22:15

transit: (*cont.*):
t. *gloria mundi* THOM 692:3
transitory: Action is t. WORD 743:7
in this t. life are in trouble BOOK 122:3
translate: as well as t. Epictetus JOHN 371:6
such as cannot write, t. DENH 236:20
translated: thou art t. SHAK 611:25
T. Daughter, come down AUDEN 34:2
t. into another tongue BIBLE 87:7
t. into Italian WHAR 730:2
translation: be a mistake in the t. VANB 708:2
only a *t.* of the Bible WHAT 730:12
Poetry is what is lost in t. FROST 295:19
t. is no translation unless SYNGE 677:8
t.'s thief that addeth MARV 451:5
unfaithful to the t. BORG 136:9
vanity of t. SHEL 644:4
translations: t. not unlike HOW 353:3
transmigrates: elements once out of it, it t. SHAK 565:15
transmutations: delighted with t. NEWT 494:1
transport: T. of Delight FLAN 285:14
wished to share the t. WORD 748:6
transported: t. and ravished me TRAH 701:14
trapeze: young man on the flying t. LEYB 421:11
trappings: t. and suits of woe SHAK 572:10
traps: t. and a lion to frighten MACH 438:10
trash: peasants their vile t. SHAK 593:6
society founded on t. SAY 557:14
steals my purse steals t. SHAK 616:12
trau: *Weil ich ihm nicht t.* BREC 140:8
Traum: *schreit im T. um Hilfe* CAN 178:2
traurig: *Dass ich so t. bin* HEINE 330:15
travail: had my labour for my t. SHAK 627:4
travaileth: groaneth and t. in pain BIBLE 99:37
travel: discover we must t. too FITZ 284:6
Englishman does not t. STER 664:3
have discredited your t. SHAK 564:20
heart turns to t. POUND 527:11
in a moment t. thither WORD 746:5
I t. for travel's sake STEV 667:20
preserve all that t. by land SWIFT 674:8
real way to t. GRAH 314:3
school, and not to t. BACON 44:35
That ever thought the t. long ROYD 549:15
there are two classes of t. BENC 62:11
tired with labour of far t. CAT 186:3
t. by land or by water BOOK 120:1
t. from Dan to Beersheba STER 664:4
t. hopefully STEV 667:29
t. in the direction of our fear BERR 66:17
T. light and you can sing JUV 384:5
would *not* t. due West CARR 184:3
travelled: care which way he t. BEAV 57:6
I took the one less t. FROST 295:9
I t. among unknown men WORD 744:14
traveller: Come, O thou T. unknown WESL 728:8
I met a t. from an antique land SHEL 642:3
lost t.'s dream under BLAKE 111:23
No t. returns, puzzles SHAK 575:16
Now spurs the lated t. apace SHAK 603:6
Sun cannot forget his fellow t. ANON 18:7
thrown off this t.'s trance DAY-L 233:3
To the misled and lonely t. MILT 463:20
t. betwixt life and death WORD 747:19
t., by the faithful hound LONG 426:20
T., knocking on the moonlit DE L 236:6
t. need have no scruple BAED 46:6
Where the t.'s journey is done BLAKE 114:5
World-besotted t. YEATS 753:11
Travellers: 'The T.' Rest' HARDY 326:1
t. must be content SHAK 560:2
travelleth: poverty come as one that t. BIBLE 78:14
travelling: no flute exemplify its t. WILB 734:4
t. at twenty miles a second EDD 266:4
T. is the ruin of all happiness BURN 160:14
travels: t. fastest who travels KIPL 399:18
t. the world in search MOORE 482:9
Tray: my poor dog T. CAMP 176:13
T., Blanch, Sweet-heart SHAK 596:19

treachery: fear their subjects' t. SHAK 588:2
justly killed with my own t. SHAK 579:6
t. of the intellectuals BENDA 62:14
which even t. cannot trust JUN 383:9
tread: Doth close behind him t. COL 211:14
face with an undaunted t. STEV 668:17
May we t. rejoicingly WILL 737:14
t. on classic ground ADD 4:2
t. safely into the unknown HASK 328:1
T. softly because you tread YEATS 751:22
Were it ever so airy a t. TENN 686:20
Where'er you t. POPE 523:13
treason: bloody t. flourished over us SHAK 592:14
cannot commit t. COKE 209:3
condoned high t. DISR 247:18
hate traitors and the t. DRYD 260:27
If *this* be t. HENRY 333:5
It were t. to our love THOR 697:11
like this, is a sort of t. BURKE 157:8
none dare call it t. HAR 326:12
reason why gunpowder t. ANON 17:11
state hireling for t. JOHN 368:5
Such popular humanity is t. ADD 3:20
temptation is the greatest t. ELIOT 272:10
though they love the t. DAN 230:4
t. can but peep to what SHAK 578:5
t. enough for God's sake SHAK 602:9
T. has done his worst SHAK 603:3
t. is not owned when 'tis DRYD 261:7
'Twixt t. and convenience CLEV 206:13
treasonous: their t. parles BROW 151:5
treasons: fit for t., stratagems SHAK 610:3
treasure: hearts' t. fixed ROCH 543:9
he that has stolen the t. CONG 215:10
preserve it as your chiefest t. BELL 60:21
purest t. mortal times afford SHAK 619:7
pure t. without measure SCOTT 559:1
She is your t. SHAK 624:13
this t. in earthen vessels BIBLE 101:17
thought my t. to dispose AST 32:6
thou shalt have t. BIBLE 91:23
t. in the world can countervail GRIM 318:12
t. of our tongue DAN 230:2
Where your t. is BIBLE 89:7
witty woman is a t. MER 457:17
yet liking his t. THOM 694:7
treasures: t. from an earthen pot HERB 334:10
t. upon earth BIBLE 89:6
t. we up-lay BOLT 117:16
Whan alle t. arn tried LANG 408:23
treasuries: sunken wrack and sumless t. SHAK 584:21
Treasury: plaintive treble of the T. DISR 247:2
T. is the spring BAG 46:14
T. were to fill old bottles KEYN 395:9
treat: compelled to t. themselves first THOM 694:10
I t. 'em just the same DUREM 264:10
Nor t. with virtuous scorn GILB 304:8
Talk about a t. COLL 213:6
t. if met where any bar HARDY 325:12
treaties: T. are like girls DE G 235:4
treatment: scientific t. for all diseases SHAW 636:10
suitable case for t. MERC 457:12
treaty: signed the t. bred a fever THOM 693:10
This is not a peace t. FOCH 288:7
treble: childish t. SHAK 568:16
plaintive t. of the Treasury DISR 247:2
trebled: t. twenty times myself SHAK 609:2
tree: A-hanging on the t. CART 184:12
An' there vor me the apple t. BARN 53:13
billboard lovely as a t. NASH 490:20
But there's a t., of many one WORD 745:14
If he finds that this t. KNOX 403:10
I must climb the t. HERB 335:18
I shall be like that t. SWIFT 675:17
I thocht it was a trustie t. BALL 51:2
it is a t. of life BIBLE 78:26
It is not growing like a t. JONS 379:21
Lawyers may revere that t. FERG 281:11

tree: *(cont.)*:

live on this Crumpetty T.	LEAR 414:19
more to my mind than a t.	MORR 485:4
O blest unfabled Incense T.	DARL 231:2
on the t. of life	MILT 471:1
place where the t. falleth	BIBLE 80:26
poem lovely as a t.	KILM 396:2
she gave me of the t.	BIBLE 70:11
Should we miss but a t.	BLAM 114:20
some single herb or t.	MARV 450:5
spare the beechen t.	CAMP 176:11
these things in a green t.	BIBLE 95:24
three ravens sat on a t.	BALL 50:18
Till the t. die	SHAK 571:20
time the river in the t.	DICK 245:5
Too happy, happy t.	KEATS 387:32
t. about which did not know	COWL 221:20
t. by a river a little	GILB 305:11
t. did end their race	MARV 450:8
t. is known by his fruit	BIBLE 90:31
t. of actual life springs	GOET 309:5
T. of Knowledge is not	BYRON 172:16
t. of knowledge of good	BIBLE 70:2
t. of liberty must be refreshed	JEFF 364:9
t. of life also	BIBLE 70:2
t. of the knowledge	BIBLE 70:3
t. on which our mischief	DRAY 258:3
t.'s inclined	POPE 520:27
t. that a wise man sees	BLAKE 112:19
t. were for the healing	BIBLE 107:23
Under the greenwood t.	SHAK 568:8
wish I were a t.	HERB 334:4
Woodman, spare that t.	MORR 485:8

treen: t. priests and golden chalices

	JEWEL 366:7

trees: all the t. are green

And with the t. to newer birth	GREN 318:2
Bosomed high in tufted t.	MILT 465:11
climbing t. in the Hesperides	SHAK 598:20
did gently kiss the t.	SHAK 609:23
die when the t. were green	CLARE 204:17
Generations pass while some t.	BROW 145:21
green grass and bursting t.	GREN 318:2
I see men as t., walking	BIBLE 93:13
Loveliest of t., the cherry now	HOUS 352:5
music of its t. at dawn	ARN 27:16
Orpheus with his lute made t.	SHAK 588:15
selected the felling of t.	CHUR 201:17
shady t. cover him	BIBLE 78:3
tall ancestral t.	HEM 331:11
t. I see barren of leaves	SHAK 633:4
t. of the Lord also	BOOK 132:8
t. so shattered	SACK 552:12
t. that grow so fair	KIPL 400:10
t. to speak	SHAK 603:13
t. when I saw them first	TRAH 701:14
T., where you sit	POPE 523:13
t. will never get across	FROST 295:4
unto the root of the t.	BIBLE 88:16
upon the t. that are therein	BOOK 134:17
We harden like t.	MONT 480:6
With rocks, and stones, and t.	WORD 748:1

Trelawny: And shall T. die | HAWK 328:4

tremble: I pant, I sink, I t. | SHEL 640:11

made great Olympus t.	HOMER 343:1
shall t. at the look of him	BOOK 132:10
start and t. under her feet	TENN 686:20
That t. into thought	COL 209:20
t. and despoil themselves	SHEL 641:17
t. for my country when	JEFF 364:18
t. like a guilty thing	WORD 746:3

trembled: t. with fear at your frown

	ENGL 277:24
Laugh at all you t. at	COWP 223:7
T. the mariners	ANAT 11:6

tremblers: boding t. learned | GOLD 310:12

trembles: he t. as I do | WELL 727:2

t. on the brink of a lovely song | HAMM 322:14

trembling: Enter every t. heart | WESL 728:14

salvation with fear and t.	BIBLE 103:6
They brought the t. woman	BLAKE 111:19
T., hoping, ling'ring, flying	POPE 519:13
T. in her soft and chilly nest	KEATS 387:7

trembling: *(cont.)*:

t. most, maintain a dignity	WALP 720:6
t. seizes all of me	SAPP 556:1

tremulous: behind my t. stay | HARDY 324:22

trenchant: t. blade, Toledo | BUTL 166:8

trencher: Dead Caesar's t. | SHAK 565:20

trencher-friends: t., time's flies | SHAK 626:12

trencher-man: very valiant t. | SHAK 613:7

trenches: t. and trying on gas-masks

	CHAM 189:7
t. in thy beauty's field	SHAK 633:1

Trent: o'er the wide vale of T. | MAC 436:2

trespass: And t. there and go | HOUS 352:1

trespasses: forgive us our t. | BOOK 118:10

tress: A little stolen t. | YEATS 753:4

tresses: or t. like the morn | MILT 464:8

t. deep'ning in the sun	BYRON 168:4
t. man's imperial race insnare	POPE 523:21

trial: In the years of t. | PAST 508:10

t. by juries impartially	JEFF 364:6
t. by jury itself	DENM 237:1
t. if I recognize it as such	KAFKA 384:16
t. is by what is contrary	MILT 475:7
t. of which you can have	SHAW 636:23
t. through which we pass	LINC 422:5

triangle: eternal t. | ANON 13:2

t. in a quadrangle | AUBR 33:4

triangles: t. make a God | MONT 481:14

tribal: constructing t. lays | KIPL 399:11

t. God who has made	BURR 164:6
t., intimate revenge	HEAN 329:20

tribe: All that t. | HOR 351:1

badge of all our t.	SHAK 607:22
Richer than all his t.	SHAK 618:20
To purify the dialect of the t.	ELIOT 271:5

tribeless: t., and nationless | SHEL 642:18

tribes: Formed of two mighty t. | BYRON 171:27

For thither the t. go up | BOOK 133:25

tribulation: In all time of our t. | BOOK 119:18

which came out of great t.	BIBLE 106:21
world ye shall have t.	BIBLE 97:21

tribunal: There's a new t. now | BROW 152:23

tribute: pay his t. to the Sea | DENH 236:16

To his feet thy t. bring	LYTE 433:17
tribute to whom t.	BIBLE 100:9
t. vice pays to virtue	LA R 410:16

trick: conjuring t. with bones | JENK 365:4

dream when the long t.'s over	MAS 453:9
I know a t. worth two	SHAK 580:3
play fair to win the t.	LAB 404:17
pleasing to t. the trickster	LA F 405:10
t. for trick expect	BEHN 60:11
T. that everyone abhors	BELL 61:7
When in doubt, win the t.	HOYLE 353:8

tricks: And for t. that are vain | HARTE 327:17

Frustrate their knavish t.	ANON 13:19
shaped for sportive t.	SHAK 621:15
t. are either knavish	JOHN 375:9
t. in plain and simple	SHAK 592:25
Women are like t. by slight	CONG 215:11

tried: she for a little t. | WOTT 749:4

t. a little, failed much	STEV 667:7
t. at least once	BENN 63:1
t. and found wanting	CHES 199:23
when he is t.	BIBLE 104:25

trifle: As 'twere a careless t. | SHAK 600:14

t. with the spoon | POPE 521:1

trifles: She who t. with all | GAY 299:28

snapper-up of unconsidered t.	SHAK 631:25
T. light as air	SHAK 616:18
t. were worth something	CAT 185:11
write t. with dignity	JOHN 375:19

trigger: whose finger do you want on the t.

	ANON 19:21

triglyph: now that t.'s here | CUMM 228:8

Trinity: strong name of the T. | ALEX 8:15

Three Persons, blessèd T.	HEBER 330:5
worship one God in T.	BOOK 119:13

trinket: jest, and joy's a t. | STEP 663:16

trinkets: ye returned to your t. | KIPL 399:13

trip: Come, and t. it as ye go | MILT 466:5

fairy t. upon the green	SHAK 635:12
look forward to the t.	STIN 669:11

trip: *(cont.)*:

nimble and airy servitors t.	MILT 475:1
To t. it, trip it, trip	ANON 12:25
t. the victor ship comes	WHIT 732:7
t. through a sewer	MIZN 478:12

triple: breast, and t. bronze | HOR 349:2

There be t. ways to take	KIPL 399:17
t. cord, which no man	BURKE 157:7
t. sight in blindness keen	KEATS 390:24

triple-towered: t. sky | DAY-L 233:4

triplex: Illi robur et aes t. | HOR 349:2

trippingly: t. on the tongue | SHAK 576:5

trips: t. he must be sustained | CHUR 203:4

triste: Caballero de la T. Figura | CERV 188:8

île t. et noire	BAUD 55:10
jamais t. archy jamais triste	MARQ 448:14

tristesse: Adieu t. | É.LUA 276:3

Tristram: call him T. | MAL 443:5

Tristram Shandy: T. did not last | JOHN 374:9

T.; the great humour of which | WALP 719:6

Triton: this T. of the minnows | SHAK 570:11

T. blow his wreathèd horn | WORD 748:16

triumph: And t. evermore | WESL 728:13

are t. and defeat	LONG 427:6
forth in t. from the north	MAC 436:4
meet with t. and disaster	KIPL 400:14
nothing for evil to t.	BURKE 160:4
Now is the Victor's t. won	POTT 525:9
our career and our t.	VANZ 708:11
pedestalled in t.	BROW 152:21
Swell the t. of His train	WESL 728:15
there is no glory in the t.	CORN 218:15
thy t. over death and sin	SPEN 659:9
T. in God above	GURN 320:4
t. o'er the timid hare	THOM 696:9
t. of hope over experience	JOHN 373:12
t. of modern science	WAUGH 724:9
t. of the embalmer's art	VIDAL 711:3
uncircumcised t.	BIBLE 75:8
We shall not see the t.	DICK 244:5
When learning's t. o'er	JOHN 370:11

triumphant: bound in with the t. sea

	SHAK 619:18
With a t. noise	WESL 728:12

triumphantes: laeti t. | ANON 21:18

triumphs: He sickened at all t. | CHUR 201:9

trivial: away all t. fond records | SHAK 573:22

mighty contests rise from t.	POPE 523:15
t. and vulgar way of coition	BROW 146:16
t. people should muse	LAWR 412:23
t. personalities decomposing	WOOLF 742:5
t. round, the common task	KEBLE 392:20

trivialities: t. where opposites | BOHR 117:1

trod: t., as on the four winds | MARV 450:18

T. beside me, close and | HOUS 352:16

trodden: little fire is quickly t. | SHAK 588:5

troika: t. nothing can overtake | GOGOL 310:2

Trojan: T. 'orses will jump out | BEVIN 69:16

Trojans: T. and the well-greaved Achaeans

	HOMER 343:2
We T. are at an end	VIRG 712:20

tromper: t. le trompeur | LA F 405:10

troops: charged the t. of error | BROW 145:29

her Aeneas shall want t.	SHAK 566:9
In solemn t., and sweet	MILT 466:14

troopship: t. leaving Bombay | HUGH 353:16

trope: out there flew a t. | BUTL 165:25

tropes: ranged his t., and preached

	PRIOR 529:10

trophies: among her cloudy t. hung

	KEATS 389:7
her weedy t. and herself	SHAK 578:13
t. o'er the garden gates	POPE 522:25
t. unto the enemies	BROW 145:29

tropic: t. is our language spoke | WALL 718:20

tropical: night of t. splendour | PORT 524:21

Trostmittel: Selbstmord ist ein starkes T.

	NIET 495:14

troth: thereto I give thee my t. | BOOK 123:20

trouble: deliver him in the time of t.

	BOOK 126:27
Double, double toil and t.	SHAK 603:17
few days, and full of t.	BIBLE 77:21

trouble: (*cont.*):
For a charm of powerful t.   SHAK 603:18
Gold? a transient, shining t.   GRAI 314:4
Go t. younger hearts   WYATT 749:16
In t. and in joy   TATE 678:17
Is to have your t. doubled   DEFOE 234:12
Man is born unto t.   BIBLE 77:12
present help in time of t.   ANON 11:16
There may be t. ahead   BERL 65:16
To-day the Roman and his t.   HOUS 352:13
to save t. I wed again   CLARE 204:19
transcendent capacity of taking t.
                                    CARL 180:18
transitory life are in t.   BOOK 122:3
t. deaf heaven   SHAK 633:10
t. enough of its own   WILC 734:7
t. myself I am learning   VIRG 712:11
Wenlock Edge the wood's in t.   HOUS 352:12
When in t., delegate   BOREN 136:7
when it is not our t.   MARQ 448:16
When there's t. brewing   KNIG 402:22
when we are in bad t.   DID 246:1
women and care and t.   WARD 721:21
You took the t. to be born   BEAU 56:12
troubled: calms the t. breast   NEWT 494:10
calm the t. mind   CONG 216:5
heart be t.   BIBLE 97:10
Like a bridge over t. water   SIMON 647:18
meteor, to the t. air   GRAY 315:7
sacrifice of God is a t. spirit   BOOK 128:8
see that ye be not t.   BIBLE 92:8
t. with her lonely life   PEPYS 512:10
troubles: against a sea of t.   SHAK 575:16
From t. of the world   HARV 327:23
house that has got over its t.   JER 365:15
neighbourhood had 't.'   WHAR 730:4
our t. and adversities   BOOK 120:3
pack up your t. in your old   ASAF 30:17
sleep with a woman whose t.   ALGR 9:5
t. of our proud and angry   HOUS 351:18
written t. of the brain   SHAK 604:22
troublesome: refined sentiments most t.
                                    KELLY 393:3
troubling: t. her mind   WALK 717:11
wicked cease from t.   BIBLE 77:8
trouser-clip: t. for bicyclists MORT 486:15
trousers: bottoms of my t. rolled ELIOT 272:6
like a steam-engine in t.   SMITH 653:14
not a man, but—a cloud in t.   MAY 454:17
shall wear white flannel t.   ELIOT 272:6
t. on when you go out   IBSEN 359:2
trout: t. that must be caught   SHAK 629:23
Where the grey t. lies asleep   HOGG 341:16
you find a t. in the milk   THOR 696:23
trovato: è molto ben t.   ANON 21:17
trowel: She lays it on with a t. CONG 215:3
should lay it on with a t.   DISR 249:11
With his t. point   HEAN 329:17
Troy: And heard T. doubted   BYRON 171:10
another T. for her to burn   YEATS 752:15
Greece is fallen and T. town   COL 209:8
night when T. was sacked   ROWE 549:6
ringing plains of windy T.   TENN 690:1
sacked T.'s sacred city   HOMER 343:11
T. came destined an exile   VIRG 711:18
Where's T., and where's   BRAM 139:16
truant: every t. knew   GOLD 310:12
I have a t. been to chivalry   SHAK 581:29
t. disposition, good my lord   SHAK 572:14
trucks: lot to learn about t.   AWDRY 40:6
true: Ah, love, let us be t.   ARN 27:1
And is it t.? And is it true   BETJ 67:4
called Faithful and T.   BIBLE 107:12
dark and t. and tender   TENN 088.6
heart of a t. Englishman   ADD 4:15
He said t. things, but called   BROW 148:6
If it is not t., it is a happy   ANON 21:17
If t., here only   MILT 471:2
I know what t. love   TENN 682:2
in her ear, 'You are not t.'   WILB 734:3
itself do rest but t.   SHAK 594:16
Let God be t.   BIBLE 99:20
man would like to be t.   BACON 45:19

true: (*cont.*):
minding t. things by what   SHAK 585:18
my shape as t.   SHAK 594:26
My t. love was true   HARB 323:9
Of t. wood, of yew wood   DOYLE 257:3
only things that are t.   SHAW 636:2
pessimist fears this is t.   CAB 174:12
ring in the t.   TENN 684:10
should always say what's t.   STEV 668:20
speak t., right wrong   TENN 681:22
spirit is the t. self   CIC 204:4
state by proportions t.   MARV 450:4
tell you three times is t.   CARR 183:27
think what is t. and do   HUXL 358:5
thou wast as t. a lover   SHAK 568:3
to thine own self be t.   SHAK 573:4
t. as truth's simplicity   SHAK 627:18
t. because a man dies   WILDE 735:24
t. beginning of our end   SHAK 612:22
t. love hath my heart   SIDN 646:14
t. love never did run   SHAK 610:21
T. patriots we   CART 184:11
t. proposition is more   WHIT 701:10
t. thy chartered freemen   JOHN 377:14
t. to thyself as thou   BACON 45:6
unfaithful kept him falsely t.   TENN 682:3
we are sure they are t.   SHAK 632:8
What! can the devil speak t.   SHAK 600:9
Whatsoever things are t.   BIBLE 103:13
what we are saying is t.   RUSS 551:17
words are t. and faithful   BIBLE 107:18
true-love: do as much for my t. BALL 51:1
truer: And nothing's t.   DICK 239:33
truest: paint 'em t. praise 'em ADD 3:15
truffles: Thy t., Perigord!   POPE 519:9
trump: at the last t.   BIBLE 101:14
with the sound of the t.   BOOK 127:20
trumpet: And blow your own t.   GILB 306:16
Blow t., for the world   TENN 681:21
blow up the t.   BOOK 130:14
flute and the t.   AUDEN 35:3
great voice as of a t.   BIBLE 105:33
heard the sound of the t.   BIBLE 73:30
he blew a t.   BIBLE 74:8
He shifted his t.   GOLD 311:7
moved more than with a t.   SIDN 647:10
shrill t. sound   CIBB 203:22
t. give an uncertain sound   BIBLE 101:2
t. in terrible tones went   ENN 278:3
t. shall sound   BIBLE 101:14
t. shall be heard on high   DRYD 261:26
t. shrill hath thrice already   SPEN 659:8
t.'s silver sound is still   SCOTT 560:1
t. summons us again   KENN 394:1
t. will fling out a wonderful   MISS 477:12
Yet ever and anon a t. sounds   THOM 695:6
trumpeter: tongue our t.   SHAK 570:3
trumpets: eagles and the t.   ELIOT 270:10
foie gras to the sound of t.   SMITH 653:23
He saith among the t.   BIBLE 77:39
snarling t. 'gan to chide   KEATS 386:22
Sound the t., beat the drums   MOR 484:17
t. en de bangin' er de   HARR 327:9
t. sounded for him   BUNY 156:16
t. to announce the beginning   MANN 445:1
t. which sing to battle   SHEL 644:8
uplifted angel t. blow   MILT 463:10
With t. also, and shawms   BOOK 131:14
trumps: If dirt were t.   LAMB 407:10
Let spades be t.! she said   POPE 523:27
turn out the ace of t.   CHUR 201:21
trunk: So large a t. before   BELL 60:22
trunkless: t. legs of stone   SHEL 642:3
trust: Because I don't t. him   BREC 140:8
built an absolute t.   SHAK 600:14
even treachery cannot t.   JUN 383:9
for the best, and t. in God   SMITH 653:9
frail mortality shall t.   BACON 45:28
he might t. in the flesh   BIBLE 103:7
I felt I did t. in Christ   WESL 728:19
In t. I have found treason   ELIZ 292:7
man assumes a public t.   JEFF 364:21
my sure t. is in thee   BOOK 129:16

trust: (*cont.*):
never should t. experts   SAL 554:2
Never t. the artist   LAWR 412:8
no more than power in t.   DRYD 259:5
not inclined to t. them   VIRG 715:7
Now t. in Christ his death   GILB 303:11
O put thy t. in God   BOOK 127:8
put no t. in the future   HOR 349:9
put not your t. in princes   BOOK 135:8
put their t. in chariots   BOOK 125:7
Put your t. in God   BLAC 110:9
still to those that t. 'em   WYCH 750:5
that all power is a t.   DISR 248:35
that put their t. in him   BOOK 124:11
T. his sworn brother   SHAK 632:12
t. me not at all or all in all   TENN 682:11
t. no man living with power   ADAMS 2:26
T. none, for oaths are straws   SHAK 585:6
T. one who has gone through it   VIRG 714:9
t. people is a luxury   FORS 290:9
t. that good shall fall   TENN 683:19
t. themselves with men   SHAK 626:7
T. the train, Mademoiselle   CHR 200:9
t. was with the eternal   MILT 469:11
was not properly but a t.   FOX 291:17
Whose t., ever childlike   STR 671:1
with pains that conquer t.   TENN 683:16
yet will I t. in him   BIBLE 77:20
trusted: armour wherein he t.   BIBLE 94:19
familiar friend, whom I t.   BOOK 127:1
He t. in God, that he would   BOOK 125:10
in thee have I t.   BOOK 118:14
Let no such man be t.   SHAK 610:3
unfit to be t.   CHES 198:23
trustest: t. upon the staff of this BIBLE 76:31
trusteth: blessed is the man that t. BOOK 126:13
trustie: I thocht it was a t. tree BALL 51:2
trusting: no t. appearances   SHER 645:21
trusts: that t. in the tameness SHAK 596:18
trustworthiness: With Carthaginian t.
                                    SALL 554:15
trusty: that t. Achates carried VIRG 712:4
T., dusky, vivid, true   STEV 669:1
truth: abode not in the t.   BIBLE 96:33
among seekers after t.   AUCT 33:23
And love of t.   TENN 681:25
And simple t. his utmost skill   WOTT 748:21
And t. thee shal delivere   CHAU 196:5
Art is not t.   PIC 514:9
As t. will paint it   CRAB 225:13
Beauty is t., truth beauty   KEATS 389:3
best test of t.   CHES 198:20
Bigotry tries to keep t.   TAG 678:6
bread of sincerity and t.   BIBLE 100:22
bright countenance of t.   MILT 476:7
bring t. to light   SHAK 632:23
But divine melodious t.   KEATS 386:8
'But love,' quoth he, 'says t.'   GREE 317:10
But that his simple t. must   SHAK 621:20
cancels everything but t.   HAZL 329:8
Christianity better than T.   COL 211:26
Church with the spirit of t.   BOOK 121:22
Cleared some great t.   TICK 698:4
Commencing in a t.   SHAK 600:12
consecrate to t. and liberty   SHEL 643:25
dared to speak the t. to me   TROL 703:11
dead we owe only t.   VOLT 717:1
dearer still is t.   ARIS 26:3
diminution of the love of t.   JOHN 368:8
does t. sound bitter   BROW 151:3
economical with the t.   ARMS 26:13
everybody can tell you the t.   MACH 438:12
exaggeration of t. that has lost   GIBR 303:4
experience, rooted in t.   HUNT 356:19
fable becomes the t.   COCT 208:7
face of t. suffer wrong   SCOTT 559:2
fiction lags after t.   BURKE 157:20
fight for freedom and t.   IBSEN 359:2
For t. to o'erpeer   SHAK 570:10
full of grace and t.   BIBLE 96:4
further to discover t.   BACON 45:1
Great is t., and it prevails   BIBLE 108:18
Great is T., and mighty   BIBLE 86:21

truth: (*cont.*):

great is t., and shall	BROO 144:5
Grey T. is now her painted toy	YEATS 753:7
have not maintained for t.	SWIFT 673:14
here have Pride and T.	YEATS 752:17
He who does not bellow the t.	PÉGUY 511:6
His t. is marching on	HOWE 353:2
I just tell the t.	TRUM 704:17
improbable, must be the t.	DOYLE 256:18
inquiry of t.	BACON 45:2
irreconcilable foes to t.	BUCK 154:8
is and will be beautiful is T.	TOLS 700:10
Is there in t. no beauty	HERB 335:6
It is the light of T.	DICK 239:10
knew T. put to the worse	MILT 475:16
lawyer interprets the t.	GIR 307:3
least touch of t.	BYRON 174:1
lie which is part a t.	TENN 681:11
like open t. to cover lies	CONG 215:5
loins girt about with t.	BIBLE 103:1
love of t. and right	TENN 684:11
love Scotland better than t.	JOHN 368:12
mainly he told the t.	TWAIN 706:1
men of less t. than tongue	SHAK 633:5
Mercy and t. are met together	BOOK 130:20
Ministers are wedded to the t.	SAKI 553:15
mistook disenchantment for t.	SART 556:12
neither T. nor Falsehood	HOBB 339:17
never ending battle for t.	ANON 13:8
new scientific t.	PLAN 516:1
noble end of glorious t.	IRWIN 360:20
Now I may wither into the t.	YEATS 754:9
one way possible of speaking t.	BROW 152:25
opposite is also a profound t.	BOHR 117:1
oratory alone is not t.	MAC 434:8
parsons do not care for t.	STUB 671:2
plain t. for plain people	WESL 728:22
platitude is simply a t.	BALD 48:8
positive in error as in t.	LOCKE 425:1
possesses not only t.	RUSS 551:20
possession of t.	LOCKE 424:19
possession of t. as of a city	BROW 146:1
Pure t., and perfect change	CORY 220.1
relationship with beauty and t.	KEATS 391:9
sad friends of T.	MILT 475:9
saith unto him, What is t.	BIBLE 97:24
send out thy light and thy t.	BOOK 127.7
shall follow t. too near	RAL 536:5
speaketh the t. from his	BOOK 124:28
spirit and in t.	BIBLE 96:17
Spirit that strove for t.	SHEL 643:6
stark naked t.	CLEL 206:4
still closing up t. to truth	MILT 475:10
Stretch age's t. sometimes	JONS 378:7
Strict Regard for T.	BELL 61:6
strife of T. with Falsehood	LOW 430:3
stupendous t. believed	SMART 650:4
sweet ornament which t.	SHAK 633:17
takes two to speak the t.	THOR 697:10
telling the t. about them	STEV 666:15
than a t. misunderstood	JAMES 363:18
that I have looked on t.	SHAK 634:21
that she is made of t.	SHAK 635:5
That t. lies somewhere	COWP 222:11
there *is* such a thing as t.	BAG 46:10
thy t. then be thy dower	SHAK 594:19
To forsake this t.	ROS 546:19
true as t.'s simplicity	SHAK 627:18
truer than the t.	ANOU 23:8
trusted to speak the t.	BALF 48:19
t. 24 times per second	GOD 308:4
T. and honour, fredom	CHAU 192:8
t. and untruth together	BACON 43:20
t. at all times firmly	KETHE 394:13
T. beareth away the victory	BIBLE 86:20
T. belongs to Thee alone	LESS 419:14
t. by consecutive reasoning	KEATS 391:6
T. can never be told	BLAKE 112:29
T. exists; only lies are	BRAQ 139:18
T. forever on the scaffold	LOW 430:4
T., for its own sake	KING 398:4
T. from his lips prevailed	GOLD 310:11
T. has no special time	SCHW 558:15

truth: (*cont.*):

t. has such a face	DRYD 260:20
t. in masquerade	BYRON 171:20
t. in the groves of Academe	HOR 348:19
t. in the inward parts	BOOK 128:5
t. in whores and ease	WRIG 749:13
t. is always strange	BYRON 171:29
T. is a pathless land	KRIS 404:1
t. is cruel, but it can be loved	SANT 555:20
t. is not in us	BIBLE 105:25
t. is often a terrible weapon	ADLER 5:7
t. is pulling its boots on	SPUR 661:16
t. is rarely pure	WILDE 734:11
T. is staring at the sun	BELL 60:25
T. is the beste	LANG 408:23
T. is the cry of all	BERK 65:9
T. is the first casualty	JOHN 368:8
T. is the hyeste thyng	CHAU 193:15
T. is the most valuable	TWAIN 706:7
t. lay all undiscovered	NEWT 494:7
t. lies in the presentation	CONR 217:18
T. lies within a little	BOL 117:10
T., like a torch, the more	HAM 322:12
T. may bear all lights	SHAF 563:22
t. never hurts the teller	BROW 149:22
T. never is undone	ROET 544:2
t. of imagination	KEATS 391:5
t. serve as a stalking-horse	BOL 117:7
t. shall be thy warrant	RAL 535:15
t. shall make you free	BIBLE 96:32
T., Sir, is a cow	JOHN 372:11
T. sits upon the lips	ARN 28:16
T. stands, and he that will reach	
	DONNE 251:15
t. that's told with bad	BLAKE 111:6
T. to her old cavern fled	POPE 519:10
t. to their fictions	HUME 355:19
t. universally acknowledged	AUST 39:9
T. *was buried deep below*	DAV 232:3
T., when witty	HARE 326:6
t. which cunning times	SHAK 609:1
t. which he has laid within	LOCKE 424:21
t. which hovers o'er	BYRON 171:7
t. which makes men free	AGAR 5:13
t. which you cannot contradict	SOCR 655:3
T. will come to light	SHAK 608:8
t. with gold she weighs	POPE 518:14
t. within thy mind rehearse	TENN 689:16
unto the enemies of t.	BROW 145:29
utter what he thinks t.	JOHN 375:13
very few lovers of t.	LOCKE 424:20
War told me t.	GURN 320:2
was all the test of t.	CRAB 224:22
way, the t., and the life	BIBLE 97:12
We'd see t. dawn together	BROW 148:10
What is t.?	BACON 44:36
Which heavenly t. imparts	KEBLE 392:21
white star of T.	ARN 28:9
Who its t. believeth	BAKER 47:19
whose subject is not t.	CHAP 191:2
would keep abreast of T.	LOW 430:5
yet friend to T.	POPE 520:32
you live so close to t.	STOP 670:12

truthful: my name is T. James HARTE 327.20
truths: Flat and flexible t. BROW 145:9
hold these t. to be self-evident ANON 19:7
instruments of darkness tell us t.
	SHAK 600:10
Irrationally held t.	HUXL 358:10
necessary and eternal t.	LEIB 416:14
repetition of unpalatable t.	SUMM 672:1
Some random t. he can impart	WORD 746:16
tell him disagreeable t.	BULW 155:6
There are no new t.	MCC 436:22
There are no whole t.	WHIT 731:11
T. as refined as ever Athens	ARMS 26:8
t. begin as blasphemies	SHAW 635:19
t. being in and out	FROST 294:12
t. lacking which any story	FAUL 281:2
T. that become old become	OUSP 502:9
t. that wake, to perish never	WORD 746:4
t. to begin as heresies	HUXL 358:9
t. to be sacred and undeniable	JEFF 364:2

truths: (*cont.*):

t. which must serve	KENN 394:7
t. without a recognition	BELL 60.20
two sorts of t.	BOHR 117:1
Two t. are told	SHAK 600:11
try: Guiltier than him they t.	SHAK 605:12
I'll t. the whole cause	CARR 182:2
Let the end t. the man	SHAK 583:6
To t. me with affliction	SHAK 617:15
t. him afterwards	MOL 479:8
T. me, O God, and seek	BOOK 134:22
T. not the Pass	LONG 426:19
t. out my reins	BOOK 125:21
t. the soul's strength	BROW 150:12
trying: business without really t.	MEAD 455:12
He just goes on t. other things	PIC 514:10
I am t., and you can't help it	SMITH 651:15
tryout: bad variant nor a t.	HUGH 354:6
tryst: T. with the moon	DRIN 258:10
tub: mere tale of a t.	WEBS 726:3
tuba: *T. mirum spargens sonum*	MISS 477:12
t. terribili sonitu tarantantara	ENN 278:3
tube: artificial inlet—a t.	FOST 291:9
toothpaste is out of the t.	HALD 321:4
tuberose: and the sweet t.	SHEL 643:1
tubers: little life with dried t.	ELIOT 272:21
tuckoo: boy named baby t.	JOYCE 381:9
Tucson: T. and Deadwood	BENÉT 62:15
Tudor: Love, my sweet T.	DRAY 257:18
Tuesday: spelling T. simply doesn't count	
	MILNE 462:10
tug: then was the t. of war	LEE 416:5
tumble: They t. headlong down	MARL 447:8
tumbled: Egypt's might is t. down	COL 209:8
tumbler: clean t., and a corkscrew	DICK 242:13
tumour: sort of t. that ends	ADAMS 2:11
when it ripens in a t.	ABSE 1:2
tumult: depth, and not the t.	WORD 744:17
Shedding white rings of t.	CRANE 225:25
t. and the shouting dies	KIPL 400:11
t. and the shouting dies	KNOX 403:7
t. dwindled to a calm	BYRON 173:19
t. in the clouds	YEATS 752:6
tun: t. of man is thy companion	SHAK 580:30
tune: And the blackbird's t.	BROW 149:13
dost thou like this t.	SHAK 629:13
ev'ry warbler has his t.	COWP 223:15
I am incapable of a t.	LAMB 406:7
out of t. and harsh	SHAK 576:4
Singeth a quiet t.	COL 211:13
That's sweetly play'd in t.	BURNS 162:27
thinkin'll turn into a t.	HUBB 353:12
t. in and drop out	LEARY 415:1
t. is catching and will	AUDEN 34:7
t. the instrument here	DONNE 251:6
we complain about the t.	BEVAN 68:17
tuneable: more t. than lark	SHAK 610:24
tunes: chanted snatches of old t.	SHAK 578:13
Dance they to the t. of Handel	SITW 648:19
found out musical t.	BIBLE 88:1
Of Cathedral T.	DICK 244:20
should have all the good t.	HILL 338:15
tunic: closest, all-concealing t.	SHEL 642:6
soldier's ribbon on a t.	ABSE 1:3
tunnel: big busy world by a t.	AUDEN 35:1
Down some profound dull t.	OWEN 503:18
light at the end of the t.	DICK 245:9
light at the end of the t.	LOW 430:19
tuppence: t. for all of the rest	FLAN 285:13
t. for your old watch chain	COLL 213:6
turbid: t. look most profound	LAND 408:12
turbot: by way of t.	SMITH 653:6
'T., Sir,' said the waiter	WELBY 726:21
turbulent: rid me of this t. priest	HENR 332:14
Sagacious, bold, and t. of wit	DRYD 259:1
turd: rymyng is nat worth a t.	CHAU 194:18
turf: At his head a grass-green t.	SHAK 577:35
blue ribbon of the t.	DISR 248:18
Green be the t. above thee	HALL 322:6
green t. beneath my feet	HAZL 329:14
Oft on the dappled t. at ease	WORD 748:11
t. in many a mouldering	GRAY 315:12
Turk: French, or T., or Proosian	GILB 306:5

Turk: (cont.):
Nose of T., and Tartar's lips   SHAK 603:19
take the T. by the beard   SHAK 587:2
woman out-paramoured the T.   SHAK 596:9
turkey: It was a t.!   DICK 239:19
myrtle and t. part of it   AUST 38:18
T. is a dying man   NICH 494:11
turkey-cock: Contemplation makes a rare t.   SHAK 630:1
Turkish: not the T. court   SHAK 584:7
T. this side—Virginia that   SAP 555:22
Turks: like those wicked T.   DICK 240:21
T. now carry away   GLAD 307:10
turn: And I t. the page   BROW 148:22
Because I do not hope to t.   ELIOT 270:5
goodnight and quickly t.   YEATS 751:20
I keep, and pass, and t. again   EMER 276:5
It is my t. now   NELS 491:9
I t. to ducks   HARV 327:23
neither t. again to cover   BOOK 132:7
t. down an empty glass   FITZ 284:17
t. on, tune in and drop out   LEARY 415:1
T. our captivity, O Lord   BOOK 134:5
t. over a new life   FLEM 287:3
T. that off   WILL 737:8
t. thee behind me   BIBLE 76:25
t. the other cheek   HOLM 342:15
t. to him the other also   BIBLE 88:32
T. up the lights   HENRY 333:4
T. us again, O God   BOOK 130:13
T. wheresoe'er I may   WORD 745:10
Wilt thou not t. again   BOOK 130:19
turned: in case anything t. up   DICK 239:27
night be t. to day   BOOK 134:19
once t. round walks   COL 211:14
t. again the captivity   BOOK 134:4
t. my back upon Don   TENN 689:2
t. out of the Realm   ELIZ 274:1
t. us around like this   RILKE 541:2
we have t. every one   BIBLE 84:12
turning: gate where they're t.   AUDEN 35:15
neither shadow of t.   BIBLE 104:26
still point of the t. world   ELIOT 270:16
t. before we have learnt   CONN 216:15
t. in the widening gyre   YEATS 753:1
turnip: candle in that great t.   CHUR 203:14
getting blood out of a t.   MARR 449:2
Have a t. than his father   JOHN 377:4
turnpike: consider supper as a t.   EDW 267:10
turns: Times go by t.   SOUT 658:2
turpe: T. paras, nec tu pueri   JUV 384:14
turpissimus: Nemo repente fuit t.   JUV 383:18
turrets: half-glimpsèd t.   THOM 695:6
her t. split the sky   LAND 408:3
turtle: t. lives 'twixt plated   NASH 490:8
voice of the t. is heard   BIBLE 81:9
turtle-dove: soul of thy t.   BOOK 130:3
Tuscany: even the ranks of T.   MAC 436:15
Tusculum: T. (beautiful T.)   DICK 240:15
tush: T., I shall never be cast   BOOK 124:22
T., say they, how should   BOOK 130:1
TV: T. — a clever contraction   ACE 1:5
twain: go with him t.   BIBLE 88:33
with t. he covered his face   BIBLE 82:19
twang: most melodious t.   AUBR 33:13
twangs: t. and breaks at the end   MACN 442:15
Tweed: Says T. to Till   ANON 17:17
Tweedledum: 'Twixt T. and   BYROM 167:15
twelve: At t. noon, the natives   COW 220:14
just turned t. years old   VIRG 715:4
sworn t. have a thief or two   SHAK 605:12
ten or t. strokes of havoc   HOPK 345:5
T. for the twelve apostles   ANON 15:1
t. good men into a box   BROU 144:7
t. great shocks of sound   TENN 681:8
t. honest men have decided   PULT 531:6
T. men are marching through   BLOK 115:6
will ruin himself in t. months   GEOR 301:5
twelvemonth: t. and a day   BALL 51:1
twenty: At t. years of age   FRAN 292:16
It means t. things   BENN 63:16
Let t. pass   BROW 149:2
t. men crossing twenty   STEV 666:1

twenty: (cont.):
t. years are the longest   SOUT 657:19
twenty-four: we shall be t.   HOUS 351:17
twenty-three: chaste, and t.   BYRON 170:5
twenty-twenty: Hindsight is always t.   WILD 736:14
twice: He gives t. who gives soon   PUBL 531:2
it is t. blessed   SHAK 609:13
t. I have also heard   BOOK 128:20
t. into the same river   HER 333:11
women do they must do t.   WHIT 733:12
twice-told: tedious as a t. tale   SHAK 594:5
twig: Just as the t. is bent   POPE 520:27
t.'s having lashed across   FROST 294:10
twilight: disastrous t.   MILT 469:2
full Surrey t.   BETJ 68:7
In a t. dim with rose   DE L 236:10
long t. struggle   KENN 394:1
rises 'midst the t. path   COLL 213:11
see'st the t. of such day   SHAK 634:6
they ever fly by t.   BACON 44:31
twilights: ancient shadows and t.   Æ 5:10
twining: like the t. vine   COL 209:16
twinkle: roguish t. in his eye   THOM 695:9
Twinkle, t., little bat   CARR 182:7
T., twinkle, little star   TAYL 679:14
twinkling: t. of a bed-staff   SHAD 563:17
t. of an eye   BIBLE 101:14
t. of an eye   BOOK 126:5
twins: Clara threw the t. she nursed   GRAH 313:9
good and evil as two t.   MILT 475:6
to have been born t.   MADAN 441:8
t. of learning that he raised   SHAK 589:11
whereof every one bear t.   BIBLE 81:13
twirled: ships are t. and spun   HODG 340:18
twirling: t. in thy hand a withered   ARN 28:6
twirp: many a t. signing on   HUGH 353:16
twist: I have NO MORE T.   POTT 525:11
Let him t. slowly   EHRL 267:14
pale death your vital t.   DAV 232:7
t. the sinews of thy heart   BLAKE 114:14
twisted: You silly t. boy   MILL 462:4
two: Can t. walk together   BIBLE 86:10
game at which t. can play   BEER 59:19
He took out t. pence   BIBLE 94:15
If t. lives join   BROW 148:26
learn t. things   BOOK 123:5
tea for t. and two for tea   CAES 174:13
think for t. minutes together   SMITH 653:1
twice t. be not four   TURG 705:11
t. and one are three   STEP 663:17
T. and two only supreme   NEWM 492:14
t. and two unto Noah   BIBLE 70:26
t. and two would continue   WHIS 730:20
t. ears of corn or two   SWIFT 673:12
t. glasses and two chairs   MACN 440:19
t. hours' traffick of our   SHAK 622:18
t. meanings packed into one word   CARR 183:13
T. nations   DISR 248:26
t. or three are gathered   BIBLE 91:20
t. or three are gathered   BOOK 119:9
t. people miserable instead   BUTL 166:29
t. things about the horse   ROYD 549:13
t. things believed of any man   TARK 678:14
T. voices are there   STEP 663:17
with t. seeming bodies   SHAK 612:3
worth t. in the street   WEST 729:6
two-and-twenty: sweet t.   BYRON 173:8
two-edged: t. sword   BIBLE 106:1
t. sword   BOOK 135:16
two-legged: unfeathered t. thing   DRYD 259:2
two o'clock: t. in the morning courage   NAP 490:2
twopence: t. every day of my life   STEV 667:21
Tyburn: a damned T.-face   CONG 215:7
Tyne: from the Severn to the T.   KIPL 398:12
type: So careful of the t.   TENN 683:20
t. nowhere existing   SPEN 658:13
who wasn't even my t.   PROU 530:9
types: by device of Movable T.   CARL 181:4
Seven t. of ambiguity   EMPS 277:21

types: (cont.):
shadows and t. to the reality   NEWM 493:17
T. and shadows have   THOM 692:14
typist: t. home at teatime   ELIOT 273:8
tyranne: tute Tati tibi tanta t.   ENN 277:25
tyranni: Non vultus instantis t.   HOR 350:1
tyrannis: semper t.   BOOTH 136:4
tyrannous: t. to use it like a giant   SHAK 605:17
tyranny: against a monstrous t.   CHUR 202:9
are the worst sort of t.   BURKE 158:34
caused by some one's t.   BAG 46:13
Ecclesiastic t.'s the worst   DEFOE 234:25
human nature against t.   JOHN 373:17
lightened the burden of t.   SHAW 637:20
long dark night of t.   MURR 488:12
straining order into t.   GODW 308:13
submission to an unnecessary t.   RUSS 551:11
T. entrenches itself within   SHEL 644:10
T. is always better organised   PÉ.GUY 511:7
under conditions of t.   AREN 24:17
under monarchy, call it t.   HOBB 340:9
until this t. be over-past   BOOK 128:14
without representation is t.   OTIS 502:7
tyrant: loses the king in the t.   MAYH 455:10
O t. Titus Tatius   ENN 277:25
spurned a t.'s chain   BARB 52:2
Thou art past the t.'s stroke   SHAK 571:16
Thou t. of the mind   DRYD 260:36
Thou t. whom I will not name   WRIG 749:13
titles for T. and Hector   BARB 52:6
t. custom, most grave   SHAK 615:7
t. duke unto a tyrant brother   SHAK 567:21
t. of his fields withstood   GRAY 315:15
t.'s authority for crime   BIER 109:9
t. spell has bound me   BRON 142:11
t. staring him in the face   HOR 350:1
t.'s vein   SHAK 611:6
tyrants: all men would be t.   ADAMS 1:11
all men would be t.   DEFOE 234:17
argument of t.   PITT 515:15
blood of patriots and t.   JEFF 364:9
curry favour with t.   ZAP 755:8
intercourse between t. and slaves   GOLD 311:17
Kings will be t. from policy   BURKE 158:17
Rebellion to t. is obedience   BRAD 139:9
sceptre from t.   TURG 705:13
t.' crests and tombs   SHAK 634:20
T. seldom want pretexts   BURKE 157:4
with the barbarity of t.   SMITH 652:24
Tyre: one with Nineveh, and T.   KIPL 400:12
which men still call T.   FLEC 286:12
Tyrian: silver-white, and budded T.   KEATS 389:18
Tyrone: steeples of Fermanagh and T.   CHUR 202:2

U

U: U and Non-U   ROSS 547:1
ubi: U. Petrus, ibi ergo ecclesia   AMBR 10:5
ubique: Quod u., quod semper   VINC 711:17
ubiquities: blazing u.   EMER 277:16
Ucalegon: U. burns very near   VIRG 712:19
uffish: as in u. thought he stood   CARR 182:19
ugly: be good than to be u.   WILDE 735:20
Despised, if u.   LEAP 413:16
hypothesis by an u. fact   HUXL 358:3
made the world u. and bad   NIET 495:11
never saw an u. thing in my life   CONS 217:23
Once sex rears its u. 'ead   ALL 9:20
solid rock the u. houses stand   MILL 461:8
u., heavy and complex   FLAU 286:5
u. mathematics   HARDY 324:4
world's as u., ay, as sin   LOCK 425:12
uita: Siquidem u. breuis   JOHN 366:15
Ulster: betrayal of U.   CAIR 175:2
U. will fight   CHUR 201:19
ulterioris: Tendebantque manus ripae u.   VIRG 713:15
ultima: U. Cumaei venit iam carminis   VIRG 714:22

ultima: (*cont.*):
  U. Thule   VIRG 715:10
ultimate: u. decency of things   STEV 668:12
ultio: *voluptas U.*   JUV 384:13
ultor: *aliquis nostris ex ossibus u.* VIRG 713:8
ultrices: *Luctus et u. posuere cubilia* VIRG 713:14
ulubris: *Est U.*   HOR 348:9
Ulysses: Happy he who like U.   DU B 263:1
'umble: We are so very u.   DICK 239:30
umbra: But it is but *U. Mortis*   LAUD 411:4
  Stat magni nominis u.   LUCAN 431:5
umbrage: Americans have taken u.
                                      PUNCH 531:19
  Beauteous the garden's u. mild SMART 650:3
  u. of the walls of Eden   BYRON 168:1
umbrella: u. might pacify barbarians
                                      PLOM 517:11
  u. to keep the scorching   FLET 287:18
  unjust steals the just's u.   BOWEN 138:4
umbris: *u. et imaginibus in veritatem*
                                      NEWM 493:17
umpire: Chaos u. sits   MILT 470:11
  u., the pavilion cat   LANG 408:15
una: *iuvat spinis de pluribus u.*   HOR 348:21
unacceptable: u. face of capitalism
                                      HEATH 329:23
unadvisedly: u., lightly, or wantonly
                                      BOOK 123:16
unaffected: Affecting to seem u.   CONG 216:4
unafraid: ruins strike him u.   HOR 350:2
unarm: U., Eros   SHAK 566:8
unassailable: u. holds on his rank SHAK 591:12
unattempted: u. yet in prose or rhyme
                                      MILT 467:20
unattractive: most u. old thing   GILB 305:10
  not against the u.   GREE 316:22
unbearable: in victory u.   CHUR 203:13
  u. lightness of being   KUND 404:9
unbeatable: in defeat u.   CHUR 203:13
unbeautiful: furnished souls are u.
                                      CUMM 228:17
unbecoming: conduct u.   ANON 12:5
  u. men that strove   TENN 690:4
unbelief: Blind u. is sure to err COWP 222:17
  help thou mine u.   BIBLE 93:15
  u. is blind   MILT 464:2
unbelievable: how u. the *second* ELIOT 270:4
unbeliever: John Henderson, an u. BELL 61:13
unbelieving: u. husband   BIBLE 100:25
unbends: nothing u. the mind like women
                                      GAY 299:21
unbent: u. her mind afterwards   LAMB 406:9
un-birthday: u. present   CARR 183:10
unborn: talk to the u.   BARZ 54:23
  Ventriloquizing for the u.   GRAV 315:2
unborrowed: U. from the eye   WORD 744.21
unbought: u. grace of life   BURKE 158:14
unbounded: He was a man of an u. stomach
                                      SHAK 589:7
  Pure u. love thou art   WESL 728:14
unbowed: bloody, but u.   HENL 332:6
unbribed: man will do u.   WOLFE 741:1
unbuild: I arise and u. it again   SHEL 640:7
unburied: bodies of u. men   WEBS 726:7
unbutton: u. here   SHAK 596:11
uncertain: little information, and u.
  temper   AUST 39:10
  trumpet give an u. sound   BIBLE 101:2
  U., coy, and hard to please   SCOTT 560:9
uncertainty: u. principle   HAWK 328:6
uncharitableness: from all u.   BOOK 119:17
unchaste: No u. action   SHAK 594:22
uncircumcised: daughters of the u. triumph
                                      BIBLE 75:8
uncircumscribed: Sceptreless, free, u.
                                      SHEL 642:18
unclad: u. and incomplete   MCL 439:16
unclassed: Equal, u., tribeless   SHEL 642:18
uncle: married with mine u.   SHAK 572:12
  O my prophetic soul! My u.!   SHAK 573:18
  nor u. me no uncle   SHAK 619:21
  O My agèd U. Arly   LEAR 414:2

unclean: he is u. to you   BIBLE 73:1
  people of u. lips   BIBLE 82:20
  u. spirit is gone out   BIBLE 90:36
uncleanness: all u., or covetousness
                                      BIBLE 102:20
  men's bones, and of all u.   BIBLE 92:6
unclouded: u. blaze of living light
                                      BYRON 169:25
unclubbable: very u. man   JOHN 372:23
uncoffined: u. and unknown   BYRON 169:15
uncomfortable: moral when he is only u.
                                      SHAW 637:12
uncompacted: depth of its u. lightness
                                      BRID 141:4
unconcerned: Thou u. canst hear POPE 519:26
unconditional: u. and immediate surrender
                                      GRANT 314:7
unconquerable: man's u. mind   WORD 748:13
  Still nursing the u. hope   ARN 28:10
  u. will   MILT 468:5
unconscionable: u. time dying   CHAR 191:20
unconscious: deep well of u. cerebration
                                      JAMES 362:13
  personal u.   JUNG 382:12
  u. activities of the mind   FREUD 293:20
  u. hodmen of the men of ideas HEINE 331:3
unconsidered: snapper-up of u. trifles
                                      SHAK 631:25
unconvincing: bald and u. narrative
                                      GILB 305:8
uncorrupt: leadeth an u. life   BOOK 124:28
uncouth: His u. way   MILT 469:20
  U. unkist, said the old poet   SPEN 660:28
uncouther: The better the u.   BROW 153:12
uncreated: one u., one incomprehensible
                                      BOOK 119:14
  wide womb of u. night   MILT 469:14
uncreating: before thy u. word   POPE 519:12
unction: not that flattering u. SHAK 577:18
  Thy blessed U. from above   BOOK 135:21
undefiled: Lord is an u. law   BOOK 125:5
  my love, my dove, my u.   BIBLE 81:17
  Pure religion and u. before   BIBLE 104:28
under: get out and get u.   CLAR 205:11
  they shall go u. the earth   BOOK 128:22
  U. a spreading chestnut tree   LONG 428:2
  U. Mirabeau Bridge flows   APOL 23:15
underachiever: basically an u.   ALLEN 9:12
underbelly: u. of the Axis   CHUR 202:18
underdogs: Englishman among the u.
                                      WAUGH 723:22
undergraduates: U. owe their happiness
                                      BEER 59:12
underground: As Johnny u.   PUDN 531:5
under-labourer: u. in clearing ground
                                      LOCKE 424:15
underlings: we are u.   SHAK 590:3
underneath: U. the Arches   FLAN 285:8
  what u. him lies   GREV 318:5
under-peep: would u. her lids   SHAK 571:1
undersized: He's a bit u.   GILB 304:16
undersold: Never knowingly u. LEWIS 420:20
understand: confused doesn't really u.
                                      MURR 488:13
  could u. what she said   BUNY 156:15
  gaze of dogs who don't u.   CALV 175:17
  grown-ups never u. anything   DE S 553:2
  It's all they can u.   MELBA 456:4
  make me to u. wisdom secretly BOOK 128:5
  Nor can anyone u. Ein   ANON 14:14
  nor to hate them but to u. them SPIN 661:3
  One has to u. the country   LESS 419:8
  said to u. one another   CHAM 189:14
  sex I don't u. too hot   SAL 553:16
  still the less they u.   BUTL 166:16
  Then thought I to u. this   BOOK 130:2
  to admire we should not u.   CONG 215:11
  u. what is happening   CHAM 189:5
  what they failed to u.   MOORE 482:11
  What you can't u.   DYLAN 265:23
understanded: tongue not u. of the people
                                      BOOK 135:24

understandeth: u. thee not, loves thee not
                                      SHAK 598:16
understanding: because they appeal to the u.
                                      BAG 47:5
  declare, if thou hast u.   BIBLE 77:34
  evidence against their own u. HAL 321:13
  Give it an u., but no tongue SHAK 572:22
  good u. have all they   BOOK 133:5
  length of days u.   BIBLE 77:19
  likely to propagate u.   JOHN 377:6
  obliged to find you an u.   JOHN 376:15
  pass man's u.   BOOK 121:4
  shall light a candle of u.   BIBLE 86:24
  sketchy u. of life itself   CRICK 226:20
  spirit of wisdom and u.   BIBLE 83:1
  they pass all u.   JAM 362:6
  u. makes one very indulgent STAEL 662:1
  where is the place of u.   BIBLE 77:27
  which have no u.   BOOK 126:10
  which passeth all u.   BIBLE 103:12
  with all thy getting get u.   BIBLE 78:10
  yourself ignorant of his u.   COL 211:27
understandings: cold hearts and muddy u.
                                      BURKE 158:16
understands: Reads verse and thinks she u.
                                      BROW 149:15
  will support it as he u. it   JACK 361:1
understonde: That thow be u., God I biseche
                                      CHAU 195:26
understood: been u. no longer exists
                                      ÉLUA 276:4
  be told so as to be u.   BLAKE 112:29
  be u. by my country   MAY 455:4
  but is u. by no body   DEFOE 233:15
  how well they u.   AUDEN 35:6
  I have u. you   DE G 235:2
  not as it is u.   JACK 361:1
  something u.   HERB 335:13
undertakers: As u.—walk before the hearse
                                      GARR 298:8
Underworld: down to the U.   VIRG 713:11
undeservedly: no books are u. forgotten
                                      AUDEN 36:17
undeserving: u. poor   SHAW 638:18
undeveloped: u. hearts   FORS 289:20
undevotional: Dirty, dark, and u. VICT 711:1
undid: And what they u. did   SHAK 565:5
undiscovered: u. country   SHAK 575:16
undivided: Alone and u.   SHIP 646:1
undo: for thee alone she u. herself MIDD 460:1
  mark me how I will u.   SHAK 620:21
  Pray you, u. this button   SHAK 598:3
  should u. a man   SHAK 587:24
  Some to u., and some   DRYD 262:5
  To u. the folded lie   AUDEN 36:1
undone: And yet, so soon u.   WILB 734:6
  death had u. so many   ELIOT 273:1
  I am u. tonight   JONS 379:15
  Is not to leave't u.   SHAK 616:14
  John Donne, Anne Donne, U. DONNE 253:15
  left u. those things which we BOOK 118:8
  petty done, the u. vast   BROW 150:23
  some to be u.   DRYD 262:5
  'tis we must be u.   BEHN 60:9
  Weather and rain have u.   KIPL 400:17
  Woe is me! for I am u.   BIBLE 82:20
undress: But I, when I u. me FIELD 281:13
undulate: U. round the world   WHIT 733:4
undulating: and an u. throat BELL 61:17
undulations: Ambiguous u.   STEV 666:11
unearned: u. increment of rent MILL 460:12
uneasy: from u. dreams   KAFKA 384:18
  U. lies the head that wears SHAK 583:12
uneatable: pursuit of the u. WILDE 735:27
uneconomic: shown it to be 'u.' SCH 558:11
uneducated: government by the u.
                                      CHES 199:18
unemancipated: u. woman   LOW 430:10
unembroidered: U. by your high, soft voice
                                      MERR 458:13
unendurable: *this* be u.   BRON 142:5
unequal: equal division of u. earnings
                                      ELL 275:12

unespied: In ocean's bosom u.   MARV 449:18
unexamined: u. life   SOCR 654:14
unexpected: Old age the most u.
  of all things   TROT 704:11
unexpert: More u., I boast not   MILT 469:12
unexplained: you're u. as yet   HALL 322:4
unextinguishable: that u. laugh   BROW 145:7
unfabled: blest u. incense Tree   DARL 231:2
unfaithful: faith u. kept him falsely true
     TENN 682:3
  u. to his wife away from home   PYM 533:9
  u. to the translation   BORG 136:9
unfathomable: u. deep   THOM 694:3
unfathomed: Whose depth u.   WESL 728:16
unfed: houseless heads and u.   SHAK 596:6
unfeeling: Th' u. for his own   GRAY 316:3
unfeignedly: that u. love thee   BOOK 121:13
unfinished: Liberty is always u.
  business   ANON 15:17
unfit: all things u.   GOLD 311:4
  chosen from the u.   ANON 12:26
  u. to be trusted   CHES 198:23
  U. to hear moral philosophy   SHAK 627:13
unforeseen: contingent and u.   FISH 283:1
unforgiveness: alp of u. grew   PLOM 517:10
unforgiving: If you can fill the
  u. minute   KIPL 400:15
  u. eye, and   SHER 645:19
unfortunate: u. man is one who   BOET 116:12
unfruitful: he becometh u.   BIBLE 91:2
unfurnished: head that's to be let u.   BUTL 166:5
ungained: prize the thing u.   SHAK 627:5
ungodliness: tents of u.   BOOK 130:18
ungodly: counsel of the u.   BOOK 124:6
  For the hope of the u.   BIBLE 87:5
  fret not thyself because of the u.   BOOK 126:18
  plagues remain for the u.   BOOK 126:10
  seen the u. in great power   BOOK 126:21
  upon the u. he shall rain   BOOK 124:23
ungratefulness: call virtue there u.   SIDN 646:17
unguem: Ad u. Factus   HOR 351:4
unguessed: tread on Earth u.   ARN 28:13
ungula: putrem sonitu quatit u.   VIRG 714:5
unhanged: three good men u. in
  England   SHAK 580:15
unhappily: bad end u.   STOP 670:5
  result of being u. married   PARK 507:6
unhappiness: loyalty we all feel to u.
     GREE 316:25
  Man's u., as I construe   CARL 181:10
  u. develops the forces   PROU 530:17
  u. for another time   GREE 316:21
  vocation of u.   SIM 647:17
  volatile spirits prefer u.   SANT 555:17
unhappy: better that some should be u.
     JOHN 374:16
  big words which make us so u.   JOYCE 381:21
  cannot be made u.   LUCR 432:3
  different from that of the u.   WITT 740:6
  in mourning for my life, I'm u.   CHEK 196:11
  learning to care for the u.   VIRG 712:11
  Men who are u., like men   RUSS 551:8
  moral as soon as one is u.   PROU 530:10
  never as u. as one thinks   LA R 410:23
  None think the great u.   YOUNG 754:7
  old, u., far-off things   WORD 748:4
  one is respectable or u.   WHIT 732:18
  only listen when I am u.   SMITH 652:16
  only the u. can give or take   RHYS 539:20
  soft, u. sex   BEHN 60:17
  stupid and profoundly u.   CHEK 196:7
  to thy self u. chief   BRET 140:17
  u. family is unhappy   TOLS 700:5
  U. the land that needs   BREC 140:6
unhasting: unresting, u., and   SMITH 653:31
unhealthy: men for u. women   BEEC 59:4
unheard: language of the u.   KING 397:4
  those u. are sweeter   KEATS 388:25
unheavenly: strange u. glare   BRID 141:4
unholy: anything unjust or u.   SOCR 654:13
  Not u. names, I hope   DICK 241:10
  shrieks, and sights u.   MILT 465:3

unhonoured: Mindful of th' u. dead
     GRAY 315:19
  Unwept, u., and unsung   SCOTT 559:17
unhoused: U., disappointed   SHAK 573:20
unicorn: rarer than the u.   JONG 378:3
  Sirion, like a young u.   BOOK 126:2
uniform: Should be more u.   HOOD 343:19
  u. 'e wore   KIPL 399:9
  u. must work its way   DICK 243:22
uniformity: preferred before u.   BACON 42:32
  towards u. [of opinion]   JEFF 364:17
uninitiated: keep far off, you u.   VIRG 713:12
unintelligible: rapid, u. patter   GILB 306:20
  this u. world   WORD 744:20
union: But yet an u. in partition   SHAK 612:3
  Federal U. must be preserved   JACK 361:2
  indestructible U. composed of   CHASE 192:3
  Liberty and U., now and   WEBS 725:6
  O U., strong and great   LONG 426:11
  our u. is perfect   DICK 245:7
  perfect U., one and   PAGE 504:4
  struggle is to save the U.   LINC 422:12
  u. of gin and vermouth   DE V 239:2
  u. of hands and hearts   TAYL 679:21
  U. of these States   WHIT 733:2
unionists: are trades u. at heart   JEV 366:6
unions: u. and the industrialists   NIEM 495:2
unit: Misses an u.   BROW 150:1
unite: Workers of the world, u.   MARX 452:14
united: U. Metropolitan   DICK 241:30
  U. thoughts and counsels   MILT 468:3
United States: rise of the U.   STEV 667:8
  so close to the U.   DIAZ 238:10
  U. helpless and contemptible   WILS 738:15
  U. as a government   PAGE 504:4
  U. themselves are essentially   WHIT 733:5
unities: u. are a completeness   DICK 242:11
uniting: By u. we stand   DICK 245:8
unity: dwell together in u.   BOOK 134:14
  preserve the u. of the empire   BURKE 157:31
  that is at u. in itself   BOOK 133:25
  Trinity in U.   BOOK 119:13
  truth, u., and concord   BOOK 121:22
  u. of the faith   BIBLE 102:17
universal: All Nature wears one u. grin
     FIEL 282:16
  All partial evil, u. good   POPE 522:8
  has a kind of u. genius   DRYD 262:9
  ill by a u. accident   TRIL 702:16
  maxim should become a u. law   KANT 385:6
  u. dovetailedness   DICK 242:11
  u. frame is without a mind   BACON 42:22
  u. monarchy of wit   CAREW 179:4
  writer must be u.   BARN 53:6
universe: better ordering of the u.   ALF 9:2
  build u. from one tiny part   BENÉT 62:18
  cover the u. with mud   FORS 290:8
  good u. next door   CUMM 228:12
  Great Architect of the U.   JEANS 363:27
  Life, the U. and Everything   ADAMS 2:1
  mingle with the u., and feel   BYRON 169:13
  our world, our u.   KUMAR 404:8
  Put back thy u.   JONES 377:18
  repetitious mechanism of the U.   WHIT 731:9
  that we and the u. exist   HAWK 328:7
  torrents of her myriad u.   TENN 686:3
  u. and does not know himself   LA F 405:12
  u. is not hostile   HOLM 342:6
  u. is not only queerer   HALD 321:2
  u. sleeps, resting a huge ear   MAY 455:1
  u.'s very existence made known   PENR 512:1
  visible u. was an illusion   BORG 136:10
  Which is the measure of the u.   SHEL 642:16
  World, Nature, U.'s Essence   PAST 509:1
universities: discipline of colleges and u.
     SMITH 651:3
  U. incline wits to sophistry   BACON 45:14
university: benefiting from u.   AMIS 10:11
  French letters to the u.   JOYCE 382:5
  gained in the U. of Life   BOTT 137:13
  servant to be bred at an U.   CONG 215:14
  U. as a whole   COL 209:7

university: (cont.):
  U. of these days is a collection   CARL 180:28
  U. printing presses exist   CORN 219:6
  U. should be a place   DISR 247:22
  We are the U.   SPR 661:11
unjust: commended the u. steward   BIBLE 95:6
  do anything u. or unholy   SOCR 654:13
  just and on the u.   BIBLE 88:34
  u. steals the just's umbrella   BOWEN 138:4
unjustly: They teach to talk u.   ARIS 25:3
unkempt: U. about those hedges blows
     BROO 143:10
unkind: called deformed but the u.
     SHAK 630:30
  sayin' you treated me u.   DYLAN 265:13
  Tell me not, Sweet, I am u.   LOV 429:6
  That are sodden and u.   BELL 61:28
unkindest: most u. cut of all   SHAK 592:14
unkindness: his u. may defeat my life
     SHAK 617:20
unking: u. himself   MAYH 455:10
unkist: Uncouth u.   SPEN 660:28
  Unknowe, u., and lost   CHAU 195:10
unknit: u. that threatening
  unkind brow   SHAK 624:21
unknowable: O world u., we know thee
     THOM 695:9
unknowe: U., unkist, and lost   CHAU 195:10
unknowing: cloud of u.   ANON 12:22
  u. and unknown   BURNS 162:16
unknown: buried the U. Prime Minister
     ASQ 31:18
  dies to himself u.   SEN 563:3
  from the known and the u.   PINT 515:1
  glorious and the u.   FORS 290:8
  holier lot to be u.   HOPK 346:18
  I travelled among u. men   WORD 744:14
  My songs is love u.   CROS 228:2
  O friend unseen, unborn, u.   FLEC 286:15
  She lived u., and few could   WORD 747:18
  side of the U. Soldier   ASQ 31:18
  Through the u., we'll   BAUD 55:11
  Thus let me live, unseen, u.   POPE 523:12
  To that u. and silent shore   LAMB 407:6
  TO THE U. GOD   BIBLE 98:31
  tread safely into the u.   HASK 328:1
  uncoffined, and u.   BYRON 169:15
  undone, but keep't u.   SHAK 616:14
  unknowing and u.   BURNS 162:16
  u. is held to be glorious   TAC 677:19
  u. regions preserved   ELIOT 269:13
  unmourned and u.   HOR 350:18
unleavened: u. bread of sincerity   BIBLE 100:22
unleaving: Over Goldengrove u.   HOPK 346:2
unlocked: u. to your occasions   SHAK 607:9
unloose: I am not worthy to u.   BIBLE 96:6
unlovely: in the long u. street   TENN 683:5
unluckily: the good u.   STOP 670:5
unlucky: born who is so u.   MARQ 448:19
unmannerly: untaught knaves, u.
     SHAK 579:30
unmapped: u. country within us   ELIOT 268:23
unmask: To u. falsehood   SHAK 632:23
  u. her beauty to the moon   SHAK 573:1
unmeaning: u. thing they call
  a thought   POPE 521:15
unmeritable: slight u. man   SHAK 592:24
unmixed: Nothing is an u. blessing   HOR 349:20
unmourned: u. and unknown   HOR 350:18
unmourning: by the u. water   THOM 693:14
unmovèd: U., cold   SHAK 634:14
unnatural: breed u. troubles   SHAK 604:17
  foul and most u. murder   SHAK 573:15
  Foul disposition, thoughts u.   SHAK 616:15
  Let me be cruel, not u.   SHAK 577:1
  most u. of all the sexual   HUXL 357:15
  this u. scene   SHAK 570:26
unnecessary: curious in u. matters   BIBLE 87:10
  thou u. letter   SHAK 595:12
  unfit, to do the u.   ANON 12:26
unnoticed: pathway of a life u.   HOR 348:14
unofficial: English u. rose   BROO 143:10
  It is the u. force   DOYLE 256:20

useful: (cont.):
  equally u.   GIBB 301:18
  or at some u. work   THOM 692:7
  Really U. Engine   AWDRY 40:6
  u. or believe to be beautiful MORR 485:16
useless: Lodged with me u. MILT 474:24
  may never live to be u. WESL 728:21
  Music is essentially u. SANT 555:19
  u. and irrational character DOST 255:2
  most u.; peacocks and lilies RUSK 550:24
uses: things for mean or no u. LOCKE 424:17
usquebae: Wi' u., we'll face the devil
                   BURNS 163:8
USSR: Back in the U. LENN 417:15
usual: Not kind sir quite u. ASHF 31:8
usura: U. slayeth child in womb POUND 526:4
  with u. hath no man a house POUND 526:3
usurp: None can u. this height KEATS 387:15
usury: money upon u. BOOK 124:29
  u. is contrary to Scripture TAWN 679:2
usus: *si volet u.* HOR 347:6
uti: *Muneribus sapienter u.* HOR 350:19
utile: *miscuit u. dulci* HOR 347:15
utility: extension which lends u. SANT 556:10
  Losing both beauty and u. SHAK 586:17
utmost: does the u. that he can BURNS 163:18
Utopia: Not in U. WORD 747:7
  possibly be attained in U. GLAD 307:13
  than a principality in U. MAC 435:2
Utopian: retrospective or u. ARON 30:15
Utopias: U. and the farmyard civilization
                   INGE 359:13
utterance: u. of the early gods KEATS 387:25
utterly: should u. have fainted BOOK 126:1
uttermost: u. parts of the sea BOOK 134:19

V

V: with a "V" or a "W" DICK 243:19
vacancies: v. to be obtained JEFF 364:12
vacancy: In chaos of u. shone DE L 236:3
vacant: In v. or in pensive mood WORD 744:16
  laugh that spoke the v. mind GOLD 310:8
  Stuffs out his v. garments SHAK 594:4
  V. heart and hand, and eye SCOTT 560:15
  v. interstellar spaces ELIOT 270:21
vacations: No extras, no v. DICK 241:31
vacuum: Nature abhors a v. RAB 534:18
  v. is a hell of a lot better WILL 737:4
  v. or space in which there is DESC 237:19
  women out from behind the v. GREER 317:15
vadis: *Quo v.?* BIBLE 108:13
vagrant: v. opinion without visible BIER 109:14
vagueness: no hypocrisy and no v. STEN 663:14
vaguery: For V. in the Field OSB 501:13
vain: And for tricks that are v. HARTE 327:17
  death, and all is v. ROSS 548:4
  deceive you with v. words BIBLE 102:21
  disquieteth himself in v. BOOK 126:23
  have not lived in v. BYRON 169:7
  knowledge that he lived in v. BYRON 168:18
  laboured in v. BIBLE 108:4
  Lord thy God in v. BIBLE 72:16
  nothing is in v. HERB 333:20
  people imagine a v. thing BOOK 124:7
  sealed in v. SHAK 606:17
  this man's religion is v. BIBLE 104:28
  Use not v. repetitions BIBLE 89:4
  V. man, said she SPEN 659:11
  V. the ambition of kings WEBS 725:13
  v. thing to save a man BOOK 126:12
  V. wisdom all, and false MILT 470:1
  watchman waketh but in v. BOOK 134:8
Vainglory: born in the land of V. BUNY 155:15
  v., and hypocrisy BOOK 119:17
vainly: How v. men themselves amaze
                   MARV 450:5
  V. begot, and yet forbidden GREV 318:8
  v. flapped its tinsel wing MARV 450:2
vale: cool sequestered v. of life GRAY 315:17
  frater, ave atque v. CAT 187:1

vale: (cont.):
  Into the v. of years SHAK 616:16
  shady sadness of a v. KEATS 387:22
  To meet thee in that hollow v. KING 396:11
  v. of misery use it for a well BOOK 130:17
  v. of soul-making KEATS 392:7
  V., the three lone weirs ARN 28:24
  weeping in this v. of tears ANON 22:14
  world as a v. of tears BROW 149:8
Valentine: Bishop V., whose day DONNE 250:17
valere: *sed v. vita est* MART 449:15
vales: lily-silver'd v. POPE 519:6
  Making all the v. rejoice BLAKE 113:21
valet: No man a hero to his v. CORN 219:10
  very v. seemed a hero BYRON 167:22
valiant: As he was v., I honour SHAK 592:3
  Queen and Faith like a v. TENN 689:5
  Ring in the v. man and free TENN 684:11
  therefore more v. SHAK 580:33
  v. never taste of death SHAK 591:5
  with a piece of v. dust SHAK 613:13
validity: Of what v. and pitch SHAK 628:9
valley: All in the v. of Death TENN 680:13
  Down in the v. drumming AUDEN 35:14
  Every v. shall be exalted BIBLE 83:26
  For Love is of the v. TENN 688:15
  heard a maid sing in the v. ANON 12:34
  He paweth in the v. BIBLE 77:38
  How green was my v. LLEW 423:14
  into the v. of Humiliation BUNY 155:16
  multitudes in the v. of decision BIBLE 86:9
  through the v. of the shadow BOOK 125:15
  To bicker down a v. TENN 680:11
  V. and lowland, sing OAKL 497:8
  v. of its saying where AUDEN 34:14
  v. which was full of bones BIBLE 85:25
  was beneath him in the v. BIBLE 74:9
valleys: lily of the v. BIBLE 81:8
  Piping down the v. wild BLAKE 113:16
  rain into the little v. BOOK 129:3
  That v., groves, hills MARL 447:17
  v. also shall stand BOOK 129:3
Vallombrosa: brooks in V. MILT 468:15
valour: birth-place of v. BURNS 162:23
  for contemplation he and v. formed
                   MILT 471:5
  For v., is not love a Hercules SHAK 598:20
  My v. is certainly going SHER 645:12
  quarrel there is no true v. SHAK 614:14
  thou mighty man of v. BIBLE 74:7
  v. in this Welshman SHAK 586:2
  v.'s minion carved out SHAK 599:15
  Who would true v. see BUNY 156:14
valourous: childish v. than MARL 448:8
valuable: Truth is the most v. thing
                   TWAIN 706:7
value: and the v. of nothing WILDE 735:12
  Its v. depends on what POUND 527:14
  more v. than many sparrows BIBLE 90:19
  nothing has v. FORS 290:24
  Though we v. none AUDEN 36:10
  unique v. in her KEYN 395:2
  v. of fortune by the persons STEE 662:21
  v. of life lies not MONT 480:17
  V. yourselves, men despise CHUD 200:13
values: moneys are for v. BACON 42:4
  not of facts but of v. INGE 360:1
valves: V. of her attention DICK 244:18
van: man said, 'Follow the v.' COLL 213:7
Vanbrugh: V.'s house of clay EVANS 279:4
Vandyke: V. is of the company GAIN 296:14
vanish: should v. with the rose FITZ 284:16
  softly and suddenly v. CARR 184:4
vanished: touch of a v. hand TENN 680:10
  v. like a dream CARL 180:27
vanishes: then v. into the dark MOT 487:1
vanishest: If thus thou v. SHAK 567:10
vanisheth: then v. away BIBLE 105:4
vanishings: Fallings from us, v. WORD 746:3
vanitas: V. vanitatum BIBLE 108:6
  V. Vanitatum THAC 691:20
vanities: bonfire of the v. WOLFE 741:6
  Guides us by v. ELIOT 271:11

vanity: administering to the v. AUST 38:23
  all ye that work v. BOOK 124:19
  altogether lighter than v. BOOK 128:20
  And speckled v. MILT 467:8
  As lick up every idle v. JONS 378:21
  fruit of my v. is shame PETR 513:10
  God's revenge against v. FOOTE 288:18
  no love, but v., sets love HUNT 356:7
  Oh, V. of vanities THAC 691:22
  pomps and v. of this wicked world
                   BOOK 123:4
  Pull down thy v. POUND 527:7
  that v. in years SHAK 580:31
  they talk of v. every one BOOK 124:24
  v. and vexation of spirit BIBLE 80:2
  V., like murder, will out COWL 221:23
  v. of human hopes JOHN 369:16
  V. of vanities, said BIBLE 108:6
  V. of vanities, saith BIBLE 79:36
  whose mouth talketh of v. BOOK 135:4
  yet forbidden v. GREV 318:8
Vanity-Fair: name of V. BUNY 155:18
  lions, or V., he feared not BUNY 156:11
vanquish: v., not my Accuser NEWM 492:13
vanquished: Quite v. him SHAK 592:14
  Valiantly v. SHAK 566:14
vans: v. to beat the air ELIOT 270:6
vantage: nor coign of v. SHAK 601:1
vanum: *v. laboraverunt qui* BIBLE 108:4
vapour: It is even a v. BIBLE 105:4
  like v. over shrines BROW 147:23
  street-bred people that v. KIPL 399:2
  take to be a deceitful v. SMOL 654:3
  v. and return it as a flood GLAD 308:1
  v. sometime like a bear SHAK 566:6
vapours: congregation of v. SHAK 574:28
  snow and v. BOOK 135:14
  v. weep their burthen TENN 689:10
variable: And v. as the shade SCOTT 560:9
  love prove likewise v. SHAK 623:2
variableness: with whom is no v. BIBLE 104:26
variant: bad v. nor a tryout HUGH 354:6
variation: admitting any v. BOOK 118:3
  swimming on a v. LOW 430:8
variegated: v., dramatic life PATER 509:7
variety: Her infinite v. SHAK 565:8
  one because it admits v. FORS 290:30
  source of pleasure is v. JOHN 368:21
  V. is the soul of pleasure BEHN 60:13
  V.'s the very spice of life COWP 223:22
  Where order in v. we see POPE 523:33
variorum: Life is all a v. BURNS 162:14
various: are lovely, so be v. GRAV 314:22
  constant as v. GRAV 314:22
  drunkenness of things being v. MACN 441:2
varium: *V. et mutabile semper* VIRG 713:7
Varsovie: *L'ordre règne à V.* ANON 21:2
vase: v. fills to the brim ROET 544:7
  you may shatter the v. MOORE 483:4
vassals: v. and serfs at my side BUNN 155:7
vast: down the v. edges drear ARN 27:1
  v. and middle of the night SHAK 572:18
vasty: v. hall of death ARN 27:20
vate: *carent quia v. sacro* HOR 350:18
vats: parcel of boilers and v. JOHN 375:23
  spirted purple of the v. TENN 688:15
vatum: *placem genus irritabile v.* HOR 348:20
vaudeville: Terrible V. ACE 1:5
vault: green sea and azured v. SHAK 626:1
  v. for funeral Monday Dorset BEER 59:18
vaulted: v. with such ease SHAK 581:20
vaulting: V. ambition, which o'erleaps
                   SHAK 601:3
vaunting: V. aloud, but racked MILT 468:7
veal: Bellamy's v. pies PITT 515:19
vécu: *J'ai v.* SIEY 647:14
veels: V. vithin veels DICK 243:23
Vega: V. conspicuous overhead AUDEN 35:13
vegetable: My v. love should MARV 451:2
  passion of a v. fashion GILB 305:17
  v., animal, and mineral GILB 306:9
vegetarian: often with v. leanings ORW 500:21

vogue: (*cont.*):
he'd be working for *V.* — UST 707:15

voi: *Siete v. qui* — DANTE 230:14

voice: against the v. of a nation — RUSS 552:1
Aghast the v. of Time — DYER 265:8
All I have is a v. — AUDEN 36:1
And a v. less loud — BROW 151:7
And utter forth a glorious v. — ADD 4:20
A sweet and potent v. — COL 209:15
At once a v. outburst among — HARDY 325:5
audible v. of the Past — CARL 180:27
candent v. which was more — ROLFE 545:8
dread v. is past — MILT 466:10
Gave thee such a tender v. — BLAKE 113:21
good the supplicating v. — JOHN 370:22
great v. as of a trumpet — BIBLE 105:33
heard a v. from heaven — BIBLE 107:2
Hear the v. of the Bard — BLAKE 114:4
hear the v. of the charmer — BOOK 128:17
heart, lift up your v. — WESL 728:13
Her v. is full of money — FITZ 285:2
her v. the harmony of the — HOOK 344:14
Her v. was ever soft — SHAK 598:2
his big manly v. — SHAK 568:16
his v. as the sound of many — BIBLE 106:1
his v. was propertied — SHAK 566:20
I have lost my v. — WEBS 726:14
inexhaustible v. — FAUL 281:3
inner v. which warns — MENC 457:9
In Rama was there a v. — BIBLE 88:11
I see a v. — SHAK 612:24
Is not your v. broken — SHAK 582:20
know thy v., and suddenly — SHEL 641:17
let thy v. rise like a — TENN 682:24
Lord, hear my v. — BIBLE 108:5
Lord, hear my v. — BOOK 134:11
Mountain's slumberous v. — SHEL 641:13
my v., I have lost it — SHAK 582:21
No v.; but oh! the silence — COL 211:15
No v. divine the storm allayed — COWP 221:25
only a look and a v. — LONG 428:1
Out of the air a v. without — AUDEN 36:2
people's v. is odd — POPE 523:2
pure heart and humble v. — BOOK 118:6
safe I sing with mortal v. — MILT 472:6
seasoned with a gracious v. — SHAK 608:26
shall tune her sacred v. — JOHN 370:6
sisters, V., and Verse — MILT 463:9
so silvery is thy v. — HERR 337:10
sound of a v. that is still — TENN 680:10
still small v. — BIBLE 76:7
Sweeter thy v. — TENN 688:16
Sweet v., sweet lips — KEATS 386:11
that tone of v. — PUNCH 532:3
They hear a v. in every wind — GRAY 316:1
thou v. of my heart — CRAW 226:16
tones of a loved v. — ARN 26:17
up at the v. of the bird — BIBLE 81:1
v. and nothing more — ANON 23:1
v. I hear this passing night — KEATS 389:15
v. intimidated by an excess — ALAI 71:17
v. is Jacob's voice — BIBLE 71:11
V. is round me like a bursting — THOM 695:7
v. of Doris Day — FISH 283:7
v. of him that crieth — BIBLE 83:26
v. of my beloved that — BIBLE 81:17
v. of one crying — BIBLE 88:13
v. of Rome is the consent — JONS 378:12
v. of that wayward song — LONG 427:4
v. of the dead was a living — TENN 684:18
v. of the Lord breaketh — BOOK 126:2
v. of the Lord God walking — BIBLE 70:10
v. of the Lord maketh — BOOK 126:3
v. of the people — ALC 8:2
v. of the sluggard — WATTS 722:18
v. of the turtle is heard — BIBLE 81:9
v. of thy brother's blood — BIBLE 70:19
v. of your eyes is deeper — CUMM 228:15
v. revives the leaden strings — CAMP 177:5
v. said in mastery while — BROW 147:18
v. so sweet, the words — JONS 379:6
v. that breathed o'er Eden — KEBLE 392:22
v. to come in as by chance — BACON 43:5

voice: (*cont.*):
v. we heard was Churchill's — ATTL 32:14
v. will run from hedge to hedge — KEATS 390:5
your high, soft v. — MERR 458:13

voices: Ancestral v. prophesying war — COL 210:12
Other v., other rooms — CAP 178:14
Two v. are there — STEP 663:17
Two V. are there — WORD 748:9
v. of children are heard — BLAKE 114:2

void: captive v. of noble rage — TENN 683:11
conscience v. of offence — BIBLE 99:7
fill an enormous v. — COL 212:21
habitation be v. — BOOK 129:13
v. left aching in the breast — POPE 519:19
without form, and v. — BIBLE 69:20

voids: attempts to fill v. — WEIL 726:18

vol: *suspend ton v.* — LAM 406:1

volat: *v. irrevocabile verbum* — HOR 348:12

volatile: v. spirits prefer unhappiness — SANT 555:17

volcanic: this sweet v. cone — LOW 430:22

volcano: dancing not on a v. — FLAU 285:17
over a v. of revolution — ELLIS 275:16

volcanoes: range of exhausted v. — DISR 247:20
religious factions are v. — BURKE 159:7

vole: passes the questing v. — WAUGH 724:2

volenti: *V. non fit iniuria* — ULP 707:1

volitional: His errors are v. — JOYCE 382:2

Volk: *Ein Reich, ein V.* — ANON 21:10

volley: A v. of the sun — WILB 734:6

volleying: v. rain and tossing breeze — ARN 28:26

volo: *Hoc v., sic iubeo* — JUV 384:1

volonte: *la sua v. è nostra pace* — DANTE 230:19

Volscians: Fluttered your V. in — SHAK 570:27

Voltaire: Jesus wept; V. smiled — HUGO 355:2
mock on V. Rousseau — BLAKE 113:5

volubility: commend her v. — SHAK 624:14

voluisse: *magnis et v. sat est* — PROP 530:1

volume: destroyed this world in one v. — SMITH 652:26
I am the entire v. — MITT 478:9
In the v. of the book — BOOK 126:25
take in our hand any v. — HUME 355:4

volumes: compressed in thirty fine v. — MORL 485:15
creators of odd v. — LAMB 406:13
I am for whole v. in folio — SHAK 598:9
scholar all Earth's v. carry — CHAP 191:4
To their subsequent v. — SHAK 627:11

volunt: *homines id quod v. credunt* — CAES 174:15

voluntary: neighbourhood of v. spies — AUST 39:1

voluntas: *fiat v. tua sicut in coelo* — MISS 477:3
sit pro ratione v. — JUV 384:1
tamen est laudanda v. — OVID 502:18

voluptas: *Trahit sua quemque v.* — VIRG 714:17

volupté: *Luxe, calme et v.* — BAUD 55:9

voluptuous: V. as the first approach — BYRON 172:13

vomit: dog is turned to his own v. — BIBLE 105:24
dog returneth to his v. — BIBLE 79:21
dog returns to his v. — KIPL 399:8
v. forth into the air — MARL 447:2

Vorsprung: *V. durch Technik* — ANON 21:12

vortex: v. of immensity — DICK 241:22

votaress: imperial v. passed — SHAK 611:17

votarist: sad v. in palmer's weed — MILT 463:19

votary: A v. of the desk — LAMB 406:10

vote: Don't buy a single v. — KENN 393:10
I never v. *for* anybody — FIEL 282:23
One man shall have one v. — CART 184:14
v. against somebody rather — ADAMS 2:5
V. early and vote often — BILL 109:19
V. for the man who promises — BAR 54:21
v. just as their leaders — GILB 304:11

voted: v. at my party's call — GILB 306:1
v. cent per cent — BYRON 167:20

voter: Every intelligent v. — ADAMS 2:3
v. who uses his money — SAM 555:1

votes: Tradition means giving v. — CHES 199:19
who uses his money as v. — SAM 555:1

voting: v. that's democracy — STOP 669:14

votis: *Hoc erat in v.* — HOR 351:9

votive: Venus, take my v. glass — PRIOR 529:8

vouchsafe: V., O Lord — BOOK 118:14

vow: I v. to thee, my country — SPR 661:8
That great v. — SHAK 591:1
v. be performed in Jerusalem — BOOK 128:23

vowels: v., some day I will tell — RIMB 541:10

vows: cancel all our v. — DRAY 258:1
falser than v. made in wine — SHAK 569:14
honey of his music v. — SHAK 576:4
Much in our v., but little — SHAK 629:20
our moist v. denied — MILT 466:12
V. can't change nature — BROW 152:14
V. for thee broke deserve — SHAK 598:18
v. now in the presence — BOOK 133:14
v. sworn by two creatures — DID 245:11
V. with so much passion — LEE 416:2

vox: *V. et praeterea nihil* — ANON 23:1
V. populi, vox Dei — ALC 8:2

voyage: about to take my last v. — HOBB 340:14
all the v. of their life — SHAK 593:12
In life's uncertain v. — SHAK 626:20
its v. closed and done — WHIT 732:7
Ulysse a fait un beau v. — DU B 263:1
v. over and they reached — VIRG 713:15

voyaging: V. through strange seas — WORD 747:2

vrai: *plus vrai que le v.* — ANOU 23:8

Vulcan: V.'s stithy — SHAK 576:8

vulgar: administered in the v. tongue — BOOK 122:19
Both the great v., and the small — COWL 221:10
let the v. stuff alone — BELL 62:4
money-spending always 'v.' — GASK 299:2
takes place with the v. — BACON 42:13
'tis such a v. expression — CONG 215:1
trivial and v. way of coition — BROW 146:16
work upon the v. with fine sense — POPE 524:3
worse than wicked, it's v. — PUNCH 531:23

vulgarity: Jacksonian v. — POTT 525:14
v., concealing something — FORS 290:19

vulpes: *v. aegroto cauta leoni* — HOR 348:1

W

wabe: gyre and gimble in the w. — CARR 182:18

wade: should I w. no more — SHAK 603:14

waded: w. thro' red blude — BALL 50:17

wafer-cakes: men's faiths are w. — SHAK 585:6

Waffen: *In gute Wehr und W.* — LUTH 432:13

wag: ambition to be a w. — JOHN 376:24
W. as it will the world for me — BYROM 167:13

wage: give themselves for w. — YEATS 752:17
I w. war — CLEM 206:6

wager: I have lost the w. — SHAK 570:28

wages: better w. and shorter hours — ORW 500:22
Home art gone and ta'en thy w. — SHAK 571:16
honours for w. — GAR 298:1
My w. taken, and in my heart — HENL 332:8
took their w. and are dead — HOUS 351:22
w. of sin is death — BIBLE 99:30
w. to put it into a bag — BIBLE 86:18

wagged: tail that w. contempt — WATS 722:10

Wagner: has lovely moments — ROSS 548:9
W.'s music better than it sounds — NYE 497:7

wagon: Hitch your w. to a star — EMER 277:13
w. of his 'Plan' — PAST 508:12

Wahrheit: *Die W. hat keine Stunde* — SCHW 558:15

wail: kindreds of earth shall w. — BIBLE 105:32
mirth to w. a week — SHAK 632:22
woes new w. my dear times — SHAK 633:11
wrynge, and w. — CHAU 193:12

wailing: w. for her demon-lover — COL 210:10

wain: wheels of Phoebus' w. — MILT 463:19

wainscot: w. tubs to seek out worlds — DRAY 258:3
wall, the w. and the mouse — ELIOT 271:4

waist: her slender w. confined — WALL 718:14
Then you live about her w. — SHAK 574:25

waistcoat: open your w. to receive a knock-down blow — HUNT 356:14

war: (*cont.*):

All whom w., dearth	DONNE 250:21
Ancestral voices prophesying w.	COL 210:12
As soon as w. is declared	GIR 307:2
as well that w. is so terrible	LEE 416:8
been no declaration of w.	EDEN 266:7
brought to the verge of w.	DULL 263:11
But w.'s a game	COWP 224:3
But when the blast of w.	SHAK 585:7
can wage a pitiless w.	GREE 316:22
cheeks strained by w.	BLOK 115:5
condemn recourse to w.	BRIA 141:1
condition which is called w.	HOBB 340:5
cudgel of the people's w.	TOLS 700:12
day w. broke out	WILT 738:22
delays are dangerous in w.	DRYD 261:34
desolation of w.	GEOR 301:3
either w. is obsolete or men	FULL 295:27
endless w. still breed	MILT 466:19
essence of w. is violence	MAC 434:11
ever another w. in Europe	BISM 110:7
except the British W. Office	SHAW 636:9
First World W. had begun	TAYL 679:6
flinty and steel couch of w.	SHAK 615:7
For w. breeds war again	DAV 231:23
France has not lost the w.	DE G 234:28
From the w. of nature	DARW 231:10
garland of the w.	SHAK 566:15
gave a w. & Nobody came	GINS 306:27
give a w. and nobody will	SAND 555:9
gone wrong since the W.	AMIS 10:12
good w. makes a good peace	HERB 336:3
great battle-plans of w.	LUCR 431:15
great protection against w.	BEVIN 69:14
guarantee success in w.	CHUR 202:14
hath all this w. been wrought	MAL 443:11
having w. in his heart	BOOK 128:12
Horses and Power and W.	KIPL 398:14
I am the tongue of w.	VOZN 717:8
If you want peace, prepare for w.	VEGE 710:1
I have seen war . . . I hate w.	ROOS 545:18
image of w. without its guilt	SURT 672:8
Image of w., without its guilt	SOM 655:12
In a pattern called a w.	LOW 429:12
infection and the hand of w.	SHAK 619:18
In w.: resolution	CHUR 203:3
In w., three-quarters turns	NAP 489:12
In w., whichever side may	CHAM 189:6
It is easier to make w.	CLEM 206:7
it is not w.	BOSQ 136:4
Laws are silent in time of w.	CIC 204:11
Let me have w.	SHAK 570:18
let slip the dogs of w.	SHAK 591:24
Let w. yield to peace	CIC 204:2
like to the morning's w.	SHAK 587:29
liking for w.	BENN 63:6
long without a w. here	BREC 140:7
looks on w. as all glory	SHER 645:27
Lord is a man of w.	BIBLE 72:14
lordship that this is w.	ADAMS 1:14
lose the w. in an afternoon	CHUR 203:6
midst of a cold w.	BAR 54:19
Minstrel Boy to the w.	MOORE 483:7
money the sinews of w.	BACON 44:33
must take chances in w.	DULL 263:11
My subject is W.	OWEN 503:10
never has been a w. yet	BEVIN 69:14
no discharge in that w.	BIBLE 80:16
no less than w. to waste	MILT 473:10
No w., or battle's sound	MILT 467:3
Now tell us all about the w.	SOUT 657:5
Oh what a lovely w.	LITT 423:10
Older men declare w.	HOOV 344:20
Once lead this people into w.	WILS 738:21
only w. creates order	BREC 140:7
Out of that bungled, unwise w.	PLOM 517:10
prepare for the last w.	TUCH 704:23
quaint and curious w.	HARDY 325:12
quickest way of ending a w.	ORW 500:18
rich wage w. it's the poor	SART 556:6
right determined without w.	HOBB 340:10
sentence is for open w.	MILT 469:12
Set roaring w.—to the dread	SHAK 626:1

war: (*cont.*):

Shakes pestilence and w.	MILT 470:7
shall they learn w. any more	BIBLE 82:11
sinews of w.	CIC 204:10
so the nature of w. consisteth	HOBB 340:6
state of w. by nature	SWIFT 675:5
still seek no wider w.	JOHN 367:9
testament of bleeding w.	SHAK 620:10
that devil's madness—W.	SERV 563:7
that first invented w.	MARL 447:23
that made this great w.	LINC 422:17
There ain't gonna be no w.	MACM 440:2
There never was a good w.	FRAN 293:2
there was w. in heaven	BIBLE 106:30
Though in the trade of w.	SHAK 614:26
time of peace thinks of w.	ANON 14:1
time of w., and a time	BIBLE 80:5
To w. and arms I fly	LOV 429:6
under the shadow of a w.	SPEN 659:7
used to w.'s alarms	HOOD 343:17
very well out of the w.	BALD 48:13
w. against a monstrous	CHUR 202:9
W. always finds a way	BREC 140:10
w. and peace	ARIS 25:6
w. between men and women	THUR 697:16
w. for its consequences	FOSD 291:4
w. has its laws	NEWM 492:12
W. hath no fury like a non-combatant	
	MONT 480:12
w. hath smoothed his wrinkled	SHAK 021:15
W., he sung, is toil	DRYD 259:21
w. is a necessary part	MOLT 479:17
W. is capitalism	STOP 670:8
W. is the continuation of politics	
	CLAU 205:16
W. is peace	ORW 500:10
W. is the national industry	MIR 476:10
W. is the trade of kings	DRYD 260:33
W. is the universal perversion	RAE 535:9
W. is too serious a matter	CLEM 206:5
W. its thousands slays	PORT 525:7
W. makes rattling good history	HARDY 324:6
w. may be jointly numbered	JOHN 368:8
w. on a kindred nation	BETH 67:2
w. on the heels of small	LOW 430:22
w. our fate has consummation	MAND 444:6
w. poet whose right	GURN 320:1
W.'s annals will cloud	HARDY 325:10
W. settles *nothing*	CHR 200:7
W.'s glorious art	YOUNG 754:10
w. that drags on indecisively	WAUGH 724:3
w. that has ever scourged	LLOY 424:7
w. that we may live in peace	ARIS 25:10
w. that will end war	WELLS 727:23
W. That Would Not Boil	TAYL 679:10
w. they kill you in a new way	ROG 544:5
W. told me truth	GURN 320:2
W. to the knife	PAL 505:4
W. will cease when men	ANON 19:5
w. will put an end to mankind	KENN 394:3
w. with a heart of fire	TENN 687:5
w. without bloodshed	MAO 445:13
w. with women	SOUT 657:12
waste of God, W.!	STUD 671:3
weapons of w.	BIBLE 75:9
We hear w. called murder	MACD 437:12
We've an, an' a debt	LOW 429:17
what can w., but endless war	MILT 466:19
when there was w., he went	AUDEN 36:11
When w. enters a country	ANON 21:11
which enable it to make w.	WEIL 726:19
who is able to make w. with	BIBLE 106:31
who wasn't against w.	LOW 429:9
with himself at w.	SHAK 589:25
Work at w. speed	MORR 485:18
warble: W., child	SHAK 598:12
warbled: Such notes as w. to the string	
	MILT 464:23
warbler: Attic w. pours her throat	GRAY 316:5
w. has his tune by heart	COWP 223:15
warbling: w. his Doric lay	MILT 466:15
Warburton: worst of W.	JOHN 371:22
warder: w. silent on the hill	SCOTT 560:1

wardrobe: silken dalliance in the w.	
	SHAK 585:1
war-drum: w. throbbed no longer	TENN 685:13
wards: W. in Jarndyce	DICK 239:15
Ware: enough for the bed of W.	SHAK 630:15
There was an old person of W.	LEAR 414:7
ware: w. that will not keep	HOUS 352:7
warfare: Armed w. must be	ZIN 755:12
her w. is accomplished	BIBLE 83:25
of w., and of laws	DU B 262:23
such a thing as legitimate w.	NEWM 492:12
Who goeth a w.	BIBLE 100:28
warm: Be w., but pure	BYRON 172:7
earth is w. with Spring	GREN 318:2
Her heart was w. and gay	HAMM 322:15
O! she's w.	SHAK 632:17
She winters and keeps w.	CAREW 179:12
This is too w. work	NELS 491:17
w. and capable	KEATS 390:16
w. and still to be enjoyed	KEATS 388:28
W. beds: w. full blooded life	JOYCE 381:27
w. kind world is all	CORY 220:1
w. to understand one who's	SOLZ 655:10
w. what is cold, guide	LANG 409:9
warmed: my heart strangely w.	WESL 728:19
w. and cooled by the same	SHAK 608:22
warmer: w. than after watry cloudes	
	LANG 409:6
warming: w. his five wits	TENN 689:9
warming pans: heroes were as	
good as w.	MER 457:16
warmth: Colour and W. and Light	GREN 318:2
comes native with the w.	KEATS 390:8
His vigorous w. did	DRYD 258:17
Now Spring restores balmy w.	CAT 186:5
w. about my heart like	KEATS 391:21
w. and colour which I found	TENN 681:26
w. to swell the grain	CAMP 176:4
warn: All a poet can do is w.	OWEN 503:11
right to w.	BAG 47:8
w. you not to be ordinary	KINN 398:9
warning: w. to the world	SHAK 634:5
With horrid w. gapèd wide	KEATS 388:13
warns: w. the heads of parties	ARB 24:7
warp: Weave the w.	GRAY 315:8
war-proof: fathers of w.	SHAK 585:8
warring: W. in heaven	MILT 470:23
warrior: Here lies a valiant w.	ANON 14:5
Home they brought her w. dead	TENN 688:9
painful w. famousèd for fight	SHAK 633:9
w. that is rapt with love	MARL 448:4
Who is the happy W.?	WORD 743:8
wars: All skilful in the w.	VAUG 708:17
All w. are planned by old men	RICE 540:2
And as for war, my w.	REED 538:2
armaments that cause w.	MAD 441:13
beginnings of all w.	ROOS 546:7
Between the w.	PLOM 517:11
came to an end all w.	LLOY 424:7
clucked thee to the w.	SHAK 570:25
Continual w. and wives are	HUGH 354:3
For all their w. are merry	CHES 198:28
he maketh w. to cease	BOOK 127:17
History is littered with the w.	POW 528:9
I see w., horrible wars	VIRG 713:10
occasion of all w.	FOX 292:2
sent into any foreign w.	ROOS 546:1
serve in the w.	BOOK 136:1
stick i' the w.	SHAK 570:24
thousand w. of old	TENN 684:11
Thy w. brought nothing about	DRYD 261:21
tumultuous w. shall kin	SHAK 620:17
w. and faithful loves shall	SPEN 659:19
w. and lechery	SHAK 628:5
w. and rumours of wars	BIBLE 92:8
W. cannot be fought	MOUN 487:6
Warsaw: Order reigns in W.	ANON 21:2
warship: every w. launched	EIS 268:10
warts: w., and everything	CROM 227:16
war-war: jaw-jaw better than to w.	
	CHUR 203:1
Warwick: impudent and shameless W.	
	SHAK 588:4

wary: craves w. walking   SHAK 590:13
was: ne'er w., nor is   POPE 521:10
  picked the w. of shall   CUMM 228:13
wash: And It-will-w.-no-more   TRAI 702:2
  Bid them w. their faces   SHAK 570:8
  every night w. I my bed   BOOK 124:18
  half-glimpsèd turrets slowly w.   THOM 695:6
  Lord, dost thou w. my feet   BIBLE 97:8
  tears w. out a word of it   FITZ 284:0
  w. me and I shall be made   BIBLE 107:28
  W. me throughly from   BOOK 128:4
  w. my hands in innocency   BOOK 125:22
  w. the balm from an anointed   SHAK 620:3
  w. their feet in soda water   ELIOT 273:7
  w. the wind   ELIOT 272:11
  W. what is dirty   LANG 409:9
  Where air might w.   SWIN 676:27
washed: have w. their robes   BIBLE 106:21
  W. by the rivers, blest   BROO 143:18
  w. himself with oriental   JOHN 369:4
  w. his ha. ds before   BIBLE 93:3
  w. in the blood   LIND 423:3
washing: country w.   BRUM 153:22
  taking in one another's w.   ANON 13:1
  w. ain't done nor sweeping   ANON 14:4
  w. on the Siegfried Line   KENN 393:9
  which came up from the w.   BIBLE 81:13
Washington: Government at W.   GARF 297:16
Washingtonian: W. dignity for
  the Jeffersonian   POTT 525:14
wash-pot: Moab is my w.   BOOK 128:18
wasps: let w. and hornets   SWIFT 673:5
wassails: Hock-carts, w.   HERR 336:6
waste: art of how to w. space   JOHN 367:16
  because thou none should w.   BARC 52:9
  haste makes w.   GASC 298:19
  I love all w.   SHEL 640:20
  make us mortal, and thee w.   MARV 451:8
  no less than war to w.   MILT 473:10
  now doth time w. me   SHAK 621:12
  spirit in a w. of shame   SHAK 635:1
  this world's perplexing w.   BYRON 172:1
  wail my dear times' w.   SHAK 633:11
  w. any time in mourning   HILL 338:13
  w. his whole heart in one   TENN 689:8
  w. howling   BIBLE 73:21
  w. of breath the years behind   YEATS 752:6
  w. of goods   VEBL 709:16
  w. remains and kills   EMPS 277:20
  we lay w. our powers   WORD 748:15
  were glimpsed in the w.   VIRG 712:3
  What a w., what a waste   DURY 264:13
  what purpose is this w.   BIBLE 92:22
  ye w. places of Jerusalem   BIBLE 84:9
wasted: Nothing is w., nothing   HERB 333:20
  there w. his substance   BIBLE 95:2
  w. my precious time   DYLAN 265:13
wasteful: w., blundering, low   DARW 231:11
wastefulness: conspicuous w.   VEBL 709:17
waste-paper: Marriage is the w. basket
   WEBB 724:17
wastes: W. beyond wastes   BRON 142:11
  W. without springs   CLARE 204:23
wasting: nor wanting, nor w.   SMITH 653:31
watch: before the morning w.   BOOK 134:12
  could ye not w. with me   BIBLE 92:29
  done much better by a w.   BELL 61:25
  everlasting w. and moveless   BROW 147:14
  For some must w., while   SHAK 576:20
  going like a fat gold w.   PLATH 516:7
  if you'd w. a dinner out   BROW 148:10
  keeping w. above his own   LOW 430:4
  like little w. springs   SPEN 659:4
  like your w. in a private   CHES 198:13
  Lord w. between me   BIBLE 71:17
  man who knew how a w.   JOHN 372:28
  No longer w. you as you sit   BROW 148:23
  or my w. has stopped   MARX 451:17
  past as a w. in the night   BOOK 130:23
  Set a w., O Lord, before   BOOK 135:1
  She shall w. all night   SHAK 624:17
  Thence to a w., thence   SHAK 574:17

watch: (*cont.*):
  To any w. they keep   FROST 295:6
  to w. for her! to pray for her!   SHAK 598:14
  W. and pray   ELL 275:11
  W. and pray, that ye enter   BIBLE 92:30
  w. in the night against   SMART 649:14
  w. not one another out   DONNE 252:5
  w. of the night Jesus went   BIBLE 91:6
  w. over their flock   BIBLE 93:26
  w. that ends the night   WATTS 723:7
  W. the parkin' meters   DYLAN 265:22
  W. therefore   BIBLE 92:15
  W. the wall, my darling   KIPL 400:9
  w. upon the ground   PALEY 505:5
  W. ye therefore   BIBLE 93:19
  whispers of each other's w.   SHAK 585:14
  why not carry a w.   TREE 702:6
  winding up the w. of his wit   SHAK 625:14
watch-chain: too large to hang on a w.
   ANON 19:3
watchdog: w.'s voice that bayed   GOLD 310:8
watched: He w. the ads   NASH 490:13
watcher: like some w. of the skies   KEATS 390:3
  posted presence of the w.   JAMES 363:5
watches: He w. from his mountain walls
   TENN 681:1
  still you w. of the element   MARL 447:7
  That w. and receives   WORD 748:8
watchful: And w. at his gate   DODD 250:1
  occasion's forelock w.   MILT 473:17
watching: BIG BROTHER IS W. YOU   ORW 500:9
  My tiny w. eye   DE L 236:12
  Weeping and w. for the morrow   GOET 309:15
watchmaker: it is the *blind* w.   DAWK 232:17
watchman: w. on the lonely tower
   SCOTT 559:19
  w. waketh but in vain   BOOK 134:6
  w. watches in vain   BIBLE 108:4
  W., what of the night   BIBLE 83:6
watchmen: w. that went about   BIBLE 81:18
watchword: Our w. is security   PITT 515:14
water: are as w. spilt   BIBLE 75:14
  As w. is in water   SHAK 566:7
  Beat the clear and sunny w.   LONG 427:15
  blackens all the w. about   ADD 4:22
  bucket of perfectly lucid w.   WILB 734:2
  But W.'s wider   HUXL 357:22
  By w. and the word   STONE 669:12
  Christ walking on the w.   THOM 695:10
  conscious w. saw its God   CRAS 226:2
  don't care where the w. goes   CHES 199:12
  drank rapidly a glass of w.   CUMM 228:6
  dry land where no w.   BOOK 128:21
  ever-flowing w. near the house   HOR 351:9
  feet are always in the w.   AMES 10:9
  fountain of the w. of life   BIBLE 107:19
  hands than w. like Pilate   GREE 316:20
  He asked w., and she gave him milk
   BIBLE 74:4
  I am poured out like w.   BOOK 125:12
  I came like w., and like   FITZ 284:2
  if I were under w.   KEATS 391:19
  King over the W.   ANON 15:14
  Lay a great w.   TENN 682:19
  Let the w. and the blood   TOPL 701:4
  like w. held   MACN 441:1
  limns the w., or but writes   BACON 45:28
  makes w. I makes water   JOYCE 381:20
  Minnehaha, Laughing W.   LONG 427:16
  more w. glideth by the mill   SHAK 626:22
  No more w., the fire next time   ANON 13:17
  Of that wide w., inescapable   STEV 666:11
  Or w. but the desert   BYRON 169:4
  presence of still w.   BERRY 66:13
  pure river of w. of life   BIBLE 107:22
  ready by w. as by land   ELST 276:1
  safe to go back in the w.   ANON 15:13
  Shall come of w. and of mud   BROO 143:7
  should go across salt w.   DICK 244:3
  sound of w.'s murmuring   SHEL 642:22
  sweet w. and bitter   BIBLE 105:3
  [Tar w.] is of a nature   BERK 65:8
  Too much of w. hast thou   SHAK 578:14

water: (*cont.*):
  travel by land or by w.   BOOK 120:1
  Unstable as w., thou shalt   BIBLE 71:33
  w. clears us of this deed   SHAK 602:7
  w. comes ashore   FROST 295:6
  w. escaping from mill-dams   CONS 217:22
  w. flowed in it dazzled   BALL 49:11
  w. hollows out a stone   OVID 502:19
  w. in the rough rude sea   SHAK 620:3
  W. is best   PIND 514:13
  W. like a stone   ROSS 547:4
  w. must o'erwhelm thy corpse   SHAK 619:3
  w. my couch   BOOK 124:18
  w. penetrates my wooden   RIMB 541:4
  w. under the earth   BIBLE 72:16
  W., water, everywhere   COL 211:1
  w. what is dry, heal what   LANG 409:9
  w. which receives and reflects   ADAMS 2:13
  We'll o'er the w. to Charlie   HOGG 341:18
  We write in w.   SHAK 589:9
  What dreadful noise of w.   SHAK 621:23
  which makes my teath w.   FLEM 287:3
  whose name was writ in w.   KEATS 392:17
  will hardly w. the ground   BACON 44:4
  wind and swift-flowing w.   CAT 186:10
  with w. and a crust   KEATS 388:16
  with w. of affliction   BIBLE 76:13
  wood and drawers of w.   BIBLE 73:31
  written by drinkers of w.   HOR 348:15
water-brooks: desireth the w.   BOOK 127:2
water-colour: w. shows the innocent
   STEV 668:2
water-drops: not women's weapons, w.
   SHAK 595:18
watered: Apollos w.   BIBLE 100:17
  w. heaven with their tears   BLAKE 114:15
  w. our houses in Helicon   CHAP 190:18
waterfall: From the w. he named her
   LONG 427:16
water-floods: great w. they   BOOK 126:9
water-lily: saw the w. bloom   TENN 685:4
Waterloo: at Austerlitz and W.   SAND 555:6
  On W.'s ensanguined plain   ANON 17:7
  That world-earthquake, W.   TENN 687:17
  W. was won on the playing   WELL 727:7
  W. was won on the playing   ORW 500:7
waterman: great-grandfather was
  but a w.   BUNY 155:20
watermelons: down by the w.   GINS 306:29
watermen: Like w., that row one way
   BURT 164:17
water-mill: noise like that of a w.   SWIFT 673:9
water-pipes: noise of the w.   BOOK 127:4
water-rats: land-rats and w.   SHAK 607:18
waters: Across the waste of w. die   BETJ 67:10
  all that move in the w.   BOOK 118:21
  And the w. as they flow   ARMS 26:5
  And the w. murmuring   MILT 464:25
  beside the w. of comfort   BOOK 125:14
  bounded w. should lift their   SHAK 627:8
  Cast thy bread upon the w.   BIBLE 80:25
  cold w. to a thirsty soul   BIBLE 79:19
  come ye to the w.   BIBLE 84:15
  crept by me upon the w.   SHAK 625:9
  Glides on, with pomp of w.   DAN 229:11
  he made the w. to stand   BOOK 130:10
  his chambers in the w.   BOOK 132:6
  His luminous home of w.   ARN 28:18
  hitherandthithering w.   JOYCE 381:4
  in perils of w.   BIBLE 102:1
  knowledge of man is as the w.   BACON 42:2
  lilies by the rivers of w.   BIBLE 88:4
  Many w. cannot quench love   BIBLE 82:6
  mighty w. rolling evermore   WORD 746:5
  Once more upon the w.   BYRON 168:12
  Over the rolling w. go   TENN 687:27
  quiet w. by   SCOT 561:8
  small w. seeping upward   ROET 544:3
  sound of many w.   BIBLE 106:1
  Stolen w. are sweet   BIBLE 78:19
  than all the w. of Israel   BIBLE 76:21
  that sitteth upon many w.   BIBLE 107:27
  their business in great w.   BOOK 133:1

waters: (cont.):

Though thou the w. warp	SHAK 568:17
voice of many w.	BIBLE 107:2
walks the fields and the w.	MER 457:29
w. at their priestlike task	KEATS 386:9
w. cover the sea	AING 6:3
w. cover the sea	BIBLE 83:3
w. of affliction	BIBLE 83:15
w. of Babylon we sat down	BOOK 134:17
w. of Babylon we sit down	WALP 719:17
w. of the crispèd spring	DEKK 235:16
w. of the heart	THOM 693:11
W. on a starry night	WORD 745:10
w. stand in the hills	BOOK 132:6
W. that be above the Firmament	BOOK 118:16
w. were his winding sheet	BARN 53:16
w. where we used to dwell	HOPE 345:3
While the nearer w. roll	WESL 728:6
why his w. never run dry	FLAU 286:2
wilderness shall w. break	BIBLE 83:21

watery: be beneath the w. floor

	MILT 466:13
Dotting the shoreless w. wild	ARN 29:3
That crown the w. glade	GRAY 315:21
weder warmer than after w.	LANG 409:6
With w. if not flaming sword	MARV 451:8

Wattle: ever hear of Captain W.   DIBD 238:11
wattles: of clay and w. made   YEATS 752:7
waukin: W. still and weary   BURNS 161:8
waul: We w. and cry   SHAK 597:10
wave: age is rocking the w.   MAND 444:4

chin upon an orient w.	MILT 467:12
cool, translucent w.	MILT 464:10
I wish you a w. o' the sea	SHAK 632:5
Oh, lift me as a w.	SHEL 641:18
or swallowing w.	LOV 429:5

Shakespeare would have grasped w.

	MCEW 437:15
third great religious w.	WOLFE 741:8
w. rolls nightly on deep	BYRON 169:28
w. that echoes round	TENN 682:9
within the w.'s intenser day	SHEL 641:16

waved: w. her lily hand   GAY 300:17
Waverley: W. pen   ANON 18:16
waves: all thy w. and storms   BOOK 127:4

And spurns the w.	DAN 229:12
Countless chuckles of the w.	AESC 5:12
floods lift up their w.	BOOK 131:7
Him that walked the w.	MILT 466:13
I see the w. upon the shore	SHEL 643:9
longed-for dash of w. is heard	ARN 28:18
lute-resounding w.	POPE 519:7
noise of his w.	BOOK 129:1
only on the w. behind us	COL 212:14
righteousness as the w.	BIBLE 84:5
w. and washèd it away	SPEN 659:11
w. bound beneath me	BYRON 168:12
w. make towards the pebbled	SHAK 633:20
w. of thy sweet singing	SHEL 641:14
w. over us all in the spring	PAST 508:11
w. that beat on heavens	BLAKE 111:7
w. thereof are still	BOOK 133:2
What are the wild w. saying	CARP 181:21

What the w. were always saying   DICK 240:17
waving: not w. but drowning   SMITH 652:17

than w. me farewell	HOPE 345:3

wax: didn't w. his moustache   KIPL 402:11

even like melting w.	BOOK 125:12
hives with honey and w.	SWIFT 673:4
moons shall w. and wane	WATTS 723:8
My faith shall w.	DAN 229:15
Of wyne and w., of gamyn	WYNT 750:10
suffocated in its own w.	FORS 290:7
they all shall w. old	BOOK 132:1
times begin to w. old	BIBLE 86:23
w. is preparing	BYRON 173:24
W. to receive	BYRON 167:23

waxworks: you think we're w.   CARR 182:23
way: all gone out of the w.   BOOK 124:27

ask that your w. be long	CAV 187:4
broad is the w.	BIBLE 89:21
but I'm on the w.	SAND 555:8
care which w. he travelled	BEAV 57:6

way: (cont.):

dirty, dangerous w.	GOLD 311:24
each thing give him w.	SHAK 564:23
every one to his own w.	BIBLE 84:12
Every which w. but loose	KRON 404:4
flowers to strew Thy w.	HERB 334:15
gentleman's w. of thinking	ANON 22:9
given us one w. in to life	SEN 563:1
God moves in a mysterious w.	COWP 222:17
gull's w. and the whale's w.	MAS 453:9
I am the w., the truth	BIBLE 97:12
I have no w., and therefore	SHAK 596:24
indirect w. to plant religion	BROW 146:9
Is there no w. out of the mind	PLATH 516:3
It's a long w. to Tipperary	JUDGE 382:8
it's the w. they say it	STEI 663:9
known and common w.	WINC 739:4
more a w. of life	ANON 16:23
mystical w. of Pythagoras	BROW 146:5
Never in the w.	CHAR 191:18
nice to people on your w. up	MIZN 478:10
perish from the right w.	BOOK 124:11
Poetry is a w. of taking	FROST 295:18
Prepare ye the w. of the Lord	BIBLE 83:26
Prepare ye the w. of the Lord	BIBLE 88:15
shows the w. to others	GAND 297:9
talked with us by the w.	BIBLE 95:32
Teach me thy w., O Lord	BOOK 125:25
teach thee in the w.	BOOK 126:10
That was a w. of putting it	ELIOT 270:10
Their w., however straight	THOM 694:3
There is no w. to peace	MUSTE 488:19
there was a w. to Hell	BUNY 156:6
they kill you in a new w.	ROG 545:4
this is the w. of them	BOOK 127:24
This is the w. the world ends	ELIOT 271:14
This is the w., walk ye in it	BIBLE 83:16
Thou art my w.	QUAR 534:1
War always finds a w.	BREC 140:10
washy w. of true tragedy	KAV 386:4
W. down upon the Swanee	FOST 291:14
w. is commonly the foulest	BACON 42:9
w. may be known upon earth	BOOK 129:4
w. of all the earth	BIBLE 73:33
w. of a man with a maid	BIBLE 79:33
w. of a man with a maid	KIPL 399:17
w. of transgressors	BIBLE 78:27
w. out is always through	FROST 295:12
w. plain before my face	BOOK 124:16
w. she disposed of an empire	HARL 326:3
w. to dusty death	SHAK 605:1
w. to the Better there be	HARDY 325:6
w. you wear your hat	GERS 301:16

ways: at the parting of the w.   BIBLE 85:24

chief of the w.	BIBLE 78:2
for w. that are dark	HARTE 327:1
her w. to roam	BROO 143:18
in whose heart are thy w.	BOOK 130:17
I wander in the w. of men	BURNS 162:16
justify the w. of God	MILT 467:21
keep thee in all thy w.	BOOK 131:4
Let all her w. be unconfined	PRIOR 529:5
Let me count the w.	BROW 147:20
maintain mine own w.	BIBLE 77:20
neither are your ways my w.	BIBLE 84:17
still dazzled by the w. of God	LIND 423:4
vastly more w. of being dead	DAWK 232:18
vindicate the w. of God to man	POPE 521:27
w. and means	ARIS 25:6
w. are ways of pleasantness	BIBLE 78:9
w. deep and the weather	ELIOT 271:17

wayside: seeds fell by the w.   BIBLE 91:1
wayward: voice of that w. song   LONG 427:4

w. is this foolish love	SHAK 631:3

we: still it is not w.   CHES 199:8

W. are the hollow men	ELIOT 271:14
W. never closed	VAN D 708:8
W. shall not be moved	ANON 19:10
W. shall not pretend	ANON 19:11
W. shall overcome	ANON 19:12

weak: but the flesh is w.   BIBLE 92:30

concessions of the w.	BURKE 157:19
earth is w., and all	BOOK 130:4

weak: (cont.):

found him w. in chemistry	WELLS 727:15
How very w. the very wise	THAC 691:22
Made w. by time and fate	TENN 690:4
pondered, w. and weary	POE 518:6
refuge of the world	CHES 198:18
Repentance is the virtue of w.	DRYD 260:30
Strengthen ye the w. hands	BIBLE 83:20
surely the W. shall perish	SERV 563:6
that are otherwise w. men	BACON 43:4
to be w. is miserable	MILT 468:7
w. alone repent	BYRON 169:21
w. always have to decide	BONH 118:1
w. from your loveliness	BETJ 68:6
w. have one weapon	BID 109:1
w. men he laid an exaggerated	MAUG 454:10
W. men must fall, for heaven	SHAK 620:3
w. piping time of peace	SHAK 621:15
w. things of the world	BIBLE 100:16

weaken: great life if you don't w.   BUCH 154:1
weaker: to the w. side inclined   BUTL 166:19

unto the w. vessel	BIBLE 105:17
w. sex, to piety more prone	ALEX 9:1

weakest: w. kind of fruit   SHAK 609:11
weak-hearted: comfort and help the w.

	BOOK 119:20

weakness: All w. which impairs   ARN 28:13

Girt round with w.	SHEL 639:20
Is it w. of intellect	GILB 305:12
makes our w. weaker	BALZ 51:9
oh! w. of joy	BETJ 68:6
strength is made perfect in w.	BIBLE 102:3
Stronger by w., wiser men	WALL 718:13
thence into a w.	SHAK 574:17
wade into the w. of Princes	JAM 362:3
w. for the stoic's pride	POPE 522:9
w. of our mortal nature	BOOK 121:1

weaknesses: w. with a delicate hand

	GOLD 311:15

weal: according to the common w.   JAM 362:5
wealth: all time of our w.   BOOK 119:18

by promoting the w.	BURKE 158:2
care for the acquisition of w.	SOCR 654:11
consume w. without producing	SHAW 636:1
cunning purchase of my w.	JONS 379:2
gained great w. by delinquency	VEBL 709:16
get w. and place	POPE 522:27
greater the w.	GALB 297:2
health and w. long to live	BOOK 119:6
He gave the w. he had	SWIFT 675:13
His w. a well-spent age	CAMP 177:7
I'm a man of w. and taste	JAGG 361:13
insolence of w. will	JOHN 375:2
In squandering w. was	DRYD 259:9
Let w. and commerce	MANN 445:6
love remembered such w.	SHAK 633:10
poor man's w.	SIDN 646:18
riches, ignorance of w.	GOLD 310:6
rule of w.	BAG 46:21
Say that health and w. have	HUNT 356:9
smoke and w. and din of Rome	HOR 350:8
so much power and w.	SMIL 650:10
Swim'st thou in w.	DEKK 235:16
There is no road to w.	TROL 703:12
There is no w. but life	RUSK 551:7
Thirst of w. no quiet knows	WINC 738:23
w. a libel on its possessor	SHEL 644:3
w. around them makes them	CRAB 225:14
w. is a sacred thing	FRAN 292:6
W. I seek, hope nor love	STEV 669:5
w. of Ormuz and of Ind	MILT 469:10
w. of thy wit in an instant	SHAK 609:6
w. piled by the bond-man's	LINC 422:8
w. to me the show had brought	WORD 744:16
w. will compensate them	TAWN 679:3
w. within the fencèd town	DRAY 258:3
w. ye find, another keeps	SHEL 643:4
Where w. accumulates	GOLD 310:6

wealthy: business of the w.   BELL 61:20

w. and others have nothing	ARIS 25:18
w. curlèd darlings	SHAK 614:28
[w.] in a religious diving-bell	FOST 291:9

weaned: w. child shall — BIBLE 83:3
w. on a pickle — ANON 18:19
were we not w. till then — DONNE 252:4
weapon: art is not a w. — KENN 394:8
bayonet is a w. with a worker — ANON 12:10
folly and his w. wit — HOPE 344:24
Innocence is no earthly w. — HILL 338:11
Loyalty is the Tory's secret w. — KILM 396:4
other hand held a w. — BIBLE 76:34
Skill in the w. is nothing — SHAK 583:27
terrible is our w. of aggression — ADLER 5:7
trusty shield and w. — LUTH 432:13
weak have one w. — BID 109:1
weaponless: And, w. himself — MILT 474:4
weapons: books are w. — ROOS 546:5
fought with nuclear w. — MOUN 487:6
get your w. ready — WHIT 732:9
let not women's w. — SHAK 595:18
Spare us all word of the w. — WILB 734:1
w. and virtues of all prisoners — COL 212:20
w. of war perished — BIBLE 75:9
wear w., and serve — BOOK 136:1
wear: I will w. him in my heart's core — SHAK 576:7
Should so w. out to nought — SHAK 597:5
such qualities as would w. — GOLD 311:29
w. ourselves and never — MARL 448:1
w. out than to rust out — CUMB 228:4
w. them out in practice — BEAU 56:8
worth the w. of winning — BELL 62:3
weariest: w. and most loathèd worldly — SHAK 606:11
weariness: Art thou pale for w. — SHEL 643:24
For w. of thee — DONNE 252:15
for w. of-walked — LANG 408:20
In hours of w., sensations — WORD 744:19
much study is a w. — BIBLE 81:3
W. can snore upon the flint — SHAK 571:12
w. may toss him to my breast — HERB 335:16
w., the fever, and the fret — KEATS 389:10
w. treads on desire — PETR 513:15
wearing: not linen you're w. out — HOOD 344:8
w. armchairs tight about — WOD 740:19
w.' o' the Green — ANON 15:4
w. such a conscience-stricken — HOUS 351:13
wearisome: make them w. — SHAK 619:19
wears: so w. she to him — SHAK 629:14
w. man's smudge and shares — HOPK 345:12
weary: Age shall not w. them — BINY 109:20
All with w. task fordone — SHAK 613:1
And I sae w. fu' o' care — BURNS 164:7
And to the w. rest — NEWT 494:10
eyelids are a little w. — PATER 509:4
For I'm w. wi' hunting — BALL 49:17
How w., stale, flat — SHAK 572:12
I am w. of my groaning — BOOK 124:18
not be w. in well doing — BIBLE 102:9
Oh the w. haunt for me — KING 397:8
O, w. reckoning — SHAK 617:5
rock in a w. land — BIBLE 83:17
rosy garland and a w. head — SIDN 646:19
shall run, and not be w. — BIBLE 84:1
So w. with disasters — SHAK 603:1
there the w. be at rest — BIBLE 77:8
Waukin still and w. — BURNS 161:8
w. warl goes round — BLAM 114:19
weasel: as a w. sucks eggs — SHAK 568:9
w. took the cork out — FIEL 282:21
w. under the cocktail cabinet — PINT 515:2
weather: All in the blue unclouded w. — TENN 685:3
but the w. turned around — THOM 693:13
But winter and rough w. — SHAK 568:8
first tale is of the w. — JOHN 368:7
her madness and her w. — AUDEN 34:14
In sad or singing w. — SWIN 677:1
It will be fair w. — BIBLE 91:12
Jolly boating w. — CORY 219:13
not in fine w. — CLOU 207:8
Stormy w. — KOEH 403:17
'Tis the hard grey w. — KING 397:11
W. and rain have undone — KIPL 400:17

weather: (cont.):
w. gynneth clere — CHAU 195:11
w. is always doing something — TWAIN 706:24
w. on the outward wall — SHAK 608:16
w. the cuckoo likes — HARDY 326:1
you won't hold up the w. — MACN 440:15
weather-wise: Some are w., some are otherwise — FRAN 292:14
weave: O what a tangled web we w. — SCOTT 560:8
w. but nets to catch the wind — WEBS 725:13
w. their thread with bones — SHAK 629:16
w. the sunlight — ELIOT 271:19
W. the warp, and weave — GRAY 315:8
weaver: swifter than a w.'s shuttle — BIBLE 77:13
weaving: thread of my own hand's w. — KEATS 387:31
web: cool w. of language — GRAV 314:18
O what a tangled web we weave — SCOTT 560:8
She left the w. — TENN 685:4
there's magic in the w. — SHAK 617:3
w. as this will I ensnare — SHAK 615:19
w., then, or the pattern — STEV 667:10
We wove a w. in childhood — BRON 142:2
Webb: Captain W. the Dawley man — BETJ 68:4
webs: By the dark w., her nape — YEATS 752:10
laws are like spider's w. — ANAC 11:5
With swarthy w. — TENN 682:26
Webster: Like W.'s Dictionary — BURKE 160:6
W. struck me much like — SMITH 653:14
W. was much possessed by death — ELIOT 273:15
wed: And think to w. it — SHAK 564:1
any good yeman to w. — CHAU 193:29
Cristen man shall w. me anon — CHAU 194:20
December when they w. — SHAK 569:18
I w. again, and made — CLARE 204:19
w. the fair Ellen — SCOTT 560:5
With this Ring I thee w. — BOOK 123:21
wedded: art w. to calamity — SHAK 623:18
I have w. fyve — CHAU 194:20
Ministers are w. to the truth — SAKI 553:15
this Woman to thy w. wife — BOOK 123:19
w. love, mysterious law — MILT 471:15
w. man so hardy be t'assaille — CHAU 193:10
wedding: bidden of any man to a w. — BIBLE 94:26
get the w. dresses ready — BYRON 171:22
has bought her w. clothes — ADD 4:21
she did her w. gown — GOLD 311:29
That earliest w.-day — KEBLE 392:22
wedding cake: enough white lies to ice a w. — ASQ 32:3
like a w. left out in the rain — AUDEN 36:19
wedding guest: W. here beat his breast — COL 210:20
wedding ring: small circle of a w. — CIBB 203:18
wedlock: consented together in holy w. — BOOK 123:23
W., indeed, hath oft compared — DAV 232:1
w.'s the devil — BYRON 173:11
Wednesday: W. in Wheeson week — SHAK 583:4
wee: Of the 'w. six' I sing — HEAN 329:21
There's nae w. wifie waitin' — MORR 486:2
W., sleekit, cow'rin' — BURNS 163:15
W. Willie Winkie — MILL 462:3
weed: gather honey from the w. — SHAK 585:20
Ignorance is an evil w. — BEV 69:8
Less than the w., that grows — HOPE 345:4
not w. their own minds — WALP 719:22
O thou w. — SHAK 617:16
ought law to w. it out — BACON 44:15
Pernicious w. — COWP 222:3
should'st thou be than the fat w. — SHAK 573:17
w. outbraves his dignity — SHAK 634:15
w. out the fault without — GOLD 311:15
w. sways in the stream — ARN 27:8
w. that grows in every soil — BURKE 157:30
What is a w.? A plant whose — EMER 277:9
weeded: W. and worn the ancient thatch — TENN 686:6
weeds: all the idle w. that grow — SHAK 596:31

weeds: (cont.):
coronet w. clambering to hang — SHAK 578:13
smell far worse than w. — SHAK 634:15
they come up like w. — WALK 717:11
w. and tares of mine own — BROW 146:10
w. and the wilderness yet — HOPK 345:15
w. from gravel paths — KIPL 399:7
w. spontaneous rise — IRWIN 360:19
week: A w. is a long time in politics — WILS 738:6
be accomplished in a w. — STEV 667:25
he had to die in my w. — JOPL 380:12
keep a w. away — SHAK 617:5
Middle of Next W. — CARR 184:8
minute's mirth to wail a w. — SHAK 632:22
No admittance till the w. after — CARR 183:24
w. of death, seven days — DONNE 253:1
weekend: go away for the w. — WHITE 731:7
going away for the w. — JENK 365:2
weeks: fou for w. thegither — BURNS 163:4
weep: As make the angels w. — SHAK 605:18
Babylon we sit down and w. — WALP 719:17
But milk my ewes and w. — SHAK 632:10
But she would w. to see today — DOUG 255:13
Doth w. full sore, and sheddeth — SPEN 659:27
fear of having to w. — BEAU 56:10
If it could w., it could — BROW 147:14
If you want me to w. — HOR 347:9
I saw my lady w. — ANON 15:6
I w. for Adonais—he is dead — SHEL 639:11
I w. like a child — LAWR 412:17
now you w., and I perceive — SHAK 592:14
scarcely cry weep weep w. — BLAKE 113:17
She must w. or she will die — TENN 688:9
She wolde w., if that she — CHAU 192:15
time to w., and a time to laugh — BIBLE 80:5
'Tis that I may not w. — BYRON 171:8
to w. on your own grave — GRAV 315:2
w., and wrynge — CHAU 193:12
W., and you weep alone — WILC 734:7
w. at joy — SHAK 613:6
W., children, you no longer — NERV 492:1
W. me not dead — DONNE 252:23
W. not for little Léonie — GRAH 313:8
w. over Saul, who clothed — BIBLE 75:9
w. when they have done — CONS 217:20
weep with them that w. — BIBLE 100:4
W. you no more, sad fountains — ANON 19:6
Wherefore w. you — SHAK 625:21
women must w. — KING 397:16
you will w. and know why — HOPK 346:3
weepest: Woman, why w. thou — BIBLE 97:33
weeping: Doth that bode w. — SHAK 617:23
have full cause of w. — SHAK 595:18
hearers to their beds — SHAK 621:5
now goeth on his way w. — BOOK 134:5
Rachel w. for her children — BIBLE 88:11
remembrance of a w. queen — SHAK 620:16
w. and gnashing of teeth — BIBLE 89:32
w. and the laughter — DOWS 256:3
W. and watching for the morrow — GOET 309:15
W. as fast as they stream — SHAK 591:21
With w. and with laughter — MAC 436:16
ye hear the children w. — BROW 147:11
wee-things: Th' expectant w. — BURNS 161:5
Weib: W. und Gesang — LUTH 432:17
Weibliche: Das Ewig-W. zieht uns hinan — GOET 309:8
weigh: more people see than w. — CHES 198:21
w. and consider — BACON 44:26
w. thy words in a balance — BIBLE 87:28
weighed: Thou art w. in the balances — BIBLE 85:31
weighing: not w. our merits — BOOK 122:13
weighs: Which w. upon the heart — SHAK 604:22
weight: heavy and the weary w. — WORD 744:20
let us lay aside every w. — BIBLE 104:17
oppression of their prodigal w. — SHAK 620:14
w. in other people's patience — UPD 707:4
w. of rages will press — SPOO 661:6
words are of less w. — BACON 43:5
weightier: w. matters of the law — BIBLE 92:5
weights: deceitful upon the w. — BOOK 128:20

weights: (cont.):
w. and measures   NAP 489:14
weighty: reserve the more w. voice
   BACON 43:5
weilest: wo w. *du*   WAGN 717:10
Wein: *Wer nicht liebt W.*   LUTH 432:17
weinend: *seinem Bette w. sass*   GOET 309:15
weird: w. sisters   SHAK 600:3
w. women promised   SHAK 602:21
weirs: three lone w.   ARN 28:24
welcome: Advice is seldom w.   CHES 198:12
And aye be w. back again   BURNS 163:12
bear w. in your eye   SHAK 600:17
effusive w. of the pier   AUDEN 34:6
Love bade me w.   HERB 335:8
silence yet I picked a w.   SHAK 612:21
terrible events are w.   SHAK 566:11
That ever with a frolic w. took   TENN 690:4
warmest w., at an inn   SHEN 644:13
W., all wonders in one sight   CRAS 226:8
w. day   BUNY 156:15
w. ever smiles   SHAK 627:21
W., O life! I go to encounter   JOYCE 381:15
W. the coming, speed   POPE 522:24
W. the sixte   CHAU 194:20
W. to your gory bed   BURNS 163:1
Yet hath outstayed his w.   COL 211:25
welcomes: w. at once all the world   ANST 23:12
welcomest: w. when they are gone   SHAK 587:7
welfare: most anxious for its w.   BURKE 157:14
w. of this realm   CHAR 191:11
with the w. of the country   WILS 737:18
welkin: how all the w. rings   WESL 728:3
let the w. roar   SHAK 583:8
well: alive and w. and living   ANON 15:11
all men shall speak w.   BIBLE 94:5
all shall be w.   ELIOT 271:9
all shall be w.   JUL 382:10
as w. said as if I had said   SWIFT 674:7
being alive, but being w.   MART 449:15
By day I shall be w. again   ARN 27:5
chiefly lies in acting w.   CHUR 200:16
do I drink from every w.   CALL 175:7
doing w. that which should   VIDAL 711:2
feeling very w. myself   PUNCH 532:5
foolish thing w. done   JOHN 373:20
golden crown like a deep w.   SHAK 620:19
He does himself extremely w.   ANON 16:18
Here lies one who meant w.   STEV 667:7
If what I do prove w.   BRAD 139:10
Is it w. with the child   BIBLE 76:18
It is not done w.   JOHN 372:18
Live w., how long or short   MILT 473:8
looking w. can't move her   SUCK 671:6
loved not wisely but too w.   SHAK 618:20
misery use it for a w.   BOOK 130:17
not so deep as a w.   SHAK 623:13
place to make it w.   TAYL 679:13
speaks w. of me herself   CONG 215:19
spent one whole day w.   THOM 692:9
W. done, thou good   BIBLE 92:16
W. of Loneliness   HALL 322:4
w. of love, a spring   COL 209:6
w. of unconscious cerebration   JAMES 362:13
when ye do w., and suffer   BIBLE 105:14
where nobody is w.   AUDEN 36:18
well-aired: morning w.   BRUM 153:21
well-beloved: myrrh is my w.   BIBLE 81:7
w. hath a vineyard   BIBLE 82:13
well-born: w. and unhappy woman
   ELIOT 269:5
well-bred: Conscience is thoroughly w.
   BUTL 167:8
w. as if we were not married   CONG 216:1
w. resignation or well-bred   TURG 705:7
well-connected: scorn the w.   GILB 304:8
well-content: Sweet Stay-at-Home, sweet W.
   DAV 232:14
well-dressed: sense of being w.   FORB 288:19
well-informed: come with a w mind
   AUST 38:23
well-looking: one of my w. days   GOLD 311:21
well-nourished: w. love   COL 212:22

wells: go about and poison w.   MARL 447:14
poison the w.   NEWM 492:12
well-shaped: handsome, w. man   AUBR 33:12
well-spent: as rare as a w. one   CARL 180:8
well-tuned: w. cymbals   BOOK 135:17
well-written: w. Life is almost as rare
   CARL 180:8
Welsh: devil understands W.   SHAK 581:10
Makes W. as sweet as ditties   SHAK 581:9
Welshman: care and valour in this W.
   SHAK 586:2
Welt: *Die W. ist alles*   WITT 740:4
welter: w. to the parching wind   MILT 465:20
Weltgeschichte: *Die W. ist das Weltgericht*
   SCH 558:4
wen: great w. of all   COBB 208:2
wench: O ill-starred w.   SHAK 618:18
w. is dead   MARL 447:15
Wenlock: On W. Edge the wood   HOUS 352:12
wept: Babylon we sat down and w.
   BOOK 134:17
Jesus w.   BIBLE 97:5
So I piped, he w. to hear   BLAKE 113:16
Station I sat down and w.   SMART 650:6
that I have sometimes w.   MUSS 488:16
W. over her, carved in stone   TENN 686:11
w. she if oon of hem were   CHAU 192:15
w. to see the dolour   MAL 443:12
Werther: W. had a love for Charlotte
   THAC 691:21
Wesley: W.'s conversation   JOHN 374:26
west: another one down in the w.   BOUL 137:16
Cincinnatus of the W.   BYRON 172:23
east is from the w.   BOOK 132:5
east, nor from the w.   BOOK 130:5
gardens of the W.   CONN 216:14
gathered to the quiet w.   HENL 332:8
Gigantic daughter of the W.   TENN 681:14
Go W., young man   GREE 316:15
Go W., young man   SOULE 656:19
Lochinvar is come out of the w.   SCOTT 560:3
longest running farce in the W. End
   SMITH 651:8
Or w. to the Golden Gate   KIPL 399:20
safeguard of the w.   WORD 746:11
sailing away to the w.   KING 397:15
That's where the W. begins   CHAP 190:10
This lady of the W. Country   DE L 236:1
W. of these out to seas   FLEC 286:7
w. yet glimmers   SHAK 603:6
would *not* travel west   CARR 184:3
wester: rainy Pleiads w.   HOUS 352:2
western: All quiet on the w. front   REM 538:16
delivered by W. Union   GOLD 312:5
Playboy of the W. world   SYNGE 677:9
Swiftly walk o'er the w. wave   SHEL 643:22
This spray of W. pine   HARTE 328:7
when you've seen one W.   WHIT 731:20
Westminster: W.'s whole year be holiday
   POPE 518:22
Westminster Abbey: peerage, or W.
   NELS 491:11
westward: stepping w.   WORD 748:5
w., look, the land   CLOU 207:25
W. the course of empire   BERK 65:13
wet: Of w. and wildness   HOPK 345:15
out of these w. clothes   ANON 15:16
so w. you could shoot snipe   POW 528:7
w. sheet and a flowing sea   CUNN 229:2
wether: tainted w. of the flock   SHAK 609:11
whacks: gave her mother forty w.   ANON 15:22
whale: all-destroying unconquering w.
   MELV 456:20
belching w.   SHAK 619:3
confound the prophet with the w.
   DICK 241:23
enormous w.   SMART 650:1
whales: O ye W.   BOOK 118:21
Where great w. come sailing   ARN 27:9
whaleship: w. was my Yale   MELV 456:17
whaling: w. a universal metaphor
   LODGE 425:20

wharfs: Of the adjacent w.   SHAK 565:6
remember the black w.   LONG 427:4
what: He knew what's w.   BUTL 166:4
my own self w. am   HILL 339:2
tell us w. the soldier   DICK 243:20
W. and Why and When   KIPL 401:22
W. does a woman want   FREUD 294:1
w. has been, has been   DRYD 262:2
W. is this that thou hast done   BIBLE 70:12
W. is to be done   LENIN 417:8
W. of the bow   DOYLE 257:3
W. was he doing, the great   BROW 147:17
Whence and w. art thou   MILT 470:6
Who, or why, or which, or w.   LEAR 413:17
what's-his-name: no W. but
Thingummy   DICK 240:21
whatsoever: W. things are true   BIBLE 103:13
wheat: orient and immortal w.   TRAH 701:13
packed like squares of w.   LARK 410:10
separate the w. from the chaff   HUBB 353:11
That sleep among the w.   CARR 183:22
w. set about with lilies   BIBLE 82:2
When w. is green   SHAK 610:24
wheel: beneath thy Chariot w.   HOPE 345:4
breaks a butterfly upon a w.   POPE 520:2
female spirit begot the w.   LAWR 412:6
in thy w. there is a point   MARL 447:8
On a round slippery w.   DAV 232:7
sees the ever-whirling w.   SPEN 660:17
w. broken at the cistern   BIBLE 81:1
w. of life run long   STER 664:29
w. the sofa round   COWP 223:31
wheeling: trees and the houses go w.
   THOM 696:18
wheels: all the w. of Being slow   TENN 683:16
apparently rolled along on w.   HUXL 357:18
his w. as burning fire   BIBLE 86:1
none of the w. of trade   HUME 355:9
tarry the w. of his chariots   BIBLE 74:6
under the w. of black Marias   AKHM 6:12
when: forgotten to say 'W.   WOD 740:23
If not now w.   HILL 339:2
w. a man should marry   BACON 44:6
w. did you last see your   YEAM 750:15
W. I am dead   BELL 61:26
W. I was a little boy   ANON 19:17
w. or how I cannot tell   ROSS 548:8
W. you call me that, *smile*   WIST 739:12
W. you go home, tell them   EDM 267:1
whence: from w. cometh my help   BOOK 133:23
W. and what art thou   MILT 470:6
W. are we, and why   SHEL 639:19
w. came they   BIBLE 106:20
W. did he whence   LENO 418:5
w. it cometh   BIBLE 96:14
you know not w. you   FITZ 284:11
where: they fixed the w. and when   HAWK 328:4
W. did you come from   MACD 437:9
W. do they all come from   LENN 417:18
W. is now thy God   BOOK 127:5
w. is your comforting   HOPK 345:16
W. Peter is, there must   AMBR 10:5
w.'s the bloody horse   CAMP 176:8
whereabout: The very stones prate
of my w.   SHAK 601:13
whereabouts: conceal our w.   SAKI 553:12
wherefore: For every why he had a w.
   BUTL 166:3
w. art thou Romeo   SHAK 622:29
W. does he why   LENO 418:5
whereof: knoweth w. we are made   BOOK 132:5
wheresome'er: with him, w.   SHAK 585:4
whetstone: There is no such w.   ASCH 31:1
whiff: w. of grapeshot   CARL 180:19
whiffling: w. through the tulgey wood
   CARR 182:19
Whig: first W. was the Devil   JOHN 375:4
he hated a w.   JOHN 377:5
see a W. in any dress   JOHN 370:28
Tory and W. in turns shall   SMITH 653:4
Tory men and W. measures   DISR 248:4
wise Tory and a wise W.   JOHN 375:28

Whigs: caught the W. bathing   DISR 246:18
  W. admit no force but   BROW 146:25
while: A little w., and ye shall   BIBLE 97:20
  But it's a long, long w.   AND 11:8
whim: conviction begins as w.   BROUN 144:10
whimper: Not with a bang but a w.   ELIOT 271:16
whims: w. of an egotist   KEATS 391:12
whimsies: they have my w.   PRIOR 529:4
whin: three w. bushes   KAV 386:2
whine: do not sweat and w.   WHIT 732:18
  w. of hysteria is heard   DID 246:1
whining: w. of a door   DONNE 253:9
whip: Do not forget the w.   NIET 495:4
whipped: w. the offending Adam   SHAK 584:18
whippersnapper: Critic and w.   BROW 148:9
whipping: top which w. Sorrow   GREV 318:6
  who should 'scape w.   SHAK 575:7
whips: Chamber selected by W.   FOOT 288:12
  hath chastised you with w.   BIBLE 75:28
  w. and scorns of time   SHAK 575:16
whirligig: w. of time   SHAK 630:35
whirling: by the w. rim I've found   BLAM 114:19
whirlwind: comfort serves in a w.   HOPK 345:18
  Rides in the w., and directs   ADD 3:14
  sweeping w.'s sway   GRAY 315:9
  they shall reap the w.   BIBLE 86:4
  went up by a w. into heaven   BIBLE 76:15
  w. hath blown the dust   DONNE 253:7
whiskers: Runcible Cat with crimson w.   LEAR 414:18
whisky: drinkin' w. and rye   MCL 439:8
  Freedom and W.   BURNS 161:7
  will give you a tot of w.   HEAT 330:1
whisper: w. to their souls, to go   DONNE 252:21
  Hush! Hush! W. who dares   MILNE 462:1
  Or the dry w. of unseen wings   THOM 694:9
  remonstrative w. to a mob   HUNT 356:15
  that w. softness in chambers   MILT 475:8
  To w. at the grates   LOV 429:1
  w. music on those strings   ELIOT 273:13
  w. of a faction   RUSS 552:1
  w. of the south-wind   TENN 685:13
  w. to the tourist the last   BEER 59:14
  w. was already born   MAND 444:7
whispered: w. every where   CONG 215:9
whispering: w. in her mouth   MARX 451:15
  w. sound of the cool colonnade   COWP 222:29
whisperings: Foul w.   SHAK 604:17
  It keeps eternal w. around   KEATS 390:6
  w. and the champagne   FITZ 285:1
whispers: but what he w.   SMITH 652:11
  W. the o'er-fraught heart   SHAK 604:8
whist: W. upon whist   BETJ 67:9
whistle: So was hir joly w.   CHAU 194:15
  until a shrimp learns to w.   KHR 395:14
  W. and she'll come to you   FLET 287:22
  w., an' I'll come to you   BURNS 162:26
  w. her off   SHAK 616:16
whistled: And w. as he went   DRYD 260:12
whistles: And w. in his sound   SHAK 568:16
  W. o'er the furrowed land   MILT 466:12
whistling: blackbird w.   STEV 666:12
  W. aloud to keep his courage   BLAIR 110:15
white: arrayed in w. robes   BIBLE 106:20
  behold a w. horse   BIBLE 107:12
  beloved is w. and ruddy   BIBLE 81:19
  be the w. man's brother   KING 396:14
  bluebirds over the w. cliffs   BURT 164:10
  called the chess-board w.   BROW 148:12
  hairs were w. like wool   BIBLE 106:1
  Is tupping your w. ewe   SHAK 614:22
  Lawn as w. as driven snow   SHAK 632:7
  look ahead up the w. road   ELIOT 273:12
  many a head has turned w.   MÜLL 487:16
  moment w.—then melts   BURNS 163:6
  Nor grew it w. in a single night   BYRON 173:2
  nor w. so very white   CANN 178:5
  no 'w.' or 'coloured'   KENN 394:5
  Now the wild w. horses play   ARN 27:7
  pluck a w. rose with me   SHAK 587:9
  read'st black where I read w.   BLAKE 111:14

white: (cont.):
  see the w. of their eyes   PUTN 533:6
  severed signs I w. and liquid   CONS 217:21
  she always goes into w. satin   SHER 644:24
  Shedding w. rings of tumult   CRANE 225:25
  some of my best friends are w.   DUREM 264:10
  So purely w. they were   SPEN 660:24
  Take up the W. Man's burden   KIPL 401:11
  they shall be as w. as snow   BIBLE 82:10
  Wearing w. for Eastertide   HOUS 352:5
  w. and hairless as an egg   HERR 336:22
  W. as an angel is the English   BLAKE 114:1
  W. as an orchid she rode   AUDEN 34:1
  w., candent voice   ROLFE 545:8
  w., celestial thought   VAUG 709:1
  w. hairs become a fool   SHAK 584:12
  w. in the blood   BIBLE 106:21
  w. men with horrible looks   EQUI 278:11
  w. might make thee nice   BARC 52:9
  w. moderate who is more   KING 396:16
  w. of egg in their veins   LAWR 412:24
  W. Peace   FANS 280:2
  w. race is the cancer   SONT 656:7
  w. races are really pinko-grey   FORS 290:20
  w. shall not neutralize   BROW 152:22
  whose garment was w.   BIBLE 86:1
  with w. and bristly beard   SHAK 633:4
  world is w. with May   TENN 681:21
  your w. hand   WEBS 725:17
white-collar: w. people   WHYTE 733:14
whited: like unto w. sepulchres   BIBLE 92:6
Whitefoot: W., come uppe Lightfoot   ING 360:5
Whitehall: gentleman in W.   JAY 363:24
White House: Log-cabin to W.   THAY 691:28
  no whitewash at the W.   NIXON 496:4
  on the way to the W.   STEV 667:1
  Operative W. Position   ZIEG 755:11
whiter: I shall be w. than snow   BOOK 128:5
  Turned a w. shade of pale   REID 538:15
  W. than new snow on a raven's   SHAK 623:17
whitewash: no w. at the White House   NIXON 496:4
whitewashed: w. wall, the nicely sanded   GOLD 310:15
whither: and w. it goeth   BIBLE 96:14
  W. is he withering   LENO 418:5
  W. shall I go then   BOOK 134:19
whiting: said a w. to a snail   CARR 180:11
  w. said with its tail   HOOD 344:11
Whitman: Walt W.   CRANE 225:19
  W. who laid end to end   LODGE 425:20
whizzing: W. them over the net   BETJ 68:3
who: O, w. am I, that for my   CROS 228:2
  that can tell me w. I am   SHAK 595:8
  W. dares wins   ANON 19:20
  W. is on my side   BIBLE 76:29
  W., or why, or which, or what   LEAR 413:17
  W.? Whom?   LENIN 417:9
whole: had I stol'n the w.   STEV 669:6
  half is greater than the w.   HES 337:14
  nothing can be sole or w.   YEATS 751:8
  parts shall slide into a w.   POPE 520:20
  seeing the w. of them   RUSK 550:29
  shall be the w. of the Law   CROW 228:3
  Thy faith hath made thee w.   BIBLE 90:9
  we shall be w.   BOOK 130:13
  what a w. Oxford is   COL 209:7
  w. man in himself   HOR 351:11
  w. need not a physician   BIBLE 90:6
  w. I planned, youth shows but   BROW 152:6
wholesome: cheap but w. salad   COWP 224:7
  labour spread her w. store   GOLD 310:6
  nights are w.   SHAK 572:2
  steal out of his w. bed   SHAK 590:22
wholly: w. in Peter Pan   TYNAN 706:28
whom: W. are you   ADE 5:6
  W. the gods love die young   BYRON 171:9
  Who? W.?   LENIN 417:9
whooping: out of all w.   SHAK 569:4
whopping: Latin for a w.   ANST 23:13
whore: cunning w. of Venice   SHAK 617:18
  Fortune's a right w.   WEBS 726:1
  I am the Protestant w.   GWYN 320:6

whore: (cont.):
  I' the posture of a w.   SHAK 567:1
  judgement of the great w.   BIBLE 107:9
  lash that w.   SHAK 597:7
  like a chaste w.   MUGG 487:10
  or a w.'s oath   SHAK 596:18
  teach the morals of a w.   JOHN 371:16
  w. and gambler   BLAKE 111:9
  young man's w.   JOHN 372:26
whoremaster: admirable evasion of w.   SHAK 595:2
whoremongers: w., and murderers   BIBLE 107:25
whores: sherry flowing into second-rate w.   PLOM 517:12
  truth in w. and ease   WRIG 749:13
  w. for Eleusis   POUND 526:4
whore-shops: Madhouses, prisons, w.   CLARE 204:18
whoring: went a w.   BOOK 132:14
whose: W. finger do you want   ANON 19:21
whoso: W. doeth these things   BOOK 124:29
whosoever: W. will be saved   BOOK 119:12
why: could he see you now, ask w.   AUDEN 34:9
  for every w. he had a wherefore   BUTL 166:3
  I can't tell you w.   MART 449:12
  shall and finding only w.   CUMM 228:13
  Whence are we, and w. are we   SHEL 639:19
  W. do you walk through   CORN 219:4
  W., Edward, tell me why   WORD 743:6
  W. in the name of Glory   KEATS 388:1
  W., man of morals, tell me w.   COWL 221:8
wibrated: had better not be w.   DICK 238:20
wicked: August is a w. month   O'BR 497:10
  better than one of the w.   SHAK 579:25
  born w., and grow worse   ANON 16:7
  desperately w.   BIBLE 85:12
  equally w. and corrupt   BURKE 159:14
  fiery darts of the w.   BIBLE 103:1
  from the deceitful and w.   BOOK 127:6
  God help the w.   SHAK 580:32
  It's worse than w.   PUNCH 531:23
  make me sick and w.   AUST 40:3
  mercies of the w. are cruel   BIBLE 78:25
  more w. than a woman once   BALL 50:7
  not that men are w.   DU B 263:5
  pomps and vanity of this w.   BOOK 123:4
  pretending to be w.   WILDE 734:17
  seven other spirits more w.   BIBLE 90:37
  Something w. this way comes   SHAK 603:20
  'There is no God,' the w. saith   CLOU 207:14
  unto the w.   BIBLE 84:6
  w. cease from troubling   BIBLE 77:8
  w. flee when no man pursueth   BIBLE 79:28
  w., wicked plant   KYD 404:15
  With a w. pack of cards   ELIOT 272:24
wickedness: I was shapen in w.   BOOK 128:5
  leaven of malice and w.   BOOK 120:17
  loose the bands of w.   BIBLE 84:22
  our manifold sins and w.   BOOK 118:5
  quite capable of every w.   CONR 217:16
  shape history than human w.   TAYL 679:8
  spiritual w. in high places   BIBLE 103:1
  That is the Path of W.   BALL 50:16
  [w.] is not punished   COMP 214:19
  W. is the root of despotism   ROB 542:5
  w. of the world is print   DICK 241:18
  w. that he hath committed   BIBLE 85:23
  w. that hinders loving   BROW 151:16
wicket: flannelled fools at the w.   KIPL 399:13
wictim: w. o' connubiality   DICK 243:11
Widdicombe Fair: to go to W.   BALL 51:4
wide: how w. also the east is from   BOOK 132:5
  nor so w. as a church door   SHAK 623:13
  Not deep the Poet sees, but w.   ARN 27:21
  W. is the gate, and broad   BIBLE 89:21
widely: W. as his mercy flows   LYTE 433:17
wideness: There's a w. in God's mercy   FABER 279:14
widening: turning in the w. gyre   YEATS 753:1
wider: seek no w. war   JOHN 367:9
  thrice w. than for other men   SHAK 584:13
  W. still and wider   BENS 63:23

wind: (*cont.*):
clouds and w. without rain — BIBLE 79:16
drown the w. — SHAK 601:3
east w. made flesh — APPL 23:18
Fair stood the w. for France — DRAY 258:8
fall upon it out of the w. — STEV 666:5
fires flare up in a w. — FRAN 292:10
fluttering in the w. — BROW 150:21
For the gentle w. does move — BLAKE 113:15
Frosty w. made moan — ROSS 547:4
God tempers the w. — STER 664:9
gone with the w. — DOWS 256:2
hiding place from the w. — BIBLE 83:17
impatient as the w. — WORD 748:6
large a charter as the w. — SHAK 568:15
let her down the w. — SHAK 616:16
light w. lives or dies — KEATS 390:20
like a rag blown by the w. — WORD 742:20
like w. I go — FITZ 284:2
likewise a w. on the heath — BORR 136:14
Loose as the w., as large — HERB 334:11
Lord was not in the w. — BIBLE 76:7
nets to catch the w. — WEBS 725:13
Nor ever w. blows loudly — TENN 682:25
not I, but the w. — LAWR 412:22
no w. is favourable — SEN 562:28
observeth the w. shall not sow — BIBLE 80:27
Only w. it into a ball — BLAKE 112:7
O wild West W., thou breath — SHEL 641:14
O w., the weder gynneth — CHAU 195:11
pass by me as the idle w. — SHAK 593:5
piffle before the w. — ASHF 31:10
Pity from blust'ring w. — LOV 429:5
reed shaken with the w. — BIBLE 90:25
rushing mighty w. — BIBLE 98:6
sand against the w. — BLAKE 113:5
Sits the w. in that corner — SHAK 613:25
slowly in the w. — EHRL 267:14
solidity to pure w. — ORW 501:2
Their substance is but only w. — WYATT 750:1
They have sown the w. — BIBLE 86:4
They hear a voice in every w. — GRAY 316:1
Unhelped by any w. — COL 210:3
upon the wings of the w. — BOOK 125:1
upon the wings of the w. — BOOK 132:6
wash the w. — ELIOT 272:11
welter to the parching w. — MILT 465.20
Western w., when will thou — ANON 19:14
Whenever the w. is high — STEV 668:21
when the w. blew due East — CARR 184:3
when the w. is southerly — SHAK 575:1
wherever the w. takes — HOR 347:20
which way the w. is — SELD 562:6
whistling mane of every w. — THOM 695:4
Whose sound dies on the w. — APOL 23:14
w. and storm, fulfilling — BOOK 135:14
w. and the rain — SHAK 596:3
w. and the rain — SHAK 630:37
w. and wave and oar — TENN 686:2
w. bloweth where it listeth — BIBLE 96:14
w. blows through it — STOP 670:7
w. blow the earth — SHAK 595:19
w. did gently kiss — SHAK 609:23
w. doth blow to-day — BALL 51:1
w. extinguishes candles — LA R 410:19
w. goeth over it — BOOK 132:5
w. is to put on your overcoat — LOW 430:7
w. it plies the saplings — HOUS 352:12
w. of change is blowing — MACM 440:5
W. of the western sea — TENN 687:27
w. plays up — BLOK 115.6
w.'s feet shine along — SWIN 676:27
w.'s in the east — DICK 239:3
w.'s like a whetted knife — MAS 453:9
w. that blows, the ship that — DIBD 238:14
w. that follows fast — CUNN 229:2
w. up the sun and moon — BYRON 173:13
w. was wild and dank — KING 397:13
with every w. of doctrine — BIBLE 102:17
With His hammer of w. — THOM 695:13
Woord is but w. — LYDG 433:5
winding: England's w. sheet — BLAKE 111:9
good structure in a w. stair — HERB 335:6

winding: (*cont.*):
In notes, with many a w. bout — MILT 465:17
place is by a w. stair — BACON 43:31
waters were his w. sheet — BARN 53:16
w. sheet in our mother's — DONNE 252:26
w.-sheet of Edward's race — GRAY 315:8
w. up the watch — SHAK 625:14
windings: deep w. of the grove — BEAT 56:6
such w. and such shade — WING 739:2
windmill: cheese and garlic in a w. — SHAK 581:7
window: at a w. Pippa passes — BEER 59:13
argument of the broken w. — PANK 506:1
clapte the w. to — CHAU 194:1
der, w., a casement — DICK 242:5
eating or opening a w. — AUDEN 35:6
Good prose is like a w.-pane — ORW 499:21
hole in a stained glass w. — CHAN 190:2
kiss my ass in Macy's w. — JOHN 367:11
light through yonder w. breaks — SHAK 622:27
little w. where the sun — HOOD 343:21
looked out at a w. — BIBLE 76:27
not one w., but a million — JAMES 363:5
out at the w. the next — DICK 243:5
Sisera looked out at a w. — BIBLE 74:6
stained-glass w.'s hue — BETJ 67:4
throw it out of the w. — BECK 57:17
Waits at the w., wearing — LENN 417:18
which spins against my w. — MOT 487:1
will return through the w. — FRED 293:10
window-glass: Dash the w. to shivers — SCOTT 560:19
windows: And then the W. failed — DICK 244:15
By breaking of w. — MORE 483:19
flushing runneth from w. — BETJ 68:1
Great w. open to the south — YEATS 752:2
open w. into men's souls — ELIZ 274:18
storied w. richly dight — MILT 465:1
This life's dim w. of the soul — BLAKE 111:17
thought of high w. — LARK 409:18
Through w., and through — DONNE 252:16
winds: beteem the w. of heaven — SHAK 572:12
called forth the mutinous w. — SHAK 626:1
For us the w. do blow — HERB 335:10
great w. shorewards blow — ARN 27:7
howling w. drive devious — COWP 222:27
imprisoned in the viewless w. — SHAK 606:11
Now the w. are all compusure — SMART 649:7
O ye W. of God, bless ye — BOOK 118:17
the stormy w. did blow — ANON 17:6
wild w. coldly blow — BRON 142:11
w. blew, and beat upon — BIBLE 89:26
w. of heaven mix for ever — SHEL 641:9
Where the w. are all asleep — ARN 27:8
w., and crack your cheeks — SHAK 595:20
w. come to me from — WORD 745:12
w. kiss my parchèd lips — SHAK 594:15
w. of March with beauty — SHAK 632:4
W. of the World, give answer — KIPL 399:2
w. were love-sick — SHAK 565:5
w. will blow the profit — MACN 440:15
w. will call the darkness — SHEL 643:8
with the light-foot w. — GREN 318:2
windscreen: w. yellowing with crushed — CONN 216:20
windward: w. of the law — CHUR 200:21
windy: w. night a rainy morrow — SHAK 634:13
w. side of the law — SHAK 630:26
wine: And blood and w. were — WILDE 735:33
And I'll not look for w. — JONS 379:20
are lordliest in their w. — MILT 474:12
Be not drunk with w. — BIBLE 102:23
best fits my little w. — HERR 336:25
bin of a w., a spice of wit — STEV 669:8
but I, as w. — HERB 334:6
buy w. and milk without — BIBLE 84:15
can with w. dispense — CRAB 224:24
carouses in this costly w. — DRAY 257:20
days of w. and roses — DOWS 256:3
doesn't get into the w. — CHES 199:12
Drinking the blude-red w. — BALL 50:10
drink one cup of w. — SCOTT 560:7
drunk old w. straightway — BIBLE 94:4

wine: (*cont.*):
drynken strong w. — CHAU 193:6
falser than vows made in w. — SHAK 569:14
feast of w. on the lees — BIBLE 83:8
flask of w., a book — FITZ 283:13
flown with insolence and w. — MILT 468:21
giant refreshed with w. — BOOK 130:12
Gin by pailfuls, w. in rivers — SCOTT 560:19
Go fetch to me a pint o' w. — BURNS 162:21
he drinks no w. — SHAK 583:26
Here is w. — KEATS 386:17
honest talk and wholesome w. — TENN 689:13
invisible spirit of w. — SHAK 616:5
last companion, W. — BELL 61:12
Let us have w. and women — BYRON 170:18
like generous w. — BUTL 166:21
Like the best w. — BIBLE 82:4
love is better than w. — BIBLE 81:5
man that is without w. — BIBLE 87:31
mellow, like good w. — PHIL 514:7
mine host's Canary w. — KEATS 388:20
mouth do crush their w. — MARV 450:9
new friend is as new w. — BIBLE 87:16
new w. into old bottles — ATTL 32:15
new w. into old bottles — BIBLE 90:8
Not given to w., no striker — BIBLE 103:26
not old w. wholesomest — WEBS 725:26
not to be rinsed with w. — HOPK 345:13
not woman, w., and song — LUTH 432:17
Of w. and wax, of gamyn — WYNT 750:10
out-did the frolic w. — HERR 336:21
pass the rosy w. — DICK 242:18
Sans w., sans song — FITZ 283:18
Sure there was w. — HERB 334:11
sweet white w. — MAS 453:2
Sweet w. of youth — BROO 143:3
temptations in w. and women — KITC 402:17
thou hast kept the good w. — BIBLE 96:11
thy w. with a merry heart — BIBLE 80:19
upon the w. when it is red — BIBLE 79:13
When the w. is in, the wit — BECON 58:7
When thirsty grief in w. — LOV 429:3
w. and women, which have — BURT 164:21
w. by his own fireside — SHER 645:23
w. diluted by a very large — SAL 554:2
w. is a good familiar creature — SHAK 616:7
W. is a mocker, strong — BIBLE 79:4
W. is the strongest — BIBLE 86:20
W. loved I deeply — SHAK 596:9
W. maketh merry — BIBLE 80:24
W., not water, binds the lover — SANS 555:14
w. of life is drawn — SHAK 602:17
w. of Shiraz into urine — DIN 246:10
w. that is in love — GUM 319:15
w. that maketh glad — BOOK 132:8
w. that tasted of the tar — BELL 62:1
w. unto those — BIBLE 79:34
w. was a farce — POW 528:3
w. with not a drop of allaying — SHAK 570:7
With seas of wine, like w. — TRAH 702:1
Women and w. should life — GAY 299:19
wine-lees: w. and democracy — BROW 148:5
wine-pots: broken and castaway w. — CLOU 206:17
wines: Soused in high-country w. — JONS 378:6
wing: by Conquest's crimson w. — GRAY 315:6
Comin' in on a w. and a pray'r — ADAM 3:11
flits by on leathern w. — COLL 213:11
headlong joy is ever on the w. — MILT 473:24
hilarity with the w. — DICK 242:18
I've got to take under my w. — GILB 305:10
Nor knowst'ou w. from tail — POUND 527:8
so long on a broken w. — TENN 687:3
stone, and start a w. — THOM 695:10
vainly flapped its tinsel w. — MARV 450:2
years damp my intended w. — MILT 472:18
winged: Time's w. chariot — MARV 451:3
w. life destroy — BLAKE 113:11
w. squadrons of the sky — MILM 462:7
W. words — HOMER 342:23
wings: Beneath thy own almighty w. — KEN 393:7
birds their w. to fly away — CLARE 204:20

wings: (cont.):

Clap her broad w., and soaring	FRERE 293:17
covered with silver w.	BOOK 129:8
darkness, on extended w.	STEV 666:11
Death spread his w.	BYRON 169:29
defend thee under his w.	BOOK 131:3
downy w. over the nest	FANS 280:2
great w. beating still	YEATS 752:10
hear the beating of his w.	BRIG 141:6
Ill news hath w.	DRAY 257:15
it imped the w. of fame	CAREW 179:6
Love without his w.	BYRON 172:15
many light hearts and w.	VAUG 709:10
mount up with w. as eagles	BIBLE 84:1
O, for a horse with w.	SHAK 571:7
On w. of song	HEINE 330:14
take the w. of the morning	BOOK 134:19
that I had w. like a dove	BOOK 128:10
thy w. shall be my refuge	BOOK 128:14
upon the w. of the wind	BOOK 125:1
upon the w. of the wind	BOOK 132:6
viewless w. of Poesy	KEATS 389:11
void his luminous w.	ARN 29:21
When Love with unconfinèd w.	LOV 429:1
w. like he'd come from	JOYCE 381:8
with ah! bright w.	HOPK 345:11
with healing in his w.	BIBLE 86:19
with their woven w.	SHAK 607:2

wingy: w. mysteries in divinity — BROW 146:2

wink: w. a reputation down — SWIFT 674:27

winners: no w., but all are losers — CHAM 189:6

winning: lips ne'er act the w. — HERR 336:14

nothing worth the wear of w.	BELL 62:3
O the glory of the w.	MER 458:5
w. cause pleased the gods	LUCAN 431:4
w. isn't everything	SAND 555:13
world be worth thy w.	DRYD 259:21

winnowing: soft-lifted by the w. wind — KEATS 390:18

wins: Who dares w. — ANON 19:20

winter: Come, rich and lovely W.'s Eve — DAV 232:13

English w.—ending in July	BYRON 171:26
every w. change to spring	TENN 683:19
From w., plague and pestilence	NASHE 491:2
furious w. blowing	RANS 536:15
go south in the w.	ELIOT 272:22
have with one w.'s brush	SHAK 626:16
If W. comes, can Spring	SHEL 642:1
In w. I get up at night	STEV 668:13
it was the w. of despair	DICK 244:1
It was the w. wild	MILT 467:2
lonely w. seem long	HAMM 322:14
mountains by the w.	TENN 682:18
my age is as a lusty w.	SHAK 567:28
Nor the furious w.'s rages	SHAK 571:16
Now is the w. of our discontent	SHAK 621:14
old man upon a w.'s night	YEATS 750:14
Our severest w., commonly	COWP 224:17
out in the Middle of W.	ADD 4:11
sad tale's best for w.	SHAK 631:17
See, amid the w.'s snow	CASW 185:4
Seeming and savour all the w.	SHAK 631:29
spring are on w.'s traces	SWIN 675:21
very dead of W.	ANDR 11:13
very dead of w.	ELIOT 271:17
whether it's summer or w.	CHEK 197:3
W. Afternoons	DICK 244:20
w. and rough weather	SHAK 568:8
W. comes to rule the varied	THOM 696:11
w. going into winter again	BEDE 58:13
w. hath my absence been	SHAK 634:16
W. is come and gone	SHEL 639:16
W. is icummen	POUND 526:2
w. is past, the rain	BIBLE 81:9
W. kept us warm, covering	ELIOT 272:21
w. of this year	ALAI 7:5
w.'s rains and ruins	SWIN 675:22
w.'s tedious nights sit	SHAK 621:5
W. suddenly was changed	SHEL 642:22
wrathful as w., 'proaching	SACK 542:17
you will bid the w. come	SHAK 594:15

winters: forty w. shall besiege — SHAK 633:1

winters: (cont.):

w. and keeps warm her note	CAREW 179:12
wintry: bent by same w. fever	THOM 693:7
chariotest to their dark w.	SHEL 641:14
long, long w. nights	LEAR 413:20
wipe: Gives it a w.	HOOD 343:22
Let me w. it first	SHAK 597:5
Must often w. a bloody nose	GAY 300:2
shall w. away all tears	BIBLE 106:23
shall w. away all tears	BIBLE 107:18
w. the tears for ever from	MILT 466:14
wiped: name be w. out likewise	SPEN 659:11
w. out of the book	BOOK 129:14
wipes: anheling, w.	HOLM 342:9
mind it w. its shoes	THOM 693:18
wire: electric w. the message came	ANON 17:4
wires: If hairs be w.	SHAK 635:2
wisdom: ancient is w.	BIBLE 77:19
apply our hearts unto w.	BOOK 131:2
be famous then by w.	MILT 473:19
beginning in w., dying	LOW 430:21
beginning of w.	BOOK 133:5
But joy is w., Time	YEATS 752:9
Can w. be put in a silver rod	BLAKE 111:11
delight and ends in w.	FROST 295:14
Eternal W. how to rule	POPE 522:11
giveth w. unto the simple	BOOK 125:5
Here is w.	COR 219:11
How can he get w. . . . . whose	BIBLE 87:36
In action W. goes by majorities	MER 457:27
increased in w. and stature	BIBLE 93:31
infallible criterion of w.	BURKE 157:2
leads to the palace of w.	BLAKE 112:16
Love is the w. of the fool	JOHN 376:25
man's wit and all men's w.	RUSS 552:4
Nature say one thing and W.	BURKE 159:22
Of highest w. brings about	MILT 474:19
price of w. is above rubies	BIBLE 77:28
privilege of w. to listen	HOLM 342:8
pursue righteousness with w.	PLATO 517:1
Solomon's w.	BIBLE 75:23
special evidences of our w.	TROL 703:20
teach his senators w.	BOOK 132:12
Thy w., less thy certainty	STEP 663:16
upon the score of their w.	SWIFT 673:14
we had power, we had w.	BENÉT 62:17
what is bettre than w.	CHAU 193:28
where shall w. be found	BIBLE 77:27
where w. makes the way	GASC 298:19
W. and goodness	SHAK 596:29
w. and truth and the perfection	SOCR 654:11
w. and understanding	BIBLE 83:1
W. and Wit are little seen	BRER 140:14
w. at one entrance quite shut	MILT 470:16
W. denotes the pursuing	HUTC 357:5
W. excelleth folly	BIBLE 80:4
W. has taught us	HOLM 342:15
w. hast thou made them	BOOK 132:9
W. hath builded her house	BIBLE 78:18
W. in minds attentive	COWP 224:4
W. is humble that he knows	COWP 224:5
W. is justified of her	BIBLE 90:27
W. is the principal thing	BIBLE 78:16
w. lingers	TENN 685:16
W. must bear what our flesh	GREV 318:6
w. of a great minister	JUN 383:5
w. of a learned man cometh	BIBLE 87:35
w. of the crocodiles	BACON 45:8
w. shall die	BIBLE 77:18
W.'s self oft seeks	MILT 463:27
w. the world is governed	OXEN 503:21
w. to provide for human	BURKE 158:12
w. we have lost in knowledge	ELIOT 272:15
w. wishes to appear most	SHAK 606:5
With them the seed of w.	FITZ 284:2
wrath of the lion is the w.	BLAKE 112:24

wise: All things w. and wonderful — ALEX 8:9

art of being w.	JAMES 363:17
be fortunate than w.	WEBS 726:10
being darkly w.	POPE 522:9
be lowly w.	MILT 472:12
be proud if you'll be w.	CHUD 200:13
Be w., be wise, and do not try	SOUT 657:3

wise: (cont.):

be w. in his own conceit	BIBLE 79:20
Be w. to-day	YOUNG 754:15
Be w. with speed	YOUNG 754:8
both to the w. and to the unwise	BIBLE 99:15
business shall become w.	BIBLE 87:35
by the wisest of the w.	TENN 686:5
consider her ways, and be w.	BIBLE 78:13
cunning men pass for w.	BACON 43:7
deemed him wondrous w.	BEAT 56:4
errors of a w. man make	BLAKE 113:9
follies of the w.	JOHN 370:20
fools and the beacons of w.	HUXL 358:11
from letters, to be w.	JOHN 370:15
Great men are not always w.	BIBLE 77:32
Had you been as w. as bold	SHAK 608:14
he is a w. man or a fool	BLAKE 112:10
How very weak the very w.	THAC 691:22
I heard a w. man say	HOUS 352:9
leave the w. to talk	FITZ 284:1
Let me smile with the w.	JOHN 373:2
man w. in his own conceit	BIBLE 79:22
men w. for not believing	BLAKE 111:21
Nature is always w.	THUR 697:22
Nor ever did a w. one	ROCH 543:5
not w. in you own conceits	BIBLE 100:5
Obscurely w., and coarsely	JOHN 375:29
only wretched are the w.	PRIOR 529:14
or more w. when he had	JOHN 375:17
reputed w. for saying nothing	SHAK 607:6
same tree that a w. man	BLAKE 112:19
So w. so young, they say	SHAK 622:1
so witty and so w.	ROCH 543:12
teachings of the w.	LUCR 431:15
that's a w. man and a fool	SHAK 595:24
therefore w. as serpents	BIBLE 90:16
think as w. men do	ASCH 31:3
'Tis folly to be w.	GRAY 316:3
To be w. and eke to love	SPEN 660:25
To be w., and love	SHAK 627:17
valorous than manly w.	MARL 448:8
virtuous, or a w. man	LOCKE 425:11
were all like that w. bird	PUNCH 531:22
wherefore thou be w.	TENN 680:8
which speak to the w.	PIND 514:14
Who can be w., amazèd	SHAK 602:18
w. enough to play the fool	SHAK 630:8
w. father that knows	SHAK 608:7
w., for cure, on exercise	DRYD 260:16
w. forgive but do not forget	SZASZ 677:13
w. is he that kan hymselven	CHAU 194:3
W. men also die, and perish	BOOK 127:24
w. men from the east	BIBLE 88:8
w. men promised has not	MELB 456:10
w. men there have received	LUIS 432:7
w. son maketh a glad father	BIBLE 78:20
w. want love	SHEL 642:11
word is enough for the w.	PLAU 517:4
words of the w. are as goads	BIBLE 81:2
world to confound the w.	BIBLE 100:16

wise-cracking: between w. and wit — PARK 506:22

wisely: Be w. worldly — QUAR 533:18

he spake w., and could	BIBLE 87:21
men and nations behave w.	EBAN 266:1
not w. but too well	SHAK 618:20

wiser: Are w. and nicer — AUDEN 35:12

be guided by the w.	CARL 180:1
French w. than they seem	BACON 44:22
looked w. when he was seated	KEYN 395:3
not the w. grow	POMF 518:11
sadder and a w. man	COL 211:18
w. in his own conceit	BIBLE 79:23
w. mind mourns less	WORD 744:4
w. than the children of light	BIBLE 95:6
w. than thou art ware	SHAK 568:6
w. to-day than yesterday	POPE 524:4
young man will be w.	TENN 681:19

wisest: gretteste clerkes been noght w. — CHAU 194:14

grief for which the w.	RAL 535:14
Rules e'en the w.	CRAB 225:1
Seems w., virtuousest	MILT 472:15

wisest: (cont.):
than the w. man can answer	COLT 214:8
w. and justest and best	PLATO 516:12
w. fool in Christendom	HENR 332:13
W. men have erred	MILT 474:5
w. of all moral men	DAV 232:3
w. of men in all ages	STER 664:14
w. of them all professed	MILT 473:21

wish: believe what they w. CAES 174:16
earnest w. to escape from it	FOST 291:8
I do w. he did not look	ANON 18:19
If otherwise w. I	SHAW- 639:3
I w. I loved the Human Race	RAL 536:12
I w. I were in love again	HART 327:11
live, not as we w.	MEN 457:3
Thy w. was father, Harry	SHAK 584:3
To w. myself much better	SHAK 609:2
Whoever hath her w.	SHAK 635:4
w. for prayer is a prayer	BERN 66:6
w. for what I faintly hope	DRYD 261:18
w. thee all thy mother's	CORB 218:14
w. 'twere done	ARN 27:15

wished: He whom I w. to see KEPP 394:11
wishes: all made of w. SHAK 569:21
there is exact to my w.	ANON 14:4

wision: you see my w.'s limited DICK 243:21
wist: But had I w., before I kist WILDE 735:34
wistful: With such a w. eye WILDE 735:34
wit: accepted w. has but to say GILB 306:25
age is in, the w. is out	SHAK 614:6
at their w.'s end	BOOK 133:2
at thirty, the w.	FRAN 292:16
attire doth show her w.	ANON 16:14
baiting place of w.	SIDN 646:18
Beauty, w.	SHAK 627:22
be w. in all languages	DRYD 262:10
bin of wine, a spice of w.	STEV 669:8
brevity, and w. its soul	COL 209:21
Brevity is the soul of w.	SHAK 574:11
could not steal their w.	CAV 187:11
deemed there but want of w.	SIDN 646:17
Devise, w.; write, pen	SHAK 598:9
effusions of w. and humour	AUST 38:21
fancy w. will come	POPE 519:22
folly and his weapon w.	HOPE 344:24
fool than a foolish w.	SHAK 628:18
For I have neither w.	SHAK 592:16
grave or tomb of w.	CAV 187:12
heart did do it and not my w.	TANF 678:13
he but have drawn his w.	JONS 379:18
He that has a little tiny w.	SHAK 596:3
highest reaches of a human w.	MARL 448:3
His fine w.	SHEL 641:5
his whole w. in a jest	BEAU 56:14
How the w. brightens	POPE 521:19
I had but a little w.	ANON 19:17
Impropriety is the soul of w.	MAUG 454:7
In w., a man	POPE 521:3
mechanic part of w.	ETH 278:18
mingled with a little w.	DRYD 260:24
nature by her mother w.	SPEN 660:13
nature of w.	MILL 460:25
neither a w. in his own eye	CONG 215:13
no free and splendid w.	MILT 476:6
nor all thy piety nor w.	FITZ 284:9
not his pointed w.	POPE 521:3
o'erflowing of unbounded w.	WINC 738:24
Of w. or arms	MILT 465:16
O incredulity! the w. of fools	CHAP 190:16
old blind *débauchée* of w.	WALP 719:8
Old Mother W.	DENH 236:19
only a w. among Lords	JOHN 371:15
pick-purse of another's w.	SIDN 647:1
pleasant smooth w.	AUBR 33:12
plentiful lack of w.	SHAK 574:22
proverb is one man's w.	RUSS 552:4
sharpen a good w.	ASCH 31:1
Staircase w.	DID 245:12
that he shoots his w.	SHAK 569:28
Their only idea of w.	SMITH 653:7
thy w. in an instant	SHAK 609:6
too proud for a w.	GOLD 311:4
universal monarchy of w.	CAREW 179:4

wit: (cont.):
use my w. as a pitchfork	LARK 410:8
wears his w. in his belly	SHAK 627:12
well craves a kind of w.	SHAK 630:8
winding up the watch of his w.	SHAK 625:14
wine is in, the w. is out	BECON 58:7
Wisdom and W. are little seen	BRER 140:14
w. be like the coruscations	GOUL 313:1
w. enough to keep it sweet	JOHN 376:17
W. has truth in it	PARK 506:22
w. invites you by his looks	COWP 222:4
w. is Nature to advantage	POPE 521:11
w. may wander ere he die	TENN 681:19
w. of man to say what dream	SHAK 612:15
w. on other souls may fall	DRYD 261:2
w.'s a feather	POPE 522:20
W.'s empire now shall know	EGER 267:13
W.'s forge and fire-blast	COL 210:16
w.'s the noblest frailty	SHAD 563:14
w. than a Christian	SHAK 628:12
W. the epitaph of an emotion	NIET 495:16
w. till I break my shins	SHAK 568:7
w. to become an author	LA BR 405:5
W. will shine	DRYD 261:31
w. with dunces	POPE 519:1
your w. single	SHAK 582:20
Your w.'s too hot, it speeds	SHAK 598:11

witchcraft: no w. charm thee SHAK 571:16
rebellion is as the sin of w.	BIBLE 74:37
w. celebrates	SHAK 601:13

witches: burnt at the stake as w. SMITH 652:18
witching: w. time of night SHAK 576:25
with: I am w. you alway BIBLE 93:6
thou art w. me	BOOK 125:15

withdrawing: melancholy, long, w. roar ARN 27:1
withdrawn: yawn and be w. DURY 264:13
withdrew: he w., he strode off CIC 204:7
wither: Age cannot w. her SHAK 565:8
And w. and perish	SMITH 653:32
Now I have w. into the truth	YEATS 751:4
Soon w., vanish, fade	BOLT 117:16
w. slowly in thine arms	TENN 689:10

withered: And w. in my hand HERB 335:7
Are they w. in the sod	BRON 142:2
dried up, and w	BOOK 130:23
flowers . . . are w. away	COCK 208:4
no root, they w. away	BIBLE 91:1
So w., and so wild	SHAK 600:5
w. is the garland	SHAK 566:15

withereth: Fast w. too KEATS 388:8
withers: it w. away ENG 277:22
our w. are unwrung	SHAK 576:18

withhold: in the evening w. not thine hand BIBLE 80:28
within: oh, he never went w. COWL 221:13
outside who ne'er look w.	COWP 222:5
that w. which passeth show	SHAK 572:10
thou wert w. me	AUG 37:2
w. would fain go out	DAV 232:1

without: are w. would fain go DAV 232:1
forasmuch as w. thee	BOOK 121:7
How many things I can do w.	SOCR 654:9
live with you—or w. you	MART 449:16
those things that are w.	BIBLE 102:1
W. ceasing I make mention	BIBLE 99:14

withstand: we w. Barabbas now BROW 150:4
w. in the evil day	BIBLE 103:1

witness: bear w. of that Light BIBLE 96:2
shalt not bear false w.	BIBLE 72:16
w. against you this day	BIBLE 73:13

witnesses: silent w. to the desolation GEOR 301:3
so great a cloud of w.	BIBLE 104:17
w. laid down their clothes	BIBLE 98:12

wits: composed in their w. ARN 29:23
incline w. to sophistry	BACON 45:14
O born in days when w. were	ARN 28:9
Some have at first for w.	POPE 521:5
they cast on female w.	BRAD 139:10
They have stolen his w. away	DE L 235:21
Tiring thy w. and toiling	DAN 229:17
warming his five w.	TENN 689:9

wits: (cont.):
Whilst our hopes our w.	WOTT 749:5
W. are gamecocks to one	GAY 299:32
w. are sure to madness	DRYD 259:1
w. may sometimes gloriously	POPE 521:7
youth have ever homely w.	SHAK 630:38

wittiest: w. of all things HARE 326:6
wittles: I live on broken w. DICK 239:24
They're w. and drink	DICK 239:31

witty: am not only w. in myself SHAK 582:14
fancy my self mighty w.	FARQ 280:24
so w. and so wise	ROCH 543:12
w. and it sha'n't be long	CHES 197:14
w. woman is a treasure	MER 457:17

Witz: W. ist das Epigramm auf NIET 495:16
wives: And many, many w. NAYL 491:3
changes when they are w.	SHAK 569:18
Continual wars and w.	HUGH 354:3
divides the w. of aldermen	SMITH 650:15
Fair be their w., right	ANON 16:2
Husbands, love your w.	BIBLE 103:17
Our loves into corpses or w.	SWIN 676:12
profane and old w.' fables	BIBLE 104:1
sklendre w., fieble as	CHAU 193:11
That have revolted w.	SHAK 631:15
We have children we have w.	TENN 689:4
W. are young men's mistresses	BACON 44:5
w. have sense like them	SHAK 618:2
W. in the avocados	GINS 306:29
w. pacience in trust	CHAU 193:10

wizards: w. haste with odours sweet MILT 467:1
wobbles: good spelling but it W. MILNE 463:5
woe: Can I see another's w. BLAKE 114:3
come away: the song of w.	TENN 683:23
Companions of our w.	WALSH 720:18
deep, unutterable w.	AYT 41:4
discover sights of w.	MILT 468:1
Europe made his w. her own	ARN 28:21
friend of W.	SOUT 657:8
groan of the martyr's w.	BLAKE 112:5
Her face was full of w.	ANON 15:6
hideous notes of w.	BYRON 171:28
Joy and w. are woven fine	BLAKE 111:6
life protracted is protracted w.	JOHN 370:18
my bliss, and all my w.	GOLD 310:19
Oft in danger, oft in w.	WHITE 731:4
rearward of a conquered w.	SHAK 634:13
source of softer w.	SCOTT 559:12
Teach me to feel another's w.	POPE 523:32
trappings and the suits of w.	SHAK 572:10
watch and moveless w.	BROW 147:14
wit, the balm of w.	SIDN 646:18
W. is me	BIBLE 82:20
w. that is in mariage	CHAU 194:19
W. to her that is filthy	BIBLE 86:17
W. to the bloody city	BIBLE 86:15
W. to thee, O land	BIBLE 80:23
W. to the land that's governed	SHAK 621:25
W. unto him that striveth	BIBLE 84:3
W. unto them that join	BIBLE 82:16
W. weeps out her division	JONS 378:14
works gave signs of w.	MILT 472:24

woeful: New-hatched to the w. time SHAK 602:13
Oh, w. state, oh danger deep	GILB 303:11

woes: exordium of our w. DRAY 258:3
self-consumer of my w.	CLARE 204:25
spring of w. unnumbered	HOMER 342:22
w. new wail my dear times'	SHAK 633:11
w. that wait on age	BYRON 168:11
w. which Hope thinks infinite	SHEL 642:20

woke: W. to my hearing from THOM 693:12
Woking: playing for W. BETJ 68:3
wolf: by his sentinel, the w. SHAK 601:13
grim w. with privy paw	MILT 466:9
have the w. by the ears	JEFF 364:20
like the w. on the fold	BYRON 169:28
man is a w.	PLAU 517:3
tameness of a w.	SHAK 596:18
which man was w. to the man	VANZ 708:10
while the w. remains	INGE 359:16
w. also shall dwell	BIBLE 83:20

women: (*cont.*):

blessed art thou among w.	BIBLE 93:21
by bad w. been deceived	MILT 474:5
claim our right as w.	PANK 505:18
concern for the rights of w.	COPE 218:10
Dream of Fair W.	TENN 680:20
even spoiled the w.'s chats	BROW 151:26
far from me, you grim w.	OVID 502:12
fondness for persons of w.	MORE 484:4
Framed to make w. false	SHAK 615:12
generally like w.'s letters	HAZL 328:12
girls turn into American w.	HAMP 323:3
Good w. always think	BROO 143:20
Half the sorrows of w.	ELIOT 269:23
hand of Nature and we w.	GIBB 302:23
happiest w.	ELIOT 269:24
he hid himself among w.	BROW 145:19
hell for w., as the diverb	BURT 165:12
human kind, wine and w.	BURT 164:21
I must have w.	GAY 299:21
In the room the w. come and	ELIOT 272:1
let not w.'s weapons	SHAK 595:18
Let us have wine and w.	BYRON 170:18
many w., and many children	JOHN 372:1
married beneath me, all w. do	ASTOR 32:11
Men don't know w.	TROL 703:11
men for unhealthy w.	BEEC 59:4
men that w. marry	LONG 427:3
men, w., and Herveys	MONT 480:8
Monstrous Regiment of W.	KNOX 403:4
more interesting than w.	WALL 718:3
Music and w. I cannot	PEPYS 512:17
on the conduct of the w.	MORE 484:2
other w. cloy	SHAK 565:8
our chilly w.	BYRON 167:24
paradise of w.	FLOR 288:5
passing the love of w.	BIBLE 75:9
personal search of w.	BURKE 159:2
place w.'s hearts	WEBS 725:15
Plain w. he regarded	ELIOT 269:15
proper function of w.	ELIOT 269:26
revenge—especially to w.	BYRON 170:11
Say, are not w. truly then	JONS 379:19
say that w. have no soul	AST 32:5
simple w. only fit	LEWIS 420:18
Single w. have a dreadful	AUST 40:2
Solomon loved many strange w.	BIBLE 75:26
Some w.'ll stay in a man's	KIPL 402:12
stir up the zeal of w.	MILL 461:3
sung w. in three cities	POUND 526:6
thing that is writ by W.	CENT 188:7
Though w. all above	SHAK 597:5
tide in the affairs of w.	BYRON 171:15
To w. their original must owe	COLL 213:2
war between men and w.	THUR 697:16
weird w. promised	SHAK 602:21
Were w. never so fair	LYLY 433:7
What is it w. do in men	BLAKE 113:12
wine and w.	KITC 402:17
with many w. I doubt	TROL 703:19
with w. nor with priests	SOUT 657:12
w. and care and trouble	WARD 721:21
W., and Champagne	BELL 61:24
w. and children could work	SELL 562:25
w., and clergymen	SMITH 653:13
W. and fortune are truest	WYCH 750:5
W. and Horses and Power	KIPL 398:14
W. and wine should life	GAY 299:19
w. are in furious secret	SHAW 636:15
W. are like tricks by slight	CONG 215:11
w. are not educated	CAV 187:14
w. are not so young	BEER 59:20
W. are really much nicer	AMIS 11:2
W. are strongest	BIBLE 86:20
w. become like their mothers	WILDE 734:15
w. be denied the benefits	DEFOE 234:2
w. born slaves	WOLL 741:18
W. can't forgive failure	CHEK 196:13
w. can true converts make	FARQ 280:19
w. come out to cut up what	KIPL 401:12
w. come to see the show	OVID 502:13
W. desiren to have sovereynetee	
	CHAU 194:26

women: (*cont.*):

W. do not find it difficult	MACK 439:3
W. don't seem to think	AMIS 11:1
w. do they must do twice	WHIT 733:12
W. enjoyed	SUCK 671:5
w. feel just as men feel	BRON 142:4
W. have positive moral sense	ADAMS 2:8
W. have no wilderness	BOGAN 116:13
W. have served all these	WOOLF 742:11
w. in a drawing-room	WOOLF 742:13
w. in a state of ignorance	KNOX 403:16
w. in general are very	REED 538:3
w. Italian, to men French	CHAR 191:21
w. like that part	WEBS 725:14
w. must be half-workers	SHAK 571:4
W. never have young minds	DEL 236:13
w. never look so well	SURT 672:20
w. of good carriage	SHAK 622:22
W., of kynde, desiren libertee	CHAU 193:13
w. of that ever-fresh terrain	AMIS 11:4
W.—one half the human race	BAG 47:4
w. out from behind the vacuum cleaner	
	GREER 317:15
w. remain the slaves	WOLL 741:16
w.'s eyes this doctrine	SHAK 598:19
w.'s eyes this doctrine	SHAK 599:1
w. should be struck regularly	COW 221:5
w.'s rights is the basic	FOUR 291:16
W., then, are only children	CHES 198:16
w. to keep counsel	SHAK 591:9
W. what they are	BRAD 139:11
W. who love the same man	BEER 59:16
work, and w. must weep	KING 397:16
work its way with the w.	DICK 243:22
works of w. are symbolical	BROW 152:6
You are going to w.	NIET 495:4
you have to kill more w.	BALD 48:9
won: ground w. today	ARN 28:8
has w. it bear the palm	JORT 380:14
he can court, or you be w.	SOUT 667:3
I w. the count	SOM 655:14
never lost till w.	CRAB 225:8
not that you w. or lost	RICE 540:1
our Lord the field is w.	MORE 484:12
prize we sought is w.	WHIT 732:6
therefore to be w.	SHAK 587:13
Things w. are done	SHAK 627:5
Where you will never w.	BALL 49:6
woman in this humour w.	SHAK 621:19
woman, therefore may be w.	SHAK 626:2
w. but to have fought well	COUB 220:4
wonder: all the w. that would	TENN 685:13
And all a w. and a wild desire	BROW 152:15
And w. what you've missed	AUDEN 34:4
appeared a great w. in heaven	BIBLE 106:29
For all knowledge and w.	BACON 41:14
Have eyes to w., but lack	SHAK 634:18
I w. by my troth, what thou	DONNE 252:4
I w. who's kissing her now	ADAMS 2:2
may w. at the workmanship	MILT 464:8
One can only w.	BENT 64:18
one w. at the least	MARL 448:3
see the boneless w.	CHUR 202:3
Smiling w. of a day	WRIG 749:12
still the w. grew	GOLD 310:14
To work a w., God would	HERR 323:11
w. any man alive	GAY 299:11
w. at ourselves like men	WORD 743:7
W. hinders love and hate	GREV 318:5
W. is the first principle	SMITH 650:14
w. of our age	DYER 264:14
w. of our state	JONS 380:1
Worship is transcendent w.	CARL 180:25
wonderful: All things wise and w.	ALEX 8:9
most w. wonderful	SHAK 569:4
My God, how w. Thou art	FABER 279:12
name shall be called W.	BIBLE 82:27
passing strange and w.	SHEL 640:8
such strange and w. things	TRAH 701:14
There are many w. things	SOPH 656:13
too w. and excellent	BOOK 134:19
which are too w. for me	BIBLE 79:33
w. piece of work	SHAK 564:20

wonderful: (*cont.*):

w. works of God	BIBLE 98:7
wonderfully: fearfully and w. made	
	BOOK 134:20
wonders: carry within us the w.	BROW 146:6
declare the w.	BOOK 132:15
Except ye see signs and w.	BIBLE 96:18
his w. in the deep	BOOK 133:1
His w. to perform	COWP 222:17
multiply my signs and my w.	BIBLE 72:3
Seven W. of the World	ADD 4:15
then I do w.	KYD 404:13
Welcome, all w. in one sight	CRAS 226:8
wondrous: all thy w. works	BOOK 125:22
What w. life is this I lead	MARV 450:9
When I survey the w. cross	WATTS 723:2
Who w. things hath done	WINK 739:6
won't: if she w., she won't	ANON 19:18
woo: are April when they w.	SHAK 569:18
Come, w. me, woo me	SHAK 569:16
wood: bows down to w. and stone	KIPL 398:19
Bows down to w. and stone	HEBER 330:4
cleave the w. and there	ANON 17:16
deep and gloomy w.	WORD 744:21
hewers of w. and drawers	BIBLE 73:31
In a dark w. I saw	ROET 544:6
lath of w. painted	BISM 110:8
old w. burn brightest	WEBS 725:26
On Wenlock Edge the w.'s	HOUS 352:12
Out of this w. do not desire	SHAK 611:27
set out to plant a w.	SWIFT 674:25
whiffling through the tulgey w.	CARR 182:19
w. of English bows	DOYLE 257:3
w. the furious winter blowing	RANS 536:15
You are not w.	SHAK 592:12
woodbine: luscious w.	SHAK 611:19
well-attired w.	MILT 466:11
w. spices are wafted abroad	TENN 686:17
woodcock: Spirits of well-shot w.	BETJ 67:6
w. near the gin	SHAK 630:2
w. to mine own springe	SHAK 579:6
woodcocks: Ay, springes to catch w.	
	SHAK 573:6
wooden: literary man—with a w. leg	
	DICK 242:31
Sailed off in a w. shoe	FIELD 281:14
this w. O the very casques	SHAK 584:17
w. walls are the best	COV 220:7
woodland: and a bit of w.	HOR 351:9
And stands about the w. ride	HOUS 352:5
woodlanded: by w. ways	BETJ 68:7
woodlands: About the w. I will go	HOUS 352:6
woodman: W., spare that tree	MORR 485:8
w., spare the beechen tree	CAMP 176:11
wood-notes: Warble his native w. wild	
	MILT 465:17
woods: Are not these w.	SHAK 567:24
Flow down the w. and stipple	SACK 552:16
green-robed senators of mighty w.	
	KEATS 387:27
If you go down in the w. today	BRAT 140:1
In w. and groves	WITH 739:13
lived in the w. like me	VIRG 714:16
Love-whisp'ring w.	POPE 519:7
once a road through the w.	KIPL 400:17
pleasure in the pathless w.	BYRON 169:13
there is a spirit in the w.	WORD 745:9
these wild w. forlorn	MILT 472:26
through the Wet Wild W.	KIPL 401:19
We'll to the w. no more	ANON 21:3
w. against the world	BLUN 116:2
w., and desert caves	MILT 466:2
w. are lovely	FROST 295:13
w. decay and fall	TENN 689:10
w. go seaward	HUNT 356:11
w. of consular dignity	VIRG 714:22
woodshed: nasty in the w.	GIBB 302:24
wooed: therefore may be w.	SHAK 626:22
therefore to be w.	SHAK 587:13
woof: weave the w.	GRAY 315:8
We know her w., her texture	KEATS 388:19
wooing: w. mind	SHAK 599:8
W., so tiring	MITF 478:7

wool: hairs were white like w. — BIBLE 106:1
He giveth snow like w. — BOOK 135:13
his head like the pure w. — BIBLE 86:1
tease the housewife's w. — MILT 464:8
woollen: Odious! in w.! — POPE 520:29
woolly: blushing apricot and w. peach — JONS 380:7
silent was the flock in w. — KEATS 386:20
Softest clothing w. bright — BLAKE 113:21
Woolworth: live a W. life — NIC 494:15
paying a visit to W.'s — BEVAN 69:3
Wops: better than Huns or W. — MITF 478:8
word: And the W. was made flesh — BIBLE 96:4
And torture one poor w. — DRYD 261:3
And what the w. did make it — ELIZ 274:11
And w. spake never more — MALL 443:1
At every w., methought — HERB 334:12
been a time for such a w. — SHAK 605:1
be ye doers of the w. — BIBLE 104:27
by every w. that proceedeth — BIBLE 88:18
choke the w. — BIBLE 91:2
comfort of thy holy W. — BOOK 120:11
Every idle w. that men shall — BIBLE 90:33
every w. she writes is a lie — MCC 437:1
father answered never a w. — LONG 428:4
fool can play upon the w. — SHAK 609:5
fulfilling his w. — BOOK 135:14
Greeks had a w. for it — AKINS 6:13
have not the w. because — ARN 29:18
honour his own w. as if — TENN 681:24
In the beginning was the W. — ELIOT 272:8
it darts without the w. — WILB 734:4
Let the w. go forth from — KENN 393:12
Lord gave the w. — BOOK 129:8
Lord, thy w. abideth — BAKER 47:19
Man's w. is God in man — TENN 681:17
many a w., at random — SCOTT 559:18
meanings packed into one w. — CARR 183:13
meekness the engrafted w. — BIBLE 104:27
nat o w. wol he faille — CHAU 194:4
once familiar w. — BAYLY 56:3
plainly repugnant to the W. — BOOK 135:24
power of the written w. — CONR 217:9
say only the w. — MISS 477:6
should leave the w. of God — BIBLE 98:11
sincere milk of the w. — BIBLE 105:10
sincere milk of the w. — BIBLE 108:17
sometimes w. for word — ALFR 9:3
suit the action to the w. — SHAK 576:6
Thou, whose eternal W. — MARR 449:1
thy tears wash out a w. — FITZ 284:9
time lies in one little w. — SHAK 619:10
truth of thy holy W. — BOOK 121:22
understanding of thy W. — BOOK 119:19
Was the mighty w. — NOEL 496:9
What is that w., honour — SHAK 582:1
When *I* use a w. — CARR 183:11
w. about oral contraception — ALLEN 9:14
w. even may be a spark — SHEL 644:6
w. fitly spoken is like — BIBLE 79:15
w. is a lantern unto — BOOK 133:20
W. is but wynd — LYDG 433:5
w. is enough for the wise — PLAU 517:4
w. is the Verb — HUGO 354:13
w. mightier than they — MILT 472:4
w. of Caesar — SHAK 592:11
w. spoken in due season — BIBLE 78:36
w. takes wing beyond recall — HOR 348:12
w. touch his keen hearing — PUSH 533:3
W. WAS MADE FLESH — MISS 477:9
W. was with God — BIBLE 95:35
w. which should never come — FLEM 287:2
W. without a word — ANDR 11:12
wordless: poem should be w. — MACL 435:9
words: all w. of tongue and pen — HARTE 327:19
artillery of w. — SWIFT 674:29
barren superfluity of w. — GARTH 298:15
big w. for little matters — JOHN 372:21
But for your w., they rob — SHAK 593:14
But w. are words — SHAK 615:6
But w. came halting forth — SIDN 646:15
by w. without knowledge — BIBLE 77:33

words: (*cont.*):
coiner of sweet w. — ARN 28:14
conceal a fact with w. — MACH 438:5
deceive you with vain w. — BIBLE 102:21
dressing old w. new — SHAK 634:7
even from good w. — BOOK 126:22
fool and his w. are soon — SHEN 644:15
For of all sad w. of tongue — WHIT 733:8
For the idiom of w. — PRIOR 529:7
For w. divide and rend — SWIN 676:2
For w., like Nature — TENN 682:31
Give 'em w. — JONS 379:3
Give sorrow w. — SHAK 604:8
gloton of w. — LANG 408:22
good food and not fine w. — MOL 478:22
gotta use w. when I talk — ELIOT 272:19
Hear what comfortable w. — BOOK 122:7
He speaks the kindest w. — LEE 416:2
He w. me, girls, he words — SHAK 566:21
his paint-pots and his w. — HOR 347:8
His w. came feebly — WORD 747:12
Hold fast the form of sound w. — BIBLE 104:6
idea within a wall of w. — BUTL 167:3
I fear those big w. — JOYCE 381:21
In all his w. most wonderful — NEWM 493:13
kindest w. I'll ever know — RODG 544:1
Let the w. of my mouth — BOOK 125:6
like others been all w. — MASS 453:15
Melting melodious w. — HERR 337:10
Men of few w. are the best — SHAK 585:12
mere w., no matter — SHAK 628:6
misused w. generate — SPEN 658:18
my w. among mankind — SHEL 642:1
my w. are my own — CHAR 191:12
My w. echo thus — ELIOT 270:14
nor w., nor worth — SHAK 592:16
not even with w. — BROO 144:1
no use indicting w. — BECK 57:16
Of every four w. I write — BOIL 117:5
on the alms-basket of w. — SHAK 599:4
poetry = *best* w. in the best order — COL 212:9
Proper w. in proper places — SWIFT 673:22
Rather than w. comes — LARK 409:18
Read out my w. at night — FLEC 286:15
repeats his w. — SHAK 594:4
say a few w. of my own — EDW 267:5
so sweet, the w. so fair — JONS 379:16
their w. than their reason — CAV 187:14
therefore let thy w. be few — BIBLE 80:9
These two w. have undone — SELD 562:2
these w. are true — BIBLE 107:18
they give good w. — BOOK 128:19
through the archèd roof in w. — MILT 467:11
twist w. and meanings as you — GAY 300:5
unpleasant'st w. — SHAK 609:3
weigh thy w. in a balance — BIBLE 87:28
We should need new w. — AUST 40:4
Whate'er you think, good w. — SHAK 594:14
when we say 'w. fail us' — AUST 40:4
While w. of learned length — GOLD 310:14
who laid end to end w. — LODGE 425:20
whose w. are of less weight — BACON 43:5
wild and whirling w. — SHAK 574:2
Winged w. — HOMER 342:23
With w. and meanings — ELIOT 270:19
w. are but the signs — JOHN 367:20
w. are images of thoughts — KEATS 390:7
W. are men's daughters — MADD 441:14
w. are quick and vain — SHEL 642:9
w. are slippery and thought — ADAMS 2:24
w. are sometimes allowed — BAUD 55:8
w. are the daughters — JOHN 367:20
W. are the tokens current — BACON 42:4
W. are wise men's counters — HOBB 340:1
w. as they are used — COMP 214:18
w. but wind — BUTL 166:15
w. clothed in reason's — MILT 469:16
w. enough a man shall find — WYATT 733:6
w. like stones — SPEN 659:2
W. may be false and full — SHAD 563:13
w. move slow — POPE 521:17
w. no virtue can digest — MARL 448:3
w. of his mouth were softer — BOOK 128:12

words: (*cont.*):
w. of Mercury are harsh — SHAK 599:12
w. oft creep in one dull — POPE 521:14
W. of the fragrant portals — STEV 665:21
w. of the wise are as goads — BIBLE 81:2
w. once spoke can never — DILL 246:2
w. or I shall burst — FARQ 280:18
w. refuse before the crowd — CLARE 204:22
w. seemed to them as idle — BIBLE 95:31
w. shall not pass away — BIBLE 92:12
W. strain — ELIOT 270:17
w. that burn — GRAY 316:8
w. that have been so nimble — BEAU 56:14
w. tho that hadden pris — CHAU 195:12
W. to the heat of deeds — SHAK 601:13
w. to trampling horses' — SIDN 647:2
w. which express what they — SHEL 644:8
w. will follow — CATO 185:9
W. without thoughts never — SHAK 577:5
W., words, words — SHAK 574:21
worth ten thousand w. — BARN 53:4
you can drug, with w. — LOW 429:14
Wordsworth: better scholar than W. — HOUS 353:1
Out-babying W. — BULW 155:4
what daffodils were for W. — LARK 410:12
W., both are thine — STEP 663:17
W. chime his childish verse — BYRON 172:11
W.'s genius is a pure emanation — HAZL 329:11
W. sometimes wakes — BYRON 171:5
W.—stupendous genius — BYRON 174:3
W., Tennyson and Browning — BAG 47:15
Wordsworthian: W. or egotistical sublime — KEATS 391:23
wore: W. it in the world's eye — YEATS 751:3
work: All hands to w. — ANON 20:2
All out of w., and cold — SHAK 584:20
All that matters is love and w. — FREUD 294:2
breed one w. that wakes — HOPK 346:9
canst w. i' the earth — SHAK 574:3
days when w. was scrappy — CHES 199:9
Did he smile his w. to see — BLAKE 114:15
do the hard and dirty w. — RUSK 550:19
Do the w. that's nearest — KING 397:10
earnestly are you set a-w. — SHAK 628:8
For men must w., and women — KING 397:16
goeth forth to his w. — BOOK 132:9
good idea but it won't w. — ROG 545:1
hands wrought in the w. — BIBLE 76:34
has plenty of w. to do — JER 365:13
He has to w. to keep alive — BELL 61:22
Her noblest w. she classes — BURNS 162:2
his six days' w. — MILT 472:10
If any would not w. — BIBLE 103:24
I have finished the w. — OVID 503:2
immortality through my w. — ALLEN 9:19
its hands and goes to w. — SAND 555:12
I want w. — SHAK 580:14
Let no one else's w. evade — LEHR 416:11
life, or of the w. — YEATS 751:6
Look at the end of w. — BROW 150:23
love my w. and my children — HILL 338:11
man according to his w. — BOOK 128:20
My medicine, w.! — SHAK 617:7
my w. is done — ANON 16:14
Nice w. if you can get it — GERS 301:12
no immortal w. behind me — KEATS 392:13
Nothing to do but w. — KING 396:9
Old Kaspar's w. was done — SOUT 657:4
one shall w. for money — KIPL 401:9
our w. is never done — DUCK 263:7
patience have her perfect w. — BIBLE 104:24
piece of w. is a man — SHAK 574:28
sport as tedious as to w. — SHAK 579:29
stomach sets us to w. — ELIOT 269:8
sublimation of the w. — LODGE 425:21
till our w. is done — COLL 212:23
very thing to w. on — AUST 39:26
We w. in the dark — JAMES 363:1
when no man can w. — BIBLE 96:34
Who first invented w. — LAMB 407:3
whose w. is not born with him — LOW 429:14
Why should I let the toad w. — LARK 410:8

work: (*cont.*):

with care our w. attend	COLL 212:23
woman is the w. of God	BLAKE 112:24
wonderful piece of w.	SHAK 564:20
W. and pray, live on hay	HILL 338:12
W. apace	DEKK 235:16
w. by the sweat of his brow	CHEK 197:2
w. does what he wants to do	COLL 213:5
W. expands so as to fill	PARK 507:3
W. is love made visible	GIBR 303:3
W. is of two kinds	RUSS 551:15
w. is terribly important	RUSS 551:10
W. is the call	MORR 485:18
W. is the curse of the drinking	WILDE 736:10
w. is to represent the age	BROW 147:5
W. is x; y is play	EINS 268:5
w. itself shall not be lost	FRAN 293:6
W. liberates	ANON 21:9
w. more and dispute less	TAWN 679:1
w. of an absolutely useless	DOST 255:2
W. out your own salvation	BIBLE 103:6
W. seethes in the hands	PAST 508:9
w. terribly hard at playing	MORT 486:6
w. till most of those whom	JOHN 371:20
w. together for good	BIBLE 99:38
W. was like a stick	SOLZ 655:9
W. without hope draws nectar	COL 211:24

worked: on we w., and waited   ROB 542:11

worker: sociable w.   BEHAN 60:3

weapon with a w. at each end	ANON 12:10
w. can be lulled by fine	KHR 395:16
w. is the slave of capitalist	CONN 216:24
w. would sooner have	BLYT 116:10

workers: men w., ever reaping   TENN 685:13

They are not the w.	WHYTE 733:14
we, the w., all demand	SERV 563:7
w. are perfectly free	ENG 277:23
w. of the country are our	SHIN 645:29
w. of the world, unite	MARX 452:14

workhouse: Christmas Day in the W.
         SIMS 648:7

prison and the woman's w.   SHAW 638:1

working: according to the mighty w.
         BOOK 124:5

And I've been w. like a dog	LENN 417:20
choice of w. or starving	JOHN 367:18
each for the joy of the w.	KIPL 401:9
I killin' meself w.	O'CAS 497:14
they can't be alwayth a w.	DICK 240:34
will protect a w.-girl	SMITH 651:30
w. about six weeks in a year	THOR 697:1
W. and wandrynge	LANG 408:21

working class: w. where we belong
         ORW 500:24

w., raw and half-developed   ARN 29:11

working-day: full of briers is this w.
         SHAK 567:22

working-house: forge and w. of thought
         SHAK 586:13

workings: inscrutable w. of Providence
         SMITH 651:14

workmanship: Inscrutable w.   WORD 746:21

most may wonder at the w.   MILT 464:8

works: all thy wondrous w.   BOOK 125:22

cast away the w. of darkness	BOOK 120:10
cast off the w. of darkness	BIBLE 100:10
devil and all his w.	BOOK 123:4
even of the greatest w.	JONS 378:5
even the w. of thy fingers	BOOK 124:20
Faith without w. is dead	BIBLE 104:29
forth the fruit of good w.	BOOK 121:11
God now accepteth thy w.	BIBLE 80:19
her w. gay nature grieves	SMART 649:16
how manifold are thy w.	BOOK 132:9
I know thy w.	BIBLE 106:7
immediately upon your w.	GRANT 314:7
into my w. is my talent	WILDE 736:7
Look on my w., ye Mighty	SHEL 642:4
man according to their w.	BIBLE 107:16
not me, believe the w.	BIBLE 97:3
O all ye W. of the Lord	BOOK 118:15
proved me, and saw my w.	BOOK 131:10
seen the future; and it w.	STEF 663:1

works: (*cont.*):

stained with their own w.	BOOK 132:14
that in all our w.	BOOK 122:17
their w. do follow	BIBLE 107:5
they may see your good w.	BIBLE 88:26
W. done least rapidly	BROW 151:15
w. of idleness and impotent	BLUNT 116:6
w. of women are symbolical	BROW 147:1

workshop: any other nation may be its w.
         CHAM 189:3

not a temple but a w.	TURG 705:5
not suffer England to be the w.	DISR 246:15
wrong since the War, it's W.	AMIS 10:12

world: absurd w.   DUH 263:10

after the w.'s opinion	EMER 277:1
All's right with the w.	BROW 151:28
All the mighty w.	WORD 745:2
all the w. and his wife	ANST 23:12
All the w. is sad and dreary	FOST 291:15
All the w.'s a stage	SHAK 568:16
all the w. was gay	POPE 523:22
all this visible w.	BYRON 172:17
anarchy is loosed upon the w.	YEATS 753:1
And naked shingles of the w.	ARN 27:1

And when Rome falls—the W.
         BYRON 169:10

And win the w. with liberality	GASC 298:17
appointment at the end of the w.	DIN 246:7
at which the w. grew pale	JOHN 370:17
away from the whole w.	VIRG 714:13
become fit for this w.	KEATS 391:8
bestride the narrow w.	SHAK 590:3
blynde w.	CHAU 195:7
bottom of the monstrous w.	MILT 466:12
brave new w.	SHAK 626:3
breaks through from another w.	GUM 319:16
brought nothing into this w.	BIBLE 104:2
bubble burst, and now a w.	POPE 521:29
But in the very w.	WORD 747:7
citizen of the w.	BACON 43:26
corners of the w. in arms	SHAK 594:16
create the wondrous w.	YOUNG 754:20
dark w. of sin	DICK 108.22
deceits of the w.	BOOK 119:17
Deceiving w.	GREE 317:8
decide the fate of the w.	DE G 235:3
despise this wrecched w.	CHAU 196:1
Dissatisfaction with the w.	DICK 245:6
dream of the actual w.	SANT 555:18
drives him to the w. without	ARN 20:22
entire combustible w.	YEATS 752:4
excellent foppery of the w.	SHAK 595:2
fashion of this w. passeth	BIBLE 100:26
filling the w., and emptying	SCOTT 560:16
flood unto the w.'s end	BOOK 129:20
For the w., I count it	BROW 146:19
foutra for the w.	SHAK 584:11
frame of the w.	BERK 65:12
From this vile w.	SHAK 634:5
God so loved the w.	BIBLE 96:15
Good-bye, proud w.	EMER 276:8
good deed in a naughty w.	SHAK 610:4
had my w. as in my time	CHAU 194:22
Had we but w. enough	MARV 451:2
happiness of the next w.	BROW 145:17
hell of this w. to enjoy	BECK 58:4
Here's a w. of pomp and state	BEAU 56:15
her w. is brazen	SIDN 647:6
his six days' work, a w.	MILT 472:10
how dry a cinder this w.	DONNE 250:8
If the w. be worth thy winning	DRYD 259:21
I have not loved the w.	BYRON 168:27
immense w. of delight	BLAKE 112:30
in all the towns in all the w.	EPST 278:6
In a w. I never made	HOUS 351:20
I nothing in this w. did know	TRAH 702:1
In this w. and the next	WINK 739:6
Into a w. which, wanting thee	WALL 718:18
into the ends of the w.	BOOK 125:4
into the history of the w.	POPP 524:13
Is all the sad w. needs	WILC 734:8
journey to the w.	SOCR 655:1
kingdoms of the w.	BIBLE 88:20

world: (*cont.*):

knack of so arranging the w.	FRIS 294:4
knowledge of the w.	CHES 198:6
leave the w. unseen	KEATS 389:9
light of the w.	BIBLE 88:25
Little Friend of all the W.	KIPL 402:4
little w. made cunningly	DONNE 251:1
lost the w. for love	DRYD 261:11
lover's quarrel with the w.	FROST 295:2
Mad w.	SHAK 593:29
make one half the w. fools	JEFF 364:17
making the w. safe for	WOLFE 741:5
Man is one w., and hath	HERB 335:11
mean the limits of my w.	WITT 740:5
monk who shook the w.	MONT 481:20
month in which the w. bigan	CHAU 194:7
much respect upon the w.	SHAK 607:3
My country is the w.	PAINE 505:1
my pains a w. of sighs	SHAK 615:2
myself create my little w.	BEDD 58:10
nature makes the whole w. kin	SHAK 627:22
need of a w. of men	BROW 150:17
never enjoy the w. aright	TRAH 701:9
never have a quiet w. till	SHAW 638:11
not as the w. giveth	BIBLE 97:15
nourish all the w.	SHAK 599:1
no w., but mass of public	KYD 404:11
Of a grey silent w.	HUGH 354:5
Of the very w. he made	SMART 649:9
one grows tired of the w.	WALP 719:9
only interpreted the w.	MARX 452:8
our country is the w.	GARR 298:12
out of the w. as out of fashion	CIBB 203:19
O w. invisible, we view thee	THOM 695:9
passing w. to turn thine eyes	JOHN 370:15
pass through this w. but once	GREL 317:19
places to learn the w.	CHES 198:8
Poor W.	CRAS 226:7
poor w. in a blue funk	CRANE 225:22
present were the w.'s last night	DONNE 251:2
rack of this tough w.	SHAK 598:4
remember of this unstable w.	MAL 443:8
round the habitable w.	DRYD 262:4
Round the w. for ever and aye	ARN 27:9
round w. so sure	BOOK 131:6
say the w. will end in fire	FROST 294:17
secure amidst a falling w.	ADD 4:5
shall gain the whole w.	BIBLE 93:14
shows how small the w.	GROS 319:3
Sob, heavy w.	AUDEN 33:28
something is, somehow, the w.	POPP 524:17
something that infects the w.	ARN 27:23
spectacle of the w.	BIBLE 100:19
start of the majestic w.	SHAK 590:2
Stop the w., I want to get off	NEWL 492:10
Strayed up from a dead w.	HEAT 329:24
Syllables govern the w.	SELD 562:12
Ten days that shook the w.	REED 538:11
Than this w. dreams of	TENN 682:24
Their w. gives way and dies	MACN 440:17
There is a w. elsewhere	SHAK 570:15
they only saved the w.	CHES 199:1
thick rotundity o' the w.	SHAK 595:20
things of this w.	MANN 444:13
This gewgaw w.	DRYD 259:26
This is the way the w. ends	ELIOT 271:14
this small-talking w.	FRY 295:23
This warm kind w. is all	CORY 220:1
this w. goes with no eyes	SHAK 597:6
This w., if we can enjoy it	RICH 540:14
This w. is bad enough	CLOU 207:11
This w.'s no blot for us	BROW 149:25
though the w. perish	FERD 281:9
Thou seest the w., Volumnius	SHAK 593:21
Thus passes the glory of the w.	ANON 22:15
To know the w., not love	YOUNG 754:21
too late to seek a newer w.	TENN 690:4
To see a w. in a grain of sand	BLAKE 110:18
triple pillar of the w.	SHAK 564:12
turning w.	ELIOT 270:16
undercuts the problematical w.	FRY 295:22
unshook amidst a bursting w.	POPE 519:26
upstairs into the w.	CONG 215:8

world: (*cont.*):

Wag as it will the w. for me	BYROM 167:13
way of coming into the w.	SWIFT 674:9
were the youth of the w.	BACON 42:11
What a w. is this	BOL 117:11
What is the w., O soldiers	DE L 236:9
What is this w.? what asketh	CHAU 193:23
what once it was, the w.	MARV 451:12
What would the w.	HOPK 345:15
When all the w. is young, lad	KING 397:17
When the w. was begun	CART 184:13
whereby the w. will be judged	MISS 477:12
where he suspends the w.	BYRON 167:18
where I live unto the w.	SHAK 621:10
which the w. cannot give	BOOK 119:10
whole w. is not sufficient	QUAR 533:15
whole w. to the scratching	HUME 356:1
whole w. turn to coal	HERB 336:2
whoso hath this w.'s good	BIBLE 105:26
wilderness of this w.	BUNY 155:13
wish the estate o' the w.	SHAK 605:2
With this w. will I fight	ASKEW 31:15
woods against the w.	BLUN 116:2
words have undone the w.	SELD 562:2
w. and all her train were hurled	VAUG 709:11
w. and love were young	RAL 535:11
W. AND WE WANT IT NOW	MORR 486:1
w. as a meadow in May	BABEL 41:13
w. as a sort of metaphysical	KOES 403:18
w. as a vale of tears	BROW 149:8
w. but as the world	SHAK 607:4
w. can only be grasped	BRON 141:17
w. do frown at my retire	ALAB 7:1
w. empty of people	LAWR 412:10
w. equally wicked and corrupt	BURKE 159:14
w. forgetting	POPE 519:21
w. has achieved brilliance	BRAD 139:8
w. has grown grey from	SWIN 676:21
w. has lost his youth	BIBLE 86:23
w. in arms is not spending	EIS 268:10
w. in one volume octavo	SMITH 652:26
w. in solemn stillness lay	SEARS 561:12
w. is a comedy to those	WALP 719:18
w. is an oyster	MILL 461:15
w. is becoming like a lunatic	LLOY 424:12
w. is charged	HOPK 345:10
W. is crazier and more of it	MACN 441:2
w. is everything	WITT 740:4
w. is full of care	WARD 721:21
w. is given over	LE G 416:9
w. is growing old	HAZL 329:9
w. is not a 'prison house'	ROB 542:12
w. is not thy friend	SHAK 624:4
w. is not yet prepared	DOYLE 256:9
w. is so full of a number	STEV 668:14
w. is still deceived	SHAK 608:26
w. is the best of all possible	BRAD 139:4
w. is too much with us	WORD 748:15
w. is weary of the past	SHEL 640:16
w. is white	TENN 681:21
w. knew him not	BIBLE 96:3
w. locks up its spoons	SHAW 637:16
w. may end tonight	BROW 150:20
w. must be made safe	WILS 738:17
w. must be peopled	SHAK 613:27
W., Nature, Universe's	PAST 509:1
w. of the emotions	COL 212:19
w. of the happy	WITT 740:6
w. on dreaming fed	YEATS 753:7
w.'s a bubble	BACON 45:27
w.'s a jest, and joy's	STEP 663:16
w.'s an inn	DRYD 261:13
w.'s a scene of changes	COWL 221:14
w.'s as ugly, ay, as sin	LOCK 425:12
w.'s at an end	D'AV 231:17
w.'s great age begins anew	SHEL 640:15
w.'s grown honest	SHAK 574:25
w.'s history is world's judgement	SCH 558:4
w. should be taxed	BIBLE 93:25
w. should break and fall	HOR 350:2
w.'s mine oyster	SHAK 610:14
w. spin for ever down	TENN 685:19
w.'s slow stain	SHEL 640:1

world: (*cont.*):

w.'s storm-troubled sphere	BRON 142:12
w. surely is wide enough	STER 664:22
w.'s whole sap is sunk	DONNE 252:12
w.'s worst wound	SASS 557:13
w. that passeth soone	CHAU 196:2
w. to me is but a ceaseless	SHAK 619:4
w. to which we turn	STEV 669:13
w. upon him falsely smiled	FANS 280:1
w. upside down	BIBLE 98:28
w. was all before them	MILT 473:14
w. was not worthy	BIBLE 104:16
w. will little note	LINC 422:10
w. will not narrow	JOHN 367:7
w. without end	BIBLE 102:15
w. without end	BOOK 118:11
w. without end	BOOK 130:22
w. would smell like what it is	SHEL 641:3
W., you have kept faith	HARDY 325:7
wrecched w.'s appetites	CHAU 196:2
worldly: breath of w. men	SHAK 620:3
clear from w. cares	VAUX 709:13
These were all his w. goods	LEAR 413:19
weary of these w. bars	SHAK 590:12
with all my w. goods	BOOK 123:21
worldly, be not w. wise	QUAR 533:18
worlds: best of all possible w.	OAD 174:12
best of all possible w.	VOLT 716:1
Between two w. life hovers	BYRON 171:33
both w. at once they view	WALL 718:13
Exhausted w.	JOHN 370:11
more w. than all the world can	GREV 318:9
wainscot tubs to seek out w.	DRAY 258:3
Wandering between two w.	ARN 28:20
what w. away	BROW 148:25
w. beyond this world's	BYRON 172:1
w. of wanwood leafmeal	HOPK 346:3
worm: am but as a crushed w.	PUNCH 531:26
And the w. that never dies	BROO 143:8
goes the same crooked w.	THOM 693:8
has made the laily w.	BALL 49:16
I am a w., and no man	BOOK 125:10
invisible w.	BLAKE 114:12
I wish you all joy of the w.	SHAK 567:5
lest in the w. you crush	BARB 52:3
like a w. i' the bud	SHAK 629:20
man may fish with the w.	SHAK 577:29
needlessly sets foot upon a w.	COWP 224:8
w. at one end and a fool	JOHN 377:1
w. in your little inside	GILB 305:12
W. nor snail, do no offence	SHAK 611:21
w., the canker	BYRON 173:1
worms: Among the hungry w. I sleep	BALL 49:4
Flies, w., and flowers	WATTS 722:14
He was eaten of w.	BIBLE 98:22
Impaling w. to torture fish	COLM 214:5
politic w. are e'en at him	SHAK 577:28
then w. shall try	MARV 451:3
with vilest w. to dwell	SHAK 634:5
W. as there are tiles	LUTH 434:1
w. destroy this body	BIBLE 77:25
w. that are thy chambermaids	SHAK 624:9
w. were hallowed	SHAK 617:3
wormwood: her end is bitter as w.	BIBLE 78:12
star is called W.	BIBLE 106:25
w. and the gall	BIBLE 85:17
worn: padded, too severely w.	DRAB 257:7
When we're w., hacked hewn	SOUT 657:2
worried: w. into being	FROST 295:16
worry: Leave your w. on the doorstep	FIEL 282:19
worrying: What's the use of w.	ASAF 30:17
W. the carcase of an old song	THOM 694:15
worse: Defend the bad against the w.	DAY-L 233:7
even from w. to better	JOHN 367:19
finding something w.	BELL 61:2
for better for w.	BOOK 123:20
greater feeling to the w.	SHAK 619:14
I follow the w.	OVID 502:24
I mean the W. one	ARIS 25:3
It is w. than a crime	BOUL 137:15

worse: (*cont.*):

Many w., better few	LOCK 425:16
More will mean w.	AMIS 10:11
my books had been any w.	CHAN 190:6
one penny the w.	BARH 52:15
Or is it something w.	SPR 661:15
state of that man is w.	BIBLE 90:37
w. appear the better reason	MILT 469:13
w. to better hath in it	HOOK 344:15
worst are no w.	SHAK 612:25
worser: throw away the w. part	SHAK 577:21
worship: And we w. thy Name	BOOK 118:14
are come to w. him	BIBLE 88:8
find someone to w.	DOST 254:7
heaven and earth doth w. thee	BOOK 118:12
let us w. and fall down	BOOK 131:10
only object of w.	ANON 12:3
O w. the King, all-glorious	GRANT 314:6
Rich in the simple w. of a day	KEATS 388:22
therefore ye ignorantly w.	BIBLE 98:31
they w. Truth	BROO 143:14
various modes of w.	GIBB 301:18
with my body I thee w.	BOOK 123:21
w. God in his own way	ROOS 546:3
w. her by years of noble	TENN 681:25
w. him in spirit	BIBLE 96:17
W. is transcendent wonder	CARL 180:25
w. of the bitch-goddess success	JAMES 363:14
w. the beast and his image	BIBLE 107:4
w. the Lord in the beauty	BOOK 131:11
w. the Lord in the beauty	MONS 480:2
Your w. is your furnaces	BOTT 137:11
worshipped: W. and served the creature	BIBLE 99:17
worships: East he w. in his way	SMART 649:13
worst: And the best and the w.	SWIN 676:24
be good to know the w.	BRAD 139:5
be the w. of the company	SWIFT 673:19
Cheer up! the w. is yet to come	JOHN 367:15
exacts a full look at the w.	HARDY 325:6
His w. is better	HAZL 329:10
In the worst inn's w. room	POPE 520:18
it was the w. of times	DICK 244:1
No w., there is none	HOPK 345:16
so much good in the w.	ANON 18:13
This is the w.	SHAK 596:26
To-morrow do thy w.	DRYD 262:1
world's w. wound	SASS 557:13
w. are full of passionate	YEATS 753:1
w. form of Government	CHUR 202:23
w. is death	SHAK 620:6
w. is that which delays	LLOY 424:9
w. returns to laughter	SHAK 596:23
w. speaks something good	HERB 334:10
w. time of the year	ANDR 11:13
worth: charter of thy w.	SHAK 634:11
contract isn't w. the paper	GOLD 312:3
his worldly w. for this	TENN 689:8
if a thing is w. doing	CHES 199:24
Is w. an age without a name	MORD 483:18
man's w. something	BROW 148:15
nor words, nor w.	SHAK 592:16
not w. going to see	JOHN 375:10
Slow rises w., by poverty	JOHN 370:9
think my trifles were w.	CAT 185:11
w. and spiritual reality	HEGEL 330:8
w. of a man by the number	FLAU 285:19
w. than his chambermaid	GODW 308:10
w. the dust which the rude	SHAK 596:28
Worthington: Mrs W.	COW 220:15
worthless: this w. man	EPH 278:4
worthy: found them w.	BIBLE 86:28
labourer is w. of his hire	BIBLE 94:10
latchet I am not w. to unloose	BIBLE 96:6
nameless in w. deeds exceeds	BROW 145:22
Of whom the world was not w.	BIBLE 104:16
there be ninc w.	CAXT 188:2
w. of serious attention	ARIS 25:13
w. of the vocation wherewith	BIBLE 102:16
w. that thou shouldest	BIBLE 89:29
w. that thou shouldest	MISS 477:6
W. the Lamb that died	WATTS 722:19

worthy: (*cont.*):
w. to be called thy son   BIBLE 95:3
w. to open the book   BIBLE 106:13
wot: W. prawce Selvytion nah   SHAW 636:31
wotthehell: w. archy   MARQ 448:12
would: He w., wouldn't he?   RIC 540:6
what we w., we know   ARN 26:17
W. I were with him   SHAK 585:4
wound: annual w. in Lebanon   MILT 468:20
Earth felt the w.   MILT 472:24
felt a stain like a w.   BURKE 158:14
first did help to w. itself   SHAK 594:16
heal me of my grievous w.   TENN 682:25
Hearts w. up with love   SPEN 659:4
In every w. of Caesar   SHAK 592:17
In one long yellow string I w.   BROW 152:3
keen knife see not the w.   SHAK 600:16
Makes such a w., the knife   SHEL 641:5
now purple with love's w.   SHAK 611:17
that never felt a w.   SHAK 622:27
that w. for many years   MAL 443:4
Willing to w., and yet afraid   POPE 519:32
world's worst w.   SASS 557:13
w. did ever heal   SHAK 616:8
w. for wound   BIBLE 72:17
wounded: makes the w. spirit whole
  NEWT 494:10
w. spirit who can bear?   BIBLE 79:2
w. and left on Afghanistan's   KIPL 401:12
w. for our transgressions   BIBLE 84:12
You're w.!   BROW 150:14
Wounded Knee: Bury my heart at W.
  BENÉT 62:16
wounding: wounded is the w. heart
  CRAS 226:3
wounds: bathe in reeking w.   SHAK 599:16
Faithful are the w. of a friend   BIBLE 79:26
heals his w., and drives away   NEWT 494:10
makes my old w. bleed anew   WALL 721:13
many eyes as thou hast w.   SHAK 591:21
not to heed the w.   IGN 359:8
revenge keeps his own w.   BACON 44:16
see in me the w. thou madest   DAN 229:15
soldier details his w.   PROP 529:22
w. I had on Crispin's day   SHAK 586:11
w. whose only bandage might   BYRON 172:14
woven: with their w. wings   SHAK 607:2
wrack: with sunken w.   SHAK 584:21
Wragg: W. is in custody   ARN 29:16
wrang: may gang a kennin w.   BURNS 161:1
wrangle: shall we begin to w.   ANON 17:21
wrap: And w. me in a gown   HERB 334:3
wrapped: meanly w.   MILT 467:2
w. him in swaddling clothes   BIBLE 93:26
wrath: between the dragon and his w.
  SHAK 594:20
Envy and w. shorten the life   BIBLE 87:29
flee from the w. to come   BIBLE 88:15
from the w. of the Lamb   BIBLE 106:17
grapes of w. are stored   HOWE 353:2
great day of his w.   BIBLE 106:17
He who the ox to w.   BLAKE 111:4
if his w. be kindled   BOOK 124:11
I told my wrath, my w. did end   BLAKE 114:11
not your children to w.   BIBLE 102:24
slow to speak, slow to w.   BIBLE 104:27
soft answer turneth away w.   BIBLE 78:33
sun go down upon your w.   BIBLE 102:19
That day, the day of w.   MISS 477:11
tygers of w. are wiser   BLAKE 112:25
Unto whom I sware in my w.   BOOK 131:10
verge of heaven, eternal w.   MILT 472:5
w. endureth but the twinkling   BOOK 126:5
w. of God upon the children   BIBLE 102:21
w. of the lion is the wisdom   BLAKE 112:24
wreath: place a tin w.   POUND 526:15
wreathed: w. the rod of criticism   D'ISR 249:16
wreaths: laurel w. entwine   HARTE 327:16
wreck: Of that colossal w.   SHEL 642:4
wreckage: w. of men who have minded
  WOOLF 742:12
wrecks: w. of a dissolving dream   SHEL 640:15
Vomits its w.   SHEL 641:2

Wrekin: forest fleece the W.   HOUS 352:12
Wren: Sir Christopher W.   BARH 52:10
Four Larks and a W.   LEAR 413:18
He who shall hurt the little w.   BLAKE 111:4
Mr Christopher W.   EVEL 279:7
musician than the w.   SHAK 610:5
poor w.   SHAK 604:4
robin-red-breast and the w.   WEBS 726:7
Sir Christopher W.   BENT 64:17
w. goes to't   SHAK 597:4
youngest w. of nine   SHAK 630:17
wrest: W. once the law   SHAK 609:15
wrestle: with the intolerable w.   ELIOT 270:19
w. not against flesh   BIBLE 103:1
wrestled: w. with him   WALT 721:13
you have w. well   SHAK 567:19
wrestles: he that w. with us   BURKE 158:24
wrestling: W., I will not let thee go   WESL 728:9
w. with (my God!)   HOPK 345:8
wretch: That w., if such a wretch   WRIG 749:13
w. that dares not die   BURNS 162:17
w. whom thou wouldest not   DONNE 253:7
wretched: All men hate the w.   SHEL 639:7
grief as age; w. in both   SHAK 595:17
ladies most deject and w.   SHAK 576:4
Most w. men   SHEL 641:1
only w. are the wise   PRIOR 529:14
proud and yet a w. thing   DAV 232:4
wretchedness: our w. is irremediable
  EDG 266:13
w. that glory brings us   SHAK 626:14
wretches: feel what w. feel   SHAK 596:7
gaping w. of the sea   HUNT 356:6
How shall w. live like us   GODL 308:7
Poor naked w.   SHAK 596:6
wriggles: He w. and giggles   HOFF 341:3
wring: soon w. their hands   WALP 720:13
wrinkle: w. and the reputation   DRYD 261:4
w. deeper on the brow   BYRON 168:11
wrinkled: w. deep in time   SHAK 565:2
wrinkles: w. will devour   NASHE 491:1
writ: censure this mysterious w.   DRYD 260:24
Hooly w. is the scripture   JER 365:12
I never w., nor no man ever   SHAK 634:24
name was w. in water   KEATS 392:17
Presbyter is but old *Priest* w.   MILT 467:14
w. with me in sour   SHAK 624:6
write: A baseness to w. fair   SHAK 579:1
And he said unto me, W.   BIBLE 107:18
And w. about it, Goddess   POPE 519:4
But those who cannot w.   POPE 523:3
can w. the life of a man   JOHN 373:15
comfortable I sit down to w.   KEATS 392:11
could w. and cypher too   GOLD 310:13
decided to w. for posterity   ADE 5:4
does not w. himself down   HAZL 329:10
Enraged I w.   DYER 264:14
I always w. of you   SHAK 634:7
I have to w.   HERR 336:16
I love to w. to the moment   RICH 540:11
it is best to w. in wind   CAT 186:10
I w. like a distinguished   NAB 489:3
I w. of melancholy   BURT 164:13
Learn to w. well, or not   BUCK 154:11
look in thy heart and w.   SIDN 646:15
man may w. at any time   JOHN 371:9
men w. in place lite   CHAU 195:25
much as a man ought to w.   TROL 703:5
Muse invoked, sit down to w.   SWIFT 675:1
not enough for me to w.   LYLY 433:13
people that w.   SHEN 644:16
people who can't w.   ZAPPA 755:9
read a novel, I w. one   DISR 249:9
reading, in order to w.   JOHN 374:1
restraint with which they w.   CAMP 176:8
Some praise in peers to w.   BYRON 172:10
Some who can't w.   CHUR 201:1
such as cannot w.   DENH 236:20
They w. about it   AMIS 11:1
Though an angel should w.   MOORE 482:19
To make me w. too much   DAN 230:3
We w. in water   SHAK 589:9

write: (*cont.*):
When men w. for profit   WALP 719:21
whether I should w. or send   HAR 326:10
w. and read comes by nature   SHAK 614:2
w. for the sake of writing   KEATS 392:4
w. in a book, and send   BIBLE 105:34
W. me as one that loves   HUNT 356:5
W. sorrow on the bosom   SHAK 620:7
w. such stuff for ever   JOHN 376:5
w. trifles with dignity   JOHN 375:19
w. upon him my new name   BIBLE 106:6
w. when I feel spiteful   LAWR 412:26
yet hate all who w.   WYCH 750:8
You w. with ease, to show   SHER 645:22
writer: concealed beauties of a w.   ADD 4:12
every great and original w.   WORD 748:20
modern hardback w.   TRIL 702:15
No tears in the w.   FROST 295:15
original w. is not   CHAT 192:4
pen: of a ready w.   BOOK 127:10
plain, rude w. . . . I call   BURT 164:15
successful w. or picture-painter   LEWIS 421:4
understand a w.'s ignorance   COL 211:27
was the book and w. too   DANTE 230:13
w. has to rob his mother   FAUL 281:4
w. must be as objective   CHEK 197:9
w. must be universal   BARN 53:6
w. must refuse   SART 556:7
[w.] must teach himself   FAUL 281:2
w. of it be a black man   ADD 4:6
w.'s ambition   KOES 403:22
w. should imagine   BARN 53:9
w.'s only responsibility   FAUL 281:4
writers: Clear w., like clear   LAND 408:12
dead w. are remote   ELIOT 273:19
W., like teeth, are divided   BAG 47:10
writes: entire man that w.   HUNT 356:18
or but w. in dust   BACON 45:28
w. as fast as they can   HAZL 329:10
writhed: W. not of passèd joy   KEATS 387:33
writing: And some for w. verses   LOCK 425:14
angel w. in a book of gold   HUNT 356:4
any style of w. untouched   JOHN 374:21
art of w.   D'ISR 249:17
as I had in the w.   QUAR 533:14
ease in w. comes from art   POPE 521:16
fine w. next to fine doing   KEATS 392:10
future of my kind of w.   PYM 533:11
God is love, but get it in w.   LEE 415:15
had no talent for w.   BENC 62:12
happy I live and despise w.   SMITH 652:16
incurable disease of w.   JUV 384:3
manner of w. [prose]   MILT 476:4
only end of w.   JOHN 368:6
recited verses in w.   BIBLE 88:1
sign the w.   BIBLE 85:32
That fairy kind of w.   DRYD 260:32
thought *nothing* of her w.   SITW 648:16
w. an exact man   BACON 44:28
w. *at once*   GIDE 303:8
w. increaseth rage   DYER 264:14
W. is not a profession   SIM 647:17
w. of oure tonge   CHAU 195:26
W., when properly managed   STER 664:21
writing-book: lost your w.   HOFF 341:5
written: as well w. as prose   POUND 527:16
Books are well w. or badly   WILDE 735:14
in which anything may be w.   TRAH 701:8
large a letter I have w.   BIBLE 102:12
power of the w. word   CONR 217:9
something so w. to aftertimes   MILT 476:5
until he has w. a book   JOW 380:17
volume of the book it is w.   BOOK 126:25
were all my members w.   BOOK 134:21
What I have written I have w.   BIBLE 97:26
w. by mere man that was   JOHN 377:9
w. exceptionally well if   HOR 347:5
w. out of reputation   BENT 65:1
w. such volumes of stuff   LEAR 414:10
w. three books on the soul   BROW 149:7
w. without effort   JOHN 377:11
w. word as unlike as possible   CONN 216:13
wrong: absent are always in the w.   DEST 238:2

X

Y

you: (*cont.*):

it was y. and me	JAGG 361:14
y. ain't heard nuttin' yet	JOLS 377:17
Y.'ve got to be carefully taught	HAMM 323:2

young: America is a country of y. men

	EMER 277:15
And y. men glittering	TRAH 701:15
being y. and foolish	YEATS 751:11
But to be y. was very heaven	WORD 744:5
castigator and censor of the y.	HOR 347:14
crime of being a y. man	PITT 515.5
dared be radical when y.	FROST 295:8
denunciation of the y.	SMITH 652:2
fat and look y. till forty	DRYD 261:4
get out while we're y.	SPR 661:14
heads on your y. shoulders	SPARK 658:5
her six y. on the rail	BROW 150:16
hinds to bring forth y.	BOOK 126:3
I have been y., and now	BLUN 116:4
I have been y., and now	BOOK 126:20
I was a poet, I was y.	FLEC 286:15
I was so y., I loved him	BROW 148:19
love's y. dream	MOORE 483:6
Most women are not so y.	BEER 59:20
Not so y., sir, to love	SHAK 595:5
Old and y., we are all	STEV 667:28
O y., fresshe folkes	CHAU 196:2
panting, and for ever y.	KEATS 388:28
proper y. men	BURNS 162:11
sight to make an old man y.	TENN 681:6
So wise so y., they say	SHAK 622:1
So y., and so untender	SHAK 594:19
think it is, and we were y.	HOUS 352:3
those that are with y.	BIBLE 83:28
too y. to fall asleep for ever	SASS 557:8
too y. to take up golf	ADAMS 2:4
When I was y.	YEATS 750:17
When thou wast y., thou	BIBLE 98:2
Whom the gods love dies y.	MEN 457:2
world and love were y.	RAL 535:11
y. a body with so old a head	SHAK 609:12
y. and easy under the apple	THOM 693:5
y. and handsome as I was	MARL 446:10
y. and lusty as an eagle	BOOK 132:3
y and sweating devil here	SHAK 617:1
y. can do for the old	SHAW 636:13
y. fellow that is neither	CONG 215:13
Y., gifted and black	IRV 360:13
y. had discovered what	MAUG 454:3
Y. in limbs, in judgement old	SHAK 608:14
y. lassie do wi' an auld	BURNS 164:2
y. man cleanse his way	BOOK 133:18
y. man not yet	BACON 44:6
y. man will be wiser	TENN 681:19
Y. men and maidens	BOOK 135:15
Y. men are fitter to invent	BACON 45:9
y. men have more virtue	JOHN 372:12
y. men shall see visions	BIBLE 86:8
y. men's vision	DRYD 259:4
y. think too little	WALP 719:13
y. wife and a good brain	JONS 378:7
you yet call yourself y.	SHAK 582:20

younger: I'm y. than that now

	DYLAN 265:19
let thy love be y.	SHAK 629:15
y. son gathered all together	BIBLE 95:2

younger: (*cont.*):

Y. than she are happy mothers	SHAK 622:20

youngman: die a y.'s death — MCG 438:2

yours: never y., Augustus — DICK 241:29

What I have done is y.	SHAK 632:20
Y. till Hell freezes	FISH 283:6

yourselves: honey not for y. — VIRG 715:20

youth: against me from my y. — BOOK 134:9

Age is deformed, y. unkind	BAST 55:3
All the flattering y. defy	ROCH 543:17
April of your y.	HERB 334:2
bear the yoke in his y.	BIBLE 85:18
Crabbed age and y. cannot	SHAK 632:18
Creator in the days of thy y.	BIBLE 81:1
days of our y. are the days	BYRON 173:8
eagle mewing her mighty y.	MILT 475:14
flourish set on y.	SHAK 633:21
flower of their y.	VIRG 715:3
Froude informs the Scottish y.	STUB 671:2
happiest y., viewing	SHAK 583:14
have y. and a little beauty	WEBS 725:16
heart is evil from his y.	BIBLE 70:28
He wears the rose of y.	SHAK 565:17
How beautiful is y.	MED 456:3
idle y. go use thy property	WYATT 749:16
I do abhor thee, y.	SHAK 632:19
If y. knew; if age could	EST 278:15
In lusty y., or when	SURR 672:4
in the days of thy y.	BIBLE 80:30
In y. is pleasure, in youth	WEVER 730:1
it is y. who must fight	HOOV 344:20
knew a phoenix in my y.	YEATS 752:1
Let age approve of it	BROW 152:13
many a y., and many a maid	MILT 465:13
melted down thy y.	SHAK 626:16
my ill adventured y.	DAN 229:16
Or the feature, or the y.	JONS 379:14
perform the promises of y.	JOHN 369:18
rigorous teachers seized my y.	ARN 28:19
shake their wicked sides at y.	YEATS 752:17
sign of an ill-spent y.	ROUP 549:1
sins and offences of my y.	BOOK 125:19
sowed in y. a mustard seed	BRON 142:2
spice-islands of Y. and Hope	COL 212:17
subtle thief of y.	MILT 474:21
tender years of y. into harsh	GOGOL 309:21
That miracle of a y.	EVEL 279:7
things Y. needed not	WORD 748:2
thoughts of y. are long	LONG 427:4
Thou hast nor y. nor age	SHAK 606:8
To y. and age in common	AHN 29:6
traitorously corrupted the y.	SHAK 587:26
Upon my y., and on my jolitee	CHAU 194:22
very riband in the cap of y.	SHAK 578:11
well-beloved y.	BALL 48:20
when Y. and Pleasure meet	BYRON 168:16
Where y. grows pale	KEATS 389:10
world has lost his y.	BIBLE 86:23
y. and the feeling that it will	CONR 217:17
Y. are boarded, clothed	DICK 241:31
Y., beauty, graceful action	DRYD 259:10
y. did dress themselves	SHAK 583:7
Y. is a blunder	DISR 248:5
y. is bent by the same	THOM 693:7
y. is the season of credulity	PITT 515:7

youth: (*cont.*):

Y. means love	BROW 152:14
y. of America	WILDE 735:26
Y. of a Nation	DISR 248:29
y. of a state arms do flourish	BACON 45:5
y. of England are on fire	SHAK 585:1
y. of labour with an age	GOLD 310:7
y. of the world	BACON 42:11
Y. on the prow, and Pleasure	GRAY 315:9
Y. pined away with desire	BLAKE 114:5
y. replies, I can	EMER 276:14
Y.'s a stuff will not endure	SHAK 629:4
Y. shows but half	BROW 152:6
y.'s sweet-scented manuscript	FITZ 284:16
Y.'s the season made for joys	GAY 299:22
y. that he cannot endure	SHAK 613:26
y. to fortune and to fame	GRAY 315:20
y. to the gallows	PAINE 504:21
y. waneth by increasing	PEELE 511:5
Y., what man's age is like	DENH 236:18
Y., which is forgiven everything	SHAW 638:3
y., who daily farther	WORD 745:14
Y. will be served	BORR 136:17

youthful: y. passion for abstracted

	JOHN 372:25

Yvetot: There was a king of Y. — BÉR 65:3

Z

Zadok: Z. the priest — BIBLE 75:21

zany: mountebank and his z. — WALP 719:24

Zauber: *Deine Z. binden wieder* — SCH 558:1

zeal: all z., Mr Easy — MARR 449:5

emotion and take it for z.	THOM 692:10
not the slightest z.	TALL 678:8
Tell z. it wants devotion	RAL 535:16
tempering bigot z.	KNOX 403:5
z. in politics as well	JUN 383:6
z. of the Lord of hosts	BIBLE 82:28
z. of thine house	BOOK 129:11
z. of women themselves	MILL 461:3

zealous: A very z. man — BUNY 156:11

zed: Thou whoreson z.! — SHAK 595:12

Zeit: *aus dem Schosse der Z.* — HEINE 331:3

Zen: Z. and the Art — PIRS 515:4

zenith: z. like a falling star — MILT 469:7

zephyr: soft the z. blows — GRAY 315:9

Zephyrus: breathing Z. did softly play

	SPEN 660:23

zest: z. goes out of a beautiful — GREN 318:1

Zion: songs of peaceful Z. — DIX 249:18

Z., city of our God	NEWT 494:9
Z. is left as a cottage	BIBLE 82:8

zipless: z. fuck — JONG 378:3

Zitronen: *wo die Z. blühn* — GOET 309:16

zodiac: Mermaid in the Z. — KEATS 388:21

zone: torrid or the frozen z. — CAREW 179:9

zoo: human z. — MORR 485:5

Zuleika: Such was Z. — BYRON 167:27

Zurich: little gnomes in Z. — WILS 737:19

Zweck: *jederzeit zugleich als Z.* — KANT 385:10

Wer den Z. will	KANT 385:8